LAUREL EDITIONS

CASSELL has published outstanding dictionaries for virtually every major foreign language. Now, for the first time, many of them are being made available in compact, paperback editions. Besides the present German–English, English–German dictionary, the Dell series includes the Cassell's New Compact French–English, Spanish–English, and Latin–English dictionaries. These handy reference books are invaluable aids for students in foreign-language courses or for those who want to polish up their language skills on their own. Additionally, they are designed for the traveler and the reader of contemporary literature, newspapers, and magazines.

CASSELL'S NEW COMPACT

German-English
English-German
Dictionary

Compiled by
H.-C. SASSE, M.A., M.Litt.
Lecturer in German at the
University of Newcastle upon Tyne

DR. J. HORNE
Lecturer in German at the
University of Birmingham

DR. CHARLOTTE DIXON

Contents

Preface

Among the difficulties that arise in the compilation of a Compact Dictionary that of the selection of words is undoubtedly the most formidable one. The decision as to what to include and, much more difficult, what to exclude, must to a considerable extent depend on the type of student of a foreign language who is most likely to use it. Primarily a dictionary of this kind is intended for the student in the earlier stages of learning German, whether at school or university. As the study of German, even at an early stage, is likely to include the reading of literary texts from the eighteenth century onwards, it was felt that some attention at least must be paid to the inclusion of words no longer in common use today but frequently found in the prescribed texts, whether poetry, drama or prose. That in this respect severe limitations are imposed by the very concept of a 'Compact' Dictionary is of course obvious, but an attempt has been made to include at least some of the most common literary and poetical terms. However, the main emphasis throughout must of course be on straightforward contemporary German. In addition to the needs of the student, those of the traveller and the tourist, of the reader of contemporary literature and of newspapers and magazines, have been kept in mind. It is hoped that the student of science and technology too will find the dictionary useful, though in his case additional reference must of course be made to one of the growing number of specialized works dealing with the technical vocabulary of his particular discipline.

The aim of a Compact Dictionary must be to achieve some kind of viable compromise between conciseness on the one hand and completeness on the other. To make the dictionary as helpful as possible—given only a limited amount of space—certain economies were called for. Omissions were inevitable. What is similarly inevitable is that, except in the most obvious cases, no two experts are likely

to agree as to what may safely be omitted unless (as was attempted here) one makes frequency of usage and general usefulness the main criteria.

It should be remembered, lastly, that this is a concise dictionary which cannot remotely hope to do justice to all the finer meanings and nuances of two highly developed and complex languages. But it is hoped that the student and reader of German, especially in the earlier stages of learning the language, will find here all the help he needs.

For more detailed reference the user will find Cassell's New German Dictionary (ed. Dr. H. T. Betteridge) of considerable help, while the Duden works of reference on German are regarded as the authoritative last word on matters of controversy. In the final analysis there will always be areas of doubt and dispute. That is the prerogative of a living and developing language.

Finally, thanks are due on behalf of the publishers to Prof. W. E. Collinson, late of the University of Liverpool, who acted in a consultative capacity.

H.-C. Sasse

Advice to the User

As a guide to the nature of words which have inevitably been omitted from a dictionary of this size, it may be helpful to state that, when a German *Fremdwort* is identical with the corresponding English term and possesses no grammatical peculiarities, it appears only in the English–German section. For example, it was felt that the word *Atom* (and *a fortiori* derivative compounds such as *Atomphysik*) was unlikely to perplex any English reader and it has therefore been omitted from the German–English, but included in the English–German, section. For the same reason, a somewhat similar plan has been followed with regard to the names of countries. These have mostly been given in German–English only, whereas the corresponding nouns and adjectives of nationality or race are given in English–German only.

Arrangement of Entries

Strict alphabetical order seemed to be most helpful in a dictionary intended primarily for readers in the earlier stages of acquiring a knowledge of German. Within the entries themselves literal meanings and frequency of usage determine the sequence of definitions. Admittedly the second criterion is to a considerable extent a matter of personal linguistic judgment, indeed of *Sprachgefühl*, but it is hoped that in most cases the reader will thereby more readily discover the meaning of any particular word. It can generally be assumed that definitions separated by commas have much the same meaning, whereas differences in meaning or usage are marked by semicolons. Where it was thought desirable and feasible to include idiomatic phrases, relative frequency of usage appeared a more helpful criterion than strict alphabetic sequence.

Words which are spelt alike but are etymologically distinct

Zur Benutzung des Wörterbuches

Ein Hinweis auf die Art der Wörter, auf die in einem Taschenwörterbuch unweigerlich verzichtet werden muss, wird dem Leser die Anwendung dieses Nachschlagwerkes gewiss erleichtern: Ein deutsches Fremdwort, das mit dem entsprechenden englischen Ausdruck identisch ist und keine grammatikalischen Besonderheiten aufweist, erscheint als Stichwort nicht in beiden Sprachen, sondern wird nur im englisch–deutschen Teil aufgeführt. Man darf wohl annehmen, dass ein Wort wie z.B. *Atom* (und *a fortiori* abgeleitete Zusammensetzungen wie *Atomphysik*) einen englischen Leser kaum verwirren wird, weshalb es denn auch im deutsch–englischen Teil weggelassen, indessen im englisch-deutschen Teil berücksichtigt wurde. Aus dem gleichen Grunde wurde bei den Namen von Ländern ein ähnliches Prinzip beachtet. Diese wurden in der Regel nur im deutsch-englischen Teil aufgeführt, während die entsprechenden Substantive und Adjektive der Nationalität oder Rasse nur im englisch–deutschen Teil erscheinen.

Anordnung der Stichwörter

Die strikte alphabetische Reihenfolge schien vorteilhaft für ein Nachschlagwerk, das in erster Linie für Lernende gedacht ist, die die deutsche Sprache noch nicht völlig beherrschen. Bei den gegebenen Übersetzungen eines Stichwortes bestimmen die wörtliche Übertragung sowie die Häufigkeit des Gebrauches die Folge der Definitionen. Gewiss ist das zweite Kriterium weitgehend eine Angelegenheit der persönlichen linguistischen Beurteilung, in der Tat des Sprachgefühls. Doch ist zu hoffen, dass der Leser in den meisten Fällen gerade dadurch der Bedeutung eines Begriffes näher kommt. Allgemein gilt, dass durch ein Komma getrennte Wörter eine annähernd gleiche Bedeutung haben, während Unterschiede in Bedeutung oder Anwendung

Advice to the User

have been given separate, numbered entries for the sake of clarity.

A word should be added on the subject of compounds. Most students of German come to realize before long that the notoriously long German nouns, far from complicating the understanding of the language, are merely a matter of syntactical and grammatical convenience, a device for structural conciseness within a given sentence construction. In a 'Compact' Dictionary only such compounds can be given which have a meaning which can be arrived at only with difficulty or not at all. Where a compound is not given, the constituent parts of the word should be looked up. The meaning should then become self-evident.

Grammar

Parts of Speech. These are indicated by abbreviations in italics (*adj.*, *v.a.* etc.), the meaning of which will be found in the List of Abbreviations. It has not been felt necessary to indicate the nature of English proper names.

Genders. In the German-English section nouns are denoted by their gender (*m.*, *f.* or *n.*). In the English-German section gender is shown by the definite article preceding the noun; in a series of nouns the gender is sometimes omitted when it is the same as that of the preceding noun or nouns.

Declension. The Genitive singular and Nominative plural of German nouns are given in parentheses after the gender. The plurals of English nouns are not given, except for certain very irregular forms. The cases governed by prepositions have been included.

Verbs. In both German and English the indication *irr.* refers the user to the tables of Irregular Verbs. Where a compound irregular verb is not given, its forms are identical with those of the simple irregular verb in the table. "To" is omitted from English infinitives throughout. German inseparable verbs are described as such only when there is any possibility of doubt, *e.g.* in the case of prepositional prefixes. Where prefixes are axiomatically always part of an

durch ein Semikolon markiert sind. Wo es als notwendig und durchführbar erachtet wurde, idiomatische Redewendungen zu zitieren, schien die relative Häufigkeit der Anwendung ein nützlicheres Kriterium als die strenge alphabetische Folge. Orthographisch gleiche Wörter, die sich durch ihre etymologische Herkunft unterscheiden, wurden um der Klarheit willen als einzelne Stichwörter aufgeführt und mit Ziffern versehen. Noch ein Wort zum Thema der Wortzusammensetzungen: Die meisten Deutschlernenden werden bald erkennen, dass die berüchtigt langen deutschen Substantive das Verständnis der Sprache keineswegs erschweren. Sie sind lediglich eine Sache syntaktischer und grammatikalischer Vereinfachung, ein Hilfsmittel zu struktureller Kürze und Prägnanz innerhalb einer gegebenen Satzbildung. In einem Taschenwörterbuch können allein solche Wortverbindungen berücksichtigt werden, die nur mit Mühe oder überhaupt nicht abzuleiten sind. Ist eine Wortverbindung nicht angeführt, so sollten die einzelnen Bestandteile nachgesehen werden. Auf diese Weise wird sich der Sinn der Zusammensetzung von selbst ergeben.

Grammatik

Wortarten. Sie sind in abgekürzter Form durch Kursivschrift gekennzeichnet (*adj.*, *v.a.* etc.). Eine Erläuterung der Abkürzungen findet sich im Verzeichnis der Abkürzungen. Es wurde nicht für nötig befunden, die Zugehörigkeit von Eigennamen anzuzeigen.

Geschlecht. Im deutsch–englischen Teil sind die Substantive mit ihrem Geschlecht (*m.*, *f.* oder *n.*) gekennzeichnet. Im englisch–deutschen Teil ist das Geschlecht durch den bestimmten Artikel vor dem Substantiv angegeben. In einer Reihe aufeinanderfolgender Definitionen wurde der Artikel dort weggelassen, wo er mit dem vorhergehenden übereinstimmt.

Deklination. Die Endungen des Genitiv Singular und des Nominativ Plural deutscher Substantive sind in Klammern nach der Bezeichnung des Geschlechtes eingefügt. Der

inseparable verb (*be-*, *ent-*, *zer-* etc.) no such information is given, as it is assumed that the student will be familiar with the function of these prefixes long before he comes to use a dictionary.

Phonetics. Phonetic transcriptions, using the symbols of the International Phonetic Association, are given throughout for all entries in both sections of the dictionary as a help to correct pronunciation. The mark ′ precedes the syllable which carries the stress. The glottal stop is not indicated.

Numbers. Only the most common numerals appear in the body of the dictionary. However, fuller coverage is given in the separate Numerical Tables.

Zur Benutzung des Wörterbuches

Plural englischer Substantive wurde nicht berücksichtigt ausser bei einigen stark unregelmässigen Formen. Fälle, die von Präpositionen regiert werden, wurden aufgenommen.

Verben. Im Deutschen wie im Englischen weist die Anmerkung *irr.* den Leser auf die Tabellen unregelmässiger Verben hin. Ist ein zusammengesetztes Verb nicht angeführt, so sind seine Formen mit denen des einfachen Verbs in der Tabelle identisch. "To" vor englischen Infinitiv–formen wurde durchgehend weggelassen. Deutsche untrennbare Verben werden nur dort als solche gekennzeichnet, wo Zweifel möglich sind, also bei Verben mit präpositionalen Vorsilben. Wo Vorsilben grundsätzlich Teile eines untrennbaren Verbes (*be-*, *ent-*, *zer-* etc.) bilden, ist kein solcher Hinweis angebracht, da angenommen werden darf, dass der Lernende die Funktion dieser Vorsilben kennt, lange bevor er dazu kommt, ein Wörterbuch zu konsultieren.

Phonetik. Jedes einzelne Stichwort ist auch in seiner phonetischen Transkription wiedergegeben. Dabei wurden die phonetischen Symbole der *International Phonetic Association* benutzt. Der Akzent ' steht jeweils unmittelbar vor der betonten Silbe. Der Knacklaut ist indessen nicht markiert.

Zahlwörter. Nur die gebräuchlichsten Zahlen erscheinen im Hauptteil des Wörterbuches. Eine ausführliche Zusammenstellung findet sich in den besonderen Zahlentabellen.

Key to Pronunciation

Vowels

Phonetic Symbol	German Example	Phonetic Symbol	English Example
a	lassen ['lasən]	i:	seat [si:t]
a:	haben ['ha:bən], Haar [ha:r]	i	finish ['finiʃ], physic ['fizik]
ɛ	häßlich ['hɛslɪç], Geld [gɛlt]	e	neck [nɛk]
ɛ:	Märchen ['mɛ:rçən], Zähne ['tsɛ:nə]	æ	man [mæn], malefactor ['mælifæktə]
e	Medizin [medi'tsi:n]	ɑ:	father ['fɑ:ðə], task [tɑ:sk]
e:	leben ['le:bən], See [ze:], lehnen ['le:nən]	ɔ	block [blɔk], waddle [wɔdl]
ə	rufen ['ru:fən]	ɔ:	shawl [ʃɔ:l], tortoise ['tɔ:təs]
ɪ	Fisch [fɪʃ], Mystik ['mɪstɪk]	o	domain [do'mein]
i	Militär [mili'tɛ:r]	u	good [gud], July [dʒu'lai]
i:	Berlin [bɛr'li:n], Liebe ['li:bə], ihm [i:m]	u:	moon [mu:n], tooth [tu:θ]
ɔ	Kopf [kɔpf]	ʌ	cut [kʌt], somewhere ['sʌmwɛə]
o	mobil [mo'bi:l]	ə:	search [sə:tʃ], surgeon ['sə:dʒən]
o:	Rose ['ro:zə], Boot [bo:t], ohne ['o:nə]	ə	cathedral [kə'θi:drəl], never ['nevə]
œ	Mörder ['mœrdər]		
ø	möblieren [mø'bli:rən]		
ø:	Löwe ['lø:və], Röhre ['rø:rə]		
u	Hund [hunt]		
u:	gut [gu:t], Uhr [u:r]		
y	fünf [fynf], Symbol [zym'bo:l]		
y:	Lübeck ['ly:bɛk], Mühe ['my:ə]		

Diphthongs

aɪ	Eis [aɪs], Waise ['vaɪzə]	ei	great [greit]
au	Haus [haus]	ou	show [ʃou]
ɔy	Beute ['bɔytə], Gebäude [gə'bɔydə]	ai	high [hai]
		au	crowd [kraud]
		ɔi	boy [bɔi]
		iə	steer [stiə]
		ɛə	hair [hɛə]
		uə	moor [muə]

Consonants

Phonetic Symbol	German Example	Phonetic Symbol	English Example
ç	Blech [blɛç], ich [ıç]	p	paper ['peipə]
f	Vater ['fa:tər]	b	ball [bɔ:l]
j	ja [ja:]	t	tea [ti:], train [trein]
ŋ	bringen ['brıŋən]	d	deed [di:d]
s	beißen ['baısən], wißen ['vısən], los [lo:s]	k	cake [keik], quest [kwest]
ʃ	schon [ʃo:n]	g	game [geim]
ts	Cäcilie [tsɛ'tsi:ljə], Zimmer ['tsımər]	m	mammoth ['mæmɵθ]
v	weiß [vaıs]	n	nose [nouz], nanny ['næni]
x	Bach [bax], kochen ['kɔxən], ruchbar ['ru:xba:r]	ŋ	bring [briŋ], finger ['fiŋgə]
z	lesen ['le:zən]	f	fair [fɛə], far [fɑ:]
b	Biene ['bi:nə]	v	vine [vain]
d	Dach [dax]	θ	thin [θin], bath [bɑ:θ]
g	geben ['ge:bən]	ð	thine [ðain], bathe [beið]
h	hier [hi:r]		
k	Koch [kɔx], quartieren [kwar'ti:rən]	s	since [sins]
l	Lied [li:t]	z	busy ['bizi]
m	Mirakel [mi'ra:kəl]	l	land [lænd], hill [hil]
n	Nase ['na:zə]	ʃ	shield [ʃi:ld], sugar ['ʃugə]
p	Probe ['pro:bə]	ʒ	vision ['viʒən]
r	rot [ro:t]	r	rat [ræt], train [trein]
t	Tisch [tıʃ]	h	here [hiə], horse [hɔ:s]
		x	coronach ['kɔrənæx], loch [lɔx]

Semi-Consonants

j	yellow ['jelou], yes [jes]
w	wall [wɔ:l]

List of Abbreviations

abbr.	abbreviation (of), abbreviated	*m.*	masculine
Acc.	Accusative	*Maths.*	Mathematics
adj.	adjective	*Meas.*	Measurement
adv.	adverb	*Mech.*	Mechanics
Agr.	agriculture	*Med.*	Medicine
Am.	American(ism)	*Met.*	Meteorology
Anat.	Anatomy	*Metall.*	Metallurgy
Archæol.	Archæology	*Mil.*	Military
Archit.	Architecture	*Min.*	Mining
Arith.	Arithmetic	*Motor.*	Motoring
art.	article	*Mount.*	Mountaineering
Astrol.	Astrology	*Mus.*	Music
Astron.	Astronomy	*Myth.*	Mythology
Austr.	Austrian	*n.*	neuter
aux.	auxiliary	*Naut.*	Nautical
Aviat.	Aviation	*Nav.*	Navigation
Bibl.	Biblical	*o.('s)*	one('s)
Bot.	Botany	*o.s.*	oneself
Br.	British	*obs.*	obsolete
Build.	Building	*Orn.*	Ornithology
Carp.	Carpentry	*p.*	person
Chem.	Chemistry	*Parl.*	Parliament
coll.	colloquial	*part.*	particle
collec.	collective	*pej.*	pejorative
Comm.	Commerce	*pers.*	person(al)
comp.	comparative	*Phil.*	Philosophy
conj.	conjunction	*Phonet.*	Phonetics
Cul.	Culinary	*Phot.*	Photography
Dat.	Dative	*Phys.*	Physics
def.	definite	*Physiol.*	Physiology
defect.	defective	*pl.*	plural
dem.	demonstrative	*Poet.*	Poetical
dial.	dialect	*Pol.*	Political
Eccl.	Ecclesiastical	*poss.*	possessive
Econ.	Economics	*p.p.*	past participle
Elec.	Electricity	*prec.*	preceded
emph.	emphatic	*pred.*	predicative
Engin.	Engineering	*prep.*	preposition
Ent.	Entomology	*pron.*	pronoun
excl.	exclamation	*Psych.*	Psychology
f.	feminine	*r.*	reflexive
fig.	figurative	*Rad.*	Radio
Fin.	Finance	*Railw.*	Railways
Footb.	Football	*reg.*	regular
Genit.	Genitive	*Rel.*	Religion
Geog.	Geography	*rel.*	relative
Geol.	Geology	*s.*	substantive
Geom.	Geometry	*Sch.*	School
Gram.	Grammar	*Scot.*	Scottish
Gymn.	Gymnastics	*sing.*	singular
Her.	Heraldry	*sl.*	slang
Hist.	History	*s.th.*	something
Hunt.	Hunting	*Tail.*	Tailoring
imper.	imperative	*Tech.*	Technical
impers.	impersonal	*Teleph.*	Telephone
Ind.	Industry	*temp.*	temporal
indecl.	indeclinable	*Text.*	Textiles
indef.	indefinite	*Theat.*	Theatre
infin.	infinitive	*Theol.*	Theology
insep.	inseparable	*Transp.*	Transport
int.	interjection	*Typ.*	Typography
interr.	interrogative	*Univ.*	University
intim.	intimate	*us.*	usually
iron.	ironical	*v.a.*	active *or* transitive verb
irr.	irregular	*v.n.*	neuter *or* intransitive verb
Ling.	Linguistics	*v.r.*	reflexive verb
Lit.	Literary	*Vet.*	Veterinary Science
Log.	Logic	*vulg.*	vulgar
		Zool.	Zoology

A

A, a [aː], *n. das A* (des **—s, die —s**) the letter A; (*Mus.*) the note A; *A Dur*, A major; *A Moll*, A minor.

Aal [aːl], *m.* (**—s,** *pl.* **—e**) eel.

Aas [aːs], *n.* (**—es,** *pl.* **Äser** *or* **—e**) carcass, carrion.

ab [ap], *adv.* off; down; away; (*Theat.*) exit *or* exeunt, — *und zu*, now and again, occasionally; *auf und* —, up and down, to and fro. — *prep.* from; — *Hamburg*, from Hamburg.

abändern ['apɛndərn], *v.a.* alter.

Abart ['apaːrt], *f.* (**—,** *pl.* **—en**) variety, species.

Abbau ['apbau], *m.* (**—s,** *no pl.*) demolition, dismantling; reduction (of staff).

abberufen ['apbəruːfən], *v.a. irr.* recall.

abbestellen ['apbəʃtɛlən], *v.a.* countermand, annul, cancel (an order).

Abbild ['apbɪlt], *n.* (**—es,** *pl.* **—er**) copy, image.

Abbildung ['apbɪlduŋ], *f.* (**—,** *pl.* **—en**) illustration.

Abbitte ['apbɪtə], *f.* (**—,** *pl.* **—n**) apology; — *leisten*, — *tun*, apologise.

abblenden ['apblɛndən], *v.a.* dim (lights).

Abbruch ['apbrux], *m.* (**—s,** *pl.* **⁓e**) breaking off; demolition; *einer Sache* — *tun*, damage s.th.

abdanken ['apdaŋkən], *v.n.* resign, abdicate, retire (from office).

abdecken ['apdɛkən], *v.a.* uncover, unroof; clear (the table).

Abdruck ['apdruk], *m.* (**—s,** *pl.* **—e**) impression, copy, reprint, cast.

Abend ['aːbənt], *m.* (**—s,** *pl.* **—e**) evening, eve.

Abendbrot ['aːbəntbroːt], *n.* (**—s,** *no pl.*) evening meal, (*Am.*) supper.

Abendland ['aːbəntlant], *n.* (**—es,** *no pl.*) occident, west.

Abendmahl ['aːbəntmaːl], *n.* (**—s,** *no pl.*) supper; *das heilige* —, Holy Communion, the Lord's Supper.

abends ['aːbənts], *adv.* in the evening, of an evening.

Abenteuer ['aːbəntɔyər], *n.* (**—s,** *pl.* **—**) adventure.

aber ['aːbər], *conj.* but, however; (*emphatic*) — *ja!* yes, indeed! of course! —*prefix.* again, once more.

Aberglaube ['aːbərglaubə], *m.* (**—ns,** *no pl.*) superstition.

abermals ['aːbərmaːls], *adv.* again, once more.

Abessinien [abɛˈsiːniən], *n.* Abyssinia.

abfahren ['apfaːrən], *v.n. irr.* (*aux.* sein) set out, depart, drive off.

Abfall ['apfal], *m.* (**—s,** *pl.* **⁓e**) scrap, remnant; secession; slope; (*pl.*) waste, refuse.

abfallen ['apfalən], *v.n. irr.* (*aux.* sein) fall off; desert; slope.

abfällig ['apfɛlɪç], *adj.* derogatory.

abfangen ['apfaŋən], *v.a. irr.* intercept, catch.

abfärben ['apfɛrbən], *v.n.* (*colours*) run; stain; lose colour.

abfassen ['apfasən], *v.a.* compose, draft.

abfertigen ['apfɛrtɪgən], *v.a.* despatch; deal with, serve (a customer *or* client).

abfeuern ['apfɔyərn], *v.a.* fire (off), launch (rocket, missile).

abfinden ['apfɪndən], *v.a. irr.* indemnify, compound with (o.'s creditors). — *v.r. sich* — *mit*, put up with, come to terms with.

Abflug ['apfluːk], *m.* (**—s,** *pl.* **⁓e**) takeoff, departure (by air).

Abfluß ['apfluːs], *m.* (**—sses,** *pl.* **⁓sse**) flowing off; drain.

Abfuhr ['apfuːr], *f.* (**—,** *pl.* **—en**) removal, collection (of refuse); (*coll.*) rebuff.

abführen ['apfyːrən], *v.a.* arrest, lead away. —*v.n.* (*Med.*) act as a purgative.

Abführmittel ['apfyːrmɪtəl], *n.* (**—s,** *pl.* **—**) purgative, laxative.

Abgabe ['apgaːbə], *f.* (**—,** *pl.* **—n**) delivery, tax, duty, levy.

abgabepflichtig ['apgaːbəpflɪçtɪç], *adj.* taxable, subject to duty.

Abgang ['apgaŋ], *m.* (**—(e)s,** *pl.* **⁓e**) wastage, loss; departure; *Schul*—, school-leaving.

abgängig ['apgɛŋɪç], *adj.* lost, missing; (*of goods*) saleable.

abgeben ['apgeːbən], *v.a. irr.* deliver, cede; give (an opinion). — *v.r. sich mit etwas*, — concern o.s. with s.th.

abgedroschen ['apgədrɔʃən], *adj.* (*phrases etc.*) trite, hackneyed.

abgefeimt ['apgəfaimt], *adj.* cunning, crafty.

abgegriffen ['apgəgrɪfən], *adj.* well thumbed, worn.

abgehen ['apgeːən], *v.n. irr.* (*aux.* sein) leave, retire; branch off; (*Theat.*) make an exit.

abgelebt ['apgəleːpt], *adj.* (*of humans*) decrepit, worn out.

abgelegen ['apgəleːgən], *adj.* remote, distant.

abgemacht ['apgəmaxt], *adj., int.* agreed! done!

abgeneigt ['apgənaikt], *adj.* disinclined, averse.

Abgeordnete ['apgəɔrdnətə], *m., f.* (**—n,** *pl.* **—n**) political representative, deputy, Member of Parliament.

Abgesandte ['apgəzantə], *m., f.* (**—n,** *pl.* **—n**) delegate, ambassador.

abgeschieden [ˈapgəʃiːdən], *adj.* secluded, remote; deceased.

abgeschmackt [ˈapgəʃmakt], *adj.* insipid.

abgesehen [ˈapgəzeːən], *adv.* — *von*, apart from, except for.

abgespannt [ˈapgəʃpant], *adj.* worn out, run down, exhausted.

abgestorben [ˈapgəʃtɔrbən], *adj.* dead, numb.

abgetan [ˈapgətaːn], *adj.* finished, over, done with; *damit ist die Sache* —, that finishes the matter.

abgetragen [ˈapgətraːgən], *adj.* (*clothes*) shabby, threadbare.

abgewöhnen [ˈapgəvøːnən], *v.a. einem etwas* —, free (rid) s.o. from (of) a habit, wean from.

abgrasen [ˈapgraːzən], *v.a.* (*animals*) graze.

Abgrund [ˈapgrunt], *m.* (—es, *pl.* ⁓e) abyss, precipice.

Abguss [ˈapgus], *m.* (—es, *pl.* ⁓e) cast, plaster-cast, mould.

abhalten [ˈaphaltən], *v.a. irr.* restrain, hold back; hold (meeting etc.).

abhandeln [ˈaphandəln], *v.a. einem etwas* —, bargain for s.th.

abhanden [apˈhandən], *adv.* mislaid; — *kommen*, get lost.

Abhandlung [ˈaphandluŋ], *f.* (—, *pl.* —en) treatise, dissertation; (*pl.*) proceedings.

Abhang [ˈaphaŋ], *m.* (—es, *pl.* ⁓e) slope; declivity.

abhängen [ˈaphɛŋən], *v.a. irr.* take off, unhook; *von etwas oder jemandem* —, depend on s.th. *or* s.o.

abhärten [ˈaphɛrtən], *v.a.* inure against rigours, toughen.

abheben [ˈapheːbən], *v.a. irr.* draw (money from bank).

abhold [ˈaphɔlt], *adj.* averse to (*Dat.*).

abholen [ˈaphoːlən], *v.a. etwas* —, fetch, collect s.th.; *einen* —, meet s.o. (at the station etc.).

Abitur [abiˈtuːr], *n.* (—s, *no pl.*) matriculation examination.

Abiturient [abituˈrjɛnt], *m.* (—en, *pl.* —en) matriculation candidate.

Abkehr [ˈapkeːr], *f.* (—, *no pl.*) turning away, renunciation.

abklären [ˈapklɛːrən], *v.a.* (*Chem.*) filter, clear.

Abkommen [ˈapkɔmən], *n.* (—s, *pl.* —) treaty, agreement, contract.

Abkömmling [ˈapkœmliŋ], *m.* (—s, *pl.* —e) descendant.

abkühlen [ˈapkyːlən], *v.a.* cool, chill.

Abkunft [ˈapkunft], *f.* (—, *no pl.*) descent, origin.

abkürzen [ˈapkyrtsən], *v.a.* shorten, abridge, curtail.

abladen [ˈapladən], *v.a. irr.* unload, dump.

Ablaß [ˈaplas], *m.* (—sses, *pl.* ⁓sse) (*Eccl.*) indulgence.

ablassen [ˈaplasən], *v.n. irr. von etwas* —, desist from, refrain from s.th.— *v.a. einem etwas billig* —, reduce the

price of s.th. for s.o.

Ablauf [ˈaplauf], *m.* (—es, *no pl.*) (*water*) drainage; (*ticket*) expiration; lapse (of time); (*bill*) maturity.

ablaufen [ˈaplaufən], *v.n. irr.* (*aux.* sein) (*water*) run off; (*ticket*) expire; *gut* —, turn out well.

Ableben [ˈapleːbən], *n.* (—s, *no pl.*) decease, death.

ablegen [ˈapleːgən], *v.a.* (*clothes*) take off; (*documents*) file; *Rechenschaft* —, account for; *eine Prüfung* —, take an examination.

Ableger [ˈapleːgər], *m.* (—s, *pl.* —) (*Hort.*) cutting.

Ablegung [ˈapleːguŋ], *f.* (—, *no pl.*) making (of a vow); taking (of an oath).

ablehnen [ˈapleːnən], *v.a.* refuse, decline.

ableiten [ˈaplaɪtən], *v.a.* divert, draw off; (*water*) drain; (*words*) derive from.

ablenken [ˈaplɛŋkən], *v.a.* (*aux.* haben) *einen von etwas* —, divert s.o.'s attention from s.th., distract.

ablesen [ˈapleːzən], *v.a. irr.* (*meter*) read off; (*field*) glean.

abliefern [ˈapliːfərn], *v.a.* deliver.

ablösen [ˈapløːzən], *v.a. einen* —, take the place of s.o., (*Mil.*) relieve; detach (a stamp from a letter etc.).

abmachen [ˈapmaxən], *v.a.* undo, detach; settle, arrange.

abmagern [ˈapmaːgərn], *v.n.* (*aux.* sein) get thinner, waste away.

Abmarsch [ˈapmarʃ], *m.* (—es, *no pl.*) (*Mil.*) marching off.

abmelden [ˈapmɛldən], *v.r. sich* —, give notice of departure.

abmessen [ˈapmɛsən], *v.a. irr.* measure (off), gauge.

abmühen [ˈapmyːən], *v.r. sich* —, exert o.s., strive.

Abnahme [ˈapnaːmə], *f.* (—, *pl.* —n) decline, loss of weight; (*moon*) waning; (*goods*) taking delivery.

abnehmen [ˈapneːmən], *v.n. irr.* lose weight; (*moon*) wane. — *v.a.* (*hat*) take off; *einem etwas* —, relieve s.o. (of trouble *or* work).

Abneigung [ˈapnaɪguŋ], *f.* (—, *pl.* —en) antipathy, dislike.

abnutzen [ˈapnutsən], *v.a.* wear out by use.

Abonnement [abɔnəˈmaŋ], *n.* (—s, *pl.* —s) (*newspaper*) subscription; (*railway*) season-ticket.

Abonnent [abɔˈnɛnt], *m.* (—en, *pl.* —en) subscriber.

abonnieren [abɔˈniːrən], *v.a.* subscribe to (a paper).

Abordnung [ˈapɔrdnuŋ], *f.* (—, *pl.* —en) delegation, deputation.

Abort [aˈbɔrt], *m.* (—s, *pl.* —e) lavatory, toilet.

Abortus [aˈbɔrtus], *m.* (—us, *no pl.*) (*Med.*) abortion.

abplagen [ˈapplaːgən], *v.r. sich* —, slave, toil.

abprallen [ˈappr,alən], *v.n.* (*aux.* sein) *von etwas* —, bounce off, rebound.

abquälen ['apkvɛ:lən], *v.r. sich —*, toil, make o.s. weary (*mit*, with).

abraten ['apra:tən], *v.n. irr. einem von etwas —*, dissuade s.o. from, advise *or* warn s.o. against.

abräumen ['aprɔymən], *v.a.* remove; *den Tisch —*, clear the table.

abrechnen ['aprɛçnən], *v.a.* reckon up. *— v.n. mit einem —*, settle accounts with s.o., (*coll.*) get even with s.o.

Abrede ['apre:də], *f.* (*—, pl. —n*) agreement, arrangement; *in — stellen*, deny.

abreißen ['apraɪsən], *v.a. irr.* tear off.

abrichten ['apriçtən], *v.a.* (*dogs*) train, (*horses*) break in.

abriegeln ['apri:gəln], *v.a.* bolt, bar.

Abriß ['apris], *m.* (*—sses, pl. —sse*) sketch; summary, synopsis.

abrollen ['aprɔlən], *v.a.* uncoil. *— v.n.* (*aux.* sein) roll off.

abrücken ['aprykən], *v.a.* move away. *—v.n. (aux. sein)* (*Mil.*) march off.

Abruf ['apru:f], *m.* (*—es, no pl.*) recall (from a post).

abrunden ['aprundən], *v.a.* round off.

abrupfen ['aprupfən], *v.a.* (*feathers*) pluck; (*flowers*) pluck off.

abrüsten ['aprystən], *v.n.* disarm.

Abrüstung ['aprystuŋ], *f.* (*—, no pl.*) disarmament.

abrutschen ['aprutʃən], *v.n.* (*aux.* sein) slide, slither down.

Absage ['apza:gə], *f.* (*—, pl. —n*) cancellation, refusal.

absagen ['apza:gən], *v.n.* refuse, beg to be excused, decline (an invitation).

Absatz ['apzats], *m.* (*—es, pl. ⁻e*) (*shoe*) heel; (*letter*) paragraph; (*Comm.*) *guter —*, ready sale.

abschaffen ['apʃafən], *v.a.* abolish, do away with.

abschälen ['apʃɛ:lən], *v.a.* peel. *— v.r. sich —*, peel off.

abschätzen ['apʃɛtsən], *v.a.* estimate, appraise; (*taxes*) assess.

Abschaum ['apʃaum], *m.* (*—es, no pl.*) scum.

Abscheu ['apʃɔy], *m.* (*—s, no pl.*) abhorrence, detestation, loathing.

abscheulich ['apʃɔylɪç], *adj.* abominable, repulsive.

abschieben ['apʃi:bən], *v.a. irr.* shove off, push off; *schieb ab!* scram!

Abschied ['apʃi:t], *m.* (*—s, pl. —e*) leave, departure, farewell; discharge; resignation.

abschießen ['apʃi:sən], *v.a. irr.* shoot off; discharge; (*gun*) fire; *den Vogel —*, win the prize.

abschinden ['apʃɪndən], *v.r. irr. sich —*, exhaust o.s. with hard work.

abschirren ['apʃɪrən], *v.a.* unharness.

abschlagen ['apʃla:gən], *v.a. irr.* (*attack*) beat off; (*branches*) lop off; *einem etwas —*, deny s.o. s.th.; *eine Bitte —*, refuse a request.

abschlägig ['apʃlɛgɪç], *adj.* negative.

Abschlagszahlung ['apʃlakstsa:luŋ], *f.* (*—, pl. —en*) payment by instalments.

abschleifen ['apʃlaifən], *v.a. irr.* grind off.

abschleppen ['apʃlɛpən], *v.a.* (*car*) tow (away). *— v.r. sich —*, wear o.s. out by carrying heavy loads.

abschließen ['apʃli:sən], *v.a. irr.* lock up; (*work*) conclude; (*accounts*) balance; *einen Vertrag —*, conclude an agreement.

Abschluß ['apʃlus], *m.* (*—sses, pl. ⁻sse*) settlement, winding-up.

abschneiden ['apʃnaidən], *v.a. irr.* cut off. *— v.n. gut —*, come off well.

Abschnitt ['apʃnit], *m.* (*—es, pl. —e*) section; (*book*) paragraph.

abschnüren ['apʃny:rən], *v.a.* lace up, tie up.

abschrecken ['apʃrɛkən], *v.a.* deter, frighten.

abschreiben ['apʃraibən], *v.a. irr.* copy, transcribe; crib; *eine Schuld —*, write off a debt.

Abschrift ['apʃrift], *f.* (*—, pl. —en*) copy, transcript, duplicate; *beglaubigte —*, certified copy.

Abschuß ['apʃus], *m.* (*—sses, pl. ⁻sse*) act of firing (a gun), shooting down (aircraft).

abschüssig ['apʃysiç], *adj.* steep.

abschütteln ['apʃytəln], *v.a.* shake off, cast off.

abschwächen ['apʃvɛçən], *v.a.* weaken, diminish.

abschweifen ['apʃvaifən], *v.n.* (*aux.* sein) digress (from), deviate.

abschwenken ['apʃvɛŋkən], *v.n.* (*aux.* sein) wheel off (*or* aside).

abschwören ['apʃvø:rən], *v.a. irr.* abjure, renounce by oath.

absehbar ['apze:ba:r], *adj.* imaginable, conceivable, foreseeable.

absehen ['apze:ən], *v.a., v.n. irr. einem etwas —*, copy s.th. from s.o.; *auf etwas —*, aim at s.th.; *von etwas —*, waive s.th.; refrain from s.th.

abseits ['apzaits], *adv., prep.* (*Genit.*) aside; *— von*, away from.

Absender ['apzɛndər], *m.* (*—s, pl.—*) sender; (*Comm.*) consigner.

absetzen ['apzɛtsən], *v.a.* set down; dismiss, deprive of office; depose; (*Comm.*) sell, dispose of.

Absicht ['apziçt], *f.* (*—, pl. —en*) intention, purpose, aim.

absondern ['apzɔndərn], *v.a.* separate, set apart; (*Med.*) secrete. *— v.r. sich —*, seclude o.s. from.

abspannen ['apʃpanən], *v.a.* unharness.

absparen ['apʃpa:rən], *v.n. sich etwas vom Munde —*, stint o.s. for s.th.

abspenstig ['apʃpɛnstiç], *adj. —machen*, alienate s.o.'s affections, entice s.o. away; *— werden*, desert.

absperren ['apʃpɛrən], *v.a.* (*door*) lock, shut up; (*street*) close, barricade; (*gas, water*) turn off.

absprechen ['apʃprɛçən], *v.a. irr. einem das Recht —*, deprive s.o. of the right to do s.th.

abspülen

abspülen ['apʃpy:lən], *v.a.* wash up, rinse.

abstammen ['apʃtamən], *v.n.* (aux. sein) descend from, originate from.

Abstand ['apʃtant], *m.* (—es, pl. ⸚e) distance; *von etwas — nehmen*, refrain from doing s.th.

abstatten ['apʃtatən], *v.a. einen Besuch* —, pay a visit; *einen Bericht* —, report on; *Dank* —, return thanks.

abstechen ['abʃtɛçən], *v.a. irr. Tiere* —, slaughter animals. — *v.n. von etwas* —, contrast with s.th.

Abstecher ['apʃtɛçər], *m.* (—s, pl. —) short trip, excursion; detour.

abstecken ['apʃtɛkən], *v.a.* mark off, peg out.

absteigen ['apʃtaigən], *v.n. irr.* (aux. sein) descend, alight, dismount.

abstellen ['apʃtɛlən], *v.a.* put s.th. down; (*gas, water*) turn off.

absterben ['apʃtɛrbən], *v.n. irr.* (aux. sein) wither; die.

Abstieg ['apʃti:k], *m.* (—es, no pl.) descent.

Abstimmung ['apʃtɪmuŋ], *f.* (—, pl. —en) (*Parl.*) division; referendum, voting.

abstoßen ['apʃto:sən], *v.a. irr.* push off, kick off. —*v.n.* (*Naut.*) set sail.

abstoßend ['apʃto:sənt], *adj.* repulsive, repugnant.

abstreifen ['apʃtraifən], *v.a. irr.* strip off, pull off; cast, shed.

abstufen ['apʃtu:fən], *v.a.* grade.

abstumpfen ['apʃtumpfən], *v.a.* blunt, dull, take the edge off.

abstürzen ['apʃtyrtsən], *v.n.* (aux. sein) (*person*) fall; fall down; (*Aviat.*) crash.

Abt [apt], *m.* (—es, pl. ⸚e) abbot.

Abtei ['aptai], *f.* (—, pl. —en) abbey.

Abteil ['aptail], *n.* (—s, pl. —e) compartment.

abteilen ['aptailən], *v.a.* divide, partition.

Abteilung ['aptailuŋ], *f.* (—, pl. —en) section, department.

Äbtissin [ɛp'tɪsɪn], *f.* (—, pl. —nen) abbess.

abtöten ['apto:tən], *v.a.* mortify, deaden.

abtragen ['aptra:gən], *v.a. irr.* carry away; (*building*) demolish; (*dress, shoes*) wear out; *eine Schuld* —, pay a debt.

abtreiben ['aptraibən], *v.a. irr.* (*cattle*) drive off; procure an abortion. — *v.n.* (aux. sein) (*ship*) drift off.

Abtreibung ['aptraibuŋ], *f.* (—, pl. —en) abortion.

abtrennen ['aptrɛnən], *v.a.* (s.th. sewn) unpick; separate.

Abtretung ['aptre:tuŋ], *f.* (—, pl. —en) cession; conveyance.

Abtritt ['aptrɪt], *m.* (—es, pl. —e) W.C.; (*Theat.*) exit or exeunt.

abtrocknen ['aptrɔknən], *v.a.* dry.

abtrünnig ['aptrynɪç], *adj.* disloyal, faithless.

aburteilen ['apurtailən], *v.a.* pass judgment on.

abwägen ['apvɛ:gən], *v.a. gegeneinander* —, weigh against each other.

abwälzen ['apvɛltsən], *v.a. etwas von sich* —, clear o.s. from s.th.

abwandeln ['apvandəln], *v.a.* change; (*verbs*) conjugate; (*nouns*) decline.

abwärts ['apvɛrts], *prep., adv.* downward.

abwaschen ['apvaʃən], *v.a. irr.* wash up.

abwechseln ['apvɛksəln], *v.a.* vary, alternate.

Abweg ['apvɛ:k], *m.* (—es, pl. —e) wrong way; *auf —e geraten*, go astray.

abwehren ['apvɛ:rən], *v.a.* ward off, parry.

abweichen ['apvaiçən], *v.n. irr.* (aux. sein) — *von*, deviate from.

abweisen ['apvaizən], *v.a. irr.* refuse admittance to, rebuff.

abwenden ['apvɛndən], *v.a. irr.* avert, prevent. — *v.r. sich* —, turn away from.

abwesend ['apvɛ:zənt], *adj.* absent.

Abwesenheit ['apvɛ:zənhait], *f.* (—, pl. —en) absence.

abwickeln ['apvɪkəln], *v.a.* uncoil; (*business*) wind up.

abwischen ['apvɪʃən], *v.a.* wipe clean; *sich die Stirn* —, mop o.'s brow.

abzahlen ['aptsa:lən], *v.a.* pay off; pay by instalments.

abzehren ['aptse:rən], *v.n.* (aux. sein) waste away.

Abzeichen ['aptsaiçən], *n.* (—s, pl. —) badge, insignia.

abzeichnen ['apsaiçnən], *v.a.* sketch, draw from a model. — *v.r. sich* —, become clear.

abziehen ['aptsi:ən], *v.a. irr.* deduct, subtract; (*knife*) sharpen; strip (a bed). — *v.n.* (aux. sein) depart; (*Mil.*) march off.

Abzug ['aptsu:k], *m.* (—es, pl. ⸚e) retreat, departure; photographic copy; — *der Kosten*, deduction of charges; (*steam, air*) outlet.

abzweigen ['aptsvaigən], *v.n.* (aux. sein) fork off, branch off.

Achsel ['aksəl], *f.* (—, pl. —n) shoulder; *die —n zucken*, shrug o.'s shoulders.

Acht [axt], *f.* (—, no pl.) attention, care, caution, heed; *achtgeben*, pay attention; *sich in — acht nehmen*, be careful; ban, excommunication, outlawry; *in — und Bann tun*, outlaw, proscribe.

acht [axt], *num. adj.* eight; *in — Tagen*, in a week; *vor — Tagen*, a week ago.

achtbar ['axtba:r], *adj.* respectable.

achten ['axtən], *v.a.* hold in esteem, value; — *auf*, pay attention to, keep an eye on.

ächten ['ɛxtən], *v.a.* ban, outlaw, proscribe.

achtlos ['axtlo:s], *adj.* inattentive, negligent.

achtsam ['axtza:m], *adj.* attentive, careful.

Achtung ['axtuŋ], *f.* (—, no pl.) esteem, regard; (*Mil.*) attention!

Ächtung ['ɛxtuŋ], *f.* (—, no pl.) ban, proscription.

achtzehn ['axtse:n], *num. adj.* eighteen.

achtzig ['axtsɪç], *num. adj.* eighty.
ächzen ['ɛçtsən], *v.n.* groan.
Acker ['akər], *m.* (—s, *pl.* ̈) field, arable land; *den — bestellen,* till the soil.
ackern ['akərn], *v.n.* till (the land).
addieren [a'di:rən], *v.a.* add, add up.
Adel ['a:dəl], *m.* (—s, *no pl.*) nobility, aristocracy.
ad(e)lig ['a:dlɪç], *adj.* of noble birth, aristocratic.
Ader ['a:dər], *f.* (—, *pl.* —n) vein; *zu — lassen,* bleed s.o.
Adler ['a:dlər], *m.* (—s, *pl.* —) eagle.
Adresse [a'drɛsə], *f.* (—, *pl.* —n) address.
adrett [a'drɛt], *adj.* neat, adroit, smart.
Affe ['afə], *m.* (—n, *pl.* —n) ape, monkey; *(fig.)* fool.
affektiert [afɛk'ti:rt], *adj.* affected, giving o.s. airs.
äffen ['ɛfən], *v.a.* ape, mimic.
Afghanistan [af'ganistan], *n.* Afghanistan.
Afrika ['a:frika], *n.* Africa.
After ['aftər], *m.* (—s, *pl.* —) anus.
Agentur [agɛn'tu:r], *f.* (—, *pl.* —en) agency.
Agraffe [a'grafə], *f.* (—, *pl.* —n) brooch, clasp.
Agrarier [a'gra:rjər], *m.* (—s, *pl.* —) landed proprietor.
Ägypten [ɛ'gyptən], *n.* Egypt.
Ahle ['a:lə], *f.* (—, *pl.* —n) awl, bodkin.
Ahn [a:n], *m.* (—en, *pl.* —en) ancestor, forefather.
ahnden ['a:ndən], *v.a.* avenge, punish.
Ahne ['a:nə] *see* **Ahn**.
ähneln ['ɛ:nəln], *v.a.* resemble, look like.
ahnen ['a:nən], *v.a., v.n.* have a presentiment, foresee, have a hunch.
ähnlich ['ɛ:nlɪç], *adj.* resembling, like, similar.
Ahnung ['a:nuŋ], *f.* (—, *pl.* —en) foreboding, presentiment, idea, *(Am.)* hunch.
Ahorn ['a:hɔrn], *m.* (—s, *pl.* —e) *(Bot.)* maple.
Ähre ['ɛ:rə], *f.* (—, *pl.* —n) ear of corn.
Akademiker [aka'de:mɪkər], *m.* (—s, *pl.* —) university graduate.
akademisch [aka'de:mɪʃ], *adj.* academic; *— gebildet,* with a university education.
Akazie [a'ka:tsjə], *f.* (—, *pl.* —n) *(Bot.)* acacia.
akklimatisieren [aklimati'zi:rən], *v.r. sich —,* become acclimatised.
Akkord [a'kɔrt], *m.* (—es, *pl.* —e) *(Mus.)* chord; *in — arbeiten,* work on piece-rates.
Akt [akt], *m.* (—es, *pl.* —e) deed, action; *(Theat.)* act; *(Art)* (depiction of the nude.
Akte ['aktə], *f.* (—, *pl.* —n) document, deed; *(pl.)* records, files; *zu den —n legen,* pigeonhole, shelve.
Aktenstück ['aktənʃtyk], *n.* (—es, *pl.* —e) official document, file.
Aktie ['aktsjə], *f.* (—, *pl.* —n) *(Comm.)* share, *(Am.)* stock.

Aktiengesellschaft ['aktsjəngəzɛlʃaft], *f.* (—, *pl.* —en) joint stock company.
Aktionär [aktsjo'nɛ:r], *m.* (—s, *pl.* —e) shareholder, *(Am.)* stockholder.
Aktiv ['akti:f], *n.* (—s, *pl.* —e) *(Gram.)* active voice.
Aktiva [ak'ti:va], *n. pl. (Comm.)* assets.
aktuell [aktu'ɛl], *adj.* topical.
akzentuieren [aktsɛntu'i:rən], *v.a.* accentuate, stress, emphasize.
Albanien [al'ba:njən], *n.* Albania.
albern ['albərn], *adj.* silly, foolish.
Aliment [ali'mɛnt], *n.* (—es, *pl.* —e) *(usually pl.—e)* alimony, maintenance.
Alkali [al'ka:li], *n.* (—s, *pl.* —en) alkali.
Alkohol ['alkoho:l], *m.* (—s, *no pl.)* alcohol.
Alkoholiker [alko'ho:lɪkər], *m.* (—s, *pl.* —) drunkard, alcoholic.
All [al], *n.* (—s, *no pl.)* the universe, (outer) space.
all [al], *adj.* all, entire, whole; every, each, any.
alle ['alə], *adj.* all, everybody; *— beide,* both of them.
Allee [a'le:], *f.* (—, *pl.* —n) tree-lined walk, avenue.
allein [a'laɪn], *adj.* alone, sole. — *adv.* solely, only, merely. — *conj. (obs.)* only, but, however.
alleinig [a'laɪnɪç], *adj.* sole, only, exclusive.
allenfalls [alən'fals], *adv.* possibly, perhaps, if need be.
allenthalben [alənt'halbən], *adv.* everywhere, in all places.
allerdings [alər'dɪŋs], *adv.* of course, indeed, nevertheless.
allerhand [alər'hant], *adj.* of all sorts or kinds, various; *das ist ja —!* I say!
Allerheiligen [alər'haɪlɪgən], *pl.* All Saints' Day.
allerlei [alər'laɪ], *adj.* miscellaneous, various.
allerliebst [alər'li:pst], *adj. (Am.)* cute; charming.
allerseits ['alərzaɪts], *adv.* generally, on all sides, universally.
alles ['aləs], *adj.* everything, all.
allgemein [algə'maɪn], *adj.* universal, common, general.
alliieren [ali'i:rən], *v.a., v.n.* ally (o.s.).
allmächtig [al'mɛçtɪç], *adj.* omnipotent.
allmählich [al'mɛ:lɪç], *adj.* by degrees, gradual.
allseitig ['alzaɪtɪç], *adj.* universal, *(Am.)* all-round.
Alltag ['alta:k], *m.* (—s, *pl.* —e) working day, week-day.
allwissend [al'vɪsənt], *adj.* omniscient.
allzu ['altsu:], *adv.* too, much too.
Alm [alm], *f.* (—, *pl.* —en) Alpine meadow.
Almosen ['almo:zən], *n.* (—s, *pl.* —) alms, charity.
Alp [alp], *f.* (—, *pl.* —en) *(mostly pl.)* mountain(s), Alps.
Alpdrücken ['alpdrykən], *n.* (—s, *no pl.*) nightmare.

5

als [als], *conj.* than; (*after comparatives*) than; as, like; but; *er hat nichts — Schulden*, he has nothing but debts; (*temp.*) when, as.

alsbald [als'balt], *adv.* forthwith.

also ['alzo:], *adv.* thus, so, in this manner. — *conj.* consequently, therefore.

Alt [alt], *m.* (—**s**, *pl.* —**e**) (*Mus.*) alto.

alt [alt], *adj.* old, ancient; aged; antique.

Altan [al'ta:n], *m.* (—**s**, *pl.* —**e**) balcony, gallery.

Altar [al'ta:r], *m.* (—**s**, *pl.* ⁀e) altar.

altbacken ['altbakən], *adj.* stale.

Alter ['altər], *n.* (—**s**, *no pl.*) age, old age; epoch.

altern ['altərn], *v.n.* (*aux.* sein) grow old.

Altertum ['altərtu:m], *n.* (—**s**, *pl.* ⁀er) antiquity.

Altistin [al'tɪstɪn], *f.* (—, *pl.* —**nen**) (*Mus.*) contralto.

altklug ['altklu:k], *adj.* precocious.

ältlich ['ɛltlɪç], *adj.* elderly.

Altweibersommer [alt'vaɪbərzɔmər], *m.* (—**s**, *pl.* —) Indian summer.

Amboß ['ambɔs], *m.* (—**sses**, *pl.* —**sse**) anvil.

Ameise ['a:maɪzə], *f.* (—, *pl.* —**n**) (*Ent.*) ant.

Amerika [a'me:rika], *n.* America.

Amme ['amə], *f.* (—, *pl.* —**n**) wet nurse.

Ammoniak [amon'jak], *n.* (—**s**, *no pl.*) ammonia.

Ampel ['ampəl], *f.* (—, *pl.* —**n**) (hanging) light, lamp, lantern; traffic light.

Ampfer ['ampfər], *m.* (—**s**, *pl.* —) (*Bot.*) sorrel, dock.

Amsel ['amzəl], *f.* (—, *pl.* —**n**) (*Orn.*) blackbird.

Amt [amt], *n.* (—**es**, *pl.* ⁀er) office, post, employment; administration, domain, jurisdiction; place of public business.

amtlich ['amtlɪç], *adj.* official.

Amtmann ['amtman], *m.* (—**s**, *pl.* ⁀er) bailiff.

Amtsblatt ['amtsblat], *n.* (—**es**, *pl.* ⁀er) official gazette.

Amtsgericht ['amtsgərɪçt], *n.* (—**s**, *pl.* —**e**) county court; (*Am.*) district court.

amüsieren [amy'zi:rən], *v.a.* amuse.— *v.r. sich* —, enjoy o.s.

an [an], *prep.* (*Dat.* or *Acc.*), at, to, on.

analog [ana'lo:k], *adj.* analogous.

Ananas ['ananas], *f.* (—, *pl.* —) pineapple.

Anatom [ana'to:m], *m.* (—**en**, *pl.* —**en**) anatomist.

anbahnen ['anba:nən], *v.a.* initiate, open up, pave the way for.

anbändeln ['anbɛndəln], *v.n.* — *mit*, flirt with, make up to.

Anbau ['anbau], *m.* (—**s**, *pl.* —**ten**) (*grain*) cultivation; annex(e), wing (of building).

anbauen ['anbauən], *v.a.* cultivate; add to a building.

anbei [an'baɪ], *adv.* enclosed (in letter).

anbeißen ['anbaɪsən], *v.a. irr.* bite at,

take a bite of. — *v.n.* (*fish*) bite; (*coll.*) take the bait.

anbelangen ['anbəlaŋən], *v.a.* concern.

anberaumen ['anbəraumən], *v.a.* fix (a date).

anbeten ['anbe:tən], *v.a.* worship, adore, idolise.

anbiedern ['anbi:dərn], *v.r. sich mit einem —,* chum up with s.o.

anbieten ['anbi:tən], *v.a. irr.* offer.

anbinden ['anbɪndən], *v.a. irr.* tie on, bind to; *kurz angebunden sein,* be curt.

Anblick ['anblɪk], *m.* (—**s**, *no pl.*) view, sight, aspect, spectacle.

anbrechen ['anbrɛçən], *v.a. irr.* begin; break; start on. — *v.n.* dawn.

anbrennen ['anbrɛnən], *v.a. irr.* light, set fire to, burn. — *v.n.* (*aux.* sein) catch fire; burn.

anbringen ['anbrɪŋən], *v.a. irr.* fit to, place.

Anbruch ['anbrux], *m.* (—**s**, *no pl.*) beginning; — *der Nacht,* night-fall.

anbrüllen ['anbrylən], *v.a.* roar at.

Andacht ['andaxt], *f.* (—, *pl.* —**en**) (*Eccl.*) devotion(s).

andächtig ['andɛxtɪç], *adj.* devout.

andauern ['andauərn], *v.n.* last, continue.

Andenken ['andɛŋkən], *n.* (—**s**, *pl.* —) memory; keepsake; souvenir.

anderer ['andərər], *adj.* other, different; *ein —,* another.

andermal ['andərma:l], *adv. ein —,* another time.

ändern ['ɛndərn], *v.a.* alter, change.

andernfalls ['andərnfals], *adv.* otherwise, or else.

anders ['andərs], *adv.* differently, in another manner, otherwise.

anderthalb ['andərthalp], *adj.* one and a half.

anderweitig ['andərvaɪtɪç], *adj.* elsewhere.

andeuten ['andɔytən], *v.a.* hint at, intimate, indicate.

Andrang ['andraŋ], *m.* (—**es**, *no pl.*) throng, crowd.

aneignen ['anaɪgnən], *v.r. sich etwas —,* appropriate s.th.; (*an opinion*) adopt.

anekeln ['ane:kəln], *v.a.* disgust.

Anerbieten ['anɛrbi:tən], *n.* (—**s**, *pl.* —) offer.

anerkennen ['anɛrkɛnən], *v.a. irr.* acknowledge, appreciate, recognize, accept.

anfachen ['anfaxən], *v.a.* kindle (a flame).

Anfahrt ['anfa:rt], *f.* (—, *pl.* —**en**) drive; (*down a mine*) descent; (*Am.*) drive-way.

Anfall ['anfal], *m.* (—**s**, *pl.* ⁀e) attack, assault; (*Med.*) seizure, fit; (*mood*) fit, burst.

anfallen ['anfalən], *v.a. irr. einen —,* attack s.o.

Anfang ['anfaŋ], *m.* (—**s**, *pl.* ⁀e) beginning, start, commencement.

anfangen [ˈanfaŋən], *v.a. irr.* begin, start. — *v.n.* begin, originate.

Anfänger [ˈanfɛŋər], *m.* (**—s**, *pl.* **—**) beginner, novice.

anfänglich [ˈanfɛŋlɪç], *adv.* in the beginning, at first, initially.

anfassen [ˈanfasən], *v.a.* take hold of; touch; seize.

anfechtbar [ˈanfɛçtbaːr], *adj.* disputable, refutable, debatable.

anfechten [ˈanfɛçtən], *v.a.* (*a will, a verdict*) contest; (*jurors*) challenge.

anfeinden [ˈanfaɪndən], *v.a.* show enmity to.

anfertigen [ˈanfɛrtɪgən], *v.a.* make, manufacture, prepare; (*a list*) draw up.

anflehen [ˈanfleːən], *v.a.* implore, beseech.

Anflug [ˈanfluːk], *m.* (**—s**, *pl.* ⁀e) (*Aviat.*) approach; (*beard*) down; touch.

anfordern [ˈanfɔrdərn], *v.a.* demand, claim.

Anfrage [ˈanfraːgə], *f.* (**—**, *pl.* **—n**) enquiry.

anfügen [ˈanfyːgən], *v.a.* join to, annex.

anführen [ˈanfyːrən], *v.a.* lead; adduce, quote (examples), cite; *einen* —, dupe s.o., take s.o. in.

Anführungszeichen [ˈanfyːruŋstsaɪçən], *n.* (**—s**, *pl.* **—**) inverted commas, quotation marks.

anfüllen [ˈanfylən], *v.a. wieder* —, replenish.

Angabe [ˈanɡaːbə], *f.* (**—**, *pl.* **—n**) declaration, statement; data; instruction; bragging.

angeben [ˈanɡeːbən], *v.a. irr.* declare, state; *den Ton* —, lead the fashion; *den Wert* —, declare the value of.— *v.n. groß* —, brag, show off.

Angeber [ˈanɡeːbər], *m.* (**—s**, *pl.* **—**) informer; braggart.

Angebinde [ˈanɡəbɪndə], *n.* (**—s**, *pl.* **—**) (*obs.*) present, gift.

angeblich [ˈanɡeːplɪç], *adj.* ostensible, alleged, so-called.

angeboren [ˈanɡəboːrən], *adj.* innate, inborn.

Angebot [ˈanɡəboːt], *n.* (**—es**, *pl.* ⁀e) offer, tender, bid; (*Comm.*) — *und Nachfrage*, supply and demand.

angebracht [ˈanɡəbraxt], *adj.* apt, appropriate, opportune.

angedeihen [ˈanɡədaɪən], *v.n. einem etwas* — *lassen*, bestow s.th. on s.o.

angegossen [ˈanɡəɡosən], *adj. das sitzt wie* —, it fits like a glove.

angehen [ˈanɡeːən], *v.a. irr. einen um etwas* —, apply to s.o. for s.th.; *das geht Dich nichts an*, that is none of your business.

angehören [ˈanɡəhøːrən], *v.n.* belong to.

Angehörige [ˈanɡəhøːrɪgə], *m., f.* (**—n**, *pl.* **—n**) near relative; next of kin.

Angeklagte [ˈanɡəklaːktə], *m., f.* (**—n**, *pl.* **—n**) the accused, defendant, prisoner at the bar.

Angel [ˈaŋəl], *f.* (**—**, *pl.* **—n**) fishing-rod; (*door*) hinge, pivot; *zwischen Tür und* —, in passing.

angelegen [ˈanɡəleːgən], *adj. sich etwas* — *sein lassen*, interest o.s. in s.th., concern o.s. in s.th.; *ich werde es mir* — *sein lassen*, I shall make it my business.

Angelegenheit [ˈanɡələgənhaɪt], *f.* (**—**, *pl.* **—en**) concern, matter, affair.

angeln [ˈaŋəln], *v.a.* fish, angle.

angemessen [ˈanɡəmɛsən], *adj.* proper, suitable, appropriate.

angenehm [ˈanɡəneːm], *adj.* acceptable, agreeable, pleasing, pleasant.

angenommen [ˈanɡənɔmən], *conj.* — *daß*, given that, supposing that, say.

Anger [ˈaŋər], *m.* (**—s**, *pl.* **—**) grassplot; green, common.

angesehen [ˈanɡəzeːən], *adj.* respected, esteemed, distinguished.

Angesicht [ˈanɡəzɪçt], *n.* (**—s**, *pl.* **—er**) face, countenance.

angestammt [ˈanɡəʃtamt], *adj.* ancestral, hereditary.

Angestellte [ˈanɡəʃtɛltə], *m., f.* (**—n**, *pl.* **—n**) employee; (*pl.*) staff.

Angler [ˈaŋlər], *m.* (**—s**, *pl.* **—**) angler, fisherman.

angliedern [ˈanɡliːdərn], *v.a.* annex, attach.

Anglist [aŋˈɡlɪst], *m.* (**—en**, *pl.* **—en**) (*Univ.*) professor or student of English.

angreifen [ˈanɡraɪfən], *v.a. irr.* handle, touch; (*capital*) break into; attack, assail; *es greift mich an*, it taxes my strength.

angrenzen [ˈanɡrɛntsən], *v.n.* border upon, adjoin.

Angriff [ˈanɡrɪf], *m.* (**—s**, *pl.* **—e**) offensive, attack, assault.

Angst [aŋst], *f.* (**—**, *pl.* ⁀e) anxiety; fear; anguish.

ängstigen [ˈɛŋstɪgən], *v.a.* alarm, frighten. — *v.r. sich* —, feel uneasy, be afraid.

angucken [ˈanɡukən], *v.a.* look at.

anhaben [ˈanhaːbən], *v.a. irr.* have on, be dressed in, wear; *einem etwas* —, hold s.th. against s.o.

anhaften [ˈanhaftən], *v.n.* stick to, adhere to.

Anhalt [ˈanhalt], *m.* (**—es**, *no pl.*) support, basis.

anhalten [ˈanhaltən], *v.a. irr. einen* —, stop s.o. — *v.n.* stop, pull up, halt; *um ein Mädchen* —, ask for a girl's hand in marriage. — *v.r. sich an etwas halten*, cling to, hang on to s.th.

Anhaltspunkt [ˈanhaltspuŋkt], *m.* (**—es**, *pl.* **—e**) clue, (*Am.*) lead.

Anhang [ˈanhaŋ], *m.* (**—s**, *pl.* ⁀e) appendix, supplement.

anhängen [ˈanhɛŋən], *v.a. irr.* hang on, fasten to, attach.

Anhänger [ˈanhɛŋər], *m.* (**—s**, *pl.* **—**) follower, adherent; (*Footb.*) supporter; pendant (on a necklace); label; (*Transp.*) trailer.

anhänglich [ˈanhɛŋlɪç], *adj.* attached, affectionate.

Anhängsel [ˈanhɛŋsəl], *n.* (—s, *pl.* —) appendage.

anhauchen [ˈanhauxən], *v.a.* breathe upon.

anhäufen [ˈanhɔyfən], *v.a.* heap up, pile up, amass. —*v.r. sich* —, accumulate.

anheben [ˈanheːbən], *v.a. irr.* lift. — *v.n.* (*obs.*) begin.

anheim [anˈhaɪm], *adv.* — *stellen*, leave to s.o.'s discretion.

anheimeln [ˈanhaɪməln], *v.a.* remind one of home.

anheischig [ˈanhaɪʃɪç], *adj. sich* — *machen*, undertake, pledge o.s.

Anhieb [ˈanhiːp], *m.* (—s, *pl.* —e) (*fencing*) first stroke; *auf* —, at the first attempt.

Anhöhe [ˈanhøːə], *f.* (—, *pl.* —n) hill, rising ground.

anhören [ˈanhøːrən], *v.a.* listen to; tell by s.o.'s voice *or* accent.

animieren [aniˈmiːrən], *v.a.* instigate, egg on.

ankämpfen [ˈankɛmpfən], *v.n. gegen etwas* —, struggle against s.th.

ankaufen [ˈankaufən], *v.a.* purchase, buy. — *v.r. sich irgendwo* —, buy land somewhere.

Anker [ˈaŋkər], *m.* (—s, *pl.* —) (*Naut.*) anchor; *den* — *auswerfen*, cast anchor.

ankern [ˈaŋkərn], *v.a., v.n.* anchor, cast anchor.

Anklage [ˈanklaːgə], *f.* (—, *pl.* —n) accusation; *gegen einen* — *erheben*, bring a charge against s.o.

Ankläger [ˈanklɛːgər], *m.* (—s, *pl.* —) accuser, prosecutor; plaintiff.

Anklang [ˈanklaŋ], *m.* (—s, *pl.* —e) reminiscence; — *finden*, please, meet with approval.

ankleben [ˈankleːbən], *v.a.* stick to, glue to, paste on.

ankleiden [ˈanklaɪdən], *v.a.* dress. — *v.r. sich* —, dress o.s., get dressed.

anklingeln [ˈanklɪŋəln], *v.a.* (*coll.*) *einen* —, ring s.o. up (on the telephone).

anklopfen [ˈanklɔpfən], *v.n.* knock.

anknüpfen [ˈanknypfən], *v.a.* tie; join on to; *ein Gespräch* —, start a conversation; *wieder* —, resume.

ankommen [ˈankɔmən], *v.n. irr.* (*aux.* sein) arrive; *es kommt darauf an*, it depends upon.

ankreiden [ˈankraɪdən], *v.a.* chalk up.

ankündigen [ˈankyndɪgən], *v.a.* announce, advertise, give notice of, proclaim.

Ankunft [ˈankunft], *f.* (—, *no pl.*) arrival.

ankurbeln [ˈankurbəln], *v.a.* (*Motor.*) crank up.

Anlage [ˈanlaːgə], *f.* (—, *pl.* —n) (*capital*) investment; enclosure (*with a letter*); (*industrial*) plant; (*building*) lay-out; *öffentliche* —, pleasure grounds; talent.

anlangen [ˈanlaŋən], *v.n.* (*aux.* sein) arrive; concern; *was das anlangt*, as far as this is concerned.

Anlaß [ˈanlas], *m.* (—sses, *pl.* —sse) cause, occasion, motive.

anlassen [ˈanlasən], *v.a. irr.* keep on; (*Motor.*) start. — *v.r. sich gut* —, promise well.

Anlasser [ˈanlasər], *m.* (—s, *pl.* —) (*Motor.*) starter.

anläßlich [ˈanlɛslɪç], *prep.* (*Genit.*) à propos of, on the occasion of.

Anlauf [ˈanlauf], *m.* (—s, *pl.* —e) start, run, (*Aviat.*) take-off run.

anlaufen [ˈanlaufən], *v.n. irr.* tarnish; call at (port).

anlegen [ˈanleːgən], *v.a. Geld* —, invest money; *Kleider* —, don clothes; *einen Garten* —, lay out a garden; *Hand* —, give a helping hand; *auf einen* —, take aim at s.o.; (*Naut.*) land, dock.

Anlegestelle [ˈanleːgəʃtɛlə], *f.* (—, *pl.* —n) landing place.

anlehnen [ˈanleːnən], *v.r. sich an etwas* —, lean against s.th.

Anleihe [ˈanlaɪə], *f.* (—, *pl.* —n) loan, *öffentliche* —, government loan; *eine* — *machen*, raise a loan.

anleiten [ˈanlaɪtən], *v.a.* train, instruct.

anlernen [ˈanlɛrnən], *v.a. einen* —, train, apprentice s.o. (in a craft).

Anliegen [ˈanliːgən], *n.* (—s, *pl.* —) request, petition, concern.

anmachen [ˈanmaxən], *v.a.* fix, fasten; light (a fire).

anmaßen [ˈanmaːsən], *v.a. sich etwas* —, arrogate s.th.

anmaßend [ˈanmaːsənt], *adj.* arrogant.

anmelden [ˈanmɛldən], *v.a.* announce, (*claim*) give notice of. — *v.r. sich* —, notify o.'s arrival, make an appointment; *sich* — *lassen*, send in o.'s name.

Anmeldungsformular [anˈmɛlduŋsfɔrmulaːr], *n.* (—s, *pl.* —e) registration form.

Anmerkung [ˈanmɛrkuŋ], *f.* (—, *pl.* —en) remark, annotation, footnote.

anmessen [ˈanmɛsən], *v.a. irr.* measure (s.o. for a garment).

Anmut [ˈanmuːt], *f.* (—, *no pl.*) grace, charm.

annähen [ˈannɛːən], *v.a.* sew on (to).

annähern [ˈannɛːərn], *v.r. sich* —, approach, draw near; (*Maths.*) approximate.

Annäherung [ˈannɛːəruŋ], *f.* (—, *pl.* —en) approach; (*Maths.*) approximation.

Annahme [ˈannaːmə], *f.* (—, *pl.* —n) acceptance; assumption, hypothesis.

annehmbar [ˈannɛːmbaːr], *adj.* acceptable; *ganz* —, passable.

annehmen [ˈannɛːmən], *v.a. irr.* take, accept, take delivery of; suppose, assume, presume; *an Kindes Statt* —, adopt.

Annehmlichkeit [ˈannɛːmlɪçkaɪt], *f.* (—, *pl.* —en) amenity, comfort.

Annonce [anˈnɔ̃ːsə], *f.* (—, *pl.* —n) (classified) advertisement (in newspaper).

anordnen [ˈanɔrdnən], *v.a.* arrange, regulate; order, direct.

anorganisch ['anɔrgaːnɪʃ], *adj.* inorganic.

anpacken ['anpakən], *v.a.* get hold of, seize, grasp.

anpassen ['anpasən], *v.a.* fit, suit. — *v.r. sich —*, adapt o.s.

anpflanzen ['anpflantsən], *v.a.* plant, grow.

Anprall ['anpral], *m.* (—s, *no pl.*) impact, bounce, shock.

anpumpen ['anpumpən], *v.a.* (*coll.*) *einen —*, borrow money from s.o.

anrechnen ['anrɛçnən], *v.a. einem etwas —*, charge s.o. with s.th.; *einem etwas hoch —*, think highly of a person for s.th.

Anrecht ['anrɛçt], *n.* (—es, *no pl.*) — *auf*, title to, claim to.

Anrede ['anreːdə], *f.* (—, *pl.* —n) (form of) address, title.

anreden ['anreːdən], *v.a.* address (s.o.).

anregen ['anreːgən], *v.a.* stimulate (s.o.); suggest (s.th.).

Anregung ['anreːguŋ], *f.* (—, *pl.* —en) suggestion, hint.

Anreiz ['anraɪts], *m.* (—es, *no pl.*) incentive; impulse.

Anrichte ['anrɪçtə], *f.* (—, *pl.* —n) dresser, sideboard.

anrichten ['anrɪçtən], *v.a.* (*meal*) prepare, serve (up); *Unheil —*, make mischief.

anrüchig ['anryːçɪç], *adj.* disreputable.

anrücken ['anrykən], *v.a.* bring near to. — *v.n.* (*aux.* sein) approach.

Anruf ['anruːf], *m.* (—s, *pl.* —e) (*by sentry*) challenge; telephone call.

anrufen ['anruːfən], *v.a. irr.* call to, challenge; implore; ring up; *Gott —*, invoke God.

anrühren ['anryːrən], *v.a.* handle, touch; (*Cul.*) mix.

Ansage ['anzaːgə], *f.* (—, *pl.* —n) announcement.

ansagen ['anzaːgən], *v.a.* announce, notify.

Ansager ['anzaːgər], *m.* (—s, *pl.* —) announcer; compère.

ansammeln ['anzaməln], *v.a.* accumulate, gather. — *v.r. sich —*, gather, foregather, congregate, collect.

ansässig ['anzɛsɪç], *adj.* domiciled, resident; *sich — machen*, settle.

Ansatz ['anzats], *m.* (—es, *pl.* —e) start; (*Maths.*) construction; disposition (to), tendency (to).

anschaffen ['anʃafən], *v.a.* buy, purchase, get.

anschauen ['anʃauən], *v.a.* look at, view.

anschaulich ['anʃaulɪç], *adj.* clear; *einem etwas — machen*, give s.o. a clear idea of s.th.

Anschauung ['anʃauuŋ], *f.* (—, *pl.* —en) view, perception; *nach meiner —*, in my opinion.

Anschein ['anʃaɪn], *m.* (—s, *no pl.*) appearance, semblance.

anscheinend ['anʃaɪnənt], *adj.* apparent, ostensible, seeming.

anschicken ['anʃɪkən], *v.r. sich — zu*, prepare for, get ready for.

anschirren ['anʃɪrən], *v.a.* (*horses*) harness.

Anschlag ['anʃlaːk], *m.* (—s, *pl.* —e) poster, placard; — *auf das Leben*, attempt at assassination.

Anschlagbrett ['anʃlaːkbrɛt], *n.* (—es, *pl.* —er) notice-board.

anschlagen ['anʃlaːgən], *v.a. irr.* (*keys of piano or typewriter*) strike, touch; (*knitting*) cast on; *zu hoch —*, overestimate.

anschließen ['anʃliːsən], *v.a. irr.* fasten with a lock. — *v.r. sich —*, join in; (*club*) join.

Anschluß ['anʃlus], *m.* (—sses, *pl.* —sse) (*Railw., telephone*) connection; (*Pol.*) annexation.

Anschlußpunkt ['anʃluspuŋkt], *m.* (—es, *pl.* —e) junction; (*Elec.*) inlet point, power point.

anschmiegen ['anʃmiːgən], *v.r. sich —*, nestle closely to.

anschmieren ['anʃmiːrən], *v.a. einen —*, (*coll.*) deceive, cheat s.o.

anschnallen ['anʃnalən], *v.a.* buckle on.

anschnauzen ['anʃnautsən], *v.a.* snarl at, snap at.

anschneiden ['anʃnaɪdən], *v.a. irr.* cut into; *ein Thema —*, broach a subject.

Anschrift ['anʃrɪft], *f.* (—, *pl.* —en) address.

anschwellen ['anʃvɛlən], *v.n.* (*aux.* sein) swell.

Ansehen ['anzeːən], *n.* (—s, *no pl.*) respect; reputation; authority.

ansehen ['anzeːən], *v.a. irr.* look at *or* upon, consider, regard.

ansehnlich ['anzeːnlɪç], *adj.* considerable, appreciable.

anseilen ['anzaɪlən], *v.a.* (*Mount.*) rope together.

ansetzen ['anzɛtsən], *v.a.* join to; (*Maths.*) start, write out (an equation).

Ansicht ['anzɪçt], *f.* (—, *pl.* —en) opinion; view; (*Comm.*) approval.

ansichtig ['anzɪçtɪç], *adj.* — *werden*, get a glimpse of.

Ansichts(post)karte ['anzɪçts(post)kartə], *f.* (—, *pl.* —n) picture postcard.

ansiedeln ['anziːdəln], *v.r. sich —*, settle (down), colonize.

Ansinnen ['anzɪnən], *n.* (—s, *pl.* —) demand, suggestion.

anspannen ['anʃpanən], *v.a.* tighten yoke, stretch; harness.

anspielen ['anʃpiːlən], *v.n.* (*Game, Sport*) lead off; *auf etwas —*, allude to s.th.

Ansporn ['anʃpɔrn], *m.* (—s, *no pl.*) spur, incentive.

Ansprache ['anʃpraːxə], *f.* (—, *pl.* —n) address, speech, talk.

ansprechen ['anʃprɛçən], *v.a. irr.* address, accost; please.

anspringen ['anʃprɪŋən], *v.a. irr.* leap at. — *v.n.* (*Motor.*) start.

9

Anspruch [ˈanʃprux], *m.* (**—s**, *pl.* ˙ˈe) (*Law*) claim, title.

anspruchsvoll [ˈanʃpruxsfɔl], *adj.* demanding, hard to please.

anstacheln [ˈanʃtaxəln], *v.a.* goad, prod.

Anstalt [ˈanʃtalt], *f.* (**—**, *pl.* **—en**) institution, establishment; *—en treffen*, make arrangements (for).

Anstand [ˈanʃtant], *m.* (**—es**, *no pl.*) propriety; politeness, good manners, good grace; decency; (*Hunt.*) stand, butts.

anständig [ˈanʃtɛndɪç], *adj.* decent, proper, respectable.

Anstandsbesuch [ˈanʃtantsbəzu:x], *m.* (**—es**, *pl.* **—e**) formal visit.

anstandshalber [ˈanʃtantshalbər], *adv.* for decency's sake.

anstandslos [ˈanʃtantslo:s], *adv.* unhesitatingly.

anstarren [ˈanʃtarən], *v.a.* stare at.

anstatt [anˈʃtat], *prep.* (*Genit.*), *conj.* instead of, in lieu of, in the place of.

anstecken [ˈanʃtɛkən], *v.a.* pin on; set fire to; infect.

Ansteckung [ˈanʃtɛkuŋ], *f.* (**—**, *pl.* **—en**) infection, contagion.

anstehen [ˈanʃte:ən], *v.n. irr.* stand in a queue; *— lassen*, put off, delay.

ansteigen [ˈanʃtaɪɡən], *v.n.* (*aux.* sein) rise, increase.

anstellen [ˈanʃtɛlən], *v.a. einen —*, appoint s.o. to a post; employ; *Betrachtungen —*, speculate. *— v.r. sich —*, form a queue, line up.

anstellig [ˈanʃtɛlɪç], *adj.* able, skilful, adroit.

Anstellung [ˈanʃtɛluŋ], *f.* (**—**, *pl.* **—en**) appointment, employment.

anstiften [ˈanʃtɪftən], *v.a.* instigate.

anstimmen [ˈanʃtɪmən], *v.a.* intone.

Anstoß [ˈanʃto:s], *m.* (**—es**, *pl.* ˙ˈe) (*Footb.*) kick-off; *Fehler —*, mark wrong.

Anstreicher [ˈanʃtraɪçər], *m.* (**—s**, *pl.* **—**) house-painter.

anstrengen [ˈanʃtrɛŋən], *v.a.* strain, exert; *eine Klage gegen einen —*, bring an action against s.o. *— v.r. sich —*, exert o.s.

Anstrengung [ˈanʃtrɛŋuŋ], *f.* (**—**, *pl.* **—en**) exertion, effort.

Anstrich [ˈanʃtrɪç], *m.* (**—s**, *pl.* **—e**) coat of paint.

Ansturm [ˈanʃturm], *m.* (**—s**, *no pl.*) attack, assault, charge.

Ansuchen [ˈanzu:xən], *n.* (**—s**, *pl.* **—**) application, request, petition.

ansuchen [ˈanzu:xən], *v.n. bei einem um etwas —*, apply to s.o. for s.th.

Anteil [ˈantaɪl], *m.* (**—s**, *pl.* **—e**) share, portion; sympathy.

Anteilnahme [ˈantaɪlna:mə], *f.* (**—**, *no pl.*) sympathy.

Antenne [anˈtɛnə], *f.* (**—**, *pl.* **—n**) aerial; antenna.

antik [anˈti:k], *adj.* antique, ancient, classical.

Antike [anˈti:kə], *f.* (**—**, *pl.* **—en**) (classical) antiquity; ancient work of art (statue etc.).

Antiquar [antiˈkva:r], *m.* (**—s**, *pl.* **—e**) second-hand dealer; antiquary.

Antiquariat [antikvaˈrja:t], *n.* (**—s**, *pl.* **—e**) second-hand bookshop.

antiquarisch [antiˈkva:rɪʃ], *adj.* antiquarian, second-hand.

Antlitz [ˈantlɪts], *n.* (**—es**, *pl.* **—e**) countenance, (*Poet.*) face.

Antrag [ˈantra:k], *m.* (**—s**, *pl.* ˙ˈe) proposition, proposal, application; *einen — stellen*, bring in a motion; make application.

antragen [ˈantra:ɡən], *v.a. irr.* propose, make a proposal, offer to.

Antragsformular [ˈantra:ksfɔrmula:r], *n.* (**—s**, *pl.* **—e**) (*Insurance*) proposal form; application form.

Antragsteller [ˈantra:kʃtɛlər], *m.* (**—s**, *pl.* **—**) applicant, mover of a resolution.

antreten [ˈantre:tən], *v.a. irr. ein Amt —*, enter upon an office; *eine Reise —*, set out on a journey. *— v.n.* (*aux.* sein) (*Mil.*) fall in.

Antrieb [ˈantri:p], *m.* (**—s**, *pl.* **—e**) impulse, motive; incentive; *aus eigenem —*, voluntarily.

Antritt [ˈantrɪt], *m.* (**—s**, *no pl.*) start, commencement.

Antrittsvorlesung [ˈantrɪtsforle:zuŋ], *f.* (*Univ.*) inaugural lecture.

antun [ˈantu:n], *v.a. irr. einem etwas —*, do s.th. to s.o.

Antwort [ˈantvɔrt], *f.* (**—**, *pl.* **—en**) answer, reply; *abschlägige —*, refusal, rebuff.

antworten [ˈantvɔrtən], *v.a.* answer, reply to.

anvertrauen [ˈanfɛrtrauən], *v.a. einem etwas —*, entrust s.o. with s.th.; confide in s.o.

anverwandt [ˈanfɛrvant] *see* **verwandt**.

Anwalt [ˈanvalt], *m.* (**—s**, *pl.* ˙ˈe) lawyer, barrister, solicitor, attorney, advocate.

anwandeln [ˈanvandəln], *v.a.* befall.

Anwandlung [ˈanvandluŋ], *f.* (**—**, *pl.* **—en**) fit, turn.

Anwartschaft [ˈanvartʃaft], *f.* (**—**, *pl.* **—en**) (*Law*) reversion; candidacy.

anweisen [ˈanvaɪzən], *v.a. irr.* instruct, direct; *angewiesen sein auf*, depend upon.

Anweisung [ˈanvaɪzuŋ], *f.* (**—**, *pl.* **—en**) instruction, advice, method; (*Comm.*) voucher, credit voucher, cheque.

anwenden [ˈanvɛndən], *v.a. irr.* use, make use of, apply.

Anstoßen [ˈanʃto:sən], *v.a. irr.* knock against, push against; give offence; clink (glasses); border on; *mit der Zunge —*, lisp.

anstößig [ˈanʃtø:sɪç], *adj.* shocking, offensive.

anstreichen [ˈanʃtraɪçən], *v.a. irr.* paint; *Fehler —*, mark wrong.

anwerben ['anverbən], *v.a. irr.* (*Mil.*) recruit; *sich — lassen*, enlist.

anwesend ['anve:zənt], *adj.* at hand, present.

Anwesenheit ['anve:zənhaɪt], *f.* (—, *no pl.*) presence, attendance.

anwidern ['anvi:dərn], *v.a.* disgust.

Anzahl ['antsa:l], *f.* (—, *no pl.*) number, quantity.

anzahlen ['antsa:lən], *v.a.* pay a deposit.

Anzahlung ['antsa:luŋ], *f.* (—, *pl.* —en) deposit.

Anzeichen ['antsaɪçən], *n.* (—s, *pl.* —) indication, omen.

Anzeige ['antsaɪgə], *f.* (—, *pl.* —n) notice, (classified) advertisement; denunciation; — *erstatten*, to lay information.

anzeigen ['antsaɪgən], *v.a.* point out, indicate; announce; notify; advertise; denounce.

Anzeiger ['antsaɪgər], *m.* (—s, *pl.* —) indicator; (*newspaper*) advertiser.

anzetteln ['antsɛtəln], *v.a.* plot, contrive.

anziehen ['antsi:ən], *v.a. irr.* pull, draw tight, give a tug; attract; stretch; dress; (*screws*) tighten. —, *v.r. sich* —, dress, put on o.'s clothes.

anziehend ['antsi:ənt], *adj.* attractive.

Anziehung ['antsi:uŋ], *f.* (—, *no pl.*) attraction.

Anzug ['antsu:k], *m.* (—s, *pl.* ⸚e) (man's) suit; approach.

anzüglich ['antsy:klɪç], *adj.* allusive; suggestive; — *werden*, become offensive.

anzünden ['antsyndən], *v.a.* kindle, ignite.

apart [a'part], *adj.* charming, delightful; (*Am.*) cute.

Apfel ['apfəl], *m.* (—s, *pl.* ⸚) apple.

Apfelmost ['apfəlmɔst], *m.* (—s, *no pl.*) cider.

Apfelsine [apfəl'zi:nə], *f.* (—, *pl.* —n) orange.

Apostel [a'pɔstəl], *m.* (—s, *pl.* —) apostle.

Apotheke [apo'te:kə], *f.* (—, *pl.* —n) dispensary, pharmacy, chemist's shop; (*Am.*) drugstore.

Apparat [apa'ra:t], *m.* (—s, *pl.* —e) apparatus; radio *or* television set; telephone.

appellieren [apɛ'li:rən], *v.n.* — *an*, appeal to.

appetitlich [ape'ti:tlɪç], *adj.* appetising, dainty.

Aprikose [apri'ko:zə], *f.* (—, *pl.* —n) apricot.

Aquarell [akva'rɛl], *n.* (—s, *pl.* —e) water-colour (painting).

Ära ['ɛ:ra], *f.* (—, *no pl.*) era.

Arabien [a'ra:bjən], *n.* Arabia.

Arbeit ['arbaɪt], *f.* (—, *pl.* —en) work, labour; job; employment; workmanship; *an die* — *gehen*, set to work.

arbeiten ['arbaɪtən], *v.a., v.n.* work, labour, toil.

Arbeiter ['arbaɪtər], *m.* (—s, *pl.* —) worker, workman, labourer, hand.

Arbeiterschaft ['arbaɪtərʃaft], *f.* (—, *no pl.*) working men; workers.

arbeitsam ['arbaɪtsa:m], *adj.* industrious, diligent.

Arbeitsamt ['arbaɪtsamt], *n.* (—s, *pl.* ⸚er) labour exchange.

arbeitsfähig ['arbaɪtsfɛ:ɪç], *adj.* capable of working, able-bodied.

arbeitslos ['arbaɪtslo:s], *adj.* unemployed, out of work.

Arbeitslosigkeit ['arbaɪtslo:zɪçkaɪt], *f.* (—, *no pl.*) unemployment.

Arbeitsnachweis ['arbaɪtsnaxvaɪs], *m.* (—es, *no pl.*) labour exchange; (*Am.*) labour registry-office.

Arbeitssperre ['arbaɪtsʃpɛrə], *f.* (—, *pl.* —n) (*Ind.*) lock-out.

Archäologe [arçɛo'lo:gə], *m.* (—n, *pl.* —n) archaeologist.

Arche ['arçə], *f.* (—, *pl.* —n) ark.

Archipel [arçi'pe:l], *m.* (—s, *pl.* —e) archipelago.

architektonisch [arçitɛk'to:nɪʃ], *adj.* architectural.

Archivar [arçi'va:r], *m.* (—s, *pl.* —e) keeper of archives.

arg [ark], *adj.* bad, wicked, mischievous.

Argentinien [argən'ti:njən], *n.* Argentina.

Ärger ['ɛrgər], *m.* (—s, *no pl.*) anger, annoyance.

ärgerlich ['ɛrgərlɪç], *adj.* annoying, aggravating, vexing; angry.

ärgern ['ɛrgərn], *v.a.* annoy, vex, make angry. — *v.r. sich* —, get annoyed.

Ärgernis ['ɛrgərnɪs], *n.* (—ses, *pl.* —se) scandal, nuisance.

arglistig ['arklɪstɪç], *adj.* crafty, sly.

arglos ['arklo:s], *adj.* unsuspecting, guileless, naive.

Argwohn ['arkvo:n], *m.* (—s, *no pl.*) mistrust, suspicion.

argwöhnisch ['arkvo:nɪʃ], *adj.* suspicious, distrustful.

Arie ['a:rjə], *f.* (—, *pl.* —n) (*Mus.*) aria.

Arm [arm], *m.* (—s, *pl.* —e) arm.

arm [arm], *adj.* poor, indigent, needy.

Armaturenbrett [arma'tu:rənbrɛt], *n.* (—s, *no pl.*) dashboard.

Armband ['armbant], *n.* (—s, *pl.* ⸚er) bracelet.

Armbanduhr ['armbantu:r], *f.* (—, *pl.* —en) wrist-watch.

Armbrust ['armbrust], *f.* (—, *pl.* —e) cross-bow.

Ärmel ['ɛrməl], *m.* (—s, *pl.* —) sleeve.

Ärmelkanal ['ɛrməlkana:l], *m.* (—s, *no pl.*) English Channel.

Armenien [ar'me:njən], *n.* Armenia.

Armenhaus ['armənhaus], *n.* (—es, *pl.* ⸚er) poor-house, almshouse.

Armenpfleger ['armənpfle:gər], *m.* (—s, *pl.* —) almoner.

Armesündermiene [armə'zyndərmi:nə], *f.* (—, *pl.* —n) hangdog look.

ärmlich ['ɛrmlɪç], *adj.* poor, shabby, scanty.

armselig ['armze:lɪç], *adj.* poor, miserable, wretched; paltry.

Armut ['armuːt], f. (—, *no pl.*) poverty; *in — geraten*, be reduced to penury.

Arsch [arʃ], m. (—es, ˙ˑe) (*vulg.*) arse.

Arsen(ik) [ar'zeːn(ɪk)], n. (—s, *no pl.*) arsenic.

Art [aːrt], f. (—, *pl.* —en) kind, species; race; sort; method, way, manner.

artig ['aːrtɪç], adj. well-behaved, civil.

Artigkeit ['aːrtɪçkaɪt], f. (—, *pl.* —en) politeness, courtesy.

Artikel [ar'tiːkəl], m. (—s, *pl.* —) article; commodity.

Artist [ar'tɪst], m. (—en, *pl.* —en) artiste (circus, variety).

Arznei [arts'naɪ], f. (—, *pl.* —en) medicine.

Arzneimittel [arts'naɪmɪtəl], n. (—s, *pl.*—) medicine, drug.

Arzt [aːrtst], m. (—es, *pl.* ˙ˑe) doctor, physician; *praktischer —*, general practitioner.

ärztlich ['ɛrtstlɪç], adj. medical.

As (1) [as], n. (—ses, *pl.*—se) (*Mus.*) A flat; — *Dur*, A flat major, — *Moll*, A flat minor.

As (2) [as], n. (—sses, *pl.*—sse) (*Sport*, *cards*) ace.

Asbest [as'bɛst], m. (—s, *no pl.*) asbestos.

Asche ['aʃə], f. (—, *no pl.*) ashes.

Aschenbecher ['aʃənbɛçər], m. (—s, *pl.* —) ash-tray.

Aschenbrödel ['aʃənbrøːdəl]*or* **Aschenputtel** ['aʃənputəl], n. Cinderella.

Aschkraut ['aʃkraut], n. (—s, *pl.* ˙ˑer) (*Bot.*) cineraria.

Askese [as'keːzə], f. (—, *no pl.*) asceticism.

Asket [as'keːt], m. (—en, *pl.* —en) ascetic.

Assessor [a'sɛsɔr], m. (—s, *pl.* —en) assistant; assistant judge.

Ast [ast], m. (—es, *pl.* ˙ˑe) branch, bough.

Aster ['astər], f. (—, *pl.*—n) (*Bot.*) aster.

Astronaut [astro'naut], m. (—en, *pl.* —en) astronaut.

Astronom [astro'noːm], m. (—en, *pl.* —en) astronomer.

Asyl [a'zyːl], n. (—s, *pl.* —e) asylum, sanctuary.

Atem ['aːtəm], m. (—s, *no pl.*) breath, breathing, respiration.

Atemzug ['aːtəmtsuːk], m. (—s, *pl.* ˙ˑe) breath.

Äthiopien [ɛti'oːpjən], n. Ethiopia.

Atlas (1) ['atlas], m. (—sses, *pl.* —sse *and* **Atlanten**) atlas, book of maps.

Atlas (2) ['atlas], m. (—sses, *pl.*—asse) satin.

atmen ['aːtmən], v.n. breathe.

atomar [ato'maːr], adj. atomic.

Attentat [atɛn'taːt], n. (—s, *pl.* —e) attempt on s.o.'s life.

Attest [a'tɛst], n. (—s, *pl.* —e) (*Med.*) certificate.

ätzen ['ɛtsən], v.a. corrode; (*Art*) etch; (*Med.*) cauterise.

auch [aux], *conj.*, *adv.* also, too, likewise, as well.

Au(e) ['au(ə)], f. (—, *pl.* —en) green meadow, pasture.

auf [auf], *prep.* on, upon; *— der Straße*, in the road; *— deine Gefahr*, at your own risk; *— Befehl*, by order; *— einige Tage*, for a few days; *— dem Lande*, in the country; *— keinen Fall*, on no account.

aufatmen ['aufaːtmən], v.n. breathe a sigh of relief.

Aufbau ['aufbau], m. (—s, *no pl.*) building; (*Lit.*) composition, structure.

aufbauen ['aufbauən], v.a. erect, build, construct.

aufbäumen ['aufbɔʏmən], v.r. sich —, (horses) rear.

aufbewahren ['aufbəvaːrən], v.a. keep, store; (*luggage*) take charge of.

Aufbewahrung ['aufbəvaːrun], f. (—, *pl.* —en) storage, safe keeping.

aufbieten ['aufbiːtən], v.a. irr. call up for service; exert (*energies*).

aufbinden ['aufbɪndən], v.a. irr. untie; *einem einen Bären —*, to hoax s.o.

aufblähen ['aufblɛːən], v.a. puff up, swell, inflate.

aufblühen ['aufblyːən], v.n. (*aux.* sein) flourish, unfold.

aufbrausen ['aufbrauzən], v.n. (*aux.* sein) fly into a rage.

aufbringen ['aufbrɪŋən], v.a. irr. bring up; afford; annoy (s.o.).

Aufbruch ['aufbrux], m. (—s, *no pl.*) departure.

aufbürden ['aufbyrdən], v.a. *einem eine Last —*, burden s.o. with a thing.

aufdecken ['aufdɛkən], v.a. uncover, unveil.

aufdonnern ['aufdɔnərn], v.r. sich — dress up showily.

aufdrängen ['aufdrɛŋən], v.a. *einem etwas —*, press s.th. upon s.o. — *v.r. sich —*, force o.'s company on s.o.

aufdrehen ['aufdreːən], v.a. (tap) turn on.

aufdringlich ['aufdrɪŋlɪç], adj. importunate, officious, obtrusive.

Aufdruck ['aufdruk], m. (—s, *pl.* —e) imprint.

aufdrücken ['aufdrykən], v.a. press open; press on s.th.

Aufenthalt ['aufɛnthalt], m. (—s, *pl.* —e) stay, sojourn; delay; stop.

auferlegen ['auferleːgən], v.a. impose; enjoin.

auferstehen ['auferʃteːən], v.n. irr. (*aux.* sein) (*Rel.*) rise from the dead.

auffahren ['auffaːrən], v.n. irr. (*aux.* sein) start (from o.'s sleep); mount; flare up (in anger).

Auffahrt ['auffaːrt], f. (—, *pl.* —en) ascent; approach to a house, drive.

auffallen ['auffalən], v.n. irr. (*aux.* sein) strike the ground; *einem —*, strike s.o., astonish.

auffangen ['auffaŋən], v.a. irr. (*ball*) catch; (*blow*) parry, ward off; (*letter*) intercept.

auffassen ['auffasən], v.a. take in, comprehend.

Auffassung ['auffasuŋ], f. (—, pl. —en) conception, interpretation; view.

aufflackern ['aufflakərn],v.n. (aux. sein) flare up, flicker.

auffordern ['auffɔrdərn], v.a. summon, request, ask, invite.

aufforsten ['auffɔrstən], v.a. afforest.

auffressen ['auffrɛsən], v.a. irr. devour; (of animals) eat up.

auffrischen ['auffrɪʃən], v.a. renew, redecorate; (fig.) brush up.

aufführen ['auffy:rən], v.a. (Theat.) perform; einzeln —, specify, particularise. — v.r. sich —, behave, conduct o.s.

Aufführung ['auffy:ruŋ], f. (—, pl. —en) (Theat.) performance.

Aufgabe ['aufga:bə], f. (—, pl. —n) giving up, abandonment; (letters, telegrams) posting, despatch; (work) task; (Sch.) exercise; (Maths.) problem.

aufgabeln ['aufga:bəln], v.a. (sl.) pick up.

Aufgang ['aufgaŋ], m. (—s, pl. ⁓e) ascent, stairs.

aufgeben ['aufge:bən], v.a. irr. give up, abandon, relinquish; (Am.) quit; (luggage) check.

aufgeblasen ['aufgəbla:zən], adj. conceited, stuck up.

Aufgebot ['aufgəbo:t], n. (—s, pl. —e) (marriage) banns; (Mil.) levy; mit aller Kräfte, with the utmost exertion.

aufgebracht ['aufgəbraxt], adj. angry, annoyed.

aufgedunsen ['aufgədunzən], adj. bloated, sodden.

aufgehen ['aufge:ən], v.n. irr. (aux. sein) (knot) come undone; (sun) rise; (dough) swell, rise; (Maths.) leave no remainder, cancel out.

aufgehoben ['aufgəho:bən], adj. gut — sein, be in good hands.

aufgelegt ['aufgəle:kt], adj. disposed, inclined.

aufgeräumt ['aufgərɔymt], adj. merry, cheerful, in high spirits.

aufgeweckt ['aufgəvɛkt], adj. bright, clever, intelligent.

aufgießen ['aufgi:sən], v.a. irr. Kaffee —, make coffee.

aufgreifen ['aufgraɪfən], v.a. irr. seize.

Aufguß ['aufgus], m. (—sses, pl. ⁓sse) infusion.

aufhalsen ['aufhalzən], v.a. einem etwas —, (coll.) saddle s.o. with s.th.

aufhalten ['aufhaltən], v.a. irr. (door) hold open; einen —, delay s.o. — v.r. sich an einem Ort —, stay at a place; sich über etwas —, find fault with s.th.

aufhängen ['aufhɛŋən], v.a. irr. hang (up).

aufhäufen ['aufhɔyfən], v.a. pile up. — v.r. sich —, accumulate.

Aufheben ['aufhe:bən], n. (—s, no pl.) lifting up; ado; viel —s machen, make a great fuss.

aufheben ['aufhe:bən], v.a. irr. lift (up), pick up; keep, preserve; (laws) repeal, abolish; (agreements) rescind, annul.

Aufhebung ['aufhe:buŋ], f. (—, pl. —en) abolition, abrogation, annulment, repeal.

aufheitern ['aufhaɪtərn], v.a. cheer up; amuse. — v.r. sich —, (weather) brighten, clear up.

aufhelfen ['aufhɛlfən], v.n. irr. einem —, help s.o. up.

aufhellen ['aufhɛlən], v.r. sich —, (weather) clear up; (face) brighten up.

aufhetzen ['aufhɛtsən],v.a. rouse (s.o.); einen — gegen, incite s.o. against.

aufhorchen ['aufhɔrçən], v.n. prick up o.'s ears.

aufhören ['aufhø:rən], v.n. cease, stop; (Am.) quit; ohne aufzuhören, incessantly; da hört sich doch alles auf! that is the limit!

aufklären ['aufklɛ:rən], v.a. enlighten; clear up; einen —, enlighten s.o. —v.r. sich —, (weather) brighten.

Aufklärung ['aufklɛ:ruŋ], f. (—, no pl.) (age of) Enlightenment.

aufknacken ['aufknakən], v.a. crack (open).

aufknöpfen ['aufknœpfən], v.a. unbutton; aufgeknöpft sein, be in a talkative mood.

aufkommen ['aufkɔmən],v.n. irr. (aux. sein) come into use, spring up; für etwas —, pay for s.th.; einen nicht — lassen, give s.o. no chance.

aufkrempeln ['aufkrɛmpəln],v.a.(coll.) roll up (o.'s sleeves).

aufkündigen ['aufkyndɪgən], v.a. (money) recall; einem die Freundschaft —, break with s.o.

Auflage ['aufla:gə], f. (—, pl. —n) (tax) impost, duty, levy; (book) edition, impression; circulation.

auflassen ['auflasən], v.a. irr. leave open; (Law) cede.

auflauern ['auflauərn], v.n. einem —, lie in wait for s.o., waylay s.o.

Auflauf ['auflauf], m. (—s, pl. ⁓e) tumult, noisy street gathering, soufflé.

auflaufen ['auflaufən], v.n. irr. (aux. sein) swell, increase; (ship) run aground.

aufleben ['aufle:bən], v.n. (aux. sein) wieder —, revive.

auflegen ['aufle:gən], v.a. lay upon, put on; (book) publish; (tax, punishment) impose, inflict.

auflehnen ['aufle:nən], v.r. sich gegen einen (or etwas) —, rebel against, mutiny, oppose.

auflesen ['aufle:zən], v.a. irr. pick up, gather.

aufleuchten ['auflɔyçtən], v.n. light up; (eyes) shine.

auflockern ['auflɔkərn], v.a. loosen.

auflodern ['auflo:dərn], v.n. (aux. sein) flare up, blaze up.

auflösen ['aʊflø:zən], *v.a.* dissolve, loosen; (*puzzle*) solve, guess; (*meeting*) break up; (*business*) wind up; (*partnership*) dissolve; (*army*) disband. — *v.r. sich* —, melt, dissolve, be broken up.

aufmachen ['aʊfmaxən], *v.a.* (*door, packet*) open; (*knot*) undo; *gut* —, pack nicely. — *v.r. sich* —, get going, set out for.

Aufmachung ['aʊfmaxuŋ], *f.* (—, *pl.* —en) outward appearance, make-up, get-up.

Aufmarsch ['aʊfmarʃ], *m.* (—es, *pl.* ⁻e) (*Mil.*) parade.

aufmerksam ['aʊfmɛrkza:m], *adj.* attentive, observant; civil, kind; *einen* — *machen auf*, draw s.o.'s attention to.

aufmuntern ['aʊfmʊntərn], *v.a.* encourage, cheer up.

Aufnahme ['aʊfna:mə], *f.* (—, *pl.* —n) reception; (*Phot.*) snap, photograph; (*Geog.*) mapping out, survey; (*Mus.*) recording.

aufnehmen ['aʊfne:mən], *v.a. irr.* take up; receive, give shelter to; (*Phot.*) photograph, film; (*Mus.*) record; (*money*) raise, borrow; (*minutes*) draw up; *den Faden wieder* —, take up the thread; *die Arbeit wieder* —, return to work, resume work; *die Fährte* —, (*Hunt.*) recover the scent; *es mit einem* —, be a match for s.o.; (*Comm.*) *Inventar* —, take stock, draw up an inventory.

aufnötigen ['aʊfnø:tɪgən], *v.a. einem etwas* —, force s.th. upon s.o.

aufpassen ['aʊfpasən], *v.n.* attend to, pay attention to, take notice of, take care of.

aufpeitschen ['aʊfpaɪtʃən], *v.a.* whip up.

aufpflanzen ['aʊfpflantsən], *v.a.* mount, erect. — *v.r. sich vor einem* —, plant o.s. in front of s.o.; *mit aufgepflanztem Bajonett*, with bayonets fixed.

Aufputz ['aʊfputs], *m.* (—es, *no pl.*) finery, trimmings.

aufraffen ['aʊfrafən], *v.a.* snatch up, rake up. — *v.r. sich wieder* —, pull o.s. together.

aufräumen ['aʊfrɔʏmən], *v.a.* put in order, clear away; (*room*) tidy up; *mit etwas* —, make a clean sweep of s.th.; *aufgeräumt sein*, be in a jolly mood.

aufrechnen ['aʊfrɛçnən], *v.a.* reckon up; set off against.

aufrecht ['aʊfrɛçt], *adj.* upright, erect; *etwas* — *erhalten*, maintain s.th.; (*opinion*) stick to, adhere to, uphold.

Aufrechterhaltung ['aʊfrɛçtərhaltuŋ], *f.* (—, *no pl.*) maintenance, preservation.

aufregen ['aʊfre:gən], *v.a.* excite, enrage.

aufreiben ['aʊfraɪbən], *v.a. irr.* rub sore; (*Mil.*) destroy, wipe out. — *v.r. sich* —, exhaust o.s. with worry (*or* work).

aufreizen ['aʊfraɪtsən], *v.a.* incite, provoke.

aufrichten ['aʊfrɪçtən], *v.a.* raise, erect, set upright; (*fig.*) comfort, console. — *v.r. sich* —, rise, sit up.

aufrichtig ['aʊfrɪçtɪç], *adj.* sincere, frank.

aufriegeln ['aʊfri:gəln], *v.a.* unbolt.

Aufriß ['aʊfrɪs], *m.* (—sses, *pl.* —sse) sketch, draft; (*Archit.*) elevation, section.

aufrücken ['aʊfrʏkən], *v.n.* (*aux.* sein) rise, be promoted (in rank), advance.

Aufruf ['aʊfru:f], *m.* (—s, *pl.* —e) summons, proclamation, appeal; (*Law*) citation.

aufrufen ['aʊfru:fən], *v.a. irr.* summons; (*Sch.*) call upon.

Aufruhr ['aʊfru:r], *m.* (—s, *pl.* —e) uproar, riot, tumult, rebellion, mutiny.

aufrühren ['aʊfry:rən], *v.a.* stir up, agitate, rouse to rebellion.

Aufrüstung ['aʊfrʏstuŋ], *f.* (—, *no pl.*) (*Mil.*) (re-)armament.

aufrütteln ['aʊfrʏtəln], *v.a.* rouse, shake s.o. out of his lethargy.

aufsagen ['aʊfza:gən], *v.a.* recite.

aufsässig ['aʊfzɛsɪç], *adj.* refractory, rebellious.

Aufsatz ['aʊfzats], *m.* (—es, *pl.* ⁻e) top, head-piece, table centre-piece; (*Sch.*) composition, essay; (*newspaper*) article.

aufscheuchen ['aʊfʃɔʏçən], *v.a.* flush (game), startle.

aufschichten ['aʊfʃɪçtən], *v.a.* stack, pile up in layers.

aufschieben ['aʊfʃi:bən], *v.a. irr.* push open; delay, postpone, adjourn; (*Parl.*) prorogue.

Aufschlag ['aʊfʃla:k], *m.* (—s, *pl.* ⁻e) impact, striking; (*sleeve*) cuff; turn-up; (*uniform*) facings; (*Comm.*) increase in price; (*Tennis*) service.

aufschlagen ['aʊfʃla:gən], *v.n. irr.* (*aux.* sein) hit, strike (open); (*Tennis*) serve. — *v.a. die Augen* —, open o.'s eyes; *ein Lager* —, pitch camp; *ein Buch* —, open a book.

aufschlitzen ['aʊfʃlɪtsən], *v.a.* rip open, slit open.

Aufschluß ['aʊfʃlus], *m.* (—sses, *pl.* ⁻sse) disclosure, information.

aufschneiden ['aʊfʃnaɪdən], *v.a. irr.* cut open. — *v.n.* brag, boast.

Aufschneider ['aʊfʃnaɪdər], *m.* (-s, *pl.* —) swaggerer, braggart.

Aufschnitt ['aʊfʃnɪt], *m.* (—s, *no pl.*) slice of cold meat *or* sausage.

aufschnüren ['aʊfʃny:rən], *v.a.* unlace, untie.

Aufschrei ['aʊfʃraɪ], *m.* (—s, *pl.* —e) outcry, screech, scream, shout, shriek.

Aufschrift ['aʊfʃrɪft], *f.* (—, *pl.* —en) inscription, address; heading.

Aufschub ['aʊfʃu:p], *m.* (—s, *pl.* ⁻e) delay, adjournment, postponement.

aufschütten ['aʊfʃʏtən], *v.a.* (*liquid*) pour upon; (*dam*) raise.

14

aufschwingen ['auf∫vɪŋən], v.r. irr. sich —, soar, rise; *ich kann mich dazu nicht —*, I cannot rise to that.

Aufschwung ['auf∫vʊŋ], m. (—s, no pl.) flight, rising; (*Comm.*) improvement, boom.

Aufsehen ['aufze:ən], n. (—s, no pl.) sensation, stir.

Aufseher ['aufze:ər], m. (—s, pl. —) overseer, inspector.

aufsein ['aufzaɪn], v.n. irr. (aux. sein) be out of bed, be up and about.

aufsetzen ['aufzɛtsən], v.a. (hat) put on; (*letter, essay*) draft.

Aufsicht ['aufzɪçt], f. (—, no pl.) inspection, supervision, control.

Aufsichtsrat ['aufzɪçtsra:t], m. (—s, pl. ⁓e) (*Comm.*) board of directors.

aufsitzen ['aufzɪtsən], v.n. irr. sit up, wait up at night; (*horse*) mount.

aufspannen ['auf∫panən], v.a. (umbrella) put up; (tent) pitch.

aufspeichern ['auf∫paɪçərn], v.a. store (up), warehouse.

aufsperren ['auf∫pɛrən], v.a. open wide, unlock.

aufspielen ['auf∫pi:lən], v.n. zum Tanz —, play music for dancing. — v.r. sich groß —, give o.s. airs.

aufspießen ['auf∫pi:sən], v.a. pierce on a spit; (joint) skewer.

aufspringen ['auf∫prɪŋən], v.n. irr. (aux. sein) leap up, jump up; (door) fly open; (hands in winter) chap.

aufspüren ['auf∫py:rən], v.a. track, trace.

aufstacheln ['auf∫taxəln], v.a. goad, incite.

Aufstand ['auf∫tant], m. (—s, pl. ⁓e) insurrection, revolt, sedition.

aufstapeln ['auf∫ta:pəln], v.a. pile up, stack, store.

aufstechen ['auf∫tɛçən], v.a. irr. (*Med.*) lance.

aufstehen ['auf∫te:ən], v.n. irr. (aux. sein) (door) stand open; stand up; get up (from bed); rise (from a chair).

aufstellen ['auf∫tɛlən], v.a. set up, arrange; erect; (*Pol.*) put forward (candidate).

Aufstellung ['auf∫tɛluŋ], f. (—, pl. —en) arrangement; statement; inventory; (*Pol.*) nomination.

aufstemmen ['auf∫tɛmən], v.a. prise open.

Aufstieg ['auf∫ti:k], m. (—s, pl. —e) ascent, rise.

aufstöbern ['auf∫tø:bərn], v.a. stir (up); start; (fig.) discover, ferret out.

aufstoßen ['auf∫to:sən], v.a. push open; bump against. — v.n. belch.

aufstreben ['auf∫tre:bən], v.n. soar; (fig.) aspire.

aufstreichen ['auf∫traɪçən], v.a. irr. (paint) lay on; (butter) spread.

aufstülpen ['auf∫tylpən], v.a. turn up; (hat) clap on o.'s head.

auftakeln ['aufta:kəln], v.a. (*Naut.*) rig.

Auftakt ['auftakt], m. (—s, pl. —e) (*Mus.*) arsis; (fig.) opening, prelude.

auftauchen ['auftauxən], v.n. (aux. sein) appear, emerge, surface.

auftauen ['auftauən], v.n. (aux. sein) thaw; (fig.) lose o.'s reserve.

auftischen ['auftɪ∫ən], v.a. dish up.

Auftrag ['auftra:k], m. (—s, pl. ⁓e) assignment, commission, errand; *im — von*, on behalf of.

auftragen ['auftra:gən], v.a. irr. (food) serve up; (paint) apply; *einem etwas —*, charge s.o. with a job; *stark —*, lay it on thick.

auftreiben ['auftraɪbən], v.a. irr. raise (money); procure, obtain. — v.n. (aux. sein) (ship) run aground.

auftrennen ['auftrɛnən], v.a. unstitch; (hem) unpick.

Auftreten ['auftre:tən], n. (—s, no pl.) (*Theat.*) appearance; behaviour.

auftreten ['auftre:tən], v.n. irr. (aux. sein) tread upon, step upon; (*Theat.*) appear, come on; *energisch —*, take strong measures, put o.'s foot down.

Auftritt ['auftrɪt], m. (—s, pl. —e) (*Theat.*) scene; altercation, row.

auftun ['auftu:n], v.a. irr. open; *den Mund —*, speak. — v.r. sich —, (abyss) yawn.

auftürmen ['auftyrmən], v.a. pile up, heap up. — v.r. sich —, tower.

aufwachen ['aufvaxən], v.n. (aux. sein) awake, wake up.

aufwallen ['aufvalən], v.n. (aux. sein) boil up, bubble up, rage.

Aufwand ['aufvant], m. (—s, no pl.) expense, expenditure; sumptuousness.

aufwarten ['aufvartən], v.n. wait upon, attend on.

aufwärts ['aufvɛrts], adv. upward(s), aloft.

Aufwartung ['aufvartuŋ], f. (—, pl. —en) attendance; *seine — machen*, pay a (formal) visit.

aufwaschen ['aufva∫ən], v.a. irr. wash the dishes.

aufweisen ['aufvaɪzən], v.a. irr. show, produce.

aufwenden ['aufvɛndən], v.a. irr. spend upon, expend upon.

aufwickeln ['aufvɪkəln], v.a. wind up; unwind.

aufwiegeln ['aufvi:gəln], v.a. stir up, incite to rebellion.

aufwiegen ['aufvi:gən], v.a. irr. outweigh, counter-balance, make up for.

aufwischen ['aufvɪ∫ən], v.a. wipe away, mop up.

aufwühlen ['aufvy:lən], v.a. dig, root up, (fig.) stir.

aufzählen ['auftsɛ:lən], v.a. count up, enumerate, list.

aufzäumen ['auftsɔymən], v.a. bridle (horses).

aufzehren ['auftse:rən], v.a. eat up, consume.

aufzeichnen ['auftsaɪçnən], v.a. write down, take a note of, record.

aufziehen [ˈauftsiːən], *v.a. irr.* draw up, pull up; pull open; (*pennant*) hoist; (*clock*) wind up; (*child*) bring up, rear; *einen —*, tease s.o.; *gelindere Saiten —*, be more lenient.

Aufzucht [ˈauftsuxt], *f.* (—, *no pl.*) breeding, rearing.

Aufzug [ˈauftsuːk], *m.* (—s, *pl.* ⸚e) lift; (*Am.*) elevator; (*Theat.*) act; dress, array, attire.

aufzwingen [ˈauftsvɪŋən], *v.a. irr.* *einem etwas —*, force s.th. on s.o.

Augapfel [ˈaukapfəl], *m.* (—s, *pl.* ⸚) eye-ball; (*fig.*) apple of o.'s eye.

Auge [ˈaugə], *n.* (—s, *pl.* —n) eye; *aus den —n, aus dem Sinn*, out of sight, out of mind; *mit einem blauen — davonkommen*, escape by the skin of o.'s teeth, get off cheaply; *es wird mir schwarz vor den —n*, I feel faint.

Augenblick [ˈaugənblɪk], *m.* (—s, *pl.* —e) moment, instant; *jeden —*, at any moment.

augenblicklich [augənˈblɪklɪç], *adj.* momentary, instantaneous.— *adv.* at present, for the moment, immediately.

Augenbraue [ˈaugənbrauə], *f.* (—, *pl.* —n) eye-brow.

augenfällig [ˈaugənfɛlɪç], *adj.* visible, evident, conspicuous.

Augenglas [ˈaugənglas], *n.* (—es, *pl.* ⸚er) eye-glass.

Augenhöhle [ˈaugənhøːlə], *f.* (—, *pl.* —n) eye-socket.

Augenlicht [ˈaugənlɪçt], *n.* (—s *no pl.*) eye-sight.

Augenlid [ˈaugənliːt], *n.* (—s, *pl.* —er) eye-lid.

Augenmaß [ˈaugənmaːs], *n.* (—es, *no pl.*) *gutes —*, good measuring ability with the eye, a sure eye.

Augenmerk [ˈaugənmɛrk], *n.* (—s, *no pl.*) attention; *sein — auf etwas richten*, focus o.'s attention on s.th.

Augenschein [ˈaugənʃain], *m.* (—s, *no pl.*) appearance; *in — nehmen*, view.

augenscheinlich [ˈaugənʃainlɪç], *adj.* apparent, evident.

Augenweide [ˈaugənvaidə], *f.* (—, *pl.* —n) delight to the eye, s.th. lovely to look at.

Augenwimper [ˈaugənvɪmpər], *f.* (—, *pl.* —n) eye-lash.

Augenzeuge [ˈaugəntsɔygə], *m.* (—n, *pl.* —n) eye-witness.

August [auˈgust], *m.* (—s, *no pl.*) (*month*) August.

Augustiner [auguˈstiːnər], *m.* (—s, *pl.* —) (*Eccl.*) Augustinian.

auktionieren [auktsjoˈniːrən], *v.a.* auction(eer), sell by auction.

Aula [ˈaula], *f.* (—, *pl.* —len) (*Sch., Univ.*) great hall; auditorium maximum.

Aurikel [auˈriːkəl], *f.* (—, *pl.* —n) (*Bot.*) auricula.

aus [aus], *prep.* (*Dat.*) from, out of, off. — *adv.* out, over, finished, done with, spent; *es ist alles —*, it is over and done with; *ich weiß weder ein noch —*, I am at my wits' end.

ausarten [ˈausartən], *v.n.* (*aux.* sein) degenerate; (*fig.*) deteriorate.

Ausbau [ˈausbau], *m.* (—s, *no pl.*) enlargement, extension.

ausbauen [ˈausbauən], *v.a.* enlarge (a house); improve on.

ausbedingen [ˈausbədɪŋən], *v.a. sich etwas —*, stipulate.

ausbessern [ˈausbɛsərn], *v.a.* (*garment*) mend, repair.

Ausbeute [ˈausbɔytə], *f.* (—, *no pl.*) gain, profit, produce.

Ausbeutung [ˈausbɔytuŋ], *f.* (—, *no pl.*) exploitation, sweating; (*Min.*) working.

ausbezahlen [ˈausbətsaːlən], *v.a.* pay in full.

ausbilden [ˈausbɪldən], *v.a.* develop, train; (*Mil.*) drill.

Ausbildung [ˈausbɪlduŋ], *f.* (—, *pl.* —en) training, education.

ausbleiben [ˈausblaibən], *v.n. irr.* (*aux.* sein) fail to appear, be absent.

Ausblick [ˈausblɪk], *m.* (—s, *pl.* —e) view (from window); (*fig.*) prospect, outlook.

ausborgen [ˈausbɔrgən], *v.a.* (*sich*) *etwas —*, borrow s.th. from.

ausbreiten [ˈausbraitən], *v.a.* spread (things); stretch out (o.'s arms). — *v.r. sich —*, spread, extend.

Ausbreitung [ˈausbraituŋ], *f.* (—, *no pl.*) spreading, extension, distribution, expansion.

ausbringen [ˈausbrɪŋən], *v.a. irr. einen Toast auf einen —*, drink s.o.'s health.

Ausbruch [ˈausbrux], *m.* (—s, *pl.* ⸚e) breaking out, outbreak, eruption, burst (of laughter).

ausbrüten [ˈausbryːtən], *v.a.* hatch; (*fig.*) plot.

Ausbund [ˈausbunt], *m.* (—s, *pl.* ⸚e) paragon, embodiment.

Ausdauer [ˈausdauər], *f.* (—, *no pl.*) perseverance, persistence, stamina.

ausdehnen [ˈausdeːnən], *v.a.* extend, stretch, distend; (*fig.*) prolong, protract. — *v.r. sich —*, expand, extend, stretch.

Ausdehnung [ˈausdeːnuŋ], *f.* (—, *pl.* —en) extension, expansion; dilation; (*Phys.*) dimension.

ausdenken [ˈausdɛŋkən], *v.a. irr.* think out. — *v.r. sich etwas —*, devise s.th., invent s.th.; *das ist gar nicht auszudenken*, that is unimaginable, inconceivable.

Ausdeutung [ˈausdɔytuŋ], *f.* (—, *pl.* —en) interpretation, explanation.

ausdörren [ˈausdœrən], *v.a.* parch, dry (up).

ausdrehen [ˈausdreːən], *v.a.* (*gas, light, water*) turn off, switch off.

Ausdruck [ˈausdruk], *m.* (—s, *pl.* ⸚e) expression, phrase.

ausdrücken [ˈausdrykən], *v.a.* squeeze out, press out; (*fig.*) express.

ausdrücklich [ˈausdryklɪç], *adj.* express, explicit.

Ausdrucksweise (ˈausdruksvaɪzə], f. (—, pl. —n) enunciation, manner of speech, (mode of) expression, style.

ausdünsten [ˈausdynstən], v.a. exhale, perspire.

auseinander [ausaɪnˈandər], adv. asunder, apart.

Auseinandersetzung [ausaɪnˈandərzɛtsuŋ], f. (—, pl. —en) altercation; discussion, explanation.

auserkoren [ˈauserkoːrən], adj. elect, chosen, selected.

auserlesen [ˈauserleːzən], adj. choice, picked, excellent, first class.

auserwählen [ˈauservɛːlən], v.a. choose, select.

Ausfahrt [ˈausfaːrt], f. (—, pl. —en) drive; gateway; exit.

Ausfall [ˈausfal], m. (—s, pl. ⁓e) falling out; (radioactivity) fall-out; sortie, sally; deficiency, loss, cancellation; result, outcome.

ausfallen [ˈausfalən], v.n. irr. (aux. sein) drop out, fall out; be cancelled, be omitted, fail to take place; turn out (well etc.).

ausfallend [ˈausfalənt], adj. offensive, abusive; — werden, become insulting.

ausfertigen [ˈausfertɪgən], v.a. despatch, draw up, make out, issue.

ausfindig [ˈausfɪndɪç], adj. — machen, find out, locate, discover.

ausflicken [ˈausflɪkən], v.a. mend, patch.

Ausflucht [ˈausfluxt], f. (—, pl. ⁓e) evasion, excuse, subterfuge.

Ausflug [ˈausfluːk], m. (—s, pl. ⁓e) trip, excursion, outing.

Ausfluß [ˈausflus], m. (—sses, pl. ⁓sse) (Engin.) outflow, outlet; (Med.) discharge, suppuration.

ausfragen [ˈausfraːgən], v.a. einen —, question, quiz s.o.

Ausfuhr [ˈausfuːr], f. (—, pl. —en) export.

ausführbar [ausfyˈrbaːr], adj. practicable, feasible; exportable.

ausführen [ˈausfyːrən], v.a. take out; lead out; export; carry out, perform, fulfil; point out.

ausführlich [ausˈfyːrlɪç], adj. detailed, full.

Ausführung [ˈausfyːruŋ], f. (—, pl. —en) execution, carrying out; finish; workmanship.

ausfüllen [ˈausfylən], v.a. (forms) fill up, fill in, complete.

ausfüttern [ˈausfytərn], v.a. line (a dress).

Ausgabe [ˈausgaːbə], f. (—, pl. —en) issue, distribution; (goods) dispatch, issuing counter; delivery; (book) edition; (pl.) expenses, expenditure.

Ausgang [ˈausgaŋ], m. (—s, pl. ⁓e) going out; exit; result, upshot; end, conclusion; time off (from duty).

Ausgangspunkt [ˈausgaŋspunkt], m. (—s, pl. —e) starting-point; point of departure.

ausgären [ˈausgɛːrən], v.n. irr. (aux. sein) ferment; ausgegoren sein, have fermented.

ausgeben [ˈausgeːbən], v.a. irr. (work) give out, distribute; (money) expend, spend; (tickets) issue. —v.r. sich — für, pass o.s. off as.

ausgebreitet [ˈausgəbraɪtət], adj. extensive, widespread.

Ausgeburt [ˈausgəburt], f. (—, pl. —en) monstrosity; — des Hirns, figment of the imagination.

ausgefahren [ˈausgəfaːrən], adj. (street) rutted, well-worn.

ausgehen [ˈausgeːən], v.n. irr. (aux. sein) go out; (hair) to fall out; (colour) come off, fade; (breath, patience, money) become exhausted; result, end in.

ausgelassen [ˈausgəlasən], adj. boisterous, exuberant, frolicsome, merry, jolly, unbridled.

ausgemacht [ˈausgəmaxt], adj. arranged, settled, decided; eine — Sache, a matter of course, a foregone conclusion; ein —er Schurke, a downright scoundrel.

ausgeschlossen [ˈausgəʃlosən], p.p. das ist —, that is impossible, out of the question.

ausgewachsen [ˈausgəvaksən], adj. full-grown, fully grown.

ausgezeichnet [ˈausgətsaɪçnət], adj. excellent, first rate, distinguished.

ausgiebig [ˈausgiːbɪç], adj. abundant, plentiful; (soil) fertile, rich.

ausgießen [ˈausgiːsən], v.a. irr. pour out.

Ausgleich [ˈausglaɪç], m. (—s, no pl.) settlement, compromise, compensation, equalisation.

ausgleichen [ˈausglaɪçən], v.a. irr. make even, balance, equalise, compensate; (sport) equalise, draw.

ausgraben [ˈausgraːbən], v.a. irr. dig out, dig up, excavate, exhume.

Ausguck [ˈausguk], m. (—s, pl. —e) look-out; (Naut.) crow's nest.

Ausguß [ˈausgus], m. (—sses, pl. ⁓sse) sink, gutter.

aushalten [ˈaushaltən], v.a. irr. sustain, endure, bear, stand.

aushändigen [ˈaushɛndɪgən], v.a. deliver up, hand over.

Aushang [ˈaushaŋ], m. (—s, pl. ⁓e) sign, sign-board, placard.

ausharren [ˈausharən], v.n. persevere, hold out, wait patiently.

aushecken [ˈaushɛkən], v.a. hatch (a plot).

aushelfen [ˈaushɛlfən], v.n. irr. help out.

Aushilfe [ˈaushɪlfə], f. (—, pl. —n) help, aid, assistance.

aushilfsweise [ˈaushɪlfsvaɪzə], adv. temporarily, as a stop-gap.

aushöhlen [ˈaushoːlən], v.a. hollow out, excavate.

ausholen [ˈaushoːlən], v.a. pump, sound s.o. — v.n. strike out; weit —, go far back (in a narration).

auskehren ['auske:rən], *v.a.* sweep out.

auskennen ['auskɛnən], *v.r. irr. sich in etwas* —, know all about s.th.

auskleiden ['ausklaɪdən], *v.a.* undress.

ausklingen ['ausklɪŋən], *v.n. irr. (aux. sein) (sound)* die away.

ausklügeln ['auskly:gəln], *v.a.* puzzle out, contrive.

auskneifen ['ausknaɪfən], *v.n. irr. (aux. sein) (coll.)* bolt, run away.

Auskommen ['auskɔmən], *n.* (—s, *no pl.*) sufficiency, subsistence, livelihood; *mit dem ist kein* —, there is no getting on with him.

auskommen ['auskɔmən], *v.n. irr. (aux. sein) mit etwas* —, have enough *or* sufficient of s.th., manage; *mit einem gut* —, be on good terms with s.o., get on well with s.o.

auskömmlich ['auskœmlɪç], *adj.* sufficient.

auskosten ['auskɔstən], *v.a.* taste *or* enjoy to the full.

auskramen ['auskra:mən], *v.a.* rummage out; *(fig.)* reminisce; talk freely.

auskundschaften ['auskuntʃaftən], *v.a.* spy out, reconnoitre, explore.

Auskunft ['auskunft], *f.* (—, *pl.* ⸚e) information; *(Tel.)* enquiries; *(Mil.)* intelligence, enquiry.

auslachen ['auslaxən], *v.a.* laugh at, deride.

ausladen ['ausla:dən], *v.a. irr.* unload, discharge; cancel (invitation).

Auslage ['ausla:gə], *f.* (—, *pl.* —n) outlay, expenses, advance; shop-window display.

Ausland ['auslant], *n.* (—s, *no pl.*) foreign country; *ins* — *fahren*, go abroad.

Ausländer ['auslɛndər], *m.* (—s, *pl.* —) foreigner, alien.

auslassen ['auslasən], *v.a. irr.* let off (steam); let out (a dress); melt (butter); leave off, omit. — *v.r. sich über etwas* —, speak o.'s mind about s.th.

Auslassung ['auslasuŋ], *f.* (—, *pl.* —en) utterance; omission.

auslaufen ['auslaufən], *v.n. irr. (aux. sein)* run out, leak out; *(ship)* put to sea; *(result)* turn out.

Ausläufer ['auslɔyfər], *m.* (—s, *pl.* —) errand boy; *(mountain)* spur.

Auslaut ['auslaut], *m.* (—s, *pl.* —e) *(Phonet.)* final sound.

auslegen ['ausle:gən], *v.a.* lay out, spread out, display; interpret; *(money)* advance.

ausleihen ['auslaɪən], *v.a. irr.* lend, hire out. — *v.r. sich etwas* —, borrow s.th.

auslernen ['auslɛrnən], *v.n.* end o.'s apprenticeship.

ausliefern ['ausli:fərn], *v.a.* hand over, deliver; surrender, give up, extradite.

auslöschen ['ausloeʃən], *v.a.* extinguish, put out (fire).

auslosen ['auslo:zən], *v.a.* raffle, draw lots for.

auslösen ['auslø:zən], *v.a.* redeem, ransom, recover; *(fig.)* produce; arouse.

Auslosung ['auslo:zuŋ], *f.* (—, *pl.* —en) raffle, draw.

Auslösung ['auslø:zuŋ], *f.* (—, *pl.* —en) ransom.

auslüften ['auslyftən], *v.a.* air, ventilate.

ausmachen ['ausmaxən], *v.a.* decide, settle; amount to; *etwas mit einem* —, arrange s.th. with s.o.; *es macht nichts aus*, it does not matter; *wieviel macht das aus?* how much is this? *würde es Ihnen etwas* —? would you mind?

Ausmaß ['ausma:s], *n.* (—es, *pl.* —e) dimension, amount, extent, scale.

ausmeißeln ['ausmaɪsəln], *v.a.* chisel out, carve out.

ausmerzen ['ausmertsən], *v.a.* expunge, eradicate.

ausmisten ['ausmɪstən], *v.a.* clean, clear up (mess).

ausmustern ['ausmustərn], *v.a.* eliminate, reject; *(Mil.)* discharge.

Ausnahme ['ausna:mə], *f.* (—, *pl.* —n) exception.

ausnehmen ['ausne:mən], *v.a. irr.* except, exclude; *(poultry)* draw; *(fish)* clean.

ausnutzen ['ausnutsən], *v.a.* make the most of s.th.; take advantage of s.th.

ausnützen ['ausnytsən], *v.a.* exploit.

auspacken ['auspakən], *v.a.* unpack. — *v.n.* talk freely; *(coll.)* open up.

auspfeifen ['auspfaɪfən], *v.a. irr. (Theat.)* hiss at, cat-call.

auspolstern ['auspɔlstərn], *v.a.* stuff.

ausprägen ['auspre:gən], *v.a.* stamp, impress, coin.

ausprobieren ['ausprobi:rən], *v.a.* try out.

Auspuff ['auspuf], *m.* (—s, *no pl.*) *(Motor.)* exhaust.

auspusten ['auspu:stən], *v.a.* blow out.

ausputzen ['ausputsən], *v.a.* clean out; adorn.

ausquartieren ['auskvarti:rən], *v.a. (Mil.)* billet out.

ausquetschen ['auskvetʃən], *v.a.* squeeze out.

ausradieren ['ausradi:rən], *v.a.* erase.

ausrangieren ['ausranʒi:rən], *v.a.* cast off, sort out.

ausräuchern ['ausrɔyçərn], *v.a.* fumigate.

ausraufen ['ausraufən], *v.a. (obs.)* tear *or* pull out (hair).

ausräumen ['ausrɔymən], *v.a.* clear out, clear away.

ausrechnen ['ausrɛçnən], *v.a.* reckon, compute, calculate; *ausgerechnet du*, *(emph.)* you of all people.

ausrecken ['ausrɛkən], *v.a. sich den Hals* —, crane o.'s neck.

Ausrede ['ausre:də], *f.* (—, *pl.* —n) evasion, excuse, subterfuge.

ausreden ['ausre:dən], *v.a. einem etwas* —, dissuade s.o. from s.th. — *v.n.* finish speaking; *einen* — *lassen*, allow s.o. to finish speaking.

ausreichen ['ausraiçən], v.n. suffice.

ausreißen ['ausraisən], v.a. irr. pluck, pull out. — v.n. (aux. sein) run away, bolt.

ausrenken ['ausreŋkən], v.a. dislocate, sprain.

ausrichten ['ausriçtən], v.a. adjust, make straight; deliver (a message); accomplish; (Mil.) dress.

ausrotten ['ausrotən], v.a. root up; exterminate, extirpate.

ausrücken ['ausrykən], v.n. (aux. sein) (Mil.) march out; (coll.) decamp.

Ausruf ['ausru:f], m. (—s, pl. —e) exclamation, interjection, outcry; (public) proclamation.

Ausruf(ungs)zeichen ['ausru:f(uŋs)-tsaiçən], n. (—s, pl. —) exclamation mark.

ausruhen ['ausru:ən], v.r. sich —, rest, take a rest.

ausrüsten ['ausrystən], v.a. furnish, fit out, equip.

Ausrutschen ['ausrutʃən], v.n. (aux. sein) slip.

Aussage ['ausza:gə], f. (—, pl. —n) declaration, statement, evidence; (Law) deposition, affidavit; (Gram.) predicate.

aussagen ['ausza:gən], v.a. say, state, utter, declare; (Law) depose, give evidence.

Aussatz ['auszats], m. (—es, no pl.) leprosy.

Aussätzige ['auszetsigə], m. (—n, pl. —n) leper.

aussaugen ['auszaugən], v.a. suck dry.

ausschalten ['ausʃaltən], v.a. switch off.

Ausschank ['ausʃank], m. (—s, no pl.) pub, bar.

Ausschau ['ausʃau], f. (—, no pl.) watch; — halten, look out for.

ausscheiden ['ausʃaidən], v.a. irr. separate; (Med.) secrete. — v.n. (aux. sein) withdraw from, retire, secede.

Ausscheidung ['ausʃaiduŋ], f. (—, pl. —en) retirement, withdrawal; (Med.) secretion.

Ausschlag ['ausʃla:k], m. (—s, pl. ˙-e) turn (of the scales); deflection (of the magnetic needle); (Med.) rash, eczema; den — geben, clinch the matter; give the casting vote.

ausschlagen ['ausʃla:gən], v.a. irr. knock out; refuse, decline (an invitation); das schlägt dem Faß den Boden aus, that is the last straw. — v.n. (aux. sein) (Hort.) bud, shoot; gut —, turn out well.

ausschlaggebend ['ausʃla:kge:bənt], adj. decisive; (vote) casting.

ausschließen ['ausʃli:sən], v.a. irr. lock out; exclude.

ausschließlich ['ausʃli:sliç], adj. exclusive, sole.

ausschlüpfen ['ausʃlypfən], v.n. (aux. sein) hatch out.

Ausschluß ['ausʃlus], m. (—sses, pl. ˙-sse) exclusion; unter — der Öffentlichkeit, in camera.

ausschmücken ['ausʃmykən], v.a. adorn, decorate, embellish.

Ausschnitt ['ausʃnit], m. (—s, pl. —e) cutting out; (newspaper) cutting; (dress) neck (line).

ausschreiben ['ausʃraibən], v.a. irr. write down in full; make out a bill; advertise (post) as vacant.

ausschreiten ['ausʃraitən], v.n. irr. (aux. sein) step out, stride along.

Ausschreitungen ['ausʃraituŋən], f. pl. rioting; excesses.

Ausschuß ['ausʃus], m. (—sses, pl. ˙-sse) dross, refuse, rejects, low quality goods; committee, commission, board.

ausschweifend ['ausʃvaifənt], adj. extravagant; licentious, dissolute.

aussehen ['ausze:ən], v.n. irr. look; look like, appear.

außen ['ausən], adv. outside, abroad, outward, without.

Außenhandel ['ausənhandəl], m. (—s, no pl.) export trade.

Außenministerium ['ausənministe:rjum], n. (—s, pl. —terien) Ministry of Foreign Affairs; (U.K.) Foreign Office, (U.S.) State Department.

Außenstände ['ausənʃtendə], m. pl. outstanding claims, liabilities.

außer ['ausər], prep. (Dat.) in addition to, besides, apart from; out of, at the outside of, beside, without; — Dienst, retired. — conj. except, save, but.

außerdem ['ausərde:m], adv. besides, moreover, furthermore.

Äussere ['oysərə], n. (—n, no pl.) exterior.

außerehelich ['ausəre:əliç], adj. illegitimate.

außergewöhnlich ['ausərgəvø:nliç], adj. unusual, exceptional.

außerhalb ['ausərhalp], prep. outside.

äußerlich ['oysərliç], adj. external.

Äußerlichkeit ['oysərliçkait], f. (—, pl. —en) formality.

äußern ['oysərn], v.a. utter, express. — v.r. sich zu etwas —, give o.'s opinion on some question; express o.s. on some subject.

außerordentlich [ausər'ordəntliç], adj. extraordinary, unusual; (Univ.) —er Professor, senior lecturer or reader; (Am.) associate professor.

äußerst ['oysərst], adj. outermost, most remote; extreme, utmost.

außerstande ['ausərʃtandə], adj. unable.

Äußerung ['oysəruŋ], f. (—, pl. —en) utterance, remark, observation.

aussetzen ['auszetsən], v.a. set out, put out; offer (a reward); suspend; etwas an einer Sache —, find fault with s.th.; sich einer Gefahr —, expose o.s. to danger, run a risk. — v.n. pause, discontinue; (Motor.) stop, misfire.

Aussicht ['auszuçt], f. (—, pl. —en) view, panorama; prospect, chance; etwas in — stellen, hold out the prospect of s.th.; in — nehmen, intend.

aussinnen ['auszɪnən],*v. a. irr.* imagine, invent, devise.

aussöhnen ['auszø:nən], *v.r. sich mit einem —*, become reconciled with s.o.

aussondern ['auszɔndərn], *v.a.* single out.

ausspannen ['ausʃpanən], *v.a. (animals)* unharness. — *v.n. (coll.)* relax.

ausspeien ['ausʃpaiən], *v.a.* spit out, vomit.

aussperren ['ausʃpɛrən], *v.a.* shut out; *(industrial)* lock out.

ausspielen ['ausʃpi:lən], *v.n.* finish playing; *(Sport, Game)* lead (off).

Aussprache ['ausʃpra:xə], *f.* (—, *no pl.*) pronunciation; discussion; confidential talk.

aussprechen ['ausʃprɛçən], *v.a. irr.* have o.'s say; utter; pronounce. — *v.r. sich —*, speak o.'s mind.

Ausspruch ['ausʃprux], *m.* (—s, *pl.* ¨e) utterance, dictum.

ausspüren ['ausʃpy:rən], *v.a. (Hunt.)* track down.

ausstaffieren ['ausʃtafi:rən],*v.a.*furnish, equip.

Ausstand ['ausʃtant], *m.* (—s, *pl.* ¨e) *(industry)* strike; *(pl.)* outstanding debts, arrears.

ausständig ['ausʃtɛndɪç], *adj.* outstanding; on strike.

ausstatten ['ausʃtatən], *v.a.* endow with, provide with, equip.

Ausstattung ['ausʃtatuŋ], *f.* (—, *pl.* —en) outfit; (bridal) trousseau; *(coll.)* get-up.

ausstechen ['ausʃtɛçən], *v.a. irr.* pierce; *einen —*, (*fig.*) excel s.o.

ausstehen ['ausʃte:ən], *v.n. irr.* stand out; *(money)* be overdue. — *v.a.* endure, suffer, bear, undergo; *ich kann ihn nicht —*, I cannot stand him.

aussteigen ['ausʃtaigən], *v.n. irr. (aux. sein)* get out, alight; disembark.

ausstellen ['ausʃtɛlən], *v.a.* exhibit; display; make out (bill etc.).

Aussteller ['ausʃtɛlər], *m.* (—s, *pl.* —) drawer (of a cheque); exhibitor.

Ausstellung ['ausʃtɛluŋ], *f.* (—, *pl.* —en) exhibition; *(Am.)* exposition.

Aussteuer ['ausʃtɔyər], *f.* (—, *pl.* —n) trousseau.

ausstopfen ['ausʃtɔpfən], *v.a.* stuff.

ausstoßen ['ausʃtosən], *v.a. irr.* push out, expel; utter.

Ausstrahlung ['ausʃtra:luŋ], *f.* (—, *pl.* —en) radiation.

ausstrecken ['ausʃtrɛkən], *v.a.* stretch out, reach out, extend.

ausstreichen ['ausʃtraiçən], *v.a. irr.* strike out, erase, delete; smoothe.

ausstreuen ['ausʃtrɔyən], *v.a.* scatter, spread, sprinkle; *Gerüchte —*, circulate rumours.

ausstudieren ['ausʃtudi:rən], *v.n.* finish o.'s studies, graduate.

aussuchen ['auszu:xən], *v.a.* select.

Austausch ['austauʃ], *m.* (—es, *pl.* —e) barter, exchange; *(thoughts, letters)* interchange.

austauschen ['austauʃən], *v.a.* barter, exchange; *(thoughts, letters)* interchange.

austeilen ['austailən], *v.a.* distribute, allocate.

Auster ['austər], *f.* (—, *pl.* —n) oyster.

Austerbank ['austərbaŋk], *f.* (—, *pl.* ¨e) oyster-bed.

austilgen ['austilgən], *v.a.* exterminate, eradicate, extirpate.

Australien [au'stra:ljən], *n.* Australia.

austreiben ['austraibən], *v.a. irr.* drive out, expel; exorcise.

austreten ['austre:tən], *v.a. irr.* tread out; stretch (shoes) by walking; *ausgetretene Stufen*, worn steps. — *v.n. (aux. sein)* retire (from business); withdraw (from a club); *(coll.)* go to the lavatory.

Austritt ['austrɪt], *m.* (—s, *pl.* —e) withdrawal, retirement.

ausüben ['ausy:bən], *v.a.* exercise, practise; exert, commit.

Ausverkauf ['ausfɛrkauf], *m.* (—s, *pl.* ¨e) selling-off, clearance sale.

Auswahl ['ausva:l], *f.* (—, *pl.* —en) choice, selection.

Auswanderer ['ausvandərər], *m.* (—s, *pl.* —) emigrant.

auswärtig ['ausvɛrtɪç], *adj.* foreign, away.

auswärts ['ausvɛrts], *adv.* outward(s), away from home.

auswechseln ['ausvɛksəln], *v.a.* exchange; fit (spare parts).

Ausweg ['ausve:k], *m.* (—s, *pl.* —e) expedient; way out; *ich weiß keinen —*, I am at my wits' end.

ausweichen ['ausvaiçən], *v.n. irr. (aux. sein)* give way; evade, parry.

Ausweis ['ausvais], *m.* (—es, *pl.* —e) proof of identity, identity card.

ausweisen ['ausvaizən], *v.a. irr.* turn out, banish, exile, deport. — *v.r. (aux. haben) sich —*, show proof of o.'s identity.

auswendig ['ausvendɪç], *adj.* by heart.

auswirken ['ausvɪrkən], *v.r. sich gut —*, work out well, have a good effect.

Auswuchs ['ausvu:ks], *m.* (—es, *pl.* ¨e) sprouting, outgrowth, (*fig.*) excrescence.

Auswurf ['ausvurf], *m.* (—s, *pl.* ¨e) excretion; expectoration; — *der Menschheit*, scum of the earth.

auszählen ['austse:lən], *v.n.* count, number. — *v.a.* count out.

Auszahlung ['austsa:luŋ], *f.* (—, *pl.* —en) payment.

auszanken ['austsaŋkən], *v.a.* scold, chide.

auszehren ['austse:rən], *v.n. (aux. sein)* waste away, be consumed.

auszeichnen ['austsaiçnən], *v.a.* mark out, honour, decorate. — *v.r. sich —*, distinguish o.s.

Auszeichnung ['austsaiçnuŋ], *f.* (—, *pl.* —en) distinction, medal.

ausziehen [ˈaustsiːən], v.a. irr. undress, take off (clothes); (Chem.) extract; stretch. — v.n. (aux. sein) move out. — v.r. sich —, undress.

auszischen [ˈaustsiʃən], v.a. (Theat.) hiss, cat-call.

Auszug [ˈaustsuːk], m. (—s, ⁓e) removal (from home); marching off; exodus; extract (from a book), abstract (from a deed).

Auto [ˈauto], n. (—s, pl. —s) motorcar, (Am.) automobile.

Autogramm [autoˈgram], n. (—s, pl. —e) autograph.

Automat [autoˈmaːt], m. (—en, pl. —en) slot machine.

Autor [ˈautor], m. (—s, pl. —en) author, writer.

Autorität [autoriˈtɛːt], f. (—, pl. —en) authority.

avisieren [aviˈziːrən], v.a. notify, advise.

Axt [akst], f. (—, pl. ⁓e) axe.

Azur [aˈtsuːr], m. (—s, no pl.) azure.

B

B [beː], n. (—s, pl.—s) the letter B; (Mus.) B flat; — Dur, B flat major; — Moll, B flat minor.

Bach [bax], m. (—es, pl. ⁓e) brook, rivulet.

Bachstelze [ˈbaxʃtɛltsə], f. (—, pl. —n) wagtail.

Backe [ˈbakə], f. (—, pl. —n) cheek.

backen [ˈbakən], v.a. bake.

Backenstreich [ˈbakənʃtraiç], m. (—s, pl. —e) box on the ear.

Bäcker [ˈbɛkər], m. (—s, pl. —) baker.

Backfisch [ˈbakfiʃ], m. (—es, pl. —e) (fig.) teenage girl.

Backhuhn [ˈbakhuːn], n. (—s, pl. ⁓er) fried chicken.

Backobst [ˈbakopst], n. (—es, no pl.) dried fruit.

Backpfeife [ˈbakpfaifə], f. (—, pl. —n) box on the ear.

Backpflaume [ˈbakpflaumə], f. (—, pl. —n) prune.

Backstein [ˈbakʃtain], m. (—s, pl. —e) brick.

Backwerk [ˈbakvɛrk], n. (—s, no pl.) pastry.

Bad [baːt], n. (—es, pl. ⁓er) bath; spa, watering-place.

Badeanstalt [ˈbaːdəanʃtalt], f. (—, pl. —en) public baths.

baden [ˈbaːdən], v.n. bathe, have a bath.

Badewanne [ˈbaːdəvanə], f. (—, pl. —n) bath-tub.

Bagage [baˈgaːʒə], f. (—, no pl.) luggage; (Am.) baggage; (sl.) mob, rabble.

Bagger [ˈbagər], m. (—s, pl. —) dredger, dredging-machine.

baggern [ˈbagərn], v.a. dredge.

Bahn [baːn], f. (—, pl. —en) road, path, course; (Astr.) orbit; railway(-line); — brechen, open a path.

bahnbrechend [ˈbaːnbrɛçənt], adj. pioneering, epoch-making.

bahnen [ˈbaːnən], v.a. make passable; pave (the way).

Bahngleis [ˈbaːnglais], n. (—es, pl. —e) railway-line, railway-track; (Am.) railroad-line, railroad-track.

Bahnhof [ˈbaːnhoːf], m. (—s, pl. ⁓e) railway-station, (Am.) depot.

Bahnsteig [ˈbaːnʃtaik], m. (—s, pl. —e) platform.

Bahnwärter [ˈbaːnvɛrtər], m. (—s, pl. —) signal-man.

Bahre [ˈbaːrə], f. (—, pl. —n) litter, stretcher; bier.

Bahrtuch [ˈbaːrtuːx], n. (—s, pl. ⁓er) pall, shroud.

Bai [bai], f. (—, pl. —en) bay, cove.

Baisse [ˈbɛsə], f. (—, pl. —n) (Comm.) fall in share prices.

Bakkalaureat [bakalaurɛˈaːt], n. (—s, pl. —e) bachelor's degree.

Bakterie [bakˈteːrjə], f. (—, pl. —n) bacterium.

bald [balt], adv. soon, shortly, directly, presently.

Baldachin [ˈbaldaxin], m. (—s, pl. —e) canopy.

baldig [ˈbaldiç], adj. quick, speedy; auf —es Wiedersehen, see you again soon.

Baldrian [ˈbaldriaːn], m. (—s, no pl.) valerian.

Balearen, die [baleˈaːrən, diː], pl. Balearic Islands.

Balg (1) [balk], m. (—s, pl. ⁓e) skin, slough, husk; bellows (of organ or forge).

Balg (2) [balk], n. (—s, pl. ⁓er) brat; naughty child.

balgen [ˈbalgən], v.r. sich —, (children) fight, romp.

Balgerei [balgəˈrai], f. (—, pl. —en) scuffle, scrimmage.

Balken [ˈbalkən], m. (—s, pl. —) beam, joist, rafter.

Balkenwerk [ˈbalkənvɛrk], n. (—s, no pl.) building-frame, timbers, woodwork.

Balkon [balˈkɔ̃], m. (—s, pl. —s, —e) balcony.

Ball [bal], m. (—s, pl. ⁓e) ball; globe; sphere; dance.

ballen [ˈbalən], v.a. form into a ball; clench (o.'s fist).

Ballen [ˈbalən], m. (—s, pl. —) bale, bundle, package; ball (of the hand or foot).

ballförmig [ˈbalfœrmiç], adj. spherical.

Ballistik [baˈlistik], f. (—, no pl.) ballistics.

Ballon [baˈlɔ̃], m. (—s, pl. —s, —e) balloon.

Balsam [ˈbalzaːm], m. (—s, pl. —e) balm, balsam.

Baltikum [ˈbaltikum], n. (—s, no pl.) the Baltic countries.

Bambusrohr ['bambusro:r], *n.* (—s, *pl.* —e) bamboo (cane).

Banane [ba'na:nə], *f.* (—, *pl.* —n) banana.

Banause [ba'nauzə], *m.* (—n, *pl.* —n) narrow-minded person, philistine.

Band (1) [bant], *n.* (—s, *pl.* ¨er) ribbon, riband, tape; string; (*Bot.*) band; hoop (*for a cask*); (*Anat.*) ligament, tendon.

Band (2) [bant], *n.* (—s, *pl.* —e) (*fig.*) bond, fetter, chain, (*pl.*) bonds, ties (*of friendship*).

Band (3) [bant], *m.* (—es, *pl.* ¨e) volume.

Bändchen ['bɛntçən], *n.* (—s, *pl.* —) small ribbon, small piece of string; (*book*) small volume.

Bande ['bandə], *f.* (—, *pl.* —n) horde, gang, set.

bändigen ['bɛndɪgən], *v.a.* tame, subdue.

Bandmaß ['bantma:s], *n.* (—es, *pl.* —e) tape-measure.

Bandwurm ['bantvurm], *m.* (—s, *pl.* ¨er) (*Zool.*) tape-worm.

bange ['baŋə], *adj.* afraid, worried, alarmed.

Bangigkeit ['baŋɪçkaɪt], *f.* (—, *no pl.*) uneasiness, anxiety.

Bank (1) [baŋk], *f.* (—, *pl.* ¨e) bench, seat (in a park); *auf die lange — schieben,* delay, shelve; *durch die —,* without exception.

Bank (2) [baŋk], *f.* (—, *pl.* —en) bank; *die — sprengen,* break the bank.

Bänkelsänger ['bɛŋkəlzɛŋər], *m.* (—s, *pl.* —) ballad singer.

bank(e)rott [baŋk'rɔt], *adj.* bankrupt.

Bankett [baŋ'kɛt], *n.* (—s, *pl.* —e) banquet.

Bankkonto ['baŋkkɔnto], *n.* (—s, *pl.* —ten) bank-account.

Bann [ban], *m.* (—s, *no pl.*) ban, exile; (*Eccl.*) excommunication; *in den — tun,* outlaw, (*Eccl.*) excommunicate; (*fig.*) charm, spell.

bannen ['banən], *v.a.* banish, exile, cast out.

Banner ['banər], *n.* (—s, *pl.* —) banner, standard.

Bannmeile ['banmaɪlə], *f.* (—, *pl.* —n) boundary.

bar [ba:r], *adv.* in cash, ready money.

Bar [ba:r], *f.* (—, *pl.* —s) bar (for selling drinks etc.).

Bär [bɛ:r], *m.* (—en, *pl.* —en) (*Zool.*) bear; *einem einen —en aufbinden,* to lead s.o. up the garden-path.

Barauslagen ['barausla:gən], *f.* *pl.* cash expenses.

Barbar [bar'ba:r], *m.* (—en, *pl.* —en) barbarian, vandal.

barbarisch [bar'ba:rɪʃ], *adj.* barbarous.

Barbestand ['ba:rbəʃtant], *m.* (—s, *pl.* ¨e) cash reserve, cash balance.

bärbeißig ['bɛ:rbaɪsɪç], *adj.* surly, morose.

Barchent ['barçənt], *m.* (—s, *no pl.*) fustian.

Barde ['bardə], *m.* (—n, *pl.* —n) bard, minstrel.

Bärenfell ['bɛ:rənfɛl], *n.* (—s, *pl.* —e) bear-skin.

Bärenmütze ['bɛ:rənmʏtsə], *f.* (—, *pl.* —n) (*Mil.*) busby.

Bärenzwinger ['bɛ:rəntsvɪŋər], *m.* (—s, *pl.* —) bear-garden.

Barett [ba'rɛt], *n.* (—s, *pl.* —e) cap, beret; (*Eccl.*) biretta.

barfuß ['barfus], *adj.* barefoot(ed).

Bargeld ['bargɛlt], *n.* (—(e)s, *no pl.*) cash.

barhäuptig ['barhɔyptɪç], *adj.* bareheaded.

Barkasse [bar'kasə], *f.* (—, *pl.* —n) launch.

Barke ['barkə], *f.* (—, *pl.* —n) barge, lighter.

barmherzig [barm'hɛrtsɪç], *adj.* merciful, charitable, compassionate.

Barock [ba'rɔk], *n.* (—s, *no pl.*) Baroque.

Baronin [ba'ro:nɪn], *f.* (—, *pl.* —nen) baroness.

Barren ['barən], *m.* (—s, *pl.* —) parallel bars.

Barsch [barʃ], *m.* (—es, *pl.* —e) (*Zool.*) perch.

barsch [barʃ], *adj.* rough, harsh, sharp, abrupt, unfriendly.

Barschaft ['ba:rʃaft], *f.* (—, *pl.* —en) ready money.

Bart [ba:rt], *m.* (—s, *pl.* ¨e) beard; (*key*) ward.

Bartflechte ['ba:rtflɛçtə], *f.* (—, *pl.* —n) barber's itch.

bärtig ['bɛ:rtɪç], *adj.* bearded.

Basalt [ba'zalt], *m.* (—s, *pl.* —e) (*Min.*) basalt.

Base ['ba:zə], *f.* (—, *pl.* —n) female cousin; (*Chem.*) base.

Basis ['ba:zɪs], *f.* (—, *pl.* **Basen**) base, foundation.

Baskenmütze ['baskənmʏtsə], *f.* (—, *pl.* —n) tam-o'-shanter, beret.

Baß [bas], *m.* (—sses, *pl.* ¨sse) (*Mus.*) bass.

Baßschlüssel ['basʃlʏsəl], *m.* (—s, *pl.* —) (*Mus.*) bass-clef.

Bassin [ba'sɛ̃], *n.* (—s, *pl.* —s) basin, reservoir.

Bast [bast], *m.* (—es, *pl.* —e) inner bark, fibre (*of trees etc.*); bast.

basta ['basta], *int.* and that's that!

Bastei [bas'taɪ], *f.* (—, *pl.* —en) bastion.

basteln ['bastəln], *v.a.* work on a hobby, tinker.

Batist [ba'tɪst], *m.* (—s, *pl.* —e) cambric.

Bau [bau], *m.* (—es, *pl.* —ten) building, structure, edifice; act of building; *im — begriffen,* in course of construction.

Bauart ['bauart], *f.* (—, *pl.* —en) (architectural) style, structure.

Bauch [baux], *m.* (—es, *pl.* ¨e) belly, stomach.

Bauchfell ['bauxfɛl], *n.* (—s, *pl.* —e) peritoneum.

bauchig ['bauçɪç], *adj.* bulgy.

Bauchredner ['bauxre:dnər], *m.* (—s, *pl.* —) ventriloquist.

bauen ['bauən], *v.a.* build, construct, erect. — *v.n. auf etwas* —, (*fig.*) rely on s.th., count on s.th.

Bauer (1) ['bauər], *m.* (—n, *pl.* —n) farmer, peasant; (*chess*) pawn.

Bauer (2) ['bauər], *n.* (—s, *pl.* —) (*bird*) cage.

Bauernfänger ['bauərnfɛŋər], *m.*°(—s, *pl.* —) sharper, rook, confidence-trickster.

Bäuerin ['bɔyərɪn], *f.* (—, *pl.* —nen) farmer's wife.

Bauernstand ['bauərnʃtant], *m.* (—s, *pl.* ·e) peasantry.

baufällig ['baufɛlɪç], *adj.* dilapidated, ramshackle.

Baugerüst ['baugəryst], *n.* (—s, *pl.* -e) scaffolding.

Baugewerbe ['baugəvɛrbə], *n.* (—s, *no pl.*) building trade.

Baukunst ['baukunst], *f.* (—, *no pl.*) architecture.

Baum [baum], *m.* (—(e)s, *pl.* ·e) tree.

Baumeister ['baumaɪstər], *m.* (—s, *pl.* —) architect; master-builder.

baumeln ['bauməln], *v.n.* dangle.

Baumkuchen ['baumku:xən], *m.* (—s, *pl.* —) pyramid-cake.

Baumschule ['baumʃu:lə], *f.* (—, *pl.* —n) plantation of trees, orchard, tree nursery.

Baumstamm ['baumʃtam], *m.* (—s, *pl.* ·e) stem, trunk.

Baumwolle ['baumvɔlə], *f.* (—, *pl.* —n) cotton.

Bauriß ['baurɪs], *m.* (—sses, *pl.* —sse) plan, architect's drawing.

Bausch [bauʃ], *m.* (—es, *pl.* ·e) pad, bolster; *in* — *und Bogen*, in the lump: all at once.

bauschig ['bauʃɪç], *adj.* baggy.

Bauwerk ['bauvɛrk] *see* **Gebäude**

Bayern ['baɪərn], *n.* Bavaria.

Bazar [ba'za:r], *m.* (—s, *pl.* —e) bazaar, fair, emporium.

beabsichtigen [bə'apzɪçtɪgən], *v.a.* aim at, intend, have in view.

beachten [bə'axtən], *v.a.* observe, pay attention to.

Beamte [bə'amtə], *m.* (—n, *pl.* —n) official, officer, civil servant.

Beamtin [bə'amtɪn], *f.* (—, *pl.* —nen) female official, female civil servant.

beängstigen [bə'ɛŋstɪgən], *v.a.* alarm, make afraid.

beanspruchen [bə'anʃpruxən], *v.a.* demand, claim, lay claim to.

beanstanden [bə'anʃtandən], *v.a.* object to, raise objections to, query.

beantragen [bə'antra:gən], *v.a.* move, apply, lodge an application.

beantworten [bə'antvɔrtən], *v.a.* answer, reply to.

bearbeiten [bə'arbaɪtən], *v.a.* work (on); (*book, play*) adapt, arrange, revise; (*Agr.*) cultivate; (*fig.*) *einen* —, try to influence s.o., try to convince s.o.

Bearbeitung [bə'arbaɪtuŋ], *f.* (—, *pl.* —en) working, manipulation, operation; (*Agr.*) culture, cultivation; (*book, play*) adaptation, revision, arrangement.

beargwöhnen [bə'arkvø:nən], *v.a.* suspect, view with suspicion.

beaufsichtigen [bə'aufzɪçtɪgən], *v.a.* control, supervise, superintend.

beauftragen [bə'auftra:gən], *v.a.* commission, charge, authorize.

bebauen [bə'bauən], *v.a.* build upon; (*Agr.*) cultivate.

beben ['be:bən], *v.n.* shake, quake, tremble; *vor Kälte* —, shiver with cold.

Becher ['bɛçər], *m.* (—s, *pl.* —) beaker, cup, goblet, mug; (*dice*) box.

Becken ['bɛkən], *n.* (—s, *pl.* —) basin, bowl; (*Anat.*) pelvis; (*Mus.*) cymbal.

Bedacht [bə'daxt], *m.* (—s, *no pl.*) consideration; *mit* —, deliberately; *ohne* —, thoughtlessly.

bedächtig [bə'dɛçtɪç], *adj.* circumspect, deliberate, cautious, slow.

bedanken [bə'daŋkən], *v.r. sich für etwas* —, thank s.o. for s.th., decline with thanks (*also iron.*).

Bedarf [bə'darf], *m.* (—s, *no pl.*) need, requirement, demand.

bedauerlich [bə'dauərlɪç], *adj.* regrettable, deplorable.

bedauern [bə'dauərn], *v.a.* pity, commiserate, regret; *ich bedaure, daß*, I am sorry that . . .

bedecken [bə'dɛkən], *v.a.* cover (up); *sich mit Ruhm* —, cover o.s. with glory.

bedeckt [bə'dɛkt], *adj.* (*sky*) overcast.

bedenken [bə'dɛŋkən], *v.a. irr.* consider, bear in mind. — *v.r. sich* —, deliberate, hesitate; *sich anders* —, change o.'s mind.

bedenklich [bə'dɛŋklɪç], *adj.* (*persons*) doubtful, dubious; (*things*) risky, delicate, precarious; (*illness*) serious, grave.

Bedenkzeit [bə'dɛŋktsaɪt], *f.* (—, *pl.* —en) time to consider, respite.

bedeuten [bə'dɔytən], *v.a.* signify, mean, imply; direct, order.

bedeutend [bə'dɔytənt], *adj.* important, eminent, considerable, outstanding.

bedeutsam [bə'dɔytza:m], *adj.* significant.

Bedeutung [bə'dɔytuŋ], *f.* (—, *pl.* —en) significance, meaning; consequence, importance; *nichts von* —, nothing to speak of.

bedienen [bə'di:nən], *v.a.* serve, attend to, wait on; (*machine*) operate; (*Cards*) follow suit. — *v.r. sich* —, help o.s., make use of.

Bediente [bə'di:ntə], *m.* (—n, *pl.* —n) servant, attendant, footman, lackey.

Bedienung [bə'di:nuŋ], *f.* (—, *pl.* —en) service, attendance.

bedingen [bə'dɪŋən], *v.a.* stipulate, postulate, condition, cause.

23

bedingt [bə'dıŋkt], *adj.* conditional.
Bedingung [bə'dıŋuŋ], *f.* (—, *pl.* —en) stipulation, condition, term; *unter keiner* —, on no account.
bedingungsweise [bə'dıŋuŋsvaızə], *adv.* on condition, conditionally.
bedrängen [bə'drɛŋən], *v.a.* oppress; press hard, afflict.
Bedrängnis [bə'drɛŋnıs], *n.* (—ses, *pl.* —se) oppression, distress.
bedrohen [bə'dro:ən], *v.a.* threaten, menace.
bedrohlich [bə'dro:lıç], *adj.* threatening, menacing, ominous.
bedrücken [bə'drykən], *v.a.* oppress, harass, depress.
Beduine [bedu'i:nə], *m.* (—n, *pl.* —n) Bedouin.
bedünken [bə'dyŋkən], *v.a.* appear, seem; *es bedünkt mich,* methinks.
bedürfen [bə'dyrfən], *v.n. irr.* want, need, be in need of.
Bedürfnis [bə'dyrfnıs], *n.* (—ses, *pl.* —se) want, need, requirement, necessity; *es ist mir ein* —, I cannot but: *einem dringenden* — *abhelfen,* meet an urgent want *or* need; *ein* — *haben,* (coll.) need to relieve o.s.
Bedürfnisanstalt [bə'dyrfnısanʃtalt], *f.* (—, *pl.* —en) public lavatory, public convenience.
bedürftig [bə'dyrftıç], *adj.* needy, indigent, poor.
beeidigen [bə'aıdıgən], *v.a.* confirm by oath, swear in.
beeifern [bə'aıfərn], *v.r. sich* —, exert o.s., strive, be zealous.
beeilen [bə'aılən], *v.r. sich* —, hurry, hasten, make haste.
beeindrucken [bə'aındrukən], *v.a.* impress.
beeinflussen [bə'aınflusən], *v.a.* influence.
beeinträchtigen [bə'aıntrɛçtıgən], *v.a.* injure, lessen, diminish, detract from, curtail.
beenden [bə'ɛndən], *v.a.* end, finish, terminate, conclude.
beendigen [bə'ɛndıgən], *v.a.* end, finish, terminate, conclude.
beengen [bə'ɛŋən], *v.a.* cramp, narrow.
beerben [bə'ɛrbən], *v.a. einen* —, inherit from s.o.
beerdigen [bə'e:rdıgən], *v.a.* bury, inter.
Beere ['be:rə], *f.* (—, *pl.* —n) berry.
Beet [be:t], *n.* (—es, *pl.* —e) (flower) bed.
befähigen [bə'fɛ:ıgən], *v.a.* fit, enable, qualify.
Befähigung [bə'fɛ:ıguŋ], *f.* (—, *pl.* —en) qualification, capacity, aptitude.
befahren [bə'fa:rən], *v.a. irr.* pass over, travel over; (*Naut.*) navigate.
befallen [bə'falən], *v.a. irr.* befall, fall on; *von Traurigkeit* — *sein,* be overcome by sadness.
befangen [bə'faŋən], *adj.* biased, prejudiced; bashful, embarrassed.

befassen [bə'fasən], *v.a.* touch, handle. — *v.r. sich mit etwas* —, occupy o.s. with s.th.
befehden [bə'fe:dən], *v.a.* make war upon, show enmity towards.
Befehl [bə'fe:l], *m.* (—s, *pl.* —e) order, command; (*Mil.*) *zu* —, very good, sir; (*Mil.*) *den* — *führen über,* command.
befehlen [bə'fe:lən], *v.ä. irr.* order, command.
befehligen [bə'fe:lıgən], *v.a.* (*Mil.*) command, head.
Befehlshaber [bə'fe:lsha:bər], *m.* (—s, *pl.* —) commander, commanding officer, chief.
befehlswidrig [bə'fe:lsvi:drıç], *adj.* contrary to orders.
befestigen [bə'fɛstıgən], *v.a.* fasten, fix, attach, affix; (*Mil.*) fortify; strengthen.
befeuchten [bə'fɔyçtən], *v.a.* wet, moisten, dampen.
Befinden [bə'fındən], *n.* (—s, *no pl.*) state of health.
befinden [bə'fındən], *v.a. irr.* think, deem, find. — *v.r. sich an einem Ort* —, be in some place; *sich wohl* —, feel well.
befindlich [bə'fıntlıç], *adj.* existing — *sein,* be contained in.
beflecken [bə'flɛkən], *v.a.* stain, spot, blot; defile, pollute.
befleißigen [bə'flaısıgən], *v.r. sich* —, devote o.s. to, take pains to.
beflissen [bə'flısən], *adj.* eager to serve, assiduous.
beflügeln [bə'fly:gəln], *v.a.* give wings; (*fig.*) accelerate, animate.
befolgen [bə'fɔlgən], *v.a.* follow, obey; *einen Befehl* —, comply with an order.
befördern [bə'fœrdərn], *v.a.* despatch, forward, send, post, mail, transmit; promote, advance.
Beförderung [bə'fœrdəruŋ], *f.* (—, *pl.* —en) forwarding, transmission; (*office*) promotion, advancement.
Beförderungsmittel [bə'fœrdəruŋsmı-təl], *n.* (—s, *pl.* —) conveyance, means of transport.
befragen [bə'fra:gən], *v.a.* question, interrogate, examine.
befreien [bə'fraıən], *v.a.* free, liberate.
befremden [bə'frɛmdən], *v.a.* appear strange, astonish, surprise.
befreunden [bə'frɔyndən], *v.a.* befriend. — *v.r. sich mit einem* —, make friends with s.o.
befriedigen [bə'fri:dıgən], *v.a.* content, satisfy; appease, calm.
befruchten [bə'fruxtən], *v.a.* fertilise; impregnate.
Befugnis [bə'fu:knıs], *f.* (—, *pl.* —se) authority, right, warrant.
Befund [bə'funt], *m.* (—s, *pl.* —e) (*Med.*) diagnosis, findings.
befürchten [bə'fyrçtən], *v.a.* fear, be afraid of.
befürworten [bə'fy:rvɔrtən], *v.a.* support, second.

begabt [bə'ga:pt], *adj.* gifted, talented, able.

Begabung [bə'ga:buŋ], *f.* (—, *pl.* —en) ability, talent, gift.

begaffen [bə'gafən], *v.a.* stare at, gape at.

begatten [bə'gatən], *v.r.* sich —, (*Zool.*) copulate.

begeben [bə'ge:bən], *v.r. irr.* sich an einen Ort —, go to a place, betake o.s. to a place; happen, occur.

Begebenheit [bə'ge:bənhaɪt], *f.* (—, *pl.* —en) happening, event, occurrence.

begegnen [bə'ge:gnən], *v.n.* (*aux.* sein) meet, meet with, encounter, befall, happen.

begehen [bə'ge:ən], *v.a. irr.* (*road*) walk along, go over; (*festival*) celebrate; (*crime*) commit, perpetrate.

begehren [bə'ge:rən], *v.a.* desire, wish, covet, want.—*v.n.* nach etwas —, long for s.th.

begehrlich [bə'ge:rlɪç], *adj.* covetous, greedy, desirous.

begeifern [bə'gaɪfərn], *v.a.* spit at; (*fig.*) vilify, besmirch.

begeistern [bə'gaɪstərn], *v.a.* inspire, fill with enthusiasm, enrapture.— *v.r.* sich für etwas —, become enthusiastic about s.th.

Begier(de) [bə'gi:r(də)], *f.* (—, *pl.* —den) desire, lust, appetite.

begierig [bə'gi:rɪç], *adj.* desirous, lustful; anxious; curious (for news).

begießen [bə'gi:sən], *v.a. irr.* (*plants*) water; (*meat etc.*) baste; etwas festlich —, celebrate s.th. by drinking; sich die Nase —, (*coll.*) get tight.

Beginn [bə'gɪn], *m.* (—s, *no pl.*) beginning, commencement, start.

beginnen [bə'gɪnən], *v.a.,v.n. irr.* begin, commence, start.

beglaubigen [bə'glaubɪgən], *v.a.* attest, certify, verify; accredit (an ambassador).

Beglaubigungsschreiben [bə'glaubɪguŋsʃraɪbən], *n.* (—s, *pl.* —) credentials.

begleichen [bə'glaɪçən], *v.a. irr.* (*bill*) pay, settle.

begleiten [bə'glaɪtən], *v.a.* accompany, escort, see s.o. off, home etc.

Begleiter [bə'glaɪtər], *m.* (—s, *pl.* —) companion, escort; (*Mus.*) accompanist.

Begleiterscheinung [bə'glaɪtərʃaɪnuŋ], *f.* (—, *pl.* —en) concomitant; (*Med.*) complication, attendant symptom.

Begleitung [bə'glaɪtuŋ], *f.* (—, *pl.* —en) company; (*Mus.*) accompaniment.

beglücken [bə'glykən], *v.a.* make happy.

beglückwünschen [bə'glykvynʃən], *v.a.* congratulate.

begnadet [bə'gna:dət], *adj.* highly talented.

begnadigen [bə'gna:dɪgən], *v.a.* pardon, reprieve.

begnügen [bə'gny:gən], *v.r.* sich mit etwas —, content o.s. with s.th.

Begonie [bə'go:njə], *f.* (—, *pl.* —n) (*Bot.*) begonia.

begraben [bə'gra:bən], *v.a. irr.* bury, inter.

Begräbnis [bə'grɛ:pnɪs], *n.* (—ses, *pl.* —se) burial, funeral, interment.

begreifen [bə'graɪfən], *v.a. irr.* understand, comprehend, conceive.

begreiflich [bə'graɪflɪç], *adj.* comprehensible, conceivable, understandable.

begrenzen [bə'grɛntsən], *v.a.* bound, border, limit.

Begriff [bə'grɪf], *m.* (—s, *pl.* —e) notion, concept, idea, conception; im — sein, be about to . . . .

begriffen [bə'grɪfən], *adj.* — sein in, be engaged in.

begriffsstutzig [bə'grɪfsʃtutsɪç], *adj.* obtuse, dense, slow in the uptake.

begründen [bə'gryndən], *v.a.* base on, justify, found, establish.

begrüßen [bə'gry:sən], *v.a.* greet, salute, welcome.

begünstigen [bə'gynstɪgən], *v.a.* favour, prefer.

Begutachter [bə'gu:taxtər], *m.* (—s, *pl.* —) expert; (*Sch.*) assessor, second examiner.

Begutachtung [bə'gu:taxtuŋ], *f.* (—, *pl.* —en) expert opinion, assessment, report.

begütert [bə'gy:tərt], *adj.* wealthy, rich, well-to-do.

behaart [bə'ha:rt], *adj.* covered with hair, hairy.

behäbig [bə'hɛ:bɪç], *adj.* comfortable, corpulent, portly.

behaften [bə'haftən], *v.a.* charge, burden.

behagen [bə'ha:gən], *v.n.* please, be agreeable; es behagt mir nicht, I do not like it.

behaglich [bə'ha:klɪç], *adj.* cosy, comfortable, snug.

behalten [bə'haltən], *v.a. irr.* retain, keep.

Behälter [bə'hɛltər], *m.* (—s, *pl.* —) container; box, bin; (*water*) reservoir; tank.

behandeln [bə'handəln], *v.a.* treat, use; (*Med.*) treat; (*subject*) treat; handle.

Behandlung [bə'handluŋ], *f.* (—, *pl.* —en) treatment, use; (*Med.*) treatment.

Behang [bə'haŋ], *m.* (—es, *pl.* ⁖e) hanging(s); appendage.

behängen [bə'hɛŋən], *v.a. irr.* festoon with, drape.

beharren [bə'harən], *v.n.* persevere, persist, insist.

beharrlich [bə'harlɪç], *adj.* persevering, persistent, constant, firm.

behauen [bə'hauən], *v.a.* (*stones*) hew, cut.

behaupten [bə'hauptən], *v.a.* claim, assert, affirm, maintain.

Behauptung [bə'haυptυŋ], *f.* (—, *pl.* —en) claim, assertion, affirmation.

Behausung [bə'haυzυŋ], *f.* (—, *pl.* —en) habitation, housing.

behelfen [bə'hɛlfən], *v.r. irr.* sich — mit, make do with.

behelfsmäßig [bə'hɛlfsmɛ:sɪç], *adj.* makeshift, temporary.

behelligen [bə'hɛlɪgən], *v.a.* trouble, molest, disturb.

behend(e) [bə'hɛndə], *adj.* quick, nimble, agile.

beherbergen [bə'hɛrbɛrgən], *v.a.* give shelter to, put up, harbour.

beherrschen [bə'hɛrʃən], *v.a.* rule, govern, dominate; *eine Sache* —, master a subject. — *v.r.* sich —, control o.s.

Beherrschung [bə'hɛrʃυŋ], *f.* (—, *pl.* (*rare*) —en) domination, sway; (*subject*) grasp; (*languages*) command.

beherzigen [bə'hɛrtsɪgən], *v.a.* take to heart, follow, heed.

Beherztheit [bə'hɛrtsthaɪt], *f.* (—, *no pl.*) courage, spirit.

behexen [bə'hɛksən], *v.a.* bewitch.

behilflich [bə'hɪlflɪç], *adj.* helpful, useful.

behindern [bə'hɪndərn], *v.a.* hinder, hamper.

Behörde [bə'hœrdə], *f.* (—, *pl.* —n) the authorities.

behufs [bə'hu:fs], *prep.* (*Genit.*) in order to, with a view to.

behüten [bə'hy:tən], *v.a.* guard, protect; *Gott behüte!* Heaven forbid!

behutsam [bə'hu:tza:m], *adj.* careful, cautious.

bei [baɪ], *prep.* (*Dat.*) (*locally*) near by, close by, next to, at.

beibehalten ['baɪbəhaltən], *v.a. irr.* keep, retain.

Beiblatt ['baɪblat], *n.* (—s, *pl.* ‒er) supplement (to a newspaper).

beibringen ['baɪbrɪŋən], *v.a. irr.* adduce (proof); produce (witnesses); (*fig.*) teach; impart to.

Beichte ['baɪçtə], *f.* (—, *pl.* —n) confession.

Beichtstuhl ['baɪçtʃtu:l], *m.* (—s, *pl.* ‒e) confessional.

beide ['baɪdə], *adj.* both, either, the two.

beiderlei ['baɪdərlaɪ], *adj.* of both kinds.

beidrehen ['baɪdre:ən], *v.n.* (*Naut.*) heave to.

Beifall ['baɪfal], *m.* (—s, *no pl.*) (*verbal*) approbation; (*shouting*) acclamation, acclaim; (*clapping*) applause.

beifällig ['baɪfɛlɪç], *adj.* favourable, approving, assenting.

beifügen ['baɪfy:gən], *v.a.* enclose, attach.

Beifuß ['baɪfu:s], *m.* (—es, *no pl.*) (*Bot.*) mugwort.

beigeben ['baɪge:bən], *v.a. irr.* add, join to. — *v.n. klein* —, give in.

Beigeschmack ['baɪgəʃmak], *m.* (—s, *no pl.*) aftertaste, tang.

beigesellen ['baɪgəzɛlən], *v.r.* sich —, associate with.

Beihilfe ['baɪhɪlfə], *f.* (—, *pl.* —n) aid, assistance, subsidy.

beikommen ['baɪkɔmən], *v.n. irr.* (*aux.* sein) *einer Sache* —, to grapple with s.th.; *ich kann ihm nicht* —, I cannot catch him out, get at him.

Beil [baɪl], *n.* (—s, *pl.* —e) hatchet, axe.

Beilage ['baɪla:gə], *f.* (—, *pl.* —n) enclosure (with a letter); supplement (to a newspaper); *Braten mit* —, joint with vegetables.

beiläufig ['baɪlɔyfɪç], *adv.* by the way, incidentally.

beilegen ['baɪle:gən], *v.a.* add, join; enclose (in letter).

beileibe [baɪ'laɪbə], *int.* — *nicht!* on no account!

Beileid ['baɪlaɪt], *n.* (—s, *no pl.*) condolence, sympathy.

beiliegen ['baɪli:gən], *v.n. irr.* be enclosed with.

beimengen ['baɪmɛŋən], *v.a.* (*Cul.*) mix with, add.

beimessen ['baɪmɛsən], *v.a. irr. einem etwas* —, impute s.th. to s.o.; *einem Glauben* —, credit s.o., give credence to.

Bein [baɪn], *n.* (—s, *pl.* —e) leg; *einem auf die* — *helfen*, give a helping hand to s.o.

beinahe [baɪ'na:ə], *adv.* almost, nearly.

Beiname ['baɪna:mə], *m.* (—ns, *pl.* —n) surname; nickname.

Beinbruch ['baɪnbrux], *m.* (—s, *pl.* ‒e) fracture of the leg; (*coll.*) *Hals- und Beinbruch!* good luck!

Beinkleider ['baɪnklaɪdər], *n. pl.* (*obs.*) pants, trousers.

beipflichten ['baɪpflɪçtən], *v.n. einem* —, agree with s.o.

beirren [bə'ɪrən], *v.a. sich nicht* — *lassen*, not let o.s. be dissuaded *or* put off.

beisammen [baɪ'zamən], *adv.* together.

Beischlaf ['baɪʃla:f], *m.* (—s, *no pl.*) cohabitation, coition.

Beisein ['baɪzaɪn], *n.* (—s, *no pl.*) *im* — *von*, in the presence of.

beiseite [baɪ'zaɪtə], *adv.* apart, aside; (*Theat.*) aside.

beisetzen ['baɪzɛtsən], *v.a.* bury, inter, entomb.

Beispiel ['baɪʃpi:l], *n.* (—s, *pl.* —e) example, instance; *zum* — (*abbr.* z.B.), for instance, for example.

beißen ['baɪsən], *v.a. irr.* bite; (*pepper, smoke*) burn, sting.

Beißzange ['baɪstsaŋə], *f.* (—, *pl.* —n) pair of pincers *or* nippers.

Beistand ['baɪʃtant], *m.* (—s, *pl.* ‒e) assistance, help; (*Law*) counsel; — *leisten*, give assistance.

beistehen ['baɪʃte:ən], *v.n. irr. einem* —, stand by s.o., help s.o.

beisteuern ['baɪʃtɔyərn], *v.a. zu etwas* —, contribute to s.th.

beistimmen ['baɪʃtɪmən], *v.n.* agree with, assent.

Beistrich ['baɪʃtrɪç], *m.* (—(e)s, *pl.* —e) comma.

beitragen ['baɪtra:gən], *v.a. irr.* contribute; be conducive to.

beitreten ['baɪtre:tən], *v.n. irr.* (*aux.* sein) join (a club); enter into partnership with (a firm).

Beitritt ['baɪtrɪt], *m.* (—s, *no pl.*) accession, joining.

Beiwagen ['baɪva:gən], *m.* (—s, *pl.* —) trailer, sidecar (on motor cycle).

beiwohnen ['baɪvo:nən], *v.n.* be present at, attend.

Beiwort ['baɪvɔrt], *n.* (—s, *pl.* ˙er) adjective, epithet.

Beize ['baɪtsə], *f.* (—, *pl.* —n) caustic fluid; (*wood*) stain.

beizeiten [baɪ'tsaɪtən], *adv.* betimes, early, in good time.

beizen ['baɪtsən], *v.a.* cauterise; (*wood*) stain.

bejahen [bə'ja:ən], *v.a.* answer in the affirmative.

bejahrt [bə'ja:rt], *adj.* aged, elderly, old.

bejammern [bə'jamərn], *v.a.* bemoan, bewail.

bekannt [bə'kant], *adj.* known, well-known; — *mit*, acquainted with.

Bekannte [bə'kantə], *m.* (—n, *pl.* —n) acquaintance.

bekanntlich [bə'kantlɪç], *adv.* as is well known.

Bekanntmachung [bə'kantmaxuŋ], *f.* (—, *pl.* —en) publication, announcement.

Bekanntschaft [bə'kantʃaft], *f.* (—, *pl.* —en) — *mit einem machen*, strike up an acquaintance with s.o.

bekehren [bə'ke:rən], *v.a.* convert. — *v.r. sich* —, be converted *or* become a convert (to); reform.

bekennen [bə'kɛnən], *v.a. irr.* confess, profess; admit, own up to.

Bekenner [bə'kɛnər], *m.* (—s, *pl.* —) Confessor (as title).

Bekenntnis [bə'kɛntnɪs], *n.* (—ses, *pl.* —se) confession (of faith), avowal, creed.

beklagen [bə'kla:gən], *v.a.* lament, bewail, deplore. — *v.r. sich* — *über*, complain of.

Beklagte [bə'kla:ktə], *m.* (—n, *pl.* —n) (*Law*) defendant.

bekleiden [bə'klaɪdən], *v.a.* clothe, dress, cover; (*office*) hold.

Bekleidung [bə'klaɪduŋ], *f.* (—, *no pl.*) clothing, clothes; (*office*) administration, holding, exercise.

beklemmen [bə'klɛmən], *v.a. irr.* oppress.

Beklemmung [bə'klɛmuŋ], *f.* (—, *pl.* —en) oppression, anguish.

beklommen [bə'klɔmən], *adj.* anxious, uneasy.

bekommen [bə'kɔmən], *v.a. irr.* obtain, get, receive.

bekömmlich [bə'kœmlɪç], *adj.* beneficial; digestible, wholesome.

beköstigen [bə'kœstɪgən], *v.a.* board; feed.

bekräftigen [bə'krɛftɪgən], *v.a.* aver, corroborate, confirm.

bekränzen [bə'krɛntsən], *v.a.* wreathe, crown (with a garland).

bekreuzigen [bə'krɔytsɪgən], *v.r. sich* —, make the sign of the cross, cross o.s.

bekriegen [bə'kri:gən], *v.a.* make war on.

bekritteln [bə'krɪtəln], *v.a.* criticise, carp at, find fault with.

bekritzeln [bə'krɪtsəln], *v.a.* scrawl on, doodle on.

bekümmern [bə'kymərn], *v.a.* grieve, distress, trouble. — *v.r.* trouble o.s. about, grieve over.

bekunden [bə'kundən], *v.a.* manifest, show; declare.

beladen [bə'la:dən], *v.a. irr.* load.

Belag [bə'la:k], *m.* (—s, *pl.* ˙e) covering, layer; spread (on sandwiches); fur (on the tongue).

belagern [bə'la:gərn], *v.a.* besiege.

Belang [bə'laŋ], *m.* (—s, *pl.* —e) importance; *von* —, of great moment *or* consequence; (*pl.*) concerns, interests.

belangen [bə'laŋən], *v.a.* (*Law*) sue, prosecute.

belanglos [bə'laŋlo:s], *adj.* of small account; irrelevant, unimportant.

belassen [bə'lasən], *v.a. irr. es dabei* —, leave things as they are.

belasten [bə'lastən], *v.a.* load, burden; (*Comm.*) debit, charge; (*Law*) incriminate.

belästigen [bə'lɛstɪgən], *v.a.* bother, pester, molest.

Belastung [bə'lastuŋ], *f.* (—, *pl.* —en) load, burden; (*Comm.*) debiting; (*house*) mortgage; *erbliche* —, hereditary disposition.

Belastungszeuge [bə'lastuŋstsɔygə], *m.* (—n, *pl.* —n) witness for the prosecution.

belaubt [bə'laupt], *adj.* covered with leaves, leafy.

belaufen [bə'laufən], *v.r. irr. sich* — *auf*, amount to, come to.

belauschen [bə'lauʃən], *v.a.* eavesdrop, overhear.

beleben [bə'le:bən], *v.a.* animate, enliven.

Belebtheit [bə'le:pthaɪt], *f.* (—, *no pl.*) animation, liveliness.

Beleg [bə'le:k], *m.* (—s, *pl.* —e) document, proof, receipt, voucher.

belegen [bə'le:gən], *v.a.* cover, overlay; reserve, book (*seat*); support by documents, authenticate, prove.

Belegschaft [bə'le:kʃaft], *f.* (—, *pl.* —en) workers, personnel, staff; (*Min.*) gang, shift.

belegt [bə'le:kt], *adj.* (*tongue*) furred; —*es Brot*, sandwich.

belehnen [bə'le:nən], *v.a.* enfeoff; invest (with a fief).

belehren [bə'le:rən], *v.a.* instruct, advise, inform.

Belehrung [bə'le:ruŋ], *f.* (—, *pl.* —en) information, instruction, advice.

beleibt [bə'laɪpt], *adj.* stout, corpulent, obese.

beleidigen [bə'laɪdɪgən], *v.a.* insult, offend, give offence to.

belesen [bə'le:zən], *adj.* well-read.

beleuchten [bə'lɔyçtən], *v.a.* illumine, illuminate; (*fig.*) throw light on, elucidate.

Beleuchtungskörper [bə'lɔyçtuŋskœr-pər], *m.* (—s, *pl.* —) lighting fixture, lamp.

Belgien ['bɛlgjən], *n.* Belgium.

belichten [bə'lɪçtən], *v.a.* (*Phot.*) expose.

belieben [bə'li:bən], *v.a.*, *v.n.* please, like, choose.

beliebig [bə'li:bɪç], *adj.* optional; any, whatever.

beliebt [bə'li:pt], *adj.* popular, well-liked.

Beliebtheit [bə'li:pthaɪt], *f.* (—, *no pl.*) popularity.

bellen ['bɛlən], *v.n.* bark.

beloben [bə'lo:bən], *v.a.* praise, approve.

belohnen [bə'lo:nən], *v.a.* reward, recompense.

belügen [bə'ly:gən], *v.a. irr. einen* —, tell lies to s.o., deceive s.o. by lying.

belustigen [bə'lustɪgən], *v.a.* amuse, divert, entertain.

bemächtigen [bə'mɛçtɪgən], *v.r. sich einer Sache* —, take possession of s.th.

bemäkeln [bə'mɛ:kəln], *v.a.* find fault with.

bemalen [bə'ma:lən], *v.a.* paint (over).

bemängeln [bə'mɛŋəln], *v.a.* find fault with.

bemannen [bə'manən], *v.a.* man.

bemänteln [bə'mɛntəln], *v.a.* cloak, hide.

bemeistern [bə'maɪstərn], *v.a.* master.

bemerkbar [bə'mɛrkbaːr], *adj.* perceptible, noticeable.

bemerken [bə'mɛrkən], *v.a.* observe, perceive, notice.

Bemerkung [bə'mɛrkuŋ], *f.* (—, *pl.* —en) remark, observation, note.

bemessen [bə'mɛsən], *v.a. irr.* measure; curtail.

bemitleiden [bə'mɪtlaɪdən], *v.a.* pity, be sorry for.

bemittelt [bə'mɪtəlt], *adj.* well-off, well-to-do.

bemoost [bə'mo:st], *adj.* mossy.

bemühen [bə'my:ən], *v.a.* trouble, give trouble (to). — *v.r. sich* —, take pains, strive, endeavour.

bemüht [bə'my:t], *adj.* studious; — *sein*, endeavour, try to.

bemuttern [bə'mutərn], *v.a.* mother.

benachbart [bə'naxba:rt], *adj.* neighbouring, adjacent.

benachrichtigen [bə'naxrɪçtɪgən], *v.a.* inform, give notice of, notify.

benachteiligen [bə'naxtaɪlɪgən], *v.a.* prejudice, discriminate against, handicap.

benagen [bə'na:gən], *v.a.* gnaw at.

benebeln [bə'ne:bəln], *v.a.* befog, cloud; (*fig.*) dim, intoxicate.

benedeien [bene'daɪən], *v.a.* bless, glorify.

Benediktiner [benedɪk'ti:nər], *m.* (—s, *pl.* —) (monk) Benedictine; Benedictine liqueur.

Benefiz [bene'fi:ts], *n.* (—es, *pl.* —e) benefit; benefit performance.

Benehmen [bə'ne:mən], *n.* (—s, *no pl.*) conduct, behaviour.

benehmen [bə'ne:mən], *v.r. irr. sich* —, behave, conduct o.s.

beneiden [bə'naɪdən], *v.a. einen* — *um*, envy s.o. (s.th.).

benennen [bə'nɛnən], *v.a.* name.

benetzen [bə'nɛtsən], *v.a.* moisten.

Bengel ['bɛŋəl], *m.* (—s, *pl.* —) naughty boy, scamp; rascal, lout.

benommen [bə'nɔmən], *adj.* dazed, giddy.

benötigen [bə'nø:tɪgən], *v.a.* be in need of, require.

benutzen [bə'nutsən], *v.a.* make use of, utilise.

Benzin [bɛnt'si:n], *n.* (—s, *no pl.*) benzine; (*Motor.*) petrol; (*Am.*) gas, gasoline.

beobachten [bə'o:baxtən], *v.a.* watch, observe.

bequem [bə'kve:m], *adj.* comfortable, easy; convenient; indolent, lazy.

bequemen [bə'kve:mən], *v.r. sich* —, condescend (to), comply (with).

Bequemlichkeit [bə'kve:mlɪçkaɪt], *f.* (—, *pl.* —en) convenience, ease; indolence.

beraten [bə'ra:tən], *v.a. irr.* advise, assist with advice, counsel. — *v.r. sich* — *mit*, confer with, consult with.

beratschlagen [bə'ra:tʃla:gən], *v.n.* deliberate with.

Beratung [bə'ra:tuŋ], *f.* (—, *pl.* —en) council, deliberation, consultation.

berauben [bə'raubən], *v.a.* rob, deprive (s.o.) of (s.th.).

berauschen [bə'rauʃən], *v.a.* intoxicate.

berechnen [bə'rɛçnən], *v.a.* compute, charge, calculate, estimate.

berechtigen [bə'rɛçtɪgən], *v.a. einen zu etwas* —, entitle s.o. to s.th.; authorise s.o. to have or do s.th.

beredsam [bə're:tza:m], *adj.* eloquent.

beredt [bə're:t], *adj.* eloquent.

Bereich [bə'raɪç], *m. & n.* (—s, *pl.* —e) extent, realm, sphere, scope.

bereichern [bə'raɪçərn], *v.a.* enrich, enlarge.

bereisen [bə'raɪzən], *v.a.* travel over or through, tour (a country).

bereit [bə'raɪt], *adj.* ready, prepared.

bereiten [bə'raɪtən], *v.a.* prepare, get ready.

bereits [bə'raɪts], *adv.* already.

Bereitschaft [bə'raɪtʃaft], *f.* (—, *no pl.*) readiness, preparedness.

bereitwillig [bə'raɪtvɪlɪç], *adj.* willing, ready, obliging.

bereuen [bə'rɔyən], *v.a.* repent, be sorry for, regret.

Berg [bɛrk], *m.* (**—es**, *pl.* **—e**) mountain, hill.

bergab [bɛrk'ap], *adj.* downhill.

Bergamt ['bɛrkamt], *n.* (**—s**, *pl.* ˙er) mining-office, mine authority.

bergan [bɛrk'an], *adj.* uphill.

Bergarbeiter ['bɛrkarbaɪtər], *m.* (**—s**, *pl.* **—**) miner, collier.

bergauf [bɛrk'auf], *adj.* uphill.

Bergbau ['bɛrkbau], *m.* (**—s**, *no pl.*) mining, mining industry.

bergen ['bɛrgən], *v.a. irr.* shelter, protect, save; (*flotsam*) save, recover, salvage.

bergig ['bɛrgɪç], *adj.* mountainous, hilly.

Bergkristall ['bɛrkkrɪstal], *m.* (**—s**, *pl.* **—e**) rock-crystal.

Bergleute ['bɛrklɔytə], *pl.* miners, colliers.

Bergmann ['bɛrkman], *m.* (**—s**, *pl.* **Bergleute**) miner, collier.

Bergpredigt ['bɛrkpreːdɪçt], *f.* (**—**, *no pl.*) Sermon on the Mount.

Bergschlucht ['bɛrkʃluxt], *f.* (**—**, *pl.* **—en**) ravine, gorge.

Bergsteiger ['bɛrkʃtaɪgər], *m.* (**—s**, *pl.* **—**) mountaineer.

Bergstock ['bɛrkʃtɔk], *m.* (**—s**, *pl.* ˙e) alpenstock.

Bergsturz ['bɛrkʃturts], *m.* (**—es**, *pl.* ˙e) landslip, landslide.

Bergung ['bɛrgun], *f.* (**—**, *pl.* **—en**) sheltering, salvaging; rescue operation.

Bergwerk ['bɛrkvɛrk], *n.* (**—s**, *pl.* **—e**) mine, pit.

Bericht [bə'rɪçt], *m.* (**—s**, *pl.* **—e**) report, account, statement; — *erstatten*, report, give an account of.

Berichterstatter [bə'rɪçtərʃtatər], *m.* (**—s**, *pl.* **—**) reporter.

berichtigen [bə'rɪçtɪgən], *v.a.* set right, correct, rectify, amend.

berieseln [bə'riːzəln], *v.a.* irrigate.

beritten [bə'rɪtən], *adj.* mounted on horseback.

Berlin [bɛr'liːn], *n.* Berlin; —*er Blau*, Prussian blue.

Bern [bɛrn], *n.* Berne.

Bernhardiner [bɛrnhar'diːnər], *m.* (**—s**, *pl.* **—**) Cistercian monk; Newfoundland dog; St. Bernard dog.

Bernstein ['bɛrnʃtaɪn], *m.* (**—s**, *no pl.*) amber.

bersten ['bɛrstən], *v.n. irr.* (*aux.* sein) burst.

berüchtigt [bə'rʏçtɪçt], *adj.* notorious, infamous.

berücken [bə'rʏkən], *v.a.* enchant, fascinate.

berücksichtigen [bə'rʏksɪçtɪgən], *v.a.* have regard to, take into consideration, allow for.

Beruf [bə'ruːf], *m.* (**—s**, *pl.* **—e**) profession, occupation, calling, trade.

berufen [bə'ruːfən], *v.a. irr.* (*meeting*) call, convene; appoint (to an office). — *v.r. sich — auf*, appeal to, refer to. — *adj.* competent, qualified.

berufsmäßig [bə'ruːfsmɛːsɪç], *adj.* professional.

Berufung [bə'ruːfun], *f.* (**—**, *pl.* **—en**) call, vocation, appointment; (*Law*) appeal.

beruhen [bə'ruːən], *v.n. auf etwas —*, be based on, be founded on.

beruhigen [bə'ruːɪgən], *v.a.* calm, pacify; comfort, console, set at rest.

Beruhigung [bə'ruːɪgun], *f.* (**—**, *pl.* **—en**) reassurance, quieting, calming.

berühmt [bə'ryːmt], *adj.* famous, celebrated, illustrious, renowned.

berühren [bə'ryːrən], *v.a.* touch, handle; (*subject*) mention, touch upon; *peinlich berührt*, unpleasantly affected.

berußt [bə'ruːst], *adj.* sooty.

Beryll [be'rʏl], *m.* (**—s**, *pl.* **—e**) beryl.

besagen [bə'zaːgən], *v.a.* mean, signify.

besagt [bə'zaːkt], *adj.* aforesaid, above-mentioned.

besaiten [bə'zaɪtən], *v.a.* fit with strings.

Besan [bə'zaːn], *m.* (**—s**, *pl.* **—e**) (*Naut.*) miz(z)en.

besänftigen [bə'zɛnftɪgən], *v.a.* calm, appease, pacify.

Besatz [bə'zats], *m.* (**—es**, *pl.* ˙e) trimming, border.

Besatzung [bə'zatsun], *f.* (**—**, *pl.* **—en**) crew; (*Mil.*) garrison, occupation.

besaufen [bə'zaufən], *v.r. irr.* (*vulg.*) *sich —*, get drunk.

beschädigen [bə'ʃɛːdɪgən], *v.a.* damage.

beschaffen [bə'ʃafən], *v.a.* procure, get. — *adj.* conditioned, constituted.

Beschaffenheit [bə'ʃafənhaɪt], *f.* (**—**, *no pl.*) nature, kind, quality, condition.

beschäftigen [bə'ʃɛftɪgən], *v.a.* occupy, employ.

beschämen [bə'ʃɛːmən], *v.a.* make ashamed, shame.

beschatten [bə'ʃatən], *v.a.* shade, shadow; follow (s.o.).

Beschau [bə'ʃau], *f.* (**—**, *no pl.*) examination; inspection.

beschauen [bə'ʃauən], *v.a.* view, look at.

beschaulich [bə'ʃaulɪç], *adj.* tranquil, contemplative.

Beschaulichkeit [bə'ʃaulɪçkaɪt], *f.* (**—**, *pl.* **—en**) contemplation, contemplation.

Bescheid [bə'ʃaɪt], *m.* (**—s**, *pl.* **—e**) answer, information; (*Law*) decision; — *wissen*, know o.'s way about; know what's what.

bescheiden [bə'ʃaɪdən], *v.a. irr.* inform (s.o.); *einen zu sich —*, send for s.o. — *adj.* modest, unassuming.

Bescheidenheit [bə'ʃaɪdənhaɪt], *f.* (**—**, *no pl.*) modesty.

bescheinen [bə'ʃaɪnən], *v.a. irr.* shine upon.

bescheinigen [bə'ʃaɪnɪgən], *v.a. einem etwas —*, attest, certify.

beschenken [bə'ʃɛŋkən], *v.a.* give a present to.

bescheren [bə'ʃeːrən], *v.a.* give (a present to), bestow (s.th. on s.o.).

Bescherung [bə'ʃeːruŋ], *f.* (—, *pl.* —en) giving (of present); *das ist eine schöne —*, (*fig.*) this is a nice mess!

beschicken [bə'ʃikən], *v.a. eine Ausstellung —*, contribute to an exhibition.

beschießen [bə'ʃiːsən], *v.a. irr.* shoot at, fire upon, bombard.

beschiffen [bə'ʃifən], *v.a.* navigate, sail.

beschimpfen [bə'ʃimpfən], *v.a.* insult, abuse, revile.

beschirmen [bə'ʃirmən], *v.a.* protect, shelter, defend.

Beschlag [bə'ʃlaːk], *m.* (—s, *pl.* ⸚e) mounting; metal fitting; (*on stick*) ferrule; *etwas mit — belegen*, or *in — nehmen*, sequestrate, confiscate, seize.

beschlagen [bə'ʃlaːgən], *v.a. irr.* shoe (a horse). — *v.n.* (*window*) mist over.

Beschlagnahme [bə'ʃlaːknaːmə], *f.* (—, *pl.* —n) confiscation, seizure.

beschleunigen [bə'ʃlɔynigən], *v.a.* hasten, speed up, accelerate.

beschließen [bə'ʃliːsən], *v.a. irr.* shut, lock up; close, conclude, finish; decide, resolve upon.

Beschluß [bə'ʃlus], *m.* (—sses, *pl.* ⸚sse) determination, resolution, decree.

beschmieren [bə'ʃmiːrən], *v.a.* soil, smear.

beschmutzen [bə'ʃmutsən], *v.a.* soil, dirty, foul.

beschneiden [bə'ʃnaidən], *v.a. irr.* cut, clip; (*Hort.*) lop, prune; (*animals*) crop; circumcise.

Beschneidung [bə'ʃnaiduŋ], *f.* (—, *pl.* —en) lopping, pruning; circumcision.

beschönigen [bə'ʃøːnigən], *v.a.* palliate, excuse.

beschränken [bə'ʃrɛnkən], *v.a.* limit, restrict.

beschränkt [bə'ʃrɛnkt], *adj.* limited; *etwas —*, a little stupid; *Gesellschaft mit —er Haftung*, limited (liability) company.

Beschränkung [bə'ʃrɛnkuŋ], *f.* (—, *pl.* —en) limitation, restriction.

beschreiben [bə'ʃraibən], *v.a. irr.* describe; write upon.

beschreiten [bə'ʃraitən], *v.a. irr.* tread on.

beschuldigen [bə'ʃuldigən], *v.a.* charge (s.o.), accuse.

beschützen [bə'ʃytsən], *v.a.* protect, shelter, guard.

Beschützer [bə'ʃytsər], *m.* (—s, *pl.* —) protector, defender.

Beschwerde [bə'ʃveːrdə], *f.* (—, *pl.* —en) trouble, hardship, difficulty; complaint, grievance.

beschweren [bə'ʃveːrən], *v.a.* make heavier, weight. — *v.r. sich über etwas —*, complain of s.th.

beschwerlich [bə'ʃveːrliç], *adj.* burdensome, hard, troublesome.

beschwichtigen [bə'ʃviçtigən], *v.a.* soothe, appease, still.

beschwindeln [bə'ʃvindəln], *v.a.* cheat, swindle (s.o.).

beschwingt [bə'ʃviŋkt], *adj.* winged, light-footed.

beschwipst [bə'ʃvipst], *adj.* (*coll.*) tipsy.

beschwören [bə'ʃvøːrən], *v.a. irr.* testify on oath; *einen —*, implore s.o.; conjure (up) (ghosts etc.); exorcize.

beseelen [bə'zeːlən], *v.a.* animate.

besehen [bə'zeːən], *v.a. irr.* look at, inspect.

beseitigen [bə'zaitigən], *v.a.* remove.

beseligt [bə'zeːliçt], *adj.* enraptured, beatified.

Besen ['beːzən], *m.* (—s, *pl.* —) broom, besom.

Besenstiel ['beːzənʃtiːl], *m.* (—s, *pl.* —e) broom-stick.

besessen [bə'zɛsən], *adj.* possessed, obsessed, mad.

besetzen [bə'zɛtsən], *v.a.* (*dress*) lace; (*Mil.*) occupy, garrison; (*office*) fill; (*Theat.*) cast; (*seat*) occupy, take; *besetzt*, engaged.

Besetzung [bə'zɛtsuŋ], *f.* (—, *pl.* —en) lacing, trimming; appointment (to post); (*Theat.*) cast.

besichtigen [bə'ziçtigən], *v.a.* view, go over, inspect, examine.

besiedeln [bə'ziːdəln], *v.a.* colonise.

besiegeln [bə'ziːgəln], *v.a.* seal, set o.'s seal to.

besiegen [bə'ziːgən], *v.a.* vanquish, conquer, overcome.

besinnen [bə'zinən], *v.r. irr.* reflect; *sich auf etwas —*, recollect, remember, think of.

besinnungslos [bə'zinuŋsloːs], *adj.* insensible, unconscious.

Besitz [bə'zits], *m.* (—es, *no pl.*) possession, property.

besitzanzeigend [bə'zitsantsaigənt], *adj.* (*Gram.*) possessive.

besitzen [bə'zitsən], *v.a. irr.* possess, own, have.

Besitzergreifung [bə'zitsɛrgraifuŋ], *f.* (—, *no pl.*) occupation, taking possession (of).

besoffen [bə'zɔfən], *adj.* (*vulg.*) drunk.

besohlen [bə'zoːlən], *v.a.* sole (shoes).

besolden [bə'zɔldən], *v.a.* give a salary to, pay.

besonder [bə'zɔndər], *adj.* special, particular.

Besonderheit [bə'zɔndərhait], *f.* (—, *pl.* —en) particularity, peculiarity, strangeness.

besonders [bə'zɔndərs], *adv.* especially.

besonnen [bə'zɔnən], *adj.* prudent, cautious, collected, circumspect.

besorgen [bə'zɔrgən], *v.a.* take care of, provide, procure.

Besorgnis [bə'zɔrknis], *f.* (—, *pl.* —se) care, concern, anxiety, fear.

besorgt [bə'zɔrkt], *adj.* apprehensive, anxious, worried.

Besorgung [bə'zɔrguŋ], *f.* (—, *pl.* —en) care, management; purchase, commission; —*en machen*, go shopping.

bespannen [bə'ʃpanən], *v.a.* string (a musical instrument); put horses (to a carriage).

bespötteln [bə'ʃpœtəln], *v.a.* ridicule.

besprechen [bə'ʃprɛçən], *v.a. irr.* discuss, talk over; (book) review. — *v.r. sich — mit*, confer with.

bespritzen [bə'ʃprɪtsən], *v.a.* sprinkle, splash.

besser ['bɛsər], *adj.* better; *um so —*, so much the better; *je mehr desto —*, the more the better; *— sein als*, be better than, be preferable to; *— werden*, (*weather*) clear up; (*health*) improve.

bessern ['bɛsərn], *v.a.* better, improve. — *v.r. sich —*, reform, improve, mend o.'s ways.

Besserung ['bɛsəruŋ], *f.* (—*pl.* —en) improvement, amendment, reform; (*Med.*) recovery; *gute —*, get well soon.

Besserungsanstalt ['bɛsəruŋsanʃtalt], *f.* (—, *pl.* —en) reformatory.

best ['bɛst], *adj.* best.

bestallen [bə'ʃtalən], *v.a.* appoint.

Bestand [bə'ʃtant], *m.* (—s, *pl.* ⸚e) continuance, duration; stock; balance of cash; *— haben*, endure.

Bestandaufnahme [bə'ʃtantaufna:mə], *f.* (—, *pl.* —n) (*Comm.*) stock-taking.

beständig [bə'ʃtɛndɪç], *adj.* continual, perpetual; (*persons*) steady, steadfast, constant.

Bestandteil [bə'ʃtanttail], *m.* (—s, *pl.* —e) constituent part, component, ingredient, essential part.

bestärken [bə'ʃtɛrkən], *v.a.* confirm, strengthen.

bestätigen [bə'ʃtɛːtɪgən], *v.a.* confirm, ratify, bear out, sanction; *den Empfang eines Briefes —*, acknowledge receipt of a letter.

bestatten [bə'ʃtatən], *v.a.* bury, inter.

bestäuben [bə'ʃtɔybən], *v.a.* cover with dust, spray; (*Bot.*) pollinate.

bestechen [bə'ʃtɛçən], *v.a. irr.* bribe, corrupt; (*fig.*) captivate.

bestechlich [bə'ʃtɛçlɪç], *adj.* corruptible.

Bestechung [bə'ʃtɛçuŋ], *f.* (—, *pl.* —en) corruption, bribery.

Besteck [bə'ʃtɛk], *n.* (—s, *pl.* —e) set of knife, fork and spoon; set *or* case (of instruments).

Bestehen [bə'ʃteːən], *n.* (—s, *no pl.*) existence.

bestehen [bə'ʃteːən], *v.a. irr.* undergo, endure, pass (an examination). — *v.n.* exist; *aus etwas —*, consist of s.th.; be composed of s.th.; *auf* (*Dat.*) —, insist upon s.th.

besteigen [bə'ʃtaigən], *v.a. irr.* ascend, mount, climb.

bestellen [bə'ʃtɛlən], *v.a.* order, book; appoint; put in order; (*letter, message*) deliver; (*field*) till.

Bestellung [bə'ʃtɛluŋ], *f.* (—, *pl.* —en) order, commission, delivery (of letter); tilling (of field); appointment; *auf —*, to order.

bestens ['bɛstəns], *adv.* in the best manner.

besteuern [bə'ʃtɔyərn], *v.a.* tax.

bestialisch [bɛstɪ'aːlɪʃ], *adj.* beastly, bestial.

Bestie ['bɛstjə], *f.* (—, *pl.* —n) beast, brute.

bestimmen [bə'ʃtɪmən], *v.a.* fix, settle; decide (s.th.); determine, define.

bestimmt [bə'ʃtɪmt], *adj.* decided, fixed, appointed; *ganz —*, positively, most decidedly.

Bestimmtheit [bə'ʃtɪmthait], *f.* (—, *no pl.*) certainty.

Bestimmung [bə'ʃtɪmuŋ], *f.* (—, *pl.* —en) settlement, decision, determination; provision; destiny.

bestrafen [bə'ʃtraːfən], *v.a.* punish, chastise.

bestrahlen [bə'ʃtraːlən], *v.a.* irradiate; (*Med.*) treat by radiotherapy.

bestreben [bə'ʃtreːbən], *v.r. sich —*, exert o.s., strive (for), endeavour.

Bestrebung [bə'ʃtreːbuŋ], *f.* (—, *pl.* —en) effort, endeavour, exertion.

bestreichen [bə'ʃtraiçən], *v.a. irr.* spread.

bestreiten [bə'ʃtraitən], *v.a. irr.* contest, deny, dispute; defray (costs).

bestreuen [bə'ʃtrɔyən], *v.a.* sprinkle, strew, powder.

bestricken [bə'ʃtrɪkən], *v.a.* ensnare, entangle.

bestürmen [bə'ʃtyrmən], *v.a.* storm, assail; (*fig.*) importune.

bestürzen [bə'ʃtyrtsən], *v.a.* dismay, confound, perplex.

Besuch [bə'zuːx], *m.* (—s, *pl.* —e) visit; (*person*) visitor.

besuchen [bə'zuːxən], *v.a.* visit, call on: attend; frequent.

besudeln [bə'zuːdəln], *v.a.* soil, foul.

betagt [bə'taːkt], *adj.* aged, elderly.

betätigen [bə'tɛːtɪgən], *v.a.* practise, operate. — *v.r. sich —*, take an active part, work, participate (in).

betäuben [bə'tɔybən], *v.a.* deafen; stun, benumb, anaesthetize.

Betäubung [bə'tɔybuŋ], *f.* (—, *pl.* —en) stupor, stupefaction; *örtliche —*, local anaesthetic.

beteiligen [bə'tailɪgən], *v.a.* einen an etwas —, give s.o. a share of s.th. — *v.r. sich an etwas —*, participate in s.th.; (*Comm.*) have shares in s.th.

Beteiligte [bə'tailɪçtə], *m.* (—n, *pl.* —n) person concerned.

Beteiligung [bə'tailɪguŋ], *f.* (—, *pl.* —en) participation, interest.

beten ['beːtən], *v.n.* pray, say o.'s prayers.

beteuern [bə'tɔyərn], *v.a.* aver, affirm solemnly.

betiteln [bə'tiːtəln], *v.a.* entitle, name.

Beton [be'tɔ̃], *m.* (—s, *no pl.*) concrete.

betonen [bə'to:nən], *v.a.* accentuate, stress, emphasise.

Betonung [bə'to:nuŋ], *f.* (—, *pl.* —en) accentuation, emphasis, stress.

betören [bə'tø:rən], *v.a.* delude, infatuate.

Betracht [bə'traxt], *m.* (—s, *no pl.*) consideration, respect, regard.

betrachten [bə'traxtən], *v.a.* consider, look at, view; *etwas aufmerksam* —, contemplate s.th.

beträchtlich [bə'trɛçtlɪç], *adj.* considerable.

Betrachtung [bə'traxtuŋ], *f.* (—, *pl.* —en) contemplation, consideration.

Betrag [bə'tra:k], *m.* (—s, *pl.* ⁻e) amount, sum total.

betragen [bə'tra:gən], *v.a. irr.* amount to, come to. — *v.r. sich* —, behave, conduct o.s.

Betragen [bə'tra:gən], *n.* (—s, *no pl.*) behaviour, conduct, demeanour.

betrauen [bə'trauən], *v.a. einen mit etwas* —, entrust s.o. with s.th.

betrauern [bə'trauərn], *v.a.* mourn for, bemoan.

Betreff [bə'trɛf], *m.* (—s, *no pl.*) reference; *in* —, with regard to.

betreffen [bə'trɛfən], *v.a. irr.* concern, affect, relate to.

Betreiben [bə'traɪbən], *n.* (—s, *no pl.*) *auf* — *von*, at the instigation of.

betreiben [bə'traɪbən], *v.a. irr.* (*business*) carry on; (*factory*) run; (*trade*) follow, practise.

Betreten [bə'tre:tən], *n.* (—s, *no pl.*) entry, entering.

betreten [bə'tre:tən], *v.a. irr.* step upon, set foot on, enter. — *adj.* disconcerted, embarrassed.

betreuen [bə'trɔyən], *v.a.* care for, attend to.

Betrieb [bə'tri:p], *m.* (—s, *pl.* —e) management, business, factory, plant; *den* — *einstellen*, close down; *in* — *sein*, be in operation; *in* — *setzen*, start working.

betriebsam [bə'tri:pza:m], *adj.* active, busy, industrious, diligent.

Betriebsamkeit [bə'tri:pza:mkaɪt], *f.* (—, *pl.* —en) activity, industry, bustle.

betriebsfertig [bə'tri:psfɛrtɪç], *adj.* ready for service; operational.

Betriebsmaterial [bə'tri:psmaterja:l], *n.* (—s, *pl.* —ien) (*Railw.*) rolling-stock; (*factory*) working-stock.

Betriebspersonal [bə'tri:psperzona:l], *n.* (—s, *no pl.*) workmen, employees, staff.

betrinken [bə'trɪŋkən], *v.r. irr. sich* —, get drunk.

betroffen [bə'trɔfən], *adj.* perplexed, confounded.

betrüben [bə'try:bən], *v.a.* afflict, grieve.

Betrübnis [bə'try:pnɪs], *f.* (—ses, *pl.* —se) affliction, grief, distress, sorrow.

betrübt [bə'try:pt], *adj.* sad, grieved.

Betrug [bə'tru:k], *m.* (—s, *pl.* ⁻ereien) fraud, deceit, deception, imposture; *einen* — *begehen*, commit a fraud.

betrügen [bə'try:gən], *v.a. irr.* cheat, deceive.

Betrüger [bə'try:gər], *m.* (—s, —) swindler, cheat, deceiver, impostor.

betrunken [bə'truŋkən], *adj.* drunk, drunken, tipsy.

Bett [bɛt], *n.* (—(e)s, *pl.* —en) bed; (*river*) bed, channel.

Bettdecke ['bɛtdɛkə], *f.* (—, *pl.* —n) counterpane; (*Am.*) bedspread; *wollene* —, blanket; *gesteppte* —, quilt.

Bettel ['bɛtəl], *m.* (—s, *no pl.*) trash, trifle.

bettelarm ['bɛtəlarm], *adj.* destitute.

Bettelei [bɛtə'laɪ], *f.* (—, *pl.* —en) begging, beggary, penury.

betteln ['bɛtəln], *v.a.* beg, ask alms.

betten ['bɛtən], *v.a.* bed, lay to rest. — *v.r.* (*fig.*) *sich* —, make o.'s bed.

bettlägerig ['bɛtlɛgərɪç], *adj.* bedridden.

Bettlaken ['bɛtla:kən], *n.* (—s, *pl.* —) sheet.

Bettler ['bɛtlər], *m.* (—s, *pl.* —) beggar.

Bettstelle ['bɛtʃtɛlə], *f.* (—, *pl.* —n) bedstead.

Bettvorleger ['bɛtfo:rle:gər], *m.* (—s, *pl.* —) bedside-carpet *or* rug.

Bettwäsche ['bɛtvɛʃə], *f.* (—, *no pl.*) bed linen, bed clothes.

Bettzeug ['bɛttsɔyk], *n.* (—s, *no pl.*) bedding.

beugen ['bɔygən], *v.a.* bend, bow. — *v.r. sich* —, bend down, stoop.

Beugung ['bɔyguŋ], *f.* (—, *pl.* —en) (*Gram.*) inflection.

Beule ['bɔylə], *f.* (—, *pl.* —n) bruise, bump, swelling, boil.

beunruhigen [bə'unru:ɪgən], *v.a.* alarm, trouble, disquiet.

beurkunden [bə'u:rkundən], *v.a.* authenticate, verify.

beurlauben [bə'u:rlaubən], *v.a.* grant leave of absence. — *v.r. sich* —, take leave.

beurteilen [bə'urtaɪlən], *v.a.* judge, criticise.

Beute ['bɔytə], *f.* (—, *no pl.*) booty, loot; (*animals*) prey; (*Hunt.*) bag.

Beutel ['bɔytəl], *m.* (—s, *pl.* —) bag; (*money*) purse; (*Zool.*) pouch.

Beuteltier ['bɔytəlti:r], *n.* (—s, *pl.* —e) marsupial.

bevölkern [bə'fœlkərn], *v.a.* people, populate.

Bevölkerung [bə'fœlkəruŋ], *f.* (—, *pl.* —en) population.

bevollmächtigen [bə'fɔlmɛçtɪgən], *v.a.* empower, authorise.

bevor [bə'fo:r], *conj.* before, ere, beforehand.

bevormunden [bə'fo:rmundən], *v.a. insep.* act as guardian to; (*fig.*) browbeat.

bevorrechtigt [bə'fo:rrɛçtɪçt], *adj.* privileged.

bevorstehen [bə'fo:rʃteːən], *v.n. irr.* impend, lie ahead, be imminent; *einem —*, be in store for s.o.

bevorzugen [bə'fo:rtsuːgən], *v.a. insep.* prefer, favour.

bewachen [bə'vaxən], *v.a.* watch over, guard.

bewachsen [bə'vaksən], *adj.* overgrown.

bewaffnen [bə'vafnən], *v.a.* arm, supply with arms.

Bewahranstalt [bə'va:ranʃtalt], *f.* (—, *pl.* —en) kindergarten, nursery.

bewahren [bə'va:rən], *v.a.* preserve, keep, take care of.

bewähren [bə've:rən], *v.r. sich —*, prove o.s.

bewahrheiten [bə'va:rhaitən], *v.r. sich —*, turn out to be true.

bewährt [bə've:rt], *adj.* proved.

Bewährung [bə've:ruŋ], *f.* (—, *no pl.*) proof, verification.

Bewährungsfrist [bə've:ruŋsfrist], *f.* (—, *pl.* —en) probation.

bewaldet [bə'valdət], *adj.* wooded, woody.

bewältigen [bə'vɛltigən], *v.a.* overcome; manage, master; cope or deal with.

bewandert [bə'vandərt], *adj.* versed, skilled, experienced, conversant.

bewandt [bə'vant], *adj.* such: *damit ist es so —*, it is like this.

Bewandtnis [bə'vantnis], *f.* (—, *pl.* —se) circumstance, condition, state; *es hat damit folgende —*, the circumstances are as follows.

bewässern [bə'vɛsərn], *v.a.* water, irrigate.

bewegen [bə've:gən], *v.a., v.r.* move, stir; take exercise. — *v.a. irr.* persuade, induce.

Beweggrund [bə've:kgrunt], *m.* (—es, *pl.* ‐e) motive, reason, motivation.

beweglich [bə've:kliç], *adj.* movable; agile, brisk, sprightly.

Bewegung [bə've:gun], *f.* (—, *pl.* —en) motion, movement; (*mind*) emotion, agitation.

beweinen [bə'vainən], *v.a.* lament, bemoan, deplore.

Beweis [bə'vais], *m.* (—es, *pl.* —e) proof, evidence; (*Maths.*) demonstration.

beweisen [bə'vaizən], *v.a. irr.* prove, show, demonstrate.

Beweiskraft [bə'vaiskraft], *f.* (—, *no pl.*) (*Law*) probative force.

Beweismittel [bə'vaismitəl], *n.* (—s, *pl.* —) evidence, proof.

Bewenden [bə'vendən], *n.* (—s, *no pl.*) *es hat damit sein —*, there the matter rests.

bewenden [bə'vendən], *v.n. irr. es dabei — lassen*, leave it at that.

bewerben [bə'vɛrbən], *v.r. irr. sich um etwas —*, apply for s.th.

Bewerber [bə'vɛrbər], *m.* (—s, *pl.* —) applicant, candidate; (*marriage*) suitor.

Bewerbung [bə'vɛrbuŋ], *f.* (—, *pl.* —en) application, candidature; (*marriage*) courtship.

bewerkstelligen [bə'vɛrkʃtɛligən], *v.a.* perform, bring about.

bewerten [bə'vɛrtən], *v.a.* estimate, value.

bewilligen [bə'viligən], *v.a.* grant, allow, permit.

bewillkommnen [bə'vilkəmnən], *v.a.* welcome.

bewirken [bə'virkən], *v.a.* effect, bring about.

bewirten [bə'virtən], *v.a.* entertain, act as host (to).

bewirtschaften [bə'virtʃaftən], *v.a.* manage.

bewohnen [bə'vo:nən], *v.a.* inhabit, occupy.

Bewohner [bə'vo:nər], *m.* (—s, *pl.* —) inhabitant, tenant, resident.

bewölken [bə'vœlkən], *v.r. sich —*, become overcast, become cloudy.

bewundern [bə'vundərn], *v.a.* admire.

bewundernswert [bə'vundərnsvert], *adj.* admirable.

bewußt [bə'vust], *adj.* conscious, aware; *es war mir nicht —*, I was not aware of.

bewußtlos [bə'vustlo:s], *adj.* unconscious; *— werden*, faint, lose consciousness.

Bewußtsein [bə'vustzain], *n.* (—s, *no pl.*) consciousness; *einem etwas zum — bringen*, bring s.th. home to s.o.

bezahlbar [bə'tsa:lba:r], *adj.* payable.

bezahlen [bə'tsa:lən], *v.a.* pay; (*bill*) settle.

bezähmen [bə'tsɛ:mən], *v.a.* tame, restrain. — *v.r. sich —*, restrain o.s., control o.s.

bezaubern [bə'tsaubərn], *v.a.* bewitch, enchant, fascinate.

bezeichnen [bə'tsaiçnən], *v.a.* mark, denote, indicate, designate.

bezeichnend [bə'tsaiçnənt], *adj.* indicative, characteristic, significant.

bezeigen [bə'tsaigən], *v.a.* manifest, show.

bezeugen [bə'tsɔygən], *v.a.* attest, bear witness, testify.

bezichtigen [bə'tsiçtigən], *v.a.* accuse (s.o.) of (s.th.).

beziehbar [bə'tsi:ba:r], *adj.* (*goods*) obtainable; (*house*) ready for occupation.

beziehen [bə'tsi:ən], *v.a. irr.* cover; (*house etc.*) move into; (*instrument*) string; make up (a bed); *die Wache —*, mount guard. — *v.r. sich —*, (*sky*) cloud over; *sich auf etwas —*, refer to s.th.

Bezieher [bə'tsi:ər], *m.* (—s, *pl.* —) customer; (*newspaper*) subscriber.

Beziehung [bə'tsi:uŋ], *f.* (—, *pl.* —en) relation, connection; reference, bearing; *in dieser —*, in this respect; (*Comm.*) *unter — auf*, with reference to.

beziehungsweise [bə'tsi:uŋsvaizə], *adv.* respectively, as the case may be, or.

beziffern [bə'tsɪfərn], *v.a.* number.
Bezirk [bə'tsɪrk], *m.* (—s, *pl.* —e)
district; (*Am.*) precinct; (*Parl.*)
constituency; (*Law*) circuit.
Bezirksgericht [bə'tsɪrksgərɪçt], *n.*
(—s, *pl.* —e) county court.
Bezug [bə'tsu:k], *m.* (—s, *pl.* ⁝e)
(*pillow*) case, cover; (*goods*) order,
purchase; (*fig.*) relation; — **haben auf**,
refer to; **mit — auf**, referring to;
(*pl.*) emoluments, income.
bezüglich [bə'tsy:klɪç], *adj.* with regard
to, regarding.
Bezugnahme [bə'tsu:kna:mə], *f.* (—,
pl. —n) reference; **unter — auf**, with
reference to.
Bezugsbedingung [bə'tsu:ksbədɪŋuŋ],
f. (—, *pl.* —en) (*usually pl.*) (*Comm.*)
conditions *or* terms of delivery.
Bezugsquelle [bə'tsu:kskvɛlə], *f.* (—,
pl. —n) source of supply.
bezwecken [bə'tsvɛkən], *v.a.* aim at,
intend.
bezweifeln [bə'tsvaɪfəln], *v.a.* doubt,
question.
bezwingen [bə'tsvɪŋən], *v.a. irr.* subdue,
conquer. — *v.r. sich* —, restrain o.s.
Bibel [bi:bəl], *f.* (—, *pl.* —n) Bible.
Bibelauslegung ['bi:bəlauslə:guŋ], *f.*
(—, *pl.* —en) (Biblical) exegesis.
Biber [bi:bər], *m.* (—s, *pl.* —) (*Zool.*)
beaver.
Bibliothek [biblio'te:k], *f.* (—, *pl.* —en)
library.
Bibliothekar [bibliote'ka:r], *m.* (—s,
pl. —e) librarian.
biblisch ['bi:blɪʃ], *adj.* biblical, scrip-
tural.
Bickbeere ['bɪkbe:rə], *f.* (—, *pl.* —n)
bilberry.
bieder ['bi:dər], *adj.* upright, honest,
decent.
Biederkeit ['bi:dərkaɪt], *f.* (—, *no pl.*)
uprightness, probity.
Biedermann ['bi:dərman], *m.* (—s, *pl.*
⁝er) honourable man; (*iron.*) Philistine.
biegen ['bi:gən], *v.a. irr.* bend, bow.
— *v.n.* (*aux.* sein) *um die Ecke* —,
turn the corner. — *v.r. sich* —, curve;
— *oder brechen*, by hook or by
crook.
biegsam ['bi:kza:m], *adj.* flexible,
supple, pliant.
Biegung ['bi:guŋ], *f.* (—, *pl.* —en)
curve, bend; (*Gram.*) inflexion.
Biene ['bi:nə], *f.* (—, *pl.* —n) bee.
Bienenhaus ['bi:nənhaus], *n.* (—es,
pl. ⁝er) apiary.
Bienenkorb ['bi:nənkɔrp], *m.* (—s, *pl.*
⁝e) beehive.
Bienenzüchter ['bi:nəntsyçtər], *m.*
(—s, *pl.* —) apiarist, bee-keeper.
Bier ['bi:r], *n.* (—(e)s, *pl.* —e) beer.
Bierkanne ['bi:rkanə], *f.* (—, *pl.* —n)
tankard.
Biest [bi:st], *n.* (—es, *pl.* —er) brute,
beast.
bieten ['bi:tən], *v.a. irr.* offer; (*auction*)
bid.

Bieter ['bi:tər], *m.* (—s, *pl.* —) (*auction*)
bidder.
Bigotterie [bɪgɔtə'ri:], *f.* (—, *no pl.*)
bigotry.
Bijouterie [bɪʒutə'ri:], *f.* (—, *pl.* —n)
trinkets, dress-jewellery.
Bilanz [bɪ'lants], *f.* (—, *pl.* —en)
(*Comm.*) balance; (*financial*) statement.
Bild, *n.* (—es, *pl.* —er) picture,
painting, portrait, image; idea; (*coins*)
effigy; (*Cards*) court card; (*books*)
illustration; (*speech*) figure of speech,
metaphor.
bilden ['bɪldən], *v.c.* form, shape;
(*mind*) cultivate. — *v.r. sich* —,
improve o.'s mind, educate o.s.
bildend ['bɪldənt], *adj.* instructive,
civilising; *die —en Künste*, the fine
arts.
bilderreich ['bɪldəraɪç], *adj.* —e
Sprache, flowery language, figurative
style.
Bilderschrift ['bɪldərʃrɪft], *f.* (—, *pl.*
—en) hieroglyphics.
Bilderstürmer ['bɪldərʃtyrmər], *m.*
(—s, *pl.* —) iconoclast.
Bildhauer ['bɪlthauər], *m.* (—s, *pl.*
—) sculptor.
bildhübsch ['bɪlthypʃ], *adj.* as pretty
as a picture.
bildlich ['bɪltlɪç], *adj.* figurative.
Bildnis ['bɪltnɪs], *n.* (—ses, *pl.* —se)
portrait, figure, image, effigy.
bildsam ['bɪltza:m], *adj.* plastic, ductile.
bildschön ['bɪltʃø:n], *adj.* very beautiful.
Bildseite ['bɪltzaɪtə], *f.* (—, *pl.* —n)
(*coin*) face, obverse.
Bildung ['bɪlduŋ], *f.* (—, *pl.* (*rare*)
—en) formation; (*mind*) education,
culture; knowledge, learning, accom-
plishments, attainments.
Billard ['bɪljart], *n.* (—s, *pl.* —s)
billiards.
Billett [bɪl'jet], *n.* (—s, *pl.* —s)
ticket.
billig ['bɪlɪç], *adj.* cheap, inexpensive;
equitable, just, fair, reasonable.
billigen ['bɪlɪgən], *v.a.* sanction,
approve of, consent to.
Billigkeit ['bɪlɪçkaɪt], *f.* (—, *no pl.*)
cheapness; fairness, equitableness,
reasonableness.
Billigung ['bɪlɪguŋ], *f.* (—, *no pl.*)
approbation, approval, sanction.
Bilsenkraut ['bɪlzənkraut], *n.* (—s, *pl.*
⁝er) henbane.
bimmeln ['bɪməln], *v.n.* (*coll.*) tinkle.
Bimsstein ['bɪmsʃtain], *m.* (—s, *pl.*
—e) pumice stone.
Binde ['bɪndə], *f.* (—, *pl.* —n) band,
bandage; tie; ligature; sanitary towel.
Bindeglied ['bɪndəgli:t], *n.* (—s, *pl.*
—er) connecting link.
Bindehaut ['bɪndəhaut], *f.* (—, *pl.* ⁝e)
(*Anat.*) conjunctiva.
Bindehautentzündung ['bɪndəhaut-
entsynduŋ], *f.* (—, *pl.* —en) conjunctivitis.

binden ['bɪndən], *v.a. irr.* bind, tie, fasten.

Bindestrich ['bɪndeʃtrɪç], *m.* (—(e)s, *pl.* —e) hyphen.

Bindewort ['bɪndəvɔrt], *n.* (—s, *pl.* ˙er) conjunction.

Bindfaden ['bɪntfa:dən], *m.* (—s, *pl.* ˙) string, twine.

Bindung ['bɪnduŋ], *f.* (—, *pl.* —en) binding, bond; obligation; (*Mus.*) ligature.

binnen ['bɪnən], *prep.* (Genit. & Dat.), *adv.* within.

Binnenhafen ['bɪnənha:fən], *m.* (—s, *pl.* ˙) inland harbour.

Binnenhandel ['bɪnənhandəl], *m.* (—s, *no pl.*) inland trade.

Binse ['bɪnzə], *f.* (—, *pl.* —n) (*Bot.*) rush, reed.

Biographie [biogra'fi:], *f.* (—, *pl.* —n) biography.

Birke ['bɪrkə], *f.* (—, *pl.* —n) (*Bot.*) birch, birch-tree.

Birma ['bɪrma:], *n.* Burma.

Birnbaum ['bɪrnbaum], *m.* (—s, *pl.* ˙e) pear-tree.

Birne ['bɪrnə], *f.* (—, *pl.* —n) pear; (*Elec.*) bulb.

birnförmig ['bɪrnfœrmɪç], *adj.* pear-shaped.

bis [bɪs], *prep.* (*time*) till, until; by; (*place*) to, up to; — auf, with the exception of — *conj.* till, until.

Bisam ['bi:zam], *m.* (—s, *pl.* —e) musk.

Bischof ['bɪʃɔf], *m.* (—s, *pl.* ˙e) bishop.

bischöflich ['bɪʃœflɪç], *adj.* episcopal.

Bischofsstab ['bɪʃɔfsʃta:p], *m.* (—s, *pl.* ˙e) crosier.

bisher ['bɪshe:r], *adv.* hitherto, till now.

bisherig [bɪs'he:rɪç], *adj.* up to this time, hitherto existing.

Biskayischer Meerbusen [bɪs'ka:ɪʃər 'me:rbu:zən], Bay of Biscay.

Biß [bɪs], *m.* (—sses, *pl.* —sse) bite, sting.

Bißchen ['bɪsçən], *n.* (—s, *pl.* —) morsel; little bit.

Bissen ['bɪsən], *m.* (—s, *pl.* —) bite, morsel.

bissig ['bɪsɪç], *adj.* biting, cutting; sharp, vicious; sarcastic.

Bistum ['bɪstum], *n.* (—s, *pl.* ˙er) bishopric, diocese; see.

bisweilen [bɪs'vaɪlən], *adv.* sometimes, now and then, occasionally.

Bitte ['bɪtə], *f.* (—, *pl.* —n) request, entreaty.

bitte ['bɪtə], *int.* please.

bitten ['bɪtən], *v.a. irr.* ask; request.

bitter ['bɪtər], *adj.* bitter.

Bitterkeit ['bɪtərkaɪt], *f.* (—, *no pl.*) bitterness.

bitterlich ['bɪtərlɪç], *adv.* (*fig.*) bitterly.

Bittersalz ['bɪtərzalts], *n.* (—es, *no pl.*) Epsom salts.

Bittgang ['bɪtgaŋ], *m.* (—(e)s, *pl.* ˙e) (*Eccl.*) procession.

Bittsteller ['bɪtʃtɛlər], *m.* (—s, *pl.* —) petitioner, suppli(c)ant.

Biwak ['bi:vak], *m.* (—s, *pl.* —s) bivouac.

blähen ['blɛ:ən], *v.a.* inflate, puff up, swell.

Blähung ['blɛ:uŋ], *f.* (—, *pl.* —en) (*Med.*) flatulence.

blaken ['bla:kən], *v.n.* smoulder; smoke.

Blamage [bla'ma:ʒə], *f.* (—, *pl.* —n) shame, disgrace.

blamieren [bla'mi:rən], *v.a., v.r.* make (o.s.) ridiculous, make a fool of o.s.

blank [blaŋk], *adj.* shining, bright, smooth, polished.

Bläschen ['blɛ:sçən], *n.* (—s, *pl.* —) little bubble, blister; (*Med.*) vesicle.

Blase ['bla:zə], *f.* (—, *pl.* —n) (*soap*) bubble; (*skin*) blister; (*Anat.*) bladder.

Blasebalg ['bla:zəbalk], *m.* (—s, *pl.* ˙e) pair of bellows.

blasen ['bla:zən], *v.a. irr.* blow; (*Mus.*) sound.

Bläser ['blɛ:zər], *m.* (—s, *pl.* —) (*glass*) blower; (*Mus.*) wind player.

blasiert [bla'zi:rt], *adj.* blasé, haughty.

Blasrohr ['bla:sro:r], *n.* (—s, *pl.* —e) blow-pipe, pea-shooter.

blaß [blas], *adj.* pale, wan, pallid.

Blässe ['blɛsə], *f.* (—, *no pl.*) paleness, pallor.

Blatt [blat], *n.* (—s, *pl.* ˙er) leaf; (*paper*) sheet; blade.

Blatter ['blatər], *f.* (—, *pl.* —n) pustule; (*pl.*) smallpox.

blättern ['blɛtərn], *v.a.* turn the leaves (of a book).

Blätterteig ['blɛtərtaɪk], *m.* (—s, *no pl.*) puff pastry.

Blattgold ['blatgɔlt], *n.* (—es, *no pl.*) gold-leaf.

Blattlaus ['blatlaus], *f.* (—, *pl.* ˙e) (*Ent.*) plant-louse.

Blattpflanze ['blatpflantsə], *f.* (—, *pl.* —n) leaf-plant.

blau [blau], *adj.* blue; —en Montag machen, stay away from work; sein —es Wunder erleben, be amazed.

blauäugig ['blauɔygɪç], *adj.* blue-eyed.

Blaubeere ['blaube:rə], *f.* (—, *pl.* —n) bilberry, blueberry.

blaublütig ['blaubly:tɪç], *adj.* aristocratic.

bläuen ['blauən], *v.a.* dye blue, rinse in blue.

bläulich ['blɔylɪç], *adj.* pale blue, bluish.

Blausäure ['blauzɔyrə], *f.* (—, *no pl.*) prussic acid.

Blaustrumpf ['blauʃtrumpf], *m.* (—s, *pl.* ˙e) blue-stocking.

Blech [blɛç], *n.* (—s, *pl.* —e) tinplate, sheet metal.

blechen ['blɛçən], *v.n.* (*coll.*) fork out money.

blechern ['blɛçərn], *adj.* made of tin, tinny.

Blechinstrument ['blɛçɪnstrumɛnt], *n.* (—s, *pl.* —e) (*Mus.*) brass instrument.

Blei

Blei [blaɪ], *n.* (—s, *no pl.*) lead.
bleiben ['blaɪbən], *v.n. irr.* (*aux.* sein) remain, stay.
bleich [blaɪç], *adj.* pale, wan, pallid.
Bleiche ['blaɪçə], *f.* (—, *pl.* —n) pallor; (*laundry*) bleaching-place.
bleichen ['blaɪçən], *v.a. irr.* bleach, whiten.
Bleichsucht ['blaɪçzuxt], *f.* (—, *no pl.*) chlorosis, anaemia.
bleiern ['blaɪərn], *adj.* leaden.
Bleiglanz ['blaɪglants], *m.* (—es, *no pl.*) (*Min.*) lead sulphide.
Bleisoldat ['blaɪzɔlda:t], *m.* (—en, *pl.* —en) tin soldier.
Bleistift ['blaɪʃtɪft], *m.* (—s, *pl.* —e) pencil.
Blende ['blɛndə], *f.* (—, *no pl.*) blind; (*Min.*) blende; (*Phot.*) shutter.
blenden ['blɛndən], *v.a.* dazzle, blind.
Blendlaterne ['blɛntlatɛrnə], *f.* (—, *pl.* —n) dark-lantern.
Blendung ['blɛnduŋ], *f.* (—, *pl.* —en) blinding, dazzling.
Blendwerk ['blɛntvɛrk], *n.* (—s, *no pl.*) (optical) illusion, false show.
Blick [blɪk], *m.* (—s, *pl.* —e) glance, look, glimpse.
blicken ['blɪkən], *v.n.* look, glance.
blind [blɪnt], *adj.* blind, sightless; —*er Passagier*, stowaway.
Blinddarm ['blɪntdarm], *m.* (—s, *pl.* Ꞌe) appendix.
Blinddarmentzündung ['blɪntdarmɛntsynduŋ], *f.* (—, *pl.* —en) appendicitis.
Blindekuh [blɪndəꞋku:], *f.* (—, *no pl.*) blind man's buff.
Blindgänger ['blɪntgɛŋər], *m.* (—s, *pl.* —) misfire, dud, blind.
Blindheit ['blɪnthaɪt], *f.* (—, *no pl.*) blindness.
blindlings ['blɪntlɪŋs], *adv.* blindly; at random.
Blindschleiche ['blɪntʃlaɪçə], *f.* (—, *pl.* —n) (*Zool.*) blind-worm.
blinken ['blɪŋkən], *v.n.* blink, flash, glitter, gleam.
blinzeln ['blɪntsəln], *v.n.* blink.
Blitz [blɪts], *m.* (—es, *pl.* —e) lightning, flash.
Blitzableiter ['blɪtsaplaɪtər], *m.* (—s, *pl.* —) lightning-conductor.
blitzblank ['blɪtsblaŋk], *adj.* as bright as a new pin; shining.
blitzen ['blɪtsən], *v.n.* flash; *es blitzt*, it is lightning; glitter, shine.
Blitzesschnelle ['blɪtsəsʃnɛlə], *f.* (—, *no pl.*) lightning-speed.
Blitzlicht ['blɪtslɪçt], *n.* (—s, *no pl.*) flashlight.
Blitzschlag ['blɪtsʃla:k], *m.* (—s, *pl.* Ꞌe) flash of lightning.
Blitzstrahl ['blɪtsʃtra:l], *m.* (—s, *pl.* —en) flash of lightning.
Block [blɔk], *m.* (—s, *pl.* Ꞌe) block, log; pad.
Blockhaus ['blɔkhaus], *n.* (—es, *pl.* Ꞌer) log-cabin.

blockieren [blɔꞋki:rən], *v.a.* block (up); (*Mil.*) blockade.
blöde ['blø:də], *adj.* stupid, dull, thick-headed, dim.
Blödsinn ['blø:tsɪn], *m.* (—s, *no pl.*) nonsense, idiocy.
blöken ['blø:kən], *v.n.* bleat; (*cows*) low.
blond [blɔnt], *adj.* blond, fair, fair-headed.
bloß [blo:s], *adj.* naked, uncovered; bare, mere.
Blöße ['blø:sə], *f.* (—, *pl.* —n) nakedness, bareness; (*fig.*) weak point.
bloßlegen ['blo:sle:gən], *v.a.* uncover, lay bare; (*fig.*) reveal, expose.
bloßstellen ['blo:sʃtɛlən], *v.a.* compromise, show up. — *v.r. sich* —, compromise o.s.
blühen ['bly:ən], *v.n.* bloom, blossom, flower, flourish.
Blümchen ['bly:mçən], *n.* (—s, *pl.* —) small flower.
Blume ['blu:mə], *f.* (—, *pl.* —n) flower, bloom; (*wine*) bouquet; (*beer*) froth.
Blumenblatt ['blu:mənblat], *n.* (—s, *pl.* Ꞌer) petal.
Blumenerde ['blu:məne:rdə], *f.* (—, *no pl.*) garden mould.
Blumenkelch ['blu:mənkɛlç], *m.* (—es, *pl.* —e) calyx.
Blumenkohl ['blu:mənko:l], *m.* (—s, *pl.* —e) cauliflower.
Blumenstaub ['blu:mənʃtaup], *m.* (—s, *no pl.*) pollen.
Blumenstrauß ['blu:mənʃtraus], *m.* (—es, *pl.* Ꞌe) bunch of flowers, posy, nosegay.
Blumenzucht ['blu:məntsuxt], *f.* (—, *no pl.*) floriculture.
Bluse ['blu:zə], *f.* (—, *pl.* —n) blouse.
Blut [blu:t], *n.* (—es, *no pl.*) blood.
blutarm ['blu:tarm], *adj.* anæmic; (*fig.*) very poor.
Blutbad ['blu:tba:t], *n.* (—es, *pl.* Ꞌer) massacre.
blutdürstig ['blu:tdyrstɪç], *adj.* bloodthirsty.
Blüte ['bly:tə], *f.* (—, *pl.* —n) blossom, flower, bloom.
Blutegel ['blu:te:gəl], *m.* (—s, *pl.* —) leech.
bluten ['blu:tən], *v.n.* bleed.
Bluterguß ['blu:tɛrgus], *m.* (—es, *pl.* Ꞌe) effusion of blood.
Blutgefäß ['blu:tgəfɛ:s], *n.* (—es, *pl.* —e) blood-vessel.
blutig ['blu:tɪç], *adj.* bloody; cruel.
blutjung ['blu:tjuŋ], *adj.* very young.
Blutkörperchen ['blu:tkœrpərçən], *n.* (—s, *pl.* —) blood-corpuscle.
Blutlassen ['blu:tlasən], *n.* (—s, *no pl.*) (*Med.*) bloodletting.
Blutrache ['blu:traxə], *f.* (—, *no pl.*) vendetta.
Blutsauger ['blu:tzaugər], *m.* (—s, *pl.* —) vampire.
Blutschande ['blu:tʃandə], *f.* (—, *no pl.*) incest.

blutstillend ['blu:ʃtɪlənt], *adj.* styptic, blood-stanching.

Blutsturz ['blu:tʃturts], *m.* (**—es**, *no pl.*) haemorrhage; *einen — haben*, burst a blood-vessel.

Blutsverwandte ['blu:tsfɛrvantə], *m.* or *f.* (**—n**, *pl.* **—n**) blood-relation.

Blutvergießen ['blu:tfɛrgi:sən], *n.* (**—s**, *no pl.*) bloodshed.

Blutvergiftung ['blu:tfɛrgɪftuŋ], *f.* (**—**, *pl.* **—en**) blood poisoning.

Blutwurst ['blu:tvurst], *f.* (**—**, *pl.* ⁺e) black-pudding.

Blutzeuge ['blu:ttsɔygə], *m.* (**—n**, *pl.* **—n**) martyr.

Bö [bø:], *f.* (**—**, *pl.* **—en**) (*Naut.*) squall, gust of wind.

Bock [bɔk], *m.* (**—s**, *pl.* ⁺e) buck; he-goat; (*Gymn.*) horse; (*horse-drawn carriage*) box seat.

bockbeinig ['bɔkbaɪnɪç], *adj.* bow-legged; pigheaded, obstinate.

Bockbier ['bɔkbi:r], *n.* (**—s**, *no pl.*) bock beer.

bocken ['bɔkən], *v.n.* kick, be refractory; sulk.

Bockfell ['bɔkfɛl], *n.* (**—s**, *pl.* **—e**) buckskin.

bockig ['bɔkɪç], *adj.* pigheaded, obstinate.

Bocksbeutel ['bɔksbɔytəl], *m.* (**—s**, *pl.* **—**) leather bag; Franconian wine (bottle).

Bockshorn ['bɔkshɔrn], *n.* (**—s**, *pl.* ⁺er) buck horn; *einen ins — jagen*, intimidate s.o.

Boden ['bo:dən], *m.* (**—s**, *pl.* ⁺) ground, bottom, soil, floor; garret, loft.

Bodenfenster ['bo:dənfɛnstər], *n.* (**—s**, *pl.* **—**) attic window.

Bodenkammer ['bo:dənkamər], *f.* (**—**, *pl.* **—n**) garret, attic.

bodenlos ['bo:dənlo:s], *adj.* bottomless; (*fig.*) unimaginable, enormous.

Bodensatz ['bo:dənzats], *m.* (**—es**, *pl.* ⁺e) sediment, dregs, deposit.

Bodensee ['bo:dənze:], *m.* Lake Constance.

Bogen ['bo:gən], *m.* (**—s**, *pl.* **—**, ⁺) arch, vault, curve; (*Maths.*) arc; (*violin*) bow; (*paper*) sheet; (*Mus.*) ligature.

bogenförmig ['bo:gənfœrmɪç], *adj.* arch-shaped, arched.

Bogenführung ['bo:gənfy:ruŋ], *f.* (**—**, *no pl.*) (*Mus.*) bowing (technique).

Bogengang ['bo:gəngaŋ], *m.* (**—es**, *pl.* ⁺e) arcade.

Bogenlampe ['bo:gənlampə], *f.* (**—**, *pl.* **—n**) arc-lamp.

Bogenschütze ['bo:gənʃytsə], *m.* (**—n**, *pl.* **—n**) archer.

bogig ['bo:gɪç], *adj.* bent, curved, arched.

Bohle ['bo:lə], *f.* (**—**, *pl.* **—n**) board, plank.

Böhmen ['bø:mən], *n.* Bohemia.

Bohne ['bo:nə], *f.* (**—**, *pl.* **—n**) bean; *grüne —n*, French (*Am.* string) beans; *dicke —n*, broad beans; *blaue —n*, (*fig.*) bullets.

Bohnenstange ['bo:nənʃtaŋə], *f.* (**—**, *pl.* **—n**) bean-pole.

Bohnerbürste ['bo:nərbyrstə], *f.* (**—**, *pl.* **—n**) polishing-brush.

bohnern ['bo:nərn], *v.a.* polish, wax.

bohren ['bo:rən], *v.a.* bore, pierce, drill.

Bohrer ['bo:rər], *m.* (**—s**, *pl.* **—**) gimlet; drill.

Bohrturm ['bo:rturm], *m.* (**—s**, *pl.* ⁺e) derrick.

Boje ['bo:jə], *f.* (**—**, *pl.* **—n**) (*Naut.*) buoy.

Bolivien [bo'li:vjən], *n.* Bolivia.

Böller ['bœlər], *m.* (**—s**, *pl.* **—**) (*Mil.*) small mortar.

Bollwerk ['bɔlvɛrk], *n.* (**—s**, *pl.* **—e**) bulwark.

Bolzen ['bɔltsən], *m.* (**—s**, *pl.* **—**) bolt, arrow, pin; (*smoothing iron*) heater.

Bombe ['bɔmbə], *f.* (**—**, *pl.* **—n**) bomb, bomb-shell.

Bombenerfolg ['bɔmbənɛrfɔlk], *m.* (**—(e)s**, *pl.* **—e**) (*Theat.*) smash hit.

Bonbon [bɔ̃'bɔ̃], *m.* (**—s**, *pl.* **—s**) sweet(s), bonbon; (*Am.*) candy.

Bonbonniere [bɔ̃bɔ'njɛ:rə], *f.* (**—**, *pl.* **—n**) box of sweets.

Bonze ['bɔntsə], *m.* (**—n**, *pl.* **—n**) (*coll.*) bigwig, (*Am.*) big shot.

Boot [bo:t], *n.* (**—s**, *pl.* **—e**) boat.

Bootsanker ['bo:tsaŋkər], *m.* (**—s**, *pl.* **—**) grapnel.

Bootsleine ['bo:tslaɪnə], *f.* (**—**, *pl.* **—n**) tow-rope.

Bor [bo:r], *n.* (**—s**, *no pl.*) (*Chem.*) boron.

Bord [bɔrt], *m.* (**—s**, *pl.* **—e**) rim; (*Naut.*) board.

Bordell [bɔr'dɛl], *n.* (**—s**, *pl.* **—e**) brothel.

borgen ['bɔrgən], *v.a.*, *v.n.* borrow; borrow (*von*, from); lend (*Dat.*, to).

Borke ['bɔrkə], *f.* (**—**, *pl.* **—n**) bark, rind.

Born [bɔrn], *m.* (**—es**, *pl.* **—e**) (*Poet.*) bourn, spring, well, source.

borniert [bɔr'ni:rt], *adj.* narrow-minded

Borsäure ['bo:rzɔyrə], *f.* (**—**, *no pl.*) boric acid.

Börse ['bœrzə], *f.* (**—**, *pl.* **—n**) purse; (*Comm.*) stock-exchange, bourse.

Börsenbericht ['bœrzənbərɪçt], *m.* (**—s**, *pl.* **—e**) stock-market report.

Borste ['bɔrstə], *f.* (**—**, *pl.* **—n**) bristle.

borstig ['bɔrstɪç], *adj.* bristly; (*fig.*) irritable.

Borte ['bɔrtə], *f.* (**—**, *pl.* **—n**) order, trimming.

bösartig ['bø:sartɪç], *adj.* malevolent, malicious, vicious; (*disease*) malignant.

Böschung ['bøʃuŋ], *f.* (**—**, *pl.* **—en**) slope, scarp.

böse ['bø:zə], *adj.* bad, wicked; evil; angry, cross (with, *Dat.*); *— auf* (*Acc.*), angry with s.o., (*Am.*) mad at s.o.

Bösewicht ['bø:zəvɪçt], *m.* (**—s**, *pl.* **—er**) villain, ruffian; wretch.

boshaft

boshaft [ˈboːshaft], *adj.* spiteful, malicious.
Bosheit [ˈboːshaɪt], *f.* (—, *pl.* —en) malice.
böswillig [ˈbøːsvɪlɪç], *adj.* malevolent.
Botanik [boˈtaːnɪk], *f.* (—, *no pl.*) botany.
Botaniker [boˈtaːnɪkər], *m.* (—s, *pl.* —) botanist.
Botanisiertrommel [botanɪˈziːrtrɔməl], *f.* (—, *pl.* —n) specimen-box.
Bote [ˈboːtə], *m.* (—n, *pl.* —n) messenger.
Botengang [ˈboːtəngaŋ], *m.* (—s, *pl.* ⁓e) errand.
botmäßig [ˈboːtmɛːsɪç], *adj.* subject, subordinate.
Botschaft [ˈboːtʃaft], *f.* (—, *pl.* —en) message; (*Pol.*) embassy; **gute —,** glad tidings.
Botschafter [ˈboːtʃaftər], *m.* (—s, *pl.* —) ambassador.
Böttcher [ˈbœtçər], *m.* (—s, *pl.* —) cooper.
Bottich [ˈbɔtɪç], *m.* (—s, *pl.* —e) vat, tub.
Bouillon [buˈljɔ], *f.* (—, *no pl.*) broth, meat soup.
Bowle [ˈboːlə], *f.* (—, *no pl.*) bowl; spiced wine.
boxen [ˈbɔksən], *v.n.* box.
brach [braːx], *adj.* fallow, unploughed, untilled.
Brand [brant], *m.* (—es, *pl.* ⁓e) burning, fire, combustion, conflagration; (*Med.*) gangrene.
Brandblase [ˈbrantblaːzə], *f.* (—, *pl.* —n) blister.
branden [ˈbrandən], *v.n.* surge, break (waves).
brandig [ˈbrandɪç], *adj.* blighted; (*Med.*) gangrenous.
Brandmal [ˈbrantmaːl], *n.* (—es, *pl.* —e) burn mark; brand (cattle); (*fig.*) stigma.
brandmarken [ˈbrantmarkən], *v.a.* brand; (*fig.*) stigmatise.
Brandmauer [ˈbrantmauər], *f.* (—, *pl.* —n) fire-proof wall.
brandschatzen [ˈbrantʃatsən], *v.a.* levy contributions (from); pillage, plunder.
Brandsohle [ˈbrantzoːlə], *f.* (—, *pl.* —n) inner sole, welt (of shoe).
Brandstifter [ˈbrantʃtɪftər], *m.* (—s, *pl.* —) incendiary, fire-raiser.
Brandstiftung [ˈbrantʃtɪftuŋ], *f.* (—, *pl.* —en) arson.
Brandung [ˈbranduŋ], *f.* (—, *pl.* —en) breakers, surf, surge (of sea).
Branntwein [ˈbrantvaɪn], *m.* (—s, *pl.* —e) brandy.
Brasilien [braˈziːljən], *n.* Brazil.
Braten [ˈbraːtən], *m.* (—s, *pl.* —) roast (meat), joint.
braten [ˈbraːtən], *v.a. reg. & irr.* roast, broil, bake, fry, grill. — *v.n.* (*coll.*) bask (in sun), roast.
Brathering [ˈbraːtheːrɪŋ], *m.* (—s, *pl.* —e) grilled herring.

Brathuhn [ˈbraːthuːn], *n.* (—s, *pl.* ⁓er) roast chicken.
Bratkartoffeln [ˈbraːtkartɔfəln], *f. pl.* roast *or* fried potatoes.
Bratpfanne [ˈbraːtpfanə], *f.* (—, *pl.* —n) frying pan.
Bratsche [ˈbraːtʃə], *f.* (—, *pl.* —n) (*Mus.*) viola.
Bratspieß [ˈbraːtʃpiːs], *m.* (—es, *pl.* —e) spit (roasting).
Bratwurst [ˈbraːtvurst], *f.* (—, *pl.* ⁓e) sausage for frying; fried sausage.
Brau [brau], **Bräu,** [brɔy], *n. & m.* (—s, *no pl.*) brew.
Brauch [braux], *m.* (—es, *pl.* ⁓e) usage, custom, habit.
brauchbar [ˈbrauxbaːr], *adj.* useful, serviceable.
brauchen [ˈbrauxən], *v.a.* make use of, employ; need, require, want; (*time*) take.
Braue [ˈbrauə], *f.* (—, *pl.* —n) brow, eye-brow.
brauen [ˈbrauən], *v.a.* brew.
Brauer [ˈbrauər], *m.* (—s, *pl.* —) brewer.
Brauerei [ˈbrauəraɪ], *f.* (—, *pl.* —en) brewery.
Brauhaus [ˈbrauhaus], *n.* (—es, *pl.* ⁓er) brewery.
braun [braun], *adj.* brown.
bräunen [ˈbrɔynən], *v.a.* make brown, tan.
Braunkohl [ˈbraunkoːl], *m.* (—s, *no pl.*) (*Bot.*) broccoli.
Braunschweig [ˈbraunʃvaɪk], *n.* Brunswick.
Braus [braus], *m.* (—es, *no pl.*) bustle, tumult; *in Saus und —* **leben,** lead a riotous life.
Brause [ˈbrauzə], *f.* (—, *pl.* —n) shower (bath); effervescence, (*coll.*) fizzy drink.
Brausekopf [ˈbrauzəkɔpf], *m.* (—es, *pl.* ⁓e) hothead.
Brauselimonade [ˈbrauzəlimonaːdə], *f.* (—, *pl.* —n) effervescent *or* fizzy lemonade.
brausen [ˈbrauzən], *v.n.* roar, bluster, rush; effervesce.
Brausepulver [ˈbrauzəpulvər], *n.* (—s, *pl.* —) effervescent powder.
Braut [braut], *f.* (—, *pl.* ⁓e) bride, betrothed, fiancée.
Brautführer [ˈbrautfyːrər], *m.* (—s, *pl.* —) best man.
Bräutigam [ˈbrɔytɪgam], *m.* (—s, *pl.* —e) bridegroom, betrothed, fiancé.
Brautjungfer [ˈbrautjuŋfər], *f.* (—, *pl.* —) bridesmaid.
bräutlich [ˈbrɔytlɪç], *adj.* bridal.
Brautpaar [ˈbrautpaːr], *n.* (—es, *pl.* —e) engaged couple.
Brautschau [ˈbrautʃau], *f.* (—, *no pl.*) (*obs.*) search for a wife.
brav [braːf], *adj.* honest, upright, worthy, honourable; well-behaved, good.
bravo! [ˈbraːvo], *int.* well done!

Bravourstück [bra'vu:rʃtyk], *n.* (—s, *pl.* —e) feat of valour.

Brechbohnen ['brɛçbo:nən], *f. pl.* kidney-beans.

Brecheisen ['brɛçaɪzən], *n.* (—s, *pl.* —) jemmy.

brechen ['brɛçən], *v.a. irr.* break; (*flowers*) pluck, pick; vomit. — *v.n.* (*aux.* sein) break.

Brechmittel ['brɛçmɪtəl], *n.* (—s, *pl.* —) emetic.

Brechruhr ['brɛçru:r], *f.* (—, *no pl.*) cholera.

Brechstange ['brɛçʃtaŋə], *f.* (—, *pl.* —n) crow-bar.

Brechung ['brɛçuŋ], *f.* (—, *pl.* —en) breaking; (*Phys.*) refraction.

Brei [braɪ], *m.* (—s, *pl.* —e) pap, pulp, porridge.

breiartig ['braɪa:rtɪç], *adj.* pulpy.

breiig ['braɪɪç], *adj.* pappy.

breit [braɪt], *adj.* broad, wide.

breitbeinig ['braɪtbaɪnɪç], *adj.* straddle-legged.

Breite ['braɪtə], *f.* (—, *pl.* —n) breadth, width; (*Geog.*) latitude.

Breitengrad ['braɪtəngra:t], *m.* (—es, *pl.* —e) (*Geog.*) degree of latitude.

Breitenkreis ['braɪtənkraɪs], *m.* (—es, *pl.* —e) (*Geog.*) parallel.

breitschultrig ['braɪtʃultrɪç], *adj.* broad-shouldered.

Bremse ['brɛmzə], *f.* (—, *pl.* —n) (*Ent.*) gad-fly; (*Motor.*) brake; (*horse*) barnacle.

bremsen ['brɛmzən], *v.a.* brake, pull up.

brennbar ['brɛnba:r], *adj.* combustible.

Brenneisen ['brɛnaɪzən], *n.* (—s, *pl.* —) branding iron.

brennen ['brɛnən], *v.a. irr.* burn; (*Med.*) cauterise; (*alcohol*) distil; (*hair*) curl; (*coffee*) roast; (*coal*) char; (*bricks*) bake. — *v.n.* burn; (*fig.*) sting; (*eyes*) smart.

Brenner ['brɛnər], *m.* (—s, *pl.* —) (*person*) distiller; (*Tech.*) burner.

Brennerei [brɛnə'raɪ], *f.* (—, *pl.* —en) distillery.

Brennessel ['brɛnnɛsəl], *f.* (—, *pl.* —n) stinging nettle.

Brennholz ['brɛnholts], *n.* (—es, *no pl.*) firewood.

Brennmaterial ['brɛnmaterja:l], *n.* (—s, *pl.* —ien) fuel.

Brennofen ['brɛno:fən], *m.* (—s, *pl.* ⸚n) kiln.

Brennpunkt ['brɛnpuŋkt], *m.* (—es, *pl.* —e) focus.

Brennschere ['brɛnʃe:rə], *f.* (—, *pl.* —n) curling-irons.

Brennstoff ['brɛnʃtof], *m.* (—(e)s, *pl.* —e) fuel.

brenzlich ['brɛntslɪç], *adj.* smelling (*or* tasting) of burning; (*fig.*) ticklish.

Bresche ['brɛʃə], *f.* (—, *pl.* —n) breach, gap.

Brett [brɛt], *n.* (—s, *pl.* —er) board, plank, shelf.

Brettspiel ['brɛtʃpi:l], *n.* (—s, *pl.* —e) table-game.

Brevier [bre'vi:r], *n.* (—s, *pl.* (*rare*) —e) breviary.

Brezel ['bre:tsəl], *f.* (—, *pl.* —n) cracknel, pretzel.

Brief [bri:f], *m.* (—es, *pl.* —e) letter; epistle.

Briefanschrift ['bri:fanʃrɪft], *f.* (—, *pl.* —en) address.

Briefbeschwerer ['bri:fbəʃve:rər], *m.* (—s, *pl.* —) letter-weight, paper-weight.

Briefbogen ['bri:fbo:gən], *m.* (—s, *pl.* —) sheet of notepaper.

Briefkasten ['bri:fkastən], *m.* (—s, *pl.* ⸚) (*house*) letter-box; (*street*) pillar-box, (*Am.*) post-box.

brieflich ['bri:flɪç], *adv.* by letter, in writing.

Briefmarke ['bri:fmarkə], *f.* (—, *pl.* —n) postage stamp.

Briefpapier ['bri:fpapi:r], *n.* (—s, *no pl.*) notepaper.

Briefporto ['bri:fporto], *n.* (—s, *pl.* —ti) postage.

Brieftasche ['bri:ftaʃə], *f.* (—, *pl.* —n) portfolio, wallet; (*Am.*) pocket-book.

Brieftaube ['bri:ftaubə], *f.* (—, *pl.* —n) carrier pigeon.

Briefträger ['bri:ftrɛ:gər], *m.* (—s, *pl.* —) postman.

Briefumschlag ['bri:fumʃla:k], *m.* (—s, *pl.* ⸚e) envelope.

Briefwechsel ['bri:fvɛksəl], *m.* (—s, *no pl.*) correspondence.

Brillant [bril'jant], *m.* (—en, *pl.* —en) brilliant, diamond. — *adj.* brilliant.

Brille ['brɪlə], *f.* (—, *pl.* —n) spectacles, glasses.

Brillenschlange ['brɪlənʃlaŋə], *f.* (—, *pl.* —n) (*Zool.*) hooded cobra.

bringen ['brɪŋən], *v.a. irr.* bring, fetch, carry to, take to, conduct to.

Brise ['bri:zə], *f.* (—, *pl.* —n) breeze, light wind.

Britannien [brɪ'tanjən], *n.* Britain.

bröckeln ['brœkəln], *v.a., v.n.* crumble.

Brocken ['brɔkən], *m.* (—s, *pl.* —) bit, piece, fragment, scrap; (*bread*) crumb.

bröcklig ['brœklɪç], *adj.* crumbling.

brodeln ['bro:dəln], *v.n.* bubble, simmer.

Brodem ['bro:dəm], *m.* (—s, *no pl.*) (*Poet.*) steam, vapour, exhalation.

Brokat [bro'ka:t], *m.* (—s, *pl.* —e) brocade.

Brom [bro:m], *n.* (—s, *no pl.*) (*Chem.*) bromine.

Brombeere ['brombe:rə], *f.* (—, *pl.* —n) blackberry, bramble.

Bronze ['brɔ̃:zə], *f.* (—, *pl.* —n) bronze.

Brosamen [bro'za:mən], *pl.* crumbs.

Brosche ['brɔʃə], *f.* (—, *pl.* —n) brooch.

Broschüre [brɔ'ʃy:rə], *f.* (—, *pl.* —n) pamphlet, brochure, folder.

Brösel ['brø:zəl], *m.* (—s, *pl.* —) crumb.

Brot [bro:t], *n.* (—es, *pl.* —e) bread, loaf; (*fig.*) livelihood.

Brötchen ['brø:tçən], *n.* (—s, *pl.* —) roll, bread-roll.

Broterwerb ['broːtərvɛrp], *m.* (—s, *no pl.*) livelihood.

Brotgeber ['broːtgeːbər], *m.* (—s, *pl.* —) employer, master.

Brotherr ['broːthɛr], *m.* (—n, *pl.* —en) employer, master.

Brotkorb ['broːtkɔrp], *m.* (—s, *pl.* ∵e) bread-basket.

brotlos ['broːtloːs], *adj.* unemployed; (*fig.*) unprofitable.

Brotneid ['broːtnaɪt], *m.* (—s, *no pl.*) professional jealousy.

Bruch [brux], *m.* (—s, *pl.* ∵e) breakage; rupture; (*Med.*) fracture, rupture, hernia; (*Maths.*) fraction.

Bruchband ['bruxbant], *f.* (—es, *pl.* ∵er) abdominal belt, truss.

brüchig ['bryçɪç], *adj.* brittle, full of flaws.

Bruchlandung ['bruxlanduŋ], *f.* (—, —en) (*Aviat.*) crash-landing.

Bruchrechnung ['bruxrɛçnuŋ], *f.* (—, *pl.* —en) (*Arith.*) fractions.

Bruchstück ['bruxʃtyk], *n.* (—s, *pl.* —e) fragment, scrap.

Bruchteil ['bruxtaɪl], *m.* (—s, *pl.* —e) fraction.

Brücke ['brykə], *f.* (—, *pl.* —n) bridge.

Brückenpfeiler ['brykənpfaɪlər], *m.* (—s, *pl.* —) pier.

Bruder ['bruːdər], *m.* (—s, *pl.* ∵) brother; (*Eccl.*) friar.

brüderlich ['bryːdərlɪç], *adj.* fraternal, brotherly.

Bruderschaft ['bruːdərʃaft], *f.* (—, *pl.* —en) fraternity, brotherhood.

Brügge ['brygə], *n.* Bruges.

Brühe ['bryːə], *f.* (—, *pl.* —n) broth, meat-soup.

brühen ['bryːən], *v.a.* scald.

Brühkartoffeln ['bryːkartɔfəln], *f. pl.* potatoes cooked in broth.

brüllen ['brylən], *v.n.* roar, howl, yell; (*cows*) low, bellow.

Brummbaß ['brumbas], *m.* (—sses, *pl.* ∵sse) (*Mus.*) double-bass.

Brummeisen ['brumaɪzən], *n.* (—s, *pl.* —) Jew's harp.

brummen ['brumən], *v.n.* growl, grumble, hum.

Brummer ['brumər], *n.* (—s, *pl.* —) (*Ent.*) blue-bottle.

Brunnen ['brunən], *m.* (—s, *pl.* —) well, fountain, spring.

Brunnenkur ['brunənkuːr], *f.* (—, *pl.* —en) taking of mineral waters.

Brunst [brunst], *f.* (—, *pl.* ∵e) (*Zool.*) rut, heat.

Brust [brust], *f.* (—, *pl.* ∵e) breast; chest; bosom.

Brustbein ['brustbaɪn], *n.* (—s, *pl.* —e) breastbone, sternum.

Brustbild ['brustbɪlt], *n.* (—s, *pl.* —er) half-length portrait.

brüsten ['brystən], *v.r. sich* —, boast, brag, plume o.s.

Brustfell ['brustfɛl], *n.* (—s, *pl.* —e) pleura.

Brustfellentzündung ['brustfɛlɛntsynduŋ], *f.* (—, *no pl.*) pleurisy.

Brusthöhle ['brusthøːlə], *f.* (—, *pl.* —n) thoracic cavity.

Brustkasten ['brustkastən], *m.* (—s, *pl.* ∵n) chest.

Brusttee ['brusteː], *m.* (—s, *no pl.*) pectoral (herbal) tea.

Brüstung ['brystuŋ], *f.* (—, *pl.* —en) parapet.

Brustwarze ['brustvartsə], *f.* (—, *pl.* —n) nipple.

Brustwehr ['brustveːr], *f.* (—, *pl.* —en) breastwork, parapet.

Brut [bruːt], *f.* (—, *no pl.*) brood; (*fish*) fry.

brutal [bruˈtaːl], *adj.* brutal.

brüten ['bryːtən], *v.a.* brood, hatch.

Brutofen ['bruːtoːfən], *m.* (—s, *pl.* ∵) incubator.

brutto ['bruto], *adv.* (*Comm.*) gross.

Bube ['buːbə], *m.* (—n, *pl.* —n) boy, lad; (*cards*) knave, (*Am.*) jack; rogue, rascal.

Bubenstreich ['buːbənʃtraɪç], *m.* (—s, *pl.* —e) boyish prank; knavish trick.

Bubikopf ['buːbɪkɔpf], *m.* (—(e)s, *pl.* ∵e) bobbed hair.

Buch [buːx], *n.* (—s, *pl.* ∵er) book; quire (of paper).

Buchdruckerei ['buːxdrukəraɪ], *f.* (—, —en) printing works, printing office.

Buche ['buːxə], *f.* (—, *pl.* —n) beech (tree).

buchen ['buːxən], *v.a.* book, enter, reserve; (*fig.*) score.

Bücherei ['byçəˈraɪ], *f.* (—, *pl.* —en) library.

Buchesche ['buːxɛʃə], *f.* (—, *pl.* —n) hornbeam.

Buchfink ['buːxfɪŋk], *m.* (—en, *pl.* —en) (*Orn.*) chaffinch.

Buchhalter ['buːxhaltər], *m.* (—s, *pl.* —) book-keeper.

Buchhändler ['buːxhɛndlər], *m.* (—s, *pl.* —) bookseller.

Buchmarder ['buːxmardər], *m.* (—s, *pl.* —) (*Zool.*) pine-marten.

Buchsbaum ['buksbaum], *m.* (—s, *pl.* ∵e) (*Bot.*) box-tree.

Büchse ['byksə], *f.* (—, *pl.* —n) box, case; tin, can; rifle, gun.

Büchsenfleisch ['byksənflaɪʃ], *n.* (—es, *no pl.*) tinned meat.

Büchsenlauf ['byksənlauf], *m.* (—s, *pl.* ∵e) gun-barrel.

Büchsenöffner ['byksənœfnər], *m.* (—s, *pl.* —) tin-opener.

Buchstabe ['buːxʃtaːbə], *m.* (—n, *pl.* —n) letter, character; *großer* —, capital (letter).

Buchstabenrätsel ['buːxʃtaːbənrɛtsəl], *n.* (—s, *pl.* —) anagram.

buchstabieren [buːxʃtaˈbiːrən], *v.a.* spell (out).

buchstäblich ['buːxʃtɛplɪç], *adj.* literal.

Bucht [buxt], *f.* (—, *pl.* —en) inlet, bay, creek, bight.

Buchung ['buːxuŋ], *f.* (—, *pl.* —en) (*Comm.*) entry (in a book); booking (of tickets).

Buchwissen ['bu:xvɪsən], *n.* (—s, *no pl.*) book-learning.

Buckel ['bukəl], *m.* (—s, *pl.* —) hump, humpback; boss, stud; (*coll.*) back.

bücken ['bykən], *v.r. sich* —, stoop, bow.

bucklig ['buklɪç], *adj.* humpbacked.

Bückling ['byklɪŋ], *m.* (—s, *pl.* —e) smoked herring; kipper.

buddeln ['budəln], *v.n.* (*coll.*) dig.

Bude ['bu:də], *f.* (—, *pl.* —n) shack, stall; (*coll.*) room; (*student's*) digs.

Büfett [by'fɛt], *n.* (—s, *pl.* —s) sideboard; buffet.

Büffel ['byfəl], *m.* (—, *pl.* —) buffalo.

büffeln ['byfəln], *v.n.* (*coll.*) cram (for an examination), swot.

Bug [bu:k], *m.* (—s, *pl.* ⸚e, —e) (*Naut.*) bow, (*Aviat.*) nose.

Buganker ['bu:kaŋkər], *m.* (—s, *pl.* —) bow-anchor.

Bügel ['bygəl], *m.* (—s, *pl.* —) coathanger; (*trigger*) guard; (*horse*) stirrup.

bügeln ['bygəln], *v.a.* iron, smoothe, press.

bugsieren [buk'si:rən], *v.a.* tow.

Bugspriet ['bu:kʃpri:t], *n.* (—s, *pl.* —e) bowsprit.

Buhle ['bu:lə], *m.* or *f.* (—n, *pl.* —n) (*Poet.*) paramour, lover.

buhlen ['bu:lən], *v.n.* (*Poet.*) woo, make love (to).

buhlerisch ['bu:lərɪʃ], *adj.* (*Poet.*) amorous, wanton, lewd.

Bühne ['by:nə], *f.* (—, *pl.* —n) (*Theat.*) stage; scaffold, platform.

Bühnenbild ['by:nənbɪlt], *n.* (—es, *pl.* —er) scenery.

Bukett [bu'kɛt], *n.* (—s, *pl.* —s) bunch of flowers, bouquet; bouquet (*wine*).

Bulgarien [bul'ga:rjən], *n.* Bulgaria.

Bulldogge ['buldɔgə], *f.* (—, *pl.* —n) bulldog.

Bulle (1) ['bulə], *m.* (—n, *pl.* —n) bull, bullock.

Bulle (2) ['bulə], *f.* (—, *pl.* —n) (*Eccl.*) (Papal) Bull.

bumm [bum], *int.* boom! bang!

Bummel ['buməl], *m.* (—s, *pl.* —) stroll.

Bummelei [bumə'laɪ], *f.* (—, *pl.* —en) idleness, negligence, casualness, carelessness.

bummeln ['buməln], *v.n.* lounge, waste o.'s time, dawdle; stroll.

Bummelzug ['buməltsu:k], *m.* (—s, *pl.* ⸚e) slow train.

bums [bums], *int.* bang! crash!

Bund (1) [bunt], *m.* (—es, *pl.* ⸚e) bond, tie, league, alliance, federation, confederacy; (*Eccl.*) covenant.

Bund (2) [bunt], *n.* (—es, *pl.* ⸚e) bundle, bunch (of keys).

Bündel ['byndəl], *n.* (—s, *pl.* —) bundle, package.

Bundesgenosse ['bundəsgənɔsə], *m.* (—n, *pl.* —n) confederate, ally.

Bundesstaat ['bundəsʃta:t], *m.* (—es, *pl.* —en) federal state; federation.

Bundestag ['bundəsta:k], *m.* (—es, *pl.* —e) federal parliament.

Bundeswehr ['bundəsve:r], *f.* (—, *no pl.*) federal defence; armed forces.

bündig ['byndɪç], *adj.* binding; *kurz und* —, concise, terse, to the point.

Bündnis ['byntnɪs], *n.* (—ses, *pl.* —se) alliance.

Bundschuh ['buntʃu:], *m.* (—s, *pl.* —e) clog, sandal.

bunt [bunt], *adj.* many-coloured, chequered, variegated, motley; *das ist mir zu* —, this is going too far.

buntscheckig ['buntʃekɪç], *adj.* dappled, spotted.

Buntspecht ['buntʃpɛçt], *m.* (—s, *pl.* —e) (*Orn.*) (spotted) woodpecker.

Bürde ['byrdə], *f.* (—, *pl.* —n) load, burden.

Bure ['bu:rə], *m.* (—n, *pl.* —n) Boer.

Burg [burk], *f.* (—, *pl.* —en) castle, fortress, citadel, stronghold.

Bürge ['byrgə], *m.* (—n, *pl.* —n) surety, bail, guarantee; *einen* —*n stellen*, offer bail.

bürgen ['byrgən], *v.n.* give security, vouch (for), go bail (for).

Bürger ['byrgər], *m.* (—s, *pl.* —) citizen, townsman, bourgeois, commoner.

bürgerlich ['byrgərlɪç], *adj.* civic; middle-class, bourgeois; —*e Küche*, plain cooking.

Bürgermeister ['byrgərmaɪstər], *m.* (—s, *pl.* —) burgomaster, mayor.

Burggraf ['burkgra:f], *m.* (—en, *pl.* —en) burgrave.

Bürgschaft ['byrkʃaft], *f.* (—, *pl.* —en) bail, surety, guarantee; — *leisten*, provide security.

Burgund [bur'gunt], *n.* Burgundy.

Burgvogt ['burkfo:kt], *m.* (—s, *pl.* —e) (*obs.*) castellan, bailiff.

Burgwarte ['burkvartə], *f.* (—, *pl.* —n) watch-tower.

Büro [by'ro:], *n.* (—s, *pl.* —s) office, bureau, (professional) chambers.

Bursche ['burʃə], *m.* (—n, *pl.* —n) lad, boy, fellow; student; (*Mil.*) batman.

Burschenschaft ['burʃənʃaft], *f.* (—, *pl.* —en) students' association.

Bürste ['byrstə], *f.* (—, *pl.* —n) brush.

Burundi [bu'rundi], *n.* Burundi.

Busch [buʃ], *m.* (—es, *pl.* ⸚e) bush, shrub, copse, thicket.

Büschel ['byʃəl], *n.* (—s, *pl.* —) bunch; (*hair*) tuft.

buschig ['buʃɪç], *adj.* bushy, tufted.

Buschklepper ['buʃklɛpər], *m.* (—s, *pl.* —) bushranger.

Busen ['bu:zən], *m.* (—s, *pl.* —) bosom, breast; (*Geog.*) bay, gulf.

Bussard ['busart], *m.* (—s, *pl.* —e) (*Orn.*) buzzard.

Buße ['bu:sə], *f.* (—, *pl.* —n) penance; repentance; penalty.

büßen ['by:sən], *v.a., v.n.* repent, atone, expiate, make amends.

bußfertig ['bu:sfɛrtɪç], *adj.* penitent, repentant.

Büste

Büste ['bystə], f. (—, pl. —n) bust.
Büstenhalter ['bystənhaltər], m. (—s, pl. —) brassière.
Bütte ['bytə], f. (—, pl. —n) tub.
Büttel ['bytəl], m. (—s, pl. —) beadle; bailiff.
Büttenpapier ['bytənpapi:r], n. (—s, no pl.) hand-made paper.
Butter ['butər], f. (—, no pl.) butter.
Butterblume ['butərblu:mə], f. (—, pl. —n) buttercup.
Butterbrot ['butərbro:t], n. (—s, pl. —e) bread and butter.
buttern ['butərn], v.a., v.n. smear with butter; churn.
Butterteig ['butərtaɪk], m. (—es, pl. —e) puff-pastry.
Butzenscheibe ['butsənʃaɪbə], f. (—, pl. —n) bull's-eyed pane.
Byzanz [by'tsants], n. Byzantium, Constantinople.

C

C [tse:], n. (—s, pl. —s) the letter C; (Mus.) C dur, C major; C Moll, C minor; C-Schlüssel, C clef.
Cäsar ['tsɛ:zar], m. Cæsar.
Ceylon ['tseɪlɔn], n. Ceylon.
Chaiselongue [ʃɛ:zə'lɔ̃:g], f. (—, pl. —s) couch, settee, sofa.
Champagner [ʃam'panjər], m. (—s, pl. —) champagne.
Champignon [ʃampɪn'jɔ̃], m. (—s, pl. —s) mushroom.
chaotisch [ka'o:tɪʃ], adj. chaotic.
Charakter [ka'raktər], m. (—s, pl. —e) character; mental make-up, disposition.
Charakteristik [karaktər'ɪstɪk], f. (—, pl. —en) characterisation.
charakteristisch [karaktər'ɪstɪʃ], adj. characteristic; typical.
Charge ['ʃarʒə], f. (—, pl. —n) office, appointment; (pl.) (Mil.) non-commissioned officers.
Chaussee [ʃɔ'se:], f. (—, pl. —n) main road, highway.
Chef [ʃef], m. (—s, pl. —s) chief, head, employer; (coll.) boss.
Chefredakteur ['ʃɛfredaktø:r], m. (—s, pl. —e) editor-in-chief.
Chemie [çe'mi:], f. (—, no pl.) chemistry.
Chemikalien [çemɪ'ka:ljən], f. pl. chemicals.
Chemiker ['çe:mɪkər], m. (—s, pl. —) (analytical) chemist.
chemisch ['çe:mɪʃ], adj. chemical; — gereinigt, dry-cleaned.
Chiffre ['ʃɪfər], f. (—, pl. —n) cipher.
chiffrieren [ʃɪ'fri:rən], v.a. encipher.
Chile ['tʃi:lə, 'çi:lə], n. Chile.

China ['çi:na], n. China.
Chinarinde [çi:na'rɪndə], f. (—, no pl.) Peruvian bark.
Chinin [çi'ni:n], n. (—s, no pl.) quinine.
Chirurg [çi'rurk], m. (—en, pl. —en) surgeon.
Chirurgie [çirur'gi:], f. (—, no pl.) surgery.
Chlor [klo:r], n. (—s, no pl.) chlorine.
Chlorkalk ['klo:rkalk], m. (—s, no pl.) chloride of lime.
Chlornatrium [klo:r'na:trjum], n. (—s, no pl.) sodium chloride.
Choleriker [ko'le:rɪkər], m. (—s, pl. —) irascible person.
Chor [ko:r], m. (—s, pl. ̈e) chorus; choir; (Archit.) choir, chancel.
Choral [ko'ra:l], m. (—s, pl. ̈e) hymn, chorale.
Choramt ['ko:ramt], n. (—s, pl. ̈er) cathedral service.
Chorgesang ['ko:ɡəsaŋ], m. (—s, pl. ̈e) chorus, choral singing.
Chorhemd ['ko:rhɛmt], n. (—s, pl. —en) surplice.
Chorherr ['ko:rhɛr], m. (—n, pl. —en) canon, prebendary.
Christ [krɪst], m. (—en, pl. —en) Christian.
Christbaum ['krɪstbaum], m. (—s, pl. ̈e) Christmas tree.
Christentum ['krɪstəntu:m], n. (—s, no pl.) Christendom, Christianity.
Christkind ['krɪstkɪnt], n. (—s, no pl.) Infant Christ, Christ child.
christlich ['krɪstlɪç], adj. Christian.
Christmette ['krɪstmɛtə], f. (—, pl. —n) Christmas matins; midnight mass.
Christus ['krɪstus], m. (—i) Christ; vor —, B.C.; nach —, A.D.
Chrom [kro:m], n. (—s, no pl.) chrome.
chromatisch [kro'ma:tɪʃ], adj. chromatic.
chromsauer ['kro:mzauər], adj. — chromate of; —es Salz, chromate.
Chronik ['kro:nɪk], f. (—, pl. —en) chronicle.
chronisch ['kro:nɪʃ], adj. chronic.
Chronist [kro'nɪst], m. (—en, pl. —en) chronicler.
Chrysantheme [kryzan'te:mə], f. (—, pl. —n) chrysanthemum.
Cis [tsɪs], n. (Mus.) C sharp.
Clique ['klɪkə], f. (—, pl. —n) clique, set.
Coeur [kø:r], n. (Cards) hearts.
coulant [ku'lant], adj. polite, friendly; (Comm.) fair, obliging.
Couleur [ku'lø:r], f. (—, pl. —en) colour; students' corporation.
Coupé [ku'pe:], n. (—s, pl. —s) (train) compartment.
Couplet [ku'ple:], n. (—s, pl. —s) comic song.
Coupon [ku'pɔ̃], m. (—s, pl. —s) coupon, check, dividend voucher.
Cour [ku:r], f. (—, no pl.) einem Mädchen die — machen, court a girl.

42

Courtage [kur'ta:ʒə], *f.* (—, *pl.* —n) brokerage.

Cousin [ku'zē], *m.* (—s, *pl.* —s) cousin.

Cousine [ku'zi:nə], *f.* (—, *pl.* —n) (female) cousin.

Cutaway ['katave:], *m.* (—s, *pl.* —s) morning coat.

Czar [tsa:r], *m.* (—en, *pl.* —en) Tsar, Czar.

D

D [de:], *n.* (—s, *pl.* —s) the letter D; (*Mus.*) *D dur*, D major; *D moll*, D minor; *D-Zug*, express train.

da [da:], *adv.* (*local*) there; here; (*temporal*) then, at that moment; (*Mil.*) *wer* —? who goes there? (*Poet. obs.*) where. — *conj.* (*temporal*) when, as; (*causal*) as, because, since.

dabei [da'baɪ], *adv.* nearby; besides, moreover; as well; —*sein*, be present, be about to (*infin.*); — *bleiben*, persist in.

Dach [dax], *n.* (—es, *pl.* —er) roof.

Dachboden ['daxbo:dən], *m.* (—s, *pl.* —) loft.

Dachdecker ['daxdɛkər], *m.* (—s, *pl.* —) slater, tiler.

Dachgiebel ['daxgi:bəl], *m.* (—s, *pl.* —) gable.

Dachluke ['daxlu:kə], *f.* (—, *pl.* —n) dormer window.

Dachpappe ['daxpapə], *f.* (—, *pl.* —n) roofing felt.

Dachrinne ['daxrɪnə], *f.* (—, *pl.* —n) gutter.

Dachs [daks], *m.* (—es, *pl.* —e) badger.

Dachstube ['daxʃtu:bə], *f.* (—, *pl.* —n) garret, attic (room).

Dachtraufe ['daxtraufə], *f.* (—, *pl.* —n) eaves.

dadurch [da'durç], *adv.* (*local*) through it; in that way; (*causal*) thereby.

dafür [da'fy:r], *adv.* for it; instead of it, in return for it; *ich kann nichts* —, it is not my fault, I can't help it.

Dafürhalten [da'fy:rhaltən], *n.* (—s, *no pl.*) opinion.

dagegen [da'ge:gən], *adv.* against it, compared to it. — *conj.* on the other hand.

daheim [da'haɪm], *adv.* at home.

daher [da'he:r], *adv.* thence, from that. — *conj.* therefore, for that reason.

dahin [da'hɪn], *adv.* thither, to that place; there; *bis* —, (*local*) thither; (*temporal*) till then; over, past, lost, gone.

dahinbringen [da'hɪnbrɪŋən], *v.a. irr.* *jemanden* —, induce s.o. to; *es* —, succeed in, manage to.

dahinsiechen [da'hɪnzi:çən], *v.n.* (*aux. sein*) pine away, be failing (in health).

dahinter [da'hɪntər], *adv.* behind that.

Dahlie ['da:ljə], *f.* (—, *pl.* —n) (*Bot.*) dahlia.

Dahome ['daome:], *n.* Dahomey.

damalig ['da:maliç], *adj.* then; of that time; past.

damals ['da:mals], *adv.* then, at that time.

Damast [da'mast], *m.* (—s, *no pl.*) damask.

Damaszener [damas'tse:nər], *m.* (—s, *pl.* —) Damascene. — *adj.* — *Stahl*, Damascus steel, dagger.

Dame ['da:mə], *f.* (—, *pl.* —n) lady; (*cards, chess*) queen; draughts (*game*).

damit [da'mɪt], *adv.* therewith, with that, with it; *und* — *basta!* and that's all there is to it. — *conj.* in order that, so that; — *nicht*, lest.

dämlich ['dɛ:mlɪç], *adj.* (*coll.*) foolish, silly.

Damm [dam], *m.* (—es, *pl.* ⸚e) dam, dyke, mole; (*street*) roadway, causeway; (*rail*) embankment.

dämmen ['dɛmən], *v.a.* dam; (*fig.*) stop, restrain.

dämmerig ['dɛmərɪç], *adj.* dusky.

dämmern ['dɛmərn], *v.n.* grow dusky; dawn.

dämonisch [dɛ'mo:nɪʃ], *adj.* demoniac-(al), demonlike.

Dampf [dampf], *m.* (—es, *pl.* ⸚e) vapour, steam, mist, fume; smoke.

dampfen ['dampfən], *v.n.* smoke, fume, steam.

dämpfen ['dɛmpfən], *v.a.* damp, smother, steam; subdue, deaden, muffle, soften down.

Dampfer ['dampfər], *m.* (—s, *pl.* —) steamer.

Dämpfer ['dɛmpfər], *m.* (—s, *pl.* —) damper; (*Mus.*) mute.

Dampfkessel ['dampfkɛsəl], *m.* (—s, *pl.* —) boiler.

Dämpfung ['dɛmpfuŋ], *f.* (—, *pl.* —en) damping, smothering, suppression; (*Aviat.*) stabilization.

danach [da'na:x], *adv.* after that, thereafter; accordingly, according to that.

daneben [da'ne:bən], *adv.* near it, by it, close by; *es geht* —, it goes amiss. — *conj.* besides.

Dänemark ['dɛ:nəmark], *n.* Denmark.

Dank [daŋk], *m.* (—es, *no pl.*) thanks, gratitude; reward; *Gott sei* —, thank heaven!

dank [daŋk], *prep.* (*Dat.*) owing to, thanks to.

dankbar ['daŋkba:r], *adj.* grateful; thankful.

danken ['daŋkən], *v.n.* (*Dat.*) thank. — *v.a.* owe.

Dankgebet ['daŋkgəbe:t], *n.* (—s, *pl.* —e) (prayer of) thanksgiving.

dann [dan], *adv.* then, at that time, in that case; — *und wann*, now and then, occasionally.

Danzig ['dantsiç], *n.* Dantzig.

daran

daran, dran ['da'ran, dran], *adv.* on it, at it, near that; thereon, thereby; *was liegt* —? what does it matter?

darauf, drauf [da'rauf, drauf], *adv.* (*local*) upon it, on it; (*temporal*) thereupon, thereon, thereafter.

daraufhin [darauf'hɪn], *adv.* thereupon; on the strength of that.

daraus, draus [da'raus, draus], *adv.* therefrom, hence, from that; *ich mache mir nichts* —, I do not care for it.

darben ['darbən], *v.n.* suffer want, go short; famish.

darbieten ['da:rbi:tən], *v.a. irr.* offer, tender, present.

Darbietung ['da:rbi:tuŋ], *f.* (—, *pl.* —en) offering, presentation, performance.

darbringen ['da:rbrɪŋən], *v.a. irr.* bring, present, offer.

darein, drein [da'raɪn, draɪn], *adv.* into it, therein.

darin, drin [da'rɪn, drɪn], *adv.* therein, in it, within.

darinnen, drinnen [da'rɪnən, 'drɪnən], *adv.* inside, in there.

darlegen ['da:rle:gən], *v.a.* demonstrate, explain; expound.

Darlehen ['da:rle:ən], *n.* (—s, *pl.* —) loan.

Darm [darm], *m.* (—s, *pl.* ⁓e) gut; (*pl.*) intestines, bowels.

Darmsaite ['darmzaɪtə], *f.* (—, *pl.* —n) catgut, gut-string.

darob [da'rɔp], *adv.* (*obs.*) on that account, on account of it.

darreichen ['da:raɪçən], *v.a.* offer, tender, present; (*Eccl.*) administer (sacraments).

darstellen ['da:rʃtɛlən], *v.a.* represent, delineate; (*Theat.*) perform.

Darstellung ['da:rʃtɛluŋ], *f.* (—, *pl.* —en) representation, exhibition, presentation; (*Theat.*) performance.

dartun ['da:rtu:n], *v.a. irr.* prove, demonstrate.

darüber, drüber [dar'y:bər, 'dry:bər], *adv.* over that, over it; concerning that.

darum, drum [da'rum, drum], *adv.* around it, around that, thereabout; therefore, for that reason.

darunter, drunter [da'runtər, 'druntər], *adv.* under that; thereunder; among; — *und drüber*, topsy-turvy.

das [das], *def. art. n.* the. — *dem. pron., dem. adj.* that, this. —*rel. pron.* which.

Dasein ['da:zaɪn], *n.* (—s, *no pl.*) presence, being, existence.

daselbst [da:'zɛlpst], *adv.* there, in that very place.

daß [das], *conj.* that; *es sei denn* —, unless; — *nicht*, lest.

dastehen ['da:ʃte:ən], *v.n. irr.* stand (there).

datieren [da'ti:rən], *v.a.* date, put a date to.

Dativ ['da:ti:f], *m.* (—s, *pl.* —e) dative.

dato [da'to], *adv. bis* —, till now, hitherto.

Dattel ['datəl], *f.* (—, *pl.* —n) (*Bot.*) date.

Datum ['da:tum], *n.* (—s, *pl.* **Daten**) date (*calendar*).

Dauer ['dauər], *f.* (—, *no pl.*) duration, length of time; continuance; permanence.

dauerhaft ['dauərhaft], *adj.* durable, lasting; (*colours*) fast.

Dauerkarte ['dauərkartə], *f.* (—, *pl.* —n) season ticket; (*Am.*) commutation ticket.

dauern ['dauərn], *v.n.* continue, last, endure.— *v.a.* move to pity; *er dauert mich*, I am sorry for him.

Dauerpflanze ['dauərpflantsə], *f.* (—, *pl.* —n) perennial plant.

Dauerwelle ['dauərvɛlə], *f.* (—, *pl.* —n) permanent wave, (*coll.*) perm.

Daumen ['daumən], *m.* (—s, *pl.* —) thumb; *einem den* — *halten*, wish s.o. well, keep o.'s fingers crossed for s.o.

Daune ['daunə], *f.* (—, *pl.* —n) down.

davon [da'fɔn], *adv.* thereof, therefrom, from that; off, away.

davonkommen [da'fɔnkɔmən], *v.n. irr.* (*aux. sein*) get off; *mit einem blauen Auge* —, get off lightly.

davor [da'fo:r], *adv.* before that, before it.

dawider [da'vi:dər], *adv.* against it.

dazu [da'tsu:], *adv.* thereto, to that, to it; in addition to that; for that purpose; *noch* —, besides.

dazumal ['da:tsuma:l], *adv.* then, at that time.

dazwischen [da'tsvɪʃən], *adv.* between, among; — *kommen*, intervene, interfere; — *treten*, intervene.

debattieren [deba'ti:rən], *v.a., v.n.* debate.

Debet ['de:bɛt], *n.* (—s, *pl.* —s) debit.

Debüt [de'by:], *n.* (—s, *pl.* —s) first appearance, début.

Dechant [de'çant], *m.* (—en, *pl.* —en) (*Eccl.*) dean.

dechiffrieren [deʃɪf'ri:rən], *v.a.* decode, decipher.

Deck [dɛk], *n.* (—s, *pl.* —e) (*Naut.*) deck.

Deckbett ['dɛkbɛt], *n.* (—s, *pl.* —en) coverlet.

Deckblatt ['dɛkblat], *n.* (—s, *pl.* ⁓er) (*Bot.*) bractea; (*cigar*) wrapper.

Decke ['dɛkə], *f.* (—, *pl.* —n) cover; blanket, rug; (*bed*) coverlet; (*room*) ceiling.

Deckel ['dɛkəl], *m.* (—s, *pl.* —) lid, top; (*book*) cover; (*coll.*) hat.

decken ['dɛkən], *v.a.* cover; (*Comm.*) secure, reimburse. — *v.r. sich* —, (*Maths.*) coincide; (*fig.*) square, tally.

Deckfarbe ['dɛkfarbə], *f.* (—, *pl.* —n) body colour.

Deckmantel ['dɛkmantəl], *m.* (—s, *pl.* ⁓) cloak, disguise.

Deckung ['dɛkuŋ], *f.* (—, *pl.* —en) covering, protection; (*Comm.*) reimbursement; security; (*Mil.*) cover.

dedizieren [dedɪ'tsi:rən], *v.a.* dedicate.

deduzieren [dedu′tsi:rən], *v.a.* deduce.

defekt [de′fɛkt], *adj.* defective, incomplete, imperfect.

defilieren [defɪ′li:rən], *v.n.* (*Mil.*) pass in review, march past.

definieren [defɪ′ni:rən], *v.a.* define.

Degen [′de:gən], *m.* (—s, *pl.* —) sword; (*fig.*) brave warrior.

degradieren [degra′di:rən], *v.a.* degrade, demote.

dehnbar [′de:nba:r], *adj.* extensible, ductile.

dehnen [′de:nən], *v.a.* extend, expand, stretch. — *v.r. sich —*, stretch o.s.

Deich [daɪç], *m.* (—es, *pl.* —e) dike, dam, embankment.

Deichsel [′daɪksəl], *f.* (—, *pl.* —n) thill, shaft, pole.

deichseln [′daɪksəln], *v.a.* (*fig.*) engineer; (*coll.*) manage; wangle.

dein [daɪn], *poss. adj.* your; (*Poet.*) thy. — *poss. pron.* yours; (*Poet.*) thine.

deinesgleichen [daɪnəs′glaɪçən], *adj. pron.* the like of you, such as you.

deinethalben [′daɪnəthalbən], *adv.* on your account, for your sake, on your behalf.

deinetwegen [′daɪnətve:gən], *adv.* because of you, on your account, for your sake, on your behalf.

deinetwillen [′daɪnətvɪlən], *adv. um* —, on your account, for your sake, on your behalf.

deinige [′daɪnɪgə], *poss. adj.* your; (*Poet.*) thy. — *poss. pron.* yours; (*Poet.*) thine.

Dekan [de′ka:n], *m.* (—s, *pl.* —e) (*Eccl., Univ.*) dean.

Dekanat [deka′na:t], *n.* (—s, *pl.* —e) (*Eccl., Univ.*) deanery, office of dean.

deklamieren [dekla′mi:rən], *v.a., v.n.* recite, declaim.

deklarieren [dekla′ri:rən], *v.a.* declare (for customs duty).

Deklination [deklina′tsjo:n], *f.* (—, *pl.* —en) (*Gram.*) declension; (*Phys.*) declination.

deklinieren [deklɪ′ni:rən], *v.a.* (*Gram.*) decline.

dekolletiert [dekɔle′ti:rt], *adj.* décolleté, low-necked.

Dekret [de′kre:t], *n.* (—s, *pl.* —e) decree, edict, official regulation.

dekretieren [dekre′ti:rən], *v.a.* decree, ordain.

delegieren [dele′gi:rən], *v.a.* delegate.

Delegierte [dele′gi:rtə], *m.* (—n, *pl.* —n) delegate.

delikat [delɪ′ka:t], *adj.* subtle, dainty; tasty; (*coll.*) tricky, difficult.

Delikatesse [delɪka′tɛsə], *f.* (—, *pl.* —n) delicacy, dainty; (*pl.*) (*Am.*) delicatessen.

Delikt [de′lɪkt], *n.* (—s, *pl.* —e) (*Law*) crime; misdemeanour.

Delle [′dɛlə], *f.* (—, *pl.* —n) dent.

Delphin [dɛl′fi:n], *m.* (—s, *pl.* —e) dolphin.

deltaförmig [′dɛltafœrmɪç], *adj.* deltoid.

dem [de:m], *def. art. Dat.* to the. — *dem. adj.* to this, to that: — *dem. pron.* to this, to that; *wie* — *auch sei,* however that may be. — *rel. pron.* to whom, to which.

demarkieren [demar′ki:rən], *v.a.* mark, demarcate.

Dementi [de′mɛnti], *n.* (—s, *pl.* —s) (*official*) denial.

dementieren [demɛn′ti:rən], *v.a.* (*Pol.*) deny, contradict.

demgemäß [′de:mgəmɛ:s], *adv.* accordingly.

demnach [′de:mnax], *conj.* therefore, consequently, in accordance with that.

demnächst [′de:mnɛ:çst], *adv.* shortly, soon, in the near future.

demokratisch [demo′kra:tɪʃ], *adj.* democratic.

demolieren [demo′li:rən], *v.a.* demolish.

demonstrieren [demɔn′stri:rən], *v.a., v.n.* demonstrate.

Demut [′de:mu:t], *f.* (—, *no pl.*) humility, meekness.

demütig [′de:mytɪç], *adj.* humble, meek, submissive.

demütigen [′de:mytɪgən], *v.a.* humble, humiliate, subdue.

Denkart [′dɛŋka:rt], *f.* (—, *pl.* —en) way of thinking.

denken [′dɛŋkən], *v.a., v.n. irr.* think, reflect (upon); imagine; (*coll.*) guess.

Denker [′dɛŋkər], *m.* (—s, *pl.* —) thinker, philosopher.

Denkmal [′dɛŋkma:l], *n.* (—s, *pl.* ″er) monument.

Denkmünze [′dɛŋkmyntsə], *f.* (—, *pl.* —n) (commemorative) medal.

Denkschrift [′dɛŋkʃrɪft], *f.* (—, *pl.* —en) memorandum, memoir.

Denkspruch [′dɛŋkʃprux], *m.* (—s, *pl.* ″e) aphorism, maxim, motto.

Denkungsart [′dɛŋkuŋsart], *f.* (*pl.* —en) *see* **Denkart.**

Denkweise [′dɛŋkvaɪzə], *f.* (—, *pl.* —n) *see* **Denkart.**

denkwürdig [′dɛŋkvyrdɪç], *adj.* memorable.

Denkzettel [′dɛŋktsɛtəl], *m.* (—s, *pl.* —) (*fig.*) reminder, punishment, lesson; *einem einen* — *geben,* give s.o. s.th. to think about *or* a sharp reminder.

denn [dɛn], *conj.* for. — *adv.* then; (*after comparatives*) than; *es sei* — *dass,* unless.

dennoch [′dɛnɔx], *conj.* yet, nevertheless, notwithstanding.

Denunziant [denun′tsjant], *m.* (—en, *pl.* —en) informer.

denunzieren [denun′tsi:rən], *v.a.* inform against, denounce.

Depesche [de′pɛʃə], *f.* (—, *pl.* —n) dispatch; telegram, wire.

deponieren [depo′ni:rən], *v.a.* deposit; (*Law*) depose.

Depositenbank [depo′zi:tənbaŋk], *f.* (—, *pl.* —en) deposit-bank.

deprimieren [depri'mi:rən], *v.a.* depress.

Deputierte [depu'ti:rtə], *m.* (**—n,** *pl.* **—n**) deputy.

der [de:r], *def. art. m.* the. — *dem. adj., dem. pron.* this, that. — *rel. pron.* who, which, that.

derart ['de:ra:rt], *adv.* so, in such a manner.

derartig ['de:ra:rtɪç], *adj.* such.

derb [dɛrp], *adj.* firm, solid, coarse, blunt, uncouth; strong, robust.

dereinst [de:r'aɪnst], *adv.* one day (in future).

derenthalben ['de:rənthalbən], *adv.* for her (their) sake, on her (their) account, on whose account.

derentwegen ['de:rəntve:gən], *adv. see* **derenthalben.**

derentwillen ['de:rəntvɪlən], *adv. see* **derenthalben.**

dergestalt ['de:rgəʃtalt], *adv.* in such a manner; so.

dergleichen [de:r'glaɪçən], *adv.* such, such as, suchlike.

derjenige ['de:rje:nɪgə], *dem. adj., dem. pron.* that, this; — *welcher,* he who.

derlei ['de:rlaɪ], *adj.* of that sort.

dermaßen [de:r'ma:sən], *adv.* to such an extent, to such a degree.

derselbe [de:r'zɛlbə], *pron.* the same.

derweilen [de:r'vaɪlən], *adv.* meanwhile.

Derwisch ['dɛrvɪʃ], *m.* (**—(e)s,** *pl.* **—e**) dervish.

derzeit ['de:rtsaɪt], *adv.* at present.

Des [dɛs], *n.* (**—,** *pl.* **—**) *(Mus.)* D flat; — *Dur,* D flat major; — *Moll,* D flat minor.

des [dɛs], *def. art. m. & n. Genit. sing.* of the.

desgleichen [dɛs'glaɪçən], *adj.* such, suchlike. — *adv.* likewise, ditto.

deshalb ['dɛshalp], *adv., conj.* therefore.

desinfizieren [dɛsɪnfit'si:rən], *v.a.* disinfect.

dessen ['dɛsən], *dem. pron. m & n. Genit. sing.* of it, of that. — *rel. pron. m. & n. Genit. sing.* whose, of whom, of which, whereof.

dessenungeachtet [dɛsənungə'axtət], *conj.* notwithstanding that, for all that, despite all that.

Destillateur [dɛstɪla'tø:r], *m.* (**—s,** *pl.* **—e**) distiller.

destillieren [dɛstɪ'li:rən], *v.a.* distil.

desto ['dɛsto], *adv.* the; — *besser,* so much the better; *je . . . —,* the . . . the.

deswegen ['dɛsve:gən], *adv., conj.* therefore.

Detaillist [deta'jɪst], *m.* (**—en,** *pl.* **—en**) retailer.

deucht [dɔyçt] *see* **dünken;** *(obs.) mich deucht,* methinks.

deuten ['dɔytən], *v.a.* point to, show; explain, interpret.

deutlich ['dɔytlɪç], *adj.* clear, distinct; evident, plain.

deutsch [dɔytʃ], *adj.* German.

Deutschland ['dɔytʃlant], *n.* Germany.

Deutschmeister ['dɔytʃmaɪstər], *m.* (**—s,** *pl.* **—**) Grand Master of the Teutonic Order.

Deutschtum ['dɔytʃtu:m], *n.* (**—s,** *no pl.*) German nationality, German customs, German manners.

Deutung ['dɔytuŋ], *f.* (**—,** *pl.* **—en**) explanation, interpretation.

Devise [de'vi:zə], *f.* (**—,** *pl.* **—n**) device, motto; *(pl.)* foreign currency.

devot [de'vo:t], *adj.* submissive, respectful, humble.

Dezember [de'tsɛmbər], *m.* December.

dezent [de'tsɛnt], *adj.* modest, decent; unobtrusive.

Dezernent [detsɛr'nɛnt], *m.* (**—en,** *pl.* **—en**) head of section in ministry or city administration.

dezimieren [detsi'mi:rən], *v.a.* decimate, reduce.

Diagramm [dia'gram], *n.* (**—s,** *pl.* **—e**) diagram, graph.

Diakon [dia'ko:n], *m.* (**—s,** *pl.* **—e**) *(Eccl.)* deacon.

Diakonisse, Diakonissin [diako'nɪsə, diako'nɪsɪn], *f.* (**—,** *pl.* **—nen**) deaconess.

Dialektik [dia'lɛktɪk], *f.* (**—,** *no pl.*) dialectics.

Diamant [dia'mant], *m.* (**—en,** *pl.* **—en**) diamond.

diametral [diame'tra:l], *adj.* diametrical.

Diapositiv [diapozi'ti:f], *n.* (**—s,** *pl.* **—e**) *(lantern, Phot.)* slide.

Diät [di'ɛ:t], *f.* (**—,** *pl.* **—en**) diet; *(pl.)* daily allowance.

dich [dɪç], *pers. pron.* you. — *refl. pron.* yourself.

dicht [dɪçt], *adj.* tight; impervious (to water); dense, compact, solid, firm; — *bei,* hard by, close to.

Dichte ['dɪçtə], *f.* (**—,** *no pl.*) density.

dichten ['dɪçtən], *v.a., v.n.* write poetry, compose *(verses etc.);* *(Tech.)* tighten; *(Naut.)* caulk.

Dichter ['dɪçtər], *m.* (**—s,** *pl.* **—**) poet.

dichterisch ['dɪçtərɪʃ], *adj.* poetic(al).

Dichtigkeit ['dɪçtɪçkaɪt], *f.* (**—,** *no pl.*) closeness, compactness, thickness, density.

Dichtkunst ['dɪçtkunst], *f.* (**—,** *no pl.*) (art of) poetry.

Dichtung ['dɪçtuŋ], *f.* (**—,** *pl.* **—en**) poetry, poem; fiction; *(Tech.)* caulking; washer, gasket.

dick [dɪk], *adj.* thick; fat; *(books)* bulky; voluminous, stout, obese, corpulent.

Dicke ['dɪkə], *f.* (**—,** *no pl.*) thickness, stoutness.

dickfellig ['dɪkfɛlɪç], *adj.* thick-skinned.

Dickicht ['dɪkɪçt], *n.* (**—s,** *pl.* **—e**) thicket.

die [di:], *def. art. f. & pl.* the. — *dem. adj., dem. pron. f. & pl.* this, these. — *rel. pron. f. & pl.* who, that which.

Dieb [di:p], *m.* (**—s,** *pl.* **—e**) thief.

Diebstahl ['di:pʃta:l], *m.* (**—s,** *pl.* ``e**) theft.

Diele ['di:lə], *f.* (—, *pl.* —n) floor; (entrance) hall.

dielen ['di:lən], *v.a.* board, floor.

dienen ['di:nən], *v.n. einem —,* serve (s.o.); help (s.o.).

Diener ['di:nər], *m.* (—s, *pl.* —) servant, attendant; (*coll.*) bow.

dienlich ['di:nlɪç], *adj.* serviceable, useful; *für — halten,* think fit.

Dienst [di:nst], *m.* (—es, *pl.* —e) service, employment, duty; — *haben,* be on duty.

Dienstag ['di:nsta:k], *m.* (—s, *pl.* —e) Tuesday.

Dienstalter ['di:nstaltər], *n.* (—s, *pl.* —) seniority.

dienstbar ['di:nstba:r], *adj.* subject, subservient.

Dienstbarkeit ['di:nstba:rkaɪt], *f.* (—, *no pl.*) bondage, servitude.

dienstbeflissen ['di:nstbəflɪsən], *adj.* assiduous.

Dienstbote ['di:nstbo:tə], *m.* (—n, *pl.* —n) domestic servant.

dienstfertig ['di:nstfɛrtɪç], *adj.* obliging, ready to serve.

Dienstleistung ['di:nstlaɪstuŋ], *f.* (—, *pl.* —en) service.

dienstlich ['di:nstlɪç], *adj.* official.

Dienstmädchen ['di:nstmɛ:tçən], *n.* (—s, pl. —) maidservant.

Dienstmann ['di:nstman], *m.* (—s, *pl.* ⁻er) commissionaire, porter.

Dienstpflicht ['di:nstpflɪçt], *f.* (—, *no pl.*) official duty, liability to serve; (*Mil.*) (compulsory) military service.

Dienststunden ['di:nstʃtundən] *f. pl.* office hours.

diensttauglich ['di:nsttauklɪç], *adj.* (*Mil.*) fit for service.

Dienstverhältnis ['di:nstfɛrhɛltnɪs], *n.* (—ses, *pl.* —se) (*pl.*) terms of service.

dies [di:s], *abbr.* **dieses.**

diesbezüglich ['di:sbətsy:klɪç], *adj.* concerning this, relating to this matter.

diese ['di:zə], *dem. adj., dem. pron. f. & pl.* this, these.

dieser ['di:zər], *dem. adj., dem. pron. m.* this.

dieses ['di:zəs], *dem. adj., dem. pron. n.* this.

diesjährig ['di:sjɛ:rɪç], *adj.* of this year, this year's.

diesmal ['di:sma:l], *adv.* this time, for this once.

Dietrich (1) ['di:trɪç], *m.* Derek.

Dietrich (2) ['di:trɪç], *m.* (—s, *pl.* —e) pick lock, master-key, skeleton key.

Differentialrechnung [dɪfərɛnts'ja:l-rɛçnuŋ], *f.* (—, *pl.* —en) differential calculus.

Differenz [dɪfə'rɛnts], *f.* (—, *pl.* —en) difference; quarrel.

Diktat [dɪk'ta:t], *n.* (—s, *pl.* —e) dictation.

diktatorisch [dɪkta'to:rɪʃ], *adj.* dictatorial.

Diktatur [dɪkta'tu:r], *f.* (—, *pl.* —en) dictatorship.

diktieren [dɪk'ti:rən], *v.a.* dictate.

Ding [dɪŋ], *n.* (—s, *pl.* —e) thing, object, matter.

dingen ['dɪŋən], *v.a.* hire, engage (a manual worker).

dingfest ['dɪŋfɛst], *adj.* — *machen,* arrest.

dinglich ['dɪŋlɪç], *adj.* real.

dinieren [di'ni:rən], *v.n.* dine.

Diözese [diø'tsɛ:zə], *f.* (—, *pl.* —n) diocese.

Diphtherie [dɪfta'ri:], *f.* (—, *no pl.*) diphtheria.

Diplom [di'plo:m], *n.* (—s, *pl.* —e) diploma.

Diplomatie [dɪploma'ti:], *f.* (—, *no pl.*) diplomacy.

dir [di:r], *pers. pron. Dat.* to you.

direkt [di'rɛkt], *adj.* direct; —*er Wagen,* (*railway*) through carriage; — *danach,* immediately afterwards.

Direktion [dɪrɛk'tsjo:n], *f.* (—, *pl.* —en) direction, management.

Direktor [di'rɛktər], *m.* (—s, *pl.* —en) (managing) director, manager; headmaster, principal.

Direktorium [dɪrɛk'to:rjum], *n.* (—s, *pl.* —rien) directorate, board of directors.

Direktrice [dɪrɛk'tri:sə], *f.* (—, *pl.* —n) manageress.

Dirigent [diri'gɛnt], *m.* (—en, *pl.* —en) (*Mus.*) conductor; (*Austr. Admin.*) head of section in Ministry.

dirigieren [diri'gi:rən], *v.a.* direct, manage; (*Mus.*) conduct.

Dirndl ['dɪrndl], *n.* (—s, *pl.* —) (*dial.*) young girl, country wench; (*fig.*) peasant dress, dirndl.

Dirne ['dɪrnə], *f.* (—, *pl.* —n) (*Poet.*) girl; prostitute.

Dis [dɪs], *n.* (—, *no pl.*) (*Mus.*) D sharp.

disharmonisch [dɪshar'mo:nɪʃ], *adj.* discordant.

Diskant [dɪs'kant], *m.* (—s, *pl.* —e) (*Mus.*) treble, soprano.

Diskont [dɪs'kɔnt], *m.* (—(e)s, *pl.* —e) discount, rebate.

diskret [dɪs'kre:t], *adj.* discreet.

Diskurs [dɪs'kurs], *m.* (—es, *pl.* —e) discourse.

diskutieren [dɪsku'ti:rən], *v.a.* discuss, debate.

Dispens [dɪs'pɛns], *m.* (—es, *pl.* —e) dispensation.

dispensieren [dɪspɛn'zi:rən], *v.a.* dispense (from), exempt (from).

disponieren [dɪspo'ni:rən], *v.n.* — *über,* dispose of; make plans about.

Dissident [dɪsi'dɛnt], *m.* (—en, *pl.* —en) dissenter, nonconformist.

distanzieren [dɪstan'tsi:rən], *v.r. sich — von,* keep o.'s distance from; dissociate o.s. from.

Distel ['dɪstəl], *f.* (—, *pl.* —n) thistle.

Distelfink ['dɪstəlfɪŋk], *m.* (—s, *pl.* —e) (*Orn.*) gold-finch.

disziplinarisch [dɪstsipli'na:rɪʃ], *adj.* diciplinary.

dito ['di:to], *adv.* ditto.

47

dividieren [dɪvɪˈdiːrən], *v.a.* divide.
Diwan [ˈdiːvan], *m.* (—s, *pl.* —e) divan, sofa, couch.
doch [dɔx], *adv., conj.* however, though, although, nevertheless, yet, but; after all, (*emphatic*) yes.
Docht [dɔxt], *m.* (—es, *pl.* —e) wick.
Dock [dɔk], *n.* (—s, *pl.* —s, —e) dock.
Dogge [ˈdɔgə], *f.* (—, *pl.* —n) bulldog, mastiff; Great Dane.
Dogmatiker [dɔgˈmaːtɪkər], *m.* (—s, *pl.* —) dogmatist.
dogmatisch [dɔgˈmaːtɪʃ], *adj.* dogmatic, doctrinal.
Dohle [ˈdoːlə], *f.* (—, *pl.* —n) (*Orn.*) jackdaw.
Doktor [ˈdɔktɔr], *m.* (—s, *pl.* —en) doctor; physician, surgeon.
Dolch [dɔlç], *m.* (—es, *pl.* —e) dagger, dirk.
Dolde [ˈdɔldə], *f.* (—, *pl.* —n) (*Bot.*) umbel.
Dolmetscher [ˈdɔlmɛtʃər], *m.* (—s, *pl.* —) interpreter.
dolmetschen [ˈdɔlmɛtʃən], *v.a.* interpret.
Dolomiten [doloˈmiːtən], *pl.* Dolomites.
Dom [doːm], *m.* (—s, *pl.* —e) cathedral; dome, cupola.
Domherr [ˈdoːmhɛr], *m.* (—n, *pl.* —en) canon, prebendary.
dominieren [domiˈniːrən], *v.a.* dominate, domineer.
Dominikaner [dominiˈkaːnər], *m.* (—s, *pl.* —) Dominican friar.
dominikanische Republik [dominiˈkaːnɪʃə repuˈbliːk], *f.* Dominican Republic.
Domizil [domiˈtsiːl], *n.* (—s, *pl.* —e) domicile, residence, address.
Domkapitel [ˈdoːmkapiːtəl], *n.* (—s, *pl.* —) dean and chapter.
Dompfaff [ˈdɔmpfaf], *m.* (—s, *pl.* —en) (*Orn.*) bullfinch.
Dompropst [ˈdoːmproːpst], *m.* (—es, *pl.* ˙e) provost.
Donau [ˈdoːnau], *f.* (—, *no pl.*) Danube.
Donner [ˈdɔnər], *m.* (—s, *no pl.*) thunder.
donnern [ˈdɔnərn], *v.n.* thunder; (*fig.*) storm, rage.
Donnerschlag [ˈdɔnərʃlaːk], *m.* (—s, *pl.* ˙e) thunderclap.
Donnerstag [ˈdɔnərstaːk], *m.* (—s, *pl.* —e) Thursday; **Grün —**, Maundy Thursday.
Donnerwetter [ˈdɔnərvɛtər], *n.* (—s, *pl.* —) thunderstorm; *zum —* (*nochmal*)! hang it all, confound it!
doppeldeutig [ˈdɔpəldɔytɪç], *adj.* ambiguous.
Doppelgänger [ˈdɔpəlgɛŋər], *m.* (—s, *pl.* —) double.
Doppellaut [ˈdɔpəllaut], *m.* (—s, *pl.* —e) diphthong.
doppeln [ˈdɔpəln] *see* **verdoppeln**.
doppelsinnig [ˈdɔpəlzɪnɪç] *see* **doppeldeutig**.
doppelt [ˈdɔpəlt], *adj.* double, twofold.

Doppelzwirn [ˈdɔpəltsvɪrn], *m.* (—s, *no pl.*) double-thread.
Dorf [dɔrf], *n.* (—es, *pl.* ˙er) village.
dörflich [ˈdœrflɪç], *adj.* rural, rustic.
dorisch [ˈdoːrɪʃ], *adj.* Doric.
Dorn [dɔrn], *m.* (—s, *pl.* —en) thorn, prickle; (*Bot.*) spine; (*buckle*) tongue.
dornig [ˈdɔrnɪç], *adj.* thorny.
Dornröschen [ˈdɔrnrøːsçən], *n.* (—s, *pl.* —) Sleeping Beauty.
Dorothea [doroˈteːa], *f.* Dorothea, Dorothy.
dorren [ˈdɔrən] *see* **verdorren**.
dörren [ˈdœrən], *v.a.* dry, make dry, parch.
Dörrobst [ˈdœrrobst], *n.* (—es, *no pl.*) dried fruit.
Dorsch [dɔrʃ], *m.* (—es, *pl.* —e) cod, codfish.
dort [dɔrt], (*Austr.*) **dorten** [ˈdɔrtən], *adv.* yonder, there; *von — aus*, from that point, from there.
dorther [ˈdɔrtheːr], *adv.* from there, therefrom, thence.
dorthin [ˈdɔrthɪn], *adv.* to that place, thereto, thither.
dortig [ˈdɔrtɪç], *adj.* of that place, local.
Dose [ˈdoːzə], *f.* (—, *pl.* —n) box, tin, can.
dösen [ˈdøːzən], *v.n.* doze, daydream.
Dosis [ˈdoːzɪs], *f.* (—, *pl.* **Dosen**) dose.
Dotter [ˈdɔtər], *n.* (—s, *pl.* —) yolk (of egg).
Dozent [doˈtsɛnt], *m.* (—en, *pl.* —en) university lecturer; (*Am.*) Assistant Professor.
dozieren [doˈtsiːrən], *v.n.* lecture.
Drache [ˈdraxə], *m.* (—n, *pl.* —n) dragon; kite; (*fig.*) termagant, shrew.
Dragoner [draˈgoːnər], *m.* (—s, *pl.* —) dragoon.
Draht [draːt], *m.* (—es, *pl.* ˙e) wire.
drahten [ˈdraːtən], *v.a.* wire, telegraph.
Drahtgewebe [ˈdraːtgəveːbə], *n.* (—s, *pl.* —) wire-gauze.
Drahtgitter [ˈdraːtgɪtər], *m.* (—s, *pl.* —) wire grating.
drahtlos [ˈdraːtloːs], *adj.* wireless.
Drahtseilbahn [ˈdraːtzailbaːn], *f.* (—, *pl.* —en) cable (funicular) railway.
Drahtzange [ˈdraːttsaŋə], *f.* (—, *pl.* —n) pliers.
drall [dral], *adj.* buxom, plump.
Drama [ˈdraːma], *n.* (—s, *pl.* —men) drama.
Dramatiker [draˈmaːtɪkər], *m.* (—s, *pl.* —) dramatist.
dramatisch [draˈmaːtɪʃ], *adj.* dramatic.
dran [dran] *see* **daran**.
Drang [draŋ], *m.* (—s, *no pl.*) urge; rush; throng; pressure; impulse.
drängeln [ˈdrɛŋəln], *v.a.* jostle.
drängen [ˈdrɛŋən], *v.a.* press, urge; *die Zeit drängt*, time presses; *es drängt mich*, I feel called upon.
Drangsal [ˈdraŋzaːl], *f. or n.* (—s, *pl.* —e *or* —en) distress, misery.
drapieren [draˈpiːrən], *v.a.* drape.

drastisch ['drastɪʃ], *adj.* drastic.
drauf [drauf] *see* **darauf.**
Draufgänger ['draufgɛŋər], *m.* (—s, *pl.* —) daredevil.
draußen ['drausən], *adv.* outside, without, out of doors.
drechseln ['drɛksəln], *v.a.* turn (on a lathe); *Phrasen —,* turn phrases.
Drechsler ['drɛkslər], *m.* (—s, *pl.* —) turner.
Dreck [drɛk], *m.* (—s, *no pl.*) dirt, mire, dust, filth, dung.
dreckig ['drɛkɪç], *adj.* dirty, filthy, muddy.
drehbar ['dre:ba:r], *adj.* revolving, swivelling.
Drehbuch ['dre:bu:x], *n.* (—s, *pl.* ̈er) (*film*) script.
drehen ['dre:ən], *v.a.* turn; (*film*) shoot. — *v.n.* turn round, veer.
Drehorgel ['dre:ɔrgəl], *f.* (—, *pl.* —n) barrel-organ.
Drehrad ['dre:ra:t], *n.* (—s, *pl.* ̈er) fly-wheel.
Drehung ['dre:uŋ], *f.* (—, *pl.* —en) rotation, turn, revolution.
drei [draɪ], *num. adj.* three.
dreiblätterig ['draɪblɛtərɪç], *adj.* trifoliate.
Dreieck ['draɪɛk], *n.* (—s, *pl.* —e) triangle.
dreieckig ['draɪɛkɪç], *adj.* triangular, three-cornered.
dreieinig [draɪ'aɪnɪç], *adj.* (*Theol.*) triune.
dreifach ['draɪfax], *adj.* threefold, triple.
Dreifaltigkeit [draɪ'faltɪçkaɪt], *f.* (—, *no pl.*) (*Theol.*) Trinity.
Dreifuß ['draɪfu:s], *m.* (—es, *pl.* ̈e) tripod.
dreijährlich ['draɪjɛrlɪç], *adj.* triennial.
Dreikönigsfest [draɪ'kø:nɪksfɛst], *n.* (—es, *no pl.*) Epiphany.
dreimonatlich ['draɪmo:natlɪç], *adj.* quarterly.
Dreirad ['draɪra:t], *n.* (—s, *pl.* ̈er) tricycle.
dreiseitig ['draɪzaɪtɪç], *adj.* trilateral.
dreißig ['draɪsɪç], *num. adj.* thirty.
dreist [draɪst], *adj.* bold, audacious; impudent.
dreistellig ['draɪʃtɛlɪç], *adj.* —*e Zahl,* number of three figures.
dreistimmig ['draɪʃtɪmɪç], *adj.* for three voices.
Dreistufenrakete ['draɪʃtu:fənra'ke:tə], *f.* (—, *pl.* —n) three-stage rocket.
dreistündig ['draɪʃtyndɪç], *adj.* lasting three hours.
dreitägig ['draɪtɛ:gɪç], *adj.* lasting three days.
dreiteilig ['draɪtaɪlɪç], *adj.* tripartite; three-piece.
dreizehn ['draɪtse:n], *num. adj.* thirteen.
Drell [drɛl], *m.* (—s, *no pl.*) *see* **Drillich.**
Dresche ['drɛʃə], *f.* (—, *no pl.*) thrashing, beating.
dreschen ['drɛʃən], *v.a. irr.* (*corn*) thresh; (*person*) thrash.

Dreschflegel ['drɛʃfle:gəl], *m.* (—s, *pl.* —) flail.
dressieren [drɛ'si:rən], *v.a.* (*animal*) train; break in.
Dressur [drɛ'su:r], *f.* (—, *pl.* —en) training, breaking-in.
Drillbohrer ['drɪlbo:rər], *m.* (—s, *pl.* —) drill.
drillen ['drɪlən], *v.a.* (*a hole*) bore; (*soldiers*) drill.
Drillich ['drɪlɪç], *m.* (—s, *pl.* —e) drill, canvas.
Drilling ['drɪlɪŋ], *m.* (—s, *pl.* —e) three-barrelled gun; (*pl.*) triplets.
drin [drɪn] *see* **darin.**
dringen ['drɪŋən], *v.n. irr.* penetrate, force o.'s way through; *auf etwas —,* insist on s.th.
dringlich ['drɪŋlɪç], *adj.* urgent, pressing.
drinnen ['drɪnən], *adv.* inside, within.
drittens ['drɪtəns], *adv.* thirdly.
droben ['dro:bən], *adv.* up there, above, aloft, overhead.
Droge ['dro:gə], *f.* (—, *pl.* —n) drug.
Drogerie [dro:gə'ri:], *f.* (—, *pl.* —n) druggist's shop, chemist's; (*Am.*) drugstore.
drohen ['dro:ən], *v.a., v.n.* threaten, menace.
Drohne ['dro:nə], *f.* (—, *pl.* —n) drone.
dröhnen ['drø:nən], *v.n.* boom, roar.
Drohung ['dro:uŋ], *f.* (—, *pl.* —en) threat, menace.
drollig ['drɔlɪç], *adj.* droll, odd, quaint.
Dromedar [dromə'da:r], *n.* (—s, *pl.* —e) dromedary.
Droschke ['drɔʃkə], *f.* (—, *pl.* —n) cab, hansom, taxi.
Drossel ['drɔsəl], *f.* (—, *pl.* —n) thrush.
Drosselader ['drɔsəla:dər], *f.* (—, *pl.* —n) jugular vein.
Drosselbein ['drɔsəlbaɪn], *n.* (—s, *pl.* —e) collar-bone.
drosseln ['drɔsəln], *v.a.* throttle. *See also* **erdrosseln.**
drüben ['dry:bən], *adv.* over there, on the other side.
drüber ['dry:bər] *see* **darüber.**
Druck [druk], *m.* (—s, ̈e, —e) pressure, squeeze; (*Phys.*) compression; (*Typ.*) impression, print; (*fig.*) hardship.
Druckbogen ['drukbo:gən], *m.* (—s, *pl.* —) proof-sheet, proof.
Druckbuchstabe ['drukbu:xʃta:bə], *m.* (—n, *pl.* —n) letter, type.
Drückeberger ['drykəbɛrgər], *m.* (—s, *pl.* —) slacker, shirker.
drucken ['drukən], *v.a.* print.
drücken ['drykən], *v.a.* press, squeeze; trouble, oppress; *v.r. sich —,* sneak away, shirk.
Drucker ['drukər], *m.* (—s, *pl.* —) printer.
Drücker ['drykər], *m.* (—s, *pl.* —) (*door*) handle, latch; (*gun*) trigger.
Druckerei ['drukəraɪ], *f.* (—, *pl.* —en) printing shop.

Druckerschwärze

Druckerschwärze ['drukərʃvertsə], *f.* (—, *no pl.*) printing-ink.

Druckfehler ['drukfe:lər], *m.* (—s, *pl.* —) misprint, printer's error.

druckfertig ['drukfertiç], *adj.* ready for press.

Drucksache ['drukzaxə], *f.* (—, *pl.* —n) (*Postal*) printed matter.

drum [drum] *see* **darum**.

drunten ['druntən], *adv.* down there, below.

drunter ['druntər] *see* **darunter**.

Drüse ['dry:zə], *f.* (—, *pl.* —n) gland.

Dschungel ['dʒuŋəl], *m.* or *n.* (—s, *pl.* —) jungle.

du [du:], *pers. pron.* thou, you.

ducken ['dukən], *v.a.* bring down, humble. — *v.r. sich* —, duck, stoop, crouch.

dudeln ['du:dəln], *v.n.* play the bagpipes; tootle.

Dudelsack ['du:dəlzak], *m.* (—s, *pl.* ⁻e) bagpipe(s).

Duft [duft], *m.* (—s, *pl.* ⁻e) scent, odour, fragrance, aroma, perfume.

duften ['duftən], *v.n.* be fragrant.

duftig ['duftiç], *adj.* fragrant, odoriferous, perfumed.

dulden ['duldən], *v.a.* suffer, endure, bear, tolerate.

duldsam ['dultza:m], *adj.* tolerant, indulgent, patient.

dumm [dum], *adj.* stupid, foolish, dull.

Dummheit ['dumhaɪt], *f.* (—, *pl.* —en) stupidity, folly.

dumpf [dumpf], *adj.* musty; (*air*) close; (*sound*) hollow; (*fig.*) gloomy.

dumpfig ['dumpfiç], *adj.* damp, musty, stuffy.

Düne ['dy:nə], *f.* (—, *pl.* —n) dune, sand-hill.

Düngemittel ['dyŋəmɪtəl], *n.* (—s, *pl.* —) fertilizer.

düngen ['dyŋən], *v.a.* manure, fertilize.

Dünger ['dyŋər], *m.* (—s, *no pl.*) compost, artificial manure.

dunkel ['duŋkəl], *adj.* dark; (*fig.*) obscure, mysterious.

Dünkel ['dyŋkəl], *m.* (—s, *no pl.*) conceit, arrogance.

dünkelhaft ['dyŋkəlhaft], *adj.* conceited, arrogant.

Dunkelheit ['duŋkəlhaɪt], *f.* (—, *no pl.*) darkness, obscurity.

dunkeln ['duŋkəln], *v.n.* grow dark.

dünken ['dyŋkən], *v.n.* (*rare*) seem, appear. — *v.r. sich* —, fancy o.s., imagine o.s.

dünn [dyn], *adj.* thin, slim, weak.

Dunst [dunst], *m.* (—es, *pl.* ⁻e) vapour, fume; exhalation; haze; *einem blauen* — *vormachen*, humbug a p.

dünsten ['dynstən], *v.a.* stew.

dunstig ['dunstiç], *adj.* misty, hazy.

Dunstkreis ['dunstkraɪs], *m.* (—es, *pl.* —e) atmosphere.

Dunstobst ['dunsto:pst], *n.* (—es, *no pl.*) stewed fruit.

duodez [duo'de:ts], *adj.* (*Typ.*) duodecimo (12mo).

Duodezfürst [duo'de:tsfyrst], *m.* (—en, *pl.* —en) petty prince, princeling.

Dur [du:r], *n.* (*Mus.*) major; sharp.

durch [durç], *prep.* (*Acc.*) (*local*) through, across; (*temporal*) during, throughout; (*manner*) by means of, by. — *adv.* thoroughly, through.

durchaus [durç'aus], *adv.* throughout, quite, by all means, absolutely.

Durchblick ['durçblik], *m.* (—s, *pl.* —e) vista, view.

durchbohren [durç'bo:rən], *v.a. insep.* perforate, pierce.

durchbrennen ['durçbrenən], *v.n. irr.* (*aux.* sein) abscond, bolt.

durchbringen ['durçbriŋən], *v.a. irr.* bring through, get through; squander (money); pull (a sick person) through. — *v.r. sich redlich* —, make an honest living.

Durchbruch ['durçbrux], *m.* (—s, *pl.* ⁻e) breach, break-through.

durchdrängen ['durçdreŋən], *v.r. sich* —, force o.'s way through.

durchdringen ['durçdriŋən], *v.n. irr. sep.* (*aux.* sein) get through. — [durç'driŋən], *v.a. irr. insep.* penetrate, pierce, permeate, pervade.

durchdrücken [durç'drykən], *v.a.* press through; (*fig.*) carry through.

durcheilen [durç'aɪlən], *v.a. insep.* hurry through.

Durcheinander [durçaɪn'andər], *n.* (—s, *no pl.*) confusion, muddle.

durcheinander [durçaɪn'andər], *adv.* in confusion, pell-mell.

Durchfall ['durçfal], *m.* (—s, *no pl.*) diarrhoea; (*exams etc.*) failure.

durchfallen ['durçfalən], *v.n. irr.* (*aux.* sein) fall through, come to nought; (*exams etc.*) fail.

durchflechten [durç'fleçtən], *v.a. irr.* interweave, intertwine.

durchfliegen [durç'fli:gən], *v.a. irr.* fly through; read superficially, skim through.

durchforschen [durç'forʃən], *v.a. insep.* explore, scrutinise, examine thoroughly.

Durchfuhr ['durçfu:r], *f.* (—, *pl.* —en) passage, transit.

durchführbar ['durçfy:rba:r], *adj.* practicable, feasible.

durchführen ['durçfy:rən], *v.a.* escort through; (*fig.*) execute, bring about, carry through.

Durchgang ['durçgaŋ], *m.* (—s, *pl.* ⁻e) passage, thoroughfare; (*Comm.*) transit.

Durchgänger ['durçgeŋər], *m.* (—s, *pl.* —) runaway horse, bolter; (*fig.*) hothead.

durchgängig ['durçgeŋɪç], *adj.* general, universal.

durchgehen ['durçge:ən], *v.n. irr.* (*aux.* sein) go through; (*fig.*) abscond; (*horse*) bolt; (*proposal*) be carried. — *v.a. irr.* (*aux.* sein) peruse, review, go over.

durchgreifen [ˈdurçgraɪfən], *v.n. irr.* act decisively, take strong action.

durchhauen [ˈdurçhauən], *v.a.* cut through; *einen —*, flog s.o.

durchkommen [ˈdurçkɔmən], *v.n. irr.* (*aux.* sein) get through; (*exams etc.*) pass.

durchkreuzen [durçˈkrɔytsən], *v.a. insep.* cross out; (*fig.*) thwart.

durchlassen [ˈdurçlasən], *v.a. irr.* let pass.

Durchlaucht [ˈdurçlauxt], *f.* (*— pl. —en*) Highness.

durchleuchten [durçˈlɔyçtən], *v.a. insep.* (*Med.*) X-ray.

durchlöchern [durçˈlœçərn], *v.a. insep.* perforate, riddle.

durchmachen [ˈdurcmaxən], *v.a.* go through, suffer.

Durchmesser [ˈdurcmɛsər], *m.* (*—s, pl. —*) diameter.

durchnässen [durçˈnɛsən], *v.a. insep.* wet to the skin, soak.

durchnehmen [ˈdurçneːmən], *v.a. irr.* go over *or* cover (a subject).

durchpausen [ˈdurçpauzən], *v.a.* trace, copy.

durchqueren [durçˈkveːrən], *v.a. insep.* cross, traverse.

Durchsage [ˈdurçzaːgə], *f.* (*—, pl. —n*) (radio) announcement.

durchschauen [durçˈʃauən], *v.a. insep. einen —*, see through s.o.

durchscheinend [ˈdurçʃaɪnənt], *adj.* transparent, translucent.

Durchschlag [ˈdurçʃlaːk], *m.* (*—s, pl. ⸚e*) strainer, sieve, colander, filter; carbon copy.

durchschlagen [durçˈʃlaːgən], *v.a. irr. insep.* strain, filter. *— v.r. irr. sich —*, fight o.'s way through.

durchschlagend [durçˈʃlaːgənt], *adj.* thorough, complete, effective.

Durchschnitt [ˈdurçʃnɪt], *m.* (*—s, pl. —e*) average; (*Med. etc.*) cross section.

durchschnittlich [ˈdurçʃnɪtlɪç], *adj.* average; ordinary.

durchschossen [durçˈʃɔsən], *adj.* interleaved; interwoven.

durchseihen [ˈdurçzaɪən], *v.a.* see **durchsieben**.

durchsetzen [durçˈzɛtsən], *v.a. insep.* intersperse; [ˈdurçzɛtsən], *v.a. sep.* have o.'s way (with s.o.). *— v.r. sep. sich —*, make o.'s way successfully, succeed.

Durchsicht [ˈdurçzɪçt], *f.* (*—, no pl.*) revision, inspection, perusal.

durchsichtig [ˈdurçzɪçtɪç], *adj.* transparent.

durchsickern [ˈdurçzɪkərn], *v.n.* (*aux.* sein) trickle through, ooze through.

durchsieben [ˈdurçziːbən], *v.a.* strain, filter, sift.

durchsprechen [ˈdurçʃprɛxən], *v.a. irr.* talk over, discuss.

durchstöbern [durçˈʃtøːbərn], *v.a. insep.* rummage through.

durchstreichen [ˈdurçʃtraɪçən], *v.a. irr.* cross out, delete.

durchstreifen [durçˈʃtraɪfən], *v.a. insep.* roam (through).

durchströmen [durçˈʃtrøːmən], *v.a. insep.* flow through, permeate.

durchsuchen [durçˈzuːxən], *v.a. insep.* search thoroughly, examine closely.

durchtrieben [durçˈtriːbən], *adj.* artful, sly, cunning, crafty.

durchweben [durçˈveːbən], *v.a.* interweave.

durchweg(s) [ˈdurçvɛk(s)], *adv.* without exception, every time, throughout.

durchwühlen [durçˈvyːlən], *v.a. insep.* search; ransack.

durchziehen [durçˈtsiːən], *v.a. irr. insep.* wander through, traverse; [ˈdurçtsiːən], *v.a. irr. sep.* interlace (with threads); draw through.

durchzucken [durçˈtsukən], *v.a. insep.* flash through, convulse.

Durchzug [ˈdurçtsuːk], *m.* (*—s, no pl.*) passage, march through; (*air*) draught.

dürfen [ˈdyrfən], *v.n. irr.* be permitted; be allowed; dare; be likely.

dürftig [ˈdyrftɪç], *adj.* paltry, insufficient, poor.

dürr [dyr], *adj.* dry, arid, withered; (*wood*) dead; (*persons*) thin, gaunt.

Dürre [ˈdyrə], *f.* (*—, pl. —n*) aridity, dryness; drought; (*persons*) thinness.

Durst [durst], *m.* (*—es, no pl.*) thirst.

dürsten [ˈdyrstən], *v.n.* thirst.

durstig [ˈdurstɪç], *adj.* thirsty.

Dusche [ˈduːʃə], *f.* (*—, pl. —n*) shower (bath).

Düse [ˈdyːzə], *f.* (*—, pl. —n*) jet.

duselig [ˈduːzəlɪç], *adj.* drowsy; silly.

düster [ˈdyːstər], *adj.* dark, gloomy; sad, mournful; sombre.

Dutzend [ˈdutsənt], *n.* (*—s, pl. —e*) dozen.

Duzbruder [ˈduːtsbruːdər], *m.* (*—s, pl. ⸚*) crony, chum; close friend.

duzen [ˈduːtsen], *v.a.* be on close terms with.

dynamisch [dyˈnaːmɪʃ], *adj.* dynamic(al).

E

E [eː], *n.* (*—s, pl. —s*) the letter E; (*Mus.*) *E Dur*, E major; *E Moll*, E minor.

Ebbe [ˈebə], *f.* (*—, pl. —n*) ebb, low tide; *— und Flut*, the tides.

ebben [ˈebən], *v.n.* ebb.

eben [ˈeːbən], *adj.* even, level, plane; (*fig.*) plain. *— adv.* precisely, exactly.

Ebenbild [ˈeːbənbɪlt], *n.* (*—es, pl. —er*) likeness, image.

ebenbürtig [ˈeːbənbyrtɪç], *adj.* of equal birth *or* rank; equal.

51

ebenda

ebenda ['e:bɔnda:], *adv.* in the same place.

ebendeswegen ['e:bɔndɛsve:gɔn], *adv.* for that very reason.

Ebene ['e:bɔnə], *f.* (—, *pl.* —n) plain; level ground; (*Maths.*) plane; *schiefe* —, inclined plane.

ebenfalls ['e:bɔnfals], *adv.* likewise, also, too, as well.

Ebenholz ['e:bɔnhɔlts], *n.* (—es, *no pl.*) ebony.

Ebenmaß ['e:bɔnma:s], *n.* (—es, *pl.* —e) symmetry.

ebenmäßig ['e:bɔnmɛ:sɪç], *adj.* symmetrical.

ebenso ['e:bɔnzo:], *adv.* in the same way; — *wie*, just as . . .

Eber ['e:bɔr], *m.* (—s, *pl.* —) (*Zool.*) boar.

Eberesche ['e:bɔrɛʃə], *f.* (—, *pl.* —n) (*Bot.*) mountain ash, rowan.

ebnen ['e:bnɔn], *v.a.* even out, level; smoothe.

echt [ɛçt], *adj.* genuine, real, true, authentic, pure.

Ecke ['ɛkə], *f.* (—, *pl.* —en) corner, nook.

eckig ['ɛkɪç], *adj.* angular.

Eckzahn ['ɛktsa:n], *m.* (—s, *pl.* ⁓e) eye tooth; canine tooth.

Eckziegel ['ɛktsi:gɔl], *m.* (—s, *pl.* —) (*Build.*) header.

edel ['e:dɔl], *adj.* noble; well-born, aristocratic; (*metal*) precious.

Edelmann ['e:dɔlman], *m.* (—s, *pl.* **Edelleute**) nobleman, aristocrat.

Edelmut ['e:dɔlmu:t], *m.* (—s, *no pl.*) generosity, magnanimity.

Edelstein ['e:dɔlʃtaɪn], *m.* (—s, *pl.* —e) precious stone, jewel.

Edeltanne ['e:dɔltanə], *f.* (—, *pl.* —n) (*Bot.*) silver fir.

Edelweiß ['e:dɔlvaɪs], *n.* (—sses, *no pl.*) (*Bot.*) edelweiss; lion's foot.

Eduard ['e:duart], *m.* Edward.

Efeu ['e:fɔy], *m.* (—s, *no pl.*) (*Bot.*) ivy.

Effekten [ɛ'fɛktɔn], *m. pl.* goods and chattels; effects; stocks, securities.

Effektenbörse [ɛ'fɛktɔnbœrzə], *f.* (—, *pl.* —n) Stock Exchange.

Effekthascherei [ɛ'fɛkthaʃɔraɪ], *f.* (—, *pl.* —en) sensationalism, clap-trap.

effektuieren [ɛfɛktu'i:rɔn], *v.a.* (*Comm.*) execute, effectuate.

egal [e'ga:l], *adj.* equal; all the same.

Egge ['ɛgə], *f.* (—, *pl.* —n) harrow.

Egoismus [ego'ɪsmus], *m.* (—, *no pl.*) selfishness, egoism.

egoistisch [ego'ɪstɪʃ], *adj.* selfish, egoistic(al).

Ehe ['e:ə], *f.* (—, *pl.* —n) marriage.

ehe ['e:ə], *conj.* before; *adv.* formerly; *je —r, desto besser*, the sooner, the better.

Ehebrecher ['e:əbrɛçɔr], *m.* (—s, *pl.* —) adulterer.

Ehebruch ['e:əbrux], *m.* (—s, *pl.* ⁓e) adultery.

Ehefrau ['e:əfrau], *f.* (—, *pl.* —en) wife, spouse, consort.

Ehegatte ['e:əgatə], *m.* (—n, *pl.* —n) husband, spouse.

ehelich ['e:əlɪç], *adj.* matrimonial; (*children*) legitimate.

Ehelosigkeit ['e:əlo:zɪçkaɪt], *f.* (—, *no pl.*) celibacy.

ehemalig ['e:əma:lɪç], *adj.* former, late.

ehemals ['e:əma:ls], *adv.* formerly, once, of old.

Ehemann ['e:əman], *m.* (—s, *pl.* ⁓er) husband.

ehern ['e:ɔrn], *adj.* brazen; of brass, of bronze.

Ehestand ['e:əʃtant], *m.* (—s, *no pl.*) matrimony.

ehestens ['e:əstəns], *adv.* as soon as possible.

Ehre ['e:rə], *f.* (—, *pl.* —n) honour, reputation, respect, distinction, glory.

ehren ['e:rɔn], *v.a.* honour, respect, esteem; *sehr geehrter Herr*, dear Sir.

Ehrenbezeigung ['e:rɔnbɔtsaɪguŋ], *f.* (—, *pl.* —en) mark of respect; (*Mil.*) salute.

Ehrenbürger ['e:rɔnbyrgɔr], *m.* (—s, *pl.* —) honorary citizen *or* freeman.

Ehrendame ['e:rɔnda:mə], *f.* (—, *pl.* —n) maid of honour.

Ehrenerklärung ['e:rɔnɛrklɛ:ruŋ], *f.* (—, *pl.* —en) reparation, apology.

Ehrengericht ['e:rɔngɔrɪçt], *n.* (—s, *pl.* —e) court of honour.

ehrenhaft ['e:rɔnhaft], *adj.* honourable, worthy.

Ehrenpreis ['e:rɔnpraɪs], *m.* (—es, *pl.* —e) prize; (*no pl.*) (*Bot.*) speedwell.

Ehrenrettung ['e:rɔnrɛtuŋ], *f.* (—, *pl.* —en) vindication.

ehrenrührig ['e:rɔnry:rɪç], *adj.* defamatory, calumnious.

ehrenvoll ['e:rɔnfɔl], *adj.* honourable.

ehrenwert ['e:rɔnvɛrt], *adj.* honourable, respectable.

ehrerbietig ['e:rɔrbi:tɪç], *adj.* reverential, respectful.

Ehrfurcht ['e:rfurçt], *f.* (—, *no pl.*) reverence, awe.

Ehrgefühl ['e:rgɔfy:l], *n.* (—s, *no pl.*) sense of honour.

Ehrgeiz ['e:rgaɪts], *m.* (—es, *no pl.*) ambition.

ehrlich ['e:rlɪç], *adj.* honest; — *währt am längsten*, honesty is the best policy.

ehrlos ['e:rlo:s], *adj.* dishonourable, infamous.

ehrsam ['e:rza:m], *adj.* respectable, honourable.

Ehrwürden ['e:rvyrdɔn], *m. & f.* (*form of address*) *Euer* —, Reverend Sir, Your Reverence.

ehrwürdig ['e:rvyrdɪç], *adj.* venerable, reverend.

Ei [aɪ], *n.* (—s, *pl.* —er) egg, ovum.

ei [aɪ], *int.* ay, indeed.

Eibe ['aɪbə], *f.* (—, *pl.* —n) (*Bot.*) yew.

Eichamt ['aɪçamt], *n.* (—s, *pl.* ⁓er) office of weights and measures; (*Am.*) bureau of standards.

52

Eichapfel ['aɪçapfəl], *m.* (—s, *pl.* ∺) oak apple.

Eiche ['aɪçə], *f.* (—, *pl.* —n) (*Bot.*) oak.

Eichel ['aɪçəl], *f.* (—, *pl.* —n) acorn; (*Anat.*) glans; (*Cards*) clubs.

eichen ['aɪçən], *v.a.* gauge, calibrate. — *adj.* made of oak.

Eichhörnchen ['aɪçhœrnçən] or **Eichkätzchen** ['aɪçkɛtsçən], *n.* (—s, *pl.* —) squirrel.

Eid [aɪt], *m.* (—es, *pl.* —e) oath; *falscher* —, perjury.

Eidam ['aɪdam], *m.* (—s, *pl.* —e) (*obs.*) son-in-law.

eidbrüchig ['aɪtbryçɪç], *adj.* guilty of perjury.

Eidechse ['aɪdɛksə], *f.* (—, *pl.* —n) lizard.

Eidesleistung ['aɪdəslaɪstuŋ], *f.* (—, *pl.* —en) affidavit.

Eidgenosse ['aɪtgənɔsə], *m.* (—n, *pl.* —n) confederate.

Eidgenossenschaft ['aɪtgənɔsənʃaft], *f.* (—, *pl.* —en) confederacy.

eidlich ['aɪtlɪç], *adj.* by oath, sworn.

Eidotter ['aɪdɔtər], *m. & n.* (—s, *pl.* —) yolk of an egg.

Eierbecher ['aɪərbɛçər], *m.* (—s, *pl.* —) egg cup.

Eierkuchen ['aɪərku:xən], *m.* (—s, *pl.* —) omelet(te), pancake.

Eierschale ['aɪərʃa:lə], *f.* (—, *pl.* —n) egg shell.

Eierspeise ['aɪərʃpaɪzə], *f.* (—, *pl.* —n) dish prepared with eggs.

Eierstock ['aɪərʃtɔk], *m.* (—s, *pl.* ∺e) ovary.

Eifer ['aɪfər], *m.* (—s, *no pl.*) zeal, eagerness, ardour, haste, passion, vehemence.

Eiferer ['aɪfərər], *m.* (—s, *pl.* —) zealot.

eifern ['aɪfərn], *v.n.* be zealous; *gegen einen* —, inveigh against s.o.

eiförmig ['aɪfœrmɪç], *adj.* oval, egg-shaped.

eifrig ['aɪfrɪç], *adj.* zealous, ardent, eager.

Eigelb ['aɪgɛlp], *n.* (—s, *no pl.*) yolk of (an) egg.

eigen ['aɪgən], *adj.* own; particular, peculiar.

Eigenart ['aɪgəna:rt], *f.* (—, *pl.* —en) peculiarity; idiosyncrasy.

eigenhändig ['aɪgənhɛndɪç], *adj.* with o.'s own hand.

Eigenheit ['aɪgənhaɪt], *f.* (—, *pl.* —en) peculiarity; idiosyncrasy.

eigenmächtig ['aɪgənmɛçtɪç], *adj.* arbitrary, autocratic, high-handed.

Eigenname ['aɪgənna:mə], *m.* (—ns, *pl.* —n) proper name.

Eigennutz ['aɪgənnuts], *m.* (—es, *no pl.*) self-interest, selfishness.

eigennützig ['aɪgənnytsɪç], *adj.* selfish, self-interested, self-seeking.

eigens ['aɪgəns], *adv.* particularly, specially.

Eigenschaft ['aɪgənʃaft], *f.* (—, *pl.* —en) quality, peculiarity; property.

Eigenschaftswort ['aɪgənʃaftsvɔrt], *n.* (—s, *pl.* ∺er) (*Gram.*) adjective.

Eigensinn ['aɪgənzɪn], *m.* (—s, *no pl.*) obstinacy.

eigentlich ['aɪgəntlɪç], *adj.* true, real; exact, literal.

Eigentum ['aɪgəntu:m], *n.* (—s, *pl.* ∺er) property, possession, estate.

Eigentümer ['aɪgənty:mər], *m.* (—s, *pl.* —) owner, proprietor.

eigenwillig ['aɪgənvɪlɪç], *adj.* self-willed.

eignen ['aɪgnən], *v.r. sich — für* (*zu*), suit, fit, be suitable *or* fit for (to).

Eilbote ['aɪlbo:tə], *m.* (—n, *pl.* —n) special messenger.

Eile ['aɪlə], *f.* (—, *no pl.*) haste, hurry.

eilen ['aɪlən], *v.n.* (*aux.* sein), *v.r.* (*sich* —), hasten, hurry; be urgent.

eilends ['aɪlənts], *adv.* hastily.

eilfertig ['aɪlfɛrtɪç], *adj.* hasty.

Eilgut ['aɪlgu:t], *n.* (—s, *pl.* ∺er) express goods.

eilig ['aɪlɪç], *adj.* hasty, speedy; pressing, urgent.

Eilzug ['aɪltsu:k], *m.* (—s, *pl.* ∺e) fast train.

Eimer ['aɪmər], *m.* (—s, *pl.* —) pail, bucket.

ein(e) ['aɪn(ə)], *indef. art.* a, an; *was für* —; what kind of a(n). — *num. adj.* one; — *jeder*, each one.

einander [aɪn'andər], *adv.* each other, one another.

einarbeiten ['aɪnarbaɪtən], *v.a.* train, familiarise s.o. with. —*v.r.* (*aux.* haben) *sich* —, familiarize o:s.

einäschern ['aɪnɛʃərn], *v.a.* reduce to ashes, incinerate; cremate.

einatmen ['aɪna:tmən], *v.a.* breathe in, inhale.

einätzen ['aɪnɛtsən], *v.a.* etch in.

einäugig ['aɪnɔygɪç], *adj.* one-eyed.

Einbahnstraße ['aɪnba:nʃtra:sə], *f.* (—, *pl.* —n) one-way street.

Einband ['aɪnbant], *m.* (—s, *pl.* ∺e) binding, cover of book.

einbändig ['aɪnbɛndɪç], *adj.* in one volume.

einbauen ['aɪnbauən], *v.a.* build in.

einbegreifen ['aɪnbəgraɪfən], *v.a. irr.* include, comprise.

einberufen ['aɪnbəru:fən], *v.a. irr.* convene, convoke; (*Mil.*) call up.

einbeziehen ['aɪnbətsi:ən], *v.a. irr.* include.

einbiegen ['aɪnbi:gən], *v.n. irr.* turn into (road).

einbilden ['aɪnbɪldən], *v.r. sich* —, imagine, fancy.

Einbildung ['aɪnbɪlduŋ], *f.* (—, *no pl.*) imagination, fancy, delusion; conceit.

einbinden ['aɪnbɪndən], *v.a. irr.* (*book*) bind.

Einblick ['aɪnblɪk], *m.* (—s, *no pl.*) insight.

Einbrecher ['aɪnbrɛçər], *m.* (—s, *pl.* —) burglar; intruder.

Einbrenne

Einbrenne [ˈaɪnbrɛnə], *f.* (—, *pl.* —n) thickening of soup.

einbringen [ˈaɪnbrɪŋən], *v.a. irr.* bring in, yield, fetch (a price); *wieder* —, retrieve.

einbrocken [ˈaɪnbrɔkən], *v.a.* crumble; *einem etwas* —, (*fig.*) get s.o. into trouble.

Einbruch [ˈaɪnbrux], *m.* (—s, *pl.* ⁓e) breaking-in; burglary, house-breaking.

Einbuchtung [ˈaɪnbuxtuŋ], *f.* (—, *pl.* —en) bight, bay.

einbürgern [ˈaɪnbyrgərn], *v.a.* naturalise.

Einbuße [ˈaɪnbuːsə], *f.* (—, *pl.* —n) loss.

einbüßen [ˈaɪnbyːsən], *v.a.* suffer a loss from, lose, forfeit.

eindämmen [ˈaɪndɛmən], *v.a.* dam in (or up).

Eindecker [ˈaɪndɛkər], *m.* (—s, *pl.* —) (*Aviat.*) monoplane.

eindeutig [ˈaɪndɔytɪç], *adj.* unequivocal, unambiguous.

eindrängen [ˈaɪndrɛŋən], *v.r. sich* —, intrude (into), force o.'s way in(to), interfere.

eindrillen [ˈaɪndrɪlən], *v.a. einem etwas* —, drum s.th. into s.o.

eindringen [ˈaɪndrɪŋən], *v.n. irr.* (*aux.* sein) enter, intrude; invade; penetrate.

eindringlich [ˈaɪndrɪŋlɪç], *adj.* forceful, urgent; impressive.

Eindruck [ˈaɪndruk], *m.* (—s, *pl.* ⁓e) impression.

eindrücken [ˈaɪndrykən], *v.a.* press in, squeeze in.

eindrucksfähig [ˈaɪndruksfɛːɪç], *adj.* impressionable.

einengen [ˈaɪnɛŋən], *v.a.* compress, limit, confine, cramp.

Einer [ˈaɪnər], *m.* (—s, *pl.* —) (*Maths.*) digit, unit.

einerlei [ˈaɪnərlaɪ], *adj.* the same, all the same.

einerseits [ˈaɪnərzaɪts], *adv.* on the one hand.

einfach [ˈaɪnfax], *adj.* single; simple, plain, uncomplicated; modest, homely.

einfädeln [ˈaɪnfɛːdəln], *v.a.* thread.

einfahren [ˈaɪnfaːrən], *v.n. irr.* (*aux.* sein) drive in, enter. — *v.a.* run in (new car).

Einfahrt [ˈaɪnfaːrt], *f.* (—, *pl.* —en) entrance, gateway, drive; (*Min.*) descent.

Einfall [ˈaɪnfal], *m.* (—s, *pl.* ⁓e) falling-in, downfall, fall; (*Mil.*) invasion; (*fig.*) idea, inspiration.

einfallen [ˈaɪnfalən], *v.n. irr.* (*aux.* sein) fall in, fall into; (*Mil.*) invade; (*fig.*) occur to s.o.

Einfalt [ˈaɪnfalt], *f.* (—, *no pl.*) simplicity; silliness.

Einfaltspinsel [ˈaɪnfaltspɪnzəl], *m.* (—s, *pl.* —) simpleton, dunce.

einfangen [ˈaɪnfaŋən], *v.a. irr.* catch, get hold of.

einfarbig [ˈaɪnfarbɪç], *adj.* of one colour; monochrome.

einfassen [ˈaɪnfasən], *v.a.* border, trim; (*diamonds*) set.

Einfassung [ˈaɪnfasuŋ], *f.* (—, *pl.* —en) bordering, trimming, edging, framing.

einfetten [ˈaɪnfɛtən], *v.a.* grease, lubricate.

einfinden [ˈaɪnfɪndən], *v.r. irr. sich* —, appear, be present.

einflechten [ˈaɪnflɛçtən], *v.a. irr.* plait; (*fig.*) insert.

einfließen [ˈaɪnfliːsən], *v.n. irr.* (*aux.* sein) flow in; — *lassen*, (*fig.*) mention casually, slip in (a word).

einflößen [ˈaɪnfløːsən], *v.a.* infuse; (*fig.*) instil, inspire with.

Einfluß [ˈaɪnflus], *m.* (—sses, *pl.* ⁓sse) influx; (*fig.*) influence.

einflußreich [ˈaɪnflusraɪç], *adj.* influential.

einflüstern [ˈaɪnflystərn], *v.n.* suggest, insinuate.

einförmig [ˈaɪnfœrmɪç], *adj.* uniform; monotonous.

einfriedigen [ˈaɪnfriːdɪgən], *v.a.* fence in, enclose.

einfügen [ˈaɪnfyːgən], *v.a.* insert, include, fit in. — *v.r. sich* —, adapt o.s., become a part of.

Einfühlungsvermögen [ˈaɪnfyːluŋsfɛrmøːgən], *n.* (—s, *no pl.*) (*Phil.*) empathy, sympathetic understanding.

Einfuhr [ˈaɪnfuːr], *f.* (—, *pl.* —en) importation, import.

einführen [ˈaɪnfyːrən], *v.a.* introduce; (*goods*) import.

Einführung [ˈaɪnfyːruŋ], *f.* (—, *pl.* —en) introduction; (*goods*) importation.

einfüllen [ˈaɪnfylən], *v.a.* fill in, pour into, bottle.

Eingabe [ˈaɪngaːbə], *f.* (—, *pl.* —n) petitition; application.

Eingang [ˈaɪngaŋ], *m.* (—s, *pl.* ⁓e) entry, entrance; arrival.

eingangs [ˈaɪngaŋs], *adv.* in or at the beginning.

eingeben [ˈaɪngeːbən], *v.a. irr.* inspire (with); (*petition*) present, deliver; (*claim*) file; (*complaint*) bring; (*medicine*) administer.

eingeboren [ˈaɪngəboːrən], *adj.* native; (*Theol.*) only-begotten.

Eingeborene [ˈaɪngəboːrənə], *m.* (—n, *pl.* —n) native.

Eingebrachte [ˈaɪngəbraxtə], *n.* (—n, *no pl.*) dowry.

Eingebung [ˈaɪngeːbuŋ], *f.* (—, *pl.* —en) inspiration.

eingedenk [ˈaɪngədɛŋk], *prep.* (*Genit.*) mindful of, remembering.

eingefleischt [ˈaɪngəflaɪʃt], *adj.* inveterate, confirmed.

eingehen [ˈaɪngeːən], *v.n. irr.* (*aux.* sein) (*Comm.*) arrive; *auf etwas* —, enter into s.th., agree to s.th.; *auf etwas näher* —, enter into the details of s.th.; (*animals, plants*) die; (*cloth*) shrink.

eingehend ['aɪngeːənt], *adj.* thorough, exhaustive.

Eingemachte ['aɪngəmaxtə], *n.* (—n, *no pl.*) preserve.

eingenommen ['aɪngənɔmən], *adj.* enthusiastic for, infatuated with; — *von sich*, conceited.

Eingeschlossenheit ['aɪngəʃlɔsənhaɪt], *f.* (—, *no pl.*) isolation, seclusion.

eingeschrieben ['aɪngəʃriːbən], *adj.* registered (letter).

eingesessen ['aɪngəzɛsən], *adj.* old-established; resident.

Eingeständnis ['aɪngəʃtɛntnɪs], *n.* (—ses, *pl.* —se) confession.

eingestehen ['aɪngəʃteːən], *v.a. irr.* confess to, avow.

Eingeweide ['aɪngəvaɪdə], *n. pl.* bowels, intestines.

eingewöhnen ['aɪngəvøːnən], *v.r. sich* —, accustom o.s. to, get used to.

eingießen ['aɪngiːsən], *v.a. irr.* pour in; pour out.

eingleisig ['aɪnglaɪzɪç], *adj.* single-track.

eingliedern ['aɪngliːdərn], *v.r. sich* —, adapt o.s., fit in.

eingreifen ['aɪngraɪfən], *v.n. irr.* intervene in; interfere with, encroach on.

Eingriff ['aɪngrɪf], *m.* (—s, *pl.* —e) intervention, encroachment, infringement; (*Med.*) operation.

Einguß ['aɪnguːs], *m.* (—sses, *pl.* ⁻sse) infusion; enema.

einhaken ['aɪnhaːkən], *v.a.* hook in. — *v.r. sich* —, (*fig.*) take a p.'s arm.

Einhalt ['aɪnhalt], *m.* (—s, *no pl.*) stop, check, prohibition, cessation; — *gebieten*, check, suppress.

einhalten ['aɪnhaltən], *v.a. irr.* observe, adhere to.

einhändigen ['aɪnhɛndɪgən], *v.a.* hand in, deliver.

einhauen ['aɪnhauən], *v.a.* hew in, break open.

Einhebung ['aɪnheːbuŋ], *f.* (—, *pl.* —en) (*taxes*) collection.

einheften ['aɪnhɛftən], *v.a.* sew in, stitch in; (*papers*) file.

einhegen ['aɪnheːgən], *v.a.* fence in, hedge in.

einheimisch ['aɪnhaɪmɪʃ], *adj.* native; (*Bot.*) indigenous.

einheimsen ['aɪnhaɪmzən], *v.a.* reap.

Einheit ['aɪnhaɪt], *f.* (—, *pl.* —en) unit, unity.

einheitlich ['aɪnhaɪtlɪç], *adj.* uniform, consistent.

einheizen ['aɪnhaɪtsən], *v.a., v.n.* heat the stove, light the fire.

einhellig ['aɪnhɛlɪç], *adj.* unanimous, harmonious.

einher [aɪn'heːr], *adv.* forth, along, on.

einholen ['aɪnhoːlən], *v.a.* obtain; catch up with. — *v.n.* go shopping.

Einhorn ['aɪnhɔrn], *n.* (—s, *pl.* ⁻er) unicorn.

einhüllen ['aɪnhylən], *v.a.* wrap up, cover, envelop.

einig ['aɪnɪç], *adj.* at one. — *adv.* in agreement.

einige ['aɪnɪgə], *adj.* some, several.

einigemal ['aɪnɪgəmaːl], *adv.* several times.

einigen ['aɪnɪgən], *v.a.* unite. — *v.r. sich* — *mit*, come to an agreement with.

einigermaßen [aɪnɪgər'maːsən], *adv.* to a certain extent.

Einigkeit ['aɪnɪçkaɪt], *f.* (—, *no pl.*) union; unity, unanimity, harmony.

Einigung ['aɪnɪguŋ], *f.* (—, *no pl.*) agreement.

einimpfen ['aɪnɪmpfən], *v.a.* inoculate, vaccinate.

einjährig ['aɪnjɛːrɪç], *adj.* one-year-old, annual.

einkassieren ['aɪnkasiːrən], *v.a.* cash (*cheque*), collect (*money*).

Einkauf ['aɪnkauf], *m.* (—s, *pl.* ⁻e) purchase, buy.

einkaufen ['aɪnkaufən], *v.a.* purchase, buy. — *v.n.* go shopping.

Einkäufer ['aɪnkɔyfər], *m.* (—s, *pl.* —) (*Comm.*) purchaser, buyer.

Einkehr ['aɪnkeːr], *f.* (—, *no pl.*) stopping (at an inn); (*fig.*) meditation.

einkehren ['aɪnkeːrən], *v.n.* (*aux. sein*) stop *or* put up (at an inn).

einkerkern ['aɪnkɛrkərn], *v.a.* imprison.

einklagen ['aɪnklaːgən], *v.a.* (*Law*) sue for (money).

einklammern ['aɪnklamərn], *v.a.* bracket, enclose in brackets.

Einklang ['aɪnklaŋ], *m.* (—s, *no pl.*) accord, unison, harmony.

einkleben ['aɪnkleːbən], *v.a.* paste in.

einkleiden ['aɪnklaɪdən], *v.a.* clothe; (*fig.*) invest; *sich — lassen*, (*Eccl.*) take the veil.

einklemmen ['aɪnklɛmən], *v.a.* squeeze in, jam in.

einkochen ['aɪnkɔxən], *v.a.* preserve. — *v.n.* (*aux. sein*) boil down.

Einkommen ['aɪnkɔmən], *n.* (—s, *no pl.*) income, revenue.

einkommen ['aɪnkɔmən], *v.n. irr.* (*aux. sein*) *bei einem wegen etwas* —, apply to s.o. for s.th.

einkreisen ['aɪnkraɪzən], *v.a.* encircle, isolate.

Einkünfte ['aɪnkynftə], *pl.* income, revenue; emoluments.

einladen ['aɪnlaːdən], *v.a. irr.* load in; invite.

Einlage ['aɪnlaːgə], *f.* (—, *pl.* —en) (*letter*) enclosure; (*Theat.*) addition to programme; (*game*) stake; (*Comm.*) investment.

einlagern ['aɪnlaːgərn], *v.a.* (*goods*) store, warehouse; (*Mil.*) billet, quarter.

Einlaß ['aɪnlas], *m.* (—sses, *no pl.*) admission, admittance; (*water*) inlet.

einlassen ['aɪnlasən], *v.a. irr.* admit, allow in; let in. — *v.r. sich auf etwas* —, engage in s.th., enter into s.th.

Einlauf ['aɪnlauf], *m.* (—s, *no pl.*) entering; (*Med.*) enema.

einlaufen

einlaufen [ˈaɪnlaufən], v.n. irr. (aux. sein) (Naut.) enter harbour, put into port; (material) shrink.

einleben [ˈaɪnleːbən], v.r. sich —, grow accustomed to, settle down, acclimatise o.s.

einlegen [ˈaɪnleːgən], v.a. put in, lay in; enclose; (money) deposit; (food) pickle, preserve; Fürbitte —, intercede; eingelegte Arbeit, inlaid work.

einleiten [ˈaɪnlaɪtən], v.a. begin, introduce; institute.

Einleitung [ˈaɪnlaɪtuŋ], f. (—, pl. —en) introduction; (book) preface; (Mus.) prelude; (Law) institution.

einlenken [ˈaɪnlɛŋkən], v.n. turn in; give in, come round.

einleuchten [ˈaɪnlɔʏçtən], v.n. become clear.

einlösen [ˈaɪnløːzən], v.a. redeem; (bill) honour; (cheque) cash.

einmachen [ˈaɪnmaxən], v.a. preserve.

einmal [ˈaɪnmaːl], adv. once; es war —, once upon a time; auf —, suddenly; noch —, once more; nicht —, not even.

Einmaleins [ˈaɪnmaːlaɪns], n. (—es, no pl.) multiplication table.

einmalig [ˈaɪnmaːlɪç], adv. unique, unrepeatable.

Einmaster [ˈaɪnmastər], m. (—s, pl. —) (Naut.) brigantine, cutter.

einmauern [ˈaɪnmauərn], v.a. wall in, immure.

einmengen [ˈaɪnmɛŋən], v.r. sich —, meddle with, interfere.

einmieten [ˈaɪnmiːtən], v.r. sich —, take lodgings.

einmischen [ˈaɪnmɪʃən], v.r. sich —, meddle (with), interfere.

einmütig [ˈaɪnmyːtɪç], adj. unanimous, in harmony, united.

Einnahme [ˈaɪnnaːmə], f. (—, pl. —n) income, revenue; receipts; (Mil.) occupation, capture.

einnehmen [ˈaɪnneːmən], v.a. irr. take in; (money) receive; (medicine) take; (taxes) collect; (place) take up, occupy; (Mil.) occupy, conquer; (fig.) captivate, fascinate.

einnehmend [ˈaɪnneːmənt], adj. fetching, engaging, charming.

einnicken [ˈaɪnnɪkən], v.n. (aux. sein) nod or doze off.

einnisten [ˈaɪnnɪstən], v.r. sich —, nestle down; (fig.) settle in a place.

Einöde [ˈaɪnøːdə], f. (—, pl. —n) desert, solitude.

einordnen [ˈaɪnɔrdnən], v.a. place in order, file, classify.

einpauken [ˈaɪnpaukən], v.a. cram.

einpferchen [ˈaɪnpfɛrçən], v.a. pen in, coop up.

einpökeln [ˈaɪnpøːkəln], v.a. salt, pickle.

einprägen [ˈaɪnprɛːgən], v.a. imprint; impress.

einquartieren [ˈaɪnkvartiːrən], v.a. (Mil.) quarter, billet.

einrahmen [ˈaɪnraːmən], v.a. frame.

einräumen [ˈaɪnrɔʏmən], v.a. stow (things) away; einem etwas —, concede s.th. to s.o.

Einrede [ˈaɪnreːdə], f. (—, pl. —n) objection.

einreden [ˈaɪnreːdən], v.a. einem etwas —, persuade s.o. to. — v.r. sich etwas —, get s.th. into o.'s head.

einreichen [ˈaɪnraɪçən], v.a. hand in, deliver; tender.

einreihen [ˈaɪnraɪən], v.a. place in line, arrange.

einreihig [ˈaɪnraɪɪç], adj. consisting of a single row; (Tail.) single-breasted (suit).

einreißen [ˈaɪnraɪsən], v.a. irr. make a tear in; (houses) pull down. — v.n. (fig.) gain ground.

einrenken [ˈaɪnrɛŋkən], v.a. (Med.) set; (fig.) settle.

einrichten [ˈaɪnrɪçtən], v.a. put in order, arrange; equip, set up; furnish.

Einrichtung [ˈaɪnrɪçtuŋ], f. (—, pl. —en) arrangement, management; furnishing; (pl.) facilities; equipment, amenities.

einrücken [ˈaɪnrykən], v.n. (aux. sein) march in. — v.a. insert (in the newspaper).

Eins [aɪns], f. (—, pl. —en, —er) one; (Sch.) top marks.

eins [aɪns], num. one; es ist mir alles —, it is all the same to me.

einsalzen [ˈaɪnzaltsən], v.a. salt, pickle, cure.

einsam [ˈaɪnzaːm], adj. lonely, solitary, secluded.

Einsamkeit [ˈaɪnzaːmkaɪt], f. (—, no pl.) loneliness, solitude, seclusion.

Einsatz [ˈaɪnzats], m. (—es, pl. ˸e) (game) stake, pool; (dress) lace inset; (Mus.) entry (of a voice), starting intonation; (Mil.) sortie, mission.

einsaugen [ˈaɪnzaugən], v.a. suck in; (fig.) imbibe.

einsäumen [ˈaɪnzɔʏmən], v.a. hem (in).

einschalten [ˈaɪnʃaltən], v.a. insert, interpolate; switch on; put in gear.

einschärfen [ˈaɪnʃɛrfən], v.a. impress s.th. on s.o.

einschätzen [ˈaɪnʃɛtsən], v.a. assess.

einschenken [ˈaɪnʃɛŋkən], v.a. pour in or out, fill.

einschieben [ˈaɪnʃiːbən], v.a. push in; interpolate, insert.

Einschiebsel [ˈaɪnʃiːpsəl], n. (—s, pl. —) interpolation; interpolated part.

einschiffen [ˈaɪnʃɪfən], v.a. embark; (goods) ship. — v.r. sich —, go aboard, embark.

einschlafen [ˈaɪnʃlaːfən], v.n. irr. (aux. sein) fall asleep, go to sleep.

einschläfern [ˈaɪnʃlɛːfərn], v.a. lull to sleep.

Einschlag [ˈaɪnʃlaːk], m. (—s, pl. ˸e) cover, envelope; (weaving) woof, weft; explosion; strike; (fig.) streak (of character); touch.

einschlagen ['aɪnʃlaːgən], *v.a. irr.* knock in; (*nail*) drive in; (*parcel*) wrap up; (*road*) take. — *v.n.* (*lightning*) strike; be a success.

einschlägig ['aɪnʃlɛːgɪç], *adj.* bearing on (the subject), pertinent.

einschleppen ['aɪnʃlɛpən], *v.a.* (*disease*) bring in, introduce.

einschließen ['aɪnʃliːsən], *v.a. irr.* lock in *or* up; (*enemy*) surround; (*fig.*) include.

einschlummern ['aɪnʃlumərn], *v.n.* (*aux.* sein) doze off, fall asleep.

Einschluß ['aɪnʃlus], *m.* (—sses, *pl.* ⸗sse) inclusion; *mit — von*, inclusive of.

einschmeicheln ['aɪnʃmaɪçəln], *v.r. sich bei einem —*, ingratiate o.s. with s.o.

einschmelzen ['aɪnʃmɛltsən], *v.a. irr.* melt down.

einschmieren ['aɪnʃmiːrən], *v.a.* smear, grease, oil; (*sore*) put ointment on.

einschneidend ['aɪnʃnaɪdənt], *adj.* important, sweeping, incisive, trenchant.

einschneidig ['aɪnʃnaɪdɪç], *adj.* single-edged.

Einschnitt ['aɪnʃnɪt], *m.* (—s, *pl.* —e) incision, cut, notch; (*verse*) caesura.

einschnüren ['aɪnʃnyːrən], *v.a.* lace up; (*parcel*) tie up.

einschränken ['aɪnʃrɛŋkən], *v.a.* confine, limit, restrict. — *v.r. sich —*, curtail o.'s expenses, economize.

einschrauben ['aɪnʃraubən], *v.a.* screw in.

einschreiben ['aɪnʃraɪbən], *v.a. irr.* write in *or* down, inscribe; (*letter*) register. — *v.r. sich —*, enter o.'s name; enrol.

Einschreibesendung ['aɪnʃraɪbəzenduŋ], *f.* (—, *pl.* —en) registered letter, registered parcel.

einschreiten ['aɪnʃraɪtən], *v.n. irr.* (*aux.* sein) step in, intervene.

einschrumpfen ['aɪnʃrumpfən], *v.n.* (*aux.* sein) shrink, shrivel.

einschüchtern ['aɪnʃʏçtərn], *v.a.* intimidate, overawe.

Einschuß ['aɪnʃus], *m.* (—sses, *pl.* ⸗sse) share, advance of capital; (*weaving*) woof, weft.

einsegnen ['aɪnzeːgnən], *v.a.* consecrate, bless; (*Eccl.*) confirm.

Einsehen ['aɪnzeːən], *n.* (—s, *no pl.*) realisation; *ein — haben*, be reasonable.

einsehen ['aɪnzeːən], *v.a. irr.* look into, glance over; (*fig.*) comprehend, realise.

einseifen ['aɪnzaɪfən], *v.a.* soap, lather; (*fig.*) take s.o. in.

einseitig ['aɪnzaɪtɪç], *adj.* one-sided; (*fig.*) one-track (mind).

Einsenkung ['aɪnzɛŋkuŋ], *f.* (—, *pl.* —en) depression (of the ground).

einsetzen ['aɪnzɛtsən], *v.a.* put in, set in; institute, establish; (*money*) stake; (*Hort.*) plant; (*office*) install s.o. — *v.n.* begin.

Einsetzung ['aɪnzɛtsuŋ], *f.* (—, *pl.* —en) (*office*) investiture, installation; institution.

Einsicht ['aɪnzɪçt], *f.* (—, *no pl.*) inspection, examination; insight, understanding.

einsichtig ['aɪnzɪçtɪç], *adj.* intelligent, sensible, judicious.

Einsichtnahme ['aɪnzɪçtnaːmə], *f. zur —*, (*Comm.*) on approval, for inspection.

Einsiedler ['aɪnziːdlər], *m.* (—s, *pl.* —) hermit, recluse.

einsilbig ['aɪnzɪlbɪç], *adj.* monosyllabic; (*fig.*) taciturn, laconic.

einspannen ['aɪnʃpanən], *v.a.* stretch in a frame; harness; (*coll.*) put to work.

Einspänner ['aɪnʃpɛnər], *m.* (—s, *pl.* —) one-horse vehicle; one-horse cab, fiacre.

einsperren ['aɪnʃpɛrən], *v.a.* lock in, shut up, imprison.

einspinnen ['aɪnʃpɪnən], *v.r. irr. sich —*, spin a cocoon.

einsprengen ['aɪnʃprɛŋən], *v.a.* sprinkle.

einspringen ['aɪnʃprɪŋən], *v.n. irr.* (*aux.* sein) *auf einen —*, leap at; (*lock*) catch, snap; *für einen —*, deputize for s.o.

Einspruch ['aɪnʃprux], *m.* (—s, *pl.* ⸗e) objection, protest; — *erheben*, protest; (*Law*) appeal (against).

einspurig ['aɪnʃpuːrɪç], *adj.* (*Railw.*) single-track line.

einst [aɪnst], *adv.* (*past*) once, once upon a time; (*future*) some day.

Einstand ['aɪnʃtant], *m.* (—s, *no pl.*) (*Tennis*) deuce.

einstecken ['aɪnʃtɛkən], *v.a.* put in; pocket; post (a letter).

einstehen ['aɪnʃteːən], *v.a. irr. zu etwas —*, answer for s.th.; *für einen —*, stand security for s.o.

einsteigen ['aɪnʃtaɪgən], *v.n. irr.* (*aux.* sein) get in, climb on; board.

einstellen ['aɪnʃtɛlən], *v.a.* put in; (*persons*) engage, hire; adjust; (*work*) stop, strike; (*payments*) stop; (*hostilities*) suspend, cease fire. — *v.r. sich —*, turn up, appear.

einstellig ['aɪnʃtɛlɪç], *adj.* (*Maths.*) of one digit.

Einstellung ['aɪnʃtɛluŋ], *f.* (—, *pl.* —en) putting in; (*persons*) engagement, hiring; adjustment; (*work*) stoppage, strike; (*payments*) suspension; (*hostilities*) suspension, cessation; (*fig.*) opinion, attitude.

einstig ['aɪnstɪç], *adj.* (*past*) former, late, erstwhile; (*future*) future, to be, to come.

einstimmen ['aɪnʃtɪmən], *v.n.* join in, chime in.

einstimmig ['aɪnʃtɪmɪç], *adj.* (*Mus.*) (for) one voice, unison; (*fig.*) unanimous.

einstmals ['aɪnstmaːls], *adv.* once, formerly.

57

einstöckig ['aɪnʃtœkɪç], *adj.* one-storied.

einstreichen ['aɪnʃtraɪçən], *v.a. irr.* (*money*) take in, pocket.

einstreuen ['aɪnʃtrɔyən], *v.a.* strew; (*fig.*) intersperse.

einstudieren ['aɪnʃtudiːrən], *v.a.* study; (*Theat., Mus.*) rehearse.

einstürmen ['aɪnʃtyrmən], *v.n.* (*aux.* sein) *auf einen —*, rush at, fall upon.

Einsturz ['aɪnʃturts], *m.* (**—es,** *pl.* **⁓e**) fall, crash; subsidence, collapse.

einstürzen ['aɪnʃtyrtsən], *v.n.* (*aux.* sein) fall in, fall into ruin, fall to pieces, collapse.

einstweilen ['aɪnstvaɪlən], *adv.* in the meantime, meanwhile, for the time being, provisionally.

einstweilig ['aɪnstvaɪlɪç], *adj.* temporary, provisional.

eintägig ['aɪntɛːgɪç], *adj.* one-day, ephemeral.

Eintagsfliege ['aɪntaːksfliːgə], *f.* (**—,** *pl.* **—n**) dayfly.

eintauschen ['aɪntauʃən], *v.a.* *— gegen,* exchange for, barter for.

einteilen ['aɪntaɪlən], *v.a.* divide; distribute; classify.

eintönig ['aɪntøːnɪç], *adj.* monotonous.

Eintracht ['aɪntraxt], *f.* (**—,** *no pl.*) concord, harmony.

einträchtig ['aɪntrɛçtɪç], *adj.* united, harmonious.

Eintrag ['aɪntraːk], *m.* (**—s,** *pl.* **⁓e**) entry (in a book); prejudice, damage, detriment.

eintragen ['aɪntraːgən], *v.a. irr.* enter (in a book), register; bring in, yield.

einträglich ['aɪntrɛklɪç], *adj.* profitable, lucrative.

Eintragung ['aɪntraːguŋ], *f.* (**—,** *pl.* **—en**) entry (in a book); enrolment.

einträufeln ['aɪntrɔyfəln], *v.a.* instil.

eintreffen ['aɪntrɛfən], *v.n. irr.* (*aux.* sein) arrive; happen, come true.

eintreiben ['aɪntraɪbən], *v.a. irr.* drive home (*cattle*); collect (debts etc.).

eintreten ['aɪntreːtən], *v.n. irr.* (*aux.* sein) step in, enter; happen, take place; *in einen Verein —,* join a club; *für einen —,* speak up for s.o.

eintrichtern ['aɪntrɪçtərn], *v.a. einem etwas —,* cram s.th. into s.o.

Eintritt ['aɪntrɪt], *m.* (**—s,** *no pl.*) entry, entrance; beginning; *kein —,* no admission.

eintrocknen ['aɪntrɔknən], *v.n.* (*aux.* sein) shrivel, dry up.

einüben ['aɪnyːbən], *v.a.* practise, exercise.

einverleiben ['aɪnfɛrlaɪbən], *v.a.* incorporate in, embody in.

Einvernahme ['aɪnfɛrnaːmə], *f.* (**—,** *pl.* **—n**) (*Austr.*) see **Vernehmung**.

Einvernehmen ['aɪnfɛrneːmən], *n.* (**—s,** *no pl.*) understanding; *im besten —,* on the best of terms.

einvernehmen ['aɪnfɛrneːmən], *v.a.* (*aux.* haben) (*Austr.*) see **vernehmen**.

einverstanden ['aɪnfɛrʃtandən], (*excl.*)

agreed! *— adj. — sein,* agree.

Einverständnis ['aɪnfɛrʃtɛntnɪs], *n.* (**—ses,** *no pl.*) consent, agreement, accord.

Einwand ['aɪnvant], *m.* (**—s,** *pl.* **⁓e**) objection, exception; *— erheben,* raise objections.

einwandern ['aɪnvandərn], *v.n.* (*aux.* sein) immigrate.

einwandfrei ['aɪnvantfraɪ], *adj.* irreproachable, unobjectionable.

einwärts ['aɪnvɛrts], *adv.* inward(s).

einwechseln ['aɪnvɛksəln], *v.a.* change, exchange.

einweichen ['aɪnvaɪçən], *v.a.* steep in water, soak.

einweihen ['aɪnvaɪən], *v.a.* dedicate; (*Eccl.*) consecrate; open (formally), inaugurate; initiate (into).

Einweihung ['aɪnvaɪuŋ], *f.* (**—,** *pl.* **—en**) (*Eccl.*) consecration; inauguration, formal opening; initiation.

einwenden ['aɪnvɛndən], *v.a. irr.* object to, raise objections, urge against.

einwerfen ['aɪnvɛrfən], *v.a. irr.* throw in; smash in; interject.

einwickeln ['aɪnvɪkəln], *v.a.* wrap up, envelop.

einwilligen ['aɪnvɪlɪgən], *v.n.* consent, assent, agree, accede.

einwirken ['aɪnvɪrkən], *v.n. auf einen —,* influence s.o.

Einwohner ['aɪnvoːnər], *m.* (**—s,** *pl.* **—**) inhabitant.

Einwohnerschaft ['aɪnvoːnərʃaft], *f.* (**—,** *no pl.*) population, inhabitants.

Einwurf ['aɪnvurf], *m.* (**—s,** *pl.* **⁓e**) (*letter box*) opening, slit; slot; objection.

einwurzeln ['aɪnvurtsəln], *v.r. sich —,* take root; *eingewurzelt,* deep-rooted.

Einzahl ['aɪntsaːl], *f.* (**—,** *no pl.*) singular.

einzahlen ['aɪntsaːlən], *v.a.* pay in, deposit.

einzäunen ['aɪntsɔynən], *v.a.* fence in.

einzeichnen ['aɪntsaɪçnən], *v.a.* draw in, sketch in. *— v.r. sich —,* enter o.'s name, sign.

Einzelhaft ['aɪntsəlhaft], *f.* (**—,** *no pl.*) solitary confinement.

Einzelheit ['aɪntsəlhaɪt], *f.* (**—,** *pl.* **—en**) detail, particular.

einzeln ['aɪntsəln], *adj.* single; isolated, detached, apart.

einziehen ['aɪntsiːən], *v.a. irr.* draw in, retract; (*Law*) confiscate, impound; (*debts*) collect, call in; (*bill of sight*) discount, cash; (*money*) withdraw (from circulation); (*sails*) furl; (*Mil.*) call up.

einzig ['aɪntsɪç], *adj.* sole, single; unique, only.

Einzug ['aɪntsuːk], *m.* (**—s,** *pl.* **⁓e**) entry, entrance; move (into new house).

einzwängen ['aɪntsvɛŋən], *v.a.* force in, squeeze in.

Eis [aɪs], *n.* (**—es,** *no pl.*) ice; ice-cream.

E-is ['eːɪs], *n.* (**—,** *pl.* **—**) (*Mus.*) E sharp.

Eisbahn ['aɪsbaːn], f. (—, pl. —en) ice-rink, skating-rink.

Eisbär ['aɪsbɛːr], m. (—en, pl. —en) polar bear, white bear.

Eisbein ['aɪsbaɪn], n. (—s, pl. —e) pig's trotters.

Eisberg ['aɪsbɛrk], m. (—s, pl. —e) iceberg.

Eisblumen ['aɪsbluːmən], f. pl. frost patterns (on glass).

Eisen ['aɪzən], n. (—s, pl. —) iron; altes —, scrap iron.

Eisenbahn ['aɪzənbaːn], f. (—, pl. —en) railway.

Eisenfleck ['aɪzənflɛk], m. (—s, pl. —e) iron mould.

Eisengießerei ['aɪzəngiːsəraɪ], f. (—, pl. —en) iron foundry, iron forge.

Eisenguß ['aɪzəngus], m. (—sses, pl. ⁼sse) cast-iron.

Eisenhändler ['aɪzənhɛndlər], m. (—s, pl. —) ironmonger.

Eisenhütte ['aɪzənhytə], f. (—, pl. —n) see **Eisengießerei**.

Eisenschlacke ['aɪzənʃlakə], f. (—, no pl.) iron dross, iron slag.

eisern ['aɪzərn], adj. made of iron; (coll. & fig.) strong; strict.

Eisgang ['aɪsgaŋ], m. (—s, pl. ⁼e) drift of ice.

eisgrau ['aɪsgrau], adj. hoary.

eiskalt ['aɪskalt], adj. icy cold.

Eislauf ['aɪslauf], m. (—s, no pl.) ice-skating.

Eismeer ['aɪsmeːr], n. (—s, pl. —e) polar sea; nördliches —, Arctic Ocean; südliches —, Antarctic Ocean.

Eispickel ['aɪspɪkəl], m. (—s, pl. —) ice axe.

Eisvogel ['aɪsfoːgəl], m. (—s, pl. ⁼) (Orn.) kingfisher.

Eiszapfen ['aɪstsapfən], m. (—s, pl. —) icicle.

eitel ['aɪtəl], adj. vain, frivolous, conceited; (obs.) pure.

Eiter ['aɪtər], m. (—s, no pl.) (Med.) pus, matter.

Eitergeschwür ['aɪtərgəʃvyːr], n. (—s, pl. —e) abscess.

eitern ['aɪtərn], v.n. suppurate.

Eiterung ['aɪtəruŋ], f. (—, pl. —en) suppuration.

eitrig ['aɪtrɪç], adj. purulent.

Eiweiß ['aɪvaɪs], n. (—es, no pl.) white of egg; albumen.

Ekel ['eːkəl], m. (—s, no pl.) nausea, disgust, distaste, aversion.

ekelhaft ['eːkəlhaft], adj. loathsome, disgusting, nauseous.

ekeln ['eːkəln], v.r. sich — vor, be disgusted (by), feel sick, loathe.

Ekuador [ɛkuaˈdɔr], n. Ecuador.

Elan [eˈlã], m. (—s, no pl.) verve, vigour.

elastisch [eˈlastɪʃ], adj. elastic, flexible, buoyant.

Elastizität [elastɪtsiˈtɛːt], f. (—, no pl.) elasticity; (mind) buoyancy.

Elch [ɛlç], m. (—s, pl. —e) (Zool.) elk.

Elegie [eleˈgiː], f. (—, pl. —n) elegy.

elektrisieren [elɛktriˈziːrən], v.a. electrify.

Elektrizität [elɛktritsiˈtɛːt], f. (—, no pl.) electricity.

Elend ['eːlɛnt], n. (—s, no pl.) misery, distress, wretchedness.

elend ['eːlɛnt], adj. miserable, wretched, pitiful; weak; sich — fühlen, feel poorly.

elendiglich ['eːlɛndɪklɪç], adv. miserably, wretchedly.

Elentier ['eːlɛntiːr], n. (—s, pl. —e) (Zool.) elk.

elf [ɛlf], num. adj. eleven.

Elfe ['ɛlfə], f. (—, pl. —n) fairy.

Elfenbein ['ɛlfənbaɪn], n. (—s, no pl.) ivory.

Elisabeth [eˈliːzabɛt], f. Elizabeth.

Ellbogen ['ɛlboːgən], m. (—s, pl. —) elbow.

Elle ['ɛlə], f. (—, pl. —n) yard, ell.

Elritze ['ɛlrɪtsə], f. (—, pl. —n) minnow.

Elsaß ['ɛlzas], n. Alsace.

Elster ['ɛlstər], f. (—, pl. —n) magpie.

Eltern ['ɛltərn], pl. parents.

Emaille [eˈmaːj], n. (—s, no pl.) enamel.

emailliert [emal(j)ˈjiːrt], adj. covered with vitreous enamel, enamelled.

Empfang [ɛmˈpfaŋ], m. (—s, pl. ⁼e) receipt; reception.

empfangen [ɛmˈpfaŋən], v.a. irr. receive, accept, take.

Empfänger [ɛmˈpfɛŋər], m. (—s, pl. —) recipient, receiver.

empfänglich [ɛmˈpfɛŋlɪç], adj. susceptible, impressionable.

Empfängnis [ɛmˈpfɛŋnɪs], f. (—, no pl.) conception.

empfehlen [ɛmˈpfeːlən], v.a. irr. commend, recommend; give compliments to. — v.r. sich —, take leave.

empfinden [ɛmˈpfɪndən], v.a. irr. feel, perceive.

empfindlich [ɛmˈpfɪntlɪç], adj. sensitive, susceptible; touchy, thin-skinned.

empfindsam [ɛmˈpfɪntsaːm], adj. sentimental.

Empfindung [ɛmˈpfɪnduŋ], f. (—, pl. —en) sensation, feeling, sentiment.

empor [ɛmˈpoːr], adv. upward(s), up.

Empore [ɛmˈpoːrə], f. (—, pl. —n) gallery (in church).

empören [ɛmˈpøːrən], v.a. excite, enrage, shock. — v.r. sich —, revolt, rebel.

Emporkömmling [ɛmˈpoːrkœmlɪŋ], m. (—s, pl. —e) upstart.

empört [ɛmˈpøːrt], adj. furious, shocked, disgusted.

Empörung [ɛmˈpøːruŋ], f. (—, pl. —en) rebellion, revolt, mutiny, insurrection; indignation, disgust.

emsig ['ɛmzɪç], adj. assiduous, industrious, busy.

Emsigkeit ['ɛmzɪçkaɪt], f. (—, no pl.) assiduity, diligence.

Ende ['ɛndə], n. (—s, pl. —n) end, conclusion.

enden

enden ['ɛndən], *v.n.* end, finish, conclude. — *v.a.* terminate, put an end to.

endgültig ['ɛntgyltɪç], *adj.* definitive, final.

Endivie [ɛn'diːvjə], *f.* (—, *pl.* —n) (*Bot.*) endive.

endlich ['ɛntlɪç], *adj.* finite, final, ultimate. — *adv.* at last, at length, finally.

endlos ['ɛntloːs], *adj.* endless, neverending, boundless.

Endung ['ɛndʊŋ], *f.* (—, *pl.* —en) (*Gram.*) ending, termination.

Endziel ['ɛntsiːl], *n.* (—s, *pl.* —e) final aim.

Energie [enɛr'giː], *f.* (—, *pl.* —n) energy.

energisch [e'nɛrgɪʃ], *adj.* energetic.

eng [ɛŋ], *adj.* narrow, tight; tightfitting.

engagieren [ãgaˈʒiːrən], *v.a.* engage, hire.

Enge ['ɛŋə], *f.* (—, *pl.* —n) narrowness, lack of space; *einen in die* — *treiben* drive s.o. into a corner.

Engel ['ɛŋəl], *m.* (—s, *pl.* —) angel.

engelhaft ['ɛŋəlhaft], *adj.* angelic.

Engelschar ['ɛŋəlʃaːr], *f.* (—, *pl.* —en) angelic host.

Engelwurzel ['ɛŋəlvʊrtsəl], *f.* (—, *pl.* —n) angelica.

engherzig ['ɛŋhɛrtsɪç], *adj.* narrowminded.

England ['ɛŋlant], *n.* England.

englisch (1) ['ɛŋlɪʃ], *adj.* (*obs.*) angelic.

englisch (2) ['ɛŋlɪʃ], *adj.* English; —*e Krankheit*, rickets.

Engpaß ['ɛŋpas], *m.* (—sses, *pl.* ᵉe) defile, narrow pass; (*fig.*) bottleneck.

engros [ãˈgroː], *adv.* wholesale.

engstirnig ['ɛŋʃtɪrnɪç], *adj.* narrowminded.

Enkel ['ɛŋkəl], *m.* (—s, *pl.* —) grandchild, grandson.

enorm [e'nɔrm], *adj.* enormous; (*coll.*) terrific.

entarten [ɛnt'artən], *v.n.* (*aux.* sein) degenerate.

entäußern [ɛnt'ɔysərn], *v.r. sich einer Sache* —, part with s.th.

entbehren [ɛnt'beːrən], *v.a.* lack, be in want of; spare.

entbehrlich [ɛnt'beːrlɪç], *adj.* dispensable, unnecessary, superfluous.

Entbehrung [ɛnt'beːrʊŋ], *f.* (—, *pl.* —en) privation, want.

entbieten [ɛnt'biːtən], *v.a. irr. Grüße* —, send o.'s respects.

entbinden [ɛnt'bɪndən], *v.a. irr. einen von etwas* —, release *or* dispense s.o. from s.th.; (*Med.*) deliver (a woman of a child).

Entbindung [ɛnt'bɪndʊŋ], *f.* (—, *pl.* —en) (*Med.*) delivery, child-birth.

entblättern [ɛnt'blɛtərn], *v.a.* strip of leaves.

entblößen [ɛnt'bløːsən], *v.a.*, *v.r.* (*sich*) —, uncover (o.s.), bare (o.s.).

entdecken [ɛnt'dɛkən], *v.a.* discover, detect.

Ente ['ɛntə], *f.* (—, *pl.* —n) duck; *junge* —, duckling; (*fig.*) hoax, fictitious newspaper report.

entehren [ɛnt'eːrən], *v.a.* dishonour, disgrace; deflower, ravish.

enterben [ɛnt'ɛrbən], *v.a.* disinherit.

Enterich ['ɛntərɪç], *m.* (—s, *pl.* —e) drake.

entfachen [ɛnt'faxən], *v.a.* set ablaze, kindle.

entfahren [ɛnt'faːrən], *v.n. irr.* (*aux.* sein) slip off, escape.

entfallen [ɛnt'falən], *v.n. irr.* (*aux.* sein) escape o.'s memory; be left off.

entfalten [ɛnt'faltən], *v.a.* unfold; display. — *v.r. sich* —, develop, open up, expand.

entfärben [ɛnt'fɛrbən], *v.r. sich* —, lose colour, grow pale.

entfernen [ɛnt'fɛrnən], *v.a.* remove. — *v.r. sich* —, withdraw.

Entfernung [ɛnt'fɛrnʊŋ], *f.* (—, *pl.* —en) removal; distance.

entfesseln [ɛnt'fɛsəln], *v.a.* unfetter; let loose.

Entfettungskur [ɛnt'fɛtʊŋskuːr], *f.* (—, —en) slimming-cure.

entflammen [ɛnt'flamən], *v.a.* inflame.

entfliegen [ɛnt'fliːgən], *v.n. irr.* (*aux.* sein) fly away.

entfliehen [ɛnt'fliːən], *v.n. irr.* (*aux.* sein) run away, escape, flee.

entfremden [ɛnt'frɛmdən], *v.a.* estrange, alienate.

entführen [ɛnt'fyːrən], *v.a.* abduct, carry off; kidnap; elope with.

entgegen [ɛnt'geːgən], *prep.* (*Dat.*), *adv.* against, contrary to; towards.

Entgegenkommen [ɛnt'geːgənkɔmən], *n.* (—s, *no pl.*) obliging behaviour, courtesy.

entgegenkommen [ɛnt'geːgənkɔmən], *v.n. irr.* (*aux.* sein) come towards s.o., come to meet s.o.; do a favour, oblige.

entgegennehmen [ɛnt'geːgənneːmən], *v.a. irr.* receive, accept.

entgegensehen [ɛnt'geːgənzeːən], *v.n. irr.* await, look forward to.

entgegnen [ɛnt'geːgnən], *v.a.* reply, retort.

Entgegnung [ɛnt'geːgnʊŋ], *f.* (—, *pl.* —en) reply, retort, rejoinder.

entgehen [ɛnt'geːən], *v.n. irr.* (*aux.* sein) (*Dat.*) escape; — *lassen*, let slip.

Entgelt [ɛnt'gɛlt], *n.* (—s, *no pl.*) remuneration, recompense.

entgelten [ɛnt'gɛltən], *v.a. irr. einen etwas* — *lassen*, make s.o. pay for s.th. *or* suffer.

entgleisen [ɛnt'glatzən], *v.n.* (*aux.* sein) run off the rails, be derailed.

enthaaren [ɛnt'haːrən], *v.a.* depilate.

enthalten [ɛnt'haltən], *v.a. irr.* hold, contain. — *v.r. sich* —, abstain from, refrain from.

enthaltsam [ɛnt'haltzaːm], *adj.* abstinent, abstemious, temperate.

Enthaltung [ɛnt'haltʊŋ], *f.* (—, *no pl.*) abstention.

enthaupten [ɛnt'haʊptən], *v.a.* behead, decapitate.

entheben [ɛnt'he:bən], *v.a. irr. einen einer Sache —*, exempt *or* dispense from, suspend from, relieve of.

entheiligen [ɛnt'haɪlɪgən], *v.a.* profane, desecrate.

enthüllen [ɛnt'hylən], *v.a.* unveil; (*fig.*) reveal.

entkleiden [ɛnt'klaɪdən], *v.a.* unclothe, undress, strip.

entkommen [ɛnt'kɔmən], *v.n. irr.* (*aux.* sein) escape, get off.

entkräften [ɛnt'krɛftən], *v.a.* enfeeble, debilitate, weaken; (*fig.*) refute (an argument).

entladen [ɛnt'la:dən], *v.a. irr.* unload, discharge. — *v.r. sich —*, burst; (*gun*) go off.

Entladung [ɛnt'la:duŋ], *f.* (—, *pl.* —en) unloading, discharge, explosion.

entlang [ɛnt'laŋ], *prep.* along.

entlarven [ɛnt'larfən], *v.a.* unmask; expose.

Entlarvung [ɛnt'larfuŋ], *f.* (—, *pl.* —en) unmasking, exposure.

entlassen [ɛnt'lasən], *v.a. irr.* dismiss; (*Am.*) fire; discharge; pension off.

Entlastung [ɛnt'lastuŋ], *f.* (—, *no pl.*) exoneration; credit (to s.o.'s bank account).

entlaufen [ɛnt'laʊfən], *v.n. irr.* (*aux.* sein) run away.

entlausen [ɛnt'lauzən], *v.a.* delouse.

entledigen [ɛnt'le:dɪgən], *v.r. sich einer Sache —*, rid o.s. of *or* get rid of a thing; *sich einer Aufgabe —*, perform a task, discharge a commission.

entleeren [ɛnt'le:rən], *v.a.* empty.

entlegen [ɛnt'le:gən], *adj.* remote, distant, far off.

entlehnen [ɛnt'le:nən], *v.a.* borrow from.

entleihen [ɛnt'laɪən], *v.a. irr.* borrow.

entlocken [ɛnt'lɔkən], *v.a.* elicit from.

entmannen [ɛnt'manən], *v.a.* castrate, emasculate.

entmündigen [ɛnt'myndɪgən], *v.a.* place under care of a guardian *or* (*Law*) trustees.

Entmündigung [ɛnt'myndɪguŋ], *f.* (—, *no pl.*) placing under legal control.

entmutigen [ɛnt'mu:tɪgən], *v.a.* discourage, dishearten.

Entnahme [ɛnt'na:mə], *f.* (—, *pl.* —n) (*money*) withdrawal.

entnehmen [ɛnt'ne:mən], *v.a. irr.* (*money*) withdraw; understand, gather *or* infer from.

entnerven [ɛnt'nɛrfən], *v.a.* enervate.

entpuppen [ɛnt'pupən], *v.r. sich —*, burst from the cocoon; (*fig.*) turn out to be.

enträtseln [ɛnt'rɛ:tsəln], *v.a.* decipher, make out.

entreißen [ɛnt'raɪsən], *v.a. irr.* snatch away from; *einer Gefahr —*, save *or* rescue from danger.

entrichten [ɛnt'rɪçtən], *v.a.* pay (off).

entrinnen [ɛnt'rɪnən], *v.n. irr.* (*aux.* sein) escape from.

entrückt [ɛnt rykt], *adj.* enraptured.

entrüsten [ɛnt'rystən], *v.a.* make angry, exasperate. — *v.r. sich —*, become angry, fly into a passion.

entsagen [ɛnt'za:gən], *v.n.* renounce; waive; abdicate.

Entsatz [ɛnt'zats], *m.* (—es, *no pl.*) (*Mil.*) relief.

entschädigen [ɛnt'ʃɛ:dɪgən], *v.a.* indemnify, compensate.

entscheiden [ɛnt'ʃaɪdən], *v.a. irr.* decide. — *v.r. sich —*, come to a decision for, decide in favour of.

Entscheidung [ɛnt'ʃaɪduŋ], *f.* (—, *pl.* —en) decision; verdict.

entschieden [ɛnt'ʃi:dən], *adj.* decided, determined, resolute, peremptory.

Entschiedenheit [ɛnt'ʃi:dənhaɪt], *f.* (—, *no pl.*) resolution, firmness, determination.

entschlafen [ɛnt'ʃla:fən], *v.n. irr.* (*aux.* sein) fall asleep; (*fig.*) die, depart this life.

entschleiern [ɛnt'ʃlaɪərn], *v.a.* unveil.

entschließen [ɛnt'ʃli:sən], *v.r. sich —*, decide (upon), resolve, make up o.'s mind.

Entschlossenheit [ɛnt'ʃlɔsənhaɪt], *f.* (—, *no pl.*) resoluteness, determination.

entschlummern [ɛnt'ʃlumərn], *v.n.* (*aux.* sein) fall asleep.

entschlüpfen [ɛnt'ʃlypfən], *v.n.* (*aux.* sein) slip away; escape.

Entschluß [ɛnt'ʃlus], *m.* (—sses, *pl.* ¨sse) resolution; *einen — fassen*, resolve (to).

entschuldigen [ɛnt'ʃuldɪgən], *v.a.* excuse. — *v.r. sich —*, apologise.

entschwinden [ɛnt'ʃvɪndən], *v.n. irr.* (*aux.* sein) disappear, vanish.

entseelt [ɛnt'ze:lt], *adj.* inanimate, lifeless.

entsenden [ɛnt'zɛndən], *v.a. irr.* send off, despatch.

Entsetzen [ɛnt'zɛtsən], *n.* (—s, *no pl.*) horror, terror.

entsetzen [ɛnt'zɛtsən], *v.a.* (*Mil.*) relieve; frighten, shock, fill with horror. — *v.r. sich — über*, be horrified at.

entsetzlich [ɛnt'zɛtslɪç], *adj.* horrible, terrible, dreadful, awful.

entsiegeln [ɛnt'zi:gəln], *v.a.* unseal.

entsinnen [ɛnt'zɪnən], *v.r. sich einer Sache —*, recollect, remember, call s.th. to mind.

entspannen [ɛnt'ʃpanən], *v.a.*, *v.r.* (*sich*) —, relax.

entspinnen [ɛnt'ʃpɪnən], *v.r. irr. sich —*, arise, begin.

entsprechen [ɛnt'ʃprɛçən], *v.n. irr.* respond to, correspond to, meet, suit.

entsprechend [ɛnt'ʃprɛçənt], *adj.* corresponding, suitable.

entsprießen [ɛnt'ʃpri:sən], *v.n. irr.* (*aux.* sein) spring up, sprout.

entspringen [ɛnt'ʃprɪŋən], *v.n. irr.* (*aux.* sein) escape, originate from; (*river*) have its source at, rise.

entstammen [ɛntˈʃtamən], *v.n.* (aux. sein) spring from, originate from.

entstehen [ɛntˈʃteːən], *v.n. irr.* (aux. sein) arise, originate, begin, result, spring from.

Entstehung [ɛntˈʃteːuŋ], *f.* (—, *no pl.*) origin, rise.

entstellen [ɛntˈʃtɛlən], *v.a.* disfigure, deform, distort; (*fig.*) garble.

entsühnen [ɛntˈzyːnən], *v.a.* free from sin, purify, purge.

enttäuschen [ɛntˈtɔyʃən], *v.a.* disappoint.

entthronen [ɛntˈtroːnən], *v.a.* dethrone.

entvölkern [ɛntˈfœlkərn], *v.a.* depopulate.

entwachsen [ɛntˈvaksən], *v.n. irr.* (aux. sein) grow out of, outgrow.

entwaffnen [ɛntˈvafnən], *v.a.* disarm.

entwässern [ɛntˈvɛsərn], *v.a.* drain.

entweder [ɛntˈveːdər], *conj.* either; — ......*oder*, either ...... or.

entweichen [ɛntˈvaiçən], *v.n. irr.* escape, run away.

entweihen [ɛntˈvaiən], *v.a.* profane, desecrate.

entwenden [ɛntˈvɛndən], *v.a.* take away, steal, embezzle.

entwerfen [ɛntˈvɛrfən], *v.a. irr.* design, sketch, plan, draw up.

entwerten [ɛntˈveːrtən], *v.a.* reduce in value, depreciate; (*stamps*) cancel.

entwickeln [ɛntˈvikəln], *v.a.* unfold, develop; (*ideas*) explain, explicate. — *v.r. sich* —, develop (into), evolve.

Entwicklung [ɛntˈvikluŋ], *f.* (—, *pl.* —en) unfolding, development, evolution.

entwinden [ɛntˈvindən], *v.a. irr.* wrench from, wrest from.

entwirren [ɛntˈvirən], *v.a.* unravel, disentangle.

entwischen [ɛntˈviʃən], *v.n.* (aux. sein) slip away, escape.

entwöhnen [ɛntˈvøːnən], *v.a.* disaccustom; break off a habit; (*baby*) wean.

entwürdigen [ɛntˈvyrdigən], *v.a.* disgrace, degrade.

Entwurf [ɛntˈvurf], *m.* (—s, *pl.* ⁝e) sketch, design, draft, plan, project.

entwurzeln [ɛntˈvurtsəln], *v.a.* uproot.

entziehen [ɛntˈtsiːən], *v.a. irr.* withdraw, take away, deprive of.

entziffern [ɛntˈtsifərn], *v.a.* decipher.

entzücken [ɛntˈtsykən], *v.a.* enchant, delight, charm.

entzündbar [ɛntˈtsyntbaːr], *adj.* inflammable.

entzünden [ɛntˈtsyndən], *v.a.* set on fire, light the fire; (*fig.*) inflame. — *v.r. sich* —, catch fire, ignite; (*Med.*) become inflamed.

Entzündung [ɛntˈtsynduŋ], *f.* (—, *pl.* —en) kindling, setting on fire; (*Med.*) inflammation.

entzwei [ɛntˈtsvai], *adv.* in two, broken.

entzweien [ɛntˈtsvaiən], *v.a.* disunite.

Enzian [ˈɛntsjan], *m.* (—s, *pl.* —e) (*Bot.*) gentian.

Enzyklopädie [ɛntsyklopɛˈdiː], *f.* (—, *pl.* —n) encyclopædia.

Epidemie [epideˈmiː], *f.* (—, *pl.* —en) epidemic.

epidemisch [epiˈdeːmiʃ], *adj.* epidemic(al).

Epik [ˈeːpik], *f.* (—, *no pl.*) epic poetry.

episch [ˈeːpiʃ], *adj.* epic.

Epos [ˈeːpɔs], *n.* (—, *pl.* Epen) epic poem.

Equipage [ekviˈpaːʒə], *f.* (—, *pl.* —n) carriage.

er [eːr], *pers. pron.* he.

Erachten [ɛrˈaxtən], *n.* (—s, *no pl.*) opinion, judgment; *meines* —*s*, in my opinion.

erachten [ɛrˈaxtən], *v.a.* think, consider.

erarbeiten [ɛrˈarbaitən], *v.a.* gain *or* achieve by working.

erb [ˈɛrb], *adj.* (*in compounds*) hereditary.

erbarmen [ɛrˈbarmən], *v.r. sich* —, have mercy (on), take pity (on).

erbärmlich [ɛrˈbɛrmliç], *adj.* miserable, pitiful; contemptible.

erbauen [ɛrˈbauən], *v.a.* build, erect; (*fig.*) edify.

erbaulich [ɛrˈbauliç], *adj.* edifying.

Erbauung [ɛrˈbauuŋ], *f.* (—, *no pl.*) building, erection; (*fig.*) edification.

Erbbesitz [ˈɛrpbazits], *m.* (—es, *pl.* —e) hereditary possession.

Erbe [ˈɛrbə], *m.* (—n, *pl.* —n) heir. *n.* (—s, *no pl.*) inheritance; heritage.

erbeben [ɛrˈbeːbən], *v.n.* (aux. sein) shake, tremble, quake.

erbeigen [ˈɛrpaigən], *adj.* inherited.

erben [ˈɛrbən], *v.a.* inherit.

erbeten [ɛrˈbeːtən], *v.a. sich etwas* —, ask for s.th. by prayer; request.

erbetteln [ɛrˈbɛtəln], *v.a.* obtain by begging.

erbeuten [ɛrˈbɔytən], *v.a.* take as booty.

Erbfeind [ˈɛrpfaint], *m.* (—s, *pl.* —e) sworn enemy.

Erbfolge [ˈɛrpfɔlgə], *f.* (—, *no pl.*) succession.

erbieten [ɛrˈbiːtən], *v.r. irr. sich* —, offer to do s.th.; volunteer; *Ehre* —, do homage.

Erbin [ˈɛrbin], *f.* (—, *pl.* —nen) heiress.

erbitten [ɛrˈbitən], *v.a. irr.* beg, request, ask for, gain by asking.

erbittern [ɛrˈbitərn], *v.a.* embitter, anger, exasperate.

erblassen [ɛrˈblasən], *v.n.* (aux. sein) turn pale.

Erblasser [ˈɛrplasər], *m.* (—s, *pl.* —) testator.

erbleichen [ɛrˈblaiçən], *v.n. irr.* (aux. sein) turn pale, lose colour.

erblich [ˈɛrpliç], *adj.* hereditary, congenital.

erblicken [ɛrˈblikən], *v.a.* perceive, behold, catch sight of.

erblinden [ɛrˈblindən], *v.n.* (aux. sein) turn blind.

erblos [ˈɛrploːs], *adj.* disinherited; without an heir.

erblühen [ɛr'bly:ən], *v.n.* (*aux.* sein) blossom (out).

Erbmasse ['ɛrpmasə], *f.* (—, *no pl.*) estate.

erbosen [ɛr'bo:zən], *v.a.* make angry. — *v.r. sich* —, become angry.

erbötig [ɛr'bø:tɪç], *adj.* — sein, be willing, be ready.

Erbpacht ['ɛrppaxt], *f.* (—, *pl.* —en) hereditary tenure.

erbrechen [ɛr'brɛçən], *v.a. irr.* break open, open by force. — *v.r. sich* —, vomit.

Erbrecht ['ɛrprɛçt], *n.* (—s, *no pl.*) law (*or* right) of succession.

Erbschaft ['ɛrpʃaft], *f.* (—, *pl.* —en) inheritance, heritage, legacy.

Erbse ['ɛrpsə], *f.* (—, *pl.* —n) pea.

Erbstück ['ɛrpʃtyk], *n.* (—s, *pl.* —e) heirloom.

Erbsünde ['ɛrpzyndə], *f.* (—, *no pl.*) original sin.

Erbteil ['ɛrptaɪl], *n.* (—s, *pl.* —e) portion of inheritance.

Erdapfel ['e:rtapfəl], *m.* (—s, *pl.* ⁼) (*Austr.*) potato.

Erdbahn ['e:rtba:n], *f.* (—, *no pl.*) orbit of the earth.

Erdball ['e:rtbal], *m.* (—s, *no pl.*) terrestrial globe.

Erdbeben ['e:rtbe:bən], *n.* (—s, *pl.* —) earthquake.

Erdbeere ['e:rtbe:rə], *f.* (—, *pl.* —n) strawberry.

Erde ['e:rdə], *f.* (—, *pl.* —n) earth, soil ground.

erden ['e:rdən], *v.a.* (*Rad.*) earth.

erdenken [ɛr'dɛŋkən], *v.a. irr.* think out; invent. — *v.r. sich etwas* —, invent s.th., devise s.th.

erdenklich [ɛr'dɛŋklɪç], *adj.* imaginable, conceivable.

Erdenleben ['e:rdənle:bən], *n.* (—s, *no pl.*) life on this earth.

Erdfall ['e:rtfal], *m.* (—s, *pl.* ⁼e) landslip.

Erdfläche ['e:rtflɛçə], *f.* (—, *no pl.*) surface of the earth.

Erdgeschoß ['e:rtgəʃɔs], *n.* (—sses, *pl.* —sse) ground floor.

Erdhügel ['e:rthy:gəl], *m.* (—s, *pl.* —) mound of earth.

erdichten [ɛr'dɪçtən], *v.a.* think out, invent, feign.

Erdkunde ['e:rtkundə], *f.* (—, *no pl.*) geography.

Erdleitung [ɛr'rtlaɪtuŋ], *f.* (—, *pl.* —en) earth circuit, earth connexion.

Erdmaus ['e:rtmaus], *f.* (—, *pl.* ⁼e) field mouse.

Erdmolch ['e:rtmɔlç], *m.* (—s, *pl.* —e) salamander.

Erdnuß ['e:rtnus], *f.* (—, *pl.* ⁼sse) groundnut, peanut.

Erdöl ['e:rtø:l], *n.* (—s, *no pl.*) petroleum, mineral oil.

erdolchen [ɛr'dɔlçən], *v.a.* stab (with a dagger).

Erdpech ['e:rtpɛç], *n.* (—s, *no pl.*) bitumen.

erdreisten [ɛr'draɪstən], *v.r. sich* —, dare, have the audacity.

erdrosseln [ɛr'drɔsəln], *v.a.* strangle, throttle.

erdrücken [ɛr'drykən], *v.a.* crush to death.

Erdrutsch ['e:rtrutʃ], *m.* (—es, *no pl.*) landslip, landslide.

Erdschicht ['e:rtʃɪçt], *f.* (—, *pl.* —en) (*Geol.*) layer, stratum.

Erdschnecke ['e:rtʃnɛkə], *f.* (—, *pl.* —n) slug, snail.

Erdscholle ['e:rtʃɔlə], *f.* (—, *pl.* —n) clod (of earth).

Erdsturz ['e:rtʃturts], *m.* (—es, *no pl.*) landslide.

erdulden [ɛr'duldən], *v.a.* suffer, endure.

Erdumseg(e)lung ['e:rtumze:g(ə)luŋ], *f.* (—, *pl.* —en) circumnavigation of the earth.

ereifern [ɛr'aɪfərn], *v.r. sich* —, become heated, get excited.

ereignen [ɛr'aɪgnən], *v.r. sich* —, happen, come to pass.

Ereignis [ɛr'aɪknɪs], *n.* (—ses, *pl.* —se) event, occurrence, happening.

ereilen [ɛr'aɪlən], *v.a.* overtake, befall.

Eremit [ere'mi:t], *m.* (—en, *pl.* —en) hermit, recluse.

erfahren [ɛr'fa:rən], *v.a. irr.* learn, hear; experience. — *adj.* experienced, practised; conversant with, versed in.

Erfahrenheit [ɛr'fa:rənhaɪt], *f.* (—, *no pl.*) experience, skill.

Erfahrung [ɛr'fa:ruŋ], *f.* (—, *pl.* —en) experience, knowledge, expertness, skill; *in* — *bringen*, ascertain, come to know.

erfahrungsgemäß [ɛr'fa:ruŋsgəmɛs], *adj.* based on *or* according to experience.

erfahrungsmäßig [ɛr'fa:ruŋsmɛsɪç], *adj.* based on experience; empirical.

erfassen [ɛr'fasən], *v.a.* get hold of, seize, comprehend, grasp.

erfinden [ɛr'fɪndən], *v.a. irr.* invent, contrive.

erfinderisch [ɛr'fɪndərɪʃ], *adj.* inventive, ingenious.

Erfindung [ɛr'fɪnduŋ], *f.* (—, *pl.* —en) invention; contrivance.

Erfolg [ɛr'fɔlk], *m.* (—s, *pl.* —e) success; result; effect; — *haben*, succeed, be successful; *keinen* — *haben*, fail.

erfolgen [ɛr'fɔlgən], *v.n.* (*aux.* sein) ensue, follow, result.

erfolgreich [ɛr'fɔlkraɪç], *adj.* successful.

erforderlich [ɛr'fɔrdərlɪç], *adj.* necessary, required.

erfordern [ɛr'fɔrdərn], *v.a.* demand, require.

Erfordernis [ɛr'fɔrdərnɪs], *n.* (—ses, *pl.* —se) necessity, requirement, requisite.

erforschen [ɛr'fɔrʃən], *v.a.* explore, investigate, conduct research into.

erfragen [ɛr'fra:gən], *v.a.* find out by asking, ascertain.

erfreuen [ɛr'frɔyən], *v.a.* gladden, cheer, delight. — *v.r. sich* — *an*, enjoy, take pleasure in.

erfreulich

erfreulich [ɛr'frɔylɪç], *adj.* pleasing, gratifying.

erfrieren [ɛr'fri:rən], *v.n. irr.* (*aux.* sein) freeze to death, die of exposure; become numb.

erfrischen [ɛr'frɪʃən], *v.a.* refresh.

erfüllen [ɛr'fylən], *v.a.* fulfil, keep (promise); comply with; perform; *seinen Zweck —,* serve its purpose. — *v.r. sich —,* come true, be fulfilled.

Erfüllung [ɛr'fylʊŋ], *f.* (—, *no pl.*) fulfilment; granting; performance; *in — gehen,* come true, be realised.

ergänzen [ɛr'gɛntsən], *v.a.* complete, complement.

Ergänzung [ɛr'gɛntsʊŋ], *f.* (—, *pl.* —en) completion; complement, supplement.

ergattern [ɛr'gatərn], *v.a.* pick up.

ergeben [ɛr'ge:bən], *v.a. irr.* give, yield, prove, show. — *v.r. sich —,* surrender (to), acquiesce (in); happen, result, follow. — *adj.* devoted, submissive, humble, obedient.

Ergebenheit [ɛr'ge:bənhaɪt], *f.* (—, *no pl.*) devotion, obedience, humility, fidelity.

ergebenst [ɛr'ge:bənst], *adj. Ihr —er* (*letter ending*), yours very truly, your obedient servant. — *adv.* respectfully.

Ergebnis [ɛr'ge:pnɪs], *n.* (—ses, *pl.* —se) outcome, result; (*Agr.*) yield.

Ergebung [ɛr'ge:bʊŋ], *f.* (—, *no pl.*) submission, resignation; surrender.

Ergehen [ɛr'ge:ən], *n.* (—s, *no pl.*) health, condition, well-being.

ergehen [ɛr'ge:ən], *v.n. irr.* (*aux.* sein) be promulgated *or* issued; — *lassen,* issue, publish; *etwas über sich — lassen,* submit to *or* suffer s.th. patiently. — *v.r. sich —,* (*obs.*) take a stroll.

ergiebig [ɛr'gi:bɪç], *adj.* rich, productive, fertile, profitable.

ergießen [ɛr'gi:sən], *v.r. irr. sich —,* discharge, flow into.

erglänzen [ɛr'glɛntsən], *v.n.* (*aux.* sein) shine forth, sparkle.

erglühen [ɛr'gly:ən], *v.n.* (*aux.* sein) glow; blush.

ergötzen [ɛr'gœtsən], *v.a.* (*obs.*) amuse, delight. — *v.r. sich — an,* delight in.

ergrauen [ɛr'grauən], *v.n.* (*aux.* sein) become grey; grow old.

ergreifen [ɛr'graɪfən], *v.a. irr.* seize, grasp, get hold of; move, touch, affect; *Maßnahmen —,* take measures.

Ergreifung [ɛr'graɪfʊŋ], *f.* (—, *no pl.*) seizure; (*measure*) adoption.

ergriffen [ɛr'grɪfən], *adj.* moved, touched, impressed.

Ergriffenheit [ɛr'grɪfənhaɪt], *f.* (—, *no pl.*) emotion.

ergrimmen [ɛr'grɪmən], *v.n.* (*aux.* sein) grow angry, be enraged.

ergründen [ɛr'gryndən], *v.a.* get to the bottom of, investigate, fathom.

Erguß [ɛr'gus], *m.* (—sses, *pl.* ˙sse) outpouring; (*fig.*) effusion.

erhaben [ɛr'ha:bən], *adj.* sublime,

exalted; majestic, elevated.

Erhabenheit [ɛr'ha:bənhaɪt], *f.* (—, *no pl.*) majesty, sublimity.

erhalten [ɛr'haltən], *v.a. irr.* receive, obtain, get, preserve; maintain, keep up. — *v.r. sich — von,* subsist on.

erhältlich [ɛr'hɛltlɪç], *adj.* obtainable.

Erhaltung [ɛr'haltʊŋ], *f.* (—, *no pl.*) preservation, conservation; (*family*) maintenance.

erhärten [ɛr'hɛrtən], *v.a.* make hard; (*fig.*) prove, confirm.

erhaschen [ɛr'haʃən], *v.a.* catch, snatch.

erheben [ɛr'he:bən], *v.a. irr.* lift up, raise; (*fig.*) elevate, exalt; *Klage —,* bring an action; *Geld —,* raise money; *Steuern —,* levy taxes. — *v.r. sich —,* rise, stand up.

erheblich [ɛr'he:plɪç], *adj.* considerable, weighty, appreciable.

Erhebung [ɛr'he:bʊŋ], *f.* (—, *pl.* —en) elevation; (*taxes*) levying; revolt, rebellion, rising.

erheischen [ɛr'haɪʃən], *v.a.* (*rare*) require, demand.

erheitern [ɛr'haɪtərn], *v.a.* cheer, exhilarate.

erhellen [ɛr'hɛlən], *v.a.* light up, illuminate; (*fig.*) enlighten. — *v.n.* become evident.

erhitzen [ɛr'hɪtsən], *v.a.* heat; (*fig.*) inflame, excite. — *v.r. sich —,* grow hot; grow angry.

erhöhen [ɛr'hø:ən], *v.a.* heighten, raise, intensify, increase; (*value*) enhance.

erholen [ɛr'ho:lən], *v.r. sich —,* recover, get better; relax (after work); take a rest.

erholungsbedürftig [ɛr'ho:lʊŋsbədyrf-tɪç], *adj.* in need of a rest.

erhören [ɛr'hø:rən], *v.a.* hear, vouchsafe, grant.

Erich ['e:rɪç], *m.* Eric.

erinnerlich [ɛr'ɪnərlɪç], *adj.* remembered; *soweit mir — ist,* as far as I can remember.

erinnern [ɛr'ɪnərn], *v.a.* remind. — *v.r. sich —,* remember, recollect, recall, call to mind.

Erinnerung [ɛr'ɪnərʊŋ], *f.* (—, *pl.* —en) remembrance; recollection; reminiscences.

erjagen [ɛr'ja:gən], *v.a.* hunt (down), chase.

erkalten [ɛr'kaltən], *v.n.* (*aux.* sein) grow cold.

erkälten [ɛr'kɛltən], *v.r. sich —,* catch cold.

Erkältung [ɛr'kɛltʊŋ], *f.* (—, *pl.* —en) cold, chill.

erkämpfen [ɛr'kɛmpfən], *v.a.* obtain by fighting; obtain by great exertion.

erkaufen [ɛr'kaufən], *v.a.* purchase; bribe, corrupt.

erkennen [ɛr'kɛnən], *v.a. irr.* recognise; perceive, distinguish, discern; (*Comm.*) credit; *zu — geben,* give to understand; *sich zu — geben,* make o.s. known. — *v.n.* (*Law*) judge; — *auf,* (*Law*) announce verdict, pass sentence.

erkenntlich [ɛr'kɛntlɪç], *adj.* grateful; (*fig.*) *sich — zeigen*, show o.s. grateful.

Erkenntlichkeit [ɛr'kɛntlɪçkaɪt], *f.* (—, *no pl.*) gratitude.

Erkenntnis [ɛr'kɛntnɪs], *f.* (—, *pl.* —e) perception, knowledge, comprehension, understanding; realisation, (*Phil.*) cognition.

Erkennung [ɛr'kɛnuŋ], *f.* (—, *no pl.*) recognition.

Erker ['ɛrkər], *m.* (—s, *pl.* —) alcove, bay, turret.

Erkerfenster ['ɛrkərfɛnstər], *n.* (—s, *pl.* —) bay-window.

erklären [ɛr'klɛːrən], *v.a.* explain, expound, account for; make a statement on, declare, state.

erklärlich [ɛr'klɛːrlɪç], *adj.* explicable.

Erklärung [ɛr'klɛːruŋ], *f.* (—, *pl.* —en) explanation; declaration, statement; (*income tax*) return.

erklecklich [ɛr'klɛklɪç], *adj.* considerable.

erklettern [ɛr'klɛtərn], *v.a.* climb.

erklimmen [ɛr'klɪmən], *v.a. irr.* climb.

erklingen [ɛr'klɪŋən], *v.n. irr.* (*aux. sein*) sound, resound.

erkoren [ɛr'koːrən], *adj.* select, chosen.

erkranken [ɛr'kraŋkən], *v.n.* (*aux. sein*) fall ill.

erkühnen [ɛr'kyːnən], *v.r. sich —*, dare, make bold, venture.

erkunden [ɛr'kundən], *v.a.* explore, find out; (*Mil.*) reconnoitre.

erkundigen [ɛr'kundɪgən], *v.r. sich —*, enquire (about), make enquiries.

erlaben [ɛr'laːbən], *v.r. sich —*, (*obs.*) refresh o.s.

erlahmen [ɛr'laːmən], *v.n.* (*aux. sein*) become lame; lose o.'s drive; grow tired.

erlangen [ɛr'laŋən], *v.a.* reach, gain, obtain; acquire; attain.

Erlaß [ɛr'las], *m.* (—sses, *pl.* ⸗sse) remission, exemption, release, dispensation; (*Comm.*) deduction; (*Law, Pol.*) proclamation, edict, decree, writ; (*Eccl.*) indulgence; remission.

erlassen [ɛr'lasən], *v.a. irr.* remit, release, let off; (*Law, Pol.*) enact, promulgate.

erläßlich [ɛr'lɛslɪç], *adj.* remissible, dispensable, venial.

erlauben [ɛr'laubən], *v.a.* permit, allow; *sich etwas —*, take the liberty of, make bold to; have the impertinence to.

Erlaubnis [ɛr'laupnɪs], *f.* (—, *no pl.*) permission, leave, permit; *die — haben*, be permitted; *um — bitten*, beg leave; *mit Ihrer —*, by your leave.

erlaucht [ɛr'lauxt], *adj.* illustrious, noble.

erlauschen [ɛr'lauʃən], *v.a.* overhear.

erläutern [ɛr'lɔytərn], *v.a.* explain, illustrate, elucidate.

Erle ['ɛrlə], *f.* (—, *pl.* —n) (*Bot.*) alder.

erleben [ɛr'leːbən], *v.a.* live to see; go through, experience.

Erlebnis [ɛr'leːpnɪs], *n.* (—sses, *pl.* —sse) experience, adventure, occurrence.

erledigen [ɛr'leːdɪgən], *v.a.* settle, finish off, clear up; dispatch; execute (commission etc.).

erledigt [ɛr'leːdɪçt], *adj.* (*coll.*) worn-out; exhausted.

erlegen [ɛr'leːgən], *v.a.* slay; pay down.

erleichtern [ɛr'laɪçtərn], *v.a.* lighten, ease, facilitate.

erleiden [ɛr'laɪdən], *v.a. irr.* suffer, endure, bear, undergo.

erlernen [ɛr'lɛrnən], *v.a.* learn, acquire.

erlesen [ɛr'leːzən], *v.a. irr.* select, choose. — *adj.* select, choice.

erleuchten [ɛr'lɔyçtən], *v.a.* illumine, illuminate, floodlight; (*fig.*) enlighten, inspire.

erliegen [ɛr'liːgən], *v.n. irr.* (*aux. sein*) succumb.

Erlkönig ['ɛrlkøːnɪç], *m.* (—s, *pl.* —e) fairy-king, elf-king.

erlogen [ɛr'loːgən], *adj.* false, untrue; trumped-up.

Erlös [ɛr'løːs], *m.* (—es, *no pl.*) proceeds.

erlöschen [ɛr'lœʃən], *v.n. irr.* (*aux. sein*) be extinguished, die out; (*fire*) go out; (*contract*) expire.

erlösen [ɛr'løːzən], *v.a.* redeem; release, save, deliver.

ermächtigen [ɛr'mɛçtɪgən], *v.a.* empower; authorise.

ermahnen [ɛr'maːnən], *v.a.* admonish, exhort, remind.

ermäßigen [ɛr'mɛːsɪgən], *v.a.* reduce.

ermatten [ɛr'matən], *v.a.* weaken, weary, tire. — *v.n.* (*aux. sein*) grow weak, become tired.

Ermessen [ɛr'mɛsən], *n.* (—s, *no pl.*) judgment, opinion.

ermitteln [ɛr'mɪtəln], *v.a.* ascertain, find out.

ermöglichen [ɛr'møːklɪçən], *v.a.* make possible.

ermorden [ɛr'mɔrdən], *v.a.* murder.

ermüden [ɛr'myːdən], *v.a.* tire, fatigue. — *v.n.* (*aux. sein*) get tired, grow weary.

ermuntern [ɛr'muntərn], *v.a.* encourage, cheer up.

ermutigen [ɛr'muːtɪgən], *v.a.* encourage.

ernähren [ɛr'nɛːrən], *v.a.* nourish, feed.

ernennen [ɛr'nɛnən], *v.a. irr.* nominate, appoint.

erneuern [ɛr'nɔyərn], *v.a.* renew, repair, renovate.

erniedrigen [ɛr'niːdrɪgən], *v.a.* humble, humiliate, degrade. — *v.r. sich —*, humble o.s., abase o.s.

Ernst (1) [ɛrnst], *m.* Ernest.

Ernst (2) [ɛrnst], *m.* (—es, *no pl.*) earnestness, seriousness.

ernst [ɛrnst], *adj.* earnest, serious.

Ernte ['ɛrntə], *f.* (—, *pl.* —n) harvest, crop.

ernüchtern [ɛr'nʏçtərn], *v.a.* sober; (*fig.*) disenchant, disillusion.

erobern [ɛr'oːbərn], *v.a.* (*Mil.*) conquer; take, win.

eröffnen [ɛr'œfnən], *v.a.* open, inaugurate; inform, reveal.

erörtern [ɛr'œrtərn], *v.a.* discuss, debate, argue.

65

erpicht [ɛrˈpɪçt], *adj.* eager for, bent on.

erpressen [ɛrˈprɛsən], *v.a.* extort, blackmail.

erquicken [ɛrˈkvɪkən], *v.a.* refresh.

erraten [ɛrˈraːtən], *v.a. irr.* guess.

erregen [ɛrˈreːgən], *v.a.* cause; stir up, excite, agitate; provoke.

erreichen [ɛrˈraɪçən], *v.a.* reach, arrive at; (*fig.*) attain, reach.

erretten [ɛrˈrɛtən], *v.a.* save, rescue.

errichten [ɛrˈrɪçtən], *v.a.* erect, raise, build.

erringen [ɛrˈrɪŋən], *v.a. irr.* obtain (by exertion), achieve.

erröten [ɛrˈrøːtən], *v.n.* (*aux.* sein) blush, redden.

Errungenschaft [ɛrˈruŋənʃaft], *f.* (—, *pl.* —en) achievement, acquisition.

Ersatz [ɛrˈzats], *m.* (—es, *no pl.*) substitute; compensation, amends; (*Mil. etc.*) replacement.

erschallen [ɛrˈʃalən], *v.n.* (*aux.* sein) resound, sound.

erschaudern [ɛrˈʃaudərn], *v.n.* (*aux.* sein) be seized with horror.

erscheinen [ɛrˈʃaɪnən], *v.n. irr.* (*aux.* sein) appear, make o.'s appearance; seem; be published.

erschießen [ɛrˈʃiːsən], *v.a. irr.* shoot dead.

erschlaffen [ɛrˈʃlafən], *v.n.* (*aux.* sein) flag, slacken.

erschlagen [ɛrˈʃlaːgən], *v.a. irr.* slay, kill.

erschließen [ɛrˈʃliːsən], *v.a. irr.* open up.

erschöpfen [ɛrˈʃœpfən], *v.a.* exhaust.

erschrecken [ɛrˈʃrɛkən], *v.a. irr.* startle, shock, terrify. — *v.n.* (*aux.* sein) be startled, be frightened, be terrified.

erschüttern [ɛrˈʃʏtərn], *v.a.* shake; (*fig.*) move, affect strongly.

erschweren [ɛrˈʃveːrən], *v.a.* (*fig.*) aggravate, make more difficult.

erschwingen [ɛrˈʃvɪŋən], *v.a.* afford, be able to pay.

erschwinglich [ɛrˈʃvɪŋlɪç], *adj.* attainable, within o.'s means.

ersehen [ɛrˈzeːən], *v.a. irr.* — *aus*, gather (from).

ersehnen [ɛrˈzeːnən], *v.a.* long for, yearn for.

ersetzen [ɛrˈzɛtsən], *v.a.* replace, take the place of; restore, make good; repair; (*money*) refund.

ersichtlich [ɛrˈzɪçtlɪç], *adj.* evident.

ersinnen [ɛrˈzɪnən], *v.a. irr.* think out; imagine, devise, contrive.

ersparen [ɛrˈʃpaːrən], *v.a.* save.

ersprießlich [ɛrˈʃpriːslɪç], *adj.* useful, profitable, beneficial.

erst [eːrst], *num. adj.* first. — *adv.* first, at first, only, but; — *jetzt*, only now; *nun — recht*, now more than ever.

erstatten [ɛrˈʃtatən], *v.a.* reimburse, compensate, repay; *Bericht —*, report.

Erstattung [ɛrˈʃtatuŋ], *f.* (—, *pl.* —en) reimbursement, restitution.

Erstaufführung [ˈeːrstauffyːruŋ], *f.* (—, *pl.* —en) (*Theat.*) first night; première.

Erstaunen [ɛrˈʃtaunən], *n.* (—s, *no pl.*) amazement, astonishment, surprise.

erstechen [ɛrˈʃtɛçən], *v.a. irr.* stab.

erstehen [ɛrˈʃteːən], *v.n. irr.* (*aux.* sein) rise, arise. — *v.a.* buy, purchase.

ersteigen [ɛrˈʃtaɪgən], *v.a. irr.* climb, mount, ascend.

ersticken [ɛrˈʃtɪkən], *v.a. irr.* choke, stifle, suffocate. — *v.n.* (*aux.* sein) choke, suffocate.

erstmalig [ˈeːrstmaːlɪç], *adj.* first. — *adv.* for the first time.

erstreben [ɛrˈʃtreːbən], *v.a.* strive after.

erstrecken [ɛrˈʃtrɛkən], *v.r. sich —*, extend, reach to.

ersuchen [ɛrˈzuːxən], *v.a.* request, ask.

ertappen [ɛrˈtapən], *v.a.* catch, detect.

erteilen [ɛrˈtaɪlən], *v.a.* bestow, impart; *einen Auftrag —*, issue an order; *Unterricht —*, instruct; *die Erlaubnis —*, give permission.

ertönen [ɛrˈtøːnən], *v.n.* (*aux.* sein) sound, resound.

Ertrag [ɛrˈtraːk], *m.* (—s, *pl.* ᵉe) produce; returns, yield; output; (*sale*) proceeds.

ertragen [ɛrˈtraːgən], *v.a. irr.* bear, suffer, endure.

ertränken [ɛrˈtrɛŋkən], *v.a.* drown.

ertrinken [ɛrˈtrɪŋkən], *v.n. irr.* (*aux.* sein) drown, be drowned.

erübrigen [ɛrˈyːbrɪgən], *v.a.* save, spare.

erwachen [ɛrˈvaxən], *v.n.* (*aux.* sein) awake, wake up.

erwachsen [ɛrˈvaksən], *adj.* grown-up, adult. — *v.n. irr.* grow up; ensue, follow, arise.

erwägen [ɛrˈvɛːgən], *v.a. irr.* weigh, ponder, consider.

erwähnen [ɛrˈvɛːnən], *v.a.* mention.

erwärmen [ɛrˈvɛrmən], *v.a.* warm (up), make warm.

erwarten [ɛrˈvartən], *v.a.* expect, await.

Erwartung [ɛrˈvartuŋ], *f.* (—, *pl.* —en) expectation.

erwecken [ɛrˈvɛkən], *v.a.* wake up, awaken, raise; rouse.

erwehren [ɛrˈveːrən], *v.r. sich —* (*Genit.*), defend o.s.; *ich kann mich des Lachens nicht —*, I cannot help laughing.

erweichen [ɛrˈvaɪçən], *v.a.* soften.

erweisen [ɛrˈvaɪzən], *v.a. irr.* prove, show; demonstrate.

erweitern [ɛrˈvaɪtərn], *v.a.* widen, enlarge, expand.

erwerben [ɛrˈvɛrbən], *v.a. irr.* acquire.

erwidern [ɛrˈviːdərn], *v.a.* reply, answer; return.

erwirken [ɛrˈvɪrkən], *v.a.* effect, secure.

erwischen [ɛrˈvɪʃən], *v.a. see* ertappen.

erwünschen [ɛrˈvʏnʃən], *v.a.* desire, wish for.

erwürgen [ɛrˈvʏrgən], *v.a.* strangle, throttle.

Erz [ɛrts], (—es, *pl.* —e) ore; brass, bronze.

erzählen [ɛrˈtsɛːlən], *v.a.* narrate, relate, tell.

Erzbischof [ˈɛrtsbɪʃɔf], *m.* (**—s**, *pl.* ⁓e) archbishop.

erzeugen [ɛrˈtsɔygən], *v.a.* engender; beget; produce; (*Elec.*) generate.

Erzherzog [ˈɛrtshɛrtsoːk], *m.* (**—s**, *pl.* ⁓e) archduke.

erziehen [ɛrˈtsiːən], *v.a. irr.* educate, train, bring up, rear.

Erziehungsanstalt [ɛrˈtsiːuŋsanʃtalt], *f.* (**—**, *pl.* **—en**) approved school, reformatory.

erzielen [ɛrˈtsiːlən], *v.a.* obtain; fetch, realize (a price); *Gewinn* —, make a profit.

erzittern [ɛrˈtsɪtərn], *v.n.* (*aux.* sein) tremble, shake.

Erzofen [ˈɛrtsoːfən], *m.* (**—s**, *pl.* ⁓n) furnace.

erzürnen [ɛrˈtsyrnən], *v.a.* make angry. — *v.r. sich* —, grow angry.

Erzvater [ˈɛrtsfaːtər], *m.* (**—s**, *pl.* ⁓) patriarch.

erzwingen [ɛrˈtsvɪŋən], *v.a. irr.* enforce, compel.

es [ɛs], *pron.* it; — *gibt*, there is; — *sind*, there are; — *lebe*, long live!

Es [ɛs], *n.* (—, *pl.* —) (*Mus.*) E flat.

Esche [ˈɛʃə], *f.* (**—**, *pl.* **—n**) (*Bot.*) ash, ashtree.

Esel [ˈeːzəl], *m.* (**—s**, *pl.* **—**) ass, donkey.

Eselsohr [ˈeːzəlsoːr], *n.* (**—s**, *pl.* **—en**) (*fig.*) dog's ear.

Eskadron [ɛskaˈdroːn], *f.* (**—**, *pl.* **—en**) squadron.

Espe [ˈɛspə], *f.* (**—**, *pl.* **—n**) (*Bot.*) asp, aspen.

eßbar [ˈɛsbaːr], *adj.* edible.

Esse [ˈɛsə], *f.* (—, *pl.* **—n**) chimney, forge.

Essen [ˈɛsən], *n.* (**—s**, *no pl.*) meal; eating.

essen [ˈɛsən], *v.a. irr.* eat, have a meal.

Essenz [ɛˈsɛnts], *f.* (—, *pl.* **—en**) essence.

Essig [ˈɛsɪç], *m.* (**—s**, *no pl.*) vinegar.

Eßlöffel [ˈɛslœfəl], *m.* (**—s**, *pl.* **—**) table-spoon.

Estland [ˈɛstlant], *n.* Estonia.

Estrade [ɛˈstraːdə], *f.* (—, *pl.* **—n**) platform.

Estrich [ˈɛstrɪç], *m.* (**—s**, *no pl.*) floor, flooring, plaster-floor.

etablieren [etaˈbliːrən], *v.a.* establish, set up (business).

Etagenwohnung [eˈtaːʒənvoːnuŋ], *f.* (—, *pl.* **—en**) flat; (*Am.*) apartment.

Etappe [eˈtapə], *f.* (—, *pl.* **—n**) stage; (*Mil.*) lines of communication.

Etat [eˈtaː], *m.* (**—s**, *pl.* **—s**) (*Parl.*) estimates, budget; (*Comm.*) statement, balance sheet.

ethisch [ˈeːtɪʃ], *adj.* ethical.

Etikett [etiˈkɛt], *n.* (**—s**, *pl.* **—s**) label, ticket, tag.

Etikette [etiˈkɛtə], *f.* (—, *no pl.*) etiquette; ceremonial.

etikettieren [etikɛˈtiːrən], *v.a.* label.

etliche [ˈɛtlɪçə], *pl. adj. & pron.* some, several, sundry.

Etui [eˈtviː], *n.* (—, *pl.* **—s**) small case, small box.

etwa [ˈɛtva], *adv.* nearly, about; perhaps, perchance, in some way.

etwaig [ˈɛtvaɪç], *adj.* possible, any, eventual.

etwas [ˈɛtvas], *indef. pron.* some, something. — *adj.* some, any. — *adv.* a little, somewhat.

Etzel [ˈɛtsəl], *m.* Attila.

euch [ɔyç], *pers. pron. pl. Dat. & Acc.* you, yourselves.

euer [ˈɔyər], *poss. adj.* your. — *poss. pron.* yours.

Eule [ˈɔylə], *f.* (—, *pl.* **—n**) owl.

eurige [ˈɔyrɪgə], *poss. pron. der, die, das* —, yours.

Europa [ɔyˈroːpa], *n.* Europe.

Euter [ˈɔytər], *n.* (**—s**, *pl.* **—**) udder.

evangelisch [evanˈgeːlɪʃ], *adj.* Evangelical, Protestant.

Evangelium [evanˈgeːljum], *n.* (**—s**, *pl.* **—lien**) gospel.

eventuell [evɛntuˈɛl], *adj.* possible.

ewig [ˈeːvɪç], *adj.* eternal; perpetual.

Ewigkeit [ˈeːvɪçkaɪt], *f.* (—, *pl.* **—en**) eternity.

explodieren [ɛksploˈdiːrən], *v.n.* explode; detonate.

exponieren [ɛkspoˈniːrən], *v.a.* set forth, explain at length.

Extemporale [ɛkstɛmpoˈraːlə], *n.* (**—s**, *pl.* **—lien**) unprepared exercise.

extrahieren [ɛkstraˈhiːrən], *v.a.* extract.

Extremitäten [ɛkstremiˈtɛːtən], *f. pl.* extremities.

F

F [ɛf], *n.* (**—s**, *pl.* **—s**) the letter F; (*Mus.*) F *Dur*, F major; F *Moll*, F minor.

Fabel [ˈfaːbəl], *f.* (—, *pl.* **—n**) fable; (*fig.*) tale, fiction; (*drama*) plot, story.

fabelhaft [ˈfaːbəlhaft], *adj.* fabulous; phenomenal, gorgeous.

fabeln [ˈfaːbəln], *v.n.* tell fables; talk nonsense.

Fabrik [faˈbriːk], *f.* (—, *pl.* **—en**) factory; plant, works.

Fabrikant [fabriˈkant], *m.* (**—en**, *pl.* **—en**) manufacturer.

fabrizieren [fabriˈtsiːrən], *v.a.* manufacture, make.

fabulieren [fabuˈliːrən], *v.n.* tell fables; (*fig.*) tell tall stories.

Fach [fax], *n.* (**—s**, *pl.* ⁓er) compartment; pigeon-hole, drawer; (*fig.*) subject of study, department, branch.

Fachausdruck [ˈfaxausdruk], *m.* (**—s**, *pl.* ⁓e) technical term.

Fächer ['fɛçər], *m.* (—s, *pl.* —) fan.

Fächertaube ['fɛçərtaubə], *f.* (—, *pl.* —n) fantail.

Fachmann ['faxman], *m.* (—s, *pl.* ̈er *or* **Fachleute**) expert, specialist.

Fachschule ['faxʃuːlə], *f.* (—, *pl.* —n) technical school.

fachsimpeln ['faxzɪmpəln], *v.n.* talk shop.

Fachwerk ['faxvɛrk], *n.* (—s, *no pl.*) timbered framework.

Fackel ['fakəl], *f.* (—, *pl.* —n) torch.

fade ['faːdə], *adj.* tasteless; boring, insipid.

Faden ['faːdən], *m.* (—s, *pl.* ̈) thread; (*measure*) fathom.

fadenscheinig ['faːdənʃaɪnɪç], *adj.* threadbare.

Fagott [fa'gɔt], *n.* (—s, *pl.* —e) (*Mus.*) bassoon.

fähig ['fɛːɪç], *adj.* able, capable; talented, gifted, competent.

fahl [faːl], *adj.* pale, sallow.

Fähnchen ['fɛːnçən], *n.* (—s, *pl.* —) small banner; pennon; (*Mil.*) (*obs.*) small troop.

fahnden ['faːndən], *v.a.* search for (officially).

Fahne ['faːnə], *f.* (—, *pl.* —n) flag, banner, standard, colours; (*weather*) vane; (*Typ.*) galley proof.

Fahnenflucht ['faːnənfluxt], *f.* (—, *no pl.*) (*Mil.*) desertion.

Fähnrich ['fɛːnrɪç], *m.* (—s, *pl.* —e) ensign.

Fahrbahn ['faːrbaːn], *f.* (—, *pl.* —en) traffic lane, roadway.

fahrbar ['faːrbaːr], *adj.* passable, navigable, negotiable.

Fähre ['fɛːrə], *f.* (—, *pl.* —n) ferry, ferry-boat.

fahren, ['faːrən], *v.a. irr.* drive. — *v.n.* (*aux.* sein) (*vehicle*) ride (in), be driven; (*vessel*) sail; go, travel.

Fahrer ['faːrər], *m.* (—s, *pl.* —) driver, chauffeur.

Fahrgast ['faːrgast], *m.* (—s, *pl.* ̈e) passenger.

fahrig ['faːrɪç], *adj.* absent-minded, giddy, thoughtless.

Fahrkarte ['faːrkartə], *f.* (—, *pl.* —n) ticket.

fahrlässig ['faːrlɛsɪç], *adj.* negligent, careless.

Fährmann ['fɛːrman], *m.* (—s, *pl.* ̈er) ferry-man.

Fahrplan ['faːrplaːn], *m.* (—s, *pl.* ̈e) timetable, railway-guide.

fahrplanmäßig ['faːrplanmɛːsɪç], *adj.* according to the timetable, scheduled.

Fahrpreis ['faːrpraɪs], *m.* (—es, *pl.* —e) cost of ticket, fare.

Fahrrad ['faːrraːt], *n.* (—s, *pl.* ̈er) cycle, bicycle.

Fahrschein ['faːrʃaɪn], *m.* (—s, *pl.* —e) ticket.

Fahrstraße ['faːrʃtrasə], *f.* (—, *pl.* —n) roadway.

Fahrstuhl ['faːrʃtuːl], *m.* (—s, *pl.* ̈e) lift; (*Am.*) elevator.

Fahrt [faːrt], *f.* (—, *pl.* —en) drive, ride, journey; (*sea*) voyage, cruise.

Fährte ['fɛːrtə], *f.* (—, *pl.* —n) track, trace, trail.

Fahrzeug ['faːrtsɔyk], *n.* (—s, *pl.* —e) vehicle, conveyance; vessel, craft.

faktisch ['faktɪʃ], *adj.* real, actual.

Faktor ['faktɔr], *m.* (—s, *pl.* —en) foreman, overseer, factor; (*Maths.*) factor, component part.

Faktura [fak'tuːra], *f.* (—, *pl.* —ren) (*Comm.*) invoice.

fakturieren [faktu'riːrən], *v.a.* (*Comm.*) invoice.

Fakultät [fakul'tɛːt], *f.* (—, *pl.* —en) (*Univ.*) faculty.

fakultativ [fakulta'tiːf], *adj.* optional.

Falbel ['falbəl], *f.* (—, *pl.* —n) flounce, furbelow.

Falke ['falkə], *m.* (—n, *pl.* —n) (*Orn.*) falcon, hawk.

Fall [fal], *m.* (—s, *pl.* ̈e) fall, falling; case; (*Geog.*) decline, incline, gradient; (*fig.*) fall, decline, downfall, failure.

Fallbaum ['falbaum], *m.* (—s, *pl.* ̈e) tollbar, turnpike.

Fallbeil ['falbaɪl], *n.* (—s, *pl.* —e) guillotine.

Fallbrücke ['falbrykə], *f.* (—, *pl.* —n) draw-bridge.

Falle ['falə], *f.* (—, *pl.* —n) trap, snare.

fallen ['falən], *v.n. irr.* (*aux.* sein) fall, drop; (*Mil.*) be killed.

fällen ['fɛlən], *v.a.* fell, cut down, hew down; *ein Urteil* —, (*Law*) pronounce judgment.

Fallensteller ['falənʃtɛlər], *m.* (—s, *pl.* —) trapper.

fallieren [fa'liːrən], *v.n.* become bankrupt.

fällig ['fɛlɪç], *adj.* due, payable.

Fälligkeit ['fɛlɪçkaɪt], *f.* (—, *pl.* —en) (*Comm.*) maturity.

Fallobst ['falo:pst], *n.* (—es, *no pl.*) windfall (of fruit).

falls [fals], *conj.* in case, if.

Fallschirm ['falʃɪrm], *m.* (—s, *pl.* —e) parachute.

Fallstrick ['falʃtrɪk], *m.* (—s, *pl.* —e) snare, trap.

Fallsucht ['falzuxt], *f.* (—, *no pl.*) (*Med.*) epilepsy.

Falltür ['faltyːr], *f.* (—, *pl.* —en) trap-door.

Fällung ['fɛluŋ], *f.* (—, *pl.* —en) cutting down.

falsch [falʃ], *adj.* false, incorrect, wrong; disloyal; counterfeit.

fälschen ['fɛlʃən], *v.a.* falsify, forge, tamper with.

Falschheit ['falʃhaɪt], *f.* (—, *pl.* —en) falsehood, deceit, disloyalty.

fälschlich ['fɛlʃlɪç], *adv.* wrongly, falsely.

Fälschung ['fɛlʃuŋ], *f.* (—, *pl.* —en) falsification; forgery.

Falte ['faltə], *f.* (—, *pl.* —n) fold, pleat; (*face*) wrinkle.

falten ['faltən], *v.a.* fold, plait, pleat; wrinkle.

Falter ['faltər], *m.* (—s, *pl.* —) (*Ent.*) butterfly.

-fältig [fɛltɪç], *suffix (following numbers).* -fold (*e.g. vierfältig,* fourfold).

Falz [falts], *m.* (—es, *pl.* —e) groove, notch; joint.

Falzbein ['faltsbaɪn], *n.* (—s, *pl.* —e) paper-folder, paper-knife.

Falzmaschine ['faltsmaʃi:nə], *f.* (—, *pl.* —n) folding-machine.

familiär [famil'jɛːr], *adj.* familiar, intimate.

Familie [fa'miːljə], *f.* (—, *pl.* —n) family.

famos [fa'moːs], *adj.* (*coll.*) excellent, splendid.

fanatisch [fa'naːtɪʃ], *adj.* fanatic(al), bigoted.

Fanatismus [fana'tɪsmŭs], *m.* (—, *no pl.*) fanaticism.

Fang [faŋ], *m.* (—es, *pl.* ᵕe) catch, capture; (*bird*) talon, claw.

fangen ['faŋən], *v.a. irr.* catch, seize.

Fangzahn ['faŋtsaːn], *m.* (—s, *pl.* ᵕe) fang, tusk.

Fant [fant], *m.* (—s, *pl.* —e) fop, cockscomb.

Farbe ['farbə], *f.* (—, *pl.* —n) colour, hue, paint, dye.

färben ['fɛrbən], *v.a.* dye, stain.

Farbenbrett ['farbənbrɛt], *n.* (—s, *pl.* —er) palette.

Farb(en)druck ['farpdruk, farbəndruk], *m.* (—s, *pl.* —e) colour-printing.

Farbenspiel ['farbənʃpiːl], *n.* (—s, *no pl.*) iridescence.

Färber ['fɛrbər], *m.* (—s, *pl.* —) dyer.

farbig ['farbɪç], *adj.* coloured.

Farbstift ['farpʃtɪft], *m.* (—s, *pl.* —e) crayon.

Farbstoff ['farpʃtɔf], *m.* (—es, *pl.* —e) dye.

Farbton ['farptoːn], *m.* (—s, *pl.* ᵕe) hue, tone, tinge, shade.

Farn [farn], *m.* (—s, *pl.* —e) (*Bot.*) fern.

Färse ['fɛrzə], *f.* (—, *pl.* —n) (*Zool.*) heifer.

Fasan [fa'zaːn], *m.* (—s, *pl.* —e) (*Orn.*) pheasant.

Fasching ['faʃɪŋ], *m.* (—s, *no pl.*) (Shrovetide) carnival.

Faschismus [fa'ʃɪsmus], *m.* (—s, *no pl.*) fascism.

Faselei [faːzə'laɪ], *f.* (—, *pl.* —en) silly talk, drivel.

faseln ['faːzəln], *v.n.* drivel.

Faser ['faːzər], *f.* (—, *pl.* —n) thread; string; fibre, filament.

fasern ['faːzərn], *v.n.* fray.

Faß [fas], *n.* (—sses, *pl.* ᵕsser) barrel, vat, tun, tub, cask, keg; *Bier vom* —, draught beer; *Wein vom* —, wine from the wood.

Fassade [fa'saːdə], *f.* (—, *pl.* —n) façade.

faßbar ['fasbaːr], *adj.* tangible.

Faßbinder ['fasbɪndər], *m.* (—s, *pl.* —) cooper.

fassen ['fasən], *v.a.* seize, take hold of, grasp; (*jewels*) set; contain, hold. — *v.r.* (*aux. haben*) *sich* —, compose o.s.; *sich kurz* —, be brief.

faßlich ['faslɪç], *adj.* comprehensible, understandable.

Fasson [fa'sɔ̃], *f.* (—, *pl.* —s) fashion; (*fig.*) cut, style.

Fassung ['fasuŋ], *f.* (—, *pl.* —en) (*jewels*) setting; (*speech*) wording, version; (*fig.*) composure.

fassungslos ['fasuŋsloːs], *adj.* bewildered, disconcerted; distraught, speechless.

fast [fast], *adv.* almost, nearly.

fasten ['fastən], *v.n.* fast.

Fastenzeit ['fastəntsaɪt], *f.* (—, *pl.* —en) time of fasting; Lent.

Fastnacht ['fastnaxt], *f.* (—, *no pl.*) Shrove Tuesday; Shrovetide.

fauchen ['fauxən], *v.n.* spit, hiss.

faul [faul], *adj.* (*food*) rotten, putrid, decayed; (*persons*) lazy, idle.

Fäule ['fɔylə], *f.* (—, *no pl.*) rot.

faulen ['faulən], *v.n.* (*aux. sein*) rot.

faulenzen ['faulɛntsən], *v.n.* laze, idle.

Faulenzer ['faulɛntsər], *m.* (—s, *pl.* —) idler, sluggard, lazybones.

Faulenzerei ['faulɛntsəraɪ], *f.* (—, *pl.* —en) idleness, laziness.

Faulheit ['faulhaɪt], *f.* (—, *no pl.*) idleness, laziness, sluggishness.

faulig ['faulɪç], *adj.* putrid, rotten.

Fäulnis ['fɔylnɪs], *f.* (—, *no pl.*) rottenness, putridity.

Faust [faust], *f.* (—, *pl.* ᵕe) fist.

Fäustchen ['fɔystçən], *n.* (—s, *pl.* —) small fist; *sich ins* — *lachen,* laugh in o.'s sleeve.

Faustkampf ['faustkampf], *m.* (—es, *pl.* ᵕe) boxing (match).

Faxen ['faksən], *f.* (—) foolery; — *machen,* play the buffoon.

Fazit ['fatsɪt], *n.* (—s, *no pl.*) sum, amount.

Februar ['feːbruaːr], *m.* (—s, *no pl.*) February.

fechten ['fɛçtən], *v.n. irr.* fight; fence; (*fig.*) beg.

Feder ['feːdər], *f.* (—, *pl.* —n) (*bird*) feather; (*hat*) plume; (*writing*) pen; (*antique*) quill; (*Tech.*) spring.

Federball ['feːdərbal], *m.* (—s, *pl.* ᵕe) shuttle-cock.

federig ['feːdərɪç], *adj.* feathery; (*Tech.*) springy, resilient.

Federlesen(s) ['feːdərleːzən(s)], *n.* (—s, *no pl.*) *nicht viel* — *machen,* make short work of.

Fee [feː], *f.* (—, *pl.* —n) fairy.

feenhaft ['feːənhaft], *adj.* fairy-like, magical.

Fegefeuer ['feːgəfɔyər], *n.* (—s, *no pl.*) purgatory.

fegen ['feːgən], *v.a.* clean, sweep. — *v.n.* (*aux. sein*) tear along.

Fehde ['feːdə], *f.* (—, *pl.* —n) feud, quarrel.

Fehdehandschuh ['feːdəhantʃuː], *m.* (—s, *pl.* —e) gauntlet.

fehlbar [ˈfeːlbaːr], *adj.* fallible.
Fehlbetrag [ˈfeːlbətraːk], *m.* (—s, *pl.* ⸚e) deficit.
fehlen [ˈfeːlən], *v.a.* miss. — *v.n.* err, do wrong; be absent; be wanting; *er fehlt mir*, I miss him.
Fehler [ˈfeːlər], *m.* (—s, *pl.* —) fault, defect; mistake, error.
Fehlgeburt [ˈfeːlɡəburt], *f.* (—, *pl.* —en) miscarriage.
Fehlschlag [ˈfeːlʃlaːk], *m.* (—s, *pl.* ⸚e) failure, disappointment.
feien [ˈfaɪən], *v.a. einen — gegen*, charm s.o. against; *gefeit*, proof.
Feier [ˈfaɪər], *f.* (—, *pl.* —n) celebration, festival, holiday, festive day.
Feierabend [ˈfaɪəraːbənt], *m.* (—s, *pl.* —e) time for leaving off work; *— machen*, knock off (work).
feierlich [ˈfaɪərlɪç], *adj.* festive, solemn, stately.
feiern [ˈfaɪərn], *v.a.* celebrate; honour, praise. — *v.n.* rest from work.
Feiertag [ˈfaɪərtaːk], *m.* (—s, *pl.* —e) holiday, festive day.
feig [faɪk], *adj.* cowardly.
Feige [ˈfaɪɡə], *f.* (—, *pl.* —n) (*Bot.*) fig.
Feigheit [ˈfaɪkhaɪt], *f.* (—, *pl.* —en) cowardice, cowardliness.
Feigling [ˈfaɪklɪŋ], *m.* (—s, *pl.* —e) coward.
Feigwurz [ˈfaɪkvurts], *m.* (—es, *no pl.*) (*Bot.*) fennel.
feil [faɪl], *adj.* (*obs.*) for sale; venal.
feilbieten [ˈfaɪlbiːtən], *v.a.* offer for sale.
Feile [ˈfaɪlə], *f.* (—, *pl.* —n) file.
feilen [ˈfaɪlən], *v.a.* file.
feilhalten [ˈfaɪlhaltən], *v.a.* have for sale, be ready to sell.
feilschen [ˈfaɪlʃən], *v.n.* bargain, haggle.
Feilspäne [ˈfaɪlʃpɛːnə], *m. pl.* filings.
fein [faɪn], *adj.* fine; neat, pretty, nice; — delicate; (*clothes*) elegant; (*behaviour*) refined, polished.
Feinbäckerei [ˈfaɪnbɛkəraɪ], *f.* (—, *pl.* —en) confectioner's shop.
Feind [faɪnt], *m.* (—es, *pl.* —e) enemy, foe, adversary.
Feindschaft [ˈfaɪntʃaft], *f.* (—, *pl.* —en) enmity, hostility.
feindselig [ˈfaɪntzeːlɪç], *adj.* hostile, malignant.
feinfühlend [ˈfaɪnfyːlənt], *adj.* delicate, sensitive.
Feinheit [ˈfaɪnhaɪt], *f.* (—, *pl.* —en) fineness, elegance, politeness, delicacy.
Feinschmecker [ˈfaɪnʃmɛkər], *m.* (—s, *pl.* —), gourmet.
Feinsliebchen [faɪnsˈliːpçən], *n.* (—, *pl.* —) (*Poet. obs.*) sweetheart.
feist [faɪst], *adj.* fat, obese.
Feld [fɛlt], *n.* (—es, *pl.* —er) field, plain; (*chess*) square; (*fig.*) sphere, province.
Feldbett [ˈfɛltbɛt], *n.* (—s, *pl.* —en) camp-bed.
Feldherr [ˈfɛlther], *m.* (—n, *pl.* —en) commander, general.

Feldmesser [ˈfɛltmɛsər], *m.* (—s, *pl.* —) land-surveyor.
Feldscher [ˈfɛltʃeːr], *m.* (—s, *pl.* —e) army-surgeon.
Feldstecher [ˈfɛltʃtɛçər], *m.* (—s, *pl.* —) field-glass(es).
Feldwebel [ˈfɛltveːbəl], *m.* (—s, *pl.* —) sergeant-major.
Feldzug [ˈfɛlttsuːk], *m.* (—es, *pl.* ⸚e) campaign, expedition.
Felge [ˈfɛlɡə], *f.* (—, *pl.* —n) (*wheel*) felloe, felly, rim.
Fell [fɛl], *n.* (—s, *pl.* —e) hide, skin, pelt.
Felsabhang [ˈfɛlsaphaŋ], *m.* (—s, *pl.* ⸚e) rocky slope.
Felsen [ˈfɛlzən], *m.* (—s, *pl.* —) rock, cliff.
Felsengebirge [ˈfɛlzənɡəbɪrɡə], *n.* Rocky Mountains.
Felsenriff [ˈfɛlzənrɪf], *n.* (—s, *pl.* —e) reef.
felsig [ˈfɛlzɪç], *adj.* rocky.
Feme [ˈfeːmə], *f.* (—, *pl.* —n) secret tribunal.
Fenchel [ˈfɛnçəl], *m.* (—s, *no pl.*) (*Bot.*) fennel.
Fenster [ˈfɛnstər], *n.* (—s, *pl.* —) window.
Fensterbrett [ˈfɛnstərbrɛt], *n.* (—s, *pl.* —er) window-sill.
Fensterflügel [ˈfɛnstərflyːɡəl], *m.* (—s, *pl.* —) (window) casement.
Fensterladen [ˈfɛnstərlaːdən], *m.* (—s, *pl.* ⸚) shutter.
Fensterscheibe [ˈfɛnstərʃaɪbə], *f.* (—, *pl.* —n) pane.
Ferien [ˈfeːrjən], *pl.* holidays.
Ferkel [ˈfɛrkəl], *n.* (—s, *pl.* —) young pig, piglet.
Fermate [fɛrˈmaːtə], *f.* (—, *pl.* —n) (*Mus.*) pause, fermata.
fern [fɛrn], *adj.* far, distant, remote.
Fernbleiben [ˈfɛrnblaɪbən], *n.* (—s, *no pl.*) absence.
Ferne [ˈfɛrnə], *f.* (—, *pl.* —n) distance, remoteness.
ferner [ˈfɛrnər], *adv.* further, furthermore, moreover.
fernerhin [ˈfɛrnərhɪn], *adv.* henceforth.
Ferngespräch [ˈfɛrnɡəʃprɛx], *n.* (—s, *pl.* —e) long-distance telephone call, trunk call.
Fernglas [ˈfɛrnɡlaːs], *n.* (—es, *pl.* ⸚er) binoculars.
fernhalten [ˈfɛrnhaltən], *v.a. irr.* keep away.
fernher [ˈfɛrnheːr], *adv. von —*, from afar.
fernliegen [ˈfɛrnliːɡən], *v.n. irr.* be far from.
Fernrohr [ˈfɛrnroːr], *n.* (—s, *pl.* —e) telescope.
Fernschreiber [ˈfɛrnʃraɪbər], *m.* (—s, *pl.* —) teleprinter.
Fernsehen [ˈfɛrnzeːən], *n.* (—s, *no pl.*) television.
fernsehen [ˈfɛrnzeːən], *v.n. irr.* watch television.

Fernsehgerät ['fɛrnze:gəre:t], *n.* (—s, —e) television set.

Fernsprechamt ['fɛrnʃprɛçamt], *n.* (—s, *pl.* ⸚er) telephone exchange.

Fernsprecher ['fɛrnʃprɛçər], *m.* (—s, *pl.* —) telephone.

Fernstehende ['fɛrnʃte:əndə], *m.* (—n, *pl.* —n) outsider.

Fernverkehr ['fɛrnfɛrke:r], *m.* (—s, *no pl.*) long-distance traffic.

Ferse ['fɛrzə], *f.* (—, *pl.* —n) heel.

Fersengeld ['fɛrzəngɛlt], *n.* (—s, *no pl.*) — *geben*, take to o.'s heels.

fertig ['fɛrtiç], *adj.* ready, finished: (*coll.*) worn-out, ruined, done for.

Fertigkeit ['fɛrtiçkait], *f.* (—, *pl.* —en) dexterity, skill.

Fes [fɛs], *n.* (—, *pl.* —) (*Mus.*) F flat.

fesch [fɛʃ], *adj.* smart, stylish; (*dial.*) good-looking.

Fessel ['fɛsəl], *f.* (—, *pl.* —n) fetter, shackle.

Fesselballon ['fɛsəlbalɔ̃], *m.* (—s, *pl.* —s) captive balloon.

Fesselbein ['fɛsəlbain], *n.* (—s, *pl.* —e) pastern-joint.

fesseln ['fɛsəln], *v.a.* fetter, shackle, chain; (*fig.*) captivate.

Fest [fɛst], *n.* (—es, *pl.* —e) feast, festival.

fest [fɛst], *adj.* fast, firm; solid, hard; sound; fixed; constant, steadfast.

Feste ['fɛstə], *f.* (—, *pl.* —n) fortress, stronghold.

festigen ['fɛstigən], *v.a.* make firm; strengthen.

Festland ['fɛstlant], *n.* (—es, *pl.* ⸚er) continent.

festlich ['fɛstliç], *adj.* festive, solemn.

festmachen ['fɛstmaxən], *v.a.* fasten.

Festnahme ['fɛstna:mə], *f.* (—, *no pl.*) apprehension, arrest.

festnehmen ['fɛstne:mən], *v.a. irr.* seize, arrest.

Festrede ['fɛstre:də], *f.* (—, *pl.* —n) formal address.

festschnallen ['fɛstʃnalən], *v.a.* buckle on, fasten.

Festschrift ['fɛstʃrift], *f.* (—, *pl.* —en) commemorative volume (in honour of a person or an occasion).

festsetzen ['fɛstzɛtsən], *v.a.* fix, decree.

Festspiel ['fɛstʃpi:l], *n.* (—s, *pl.* —e) festival (play).

feststehen ['fɛstʃte:ən], *v.n. irr.* stand firm; *es steht fest*, it is certain.

feststellen ['fɛstʃtelən], *v.a.* ascertain; state; find; determine; diagnose; establish.

Festtag ['fɛstta:k], *m.* (—s, *pl.* —e) feast-day, holiday.

Festung ['fɛstuŋ], *f.* (—, *pl.* —en) fortress, stronghold, citadel.

festziehen ['fɛsttsi:ən], *v.a. irr.* tighten.

Festzug ['fɛsttsu:k], *m.* (—s, *pl.* ⸚e) procession.

Fett [fɛt], *n.* (—s, *pl.* —e) fat, grease, lard.

fett [fɛt], *adj.* fat, greasy.

fettartig ['fɛtartiç], *adj.* fatty.

fetten ['fɛtən], *v.a.* oil, grease.

Fettfleck ['fɛtflɛk], *m.* (—s, *pl.* —e) spot of grease.

fettgedruckt ['fɛtgədrukt], *adj.* in heavy type.

fetthaltig ['fɛthaltiç], *adj.* greasy; adipose.

fettig ['fɛtiç], *adj.* greasy.

fettleibig ['fɛtlaibiç], *adj.* corpulent, obese.

Fetzen ['fɛtsən], *m.* (—s, *pl.* —) piece, rag, tatter, shred.

feucht [fɔyçt], *adj.* moist; (*weather*) muggy, wet; (*room*) damp.

Feuchtigkeit ['fɔyçtiçkait], *f.* (—, *no pl.*) moisture, humidity, dampness, wetness.

feudal [fɔy'da:l], *adj.* feudal; (*coll.*) distinguished, magnificent.

Feuer ['fɔyər], *n.* (—s, *pl.* —) fire; (*jewels*) brilliancy; (*fig.*) ardour, passion.

feuerbeständig ['fɔyərbəʃtendiç], *adj.* fire-proof.

Feuerbestattung ['fɔyərbəʃtatuŋ], *f.* (—, *pl.* —en) cremation.

Feuereifer ['fɔyəraifər], *m.* (—s, *no pl.*) ardour.

feuerfest ['fɔyərfɛst], *adj.* fire-proof, incombustible.

feuergefährlich ['fɔyərgəfɛːrliç], *adj.* inflammable.

Feuerlilie ['fɔyərli:ljə], *f.* (—, *pl.* —n) tiger lily.

Feuermal ['fɔyərma:l], *n.* (—s, *pl.* —e) burn, burn-mark.

Feuermauer ['fɔyərmauər], *f.* (—, *pl.* —n) fire-proof wall, party-wall.

Feuermelder ['fɔyərmɛldər], *m.* (—s, *pl.* —) fire-alarm.

feuern ['fɔyərn], *v.a.* (*Mil.*) fire, discharge; (*coll.*) fire, sack.

Feuerprobe ['fɔyərpro:bə], *f.* (—, *pl.* —n) ordeal by fire.

Feuerrad ['fɔyərra:t], *n.* (—s, *pl.* ⸚er) Catherine wheel.

Feuerrohr ['fɔyərro:r], *n.* (—s, *pl.* —e) gun, matchlock.

Feuersbrunst ['fɔyərsbrunst], *f.* (—, *pl.* ⸚e) (*rare*) fire, conflagration.

Feuerspritze ['fɔyərʃpritsə], *f.* (—, *pl.* —n) fire-engine.

Feuerstein ['fɔyərʃtain], *m.* (—s, *no pl.*) flint.

Feuertaufe ['fɔyərtaufə], *f.* (—, *pl.* —n) baptism of fire.

Feuerwarte ['fɔyərvartə], *f.* (—, *pl.* —en) beacon; lighthouse.

Feuerwehr ['fɔyərve:r], *f.* (—, *no pl.*) fire-brigade.

Feuerwerk ['fɔyərvɛrk], *n.* (—, *no pl.*) fireworks.

Feuerwerkskunst ['fɔyərvɛrkskunst], *f.* (—, *no pl.*) pyrotechnics.

Feuerzange ['fɔyərtsaŋə], *f.* (—, *pl.* —n) fire-tongs.

Feuerzeug ['fɔyərtsɔyk], *n.* (—s, *pl.* —e) match-box; cigarette-lighter.

feurig ['fɔyriç], *adj.* fiery, burning; (*fig.*) ardent, impassioned, fervent; (*wine*) heady.

Fiaker

Fiaker [fi'akər], *m.* (**—s**, *pl.* **—**) (*Austr.*) cab, hansom; (*Am.*) coach.

Fiasko [fi'asko:], *n.* (**—s**, *pl.* **—s**) failure.

Fibel ['fi:bəl], *f.* (**—**, *pl.* **—n**) primer, spelling-book.

Fiber ['fi:bər], *f.* (**—**, *pl.* **—n**) fibre.

Fichte ['fɪçtə], *f.* (**—**, *pl.* **—n**) (*Bot.*) pine, pine-tree.

fidel [fi'de:l], *adj.* merry, jolly.

Fidibus ['fi:dibus], *m.* (**—ses**, *pl.* **—se**) spill, fidibus.

Fidschi ['fɪdʒi:], Fiji.

Fieber ['fi:bər], *n.* (**—s**, *no pl.*) fever.

fieberhaft ['fi:bərhaft], *adj.* feverish, vehement.

fieberig ['fi:bərɪç], *adj.* feverish, racked by fever.

Fieberkälte ['fi:bərkɛltə], *f.* (**—**, *no pl.*) chill, shivering (fit).

fiebern ['fi:bərn], *v.n.* have a fever; (*fig.*) rave.

fiebrig ['fi:brɪç], *see* **fieberig**.

Fiedel ['fi:dəl], *f.* (**—**, *pl.* **—n**) (*Mus.*) fiddle, violin.

Figur [fi'gu:r], *f.* (**—**, *pl.* **—en**) figure, statue, sculpture; chessman.

figürlich [fi'gy:rlɪç], *adj.* figurative.

Filet [fi'le:], *n.* (**—s**, *pl.* **—s**) netting, net-work; (*meat*) fillet.

Filiale [fil'ja:lə], *f.* (**—**, *pl.* **—n**) branch, branch-establishment, branch-office.

Filigran [fili'gra:n], *n.* (**—s**, *no pl.*) filigree.

Film [film], *m.* (**—s**, *pl.* **—e**) film; (motion) picture.

Filter ['filtər], *m.* (**—s**, *pl.* **—**) filter.

filtrieren [fil'tri:rən], *v.a.* filter.

Filz [filts], *m.* (**—es**, *pl.* **—e**) felt; (*fig.*) niggard, miser, skinflint.

Filzlaus ['filtslaus], *f.* (**—**, *pl.* *ˉe*) crab-louse.

Finanzamt [fi'nantsamt], *n.* (**—s**, *pl.* *ˉer*) income-tax office; revenue-office.

Finanzen [fi'nantsən], *f. pl.* finances, revenue.

Findelkind ['findəlkint], *n.* (**—s**, *pl.* **—er**) foundling.

finden ['findən], *v.a. irr.* find. — *v.r. sich —, das wird sich —*, we shall see.

Finder ['findər], *m.* (**—s**, *pl.* **—**) finder.

findig ['findɪç], *adj.* resourceful, ingenious.

Findling ['fintlɪŋ], *m.* (**—s**, *pl.* **—e**) foundling.

Finger ['fiŋər], *m.* (**—s**, *pl.* **—**) finger.

Fingerabdruck ['fiŋərapdruk], *m.* (**—s**, *pl.* *ˉe*) finger-print.

fingerfertig ['fiŋərfɛrtɪç], *adj.* nimble-fingered.

Fingerhut ['fiŋərhu:t], *m.* (**—s**, *pl.* *ˉe*) thimble; (*Bot.*) foxglove.

fingern ['fiŋərn], *v.a.* touch with the fingers, finger.

Fingersatz ['fiŋərzats], *m.* (**—es**, *pl.* *ˉe*) (*Mus.*) fingering.

Fingerspitze ['fiŋərʃpitsə], *f.* (**—**, *pl.* **—n**) finger-tip.

Fingerzeig ['fiŋərtsaik], *m.* (**—s**, *pl.* **—e**) hint.

fingieren [fiŋ'gi:rən], *v.a.* sham.

fingiert [fiŋ'gi:rt], *adj.* fictitious.

Fink [fiŋk], *m.* (**—en**, *pl.* **—en**) (*Orn.*) finch.

Finne (1) ['finə], *m.* (**—n**, *pl.* **—n**) Finn.

Finne (2) ['finə], *f.* (**—**, *pl.* **—n**) pimple; (*fish*) fin.

finnig ['finɪç], *adj.* pimpled; (*fish*) finny.

Finnland ['finlant], *n.* Finland.

finster ['finstər], *adj.* dark, obscure; (*fig.*) gloomy, sinister.

Finsternis ['finstərnis], *f.* (**—**, *no pl.*) darkness, gloom.

Finte ['fintə], *f.* (**—**, *pl.* **—n**) feint; (*fig.*) pretence, trick.

Firlefanz ['firləfants], *m.* (**—es**, *no pl.*) foolery.

Firma ['firma], *f.* (**—**, *pl.* **—men**) (*business*) firm, company.

Firmung ['firmuŋ], *f.* (**—**, *pl.* **—en**) (*Eccl.*) confirmation.

Firnis ['firnis], *m.* (**—ses**, *pl.* **—se**) varnish.

firnissen ['firnisən], *v.a.* varnish.

First [first], *m.* (**—s**, *pl.* **—e**) (*house*) roof-ridge; (*mountain*) top.

Fis [fis], *n.* (**—**, *pl.* **—**) (*Mus.*) F sharp.

Fisch [fiʃ], *m.* (**—es**, *pl.* **—e**) fish.

Fischadler ['fiʃa:dlər], *m.* (**—s**, *pl.* **—**) osprey, sea-eagle.

Fischbein ['fiʃbain], *n.* (**—s**, *no pl.*) whalebone.

fischen ['fiʃən], *v.a.*, *v.n.* fish, angle.

Fischer ['fiʃər], *m.* (**—s**, *pl.* **—**) fisherman, fisher.

Fischerei [fiʃə'rai], *f.* (**—**, *no pl.*) fishing; fishery.

Fischergerät ['fiʃərgərɛ:t], *n.* (**—s**, *pl.* **—e**) fishing-tackle.

Fischgräte ['fiʃgrɛ:tə], *f.* (**—**, *pl.* **—n**) fish-bone.

Fischkelle ['fiʃkɛlə], *f.* (**—**, *pl.* **—n**) fish-slice.

Fischlaich ['fiʃlaiç], *m.* (**—s**, *no pl.*) spawn.

Fischmilch ['fiʃmilç], *f.* (**—**, *no pl.*) soft roe, milt.

Fischotter ['fiʃotər], *m.* (**—s**, *pl.* **—**) common otter.

Fischreiher ['fiʃraiər], *m.* (**—s**, *pl.* **—**) (*Orn.*) heron.

Fischreuse ['fiʃrɔyzə], *f.* (**—**, *pl.* **—n**) bow-net; weir.

Fischrogen ['fiʃro:gən], *m.* (**—s**, *no pl.*) roe.

Fischschuppe ['fiʃʃupə], *f.* (**—**, *pl.* **—n**) scale.

Fischtran ['fiʃtra:n], *m.* (**—s**, *no pl.*) train-oil.

Fischzucht ['fiʃtsuxt], *f.* (**—**, *no pl.*) fish-breeding, pisciculture.

Fiskus ['fiskus], *m.* (**—**, *pl.* **—ken**) Treasury, Exchequer.

Fisole [fi'zo:lə], *f.* (**—**, *pl.* **—n**) (*Austr.*) French bean.

Fistelstimme ['fɪstəlʃtɪmə], *f.* (—, *no pl.*) (*Mus.*) falsetto.
Fittich ['fɪtɪç], *m.* (—es, *pl.* —e) (*Poet.*) wing, pinion.
fix [fɪks], *adj.* quick, sharp; — *und fertig*, quite ready.
Fixum ['fɪksum], *n.* (—s, *pl.* —xa) fixed amount; regular salary.
flach [flax], *adj.* flat, plain, smooth, level; (*water*) shallow.
Fläche ['flɛça], *f.* (—, *pl.* —n) plain; (*Maths.*) plane; (*crystal*) face.
Flächeninhalt ['flɛçənɪnhalt], *m.* (—s, *no pl.*) area.
Flächenmaß ['flɛçənmaːs], *n.* (—es, *pl.* —e) square-measure.
Flächenraum ['flɛçənraum], *m.* (—es, *no pl.*) surface area.
Flachheit ['flaxhaɪt], *f.* (—, *no pl.*) flatness; (*fig.*) shallowness.
Flachs [[flaks], *m.* (—es, *no pl.*) flax.
flackern ['flakərn], *v.n.* flare, flicker.
Fladen ['flaːdən], *m.* (—s, *pl.* —) flat cake; cow-dung.
Flagge ['flagə], *f.* (—, *pl.* —n) flag.
Flame ['flaːmə], *m.* (—n, *pl.* —n) Fleming.
flämisch ['flɛːmɪʃ], *adj.* Flemish.
Flamme ['flamə], *f.* (—, *pl.* —n) flame; blaze.
flammen ['flamən], *v.n.* flame, blaze, sparkle.
Flammeri ['flamərɪ], *m.* (—s, *pl.* —s) blanc-mange.
Flandern ['flandərn], *n.* Flanders.
Flanell [fla'nɛl], *m.* (—s, *pl.* —e) flannel.
Flaneur [fla'nøːr], *m.* (—s, *pl.* —e) lounger, stroller.
flanieren [fla'niːrən], *v.n.* lounge, stroll.
Flanke ['flaŋkə], *f.* (—, *pl.* —n) flank; *in die — fallen*, (*Mil.*) attack in the flank.
Flasche ['flaʃə], *f.* (—, *pl.* —en) bottle, flask.
Flaschenzug ['flaʃəntsuːk], *m.* (—es, *pl.* ⁓e) pulley.
flatterhaft ['flatərhaft], *adj.* fickle, inconstant, flighty.
flattern ['flatərn], *v.n.* flutter.
flau [flau], *adj.* insipid, stale; (*fig.*) dull.
Flaum [flaum], *m.* (—s, *no pl.*) down.
Flausch [flauʃ], *m.* (—es, *no pl.*) pilot-cloth.
Flaute ['flautə], *f.* (—, *pl.* —n) (*Nav.*) calm; (*fig.*) depression.
Flechte ['flɛçtə], *f.* (—, *pl.* —n) twist, plait, braid; (*Med.*) eruption, ring-worm; (*Bot.*) lichen.
flechten ['flɛçtən], *v.a. irr.* plait; wreathe.
Flechtwerk ['flɛçtvɛrk], *n.* (—s, *no pl.*) wicker-work, basketry.
Fleck [flɛk], *m.* (—s, *pl.* —e) spot; place, piece (of ground); (*fig.*) stain, blemish.
Flecken ['flɛkən], *m.* (—s, *pl.* —) market town, small town.

fleckenlos ['flɛkənloːs], *adj.* spotless.
fleckig ['flɛkɪç], *adj.* spotted, speckled.
Fledermaus ['fleːdərmaus], *f.* (—, *pl.* ⁓e) (*Zool.*) bat.
Flederwisch ['fleːdərvɪʃ], *m.* (—es, *pl.* —e) feather-duster.
Flegel ['fleːgəl], *m.* (—s, *pl.* —) flail; (*fig.*) boor.
flegelhaft ['fleːgəlhaft], *adj.* boorish, churlish, rude.
Flegeljahre ['fleːgəljaːrə], *n. pl.* years of indiscretion; teens, adolescence.
flehen ['fleːən], *v.a., v.n.* implore, supplicate, entreat.
Fleisch [flaɪʃ], *n.* (—es, *no pl.*) (raw) flesh; (*for cooking*) meat; (*fruit*) pulp.
Fleischbrühe ['flaɪʃbryːə], *f.* (—, *pl.* —n) broth, beef-tea.
Fleischer ['flaɪʃər], *m.* (—s, *pl.* —) butcher.
fleischfressend ['flaɪʃfrɛsənt], *adj.* carnivorous.
Fleischhacker ['flaɪʃhakər], **Fleischhauer** ['flaɪʃhauər], *m.* (—s, *pl.* —) butcher.
fleischlich ['flaɪʃlɪç], *adj.* fleshly, carnal.
fleischlos ['flaɪʃloːs], *adj.* vegetarian.
Fleischpastete ['flaɪʃpasteːtə], *f.* (—, *pl.* —n) meat-pie.
Fleiß [flaɪs], *m.* (—es, *no pl.*) diligence, assiduity, industry.
fleißig ['flaɪsɪç], *adj.* diligent, assiduous, industrious, hard-working.
fletschen ['flɛtʃən], *v.a. die Zähne —*, show o.'s teeth.
Flicken ['flɪkən], *m.* (—s, *pl.* —) patch.
flicken ['flɪkən], *v.a.* patch, repair, mend; (*shoes*) cobble; (*stockings*) darn.
Flieder ['fliːdər], *m.* (—s, *pl.* —) (*Bot.*) elder, lilac.
Fliege ['fliːgə], *f.* (—, *pl.* —n) (*Ent.*) fly; (*beard*) imperial.
fliegen ['fliːgən], *v.n. irr.* (*aux.* sein) fly; (*coll.*) get the sack, be fired. — *v.a.* fly, pilot (an aircraft).
Flieger ['fliːgər], *m.* (—s, *pl.* —) airman, aviator; pilot.
fliehen ['fliːən], *v.n. irr.* (*aux.* sein) flee, run away; *zu einem —*, take refuge with s.o. — *v.a. irr.* avoid, shun (s.o.).
Fliehkraft ['fliːkraft], *f.* (—, *no pl.*) centrifugal force.
Fliese ['fliːzə], *f.* (—, *pl.* —n) floor-tile, flagstone.
Fließband ['fliːsbant], *n.* (—(e)s, *pl.* ⁓er) (*Ind.*) assembly line.
fließen ['fliːsən], *v.n. irr.* (*aux.* sein) flow.
Fließpapier ['fliːspapiːr], *n.* (—s, *no pl.*) blotting-paper.
Flimmer ['flɪmər], *m.* (—s, *no pl.*) glittering, sparkling, glimmer.
flimmern ['flɪmərn], *v.n.* glisten, glitter.
flink [flɪŋk], *adj.* brisk, agile, quick, sharp, nimble.

Flinte

Flinte ['flɪntə], *f.* (—, *pl.* —n) gun, musket, rifle.

Flitter ['flɪtər], *m.* (—s, *no pl.*) tinsel, spangle, frippery.

Flitterwochen ['flɪtərvɔxən], *f. pl.* honeymoon.

flitzen ['flɪtsən], *v.n.* (*aux.* sein) *vorbei* —, flit *or* rush past, dash along.

Flocke ['flɔkə], *f.* (—, *pl.* —n) (*snow*) flake; (*wool*) flock.

Floh [flo:], *m.* (—s, *pl.* ⁻e) (*Ent.*) flea.

Flor [flo:r], *m.* (—s, *pl.* —e) bloom; gauze, crape; *in* —, blossoming, blooming.

Florenz [flo'rɛnts], *n.* Florence.

Florett [flo'rɛt], *n.* (—s, *pl.* —e) (*fencing*) foil.

florieren [flo'ri:rən], *v.n.* flourish.

Florstrumpf ['flo:rʃtrumpf], *m.* (—s, *pl.* ⁻e) lisle stocking.

Floskel ['flɔskəl], *f.* (—, *pl.* —n) rhetorical ornament; oratorical flourish; phrase.

Floß [flo:s], *n.* (—es, *pl.* ⁻e) raft.

Flosse ['flɔsə], *f.* (—, *pl.* —n) fin.

flößen ['flø:sən], *v.a.* float.

Flößer ['flø:sər], *m.* (—s, *pl.* —) raftsman.

Flöte ['flø:tə], *f.* (—, *pl.* —n) (*Mus.*) flute.

Flötenzug ['flø:təntsu:k], *m.* (—es, *pl.* ⁻e) (*organ*) flute-stop.

flott [flɔt], *adj.* (*Naut.*) afloat, floating; (*fig.*) gay, jolly, lively, smart; — *leben*, lead a fast life.

Flotte ['flɔtə], *f.* (—, *pl.* —n) fleet, navy.

Flottille [flɔ'tɪljə], *f.* (—, *pl.* —n) flotilla, squadron.

Flöz [flø:ts], *n.* (—es, *pl.* —e) layer, stratum; (*coal*) seam.

Fluch [flu:x], *m.* (—es, *pl.* ⁻e) curse, spell; (*verbal*) curse, oath, swearword.

fluchen ['flu:xən], *v.n.* curse, swear.

Flucht [fluxt], *f.* (—, *pl.* —en) flight, fleeing; suite (of rooms).

flüchten ['flʏçtən], *v.n.* (*aux.* sein), *v.r.* flee, run away, escape.

flüchtig ['flʏçtɪç], *adj.* fugitive; (*Chem.*) volatile; (*fig.*) superficial; evanescent; hasty; slight.

Flüchtling ['flʏçtlɪŋ], *m.* (—s, *pl.* —e) fugitive, refugee.

Flug [flu:k], *m.* (—s, *pl.* ⁻e) (*Aviat.*) flight.

Flugblatt ['flu:kblat], *n.* (—s, *pl.* ⁻er) broadsheet, leaflet.

Flügel ['fly:gəl], *m.* (—s, *pl.* —) wing; (*Mus.*) grand piano; (*door*) leaf.

Flügelschlag ['fly:gəlʃla:k], *m.* (—s, *pl.* ⁻e) wing-stroke.

Flügeltür ['fly:gəlty:r], *f.* (—, *pl.* —en) folding-door.

flügge ['flygə], *adj.* fledged.

Flughafen ['flu:kha:fən], *m.* (—s, *pl.* —) airport; aerodrome.

Flugpost ['flu:kpɔst], *f.* (—, *no pl.*) air mail.

flugs [fluks], *adv.* quickly, instantly; (*Lit., obs.*) anon.

Flugsand ['flu:kzant], *m.* (—s, *no pl.*) quicksand, drifting sand.

Flugzeug ['flu:ktsɔyk], *n.* (—s, *pl.* —e) aeroplane; (*Am.*) airplane.

Flugzeugführer ['flu:ktsɔykfy:rər], *m.* (—s, *pl.* —) (*Aviat.*) pilot.

Fluidum ['flu:idum], *n.* (—s, *pl.* —da) fluid; (*fig.*) atmosphere.

Flunder ['flundər], *f.* (—, *pl.* —n) (*fish*) flounder.

Flunkerer ['fluŋkərər], *m.* (—s, *pl.* —) (*coll.*) fibber, story-teller.

Flur (1) [flu:r], *f.* (—, *pl.* —en) field, plain; *auf weiter* —, in the open.

Flur (2) [flu:r], *m.* (—s, *pl.* —e) (*house*) hall, vestibule; corridor.

Flurschaden ['flu:rʃa:dən], *m.* (—s, *pl.* ⁻) damage to crops.

Fluß [flus], *m.* (—sses, *pl.* ⁻sse) river, stream; flow, flowing; flux.

Flußbett ['flusbɛt], *n.* (—s, *pl.* —en) channel, riverbed.

flüssig ['flʏsɪç], *adj.* fluid, liquid; —*e Gelder*, ready cash; liquid assets.

flüstern ['flʏstərn], *v.a.* whisper.

Flut [flu:t], *f.* (—, *pl.* —en) flood; high-tide, high water; torrent; deluge.

fluten ['flu:tən], *v.n.* flow.

Fockseil ['fɔkzɛ:gəl], *n.* (—s, *pl.* —) foresail.

Fockmast ['fɔkmast], *m.* (—s, *pl.* —en) foremast.

Föderalismus [fø:dəra'lɪsmus], *m.* (—, *no pl.*) federalism.

Fohlen ['fo:lən], *n.* (—s, *pl.* —) foal.

fohlen ['fo:lən], *v.n.* foal.

Föhn [fø:n], *m.* (—s, *pl.* —e) (warm) Alpine wind.

Föhre ['fø:rə], *f.* (—, *pl.* —n) (*Bot.*) fir, fir-tree.

Folge ['fɔlgə], *f.* (—, *pl.* —n) succession; series, sequence; continuation; consequence.

folgen ['fɔlgən], *v.n.* (*aux.* sein) follow; succeed; result from, be the consequence of; obey.

folgendermaßen ['fɔlgəndərma:sən], *adv.* as follows.

folgenschwer ['fɔlgənʃve:r], *adj.* momentous, portentous.

folgerichtig ['fɔlgərɪçtɪç], *adj.* consistent, logical.

folgern ['fɔlgərn], *v.a.* draw a conclusion, infer, conclude, deduce.

Folgerung ['fɔlgəruŋ], *f.* (—, *pl.* —en) induction, deduction, inference.

folglich ['fɔlklɪç], *conj.* consequently, therefore.

folgsam ['fɔlkza:m], *adj.* obedient.

Foliant [fo:l'jant], *m.* (—en, *pl.* —en) folio-volume, tome.

Folie ['fo:ljə], *f.* (—, *pl.* —n) foil.

Folter ['fɔltər], *f.* (—, *pl.* —n) rack, torture.

Folterbank ['fɔltərbaŋk], *f.* (—, *pl.* ⁻e) rack.

Fond [fɔ̃:], *m.* (—s, *pl.* —s) back seat.

74

Fontäne [fɔ'tɛ:nə], *f.* (—, *pl.* —n) fountain.

foppen ['fɔpən], *v.a.* chaff, banter, tease.

Fopperei [fɔpə'raɪ], *f.* (—, *pl.* —en) chaff, banter, teasing.

forcieren [fɔr'si:rən], *v.a.* strain, overdo.

Förderer ['fœrdərər], *m.* (—s, *pl.* —) promoter, backer.

Förderkarren ['fœrdərkarən], *m.* (—s, *pl.* —) (*Min.*) truck, trolley.

förderlich ['fœrdərlɪç], *adj.* useful, conducive (to).

Fördermaschine ['fœrdərmaʃi:nə], *f.* (—, *pl.* —n) hauling-machine.

fordern ['fɔrdərn], *v.a.* demand, claim, ask for; (*duel*) challenge.

fördern ['fœrdərn], *v.a.* further, advance, promote, back; hasten; (*Min.*) haul.

Förderschacht ['fœrdərʃaxt], *m.* (—s, *pl.* -̈e) (*Min.*) winding shaft.

Forderung ['fɔrdəruŋ], *f.* (—, *pl.* —en) demand, claim; (*duel*) challenge.

Förderung ['fœrdəruŋ], *f.* (—, *no pl.*) furtherance, promotion, advancement; (*Min.*) hauling.

Forelle [fo'rɛlə], *f.* (—, *pl.* —n) trout.

Forke ['fɔrkə], *f.* (—, *pl.* —n) pitchfork, garden-fork.

Form [fɔrm], *f.* (—, *pl.* —en) form, shape, figure; manner; condition; (*casting*) mould; (*grammar*) form, voice.

Formalien [fɔr'ma:liən], *pl.* formalities.

Formalität [fɔrmalı'tɛ:t], *f.* (—, *pl.* —en) formality, form.

Format [fɔr'ma:t], *n.* (—s, *pl.* —e) (*book, paper*) size; format; (*fig.*) stature.

Formel ['fɔrməl], *f.* (—, *pl.* —n) formula.

formell [fɔr'mɛl], *adj.* formal.

Formfehler ['fɔrmfe:lər], *m.* (—s, *pl.* —) faux pas, breach of etiquette.

formieren [fɔr'mi:rən], *v.a.* form. — *v.r. sich* —, fall into line.

förmlich ['fœrmlɪç], *adj.* formal; downright.

formlos ['fɔrmlo:s], *adj.* shapeless; (*fig.*) unconventional, informal, unceremonious.

Formular [fɔrmu'la:r], *n.* (—s, *pl.* —e) (*printed*) form, schedule.

formulieren [fɔrmu'li:rən], *v.a.* formulate, word.

formvollendet ['fɔrmfɔlɛndət], *adj.* well-rounded, well-finished.

forsch [fɔrʃ], *adj.* dashing.

forschen ['fɔrʃən], *v.n.* search, enquire (after), do research.

Forschung ['fɔrʃuŋ], *f.* (—, *pl.* —en) research, investigation; search, exploration.

Forst [fɔrst], *m.* (—es, *pl.* —e) forest.

Förster ['fœrstər], *m.* (—s, *pl.* —) forester, forest-keeper; (*Am.*) ranger.

Forstfrevel ['fɔrstfre:fəl], *m.* (—s, *no pl.*) infringement of forest-laws.

Forstrevier ['fɔrstrevi:r], *n.* (—s, *pl.* —e) section of forest.

Forstwesen ['fɔrstve:zən], *n.* (—s, *no pl.*) forestry.

Forstwirtschaft ['fɔrstvɪrtʃaft], *f.* (—, *no pl.*) forestry.

fort [fɔrt], *adv.* away; lost, gone, forth, forward.

Fort [fo:rt], *n.* (—s, *pl.* —s) fort.

fortan [fɔrt'an], *adv.* henceforth.

fortbilden ['fɔrtbɪldən], *v.r. sich* —, improve o.s., receive further education.

fortbleiben ['fɔrtblaɪbən], *v.n. irr.* (*aux.* sein) stay away.

Fortdauer ['fɔrtdauər], *f.* (—, *no pl.*) continuance, duration.

fortfahren ['fɔrtfa:rən], *v.n. irr.* (*aux.* sein) drive off; (*Naut.*) set sail; (*fig.*) continue, go on.

Fortgang ['fɔrtgaŋ], *m.* (—s, *no pl.*) going away, departure; (*fig.*) continuation, progress.

Fortkommen ['fɔrtkɔmən], *n.* (—s, *no pl.*) advancement, progress; (*fig.*) livelihood.

fortkommen ['fɔrtkɔmən], *v.n. irr.* (*aux.* sein) *gut* —, prosper, succeed.

fortlassen ['fɔrtlasən], *v.a. irr.* allow to go; leave out, omit; *nicht* —, detain.

fortlaufen ['fɔrtlaufən], *v.n. irr.* (*aux.* sein) run away.

fortpflanzen ['fɔrtpflantsən], *v.r. sich* —, propagate, multiply; (*sickness*) spread.

forträumen ['fɔrtrɔymən], *v.a.* clear away, remove.

fortschaffen ['fɔrtʃafən], *v.a.* carry away, get rid of.

fortscheren ['fɔrtʃe:rən], *v.r. sich* — (*coll.*) beat it, go away.

fortscheuchen ['fɔrtʃɔyçən], *v.a.* scare away.

fortschreiten ['fɔrtʃraɪtən], *v.n. irr.* (*aux.* sein) progress, advance.

Fortschritt ['fɔrtʃrɪt], *m.* (—s, *pl.* —e) progress, advancement, proficiency.

fortsetzen ['fɔrtzɛtsən], *v.a.* continue, carry on.

fortwährend ['fɔrtvɛ:rənt], *adj.* continual, perpetual, unceasing.

Fracht [fraxt], *f.* (—, *pl.* —en) freight, cargo, load.

Frack [frak], *m.* (—s, *pl.* —s, -̈e) dress-suit, evening dress.

Frage ['fra:gə], *f.* (—, *pl.* —n) question, query.

Fragebogen ['fra:gəbo:gən], *m.* (—s, *pl.* —) questionnaire.

fragen ['fra:gən], *v.a.* ask, enquire, question.

Fragesteller ['fra:gəʃtɛlər], *m.* (—s, *pl.* —) interrogator, questioner.

fraglich ['fra:klɪç], *adj.* questionable, problematic(al).

fragwürdig ['fra:kvyrdɪç], *adj.* doubtful, questionable.

Fraktion [frak'tsjo:n], *f.* (—, *pl.* —en) (*Pol.*) party group.

Frakturschrift [frak'tu:rʃrɪft], f. (—, no pl.) (lettering) Gothic type, Old English type, Black Letter type.

Frank [fraŋk], m. (—en, pl. —en) (money) franc.

Franke ['fraŋkə], m. (—n, pl. —n) Frank, Franconian.

frankieren [fraŋ'ki:rən], v.a. (post) prepay, frank.

franko ['fraŋko], adj. post-paid; gratis und —, gratuitously.

Frankreich ['frankraɪx], n. France.

Franse ['franzə], f. (—, pl. —n) fringe.

Franzose [fran'tso:zə], m. (—n, pl. —n) Frenchman.

französisch [fran'tso:zɪʃ], adj. French.

frappant [fra'pant], adj. striking.

frappieren [fra'pi:rən], v.a. strike, astonish.

Fraß [fra:s], m. (—es, no pl.) (animals) feed, fodder; (sl.) grub.

Fratz [frats], m. (—es, pl. —en) brat, little monkey.

Fratze ['fratsə], f. (—, pl. —en) grimace, caricature.

Frau [frau], f. (—, pl. —en) woman, wife, lady; (title) Mrs.; gnädige —, Madam.

Frauenkirche ['frauənkɪrçə], f. (—, no pl.) Church of Our Lady.

Frauenzimmer ['frauəntsɪmər], n. (—s, pl.) (pej.) woman, female.

Fräulein ['frɔylaɪn], n. (—s, pl. —) young lady; (title) Miss.

frech [frɛç], adj. insolent, impudent, cheeky, pert, saucy.

Frechheit ['frɛçhaɪt], f. (—, pl. —en) insolence, impudence.

Fregatte [fre'gatə], f. (—, pl. —n) frigate.

frei [fraɪ], adj. free, exempt, unhampered, independent, disengaged; vacant; candid, frank.

Freibeuter ['fraɪbɔytər], m. (—s, pl. —) freebooter, pirate.

Freibrief ['fraɪbri:f], m. (—s, pl. —e) patent, licence; permit.

freien ['fraɪən], v.a. woo, court.

Freier ['fraɪər], m. (—s, pl. —) (obs.) suitor.

Freigabe ['fraɪga:bə], f. (—, no pl.) release.

freigeben ['fraɪge:bən], v.a. irr. release.

freigebig ['fraɪge:bɪç], adj. liberal, generous.

Freigebigkeit ['fraɪgə:bɪçkaɪt], f. (—, no pl.) liberality, munificence, generosity.

Freigut ['fraɪgu:t], n. (—s, pl. ¨er) freehold.

Freiheit ['fraɪhaɪt], f. (—, pl. —en) freedom, liberty, immunity, privilege.

Freiherr ['fraɪhɛr], m. (—n, pl. —en) baron.

Freikorps ['fraɪko:r], n. (—, no pl.) volunteer-corps.

Freilauf ['fraɪlauf], m. (—s, no pl.) (bicycle) free-wheel.

freilich ['fraɪlɪç], adv. to be sure, it is true, indeed, of course.

Freilicht- ['fraɪlɪxt], adj. (in compounds) open-air.

Freimarke ['fraɪmarkə], f. (—, pl. —n) postage stamp.

freimütig ['fraɪmy:tɪç], adj. frank, open, candid.

Freisprechung ['fraɪʃprɛçuŋ], f. (—, no pl.) acquittal; absolution.

Freistätte ['fraɪʃtɛtə], f. (—, pl. —n) refuge, asylum.

Freistoß ['fraɪʃto:s], m. (—es, pl. ¨e) (Footb.) free-kick.

Freitag ['fraɪta:k], m. (—s, pl. —e) Friday.

Freitreppe ['fraɪtrɛpə], f. (—, pl. —n) outside staircase.

Freiübung ['fraɪy:buŋ], f. (—, pl. —en) (mostly pl.) physical exercises, gymnastics.

freiwillig ['fraɪvɪlɪç], adj. voluntary, of o.'s own accord; spontaneous.

Freiwillige ['fraɪvɪlɪgə], m. (—n, pl. —n) (Mil.) volunteer.

fremd [frɛmt], adj. strange, foreign, outlandish; odd.

fremdartig ['frɛmtartɪç], adj. strange, odd.

Fremde (1) ['frɛmdə], f. (—, no pl.) foreign country; in die — gehen, go abroad.

Fremde (2) ['frɛmdə], m. (—n, pl. —n) stranger, foreigner.

Fremdheit ['frɛmthaɪt], f. (—, no pl.) strangeness.

Freßbeutel ['frɛsbɔytəl], m. (—s, pl. —) nose-bag.

Fresse ['frɛsə], f. (—, pl. —n) (vulg.) mouth, snout.

fressen ['frɛsən], v.a. irr. (animals) eat; (also fig.) devour.

Fresserei [frɛsəraɪ], f. (—, no pl.) gluttony.

Frettchen ['frɛtçən], n. (—s, pl. —) (Zool.) ferret.

Freude ['frɔydə], f. (—, pl. —n) joy, joyfulness, gladness, enjoyment, delight, pleasure.

Freudenfest ['frɔydənfɛst], n. (—s, pl. —e) feast, jubilee.

Freudenhaus ['frɔydənhaus], n. (—es, pl. ¨er) brothel.

Freudenmädchen ['frɔydənmɛːtçən], n. (—s, pl. —) prostitute.

freudig ['frɔydɪç], adj. joyful, cheerful, glad.

freudlos ['frɔytlo:s], adj. joyless.

freuen ['frɔyən], v.r. sich —, rejoice (at); be glad (of); sich auf etwas —, look forward to s.th.

Freund [frɔynt], m. (—es, pl. —e) friend.

freundlich ['frɔyntlɪç], adj. friendly, kind, affable, pleasing, cheerful, pleasant, genial.

Freundschaft ['frɔyntʃaft], f. (—, pl. —en) friendship.

Frevel ['fre:fəl], m. (—s, pl. —) crime, misdeed, offence.

76

freveln ['fre:fəln], *v.n.* do wrong, trespass, commit an outrage.

Friede(n) ['fri:də(n)], *m.* (—ns, *no pl.*) peace.

friedfertig ['fri:tfɛrtıç], *adj.* peaceable.

Friedhof ['fri:tho:f], *m.* (—s, *pl.* ⁓e) churchyard, cemetery.

friedlich ['fri:tlıç], *adj.* peaceful.

friedliebend ['fri:tli:bənt], *adj.* peaceable, peace-loving.

Friedrich ['fri:drıç], *m.* Frederic(k).

friedselig ['fri:tze:lıç], *adj.* peaceable.

frieren ['fri:rən], *v.n. irr.* feel cold, freeze.

Fries [fri:s], *m.* (—es, *pl.* —e) frieze.

Friese ['fri:zə], *m.* (—n, *pl.* —n) Frisian.

frisch [frıʃ], *adj.* fresh; new; (*weather*) crisp; (*fig.*) lively, brisk, gay.

Frische ['frıʃə], *f.* (—, *no pl.*) freshness, liveliness, gaiety.

Friseur [fri'zø:r], *m.* (—s, *pl.* —e) hairdresser, barber.

Friseuse [fri'zø:zə], *f.* (—, *pl.* —n) female hairdresser.

frisieren [fri'zi:rən], *v.a.* dress (s.o.'s) hair.

Frist [frıst], *f.* (—, *pl.* —en) time, term, period; (fixed) term; delay, respite.

fristen ['frıstən], *v.a. das Leben* —, gain a bare living.

Frisur [fri'zu:r], *f.* (—, *pl.* —en) coiffure, hair-style.

frivol [fri'vo:l], *adj.* frivolous.

Frivolität [frivo:li'tɛ:t], *f.* (—, *pl.* —en) frivolity.

froh [fro:], *adj.* glad, joyful, joyous.

frohgelaunt ['fro:gəlaunt], *adj.* good-humoured, cheerful.

fröhlich ['frø:lıç], *adj.* gay, merry.

frohlocken [fro:'lɔkən], *v.n.* (*rare*) exult.

Frohsinn ['fro:zın], *m.* (—s, *no pl.*) good humour, gaiety.

fromm [frɔm], *adj.* pious, religious, devout.

frommen ['frɔmən], *v.n.* (*obs.*) be of advantage (to s.o.).

Frömmigkeit ['frœmıçkaıt], *f.* (—, *no pl.*) piety, devoutness.

Fron [fro:n], *f.* (—, *no pl.*) (feudal) service; statute labour.

frönen ['frø:nən], *v.n.* (*fig.*) be a slave to; indulge in (*Dat.*).

Fronleichnam [fro:n'laıxna:m], *m.* (*Eccl.*) (feast of) Corpus Christi.

Front [frɔnt], *f.* (—, *pl.* —en) front, forepart; (*building*) elevation; (*Mil.*) front line.

Frosch [frɔʃ], *m.* (—es, *pl.* ⁓e) (*Zool.*) frog.

Frost [frɔst], *m.* (—es, *pl.* ⁓e) frost; coldness, chill.

Frostbeule ['frɔstbɔylə], *f.* (—, *pl.* —n) chilblain.

frösteln ['frœstəln], *v.n.* feel a chill, shiver.

frostig ['frɔstıç], *adj.* frosty; cold, chilly.

frottieren [frɔ'ti:rən], *v.a.* rub (down).

Frottiertuch [frɔ'ti:rtu:x], *n.* (—s, *pl.* ⁓er) Turkish towel, bath towel.

Frucht [fruxt], *f.* (—, *pl.* ⁓e) fruit; (*fig.*) result, effect; (*Med.*) fœtus.

fruchtbar ['fruxtba:r], *adj.* fruitful, productive, fertile.

fruchten ['fruxtən], *v.n.* produce fruit; (*fig.*) be effectual.

Fruchtknoten ['fruxtkno:tən], *m.* (—s, *pl.* —) (*Bot.*) seed-vessel.

früh(e) [fry:(ə)], *adj.* early.

Frühe ['fry:ə], *f.* (—, *no pl.*) early morning, dawn.

früher ['fry:ər], *adv.* earlier (on), formerly.

frühestens ['fry:əstəns], *adv.* at the earliest (possible moment).

Frühjahr ['fry:ja:r], *n.*, **Frühling** ['fry:lıŋ], *m.* (—s, *pl.* —e) spring.

frühreif ['fry:raıf], *adj.* precocious.

Frühschoppen ['fry:ʃɔpən], *m.* (—s, *pl.* —) morning pint (beer *or* wine).

Frühstück ['fry:ʃtyk], *n.* (—s, *pl.* —e) breakfast; *zweites* —, lunch.

Fuchs [fuks], *m.* (—es, *pl.* ⁓e) fox; chestnut (horse); (*fig.*) cunning chap; (*student*) freshman.

Fuchsbau ['fuksbau], *m.* (—s, *pl.* ⁓e) fox-hole.

Fuchseisen ['fuksaızən], *n.* (—s, *pl.* —) fox-trap.

fuchsen ['fuksən], *v.r. sich* — *über*, be annoyed about.

Fuchsie ['fuksjə], *f.* (—, *pl.* —n) (*Bot.*) fuchsia.

fuchsig ['fuksıç], *adj.* (*coll.*) very angry.

Füchsin ['fyksın], *f.* (—, *pl.* —innen) vixen.

fuchsrot ['fuksro:t], *adj.* fox-coloured, sorrel.

Fuchsschwanz ['fuksʃvants], *m.* (—es, *pl.* ⁓e) fox-brush; pad saw.

Fuchtel ['fuxtəl], *f.* (—, *pl.* —n) sword blade; rod, whip.

Fuder ['fu:dər], *n.* (—s, *pl.* —) load, cart-load; wine measure (c. 270 gallons).

Fug ['fu:k], *m.* (—s, *no pl.*) (*rare*) right, justice; *mit* — *und Recht*, with every right.

Fuge (1) ['fu:gə], *f.* (—, *pl.* —n) joint, groove.

Fuge (2) ['fu:gə], *f.* (—, *pl.* —n) (*Mus.*) fugue.

fügen ['fy:gən], *v.a.* fit together, join, dovetail. — *v.r. sich* —, submit (to), accommodate o.s. (to).

fügsam ['fy:kza:m], *adj.* pliant, submissive, yielding.

Fügung ['fy:guŋ], *f.* (—, *pl.* —en) coincidence; dispensation (of Providence); Providence.

fühlbar ['fy:lba:r], *adj.* perceptible; tangible; *sich* — *machen*, make o.s. felt.

fühlen ['fy:lən], *v.a.* feel, touch, sense, be aware of.

Fühler ['fy:lər], *m.* (—s, *pl.* —) tentacle, feeler.

Fühlhorn [ˈfyːlhɔrn], *n.* (—s, *pl.* ˍer) feeler, antenna, tentacle.

Fühlung [ˈfyːluŋ], *f.* (—, *no pl.*) — *haben mit*, be in touch with.

Fuhre [ˈfuːrə], *f.* (—, *pl.* —n) conveyance, vehicle, cart-load.

führen [ˈfyːrən], *v.a.* lead, guide, conduct, command; (*pen*) wield; (*law-suit*) carry on; (*conversation*) have, keep up; (*name, title*) bear; (*goods*) stock, deal in; *Krieg* —, wage war; *etwas im Schilde* —, have a plan; *das Wort* —, be spokesman; *einen hinters Licht* —, cheat s.o.

Führer [ˈfyːrər], *m.* (—s, *pl.* —) leader, guide; head, manager; conductor; driver, pilot.

Führerschaft [ˈfyːrərʃaft], *f.* (—, *no pl.*) leadership.

Führerschein [ˈfyːrərʃain], *m.* (—s, *pl.* —e) driving-licence.

Führersitz [ˈfyːrərzɪts], *m.* (—es, *pl.* —e) driver's seat; pilot's cockpit.

Fuhrlohn [ˈfuːrloːn], *m.* (—s, *no pl.*) cartage, carriage.

Fuhrmann [ˈfuːrman], *m.* (—s, *pl.* ˍer) carter, carrier.

Führung [ˈfyːruŋ], *f.* (—, *no pl.*) guidance; leadership; conducted tour; management, direction; behaviour, conduct.

Führungszeugnis [ˈfyːruŋstsɔyknɪs], *n.* (—sses, *pl.* —sse) certificate of good conduct.

Fuhrwerk [ˈfuːrvɛrk], *n.* (—s, *pl.* —e) carriage, vehicle, waggon.

Fuhrwesen [ˈfuːrveːzən], *n.* (—s, *no pl.*) transport services, transportation.

Fülle [ˈfylə], *f.* (—, *no pl.*) fullness; abundance, plenty.

Füllen [ˈfylən], *n.* (—s, *pl.* —) foal.

füllen [ˈfylən], *v.a.* fill, fill up; stuff.

Füllfederhalter [ˈfylfeːdərhaltər], *m.* (—s, *pl.* —) fountain-pen.

Füllung [ˈfyluŋ], *f.* (—, *pl.* —en) filling; stuffing; (*door*) panel.

fummeln [ˈfuməln], *v.n.* fumble.

Fund [funt], *n.* (—es, *pl.* —e) find; discovery.

Fundbüro [ˈfuntbyro], *n.* (—s, *pl.* —s) lost property office.

Fundgrube [ˈfuntgruːbə], *f.* (—, *pl.* —n) gold-mine, source, treasure-house.

fundieren [funˈdiːrən], *v.a.* found; establish.

fünf [fynf], *num. adj.* five.

Fünfeck [ˈfynfɛk], *n.* (—s, *pl.* —e) pentagon.

Fünffüßler [ˈfynffyːslər], *m.* (—s, *pl.* —) (*Poet.*) pentameter.

fünfjährig [ˈfynfjɛːrɪç], *num. adj.* five-year-old.

fünfjährlich [ˈfynfjɛːrlɪç], *num. adj.* quinquennial, five-yearly.

fünfzehn [ˈfynftseːn], *num. adj.* fifteen.

fünfzig [ˈfynftsɪç], *num. adj.* fifty.

fungieren [funˈgiːrən], *v.n.* — *als*, act as, officiate as.

Funk [funk], *m.* (—s, *no pl.*) radio; wireless; telegraphy.

Funke [ˈfunkə], *m.* (—n, *pl.* —n) spark, sparkle.

funkeln [ˈfunkəln], *v.n.* sparkle, glitter; (*stars*) twinkle.

funkelnagelneu [ˈfunkəlnaːgəlnɔy], *adj.* (*coll.*) brand-new.

funken [ˈfunkən], *v.a.* flash (messages); telegraph, broadcast.

Funker [ˈfunkər], *m.* (—s, *pl.* —) wireless operator.

Funksender [ˈfunkzɛndər], *m.* (—s, *pl.* —) radio-transmitter.

Funkspruch [ˈfunkʃprux], *m.* (—s, *pl.* ˍe) wireless-message.

Funktelegramm [ˈfunktelegram], *n.* (—s, *pl.* —e) radio telegram.

für [fyːr], *prep.* (*Acc.*) for, instead of; *ein — allemal*, once and for all; *an und — sich*, in itself.

Fürbitte [ˈfyːrbɪtə], *f.* (—, *pl.* —n) intercession.

Furche [ˈfurçə], *f.* (—, *pl.* —n) furrow; (*face*) wrinkle.

furchen [ˈfurçən], *v.a.* furrow; (*face*) wrinkle.

Furcht [furçt], *f.* (—, *no pl.*) fear, worry, anxiety; dread, fright, terror, apprehension.

furchtbar [ˈfurçtbaːr], *adj.* dreadful, terrible, frightful.

fürchten [ˈfyrçtən], *v.a.* fear, be afraid of. — *v.r. sich — vor*, be afraid of.

fürchterlich [ˈfyrçtərlɪç], *adj.* terrible, horrible, awful.

furchtsam [ˈfurçtzaːm], *adj.* timid, fearful, apprehensive.

Furie [ˈfuːrjə], *f.* (—, *pl.* —n) fury, virago.

fürlieb [fyrˈliːp], *adv. mit etwas — nehmen*, put up with, be content with s.th.

Furnier [furˈniːr], *n.* (—s, *pl.* —e) veneer, inlay.

Furore [fuˈroːrə], *n.* (—s, *no pl.*) — *machen*, cause a sensation, create an uproar.

Fürsorge [ˈfyːrzɔrgə], *f.* (—, *no pl.*) solicitude; provision; welfare.

fürsorglich [ˈfyːrzɔrglɪç], *adj.* thoughtful, with loving care.

Fürsprache [ˈfyːrʃpraːxə], *f.* (—, *no pl.*) advocacy, intercession.

Fürst [fyrst], *m.* (—en, *pl.* —en) prince, sovereign.

Furt [furt], *f.* (—, *pl.* —en) ford.

Furunkel [fuˈruŋkəl], *m.* (—s, *pl.* —) furuncle, boil.

Fürwort [ˈfyːrvɔrt], *n.* (—s, *pl.* ˍer) pronoun.

Fusel [ˈfuːzəl], *m.* (—s, *no pl.*) bad liquor, (*Am.*) hooch (*sl.*).

Fuß [fuːs], *m.* (—es, *pl.* ˍe) (*human*) foot; (*object*) base.

Fußangel [ˈfuːsaŋəl], *f.* (—, *pl.* —n) man-trap.

Fußball [ˈfuːsbal], *m.* (—s, *pl.* ˍe) football.

Fußboden ['fu:sbo:dən], *m.* (—s, *pl.* ∵) floor.

fußen ['fu:sən], *v.n.* — *auf*, be based upon.

fußfrei ['fu:sfraɪ], *adj.* ankle-length.

Fußgänger ['fu:sgɛŋər], *m.* (—s, *pl.* —) pedestrian.

Fußgestell ['fu:sgəʃtɛl], *n.* (—s, *pl.* —e) pedestal.

Fußpflege ['fu:spfle:gə], *f.* (—, *no pl.*) chiropody.

Fußpunkt ['fu:spuŋkt], *m.* (—s, *no pl.*) nadir.

Fußtritt ['fu:strɪt], *m.* (—s, *pl.* —e) kick.

futsch [futʃ], *excl.* (*coll.*) gone, lost.

Futter ['futər], *n.* (—s, *no pl.*) (*dress*) lining; (*animals*) fodder, feed.

Futteral [futə'ra:l], *n.* (—s, *pl.* —e) case; sheath.

Futterkräuter ['futərkrɔytər], *n. pl.* herbage.

futtern ['futərn], *v.n.* (*coll.*) feed, stuff o.s.

füttern ['fytərn], *v.a.* feed; (*garment*) line.

G

G [ge:], *n.* (—s, *pl.* —s) the letter G; (*Mus.*) G *Dur*, G major; (*Mus.*) G *Moll*, G minor; (*Mus.*) — -*Saite*, G string.

Gabe ['ga:bə], *f.* (—, *pl.* —n) gift, present; donation; *barmherzige* —, alms; (*fig.*) gift, talent.

Gabel ['ga:bəl], *f.* (—, *pl.* —n) fork; (*deer*) antler; (*cart*) shafts.

gabelig ['ga:bəlɪç], *adj.* forked.

Gabelung ['ga:bəluŋ], *f.* (—, *pl.* —en) bifurcation, branching (of road).

Gabelzinke ['ga:bəltsɪŋkə], *f.* (—, *pl.* —n) prong, tine.

Gabun [ga'bu:n], *n.* Gaboon.

gackern ['gakərn], *v.n.* cackle; (*fig.*) chatter.

gaffen ['gafən], *v.n.* gape (at), stare.

Gage ['ga:ʒə], *f.* (—, *pl.* —n) salary, pay, fee.

gähnen ['gɛ:nən], *v.n.* yawn, gape.

Galan [ga'la:n], *m.* (—s, *pl.* —e) lover, gallant.

galant [ga'lant], *adj.* polite, courteous; —*es Abenteuer*, love affair.

Galanterie [galantə'ri:], *f.* (—, *pl.* —n) courtesy.

Galanteriewaren [galantə'ri:va:rən], *f. pl.* fancy goods.

Galeere [ga'le:rə], *f.* (—, *pl.* —n) galley.

Galerie [galə'ri:], *f.* (—, *pl.* —n) gallery.

Galgen ['galgən], *m.* (—s, *pl.* —) gallows, gibbet; scaffold.

Galgenfrist ['galgənfrɪst], *f.* (—, *no pl.*) short delay, respite.

Galgenhumor ['galgənhu:mo:r], *m.* (—s, *no pl.*) wry or grim humour.

Galgenvogel ['galgənfo:gəl], *m.* (—s, *pl.* ∵) gallows-bird.

Galizien [ga'li:tsjən], *n.* Galicia.

Gallapfel ['galapfəl], *m.* (—s, *pl.* ∵) gall-nut.

Galle ['galə], *f.* (—, *pl.* —n) gall, bile.

Gallenblase ['galənbla:zə], *f.* (—, *pl.* —n) gall-bladder.

Gallert ['galərt], *n.* (—s, *no pl.*) jelly.

Gallien ['galjən], *n.* Gaul.

gallig ['galɪç], *adj.* bilious.

galvanisieren [galvanɪ'zi:rən], *v.a.* galvanize.

Gamaschen [ga'maʃən], *f. pl.* spats, gaiters.

Gang [gaŋ], *m.* (—es, *pl.* ∵e) walk, gait; (*horse*) pace; (*house*) passage, corridor; (*meal*) course, dish; (*action*) progress, course; (*sport*) round, bout; (*machine*) motion; stroke; (*Motor.*) gear.

gang [gaŋ], *adj.* — *und gäbe*, customary, usual, common.

Gangart ['gaŋa:rt], *f.* (—, *pl.* —en) gait; (*horse*) pace.

gangbar ['gaŋba:r], *adj.* marketable, saleable; (*road*) passable; practicable.

Gans [gans], *f.* (—, *pl.* ∵e) (*Orn.*) goose.

Gänseblümchen ['gɛnzəbly:mçən], *n.* (—s, *pl.*—) daisy.

Gänsefüßchen ['gɛnzəfy:sçən], *n. pl.* (*coll.*) inverted commas, quotation marks.

Gänsehaut ['gɛnzəhaut], *f.* (—, *no pl.*) goose-flesh, goose-pimples.

Gänserich ['gɛnzərɪç], *m.* (—s, *pl.* —e) (*Orn.*) gander.

ganz [gants], *adj.* whole, entire, all; complete, total.

gänzlich ['gɛntslɪç], *adj.* whole, total, entire, full, complete.

gar [ga:r], *adj.* sufficiently cooked, done. — *adv.* very, quite.

garantieren [garan'ti:rən], *v.a.* guarantee, warrant.

Garaus ['ga:raus], *m.* (—, *no pl.*) *einem den* — *machen*, finish s.o., kill s.o.

Garbe ['garbə], *f.* (—, *pl.* —n) sheaf.

Garde ['gardə], *f.* (—, *pl.* —n) guard, guards.

Garderobe [gardə'ro:bə], *f.* (—, *pl.* —n) wardrobe; cloak-room; (*Theat.*) dressing-room.

Gardine [gar'di:nə], *f.* (—, *pl.* —n) curtain.

Gardist [gar'dɪst], *m.* (—en, *pl.* —en) guardsman.

gären ['gɛ:rən], *v.n.* ferment; effervesce.

Garn [garn], *n.* (—s, *pl.* —e) yarn, thread.

Garnele [gar'ne:lə], *f.* (—, *pl.* —n) (*Zool.*) shrimp; *große* —, prawn.

garnieren [gar'ni:rən], *v.a.* trim, garnish.

Garnison [garni'zo:n], *f.* (—, *pl.* —en) garrison.

Garnitur [garni'tu:r], *f.* (—, *pl.* —en) trimming; set.

Garnröllchen ['garnrœlçən], *n.* (—s, *pl.* —) reel of thread.

garstig ['garstiç], *adj.* nasty, loathsome, ugly.

Garten ['gartən], *m.* (—s, *pl.* ⁙) garden.

Gartenlaube ['gartənlaubə], *f.* (—, *pl.* —n) bower, arbour.

Gärtner ['gɛrtnər], *m.* (—s, *pl.* —) gardener.

Gärtnerei [gɛrtnə'rai], *f.* (—, *pl.* —en) horticulture; market-garden; (plant) nursery.

Gärung ['gɛ:ruŋ], *f.* (—, *pl.* —en) fermentation, effervescence.

Gas [ga:s], *n.* (—es, —e) gas; — *geben*, (*Motor.*) accelerate.

gasartig ['ga:sartiç], *adj.* gaseous.

Gäßchen ['gɛsçən], *n.* (—s, *pl.* —) narrow alley; lane.

Gasse ['gasə], *f.* (—, *pl.* —n) alleyway, lane; (*rare*) street.

Gassenbube ['gasənbu:bə] *see* **Gassenjunge**.

Gassenhauer ['gasənhauər], *m.* (—s, *pl.* —), street-song, vulgar ballad; pop song.

Gassenjunge ['gasənjuŋə], *m.* (—n, *pl.* —n) street-urchin.

Gast [gast], *m.* (—s, *pl.* ⁙e) guest, visitor.

gastfrei ['gastfrai], *adj.* hospitable.

Gastfreund ['gastfrɔynt], *m.* (—s, *pl.* —e) guest; host.

Gastfreundschaft ['gastfrɔyntʃaft], *f.* (—, *no pl.*) hospitality.

Gastgeber ['gastge:bər], *m.* (—s, *pl.* —) host.

Gasthaus ['gasthaus], *n.* (—es, *pl.* ⁙er), **Gasthof** ['gastho:f], *m.* (—es, *pl.* ⁙e) inn, hotel, public house.

gastieren [gas'ti:rən], *v.n.* (*Theat.*) appear as a guest artist; star.

gastlich ['gastliç], *adj.* hospitable.

Gastmahl ['gastma:l], *n.* (—s, *pl.* —e) banquet, feast.

Gastrecht ['gastrɛçt], *n.* (—s, *no pl.*) right of hospitality.

Gastspiel ['gastʃpi:l], *n.* (—s, *pl.* —e) (*Theat.*) performance by visiting company.

Gaststätte ['gaststɛtə], *f.* (—, *pl.* —n) restaurant.

Gaststube ['gastʃtu:bə], *f.* (—, *pl.* —n) hotel lounge; guest room.

Gastwirt ['gastvirt], *m.* (—s, *pl.* —e) landlord.

Gastwirtin ['gastvirtin], *f.* (—, *pl.* —nen) landlady.

Gastzimmer ['gasttsimər], *n.* (—s, *pl.* —) *see* **Gaststube**; spare bedroom.

Gatte ['gatə], *m.* (—n, *pl.* —n) husband, spouse, consort.

Gatter ['gatər], *n.* (—s, *pl.* —) grate, lattice, grating.

Gattin ['gatin], *f.* (—, *pl.* —nen) wife, spouse, consort.

Gattung ['gatuŋ], *f.* (—, *pl.* —en) kind, species, sort, class; breed, genus; (*Lit.*) genre.

Gau [gau], *m.* (—s, *pl.* —e) district, province.

gaukeln ['gaukəln], *v.n.* juggle. — *v.a.* dazzle.

Gaul [gaul], *m.* (—s, *pl.* ⁙e) (old) horse, nag: *einem geschenkten — sieht man nicht ins Maul*, never look a gift horse in the mouth.

Gaumen ['gaumən], *m.* (—s, *pl.* —) palate.

Gauner ['gaunər], *m.* (—s, *pl.* —) rogue, sharper, swindler, cheat.

gaunern ['gaunərn], *v.n.* cheat, trick, swindle.

Gaunersprache ['gaunərʃpra:xə], *f.* (—, *no pl.*) thieves' slang.

Gaze ['ga:zə], *f.* (—, *pl.* —n) gauze.

Gazelle [ga'tsɛlə], *f.* (—, *pl.* —n) (*Zool.*) gazelle, antelope.

Geächtete [gə'ɛçtətə], *m.* (—n, *pl.* —n) outlaw.

Geächze [gə'ɛçtsə], *n.* (—s, *no pl.*) moaning, groaning.

Geäder [gə'ɛ:dər], *n.* (—s, *no pl.*) veins, arteries; veining.

geädert [gə'ɛdərt], *adj.* veined, streaked; grained.

-geartet [gə'a:rtət], *adj.* (*suffix in compounds*) -natured.

Gebäck [gə'bɛk], *n.* (—s, *no pl.*) pastry, rolls, cakes.

Gebälk [gə'bɛlk], *n.* (—s, *no pl.*) timberwork, timber-frame.

Gebärde [gə'bɛ:rdə], *f.* (—, *pl.* —n) gesture.

gebärden [gə'bɛ:rdən], *v.r. sich —*, behave.

Gebaren [gə'ba:rən], *n.* (—s, *no pl.*) demeanour.

gebären [gə'bɛ:rən], *v.a. irr.* bear, bring forth, give birth to, be delivered of.

Gebärmutter [gə'bɛ:rmutər], *f.* (—, *no pl.*) womb, uterus.

Gebäude [gə'bɔydə], *n.* (—s, *pl.* —) building, edifice.

Gebein [gə'bain], *n.* (—s, *pl.* —e) bones, skeleton; (*fig.*) remains.

Gebell [gə'bɛl], *n.* (—s, *no pl.*) barking.

geben ['ge:bən], *v.a. irr.* give, present; confer, bestow; yield; (*cards*) deal. — *v.r. sich —*, show o.s., behave; abate; *das gibt sich*, that won't last long; *es gibt . . .*, there is . . .; *was gibt's?* what's the matter?

Geber ['ge:bər], *m.* (—s, *pl.* —) giver, donor.

Gebet [gə'be:t], *n.* (—s, *pl.* —e) prayer; *sein — verrichten*, say o.'s prayers; *ins — nehmen*, question s.o. thoroughly.

Gebiet [gə'bi:t], *n.* (—s, *pl.* —e) district, territory; (*Am.*) precinct; jurisdiction; (*fig.*) province, field, sphere, domain.

gebieten [gə'bi:tən], *v.a. irr.* command, order.

Gebieter [gə'bi:tər], *m.* (—s, *pl.* —) lord, master, ruler.

Gebilde [gə'bɪldə], *n.* (—s, *pl.* —) form, thing; formation, structure; figment.

gebildet [gə'bɪldət], *adj.* educated, cultured, refined.

Gebirge [gə'bɪrgə], *n.* (—s, *pl.* —) mountains.

Gebirgskamm [gə'bɪrkskam], *m.* (—s, *pl.* ̈e) mountain-ridge.

Gebiß [gə'bɪs], *n.* (—sses, *pl.* —sse) set of (false) teeth, denture; (*horse*) bit.

Gebläse [gə'blɛ:zə], *n.* (—s, *pl.* —) bellows; blower.

Gebläsemaschine [gə'blɛ:zəmaʃi:nə], *f.* (—, *pl.* —n) blower.

Gebläseofen [gə'blɛ:zəo:fən], *m.* (—s, *pl.* ̈e) blast-furnace.

geblümt [gə'bly:mt], *adj.* flowered.

Geblüt [gə'bly:t], *n.* (—s, *no pl.*) blood; race, line, lineage, stock.

geboren [gə'bo:rən], *adj.* born.

geborgen [gə'bɔrgən], *adj.* saved, hidden, sheltered, rescued.

Gebot [gə'bo:t], *n.* (—s, *pl.* —e) order, decree, command; (*Bibl.*) Commandment.

geboten [gə'bo:tən], *adj.* necessary, advisable.

Gebräu [gə'brɔy], *n.* (—s, *no pl.*) brew, concoction, mixture.

Gebrauch [gə'braux], *m.* (—s, *pl.* ̈e) use; employment; custom, usage, habit, practice; (*rare*) rite.

gebrauchen [gə'brauxən], *v.a.* use, make use of, employ.

gebräuchlich [gə'brɔyçlɪç], *adj.* usual, customary, common.

Gebrauchsanweisung [gə'brauxsanvaizuŋ], *f.* (—, *pl.* —en) directions for use.

gebraucht [gə'brauxt], *adj.* used, second-hand.

Gebrechen [gə'brɛçən], *n.* (—s, *pl.* —) infirmity.

gebrechen [gə'brɛçən], *v.n. irr. es gebricht mir an,* I am in want of, I lack.

gebrechlich [gə'brɛçlɪç], *adj.* infirm, frail, weak.

gebrochen [gə'brɔxən], *adj.* broken; —*es Deutsch,* broken German.

Gebrüder [gə'bry:dər], *m. pl.* (*Comm.*) brothers.

Gebrüll [gə'bryl], *n.* (—s, *no pl.*) roaring; (*cows*) lowing.

Gebühr [gə'by:r], *f.* (—, *pl.* —en) charge, due; fee; tax, duty.

gebühren [gə'by:rən], *v.n.* be due to s.o. — *v.r. sich —, wie es sich gebührt,* as it ought to be, as is right and proper.

gebunden [gə'bundən], *adj.* (*fig.*) bound, committed; (*Poet.*) metrical.

Geburt [gə'burt], *f.* (—, *pl.* —en) birth.

gebürtig [gə'byrtɪç], *adj.* a native of.

Geburtsfehler [gə'burtsfe:lər], *m.* (—s, *pl.* —) congenital defect.

Geburtshelfer [gə'burtshɛlfər], *m.* (—s, *pl.* —) obstetrician.

Geburtshelferin [gə'burtshɛlfərɪn], *f.* (—, *pl.* —nen) midwife.

Geburtsort [gə'burtsɔrt], *m.* (—s, *pl.* —e) birthplace.

Geburtsschein [gə'burtsʃain], *m.* (—(e)s, *pl.* —e) birth certificate.

Geburtswehen [gə'burtsve:ən], *f. pl.* birthpangs; labour pains.

Gebüsch [gə'byʃ], *n.* (—es, *pl.* —e) bushes, thicket; underwood.

Geck [gɛk], *m.* (—en, *pl.* —en) fop, dandy; (*carnival*) fool.

geckenhaft ['gɛkənhaft], *adj.* foppish, dandyish.

Gedächtnis [gə'dɛçtnɪs], *n.* (—ses, *no pl.*) memory; remembrance, recollection; *im — behalten,* keep in mind.

Gedanke [gə'daŋkə], *m.* (—ns, *pl.* —n) thought, idea.

Gedankenfolge [gə'daŋkənfɔlgə], *f.* (—, *no pl.*), **Gedankengang** [gə'daŋkəngaŋ], *m.* (—s, *pl.* ̈e) sequence of thought, train of thought.

Gedankenstrich [gə'daŋkənʃtrɪç], *m.* (—s, *pl.* —e) dash; hyphen.

Gedärm [gə'dɛrm], *n.* (—s, *pl.* —e) bowels, intestines, entrails.

Gedeck [gə'dɛk], *n.* (—s, *pl.* —e) cover; menu; place laid at a table.

gedeihen [gə'daiən], *v.n. irr.* (*aux.* sein) thrive, prosper; progress.

gedeihlich [gə'dailɪç], *adj.* thriving, salutary.

gedenken [gə'dɛŋkən], *v.n. irr.* (*Genit.*) think of, remember; — *etwas zu tun,* intend to do s.th.

Gedenken [gə'dɛŋkən], *n.* (—s, *no pl.*) remembrance.

Gedenkfeier [gə'dɛŋkfaiər], *f.* (—, *pl.* —n) commemoration.

Gedicht [gə'dɪçt], *n.* (—s, *pl.* —e) poem.

gediegen [gə'di:gən], *adj.* solid, sound, genuine, true, honourable, sterling.

Gedränge [gə'drɛŋə], *n.* (—s, *no pl.*) crowd, throng; crush.

Gedrängtheit [gə'drɛŋkthait], *f.* (—, *no pl.*) conciseness.

gedrungen [gə'druŋən], *adj.* thick-set, stocky; compact; concise (style).

Geduld [gə'dult], *f.* (—, *no pl.*) patience, forbearance.

gedulden [gə'duldən], *v.r. sich —,* be patient.

geduldig [gə'duldɪç], *adj.* patient, forbearing, indulgent.

Geduld(s)spiel [gə'dult(s)ʃpi:l], *n.* (—s, *pl.* —e) puzzle; (*Cards*) patience.

gedunsen [gə'dunzən], *adj.* bloated.

geeignet [gə'aignət], *adj.* suitable, fit, appropriate, apt.

Gefahr [gə'fa:r], *f.* (—, *pl.* —en) danger, peril, hazard, risk; — *laufen,* run the risk.

gefährden [gə'fɛ:rdən], *v.a.* endanger, imperil, jeopardize.

gefährlich [gə'fɛ:rlɪç], *adj.* dangerous, perilous.

Gefährt [gə'fɛ:rt], *n.* (—s, *pl.* —e) (*obs.*) vehicle, conveyance.

Gefährte [gə'fɛ:rtə], *m.* (—en, *pl.* —en) comrade, companion, fellow.

Gefälle

Gefälle [gə'fɛlə], *n.* (—s, *pl.* —e) fall, descent, incline, gradient.

Gefallen [gə'falən], *m.* (—s, *no pl.*) pleasure, liking; favour, kindness.

gefallen (1) [gə'falən], *v.n. irr.* please; *es gefällt mir,* I like it; *wie gefällt Ihnen ...;* how do you like ....

gefallen (2) [gə'falən], *adj.* (*Mil.*) fallen, killed in action.

gefällig [gə'fɛlɪç], *adj.* pleasing, accommodating, obliging, anxious to please; *was ist —?* what can I do for you?

Gefälligkeit [gə'fɛlɪçkaɪt], *f.* (—, *pl.* —en) courtesy; favour, service, good turn.

gefälligst [gə'fɛlɪçst], *adv.* if you please.

Gefallsucht [gə'falzuxt], *f.* (—, *no pl.*) coquetry.

gefallsüchtig [gə'falzyçtɪç], *adj.* coquettish.

gefangen [gə'faŋən], *adj.* in prison, imprisoned, captive.

Gefangene [gə'faŋənə], *m.* (—n, *pl.* —n) prisoner, captive.

Gefangennahme [gə'faŋənna:mə], *f.* (—, *no pl.*) capture.

Gefangenschaft [gə'faŋənʃaft], *f.* (—, *no pl.*) captivity, imprisonment, detention; *in — geraten,* be taken prisoner.

Gefängis [gə'fɛnnɪs], *n.* (—sses, *pl.* —sse) prison, gaol.

Gefäß [gə'fɛːs], *n.* (—es, *pl.* —e) vessel.

gefaßt [gə'fast], *adj.* collected, composed, ready; calm; *sich auf etwas — machen,* prepare o.s. for s.th.

Gefecht [gə'fɛçt], *n.* (—s, *pl.* —e) fight, battle, combat; action, engagement.

gefeit [gə'faɪt], *adj.* proof against.

Gefieder [gə'fiːdər], *n.* (—s, *no pl.*) plumage, feathers.

Gefilde [gə'fɪldə], *n.* (—s, *pl.* —) (*Poet.*) fields, plain.

Geflecht [gə'flɛçt], *n.* (—s, *no pl.*) wicker-work, texture.

geflissentlich [gə'flɪsəntlɪç], *adj.* intentional, wilful, with a purpose.

Geflügel [gə'flyːgəl], *n.* (—s, *no pl.*) fowls, poultry.

geflügelt [gə'flyːgəlt], *adj.* winged; *—e Worte,* household word, familiar quotation.

Geflüster [gə'flystər], *n.* (—s, *pl.* —e) whispering, whisper.

Gefolge [gə'fɔlgə], *n.* (—s, *no pl.*) retinue, following.

gefräßig [gə'frɛːsɪç], *adj.* voracious, gluttonous.

Gefreite [gə'fraɪtə], *m.* (—n, *pl.* —n) (*Mil.*) lance-corporal.

gefrieren [gə'friːrən], *v.n. irr.* (*aux.* sein) freeze; congeal.

Gefrierpunkt [gə'friːrpuŋkt], *m.* (—s, *no pl.*) freezing point, zero.

Gefrorene [gə'froːrənə], *n.* (—n, *no pl.*) ice-cream.

Gefüge [gə'fyːgə], *n.* (—s *no pl.*) joints, structure, construction; frame.

gefügig [gə'fyːgɪç], *adj.* pliant; docile; *einen — machen,* make s.o. amenable, persuade s.o.

Gefühl [gə'fyːl], *n.* (—s, *pl.* —e) feeling, sense, sensation.

gegen ['geːgən], *prep.* (*Acc.*) against; towards; about, near; in comparison with; in the direction of; opposed to; in exchange for; *— Quittung,* against receipt. *— adv., prefix.* counter, opposing, contrary.

Gegend ['geːgənt], *f.* (—, *pl.* —en) region, country, part.

Gegengewicht ['geːgəngəvɪçt], *n.* (—s, *pl.* —e) counterweight, counterpoise.

Gegengift ['geːgəngɪft], *n.* (—s, *pl.* —e) antidote.

Gegenleistung ['geːgənlaɪstuŋ], *f.* (—, *pl.* —en) return; service in return; *Leistung und —,* give and take.

Gegenrede ['geːgənreːdə], *f.* (—, *pl.* —n) contradiction; objection.

Gegensatz ['geːgənzats], *m.* (—es, *pl.* —e) contrast, opposition, antithesis.

gegensätzlich ['geːgənzetslɪç], *adj.* contrary, adverse.

Gegenseite ['geːgənzaɪtə], *f.* (—, *pl.* —n) opposite side; (*coin*) reverse.

gegenseitig ['geːgənzaɪtɪç], *adj.* reciprocal, mutual.

Gegenstand ['geːgənʃtant], *m.* (—s, *pl.* —e) object; subject, matter.

gegenstandslos ['geːgənʃtantslo:s], *adj.* superfluous, irrelevant.

Gegenstück ['geːgənʃtyk], *n.* (—s, *pl.* —e) counterpart.

Gegenteil ['geːgəntaɪl], *n.* (—s, *no pl.*) contrary; *im —,* on the contrary.

gegenüber [geːgən'yːbər], *prep.* (*Dat.*) opposite to, facing. *— adv.* opposite.

Gegenüberstellung [geːgən'yːberʃteluŋ], *f.* (—, *pl.* —en) confrontation.

Gegenwart ['geːgənvart], *f.* (—, *no pl.*) presence; (*Gram.*) present tense.

Gegenwehr ['geːgənveːr], *f.* (—, *no pl.*) defence, resistance.

Gegenwirkung ['geːgənvɪrkuŋ], *f.* (—, *pl.* —en) reaction, counter-effect.

gegenzeichnen ['geːgəntsaɪçnən], *v.a.* countersign.

Gegner ['geːgnər], *m.* (—s, *pl.* —) opponent, adversary, antagonist.

gegnerisch ['geːgnərɪʃ], *adj.* adverse, antagonistic.

Gegnerschaft ['geːgnərʃaft], *f.* (—, *no pl.*) antagonism; opposition.

Gehalt (1) [gə'halt], *m.* (—s, *no pl.*) contents; (*fig.*) value, standard.

Gehalt (2) [gə'halt], *n.* (—s, *pl.* —er) salary, stipend; pay.

Gehaltszulage [gə'haltstsu:la:gə], *f.* (—, *pl.* —n) rise (in salary); increment; (*Am.*) raise.

gehaltvoll [gə'haltfɔl], *adj.* substantial.

Gehänge [gə'heŋə], *n.* (—s, *pl.* —) slope; festoon, garland.

geharnischt [gə'harnɪʃt], *adj.* armoured, steel-clad; (*fig.*) severe.

gehässig [gə'hesɪç], *adj.* malicious, spiteful.

Gehäuse [gə'hɔyzə], *n.* (—s, *pl.* —) casing, case; (*snail*) shell.

Gehege [gə'he:gə], *n.* (—s, *pl.* —) enclosure; *einem ins — kommen*, trespass on s.o.'s preserves.

geheim [gə'haɪm], *adj.* secret, clandestine.

Geheimnis [gə'haɪmnɪs], *n.* (—ses, *pl.* —se) secret, mystery.

geheimnisvoll [gə'haɪmnɪsfɔl], *adj.* mysterious.

Geheimrat [gə'haɪmra:t], *m.* (—s, *pl.* ∺e) Privy Councillor.

Geheimschrift [gə'haɪmʃrɪft], *f.* (—, *.pl.* —en) cryptography.

Geheimsprache [gə'haɪmʃpra:xə], *f.* (—, *pl.* —en) cipher.

Geheiß [gə'haɪs], *n.* (—es, *no pl.*) command, order, bidding.

gehen ['ge:ən], *v.n. irr.* (*aux.* sein) go, walk; (*Mach.*) work, function; (*goods*) sell; (*dough*) rise; *er lässt sich —*, he lets himself go; *er lässt es sich gut —*, he enjoys himself; *einem an die Hand —*, lend s.o. a hand, assist s.o.; *in Erfüllung —*, come true; *in sich —*, reflect; *wie geht es dir?* how are you? *es geht mir gut*, I am well.

geheuer [gə'hɔyər], *adj.* (*only in neg.*) *nicht ganz —*, creepy, eerie, uncanny; (*coll.*) fishy.

Gehilfe [gə'hɪlfə], *m.* (—n, *pl.* —n) assistant, helper.

Gehirn [gə'hɪrn], *n.* (—s, *pl.* —e) brain, brains.

Gehirnhautentzündung [gə'hɪrnhaut-ɛntsyndun], *f.* (—, *pl.* —en) meningitis, cerebral inflammation.

Gehirnschlag [gə'hɪrnʃla:k], *m.* (—s, *pl.* ∺e) apoplexy.

Gehöft [gə'hœft], *n.* (—es, *pl.* —e) farmstead.

Gehör [gə'hø:r], (—s, *no pl.*) hearing; *gutes —*, musical ear.

gehorchen [gə'hɔrçən], *v.n.* obey; *nicht —*, disobey.

gehören [gə'hø:rən], *v.n.* belong. — *v.r. sich —*, be the proper thing to do.

gehörig [gə'hø:rɪç], *adj. dazu —*, belonging to, referring to; due, fit, proper, thorough; (*fig.*) sound.

Gehörn [gə'hœrn], *n.* (—s, *pl.* —e) horns, antlers.

gehörnt [gə'hœrnt], *adj.* horned; (*fig.*) duped (husband).

Gehorsam [gə'ho:rza:m], *m.* (—s, *no pl.*) obedience; *— leisten*, show obedience; *den — verweigern*, refuse to obey.

gehorsam [gə'ho:rza:m], *adj.* obedient, dutiful, submissive.

Gehrock ['ge:rɔk], *m.* (—s, *pl.* ∺e) frock-coat.

Geier ['gaɪər], *m.* (—s, *no pl.*) (*Orn.*) vulture.

Geifer ['gaɪfər], *m.* (—s, *no pl.*) saliva, drivel; (*animals*) foam; (*fig.*) venom, rancour.

geifern ['gaɪfərn], *v.n.* slaver, drivel; (*fig.*) foam at the mouth; give vent to o.'s anger.

Geige ['gaɪgə], *f.* (—, *pl.* —n) violin, fiddle.

Geigenharz ['gaɪgənha:rts], *n.* (—es, *no pl.*) colophony; rosin.

Geigensteg ['gaɪgənʃte:k], *m.* (—s, *pl.* —e) bridge of a violin.

Geiger ['gaɪgər], *m.* (—s, *pl.* —) violin-player, violinist.

geil [gaɪl], *adj.* rank; lecherous, lascivious.

Geisel ['gaɪzəl], *f.* (—, *pl.* —n) hostage.

Geiß [gaɪs], *f.* (—, *pl.* —en) goat, she-goat.

Geißblatt ['gaɪsblat], *n.* (—s, *no pl.*) (*Bot.*) honeysuckle.

Geißbock ['gaɪsbɔk], *m.* (—s, *pl.* ∺e) billy-goat.

Geißel ['gaɪsəl], *f.* (—, *pl.* —n) scourge.

geißeln ['gaɪsəln], *v.a.* scourge, whip, flagellate.

Geist [gaɪst], *m.* (—es, *pl.* —er) spirit, mind; brains, intellect; wit; apparition, ghost.

Geisterbeschwörung ['gaɪstərbəʃvø:-run], *f.* (—, *pl.* —en) evocation (of spirits); necromancy; exorcism.

geisterhaft ['gaɪstərhaft], *adj.* ghostly, spectral, weird.

Geisterwelt ['gaɪstərvɛlt], *f.* (—, *no pl.*) world of spirits.

geistesabwesend ['gaɪstəsapve:zənt], *adj.* absent-minded.

Geistesfreiheit ['gaɪstəsfraɪhaɪt], *f.* (—, *no pl.*) freedom of thought.

Geistesgegenwart ['gaɪstəsge:gənvart], *f.* (—, *no pl.*) presence of mind.

Geisteskraft ['gaɪstəskraft], *f.* (—, *pl.* ∺e) faculty of the mind.

Geistesstörung ['gaɪstəsʃtø:run], *f.* (—, *pl.* —en) mental aberration.

Geistesverfassung ['gaɪstəsfɛrfasun], *f.* (—, *no pl.*) state of mind.

geistesverwandt ['gaɪstəsfɛrvant], *adj.* congenial.

Geistesverwirrung ['gaɪstəsfɛrvɪrun], *f.* (—, *no pl.*) bewilderment.

Geisteswissenschaften ['gaɪstəsvɪsən-ʃaftən], *f.pl.* (*Univ.*) Arts, Humanities.

Geisteszerrüttung ['gaɪstəstsɛrytun], *f.* (—, *no pl.*) mental derangement, insanity.

geistig ['gaɪstɪç], *adj.* intellectual, mental; spiritual; *—e Getränke*, alcoholic liquors.

geistlich ['gaɪstlɪç], *adj.* spiritual; religious; ecclesiastical, clerical; *—er Orden*, religious order; *—er Stand*, holy orders, the Clergy.

Geistliche ['gaɪstlɪçə], *m.* (—n, *pl.* —n) priest, clergyman, cleric; minister of religion.

Geistlichkeit ['gaɪstlɪçkaɪt], *f.* (—, *no pl.*) clergy.

geistlos ['gaɪstlo:s], *adj.* dull, stupid.

geistreich ['gaɪstraɪç], *adj.* clever, witty.

Geiz [gaɪts], *m.* (—es, *no pl.*) avarice, covetousness.

geizen ['gaɪtsən], *v.n.* be miserly.

Geizhals

Geizhals [ˈgaɪtshals], *m.* (**—es**, *pl.* ˙e) miser, niggard.

Geizkragen [ˈgaɪtskraːgən], *m.* (**—s**, *pl.* —) *see* **Geizhals**.

Gekreisch [gəˈkraɪʃ], *n.* (**—es**, *no pl.*) screaming, shrieks.

Gekritzel [gəˈkrɪtsəl], *n.* (**—s**, *no pl.*) scrawling, scribbling.

Gekröse [gəˈkrøːzə], *n.* (**—s**, *no pl.*) tripe; (*Anat.*) mesentery.

gekünstelt [gəˈkynstəlt], *adj.* artificial, affected.

Gelächter [gəˈlɛçtər], *n.* (**—s**, *no pl.*) laughter.

Gelage [gəˈlaːgə], *n.* (**—s**, *pl.* —) (*obs.*) feast, banquet.

Gelände [gəˈlɛndə], *n.* (**—s**, *pl.* —) terrain, region; landscape.

Geländer [gəˈlɛndər], *n.* (**—s**, *pl.* —) railing, balustrade, banister.

gelangen [gəˈlaŋən], *v.n.* (*aux.* sein) arrive, come (to).

Gelaß [gəˈlas], *n.* (**—sses**, *pl.* **—sse**) (*obs.*) room, chamber.

gelassen [gəˈlasən], *adj.* calm, composed, collected.

geläufig [gəˈlɔyfɪç], *adj.* fluent.

gelaunt [gəˈlaunt], *adj.* disposed.

Geläute [gəˈlɔytə], *n.* (**—s**, *no pl.*) ringing, chiming; bells.

geläutert [gəˈlɔytərt], *adj.* purified, cleansed.

gelb [gɛlp], *adj.* yellow, amber.

Gelbschnabel [ˈgɛlpʃnaːbəl], *m.* (**—s**, *pl.* ˙) (*Orn.*) fledg(e)ling; greenhorn.

Gelbsucht [ˈgɛlpzuxt], *f.* (**—**, *no pl.*) jaundice.

Geld [gɛlt], *n.* (**—es**, *pl.* **—er**) money, currency, coin; *bares* —, ready money, hard cash; *kleines* —, small change.

Geldanweisung [ˈgɛltanvaɪzuŋ], *f.* (**—**, *pl.* **—en**) money-order.

Geldbuße [ˈgɛltbuːsə], *f.* (**—**, *pl.* **—n**) fine.

Geldkurs [ˈgɛltkurs], *m.* (**—es**, *pl.* **—e**) rate of exchange.

Geldmittel [ˈgɛltmɪtəl], *n. pl.* pecuniary resources, financial resources.

Geldschrank [ˈgɛltʃraŋk], *m.* (**—s**, *pl.* ˙e) safe.

Geldstrafe [ˈgɛltʃtraːfə], *f.* (**—**, *pl.* **—n**) fine.

Geldverlegenheit [ˈgɛltferleːgənhaɪt], *f.* (**—**, *pl.* **—en**) pecuniary embarrassment, financial difficulty.

Geldwährung [ˈgɛltvɛːruŋ], *f.* (**—**, *pl.* **—en**) currency.

Geldwechsel [ˈgɛltvɛksəl], *m.* (**—s**, *no pl.*) exchange.

Gelee [ʒəˈleː], *n.* (**—s**, *pl.* **—s**) jelly.

gelegen [gəˈleːgən], *adj.* situated, situate; *das kommt mir gerade —*, that suits me; *mir ist daran —, dass*, I am anxious that.

Gelegenheit [gəˈleːgənhaɪt], *f.* (**—**, *pl.* **—en**) occasion, chance, opportunity; facility; *bei* —, one of these days.

Gelegenheitskauf [gəˈleːgənhaɪtskauf], *m.* (**—s**, *pl.* ˙e) bargain.

gelegentlich [gəˈleːgəntlɪç], *adj.* occasional.

gelehrig [gəˈleːrɪç], *adj.* docile, tractable.

Gelehrsamkeit [gəˈleːrzaːmkaɪt], *f.* (**—**, *no pl.*) learning, erudition.

gelehrt [gəˈleːrt], *adj.* learned, erudite.

Gelehrte [gəˈleːrtə], *m.* (**—n**, *pl.* **—n**) scholar, man of learning, savant.

Geleise [gəˈlaɪzə], *n.* (**—s**, *pl.* —) *see* **Gleis**.

Geleit [gəˈlaɪt], *n.* (**—s**, *no pl.*) escort, accompaniment; (*Naut.*) convoy; *sicheres* —, safe conduct.

geleiten [gəˈlaɪtən], *v.a.* accompany, conduct, escort.

Gelenk [gəˈlɛŋk], *n.* (**—s**, *pl.* **—e**) (*human*) joint; (*chain*) link.

Gelenkentzündung [gəˈlɛŋkɛnttsynduŋ], *f.* (**—**, *pl.* **—en**) (*Med.*) arthritis.

gelenkig [gəˈlɛŋkɪç], *adj.* flexible, pliant, nimble, supple.

Gelenkrheumatismus [gəˈlɛŋkrɔymatɪsmus], *m.* (**—**, *no pl.*) (*Med.*) rheumatoid arthritis, rheumatic gout.

Gelichter [gəˈlɪçtər], *n.* (**—s**, *no pl.*) riff-raff.

Geliebte [gəˈliːptə], *m.* (**—n**, *pl.* **—n**) lover, sweetheart, beloved. — *f.* (**—n**, *pl.* **—n**) mistress; beloved.

gelinde [gəˈlɪndə], *adj.* soft, smooth, gentle, mild; — *gesagt*, to say the least.

Gelingen [gəˈlɪŋən], *n.* (**—s**, *no pl.*) success.

gelingen [gəˈlɪŋən], *v.n. irr.* (*aux.* sein) succeed; *es gelingt mir*, I succeed.

gellen [ˈgɛlən], *v.n.* yell; shrill.

geloben [gəˈloːbən], *v.a.* (*aux.* haben) promise solemnly, vow; *das Gelobte Land*, the Promised Land.

Gelöbnis [gəˈløːpnɪs], *n.* (**—ses**, *pl.* **—se**) vow, promise.

gelt [gɛlt], *inter.* (*coll.*) isn't it? don't you think so?

gelten [ˈgɛltən], *v.a. irr.* be worth, cost. — *v.n.* count (as), be valid.

Geltung [ˈgɛltuŋ], *f.* (**—**, *no pl.*) value, importance.

Gelübde [gəˈlypdə], *n.* (**—s**, *pl.* —) vow, solemn promise *or* undertaking.

gelungen [gəˈluŋən], *adj.* (*coll.*) funny, capital.

Gelüst [gəˈlyst], *n.* (**—s**, *pl.* **—e**) appetite, desire.

gelüsten [gəˈlystən], *v.a.* — *nach*, long for, covet.

Gemach [gəˈmaːx], *n.* (**—es**, *pl.* ˙er) (*Poet.*) chamber, room; apartment.

gemach [gəˈmaːx], *adv.* slowly, softly, by degrees.

gemächlich [gəˈmɛçlɪç], *adj.* slow, soft, easy, unhurried, leisurely.

Gemahl [gəˈmaːl], *m.* (**—s**, *pl.* **—e**) spouse, husband, consort.

Gemahlin [gəˈmaːlɪn], *f.* (**—**, *pl.* **—nen**) spouse, wife, consort.

Gemälde [gəˈmɛːldə], *n.* (**—s**, *pl.* —) picture, painting, portrait.

gemäß [gəˈmɛːs], *prep.* (*Dat.*) in accordance with, according to.

gemäßigt [gə'mɛːsɪçt], *adj.* temperate, moderate; *—es Klima*, temperate climate.

Gemäuer [gə'mɔyər], *n.* (—s, *no pl.*) ancient walls, ruins.

gemein [gə'maɪn], *adj.* common, mean, low, vulgar, base.

Gemeinde [gə'maɪndə], *f.* (—, *pl.* —n) community, parish, municipality; (*Eccl.*) congregation.

Gemeindevorstand [gə'maɪndefɔr-ʃtant], *m.* (—es, *no pl.*) town *or* borough council.

gemeingefährlich [gə'maɪngəfɛːrlɪç], *adj.* dangerous to the public.

Gemeinheit [gə'maɪnhaɪt], *f.* (—, *pl.* —en) meanness; baseness; dirty trick.

gemeinhin [gə'maɪnhɪn], *adv.* commonly.

Gemeinplatz [gə'maɪnplats], *m.* (—es, *pl.* ⁻e) commonplace, truism.

gemeinsam [gə'maɪnzaːm], *adj.* common, joint; (*Pol.*) Common Market; *—e Sache machen*, make common cause. — *adv.* together.

Gemeinschaft [gə'maɪnʃaft], *f.* (—, *pl.* —en) community; association; *in — mit*, jointly; *in — haben*, hold in common.

gemeinschaftlich [gə'maɪnʃaftlɪç], *adj.* common. — *adv.* in common, together.

Gemeinsinn [gə'maɪnzɪn], *m.* (—s, *no pl.*) public spirit.

Gemeinwesen [gə'maɪnveːzən], *n.* (—s, *no pl.*) community.

Gemeinwohl [gə'maɪnvoːl], *n.* (—s, *no pl.*) common weal; common good.

Gemenge [gə'mɛŋə], *n.* (—s, *no pl.*) mixture; (*fig.*) scuffle.

Gemengsel [gə'mɛŋsəl], *n.* (—s, *no pl.*) medley, hotchpotch.

gemessen [gə'mɛsən], *adj.* deliberate.

Gemessenheit [gə'mɛsənhaɪt], *f.* (—, *no pl.*) precision, deliberation.

Gemetzel [gə'mɛtsəl], *n.* (—s, *no pl.*) slaughter, massacre.

Gemisch [gə'mɪʃ], *n.* (—es, *pl.* —e) mixture, motley.

Gemme ['gɛmə], *f.* (—, *pl.* —n) gem, cameo.

Gemse ['gɛmzə], *f.* (—, *pl.* —n) chamois.

Gemüse [gə'myːzə], *n.* (—s, *pl.* —) vegetables, greens.

Gemüsehändler [gə'myːzəhɛndlər], *m.* (—s, *pl.* —) greengrocer.

gemustert [gə'mustərt], *adj.* patterned, figured; (*Comm.*) *—e Sendung*, delivery as per sample.

Gemüt [gə'myːt], *n.* (—s, *pl.* —er) mind, soul, heart; disposition, nature, spirit, temper; feeling.

gemütlich [gə'myːtlɪç], *adj.* cosy, snug, comfortable; genial, friendly, pleasant.

Gemütlichkeit [gə'myːtlɪçkaɪt], *f.* (—, *no pl.*) cosiness, snugness; *da hört die — auf*, that is more than I will stand for.

gemütlos [gə'myːtloːs], *adj.* unfeeling.

Gemütsart [gə'myːtsaːrt], *f.* (—, *no pl.*) disposition; character.

Gemütsbewegung [gə'myːtsbəveːguŋ], *f.* (—, *pl.* —en) emotion.

gemütskrank [gə'myːtskraŋk], *adj.* sick in mind; melancholy.

Gemütsleben [gə'myːtsleːbən], *n.* (—s, *no pl.*) emotional life.

Gemütsmensch [gə'myːtsmɛnʃ], *m.* (—en, *pl.* —en) man of feeling *or* sentiment; (*pej.*) sentimentalist.

gemütvoll [gə'myːtfɔl], *adj.* full of feeling, sympathetic.

gen [gɛn], *prep. contraction of* **gegen**, (*Poet.*) towards, to (*Acc.*).

Genannte [gə'nantə], *m.* (—n, *pl.* —n) named person, aforesaid.

genäschig [gə'nɛʃɪç], *adj.* fond of sweets, sweet-toothed.

genau [gə'nau], *adj.* precise, exact, accurate; strict, parsimonious.

Genauigkeit [gə'nauɪçkaɪt], *f.* (—, *no pl.*) accuracy, exactitude, precision.

Gendarm [ʒãˈdarm], *m.* (—en, *pl.* —en) policeman, constable.

genehm [gə'neːm], *adj.* agreeable, acceptable, convenient.

genehmigen [gə'neːmɪgən], *v.a.* approve of, agree to, permit; (*contract*) ratify.

geneigt [gə'naɪkt], *adj.* inclined (to), disposed (to), prone (to); *einem — sein*, be well disposed towards s.o.; (*Lit.*) *der —e Leser*, gentle reader.

Geneigtheit [gə'naɪkthaɪt], *f.* (—, *no pl.*) inclination, proneness, propensity; favour, kindness.

General [genə'raːl], *m.* (—s, *pl.* —e, ⁻e) general.

Generalfeldmarschall [genə'raːlfɛlt-marʃal], *m.* (—s, *pl.* ⁻e) field marshal.

Generalkommando [genə'raːlkɔmando], *n.* (—s, *pl.* —s) general's headquarters; (*corps*) headquarters.

Generalkonsul [genə'raːlkɔnzul], *m.* (—s, *pl.* —e) consul-general.

Generalnenner [genə'raːlnɛnər], *m.* (—s, *pl.* —) (*Maths.*) common denominator.

Generalprobe [genə'raːlproːbə], *f.* (—, *pl.* —n) dress-rehearsal.

Generalvollmacht [genə'raːlfɔlmaxt], *f.* (—, *pl.* —en) (*Law*) general power of attorney.

generell [genə'rɛl], *adj.* general, common.

generös [genə'røːs], *adj.* generous, magnanimous.

genesen [gə'neːzən], *v.n. irr.* (*aux.* sein) recover, be restored to health; convalesce.

Genf [gɛnf], *n.* Geneva.

genial [gen'jaːl], *adj.* ingenious; extremely gifted.

Genick [gə'nɪk], *n.* (—s, *pl.* —e) nape, neck.

Genickstarre [gə'nɪkʃtarə], *f.* (—, *no pl.*) (*Med.*) (cerebrospinal) meningitis.

Genie [ʒe'niː], *n.* (—s, *pl.* —s) genius.

genieren [ʒeˈniːrən], v.a. trouble, embarrass, disturb. — v.r. sich —, feel embarrassed; sich nicht —, make o.s. at home.

genießbar [gəˈniːsbaːr], adj. eatable, edible, palatable; drinkable; (fig.) pleasant, agreeable.

genießen [gəˈniːsən], v.a. irr. enjoy; have the use of; (food) eat, partake of; Ansehen —, enjoy respect.

Geniestreich [ʒeˈniːʃtraɪç], m. (—s, pl. —e) stroke of genius.

Genitiv [ˈgeːnitiːf], m. (—s, pl. —e) (Gram.) genitive.

Genosse [gəˈnɔsə], m. (—n, pl. —n) comrade, mate, colleague; (crime) accomplice.

Genossenschaft [gəˈnɔsənʃaft], f. (—, pl. —en) association, company, confederacy, co-operative, union.

Genre [ˈʒãrə], n. (—s, pl. —s) genre; style, kind.

Gent [gɛnt], n. Ghent.

Genua [ˈgeːnua], n. Genoa.

genug [gəˈnuːk], indecl. adj. enough, sufficient; —! that will do!

Genüge [gəˈnyːgə], f. (—, no pl.) zur —, sufficiently; einem — leisten, give satisfaction to s.o.

genügen [gəˈnyːgən], v.n. be enough, suffice; sich etwas — lassen, be content with s.th.

genügsam [gəˈnyːkzaːm], adj. easily satisfied; temperate, sober.

Genügsamkeit [gəˈnyːkzaːmkaɪt], f. (—, no pl.) contentedness, moderation; temperateness, sobriety.

Genugtuung [gəˈnuːktuːŋ], f. (—, no pl.) satisfaction; reparation; atonement.

Genuß [gəˈnus], m. (—sses, pl. ˝sse) enjoyment; use; (food) consumption.

Genußmittel [gəˈnusmɪtəl], n. (—s, pl. —) (mostly pl.) luxuries; (Am.) delicatessen.

genußreich [gəˈnusraɪç], adj. enjoyable, delightful.

Genußsucht [gəˈnusuxt], f. (—, no pl.) thirst for pleasure.

Geograph [geoˈgraːf], m. (—en, pl. —en) geographer.

Geographie [geograˈfiː], f. (—, no pl.) geography.

Geologe [geoˈloːgə], m. (—n, pl. —n) geologist.

Geologie [geoloˈgiː], f. (—, no pl.) geology.

Geometer [geoˈmeːtər], m. (—s, pl. —) geometrician; land-surveyor.

Geometrie [geomeˈtriː], f. (—, no pl.) geometry.

Georg [geˈɔrk], m. George.

Georgine [geɔrˈgiːnə], f. (—, pl. —n) (Bot.) dahlia.

Gepäck [gəˈpɛk], n. (—s, no pl.) luggage; (Am.) baggage.

Gepäckaufbewahrung [gəˈpɛkaufbəvaːruŋ], f. (—, pl. —en) left luggage office.

Gepäckträger [gəˈpɛktrɛːgər], m. (—s, pl. —) porter.

Gepflogenheit [gəˈpfloːgənhaɪt], f. (—, pl. —en) habit, custom, wont.

Geplänkel [gəˈplɛnkəl], n. (—s, pl. —) (rare) skirmish.

Geplärr [gəˈplɛr], n. (—s, no pl.) bawling.

Geplauder [gəˈplaudər], n. (—s, no pl.) chatting; small talk.

Gepräge [gəˈprɛːgə], n. (—s, no pl.) impression, stamp.

Gepränge [gəˈprɛŋə], n. (—s, no pl.) pomp, ceremony, splendour.

Ger [geːr], m. (—s, pl. —e) (rare) spear, javelin.

Gerade [gəˈraːdə], f. (—n, pl. —n) (Maths.) straight line.

gerade [gəˈraːdə], adj. straight, direct, erect, even; (fig.) upright, honest. — adv. quite, just; jetzt —, now more than ever; fünf — sein lassen, stretch a point; — heraus, in plain terms.

geradeaus [gəˈraːdəaus], adv. straight on.

gerädert [gəˈrɛːdərt], adj. (fig.) fatigued, exhausted, worn out.

geradeswegs [gəˈraːdəsveːks], adv. straightaway, immediately.

geradezu [gəˈraːdətsuː], adv. frankly, downright; das ist — scheußlich, this is downright nasty.

Geradheit [gəˈraːthaɪt], f. (—, no pl.) straightness; (fig.) straightforwardness.

geradlinig [gəˈraːtliːnɪç], adj. rectilinear.

geradsinnig [gəˈraːtzɪnɪç], adj. honest, upright.

gerändert [gəˈrɛndərt], adj. with a milled edge.

Geranie [gəˈraːnjə], f. (—, pl. —n) (Bot.) geranium.

Gerät [gəˈrɛːt], n. (—s, pl. —e) tool, implement, device; appliance; (radio, television) set; apparatus.

geraten [gəˈraːtən], v.n. irr. (aux. sein) turn out; gut —, turn out well; — auf, come upon.

Geräteturnen [gəˈrɛːtəturnən], n. (—s, no pl.) gymnastics with apparatus.

Geratewohl [gəˈraːtəvoːl], n. (—s, no pl.) aufs —, at random.

geraum [gəˈraum], adj. —e Zeit, a long time.

geräumig [gəˈrɔymɪç], adj. spacious, large, wide, roomy.

Geräusch [gəˈrɔyʃ], n. (—es, pl. —e) noise; sound.

gerben [ˈgɛrbən], v.a. tan, taw; einem die Haut —, give s.o. a hiding.

Gerber [ˈgɛrbər], m. (—s, pl. —) tanner.

Gerbsäure [ˈgɛrbsɔyrə], f. (—, no pl.) tannin.

gerecht [gəˈrɛçt], adj. just, fair; (Bibl.) righteous; einem — werden, do justice to s.o.

Gerechtigkeit [gəˈrɛçtɪçkaɪt], f. (—, no pl.) justice, fairness; (Bibl.) righteousness.

Gerede [gə're:də], n. (—s, no pl.) talk, rumour, gossip.

gereichen [gə'raɪçən], v.n. turn out to be; *einem zur Ehre* —, redound to s.o.'s honour.

gereizt [gə'raɪtst], adj. irritated, annoyed.

gereuen [gə'rɔyən] see **reuen**.

Gerhard ['ge:rhart], m. Gerard, Gerald.

Gericht [gə'rɪçt], n. (—s, pl. —e) court of justice, tribunal; (*food*) course, dish; *das Jüngste* —, Last Judgment.

gerichtlich [gə'rɪçtlɪç], adj. judicial, legal; *einen — belangen*, sue s.o.

Gerichtsbarkeit [gə'rɪçtsbarkaɪt], f. (—, no pl.) jurisdiction.

Gerichtsdiener [gə'rɪçtsdi:nər], m. (—s, pl. —) (*law court*) usher.

Gerichtshof [gə'rɪçtsho:f], m. (—es, pl. ̈e) court of justice.

Gerichtskanzlei [gə'rɪçtskantslaɪ], f. (—, pl. —en) record office.

Gerichtskosten [gə'rɪçtskɔstən], f. pl. (*Law*) costs.

Gerichtsordnung [gə'rɪçtsɔrdnuŋ], f. (—, pl —en) legal procedure.

Gerichtstermin [gə'rɪçtstermi:n], m. (—s, pl. —e) day fixed for a hearing.

Gerichtsverhandlung [gə'rɪçtsfer-handluŋ], f. (—, pl. —en) hearing; trial.

Gerichtsvollzieher [gə'rɪçtsfɔltsi:ər], m. (—s, pl. —) bailiff.

gerieben [gə'ri:bən], adj. ground; crafty, cunning.

gering [gə'rɪŋ], adj. small, little, mean, petty, unimportant, of little value, trifling; low, base.

geringfügig [gə'rɪŋfy:gɪç], adj. small, petty, insignificant.

geringschätzig [gə'rɪŋʃɛtsɪç], adj. contemptuous, disdainful, supercilious; derogatory.

gerinnen [gə'rɪnən], v.n. irr. (*aux.* sein) coagulate, clot; curdle.

Gerinnsel [gə'rɪnzəl], n. (—s, pl. —) embolism (of the blood); clot.

Gerippe [gə'rɪpə], n. (—s, pl. —) skeleton; frame; (*Aviat.*) air-frame.

gerippt [gə'rɪpt], adj. ribbed, fluted.

gerissen [gə'rɪsən], adj. (*coll.*) sharp, cunning.

Germane [gɛr'ma:nə], m. (—n, pl. —n) Teuton.

Germanist ['germanɪst], m. (—en, pl. —en) (*Univ.*) student or expert in German language and/or literature.

gern [gɛrn], adv. gladly, willingly, readily, with pleasure; — *haben*, like.

Geröll [gə'rœl], n. (—s, no pl.) boulders, rubble.

Gerste ['gɛrstə], f. (—, no pl.) (*Bot.*) barley.

Gerstenschleim ['gɛrstənʃlaɪm], m. (—s, no pl.) barley water.

Gerte ['gɛrtə], f. (—, pl. —n) whip, switch, rod.

Geruch [gə'ru:x], m. (—s, pl. ̈e) smell, odour, scent; *guter* —, fragrance, aroma.

geruchlos [gə'ru:xlo:s], adj. scentless, odourless, without smell.

Geruchsinn [gə'ru:xzɪn], m. (—es, no pl.) sense of smell.

Gerücht [gə'ryçt], n. (—s, pl. —e) rumour, report.

Gerümpel [gə'rympəl], n. (—s, no pl.) lumber, trash.

Gerundium [gə'rundjum], n. (—s, pl. —dien) (*Gram.*) gerund.

Gerüst [gə'ryst], n. (—es, pl. —e) scaffolding.

Ges [gɛs], n. (—, pl. —) (*Mus.*) G flat.

gesamt [gə'zamt], adj. entire, all, complete.

Gesamtheit [gə'zamthaɪt], f. (—, no pl.) totality.

Gesandte [gə'zantə], m. (—n, pl. —n) messenger; ambassador, envoy; *päpstlicher* —, papal nuncio.

Gesandtschaft [gə'zantʃaft], f. (—, pl. —en) embassy, legation.

Gesang [gə'zaŋ], m. (—s, pl. ̈e) song, air; hymn; (*Lit.*) canto.

Gesangbuch [gə'zaŋbu:x], n. ̈(—s, pl. ̈er) hymnal, hymn-book.

Gesäß [gə'zɛ:s], n. (—es, pl. —e) seat, buttocks.

Geschäft [gə'ʃɛft], n. (—s, pl. —e) business; trade, commerce; affairs; occupation; shop; (*Am.*) store.

geschäftig [gə'ʃɛftɪç], adj. active, bustling, busy.

geschäftlich [gə'ʃɛftlɪç], adj. concerning business. — *adv.* on business.

Geschäftsführer [gə'ʃɛftsfy:rər], m. (—s, pl. —) manager.

Geschäftshaus [gə'ʃɛftshaus], n. (—es, pl. ̈er) firm; business premises.

geschäftskundig [gə'ʃɛftskundɪç], adj. experienced in business.

Geschäftslokal [gə'ʃɛftsloka:l], n. (—s, pl. —e) business premises, shop.

Geschäftsordnung [gə'ʃɛftsɔrdnuŋ], f. (—, pl. —en) standing orders; agenda.

Geschäftsträger [gə'ʃɛftstrɛ:gər], m. (—s, pl. —) (*Comm.*) agent; (*Pol.*) chargé d'affaires.

Geschäftsverkehr [gə'ʃɛftsferke:r], m. (—s, no pl.) business dealings.

Geschehen [gə'ʃe:ən], n. (—s, no pl.) happening.

geschehen [gə'ʃe:ən], v.n. irr. (*aux.* sein) happen, occur; take place; be done; *das geschieht dir recht*, it serves you right.

gescheit [gə'ʃaɪt], adj. clever, intelligent.

Geschenk [gə'ʃɛŋk], n. (—s, pl. —e) gift, present, donation.

Geschichte [gə'ʃɪçtə], f. (—, pl. —n) tale; story; history.

Geschichtenbuch [gə'ʃɪçtənbu:x], n. (—es, pl. ̈er) story-book.

geschichtlich [gə'ʃɪçtlɪç], adj. historical.

Geschichtsschreiber [gə'ʃɪçtsʃraɪbər], m. (—s, pl. —) historian.

Geschick [gə'ʃɪk], n. (—es, no pl.) fate, destiny; dexterity, skill, knack, aptitude.

Geschicklichkeit [gə'ʃɪklɪçkaɪt], *f.* (—, *pl.* —en) dexterity, adroitness, skill.

geschickt [gə'ʃɪkt], *adj.* skilled, skilful, clever, able.

Geschirr [gə'ʃɪr], *n.* (—s, *no pl.*) crockery, plates and dishes; (*horses*) harness.

Geschlecht [gə'ʃlɛçt], *n.* (—s, *pl.* —er) sex; kind, race, species, extraction, family; (*Gram.*) gender.

geschlechtlich [gə'ʃlɛçtlɪç], *adj.* sexual; generic.

Geschlechtsart [gə'ʃlɛçtsaːrt], *f.* (—, *pl.* —en) generic character.

Geschlechtskrankheit [gə'ʃlɛçtskraŋkhaɪt], *f.* (—, *pl.* —en) venereal disease.

Geschlechtskunde [gə'ʃlɛçtskundə], *f.* (—, *no pl.*) genealogy.

Geschlechtsreife [gə'ʃlɛçtsraɪfə], *f.* (—, *no pl.*) puberty.

Geschlechtsteile [gə'ʃlɛçtstaɪlə], *m. pl.* genitals.

Geschlechtstrieb [gə'ʃlɛçtstriːp], *m.* (—s, *no pl.*) sexual instinct.

Geschlechtswort [gə'ʃlɛçtsvɔrt], *n.* (—s, *pl.* —er) (*Gram.*) article.

geschliffen [gə'ʃlɪfən], *adj.* polished; (*glass*) cut.

Geschmack [gə'ʃmak], *m.* (—s, *pl.* ⁀er) taste, flavour.

geschmacklos [gə'ʃmakloːs], *adj.* tasteless, insipid; in bad taste.

Geschmacksrichtung [gə'ʃmaksrɪçtuŋ], *f.* (—, *pl.* —en) prevailing taste; vogue; tendency.

Geschmeide [gə'ʃmaɪdə], *n.* (—s, *pl.* —) jewels, jewellery; trinkets.

geschmeidig [gə'ʃmaɪdɪç], *adj.* flexible, pliant, supple; (*Tech.*) malleable.

Geschmeiß [gə'ʃmaɪs], *n.* (—es, *no pl.*) dung; vermin; (*fig.*) rabble.

Geschnatter [gə'ʃnatər], *n.* (—s, *no pl.*) cackling.

geschniegelt [gə'ʃniːgəlt], *adj.* spruce, dressed up.

Geschöpf [gə'ʃœpf], *n.* (—es, *pl.* —e) creature.

Geschoß [gə'ʃɔs], *n.* (—sses, *pl.* —sse) shot, shell, projectile, missile; (*house*) storey.

geschraubt [gə'ʃraupt], *adj.* (*style*) stilted, affected.

Geschrei [gə'ʃraɪ], *n.* (—s, *no pl.*) shrieking, shouting, screaming; (*fig.*) stir, great noise.

Geschreibsel [gə'ʃraɪpsəl], *n.* (—s, *no pl.*) scrawl, scribbling.

Geschütz [gə'ʃyts], *n.* (—es, *pl.* —e) artillery, guns; *schweres — auffahren*, bring o.'s. guns into play.

Geschützweite [gə'ʃytsvaɪtə], *f.* (—, *no pl.*) calibre.

Geschwader [gə'ʃvaːdər], *n.* (—s, *pl.*—) squadron.

Geschwätz [gə'ʃvɛts], *n.* (—es, *no pl.*) chatter, gossip, prattle, tittle-tattle.

geschweige [gə'ʃvaɪgə], *adv.* let alone, to say nothing of.

geschwind [gə'ʃvɪnt], *adj.* quick, nimble, fast, swift, fleet.

Geschwindigkeitsmesser [gə'ʃvɪndɪçkaɪtsmɛsər], *m.* (—s, *pl.* —) (*Motor.*) speedometer.

Geschwister [gə'ʃvɪstər], *pl.* brothers and sisters.

geschwollen [gə'ʃvɔlən], *adj.* stilted, turgid, pompous.

Geschworene [gə'ʃvoːrənə], *m.* (—n, *pl.* —n), juror, juryman; (*pl.*) jury.

Geschwulst [gə'ʃvulst], *f.* (—, *pl.* ⁀e) swelling, tumour.

Geschwür [gə'ʃvyːr], *n.* (—s, *pl.* —e) sore, ulcer, abscess.

Geselle [gə'zɛlə], *m.* (—n, *pl.* —n) journeyman; companion, comrade, mate.

gesellen [gə'zɛlən], *v.a.*, *v.r.* join, associate with, keep company with.

gesellig [gə'zɛlɪç], *adj.* sociable, companionable; gregarious.

Gesellschaft [gə'zɛlʃaft], *f.* (—, *pl.* —en) society; community; (formal) party; company, club; *geschlossene —*, private party; *einem — leisten*, keep s.o. company; (*Comm.*) — *mit beschränkter Haftung*, (abbr.) *GmbH*, limited company, (*abbr.*) Ltd.

gesellschaftlich [gə'zɛlʃaftlɪç], *adj.* social.

Gesellschaftsanzug [gə'zɛlʃaftsantsuːk], *m.* (—s, *pl.* ⁀e) evening dress.

Gesellschaftsspiel [gə'zɛlʃaftsʃpiːl], *n.* (—s, *pl.* —e) round game, party game.

Gesellschaftsvertrag [gə'zɛlʃaftsfɛrtraːk], *m.* (—es, *pl.* ⁀e) (*Law*) partnership agreement; deed of partnership.

Gesellschaftszimmer [gə'zɛlʃaftstsimər], *n.* (—s, *pl.* —) drawing-room, reception room.

Gesetz [gə'zɛts], *n.* (—es, *pl.* —e) law, statute, regulation.

Gesetzbuch [gə'zɛtsbuːx], *n.* (—es, *pl.* ⁀er) code of laws; statute book.

Gesetzentwurf [gə'zɛtsɛntvurf], *m.* (—es, *pl.* ⁀er) (*Parl.*) draft bill.

gesetzgebend [gə'zɛtsgeːbənt], *adj.* legislative.

gesetzlich [gə'zɛtslɪç], *adj.* lawful, legal.

Gesetzlichkeit [gə'zɛtslɪçkaɪt], *f.* (—, *no pl.*) lawfulness, legality.

gesetzlos [gə'zɛtsloːs], *adj.* lawless, anarchical.

gesetzmäßig [gə'zɛtsmɛːsɪç], *adj.* conforming to law, lawful, legitimate.

gesetzt [gə'zɛtst], *adj.* steady, sedate, staid; *von — em Alter*, of mature age; — *daß*, supposing that.

Gesetztheit [gə'zɛtsthaɪt], *f.* (—, *no pl.*) sedateness, steadiness.

gesetzwidrig [gə'zɛtsviːdrɪç], *adj.* illegal, unlawful.

Gesicht (1) [gə'zɪçt], *n.* (—s, *pl.* —er) face, physiognomy, look.

Gesicht (2) [gə'zɪçt], *n.* (—s, *pl.* —e) sight; vision, apparition.

Gesichtsausdruck [gə'zɪçtsausdruk], *m.* (—s, *no pl.*) face, mien; expression.

Gesichtsfeld [gəˈzɪçtsfɛlt], *n.* (**—es,** *pl.* **—er**) field of vision.

Gesichtskreis [gəˈzɪçtskraɪs], *m.* (**—es,** *pl.* **—e**) horizon.

Gesichtspunkt [gəˈzɪçtspuŋkt], *m.* (**—es,** *pl.* **—e**) point of view.

Gesichtszug [gəˈzɪçtstsuːk], *m.* (**—s,** *pl.* ˑːe) feature.

Gesims [gəˈzɪms], *n.* (**—es,** *pl.* **—e**) cornice, moulding, ledge.

Gesinde [gəˈzɪndə], *n.* (**—s,** *no pl.*) (domestic) servants.

Gesindel [gəˈzɪndəl], *n.* (**—s,** *no pl.*) mob, rabble.

gesinnt [gəˈzɪnt], *adj.* disposed.

Gesinnung [gəˈzɪnuŋ], *f.* (**—,** *pl.* **—en**) disposition, sentiment; conviction.

gesinnungslos [gəˈzɪnuŋsloːs], *adj.* unprincipled.

gesinnungstreu [gəˈzɪnuŋstrɔy], *adj.* loyal, staunch.

Gesinnungswechsel [gəˈzɪnuŋsvɛksəl], *m.* (**—s,** *no pl.*) change of opinion, volte-face.

gesittet [gəˈzɪtət], *adj.* civilised, well-mannered.

Gesittung [gəˈzɪtuŋ], *f.* (**—,** *no pl.*) (*rare*) civilisation, good manners.

gesonnen [gəˈzɔnən] *see* gesinnt.

Gespann [gəˈʃpan], *n.* (**—s,** *pl.* **—e**) team, yoke (oxen etc.).

gespannt [gəˈʃpant], *adj.* stretched; intense, thrilled; tense; filled with suspense.

Gespanntheit [gəˈʃpanthaɪt], *f.* (**—,** *no pl.*) tension, strain, suspense.

Gespenst [gəˈʃpɛnst], *n.* (**—es,** *pl.* **—er**) ghost, spectre, apparition.

gespenstisch [gəˈʃpɛnstɪʃ], *adj.* ghostly, spectral.

Gespiele [gəˈʃpiːlə], *m.* (**—n,** *pl.* **—n**) playmate.

Gespielin [gəˈʃpiːlɪn], *f.* (**—,** *pl.* **—innen**) (girl) playmate.

Gespinst [gəˈʃpɪnst], *n.* (**—es,** *pl.* **—e**) web.

Gespött [gəˈʃpœt], *n.* (**—s,** *no pl.*) mocking, mockery, jeering, derision; (*fig.*) laughing stock.

Gespräch [gəˈʃprɛːç], *n.* (**—s,** *pl.* **—e**) conversation, discourse, talk; (*phone*) call; *ein — anknüpfen*, start a conversation.

gesprächig [gəˈʃprɛːçɪç], *adj.* talkative, communicative.

gespreizt [gəˈʃpraɪtst], *adj.* wide apart; (*fig.*) affected, pompous.

gesprenkelt [gəˈʃprɛŋkəlt], *adj.* speckled.

gesprungen [gəˈʃpruŋən], *adj.* cracked (glass etc.).

Gestade [gəˈʃtaːdə], *n.* (**—s,** *pl.* **—**) shore, coast, bank.

Gestalt [gəˈʃtalt], *f.* (**—**, *pl.* **—en**) form, figure, shape; configuration; stature; fashion; manner, way.

gestalten [gəˈʃtaltən], *v.a.* form, shape, fashion, make. — *v.r. sich —*, turn out.

Gestaltung [gəˈʃtaltuŋ], *f.* (**—,** *pl.* **—en**) formation; arrangement; planning.

geständig [gəˈʃtɛndɪç], *adj.* confessing; *— sein,* confess.

Geständnis [gəˈʃtɛntnɪs], *n.* (**—ses,** *pl.* **—se**) confession, admission.

Gestank [gəˈʃtaŋk], *m.* (**—s,** *no pl.*) stink, stench.

gestatten [gəˈʃtatən], *v.a.* permit, allow, grant; *wir —,* we beg leave to; *— Sie !* pardon me, excuse me.

Geste [ˈgɛstə], *f.* (**—,** *pl.* **—n**) gesture, gesticulation.

gestehen [gəˈʃteːən], *v.a. irr.* confess, admit, own; *offen gestanden,* quite frankly.

Gestein [gəˈʃtaɪn], *n.* (**—s,** *pl.* **—e**) (*Poet.*) rock; (*Geol.*) rocks, minerals.

Gestell [gəˈʃtɛl], *n.* (**—s,** *pl.* **—e**) rack, frame; (*table*) trestle; (*books*) stand.

Gestellung [gəˈʃtɛluŋ], *f.* (**—,** *no pl.*) (*Mil.*) reporting for service.

gestern [ˈgɛstərn], *adv.* yesterday; *— abend,* last night.

gestiefelt [gəˈʃtiːfəlt], *adj.* booted; *der —e Kater,* Puss in Boots.

gestielt [gəˈʃtiːlt], *adj.* (*axe*) helved; (*Bot.*) stalked, stemmed.

gestikulieren [gɛstikuˈliːrən], *v.n.* gesticulate.

Gestirn [gəˈʃtɪrn], *n.* (**—s,** *pl.* **—e**) star, constellation.

gestirnt [gəˈʃtɪrnt], *adj.* starred, starry.

Gestöber [gəˈʃtøːbər], *n.* (**—s,** *pl.* **—**) (*snow, dust*) drift, storm, blizzard.

Gesträuch [gəˈʃtrɔyç], *n.* (**—s,** *no pl.*) bushes, shrubs; thicket.

gestreift [gəˈʃtraɪft], *adj.* striped.

gestreng [gəˈʃtrɛŋ], *adj.* (*obs.*) strict, severe.

gestrig [ˈgɛstrɪç], *adj.* of yesterday.

Gestrüpp [gəˈʃtryp], *n.* (**—s,** *no pl.*) bushes, underwood, shrubs, shrubbery.

Gestüt [gəˈʃtyːt], *n.* (**—s,** *pl.* **—e**) stud (-farm).

Gestüthengst [gəˈʃtyːthɛŋst], *m.* (**—es,** *pl.* **—e**) stallion.

Gesuch [gəˈzuːx], *n.* (**—s,** *pl.* **—e**) petition, request, application.

gesucht [gəˈzuːxt], *adj.* in demand; (*style*) far-fetched; affected; studied.

gesund [gəˈzunt], *adj.* healthy, wholesome; *der —e Menschenverstand,* common sense.

Gesundbrunnen [gəˈzuntbrunən], *m.* (**—s,** *pl.* **—**) mineral waters; spa.

gesunden [gəˈzundən], *v.n.* (*aux.* sein) recover o.'s health.

Gesundheit [gəˈzunthaɪt], *f.* (**—,** *no pl.*) health.

Gesundheitslehre [gəˈzunthaɪtsleːrə], *f.* (**—,** *no pl.*) hygiene.

Getäfel [gəˈtɛːfəl], *n.* (**—s,** *no pl.*) wainscot, wainscoting, panelling.

Getändel [gəˈtɛndəl], *n.* (**—s,** *no pl.*) (*rare*) flirting, dallying.

Getier [gəˈtiːr], *n.* (**—s,** *no pl.*) (*collective term*) animals.

Getöse [gəˈtøːzə], *n.* (**—s,** *no pl.*) loud noise, din.

Getränk [gə'trɛŋk], *n.* (**—s,** *pl.* **—e**) drink, beverage.
getrauen [gə'trauən], *v.r. sich —*, dare, venture.
Getreide [gə'traɪdə], *n.* (**—s,** *pl.* **—**) corn, grain.
getreu [gə'trɔy], *adj.* faithful, true, loyal.
getreulich [gə'trɔylɪç], *adv.* faithfully, truly, loyally.
Getriebe [gə'tri:bə], *n.* (**—s,** *pl.* **—**) machinery; (*Motor.*) gear; drive; *das — der Welt*, the bustle of life.
getrieben [gə'tri:bən], *adj.* (*Tech.*) chased (work.)
Getrödel [gə'trø:dəl], *n.* (**—s,** *no pl.*) dawdling.
getrost [gə'tro:st], *adj.* confident, cheerful; *— sein*, be of good cheer.
Getto ['gɛto], *n.* (**—s,** *pl.* **—s**) ghetto.
Getue [gə'tu:ə], *n.* (**—s,** *no pl.*) pretence, fuss.
Getümmel [gə'tyməl], *n.* (**—s,** *no pl.*) bustle, turmoil.
geübt [gə'y:pt], *adj.* skilled, versed.
Geübtheit [gə'y:pthaɪt], *f.* (**—,** *no pl.*) skill, experience, dexterity.
Gevatter [gə'fatər], *m.* (**—s,** *pl.* **—**) (*obs.*) godfather.
geviertelt [gə'fi:rtaɪlt], *adj.* quartered.
Gewächs [gə'vɛks], *n.* (**—es,** *pl.* **—e**) plant, growth; (*Med.*) excrescence.
gewachsen [gə'vaksən], *adj. einem* (*einer Sache*) *— sein*, be equal to s.o. (s.th.).
Gewächshaus [gə'vɛkshaus], *n.* (**—es,** *pl.* **¨er**) green-house, hot-house, conservatory.
gewagt [gə'va:kt], *adj.* risky, hazardous; daring.
gewählt [gə'vɛ:lt], *adj.* choice, select.
gewahr [gə'va:r], *adj. einer Sache — werden*, become aware of s.th., perceive s.th.
Gewähr [gə'vɛ:r], *f.* (**—,** *no pl.*) surety; guarantee; warranty; *— leisten*, guarantee.
gewahren [gə'va:rən], *v.a.* perceive, see, become aware of.
gewähren [gə'vɛ:rən], *v.a.* allow, grant; *einen — lassen*, let s.o. do as he pleases, let be.
Gewährleistung [gə'vɛ:rlaɪstuŋ], *f.* (**—,** *pl.* **—en**) grant of security (*or* bail); guarantee.
Gewahrsam [gə'va:rza:m], *m.* (**—s,** *no pl.*) safe-keeping, custody.
Gewährsmann [gə'vɛ:rsman], *m.* (**—es,** *pl.* **¨er**) authority; informant.
Gewährung [gə'vɛ:ruŋ,] *f.* (**—,** *no pl.*) granting (of request).
Gewalt [gə'valt], *f.* (**—,** *pl.* **—en**) power, force, might; authority; violence; *höhere —*, (*Law*) act of God, force majeure; *sich in der — haben*, have control over o.s.
Gewalthaber [gə'valtha:bər], *m.* (**—s,** *pl.* **—**) tyrant; despot, autocrat; person in authority.
gewaltig [gə'valtɪç], *adj.* powerful, mighty, enormous, stupendous.
gewaltsam [gə'valtza:m], *adj.* forcible, violent.
Gewaltstreich [gə'valtʃtraɪç], *m.* (**—s,** *pl.* **—e**) bold stroke; coup d'état.
Gewalttat [gə'valtta:t], *f.* (**—,** *pl.* **—en**) violent action, violence, outrage.
gewalttätig [gə'valttɛ:tɪç], *adj.* violent, fierce, outrageous.
Gewand [gə'vant], *n.* (**—es,** *pl.* **¨er**) (*Lit.*) garment, dress; (*Eccl.*) vestment.
gewandt [gə'vant], *adj.* nimble, deft, clever; (*mind*) versatile.
gewärtig [gə'vɛrtɪç], *adj. einer Sache — sein*, expect s.th. to happen.
Gewäsch [gə'vɛʃ], *n.* (**—es,** *no pl.*) stuff and nonsense; rubbish.
Gewässer [gə'vɛsər], *n.* (**—s,** *pl.* **—**) waters.
Gewebe [gə've:bə], *n.* (**—s,** *pl.* **—**) (*Physiol.*, *Text.*) tissue; web, weft, texture.
geweckt [gə'vɛkt], *adj.* smart, wide-awake.
Gewehr [gə've:r], *n.* (**—s,** *pl.* **—e**) gun, fire-arm, rifle.
Gewehrlauf [gə've:rlauf], *m.* (**—s,** *pl.* **¨e**) barrel.
Geweih [gə'vaɪ], *n.* (**—s,** *pl.* **—e**) horns, antlers.
geweiht [gə'vaɪt], *adj.* consecrated; holy.
gewellt [gə'vɛlt], *adj.* corrugated, wavy.
Gewerbe [gə'vɛrbə], *n.* (**—s,** *pl.* **—**) trade, profession, business; calling; industry.
Gewerbekunde [gə'vɛrbəkundə], *f.* (**—,** *no pl.*) technology.
Gewerbeschein [gə'vɛrbəʃaɪn], *m.* (**—s,** *pl.* **—e**) trade-licence.
gewerblich [gə'vɛrplɪç], *adj.* industrial.
gewerbsmäßig [gə'vɛrpsmɛ:sɪç], *adj.* professional.
Gewerkschaft [gə'vɛrkʃaft], *f.* (**—,** *pl.* **—en**) trade union.
Gewicht [gə'vɪçt], *n.* (**—s,** *pl.* **—e**) weight; *schwer ins — fallen*, carry great weight, weigh heavily.
gewichtig [gə'vɪçtɪç], *adj.* weighty, ponderous; (*fig.*) momentous, important, strong.
gewiegt [gə'vi:kt], *adj.* experienced, clever.
gewillt [gə'vɪlt], *adj.* willing.
Gewimmel [gə'vɪməl], *n.* (**—s,** *no pl.*) milling crowd, swarm, throng.
Gewinde [gə'vɪndə], *n.* (**—s,** *pl.* **—**) (*screw*) thread; (*flowers*) garland.
Gewinn [gə'vɪn], *m.* (**—s,** *pl.* **—e**) gain, profit; (*lottery*) prize; (*gambling*) winnings.
gewinnen [gə'vɪnən], *v.a. irr.* win, gain, obtain, get, earn.
gewinnend [gə'vɪnənt], *adj.* prepossessing; engaging.
Gewinnung [gə'vɪnuŋ], *f.* (**—,** *no pl.*) (*Ind.*, *Chem.*) extraction; output, production.
Gewinsel [gə'vɪnzəl], *n.* (**—s,** *no pl.*) whimpering.

Gewinst [gə'vɪnst], *m.* (—es, *pl.* —e) (*obs.*) gain, profit.

Gewirr [gə'vɪr], *n.* (—s, *no pl.*) entanglement, confusion.

gewiß [gə'vɪs], *adj.* (*Genit.*) certain, sure. — *adv.* indeed.

Gewissen [gə'vɪsən], *n.* (—s, *no pl.*) conscience.

gewissenhaft [gə'vɪsənhaft], *adj.* conscientious, scrupulous.

gewissenlos [gə'vɪsənlo:s], *adj.* unscrupulous.

Gewissensbiß [gə'vɪsənsbɪs],*m.*(—sses, *pl.* —sse) (*mostly pl.*) pangs of conscience.

gewissermaßen [gə'vɪsərma:sən], *adv.* to a certain extent, so to speak.

Gewißheit [gə'vɪshaɪt], *f.* (—, *no pl.*) certainty.

gewißlich [gə'vɪslɪç], *adv.* surely.

Gewitter [gə'vɪtər], *n.* (—s, *pl.* —) thunderstorm.

gewittern [gə'vɪtərn], *v.n.* thunder.

gewitzigt, gewitzt [gə'vɪtsɪçt, gə'vɪtst], *adj.* knowing, clever; shrewd.

gewogen [gə'vo:gən], *adj.* kindly disposed, favourable; *einem — sein*, be favourably inclined towards s.o.

Gewogenheit [gə'vo:gənhaɪt], *f.* (—, *no pl.*) kindness, favour.

gewöhnen [gə'vø:nən], *v.a.* accustom to. — *v.r. sich — an*, get used to, accustom o.s. to.

Gewohnheit [gə'vo:nhaɪt], *f.* (—, *pl.* —en) (*general*) custom, usage; (*personal*) habit.

gewohnheitsmäßig [gə'vo:nhaɪtsmɛ:sɪç], *adj.* habitual. — *adv.* by force of habit.

Gewohnheitsrecht [gə'vo:nhaɪtsrɛçt], *n.* (—s, *no pl.*) common law.

gewöhnlich [gə'vø:nlɪç], *adj.* customary, usual; (*fig.*) common, mean, vulgar.

gewohnt [gə'vo:nt], *adj.* accustomed to, used to.

Gewöhnung [gə'vø:nuŋ], *f.* (—, *no pl.*) habit, use, habituation.

Gewölbe [gə'vœlbə], *n.* (—s, *pl.* —) vault, arch.

Gewölk [gə'vœlk], *n.* (—s, *no pl.*) clouds, cloud formation.

Gewühl [gə'vy:l], *n.* (—s, *no pl.*) crowd, throng, bustle.

gewunden [gə'vundən], *adj.* tortuous.

Gewürm [gə'vyrm], *n.* (—s, *no pl.*) reptiles, worms; vermin.

Gewürz [gə'vyrts], *n.* (—es, *pl.* —e) spice.

Gewürznelke [gə'vyrtsnɛlkə], *f.* (—, *pl.* —n) clove.

Gezänk [gə'tsɛŋk], *n.* (—s, *no pl.*) quarrelling, bickering.

Gezeiten [gə'tsaɪtən], *f. pl.* tides.

Gezeter [gə'tse:tər], *n.* (—s, *no pl.*) screaming, yelling; (*fig.*) outcry.

geziemen [gə'tsi:mən], *v.r. sich für einen —*, befit or become s.o.

geziert [gə'tsi:rt], *adj.* affected.

Gezischel [gə'tsɪʃəl], *n.* (—s, *no pl.*) whispering.

Gezücht [gə'tsyçt], *n.* (—s, *no pl.*) brood, breed.

Gezweig [gə'tsvaɪk], *n.* (—s, *no pl.*) branches, boughs.

Gezwitscher [gə'tsvɪtʃər], *n.* (—s, *no pl.*) chirping.

Gezwungenheit [gə'tsvuŋənhaɪt], *f.* (—, *no pl.*) constraint.

Gicht [gɪçt], *f.* (—, *no pl.*) (*Med.*) gout.

gichtbrüchig ['gɪçtbryçɪç], *adj.* (*obs.*) paralytic; gouty.

gichtig ['gɪçtɪç], *adj.* gouty.

Giebel ['gi:bəl], *m.* (—s, *pl.* —) gable.

Giebelfenster ['gi:bəlfɛnstər], *n.* (—s, *pl.*—) gable-window, dormer-window.

gieb(e)lig ['gi:b(ə)lɪç], *adj.* gabled.

Gier [gi:r], *f.* (—, *no pl.*) greediness, eagerness.

gieren ['gi:rən], *v.n.* (*rare*) — *nach*, thirst for, yearn for.

gierig ['gi:rɪç], *adj.* eager, greedy.

Gießbach ['gi:sbax], *m.* (—s, *pl.* ⁻e) mountain-torrent.

gießen ['gi:sən], *v.a. irr.* (*liquids*) pour, shed; (*metal*) cast, found.

Gießer ['gi:sər], *m.* (—s, *pl.* —) founder.

Gießerei [gi:sə'raɪ], *f.* (—, *pl.* —en) foundry.

Gießform ['gi:sfɔrm], *f.* (—, *pl.* —en) casting-mould.

Gießkanne ['gi:skanə], *f.* (—, *pl.* —n) watering-can.

Gift [gɪft], *n.* (—es, *pl.* —e) poison, venom; (*fig.*) virulence; (*coll.*) *darauf kannst du — nehmen*, you can bet your life on it.

Giftbaum ['gɪftbaum], *m.* (—s, *pl.* ⁻e) upas-tree.

Giftdrüse ['gɪftdry:zə], *f.* (—, *pl.* —n) poison-gland.

giftig ['gɪftɪç], *adj.* poisonous; (*fig.*) venomous; (*Med.*) toxic.

Giftlehre ['gɪftle:rə], *f.* (—, *no pl.*) toxicology.

Giftpilz ['gɪftpɪlts], *m.* (—es, *pl.* —e) poisonous toadstool.

Giftschlange ['gɪftʃlaŋə], *f.* (—, *pl.* —n) poisonous snake.

Giftstoff ['gɪftʃtɔf], *m.* (—es, *pl.* —e) poison, virus.

Gigant [gɪ'gant], *m.* (—en, *pl.* —en) giant.

Gigerl ['gi:gərl], *m.* (—s, *pl.* —) (*Austr. dial.*) fop, coxcomb.

Gilde ['gɪldə], *f.* (—, *pl.* —n) guild, corporation.

Gimpel ['gɪmpəl], *m.* (—s, *pl.* —) (*Orn.*) bullfinch, chaffinch; (*fig.*) simpleton.

Ginster ['gɪnstər], *m.* (—s, *no pl.*) (*Bot.*) gorse, furze, broom.

Gipfel ['gɪpfəl], *m.* (—s, *pl.* —) summit, peak; (*fig.*) acme, culmination, height.

gipfeln ['gɪpfəln], *v.n.* culminate.

Gips [gɪps], *m.* (—, *no pl.*) gypsum, stucco, plaster of Paris.

Gipsabdruck ['gɪpsapdruk], *m.* (—s, *pl.* ⁻e) plaster-cast.

Gipsbild

Gipsbild [ˈgɪpsbɪlt], *n.* (—s, *pl.* —er) plaster-figure.

Gipsverband [ˈgɪpsfɛrbant], *m.* (—es, *pl.* ⁓e) (*Med.*) plaster of Paris dressing.

girieren [ʒiˈriːrən], *v.a.* (*Comm.*) endorse (a bill).

Girlande [gɪrˈlandə], *f.* (—, *pl.* —n) garland.

Girobank [ˈʒiːrobaŋk], *f.* (—, *pl.* —en) transfer *or* clearing bank.

Gis [gɪs], *n.* (—, *pl.* —) (*Mus.*) G sharp; — *Moll*, G sharp minor.

gischen [ˈgɪʃən], *v.n.* foam, froth.

Gischt [gɪʃt], *f.* (—, *pl.* ⁓e) foam, froth; spray.

Gitarre [giˈtarə], *f.* (—, *pl.* —n) guitar.

Gitter [ˈgɪtər], *n.* (—s, *pl.* —) trellis, grate, fence; railing; lattice; (*colour-printing*) screen.

Gitterwerk [ˈgɪtərvɛrk], *n.* (—s, *no pl.*) trellis-work.

Glacéhandschuh [glaˈseːhantʃuː], *m.* (—s, *pl.* ⁓e) kid-glove.

Glanz [glants], *m.* (—es, *no pl.*) brightness, lustre, gloss; polish, sheen; (*fig.*) splendour.

glänzen [ˈglɛntsən], *v.n.* shine, glitter, glisten; (*fig.*) sparkle.

glänzend [ˈglɛntsənt], *adj.* glossy; (*fig.*) splendid, magnificent.

Glanzfirnis [ˈglantsfɪrnɪs], *m.* (—ses, *pl.* —se) glazing varnish.

Glanzleder [ˈglantsleːdər], *n.* (—s, *no pl.*) patent leather.

Glanzleinwand [ˈglantslaɪnvant], *f.* (—, *no pl.*) glazed linen.

glanzlos [ˈglantsloːs], *adj.* lustreless, dull.

glanzvoll [ˈglantsfɔl], *adj.* splendid, brilliant.

Glanzzeit [ˈglantstsaɪt], *f.* (—, *pl.* —en) golden age.

Glas [glaːs], *n.* (—es, *pl.* ⁓er) glass, tumbler.

glasartig [ˈglaːsaːrtɪç], *adj.* vitreous, glassy.

Glaser [ˈglaːzər], *m.* (—s, *pl.* —) glazier.

Glaserkitt [ˈglaːzərkɪt], *m.* (—s, *no pl.*) putty.

gläsern [ˈglɛːzərn], *adj.* vitreous, glassy, made of glass.

Glashütte [ˈglaːshʏtə], *f.* (—, *pl.* —n) glass-works.

glasieren [glaˈziːrən], *v.a.* glaze; (*cake etc.*) ice.

glasiert [glaˈziːrt], *adj.* glazed; (*Cul.*) frosted, iced; (*Art.*) varnished.

Glasröhre [ˈglaːsrøːrə], *f.* (—, *pl.* —n) glass-tube.

Glasscheibe [ˈglaːsʃaɪbə], *f.* (—, *pl.* —n) glass-pane, sheet of glass.

Glassplitter [ˈglaːsʃplɪtər], *m.* (—s, *pl.* —) splinter of glass.

Glasur [glaˈzuːr], *f.* (—, *pl.* —en) (*potter's*) glaze, glazing; enamel, varnish; (*cake*) icing.

glatt [glat], *adj.* smooth, sleek; even, plain, glossy; glib; downright. — *adv.* entirely; — *rasiert*, close-shaven.

Glätte [ˈglɛtə], *f.* (—, *no pl.*) smoothness, evenness, slipperiness; polish.

Glatteis [ˈglataɪs], *n.* (—es, *no pl.*) slippery ice; sheet ice; (*Am.*) glaze; *einen aufs* — *führen*, lead s.o. up the garden path.

glätten [ˈglɛtən], *v.a.* smooth; (*dial.*) iron.

Glatze [ˈglatsə], *f.* (—, *pl.* —n) bald head.

glatzköpfig [ˈglatskœpfɪç], *adj.* bald, bald-pated.

Glaube(n) [ˈglaubə(n)], *m.* (—ns, *no pl.*) faith, belief; creed, religion.

glauben [ˈglaubən], *v.a.* believe; think, suppose. — *v.n. an etwas* (*Acc.*) —, believe in s.th.

Glaubensbekenntnis [ˈglaubənsbəkɛntnɪs], *n.* (—ses, *pl.* —se) confession of faith; creed.

Glaubensgericht [ˈglaubənsgərɪçt], *n.* (—es, *no pl.*) inquisition.

Glaubersalz [ˈglaubərzalts], *n.* (—es, *no pl.*) phosphate of soda, Glauber's salts.

glaubhaft [ˈglauphaft], *adj.* credible, authentic.

gläubig [ˈglɔybɪç], *adj.* believing, faithful; (*Eccl.*) *die Gläubigen*, the faithful.

Gläubiger [ˈglɔybɪgər], *m.* (—s, *pl.* —) creditor.

glaublich [ˈglauplɪç], *adj.* credible, believable.

glaubwürdig [ˈglaupvyrdɪç], *adj.* authentic, worthy of belief; plausible.

gleich [glaɪç], *adj.* same, like, equal, even; *auf —e Weise*, likewise; *es ist mir ganz* —, it is all the same to me. — *adv.* alike, at once; almost; just as; *ich komme* —, I shall be there in a moment; — *und* — *gesellt sich gern*, birds of a feather flock together.

gleichaltrig [ˈglaɪçaltrɪç], *adj.* of the same age.

gleichartig [ˈglaɪçaːrtɪç], *adj.* of the same kind, homogeneous.

gleichberechtigt [ˈglaɪçbəreçtɪçt], *adj.* entitled to equal rights.

Gleiche [ˈglaɪçə], *n.* (—n, *pl.* —n) the like; the same; *etwas ins* — *bringen*, straighten s.th. out.

gleichen [ˈglaɪçən], *v.n. irr.* be like, resemble, be equal to.

gleichermaßen [ˈglaɪçərmaːsən], *adv.* in a like manner, likewise.

gleichfalls [ˈglaɪçfals], *adv.* likewise, equally, as well; *danke* —, thanks, the same to you.

gleichförmig [ˈglaɪçfœrmɪç], *adj.* uniform; monotonous.

gleichgesinnt [ˈglaɪçgəzɪnt], *adj.* congenial, of the same mind.

Gleichgewicht [ˈglaɪçgəvɪçt], *n.* (—s, *no pl.*) balance, equilibrium.

gleichgültig [ˈglaɪçgʏltɪç], *adj.* indifferent; *es ist mir* —, it's all the same to me.

Gleichheit [ˈglaɪçhaɪt], *f.* (—, *pl.* —en) equality, likeness.

Gleichklang ['glaıçklaŋ], *m.* (—s, *pl.* ⁻e) consonance.

gleichmachen ['glaıçmaxən], *v.a.* level, equate; *dem Erdboden —,* raze to the ground.

Gleichmaß ['glaıçma:s], *n.* (—es, *no pl.*) proportion, symmetry.

gleichmäßig ['glaıçme:sıç], *adj.* proportionate, symmetrical.

Gleichmut ['glaıçmu:t], *m.* (—s, *no pl.*) equanimity, calm.

gleichmütig ['glaıçmy:tıç], *adj.* even-tempered, calm.

gleichnamig ['glaıçna:mıç], *adj.* homonymous.

Gleichnis ['glaıçnıs], *n.* (—ses, *pl.* —se) simile; (*Bibl.*) parable.

gleichsam ['glaıçza:m], *adv.* as it were, as if.

gleichschenklig ['glaıçʃeŋklıç], *adj.* (*Maths.*) isosceles.

gleichseitig ['glaıçzaıtıç], *adj.* (*Maths.*) equilateral.

Gleichsetzung ['glaıçzɛtsuŋ], *f.* (—, *no pl.*), **Gleichstellung** ['glaıçʃtɛluŋ], *f.* (—, *pl.* —en) equalisation.

Gleichstrom ['glaıçʃtro:m], *m.* (—s, *no pl.*) (*Elec.*) direct current.

gleichtun ['glaıçtu:n], *v.a. irr. es einem —,* emulate s.o.

Gleichung ['glaıçuŋ], *f.* (—, *pl.* —en) (*Maths.*) equation.

gleichwohl ['glaıçvo:l], *adv., conj.* nevertheless, however, yet.

gleichzeitig ['glaıçtsaıtıç], *adj.* simultaneous, contemporary.

Gleis [glaıs], *n.* (—es, *pl.* —e) (*Railw.*) track; rails; (*Am.*) track.

gleiten ['glaıtən], *v.n. irr.* (*aux.* sein) glide, slide, slip.

Gleitflug ['glaıtflu:k], *m.* (—es, *pl.* ⁻e) (*Aviat.*) gliding.

Gletscher ['glɛtʃər], *m.* (—s, *pl.* —) glacier.

Gletscherspalte ['glɛtʃərʃpaltə], *f.* (—, *pl.* —n) crevasse.

Glied [gli:t], *n.* (—es, *pl.* —er) limb, joint; member; link; rank, file.

Gliederlähmung ['gli:dərlɛ:muŋ], *f.* (—, *no pl.*) paralysis.

gliedern ['gli:dərn], *v.a.* articulate, arrange, form.

Gliederreißen ['gli:dərraısən], *n.* (—s, *no pl.*) pain in the limbs, rheumatism, arthritis etc.

Gliederung ['gli:dəruŋ], *f.* (—, *pl.* —en) articulation, disposition, structure, arrangement, organisation.

Gliedmaßen ['gli:tma:sən], *f. pl.* limbs.

glimmen ['glımən], *v.n. irr.* glimmer, glow, burn faintly; *—de Asche,* embers.

Glimmer ['glımər], *m.* (—s, *no pl.*) (*Min.*) mica.

glimpflich ['glımpflıç], *adj.* gentle.

glitschen ['glıtʃən], *v.n.* (*aux.* sein) (*coll.*) slide.

glitschig ['glıtʃıç], *adj.* (*coll.*) slippery.

glitzern ['glıtsərn], *v.n.* glisten, glitter.

Globus ['glo:bus], *m.* (—ses, *pl.* —se) globe.

Glöckchen ['glœkçən], *n.* (—s, *pl.* —) small bell; hand-bell.

Glocke ['glɔkə], *f.* (—, *pl.* —n) bell; *etwas an die große — hängen,* make a great fuss about s.th.

Glockenblume ['glɔkənblu:mə], *f.* (—, *pl.* —n) (*Bot.*) bluebell.

Glockengießer ['glɔkəngi:sər], *m.* (—s, *pl.* —) bell-founder.

glockenklar ['glɔkənkla:r], *adj.* as clear as a bell.

Glockenläuter ['glɔkənlɔytər], *m.* (—s, *pl.* —) bell-ringer.

Glockenspiel ['glɔkənʃpi:l], *n.* (—s, *pl.* —e) chime; (*Mus.*) glockenspiel, carillon.

Glockenstuhl ['glɔkənʃtu:l], *m.* (—s, *pl.* ⁻e) belfry.

Glockenzug ['glɔkəntsu:k], *m.* (—s, *pl.* ⁻e) bell-rope; (*Mus.*) bell-stop.

Glöckner ['glœkner], *m.* (—s, *pl.* —) bellringer, sexton.

glorreich ['glo:raıç], *adj.* glorious.

Glosse ['glɔsə], *f.* (—, *pl.* —n) gloss, comment, annotation; *—n machen über,* comment upon; find fault with; scoff at.

glotzen ['glɔtsən], *v.n.* stare wide-eyed; gape.

Glück [glyk], *n.* (—s, *no pl.*) luck, good luck, fortune, happiness; — *haben,* be in luck; *auf gut —,* at random; *zum —,* fortunately, luckily; *viel —,* good luck.

Glucke ['glukə], *f.* (—, *pl.* —n) (sitting) hen.

glücken ['glykən], *v.n.* succeed; *es ist mir geglückt,* I have succeeded in.

glücklich ['glyklıç], *adj.* fortunate, lucky, happy.

glückselig [glyk'ze:lıç], *adj.* blissful, happy.

glucksen ['gluksən], *v.n.* gurgle.

Glücksfall ['glyksfal], *m.* (—es, *pl.* ⁻e) lucky chance, windfall, stroke of good fortune.

Glückspilz ['glykspılts], *m.* (—es, *pl.* —e) (*coll.*) lucky dog.

glückverheißend ['glykfɛrhaısənt], *adj.* auspicious, propitious.

Glückwunsch ['glykvunʃ], *m.* (—es, *pl.* ⁻e) congratulation; felicitation.

glühen ['gly:ən], *v.a.* make red-hot; (*wine*) mull. — *v.n.* glow, be red-hot.

glühend ['gly:ənt], *adj.* glowing, burning; red-hot; (*coal*) live; (*fig.*) ardent, fervent.

Glühstrumpf ['gly:ʃtrumpf], *m.* (—es, *pl.* ⁻e) incandescent mantle.

Glühwein ['gly:vaın], *m.* (—s, *no pl.*) mulled wine.

Glut [glu:t], *f.* (—, *no pl.*) glowing fire; heat; (*fig.*) ardour.

glutrot ['glu:tro:t], *adj.* fiery red.

Glyzerin ['glytsəri:n], *n.* (—s, *no pl.*) glycerine.

93

Gnade

Gnade ['gna:də], *f.* (—, *pl.* —**n**) grace; favour; pardon, clemency, mercy; kindness; *Euer* —**n**, Your Grace.

Gnadenakt ['gna:dənakt], *m.* (—**s**, *pl.* —**e**) act of grace.

Gnadenbrot ['gna:dənbro:t], *n.* (—**s**, *no pl.*) *das* — *essen*, live on charity.

Gnadenfrist ['gna:dənfrist], *f.* (—, *pl.* —**en**) respite.

Gnadenort ['gna:dənɔrt], *m.* (—(**e**)**s**, *pl.* —**e**) place of pilgrimage.

Gnadenstoß ['gna:dənʃto:s], *m.* (—**es**, *pl.* ⸚**e**) finishing stroke, coup de grâce, death-blow.

gnadenvoll ['gna:dənfɔl], *adj.* merciful, gracious.

Gnadenweg ['gna:dənve:k], *m.* (—**es**, *no pl.*) act of grace; *auf dem* —, by reprieve (as an act of grace).

gnädig ['gnɛ:diç], *adj.* gracious, merciful, kind; —*e Frau*, Madam; —*er Herr*, Sir.

Gnostiker ['gnɔstikər], *m.* (—**s**, *pl.* —) gnostic.

Gnu [gnu:], *n.* (—**s**, *pl.* —**s**) (*Zool.*) gnu.

Gold [gɔlt], *n.* (—(**e**)**s**, *no pl.*) gold.

Goldammer ['gɔltamər], *f.* (—, *pl.* —**n**) (*Orn.*) yellow-hammer.

Goldamsel ['gɔltamzəl], *f.* (—, *pl.* —**n**) (*Orn.*) yellow-thrush.

Goldarbeiter ['gɔltarbaitər], *m.* (—**s**, *pl.* —) goldsmith.

Goldbarren ['gɔltbarən], *m.* (—**s**, *pl.* —) ingot of gold.

Goldbergwerk ['gɔltbɛrkvɛrk], *n.* (—**s**, *pl.* —**e**) gold-mine.

Goldfisch ['gɔltfiʃ], *m.* (—**es**, *pl.* —**e**) goldfish.

Goldgewicht ['gɔltgəviçt], *n.* (—**s**, *no pl.*) gold-weight, troy-weight.

Goldgrube ['gɔltgru:bə], *f.* (—, *pl.* —**n**) gold-mine.

goldig ['gɔltiç], *adj.* golden; (*fig.*) sweet, cute, charming.

Goldklumpen ['gɔltklumpən], *m.* (—**s**, *pl.* —) nugget (of gold).

Goldlack ['gɔltlak], *m.* (—**s**, *no pl.*) gold-coloured varnish; (*Bot.*) wall-flower.

Goldmacher ['gɔltmaxər], *m.* (—**s**, *pl.* —) alchemist.

Goldregen ['gɔltre:gən], *m.* (—**s**, *pl.* —) (*Bot.*) laburnum.

Goldscheider ['gɔltʃaidər], *m.* (—**s**, *pl.* —) gold-refiner.

Goldschmied ['gɔltʃmi:t], *m.* (—**s**, *pl.* —**e**) goldsmith.

Goldschnitt ['gɔltʃnit], *m.* (—**s**, *no pl.*) gilt edge.

Golf (1) [gɔlf], *m.* (—**s**, *pl.* —**e**) gulf.

Golf (2) [gɔlf], *n.* (—**s**, *no pl.*) golf.

Gondel ['gɔndəl], *f.* (—, *pl.* —**n**) gondola.

gondeln ['gɔndəln], *v.n.* (*aux.* sein) ride in a gondola; (*coll.*) travel, get about.

gönnen ['gœnən], *v.a. einem etwas* —, not grudge s.o. s.th.; *wir* — *es ihm*, we are happy for him.

Gönner ['gœnər], *m.* (—**s**, *pl.* —) patron, protector.

gönnerhaft ['gœnərhaft], *adj.* patronising.

Gönnerschaft ['gœnərʃaft], *f.* (—, *no pl.*) patronage.

gordisch ['gɔrdiʃ], *adj.* Gordian; *der* —*e Knoten*, the Gordian knot.

Göre ['gø:rə], *f.* (—, *pl.* —**n**) (*coll.*) brat; (*Am.*) kid.

Gosse ['gɔsə], *f.* (—, *pl.* —**n**) gutter.

Gote ['go:tə], *m.* (—**n**, *pl.* —**n**) Goth.

Gotik ['go:tik], *f.* (—, *no pl.*) Gothic style (architecture etc.).

gotisch ['go:tiʃ], *adj.* Gothic.

Gott [gɔt], *m.* (—**es**, *pl.* ⸚**er**) God, god; — *befohlen*, goodbye; *grüß* —*!* (*Austr.*) good day; — *sei Dank*, thank God, thank heaven.

gottbegnadet ['gɔtbəgna:dət], *adj.* favoured by God, inspired.

Götterbild ['gœtərbilt], *n.* (—**es**, *pl.* —**er**) image of a god.

gottergeben ['gɔterge:bən], *adj.* submissive to God's will, devout.

Götterlehre ['gœtərle:rə], *f.* (—, *pl.* —**n**) mythology.

Götterspeise ['gœtərʃpaizə], *f.* (—, *pl.* —**n**) ambrosia.

Götterspruch ['gœtərʃprux], *m.* (—**s**, *no pl.*) oracle.

Göttertrank ['gœtərtraŋk], *m.* (—**s**, *pl.* ⸚**e**) nectar.

Gottesacker ['gɔtəsakər], *m.* (—**s**, *pl.* —) God's acre, churchyard.

Gottesdienst ['gɔtəsdi:nst], *m.* (—**es**, *pl.* —**e**) divine service, public worship.

gottesfürchtig ['gɔtəsfyrçtiç], *adj.* God-fearing, pious.

Gottesgelehrsamkeit ['gɔtəsgəle:rza:mkait], *f.* (—, *no pl.*) (*rare*) theology, divinity.

Gottesgericht ['gɔtəsgəriçt], *n.* (—**s**, *pl.* —**e**) ordeal.

Gotteshaus ['gɔtəshaus], *n.* (—**es**, *pl.* ⸚**er**) house of God; (*rare*) church.

Gotteslästerer ['gɔtəslɛstərər], *m.* (—**s**, *pl.* —) blasphemer.

Gottesleugner ['gɔtəslɔygnər], *m.* (—**s**, *pl.* —) atheist.

Gottfried ['gɔtfri:t], *m.* Godfrey, Geoffrey.

gottgefällig ['gɔtgəfɛliç], *adj.* pleasing to God.

Gottheit ['gɔthait], *f.* (—, *pl.* —**en**) deity, divinity.

Göttin ['gœtin], *f.* (—, *pl.* —**nen**) goddess.

göttlich ['gœtliç], *adj.* divine, godlike; (*fig.*) heavenly.

gottlob! [gɔt'lo:p], *excl.* thank God!

gottlos ['gɔtlo:s], *adj.* godless, ungodly, impious; (*fig.*) wicked.

gottvergessen ['gɔtfergesən], *adj.* reprobate, impious.

gottverlassen ['gɔtfɛrlasən], *adj.* God-forsaken.

Götze ['gœtsə], *m.* (—**n**, *pl.* —**n**) idol, false deity.

94

Götzenbild ['gœtsənbɪlt], *n.* (**—es,** *pl.* **—er**) idol.
Götzendienst ['gœtsəndi:nst], *m.* (**—es,** *no pl.*) idolatry.
Gouvernante [guvɛr'nantə], *f.* (**—,** *pl.* **—n**) governess.
Gouverneur [guvɛr'nø:r], *m.* (**—s,** *pl.* **—e**) governor.
Grab [gra:p], *n.* (**—s,** *pl.* **—er**) grave, tomb; sepulchre.
Graben ['gra:bən], *m.* (**—s,** *pl.* **⸚**) ditch, trench.
graben ['gra:bən], *v.a. irr.* dig.
Grabgeläute ['gra:pgəlɔytə], *n.* (**—s,** *no pl.*) death-knell.
Grabhügel ['gra:phy:gəl], *m.* (**—s,** *pl.* **—**) tumulus, mound.
Grablegung ['gra:ple:gung], *f.* (**—,** *no pl.*) (*rare*) burial, interment.
Grabmal ['gra:pma:l], *n.* (**—s,** *pl.* **—e,** **⸚er**) tomb, sepulchre, monument.
Grabschrift ['gra:pʃrɪft], *f.* (**—,** *pl.* **—n**) epitaph.
Grabstichel ['gra:pʃtɪçəl], *m.* (**—s,** *pl.* **—**) graving-tool.
Grad [gra:t], *m.* (**—s,** *pl.* **—e**) degree; rank; grade; extent; point; *in gewissem —e,* to a certain degree; *im höchsten —e,* in the highest degree, extremely.
Gradeinteilung ['gra:taɪntaɪlung], *f.* (**—,** *pl.* **—en**) gradation, graduation.
Gradmesser ['gra:tmɛsər], *m.* (**—s,** *pl.* **—**) graduator; (*fig.*) index.
gradweise ['gra:tvaɪzə], *adv.* gradually, by degrees.
Graf [gra:f], *m.* (**—en,** *pl.* **—en**) count, earl.
Gräfin ['grɛfɪn], *f.* (**—,** *pl.* **—en**) countess.
gräflich ['grɛflɪç], *adj.* belonging to a count *or* earl.
Grafschaft ['gra:fʃaft], *f.* (**—,** *pl.* **—en**) county, shire.
Gral [gra:l], *m.* (**—s,** *no pl.*) Holy Grail.
Gram [gra:m], *m.* (**—s,** *no pl.*) grief, sorrow.
grämen ['grɛ:mən], *v.a.* grieve. — *v.r. sich —,* grieve, fret, worry.
gramgebeugt ['gra:mgəbɔykt], *adj.* prostrate with grief.
grämlich ['grɛ:mlɪç], *adj.* sullen, morose, ill-humoured.
Gramm [gram], *n.* (**—s,** *pl.* **—e**) gramme (15.438 grains); (*Am.*) gram.
Grammatik [gra'matɪk], *f.* (**—,** *pl.* **—en**) grammar.
grammatikalisch, **grammatisch** [gramatɪ'ka:lɪʃ, gra'matɪʃ], *adj.* grammatical.
Gran [gra:n], *n.* (**—s,** *pl.* **—e**) (*weight*) grain.
Granat [gra'na:t], *m.* (**—s,** *pl.* **—e**) garnet.
Granatapfel [gra'na:tapfəl], *m.* (**—s,** *pl.* **⸚e**) (*Bot.*) pomegranate.
Granate [gra'na:tə], *f.* (**—,** *pl.* **—n**) shell, grenade.
Grande ['grandə], *m.* (**—n,** *pl.* **—n**) grandee.

Grandezza [gran'dɛtsa], *f.* (**—,** *no pl.*) grandeur; sententiousness; pomposity.
grandios [grandɪ'o:s], *adj.* grand.
Granit [gra'ni:t], *m.* (**—s,** *pl.* **—e**) granite.
Granne ['granə], *f.* (**—,** *pl.* **—n**) (*corn*) awn, beard.
graphisch ['gra:fɪʃ], *adj.* graphic.
Graphit [gra'fi:t], *m.* (**—s,** *no pl.*) blacklead.
Gras [gra:s], *n.* (**—es,** *pl.* **—er**) grass; *ins — beißen,* bite the dust.
grasartig ['gra:sa:rtɪç], *adj.* gramineous.
grasen ['gra:zən], *v.n.* graze.
Grasfleck ['gra:sflɛk], *m.* (**—s,** *pl.* **—e**) grass-stain.
Grashalm ['gra:shalm], *m.* (**—s,** *pl.* **—e**) grass-blade.
Grashüpfer ['gra:shypfər], *m.* (**—s,** *pl.* **—**) (*Ent.*) grass-hopper.
grasig ['gra:zɪç], *adj.* grassy.
Grasmäher ['gra:smɛ:ər], *m.* (**—s,** *pl.* **—**) lawn-mower.
Grasmücke ['gra:smykə], *f.* (**—,** *pl.* **—n**) (*Orn.*) hedge-sparrow.
grassieren [gra'si:rən], *v.n.* (*epidemics etc.*) spread, rage.
gräßlich ['grɛslɪç], *adj.* hideous, horrible, ghastly.
Grasweide ['gra:svaɪdə], *f.* (**—,** *pl.* **—n**) pasture.
Grat [gra:t], *m.* (**—s,** *pl.* **—e**) edge, ridge.
Gräte ['grɛ:tə], *f.* (**—,** *pl.* **—n**) fish-bone.
Grätenstich ['grɛ:tənʃtɪç], *m.* (**—s,** *pl.* **—e**) (*embroidery*) herring-bone stitch.
grätig ['grɛ:tɪç], *adj.* full of fishbones; (*fig.*) grumpy.
gratis ['gra:tɪs], *adj.* gratis; *— und franko,* for nothing.
Gratulation [gratula'tsjo:n], *f.* (**—,** *pl.* **—en**) congratulation.
gratulieren [gratu'li:rən], *v.n.* *einem zu etwas,* congratulate s.o. on s.th.
grau [grau], *adj.* grey; (*Am.*) gray; *vor —en Zeiten,* in times of yore.
Grauen ['grauən], *n.* (**—s,** *no pl.*) horror, aversion.
grauen ['grauən], *v.n.* (*morning*) dawn; *es graut mir vor,* I shudder at.
grauenhaft ['grauənhaft], *adj.* horrible, awful, ghastly.
graulen ['graulən], *v.r. sich —,* shudder, be afraid (of ghosts etc.).
graulich ['graulɪç], *adj. mir ist ganz —,* I shudder.
Graupe ['graupə], *f.* (**—,** *pl.* **—n**) groats, peeled barley.
graupeln ['graupəln], *v.n. imp.* (*coll.*) drizzle, sleet.
Graus [graus], *m.* (**—es,** *no pl.*) horror, dread.
grausam ['grauza:m], *adj.* cruel.
Grauschimmel ['grauʃɪməl], *m.* (**—s,** *pl.* **—**) grey (horse).
grausen ['grauzən], *v.n. es graust mir vor,* I shudder at.
grausig ['grauzɪç], *adj.* dread, gruesome, horrible.

Graveur [gra'vøːr], *m.* (—s, *pl.* —e) engraver.

gravieren [gra'viːrən], *v.a.* engrave.

Gravität [gravi'tɛːt], *f.* (—, *no pl.*) gravity.

gravitätisch [gravi'tɛːtiʃ], *adj.* grave, solemn.

Grazie ['graːtsjə], *f.* (—, *pl.* —n) grace, charm; (*goddess*) Grace.

graziös [gra'tsjøːs], *adj.* graceful.

Greif [graif], *m.* (—(e)s, *pl.* —e) griffin.

greifbar ['graifbaːr], *adj.* to hand; (*fig.*) tangible, palpable.

greifen ['graifən], *v.a. irr.* grasp, seize, touch, handle; *etwas aus der Luft* —, invent s.th.; *um sich* —, gain ground.

greinen ['grainən], *v.n.* (*dial. & coll.*) cry, blubber.

Greis [grais], *m.* (—es, *pl.* —e) old man.

greisenhaft ['graizənhaft], *adj.* senile.

grell [grɛl], *adj.* (*colour*) glaring; (*light*) dazzling; (*tone*) shrill, sharp.

Grenadier [grena'diːr], *m.* (—s, *pl.* —e) grenadier.

Grenadiermütze [grena'diːrmytsə], *f.* (—, *pl.* —n) busby, bearskin.

Grenze ['grɛntsə], *f.* (—, *pl.* —n) boundary; frontier; borders; (*fig.*) limit.

grenzen ['grɛntsən], *v.n.* — *an*, border on; (*fig.*) verge on.

Grenzlinie ['grɛntsliːnjə], *f.* (—, *pl.* —n) boundary-line, line of demarcation.

Greuel ['grɔyəl], *m.* (—s, *pl.* —) horror, abomination; *das ist mir ein* —, I abominate it.

Greueltat ['grɔyəltaːt], *f.* (—, *pl.* —en) atrocity.

greulich ['grɔyliç], *adj.* horrible, dreadful, shocking, heinous.

Griebe ['griːbə], *f.* (—, *pl.* —n) (*mostly pl.*) greaves.

Griebs ['griːps], *m.* (—es, *pl.* —e) (*dial.*) (*apple*) core.

Grieche ['griːçə], *m.* (—n, *pl.* —n) Greek.

Griechenland ['griːçənlant], *n.* Greece.

Griesgram ['griːsgraːm], *m.* (—s, *pl.* —e) grumbler.

griesgrämig ['griːsgrɛːmiç], *adj.* morose, grumbling.

Grieß ['griːs], *m.* (—es, *no pl.*) groats, semolina.

Grießbrei ['griːsbrai], *m.* (—s, *pl.* —e) gruel.

Griff [grif], *m.* (—s, *pl.* —e) grip, hold, handle.

griffbereit ['grifbərait], *adj.* handy.

Grille ['grilə], *f.* (—, *pl.* —n) (*Ent.*) cricket; (*fig.*) whim; —*n haben*, be capricious; —*n fangen*, be crotchety, be depressed.

grillenhaft ['grilənhaft], *adj.* whimsical; capricious.

Grimasse [gri'masə], *f.* (—, *pl.* —n) grimace.

Grimm [grim], *m.* (—s, *no pl.*) fury, rage, wrath.

Grimmen ['grimən], *n.* (—s, *no pl.*) gripes; (*Med.*) colic.

grimmig ['grimiç], *adj.* fierce, furious; grim.

Grind [grint], *m.* (—s, *pl.* —e) scab, scurf.

grinsen ['grinzən], *v.n.* grin.

Grippe ['gripə], *f.* (—, *pl.* —n) influenza, grippe.

Grips [grips], *m.* (—es, *no pl.*) (*coll.*) sense, brains; *einen beim* —*nehmen*, take s.o. by the scruff of his neck.

grob [groːp], *adj.* coarse; rough; gross; rude, crude, uncouth, impolite; (*jewels*) rough, unpolished.

Grobheit ['groːphait], *f.* (—, *pl.* —en) rudeness; abusive language.

Grobian ['groːbjaːn], *m.* (—s, *pl.* —e) boor, rude fellow.

Grobschmied ['groːpʃmiːt], *m.* (—s, *pl.* —e) blacksmith.

Grog [grɔk], *m.* (—s, *pl.* —s) grog, toddy.

grölen ['grøːlən], *v.n.* (*coll.*) scream, squall, bawl.

Groll [grɔl], *m.* (—s, *no pl.*) resentment, anger, rancour; *einen* — *gegen einen haben*, bear s.o. a grudge.

grollen ['grɔlən], *v.n.* (*thunder*) rumble; *einem* —, bear s.o. ill-will; (*Poet.*) be angry (with).

Grönland ['grøːnlant], *n.* Greenland.

Gros (1) [groːs], *n.* (—ses, *pl.* —se) gross; twelve dozen.

Gros (2) [groː], *n.* (—s, *no pl.*) bulk, majority; *en* —, wholesale.

Groschen ['grɔʃən], *m.* (—s, *pl.* —) small coin, penny; one 100th of an Austrian shilling; ten-pfennig piece; *einen schönen* — *verdienen,* make good money.

groß [groːs], *adj.* great, big, large; tall; vast; eminent, famous; intense; —*e Augen machen*, stare; *Grosser Ozean*, Pacific (Ocean).

großartig ['groːsaːrtiç], *adj.* grand, sublime, magnificent, splendid.

Großbetrieb ['groːsbətriːp], *m.* (—s, *pl.* —e) large business; large (industrial) concern.

Großbritannien [groːsbri'tanjən], *n.* Great Britain.

Größe ['grøːsə], *f.* (—, *pl.* —n) size, largeness, greatness; height; quantity; power; celebrity, star; importance.

Großeltern ['groːsɛltərn], *pl.* grandparents.

Großenkel ['groːsɛŋkəl], *m.* (—s, *pl.* —) great-grandson.

Größenverhältnis ['grøːsənferhɛltnis], *n.* (—ses, *pl.* —se) proportion, ratio.

Größenwahn ['grøːsənvaːn], *m.* (—s, *no pl.*) megalomania; delusion of grandeur.

Großfürst ['groːsfyrst], *m.* (—en, *pl.* —en) grand-duke.

Großfürstin ['groːsfyrstɪn], *f.* (—, *pl.* —nen) grand-duchess.

Großgrundbesitz ['groːsgruntbəzɪts], *m.* (—es, *pl.* —e) large landed property, estates.

Großhandel ['groːshandəl], *m.* (—s, *no pl.*) wholesale business.

großherzig ['groːshɛrtsɪç], *adj.* magnanimous.

Grossist [grɔˈsɪst], *m.* (—en, *pl.* —en) wholesale merchant.

großjährig ['groːsjɛːrɪç], *adj.* of age; — werden, come of age.

großmächtig ['groːsmɛçtɪç], *adj.* (*fig.*) high and mighty.

großmäulig ['groːsmɔylɪç], *adj.* bragging, swaggering.

Großmut ['groːsmuːt], *f.* (—, *no pl.*) magnanimity, generosity.

Großmutter ['groːsmutər], *f.* (—, *pl.* ¨) grandmother.

Großsiegelbewahrer [groːsˈziːgəlbəvaːrər], *m.* (—s, *pl.* —) Lord Chancellor; Keeper of the Great Seal.

Großstadt ['groːsʃtat], *f.* (—, *pl.* ¨e) large town, city, metropolis.

Großtat ['groːstaːt], *f.* (—, *pl.* —en) achievement, exploit, feat.

Großtuer ['groːstuːər], *m.* (—s, *pl.* —) boaster, braggart.

großtun ['groːstuːn], *v.r. irr.* sich — mit, brag of; show off, parade.

Großvater ['groːsfaːtər], *m.* (—s, *pl.* ¨) grandfather.

großziehen ['groːstsiːən], *v.a. irr.* bring up, rear.

großzügig ['groːstsyːgɪç], *adj.* boldly conceived; grand, generous.

Grotte ['grɔtə], *f.* (—, *pl.* —n) grotto.

Grübchen ['gryːpçən], *n.* (—s, *pl.* —) dimple.

Grube ['gruːbə], *f.* (—, *pl.* —n) hole, pit; (*Min.*) mine; *in die* — *fahren*, (*Bibl.*) go down to the grave.

Grübelei ['gryːbəlaɪ], *f.* (—, *pl.* —en) brooding, musing.

grübeln ['gryːbəln], *v.n.* brood (over s.th.)

Grubenarbeiter ['gruːbənarbaɪtər], *m.* (—s, *pl.* —) miner.

Grubengas ['gruːbəngaːs], *n.* (—es, *pl.* —e) fire-damp.

Grubenlampe ['gruːbənlampə], *f.* (—, *pl.* —n) miner's lamp.

Gruft [gruft], *f.* (—, *pl.* ¨e) tomb, sepulchre; vault, mausoleum.

grün [gryːn], *adj.* green; *grüne Bohnen*, French beans, runner beans; (*fig.*) unripe, immature, inexperienced; *am* —*en Tisch*, at the conference table; (*fig.*) in theory; *auf einen* —*en Zweig kommen*, thrive, get on in the world; *einem nicht* — *sein*, dislike s.o.

Grund [grunt], *m.* (—s, *pl.* ¨e) ground, soil; earth; land; bottom; foundation, basis; valley; reason, cause, argument; motive.

Grundbedeutung ['gruntbədɔytuŋ], *f.* (—, *pl.* —en) primary meaning, basic meaning.

Grundbesitz ['gruntbəzɪts], *m.* (—es, *no pl.*) landed property.

Grundbuch ['gruntbuːx], *n.* (—s, *pl.* ¨er) land register.

grundehrlich ['gruntˈeːrlɪç], *adj.* thoroughly honest.

Grundeigentum ['gruntaɪgəntuːm], *n.* (—s, *pl.* ¨er) landed property.

Grundeis ['gruntaɪs], *n.* (—es, *no pl.*) ground-ice.

gründen ['gryndən], *v.a.* found, establish, float (a company). — *v.r.* sich — auf, be based on.

grundfalsch ['gruntfalʃ], *adj.* radically false.

Grundfarbe ['gruntfarbə], *f.* (—, *pl.* —n) primary colour.

Grundfläche ['gruntflɛçə], *f.* (—, *pl.* —n) basis, base.

Grundherr ['grunthɛr], *m.* (—n, *pl.* —en) lord of the manor, freeholder.

grundieren [grunˈdiːrən], *v.a.* prime, size, paint the undercoat.

Grundkapital ['gruntkapitaːl], *n.* (—s, *no pl.*) original stock.

Grundlage ['gruntlaːgə], *f.* (—, *pl.* —n) foundation, basis.

Grundlegung ['gruntleːguŋ], *f.* (—, *no pl.*) laying the foundation.

gründlich ['gryntlɪç], *adj.* thorough, solid.

grundlos ['gruntloːs], *adj.* bottomless; groundless, unfounded, without foundation.

Grundmauer ['gruntmauər], *f.* (—, *pl.* —n) foundation wall.

Gründonnerstag [gryːnˈdɔnərstaːk], *m.* (—s, *pl.* —e) Maundy Thursday.

Grundpfeiler ['gruntpfaɪlər], *m.* (—s, *pl.* —) (main) pillar.

Grundriß ['gruntrɪs], *m.* (—sses, *pl.* —sse) design, groundplan; compendium, elements; blueprint.

Grundsatz ['gruntzats], *m.* (—es, *pl.* ¨e) principle, maxim; axiom.

grundschlecht ['gruntʃlɛçt], *adj.* thoroughly bad.

Grundschuld ['gruntʃult], *f.* ¨(—, *pl.* —en) mortgage (on land).

Grundstein ['gruntʃtaɪn], *m.* (—s, *pl.* —e) foundation-stone.

Grundsteuer ['gruntʃtɔyər], *f.* (—, *pl.* —n) land-tax.

Grundstoff ['gruntʃtɔf], *m.* (—es, *pl.* —e) raw material.

Grundstück ['gruntʃtyk], *n.* (—s, *pl.* —e) real estate; plot of land; lot.

Grundtugend ['grunttuːgənt], *f.* (—, *pl.* —en) cardinal virtue.

Gründung ['grynduŋ], *f.* (—, *pl.* —en) foundation, establishment.

grundverschieden ['gruntfɛrʃiːdən], *adj.* radically different.

Grundwasser ['gruntvasər], *n.* (—s, *no pl.*) underground water.

Grundzahl ['grunttsaːl], *f.* (—, *pl.* —en) cardinal number.

Grundzug ['grunttsuːk], *m.* (—s, *pl.* ¨e) characteristic; distinctive feature.

Grüne

Grüne ['gry:nə], *n.* (—**n**, *no pl.*) greenness, verdure; *ins — gehen*, take a walk in the open country.

grünen ['gry:nən], *v.n.* become green; (*fig.*) flourish.

Grünfutter ['gry:nfutər], *n.* (—**s**, *no pl.*) green food.

Grünkohl ['gry:nko:l], *m.* (—**s**, *no pl.*) green kale.

Grünkramhändler ['gry:nkra:mhɛndlər], *m.* (—**s**, *pl.* —) greengrocer.

Grünschnabel ['gry:nʃna:bəl], *m.* (—**s**, *pl.* ⸚) greenhorn.

Grünspan ['gry:nʃpa:n], *m.* (—**s**, *no pl.*) verdigris.

Grünspecht ['gry:nʃpɛçt], *m.* (—**s**, *pl.* —**e**) (*Orn.*) green woodpecker.

grunzen ['gruntsən], *v.n.* grunt.

Grünzeug ['gry:ntsɔyk], *n.* (—**s**, *no pl.*) greens, herbs.

Gruppe ['grupə], *f.* (—, *pl.* —**n**) group.

gruppieren [gru'pi:rən], *v.d.* group.

gruselig ['gru:zəliç], *adj.* creepy, uncanny.

gruseln ['gru:zəln], *v.a. es gruselt mir* I shudder, it gives me the creeps.

Gruß [gru:s], *m.* (—**es**, *pl.* ⸚**e**) salutation, greeting; (*pl.*) regards; *mit herzlichem —*, with kind regards; *einen — ausrichten*, convey s.o.'s regards.

grüßen ['gry:sən], *v.a.* greet; *einen — lassen*, send o.'s regards to s.o.; — *Sie ihn von mir*, remember me to him.

Grütze ['grytsə], *f.* (—, *pl.* —**n**) peeled grain, groats; (*fig.*) (*coll.*) gumption, brains.

Guatemala [guatə'ma:la], *n.* Guatemala.

gucken ['gukən], *v.n.* look, peep.

Guinea [gɪ'ne:a], *n.* Guinea.

Gulasch ['gulaʃ], *n.* (—**s**, *no pl.*) goulash.

Gulden ['guldən], *m.* (—**s**, *pl.* —) florin, guilder.

gülden ['gyldən], *adj.* (*Poet.*) golden.

gültig ['gyltiç], *adj.* valid; (*money*) current, legal (tender).

Gummi ['gumi], *m.* (—**s**, *no pl.*) gum, rubber.

Gummiarabikum [gumia'ra:bikum], *n.* gum arabic.

gummiartig ['gumia:rtiç], *adj.* gummy; like rubber.

Gummiball ['gumibal], *m.* (—**s**, *pl.* ⸚**e**) rubber-ball.

Gummiband ['gumibant], *n.* (—**s**, *pl.* ⸚**er**) rubber-band, elastic.

Gummielastikum [gumie'lastikum], *n.* indiarubber.

gummieren [gu'mi:rən], *v.a.* gum.

Gummireifen ['gumiraifən], *m.* (—**s**, *pl.* —) tyre; (*Am.*) tire.

Gummischuhe ['gumiʃu:ə], *m. pl.* galoshes; (*Am.*) rubbers.

Gunst [gunst], *f.* (—, *no pl.*) favour; *zu seinen —*, in his favour.

Gunstbezeigung ['gunstbətsaigun], *f.* (—, *pl.* —**en**) favour, kindness, goodwill.

günstig ['gynstiç], *adj.* favourable, propitious.

Günstling ['gynstlin], *m.* (—**s**, *pl.* —**e**) favourite.

Gurgel ['gurgəl], *f.* (—, *pl.* —**n**) gullet, throat.

gurgeln ['gurgəln], *v.n.* gargle; gurgle.

Gurke ['gurkə], *f.* (—, *pl.* —**n**) (*Bot.*) cucumber; (*pickled*) gherkin.

Gurt [gurt], *m.* (—**es**, *pl.* —**e**) belt; strap; harness.

Gürtel ['gyrtəl], *m.* (—**s**, *pl.* —) girdle, belt; (*Geog.*) zone.

Guß [gus], *m.* (—**sses**, *pl.* ⸚**sse**) gush, downpour; founding, cast; (*Cul.*) icing.

Gut [gu:t], *n.* (—(**e**)**s**, *pl.* ⸚**er**) good thing, blessing; property, possession; country seat; estate; (*pl.*) goods.

gut [gu:t], *adj.* good; beneficial; kind; virtuous; — *adv.* well; *es — haben*, be well off; —*er Dinge sein*, be of good cheer; *kurz und —*, in short.

Gutachten ['gu:taxtən], *n.* (—**s**, *pl.* —) expert opinion, expert evidence.

gutartig ['gu:ta:rtiç], *adj.* good-natured; benign.

Güte ['gy:tə], *f.* (—, *no pl.*) goodness, kindness, quality.

Güterabfertigung ['gy:tərapfɛrtigun], *f.* (—, *pl.* —**en**) (*Railw.*) goods-depot, goods-office.

Güterabtretung ['gy:təraptre:tun], *f.* (—, *pl.* —**en**) cession of goods; (*Law*) surrender of an estate.

gutgelaunt ['gu:tgəlaunt], *adj.* in good spirits, good-humoured.

gutgemeint ['gu:tgəmaint], *adj.* well-meant, well-intentioned.

gutgesinnt ['gu:tgəzint], *adj.* well-intentioned.

Guthaben ['gu:tha:bən], *n.* (—**s**, *pl.* —) credit-balance, assets.

gutheißen ['gu:thaisən], *v.a. irr.* approve.

gütig ['gy:tiç], *adj.* kind, benevolent.

gütlich ['gy:tliç], *adj.* amicable, friendly; —*er Vergleich*, amicable settlement; *sich — tun*, indulge o.s.

gutmachen ['gu:tmaxən], *v.a. etwas wieder —*, make amends for s.th., compensate.

gutmütig ['gu:tmy:tiç], *adj.* good-natured, good-tempered.

Gutsbesitzer ['gu:tsbəzitsər], *m.* (—**s**, *pl.* —) landowner; proprietor of an estate.

gutschreiben ['gu:tʃraibən], *v.a. irr. einem etwas —*, enter a sum to s.o.'s credit.

Gutsverwalter ['gu:tsfɛrvaltər], *m.* (—**s**, *pl.* —) land-steward, agent, bailiff.

gutwillig ['gu:tviliç], *adj.* willing, of o.'s own free will.

Gymnasialbildung [gymnaz'ja:lbildun], *f.* (—, *no pl.*) classical *or* grammar school education.

Gymnasiast [gymnaz'jast], *m.* (—**en**, *pl.* —**en**) grammar-school pupil.

haften

Gymnasium [gym'na:zjum], *n.* (—s, *pl.* —sien) high school.
Gymnastik [gym'nastık], *f.* (—, *no pl.*) gymnastics.
gymnastisch [gym'nastıʃ], *adj.* gymnastic(al); —e Übungen, physical exercises.

H

H [ha:], *n.* (—s, *pl.* —s) the letter H; (*Mus.*) H Dur, B major; H Moll, B minor.
ha! [ha:], *excl.* ha!
Haag, Den [ha:k, de:n], *m.* The Hague.
Haar [ha:r], *n.* (—s, *pl.* —e) hair; wool; nap; aufs —, exactly, to a hair; um ein —, very nearly, within a hair's breadth.
haaren ['ha:rən], *v.r. sich* —, shed o.'s hair.
haargenau ['ha:rgənau], *adj.* (very) exactly; to a nicety.
haarig ['ha:rıç], *adj.* hairy.
Haarlocke ['ha:rlɔkə], *f.* (—, *pl.* —n) curl, ringlet.
Haarnadel ['ha:rna:dəl], *f.* (—, *pl.* —n) hairpin.
Haaröl ['ha:rø:l], *n.* (—s, *no pl.*) hair-oil.
Haarpinsel ['ha:rpınzəl], *m.* (—s, *pl.* —) camel-hair brush.
Haarröhrchen ['ha:rrø:rçən], *n.* (—s, *pl.* —) capillary tube.
Haarschleife ['ha:rʃlaıfə], *f.* (—, *pl.* —en) bow in the hair.
Haarschnitt ['ha:rʃnıt], *m.* (—s, *pl.* —e) hair-cut.
Haarschuppen ['ha:rʃupən], *f.* dandruff.
Haarspalterei ['ha:rʃpaltəraı], *f.* (—, *pl.* —en) hair-splitting.
haarsträubend ['ha:rʃtrɔybənt], *adj.* hair-raising, monstrous.
Haarwäsche ['ha:rvɛʃə], *f.* (—, *no pl.*) shampooing.
Haarwickel ['ha:rvıkəl], *m.* (—s, *pl.* —) curler.
Haarzange ['ha:rtsaŋə], *f.* (—, *pl.* —n) tweezers.
Habe ['ha:bə], *f.* (—, *no pl.*) property, belongings, effects; Hab und Gut, all o.'s belongings, goods and chattels.
Haben ['ha:bən], *n.* (—s, *no pl.*) credit: Soll und —, debit and credit.
haben ['ha:bən], *v.a. irr.* have, possess; da hast du's, there you are; es ist nicht zu —, it is not available.
Habenichts ['ha:bənıçts], *m.* (—es, *no pl.*) have-not.
Habgier ['ha:pgi:r], *f.* (—, *no pl.*) greediness, avarice, covetousness.

habhaft ['ha:phaft], *adj. einer Sache* — werden, get possession of a thing.
Habicht ['ha:bıçt], *m.* (—s, *pl.* —e) (*Orn.*) hawk.
Habichtsinseln ['ha:bıçtsınzəln], *f. pl.* the Azores.
Habichtsnase ['ha:bıçtsna:zə], *f.* (—, *pl.* —n) hooked nose, aquiline nose.
Habilitation [habilita'tsjo:n], *f.* (—, *pl.* —en) admission *or* inauguration as a university lecturer.
habilitieren [habili'ti:rən], *v.r. sich* —, qualify as a university lecturer.
Habseligkeiten ['ha:pzelıçkaıtən], *f. pl.* property, effects, chattels.
Habsucht ['ha:pzuxt], *f.* (—, *no pl.*) avarice, greediness.
Hackbeil ['hakbaıl], *n.* (—s, *pl.* —e) cleaver, chopping-knife.
Hackbrett ['hakbrɛt], *n.* (—s, *pl.* —er) chopping-board.
Hacke ['hakə], *f.* (—, *pl.* —n) hoe, mattock; heel.
Hacken ['hakən], *m.* (—s, *pl.* —) heel; sich auf die — machen, be off, take to o.'s heels.
hacken ['hakən], *v.a.* hack, chop, hoe; mince; (*birds*) peck.
Hacker ['hakər], *m.* (—s, *pl.* —) chopper.
Häckerling ['hɛkərlıŋ], *m.* (—s, *no pl.*) chopped straw.
Hackfleisch ['hakflaıʃ], *n.* (—es, *no pl.*) minced meat.
Häcksel ['hɛksəl], *n.* (—s, *no pl.*) chopped straw.
Hader ['ha:dər], *m.* (—s, *no pl.*) quarrel, dispute.
hadern ['ha:dərn], *v.n.* quarrel, have a dispute.
Hafen ['ha:fən], *m.* (—s, *pl.* ⁀) harbour, port; refuge, haven.
Hafendamm ['ha:fandam], *m.* (—s, *pl.* ⁀e) jetty, mole, pier.
Hafensperre ['ha:fɛnʃpɛrə], *f.* (—, *pl.* —n) embargo, blockade.
Hafenzoll ['ha:fəntsɔl], *m.* (—s, *no pl.*) anchorage, harbour due.
Hafer ['ha:fər], *m.* (—s, *no pl.*) oats; es sticht ihn der —, he is getting cheeky, insolent.
Haferbrei ['ha:fərbraı], *m.* (—s, *no pl.*) porridge.
Hafergrütze ['ha:fərgrytsə], *f.* (—, *no pl.*) ground-oats, oatmeal.
Haferschleim ['ha:fərʃlaım], *m.* (—s, *no pl.*) oat-gruel, porridge.
Haff [haf], *n.* (—s, *pl.* —e) bay, lagoon.
Haft [haft], *f.* (—, *no pl.*) custody, imprisonment, arrest.
haftbar ['haftba:r], *adj.* answerable; (*Law*) liable.
Haftbefehl ['haftbəfe:l], *m.* (—s, *pl.* —e) warrant for arrest.
haften ['haftən], *v.n.* stick, cling, adhere; für einen —, go bail for s.o.; für etwas —, answer for, be liable for s.th.

Häftling

Häftling ['hɛftlɪŋ], *m.* (—s, *pl.* —e) prisoner.

Haftpflicht ['haftpflɪçt], *f.* (—, *no pl.*) liability.

Haftung ['haftuŋ], *f.* (—, *no pl.*) liability, security; (*Comm.*) *Gesellschaft mit beschränkter* —, limited liability company, (*abbr.*) Ltd.

Hag [ha:k], *m.* (—es, *pl.* —e) hedge, enclosure.

Hagebuche ['ha:gəbu:xə], *f.* (—, *pl.* —n) hornbeam.

Hagebutte ['ha:gəbutə], *f.* (—, *pl.* —n) (*Bot.*) hip, haw.

Hagedorn ['ha:gədɔrn], *m.* (—s, *no pl.*) (*Bot.*) hawthorn.

Hagel ['ha:gəl], *m.* (—s, *no pl.*) hail.

hageln ['ha:gəln], *v.n.* hail.

Hagelschauer ['ha:gəlʃauər], *m.* (—s, *pl.* —) hailstorm.

hager ['ha:gər], *adj.* thin, lean, lank, gaunt.

Häher ['hɛ:ər], *m.* (—s, *pl.* —) (*Orn.*) jay.

Hahn [ha:n], *m.* (—s, *pl.* ⁀e) (*Orn.*) cockerel, cock; (*water, gas*) cock, tap, faucet; — *im Korbe sein*, rule the roost; *da kräht kein — danach*, nobody cares two hoots about it.

Hahnenbalken ['ha:nənbalkən], *m.* (—s, *pl.* —) cock-loft; hen-roost.

Hahnenfuß ['ha:nənfu:s], *m.* (—es, *no pl.*) (*Bot.*) crow-foot.

Hahnensporn ['ha:nɛnʃpɔrn], *m.* (—s, *no pl.*) cockspur.

Hahnentritt ['ha:nəntrɪt], *m.* (—s, *no pl.*) cock's tread.

Hahnrei ['ha:nrai], *m.* (—s, *pl.* —e) cuckold; *einen zum — machen*, cuckold s.o.

Hai [hai], *m.* (—s, *pl.* —e) (*Zool.*) shark.

Haifisch ['haifɪʃ], *m.* (—es, *pl.* —e) (*Zool.*) shark.

Hain [hain], *m.* (—s, *pl.* —e) (*Poet.*) grove, thicket.

Haiti [ha'iti], *n.* Haiti.

Häkchen ['hɛ:kçən], *n.* (—s, *pl.* —) small hook, crotchet; apostrophe.

häkeln ['hɛ:kəln], *v.a. v.n.* crochet; (*fig.*) tease; (*Am.*) needle (*coll.*).

Haken ['ha:kən], *m.* (—s, *pl.* —) hook, clasp; (*fig.*) hitch, snag.

Hakenkreuz ['ha:kənkrɔyts], *n.* (—es, *pl.* —e) swastika.

halb [halp], *adj.* half; *halb neun*, half past eight.

halbieren [hal'bi:rən], *v.a.* halve, divide into halves; (*Maths.*) bisect.

Halbinsel ['halpɪnzəl], *f.* (—, *pl.* —n) peninsula.

Halbmesser ['halpmɛsər], *m.* (—s, *pl.* —) radius.

halbpart ['halppart], *adj.* — *mit einem machen*, go halves with s.o.

halbstündig ['halpʃtyndɪç], *adj.* lasting half an hour.

halbstündlich ['halpʃtyntlɪç], *adj.* half-hourly, every half-hour.

halbwegs ['halpve:ks], *adv.* (*coll.*) reasonably, tolerably.

Halbwelt ['halpvɛlt], *f.* (—, *no pl.*) demi-monde.

halbwüchsig ['halpvy:ksɪç], *adj.* teenage.

Halde ['haldə], *f.* (—, *pl.* —n) declivity, hill; (*Min.*) waste-heap, slag-heap.

Hälfte ['hɛlftə], *f.* (—, *pl.* —n) half; (*obs.*) moiety.

Halfter ['halftər], *f.* (—, *pl.* —n) halter.

Hall [hal], *m.* (—s, *no pl.*) sound, echo.

Halle ['halə], *f.* (—, *pl.* —n) hall, vestibule; portico; porch.

hallen ['halən], *v.n.* sound, resound; clang.

Halm [halm], *m.* —es, *pl.* —e) stalk; (*grass*) blade.

Hals [hals], *m.* (—es, *pl.* ⁀e) neck, throat; — *über Kopf*, head over heels, hastily, hurriedly.

Halsader ['halsa:dər], *f.* (—, *pl.* —n) jugular vein.

Halsbinde ['halsbɪndə], *f.* (—, *pl.* —n) scarf, tie.

Halsentzündung ['halsɛntsynduŋ], *f.* (—, *pl.* —en) inflammation of the throat.

Halskrause ['halskrauzə], *f.* (—, *pl.* —n) frill, ruff.

halsstarrig ['halsʃtarɪç], *adj.* stubborn, obstinate.

Halsweh ['halsve:], *n.* (—s, *no pl.*) sore throat.

Halt [halt], *m.* (—es, *no pl.*) halt; stop; hold; (*also fig.*) support.

haltbar ['haltba:r], *adj.* durable, strong; tenable, valid.

halten ['haltən], *v.a. irr.* hold; keep; detain; deliver (speech, lecture); observe, celebrate. — *v.n.* stop; stand firm; insist; *halt!* stop! stop it! — *v.r. sich* —, hold out, keep, behave.

haltlos ['haltlo:s], *adj.* unprincipled; floundering, unsteady.

Haltung ['haltuŋ], *f.* (—, *pl.* —en) carriage, posture, attitude; (*fig.*) behaviour, demeanour; attitude.

Halunke [ha'luŋkə], *m.* (—n, *pl.* —n) scoundrel, rascal, scamp.

hämisch ['hɛ:mɪʃ], *adj.* malicious, spiteful.

Hammel ['haməl], *m.* (—s, *pl.* —) (*meat*) mutton.

Hammelkeule ['haməlkɔylə], *f.* (—, *pl.* —n) leg of mutton.

Hammer ['hamər], *m.* (—s, *pl.* ⁀) hammer; *unter den — kommen*, be sold by auction.

Hämorrhoiden [hɛmo'riːdən], *f. pl.* (*Med.*) piles, haemorrhoids.

Hand [hant], *f.* (—, *pl.* ⁀e) hand.

Handarbeit ['hantarbait], *f.* (—, *pl.* —en) manual labour; needlework.

Handel ['handəl], *m.* (—s, *no pl.*) trade, commerce; — *treiben*, carry on trade, do business.

Händel ['hɛndəl], *m. pl.* quarrel, difference, dispute.

handeln ['handəln], *v.n.* act; — *in*, deal in; *es handelt sich um* ... it is a question of ... ; *es handelt von* ... , it deals with ... .

handelseinig ['handəlsainiç], *adj.* — *werden*, come to terms.

Handelsgenossenschaft ['handəlsgənɔsənʃaft], *f.* (—, *pl.* —en) trading company.

Handelsgeschäft ['handəlsgəʃeft], *n.* (—es, *pl.* —e) commercial transaction.

Handelsgesellschaft ['handəlsgəzɛlʃaft], *f.* (—, *pl.* —en) trading company; joint-stock company.

Handelskammer ['handəlskamər], *f.* (—, *pl.* —n) chamber of commerce.

Handelsmarke ['handəlsmarkə], *f.* (—, *pl.* —n) trade-mark.

Handelsreisende ['handəlsraizəndə], *m.* (—n, *pl.* —n) commercial traveller.

händelsüchtig ['hendəlzyçtiç], *adj.* quarrelsome; litigious.

Handelsvertrag ['handəlsfertra:k], *m.* (—es, *pl.* ˙'e) commercial treaty; contract.

Handelszweig ['handəlstsvaik], *m.* (—es, *pl.* —e) branch of trade.

Handfeger ['hantfe:gər], *m.* (—s, *pl.* —) hand-broom, handbrush.

Handfertigkeit ['hantfertiçkait], *f.* (—, *no pl.*) dexterity, manual skill; handicrafts.

Handfessel ['hantfesəl], *f.* (—, *pl.* —n) handcuff.

handfest ['hantfest], *adj.* robust, strong.

Handgeld ['hantgelt], *n.* (—es, *no pl.*) earnest; (*money*) advance.

Handgelenk ['hantgələŋk], *n.* (—s, *pl.* —e) wrist.

handgemein ['hantgəmain], *adj.* — *werden*, come to blows.

Handgemenge ['hantgəmeŋə], *n.* (—s, *no pl.*) fray, scuffle.

handgreiflich ['hantgraifliç], *adj.* palpable; evident, plain.

Handgriff ['hantgrif], *m.* (—es, *pl.* —e) handle; (*fig.*) knack.

Handhabe ['hantha:bə], *f.* (—, *pl.* —n) (*fig.*) hold, handle.

handhaben ['hantha:bən], *v.a.* handle, manage; operate.

Handlanger ['hantlaŋər], *m.* (—s, *pl.* —) helper, carrier.

Händler ['hendlər], *m.* (—s, *pl.* —) dealer, merchant.

handlich ['hantliç], *adj.* handy, manageable.

Handlung ['handluŋ], *f.* (—, *pl.* —en) shop; (*Am.*) store; commercial house, mercantile business; action, act, deed; (*Lit.*) plot.

Handrücken ['hantrykən], *m.* (—s, *pl.* —) back of the hand.

Handschelle ['hantʃelə], *f.* (—, *pl.* —n) manacle, handcuff.

Handschlag ['hantʃla:k], *m.* (—s, *pl.* ˙'e) handshake.

Handschuh ['hantʃu:], *m.* (—s, *pl.* —e) glove; (*of iron*) gauntlet.

Handstreich ['hantʃtraiç], *m.* (—es, *pl.* —e) (*Mil.*) surprise attack, coup de main.

Handtuch ['hanttu:x], *n.* (—es, *pl.* ˙'er) towel.

Handumdrehen ['hantumdre:ən], *n.* (—s, *no pl.*) *im* —, in no time, in a jiffy.

Handwerk ['hantverk], *n.* (—s, *pl.* —e) handicraft, trade, craft.

Handwörterbuch ['hantvœrtərbu:x], *n.* (—es, *pl.* ˙'er) compact dictionary.

Handwurzel ['hantvurtsəl], *f.* (—, *pl.* —n) wrist.

Hanf [hanf], *m.* (—es, *no pl.*) hemp.

Hänfling ['henfliŋ], *m.* (—s, *pl.* —e) (*Orn.*) linnet.

Hang [haŋ], *m.* (—es, *pl.* ˙'e) slope, declivity; (*fig.*) (*no pl.*) inclination, propensity.

Hängematte ['heŋəmatə], *f.* (—, *pl.* —n) hammock.

hängen ['heŋən], *v.a.* irr. hang, suspend. — *v.r. sich* —, hang o.s. — *v.n.* hang, be suspended; be hanged (*execution*).

Hannover [ha'no:fər], *n.* Hanover.

Hänselei ['henzəlai], *f.* (—, *pl.* —en) chaffing, leg-pulling, teasing.

hänseln ['henzəln], *v.a.* tease, chaff.

Hantel ['hantəl], *f.* (—, *pl.* —n) dumbbell.

hantieren [han'ti:rən], *v.n.* busy o.s., work, occupy o.s. (with).

hapern ['ha:pərn], *v.n.* lack, be deficient; *da hapert es*, that's the snag.

Häppchen ['hepçən], *n.* (—s, *pl.* —) morsel.

Happen ['hapən], *m.* (—s, *pl.* —) mouthful.

happig ['hapiç], *adj.* greedy; excessive.

Härchen ['he:rçən], *n.* (—s, *pl.* —) short hair.

Harfe ['harfə], *f.* (—, *pl.* —n) (*Mus.*) harp.

Harke ['harkə], *f.* (—, *pl.* —n) rake.

Harm [harm], *m.* (—es, *no pl.*) grief, sorrow; injury, wrong.

härmen ['hermən], *v.r. sich* — *um*, grieve over.

harmlos ['harmlo:s], *adj.* harmless, innocuous.

Harmonielehre [harmo'ni:le:rə], *f.* (—, *pl.* —n) (*Mus.*) harmonics; harmony.

harmonieren [harmo'ni:rən], *v.n. mit einem* —, be in concord with s.o., agree with s.o.

Harmonika [har'mo:nika], *f.* (—, *pl.* —ken) (*Mus.*) accordion, concertina; mouth-organ.

Harn [harn], *m.* (—s, *no pl.*) urine.

Harnisch ['harniʃ], *m.* (—es, *pl.* —e) harness, armour; *in* — *bringen*, enrage.

Harpune [har'pu:nə], *f.* (—, *pl.* —n) harpoon.

harren ['harən], *v.n.* wait for, hope for.

harsch

harsch [harʃ], *adj.* harsh; rough; unfriendly.
hart [hart], *adj.* hard, severe, cruel, austere.
Härte ['hɛrtə], *f.* (—, *pl.* —n) hardness, severity.
härten ['hɛrtən], *v.a.* harden.
hartleibig ['hartlaibiç], *adj.* constipated.
hartnäckig ['hartnɛkiç], *adj.* stubborn, obstinate; undaunted.
Harz (1) [harts], *m.* (*Geog.*) (—es, *no pl.*) the Hartz mountains.
Harz (2) [harts], *n.* (—es, *pl.* —e) resin, rosin.
harzig ['hartsiç], *adj.* resinous.
Hasardspiel [ha'zartʃpiːl], *n.* (—es, *pl.* —e) game of chance, gamble.
Haschee [ha'ʃeː], *n.* (—s, *pl.* —s) puree, hash, mash.
haschen ['haʃən], *v.a.* catch, snatch, seize. — *v.n.* — nach, strain after, snatch at.
Häschen ['hɛːsçən], *n.* (—s, *pl.* —) (*Zool.*) small hare, leveret.
Häscher ['hɛʃər], *m.* (—s, *pl.* —) bailiff.
Hase ['haːzə], *m.* (—n, *pl.* —n) (*Zool.*) hare.
Haselrute ['haːzəlruːtə], *f.* (—, *pl.* —n) hazel-switch.
Hasenfuß ['haːzənfuːs], *m.* (—es, *no pl.*) coward.
Hasenklein ['haːzənklain], *n.* (—s, *no pl.*) jugged hare.
Hasenscharte ['haːzənʃartə], *f.* (—, *pl.* —n) hare-lip.
Haspe ['haspə], *f.* (—, *pl.* —n) hasp, hinge.
Haspel ['haspəl], *f.* (—, *pl.* —n) reel.
haspeln ['haspəln], *v.a.* wind on a reel; (*fig.*) rattle off.
Haß [has], *m.* (—sses, *no pl.*) hatred, hate, detestation.
hassen ['hasən], *v.a.* hate, detest.
haßerfüllt ['hasərfylt], *adj.* full of spite, full of hatred.
häßlich ['hɛsliç], *adj.* ugly, repulsive; (*fig.*) unpleasant, unkind; unseemly.
Hast [hast], *f.* (—, *no pl.*) haste, hurry, hastiness, rashness.
hastig ['hastiç], *adj.* hasty, hurried.
hätscheln ['hɛtʃəln], *v.a.* pamper, caress, fondle.
Hatz [hats], *f.* (—, *pl.* —en) baiting; hunt; revelry.
Haube ['haubə], *f.* (—, *pl.* —n) bonnet, cap; (*Motor.*) bonnet, (*Am.*) hood.
Haubenlerche ['haubənlɛrçə], *f.* (—, *pl.* —n) (*Orn.*) crested lark.
Haubitze [hau'bitsə], *f.* (—, *pl.* —n) howitzer.
Hauch [haux], *m.* (—es, *no pl.*) breath, whiff; (*fig.*) touch, tinge.
hauchdünn ['hauxdyn], *adj.* extremely thin.
hauchen ['hauxən], *v.n.* breathe.
Hauchlaut ['hauxlaut], *m.* (—es, *pl.* —e) (*Phonet.*) aspirate.

Haudegen ['haudeːgən], *m.* (—s, *pl.* —) broad-sword; *ein alter* —, an old bully.
Haue ['hauə], *f.* (—, *no pl.*) (*coll.*) thrashing.
hauen ['hauən], *v.a.* hew; cut; strike; hit; give a hiding to. — *v.n. über die Schnur* —, kick over the traces.
Hauer ['hauər], *m.* (—s, *pl.* —) hewer, cutter; (*animal*) fang, tusk.
Häuer ['hɔyər], *m.* (—s, *pl.* —) miner.
Haufen ['haufən], *m.* (—s, *pl.* —) heap, pile.
häufen ['hɔyfən], *v.a.* heap, pile. — *v.r. sich* —, accumulate, multiply, increase.
häufig ['hɔyfiç], *adj.* frequent, abundant. — *adv.* frequently, often.
Häufung ['hɔyfuŋ], *f.* (—, *pl.* —en) accumulation.
Haupt [haupt], *n.* (—es, *pl.* ̈er) head; leader; chief, principal; (*compounds*) main—; *aufs* — *schlagen*, inflict a total defeat on; *ein bemoostes* —, an old student.
Hauptaltar ['hauptalta:r], *m.* (—s, *pl.* —e) (*Eccl.*) high altar.
Hauptbuch ['hauptbu:x], *n.* (—es, *pl.* ̈er) ledger.
Häuptling ['hɔyptliŋ], *m.* (—s, *pl.* —e) chieftain.
Hauptmann ['hauptman], *m.* (—s, *pl.* ̈er, **Hauptleute**) (*Mil.*) captain.
Hauptnenner ['hauptnɛnər], *m.* (—s, *pl.* —) (*Maths.*) common denominator.
Hauptquartier ['hauptkvarti:r], *n.* (—es, *pl.* —e) headquarters.
Hauptsache ['hauptzaxə], *f.* (—, *pl.* —n) main thing, substance, main point; *in der* —, in the main.
hauptsächlich ['hauptzɛçliç], *adj.* chief, main, principal, essential.
Hauptsatz ['hauptzats], *m.* (—es, *pl.* ̈e) (*Gram.*) principal sentence.
Hauptschriftleiter ['hauptʃriftlaitər], *m.* (—s, *pl.* —) editor-in-chief.
Hauptschule ['hauptʃuːlə], *f.* (—, *pl.* —n) intermediate school.
Hauptstadt ['hauptʃtat], *f.* (—, *pl.* ̈e) capital, metropolis.
Haupton ['hauptoːn], *m.* (—s, *pl.* ̈e) (*Mus.*) key-note; (*Phonet.*) primary accent.
Haupttreffer ['haupttrɛfər], *m.* (—s, *pl.* —) first prize; jackpot.
Hauptverkehrsstunden ['hauptfɛrkeːrsʃtundən], *f. pl.* (*traffic etc.*) rush-hour.
Hauptwache ['hauptvaxə], *f.* (—, *pl.* —n) central guardroom.
Hauptwort ['hauptvɔrt], *n.* (—es, *pl.* ̈er) noun, substantive.
Hauptzahl ['haupttsaːl], *f.* (—, *pl.* —en) cardinal number.
Haus [haus], *n.* (—es, *pl.* ̈er) house, home; household; firm; *zu* —e, at home; *nach* —e, home.
Hausarbeit ['hausarbait], *f.* (—, *pl.* —en) housework, domestic work; homework.

Hausarrest ['hausarɛst], *m.* (**—es**, *no pl.*) house arrest.

Hausarzt ['hausartst], *m.* (**—es**, *pl.* ⸚e) family doctor.

hausbacken ['hausbakən], *adj.* home-made; homely; humdrum.

Häuschen ['hɔysçən], *n.* (**—s**, *pl.* —) small house, cottage; *ganz aus dem — sein*, be beside o.s.

Hausen ['hauzən], *m.* (**—s**, *pl.* —) sturgeon.

hausen ['hauzən], *v.n.* reside, be domiciled; *übel —*, play havoc among.

Hausflur ['hausflu:r], *m.* (**—s**, *pl.* —e) entrance hall (of a house), vestibule.

Hausfrau ['hausfrau], *f.* (**—**, *pl.* —en) housewife, mistress of the house.

Hausfriedensbruch ['hausfri:dənsbrux], *m.* (**—es**, *pl.* ⸚e) (*Law*) intrusion, trespass.

Hausgenosse ['hausgənɔsə], *m.* (**—n**, *pl.* —n) fellow-lodger.

Haushalt ['haushalt], *m.* (**—es**, *no pl.*) household.

Haushaltung ['haushaltuŋ], *f.* (**—**, *no pl.*) housekeeping.

Hausherr ['hausher], *m.* (**—n**, *pl.* —en) master of the house, householder.

Haushofmeister ['haushofmaɪstər], *m.* (**—s**, *pl.* —) steward; butler.

hausieren [hau'zi:rən], *v.n.* peddle, hawk.

Hauslehrer ['hausle:rər], *m.* (**—s**, *pl.* —) private tutor.

Häusler ['hɔyslər], *m.* (**—s**, *pl.* —) cottager.

häuslich ['hɔyslɪç], *adj.* domestic, domesticated.

Hausmädchen ['hausmɛdçən], *n.* (**—s**, *pl.* —) housemaid.

Hausmannskost ['hausmanskɔst], *f.* (**—**, *no pl.*) plain fare.

Hausmeister ['hausmaɪstər], *m.* (**—s**, *pl.* —) house-porter, caretaker.

Hausmittel ['hausmɪtəl], *n.* (**—s**, *pl.* —) household remedy.

Hausrat ['hausra:t], *m.* (**—s**, *no pl.*) household furnishings, household effects.

Hausschlüssel ['hausʃlysəl], *m.* (**—s**, *pl.* —) latch-key.

Hausschuh ['hausʃu:], *m.* (**—s**, *pl.* —e) slipper.

Hausstand ['hausʃtant], *m.* (**—es**, *pl.* ⸚e) household.

Haustier ['hausti:r], *n.* (**—es**, *pl.* —e) domestic animal.

Hausvater ['hausfa:tər], *m.* (**—s**, *pl.* ⸚) paterfamilias.

Hausverwalter ['hausfɛrvaltər], *m.* (**—s**, *pl.* —) steward, caretaker; (*Am.*) janitor.

Hauswesen ['hausve:zən], *n.* (**—s**, *no pl.*) household management *or* affairs.

Hauswirt ['hausvɪrt], *m.* (**—es**, *pl.* —e) landlord.

Hauswirtin ['hausvɪrtɪn], *f.* (**—**, *pl.* —nen) landlady.

Hauswirtschaft ['hausvɪrtʃaft], *f.* (**—**, *no pl.*) housekeeping, domestic economy.

Haut [haut], *f.* (**—**, *pl.* ⸚e) (*human*) skin; (*animal*) hide; (*fruit*) peel; (*on liquid*) skin; membrane; film; *aus der — fahren*, flare up.

Hautausschlag ['hautausʃla:k], *m.* (**—s**, *pl.* ⸚e) rash, eczema.

Häutchen ['hɔytçən], *n.* (**—s**, *pl.* —) cuticle, pellicle, membrane.

häuten ['hɔytən], *v.a.* skin, flay, strip off the skin. *— v.r. sich —*, cast off (skin) *or* slough.

Hebamme ['he:pamə], *f.* (**—**, *pl.* —n) midwife.

Hebel ['he:bəl], *m.* (**—s**, *pl.* —) lever.

heben ['he:bən], *v.a. irr.* raise, lift, hoist, heave; elevate; improve; *aus der Taufe —*, be godfather (godmother) to (s.o.).

Heber ['he:bər], *m.* (**—s**, *pl.* —) siphon.

Hebräer [he'brɛ:ər], *m.* (**—s**, *pl.* —) Hebrew.

Hechel ['heçəl], *f.* (**—**, *pl.* —n) hackle, flax-comb.

hecheln ['heçəln], *v.a.* dress flax; hackle; (*fig.*) taunt, heckle.

Hecht [heçt], *m.* (**—es**, *pl.* —e) (*Zool.*) pike; (*swimming*) dive.

Hechtsprung ['heçtʃpruŋ], *m.* header.

Heck [hek], *n.* (**—s**, *pl.* —e) (*Naut.*) stern; (*Motor.*) rear; (*Aviat.*) tail.

Heckbord ['hekbɔrt], *m.* (**—s**, *pl.* —e) (*Naut.*) taffrail.

Hecke ['hekə], *f.* (**—**, *pl.* —n) hedge.

hecken ['hekən], *v.n.* breed, bring forth.

Heckpfennig ['hekpfenɪç], *m.* (**—s**, *pl.* —e) lucky sixpence.

heda! ['he:da:], *excl.* hey, you!

Heer [he:r], *m.* (**—s**, *pl.* —e) army; multitude; *stehendes —*, regular army.

Heeresmacht ['he:rəsmaxt], *f.* (**—**, *pl.* ⸚e) armed forces, troops.

Heerschar ['he:rʃa:r], *f.* (**—**, *pl.* —en) host; corps, legion; (*Bibl.*) *der Herr der —en*, the Lord of Hosts.

Heerschau ['he:rʃau], *f.* (**—**, *pl.* —en) review, muster, parade.

Heerstraße ['he:rʃtra:sə], *f.* (**—**, *pl.* —en) military road; highway; (*Am.*) highroad.

Heerwesen ['he:rve:zən], *n.* (**—s**, *no pl.*) military affairs.

Hefe ['he:fə], *f.* (**—**, *no pl.*) yeast; dregs; sediment.

Hefeteig ['he:fətaɪk], *m.* (**—s**, *pl.* —e) leavened dough.

Heft [heft], *n.* (**—es**, *pl.* —e) exercise-book, copy-book; haft, handle, hilt.

heften ['heftən], *v.a.* fasten; baste, stitch, fix, pin.

heftig ['heftɪç], *adj.* vehement, violent.

Heftnadel ['heftna:dəl], *f.* (**—**, *pl.* —n) stitching-needle.

hegen ['he:gən], *v.a.* enclose, protect, preserve; (*fig.*) cherish; entertain; hold; *— und pflegen*, nurse carefully.

Hehl

Hehl [he:l], *n.* (**—es,** *no pl.*) concealment, secret.

hehlen ['he:lən], *v.n.* receive stolen goods.

Hehler ['hə:lər], *m.* (**—s,** *pl.* **—**) receiver of stolen goods, (*sl.*) fence.

hehr [he:r], *adj.* (*Lit.*) exalted, august, sublime.

Heide (1) ['haɪdə], *m.* (**—n,** *pl.* **—n**) heathen, pagan.

Heide (2) ['haɪdə], *f.* (**—,** *pl.* **—n**) heath.

Heidekraut ['haɪdəkraut], *n.* (**—es,** *no pl.*) heath, heather.

Heidelbeere ['haɪdəlbe:rə], *f.* (**—,** *pl.* **—n**) (*Bot.*) bilberry; (*Am.*) blueberry.

Heidenangst ['haɪdənaŋst], *f.* (**—,** *no pl.*) (*coll.*) mortal fear.

Heidenlärm ['haɪdənlɛrm], *m.* (**—es,** *no pl.*) hullaballoo.

Heidenröschen ['haɪdənrø:sçən], *n.* (**—s,** *pl.* **—**) (*Bot.*) sweet-briar.

Heidentum ['haɪdəntu:m], *n.* (**—s,** *no pl.*) paganism.

heidnisch ['haɪdnɪʃ], *adj.* pagan, heathen.

Heidschnuke ['haɪtʃnu:kə], *f.* (**—,** *pl.* **—n**) moorland sheep.

heikel ['haɪkəl], *adj.* delicate, sensitive, critical.

Heil [haɪl], *n.* (**—(e)s,** *no pl.*) safety, welfare; (*Theol.*) salvation; *sein — versuchen,* have a try, try o.'s luck. **— int.** hail! *— der Königin,* God save the Queen.

heil [haɪl], *adj.* unhurt, intact.

Heiland ['haɪlant], *m.* (**—s,** *no pl.*) Saviour, Redeemer.

Heilanstalt ['haɪlanʃtalt], *f.* (**—,** *pl.* **—en**) sanatorium, convalescent home; (*Am.*) sanitarium.

heilbar ['haɪlba:r], *adj.* curable.

heilbringend ['haɪlbrɪŋənt],*adj.*salutary.

heilen ['haɪlən], *v.a.* cure, heal. *— v.n.* (*aux. sein*) heal.

heilig ['haɪlɪç], *adj.* holy, sacred; *der Heilige Abend,* Christmas Eve; *— sprechen,* canonise; (*before name*) *der, die —s,* Saint.

Heiligenschein ['haɪlɪgənʃaɪn], *m.* (**—s,** *pl.* **—e**) halo; (*clouds*) nimbus.

Heiligkeit ['haɪlɪçkaɪt], *f.* (**—,** *no pl.*) holiness, sanctity, sacredness.

Heiligtum ['haɪlɪçtu:m], *n.* (**—s,** *pl.* **—er**) sanctuary, shrine; holy relic.

Heiligung ['haɪlɪguŋ], *f.* (**—,** *pl.* **—en**) sanctification, consecration.

heilkräftig ['haɪlkrɛftɪç], *adj.* curative, salubrious.

Heilkunde ['haɪlkundə], *f.* (**—,** *no pl.*) therapeutics.

heillos ['haɪllo:s], *adj.* wicked, mischievous; (*fig.*) awful.

Heilmittel ['haɪlmɪtəl], *n.* (**—s,** *pl.* **—**) remedy.

heilsam ['haɪlza:m], *adj.* salubrious, salutary.

Heilsamkeit ['haɪlza:mkaɪt], *f.* (**—,** *no pl.*) salubrity, salubriousness.

Heilsarmee ['haɪlsarme:], *f.* (**—,** *no pl.*) Salvation Army.

Heilslehre ['haɪlsle:rə], *f.* (**—,** *pl.* **—n**) doctrine of salvation.

Heiltrank ['haɪltraŋk], *m.* (**—es,** *no pl.*) (medicinal) potion.

Heim [haɪm], *n.* (**—es,** *pl.* **—e**) home.

heim [haɪm], *adv. prefix (to verbs)* home.

Heimat ['haɪmat], *f.* (**—,** *no pl.*) native place, home, homeland.

Heimatschein ['haɪmatʃaɪn], *m.* (**—es,** *pl.* **—e**) certificate of origin *or* domicile.

Heimchen ['haɪmçən], *n.* (**—s,** *pl.* **—**) (*Ent.*) cricket.

heimführen ['haɪmfy:rən], *v.a.* bring home (a bride); (*fig.*) marry.

Heimgang ['haɪmgaŋ], *m.* (**—es,** *no pl.*) going home; (*fig.*) decease, death.

heimisch ['haɪmɪʃ], *adj.* native, indigenous; *sich — fühlen,* feel at home.

heimkehren ['haɪmke:rən], *v.n.* return (home).

heimleuchten ['haɪmlɔyçtən], *v.n. einem —,* tell s.o. the plain truth, give s.o. a piece of o.'s mind.

heimlich ['haɪmlɪç], *adj.* secret, clandestine, furtive.

heimsuchen ['haɪmzu:xən], *v.a.* visit; afflict, punish.

Heimtücke ['haɪmtykə], *f.* (**—,** *no pl.*) malice.

heimwärts ['haɪmvɛrts], *adv.* homeward.

Heimweh ['haɪmve:], *n.* (**—s,** *no pl.*) homesickness; nostalgia.

heimzahlen ['haɪmtsa:lən], *v.a.* pay back, retaliate.

Hein [haɪn], *m.* (*coll.*) *Freund —,* Death.

Heinzelmännchen ['haɪntsəlmɛnçən], *n.* (**—s,** *pl.* **—**) goblin, brownie, imp.

Heirat ['haɪra:t], *f.* (**—,** *pl.* **—en**) marriage, wedding.

heiraten ['haɪra:tən], *v.a.* marry, wed.

Heiratsgut ['haɪra:tsgu:t], *n.* (**—es,** *pl.* **—er**) dowry.

heischen ['haɪʃən], *v.a.* (*Poet.*) ask, demand.

heiser ['haɪzər], *adj.* hoarse.

heiß [haɪs], *adj.* hot; (*fig.*) ardent; (*climate*) torrid.

heißen ['haɪsən], *v.a. irr.* bid, command. *— v.n.* be called; be said; signify, mean; *es heißt,* it is said; *das heißt (d.h.),* that is to say; *wie — Sie?* what is your name?

heißgeliebt ['haɪsgəli:pt], *adj.* dearly beloved.

heiter ['haɪtər], *adj.* clear; serene; cheerful.

Heiterkeit ['haɪtərkaɪt], *f.* (**—,** *no pl.*) serenity; cheerfulness.

heizen ['haɪtsən], *v.a. v.n.* heat.

Heizkissen ['haɪtskɪsən], *n.* (**—s,** *pl.* **—**) electric pad *or* blanket.

Heizkörper ['haɪtskœrpər], *m.* (**—s,** *pl.* **—**) radiator; heater.

Heizung ['haɪtsuŋ], *f.* (**—,** *pl.* **—en**) heating.

hektisch ['hɛktɪʃ], *adj.* hectic.

hektographieren [hɛktogra'fiːrən], *v.a.* stencil, duplicate.

Hektoliter ['hɛktoliːtər], *m.* (—s, *pl.* —) hectolitre (22 gallons).

Held [hɛlt], *m.* (—en, *pl.* —en) hero.

Heldengedicht ['hɛldəngədɪçt], *n.* (—es, *pl.* —e) heroic poem, epic.

heldenhaft ['hɛldənhaft], *adj.* heroic. — *adv.* heroically.

Heldenmut ['hɛldənmuːt], *m.* (—es, *no pl.*) heroism.

helfen ['hɛlfən], *v.n. irr.* (*Dat.*) help, aid, assist.

Helfershelfer ['hɛlfərshɛlfər], *m.* (—s, *pl.* —) accomplice, accessory.

Helgoland ['hɛlgolant], *n.* Heligoland.

hell [hɛl], *adj.* clear, bright, light; (*coll.*) clever, wide awake.

Helldunkel ['hɛldʊŋkəl], *n.* (—s, *no pl.*) twilight; (*Art*) chiaroscuro.

Helle ['hɛlə], *f.* (—, *no pl.*) clearness; brightness; daylight.

Heller ['hɛlər], *m.* (—s, *pl.* —) small coin, farthing.

hellhörig ['hɛlhøːrɪç], *adj.* keen of hearing.

Helligkeit ['hɛlɪçkaɪt], *f.* (—, *no pl.*) clearness; daylight.

Hellseher ['hɛlzeːər], *m.* (—s, *pl.* —) clairvoyant.

hellsichtig ['hɛlzɪxtɪç], *adj.* clairvoyant; clear-sighted.

Helm [hɛlm], *m.* (—es, *pl.* —e) helmet.

Helmbusch ['hɛlmbuʃ], *m.* (—es, *pl.* ∹e) crest (of helmet).

Helmgitter ['hɛlmgɪtər], *n.* (—s, *pl.* —) eye-slit (in helmet).

Helsingfors ['hɛlzɪŋfors], *n.* Helsinki.

Helsingör [hɛlzɪŋ'øːr], *n.* Elsinore.

Hemd [hɛmt], *n.* (—es, *pl.* —en) shirt; vest.

Hemdenstoff ['hɛmdənʃtof], *m.* (—es, *pl.* —e) shirting.

hemmen ['hɛmən], *v.a.* stop, hamper, hinder, restrain; (*fig.*) inhibit.

Hemmschuh ['hɛmʃuː], *m.* (—s, *pl.* —e) brake; (*fig.*) drag, obstruction.

Hemmung ['hɛmʊŋ], *f.* (—, *pl.* —en) stoppage, hindrance, restraint; (*watch*) escapement; (*fig.*) inhibition, reluctance.

Hengst [hɛŋkst], *m.* (—es, *pl.* —e) stallion.

Henkel ['hɛŋkəl], *m.* (—s, *pl.* —) handle.

henken ['hɛŋkən], *v.a* hang (s.o.).

Henker ['hɛŋkər], *m.* (—s, *pl.* —) hangman, executioner.

Henne ['hɛnə], *f.* (—, *pl.* —n) (*Zool.*) hen; *junge* —, pullet.

her [heːr], *adv.* hither, here, to me; (*temp.*) since, ago; *von alters* —, from olden times; *von je* —, from time immemorial; *wo kommst du* —? where do you come from? *wie lange ist es* —? how long ago is it?

herab [hɛ'rap], *adv.* downwards, down to; *die Treppe* —, downstairs.

herablassen [hɛ'raplasən], *v.r. irr. sich* — *etwas zu tun*, condescend to do s.th.

herabsehen [hɛ'rapzeːən], *v.n. irr.* look down; (*fig.*) look down upon s.o.

herabsetzen [hɛ'rapzɛtsən], *v.a.* put down; degrade; (*value*) depreciate; (*price*) reduce, lower; (*fig.*) disparage.

herabwürdigen [hɛ'rapvyrdɪgən], *v.a.* degrade, abase.

herabziehen [hɛ'raptsiːən], *v.a. irr.* pull down.

Heraldik [he'raldɪk], *f.* (—, *no pl.*) heraldry.

heran [hɛ'ran], *adv.* up to, on, near.

heranbilden [hɛ'ranbɪldən], *v.a.* train. — *v.r. sich* —, train, qualify.

herangehen [hɛ'rangeːən], *v.n. irr.* (*aux.* sein) approach, sidle up (to); *an etwas* —, set to work on s.th.

heranmachen [hɛ'ranmaxən], *v.r. sich an etwas* —, set to work on s.th., set about s.th.

herannahen [hɛ'rannaːən], *v.n.* (*aux.* sein) approach, draw near.

heranrücken [hɛ'ranrykən], *v.a.* move near. — *v.n.* (*aux.* sein) advance, draw near.

heranschleichen [hɛ'ranʃlaɪçən], *v.r. irr. sich* — *an*, sneak up to.

heranwachsen [hɛ'ranvaksən], *v.n. irr.* (*aux.* sein) grow up.

heranwagen [hɛ'ranvaːgən], *v.r. sich* —, venture near.

heranziehen [hɛ'rantsiːən], *v.a. irr.* draw near; *als Beispiel* —, cite as an example; (*fig.*) enlist (s.o.'s aid). — *v.n.* (*aux.* sein) draw near, approach.

herauf [hɛ'rauf], *adv.* up, upwards.

heraufbeschwören [hɛ'raufbeʃvøːrən], *v.a.* conjure up.

heraus [hɛ'raus], *adv.* out, out of.

herausfordern [hɛ'rausfordərn], *v.a.* challenge.

Herausgabe [hɛ'rausgaːbə], *f.* (—, *pl.* —n) delivery; (*book*) publication; editing.

herausgeben [hɛ'rausgeːbən], *v.a. irr.* give out, deliver; (*money*) give change; (*book*) publish, edit.

Herausgeber [hɛ'rausgeːbər], *m.* (—s, *pl.* —) publisher; editor.

heraushaben [hɛ'raushaːbən], *v.a. irr. etwas* —, have the knack of s.th.

herausputzen [hɛ'rausputsən], *v.r. sich* —, dress up.

herausrücken [hɛ'rausrykən], *v.n. mit Geld* —, fork out money; *mit der Sprache* —, speak out, come out with.

herausschlagen [hɛ'rausʃlaːgən], *v.a. irr. die Kosten* —, recover expenses; *viel* —, make the most of; profit by.

herausstellen [hɛ'rausʃtɛlən], *v.a.* put out, expose. — *v.r. sich* — *als*, turn out to be.

herausstreichen [hɛ'rausʃtraɪçən], *v.a. irr.* extol, praise.

heraussuchen [hɛ'rauszuːxən], *v.a.* pick out.

herauswollen

herauswollen [hɛˈrausvɔlən], *v.n. nicht mit der Sprache —*, hesitate to speak out.

herb [hɛrp], *adj.* sour, sharp, tart, acrid; (*fig.*) austere, harsh, bitter; (*wine*) dry.

herbei [hɛrˈbaɪ], *adv.* hither, near.

herbeischaffen [hɛrˈbaɪʃafən], *v.a.* procure.

herbeiströmen [hɛrˈbaɪʃtrøːmən], *v.n.* (*aux.* sein) crowd, flock.

Herberge [ˈhɛrbɛrɡə], *f.* (—, *pl.* —n) shelter, lodging, inn.

Herbst [hɛrpst], *m.* (—es, *pl.* —e) autumn; (*Am.*) fall.

Herbstrose [ˈhɛrpstroːzə], *f.* (—, *pl.* —n) (*Bot.*) hollyhock.

Herbstzeitlose [ˈhɛrpstsaɪtloːzə], *f.* (—, *pl.* —n) (*Bot.*) meadow-saffron.

Herd [heːrt], *m.* (—es, *pl.* —e) hearth, fireplace; cooking-stove; (*fig.*) focus.

Herde [ˈheːrdə], *f.* (—, *pl.* —n) flock, herd; (*fig.*) troop.

herein [heˈraɪn], *adv.* in, inside. — *int.* —! come in!

hereinbrechen [heˈraɪnbrɛçən], *v.n. irr.* (*aux.* sein) *über einen —*, befall s.o., overtake s.o.; (*night*) close in.

hereinfallen [heˈraɪnfalən], *v.n. irr.* (*aux.* sein) (*fig.*) be taken in, fall for s.th.

herfallen [ˈheːrfalən], *v.n. irr.* (*aux.* sein) *über einen —*, go for s.o., set upon s.o.

Hergang [ˈheːrɡaŋ], *m.* (—es, *no pl.*) proceedings, course of events; circumstances; story, plot.

hergeben [ˈheːrɡeːbən], *v.a. irr.* give up, surrender.

hergebracht [ˈheːrɡəbraxt], *adj.* traditional, time-honoured.

hergehen [ˈheːrɡeːən], *v.n. irr.* (*aux.* sein) proceed; *es geht lustig her*, they are having a gay time.

hergelaufen [ˈheːrɡəlaufən], *adj. ein —er Kerl*, an adventurer, an upstart.

herhalten [ˈheːrhaltən], *v.n. irr.* suffer, serve (as a butt).

Hering [ˈheːrɪŋ], *m.* (—s, *pl.* —e) (*Zool.*) herring; *geräucherter —*, smoked herring, bloater; *gesalzener —*, pickled herring.

herkommen [ˈheːrkɔmən], *v.n. irr.* (*aux.* sein) come here; be derived from, descend from.

herkömmlich [ˈheːrkœmlɪç], *adj.* traditional, customary, usual.

Herkunft [ˈheːrkunft], *f.* (—, *no pl.*) descent, extraction; origin.

herleiern [ˈheːrlaɪərn], *v.a.* recite monotonously; reel off.

herleiten [ˈheːrlaɪtən], *v.a.* derive from.

Hermelin [hɛrməˈliːn], *m.* (—s, *no pl.*) ermine (*fur*).

hermetisch [hɛrˈmeːtɪʃ], *adj.* hermetical.

hernach [hɛrˈnaːx], *adv.* after, afterwards; hereafter.

hernehmen [ˈheːrneːmən], *v.a. irr.* take, get (from); take (s.o.) to task.

hernieder [hɛrˈniːdər], *adv.* down.

Herr [hɛr], *m.* (—n, *pl.* —en) master; lord; nobleman; gentleman; (*Theol.*) Lord; principal, governor; *mein —*, Sir; *meine Herren*, gentlemen; — *Schmidt*, Mr. Smith; *einer Sache — werden*, master s.th.

Herrenhaus [ˈhɛrənhaus], *n.* (—es, *pl.* ̈er) mansion, manor house; (*Parl.*) House of Lords.

Herrenhof [ˈhɛrənhoːf], *m.* (—es, *pl.* ̈e) manor, country-seat.

Herrenstand [ˈhɛrənʃtant], *m.* (—es, *no pl.*) nobility, gentry.

Herrenzimmer [ˈhɛrəntsɪmər], *n.* (—s, *pl.* —) study.

Herrgott [ˈhɛrɡɔt], the Lord God.

herrichten [ˈheːrɪçtən], *v.a.* prepare, fix up.

Herrin [ˈhɛrɪn], *f.* (—, *pl.* —innen) mistress, lady.

herrisch [ˈhɛrɪʃ], *adj.* imperious, lordly.

herrlich [ˈhɛrlɪç], *adj.* magnificent, splendid, glorious, excellent.

Herrnhuter [ˈhɛrnhuːtər], *m.* (—s, *pl.* —) Moravian; (*pl.*) Moravian brethren.

Herrschaft [ˈhɛrʃaft], *f.* (—, *pl.* —en) mastery, rule, dominion; master, mistress; *meine —en!* ladies and gentlemen!

herrschaftlich [ˈhɛrʃaftlɪç], *adj.* belonging to a lord; (*fig.*) elegant, fashionable, distinguished.

herrschen [ˈhɛrʃən], *v.n.* rule, govern, reign.

Herrscher [ˈhɛrʃər], *m.* (—s, *pl.* —) ruler.

herrühren [ˈheːryrən], *v.n.* come from, originate in.

hersagen [ˈheːrzaːɡən], *v.a.* recite, reel off.

herschaffen [ˈheːrʃafən], *v.a.* procure.

herstammen [ˈheːrʃtamən], *v.n.* come from, stem from, originate from; be derived from.

herstellen [ˈheːrʃtɛlən], *v.a.* place here; manufacture; *wieder —*, restore; (*sick person*) restore to health.

Herstellung [ˈheːrʃtɛluŋ], *f.* (—, *no pl.*) manufacture, production.

herstürzen [ˈheːrʃtyrtsən], *v.n.* (*aux.* sein) *über einen —*, rush at s.o.

herüber [hɛˈryːbər], *adv.* over, across; — *und hinüber*, there and back.

herum [hɛˈrum], *adv.* round, about; around.

herumbalgen [hɛˈrumbalɡən], *v.r. sich —*, scrap; scuffle.

herumbekommen [hɛˈrumbəkɔmən], *v.a. irr.* (*coll.*) talk s.o. over, win s.o. over.

herumbummeln [hɛˈrumbuməln], *v.n.* loaf about.

herumstreichen [hɛˈrumʃtraɪçən], *v.n. irr.* (*aux.* sein) gad about.

herumtreiben [hɛˈrumtraɪbən], *v.r. irr. sich —*, loaf about, gad about.

herumzanken [hɛˈrumtsaŋkən], *v.r. sich —*, squabble, quarrel; live like cat and dog.

herumziehen [he'rumtsiːən], *v.a. irr.* drag about. — *v.n.* (*aux.* sein) wander about, move from place to place.

herunter [he'runtər], *adj.* down, downward; *ich bin ganz —*, I feel poorly.

heruntergekommen [he'runtərgəkɔmən], *adj.* decayed, broken down; in straitened circumstances; depraved.

herunterhandeln [he'runtərhandəln], *v.a. einem etwas —*, beat s.o. down (in price).

herunterwürgen [he'runtervyrgən], *v.a.* swallow s.th. with dislike.

hervor [her'foːr], *adv.* forth, forward, out.

hervorheben [her'foːrheːbən], *v.a. irr.* emphasize, stress.

hervorragen [her'foːrraːgən], *v.n.* stand out, project; (*fig.*) be distinguished, excel.

hervorragend [her'foːrraːgənt], *adj.* prominent; (*fig.*) outstanding, excellent.

hervorrufen [her'foːrruːfən], *v.a. irr.* call forth; (*fig.*) evoke, bring about, create, cause.

hervorstechen [her'foːrʃteçən], *v.n. irr.* be predominant, stand out.

hervortun [her'foːrtuːn], *v.r. irr. sich —*, distinguish o.s.

Herz [herts], *n.* (—*ens*, *pl.* —*en*) heart; courage; mind; spirit; feeling; core; (*Cards*) hearts; (*coll.*) darling; *einem etwas ans — legen*, impress s.th. upon s.o.; *von —en gern*, with all my heart; *sich etwas zu —en nehmen*, take s.th. to heart.

herzählen [he:rtsɛːlən], *v.a.* enumerate.

Herzanfall ['hɛrtsanfal], *m.* (—*s*, *pl.* ⁚e) (*Med.*) heart attack.

Herzbube ['hɛrtsbuːbə], *m.* (—*n*, *pl.* —*n*) (*Cards*) knave *or* jack of hearts.

Herzdame ['hɛrtsdaːmə], *f.* (—, *pl.* —*n*) (*Cards*) queen of hearts.

Herzeleid ['hɛrtsəlaɪt], *n.* (—*es*, *no pl.*) heartbreak, sorrow, anguish, grief.

herzen ['hɛrtsən], *v.a.* hug.

Herzenseinfalt ['hɛrtsənsaɪnfalt], *f.* (—, *no pl.*) simple-mindedness.

Herzensgrund ['hɛrtsənsgrunt], *m.* (—*es*, *no pl.*) *aus —*, with all my heart.

Herzenslust ['hɛrtsənslust], *f.* (—, *no pl.*) heart's delight; *nach —*, to o.'s heart's content.

Herzfehler ['hɛrtsfeːlər], *m.* (—*s*, *pl.* —) (*Med.*) cardiac defect; organic heart disease.

Herzfell ['hɛrtsfɛl], *n.* (—*s*, *pl.* —*e*) pericardium.

herzförmig ['hɛrtsfœrmɪç], *adj.* heart-shaped.

herzhaft ['hɛrtshaft], *adj.* stout-hearted; courageous, bold; resolute; hearty.

herzig ['hɛrtsɪç], *adj.* lovely, charming, sweet; (*Am.*) cute.

Herzkammer ['hɛrtskamər], *f.* (—, *pl.* —*n*) ventricle (of the heart).

Herzklappe ['hɛrtsklapə], *f.* (—, *pl.* —*n*) valve of the heart.

Herzklopfen ['hɛrtsklɔpfən], *n.* (—*s*, *no pl.*) palpitations.

herzlich ['hɛrtslɪç], *adj.* hearty, cordial, affectionate; *— gern*, with pleasure; *—e Grüße*, kind regards.

Herzog ['hɛrtsoːk], *m.* (—*s*, *pl.* ⁚e) duke.

Herzogtum ['hɛrtsoːktuːm], *n.* (—*s*, *pl.* ⁚er) duchy, dukedom.

Herzschlag ['hɛrtsʃlaːk], *m.* (—*es*, *pl.* ⁚e) heartbeat; (*Med.*) heart attack, cardiac failure.

Hetäre [he'tɛːrə], *f.* (—, *pl.* —*n*) courtesan.

Hetzblatt ['hɛtsblat], *n.* (—*s*, *pl.* ⁚er) gutter press.

Hetze ['hɛtsə], *f.* (—, *pl.* —*n*) chase, hunt, hurry, rush; agitation.

hetzen ['hɛtsən], *v.a.* bait, fluster, chase, hunt, incite. — *v.n. herum —*, rush around.

Hetzer ['hɛtsər], *m.* (—*s*, *pl.* —) instigator, rabble-rouser.

Heu [hɔy], *n.* (—*s*, *no pl.*) hay.

Heuboden ['hɔyboːdən], *m.* (—*s*, *pl.* ⁚) hayloft.

Heuchelei [hɔyçə'laɪ], *f.* (—, *pl.* —*en*) hypocrisy.

heucheln ['hɔyçəln], *v.n.* play the hypocrite, dissemble. — *v.a.* simulate, affect, feign.

Heuchler ['hɔyçlər], *m.* (—*s*, *pl.* —) hypocrite.

Heuer ['hɔyər], *f.* (—, *pl.* —*n*) (*Naut.*) engagement; hire, wages.

heuer ['hɔyər], *adv.* (*dial.*) this year, this season.

heuern ['hɔyərn], *v.a.* (*Naut.*) engage, hire.

Heugabel ['hɔygaːbəl], *f.* (—, *pl.* —*n*) pitchfork.

heulen ['hɔylən], *v.n.* howl; roar; cry, yell, scream.

Heupferd ['hɔypfɛrt], *n.* (—*es*, *pl.* —*e*) (*Ent.*) grasshopper.

heurig ['hɔyrɪç], *adj.* of this year, this year's (*wine etc.*).

Heuschnupfen ['hɔyʃnupfən], *m.* (—*s*, *no pl.*) hay-fever.

Heuschober ['hɔyʃoːbər], *m.* (—*s*, *pl.* —) hayrick.

Heuschrecke ['hɔyʃrɛkə], *f.* (—, *pl.* —*n*) (*Ent.*) locust.

heute ['hɔytə], *adv.* today, this day; *— in acht Tagen*, today week, a week today; *— abend*, tonight.

heutig ['hɔytɪç], *adj.* today's, this day's; modern.

heutzutage ['hɔytsutaːgə], *adv.* nowadays.

Hexe ['hɛksə], *f.* (—, *pl.* —*n*) witch, sorceress, hag.

hexen ['hɛksən], *v.n.* use witchcraft; practise sorcery.

Hexenschuß ['hɛksənʃus], *m.* (—*sses*, *no pl.*) (*Med.*) lumbago.

Hexerei

Hexerei [hɛksə'raɪ], *f.* (—, *pl.* —en) witchcraft, sorcery, juggling.

hie [hi:], *adv.* (*dial.*) here.

Hieb [hi:p], *m.* (—es, *pl.* —e) cut, stroke; hit, blow; (*pl.*) a thrashing.

hienieden [hi:'ni:dən], *adv.* here below, down here.

hier [hi:r], *adv.* here, in this place.

Hiersein ['hi:rzaɪn], *n.* (—s, *no pl.*) presence, attendance.

hiesig ['hi:zɪç], *adj.* of this place, of this country, local.

Hifthorn ['hɪfthɔrn], *n.* (—s, *pl.* ̈er) hunting-horn.

Hilfe ['hɪlfə], *f.* (—, *pl.* —n) help, aid, assistance, succour, relief.

hilflos ['hɪlflo:s], *adj.* helpless.

hilfreich ['hɪlfraɪç], *adj.* helpful.

Hilfsmittel ['hɪlfsmɪtəl], *n.* (—s, *pl.* —) expedient, remedy.

Hilfsschule ['hɪlfsʃu:lə], *f.* (—, *pl.* —n) school for backward children.

Hilfszeitwort ['hɪlfstsaɪtvɔrt], *n.* (—s, *pl.* ̈er) (*Gram.*) auxiliary verb.

Himbeere ['hɪmbe:rə], *f.* (—, *pl.* —n) raspberry.

Himmel ['hɪməl], *m.* (—s, *pl.* —) heaven, heavens; sky; firmament.

himmelan [hɪmə'lan], *adv.* heavenward.

himmelangst ['hɪməlaŋkst], *adv.* *ihm war —*, he was panic-stricken.

Himmelbett ['hɪməlbɛt], *n.* (—s, *pl.* —en) fourposter.

himmelblau ['hɪməlblau], *adj.* sky-blue.

Himmelfahrt ['hɪməlfa:rt], *f.* (—, *no pl.*) Ascension.

Himmelschlüssel ['hɪməlʃlysəl], *m.* (—s, *pl.* —) (*Bot.*) primrose.

himmelschreiend ['hɪməlʃraɪənt], *adj.* atrocious, revolting.

Himmelsgewölbe ['hɪməlsgəvœlbə], *n.* (—s, *pl.* —) firmament.

Himmelsstrich ['hɪməlsʃtrɪç], *m.* (—s, *pl.* —e) climate, zone.

Himmelszeichen ['hɪməlstsaɪçən], *n.* (—s, *pl.* —) sign of the zodiac.

himmelweit ['hɪməlvaɪt], *adv.* enormous; — *entfernt*, poles apart.

himmlisch ['hɪmlɪʃ], *adj.* celestial, heavenly.

hin [hɪn], *adv.* there, towards that place; finished, gone; ruined; — *und her*, to and fro.

hinab [hɪn'ap], *adv.* down.

hinan [hɪn'an], *adv.* up.

hinarbeiten ['hɪnarbaɪtən], *v.n. auf etwas —*, work towards s.th.

hinauf [hɪn'auf], *adv.* up, up to.

hinaus [hɪn'aus], *adv.* out, out of; *es kommt auf dasselbe —*, it comes to the same thing.

hinauswollen [hɪn'ausvɔlən], *v.n.* wish to go out; (*fig.*) *hoch —*, aim high.

hinausziehen [hɪn'austsi:ən], *v.a. irr.* draw out; drag on; (*fig.*) protract.

Hinblick ['hɪnblɪk], *m.* (—es, *no pl.*) *im — auf*, in consideration of, with regard to.

hinbringen ['hɪnbrɪŋən], *v.a. irr.* bring to; escort; *Zeit —*, while away time.

hinderlich ['hɪndərlɪç], *adj.* obstructive, cumbersome.

hindern ['hɪndərn], *v.a.* hinder, obstruct, hamper, impede.

hindeuten ['hɪndɔytən], *v.n. auf etwas —*, point to s.th., hint at s.th.

Hindin ['hɪndɪn], *f.* (—, *pl.* —innen) (*Poet.*) hind.

hindurch [hɪn'durç], *adv.* through; throughout; *die ganze Zeit —*, all the time.

hinein [hɪn'aɪn], *adv.* in, into; *in den Tag — leben*, live for the present, lead a life of carefree enjoyment.

hineinfinden [hɪn'aɪnfɪndən], *v.r. irr. sich in etwas —*, reconcile or adapt o.s. to s.th.

hinfällig ['hɪnfɛlɪç], *adj.* frail, feeble, weak; shaky, void, invalid.

Hingabe ['hɪnga:bə], *f.* (—, *no pl.*) surrender; (*fig.*) devotion.

hingeben ['hɪnge:bən], *v.a. irr.* give up, surrender. — *v.r. sich einer Sache —*, devote o.s. to a task.

hingegen [hɪn'ge:gən], *adv.* on the other hand.

hinhalten ['hɪnhaltən], *v.a. irr.* (*thing*) hold out; (*person*) keep in suspense, put off.

hinken ['hɪŋkən], *v.n.* limp.

hinlänglich ['hɪnlɛŋlɪç], *adj.* sufficient.

hinlegen ['hɪnle:gən], *v.a.* lay down, put away. — *v.r. sich —*, lie down, go to bed.

hinnehmen ['hɪnne:mən], *v.a. irr.* take, submit to, accept.

hinreichen ['hɪnraɪçən], *v.a.* pass to. — *v.n.* suffice, be sufficient.

Hinreise ['hɪnraɪzə], *f.* (—, *pl.* —n) outward journey.

hinreißen ['hɪnraɪsən], *v.r. irr. sich — lassen*, allow o.s. to be carried away.

hinreißend ['hɪnraɪsənt], *adj.* charming, ravishing, enchanting.

hinrichten ['hɪnrɪçtən], *v.a.* execute, put to death.

hinscheiden ['hɪnʃaɪdən], *v.n. irr.* die, pass away.

hinschlängeln ['hɪnʃlɛŋəln], *v.r. sich —*, meander, wind along.

Hinsicht ['hɪnzɪçt], *f.* (—, *no pl.*) view, consideration, regard.

hinsichtlich ['hɪnzɪçtlɪç], *prep.* (*Genit.*) with regard to.

hinstellen ['hɪnʃtɛlən], *v.a.* put down; make out to be.

hinten ['hɪntən], *adv.* behind; *von —*, from behind.

hinter ['hɪntər], *prep.* (*Dat.*) behind, after.

Hinterachse ['hɪntəraksə], *f.* (—, *pl.* —n) (*Motor.*) rear-axle.

Hinterbein ['hɪntərbaɪn], *n.* (—s, *pl.* —e) hind-leg; (*fig.*) *sich auf die —e stellen*, get up on o.'s hind-legs.

Hinterbliebene [hɪntər'bliːbənə], *m.* (—n, *pl.* —n) survivor; mourner; (*pl.*) the bereaved.

hinterbringen [hɪntər'brɪŋən], *v.a. irr.* give information about, (*coll.*) tell on.

Hinterdeck ['hɪntərdɛk], *n.* (—s, *no pl.*) (*Naut.*) quarter deck.

hinterdrein ['hɪntərdraɪn], *adv.* afterwards, after; behind.

hintereinander [hɪntəraɪn'andər], *adv.* in succession, one after another.

Hintergedanke ['hɪntərgədaŋkə], *m.* (—n, *pl.* —n) mental reservation, ulterior motive.

hintergehen [hɪntər'geːən], *v.a. irr.* deceive, circumvent.

Hintergrund ['hɪntərgrunt], *m.* (—es, *pl.* ⁝e) background; (*Theat.*) back-cloth, back-drop.

Hinterhalt ['hɪntərhalt], *m.* (—s, *pl.* —e) ambush; (*fig.*) reserve.

hinterhältig ['hɪntərhɛltɪç], *adj.* furtive, secretive; insidious.

hinterher [hɪntər'heːr], *adv.* behind; in the rear; afterwards.

Hinterindien ['hɪntərɪndjən], *n.* Indo-China.

Hinterkopf ['hɪntərkɔpf], *m.* (—es, *pl.* ⁝e) occiput, back of the head.

Hinterlader ['hɪntərlaːdər], *m.* (—s, *pl.* —) breech-loader.

hinterlassen [hɪntər'lasən], *v.a. irr.* leave (a legacy), bequeath; leave (word).

Hinterlassenschaft [hɪntər'lasənʃaft], *f.* (—, *pl.* —en) inheritance, bequest.

Hinterlegung [hɪntər'leːguŋ], *f.* (—, *pl.* —en) deposition.

Hinterlist ['hɪntərlɪst], *f.* (—, *no pl.*) fraud, deceit; cunning.

hinterrücks [hɪntər'ryks], *adv.* from behind; (*fig.*) treacherously, behind s.o.'s back.

Hintertreffen ['hɪntərtrɛfən], *n.* (—s, *no pl.*) ins — geraten, be left out in the cold, fall behind.

hintertreiben [hɪntər'traɪbən], *v.a. irr.* prevent, frustrate.

Hintertreppe ['hɪntərtrɛpə], *f.* (—, *pl.* —n) back-stairs.

Hintertreppenroman ['hɪntərtrepənromaːn], *m.* (—s, *pl.* —e) (*Lit.*) cheap thriller.

hinterziehen ['hɪntərtsiːən], *v.a. irr. insep.* defraud.

hinträumen ['hɪntrɔʏmən], *v.n.* vor sich —, daydream.

hinüber [hɪn'yːbər], *adv.* over, across.

hinunter [hɪn'untər], *adv.* down; den Berg —, downhill.

hinweg [hɪn'vɛk], *adv.* away, off.

hinwegsetzen [hɪn'vɛkzɛtsən], *v.r. sich über etwas —,* make light of s.th.

Hinweis ['hɪnvaɪs], *m.* (—es, *pl.* —e) hint, indication, reference; unter — auf, with reference to.

hinweisen ['hɪnvaɪzən], *v.a. irr.* auf etwas —, refer to, point to s.th.

hinwerfen ['hɪnvɛrfən], *v.a. irr.* throw down; hingeworfene Bemerkung, casual remark.

hinziehen ['hɪntsiːən], *v.a. irr.* draw along; attract. — *v.n.* (*aux. sein*) march along. — *v.r. sich —,* drag on.

hinzielen ['hɪntsiːlən], *v.n. auf etwas —,* aim at s.th., have s.th. in mind.

hinzu [hɪn'tsuː], *adv.* to, near; besides; in addition.

hinzufügen [hɪn'tsuːfyːgən], *v.a.* add.

hinzukommen [hɪn'tsuːkɔmən], *v.n. irr.* (*aux. sein*) be added.

hinzuziehen [hɪn'tsutsiːən], *v.a. irr.* include, add; call in (expert).

Hiobsbotschaft ['hiːɔpsboːtʃaft], *f.* (—, *no pl.*) bad news.

Hirn [hɪrn], *n.* (—s, *pl.* —e) brain, brains. See also **Gehirn**.

Hirngespinst ['hɪrngəʃpɪnst], *n.* (—es, *pl.* —e) fancy, chimera, illusion, figment of the imagination.

hirnverbrannt ['hɪrnfɛrbrant], *adj.* crazy, insane, mad; (*coll.*) crackbrained.

Hirsch [hɪrʃ], *m.* (—es, *pl.* —e) (*Zool.*) stag, hart.

Hirschbock ['hɪrʃbɔk], *m.* (—s, *pl.* ⁝e) (*Zool.*) stag.

Hirschfänger ['hɪrʃfɛŋər], *m.* (—s, *pl.* —) hunting-knife.

Hirschgeweih ['hɪrʃgəvaɪ], *n.* (—s, *pl.* —e) horns, antlers.

Hirschhorn ['hɪrʃhɔrn], *n.* (—s, *no pl.*) (*Chem.*) hartshorn.

Hirschkäfer ['hɪrʃkɛːfər], *m.* (—s, *pl.* —) (*Ent.*) stag beetle.

Hirschkeule ['hɪrʃkɔʏlə], *f.* (—, *pl.* —n) haunch of venison.

Hirschkuh ['hɪrʃkuː], *f.* (—, *pl.* ⁝e) (*Zool.*) hind, doe.

Hirse ['hɪrzə], *f.* (—, *no pl.*) (*Bot.*) millet.

Hirt [hɪrt], *m.* (—en, *pl.* —en) shepherd, herdsman.

Hirtenbrief ['hɪrtənbriːf], *m.* (—s, *pl.* —e) (*Eccl.*) pastoral letter.

His [hɪs], *n.* (—, *pl.* —) (*Mus.*) B sharp.

hissen ['hɪsən], *v.a.* hoist (the flag).

Historiker [hɪ'stoːrɪkər], *m.* (—s, *pl.* —) historian.

historisch [hɪ'stoːrɪʃ], *adj.* historical.

Hitzblase ['hɪtsblaːzə], *f.* (—, *pl.* —n) blister, heat-rash.

Hitze ['hɪtsə], *f.* (—, *no pl.*) heat, hot weather.

hitzig ['hɪtsɪç], *adj.* hot-headed, hasty, passionate.

Hitzschlag ['hɪtsʃlaːk], *m.* (—es, *pl.* ⁝e) sunstroke, heat-stroke.

Hobel ['hoːbəl], *m.* (—s, *pl.* —) (*tool*) plane.

Hoch [hoːx], *n.* (—s, *no pl.*) toast (*drink*); (*Met.*) high.

hoch, hoh [hoːx, hoː], *adj.* high; (*fig.*) eminent, sublime.

Hochachtung ['hoːxaxtuŋ], *f.* (—, *no pl.*) esteem, regard, respect.

hochachtungsvoll ['hoːxaxtuŋsfɔl], *adj., adv.* (*letters*) yours faithfully.

Hochamt

Hochamt ['ho:xamt], *n.* (—**es**, *pl.* ̈**er**) (*Eccl.*) High Mass.

Hochbau ['ho:xbau], *m.* (—**s**, *pl.* —**ten**) superstructure.

hochbetagt ['ho:xbəta:kt], *adj.* advanced in years.

Hochburg ['ho:xburk], *f.* (—, *pl.* —**en**) (*fig.*) stronghold, citadel.

Hochebene ['ho:xe:bənə], *f.* (—, *pl.* —**n**) table-land, plateau.

hochfahrend ['ho:xfa:rənt], *adj.* haughty, high-flown; (*coll.*) stuck-up.

Hochgefühl ['ho:xgəfy:l], *n.* (—**s**, *no pl.*) exaltation.

Hochgenuß ['ho:xgənus], *m.* (—**sses**, *pl.* ̈**sse**) exquisite enjoyment; treat.

Hochgericht ['ho:xgərɪçt], *n.* (—**s**, *pl.* —**e**) place of execution, scaffold.

hochherzig ['ho:xhɛrtsɪç], *adj.* magnanimous.

Hochmeister ['ho:xmaɪstər], *m.* (—**s**, *pl.* —) Grand Master.

Hochmut ['ho:xmu:t], *m.* (—**s**, *no pl.*) haughtiness, pride.

hochnäsig ['ho:xnɛ:zɪç], *adj.* supercilious, stuck-up.

hochnotpeinlich ['ho:xno:tpaɪnlɪç], *adj.* (*obs.*) penal, criminal; —**es** *Verhör*, criminal investigation.

Hochofen ['ho:xo:fən], *m.* (—**s**, *pl.* ̈) blast-furnace.

Hochschule ['ho:xʃu:lə], *f.* (—, *pl.* —**n**) academy; university.

Hochschüler ['ho:xʃy:lər], *m.* (—**s**, *pl.* —) student, undergraduate.

höchst [hœ:çst], *adj.* highest, most. — *adv.* most, extremely.

Hochstapler ['ho:xʃta:plər], *m.* (—**s**, *pl.* —) confidence trickster, swindler.

höchstens ['hœ:çstəns], *adv.* at most, at best.

hochtrabend ['ho:xtra:bənt], *adj.* (*horse*) high-stepping; (*fig.*) high-sounding, bombastic.

hochverdient ['ho:xfɛrdi:nt], *adj.* highly meritorious.

Hochverrat ['ho:xfɛra:t], *m.* (—**s**, *no pl.*) high treason.

Hochwild ['ho:xvɪlt], *n.* (—**es**, *no pl.*) deer; big game.

hochwohlgeboren ['ho:xvo:lgəbo:rən], *adj.* (*obs.*) noble; *Euer Hochwohlgeboren*, Right Honourable Sir.

hochwürden ['ho:xvyrdən], *adj. Euer Hochwürden*, Reverend Sir.

Hochzeit ['hɔxtsaɪt], *f.* (—, *pl.* —**en**) wedding; nuptials.

hochzeitlich ['hɔxtsaɪtlɪç], *adj.* nuptial, bridal.

Hochzeitsreise ['hɔxtsaɪtsraɪzə], *f.* (—, *pl.* —**n**) honeymoon.

Hocke ['hɔkə], *f.* (—, *pl.* —**n**) squatting posture; shock, stook.

hocken ['hɔkən], *v.n.* crouch, squat; *zu Hause* —, be a stay-at-home.

Hocker ['hɔkər], *m.* (—**s**, *pl.* —) stool.

Höcker ['hœkər], *m.* (—**s**, *pl.* —) hump.

höckerig ['hœkərɪç], *adj.* hump-backed, hunch-backed.

Hode ['ho:də], *f.* (—, *pl.* —**n**) testicle.

Hof [ho:f], *m.* (—**es**, *pl.* ̈**e**) yard, courtyard; farm(stead); (*royal*) court; (*moon*) halo; *einem den* — *machen*, court s.o.

Hofarzt ['ho:fartst], *m.* (—**es**, *pl.* ̈**e**) court physician.

hoffähig ['ho:ffɛ:ıç], *adj.* presentable at court.

Hoffart ['hɔfart], *f.* (—, *no pl.*) pride, arrogance.

hoffärtig ['hɔfɛrtɪç], *adj.* proud, arrogant.

hoffen ['hɔfən], *v.n.* hope; *fest auf etwas* —, trust.

hoffentlich ['hɔfəntlɪç], *adv.* as I hope, I trust that.

Hoffnung ['hɔfnuŋ], *f.* (—, *pl.* —**en**) hope, expectation, anticipation, expectancy; *guter* — *sein*, be full of hope; be expecting a baby; *sich* — *machen auf*, cherish hopes of.

hoffnungslos ['hɔfnuŋslo:s], *adj.* hopeless, past hope.

hofieren [ho'fi:rən], *v.a.* court.

höfisch ['hø:fɪʃ], *adj.* courtlike, courtly.

höflich ['hø:flɪç], *adj.* courteous, civil, polite.

Hoflieferant ['ho:fli:fərant], *m.* (—**en**, *pl.* —**en**) purveyor to His *or* Her Majesty.

Höfling ['hø:flɪŋ], *m.* (—**s**, *pl.* —**e**) courtier.

Hofmarschall ['ho:fmarʃal], *m.* (—**s**, *pl.* —**e**) Lord Chamberlain.

Hofmeister ['ho:fmaɪstər], *m.* (—**s**, *pl.* —) (*obs.*) steward; tutor.

Hofnarr ['ho:fnar], *m.* (—**en**, *pl.* —**en**) court jester, court fool.

Hofrat ['ho:fra:t], *m.* (—**s**, *pl.* ̈**e**) Privy Councillor.

Hofschranze ['ho:fʃrantsə], *m.* (—**n**, *pl.* —**n**) courtier; flunkey.

Hofsitte ['ho:fzɪtə], *f.* (—, *pl.* —**n**) court etiquette.

Höhe ['hø:ə], *f.* (—, *pl.* —**n**) height, altitude; *bis zur* —, up to the level of; *in die* —, upwards; *in die* — *fahren*, give a start, get excited.

Hoheit ['ho:haɪt], *f.* (—, *pl.* —**en**) grandeur; sovereignty; (*title*) Highness.

Hohelied [ho:ə'li:t], *n.* (—**s**, *no pl.*) Song of Solomon.

Höhenmesser ['hø:ənmɛsər], *m.* (—**s**, *pl.* —) (*Aviat.*) altimeter.

Höhensonne ['hø:ənzɔnə], *f.* (—, *pl.* —**n**) Alpine sun; (*Med.*) ultra-violet lamp.

Höhenzug ['hø:əntsu:k], *m.* (—**s**, *pl.* ̈**e**) mountain range.

Höhepunkt ['hø:əpuŋkt], *m.* (—**s**, *pl.* —**e**) climax, culmination, acme; peak.

höher ['hø:ər], *comp. adj.* higher.

hohl [ho:l], *adj.* hollow; (*tooth*) decayed, hollow.

Höhle ['hø:lə], *f.* (—, *pl.* —**n**) cave, cavern, den.

Hörsaal

hohlgeschliffen ['ho:lgəʃlɪfən], _adj._ concave, hollow-ground.

Hohlheit ['ho:lhaɪt], _f._ (—, _no pl._) hollowness.

Hohlleiste ['ho:llaɪstə], _f._ (—, _pl._ —n) groove, channel.

Hohlmaß ['ho:lma:s], _n._ (—es, _pl._ —e) dry measure.

Hohlmeißel ['ho:lmaɪsəl], _m._ (—s, _pl._ —) gouge.

Hohlsaum ['ho:lzaum], _m._ (—s, _pl._ ˙e) hemstitch.

Hohlspiegel ['ho:lʃpi:gəl], _m._ (—s, _pl._ —) concave mirror.

Höhlung ['hø:luŋ], _f._ (—, _pl._ —en) hollow, cavity.

Hohlziegel ['ho:ltsi:gəl], _m._ (—s, _pl._ —) hollow brick.

Hohn [ho:n], _m._ (—s, _no pl._) scorn, derision, mockery; sneer.

höhnen ['hø:nən], _v.a._ deride, sneer at; _see_ **verhöhnen.**

Höker ['hø:kər], _m._ (—s, _pl._ —) hawker, huckster.

hold [hɔlt], _adj._ kind, friendly; gracious; graceful; sweet.

Holder ['hɔldər] _see_ **Holunder.**

holdselig ['hɔltze:lɪç], _adj._ sweet, charming, gracious.

holen ['ho:lən], _v.a._ fetch, collect, get.

Holland ['hɔlant], _n._ Holland.

Hölle ['hœlə], _f._ (—, _no pl._) hell.

Holm [hɔlm], _m._ (—es, _pl._ —e) islet, holm; (_Gymn._) bar.

holperig ['hɔlpərɪç], _adj._ rough, bumpy.

holpern ['hɔlpərn], _v.n._ jolt, stumble; (_fig._) falter.

Holunder [ho'lundər], _m._ (—s, _pl._ —) (_Bot._) elder; _spanischer_ —, lilac.

Holz [hɔlts], _n._ (—es, _pl._ ˙er) wood, timber; (_Am._) lumber; (_no pl._) forest; bush.

Holzapfel ['hɔltsapfəl], _m._ (—s, _pl._ ˙) (_Bot._) crab-apple.

holzartig ['hɔltsartɪç], _adj._ woody, ligneous.

holzen ['hɔltsən], _v.a._ cut _or_ gather wood.

hölzern ['hœltsərn], _adj._ wooden; (_fig._) stiff.

Holzhändler ['hɔltshɛndlər], _m._ (—s, _pl._ —) timber-merchant; (_Am._) lumber merchant.

Holzhauer ['hɔltshauər], _m._ (—s, _pl._ —) wood-cutter.

holzig ['hɔltsɪç], _adj._ woody, wooded; (_asparagus_) woody, hard; (_beans_) stringy.

Holzkohle ['hɔltsko:lə], _f._ (—, _no pl._) charcoal.

Holzscheit ['hɔltsʃaɪt], _n._ (—s, _pl._ —e) log of wood.

Holzschlag ['hɔltsʃla:k], _m._ (—es, _pl._ ˙e) clearing; felling area.

Holzschnitt ['hɔltsʃnɪt], _m._ (—es, _pl._ —e) wood-cut.

Holzschuh ['hɔltsʃu:], _m._ (—s, _pl._ —e) clog.

Holzweg ['hɔltsve:k], _m._ (—s, _pl._ —e) timbertrack; (_fig._) _auf dem_ — _sein_, be on the wrong tack.

Holzwolle ['hɔltsvɔlə], _f._ (—, _no pl._) wood shavings.

homogen [homo'ge:n], _adj._ homogeneous.

homolog [homo'lo:g], _adj._ homologous.

honett [ho'nɛt], _adj._ (_obs._) respectable, genteel.

Honig ['ho:nɪç], _m._ (—s, _no pl._) honey.

Honigkuchen ['ho:nɪçku:xən], _m._ (—s, _pl._ —) ginger-bread.

Honigwabe ['ho:nɪçva:bə], _f._ (—, _pl._ —n) honeycomb.

Honorar [hono'ra:r], _n._ (—s, _pl._ —e) remuneration; (_professional_) fee; honorarium.

Honoratioren [honora'tsjo:rən], _m. pl._ people of rank; dignitaries.

honorieren [hono'ri:rən], _v.a._ pay a fee to, remunerate.

Hopfen ['hɔpfən], _m._ (—s, _no pl._) (_Bot._) hop, hops; _an dem ist_ — _und Malz verloren_, he is beyond help.

Hopfenstange ['hɔpfənʃtaŋə], _f._ (—, _pl._ —n) hop-pole; (_fig._) tall thin person.

hopsen ['hɔpsən], _v.n._ (_aux._ sein) (_coll._) hop, jump.

hörbar ['hø:rba:r], _adj._ audible.

horchen ['hɔrçən], _v.n._ listen, eavesdrop.

Horde ['hɔrdə], _f._ (—, _pl._ —n) horde.

hören ['hø:rən], _v.a._, _v.n._ hear.

Hörer ['hø:rər], _m._ (—s, _pl._ —) listener; (_Univ._) student; (_telephone_) receiver.

Hörerin ['hø:rərɪn], _f._ (—, _pl._ —innen) female listener; (_Univ._) woman student.

Hörerschaft ['hø:rərʃaft], _f._ (—, _no pl._) audience.

Hörgerät ['hø:rgere:t], _n._ (—es, _pl._ —e) hearing aid.

hörig ['hø:rɪç], _adj._ in bondage, a slave to.

Horizont [hori'tsɔnt], _m._ (—es, _pl._ —e) horizon.

Horizontale [horitsɔn'ta:lə], _f._ (—, _pl._ —n) horizontal line.

Horn [hɔrn], _n._ (—s, _pl._ ˙er) horn; (_Mus._) French horn.

Hörnchen ['hœrnçən], _n._ (—s, _pl._ —) French roll, croissant.

hörnern ['hœrnərn], _adj._ horny, made of horn.

Hornhaut ['hɔrnhaut], _f._ (—, _pl._ ˙te) horny skin; (_eye_) cornea.

Hornhautverpflanzung ['hɔrnhautfɛrpflantsuŋ], _f._ (—, _no pl._) corneal graft.

hornig ['hɔrnɪç], _adj._ hard, horny.

Hornisse [hɔr'nɪsə], _f._ (—, _pl._ —n) (_Ent._) hornet.

horrend [hɔ'rɛnt], _adj._ exorbitant; stupendous.

Hörrohr ['hø:rro:r], _n._ (—s, _pl._ —e) ear trumpet.

Hörsaal ['hø:rza:l], _m._ (—s, _pl._ —säle) auditorium, lecture room.

Hörspiel [ˈhøːrʃpiːl], *n.* (**—s**, *pl.* **—e**) radio play.

Horst [hɔrst], *m.* (**—es**, *pl.* **—e**) eyrie.

Hort [hɔrt], *m.* (**—es**, *pl.* **—e**) (*Poet.*) treasure; stronghold.

Hortensie [hɔrˈtɛnzjə], *f.* (**—**, *pl.* **—n**) (*Bot.*) hydrangea.

Hose [ˈhoːzə], *f.* (**—**, *pl.* **—n**) trousers, pants, breeches; (*women*) slacks.

Hosenband [ˈhoːzənbant], *n.* (**—es**, *pl.* ˙er) garter.

Hosenträger [ˈhoːzəntrɛɡər], *m. pl.* braces, suspenders.

Hospitant [hɔspiˈtant], *m.* (**—en**, *pl.* **—en**) (*Univ.*) temporary student, non-registered student.

hospitieren [hɔspiˈtiːrən], *v.n.* attend lectures as a visitor.

Hostie [ˈhɔstjə], *f.* (**—**, *pl.* **—n**) (*Eccl.*) the Host.

hüben [ˈhyːbən], *adv.* on this side; *— und drüben*, on either side.

hübsch [hypʃ], *adj.* pretty, attractive; handsome; good-looking.

Hubschrauber [ˈhuːpʃraubər], *m.* (**—s**, *pl.* **—**) (*Aviat.*) helicopter.

huckepack [ˈhukəpak], *adv. — tragen,* carry pick-a-back.

Huf [huːf], *m.* (**—es**, *pl.* **—e**) hoof.

Hufe [ˈhuːfə], *f.* (**—**, *pl.* **—n**) hide (of land).

Hufeisen [ˈhuːfaizən], *n.* (**—s**, *pl.* **—**) horseshoe.

Huflattich [ˈhuːflatiç], *m.* (**—s**, *pl.* **—e**) (*Bot.*) colt's foot.

Hufschlag [ˈhuːfʃlaːk], *m.* (**—s**, *pl.* ˙e) (*of a horse*) hoof-beat.

Hüfte [ˈhyftə], *f.* (**—**, *pl.* **—n**) (*Anat.*) hip; (*animals*) haunch.

Hügel [ˈhyːɡəl], *m.* (**—s**, *pl.* **—**) hill, hillock.

hügelig [ˈhyːɡəliç], *adj.* hilly.

Huhn [huːn], *n.* (**—s**, *pl.* ˙er) fowl; hen.

Hühnchen [ˈhyːnçən], *n.* (**—s**, *pl.* **—**) pullet, chicken.

Hühnerauge [ˈhyːnərauɡə], *n.* (**—s**, *pl.* **—n**) corn (*on the foot*).

Huld [hult], *f.* (**—**, *no pl.*) grace, favour.

huldigen [ˈhuldiɡən], *v.n.* pay homage.

huldvoll [ˈhultfɔl], *adj.* gracious.

Hülle [ˈhylə], *f.* (**—**, *pl.* **—n**) cover, covering; veil; *in — und Fülle*, in abundance, in profusion.

hüllen [ˈhylən], *v.a.* cover, veil, wrap.

Hülse [ˈhylzə], *f.* (**—**, *pl.* **—n**) hull, husk, shell; cartridge-case.

Hülsenfrucht [ˈhylzənfruxt], *f.* (**—**, *pl.* ˙e) (*Bot.*) leguminous plant.

human [huˈmaːn], *adj.* humane.

humanistisch [humaˈnistiʃ], *adj.* classical; humanistic.

Hummel [ˈhuməl], *f.* (**—**, *pl.* **—n**) (*Ent.*) bumble-bee.

Hummer [ˈhumər], *m.* (**—s**, *pl.* **—**) (*Zool.*) lobster.

Humor [huˈmoːr], *m.* (**—s**, *no pl.*) humour.

humoristisch [humoˈristiʃ], *adj.* humorous, witty.

humpeln [ˈhumpəln], *v.n.* hobble, limp.

Humpen [ˈhumpən], *m.* (**—s**, *pl.* **—**) deep drinking-cup, bowl, tankard.

Humus [ˈhuːmus], *m.* (**—**, *no pl.*) garden-mould, humus.

Hund [hunt], *m.* (**—es**, *pl.* **—e**) dog; (*hunting*) hound; (*fig.*) rascal, scoundrel.

Hundehaus [ˈhundəhaus], *n.* (**—es**, *pl.* ˙er) dog-kennel.

hundert [ˈhundərt], *num. adj.* a hundred, one hundred.

Hündin [ˈhyndin], *f.* (**—**, *pl.* **—innen**) bitch.

Hundstage [ˈhuntstaːɡə], *m. pl.* dog days (July to August).

Hundszahn [ˈhuntstsaːn], *m.* (**—es**, *pl.* ˙e) (*Bot.*) dandelion.

Hüne [ˈhyːnə], *m.* (**—n**, *pl.* **—n**) giant, colossus; (*fig.*) tall man.

Hünengrab [ˈhyːnəngraːp], *n.* (**—es**, *pl.* ˙er) tumulus, burial mound, barrow, cairn.

Hunger [ˈhuŋər], *m.* (**—s**, *no pl.*) hunger; starvation.

hungern [ˈhuŋərn], *v.n.* hunger, be hungry.

Hungertuch [ˈhuŋərtuːx], *n.* (**—es**, *no pl.*) *am — nagen,* go without food; live in poverty.

hungrig [ˈhuŋriç], *adj.* hungry; (*fig.*) desirous (of).

Hupe [ˈhuːpə], *f.* (**—**, *pl.* **—n**) motor-horn, hooter (of a car).

hüpfen [ˈhypfən], *v.n.* (*aux.* sein) hop, skip.

Hürde [ˈhyrdə], *f.* (**—**, *pl.* **—n**) hurdle.

Hure [ˈhuːrə], *f.* (**—**, *pl.* **—n**) whore, prostitute, harlot; (*coll.*) tart.

hurtig [ˈhurtiç], *adj.* nimble, agile; quick, speedy, swift.

Husar [huˈzaːr], *m.* (**—en**, *pl.* **—en**) hussar.

husch! [huʃ], *excl.* quick!

huschen [ˈhuʃən], *v.n.* (*aux.* sein) scurry, slip away.

hüsteln [ˈhyːstəln], *v.n.* cough slightly; clear o.'s throat.

husten [ˈhuːstən], *v.n.* cough.

Hut (1) [huːt], *m.* (**—es**, *pl.* ˙e) hat; *steifer —,* bowler.

Hut (2) [huːt], *f.* (**—**, *no pl.*) guard, keeping, care.

hüten [ˈhyːtən], *v.a.* guard, tend, care for; *Kinder —,* baby-sit; *das Bett —,* be confined to o.'s bed, be ill in bed. *— v.r. sich — vor,* be on o.'s guard against, beware of.

Hüter [ˈhyːtər], *m.* (**—s**, *pl.* **—**) guardian, keeper; (*cattle*) herdsman.

Hutkrempe [ˈhuːtkrɛmpə], *f.* (**—**, *pl.* **—n**) hat-brim.

Hütte [ˈhytə], *f.* (**—**, *pl.* **—n**) hut, cottage; (*Tech.*) furnace, forge, foundry.

Hüttenarbeiter [ˈhytənarbaitər], *m.* (**—s**, *pl.* **—**) smelter, foundry worker.

Hyäne [hyˈɛːnə], *f.* (**—**, *pl.* **—n**) (*Zool.*) hyena.

Hyazinthe [hyat'sɪntə], *f.* (—, *pl.* —n) (*Bot.*) hyacinth.

Hyperbel [hy'pɛrbəl], *f.* (—, *pl.* —n) hyperbola.

hypnotisch [hyp'no:tɪʃ], *adj.* hypnotic.

hypnotisieren [hypnoti'zi:rən], *v.a.* hypnotise.

Hypochonder [hypo'xɔndər], *m.* (—s, *pl.* —) hypochondriac.

Hypothek [hypo'te:k], *f.* (—, *pl.* —en) mortgage.

Hysterie [hyste'ri:], *f.* (—, *no pl.*) hysterics, hysteria.

hysterisch [hys'te:rɪʃ], *adj.* hysterical.

I

I [i:], *n.* (—, *no pl.*) the letter I. — *excl. i wo!* (*dial.*) certainly not, of course not.

ich [ɪç], *pers. pron.* I, myself.

ideal [ide'a:l], *adj.* ideal.

idealisieren [ideali'zi:rən], *v.a.* idealise.

Idealismus [idea'lɪsmus], *m.* (—, *no pl.*) idealism.

Idee [i'de:], *f.* (—, *pl.* —n) idea, notion, conception.

identifizieren [identifi'tsi:rən], *v.a.* identify.

identisch [i'dɛntɪʃ], *adj.* identical.

Identität [identi'tɛ:t], *f.* (—, *no pl.*) identity.

idiomatisch [idio'ma:tɪʃ], *adj.* idiomatic.

Idyll [i'dyl], *n.* (—s, *pl.* —e) idyll.

Idylle [i'dylə], *f.* (—, *pl.* —n) idyll.

idyllisch [i'dylɪʃ], *adj.* idyllic.

Igel [i'i:gəl], *m.* (—s, *pl.* —) (*Zool.*) hedgehog.

ignorieren [ɪgno'ri:rən], *v.a.* ignore, take no notice of.

ihm [i:m], *pers. pron. Dat.* to him, it.

ihn [i:n], *pers. pron. Acc.,* him, it.

Ihnen [i:nən], *pers. pron. Dat.* you, to you.

ihnen [i:nən], *pers. pron. pl. Dat.* them, to them.

Ihr [i:r], *poss. adj.* your; of your. —, *poss. pron.* yours.

ihr [i:r], *pers. pron.* to her; (*pl.*) (*intim.*) you. — *poss. adj.* her, their. — *poss. pron.* hers, theirs.

Ihrer [i:rər], *pers. pron.* of you. — *poss. adj.* of your.

ihrer [i:rər], *pers. pron.* of her, of it; (*pl.*) of them. — *poss. adj* of her; to her; (*pl.*) of their.

ihresgleichen [i:rəsglaıçən], *adv.* of her, its *or* their kind.

ihrethalben [i:rəthalbən], *adv.* for her sake, for their sake, on her account, on their account.

ihretwegen [i:rətve:gən] *see* **ihrethalben.**

ihretwillen [i:rətvɪlən] *see* **ihrethalben.**

Ihrige [i:rɪgə], *poss. pron.* yours.

ihrige [i:rɪgə], *poss. pron.* hers, its, theirs.

illegitim [ɪlegi'ti:m], *adj.* illegitimate.

illuminieren [ɪlumi'ni:rən], *v.a.* illuminate, floodlight.

illustrieren [ɪlu'stri:rən], *v.a.* illustrate.

Iltis [ɪltɪs], *m.* (—ses, *pl.* —se) (*Zool.*) polecat, fitchet.

im [ɪm], *contraction of* **in dem,** in the.

Imbiß [ɪmbɪs], *m.* (—sses, *pl.* —sse) snack, refreshment, light meal.

Imker [ɪmkər], *m.* (—s, *pl.* —) beekeeper.

immatrikulieren [ɪmmatriku'li:rən], *v.a.* (*Univ.*) matriculate, enrol.

Imme [ɪmə], *f.* (—, *pl.* —n) (*dial., Poet.*) bee.

immer [ɪmər], *adv.* always, ever; — *mehr,* more and more; — *noch,* still; — *wieder,* time and again: — *größer,* larger and larger; *auf* —, for ever.

immerdar [ɪmərda:r], *adv.* for ever.

immerhin [ɪmərhɪn], *adv.* nevertheless, still, after all.

immerzu [ɪmərtsu:], *adv.* always, constantly.

Immobilien [ɪmo'bi:ljən], *pl.* real estate.

Immortelle [ɪmor'tɛlə], *f.* (—, *pl.* —n) (*Bot.*) everlasting flower.

immun [ɪ'mu:n], *adj.* immune.

impfen [ɪmpfən], *v.a.* vaccinate, inoculate; (*Hort.*) graft.

imponieren [ɪmpo'ni:rən], *v.n.* impress.

Import [ɪm'pɔrt], *m.* (—s, *pl.* —e) import, importation.

imposant [ɪmpo'zant], *adj.* imposing, impressive.

imstande [ɪm'ʃtandə], *adv.* capable, able; — *sein,* be able.

in [ɪn], *prep.* (*Dat., Acc.*) in, into; at; within.

Inangriffnahme [ɪn'angrɪfna:mə], *f.* (—, *no pl.*) start, beginning, inception.

Inbegriff [ɪnbəgrɪf], *m.* (—es, *no pl.*) essence, epitome.

inbegriffen [ɪnbəgrɪfən], *adv.* inclusive.

Inbrunst [ɪnbrunst], *f.* (—, *no pl.*) ardour, fervour.

indem [ɪn'de:m], *adv.* meanwhile. — *conj.* while, whilst; as, because, in that.

indessen [ɪn'dɛsən], *adv.* meanwhile, in the meantime. — *conj.* however, nevertheless, yet.

Indien [ɪndjən], *n.* India.

Individualität [ɪndividuali'tɛ:t], *f.* (—, *pl.* —en) individuality, personality.

individuell [ɪndividu'ɛl], *adj.* individual.

Individuum [ɪndi'vi:duum], *n.* (—s, *pl.* —duen) individual.

Indizienbeweis [ɪn'di:tsjənbəvaɪs], *m.*
(—es, *pl.* —e) (*Law*) circumstantial
evidence *or* proof.

indossieren [ɪndɔ'si:rən], *v.a.* endorse.

Industrie [ɪndus'tri:], *f.* (—, *pl.* —n)
industry; manufacture.

industriell [ɪndustri'ɛl], *adj.* industrial.

Industrielle [ɪndustri'ɛlə], *m.* (—n, *pl.*
—n) manufacturer, industrialist.

ineinander [ɪnaɪ'nandər], *adv.* into
each other, into one another.

infam [ɪn'fa:m], *adj.* infamous.

Infantin [ɪn'fantɪn], *f.* (—, *pl.* —en)
Infanta.

infizieren [ɪnfi'tsi:rən], *v.a.* infect.

infolge [ɪn'fɔlgə], *prep.* (*Genit.*) in consequence of, owing to.

informieren [ɪnfɔr'mi:rən], *v.a.* inform, advise.

Ingenieur [ɪnʒɛn'jø:r], *m.* (—s, *pl.* —e)
engineer.

Ingrimm ['ɪngrɪm], *m.* (—s, *no pl.*)
anger, rage, wrath.

Ingwer ['ɪŋvər], *m.* (—s, *no pl.*) ginger.

Inhaber ['ɪnha:bər], *m.* (—s, *pl.* —)
possessor, owner; proprietor; occupant.

inhaftieren [ɪnhaf'ti:rən], *v.a.* imprison; arrest.

inhalieren [ɪnha'li:rən], *v.a.* inhale.

Inhalt ['ɪnhalt], *m.* (—(e)s, *no pl.*)
content; contents; tenor.

Inhaltsverzeichnis ['ɪnhaltsfɛrtsaɪç-
nɪs], *n.* (—ses, *pl.* —se) (table of)
contents; index.

inhibieren [ɪnhi'bi:rən], *v.a.* inhibit,
prevent.

Inkasso [ɪn'kaso], *n.* (—s, *pl.* —s)
encashment.

inklinieren [ɪnkli'ni:rən], *v.n.* be
inclined to.

inklusive [ɪnklu'zi:və], *adv.* inclusive
of, including.

inkonsequent ['ɪnkɔnzəkvɛnt], *adj.*
inconsistent.

Inkrafttreten [ɪn'krafttre:tən], *n.* (—s,
no pl.) enactment; coming into force.

Inland ['ɪnlant], *n.* (—s, *no pl.*) inland,
interior.

Inländer ['ɪnlɛndər], *m.* (—s, *pl.* —)
native.

Inlett ['ɪnlɛt], *n.* (—s, *pl.* —e) bed-tick,
ticking.

inliegend ['ɪnli:gənt], *adj.* enclosed.

inmitten [ɪn'mɪtən], *prep.* (*Genit.*) in the
midst of.

innehaben ['ɪnəha:bən], *v.a. irr.*
possess; occupy; hold.

innehalten ['ɪnəhaltən], *v.a. irr.* (*conditions*) keep to, observe; (*time*) come
promptly at. — *v.n.* stop, pause.

innen ['ɪnən], *adv.* within; *nach* —,
inwards; *von* —, from within.

Innenminister ['ɪnənmɪnɪstər], *m.*
(—s, *pl.* —) Minister for Internal
Affairs; Home Secretary; (*Am.*) Secretary of the Interior.

inner ['ɪnər], *adj.* inner, interior,
internal; intrinsic.

innerhalb ['ɪnərhalp], *prep.* (*Genit.*)
within.

innerlich ['ɪnərlɪç], *adj.* internal;
inside o.s.; inward.

innerste ['ɪnərstə], *adj.* inmost, innermost.

innewerden ['ɪnəve:rdən], *v.a. irr.*
(*aux.* sein) perceive, become aware of.

innewohnen ['ɪnəvo:nən], *v.n.* be
inherent in.

innig ['ɪnɪç], *adj.* heartfelt, cordial.

Innung ['ɪnuŋ], *f.* (—, *pl.* —en) guild,
corporation.

Insasse ['ɪnzasə], *m.* (—n, *pl.* —n)
inmate; occupant.

insbesondere [ɪnsbə'zɔndərə], *adv.*
especially, particularly, in particular.

Inschrift ['ɪnʃrɪft], *f.* (—, *pl.* —en)
inscription.

Insel ['ɪnzəl], *f.* (—, *pl.* —n) island.

Inserat [ɪnzə'ra:t], *n.* (—es, *pl.* —e)
classified advertisement; (*coll.*) (small)
ad.

inserieren [ɪnzə'ri:rən], *v.a.* advertise;
insert.

insgeheim [ɪnsgə'haɪm], *adv.* privately,
secretly.

insgesamt [ɪnsgə'zamt], *adv.* altogether, in a body.

insofern [ɪnzo'fɛrn], *conj.* — *als*, in
so far as, inasmuch as, so far as.

inspirieren [ɪnspi'ri:rən], *v.a.* inspire.

installieren [ɪnsta'li:rən], *v.a.* install,
fit.

instandhalten [ɪn'ʃtanthaltən], *v.a. irr.*
maintain, preserve, keep in repair.

inständig ['ɪnʃtɛndɪç], *adj.* urgent;
fervent.

instandsetzen [ɪn'ʃtantzɛtsən], *v.a.*
restore, repair; *einen — etwas zu tun*,
enable s.o. to do s.th.

Instanz [ɪn'ʃtants], *f.* (—, *pl.* —en)
(*Law*) instance; *letzte* —, highest
court of appeal, last resort.

Institut [ɪnsti'tu:t], *n.* (—es, *pl.* —e)
institute, institution, establishment;
(*Univ.*) department.

instruieren [ɪnstru'i:rən], *v.a.* instruct.

Insulaner [ɪnzu'la:nər], *m.* (—s, *pl.* —)
islander.

inszenieren [ɪnstse'ni:rən], *v.a.* put on
the stage, produce.

Inszenierung [ɪnstse'ni:ruŋ], *f.* (—, *pl.*
—en) (*Theat.*) production, staging.

intellektuell [ɪntɛlɛktu'ɛl], *adj.* intellectual.

Intendant [ɪntɛn'dant], *m.* (—en, *pl.*
—en) (*Theat.*) director.

interessant [ɪntərɛ'sant], *adj.* interesting.

Interesse [ɪntə'rɛsə], *n.* (—s, *pl.* —n)
interest.

Interessent [ɪntərɛ'sɛnt], *m.* (—en, *pl.*
—en) interested party.

interessieren [ɪntərɛ'si:rən], *v.a.* interest. — *v.r. sich* —, be interested
(in).

intern [ɪn'tɛrn], *adj.* internal.

Internat [ɪntɛr'na:t], *n.* (—es, *pl.* —e)
boarding-school.

Interne [ɪn'tɛrnə], *m.* (—n, *pl.* —n) resident (pupil *or* doctor), boarder.
Internist [ɪntɛr'nɪst], *m.* (—en, *pl.* —en) specialist in internal diseases.
interpunktieren [ɪntərpunk'ti:rən], *v.a.* punctuate.
Interpunktion [ɪntərpunkts'jo:n], *f.* (—, *pl.* —en) punctuation.
intim [ɪn'ti:m], *adj.* intimate; *mit einem — sein*, b : on close terms with s.o.
intonieren [ɪnto'ni:rən], *v.n.* intone.
Intrigant [ɪntri'gant], *m.* (—en, *pl.* —en) intriguer, schemer.
intrigieren [ɪntri'gi:rən], *v.n.* intrigue, scheme.
Inventar [ɪnvɛn'ta:r], *n.* (—s, *pl.* —e) inventory; *ein — aufnehmen*, draw up an inventory.
Inventur [ɪnvɛn'tu:r], *f.* (—, *pl.* —en) stock-taking.
inwärts [ɪnvɛrts], *adv.* inwards.
inwendig [ɪnvɛndɪç], *adj.* inward, internal, inner.
inwiefern [ɪnvi:'fɛrn], *adv.* to what extent.
inwieweit [ɪnvi:'vaɪt], *adv.* how far.
Inzucht [ɪntsuxt], *f.* (—, *no pl.*) in-breeding.
inzwischen [ɪn'tsvɪʃən], *adv.* meanwhile, in the meantime.
Irak [i'ra:k], *m., n.* Iraq.
Iran [i'ra:n], *n.* Iran.
irden [ɪrdən], *adj.* earthen.
irdisch [ɪrdɪʃ], *adj.* earthly, worldly; terrestrial, temporal.
irgend [ɪrgənt], *adv.* any, some; *wenn es — geht*, if it can possibly be done.
irgendein [ɪrgənt'aɪn], *pron.* any, some.
Irland [ɪrlant], *n.* Ireland.
ironisch [i'ro:nɪʃ], *adj.* ironic, ironical.
Irre (1) [ɪrə], *f.* (—, *no pl.*) *in die — gehen*, go astray.
Irre (2) [ɪrə], *m.* (—n, *pl.* —n) madman, lunatic.
irre [ɪrə], *adj.* astray; wrong, confused; crazy, demented.
irren [ɪrən], *v.n.* err, go astray, be wrong. — *v.r. sich —*, be mistaken.
Irrenarzt [ɪrənartst], *m.* (—es, *pl.* -̈e) psychiatrist.
Irrenhaus [ɪrənhaus], *n.* (—es, *pl.* -̈er) lunatic asylum, mental hospital.
Irrfahrt [ɪrfa:rt], *f.* (—, *pl.* —en) wandering.
Irrglaube [ɪrglaubə], *m.* (—ns, *no pl.*) heresy.
irrig [ɪrɪç], *adj.* erroneous.
irritieren [iri'ti:rən], *v.a.* irritate.
Irrlicht [ɪrlɪçt], *n.* (—s, *pl.* —er) will-o'-the-wisp.
Irrsinn [ɪrzɪn], *m.* (—s, *no pl.*) madness, insanity, lunacy.
irrsinnig [ɪrzɪnɪç], *adj.* insane, deranged.
Irrtum [ɪrtu:m], *m.* (—s, *pl.* -̈er) error, mistake, fault, oversight.
Irrweg [ɪrve:k], *m.* (—s, *pl.* —e) wrong track.
Irrwisch [ɪrvɪʃ], *m.* (—es, *pl.* —e) will-o'-the-wisp.

Ischias [ɪsçias], *f., m.* (*Med.*) sciatica.
Isegrim [i:zəgrɪm], *m.* (—s, *pl.* —e) (*fable*) the wolf; a bear (with a sore head) (*also fig.*).
Island [i:slant], *n.* Iceland.
isolieren [izo'li:rən], *v.a.* (*Electr.*) insulate; (*fig.*) isolate.
Isolierung [izo'li:run], *f.* (—, *pl.* —en) (*Electr.*) insulation; (*fig.*) isolation.
Italien [i'ta:ljən], *n.* Italy.

J

J [jɔt], *n.* (—, *no pl.*) the letter J.
ja [ja:], *adv., part.* yes; indeed, certainly; even; — *doch*, to be sure; — *freilich*, certainly.
Jacht [jaxt], *f.* (—, *pl.* —en) yacht.
Jacke [jakə], *f.* (—, *pl.* —n) jacket, tunic.
Jackett [ja'kɛt], *n.* (—s, *pl.* —s) jacket, short coat.
Jagd [ja:kt], *f.* (—, *pl.* —en) hunt, hunting; shooting; chase.
Jagdhund [ja:kthunt], *m.* (—es, *pl.* —e) retriever, setter; hound.
Jagdrevier [ja:ktrevi:r], *n.* (—s, *pl.* —e) hunting-ground.
jagen [ja:gən], *v.a.* hunt; chase; (*fig.*) tear along.
Jäger [jɛ:gər], *m.* (—s, *pl.* —) hunter, huntsman; game-keeper.
Jägerei [jɛ:gə'raɪ], *f.* (—, *no pl.*) huntsmanship.
jäh [jɛ:], *adj.* abrupt; steep, precipitous; (*fig.*) hasty, rash, sudden.
jählings [jɛ:lɪŋs], *adv.* abruptly, suddenly, hastily.
Jahr [ja:r], *n.* (—es, *pl.* —e) year.
jähren [jɛ:rən], *v.r. sich —*, (*anniversary*) come round.
Jahresfeier [ja:rəsfaɪər], *f.* (—, *pl.* —n) anniversary.
Jahresrente [ja:rəsrɛntə], *f.* (—, *pl.* —n) annuity.
Jahreszeit [ja:rəstsaɪt], *f.* (—, *pl.* —en) season.
Jahrgang [ja:rgaŋ], *m.* (—s, *pl.* -̈e) age group; class; year of publication; vintage.
Jahrhundert [ja:r'hundərt], *n.* (—s, *pl.* —e) century.
jährig [jɛ:rɪç], *adj.* year-old.
jährlich [jɛ:rlɪç], *adj.* yearly, annual. — *adv.* every year.
Jahrmarkt [ja:rmarkt], *m.* (—s, *pl.* -̈e) annual fair.
Jahrtausend [ja:r'tauzənt], *n.* (—s, *pl.* —e) millennium.
Jahrzehnt [ja:r'tse:nt], *n.* (—s, *pl.* —e) decade.
Jähzorn [jɛ:tsɔrn], *m.* (—s, *no pl.*) irascibility.

Jalousie

Jalousie [ʒalu'zi:], *f.* (—, *pl.* —n) Venetian blind.

Jamaika [ja'maika], *n.* Jamaica.

Jambus ['jambus], *m.* (—, *pl.* —ben) (*Poet.*) iambic foot.

Jammer ['jamər], *m.* (—s, *no pl.*) lamentation; misery; (*fig.*) pity.

jämmerlich ['jɛmərlɪç], *adj.* lamentable, miserable, wretched, piteous.

jammerschade ['jamərʃaːdə], *adv.* a thousand pities.

Jänner ['jɛnər] (*Austr.*) *see* **Januar.**

Januar ['januaːr], *m.* (—s, *pl.* —e) January.

Japan ['jaːpan], *n.* Japan.

Jaspis ['jaspɪs], *m.* (—ses, *pl.* —se) jasper.

jäten ['jeːtən], *v.a.* weed.

Jauche ['jauxə], *f.* (—, *pl.* —n) liquid manure.

jauchzen ['jauxtsən], *v.n.* exult, shout with joy.

Jauchzer ['jauxtsər], *m.* (—s, *pl.* —) shout of joy.

jawohl [ja'voːl], *int.* yes, indeed! certainly, of course.

je [jeː], *adv.* ever; at any time; at a time; each; *von — her,* always; — *nachdem,* it depends; — *zwei,* in twos; — *eher — besser,* the sooner the better.

jedenfalls ['jeːdənfals], *adv.* at all events, in any case, at any rate, anyway.

jeder, -e, -es ['jeːdər], *adj.* every, each; — *beliebige,* any. — *pron.* each, each one; everybody.

jederlei ['jeːdərlaɪ], *adj.* of every kind.

jedoch [je'dɔx], *adv.* however, nevertheless, yet, notwithstanding.

jeglicher, -e, -es ['je:klɪçər], *adj.* every, each. — *pron.* every man, each.

jemals ['jeːmals], *adv.* ever, at any time.

jemand ['jeːmant], *pron.* somebody, someone; anybody, anyone.

Jemen ['jeːmən], *n.* Yemen.

jener, -e, -es ['jeːnər], *dem. adj.* that, (*Poet.*) yonder. — *dem. pron.* that one, the former.

Jenseits ['jɛnzaɪts], *n.* (—, *no pl.*) the next world, the hereafter, the life to come.

jenseits ['jɛnzaɪts], *prep.* (*Genit.*) on the other side, beyond.

jetzig ['jɛtsɪç], *adj.* present, now existing, current, extant.

jetzt [jɛtst], *adv.* now, at this time, at present.

jeweilig ['jeːvaɪlɪç], *adj.* momentary; actual, for the time being.

Joch [jɔx], *n.* (—es, *pl.* —e) yoke.

Jochbein ['jɔxbaɪn], *n.* (—s, *pl.* —e) cheek-bone.

Jockei ['jɔkaɪ], *m.* (—s, *pl.* —s) jockey.

Jod [joːt], *n.* (—s, *no pl.*) iodine.

jodeln ['joːdəln], *v.n.* yodel.

Jodler ['joːdlər], *m.* (—s, *pl.* —) (*person*) yodeler; (*sound*) yodelling.

Johannisbeere [jo'hanɪsbeːrə], *f.* (—, *pl.* —n) (*Bot.*) red currant.

Johannisfest [jo'hanɪsfest], *n.* (—s, *pl.* —e) Midsummer Day, St. John the Baptist's Day (June 24th).

Johanniskäfer [jo'hanɪskeːfər], *m.* (—s, *pl.* —) (*Ent.*) glow-worm.

Johannisnacht [jo'hanɪsnaxt], *f.* (—, *pl.* ⁻e) Midsummer Eve.

johlen ['joːlən], *v.n.* bawl.

Joppe ['jɔpə], *f.* (—, *pl.* —n) shooting jacket.

Jota ['joːta], *n.* (—s, *pl.* —s) iota, jot.

Journalismus [ʒurna'lɪsmus], *m. see* **Journalistik.**

Journalistik [ʒurna'lɪstɪk], *f.* (—, *no pl.*) journalism.

jubeln ['juːbəln], *v.n.* rejoice, exult.

Jubilar [juːbi'laːr], *m.* (—s, *pl.* —e) person celebrating a jubilee.

Jubiläum [juːbi'lɛːum], *n.* (—s, *pl.* —läen) jubilee.

jubilieren [juːbi'liːrən], *v.n.* exult, shout with glee.

juchhe [jux'heː], *excl.* hurrah!

Juchten ['juxtən], *m.* (—, *no pl.*) Russian leather.

jucken ['jukən], *v.a.* scratch. — *v.n.* itch.

Jude ['juːdə], *m.* (—n, *pl.* —n) Jew, Israelite.

Judentum ['juːdəntuːm], *n.* (—s, *no pl.*) Judaism.

Judenviertel ['juːdənfiːrtəl], *n.* (—s, *pl.* —) Jewish quarter, ghetto.

Jüdin ['jyːdɪn], *f.* (—, *pl.* —innen) Jewess.

jüdisch ['jyːdɪʃ], *adj.* Jewish.

Jugend ['juːgənt], *f.* (—, *no pl.*) youth.

jugendlich ['juːgəntlɪç], *adj.* youthful, juvenile.

Jugoslawien [ju:go'slaːvjən], *n.* Jugoslavia.

Julfest ['juːlfest], *n.* (—es, *pl.* —e) Yule.

Juli ['juːli], *m.* (—s, *pl.* —s) July.

jung [juŋ], *adj.* young.

Junge (1) ['juŋə], *m.* (—n, *pl.* —n) boy, lad.

Junge (2) ['juŋə], *n.* (—n, *pl.* —n) young animal.

jungenhaft ['juŋənhaft], *adj.* boyish.

Jünger ['jyŋər], *m.* (—s, *pl.* —) disciple, devotee, follower.

Jungfer ['juŋfər], *f.* (—, *pl.* —n) (*obs.*) virgin, maid, maiden; lady's maid.

jüngferlich ['jyŋfərlɪç], *adj.* maidenly, coy, prim.

Jungfrau ['juŋfrau], *f.* (—, *pl.* —en) virgin.

Junggeselle ['juŋgəzɛlə], *m.* (—n, *pl.* —n) bachelor; *eingefleischter* —, confirmed bachelor.

Jüngling ['jyŋlɪŋ], *m.* (—s, *pl.* —e) young man.

jüngst [jyŋst], *adv.* lately, recently.

Juni ['juːni], *m.* (—s, *pl.* —s) June.

Junker ['juŋkər], *m.* (—s, *pl.* —) country squire; titled landowner.

Jura ['juːra], *n. pl.* jurisprudence, law; (*Univ.*) — *studieren,* read law.

Jurisprudenz [juːrɪspruˈdɛnts], *f.* (—, *no pl.*) jurisprudence.

Jurist [juːˈrɪst], *m.* (—en, *pl.* —en) lawyer, jurist.

juristisch [ju:'rɪstɪʃ], *adj.* juridical; legal.

just [just], *adv.* just now.

Justiz [jus'ti:ts], *f.* (—, *no pl.*) administration of the law *or* of justice.

Justizrat [jus'ti:tsra:t], *m.* (—s, *pl.* ̈e) (*Law*) Counsellor; King's (Queen's) Counsel.

Jute ['ju:tə], *f.* (—, *no pl.*) jute.

Juwel [ju've:l], *n.* (—s, *pl.* —en) jewel; (*pl.*) jewellery; (*Am.*) jewelry.

Juwelier [juvə'li:r], *m.* (—s, *pl.* —e) jeweller, goldsmith.

K

K [ka:], *n.* (—, *no pl.*) the letter K.

Kabel ['ka:bəl], *n.* (—s, *pl.* —) cable.

Kabeljau [kabəl'jau], *m.* (—s, *pl.* —e) (*Zool.*) cod, codfish.

kabeln ['ka:bəln], *v.n.* cable, send a cablegram.

Kabine [ka'bi:nə], *f.* (—, *pl.* —n) cabin, cubicle.

Kabinett [kabi'nɛt], *n.* (—s, *pl.* —e) closet; cabinet.

Kabinettsrat [kabi'nɛtsra:t], *m.* (—s, *pl.* ̈e) cabinet *or* ministerial committee; political adviser.

Kabüse [ka'by:zə], *f.* (—, *pl.* —n) ship's galley.

Kachel ['kaxəl], *f.* (—, *pl.* —n) glazed tile.

Kadaver [ka'da:vər], *m.* (—s, *pl.* —) carrion, carcass; corpse.

Kadenz [ka'dɛnts], *f.* (—, *pl.* —en) (*Mus.*) cadenza.

Kadett [ka'dɛt], *m.* (—en, *pl.* —en) cadet.

Käfer ['kɛ:fər], *m.* (—s, *pl.* —) (*Ent.*) beetle, (*Am.*) bug.

Kaffee ['kafe], *m.* (—s, *no pl.*) coffee.

Käfig ['kɛ:fɪç], *m.* (—s, *pl.* —e) cage.

kahl [ka:l], *adj.* bald; (*trees*) leafless; (*landscape*) barren; — geschoren, close-cropped.

Kahn ['ka:n], *m.* (—s, *pl.* ̈e) boat; punt.

Kai [kaɪ], *m.* (—s, *pl.* —s) quay, wharf, landing-place.

Kaimeister ['kaɪmaɪstər], *m.* (—s, *pl.* —) wharfinger.

Kaiser ['kaɪzər], *m.* (—s, *pl.* —) emperor; *um des —s Bart streiten,* quarrel about nothing.

kaiserlich ['kaɪzərlɪç], *adj.* imperial.

Kaiserschnitt ['kaɪzərʃnɪt], *m.* (—es, *pl.* —e) (*Med.*) Caesarean operation.

Kajüte [ka'jy:tə], *f.* (—, *pl.* —n) cabin.

Kakadu [ka'kadu:], *m.* (—s, *pl.* —s) (*Orn.*) cockatoo.

Kakao [ka'ka:o], *m.* (—s, *no pl.*) cocoa.

Kalauer ['ka:lauər], *m.* (—s, *no pl.*) pun; stale joke.

Kalb [kalp], *n.* (—es, *pl.* ̈er) calf; (*roe*) fawn; (*fig.*) colt, calf.

Kalbfleisch ['kalpflaɪʃ], *n.* (—es, *no pl.*) veal.

Kälberei [kɛlbə'raɪ], *f.* (—, *pl.* —en) friskiness.

kälbern ['kɛlbərn], *v.n.* frisk, frolic.

Kalbsbraten ['kalpsbra:tən], *m.* (—s, *pl.* —) roast veal.

Kalbshaxe ['kalpshaksə], *f.* (—, *pl.* —n) knuckle of veal.

Kalbskeule ['kalpskɔylə], *f.* (—, *pl.* —n) leg of veal.

Kalbsmilch ['kalpsmɪlç], *f.* (—, *no pl.*) sweetbread.

Kaldaunen [kal'daunən], *f. pl.* (*dial.*) tripe.

Kalesche [ka'lɛʃə], *f.* (—, *pl.* —n) chaise, light carriage.

Kali ['ka:li], *n.* (—s, *no pl.*) potash.

Kaliber [ka'li:bər], *n.* (—s, *pl.* —) calibre; (*fig.*) sort, quality.

kalibrieren [kali'bri:rən], *v.a.* (*Tech.*) calibrate, graduate, gauge.

Kalifornien [kali'fɔrnjən], *n.* California.

Kalium ['ka:ljum], *n.* (—s, *no pl.*) (*Chem.*) potassium.

Kalk [kalk], *m.* (—s, *pl.* —e) lime; *gebrannter —,* quicklime; *mit — bewerfen,* rough-cast.

kalkartig ['kalka:rtɪç], *adj.* calcareous.

Kalkbewurf ['kalkbəvurf], *m.* (—es, *pl.* ̈e) coat of plaster.

kalken ['kalkən], *v.a.* whitewash; (*Agr.*) lime.

kalkig ['kalkɪç], *adj.* limy, calcareous.

kalkulieren [kalku'li:rən], *v.n.* calculate, reckon.

kalt [kalt], *adj.* cold, frigid; *mir ist —,* I am cold.

kaltblütig ['kaltbly:tɪç], *adj.* cold-blooded, cool.

Kälte ['kɛltə], *f.* (—, *no pl.*) cold, coldness.

Kaltschale ['kaltʃa:lə], *f.* (—, *pl.* —n) cold beer (*or* wine) soup.

Kambodscha [kam'bɔtʃa], *f.* Cambodia.

Kamee [ka'me:], *f.* (—, *pl.* ̈n) cameo.

Kamel [ka'me:l], *n.* (—s, *pl.* —e) (*Zool.*) camel.

Kamelziege [ka'me:ltsi:gə], *f.* (—, *pl.* —n) (*Zool.*) Angora-goat, llama.

Kamerad [kamə'ra:t], *m.* (—en, *pl.* —en) comrade, companion, mate.

Kameradschaft [kamə'ra:tʃaft], *f.* (—, *pl.* —en) comradeship, fellowship.

Kamerun [kamə'ru:n], *n.* the Cameroons.

Kamille [ka'mɪlə], *f.* (—, *pl.* —n) camomile.

Kamin [ka'mi:n], *m.* (—s, *pl.* —e) chimney; funnel; fireplace, fireside.

Kaminaufsatz [ka'mi:naufzats], *m.* (—es, *pl.* ̈e) mantel-piece, overmantel.

Kaminfeger [ka'mi:nfe:gər], *m.* (—s, *pl.* —) chimney-sweep.

117

Kaminsims

Kaminsims [ka'mi:nzims], *m.* or *n.* (—es, *pl.* —e) mantel-piece.

Kamm [kam], *m.* (—es, *pl.* ⁻e) comb; (*cock*) crest; (*mountains*) ridge.

kämmen ['kɛmən], *v.a.* comb; (*wool*) card.

Kammer ['kamər], *f.* (—, *pl.* —n) chamber, small room; (*Am.*) closet; (*authority*) board; (*Parl. etc.*) chamber.

Kammerdiener ['kamərdi:nər], *m.* (—s, *pl.* —) valet.

Kämmerer ['kɛmərər], *m.* (—s, *pl.* —) Chamberlain, Treasurer.

Kammergericht ['kamərgərɪçt], *n.* (—s, *pl.* —e) Supreme Court of Justice.

Kammergut ['kamərgu:t], *n.* (—s, *pl.* ⁻er) domain, demesne; crown land.

Kammerherr ['kamərher], *m.* (—n, *pl.* —en) chamberlain.

Kammersänger ['kamərzɛŋər], *m.* (—s, *pl.* —) court singer; title given to prominent singers.

Kammgarn ['kamgarn], *n.* (—s, *no pl.*) worsted.

Kammwolle ['kamvɔlə], *f.* (—, *no pl.*) carded wool.

Kampagne [kam'panjə], *f.* (—, *pl.* —n) (*Mil.*) campaign.

Kämpe ['kɛmpə], *m.* (—n, *pl.* —n) (*Poet.*) champion, warrior; *alter* —, old campaigner.

Kampf [kampf], *m.* (—es, *pl.* ⁻e) combat, fight, struggle; (*fig.*) conflict.

kämpfen ['kɛmpfən], *v.n.* fight, combat, struggle.

Kampfer ['kampfər], *m.* (—s, *no pl.*) camphor.

Kämpfer ['kɛmpfər], *m.* (—s, *pl.* —) fighter, combatant.

kampfunfähig ['kampfunfɛ:ɪç], *adj.* (*Mil.*) disabled; — *machen*, disable, put out of action.

kampieren [kam'pi:rən], *v.n.* be encamped, camp.

Kanada ['kanada], *n.* Canada.

Kanal [ka'na:l], *m.* (—s, *pl.* ⁻e) (*natural*) channel; (*artificial*) canal; sewer; *der Ärmelkanal*, the English Channel.

kanalisieren [kanali'zi:rən], *v.a.* canalise; (*streets*) drain by means of sewers.

Kanapee ['kanape:], *n.* (—s, *pl.* —s) sofa, divan.

Kanarienvogel [ka'na:rjənfo:gəl], *m.* (—s, *pl.* ⁻) (*Orn.*) canary.

Kanarische Inseln [ka'na:rɪʃə 'ɪnzəln], *f.pl.* Canary Islands.

Kandare [kan'da:rə], *f.* (—, *pl.* —n) bridle, bit.

Kandelaber [kandə'la:bər], *m.* (—s, *pl.* —) candelabrum, chandelier.

kandidieren [kandi'di:rən], *v.n.* be a candidate (for), apply (for) (*post*); (*Parl.*) stand (for), (*Am.*) run (for election).

kandieren [kan'di:rən], *v.a.* candy.

Kandiszucker ['kandɪstsukər], *m.* (—, *no pl.*) sugar-candy.

Kanevas ['kanəvas], *m.* (—ses, *pl.* —se) canvas.

Känguruh ['kɛŋguru:], *n.* (—s, *pl.* —s) (*Zool.*) kangaroo.

Kaninchen [ka'ni:nçən], *n.* (—s, *pl.* —) (*Zool.*) rabbit.

Kaninchenbau [ka'ni:nçənbau], *m.* (—s, *pl.* —e) rabbit-warren, burrow.

Kanne ['kanə], *f.* (—, *pl.* —n) can, tankard, mug; jug; pot; quart.

Kannegießer ['kanəgi:sər], *m.* (—s, *pl.* —) pot-house politician.

kannelieren [kanə'li:rən], *v.a.* flute; channel.

Kannibale [kani'ba:lə], *m.* (—n, *pl.* —n) cannibal.

Kanoe [ka'nu:], *n. see* Kanu.

Kanone [ka'no:nə], *f.* (—, *pl.* —n) cannon, gun; *unter aller* —, beneath contempt; beneath criticism.

Kanonier [kano'ni:r], *m.* (—s, *pl.* —e) gunner.

Kanonikus [ka'no:nikus], *m.* (—, *pl.* —ker) canon, prebendary.

kanonisieren [kanoni'zi:rən], *v.a.* canonise.

Kante ['kantə], *f.* (—, *pl.* —n) edge, rim, brim, brink, ledge; (*cloth*) list, selvedge.

Kanten ['kantən], *m.* (—s, *pl.* —) (*bread*) crust.

kanten ['kantən], *v.a.* edge, tilt.

Kanthaken ['kantha:kən], *m.* (—s, *pl.* —) cant-hook; grapple; grappling hook.

kantig ['kantɪç], *adj.* angular.

Kantine [kan'ti:nə], *f.* (—, *pl.* —n), canteen, mess.

Kanton [kan'to:n], *m.* (—s, *pl.* —e) (*Swiss*) canton; district, region.

Kantonist [kanto'nɪst], *m.* (—en, *pl.* —en) *unsicherer* —, shifty fellow.

Kantor ['kantɔr], *m.* (—s, *pl.* —en) precentor, organist; cantor.

Kanu ['kanu:], *n.* (—s, *pl.* —s) canoe.

Kanzel ['kantsəl], *f.* (—, *pl.* —n) pulpit; (*Aviat.*) cockpit.

Kanzlei [kants'lai], *f.* (—, *pl.* —en) office, secretariat; chancellery; chancery office; lawyer's office.

Kanzleipapier [kants'laipapi:r], *n.* (—s, *no pl.*) foolscap (paper).

Kanzleistil [kants'laiʃti:l], *m.* (—s, *no pl.*) legal jargon.

Kanzler ['kantslər], *m.* (—s, *pl.* —) Chancellor.

Kanzlist [kants'lɪst], *m.* (—en, *pl.* —en) chancery clerk; copying clerk.

Kap [kap], *n.* (—s, *pl.* —s) (*Geog.*) cape, promontory.

Kapaun [ka'paun], *m.* (—s, *pl.* —e) capon.

Kapazität [kapatsi'tɛ:t], *f.* (—, *pl.* —en) capacity; (*fig.*) (*person*) authority.

Kapelle [ka'pɛlə], *f.* (—, *pl.* —n) chapel; (*Mus.*) band.

Kapellmeister [ka'pɛlmaistər], *m.* (—s, *pl.* —) (*Mus.*) band leader, conductor.

Kaper ['ka:pər], *f.* (—, *pl.* —n) (*Bot.*) caper.

kapern [ˈkaːpərn], *v.a.* capture, catch.
kapieren [kaˈpiːrən], *v.a.* (*coll.*) understand, grasp.
Kapital [kapiˈtaːl], *n.* (—s, *pl.* —ien) (*money*) capital, stock.
Kapitäl, Kapitell [kapiˈtɛːl, kapiˈtɛl], *n.* (—s, *pl.* —e) (*Archit.*) capital.
Kapitalanlage [kapiˈtaːlanlaːɡə], *f.* (— *pl.* —n) investment.
kapitalisieren [kapitaliˈziːrən], *v.a.* capitalise.
kapitalkräftig [kapiˈtaːlkrɛftɪç], *adj.* wealthy, moneyed, affluent; (*business, firm*) sound.
Kapitalverbrechen [kapiˈtaːlfɛrbreçən], *n.* (—s, *pl.* —) capital offence.
Kapitän [kapiˈtɛːn], *m.* (—s, *pl.* —e) captain (of a ship), master.
Kapitel [kaˈpɪtəl], *n.* (—s, *pl.* —) chapter.
Kapitulation [kapitulatsˈjoːn], *f.* (—, *pl.* —en) surrender.
kapitulieren [kapituˈliːrən], *v.n.* surrender; capitulate.
Kaplan [kapˈlaːn], *m.* (—s, *pl.* ˙ːe) chaplain; assistant priest.
Kapotte [kaˈpɔtə], *f.* (—, *pl.* —n) hood.
Kappe [ˈkapə], *f.* (—, *pl.* —n) cap, bonnet; (*shoe*) toe-cap.
Käppi [ˈkɛpi], *n.* (—s, *pl.* —s) military cap.
Kapriole [kapriˈoːlə], *f.* (—, *pl.* —n) caper.
kaprizieren [kapriˈtsiːrən], *v.r. sich auf etwas —*, set o.'s heart on s.th., be obstinate about s.th.
kapriziös [kapriˈtsjøːs], *adj.* whimsical, capricious.
Kapsel [ˈkapsəl], *f.* (—, *pl.* —n) capsule.
kaputt [kaˈput], *adj.* broken, ruined, done for; — *machen*, break, ruin.
Kapuze [kaˈpuːtsə], *f.* (—, *pl.* —n) hood; monk's cowl.
Kapuziner [kaputˈsiːnər], *m.* (—s, *pl.* —) Capuchin (friar); (*coffee*) cappuccino.
Kapuzinerkresse [kaputˈsiːnərkrɛsə], *f.* (—, *no pl.*) nasturtium.
Karabiner [karaˈbiːnər], *m.* (—s, *pl.* —) (*rifle*) carbine.
Karaffe [kaˈrafə], *f.* (—, *pl.* —n) carafe; decanter.
Karambolage [karamboˈlaːʒə], *f.* (—, *pl.* —n) collision; (*billiards*) cannon.
Karawane [karaˈvaːnə], *f.* (—, *pl.* —n) convoy; caravan.
Karbol [karˈboːl], *n.* (—s, *no pl.*) carbolic acid.
Karbunkel [karˈbuŋkəl], *m.* (—s, *pl.* —) (*Med.*) carbuncle.
Karfreitag [karˈfraɪtaːk], *m.* Good Friday.
Karfunkel [karˈfuŋkəl], *m.* (—s, *pl.* —) (*Min.*) carbuncle.
karg [kark], *adj.* scant; meagre; parsimonious.
kargen [ˈkarɡən], *v.n.* be stingy, be niggardly.
kärglich [ˈkɛrklɪç], *adj.* sparing, scanty, poor, paltry.

karieren [kaˈriːrən], *v.a.* checker.
kariert [kaˈriːrt], *adj.* checked, checkered.
Karikatur [karikaˈtuːr], *f.* (—, *pl.* —en) caricature, cartoon.
karikieren [kariˈkiːrən], *v.a.* caricature, distort.
Karl [karl], *m.* Charles; — *der Grosse*, Charlemagne.
Karmeliter [karmeˈliːtər], *m.* (—s, *pl.* —) Carmelite (friar).
karminrot [karˈmiːnrɔːt], *adj.* carmine.
karmoisin [karmoaˈziːn], *adj.* crimson.
Karneol [karneˈoːl], *m.* (—s, *pl.* —e) (*Min.*) cornelian, carnelian.
Karneval [ˈkarnəval], *m.* (—s, *pl.* —s) carnival; Shrovetide festivities.
Karnickel [karˈnɪkəl], *n.* (—s, *pl.* —) rabbit; *er war das* —, he was to blame.
Kärnten [ˈkɛrntən], *n.* Carinthia.
Karo [ˈkaːro], *n.* (—s, *pl.* —s) check, square; (*cards*) diamonds.
Karosse [kaˈrɔsə], *f.* (—, *pl.* —n) statecoach.
Karosserie [karɔsəˈriː], *f.* (—, *pl.* —n) (*Motor.*) body(-work).
Karotte [kaˈrɔtə], *f.* (—, *pl.* —n) (*Bot.*) carrot.
Karpfen [ˈkarpfən], *m.* (—s, *pl.* —) (*fish*) carp.
Karre [ˈkarə], *f.* (—, *pl.* —n) cart, wheelbarrow.
Karren [ˈkarən], *m.* (—s, *pl.* —) cart, wheelbarrow, dray.
Karrete [kaˈreːtə], *f.* (—, *pl.* —n) (*Austr.*) rattletrap, rickety coach.
Karriere [kaˈrjɛːrə], *f.* (—, *pl.* —n) career; — *machen*, get on well.
Kärrner [ˈkɛrnər], *m.* (—s, *pl.* —) (*obs.*) carter.
Karst [karst], *m.* (—s, *pl.* —e) mattock.
Karthago [karˈtaːgo], *n.* Carthage.
Kartätsche [karˈtɛːtʃə], *f.* (—, *pl.* —n) grape-shot, shrapnel.
Kartäuser [karˈtɔyzər], *m.* (—s, *pl.* —) Carthusian (monk).
Karte [ˈkartə], *f.* (—, *pl.* —n) card; ticket; map; chart; (*pl.*) pack ((*Am.*) deck) of cards.
Kartei [karˈtaɪ], *f.* (—, *pl.* —en) card index.
Kartell [karˈtɛl], *n.* (—s, *pl.* —e) cartel; ring; syndicate.
Kartoffel [karˈtɔfəl], *f.* (—, *pl.* —n) (*Bot.*) potato.
Kartoffelpuffer [karˈtɔfəlpufər], *m.* —s, *pl.* —) potato-pancake.
Karton [karˈtɔŋ], *m.* (—s, *pl.* —s) carton, cardboard-box; (*material*) cardboard, paste-board; cartoon.
Kartusche [karˈtuʃə], *f.* (—, *pl.* —n) cartridge.
Karussell [karuˈsɛl], *n.* (—s, *pl.* —e) merry-go-round.
Karwoche [ˈkaːrvɔxə], *f.* Holy Week.
Karzer [ˈkartsər], *m.* (—s, *pl.* —) lock-up, prison.
Kaschmir [ˈkaʃmiːr], *m.* (—s, *no pl.*) cashmere.

Käse

Käse [ˈkɛːzə], *m.* (—s, *pl.* —) cheese.
käseartig [ˈkɛːzəaˌrtɪç], *adj.* like cheese; caseous.
Kaserne [kaˈzɛrnə], *f.* (—, *pl.* —n) barracks.
kasernieren [kazɛrˈniːrən], *v.a.* put into barracks.
Käsestoff [ˈkɛːzəʃtɔf], *m.* (—s, *pl.* —e) casein.
käseweiß [ˈkɛːzəvaɪs], *adj.* deathly pale.
käsig [ˈkɛːzɪç], *adj.* cheese-like, cheesy, caseous; (*fig.*) pale.
Kasperle [ˈkaspɛrlə], *n.* (—s, *pl.* —) Punch.
Kasperl(e)theater [ˈkaspɛrl(ə)teaˌtər], *n.* (—s, *pl.* —) Punch-and-Judy show.
Kaspisches Meer [ˈkaspɪʃəsmeːr], *n.* Caspian Sea.
Kasse [ˈkasə], *f.* (—, *pl.* —n) money-box, till; cash-desk; box-office; cash, ready money.
Kassenanweisung [ˈkasənanvaɪzuŋ], *f.* (—, *pl.* —en) treasury-bill; cash voucher.
Kassenbuch [ˈkasənbuːx], *n.* (—es, *pl.* ⁝er) cash-book.
Kassenschrank [ˈkasənʃraŋk], *m.* (—s, *pl.* ⁝e) strong-box, safe.
Kasserolle [kasəˈrɔlə], *f.* (—, *pl.* —n) stew-pot, casserole.
Kassette [kaˈsɛtə], *f.* (—, *pl.* —n) deed-box; casket; (*Phot.*) plate-holder.
kassieren [kaˈsiːrən], *v.a.* cash, collect (money); cashier, annul, discharge.
Kastagnette [kastanˈjɛtə], *f.* (—, *pl.* —n) castanet.
Kassierer [kaˈsiːrər], *m.* (—s, *pl.* —) cashier; teller.
Kastanie [kasˈtanjə], *f.* (—, *pl.* —n) (*Bot.*) chestnut, (*coll.*) conker; chestnut-tree.
Kästchen [ˈkɛstçən], *n.* (—s, *pl.* —) casket, little box.
Kaste [ˈkastə], *f.* (—, *pl.* —n) caste.
kasteien [kasˈtaɪən], *v.r. sich* —, castigate *or* mortify o.s.
Kastell [kasˈtɛl], *n.* (—s, *pl.* —e) citadel, small fort; castle.
Kastellan [kastɛˈlaːn], *m.* (—s, *pl.* —e) castellan; caretaker.
Kasten [ˈkastən], *m.* (—s, *pl.* ⁝) box, chest, case, crate.
Kastengeist [ˈkastəngaɪst], *m.* (—es, *no pl.*) exclusiveness; class consciousness.
Kastilien [kasˈtiːljən], *n.* Castile.
Kastrat [kasˈtraːt], *m.* (—en, *pl.* —en) eunuch.
kastrieren [kasˈtriːrən], *v.a.* castrate.
Katafalk [kataˈfalk], *m.* (—s, *pl.* —e) catafalque.
katalogisieren [katalogiˈziːrən], *v.a.* catalogue.
Katarakt [kataˈrakt], *m.* (—es, *pl.* —e) cataract; waterfall.
Katasteramt [kaˈtastəramt], *n.* (—es, *pl.* ⁝er) land-registry office.
katechisieren [kateçiˈziːrən], *v.a.* catechise, instruct.

kategorisch [kateˈgoːrɪʃ], *adj.* categorical, definite.
Kater [ˈkaːtər], *m.* (—s, *pl.* —) tom-cat; (*fig.*) hangover; *der gestiefelte* —, Puss-in-Boots.
Katheder [kaˈteːdər], *n.* (—s, *pl.* —) desk; rostrum; lecturing-desk; (*fig.*) professorial chair.
Kathedrale [kateˈdraːlə], *f.* (—, *pl.* —n) cathedral.
Katholik [katoˈliːk], *m.* (—en, *pl.* —en) (Roman) Catholic.
katholisch [kaˈtoːlɪʃ], *adj.* (Roman) Catholic.
Kattun [kaˈtuːn], *m.* (—s, *pl.* —e) calico, cotton.
Kätzchen [ˈkɛtsçən], *n.* (—s, *pl.* —) kitten; (*Bot.*) catkin.
Katze [ˈkatsə], *f.* (—, *pl.* —n) cat; *die — im Sack kaufen*, buy a pig in a poke; *für die* —, no good at all, useless.
katzenartig [ˈkatsənaˌrtɪç], *adj.* cat-like, feline.
Katzenauge [ˈkatsənaugə], *n.* (—s, *pl.* —n) cat's-eye.
Katzenbuckel [ˈkatsənbukəl], *m.* (—s, *pl.* —) arched back of a cat.
Katzenjammer [ˈkatsənjamər], *m.* (—s, *pl.* —) hangover.
Katzenmusik [ˈkatsənmuziːk], *f.* (—, *no pl.*) caterwauling; cacophony, discordant music.
Katzensprung [ˈkatsənʃpruŋ], *m.* (—es, *no pl.*) (*fig.*) stone's throw.
Kauderwelsch [ˈkaudərvɛlʃ], *n.* (—es, *no pl.*) gibberish, double-Dutch.
kauen [ˈkauən], *v.a., v.n.* chew.
kauern [ˈkauərn], *v.n.* cower, squat, crouch.
Kauf [kauf], *m.* (—es, *pl.* ⁝e) purchase, buy; bargain.
Kaufbummel [ˈkaufbuməl], *m.* (—s, *no pl.*) shopping-spree.
kaufen [ˈkaufən], *v.a.* (*things*) buy, purchase; (*persons*) bribe.
Käufer [ˈkɔyfər], *m.* (—s, *pl.* —) buyer, purchaser.
Kaufhaus [ˈkaufhaus], *n.* (—es, *pl.* ⁝er) department store, emporium.
Kaufladen [ˈkauflaːdən], *m.* (—s, *pl.* ⁝) shop.
käuflich [ˈkɔyflɪç], *adj.* (*things*) purchasable, marketable; (*persons*) open to bribery, venal.
Kaufmann [ˈkaufman], *m.* (—s, *pl.* **Kaufleute** [ˈkauflɔytə]) merchant; shopkeeper; (*Am.*) store-keeper.
kaufmännisch [ˈkaufmɛnɪʃ], *adj.* commercial, mercantile.
Kaugummi [ˈkauɡumi], *m.* (—s, *no pl.*) chewing gum.
Kaukasus [ˈkaukazus], *m.* Caucasus (Mountains).
Kaulquappe [ˈkaulkvapə], *f.* (—, *pl.* —n) (*Zool.*) tadpole.
kaum [kaum], *adv.* scarcely, hardly; no sooner.
Kaurimuschel [ˈkaurimuʃəl], *f.* (—, *pl.* —n) (*Zool.*) cowrie shell.

Kautabak ['kautabak], *m.* (—s, *no pl.*) chewing-tobacco.

Kaution [kau'tsjo:n], *f.* (—, *pl.* —en) security, bail, surety; *eine — stellen,* go, give *or* stand bail.

Kautschuk ['kautʃuk], *m.* (—s, *no pl.*) caoutchouc, India-rubber.

Kauz [kauts], *m.* (—es, *pl.* ⁓e) (*Orn.*) screech-owl; (*fig.*) *komischer —,* queer customer.

Käuzchen ['kɔytsçən], *n.* (—s, *pl.* —) little owl; (*fig.*) imp.

Kavalier [kava'li:r], *m.* (—s, *pl.* —e) gentleman; lady's man.

keck [kɛk], *adj.* bold, daring; pert, saucy.

Kegel ['ke:gəl], *m.* (—s, *pl.* —) ninepin, skittle; (*Geom.*) cone; *mit Kind und —,* bag and baggage.

Kegelbahn ['ke:gəlba:n], *f.* (—, *pl.* —en) skittle-alley, bowling-alley.

kegelförmig ['ke:gəlfœrmɪç], *adj.* conical.

kegeln ['ke:gəln], *v.n.* bowl, play at ninepins.

Kehle ['ke:lə], *f.* (—, *pl.* —n) throat, windpipe.

Kehlkopf ['ke:lkɔpf], *m.* (—es, *pl.* ⁓e) larynx.

Kehllaut ['ke:llaut], *m.* (—es, *pl.* —e) (*Phonet.*) guttural sound.

Kehlung ['ke:luŋ], *f.* (—, *pl.* —en) channel, flute, groove.

Kehraus ['ke:raus], *m.* (—, *no pl.*) last dance; (*fig.*) break-up, end.

kehren ['ke:rən], *v.a.* sweep; turn; *den Rücken —,* turn o.'s back. — *v.r. sich — an,* pay attention to, regard.

Kehricht ['ke:rɪçt], *m.* (—s, *no pl.*) sweepings; rubbish.

Kehrreim ['ke:rraɪm], *m.* (—s, *pl.* —e) refrain.

Kehrseite ['ke:rzaɪtə], *f.* (—, *pl.* —n) reverse.

kehrtmachen ['ke:rtmaxən], *v.n.* turn around; (*Mil.*) face about; turn back.

keifen ['kaɪfən], *v.n.* scold, nag.

Keil [kaɪl], *m.* (—s, *pl.* —e) wedge.

Keile ['kaɪlə], *f.* (—, *no pl.*) blows; (*coll.*) hiding; — *kriegen,* get a thrashing.

keilen ['kaɪlən], *v.a.* wedge; (*coll.*) thrash.

Keilerei [kaɪlə'raɪ], *f.* (—, *pl.* —en) brawl, fight.

keilförmig ['kaɪlfœrmɪç], *adj.* wedge-shaped.

Keilschrift ['kaɪlʃrɪft], *f.* (—, *pl.* —en) cuneiform writing.

Keim [kaɪm], *m.* (—es, *pl.* —e) germ, seed.

keimen ['kaɪmən], *v.n.* germinate.

keimfrei ['kaɪmfraɪ], *adj.* sterile, germ-free.

keiner, -e, -es [kaɪnər], *adj.* no, not a, not any. — *pron.* no one, none.

keinerlei ['kaɪnərlaɪ], *adj.* no, of no sort, no ... whatever.

keineswegs ['kaɪnəsve:ks], *adv.* by no means, on no account.

Keks [ke:ks], *m.* (—es, *pl.* —e) biscuit.

Kelch [kɛlç], *m.* (—es, *pl.* —e) cup; (*Eccl.*) chalice; (*Bot.*) calyx.

Kelchblatt ['kɛlçblat], *n.* (—es, *pl.* ⁓er) sepal.

kelchförmig ['kɛlçfœrmɪç], *adj.* cup-shaped.

Kelle ['kɛlə], *f.* (—, *pl.* —n) ladle; (*mason*) trowel.

Keller ['kɛlər], *m.* (—s, *pl.* —) cellar, basement.

Kellergewölbe ['kɛlərgəvœlbə], *n.* (—s, *pl.* —) vault.

Kellner ['kɛlnər], *m.* (—s, *pl.* —) waiter.

keltern ['kɛltərn], *v.a.* press (grapes).

Kenia ['ke:nja], *n.* Kenya.

kennbar ['kɛnba:r], *adj.* recognisable, conspicuous.

kennen ['kɛnən], *v.a. irr.* know, be acquainted with.

Kenner ['kɛnər], *m.* (—s, *pl.* —) connoisseur, expert.

Kennkarte ['kɛnkartə], *f.* (—, *pl.* —n) identity card.

kenntlich ['kɛntlɪç], *adj.* distinguishable.

Kenntnis ['kɛntnɪs], *f.* (—, *pl.* —se) knowledge; (*language*) command.

Kennzeichen ['kɛntsaɪxən], *n.* (—s, *pl.* —) characteristic, distinguishing mark; sign; symptom; criterion.

Kenterhaken ['kɛntərha:kən], *m.* (—s, *pl.* —) grappling-iron.

kentern ['kɛntərn], *v.n.* (*aux.* sein) capsize.

keramisch [ke'ra:mɪʃ], *adj.* ceramic.

Kerbe ['kɛrbə], *f.* (—, *pl.* —n) notch, indentation.

kerben ['kɛrbən], *v.a.* notch.

Kerbholz ['kɛrphɔlts], *n.* (—es, *no pl.*) tally; *auf dem —,* on o.'s conscience, charged against o.

Kerbtier ['kɛrpti:r], *n.* (—es, *pl.* —e) insect.

Kerker ['kɛrkər], *m.* (—s, *pl.* —) prison, jail, gaol; dungeon.

Kerl [kɛrl], *m.* (—s, *pl.* —e) fellow, chap; (*Am.*) guy (*coll.*).

Kern [kɛrn], *m.* (—es, *pl.* —e) (*nut*) kernel; (*fruit*) stone; (*fig.*) heart, crux; pith; (*Phys.*) nucleus.

kerngesund ['kɛrngəzunt], *adj.* hale and hearty, fit as a fiddle.

kernig ['kɛrnɪç], *adj.* solid, pithy.

Kernphysik ['kɛrnfyzi:k], *f.* (—, *no pl.*) nuclear physics.

Kernpunkt ['kɛrnpuŋkt], *m.* (—es, *pl.* —e) gist, essential point.

Kernwaffe ['kɛrnvafə], *f.* (—, *pl.* —n) nuclear weapon.

Kerze ['kɛrtsə], *f.* (—, *pl.* —n) candle.

Kessel ['kɛsəl], *m.* (—s, *pl.* —) kettle, cauldron; (*steam*) boiler.

Kesselschmied ['kɛsəlʃmi:t], *m.* (—s, *pl.* —e) boiler maker.

Kesselstein ['kɛsəlʃtaɪn], *m.* (—s, *no pl.*) fur, deposit, scale (on boiler).

Kette ['kɛtə], *f.* (—, *pl.* —n) chain.

ketten ['kɛtən], *v.a.* chain, fetter.

Kettenstich ['kɛtənʃtɪç], *m.* (—es, *pl.* —e) chain stitch; (*Naut.*) chain knot.

Ketzer

Ketzer ['kɛtsər], *m.* (—s, *pl.* —) heretic.
Ketzerei [kɛtsə'raɪ], *f.* (—, *pl.* —en) heresy.
ketzerisch ['kɛtsərɪʃ], *adj.* heretical.
keuchen ['kɔyçən], *v.n.* pant, puff, gasp.
Keuchhusten ['kɔyçhu:stən], *m.* (—s, *no pl.*) whooping-cough.
Keule ['kɔylə], *f.* (—, *pl.* —n) club; (*meat*) leg.
keusch [kɔyʃ], *adj.* chaste, pure.
kichern ['kɪçərn], *v.n.* titter, giggle.
Kiebitz ['ki:bɪts], *m.* (—es, *pl.* —e) (*Orn.*) lapwing, peewit; (*fig.*) onlooker; (*coll.*) rubber-neck (at chess or cards).
Kiefer (1) ['ki:fər], *m.* (—s, *pl.* —) jaw, jaw-bone.
Kiefer (2) ['ki:fər], *f.* (—, *pl.* —n) (*Bot.*) pine.
Kiel [ki:l], *m.* (—es, *pl.* —e) keel; (*pen*) quill.
Kielwasser ['ki:lvasər], *n.* (—s, *no pl.*) wake.
Kieme ['ki:mə], *f.* (—, *pl.* —n) (*fish*) gill.
Kien [ki:n], *m.* (—s, *no pl.*) pine-resin, resinous pinewood.
Kienspan ['ki:nʃpa:n], *m.* (—s, *pl.* ⸚e) pine-splinter.
Kiepe ['ki:pə], *f.* (—, *pl.* —n) (*dial.*) creel, wicker basket.
Kies [ki:s], *m.* (—es, *no pl.*) gravel.
Kiesel ['ki:zəl], *m.* (—s, *pl.* —) pebble; flint.
Kieselsäure ['ki:zəlzɔyrə], *f.* (—, *no pl.*) silicic acid.
Kieselstein ['ki:zəlʃtaɪn], *m.* (—s, *pl.* —e) pebble.
Kilogramm ['ki:logram], *n.* (—s, *pl.* —e) kilogram (1000 grammes).
Kilometer ['ki:lome:tər], *n.* (—s, *pl.* —) kilometre; (*Am.*) kilometer (1000 metres).
Kimme ['kɪmə], *f.* (—, *pl.* —n) notch.
Kind [kɪnt], *n.* (—es, *pl.* —er) child; (*law*) infant; — *und Kegel*, bag and baggage.
Kind(e)l ['kɪnd(ə)l], *n.* (—s, *pl.* —) (*dial.*) small child, baby; *Münchner* —, Munich beer.
Kinderei [kɪndə'raɪ], *f.* (—, *pl.* —en) childishness; childish prank.
Kinderfräulein ['kɪndərfrɔylaɪn], *n.* (—s, *pl.* —) nurse, (*coll.*) nannie.
Kindergarten ['kɪndərgartən], *m.* (—s, *pl.* ⸚) kindergarten, infant-school.
Kinderhort ['kɪndərhɔrt], *m.* (—s, *pl.* —e) crèche.
kinderleicht ['kɪndərlaɪçt], *adj.* extremely easy, child's play.
Kindermärchen ['kɪndərmɛːrçən], *n.* (—s, *pl.* —) fairy-tale.
Kinderstube ['kɪndərʃtu:bə], *f.* (—, *pl.* —n) nursery; *eine gute* —, a good upbringing.
Kinderwagen ['kɪndərva:gən], *m.* (—s, *pl.* —) perambulator, pram.
Kindesbeine ['kɪndəsbaɪnə], *n. pl. von* —*n an*, from infancy.

Kindeskind ['kɪndəskɪnt], *n.* (—es, *pl.* —er) (*obs.*) grandchild.
Kindheit ['kɪnthaɪt], *f.* (—, *no pl.*) childhood, infancy.
kindisch ['kɪndɪʃ], *adj.* childish.
kindlich ['kɪntlɪç], *adj.* childlike; naïve.
Kinn [kɪn], *n.* (—s, *pl.* —e) chin.
Kinnbacken ['kɪnbakən], *m.* (—s, *pl.* —) (*Anat.*) jaw-bone.
Kinnbackenkrampf ['kɪnbakənkrampf], *m.* (—s, *pl.* ⸚e) (*Med.*) lock-jaw.
Kinnlade ['kɪnla:də], *f.* (—, *pl.* —n) (*Anat.*) jaw-bone.
Kino ['ki:no], *n.* (—s, *pl.* —s) cinema; (*coll.*) pictures; (*Am.*) motion picture theatre; motion pictures, (*coll.*) movies.
Kipfel ['kɪpfəl], *n.* (—s, *pl.* —) (*dial.*) roll, croissant.
kippen ['kɪpən], *v.a.* tilt, tip over.
Kirche ['kɪrçə], *f.* (—, *pl.* —n) church.
Kirchenbann ['kɪrçənban], *m.* (—s, *no. pl.*) excommunication.
Kirchenbuch ['kɪrçənbu:x], *n.* (—es, *pl.* ⸚er) parish-register.
Kirchengut ['kɪrçəngu:t], *n.* (—es, *pl.* ⸚er) church-property.
Kirchenlicht ['kɪrçənlɪçt], *n.* (—es, *pl.* —er) (*fig.*) shining light, bright spark.
Kirchenrecht ['kɪrçənrɛçt], *n.* (—es, *no pl.*) canon law.
Kirchenschiff ['kɪrçənʃɪf], *n.* (—es, *pl.* —e) nave.
Kirchenstuhl ['kɪrçənʃtu:l], *m.* (—es, *pl.* ⸚e) pew.
Kirchenversammlung ['kɪrçənfɛrzamluŋ], *f.* (—, *pl.* —en) synod; convocation.
Kirchenvorsteher ['kɪrçənfɔrʃte:ər], *m.* (—s, *pl.* —) churchwarden.
kirchlich ['kɪrçlɪç], *adj.* ecclesiastic(al), religious.
Kirchspiel ['kɪrçʃpi:l], *n.* (—es, *pl.* —e) parish.
Kirchsprengel ['kɪrçʃprɛŋəl], *m.* (—s, *pl.* —) diocese.
Kirchturm ['kɪrçturm], *m.* (—es, *pl.* ⸚e) steeple.
Kirchweih ['kɪrçvaɪ], *f.* (—, *pl.* —en) consecration (of a church); church fair.
Kirmes ['kɪrmɛs], *f.* (—, *pl.* —sen) *see* **Kirchweih**.
kirre ['kɪrə], *adj.* tame; (*fig.*) amenable.
kirren ['kɪrən], *v.a.* tame, allure; *v.n.* coo.
Kirsch(branntwein) [kɪrʃ(brantvaɪn)], *m.* (—s, *no pl.*) cherry-brandy.
Kirsche ['kɪrʃə], *f.* (—, *pl.* —n) (*Bot.*) cherry; *mit ihr ist nicht gut* —*n essen*, she is hard to get on with or not pleasant to deal with.
Kirschsaft ['kɪrʃzaft], *m.* (—es, *no pl.*) cherry-juice.
Kirschwasser ['kɪrʃvasər], *n.* (—s, *no pl.*) cherry-brandy.
Kissen ['kɪsən], *n.* (—s, *pl.* —) cushion, pillow.

Kiste ['kɪstə], *f.* (—, *pl.* —n) box, case, chest; crate; coffer.

Kitsch [kɪtʃ], *m.* (—es, *no pl.*) trash; rubbish.

Kitt [kɪt], *m.* (—s, *pl.* —e) cement; (*Glazing*) putty.

Kittel ['kɪtəl], *m.* (—s, *pl.* —) smock; overall, tunic; frock.

kitten ['kɪtən], *v.a.* cement, glue.

Kitzchen ['kɪtsçən], *n.* (—s, *pl.* —) kid; fawn; kitten.

Kitzel ['kɪtsəl], *m.* (—s, *no pl.*) tickling, titillation; itch; (*fig.*) desire, appetite.

kitzeln ['kɪtsəln], *v.a.* tickle, titillate.

kitzlich ['kɪtslɪç], *adj.* ticklish; (*fig.*) delicate.

Kladderadatsch ['kladəradatʃ], *m.* (—es, *no pl.*) bang; mess, muddle.

klaffen ['klafən], *v.n.* gape, yawn.

kläffen ['klɛfən], *v.n.* bark, yelp.

Klafter ['klaftər], *f.* (—, *pl.* —n) fathom; (*wood*) cord.

klagbar ['kla:kba:r], *adj.* (*Law*) actionable.

Klage ['kla:gə], *f.* (—, *pl.* —n) complaint; (*Law*) suit, action.

Klagelied ['kla:gəli:t], *n.* (—es, *pl.* —er) dirge, lamentation.

klagen ['kla:gən], *v.n.* complain, lament; (*Law*) sue.

Kläger ['klɛ:gər], *m.* (—s, *pl.* —) complainant; (*Law*) plaintiff.

Klageschrift ['kla:gəʃrɪft], *f.* (—, *pl.* —en) bill of indictment; written complaint.

kläglich ['klɛ:klɪç], *adj.* woeful, pitiful, deplorable.

klaglos ['kla:klo:s], *adj.* uncomplaining.

Klamm [klam], *f.* (—, *pl.* —en) gorge, ravine.

klamm [klam], *adj.* tight, narrow; numb; clammy.

Klammer ['klamər], *f.* (—, *pl.* —n) clamp, clasp, hook; peg; clip; bracket, parenthesis.

klammern ['klamərn], *v.a.* fasten, peg. — *v.r. sich — an,* cling to.

Klang [klaŋ], *m.* (—es, *pl.* ⁔e) sound, tone; *ohne Sang und —,* unheralded and unsung.

klanglos ['klaŋlo:s], *adj.* soundless.

klangnachahmend ['klaŋnaxa:mənt], *adj.* onomatopoeic.

klangvoll ['klaŋfɔl], *adj.* sonorous.

Klappe ['klapə], *f.* (—, *pl.* —en) flap; (*Tech.*) valve; (*vulg.*) *halt die — !* shut up!

klappen ['klapən], *v.n.* flap; (*fig.*) tally, square; *es hat geklappt,* it worked.

Klapper ['klapər], *f.* (—, *pl.* —n) rattle.

klappern ['klapərn], *v.n.* rattle; (*teeth*) chatter.

Klapperschlange ['klapərʃlaŋə], *f.* (—, *pl.* —n) (*Zool.*) rattle-snake.

Klapphut ['klaphu:t], *m.* (—es, *pl.* ⁔e) opera-hat; chapeau-claque.

Klapps [klaps], *m.* (—es, *pl.* ⁔e) slap, smack; (*fig.*) touch of madness, kink.

Klappstuhl ['klapʃtu:l], *m.* (—s, *pl.* ⁔e) camp-stool, folding-chair.

Klapptisch ['klaptɪʃ], *m.* (—es, *pl.* ⁔e) folding-table.

klar [kla:r], *adj.* clear; bright; (*fig.*) evident; plain, distinct.

Kläranlage ['klɛ:ranla:gə], *f.* (—, *pl.* —n) sewage-farm; filter plant.

klären ['klɛ:rən], *v.a.* clear.

Klarheit ['kla:rhaɪt], *f.* (—, *no pl.*) clearness, plainness.

Klarinette [klari'netə], *f.* (—, *pl.* —n) (*Mus.*) clarinet.

Klärmittel ['klɛ:rmɪtəl], *n.* (—s, *pl.* —) clarifier.

Klärung ['klɛ:ruŋ], *f.* (—, *pl.* —en) clarification; (*fig.*) elucidation.

Klasse ['klasə], *f.* (—, *pl.* —n) class, order; (*Sch.*) form.

klassifizieren [klasifi'tsi:rən], *v.a.* classify.

Klassiker ['klasɪkər], *m.* (—s, *pl.* —) classic.

klassisch ['klasɪʃ], *adj.* classic(al), standard.

Klatsch [klatʃ], *m.* (—es, *no pl.*) gossip, scandal.

klatschen ['klatʃən], *v.n.* clap; gossip; (*rain*) patter; *Beifall —,* applaud.

Klatscherei [klatʃə'raɪ], *f.* (—, *pl.* —en) gossip, scandalmongering.

klauben ['klaubən], *v.a.* pick.

Klaue ['klauə], *f.* (—, *pl.* —n) claw, talon; paw.

klauen ['klauən], *v.a.* steal, (*coll.*) pinch.

Klauenseuche ['klauənzɔyçə], *f.* (—, *pl.* —n) *Maul und —,* foot and mouth disease.

Klause ['klauzə], *f.* (—, *pl.* —n) cell, hermitage; (*coll.*) den.

Klausel ['klauzəl], *f.* (—, *pl.* —n) clause, paragraph.

Klausner ['klausnər], *m.* (—s, *pl.* —) hermit, recluse, anchorite.

Klausur [klau'zu:r], *f.* (—, *pl.* —en) seclusion; written examination.

Klaviatur [klavja'tu:r], *f.* (—, *pl.* —en) keyboard.

Klavier [kla'vi:r], *n.* (—s, *pl.* —e) piano, pianoforte.

Klavierstück [kla'vi:rʃtyk], *n.* (—s, *pl.* —e) piece of piano music.

Klebemittel ['kle:bemɪtəl], *n.* (—s, *pl.* —) adhesive, glue.

kleben ['kle:bən], *v.a.* paste, stick, glue. — *v.n.* stick, adhere.

klebrig ['kle:brɪç], *adj.* sticky; clammy.

Klebstoff ['kle:pʃtɔf], *m.* (—es, *no pl.*) gum; glue.

Klecks [klɛks], *m.* (—es, *pl.* —e) blot; blotch.

Kleckser ['klɛksər], *m.* (—s, *pl.* —) scrawler; (*painter*) dauber.

Klee [kle:], *m.* (—s, *no pl.*) (*Bot.*) clover, trefoil.

Kleid [klaɪt], *n.* (—es, *pl.* —er) frock, garment, dress, gown; (*Poet.*) garb; (*pl.*) clothes; —er *machen Leute,* clothes make the man.

Kleidchen ['klaɪtçən], *n.* (—s, *pl.* —) child's dress.

kleiden ['klaɪdən], *v.a.* dress, clothe.

Kleiderbügel

Kleiderbügel [′klaɪdərby:gəl], *m.* (—s, *pl.* —) coat-hanger.

Kleiderpuppe [′klaɪdərpupə], *f.* (—, *pl.* —n) tailor's dummy.

Kleiderschrank [′klaɪdərʃraŋk], *m.* (—s, *pl.* ″e) wardrobe.

kleidsam [′klaɪtza:m], *adj.* becoming; well-fitting, a good fit.

Kleidung [′klaɪduŋ], *f.* (—, *no pl.*) clothing, clothes, dress.

Kleie [′klaɪə], *f.* (—, *no pl.*) bran.

klein [klaɪn], *adj.* little, small; minute; petty; *ein — wenig*, a little bit.

Kleinasien [klaɪn′a:zjən], *n.* Asia Minor.

Kleinbahn [′klaɪnba:n], *f.* (—, *pl.* —en) narrow-gauge railway.

kleinbürgerlich [′klaɪnbyrgərlɪç], *adj.* (petit) bourgeois.

Kleingeld [′klaɪngɛlt], *n.* (—(e)s, *no pl.*) small change.

kleingläubig [′klaɪnglɔybɪç], *adj.* faint-hearted.

Kleinhandel [′klaɪnhandəl], *m.* (—s, *no pl.*) retail-trade.

Kleinigkeit [′klaɪnɪçkaɪt], *f.* (—, *pl.* —en) trifle, small matter.

Kleinkram [′klaɪnkra:m], *m.* (—s, *no pl.*) trifles.

kleinlaut [′klaɪnlaut], *adj.* subdued, dejected, low-spirited.

kleinlich [′klaɪnlɪç], *adj.* petty; mean; narrow-minded; pedantic.

Kleinmut [′klaɪnmu:t], *m.* (—es, *no pl.*) faint-heartedness; dejection.

Kleinod [′klaɪno:t], *n.* (—s, *pl.* —ien) jewel; trinket.

Kleinstadt [′klaɪnʃtat], *f.* (—, *pl.* ″e) small town.

Kleister [′klaɪstər], *m.* (—s, *no pl.*) paste.

Klemme [′klɛmə], *f.* (—, *pl.* —n) (*Tech.*) vice; clamp; (*fig.*) difficulty, straits; (*coll.*) fix, jam.

klemmen [′klɛmən], *v.a.* pinch, squeeze, jam.

Klemmer [′klɛmər], *m.* (—s, *pl.*—) (*eye*) glasses, pince-nez.

Klempner [′klɛmpnər], *m.* (—s, *pl.*—) tin-smith; plumber.

Klerus [′kle:rus], *m.* (—, *no pl.*) clergy.

Klette [′klɛtə], *f.* (—, *pl.* —n) burdock, bur(r); (*fig.*) hanger-on.

klettern [′klɛtərn], *v.n.* (*aux.* sein) climb, clamber.

Klima [′kli:ma], *n.* (—s, *pl.* —s) climate.

Klimaanlage [′kli:maanla:gə], *f.* (—, *pl.* —n) air conditioning plant.

Klimbim [′klɪm′bɪm], *m.* (—s, *no pl.*) goings-on; festivity; fuss; *der ganze —*, the whole caboodle.

klimpern [′klɪmpərn], *v.n.* (*piano*) strum; (*money*) jingle.

Klinge [′klɪŋə], *f.* (—, *pl.* —n) blade.

Klingel [′klɪŋəl], *f.* (—, *pl.* —n) (*door, telephone*) bell.

Klingelbeutel [′klɪŋəlbɔytəl], *m.* (—s, *pl.*—) collecting-bag.

klingeln [′klɪŋəln], *v.n.* ring, tinkle.

Klingelzug [′klɪŋəltsu:k], *m.* . (—es, *pl.* ″e) bell-rope, bell-pull.

klingen [′klɪŋən], *v.n. irr.* sound; (*metals*) clang; (*ears*) tingle; *—de Münze*, hard cash, ready money.

Klinke [′klɪŋkə], *f.* (—, *pl.* —en) (*door*) handle, latch.

klipp [klɪp], *adv.* — *und klar*, as clear as daylight.

Klippe [′klɪpə], *f.* (—, *pl.* —n) cliff, crag, rock.

klirren [′klɪrən], *v.n.* clatter, rattle.

Klischee [klɪ′ʃe:], *n.* (—s, *pl.* —s) (*Typ.*) plate, printing-block; (*fig.*) cliché, hackneyed expression, tag.

Klistier [klɪ′sti:r], *n.* (—s, *pl.* —e) (*Med.*) enema.

Kloake [klo′a:kə], *f.* (—, *pl.* —n) sewer, drain.

Kloben [′klo:bən], *m.* (—s, *pl.* —) log, block (of wood); pulley.

klopfen [′klɔpfən], *v.a., v.n.* knock, beat.

Klöppel [′klœpəl], *m.* (—s, *pl.* —) mallet; (*bell*) tongue, clapper; (*drum*) stick; (*lace*) bobbin.

klöppeln [′klœpəln], *v.a* make (bone) lace.

Klöppelspitze [′klœpəlʃpɪtsə], *f.* (—, *no pl.*) bone-lace.

Klops [klɔps], *m.* (—es, *pl.* —e) meat-dumpling.

Klosett [klo′zet], *n.* (—s, *pl.* —e) lavatory, water-closet, toilet.

Kloß [klo:s], *m.* (—es, *pl.* ″e) dumpling.

Kloster [′klo:stər], *n.* (—s, *pl.* ″) cloister; monastery; convent.

Klostergang [′klo:stərgaŋ], *m.* (—es, *pl.* ″e) cloisters.

Klotz [klɔts], *m.* (—es, *pl.* ″e) block, trunk, stump; (*fig.*) *ein grober —*, a great lout.

klotzig [′klɔtsɪç], *adj.* cloddy; lumpish; (*sl.*) enormous.

Klub [klup], *m.* (—s, *pl.* —s) club.

Kluft [kluft], *f.* (—, *pl.* ″e) gap; gulf, chasm; (*fig.*) cleavage.

klug [klu:k], *adj.* clever, wise, prudent, judicious, sagacious; *ich kann daraus nicht — werden*, I cannot make head nor tail of it.

klügeln [′kly:gəln], *v.n.* ponder; quibble.

Klugheit [′klu:khaɪt], *f.* (—, *no pl.*) cleverness, wisdom, prudence, judiciousness.

Klumpfuß [′klumpfu:s], *m.* (—es, *pl.* ″e) club-foot.

Klumpen [′klumpən], *m.* (—s, *pl.* —) lump, mass, clod; (*blood*) clot; (*metal*) ingot; (*gold*) nugget.

Klüngel [′klyŋəl], *m.* (—s, *pl.* —) clique, set.

knabbern [′knabərn], *v.n.* nibble.

Knabe [′kna:bə], *m.* (—n, *pl.* —n) boy.

Knäblein [′knɛblaɪn], *n.* (—s, *pl.* —) (*Poet.*) baby boy, small boy.

knack [knak], *int.* crack! snap!

Knäckebrot [′knɛkəbro:t], *n.* (—es, *no pl.*) crispbread.

knacken [′knakən], *v.a.* crack.

Knackmandel ['knakmandəl], *f.* (—, *pl.* —n) shell-almond.

Knackwurst ['knakvurst], *f.* (—, *pl.* ⁝e) saveloy.

Knacks [knaks], *m.* (—es, *pl.* —e) crack.

knacksen ['knaksən], *v.n.* (*coll.*) crack.

Knall [knal], *m.* (—es, *pl.* —e) report, bang, detonation; — *und Fall,* quite suddenly, then and there.

Knallbüchse ['knalbyksə], *f.* (—, *pl.* —n) pop-gun.

Knalleffekt ['knalɛfɛkt], *m.* (—s, *pl.* —e) coup de théâtre; sensation.

knallen ['knalən], *v.n.* pop, explode, crack.

Knallgas ['knalga:s], *n.* (—es, *no pl.*) oxyhydrogen gas.

knallrot ['knalro:t], *adj.* scarlet; glaring red.

knapp [knap], *adj.* tight; scarce, insufficient; (*style*) concise; (*majority*) narrow, bare.

Knappe ['knapə], *m.* (—n, *pl.* —n) esquire, shield-bearer; miner.

Knappheit ['knaphait], *f.* (—, *no pl.*) scarcity, shortage.

Knappschaft ['knapʃaft], *f.* (—, *pl.* —en) miners' association.

Knarre ['knarə], *f.* (—, *pl.* —n) rattle.

knarren ['knarən], *v.n.* rattle, creak.

Knaster ['knastər], *m.* (—s, *pl.* —) tobacco.

knattern ['knatərn], *v.n.* crackle.

Knäuel ['knɔyəl], *m., n.* (—s, *pl.* —) skein, clew, ball.

Knauf [knauf], *m.* (—es, *pl.* ⁝e) (*stick*) knob, head; (*Archit.*) capital.

Knauser ['knauzər], *m.* (—s, *pl.* —) niggard, skinflint.

knausern ['knauzərn], *v.n.* be stingy, scrimp.

Knebel ['kne:bəl], *m.* (—s, *pl.* —) cudgel, gag.

knebeln ['kne:bəln], *v.a.* tie, bind; gag; (*fig.*) muzzle.

Knecht [knɛçt], *m.* (—es, *pl.* —e) servant, farm hand, menial; vassal, slave.

Knechtschaft ['knɛçtʃaft], *f.* (—, *no pl.*) servitude, slavery.

kneifen ['knaifən], *v.a. irr.* pinch. — *v.n.* (*fig. coll.*) back out (of), shirk.

Kneifer ['knaifər], *m.* (—s, *pl.* —) pince-nez.

Kneifzange ['knaiftsaŋə], *f.* (—, *pl.* —n) pincers.

Kneipe ['knaipə], *f.* (—, *pl.* —n) pub; saloon.

kneten ['kne:tən], *v.a.* knead; massage.

knick(e)beinig ['knɪk(ə)bainɪç], *adj.* knock-kneed.

knicken ['knɪkən], *v.a.* crack, break.

Knicks [knɪks], *m.* (—es, *pl.* —e) curtsy.

knicksen ['knɪksən], *v.n.* curtsy.

Knie [kni:], *n.* (—s, *pl.* —) knee; *etwas übers — brechen,* make short work of.

Kniekehle ['kni:ke:lə], *f.* (—, *pl.* —n) hollow of the knee.

knien ['kni:ən], *v.n.* kneel.

Kniescheibe ['kni:ʃaibə], *f.* (—, *pl.* —n) knee-cap.

Kniff [knɪf], *m.* (—es, *pl.* —e) fold; (*fig.*) trick, knack, dodge.

knipsen ['knɪpsən], *v.a.* (*tickets*) clip, punch; (*Phot.*) take a snap of.

Knirps [knɪrps], *m.* (—es, *pl.* —e) pigmy; (*fig.*) urchin.

knirschen ['knɪrʃən], *v.n.* crunch, grate, gnash (teeth).

knistern ['knɪstərn], *v.n.* crackle.

knittern ['knɪtərn], *v.a.* rumple, wrinkle, crinkle, crease.

Knobel ['kno:bəl], *m. pl.* dice.

Knoblauch ['kno:blaux], *m.* (—s, *no pl.*) (*Bot.*) garlic.

Knöchel ['knœçəl], *m.* (—s, *pl.* —) knuckle, joint; ankle.

Knochen ['knɔxən], *m.* (—s, *pl.* —) bone.

Knochengerüst ['knɔxəngəryst], *n.* (—es, *pl.* —e) skeleton.

knöchern ['knœçərn], *adj.* made of bone.

knochig ['knɔxɪç], *adj.* bony.

Knödel ['knø:dəl], *m.* (—s, *pl.* —) dumpling.

Knollen ['knɔlən], *m.* (—s, *pl.* —) lump, clod; (*Bot.*) tuber, bulb.

knollig ['knɔlɪç], *adj.* knobby, bulbous.

Knopf [knɔpf], *m.* (—es, *pl.* ⁝e) button; stud; (*stick*) head, knob.

knöpfen ['knœpfən], *v.a.* button.

Knorpel ['knɔrpəl], *m.* (—s, *pl.* —) gristle, cartilage.

knorplig ['knɔrplɪç], *adj.* gristly.

knorrig ['knɔrɪç], *adj.* knotty, gnarled.

Knospe ['knɔspə], *f.* (—, *pl.* —n) bud.

Knote ['kno:tə], *m.* (—n, *pl.* —n) (*fig.*) bounder; lout.

Knoten ['kno:tən], *m.* (—s, *pl.* —) knot; (*fig.*) difficulty; (*Theat.*) plot.

Knotenpunkt ['kno:tənpuŋkt], *m.* (—es, *pl.* —e) (*Railw.*) junction.

Knotenstock ['kno:tənʃtɔk], *m.* (—es, *pl.* ⁝e) knotty stick.

knotig ['kno:tɪç], *adj.* knotty, nodular.

knüllen ['knylən], *v.a.* crumple.

knüpfen ['knypfən], *v.a.* tie; knot; form (a friendship etc.).

Knüppel ['knypəl], *m.* (—s, *pl.* —) cudgel.

knurren ['knurən], *v.n.* grunt, snarl; (*fig.*) growl, grumble.

knurrig ['knurɪç], *adj.* surly, grumpy.

knusprig ['knusprɪç], *adj.* crisp, crunchy.

Knute ['knu:tə], *f.* (—, *pl.* —n) knout.

knutschen ['knu:tʃən], *v.r. sich* —, (*coll.*) cuddle; (*Am.*) neck.

Knüttel [knytəl], *m.* (—s, *pl.* —) cudgel, bludgeon.

Knüttelvers ['knytəlfɛrs], *m.* (—es, *pl.* —e) doggerel, rhyme.

Kobalt ['ko:balt], *m.* (—s, *no pl.*) cobalt.

Kobaltblau ['ko:baltblau], *n.* (—s, *no pl.*) smalt.

Koben

Koben [ˈkoːbən], *m.* (—s, *pl.* —) pig-sty.

Kober [ˈkoːbər], *m.* (—s, *pl.* —) (*dial.*) basket, hamper.

Kobold [ˈkoːbɔlt], *m.* (—(e)s, *pl.* —e) goblin, hobgoblin.

Koch [kɔx], *m.* (—es, *pl.* ⁓e) cook, chef.

kochen [ˈkɔxən], *v.a.* cook, boil. — *v.n.* boil; (*fig.*) seethe.

Kocher [ˈkɔxər], *m.* (—s, *pl.* —) boiler.

Köcher [ˈkœçər], *m.* (—s, *pl.* —) quiver.

Köchin [ˈkœçɪn], *f.* (—, *pl.* —innen) (female) cook.

Kochsalz [ˈkɔxzalts], *n.* (—es, *no pl.*) common salt.

Köder [ˈkøːdər], *m.* (—s, *no pl.*) bait, lure; (*fig.*) decoy.

ködern [ˈkøːdərn], *v.a.* bait; (*fig.*) decoy.

Kodex [ˈkoːdeks], *m.* (—es, *pl.* —e) codex; old MS.; (*Law*) code.

kodifizieren [kodifiˈtsiːrən], *v.a.* codify.

Koffein [kɔfɛˈiːn], *n.* (—s, *no pl.*) caffeine.

Koffer [ˈkɔfər], *m.* (—s, *pl.* —) box, trunk, suitcase, portmanteau.

Kofferradio [ˈkɔfərraːdjo], *n.* (—s, *pl.* —s) portable radio.

Kofferraum [ˈkɔfərraum], *m.* (—s, *no pl.*) (*Motor.*) boot, (*Am.*) trunk.

Kohl [koːl], *m.* (—s, *no pl.*) (*Bot.*) cabbage; (*fig.*) nonsense, rot.

Kohle [ˈkoːlə], *f.* (—, *pl.* —n) coal.

Kohlenflöz [ˈkoːlənføːts], *n.* (—es, *pl.* —e) coal-seam.

Kohlenoxyd [ˈkoːlənɔksyːt], *n.* (—s, *no pl.*) carbon monoxide.

Kohlensäure [ˈkoːlənzɔyrə], *f.* (—, *no pl.*) carbolic acid.

Kohlenstift [ˈkoːlənʃtɪft], *m.* (—es, *pl.* —e) charcoal-crayon.

Köhler [ˈkøːlər], *m.* (—s, *pl.* —) charcoal-burner.

Koje [ˈkoːjə], *f.* (—, *pl.* —n) (*Naut.*) berth, bunk.

Kokarde [koˈkardə], *f.* (—, *pl.* —n) cockade.

kokett [koˈket], *adj.* coquettish.

Kokette [koˈketə], *f.* (—, *pl.* —n) coquette, flirt.

kokettieren [kokeˈtiːrən], *v.n.* flirt.

Kokon [koˈkɔ̃], *m.* (—s, *pl.* —s) cocoon.

Kokosnuß [ˈkoːkosnus], *f.* (—, *pl.* ⁓sse) (*Bot.*) coconut.

Koks [koːks], *m.* (—es, *no pl.*) coke.

Kolben [ˈkɔlbən], *m.* (—s, *pl.* —) club; (*rifle*) butt-end; (*engine*) piston; (*Chem.*) retort.

Kolbenstange [ˈkɔlbənʃtaŋə], *f.* (—, *pl.* —n) piston-rod.

Kolibri [ˈkoːlibriː], *m.* (—s, *pl.* —s) (*Orn.*) humming-bird.

Kolkrabe [ˈkɔlkraːbə], *m.* (—n, *pl.* —n) (*Orn.*) raven.

Kolleg [kɔˈleːk], *n.* (—s, *pl.* —ien) course of lectures; lecture.

Kollege [kɔˈleːɡə], *m.* (—n, *pl.* —n) colleague.

Kollekte [kɔˈlɛktə], *f.* (—, *pl.* —n) collection; (*Eccl.*) collect.

Koller [ˈkɔlər], *m.* (—s, *no pl.*) frenzy, rage.

kollidieren [kɔliˈdiːrən], *v.n.* collide.

Köln [kœln], *n.* Cologne.

kölnisch [ˈkœlnɪʃ], *adj.* of Cologne; —*Wasser*, eau de Cologne.

kolonisieren [koloniˈziːrən], *v.a.* colonise.

Kolonnade [koloˈnaːdə], *f.* (— *pl.* —n) colonnade.

Koloratur [koloraˈtuːr], *f.* (—, *pl.* —n) coloratura.

kolorieren [koloˈriːrən], *v.a.* colour.

Koloß [koˈlɔs], *m.* (—sses, *pl.* —sse) colossus.

Kolportage [kɔlpɔrˈtaːʒə], *f.* (—, *pl.* —n) colportage, door-to-door sale of books; sensationalism.

Kolportageroman [kɔlpɔrˈtaːʒəromaːn], *m.* (—s, *pl.* —e) penny dreadful, shocker.

kolportieren [kɔlpɔrˈtiːrən], *v.a.* hawk; spread, disseminate.

Kombinationsgabe [kɔmbinaˈtsjoːnsɡaːbə], *f.* (—, *pl.* —en) power of deduction.

kombinieren [kɔmbiˈniːrən], *v.a.* combine; deduce.

Kombüse [kɔmˈbyːzə], *f.* (— *pl.* —n) galley, caboose.

Komik [ˈkoːmɪk], *f.* (—, *no pl.*) comicality; humour; funny side.

Komiker [ˈkoːmɪkər], *m.* (—s, *pl.* —) comedian.

komisch [ˈkoːmɪʃ], *adj.* comical, funny; peculiar, strange, odd.

Kommandantur [kɔmandanˈtuːr], *f.* (—, *pl.* —en) commander's office; garrison headquarters.

kommandieren [kɔmanˈdiːrən], *v.a.* command.

Kommanditgesellschaft [kɔmanˈdiːtɡəzelʃaft], *f.* (—, *pl.* —en) limited partnership.

Kommando [kɔˈmando], *n.* (—s, *pl.* —s) command.

kommen [ˈkɔmən], *v.n. irr.* (*aux.* sein) come, arrive; come about; *um etwas* —, lose s.th.; *zu etwas* —, come by s.th.; *zu sich* —, come to, regain consciousness.

Kommentar [kɔmenˈtaːr], *m.* (—s, *pl.* —e) comment, commentary.

Kommers [kɔˈmers], *m.* (—es, *pl.* —e) students' festivity; drinking party.

Kommersbuch [kɔˈmersbuːx], *n.* (—es, *pl.* ⁓er) students' song-book.

kommerziell [kɔmertsˈjel], *adj.* commercial.

Kommerzienrat [kɔˈmertsjənraːt], *m.* (—s, *pl.* ⁓e) Councillor to the Chamber of Commerce.

Kommilitone [kɔmiliˈtoːnə], *m.* (—n, *pl.* —n) fellow-student.

Kommis [kɔˈmiː], *m.* (—, *pl.* —) clerk.

Kommiß [kɔˈmɪs], *m.* (—sses, *pl.* —) military fatigue-dress; (*fig.*) military service.

Kommißbrot [kɔ'mɪsbroːt], *n.* (—es, *no pl.*) (coarse) army bread.
Kommissar [kɔmɪ'saːr], *m.* (—s, *pl.* —e) commissioner.
Kommissariat [kɔmɪsar'jaːt], *n.* (—s, *pl.* —e) commissioner's office.
Kommission [kɔmɪs'joːn], *f.* (—, *pl.* —en) commission, mission, committee.
kommod [kɔ'moːd], *adj.* (*coll.*) snug, comfortable.
Kommode [kɔ'moːdə], *f.* (—, *pl.* —n) chest of drawers.
Kommune [kɔ'muːnə], *f.* (—, *pl.* —n) (*coll.*) Communist Party; Reds.
Kommunismus [kɔmu'nɪsmus], *m.* (—, *no pl.*) Communism.
kommunistisch [kɔmu'nɪstɪʃ], *adj.* Communist.
Komödiant [kɔmød'jant], *m.* (—en, *pl.* —en) comedian, player; humbug.
Komödie [kɔ'møːdjə], *f.* (—, *pl.* —n) comedy, play; make-believe; — *spielen*, (*fig.*) sham, pretend, play-act.
Kompagnon ['kɔmpanjõ], *m.* (—s, *pl.* —s) partner, associate.
Kompanie [kɔmpa'niː], *f.* (—, *pl.* —n) (*Mil.*) company; (*Comm.*) partnership, company.
Kompaß ['kɔmpas], *m.* (—sses, *pl.* —sse) compass.
Kompaßrose ['kɔmpasroːzə], *f.* (—, *pl.* —n) compass-card.
kompensieren [kɔmpɛn'ziːrən], *v.a.* compensate.
komplementär [kɔmpləmɛn'tɛːr], *adj.* complementary.
komplett [kɔm'plɛt], *adj.* complete.
komplimentieren [kɔmplimɛn'tiːrən], *v.a.* compliment, flatter.
Komplize [kɔm'pliːtsə], *m.* (—n, *pl.* —n) accomplice.
kompliziert [kɔmpli'tsiːrt], *adj.* complicated.
Komplott [kɔm'plɔt], *n.* (—s, *pl.* —e) plot, conspiracy.
Komponente [kɔmpo'nɛntə], *f.* (—, *pl.* —n) component part; constituent.
komponieren [kɔmpo'niːrən], *v.a.* compose, set to music.
Komponist [kɔmpo'nɪst], *m.* (—en, *pl.* —en) composer.
Kompositum [kɔm'poːzɪtum], *n.* (—s, *pl.* —ta) (*Gram.*) compound word.
Kompott [kɔm'pɔt], *n.* (—s, *pl.* —e) stewed fruit, compote; sweet, dessert.
Kompresse [kɔm'prɛsə], *f.* (—, *pl.* —n) compress.
komprimieren [kɔmpri'miːrən], *v.a.* compress.
Kompromiß [kɔmpro'mɪs], *m.* (—sses, *pl.* —sse) compromise, settlement.
kompromittieren [kɔmpromɪ'tiːrən], *v.a.* compromise. — *v.r. sich* —, compromise o.s.
kondensieren [kɔndɛn'ziːrən], *v.a.* condense.
Konditor [kɔn'diːtɔr], *m.* (—s, *pl.* —en) confectioner, pastry-cook.

Konditorei [kɔnditɔ'raɪ], *f.* (—, *pl.* —en) confectioner's shop, pastry-shop; café.
kondolieren [kɔndo'liːrən], *v.n.* condole with s.o.
Kondukteur [kɔnduk'tøːr], *m.* (—s, *pl.* —e) (*Swiss & Austr. dial.*) guard (on train), conductor (on tram *or* bus).
Konfekt [kɔn'fɛkt], *n.* (—s, *pl.* —e) chocolates; (*Am.*) candy.
Konfektion [kɔnfɛk'tsjoːn], *f.* (—, *no pl.*) ready-made clothes; outfitting.
Konfektionär [kɔnfɛktsjo'nɛːr], *m.* (—s, *pl.* —e) outfitter.
Konferenz [kɔnfe'rɛnts], *f.* (—, *pl.* —en) conference.
konfessionell [kɔnfɛsjo'nɛl], *adj.* denominational, confessional.
Konfirmand [kɔnfɪr'mant], *m.* (—en, *pl.* —en) confirmation candidate.
konfirmieren [kɔnfɪr'miːrən], *v.a.* (*Eccl.*) confirm.
konfiszieren [kɔnfɪs'tsiːrən], *v.a.* confiscate.
Konfitüren [kɔnfi'tyːrən], *f. pl.* confectionery, candied fruit, preserves.
konform [kɔn'fɔrm], *adj.* in comformity (with).
konfus [kɔn'fuːs], *adj.* confused, puzzled, disconcerted.
Kongo ['kɔŋgo], *m.* Congo.
Kongruenz [kɔŋgru'ɛnts], *f.* (—, *no pl.*) congruity.
König ['køːnɪç], *m.* (—s, *pl.* —e) king.
Königin ['køːnɪgɪn], *f.* (—, *pl.* —nen) queen.
königlich ['køːnɪglɪç], *adj.* royal, regal, kingly, king-like.
Königreich ['køːnɪçraɪç], *n.* (—(e)s, *pl.* —e) kingdom.
Königsadler ['køːnɪçsaːdlər], *m.* (—s, *pl.* —) golden eagle.
Königsschlange ['køːnɪçsʃlaŋə], *f.* (—, *pl.* —n) (*Zool.*) boa constrictor.
Königstiger ['køːnɪçstiːgər], *m.* (—s, *pl.* —) (*Zool.*) Bengal tiger.
Königtum ['køːnɪçtuːm], *n.* (—s, *no pl.*) kingship.
Konjunktur [kɔnjunk'tuːr], *f.* (—, *pl.* —en) state of the market, (*coll.*) boom.
Konkordat [kɔnkɔr'daːt], *n.* (—s, *pl.* —e) concordat.
konkret [kɔn'kreːt], *adj.* concrete.
Konkurrent [kɔnku'rɛnt], *m.* (—en, *pl.* —en) competitor, (business) rival.
Konkurrenz [kɔnku'rɛnts], *f.* (—, *no pl.*) competition.
konkurrieren [kɔnku'riːrən], *v.n.* compete.
Konkurs [kɔn'kurs], *m.* (—es, *pl.* —e) bankruptcy.
Konkursmasse [kɔn'kursmasə], *f.* (—, *pl.* —n) bankrupt's estate, bankrupt's stock.
Können ['kœnən], *n.* (—s, *no pl.*) ability; knowledge.
können ['kœnən], *v.a., v.n. irr.* be able to, be capable of; understand; *ich kann*, I can; *er kann Englisch*, he speaks English.

konsequent

konsequent [kɔnze'kvɛnt], *adj.* consistent.

Konsequenz [kɔnze'kvɛnts], *f.* (—, *pl.* —en) (*characteristic*) consistency; (*result*) consequence.

Konservatorium [kɔnzɛrva'to:rjum], *n.* (—s, *pl.* —rien) (*Mus.*) conservatoire, conservatorium.

Konserve [kɔn'zɛrvə], *f.* (—, *pl.* —n) preserve; tinned, *or* (*Am.*) canned food.

konservieren [kɔnzɛr'vi:rən], *v.a.* preserve.

Konsistorium [kɔnzɪs'to:rjum], *n.* (—s, *pl.* —rien) (*Eccl.*) consistory.

Konsole [kɔn'zo:lə], *f.* (—, *pl.* —n) bracket.

konsolidieren [kɔnzoli'di:rən], *v.a.* consolidate.

Konsonant [kɔnzo'nant], *m.* (—en, *pl.* —en) (*Phonet.*) consonant.

Konsorte [kɔn'zɔrtə], *m.* (—n, *pl.* —n) associate, accomplice.

Konsortium [kɔn'zɔrtsjum], *n.* (—s, *pl.* —tien) syndicate.

konstatieren [kɔnsta'ti:rən], *v.a.* state, note, assert.

konsternieren [kɔnstɛr'ni:rən], *v.a.* dismay, disconcert.

konstituieren [kɔnstitu'i:rən], *v.a.* constitute.

konstitutionell [kɔnstitutsjo'nɛl], *adj.* constitutional.

konstruieren [kɔnstru'i:rən], *v.a.* construct; (*Gram.*) construe.

konsularisch [kɔnzu'la:rɪʃ], *adj.* consular.

Konsulat [kɔnzu'la:t], *n.* (—s, *pl.* —e) consulate.

Konsulent [kɔnzu'lɛnt], *m.* (—en, *pl.* —en) (*Law*) counsel; consultant.

konsultieren [kɔnzul'ti:rən], *v.a.* consult.

Konsum [kɔn'zu:m], *m.* (—s, *no pl.*) (*Econ.*) consumption.

Konsumverein [kɔn'zu:mfɛraɪn], *m.* (—s, *pl.* —e) cooperative society.

konsumieren [kɔnzu'mi:rən], *v.a.* consume.

Konterbande [kɔntər'bandə], *f.* (—, *no pl.*) contraband.

Konterfei [kɔntər'faɪ], *n.* (—s, *pl.* —e) (*obs.*) portrait, likeness.

Kontertanz ['kɔntərtants], *m.* (—es, *pl.* ̈e) square dance, quadrille.

kontinuierlich [kɔntinu'i:rlɪç], *adj.* continuous.

Kontinuität [kɔntinui'tɛ:t], *f.* (—, *no pl.*) continuity.

Konto ['kɔnto], *n.* (—s, *pl.* —ten) (*bank*) account; à —, on account.

Kontokorrent [kɔntoko'rɛnt], *n.* (—s, *pl.* —e) current account.

Kontor [kɔn'to:r], *n.* (—s, *pl.* —e) (*obs.*) office.

Kontorist [kɔnto'rɪst], *m.* (—en, *pl.* —en) clerk.

Kontrabaß ['kɔntrabas], *m.* (—sses, *pl.* ̈sse) double-bass.

Kontrapunkt ['kɔntrapuŋkt], *m.* (—es, *pl.* —e) (*Mus.*) counterpoint.

kontrastieren [kɔntras'ti:rən], *v.a.*, *v.n.* contrast.

kontrollieren [kɔntro'li:rən], *v.a.* check, verify.

Kontroverse [kɔntro'vɛrzə], *f.* (—, *pl.* —n) controversy.

Kontur [kɔn'tu:r], *f.* (—, *pl.* —en) outline, (*pl.*) contours.

Konvent [kɔn'vɛnt], *m.* (—s, *pl.* —e) convention, assembly, congress.

konventionell [kɔnvɛntsjo'nɛl], *adj.* conventional, formal.

Konversationslexikon [kɔnvɛrza-'tsjo:nslɛksɪkɔn], *n.* (—s, *pl.* —s) encyclopaedia.

konvertieren [kɔnvɛr'ti:rən], *v.a.*, *v.n.* convert.

Konvertit [kɔnvɛr'tɪt], *m.* (—en, *pl.* —en) convert.

Konvolut [kɔnvo'lu:t], *n.* (—s, *pl.* —e) bundle; scroll.

konvulsivisch [kɔnvul'zi:vɪʃ], *adj.* convulsive.

konzentrieren [kɔntsɛn'tri:rən], *v.a.*, *v.r.* concentrate; *auf etwas* —, centre upon.

konzentrisch [kɔn'tsɛntrɪʃ], *adj.* concentric.

Konzept [kɔn'tsɛpt], *n.* (—es, *pl.* —e) rough draft, sketch; *aus dem* — *bringen*, unsettle, disconcert.

Konzeptpapier [kɔn'tsɛptpapi:r], *n.* (—s, *no pl.*) scribbling paper.

Konzern [kɔn'tsɛrn], *m.* (—s, *pl.* —e) (*Comm.*) combine.

Konzert [kɔn'tsɛrt], *n.* (—es, *pl.* —e) concert, (*musical*) recital.

Konzertflügel [kɔn'tsɛrtfly:gəl], *m.* (—s, *pl.* —) grand piano.

konzertieren [kɔntsɛr'ti:rən], *v.n.* give recitals; play in a concert.

Konzertmeister [kɔn'tsɛrtmaɪstər], *m.* (—s, *pl.* —) impresario.

Konzession [kɔntse'sjo:n], *f.* (—, *pl.* —en) concession, licence.

konzessionieren [kɔntsesjo'ni:rən], *v.a.* license.

Konzil [kɔn'tsi:l], *n.* (—s, *pl.* —ien) (*Eccl.*) council.

konzipieren [kɔntsi'pi:rən], *v.a.* draft, plan.

Koordinierung [ko:ɔrdi'ni:ruŋ], *f.* (—, *pl.* —en) co-ordination.

Kopf [kɔpf], *m.* (—es, *pl.* ̈e) head; top; heading; (*fig.*) mind, brains, judgment; *aus dem* —, by heart.

köpfen ['kœpfən], *v.a.* behead, decapitate; (*Bot.*) lop.

Kopfhaut ['kɔpfhaut], *f.* (—, *no pl.*) scalp.

Kopfhörer ['kɔpfhø:rər], *m.* (—s, *pl.* —) headphone, receiver.

Kopfkissen ['kɔpfkɪsən], *n.* (—s, *pl.* —) pillow.

Kopfsalat ['kɔpfzala:t], *m.* (—s, *pl.* —e) (*garden*) lettuce.

kopfscheu ['kɔpfʃɔy], *adj.* afraid; alarmed, timid; — *machen*, scare; — *werden*, take fright, jib.

Kopfschmerz ['kɔpfʃmɛrts], *m.* (**—es**, *pl.* **—en**) (*mostly pl.*) headache.

Kopfsprung ['kɔpfʃpruŋ], *m.* (**—s**, *pl.* ∵e) (*diving*) header.

kopfüber [kɔpf'y:bər], *adv.* head over heels; headlong.

Kopfweh ['kɔpfve:], *n.* (**—s**, *no pl.*) headache.

Kopfzerbrechen ['kɔpftsɛrbrɛçən], *n.* (**—s**, *no pl.*) racking o.'s brains.

Kopie [ko'pi:] *f.* (**—**, *pl.* **—n**) copy, duplicate.

kopieren [ko'pi:rən], *v.a.* copy, ape, mimic, take off.

Koppe ['kɔpə], *f. see* **Kuppe**.

Koppel ['kɔpəl], *f.* (**—**, *pl.* **—n**) (*dogs*) couple, leash; (*ground*) enclosure, paddock.

koppeln ['kɔpəln], *v.a.* couple, leash.

kopulieren [kopu'li:rən], *v.a.* (*obs.*) marry; pair; (*Hort.*) graft.

Koralle [ko'ralə], *f.* (**—**, *pl.* **—n**) coral.

Korallenriff [ko'ralənrɪf], *n.* (**—es**, *pl.* **—e**) coral-reef.

Korb [kɔrp], *m.* (**—s**, *pl.* ∵e) basket, hamper; *einen — geben*, turn s.o. down, refuse an offer of marriage.

Korbweide ['kɔrpvaɪdə], *f.* (**—**, *pl.* **—n**) (*Bot.*) osier.

Kord [kɔrt], *m.* (**—s**, *no pl.*) corduroy.

Kordel ['kɔrdəl], *f.* (**—**, *pl.* **—n**) cord, twine, thread.

Korea [ko're:a], *n.* Korea.

Korinthe [ko'rɪntə], *f.* (**—**, *pl.* **—n**) (*Bot.*) currant.

Korken ['kɔrkən], *m.* (**—s**, *pl.* **—**) cork, stopper.

Korkenzieher ['kɔrkəntsi:ər], *m.* (**—s**, *pl.* **—**) cork-screw.

Korn [kɔrn], *n.* (**—s**, *pl.* **—e**, ∵er) (*Bot.*) corn, grain, cereal, rye; (*gun*) sight, *aufs — nehmen*, take aim at.

Kornblume ['kɔrnblu:mə], *f.* (**—**, *pl.* **—n**) (*Bot.*) corn-flower.

Kornbranntwein ['kɔrnbrantvaɪn], *m.* (**—s**, *no pl.*) corn-brandy, whisky.

Kornett [kɔr'nɛt], *m.* (**—s**, *pl.* **—e**) (*Mil.*, *Mus.*) cornet.

körnig ['kœrnɪç], *adj.* granular, granulous; grained.

Kornrade ['kɔrnra:də], *f.* (**—**, *pl.* **—n**) (*Bot.*) corn-cockle.

Kornspeicher ['kɔrnʃpaɪçər], *m.* (**—s**, *pl.* **—**) granary, corn-loft.

Körper ['kœrpər], *m.* (**—s**, *pl.* **—**) body; (*Phys.*) solid.

Körperbau ['kœrpərbau], *m.* (**—s**, *no pl.*) build, frame.

Körpergeruch ['kœrpərgəru:x], *m.* (**—s**, *no pl.*) body odour.

körperlich ['kœrpərlɪç], *adj.* bodily, physical; *—e Züchtigung*, corporal punishment.

Körpermaß ['kœrpəra:s], *n.* (**—es**, *pl.* **—e**) cubic measure.

Körperschaft ['kœrpərʃaft], *f.* (**—**, *pl.* **—en**) corporation.

Korps [ko:r], *n.* (**—**, *pl.* **—**) (*Mil.*) corps; students' corporation.

Korrektheit [kɔ'rɛkthaɪt], *f.* (**—**, *no pl.*) correctness.

Korrektionsanstalt [kɔrɛk'tsjo:nsan-ʃtalt], *f.* (**—**, *pl.* **—en**) penitentiary, Borstal institution.

Korrektor [kɔ'rɛktor], *m.* (**—s**, *pl.* **—en**) proof-reader.

Korrektur [kɔrɛk'tu:r], *f.* (**—**, *pl.* **—en**) correction; proof-correction; revision.

Korrekturbogen [kɔrɛk'tu:rbo:gən], *m.* (**—s**, *pl.*) (*Typ.*) proof-sheet, galley.

Korrespondenzkarte [kɔrɛspɔn'dɛnts-kartə], *f.* (**—**, *pl.* **—n**) post-card.

korrigieren [kɔri'gi:rən], *v.a.* correct, revise; read (proofs).

Korsett [kɔr'zɛt], *n.* (**—s**, *pl.* **—s**) corset, bodice, stays.

Koryphäe [kɔri'fɛ:ə], *m.* (**—n**, *pl.* **—n**) celebrity, authority, master mind.

Koseform ['ko:zəfɔrm], *f.* (**—**, *pl.* **—en**) term of endearment, pet-name, diminutive.

kosen ['ko:zən], *v.a.*, *v.n.* caress, fondle; make love (to).

Kosinus ['ko:zinus], *m.* (**—**, *pl.* **—**) (*Maths.*) cosine.

Kosmetik [kɔs'me:tɪk], *f.* (**—**, *no pl.*) cosmetics.

kosmetisch [kɔs'me:tɪʃ], *adj.* cosmetic.

kosmisch ['kɔzmɪʃ], *adj.* cosmic.

Kosmopolit [kɔsmopo'li:t], *m.* (**—en**, *pl.* **—en**) cosmopolitan.

kosmopolitisch [kɔsmopo'li:tɪʃ], *adj.* cosmopolitan.

Kost [kɔst], *f.* (**—**, *no pl.*) food, fare; board.

Kostarika [kɔsta'rika], *n.* Costa Rica.

kostbar ['kɔstba:r], *adj.* valuable, precious, costly.

Kostbarkeit ['kɔstba:rkaɪt], *f.* (**—**, *pl.* **—en**) costliness, preciousness; (*pl.*) (*goods*) valuables.

Kosten ['kɔstən], *pl.* cost(s), expenses, charges; (*Law*) costs.

kosten ['kɔstən], *v.a.* taste; (*money*) cost; take, require; *was kostet das?* how much is this?

Kosten(vor)anschlag ['kɔstən(for)an-ʃla:k], *m.* (**—s**, *pl.* **—e**) estimate.

Kostenaufwand ['kɔstənaufvant], *m.* (**—s**, *pl.* **—e**) expenditure.

Kostenersatz ['kɔstənerzats], *m.* (**—s**, *no pl.*) refund of expenses, compensation.

kostenfrei ['kɔstənfraɪ], *adj.* free (of charge), gratis.

kostenlos ['kɔstənlo:s], *see* **kostenfrei**.

Kostgänger ['kɔstgɛŋər], *m.* (**—s**, *pl.* **—**) boarder.

Kostgeld ['kɔstgɛlt], *n.* (**—es**, *no pl.*) maintenance or board allowance.

köstlich ['kœstlɪç], *adj.* excellent, precious; delicious; *ein —er Witz*, a capital joke.

kostspielig ['kɔstʃpi:lɪç], *adj.* expensive, costly.

Kostüm [kɔ'sty:m], *n.* (**—s**, *pl.* **—e**) costume; fancy dress.

Kostümfest [kɔ'sty:mfɛst], *n.* (**—s**, *pl.* **—e**) fancy-dress ball.

129

kostümieren [kɔsty'miːrən], *v.a.* dress up.

Kot [koːt], *m.* (**—es**, *no pl.*) mud, dirt; filth, mire; excrement.

Kotelett [kɔt'lɛt], *n.* (**—s,** *pl.* **—s**) cutlet.

Köter ['køːtər], *m.* (**—s,** *pl.* **—**) cur, mongrel.

Koterie [koːtə'riː], *f.* (**—,** *pl.* **—n**) clique, set, coterie.

Kotflügel ['koːtflyːgəl], *m.* (**—s,** *pl.* **—**) (*Motor.*) mudguard.

kotig ['koːtɪç], *adj.* dirty, miry.

kotzen ['kɔtsən], *v.n.* (*vulg.*) vomit.

Koweit ['koːvaɪt], *n.* Kuwait.

Krabbe ['krabə], *f.* (**—,** *pl.* **—n**) (*Zool.*) crab; shrimp; (*fig.*) brat, imp.

krabbeln ['krabəln], *v.n.* crawl.

Krach [krax], *m.* (**—es,** *pl.* **—e**) crack, crash; din, noise; (*Comm.*) slump; quarrel, row.

krachen ['kraxən], *v.n.* crack, crash.

krächzen ['krɛçtsən], *v.n.* croak.

Kraft [kraft], *f.* (**—,** *pl.* **⸚e**) strength, vigour; force; power, energy; intensity; *in — treten*, come into force.

kraft [kraft], *prep.* (*Genit.*) by virtue of, by authority of, on the strength of.

Kraftausdruck ['kraftausdruk], *m.* (**—s,** *pl.* **⸚e**) forcible expression; expletive.

Kraftbrühe ['kraftbryːə], *f.* (**—,** *pl.* **—n**) meat-soup, beef-tea.

Kraftfahrer ['kraftfaːrər], *m.* (**—s,** *pl.* **—**) motorist.

kräftig ['krɛftɪç], *adj.* strong, powerful, vigorous, energetic; (*food*) nourishing.

Kraftlehre ['kraftleːrə], *f.* (**—,** *no pl.*) dynamics.

kraftlos ['kraftloːs], *adj.* weak, feeble.

Kraftwagen ['kraftvaːgən], *m.* (**—s,** *pl.* **—**) motor car, automobile, car, lorry, truck.

Kragen ['kraːgən], *m.* (**—s,** *pl.* **—**) collar; *es geht mir an den —*, it will cost me dearly.

Krähe ['krɛːə], *f.* (**—,** *pl.* **—n**) (*Orn.*) crow.

krähen ['krɛːən], *v.n.* crow.

Krähenfüße ['krɛːənfyːsə], *m. pl.* crow's feet (wrinkles).

Krakau ['kraːkau], *n.* Cracow.

krakeelen [kra'keːlən], *v.n.* (*coll.*) kick up a row.

Kralle ['kralə], *f.* (**—,** *pl.* **—n**) claw, talon.

Kram [kraːm], *m.* (**—s,** *no pl.*) small wares (trade); stuff, rubbish, litter; *es paßt mir nicht in den —*, it does not suit my purpose.

kramen ['kraːmən], *v.n.* rummage.

Krämer ['krɛːmər], *m.* (**—s,** *pl.* **—**) retailer, general dealer, shopkeeper.

Kramladen ['kraːmlaːdən], *m.* (**—s,** *pl.* **⸚**) small retail-shop, general shop *or* store.

Krampe ['krampə], *f.* (**—,** *pl.* **—n**) staple.

Krampf [krampf], *m.* (**—es,** *pl.* **⸚**) cramp, spasm, convulsion.

Krampfader ['krampfaːdər], *f.* (**—,** *pl.* **—n**) varicose vein.

krampfartig ['krampfaːrtɪç], *adj.* spasmodic.

krampfhaft ['krampfhaft], *adj.* convulsive.

Kran [kraːn], *m.* (**—s,** *pl.* **⸚e**) (*Engin.*) crane.

Kranich ['kraːnɪç], *m.* (**—s,** *pl.* **—e**) (*Orn.*) crane.

krank [kraŋk], *adj.* sick, ill.

kränkeln ['krɛŋkəln], *v.n.* be ailing, be in poor health.

kranken ['kraŋkən], *v.n. an etwas —*, suffer from s.th., be afflicted with s.th.

kränken ['krɛŋkən], *v.a.* vex, grieve, offend, insult.

Krankenbahre ['kraŋkənbaːrə], *f.* (**—,** *pl.* **—n**) stretcher.

Krankenhaus ['kraŋkənhaus], *n.* (**—es,** *pl.* **⸚er**) hospital.

Krankenkasse ['kraŋkənkasə], *f.* (**—,** *pl.* **—n**) sick-fund; health insurance.

Krankenkost ['kraŋkənkɔst], *f.* (**—,** *no pl.*) invalid diet.

Krankenschwester ['kraŋkənʃvɛstər], *f.* (**—,** *pl.* **—n**) nurse.

Krankenstuhl ['kraŋkənʃtuːl], *m.* (**—s,** *pl.* **⸚e**) invalid chair.

Krankenversicherung ['kraŋkənfɛrzɪçəruŋ], *f.* (**—,** *pl* **—en**) health insurance.

Krankenwärter ['kraŋkənvɛrtər], *m.* (**—s,** *pl.* **—**) attendant, male nurse.

krankhaft ['kraŋkhaft], *adj.* morbid.

Krankheit ['kraŋkhaɪt], *f.* (**—,** *pl.* **—en**) illness, sickness, disease, malady; complaint; *englische —*, rickets.

Krankheitserscheinung ['kraŋkhaɪtsɛrʃaɪnuŋ], *f.* (**—,** *pl.* **—en**) symptom.

kränklich ['krɛŋklɪç], *adj.* sickly, infirm, in poor health.

Kränkung ['krɛŋkuŋ], *f.* (**—,** *pl.* **—en**) grievance, annoyance; offence, insult.

Kranz [krants], *m.* (**—es,** *pl.* **⸚e**) wreath, garland.

Kränzchen ['krɛntsçən], *n.* (**—s,** *pl.* **—**) little garland; (*fig.*) (ladies') weekly tea party; circle, club.

kränzen ['krɛntsən], *v.a.* garland, wreathe.

Krapfen ['krapfən], *m.* (**—s,** *pl.* **—**) doughnut.

kraß [kras], *adj.* crass, crude.

Krater ['kraːtər], *m.* (**—s,** *pl.* **—**) crater.

Kratzbürste ['kratsbyrstə], *f.* (**—,** *pl.* **—n**) scraper; (*fig.*) cross-patch, irritable person.

Krätze ['krɛtsə], *f.* (**—,** *no pl.*) (*Med.*) scabies, itch, mange.

kratzen ['kratsən], *v.a., v.n.* scratch, scrape, itch.

krauen ['krauən], *v.a.* scratch softly.

kraus [kraus], *adj.* frizzy, curly; crisp, fuzzy; creased; (*fig.*) abstruse; *die Stirn — ziehen*, frown, knit o.'s brow.

Krause ['krauzə], *f.* (**—,** *pl.* **—n**) ruff.

kräuseln ['krɔyzəln], *v.a., v.r.* crisp, curl; ripple.

Krauskohl ['krauskoːl], *m.* (**—s,** *no pl.*) Savoy cabbage.

Kraut [kraut], *n.* (—es, *pl.* ¨er) herb; plant; (*dial.*) cabbage; ·wie — und *Rüben*, higgledy-piggledy.

krautartig ['krauta:rtıç], *adj.* herbaceous.

Kräuterkäse ['krɔytərke:zə], *m.* (—s, *pl.* —) green cheese.

Kräutertee ['krɔytərte:], *m.* (—s, *no pl.*) herb-tea, infusion of herbs.

Krawall [kra'val], *m.* (—s, *pl.* —e) (*coll.*) row, uproar; shindy.

Krawatte [kra'vatə], *f.* (—, *pl.* —n) cravat, tie.

kraxeln ['kraksəln], *v.n.* (*coll.*) climb, clamber.

Krebs [kre:ps], *m.* (—es, *pl.* —e) (*Zool.*) crayfish, crab; (*Med.*) cancer, carcinoma; (*Geog.*) Tropic of Cancer.

krebsartig ['kre:psa:rtıç], *adj.* cancerous.

Krebsbutter ['kre:psbutər], *f.* (—, *no pl.*) crab-cheese.

Krebsgang ['kre:psgaŋ], *m.* (—es, *no pl.*) crab's walk, sidling; *den — gehen*, retrograde, decline.

Krebsschaden ['kre:psʃa:dən], *m.* (—s, *pl.* ¨-) cancerous sore *or* affection; (*fig.*) canker, inveterate evil.

Kredenz [kre'dɛnts], *f.* (—, *pl.* —en) buffet, serving table, sideboard.

kredenzen [kre'dɛntsən], *v.a.* taste (*wine*); (*obs.*) present, offer.

kreditieren [kredi'ti:rən], *v.a.* *einem etwas* —, credit s.o. with s.th.

Kreide ['kraıdə], *f.* (—, *pl.* —n) chalk; (*Art*) crayon.

kreieren [kre'i:rən], *v.a.* create.

Kreis [kraıs], *m.* (—es, *pl.* —e) circle; (*Astron.*) orbit; district; range; sphere.

Kreisabschnitt ['kraısapʃnıt], *m.* (—s, *pl.* —e) segment.

Kreisausschnitt ['kraısausʃnıt], *m.* (—s, *pl.* —e) sector.

Kreisbogen ['kraısbo:gən], *m.* (—s, *pl.* ¨) arc.

kreischen ['kraıʃən], *v.n.* scream, shriek.

Kreisel ['kraızəl], *m.* (—s, *pl.* —) (*toy*) (spinning) top; gyroscope.

kreisen ['kraızən], *v.n.* circle, revolve; circulate.

Kreislauf ['kraıslauf], *m.* (—es, *pl.* ¨e) circular course; (*Astron.*) orbit; (*blood*) circulation.

kreißen ['kraısən], *v.n.* (*Med.*) be in labour.

Kreisstadt ['kraısʃtat], *f.* (—, *pl.* ¨e) county town.

Kreisumfang ['kraısumfaŋ], *m.* (—s, *pl.* ¨e) circumference.

Kreml ['krɛml], *m.* (—s, *no pl.*) the Kremlin.

Krempe ['krɛmpə], *f.* (—, *pl.* —n) (*hat*) brim.

Krempel ['krɛmpəl], *m.* (—s, *no pl.*) (*coll.*) refuse, rubbish; stuff.

Kren [kre:n], *m.* (—s, *no pl.*) (*Austr.*) horse-radish.

krepieren [kre'pi:rən], *v.n.* (*aux.* sein) (*animals*) die; (*humans*) (*coll.*) perish miserably; explode.

Krepp [krɛp], *m.* (—s, *no pl.*) crape, crêpe.

Kresse ['krɛsə], *f.* (—, *pl.* —n) cress.

Kreta ['kre:ta], *n.* Crete.

Kreuz [krɔyts], *n.* (—es, *pl.* —e) cross, crucifix; (*Anat.*) small of the back; (*fig.*) calamity; affliction; *kreuz und quer*, in all directions.

Kreuzband ['krɔytsbant], *n.* (—es, *pl.* ¨er) wrapper (for printed matter).

kreuzbrav ['krɔytsbra:f], *adj.* as good as gold.

kreuzen ['krɔytsən], *v.a.* cross. — *v.r. sich* —, make the sign of the cross.

Kreuzfahrer ['krɔytsfa:rər], *m.* (—s, *pl.* —) crusader.

kreuzfidel ['krɔytsfide:l], *adj.* jolly, merry, as merry as a cricket.

Kreuzgang ['krɔytsgaŋ], *m.* (—es, *pl.* ¨e) cloisters.

kreuzigen ['krɔytsıgən], *v.a.* crucify.

Kreuzritter ['krɔıtsrıtər], *m.* (—s, *pl.* —) Knight of the Cross; crusader.

Kreuzschmerzen ['krɔytsʃmɛrtsən], *m. pl.* lumbago.

Kreuzstich ['krɔytsʃtıç], *m.* (—es, *no pl.*) (*Embroidery*) cross-stitch.

Kreuzung ['krɔytsuŋ], *f.* (—, *pl.* —en) (*road*) crossing; (*animals*) cross-breeding.

Kreuzverhör ['krɔytsferhø:r], *n.* (—s, *pl.* —e) cross-examination.

Kreuzweg ['krɔytsve:k], *m.* (—s, *pl.* —e) crossroads; (*Eccl.*) Stations of the Cross.

Kreuzworträtsel ['krɔytsvɔrtrɛ:tsəl], *n.* (—s, *pl.* —) crossword-puzzle.

Kreuzzug ['krɔytstsu:k], *m.* (—es, *pl.* ¨e) crusade.

kriechen ['kri:çən], *v.n. irr.* (*aux.* sein) creep, crawl; (*fig.*) cringe, fawn.

kriecherisch ['kri:çərıʃ], *adj.* fawning, cringing.

Kriechtier ['kri:çti:r], *n.* (—s, *pl.* —e) reptile.

Krieg [kri:k], *m.* (—es, *pl.* —e) war.

kriegen ['kri:gən], *v.a.* get, obtain.

Krieger ['kri:gər], *m.* (—s, *pl.* —) warrior.

kriegerisch ['kri:gərıʃ], *adj.* warlike, martial.

kriegführend ['kri:kfy:rənt], *adj.* belligerent.

Kriegsfuß ['kri:ksfu:s], *m.* (—es, *no pl.*) *auf* —, at logger-heads.

Kriegsgewinnler ['kri:ksgəvınlər], *m.* (—s, *pl.* —) war-profiteer.

Kriegslist ['kri:kslıst], *f.* (—, *pl.* —en) stratagem.

Kriegsschauplatz ['kri:ksʃauplats], *m.* (—es, *pl.* ¨e) theatre of war.

Kriegsschiff ['kri:ksʃif], *n.* (—es, *pl.* —e) man-of-war, warship.

Kriegswesen ['kri:ksve:zən], *n.* (—s, *no pl.*) military affairs.

Kriegszug ['kri:kstsu:k], *m.* (—es, *pl.* ¨e) campaign.

Krim [krim], *f.* the Crimea.

Kriminalbeamte [krımi'na:lbəamtə], *m.* (—n, *pl.* —n) crime investigator.

Kriminalprozeß

Kriminalprozeß [krɪmiˈnaːlprotsɛs], *m.* (—sses, *pl.* —sse) criminal procedure *or* trial.

Krimskrams [ˈkrɪmskrams], *m.* (—, *no pl.*) whatnots, knick-knacks, medley.

Krippe [ˈkrɪpə], *f.* (—, *pl.* —n) crib, manger; crèche.

Krise [ˈkriːzə], *f.* (—, *pl.* —n) crisis.

Kristall [krɪˈstal], *m.* (—s, *pl.* —e) crystal; cut glass.

kristallartig [krɪˈstalaːrtɪç], *adj.* crystalline.

kristallisieren [krɪstaliˈziːrən], *v.a., v.n.* (*aux.* sein), crystallise.

Kristallkunde [krɪˈstalkundə], *f.* (—, *no pl.*) crystallography.

Kriterium [kriˈteːrjum], *n.* (—s, *pl.* —rien) criterion, test.

Kritik [kriˈtiːk], *f.* (—, *pl.* —en) criticism, review; *unter aller* —, extremely bad.

Kritiker [ˈkriːtɪkər], *m.* (—s, *pl.* —) critic.

kritisch [ˈkriːtɪʃ], *adj.* critical; precarious, crucial.

kritisieren [kritiˈziːrən], *v.a.* criticise; review; censure.

kritteln [ˈkrɪtəln], *v.n.* cavil (at), find fault.

Krittler [ˈkrɪtlər], *m.* (—s, *pl.* —) caviller, fault-finder.

Kritzelei [krɪtsəˈlaɪ], *f.* (—, *pl.* —en) scrawling, scribbling.

kritzeln [ˈkrɪtsəln], *v.a.* scrawl, scribble.

Kroatien [kroˈaːtsjən], *n.* Croatia.

Krokodil [krokoˈdiːl], *n.* (—s, *pl.* —e) (*Zool.*) crocodile.

Kronbewerber [ˈkroːnbevɛrbər], *m.* (—s, *pl.* —) aspirant to the crown, pretender.

Krone [ˈkroːnə], *f.* (—, *pl.* —n) crown; (*Papal*) tiara; (*fig.*) head, top, flower.

krönen [ˈkrøːnən], *v.a.* crown.

Kronerbe [ˈkroːnɛrbə], *m.* (—n, *pl.* —n) heir apparent.

Kronleuchter [ˈkroːnlɔʏçtər], *m.* (—s, *pl.* —) chandelier.

Kronsbeere [ˈkroːnsbeːrə], *f.* (—, *pl.* —n) (*Bot.*) cranberry.

Krönung [ˈkrøːnuŋ], *f.* (—, *pl.* —en) coronation.

Kropf [krɔpf], *m.* (—es, *pl.* ⸚e) (*human*) goitre, wen; (*birds*) crop, craw.

kropfartig [ˈkrɔpfaːrtɪç], *adj.* goitrous.

kröpfen [ˈkrœpfən], *v.a.* (*birds*) cram.

Kropftaube [ˈkrɔpftaubə], *f.* (—, *pl.* —n) (*Orn.*) pouter-pigeon.

Kröte [ˈkrøːtə], *f.* (—, *pl.* —n) toad. (*fig.*) frog.

Krücke [ˈkrykə], *f.* (—, *pl.* —n) crutch; (*fig.*) rake.

Krückstock [ˈkrykʃtɔk], *m.* (—s, *pl.* ⸚e) crutch.

Krug [kruːk], *m.* (—es, *pl.* ⸚e) jug, pitcher, mug; (*fig.*) pub, inn.

Krüger [ˈkryːgər], *m.* (—s, *pl.* —) pub-keeper, tapster.

Krume [ˈkruːmə], *f.* (—, *pl.* —n) crumb.

krüm(e)lig [ˈkryːm(ə)lɪç], *adj.* crumbly, crumby.

krümeln [ˈkryːmeln], *v.n.* crumble.

krumm [krum], *adj.* crooked, curved; *etwas — nehmen*, take s.th. amiss.

krummbeinig [ˈkrumbaɪnɪç], *adj.* bandy-legged.

krümmen [ˈkrymən], *v.a.* crook, bend, curve. — *v.r. sich —*, (*fig.*) writhe, cringe.

Krummholz [ˈkrumhɔlts], *n.* (—es, *no pl.*) (*Bot.*) dwarf-pine.

Krummschnabel [ˈkrumʃnaːbəl], *m.* (—s, *pl.* ⸚) (*Orn.*) curlew, crook-bill.

Krümmung [ˈkrymuŋ], *f.* (—, *pl.* —en) curve; turning, winding.

Krüppel [ˈkrypəl], *m.* (—s, *pl.* —) cripple.

krüppelhaft [ˈkrypəlhaft], *adj.* crippled, lame.

krüpp(e)lig [ˈkryp(ə)lɪç], *adj.* crippled, lame.

Kruste [ˈkrustə], *f.* (—, *pl.* —n) crust.

Kübel [ˈkyːbəl], *m.* (—s, *pl.* —) tub, bucket.

Kubikfuß [kuˈbiːkfuːs], *m.* (—es, *pl.* —) cubic foot.

Kubikinhalt [kuˈbiːkɪnhalt], *m.* (—s, *no pl.*) cubic content.

Kubismus [kuˈbɪsmus], *m.* (—, *no pl.*) cubism.

Küche [ˈkyçə], *f.* (—, *pl.* —n) (*room*) kitchen; (*food*) cooking, cookery, cuisine.

Kuchen [ˈkuːxən], *m.* (—s, *pl.* —) cake.

Küchengeschirr [ˈkyçəngəʃɪr], *n.* (—s, *no pl.*) kitchen utensils.

Küchenherd [ˈkyçənheːrt], *m.* (—es, *pl.* —e) kitchen-range.

Küchenlatein [ˈkyçənlataɪn], *n.* (—s, *no pl.*) dog-Latin.

Küchenmeister [ˈkyçənmaɪstər], *m.* (—s, *pl.* —) chef, head cook.

Küchenschrank [ˈkyçənʃraŋk], *m.* (—s, *pl.* ⸚e) dresser.

Kuchenteig [ˈkuːxəntaɪk], *m.* (—s, *pl.* —e) dough (for cake).

Küchenzettel [ˈkyçəntsɛtəl], *m.* (—s, *pl.* —) bill of fare.

Küchlein [ˈkyːçlaɪn], *n.* (—s, *pl.* —) young chicken, pullet.

Kücken [ˈkykən], *n.* (—s, *pl.* —) young chicken, pullet.

Kuckuck [ˈkukuk], *m.* (—s, *pl.* —e) (*Orn.*) cuckoo; *scher Dich zum —!* go to blazes!

Kufe [ˈkuːfə], *f.* (—, *pl.* —n) tub, vat; (*sleigh*) runner; (*cradle*) rocker.

Küfer [ˈkyːfər], *m.* (—s, *pl.* —) cooper.

Kugel [ˈkuːgəl], *f.* (—, *pl.* —n) ball, bullet, sphere; globe.

kugelfest [ˈkuːgəlfɛst], *adj.* bullet-proof.

kugelförmig [ˈkuːgəlfœrmɪç], *adj.* spherical, globular.

Kugelgelenk [ˈkuːgəlgəlɛŋk], *n.* (—s, *pl.* —e) ball and socket joint.

Kugellager [ˈkuːgəllaːgər], *n.* (—s, *pl.* —s) ball-bearing.

Kugelmaß [ˈkuːgəlmaːs], *n.* (—es, *pl.* —e) ball-calibre.

kugeln [ˈkuːgəln], *v.a.* roll; bowl.

Kugelregen ['ku:gəlre:gən], *m.* (**—s,** *no pl.*) hail of bullets.

kugelrund ['ku:gəlrunt], *adj.* round as a ball, well-fed.

Kugelschreiber ['ku:gəlʃraɪbər], *m.* (**—s,** *pl.* **—**) ball-point pen.

Kuh [ku:] *f.* (**—,** *pl.* **:e**) cow; *junge —,* heifer.

Kuhblattern ['ku:blatərn], *f. pl.* cow-pox.

Kuhblume ['ku:blu:mə], *f.* (**—,** *pl.* **—n**) (*Bot.*) marigold.

Kuhfladen ['ku:fla:dən], *m.* (**—s,** *pl.* **—**) cow-dung.

Kuhhaut ['ku:haut], *f.* (**—,** *pl.* **:e**) cow-hide; *das geht auf keine —,* that defies description.

kühl [ky:l], *adj.* cool, fresh; (*behaviour*) reserved.

Kühle ['ky:lə], *f.* (**—,** *no pl.*) coolness, freshness; (*behaviour*) reserve.

kühlen ['ky:lən], *v.a.* cool, freshen.

Kühlraum ['ky:lraum], *m.* (**—es,** *pl.* **:e**) refrigerating-chamber.

Kühlschrank ['ky:lʃraŋk], *m.* (**—s,** *pl.* **:e**) refrigerator, (*coll.*) fridge.

Kühltruhe ['ky:ltru:ə], *f.* (**—,** *pl.* **—n**) deep freeze.

Kühlung ['ky:luŋ], *f.* (**—,** *pl.* **—en**) refrigeration.

Kuhmist ['ku:mɪst], *m.* (**—s,** *no pl.*) cow-dung.

kühn [ky:n], *adj.* bold, daring, audacious.

Kühnheit ['ky:nhaɪt], *f.* (**—,** *no pl.*) boldness, daring, audacity.

Kujon [ku'jo:n], *m.* (**—s,** *pl.* **—e**) bully, scoundrel.

kujonieren [kujo'ni:rən], *v.a.* bully, exploit.

Kukuruz ['kukuruts], *m.* (**—es,** *no pl.*) (*Austr.*) maize.

kulant [ku'lant], *adj.* obliging; (*terms*) easy.

Kulanz [ku'lants], *f.* (**—,** *no pl.*) accommodating manner.

Kuli ['ku:li:], *m.* (**—s,** *pl.* **—s**) coolie.

kulinarisch [kuli'na:rɪʃ], *adj.* culinary.

Kulisse [ku'lɪsə], *f.* (**—,** *pl.* **—n**) (*Theat.*) back-drop, side-scene, wings.

Kulissenfieber [ku'lɪsənfi:bər], *n.* (**—s,** *no pl.*) stage-fright.

kulminieren [kulmi'ni:rən], *v.n.* culminate.

kultivieren [kulti'vi:rən], *v.a.* cultivate.

Kultur [kul'tu:r], *f.* (**—,** *pl.* **—en**) (*Agr.*) cultivation; (*fig.*) culture, civilization.

Kultus ['kultus], *m.* (**—,** *pl.* Kulte) cult, worship.

Kultusministerium ['kultusmɪnɪste:rjum], *n.* (**—s,** *pl.* **—rien**) Ministry of Education.

Kümmel ['kyməl], *m.* (**—s,** *no pl.*) caraway-seed; (*drink*) kümmel.

Kummer ['kumər], *m.* (**—s,** *no pl.*) grief, sorrow, trouble.

kümmerlich ['kymərlɪç], *adj.* miserable, pitiful.

kummerlos ['kumərlo:s], *adj.* untroubled.

kümmern ['kymərn], *v.r. sich — um,* mind, look after, be worried about, care for.

Kümmernis ['kymərnɪs], *f.* (**—,** *pl.* **—se**) grief, sorrow.

kummervoll ['kumərfɔl], *adj.* sorrowful, painful, grievous.

Kumpan [kum'pa:n], *m.* (**—s,** *pl.* **—e**) companion; mate; *lustiger —,* jolly fellow, good companion.

kund [kunt], *adj.* known, public; *etwas — tun,* make s.th. public; *— und zu wissen sei hiermit,* (*obs.*) we hereby give notice.

kundbar ['kuntba:r], *adj.* known; *etwas — machen,* announce s.th., make s.th. known.

kündbar ['kyntba:r], *adj.* (*loan, capital etc.*) redeemable; capable of being called in, terminable.

Kunde (1) ['kundə], *m.* (**—n,** *pl.* **—n**) customer; *ein schlauer —,* an artful dodger.

Kunde (2) ['kundə], *f.* (**—,** *pl.* **—n**) news; information, notification; (*compounds*) science.

Kundgebung ['kuntge:buŋ], *f.* (**—,** *pl.* **—en**) publication; rally; demonstration.

kundig ['kundɪç], *adj.* versed in, conversant with.

Kundige ['kundɪgə], *m.* (**—n,** *pl.* **—n**) expert, initiate.

kündigen ['kyndɪgən], *v.n.* give notice (*Dat.*).

Kundmachung ['kuntmaxuŋ], *f.* (**—,** *pl.* **—en**) publication.

Kundschaft ['kuntʃaft], *f.* (**—,** *no pl.*) clientele, customers; information, reconnaissance.

kundschaften ['kuntʃaftən], *v.n.* reconnoitre, scout.

künftig ['kynftɪç], *adj.* future, prospective, to come.

Kunst [kunst], *f.* (**—,** *pl.* **:e**) art; skill.

Kunstbutter ['kunstbutər], *f.* (**—,** *no pl.*) margarine.

Künstelei [kynstə'laɪ], *f.* (**—,** *pl.* **—en**) affectation, mannerism.

kunstfertig ['kunstfɛrtɪç], *adj.* skilled, skilful.

Kunstfreund ['kunstfrɔynt], *m.* (**—es,** *pl.* **—e**) art-lover.

kunstgerecht ['kunstgərɛçt], *adj.* workmanlike.

Kunstgewerbe ['kunstgəvɛrbə], *n.* (**—s,** *no pl.*) arts and crafts.

Kunstgriff ['kunstgrɪf], *m.* (**—es,** *pl.* **—e**) trick, dodge, artifice, knack.

Kunsthändler ['kunsthɛndlər], *m.* (**—s,** *pl.* **—**) art-dealer.

Kunstkenner ['kunstkɛnər], *m.* (**—s,** *pl.* **—**) connoisseur.

Künstler ['kynstlər], *m.* (**—s,** *pl.* **—**) artist, performer.

künstlerisch ['kynstlərɪʃ], *adj.* artistic, elaborate, engrossing.

künstlich ['kynstlɪç], *adj.* artificial.

kunstlos ['kunstlo:s], *adj.* artless, unaffected.

kunstreich

kunstreich ['kunstraıç], *adj.* ingenious.
Kunstseide ['kunstzaıdə], *f.* (—, *no pl.*) artificial silk.
Kunststickerei ['kunstʃtıkəraı], *f.* (—, *no pl.*) art needlework.
Kunststoff ['kunstʃtɔf], *m.* (—es, *pl.* —e) plastics.
Kunststopfen ['kunstʃtɔpfən], *n.* (—s, *no pl.*) invisible mending.
Kunststück ['kunstʃtyk], *n.* (—es, *pl.* —e) trick, feat.
Kunstverständige ['kunstfɛrʃtɛndıgə], *m.* (—n, *pl.* —n) art expert.
Küpe ['ky:pə], *f.* (—, *pl.* —n) large tub; (dyeing) copper.
Kupfer ['kupfər], *n.* (—s, *no pl.*) copper.
Kupferblech ['kupfərblɛç], *n.* (—es, *no pl.*) copper-sheet.
Kupferdraht ['kupfərdra:t], *m.* (—es, *pl.* ⁀e) copper-wire.
kupferhaltig ['kupfərhaltıç], *adj.* containing copper.
Kupferrost ['kupfərrɔst], *m.* (—es, *no pl.*) verdigris.
Kupferstecher ['kupfərʃtɛçər], *m.* (—s, *pl.* —) (copperplate) engraver.
kupieren [ku'pi:rən], *v.a.* (*rare*) (*ticket*) punch; (*Austr.*) (*horse*) dock.
Kuppe ['kupə], *f.* (—, *pl.* —n) (*hill*) top, summit.
Kuppel ['kupəl], *f.* (—, *pl.* —n) cupola, dome.
kuppeln ['kupəln], *v.n.* procure, pimp; make a match.
Kuppler ['kuplər], *m.* (—s, *pl.* —) procurer, pimp; matchmaker.
Kupplung ['kuplun], *f.* (—, *pl.* —en) (*Railw.*) coupling, joint; (*Motor.*) clutch.
Kur [ku:r], *f.* (—. *pl.* —en) cure; *eine — machen,* undergo medical treatment.
Kuranstalt ['ku:ranʃtalt], *f.* (—, *pl.* —en) sanatorium; (*Am.*) sanitarium.
Küraß ['ky:ras], *m.* (—sses, *pl.* —sse) cuirass.
Kuratel [kura'tɛl], *f.* (—, *pl.* —en) guardianship, trusteeship.
Kuratorium [kura'to:rjum], *n.* (—s, *pl.* —rien) board of guardians *or* trustees; council, governing body.
Kurbel ['kurbəl], *f.* (—, *pl.* —n) crank, winch.
Kurbelstange ['kurbəlʃtaŋə], *f.* (—, *pl.* —n) connecting rod.
Kurbelwelle ['kurbəlvɛlə], *f.* (—, *pl.* —n) crankshaft.
Kürbis ['kyrbıs], *m.* (—ses, *pl.* —se) (*Bot.*) pumpkin, gourd.
küren ['ky:rən], *v.a. irr.* (*Poet.*) choose, elect.
Kurfürst ['ku:rfyrst], *m.* (—en, *pl.* —en) Elector (of the Holy Roman Empire).
Kurhaus ['ku:rhaus], *n.* (—es, *pl.* ⁀er) spa; hotel; pump room.
Kurie ['ku:rjə], *f.* (—, *pl.* —n) (*Eccl.*) Curia; Papal Court.

Kurier [ku'ri:r], *m.* (—s, *pl.* —e) courier.
kurieren [ku'ri:rən], *v.a.* cure.
kurios [kur'jo:s], *adj.* curious, queer, strange.
Kuriosität [kurjozi'tɛ:t], *f.* (—, *pl.* —en) curio, curiosity.
Kurort ['ku:rɔrt], *m.* (—es, *pl.* —e) spa, watering-place, health-resort.
Kurrentschrift [ku'rɛntʃrıft], *f.* (—, *no pl.*) running hand, cursive writing.
Kurs [kurs], *m.* (—es, *pl.* —e) rate of exchange; quotation; circulation; course.
Kursaal ['ku:rza:l], *m.* (—s, *pl.* —säle) hall, (*spa*) pump-room, casino.
Kursbericht ['kursbərıçt], *m.* (—es, *pl.* —e) market report.
Kursbuch ['kursbu:x], *n.* (—es, *pl.* ⁀er) railway-guide, time-table.
Kürschner ['kyrʃnər], *m.* (—s, *pl.* —) furrier, skinner.
kursieren [kur'zi:rən], *v.n.* be current, circulate.
Kursivschrift [kur'zi:fʃrıft], *f.* (—, *no pl.*) italics.
Kursstand ['kursʃtant], *m.* (—es, *no pl.*) rate of exchange.
Kursus ['kurzus], *m.* (—, *pl.* Kurse) course of lectures).
Kurszettel ['kursʦɛtəl], *m.* (—s, *pl.* —) quotation-list.
Kurve ['kurvə], *f.* (—, *pl.* —n) curve.
kurz [kurts], *adj.* short, brief, concise; curt, abrupt.
kurzangebunden [kurts'aŋəbundən], *adj.* terse, abrupt, curt.
kurzatmig ['kurtsa:tmıç], *adj.* short-winded, short of breath.
Kürze ['kyrtsə], *f.* (—, *no pl.*) shortness, brevity.
kürzen ['kyrtsən], *v.a.* shorten, abbreviate, condense; (*Maths.*) reduce.
kürzlich ['kyrtslıç], *adv.* lately, recently, the other day.
Kurzschluß ['kurtsʃlus], *m.* (—sses, *pl.* ⁀sse) short circuit.
Kurzschrift ['kurtsʃrıft], *f.* (—, *no pl.*) shorthand.
kurzsichtig ['kurtszıçtıç], *adj.* short-sighted.
kurzum [kurts'um], *adv.* in short.
Kürzung ['kyrtsun], *f.* (—, *pl.* —en) abbreviation, abridgement.
Kurzwaren ['kurtsva:rən], *f. pl.* haberdashery.
kurzweg [kurts've:k], *adv.* simply, off-hand, briefly.
Kurzweil ['kurtsvaıl], *f.* (—, *no pl.*) pastime.
kurzweilig ['kurtsvaılıç], *adj.* amusing, diverting, entertaining.
kusch! [kuʃ], *excl.* (*to dogs*) lie down!
kuschen ['kuʃən], *v.n., v.r.* crouch, lie down.
Kuß [kus], *m.* (—sses, *pl.* ⁀sse) kiss.
küssen ['kysən], *v.a., v.n., v.r.* kiss.
Küste ['kystə], *f.* (—, *pl.* —n) coast, shore.

Küstenstadt ['kystənʃtat], f. (—, pl. ⁻e) seaside town.
Küster ['kystər], m. (—s, pl. —) sacristan, sexton, verger.
Kustos ['kustɔs], m. (—, pl. **—oden**) custodian; director of museum.
Kutschbock ['kutʃbɔk], m. (—s, pl. ⁻e) box(-seat).
Kutsche ['kutʃə], f. (—, pl. **—n**) coach, carriage.
kutschieren [kut'ʃiːrən], v.n. drive a coach.
Kutte ['kutə], f. (—, pl. **—n**) cowl.
Kutter ['kutər], m. (—s, pl. —) (Naut.) cutter.
Kuvert [ku'vɛːr], n. (—s, pl. **—s**) envelope; (dinner) place laid.
kuvertieren [kuvɛr'tiːrən], v.a. envelop, wrap.
Kux [kuks], m. (—es, pl. **—e**) share in a mining concern.
Kybernetik [kyːbɛr'neːtɪk], f. (—, no pl.) cybernetics.

L

L [ɛl], n. (—, pl. —) the letter L.
Lab [la:p], n. (—es, pl. **—e**) rennet.
labbern ['labərn], v.a., v.n. dribble, slobber; blab.
Labe ['la:bə], f. (—, no pl.) (Poet.) refreshment; comfort.
laben ['la:bən], v.a. refresh, restore, revive.
labil [la'bi:l], adj. unstable.
Laborant [labo'rant], m. (—en, pl. **—en**) laboratory assistant.
Laboratorium [labora'to:rjum], n. (—s, pl. **—rien**) laboratory.
laborieren [labo'ri:rən], v.n. experiment; suffer (from).
Labsal ['la:pza:l], n. (—s, pl. **—e**) restorative, refreshment.
Labung ['la:bun], f. (—, pl. **—en**) refreshment, comfort.
Lache ['laxə], f. (—, pl. **—n**) pool, puddle.
Lächeln ['lɛçəln], n. (—s, no pl.) smile; albernes —, smirk; höhnisches —, sneer.
lächeln ['lɛçəln], v.n. smile.
Lachen ['laxən], n. (—s, no pl.) laugh, laughter.
lachen ['laxən], v.n. laugh.
lächerlich ['lɛçərlɪç], adj. laughable, ridiculous; preposterous; ludicrous; sich — machen, make a fool of o.s.; etwas — machen, ridicule s.th.
Lachgas ['laxga:s], n. (—es, no pl.) nitrous oxide, laughing-gas.
lachhaft ['laxhaft], adj. laughable, ridiculous.

Lachkrampf ['laxkrampf], m. (—es, pl. ⁻e) hysterical laughter, a fit of laughter.
Lachs [laks], m. (—es, pl. **—e**) salmon.
Lachsalve ['laxzalvə], f. (—, pl. **—n**) peal of laughter.
Lack [lak], m. (—s, pl. **—e**) lac, lacquer, varnish.
lackieren [la'ki:rən], v.a. lacquer, varnish.
Lackmus ['lakmus], n. (—, no pl.) litmus.
Lackschuh ['lakʃu:], m. (—s, pl. **—e**) patent-leather shoe.
Lackwaren ['lakva:rən], f. pl. japanned goods.
Lade ['la:də], f. (—, pl. **—n**) box, chest, case, drawer.
Ladebaum ['la:dəbaum], m. derrick.
Ladefähigkeit ['la:dəfɛːɪçkaɪt], f. (—, pl. **—en**), carrying capacity, loading capacity; tonnage.
Ladegeld ['la:dəgɛlt], n. (—es, pl. **—er**) loading charges.
Laden ['la:dən], m. (—s, pl. ⁻) (window) shutter; shop, store.
laden ['la:dən], v.a. irr. load; (Elec.) charge; (Law) summon; (fig.) incur.
Ladenhüter ['la:dənhyːtər], m. (—s, pl. —) unsaleable article.
Ladenpreis ['la:dənpraɪs], m. (—es, pl. **—e**) retail-price.
Ladentisch ['la:dəntɪʃ], m. (—es, pl. **—e**) counter.
Ladeschein ['la:dəʃaɪn], m. (—s, pl. **—e**) bill of lading.
Ladestock ['la:dəʃtɔk], m. (—es, pl. ⁻e) ramrod.
Ladung ['la:dun], f. (—, pl. **—en**) loading, lading, freight; shipment, cargo; (gun) charge; (Law) summons.
Laffe ['lafə], m. (—n, pl. **—n**) fop.
Lage ['la:gə], f. (—, pl. **—n**) site, position, situation; state, condition; stratum, layer.
Lager ['la:gər], n. (—s, pl. —) couch, bed, divan; (Geol.) seam, vein; (Tech.) bearing; (Comm.) warehouse, store; camp.
Lageraufnahme ['la:gəraufna:mə], f. (—, pl. **—n**) stock-taking, inventory.
Lager(bier) ['la:gər(bi:r)], n. (—s, pl. **—e**) lager.
Lagergeld ['la:gərgɛlt], n. (—es, pl. **—er**) storage charge.
Lagerist [la:gə'rɪst], m. (—en, pl. **—en**) warehouse-clerk.
lagern ['la:gərn], v.a. store, warehouse.
Lagerstätte ['la:gərʃtɛtə], f. (—, pl. **—n**) couch, resting-place; camp site.
Lagerung ['la:gərun], f. (—, pl. **—en**) encampment; storage; stratification.
Lagune [la'gu:nə], f. (—, pl. **—n**) lagoon.
lahm [la:m], adj. lame, paralysed, crippled.
lahmen ['la:mən], v.n. be lame, limp.
lähmen ['lɛːmən], v.a. paralyse.
lahmlegen ['la:mle:gən], v.a. paralyse.

Lähmung

Lähmung ['lɛːmuŋ], *f.* (—, *pl.* —en) paralysis.

Laib [laɪp], *m.* (—es, *pl.* —e) (*bread*) loaf.

Laich [laɪç], *m.* (—es, *pl.* —e) spawn.

laichen ['laɪçən], *v.n.* spawn.

Laie ['laɪə], *m.* (—n, *pl.* —n) layman, (*pl.*) laity.

Lakai [la'kaɪ], *m.* (—en, *pl.* —en) lackey, flunkey, footman.

Lake ['laːkə], *f.* (—, *pl.* —n) brine, pickle.

Laken ['laːkən], *n.* (—s, *pl.* —) (*bed*) sheet.

lakonisch [la'koːnɪʃ], *adj.* laconic.

Lakritze [la'krɪtsə], *f.* (—, *pl.* —n) liquorice.

lallen ['lalən], *v.a., v.n.* stammer; babble.

Lama (1) ['laːmaː], *n.* (—s, *pl.* —s) (*animal*) llama.

Lama (2) ['laːmaː], *n.* (—s, *pl.* —s) (*priest*) lama.

lamentieren [lamɛn'tiːrən], *v.n.* lament, wail.

Lamm [lam], *n.* (—es, *pl.* ̈er) (*Zool.*) lamb.

Lämmchen ['lɛmçən], *n.* (—s, *pl.* —) (*Zool.*) lambkin.

Lämmergeier ['lɛmərgaɪər], *m.* (—s, *pl.* —) (*Orn.*) great bearded vulture.

Lampe ['lampə], *f.* (—, *pl.* —n) lamp.

Lampenfieber ['lampənfiːbər], *n.* (—s, *no pl.*) stage-fright.

Lampenputzer ['lampənputsər], *m.* (—s, *pl.* —) lamplighter.

Lampenschirm ['lampənʃɪrm], *m.* (—s, *pl.* —e) lampshade.

Lampion [lam'pjõ], *m. & n.* (—s, *pl.* —s) Chinese lantern.

lancieren [lãˈsiːrən], *v.a.* thrust; launch.

Land [lant], *n.* (—es, *pl.* —e (*Poet.*) and ̈er) land, country; state; ground, soil; *das Gelobte* —, the Promised Land; *an* — *gehen*, go ashore; *aufs* — *gehen*, go into the country.

Landadel ['lantaːdəl], *m.* (—s, *no pl.*) landed gentry.

Landarbeiter ['lantarbaɪtər], *m.* (—s, *pl.* —) farm-worker.

Landauer ['landauər], *m.* (—s, *pl.* —) landau.

Landebahn ['landəbaːn], *f.* (—, *pl.* —en) (*Aviat.*) runway.

landen ['landən], *v.n.* (*aux. sein*) land, disembark; (*aircraft*) land, touch down.

Landenge ['lantɛŋə], *f.* (—, *pl.* —n) isthmus.

Ländereien ['lɛndəraɪən], *f. pl.* landed property, estate.

Landeserzeugnis ['landəsɛrtsɔyknɪs], *n.* (—sses, *pl.* —sse) home produce.

Landesfürst ['landəsfyrst], *m.* (—en, *pl.* —en) sovereign.

Landesherr ['landəshɛr], *m.* (—n, *pl.* —en) (reigning) prince; sovereign.

Landeshoheit ['landəshohaɪt], *f.* (—, *no pl.*) sovereignty.

Landeskirche ['landəskɪrçə], *f.* (—, *pl.* —n) established church; national church.

Landesschuld ['landəsʃult], *f.* (—, *no pl.*) national debt.

Landessprache ['landəsʃpraːxə], *f.* (—, *pl.* —n) vernacular.

Landestracht ['landəstraxt], *f.* (—, *pl.* —en) national costume.

landesüblich ['landəsyːplɪç], *adj.* conventional, usual, customary.

Landesverweisung ['landəsfɛrvaɪzuŋ], *f.* (—, *pl.* —en) exile, banishment.

landflüchtig ['lantflyçtɪç], *adj.* fugitive.

Landfrieden ['lantfriːdən], *m.* (—s, *no pl.*) King's (*or* Queen's) peace; (*medieval*) public peace.

Landgericht ['lantgərɪçt], *n.* (—es, *pl.* —e) district court; county court.

Landgraf ['lantgraːf], *m.* (—en, *pl.* —en) landgrave, count.

Landhaus ['lanthaus], *n.* (—es, *pl.* ̈er) country house.

Landjunker ['lantjuŋkər], *m.* (—s, *pl.* —) country squire.

Landkarte ['lantkartə], *f.* (—, *pl.* —n) map.

landläufig ['lantlɔyfɪç], *adj.* customary, conventional.

ländlich ['lɛntlɪç], *adj.* rural, rustic.

Landmann ['lantman], *m.* (—es, *pl.* **Landleute**) rustic, peasant.

Landmesser ['lantmɛsər], *m.* (—s, *pl.* —) surveyor.

Landpartie ['lantparti:], *f.* (—, *pl.* —n) country excursion, picnic.

Landplage ['lantplaːgə], *f.* (—, *pl.* —n) scourge, calamity; *eine richtige* —, a public nuisance.

Landrat ['lantraːt], *m.* (—s, *pl.* ̈e) district president *or* magistrate.

Landratte ['lantratə], *f.* (—, *pl.* —n) landlubber.

Landrecht ['lantrɛçt], *n.* (—es, *no pl.*) common law.

Landregen ['lantreːgən], *m.* (—s, *no pl.*) steady downpour; persistent rain.

Landschaft ['lantʃaft], *f.* (—, *pl.* —en) landscape.

landschaftlich ['lantʃaftlɪç], *adj.* scenic.

Landsknecht ['lantsknɛçt], *m.* (—es, *pl.* —e) mercenary; hired soldier.

Landsmann ['lantsman], *m.* (—es, *pl.* **Landsleute**) fellow-countryman, compatriot.

Landspitze ['lantʃpɪtsə], *f.* (—, *pl.* —n) cape, headland, promontory.

Landstraße ['lantʃtraːsə], *f.* (—, *pl.* —n) open road, main road, highway.

Landstreicher ['lantʃtraɪçər], *m.* (—s, *pl.* —) vagabond, tramp, (*Am.*) hobo.

Landstrich ['lantʃtrɪç], *m.* (—es, *pl.* —e) tract of land.

Landsturm ['lantʃturm], *m.* (—s, *no pl.*) (*Milit.*) militia; Home Guard.

Landtag ['lanttaːk], *m.* (—s, *pl.* —e) (*Parl.*) diet.

Landung ['landuŋ], *f.* (—, *pl.* —en) landing.

Landvermesser *see* **Landmesser**.

Landvogt ['lantfoːkt], *m.* (**—es**, *pl.* ⸚e) (provincial) governor.

Landweg ['lantveːk], *m.* (**—s**, *pl.* **—e**) overland route.

Landwehr ['lantveːr], *f.* (**—**, *pl.* **—en**) militia.

Landwirt ['lantvɪrt], *m.* (**—s**, *pl.* **—e**) farmer, husbandman.

Landwirtschaft ['lantvɪrtʃaft], *f.* (**—**, *no pl.*) agriculture.

Landzunge ['lanttsuŋə], *f.* (**—**, *pl.* **—n**) spit of land.

lang [laŋ], *adj.* long, tall. — *adv.*, *prep.* (*prec. by Acc.*) for, during, long.

langatmig ['laŋaːtmɪç], *adj.* long-winded.

lange ['laŋə], *adv.* a long time; *wie —?* how long? *so — wie*, as long as.

Länge ['lɛŋə], *f.* (**—**, *pl.* **—n**) length; (*Geog.*) longitude.

langen ['laŋən], *v.a.* reach, hand, give s.o. s.th. — *v.n.* suffice, be enough.

Längengrad ['lɛŋəngraːt], *m.* (**—s**, *pl.* **—e**) degree of longitude.

Längenkreis ['lɛŋənkraɪs], *m.* (**—es**, *pl.* **—e**) meridian.

Längenmaß ['lɛŋənmaːs], *n.* (**—es**, *pl.* **—e**) linear measure.

Langeweile ['laŋəvaɪlə], *f.* (**—**, *no pl.*) boredom, ennui.

Langfinger ['laŋfɪŋər], *m.* (**—s**, *pl.* **—**) pickpocket.

langjährig ['laŋjɛːrɪç], *adj.* of long standing.

Langlebigkeit ['laŋleːbɪçkaɪt], *f.* (**—**, *no pl.*) longevity.

länglich ['lɛŋlɪç], *adj.* oblong.

Langmut ['laŋmuːt], *f.* (**—**, *no pl.*) forbearance, patience.

längs [lɛŋs], *prep.* (*Genit.*, *Dat.*) along.

langsam ['laŋzaːm], *adj.* slow; deliberate.

längst [lɛŋst], *adv.* long ago, long since.

längstens ['lɛŋstəns], *adv.* at the longest; at the latest.

Languste [laŋ'gustə], *f.* (**—**, *pl.* **—n**) (*Zool.*) spiny lobster.

langweilen ['laŋvaɪlən], *v.a.*(*insep.*) bore, tire. — *v.r. sich —*, feel bored, be bored.

langwierig ['laŋviːrɪç], *adj.* lengthy, protracted, wearisome.

Lanze ['lantsə], *f.* (**—**, *pl.* **—n**) lance, spear; *eine — brechen*, take up the cudgels, stand up for (s.th. *or* s.o.).

Lanzenstechen ['lantsənʃtɛçən], *n.* (**—s**, *no pl.*) tournament.

Lanzette [lan'tsɛtə], *f.* (**—**, *pl.* **—n**) lancet.

Lanzknecht ['lantsknɛçt], *m.* (**—es**, *pl.* **—e**) *see* **Landsknecht**.

Laos ['laːɔs], *n.* Laos.

Lappalie [la'paːljə], *f.* (**—**, *pl.* **—n**) trifle.

Lappen ['lapən], *m.* (**—s**, *pl.* **—**) rag, duster, patch; (*ear*) lobe.

Läpperschulden ['lɛpərʃuldən], *f. pl.* petty debts.

läppisch ['lɛpɪʃ], *adj.* silly, foolish, trifling.

Lappland ['lapland], *n.* Lapland.

Lärche ['lɛrçə], *f.* (**—**, *pl.* **—n**) (*Bot.*) larch.

Lärm [lɛrm], *m.* (**—s**, *no pl.*) noise, din.

lärmen ['lɛrmən], *v.n.* make a noise, brawl.

Larve ['larfə], *f.* (**—**, *pl.* **—n**) mask; (*Ent.*) grub, larva.

lasch [laʃ], *adj.* limp; insipid.

Lasche ['laʃə], *f.* (**—**, *pl.* **—n**) flap; (*shoe*) gusset, strip.

lassen ['lasən], *v.a.*, *v.n. irr.* let, allow, suffer, permit; leave; make, cause; order, command; desist.

läßlich ['lɛslɪç], *adj.* (*Eccl.*) venial (*sin*).

lässig ['lɛsɪç], *adj.* indolent, sluggish, inactive.

Lässigkeit ['lɛsɪçkaɪt], *f.* (**—**, *no pl.*) lassitude, inaction, indolence; negligence.

Last [last], *f.* (**—**, *pl.* **—en**) load, burden, weight, charge.

lasten ['lastən], *v.n.* be heavy; weigh (on).

lastenfrei ['lastənfraɪ], *adj.* unencumbered.

Laster ['lastər], *n.* (**—s**, *pl.* **—**) vice.

Lästerer ['lɛstərər], *m.* (**—s**, *pl.* **—**) slanderer, calumniator; blasphemer.

lasterhaft ['lastərhaft], *adj.* vicious, wicked; corrupt.

Lasterhöhle ['lastərhøːlə], *f.* (**—**, *pl.* **—n**) den of vice.

lästerlich ['lɛstərlɪç], *adj.* blasphemous.

lästern ['lɛstərn], *v.a.* slander, defame; blaspheme.

lästig ['lɛstɪç], *adj.* tiresome, troublesome.

Lasttier ['lasttiːr], *n.* (**—es**, *pl.* **—e**) beast of burden.

Lastwagen ['lastvaːgən], *m.* (**—s**, *pl.* **—**) lorry, (*Am.*) truck.

Lasur [la'zuːr], *m.* (**—s**, *pl.* **—e**) lapis-lazuli; ultramarine.

Latein [la'taɪn], *n.* (**—s**, *no pl.*) Latin.

lateinisch [la'taɪnɪʃ], *adj.* Latin.

Laterne [la'tɛrnə], *f.* (**—**, *pl.* **—n**) lantern; (*street*) lamp.

latschen [la'tʃən], *v.n.* shuffle along.

Latte ['latə], *f.* (**—**, *pl.* **—n**) lath, batten; *eine lange —*, lanky person.

Lattich ['latɪç], *m.* (**—s**, *pl.* **—e**) lettuce.

Latz [lats], *m.* (**—es**, *pl.* ⸚e) flap, bib; pinafore.

lau [lau], *adj.* tepid, lukewarm, insipid; (*fig.*) half-hearted.

Laub [laup], *n.* (**—es**, *no pl.*) foliage, leaves.

Laube ['laubə], *f.* (**—**, *pl.* **—n**) arbour, summer-house.

Laubengang ['laubəngaŋ], *m.* (**—es**, *pl.* ⸚e) arcade, covered walk.

Laubfrosch ['laupfrɔʃ], *m.* (**—es**, *pl.* ⸚e) (*Zool.*) tree-frog.

Laubsäge ['laupzɛːgə], *f.* (**—**, *pl.* **—n**) fret-saw.

Lauch [laux], *m.* (**—es**, *no pl.*) (*Bot.*) leek.

Lauer ['lauər], *f.* (**—**, *no pl.*) ambush, hiding-place; *auf der — sein*, lie in wait.

lauern

lauern ['lauərn], *v.n.* lurk, lie in wait (for), watch (for).

Lauf [lauf], *m.* (—es, *pl.* ⸚e) course, run; running; operation; (*river*) current; (*gun*) barrel; (*fig.*) rein.

Laufbahn ['laufbaːn], *f.* (—, *pl.* —en) career, *die medizinische — einschlagen*, enter upon a medical career.

Laufband ['laufbant], *n.* (—s, *pl.* ⸚er) (*baby*) rein, leading-string; (*Tech.*) conveyor-belt.

Laufbrücke ['laufbrykə], *f.* (—, *pl.* —n) gangway.

Laufbursche ['laufburʃə], *m.* (—n, *pl.* —n) errand-boy.

laufen ['laufən], *v.n. irr.* (*aux.* sein) run; walk; (*wheel*) turn; flow, trickle down.

laufend ['laufənt], *adj.* current.

Läufer ['lɔyfər], *m.* (—s, *pl.* —) runner; (*carpet*) rug; (*Chess*) bishop; (*Footb.*) half-back.

Lauffeuer ['lauffɔyər], *n.* (—s, *no pl.*) wildfire.

Laufgraben ['laufgraːbən], *m.* (—s, *pl.* ⸚) trench.

läufig ['lɔyfɪç], *adj.* (*animals*) ruttish.

Laufpaß ['laufpas], *m.* (—sses, *no pl.*) *den — geben*, give (s.o.) the sack.

Laufschritt ['laufʃrɪt], *m.* (—es, *pl.* —e) march; *im —*, at the double.

Laufzeit ['laufsait], *f.* (—, *pl.* —en) running-time; currency; (*animals*) rutting time.

Lauge ['laugə], *f.* (—, *pl.* —en) (*Chem.*) lye, alkali.

Lauheit ['lauhait], *f.* (—, *no pl.*) tepidity, lukewarmness; (*fig.*) half-heartedness.

Laune ['launə], *f.* (—, *pl.* —n) humour, temper, mood, whim.

launenhaft ['launənhaft], *adj.* moody.

launig ['launɪç], *adj.* humorous.

launisch ['launɪʃ], *adj.* moody, fitful, bad-tempered.

Laus [laus], *f.* (—, *pl.* ⸚e) (*Zool.*) louse.

Lausbub ['lausbuːp], *m.* (—en, *pl.* —en) young scamp, rascal.

lauschen ['lauʃən], *v.n.* listen, eavesdrop.

Lausejunge ['lauzəjuŋə], *m.* (—n, *pl.* —n) rascal, lout.

lausig ['lauzɪç], *adj.* (*vulg.*) sordid, lousy.

laut [laut], *adj.* loud, noisy, audible, clamorous. — *prep.* (*Genit.*) as per, according to, in virtue of.

Laut [laut], *m.* (—es, *pl.* —e) sound.

lautbar ['lautbaːr], *adj.* — *machen*, make known.

Laute ['lautə], *f.* (—, *pl.* —n) (*Mus.*) lute.

lauten ['lautən], *v.n.* purport, run, read.

läuten ['lɔytən], *v.a., v.n.* ring; toll; *es läutet*, the bell is ringing.

lauter ['lautər], *adj.* clear, pure; (*fig.*) single-minded; genuine; nothing but. — *adv.* merely.

Lauterkeit ['lautərkait], *f.* (—, *no pl.*) clearness, purity; (*fig.*) single-mindedness, integrity.

läutern ['lɔytərn], *v.a.* clear, purify; refine.

Läuterung ['lɔytəruŋ], *f.* (—, *pl.* —en) clearing, purification; refinement.

lautieren [lau'tiːrən], *v.a.* read phonetically.

Lautlehre ['lautleːrə], *f.* (—, *no pl.*) phonetics.

lautlich ['lautlɪç], *adj.* phonetic.

lautlos ['lautloːs], *adj.* mute, silent; noiseless.

Lautmalerei ['lautmaːlərai], *f.* (—, *no pl.*) onomatopoeia.

Lautsprecher ['lautʃpreçər], *m.* (—s, *pl.* —) loudspeaker.

Lautverschiebung ['lautfərʃiːbuŋ], *f.* (—, *pl.* —en) sound shift.

lauwarm ['lauvarm], *adj.* lukewarm, tepid; (*fig.*) half-hearted.

Lava ['laːva], *f.* (—, *no pl.*) lava.

Lavendel [la'vɛndəl], *m.* (—s, *no pl.*) (*Bot.*) lavender.

lavieren [la'viːrən], *v.n.* tack; (*fig.*) wangle.

Lawine [la'viːnə], *f.* (—, *pl.* —n) avalanche.

lax [laks], *adj.* lax, loose.

Laxheit ['lakshait], *f.* (—, *pl.* —en) laxity.

Laxiermittel [lak'siːrmɪtəl], *n.* (—s, *pl.* —) laxative, aperient.

Lazarett [latsa'rɛt], *n.* (—s, *pl.* —e) infirmary, military hospital.

Lebemann ['leːbəman], *m.* (—es, *pl.* ⸚er) man about town.

Leben ['leːbən], *n.* (—s, *pl.* —) life; (*fig.*) existence; activity; animation, bustle, stir.

leben ['leːbən], *v.n.* live, be alive.

lebend ['leːbənt], *adj.* alive, living; (*language*) modern.

lebendig [le'bɛndɪç], *adj.* living, alive, quick.

Lebensanschauung ['leːbənsanʃauuŋ], *f.* (—, *pl.* —en) conception of life, philosophy of life.

Lebensart ['leːbənsaːrt], *f.* (—, *no pl.*) way of living; (*fig.*) behaviour; *gute —*, good manners.

lebensfähig ['leːbənsfɛːɪç], *adj.* capable of living, viable.

lebensgefährlich ['leːbənsgəfɛːrlɪç], *adj.* perilous, extremely dangerous.

Lebensgeister ['leːbənsgaistər], *m. pl.* spirits.

lebensgroß ['leːbənsgroːs], *adj.* life-size.

lebenslänglich ['leːbənslɛŋlɪç], *adj.* lifelong, for life; — *e Rente*, life annuity.

Lebenslauf ['leːbənslauf], *m.* (—es, *pl.* ⸚e) curriculum vitae.

Lebensmittel ['leːbənsmɪtəl], *n. pl.* food, provisions, victuals.

lebensmüde ['leːbənsmyːdə], *adj.* weary of life.

Lebensunterhalt ['leːbənsuntərhalt], *m.* (—s, *no pl.*) livelihood.

Lebenswandel ['leːbənsvandəl], *m.* (—s, *no pl.*) conduct, mode of life.

Leibarzt

Lebensweise ['le:bənsvaɪzə], *f.* (—, *no pl.*) habits, way of life.
Leber ['le:bər], *f.* (—, *pl.* —n) liver; *frisch von der — weg*, frankly, without mincing matters.
Leberblümchen ['le:bərbly:mçən], *n.* (—s, *pl.* —) (*Bot.*) liverwort.
Leberfleck ['le:bərflɛk], *m.* (—s, *pl.* —e) mole.
Lebertran ['le:bərtra:n], *m.* (—s, *no pl.*) cod-liver oil.
Leberwurst ['le:bərvurst], *f.* (—, *pl.* ⁓e) liver sausage.
Lebewesen ['le:bəve:zən], *n.* (—s, *pl.* —) living creature.
Lebewohl ['le:bəvo:l], *n.*, *excl.* farewell, good-bye; *— sagen*, bid farewell.
lebhaft ['le:phaft], *adj.* lively, vivacious, brisk, animated.
Lebkuchen ['le:pku:xən], *m.* (—s, *pl.* —) gingerbread.
Lebzeiten ['le:ptsaɪtən], *f. pl. zu — von* (*Genit.*), in the lifetime of.
lechzen ['lɛçtsən], *v.n.* be parched with thirst; *nach etwas —*, (*fig.*) long for s.th., pine for s.th.
Leck [lɛk], *n.* (—s, *pl.* —e) leak; *ein — bekommen*, spring a leak.
leck [lɛk], *adj.* leaky.
lecken ['lɛkən], *v.a.* lick, lap.
lecker ['lɛkər], *adj.* delicate, delicious, dainty.
Leckerbissen ['lɛkərbɪsən], *m.* (—s, *pl.* —) delicacy; dainty, tit-bit.
Leckerei [lɛkə'raɪ], *f.* (—, *pl.* —en) delicacy.
Leder ['le:dər], *n.* (—s, *no pl.*) leather.
ledern ['le:dərn], *adj.* (of) leather, leathery; (*fig.*) dull, boring.
ledig ['le:dɪç], *adj.* unmarried, single; (*fig.*) rid of, free from.
lediglich ['le:dɪklɪç], *adv.* merely, only, solely.
leer [le:r], *adj.* empty, void; blank; (*fig.*) hollow, futile, empty, vain, inane.
Leere ['le:rə], *f.* (—, *no pl.*) emptiness, void, vacuum.
leeren ['le:rən], *v.a.* empty, evacuate.
Leerlauf ['le:rlauf], *m.* (—s, *no pl.*) (*Motor.*) idling; (*gear*) neutral.
legalisieren [legali'zi:rən], *v.a.* legalise, authenticate.
Legat (1) [le'ga:t], *m.* (—en, *pl.* —en) legate.
Legat (2) [le'ga:t], *n.* (—s, *pl.* —e) legacy, bequest.
Legationsrat [lega'tsjo:nsra:t], *m.* (—s, *pl.* ⁓e) counsellor in a legation.
legen ['le:gən], *v.a.* lay, put, place. *— v.r. sich —*, lie down; cease, subside.
Legende [le'gɛndə], *f.* (—, *pl.* —n) legend.
Legierung [lə'gi:ruŋ], *f.* (—, *pl.* —en) alloy.
Legion [le'gjo:n], *f.* (—, *pl.* —en) legion.
Legionär [le:gjo'nɛ:r], *m.* (—s, *pl.* —e) legionary.
legitim [legi'ti:m], *adj.* legitimate.

Legitimation [legitima'tsjo:n], *f.* (—, *pl.* —en) proof of identity.
legitimieren [legiti'mi:rən], *v.a.* legitimise. *— v.r. sich —*, prove o.'s identity.
Lehen ['le:ən], *n.* (—s, *pl.* —) fief; *zu — geben*, invest with, enfeoff; *zu — tragen*, hold in fee.
Lehensdienst *see* **Lehnsdienst.**
Lehenseid *see* **Lehnseid.**
Lehensmann *see* **Lehnsmann.**
Lehm [le:m], *m.* (—s, *no pl.*) loam, clay, mud.
lehmig ['le:mɪç], *adj.* clayey, loamy.
Lehne ['le:nə], *f.* (—, *pl.* —n) support, prop; (*chair*) back, arm-rest.
lehnen ['le:nən], *v.a., v.n.* lean. *— v.r. sich — an*, lean against.
Lehnsdienst ['le:nsdi:nst], *m.* (—es, *pl.* —e) feudal service.
Lehnseid ['le:nsaɪt], *m.* (—es, *pl.* —e) oath of allegiance.
Lehnsmann ['le:nsman], *m.* (—es, *pl.* ⁓er) feudal tenant, vassal.
Lehnstuhl ['le:nʃtu:l], *m.* (—s, *pl.* ⁓e) armchair, easy chair.
Lehramt ['le:ramt], *n.* (—es, *pl.* ⁓er) professorship; teaching post *or* profession.
Lehrbrief ['le:rbri:f], *m.* (—es, *pl.* —e) apprentice's indentures; certificate of apprenticeship.
Lehrbuch ['le:rbu:x], *n.* (—es, *pl.* ⁓er) textbook, manual.
Lehre ['le:rə], *f.* (—, *pl.* —n) teaching, advice, rule, doctrine, dogma, moral; (*craft*) apprenticeship.
lehren ['le:rən], *v.a.* teach, inform, instruct; profess.
Lehrer ['le:rər], *m.* (—s, *pl.* —) teacher, instructor, schoolmaster.
Lehrgang ['le:rgaŋ], *m.* (—es, *pl.* ⁓e) course (of instruction).
Lehrgegenstand ['le:rge:gənʃtant], *m.* (—es, *pl.* ⁓e) subject of instruction; branch of study.
Lehrgeld ['le:rgɛlt], *n.* (—es, *pl.* —er) premium for apprenticeship; *— zahlen*, (*fig.*) pay for o.'s experience.
Lehrkörper ['le:rkœrpər], *m.* (—s, *no pl.*) teaching staff; (*Univ.*) faculty.
Lehrling ['le:rlɪŋ], *m.* (—s, *pl.* —e) apprentice.
Lehrmädchen ['le:rmɛ:tçən], *n.* (—s, *pl.* —) girl apprentice.
Lehrmeister ['le:rmaɪstər], *m.* (—s, *pl.* —) teacher, instructor, master.
Lehrmittel ['le:rmɪtəl], *n.* (—s, *pl.* —) teaching appliance *or* aid.
lehrreich ['le:rraɪç], *adj.* instructive.
Lehrsatz ['le:rzats], *m.* (—es, *pl.* ⁓e) tenet, dogma, rule; (*Maths.*) theorem.
Lehrstuhl ['le:rʃtu:l], *m.* (—s, *pl.* ⁓e) (*Univ.*) chair; professorship.
Lehrzeit ['le:rtsaɪt], *f.* (—, *pl.* —en) apprenticeship.
Leib [laɪp], *m.* (—es, *pl.* —er) body; abdomen; womb.
Leibarzt ['laɪpa:rtst], *m.* (—es, *pl.* ⁓e) court surgeon.

139

Leibbinde

Leibbinde ['laɪpbɪndə], *f.* (—, *pl.* —n) abdominal belt.

Leibchen ['laɪpçən], *n.* (—s, *pl.* —) bodice, corset; vest.

leibeigen [laɪp'aɪgən], *adj.* in bondage, in thraldom, in serfdom.

Leibeserbe ['laɪbəsɛrbə], *m.* (—n, *pl.* —n) heir, descendant, offspring; (*pl.*) issue.

Leibesfrucht ['laɪbəsfruxt], *f.* (—, *pl.* ⁓e) embryo, foetus.

Leibeskraft ['laɪbəskraft], *f.* (—, *pl.* ⁓e) bodily strength; *aus* —en, with might and main.

Leibesübung ['laɪbəsyːbuŋ], *f.* (—, *pl.* —en) physical exercise; (*pl.*) gymnastic exercises.

Leibgericht ['laɪpgərɪçt], *n.* (—s, *pl.* —e) favourite dish.

leibhaftig [laɪp'haftɪç], *adj.* real, incarnate, in person.

leiblich ['laɪplɪç], *adj.* bodily, corporeal.

Leibrente ['laɪprɛntə], *f.* (—, *pl.* —n) life-annuity.

Leibschmerzen ['laɪpʃmɛrtsən], *m. pl.* stomach-ache.

Leibspeise ['laɪpʃpaɪzə], *f.* (—, *pl.* —n) favourite dish.

Leibwache ['laɪpvaxə], *f.* (—, *no pl.*) body-guard.

Leibwäsche ['laɪpvɛʃə], *f.* (—, *no pl.*) underwear.

Leiche ['laɪçə], *f.* (—, *pl.* —n) (dead) body, corpse; (*dial.*) funeral.

Leichenbegängnis ['laɪçənbəgɛŋnɪs], *n.* (—ses, *pl.* —se) funeral, burial, interment.

Leichenbeschauer ['laɪçənbəʃauər], *m.* (—s, *pl.* —) coroner.

Leichenbestatter ['laɪçənbəʃtater], *m.* (—s, *pl.* —) undertaker; (*Am.*) mortician.

leichenhaft ['laɪçənhaft], *adj.* corpselike, cadaverous.

Leichenschau ['laɪçənʃau], *f.* (—, *no pl.*) post mortem (examination), (coroner's) inquest.

Leichentuch ['laɪçəntuːx], *n.* (—es, *pl.* ⁓er) shroud, pall.

Leichenverbrennung ['laɪçənfɛrbrɛnun], *f.* (—, *pl.* —en) cremation.

Leichenwagen ['laɪçənvaːgən], *m.* (—s, *pl.* —) hearse.

Leichenzug ['laɪçəntsuːk], *m.* (—es, *pl.* ⁓e) funeral procession.

Leichnam ['laɪçnaːm], *m.* (—s, *pl.* —e) (dead) body, corpse.

leicht [laɪçt], *adj.* light; slight; weak; easy.

leichtfertig ['laɪçtfɛrtɪç], *adj.* frivolous, irresponsible.

leichtgläubig ['laɪçtglɔybɪç], *adj.* credulous, gullible.

leichthin ['laɪçthɪn], *adv.* lightly.

Leichtigkeit ['laɪçtɪçkaɪt], *f.* (—, *no pl.*) ease, facility.

Leichtsinn ['laɪçtzɪn], *m.* (—s, *no pl.*) thoughtlessness, carelessness; frivolity.

Leid [laɪt], *n.* (—es, *no pl.*) sorrow, grief; harm, hurt; *einem etwas zu —e tun*, harm s.o.

leid [laɪt], *adj.* *es tut mir —*, I am sorry; *du tust mir —*, I am sorry for you.

Leiden ['laɪdən], *n.* (—s, *pl.* —) suffering, misfortune; (*illness*) affliction, complaint; *das — Christi*, the Passion.

leiden ['laɪdən], *v.a., v.n. irr.* suffer, bear, endure, undergo.

Leidenschaft ['laɪdənʃaft], *f.* (—, *pl.* —en) passion.

leider ['laɪdər], *adv.* unfortunately.

leidig ['laɪdɪç], *adj.* tiresome, unpleasant.

leidlich ['laɪtlɪç], *adj.* tolerable, moderate.

leidtragend ['laɪttraːgənt], *adj.* in mourning.

Leidtragende ['laɪttraːgəndə], *m. or f.* (—n, *pl.* —n) mourner.

Leidwesen ['laɪtveːzən], *n.* (—s, *no pl.*) *zu meinem —*, to my regret.

Leier ['laɪər], *f.* (—, *pl.* —n) lyre.

Leierkasten ['laɪərkastən], *m.* (—s, *pl.* ⁓) barrel organ.

leiern ['laɪərn], *v.n.* drone, drawl on.

leihen ['laɪən], *v.a. irr. einem etwas —*, lend s.o. s.th.; *von einem etwas —*, borrow s.th. from s.o.

Leim [laɪm], *m.* (—s, *no pl.*) glue; *einem auf den — gehen*, be taken in by s.o., fall for s.th.

Leimfarbe ['laɪmfarbə], *f.* (—, *pl.* —en) water-colour, distemper.

Lein [laɪn], *m.* (—s, *pl.* —e) linseed, flax.

Leine ['laɪnə], *f.* (—, *pl.* —n) line, cord.

Leinen ['laɪnən], *n.* (—s, *no pl.*) linen.

Leinöl ['laɪnøːl], *n.* (—s, *no pl.*) linseed oil.

Leintuch ['laɪntuːx], *n.* (—es, *pl.* ⁓er) linen sheet, sheeting.

Leinwand ['laɪnvant], *f.* (—, *no pl.*) linen, sheeting; (*Art*) canvas; (*film*) screen.

leise ['laɪzə], *adj.* low, soft, gentle, faint, slight; delicate.

Leiste ['laɪstə], *f.* (—, *pl.* —n) ledge, border; groin.

Leisten ['laɪstən], *m.* (—s, *pl.* —) (*shoe*) last, form.

leisten ['laɪstən], *v.a.* do, perform; accomplish; *ich kann es mir nicht —*, I cannot afford it.

Leistenbruch ['laɪstənbrux], *m.* (—es, *pl.* ⁓e) hernia, rupture.

Leistung ['laɪstuŋ], *f.* (—, *pl.* —en) performance, accomplishment, achievement.

leistungsfähig ['laɪstuŋksfɛːɪç], *adj.* efficient.

leiten ['laɪtən], *v.a.* lead, guide, manage; preside over.

Leiter (1) ['laɪtər], *m.* (—s, *pl.* —) leader, manager; conductor; head.

Leiter (2) ['laɪtər], *f.* (—, *pl.* —n) ladder.

Leiterwagen ['laɪtərvaːgən], *m.* (—s, *pl.* —) rack-wagon; (*Austr.*) small hand-cart.

Leitfaden ['laɪtfaːdən], m. (—s, pl. ⁃) (book) manual, textbook, guide.

Leitstern ['laɪtʃtɛrn], m. (—s, pl. —e) pole-star; (fig.) lodestar, guiding star.

Leitung ['laɪtuŋ], f. (—, pl. —en) management, direction; (Elec.) lead, connection; line; (water- or gas-) main(s); pipeline; eine lange — haben, be slow in the uptake.

Leitungsvermögen ['laɪtuŋsfɛrmøː-gən], n. (—s, no pl.) conductivity.

Leitwerk ['laɪtvɛrk], n. (—s, no pl.) (Aviat.) tail unit.

Lektion [lɛkts'joːn], f. (—, pl. —en) lesson; einem eine — geben, lecture s.o.

Lektor ['lɛktɔr], m. (—s, pl. —en) publisher's reader; teacher, lector.

Lektüre [lɛk'tyːrə], f. (—, pl. —n) reading matter, books.

Lende ['lɛndə], f. (—, pl. —n) (Anat.) loin.

lendenlahm ['lɛndənlaːm], adj. weak-kneed, lame.

lenkbar ['lɛŋkbaːr], adj. dirigible, manageable, tractable, governable.

lenken ['lɛŋkən], v.a. drive, steer; (fig.) direct, rule, manage.

Lenkstange ['lɛŋkʃtaŋə], f. (—, pl. —n) connecting-rod; (bicycle) handle-bar.

Lenz [lɛnts], m. (—es, pl. —e) (Poet.) spring.

Lepra ['leːpra], f. (—, no pl.) leprosy.

Lerche ['lɛrçə], f. (—, pl. —n) (Orn.) lark, skylark.

lernbegierig ['lɛrnbəgiːrɪç], adj. studious, eager to learn.

lernen ['lɛrnən], v.a. learn; study; einen kennen —, make s.o.'s acquaintance; auswendig —, learn by heart.

Lesart ['leːsaːrt], f. (—, pl. —en) reading, version.

lesbar ['leːsbaːr], adj. legible; readable.

Lese ['leːzə], f. (—, pl. —n) gathering (of fruit); vintage.

lesen ['leːzən], v.a. irr. gather; glean; read; die Messe —, celebrate or say mass; über etwas —, (Univ.) lecture on s.th.

lesenswert ['leːzənsvɛrt], adj. worth reading.

Leser ['leːzər], m. (—s, pl. —) gatherer, gleaner; reader.

leserlich ['leːzərlɪç], adj. legible.

Lettland ['lɛtlant], n. Latvia.

letzen ['lɛtsən], v.a. (Poet.) comfort, cheer, refresh.

letzt [lɛtst], adj. last, extreme, ultimate, final.

letztens ['lɛtstəns], adv. lastly, in the end.

letztere ['lɛtstərə], adj. latter.

letzthin ['lɛtsthɪn], adv. (rare) lately, the other day, recently.

Leu [lɔy], m. (—en, pl. —en) (Poet.) lion.

Leuchte ['lɔyçtə], f. (—, pl. —n) light, lamp, lantern; (fig.) luminary, star.

leuchten ['lɔyçtən], v.n. light, shine.

leuchtend ['lɔyçtənt], adj. shining, bright; luminous.

Leuchter ['lɔyçtər], m. (—s, pl. —) candlestick, candelabrum.

Leuchtrakete ['lɔyçtrakeːtə], f. (—, pl. —n) Roman candle; flare.

Leuchtturm ['lɔyçtturm], m. (—s, pl. ⁃e) lighthouse.

leugnen ['lɔygnən], v.a. deny, disclaim; nicht zu —, undeniable.

Leumund ['lɔymunt], m. (—es, no pl.) renown, reputation.

Leute ['lɔytə], pl. persons, people, men; servants, domestic staff.

Leutnant ['lɔytnant], m. (—s, pl. —s) lieutenant.

leutselig ['lɔytzeːlɪç], adj. affable, friendly; condescending.

Levkoje [lɛf'koːjə], f. (—, pl. —n) (Bot.) stock.

Lexikon ['lɛksikɔn], n. (—s, pl. —s, —ka) dictionary, lexicon, encyclopaedia.

Libanon ['liːbanɔn], m. Lebanon.

Libelle [li'bɛlə], f. (—, pl. —n) (Ent.) dragonfly.

Liberia [li'beːria], n. Liberia.

Libyen ['liːbɪən], n. Libya.

Licht [lɪçt], n. (—es, pl. —er) light, candle; luminary.

licht [lɪçt], adj. light, clear, open.

Lichtbild ['lɪçtbɪlt], n. (—es, pl. —er) photograph.

Lichtbrechung ['lɪçtbrɛçuŋ], f. (—, pl. —en) refraction of light.

lichten ['lɪçtən], v.a. clear, thin; den Anker —, weigh anchor.

lichterloh ['lɪçtərloː], adj. blazing, ablaze.

Lichthof ['lɪçthoːf], m. (—s, pl. ⁃e) well of a court, quadrangle.

Lichtmeß ['lɪçtmɛs], f. (—, no pl.) (Eccl.) Candlemas.

Lichtschirm ['lɪçtʃɪrm], m. (—s, pl. —e) screen, lamp-shade.

Lichtspieltheater ['lɪçtʃpiːlteaːtər], n. (—s, pl. —) cinema.

Lichtung ['lɪçtuŋ], f. (—, pl. —en) glade, clearing.

Lid [liːt], n. (—s, pl. —er) eye-lid.

lieb [liːp], adj. dear; beloved; good; das ist mir —, I am glad of it; der —e Gott, God; unsere —e Frau, Our Lady; bei einem — Kind sein, be a favourite with s.o., curry favour with s.o.

liebäugeln ['liːpɔygəln], v.n. insep. ogle.

Liebchen ['liːpçən], n. (—s, pl. —) sweetheart, love, darling.

Liebe ['liːbə], f. (—, no pl.) love.

Liebelei [liːbə'laɪ], f. (—, pl. —en) flirtation.

lieben ['liːbən], v.a. love, like, be fond of.

liebenswürdig ['liːbənsvyrdɪç], adj. amiable, kind, charming.

lieber ['liːbər], adv. rather, better, sooner; etwas — tun, prefer to do s.th.

Liebhaber ['liːphaːbər], m. (—s, pl. —) lover; (fig.) amateur, dilettante; (Theat.) leading man.

Liebhaberin ['liːphabərɪn], f. leading lady.

liebkosen

liebkosen ['liːpkoːzən], *v.a. insep.* fondle, caress.

lieblich ['liːplɪç] *adj.* lovely, charming, sweet.

Liebling ['liːplɪŋ], *m.* (**—s**, *pl.* **—e**) darling, favourite.

lieblos ['liːploːs], *adj.* hard-hearted; unkind.

Liebreiz ['liːpraɪts], *m.* (**—es**, *no pl.*) charm, attractiveness.

liebreizend ['liːpraɪtsənt], *adj.* charming.

Liebschaft ['liːpʃaft], *f.* (**—**, *pl.* **—en**) love affair.

Lied [liːt], *n.* (**—es**, *pl.* **—er**) song, air, tune; *geistliches* **—**, hymn.

liederlich ['liːdərlɪç], *adj.* careless, slovenly; dissolute, debauched; *—es Leben*, profligacy.

Lieferant [liːfəˈrant], *m.* (**—en**, *pl.* **—en**) supplier, purveyor, contractor; *Eingang für* **—en**, tradesmen's entrance.

liefern ['liːfərn], *v.a.* deliver, furnish, supply.

Lieferschein ['liːfərʃaɪn], *m.* (**—s**, *pl.* **—e**) delivery note.

liegen ['liːgən], *v.n. irr.* lie; be situated; *es liegt mir daran*, it is of importance to me, I have it at heart; *es liegt mir nichts daran*, it is of no consequence to me.

Liegenschaft ['liːgənʃaft], *f.* (**—**, *pl.* **—en**) landed property, real estate.

Liga ['liːgaː], *f.* (**—**, *pl.* **—gen**) league.

Liguster [liˈgustər], *m.* (**—s**, *no pl.*) privet.

liieren [liˈiːrən], *v.r.* (*aux.* haben) *sich — mit*, unite with, combine with.

Likör [liˈkøːr], *m.* (**—s**, *pl.* **—e**) liqueur.

lila ['liːla] *adj.* (*colour*) lilac.

Lilie ['liːljə], *f.* (**—**, *pl.* **—n**) (*Bot.*) lily.

Limonade [limoˈnaːdə], *f.* (**—**, *pl.* **—n**) lemonade.

lind [lɪnt], *adj.* soft, gentle, mild.

Linde ['lɪndə], *f.* (**—**, *pl.* **—n**) (*Bot.*) lime-tree, linden.

lindern ['lɪndərn], *v.a.* soften, assuage, mitigate, soothe, allay.

Lindwurm ['lɪntvurm], *m.* (**—s**, *pl.* **er**) (*Poet.*) dragon.

Lineal [lineˈaːl], *n.* (**—s**, *pl.* **—e**) ruler, rule.

Linie ['liːnjə], *f.* (**—**, *pl.* **—n**) line; lineage, descent; *in erster* **—**, in the first place.

Linienschiff ['liːnjənʃɪf], *n.* (**—es**, *pl.* **—e**) (*Naut.*) liner.

lin(i)ieren [lin'(i)iːrən], *v.a.* rule.

linkisch ['lɪŋkɪʃ], *adj.* awkward, clumsy.

links [lɪŋks], *adv.* to the left, on the left-hand side; *—um!* left about turn!

Linnen ['lɪnən], *n.* (**—s**, *no pl.*) (*Poet.*) linen.

Linse ['lɪnzə], *f.* (**—**, *pl.* **—n**) (*vegetable*) lentil; (*optical*) lens.

linsenförmig ['lɪnzənfœrmɪç], *adj.* lens-shaped.

Linsengericht ['lɪnzəngərɪçt], *n.* (**—es**, *pl.* **—e**) (*Bibl.*) mess of pottage.

Lippe ['lɪpə], *f.* (**—**, *pl.* **—n**) lip; (*coll.*) *eine — riskieren*, be cheeky.

Lippenlaut ['lɪpənlaut], *m.* (**—s**, *pl.* **—e**) (*Phonet.*) labial.

Lippenstift ['lɪpənʃtift], *m.* (**—s**, *pl.* **—e**) lipstick.

liquidieren [lɪkviˈdiːrən], *v.a.* liquidate, wind up, settle; charge.

lispeln ['lɪspəln], *v.n.* lisp.

Lissabon [lɪsaˈbɔn], *n.* Lisbon.

List [lɪst], *f.* (**—**, *pl.* **—en**) cunning, craft; trick, stratagem, ruse.

Liste ['lɪstə], *f.* (**—**, *pl.* **—n**) list, roll, catalogue.

listig ['lɪstɪç], *adj.* cunning, crafty, sly.

Listigkeit ['lɪstɪçkaɪt], *f.* (**—**, *no pl.*) slyness, craftiness.

Litanei [litaˈnaɪ], *f.* (**—**, *pl.* **—en**) litany.

Litauen ['liːtauən], *n.* Lithuania.

Liter ['liːtər], *m. & n.* (**—s**, *pl.* **—**) litre.

literarisch [lɪkvaˈraːrɪʃ], *adj.* literary.

Literatur [lɪtəraˈtuːr], *f.* (**—**, *pl.* **—en**) literature, letters.

Litfaßsäule ['lɪtfaszɔylə], *f.* (**—**, *pl.* **—n**) advertisement pillar.

Liturgie [lɪturˈgiː], *f.* (**—**, *pl.* **—n**) liturgy.

Litze ['lɪtsə], *f.* (**—**, *pl.* **—n**) lace, braid, cord; (*Elec.*) flex.

Livland ['liːflant], *n.* Livonia.

Livree [liˈvreː], *f.* (**—**, *pl.* **—n**) livery.

Lizenz [liˈtsɛnts], *f.* (**—**, *pl.* **—en**) licence.

Lob [loːp], *n.* (**—es**, *no pl.*) praise, commendation.

loben ['loːbən], *v.a.* praise, commend.

lobesam ['loːbəzaːm], *adj.* (*Poet.*) worthy, honourable.

Lobgesang ['loːpgəzaŋ], *m.* (**—s**, *pl.* **e**) hymn of praise.

Lobhudelei [loːphuːdəˈlaɪ], *f.* (**—**, *pl.* **—en**) adulation, flattery, toadying.

löblich ['løːplɪç], *adj.* laudable, commendable, meritorious.

lobpreisen ['loːppraɪzən], *v.a. insep.* eulogise, extol.

Lobrede ['loːpreːdə], *f.* (**—**, *pl.* **—n**) panegyric, eulogy.

Loch [lɔx], *n.* (**—es**, *pl.* **er**) hole.

Lochbohrer ['lɔxboːrər], *m.* (**—s**, *pl.* **—**) auger.

lochen ['lɔxən], *v.a.* perforate, punch.

Locher ['lɔxər], *m.* (**—s**, *pl.* **—**) perforator, punch.

löcherig ['lœçərɪç], *adj.* full of holes.

Lochmeißel ['lɔxmaɪsəl], *m.* (**—s**, *pl.* **—**) mortice-chisel.

Locke ['lɔkə], *f.* (**—**, *pl.* **—n**) curl, lock, ringlet, tress.

locken ['lɔkən], *v.a.* allure, decoy, entice.

locker ['lɔkər], *adj.* loose; slack; spongy; dissolute; *nicht — lassen*, stick to o.'s guns.

lockern ['lɔkərn], *v.a.* loosen.

lockig ['lɔkɪç], *adj.* curled, curly.

Lockmittel ['lɔkmɪtəl], *n.* (**—s**, *pl.* **—**) inducement, lure, bait.

Lockspeise ['lɔkʃpaɪzə], *f.* (**—**, *pl.* **—n**) lure, bait.

Lockung ['lɔkuŋ], *f.* (—, *pl.* —en) allurement, enticement.

Lockvogel ['lɔkfo:gəl], *m.* (—s, *pl.* ⁓) decoy-bird.

Loden ['lo:dən], *m.* (—s, *pl.* —) coarse cloth, frieze.

lodern ['lo:dərn], *v.n.* blaze, flame.

Löffel ['lœfəl], *m.* (—s, *pl.* —) spoon; (*animal*) ear; *einen über den — barbieren*, take s.o. in.

Logarithmus [loga'rıtmus], *m.* (—, *pl.* —men) logarithm.

Logbuch ['lɔkbu:x], *n.* (—es, *pl.* ⁓er) logbook.

Loge ['lo:ʒə], *f.* (—, *pl.* —n) (*Theat.*) box; (*Freemasonry*) lodge.

Logenschließer ['lo:ʒənʃli:sər], *m.* (—s, *pl.* —) (*Theat.*) attendant.

logieren [lo'ʒi:rən], *v.n.* board (with).

Logis [lo'ʒi:], *n.* (—, *pl.* —) lodgings.

logisch ['lo:gıʃ], *adj.* logical.

Lohe ['lo:hə], *f.* (—, *pl.* —n) tanning bark; flame.

Lohgerber ['lo:gɛrbər], *m.* (—s, *pl.* —) tanner.

Lohn [lo:n], *m.* (—s, *pl.* ⁓e) wages, pay; reward; recompense.

lohnen ['lo:nən], *v.a.* reward, recompense, remunerate; pay wages to; *es lohnt sich nicht*, it is not worth while.

Lohnstopp ['lo:nʃtɔp], *m.* (—s, *pl.* —s) pay pause, wage freeze.

Löhnung ['lø:nuŋ], *f.* (—, *pl.* —en) pay, payment.

Lokal [lo'ka:l], *n.* (—s, *pl* —e) locality, premises; inn, pub, café.

lokalisieren [lokali'zi:rən], *v.a.* localise.

Lokalität [lokali'tɛ:t], *f.* (—, *pl.* —en) *see* Lokal.

Lokomotive [lokomo'ti:və], *f.* (—, *pl.* —n) (*Railw.*) locomotive, engine.

Lokomotivführer [lokomo'ti:ffy:rər], *m.* (—s, *pl.* —) (*Railw.*) engine-driver.

Lombard [lɔm'bart], *m.* (—s, *pl.* —) deposit-bank, loan bank.

Lombardei [lɔmbar'daı], *f.* Lombardy.

Lorbeer ['lɔrbe:r], *m.* (—s, *pl.* —en) laurel.

Lorbeerbaum ['lɔrbe:rbaum], *m.* (—s, *pl.* ⁓e) laurel-tree, bay-tree.

Lorbeerspiritus ['lɔrbe:rʃpi:ritus], *m.* (—, *no pl.*) bay rum.

Lorgnon [lɔrn'jõ], *n.* (—s, *pl.* —e) monocle, eye-glass.

Los [lo:s], *n.* (—es, *pl.* —e) share, ticket; lot, fate; *das große —*, first prize.

los [lo:s], *adj.* loose, untied; free from, released from, rid of; (*Am.*) quit of; *was ist los?* what is going on? what's the matter? *etwas — werden*, get rid of s.th.; *schieß los!* fire away!

lösbar ['lø:sba:r], *adj.* (*question, riddle*) soluble.

losbinden ['lo:sbındən], *v.a. irr.* untie, unbind, loosen.

losbrechen ['lo:sbrɛçən], *v.a. irr.* break off. — *v.n.* (*aux.* sein) break loose.

Löschblatt ['lœʃblat], *n.* (—es, *pl.* ⁓er) blotting-paper.

Löscheimer ['lœʃaımər], *m.* (—s, *pl.* —) fire-bucket.

löschen ['lœʃən], *v.a.* put out; extinguish; (*debt*) cancel; (*writing*) efface, blot; (*freight*) (*Naut.*) unload; (*thirst*) quench.

Löschpapier ['lœʃpapi:r], *n.* (—s, *no pl.*) blotting-paper.

Löschung ['lœʃuŋ], *f.* (—, *pl.* —en) (*freight*) (*Naut.*) discharging, landing, unloading.

losdrücken ['lo:sdrykən], *v.n.* discharge, fire.

lose ['lo:zə], *adj.* loose, slack; (*fig.*) dissolute; *—s Maul*, malicious tongue.

losen ['lo:zən], *v.n.* draw lots.

lösen ['lø:zən], *v.a.* loosen, untie; absolve, free, deliver; dissolve; solve; (*relations*) break off; (*tickets*) take, buy.

losgehen ['lo:sge:ən], *v.n. irr.* (*aux.* sein) begin; (*gun*) go off; *auf einen —*, go for s.o.; *jetzt kann's —*, now for it.

loskaufen ['lo:skaufən], *v.a.* redeem, ransom.

loskommen ['lo:skɔmən], *v.n. irr.* (*aux.* sein) come loose; *von etwas —*, get rid of s.th.

löslich ['lø:slıç], *adj.* (*Chem.*) soluble.

loslösen ['lo:slø:zən], *v.a.* detach.

losmachen ['lo:smaxən], *v.a.* free from. — *v.r. sich — von*, disengage o.s. from.

losreißen ['lo:sraısən], *v.a. irr.* pull away, separate. — *v.n.* (*aux.* sein), break loose. — *v.r. sich — von*, tear o.s. away from.

lossagen ['lo:sza:gən], *v.r. sich — von*, renounce s.th., dissociate o.s. from s.th.

losschlagen ['lo:sʃla:gen], *v.a.* knock loose; let fly; (*fig.*) sell, dispose of.

lossprechen ['lo:sʃprɛçən], *v.a. irr.* (*Eccl.*) absolve; (*Law*) acquit.

lossteuern ['lo:sʃtɔyərn], *v.n.* — *auf*, make for.

Losung ['lo:zuŋ], *f.* (—, *pl.* —en) watchword, motto, password, slogan.

Lösung ['lø:zuŋ], *f.* (—, *pl.* —en) loosening; solution.

losziehen ['lo:stsi:ən], *v.n. irr.* (*Mil.*) set out; *gegen einen —*, inveigh against s.o.; (*fig., coll.*) run s.o. down.

Lot [lo:t], *n.* (—es, *pl.* —e) lead, plummet; (*weight*) half an ounce; (*Maths.*) perpendicular (line).

Löteisen ['lø:taızən], *n.* (—s, *pl.* —) soldering iron.

loten ['lo:tən], *v.a., v.n.* (*Naut.*) take soundings, plumb.

löten ['lø:tən], *v.a.* solder.

Lothringen ['lo:trıŋən], *n.* Lorraine.

Lötkolben ['lø:tkɔlbən], *m.* (—s, *pl.* —) soldering iron.

Lotleine ['lo:tlaınə], *f.* (—, *pl.* —n) sounding-line.

Lotrechtstarter ['lo:trɛçtʃtartər], *m.* (—s, *pl.* —) (*Aviat.*) vertical take-off plane (V.T.O.L.).

Lötrohr

Lötrohr ['lø:tro:r], *n.* (—s, *pl.* —e) soldering-pipe.

Lotse ['lo:tsə], *m.* (—n, *pl.* —n) (*Naut.*) pilot.

Lotterbett ['lɔtərbɛt], *n.* (—es, *pl.* —en) bed of idleness; (*obs.*) couch.

Lotterie [lɔtə'ri:], *f.* (—, *pl.* —n) lottery, sweep-stake.

Lotterleben ['lɔtərle:bən], *n.* (—s, *no pl.*) dissolute life.

Löwe ['lø:və], *m.* (—n, *pl.* —n) (*Zool.*) lion.

Löwenbändiger ['lø:vənbɛndɪgər], *m.* (—s, *pl.*—) lion tamer.

Löwengrube ['lø:vəngru:bə], *f.* (—, *pl.* —n) lion's den.

Löwenmaul ['lø:vənmaul], *n.* (—s, *no pl.*) (*Bot.*) snapdragon.

Löwenzahn ['lø:vəntsa:n], *m.* (—s, *no pl.*) (*Bot.*) dandelion.

Löwin ['lø:vɪn], *f.* (—, *pl.* —nen) (*Zool.*) lioness.

Luchs [luks], *m.* (—es, *pl.* —e) lynx.

Lücke ['lykə], *f.* (—, *pl.* —n) gap, breach; (*fig.*) omission, defect, blank.

Lückenbüßer ['lykənby:sər], *m.* (—s, *pl.* —) stop-gap, stand-in.

lückenhaft ['lykənhaft], *adj.* fragmentary, incomplete, imperfect.

Luder ['lu:dər], *n.* (—s, *pl.* —) (*rare*) carrion; (*vulg.*) beast, trollop; *dummes* —, silly ass, fathead.

Luderleben ['lu:dərle:bən], *n.* (—s, *no pl.*) dissolute life.

ludern ['lu:dərn], *v.n.* lead a dissolute life.

Luft [luft], *f.* (—, *pl.* ⁓e) air.

Luftbrücke ['luftbrykə], *f.* (—, *no pl.*) air-lift.

Lüftchen ['lyftçən], *n.* (—s, *pl.* —) gentle breeze.

luftdicht ['luftdɪçt], *adj.* airtight.

Luftdruck ['luftdruk], *m.* (—s, *no pl.*) air pressure, atmospheric pressure; blast.

Luftdruckmesser ['luftdrukmɛsər], *m.* (—s, *pl.* —) barometer, pressure-gauge.

lüften ['lyftən], *v.a.* air, ventilate.

luftförmig ['luftfœrmɪç], *adj.* gaseous.

luftig ['luftɪç], *adj.* airy, windy.

Luftklappe ['luftklapə], *f.* (—, *pl.* —n) air-valve.

Luftkurort ['luftku:rɔrt], *m.* (—s, *pl.* —e) health resort.

Luftlinie ['luftli:njə], *f.* (—, *pl.*—n) beeline; *in der* —, as the crow flies; (*Aviat.*) airline.

Luftloch ['luftlɔx], *n.* (—s, *pl.* ⁓er) air-pocket.

Luftraum ['luftraum], *m.* (—s, *no pl.*) atmosphere; air space.

Luftröhre ['luftrø:rə], *f.* (—, *pl.* —n) windpipe.

Luftschiff ['luftʃɪf], *n.* (—es, *pl.* —e) air-ship.

Luftschiffahrt ['luftʃɪfa:rt], *f.* (—, *no pl.*) aeronautics.

Luftspiegelung ['luftʃpi:gəluŋ], *f.* (—, *pl.* —en) mirage.

Luftsprung ['luftʃpruŋ], *m.* (—s, *pl.* ⁓e) caper, gambol; ⁓e *machen*, caper, gambol.

Lüftung ['lyftuŋ], *f.* (—, *no pl.*) airing, ventilation.

Lug [lu:k], *m.* (—s, *no pl.*) (*obs.*) lie; — *und Trug*, a pack of lies.

Lüge ['ly:gə], *f.* (—, *pl.* —n) lie, falsehood, fib; *einen* — *strafen*, give s.o. the lie.

lügen ['ly:gən], *v.n. irr.* lie, tell a lie.

lügenhaft ['ly:gənhaft], *adj.* lying, false, untrue.

Lügner ['ly:gnər], *m.* (—s, *pl.* —) liar.

Luke ['lu:kə], *f.* (—, *pl.* —n) dormerwindow; (*ship*) hatch.

Lümmel ['lyməl], *m.* (—s, *pl.* —) lout; hooligan.

Lump [lump], *m.* (—s, —en, *pl.* —e, —en) scoundrel, blackguard.

Lumpen ['lumpən], *m.* (—s, *pl.* —) rag, tatter.

Lumpengesindel ['lumpəngəzindəl], *n.* (—s, *no pl.*) rabble, riffraff.

Lumpenpack ['lumpənpak], *n.* (—s, *no pl.*) rabble, riffraff.

Lumpensammler ['lumpənzamlər], *m.* (—s, *pl.* —) rag-and-bone-man.

Lumperei [lumpə'rai], *f.* (—, *pl.* —en) shabby trick; meanness; trifle.

lumpig ['lumpɪç], *adj.* ragged; (*fig.*) shabby, mean.

Lunge ['luŋə], *f.* (—, *pl.* —n) (*human*) lung; (*animals*) lights.

Lungenentzündung ['luŋənentsyn-duŋ], *f.* (—, *no pl.*) pneumonia.

Lungenkrankheit ['luŋənkraŋkhait], *f.* (—, *pl.* —en) pulmonary disease.

Lungenkraut ['luŋənkraut], *n.* (—s, *pl.* ⁓er) lungwort.

Lungenschwindsucht ['luŋənʃvint-zuxt], *f.* (—, *no pl.*) pulmonary consumption, tuberculosis.

lungern ['luŋərn], *v.n.* idle, loiter.

Lunte ['luntə], *f.* (—, *pl.* —n) fuse, slow-match; — *riechen*, smell a rat.

Lupe ['lu:pə], *f.* (—, *pl.* —n) magnifying glass, lens; *etwas durch die* — *besehen*, examine s.th. closely, scrutinise s.th.; *unter die* — *nehmen*, examine closely.

lüpfen ['lypfən], *v.a.* lift.

Lupine [lu'pi:nə], *f.* (—, *pl.* —n) (*Bot.*) lupin.

Lust [lust], *f.* (—, *pl.* ⁓e) enjoyment, pleasure, delight; desire, wish, inclination, liking; — *bekommen zu*, feel inclined to; — *haben auf*, have a mind to, feel like; *nicht übel* — *haben*, have half a mind to.

Lustbarkeit ['lustba:rkait], *f.* (—, *pl.* —en) amusement, diversion, entertainment, pleasure.

Lustdirne ['lustdɪrnə], *f.* (—, *pl.* —n) prostitute.

lüstern ['lystərn], *adj.* lustful, lascivious.

lustig ['lustɪç], *adj,* gay, merry, cheerful, amusing, funny; — *sein*, make merry; *sich über einen* — *machen*, poke fun at s.o.

Lüstling ['lystlɪŋ], *m.* (—s, *pl.* —e) libertine, lecher.
Lustmord ['lustmɔrt], *m.* (—es, *pl.* —e) sex murder.
Lustreise ['lustraɪzə], *f.* (—, *pl.* —n) pleasure trip.
Lustschloß ['lustʃlɔs], *n.* (—sses, *pl.* ̈sser) country house, country seat.
Lustspiel ['lustʃpiːl], *n.* (—s, *pl.* —e) comedy.
lustwandeln ['lustvandəln], *v.n. insep.* (*aux.* sein) stroll, promenade.
Lutherisch ['lutərɪʃ], *adj.* Lutheran.
lutschen ['lutʃən], *v.a.* suck.
Lüttich ['lytɪç], *n.* Liège.
Luxus ['luksus], *m.* (—, *no pl.*) luxury.
Luzern [lu'tsɛrn], *n.* Lucerne.
Luzerne [lut'sɛrnə], *f.* (—, *pl.* —n) (*Bot.*) lucerne.
Lymphe ['lymfə], *f.* (—, *pl.* —n) lymph.
lynchen ['lynçən], *v.a.* lynch.
Lyrik ['lyːrɪk], *f.* (—, *no pl.*) lyric poetry.
lyrisch ['lyːrɪʃ], *adj.* lyric(al).
Lyzeum [ly'tseːum], *n.* (—s, *pl.* **Lyzeen**) lyceum, grammar school *or* high school for girls.

M

M [ɛm], *n.* (—s, *pl.* —s) the letter M.
Maas [maːs], *f.* River Meuse.
Maat [maːt], *m.* (—s, *pl.* —s, —en) (*Naut.*) mate.
Mache ['maxə], *f.* (—, *no pl.*) put-up job, humbug, sham, eyewash.
machen ['maxən], *v.a.* make, do, produce, manufacture; cause; amount to; *mach schon*, be quick; *das macht nichts*, it does not matter; *mach's kurz*, cut it short; *etwas — lassen*, have s.th. made; *sich auf den Weg —*, set off; *sich viel (wenig) aus etwas —*, care much (little) for s.th.; *mach, daß du fortkommst*, get out, scram.
Macherlohn ['maxərloːn], *m.* (—es, *pl.* ̈e) charge for making s.th.
Macht [maxt], *f.* (—, *pl.* ̈e) might, power; force, strength; authority; *mit aller —*, with might and main.
Machtbefugnis ['maxtbəfuːknɪs], *f.* (—, *pl.* —se) competence.
Machtgebot ['maxtgəboːt], *n.* (—s, *pl.* —e) authoritative order.
Machthaber ['maxthaːbər], *m.* (—s, *pl.* ̈e) potentate, ruler.
mächtig ['mɛçtɪç], *adj.* mighty, powerful; *einer Sache — ̈sein*, to have mastered s.th.
machtlos ['maxtloːs], *adj.* powerless.
Machtspruch ['maxtʃprux], *m.* (—s, *pl.* ̈e) authoritative dictum; command; decree.

Machtvollkommenheit ['maxtfɔlkə-mənhaɪt], *f.* (—, *pl.* —en) absolute power; sovereignty; *aus eigner —*, of o.'s own authority.
Machtwort ['maxtvɔrt], *n.* (—es, *pl.* —e) word of command, fiat; *ein — sprechen*, bring o.'s authority to bear, speak with authority.
Machwerk ['maxvɛrk], *n.* (—s, *pl.* —e) shoddy product; bad job; concoction; (*story*) pot-boiler.
Madagaskar [mada'gaskar], *n.* Madagascar.
Mädchen ['mɛːtçən], *n.* (—s, *pl.* —) girl; (*servant*) maid; *— für alles*, maid-of-all-work.
mädchenhaft ['mɛːtçənhaft], *adj.* girlish, maidenly.
Mädchenhandel ['mɛːtçənhandəl], *m.* (—s, *no pl.*) white slave trade.
Made ['maːdə], *f.* (—, *pl.* —n) maggot, mite.
Mädel ['mɛːdəl], *n.* (—s, *pl.* —) (*coll.*) *see* **Mädchen**.
madig ['maːdɪç], *adj.* maggoty.
Magazin [maga'tsiːn], *n.* (—s, *pl.* —e) warehouse, storehouse; journal.
Magd [maːkt], *f.* (—, *pl.* ̈e) maid, maidservant; (*Poet.*) maiden.
Magen ['maːgən], *m.* (—s, *pl.* —) (*human*) stomach; (*animals*) maw.
Magengrube ['maːgəngruːbə], *f.* (—, *pl.* —n) pit of the stomach.
Magensaft ['maːgənzaft], *m.* (—es, *pl.* ̈e) gastric juice.
mager ['maːgər], *adj.* lean, thin, slender, slim; (*fig.*) meagre.
Magerkeit ['maːgərkaɪt], *f.* (—, *no pl.*) leanness, thinness, slenderness.
Magie [ma'giː], *f.* (—, *no pl.*) magic.
Magier ['maːgjər], *m.* (—s, *pl.* —) magician.
Magister [ma'gɪstər], *m.* (—s, *pl.* —) schoolmaster; (*Univ.*) Master; *— der freien Künste*, Master of Arts.
Magistrat [magɪs'traːt], *m.* (—s, *pl.* —e) municipal board, local authority.
magnetisch [mag'neːtɪʃ], *adj.* magnetic.
magnetisieren [magneti'ziːrən], *v.a.* magnetise.
Magnetismus [magne'tɪsmus], *m.* (—, *pl.* —men) magnetism; (*person*) mesmerism; *Lehre vom —*, magnetics.
Magnifizenz [magnifi'tsɛnts], *f.* (—, *pl.* —en) magnificence; *seine —*, (*Univ.*) title of Vice-Chancellor.
Mahagoni [maha'goːni], *n.* (—s, *no pl.*) mahogany.
Mahd [maːt], *f.* (—, *pl.* —en) mowing.
mähen ['mɛːən], *v.a.* mow.
Mäher ['mɛːər], *m.* (—s, *pl.* —) mower.
Mahl [maːl], *n.* (—s, *pl.* —e, ̈er) meal, repast.
mahlen ['maːlən], *v.a.* grind.
Mahlstrom ['maːlʃtroːm], *m.* (—s, *no pl.*) maelstrom, whirlpool, eddy.
Mahlzahn ['maːltsaːn], *m.* (—s, *pl.* ̈e) molar, grinder.

Mahlzeit ['ma:ltsaɪt], *f.* (—, *pl.* **—en**) meal, repast.

Mähmaschine ['mɛ:maʃi:nə], *f.* (—, *pl.* **—n**) reaping-machine; lawn-mower.

Mähne ['mɛ:nə], *f.* (—, *pl.* **—n**) mane.

mahnen ['ma:nən], *v.a.* remind, admonish, warn; (*debtor*) demand payment, dun.

Mähre ['mɛ:rə], *f.* (—, *pl.* **—n**) mare.

Mähren ['mɛ:rən], *n.* Moravia.

Mai [maɪ], *m.* (**—s**, *pl.* **—e**) May.

Maid [maɪt], *f.* (—, *no pl.*) (*Poet.*) maiden.

Maiglöckchen ['maɪɡlœkçən], *n.* (**—s**, *pl.* —) (*Bot.*) lily of the valley.

Maikäfer ['maɪkɛ:fər], *m.* (**—s**, *pl.* —) (*Ent.*) cockchafer.

Mailand ['maɪlant], *n.* Milan.

Mais [maɪs], *m.* (**—es**, *no pl.*) (*Bot.*) maize, Indian corn.

Majestät [majɛs'tɛ:t], *f.* (—, *pl.* **—en**) majesty.

majestätisch [majɛs'tɛ:tiʃ], *adj.* majestic.

Major [ma'jo:r], *m.* (**—s**, *pl.* **—e**) (*Mil.*) major.

Majoran [majo'ra:n], *m.* (**—s**, *no pl.*) (*Bot.*) marjoram.

Majorat [majo'ra:t], *n.* (**—s**, *pl.* **—e**) primogeniture; entail.

majorenn [majo'rɛn], *adj.* (*obs.*) of age, over twenty-one.

Majorität [majori'tɛ:t], *f.* (—, *pl.* **—en**) majority.

Makel ['ma:kəl], *m.* (**—s**, *pl.* —) spot, blot; (*fig.*) blemish, flaw, defect.

Mäkelei [mɛ:kə'laɪ], *f.* (—, *pl.* **—en**) fault-finding, carping; fastidiousness.

makellos ['ma:kəllo:s], *adj.* spotless, immaculate.

mäkeln ['mɛ:kəln], *v.n.* find fault (with), cavil (at).

Makkabäer [maka'bɛ:ər], *m.* Maccabee.

Makler ['ma:klər], *m.* (**—s**, *pl.* —) broker.

Mäkler ['mɛ:klər], *m.* (**—s**, *pl.* —) fault-finder, caviller.

Maklergebühr [ma:klərɡəby:r], *f.* (—, *pl.* **—en**) brokerage.

Makrele [ma'kre:lə], *f.* (—, *pl.* **—n**) (*Zool.*) mackerel.

Makrone [ma'kro:nə], *f.* (—, *pl.* **—n**) macaroon.

Makulatur [makula'tu:r], *f.* (—, *no pl.*) waste paper.

Mal [ma:l], *n.* (**—s**, *pl.* **—e**) mark, sign, token; monument; mole, birthmark; stain; time; *dieses* —, this time, this once; *manches* —, sometimes; *mehrere* **—e**, several times; *mit einem* —, all of a sudden.

mal [ma:l], *adv. & part.* once; *noch*—, once more; (*coll.*) *hör* —, I say.

Malaya [ma'laɪa], *n.* Malaya.

malen ['ma:lən], *v.a.* paint.

Maler ['ma:lər], *m.* (**—s**, *pl.* —) painter.

Malerei [ma:lə'raɪ], *f.* (—, *pl.* **—en**) painting; picture.

malerisch ['ma:lərɪʃ], *adj.* picturesque.

Malerleinwand ['ma:lərlaɪnvant], *f.* (—, *no pl.*) canvas.

Malheur [ma'lø:r], *n.* (**—s**, *pl.* **—e**) misfortune, mishap.

Mali [ma:li] *n.* Mali.

maliziös [mali'tsjø:s], *adj.* malicious.

Malkasten ['ma:lkastən], *m.* (**—s**, *pl.* **⁻**) paint-box.

Malstein ['ma:lʃtaɪn], *m.* (**—s**, *pl.* **—e**) monument; boundary stone.

Malstock ['ma:lʃtɔk], *m.* (**—s**, *pl.* **⁻e**) maulstick, mahlstick.

Malteserorden [mal'te:zərɔrdən], *m.* (**—s**, *no pl.*) Order of the Knights of Malta.

malträtieren [maltrɛ'ti:rən], *v.a.* illtreat.

Malve ['malvə], *f.* (—, *pl.* **—n**) (*Bot.*) mallow.

Malz [malts], *n.* (**—es**, *no pl.*) malt; *an ihm ist Hopfen und — verloren,* he is hopeless.

Malzbonbon ['maltsbɔbɔ̃], *m.* (**—s**, *pl.* **—s**) cough-lozenge, malt drop.

Mälzer ['mɛltsər], *m.* (**—s**, *pl.* —) maltster.

Mama [ma'ma:], *f.* (—, *pl.* **—s**) (*fam.*) mummy, mum, (*Am.*) ma.

Mammon ['mamɔn], *m.* (**—s**, *no pl.*) mammon; *schnöder* —, filthy lucre.

Mammut ['mamut], *n.* (**—s**, *pl.* **—e**) mammoth.

Mamsell [mam'zɛl], *f.* (—, *pl.* **—en**) housekeeper.

man [man], *indef. pron.* one, they, people, men; — *sagt,* they say.

manch [manç], *pron.* (**—er**, **—e**, **—es**) many a, some, several.

mancherlei [mançər'laɪ], *adj.* several; of several kinds.

Manchester [man'çɛstər], *m.* (**—s**, *no pl.*) corduroy.

manchmal ['mançma:l], *adv.* sometimes.

Mandant [man'dant], *m.* (**—en**, *pl.* **—en**) client.

Mandantin [man'dantin], *f.* (—, *pl.* **—innen**) female client.

Mandarine [manda'ri:nə], *f.* (—, *pl.* **—n**) mandarin (orange), tangerine.

Mandat [man'da:t], *n.* (**—s**, *pl.* **—e**) mandate.

Mandel ['mandəl], *f.* (—, *pl.* **—n**) almond; (*Anat.*) tonsil; (*quantity*) fifteen; *eine* — *Eier,* fifteen eggs.

Mandoline [mando'li:nə], *f.* (—, *pl.* **—n**) mandolin.

Mangan [maŋ'ga:n], *n.* (**—s**, *no pl.*) (*Chem.*) manganese.

Mangel (1) ['maŋəl], *f.* (—, *pl.* **—n**) mangle, wringer.

Mangel (2) ['maŋəl], *m.* (**—s**, *pl.* **⁻**) deficiency, defect; blemish; lack, shortage, want; *aus* —, for want of; — *haben an,* be short of, lack (s.th.).

mangelhaft ['maŋəlhaft], *adj.* defective, imperfect.

mangeln (1) ['maŋəln], *v.a.* (*laundry*) mangle.

mangeln (2) ['maŋəln], *v.n.* be in want of, be short of; *es —t uns an . . .*, we lack . . . .

mangels ['maŋəls], *prep.* (*Genit.*) for lack of, for want of.

Mangold ['maŋɔlt], *m.* (**—s**, *no pl.*) (*Bot.*) beet, mangel-wurzel.

Manie [ma'ni:], *f.* (**—**, *pl.* **—n**) mania, craze.

Manier [ma'ni:r], *f.* (**—**, *pl.* **—en**) manner, habit; *gute —en haben*, have good manners.

manieriert [mani'ri:rt], *adj.* affected; (*Art*) mannered.

manierlich [ma'ni:rlɪç], *adj.* well behaved, civil, polite.

manipulieren [manipu'li:rən], *v.a.* manipulate.

Manko ['maŋko:], *n.* (**—s**, *pl.* **—s**) deficit, deficiency.

Mann [man], *m.* (**—(e)s**, *pl.* ˙er, (*Poet.*) **—en**) man; husband; *etwas an den — bringen*, get s.th. off o.'s hands, dispose of s.th.; *seinen — stellen*, hold o.'s own; *bis auf den letzten —*, to a man.

Mannbarkeit ['manba:rkaɪt], *f.* (**—**, *no pl.*) puberty; marriageable age.

Männchen ['mɛnçən], *n.* (**—s**, *pl.* **—**) little man, manikin; (*Zool.*) male; *mein —*, (*coll.*) my hubby; *— machen*, (*dogs*) sit on the hindlegs, beg.

mannhaft ['manhaft], *adj.* manly, stout, valiant.

mannigfaltig ['manɪçfaltɪç], *adj.* manifold, multifarious.

männlich ['mɛnlɪç], *adj.* male; (*fig.*) manly; (*Gram.*) masculine.

Mannsbild ['mansbɪlt], *n.* (**—es**, *pl.* **—er**) (*coll.*) man, male person.

Mannschaft ['manʃaft], *f.* (**—**, *pl.* **—en**) men; crew, team.

mannstoll ['manstɔl], *adj.* man-mad.

Mannszucht ['manstsuxt], *f.* (**—**, *no pl.*) discipline.

Manöver [ma'nø:vər], *n.* (**—s**, *pl.* **—**) manoeuvre.

manövrieren [manø'vri:rən], *v.a.* manoeuvre.

Mansarde [man'zardə], *f.* (**—**, *pl.* **—n**) garret, attic.

manschen ['manʃən], *v.a., v.n.* dabble; splash (about).

Manschette [man'ʃɛtə], *f.* (**—**, *pl.* **—n**) cuff.

Mantel ['mantəl], *m.* (**—s**, *pl.* ˙) cloak, overcoat, coat, mantle, wrap; *den — nach dem Winde hängen*, be a timeserver.

Manufaktur [manufak'tu:r], *f.* (**—**, *pl.* **—en**) manufacture.

Mappe ['mapə], *f.* (**—**, *pl.* **—n**) portfolio, case, file.

Mär [mɛ:r], *f.* (**—**, *pl.* **—en**) (*Poet.*) tale, tidings, legend.

Märchen ['mɛ:rçən], *n.* (**—s**, *pl.* **—**) fairy-tale, fable; fib.

märchenhaft ['mɛ:rçənhaft], *adj.* fabulous, legendary; (*coll.*) marvellous.

Marder ['mardər], *m.* (**—s**, *pl.* **—**) (*Zool.*) marten.

Maria [ma'ri:a], *f.* Mary; *die Jungfrau —*, the Virgin Mary.

Marienbild [ma'ri:ənbɪlt], *n.* (**—es**, *pl.* **—er**) image of the Virgin Mary.

Marienblume [ma'ri:ənblu:mə], *f.* (**—**, *pl.* **—n**) (*Bot.*) daisy.

Marienglas [ma'ri:ənglas], *n.* (**—es**, *no pl.*) mica.

Marienkäfer [ma'ri:ənkɛ:fər], *m.* (**—s**, *pl.* **—**) (*Ent.*) lady-bird.

Marine [ma'ri:nə], *f.* (**—**, *pl.* **—n**) navy.

marinieren [mari'ni:rən], *v.a.* pickle.

Marionette [mario'netə], *f.* (**—**, *pl.* **—n**) puppet, marionette.

Mark (1) [mark], *n.* (**—s**, *no pl.*) (*bone*) marrow; (*fruit*) pith, pulp.

Mark (2) [mark], *f.* (**—**, *pl.* **—en**) boundary, frontier province.

Mark (3) [mark], *f.* (**—**, *pl.* **—**) (*coin*) mark.

markant [mar'kant], *adj.* striking, prominent; (*remark*) pithy.

Marke ['markə], *f.* (**—**, *pl.* **—n**) (*trade*) mark, brand; (*postage*) stamp; (*game*) counter.

markieren [mar'ki:rən], *v.a.* mark.

markig ['markɪç], *adj.* marrowlike; (*fig.*) pithy, strong.

Markise [mar'ki:zə], *f.* (**—**, *pl.* **—n**) (sun)blind, awning.

Markt [markt], *m.* (**—es**, *pl.* ˙e) market, market-square, fair.

Marktflecken ['marktflɛkən], *m.* (**—s**, *pl.* **—**) borough; (small) market town.

Marktschreier ['marktʃraɪər], *m.* (**—s**, *pl.* **—**) cheap-jack, quack, charlatan.

Markus ['markus], *m.* Mark.

Marmel ['marməl], *f.* (**—**, *pl.* **—n**) (*obs.*) marble.

Marmelade [marmə'la:də], *f.* (**—**, *pl.* **—n**) marmalade, jam.

Marmor ['marmɔr], *m.* (**—s**, *no pl.*) marble.

Marokko [ma'rɔko], *n.* Morocco.

Marone [ma'ro:nə], *f.* (**—**, *pl.* **—n**) sweet chestnut.

Maroquin [maro'kɛ̃], *n.* (**—s**, *no pl.*) Morocco leather.

Marotte [ma'rɔtə], *f.* (**—**, *pl.* **—n**) whim; fad.

Marquise [mar'ki:zə], *f.* (**—**, *pl.* **—n**) marchioness.

Marsch (1) [marʃ], *m.* (**—es**, *pl.* ˙e) march; *sich in — setzen*, set out; march off.

Marsch (2) [marʃ], *f.* (**—**, *pl.* **—en**) fen, marsh.

marsch! [marʃ], *int.* march! be off! get out!

Marschboden ['marʃbo:dən], *m.* (**—s**, *no pl.*) marshy soil, marshland.

marschieren [mar'ʃi:rən], *v.n.* (*aux.* sein) march.

Marstall ['marʃtal], *m.* (**—s**, *pl.* ˙e) royal stud.

Marter ['martər], *f.* (**—**, *pl.* **—n**) torture, torment.

martern

martern ['martərn], *v.a.* torture, torment.

Märtyrer ['mɛrtyrər], *m.* (—s, *pl.* —) martyr.

Martyrium [mar'ty:rjum], *n.* (—s, *pl.* —rien) martyrdom.

März [mɛrts]. *m.* (—es, *pl.* —e) (*month*) March.

Masche ['maʃə], *f.* (—, *pl.* —n) mesh; (*knitting*) stitch; (*dial.*) bow tie; (*coll.*) racket.

Maschine [ma'ʃi:nə], *f.* (—, *pl.* —n) machine; engine; *mit der* — *geschrieben*, typewritten.

Maschinengarn [ma'ʃi:nəngarn], *n.* (—s, *no pl.*) twist.

Maschinerie [maʃinə'ri:], *f.* (—, *pl.* —en) machinery.

Maser ['ma:zər], *f.* (—, *pl.* —n) (*wood*) vein, streak.

Masern ['ma:zərn], *f. pl.* measles.

Maske ['maskə], *f.* (—, *pl.* —n) mask, visor.

Maskerade [maskə'ra:də], *f.* (—, *pl.* —n) masquerade.

maskieren [mas'ki:rən], *v.a.* mask. — *v.r. sich* —, put on a mask.

Maß (1) [ma:s], *n.* (—es, *pl.* —e) measure, size; moderation, propriety; degree, extent; proportion; — *halten*, be moderate; *einem* — *nehmen*, measure s.o. (for); *in starkem* —, to a high degree; *mit* —, in moderation; *nach* —, to measure; *ohne* — *und Ziel*, immoderately, with no holds barred; *über alle* —*en*, exceedingly.

Maß (2) [ma:s], *m. & f.* (—, *pl.* —e) (*drink*) quart.

massakrieren [masa'kri:rən], *v.a.* massacre, slaughter.

Maßarbeit ['ma:sarbaɪt], *f.* (—, *pl.* —en) (*work*) made to measure; bespoke tailoring.

Masse ['masə], *f.* (—, *pl.* —n) mass, bulk; multitude; *eine* —, a lot.

Maßeinheit ['ma:saɪnhaɪt], *f.* (—, *pl.* —n) measuring-unit.

massenhaft ['masənhaft], *adj.* abundant.

Maßgabe ['ma:sga:bə], *f.* (—, *pl.* —n) *nach* —, according to, in proportion to.

maßgebend ['ma:sge:bənt], *adj.* standard; (*fig.*) authoritative.

massieren [ma'si:rən], *v.a.* massage.

mäßig ['mɛ:sɪç], *adj.* moderate, temperate, frugal.

Mäßigkeit ['mɛ:sɪçkaɪt], *f.* (—, *no pl.*) moderation, temperance, frugality.

Mäßigung ['mɛ:sɪguŋ], *f.* (—, *no pl.*) moderation.

Massiv [ma'si:f], *n.* (—s, *pl.* —e) (*mountains*) massif, range.

Maßliebchen ['ma:sli:pçən], *n.* (—s, *pl.* —) (*Bot.*) daisy.

maßlos ['ma:slo:s], *adj.* immoderate; (*fig.*) extravagant.

Maßnahme ['ma:sna:mə], *f.* (—, *pl.* —n) measure; —*n ergreifen*, take steps.

Maßregel ['ma:sre:gəl], *f.* (—, *pl.* —n) measure.

maßregeln ['ma:sre:gəln], *v.a.* reprove, reprimand.

Maßstab ['ma:sʃta:p], *m.* (—es, *pl.* -̈e) standard; (*maps*) scale; *in kleinem* (*großem*) —, on a small (large) scale.

maßvoll ['ma:sfɔl], *adj.* moderate.

Mast (1) [mast], *m.* (—es, *pl.* —e) mast; pylon.

Mast (2) [mast], *f.* (—, *no pl.*) fattening.

Mastbaum ['mastbaum], *m.* (—s, *pl.* -̈e) mast.

Mastdarm ['mastdarm], *m.* (—s, *pl.* -̈e) rectum.

mästen ['mɛstən], *v.a.* feed, fatten.

Mastkorb ['mastkɔrp], *m.* (—s, *pl.* -̈e) masthead.

Mästung ['mɛstuŋ], *f.* (—, *no pl.*) fattening, cramming.

Materialwaren [mate'rjalva:rən], *f. pl.* groceries; household goods.

materiell [mate'rjɛl], *adj.* material, real; materialistic.

Mathematik [matema'ti:k], *f.* (—, *no pl.*) mathematics.

mathematisch [mate'ma:tɪʃ], *adj.* mathematical.

Matratze [ma'tratsə], *f.* (—, *pl.* —n) mattress.

Matrikel [ma'tri:kəl], *f.* (—, *pl.* —n) register, roll.

Matrize [ma'tri:tsə], *f.* (—, *pl.* —n) matrix, die, stencil.

Matrose [ma'tro:zə], *m.* (—n, *pl.* —n) sailor, seaman.

Matsch [matʃ], *m.* (—es, *no pl.*) slush; mud.

matt [mat], *adj.* tired, exhausted, spent; languid; weak, feeble; (*light*) dim; (*gold*) dull; (*silver*) tarnished; (*Chess*) (check-)mate; — *setzen*, (*Chess*) to (check-)mate.

Matte ['matə], *f.* (—, *pl.* —n) mat, matting.

Matthäus [ma'tɛ:us], *m.* Matthew.

Mattheit ['mathaɪt], *f.* (—, *no pl.*) tiredness, exhaustion, languor, feebleness; (*light*) dimness; (*gold*) dullness.

mattherzig ['mathɛrtsɪç], *adj.* poorspirited, faint-hearted.

Matura [ma'tu:ra], *f.* (—, *pl.* —en) (*Austr.*) school-leaving *or* matriculation examination.

Mätzchen ['mɛtsçən], *n.* (—s, *pl.* —) nonsense; trick; *mach keine* —, don't be silly.

Mauer ['mauər], *f.* (—, *pl.* —n) wall.

Mauerkelle ['mauərkɛlə], *f.* (—, *pl.* —n) trowel.

mauern ['mauərn], *v.a.* build. — *v.n.* lay bricks, construct a wall.

Mauerwerk ['mauərvɛrk], *n.* (—s, *no pl.*) brick-work.

Maul [maul], *n.* (—es, *pl.* -̈er) (*animals*) mouth, muzzle; (*vulg.*) mouth; *das* — *halten*, shut up, hold o.'s tongue; *ein loses* — *haben*, have a loose tongue; *nicht aufs* — *gefallen sein*, have a quick tongue; (*vulg.*) *halt's* —, shut up.

Maulaffe ['maulafə], *m.* (—n, *pl.* —n) booby; —n feilhalten, stand gaping.
Maulbeere ['maulbe:rə], *f.* (—, *pl.* —n) (*Bot.*) mulberry.
maulen ['maulən], *v.n.* pout, sulk.
Maulesel ['maule:zəl], *m.* (—s, *pl.* —) (*Zool.*) mule.
maulfaul ['maulfaul], *adj.* tongue-tied; taciturn.
Maulheld ['maulhɛlt], *m.* (—en *pl.* —en) braggart.
Maulkorb ['maulkɔrp], *m.* (—s, *pl.* ̈e) muzzle.
Maulschelle ['maulʃɛlə], *f.* (—, *pl.* —n) box on the ear.
Maultier ['maulti:r], *n.* (—s, *pl.* —e) (*Zool.*) mule.
Maulwerk ['maulvɛrk], *n.* (—s, *no pl.*) ein großes — haben, (*coll.*) have the gift of the gab.
Maulwurf ['maulvurf], *m.* (—s, *pl.* ̈e) (*Zool.*) mole.
Maurer ['maurər], *m.* (—s, *pl.* —) mason, bricklayer.
Maus [maus], *f.* (—, *pl.* ̈e) mouse.
Mausefalle ['mauzəfalə], *f.* (—, *pl.* —n) mouse-trap.
mausen ['mauzən], *v.n.* catch mice. — *v.a.* (*fig.*) pilfer, pinch.
Mauser ['mauzər], *f.* (—, *no pl.*) moulting.
mausern ['mauzərn], *v.r. sich* —, moult.
mausetot ['mauzəto:t], *adj.* dead as a door-nail.
mausig ['mauzɪç], *adj. sich* — machen, put on airs.
Maxime [mak'si:mə], *f.* (—, *pl.* —n) maxim, motto, device.
Mazedonien [matsə'do:njən], *n.* Macedonia.
Mäzen [mɛ:'tse:n], *m.* (—s, *pl.* —e) patron of the arts, Maecenas.
Mechanik [me'ça:nɪk], *f.* (—, *no pl.*) mechanics.
Mechaniker [me'ça:nɪkər], *m.* (—s, *pl.* —) mechanic.
mechanisch [me'ça:nɪʃ], *adj.* mechanical.
meckern ['mɛkərn], *v.n.* bleat; (*fig.*) grumble, complain.
Medaille [me'daljə], *f.* (—, *pl.* —n) medal.
Medaillon [medal'j5], *n.* (—s, *pl.* —s) locket.
meditieren [medi'ti:rən], *v.n.* meditate.
Medizin [medi'tsi:n], *f.* (—, *pl.* —en) medicine, physic.
Mediziner [medi'tsi:nər], *m.* (—s, *pl.* —) physician, medical practitioner, student of medicine.
medizinisch [medi'tsi:nɪʃ], *adj.* medical, medicinal.
Meer [me:r], *n.* (—es, *pl.* —e) sea, ocean; offnes —, high seas; am —, at the seaside; auf dem —, at sea; übers —, overseas.
Meerbusen ['me:rbu:zən], *m.* (—s, *pl.* —) bay, gulf, bight.

Meerenge ['me:rɛŋə], *f.* (—, *pl.* —n) straits.
Meeresspiegel ['me:rəsʃpi:gəl], *m.* (—s, *no pl.*) sea-level.
Meerkatze ['me:rkatsə], *f.* (—, *pl.* —n) long-tailed monkey.
Meerrettich ['me:rrettɪç], *m.* (—s, *pl.* —e) (*Bot.*) horse-radish.
Meerschaum ['me:rʃaum], *m.* (—s, *no pl.*) sea-foam; (*pipe*) meerschaum.
Meerschwein ['me:rʃvain], *n.* (—s, *pl.* —e) (*Zool.*) porpoise.
Meerschweinchen ['me:rʃvainçən], *n.* (—s, *pl.* —) (*Zool.*) guinea-pig.
Mehl [me:l], *n.* (—es, *no pl.*) flour; meal; dust, powder.
Mehlkleister ['me:lklaistər], *m.* (—s, *no pl.*) flour paste.
Mehlspeise ['me:lʃpaizə], *f.* (—, *pl.* —n) (*dial.*) pudding, sweet.
mehr [me:r], *indecl. adj., adv.* more; umso —, all the more; immer —, more and more; — als genug, enough and to spare.
Mehrbetrag ['me:rbətra:k], *m.* (—s, *pl.* ̈e) surplus.
mehrdeutig ['me:rdɔytɪç], *adj.* ambiguous.
mehren ['me:rən], *v.r. sich* —, multiply, increase in numbers.
mehrere ['me:rərə], *pl. adj.* several.
mehrfach ['me:rfax], *adj.* repeated.
Mehrheit ['me:rhait], *f.* (—, *pl.* —en) majority.
mehrmals ['me:rma:ls], *adv.* several times.
Mehrzahl ['me:rtsa:l], *f.* (—, *no pl.*) (*Gram.*) plural; majority, bulk.
meiden ['maidən], *v.a. irr.* shun, avoid.
Meierei [maiə'rai], *f.* (—, *pl.* —en) (*dairy*) farm.
Meile ['mailə], *f.* (—, *pl.* —n) mile; league.
Meiler ['mailər], *m.* (—s, *pl.* —) charcoal-kiln, charcoal-pile.
mein(e) ['main(ə)], *poss. adj. my.* — *poss. pron.* mine.
Meineid ['mainait], *m.* (—s, *pl.* —e) perjury; einen — schwören, perjure o.s.
meineidig ['mainaidɪç], *adj.* perjured, forsworn.
meinen ['mainən], *v.a.* mean, intend, think.
meinerseits ['mainərzaits], *adv.* I, for my part.
meinethalben ['mainəthalbən], *adv.* on my account, speaking for myself, for my sake; I don't care, I don't mind.
meinetwegen ['mainətve:gən], *adv. see* meinethalben.
meinetwillen ['mainətvilən], *adv. um* —, for my sake, on my behalf.
meinige ['mainigə], *poss. pron.* mine.
Meinung ['mainuŋ], *f.* (—, *pl.* —en) opinion; meaning; notion; öffentliche —, public opinion; der — sein, be of the opinion, hold the opinion; einem die — sagen, give s.o. a piece of o.'s mind; meiner — nach, in my opinion.

Meinungsverschiedenheit ['maɪnuŋs-ferʃi:dənhaɪt], *f.* (—, *pl.* —en) difference of opinion, disagreement.

Meise ['maɪzə], *f.* (—, *pl.* —n) (*Orn.*) titmouse.

Meißel ['maɪsəl], *m.* (—s, *pl.* —) chisel.

meißeln ['maɪsəln], *v.a.* chisel, sculpt.

meist [maɪst], *adj.* most. — *adv.* usually, generally.

meistens ['maɪstəns], *adv.* mostly.

Meister ['maɪstər], *m.* (—s, *pl.* —) (*craft*) master; (*sport*) champion; *seinen — finden,* meet o.'s match.

meisterhaft ['maɪstərhaft], *adj.* masterly.

meisterlich ['maɪstərlɪç], *adj.* masterly.

meistern ['maɪstərn], *v.a.* master.

Meisterschaft ['maɪstərʃaft], *f.* (—, *pl.* —en) mastery; (*sport*) championship.

Mekka ['mɛka], *n.* Mecca.

Meldeamt ['mɛldəamt], *n.* (—s, *pl.* –er) registration office.

melden ['mɛldən], *v.a.* announce, inform, notify; (*Mil.*) report. — *v.r. sich —,* answer the phone; *sich lassen,* send in o.'s name, have o.s. announced; *sich zu etwas —,* apply for s.th.

Meldezettel ['mɛldətsetəl], *m.* (—s, *pl.* —) registration form.

meliert [me'li:rt], *adj.* mixed; (*hair*) iron grey, streaked with grey.

melken ['mɛlkən], *v.a. irr.* milk.

Melodie [melo'di:], *f.* (—, *pl.* —n) melody, tune.

Melone [me'lo:nə], *f.* (—, *pl.* —n) (*Bot.*) melon; (*coll.*) bowler hat.

Meltau ['me:ltau], *m.* (—s, *no pl.*) mildew.

Membrane [mɛm'bra:nə], *f.* (—, *pl.* —n) membrane, diaphragm.

Memme ['mɛmə], *f.* (—, *pl.* —n) coward, poltroon.

memorieren [memo'ri:rən], *v.a.* memorise, learn by heart.

Menage [me'na:ʒə], *f.* (—, *pl.* —n) household.

Menge ['mɛŋə], *f.* (—, *pl.* —n) quantity, amount; multitude, crowd; *eine —,* a lot.

mengen ['mɛŋən], *v.a.* mix. — *v.r. sich — in,* interfere in.

Mensch (1) [mɛnʃ], *m.* (—en, *pl.* —en) human being; man; person; *kein —,* nobody.

Mensch (2) [mɛnʃ], *n.* (—es, *pl.* —er) (*vulg.*) wench.

Menschenfeind ['mɛnʃənfaɪnt], *m.* (—es, *pl.* —e) misanthropist.

Menschenfreund ['mɛnʃənfrɔynt], *m.* (—es, *pl.* —e) philanthropist.

Menschengedenken ['mɛnʃəngədɛŋkən], *n.* (—s, *no pl.*) *seit —,* from time immemorial.

Menschenhandel ['mɛnʃənhandəl], *m.* (—s, *no pl.*) slave-trade.

Menschenkenner ['mɛnʃənkɛnər], *m.* (—s, *pl.* —) judge of character.

Menschenmenge ['mɛnʃənmɛŋə], *f.* (—, *no pl.*) crowd.

Menschenraub ['mɛnʃənraup], *m.* (—s, *no pl.*) kidnapping.

Menschenverstand ['mɛnʃənferʃtant], *m.* (—es, *no pl.*) human understanding; *gesunder —,* commonsense.

Menschheit ['mɛnʃhaɪt], *f.* (—, *no pl.*) mankind, human race.

menschlich ['mɛnʃlɪç], *adj.* human.

Menschwerdung ['mɛnʃverduŋ], *f.* (—, *no pl.*) incarnation.

Mensur [mɛn'zu:r], *f.* (—, *pl.* —en) students' duel.

Mergel ['mɛrgəl], *m.* (—s, *no pl.*) marl.

merkbar ['mɛrkba:r], *adj.* perceptible, noticeable.

merken ['mɛrkən], *v.a.* note, perceive, observe, notice; *sich etwas —,* bear in mind; *sich nichts — lassen,* show no sign.

merklich ['mɛrklɪç], *adj.* perceptible, appreciable.

Merkmal ['mɛrkma:l], *n.* (—s, *pl.* —e) mark, characteristic, feature.

merkwürdig ['mɛrkvyrdɪç], *adj.* remarkable, curious, strange.

Merle ['mɛrlə], *f.* (—, *pl.* —n) (*dial.*) blackbird.

Mesner ['mɛsnər], *m.* (—s, *pl.* —) sexton, sacristan.

meßbar ['mɛsba:r], *adj.* measurable.

Meßbuch ['mɛsbu:x], *n.* (—es, *pl.* –er) missal.

Messe ['mɛsə], *f.* (—, *pl.* —n) (*Eccl.*) Mass; *stille —,* Low Mass; (*Comm.*) fair; (*Mil.*) mess.

messen ['mɛsən], *v.a. irr.* measure, gauge. — *v.r. sich mit einem —,* pit oneself against s.o.

Messer (1) ['mɛsər], *m.* (—s, *pl.* —) gauge, meter.

Messer (2) ['mɛsər], *n.* (—s, *pl.* —) knife.

Messerheld ['mɛsərhɛlt], *m.* (—en, *pl.* —en) cut-throat, hooligan, rowdy.

Messias [mɛ'si:as], *m.* Messiah.

Meßgewand ['mɛsgəvant], *n.* (—es, *pl.* ·er) chasuble, vestment.

Meßkunst ['mɛskunst], *f.* (—, *no pl.*) surveying.

Messing ['mɛsɪŋ], *n.* (—s, *no pl.*) brass; *aus —,* brazen.

Metall [me'tal], *n.* (—s, *pl.* —e) metal; *unedle —e,* base metals.

Metallkunde [me'talkundə], *f.* (—, *no pl.*) metallurgy.

meteorologisch [meteoro'lo:gɪʃ], *adj.* meteorological.

Meter ['me:tər], *n. & m.* (—s, *pl.* —) (*linear measure*) metre; (*Am.*) meter; (*Poet.*) metre.

methodisch [me'to:dɪʃ], *adj.* methodical.

Metrik ['me:trɪk], *f.* (—, *no pl.*) prosody, versification.

Mette ['mɛtə], *f.* (—, *pl.* —n) (*Eccl.*) matins.

Metze ['mɛtsə], *f.* (—, *pl.* —n) (*obs.*) prostitute.

Metzelei [mɛtsə'laɪ], *f.* (—, *pl.* —en) slaughter, massacre.

metzeln ['mɛtsəln], *v.a.* massacre, butcher.

Metzger ['mɛtsgər], *m.* (—s, *pl.* —) butcher.

Meuchelmörder ['mɔyçəlmœrdər], *m.* (—s, *pl.* —) assassin.

meucheln ['mɔyçəln], *v.a.* assassinate.

meuchlings ['mɔyçlɪŋs], *adv.* treacherously, insidiously.

Meute ['mɔytə], *f.* (—, *pl.* —n) pack of hounds; (*fig.*) gang.

Meuterei [mɔytə'raɪ], *f.* (—, *pl.* —en) mutiny, sedition.

meutern ['mɔytərn], *v.n.* mutiny.

Mezzanin ['mɛtsanɪn], *n.* (—s, *pl.* —e) half-storey, mezzanine.

miauen [mi'auən], *v.n.* mew.

mich [mɪç], *pers. pron.* me, myself.

Michaeli(s) [mɪça'e:li(s)], *n.* Michaelmas.

Michel ['mɪçəl], *m.* Michael; *deutscher* —, plain honest German.

Mieder ['mi:dər], *n.* (—s, *pl.* —) bodice.

Miene ['mi:nə], *f.* (—, *pl.* —n) mien, air; (facial) expression.

Miete ['mi:tə], *f.* (—, *pl.* —n) rent; (*corn*) rick, stack.

mieten ['mi:tən], *v.a.* rent, hire.

Mieter ['mi:tər], *m.* (—s, *pl.* —) tenant, lodger.

Mietskaserne ['mi:tskazɛrnə], *f.* (—, *pl.* —en) tenement house.

Mietszins ['mi:tstsɪns], *m.* (—es, *pl.* —e) rent.

Milbe ['mɪlbə], *f.* (—, *pl.* —n) mite.

Milch [mɪlç], *f.* (—, *no pl.*) milk; (*fish*) soft roe; *abgerahmte* —, skim(med) milk; *geronnene* —, curdled milk.

Milchbart ['mɪlçba:rt], *m.* (—s, *pl.* ⁻e) milksop.

Milchbruder ['mɪlçbru:dər], *m.* (—s, *pl.* ⁻) foster-brother.

milchen ['mɪlçən], *v.n.* yield milk.

Milcher ['mɪlçər], *m.* (—s, *pl.* —) (*fish*) milter.

Milchgesicht ['mɪlçgəzɪçt], *n.* (—es, *pl.* —er) baby face; smooth complexion.

Milchglas ['mɪlçglas], *n.* (—es, *no pl.*) opalescent glass, frosted glass.

Milchstraße ['mɪlçʃtra:sə], *f.* (—, *no pl.*) Milky Way.

Milde ['mɪldə], *f.* (—, *no pl.*) mildness, softness; (*fig.*) gentleness, (*rare*) charity, generosity.

mildern ['mɪldərn], *v.a.* soften, alleviate, mitigate, soothe, allay; —*de Umstände,* extenuating circumstances.

Milderung ['mɪldəruŋ], *f.* (—, *pl.* —en) mitigation, mollifying; soothing.

mildtätig ['mɪltte:tɪç], *adj.* charitable, benevolent, munificent.

Militär [mili'te:r], *n.* (—s, *no pl.*) military, army; *beim* — *sein,* serve in the army.

Miliz [mi'li:ts], *f.* (—, *no pl.*) militia.

Milliarde [mɪl'jardə], *f.* (—, *pl.* —n) a thousand millions; (*Am.*) billion.

Million [mɪl'jo:n], *f.* (—, *pl.* —en) million.

Millionär [mɪljo'ne:r], *m.* (—s, *pl.* —e) millionaire.

Milz [mɪlts], *f.* (—, *pl.* —en) spleen.

Mime ['mi:mə], *m.* (—n, *pl.* —n) mime, actor.

Mimik ['mi:mɪk], *f.* (—, *no pl.*) mime, miming.

Mimiker ['mi:mɪkər], *m.* (—s, *pl.* —) mimic.

Mimose [mi'mo:zə], *f.* (—, *pl.* —n) (*Bot.*) mimosa.

minder ['mɪndər], *adj.* lesser, smaller, minor, inferior.

Minderheit ['mɪndərhaɪt], *f.* (—, *pl.* —en) minority.

minderjährig ['mɪndərjɛ:rɪç], *adj.* (*Law*) under age.

mindern ['mɪndərn], *v.a.* diminish, lessen.

minderwertig ['mɪndərvɛrtɪç], *adj.* inferior, of poor quality.

Minderwertigkeitskomplex ['mɪndərvɛrtɪçkaɪtskɔmplɛks], *m.* (—es, *pl.* —e) inferiority complex.

mindest ['mɪndəst], *adj.* least, smallest, minimum, lowest; *nicht im* —*en,* not in the least, not at all.

mindestens ['mɪndəstəns], *adv.* at least.

Mine ['mi:nə], *f.* (—, *pl.* —n) mine; (*ball point pen*) refill; (*pencil*) lead.

minimal [mini'ma:l], *adj.* infinitesimal, minimum.

Ministerialrat [minister'ja:lra:t], *m.* (—s, *pl.* ⁻e) senior civil servant.

ministeriell [mɪnɪster'jɛl], *adj.* ministerial.

Ministerium [mini'ste:rjum], *n.* (—s, *pl.* —rien) ministry.

Ministerpräsident [mi'nɪstərprɛ:zident], *m.* (—en, *pl.* —en) prime minister; premier.

Ministerrat [mi'nɪstərra:t], *m.* (—s, *pl.* ⁻e) cabinet, council of ministers.

Ministrant [mini'strant], *m.* (—en, *pl.* —en) acolyte; sacristan.

Minne ['mɪnə], *f.* (—, *no pl.*) (*obs.,* *Poet.*) love.

Minnesänger [mɪnə'zɛŋər], *m.* (—s, *pl.* —) minnesinger; troubadour, minstrel.

Minus ['mi:nus], *n.* (—, *no pl.*) deficit.

Minze ['mɪntsə], *f.* (—, *pl.* —n) (*Bot.*) mint.

mir [mi:r], *pers. pron.* to me.

Mirakel [mi'ra:kəl], *n.* (—s, *pl.* —) miracle, marvel, wonder.

mischen ['mɪʃən], *v.a.* mix; (*Cards*) shuffle; (*coffee, tea*) blend.

Mischling ['mɪʃlɪŋ], *m.* (—s, *pl.* —e) mongrel, hybrid.

Mischrasse ['mɪʃrasə], *f.* (—, *pl.* —n) cross-breed.

Mischung ['mɪʃuŋ], *f.* (—, *pl.* —en) mixture, blend.

Misere [mi'ze:rə], *f.* (—, *no pl.*) unhappiness, misery.

Mispel ['mɪspəl], *f.* (—, *pl.* —n) (*Bot.*) medlar (tree).

mißachten [mɪs'axtən], *v.a.* disregard, despise.

mißarten [mɪs'a:rtən], *v.n.* (*aux.* sein) degenerate.

Mißbehagen ['mɪsbəha:gən], *n.* (—s, *no pl.*) displeasure, uneasiness.

mißbilligen [mɪs'bɪlɪgən], *v.a.* object (to), disapprove (of).

Mißbrauch ['mɪsbraux], *m.* (—s, *pl.* ⸚e) abuse, misuse.

missen ['mɪsən], *v.a.* lack, be without, feel the lack of.

Missetat ['mɪsəta:t], *f.* (—, *pl.* —en) misdeed, felony.

mißfallen [mɪs'falən], *v.n. irr.* displease.

mißförmig ['mɪsfœrmɪç], *adj.* deformed, misshapen.

Mißgeburt ['mɪsgəburt], *f.* (—, *pl.* —en) abortion; monster.

mißgelaunt ['mɪsgəlaunt], *adj.* ill-humoured.

Mißgeschick ['mɪsgəʃɪk], *n.* (—s, *no pl.*) mishap, misfortune.

mißgestimmt ['mɪsgəʃtɪmt], *adj.* grumpy, out of sorts.

mißglücken [mɪs'glykən], *v.n.* (*aux.* sein) fail, be unsuccessful.

Mißgriff ['mɪsgrɪf], *m.* (—s, *pl.* —e) blunder, mistake.

Mißgunst ['mɪsgunst], *f.* (—, *no pl.*) jealousy, envy.

mißhandeln [mɪs'handəln], *v.a.* ill-treat.

Missionar [mɪsjo'na:r], *m.* (—s, *pl.* —e) missionary.

mißlich ['mɪslɪç], *adj.* awkward; difficult, unpleasant.

mißliebig ['mɪsli:bɪç], *adj.* unpopular, odious.

mißlingen [mɪs'lɪŋən], *v.n. irr.* (*aux.* sein) miscarry, go wrong, misfire, prove a failure, turn out badly.

mißraten [mɪs'ra:tən], *v.n. irr.* (*aux.* sein) miscarry, turn out badly.

Mißstand ['mɪsʃtant], *m.* (—es, *pl.* ⸚e) grievance, abuse.

Mißton ['mɪsto:n], *m.* (—s, *pl.* ⸚e) dissonance.

mißtrauen [mɪs'trauən], *v.n.* distrust, mistrust.

Mißverhältnis ['mɪsfɛrhɛltnɪs], *n.* (—ses, *no pl.*) disproportion.

Mißverständnis ['mɪsfɛrʃtɛntnɪs], *n.* (—ses, *pl.* —se) misunderstanding.

Mist [mɪst], *m.* (—es, *no pl.*) dung, manure, muck; (*fig.*) rubbish.

Mistel ['mɪstəl], *f.* (—, *pl.* —n) (*Bot.*) mistletoe.

Mistfink ['mɪstfɪŋk], *m.* (—s, *pl.* —e) (*fig.*) dirty child; mudlark.

mit [mɪt], *prep.* (*Dat.*) with. — *adv.* also, along with.

mitarbeiten ['mɪtarbaɪtən], *v.n.* collaborate, cooperate; (*lit. work*) contribute.

mitbringen ['mɪtbrɪŋən], *v.a. irr.* bring along.

Mitbürger ['mɪtbyrgər], *m.* (—s, *pl.* —) fellow-citizen.

mitempfinden ['mɪtɛmpfɪndən], *v.a. irr.* sympathise with.

Mitesser ['mɪtɛsər], *m.* (—s, *pl.* —) (*Med.*) blackhead.

mitfahren ['mɪtfa:rən], *v.n. irr.* (*aux.* sein) ride with s.o.; *einen — lassen*, give s.o. a lift.

mitfühlen ['mɪtfy:lən], *v.n.* sympathise.

mitgehen ['mɪtge:ən], *v.n. irr.* (*aux.* sein) go along (with), accompany (s.o.); *etwas — heißen* or *lassen*, pilfer, pocket, pinch.

Mitgift ['mɪtgɪft], *f.* (—, *no pl.*) dowry.

Mitglied ['mɪtgli:t], *n.* (—s, *pl.* —er) member, fellow, associate.

mithin [mɪt'hɪn], *adv., conj.* consequently, therefore.

Mitläufer ['mɪtlɔyfər], *m.* (—s, *pl.* —) (*Polit.*) fellow-traveller.

Mitlaut ['mɪtlaut], *m.* (—s, *pl.* —e) (*Phonet.*) consonant.

Mitleid ['mɪtlaɪt], *n.* (—s, *no pl.*) compassion, sympathy, pity; *mit einem — haben*, take pity on s.o.

Mitleidenschaft ['mɪtlaɪdənʃaft], *f.* (—, *no pl.*) *einen in — ziehen*, involve s.o., implicate s.o.

mitmachen ['mɪtmaxən], *v.a., v.n.* join in, participate (in), do as others do; go through, suffer.

Mitmensch ['mɪtmɛnʃ], *m.* (—en, *pl.* —en) fellow-man; fellow-creature.

mitnehmen ['mɪtne:mən], *v.a. irr.* take along, take with o.; strain, take it out of o., weaken.

mitnichten [mɪt'nɪçtən], *adv.* by no means.

mitreden ['mɪtre:dən], *v.n.* join in a conversation; contribute.

mitsamt [mɪt'zamt], *prep.* (*Dat.*) together with.

Mitschuld ['mɪtʃult], *f.* (—, *no pl.*) complicity.

Mitschüler ['mɪtʃy:lər], *m.* (—s, *pl.* —) schoolfellow, fellow-pupil, fellow-student, classmate.

Mittag ['mɪta:k], *m.* (—s, *pl.* —e) midday, noon, noontide; *zu — essen*, have dinner or lunch.

Mittagessen ['mɪta:kɛsən], *n.* (—s, *pl.* —) lunch, luncheon.

Mittagsseite ['mɪta:kszaɪtə], *f.* (—, *no pl.*) south side.

Mittäter ['mɪttɛːtər], *m.* (—s, *pl.* —) accomplice.

Mitte ['mɪtə], *f.* (—, *no pl.*) middle, midst.

mitteilen ['mɪttaɪlən], *v.a.* (*Dat.*) communicate, inform, impart.

mitteilsam ['mɪttaɪlzaːm], *adj.* communicative.

Mitteilung ['mɪttaɪluŋ], *f.* (—, *pl.* —en) communication.

Mittel ['mɪtəl], *n.* (—s, *pl.*) means, expedient, way, resource; remedy; (*pl.*) money, funds; *als — zum Zweck*, as a means to an end; *sich ins — legen*, mediate, intercede.

Mittelalter ['mɪtəlaltər], *n.* (—s, *no pl.*) Middle Ages.

mittelbar ['mɪtəlbaːr], *adj.* indirect.

Mittelding ['mɪtəldɪŋ], *n.* (—s, *pl.* —e) medium; something in between.

Mittelgebirge ['mɪtəlgəbɪrgə], *n.* (—s, *pl.* —) hills; (subalpine) mountains.

mittelländisch ['mɪtəllɛndɪʃ], *adj.* Mediterranean.

mittellos ['mɪtəlloːs], *adj.* penniless, impecunious.

Mittelmaß ['mɪtəlmaːs], *n.* (—es, *pl.* —e) average.

mittelmäßig ['mɪtəlmɛːsɪç], *adj.* mediocre.

Mittelmeer ['mɪtəlmeːr], *n.* (—s, *no pl.*) Mediterranean.

Mittelpunkt ['mɪtəlpuŋkt], *m.* (—s, *pl.* —e) centre; focus.

mittels ['mɪtəls], *prep.* (*Genit.*) by means of.

Mittelschule ['mɪtəlʃuːlə], *f.* (—, *pl.* —n) secondary (intermediate) school; (*Austr.*) grammar school; (*Am.*) high school.

Mittelstand ['mɪtəlʃtant], *m.* (—es, *no pl.*) middle class.

mittelste ['mɪtəlstə], *adj.* middlemost, central.

Mittelstürmer ['mɪtəlʃtyrmər], *m.* (—s, *pl.* —) (*Footb.*) centre-forward.

Mittelwort ['mɪtəlvɔrt], *n.* (—es, *pl.* ⸚er) (*Gram.*) participle.

mitten ['mɪtən], *adv.* in the midst; *— am Tage*, in broad daylight.

Mitternacht ['mɪtərnaxt], *f.* (—, *no pl.*) midnight.

Mittler ['mɪtlər], *m.* (—s, *pl.* —) mediator.

mittlere ['mɪtlərə], *adj.* middle; average; mean.

Mittwoch ['mɪtvɔx], *m.* (—s, *pl.* —e) Wednesday.

mitunter [mɪt'untər], *adv.* now and then, occasionally, sometimes.

mitunterzeichnen ['mɪtuntərtsaɪçnən], *v.a., v.n.* countersign; add o.'s signature (to).

Miturheber ['mɪtuːrheːbər], *m.* (—s, *pl.* —) co-author.

Mitwelt ['mɪtvɛlt], *f.* (—, *no pl.*) the present generation, contemporaries, our own times; the world outside.

mitwirken ['mɪtvɪrkən], *v.n.* cooperate.

Mnemotechnik [mne:mo'tɛçnɪk], *f.* (—, *no pl.*) mnemonics.

Möbel ['møːbəl], *n.* (—s, *pl.* —) piece of furniture; (*pl.*) furniture.

mobil [mo'biːl], *adj.* mobile, active, quick; *— machen*, mobilise, put in motion.

Mobiliar [mobil'jaːr], *n.* (—s, *pl.* **Mobilien**) furniture, movables.

mobilisieren [mobili'ziːrən], *v.a.* mobilise.

möblieren [mø'bliːrən], *v.a.* furnish; *neu —*, refurnish.

Mode ['moːdə], *f.* (—, *pl.* —n) mode, fashion; custom, use; *in der —*, in fashion, in vogue.

Modell [mo'dɛl], *n.* (—s, *pl.* —e) model; *— stehen*, model; (*fig.*) be the prototype.

modellieren [modɛ'liːrən], *v.a.* (*dresses*) model; (*Art*) mould.

Moder ['moːdər], *m.* (—s, *no pl.*) mould.

moderig ['moːdrɪç] *see* **modrig**.

modern (1) ['moːdərn], *v.n.* moulder, rot.

modern (2) [mo'dɛrn], *adj.* modern, fashionable, up-to-date.

modernisieren [modɛrni'ziːrən], *v.a.* modernise.

modifizieren [modifi'tsiːrən], *v.a.* modify.

modisch ['moːdɪʃ], *adj.* stylish, fashionable.

Modistin [mo'dɪstɪn], *f.* (—, *pl.* —nen) milliner.

modrig ['moːdrɪç], *adj.* mouldy.

modulieren [modu'liːrən], *v.a.* modulate.

Modus ['moːdus], *m.* (—, *pl.* **Modi**) (*Gram.*) mood; mode, manner.

mogeln ['moːgəln], *v.n.* cheat.

mögen ['møːgən], *v.n. irr.* like, desire, want, be allowed, have a mind to; (*modal auxiliary*) may, might; *ich möchte gern*, I should like to.

möglich ['møːklɪç], *adj.* possible, practicable; feasible; *sein —stes tun*, do o.'s utmost; *nicht —!* you don't say (so)!

Möglichkeit ['møːklɪçkaɪt], *f.* (—, *pl.* —en) possibility, feasibility, practicability; (*pl.*) potentialities; contingencies, prospects (of career).

Mohn [moːn], *m.* (—es, *no pl.*) poppy-(seed).

Mohr [moːr], *m.* (—en, *pl.* —en) Moor; negro.

Möhre ['møːrə], *f.* (—, *pl.* —n) carrot.

Mohrenkopf ['moːrənkɔpf], *m.* (—s, *pl.* ⸚e) chocolate éclair.

Mohrrübe ['moːrryːbə], *f.* (—, *pl.* —n) carrot.

mokieren [mɔ'kiːrən], *v.r. sich — über*, sneer at, mock at, be amused by.

Mokka ['mɔka], *m.* (—s, *no pl.*) Mocha coffee.

Molch [mɔlç], *m.* (—es, *pl.* —e) (*Zool.*) salamander.

Moldau ['mɔldau], *f.* Moldavia.

Mole ['moːlə], *f.* (—, *pl.* —n) breakwater, jetty, pier.

Molekül [mole'kyːl], *n.* (—s, *pl.* —e) molecule.

Molke ['mɔlkə], *f.* (—, *pl.* —n) whey.

Molkerei [mɔlkə'raɪ], *f.* (—, *pl.* —en) dairy.

moll [mɔl], *adj.* (*Mus.*) minor.

Molluske

Molluske [mɔ'luskə], *f.* (—, *pl.* —n) (*Zool.*) mollusc.

Moment (1) [mo'mɛnt], *m.* (—s, *pl.* —e) moment, instant.

Moment (2) [mo'mɛnt], *n.* motive, factor; (*Phys.*) momentum.

Momentaufnahme [mo'mɛntaufna:-ma], *f.* (—, *pl.* —n) snapshot.

momentan [momɛn'ta:n], *adv.* at the moment, for the present, just now.

Monarch [mo'narç], *m.* (—en, *pl.* —en) monarch.

Monarchie [monar'çi:], *f.* (—, *pl.* —n) monarchy.

Monat [mo:nat], *m.* (—s, *pl.* —e) month.

monatlich ['mo:natlɪç], *adj.* monthly.

Monatsfluß ['mo:natsflus], *m.* (—sses, *pl.* ⁖sse) menses.

Monatsschrift ['mo:natsʃrɪft], *f.* (—, *pl.* —en) monthly (*journal*).

Mönch [mœnç], *m.* (—es, *pl.* —e) monk, friar.

Mönchskappe ['mœnçskapə], *f.* (—, *pl.* —n) cowl, monk's hood.

Mönchskutte ['mœnçskutə], *f.* (—, *pl.* —n) cowl.

Mond [mo:nt], *m.* (—es, *pl.* —e) moon; *zunehmender* —, waxing moon; *abnehmender* —, waning moon.

Mondfinsternis ['mo:ntfɪnstərnɪs], *f.* (—, *pl.* —se) eclipse of the moon.

mondsüchtig ['mo:ntzyçtɪç], *adj.* given to sleep-walking; (*fig.*) moon-struck.

Mondwandlung ['mo:ntvandluŋ], *f.* (—, *pl.* —en) phase of the moon.

Moneten [mo'ne:tən], *pl.* (*sl.*) money, cash, funds.

Mongolei [mɔŋgo'lai], *f.* Mongolia.

monieren [mo'ni:rən], *v.a.* remind (a debtor); censure.

monogam [mono'ga:m], *adj.* monogamous.

Monopol [mono'po:l], *n.* (—s, *pl.* —e) monopoly.

monoton [mono'to:n], *adj.* monotonous.

Monstrum ['mɔnstrum], *n.* (—s, *pl.* Monstra) monster, monstrosity.

Monsun [mɔn'zu:n], *m.* (—s, *pl.* —e) monsoon.

Montag ['mo:nta:k], *m.* (—s, *pl.* —e) Monday; *blauer* —, Bank Holiday Monday.

Montage [mɔn'ta:ʒə], *f.* (—, *pl.* —n) fitting (up), setting up, installation, assembling.

Montanindustrie [mɔn'ta:nɪndustri:], *f.* (—, *no pl.*) mining industry.

Montanunion [mɔn'ta:nunjo:n], *f.* (—, *no pl.*) (*Pol.*) European Coal and Steel Community.

Monteur [mɔn'tø:r], *m.* (—s, *pl.* —e) fitter.

montieren [mɔn'ti:rən], *v.a.* fit (up), set up, mount, install.

Montur [mɔn'tu:r], *f.* (—, *pl.* —en) uniform, livery.

Moor [mo:r], *n.* (—es, *pl.* —e) swamp, fen, bog.

Moos [mo:s], *n.* (—es, *pl.* —e) moss; (*sl.*) cash.

Moped ['mo:pɛt], *n.* (—s, *pl.* —s) moped, motorised pedal cycle.

Mops [mɔps], *m.* (—es, *pl.* ⁖e) pug (dog).

mopsen ['mɔpsən], *v.r. sich* —, feel bored.

Moral [mo'ra:l], *f.* (—, *no pl.*) moral, morals.

moralisch [mo'ra:lɪʃ], *adj.* moral.

Morast [mo'rast], *m.* (—es, *pl.* ⁖e) morass, bog, fen, mire.

Moratorium [mora'to:rjum], *n.* (—s, *pl.* —rien) (*payments etc.*) respite.

Morchel ['mɔrçəl], *f.* (—, *pl.* —n) (*Bot.*) morel (edible fungus).

Mord [mɔrt], *m.* (—es, *pl.* —e) murder.

morden ['mɔrdən], *v.a.*, *v.n.* murder.

Mörder ['mœrdər], *m.* (—s, *pl.* —) murderer.

Mordsgeschichte ['mɔrtsgəʃɪçtə], *f.* (—, *pl.* —n) (*coll.*) cock-and-bull story.

Mordskerl ['mɔrtskɛrl], *m.* (—s, *pl.* —e) devil of a fellow; (*Am.*) great guy.

Mordtat ['mɔrtta:t], *f.* (—, *pl.* —en) murder.

Morelle [mo'rɛlə], *f.* (—, *pl.* —n) (*Bot.*) morello cherry.

Morgen ['mɔrgən], *m.* (—s, *pl.* —) morning, daybreak; (*Poet.*) east; measure of land; *eines* —s, one morning.

morgen ['mɔrgən], *adv.* tomorrow; — *früh*, tomorrow morning; *heute* —, this morning.

Morgenblatt ['mɔrgənblat], *n.* (—s, *pl.* ⁖er) morning paper.

morgendlich ['mɔrgəntlɪç], *adj.* of or in the morning; matutinal.

Morgenland ['mɔrgənlant], *n.* (—es, *pl.* —) orient, east.

Morgenrot ['mɔrgənro:t], *n.* (—s, *no pl.*) dawn, sunrise.

morgens ['mɔrgəns], *adv.* in the morning.

morgig ['mɔrgɪç], *adj.* tomorrow's.

Morphium ['mɔrfjum], *n.* (—s, *no pl.*) morphia, morphine.

morsch [mɔrʃ], *adj.* brittle, rotten, decayed.

Mörser ['mœrzər], *m.* (—s, *pl.* —) mortar.

Mörserkeule ['mœrzərkɔylə], *f.* (—, *pl.* —n) pestle.

Mörtel ['mœrtəl], *m.* (—s, *no pl.*) mortar, plaster.

Mörtelkelle ['mœrtəlkɛlə], *f.* (—, *pl.* —n) trowel.

Mosaik [moza'i:k], *n.* (—s, *pl.* —e) mosaic (work); inlaid work.

mosaisch [mo'za:ɪʃ], *adj.* Mosaic.

Moschee [mo'ʃe:], *f.* (—, *pl.* —n) mosque.

Moschus ['mɔʃus], *m.* (—, *no pl.*) musk.

Mosel ['mo:zəl], *f.* Moselle.

Moskau ['mɔskau], *n.* Moscow.

Moskito [mɔs'ki:to], *m.* (—s, *pl.* —s) (*Ent.*) mosquito.

Most [mɔst], *m.* (—es, *no pl.*) new wine, cider.

Mostrich ['mɔstrɪç], *m.* (—s, *no pl.*) mustard.

Motiv [mo'ti:f], *n.* (—es, *pl.* —e) motive; (*Mus., Lit.*) motif, theme.

motivieren [moti'vi:rən], *v.a.* motivate.

Motorrad ['mo:tɔrra:t], *n.* (—es, *pl.* ⁻er) motor-cycle.

Motte ['mɔtə], *f.* (—, *pl.* —n) (*Ent.*) moth.

moussieren [mu'si:rən], *v.n.* effervesce, sparkle.

Möwe ['mø:və], *f.* (—, *pl.* —n) (*Orn.*) seagull.

Mucke ['mukə], *f.* (—, *pl.* —n) whim, caprice; obstinacy.

Mücke ['mykə], *f.* (—, *pl.* —n) (*Ent.*) gnat, fly, mosquito.

Muckerei [mukə'raɪ], *f.* (—, *pl.* —en) cant.

mucksen ['muksən], *v.n.* stir, move, budge.

müde ['my:də], *adj.* tired, weary; — *machen*, tire.

Muff [muf], *m.* (—es, *pl.* —e) muff.

muffig ['mufɪç], *adj.* musty, fusty, stuffy.

Mühe ['my:ə], *f.* (—, *pl.* —n) trouble, pains; effort, labour, toil; *sich* — *geben*, take pains.

mühelos ['my:əlo:s], *adj.* effortless, easy.

mühen ['my:ən], *v.r. sich* —, exert o.s., take pains.

Mühewaltung ['my:əvaltuŋ], *f.* (—, *pl.* —en) exertion, effort.

Mühle ['my:lə], *f.* (—, *pl.* —n) (*flour*) mill; (*coffee*) grinder; game.

Muhme ['mu:mə], *f.* (—, *pl.* —n) (*obs.*) aunt.

Mühsal ['my:za:l], *f.* (—, *pl.* —e) hardship, misery, toil.

mühsam ['my:za:m], *adj.* troublesome, laborious.

mühselig ['my:ze:lɪç], *adj.* painful, laborious; miserable.

Mulatte [mu'latə], *m.* (—n, *pl.* —n) mulatto.

Mulde ['muldə], *f.* (—, *pl.* —n) trough.

muldenförmig ['muldənfœrmɪç], *adj.* trough-shaped.

Mull [mul], *m.* (—s, *no pl.*) Indian muslin.

Müll [myl], *m.* (—s, *no pl.*) dust, rubbish; (*Am.*) garbage.

Müller ['mylər], *m.* (—s, *pl.* —) miller.

mulmig ['mulmɪç], *adj.* dusty, mouldy, decayed.

multiplizieren [multipli'tsi:rən], *v.a.* multiply.

Mumie ['mu:mjə], *f.* (—, *pl.* —n) (*Archæol.*) mummy.

Mummenschanz ['mumənʃants], *m.* (—es, *no pl.*) mummery, masquerade.

München ['mynçən], *n.* Munich.

Mund [munt], *m.* (—es, *pl.* —e, ⁻er) mouth; *den* — *halten*, keep quiet; *einen großen* — *haben*, talk big; *sich den* — *verbrennen*, put o.'s foot in it.

Mundart ['munta:rt], *f.* (—, *pl.* —en) (local) dialect.

Mündel ['myndəl], *m.*, *f.* & *n.* (—s, *pl.* —) ward, minor, child under guardianship.

mündelsicher ['myndəlzɪçər], *adj.* gilt-edged.

munden ['mundən], *v.n. es mundet mir*, I like the taste, I relish it.

münden ['myndən], *v.n.* discharge (into), flow (into).

mundfaul ['muntfaul], *adj.* tonguetied; taciturn.

mundgerecht ['muntgərɛçt], *adj.* palatable; (*fig.*) suitable.

Mundharmonika ['muntharmo:nɪka], *f.* (—, *pl.* —kas, —ken) mouth organ.

mündig ['myndɪç], *adj.* of age; — *werden*, come of age.

mündlich ['myntlɪç], *adj.* verbal, oral, by word of mouth; (*examination*) viva voce.

Mundschenk ['muntʃɛŋk], *m.* (—s, *pl.* —e) cupbearer.

mundtot ['muntto:t], *adj.* — *machen*, silence, gag.

Mündung ['mynduŋ], *f.* (—, *pl.* —en) (*river*) estuary, mouth; (*gun*) muzzle.

Mundvorrat ['muntfɔrra:t], *m.* (—s, *pl.* ⁻e) provisions, victuals.

Mundwerk ['muntvɛrk], *n.* (—s, *no pl.*) mouth; (*fig.*) gift of the gab.

Munition [muni'tsjo:n], *f.* (—, *no pl.*) ammunition.

munkeln ['muŋkəln], *v.n.* whisper; *man munkelt*, it is rumoured.

Münster ['mynstər], *n.* (—s, *pl.* —) minster, cathedral.

munter ['muntər], *adj.* awake; lively, active, sprightly, vivacious, cheerful, gay.

Münze ['myntsə], *f.* (—, *pl.* —n) coin.

Münzeinheit ['myntsaɪnhaɪt], *f.* (—, *no pl.*) monetary unit.

Münzfälscher ['myntsfɛlʃər], *m.* (—s, *pl.* —) (counterfeit) coiner.

Münzkunde ['myntskundə], *f.* (—, *no pl.*) numismatics.

Münzprobe ['myntspro:bə], *f.* (—, *pl.* —n) assay of a coin.

mürbe ['myrbə], *adj.* mellow; (*meat*) tender; (*cake*) crisp; brittle; *einen* — *machen*, soften s.o. up, force s.o. to yield.

Murmel ['murməl], *f.* (—, *pl.* —n) (*toy*) marble.

murmeln ['murməln], *v.n.* murmur, mutter.

Murmeltier ['murməlti:r], *n.* (—s, *pl.* —e) (*Zool.*) marmot; *wie ein* — *schlafen*, sleep like a log.

murren ['murən], *v.n.* grumble, growl.

mürrisch ['myrɪʃ], *adj.* morose, surly, sulky, peevish, sullen.

Mus [mu:s], *n.* (—es, *no pl.*) purée, (apple) sauce; pulp.

Muschel ['muʃəl], *f.* (—, *pl.* —n) mussel, shell; (*telephone*) ear-piece.

Muse ['mu:zə], *f.* (—, *pl.* —n) muse.

Muselman ['mu:zəlman], *m.* (—en, *pl.* —en) Muslim, Moslem.

Musik [mu'zi:k], *f.* (—, *no pl.*) music.

musikalisch [muzi'ka:lɪʃ], *adj.* musical.

Musikant [muzi'kant], *m.* (—en, *pl.* —en) musician; performer.

Musiker ['mu:zɪkər], *m.* (—s, *pl.* —) musician.

musizieren [muzi'tsi:rən], *v.n.* play music.

Muskateller [muska'tɛlər], *m.* (—s, *no pl.*) muscatel (wine).

Muskatnuß [mus'ka:tnus], *f.* (—, *pl.* ⁺sse) nutmeg.

Muskel ['muskəl], *m.* (—s, *pl.* —n) muscle.

muskelig ['musklɪç] *see* **musklig**

Muskete [mus'ke:tə], *f.* (—, *pl.* —n) musket.

Musketier [muske'ti:r], *m.* (—s, *pl.* —e) musketeer.

musklig ['musklɪç], *adj.* muscular.

muskulös [musku'lø:s], *adj.* muscular.

Muße ['mu:sə], *f.* (—, *no pl.*) leisure; *mit* —, leisurely, at leisure.

Musselin [musə'li:n], *m.* (—s, *pl.* —e) muslin.

müssen ['mysən], *v.n. irr.* have to, be forced, be compelled, be obliged; *ich muß*, I must, I have to.

müßig ['my:sɪç], *adj.* idle, lazy, unemployed.

Müßiggang ['my:sɪçgaŋ], *m.* (—s, *no pl.*) idleness, laziness, sloth.

Muster ['mustər], *n.* (—s, *pl.* —) sample; pattern; (proto-)type; (*fig.*) example.

Musterbild ['mustərbɪlt], *n.* (—s, *pl.* —er) paragon.

mustergültig ['mustərgyltɪç], *adj.* exemplary; standard; excellent.

musterhaft ['mustərhaft], *adj.* exemplary.

mustern ['mustərn], *v.a.* examine, muster, scan; (*troops*) review, inspect.

Musterung ['mustəruŋ], *f.* (—, *pl.* —en) review; examination, inspection.

Mut ['mu:t], *m.* (—es, *no pl.*) courage, spirit; — *fassen*, take heart, muster up courage.

Mutation [muta'tsjo:n], *f.* (—, *pl.* —en) change.

mutieren [mu'ti:rən], *v.n.* change; (*voice*) break.

mutig ['mu:tɪç], *adj.* courageous, brave.

mutlos ['mu:tlo:s], *adj.* discouraged, dejected, despondent.

mutmaßen ['mu:tma:sən], *v.a. insep.* surmise, suppose, conjecture.

Mutter ['mutər], *f.* (—, *pl.* ⁺) mother; (*screw*) nut.

Mutterkorn ['mutərkɔrn], *n.* (—s, *no pl.*) ergot.

Mutterkuchen ['mutərku:xən], *m.* (—s, *pl.* —) placenta, after-birth.

Mutterleib ['mutərlaip], *m.* (—s, *no pl.*) womb, uterus.

Muttermal ['mutərma:l], *n.* (—s, *pl.* —e) birth-mark.

Mutterschaft ['mutərʃaft], *f.* (—, *no pl.*) motherhood, maternity.

mutterseelenallein ['mutərze:lən-alain], *adj.* quite alone; (*coll.*) all on o.'s own.

Muttersöhnchen ['mutərzø:nçən], *n.* (—s, *pl.* —) mother's darling, spoilt child.

Mutterwitz ['mutərvɪts], *m.* (—es, *no pl.*) mother-wit, native wit, common sense.

Mutwille ['mu:tvɪlə], *m.* (—ns, *no pl.*) mischievousness, wantonness.

Mütze ['mytsə], *f.* (—, *pl.* —n) cap; bonnet; beret.

Myrrhe ['mɪrə], *f.* (—, *pl.* —n) myrrh.

Myrte ['mɪrtə], *f.* (—, *pl.* —n) (*Bot.*) myrtle.

Mysterium [mɪs'te:rjum], *n.* (—s, *pl.* —rien) mystery.

Mystik ['mɪstɪk], *f.* (—, *no pl.*) mysticism.

Mythologie [mytolo'gi:], *f.* (—, *pl.* —n) mythology.

Mythus ['mytus], *m.* (—, *pl.* **Mythen**) myth.

N

N [ɛn], *n.* (—s, *pl.* —s) the letter N.

na [na], *int.* well, now; —*nu!* well, I never! — *und?* so what?

Nabe ['na:bə], *f.* (—, *pl.* —n) hub.

Nabel ['na:bəl], *m.* (—s, *pl.* —) navel.

Nabelschnur ['na:bəlʃnu:r], *f.* (—, *pl.* ⁺e) umbilical cord.

nach [na:x], *prep.* (*Dat.*) after, behind, following; to, towards; according to, in conformity *or* accordance with; in imitation of. — *adv.*, *prefix.* after, behind; afterwards, later; — *und* —, little by little, by degrees, gradually.

nachäffen ['na:xɛfən], *v.a.* ape, mimic, imitate; (*coll.*) take off.

nachahmen ['na:xa:mən], *v.a.* imitate, copy; counterfeit.

nacharbeiten ['na:xarbaitən], *v.n.* work after hours *or* overtime. — *v.a.* copy (*Dat.*).

nacharten ['na:xa:rtən], *v.n.* (*aux.* sein) resemble, (*coll.*) take after.

Nachbar ['naxba:r], *m.* (—s, —n, *pl.* —n) neighbour.

Nachbarschaft ['naxba:rʃaft], *f.* (—, *no pl.*) neighbourhood, vicinity; (*people*) neighbours.

nachbestellen ['na:xbəʃtɛlən], *v.a.* order more, re-order.

nachbilden ['na:xbɪldən], *v.a.* copy, reproduce.

nachdem [na:x'de:m], *adv.* afterwards, after that. — *conj.* after, when; *je* —, according to circumstances, that depends.

nachdenken ['na:xdɛŋkən], *v.n. irr.* think (over), meditate, muse, ponder.

nachdenklich ['na:xdɛŋklɪç], *adj.* reflective, pensive, wistful; — *stimmen*, set thinking.

Nachdruck ['na:xdruk], *m.* (—s, *pl.* —e) reprint; stress, emphasis.

nachdrucken ['na:xdrukən], *v.a.* reprint.

nachdrücklich ['na:xdryklɪç], *adj.* emphatic; — *betonen*, emphasise.

nacheifern ['na:xaɪfərn], *v.n. einem* —, emulate s.o.

nacheinander ['na:xaɪnandər], *adv.* one after another.

nachempfinden ['na:xɛmpfɪndən], *v.a. irr.* sympathize with, feel for.

Nachen ['naxən], *m.* (—s, *pl.* —) (*Poet.*) boat, skiff.

Nachfolge ['na:xfɔlgə], *f.* (—, *pl.* —n) succession.

nachfolgend ['na:xfɔlgənt], *adj.* following, subsequent.

Nachfolger ['na:xfɔlgər], *m.* (—s, *pl.* —) successor.

nachforschen ['na:xfɔrʃən], *v.a.* search after; enquire into, investigate.

Nachfrage ['na:xfra:gə], *f.* (—, *no pl.*) enquiry; (*Comm.*) demand; *Angebot und* —, supply and demand.

nachfühlen ['na:xfy:lən], *v.a. einem etwas* —, enter into s.o.'s feelings, sympathize with s.o.

nachfüllen ['na:xfylən], *v.a.* replenish, fill up.

nachgeben ['na:xge:bən], *v.n. irr.* relax, slacken, yield; give in, relent, give way.

nachgehen ['na:xge:ən], *v.n. irr.* (*aux.* sein) *einem* —, follow s.o., go after s.o.; (*clock*) be slow; follow up, investigate.

nachgerade ['na:xgəra:də], *adv.* by this time, by now; gradually.

nachgiebig ['na:xgi:bɪç], *adj.* yielding, compliant.

nachgrübeln ['na:xgry:bəln], *v.n.* speculate.

Nachhall ['na:xhal], *m.* (—s, *no pl.*) echo, resonance.

nachhaltig ['na:xhaltɪç], *adj.* lasting, enduring.

nachhängen ['na:xhɛŋən], *v.n. irr. seinen Gedanken* —, muse.

nachher ['na:xhe:r], *adv.* afterwards, later on.

nachherig ['na:xhe:rɪç], *adj.* subsequent, later.

Nachhilfestunde ['na:xhɪlfəʃtundə], *f.* (—, *pl.* —n) private coaching.

nachholen ['na:xho:lən], *v.a.* make good; make up for.

Nachhut ['na:xhu:t], *f.* (—, *no pl.*) (*Mil.*) rearguard.

nachjagen ['na:xja:gən], *v.n.* (*aux* sein) pursue.

Nachklang ['na:xklaŋ], *m.* (—s, *pl.* ⁻e) echo; (*fig.*) after-effect, reminiscence.

Nachkomme ['na:xkɔmə], *m.* (—n, *pl.* —n) descendant, offspring.

nachkommen ['na:xkɔmən], *v.n. irr.* (*aux.* sein) come after, follow; *seiner Pflicht* —, do o.'s duty; comply with; *einem Versprechen* —, keep a promise; *seinen Verpflichtungen nicht — können*, be unable to meet o.'s commitments.

Nachkommenschaft ['na:xkɔmənʃaft], *f.* (—, *no pl.*) descendants, offspring, issue, progeny.

Nachlaß ['na:xlas], *m.* (—sses, *pl.* ⁻sse) inheritance, estate, bequest; remission, discount, allowance.

nachlassen ['na:xlasən], *v.a. irr.* leave behind, bequeath; (*trade*) give a discount of. — *v.n.* abate, subside, slacken.

nachlässig ['na:xlɛsɪç], *adj.* negligent, remiss, careless.

nachlaufen ['na:xlaufən], *v.n. irr.* (*aux.* sein) *einem* —, run after s.o.

Nachlese ['na:xle:zə], *f.* (—, *pl.* —n) gleaning.

nachliefern ['na:xli:fərn], *v.a.* supply subsequently, complete delivery of.

nachmachen ['na:xmaxən], *v.a.* copy, imitate; counterfeit, forge.

nachmals ['na:xma:ls], *adv.* afterwards, subsequently.

Nachmittag ['na:xmɪta:k], *m.* (—s, *pl.* —e) afternoon.

Nachnahme ['na:xna:mə], *f.* (—, *no pl.*) *per* —, cash *or* (*Am.*) collect (payment) on delivery (*abbr.* C.O.D.).

nachplappern ['na:xplapərn], *v.a.* repeat mechanically.

Nachrede ['na:xre:də], *f.* (—, *pl.* —n) epilogue; *üble* —, slander.

Nachricht ['na:xrɪçt], *f.* (—, *pl.* —en) news, information; (*Mil.*) intelligence; — *geben*, send word.

nachrücken ['na:xrykən], *v.n.* (*aux.* sein) move up.

Nachruf ['na:xru:f], *m.* (—s, *pl.* —e) obituary.

nachrühmen ['na:xry:mən], *v.a. einem etwas* —, speak well of s.o.

Nachsatz ['na:xzats], *m.* (—es, *pl.* ⁻e) concluding clause; postscript.

nachschauen ['na:xʃauən], *v.n. jemandem* —, gaze after s.o.

nachschlagen ['na:xʃla:gən], *v.a. irr.* look up, consult (a book).

Nachschlagewerk ['na:xʃla:gəvɛrk], *n.* (—s, *pl.* —e) work of reference, reference book.

Nachschlüssel ['na:xʃlysəl], *m.* (—s, *pl.* —) master-key, skeleton-key.

Nachschrift ['na:xʃrɪft], *f.* (—, *pl.* —en) postscript, (*abbr.* P.S.).

Nachschub ['na:xʃu:p], *m.* (—s, *pl.* ⁻e) (fresh) supply; (*Mil.*) reinforcements.

Nachsehen ['na:xze:ən], *n.* (—s, *no pl.*) *das — haben*, be left out in the cold.

nachsehen

nachsehen ['na:xze:ən], *v.a., v.n. irr.*
look for, look s.th. up, refer to s.th.;
einem etwas —, be indulgent with s.o.

Nachsicht ['na:xzɪçt], *f.* (—, *no pl.*)
forbearance, indulgence.

Nachsilbe ['na:xzɪlbə], *f.* (—, *pl.* —n)
suffix.

nachsinnen ['na:xzɪnən], *v.n.* muse,
reflect.

nachsitzen ['na:xzɪtsən], *v.n.* be kept
in after school.

Nachsommer ['na:xzɔmər], *m.* (—s,
pl. —) Indian summer.

Nachspeise ['na:xʃpaɪzə], *f.* (—, *pl.* —n)
dessert.

nachspüren ['na:xʃpy:rən], *v.n. einem*
—, trace, track.

nächst [nɛːçst], *prep.* (*Dat.*) next to,
nearest to. — *adj.* next.

Nächste ['nɛːçstə], *m.* (—n, *pl.* —n)
fellow-man, neighbour.

nachstehen ['na:xʃte:ən], *v.n. irr.*
einem —, be inferior to s.o.; *keinem*
—, be second to none.

nachstehend ['na:xʃte:ənt], *adv.* below,
hereinafter. — *adj.* following.

nachstellen ['na:xʃtɛlən], *v.n. einem* —,
lie in wait for s.o.

Nachstellung ['na:xʃtɛluŋ], *f.* (—, *pl.*
—en) persecution, ambush; (*Gram.*)
postposition.

nächstens ['nɛːçstəns], *adv.* soon,
shortly.

nachstöbern ['na:xʃtøːbərn], *v.n.* rummage.

nachströmen ['na:xʃtrøːmən], *v.n.*
(*aux.* sein) crowd after.

Nacht [naxt], *f.* (—, *pl.* ⸚e) night;
die ganze — *hindurch,* all night;
bei —, at night; *gute* — *wünschen,*
bid goodnight; *über* —, overnight;
in der —, during the night; *bei* — *und
Nebel,* in the dead of night.

Nachteil ['na:xtaɪl], *m.* (—s, *pl.* —e)
disadvantage, damage.

Nachtessen ['naxtɛsən], *n.* (—s, *pl.* —)
supper; evening meal.

Nachtfalter ['naxtfaltər], *m.* (—s, *pl.* —)
(*Ent.*) moth.

Nachtgeschirr ['naxtgəʃɪr], *n.* (—s,
pl. —e) chamber-pot.

Nachtgleiche ['naxtglaɪçə], *f.* (—, *pl.*
—n) equinox.

Nachthemd ['naxthɛmt], *n.* (—es, *pl.*
—en) night-dress, night-gown.

Nachtigall ['naxtɪgal], *f.* (—, *pl.* —en)
(*Orn.*) nightingale.

nächtigen ['nɛçtɪgən], *v.n.* spend the
night.

Nachtisch ['naxtɪʃ], *m.* (—es, *pl.* —e)
dessert.

Nachtlager ['naxtla:gər], *n.* (—s, *pl.*
—) lodgings for the night; (*Mil.*)
bivouac.

Nachtmahl ['naxtma:l], *n.* (—s, *pl.*
—e) (*Austr.*) supper.

nachtönen ['na:xtøːnən], *v.n.* resound.

Nachtrag ['na:xtra:k], *m.* (—s, *pl.* ⸚e)
supplement, postscript, addition; (*pl.*)
addenda.

nachtragen ['na:xtra:gən], *v.a. irr.*
carry after; add; (*fig.*) *einem etwas* —,
bear s.o. a grudge.

nachträglich ['na:xtrɛːklɪç], *adj.* subsequent; supplementary; additional;
further; later.

Nachtrupp ['na:xtrup], *m.* (—s, *no pl.*)
rearguard.

Nachtschwärmer ['naxtʃvɛrmər], *m.*
(—s, *pl.* —) night-reveller.

Nachttisch ['naxttɪʃ], *m.* (—es, *pl.* —e)
bedside-table.

nachtun ['na:xtu:n], *v.a. irr. einem
etwas* —, imitate s.o., emulate s.o.

Nachtwächter ['naxtvɛçtər], *m.* (—s,
pl. —) night-watchman.

Nachtwandler ['naxtvandlər], *m.* (—s,
pl. —) sleep-walker, somnambulist.

Nachwahl ['na:xva:l], *f.* (—, *pl.* —en)
by(e)-election.

Nachwehen ['na:xve:ən], *f. pl.* after-
math; unpleasant consequences.

Nachweis ['na:xvaɪs], *m.* (—es, *pl.*
—e) proof; (*Lit.*) reference; agency.

nachweisen ['na:xvaɪzən], *v.a. irr.*
prove, establish; (*Lit.*) refer.

Nachwelt ['na:xvɛlt], *f.* (—, *no pl.*)
posterity.

Nachwort ['na:xvɔrt], *n.* (—es, *pl.* —e)
epilogue.

Nachwuchs ['na:xvu:ks], *m.* (—es, *no
pl.*) coming generation; recruits.

Nachzahlung ['na:xtsa:luŋ], *f.* (—, *pl.*
—en) additional payment, supplementary payment.

Nachzählung ['na:xtsɛːluŋ], *f.* (—, *pl.*
—en) recount.

nachziehen ['na:xtsi:ən], *v.a. irr.*
drag, tow; tighten; trace, pencil. —
v.n. follow.

Nachzügler ['na:xtsyːglər], *m.* (—s, *pl.*
—) straggler.

Nacken ['nakən], *m.* (—s, *pl.* —) nape,
scruff of the neck.

nackend ['nakənt], *adj.* naked.

nackt [nakt], *adj.* nude, naked; (*bird*)
callow; (*fig.*) bare; *sich* — *ausziehen,*
strip.

Nadel ['na:dəl], *f.* (—, *pl.* —n) needle,
pin; *wie auf* —n *sitzen,* be on tenterhooks.

Nadelöhr ['na:dəlø:r], *n.* (—s, *pl.* —e)
eye of a needle.

Nagel ['na:gəl], *m.* (—s, *pl.* ⸚) nail;
(*wooden*) peg; (*ornament*) stud; *etwas
an den* — *hängen,* lay s.th. aside, give
s.th. up.

nagelneu ['na:gəlnɔy], *adj.* brand new.

nagen ['na:gən], *v.a., v.n.* gnaw; (*fig.*)
rankle.

Näharbeit ['nɛːarbaɪt], *f.* (—, *pl.* —en)
sewing, needlework.

nahe ['na:ə], *adj., adv.* near, close, nigh;
— *bei,* close to; — *daran sein,* be on
the point of; *es geht mir* —, it grieves
me, it touches me; *einem* — *zu-
treten,* hurt s.o.'s feelings; *es liegt* —,
it is obvious, it suggests itself.

Nähe ['nɛːə], *f.* (—, *no pl.*) nearness,
proximity; *in der* —, at hand, close by.

nahen ['na:ən], *v.n.* (*aux.* sein) draw near, approach.

nähen ['nɛ:ən], *v.a.* sew, stitch.

Nähere ['nɛ:ərə], *n.* (—n, *no pl.*) details, particulars.

Näherin ['nɛ:ərɪn], *f.* (—, *pl.* — innen) seamstress, needlewoman.

nähern ['nɛ:ərn], *v.r. sich —,* draw near, approach.

nahestehen ['na:əʃte:ən], *v.n.* be closely connected *or* friendly (with s.o.).

Nährboden ['nɛ:rbo:dən], *m.* (—s, *pl.* ⁓) rich soil; (*Med., Biol.*) culture-medium.

nähren ['nɛ:rən], *v.a.* nourish, feed. — *v.r. sich — von,* feed on; (*fig.*) gain a livelihood.

nahrhaft ['na:rhaft], *adj.* nourishing, nutritive, nutritious.

Nährstand ['nɛ:rʃtant], *m.* (—es, *no pl.*) peasants, producers.

Nahrung ['na:rʊŋ], *f.* (—, *no pl.*) nourishment.

Nahrungsmittel ['na:rʊŋsmɪtəl], *n.* (—s, *pl.* —) food, provisions, victuals.

Naht [na:t], *f.* (—, *pl.* ⁓e) seam.

Nähzeug ['nɛ:tsɔyk], *n.* (—s, *no pl.*) sewing kit, work box.

naiv [na'i:f], *adj.* naïve, artless, guileless.

Naivität [naivi'tɛ:t], *f.* (—, *no pl.*) artlessness, guilelessness, naïveté.

Name ['na:mə], *m.* (—ns, *pl.* —n) name; *guter —,* good name, renown; *reputation; dem — nach,* by name; *etwas beim rechten —n nennen,* call a spade a spade.

namens ['na:məns], *adv.* called; by the name of.

Namensvetter ['na:mənsfɛtər], *m.* (—s, *pl.* —n) namesake.

namentlich ['na:məntlɪç], *adj.* by name; particularly.

Namenverzeichnis ['na:mɛnfɛrtsaɪçnɪs], *n.* (—ses, *pl.* —se) list of names; (*scientific*) nomenclature.

namhaft ['na:mhaft], *adj.* distinguished, renowned; considerable; — *machen,* name.

nämlich ['nɛ:mlɪç], *adv.* namely, to wit.

Napf [napf], *m.* (—es, *pl.* ⁓e) bowl, basin.

Napfkuchen ['napfku:xən], *m.* (—s, *pl.* —) pound-cake, large cake.

Narbe ['narbə], *f.* (—, *pl.* —n) scar; (*leather*) grain.

Narkose [nar'ko:zə], *f.* (—, *pl.* —n) anaesthesia; narcosis.

Narr [nar], *m.* (—en, *pl.* —en) fool; jester, buffoon; *einen zum —en haben,* make a fool of s.o.; *an einem einen —en gefressen haben,* dote on, be infatuated with s.o.

Narrheit ['narhaɪt], *f.* (—, *pl.* —en) foolishness, folly.

närrisch ['nɛrɪʃ], *adj.* foolish, comical; odd; merry; eccentric, mad; — *werden,* go mad.

Narzisse [nar'tsɪsə], *f.* (—, *pl.* —n) (*Bot.*) narcissus; *gelbe —,* daffodil.

naschen ['naʃən], *v.a., v.n.* pilfer titbits; nibble at, eat sweets.

Näscherei [nɛʃər'aɪ], *f.* (—, *pl.* —en) sweets, dainties, sweetmeats.

naschhaft ['naʃhaft], *adj.* sweet-toothed.

Naschkatze ['naʃkatsə], *f.* (—, *pl.* —n) sweet tooth.

Nase ['na:zə], *f.* (—, *pl.* —n) nose; (*animal*) snout; scent; *stumpfe —,* snub nose; *gebogene —,* Roman nose; *immer der — nach,* follow your nose; *die — hoch tragen,* be stuck-up; *eine feine (gute) — haben,* be good at; not miss much; *die — rümpfen,* turn up o.'s nose; *seine — in alles stecken,* poke o.'s nose into everything; *einem etwas unter die — reiben,* bring s.th. home to s.o.

näseln ['nɛ:zəln], *v.n.* speak with a twang.

Nasenbein ['na:zənbaɪn], *n.* (—s, *pl.* —e) nasal bone.

Nasenbluten ['na:zənblu:tən], *n.* (—s, *no pl.*) nose-bleed.

Nasenflügel ['na:zənfly:gəl], *m.* (—s, *pl.* —) side of the nose; nostril.

naseweis ['na:zəvaɪs], *adj.* pert, saucy.

Nashorn ['na:shɔrn], *n.* (—s, *pl.* ⁓er) (*Zool.*) rhinoceros.

Naß [nas], *n.* (—sses, *no pl.*) (*Poet.*) fluid.

naß [nas], *adj.* wet, moist, damp.

Nässe ['nɛsə], *f.* (—, *no pl.*) wetness, dampness, moisture, humidity.

nationalisieren [natsjonali'zi:rən], *v.a.* nationalise.

Nationalität [natsjonali'tɛ:t], *f.* (—, *pl.* —en) nationality.

Natrium ['na:trjum], *n.* (—s, *no pl.*) sodium.

Natron ['natrɔn], *n.* (—s, *no pl.*) sodium carbonate; *doppelkohlensaures —,* sodium bicarbonate; bicarbonate of soda.

Natter ['natər], *f.* (—, *pl.* —n) (*Zool.*) adder, viper.

Natur [na'tu:r], *f.* (—, *pl.* —en) nature; (*body*) constitution; (*mind*) disposition; *von —,* by nature, constitutionally; *nach der — zeichnen,* draw from nature.

naturalisieren [naturali'zi:rən], *v.a.* naturalise.

Naturalleistung [natu'ra:llaɪstʊŋ], *f.* (—, *pl.* —en) payment in kind.

Naturell [natu'rɛl], *n.* (—s, *pl.* —e) natural disposition, temper.

Naturforscher [na'tu:rfɔrʃər], *m.* (—s, *pl.* —) naturalist.

naturgemäß [na'tu:rgəmɛ:s], *adj.* natural.

Naturgeschichte [na'tu:rgəʃɪçtə], *f.* (—, *no pl.*) natural history.

naturgetreu [na'tu:rgətrɔy], *adj.* true to nature, lifelike.

Naturkunde [na'tu:rkundə], *f.* (—, *no pl.*) natural history.

Naturlehre [na'tu:rle:rə], *f.* (—, *no pl.*) natural philosophy; physics.

natürlich

natürlich [na'ty:rlıç], *adj.* natural; innate, inherent; unaffected, artless. — *adv.* of course, naturally.

Naturspiel [na'tu:rʃpi:l], *n.* (—s, *pl.* —e) freak of nature.

Naturtrieb [na'tu:rtri:p], *m.* (—s, *no pl.*) natural impulse, instinct.

naturwidrig [na'tu:rvi:drıç], *adj.* contrary to nature, unnatural.

Naturwissenschaft [na'tu:rvisənʃaft], *f.* (—, *pl.* —en) (natural) science.

naturwüchsig [na'tu:rvy:ksıç], *adj.* original; unsophisticated.

Nautik ['nautık], *f.* (—, *no pl.*) nautical science.

nautisch ['nautıʃ], *adj.* nautical.

Nazi ['na:tsi], *abbr.* National Socialist.

Neapel [ne'a:pəl], *n.* Naples.

Nebel ['ne:bəl], *m.* (—s, *pl.* —) fog; *leichter* —, haze, mist; *dichter* —, (*London*) pea-souper; (*with soot*) smog.

Nebelschicht ['ne:bəlʃıçt], *f.* (—, *pl.* —n) fog-bank.

neben ['ne:bən], *prep.* (*Dat.*, *Acc.*) near, by, beside, besides, close to, next to; (*in compounds*) secondary, subsidiary, side-. — *adv.* beside, besides.

nebenan [ne:bən'an], *adv.* next door, nearby.

nebenbei [ne:bən'bai], *adv.* besides, by the way, incidentally.

Nebenbuhler [ne:bənbu:lər], *m.* (—s, *pl.* —) rival.

nebeneinander [ne:bənain'andər], *adv.* side by side, abreast.

Nebenfluß ['ne:bənflus], *m.* (—sses, *pl.* ⁓sse) tributary, affluent.

nebenher [ne:bən'he:r], *adv.* by the side of, along with.

Nebenmensch ['ne:bənmɛnʃ], *m.* (—en, *pl.* —en) fellow creature.

Nebensatz ['ne:bənzats], *m.* (—es, *pl.* ⁓e) (*Gram.*) subordinate clause.

Nebenzimmer ['ne:bəntsımər], *n.* (—s, *pl.* —) adjoining room.

neblig ['ne:blıç], *adj.* foggy, misty, hazy.

nebst [ne:pst], *prep.* (*Dat.*) together with, including.

necken ['nɛkən], *v.a.* tease, chaff, banter.

neckisch ['nɛkıʃ], *adj.* droll, playful, arch.

Neffe ['nɛfə], *m.* (—n, *pl.* —n) nephew.

Neger ['ne:gər], *m.* (—s, *pl.* —) Negro.

negerartig ['ne:gəra:rtıç], *adj.* Negroid.

negieren [ne'gi:rən], *v.a.* deny, negate, negative.

nehmen ['ne:mən], *v.a. irr.* take, seize; receive, accept; *einem etwas* —, take s.th. from s.o.; *das lasse ich mir nicht* —, I insist on that, I am not to be done out of that; *ein Ende* —, come to an end; *etwas in die Hand* —, take s.th. in hand; *Schaden* —, suffer damage; *einen beim Wort* —, take s.o. at his word; *sich in acht* —, take care.

Nehrung ['ne:ruŋ], *f.* (—, *pl.* —en) narrow tongue of land, spit.

Neid [nait], *m.* (—es, *no pl.*) envy, grudge.

Neidhammel ['naithaməl], *m.* (—s, *pl.* —) dog in the manger.

neidisch ['naidıʃ], *adj.* envious, grudging, jealous.

Neige ['naigə], *f.* (—, *pl.* —n) remnant, sediment; *zur* — *gehen*, be on the decline, run short, dwindle.

neigen ['naigən], *v.a., v.n.* incline, bow, bend; *zu etwas* —, be inclined to, be prone to. — *v.r. sich* —, bow.

Neigung ['naiguŋ], *f.* (—, *pl.* —en) inclination, proneness; affection; (*ground*) dip, slope, gradient; (*ship*) list.

Neigungsfläche ['naiguŋsflɛçə], *f.* (—, *pl.* —n) inclined plane.

nein [nain], *adv.* no.

Nekrolog [nekro'lo:k], *m.* (—(e)s, *pl.* —e) obituary.

Nelke ['nɛlkə], *f.* (—, *pl.* —n) (*Bot.*) pink, carnation; (*condiment*) clove.

nennen ['nɛnən], *v.a. irr.* name, call by name, term, style.

Nenner ['nɛnər], *m.* (—s, *pl.* —) denominator.

Nennung ['nɛnuŋ], *f.* (—, *pl.* —en) naming, mentioning.

Nennwert ['nɛnve:rt], *m.* (—s, *pl.* —e) nominal value.

Nepal ['ne:pal], *n.* Nepal.

Nerv [nɛrf], *m.* (—s, *pl.* —en) nerve, sinew; *einem auf die* —en *gehen*, get on s.o.'s nerves.

Nervenlehre ['nɛrfənle:rə], *f.* (—, *no pl.*) neurology.

nervig ['nɛrvıç], *adj.* strong; (*fig.*) pithy.

nervös [nɛr'vø:s], *adj.* nervous, irritable, fidgety.

Nerz [nɛrts], *m.* (—es, *pl.* —e) mink.

Nessel ['nɛsəl], *f.* (—, *pl.* —n) nettle.

Nesseltuch ['nɛsəltu:x], *n.* (—es, *no pl.*) muslin.

Nest [nɛst], *n.* (—es, *pl.* —er) nest; (*eagle*) eyrie; *kleines* —, small town.

Nesthäkchen ['nɛsthɛːkçən], *n.* (—s, *pl.* —) youngest child.

nett [nɛt], *adj.* nice, kind, friendly; neat, trim.

netto ['nɛto], *adv.* (*Comm.*) net, clear.

Netz [nɛts], *n.* (—es, *pl.* —e) net; (*Electr.*) grid; *Eisenbahn* —, railway network or system.

netzen ['nɛtsən], *v.a.* (*obs.*, *Poet.*) wet, moisten.

Netzhaut ['nɛtshaut], *f.* (—, *pl.* ⁓e) retina.

neu [nɔy], *adj.* new, fresh; modern; recent; *aufs* —e, *von* —em, anew, afresh; —e, —ere *Sprachen*, modern languages.

Neuenburg ['nɔyənburk], *n.* Neuchâtel.

neuerdings ['nɔyərdıŋs], *adv.* newly, lately.

Neuerer ['nɔyərər], *m.* (—s, *pl.* —) innovator.

neuerlich ['nɔyərlɪç], *adj.* late, repeated.

Neufundland [nɔy'funtlant], *n.* Newfoundland.

Neugier(de) ['nɔygi:r(də)], *f.* (—, *no pl.*) inquisitiveness, curiosity.

neugierig ['nɔygi:rɪç], *adj.* curious, inquisitive.

Neuheit ['nɔyhaɪt], *f.* (—, *pl.* —en) novelty.

Neuigkeit ['nɔyɪçkaɪt], *f.* (—, *pl.* —en) piece of news.

neulich ['nɔylɪç], *adv.* lately, recently.

Neuling ['nɔylɪŋ], *m.* (—s, *pl.* —e) novice, beginner, tyro, newcomer; (*Am.*) greenhorn.

neumodisch ['nɔymo:dɪʃ], *adj.* newfangled, in vogue.

Neumond ['nɔymo:nt], *m.* (—s, *pl.* —e) new moon.

neun [nɔyn], *num. adj.* nine.

Neunauge ['nɔynaugə], *n.* (—s, *pl.* —n) river lamprey.

neunzehn ['nɔyntse:n], *num. adj.* nineteen.

neunzig ['nɔyntsɪç], *num. adj.* ninety.

Neuregelung ['nɔyre:gəluŋ], *f.* (—, *pl.* —en) rearrangement.

Neuseeland [nɔy'ze:lant], *n.* New Zealand.

neutralisieren [nɔytrali'zi:rən], *v.a.* neutralise.

Neutralität [nɔytrali'tɛ:t], *f.* (—, *no pl.*) neutrality.

Neutrum ['nɔytrum], *n.* (—s, *pl.* —ren) (*Gram.*) neuter.

Neuzeit ['nɔytsaɪt], *f.* (—, *no pl.*) modern times.

nicht [nɪçt], *adv.* not; *auch* —, nor; — *doch*, don't; — *einmal*, not even; *durchaus* —, not at all, by no means; — *mehr*, no more, no longer; not any more; *noch* —, not yet; — *wahr?* isn't it? aren't you? (*in compounds*) non-, dis-, a- (*negativing*).

Nichte ['nɪçtə], *f.* (—, *pl.* —n) niece.

nichten ['nɪçtən], *adv.* (*obs.*) *mit* —, by no means, not at all.

nichtig ['nɪçtɪç], *adj.* null, void, invalid.

Nichtigkeit ['nɪçtɪçkaɪt], *f.* (—, *no pl.*) invalidity, nullity.

nichts [nɪçts], *pron.* nothing, nought; — *als*, nothing but.

nichtsdestoweniger [nɪçtsdɛsto've:nɪgər], *adv.* nevertheless.

Nichtsnutz ['nɪçtsnuts], *m.* (—es, *pl.* —e) good for nothing.

Nickel ['nɪkəl], *n.* (—s, *no pl.*) (*metal*) nickel.

nicken ['nɪkən], *v.n.* nod.

nie [ni:], *adv.* never, at no time.

nieder ['ni:dər], *adj.* low, lower, nether; mean, inferior. — *adv.* down.

niedergeschlagen ['ni:dərgəʃla:gən], *adj.* dejected, low-spirited, depressed.

niederkommen ['ni:dərkɔmən], *v.n. irr.* (*aux. sein*) be confined.

Niederkunft ['ni:dərkunft], *f.* (—, *no pl.*) confinement, childbirth.

Niederlage ['ni:dərla:gə], *f.* (—, *pl.* —n) (*enemy*) defeat, overthrow; (*goods*) depot, warehouse; agency.

Niederlande ['ni:dərlandə], *n. pl.* the Netherlands.

niederlassen ['ni:dərlasən], *v.a. irr.* let down. — *v.r. sich* —, sit down, take a seat; settle; establish o.s. in business.

Niederlassung ['ni:dərlasuŋ], *f.* (—, *pl.* —en) establishment; settlement, colony; branch, branch establishment.

niederlegen ['ni:dərle:gən], *v.a.* lay down, put down; (*office*) resign, abdicate. — *v.r. sich* —, lie down.

Niederschlag ['ni:dərʃla:k], *m.* (—s, *pl.* ꞏe) precipitation, sediment, deposit; rain.

niederschlagen ['ni:dərʃla:gən], *v.a. irr.* strike down; (*fig.*) depress, discourage; (*Law*) quash, cancel; (*eyes*) cast down; (*Chem.*) precipitate; (*Boxing*) knock out.

Niedertracht ['ni:dərtraxt], *f.* (—, *no pl.*) baseness, meanness, villainy, beastliness.

Niederung ['ni:dəruŋ], *f.* (—, *pl.* —en) low ground, marsh.

niedlich ['ni:tlɪç], *adj.* pretty, dainty; (*Am.*) cute.

niedrig ['ni:drɪç], *adj.* low; (*fig.*) base, vile.

niemals ['ni:ma:ls], *adv.* never, at no time.

niemand ['ni:mant], *pron.* nobody, no one.

Niere ['ni:rə], *f.* (—, *pl.* —n) kidney.

Nierenbraten ['ni:rənbra:tən], *m.* (—s, *no pl.*) roast loin.

Nierenfett ['ni:rənfɛt], *n.* (—s, *no pl.*) suet.

nieseln ['ni:zəln], *v.n. imp.* drizzle.

niesen ['ni:zən], *v.n.* sneeze.

Nießbrauch ['ni:sbraux], *m.* (—s, *no pl.*) usufruct, benefit.

Niete ['ni:tə], *f.* (—, *pl.* —n) blank; (*Engin.*) rivet; failure.

Niger ['ni:gər], *n.* Niger.

Nigeria [ni'ge:rja], *n.* Nigeria.

Nikaragua [nika'ra:gua], *n.* Nicaragua.

Nikolaus ['nɪkolaus], *m.* Nicholas; *Sankt* —, Santa Claus.

Nil [ni:l], *m.* (—s, *no pl.*) Nile.

Nilpferd ['ni:lpfe:rt], *n.* (—s, *pl.* —e) (*Zool.*) hippopotamus.

nimmer (mehr) ['nɪmər (me:r)], *adv.* never, never again.

nippen ['nɪpən], *v.a., v.n.* sip, (take a) nip (of).

Nippsachen ['nɪpzaxən], *f. pl.* knickknacks.

nirgends ['nɪrgənts], *adv.* nowhere.

Nische ['ni:ʃə], *f.* (—, *pl.* —n) niche.

Nisse ['nɪsə], *f.* (—, *pl.* —n) nit.

nisten ['nɪstən], *v.n.* nest.

Niveau [ni'vo:], *n.* (—s, *pl.* —s) level, standard.

nivellieren [nivɛ'li:rən], *v.a.* level.

Nixe ['nɪksə], *f.* (—, *pl.* —n) waternymph, mermaid, water-sprite.

Nizza

Nizza ['nɪtsa], *n.* Nice.
nobel ['noːbəl], *adj.* noble, smart; (*Am.*) swell; munificent, open-handed, magnanimous.
noch [nɔx], *adv.* still, yet; — *einmal*, — *mals*, once more; *weder* . . . — . . ., neither . . . nor . . .; — *nicht*, not yet; — *nie*, never yet; never before.
nochmalig ['nɔxmaːlɪç], *adj.* repeated.
Nomade [noˈmaːdə], *m.* (—n, *pl.* —n) nomad.
nominell [nomiˈnɛl], *adj.* nominal.
nominieren [nomiˈniːrən], *v.a.* nominate.
Nonne ['nɔnə], *f.* (—, *pl.* —n) nun.
Noppe ['nɔpə], *f.* (—, *pl.* —n) nap.
Norden ['nɔrdən], *m.* (—s, *no pl.*) north.
nördlich ['nœrtlɪç], *adj.* northern, northerly.
Nordsee ['nɔrtzeː], *f.* North Sea.
nörgeln ['nœrgəln], *v.n.* find fault, cavil, carp, nag.
Norm ['nɔrm], *f.* (—, *pl.* —en) standard, rule, norm.
normal [nɔrˈmaːl], *adj.* normal, standard.
Norwegen ['nɔrveːgən], *n.* Norway.
Not [noːt], *f.* (—, *pl.* ⁻e) need, necessity; misery, want, trouble, distress; (*in compounds*) emergency.
not [noːt], *pred. adj.* — *tun*, be necessary.
Nota ['noːta], *f.* (—, *pl.* —s) bill, statement.
Notar [noˈtaːr], *m.* (—s, *pl.* —e) notary.
Notdurft ['noːtdurft], *f.* (—, *pl.* ⁻e) want, necessaries, necessity; *seine* — *verrichten*, ease o.s.
notdürftig ['noːtdyrftɪç], *adj.* scanty, makeshift.
Note ['noːtə], *f.* (—, *pl.* —n) note; (*Mus.*) note; (*School*) mark(s); *nach* —*n*, (*fig.*) with a vengeance.
Notenbank ['noːtənbaŋk], *f.* (—, *pl.* —en) bank of issue.
Notenblatt ['noːtənblat], *n.* (—s, *pl.* ⁻er) sheet of music.
notgedrungen ['noːtgədruŋən], *adj.* compulsory, forced; perforce.
Nothelfer ['noːthɛlfər], *m.* (—s, *pl.* —) helper in time of need.
notieren [noˈtiːrən], *v.a.* note, book; (*Comm.*) quote.
notifizieren [notifiˈtsiːrən], *v.a.* notify.
nötig ['noːtɪç], *adj.* necessary; — *haben*, want, need.
nötigen ['noːtɪgən], *v.a.* compel, press, force, urge; necessitate; *sich* — *lassen*, stand upon ceremony.
Notiz [noˈtiːts], *f.* (—, *pl.* —en) note, notice; — *nehmen von*, take notice of; (*pl.*) notes, jottings.
notleidend ['noːtlaɪdənt], *adj.* financially distressed, indigent, needy.
notorisch [noˈtoːrɪʃ], *adj.* notorious.
Notstand ['noːtʃtant], *m.* (—s, *no pl.*) state of distress; emergency.

Notverband ['noːtfɛrbant], *m.* (—es, *pl.* ⁻e) first-aid dressing.
Notwehr ['noːtveːr], *f.* (—, *no pl.*) self-defence.
notwendig ['noːtvɛndɪç], *adj.* necessary, essential, needful.
Notzucht ['noːttsuxt], *f.* (—, *no pl.*) rape, violation.
Novelle [noˈvɛlə], *f.* (—, *pl.* —n) (*Lit.*) novella, short story, short novel.
Novize [noˈviːtsə], *m.* (—n, *pl.* —n) or *f.* (—, *pl.* —n) novice.
Nu [nuː], *m. & n.* (—, *no pl.*) moment; *im* —, in no time, in an instant.
Nubien ['nuːbjən], *n.* Nubia.
nüchtern ['nyçtərn], *adj.* fasting; sober; jejune; (*fig.*) dry, matter-of-fact, realistic.
Nüchternheit ['nyçtərnhaɪt], *f.* (—, *no pl.*) sobriety; (*fig.*) dryness.
Nudel ['nuːdəl], *f.* (—, *pl.* —n) noodles, macaroni, vermicelli; *eine komische* —, a funny person.
Null [nul], *f.* (—, *pl.* —en) nought, zero; (*fig.*) nonentity.
null [nul], *adj.* null; nil; — *und nichtig*, null and void; *etwas für* — *und nichtig erklären*, annul.
numerieren [numeˈriːrən], *v.a.* number.
Nummer ['numər], *f.* (—, *pl.* —n) number, size, issue.
nun [nuːn], *adv., conj.* now, at present; since; —! now! well! *von* — *an*, henceforth; — *und nimmermehr*, nevermore; *was* —? what next?
nunmehr ['nuːnmeːr], *adv.* now, by this time.
Nunzius ['nuntsjus], *m.* (—, *pl.* —zien) (Papal) nuncio.
nur [nuːr], *adv.* only, solely, merely, but; *wenn* —, if only, provided that; — *das nicht*, anything but that; — *zu*, go to it!
Nürnberg ['nyrnbɛrk], *n.* Nuremberg.
Nuß [nus], *f.* (—, *pl.* ⁻sse) nut.
Nußhäher ['nushɛːər], *m.* (—s, *pl.* —) (*Orn.*) jay.
Nüster ['nystər], *f.* (—, *pl.* —n) (*horse*) nostril.
Nutzanwendung ['nutsanvɛnduŋ], *f.* (—, *pl.* —en) practical application.
nutzbar ['nutsbaːr], *adj.* useful, usable, productive.
nütze ['nytsə], *adj.* useful, of use.
Nutzen ['nutsən], *m.* (—s, *pl.* —) use, utility; profit, gain, advantage, benefit; — *bringen*, yield profit; — *ziehen aus*, derive profit from.
nützen ['nytsən], *v.a.* make use of, use. — *v.n.* be of use, serve, be effective, work.
nützlich ['nytslɪç], *adj.* useful.
nutzlos ['nutsloːs], *adj.* useless.
Nutznießer ['nutsniːsər], *m.* (—s, *pl.* —) beneficiary, usufructuary.
Nymphe ['nymfə], *f.* (—, *pl.* —en) nymph.

162

O

O [o:], *n*, (**—s**, *pl.* **—s**) the letter O.
o! [o:], *excl.* oh!
Oase [o'a:zə], *f.* (**—**, *pl.* **—n**) oasis.
ob [ɔp], *conj.* whether; if; *als* **—**, as if; *und* **—**! rather! yes, indeed! **—** *prep.* (*Genit.*, *Dat.*) on account of; upon, on.
Obacht ['o:baxt], *f.* (**—**, *no pl.*) heed, care; **—** *geben*, pay attention, look out.
Obdach ['ɔpdax], *n.* (**—es**, *no pl.*) shelter, lodging.
Obduktion ['ɔpdukts'jo:n], *f.* (**—**, *pl.* **—en**) post-mortem examination.
oben [o:bən], *adv.* above, aloft, on top; (*house*) upstairs; (*water*) on the surface; *von* **—** *bis unten*, from top to bottom; *von* **—** *herab*, from above; (*fig.*) haughtily, superciliously.
obendrein [o:bən'draɪn], *adv.* besides, into the bargain.
obengenannt ['o:bəngənant], *adj.* above-mentioned.
Ober ['o:bər], *m.* (**—s**, *pl.* **—**) head waiter; *Herr* **—**!, waiter!; (*in compounds*) upper, chief.
ober ['o:bər], *adj.* upper, higher; chief; superior.
Oberfläche ['o:bərflɛçə], *f.* (**—**, *pl.* **—n**) surface.
oberflächlich ['o:bərflɛçlɪç], *adj.* superficial, casual.
oberhalb ['o:bərhalp], *adv.*, *prep.* (*Genit.*) above.
Oberin ['o:bərɪn], *f.* (**—**, *pl.* **—innen**) (*Eccl.*) Mother Superior; hospital matron.
Oberschule ['o:bərʃu:lə], *f.* (**—**, *pl.* **—n**) high school, secondary school.
Oberst ['o:bərst], *m.* (**—en**, *pl.* **—en**) colonel.
Oberstaatsanwalt ['o:bərʃta:tsanvalt], *m.* (**—s**, *pl.* ⏜**e**) Attorney-General.
oberste ['o:bərstə], *adj.* uppermost, highest, supreme.
Oberstimme ['o:bərʃtɪmə], *f.* (**—**, *pl.* **—n**) treble, soprano.
Oberstübchen ['o:bərʃty:pçən], *n.* (**—s**, *pl.* **—**) (*fig.*) *nicht richtig im* **—** *sein*, have bats in the belfry.
Obervolta ['o:bərvɔltə], *n.* Upper Volta.
obgleich [ɔp'glaɪç], *conj.* though, although.
Obhut ['ɔphu:t], *f.* (**—**, *no pl.*) keeping, care, protection.
obig ['o:bɪç], *adj.* foregoing, above-mentioned, aforementioned, aforesaid.
objektiv [ɔpjɛk'ti:f], *adj.* objective, impartial, unprejudiced.
Oblate [o'bla:tə], *f.* (**—**, *pl.* **—n**) wafer; (*Eccl.*) Host.

obliegen ['ɔpli:gən], *v.n. irr.* be incumbent upon s.o.; be o.'s duty; apply o.s. to.
Obmann ['ɔpman], *m.* (**—es**, *pl.* ⏜**er**) chairman; (*jury*) foreman.
Obrigkeit ['o:brɪçkaɪt], *f.* (**—**, *pl.* **—en**) authorities.
obschon [ɔp'ʃo:n] *see under* **obwohl**.
Observatorium ['ɔpzɛrva'to:rjum], *n.* (**—s**, *pl.* **—rien**) observatory.
obsiegen ['ɔpzi:gən], *v.n.* (*rare*) be victorious.
Obst [o:pst], *n.* (**—es**, *no pl.*) fruit.
obszön [ɔps'tsø:n], *adj.* obscene.
obwalten ['ɔpvaltən], *v.n.* (*rare*) exist, prevail, obtain; *unter den* **—den** *Umständen*, in the circumstances, as matters stand.
obwohl [ɔp'vo:l] (also **obschon** [ɔp'ʃo:n], **obzwar** [ɔp'tsva:r]), *conj.* though, although.
Ochse ['ɔksə], *m.* (**—n**, *pl.* **—n**) (*Zool.*) ox; bullock; (*fig.*) blockhead.
ochsen ['ɔksən], *v.n.* (*sl.*) swot, cram.
Ochsenauge ['ɔksənaugə], *n.* (**—s**, *pl.* **—n**) ox-eye, bull's eye; (*Archit.*) oval dormer window; porthole light.
Ochsenziemer ['ɔksəntsi:mər], *m.* (**—s**, *pl.* **—**) (*obs.*) horse-whip.
Ocker ['ɔkər], *m.* (**—s**, *no pl.*) ochre.
Öde ['ø:də], *f.* (**—**, *pl.* **—n**) wilderness.
öde ['ø:də], *adj.* desolate, bleak, dreary.
Odem ['o:dəm], *m.* (**—s**, *no pl.*) (*Poet.*) breath.
oder ['o:dər], *conj.* or; **—** *auch*, or else; **—** *aber*, or rather.
Ofen ['o:fən], *m.* (**—s**, *pl.* ⏜) stove; oven, furnace.
Ofenpest [o:fən'pɛst], *n.* Budapest.
offen ['ɔfən], *adj.* open; (*fig.*) candid, sincere, frank; **—** *gestanden*, frankly speaking.
offenbar [ɔfən'ba:r], *adj.* obvious, manifest, evident.
offenbaren [ɔfən'ba:rən], *v.a. insep.* make known, reveal, disclose. **—** *v.r. sich einem* **—**, open o.'s heart to s.o.; unbosom o.s.
Offenheit ['ɔfənhaɪt], *f.* (**—**, *pl.* **—en**) frankness, candour.
offenkundig ['ɔfənkundɪç], *adj.* obvious, manifest.
offensichtlich ['ɔfənzɪçtlɪç], *adj.* obvious; apparent.
öffentlich ['œfəntlɪç], *adj.* public.
offerieren [ɔfe'ri:rən], *v.a.* offer.
Offerte [ɔ'fɛrtə], *f.* (**—**, *pl.* **—n**) offer, tender.
offiziell [ɔfi'tsjɛl], *adj.* official.
Offizier [ɔfi'tsi:r], *m.* (**—s**, *pl.* **—e**) officer, lieutenant.
Offizierspatent [ɔfi'tsi:rspatɛnt], *n.* (**—s**, *pl.* **—e**) (*Mil.*) commission.
offiziös [ɔfi'tsjø:s], *adj.* semi-official.
öffnen ['œfnən], *v.a.* open.
oft [ɔft], **oftmals** ['ɔftma:ls], *adv.* often, frequently.
öfters ['œftərs], *adv.* often, frequently.

Oheim

Oheim ['oːhaɪm], *m.* (—s, *pl.* —e) (*Poet.*) uncle.

ohne ['oːnə], *prep.* (*Acc.*) without, but for, except.

ohnehin ['oːnəhɪn], *adv.* as it is.

Ohnmacht ['oːnmaxt], *f.* (—, *pl.* —en) fainting-fit, swoon; impotence; *in — fallen*, faint.

Ohr [oːr], *n.* (—es, *pl.* —en) ear; *bis über beide —en*, head over heels; *die —en spitzen*, prick up o.'s ears.

Ohrenbläser ['oːrənblɛːzər], *m.* (—s, *pl.* —) tale-bearer.

Ohrensausen ['oːrənzauzən], *n.* (—s, *no pl.*) humming in the ears.

Ohrenschmaus ['oːrənʃmaus], *m.* (—es, *no pl.*) musical treat.

Ohrfeige ['oːrfaɪɡə], *f.* (—, *pl.* —n) box on the ear.

Ohrläppchen ['oːrlɛpçən], *n.* (—s, *pl.* —) lobe of the ear.

Ohrmuschel ['oːrmuʃəl], *f.* (—, *pl.* —n) auricle.

oktav [ɔk'taːf], *adj.* octavo.

Oktober [ɔk'toːbər], *m.* (—s, *pl.* —) October.

oktroyieren [ɔktroa'jiːrən], *v.a.* dictate, force s.th. upon s.o.

okulieren [oku'liːrən], *v.a.* (*trees*) graft.

Öl [øːl], *n.* (—s, *pl.* —e) oil; (*rare*) olive-oil.

Ölanstrich ['øːlanʃtrɪç], *m.* (—s, *pl.* —e) coat of oil-paint.

ölen ['øːlən], *v.a.* oil, lubricate; (*rare*) anoint.

Ölgemälde ['øːlɡəmɛːldə], *n.* (—s, *pl.* —) oil painting.

Ölung ['øːluŋ], *f.* (—, *pl.* —en) oiling; anointing; (*Eccl.*) *die letzte —*, Extreme Unction.

Olymp [o'lʏmp], *m.* Mount Olympus.

olympisch [o'lʏmpɪʃ], *adj.* Olympian.

Omelett [oməˈlɛt], *n.* (—s, *pl.* —s) omelette.

Onkel ['ɔŋkəl], *m.* (—s, *pl.* —) uncle.

Oper ['oːpər], *f.* (—, *pl.* —n) opera.

operieren [opə'riːrən], *v.a.*, *v.n.* operate (on); *sich — lassen*, be operated on; undergo an operation.

Opfer ['ɔpfər], *n.* (—s, *pl.* —) sacrifice; victim.

opfern ['ɔpfərn], *v.a.*, *v.n.* offer (up), sacrifice, immolate.

opponieren [ɔpo'niːrən], *v.n.* oppose.

Optiker ['ɔptikər], *m.* (—s, *pl.* —) optician.

oratorisch [ora'toːrɪʃ], *adj.* oratorical.

Orchester [ɔr'kɛstər], *n.* (—s, *pl.* —) orchestra, band.

orchestrieren [ɔrkɛs'triːrən], *v.a.* orchestrate, score for orchestra.

Orchidee [ɔrçi'deː], *f.* (—, *pl.* —n) (*Bot.*) orchid.

Orden ['ɔrdən], *m.* (—s, *pl.* —) medal; (*Eccl.*) (religious) order.

ordentlich ['ɔrdəntlɪç], *adj.* orderly, tidy, methodical, neat; regular; respectable, steady; sound; *—er Professor*, (full) professor.

Order ['ɔrdər], *f.* (—, *pl.* —s) (*Comm.*) order.

Ordinarius [ɔrdi'naːrjus], *m.* (—, *pl.* —ien) (*Univ.*) professor; (*Eccl.*) ordinary.

ordinär [ɔrdi'nɛːr], *adj.* common, vulgar.

ordnen ['ɔrdnən], *v.a.* put in order, tidy, arrange, dispose.

Ordnung ['ɔrdnuŋ], *f.* (—, *pl.* —en) order, arrangement, disposition, routine; tidiness; class, rank; *in —*, all right, in good trim; *nicht in —*, out of order, wrong.

ordnungsgemäß ['ɔrdnuŋsɡəmɛːs], *adv.* duly.

ordnungsmäßig ['ɔrdnuŋsmɛːsɪç], *adj.* regular.

ordnungswidrig ['ɔrdnuŋsviːdrɪç], *adj.* irregular.

Ordnungszahl ['ɔrdnuŋstsaːl], *f.* (—, *pl.* —en) ordinal number.

Ordonnanz [ɔrdo'nants], *f.* (—, *pl.* —en) ordinance; (*Mil.*) orderly.

Organ [ɔr'ɡaːn], *n.* (—s, *pl.* —e) organ.

organisieren [ɔrɡani'ziːrən], *v.a.* organise.

Orgel ['ɔrɡəl], *f.* (—, *pl.* —n) (*Mus.*) organ.

Orgelzug ['ɔːrɡəltsuːk], *m.* (—s, *pl.* ̈e) organ-stop.

Orgie ['ɔrɡiə], *f.* (—, *pl.* —n) orgy.

orientalisch [ɔrjɛn'taːlɪʃ], *adj.* oriental, eastern.

orientieren [ɔrjɛn'tiːrən], *v.a.* inform, orientate; set s.o. right. — *v.r. sich — über*, orientate o.s., find out about; get o.'s bearings.

Orkan [ɔr'kaːn], *m.* (—s, *pl.* —e) hurricane, gale, typhoon.

Ornat [ɔr'naːt], *m.* (—es, *pl.* —e) official robes; vestments.

Ort [ɔrt], *m.* (—es, *pl.* —e, ̈er) place, spot; region; (*in compounds*) local.

örtlich ['œrtlɪç], *adj.* local.

Ortschaft ['ɔrtʃaft], *f.* (—, *pl.* —en) place, township, village.

Öse ['øːzə], *f.* (—, *pl.* —n) loop; *Haken und —n*, hooks and eyes.

Ostasien ['ɔstaːzjən], *n.* Eastern Asia, the Far East.

Ost(en) ['ɔst(ən)], *m.* (—s, *no pl.*) east.

ostentativ [ɔstɛnta'tiːf], *adj.* ostentatious.

Osterei ['oːstəraɪ], *n.* (—s, *pl.* —er) Easter egg.

Ostern ['oːstərn], *f. pl.* (used as *n. sing.*) Easter.

Österreich ['øːstərraɪç], *n.* Austria.

Ostindien ['ɔstɪndjən], *n.* the East Indies.

östlich ['œstlɪç], *adj.* eastern, easterly.

Oxyd [ɔk'syːt], *n.* (—es, *pl.* —e) oxide.

oxydieren [ɔksy'diːrən], *v.a.*, *v.n.* oxidise.

Ozean ['oːtsea:n], *m.* (—s, *pl.* —e) ocean, sea; *Grosser —*, Pacific (Ocean).

Ozon [o'tsoːn], *n.* (—s, *no pl.*) ozone.

P

P [peː], *n.* (—s, *pl.* —s) the letter P.
Paar [paːr], *n.* (—es, *pl.* —e) pair, couple.
paar [paːr], *adj.* ein —, a few, some.
Pacht [paxt], *f.* (—, *pl.* —en) lease; *in — nehmen*, take on lease.
Pachthof ['paxthoːf], *m.* (—s, *pl.* ⁻e) leasehold estate, farm.
Pack (1) [pak], *m.* (—s, *pl.* ⁻e) pack, bale, packet; *mit Sack und —*, (with) bag and baggage.
Pack (2) [pak], *n.* (—s, *no pl.*) rabble, mob.
Päckchen ['pɛkçən], *n.* (—s, *pl.* —) pack, packet; (small) parcel.
packen ['pakən], *v.a.* pack; seize; (*fig.*) —d, thrilling; *pack dich!* be off! scram!
pädagogisch [pɛːda'goːgiʃ], *adj.* educational, pedagogic(al).
paddeln ['padəln], *v.n.* paddle.
paff [paf], *excl.* bang! *ich bin ganz —,* I am astounded.
paffen ['pafən], *v.n.* puff; draw (at a pipe).
Page ['paːʒə], *m.* (—n, *pl.* —n) page-boy.
Paket [pa'keːt], *n.* (—s, *pl.* —e) packet, package, parcel.
paktieren [pak'tiːrən], *v.n.* come to terms.
Palast [pa'last], *m.* (—es, *pl.* ⁻e) palace.
Palästina [palɛ'stiːna], *n.* Palestine.
Paletot ['palətoː], *m.* (—s, *pl.* —s) overcoat.
Palisanderholz [pali'zandərhɔlts], *n.* (—es, *no pl.*) rosewood.
Palme ['palmə], *f.* (—, *pl.* —n) (*Bot.*) palm-tree.
Palmkätzchen ['palmkɛtsçən], *n.* (—s, *pl.* —) (*Bot.*) catkin.
Palmwoche ['palmvɔxə], *f.* Holy Week.
Pampelmuse ['pampəlmuːzə], *f.* (—, *pl.* —n) (*Bot.*) grapefruit.
Panama ['paːnama], *n.* Panama.
Panier [pa'niːr], *n.* (—s, *pl.* —e) standard, banner.
panieren [pa'niːrən], *v.a.* dress (*meat etc.*), roll in bread-crumbs.
Panne ['panə], *f.* (—, *pl.* —n) puncture; (*Motor.*) break-down; mishap.
panschen ['panʃən], *v.n.* splash about in water. — *v.a.* adulterate.
Pantoffel [pan'tɔfəl], *m.* (—s, *pl.* —n) slipper; *unter dem — stehen,* be henpecked.
Pantoffelheld [pan'tɔfəlhɛlt], *m.* (—en, *pl.* —en) henpecked husband.

Panzer ['pantsər], *m.* (—s, *pl.* —) armour, breast-plate, coat of mail; (*Mil.*) tank.
Papagei [papa'gaɪ], *m.* (—s, *pl.* —en) (*Orn.*) parrot.
Papier [pa'piːr], *n.* (—s, *pl.* —e) paper; (*Comm.*) stocks; (*pl.*) papers, documents; *ein Bogen —,* a sheet of paper.
Papierkrieg [pa'piːrkriːk], *m.* (—s, *no pl.*) (*coll.*) red tape.
Papierwaren [pa'piːrvaːrən], *f. pl.* stationery.
Pappdeckel ['papdɛkəl], *m.* (—s, *pl.* —) pasteboard.
Pappe ['papə], *f.* (—, *no pl.*) paste, cardboard, pasteboard.
Pappel ['papəl], *f.* (—, *pl.* —n) poplar.
pappen ['papən], *v.a.* stick; glue, paste.
Pappenstiel ['papənʃtiːl], *m.* (—s, *pl.* —e) trifle.
papperlapapp ['papərlapap], *excl.* fiddlesticks! nonsense!
Papst [paːpst], *m.* (—es, *pl.* ⁻e) Pope.
päpstlich ['pɛːpstlɪç], *adj.* papal; *—er als der Papst,* fanatically loyal, outheroding Herod; over-zealous.
Parabel [pa'raːbəl], *f.* (—, *pl.* —n) parable; (*Maths.*) parabola.
paradieren [para'diːrən], *v.n.* parade, make a show.
Paradies [para'diːs], *n.* (—es, *pl.* —e) paradise.
paradox [para'dɔks], *adj.* paradoxical.
Paragraph [para'graːf], *m.* (—en, *pl.* —en) paragraph, article, clause, section.
Paraguay ['paragvaɪ, para'gua:ɪ], *n.* Paraguay.
Paralyse [para'lyːzə], *f.* (—, *pl.* —n) paralysis.
parat [pa'raːt], *adj.* prepared, ready.
Pardon [par'dɔ], *m.* (—s, *no pl.*) pardon, forgiveness.
Parfüm [par'fyːm], *n.* (—s, *pl.* —e) perfume, scent.
pari ['paːriː], *adv.* at par.
parieren [pa'riːrən], *v.a.* parry, keep off. — *v.n.* obey; *aufs Wort —,* obey implicitly *or* to the letter.
Parität [pari'tɛːt], *f.* (—, *no pl.*) parity; (religious) equality.
Parkanlagen [park'anlaːgən], *f. pl.* parks; public gardens.
parken ['parkən], *v.a.* park.
Parkett [par'kɛt], *n.* (—s, *pl.* —e) parquet flooring; (*Theat.*) stalls.
Parkuhr [park'uːr], *f.* (—, *pl.* —en) parking-meter.
Parlament [parla'mɛnt], *n.* (—s, *pl.* —e) parliament.
Parlamentär [parlamɛn'tɛːr], *m.* (—s, *pl.* —e) officer negotiating a truce.
Parlamentarier [parlamɛn'taːrjər], *m.* (—s, *pl.* —) parliamentarian, member of a parliament.
Parole [pa'roːlə], *f.* (—, *pl.* —n) watchword, cue, motto, slogan, password.

Partei

Partei [par'taɪ], *f.* (—, *pl.* **—en**) party, faction; — *nehmen für*, side with.

Parteigänger [par'taɪɡɛŋər], *m.* (—s, *pl.* —) partisan.

Parteigenosse [par'taɪɡənɔsə], *m.* (—n, *pl.* —n) party member (especially National Socialist); comrade.

parteilisch [par'taɪlɪʃ], *adj.* partial, biased, prejudiced.

Parteinahme [par'taɪnɑːmə], *f.* (—, *no pl.*) partisanship.

Parteitag [par'taɪtaːk], *m.* (—s, *pl.* —e) party conference; congress.

Parterre [par'tɛra], *n.* (—s, *pl.* —s) ground floor; (*Theat.*) pit; stalls.

Partie [par'tiː], *f.* (—, *pl.* —n) (*Comm.*) parcel; (*marriage*) match; (*chess etc.*) game; (*bridge*) rubber; outing, excursion, trip.

Partitur [parti'tuːr], *f.* (—, *pl.* —en) (*Mus.*) score.

Partizip [parti'tsiːp], *n.* (—s, *pl.* —e, —ien) (*Gram.*) participle.

Parzelle [par'tsɛlə], *f.* (—, *pl.* —n) allotment, lot, parcel.

paschen ['paʃən], *v.a.* smuggle.

Paß [pas], *m.* (**—sses**, *pl.* **˙sse**) (*mountain*) pass; (*travelling*) passport; (*horse*) amble.

Passagier [pasa'ʒiːr], *m.* (—s, *pl.* —e) passenger; *blinder* —, stowaway.

Passant [pa'sant], *m.* (—en, *pl.* —en) passer-by.

Passatwind [pa'saːtvɪnt], *m.* (—s, *pl.* —e) trade-wind.

passen ['pasən], *v.n.* fit, suit, be suitable, be convenient; (*Cards*) pass.

passieren [pa'siːrən], *v.a.* sieve; (*road*) pass, cross, negotiate. — *v.n.* (*aux. sein*) pass; happen, take place, come about.

Passif, Passivum [pa'siːf *or* 'pasiːf, pa'siːvum], *n.* (—s, *pl.* —e, —, *pl.* —va) (*Gram.*) passive voice; (*Comm.*) (*pl.*) debts, liabilities.

Passus ['pasus], *m.* (—, *pl.* —) passage (in book).

Pasta, Paste ['pasta, 'pastə], *f.* (—, *pl.* —ten) paste.

Pastell [pa'stɛl], *m.* (—s, *pl.* —e) pastel, crayon; — *malen*, draw in pastel.

Pastete [pa'steːtə], *f.* (—, *pl.* —n) pie, pastry.

Pastille [pa'stɪlə], *f.* (—, *pl.* —n) lozenge, pastille.

Pastor ['pastɔr], *m.* (—s, *pl.* —en) minister, pastor; parson; vicar, rector.

Pate ['paːtə], *m.* (—n, *pl.* —n) godparent; — *stehen*, be godfather to.

patent [pa'tɛnt], *adj.* fine, grand, (*sl.*) smashing.

Patent [pa'tɛnt], *n.* (—(e)s, *pl.* —e) patent; charter, licence.

patentieren [patɛn'tiːrən], *v.a.* patent, license.

pathetisch [pa'teːtɪʃ], *adj.* elevated, solemn, moving.

Patin ['paːtɪn], *f.* (—, *pl.* **—innen**) godmother.

patriotisch [patri'oːtɪʃ], *adj.* patriotic.

Patrone [pa'troːnə], *f.* (—, *pl.* —n) cartridge; stencil, pattern.

Patrouille [pa'truljə], *f.* (—, *pl.* —n) (*Mil.*) patrol.

Patsche ['patʃə], *f.* (—, *pl.* —n) (*dial.*) hand; (*fig.*) mess, pickle; *in eine* — *geraten*, get into a jam.

patschen ['patʃən], *v.n.* (*aux. sein*) splash.

Patt [pat], *n.* (—s, *pl.* —s) (*Chess*) stalemate.

patzig ['patsɪç], *adj.* rude; cheeky, saucy.

Pauke ['paukə], *f.* (—, *pl.* —n) kettledrum; *mit* —n *und Trompeten*, with drums beating and colours flying.

pauken ['paukən], *v.n.* beat the kettledrum; (*coll.*) swot, plod, grind; fight a duel.

pausbackig ['pausbakɪç], *adj.* chubby-faced, bonny.

Pauschale [pau'ʃaːlə], *f.* (—, *pl.* —n) lump sum.

Pause ['pauzə], *f.* (—, *pl.* —n) pause, stop; (*Theat.*) interval; (*Sch.*) playtime, break; (*Tech.*) tracing.

pausen ['pauzən], *v.a.* trace.

pausieren [pau'ziːrən], *v.n.* pause.

Pavian ['paːvjaːn], *m.* (—s, *pl.* —e) (*Zool.*) baboon.

Pech [pɛç], *n.* (—es, *no pl.*) pitch; (*shoemaker's*) wax; (*fig.*) bad luck, rotten luck.

pechschwarz ['pɛçʃvarts], *adj.* black as pitch.

Pechvogel ['pɛçfoːɡəl], *m.* (—s, *pl.* ˙-) unlucky fellow.

Pedell [pe'dɛl], *m.* (—s, *pl.* —e) beadle; porter, caretaker; (*Univ. sl.*) bulldog.

Pegel ['peːɡəl], *m.* (—s, *pl.* —) water-gauge.

peilen ['paɪlən], *v.a., v.n.* sound, measure, take bearings (of).

Pein [paɪn], *f.* (—, *no pl.*) pain, torment.

peinigen ['paɪnɪɡən], *v.a.* torment; harass, distress.

peinlich ['paɪnlɪç], *adj.* painful, disagreeable; embarrassing; delicate; strict, punctilious; (*Law*) capital, penal.

Peitsche ['paɪtʃə], *f.* (—, *pl.* —n) whip.

pekuniär [pekun'jɛːr], *adj.* financial.

Pelerine [pelə'riːnə], *f.* (—, *pl.* —n) cape.

Pelle ['pɛlə], *f.* (—, *pl.* —n) peel, husk.

Pellkartoffeln ['pɛlkartɔfəln], *f. pl.* potatoes in their jackets.

Pelz [pɛlts], *m.* (—es, *pl.* —e) pelt, fur; fur coat.

pelzig ['pɛltsɪç], *adj.* furry.

Pendel ['pɛndəl], *n.* (—s, *pl.* —) pendulum.

pendeln ['pɛndəln], *v.n.* swing, oscillate.

pennen ['pɛnən], *v.n.* (*sl.*) sleep.

Pension [pã'sjo:n], *f.* (—, *pl.* —**en**) pension; boarding-house; board and lodging.

Pensionat [pãsjo'na:t], *n.* (—**s**, *pl.* —**e**) boarding-school.

pensionieren [pãsjo'ni:rən], *v.a.* pension off; *sich — lassen*, retire.

Pensum ['pɛnzum], *n.* (—**s**, *pl.* —**sen**) task; curriculum, syllabus.

per [pɛr], *prep.* — *Adresse*, care of.

Perfekt [per'fɛkt], *n.* (—**s**, *pl.* —**e**) (*Gram.*) perfect (tense).

perforieren [pɛrfo'ri:rən], *v.a.* perforate, punch.

Pergament [pɛrga'mɛnt], *n.* (—**s**, *pl.* —**e**) parchment, vellum.

Perle ['pɛrlə], *f.* (—, *pl.* —**n**) pearl; (*glass*) bead; (*fig.*) gem, treasure.

perlen ['pɛrlən], *v.n.* sparkle.

Perlgraupe ['pɛrlgraupə], *f.* (—, *no pl.*) (*Bot.*) pearl-barley.

Perlhuhn ['pɛrlhu:n], *n.* (—**s**, *pl.* ⁻er) (*Zool.*) guinea-fowl.

Perlmutter [pɛrlmutər], *f.* (—, *no pl.*) mother-of-pearl.

Perpendikel [pɛrpən'dikəl], *m. & n.* (—**s**, *pl.* —) pendulum.

Perser ['pɛrzər], *m.* (—**s**, *pl.* —) Persian; *echter* —, genuine Persian carpet.

Persien ['pɛrzjən], *n.* Persia.

Personal [pɛrzo'na:l], *n.* (—**s**, *no pl.*) personnel, staff.

Personalien [pɛrzo'na:ljən], *n. pl.* particulars (of a person).

Personenverkehr [pɛr'zo:nənfɛrke:r], *m.* (—**s**, *no pl.*) passenger-traffic.

Personenzug [pɛr'zo:nəntsu:k], *m.* (—**s**, *pl.* ⁻e) (slow) passenger train.

personifizieren [pɛrzonifi'tsi:rən], *v.a.* personify, embody, impersonate.

Persönlichkeit [pɛr'zø:nlıçkaıt], *f.* (—, *pl.* —**en**) personality, person.

perspektivisch [pɛrspɛk'ti:vıʃ], *adj.* perspective.

Peru [pe'ru:], *n.* Peru.

Perücke [pɛ'rykə], *f.* (—, *pl.* —**n**) wig.

Pest [pɛst], *f.* (—, *no pl.*) plague, pestilence.

pestartig ['pɛsta:rtıç], *adj.* pestilential.

Petersilie [petər'zi:ljə], *f.* (—, *no pl.*) (*Bot.*) parsley.

petitionieren [petitsjo'ni:rən], *v.a.* petition.

Petschaft ['pɛtʃaft], *n.* (—**s**, *pl.* —**e**) seal, signet.

Petz [pɛts], *m.* (—**es**, *pl.* —**e**) *Meister* —, Bruin (the bear).

petzen ['pɛtsən], *v.n.* tell tales (about), sneak.

Pfad [pfa:t], *m.* (—**es**, *pl.* —**e**) path.

Pfadfinder ['pfa:tfɪndər], *m.* (—**s**, *pl.* —) Boy Scout.

Pfaffe ['pfafə], *m.* (—**n**, *pl.* —**n**) (*pej.*) cleric, priest.

Pfahl [pfa:l], *m.* (—**s**, *pl.* ⁻e) post, stake.

Pfahlbauten ['pfa:lbautən], *m. pl.* lake dwellings.

pfählen ['pfɛ:lən], *v.a.* fasten with stakes; impale.

Pfand [pfant], *n.* (—**s**, *pl.* ⁻er) pawn, pledge; security; (*game*) forfeit; *ein — einlösen*, redeem a pledge.

pfänden ['pfɛndən], *v.a.* take in pledge; seize.

Pfänderspiel ['pfɛndərʃpi:l], *n.* (—**s**, *pl.* —**e**) game of forfeits.

Pfandgeber ['pfantge:bər], *m.* (—**s**, *pl.* —) pawner.

Pfandleiher ['pfantlaıər], *m.* (—**s**, *pl.* —) pawnbroker.

Pfandrecht ['pfantrɛçt], *n.* (—**s**, *no pl.*) lien.

Pfändung ['pfɛnduŋ], *f.* (—, *pl.* —**en**) seizure, attachment, distraint.

Pfanne ['pfanə], *f.* (—, *pl.* —**n**) pan, frying-pan.

Pfannkuchen ['pfanku:xən], *m.* (—**s**, *pl.* —) pancake; *Berliner* —, doughnut.

Pfarre ['pfarə], *f.* (—, *pl.* —**n**) living, parish; (*house*) vicarage, parsonage, manse.

Pfarrer ['pfarər], *m.* (—**s**, *pl.* —) parson; vicar, (parish) priest.

Pfau [pfau], *m.* (—**en**, *pl.* —**en**) (*Orn.*) peacock.

Pfauenauge ['pfauənaugə], *n.* (—**s**, *pl.* —**n**) (*Ent.*) peacock butterfly.

Pfeffer ['pfɛfər], *m.* (—**s**, *no pl.*) pepper; *spanischer* —, red pepper, cayenne.

Pfefferkuchen ['pfɛfərku:xən], *m.* (—**s**, *pl.* —) gingerbread, spiced cake.

Pfefferminz ['pfɛfərmɪnts], *n.* (—, *no pl.*) peppermint.

Pfeife ['pfaıfə], *f.* (—, *pl.* —**n**) whistle, fife; pipe.

pfeifen ['pfaıfən], *v.a., v.n. irr.* whistle, play the fife; (*Theat.*) boo, hiss; (*bullets*) whiz(z).

Pfeifenrohr ['pfaıfənro:r], *n.* (—**s**, *pl.* —**e**) pipe-stem.

Pfeil [pfaıl], *m.* (—**es**, *pl.* —**e**) arrow, dart, bolt.

Pfeiler ['pfaılər], *m.* (—**s**, *pl.* —) pillar.

Pfeilwurz ['pfaılvurts], *f.* (—, *no pl.*) (*Bot.*) arrow root.

Pfennig ['pfɛnıç], *m.* (—**s**, *pl.* —**e**) one hundredth of a mark; (*loosely*) penny.

Pferch [pfɛrç], *m.* (—**es**, *pl.* —**e**) fold, pen.

Pferd [pfe:rt], *n.* (—**es**, *pl.* —**e**) horse; *zu* —, on horseback; *vom — steigen*, dismount.

Pferdeknecht ['pfe:rdəknɛçt], *m.* (—**es**, *pl.* —**e**) groom.

Pferdestärke ['pfe:rdəʃtɛrkə], *f.* (—, *no pl.*) horse-power (*abbr.* PS).

Pfiff [pfɪf], *m.* (—**es**, *pl.* —**e**) whistle.

Pfifferling ['pfɪfərlıŋ], *m.* (—**s**, *pl.* —**e**) (*Bot.*) mushroom; chanterelle; *einen — wert*, worthless.

pfiffig ['pfɪfıç], *adj.* cunning, sly, crafty.

Pfiffikus ['pfɪfıkus], *m.* (—, *pl.* —**se**) (*coll.*) sly dog.

Pfingsten ['pfɪŋkstən], *n.* Whitsun (-tide), Pentecost.

Pfingstrose ['pfɪŋkstro:zə], *f.* (—, *pl.* (*Bot.*) peony.

Pfirsich ['pfɪrzɪç], *m.* (—s, *pl.* —e) (*Bot.*) peach.

Pflanze ['pflantsə], *f.* (—, *pl.* —n) plant.

pflanzen ['pflantsən], *v.a.* plant.

Pflanzer ['pflantsər], *m.* (—s, *pl.* —) planter.

pflanzlich ['pflantslɪç], *adj.* vegetable, botanical.

Pflänzling ['pflɛntslɪŋ], *m.* (—s, *pl.* —e) seedling, young plant.

Pflanzung ['pflantsuŋ], *f.* (—, *pl.* —en) plantation.

Pflaster ['pflastər], *n.* (—s, *pl.* —) (*Med.*) plaster; (*street*) pavement; *ein teures* —, an expensive place to live in.

Pflaume ['pflaumə], *f.* (—, *pl.* —n) plum; *getrocknete* —, prune.

Pflege ['pfle:gə], *f.* (—, *no pl.*) care, attention, nursing, fostering.

Pflegeeltern ['pfle:gəɛltərn], *pl.* foster-parents.

pflegen ['pfle:gən], *v.a.* nurse, look after, take care of; *Umgang* — *mit*, associate with. — *v.n.* be used to, be in the habit of.

Pflegling ['pfle:klɪŋ], *m.* (—s, *pl.* —e) foster-child, ward.

Pflicht [pflɪçt], *f.* (—, *pl.* —en) duty, obligation.

Pflichtgefühl ['pflɪçtgəfy:l], *n.* (—s, *no pl.*) sense of duty.

pflichtgemäß ['pflɪçtgəmɛ:s], *adj.* dutiful.

pflichtschuldig ['pflɪçtʃuldɪç], *adj.* in duty bound.

Pflock [pflɔk], *m.* (—s, *pl.* ⸚e) plug, peg.

pflücken ['pflykən], *v.a.* pluck, pick, gather.

Pflug [pflu:k], *m.* (—es, *pl.* ⸚e) plough.

Pflugschar ['pflu:kʃa:r], *f.* (—, *pl.* —en) ploughshare.

Pforte ['pfɔrtə], *f.* (—, *pl.* —n) gate, door, porch.

Pförtner ['pfœrtnər], *m.* (—s, *pl.* —) door-keeper, porter.

Pfosten ['pfɔstən], *m.* (—s, *pl.* —) post, stake; (*door*) jamb.

Pfote ['pfo:tə], *f.* (—, *pl.* —n) paw.

Pfriem [pfri:m], *m.* (—es, *pl.* —e) awl.

Pfropf(en) ['pfrɔpf(ən)], *m.* (—s, *pl.* —en) cork, stopper; (*gun*) wad.

pfropfen ['pfrɔpfən], *v.a.* graft; cork.

Pfründe ['pfryndə], *f.* (—, *pl.* —n) living, benefice.

Pfuhl [pfu:l], *m.* (—es, *pl.* —e) pool, puddle.

Pfühl [pfy:l], *m.* (—es, *pl.* —e) (*Poet.*) bolster, pillow, cushion.

pfui! [pfui], *excl.* shame! ugh! — *Teufel!* shame! a damned shame!

Pfund [pfunt], *n.* (—es, *pl.* —e) pound.

pfuschen ['pfuʃən], *v.n.* botch; *einem ins Handwerk* —, poach on s.o. else's preserve.

Pfütze ['pfytsə], *f.* (—, *pl.* —n) puddle.

Phänomen [fɛno'me:n], *n.* (—s, *pl.* —e) phenomenon.

Phantasie [fanta'zi:], *f.* (—, *pl.* —n) fancy, imagination; (*Mus.*) fantasia.

phantasieren [fanta'zi:rən], *v.n.* indulge in fancies; (*sick person*) rave, wander, be delirious; (*Mus.*) improvise.

Phantast [fan'tast], *m.* (—en, *pl.* —en) dreamer, visionary.

Pharisäer [fari'zɛ:ər], *m.* (—s, *pl.* —) Pharisee.

Phase ['fa:zə], *f.* (—, *pl.* —n) phase, stage (of process or development).

Philippinen [fili'piːnən], *f. pl.* Philippines.

Philister [fi'lɪstər], *m.* (—s, *pl.* —) Philistine.

philisterhaft [fi'lɪstərhaft], *adj.* philistine, narrow-minded, conventional.

Philologie [filolo'gi:], *f.* (—, *no pl.*) philology; study of languages.

Philosoph [filo'zo:f], *m.* (—en, *pl.* —en) philosopher.

Philosophie [filozo'fi:], *f.* (—, *pl.* —n) philosophy.

Phiole [fi'o:lə], *f.* (—, *pl.* —n) phial, vial.

Phlegma ['flɛgma], *n.* (—s, *no pl.*) phlegm.

Phonetik [fo'ne:tɪk], *f.* (—, *no pl.*) phonetics.

photogen [foto'ge:n], *adj.* photogenic.

Photograph [foto'gra:f], *m.* (—en, *pl.* —en) photographer.

Photographie [fotogra'fi:], *f.* (—, *pl.* —n) photograph, photo; (*Art*) photography.

photographieren [fotogra'fi:rən], *v.a.* photograph.

Physik [fy'zi:k], *f.* (—, *no pl.*) physics.

physikalisch [fyzi'ka:lɪʃ], *adj.* physical (of physics).

Physiker ['fy:zɪkər], *m.* (—s, *pl.* —) physicist.

Physiologe [fy:zjo'lo:gə], *m.* (—en, *pl.* —en) physiologist.

physiologisch [fy:zjo'lo:gɪʃ], *adj.* physiological.

physisch ['fy:zɪʃ], *adj.* physical.

Picke ['pɪka], *f.* (—, *pl.* —n) pickaxe, axe.

Pickel ['pɪkəl], *m.* (—s, *pl.* —) pimple.

Piedestal ['pje:dɛsta:l], *n.* (—s, *pl.* —e) pedestal.

piepen ['pi:pən], *v.n.* squeak, chirp.

piepsen ['pi:psən], *v.n.* squeak, chirp.

Pietät [pie'tɛ:t], *f.* (—, *no pl.*) piety, reverence.

Pik [pi:k], *n.* (—s, *pl.* —s) (*cards*) spades.

pikant [pi'kant], *adj.* piquant, spicy; (*fig.*) risqué.

Pikee [pi'ke:], *m.* (—s, *pl.* —s) piqué.

pikiert [pi'ki:rt], *adj.* irritated, annoyed, piqued.

Pikkolo ['pɪkolo], *m.* (—s, *pl.* —s) apprentice waiter, boy (waiter); (*Mus.*) piccolo, flute.

Pilger ['pɪlgər], *m.* (—s, *pl.* —) pilgrim.
Pille ['pɪlə], *f.* (—, *pl.* —n) pill.
Pilz [pɪlts], *m.* (—es, *pl.* —e) fungus, mushroom.
Piment [pi'mɛnt], *n.* (—s, *pl.* —e) pimento, Jamaican pepper, all-spice.
pimplig ['pɪmplɪç], *adj.* effeminate.
Pinguin ['pɪŋguˈiːn], *m.* (—s, *pl.* —e) (*Orn.*) penguin.
Pinie ['piːnjə], *f.* (—, *pl.* —n) (*Bot.*) stone-pine.
Pinne ['pɪnə], *f.* (—, *pl.* —n) drawing-pin; peg.
Pinscher ['pɪnʃər], *m.* (—s, *pl.* —) terrier.
Pinsel ['pɪnzəl], *m.* (—s, *pl.* —) (*Painting*) brush, pencil; (*fig.*) simpleton.
Pinzette [pɪn'tsɛtə], *f.* (—, *pl.* —n) pincers, tweezers.
Pirsch [pɪrʃ], *f.* (—, *no pl.*) (deer-) stalking.
Piste ['pɪstə], *f.* (—, *pl.* —n) track; (*Aviat.*) runway.
pittoresk [pɪto'rɛsk], *adj.* picturesque.
placken ['plakən], *v.r. sich* —, toil, drudge.
plädieren [plɛ'diːrən], *v.n.* plead.
Plädoyer [plɛ:doaˈjeː], *n.* (—s, *pl.* —s) speech for the prosecution *or* the defence (in a court of law), plea, pleading.
Plage ['plaːgə], *f.* (—, *pl.* —n) torment, trouble; calamity; plague.
plagen ['plaːgən], *v.a.* plague, trouble, torment, vex. — *v.r. sich* —, toil.
Plagiat [plagˈjaːt], *n.* (—es, *pl.* —e) plagiarism.
Plaid [plɛːt], *n.* (—s, *pl.* —s) travelling-rug.
Plakat [pla'kaːt], *n.* (—(e)s, *pl.* —e) poster, placard, bill.
Plan [plaːn], *n.* (—es, *pl.* ˙e) plan, scheme, plot; map, ground-plan.
Plane ['plaːnə], *f.* (—, *pl.* —n) awning, cover.
planieren [pla'niːrən], *v.a.* level, plane down; bulldoze, flatten.
Planke ['plaŋkə], *f.* (—, *pl.* —n) plank, board.
Plänkelei [plɛnkə'laɪ], *f.* (—, *pl.* —en) skirmish.
planmäßig ['plaːnmɛːsɪç], *adj.* according to plan.
planschen ['planʃən], *v.n.* splash; paddle.
Plantage [plan'taːʒə], *f.* (—, *pl.* —n) plantation.
planvoll ['plaːnfɔl], *adj.* systematic, well-planned.
Planwagen ['plaːnvaːgən], *m.* (—s, *pl.* —) tilt-cart.
plappern ['plapərn], *v.n.* prattle, chatter.
plärren ['plɛrən], *v.n.* blubber, bawl.
Plastik ['plastɪk], *f.* (—, *pl.* —en) plastic art; plastic (material).
Platane [pla'taːnə], *f.* (—, *pl.* —n) plane-tree.

Platin ['plaːtiːn], *n.* (—s, *no pl.*) platinum.
platonisch [pla'toːnɪʃ], *adj.* platonic.
plätschern ['plɛtʃərn], *v.n.* splash about.
platt [plat], *adj.* flat, level, even; insipid; downright; —e *Redensart*, commonplace, platitude; (*coll.*) *ich bin ganz* —, I am astonished *or* dumbfounded.
Plättbrett ['plɛtbrɛt], *n.* (—es, *pl.* —er) ironing board.
plattdeutsch ['platdɔytʃ], *adj.* Low German.
Platte ['platə], *f.* (—, *pl.* —n) plate; dish; board; slab; sheet; ledge; (*fig.*) bald head; (*Mus.*) gramophone record.
plätten ['plɛtən], *v.a.* iron (clothes).
Plattfisch ['platfɪʃ], *m.* (—es, *pl.* —e) (*Zool.*) plaice.
Plattfuß ['platfuːs], *n.* (—es, *pl.* ˙e) flat foot.
Plattheit ['plathaɪt], *f.* (—, *pl.* —en) flatness; (*fig.*) platitude.
Platz [plats], *m.* (—es, *pl.* ˙e) place, town, spot, site; space, room; (*town*) square; seat; — *nehmen*, take a seat, be seated.
Platzanweiserin ['platsanvaɪzərɪn], *f.* (—, *pl.* —nen) usherette.
Plätzchen ['plɛtsçən], *n.* (—s, *pl.* —) small place; drop; biscuit.
platzen ['platsən], *v.n.* (*aux.* sein) burst, explode.
Platzregen ['platsreːgən], *m.* (—s, *no pl.*) downpour, heavy shower.
Plauderei [plaudə'raɪ], *f.* (—, *pl.* —en) chat.
Plaudertasche ['plaudərtaʃə], *f.* (—, *pl.* —n) chatterbox.
Pleite ['plaɪtə], *f.* (—, *pl.* —n) (*coll.*) bankruptcy; — *machen*, go bankrupt.
Plenum ['pleːnum], *n.* (—s, *no pl.*) plenary session.
Pleuelstange ['plɔyəlʃtaŋə], *f.* (—, *pl.* —n) connecting-rod.
Plinsen ['plɪnzən], *f. pl.* (*Austr.*) fritters.
Plissee [plɪ'seː], *n.* (—s, *pl.* —s) pleating.
Plombe ['plɔmbə], *f.* (—, *pl.* —n) lead, seal; (*teeth*) filling.
plombieren [plɔm'biːrən], *v.a.* seal with lead; (*teeth*) fill.
plötzlich ['plœtslɪç], *adj.* sudden.
plump [plump], *adj.* clumsy, ungainly, awkward; crude, coarse.
plumps [plumps], *excl.* bump! oops!
Plunder ['plundər], *m.* (—s, *no pl.*) lumber, trash.
plündern ['plyndərn], *v.a.* plunder, pillage.
Plüsch [plyːʃ], *m.* (—es, *no pl.*) plush.
pneumatisch [pnɔy'maːtɪʃ], *adj.* pneumatic.
Pöbel ['pøːbəl], *m.* (—s, *no pl.*) mob, rabble.
pochen ['pɔxən], *v.a., v.n.* knock, beat, throb.

Pocke

Pocke ['pɔkə], *f.* (—, *pl.* —n) pock-mark; (*pl.*) smallpox.
pockennarbig ['pɔkənnarbıç], *adj.* pockmarked.
Podagra ['po:dagra:], *n.* (—s, *no pl.*) (*Med.*) gout.
Pointe [po'ɛ̃tə], *f.* (—, *pl.* —n) (*of a story*) point.
Pokal [po'ka:l], *m.* (—s, *pl.* —e) goblet, cup; trophy.
Pökelfleisch ['pø:kəlflaıʃ], *n.* (—es, *no pl.*) salted meat.
Pol [po:l], *m.* (—s, *pl.* —e) pole.
polemisch [po'le:mıʃ], *adj.* polemic(al), controversial.
Polen ['po:lən], *n.* Poland.
Police [po'li:sə], *f.* (—, *pl.* —n) insurance policy.
polieren [po'li:rən], *v.a.* polish, furbish, burnish.
Poliklinik ['po:likli:nık], *f.* (—, *pl.* —en) (*Med.*) out-patients' department.
Politik [poli'ti:k], *f.* (—, *no pl.*) politics; policy.
politisieren [politi'zi:rən], *v.n.* talk politics.
Politur [poli'tu:r], *f.* (—, *no pl.*) polish, gloss.
Polizei [poli'tsaı], *f.* (—, *no pl.*) police.
polizeilich [poli'tsaılıç], *adj.* of the police.
Polizeistunde [poli'tsaıʃtundə], *f.* (—, *no pl.*) closing time.
Polizeiwache [poli'tsaıvaxə], *f.* (—, *pl.* —n) police station.
Polizist [poli'tsıst], *m.* (—en, *pl.* —en) policeman, constable.
Polizze [po'lıtsə], *f.* (—, *pl.* —n) (*Austr. dial.*) insurance policy.
polnisch ['pɔlnıʃ], *adj.* Polish.
Polster ['pɔlstər], *n.* (—s, *pl.* —) cushion, bolster.
Polterabend ['pɔltəra:bənt], *m.* (—s, *pl.* —e) wedding-eve party.
Poltergeist ['pɔltərgaıst], *m.* (—es, *pl.* —er) poltergeist, hobgoblin.
poltern ['pɔltərn], *v.n.* rumble; make a noise; bluster.
Polyp [po'ly:p], *m.* (—en, *pl.* —en) (*Zool.*) polyp; (*Med.*) polypus.
Pomeranze [pomə'rantsə], *f.* (—, *pl.* —n) (*Bot.*) orange.
Pommern ['pɔmərn], *n.* Pomerania.
Pope ['po:pə], *m.* (—n, *pl.* —n) Greek Orthodox priest.
Popo [po'po:], *m.* (—s, *pl.* —s) (*coll.*) backside, bottom.
populär [popu'lɛ:r], *adj.* popular.
porös [po'rø:s], *adj.* porous.
Porree ['pɔre:], *m.* (—s, *no pl.*) leek.
Portefeuille [pɔrt'fœj], *n.* (—s, *pl.* —s) portfolio.
Portier [pɔr'tje:], *m.* (—s, *pl.* —s) doorkeeper, caretaker; porter.
Porto ['pɔrto:], *n.* (—s, *pl.* Porti) postage.
Porzellan [pɔrtsɛ'la:n], *n.* (—s, *pl.* —e) china, porcelain; *Meißner* —, Dresden china.

Posamenten [poza'mɛntən], *n. pl.* trimmings.
Posaune [po'zaunə], *f.* (—, *pl.* —n) (*Mus.*) trombone.
Positur [pozi'tu:r], *f.* (—, *pl.* —en) posture; *sich in — setzen*, strike an attitude.
Posse ['pɔsə], *f.* (—, *pl.* —n) (*Theat.*) farce, skit.
Possen ['pɔsən], *m.* (—s, *pl.* —) trick; *einem einen — spielen*, play a trick on s.o.
possierlich [pɔ'si:rlıç], *adj.* droll, funny, comic(al).
Post [pɔst], *f.* (—, *pl.* —en) post, mail; (*building*) post-office.
Postament [pɔsta'mɛnt], *n.* (—s, *pl.* —e) plinth, pedestal.
Postanweisung ['pɔstanvaızuŋ], *f.* (—, *pl.* —en) postal order, money order.
Posten ['pɔstən], *m.* (—s, *pl.* —) post, station; place; (*goods*) parcel, lot, job lot; (*Comm.*) item; (*Mil.*) outpost; *— stehen*, stand sentry; *nicht auf dem — sein*, be unwell.
Postfach ['pɔstfax], *n.* (—es, *pl.* ⁻er) post-office box.
postieren [pɔs'ti:rən], *v.a.* post, place, station.
postlagernd ['pɔstla:gərnt], *adj.* poste restante, to be called for.
Postschalter ['pɔstʃaltər], *m.* (—s, *pl.* —) post-office counter.
postulieren [pɔstu'li:rən], *v.a.* postulate.
postwendend ['pɔstvɛndənt], *adj.* by return of post.
Postwertzeichen ['pɔstve:rttsaıçən], *n.* (—s, *pl.* —) stamp.
Potenz [po'tɛnts], *f.* (—, *pl.* —en) (*Maths.*) power; *zur dritten —*, cubed, to the power of three.
potenzieren [potɛn'tsi:rən], *v.a.* (*Math.*) raise; intensify.
Pottasche ['pɔtaʃə], *f.* (—, *no pl.*) potash.
potzblitz ['pɔtsblıts], *excl.* good Heavens! good gracious!
potztausend ['pɔtstauzənt], *excl.* great Scott! good Heavens!
Pracht [praxt], *f.* (—, *no pl.*) splendour, magnificence; (*in compounds*) de luxe.
prächtig ['prɛ:çtıç], *adj.* splendid, magnificent, sumptuous.
prachtvoll ['praxtfɔl], *adj.* gorgeous, magnificent.
Prädikat [prɛ:di'ka:t], *n.* (—s, *pl.* —e) mark; (*Gram.*) predicate.
Prag [pra:k], *n.* Prague.
prägen ['prɛ:gən], *v.a.* coin, mint, stamp.
prägnant [prɛg'nant], *adj.* meaningful, precise.
prahlen ['pra:lən], *v.n.* boast, brag, talk big, show off.
Praktikant [prakti'kant], *m.* (—en, *pl.* —en) probationer; apprentice.
Praktiken ['praktıkən], *f. pl.* machinations.

praktisch ['praktɪʃ], *adj.* practical; —*er Arzt*, general practitioner.

praktizieren [prakti'tsi:rən], *v.a.* practise.

Prall [pral], *m.* (—**es**, *pl.* —**e**) impact.

prall [pral], *adj.* tense, tight; (*cheeks*) chubby.

prallen ['pralən], *v.n.* (*aux.* sein) *auf etwas* —, bounce against s.th.

Prämie ['prɛ:mjə], *f.* (—, *pl.* —**n**) prize; (*insurance*) premium; (*dividend*) bonus.

prangen ['praŋən], *v.n.* shine, glitter, make a show.

Pranger ['praŋər], *m.* (—**s**, *pl.* —) pillory; *etwas an den* — *stellen*, expose s.th., pillory.

präparieren [prɛpa'ri:rən], *v.a.*, *v.r.* prepare.

Präsens ['prɛ:zɛns], *n.* (—, *pl.* —**ntia**) (*Gram.*) present tense.

präsentieren [prɛzɛn'ti:rən], *v.a.* present; *präsentiert das Gewehr!* present arms!

prasseln ['prasəln], *v.n.* (*fire*) crackle; rattle.

prassen ['prasən], *v.n.* revel, gorge (o.s.), guzzle, feast.

Prätendent [prɛtɛn'dɛnt], *m.* (—**en**, *pl.* —**en**) pretender, claimant.

Präteritum [prɛ'te:ritum], *n.* (—**s**, *pl.* —**ta**) (*Gram.*) preterite, past tense.

Praxis ['praksɪs], *f.* (—, *no pl.*) practice.

präzis [prɛ'tsi:s], *adj.* precise, exact.

präzisieren [prɛtsi'zi:rən], *v.a.* define exactly.

predigen ['pre:dɪgən], *v.a.*, *v.n.* preach.

Predigt ['pre:dɪçt], *f.* (—, *pl.* —**en**) sermon; (*fig.*) homily, lecture.

Preis [praɪs], *m.* (—**es**, *pl.* —**e**) price, rate, value; (*reward*) prize; praise; *um jeden* —, at any price, at all costs; *um keinen* —, not for all the world; *feste* —*e*, fixed prices; no rebate, no discount.

Preisausschreiben ['praɪsausʃraɪbən], *n.* (—**s**, *pl.* —) prize competition.

Preiselbeere ['praɪzɛlbe:rə], *f.* (—, *pl.* —**n**) (*Bot.*) bilberry, cranberry.

preisen ['praɪzən], *v.a. irr.* praise, laud; glorify.

preisgeben ['praɪsge:bən], *v.a. irr.* give up, abandon, part with; *dem Spott preisgegeben sein*, become a laughing-stock.

Preisunterbietung ['praɪsuntərbi:-tuŋ], *f.* (—, *pl.* —**en**) under-cutting.

Prellbock ['prɛlbɔk], *m.* (—**s**, *pl.* ⸚**e**) buffer (-block).

prellen ['prɛlən], *v.a.* cheat, defraud.

Prellstein ['prɛlʃtaɪn], *m.* (—**s**, *pl.* —**e**) kerbstone.

pressant [prɛ'sant], *adj.* (*Austr.*) urgent.

Presse ['prɛsə], *f.* (—, *pl.* —**n**) press; newspapers; (*coll.*) coaching establishment, crammer.

pressieren [prɛ'si:rən], *v.n.* be urgent.

Preßkohle ['prɛsko:lə], *f.* (—, *no pl.*) briquette(s).

Preßkolben ['prɛskɔlbən], *m.* (—**s**, *pl.* —) piston.

Preßluft ['prɛsluft], *f.* (—, *no pl.*) compressed air.

Preußen ['prɔysən], *n.* Prussia.

prickeln ['prɪkəln], *v.n.* prick, prickle, sting, tickle.

Prieme ['pri:mə], *f.* (—, *pl.* —**n**) chew, quid.

Priester ['pri:stər], *m.* (—**s**, *pl.* —) priest; *zum* — *weihen*, ordain to the priesthood.

Prima ['pri:ma:], *f.* (—, *pl.* **Primen**) highest form at a grammar school (sixth form).

prima ['pri:ma:], *adj.* excellent, splendid, first-rate.

Primaner [pri'ma:nər], *m.* (—**s**, *pl.* —) pupil in the highest form at a grammar school, sixth form boy.

Primel ['pri:məl], *f.* (—, *pl.* —**n**) (*Bot.*) primrose, primula.

Primus ['pri:mus], *m.* (—, *no pl.*) (*School*) head boy, captain of the school.

Prinzip [prɪn'tsi:p], *n.* (—**s**, *pl.* —**ien**) principle.

Priorität [priori'tɛ:t], *f.* (—, *no pl.*) priority, precedence.

Prise ['pri:zə], *f.* (—, *pl.* —**n**) pinch of snuff.

Prisma ['prɪsma:], *n.* (—**s**, *pl.* —**men**) prism.

Pritsche ['prɪtʃə], *f.* (—, *pl.* —**n**) plank-bed.

Privatdozent [pri'va:tdotsɛnt], *m.* (—**en**, *pl.* —**en**) (*Univ.*) (unsalaried) lecturer.

privatisieren [privati'zi:rən], *v.n.* have private means.

Probe ['pro:bə], *f.* (—, *pl.* —**n**) experiment, trial, probation, test; (*Theat.*, *Mus.*) rehearsal; sample, pattern; *auf* —, on trial; *auf die* — *stellen*, put to the test *or* on probation.

Probeabzug ['pro:baaptsu:k], *m.* (—**s**, *pl.* ⸚**e**) (*Printing*) proof.

proben ['pro:bən], *v.a.* rehearse.

probieren [pro'bi:rən], *v.a.* try, attempt; taste.

Probst [pro:pst], *m.* (—**es**, *pl.* ⸚**e**) provost.

Produzent [produ'tsɛnt], *m.* (—**en**, *pl.* —**en**) producer (of goods), manufacturer.

produzieren [produ'tsi:rən], *v.a.* produce (goods); — *v.r. sich* —, perform, show off.

profanieren [profa'ni:rən], *v.a.* desecrate, profane.

Professur [profɛ'su:r], *f.* (—, *pl.* —**en**) (*Univ.*) professorship, Chair.

profitieren [profi'ti:rən], *v.a.*, *v.n.* profit (by), take advantage (of).

projizieren [proji'tsi:rən], *v.a.* project.

Prokura [pro'ku:ra:], *f.* (—, *no pl.*) (*Law*) power of attorney.

Prokurist [proku'rɪst], *m.* (—**en**, *pl.* —**en**) confidential clerk; company secretary.

171

prolongieren

prolongieren [prolɔŋ'giːrən], *v.a.* prolong, extend.

promenieren [prɔməˈniːrən], *v.n.* take a stroll.

Promotion [promoˈtsjoːn], *f.* (—, *pl.* —en) graduation, degree ceremony.

promovieren [promoˈviːrən], *v.n.* graduate, take a degree.

promulgieren [promulˈgiːrən], *v.a.* promulgate.

Pronomen [proˈnoːmɛn], *n.* (—s, *pl.* —mina) (*Gram.*) pronoun.

prophezeien [profeˈtsaɪən], *v.a.* prophesy, predict, forecast.

prophylaktisch [profyˈlaktɪʃ], *adj.* preventive, prophylactic.

Propst [proːpst], *m.* (—es, *pl.* ⁻e) provost.

Prosa [ˈproːzaː], *f.* (—, *no pl.*) prose.

prosit [ˈproːzɪt], *excl.* cheers! here's to you! your health!

Prospekt [proˈspɛkt], *m.* (—es, *pl.* —e) prospect; (*booklet*) prospectus.

Prostituierte [prostituˈiːrtə], *f.* (—n, *pl.* —n) prostitute; (*coll.*) tart.

protegieren [proteˈʒiːrən], *v.a.* favour, patronize.

Protektion [protɛkˈtsjoːn], *f.* (—, *no pl.*) patronage, favouritism.

protestieren [protɛsˈtiːrən], *v.n.* make a protest, protest (against s.th.).

Protokoll [protoˈkɔl], *n.* (—en, *pl.* —e) minutes, record; protocol; regulations.

Protokollführer [protoˈkɔlfyːrər], *m.* (—s, *pl.* —) recorder, clerk of the minutes.

Protz [prɔts], *m.* (—en, *pl.* —en) snob, upstart; show-off.

Proviant [proˈvjant], *m.* (—s, *no pl.*) provisions, stores.

provinziell [provɪnˈtsjɛl], *adj.* provincial.

Provinzler [proˈvɪntslər], *m.* (—s, *pl.* —) provincial.

Provision [proviˈzjoːn], *f.* (—, *pl.* —en) (*Comm.*) commission, brokerage.

Provisor [proˈviːzɔr], *m.* (—s, *pl.* —en) dispenser.

provisorisch [proviˈzoːrɪʃ], *adj.* provisional, temporary.

provozieren [provoˈtsiːrən], *v.a.* provoke.

Prozedur [protseˈduːr], *f.* (—, *pl.* —en) proceedings, procedure.

Prozent [proˈtsɛnt], *m. & n.* (—s, *pl.* —e) per cent.

Prozentsatz [proˈtsɛntzats], *m.* (—es, *pl.* ⁻e) percentage, rate of interest.

Prozeß [proˈtsɛs], *m.* (—es, *pl.* —e) process; lawsuit, litigation; trial; *mit etwas kurzen — machen*, deal summarily with.

Prozeßwesen [proˈtsɛsveːzən], *n.* (—s, *no pl.*) legal procedure.

prüde [ˈpryːdə], *adj.* prudish, prim.

prüfen [ˈpryːfən], *v.a.* test, examine.

Prüfung [ˈpryːfuŋ], *f.* (—, *pl.* —en) trial, test; examination; (*fig.*) temptation, affliction.

Prügel [ˈpryːgəl], *m.* (—s, *pl.* —) cudgel; (*pl.*) thrashing; *eine Tracht —*, a good hiding.

prügeln [ˈpryːgəln], *v.a.* beat, give a hiding to.

Prunk [pruŋk], *m.* (—(e)s, *no pl.*) splendour, ostentation, pomp.

prusten [ˈpruːstən], *v.n.* snort.

Psalm [psalm], *m.* (—es, *pl.* —e) psalm.

Psalter [ˈpsaltər], *m.* (—s, *pl.* —) (*book*) psalter; (*instrument*) psaltery.

Psychiater [psyçiˈaːtər], *m.* (—s, *pl.* —) psychiatrist.

Psychologe [psyçoˈloːgə], *m.* (—n, *pl.* —n) psychologist.

Pubertät [pubɛrˈtɛːt], *f.* (—, *no pl.*) puberty.

Publikum [ˈpuːblɪkum], *n.* (—s, *no pl.*) public; (*Theat.*) audience.

publizieren [publiˈtsiːrən], *v.a.* publish; promulgate.

Pudel [ˈpuːdəl], *m.* (—s, *pl.* —) poodle; *des —s Kern*, the gist of the matter.

Puder [ˈpuːdər], *m.* (—s, *no pl.*) powder, face-powder.

pudern [ˈpuːdərn], *v.a.* powder.

Puff [puf], *m.* (—es, *pl.* ⁻e) cuff, thump.

puffen [ˈpufən], *v.a.* cuff, thump.

Puffer [ˈpufər], *m.* (—s, *pl.* —) buffer.

Puffspiel [ˈpufʃpiːl], *n.* (—s, *pl.* —e) backgammon.

pullen [ˈpulən], *v.n.* rein in (a horse); (*coll.*) piddle.

Pulsader [ˈpulsaːdər], *f.* (—, *pl.* —n) artery; aorta.

pulsieren [pulˈziːrən], *v.n.* pulsate; pulse, throb.

Pulsschlag [ˈpulsʃlaːk], *m.* (—s, *pl.* ⁻e) pulse-beat; pulsation.

Pult [pult], *n.* (—es, *pl.* —e) desk, writing-table; lectern.

Pulver [ˈpulvər], *n.* (—s, *pl.* —) powder.

Pump [pump], *m.* (—s, *no pl.*) (*sl.*) credit; *auf —*, on tick.

pumpen [ˈpumpən], *v.a., v.n.* pump; (*fig.*) (*sl.*) *sich etwas —*, borrow s.th., touch s.o. for s.th.; lend.

Pumpenschwengel [ˈpumpənʃvɛŋəl], *m.* (—s, *pl.* —) pump-handle.

Pumpernickel [ˈpumpərnɪkəl], *m.* (—s, *pl.* —) black bread, Westphalian rye-bread.

Pumphosen [ˈpumphoːzən], *f. pl.* plus-fours.

Punkt [puŋkt], *m.* (—es, *pl.* —e) point, dot, spot; (*Gram.*) full stop.

punktieren [puŋkˈtiːrən], *v.a.* dot, punctuate.

pünktlich [ˈpyŋktlɪç], *adj.* punctual.

punktum [ˈpuŋktum], *excl. und damit —*, that's the end of it; that's it.

Puppe [ˈpupə], *f.* (—, *pl.* —n) doll; (*Ent.*) pupa, chrysalis.

pur [puːr], *adj.* pure, sheer; (*drink*) neat.

172

Puritaner [puri'ta:nər], *m.* (—s, *pl.* —) puritan.

Purpur ['purpur], *m.* (—s, *no pl.*) purple.

Purzelbaum ['purtsəlbaum], *m.* (—s, *pl.* ̈e) somersault.

purzeln ['purtsəln], *v.n.* tumble.

Pustel ['pustəl], *f.* (—, *pl.* —n) pustule.

pusten ['pu:stən], *v.n.* puff, blow.

Pute ['pu:tə], *f.* (—, *pl.* —n) (*Orn.*) turkey-hen; *dumme —*, silly goose.

Puter ['pu:tər], *m.* (—s, *pl.* —) turkey-cock.

puterrot ['pu:tərro:t], *adj.* as red as a turkey-cock.

Putsch [putʃ], *m.* (—es, *pl.* —e) coup de main, insurrection, riot.

Putz [puts], *m.* (—es, *no pl.*) finery; cleaning; rough-cast.

putzen ['putsən], *v.a.* polish, shine; clean. — *v.r. sich —*, dress up.

Putzfrau ['putsfrau], *f.* (—, *pl.* —en) charwoman.

Putzmacherin ['putsmaxərin], *f.* (—, *pl.* —nen) milliner.

Pyramide [pyra'mi:də], *f.* (—, *pl.* —n) pyramid.

Pyrenäen [pyrə'nɛ:ən], *pl.* Pyrenees; *—halbinsel*, Iberian Peninsula.

Q

Q [ku:], *n.* (—s, *pl.* —s) the letter Q.

quabbeln ['kvabəln], *v.n.* shake, wobble.

Quacksalber ['kvakzalbər], *m.* (—s, *pl.* —) quack, mountebank.

Quacksalberei [kvakzalbə'rai], *f.* (—, *pl.* —en) quackery.

Quaderstein ['kva:dərʃtain], *m.* (—s, *pl.* —e) ashlar, hewn stone.

Quadrat [kva'dra:t], *n.* (—es, *pl.* —e) square; *zum* (or *ins*) *— erheben*, square (a number).

Quadratur [kvadra'tu:r], *f.* (—, *pl.* —en) quadrature; *die — des Kreises finden*, square the circle.

quadrieren [kva'dri:rən], *v.a.* square.

quaken ['kva:kən], *v.n.* (*frog*) croak; (*duck*) quack.

quäken ['kvɛ:kən], *v.n.* squeak.

Quäker ['kvɛ:kər], *m.* (—s, *pl.* —) Quaker.

Qual [kva:l], *f.* (—, *pl.* —en) anguish, agony, torment.

quälen ['kvɛ:lən], *v.a.* torment, torture, vex. — *v.r. sich —*, toil.

qualifizieren [kvalifi'tsi:rən], *v.a.* qualify.

Qualität [kvali'tɛ:t], *f.* (—, *pl.* —en) quality.

Qualle ['kvalə], *f.* (—, *pl.* —n) (*Zool.*) jelly-fish.

Qualm [kvalm], *m.* (—es, *no pl.*) dense smoke.

Quantität [kvanti'tɛ:t], *f.* (—, *pl.* —en) quantity.

Quantum ['kvantum], *n.* (—s, *pl.* —ten) portion, quantity.

Quappe ['kvapə], *f.* (—, *pl.* —n) (*Zool.*) tadpole.

Quarantäne [kvaran'tɛ:nə], *f.* (—, *no pl.*) quarantine.

Quark [kvark], *m.* (—s, *no pl.*) curds; cream-cheese; (*fig.*) trash, rubbish, nonsense, bilge.

Quarta ['kvarta:], *f.* (—, *no pl.*) fourth form.

Quartal [kvar'ta:l], *n.* (—s, *pl.* —e) quarter of a year; term.

Quartier [kvar'ti:r], *n.* (—s, *pl.* —e) quarters, lodging; (*Mil.*) billet.

Quarz [kvarts], *m.* (—es, *no pl.*) quartz.

Quaste ['kvastə], *f.* (—, *pl.* —n) tassel.

Quatember [kva'tembər], *m.* (—s, *pl.* —) quarter day; (*Eccl.*) Ember Day.

Quatsch [kvatʃ], *m.* (—es, *no pl.*) nonsense, drivel.

Quecke ['kvekə], *f.* (—, *pl.* —n) couch-grass, quick-grass.

Quecksilber ['kvekzilbər], *n.* (—s, *no pl.*) quicksilver, mercury.

Quelle ['kvelə], *f.* (—, *pl.* —n) well, spring, fountain; (*fig.*) source; *aus sicherer —*, on good authority.

Quentchen ['kventçən], *n.* (—s, *pl.* —) small amount, dram.

quer [kve:r], *adj.* cross, transverse, oblique, diagonal. — *adv.* across; *kreuz und —*, in all directions.

Querbalken ['kve:rbalkən], *m.* (—s, *pl.* —) cross-beam.

querdurch ['kve:rdurç], *adv.* across.

querfeldein ['kve:rfeltain], *adv.* cross-country.

Querkopf ['kve:rkɔpf], *m.* (—es, *pl.* ̈e) crank.

Quersattel ['kve:rzatəl], *m.* (—s, *pl.* ̈) side-saddle.

Querschiff ['kve:rʃif], *n.* (—es, *pl.* —e) (*church*) transept.

Querschnitt ['kve:rʃnit], *m.* (—s, *pl.* —e) cross-section; (*fig.*) average.

Querulant [kveru'lant], *m.* (—en, *pl.* —en) grumbler.

quetschen ['kvetʃən], *v.a.* squeeze, crush, mash; bruise.

Queue [kø:], *n.* (—s, *pl.* —s) (*Billiards*) cue.

quieken ['kvi:kən], *v.n.* squeak.

Quinta ['kvinta:], *f.* (—, *no pl.*) fifth form.

Quinte ['kvintə], *f.* (—, *pl.* —n) (*Mus.*) fifth.

Quirl [kvirl], *m.* (—s, *pl.* —e) whisk; (*Bot.*) whorl.

quitt [kvit], *adj.* *— sein*, be quits.

Quitte ['kvitə], *f.* (—, *pl.* —n) (*Bot.*) quince.

quittegelb [ˈkvɪtəgɛlp], *adj.* bright yellow.

quittieren [kvɪˈtiːrən], *v.a.* receipt; give a receipt; *den Dienst* —, leave the service.

Quittung [ˈkvɪtuŋ], *f.* (—, *pl.* —en) receipt.

Quodlibet [ˈkvɔdlibɛt], *n.* (—s, *pl.* —s) medley.

Quote [ˈkvoːtə], *f.* (—, *pl.* —n) quota, share.

quotieren [kvoˈtiːrən], *v.a.* (*stock exchange*) quote (prices).

R

R [ɛr], *n.* (—s, *pl.* —s) the letter R.

Rabatt [raˈbat], *m.* (—s, *pl.* —e) rebate, discount.

Rabatte [raˈbatə], *f.* (—, *pl.* —n) flower-border.

Rabbiner [raˈbiːnər], *m.* (—s, *pl.* —) rabbi.

Rabe [ˈraːbə], *m.* (—n, *pl.* —n) (*Orn.*) raven; *ein weißer* —, a rare bird.

Rabenaas [ˈraːbənaːs], *n.* (—es, *pl.* —e) carrion.

rabiat [raˈbjaːt], *adj.* furious, rabid.

Rache [ˈraxə], *f.* (—, *no pl.*) revenge, vengeance.

Rachen [ˈraxən], *m.* (—s, *pl.* —) jaws, throat.

rächen [ˈrɛːçən], *v.a.* avenge. — *v.r. sich* —, avenge o.s., take vengeance.

Rachenbräune [ˈraxənbrɔynə], *f.* (—, *no pl.*) croup, quinsy.

Rachitis [raˈxiːtɪs], *f.* (—, *no pl.*) (*Med.*) rickets.

rachsüchtig [ˈraxzyçtɪç], *adj.* vindictive, vengeful.

rackern [ˈrakərn], *v.r. sich* —, (*coll.*) toil, work hard.

Rad [raːt], *n.* (—es, *pl.* —er) wheel; bicycle; *ein* — *schlagen*, turn a cart-wheel; (*peacock*) spread the tail.

Radau [raˈdau], *m.* (—s, *no pl.*) noise, din, shindy.

Rade [ˈraːdə], *f.* (—, *pl.* —n) corn-cockle.

radebrechen [ˈraːdəbrɛçən], *v.a. insep.* murder a language.

radeln [ˈraːdəln], *v.n.* (*aux.* sein) (*coll.*) cycle.

Rädelsführer [ˈrɛːdəlsfyːrər], *m.* (—s, *pl.* —) ringleader.

rädern [ˈrɛːdərn], *v.a.* break on the wheel; *gerädert sein*, (*fig.*) ache in all o.'s bones, be exhausted.

Radfahrer [ˈraːtfaːrər], *m.* (—s, *pl.* —) cyclist.

radieren [raˈdiːrən], *v.n.* erase; etch.

Radierung [raˈdiːruŋ], *f.* (—, *pl.* —en) etching.

Radieschen [raˈdiːsçən], *n.* (—s, *pl.* —) (*Bot.*) radish.

Radio [ˈraːdjo], *n.* (—s, *pl.* —s) wireless, radio.

raffen [ˈrafən], *v.a.* snatch up, gather up.

Raffinade [rafiˈnaːdə], *f.* (—, *no pl.*) refined sugar.

Raffinement [rafinəˈmãː], *n.* (—s, *no pl.*) elaborateness.

raffinieren [rafiˈniːrən], *v.a.* refine.

raffiniert [rafiˈniːrt], *adj.* refined; elaborate, crafty, wily, cunning.

ragen [ˈraːgən], *v.n.* tower, soar.

Rahm [raːm], *m.* (—es, *no pl.*) cream; *den* — *abschöpfen*, skim; (*fig.*) skim the cream off.

Rahmen [ˈraːmən], *m.* (—s, *pl.* —) frame; milieu, limit, scope, compass; *im* — *von*, within the framework of.

rahmig [ˈraːmɪç], *adj.* creamy.

raisonnieren [rɛzɔˈniːrən], *v.n.* reason, argue; (*fig.*) grumble, answer back.

Rakete [raˈkeːtə], *f.* (—, *pl.* —n) rocket, sky-rocket.

Rakett [raˈkɛt], *n.* (—s, *pl.* —s) (*tennis*) racket.

rammen [ˈramən], *v.a.* ram.

Rampe [ˈrampə], *f.* (—, *pl.* —n) ramp, slope; platform; (*Theat.*) apron.

ramponiert [rampoˈniːrt], *adj.* battered, damaged.

Ramsch [ramʃ], *m.* (—es, *pl.* ⁓e) odds and ends; (*Comm.*) job lot.

Rand [rant], *m.* (—es, *pl.* ⁓er) edge, border, verge, rim; (*book*) margin; (*hat*) brim; *am* — *des Grabes*, with one foot in the grave; *außer* — *und Band geraten*, get completely out of hand.

randalieren [randaˈliːrən], *v.n.* kick up a row.

Randbemerkung [ˈrantbəmɛrkuŋ], *f.* (—, *pl.* —en) marginal note, gloss.

rändern [ˈrɛndərn], *v.a.* border, edge, mill.

Ränftchen [ˈrɛnftçən], *n.* (—s, *pl.* —) crust (of bread).

Rang [raŋ], *m.* (—es, *pl.* ⁓e) rank, grade, rate; order, class; standing (in society); (*Theat.*) circle, tier, gallery.

Range [ˈraŋə], *m.* (—n, *pl.* —n) scamp, rascal. — *f.* (—, *pl.* —n) tomboy, hoyden.

rangieren [rãˈʒiːrən], *v.a.* (*Railw.*) shunt. — *v.n.* rank.

Ranke [ˈraŋkə], *f.* (—, *pl.* —n) tendril, shoot.

Ränke [ˈrɛŋkə], *m. pl.* intrigues, tricks.

ranken [ˈraŋkən], *v.r.* (*aux.* haben) *sich* —, (*plant*) climb (with tendrils).

Ränkeschmied [ˈrɛŋkəʃmiːt], *m.* (—es, *pl.* —e) plotter, intriguer.

Ranzen [ˈrantsən], *m.* (—s, *pl.* —) satchel, knapsack, rucksack.

ranzig [ˈrantsɪç], *adj.* rancid, rank.

Rappe [ˈrapə], *m.* (—n, *pl.* —n) black horse.

Rappel ['rapəl], *m.* (—s, *no pl.*) (*coll.*) slight madness; rage, fit.

Rappen ['rapən], *m.* (—s, *pl.* —) small Swiss coin; centime.

rapportieren [rapɔr'tiːrən], *v.a.* report.

Raps [raps], *m.* (—es, *no pl.*) rapeseed.

rar [raːr], *adj.* rare, scarce; exquisite.

rasch [raʃ], *adj.* quick, swift.

rascheln ['raʃəln], *v.n.* rustle.

Rasen ['raːzən], *m.* (—s, *pl.* —) lawn, turf, sod.

rasen ['raːzən], *v.n.* rave, rage, be delirious; rush, speed; *in — der Eile*, in a tearing hurry.

Raserei [raːzə'raɪ], *f.* (—, *pl.* —en) madness; (*fig.*) fury.

Rasierapparat [ra'ziːrapara:t], *m.* (—s, *pl.* —e) (safety-)razor; shaver.

rasieren [ra'ziːrən], *v.a.* shave; *sich — lassen*, be shaved, get a shave.

Rasierzeug [ra'ziːrtsɔyk], *n.* (—s, *no pl.*) shaving-tackle.

Raspel ['raspəl], *f.* (—, *pl.* —n) rasp.

Rasse ['rasə], *f.* (—, *pl.* —n) race; breed; *reine —*, thoroughbred; *gekreuzte —*, cross-breed.

Rassel ['rasəl], *f.* (—, *pl.* —n) rattle.

rasseln ['rasəln], *v.n.* rattle, clank.

Rassendiskriminierung ['rasəndɪskrɪmi:ruŋ], *f.* (—, *no pl.*) racial discrimination.

Rast [rast], *f.* (—, *no pl.*) rest, repose.

rasten ['rastən], *v.n.* rest, take a rest; halt.

Raster ['rastər], *m.* (—s, *pl.* —) (*Phot.*) screen.

rastlos ['rastloːs], *adj.* restless.

Rat (1) [raːt], *m.* (—es, *pl.* —schläge) advice, counsel; deliberation.

Rat (2) [raːt], *m.* (—es, *pl.* ˙e) council, councillor; *mit — und Tat*, with advice and assistance; *einem einen — geben*, give s.o. advice, counsel s.o.; *einen um — fragen*, consult s.o.; *— schaffen*, find ways and means.

Rate ['raːtə], *f.* (—, *pl.* —n) instalment, rate.

raten ['raːtən], *v.a., v.n. irr.* advise; guess, conjecture.

Ratgeber ['raːtgeːbər], *m.* (—s, *pl.* —) adviser, counsellor.

Rathaus ['raːthaus], *n.* (—es, *pl.* ˙er) town-hall.

Ratifizierung [ratifi'tsiːruŋ], *f.* (—, *pl.* —en) ratification.

Ration [ra'tsjoːn], *f.* (—, *pl.* —en) ration, share, portion.

rationell [ratsjo'nɛl], *adj.* rational.

ratlos ['raːtloːs], *adj.* helpless, perplexed.

ratsam ['raːtzaːm], *adj.* advisable.

Ratschlag ['raːtʃlaːk], *m.* (—s, *pl.* ˙e) advice, counsel.

Ratschluß ['raːtʃlus], *m.* (—sses, *pl.* ˙sse) decision, decree.

Ratsdiener ['raːtsdiːnər], *m.* (—s, *pl.* —) beadle, tipstaff, summoner.

Rätsel ['rɛːtsəl], *n.* (—s, *pl.* —) riddle, puzzle, mystery, enigma, conundrum.

Ratsherr ['raːtshɛr], *m.* (—n, *pl.* —en) alderman, (town-)councillor, senator.

Ratte ['ratə], *f.* (—, *pl.* —n) (*Zool.*) rat.

Raub [raup], *m.* (—es, *no pl.*) robbery; booty, prey.

rauben ['raubən], *v.a.* rob, plunder; *es raubt mir den Atem*, it takes my breath away.

Räuber ['rɔybər], *m.* (—s, *pl.* —) robber, thief; highwayman; *— und Gendarm*, cops and robbers.

Raubgier ['raupgiːr], *f.* (—, *no pl.*) rapacity.

Rauch [raux], *m.* (—s, *no pl.*) smoke, vapour.

Rauchen ['rauxən], *n.* (—s, *no pl.*) smoking; *— verboten*, no smoking.

rauchen ['rauxən], *v.a., v.n.* smoke.

räuchern ['rɔyçərn], *v.a.* (*meat, fish*) smoke-dry, cure; (*disinfect*) fumigate. *— v.n.* (*Eccl.*) burn incense.

Rauchfang ['rauxfaŋ], *m.* (—s, *pl.* ˙e) chimney-flue.

Räude ['rɔydə], *f.* (—, *no pl.*) mange.

Raufbold ['raufbɔlt], *m.* (—s, *pl.* —e) brawler, bully.

raufen ['raufən], *v.a.* (*hair*) tear out, pluck. *— v.n.* fight, brawl. *— v.r. sich — mit*, scuffle with, fight, have a scrap with.

rauh [rau], *adj.* rough; (*fig.*) harsh, rude; hoarse; (*weather*) raw, inclement.

Rauheit ['rauhaɪt], *f.* (—, *no pl.*) roughness; hoarseness; (*fig.*) harshness, rudeness; (*weather*) inclemency; (*landscape*) ruggedness.

rauhen ['rauən], *v.a.* (*cloth*) nap.

Raum [raum], *m.* (—es, *pl.* ˙e) space, room; outer space; (*fig.*) scope; *dem Gedanken — geben*, entertain an idea.

räumen ['rɔymən], *v.a.* clear, empty; quit, leave; *das Feld —*, abandon the field, clear out.

Rauminhalt ['raumɪnhalt], *m.* (—s, *no pl.*) volume.

räumlich ['rɔymlɪç], *adj.* spatial; (*in compounds*) space-.

Räumlichkeiten ['rɔymlɪçkaɪtən], *pl.* premises.

Raumschiff ['raumʃɪf], *n.* (—es, *pl.* —e) spaceship, spacecraft.

Räumung ['rɔymuŋ], *f.* (—, *pl.* —en) evacuation.

raunen ['raunən], *v.a., v.n.* whisper.

Raupe ['raupə], *f.* (—, *pl.* —n) (*Ent.*) caterpillar.

Rausch [rauʃ], *m.* (—es, *pl.* ˙e) intoxication; delirium, frenzy; *einen — haben*, be drunk, intoxicated; *seinen — ausschlafen*, sleep it off.

rauschen ['rauʃən], *v.n.* rustle, rush, roar.

Rauschgift ['rauʃgɪft], *n.* (—es, *pl.* —e) drug; narcotic.

Rauschgold ['rauʃgɔlt], *n.* (—es, *no pl.*) tinsel.

räuspern ['rɔyspərn], *v.r. sich —*, clear o.'s throat.

Raute ['rautə], *f.* (—, *pl.* —n) (*Maths.*) rhombus; lozenge; (*Bot.*) rue.

Razzia ['ratsja], *f.* (—, *pl.* —zzien) (police-)raid, swoop.

reagieren [rea'gi:rən], *v.n.* react (on).

realisieren [reali'zi:rən], *v.a.* convert into money, realise.

Realschule [re'a:lʃu:lə], *f.* (—, *pl.* —n) technical grammar school; secondary modern school.

Rebe ['re:bə], *f.* (—, *pl.* —n) vine.

Rebell [re'bɛl], *m.* (—en, *pl.* —en) rebel, mutineer, insurgent.

Rebensaft ['re:bənzaft], *m.* (—s, *pl.* ⁻e) grape-juice, wine.

Rebhuhn ['re:phu:n], *n.* (—s, *pl.* ⁻er) (*Orn.*) partridge.

Reblaus ['re:plaus], *f.* (—, *pl.* ⁻e) (*Ent.*) phylloxera.

Rechen ['rɛçən], *m.* (—s, *pl.* —) (*garden*) rake; (*clothes*) rack.

Rechenaufgabe ['rɛçənaufga:bə], *f.* (—, *pl.* —n) sum; mathematical *or* arithmetical problem.

Rechenmaschine ['rɛçənmaʃi:nə], *f.* (—, *pl.* —n) calculating machine, adding-machine.

Rechenschaft ['rɛçənʃaft], *f.* (—, *no pl.*) account; — *ablegen*, account for; *zur* — *ziehen*, call to account.

Rechenschieber ['rɛçənʃi:bər], *m.* (—s, *pl.* —) slide-rule.

Rechentabelle ['rɛçəntabɛlə], *f.* (—, *pl.* —n) ready reckoner.

rechnen ['rɛçnən], *v.a., v.n.* reckon, calculate, do sums; compute; *auf etwas* —, count on s.th.; *auf einen* —, rely on s.o.

Rechnung ['rɛçnuŋ], *f.* (—, *pl.* —en) reckoning, account, computation; (*document*) invoice, bill, statement, account; *einer Sache* — *tragen*, make allowances for s.th.; take s.th. into account; *einem einen Strich durch die* — *machen*, put a spoke in s.o.'s wheel; *eine* — *begleichen*, settle an account.

Rechnungsabschluß ['rɛçnuŋsapʃlus], *m.* (—sses, *pl.* ⁻sse) balancing of accounts, balance-sheet.

Rechnungsprüfer ['rɛçnuŋspry:fər], *m.* (—s, *pl.* —) auditor.

Rechnungsrat ['rɛçnuŋsra:t], *m.* (—s, *pl.* ⁻e) member of the board of accountants, (senior government) auditor.

Recht [rɛçt], *n.* (—es, *pl.* —e) right, justice; claim on, title to; law, jurisprudence; *von* —*s wegen*, by right; — *sprechen*, administer justice; *die* —*e studieren*, study law.

recht [rɛçt], *adj.* right; just; real, true; suitable; proper; *zur* —*en Zeit*, in time; *es geht nicht mit* —*en Dingen zu*, there is s.th. queer about it; *was dem einen* —, *ist dem andern billig*, what is sauce for the goose is sauce for the gander; *einem* — *geben*, agree with s.o.; — *haben*, be (in the) right.

Rechteck ['rɛçtɛk], *n.* (—s, *pl.* —e) rectangle.

rechten ['rɛçtən], *v.n. mit einem* —, dispute, remonstrate with s.o.

rechtfertigen ['rɛçtfɛrtigən], *v.a. insep.* justify. — *v.r. sich* —, exculpate o.s.

rechtgläubig ['rɛçtglɔybiç], *adj.* orthodox.

rechthaberisch ['rɛçtha:bəriʃ], *adj.* stubborn, obstinate.

rechtlich ['rɛçtliç], *adj.* legal, lawful, legitimate; (*Law*) judicial, juridical.

rechtmäßig ['rɛçtmɛ:siç], *adj.* lawful, legitimate, legal.

rechts [rɛçts], *adv.* to the right, on the right.

Rechtsabtretung ['rɛçtsaptre:tuŋ], *f.* (—, *pl.* —en) cession, assignment.

Rechtsanwalt ['rɛçtsanvalt], *m.* (—s, *pl.* ⁻e) lawyer, solicitor, attorney.

Rechtsbeistand ['rɛçtsbaiʃtant], *m.* (—s, *pl.* ⁻e) (legal) counsel.

rechtschaffen ['rɛçtʃafən], *adj.* upright, honest, righteous.

Rechtschreibung ['rɛçtʃraibuŋ], *f.* (—, *no pl.*) orthography, spelling.

Rechtshandel ['rɛçtshandəl], *m.* (—s, *pl.* ⁻) action, case, lawsuit.

rechtskräftig ['rɛçtskrɛftiç], *adj.* legal, valid.

Rechtslehre ['rɛçtsle:rə], *f.* (—, *pl.* —n) jurisprudence.

Rechtsspruch ['rɛçtsʃprux], *m.* (—(e)s, *pl.* ⁻e) verdict.

Rechtsverhandlung ['rɛçtsfɛrhand-luŋ], *f.* (—, *pl.* —en) legal proceedings.

Rechtsweg ['rɛçtsve:k], *m.* (—(e)s, *pl.* —e) course of law.

rechtswidrig ['rɛçtsvi:driç], *adj.* against the law, illegal.

Rechtszuständigkeit ['rɛçtstsu:ʃten-diçkait], *f.* (—, *pl.* —en) (legal) competence.

rechtwinklig ['rɛçtviŋkliç], *adj.* rectangular.

rechtzeitig ['rɛçttsaitiç], *adj.* opportune. — *adv.* in time, at the right time.

Reck [rɛk], *n.* (—s, *pl.* —e) horizontal bar.

Recke ['rɛkə], *m.* (—n, *pl.* —n) (*Poet.*) hero.

recken ['rɛkən], *v.a.* stretch, extend.

Redakteur [redak'tø:r], *m.* (—s, *pl.* —e) editor (newspaper, magazine).

Redaktion [redak'tsjo:n], *f.* (—, *pl.* —en) editorship, editorial staff; (*room*) editorial office.

Rede ['re:də], *f.* (—, *pl.* —n) speech, oration; address; *es geht die* —, people say; *es ist nicht der* — *wert*, it is not worth mentioning; *eine* — *halten*, deliver a speech; *zur* — *stellen*, call to account.

reden ['re:dən], *v.a.* speak, talk, discourse; *einem nach dem Munde* —, humour s.o.; *in den Wind* —, speak in vain, preach to the winds; *mit sich* — *lassen*, be amenable to reason.

Redensart ['re:dənsa:rt], *f.* (—, *pl.* —en) phrase, idiom; cliché; *einen mit leeren — en abspeisen*, put s.o. off with fine words.

Redewendung ['re:dəvɛnduŋ], *f.* (—, *pl.* —en) turn of phrase.

redigieren [redi'gi:rən], *v.a.* edit.

redlich ['re:tlıç], *adj.* honest, upright.

Redner ['re:dnər], *m.* (—s, *pl.* —) speaker, orator.

Reede ['re:də], *f.* (—, *pl.* —n) (*Naut.*) roadstead.

Reederei [re:də'raı], *f.* (—, *pl.* —en) shipping-business.

reell [re'ɛl], *adj.* honest, fair, sound, bona fide.

Reep [re:p], *n.* (—s, *pl.* —e) (*Naut.*) rope.

Referat [refe'ra:t], *n.* (—s, *pl.* —e) report; paper (to a learned society), lecture.

Referendar [referɛn'da:r], *m.* (—s, *pl.* —e) junior barrister or teacher.

Referent [refe'rɛnt], *m.* (—en, *pl.* —en) reporter, reviewer; lecturer; expert (adviser).

Referenz [refe'rɛnts], *f.* (—, *pl.* —en) reference (to s.o. or s.th.).

referieren [refe'ri:rən], *v.a.*, *v.n.* report (on), give a paper (on).

reflektieren [reflɛk'ti:rən], *v.a.* reflect. — *v.n. auf etwas* —, be a prospective buyer of s.th., have o.'s eye on s.th.

Reformator [refɔr'ma:tɔr], *m.* (—s, *pl.* —en) reformer.

reformieren [refɔr'mi:rən], *v.a.* reform.

Regal [re'ga:l], *n.* (—s, *pl.* —e) shelf.

rege ['re:gə], *adj.* brisk, lively, animated.

Regel ['re:gəl], *f.* (—, *pl.* —n) rule, precept, principle; *in der* —, as a rule, generally.

regelmäßig ['re:gəlmɛ:sıç], *adj.* regular.

regeln ['re:gəln], *v.a.* regulate, arrange, order.

Regelung ['re:gəluŋ], *f.* (—, *pl.* —en) regulation.

regelwidrig ['re:gəlvi:drıç], *adj.* contrary to rule, irregular, foul.

Regen ['re:gən], *m.* (—s, *no pl.*) rain.

regen ['re:gən], *v.r. sich* —, move, stir.

Regenbogen ['re:gənbo:gən], *m.* (—s, *pl.* —) rainbow.

Regenbogenhaut ['re:gənbo:gənhaut], *f.* (—, *pl.* —e) (*eye*) iris.

Regenguß ['re:gəngus], *m.* (—sses, *pl.* —sse) downpour, violent shower.

Regenmantel ['re:gənmantəl], *m.* (—s, *pl.* —) waterproof, raincoat, mac.

Regenpfeifer ['re:gənpfaıfər], *m.* (—s, *pl.* —) (*Orn.*) plover.

Regenrinne ['re:gənrınə], *f.* (—, *pl.* —n) eaves.

Regenschirm ['re:gənʃırm], *m.* (—s, *pl.* —e) umbrella.

Regentschaft [re'gɛntʃaft], *f.* (—, *pl.* —en) regency.

Regie [re'ʒi:], *f.* (—, *pl.* —n) stage management, production, direction.

regieren [re'gi:rən], *v.a.* rule, reign over, govern. — *v.n.* reign; (*fig.*) prevail, predominate.

Regierung [re'gi:ruŋ], *f.* (—, *pl.* —en) government; reign.

Regierungsrat [re'gi:ruŋsra:t], *m.* (—s, *pl.* —e) government adviser.

Regiment (1) [regi'mɛnt], *n.* (—s, *pl.* —e) rule, government.

Regiment (2) [regi'mɛnt], *n.* (—s, *pl.* —er) (*Mil.*) regiment.

Regisseur [reʒi'sø:r], *m.* (—s, *pl.* —e) stage-manager, producer, director.

Registrator [regıs'tra:tɔr], *m.* (—s, *pl.* —en) registrar, recorder; registering machine.

Registratur [regıstra'tu:r], *f.* (—, *pl.* —en) record office, registry; filing-cabinet.

registrieren [regıs'tri:rən], *v.a.* register, record, file.

reglos ['re:klo:s], *adj.* motionless.

regnen ['re:gnən], *v.n.* rain; *es regnet in Strömen*, it is raining cats and dogs.

Regreß [re'grɛs], *m.* (—sses, *pl.* —sse) recourse, remedy.

regsam ['re:kza:m], *adj.* quick, alert, lively.

regulieren [regu'li:rən], *v.a.* regulate.

Regung ['re:guŋ], *f.* (—, *pl.* —en) movement; impulse.

Reh [re:], *n.* (—(e)s, *pl.* —e) doe, roe.

rehabilitieren [rehabili'ti:rən], *v.a.* rehabilitate.

Rehbock ['re:bɔk], *m.* (—s, *pl.* —e) (*Zool.*) roe-buck.

Rehkeule ['re:kɔylə], *f.* (—, *pl.* —n) haunch of venison.

reiben ['raıbən], *v.a. irr.* rub, grate, grind; *einem etwas unter die Nase* —, throw s.th. in s.o.'s teeth, bring s.th. home to s.o.

Reibung ['raıbuŋ], *f.* (—, *pl.* —en) friction.

Reich [raıç], *n.* (—(e)s, *pl.* —e) kingdom, realm, empire, state.

reich [raıç], *adj.* rich, wealthy, opulent.

reichen ['raıçən], *v.a.* reach, pass, hand; *einem die Hand* —, shake hands with s.o. — *v.n.* reach, extend; be sufficient.

reichhaltig ['raıçhaltıç], *adj.* abundant, copious.

reichlich ['raıçlıç], *adj.* ample, plentiful.

Reichskammergericht [raıçs'kamərgərıçt], *n.* (—s, *no pl.*) Imperial High Court of Justice (*Holy Roman Empire*).

Reichskanzlei ['raıçskantslaı], *f.* (—, *pl.* —en) (Imperial) Chancery.

Reichskanzler ['raıçskantslər], *m.* (—s, *pl.* —) (Imperial) Chancellor.

Reichsstände ['raıçsʃtɛndə], *m. pl.* Estates (of the Holy Roman Empire).

Reichstag ['raıçsta:k], *m.* (—s, *pl.* —e) Imperial Parliament, Reichstag, Diet.

Reichtum ['raɪçtu:m], *m.* (—s, *pl.* ˙er) riches, wealth, opulence.

Reif (1) [raɪf], *m.* (—s, *no pl.*) hoarfrost.

Reif (2) [raɪf], *m.* (—s, *pl.* —e) ring.

reif [raɪf], *adj.* ripe, mature.

Reifen ['raɪfən], *m.* (—s, *pl.* —) hoop; tyre; — *schlagen*, trundle a hoop.

reifen ['raɪfən], *v.n.* (*aux.* sein) ripen, mature, grow ripe.

Reifeprüfung ['raɪfəpry:fuŋ], *f.* (—, *pl.* —en) matriculation examination.

reiflich ['raɪflɪç], *adj. sich etwas — überlegen*, give careful consideration to s.th.

Reigen ['raɪgən], *m.* (—s, *pl.* —) round-dance, roundelay.

Reihe ['raɪə], *f.* (—, *pl.* —n) series; file; row; progression, sequence; (*Theat.*) tier; *in — und Glied*, in closed ranks; *nach der —*, in turns; *ich bin an der —*, it is my turn.

Reihenfolge ['raɪənfɔlgə], *f.* (—, *no pl.*) succession.

Reiher ['raɪər], *m.* (—s, *pl.* —) (*Orn.*) heron.

Reim [raɪm], *m.* (—(e)s, *pl.* —e) rhyme.

rein [raɪn], *adj.* clean, pure, clear, neat; —*e Wahrheit*, plain truth; *ins —e bringen*, settle, clear up; *ins —e schreiben*, make a fair copy of; *einem —en Wein einschenken*, have a straight talk with s.o.

Reineke ['raɪnəkə], *m.* (—, *no pl.*) — *Fuchs*, Reynard the Fox.

Reinertrag ['raɪnɛrtra:k], *m.* (—(e)s, *pl.* ˙e) net proceeds.

Reinfall ['raɪnfal], *m.* (—s, *pl.* ˙e) sell, wild-goose chase; disappointment.

reinfallen ['raɪnfalən], *v.n. irr.* (*aux.* sein) be unsuccessful.

Reingewinn ['raɪngəvɪn], *m.* (—s, *pl.* —e) net proceeds.

Reinheit ['raɪnhaɪt], *f.* (—, *no pl.*) purity.

reinigen ['raɪnɪgən], *v.a.* clean, cleanse; dry-clean; purge.

Reinigung ['raɪnɪguŋ], *f.* (—, *pl.* —en) cleaning; (*fig.*) purification, cleansing; *chemische —*, dry-cleaning.

reinlich ['raɪnlɪç], *adj.* clean, neat.

Reis (1) [raɪs], *m.* (—, *no pl.*) rice.

Reis (2) [raɪs], *n.* (—es, *pl.* —er) twig, sprig; scion; cutting.

Reisbesen ['raɪsbe:zən], *m.* (—s, *pl.* —) birch-broom, besom.

Reise ['raɪzə], *f.* (—, *pl.* —n) tour, trip, journey, travels; voyage; *gute —!* bon voyage!

reisefertig ['raɪzəfɛrtɪç], *adj.* ready to start.

Reisegeld ['raɪzəgɛlt], *n.* (—es, *pl.* —er) travel allowance.

reisen ['raɪzən], *v.n.* (*aux.* sein) travel, tour, journey, take a trip.

Reisende ['raɪzəndə], *m.* (—n, *pl.* —n) traveller; commercial traveller.

Reisig ['raɪzɪç], *n.* (—s, *no pl.*) brushwood.

Reisige ['raɪzɪgə], *m.* (—n, *pl.* —n) (*obs.*) trooper, horseman.

Reißaus [raɪs'aʊs], *n.* (—, *no pl.*) — *nehmen*, take to o.'s heels.

Reißbrett ['raɪsbrɛt], *n.* (—es, *pl.* —er) drawing-board.

reißen ['raɪsən], *v.a. irr.* tear; rend; pull; snatch; *etwas an sich —*, seize s.th., usurp.

reißend ['raɪsənt], *adj.* rapid; ravening; carnivorous; (*Comm.*) brisk, rapid (sales).

Reißnagel ['raɪsna:gəl], *m.* see **Reißzwecke.**

Reißschiene ['raɪsʃi:nə], *f.* (—, *pl.* —n) T-square.

Reißverschluß ['raɪsfɛrʃlus], *m.* (—sses, *pl.* ˙sse) zip-fastener.

Reißzwecke ['raɪstsvɛkə], *f.* (—, *pl.* —n) drawing-pin.

reiten ['raɪtən], *v.a. irr.* ride (a horse). — *v.n.* (*aux.* sein) ride, go on horseback.

Reiterei [raɪtə'raɪ], *f.* (—, *pl.* —en) cavalry.

Reitknecht ['raɪtknɛçt], *m.* (—es, *pl.* —e) groom.

Reiz [raɪts], *m.* (—es, *pl.* —e) charm, attraction, fascination, allure; stimulus; irritation; (*Phys.*) impulse.

reizbar ['raɪtsba:r], *adj.* susceptible; irritable.

reizen ['raɪtsən], *v.a.* irritate; stimulate, charm, entice.

reizend ['raɪtsənt], *adj.* charming.

Reizmittel ['raɪtsmɪtəl], *n.* (—s, *pl.* —) stimulant; irritant.

rekeln ['re:kəln], *v.r.* (*dial.*) *sich —*, loll about.

Reklame [re'kla:mə], *f.* (—, *pl.* —n) propaganda, advertisement, advertising, publicity.

reklamieren [rekla'mi:rən], *v.a.* claim, reclaim. — *v.n.* complain.

rekognoszieren [rekɔgnɔs'tsi:rən], *v.a.* reconnoitre.

rekommandieren [rekɔman'di:rən], *v.a.* (*Austr.*) register (a letter).

Rekonvaleszent [rekɔnvalɛs'tsɛnt], *m.* (—en, *pl.* —en) convalescent.

Rekrut [re'kru:t], *m.* (—en, *pl.* —en) recruit.

rekrutieren [rekru'ti:rən], *v.a.* recruit. — *v.r. sich — aus*, be recruited from.

rektifizieren [rɛktifi'tsi:rən], *v.a.* rectify.

Rektor ['rɛktɔr], *m.* (—s, *pl.* —en) (school) principal; (*Univ.*) president.

Rektorat [rɛkto'ra:t], *n.* (—es, *pl.* —e) rectorship, presidency.

relativ [rela'ti:f], *adj.* relative, comparative.

relegieren [rele'gi:rən], *v.a.* expel; (*Univ.*) send down, rusticate.

Relief [rel'jɛf], *n.* (—s, *pl.* —s) (*Art*) relief.

religiös [reli'gjø:s], *adj.* religious.

Reliquie [re'li:kvjə], *f.* (—, *pl.* —n) (*Rel.*) relic.

Remise [re'mi:zə], *f.* (—, *pl.* —n) coach-house.

Remittent [remɪ'tɛnt], *m.* (—en, *pl.* —en) remitter.

Renegat [rene'ga:t], *m.* (—en, *pl.* —en) renegade.

Renette [re'nɛtə], *f.* (—, *pl.* —n) rennet(-apple).

renken ['rɛŋkən], *v.a.* wrench, bend, twist.

Rennbahn ['rɛnba:n], *f.* (—, *pl.* —en) race-course; (cinder)-track; (*Motor.*) racing-circuit.

rennen ['rɛnən], *v.n. irr.* (*aux.* sein) run, race, rush.

Renommé [renɔ'me:], *n.* (—s, *no pl.*) renown, repute, reputation.

renommieren [renɔ'mi:rən], *v.n.* brag, boast.

renovieren [reno'vi:rən], *v.a.* renovate, restore, redecorate, renew.

rentabel [rɛn'ta:bəl], *adj.* profitable, lucrative.

Rente ['rɛntə], *f.* (—, *pl.* —n) pension, annuity.

Rentier [rɛn'tje:], *m.* (—s, *pl.* —s) rentier, person of independent means.

rentieren [rɛn'ti:rən], *v.r. sich* —, be profitable, be worthwhile, pay.

Rentner ['rɛntnər], *m.* (—s, *pl.* —) pensioner.

Reparatur [repara'tu:r], *f.* (—, *pl.* —en) repair.

reparieren [repa'ri:rən], *v.a.* repair.

Repräsentant [reprɛzɛn'tant], *m.* (—en, *pl.* —en) representative.

Repräsentantenkammer [reprɛzɛn-'tantənkamər], *f.* (—, *pl.* —n) (*Am.*) House of Representatives.

Repressalien [reprɛ'sa:ljən], *f. pl.* reprisals, retaliation.

reproduzieren [reprodu'tsi:rən], *v.a.* reproduce.

Republikaner [republi'ka:nər], *m.* (—s, *pl.* —) republican.

requirieren [rekvi'ri:rən], *v.a.* requisition.

Reseda [re'ze:da], *f.* (—, *pl.* —s) (*Bot.*) mignonette.

Reservat [rezɛr'va:t], *n.* (—es, *pl.* —e) reservation, reserve.

Residenz [rezi'dɛnts], *f.* (—, *pl.* —en) residence, seat of the Court.

residieren [rezi'di:rən], *v.n.* reside.

Residuum [re'zi:duum], *n.* (—s, *pl.* —duen) residue, dregs.

resignieren [rezɪg'ni:rən], *v.n., v.r.* resign; be resigned (to s.th.); give up.

Respekt [re'spɛkt], *m.* (—es, *no pl.*) respect, regard; *mit* — *zu sagen*, with all due respect.

respektieren [respɛk'ti:rən], *v.a.* respect, honour.

Ressort [rɛ'so:r], *n.* (—s, *pl.* —s) department, domain.

Rest [rɛst], *m.* (—es, *pl.* —e) rest, residue, remainder; remnant; (*money*) balance.

restaurieren [rɛsto'ri:rən], *v.a.* restore, renovate.

Resultat [rezul'ta:t], *n.* (—es, *pl.* —e) result, outcome.

Resümee [rezy'me:], *n.* (—s, *pl.* —s) résumé, précis, digest, summary, synopsis, abstract.

retten ['rɛtən], *v.a.* save, preserve; rescue, deliver; *die Ehre* —, vindicate o.'s honour.

Rettich ['rɛtɪç], *m.* (—s, *pl.* —e) radish.

Rettung ['rɛtuŋ], *f.* (—, *pl.* —en) saving, rescue, deliverance.

retuschieren [retu'ʃi:rən], *v.a.* re-touch.

Reue ['rɔyə], *f.* (—, *no pl.*) repentance, remorse, contrition.

reuen ['rɔyən], *v.a., v.n.* repent, regret; *es reut mich*, I am sorry.

Reugeld ['rɔygɛlt], *n.* (—es, *pl.* —er) forfeit-money, penalty.

reüssieren [rey'si:rən], *v.n.* succeed.

Revanche [re'vã:ʃə], *f.* (—, *pl.* —n) revenge; (*fig.*) return.

revanchieren [revã'ʃi:rən], *v.r. sich* —, repay a service, have *or* take o.'s revenge.

Reverenz [reve'rɛnts], *f.* (—, *pl.* —en) bow, curtsy.

revidieren [revi'di:rən], *v.a.* revise, check.

Revier [re'vi:r], *n.* (—s, *pl.* —e) district, precinct, quarter; preserve.

Revisor [re'vi:zɔr], *m.* (—s, *pl.* —en) accountant, auditor.

revoltieren [revɔl'ti:rən], *v.n.* rise, revolt.

revolutionieren [revolutsjo'ni:rən], *v.a.* revolutionise.

Revolverblatt [re'vɔlvərblat], *n.* (—s, *pl.* ⸚er) gutter press.

Revue [re'vy:], *f.* (—, *pl.* —n) revue; review; — *passieren lassen*, pass in review.

Rezensent [retsɛn'zɛnt], *m.* (—en, *pl.* —en) reviewer, critic.

rezensieren [retsɛn'zi:rən], *v.a.* review.

Rezept [re'tsɛpt], *n.* (—es, *pl.* —e) (*Med.*) prescription; (*Cul.*) recipe.

rezitieren [retsi'ti:rən], *v.a.* recite.

Rhabarber [ra'barbər], *m.* (—s, *no pl.*) (*Bot.*) rhubarb.

Rhein [rain], *m.* (—s, *no pl.*) (River) Rhine.

Rhodesien [ro'de:zjən], *n.* Rhodesia.

Rhodus ['ro:dus], *n.* Rhodes.

Rhythmus ['rytmus], *m.* (—, *pl.* —men) rhythm.

Richtbeil ['rɪçtbail], *n.* (—s, *pl.* —e) executioner's axe.

richten ['rɪçtən], *v.a., v.n.* direct, point at; prepare; *die Augen* — *auf*, fix o.'s eyes upon; *einen zugrunde* —, ruin s.o.; judge, try, pass sentence on, condemn. —*v.r. sich nach* (*Dat.*) —, be guided by.

Richter ['rɪçtər], *m.* (—, *pl.* —) judge; justice.

richtig ['rɪçtɪç], *adj.* right, correct, exact, true; *nicht ganz* — *sein*, be not quite right in the head.

Richtlot ['rɪçtlo:t], *n.* (—s, *pl.* —e) plumb-line.

Richtschnur ['rɪçtʃnu:r], *f.* (—, *pl.* —en) plumb-line; (*fig.*) rule, precept.

Richtung ['rɪçtuŋ], *f.* (—, *pl.* —en) direction.

riechen ['ri:çən], *v.a., v.n. irr.* smell, scent, reek; *Lunte* —, smell a rat.

Riege ['ri:gə], *f.* (—, *pl.* —n) row, section.

Riegel ['ri:gəl], *m.* (—s, *pl.* —) bar, bolt; *ein* — *Schokolade*, a bar of chocolate.

Riemen ['ri:mən], *m.* (—s, *pl.* —) strap, thong; oar.

Ries [ri:s], *n.* (—es, *pl.* —e) (*paper*) ream.

Riese ['ri:zə], *m.* (—n, *pl.* —n) giant.

rieseln ['ri:zəln], *v.n.* murmur, babble, ripple, trickle; drizzle.

Riesenschlange ['ri:zənʃlaŋə], *f.* (—, *pl.* —n) anaconda.

Riff [rɪf], *n.* (—es, *pl.* —e) reef.

rigoros [rigo'ro:s], *adj.* strict, rigorous.

Rille ['rɪlə], *f.* (—, *pl.* —n) groove, small furrow; (*Archit.*) flute, chamfer.

Rind [rɪnt], *n.* (—es, *pl.* —er) ox, cow; (*pl.*) cattle, horned cattle, head of cattle.

Rinde ['rɪndə], *f.* (—, *pl.* —n) rind, bark, peel; (*bread*) crust.

Rinderbraten ['rɪndərbra:tən], *m.* (—s, *pl.* —) roast beef.

Rindfleisch ['rɪntflaɪʃ], *n.* (—es, *no pl.*) beef.

Rindvieh ['rɪntfi:], *n.* (—s, *no pl.*) cattle; (*fig.*) blockhead, ass.

Ring [rɪŋ], *m.* (—(e)s, *pl.* —e) ring; (*chain*) link; (*under the eye*) dark circle; (*Comm.*) syndicate, trust.

Ringelblume ['rɪŋəlblu:mə], *f.* (—, *pl.* —n) (*Bot.*) marigold.

ringeln ['rɪŋəln], *v.r. sich* —, curl.

ringen ['rɪŋən], *v.a. irr.* wring. — *v.n.* wrestle.

Ringer [rɪŋər], *m.* (—s, *pl.* —) wrestler.

Ringmauer ['rɪŋmauər], *f.* (—, *pl.* —n) city *or* town wall.

rings [rɪŋs], *adv.* around.

ringsum(her) [rɪŋ'sum(he:r)], *adv.* round about.

Rinne ['rɪnə], *f.* (—, *pl.* —n) furrow, gutter; groove.

rinnen ['rɪnən], *v.n. irr.* (*aux*, sein) run, leak, drip.

Rinnsal ['rɪnza:l], *n.* (—s, *pl.* —e) channel, water-course.

Rinnstein ['rɪnʃtain], *m.* (—s, *pl.* —e) gutter.

Rippe ['rɪpə], *f.* (—, *pl.* —n) rib.

Rippenfellentzündung ['rɪpənfɛlɛnt-tsyndun], *f.* (—, *pl.* —en) pleurisy.

Rippenspeer ['rɪpənʃpe:r], *m.* (—, —e) (*Casseler*) —, spare-rib, ribs of pork.

Rippenstoß ['rɪpənʃto:s], *m.* (—es, *pl.* ‾e) dig in the ribs, nudge.

Rips [rɪps], *m.* (—es, *no pl.*) rep.

Risiko ['ri:ziko], *n.* (—s, *pl.* —ken) risk.

riskant [rɪs'kant], *adj.* risky.

riskieren [rɪs'ki:rən], *v.a.* risk.

Riß [rɪs], *m.* (—sses, *pl.* —sse) rent, tear; sketch, design, plan.

rissig ['rɪsɪç], *adj.* cracked, torn.

Ritt [rɪt], *m.* (—(e)s, *pl.* —e) ride.

Ritter ['rɪtər], *m.* (—s, *pl.* —) knight; *einen zum* — *schlagen*, dub s.o. a knight.

ritterlich ['rɪtərlɪç], *adj.* knightly; (*fig.*) chivalrous, valiant, gallant.

Ritterschlag ['rɪtərʃla:k], *m.* (—(e)s, *pl.* ‾e) accolade.

Rittersporn ['rɪtərʃpɔrn], *m.* (—s, *pl.* —e) (*Bot.*) larkspur.

rittlings ['rɪtlɪŋs], *adv.* astride.

Rittmeister ['rɪtmaistər], *m.* (—s, *pl.* —) captain (of cavalry).

Ritus ['ri:tus], *m.* (—, *pl.* **Riten**) rite.

Ritz [rɪts], *m.* (—es, *pl.* —e) chink, fissure, cleft, crevice; (*glacier*) crevasse.

ritzen ['rɪtsən], *v.a.* scratch.

Rivale [ri'va:lə], *m.* (—n, *pl.* —n) rival.

Rivalität [rivali'tε:t], *f.* (—, *pl.* —en) rivalry.

Rizinusöl ['ri:tsinusø:l], *n.* (—s, *no pl.*) castor oil.

Robbe ['rɔbə], *f.* (—, *pl.* —n) (*Zool.*) seal.

Robe ['ro:bə], *f.* (—, *pl.* —n) dress, robe; gown.

röcheln ['rœçəln], *v.n.* rattle in o.'s throat.

rochieren [rɔ'xi:rən], *v.n.* (*Chess*) castle.

Rock [rɔk], *m.* (—(e)s, *pl.* ‾e) (*woman*) skirt; (*man*) coat.

rodeln ['ro:dəln], *v.n.* (*aux.* haben & sein) toboggan.

roden ['ro:dən], *v.a.* clear, weed, thin out (plants).

Rogen ['ro:gən], *m.* (—s, *no pl.*) (*fish*) roe, spawn.

Roggen ['rɔgən], *m.* (—s, *no pl.*) rye.

roh [ro:], *adj.* raw; rough, rude, coarse, crude; *ein* —*er Mensch*, a brute; (*in compounds*) rough—; preliminary, unrefined.

Rohbilanz ['ro:bilants], *f.* (—, *pl.* —en) trial balance.

Roheisen ['ro:aizən], *n.* (—s, *no pl.*) pig-iron.

Roheit ['ro:hait], *f.* (—, *pl.* —en) coarseness, rudeness, crudity.

Rohr [ro:r], *n.* (—es, *pl.* —e, ‾e) tube, pipe; reed, cane; (*gun*) barrel.

Rohrdommel ['ro:rdɔməl], *f.* (—, *pl.* —n) (*Orn.*) bittern.

Röhre ['rø:rə], *f.* (—, *pl.* —n) tube, pipe; (*Radio*) valve.

Röhricht ['rø:rɪçt], *n.* (—s, *pl.* —e) reeds.

Rohrpfeife ['ro:rpfaifə], *f.* (—, *pl.* —n) reed-pipe.

Rohrpost ['ro:rpɔst], *f.* (—, *no pl.*) pneumatic post.

Rohrzucker ['ro:rtsukər], *m.* (—s, *no pl.*) cane-sugar.

Rolladen ['rɔladən], *m.* (**—s**, *pl.* ∴) sliding shutter, roller blind.

Rollbahn ['rɔlba:n], *f.* (**—**, *pl.* **—en**) (*Aviat.*) runway.

Rolle ['rɔlə], *f.* (**—**, *pl.* **—n**) reel, roll; pulley; (*Theat.*) part; rôle; (*laundry*) mangle.

rollen ['rɔlən], *v.a.* roll, reel; (*laundry*) mangle. — *v.n.* (*aux.* sein) roll (along); (*thunder*) roar, roll.

Roller ['rɔlər], *m.* (**—s**, *pl.* **—**) scooter.

Rollmops ['rɔlmɔps], *m.* (**—es**, *pl.* ∴e) soused herring.

Rollschuh ['rɔlʃu:], *m.* (**—s**, *pl.* **—e**) roller-skate.

Rollstuhl ['rɔlʃtu:l], *m.* (**—s**, *pl.* ∴e) wheel-chair, bath-chair.

Rolltreppe ['rɔltrɛpə], *f.* (**—**, *pl.* **—n**) escalator, moving staircase.

Rom [ro:m], *n.* Rome.

Roman [ro'ma:n], *m.* (**—s**, *pl.* **—e**) novel.

romanisch [ro'ma:nɪʃ], *adj.* Romanesque.

Romanliteratur [ro'ma:nlitəratu:r], *f.* (**—**, *no pl.*) fiction.

Romanschriftsteller [ro'ma:nʃrɪftʃtelər], *m.* (**—s**, *pl.* **—**) novelist.

Römer ['rø:mər], *m.* (**—s**, *pl.* **—**) Roman; (*glass*) rummer.

Rondell [rɔn'dɛl], *n.* (**—s**, *pl.* **—e**) circular flower-bed.

Röntgenstrahlen ['rœntgənʃtra:lən], *m. pl.* X-rays.

rosa ['ro:za:], *adj.* pink, rose-coloured.

Rose ['ro:zə], *f.* (**—**, *pl.* **—n**) rose.

Rosenkranz ['ro:zənkrants], *m.* (**—es**, *pl.* ∴e) garland of roses; (*Eccl.*) rosary.

Rosenkreuzer ['ro:zənkrɔytsər], *m.* (**—s**, *pl.* **—**) Rosicrucian.

Rosine [ro'zi:nə], *f.* (**—**, *pl.* **—n**) sultana, raisin.

Rosmarin ['rɔsmari:n], *m.* (**—s**, *no pl.*) (*Bot.*) rosemary.

Roß [rɔs], *n.* (**—sses**, *pl.* **—sse**) horse, steed.

Roßbremse ['rɔsbrɛmzə], *f.* (**—**, *pl.* **—n**) (*Ent.*) horsefly, gadfly.

Rössel ['rœsəl], *n.* (**—s**, *pl.* **—**) (*Chess*) knight.

Roßhaarmatratze ['rɔsha:rmatratsə], *f.* (**—**, *pl.* **—n**) hair-mattress.

Roßkastanie ['rɔskasta:njə], *f.* (**—**, *pl.* **—n**) (*Bot.*) horse-chestnut.

Rost (1) [rɔst], *m.* (**—es**, *no pl.*) rust.

Rost (2) [rɔst], *m.* (**—s**, *pl.* **—e**) grate; gridiron.

Rostbraten ['rɔstbra:tən], *m.* (**—s**, *pl.* **—**) roast meat.

rosten ['rɔstən], *v.n.* go rusty; rust; *alte Liebe rostet nicht*, love that's old rusts not away.

rösten ['rø:stən], *v.a.* toast, roast, grill.

rot [ro:t], *adj.* red; **—** *werden*, redden, blush.

Rotauge ['ro:taugə], *n.* (**—s**, *pl.* **—n**) (*Zool.*) roach.

Röte ['rø:tə], *f.* (**—**, *no pl.*) redness, red colour.

Röteln ['rø:təln], *m. pl.* (*Med.*) German measles, rubella.

Rotfink ['ro:tfɪŋk], *m.* (**—en**, *pl.* **—en**) (*Orn.*) bullfinch.

Rotfuchs ['ro:tfuks], *m.* (**—es**, *pl.* ∴e) (*Zool.*) sorrel horse.

rotieren [ro'ti:rən], *v.n.* rotate.

Rotkäppchen ['ro:tkɛpçən], *n.* Little Red Riding Hood.

Rotkehlchen ['ro:tke:lçən], *n.* (**—s**, *pl.* **—**) robin.

Rotlauf ['ro:tlauf], *m.* (**—s**, *no pl.*) (*Med.*) erysipelas.

Rotschimmel ['ro:tʃɪməl], *m.* (**—s**, *pl.* **—**) roan-horse.

Rotspon ['ro:tʃpo:n], *m.* (**—s**, *no pl.*) (*dial.*) claret.

Rotte ['rɔtə], *f.* (**—**, *pl.* **—n**) band, gang, rabble; (*Mil.*) file, squad.

Rotwild ['ro:tvɪlt], *n.* (**—s**, *no pl.*) red deer.

Rotz [rɔts], *m.* (**—es**, *no pl.*) (*vulg.*) mucus; snot.

Rouleau [ru'lo:], *n.* (**—s**, *pl.* **—s**) sun-blind, roller-blind.

routiniert [ruti'ni:rt], *adj.* smart; experienced.

Rübe ['ry:bə], *f.* (**—**, *pl.* **—n**) (*Bot.*) turnip; *rote* **—**, beetroot; *gelbe* **—**, carrot.

Rubel ['ru:bəl], *m.* (**—s**, *pl.* **—**) rouble.

Rübenzucker ['ry:bəntsukər], *m.* (**—s**, *no pl.*) beet-sugar.

Rubin [ru'bi:n], *m.* (**—s**, *pl.* **—e**) ruby.

Rubrik [ru'bri:k], *f.* (**—**, *pl.* **—en**) rubric; title, heading, category, column.

Rübsamen ['ry:pza:mən], *m.* (**—s**, *no pl.*) rape-seed.

ruchbar ['ru:xba:r], *adj.* manifest, known, notorious.

ruchlos ['ru:xlo:s], *adj.* wicked, profligate, vicious.

Ruck [ruk], *m.* (**—(e)s**, *pl.* **—e**) pull, jolt, jerk.

Rückblick ['rykblɪk], *m.* (**—s**, *pl.* **—e**) retrospect, retrospective view.

Rücken ['rykən], *m.* (**—s**, *pl.* **—**) back; (*mountains*) ridge; *einem den* — *kehren*, turn o.'s back upon s.o.

rücken ['rykən], *v.a.* move, push. — *v.n.* move along.

Rückenmark ['rykənmark], *n.* (**—s**, *no pl.*) spinal marrow.

Rückenwirbel ['rykənvɪrbəl], *m.* (**—s**, *pl.* **—**) dorsal vertebra.

rückerstatten ['rykərʃtatən], *v.a.* refund.

Rückfahrkarte ['rykfa:rkartə], *f.* (**—**, *pl.* **—n**) return ticket.

Rückfall ['rykfal], *m.* (**—s**, *pl.* ∴e) relapse.

rückgängig ['rykgɛŋɪç], *adj.* — *machen*, cancel, annul, reverse (a decision).

Rückgrat ['rykgra:t], *n.* (**—s**, *pl.* **—e**) backbone, spine.

Rückhalt ['rykhalt], *m.* (**—s**, *no pl.*) reserve; support, backing.

Rückkehr

Rückkehr ['rykke:r], *f.* (—, *no pl.*) return.

Rücklicht ['ryklɪçt], *n.* (—s, *pl.* —er) (*Motor. etc.*) tail-light.

rücklings ['ryklɪŋks], *adv.* from behind.

Rucksack ['rukzak], *m.* (—s, *pl.* ⸚e) rucksack; knapsack.

Rückschritt ['rykʃrɪt], *m.* (—es, —e) step backward, retrograde step, regression.

Rücksicht ['rykzɪçt], *f.* (—, *pl.* —en) consideration, regard.

Rücksprache ['rykʃpra:xə], *f.* (—, *pl.* —n) conference, consultation; — *nehmen mit*, consult, confer with.

rückständig ['rykʃtɛndɪç], *adj.* outstanding; old-fashioned; backward.

Rücktritt ['ryktrɪt], *m.* (—s, *no pl.*) resignation.

ruckweise ['rukvaɪzə], *adv.* by fits and starts; jerkily.

Rückwirkung ['rykvɪrkuŋ], *f.* (—, *pl.* —en) reaction, retroaction.

Rüde ['ry:də], *m.* (—n, *pl.* —n) male (dog, fox etc.).

Rudel ['ru:dəl], *n.* (—s, *pl.* —) flock, herd, pack.

Ruder ['ru:dər], *n.* (—s, *pl.* —) oar, rudder, paddle; *am* — *sein*, be at the helm; (*Pol.*) be in power.

rudern ['ru:dərn], *v.a., v.n.* row.

Ruf [ru:f], *m.* (—(e)s, *pl.* —e) call; shout; reputation, renown; *einen guten (schlechten)* — *haben*, have a good (bad) reputation, be well (ill) spoken of.

rufen ['ru:fən], *v.a., v.n. irr.* call, shout; *einen* — *lassen*, send for s.o.

Rüffel ['ryfəl], *m.* (—s, *pl.* —) (*coll.*) reprimand; (*sl.*) rocket.

Rüge ['ry:gə], *f.* (—, *pl.* —n) censure, blame, reprimand.

Ruhe ['ru:ə], *f.* (—, *no pl.*) rest, repose; quiet, tranquillity; *sich zur* — *setzen*, retire (from business etc.).

Ruhegehalt ['ru:əgəhalt], *n.* (—es, *pl.* ⸚er) retirement pension, superannuation.

ruhen ['ru:ən], *v.n.* rest, repose, take a rest.

Ruhestand ['ru:əʃtant], *m.* (—es, *no pl.*) retirement.

ruhig ['ru:ɪç], *adj.* quiet, tranquil, peaceful, calm; *sich* — *verhalten*, keep quiet.

Ruhm [ru:m], *m.* (—(e)s, *no pl.*) glory, fame, renown; *einem zum* — *gereichen*, be or redound to s.o.'s credit.

rühmen ['ry:mən], *v.a.* praise, extol, glorify; — *v.r. sich* —, boast.

Ruhr [ru:r], *f.* (River) Ruhr.

Ruhr (2) [ru:r], *f.* (—, *no pl.*) dysentery.

Rührei ['ry:rai], *n.* (—s, *pl.* —er) scrambled egg.

rühren ['ry:rən], *v.a.* stir, move, touch; — *v.r. sich* —, move, stir; get a move on.

rührig ['ry:rɪç], *adj.* active, alert.

rührselig ['ry:rze:lɪç], *adj.* oversentimental; lachrymose.

Rührung ['ry:ruŋ], *f.* (—, *no pl.*) emotion.

Ruin [ru'i:n], *m.* (—s, *no pl.*) (*fig.*) ruin; decay; bankruptcy.

Ruine [ru'i:nə], *f.* (—, *pl.* —n) ruin(s).

rülpsen ['rylpsən], *v.n.* belch.

Rum [rum], *m.* (—s, *no pl.*) rum.

Rumänien [ru'mɛ:njən], *n.* Rumania.

Rummel ['ruməl], *m.* (—s, *no pl.*) tumult, row, hubbub.

Rumor [ru'mo:r], *m.* (—s, *no pl.*) noise; rumour.

rumoren [ru'mo:rən], *v.n.* make a noise.

Rumpelkammer ['rumpəlkamər], *f.* (—, *pl.* —n) lumber-room, junk-room.

rumpeln ['rumpəln], *v.n.* rumble.

Rumpf [rumpf], *m.* (—(e)s, *pl.* ⸚e) (*Anat.*) trunk; (*ship*) hull; (*Aviat.*) fuselage.

rümpfen ['rympfən], *v.a. die Nase* —, turn up o.'s nose.

rund [runt], *adj.* round, rotund; — *heraus*, flatly; *etwas* — *abschlagen*, refuse s.th. flatly; — *herum*, round about.

Runde ['rundə], *f.* (—, *pl.* —n) round; (*Sport*) round, bout; *die* — *machen*, (*watchman*) patrol.

Rundfunk ['runtfuŋk], *m.* (—s, *no pl.*) broadcasting, wireless; radio.

Rundgang ['runtgaŋ], *m.* (—s, *pl.* ⸚e) round, tour (of inspection).

rundlich ['runtlɪç], *adj.* plump.

Rundschau ['runtʃau], *f.* (—, *no pl.*) panorama; review, survey.

Rundschreiben ['runtʃraɪbən], *n.* (—s, *pl.* —) circular letter.

rundweg ['runtve:k], *adv.* flatly, plainly.

Rune ['ru:nə], *f.* (—, *pl.* —n) rune; runic writing.

Runkelrübe ['ruŋkəlry:bə], *f.* (—, *pl.* —n) beetroot.

Runzel ['runtsəl], *f.* (—, *pl.* —n) wrinkle, pucker.

Rüpel ['ry:pəl], *m.* (—s, *pl.* —) bounder, lout.

rupfen ['rupfən], *v.a.* pluck; *einen* —, (*fig.*) fleece s.o.

Rupie ['ru:pjə], *f.* (—, *pl.* —n) rupee.

ruppig ['rupɪç], *adj.* unfriendly, rude; scruffy.

Ruprecht ['ru:prɛçt], *m. Knecht* —, Santa Claus.

Rüsche ['ry:ʃə], *f.* (—, *pl.* —n) ruche.

Ruß [ru:s], *m.* (—s, *no pl.*) soot.

Rüssel ['rysəl], *m.* (—s, *pl.* —) snout; (*elephant*) trunk.

Rußland ['ruslant], *n.* Russia.

rüsten ['rystən], *v.a.* prepare, fit (out); equip; (*Mil.*) arm, mobilise.

Rüster ['rystər], *f.* (—, *pl.* —n) elm.

rüstig ['rystɪç], *adj.* vigorous, robust.

Rüstung ['rystuŋ], *f.* (—, *pl.* —en) armour; preparation; (*Mil.*) armament.

Rüstzeug ['rysttsɔyk], *n.* (—s, *no pl.*) equipment.
Rute ['ru:tə], *f.* (—, *pl.* —n) rod, twig; (*fox*) brush.
Rutengänger ['ru:təngɛŋər], *m.* (—s, *pl.* —) water-diviner.
rutschen ['rutʃən], *v.n.* (*aux.* sein) slip, slide, skid, slither.
rütteln ['rytəln], *v.a., v.n.* shake, jolt.

S

S [ɛs], *n.* (—s, *pl.* —s) the letter S.
Saal [za:l], *m.* (—(e)s, *pl.* **Säle**) hall, large room.
Saat [za:t], *f.* (—, *pl.* —en) seed; sowing; standing corn.
Sabbat ['zabat], *m.* (—s, *pl.* —e) sabbath.
sabbern ['zabərn], *v.n.* (*sl.*) slaver, drivel.
Säbel ['zɛ:bəl], *m.* (—s, *pl.* —) sabre; *krummer* —, falchion, scimitar.
säbeln ['zɛ:bəln], *v.a.* sabre, hack at.
sachdienlich ['zaxdi:nlɪç], *adj.* relevant, pertinent.
Sache ['zaxə], *f.* (—, *pl.* —n) thing, matter, affair; (*Law*) action, case; *die — ist* (*die*) *daß*, the fact is that; *das gehört nicht zur* —, that is beside the point; *bei der — sein*, pay attention to the matter in hand; *das ist meine* —, that is my business; *die — der Unterdrückten verteidigen*, take up the cause of the oppressed.
Sachlage ['zaxla:gə], *f.* (—, *no pl.*) state of affairs.
sachlich ['zaxlɪç], *adj.* pertinent; objective.
sächlich ['zɛçlɪç], *adj.* (*Gram.*) neuter.
Sachse ['zaksə], *m.* (—n, *pl.* —n) Saxon.
Sachsen ['zaksən], *n.* Saxony.
sachte ['zaxtə], *adj.* soft, slow, quiet, careful, gentle.
Sachverhalt ['zaxfɛrhalt], *m.* (—s, *no pl.*) facts (of a case), state of things, circumstances.
sachverständig ['zaxfɛrʃtɛndɪç], *adj.* expert, competent, experienced.
Sachwalter ['zaxvaltər], *m.* (—s, *pl.* —) manager, counsel, attorney.
Sack [zak], *m.* (—(e)s, *pl.* —e) sack, bag; *mit — und Pack,* (with) bag and baggage.
Säckel ['zɛkəl], *m.* (—s, *pl.* —) purse.
Sackgasse ['zakgasə], *f.* (—, *pl.* —n) cul-de-sac, blind alley; *einen in eine — treiben,* corner s.o.
Sackpfeife ['zakpfaifə], *f.* (—, *pl.* —n) bagpipe.
Sacktuch ['zaktu:x], *n.* (—es, *pl.* —er) sacking; (*dial.*) pocket-handkerchief.

säen ['zɛ:ən], *v.a.* sow.
Saffian ['zafja:n], *m.* (—s, *no pl.*) morocco-leather.
Saft [zaft], *m.* (—(e)s, *pl.* —e) juice; (*tree*) sap; (*meat*) gravy; *ohne — und Kraft,* insipid; *im eigenen — schmoren,* stew in o.'s own juice.
Sage ['za:gə], *f.* (—, *pl.* —n) legend, fable, myth; *es geht die* —, it is rumoured.
Säge ['zɛ:gə], *f.* (—, *pl.* —n) saw.
sagen ['za:gən], *v.a.* say, tell; *einem etwas — lassen,* send word to s.o.; *es hat nichts zu* —, it does not matter; *was Du nicht sagst!* you don't say (so)!
sägen ['zɛ:gən], *v.a., v.n.* saw; (*fig.*) snore.
sagenhaft ['za:gənhaft], *adj.* legendary, mythical, (*fig.*) fabulous.
Sahne ['za:nə], *f.* (—, *no pl.*) cream.
Saite ['zaitə], *f.* (—, *pl.* —n) string; *strengere —n aufziehen,* (*fig.*) take a stricter line.
Sakko ['zako], *m.* (—s, *pl.* —s) lounge jacket.
Sakristei [zakrɪ'stai], *f.* (—, *pl.* —en) vestry.
Salat [za'la:t], *m.* (—(e)s, *pl.* —e) salad; (*plant*) lettuce; (*sl.*) mess.
salbadern ['zalba:dərn], *v.n.* prate, talk nonsense.
Salbe ['zalbə], *f.* (—, *pl.* —n) ointment, salve.
Salbei ['zalbai], *m.* (—s, *no pl.*) (*Bot.*) sage.
salben ['zalbən], *v.a.* anoint.
salbungsvoll ['zalbuŋsfɔl], *adj.* unctuous.
Saldo ['zaldo], *m.* (—s, *pl.* —s) balance.
Saline [za'li:nə], *f.* (—, *pl.* —n) saltmine, salt-works.
Salkante ['za:lkantə], *f.* (—, *pl.* —n) selvedge, border.
Salm [zalm], *m.* (—s, *pl.* —e) (*Zool.*) salmon.
Salmiakgeist ['zalmjakgaist], *m.* (—s, *no pl.*) ammonia.
Salon [za'lɔ̃], *m.* (—s, *pl.* —s) salon; saloon; drawing-room.
salonfähig [za'lɔ̃fɛ:ɪç], *adj.* presentable, socially acceptable.
salopp [za'lɔp], *adj.* careless, slovenly, shabby, sloppy.
Salpeter [zal'pe:tər], *m.* (—s, *no pl.*) nitre, saltpetre.
salutieren [zalu'ti:rən], *v.a., v.n.,* salute.
Salve ['zalvə], *f.* (—, *pl.* —n) volley, discharge, salute.
Salz [zalts], *n.* (—es, *pl.* —e) salt.
Salzfaß ['zaltsfas], *n.* (—sses, *pl.* —sser) salt-cellar.
Salzlake ['zaltsla:kə], *f.* (—, *pl.* —n) brine.
Salzsäure ['zaltszɔyrə], *f.* (—, *no pl.*) hydrochloric acid.
Sämann ['zɛ:man], *m.* (—s, *pl.* —ner) sower.
Sambia ['zambia], *n.* Zambia.

Same(n)

Same(n) ['zaːmə(n)], *m.* (**—ns,** *pl.* **—n**) seed; sperm; spawn.

Samenstaub ['zaːmənʃtaup], *m.* (**—s,** *no pl.*) pollen.

Sämereien [zɛːməˈraɪən], *f. pl.* seeds, grain.

sämisch ['zɛːmɪʃ], *adj.* chamois.

Sammelband ['zaməlbant], *m.* (**—es,** *pl.* ⸚e) miscellany, anthology.

sammeln ['zaməln], *v.a.* collect, gather. — *v.r. sich —,* meet; collect o.'s thoughts, compose o.s.

Sammler ['zamlər], *m.* (**—s,** *pl.* **—**) collector; accumulator.

Samstag ['zamstaːk], *m.* (**—s,** *pl.* **—e**) Saturday.

Samt [zamt], *m.* (**—(e)s,** *pl.* **—e**) velvet.

samt [zamt], *adv.* together, all together; *— und sonders,* jointly and severally.— *prep.* (*Dat.*) together with.

sämtlich ['zɛmtlɪç], *adj.* each and every.

Sand [zant], *m.* (**—es,** *no pl.*) sand; *feiner —,* grit; *grober —,* gravel.

Sandtorte ['zanttɔrtə], *f.* (**—,** *pl.* **—n**) sponge-cake, madeira-cake.

Sanduhr ['zantuːr], *f.*, (**—,** *pl.* **—en**) hour-glass.

sanft [zanft], *adj.* soft, gentle.

Sänfte ['zɛnftə], *f.* (**—,** *pl.* **—n**) sedan-chair.

Sang [zaŋ], *m.* (**—es,** *pl.* **Gesänge**) song; *ohne — und Klang,* un-ostentatiously, without fuss, without ceremony.

sanieren [zaˈniːrən], *v.a.* cure; (*company*) reconstruct, put on a sound financial basis.

sanitär [zaniˈtɛːr], *adj.* sanitary.

Sanitäter [zaniˈtɛːtər], *m.* (**—s,** *pl.*—) medical orderly; ambulance man.

Sankt [zaŋkt], *indecl. adj.* Saint; (*abbr.*) St.

sanktionieren [zaŋktsjoˈniːrən], *v.a.* sanction.

Sansibar ['zanzibaːr], *n.* Zanzibar.

Sardelle [zarˈdɛlə], *f.* (**—,** *pl.* **—n**) (*Zool.*) anchovy.

Sardinien [zarˈdiːnjən], *n.* Sardinia.

Sarg [zark], *m.* (**—es,** *pl.* ⸚e) coffin.

sarkastisch [zarˈkastɪʃ], *adj.* sarcastic.

Satellit [zatəˈliːt], *m.* (**—en,** *pl.* **—en**) satellite.

Satiriker [zaˈtiːrɪkər], *m.* (**—s,** *pl.* —) satirist.

satt [zat], *adj.* sated, satiated, satisfied; (*colours*) deep, rich; *sich — essen,* eat o.'s fill; *einer Sache — sein,* be sick of s.th., have had enough of s.th.

Sattel ['zatəl], *m.* (**—s,** *pl.* ⸚) saddle; *einen aus dem — heben,* (*fig.*) oust s.o.; *fest im — sitzen,* (*fig.*) be master of a situation; *in allen —n gerecht,* versatile.

satteln ['zatəln], *v.a.* saddle.

Sattheit ['zathaɪt], *f.* (**—,** *no pl.*) satiety.

sättigen ['zɛtɪgən], *v.a.* satisfy, sate, satiate; (*Chem.*) saturate.

sattsam ['zatzaːm], *adv.* enough, sufficiently.

saturieren [zatuˈriːrən], *v.a.* (*Chem.*) saturate.

Satz [zats], *m.* (**—es,** *pl.* ⸚e) sentence; proposition; thesis; (*Mus.*) movement; (*Typ.*) composition; (*dregs*) sediment; (*gambling*) stake; *mit einem —,* with one leap (*or* jump *or* bound).

Satzbildung ['zatsbɪlduŋ], *f.* (**—,** *pl.* **—en**) (*Gram.*) construction; (*Chem.*) sedimentation.

Satzlehre ['zatsleːrə], *f.* (**—,** *no pl.*) syntax.

Satzung ['zatsuŋ], *f.* (**—,** *pl.* **—en**) statute.

Satzzeichen ['zatstsaɪçən], *n.* (**—s,** *pl.* —) punctuation-mark.

Sau [zau], *f.* (**—,** *pl.* ⸚e) sow; (*vulg.*) dirty person, slut.

sauber ['zaubər], *adj.* clean, neat, tidy.

säubern ['zɔybərn], *v.a.* clean, cleanse; (*fig.*) purge.

Saubohne ['zauboːnə], *f.* (**—,** *pl.* **—n**) broad bean.

Saudiarabien ['zaudiaraːbjən], *n.* Saudi Arabia.

sauer ['zauər], *adj.* sour, acid; (*fig.*) troublesome; morose.

Sauerbrunnen ['zauərbrunən], *m.* (**—s,** *pl.* —) mineral water.

Sauerei [zauəˈraɪ], *f.* (**—,** *pl.* **—en**) (*sl.*) filthiness; mess.

Sauerkraut ['zauərkraut], *n.* (**—s,** *no pl.*) pickled cabbage.

säuerlich ['zɔyərlɪç], *adj.* acidulous.

Sauerstoff ['zauərʃtɔf], *m.* (**—(e)s,** *no pl.*) oxygen.

Sauerteig ['zauərtaɪk], *m.* (**—(e)s,** *pl.* **—e**) leaven.

sauertöpfisch ['zauərtœpfɪʃ], *adj.* morose, peevish.

saufen ['zaufən], *v.a., v.n. irr.* (*animals*) drink; (*humans*) drink to excess.

Säufer ['zɔyfər], *m.* (**—s,** *pl.* —) drunkard, drinker, alcoholic.

saugen ['zaugən], *v.a., v.n.* suck.

säugen ['zɔygən], *v.a.* suckle.

Säugetier ['zɔygətiːr], *n.* (**—s,** *pl.* **—e**) mammal.

Saugheber ['zaukheːbər], *m.* (**—s,** *pl.* —) suction-pump; siphon.

Säugling ['zɔyklɪŋ], *m.* (**—s,** *pl.* **—e**) suckling, baby.

Saugwarze ['zaukvartsə], *f.* (**—,** *pl.* **—n**) nipple.

Säule ['zɔylə], *f.* (**—,** *pl.* **—n**) pillar, column.

Säulenbündel ['zɔylənbyndəl], *n.* (**—s,** *pl.* —) (*Archit.*) clustered column.

Säulenfuß ['zɔylənfuːs], *m.* (**—es,** *pl.* ⸚e) (*Archit.*) base, plinth.

Säulengang ['zɔyləngaŋ], *m.* (**—s,** *pl.* ⸚e) colonnade.

Saum [zaum], *m.* (**—(e)s,** *pl.* ⸚e) seam, hem, border, edge; selvedge.

saumäßig ['zaumɛːsɪç], *adj.* (*sl.*) beastly, filthy, piggish; enormous.

säumen (1) ['zɔymən], *v.a.* hem.

säumen (2) ['zɔymən], *v.n.* delay, tarry.

säumig ['zɔymɪç], *adj.* tardy, slow, dilatory.

Saumpferd [ˈzaumpfeːrt], *n.* (—s, *pl.* —e) pack-horse.

saumselig [ˈzaumzeːlɪç], *adj.* tardy, dilatory.

Säure [ˈzɔyrə], *f.* (—, *pl.* —n) acid; (*Med.*) acidity.

Saurier [ˈzaurjər], *m.* (—s, *pl.* —) saurian.

Saus [zaus], *m.* (—es, *no pl.*) rush; revel, riot; *in — und Braus leben*, live a wild life, live riotously.

säuseln [ˈzɔyzəln], *v.n.* rustle, murmur.

sausen [ˈzauzən], *v.n.* bluster, blow, howl, whistle; (*coll.*) rush, dash.

Saustall [ˈzauʃtal], *m.* (—s, *pl.* ⸚e) pigsty.

Schabe [ˈʃaːbə], *f.* (—, *pl.* —n) (*Ent.*) cockroach.

schaben [ˈʃaːbən], *v.a.* scrape, shave, rub.

Schabernack [ˈʃaːbərnak], *m.* (—s, *pl.* —e) practical joke, trick.

schäbig [ˈʃɛːbɪç], *adj.* shabby.

Schablone [ʃaˈbloːnə], *f.* (—, *pl.* —n) model, mould, pattern, stencil; (*fig.*) routine.

Schach [ʃax], *n.* (—(e)s, *no pl.*) chess; — *bieten*, check; — *spielen*, play chess; *in — halten*, keep in check.

Schacher [ˈʃaxər], *m.* (—s, *no pl.*) haggling, bargaining, barter.

Schächer [ˈʃɛçər], *m.* (—s, *pl.* —) wretch, felon, robber.

Schacht [ʃaxt], *m.* (—(e)s, *pl.* ⸚e) shaft.

Schachtel [ˈʃaxtəl], *f.* (—, *pl.* —n) box, (cardboard) box, (small) case.

Schachtelhalm [ˈʃaxtəlhalm], *m.* (—s, *pl.* —e) (*grass*) horse-tail.

Schächter [ˈʃɛçtər], *m.* (—s, *pl.* —) (kosher) butcher.

schade [ˈʃaːdə], *int.* a pity, a shame, unfortunate; *wie* —, what a pity; *sehr* —, a great pity.

Schädel [ˈʃɛːdəl], *m.* (—s, *pl.* —) skull.

Schaden [ˈʃaːdən], *m.* (—s, *pl.* ⸚) damage, injury, detriment; *zu — kommen*, come to grief.

schaden [ˈʃaːdən], *v.n.* do harm, do damage, do injury; *es schadet nichts*, it does not matter.

Schadenersatz [ˈʃaːdənɛrzats], *m.* (—es, *no pl.*) indemnity, compensation, indemnification; (*money*) damages.

Schadenfreude [ˈʃaːdənfrɔydə], *f.* (—, *no pl.*) malicious pleasure.

Schadensforderung [ˈʃaːdənsfɔrdəruŋ], *f.* (—, *pl.* —en) claim (for damages).

schadhaft [ˈʃaːthaft], *adj.* defective, faulty.

schädlich [ˈʃɛːtlɪç], *adj.* injurious, noxious, pernicious, noisome.

schadlos [ˈʃaːtloːs], *adj.* indemnified; *einen — halten*, indemnify s.o., compensate s.o.; *sich an einem — halten*, recoup o.s. from s.o.

Schadlosigkeit [ˈʃaːtloːzɪçkaɪt], *f.* (—, *no pl.*) harmlessness.

Schaf [ʃaːf], *n.* (—(e)s, *pl.* —e) sheep.

Schafblattern [ˈʃaːfblatərn], *f. pl.* (*Med.*) chicken-pox.

Schafdarm [ˈʃaːfdarm], *m.* (—s, *pl.* ⸚e) sheep-gut.

Schäfer [ˈʃɛːfər], *m.* (—s, *pl.* —) shepherd.

Schäferstündchen [ˈʃɛːfərʃtyntçən], *n.* (—s, *pl.* —) tryst; rendezvous.

schaffen [ˈʃafən], *v.a., v.n. irr.* make, produce, create. — *v.a. reg.* provide; manage; *aus dem Wege* —, remove. — *v.n. reg.* work; *einem zu — machen*, give s.o. trouble.

Schaffner [ˈʃafnər], *m.* (—s, *pl.* —) (*Railw. etc.*) guard, conductor.

Schafgarbe [ˈʃaːfgarbə], *f.* (—, *pl.* —n) (*Bot.*) common yarrow.

Schafhürde [ˈʃaːfhyrdə], *f.* (—, *pl.* —n) sheep-fold.

Schafott [ʃaˈfɔt], *n.* (—(e)s, *pl.* —e) scaffold.

Schafschur [ˈʃaːfʃuːr], *f.* (—, *pl.* —en) sheep-shearing.

Schaft [ʃaft], *m.* (—(e)s, *pl.* ⸚e) shaft; (*gun*) stock.

Schafwolle [ˈʃaːfvɔlə], *f.* (—, *no pl.*) sheep's wool, fleece.

Schakal [ʃaˈkaːl], *m.* (—s, *pl.* —e) (*Zool.*) jackal.

Schäkerei [ʃɛːkəˈraɪ], *f.* (—, *pl.* —en) playfulness, teasing, dalliance, flirtation.

Schal [ʃaːl], *m.* (—s, *pl.* —e) scarf, shawl.

schal [ʃaːl], *adj.* stale, flat, insipid.

Schale [ˈʃaːlə], *f.* (—, *pl.* —n) (*nut, egg*) shell; (*fruit*) peel, rind; dish, bowl; (*Austr.*) cup; (*fig.*) outside.

schälen [ˈʃɛːlən], *v.a.* shell; peel.

Schalk [ʃalk], *m.* (—(e)s, *pl.* —e) knave; rogue; wag, joker.

Schall [ʃal], *m.* (—(e)s, *no pl.*) sound.

Schallbecken [ˈʃalbɛkən], *n.* (—s, *pl.* —) cymbal.

Schallehre [ˈʃalleːrə], *f.* (—, *no pl.*) acoustics.

schallen [ˈʃalən], *v.n.* sound, reverberate.

Schalmei [ʃalˈmaɪ], *f.* (—, *pl.* —en) (*Poet., Mus.*) shawm.

Schallplatte [ˈʃalplatə], *f.* (—, *pl.* —n) (gramophone) record.

schalten [ˈʃaltən], *v.n.* rule; switch; (*Motor.*) change gear; — *und walten*, manage.

Schalter [ˈʃaltər], *m.* (—s, *pl.* —) (*Elec.*) switch; booking-office; counter.

Schalthebel [ˈʃaltheːbəl], *m.* (—s, *pl.* —) (*Motor.*) gear lever.

Schaltier [ˈʃalˈtiːr], *n.* (—s, *pl.* —e) (*Zool.*) crustacean.

Schaltjahr [ˈʃaltjaːr], *n.* (—s, *pl.* —e) leap year.

Schalttafel [ˈʃalttaːfəl], *f.* (—, *pl.* —n) switch-board.

Scham [ʃaːm], *f.* (—, *no pl.*) shame, modesty; private parts.

schämen [ˈʃɛːmən], *v.r. sich* —, be ashamed (of).

schamlos [ˈʃaːmloːs], *adj.* shameless.

schamrot [ˈʃaːmroːt], *adj.* blushing; — *werden*, blush.

schandbar [ˈʃantbaːr], *adj.* ignominious, infamous.

Schande [ˈʃandə], *f.* (—, *no pl.*) shame, disgrace; dishonour, ignominy.

schänden [ˈʃɛndən], *v.a.* dishonour, disgrace; violate, ravish.

Schandfleck [ˈʃantflɛk], *m.* (—s, *pl.* —e) stain, blemish.

schändlich [ˈʃɛntlɪç], *adj.* shameful, disgraceful, infamous.

Schändung [ˈʃɛnduŋ], *f.* (—, *pl.* —en) violation.

Schank [ˈʃaŋk], *m.* (—s, *no pl.*) sale of liquor.

Schanzarbeiter [ˈʃantsarbaɪtər], *m.* (—s, *pl.* —) sapper.

Schanze [ˈʃantsə], *f.* (—, *pl.* —n) redoubt, bulwark; *in die* — *schlagen*, risk, venture.

Schar [ʃaːr], *f.* (—, *pl.* —en) troop, band; host.

Scharade [ʃaˈraːdə], *f.* (—, *pl.* —n) charade.

scharen [ˈʃaːrən], *v.r. sich* — *um*, assemble, congregate, gather round.

Schären [ˈʃɛːrən], *f. pl.* reefs, skerries.

scharf [ʃarf], *adj.* sharp, keen, acute, acrid, pungent; piercing; (*fig.*) severe, rigorous.

Schärfe [ˈʃɛrfə], *f.* (—, *no pl.*) sharpness, keenness, acuteness; pungency, acridness; severity, rigour.

schärfen [ˈʃɛrfən], *v.a.* sharpen, whet; (*fig.*) strengthen, intensify.

Scharfrichter [ˈʃarfrɪçtər], *m.* (—s, *pl.* —) executioner.

scharfsichtig [ˈʃarfzɪçtɪç], *adj.* sharp-eyed, (*fig.*) penetrating, astute.

scharfsinnig [ˈʃarfzɪnɪç], *adj.* clear-sighted, sagacious, ingenious.

Scharlach [ˈʃarlax], *m.* (—s, *no pl.*) scarlet; (*Med.*) scarlet-fever.

Scharlatan [ˈʃarlataːn], *m.* (—s, *pl.* —e) charlatan, humbug.

scharmant [ʃarˈmant], *adj.* charming.

Scharmützel [ʃarˈmytsəl], *n.* (—s, *pl.* —) skirmish.

Scharnier [ʃarˈniːr], *n.* (—s, *pl.* —e) hinge, joint.

Schärpe [ˈʃɛrpə], *f.* (—, *pl.* —n) sash.

Scharpie [ʃarˈpiː], *f.* (—, *no pl.*) lint.

scharren [ˈʃarən], *v.a., v.n.* scrape, rake.

Scharte [ˈʃartə], *f.* (—, *pl.* —n) notch, crack; *eine* — *auswetzen*, repair a mistake, make up for s.th.

Scharteke [ʃarˈteːkə], *f.* (—, *pl.* —n) worthless book, trash; *eine alte* —, an old fuddy-duddy, frump.

scharwenzeln [ʃarˈvɛntsəln], *v.n.* dance attendance, be obsequious.

Schatten [ˈʃatən], *m.* (—s, *pl.* —) shade, shadow.

Schattenbild [ˈʃatənbɪlt], *n.* (—s, *pl.* —er) silhouette.

Schattenriß [ˈʃatənrɪs], *m.* (—sses, *pl.* —sse) silhouette.

schattieren [ʃaˈtiːrən], *v.a.* shade (drawing).

schattig [ˈʃatɪç], *adj.* shady.

Schatulle [ʃaˈtulə], *f.* (—, *pl.* —n) cash-box; privy purse.

Schatz [ʃats], *m.* (—es, *pl* ¨e) treasure; (*fig.*) sweetheart, darling.

Schatzamt [ˈʃatsamt], *n.* (—s, *pl.* ¨er) Treasury, Exchequer.

schätzbar [ˈʃɛtsbaːr], *adj.* estimable.

Schätzchen [ˈʃɛtsçən], *n.* (—s, *pl.* —) (*coll.*) sweetheart.

schätzen [ˈʃɛtsən], *v.a.* value, estimate; esteem; reckon at.

Schatzkammer [ˈʃatskamər], *f.* (—, *pl.* —n) treasury.

Schatzmeister [ˈʃatsmaɪstər], *m.* (—s, *pl.* —) treasurer.

Schätzung [ˈʃɛtsuŋ], *f.* (—, *pl.* —en) valuation, estimate; (*fig.*) esteem.

Schau [ʃau], *f.* (—, *pl.* —en) show, view, spectacle; *zur* — *stellen*, display; parade.

Schauder [ˈʃaudər], *m.* (—s, *pl.* —) shudder, shiver; horror.

schaudern [ˈʃaudərn], *v.n.* shudder, shiver.

schauen [ˈʃauən], *v.a.* see, view. — *v.n.* look, gaze (*auf*, at), *schau mal*, look here.

Schauer [ˈʃauər], *m.* (—s, *pl.* —) shiver, paroxysm; (*fig.*) thrill, awe; (*rain*) shower.

schauern [ˈʃauərn], *v.n.* shudder, shiver; (*rain*) shower.

Schauerroman [ˈʃauərroːmaːn], *m.* (—s, *pl.* —e) (*novel*) penny dreadful, thriller.

Schaufel [ˈʃaufəl], *f.* (—, *pl.* —n) shovel.

Schaufenster [ˈʃaufɛnstər], *n.* (—s, *pl.* —) shop-window.

Schaukel [ˈʃaukəl], *f.* (—, *pl.* —n) swing.

schaulustig [ˈʃaulustɪç], *adj.* curious.

Schaum [ʃaum], *m.* (—es, *pl.* ¨e) foam, froth; bubbles; scum; — *schlagen*, whip cream.

schäumen [ˈʃɔymən], *v.n.* foam, froth, sparkle.

Schauplatz [ˈʃauplats], *m.* (—es, *pl.* ¨e) scene, stage.

schaurig [ˈʃaurɪç], *adj.* grisly, horrid, horrible.

Schauspiel [ˈʃauʃpiːl], *n.* (—s, *pl.* —e) spectacle; drama, play.

Schauspieler [ˈʃauʃpiːlər], *m.* (—s, *pl.* —) actor, player.

Schaustellung [ˈʃauʃtɛluŋ], *f.* (—, *pl.* —en) exhibition.

Scheck [ʃɛk], *m.* (—s, *pl.* —s) cheque.

scheckig [ˈʃɛkɪç], *adj.* piebald, spotted, dappled.

scheel [ʃeːl], *adj.* squint-eyed; envious; *einen* — *ansehen*, look askance at s.o.

Scheffel [ˈʃɛfəl], *m.* (—s, *pl.* —) bushel.

scheffeln [ˈʃɛfəln], *v.a.* rake in; accumulate.

Scheibe [ˈʃaɪbə], *f.* (—, *pl.* —n) disc; (*window*) pane; (*shooting*) target; (*bread*) slice.

Scheibenhonig [ˈʃaɪbənhoːnɪç], *m.* (—s, *no pl.*) honey in the comb.

Scheibenschießen ['ʃaɪbənʃiːsən], *n.* (—s, *no pl.*) target-practice.

Scheich [ʃaɪç], *m.* (—s, *pl.* —e) sheikh.

Scheide ['ʃaɪdə], *f.* (—, *pl.* —n) sheath, scabbard; (*Anat.*) vagina.

Scheidemünze ['ʃaɪdəmyntsə], *f.* (—, *pl.* —n) small coin, change.

scheiden ['ʃaɪdən], *v.a. irr.* divide; separate, divorce; *sich — lassen*, obtain a divorce. — *v.n.* (*aux.* sein) part, depart; *aus dem Amte —*, resign office.

Scheidewand ['ʃaɪdəvant], *f.* (—, *pl.* ∸e) partition-wall.

Scheideweg ['ʃaɪdəveːk], *m.* (—s, *pl.* —e) cross-roads; *am — stehen*, be at the parting of the ways.

Scheidung ['ʃaɪduŋ], *f.* (—, *pl.* —en) divorce.

Schein [ʃaɪn], *m.* (—(e)s, *no pl.*) shine, sheen, lustre, splendour; semblance, pretence; *den — wahren*, keep up appearances; *der — trügt*, appearances are deceptive; (*in compounds*) mock, would-be, apparent; (*pl.* —e) (piece of) paper, chit, note; (*fig.*) attestation, certificate.

scheinbar ['ʃaɪnbaːr], *adj.* apparent; ostensible, specious. — *adv.* seemingly.

scheinen ['ʃaɪnən], *v.n. irr.* shine, sparkle; seem, appear.

scheinheilig ['ʃaɪnhaɪlɪç], *adj.* hypocritical.

Scheinheiligkeit ['ʃaɪnhaɪlɪçkaɪt], *f.* (—, *no pl.*) hypocrisy.

scheintot ['ʃaɪntoːt], *adj.* in a cataleptic trance; seemingly dead.

Scheinwerfer ['ʃaɪnvɛrfər], *m.* (—s, *pl.* —) headlight; searchlight; floodlight.

Scheit [ʃaɪt], *n.* (—(e)s, *pl.* —e) piece of wood, billet.

Scheitel ['ʃaɪtəl], *m.* (—s, *pl.* —) (*hair*) parting; top, vertex.

Scheiterhaufen ['ʃaɪtərhaufən], *m.* (—s, *pl.* —) stake; funeral pyre.

scheitern ['ʃaɪtərn], *v.n.* (*aux.* sein) (*ship*) founder, be wrecked; (*fig.*) miscarry, fail.

Schelle ['ʃɛlə], *f.* (—, *pl.* —n) bell.

Schellen ['ʃɛlən], *f. pl.* (*Cards*) diamonds.

schellen ['ʃɛlən], *v.n.* ring the bell.

Schellfisch ['ʃɛlfɪʃ], *m.* (—es, *pl.* —e) (*Zool.*) haddock.

Schelm [ʃɛlm], *m.* (—(e)s, *pl.* —e) rogue, knave, villain.

schelten ['ʃɛltən], *v.a. irr.* scold, chide, rebuke, reprimand.

Schema ['ʃeːma], *n.* (—s, *pl.* —s) schedule, model, plan, scheme.

Schemel ['ʃeːməl], *m.* (—s, *pl.* —) foot-stool.

Schenk [ʃɛŋk], *m.* (—en, *pl.* —en) cupbearer; publican.

Schenke ['ʃɛŋkə], *f.* (—, *pl.* —n) alehouse, tavern, pub.

Schenkel ['ʃɛŋkəl], *m.* (—s, *pl.* —) thigh, (*Geom.*) side of triangle.

schenken ['ʃɛŋkən], *v.a.* present s.o. with, donate, give.

Schenkstube ['ʃɛŋkʃtuːbə], *f.* (—, *pl.* —n) tap-room.

Scherbe ['ʃɛrbə], *f.* (—, *pl.* —n) potsherd; fragment of glass etc.

Schere ['ʃeːrə], *f.* (—, *pl.* —n) scissors; (*garden*) shears; (*crab*) claw.

scheren ['ʃeːrən], *v.a.* shave; clip, shear; bother, concern. — *v.r. sich —*, clear off; *scher dich zum Teufel!* go to blazes!

Scherereien [ʃerə'raɪən], *f. pl.* vexation, bother, trouble.

Scherflein ['ʃɛrflaɪn], *n.* (—s, *pl.* —) mite; *sein — beitragen*, contribute o.'s share.

Scherge ['ʃɛrgə], *m.* (—n, *pl.* —n) (*obs.*) beadle.

Scherz [ʃɛrts], *m.* (—es, *pl.* —e) jest, joke; *— beiseite*, joking apart.

scheu [ʃɔy], *adj.* shy, bashful, timid; skittish.

scheuchen ['ʃɔyçən], *v.a.* scare away.

scheuen ['ʃɔyən], *v.a.* shun, avoid, fight shy of, fear. — *v.n.* take fright.

Scheuer ['ʃɔyər], *f.* (—, *pl.* —n) barn.

scheuern ['ʃɔyərn], *v.a.* scour, scrub.

Scheuklappe ['ʃɔyklapə], *f.* (—, *pl.* —n) blinker.

Scheune ['ʃɔynə], *f.* (—, *pl.* —n) barn.

Scheusal ['ʃɔyzaːl], *n.* (—s, *pl.* —e) monster.

scheußlich ['ʃɔyslɪç], *adj.* frightful, dreadful, abominable, hideous.

Schicht [ʃɪçt], *f.* (—, *pl.* —en) layer, stratum, seam; (*society*) class; (*work*) shift.

schick [ʃɪk], *adj.* stylish, chic.

schicken ['ʃɪkən], *v.a.* send, despatch, convey. — *v.r. sich —*, be proper; *sich in etwas —*, put up with s.th., resign o.s. to s.th.

schicklich ['ʃɪklɪç], *adj.* proper, becoming, suitable, seemly.

Schicksal ['ʃɪkzaːl], *n.* (—s, *pl.* —e) fate, destiny, lot.

Schickung ['ʃɪkuŋ], *f.* (—, *pl.* —en) Divine Will, Providence.

schieben ['ʃiːbən], *v.a. irr.* shove, push; *die Schuld auf einen —*, put the blame on s.o.

Schieber ['ʃiːbər], *m.* (—s, *pl.* —) bolt, slide; (*fig.*) profiteer, spiv.

Schiedsgericht ['ʃiːtsgərɪçt], *n.* (—es, *pl.* —e) arbitration tribunal.

Schiedsrichter ['ʃiːtsrɪçtər], *m.* (—s, *pl.* —) referee, umpire, arbiter.

schief [ʃiːf], *adj.* slanting, oblique, bent, crooked; wry; *—e Ebene*, inclined plane; *— gehen*, go wrong.

Schiefe ['ʃiːfə], *f.* (—, *no pl.*) obliquity.

Schiefer ['ʃiːfər], *m.* (—s, *no pl.*) slate.

schiefrig ['ʃiːfrɪç], *adj.* slaty.

schielen ['ʃiːlən], *v.n.* squint, be cross-eyed.

Schienbein ['ʃiːnbaɪn], *n.* (—s, *pl.* —e) shin-bone, shin.

Schiene

Schiene [ˈʃiːnə], *f.* (—, *pl.* —**n**) rail; (*Med.*) splint.

schier [ʃiːr], *adj.* (*rare*) sheer, pure. — *adv.* almost, very nearly.

Schierling [ˈʃiːrlɪŋ], *m.* (—**s**, *pl.* —**e**) (*Bot.*) hemlock.

schießen [ˈʃiːsən], *v.a.*, *v.n. irr.* shoot, fire, discharge; (*fig.*) rush; *etwas — lassen,* let go of s.th.; *die Zügel — lassen,* loosen o.'s hold on the reins; *ein Kabel — lassen,* pay out a cable; *das ist zum —,* that's very funny.

Schiff [ʃɪf], *n.* (—(**e**)**s**, *pl.* —**e**) ship, vessel, boat; (*church*) nave.

schiffbar [ˈʃɪfbaːr], *adj.* navigable.

Schiffbruch [ˈʃɪfbrux], *m.* (—**s**, *pl.* ⸚**e**) shipwreck.

Schiffbrücke [ˈʃɪfbrykə], *f.* (—, *pl.* —**n**) pontoon-bridge.

schiffen [ˈʃɪfən], *v.n.* sail; navigate.

Schiffsboden [ˈʃɪfsboːdən], *m.* (—**s**, *pl.* ⸚) (ship's) hold.

Schiffsmaat [ˈʃɪfsmaːt], *m.* (—**s**, *pl.* —**e**) shipmate.

Schiffsrumpf [ˈʃɪfsrumpf], *m.* (—**es**, *pl.* ⸚**e**) hull.

Schiffsschnabel [ˈʃɪfsʃnaːbəl], *m.* (—**s**, *pl.* ⸚) prow, bows.

Schiffsvorderteil [ˈʃɪfsfɔrdərtaɪl], *n.* (—**s**, *pl.* —**e**) forecastle, prow.

Schiffszwieback [ˈʃɪfstsviːbak], *m.* (—**s**, *no pl.*) ship's biscuit.

Schikane [ʃiˈkaːnə], *f.* (—, *pl.* —**n**) chicanery.

Schild (1) [ʃɪlt], *m.* (—(**e**)**s**, *pl.* —**e**) shield, buckler, escutcheon; *etwas im — führen,* have designs on s.th., plan s.th.

Schild (2) [ʃɪlt], *n.* (—**s**, *pl.* —**er**) signboard, plate.

Schilderhaus [ˈʃɪldərhaus], *n.* (—**es**, *pl.* ⸚**er**) sentry-box.

Schildermaler [ˈʃɪldərmaːlər], *m.* (—**s**, *pl.* —) sign-painter.

schildern [ˈʃɪldərn], *v.a.* describe, depict.

Schildknappe [ˈʃɪltknapə], *m.* (—**n**, *pl.* —**n**) shield-bearer, squire.

Schildkrot [ˈʃɪltkroːt], *n.* (—**s**, *no pl.*) tortoise-shell.

Schildkröte [ˈʃɪltkrøːtə], *f.* (—, *pl.* —**n**) (*Zool.*) turtle, tortoise.

Schildpatt [ˈʃɪltpat], *n.* (—**s**, *no pl.*) tortoise-shell.

Schildwache [ˈʃɪltvaxə], *f.* (—, *pl.* —**n**) sentinel, sentry; — *stehen,* be on sentry duty, stand guard.

Schilf(rohr) [ˈʃɪlf(roːr)], *n.* (—(**e**)**s**, *no pl.*) (*Bot.*) reed, rush, sedge.

schillern [ˈʃɪlərn], *v.n.* opalesce, glitter, change colour, be iridescent.

Schilling [ˈʃɪlɪŋ], *m.* (—**s**, *pl.* —**e**) Austrian coin; shilling.

Schimmel (1) [ˈʃɪməl], *m.* (—**s**, *pl.* —) white horse.

Schimmel (2) [ˈʃɪməl], *m.* (—**s**, *no pl.*) mould, mustiness.

schimmeln [ˈʃɪməln], *v.n.* (*aux.* sein) go mouldy, moulder.

Schimmer [ˈʃɪmər], *m.* (—**s**, *pl.* —) glitter, gleam; *ich habe keinen —,* I haven't a clue.

schimmlig [ˈʃɪmlɪç], *adj.* mouldy, musty, mildewed.

Schimpanse [ʃɪmˈpanzə], *m.* (—**n**, *pl.* —**n**) (*Zool.*) chimpanzee.

Schimpf [ʃɪmpf], *m.* (—**es**, *no pl.*) abuse, affront, insult; *mit — und Schande,* in disgrace.

schimpfen [ˈʃɪmpfən], *v.n.* curse, swear; — *auf,* (*fig.*) run (s.o.) down. — *v.a.* insult (s.o.), call (s.o.) names; scold.

Schindel [ˈʃɪndəl], *f.* (—, *pl.* —**n**) shingle.

schinden [ˈʃɪndən], *v.a. irr.* flay; (*fig.*) grind, oppress, sweat. — *v.r. sich —,* slave, drudge.

Schindluder [ˈʃɪntluːdər], *n.* (—**s**, *pl.* —) worn-out animal; *mit einem — treiben,* exploit s.o.

Schinken [ˈʃɪŋkən], *m.* (—**s**, *pl.* —) ham.

Schinkenspeck [ˈʃɪŋkənʃpɛk], *m.* (—**s**, *no pl.*) bacon.

Schippe [ˈʃɪpə], *f.* (—, *pl.* —**n**) shovel, spade.

Schirm [ʃɪrm], *m.* (—(**e**)**s**, *pl.* —**e**) screen; umbrella; parasol, sunshade; lampshade; (*fig.*) shield, shelter, cover.

schirmen [ˈʃɪrmən], *v.a.* protect (from), shelter.

Schirmherr [ˈʃɪrmhɛr], *m.* (—**n**, *pl.* —**en**) protector, patron.

Schlacht [ʃlaxt], *f.* (—, *pl.* —**en**) battle; fight; *eine — liefern,* give battle; *die — gewinnen,* carry the day, win the battle.

Schlachtbank [ˈʃlaxtbaŋk], *f.* (—, *pl.* ⸚**e**) shambles; *zur — führen,* lead to the slaughter.

schlachten [ˈʃlaxtən], *v.a.* kill, butcher, slaughter.

Schlachtenbummler [ˈʃlaxtənbumlər], *m.* (—**s**, *pl.* —) camp follower.

Schlachtfeld [ˈʃlaxtfɛlt], *n.* (—**s**, *pl.* —**er**) battlefield.

Schlachtruf [ˈʃlaxtruːf], *m.* (—**s**, *pl.* —**e**) battle-cry.

Schlacke [ˈʃlakə], *f.* (—, *pl.* —**n**) slag, clinker, dross.

Schlackwurst [ˈʃlakvurst], *f.* (—, *pl.* ⸚**e**) (*North German*) sausage.

Schlaf [ʃlaːf], *m.* (—(**e**)**s**, *no pl.*) sleep; slumber, rest; *in tiefem —,* fast asleep; *in den — wiegen,* rock to sleep.

Schläfchen [ˈʃlɛːfçən], *n.* (—**s**, *pl.* —) nap; *ein — machen,* have forty winks.

Schläfe [ˈʃlɛːfə], *f.* (—, *pl.* —**n**) temple.

schlafen [ˈʃlaːfən], *v.n. irr.* sleep; *schlaf wohl,* sleep well; — *gehen,* go to bed.

schlaff [ʃlaf], *adj.* slack, loose, lax, flabby; weak; remiss.

schlaflos [ˈʃlaːfloːs], *adj.* sleepless.

Schlafmittel [ˈʃlaːfmɪtəl], *n.* (—**s**, *pl.* —) soporific, sleeping tablet, sleeping draught.

schläfrig [ˈʃlɛːfrɪç], *adj.* drowsy, sleepy.

Schlafrock ['ʃlaːfrɔk], s. (—s, pl. ̈e) dressing-gown; *Äpfel im —*, apple fritters.

schlafwandeln ['ʃlaːfvandəln], v.n. (aux. sein) walk in o.'s sleep, sleep-walk.

Schlag [ʃlaːk], m. (—(e)s, pl. ̈e) blow, stroke; beat; (*Elec.*) shock; *ein Mann von gutem —*, a good type of man; *vom — gerührt*, struck by apoplexy; *— fünf*, at five o'clock sharp.

Schlagader ['ʃlaːkaːdər], f. (—, pl. —n) artery.

Schlaganfall ['ʃlaːkanfal], m. (—s, pl. ̈e) stroke, apoplexy.

Schlagballspiel ['ʃlaːkbalʃpiːl], n. (—s, pl. —e) rounders.

Schlagbaum ['ʃlaːkbaum], m. (—s, pl. ̈e) turnpike.

schlagen ['ʃlaːgən], v.a. irr. beat, strike, hit; (*tree*) fell; (*money*) coin; *Alarm —*, sound the alarm; *ans Kreuz —*, crucify; *ein Kreuz —*, make the sign of the cross. — v.n. (*clock*) strike; (*birds*) warble; *aus der Art —*, degenerate. — v.r. *sich —*, fight; *sich auf Säbel —*, fight with sabres; *sich an die Brust —*, beat o.'s breast.

Schlager ['ʃlaːgər], m. (—s, pl. —) hit, pop song; (*fig.*) success.

Schläger ['ʃlɛːgər], m. (—s, pl. —) rapier; bat; (*tennis-*)racket; (*golf-*)club.

Schlägerei [ʃlɛːgəˈraɪ], f. (—, pl. —en) fray, scuffle.

schlagfertig ['ʃlaːkfɛrtɪç], adj. quick-witted.

Schlagkraft ['ʃlaːkkraft], f. (—, no pl.) striking power.

Schlaglicht ['ʃlaːklɪçt], n. (—s, pl. —er) strong direct light.

Schlagsahne ['ʃlaːkzaːnə], f. (—, no pl.) double cream, raw cream; whipped cream.

Schlagschatten ['ʃlaːkʃatən], m. (—s, pl. —) deep shadow.

Schlagseite ['ʃlaːkzaɪtə], f. (—, no pl.) *— bekommen*, (*Naut.*) list.

Schlagwort ['ʃlaːkvɔrt], n. (—s, pl. ̈er) catchword, slogan; trite saying.

Schlagzeile ['ʃlaːktsaɪlə], f. (—, pl. —n) headline.

Schlamm [ʃlam], m. (—(e)s, no pl.) mud, mire.

Schlampe ['ʃlampə], f. (—, pl. —n) slut.

Schlange ['ʃlaŋə], f. (—, pl. —n) snake, serpent; (*fig.*) queue.

schlängeln ['ʃlɛŋəln], v.r. *sich —*, wind, meander.

schlangenartig ['ʃlaŋənaːrtɪç], adj. snaky, serpentine.

schlank [ʃlaŋk], adj. slim, slender.

schlapp [ʃlap], adj. limp, tired, weak, slack; *— machen*, break down, collapse.

Schlappe ['ʃlapə], f. (—, pl. —n) reverse, defeat; *eine — erleiden*, suffer a setback.

Schlappschwanz ['ʃlapʃvants], m. (—es, pl. ̈e) weakling; milksop.

Schlaraffenland [ʃlaˈrafənlant], n. (—(e)s, pl. ̈er) land of milk and honey.

schlau [ʃlau], adj. cunning, crafty, sly, shrewd.

Schlauch [ʃlaux], m. (—(e)s, pl. ̈e) hose; tube.

Schlaukopf ['ʃlaukɔpf], m. (—(e)s, pl. ̈e) slyboots; (*Am.*) wiseacre.

schlecht [ʃlɛçt], adj. bad, evil, wicked; poor; *mir ist —*, I feel ill; *—e Zeiten*, hard times; *—es Geld*, base money.

schlechterdings ['ʃlɛçtərdɪŋs], adv. simply, positively, absolutely.

schlechthin ['ʃlɛçthɪn], adv. simply, plainly.

Schlechtigkeit ['ʃlɛçtɪçkaɪt], f. (—, pl. —en) wickedness, baseness.

Schlegel ['ʃleːgəl], m. (—s, pl. —) mallet; drumstick; (*bell*) clapper.

Schlehdorn ['ʃleːdɔrn], m. (—s, pl. —e) blackthorn, sloe-tree.

schleichen ['ʃlaɪçən], v.n. irr. (aux. sein) sneak, prowl, slink; *—de Krankheit*, lingering illness.

Schleichhandel ['ʃlaɪçhandəl], m. (—s, pl. ̈) smuggling, black marketeering.

Schleie ['ʃlaɪə], f. (—, pl. —n) tench.

Schleier ['ʃlaɪər], m. (—s, pl. —) veil.

Schleife ['ʃlaɪfə], f. (—, pl. —n) bow, loop, noose.

schleifen ['ʃlaɪfən], v.a. irr. drag along, trail; grind, polish, sharpen, whet, hone; cut.

Schleim [ʃlaɪm], m. (—(e)s, no pl.) slime, mucus, phlegm.

Schleimhaut ['ʃlaɪmhaut], f. (—, pl. ̈e) mucous membrane.

Schleimsuppe ['ʃlaɪmzupə], f. (—, pl. —n) gruel.

schleißen ['ʃlaɪsən], v.a. irr. split, slit; (*feathers*) strip.

schlemmen ['ʃlɛmən], v.n. carouse, gormandise.

schlendern ['ʃlɛndərn], v.n. (aux. sein) saunter along, stroll.

Schlendrian ['ʃlɛndriaːn], m. (—s, no pl.) old jog-trot, routine.

schlenkern ['ʃlɛŋkərn], v.a. dangle, swing.

Schleppdampfer ['ʃlɛpdampfər], m. (—s, pl. —) steam-tug, tug-boat, tow-boat.

Schleppe ['ʃlɛpə], f. (—, pl. —n) train (of a dress).

schleppen ['ʃlɛpən], v.a. carry (s.th. heavy), drag, tow.

Schleppenträger ['ʃlɛpəntrɛːgər], m. (—s, pl. —) train-bearer.

Schleppnetz ['ʃlɛpnɛts], n. (—es, pl. —e) dragnet.

Schlesien ['ʃleːzjən], n. Silesia.

Schleuder ['ʃlɔydər], f. (—, pl. —n) sling; catapult.

schleudern ['ʃlɔydərn], v.a. sling, throw, fling away. — v.n. (*Motor.*) skid; (*Comm.*) sell cheaply, undersell.

schleunigst [ˈʃlɔynɪçst], *adv.* very quickly, with the utmost expedition, promptly.

Schleuse [ˈʃlɔyzə], *f.* (—, *pl.* —n) sluice, flood-gate, lock.

Schlich [ʃlɪç], *m.* (—es, *pl.* —e) trick, dodge; *einem hinter seine —e kommen*, be up to s.o.'s tricks.

schlicht [ʃlɪçt], *adj.* plain, simple, homely; *—er Abschied*, curt dismissal.

schlichten [ˈʃlɪçtən], *v.a.* level; (*argument*) settle; adjust, compose.

Schlichtheit [ˈʃlɪçthaɪt], *f.* (—, *no pl.*) plainness, simplicity, homeliness.

schließen [ˈʃliːsən], *v.a. irr.* shut, close; contract; *etwas — aus*, conclude s.th. from; (*meeting*) close; *Frieden —*, make peace; *einen in die Arme —*, embrace s.o.; *etwas in sich —*, imply, entail.

Schließer [ˈʃliːsər], *m.* (—s, *pl.* —) doorkeeper; (*prison*) jailer, turnkey.

schließlich [ˈʃliːslɪç], *adv.* lastly, finally, in conclusion.

Schliff [ʃlɪf], *m.* (—(e)s, *no pl.*) polish, refinement.

schlimm [ʃlɪm], *adj.* bad, evil, ill; sad; serious, sore; disagreeable; naughty; *um so —er*, so much the worse, worse luck.

Schlinge [ˈʃlɪŋə], *f.* (—, *pl.* —n) loop, knot; noose, snare.

Schlingel [ˈʃlɪŋəl], *m.* (—s, *pl.* —) little rascal.

schlingen [ˈʃlɪŋən], *v.a. irr.* sling, wind; swallow, devour.

Schlips [ʃlɪps], *m.* (—es, *pl.* —e) (neck-)tie, cravat.

Schlitten [ˈʃlɪtən], *m.* (—s, *pl.* —) sledge, sled, sleigh.

Schlittschuh [ˈʃlɪtʃuː], *m.* (—s, *pl.* —e) skate; *— laufen*, skate.

Schlitz [ʃlɪts], *m.* (—es, *pl.* —e) slit.

schlohweiß [ˈʃloːvaɪs], *adj.* white as sloe-blossom, snow-white.

Schloß [ʃlɔs], *n.* (—sses, *pl.* ⸚sser) (*door*) lock, padlock; (*gun*) lock; palace, castle; *unter — und Riegel*, under lock and key.

Schloße [ˈʃloːsə], *f.* (—, *pl.* —n) hailstone.

Schlosser [ˈʃlɔsər], *m.* (—s, *pl.* —) locksmith.

Schlot [ʃloːt], *m.* (—(e)s, *pl.* —e) chimney, funnel.

schlottern [ˈʃlɔtərn], *v.n.* wobble, dodder; tremble.

Schlucht [ʃluxt], *f.* (—, *pl.* —en) deep valley, defile, cleft, glen, ravine, gorge.

schluchzen [ˈʃluxtsən], *v.n.* sob.

schlucken [ˈʃlukən], *v.a.* gulp down, swallow. — *v.n.* hiccup.

Schlucker [ˈʃlukər], *m.* (—s, *pl.* —) *armer —*, poor wretch.

Schlummer [ˈʃlumər], *m.* (—s, *no pl.*) slumber.

Schlumpe [ˈʃlumpə], *f.* (—, *pl.* —n) slut, slattern.

Schlund [ʃlunt], *m.* (—(e)s, *pl.* ⸚e) throat, gorge, gullet; gulf, abyss.

schlüpfen [ˈʃlypfən], *v.n.* (*aux.* sein) slip, slide, glide.

Schlüpfer [ˈʃlypfər], *m.* *pl.* knickers.

schlüpfrig [ˈʃlypfrɪç], *adj.* slippery; (*fig.*) obscene, indecent.

schlürfen [ˈʃlyrfən], *v.a.* drink noisily, lap up. — *v.n.* (*aux.* sein) (*dial.*) shuffle along.

Schluß [ʃlus], *m.* (—sses, *pl.* ⸚sse) end, termination; conclusion.

Schlüssel [ˈʃlysəl], *m.* (—s, *pl.* —) key; (*Mus.*) clef.

Schlüsselbein [ˈʃlysəlbaɪn], *n.* (—s, *pl.* —e) collar-bone.

Schlüsselblume [ˈʃlysəlbluːmə], *f.* (—, *pl.* —n) (*Bot.*) cowslip, primrose.

Schlußfolgerung [ˈʃlusfɔlgəruŋ], *f.* (—, *pl.* —en) conclusion, inference, deduction.

schlüssig [ˈʃlysɪç], *adj.* resolved, determined; sure; (*Law*) well-grounded; *sich — werden über*, resolve on.

Schmach [ʃmaːx], *f.* (—, *no pl.*) disgrace, ignominy.

schmachten [ˈʃmaxtən], *v.n.* languish, pine.

schmächtig [ˈʃmɛçtɪç], *adj.* slender, slim, spare.

schmackhaft [ˈʃmakhaft], *adj.* tasty, savoury.

schmähen [ˈʃmɛːən], *v.a.* revile, abuse, calumniate.

Schmähschrift [ˈʃmɛːʃrɪft], *f.* (—, *pl.* —en) lampoon.

schmal [ʃmaːl], *adj.* narrow.

schmälen [ˈʃmɛːlən], *v.a.* chide, scold.

schmälern [ˈʃmɛːlərn], *v.a.* lessen, diminish, curtail; detract from, belittle.

Schmalz [ʃmalts], *n.* (—es, *no pl.*) grease, fund, fat.

schmarotzen [ʃmaˈrɔtsən], *v.n.* sponge on others.

Schmarren [ˈʃmarən], *m.* (—s, *pl.* —) trash; (*dial.*) omelette.

Schmatz [ʃmats], *m.* (—es, *pl.* ⸚e) (*dial.*) smacking kiss.

schmauchen [ˈʃmauxən], *v.a.*, *v.n.* smoke.

Schmaus [ʃmaus], *m.* (—es, *pl.* —e) feast, banquet.

schmecken [ˈʃmɛkən], *v.a.* taste. — *v.n.* taste; *es schmeckt mir*, I like it.

Schmeichelei [ʃmaɪçəˈlaɪ], *f.* (—, *pl.* —en) flattery, adulation.

schmeicheln [ˈʃmaɪçəln], *v.n.* flatter; fondle, pet.

schmeißen [ˈʃmaɪsən], *v.a. irr.* throw, hurl, fling; (*sl.*) *ich werde die Sache schon —*, I shall pull it off.

Schmeißfliege [ˈʃmaɪsfliːgə], *f.* (—, *pl.* —n) (*Ent.*) bluebottle.

Schmelz [ʃmɛlts], *m.* (—es, *no pl.*) enamel; melting; (*voice*) mellowness.

schmelzbar [ˈʃmɛltsbaːr], *adj.* fusible.

schmelzen [ˈʃmɛltsən], *v.a. irr.* smelt, melt. — *v.n.* (*aux.* sein) (*ice*) melt; (*fig.*) decrease, diminish.

Schmelztiegel ['ʃmɛltsti:gəl], *m.* (**—s,** *pl.* **—**) crucible; melting pot.
Schmelztopf ['ʃmɛltstɔpf], *m. see* **Schmelztiegel.**
Schmerbauch ['ʃme:rbaux], *m.* (**—(e)s,** *pl.* **⸚e**) (*coll.*) paunch, belly.
Schmerz [ʃmɛrts], *m.* (**—es,** *pl.* **—en**) ache, pain; grief, sorrow; *einem —en verursachen,* give *or* cause s.o. pain.
schmerzlich ['ʃmɛrtslɪç], *adj.* painful, distressing.
Schmetterling ['ʃmɛtərlɪŋ], *m.* (**—s,** *pl.* **—e**) (*Ent.*) butterfly, moth.
schmettern ['ʃmɛtərn], *v.n.* resound; (*trumpets*) blare; (*bird*) warble.
Schmied [ʃmi:t], *m.* (**—s,** *pl.* **—e**) (black)smith.
Schmiede ['ʃmi:də], *f.* (**—,** *pl.* **—n**) forge, smithy.
schmiegen ['ʃmi:gən], *v.r. sich —,* bend, yield; *sich an einen —,* cling to s.o., nestle against s.o.
Schmiere ['ʃmi:rə], *f.* (**—,** *pl.* **—n**) grease, salve; (*Theat.*) troop of strolling players.
schmieren ['ʃmi:rən], *v.a.* smear, grease, spread; (*fig.*) bribe; (*bread*) butter. — *v.n.* scrawl, scribble.
Schmierfink ['ʃmi:rfɪŋk], *m.* (**—en,** *pl.* **—en**) dirty person; muckraker.
Schmiermittel ['ʃmi:rmɪtəl], *n.* (**—s,** *pl.* **—**) lubricant.
Schmierseife ['ʃmi:rzaɪfə], *f.* (**—,** *no pl.*) soft soap.
Schminke ['ʃmɪŋkə], *f.* (**—,** *pl.* **—n**) greasepaint; rouge; make-up, cosmetics.
Schmirgel ['ʃmɪrgəl], *m.* (**—s,** *no pl.*) emery.
Schmiß [ʃmɪs], *m.* (**—sses,** *pl.* **—sse**) cut in the face, (duelling) scar; (*fig.*) smartness, verve.
Schmöker ['ʃmø:kər], *m.* (**—s,** *pl.* **—**) trashy book.
schmollen ['ʃmɔlən], *v.n.* sulk, pout.
Schmorbraten ['ʃmo:rbra:tən], *m.* (**—s,** *pl.* **—**) stewed meat.
Schmuck [ʃmuk], *m.* (**—(e)s,** *pl.* **—stücke**) ornament, jewels, jewellery; (*Am.*) jewelry.
schmuck [ʃmuk], *adj.* neat, spruce, dapper, smart.
schmücken ['ʃmykən], *v.a.* adorn, embellish.
Schmucksachen ['ʃmukzaxən], *f. pl.* jewels, finery, jewellery, articles of adornment; (*Am.*) jewelry.
schmuggeln ['ʃmugəln], *v.a.* smuggle.
schmunzeln ['ʃmuntsəln], *v.n.* smirk, grin.
Schmutz [ʃmuts], *m.* (**—es,** *no pl.*) dirt, filth.
schmutzen ['ʃmutsən], *v.n.* get soiled, get dirty.
Schmutzkonkurrenz ['ʃmutskɔnkurɛnts], *f.* (**—,** *no pl.*) unfair competition.
Schnabel ['ʃna:bəl], *m.* (**—s,** *pl.* **⸚**) bill, beak; (*ship*) prow; *halt den —,* keep your mouth shut; *er spricht, wie ihm der — gewachsen ist,* he calls a spade a spade.
Schnabeltier ['ʃna:bəlti:r], *n.* (**—s,** *pl.* **—e**) duck-bill, duck-billed platypus.
Schnaderhüpfel ['ʃna:dərhypfəl], *n.* (**—s,** *pl.* **—**) (*dial.*) Alpine folk-song.
Schnalle ['ʃnalə], *f.* (**—,** *pl.* **—n**) buckle.
schnalzen ['ʃnaltsən], *v.n.* click; snap.
schnappen ['ʃnapən], *v.n.* snap; snatch at s.th.; *nach Luft —,* gasp for breath.
Schnaps [ʃnaps], *m.* (**—es,** *pl.* **⸚e**) spirits, brandy, gin.
schnarchen ['ʃnarçən], *v.n.* snore.
Schnarre ['ʃnarə], *f.* (**—,** *pl.* **—n**) rattle.
schnattern ['ʃnatərn], *v.n.* cackle; gabble; chatter.
schnauben ['ʃnaubən], *v.n.* puff and blow; snort; *vor Zorn —,* fret and fume.
schnaufen ['ʃnaufən], *v.n.* breathe heavily, pant.
Schnauze ['ʃnautsə], *f.* (**—,** *pl.* **—n**) (*animals*) snout; (*vulg.*) mouth, trap; nozzle.
schnauzen ['ʃnautsən], *v.n.* snarl, shout (at).
Schnecke ['ʃnɛkə], *f.* (**—,** *pl.* **—n**), (*Zool.*) snail, slug.
Schnee [ʃne:], *m.* (**—s,** *no pl.*) snow.
Schneegestöber ['ʃne:gəʃtø:bər], *n.* (**—s,** *pl.* **—**) snow-storm.
Schneeglöckchen ['ʃne:glœkçən], *n.* (**—s,** *pl.* **—**) (*Bot.*) snowdrop.
Schneeschläger ['ʃne:ʃlɛ:gər], *m.* (**—s,** *pl.* **—**) whisk.
Schneetreiben ['ʃne:traɪbən], *n.* (**—s,** *no pl.*) snow-storm, blizzard.
Schneewittchen [ʃne:'vɪtçən], *n.* (**—s,** *no pl.*) Snow White.
Schneid [ʃnaɪt], *m.* (**—s,** *no pl.*) go, push, dash, courage.
Schneide ['ʃnaɪdə], *f.* (**—,** *pl.* **—n**) edge.
Schneidebohne ['ʃnaɪdəbo:nə], *f.* (**—,** *pl.* **—n**) French bean, string-bean.
Schneidemühle ['ʃnaɪdəmy:lə], *f.* (**—,** *pl.* **—n**) saw mill.
schneiden ['ʃnaɪdən], *v.a. irr.* cut, trim, carve; (*fig.*) ignore, cut; *Gesichter —,* make faces. — *v.r. sich —,* cut o.s.; (*Maths.*) intersect; *sich die Haare — lassen,* have o.'s hair cut.
Schneider ['ʃnaɪdər], *m.* (**—s,** *pl.* **—**) tailor.
Schneiderei [ʃnaɪde'raɪ], *f.* (**—,** *no pl.*) tailoring; dressmaking.
Schneidezahn ['ʃnaɪdətsa:n], *m.* (**—s,** *pl.* **⸚e**) incisor.
schneidig ['ʃnaɪdɪç], *adj.* dashing.
schneien ['ʃnaɪən], *v.n.* snow.
Schneise ['ʃnaɪzə], *f.* (**—,** *pl.* **—n**) (*forest*) glade, cutting.
schnell [ʃnɛl], *adj.* quick, swift, speedy, fast, rapid; *mach —,* hurry up.
Schnelle ['ʃnɛlə], *f.* (**—,** *pl.* **—n**) (*river*) rapids.
schnellen ['ʃnɛlən], *v.n.* spring, jump.

Schnelligkeit

Schnelligkeit [ˈʃnɛlɪçkaɪt], *f.* (—, *no pl.*) quickness, speed, swiftness, rapidity; (*Tech.*) velocity.

Schnepfe [ˈʃnɛpfə], *f.* (—, *pl.* —n) (*Orn.*) snipe, woodcock.

schneuzen [ˈʃnɔytsən], *v.r.* sich (*die Nase*) —, blow o.'s nose.

schniegeln [ˈʃniːgəln], *v.r.* sich —, (*coll.*) dress up, deck out; *geschniegelt und gebügelt*, spick and span.

Schnippchen [ˈʃnɪpçən], *n.* (—s, *pl.* —) *einem ein* — *schlagen*, play a trick on s.o.

schnippisch [ˈʃnɪpɪʃ], *adj.* pert, perky.

Schnitt [ʃnɪt], *m.* (—(e)s, *pl.* —e) cut, incision; section; (*beer*) small glass; (*dress*) cut-out pattern; (*book*) edge.

Schnittbohne [ˈʃnɪtboːnə], *f.* (—, *pl.* —n) (*Bot.*) French bean.

Schnitte [ˈʃnɪtə], *f.* (—, *pl.* —n) slice (of bread).

Schnitter [ˈʃnɪtər], *m.* (—s, *pl.* —) reaper.

Schnittlauch [ˈʃnɪtlaux], *m.* (—s, *no pl.*) (*Bot.*) chives.

Schnittmuster [ˈʃnɪtmʊstər], *n.* (—s, *pl.* —) cut-out pattern.

Schnittwaren [ˈʃnɪtvaːrən], *f. pl.* dry goods, drapery.

Schnitzel [ˈʃnɪtsəl], *n.* (—s, *pl.* —) (*Cul.*) cutlet; *Wiener* —, veal cutlet; snip; (*pl.*) shavings.

schnitzen [ˈʃnɪtsən], *v.a.* carve (in wood).

schnodd(e)rig [ˈʃnɔd(ə)rɪç], *adj.* (*coll.*) cheeky, insolent.

schnöde [ˈʃnøːdə], *adj.* base, heinous, mean, vile; —*r Mammon*, filthy lucre; —*r Undank*, rank ingratitude.

Schnörkel [ˈʃnœrkəl], *m.* (—s, *pl.* —) (*writing*) flourish.

schnorren [ˈʃnɔrən], *v.n.* (*rare*) cadge, beg.

schnüffeln [ˈʃnyfəln], *v.n.* sniff; (*fig.*) pry, snoop.

Schnuller [ˈʃnʊlər], *m.* (—s, *pl.* —) baby's dummy; (*Am.*) pacifier.

Schnupfen [ˈʃnʊpfən], *m.* (—s, *pl.* —) cold (in the head); *den* — *haben*, have a (running) cold; *den* — *bekommen*, catch cold.

schnupfen [ˈʃnʊpfən], *v.a., v.n.* take snuff.

Schnupftuch [ˈʃnʊpftuːx], *n.* (—(e)s, *pl.* ̈er) (*dial.*) (pocket-) handkerchief.

schnuppe [ˈʃnʊpə], *adj.* (*sl.*) *mir ist alles* —, it is all the same to me, I don't care.

schnuppern [ˈʃnʊpərn], *v.n.* smell, snuffle.

Schnur [ʃnuːr], *f.* (—, *pl.* —en, ̈e) twine, cord, string; (*Elec.*) lead, extension cord.

Schnurrbart [ˈʃnurbaːrt], *m.* (—s, *pl.* ̈e) moustache; *sich einen* — *wachsen lassen*, grow a moustache.

Schnürchen [ˈʃnyːrçən], *n.* (—s, *pl.* —) *wie am* —, like clockwork.

schnüren [ˈʃnyːrən], *v.a.* lace, tie up; *sein Ränzel* —, pack o.'s bag.

Schnurre [ˈʃnurə], *f.* (—, *pl.* —n) funny story, yarn.

schnurren [ˈʃnurən], *v.n.* purr.

Schnürsenkel [ˈʃnyːrzɛnkəl], *m.* (—s, *pl.* —) (*shoe*) lace.

schnurstracks [ˈʃnuːrʃtraks], *adv.* directly, immediately, on the spot.

Schober [ˈʃoːbər], *m.* (—s, *pl.* —) stack, rick.

Schock (1) [ʃɔk], *n.* (—(e)s, *pl.* —e) sixty, three score.

Schock (2) [ʃɔk], *m.* (—(e)s, *pl.* —s) shock; blow; stroke.

Schöffe [ˈʃœfə], *m.* (—n, *pl.* —n) (*Law*) juror; member of jury.

Schokolade [ʃokoˈlaːdə], *f.* (—, *pl.* —n) chocolate; *eine Tafel* —, a bar of chocolate.

Scholle [ˈʃɔlə], *f.* (—, *pl.* —n) plaice; (*ice*) floe; clod; soil.

schon [ʃoːn], *adv.* already; indeed; yet; *na wenn* —, so what; — *gut*, that'll do; — *gestern*, as early as yesterday.

schön [ʃøːn], *adj.* beautiful, fair, handsome, lovely; —*e Literatur*, belles-lettres, good books.

schonen [ˈʃoːnən], *v.a.* spare, save; treat considerately.

Schoner [ˈʃoːnər], *m.* (—s, *pl.* —) antimacassar; (*Naut.*) schooner.

Schönheit [ˈʃøːnhaɪt], *f.* (—, *no pl.*) beauty.

Schonung [ˈʃoːnun], *f.* (—, *pl.* —en) forbearance, considerate treatment; (*forest*) plantation of young trees.

Schonzeit [ˈʃoːntsaɪt], *f.* (—, *pl.* —en) close season.

Schopf [ʃɔpf], *m.* (—es, *pl.* ̈e) tuft, head of hair; (*bird*) crest; *das Glück beim* —*e fassen*, take time by the forelock, make hay while the sun shines.

Schöpfbrunnen [ˈʃœpfbrunən], *m.* (—s, *pl.* —) (draw-)well.

schöpfen [ˈʃœpfən], *v.a.* (*water*) draw; derive; *Verdacht* —, become suspicious; *frische Luft* —, get a breath of fresh air; *Mut* —, take heart.

Schöpfer [ˈʃœpfər], *m.* (—s, *pl.* —) creator.

Schöpfkelle [ˈʃœpfkɛlə], *f.* (—, *pl.* —n) scoop.

Schopflerche [ˈʃɔpflɛrçə], *f.* (—, *pl.* —n) (*Orn.*) crested lark.

Schöpfung [ˈʃœpfun], *f.* (—, *pl.* —en) creation.

Schoppen [ˈʃɔpən], *m.* (—s, *pl.* —) (*approx.*) half a pint.

Schöps [ʃœps], *m.* (—es, *pl.* —e) (*Zool.*) wether; (*fig.*) simpleton.

Schorf [ʃɔrf], *m.* (—(e)s, *pl.* —e) scab, scurf.

Schornstein [ˈʃɔrnʃtaɪn], *m.* (—s, *pl.* —e) chimney; (*ship*) funnel.

Schoß [ʃoːs], *m.* (—es, *pl.* ̈e) lap; (*Poet.*) womb; skirt, tail; *die Hände in den* — *legen*, be idle, fold o.'s arms, twiddle o.'s thumbs.

Schößling [ˈʃœslɪŋ], *m.* (—s, *pl.* —e) shoot, sprig.

Schote [ˈʃoːtə], *f.* (—, *pl.* —n) pod, husk, shell; (*pl.*) green peas.

Schotter [ˈʃɔtər], *m.* (—s, *no pl.*) road-metal, broken stones, gravel.

Schottland [ˈʃɔtlant], *n.* Scotland.

schraffieren [ʃraˈfiːrən], *v.a.* (*Art*) hatch.

schräg [ˈʃrɛːk], *adj.* oblique, sloping, slanting, diagonal.

Schramme [ˈʃramə], *f.* (—, *pl.* —n) scratch, scar.

Schrank [ʃraŋk], *m.* (—(e)s, *pl.* ⸚e) cupboard, wardrobe.

Schranken [ˈʃraŋkən], *f. pl.* barriers, (level crossing) gates, limits, bounds; *in* — *halten*, limit, keep within bounds.

schränken [ˈʃrɛŋkən], *v.a.* cross; fold.

Schranze [ˈʃrantsə], *m.* (—n, *pl.* —n) sycophant, toady.

Schraube [ˈʃraubə], *f.* (—, *pl.* —n) screw; bolt; propeller.

Schraubengewinde [ˈʃraubəngəvɪndə], *n.* (—s, *pl.* —) thread of a screw.

Schraubenmutter [ˈʃraubənmutər], *f.* (—, *pl.* —n) female screw, nut.

Schraubenzieher [ˈʃraubəntsiːər], *m.* (—s, *pl.* —) screw-driver.

Schraubstock [ˈʃraupʃtɔk], *m.* (—s, *pl.* ⸚e) (*tool*) vise.

Schreck(en) [ˈʃrɛk(ən)], *m.* (—s, *pl.* —) fright, terror, alarm, horror; shock.

Schrecknis [ˈʃrɛknɪs], *n.* (—ses, *pl.* —se) terror, horror.

Schrei [ʃraɪ], *m.* (—s, *pl.* —e) cry; scream.

Schreiben [ˈʃraɪbən], *n.* (—s, *pl.* —) letter, missive.

schreiben [ˈʃraɪbən], *v.a. irr.* write; *ins Reine* —, make a fair copy.

Schreibfehler [ˈʃraɪpfeːlər], *m.* (—s, *pl.* —) slip of the pen.

Schreibkrampf [ˈʃraɪpkrampf], *m.* (—(e)s, *pl.* ⸚e) writer's cramp.

Schreibmaschine [ˈʃraɪpmaʃiːnə], *f.* (—, *pl.* —n) typewriter.

Schreibwaren [ˈʃraɪpvaːrən], *f. pl.* stationery.

Schreibweise [ˈʃraɪpvaɪzə], *f.* (—*pl.* —n) style; spelling.

schreien [ˈʃraɪən], *v.a., v.n. irr.* cry, shout, scream, yell.

Schreihals [ˈʃraɪhals], *m.* (—es, *pl.* ⸚e) cry-baby, noisy child.

Schrein [ʃraɪn], *m.* (—(e)s, *pl.* —e) box, chest; shrine.

schreiten [ˈʃraɪtən], *v.n. irr.* (*aux. sein*) stride, step, pace.

Schrift [ʃrɪft], *f.* (—, *pl.* —en) writing; handwriting, calligraphy; publication; type; *Heilige* —, Holy Writ, Holy Scripture.

Schriftführer [ˈʃrɪftfyːrər], *m.* (—s, *pl.* —) secretary.

Schriftgießerei [ˈʃrɪftgiːsəraɪ], *f.* (—, *pl.* —en) type-foundry.

Schriftleiter [ˈʃrɪftlaɪtər], *m.* (—s, *pl.* —) editor.

schriftlich [ˈʃrɪftlɪç], *adj.* written. — *adv.* in writing, by letter.

Schriftsetzer [ˈʃrɪftzɛtsər], *m.* (—s, *pl.* —) compositor.

Schriftsteller [ˈʃrɪftʃtɛlər], *m.* (—s, *pl.* —) writer, author.

Schriftstück [ˈʃrɪftʃtyk], *n.* (—s, *pl.* —e) document, deed.

Schriftwechsel [ˈʃrɪftvɛksəl], *m.* (—s, *no pl.*) exchange of notes, correspondence.

Schriftzeichen [ˈʃrɪftsaɪçən], *n.* (—s, *pl.* —) character, letter (of alphabet).

schrill [ʃrɪl], *adj.* shrill.

Schritt [ʃrɪt], *m.* (—(e)s, *pl.* —e) step, pace, move; *lange* — *machen*, stride; — *halten*, keep pace; — *fahren*, drive slowly, drive at walking pace; *aus dem* —, out of step; *in einer Sache* —*e tun*, make a move *or* take steps about s.th.

schrittweise [ˈʃrɪtvaɪzə], *adv.* step by step, gradually.

schroff [ˈʃrɔf], *adj.* steep, precipitous; (*fig.*) gruff, blunt, rough, harsh.

schröpfen [ˈʃrœpfən], *v.a.* (*Med.*) cup; (*fig.*) fleece.

Schrot [ʃroːt], *m. & n.* (—(e)s, *pl.* —e) grape-shot, small shot; *ein Mann vom alten* —, a man of the utmost probity.

Schrotbrot [ˈʃroːtbroːt], *n.* (—es, *no pl.*) wholemeal bread.

Schrott [ʃrɔt], *m.* (—(e)s, *pl.* —e), old iron, scrap metal.

Schrulle [ˈʃrulə], *f.* (—, *pl.* —n) fad, whim.

schrumpfen [ˈʃrumpfən], *v.n.* (*aux. sein*) shrink, shrivel.

Schub [ʃup], *m.* (—s, *pl.* ⸚e) shove, push; batch.

Schubkarren [ˈʃupkarən], *m.* (—s, *pl.* —) wheelbarrow.

Schublade [ˈʃuplaːdə], *f.* (—, *pl.* —n) drawer.

schüchtern [ˈʃyçtərn], *adj.* shy, bashful, timid.

Schuft [ʃuft], *m.* (—(e)s, *pl.* —e) blackguard, scoundrel.

schuften [ˈʃuftən], *v.n.* work hard, toil.

Schufterei [ʃuftəˈraɪ], *f.* (—, *no pl.*) drudgery.

schuftig [ˈʃuftɪç], *adj.* rascally, mean.

Schuh [ʃuː], *m.* (—s, *pl.* —e) shoe; *einem etwas in die* — *schieben*, lay the blame at s.o.'s door.

Schuhwerk [ˈʃuːvɛrk], *n.* (—s, *no pl.*) footwear.

Schuhwichse [ˈʃuːvɪksə], *f.* (—, *no pl.*) shoe-polish.

Schuld [ʃult], *f.* (—, *pl.* —en) guilt, offence, sin; fault; blame; cause; (*money*) debt; *in* —*en geraten*, run into debt.

schuld [ʃult], *adj. ich bin* —, it is my fault, I am to blame.

schulden [ˈʃuldən], *v.a.* owe, be indebted to.

schuldig [ˈʃuldɪç], *adj.* guilty, culpable; *sich* — *bekennen*, plead guilty; *einen* — *sprechen*, pronounce s.o. guilty;

ihm ist Anerkennung —, appreciation is due to him.

Schuldigkeit [ˈʃuldɪçkaɪt], *f.* (—, *no pl.*) obligation, duty.

schuldlos [ˈʃultloːs], *adj.* innocent, guiltless.

Schuldner [ˈʃuldnər], *m.* (—s, *pl.* —) debtor.

Schule [ˈʃuːlə], *f.* (—, *pl.* —n) school; *in die* — *gehen*, go to school, attend school; *die* — *schwänzen*, play truant; *hohe* —, (*Riding*) advanced horsemanship.

schulen [ˈʃuːlən], *v.a.* train, instruct.

Schüler [ˈʃyːlər], *m.* (—s, *pl.* —) schoolboy, pupil, student, scholar.

Schulklasse [ˈʃuːlklasə], *f.* (—, *pl.* —n) class, form.

Schulleiter [ˈʃuːllaɪtər], *m.* (—s, *pl.* —) headmaster.

Schulrat [ˈʃuːlraːt], *m.* (—s, *pl.* ⸚e) school-inspector.

Schulter [ˈʃultər], *f.* (—, *pl.* —n) shoulder.

Schulterblatt [ˈʃultərblat], *n.* (—s, *pl.* ⸚er) shoulder-blade.

Schultheiß [ˈʃulthaɪs], *m.* (—en, *pl.* —en) village magistrate, mayor.

Schulunterricht [ˈʃuːluntərrɪçt], *m.* (—s, *no pl.*) school teaching, lessons.

schummeln [ˈʃuməln], *v.n.* (*coll.*) cheat.

Schund [ʃunt], *m.* (—(e)s, *no pl.*) trash.

Schuppe [ˈʃupə], *f.* (—, *pl.* —n) scale; (*pl.*) dandruff.

Schuppen [ˈʃupən], *m.* (—s, *pl.* —) shed.

Schuppentier [ˈʃupəntiːr], *m.* (—s, *pl.* —e) (*Zool.*) armadillo.

Schur [ʃuːr], *f.* (—, *pl.* —en) shearing.

schüren [ˈʃyːrən], *v.a.* (*fire*) poke, rake; (*fig.*) stir up, fan, incite.

schürfen [ˈʃyrfən], *v.a.* scratch. — *v.n.* (*Min.*) prospect.

schurigeln [ˈʃuːrɪgəln], *v.a.* bully, pester.

Schurke [ˈʃurkə], *m.* (—n, *pl.* —n) scoundrel, villain, blackguard.

Schurz [ʃurts], *m.* (—es, *pl.* —e) apron, overall.

Schürze [ˈʃyrtsə], *f.* (—, *pl.* —n) apron, pinafore.

schürzen [ˈʃyrtsən], *v.a.* tuck up, pin up.

Schürzenjäger [ˈʃyrtsənjɛːgər], *m.* (—s, *pl.* —) ladies' man.

Schurzfell [ˈʃurtsfɛl], *n.* (—s, *pl.* —e) leather apron.

Schuß [ʃus], *m.* (—sses, *pl.* ⸚sse) shot, report; dash; *weit vom* —, out of harm's way; *wide of the mark.*

Schüssel [ˈʃysəl], *f.* (—, *pl.* —n) dish.

Schußwaffe [ˈʃusvafə], *f.* (—, *pl.* —n) fire-arm.

Schuster [ˈʃuːstər], *m.* (—s, *pl.* —) shoemaker, cobbler; *auf* —*s Rappen*, on Shanks's pony.

schustern [ˈʃuːstərn], *v.n.* cobble, make *or* mend shoes.

Schutt [ʃut], *m.* (—(e)s, *no pl.*) rubbish, refuse; rubble; — *abladen*,

dump refuse.

Schütte [ˈʃytə], *f.* (—, *pl.* —n) (*dial.*) bundle, truss.

schütteln [ˈʃytəln], *v.a.* shake, jolt.

schütten [ˈʃytən], *v.a.* shoot, pour; pour out.

schütter [ˈʃytər], *adj.* (*dial.*) (*hair*) thin; scarce.

Schutz [ʃuts], *m.* (—es, *no pl.*) protection, shelter, cover; *einen in* — *nehmen gegen*, defend s.o. against.

Schutzbefohlene [ˈʃutsbəfoːlənə], *m.* (—n, *pl.* —n) charge, person in o.'s care, ward.

Schutzbündnis [ˈʃutsbyntnɪs], *n.* (—ses, *pl.* —se) defensive alliance.

Schütze [ˈʃytsə], *m.* (—n, *pl.* —n) rifleman, sharpshooter, marksman; (*Astrol.*) Sagittarius.

schützen [ˈʃytsən], *v.a.* protect, shelter, defend. — *v.r. sich* — *vor*, guard o.s. against.

Schützengraben [ˈʃytsəngraːbən], *m.* (—s, *pl.* ⸚) trench.

Schutzgebiet [ˈʃutsgəbiːt], *n.* (—s, *pl.* —e) protectorate.

Schutzgitter [ˈʃutsgɪtər], *n.* (—s, *pl.* —) grid, guard.

Schutzheilige [ˈʃutshaɪlɪgə], *m.* (—n, *pl.* —n) patron saint.

Schützling [ˈʃytslɪŋ], *m.* (—s, *pl.* —e) protégé, charge.

Schutzmann [ˈʃutsman], *m.* (—s, *pl.* ⸚er, **Schutzleute**) policeman, constable.

Schutzmarke [ˈʃutsmarkə], *f.* (—, *pl.* —n) trade-mark.

Schutzzoll [ˈʃutstsɔl], *m.* (—s, *pl.* ⸚e) protective duty, tariff.

Schwaben [ˈʃvaːbən], *n.* Swabia.

Schwabenstreich [ˈʃvaːbənʃtraɪç], *m.* (—s, *pl.* —e) tomfoolery.

schwach [ʃvax], *adj.* weak, frail, feeble; (*noise*) faint; (*pulse*) low; —*e Seite*, foible; —*e Stunde*, unguarded moment.

Schwäche [ˈʃvɛçə], *f.* (—, *pl.* —n) weakness, faintness; infirmity.

schwächen [ˈʃvɛçən], *v.a.* weaken, debilitate.

Schwächling [ˈʃvɛçlɪŋ], *m.* (—s, *pl.* —e) weakling.

Schwachsinn [ˈʃvaxzɪn], *m.* (—s, *no pl.*) feeble-mindedness.

Schwächung [ˈʃvɛçuŋ], *f.* (—, *pl.* —en) weakening, lessening.

Schwadron [ʃvaˈdroːn], *f.* (—, *pl.* —en) squadron.

Schwadroneur [ʃvadroˈnøːr], *m.* (—s, *pl.* —e) swaggerer.

schwadronieren [ʃvadroˈniːrən], *v.n.* talk big, swagger.

schwafeln [ˈʃvaːfəln], *v.n.* (*sl.*) talk nonsense, waffle.

Schwager [ˈʃvaːgər], *m.* (—s, *pl.* ⸚) brother-in-law.

Schwägerin [ˈʃvɛːgərɪn], *f.* (—, *pl.* —nen) sister-in-law.

Schwalbe [ˈʃvalbə], *f.* (—, *pl.* —n) (*Orn.*) swallow.

Schwalbenschwanz [ˈʃvalbənʃvants], *m.* (—es, *pl.* ⁓e) (*butterfly*) swallow's tail; (*joinery*) dovetail.

Schwall [ʃval], *m.* (—(e)s, *no pl.*) flood; (*fig.*) deluge, torrent.

Schwamm [ʃvam], *m.* (—(e)s, *pl.* ⁓e) sponge; fungus, mushroom; dry rot.

schwammig [ˈʃvamɪç], *adj.* spongy, fungous.

Schwan [ʃvaːn], *m.* (—(e)s, *pl.* ⁓e) swan; *junger* —, cygnet.

schwanen [ˈʃvaːnən], *v.n. imp. es schwant mir,* I have a foreboding.

Schwang [ʃvaŋ], *m. im* —*e sein,* be in fashion, be the rage.

schwanger [ˈʃvaŋər], *adj.* pregnant.

schwängern [ˈʃvɛŋərn], *v.a.* make pregnant, get with child; (*fig.*) impregnate.

Schwangerschaft [ˈʃvaŋərʃaft], *f.* (—, *pl.* —en) pregnancy.

Schwank [ʃvaŋk], *m.* (—(e)s, *pl.* ⁓e) funny story, joke; (*Theat.*) farce.

schwank [ʃvaŋk], *adj.* flexible, supple; *ein* —*es Rohr,* a reed shaken by the wind.

schwanken [ˈʃvaŋkən], *v.n.* totter, stagger; (*fig.*) waver, vacillate; (*prices*) fluctuate.

Schwanz [ʃvants], *m.* (—es, *pl.* ⁓e) tail.

schwänzeln [ˈʃvɛntsəln], *v.n.* (*animal*) wag the tail; (*fig.*) fawn, cringe.

schwänzen [ˈʃvɛntsən], *v.a. die Schule* —, play truant.

Schwären [ˈʃvɛːrən], *m.* (—s, *pl.* —) ulcer, abscess.

schwären [ˈʃvɛːrən], *v.n.* fester, suppurate.

Schwarm [ʃvarm], *m.* (—(e)s, *pl.* ⁓e) (*insects*) swarm; (*humans*) crowd; (*birds*) flight.

Schwärmerei [ʃvɛrmə'raɪ], *f.* (—, *pl.* —en) enthusiasm, passion, craze.

Schwarte [ˈʃvartə], *f.* (—, *pl.* —n) rind; crust; *alte* —, (*fig.*) old volume; tome.

schwarz [ʃvarts], *adj.* black.

Schwarzamsel [ˈʃvartsamzəl], *f.* (—, *pl.* —n) (*Orn.*) blackbird.

Schwarzdorn [ˈʃvartsdɔrn], *m.* (—s, *no pl.*) (*Bot.*) blackthorn, sloe.

Schwärze [ˈʃvɛrtsə], *f.* (—, *no pl.*) blackness; printer's ink.

schwärzen [ˈʃvɛrtsən], *v.a.* blacken.

Schwarzkünstler [ˈʃvartskynstlər], *m.* (—s, *pl.* —) magician, necromancer.

Schwarzwald [ˈʃvartsvalt], *m.* Black Forest.

Schwarzwild [ˈʃvartsvɪlt], *n.* (—(e)s, *no pl.*) wild boar.

schwatzen [ˈʃvatsən], *v.n.* chat, chatter, prattle.

Schwätzer [ˈʃvɛtsər], *m.* (—s, *pl.* —) chatterbox.

Schwatzhaftigkeit [ˈʃvatshaftɪçkaɪt], *f.* (—, *no pl.*) loquacity, talkativeness.

Schwebe [ˈʃveːbə], *f.* (—, *pl.* —n) suspense; suspension.

Schwebebaum [ˈʃveːbəbaum], *m.* (—s, *pl.* ⁓e) horizontal bar.

schweben [ˈʃveːbən], *v.n.* be suspended, hover; (*fig.*) be pending; *in Gefahr* —, be in danger; *es schwebt mir auf der Zunge,* it is on the tip of my tongue.

Schwede [ˈʃveːdə], *m.* (—n, *pl.* —n) Swede; *alter* —, (*fig.*) old boy.

Schweden [ˈʃveːdən], *n.* Sweden.

Schwedenhölzer [ˈʃveːdənhœltsər], *n. pl.* (*rare*) matches.

Schwefel [ˈʃveːfəl], *m.* (—s, *no pl.*) sulphur, brimstone.

Schwefelhölzchen [ˈʃveːfəlhœltsçən], *n.* (—s, *pl.* —) (*obs.*) match.

schwefeln [ˈʃveːfəln], *v.a.* impregnate with sulphur, fumigate.

Schwefelsäure [ˈʃveːfəlzɔʏrə], *f.* (—, *no pl.*) sulphuric acid.

Schweif [ʃvaɪf], *m.* (—(e)s, *pl.* —e) tail.

schweifen [ˈʃvaɪfən], *v.n.* (*aux. sein*) ramble, stray, wander.

schweifwedeln [ˈʃvaɪfveːdəln], *v.n.* fawn.

Schweigegeld [ˈʃvaɪgəgɛlt], *n.* (—(e)s, *pl.* —er) (*coll.*) hush-money.

Schweigen [ˈʃvaɪgən], *n.* (—s, *no pl.*) silence.

schweigen [ˈʃvaɪgən], *v.n. irr.* be silent; be quiet; *ganz zu* — *von,* to say nothing of.

schweigsam [ˈʃvaɪkzaːm], *adj.* taciturn.

Schwein [ʃvaɪn], *n.* (—(e)s, *pl.* —e) pig, hog; swine; *wildes* —, boar; (*fig.*) luck, fluke; — *haben,* be lucky.

Schweinekoben [ˈʃvaɪnəkoːbən], *m.* (—s, *pl.* —) pigsty.

Schweinerei [ʃvaɪnə'raɪ], *f.* (—, *pl.* —en) filth; (*fig.*) smut, filthiness, obscenity; mess.

Schweineschmalz [ˈʃvaɪnəʃmalts], *n.* (—es, *no pl.*) lard.

Schweinigel [ˈʃvaɪnɪgəl], *m.* (—s, *pl.* —) (*Zool.*) hedgehog, porcupine; (*fig.*) dirty pig, filthy wretch.

Schweinskeule [ˈʃvaɪnskɔʏlə], *f.* (—, *pl.* —n) leg of pork.

Schweiß [ʃvaɪs], *m.* (—es, *no pl.*) sweat, perspiration.

schweißen [ˈʃvaɪsən], *v.a.* weld, solder.

Schweiz [ʃvaɪts], *f.* Switzerland.

Schweizer [ˈʃvaɪtsər], *m.* (—s, *pl.* —) Swiss; (*fig.*) dairyman.

Schweizerei [ʃvaɪtsə'raɪ], *f.* (—, *pl.* —en) dairy.

schwelen [ˈʃveːlən], *v.n.* burn slowly, smoulder.

schwelgen [ˈʃvɛlgən], *v.n.* carouse, revel.

Schwelgerei [ʃvɛlgə'raɪ], *f.* (—, *pl.* —en) revelry.

schwelgerisch [ˈʃvɛlgərɪʃ], *adj.* luxurious, voluptuous.

Schwelle [ˈʃvɛlə], *f.* (—, *pl.* —n) threshold; (*Railw.*) sleeper, tie.

schwellen [ˈʃvɛlən], *v.n. irr.* (*aux. sein*) swell; (*water*) rise.

Schwellung [ˈʃvɛluŋ], *f.* (—, *pl.* —en) swelling.

schwemmen

schwemmen [ˈʃvɛmən], *v.a.* wash, soak, carry off.

Schwengel [ˈʃvɛŋəl], *m.* (—s, *pl.* —) (*bell*) clapper; (*pump*) handle.

schwenken [ˈʃvɛŋkən], *v.a.* swing; shake, brandish; (*glasses*) rinse.

Schwenkung [ˈʃvɛŋkuŋ], *f.* (—, *pl.* —en) change; (*Mil.*) wheeling.

schwer [ʃveːr], *adj.* heavy; difficult, hard; ponderous; severe; — *von Begriff*, obtuse, slow in the uptake; —*e Speise*, indigestible food; *einem das Herz — machen*, grieve s.o.

schwerblütig [ˈʃveːrblyːtɪç], *adj.* phlegmatic.

Schwere [ˈʃveːrə], *f.* (—, *no pl.*) weight, heaviness; gravity.

Schwerenöter [ˈʃveːrənøːtər], *m.* (—s, *pl.* —) gay dog, ladies' man.

schwerfällig [ˈʃveːrfɛlɪç], *adj.* ungainly, cumbrous, unwieldy; (*fig.*) thickheaded, dense.

Schwergewicht [ˈʃveːrgəvɪçt], *n.* (—s, *no pl.*) (*Sport*) heavyweight; (*fig.*) emphasis.

schwerhörig [ˈʃveːrhøːrɪç], *adj.* hard of hearing, deaf.

Schwerkraft [ˈʃveːrkraft], *f.* (—, *no pl.*) gravity.

schwerlich [ˈʃveːrlɪç], *adv.* hardly, scarcely.

schwermütig [ˈʃveːrmyːtɪç], *adj.* melancholy.

Schwerpunkt [ˈʃveːrpuŋkt], *m.* (—s, *pl.* —e) centre of gravity.

Schwert [ʃveːrt], *n.* (—(e)s, *pl.* —er) sword.

Schwertgriff [ˈʃveːrtgrɪf], *m.* (—s, *pl.* —e) hilt.

Schwertlilie [ˈʃveːrtliːljə], *f.* (—, *pl.* —n) (*Bot.*) iris; fleur-de-lys.

Schwertstreich [ˈʃveːrtʃtraɪç], *m.* (—(e)s, *pl.* —e) sword-blow, swordstroke.

schwerwiegend [ˈʃveːrviːgənt], *adj.* weighty.

Schwester [ˈʃvɛstər], *f.* (—, *pl.* —n) sister; *barmherzige* —, sister of mercy.

Schwesternschaft [ˈʃvɛstərnʃaft], *f.* (—, *pl.* —en) sisterhood; (*Am.*) sorority.

Schwibbogen [ˈʃvɪpboːgən], *m.* (—s, *pl.* —) (*Archit.*) flying buttress.

Schwiegersohn [ˈʃviːgərzoːn], *m.* (—s, *pl.* ·̈e) son-in-law.

Schwiegertochter [ˈʃviːgərtɔxtər], *f.* (—, *pl.* ·̈) daughter-in-law.

Schwiele [ˈʃviːlə], *f.* (—, *pl.* —n) hard skin, callus, weal.

schwielig [ˈʃviːlɪç], *adj.* callous, horny.

schwierig [ˈʃviːrɪç], *adj.* difficult, hard.

Schwierigkeit [ˈʃviːrɪçkaɪt], *f.* (—, *pl.* —en) difficulty; *auf —en stoßen*, meet with difficulties.

schwimmen [ˈʃvɪmən], *v.n. irr.* (*aux.* sein) swim, float.

Schwimmer [ˈʃvɪmər], *m.* (—s, *pl.* —) swimmer.

Schwimmgürtel [ˈʃvɪmgyrtəl], *m.* (—s, *pl.* —) life-belt.

Schwindel [ˈʃvɪndəl], *m.* (—s, *pl.* —) giddiness, dizziness, vertigo; swindle, fraud.

Schwindelanfall [ˈʃvɪndəlanfal], *m.* (—s, *pl.* ·̈e) attack of giddiness, vertigo.

Schwindelei [ʃvɪndəˈlaɪ], *f.* (—, *pl.* —en) swindle, fraud, deceit.

schwindelhaft [ˈʃvɪndəlhaft], *adj.* fraudulent.

schwinden [ˈʃvɪndən], *v.n. irr.* (*aux.* sein) dwindle; disappear, vanish.

Schwindler [ˈʃvɪndlər], *m.* (—s, *pl.* —) swindler, humbug, cheat.

schwindlig [ˈʃvɪndlɪç], *adj.* dizzy, giddy.

Schwindsucht [ˈʃvɪntzuxt], *f.* (—, *no pl.*) (*Med.*) tuberculosis, consumption.

schwindsüchtig [ˈʃvɪntzyçtɪç], *adj.* (*Med.*) tubercular.

Schwinge [ˈʃvɪŋə], *f.* (—, *pl.* —n) wing.

schwingen [ˈʃvɪŋən], *v.a. irr.* brandish. — *v.n.* swing, vibrate. — *v.r. sich* —, vault; *sich auf den Thron* —, usurp or take possession of the throne.

Schwingung [ˈʃvɪŋuŋ], *f.* (—, *pl.* —en) vibration, oscillation.

Schwips [ʃvɪps], *m.* (—es, *pl.* —e) (*coll.*) tipsiness; *einen — haben*, be tipsy.

schwirren [ˈʃvɪrən], *v.n.* whir, buzz.

Schwitzbad [ˈʃvɪtsbaːt], *n.* (—es, *pl.* ·̈er) Turkish bath, steam-bath.

schwitzen [ˈʃvɪtsən], *v.n.* sweat, perspire.

schwören [ˈʃvøːrən], *v.a.*, *v.n. irr.* swear, take an oath; *darauf kannst du* —, you can be quite sure of that, you bet; *falsch* —, forswear o.s., perjure o.s.

schwül [ʃvyːl], *adj.* sultry, close.

Schwüle [ˈʃvyːlə], *f.* (—, *no pl.*) sultriness.

Schwulst [ʃvulst], *m.* (—es, *no pl.*) bombast.

schwülstig [ˈʃvyːlstɪç], *adj.* bombastic, turgid.

Schwülstigkeit [ˈʃvyːlstɪçkaɪt], *f.* (—, *pl.* —en) bombastic style, turgidity.

Schwund [ʃvunt], *m.* (—(e)s, *no pl.*) dwindling, decline; shrinkage.

Schwung [ʃvuŋ], *m.* (—(e)s, *pl.* ·̈e) swing, leap, bound; (*fig.*) verve, élan; (*Poet.*) flight, soaring.

schwunghaft [ˈʃvuŋhaft], *adj.* flourishing, soaring.

Schwungkraft [ˈʃvuŋkraft], *f.* (—, *no pl.*) centrifugal force; (*mental*) resilience.

Schwungrad [ˈʃvuŋraːt], *n.* (—s, *pl.* ·̈er) fly-wheel.

schwungvoll [ˈʃvuŋfɔl], *adj.* spirited.

Schwur [ʃvuːr], *m.* (—(e)s, *pl.* ·̈e) oath.

Schwurgericht [ˈʃvuːrgərɪçt], *n.* (—s, *pl.* —e) (*Law*) assizes.

sechs [zɛks], *num. adj.* six.

Sechseck [ˈzɛksɛk], *n.* (—s, *pl.* —e) hexagon.

sechseckig [ˈzɛksɛkɪç], *adj.* hexagonal.

Sechser ['zɛksər], *m.* (—s, *pl.* —) coin of small value.

sechsspännig ['zɛksʃpɛnɪç], *adj.* drawn by six horses.

sechzehn ['zɛçtseːn], *num. adj.* sixteen.

sechzig ['zɛçtsɪç], *num. adj.* sixty.

Sediment [zedi'mɛnt], *n.* (—s, *pl.* —e) sediment.

See (1) [zeː], *m.* (—s, *pl.* —n) lake, pool.

See (2) [zeː], *f.* (—, *no pl.*) sea, ocean; *hohe* —, high seas; *zur* — *gehen*, go to sea, become a sailor.

Seeadler ['zeːadlər], *m.* (—s, *pl.* —) (*Orn.*) osprey.

Seebad ['zeːbaːt], *n.* (—s, *pl.* ⁓er) seaside resort; bathe in the sea.

Seebär ['zeːbɛːr], *m.* (—en, *pl.* —en) (*fig.*) old salt.

Seefahrer ['zeːfaːrər], *m.* (—s, *pl.* —) mariner, navigator.

Seefahrt ['zeːfaːrt], *f.* (—, *pl.* —en) seafaring; voyage, cruise.

seefest ['zeːfɛst], *adj.* (*ship*) seaworthy; (*person*) a good sailor.

Seefischerei ['zeːfɪʃəraɪ], *f.* (—, *no pl.*) deep-sea fishing.

Seeflotte ['zeːflɔtə], *f.* (—, *pl.* —n) navy, fleet.

Seegang ['zeːgaŋ], *m.* (—s, *no pl.*) swell.

Seegras ['zeːgraːs], *n.* (—es, *no pl.*) seaweed.

Seehandel ['zeːhandəl], *m.* (—s, *no pl.*) maritime trade.

Seehund ['zeːhunt], *m.* (—s, *pl.* —e) (*Zool.*) seal.

Seeigel ['zeːiːgəl], *m.* (—s, *pl.* —) (*Zool.*) sea-urchin.

Seejungfrau ['zeːjuŋfrau], *f.* (—, *pl.* —en) mermaid.

Seekadett ['zeːkadɛt], *m.* (—en, *pl.* —en) midshipman; (naval) cadet.

Seekarte ['zeːkartə], *f.* (—, *pl.* —n) chart.

seekrank ['zeːkraŋk], *adj.* seasick.

Seekrieg ['zeːkriːk], *m.* (—s, *pl.* —e) naval war.

Seeküste ['zeːkystə], *f.* (—, *pl.* —n) sea-coast, shore, beach.

Seele ['zeːlə], *f.* (—, *pl.* —n) soul; *mit ganzer* —, with all my heart.

Seelenamt ['zeːlənamt], *n.* (—s, *pl.* ⁓er) (*Eccl.*) office for the dead, requiem.

Seelenangst ['zeːlənaŋkst], *f.* (—, *pl.* ⁓e) anguish, agony.

Seelenheil ['zeːlənhaɪl], *n.* (—s, *no pl.*) (*Theol.*) salvation.

Seelenhirt ['zeːlənhɪrt], *m.* (—en, *pl.* —en) pastor.

seelenlos ['zeːlənloːs], *adj.* inanimate.

Seelenmesse ['zeːlənmɛsə], *f.* (—, *pl.* —n) requiem; Mass for the dead.

Seelenruhe ['zeːlənruːə], *f.* (—, *no pl.*) tranquillity of mind.

seelenruhig ['zeːlənruːɪç], *adj.* cool, calm, collected, unperturbed.

Seelenstärke ['zeːlənʃtɛrkə], *f.* (—, *no pl.*) fortitude; composure.

seelenvergnügt ['zeːlənfɛrgnyːkt], *adj.* blissfully happy.

Seelenverwandtschaft ['zeːlənfɛrvantʃaft], *f.* (—, *pl.* —en) mental affinity, (mutual) understanding.

seelenvoll ['zeːlənfɔl], *adj.* wistful, soulful.

Seelenwanderung ['zeːlənvandəruŋ], *f.* (—, *no pl.*) transmigration of souls, metempsychosis.

Seeleute ['zeːlɔytə] *see under* **Seemann.**

seelisch ['zeːlɪʃ], *adj.* mental, psychological, psychic(al).

Seelsorge ['zeːlzɔrgə], *f.* (—, *no pl.*) (*Eccl.*) cure of souls; pastoral duties or work.

Seemann ['zeːman], *m.* (—s, *pl.* ⁓er, **Seeleute**) seaman, sailor, mariner.

Seemeile ['zeːmaɪlə], *f.* (—, *pl.* —n) knot, nautical mile.

Seemöwe ['zeːmøːvə], *f.* (—, *pl.* —n) (*Orn.*) seagull.

Seemuschel ['zeːmuʃəl], *f.* (—, *pl.* —n) sea-shell.

Seepflanze ['zeːpflantsə], *f.* (—, *pl.* —n) marine plant.

Seerabe ['zeːraːbə], *m.* (—n, *pl.* —n) (*Orn.*) cormorant.

Seeräuber ['zeːrɔybər], *m.* (—s, *pl.* —) pirate.

Seerose ['zeːroːzə], *f.* (—, *pl.* —n) (*Bot.*) water-lily.

Seesalz ['zeːzalts], *n.* (—es, *no pl.*) bay salt, sea salt.

Seeschlacht ['zeːʃlaxt], *f.* (—, *pl.* —en) naval engagement, naval battle.

Seestern ['zeːʃtɛrn], *m.* (—s, *pl.* —e) (*Zool.*) starfish.

Seestille ['zeːʃtɪlə], *f.* (—, *no pl.*) calm (at sea).

Seetang ['zeːtaŋ], *m.* (—s, *no pl.*) (*Bot.*) seaweed.

seetüchtig ['zeːtyçtɪç], *adj.* seaworthy.

Seeuhr ['zeːuːr], *f.* (—, *pl.* —en) marine chronometer.

Seeuntüchtigkeit ['zeːuntyçtɪçkaɪt], *f.* (—, *no pl.*) unseaworthiness.

Seewasser ['zeːvasər], *n.* (—s, *no pl.*) sea-water, brine.

Seewesen ['zeːvezən], *n.* (—s, *no pl.*) naval affairs.

Seezunge ['zeːtsuŋə], *f.* (—, *pl.* —n) sole (*fish*).

Segel ['zeːgəl], *n.* (—s, *pl.* —) sail; *großes* —, mainsail; *unter* — *gehen*, set sail, put to sea; *die* — *streichen*, strike sail.

segelfertig ['zeːgəlfɛrtɪç], *adj.* ready to sail; *sich* — *machen*, get under sail.

Segelflugzeug ['zeːgəlfluːktsɔyk], *n.* (—s, *pl.* —e) glider(-plane).

Segelschiff ['zeːgəlʃɪf], *n.* (—s, *pl.* —e) sailing-vessel.

Segelstange ['zeːgəlʃtaŋə], *f.* (—, *pl.* —n) sail-yard.

Segen ['zeːgən], *m.* (—s, *no pl.*) blessing, benediction; (*fig.*) abundance; — *sprechen*, give the blessing, say grace.

segensreich ['ze:gənsraɪç], *adj.* blessed, full of blessings; prosperous.

Segenswunsch ['ze:gənsvunʃ], *m.* (—es, *pl.* ⁓e) good wish.

segnen ['ze:gnən], *v.a.* bless.

sehen ['ze:ən], *v.a. irr.* see, behold, perceive; *etwas gern* —, like s.th., approve of s.th. — *v.n.* look, see; *sich* — *lassen,* parade, show o.s., *wir werden* —, that remains to be seen, we shall see.

sehenswert ['ze:ənsve:rt], *adj.* worth seeing.

Sehenswürdigkeit ['ze:ənsvyrdɪçkaɪt], *f.* (—, *pl.* —en) curiosity, object of interest, tourist attraction; (*pl.*) sights.

Seher ['ze:ər], *m.* (—s, *pl.* —) seer, prophet.

Sehne ['ze:nə], *f.* (—, *pl.* —n) sinew, tendon; string.

sehnig ['ze:nɪç], *adj.* sinewy, muscular; (*meat*) tough.

sehnlich ['ze:nlɪç], *adj.* earnest, passionate, eager.

Sehnsucht ['ze:nzuxt], *f.* (—, *no pl.*) longing, yearning, desire.

sehr [ze:r], *adv.* very, much, greatly, very much; *zu* —, too much; — *gut,* very good; — *wohl,* very well.

Sehweite ['ze:vaɪtə], *f.* (—, *no pl.*) range of vision.

seicht [zaɪçt], *adj.* shallow, superficial.

Seide ['zaɪdə], *f.* (—, *pl.* —n) silk.

Seidel ['zaɪdəl], *n.* (—s, *pl.* —) (*dial.*) mug, tankard; pint.

seiden ['zaɪdən], *adj.* silk, silken, silky.

Seidenpapier ['zaɪdənpapi:r], *n.* (—s, *no pl.*) tissue-paper.

Seidenraupe ['zaɪdənraupə], *f.* (—, *pl.* —n) (*Ent.*) silkworm.

Seidenstoff ['zaɪdənʃtɔf], *m.* (—es, *pl.* —e) spun silk.

Seife ['zaɪfə], *f.* (—, *pl.* —n) soap; *ein Stück* —, a cake of soap.

seifen ['zaɪfən], *v.a.* soap.

Seifenschaum ['zaɪfənʃaum], *m.* (—s, *no pl.*) lather.

Seifenwasser ['zaɪfənvasər], *n.* (—s, *no pl.*) soap-suds.

seifig ['zaɪfɪç], *adj.* soapy, saponaceous.

seihen ['zaɪən], *v.a.* strain, filter.

Seil [zaɪl], *n.* (—(e)s, *pl.* —e) rope; *straffes* —, taut rope, tight rope; *schlaffes* —, slack rope.

Seilbahn ['zaɪlba:n], *f.* (—, *pl.* —en) funicular railway; cable car.

Seilbrücke ['zaɪlbrykə], *f.* (—, *pl.* —n) rope bridge.

Seiltänzer ['zaɪltɛntsər], *m.* (—s, *pl.* —) tight-rope walker.

Seilziehen ['zaɪltsi:ən], *n.* (—s, *no pl.*) tug of war.

Seim [zaɪm], *m.* (—(e)s, *pl.* —e) strained honey.

Sein [zaɪn], *n.* (—s, *no pl.*) being, existence.

sein (1) [zaɪn], *v.n. irr.* (*aux.* sein) be, exist.

sein (2) [zaɪn], *poss. adj.* his, her, its; one's. — *pers. pron.* his.

seinerseits ['zaɪnərzaɪts], *adv.* for his part.

seinerzeit ['zaɪnərtsaɪt], *adv.* at that time, at the time, formerly.

seinesgleichen ['zaɪnəsglaɪçən], *indecl. adj. & pron.* of his sort, such as he.

seinethalben ['zaɪnəthalbən], *adv.* on his account, for his sake, on his behalf.

seinetwegen ['zaɪnətve:gən], *adv.* on his account, for his sake, on his behalf.

Seinige ['zaɪnɪgə], *n.* (—n, *pl.* —n) his, his property; (*pl.*) his family, his people; *das* — *tun,* do o.'s share.

seit [zaɪt], *prep.* (*Dat.*) since, for; — *gestern,* since yesterday, from yesterday onwards; — *einiger Zeit,* for some time past. — *conj. see* **seitdem**.

seitdem [zaɪt'de:m], *adv.* since then, since that time. — *conj.* since.

Seite ['zaɪtə], *f.* (—, *pl.* —n) side, flank; (*book*) page; *etwas auf die* — *bringen,* put s.th. aside; *ich bin auf seiner* —, I side with him, I am on his side; *er hat seine guten* —n, he has his good points.

Seitenansicht ['zaɪtənanzɪçt], *f.* (—, *pl.* —en) profile.

Seitengleis ['zaɪtənglaɪs], *n.* (—es, *pl.* ⁓e) (railway) siding.

Seitenhieb ['zaɪtənhi:p], *m.* (—s, *pl.* —e) innuendo, sly hit, dig.

seitens ['zaɪtəns], *prep.* (*Genit.*) on the part of.

Seitensprung ['zaɪtənʃpruŋ], *m.* (—s, *pl.* ⁓e) side-leap, caper; (*fig.*) (amorous) escapade.

Seitenstraße ['zaɪtənʃtra:sə], *f.* (—, *pl.* —n) side-street.

Seitenstück ['zaɪtənʃtyk], *n.* (—s, *pl.* —e) companion-piece.

Seitenzahl ['zaɪtəntsa:l], *f.* (—, *pl.* —en) page-number; number of pages.

seither [zaɪ'the:r], *adv.* since that time, since then.

seitlich ['zaɪtlɪç], *adj.* lateral.

Sekretär [zekre'tɛ:r], *m.* (—s, *pl.* —e) secretary.

Sekretariat [zekreta'rja:t], *n.* (—s, *pl.* —e) secretariat, secretary's office.

Sekt [zɛkt], *m.* (—s, *pl.* —e) champagne.

Sekte ['zɛktə], *f.* (—, *pl.* —n) sect.

Sektierer [zɛk'ti:rər], *m.* (—s, *pl.* —) sectarian.

Sektion [zɛk'tsjo:n] *f.* (—, *pl.* —en) section; (*Med.*) dissection.

Sekundaner [zekun'da:nər], *m.* (—s, *pl.* —) pupil in the second (highest) form.

Sekundant [zekun'dant], *m.* (—en, *pl.* —en) (*Duelling*) second.

sekundär [zekun'dɛ:r], *adj.* secondary.

Sekunde [ze'kundə], *f.* (—, *pl.* —n) (*time*) second.

Sekundenzeiger [ze'kundəntsaɪgər], *m.* (—s, *pl.* —) (*clock*) second-hand.

sekundieren [zekun'di:rən], *v.n. einem* —, second s.o.

selber ['zɛlbər], *indecl. adj. & pron.* self.

selb(ig) ['zɛlb(ɪg)], *adj.* the same.

selbst [zɛlpst], *indecl. adj. & pron.* self; — *ist der Mann,* depend on yourself; *von* —, of its own accord, spontaneously. — *adv.* even; — *wenn,* even if, even though; — *dann nicht,* not even then.

selbständig ['zɛlpʃtɛndɪç], *adj.* independent.

Selbstbestimmung ['zɛlpstbəʃtɪmuŋ], *f.* (—, *no pl.*) self-determination, autonomy.

selbstbewußt ['zɛlpstbəvust], *adj.* self-assertive, self-confident, conceited.

selbstherrlich ['zɛlpsthɛrlɪç], *adj.* autocratic, tyrannical.

Selbstlaut ['zɛlpstlaut], *m.* (—s, *pl.* —e) vowel.

selbstlos ['zɛlpstlo:s], *adj.* unselfish, selfless, altruistic.

Selbstlosigkeit [zɛlpst'lo:zɪçkaɪt], *f.* (—, *no pl.*) unselfishness, altruism.

Selbstmord ['zɛlpstmɔrt], *m.* (—s, *pl.* —e) suicide.

selbstredend ['zɛlpstre:dənt], *adj.* self-evident, obvious.

Selbstsucht ['zɛlpstzuxt], *f.* (—, *no pl.*) selfishness, ego(t)ism.

selbstsüchtig ['zɛlpstzyçtɪç], *adj.* selfish, ego(t)istic(al).

selbstverständlich ['zɛlpstfɛrʃtɛntlɪç], *adj.* self-evident. — *adv.* of course, obviously.

Selbstzweck ['zɛlpstsvɛk], *m.* (—s, *no pl.*) end in itself.

selig ['ze:lɪç], *adj.* blessed, blissful; (*fig.*) delighted; deceased, late; — *sprechen,* beatify.

Seligkeit ['ze:lɪçkaɪt], *f.* (—, *pl.* —en) bliss, blissfulness; (*Eccl.*) salvation, beatitude.

Seligsprechung ['ze:lɪçʃprɛçuŋ], *f.* (—, *pl.* —en) beatification.

Sellerie ['zɛləri:], *m.* (—s, *pl.* —s) (*Bot.*) celery.

selten ['zɛltən], *adj.* rare, scarce; (*fig.*) remarkable. — *adv.* seldom, rarely, infrequently.

Seltenheit ['zɛltənhaɪt], *f.* (—, *pl.* —en) rarity, curiosity, scarcity; (*fig.*) remarkableness.

Selterwasser ['zɛltərvasər], *n.* (—s, *no pl.*) soda-water.

seltsam ['zɛltza:m], *adj.* strange, unusual, odd, curious.

Semester [ze'mɛstər], *n.* (—s, *pl.* —) university term, semester.

Semit [ze'mi:t], *m.* (—en, *pl.* —en) Semite, Jew.

semmelblond ['zɛməlblɔnt], *adj.* flaxen-haired.

Semmelkloß ['zɛməlklo:s], *m.* (—es, *pl.* ⁀e) bread dumpling.

Senator [ze'na:tɔr], *m.* (—s, *pl.* —en) senator.

senden ['zɛndən], *v.a. irr.* send, despatch; (*money*) remit. — *v.a. reg.* (*Rad.*) broadcast.

Sender ['zɛndər], *m.* (—s, *pl.* —) sender; (*Rad.*) (broadcasting) station, transmitter.

Sendling ['zɛntlɪŋ], *m.* (—s, *pl.* —e) (*Poet.*) emissary.

Sendschreiben ['zɛntʃraɪbən], *n.* (—s, *pl.* —) epistle, missive.

Sendung ['zɛnduŋ], *f.* (—, *pl.* —en) (*Comm.*) shipment, consignment; (*fig.*) mission; (*Rad.*) broadcast, transmission.

Senegal ['ze:nəgal], *n.* Senegal.

Senf [zɛnf], *m.* (—s, *no pl.*) mustard.

sengen ['zɛŋən], *v.a.* singe, scorch; — *und brennen,* lay waste.

Senkblei ['zɛŋkblaɪ], *n.* (—s, *pl.* —e) plummet.

Senkel ['zɛŋkəl], *m.* (—s, *pl.* —) shoe-lace.

senken ['zɛŋkən], *v.a.* lower, sink. — *v.r. sich* —, sink, go down; dip, slope, subside.

senkrecht ['zɛŋkrɛçt], *adj.* perpendicular.

Senkung ['zɛŋkuŋ], *f.* (—, *pl.* —en) depression, dip, subsidence.

Senn(e) ['zɛn(ə)], *m.* (—n, *pl.* —(e)n) Alpine herdsman.

Sennerin ['zɛnərɪn], *f.* (—, *pl.* —nen) Alpine dairy-woman.

Senneschoten ['zɛnəʃo:tən], *f. pl.* senna pods.

Sennhütte ['zɛnhytə], *f.* (—, *pl.* —n) Alpine dairy; chalet.

sensationell [zɛnzatsjo'nɛl], *adj.* sensational.

Sense ['zɛnzə], *f.* (—, *pl.* —n) scythe.

sensibel [zɛn'zi:bəl], *adj.* sensitive.

Sentenz [zɛn'tɛnts], *f.* (—, *pl.* —en) aphorism.

sentimental [zɛntimɛn'ta:l], *adj.* sentimental.

separat [zepa'ra:t], *adj.* separate, special.

September [zɛp'tɛmbər], *m.* (—s, *pl.* —) September.

Serbien ['zɛrbjən], *n.* Serbia.

Serie ['ze:rjə], *f.* (—, *pl.* —n) series.

Service [zɛr'vi:s], *n.* (—s, *pl.* —) dinner-set, dinner-service.

servieren [zɛr'vi:rən], *v.a., v.n.* serve, wait at table.

Serviertisch [zɛr'vi:rtɪʃ], *m.* (—es, *pl.* —e) sideboard.

Sessel ['zɛsəl], *m.* (—s, *pl.* —) armchair, easy-chair; (*Austr. dial.*) chair.

seßhaft ['zɛshaft], *adj.* settled, domiciled.

setzen ['zɛtsən], *v.a.* set, put, place; (*monument*) erect; (*bet*) stake; (*Typ.*) compose. — *v.r. sich* —, sit down; (*coffee*) settle; *sich bei einem in Gunst* —, ingratiate o.s. with s.o.

Setzer ['zɛtsər], *m.* (—s, *pl.* —) compositor.

Setzling ['zɛtslɪŋ], *m.* (—s, *pl.* —e) young tree, young plant.

Seuche ['zɔʏçə], *f.* (—, *pl.* —n) pestilence; epidemic.

seufzen ['zɔʏftsən], *v.n.* sigh.

Seufzer ['zɔʏftsər], *m.* (—s, *pl.* —) sigh.

Sexta ['zɛksta:], *f.* (—, *pl.* —s) (*Sch.*) sixth form, lowest form.

Sextant [zɛks'tant], *m.* (—en, *pl.* —en) sextant.

sexuell [zɛksu'ɛl], *adj.* sexual.

sezieren [ze'tsi:rən], *v.a.* dissect.

Seziersaal [ze'tsi:rza:l], *m.* (—s, *pl.* —säle) dissecting-room.

Sibirien [zi'bi:rjən], *n.* Siberia.

sich [zɪç], *pron.* oneself, himself, herself, itself, themselves; each other.

Sichel ['zɪçəl], *f.* (—, *pl.* —n) sickle.

sicher ['zɪçər], *adj.* certain, sure, secure, safe; confident, positive; *seiner Sache — sein,* be sure of o.'s ground; — *stellen,* secure.

Sicherheit ['zɪçərhaɪt], *f.* (—, *pl.* —en) certainty; security, safety; confidence, positiveness; *in — bringen,* secure.

sichern ['zɪçərn], *v.a.* secure, make secure; assure, ensure.

Sicherung ['zɪçəruŋ], *f.* (—, *pl.* —en) securing; (*Elec.*) fuse; (*gun*) safety-catch.

Sicht [zɪçt], *f.* (—, *no pl.*) sight.

sichtbar ['zɪçtba:r], *adj.* visible; conspicuous.

sichten ['zɪçtən], *v.a.* sift, sort out; sight.

sichtlich ['zɪçtlɪç], *adv.* visibly.

Sichtwechsel ['zɪçtvɛksəl], *m.* (—s, *pl.* —) (*Banking*) sight-bill, bill payable on sight.

Sichtweite ['zɪçtvaɪtə], *f.* (—, *no pl.*) range of vision.

sickern ['zɪkərn], *v.n.* (*aux.* sein) leak, ooze, seep.

Sie [zi:], *pron.* (*formal*) you.

sie [zi:], *pers. pron.* she, her; they, them.

Sieb [zi:p], *n.* (—(e)s, *pl.* —e) sieve; riddle; colander.

sieben (1) ['zi:bən], *v.a.* (*Cul.*) sift, strain.

sieben (2) ['zi:bən], *num. adj.* seven; *meine — Sachen,* my belongings.

Siebeneck ['zi:bɛnɛk], *n.* (—s, *pl.* —e) heptagon.

Siebengestirn ['zi:bəŋgəʃtɪrn], *n.* (—s, *no pl.*) Pleiades.

siebenmal ['zi:bənma:l], *adv.* seven times.

Siebenmeilenstiefel [zi:bən'maɪlənʃti:fəl], *m. pl.* seven-league boots.

Siebenschläfer ['zi:bənʃle:fər], *m.* (—s, *pl.* —) lazy-bones.

siebzehn ['zi:ptse:n], *num. adj.* seventeen.

siebzig ['zi:ptsɪç], *num. adj.* seventy.

siech [zi:ç], *adj.* (*rare*) sick, infirm.

siechen ['zi:çən], *v.n.* be in bad health.

sieden ['zi:dən], *v.a., v.n.* boil, seethe.

siedeln ['zi:dəln], *v.n.* settle.

Siedlung ['zi:dluŋ], *f.* (—, *pl.* —en) settlement; housing estate.

Sieg [zi:k], *m.* (—(e)s, *pl.* —e) victory; *den — davontragen,* win the day.

Siegel ['zi:gəl], *m.* (—s, *pl.* —) seal; *Brief und —,* sign and seal.

Siegelbewahrer ['zi:gəlbəva:rər], *m.* (—s, *pl.* —) Lord Privy Seal; keeper of the seal.

Siegellack ['zi:gəllak], *n.* (—s, *no pl.*) sealing wax.

siegeln ['zi:gəln], *v.n.* seal.

siegen ['zi:gən], *v.n.* conquer, win, be victorious, triumph (over).

Sieger ['zi:gər], *m.* (—s, *pl.* —) victor, conqueror.

Siegesbogen ['zi:gəsbo:gən], *m.* (—s, *pl.* ⸚) triumphal arch.

Siegeszeichen ['zi:gəstsaɪçən], *n.* (—s, *pl.* —) sign of victory, trophy.

sieghaft ['zi:khaft], *adj.* victorious, triumphant.

siegreich ['zi:kraɪç], *adj.* victorious, triumphant.

siehe! ['zi:ə], *excl.* see! look! lo and behold!

Sierra Leone ['siɛra le'o:nə], *f.* Sierra Leone.

Signal [zɪg'na:l], *n.* (—s, *pl.* —e) signal.

Signalement [zɪgnalə'mã], *n.* (—s, *pl.* —s) personal description.

Signalglocke ['zɪg'na:lglɔkə], *f.* (—, *pl.* —n) warning-bell.

signalisieren [zɪgnali'zi:rən], *v.a.* signal.

Signatarmacht [zɪgna'ta:rmaxt], *f.* (—, *pl.* ⸚e) signatory power.

signieren [zɪg'ni:rən], *v.a.* sign.

Silbe ['zɪlbə], *f.* (—, *pl.* —n) syllable.

Silbenmaß ['zɪlbənma:s], *n.* (—es, *pl.* —e) (*Poet.*) metre.

Silbenrätsel ['zɪlbənrɛ:tsəl], *n.* (—s, *pl.* —) charade.

Silber ['zɪlbər], *n.* (—s, *no pl.*) silver; plate.

Silberbuche ['zɪlbərbu:xə], *f.* (—, *pl.* —n) white beech(-tree).

Silberfuchs ['zɪlbərfuks], *m.* (—es, *pl.* ⸚e) (*Zool.*) silver fox.

silbern ['zɪlbərn], *adj.* made of silver, silvery.

Silberpappel ['zɪlbərpapəl], *f.* (—, *pl.* —n) (*Bot.*) white poplar(-tree).

Silberschimmel ['zɪlbərʃiməl], *m.* (—s, *pl.* —) grey-white horse.

Silberzeug ['zɪlbərtsɔyk], *n.* (—s, *no pl.*) (silver) plate.

Silvester [zɪl'vɛstər], *m.* (—s, *pl.* —) New Year's Eve.

Similistein ['zi:miliʃtaɪn], *m.* (—s, *pl.* —e) imitation *or* paste jewellery.

Sims [zɪms], *m.* (—es, *pl.* —e) cornice, moulding, shelf, ledge.

Simulant [zimu'lant], *m.* (—en, *pl.* —en) malingerer.

simulieren [zimu'li:rən], *v.a.* simulate.

simultan [zimul'ta:n], *adj.* simultaneous.

Singapur [zɪŋga'pu:r], *n.* Singapore.

Singdrossel ['zɪŋdrɔsəl], *f.* (—, *pl.* —n) (*Orn.*) common thrush.

singen ['zɪŋən], *v.a., v.n. irr.* sing.

Singspiel ['zɪŋʃpi:l], *n.* (—s, *pl.* —e) musical comedy, light opera, opera buffa.

Singular ['zɪŋgula:r], *m.* (—s, *pl.* —e) singular.

sinken ['zɪŋkən], *v.n. irr.* (*aux.* sein) sink; (*price*) decline, drop, fall; *den Mut — lassen,* lose heart.

Sinn [zɪn], *m.* (—(e)s, *pl.* —e) sense; intellect, mind; consciousness, memory; taste, meaning, purport; wish; *etwas im — haben,* have s.th. in mind, intend s.th.; *leichter —,* lightheartedness; *andern —es werden,* change o's mind; *das hat keinen —,* there is no sense in that; *von —en sein,* be out of o.'s senses; *seine fünf —e beisammen haben,* be in o.'s right mind; *sich etwas aus dem — schlagen,* dismiss s.th. from o.'s mind; *es kommt mir in den —,* it occurs to me.

Sinnbild ['zɪnbɪlt], *n.* (—s, *pl.* —er) symbol, emblem.

sinnen ['zɪnən], *v.n. irr.* meditate, reflect.

Sinnesänderung ['zɪnəsɛndərʊŋ], *f.* (—, *pl.* —en) change of mind.

Sinnesart ['zɪnəsaːrt], *f.* (—, *no pl.*) disposition, character.

Sinnesorgan ['zɪnəsɔrgaːn], *n.* (—s, *pl.* —e) sense-organ.

Sinnestäuschung ['zɪnəstɔyʃʊŋ], *f.* (—, *pl.* —en) illusion, hallucination.

sinnfällig ['zɪnfɛlɪç], *adj.* obvious, striking.

Sinngedicht ['zɪngədɪçt], *n.* (—es, *pl.* —e) epigram.

sinnig ['zɪnɪç], *adj.* thoughtful, meaningful; judicious, fitting.

sinnlich ['zɪnlɪç], *adj.* sensual, sensuous.

Sinnlichkeit ['zɪnlɪçkaɪt], *f.* (—, *no pl.*) sensuality, sensuousness.

sinnlos ['zɪnloːs], *adj.* senseless, meaningless, pointless.

sinnreich ['zɪnraɪç], *adj.* ingenious.

Sinnspruch ['zɪnʃprux], *m.* (—es, *pl.* ⁻e) sentence, maxim, device, motto.

sinnverwandt ['zɪnfɛrvant], *adj.* synonymous.

sinnvoll ['zɪnfɔl], *adj.* meaningful, significant.

sinnwidrig ['zɪnviːdrɪç], *adj.* nonsensical, absurd.

Sintflut ['zɪntfluːt], *f.* (—, *no pl.*) (*Bibl.*) the Flood.

Sinus ['ziːnus], *m.* (—, *pl.* —se) (*Maths.*) sine.

Sippe ['zɪpə], *f.* (—, *pl.* —n) kin, tribe, family, clan.

Sippschaft ['zɪpʃaft], *f.* (—, *pl.* —en) kindred; *die ganze —,* the whole caboodle.

Sirene [ziˈreːnə], *f.* (—, *pl.* —n) siren.

Sirup ['ziːrup], *m.* (—s, *no pl.*) syrup, treacle.

Sitte ['zɪtə], *f.* (—, *pl.* —n) custom, mode, fashion; (*pl.*) manners, morals; *—n und Gebräuche,* manners and customs.

Sittengesetz ['zɪtəngəzɛts], *n.* (—es, *pl.* —e) moral law.

Sittenlehre ['zɪtənleːrə], *f.* (—, *no pl.*) moral philosophy, ethics.

sittenlos ['zɪtənloːs], *adj.* immoral, profligate, licentious.

Sittenprediger ['zɪtənpreːdɪgər], *m.* (—s, *pl.* —) moraliser.

Sittich ['zɪtɪç], *m.* (—s, *pl.* —e) (*Orn.*) budgerigar; parakeet.

sittig ['zɪtɪç], *adj.* well-behaved.

sittlich ['zɪtlɪç], *adj.* moral.

Sittlichkeit ['zɪtlɪçkaɪt], *f.* (—, *no pl.*) morality, morals.

sittsam ['zɪtzaːm], *adj.* modest, demure.

situiert [zituˈiːrt], *adj. gut* (*schlecht*) —, well (badly) off.

Sitz [zɪts], *m.* (—es, *pl.* —e) seat, chair; residence, location, place; (*Eccl.*) see.

Sitzarbeit ['zɪtsarbaɪt], *f.* (—, *pl.* —en) sedentary work.

Sitzbad ['zɪtsbaːt], *n.* (—(e)s, *pl.* ⁻er) hip bath.

sitzen ['zɪtsən], *v.n. irr.* sit, be seated; (*fig.*) be in prison; (*dress*) fit; *— lassen,* throw over, jilt; *— bleiben,* remain seated; (*school*) stay in the same class, not be moved up; be a wallflower; remain unmarried.

Sitzfleisch ['zɪtsflaɪʃ], *n.* (—es, *no pl.*) (*coll.*) *kein — haben,* be restless, lack application.

Sitzplatz ['zɪtsplats], *m.* (—es, *pl.* ⁻e) seat.

Sitzung ['zɪtsuŋ], *f.* (—, *pl.* —en) meeting, sitting, session.

Sitzungsprotokoll ['zɪtsuŋsprotokɔl], *n.* (—s, *pl.* —e) minutes (of a meeting).

Sitzungssaal ['zɪtsunszaːl], *m.* (—s, *pl.* —säle) board-room, conference room.

Sizilien [ziˈtsiːljən], *n.* Sicily.

Skala ['skaːla], *f.* (—, *pl.* —len) scale; (*Mus.*) gamut.

Skandal [skanˈdaːl], *m.* (—s, *pl.* —e) scandal; row, riot; *— machen,* kick up a row.

skandalös [skandaˈløːs], *adj.* scandalous.

skandieren [skanˈdiːrən], *v.a.* (*Poet.*) scan.

Skandinavien [skandiˈnaːvjən], *n.* Scandinavia.

Skelett [skeˈlɛt], *n.* (—s, *pl.* —e) skeleton.

Skepsis ['skɛpzɪs], *f.* (—, *no pl.*) scepticism, doubt.

skeptisch ['skɛptɪʃ], *adj.* sceptical, doubtful.

Skizze ['skɪtsə], *f.* (—, *pl.* —n) sketch.

skizzieren [skɪˈtsiːrən], *v.a.* sketch.

Sklave ['sklaːvə], *m.* (—n, *pl.* —n) slave; *zum —n machen,* enslave.

Sklavendienst ['sklaːvəndiːnst], *m.* (—es, *no pl.*) slavery.

Sklaverei [sklaːvəˈraɪ], *f.* (—, *no pl.*) slavery, thraldom.

Skonto ['skɔnto], *m. & n.* (—s, *pl.* —s) discount.

Skrupel ['skruːpəl], *m.* (—s, *pl.* —) scruple; *sich — machen,* have scruples.

skrupulös [skrupuˈløːs], *adj.* scrupulous, meticulous.

Skulptur [skulp'tu:r], *f.* (—, *pl.* —en) sculpture.

skurril [sku'ri:l], *adj.* ludicrous.

Slawe ['sla:və], *m.* (—n, *pl.* —n) Slav.

slawisch ['sla:vɪʃ], *adj.* Slav, Slavonic.

Slowake [slo'va:kə], *m.* (—n, *pl.* —n) Slovakian.

Slowene [slo've:nə], *m.* (—n, *pl.* —n) Slovenian.

Smaragd [sma'rakt], *m.* (—(e)s, *pl.* —e) emerald.

smaragden [sma'raktən], *adj.* emerald.

Smoking ['smo:kɪŋ], *m.* (—s, *pl.* —s) dinner-jacket.

so [zo:], *adv.* so, thus, in this way, like this; — ? really? — *ist es*, that is how it is; — *daß*, so that; — ... *wie*, as ... as; *na — was!* well, I never! — *conj.* then, therefore.

sobald [zo'balt], *conj.* as soon as, directly.

Socke ['zɔkə], *f.* (—, *pl.* —n) sock.

Sockel ['zɔkəl], *m.* (—s, *pl.* —) pedestal, plinth, stand, base.

Soda ['zo:da], *n.* (—s, *no pl.*) (carbonate of) soda.

sodann [zo'dan], *adv. conj.* then.

Sodbrennen ['zo:tbrɛnən], *n.* (—s, *no pl.*) heartburn.

soeben [zo'e:bən], *adv.* just now.

sofern [zo'fɛrn], *conj.* if, in case, so far as.

sofort [zo'fɔrt], *adv.* at once, immediately.

Sog [zo:k], *m.* (—(e)s, *pl.* —e) undertow, suction.

sogar [zo'ga:r], *adv.* even.

sogenannt [zogə'nant], *adj.* so-called, would-be.

sogleich [zo'glaɪç], *adv.* at once, immediately.

Sohle ['zo:lə], *f.* (—, *pl.* —n) sole; (*mine*) floor.

Sohn [zo:n], *m.* (—(e)s, *pl.* ⸚e) son; *der verlorene —*, the prodigal son.

solange [zo'laŋə], *conj.* as long as.

Solbad [zo:lba:t], *n.* (—s, *pl.* ⸚er) saline bath.

solch [zɔlç], *adj., dem. pron.* such.

solcherlei ['zɔlçərlaɪ], *adj.* of such a kind, suchlike.

Sold [zɔlt], *m.* (—(e)s, *no pl.*) army pay.

Soldat [zɔl'da:t], *m.* (—en, *pl.* —en) soldier.

Soldateska [zɔlda'teska], *f.* (—, *pl.* —s) soldiery.

Söldner ['zœldnər], *m.* (—s, *pl.* —) mercenary, hireling.

Sole ['zo:lə], *f.* (—, *pl.* —n) salt-water, brine.

Solei ['zo:laɪ], *n.* (—s, *pl.* —er) pickled egg.

solidarisch [zoli'da:rɪʃ], *adj.* joint, jointly responsible; unanimous.

Solidarität [zolidari'tɛ:t], *f.* (—, *no pl.*) solidarity.

Solist [zo'lɪst], *m.* (—en, *pl.* —en) soloist.

Soll [zɔl], *n.* (—s, *no pl.*) debit; — *und Haben*, debit and credit.

sollen ['zɔlən], *v.n. irr.* be obliged, be compelled; have to; be supposed to; (*aux.*) shall, should etc.; *ich soll*, I must, I am to; *er soll krank sein*, he is said to be ill; *ich sollte eigentlich*, I really ought to.

Söller ['zœlər], *m.* (—s, *pl.* —) loft, garret, balcony.

Somali [zo'ma:li], *n.* Somalia.

somit [zo'mɪt], *adv.* consequently, therefore, accordingly.

Sommer ['zɔmər], *m.* (—s, *pl.* —) summer.

Sommerfäden ['zɔmərfɛ:dən], *m. pl.* gossamer.

Sommerfrische ['zɔmərfrɪʃə], *f.* (—, *pl.* —n) holiday resort.

Sommergetreide ['zɔmərgətraɪdə], *n.* (—s, *no pl.*) spring corn.

Sommersonnenwende ['zɔmərzɔnənvɛndə], *f.* (—, *pl.* —n) summer solstice.

Sommersprosse ['zɔmərʃprɔsə], *f.* (—, *pl.* —n) freckle.

sonach [zo'na:x], *adv.* therefore, consequently.

Sonate [zo'na:tə], *f.* (—, *pl.* —n) sonata.

Sonde ['zɔndə], *f.* (—, *pl.* —n) sounding-lead, plummet; probe.

sonder ['zɔndər], (*obs.*) *prep.* (*Acc.*) without.

Sonderausgabe ['zɔndərausga:bə], *f.* (—, *pl.* —n) separate edition; special edition.

Sonderausschuß ['zɔndərausʃus], *m.* (—sses, *pl.* ⸚sse) select committee.

sonderbar ['zɔndərba:r], *adj.* strange, odd, queer, singular, peculiar.

sonderlich ['zɔndərlɪç], *adj.* special, especial, particular. — *adv. nicht —*, not much.

Sonderling ['zɔndərlɪŋ], *m.* (—s, *pl.* —e) freak, odd character, crank.

sondern ['zɔndərn], *v.a.* separate, distinguish, differentiate. — *conj.* but; *nicht nur*, ... — *auch*, not only ... but also.

Sonderrecht ['zɔndərrɛçt], *n.* (—s, *pl.* —e) special privilege.

sonders ['zɔndərs], *adv. samt und —*, all and each, all and sundry.

Sonderstellung ['zɔndərʃtɛluŋ], *f.* (—, *no pl.*) exceptional position.

Sonderung ['zɔndəruŋ], *f.* (—, *pl.* —en) separation.

Sonderzug ['zɔndərtsu:k], *m.* (—s, *pl.* ⸚e) special train.

sondieren [zɔn'di:rən], *v.a.* (*wound*) probe; (*ocean*) plumb; (*fig.*) sound.

Sonett [zo'nɛt], *n.* (—(e)s, *pl.* —e) sonnet.

Sonnabend ['zɔna:bənt], *m.* (—s, *pl.* —e) Saturday.

Sonne ['zɔnə], *f.* (—, *pl.* —n) sun.

sonnen ['zɔnən], *v.r. sich —*, sun o.s., bask in the sun, sunbathe.

Sonnenaufgang ['zɔnənaufgaŋ], *m.* (—s, *pl.* ⸚e) sunrise.

Sonnenbrand ['zɔnənbrant], *m.* (—s, *pl.* ⸚e) sunburn.

Sonnendeck ['zɔnəndɛk], *n.* (—s, *pl.* —e) awning.

Sonnenfinsternis ['zɔnənfɪnstərnis], *f.* (—, *pl.* —se) eclipse of the sun.

sonnenklar ['zɔnənklaːr], *adj.* very clear, as clear as daylight.

Sonnenschirm ['zɔnənʃɪrm], *m.* (—s, *pl.* —e) parasol, sunshade.

Sonnenstich ['zɔnənʃtɪç], *n.* (—(e)s, *no pl.*) sunstroke.

Sonnenuhr ['zɔnənuːr], *f.* (—, *pl.* —en) sundial.

Sonnenuntergang ['zɔnənuntərgaŋ], *m.* (—s, *pl.* ⸚e) sunset.

Sonnenwende ['zɔnənvɛndə], *f.* (—, *no pl.*) solstice.

Sonntag ['zɔntaːk], *m.* (—s, *pl.* —e) Sunday.

sonntags ['zɔntaːks], *adv.* on Sundays, of a Sunday.

Sonntagsjäger ['zɔntaːksjɛːgər], *m.* (—s, *pl.* —) amateur sportsman.

sonor [zo'noːr], *adj.* sonorous.

sonst [zɔnst], *adv.* else, otherwise, besides, at other times; — *noch etwas?* anything else?

sonstig ['zɔnstɪç], *adj.* other, existing besides.

sonstwo ['zɔnstvo], *adv.* elsewhere, somewhere else.

Sopran [zo'praːn], *m.* (—s, *pl.* —e) soprano.

Sorbett ['zɔrbɛt], *n.* (—s, *pl.* —e) sherbet.

Sorge ['zɔrgə], *f.* (—, *pl.* —n) care; grief, worry; sorrow; anxiety; concern; (*pl.*) troubles, worries; — *tragen dass* . . . , see to it that . . . ; — *tragen zu,* take care of; — *um,* concern for.

sorgen ['zɔrgən], *v.n.* else, *für,* care for, provide for, look after. — *v.r. sich — um,* worry about.

sorgenvoll ['zɔrgənfɔl], *adj.* uneasy, troubled, anxious.

Sorgfalt ['zɔrkfalt], *f.* (—, *no pl.*) care, attention.

sorgfältig ['zɔrkfɛltɪç], *adj.* careful, painstaking; elaborate.

sorglos ['zɔrkloːs], *adj.* careless, irresponsible, unconcerned, indifferent; carefree.

sorgsam ['zɔrkzaːm], *adj.* careful, heedful.

Sorte ['zɔrtə], *f.* (—, *pl.* —n) sort, kind, species, brand.

sortieren [zɔr'tiːrən], *v.a.* sort (out).

Sortiment [zɔrti'mɛnt], *n.* (—s, *pl.* —e) assortment; bookshop.

Sortimentsbuchhändler [zɔrti'mɛntsbuːxhɛndlər], *m.* (—s, *pl.* —) retail bookseller.

Soße ['zoːsə], *f.* (—, *pl.* —n) sauce, gravy.

Souffleur [suf'løːr], *m.* (—s, *pl.* —e) prompter.

Soutane [su'taːnə], *f.* (—, *pl.* —n) cassock, soutane.

Souterrain [sutɛ'rɛ̃], *n.* (—s, *pl.* —s) basement.

souverän [suːvəˈrɛːn], *adj.* sovereign; (*fig.*) supremely good.

Souveränität [suːvərɛːniˈtɛːt], *f.* (—, *no pl.*) sovereignty.

soviel [zo'fiːl], *adv.* so much; — *wie,* as much as. — *conj.* so far as; — *ich weiß,* as far as I know.

sowie [zo'viː], *conj.* as, as well as, as soon as.

Sowjet [sɔv'jɛt], *m.* (—s, *pl.* —s) Soviet.

sowohl [zo'voːl], *conj.* — *wie,* as well as.

sozial [zo'tsjaːl], *adj.* social.

sozialisieren [zotsjali'ziːrən], *v.a.* nationalis**e**.

Sozialwissenschaft [zo'tsjaːlvɪsənʃaft], *f.* (—, *pl.* —en) sociology; social science.

Sozietät [zotsje'tɛːt], *f.* (—, *pl.* —en) partnership.

Sozius ['zotsjus], *m.* (—s, *pl.* —se, *Socii*) partner; pillion-rider; —*sitz,* (*motor cycle*) pillion (seat).

sozusagen ['zoːtsuːzaːgən], *adv.* as it were, so to speak.

Spagat [ʃpa'gaːt], *m.* (—(e)s, *no pl.*) (*dial.*) string, twine; (*Dancing*) the splits.

spähen ['ʃpɛːən], *v.n.* look out, watch; (*Mil.*) scout; spy.

Späher ['ʃpɛːər], *m.* (—s, *pl.* —) scout; spy.

Spalier [ʃpa'liːr], *n.* (—s, *pl.* —e) trellis; — *bilden,* form a lane (*of people*).

Spalierobst [ʃpa'liːroːpst], *n.* (—(e)s, *no pl.*) wall-fruit.

Spalt [ʃpalt], *m.* (—(e)s, *pl.* —e) crack, rift, cleft, rent; (*glacier*) crevasse.

Spalte ['ʃpaltə], *f.* (—, *pl.* —n) (*newspaper*) column.

spalten ['ʃpaltən], *v.a.* split, cleave, slit. — *v.r. sich —* divide, break up, split up; (*in two*) bifurcate.

Spaltholz ['ʃpalthɔlts], *n.* (—es, *no pl.*) fire-wood.

Spaltpilz ['ʃpaltpɪlts], *m.* (—es, *pl.* —e) fission-fungus.

Spaltung ['ʃpaltuŋ], *f.* (—, *pl.* —en) cleavage; (*atomic*) fission; (*fig.*) dissension, rupture; (*Eccl.*) schism.

Span [ʃpaːn], *m.* (—(e)s, *pl.* ⸚e) chip, chippings, shavings.

Spange ['ʃpaŋə], *f.* (—, *pl.* —n) clasp, buckle.

Spanien ['ʃpaːnjən], *n.* Spain.

spanisch ['ʃpaːnɪʃ], *adj.* Spanish; —*e Wand,* folding screen; *es kommt mir — vor,* it is Greek to me.

Spann [ʃpan], *m.* (—(e)s, *pl.* —e) instep.

Spanne ['ʃpanə], *f.* (—, *pl.* —n) span; *eine — Zeit,* a short space of time.

spannen ['ʃpanən], *v.a.* stretch, strain, span.

spannend ['ʃpanənt], *adj.* thrilling, tense.

Spannkraft ['ʃpankraft], *f.* (—, *no pl.*) elasticity.

Spannung ['ʃpanuŋ], *f.* (—, *pl.* —en) tension, suspense, strain; (*fig.*) eager expectation, curiosity, suspense, close attention; (*Elec.*) voltage.

Sparbüchse

Sparbüchse ['ʃpaːrbyksə], *f.* (—, *pl.* —n) money-box.

sparen ['ʃpaːrən], *v.a., v.n.* save, economise, put by, lay by.

Spargel ['ʃpargəl], *m.* (—s, *pl.* —) asparagus.

Spargelder ['ʃpaːrgɛldər], *n. pl.* savings.

Sparkasse ['ʃpaːrkasə], *f.* (—, *pl.* —n) savings bank.

spärlich ['ʃpɛːrlɪç], *adj.* scant, scanty, sparse.

Sparpfennig ['ʃpaːrpfɛnɪç], *m.* (—s, *pl.* —e) nest-egg.

Sparren ['ʃparən], *m.* (—s, *pl.* —) spar, rafter; *er hat einen —,* he has a screw loose.

sparsam ['ʃpaːrzaːm], *adj.* economical, thrifty, frugal.

Spaß [ʃpaːs], *m.* (—es, *pl.* ⁻e) jest, fun, joke; *aus —, im —, zum —,* in fun; *— verstehen,* take a joke; *es macht mir —,* it amuses me, it is fun for me.

spaßen ['ʃpaːsən], *v.n.* jest, joke.

spaßhaft ['ʃpaːshaft], *adj.* funny, facetious, jocular.

Spaßverderber ['ʃpaːsfɛrdɛrbər], *m.* (—s, *pl.* —) spoil-sport.

Spaßvogel ['ʃpaːsfoːgəl], *m.* (—s, *pl.* ⁻) wag.

Spat [ʃpaːt], *m.* (—(e)s, *pl.* —e) (*Min.*) spar.

spät [ʃpɛːt], *adj.* late; *wie — ist es?* what is the time? *zu — kommen,* be late.

Spätabend ['ʃpɛːtaːbənt], *m.* (—s, *pl.* —e) latter part of the evening, late evening.

Spatel ['ʃpaːtəl], *m.* (—s, *pl.* —) spatula.

Spaten ['ʃpaːtən], *m.* (—s, *pl.* —) spade.

Spatenstich ['ʃpaːtənʃtɪç], *m.* (—(e)s, *pl.* —e) *den ersten — tun,* turn the first sod.

später ['ʃpɛːtər], *adv.* later (on), afterwards.

spätestens ['ʃpɛːtəstəns], *adv.* at the latest.

Spätling ['ʃpɛːtlɪŋ], *m.* (—s, *pl.* —e) late arrival; late fruit.

Spätsommer ['ʃpɛːtzɔmər], *m.* (—s, *pl.* —) Indian summer.

Spatz [ʃpats], *m.* (—en *pl.* —en) (*Orn.*) sparrow.

spazieren [ʃpaˈtsiːrən], *v.n.* (*aux.* sein) walk leisurely, stroll; *— gehen,* go for a walk, take a stroll; *— führen,* take for a walk.

Spazierfahrt [ʃpaˈtsiːrfaːrt], *f.* (—, *pl.* —en) (pleasure-)drive.

Spazierstock [ʃpaˈtsiːrʃtɔk], *m.* (—s, *pl.* ⁻e) walking-stick.

Spazierweg [ʃpaˈtsiːrveːk], *m.* (—(e)s, *pl.* —e) walk, promenade.

Specht [ʃpɛçt], *m.* (—(e)s, *pl.* —e) (*Orn.*) woodpecker.

Speck [ʃpɛk], *m.* (—(e)s, *no pl.*) bacon; *eine Scheibe —,* a rasher of bacon.

speckig ['ʃpɛkɪç], *adj.* fat.

Speckschwarte ['ʃpɛkʃvartə], *f.* (—, *pl.* —n) bacon-rind.

Speckseite ['ʃpɛkzaɪtə], *f.* (—, *pl.* —n) flitch of bacon.

spedieren [ʃpeˈdiːrən], *v.a.* forward; despatch.

Spediteur [ʃpediˈtøːr], *m.* (—s, *pl.* —e) forwarding agent, furniture-remover, carrier.

Spedition [ʃpediˈtsjoːn], *f.* (—, *pl.* —en) conveyance; forwarding agency.

Speer [ʃpeːr], *m.* (—(e)s, *pl.* —e) spear, lance.

Speiche ['ʃpaɪçə], *f.* (—, *pl.* —n) spoke.

Speichel ['ʃpaɪçəl], *m.* (—s, *no pl.*) spittle, saliva.

Speicher ['ʃpaɪçər], *m.* (—s, *pl.* —) granary; warehouse, storehouse; loft.

speien ['ʃpaɪən], *v.a., v.n. irr.* spit; vomit, be sick.

Speise ['ʃpaɪzə], *f.* (—, *pl.* —n) food, nourishment, dish.

Speisekammer ['ʃpaɪzəkamər], *f.* (—, *pl.* —n) larder, pantry.

Speisekarte ['ʃpaɪzəkartə], *f.* (—, *pl.* —n) bill of fare, menu.

speisen ['ʃpaɪzən], *v.a.* feed, give to eat. — *v.n.* eat, dine, sup, lunch.

Speiseröhre ['ʃpaɪzərøːrə], *f.* (—, *pl.* —n) gullet.

Speisewagen ['ʃpaɪzəvaːgən], *m.* (—s, *pl.* —) (*Railw.*) dining-car.

Spektakel [ʃpɛkˈtaːkəl], *m.* (—s, *no pl.*) uproar, hubbub; shindy, rumpus; noise, row.

Spektrum ['ʃpɛktrum], *n.* (—s, *pl.* Spektren) spectrum.

Spekulant [ʃpekuˈlant], *m.* (—en, *pl.* —en) speculator.

spekulieren [ʃpekuˈliːrən], *v.n.* speculate; theorise.

Spende ['ʃpɛndə], *f.* (—, *pl.* —n) gift, donation; bounty.

spenden ['ʃpɛndən], *v.a.* bestow, donate, contribute.

Spender ['ʃpɛndər], *m.* (—s, *pl.* —) donor, giver, benefactor.

spendieren [ʃpɛnˈdiːrən], *v.a.* (give a) treat, pay for, stand.

Sperber ['ʃpɛrbər], *m.* (—s, *pl.* —) (*Orn.*) sparrow-hawk.

Sperling ['ʃpɛrlɪŋ], *m.* (—s, *pl.* —e) (*Orn.*) sparrow.

sperrangelweit ['ʃpɛraŋəlvaɪt], *adv.* wide open.

Sperre ['ʃpɛrə], *f.* (—, *pl.* —n) shutting, closing, blockade, blocking; closure; ban; (*Railw.*) barrier.

sperren ['ʃpɛrən], *v.a.* spread out; (*Typ.*) space; shut, close, block; cut off; *ins Gefängnis —,* put in prison. — *v.r. sich — gegen,* offer resistance to.

Sperrhaken ['ʃpɛrhaːkən], *m.* (—s, *pl.* —) catch, ratchet.

Sperrsitz ['ʃpɛrzɪts], *m.* (—es, *pl.* —e) (*Theat.*) stall.

Sperrung ['ʃpɛruŋ], *f.* (—, *pl.* —en) barring, obstruction, block, blockade; (*Comm.*) embargo.

Sperrzeit ['ʃpɛrtsaɪt], *f.* (—, *pl.* —en) closing-time.

Spesen ['ʃpeːzən], *f. pl.* charges, expenses.

spesenfrei [ˈʃpeːzənfraɪ], *adj.* free of charge; expenses paid.

Spezereien [ʃpeːtsəˈraɪən], *f. pl.* spices.

spezial [ʃpeˈtsjaːl], *adj.* special, particular.

spezialisieren [ʃpetsjaliˈziːrən], *v.a.* specify. — *v.r.* sich —, specialise.

Spezialist [ʃpetsjaˈlɪst], *m.* (—en, *pl.* —en) specialist, expert.

Spezialität [ʃpetsjaliˈtɛːt], *f.* (—, *pl.* —en) speciality, (*Am.*) specialty.

Spezies [ˈʃpeːtsjɛs], *f.* (—, *pl.* —) species; (*Maths.*) rule.

Spezifikation [ʃpetsifikaˈtsjoːn], *f.* (—, *pl.* —en) specification.

spezifisch [ʃpeˈtsiːfɪʃ], *adj.* specific.

spezifizieren [ʃpetsifiˈtsiːrən], *v.a.* specify.

Spezifizierung [ʃpetsifiˈtsiːruŋ], *f.* (—, *pl.* —en) specification.

Spezimen [ˈʃpeːtsimən], *n.* (—s, *pl.* —mina) specimen.

Sphäre [ˈsfɛːrə], *f.* (—, *pl.* —n) sphere.

sphärisch [ˈsfɛːrɪʃ], *adj.* spherical.

Spickaal [ˈʃpiːkaːl], *m.* (—s, *pl.* —e) smoked eel.

spicken [ˈʃpɪkən], *v.a.* lard; *den Beutel* —, fill o.'s purse.

Spiegel [ˈʃpiːɡəl], *m.* (—s, *pl.* —) mirror, looking-glass.

spiegelblank [ˈʃpiːɡəlblaŋk], *adj.* sparkling, shiny, polished.

Spiegelei [ˈʃpiːɡəlaɪ], *n.* (—s, *pl.* —er) fried egg.

Spiegelfechterei [ˈʃpiːɡəlfɛçtəraɪ], *f.* (—, *pl.* —en) shadow-boxing, make-believe.

Spiegelfenster [ˈʃpiːɡəlfɛnstər], *n.* (—s, *pl.* —) plate-glass window.

spiegeln [ˈʃpiːɡəln], *v.n.* glitter, shine. — *v.a.* reflect. — *v.r.* sich —, be reflected.

Spiegelscheibe [ˈʃpiːɡəlʃaɪbə], *f.* (—, *pl.* —n) plate-glass pane.

Spiegelung [ˈʃpiːɡəluŋ], *f.* (—, *pl.* —en) reflection; mirage.

Spiel [ʃpiːl], *n.* (—(e)s, *pl.* —e) play; game; sport; (*Theat.*) acting, performance; (*Mus.*) playing; *ehrliches* (*unehrliches*) —, fair (foul) play; *leichtes* —, walk-over; *auf dem* — *stehen*, be at stake; *aufs* — *setzen*, stake, risk; *die Hand im* — *haben*, have a finger in the pie; *gewonnenes* — *haben*, gain o.'s point; *ein gewagtes* — *treiben*, play a bold game; *sein* — *mit einem treiben*, trifle with s.o.

Spielart [ˈʃpiːlaːrt], *f.* (—, *pl.* —en) manner of playing; variety.

Spielbank [ˈʃpiːlbaŋk], *f.* (—, *pl.* —en) casino; gambling-table.

Spieldose [ˈʃpiːldoːzə], *f.* (—, *pl.* —n) musical box.

spielen [ˈʃpiːlən], *v.a.*, *v.n.* play; gamble; (*Mus.*) play; (*Theat.*) act; *eine Rolle* —, play a part; *mit dem Gedanken* —, toy with the idea.

spielend [ˈʃpiːlənt], *adv.* easily.

Spieler [ˈʃpiːlər], *m.* (—s, *pl.* —) player; gambler; gamester.

Spielerei [ʃpiːləˈraɪ], *f.* (—, *pl.* —en) child's play; trivialities.

Spielhölle [ˈʃpiːlhœlə], *f.* (—, *pl.* —n) gambling-den.

Spielmann [ˈʃpiːlman], *m.* (—s, *pl.* **Spielleute**) musician, fiddler; (*Middle Ages*) minstrel.

Spielmarke [ˈʃpiːlmarkə], *f.* (—, *pl.* —n) counter, chip.

Spielplan [ˈʃpiːlplaːn], *m.* (—s, *pl.* ̈e) (*Theat.*) repertory.

Spielplatz [ˈʃpiːlplats], *m.* (—es, *pl.* ̈e) playground.

Spielraum [ˈʃpiːlraum], *m.* (—s, *no pl.*) elbow-room; (*fig.*) scope; margin; clearance.

Spielsache [ˈʃpiːlzaxə], *f.* (—, *pl.* —n) toy, plaything.

Spielschule [ˈʃpiːlʃuːlə], *f.* (—, *pl.* —n) infant-school, kindergarten.

Spieltisch [ˈʃpiːltɪʃ], *m.* (—es, *pl.* —e) card-table.

Spieluhr [ˈʃpiːluːr], *f.* (—, *pl.* —en) musical clock.

Spielverderber [ˈʃpiːlfɛrdɛrbər], *m.* (—s, *pl.* —) spoilsport.

Spielwaren [ˈʃpiːlvaːrən], *f. pl.* toys.

Spielzeit [ˈʃpiːltsaɪt], *f.* (—, *pl.* —en) playtime; (*Theat.*) season.

Spielzeug [ˈʃpiːltsɔyk], *n.* (—s, *pl.* —e) plaything, toy.

Spieß [ʃpiːs], *m.* (—es, *pl.* —e) spear, pike; (*Cul.*) spit.

Spießbürger [ˈʃpiːsbyrɡər], *m.* (—s, *pl.* —) Philistine.

spießen [ˈʃpiːsən], *v.a.* spear, pierce.

Spießer [ˈʃpiːsər], *m.* (—s, *pl.* —) Philistine.

Spießgeselle [ˈʃpiːsɡəzɛlə], *m.* (—n, *pl.* —n) accomplice, companion *or* partner in crime.

spießig [ˈʃpiːsɪç], *adj.* (*coll.*) Philistine, uncultured, narrow-minded.

Spießruten [ˈʃpiːsruːtən], *f. pl.* — *laufen*, run the gauntlet.

Spinat [ʃpiˈnaːt], *m.* (—s, *no pl.*) spinach.

Spind [ʃpɪnt], *n.* (—(e)s, *pl.* —e) cupboard.

Spindel [ˈʃpɪndəl], *f.* (—, *pl.* —n) spindle; distaff; (*staircase*) newel.

spindeldürr [ˈʃpɪndəldyr], *adj.* as thin as a lath.

Spindelholz [ˈʃpɪndəlhɔlts], *n.* (—es, *no pl.*) spindle-tree wood.

Spinett [ʃpiˈnɛt], *n.* (—s, *pl.* —e) spinet.

Spinne [ˈʃpɪnə], *f.* (—, *pl.* —n) spider.

spinnefeind [ˈʃpɪnəfaɪnt], *adj.* *einander* — *sein*, hate each other like poison.

spinnen [ˈʃpɪnən], *v.a.* irr. spin. — *v.n.* (*coll.*) be off o.'s head, be crazy.

Spinnerei [ʃpɪnəˈraɪ], *f.* (—, *pl.* —en) spinning-mill.

Spinngewebe [ˈʃpɪŋɡəveːbə], *n.* (—s, *pl.* —) cobweb.

Spinnrocken [ˈʃpɪnrɔkən], *m.* (—s, *pl.* —) distaff.

spintisieren [ʃpɪntiˈziːrən], *v.n.* muse, meditate.

Spion

Spion [ʃpi'oːn], *m.* (—s, *pl.* —e) spy.

spionieren [ʃpio'niːrən], *v.n.* spy, pry.

Spirale [ʃpi'raːlə], *f.* (—, *pl.* —n) spiral.

Spirituosen [ʃpiritu'oːzən], *pl.* spirits, liquors.

Spiritus [ʃpiːritus], *m.* (—, *pl.* —se) alcohol, spirits of wine; *denaturierter* —, methylated spirits.

Spiritusbrennerei [ʃpiːritusbrɛnərai], *f.* (—, *pl.* —en) distillery.

Spiritusgehalt [ʃpiːritusɡəhalt], *m.* (—s, *pl.* —e) *(alcoholic)* strength, proof.

Spital [ʃpi'taːl], *n.* (—s, *pl.* ̈er) infirmary; hospital.

Spitz [ʃpits], *m.* (—es, *pl.* —e) Pomeranian dog; *einen — haben,* (*coll.*) be slightly tipsy.

spitz [ʃpits], *adj.* pointed; (*fig.*) snappy, biting.

Spitzbart [ʃpitsbaːrt], *m.* (—s, *pl.* ̈e) imperial (beard), pointed beard.

Spitzbogen [ʃpitsboːɡən], *m.* (—s, *pl.* —) pointed arch, Gothic arch.

Spitzbogenfenster [ʃpitsboːɡənfɛnstər], *n.* (—s, *pl.* —) lancet window.

Spitzbube [ʃpitsbuːbə], *m.* (—n, *pl.* —n) rogue; rascal; scamp.

Spitzbubenstreich [ʃpitsbuːbənʃtraiç], *m.* (—(e)s, *pl.* —e) act of roguery, knavery.

spitzbübisch [ʃpitsbyːbiʃ], *adj.* roguish.

Spitze [ʃpitsə], *f.* (—, *pl.* —n) point; tip; top, peak; extremity; (*pipe*) mouthpiece; (*cigarette*) holder; (*pen*) nib; lace; *etwas auf die — treiben,* carry s.th. to extremes; *an der — stehen,* be at the head of.

Spitzel [ʃpitsəl], *m.* (—s, *pl.* —) police-agent; informer.

spitzen [ʃpitsən], *v.a.* sharpen; *die Ohren —,* prick up o.'s ears; *sich auf etwas —,* await s.th. eagerly, be all agog for s.th.

Spitzenbelastung [ʃpitsənbəlastuŋ], *f.* (—, *pl.* —en) peak load.

Spitzenleistung [ʃpitsənlaistuŋ], *f.* (—, *pl.* —en) maximum output; peak performance.

Spitzentuch [ʃpitsəntuːx], *n.* (—(e)s, *pl.* ̈er) lace scarf.

spitzfindig [ʃpitsfindiç], *adj.* subtle, crafty; hair-splitting.

Spitzhacke [ʃpitshakə], *f.* (—, *pl.* —n) pickaxe.

spitzig [ʃpitsiç], *adj.* pointed, sharp; (*fig.*) biting, poignant.

Spitzmaus [ʃpitsmaus], *f.* (—, *pl.* ̈e) (*Zool.*) shrew.

Spitzname [ʃpitsnaːmə], *m.* (—ns, *pl.* —n) nickname.

spitzwinklig [ʃpitsviŋkliç], *adj.* acute-angled.

spleißen [ʃplaisən], *v.a. irr.* split, cleave.

Splitter [ʃplitər], *m.* (—s, *pl.* —) splinter, chip.

splitternackt [ʃplitərnakt], *adj.* stark naked.

splittern [ʃplitərn], *v.n.* (*aux.* sein) splinter.

spontan [ʃpɔn'taːn], *adj.* spontaneous.

sporadisch [ʃpo'raːdiʃ], *adj.* sporadic.

Spore [ʃpoːrə], *f.* (—, *pl.* —n) spore.

Sporn [ʃpɔrn], *m.* (—s, *pl.* **Sporen**) spur.

spornstreichs [ʃpɔrnʃtraiçs], *adv.* post-haste, at once.

Sportler [ʃpɔrtlər], *m.* (—s, *pl.* —) athlete, sportsman.

sportlich [ʃpɔrtliç], *adj.* athletic; sporting.

sportsmäßig [ʃpɔrtsmɛːsiç], *adj.* sportsmanlike.

Spott [ʃpɔt], *m.* (—(e)s, *no pl.*) mockery; scorn; *Gegenstand des —s,* laughing-stock; *— treiben mit,* mock, deride; *zum Schaden den — hinzufügen,* add insult to injury.

spottbillig [ʃpɔtbiliç], *adj.* ridiculously cheap, dirt-cheap.

Spöttelei [ʃpœtə'lai], *f.* (—, *pl.* —en) sarcasm.

spötteln [ʃpœtəln], *v.n.* mock, jeer.

spotten [ʃpɔtən], *v.a., v.n.* deride, scoff (at); *es spottet jeder Beschreibung,* it defies description.

Spötter [ʃpœtər], *m.* (—s, *pl.* —) mocker, scoffer.

Spötterei [ʃpœtə'rai], *f.* (—, *pl.* —en) mockery, derision.

Spottgedicht [ʃpɔtɡədiçt], *n.* (—(e)s, *pl.* —e) satirical poem.

spöttisch [ʃpœtiʃ], *adj.* mocking, satirical, ironical, scoffing.

spottlustig [ʃpɔtlustiç], *adj.* flippant, satirical.

Spottschrift [ʃpɔtʃrift], *f.* (—, *pl.* —en) satire, lampoon.

Sprache [ʃpraːxə], *f.* (—, *pl.* —n) speech, language, tongue; expression; diction; discussion; *etwas zur — bringen,* bring a subject up; *zur — kommen,* come up for discussion; *heraus mit der —!* speak out!

Sprachfehler [ʃpraːxfeːlər], *m.* (—s, *pl.* —) impediment in o.'s speech.

sprachfertig [ʃpraːxfɛrtiç], *adj.* having a ready tongue; a good linguist, fluent.

Sprachgebrauch [ʃpraːxɡəbraux], *m.* (—(e)s, *no pl.*) (linguistic) usage.

Sprachkenner [ʃpraːxkɛnər], *m.* (—s, *pl.* —) linguist.

sprachkundig [ʃpraːxkundiç], *adj.* proficient in languages.

Sprachlehre [ʃpraːxleːrə], *f.* (—, *no pl.*) grammar.

sprachlich [ʃpraːxliç], *adj.* linguistic.

sprachlos [ʃpraːxloːs], *adj.* speechless, tongue-tied; *— dastehen,* be dumb-founded.

Sprachrohr [ʃpraːxroːr], *n.* (—s, *pl.* —e) megaphone, speaking-tube; (*fig.*) mouthpiece.

Sprachschatz [ʃpraːxʃats], *m.* (—es, *no pl.*) vocabulary.

Sprachvergleichung [ʃpraːxfɛrɡlaiçuŋ], *f.* (—, *no pl.*) comparative philology.

Sprachwerkzeug [ˈʃpraːxvərktsɔyk], *n.* (—s, *pl.* —e) organ of speech.

Sprachwissenschaft [ˈʃpraːxvisənʃaft], *f.* (—, *pl.* —en) linguistics, philology.

sprechen [ˈʃpreçən], *v.a., v.n. irr.* speak, declare, say; talk; *für einen* —, put in a good word for s.o., speak up for s.o.; *er ist nicht zu* —, he is not available; *auf einen gut zu* — *sein*, feel well disposed towards s.o.; *schuldig* —, pronounce guilty; *das Urteil* —, pass sentence.

sprechend [ˈʃpreçənt], *adj.* expressive; — *ähnlich*, strikingly alike.

Sprecher [ˈʃpreçər], *m.* (—s, *pl.* —) speaker, orator, spokesman; (*Rad.*) announcer.

Sprechstunde [ˈʃpreçʃtundə], *f.* (—, *pl.* —n) consulting hours, surgery hours; office hours.

Sprechzimmer [ˈʃpreçtsimər], *n.* (—s, *pl.*—) consulting-room.

spreizen [ˈʃpraɪtsən], *v.a.* spread open; *die Beine* —, plant o.'s legs wide apart, straddle. — *v.r. sich* —, give o.s. airs.

Sprengbombe [ˈʃprɛŋbɔmbə], *f.* (—, *pl.* —n) (high explosive) bomb.

Sprengel [ˈʃprɛŋəl], *m.* (—s, *pl.* —) diocese.

sprengen [ˈʃprɛŋən], *v.a.* sprinkle; water; burst, explode; burst open, blow up; *eine Versammlung* —, break up a meeting. — *v.n.* (*aux.* sein) ride at full speed, gallop.

Sprengpulver [ˈʃprɛŋpulvər], *n.* (—s, *no pl.*) blasting-powder.

Sprengstoff [ˈʃprɛŋʃtɔf], *m.* (—es, *pl.* —e) explosive.

Sprengwagen [ˈʃprɛŋvaːɡən], *m.* (—s, *pl.* —) sprinkler; water-cart.

sprenkeln [ˈʃprɛŋkəln], *v.a.* speckle.

Spreu [ʃprɔy], *f.* (—, *no pl.*) chaff.

Sprichwort [ˈʃpriçvɔrt], *n.* (—s, *pl.* ⁝er) proverb, adage, saying.

sprießen [ˈʃpriːsən], *v.n. irr.* sprout, shoot, germinate.

Springbrunnen [ˈʃprɪŋbrunən], *m.* (—s, *pl.*—) fountain.

springen [ˈʃprɪŋən], *v.n. irr.* (*aux.* sein) spring, leap, jump; (*glass*) burst; *etwas* — *lassen*, (*coll.*) treat s.o. to s.th.

Springer [ˈʃprɪŋər], *m.* (—s, *pl.* —) jumper, acrobat; (*Chess*) knight.

Springflut [ˈʃprɪŋfluːt], *f.* (—, *pl.* —en) spring-tide.

Springtau [ˈʃprɪŋtau], *n.* (—s, *pl.* —e) skipping-rope; (*Naut.*) slip-rope.

Sprit [ʃprɪt], *m.* (—s, *pl.* —e) spirit alcohol; (*sl.*) fuel, petrol.

Spritze [ˈʃprɪtsə], *f.* (—, *pl.* —n) squirt, syringe; fire-engine; (*coll.*) injection.

spritzen [ˈʃprɪtsən], *v.a.* squirt, spout, spray, sprinkle; (*coll.*) inject. — *v.n.* gush forth.

Spritzkuchen [ˈʃprɪtskuːxən], *m.* (—s, *pl.* —) fritter.

Spritztour [ˈʃprɪtstuːr], *f.* (—, *pl.* —en) (*coll.*) pleasure trip, outing; (*coll.*) spin.

spröde [ˈʃprøːdə], *adj.* (*material*) brittle; (*person*) stubborn; coy, prim, prudish.

Sprödigkeit [ˈʃprøːdɪçkaɪt], *f.* (—, *no pl.*) (*material*) brittleness; (*person*) stubbornness; coyness, primness, prudery.

Sproß [ʃprɔs], *m.* (—sses, *pl.* —sse) sprout, shoot, germ; (*fig.*) scion, offspring.

Sprosse [ˈʃprɔsə], *f.* (—, *pl.* —n) (*ladder*) step, rung.

Sprößling [ˈʃprœslɪŋ], *m.* (—s, *pl.* —e) scion, offspring.

Sprotte [ˈʃprɔtə], *f.* (—, *pl.* —n) sprat.

Spruch [ʃprux], *m.* (—(e)s, *pl.* ⁝e) saying, aphorism; proverb; (*obs.*) saw; (*judge*) sentence, verdict.

spruchreif [ˈʃpruxraɪf], *adj.* ripe for judgment; ready for a decision.

Sprudel [ˈʃpruːdəl], *m.* (—s, *pl.* —) bubbling spring; (*coll.*) soda water.

sprudeln [ˈʃpruːdəln], *v.n.* bubble, gush.

sprühen [ˈʃpryːən], *v.a.* sprinkle, scatter, spray. — *v.n.* sparkle, emit sparks; (*rain*) drizzle.

sprühend [ˈʃpryːənt], *adj.* (*fig.*) sparkling, scintillating, brilliant.

Sprühregen [ˈʃpryːreːɡən], *m.* (—s, *no pl.*) drizzling rain, drizzle.

Sprung [ʃpruŋ], *m.* (—(e)s, *pl.* ⁝e) leap, bound, jump; chink, crack; *nur auf einen* — *zu Besuch kommen*, pay a flying visit; *auf dem* — *sein zu*, be on the point of; *sich auf den* — *machen*, cut and run, (*coll.*) fly; *große* ⁝e *machen*, (*coll.*) live it up, cut a dash.

Sprungfeder [ˈʃpruŋfeːdər], *f.* (—, *pl.* —n) spring.

Sprungkraft [ˈʃpruŋkraft], *f.* (—, *no pl.*) springiness, elasticity, buoyancy.

Spucke [ˈʃpukə], *f.* (—, *no pl.*) spittle, saliva.

spucken [ˈʃpukən], *v.a., v.n.* spit.

Spuk [ʃpuːk], *m.* (—s, *pl.* —e) haunting; ghost, spectre, apparition; (*coll.*) spook.

spuken [ˈʃpuːkən], *v.n.* haunt; be haunted.

spukhaft [ˈʃpuːkhaft], *adj.* uncanny, phantom-like, ghost-like, spooky.

Spule [ˈʃpuːlə], *f.* (—, *pl.* —n) spool; (*Elec.*) coil.

Spüleimer [ˈʃpyːlaɪmər], *m.* (—s, *pl.* —) slop-pail.

spülen [ˈʃpyːlən], *v.a.* rinse, wash.

Spülicht [ˈʃpyːlɪçt], *n.* (—s, *no pl.*) dish-water.

Spund [ʃpunt], *m.* (—(e)s, *pl.* ⁝e) bung.

Spundloch [ˈʃpuntlɔx], *n.* (—s, *pl.* ⁝er) bung-hole.

Spur [ʃpuːr], *f.* (—, *pl.* —en) footprint, track, trail; spoor; (*fig.*) trace, vestige; *frische* —, hot scent; *einer Sache auf die* — *kommen*, be on the track of s.th.; *keine* — *von*, not a trace of, not an inkling of.

spüren [ˈʃpyːrən], *v.a.* trace, track (down); feel, sense, notice.

Spürhund [ˈʃpyːrhunt], *m.* (—s, *pl.* —e) tracker dog, setter, beagle; (*fig.*) spy, sleuth.

spurlos

spurlos ['ʃpuːrloːs], *adj.* trackless, without a trace; *es ging — an ihm vorüber*, it left no mark on him; — *verschwinden*, vanish into thin air.

Spürsinn ['ʃpyːrzɪn], *m.* (—s, *no pl.*) scent; flair; sagacity, shrewdness.

Spurweite ['ʃpuːrvaɪtə], *f.* (—, *pl.* —n) gauge, width of track.

sputen ['ʃpuːtən], *v.r. sich* —, make haste, hurry.

Staat [ʃtaːt], *m.* (—(e)s, *pl.* —en) state; government; pomp, show, parade; — *machen*, make a show of.

Staatenbund ['ʃtaːtənbunt], *m.* (—(e)s, *pl.* ⁝e) confederacy, federation.

staatlich ['ʃtaːtlɪç], *adj.* belonging to the state, public, national.

Staatsangehörige ['ʃtaːtsaŋəhøːrɪgə], *m.* (—n, *pl.* —n) citizen (of a country), subject, national.

Staatsangehörigkeit ['ʃtaːtsaŋəhøːrɪçkaɪt], *f.* (—, *pl.* —en) nationality.

Staatsanwalt ['ʃtaːtsanvalt], *m.* —s, *pl.* ⁝e) public prosecutor, Attorney-General.

Staatsbeamte ['ʃtaːtsbəamtə], *m.* (—n, *pl.* —n) civil servant, employee of the state.

Staatsbürger ['ʃtaːtsbyrgər], *m.* (—s, *pl.* —) citizen, national.

Staatsdienst ['ʃtaːtsdiːnst], *m.* (—(e)s, *pl.* —e) civil service, government service.

Staatseinkünfte ['ʃtaːtsaɪnkynftə], *f. pl.* public revenue.

Staatsgesetz ['ʃtaːtsgəzɛts], *n.* (—es, *pl.* —e) statute law.

Staatsgewalt ['ʃtaːtsgəvalt], *f.* (—, *no pl.*) executive power.

Staatshaushalt ['ʃtaːtshaushalt], *m.* (—s, *no pl.*) state finances, budget.

Staatshaushaltsanschlag ['ʃtaːtshaushaltsanʃlaːk], *m.* (—s, *pl.* ⁝e) budget estimates.

Staatskanzler ['ʃtaːtskantslər], *m.* (—s, *pl.* —) Chancellor.

Staatskasse ['ʃtaːtskasə], *f.* (—, *no pl.*) public exchequer, treasury.

Staatskörper ['ʃtaːtskœrpər], *m.* (—s, *pl.* —) body politic.

Staatskosten ['ʃtaːtskɔstən], *f. pl. auf* —, at (the) public expense.

Staatskunst ['ʃtaːtskunst], *f.* (—, *no pl.*) statesmanship; statecraft.

Staatsminister ['ʃtaːtsminɪstər], *m.* (—s, *pl.* —) cabinet minister; minister of state.

Staatsrat ['ʃtaːtsraːt], *m.* (—s, *no pl.*) council of state; (*pl.* ⁝e) councillor of state.

Staatsrecht ['ʃtaːtsrɛçt], *n.* (—(e)s, *no pl.*) constitutional law.

Staatssiegel ['ʃtaːtsziːgəl], *n.* (—s, *pl.* —) Great Seal, official seal.

Staatsstreich ['ʃtaːtsʃtraɪç], *m.* (—(e)s, *pl.* —e) coup d'état.

Staatswirtschaft ['ʃtaːtsvɪrtʃaft], *f.* (—, *no pl.*) political economy.

Staatszimmer ['ʃtaːtstsɪmər], *n.* (—s, *pl.* —) state apartment.

Stab [ʃtaːp], *m.* (—(e)s, *pl.* ⁝e) staff; stick, rod, pole; crosier; mace; (*Mil.*) field-officers, staff; *den — über einen brechen*, condemn s.o. (to death).

stabil [ʃtaˈbiːl], *adj.* steady, stable, firm.

stabilisieren [ʃtabiliˈziːrən], *v.a.* stabilise.

Stabreim ['ʃtaːpraɪm], *m.* (—s, *no pl.*) alliteration.

Stabsarzt ['ʃtaːpsartst], *m.* (—es, *pl.* ⁝e) (*Mil.*) medical officer.

Stabsquartier ['ʃtaːpskvartiːr], *n.* (—s, *pl.* —e) (*Mil.*) headquarters.

Stachel ['ʃtaxəl], *m.* (—s, *pl.* —n) (*animal*) sting; (*plant*) prickle, thorn; (*fig.*) keen edge, sting; stimulus; *wider den — löcken*, kick against the pricks.

Stachelbeere ['ʃtaxəlbeːrə], *f.* (—, *pl.* —n) (*Bot.*) gooseberry.

Stachelschwein ['ʃtaxəlʃvaɪn], *n.* (—s, *pl.* —e) (*Zool.*) hedgehog, porcupine.

stachlig ['ʃtaxlɪç], *adj.* prickly, thorny; (*fig.*) disagreeable.

Stadion ['ʃtaːdjɔn], *n.* (—s, *pl.* —dien) sports-arena, stadium.

Stadium ['ʃtaːdjum], *n.* (—s, *pl.* —dien) stage (of development), phase.

Stadt [ʃtat], *f.* (—, *pl.* ⁝e) town; city.

Stadtbahn ['ʃtatbaːn], *f.* (—, *pl.* —en) metropolitan railway.

Städtchen ['ʃtɛtçən], *n.* (—s, *pl.* —) small town, township.

Städter ['ʃtɛtər], *m.* (—s, *pl.* —) townsman.

Stadtgemeinde ['ʃtatgəmaɪndə], *f.* (—, *pl.* —n) municipality.

städtisch ['ʃtɛtɪʃ], *adj.* municipal.

Stadtmauer ['ʃtatmauər], *f.* (—, *pl.* —n) town wall, city wall.

Stadtrat ['ʃtatraːt], *m.* (—s, *no pl.*) town council; (*pl.* ⁝e) town councillor; alderman.

Stadtteil ['ʃtattaɪl], *m.* (—s, *pl.* —e) ward, district, part of a town.

Stadttor ['ʃtattoːr], *n.* (—s, *pl.* —e) city-gate.

Stadtverordnete ['ʃtatfɛrɔrdnətə], *m.* (—n, *pl.* —n) town councillor.

Stafette [ʃtaˈfɛtə], *f.* (—, *pl.* —n) courier; relay.

Staffel ['ʃtafəl], *f.* (—, *pl.* —n) step, rundle, rung, round; relay; (*fig.*) degree; (*Aviat.*) squadron.

Staffelei [ʃtafəˈlaɪ], *f.* (—, *pl.* —en) easel.

staffeln ['ʃtafəln], *v.a.* grade; differentiate; stagger.

Staffelung ['ʃtafəluŋ], *f.* (—, *pl.* —en) gradation.

stagnieren [ʃtagˈniːrən], *v.n.* stagnate.

Stahl [ʃtaːl], *m.* (—(e)s, *pl.* ⁝e) steel.

stählen ['ʃteːlən], *v.a.* steel, harden, temper; brace.

stählern ['ʃteːlərn], *adj.* made of steel, steely.

Stahlquelle ['ʃtaːlkvɛlə], *f.* (—, *pl.* —n) chalybeate spring; mineral spring.

Stahlstich ['ʃtaːlʃtɪç], *m.* (—(e)s, *pl.* —e) steel-engraving.

Stählung ['ʃtɛːluŋ], f. (—, no pl.) steeling; (fig.) bracing.

Stahlwaren ['ʃtaːlvaːrən], f. pl. hardware, cutlery.

Stall [ʃtal], m. (—(e)s, pl. ⁀e) stable; (pig) sty; (dog) kennel.

Stallbursche ['ʃtalburʃə], m. (—n, pl. —n) stable-boy, groom.

Stallungen ['ʃtaluŋən], f. pl. stabling, stables.

Stambul ['stambul], n. Istanbul.

Stamm [ʃtam], m. (—(e)s, pl. ⁀e) (tree) trunk; (people) tribe, family, race; (words) stem; root.

Stammaktie ['ʃtamaktsjə], f. (—, pl. —n) (Comm.) original share.

Stammbaum ['ʃtambaum], m. (—s, pl. ⁀e) pedigree; family tree.

Stammbuch ['ʃtambuːx], n. (—(e)s, pl. ⁀er) album.

stammeln ['ʃtaməln], v.a., v.n. stammer, stutter; falter.

stammen ['ʃtamən], v.n. (aux. sein) be descended from, spring from, originate from, stem from; be derived from.

Stammesgenosse ['ʃtaməsgənɔsə], m. (—n, pl. —n) kinsman, clansman.

Stammgast ['ʃtamgast], m. (—es, pl. ⁀e) regular customer.

Stammgut ['ʃtamguːt], n. (—s, pl. ⁀er) family estate.

Stammhalter ['ʃtamhaltər], m. (—s, pl. —) son and heir; eldest son.

Stammhaus ['ʃtamhaus], n. (—es, pl. ⁀er) ancestral mansion; (royalty) dynasty; (Comm.) business headquarters, head office.

stämmig ['ʃtɛmɪç], adj. sturdy, strong.

Stammler ['ʃtamlər], m. (—s, pl. —) stammerer, stutterer.

Stammsilbe ['ʃtamzilbə], f. (—, pl. —n) (Ling.) radical syllable.

Stammtafel ['ʃtamtaːfəl], f. (—, pl. —n) genealogical table.

Stammvater ['ʃtamfaːtər], m. (—s, pl. ⁀) ancestor, progenitor.

stammverwandt ['ʃtamfɛrvant], adj. cognate, kindred.

stampfen ['ʃtampfən], v.a. stamp, pound, ram down. — v.n. stamp, trample.

Stand [ʃtant], m. (—(e)s, pl. ⁀e) stand; (market) stall; situation, state (of affairs), condition; reading, position; rank, station (in life); (pl.) the classes, the estates.

Standarte [ʃtan'dartə], f. (—, pl. —n) standard, banner.

Standbild ['ʃtantbɪlt], n. (—(e)s, pl. —er) statue.

Ständchen ['ʃtɛntçən], n. (—s, pl. —) serenade; einem ein — bringen, serenade s.o.

Ständehaus ['ʃtɛndəhaus], n. (—es, pl. ⁀er) state assembly-hall.

Ständer ['ʃtɛndər], m. (—s, pl. —) stand, pedestal; post; (upright) desk.

Standesamt ['ʃtandəsamt], n. (—s, pl. ⁀er) registry office.

Standesbeamte ['ʃtandəsbəamtə], m. (—n, pl. —n) registrar (of births, marriages and deaths).

Standesbewußtsein ['ʃtandəsbəvustzain], n. (—s, no pl.) class-feeling, class-consciousness.

Standesperson ['ʃtandəspɛrzoːn], f. (—, pl. —en) person of rank.

Standgericht ['ʃtantgərɪçt], n. (—es, pl. —e) court-martial; summary court of justice.

standhaft ['ʃtanthaft], adj. constant, firm, steadfast.

standhalten ['ʃtanthaltən], v.n. irr. bear up, stand o.'s ground, withstand, resist.

ständig ['ʃtɛndɪç], adj. permanent.

ständisch ['ʃtɛndɪʃ], adj. relating to the estates (of the realm).

Standort ['ʃtantɔrt], m. (—s, pl. —e) location; station.

Standpauke ['ʃtantpaukə], f. (—, pl. —n) (coll.) harangue; severe reprimand.

Standpunkt ['ʃtantpuŋkt], m. (—(e)s, pl. —e) standpoint; point of view; den — vertreten, take the line; einem den — klar machen, give s.o. a piece of o.'s mind.

Standrecht ['ʃtantrɛçt], n. (—(e)s, no pl.) martial law.

Standuhr ['ʃtantuːr], f. (—, pl. —en) grandfather-clock.

Stange ['ʃtaŋə], f. (—, pl. —n) stick, pole; bei der — bleiben, stick to the point, persevere.

Stank [ʃtaŋk], m. (—s, no pl.) (dial.) stench; discord, trouble.

Stänker ['ʃtɛŋkər], m. (—s, pl. —) (coll.) mischief-maker, quarrelsome person.

stänkern ['ʃtɛŋkərn], v.n. pick quarrels; ferret about, make trouble.

Stanniol [ʃta'njoːl], n. (—s, no pl.) tinfoil.

stanzen ['ʃtantsən], v.a. punch, stamp.

Stapel ['ʃtaːpəl], m. (—s, pl. —) pile, heap; (Naut.) slipway; ein Schiff vom — lassen, launch a ship.

Stapellauf ['ʃtaːpəllauf], m. (—s, pl. ⁀e) (Naut.) launch, launching.

stapeln ['ʃtaːpəln], v.a. pile up.

Stapelnahrung ['ʃtaːpəlnaːruŋ], f. (—, no pl.) staple diet.

Stapelplatz ['ʃtaːpəlplats], m. (—es, pl. ⁀e) mart, emporium.

Stapelware ['ʃtaːpəlvaːrə], f. (—, pl. —n) staple goods.

Stapfen ['ʃtapfən], m. or f. pl. footsteps.

Star (1) [ʃtaːr], m. (—(e)s, pl. —e) (Med.) cataract; einem den — stechen, operate for cataract; (fig.) open s.o.'s eyes.

Star (2) [ʃtaːr], m. (—(e)s, pl. —en) (Orn.) starling.

stark [ʃtark], adj. strong, stout; robust; vigorous; heavy; considerable; —er Esser, hearty eater. — adv. very much.

209

Stärke [ˈʃtɛrkə], f. (—, no pl.) strength, vigour, robustness; strong point; starch.

Stärkekleister [ˈʃtɛrkəklaɪstər], m. (—s, no pl.) starch-paste.

Stärkemehl [ˈʃtɛrkəme:l], n. (—s, no pl.) starch-flour.

stärken [ˈʃtɛrkən], v.a. strengthen; corroborate; starch. — v.r. sich —, take some refreshment.

stärkend [ˈʃtɛrkənt], adj. strengthening, restorative; —es Mittel, tonic.

starkleibig [ˈʃtarklaɪbɪç], adj. corpulent, stout, obese.

Stärkung [ˈʃtɛrkuŋ], f. (—, pl. —en) strengthening, invigoration; refreshment.

starr [ʃtar], adj. stiff, rigid; fixed; inflexible; stubborn; staring; einen — ansehen, stare at s.o.

starren [ˈʃtarən], v.n. stare.

Starrheit [ˈʃtarhaɪt], f. (—, no pl.) stiffness, rigidity; fixedness; inflexibility; stubbornness.

starrköpfig [ˈʃtarkœpfɪç], adj. headstrong, stubborn, obstinate, pigheaded.

Starrkrampf [ˈʃtarkrampf], m. (—(e)s, no pl.) (Med.) tetanus.

Starrsinn [ˈʃtarzɪn], m. (—s, no pl.) stubbornness, obstinacy.

Station [ʃtaˈtsjo:n], f. (—, pl. —en) (Railw.) station; (main) terminus; stop, stopping-place; (hospital) ward; freie —, board and lodging found.

stationär [ʃtatsjoˈnɛːr], adj. stationary.

stationieren [ʃtatsjoˈniːrən], v.a. station.

Stationsvorsteher [ʃtatˈsjoːnsfɔrʃteːər], m. (—s, pl. —) station-master.

statisch [ˈʃtaːtɪʃ], adj. static.

Statist [ʃtaˈtɪst], m. (—en, pl. —en) (Theat.) extra, walking-on part; (pl.) supers.

Statistik [ʃtaˈtɪstɪk], f. (—, pl. —en) statistics.

Statistiker [ʃtaˈtɪstɪkər], m. (—s, pl. —) statistician.

Stativ [ʃtaˈtiːf], n. (—s, pl. —e) stand, tripod.

Statt [ʃtat], f. (—, no pl.) place, stead; an seiner —, in his place.

statt [ʃtat], prep. (Genit.) instead of, in lieu of.

Stätte [ˈʃtɛtə], f. (—, pl. —n) place, abode.

stattfinden [ˈʃtatfɪndən], v.n. irr. take place.

stattgeben [ˈʃtatgeːbən], v.n. irr. einer Bitte —, grant a request.

statthaft [ˈʃtathaft], adj. admissible, allowable, lawful.

Statthalter [ˈʃtathaltər], m. (—s, pl. —) governor.

stattlich [ˈʃtatlɪç], adj. stately, handsome, distinguished, comely; portly; considerable; eine — Summe, a tidy sum.

statuieren [ʃtatuˈiːrən], v.a. decree; ein Exempel —, make an example of.

Statut [ʃtaˈtuːt], n. (—s, pl. —en) statute, regulation.

Staub [ʃtaup], m. (—(e)s, no pl.) dust, powder; sich aus dem — machen, take French leave; abscond.

Stäubchen [ˈʃtɔypçən], n. (—s, pl. —) mote, particle of dust.

stauben [ˈʃtaubən], v.n. es staubt, it is dusty.

Staubgefäß [ˈʃtaupgəfɛːs], n. (—es, pl. —e) stamen.

staubig [ˈʃtaubɪç], adj. dusty.

Staubkamm [ˈʃtaupkam], m. (—s, pl. ⁓e) fine-tooth comb.

Staublappen [ˈʃtauplapən], m. (—s, pl. —) duster.

Staubmantel [ˈʃtaupmantəl], m. (—s, pl. ⁓) overall, smock; dust(er)coat, (Am.) duster.

Staubsauger [ˈʃtaupzaugər], m. (—s, pl. —) vacuum cleaner.

Staubtuch [ˈʃtauptuːx], n. (—es, pl. ⁓er) duster.

Staubwedel [ˈʃtaupveːdəl], m. (—s, pl. —) feather duster.

Staubwolke [ˈʃtaupvɔlkə], f. (—, pl. —n) cloud of dust.

Staubzucker [ˈʃtauptsukər], m. (—s, no pl.) castor-sugar, icing-sugar.

Staudamm [ˈʃtaudam], m. (—s, pl. ⁓e) dam, dyke.

Staude [ˈʃtaudə], f. (—, pl. —n) shrub, bush.

stauen [ˈʃtauən], v.a. stow; (water) dam. — v.r. sich —, be congested.

staunen [ˈʃtaunən], v.n. be astonished, be surprised, wonder (at).

Staupe [ˈʃtaupə], f. (—, pl. —n) (animals) distemper.

stäupen [ˈʃtɔypən], v.a. (obs.) scourge, flog.

Stauung [ˈʃtauuŋ], f. (—, pl. —en) stowage; (water) damming-up, swell, rising; (blood) congestion; (traffic) jam, build-up.

stechen [ˈʃtɛçən], v.a. irr. prick, sting; stab; (cards) trump.

stechend [ˈʃtɛçənt], adj. pungent, biting.

Stechmücke [ˈʃtɛçmykə], f. (—, pl. —n) (Ent.) gnat, mosquito.

Stechpalme [ˈʃtɛçpalmə], f. (—, pl. —n) (Bot.) holly.

Steckbrief [ˈʃtɛkbriːf], m. (—s, pl. —e) warrant (for arrest).

stecken [ˈʃtɛkən], v.a. stick into, put, place, fix; (plants) set, plant; in Brand —, set on fire, set fire to. — v.n. irgendwo —, be about somewhere; — bleiben, get stuck, break down; er steckt dahinter, he is at the bottom of it. — v.r. sich hinter einen —, shelter behind s.o.

Stecken [ˈʃtɛkən], m. (—s, pl. —) stick, staff.

Stecker [ˈʃtɛkər], m. (—s, pl. —) (Elec.) plug.

Steckkontakt [ˈʃtɛkkɔntakt], m. (—(e)s, pl. —e) (Elec.) plug, point.

Stecknadel [ˈʃtɛknaːdəl], f. (—, pl. —n) pin.

Steg [ʃteːk], m. (—(e)s, pl. —e) plank, foot-bridge; jetty; (violin) bridge.

Stegreif [ˈʃteːkraɪf], *m.* (—s, *pl.* —e) (*obs.*) stirrup; *aus dem* — *sprechen*, extemporise, improvise.

stehen [ˈʃteːən], *v.n. irr.* stand; be; stand still; mit einem gut —, be on good terms with s.o.; gut —, be in a fair way, look promising; was steht zu Diensten? what can I do for you? — bleiben, stand still, stop, pull up.

stehlen [ˈʃteːlən], *v.a. irr.* steal.

Steiermark [ˈʃtaɪərmark], *f.* Styria.

steif [ʃtaɪf], *adj.* stiff; (grog) strong; awkward; ceremonious, punctilious, formal. — *adv. etwas* — *und fest behaupten*, swear by all that's holy.

steifen [ˈʃtaɪfən], *v.a.* stiffen, starch.

Steifheit [ˈʃtaɪfhaɪt], *f.* (—, *no pl.*) stiffness; (fig.) formality.

Steifleinen [ˈʃtaɪflaɪnən], *n.* (—s, *no pl.*) buckram.

Steig [ʃtaɪk], *m.* (—(e)s, *pl.* —e) path, (mountain) track.

Steigbügel [ˈʃtaɪkbyːgəl], *m.* (—s, *pl.* —) stirrup.

Steigen [ˈʃtaɪgən], *n.* (—s, *no pl.*) rising, increase; (price) advance, rise; im —, on the increase.

steigen [ˈʃtaɪgən], *v.n. irr.* (aux. sein) climb, mount, ascend; (barometer) rise; (population) increase; (horse) rear; (price) advance, rise.

Steiger [ˈʃtaɪgər], *m.* (—s, *pl.* —) climber, mountaineer; mining-surveyor, overseer.

steigern [ˈʃtaɪgərn], *v.a.* (price) raise; (fig.) enhance, increase. — *v.r. sich* —, increase.

Steigerung [ˈʃtaɪgəruŋ], *f.* (—, *pl.* —en) raising; (fig.) enhancement; increase; (Gram.) comparison.

Steigung [ˈʃtaɪguŋ], *f.* (—, *pl.* —en) gradient.

steil [ʃtaɪl], *adj.* steep.

Stein [ʃtaɪn], *m.* (—(e)s, *pl.* —e) stone, rock; flint; jewel, gem; monument; (Chess) piece, chessman; (Draughts) man; (fruit) stone, kernel; — des Anstoßes, stumbling block; mir fällt ein — vom Herzen, it is a load off my mind; bei einem einen — im Brett haben, be in s.o.'s good books; einem —e in den Weg legen, put obstacles in s.o.'s way; der — des Weisen, the philosopher's stone.

Steinadler [ˈʃtaɪnaːdlər], *m.* (—s, *pl.* —) (Orn.) golden eagle.

steinalt [ˈʃtaɪnalt], *adj.* very old.

Steinbock [ˈʃtaɪnbɔk], *m.* (—s, *pl.* ⸚e) ibex; (Astrol.) Capricorn.

Steinbruch [ˈʃtaɪnbrux], *m.* (—s, *pl.* ⸚e) stone-pit, quarry.

Steinbutt [ˈʃtaɪnbut], *m.* (—s, *pl.* —e) (Zool.) turbot.

Steindruck [ˈʃtaɪndruk], *m.* (—s, *no pl.*) lithography.

steinern [ˈʃtaɪnərn], *adj.* stony; built of stone.

Steingut [ˈʃtaɪnguːt], *n.* (—s, *no pl.*) earthenware, stoneware, pottery.

Steinhagel [ˈʃtaɪnhaːgəl], *m.* (—s, *no pl.*) shower of stones.

Steinhaue [ˈʃtaɪnhauə], *f.* (—, *pl.* —n) pickaxe.

Steinhügel [ˈʃtaɪnhyːgəl], *m.* (—s, *pl.* —) cairn.

steinig [ˈʃtaɪnɪç], *adj.* stony, rocky.

steinigen [ˈʃtaɪnɪgən], *v.a.* stone.

Steinkalk [ˈʃtaɪnkalk], *m.* (—s, *no pl.*) quicklime.

Steinkohle [ˈʃtaɪnkoːlə], *f.* (—, *no pl.*) pit-coal.

Steinkrug [ˈʃtaɪnkruːk], *m.* (—s, *pl.* ⸚e) stone jar.

Steinmarder [ˈʃtaɪnmardər], *m.* (—s, *pl.* —) (Zool.) stone-marten.

Steinmetz [ˈʃtaɪnmets], *m.* (—es, *pl.* —e) stone-cutter, stone-mason.

Steinobst [ˈʃtaɪnoːpst], *n.* (—es, *no pl.*) stone-fruit.

Steinplatte [ˈʃtaɪnplatə], *f.* (—, *pl.* —n) slab, flagstone.

steinreich [ˈʃtaɪnraɪç], *adj.* as rich as Croesus.

Steinsalz [ˈʃtaɪnzalts], *n.* (—es, *no pl.*) rock-salt, mineral-salt.

Steinwurf [ˈʃtaɪnvurf], *m.* (—s, *pl.* ⸚e) einen — entfernt, within a stone's throw.

Steiß [ʃtaɪs], *m.* (—es, *pl.* —e) rump; (coll.) buttocks, posterior.

Stellage [ʃteˈlaːʒə], *f.* (—, *pl.* —n) stand, frame.

Stelldichein [ˈʃtɛldɪçaɪn], *n.* (—s, *no pl.*) assignation, rendezvous, tryst; (coll.) date.

Stelle [ˈʃtɛlə], *f.* (—, *pl.* —n) place, spot; job, position; situation; (book) passage; figure, digit; department; offene —, vacancy; auf der —, at once, immediately; an deiner —, if I were you; nicht von der — kommen, remain stationary; zur — sein, be at hand.

stellen [ˈʃtɛlən], *v.a.* put, place, set; richtig —, regulate, correct, amend; (clock) set right; seinen Mann —, play o.'s part, pull o.'s weight. — *v.r. sich* —, come forward; pretend; sich krank —, feign illness, malinger, pretend to be ill.

Stellenbewerber [ˈʃtɛlənbəvɛrbər], *m.* (—s, *pl.* —) applicant (for a job).

Stellengesuch [ˈʃtɛləngəzuːx], *n.* (—s, *pl.* —e) application (for a job).

Stellenvermittlung [ˈʃtɛlənfɛrmɪtluŋ], *f.* (—, *pl.* —en) employment office, employment exchange.

stellenweise [ˈʃtɛlənvaɪzə], *adv.* in parts, here and there.

Stellmacher [ˈʃtɛlmaxər], *m.* (—s, *pl.* —) wheelwright.

Stellung [ˈʃtɛluŋ], *f.* (—, *pl.* —en) position, posture; attitude; situation; job; (Mil.) trenches; — nehmen zu, express o.'s views on.

Stellvertreter [ˈʃtɛlfɛrtreːtər], *m.* (—s, *pl.* —) representative, deputy; substitute, supply, proxy, relief; (doctor) locum.

Stelzbein [ˈʃtɛltsbaɪn], *n.* (—s, *pl.* —e) wooden leg.

211

Stemmeisen ['ʃtemaizən], *n.* (—s, *pl.* —) crowbar.

stemmen ['ʃtemən], *v.a.* (*water*) stem, dam; (*weight*) lift. — *v.r. sich — gegen*, resist fiercely.

Stempel ['ʃtempəl], *m.* (—s, *pl.* —) stamp, rubber-stamp, die; pounder; (*Bot.*) pistil.

Stempelgebühr ['ʃtempəlgəby:r], *f.* (—, *pl.* —en) stamp-duty.

stempeln ['ʃtempəln], *v.a.* stamp, hallmark; brand; cancel (*postage stamp*). — *v.n.* (*coll.*) — *gehen*, be on the dole.

Stengel ['ʃtenəl], *m.* (—s, *pl.* —) stalk.

Stenografie [ʃtenogra'fi:], *f.* (—, *no pl.*) stenography, shorthand.

stenografisch [ʃteno'gra:fiʃ], *adj.* in shorthand.

Stenogramm [ʃteno'gram], *n.* (—s, *pl.* —e) shorthand-note.

Stenotypistin [ʃtenoty'pistin], *f.* (—, *pl.* —nen) shorthand-typist.

Stephan ['ʃtefan], *m.* Stephen.

Steppdecke ['ʃtepdekə], *f.* (—, *pl.* —n) quilt.

Steppe ['ʃtepə], *f.* (—, *pl.* —n) steppe.

steppen ['ʃtepən], *v.a.* stitch, quilt.

Sterbeglocke ['ʃterbəglɔkə], *f.* (—, *pl.* —n) passing bell, death bell.

Sterbehemd ['ʃterbəhemt], *n.* (—(e)s, *pl.* —en) shroud, winding-sheet.

sterben ['ʃterbən], *v.n. irr.* (*aux.* sein) die.

Sterbenswörtchen ['ʃterbənsvœrtçən], *n.* (—s, *pl.* —) *nicht ein* —, not a syllable.

Sterbesakramente ['ʃterbəzakramentə], *n. pl.* (*Eccl.*) last sacraments, last rites.

sterblich ['ʃterpliç], *adj.* mortal; — *verliebt*, desperately in love.

Sterblichkeit ['ʃterplickait], *f.* (—, *no pl.*) mortality.

stereotyp [stereo'ty:p], *adj.* stereotyped.

sterilisieren [sterili'zi:rən], *v.a.* sterilise.

Sterilität [sterili'tɛ:t], *f.* (—, *no pl.*) sterility.

Stern [ʃtern], *m.* (—(e)s, *pl.* —e) star; (*Typ.*) asterisk.

Sternbild ['ʃternbilt], *n.* (—s, *pl.* —er) constellation.

Sterndeuter ['ʃterndɔytər], *m.* (—s, *pl.* —) astrologer.

Sterndeutung ['ʃterndɔytuŋ], *f.* (—, *no pl.*) astrology.

Sternenschimmer ['ʃternənʃimər], *m.* (—s, *no pl.*) starlight.

sternförmig ['ʃternfœrmiç], *adj.* star-like, star-shaped.

Sterngucker ['ʃterngukər], *m.* (—s, *pl.* —) stargazer.

sternhagelvoll ['ʃternha:gəlfɔl], *adj.* (*coll.*) as drunk as a lord.

Sternkunde ['ʃternkundə], *f.* (—, *no pl.*) astronomy.

Sternkundige ['ʃternkundigə], *m.* (—n, *pl.* —n) astronomer.

Sternschnuppe ['ʃternʃnupə], *f.* (—, *pl.* —n) falling star, shooting star, meteorite.

Sternwarte ['ʃternvartə], *f.* (—, *pl.* —n) observatory.

stetig ['ʃte:tiç], *adj.* continual, continuous, constant.

stets [ʃte:ts], *adv.* always, ever, continually.

Steuer (1) ['ʃtɔyər], *n.* (—s, *pl.* —) rudder, helm, steering wheel.

Steuer (2) ['ʃtɔyər], *f.* (—, *pl.* —n) tax; (*local*) rate; (*import*) customs duty.

Steueramt ['ʃtɔyəramt], *n.* (—s, *pl.* ⸚er) inland revenue office, tax office.

Steuerbeamte ['ʃtɔyərbəamtə], *m.* (—n, *pl.* —n) revenue officer, tax collector.

Steuerbord ['ʃtɔyərbɔrt], *n.* (—s, *no pl.*) starboard.

Steuereinnehmer ['ʃtɔyərainne:mər], *m.* (—s, *pl.* —) tax collector.

steuerfrei ['ʃtɔyərfrai], *adj.* duty-free, exempt from taxes.

Steuerhinterziehung ['ʃtɔyərhintərtsi:uŋ], *f.* (—, *pl.* —en) tax evasion.

steuerlos ['ʃtɔyərlo:s], *adj.* rudderless, adrift.

Steuermann ['ʃtɔyərman], *m.* (—s, *pl.* ⸚er) mate; helmsman.

steuern ['ʃtɔyərn], *v.a.* steer; *einem Unheil* —, avoid *or* steer clear of an evil.

steuerpflichtig ['ʃtɔyərpfliçtiç], *adj.* taxable, liable to tax, dutiable.

Steuerrad ['ʃtɔyərra:t], *n.* (—s, *pl.* ⸚er) steering-wheel.

Steuerung ['ʃtɔyəruŋ], *f.* (—, *no pl.*) steering, controls.

Steuerveranlagung ['ʃtɔyərferanla:guŋ], *f.* (—, *pl.* —en) tax-assessment.

stibitzen [ʃti'bitsən], *v.a.* (*coll.*) pilfer, filch.

Stich [ʃtiç], *m.* (—(e)s, *pl.* —e) sting; prick; stitch; stab; (*Cards*) trick; (*Art*) engraving; *einen im* — *lassen*, leave s.o. in the lurch.

Stichel ['ʃtiçəl], *m.* (—s, *pl.* —) (*Art*) graver.

Stichelei [ʃtiçə'lai], *f.* (—, *pl.* —en) taunt, sneer, gibe.

sticheln ['ʃtiçəln], *v.a.* taunt, nag.

stichhaltig ['ʃtiçhaltiç], *adj.* valid, sound.

Stichhaltigkeit ['ʃtiçhaltiçkait], *f.* (—, *no pl.*) validity, cogency.

Stichprobe ['ʃtiçpro:bə], *f.* (—, *pl.* —n) sample taken at random, sampling.

Stichwahl ['ʃtiçva:l], *f.* (—, *pl.* —en) second ballot.

Stichwort ['ʃtiçvɔrt], *n.* (—s, *pl.* —e) key-word; (*Theat.*) cue.

sticken ['ʃtikən], *v.a., v.n.* embroider.

Stickerei [ʃtikə'rai], *f.* (—, *pl.* —en) embroidery.

Stickgarn ['ʃtikgarn], *n.* (—s, *pl.* —e) embroidery cotton *or* silk.

Stickhusten ['ʃtikhu:stən], *m.* (—s, *no pl.*) choking cough.

stickig ['ʃtɪkɪç], adj. stuffy.
Stickmuster ['ʃtɪkmustər], n. (—s, pl. —) embroidery-pattern.
Stickstoff ['ʃtɪkʃtɔf], m. (—(e)s, no pl.) nitrogen.
stieben ['ʃtiːbən], v.n. (aux. sein) scatter, spray; auseinander —, disperse.
Stiefbruder ['ʃtiːfbruːdər], m. (—s, pl. ⸚) step-brother.
Stiefel ['ʃtiːfəl], m. (—s, pl. —) boot.
Stiefelknecht ['ʃtiːfəlknɛçt], m. (—(e)s, pl. —e) boot-jack.
Stiefelputzer ['ʃtiːfəlputsər], m. (—s, pl. —) shoe-black; (Am.) shoe-shine; (hotel) boots.
Stiefeltern ['ʃtiːfɛltərn], pl. step-parents.
Stiefmütterchen ['ʃtiːfmytərçən], n. (—s, pl. —) (Bot.) pansy.
stiefmütterlich ['ʃtiːfmytərlɪç], adj. like a stepmother; niggardly.
Stiefsohn ['ʃtiːfzoːn], m. (—s, pl. ⸚e) stepson.
Stiege ['ʃtiːgə], f. (—, pl. —n) staircase.
Stieglitz ['ʃtiːglɪts], m. (—es, pl. —e) goldfinch.
Stiel [ʃtiːl], m. (—(e)s, pl. —e) handle; (plant) stalk.
Stier [ʃtiːr], m. (—(e)s, pl. —e) bull; junger —, bullock; (Astrol.) Taurus.
stieren ['ʃtiːrən], v.n. stare (at), goggle.
Stift (1) [ʃtɪft], m. (—(e)s, pl. —e) tack, pin, peg; pencil; (coll.) apprentice; young chap.
Stift (2) [ʃtɪft], n. (—(e)s, pl. —e) charitable or religious foundation.
stiften ['ʃtɪftən], v.a. establish, give, donate; found, set on foot, originate; Frieden —, bring about peace.
Stifter ['ʃtɪftər], m. (—s, pl. —) founder, originator, donor.
Stiftung ['ʃtɪftuŋ], f. (—, pl. —en) establishment, foundation; institution; charitable foundation; endowment, donation.
Stil [ʃtiːl], m. (—(e)s, pl. —e) style; (fig.) manner.
stilisieren [ʃtiːliˈziːrən], v.a. word, draft.
Stilistik [ʃtiːˈlɪstɪk], f. (—, no pl.) art of composition.
stilistisch [ʃtiːˈlɪstɪʃ], adj. stylistic.
still [ʃtɪl], adj. quiet, still, silent; calm; —er Teilhaber, sleeping partner; im —en, secretly, on the sly.
Stille ['ʃtɪlə], f. (—, no pl.) silence, quietness, tranquillity; calm, calmness; in der —, silently; in der — der Nacht, at dead of night.
stillen ['ʃtɪlən], v.a. allay; (blood) staunch; (baby) suckle, feed, nurse; (thirst) quench; (hunger) appease.
stillos ['ʃtiːlloːs], adj. incongruous; in bad taste.
Stillung ['ʃtɪluŋ], f. (—, no pl.) allaying; (blood) staunching; (baby) suckling, feeding, nursing; (thirst) quenching; (hunger) appeasing.

stilvoll ['ʃtiːlfɔl], adj. harmonious; stylish; in good taste.
Stimmband ['ʃtɪmbant], n. (—s, pl. ⸚er) vocal chord.
stimmberechtigt ['ʃtɪmbərɛçtɪçt], adj. entitled to vote, enfranchised.
Stimmbruch ['ʃtɪmbrux], m. (—s, no pl.) breaking of the voice.
Stimme ['ʃtɪmə], f. (—, pl. —n) voice; (election) vote, suffrage; die — abgeben, vote.
stimmen ['ʃtɪmən], v.a. (piano) tune; einen günstig —, dispose s.o. favourably towards s.th. — v.n. agree, tally (with), square (with), accord (with); vote.
Stimmeneinheit ['ʃtɪmənaɪnhaɪt], f. (—, no pl.) unanimity.
Stimmengleichheit ['ʃtɪmənglaɪçhaɪt], f. (—, no pl.) equality of votes, tie.
Stimmer ['ʃtɪmər], m. (—s, pl. —) (piano) tuner.
Stimmführer ['ʃtɪmfyːrər], m. (—s, pl. —) leader, spokesman.
Stimmgabel ['ʃtɪmgaːbəl], f. (—, pl. —n) tuning fork.
stimmhaft ['ʃtɪmhaft], adj. (Phonet.) voiced.
Stimmlage ['ʃtɪmlaːgə], f. (—, pl. —n) (Mus.) register.
stimmlos ['ʃtɪmloːs], adj. voiceless; (Phonet.) unvoiced.
Stimmrecht ['ʃtɪmrɛçt], n. (—s, no pl.) suffrage, right to vote; allgemeines —, universal suffrage.
Stimmung ['ʃtɪmuŋ], f. (—, no pl.) tuning; (fig.) disposition, humour, mood; atmosphere; in guter —, in high spirits, in gedrückter —, in low spirits.
stimmungsvoll ['ʃtɪmuŋsfɔl], adj. impressive, full of atmosphere.
Stimmwechsel ['ʃtɪmvɛksəl], m. (—s, no pl.) breaking of the voice.
Stimmzettel ['ʃtɪmtsɛtəl], m. (—s, pl. —) ballot-paper.
stinken ['ʃtɪŋkən], v.n. irr. stink, reek, smell.
Stinktier ['ʃtɪŋktiːr], n. (—s, pl. —e) (Zool.) skunk.
Stipendium [ʃtiˈpɛndjum], n. (—s, pl. —dien) scholarship.
Stirn [ʃtɪrn], f. (—, pl. —en) forehead, brow; die — runzeln, frown, knit o.'s brow; die — haben zu, have the cheek to; einem die — bieten, face s.o., defy s.o.
Stirnhöhle ['ʃtɪrnhøːlə], f. (—, pl. —en) frontal cavity.
Stirnseite ['ʃtɪrnzaɪtə], f. (—, pl. —n) front.
stöbern ['ʃtøːbərn], v.n. rummage about; (snow) drift.
stochern ['ʃtɔxərn], v.a., v.n. (food) pick (at); (teeth) pick.
Stock (1) [ʃtɔk], m. (—(e)s, pl. ⸚e) stick, cane, walking-stick; über — und Stein, over hedges and ditches.
Stock (2) [ʃtɔk], m. (—es, pl. —werke) storey, floor.

stocken

stocken ['ʃtɔkən], *v.n.* stop; *(blood)* run cold; *(linen)* go mildewed; hesitate, falter; *(conversation)* flag.

stockfinster ['ʃtɔkfɪnstər], *adj.* pitch dark.

Stockfisch ['ʃtɔkfɪʃ], *m.* (—es, *pl.* —e) dried cod; dried fish.

stöckisch ['ʃtœkɪʃ], *adj.* obstinate, stubborn.

Stockrose ['ʃtɔkro:zə], *f.* (—, *pl.* —n) *(Bot.)* hollyhock.

Stockschnupfen ['ʃtɔkʃnupfən], *m.* (—s, *no pl.*) heavy *or* chronic cold.

stocksteif ['ʃtɔkʃtaif], *adj.* stiff as a poker.

stockstill ['ʃtɔkʃtɪl], *adj.* quite still, stock-still.

stocktaub ['ʃtɔktaup], *adj.* deaf as a post.

Stockung ['ʃtɔkuŋ], *f.* (—, *pl.* —en) stagnation; hesitation; block, blockage; stopping, standstill.

Stockwerk ['ʃtɔkvɛrk], *n.* (—s, *pl.* —e) storey, floor.

Stoff [ʃtɔf], *m.* (—(e)s, *pl.* —e) fabric, material; substance; subject matter.

Stoffwechsel ['ʃtɔfvɛksəl], *m.* (—s, *no pl.*) metabolism.

stöhnen ['ʃtø:nən], *v.n.* groan, moan.

Stoiker ['sto:ikər], *m.* (—s, *pl.* —) stoic.

Stola ['sto:la:], *f.* (—, *pl.* —len) *(Eccl.)* stole.

Stollen ['ʃtɔlən], *m.* (—s, *pl.* —) fruitcake; *(Min.)* gallery, adit.

stolpern ['ʃtɔlpərn], *v.n.* *(aux.* sein*)* stumble, trip.

Stolz [ʃtɔlts], *m.* (—es, *no pl.*) haughtiness, pride.

stolz [ʃtɔlts], *adj.* haughty, proud; stuck-up, conceited; *(fig.)* majestic.

stolzieren [ʃtɔl'tsi:rən], *v.n.* *(aux.* sein*)* strut; prance.

stopfen ['ʃtɔpfən], *v.a.* stuff; fill; darn, mend; *einem den Mund —*, cut s.o. short.

Stopfgarn ['ʃtɔpfgarn], *n.* (—s, *pl.* —e) darning-thread.

Stoppel ['ʃtɔpəl], *f.* (—, *pl.* —n) stubble.

stoppeln ['ʃtɔpəln], *v.a.* glean; *etwas zusammen —*, compile s.th. badly.

Stöpsel ['ʃtœpsəl], *m.* (—s, *pl.* —) stopper, cork; *kleiner —*, little mite.

stöpseln ['ʃtœpsəln], *v.a.* cork.

Stör [ʃtø:r], *m.* (—(e)s, *pl.* —e) *(Zool.)* sturgeon.

Storch [ʃtɔrç], *m.* (—(e)s, *pl.* ⸚e) *(Orn.)* stork.

Storchschnabel ['ʃtɔrçʃna:bəl], *m.* (—s, *pl.* ⸚) stork's bill; *(Tech.)* pantograph.

stören ['ʃtø:rən], *v.a.* disturb, trouble; *(Rad.)* jam. — *v.n.* intrude, be in the way.

Störenfried ['ʃtø:rənfri:d], *m.* (—s, *pl.* —e) intruder, mischief-maker; nuisance.

Störer ['ʃtø:rər], *m.* (—s, *pl.* —) disturber.

stornieren [stɔr'ni:rən], *v.a.* cancel, annul.

störrisch ['ʃtœrɪʃ], *adj.* stubborn, obstinate.

Störung ['ʃtø:ruŋ], *f.* (—, *pl.* —en) disturbance, intrusion; *(Rad.)* jamming.

Stoß [ʃto:s], *m.* (—es, *pl.* ⸚e) push, thrust; impact; blow, stroke, jolt; *(papers)* heap, pile; *(documents)* bundle.

Stoßdegen ['ʃto:sde:gən], *m.* (—s, *pl.* —) rapier.

Stößel ['ʃtø:səl], *m.* (—s, *pl.* —) pestle; *(Motor.)* tappet.

stoßen ['ʃto:sən], *v.a. irr.* thrust, push; pound; *vor den Kopf —*, offend. — *v.n.* bump, jolt; *— an*, border upon; *auf etwas —*, come across s.th., stumble on s.th.; *ins Horn —*, blow a horn. — *v.r. sich —*, hurt o.s.; *sich an etwas —*, take offence at s.th., take exception to s.th.

Stoßseufzer ['ʃto:szɔyftsər], *m.* (—s, *pl.* —) deep sigh.

Stoßwaffe ['ʃto:svafə], *f.* (—, *pl.* —n) thrusting *or* stabbing weapon.

stoßweise ['ʃto:svaizə], *adv.* by fits and starts.

Stotterer ['ʃtɔtərər], *m.* (—s, *pl.* —) stutterer, stammerer.

stottern ['ʃtɔtərn], *v.n.* stutter, stammer.

stracks [ʃtraks], *adv.* straight away, directly.

Strafanstalt ['ʃtra:fanʃtalt], *f.* (—, *pl.* —en) penitentiary, prison.

Strafarbeit ['ʃtra:farbait], *f.* (—, *pl.* —en) *(Sch.)* imposition.

strafbar ['ʃtra:fba:r], *adj.* punishable, criminal, culpable.

Strafbarkeit ['ʃtra:fba:rkait], *f.* (—, *no pl.*) culpability.

Strafe ['ʃtra:fə], *f.* (—, *pl.* —n) punishment; *(money)* fine, penalty; *bei — von*, on pain of.

strafen ['ʃtra:fən], *v.a.* punish, rebuke; *(money)* fine.

Straferlaß ['ʃtra:fərlas], *m.* (—sses, *pl.* —sse) remission of penalty, amnesty.

straff [ʃtraf], *adj.* tight, tense, taut.

Strafgericht ['ʃtra:fgərıçt], *n.* (—es, *no pl.*) punishment; judgment; *(Law)* Criminal Court.

Strafgesetzbuch ['ʃtra:fgəzɛtsbu:x], *n.* (—(e)s, *pl.* ⸚er) penal code.

sträflich ['ʃtrɛ:flıç], *adj.* punishable; culpable; reprehensible, blameworthy.

Sträfling ['ʃtrɛ:flıŋ], *m.* (—s, *pl.* —e) convict.

Strafporto ['ʃtra:fpɔrto], *n.* (—s, *pl.* —ti) excess postage.

Strafpredigt ['ʃtra:fpredıçt], *f.* (—, *pl.* —en) severe admonition, stern reprimand.

Strafprozess ['ʃtra:fprɔtsɛs], *m.* (—es, *pl.* —e) criminal proceedings.

Strafrecht ['ʃtra:frɛçt], *n.* (—(e)s, *no pl.*) criminal law.

Strafverfahren ['ʃtra:ffɛrfa:rən], *n.* (—s, *pl.* —) criminal procedure.

Strahl [ʃtraːl], *m.* (—(e)s, *pl.* —en) beam, ray; (*water etc.*) jet, spout; (*lightning*) flash; —en werfen, emit rays.

Strahlantrieb ['ʃtraːlantriːp], *m.* (—s, *no pl.*) (*Aviat.*) jet propulsion.

strahlen ['ʃtraːlən], *v.n.* radiate, shine, beam, emit rays; (*fig.*) beam (with joy).

strählen ['ʃtrɛːlən], *v.a.* (*rare*) comb.

Strahlenbrechung ['ʃtraːlənbrɛçuŋ], *f.* (—, *pl.* —en) refraction.

strahlenförmig ['ʃtraːlənfœrmɪç], *adj.* radiate.

Strahlenkrone ['ʃtraːlənkroːnə], *f.* (—, *pl.* —n) aureole, halo.

Strahlung ['ʃtraːluŋ], *f.* (—, *pl.* —en) radiation; (*fig.*) radiance.

Strähne ['ʃtrɛːnə], *f.* (—, *pl.* —n) skein, hank; *eine — Pech*, a spell of bad luck.

Stramin [ʃtraˈmiːn], *m.* (—s, *pl.* —e) embroidery canvas.

stramm [ʃtram], *adj.* tight; rigid; sturdy, strapping.

strampeln ['ʃtrampəln], *v.n.* struggle; (*baby*) kick.

Strand [ʃtrant], *m.* (—(e)s, *pl.* —e) shore, beach, strand.

stranden ['ʃtrandən], *v.n.* be stranded, founder.

Strandkorb ['ʃtrantkɔrp], *m.* (—s, *pl.* ⁻e) beach-chair.

Strandwache ['ʃtrantvaxə], *f.* (—, *no pl.*) coast-guard.

Strang [ʃtraŋ], *m.* (—(e)s, *pl.* ⁻e) rope, cord; *über die ⁻e schlagen*, kick over the traces; *zum — verurteilen*, condemn to be hanged.

strangulieren [ʃtraŋguˈliːrən], *v.a.* strangle.

Strapaze [ʃtraˈpatsə], *f.* (—, *pl.* —n) over-exertion, fatigue, hardship.

strapazieren [ʃtrapaˈtsiːrən], *v.a.* over-exert, fatigue.

strapaziös [ʃtrapaˈtsjøːs], *adj.* fatiguing, exacting.

Straße ['ʃtraːsə], *f.* (—, *pl.* —n) (*city*) street; (*country*) road, highway; (*sea*) strait; *auf der —*, in the street; *über die — gehen*, cross the street.

Straßenbahn ['ʃtraːsənbaːn], *f.* (—, *pl.* —en) tram; tramcar, (*Am.*) street-car.

Straßendamm ['ʃtraːsəndam], *m.* (—s, *pl.* ⁻e) roadway.

Straßendirne ['ʃtraːsəndɪrnə], *f.* (—, *pl.* —n) prostitute, street-walker.

Straßenfeger ['ʃtraːsənfeːgər], *m.* (—s, *pl.* —) roadman, road-sweeper, scavenger, crossing-sweeper.

Straßenpflaster ['ʃtraːsənpflastər], *n.* (—s, *no pl.*) pavement.

Straßenraub ['ʃtraːsənraup], *m.* (—s, *no pl.*) highway-robbery.

Stratege [ʃtraˈteːgə], *m.* (—n, *pl.* —n) strategist.

sträuben ['ʃtrɔybən], *v.r. sich —*, bristle; (*fig.*) struggle (against), oppose.

Strauch [ʃtraux], *m.* (—(e)s, *pl.* ⁻er) bush, shrub.

straucheln ['ʃtrauxəln], *v.n.* (*aux.* sein) stumble.

Strauchritter ['ʃtrauxrɪtər], *m.* (—s, *pl.* —) footpad, vagabond, highwayman.

Strauß (1) [ʃtraus], *m.* (—es, *pl.* ⁻e) (*Poet.*) fight, tussle; (*flowers*) bunch, bouquet, nosegay.

Strauß (2) [ʃtraus], *m.* (—es, *pl.* —e) (*Orn.*) ostrich.

Sträußchen ['ʃtrɔysçən], *n.* (—s, *pl.* —) small bunch of flowers, nosegay.

Straußfeder ['ʃtrausfeːdər], *f.* (—, *pl.* —n) ostrich-feather.

Strazze ['ʃtratsə], *f.* (—, *pl.* —n) scrapbook.

Strebe ['ʃtreːbə], *f.* (—, *pl.* —n) buttress, prop, stay.

Strebebogen ['ʃtreːbəboːgən], *m.* (—s, *pl.* —) (*Archit.*) arch, buttress; flying buttress.

Streben ['ʃtreːbən], *n.* (—s, *no pl.*) ambition, aspiration; effort, endeavour, striving.

streben ['ʃtreːbən], *v.n.* strive, aspire, endeavour.

Streber ['ʃtreːbər], *m.* (—s, *pl.* —) pushing person, (social) climber. (*Am. coll.*) go-getter.

strebsam ['ʃtreːpzaːm], *adj.* ambitious, assiduous, industrious.

streckbar ['ʃtrɛkbaːr], *adj.* ductile, extensible.

Streckbett ['ʃtrɛkbɛt], *n.* (—s, *pl.* —en) orthopaedic bed.

Strecke ['ʃtrɛkə], *f.* (—, *pl.* —n) stretch, reach, extent; distance; tract; line; *zur — bringen*, (*Hunt.*) bag, run to earth.

strecken ['ʃtrɛkən], *v.a.* stretch, extend; (*metal*) hammer out, roll; make (s.th.) last; *die Waffen —*, lay down arms.

Streich [ʃtraɪç], *m.* (—(e)s, *pl.* —e) stroke, blow; (*fig.*) prank; trick; *dummer —*, piece of folly, lark.

streicheln ['ʃtraɪçəln], *v.a.* stroke, caress.

streichen ['ʃtraɪçən], *v.a. irr.* stroke, touch; paint, spread; cancel; strike; (*sail*) lower. — *v.n.* move past, fly past; wander.

Streichholz ['ʃtraɪçhɔlts], *n.* (—es, *pl.* ⁻er) match.

Streichinstrument ['ʃtraɪçɪnstruˌmɛnt], *n.* (—s, *pl.* —e) stringed instrument.

Streif [ʃtraɪf], *m.* (—(e)s, *pl.* —e) stripe, strip, streak.

Streifband ['ʃtraɪfbant], *n.* (—s, *pl.* ⁻er) wrapper.

Streifblick ['ʃtraɪfblɪk], *m.* (—s, *pl.* —e) glance.

Streife ['ʃtraɪfə], *f.* (—, *pl.* —n) raid; patrol (*police etc.*).

Streifen ['ʃtraɪfən], *m.* (—s, *pl.* —) stripe, streak; (*Mil.*) bar.

streifen

streifen ['ʃtraɪfən], *v.a.* graze, touch in passing; take off (*remove*). — *v.n.* (*aux.* sein) ramble, roam, rove.

streifig ['ʃtraɪfɪç], *adj.* striped, streaky.

Streik [ʃtraɪk], *m.* (—(e)s, *pl.* —s) strike; *in den* — *treten*, go on strike.

Streikbrecher ['ʃtraɪkbrɛçər], *m.* (—s, *pl.* —) blackleg.

streiken ['ʃtraɪkən], *v.n.* (*workers*) strike, be on strike.

Streit [ʃtraɪt], *m.* (—(e)s, *pl.* —e) dispute, quarrel, conflict; (*words*) argument; *einen* — *anfangen*, pick a quarrel.

Streitaxt ['ʃtraɪtakst], *f.* (—, *pl.* ⁻e) battle-axe.

streitbar ['ʃtraɪtbaːr], *adj.* warlike, martial.

streiten ['ʃtraɪtən], *v.n.* irr. quarrel, fight; —*de Kirche*, Church Militant.

Streitfrage ['ʃtraɪtfraːgə], *f.* (—, —n) moot point, point at issue; controversy.

Streithammel ['ʃtraɪthaməl], *m.* (—s, *pl.* —) squabbler.

Streithandel ['ʃtraɪthandəl], *m.* (—s, *pl.* ⁻) law-suit.

streitig ['ʃtraɪtɪç], *adj.* disputable, doubtful, at issue; *einem etwas* — *machen*, contest s.o.'s right to s.th.

Streitkräfte ['ʃtraɪtkrɛftə], *f. pl.* (*Mil.*) forces.

streitlustig ['ʃtraɪtlʊstɪç], *adj.* argumentative.

Streitschrift ['ʃtraɪtʃrɪft], *f.* (—, *pl.* —en) pamphlet, polemical treatise.

Streitsucht ['ʃtraɪtzuxt], *f.* (—, *no pl.*) quarrelsomeness; (*Law*) litigiousness.

streitsüchtig ['ʃtraɪtzyçtɪç], *adj.* quarrelsome, litigious.

streng [ʃtrɛn], *adj.* severe, strict, rigorous; —*e Kälte*, biting cold; *im* —*sten Winter*, in the depth of winter. — *adv.* —*genommen*, strictly speaking.

Strenge ['ʃtrɛnə], *f.* (—, *no pl.*) severity, rigour.

strenggläubig ['ʃtrɛnɡlɔybɪç], *adj.* strictly orthodox.

Streu [ʃtrɔy], *f.* (—, *pl.* —en) litter, bed of straw.

Streubüchse ['ʃtrɔybyksə], *f.* (—, *pl.* —n) castor.

streuen ['ʃtrɔyən], *v.a.* strew, scatter, sprinkle.

streunen ['ʃtrɔynən], *v.n.* roam (about).

Streuung ['ʃtrɔyun], *f.* (—, *pl.* —en) strewing; (*shot*) dispersion.

Streuzucker ['ʃtrɔytsukər], *m.* (—s, *no pl.*) castor-sugar.

Strich [ʃtrɪç], *m.* (—(e)s, *pl.* —e) stroke, line, dash; (*land*) tract; (*Art*) touch; region; *gegen den* —, against the grain; *einem einen* — *durch die Rechnung machen*, put a spoke in s.o.'s wheel, frustrate s.o.

Strichpunkt ['ʃtrɪçpunkt], *m.* (—s, *pl.* —e) semicolon.

Strichregen ['ʃtrɪçreːgən], *m.* (—s, *pl.* —) passing shower.

Strick [ʃtrɪk], *m.* (—(e)s, *pl.* —e) cord, line, rope; *du* —, (*fig.*) you scamp! *einem einen* — *drehen*, give s.o. enough rope to hang himself, lay a trap for s.o.

stricken ['ʃtrɪkən], *v.a., v.n.* knit.

Strickerei [ʃtrɪkə'raɪ], *f.* (—, *pl.* —en) knitting; knitting business, workshop.

Strickleiter ['ʃtrɪklaɪtər], *f.* (—, *pl.* —n) rope-ladder.

Strickzeug ['ʃtrɪktsɔyk], *n.* (—s, *pl.* —e) knitting.

Striegel ['ʃtriːgəl], *m.* (—s, *pl.* —) curry-comb.

striegeln ['ʃtriːgəln], *v.a.* curry.

Strieme ['ʃtriːmə], *f.* (—, *pl.* —n) weal, stripe.

Strippe ['ʃtrɪpə], *f.* (—, *pl.* —n) strap, band, string; cord.

strittig ['ʃtrɪtɪç], *adj.* contentious, debatable.

Stroh [ʃtroː], *n.* (—s, *no pl.*) straw; (*roof*) thatch; *mit* — *decken*, thatch; *leeres* — *dreschen*, beat the air.

Strohfeuer ['ʃtroːfɔyər], *n.* (—s, *no pl.*) (*fig.*) flash in the pan; short-lived enthusiasm.

Strohhalm ['ʃtroːhalm], *m.* (—s, *pl.* —e) straw.

Strohhut ['ʃtroːhuːt], *m.* (—s, *pl.* ⁻e) straw-hat.

Strohkopf ['ʃtroːkɔpf], *m.* (—(e)s, *pl.* ⁻e) (*coll.*) stupid person.

Strohmann ['ʃtroːman], *m.* (—s, *pl.* ⁻er) (*coll.*) man of straw; (*Cards*) dummy.

Strohmatte ['ʃtroːmatə], *f.* (—, *pl.* —n) straw-mat.

Strohwitwe ['ʃtroːvɪtvə], *f.* (—, *pl.* —n) grass-widow.

Strolch [ʃtrɔlç], *m.* (—(e)s, *pl.* —e) vagabond, (*fig.*) scamp.

Strom [ʃtroːm], *m.* (—(e)s, *pl.* ⁻e) river, torrent; (*also fig.*) flood; stream; (*also Elec.*) current; (*coll.*) electricity; *gegen den* — *schwimmen*, swim against the current, be an individualist.

stromab [ʃtroː'map], *adv.* downstream.

stromauf [ʃtroː'mauf], *adv.* upstream.

strömen ['ʃtrøːmən], *v.n.* (*aux.* sein) flow, stream; (*rain*) pour; (*people*) flock.

Stromer ['ʃtroːmər], *m.* (—s, *pl.* —) vagabond, tramp, vagrant.

Stromkreis ['ʃtroːmkraɪs], *m.* (—es, *pl.* —e) (*Elec.*) circuit.

Stromschnelle ['ʃtroːmʃnɛlə], *f.* (—, *pl.* —n) rapids.

Strömung ['ʃtrøːmun], *f.* (—, *pl.* —en) current; (*fig.*) tendency.

Strophe ['ʃtroːfə], *f.* (—, *pl.* —n) verse, stanza.

strotzen ['ʃtrɔtsən], *v.n.* be puffed up; overflow, burst, teem.

strotzend ['ʃtrɔtsənt], *adj. vor Gesundheit* —, bursting with health.

Strudel ['ʃtruːdəl], *m.* (—s, *pl.* —) whirl, whirlpool, vortex, eddy; pastry.

Struktur [ʃtruk'tuːr], *f.* (—, *pl.* —en) structure.

Strumpf [ʃtrumpf], *m.* (—(e)s, *pl.* ̈e) stocking; (*short*) sock.

Strumpfband [ʃtrumpfbant], *n.* (—(e)s, *pl.* ̈er) garter.

Strumpfwaren [ʃtrumpfvaːrən], *f. pl.* hosiery.

Strumpfwirker [ʃtrumpfvɪrkər], *m.* (—s, *pl.* —) stocking-weaver.

Strunk [ʃtruŋk], *m.* (—(e)s, *pl.* ̈e) (*tree*) stump, trunk; (*plant*) stalk.

struppig [ʃtrupɪç], *adj.* rough, unkempt, frowsy.

Stube [ʃtuːbə], *f.* (—, *pl.* —n) room, chamber; *gute* —, sitting-room.

Stubenarrest [ʃtuːbənarɛst], *m.* (—s, *pl.* —e) confinement to quarters.

Stubenhocker [ʃtuːbənhɔkər], *m.* (—s, *pl.* —) stay-at-home.

Stubenmädchen [ʃtuːbənmɛːtçən], *n.* (—s, *pl.* —) housemaid.

Stuck [ʃtuk], *m.* (—(e)s, *no pl.*) stucco, plaster.

Stück [ʃtyk], *n.* (—(e)s, *pl.* —e) piece; part; lump; (*Theat.*) play; *aus freien —en*, of o.'s own accord; *große —e auf einen halten*, think highly of s.o.

Stückarbeit [ʃtykarbaɪt], *f.* (—, *pl.* —en) piece-work.

Stückchen [ʃtykçən], *n.* (—s, *pl.* —) small piece, morsel, bit.

stückeln [ʃtykəln], *v.a.* cut in(to) pieces; patch, mend.

stückweise [ʃtykvaɪzə], *adv.* piecemeal.

Stückwerk [ʃtykvɛrk], *n.* (—s, *no pl.*) (*fig.*) patchy or imperfect work, a bungled job.

Stückzucker [ʃtyktsukər], *m.* (—s, *no pl.*) lump sugar.

Student [ʃtuˈdɛnt], *m.* (—en, *pl.* —en) (*Univ.*) student, undergraduate.

studentenhaft [ʃtuˈdɛntənhaft], *adj.* student-like.

Studentenverbindung [ʃtuˈdɛntənfɛrbɪnduŋ], *f.* (—, *pl.* —en) students' association *or* union.

Studie [ʃtuːdjə], *f.* (—, *pl.* —n) study, (*Art*) sketch; (*Lit.*) essay; (*pl.*) studies.

Studienplan [ʃtuːdjənplaːn], *m.* (—s, *pl.* ̈e) curriculum.

Studienrat [ʃtuːdjənraːt], *m.* (—s, *pl.* ̈e) grammar school teacher, assistant master.

studieren [ʃtuˈdiːrən], *v.a., v.n.* study, read (a subject); be at (the) university.

studiert [ʃtuˈdiːrt], *adj.* educated; (*fig.*) affected, deliberate, studied.

Studierte [ʃtuˈdiːrtə], *m.* (*coll.*) egghead.

Studium [ʃtuːdjum], *n.* (—s,) *pl.* —dien study, pursuit; university education.

Stufe [ʃtuːfə], *f.* (—, *pl.* —n) step; (*fig.*) degree; *auf gleicher — mit*, on a level with.

stufenweise [ʃtuːfənvaɪzə], *adv.* gradually, by degrees.

Stuhl [ʃtuːl], *m.* (—s, *pl.* ̈e) chair, seat; *der Heilige —*, the Holy See.

Stuhlgang [ʃtuːlgaŋ], *m.* (—s, *no pl.*) (*Med.*) stool, evacuation (of the bowels), movement, motion.

Stukkatur [ʃtukaˈtuːr], *f.* (—, *no pl.*) stucco-work.

Stulle [ʃtulə], *f.* (—, *pl.* —n) (*dial.*) slice of bread and butter.

Stulpe [ʃtulpə], *f.* (—, *pl.* —n) cuff.

stülpen [ʃtylpən], *v.a.* turn up, invert.

Stulpnase [ʃtulpnaːzə], *f.* (—, *pl.* —n) turned-up nose, pug-nose.

Stulpstiefel [ʃtulpʃtiːfəl], *m.* (—s, *pl.* —) top-boot.

stumm [ʃtum], *adj.* mute, dumb, silent.

Stumme [ʃtumə], *m. & f.* (—n, *pl.* —n) dumb person, mute.

Stummel [ʃtuməl], *m.* (—s, *pl.* —) stump; (*cigarette*) end, butt.

Stummheit [ʃtumhaɪt], *f.* (—, *no pl.*) dumbness.

Stümper [ʃtympər], *m.* (—s, *pl.* —) bungler, botcher.

stümperhaft [ʃtympərhaft], *adj.* bungling, botchy.

stümpern [ʃtympərn], *v.a., v.n.* bungle, botch.

Stumpf [ʃtumpf], *m.* (—(e)s, *pl.* ̈e) stump, trunk; *mit — und Stiel ausrotten*, destroy root and branch.

stumpf [ʃtumpf], *adj.* blunt; (*angle*) obtuse; (*fig.*) dull; — *machen*, blunt, dull.

Stumpfsinn [ʃtumpfzɪn], *m.* (—s, *no pl.*) stupidity, dullness.

stumpfwinklig [ʃtumpfvɪŋklɪç], *adj.* obtuse-angled.

Stunde [ʃtundə], *f.* (—, *pl.* —n) hour; lesson.

stunden [ʃtundən], *v.a.* give a respite, allow time (to pay up).

Stundenglas [ʃtundənglas], *n.* (—es, *pl.* ̈er) hour-glass.

Stundenplan [ʃtundənplaːn], *m.* (—s, *pl.* ̈e) (*Sch.*) schedule.

Stundenzeiger [ʃtundəntsaɪgər], *m.* (—s, *pl.* —) hour-hand.

Stündlein [ʃtyntlaɪn], *n.* (—s, *pl.* —) *sein — hat geschlagen*, his last hour has come.

Stundung [ʃtunduŋ], *f.* (—, *pl.* —en) respite, grace.

stupend [ʃtuˈpɛnt], *adj.* stupendous.

stur [ʃtuːr], *adj.* obdurate, unwavering, stolid, dour, stubborn.

Sturm [ʃturm], *m.* (—(e)s, *pl.* ̈e) storm, gale, tempest, hurricane; (*Mil.*) attack, assault; — *und Drang*, (*Lit.*) Storm and Stress; — *im Wasserglas*, storm in a teacup; — *laufen gegen*, storm against.

Sturmband [ʃturmbant], *n.* (—s, *pl.* ̈er) chinstrap.

Sturmbock [ʃturmbɔk], *m.* (—s, *pl.* ̈e) battering-ram.

stürmen [ʃtyrmən], *v.a.* storm, take by assault. — *v.n.* be violent, be stormy; (*Mil.*) advance.

Stürmer [ʃtyrmər], *m.* (—s, *pl.* —) assailant; (*football*) centre-forward.

Sturmglocke [ʃturmglɔkə], *f.* (—, *pl.* —n) tocsin, alarm-bell.

Sturmhaube

Sturmhaube [ˈʃturmhaubə], *f.* (—, *pl.* **-en**) (*Mil.*) morion, helmet.

stürmisch [ˈʃtyrmɪʃ], *adj.* stormy, tempestuous; (*fig.*) boisterous, turbulent, tumultuous, impetuous; —*er Beifall,* frantic applause; —*e Überfahrt,* rough crossing.

Sturmschritt [ˈʃturmʃrɪt], *m.* (—s, *no pl.*) double march.

Sturmvogel [ˈʃturmfoːgəl], *m.* (—s, *pl.* ") (*Orn.*) stormy petrel.

Sturz [ʃturts], *m.* (—es, *pl.* "e) fall, tumble; crash; collapse; (*Comm.*) failure; smash; (*government*) overthrow.

Sturzacker [ˈʃturtsakər], *m.* (—s, *pl.* ") freshly ploughed field.

Sturzbach [ˈʃturtsbax], *m.* (—(e)s, *pl.* "e) torrent.

Stürze [ˈʃtyrtsə], *f.* (—, *pl.* **-n**) pot-lid, cover.

stürzen [ˈʃtyrtsən], *v.a.* hurl, overthrow; ruin. — *v.n.* (*aux.* sein) (*person*) have a fall; (*object*) tumble down; (*business*) fail; crash; plunge; (*water*) rush. — *v.r.* throw oneself; *sich* — *auf,* rush at, plunge into.

Sturzhelm [ˈʃturtshɛlm], *m.* (—s, *pl.* —e) crash-helmet.

Sturzsee [ˈʃturtszeː], *f.* (—, *no pl.*) heavy sea.

Sturzwelle [ˈʃturtsvɛlə], *f.* (—, *pl.* —n) breaker, roller.

Stute [ˈʃtuːtə], *f.* (—, *pl.* —n) mare.

Stutzbart [ˈʃtutsbaːrt], *m.* (—s, *pl.* "e) short beard.

Stütze [ˈʃtytsə], *f.* (—, *pl.* —n) prop, support, stay.

Stutzen [ˈʃtutsən], *m.* (—s, *pl.* —) short rifle, carbine.

stutzen [ˈʃtutsən], *v.a.* (*hair*) clip, trim; (*horse*) dock, crop; (*tree*) prune, lop. — *v.n.* be taken aback, hesitate.

stützen [ˈʃtytsən], *v.a.* prop, support; base *or* found (on). — *v.r. sich* — *auf,* lean upon; (*fig.*) rely upon.

Stutzer [ˈʃtutsər], *m.* (—s, *pl.* —) dandy, fop, beau.

stutzerhaft [ˈʃtutsərhaft], *adj.* dandified.

stutzig [ˈʃtutsɪç], *adj.* startled, puzzled; — *werden,* be non-plussed, be taken aback *or* puzzled.

Stützmauer [ˈʃtytsmauər], *f.* (—, *pl.* —n) buttress, retaining wall.

Stützpunkt [ˈʃtytspuŋkt], *m.* (—s, *pl.* —e) point of support; foothold; (*Mil.*) base; (*Tech.*) fulcrum.

Subjekt [zupˈjɛkt], *n.* (—s, *pl.* —e) subject; (*fig.*) creature.

subjektiv [zupjɛkˈtiːf], *adj.* subjective, personal, prejudiced.

sublimieren [zubliˈmiːrən], *v.a.* sublimate.

Substantiv [zupstanˈtiːf], *n.* (—(e)s, *pl.* —e) (*Gram.*) substantive, noun.

subtil [zupˈtiːl], *adj.* subtle.

subtrahieren [zuptraˈhiːrən], *v.a.* subtract.

Subvention [zupvɛnˈtsjoːn], *f.* (—, *pl.* —en) subsidy, grant-in-aid.

Suche [ˈzuːxə], *f.* (—, *no pl.*) search, quest; *auf der* — *nach,* in quest of.

suchen [ˈzuːxən], *v.a., v.n.* seek, look for; attempt, endeavour.

Sucht [zuxt], *f.* (—, *pl.* "e) mania, addiction, passion.

süchtig [ˈzyxtɪç], *adj.* addicted (to).

Sud [zuːd], *m.* (—(e)s, *pl.* —e) boiling, brewing; suds.

Sudan [ˈzuːdan], *m.* the Sudan.

sudeln [ˈzuːdəln], *v.a., v.n.* smear, daub, make a mess (of).

Süden [ˈzyːdən], *m.* (—s, *no pl.*) south.

Südfrüchte [ˈzyːtfryçtə], *f. pl.* Mediterranean *or* tropical fruit.

südlich [ˈzyːtlɪç], *adj.* southern, southerly; *in* —*er Richtung,* southward.

Südosten [zyːtˈʔɔstən], *m.* (—s, *no pl.*) south-east.

Suff [zuf], *m.* (—(e)s, *no pl.*) (*sl.*) boozing, tippling.

suggerieren [zugeˈriːrən], *v.a.* suggest.

Sühne [ˈzyːnə], *f.* (—, *no pl.*) expiation, atonement.

sühnen [ˈzyːnən], *v.a.* expiate, atone for.

Sühneopfer [ˈzyːnəʔɔpfər], *n.* (—s, *pl.* —) expiatory sacrifice; atonement.

Suite [ˈsviːtə], *f.* (—, *pl.* —n) retinue, train.

sukzessiv [zuktsɛˈsiːf], *adj.* gradual, successive.

Sülze [ˈzyltsə], *f.* (—, *pl.* —n) brawn, aspic, jelly.

Summa [ˈzuˈmaː], *f.* (—, *pl.* **Summen**) — *summarum,* sum total.

summarisch [zuˈmaːrɪʃ], *adj.* summary.

Summe [ˈzumə], *f.* (—, *pl.* —n) sum, amount.

summen [ˈzumən], *v.a.* hum. — *v.n.* buzz, hum.

summieren [zuˈmiːrən], *v.a.* sum up, add up. — *v.r. sich* —, mount up.

Sumpf [zumpf], *m.* (—(e)s, *pl.* "e) bog, morass, marsh, moor, swamp.

sumpfig [ˈzumpfɪç], *adj.* boggy, marshy.

Sund [zunt], *m.* (—(e)s, *pl.* —e) straits, sound.

Sünde [ˈzyndə], *f.* (—, *pl.* —n) sin.

Sündenbock [ˈzyndənbɔk], *m.* (—s, *pl.* "e) scapegoat.

Sündenfall [ˈzyndənfal], *m.* (—s, *no pl.*) (*Theol.*) the Fall (*of man*).

Sündengeld [ˈzyndəngɛlt], *n.* (—(e)s, *no pl.*) ill-gotten gains; (*coll.*) vast sum of money.

sündenlos [ˈzyndənloːs], *adj.* sinless, impeccable.

Sündenpfuhl [ˈzyndənpfuːl], *m.* (—s, *pl.* —e) sink of iniquity.

Sünder [ˈzyndər], *m.* (—s, *pl.* —) sinner; *armer* —, poor devil; *du alter* —, you old scoundrel.

sündhaft [ˈzynthaft], *adj.* sinful, iniquitous.

sündig [ˈzyndɪç], *adj.* sinful.

sündigen [ˈzyndɪgən], *v.n.* sin, err.

Sündigkeit [ˈzyndɪçkaɪt], *f.* (—, *no pl.*) sinfulness.

Superlativ [ˈzuːpərlatiːf], *m.* (—s, *pl.* —e) superlative (degree).

Suppe ['zupə], *f.* (—, *pl.* —n) soup; *eingebrannte* —, thick soup; *einem edi — versalzen*, spoil s.o.'s little game.
Suppenfleisch ['zupənflaiʃ], *n.* (—es, *no pl.*) stock-meat.
Suppenkelle ['zupənkɛlə], *f.* (—, *pl.* —n) soup ladle.
Suppenterrine ['zupənteri:nə], *f.* (—, *pl.* —n) tureen.
Surrogat [zuro'ga:t], *n.* (—s, *pl.* —e) substitute.
süß [zy:s], *adj.* sweet.
Süße ['zy:sə], *f.* (—, *no pl.*) sweetness.
süßen ['zy:sən], *v.a.* sweeten.
Süßholz ['zy:sɔlts], *n.* (—es, *no pl.*) liquorice; — *raspeln*, talk sweet nothings, pay compliments.
Süßigkeit ['zy:sɪçkaɪt], *f.* (—, *pl.* —en) sweetness; (*pl.*) sweets.
süßlich ['zy:slɪç], *adj.* sweetish; (*fig.*) fulsome, mawkish, cloying.
Süßspeise ['zy:sʃpaɪzə], *f.* (—, *pl.* —n) dessert.
Süßwasser ['zy:svasər], *n.* (—s, *no pl.*) fresh water.
Symbolik [zym'bo:lɪk], *f.* (—, *no pl.*) symbolism.
symbolisch [zym'bo:lɪʃ], *adj.* symbolic(al).
symbolisieren [zymbɔlɪ'zi:rən], *v.a.* symbolize.
symmetrisch [zy'me:trɪʃ], *adj.* symmetrical.
Sympathie [zympa'ti:], *f.* (—, *no pl.*) sympathy.
sympathisch [zym'pa:tɪʃ], *adj.* congenial, likeable.
Synagoge [zyna'go:gə], *f.* (—, *pl.* —n) synagogue.
synchronisieren [zynkroni'zi:rən], *v.a.* synchronise.
Syndikus ['zyndikus], *m.* (—, *pl.* **Syndizi**) syndic.
Synode [zy'no:də], *f.* (—, *pl.* —n) synod.
synthetisch [zyn'te:tɪʃ], *adj.* synthetic.
Syrien [zy:rjən], *n.* Syria.
systematisch [zyste'ma:tɪʃ], *adj.* systematic(al).
Szenarium [stse'na:rjum], *n.* (—s, *pl.* —rien) scenario, stage, scene.
Szene ['stsɛ:nə], *f.* (—, *pl.* —n) scene; *in — setzen*, stage, produce; (*coll.*) get up; *sich in — setzen*, show off.
Szenerie [stsenə'ri:], *f.* (—, *pl.* —n) scenery.
szenisch ['stse:nɪʃ], *adj.* scenic.
Szepter ['stsɛptər], *n.* (—s, *pl.* —) sceptre, mace.

T

T [te:], *n.* (—, *pl.* —) the letter T.
Tabak ['ta:bak], *m.* (—s, *pl.* —e) tobacco.

Tabaksbeutel ['ta:baksbɔytəl], *m.* (—s, *pl.* —) tobacco-pouch.
Tabatiere [ta:ba'tjɛ:rə], *f.* (—, *pl.* —n) snuff-box.
tabellarisch [tabɛ'la:rɪʃ], *adj.* in tables, tabular.
Tabelle [ta'bɛlə], *f.* (—, *pl.* —n) table, index, schedule.
Tablett [ta'blɛt], *n.* (—s, *pl.* —s) tray.
Tablette [ta'blɛtə], *f.* (—, *pl.* —n) tablet, pill.
Tabulatur [tabula'tu:r], *f.* (—, *pl.* —en) tablature, tabling, index.
Tadel ['ta:dəl], *m.* (—s, *pl.* —) blame, censure, reproach; (*Sch.*) bad mark; *ohne* —, blameless.
tadellos ['ta:dəllo:s], *adj.* blameless, faultless, impeccable.
tadeln ['ta:dəln], *v.a.* blame, censure, find fault with; reprimand.
tadelnswert ['ta:dəlnsvɛ:rt], *adj.* blameworthy, culpable.
Tafel ['ta:fəl], *f.* (—, *pl.* —n) board; (*Sch.*) blackboard; slate; (*fig.*) (*obs.*) dinner, banquet; festive fare; (*chocolate*) slab, bar.
Täfelchen ['tɛ:fəlçən], *n.* (—s, *pl.* —) tablet.
tafelförmig ['ta:fəlfœrmɪç], *adj.* tabular.
tafeln ['ta:fəln], *v.n.* dine, feast.
täfeln ['tɛ:fəln], *v.a.* wainscot, panel.
Täfelung ['tɛ:fəluŋ], *f.* (—, *pl.* —en) wainscoting, panelling.
Taft, Taffet [taft, 'tafət], *m.* (—(e)s, *pl.* —e) taffeta.
Tag [ta:k], *m.* (—(e)s, *pl.* —e) day; (*fig.*) light; *der jüngste —*, Doomsday; *bei —e*, in the daytime, by daylight; *sich etwas bei —e besehen*, examine s.th. in the light of day; *für —*, day by day; *von — zu —*, from day to day; *dieser —e*, one of these days, shortly; *etwas an den — bringen*, bring s.th. to light; *in den — hinein leben*, live improvidently; *— und Nachtgleiche*, equinox.
Tagbau ['ta:kbau], *m.* (—s, *no pl.*) opencast mining.
Tageblatt ['ta:gəblat], *n.* (—s, *pl.* ⸚er) daily paper.
Tagebuch ['ta:gəbu:x], *n.* (—(e)s, *pl.* ⸚er) diary, journal.
Tagedieb ['ta:gədi:p], *m.* (—(e)s, *pl.* —e) idler, wastrel.
Tagelöhner ['ta:gəlø:nər], *m.* (—s, *pl.* —) day-labourer.
tagen ['ta:gən], *v.n.* dawn; (*gathering*) meet; (*Law*) sit.
Tagesanbruch ['ta:gəsanbrux], *m.* (—s, *pl.* ⸚e) daybreak, dawn.
Tagesbericht ['ta:gəsbərɪçt], *m.* (—(e)s, *pl.* —e) daily report.
Tagesgespräch ['ta:gəsgəʃprɛ:ç], *n.* (—(e)s, *pl.* —e) topic of the day.
Tagesordnung ['ta:gəsɔrdnuŋ], *f.* (—, *pl.* —en) agenda.
Tagewerk ['ta:gəvɛrk], *n.* (—s, *no pl.*) day's work, daily round.
täglich ['tɛ:klɪç], *adj.* daily.

tagsüber ['ta:ksy:bər], *adv.* in the daytime, during the day.

Taille ['taljə], *f.* (—, *pl.* —n) waist.

takeln ['ta:kəln], *v.a.* tackle, rig.

Takelwerk ['ta:kəlvɛrk], *n.* (—s, *no pl.*) rigging.

Takt (1) [takt], *m.* (—es, *pl.* —e) (*Mus.*) time, measure, bar; — *schlagen*, beat time.

Takt (2) [takt], *m.* (—es, *no pl.*) tact, discretion.

taktfest ['taktfɛst], *adj.* (*Mus.*) good at keeping time; (*fig.*) firm.

taktieren [tak'ti:rən], *v.n.* (*Mus.*) beat time.

Taktik ['taktɪk], *f.* (—, *pl.* —en) tactics.

Taktiker ['taktɪkər], *m.* (—s, *pl.* —) tactician.

taktisch ['taktɪʃ], *adj.* tactical.

taktlos ['taktlo:s], *adj.* tactless.

Taktmesser ['taktmɛsər], *m.* (—s, *pl.* —) metronome.

Taktstock ['taktʃtɔk], *m.* (—s, *pl.* ⁀e) baton.

Tal [ta:l], *n.* (—(e)s, *pl.* ⁀er) valley, dale, glen.

talab [ta:l'ap], *adv.* downhill.

Talar [ta'la:r], *m.* (—s, *pl.* —e) gown.

Talent [ta'lɛnt], *n.* (—(e)s, *pl.* —e) talent, accomplishment, gift.

talentiert [talən'ti:rt], *adj.* talented, gifted, accomplished.

talentvoll [ta'lɛntfɔl], *adj.* talented, gifted, accomplished.

Taler ['ta:lər], *m.* (—s, *pl.* —) old German coin; thaler.

Talfahrt ['ta:lfa:rt], *f.* (—, *pl.* —en) descent.

Talg [talk], *m.* (—(e)s, *no pl.*) tallow.

Talk [talk], *m.* (—(e)s, *no pl.*) talc.

Talkerde ['talke:rdə], *f.* (—, *no pl.*) magnesia.

Talkessel ['ta:lkɛsəl], *m.* (—s, *pl.* —) (*Geog.*) hollow, narrow valley.

Talmulde ['ta:lmuldə], *f.* (—, *pl.* —n) narrow valley, trough.

Talschlucht ['ta:lʃluxt], *f.* (—, *pl.* —en) glen.

Talsohle ['ta:lzo:lə], *f.* (—, *pl.* —n) floor of a valley.

Talsperre ['ta:lʃpɛrə], *f.* (—, *pl.* —n) dam (across valley); barrage.

Tambour ['tambu:r], *m.* (—s, *pl.* —e) drummer.

Tamtam ['tamtam], *n.* (—s, *no pl.*) tom-tom; (*fig.*) palaver.

Tand [tant], *m.* (—(e)s, *no pl.*) knick-knack, trifle; rubbish.

Tändelei [tɛndə'laɪ], *f.* (—, *pl.* —en) trifling, toying; (*fig.*) flirting.

Tändelmarkt ['tɛndəlmarkt], *m.* (—s, *pl.* ⁀e) rag-fair.

tändeln ['tɛndəln], *v.n.* trifle, dally, toy; (*fig.*) flirt.

Tang [taŋ], *m.* (—s, *pl.* —e) (*Bot.*) seaweed.

Tanganjika [taŋga'nji:ka], *n.* Tanganyika.

Tangente [taŋ'gɛntə], *f.* (—, *pl.* —n) tangent.

Tanger ['taŋər], *n.* Tangier.

Tank [taŋk], *m.* (—(e)s, *pl.* —e) tank.

tanken ['taŋkən], *v.n.* refuel; fill up (with petrol).

Tankstelle ['taŋkʃtɛlə], *f.* (—, *pl.* —n) filling-station.

Tanne ['tanə], *f.* (—, *pl.* —n) (*Bot.*) fir.

Tannenbaum ['tanənbaum], *m.* (—s, *pl.* ⁀e) (*Bot.*) fir-tree.

Tannenholz ['tanənhɔlts], *n.* (—es, *no pl.*) (*timber*) deal.

Tannenzapfen ['tanəntsapfən], *m.* (—s, *pl.* —) (*Bot.*) fir-cone.

Tansania [tanza'ni:a], *n.* Tanzania.

Tante ['tantə], *f.* (—, *pl.* —n) aunt.

Tantieme [tã'tjɛːmə], *f.* (—, *pl.* —n) royalty, share (in profits), percentage.

Tanz [tants], *m.* (—es, *pl.* ⁀e) dance.

Tanzboden ['tantsbo:dən], *m.* (—s, *pl.* ⁀) ballroom, dance-hall.

tänzeln ['tɛntsəln], *v.n.* skip about, frisk; (*horses*) amble.

tanzen ['tantsən], *v.a., v.n.* dance.

tanzlustig ['tantslustɪç], *adj.* fond of dancing.

Tapet [ta'pe:t], *n.* (—s, *no pl.*) *aufs — bringen*, broach, bring up for discussion.

Tapete [ta'pe:tə], *f.* (—, *pl.* —n) wall-paper.

tapezieren [tapə'tsi:rən], *v.a.* paper.

Tapezierer [tapə'tsi:rər], *m.* (—s, *pl.* —) paperhanger; upholsterer.

tapfer ['tapfər], *adj.* brave, valiant, gallant, courageous.

Tapferkeit ['tapfərkaɪt], *f.* (—, *no pl.*) valour, bravery, gallantry.

Tapisserie [tapɪsə'ri:], *f.* (—, *no pl.*) needlework; tapestry.

tappen ['tapən], *v.n.* grope about.

täppisch ['tɛpɪʃ], *adj.* clumsy, awkward, unwieldy.

tarnen ['tarnən], *v.a.* camouflage.

Tasche ['taʃə], *f.* (—, *pl.* —n) pocket; bag, pouch; *in die — stecken*, pocket; *in die — greifen*, pay, fork out, put o.'s hand in o.'s pocket.

Taschendieb ['taʃəndi:p], *m.* (—(e)s, *pl.* —e) pickpocket; *vor —en wird gewarnt*, beware of pickpockets.

Taschenformat ['taʃənfɔrma:t], *n.* (—s, *no pl.*) pocket-size.

Taschenspieler ['taʃənʃpi:lər], *m.* (—s, *pl.* —) juggler, conjurer.

Taschentuch ['taʃəntu:x], *n.* (—s, *pl.* ⁀er) (pocket-)handkerchief.

Taschenuhr ['taʃənu:r], *f.* (—, *pl.* —en) pocket-watch.

Tasse ['tasə], *f.* (—, *pl.* —n) cup.

Tastatur [tasta'tu:r], *f.* (—, *pl.* —en) keyboard.

Taste ['tastə], *f.* (—, *pl.* —n) (*Mus.*) key.

tasten ['tastən], *v.n.* grope about, feel o.'s way.

Tastsinn ['tastzɪn], *m.* (—s, *no pl.*) sense of touch.

technologisch

Tat [ta:t], *f.* (—, *pl.* —en) deed, act, action; feat, exploit; *in der* —, in fact, indeed; *auf frischer* —, in the very act; *einem mit Rat und* — *beistehen*, give s.o. advice and guidance, help by word and deed.

Tatbestand [ˈta:tbəʃtant], *m.* (—es, *pl.* ⁻e) (*Law*) facts of the case.

Tatendrang [ˈta:təndraŋ], *m.* (—(e)s, *no pl.*) urge for action; impetuosity.

tatenlos [ˈta:tənlo:s], *adj.* inactive.

Täter [ˈtɛ:tər], *m.* (—s, *pl.* —) perpetrator, doer; culprit.

tätig [ˈtɛ:tɪç], *adj.* active, busy.

Tätigkeit [ˈtɛ:tɪçkaɪt], *f.* (—, *pl.* —en) activity.

Tätigkeitswort [ˈtɛ:tɪçkaɪtsvɔrt], *n.* (—(e)s, *pl.* ⁻er) (*Gram.*) verb.

Tatkraft [ˈta:tkraft], *f.* (—, *no pl.*) energy.

tätlich [ˈtɛ:tlɪç], *adj.* — *werden*, become violent.

tätowieren [tɛ:toˈvi:rən], *v.a.* tattoo.

Tatsache [ˈta:tzaxa], *f.* (—, *pl.* —en) fact, matter of fact.

tatsächlich [ˈta:tzɛçlɪç], *adj.* actual. — *excl.* really!

tätscheln [ˈtɛ:tʃəln], *v.a.* fondle.

Tatterich [ˈtatərɪç], *m.* (—s, *no pl.*) (*coll.*) trembling, shakiness.

Tatze [ˈtatsə], *f.* (—, *pl.* —n) paw.

Tau (1) [tau], *m.* (—s, *no pl.*) thaw; dew.

Tau (2) [tau], *n.* (—s, *pl.* —e) rope, cable.

taub [taup], *adj.* deaf; (*nut*) hollow, empty; — *machen*, deafen; — *sein gegen*, turn a deaf ear to.

Täubchen [ˈtɔypçən], *n.* (—s, *pl.* —) little dove; (*fig.*) sweetheart.

Taube [ˈtaubə], *f.* (—, *pl.* —n) (*Orn.*) pigeon, dove.

Taubenschlag [ˈtaubənʃla:k], *m.* (—s, *pl.* ⁻e) dovecote.

Taubenschwanz [ˈtaubənʃvants], *m.* (—es, *pl.* ⁻e) (*Ent.*) hawkmoth.

Tauber [ˈtaubər], *m.* (—s, *pl.* —) (*Orn.*) cock-pigeon.

Taubheit [ˈtauphaɪt], *f.* (—, *no pl.*) deafness.

Taubnessel [ˈtaupnɛsəl], *f.* (—, *pl.* —n) (*Bot.*) deadnettle.

taubstumm [ˈtaupʃtum], *adj.* deaf and dumb, deaf-mute.

tauchen [ˈtauçən], *v.n.* (*aux.* haben & sein) dive, plunge. — *v.a.* immerse, dip.

Tauchsieder [ˈtauçzi:dər], *m.* (—s, *pl.* —) (*Elec.*) immersion heater.

tauen [ˈtauən], *v.a., v.n.* thaw, melt.

Taufbecken [ˈtaufbɛkən], *n.* (—s, *pl.* —) (baptismal) font.

Taufe [ˈtaufə], *f.* (—, *pl.* —n) baptism, christening; *aus der* — *heben*, stand godparent.

taufen [ˈtaufən], *v.a.* baptise, christen.

Taufkleid [ˈtaufklaɪt], *n.* (—s, *pl.* —er) christening robe.

Täufling [ˈtɔyflɪŋ], *m.* (—s, *pl.* —e) infant presented for baptism; neophyte.

Taufname [ˈtaufna:mə], *n.* (—ns, *pl.* —n) Christian name.

Taufpate [ˈtaufpa:tə], *m.* (—n, *pl.* —n) godfather, godmother.

Taufstein [ˈtaufʃtain], *n.* (—s, *pl.* —e) (baptismal) font.

taugen [ˈtaugən], *v.n.* be good for, be fit for; *nichts* —, be good for nothing.

Taugenichts [ˈtaugənɪçts], *m.* (—, *pl.* —e) ne'er-do-well, scapegrace, good-for-nothing.

tauglich [ˈtauklɪç], *adj.* able; useful, fit, suitable.

Taumel [ˈtauməl], *m.* (—s, *no pl.*) giddiness, dizziness, staggering; (*fig.*) whirl; ecstasy, frenzy, delirium, intoxication.

taumeln [ˈtauməln], *v.n.* (*aux.* sein) reel, stagger.

Tausch [tauʃ], *m.* (—es, *no pl.*) exchange, barter.

tauschen [ˈtauʃən], *v.a.* exchange for, barter against, swop; *die Rollen* —, change places.

täuschen [ˈtɔyʃən], *v.a.* deceive, delude. — *v.r. sich* —, be mistaken.

Tauschhandel [ˈtauʃhandəl], *m.* (—s, *no pl.*) barter.

Tauschmittel [ˈtauʃmɪtəl], *n.* (—s, *pl.* —) medium of exchange.

Täuschung [ˈtɔyʃuŋ], *f.* (—, *pl.* —en) deceit, deception; illusion.

Täuschungsversuch [ˈtɔyʃuŋsfɛrzu:ç], *m.* (—es, *pl.* —e) attempt at deception; (*Mil.*) diversion.

tausend [ˈtauzənt], *num. adj.* a thousand.

tausendjährig [ˈtauzəntjɛːrɪç], *adj.* millennial, of a thousand years; *das* —*e Reich*, the millennium.

Tausendsasa [ˈtauzəntzasa], *m.* (—s, *pl.* —) devil of a fellow.

Tautropfen [ˈtautrɔpfən], *m.* (—s, *pl.* —) dew-drop.

Tauwetter [ˈtauvɛtər], *n.* (—s, *no pl.*) thaw.

Taxameter [taksaˈme:tər], *m.* (—s, *pl.* —) taximeter.

Taxe [ˈtaksə], *f.* (—, *pl.* —n) set rate, tariff; (taxi)cab; *nach der* — *verkauft werden*, be sold *ad valorem*.

taxieren [takˈsi:rən], *v.a.* appraise, value.

Taxus [ˈtaksus,] *m.* (—, *pl.* —) (*Bot.*) yew(-tree).

Technik [ˈtɛçnik], *f.* (—, *pl.* —en) technology, engineering; technique; skill, execution.

Techniker [ˈtɛçnikər], *m.* (—s, *pl.* —) technician, technical engineer.

Technikum [ˈtɛçnikum], *n.* (—s, *pl.* —s) technical school, college.

technisch [ˈtɛçniʃ], *adj.* technical; —*er Ausdruck*, technical term; —*e Störung*, technical hitch or breakdown.

technologisch [tɛçnoˈlo:giʃ], *adj.* technological.

221

Techtelmechtel

Techtelmechtel ['tɛçtəlmɛçtəl], n. (—s, pl. —) (coll.) love affair, flirtation.

Tee [te:], m. (—s, no pl.) tea.

Teedose ['te:do:zə], f. (—, pl. —n) tea-caddy.

Teekanne ['te:kanə], f. (—, pl. —n) tea-pot.

Teelöffel ['te:lœfəl], m. (—s, pl. —) tea-spoon.

Teemaschine ['te:maʃi:nə], f. (—, pl. —n) tea-urn.

Teer [te:r], m. (—(e)s, no pl.) tar.

Teerleinwand ['te:rlaɪnvant], f. (—, no pl.) tarpaulin.

Teerose ['te:ro:zə], f. (—, pl. —n) (Bot.) tea rose.

Teerpappe ['te:rpapə], f. (—, no pl.) roofing-felt.

teeren ['te:rən], v.a. tar.

Teesieb ['te:zi:p], n. (—(e)s, pl. —e) tea-strainer.

Teich [taɪç], m. (—es, pl. —e) pond.

Teig [taɪk], m. (—(e)s, pl. —e) dough, paste.

teigig ['taɪɡɪç], adj. doughy.

Teigrolle ['taɪkrɔlə], f. (—, pl. —n) rolling-pin.

Teil [taɪl], m. & n. (—(e)s, pl. —e) part; portion; piece, component; share; edler —, vital part; zum —, partly; zu gleichen —en, share and share alike.

teilbar ['taɪlba:r], adj. divisible.

Teilchen ['taɪlçən], n. (—s, pl. —) particle.

teilen ['taɪlən], v.a. divide; share; partition off. — v.r. sich —, share in; (road) fork.

Teiler ['taɪlər], m. (—s, pl. —) divider; (Maths.) divisor.

teilhaben ['taɪlha:bən], v.n. irr. (have a) share in, participate in.

Teilhaber ['taɪlha:bər], m. (—s, pl. —) partner.

teilhaftig ['taɪlhaftɪç], adj. sharing, participating; einer Sache — werden, partake of s.th., come in for s.th.

Teilnahme ['taɪlna:mə], f. (—, no pl.) participation; (fig.) sympathy, interest.

teilnahmslos ['taɪlna:mslo:s], adj. unconcerned, indifferent.

Teilnahmslosigkeit ['taɪlna:mslo:zɪçkaɪt], f. (—, no pl.) unconcern; listlessness, indifference.

teilnahmsvoll ['taɪlna:msfɔl], adj. solicitous.

teilnehmen ['taɪlne:mən], v.n. irr. take part (in), participate, partake; (fig.) sympathise.

Teilnehmer ['taɪlne:mər], m. (—s, pl. —) member, participant; (telephone) subscriber.

teils [taɪls], adv. partly.

Teilstrecke ['taɪlʃtrɛkə], f. (—, pl. —n) section (of a railway).

Teilung ['taɪluŋ], f. (—, pl. —en) division, partition; distribution.

Teilungszahl ['taɪluŋtsa:l], f. (—, pl. —en) (Maths.) dividend; quotient.

teilweise ['taɪlvaɪzə], adv. partly, in part.

Teilzahlung ['taɪltsa:luŋ], f. (—, pl. —en) part-payment, instalment.

Teint [tɛ̃], m. (—s, no pl.) complexion.

telephonieren [telefo'ni:rən], v.a., v.n. telephone.

Telegraphie [telegra'fi:], f. (—, no pl.) telegraphy.

telegraphisch [tele'gra:fɪʃ], adj. telegraphic, by telegram.

Telegramm [tele'gram], n. (—s, pl. —e) telegram, wire, cable.

Telegrammadresse [tele'gramadrɛsə], f. (—, pl. —n) telegraphic address.

Telegrammformular [tele'gramformula:r], n. (—s, pl. —e) telegram-form.

Teleskop [teles'ko:p], n. (—s, pl. —e) telescope.

Teller ['tɛlər], m. (—s, pl. —) plate.

Tempel ['tɛmpəl], m. (—s, pl. —) temple.

Temperament [tɛmpəra'mɛnt], n. (—s, pl. —e) temperament, disposition; (fig.) spirits.

temperamentvoll [tɛmpəra'mɛntfɔl], adj. full of spirits, vivacious, lively.

Temperatur [tɛmpəra'tu:r], f. (—, pl. —en) temperature.

Temperenzler [tɛmpə'rɛntslər], m. (—s, pl. —) total abstainer, teetotaller.

temperieren [tɛmpə'ri:rən], v.a. temper.

Tempo ['tɛmpo:], n. (—s, pl. —s, Tempi) time, measure, speed.

temporisieren [tɛmpori'zi:rən], v.n. temporise.

Tendenz [tɛn'dɛnts], f. (—, pl. —en) tendency.

tendenziös [tɛndɛn'tsjø:s], adj. biased, coloured, tendentious.

Tender ['tɛndər], m. (—, pl. —) (Railw.) tender.

Tenne ['tɛnə], f. (—, pl. —n) threshing floor.

Tenor [te'no:r], m. (—s, pl. ⸚e) (Mus.) tenor.

Teppich ['tɛpɪç], m. (—s, pl. —e) carpet.

Termin [tɛr'mi:n], m. (—s, pl. —e) time, date, appointed day; einen — ansetzen, fix a day (for a hearing, examination etc.).

Termingeschäft [tɛr'mi:nɡəʃɛft], n. (—s, pl. —e) (business in) futures.

Terminologie [tɛrminolo'gi:], f. (—, pl. —n) terminology.

Terpentin [tɛrpɛn'ti:n], n. (—s, no pl.) turpentine.

Terrain [tɛ'rɛ̃], n. (—s, pl. —s) ground, terrain.

Terrasse [tɛ'rasə], f. (—, pl. —n) terrace.

Terrine [tɛ'ri:nə], f. (—, pl. —n) tureen.

territorial [tɛrɪto'rja:l], adj. territorial.

Territorium [tɛrɪ'to:rjum], n. (—s, pl. —torien) territory.

tertiär [tɛrˈtsjɛːr], *adj.* tertiary.
Terzett [tɛrˈtsɛt], *n.* (—s, *pl.* —e) trio.
Testament [tɛstaˈmɛnt], *n.* (—s, *pl.* —e) testament, will; (*Bibl.*) Testament; *ohne* —, intestate.
testamentarisch [tɛstamɛnˈtaːrɪʃ], *adj.* testamentary.
Testamentseröffnung [tɛstaˈmɛntsɛrˌœfnuŋ], *f.* (—, *pl.* —en) reading of the will.
Testamentsvollstrecker [tɛstaˈmɛntsfɔlˌʃtrɛkər], *m.* (—s, *pl.* —) executor.
teuer [ˈtɔyər], *adj.* dear; costly, expensive; *einem — zu stehen kommen*, cost s.o. dear.
Teuerung [ˈtɔyəruŋ], *f.* (—, *pl.* —en) scarcity, dearth.
Teufel [ˈtɔyfəl], *m.* (—s, *pl.* —) devil, fiend; *armer* —, poor devil; *scher dich zum* —, go to blazes; *den — an die Wand malen*, talk of the devil.
Teufelei [tɔyfəˈlaɪ], *f.* (—, *pl.* —en) devilry, devilish trick.
teuflisch [ˈtɔyflɪʃ], *adj.* devilish, diabolical.
Thailand [ˈtaɪlant], *n.* Thailand.
Theater [teˈaːtər], *n.* (—s, *pl.* —) theatre, stage.
Theaterkarte [teˈaːtərkartə], *f.* (—, *pl.* —n) theatre-ticket.
Theaterkasse [teˈaːtərkasə], *f.* (—, *pl.* —n) box-office.
Theaterstück [teˈaːtərʃtyk], *n.* (—(e)s, *pl.* —e) play, drama.
Theatervorstellung [teˈaːtərfoːrʃtɛluŋ], *f.* (—, *pl.* —en) theatre performance.
Theaterzettel [teˈaːtartsɛtəl], *m.* (—s, *pl.* —) play-bill.
theatralisch [teaˈtraːlɪʃ], *adj.* theatrical; dramatic; histrionic.
Thema [ˈteːmaː], *n.* (—s, *pl.* —men, *Themata*) theme, subject, topic.
Themse [ˈtɛmzə], *f.* Thames.
Theologe [teoˈloːgə], *m.* (—n, *pl.* —n) theologian.
Theologie [teoloˈgiː], *f.* (—, *no pl.*) theology, divinity.
theoretisch [teoˈreːtɪʃ], *adj.* theoretical.
theoretisieren [teoretiˈziːrən], *v.n.* theorise.
Theorie [teoˈriː], *f.* (—, *pl.* —n) theory.
Therapie [teraˈpiː], *f.* (—, *no pl.*) therapy.
Therme [ˈtɛrmə], *f.* (—, *pl.* —n) hot spring.
Thermometer [tɛrmoˈmeːtər], *n.* (—s, *pl.* —) thermometer.
Thermosflasche [ˈtɛrmɔsflaʃə], *f.* (—, *pl.* —n) thermos-flask.
These [ˈteːzə], *f.* (—, *pl.* —n) thesis.
Thron [troːn], *m.* (—(e)s, *pl.* —e) throne; *auf den — setzen*, place on the throne, enthrone; *vom — stoßen*, dethrone, depose.
Thronbesteigung [ˈtroːnbəʃtaɪguŋ], *f.* (—, *pl.* —en) accession (to the throne).
Thronbewerber [ˈtroːnbəvɛrbər], *m.* (—s, *pl.* —) claimant to the throne, pretender.
thronen [ˈtroːnən], *v.n.* sit enthroned.

Thronerbe [ˈtroːnɛrbə], *m.* (—n, *pl.* —n) heir apparent, crown prince.
Thronfolge [ˈtroːnfɔlgə], *f.* (—, *no pl.*) line *or* order of succession.
Thronfolger [ˈtroːnfɔlgər], *m.* (—s, *pl.* —) heir to the throne, heir apparent.
Thronhimmel [ˈtroːnhɪməl], *m.* (—s, *pl.* —) canopy.
Thronrede [ˈtroːnreːdə], *f.* (—, *pl.* —n) speech from the throne.
Thunfisch [ˈtuːnfɪʃ], *m.* (—es, *pl.* —e) (*Zool.*) tunny, (*Am.*) tuna.
Thüringen [ˈtyːrɪŋən], *n.* Thuringia.
Thymian [ˈtyːmjaːn], *m.* (—s, *no pl.*) (*Bot.*) thyme.
ticken [ˈtɪkən], *v.n.* tick.
tief [tiːf], *adj.* deep, profound, low; far; extreme; (*voice*) bass; (*fig.*) profound; *in —ster Nacht*, in the dead of night; *aus —stem Herzen*, from the bottom of o.'s heart. — *adv.* — *atmen*, take a deep breath; — *in Schulden*, head over ears in debt; — *verletzt*, cut to the quick.
Tiefbau [ˈtiːfbau], *m.* (—s, *no pl.*) underground workings.
tiefbedrückt [ˈtiːfbədrykt], *adj.* deeply distressed; very depressed.
tiefbewegt [ˈtiːfbəveːkt], *adj.* deeply moved.
Tiefe [ˈtiːfə], *f.* (—, *pl.* —en) depth; (*fig.*) profundity.
tiefgebeugt [ˈtiːfgəbɔykt], *adj.* bowed down.
tiefgreifend [ˈtiːfgraɪfənt], *adj.* radical, sweeping.
tiefschürfend [ˈtiːfʃyrfənt], *adj.* profound; thoroughgoing.
Tiefsee [ˈtiːfzeː], *f.* (—, *no pl.*) deep sea.
Tiefsinn [ˈtiːfzɪn], *m.* (—s, *no pl.*) pensiveness, melancholy.
tiefsinnig [ˈtiːfzɪnɪç], *adj.* pensive, melancholy, melancholic(al).
Tiegel [ˈtiːgəl], *m.* (—s, *pl.* —) crucible; saucepan.
Tier [tiːr], *n.* (—(e)s, *pl.* —e) animal, beast; *ein großes* —, (*coll.*) a V.I.P., a bigwig; (*Am.*) a swell, a big shot.
Tierart [ˈtiːraːrt], *f.* (—, *pl.* —en) (*Zool.*) species.
Tierarzt [ˈtiːraːrtst], *m.* (—es, *pl.* ⸚e) veterinary surgeon.
Tierbändiger [ˈtiːrbɛndɪgər], *m.* (—s, *pl.* —) animal-tamer.
Tiergarten [ˈtiːrgartən], *m.* (—s, *pl.* ⸚) zoological gardens, zoo.
tierisch [ˈtiːrɪʃ], *adj.* animal, brute, brutal, bestial.
Tierkreis [ˈtiːrkraɪs], *m.* (—es, *no pl.*) zodiac.
Tierkunde [ˈtiːrkundə], *f.* (—, *no pl.*) zoology.
Tierquälerei [ˈtiːrkvɛːləraɪ], *f.* (—, *pl.* —en) cruelty to animals.
Tierreich [ˈtiːrraɪç], *n.* (—(e)s, *no pl.*) animal kingdom.
Tierschutzverein [ˈtiːrʃutsfəraɪn], *m.* (—s, *pl.* —e) society for the prevention of cruelty to animals.

Tierwärter ['tiːrvɛrtər], *m.* (—s, *pl.* —) keeper (at a zoo).

Tiger ['tiːgər], *m.* (—s, *pl.* —) (*Zool.*) tiger.

Tigerin ['tiːgərɪn], *f.* (—, *pl.* —**nen**) (*Zool.*) tigress.

tilgbar ['tɪlkbaːr], *adj.* extinguishable; (*debt*) redeemable.

tilgen ['tɪlgən], *v.a.* strike out, efface, annul; (*debt*) discharge; (*sin*) expiate, atone for.

Tilgung ['tɪlguŋ], *f.* (—, *pl.* —**en**) striking out, obliteration; annulment; payment; redemption.

Tilgungsfonds ['tɪlguŋsfɔ̃], *m.* (—, *pl.* —) sinking fund.

Tingeltangel ['tɪŋəltaŋəl], *m. & n.* (—s, *pl.* —) (*coll.*) music-hall.

Tinktur [tɪŋk'tuːr], *f.* (—, *pl.* —**en**) tincture.

Tinte ['tɪntə], *f.* (—, *pl.* —**n**) ink; *in der — sein*, be in a jam, be in the soup.

Tintenfaß ['tɪntənfas], *n.* (—**sses**, *pl.* ·**sser**) ink-pot, ink-stand.

Tintenfisch ['tɪntənfɪʃ], *m.* (—**es**, *pl.* —**e**) (*Zool.*) cuttle-fish.

Tintenfleck ['tɪntənflɛk], *m.* (—**s**, *pl.* —**e**) blot, ink-spot.

Tintenklecks ['tɪntənklɛks], *m.* (—**es**, *pl.* —**e**) blot.

Tintenstift ['tɪntənʃtɪft], *m.* (—**s**, *pl.* —**e**) indelible pencil.

Tintenwischer ['tɪntənvɪʃər], *m.* (—**s**, *pl.* —) pen-wiper.

tippen ['tɪpən], *v.a.* tap; (*coll.*) type.

Tirol [ti'roːl], *n.* Tyrol.

Tisch [tɪʃ], *m.* (—**es**, *pl.* —**e**) table, board; *den — decken*, lay the table; *zu — gehen*, sit down to dinner.

Tischdecke ['tɪʃdɛkə], *f.* (—, *pl.* —**n**) tablecloth.

Tischgebet ['tɪʃgəbeːt], *n.* (—**s**, *pl.* —**e**) grace.

Tischler ['tɪʃlər], *m.* (—**s**, *pl.* —) joiner, cabinet-maker, carpenter.

Tischlerei [tɪʃlə'raɪ], *f.* (—, *no pl.*) joinery, cabinet-making, carpentry.

Tischrede ['tɪʃreːdə], *f.* (—, *pl.* —**n**) after-dinner speech.

Tischrücken ['tɪʃrykən], *n.* (—**s**, *no pl.*) table-turning.

Tischtennis ['tɪʃtɛnɪs], *n.* (—, *no pl.*) table-tennis, ping-pong.

Tischtuch ['tɪʃtuːx], *n.* (—(**e**)**s**, *pl.* ·**er**) tablecloth.

Tischzeit ['tɪʃtsaɪt], *f.* (—, *pl.* —**en**) mealtime.

Titane [ti'taːnə], *m.* (—**n**, *pl.* —**n**) Titan.

titanenhaft [ti'taːnənhaft], *adj.* titanic.

Titel ['tiːtəl], *m.* (—**s**, *pl.* —) title; claim; heading, headline.

Titelbild ['tiːtəlbɪlt], *n.* (—(**e**)**s**, *pl.* —**er**) frontispiece.

Titelblatt ['tiːtəlblat], *n.* (—(**e**)**s**, *pl.* ·**er**) title page.

Titelrolle ['tiːtəlrɔlə], *f.* (—, *pl.* —**n**) title role.

titulieren [titu'liːrən], *v.a.* style, address.

toben ['toːbən], *v.n.* rave; rage, roar; be furious; be wild.

tobsüchtig ['toːpzyçtɪç], *adj.* raving, mad.

Tochter ['tɔxtər], *f.* (—, *pl.* ·) daughter.

töchterlich ['tœçtərlɪç], *adj.* filial, daughterly.

Tod [toːt], *m.* (—**es**, *pl.* —**esfälle** *or* (*rare*) —**e**) death, decease, demise; *dem — geweiht*, doomed; *Kampf auf — und Leben*, fight to the death; *zum — verurteilen*, condemn to death.

Todesangst ['toːdəsaŋst], *f.* (—, *pl.* ·**e**) agony, mortal terror.

Todesanzeige ['toːdəsantsaɪgə], *f.* (—, *pl.* —**n**) announcement of death; obituary notice.

Todesfall ['toːdəsfal], *m.* (—(**e**)**s**, *pl.* ·**e**) death, decease; fatality.

Todesgefahr ['toːdəsgəfaːr], *f.* (—, *pl.* —**en**) mortal danger.

Todeskampf ['toːdəskampf], *m.* (—(**e**)**s**, *pl.* ·**e**) death agony.

todesmutig ['toːdəsmuːtɪç], *adj.* death-defying.

Todesstoß ['toːdəsʃtoːs], *m.* (—**es**, *pl.* ·**e**) death-blow.

Todesstrafe ['toːdəsʃtraːfə], *f.* (—, *no pl.*) capital punishment.

Todfeind ['toːtfaɪnt], *m.* (—**es**, *pl.* —**e**) mortal enemy.

todkrank ['toːtkraŋk], *adj.* sick unto death, dangerously *or* mortally ill.

tödlich ['tœːtlɪç], *adj.* mortal, deadly, fatal.

todmüde ['toːtmyːdə], *adj.* tired to death.

Todsünde ['toːtzyndə], *f.* (—, *pl.* —**n**) mortal sin.

Togo ['toːgo], *n.* Togo.

Toilette [toa'lɛtə], *f.* (—, *pl.* —**n**) lavatory, toilet; (*fig.*) dress.

tolerant [tole'rant], *adj.* tolerant.

Toleranz [tole'rants], *f.* (—, *no pl.*) toleration; tolerance.

tolerieren [tole'riːrən], *v.a.* tolerate.

toll [tɔl], *adj.* mad, frantic; wild; —*er Streich*, mad prank; *zum — werden*, enough to drive o. mad.

Tolle ['tɔlə], *f.* (—, *pl.* —**n**) (*dial.*) forelock, tuft of hair, top-knot.

Tollhaus ['tɔlhaus], *n.* (—**es**, *pl.* ·**er**) madhouse, lunatic asylum.

Tollheit ['tɔlhaɪt], *f.* (—, *pl.* —**en**) foolhardiness, mad prank.

Tollkirsche ['tɔlkɪrʃə], *f.* (—, *pl.* —**n**) belladonna, deadly nightshade.

Tollwut ['tɔlvuːt], *f.* (—, *no pl.*) frenzy; rabies.

Tolpatsch ['tɔlpatʃ], *m.* (—**es**, *pl.* —**e**) clumsy person.

Tölpel ['tœlpəl], *m.* (—**s**, *pl.* —) blockhead, lout, hobbledehoy.

Tölpelei [tœlpə'laɪ], *f.* (—, *pl.* —**en**) clumsiness, awkwardness.

tölpelhaft ['tœlpəlhaft], *adj.* clumsy, doltish, loutish.

Tomate [to'maːtə], *f.* (—, *pl.* —**n**) tomato.

Ton (1) [to:n], *m.* (—(e)s, *pl.* ⸚e) sound, tone, accent, note; shade; manners; *guter (schlechter)* —, good (bad) form, etiquette; *den — angeben,* set the fashion.

Ton (2) [to:n], *m.* (—s, *no pl.*) clay, potter's earth.

Tonabnehmer ['to:nabne:mər], *m.* (—s, *pl.* —) (*gramophone*) pick-up.

tonangebend ['to:nange:bənt], *adj.* leading in fashion, setting the pace; leading, fashionable.

Tonart ['to:na:rt], *f.* (—, *pl.* —en) (*Mus.*) key.

Tonbandgerät ['to:nbantgɛrɛ:t], *n.* (—s, *pl.* —e) tape-recorder.

tönen ['tø:nən], *v.n.* sound.

Tonerde ['to:ne:rdə], *f.* (—, *no pl.*) clay.

tönern ['tø:nərn], *adj.* earthen.

Tonfall ['to:nfal], *m.* (—s, *no pl.*) cadence, intonation (of voice).

Tonfolge ['to:nfɔlgə], *f.* (—, *pl.* —n) (*Mus.*) succession of notes.

Tonführung ['to:nfy:ruŋ], *f.* (—, *no pl.*) modulation.

Tonkunst ['to:nkunst], *f.* (—, *no pl.*) music.

Tonkünstler ['to:nkynstlər], *m.* (—s, *pl.* —) musician.

Tonleiter ['to:nlaɪtər], *f.* (—, *pl.* —n) scale, gamut.

Tonne ['tɔnə], *f.* (—, *pl.* —n) tun, cask, barrel; ton.

Tonnengewölbe ['tɔnəngəvœlbə], *n.* (—s, *pl.* —) cylindrical vault.

Tonpfeife ['to:npfaɪfə], *f.* (—, *pl.* —n) clay-pipe.

Tonsatz ['to:nzats], *m.* (—es, *pl.* ⸚e) (*Mus.*) composition.

Tonsur [tɔn'zu:r], *f.* (—, *pl.* —en) tonsure.

Tonwelle ['to:nvɛlə], *f.* (—, *pl.* —n) sound-wave.

Topas [to'pa:s], *m.* (—es, *pl.* —e) topaz.

Topf [tɔpf], *m.* (—(e)s, *pl.* ⸚e) pot; *alles in einen — werfen,* lump everything together.

Topfblume ['tɔpfblu:mə], *f.* (—, *pl.* —n) pot-plant.

Topfdeckel ['tɔpfdɛkəl], *m.* (—s, *pl.* —) lid of a pot.

Töpfer ['tœpfər], *m.* (—s, *pl.* —) potter.

Töpferarbeit ['tœpfərarbaɪt], *f.* (—, *pl.* —en) pottery.

Töpferscheibe ['tœpfərʃaɪbə], *f.* (—, *pl.* —n) potter's wheel.

Töpferware ['tœpfərva:rə], *f.* (—, *pl.* —n) pottery, earthenware.

Topfgucker ['tɔpfgukər], *m.* (—s, *pl.* —) busybody; inquisitive person.

Topographie [topogra'fi:], *f.* (—, *no pl.*) topography.

Tor (1) [to:r], *m.* (—en, *pl.* —en) (*obs.*) fool, simpleton.

Tor (2) [to:r], *n.* (—(e)s, *pl.* —e) gate; (*Footb.*) goal.

Torangel ['to:raŋəl], *f.* (—, *pl.* —n) hinge.

Tor(es)schluß ['to:r(əs)ʃlus], *m.* (—es, *no pl.*) shutting of the gate; *noch gerade vor —,* at the eleventh hour.

Torf [tɔrf], *m.* (—(e)s, *no pl.*) peat, turf.

Torfgrube ['tɔrfgru:bə], *f.* (—, *pl.* —n) turf-pit.

Torfmoor ['tɔrfmo:r], *n.* (—s, *pl.* —e) peat-bog.

Torfstecher ['tɔrfʃtɛçər], *m.* (—s, *pl.* —) peat-cutter.

Torheit ['to:rhaɪt], *f.* (—, *pl.* —en) foolishness, folly.

Torhüter ['to:rhy:tər], *m.* (—s, *pl.* —) gate-keeper.

töricht ['tø:rɪçt], *adj.* foolish, silly.

Törin ['tø:rɪn], *f.* (—, *pl.* —nen) (*rare*) foolish woman.

torkeln ['tɔrkəln], *v.n.* (*aux.* sein) (*coll.*) stagger, reel.

Tornister [tɔr'nɪstər], *m.* (—s, *pl.* —) knapsack, satchel.

Torpedo [tɔr'pe:do], *m.* (—s, *pl.* —s) torpedo.

Torso ['tɔrzo], *m.* (—s, *pl.* —s) trunk, torso.

Tort [tɔrt], *m.* (—s, *no pl.*) injury, wrong; *einem einen — antun,* wrong s.o.; play a trick on s.o.

Torte ['tɔrtə], *f.* (—, *pl.* —n) cake, pastry, tart.

Tortur [tɔr'tu:r], *f.* (—, *pl.* —en) torture.

Torwächter ['to:rvɛçtər], *m.* (—s, *pl.* —) gate-keeper; porter.

tosen ['to:zən], *v.n.* roar.

tot [to:t], *adj.* dead, deceased.

total [to'ta:l], *adj.* total, complete.

Totalisator [totali'za:tɔr], *m.* (—s, *pl.* —en) totalisator; (*coll.*) tote.

Totalleistung [to'ta:llaɪstuŋ], *f.* (—, *pl.* —en) full effect; total output.

Tote ['to:tə], *m.*, *f.* (—n, *pl.* —n) dead person, the deceased.

töten ['tø:tən], *v.a.* kill, put to death.

Totenacker ['to:tənakər], *m.* (—s, *pl.* ⸚) churchyard, cemetery.

Totenamt ['to:tənamt], *n.* (—s, *no pl.*) office for the dead, requiem, Mass for the dead.

Totenbahre ['to:tənba:rə], *f.* (—, *pl.* —n) bier.

Totengräber ['to:təngrɛ:bər], *m.* (—s, *pl.* —) grave-digger.

Totenhemd ['to:tənhɛmt], *n.* (—(e)s, *pl.* —en) shroud, winding-sheet.

Totenklage ['to:tənkla:gə], *f.* (—, *no pl.*) lament.

Totenschein ['to:tənʃaɪn], *m.* (—(e)s, *pl.* —e) death-certificate.

Totenstille ['to:tənʃtɪlə], *f.* (—, *no pl.*) dead calm.

Totenwache ['to:tənvaxə], *f.* (—, *no pl.*) wake.

totgeboren ['to:tgəbo:rən], *adj.* stillborn, born dead.

Totschlag ['to:tʃla:k], *m.* (—s, *no pl.*) manslaughter.

totschlagen ['to:tʃla:gən], *v.a.* irr. kill, strike dead.

Totschläger ['to:tʃlɛ:gər], *m.* (—s, *pl.* —) loaded cane, cudgel.

totschweigen ['to:tʃvaigən], *v.a. irr.* hush up.

Tötung ['tø:tuŋ], *f.* (—, *pl.* —en) killing.

Tour [tu:r], *f.* (—, *pl.* —en) tour, excursion; *in einer* —, ceaselessly; *auf —en bringen,* (coll.) (Motor.) rev up.

Tournee [tur'ne:], *f.* (—, *pl.* —n) (Theat.) tour.

Trab [tra:p], *m.* (—(e)s, *no pl.*) trot.

Trabant [tra'bant], *m.* (—en, *pl.* —en) satellite.

traben ['tra:bən], *v.n.* (aux. sein) trot.

Trabrennen ['tra:prɛnən], *n.* (—s, *pl.* —) trotting-race.

Tracht [traxt], *f.* (—, *pl.* —en) dress, costume; national costume; native dress; *eine* — *Prügel,* a good hiding.

trachten ['traxtən], *v.n.* strive, aspire, endeavour; *einem nach dem Leben* —, seek to kill s.o.

trächtig ['trɛçtɪç], *adj.* (animal) pregnant, with young.

Trafik [tra'fik], *m.* (—s, *pl.* —s) (Austr.) tobacco-kiosk.

Tragbahre ['tra:kba:rə], *f.* (—, *pl.* —n) stretcher.

Tragbalken ['tra:kbalkən], *m.* (—s *pl.*, —) girder.

tragbar ['tra:kba:r], *adj.* portable; tolerable.

träge ['trɛ:gə], *adj.* lazy, indolent, inert, sluggish.

tragen ['tra:gən], *v.a. irr.* bear, carry; (dress) wear; (fig.) bear, endure; *Bedenken* —, hesitate, have doubts; *Zinsen* —, yield interest; *einen auf Händen* —, care lovingly for s.o.

Träger ['trɛ:gər], *m.* (—s, *pl.* —) porter, carrier; girder.

Trägheit ['trɛ:khait], *f.* (—, *no pl.*) indolence, laziness, inertia.

tragisch ['tra:gɪʃ], *adj.* tragic(al).

Tragkraft ['tra:kkraft], *f.* (—, *no pl.*) carrying or load capacity; lifting power.

Tragödie [tra'gø:djə], *f.* (—, *pl.* —n) tragedy.

Tragsessel ['tra:kzɛsəl], *m.* (—s, *pl.* —) sedan-chair.

Tragweite ['tra:kvaitə], *f.* (—, *no pl.*) significance, importance, range.

trainieren [trɛ'ni:rən], *v.a.* train.

Traktat [trak'ta:t], *n.* (—s, *pl.* —e) treatise, tract.

Traktätchen [trak'tɛ:tçən], *n.* (—s, *pl.* —) (short) tract.

traktieren [trak'ti:rən], *v.a.* treat; treat badly.

trällern ['trɛlərn], *v.n.* trill, hum.

Trambahn ['tramba:n], *f.* (—, *pl.* —en) tram; (Am.) streetcar.

Trampel ['trampəl], *n.* (—s, *pl.* —) clumsy person, bumpkin; (Am.) hick.

trampeln ['trampəln], *v.n.* trample.

Trampeltier ['trampəlti:r], *n.* (—s, *pl.* —e) camel; (fig.) clumsy person.

Tran [tra:n], *m.* (—(e)s, *no pl.*) whale-oil.

tranchieren [trã'ʃi:rən], *v.a.* carve.

Tranchiermesser [trã'ʃi:rmɛsər], *n.* (—s, *pl.* —) carving-knife.

Träne ['trɛ:nə], *f.* (—, *pl.* —n) tear, teardrop; *zu* —n *gerührt,* moved to tears.

tränen ['trɛ:nən], *v.n.* (eyes) water.

Tränendrüse ['trɛ:nəndry:zə], *f.* (—, *pl.* —n) lachrymal gland.

tränenleer ['trɛ:nənle:r], *adj.* tearless.

Tränenstrom ['trɛ:nənʃtro:m], *m.* (—s, *pl.* —e) flood of tears.

tränenvoll ['trɛ:nənfɔl], *adj.* tearful.

tranig ['tra:nɪç], *adj.* dull, slow.

Trank [traŋk], *m.* (—(e)s, *pl.* —e) drink, beverage, potion.

Tränke ['trɛŋkə], *f.* (—, *pl.* —n) (horse) watering-place.

tränken ['trɛŋkən], *v.a.* give to drink, water; impregnate, saturate.

transitiv ['tranziti:f], *adj.* transitive.

Transitlager ['tranzitla:gər], *n.* (—s, *pl.* —) bonded warehouse; transit camp.

transitorisch [tranzi'to:rɪʃ], *adj.* transitory.

transpirieren [transpi'ri:rən], *v.n.* perspire.

transponieren [transpo'ni:rən], *v.a.* transpose.

Transportkosten [trans'pɔrtkɔstən], *f. pl.* shipping charges.

Transportmittel [trans'pɔrtmɪtəl], *n.* (—s, *pl.* —) means of carriage, conveyance, transport.

Trapez [tra'pe:ts], *n.* (—es, *pl.* —e) trapeze; (Maths.) trapezoid.

Tratsch [tra:tʃ], *m.* (—es, *no pl.*) (coll.) gossip, tittle-tattle.

tratschen ['tra:tʃən], *v.n.* (coll.) gossip.

Tratte ['tratə], *f.* (—, *pl.* —n) (Comm.) draft, bill of exchange.

Traube ['traubə], *f.* (—, *pl.* —n) (Bot.) grape, bunch of grapes.

Traubensaft ['traubənzaft], *m.* (—s, *pl.* —e) grape-juice; (Poet.) wine.

traubig ['traubɪç], *adj.* clustered, grape-like.

trauen ['trauən], *v.a.* marry; join in marriage; *sich* — *lassen,* get married. — *v.n. einem* —, trust s.o., confide in s.o. — *v.r. sich* —, dare, venture.

Trauer ['trauər], *f.* (—, *no pl.*) mourning; sorrow, grief.

Trauermarsch ['trauərmarʃ], *m.* (—es, *pl.* —e) funeral march.

trauern ['trauərn], *v.n.* mourn, be in mourning.

Trauerspiel ['trauərʃpi:l], *n.* (—s, *pl.* —e) tragedy.

Trauerweide ['trauərvaidə], *f.* (—, *pl.* —n) (Bot.) weeping willow.

Traufe ['traufə], *f.* (—, *pl.* —n) eaves; *vom Regen in die* —, out of the frying pan into the fire.

träufeln ['trɔyfəln], *v.a.* drip, drop.

Traufröhre ['traufrø:rə], *f.* (—, *pl.* —n) gutter-pipe.

traulich ['traulɪç], *adj.* familiar, homely, cosy.

Traum [traum], *m.* (—(e)s, *pl.* ˙e) dream; *das fällt mir nicht im* —*e ein*, I should not dream of it.

Traumbild ['traumbɪlt], *n.* (—s, *pl.* —er) vision.

Traumdeutung ['traumdɔytuŋ], *f.* (—, *no pl.*) interpretation of dreams.

träumen ['trɔymən], *v.n.* dream; *sich etwas nicht* — *lassen*, have no inkling of, not dream of s.th.; not believe s.th.

Träumer ['trɔymər], *m.* (—s, *pl.* —) dreamer; (*fig.*) visionary.

Träumerei [trɔymə'raɪ], *f.* (—, *pl.* —en) dreaming, reverie.

traumhaft ['traumhaft], *adj.* dream-like.

traurig ['trauriç], *adj.* sad, mournful, sorrowful.

Traurigkeit ['trauriçkaɪt], *f.* (—, *no pl.*) sadness, melancholy.

Trauring ['trauriŋ], *m.* (—s, *pl.* —e) wedding-ring.

Trauschein ['trauʃaɪn], *m.* (—s, *pl.* —e) marriage certificate.

traut [traut], *adj.* dear, beloved; cosy; —*es Heim Glück allein*, east, west, home's best; there's no place like home.

Trauung ['trauuŋ], *f.* (—, *pl.* —en) marriage ceremony.

Trauzeuge ['trautsɔygə], *m.* (—n, *pl.* —n) witness to a marriage.

trecken ['trɛkən], *v.a.* (*dial.*) draw, drag, tug.

Trecker ['trɛkər], *m.* (—s, *pl.* —) tractor.

Treff [trɛf], *n.* (—s, *no pl.*) (*Cards*) clubs.

Treffen ['trɛfən], *n.* (—s, *pl.* —) action, battle, fight; meeting, gathering; *etwas ins* — *führen*, put s.th. forward, urge s.th.

treffen ['trɛfən], *v.a. irr.* hit, meet; *nicht* —, miss; *wie vom Donner getroffen*, thunderstruck; *ins Schwarze* —, hit the mark, score a bull's eye. — *v.r. sich* —, happen.

treffend ['trɛfənt], *adj.* appropriate, pertinent.

Treffer ['trɛfər], *m.* (—s, *pl.* —) (*lottery*) win, prize; (*Mil.*) hit.

trefflich ['trɛflɪç], *adj.* excellent.

Treffpunkt ['trɛfpuŋkt], *m.* (—s, *pl.* —e) meeting-place.

Treffsicherheit ['trɛfsɪçərhaɪt], *f.* (—, *no pl.*) accurate aim.

Treibeis ['traɪpaɪs], *n.* (—es, *no pl.*) floating-ice, ice floe.

treiben ['traɪbən], *v.a. irr.* drive, urge; incite; (*trade*) carry on, ply; *Studien* —, study; *was treibst du?* what are you doing? *etwas zu weit* —, carry s.th. too far; *einen in die Enge* —, drive s.o. into a corner. — *v.n.* be adrift, drift.

Treiben ['traɪbən], *n.* (—s, *no pl.*) driving; doings; bustle.

Treiber ['traɪbər], *m.* (—s, *pl.* —) (*Hunt.*) driver; beater.

Treibhaus ['traɪphaus], *n.* (—es, *pl.* ˙er) hothouse, greenhouse.

Treibkraft ['traɪpkraft], *f.* (—, *no pl.*) impulse, driving power.

Treibriemen ['traɪpriːmən], *m.* (—s, *pl.* —) driving-belt.

Treibsand ['traɪpzant], *m.* (—s, *no pl.*) quicksand, shifting sand.

Treibstange ['traɪpʃtaŋə], *f.* (—, *pl.* —en) main rod, connecting-rod.

Treibstoff ['traɪpʃtɔf], *m.* (—(e)s, *pl.* —e) fuel.

treideln ['traɪdəln], *v.a.* (*Naut.*) tow.

Treidelsteig ['traɪdəlʃtaɪk], *m.* (—s, *pl.* —e) towpath.

trennbar ['trɛnbaːr], *adj.* separable.

trennen ['trɛnən], *v.a.* separate, sever. — *v.r. sich* —, part.

Trennung ['trɛnuŋ], *f.* (—, *pl.* —en) separation, segregation; parting; division.

Trennungsstrich ['trɛnuŋsʃtrɪç], *m.* (—es, *pl.* —e) (*staircase*) landing.

treppab [trɛp'ap], *adv.* downstairs.

treppauf [trɛp'auf], *adv.* upstairs.

Treppe ['trɛpə], *f.* (—, *pl.* —n) stairs, staircase, flight of stairs.

Treppenabsatz ['trɛpənapzats], *m.* (—es, *pl.* ˙e) (*staircase*) landing.

Treppengeländer ['trɛpəngələndər], *n.* (—s, *pl.* —) balustrade, banisters.

Treppenhaus ['trɛpənhaus], *n.* (—es, *pl.* ˙er) stair-well, staircase.

Treppenläufer ['trɛpənlɔyfər], *m.* (—s, *pl.* —) stair-carpet.

Treppenstufe ['trɛpənʃtuːfə], *f.* (—, *pl.* —n) step, stair.

Treppenwitz ['trɛpənvɪts], *m.* (—es, *no pl.*) afterthought, esprit de l'escalier.

Tresor [tre'zoːr], *m.* (—s, *pl.* —e) safe, strongroom.

Tresse ['trɛsə], *f.* (—, *pl.* —n) braid, lace, galloon.

treten ['treːtən], *v.a., v.n. irr.* tread, step, trample upon; go; — *Sie näher*, step this way; *in Verbindung* — *mit*, make contact with; *in den Ehestand* —, get married; *einem zu nahe* —, offend s.o.; *tread on s.o.'s toes.

treu [trɔy], *adj.* faithful, loyal, true; conscientious.

Treubruch ['trɔybrux], *m.* (—(e)s, *pl.* ˙e) breach of faith, disloyalty.

Treue ['trɔyə], *f.* (—, *no pl.*) faithfulness, loyalty, fidelity; *meiner Treu!* upon my soul! *auf Treu und Glauben*, on trust.

Treueid ['trɔyaɪt], *m.* (—s, *pl.* —e) oath of allegiance.

Treuhänder ['trɔyhɛndər], *m.* (—s, *pl.* —) trustee.

treuherzig ['trɔyhɛrtsɪç], *adj.* guileless, trusting.

treulich ['trɔylɪç], *adv.* faithfully.

treulos ['trɔyloːs], *adj.* faithless, perfidious; unfaithful.

Treulosigkeit

Treulosigkeit ['trɔylo:ziçkaɪt], *f.* (—, *no pl.*) faithlessness, perfidy, disloyalty.

Tribüne [tri'by:nə], *f.* (—, *pl.* —n) tribune, platform; (*racing*) grandstand.

Tribut [tri'bu:t], *m.* (—s, *pl.* —e) tribute.

tributpflichtig [tri'bu:tpfliçtiç], *adj.* tributary.

Trichter ['trɪçtər], *m.* (—s, *pl.* —) funnel.

trichterförmig ['trɪçtərfœrmiç], *adj.* funnel-shaped.

Trieb [tri:p], *m.* (—(e)s, *pl.* —e) (*plant*) shoot, growth; instinct, bent, propensity, inclination; (*Psych.*) drive.

Triebfeder ['tri:pfe:dər], *f.* (—, *pl.* —n) mainspring; (*fig.*) motive, guiding principle.

Triebkraft ['tri:pkraft], *f.* (—, *pl.* ⁻e) motive power.

Triebwagen ['tri:pva:gən], *m.* (—s, *pl.* —) rail-car.

Triebwerk ['tri:pvɛrk], *n.* (—s, *pl.* —e) power unit, drive.

triefen ['tri:fən], *v.n. irr. & reg.* trickle, drip; be wet through, be soaking wet.

Trient [tri'ɛnt], *n.* Trent.

Trier [tri:r], *n.* Treves.

Triest [tri'ɛst], *n.* Trieste.

Trift [trɪft], *f.* (—, *pl.* —en) pasture, pasturage, common, meadow.

triftig ['trɪftɪç], *adj.* weighty, valid, conclusive, cogent.

Trikot [tri'ko:], *m. & n.* (—s, *pl.* —s) stockinet; (*circus, ballet*) tights.

Triller ['trɪlər], *m.* (—s, *pl.* —) (*Mus.*) trill, shake.

trillern ['trɪlərn], *v.n.* trill, quaver, shake; warble.

Trinität [trini'tɛ:t], *f.* (—, *no pl.*) Trinity.

trinkbar ['trɪŋkba:r], *adj.* drinkable.

Trinkbecher ['trɪŋkbɛçər], *m.* (—s, *pl.* —) drinking-cup.

trinken ['trɪŋkən], *v.a., v.n. irr.* drink.

Trinker ['trɪŋkər], *m.* (—s, *pl.* —) drinker, drunkard.

Trinkgelage ['trɪŋkgəla:gə], *n.* (—s, *pl.* —) drinking-bout.

Trinkgeld ['trɪŋkgɛlt], *n.* (—s, *pl.* —er) tip, gratuity.

Trinkhalle ['trɪŋkhalə], *f.* (—, *pl.* —n) (*spa*) pump-room.

Trinkspruch ['trɪŋkʃprux], *m.* (—(e)s, *pl.* ⁻e) toast.

Trinkstube ['trɪŋkʃtu:bə], *f.* (—, *pl.* —n) tap-room.

Tripolis ['tri:polɪs], *n.* Tripoli.

trippeln ['trɪpəln], *v.n.* trip (daintily), patter.

Tripper ['trɪpər], *m.* (—s, *no pl.*) (*Med.*) gonorrhoea.

Tritt [trɪt], *m.* (—(e)s, *pl.* —e) step, pace; kick.

Trittbrett ['trɪtbrɛt], *n.* (—s, *pl.* —er) foot-board; carriage-step; (*organ*) pedal.

Triumph [tri'umf], *m.* (—(e)s, *pl.* —e) triumph.

Triumphzug [tri'umftsu:k], *m.* (—(e)s, *pl.* ⁻e) triumphal procession.

Trivialität [trivjali'tɛ:t], *f.* (—, *pl.* —en) triviality, platitude.

trocken ['trɔkən], *adj.* dry, arid; (*fig.*) dull, dry as dust; (*wine*) dry.

Trockenfäule ['trɔkənfɔylə], *f.*, **Trockenfäulnis** ['trɔkənfɔylnɪs], *f.* (—, *no pl.*) dry rot.

Trockenboden ['trɔkənbo:dən], *m.* (—s, *pl.* ⁻) loft.

Trockenfutter ['trɔkənfutər], *n.* (—s, *no pl.*) fodder.

Trockenfütterung ['trɔkənfytərʊŋ], *f.* (—, *pl.* —en) dry feeding.

Trockenhaube ['trɔkənhaubə], *f.* (—, *pl.* —n) hair drier.

Trockenheit ['trɔkənhaɪt], *f.* (—, *no pl.*) dryness; drought.

Trockenschleuder ['trɔkənʃlɔydər], *f.* (—, *pl.* —n) spin-drier.

trocknen ['trɔknən], *v.a., v.n.* dry, air.

Troddel ['trɔdəl], *f.* (—, *pl.* —n) tassel.

Trödel ['trø:dəl], *m.* (—s, *no pl.*) junk, lumber, rubbish.

Trödelladen ['trø:dəlla:dən], *m.* (—s, *pl.* ⁻) junk-shop.

Trödelmarkt ['trø:dəlmarkt], *m.* (—s, *no pl.*) kettle market, jumble sale.

trödeln ['trø:dəln], *v.n.* dawdle, loiter.

Trödler ['trø:dlər], *m.* (—s, *pl.* —) second-hand dealer; (*coll.*) dawdler, loiterer.

Trog [tro:k], *m.* (—(e)s, *pl.* ⁻e) trough.

Troja ['tro:ja], *n.* Troy.

trollen ['trɔlən], *v.r. sich —*, decamp, toddle off, make o.s. scarce.

Trommel ['trɔməl], *f.* (—, *pl.* —n) drum; cylinder, barrel; tin box; *die — rühren*, beat the big drum.

Trommelfell ['trɔməlfɛl], *n.* (—s, *pl.* —e) drum-skin; ear-drum.

trommeln ['trɔməln], *v.n.* drum, beat the drum.

Trommelschlegel ['trɔməlʃle:gəl], *m.* (—s, *pl.* —) drumstick.

Trommelwirbel ['trɔməlvɪrbəl], *m.* (—s, *pl.* —) roll of drums.

Trommler ['trɔmlər], *m.* (—s, *pl.* —) drummer.

Trompete [trɔm'pe:tə], *f.* (—, *pl.* —n) trumpet; *die — blasen*, blow the trumpet.

trompeten [trɔm'pe:tən], *v.n.* trumpet, sound the trumpet.

Trompetengeschmetter [trɔm'pe:təngəʃmetər], *n.* (—s, *no pl.*) flourish of trumpets.

Tropen ['tro:pən], *f. pl.* the tropics.

Tropenfieber ['tro:pənfi:bər], *n.* (—s, *no pl.*) tropical fever.

tröpfeln ['trœpfəln], *v.a., v.n.* trickle, sprinkle.

Tropfen ['trɔpfən], *m.* (—s, *pl.* —) drop; *steter — höhlt den Stein*, constant dripping wears away a stone.

tropfen ['trɔpfən], *v.n.* drop, drip.

Trophäe [tro'fɛə], *f.* (—, *pl.* —n) trophy.

tropisch ['tro:pɪʃ], *adj.* tropical, tropic.

Troß [trɔs], *m.* (—sses, *pl.* -sse) (*Mil.*) baggage-train; (*fig.*) hangers-on, camp-followers.

Troßpferd ['trɔspfe:rt], *n.* (—s, *pl.* —e) pack-horse.

Trost [tro:st], *m.* (—es, *no pl.*) consolation, comfort; *geringer* —, cold comfort; *du bist wohl nicht bei* —? have you taken leave of your senses?

trösten ['trø:stən], *v.a.* comfort, console; *tröste dich*, cheer up.

Tröster ['trø:stər], *m.* (—s, *pl.* —) comforter, consoler; (*Theol.*) Holy Ghost, Comforter.

tröstlich ['trø:stlɪç], *adj.* consoling, comforting.

trostlos ['tro:stlo:s], *adj.* disconsolate, inconsolable; desolate, bleak.

Trostlosigkeit ['tro:stlo:zɪçkaɪt], *f.* (—, *no pl.*) disconsolateness; (*fig.*) wretchedness; dreariness.

Trott [trɔt], *m.* (—s, *no pl.*) trot.

Trottel ['trɔtəl], *m.* (—s, *pl.* —) (*coll.*) idiot.

Trottoir [trɔto'a:r], *n.* (—s, *pl.* —e) pavement, footpath; (*Am.*) sidewalk.

trotz [trɔts], *prep.* (*Genit.*, *Dat.*) in spite of, despite; — *alledem*, all the same.

Trotz [trɔts], *m.* (—es, *no pl.*) defiance, obstinacy, refractoriness; *einem* — *bieten*, defy s.o.; *einem etwas zum* — *machen*, do s.th. in defiance of s.o.

trotzdem [trɔts'de:m], *conj.* notwithstanding that, albeit, although. — *adv.* nevertheless.

trotzen ['trɔtsən], *v.n.* defy; sulk, be obstinate; *Gefahren* —, brave dangers.

trotzig ['trɔtsɪç], *adj.* defiant, sulky, refractory; headstrong, stubborn, obstinate.

Trotzkopf ['trɔtskɔpf], *m.* (—(e)s, *pl.* ˙e) obstinate child; pig-headed person.

trübe ['try:bə], *adj.* dim, gloomy; (*weather*) dull, cloudy, overcast; (*water*) troubled; (*glass*) misted; —s *Lächeln*, wan smile.

Trubel ['tru:bəl], *m.* (—s, *no pl.*) tumult, turmoil, disturbance.

trüben ['try:bən], *v.a.* darken, sadden, trouble; (*glass*) mist; (*metal*) tarnish; (*fig.*) obscure.

Trübsal ['try:pza:l], *f.* (—, *pl.* —e), *n.* (—s, *pl.* —e) misery, trouble, distress; — *blasen*, mope.

trübselig ['try:pze:lɪç], *adj.* woeful, lamentable; woebegone, forlorn.

Trübsinn ['try:pzɪn], *m.* (—s, *no pl.*) sadness, dejection.

trübsinnig ['try:pzɪnɪç], *adj.* sad, dejected.

Trüffel ['tryfəl], *f.* (—, *pl.* —n) truffle.

Trug [tru:k], *m.* (—(e)s, *no pl.*) deceit, fraud; *Lug und* —, a pack of lies.

Trugbild ['tru:kbɪlt], *n.* (—es, *pl.* —er) phantom.

trügen ['try:gən], *v.a.* *irr.* deceive.

trügerisch ['try:gərɪs], *adj.* deceptive, illusory, fallacious.

Truggewebe ['tru:kgəve:bə], *n.* (—s, *pl.* —) tissue of lies.

Trugschluß ['tru:kʃlus], *m.* (—sses, *pl.* ˙sse) fallacy, false deduction.

Truhe ['tru:ə], *f.* (—, *pl.* —n) chest, trunk, coffer.

Trumm [trum], *m.* (—s, *pl.* ˙er) lump, broken piece.

Trümmer ['trymər], *m. pl.* fragments, debris, ruins; *in* — *gehen*, go to wrack and ruin; *in* — *schlagen*, wreck.

Trümmerhaufen ['trymərhaufən], *m.* (—s, *pl.* —) heap of ruins, heap of rubble.

Trumpf [trumpf], *m.* (—(e)s, *pl.* ˙e) trump, trump-card.

trumpfen ['trumpfən], *v.a.* trump.

Trumpffarbe ['trumpffarbə], *f.* (—, *pl.* —n) trump-suit.

Trunk [truŋk], *m.* (—(e)s, *pl.* ˙e) draught, potion, drinking; *sich dem* — *ergeben*, take to drink.

trunken ['truŋkən], *adj.* drunk, intoxicated; (*fig.*) elated.

Trunkenbold ['truŋkənbɔlt], *m.* (—s, *pl.* —e) drunkard.

Trunkenheit ['truŋkənhaɪt], *f.* (—, *no pl.*) drunkenness, intoxication.

Trunksucht ['truŋkzuxt], *f.* (—, *no pl.*) dipsomania, alcoholism.

trunksüchtig ['truŋkzyçtɪç], *adj.* dipsomaniac, addicted to drinking.

Trupp [trup], *m.* (—s, *pl.* —s) troop, band.

Truppe ['trupə], *f.* (—, *pl.* —n) (*Mil.*) company, troops, forces; (*actors*) troupe.

Truppengattung ['trupəngatuŋ], *f.* (—, *pl.* —en) branch of the armed forces.

Truthahn ['tru:tha:n], *m.* (—s, *pl.* ˙e) (*Orn.*) turkey cock.

Truthenne ['tru:thenə], *f.* (—, *pl.* —n) (*Orn.*) turkey hen.

Trtuhühner ['tru:thy:nər], *n. pl.* (*Orn.*) turkey-fowl.

Trutz [truts], *m.* (—es, *no pl.*) (*Poet.*) defiance; *zum Schutz und* —, offensively and defensively.

Tschad [tʃat], *n.* Chad.

Tschechoslowakei [tʃɛçoslova'kaɪ], *f.* Czechoslovakia.

Tuch (1) [tu:x], *n.* (—(e)s, *pl.* ˙er) shawl, wrap.

Tuch (2) [tu:x], *n.* (—s, *pl.* —e) cloth, fabric.

Tuchhändler ['tu:xhɛndlər], *m.* (—s, *pl.* —) draper, clothier.

tüchtig ['tyçtɪç], *adj.* able, competent, efficient. — *adv.* largely, much, heartily.

Tüchtigkeit ['tyçtɪçkaɪt], *f.* (—, *no pl.*) ability, competence, efficiency.

Tücke ['tykə], *f.* (—, *pl.* —n) malice, spite.

tückisch

tückisch ['tykɪʃ], *adj.* malicious, insidious.

Tugend ['tu:gənt], *f.* (—, *pl.* —en) virtue.

Tugendbold ['tu:gəntbɔlt], *m.* (—s, *pl.* —e) paragon.

tugendhaft ['tu:gənthaft], *adj.* virtuous.

Tugendlehre ['tu:gəntle:rə], *f.* (—, *no pl.*) ethics, morals.

Tüll [tyl], *m.* (—s, *pl.* —e) tulle.

Tulpe ['tulpə], *f.* (—, *pl.* —n) (*Bot.*) tulip.

Tulpenzwiebel ['tulpəntsvi:bəl], *f.* (—, *pl.* —n) tulip-bulb.

tummeln ['tuməln], *v.r. sich* —, romp about; make haste.

Tummelplatz ['tuməlplats], *m.* (—es, *pl.* ⸚e) playground, fairground.

Tümpel ['tympəl], *m.* (—s, *pl.* —) pond, pool, puddle.

Tun [tu:n], *n.* (—s, *no pl.*) doing; *sein — und Lassen*, his conduct.

tun [tu:n], *v.a. irr.* do, make; put; *tut nichts,* it does not matter; *viel zu — haben,* have a lot to do, be busy; *not —,* be necessary; *Buße —,* repent.

Tünche ['tynçə], *f.* (—, *pl.* —n) whitewash.

tünchen ['tynçən], *v.a.* whitewash.

Tunichtgut ['tu:nɪçtgu:t], *m.* (—s, *no pl.*) ne'er-do-well, scamp.

Tunke ['tuŋkə], *f.* (—, *pl.* —n) sauce, gravy.

tunken ['tuŋkən], *v.a.* dip, steep; (*Am.*) dunk.

tunlich ['tu:nlɪç], *adj.* feasible, practicable, expedient.

tunlichst ['tu:nlɪçst], *adv.* if possible, possibly.

Tunnel ['tunəl], *m.* (—s, *pl.* —) tunnel.

Tunnelbau ['tunəlbau], *m.* (—s, *no pl.*) tunnelling.

tüpfeln ['typfəln], *v.a.* dot, spot.

Tupfen ['tupfən], *m.* (—s, *pl.* —) dot, polka-dot.

Tür [ty:r], *f.* (—, *pl.* —en) door; *einem die — weisen,* show s.o. the door; *vor der — stehen,* be imminent; *kehr vor deiner eigenen —,* mind your own business; *put your own house in order; offene —en einrennen,* flog a willing horse; *zwischen — und Angel stecken,* be undecided.

Türangel ['ty:raŋəl], *f.* (—, *pl.* —n) door-hinge.

Türhüter ['ty:rhy:tər], *m.* (—s, *pl.* —) doorkeeper.

Türkei [tyr'kai], *f.* Turkey.

Türkensäbel ['tyrkənzɛ:bəl], *m.* (—s, *pl.* —) scimitar.

Türkis [tyr'ki:s], *m.* (—es, *pl.* —e) turquoise.

Türklinke ['ty:rklɪŋkə], *f.* (—, *pl.* —n) door-handle.

Turm [turm], *m.* (—(e)s, *pl.* ⸚e) tower; spire, steeple; belfry; (*Chess*) castle.

Turmalin [turma'li:n], *m.* (—s, *pl.* —e) tourmaline.

Türmchen ['tyrmçən], *n.* (—s, *pl.* —) turret.

türmen ['tyrmən], *v.a.* pile up. — *v.n.* (*coll.*) bolt, run away. — *v.r. sich* —, rise high, be piled high.

Turmspitze ['turmʃpitsə], *f.* (—, *pl.* —n) spire.

turnen ['turnən], *v.n.* do exercises *or* gymnastics.

Turnen ['turnən], *n.* (—s, *no pl.*) gymnastics, physical training.

Turner ['turnər], *m.* (—s, *pl.* —) gymnast.

Turngerät ['turngɛrɛ:t], *n.* (—es, *pl.* —e) gymnastic apparatus.

Turnhalle ['turnhalə], *f.* (—, *pl.* —n) gymnasium.

Turnier [tur'ni:r], *n.* (—s, *pl.* —e) tournament.

Turnübung ['turny:buŋ], *f.* (—, *pl.* —en) gymnastic exercise.

Turnverein ['turnfərain], *m.* (—s, *pl.* —e) athletics club, gymnastics club.

Türpfosten ['ty:rpfɔstən], *m.* (—s, *pl.* —) door-post.

Türriegel ['ty:rri:gəl], *m.* (—s, *pl.* —) bolt.

Türschild ['ty:rʃilt], *n.* (—(e)s, *pl.* —e) (door)plate.

Türschloß ['ty:rʃlɔs], *n.* (—sses, *pl.* ⸚sser) lock.

Türschlüssel ['ty:rʃlysəl], *m.* (—s, *pl.* —) door-key, latch-key.

Türschwelle ['ty:rʃvelə], *f.* (—, *pl.* —n) threshold.

Tusch [tuʃ], *m.* (—es, *pl.* —e) (*Mus.*) flourish.

Tusche ['tuʃə], *f.* (—, *pl.* —n) water-colour; Indian ink.

tuscheln ['tuʃəln], *v.n.* whisper.

tuschen ['tuʃən], *v.a.* draw in Indian ink.

Tuschkasten ['tuʃkastən], *m.* (—s, *pl.* ⸚) paint-box.

Tüte ['ty:tə], *f.* (—, *pl.* —n) paper bag.

Tutel [tu'te:l], *f.* (—, *no pl.*) guardianship.

tuten ['tu:tən], *v.n.* hoot, honk, blow a horn.

Tütendreher ['ty:təndre:ər], *m.* (—s, *pl.* —) (*sl.*) small shopkeeper.

Typ [ty:p], *m.* (—s, *pl.* —en) type.

Type ['ty:pə], *f.* (—, *pl.* —n) (*Typ.*) type; (*fig.*) queer fish.

Typhus ['ty:fus], *m.* (—, *no pl.*) (*Med.*) typhoid (fever).

typisch ['ty:pɪʃ], *adj.* typical.

Typus ['ty:pus], *m.* (—, *pl.* **Typen**) type.

Tyrann [ty'ran], *m.* (—en, *pl.* —en) tyrant.

Tyrannei [tyra'nai], *f.* (—, *pl.* —en) tyranny, despotism.

tyrannisch [ty'ranɪʃ], *adj.* tyrannical, despotic.

tyrannisieren [tyrani'zi:rən], *v.a.* tyrannize over, oppress, bully.

U

U [u:], *n.* (**—s**, *pl.* **—s**) the letter U.
U-Bahn ['u:ba:n], *f.* (**—**, *no pl.*) underground (railway); (*Am.*) subway.
Übel ['y:bəl], *n.* (**—s**, *pl.* **—**) evil, trouble; misfortune; disease.
übel ['y:bəl], *adj.* evil, ill, bad; *mir ist* **—**, I feel sick; *nicht* **—**, not too bad; *— daran sein*, be in a bad way, be in a mess.
übelgesinnt ['y:bəlgəzInt], *adj.* evil-minded; ill-disposed; *einem — sein*, bear s.o. a grudge.
Übelkeit ['y:bəlkaIt], *f.* (**—**, *pl.* **—en**) nausea, sickness.
übellaunig ['y:bəllaunIç], *adj.* ill-humoured, bad-tempered.
übelnehmen ['y:bəlne:mən], *v.a. irr.* take amiss, resent, be offended at.
übelnehmerisch ['y:bəlne:mərIʃ], *adj.* touchy, easily offended.
Übelstand ['y:bəlʃtant], *m.* (**—(e)s**, *pl.* ⁀**e**) inconvenience, drawback; (*pl.*) abuses.
Übeltat ['y:bəlta:t], *f.* (**—**, *pl.* **—en**) misdeed.
Übeltäter ['y:bəlte:tər], *m.* (**—s**, *pl.* **—**) evildoer, malefactor.
übelwollend ['y:bəlvɔlənt], *adj.* malevolent.
üben ['y:bən], *v.a.* practise, exercise; *Rache* **—**, wreak vengeance.
über ['y:bər], *prep.* (*Dat., Acc.*) over, above; across; about; more than, exceeding; via, by way of; concerning, on. — *adv.* over, above; *— und* **—**, all over; *— kurz oder lang*, sooner or later; *heute* **—**s *Jahr*, a year from today.
überall ['y:bəral], *adv.* everywhere, anywhere.
überanstrengen [y:bər'anʃtreŋən], *v.a. insep.* overtax s.o.'s strength, strain. — *v.r. sich* **—**, overtax o.'s strength, overexert o.s.
Überanstrengung [y:bər'anʃtreŋuŋ], *f.* (**—**, *pl.* **—en**) over-exertion, strain.
überantworten [y:bər'antvɔrtən], *v.a. insep.* deliver up, surrender.
überarbeiten [y:bər'arbaItən], *v.a. insep.* revise, do again. — *v.r. sich* **—**, overwork o.s.
überarbeitet [y:bər'arbaItət], *adj.* overwrought, overworked.
überaus ['y:bəraus], *adv.* exceedingly, extremely.
überbauen [y:bər'bauən], *v.a. insep.* build over.
überbieten [y:bər'bi:tən], *v.a. irr. insep.* outbid (s.o.); (*fig.*) surpass.

Überbleibsel ['y:bərblaIpsəl], *n.* (**—s**, *pl.* **—**) remainder, remnant, residue, rest.
Überblick ['y:bərblIk], *m.* (**—(e)s**, *pl.* **—e**) survey, general view.
überblicken [y:bər'blIkən], *v.a. insep.* survey, look over.
überbringen [y:bər'brIŋən], *v.a. irr. insep.* bear, deliver, hand in.
Überbringung [y:bər'brIŋuŋ], *f.* (**—**, *no pl.*) delivery.
überbrücken [y:bər'brykən], *v.a. insep.* bridge, span.
überdachen [y:bər'daxən], *v.a. insep.* roof (over).
überdauern [y:bər'dauərn], *v.a. insep.* outlast; tide over.
überdenken [y:bər'deŋkən], *v.a. irr. insep.* think over, consider.
überdies [y:bər'di:s], *adv.* besides, moreover.
überdrucken [y:bər'drukən], *v.a. insep.* overprint.
Überdruß ['y:bərdrus], *m.* (**—sses**, *no pl.*) weariness; disgust; *zum* **—**, ad nauseam.
überdrüssig ['y:bərdrysIç], *adj.* weary of.
Übereifer [y:bər'araIfər], *m.* (**—s**, *no pl.*) excessive zeal.
übereifrig ['y:bəraIfrIç], *adj.* excessively zealous, officious.
übereilen [y:bər'araIlən], *v.r. insep. sich* **—**, hurry too much, overshoot the mark.
übereilt [y:bər'araIlt], *adj.* overhasty, rash.
übereinkommen [y:bər'araInkɔmən], *v.n. irr.* (*aux.* sein) agree.
Übereinkunft [y:bər'araInkunft], *f.* (**—**, *pl.* ⁀**e**) agreement, convention.
übereinstimmen [y:bər'araInʃtImən], *v.n.* agree, concur, harmonize, be of one mind, be of the same opinion; (*things*) tally, square.
Übereinstimmung [y:bər'araInʃtImuŋ], *f.* (**—**, *no pl.*) accord, agreement, conformity, harmony.
überfahren (1) [y:bər'fa:rən], *v.a. irr. insep.* traverse, pass over; run over (s.o.).
überfahren (2) ['y:bərfa:rən], *v.a. irr.* ferry across. — *v.n.* (*aux.* sein) cross.
überfahren (3) ['y:bərfa:rən], *v.n.* (*aux.* sein) cross.
Überfahrt ['y:bərfa:rt], *f.* (**—**, *pl.* **—en**) passage, crossing.
Überfall ['y:bərfal], *m.* (**—s**, *pl.* ⁀**e**) sudden attack, raid.
überfallen (1) ['y:bərfalən], *v.n. irr.* (*aux.* sein) (*p.p.* übergefallen) fall over.
überfallen (2) [y:bər'falən], *v.a. irr. insep.* (*p.p.* überfallen) attack suddenly, raid.
überfliegen [y:bər'fli:gən], *v.a. irr. insep.* fly over; (*fig.*) glance over, skim.
überfließen ['y:bərfli:sən], *v.n. irr.* (*aux.* sein) overflow.

überflügeln [y:bər'fly:gəln], *v.a. insep.* surpass, outstrip.

Überfluß ['y:bərflus], *m.* (—**sses**, *no pl.*) abundance, plenty, profusion; surplus; — *haben an*, abound in, have too much of.

überflüssig ['y:bərflysiç], *adj.* superfluous, unnecessary.

überfluten [y:bər'flu:tən], *v.a. insep.* overflow, flood.

überführen (1) ['y:bərfy:rən], *v.a.* convey, conduct (across).

überführen (2) [y:bər'fy:rən], *v.a. insep.* convict; transport a coffin.

Überführung [y:bər'fy:ruŋ], *f.* (—, *pl.* —**en**) conviction (for a crime); transport (of a coffin).

Überfüllung [y:bər'fyluŋ], *f.* (—, *no pl.*) overcrowding.

Übergabe ['y:bərga:bə], *f.* (—, *no pl.*) surrender, yielding up; delivery, handing over.

Übergang ['y:bərgaŋ], *m.* (—**s**, *pl.* ⸚e) passage; (*Railw.*) crossing; (*fig.*) change-over, transition.

übergeben [y:bər'ge:bən], *v.a. irr. insep.* deliver up, hand over. — *v.r. sich* —, vomit.

übergehen (1) ['y:bərge:ən], *v.n. irr.* (*aux.* sein) (*p.p.* übergegangen) go over, change over, turn (into); *zum Feinde* —, go over to the enemy; *in andre Hände* —, change hands.

übergehen (2) [y:bər'ge:ən], *v.a. irr. insep.* (*p.p.* übergangen) pass over, pass by.

Übergehung [y:bər'ge:uŋ], *f.* (—, *no pl.*) omission; passing over.

übergeordnet ['y:bərgəɔrdnət], *adj.* superior.

Übergewicht ['y:bərgəviçt], *n.* (—(**e**)**s**, *no pl.*) overweight; (*fig.*) preponderance, superiority.

übergießen [y:bər'gi:sən], *v.a. irr. insep.* pour over, douse with.

überglücklich ['y:bərglykliç], *adj.* overjoyed.

übergreifen ['y:bərgraifən], *v.n. irr.* overlap; encroach (upon); spread.

Übergriff ['y:bərgrif], *m.* (—(**e**)**s**, *pl.* —**e**) encroachment.

übergroß ['y:bərgro:s], *adj.* excessively large, overlarge.

überhaben ['y:bərha:bən], *v.a. irr.* have enough of, be sick of.

überhandnehmen [y:bər'hantne:mən], *v.n. irr.* gain the upper hand; run riot.

überhangen ['y:bərhaŋən], *v.n. irr.* hang over.

überhängen [y:bər'hɛŋən], *v.a. irr.* cover, hang upon.

überhäufen [y:bər'hɔyfən], *v.a. insep.* overwhelm.

überhaupt [y:bər'haupt], *adv.* in general, altogether, at all.

überheben [y:bər'he:bən], *v.r. irr. insep. sich* —, strain o.s. by lifting; (*fig.*) be overbearing.

überheblich [y:bər'he:pliç], *adj.* overbearing, arrogant.

überheizen [y:bər'haitsən], *v.a. insep.* overheat.

überhitzt [y:bər'hitst], *adj.* overheated; impassioned.

überholen [y:bər'ho:lən], *v.a. insep.* overtake, out-distance; (*fig.*) overhaul.

überhören [y:bər'ho:rən], *v.a. insep.* hear s.o.'s lessons; ignore, miss (s.th.).

überirdisch ['y:bərirdiʃ], *adj.* celestial, superterrestrial.

Überkleid ['y:bərklait], *n.* (—(**e**)**s**, *pl.* —**er**) outer garment; overall.

überklug ['y:bərklu:k], *adj.* too clever by half, conceited.

überkochen ['y:bərkɔxən], *v.n.* (*aux.* sein) boil over.

überkommen [y:bər'kɔmən], *adj.* — *sein von*, be seized with.

überladen [y:bər'la:dən], *v.a. irr. insep.* overload. — *adj.* overdone, too elaborate; bombastic.

überlassen [y:bər'lasən], *v.a. irr. insep.* leave, relinquish, give up, yield.

überlasten [y:bər'lastən], *v.a. insep.* overburden.

überlaufen (1) ['y:bərlaufən], *v.a. irr.* run over; (*to the enemy*) desert.

überlaufen (2) [y:bər'laufən], *v.a. insep.* (*p.p.* überlaufen) overrun.

Überläufer ['y:bərlɔyfər], *m.* (—**s**, *pl.* —) deserter, runaway.

überleben [y:bər'le:bən], *v.a. insep.* survive, outlive; (*fig.*) live (s.th.) down; *sich überlebt haben*, be out of date, be dated.

Überlebende [y:bər'le:bəndə], *m.* (—**n**, *pl.* —**n**) survivor.

überlegen (1) ['y:bərle:gən], *v.a.* lay over, cover.

überlegen (2) [y:bər'le:gən], *v.a. insep.* (*p.p.* überlegt) think over, consider, turn over in o.'s mind. — *adj.* superior; — *sein*, outdo, be superior to.

Überlegenheit [y:bər'le:gənhait], *f.* (—, *no pl.*) superiority.

Überlegung [y:bər'le:guŋ], *f.* (—, *pl.* —**en**) consideration, deliberation; *bei näherer* —, on second thoughts, on thinking it over.

überliefern [y:bər'li:fərn], *v.a. insep.* hand down (to posterity), hand on, pass on.

Überlieferung [y:bər'li:fəruŋ], *f.* (—, *pl.* —**en**) tradition.

überlisten [y:bər'listən], *v.a. insep.* outwit.

Übermacht ['y:bərmaxt], *f.* (—, *no pl.*) superiority, superior force.

übermalen [y:bər'ma:lən], *v.a. insep.* paint over.

übermangansauer [y:bərmaŋga'nzauər], *adj.* permanganate of; —*saueres Kali*, permanganate of potash.

übermannen [y:bər'manən], *v.a. insep.* overpower.

Übermaß ['y:bərma:s], *n.* (—**es**, *no pl.*) excess; *im* —, to excess.

übermäßig ['y:bərmɛ:sɪç], *adj.* excessive, immoderate.

Übermensch ['y:bərmɛnʃ], *m.* (—en, *pl.* —en) superman.

übermenschlich ['y:bərmɛnʃlɪç], *adj.* superhuman.

übermitteln [y:bər'mɪtəln], *v.a. insep.* convey.

übermorgen ['y:bərmɔrgən], *adv.* the day after tomorrow.

Übermut ['y:bərmu:t], *m.* (—s, *no pl.*) wantonness; high spirits.

übermütig ['y:bərmy:tɪç], *adj.* wanton; full of high spirits.

übernachten [y:bər'naxtən], *v.n. insep.* pass *or* spend the night.

übernächtig [y:bər'nɛçtɪç], *adj.* haggard, tired by a sleepless night.

Übernahme ['y:bərna:mə], *f.* (—, *no pl.*) taking possession, taking charge.

übernatürlich ['y:bərnaty:rlɪç], *adj.* supernatural.

übernehmen [y:bər'ne:mən], *v.a. irr. insep.* take possession of, take upon o.s., take over. — *v.r. sich* —, overtax o.'s strength.

überordnen ['y:bərɔrdnən], *v.a. insep.* place above.

überprüfen [y:bər'pry:fən], *v.a. insep.* examine, overhaul.

überquellen ['y:bərkvɛlən], *v.n. irr. insep. (aux. sein)* bubble over.

überqueren [y:bər'kve:rən], *v.a. insep.* cross.

überragen [y:bər'ra:gən], *v.a. insep.* tower above, overtop; (*fig.*) surpass, outstrip.

überraschen [y:bər'raʃən], *v.a. insep.* surprise, take by surprise.

Überraschung [y:bər'raʃuŋ], *f.* (—, *pl.* —en) surprise.

überreden [y:bər're:dən], *v.a. insep.* persuade, talk s.o. into (s.th.).

Überredung [y:bər're:duŋ], *f.* (—, *no pl.*) persuasion.

überreichen [y:bər'raɪçən], *v.a. insep.* hand over, present formally.

überreichlich ['y:bərraɪçlɪç], *adj.* superabundant.

Überreichung [y:bər'raɪçuŋ], *f.* (—, *no pl.*) formal presentation.

überreizen [y:bər'raɪtsən], *v.a. insep.* over-excite, over-stimulate.

überrennen [y:bər'rɛnən], *v.a. irr. insep.* take by storm, overrun.

Überrest ['y:bərrɛst], *m.* (—es, *pl.* —e) remainder, remnant, residue.

überrumpeln [y:bər'rumpəln], *v.a. insep.* catch unawares, surprise.

übersättigen [y:bər'zɛtɪgən], *v.a. insep.* saturate; surfeit, cloy.

Übersättigung [y:bər'zɛtɪguŋ], *f.* (—, *no pl.*) saturation; surfeit.

Überschallgeschwindigkeit ['y:bərʃalgəʃvɪndɪçkaɪt], *f.* (—, *no pl.*) supersonic speed.

überschatten [y:bər'ʃatən], *v.a. insep.* overshadow.

überschätzen [y:bər'ʃɛtsən], *v.a. insep.* overrate, over-estimate.

überschauen [y:bər'ʃauən], *v.a. insep.* survey.

überschäumen ['y:bərʃɔymən], *v.n. (aux. sein)* bubble over.

überschäumend ['y:bərʃɔymənt], *adj.* ebullient, exuberant.

Überschlag ['y:bərʃla:k], *m.* (—s, *pl.* ⁓e) somersault; estimate.

überschlagen [y:bər'ʃla:gən], *v.a. irr. insep.* (*pages*) miss, skip; estimate, compute. — *v.r. sich* —, turn a somersault, overturn. — *adj.* tepid, lukewarm.

überschnappen ['y:bərʃnapən], *v.n. (aux. sein)* snap; (*fig., coll.*) go out of o.'s mind.

überschreiben [y:bər'ʃraɪbən], *v.a. irr. insep.* superscribe, entitle.

überschreiten [y:bər'ʃraɪtən], *v.a. irr. insep.* cross; go beyond, exceed.

Überschrift ['y:bərʃrɪft], *f.* (—, *pl.* —en) heading, headline.

Überschuß ['y:bərʃus], *m.* (—sses, *pl.* ⁓sse) surplus.

überschüssig ['y:bərʃysɪç], *adj.* surplus, remaining.

überschütten [y:bər'ʃytən], *v.a. insep.* shower with, overwhelm with.

Überschwang ['y:bərʃvaŋ], *m.* (—s, *no pl.*) exaltation, rapture.

überschwemmen [y:bər'ʃvɛmən], *v.a. insep.* flood, inundate.

Überschwemmung [y:bər'ʃvɛmuŋ], *f.* (—, *pl.* —en) inundation, flood, deluge.

überschwenglich [y:bər'ʃvɛŋlɪç], *adj.* exuberant, exalted.

Übersee ['y:bərze:], *f.* (—, *no pl.*) overseas.

übersehen [y:bər'ze:ən], *v.a. irr. insep.* survey, look over; overlook, disregard.

übersenden [y:bər'zɛndən], *v.a. irr. insep.* send, forward, transmit; (*money*) remit.

Übersendung [y:bər'zɛnduŋ], *f.* (—, *pl.* —en) sending, forwarding, transmission; remittance.

übersetzen (1) ['y:bərzɛtsən], *v.a. (p.p. übergesetzt)* ferry across, cross (a river).

übersetzen (2) [y:bər'zɛtsən], *v.a. insep. (p.p. übersetzt)* translate.

Übersetzer [y:bər'zɛtsər], *m.* (—s, *pl.* —) translator.

Übersetzung [y:bər'zɛtsuŋ], *f.* (—, *pl.* —en) translation.

Übersicht ['y:bərzɪçt], *f.* (—, *pl.* —en) survey, summary; epitome.

übersichtlich ['y:bərzɪçtlɪç], *adj.* clearly arranged, readable at a glance, lucid.

übersiedeln [y:bər'zi:dəln], *v.n. (aux. sein)* remove, move, settle in a different place.

Übersiedlung [y:bər'zi:dluŋ], *f.* (—, *pl.* —en) removal.

überspannen [y:bər'ʃpanən], *v.a. insep.* overstretch.

überspannt [y:bər'ʃpant], *adj.* eccentric, extravagant.

Überspanntheit

Überspanntheit [y:bər'ʃpanthaɪt], *f.*
(—, *pl.* —en) eccentricity.
überspringen [y:bər'ʃprɪŋən], *v.a. irr.*
insep. jump over; (*fig.*) skip.
übersprudeln ['y:bərʃpru:dəln], *v.n.*
(*aux.* sein) bubble over.
überstechen [y:bər'ʃtɛçən], *v.a. irr.*
(*cards*) trump higher.
überstehen [y:bər'ʃte:ən], *v.a. irr.*
insep. overcome, endure, get over,
weather.
übersteigen [y:bər'ʃtaɪgən], *v.a. irr.*
insep. exceed, surpass.
überstrahlen [y:bər'ʃtra:lən], *v.a. insep.*
outshine, surpass in splendour.
überstreichen [y:bər'ʃtraɪçən], *v.a. irr.*
insep. paint over.
überströmen [y:bər'ʃtrø:mən], *v.a.*
insep. flood, overflow.
Überstunde ['y:bərʃtundə], *f.* (—, *pl.*
—n) extra working time, overtime.
überstürzen [y:bər'ʃtyrtsən], *v.r. insep.*
sich —, act in haste.
übertäuben [y:bər'tɔybən], *v.a. insep.*
deafen.
überteuern [y:bər'tɔyərn], *v.a. insep.*
overcharge.
übertölpeln [y:bər'tœlpəln], *v.a. insep.*
cheat.
übertönen [y:bər'tø:nən], *v.a. insep.*
(*sound*) drown.
übertragen [y:bər'tra:gən], *v.a. irr.*
insep. transfer, hand over; convey;
broadcast; translate; (*Comm.*) carry
over; *einem ein Amt* —, confer an
office on s.o.
Übertragung [y:bər'tra:guŋ], *f.* (—, *pl.*
—en) cession; transference; handing
over; (*Comm.*) carrying over; (*Rad.*)
transmission; (*Med.*) transfusion.
übertreffen [y:bər'trɛfən], *v.a. irr.*
insep. surpass, excel, outdo.
übertreiben [y:bər'traɪbən], *v.a. irr.*
insep. exaggerate.
Übertreibung [y:bər'traɪbuŋ], *f.* (—,
pl. —en) exaggeration.
übertreten (1) ['y:bərtre:tən], *v.n. irr.*
(*aux.* sein) go over to; (*river*) overflow; (*religion*) change to, join (*church,
party*).
übertreten (2) [y:bər'tre:tən], *v.a. irr.*
insep. transgress, trespass against,
infringe, violate.
Übertretung [y:bər'tre:tuŋ], *f.* (—, *pl.*
—en) transgression, trespass, violation, infringement.
übertrieben [y:bər'tri:bən], *adj.* excessive, immoderate, exaggerated.
Übertritt ['y:bərtrɪt], *m.* (—s, *no pl.*)
defection, going over; (*Rel.*) change,
conversion.
übertünchen [y:bər'tynçən], *v.a. insep.*
whitewash, rough-cast; (*fig.*) gloss
over.
Übervölkerung [y:bər'fœlkəruŋ], *f.*
(—, *no pl.*) overpopulation.
übervoll ['y:bərfɔl], *adj.* overful, brimful, chock-full.
übervorteilen [y:bər'fo:rtaɪlən], *v.a.*
insep. cheat, defraud.

überwachen [y:bər'vaxən], *v.a. insep.*
watch over, superintend, supervise.
Überwachung [y:bər'vaxuŋ], *f.* (—,
no pl.) superintendence, supervision.
überwachsen [y:bər'vaksən], *v.a. irr.*
insep. overgrow.
überwältigen [y:bər'vɛltɪgən], *v.a.*
insep. overcome, overpower, subdue.
überwältigend [y:bər'vɛltɪgənt], *adj.*
overwhelming.
Überwältigung [y:bər'vɛltɪguŋ], *f.*
(—, *no pl.*) overpowering.
überweisen [y:bər'vaɪzən], *v.a. irr.*
insep. assign; (*money*) remit.
Überweisung [y:bər'vaɪzuŋ], *f.* (—, *pl.*
—en) assignment; (*money*) remittance.
überwerfen (1) ['y:bərvɛrfən], *v.a. irr.*
throw over; (*clothes*) slip on.
überwerfen (2) [y:bər'vɛrfən], *v.r. irr.*
insep. sich — *mit*, fall out with s.o.
überwiegen [y:bər'vi:gən], *v.n. irr.*
insep. prevail.
überwiegend [y:bər'vi:gənt], *adj.* paramount, overwhelming, predominant.
überwinden [y:bər'vɪndən], *v.a. irr.*
insep. overcome, conquer. — *v.r.*
sich —, prevail upon o.s., bring o.s.
(to).
Überwindung [y:bər'vɪnduŋ], *f.* (—,
no pl.) conquest; reluctance.
überwintern [y:bər'vɪntərn], *v.n. insep.*
winter, hibernate.
Überwinterung [y:bər'vɪntəruŋ], *f.*
(—, *no pl.*) hibernation.
überwölkt [y:bər'vœlkt], *adj.* overcast.
Überwurf ['y:bərvurf], *m.* (—s, *pl.* ⁻e)
wrap, shawl, cloak.
Überzahl [y:bər'tsa:l], *f.* (—, *no pl.*) *in
der* —, in the majority.
überzählig ['y:bərtsɛ:lɪç], *adj.* super-
numerary, surplus.
überzeichnen ['y:bərtsaɪçnən], *v.a.*
insep. (*Comm.*) over-subscribe.
überzeugen [y:bər'tsɔygən], *v.a. insep.*
convince. — *v.r. sich*—, satisfy o.s.
Überzeugung [y:bər'tsɔyguŋ], *f.* (—,
no pl.) conviction.
überziehen (1) ['y:bərtsi:ən], *v.a. irr.*
put on (a garment).
überziehen (2) [y:bər'tsi:ən], *v.a. irr.*
insep. cover; (*bed*) put fresh linen on;
(*Bank*) overdraw.
Überzieher ['y:bərtsi:ər], *m.* (—s, *pl.*
—) overcoat.
Überzug ['y:bərtsu:k], *m.* (—s, *pl.* ⁻e)
case, cover; bed-tick; coating.
üblich ['y:plɪç], *adj.* usual, customary;
nicht mehr —, out of use, obsolete.
übrig ['y:brɪç], *adj.* remaining, left
over; *die* —*en*, the others; — *bleiben*,
be left, remain; — *haben*, have left;
— *sein*, be left; *im* —*en*, for the rest;
ein —*es tun*, stretch a point; *für
einen etwas* — *haben*, like s.o.
übrigens ['y:brɪgəns], *adv.* besides,
moreover; by the way.
Übung ['y:buŋ], *f.* (—, *pl.* —en)
exercise, practice.

Ufer ['u:fər], *n.* (—s, *pl.* —) *(river)* bank; *(sea)* shore, beach.

Uganda [u'ganda], *n.* Uganda.

Uhr [u:r], *f.* (—, *pl.* —en) clock; watch; *elf* —, eleven o'clock; *wieviel* — *ist es?* what is the time?

Uhrmacher ['u:rmaxər], *m.* (—s, *pl.* —) watchmaker, clockmaker.

Uhrwerk ['u:rvɛrk], *n.* (—s, *pl.* —e) clockwork.

Uhrzeiger ['u:rtsaɪgər], *m.* (—s, *pl.* —) hand (of clock *or* watch).

Uhu ['u:hu:], *m.* (—s, *pl.* —s) *(Orn.)* eagle-owl.

ulkig ['ʊlkɪç], *adj.* funny.

Ulme ['ʊlmə], *f.* (—, *pl.* —en) *(Bot.)* elm, elm-tree.

Ultrakurzwelle ['ultrakurtsvɛlə], *f.* (—, *pl.* —n) ultra-short wave.

ultrarot ['ultraro:t], *adj.* infra-red.

Ultrastrahlung ['ultraʃtra:luŋ], *f.* (—, *pl.* —en) cosmic radiation.

ultraviolett ['ultraviolet], *adj.* ultra-violet.

um [um], *prep.* *(Acc.)* about, around; approximately, near; for, because of; by; — *Geld bitten,* ask for money; — *5 Uhr,* at five o'clock. — *conj.* to, in order to. — *adv.* up, past, upside down; round about; around.

umarbeiten ['umarbaɪtən], *v.a.* do again, remodel, revise; recast.

umarmen [um'armən], *v.a.* *insep.* embrace.

Umarmung [um'armuŋ], *f.* (—, *pl.* —en) embrace.

umbauen (1) ['umbauən], *v.a.* rebuild.

umbauen (2) [um'bauən], *v.a. insep.* surround with buildings.

umbiegen ['umbi:gən], *v.a. irr.* bend.

umbilden ['umbɪldən], *v.a.* transform, reform, recast, remould.

umbinden ['umbɪndən], *v.a. irr. sich etwas —,* tie s.th. around o.s.

umblicken ['umblɪkən], *v.r. sich —,* look round.

umbringen ['umbrɪŋən], *v.a. irr.* kill, slay, murder.

umdrehen ['umdre:ən], *v.a.* turn over, turn round, revolve. — *v.r. sich —,* turn round.

Umdrehung [um'dre:uŋ], *f.* (—, *pl.* —en) revolution, rotation.

umfahren (1) [um'fa:rən], *v.a. irr. insep.* drive round, circumnavigate.

umfahren (2) ['umfa:ren], *v.a. irr.* run down.

umfallen ['umfalən], *v.n. irr. (aux. sein)* fall down, fall over.

Umfang ['umfaŋ], *m.* (—s, *pl.* ⁓e) circumference; *(fig.)* extent.

umfangen [um'faŋən], *v.a. irr. insep.* encircle, embrace.

umfangreich ['umfaŋraɪç], *adj.* extensive, voluminous.

umfassen [um'fasən], *v.a. insep.* comprise, contain.

umfassend [um'fasənt], *adj.* comprehensive.

umfließen [um'fli:sən], *v.a. irr. insep.* surround by water.

umformen ['umfɔrmən], *v.a.* transform, remodel.

Umformung ['umfɔrmuŋ], *f.* (—, *pl.* —en) transformation, remodelling.

Umfrage ['umfra:gə], *f.* (—, *pl.* —n) enquiry, poll, quiz.

Umfriedung [um'fri:duŋ], *f.* (—, *pl.* —en) enclosure.

Umgang ['umgaŋ], *m.* (—s, *pl.* ⁓e) circuit, procession; *(fig.)* acquaintance, association; relations, connection; — *haben mit,* associate with.

umgänglich ['umgɛŋlɪç], *adj.* sociable, companionable.

Umgangsformen ['umgaŋsfɔrmən], *f. pl.* manners.

Umgangssprache ['umgaŋsʃpra:xə], *f.* (— *pl.* —en) colloquial speech.

umgeben [um'ge:bən], *v.a. irr. insep.* surround.

Umgebung [um'ge:buŋ], *f.* (—, *pl.* —en) environment, surroundings.

umgehen (1) ['umge:ən], *v.n. irr. (aux. sein)* associate with s.o.; handle s.th.; — *in,* haunt.

umgehen (2) [um'ge:ən], *v.a. irr. insep.* go round; *(flank)* turn; *(fig.)* evade, shirk.

umgehend ['umge:ənt], *adv.* immediately; *(letter)* by return mail.

Umgehung [um'ge:uŋ], *f.* (—, *pl.* —en) shirking, evasion; detour; *(Mil.)* flank movement, turning.

umgekehrt ['umgəke:rt], *adj.* reverse. — *adv.* conversely.

umgestalten ['umgəʃtaltən], *v.a.* transform, recast.

Umgestaltung ['umgəʃtaltuŋ], *f.* (—, *pl.* —en) transformation; recasting.

umgraben ['umgra:bən], *v.a. irr.* dig up.

umgrenzen [um'grɛntsən], *v.a. insep.* limit, set bounds to.

Umgrenzung [um'grɛntsuŋ], *f.* (—, *pl.* —en) boundary; limitation.

umgucken ['umgukən], *v.r. sich —,* look about o.

umhalsen [um'halzən], *v.a. insep.* hug, embrace.

Umhang ['umhaŋ], *m.* (—s, *pl.* ⁓e) shawl, cloak.

umher [um'he:r], *adv.* around, round, about.

umherblicken [um'he:rblɪkən], *v.n.* look round.

umherflattern [um'he:rflatərn], *v.n. (aux. sein)* flutter about.

umherlaufen [um'he:rlaufən], *v.n. irr. (aux. sein)* run about; roam about, ramble, wander.

umherziehend [um'he:rtsi:ənt], *adj.* itinerant.

umhüllen [um'hylən], *v.a. insep.* envelop, wrap up.

Umkehr ['umke:r], *f.* (—, *no pl.*) return; change; *(fig.)* conversion.

umkehren

umkehren ['umke:rən], *v.a.* turn (back), upset, overturn. — *v.n.* (*aux. sein*) turn back, return.

Umkehrung ['umke:ruŋ], *f.* (—, *pl.* —en) inversion.

umkippen ['umkɪpən], *v.a.* upset, overturn. — *v.n.* (*aux. sein*) capsize, tilt over.

umklammern [um'klamərn], *v.a. insep.* clasp; clutch; (*fig.*) cling to.

umkleiden (1) ['umklaɪdən], *v.r. sich —*, change o.'s clothes.

umkleiden (2) [um'klaɪdən], *v.a. insep.* cover.

umkommen ['umkɔmən], *v.n. irr.* (*aux. sein*) perish.

Umkreis ['umkraɪs], *m.* (—es, *pl.* —e) circumference, compass.

Umlauf ['umlauf], *m.* (—s, *no pl.*) circulation; *in — bringen*, put into circulation.

Umlaut ['umlaut], *m.* (—s, *pl.* —e) (*Phonet.*) modification of vowels.

umlegen ['umle:gən], *v.a.* lay down, move, shift, put about; (*sl.*) kill.

umleiten ['umlaɪtən], *v.a.* (*traffic*) divert.

umlernen ['umlɛrnən], *v.a.*, *v.n.* relearn; retrain (for new job).

umliegend ['umli:gənt], *adj.* surrounding.

ummodeln ['ummo:dəln], *v.a.* remodel, recast, change, fashion differently.

Umnachtung [um'naxtuŋ], *f.* (—, *no pl.*) mental derangement.

umpacken ['umpakən], *v.a.* repack.

umpflanzen ['umpflantsən], *v.a.* transplant.

Umpflanzung ['umpflantsuŋ], *f.* (—, *pl.* —en) transplantation.

umrahmen [um'ra:mən], *v.a. insep.* frame, surround.

umrändern [um'rɛndərn], *v.a. insep.* border, edge.

umrechnen ['umrɛçnən], *v.a.* (*figures*) reduce, convert.

umreißen (1) ['umraɪsən], *v.a. irr.* pull down, break up.

umreißen (2) [um'raɪsən], *v.a. irr. insep.* sketch, outline.

umrennen ['umrɛnən], *v.a. irr.* run down, knock over.

umringen [um'rɪŋən], *v.a. insep.* encircle, surround.

Umriß ['umrɪs], *m.* (—sses, *pl.* —sse) outline, contour.

umrühren ['umry:rən], *v.a.* (*Cul.*) stir.

umsatteln ['umzatəln], *v.n.* (*fig.*) change o.'s profession.

Umsatz ['umzats], *m.* (—es, *pl.* —e) turnover.

umschalten ['umʃaltən], *v.a.* (*Elec.*) switch (over); reverse (current).

Umschau ['umʃau], *f.* (—, *no pl.*) review, survey; *— halten*, look round, muster, review.

umschauen ['umʃauən], *v.r. sich —*, look round.

umschichtig ['umʃɪçtɪç], *adv.* turn and turn about, in turns.

umschiffen (1) ['umʃɪfən], *v.a.* tranship, transfer (cargo, passengers).

umschiffen (2) [um'ʃɪfən], *v.a. insep.* sail round, circumnavigate.

Umschlag ['umʃla:k], *m.* (—(e)s, *pl.* ⁓e) (*weather*) break, sudden change; (*letter*) envelope; (*Med.*) poultice, compress.

umschlagen ['umʃla:gən], *v.n. irr.* (*aux. sein*) (*weather*) change suddenly; capsize; turn sour.

umschließen [um'ʃli:sən], *v.a. irr. insep.* enclose, surround; comprise.

umschlingen [um'ʃlɪŋən], *v.a. irr. insep.* embrace.

umschnallen ['umʃnalən], *v.a.* buckle on.

umschreiben (1) ['umʃraɪbən], *v.a. irr. insep.* rewrite, write differently.

umschreiben (2) [um'ʃraɪbən], *v.a. irr. insep.* circumscribe, paraphrase.

Umschreibung [um'ʃraɪbuŋ], *f.* (—, *pl.* —en) paraphrase.

Umschweife ['umʃvaɪfə], *m.pl.* fuss, talk; circumlocution; *ohne —*, point-blank.

Umschwung ['umʃvuŋ], *m.* (—s, *no pl.*) sudden change, revolution.

umsegeln [um'ze:gəln], *v.a. insep.* sail round.

umsehen ['umze:ən], *v.r. irr. sich —*, look round; look out (for), cast about (for).

Umsicht ['umzɪçt], *f.* (—, *no pl.*) circumspection.

umsichtig ['umzɪçtɪç], *adj.* cautious, circumspect.

umsinken ['umzɪŋkən], *v.n. irr.* (*aux. sein*) sink down.

umsonst [um'zɔnst], *adv.* without payment, gratis, for nothing; in vain, vainly, to no purpose.

umspannen (1) ['umʃpanən], *v.a.* change horses.

umspannen (2) [um'ʃpanən], *v.a. insep.* encompass, span.

umspringen ['umʃprɪŋən], *v.n. irr.* (*aux. sein*) (*wind*) change suddenly; *mit einem —*, (*fig.*) deal with s.o.

Umstand ['umʃtant], *m.* (—s, *pl.* ⁓e) circumstance; fact; factor; (*pl.*) fuss; *in anderen ⁓en sein*, be expecting a baby; *unter keinen ⁓en*, on no account.

umständlich ['umʃtɛntlɪç], *adj.* circumstantial, ceremonious; complicated, fussy.

Umstandswort ['umʃtantsvɔrt], *n.* (—es, *pl.* ⁓er) (*Gram.*) adverb.

umstehend ['umʃte:ənt], *adv.* on the next page.

Umstehenden ['umʃte:ondən], *pl.* bystanders.

umsteigen ['umʃtaɪgən], *v.n. irr.* (*aux. sein*) change (trains etc.).

umstellen (1) ['umʃtɛlən], *v.a.* place differently, transpose, change over.

umstellen (2) [um'ʃtɛlən], *v.a. insep.* surround, beset.

Umstellung [ʹumʃtɛluŋ], *f.* (—, *pl.* —en) transposition; (*Gram.*) inversion; change of position in team.

umstimmen [ʹumʃtɪmən], *v.a.* turn s.o. from his opinion, bring s.o. round to (s.th.).

umstoßen [ʹumʃtoːsən], *v.a. irr.* knock down, upset, overthrow; (*judgment*) reverse.

umstricken [umʹʃtrɪkən], *v.a. insep.* ensnare.

umstritten [umʹʃtrɪtən], *adj.* controversial, disputed.

umstülpen [ʹumʃtylpən], *v.a.* turn up, turn upside down.

Umsturz [ʹumʃturts], *m.* (—es, *no pl.*) downfall; subversion; revolution.

umstürzen [ʹumʃtyrtsən], *v.a.* upset, overturn; overthrow.

umtaufen [ʹumtaufən], *v.a.* rename, rechristen.

Umtausch [ʹumtauʃ], *m.* (—s, *no pl.*) exchange.

umtauschen [ʹumtauʃən], *v.a.* exchange, change.

Umtriebe [ʹumtriːbə], *m. pl.* plots, goings-on, intrigues.

umtun [ʹumtuːn], *v.r. irr. sich — nach*, look for, cast about for.

Umwälzung [ʹumvɛltsuŋ], *f.* (—, *pl.* —en) turning-about; (*fig.*) revolution.

umwandeln [ʹumvandəln], *v.a.* change, transform; (*Gram.*) inflect.

umwechseln [ʹumvɛksəln], *v.a.* exchange.

Umweg [ʹumveːk], *m.* (—s, *pl.* —e) roundabout way, detour.

Umwelt [ʹumvɛlt], *f.* (—, *no pl.*) environment, milieu.

umwenden [ʹumvɛndən], *v.a. irr.* turn round; turn over.— *v.r. sich —*, turn round.

umwerben [umʹvɛrbən], *v.a. irr. insep.* court.

umwerfen [ʹumvɛrfən], *v.a. irr.* overturn, knock over, upset.

umwickeln [umʹvɪkəln], *v.a. insep.* wrap round, wind round.

umwölken [umʹvœlkən], *v.r. insep. sich —*, (*sky*) darken, become overcast.

umzäunen [umʹtsɔynən], *v.a. insep.* hedge in, fence in, enclose.

umziehen (1) [ʹumtsiːən], *v.a. irr.* change (clothes).— *v.n.* (*aux. sein*) move (abode).— *v.r. sich —*, change o.'s clothes.

umziehen (2) [umʹtsiːən], *v.r. irr. insep. sich —*, get overcast, cloud over.

umzingeln [umʹtsɪŋəln], *v.a. insep.* surround.

Umzug [ʹumtsuːk], *m.* (—s, *pl.* ⁀e) procession; removal; move.

unabänderlich [unapʹɛndərlɪç], *adj.* unalterable, irrevocable.

Unabänderlichkeit [ʹunapɛndərlɪçkaɪt], *f.* (—, *no pl.*) unchangeableness, irrevocability.

unabhängig [ʹunaphɛŋɪç], *adj.* independent, autonomous; unrelated.

Unabhängigkeit [ʹunaphɛŋɪçkaɪt], *f.* (—, *no pl.*) independence, self-sufficiency.

unabkömmlich [ʹunapkœmlɪç], *adj.* indispensable.

unablässig [ʹunaplɛsɪç], *adj.* unceasing, continual, unremitting.

unabsehbar [ʹunapzeːbaːr], *adj.* immeasurable, immense; unfathomable.

unabsichtlich [ʹunapzɪçtlɪç], *adj.* unintentional, accidental.

unabwendbar [unapʹvɛntbaːr], *adj.* irremediable; unavoidable.

unachtsam [ʹunaxtzaːm], *adj.* inattentive, inadvertent, negligent, careless.

Unachtsamkeit [ʹunaxtzaːmkaɪt], *f.* (—, *pl.* —en) inadvertence, inattention, negligence, carelessness.

unähnlich [ʹunɛːnlɪç], *adj.* unlike, dissimilar.

unanfechtbar [ʹunanfɛçtbaːr], *adj.* indisputable, incontestable.

unangebracht [ʹunangəbraxt], *adj.* out of place, inapposite.

unangefochten [ʹunangəfɔxtən], *adj.* undisputed, uncontested.

unangemeldet [ʹunangəmɛldət], *adj.* unannounced, unheralded.

unangemessen [ʹunangəmɛsən], *adj.* unsuitable, inappropriate, inadequate.

unangenehm [ʹunangəneːm], *adj.* disagreeable, unpleasant; *einen — berühren*, jar, grate on s.o.

unangetastet [ʹunangətastət], *adj.* untouched.

unangreifbar [ʹunangraɪfbaːr], *adj.* unassailable, secure.

unannehmbar [ʹunanneːmbaːr], *adj.* unacceptable.

Unannehmlichkeit [ʹunanneːmlɪçkaɪt], *f.* (—, *pl.* —en) unpleasantness, annoyance.

unansehnlich [ʹunanzeːnlɪç], *adj.* insignificant; unattractive.

unanständig [ʹunanʃtɛndɪç], *adj.* improper, indecent.

Unanständigkeit [ʹunanʃtɛndɪçkaɪt], *f.* (—, *pl.* —en) indecency, immodesty, impropriety.

unantastbar [ʹunantastbaːr], *adj.* unimpeachable.

unappetitlich [ʹunapeti:tlɪç], *adj.* distasteful, unsavoury, unappetising.

Unart [ʹunaːrt], *f.* (—, *pl.* —en) bad habit, naughtiness.

unartig [ʹunaːrtɪç], *adj.* ill-behaved, naughty.

unästhetisch [ʹunɛste:tɪʃ], *adj.* offensive, coarse; inartistic.

unauffällig [ʹunauffɛlɪç], *adj.* unobtrusive.

unaufgefordert [ʹunaufgəfɔrdərt], *adj.* unbidden.

unaufgeklärt [ʹunaufgəklɛːrt], *adj.* unexplained, unsolved.

unaufgeschnitten [ʹunaufgəʃnɪtən], *adj.* uncut.

unaufhaltsam [ʹunaufhaltzaːm], *adj.* incessant, irresistible.

unaufhörlich [ˈunaufhøːrlıç], *adj.* incessant, continual.

unauflöslich [ˈunaufløːslıç], *adj.* indissoluble.

unaufmerksam [ˈunaufmɛrkzaːm], *adj.* inattentive.

unaufrichtig [ˈunaufrıçtıç], *adj.* insincere.

unaufschiebbar [ˈunaufʃiːpbaːr], *adj.* urgent, pressing, brooking no delay.

unausbleiblich [ˈunausblaıplıç], *adj.* inevitable, unfailing.

unausführbar [ˈunausfyːrbaːr], *adj.* impracticable.

unausgebildet [ˈunausgəbıldət], *adj.* untrained, unskilled.

unausgefüllt [ˈunausgəfylt], *adj.* not filled up; (*form*) blank.

unausgegoren [ˈunausgəgoːrən], *adj.* crude; (*wine*) unfermented.

unausgesetzt [ˈunausgəzɛtst], *adj.* continual, continuous.

unausgesprochen [ˈunausgəʃprɔxən], *adj.* unsaid; (*fig.*) implied.

unauslöschlich [ˈunauslœʃlıç], *adj.* indelible, inextinguishable.

unaussprechlich [ˈunausʃpreçlıç], *adj.* inexpressible, unspeakable.

unausstehlich [ˈunausʃteːlıç], *adj.* insufferable.

unausweichlich [ˈunausvaıçlıç], *adj.* inevitable.

unbändig [ˈunbɛndıç], *adj.* intractable, unmanageable; (*fig.*) extreme.

unbarmherzig [ˈunbarmhɛrtsıç], *adj.* merciless.

unbeabsichtigt [ˈunbəapzıçtıçt], *adj.* unintentional.

unbeanstandet [ˈunbəanʃtandət], *adj.* unexceptionable; unopposed; with impunity.

unbeantwortlich [ˈunbəantvɔrtlıç], *adj.* unanswerable.

unbeaufsichtigt [ˈunbəaufzıçtıçt], *adj.* unattended to, not looked after; without supervision.

unbebaut [ˈunbəbaut], *adj.* (*Agr.*) uncultivated; undeveloped (by building).

unbedacht [ˈunbədaxt], *adj.* thoughtless.

unbedenklich [ˈunbədɛŋklıç], *adj.* harmless, innocuous. — *adv.* without hesitation.

unbedeutend [ˈunbədɔytənt], *adj.* insignificant.

unbedingt [ˈunbədıŋkt], *adj.* unconditional, unlimited, absolute. — *adv.* quite definitely; without fail.

unbeeinflußt [ˈunbəaınflust], *adj.* uninfluenced.

unbefahrbar [ˈunbəfaːrbaːr], *adj.* impassable, impracticable.

unbefangen [ˈunbəfaŋən], *adj.* unbiased, unprejudiced; easy, unselfconscious, unembarrassed, uninhibited; natural.

Unbefangenheit [ˈunbəfaŋənhaıt], *f.*

(—, *no pl.*) impartiality; ease of manner, unselfconsciousness, openness, naturalness.

unbefestigt [ˈunbəfɛstıçt], *adj.* unfortified.

unbefleckt [ˈunbəflɛkt], *adj.* immaculate; —*e Empfängnis*, Immaculate Conception.

unbefriedigend [ˈunbəfriːdıgənt], *adj.* unsatisfactory.

unbefriedigt [ˈunbəfriːdıçt], *adj.* not satisfied, unsatisfied.

unbefugt [ˈunbəfuːkt], *adj.* unauthorised.

unbegreiflich [ˈunbəgraıflıç], *adj.* incomprehensible, inconceivable.

unbegrenzt [ˈunbəgrɛntst], *adj.* unlimited, unbounded.

unbegründet [ˈunbəgryndət], *adj.* unfounded, groundless.

Unbehagen [ˈunbəhaːgən], *n.* (—*s, no pl.*) uneasiness, discomfort.

unbehaglich [ˈunbəhaːklıç], *adj.* uncomfortable; *sich — fühlen*, feel ill at ease.

unbehelligt [ˈunbəhɛlıçt], *adj.* unmolested.

unbeholfen [ˈunbəhɔlfən], *adj.* awkward, clumsy.

unbeirrt [ˈunbəırt], *adj.* unswerving, uninfluenced, unperturbed.

unbekannt [ˈunbəkant], *adj.* unknown, unacquainted; *ich bin hier —,* I am a stranger here.

unbekümmert [ˈunbəkymərt], *adj.* unconcerned, careless, indifferent.

unbelehrt [ˈunbəleːrt], *adj.* uninstructed.

unbeliebt [ˈunbəliːpt], *adj.* unpopular.

unbemannt [ˈunbəmant], *adj.* without crew, unmanned.

unbemerkbar [ˈunbəmɛrkbaːr], *adj.* unnoticeable, imperceptible.

unbemerkt [ˈunbəmɛrkt], *adj.* unnoticed.

unbemittelt [ˈunbəmıtəlt], *adj.* impecunious, poor.

unbenommen [ˈunbənɔmən], *adj.* *es bleibt dir —,* you are free to.

unbenutzt [ˈunbənutst], *adj.* unused.

unbequem [ˈunbəkveːm], *adj.* uncomfortable, inconvenient, troublesome.

Unbequemlichkeit [ˈunbəkveːmlıçkaıt], *f.* (—, *pl.* —en) inconvenience.

unberechenbar [ˈunbəreçənbaːr], *adj.* incalculable; (*fig.*) erratic.

unberechtigt [ˈunbəreçtıçt], *adj.* unwarranted, unjustified.

unberücksichtigt [ˈunbərykzıçtıçt], *adj.* disregarded; — *lassen,* ignore.

unberufen [ˈunbəruːfən], *adj.* unauthorized. — *excl.* touch wood!

unbeschadet [ˈunbəʃaːdət], *prep.* (*Genit.*) without prejudice to.

unbeschädigt [ˈunbəʃeːdıçt], *adj.* undamaged.

unbeschäftigt [ˈunbəʃɛftıçt], *adj.* unemployed, disengaged.

unbescheiden ['unbəʃaɪdən], *adj.* presumptuous, greedy, immodest; unblushing; exorbitant; arrogant.
Unbescheidenheit ['unbəʃaɪdənhaɪt], *f.* (—, *no pl.*) presumptuousness, greed.
unbescholten ['unbəʃɔltən], *adj.* irreproachable, of unblemished character.
Unbescholtenheit ['unbəʃɔltənhaɪt], *f.* (—, *no pl.*) blamelessness, good character, unsullied reputation.
unbeschränkt ['unbəʃrɛŋkt], *adj.* unlimited, unbounded; —*e Monarchie*, absolute monarchy.
unbeschreiblich ['unbəʃraɪplɪç], *adj.* indescribable.
unbeschrieben ['unbəʃriːbən], *adj.* unwritten; *ein —es Papier*, a blank sheet of paper.
unbeschwert ['unbəʃveːrt], *adj.* unburdened; easy.
unbeseelt ['unbəzeːlt], *adj.* inanimate.
unbesiegbar [unbə'ziːkbaːr], *adj.* invincible.
unbesoldet ['unbəzɔldət], *adj.* unpaid, unsalaried.
unbesonnen ['unbəzɔnən], *adj.* thoughtless, rash.
Unbesonnenheit ['unbəzɔnənhaɪt], *f.* (—, *pl.* —en) thoughtlessness.
unbesorgt ['unbəzɔrkt], *adj.* unconcerned; *sei —*, never fear.
unbeständig ['unbəʃtɛndɪç], *adj.* fickle, inconstant; (*weather*) unsettled.
unbestechlich ['unbəʃtɛçlɪç], *adj.* incorruptible.
unbestellbar ['unbəʃtɛlbaːr], *adj.* not deliverable; (*letters etc.*) address(ee) unknown.
unbestellt ['unbəʃtɛlt], *adj.* not ordered; (*Agr.*) uncultivated, untilled.
unbestimmt ['unbəʃtɪmt], *adj.* uncertain, not settled; indefinite; irresolute; vague.
unbestraft ['unbəʃtraːft], *adj.* unpunished; without previous conviction.
unbestreitbar ['unbəʃtraɪtbaːr], *adj.* indisputable, incontestable.
unbestritten ['unbəʃtrɪtən], *adj.* uncontested, undoubted, undisputed.
unbeteiligt ['unbətaɪlɪçt], *adj.* unconcerned, indifferent.
unbeträchtlich ['unbətrɛçtlɪç], *adj.* inconsiderable, trivial.
unbetreten ['unbətreːtən], *adj.* untrodden, untouched.
unbeugsam ['unbɔ̈ykzaːm], *adj.* inflexible, unyielding.
unbewacht ['unbəvaxt], *adj.* unguarded.
unbewaffnet ['unbəvafnət], *adj.* unarmed; *mit —em Auge*, with the naked eye.
unbewandert ['unbəvandərt], *adj.* unversed in, unfamiliar with.
unbezahlt ['unbətsaːlt], *adj.* unpaid.
unbezähmbar ['unbətsɛːmbaːr], *adj.* uncontrollable; indomitable.

unbezwinglich ['unbətsvɪŋlɪç], *adj.* invincible, unconquerable.
Unbildung ['unbɪldʊŋ], *f.* (—, *no pl.*) lack of education *or* knowledge *or* culture.
Unbill ['unbɪl], *f.* (—, *pl.* **Unbilden**) injustice, wrong, injury; (*weather*) inclemency.
unbillig ['unbɪlɪç], *adj.* unreasonable, unfair.
Unbilligkeit ['unbɪlɪçkaɪt], *f.* (—, *no pl.*) unreasonableness, injustice, unfairness.
unbotmäßig ['unboːtmɛːsɪç], *adj.* unruly, insubordinate.
unbußfertig ['unbuːsfɛrtɪç], *adj.* impenitent, unrepentant.
und [unt], *conj.* and; — *nicht*, nor; — *so weiter* (abbr. *u.s.w.*), etc., and so on, and so forth; — *wenn*, even if.
Undank ['undaŋk], *m.* (—s, *no pl.*) ingratitude.
undankbar ['undaŋkbaːr], *adj.* ungrateful; *eine —e Aufgabe*, a thankless task.
Undankbarkeit ['undaŋkbaːrkaɪt], *f.* (—, *no pl.*) ingratitude.
undenkbar ['undɛŋkbaːr], *adj.* unthinkable, unimaginable, inconceivable.
undenklich ['undɛŋklɪç], *adj.* seit —*en Zeiten*, from time immemorial.
undeutlich ['undɔ̈ytlɪç], *adj.* indistinct; inarticulate; (*fig.*) unintelligible.
Unding ['undɪŋ], *n.* (—s, *no pl.*) absurdity.
unduldsam ['undultzaːm], *adj.* intolerant.
undurchdringlich ['undurçdrɪŋlɪç], *adj.* impenetrable.
undurchführbar ['undurçfyːrbaːr], *adj.* impracticable, unworkable.
undurchsichtig ['undurçzɪçtɪç], *adj.* opaque, not transparent.
uneben ['uneːbən], *adj.* uneven, rugged; (*coll.*) *nicht —*, not bad.
unecht ['unɛçt], *adj.* false, not genuine, spurious, counterfeit.
unedel ['uneːdəl], *adj.* (*metal*) base.
unehelich ['uneːəlɪç], *adj.* illegitimate.
Unehre ['uneːrə], *f.* (—, *no pl.*) dishonour, disgrace, discredit.
unehrlich ['uneːrlɪç], *adj.* dishonest.
Unehrlichkeit ['uneːrlɪçkaɪt], *f.* (—, *pl.* —en) dishonesty.
uneigennützig ['unaɪgənnytsɪç], *adj.* unselfish, disinterested, public-spirited.
uneingedenk ['unaɪŋədɛŋk], *adj.* (*Genit.*) unmindful, forgetful.
uneingeschränkt ['unaɪŋəʃrɛŋkt], *adj.* unrestrained, unlimited.
uneinig ['unaɪnɪç], **uneins** ['unaɪns], *adj.* disunited, divided; — *werden*, fall out; — *sein*, disagree.
Uneinigkeit ['unaɪnɪçkaɪt], *f.* (—, *pl.* —en) disharmony, discord.
uneinnehmbar ['unaɪnneːmbaːr], *adj.* unconquerable, impregnable.

uneins

uneins *see under* **uneinig.**

unempfänglich [ˈunɛmpfɛŋlɪç], *adj.* insusceptible; unreceptive.

unempfindlich [ˈunɛmpfɪntlɪç], *adj.* insensitive, indifferent; unfeeling.

unendlich [unˈɛntlɪç], *adj.* endless, infinite.

unentbehrlich [ˈunɛntbeːrlɪç], *adj.* indispensable, (absolutely) essential.

unentgeltlich [unɛntˈgɛltlɪç], *adj.* free (of charge).

unentschieden [ˈunɛntʃiːdən], *adj.* undecided, undetermined; irresolute; (*game*) drawn, tied.

unentschlossen [ˈunɛntʃlɔsən], *adj.* irresolute.

Unentschlossenheit [ˈunɛntʃlɔsənhaɪt], *f.* (—, *no pl.*) irresolution, indecision.

unentschuldbar [unɛntˈʃultbaːr], *adj.* inexcusable.

unentstellt [ˈunɛntʃtɛlt], *adj.* undistorted.

unentwegt [ˈunɛntveːkt], *adj.* steadfast, unflinching, unswerving.

unentwickelt [ˈunɛntvɪkəlt], *adj.* undeveloped; **—e** *Länder*, underdeveloped countries.

unentwirrbar [ˈunɛntvɪrbaːr], *adj.* inextricable.

unentzifferbar [ˈunɛnttsɪfərbaːr], *adj.* indecipherable.

unentzündbar [ˈunɛnttsyntbaːr], *adj.* non-inflammable.

unerachtet [ˈunɛraxtət], *prep.* (*Genit.*) (*obs.*) notwithstanding.

unerbeten [ˈunɛrbeːtən], *adj.* unsolicited.

unerbittlich [ˈunɛrbɪtlɪç], *adj.* inexorable.

unerfahren [ˈunɛrfaːrən], *adj.* inexperienced.

unerforschlich [ˈunɛrfɔrʃlɪç], *adj.* inscrutable.

unerfreulich [ˈunɛrfrɔylɪç], *adj.* unpleasant, displeasing, disagreeable.

unerfüllbar [ˈunɛrfylbaːr], *adj.* unrealisable.

unerfüllt [ˈunɛrfylt], *adj.* unfulfilled.

unergründlich [ˈunɛrgryntlɪç], *adj.* unfathomable, impenetrable.

unerheblich [ˈunɛrheːplɪç], *adj.* trifling, unimportant.

unerhört [ˈunɛrhøːrt], *adj.* unprecedented, unheard of, shocking, outrageous; not granted; turned down.

unerkannt [ˈunɛrkant], *adj.* unrecognised.

unerkennbar [ˈunɛrkɛnbaːr], *adj.* unrecognisable.

unerklärlich [ˈunɛrkleːrlɪç], *adj.* inexplicable.

unerläßlich [ˈunɛrlɛslɪç], *adj.* indispensable.

unerlaubt [ˈunɛrlaupt], *adj.* unlawful, illicit.

unermeßlich [ˈunɛrmɛslɪç], *adj.* immense, vast.

unermüdlich [ˈunɛrmyːtlɪç], *adj.* untiring, indefatigable.

unerquicklich [ˈunɛrkvɪklɪç], *adj.* unedifying, disagreeable.

unerreichbar [ˈunɛrraɪçbaːr], *adj.* unattainable, inaccessible.

unerreicht [ˈunɛrraɪçt], *adj.* unequalled.

unersättlich [ˈunɛrzɛtlɪç], *adj.* insatiable, greedy.

unerschöpflich [ˈunɛrʃœpflɪç], *adj.* inexhaustible.

unerschöpft [ˈunɛrʃœpft], *adj.* unexhausted.

unerschrocken [ˈunɛrʃrɔkən], *adj.* intrepid, undaunted.

unerschütterlich [ˈunɛrʃytərlɪç], *adj.* imperturbable.

unerschüttert [ˈunɛrʃytərt], *adj.* unshaken, unperturbed.

unerschwinglich [ˈunɛrʃvɪŋlɪç], *adj.* prohibitive, exorbitant, unattainable.

unersetzlich [ˈunɛrzetslɪç], *adj.* irreplaceable.

unersprießlich [ˈunɛrʃpriːslɪç], *adj.* unprofitable.

unerträglich [ˈunɛrtrɛːklɪç], *adj.* intolerable, insufferable.

unerwartet [ˈunɛrvartət], *adj.* unexpected.

unerwidert [ˈunɛrvɪːdərt], *adj.* (*love*) unrequited; (*letter*) unanswered.

unerwünscht [ˈunɛrvynʃt], *adj.* undesirable, unwelcome.

unerzogen [ˈunɛrtsoːgən], *adj.* uneducated; ill-bred, unmannerly.

unfähig [ˈunfeːɪç], *adj.* incapable, unable, unfit.

Unfähigkeit [ˈunfeːɪçkaɪt], *f.* (—, *no pl.*) incapability, inability, unfitness.

Unfall [ˈunfal], *m.* (—s, *pl.* ‼e) accident.

unfaßbar [ˈunfasbaːr], *adj.* incomprehensible, inconceivable.

unfehlbar [ˈunfeːlbaːr], *adj.* inevitable; infallible.

Unfehlbarkeit [ˈunfeːlbaːrkaɪt], *f.* (—, *no pl.*) infallibility.

unfein [ˈunfaɪn], *adj.* indelicate, coarse, impolite.

unfern [ˈunfɛrn], *prep.* (*Genit., Dat.*) not far from.

unfertig [ˈunfɛrtɪç], *adj.* unfinished, unready.

unflätig [ˈunfleːtɪç], *adj.* obscene, nasty, filthy.

unfolgsam [ˈunfɔlkzaːm], *adj.* disobedient, recalcitrant.

unförmig [ˈunfœrmɪç], *adj.* deformed, ill-shaped, misshapen.

unförmlich [ˈunfœrmlɪç], *adj.* shapeless; free and easy, unceremonious.

unfrankiert [ˈunfraŋkiːrt], *adj.* (*letter*) not prepaid, unstamped, unfranked.

unfrei [ˈunfraɪ], *adj.* not free; subjugated; constrained.

unfreiwillig [ˈunfraɪvɪlɪç], *adj.* involuntary.

unfreundlich [ˈunfrɔyntlɪç], adj. unfriendly, unkind; (weather) inclement.

Unfreundlichkeit [ˈunfrɔyntlɪçkaɪt], f. (—, pl. —en) unfriendliness, unkindness; (weather) inclemency.

Unfrieden [ˈunfriːdən], m. (—s, no pl.) discord, dissension.

unfruchtbar [ˈunfruxtbaːr], adj. barren, sterile; (fig.) fruitless.

Unfug [ˈunfuːk], m. (—s, no pl.) disturbance, misconduct; mischief; grober —, public nuisance.

unfühlbar [ˈunfyːlbaːr], adj. imperceptible.

ungangbar [ˈunɡaŋbaːr], adj. impassable.

Ungarn [ˈuŋɡarn], n. Hungary.

ungastlich [ˈunɡastlɪç], adj. inhospitable.

ungeachtet [ˈunɡəaxtət], prep. (Genit.) notwithstanding.

ungeahndet [ˈunɡəaːndət], adj. unpunished, with impunity.

ungeahnt [ˈunɡəaːnt], adj. unexpected, unsuspected, undreamt of.

ungebändigt [ˈunɡəbɛndɪçt], adj. untamed.

ungebärdig [ˈunɡəbɛːrdɪç], adj. unmannerly, refractory.

ungebeten [ˈunɡəbeːtən], adj. uninvited, unbidden.

ungebleicht [ˈunɡəblaɪçt], adj. unbleached.

ungebraucht [ˈunɡəbrauxt], adj. unused.

Ungebühr [ˈunɡəbyːr], f. (—, no pl.) unseemliness, impropriety, excess.

ungebührlich [ˈunɡəbyːrlɪç], adj. unseemly.

ungebunden [ˈunɡəbundən], adj. unbound, in sheets; unrestrained, loose; unlinked; —e Rede, prose.

Ungeduld [ˈunɡədult], f. (—, no pl.) impatience.

ungeduldig [ˈunɡəduldɪç], adj. impatient.

ungeeignet [ˈunɡəaɪɡnət], adj. unfit, unsuitable.

ungefähr [ˈunɡəfɛːr], adj. approximate, rough. — adv. approximately, roughly, about, round.

ungefährlich [ˈunɡəfɛːrlɪç], adj. not dangerous, harmless, safe.

ungefällig [ˈunɡəfɛlɪç], adj. ungracious, disobliging.

ungefärbt [ˈunɡəfɛrpt], adj. uncoloured; (fig.) unvarnished.

ungefüge [ˈunɡəfyːɡə], adj. clumsy.

ungehalten [ˈunɡəhaltən], adj. indignant, angry.

ungeheißen [ˈunɡəhaɪsən], adj. unbidden. — adv. of o.'s own accord.

ungehemmt [ˈunɡəhɛmt], adj. unchecked, uninhibited.

ungeheuchelt [ˈunɡəhɔyçəlt], adj. unfeigned.

Ungeheuer [ˈunɡəhɔyər], n. (—s, pl. —) monster, monstrosity.

ungeheuer [ˈunɡəhɔyər], adj. huge, immense; atrocious, frightful.

ungehobelt [ˈunɡəhoːbəlt], adj. unplaned; (fig.) boorish, uncultured, unpolished.

ungehörig [ˈunɡəhøːrɪç], adj. unseemly, improper.

Ungehorsam [ˈunɡəhoːrzaːm], m. (—s, no pl.) disobedience.

ungehorsam [ˈunɡəhoːrzaːm], adj. disobedient; — sein, disobey.

Ungehorsamkeit [ˈunɡəhoːrzaːmkaɪt], f. (—, pl. —en) disobedience, insubordination.

ungekämmt [ˈunɡəkɛmt], adj. unkempt.

ungekünstelt [ˈunɡəkynstəlt], adj. artless, unstudied.

ungeladen [ˈunɡəlaːdən], adj. (gun) unloaded, not charged; uninvited.

ungeläutert [ˈunɡəlɔytərt], adj. unrefined; unpurified.

ungelegen [ˈunɡəleːɡən], adj. inconvenient, inopportune.

Ungelegenheit [ˈunɡəleːɡənhaɪt], f. (—, pl. —en) inconvenience, trouble.

ungelehrig [ˈunɡəleːrɪç], adj. intractable, unintelligent.

ungelenk [ˈunɡəlɛŋk], adj. clumsy, awkward; ungainly.

ungelöscht [ˈunɡəlœʃt], adj. unquenched; (lime) unslaked; (mortgage) unredeemed.

Ungemach [ˈunɡəmaːx], n. (—(e)s, no pl.) adversity, toil, privation.

ungemein [ˈunɡəmaɪn], adj. uncommon, extraordinary. — adv. very much, exceedingly.

ungemütlich [ˈunɡəmyːtlɪç], adj. uncomfortable, cheerless, unpleasant.

ungeniert [ˈunʒeniːrt], adj. free and easy, unceremonious, unabashed.

ungenießbar [ˈunɡəniːsbaːr], adj. unpalatable, uneatable, inedible.

ungenügend [ˈunɡənyːɡənt], adj. insufficient, unsatisfactory.

ungenügsam [ˈunɡənyːkzaːm], adj. insatiable, greedy.

ungeordnet [ˈunɡəɔrdnət], adj. illassorted, confused.

ungepflegt [ˈunɡəpfleːkt], adj. uncared for, neglected.

ungerade [ˈunɡəraːdə], adj. uneven; — Zahl, odd number.

ungeraten [ˈunɡəraːtən], adj. abortive, unsuccessful, spoiled; undutiful; illbred.

ungerecht [ˈunɡərɛçt], adj. unjust, unfair.

ungerechtfertigt [ˈunɡərɛçtfɛrtɪçt], adj. unwarranted, unjustified.

Ungerechtigkeit [ˈunɡərɛçtɪçkaɪt], f. (—, pl. —en) injustice.

ungeregelt [ˈunɡəreːɡəlt], adj. not regulated, irregular.

ungereimt [ˈunɡəraɪmt], adj. rhymeless; —es Zeug, nonsense, absurdity.

ungern [ˈunɡern], adv. unwillingly, reluctantly.

241

ungerufen ['ʊngəru:fən], *adj.* unbidden.

ungerührt ['ʊngəry:rt], *adj.* unmoved.

ungesäumt ['ʊngezɔymt], *adj.* unseamed, unhemmed; (*fig.*) immediate. — *adv.* immediately, without delay.

ungeschehen ['ʊngəʃe:ən], *adj.* undone; — *machen*, undo.

Ungeschick ['ʊngəʃɪk], *n.* (—s, *no pl.*) awkwardness, clumsiness.

Ungeschicklichkeit ['ʊngəʃɪklɪçkaɪt], *f.* (—, *pl.* —en) awkwardness, clumsiness.

ungeschickt ['ʊngəʃɪkt], *adj.* awkward, clumsy, unskilful.

ungeschlacht ['ʊngəʃlaxt], *adj.* uncouth, unwieldy; coarse, rude.

ungeschliffen ['ʊngəʃlɪfən], *adj.* unpolished; (*fig.*) coarse.

Ungeschliffenheit ['ʊngəʃlɪfənhaɪt], *f.* (—, *no pl.*) coarseness, uncouthness.

ungeschmälert ['ʊngəʃmɛ:lərt], *adj.* undiminished, unimpaired.

ungeschminkt ['ʊngəʃmɪŋkt], *adj.* without cosmetics *or* make-up, not made up; (*truth*) plain, unvarnished.

ungeschoren ['ʊngəʃo:rən], *adj.* unshorn; *laß mich* —, leave me alone.

ungeschult ['ʊngəʃu:lt], *adj.* untrained.

ungeschwächt ['ʊngəʃvɛçt], *adj.* unimpaired.

ungesellig ['ʊngəzɛlɪç], *adj.* unsociable.

ungesetzlich ['ʊngəzɛtslɪç], *adj.* illegal, unlawful, illicit.

ungesetzmäßig ['ʊngəzɛtsmɛ:sɪç], *adj.* illegitimate, lawless; exceptional; not regular.

ungesiegelt ['ʊngəzi:gəlt], *adj.* unsealed.

Ungestalt ['ʊngəʃtalt], *f.* (—, *no pl.*) deformity.

ungestalt ['ʊngəʃtalt], *adj.* misshapen, deformed.

ungestempelt ['ʊngəʃtɛmpəlt], *adj.* unstamped, uncancelled, not postmarked.

ungestillt ['ʊngəʃtɪlt], *adj.* unquenched, unslaked; not fed, unsatisfied.

ungestört ['ʊngəʃtø:rt], *adj.* undisturbed.

ungestraft ['ʊngəʃtra:ft], *adj.* unpunished. — *adv.* with impunity.

ungestüm ['ʊngəʃty:m], *adj.* impetuous.

Ungestüm ['ʊngəʃty:m], *m. & n.* (—s, *no pl.*) impetuosity.

ungesund ['ʊngəzunt], *adj.* unwholesome, unhealthy, sickly; (*fig.*) unnatural, morbid.

ungetan ['ʊngəta:n], *adj.* not done, left undone.

ungetreu ['ʊngətrɔy], *adj.* disloyal, faithless.

ungetrübt ['ʊngətry:pt], *adj.* untroubled.

ungewandt ['ʊngəvant], *adj.* unskilful.

ungewaschen ['ʊngəvaʃən], *adj.* unwashed; (*sl.*) *—es Mundwerk*, malicious tongue.

ungeweiht ['ʊngəvaɪt], *adj.* unconsecrated.

ungewiß ['ʊngəvɪs], *adj.* uncertain, doubtful.

Ungewißheit ['ʊngəvɪshaɪt], *f.* (—, *no pl.*) uncertainty, suspense.

Ungewitter ['ʊngəvɪtər], *n.* (—s, *pl.* —) storm, thunderstorm.

ungewöhnlich ['ʊngəvø:nlɪç], *adj.* unusual, uncommon.

Ungewohntheit ['ʊngəvo:nthaɪt], *f.* (—, *no pl.*) strangeness; want of practice.

ungezähmt ['ʊngətsɛ:mt], *adj.* untamed; (*fig.*) uncurbed.

Ungeziefer ['ʊngətsi:fər], *n.* (—s, *pl.* —) vermin.

ungeziert ['ʊngətsi:rt], *adj.* unaffected, natural.

ungezogen ['ʊngətso:gən], *adj.* illmannered, naughty.

ungezügelt ['ʊngətsy:gəlt], *adj.* unbridled; (*fig.*) unruly.

ungezwungen ['ʊngətsvuŋən], *adj.* unforced; (*fig.*) unaffected.

Ungezwungenheit ['ʊngətsvuŋənhaɪt], *f.* (—, *no pl.*) naturalness, ease.

Unglaube ['ʊnglaubə], *m.* (—ns, *no pl.*) disbelief.

unglaubhaft ['ʊnglauphaft], *adj.* unauthenticated, incredible.

ungläubig ['ʊnglɔybɪç], *adj.* incredulous, disbelieving.

Ungläubige ['ʊnglɔybɪgə], *m.* (—n, *pl.* —n) unbeliever.

unglaublich ['ʊnglauplɪç], *adj.* incredible, unbelievable.

unglaubwürdig ['ʊnglaupvyrdɪç], *adj.* unauthenticated, incredible.

ungleichartig ['ʊnglaɪça:rtɪç], *adj.* dissimilar, heterogeneous.

ungleichförmig ['ʊnglaɪçfœrmɪç], *adj.* not uniform; dissimilar.

Ungleichheit ['ʊnglaɪçhaɪt], *f.* (—, *pl.* —en) inequality; unlikeness, dissimilarity; unevenness.

ungleichmäßig ['ʊnglaɪçmɛ:sɪç], *adj.* unequal, irregular; changeable, fitful.

Unglimpf ['ʊnglɪmpf], *m.* (—(e)s, *no pl.*) harshness; insult.

Unglück ['ʊnglyk], *n.* (—s, *pl.* —sfälle) misfortune, adversity, ill-luck; accident, disaster; distress, sorrow, affliction.

unglückbringend ['ʊnglykbrɪŋənt], *adj.* disastrous, unpropitious.

unglücklich ['ʊnglyklɪç], *adj.* unfortunate, unhappy, unlucky; *—e Liebe*, unrequited love.

unglücklicherweise ['ʊnglyklɪçərvaɪzə], *adv.* unfortunately, unluckily.

Unglücksbotschaft ['ʊnglyksbo:tʃaft], *f.* (—, *pl.* —en) bad news.

unglückselig ['ʊnglykze:lɪç], *adj.* luckless, wretched, unfortunate, calamitous.

Unglücksfall ['ʊnglyksfal], *m.* (—(e)s, *pl.* ⸚e) accident.

Unglücksgefährte [ˈunglyksgəfɛːrtə], *m.* (—n, *pl.* —n) companion in misfortune.

Ungnade [ˈungnaːdə], *f.* (—, *no pl.*) disgrace.

ungültig [ˈungyltɪç], *adj.* invalid, void; — *machen*, invalidate, annul.

Ungunst [ˈungunst], *f.* (—, *no pl.*) disfavour; unpropitiousness; (*weather*) inclemency.

ungünstig [ˈungynstɪç], *adj.* unfavourable, adverse.

ungut [ˈunguːt], *adj. etwas für — nehmen*, take s.th. amiss.

unhaltbar [ˈunhaltaːr], *adj.* untenable.

Unheil [ˈunhaɪl], *n.* (—s, *no pl.*) mischief, harm; disaster.

unheilbar [ˈunhaɪlbaːr], *adj.* incurable.

unheilbringend [ˈunhaɪlbrɪŋənt], *adj.* ominous, unlucky; disastrous.

Unheilstifter [ˈunhaɪlʃtɪftər], *m.* (—s, *pl.* —) mischief-maker.

unheilvoll [ˈunhaɪlfɔl], *adj.* calamitous, disastrous.

unheimlich [ˈunhaɪmlɪç], *adj.* weird, eerie, uncanny.

unhöflich [ˈunhøːflɪç], *adj.* impolite, uncivil, discourteous.

Unhold [ˈunhɔlt], *m.* (—s, *pl.* —e) fiend, monster.

Unhörbarkeit [ˈunhøːrbaːrkaɪt], *f.* (—, *no pl.*) inaudibility.

Uniformität [uniformiˈtɛːt], *f.* (—, *no pl.*) uniformity.

Unikum [ˈuːnikum], *n.* (—s, *pl.* —s) unique thing *or* person; eccentric.

Universalmittel [univɛrˈzaːlmɪtəl], *n.* (—s, *pl.* —) panacea, universal remedy.

Universität [univɛrziˈtɛːt], *f.* (—, *pl.* —en) university.

Universitätsdozent [univɛrziˈtɛːtsdotsent], *m.* (—en, *pl.* —en) university lecturer.

Universum [uniˈvɛrzum], *n.* (—s, *no pl.*) universe.

unkaufmännisch [ˈunkaufmɛnɪʃ], *adj.* unbusinesslike.

Unke [ˈuŋkə], *f.* (—, *pl.* —n) (*Zool.*) toad; (*fig.*) grumbler, pessimist.

unken [ˈuŋkən], *v.n.* grumble, grouse.

unkenntlich [ˈunkɛntlɪç], *adj.* indiscernible, unrecognisable.

Unkenntlichkeit [ˈunkɛntlɪçkaɪt], *f.* (—, *no pl.*) *bis zur* —, past recognition.

Unkenntnis [ˈunkɛntnɪs], *f.* (—, *no pl.*) ignorance.

unklug [ˈunkluːk], *adj.* imprudent.

Unkosten [ˈunkɔstən], *f. pl.* expenses, costs, charges; overheads.

Unkraut [ˈunkraut], *n.* (—s, *no pl.*) weed(s).

unkündbar [ˈunkyntbaːr], *adj.* irredeemable; irrevocable, permanent.

unkundig [ˈunkundɪç], *adj.* ignorant (of), unacquainted (with).

unlängst [ˈunlɛŋst], *adv.* recently, lately, not long ago.

unlauter [ˈunlautər], *adj.* sordid, squalid; unfair.

unleidlich [ˈunlaɪtlɪç], *adj.* intolerable.

unleserlich [ˈunleːzərlɪç], *adj.* illegible.

unleugbar [ˈunlɔykbaːr], *adj.* undeniable, indisputable.

unlieb [ˈunliːp], *adj.* disagreeable.

unliebenswürdig [ˈunliːbənsvyrdɪç], *adj.* sullen, surly.

unlösbar [ˈunløːsbaːr], *adj.* insoluble.

unlöslich [ˈunløːslɪç], *adj.* (*substance*) indissoluble, insoluble.

Unlust [ˈunlust], *f.* (—, *no pl.*) aversion, disinclination; slackness.

unlustig [ˈunlustɪç], *adj.* averse, disinclined.

unmanierlich [ˈunmaniːrlɪç], *adj.* ill-mannered.

unmännlich [ˈunmɛnlɪç], *adj.* unmanly, effeminate.

Unmaß [ˈunmaːs], *n.* (—es, *no pl.*) excess.

Unmasse [ˈunmasə], *f.* (—, *pl.* —n) vast quantity.

unmaßgeblich [ˈunmaːsgeːplɪç], *adj.* unauthoritative, open to correction; (*fig.*) humble.

unmäßig [ˈunmɛːsɪç], *adj.* intemperate, excessive.

Unmenge [ˈunmɛŋə], *f.* (—, *pl.* —n) vast quantity.

Unmensch [ˈunmɛnʃ], *m.* (—en, *pl.* —en) brute.

unmenschlich [ˈunmɛnʃlɪç], *adj.* inhuman, brutal; (*coll.*) vast.

unmerklich [ˈunmɛrklɪç], *adj.* imperceptible.

unmeßbar [ˈunmɛsbaːr], *adj.* immeasurable.

unmittelbar [ˈunmɪtəlbaːr], *adj.* immediate, direct.

unmöglich [ˈunmøːklɪç], *adj.* impossible.

unmündig [ˈunmyndɪç], *adj.* under age, minor.

Unmündige [ˈunmyndɪgə], *m.* (—n, *pl.* —n) (*Law*) minor.

Unmündigkeit [ˈunmyndɪçkaɪt], *f.* (—, *no pl.*) minority.

Unmut [ˈunmuːt], *m.* (—s, *no pl.*) ill-humour; displeasure, indignation, petulance.

unmutig [ˈunmuːtɪç], *adj.* ill-humoured, petulant, indignant.

unnachahmlich [ˈunnaxaːmlɪç], *adj.* inimitable.

unnachgiebig [ˈunnaxgiːbɪç], *adj.* relentless, unyielding.

unnachsichtig [ˈunnaxzɪçtɪç], *adj.* unrelenting, relentless.

unnahbar [ˈunnaːbaːr], *adj.* unapproachable, stand-offish.

unnennbar [ˈunnɛnbaːr], *adj.* unutterable.

unnütz [ˈunnyts], *adj.* useless.

unordentlich [ˈunɔrdəntlɪç], *adj.* untidy, slovenly.

Unordnung [ˈunɔrdnuŋ], *f.* (—, *no pl.*) disorder, untidiness, muddle, confusion.

unparteiisch [ʹunpartaɪɪʃ], adj. impartial, unbiased, objective.

unpassend [ʹunpasənt], adj. unsuitable, inappropriate; improper.

unpassierbar [ʹunpasiːrbaːr], adj. impassable.

unpäßlich [ʹunpɛslɪç], adj. indisposed, unwell, out of sorts.

Unpäßlichkeit [ʹunpɛslɪçkaɪt], f. (—, pl. —en) indisposition.

unproportioniert [ʹunproːpɔrtsjoniːrt], adj. disproportionate; unshapely.

unqualifizierbar [ʹunkvalifitsiːrbaːr], adj. unspeakable, nameless.

Unrat [ʹunraːt], m. (—(e)s, no pl.) dirt, rubbish.

unratsam [ʹunraːtzaːm], adj. inadvisable.

Unrecht [ʹunrɛçt], n. (—(e)s, no pl.) wrong, injustice; — haben, be in the wrong.

unrecht [ʹunrɛçt], adj. wrong, unjust.

unrechtmäßig [ʹunrɛçtmɛːsɪç], adj. unlawful, illegal.

unredlich [ʹunreːtlɪç], adj. dishonest.

unregelmäßig [ʹunreːgəlmɛːsɪç], adj. irregular.

unreif [ʹunraɪf], adj. unripe, immature; (fig.) crude, raw.

Unreife [ʹunraɪfə], f. (—, no pl.) immaturity.

unrein [ʹunraɪn], adj. unclean; (fig.) impure.

Unreinheit [ʹunraɪnhaɪt], f. (—, pl. —en) impurity.

Unreinlichkeit [ʹunraɪnlɪçkaɪt], f. (—, no pl.) uncleanliness.

unrentabel [ʹunrɛntaːbəl], adj. unprofitable.

unrettbar [ʹunrɛtbaːr], adj. irretrievable, hopelessly lost.

unrichtig [ʹunrɪçtɪç], adj. incorrect, erroneous, wrong.

Unrichtigkeit [ʹunrɪçtɪçkaɪt], f. (—, no pl.) error, falsity, incorrectness.

Unruhe [ʹunruːə], f. (—, pl. —en) unrest, restlessness; disquiet, uneasiness; riot, disturbance; (clock) balance.

Unruhestifter [ʹunruːəʃtɪftər], m. (—s, pl. —) disturber (of the peace); troublemaker.

unruhig [ʹunruːɪç], adj. restless; troublesome, turbulent, uneasy (about), fidgety.

unrühmlich [ʹunryːmlɪç], adj. inglorious.

uns [uns], pers. pron. us, ourselves; to us.

unsachlich [ʹunzaxlɪç], adj. subjective; irrelevant.

unsagbar [ʹunzaːkbaːr], adj. unutterable, unspeakable.

unsanft [ʹunzanft], adj. harsh, violent.

unsauber [ʹunzaubər], adj. unclean, dirty; (fig.) squalid.

unschädlich [ʹunʃɛːtlɪç], adj. harmless, innocuous.

unschätzbar [ʹunʃɛtsbaːr], adj. invaluable.

unscheinbar [ʹunʃaɪnbaːr], adj. plain, homely, insignificant.

unschicklich [ʹunʃɪklɪç], adj. unbecoming, indecent, improper, unseemly.

unschlüssig [ʹunʃlysɪç], adj. irresolute, undecided.

Unschuld [ʹunʃult], f. (—, no pl.) innocence; verfolgte —, injured innocence.

unschuldig [ʹunʃuldɪç], adj. innocent, guiltless; chaste; —es Vergnügen, harmless pleasure.

unschwer [ʹunʃveːr], adv. easily.

Unsegen [ʹunzeːgən], m. (—s, no pl.) misfortune; curse.

unselbständig [ʹunzɛlpʃtɛndɪç], adj. dependent.

unselig [ʹunzeːlɪç], adj. unfortunate, luckless, fatal.

unser [ʹunzər], poss. adj. our. — pers. pron. of us.

unsereiner [ʹunzəraɪnər], pron. s.o. in our position; one of us, people in our position.

unserthalben, unsertwegen [ʹunzərthalbən, unzərtveːgən], adv. for our sake, on our account.

unsertwillen [ʹunzərtvilən], adv. um —, for our sake, on our account.

unsicher [ʹunzɪçər], adj. unsafe; uncertain, doubtful; (route) precarious; (hand) unsteady; (legs) shaky.

unsichtbar [ʹunzɪçtbaːr], adj. invisible.

Unsinn [ʹunzɪn], m. (—s, no pl.) nonsense.

unsinnig [ʹunzɪnɪç], adj. nonsensical; mad, insane.

Unsitte [ʹunzɪtə], f. (—, pl. —n) abuse, nuisance; bad habit.

unsittlich [ʹunzɪtlɪç], adj. immoral.

unstät, unstet [ʹunʃtɛːt, ʹunʃteːt], adj. unsteady, inconstant; restless.

unstatthaft [ʹunʃtathaft], adj. illicit.

unsterblich [ʹunʃtɛrplɪç], adj. immortal.

Unsterblichkeit [ʹunʃtɛrplɪçkaɪt], f. (—, no pl.) immortality.

unstillbar [ʹunʃtilbaːr], adj. unappeasable, unquenchable.

unstreitig [ʹunʃtraɪtɪç], adj. indisputable, unquestionable.

Unsumme [ʹunzumə], f. (—, pl. —n) vast amount (of money).

unsympathisch [ʹunzympaːtɪʃ], adj. uncongenial, disagreeable; er ist mir —, I dislike him.

untadelhaft, untadelig [ʹunta·dəlhaft, ʹunta·dəlɪç], adj. blameless, irreproachable, unimpeachable.

Untat [ʹuntaːt], f. (—, pl. —en) misdeed, crime.

untätig [ʹuntɛːtɪç], adj. inactive, idle, supine.

untauglich [ʹuntauklɪç], adj. unfit, useless; incompetent; (Mil.) disabled.

unteilbar [unʹtaɪlbaːr], adj. indivisible.

unten ['untən], *adv.* below, beneath; (*house*) downstairs.

unter ['untər], *prep.* (*Dat., Acc.*) under, beneath, below, among, between.

Unterbau ['untərbau], *m.* (—s, *pl.* —ten) substructure, foundation.

Unterbewußtsein ['untərbəvustzaın], *n.* (—s, *no pl.*) subconscious mind, subconsciousness.

unterbieten [untər'bi:tən], *v.a. irr. insep.* underbid, undersell.

Unterbilanz ['untərbilants], *f.* (—, *pl.* —en) deficit.

unterbinden [untər'bındən], *v.a. irr. insep.* tie up, bind up; (*fig.*) prevent, check.

unterbleiben [untər'blaıbən], *v.n. irr. insep.* (*aux.* sein) remain undone, be left undone, cease.

unterbrechen [untər'brɛçən], *v.a. irr. insep.* interrupt; (*journey*) break; (*speech*) cut short.

Unterbrechung [untər'brɛçuŋ], *f.* (—, *pl.* —en) interruption.

unterbreiten (1) ['untərbraıtən], *v.a.* spread under.

unterbreiten (2) [untər'braıtən], *v.a. insep.* submit, lay before.

unterbringen ['untərbrıŋən], *v.a. irr.* provide (*a place*) for; (*goods*) dispose of; (*money*) invest; (*people*) accommodate, put up.

Unterbringung ['untərbrıŋuŋ], *f.* (—, *no pl.*) provision for; (*goods*) disposal of; (*money*) investment; (*people*) accommodation.

unterdessen [untər'dɛsən], *adv., conj.* in the meantime, meanwhile.

unterdrücken [untər'drykən], *v.a. insep.* suppress, curb, check; oppress.

Unterdrückung [untər'drykuŋ], *f.* (—, *no pl.*) oppression, suppression.

untereinander [untəraın'andər], *adv.* with each other, mutually, among themselves.

unterfangen [untər'faŋən], *v.r. irr. insep. sich* —, dare, venture, presume.

Untergang ['untərgaŋ], *m.* (—s, *pl.* ⸚e) (*sun*) setting; (*ship*) sinking; (*fig.*) decline.

untergeben [untər'ge:bən], *adj.* subject, subordinate.

Untergebene [untər'ge:bənə], *m.* (—n, *pl.* —n) subordinate.

untergehen ['untərge:ən], *v.n. irr.* (*aux.* sein) (*sun*) go down, set; (*ship*) sink; (*fig.*) perish; decline.

Untergeschoß ['untərgəʃɔs], *n.* (—sses, *pl.* —sse) ground floor.

Untergestell ['untərgəʃtɛl], *n.* (—s, *pl.* —e) undercarriage, chassis.

untergraben [untər'gra:bən], *v.a. irr. insep.* undermine.

unterhalb ['untərhalp], *prep.* (*Genit.*) below, under.

Unterhalt ['untərhalt], *m.* (—s, *no pl.*) maintenance, support, livelihood.

unterhalten (1) ['untərhaltən], *v.a. irr.* hold under.

unterhalten (2) [untər'haltən], *v.a. irr. insep.* maintain, keep, support; entertain. — *v.r. sich* —, converse, make conversation; *sich gut* —, enjoy o.s.

unterhaltend [untər'haltənt], *adj.* entertaining, amusing, lively.

Unterhaltskosten ['untərhaltskɔstən], *f. pl.* maintenance; (*house*) cost of repairs.

Unterhaltung [untər'haltuŋ], *f.* (—, *pl.* —en) maintenance; conversation; amusement, entertainment.

Unterhaltungslektüre [untər'haltuŋslɛkty:rə], *f.* (—, *no pl.*) light reading, fiction.

unterhandeln [untər'handəln], *v.n. insep.* negotiate.

Unterhändler [untər'hɛndlər], *m.* (—s, *pl.* —) negotiator, mediator.

Unterhandlung [untər'handluŋ], *f.* (—, *pl.* —en) negotiation.

Unterhaus ['untərhaus], *n.* (—es, *pl.* ⸚er) ground floor; (*Parl.*) lower house; House of Commons.

Unterhemd ['untərhɛmt], *n.* (—(e)s, *pl.* —en) vest.

unterhöhlen [untər'hø:lən], *v.a. insep.* undermine.

Unterholz ['untərhɔlts], *n.* (—es, *no pl.*) undergrowth, underwood.

Unterhosen ['untərho:zən], *f. pl.* (*women*) briefs; (*men*) underpants.

unterirdisch ['untərırdıʃ], *adj.* subterranean, underground.

unterjochen [untər'jɔxən], *v.a. insep.* subjugate, subdue.

Unterkiefer ['untərki:fər], *m.* (—s, *pl.* —) lower jaw.

Unterkleid ['untərklaıt], *n.* (—s, *pl.* ⸚er) under-garment.

unterkommen ['untərkɔmən], *v.n. irr.* (*aux.* sein) find accommodation *or* shelter; (*fig.*) find employment.

Unterkommen ['untərkɔmən], *n.* (—s, *no pl.*) shelter, accommodation; (*fig.*) employment, place.

Unterkörper ['untərkœrpər], *m.* (—s, *pl.* —) lower part of the body.

unterkriegen ['untərkri:gən], *v.a.* get the better of; *lass dich nicht* —, stand firm.

Unterkunft ['untərkunft], *f.* (—, *pl.* ⸚e) shelter, accommodation; employment.

Unterlage ['untərla:gə], *f.* (—, *pl.* —n) foundation, base; blotting pad; (*pl.*) documents, files.

unterlassen [untər'lasən], *v.a. irr. insep.* omit (to do), fail (to do), neglect; forbear.

Unterlassung [untər'lasuŋ], *f.* (—, *pl.* —en) omission, neglect.

Unterlassungssünde [untər'lasuŋszyndə], *f.* (—, *pl.* —n) sin of omission.

Unterlauf ['untərlauf], *m.* (—(e)s, *pl.* ⸚e) (*river*) lower course.

Unterlaufen

unterlaufen [untər'laufən], *v.n. irr. insep. (aux. sein)* run under; *(mistake)* creep in. — *adj.* suffused, blood-shot.

unterlegen (1) ['untərle:gən], *v.a.* lay under; *einen anderen Sinn —*, put a different construction upon.

unterlegen (2) [untər'le:gən], *adj.* inferior.

Unterleib ['untərlaip], *m.* (—s, *no pl.*) abdomen.

unterliegen [untər'li:gən], *v.n. irr. insep. (aux. sein)* succumb, be overcome; be subject (to).

Untermieter ['untərmi:tər], *m.* (—s, *pl.* —) subtenant.

unterminieren [untərmi'ni:rən], *v.a. insep.* undermine.

unternehmen [untər'ne:mən], *v.a. insep.* undertake, take upon o.s., attempt.

Unternehmen [untər'ne:mən], *n.* (—s, *pl.* —) enterprise, undertaking.

unternehmend [untər'ne:mənt], *adj.* bold, enterprising.

Unternehmer [untər'ne:mər], *m.* (—s, *pl.* —) contractor, entrepreneur.

Unteroffizier [untərofitsi:r], *m.* (—s, *pl.* —e) *(army)* non-commissioned officer; *(navy)* petty officer.

unterordnen ['untərordnən], *v.a.* subordinate. — *v.r. sich —*, submit (to).

Unterordnung ['untərordnuŋ], *f.* (—, *no pl.*) subordination, submission; *(Biol.)* sub-order.

Unterpacht ['untərpaxt], *f.* (—, *no pl.*) sublease.

Unterpfand ['untərpfant], *n.* (—(e)s, *no pl.*) pawn, pledge.

Unterredung [untər're:duŋ], *f.* (—, *pl.* —en) conference, interview, talk.

Unterricht ['untərriçt], *m.* (—(e)s, *no pl.*) instruction, tuition, teaching.

unterrichten [untər'riçtən], *v.a. insep.* instruct, teach.

Unterrichtsanstalt ['untərriçtsanʃtalt], *f.* (—, *pl.* —en) educational establishment *or* institution.

Unterrichtsgegenstand ['untərriçtsge:gənʃtant], *m.* (—s, *pl.* ⸚e) subject of instruction.

Unterrock ['untərrɔk], *m.* (—s, *pl.* ⸚e) petticoat, slip; underskirt.

untersagen [untər'za:gən], *v.a. insep.* forbid; *Rauchen untersagt*, smoking prohibited.

Untersatz ['untərzats], *m.* (—es, *pl.* ⸚e) basis, holder, stand, trestle; saucer.

unterschätzen [untər'ʃɛtsən], *v.a. insep.* underrate, underestimate.

unterscheiden [untər'ʃaidən], *v.a. irr. insep.* distinguish, discriminate, discern, differentiate. — *v.r. sich —*, differ; *ich kann sie nicht —*, I cannot tell them apart.

Unterscheidung [untər'ʃaidun], *f.* (—, *pl.* —en) distinction, differentiation.

Unterscheidungsmerkmal [untər-'ʃaiduŋsmerkma:l], *n.* (—s, *pl.* —e) distinctive mark, characteristic.

Unterscheidungsvermögen [untər-'ʃaiduŋsfermø:gən], *n.* (—s, *no pl.*) power of discrimination.

Unterscheidungszeichen [untər'ʃaiduŋstsaiçən], *n.* (—s, *pl.* —) criterion.

Unterschenkel ['untərʃɛnkəl], *m.* (—s, *pl.* —) shank, lower part of the thigh.

Unterschicht ['untərʃiçt], *f.* (—, *pl.* —en) substratum, subsoil.

unterschieben (1) ['untərʃi:bən], *v.a. irr. insep.* substitute; interpolate; forge; foist upon.

unterschieben (2) [untər'ʃi:bən], *v.a. irr. insep. (fig.)* attribute falsely, pass s.o. off as.

Unterschiebung [untər'ʃi:buŋ], *f.* (—, *pl.* —en) substitution; forgery.

Unterschied ['untərʃi:t], *m.* (—(e)s, *pl.* —e) difference.

unterschiedlich ['untərʃi:tliç], *adj.* different, diverse.

unterschiedslos ['untərʃi:tslo:s], *adv.* indiscriminately.

unterschlagen [untər'ʃla:gən], *v.a. irr. insep.* embezzle, intercept.

Unterschlagung [untər'ʃla:guŋ], *f.* (—, *pl.* —en) embezzlement.

Unterschlupf ['untərʃlupf], *m.* (—es, *pl.* ⸚e) shelter, refuge.

unterschlüpfen ['untərʃlypfən], *v.n. (aux. sein)* find shelter, slip away; *(fig.)* hide.

unterschreiben [untər'ʃraibən], *v.a. irr. insep.* sign, subscribe to.

Unterschrift ['untərʃrift], *f.* (—, *pl.* —en) signature.

Unterseeboot ['untərze:bo:t], *n.* (—s, *pl.* —e) submarine.

untersetzt [untər'zɛtst], *adj.* thickset, dumpy.

untersinken ['untərziŋkən], *v.n. irr. (aux. sein)* go down.

unterst ['untərst], *adj.* lowest, undermost, bottom.

Unterstaatssekretär [untər'ʃta:tszekrete:r], *m.* (—s, *pl.* —e) undersecretary of state.

unterstehen (1) ['untərʃte:ən], *v.n. irr. (aux. sein)* find shelter (under).

unterstehen (2) [untər'ʃte:ən], *v.n. irr. insep.* be subordinate. — *v.r. sich —*, dare, venture.

unterstellen (1) ['untərʃtɛlən], *v.a.* place under. — *v.r. sich —*, take shelter (under).

unterstellen (2) [untər'ʃtɛlən], *v.a. insep.* put under the authority of; impute (s.th. to s.o.).

Unterstellung [untər'ʃtɛluŋ], *f.* (—, *pl.* —en) imputation, insinuation.

unterstreichen [untər'ʃtraiçən], *v.a. irr. insep.* underline.

Unterstreichung [untər'ʃtraiçuŋ], *f.* (—, *pl.* —en) underlining.

Unterströmung [untər'ʃtrø:muŋ], *f.* (—, *pl.* —en) undercurrent.

unterstützen [untər'ʃtytsən], *v.a. insep.* support, assist, aid; *(fig.)* countenance.

Unterstützung [untər'ʃtytsuŋ], *f.* (—, *pl.* —en) support, aid, assistance, relief.
Unterstützungsanstalt[untər'ʃtytsuŋs-anʃtalt], *f.* (—, *pl.* —en) charitable institution.
unterstützungsbedürftig [untər'ʃtyt-suŋsbədyrftiç], *adj.* indigent.
untersuchen [untər'zu:xən], *v.a. insep.* investigate, examine, look over.
Untersuchung [untər'zu:xuŋ], *f.* (—, *pl.* —en) investigation, inquiry; *(medical)* examination.
Untersuchungshaft [untər'zu:xuŋs-haft], *f.* (—, *no pl.*) imprisonment pending investigation.
Untersuchungsrichter [untər'zu:-xuŋsriçtər], *m.* (—s, *pl.* —) examining magistrate.
Untertan ['untərta:n], *m.* (—s, *pl.* —en) subject, vassal.
untertan ['untərta:n], *adj.* subject.
untertänig ['untərte:niç], *adj.* humble, obsequious, submissive, servile.
Untertasse ['untərtasə], *f.* (—, *pl.* —n) saucer.
untertauchen ['untərtauxən], *v.a.* dip, duck, submerge. — *v.n.* (*aux.* sein) dive.
unterwegs [untər've:ks], *adv.* on the way.
unterweisen [untər'vaizən], *v.a. irr. insep.* teach, instruct.
Unterweisung [untər'vaizuŋ], *f.* (—, *pl.* —en) instruction, teaching.
Unterwelt ['untərvɛlt], *f.* (—, *no pl.*) Hades, the underworld.
unterwerfen [untər'vɛrfən], *v.a. irr. insep.* subject, subdue. — *v.r. sich* —, submit (to), resign o.s. (to).
Unterwerfung [untər'vɛrfuŋ], *f.* (—, *no pl.*) subjection, submission.
unterwühlen [untər'vy:lən], *v.a. insep.* root up; *(fig.)* undermine.
unterwürfig [untər'vyrfiç], *adj.* submissive, subject; obsequious.
Unterwürfigkeit [untər'vyrfiçkait], *f.* (—, *no pl.*) submissiveness; obsequiousness.
unterzeichnen [untər'tsaiçnən], *v.a. insep.* sign.
Unterzeichner [untər'tsaiçnər], *m.* (—s, *pl.* —) signatory; *(insurance)* underwriter.
Unterzeichnete [untər'tsaiçnətə], *m.* (—n, *pl.* —n) undersigned.
Unterzeichnung [untər'tsaiçnuŋ], *f.* (—, *pl.* —en) signature.
unterziehen [untər'tsi:ən], *v.r. irr. insep. sich* —, submit to, undertake; *(operation)* undergo.
Untiefe ['unti:fə], *f.* (—, *pl.* —n) shallow water, flat, shoal, sands.
Untier ['unti:r], *n.* (—s, *pl.* —e) monster.
untilgbar ['untilkba:r], *adj.* indelible; *(debt)* irredeemable.
untrennbar ['untrɛnba:r], *adj.* inseparable.
untreu ['untrɔy], *adj.* faithless, unfaithful, disloyal, perfidious.

Untreue ['untrɔyə], *f.* (—, *no pl.*) faithlessness, unfaithfulness, disloyalty, perfidy.
untröstlich ['untrø:stliç], *adj.* inconsolable, disconsolate.
untrüglich ['untry:kliç], *adj.* unmistakable, infallible.
untüchtig ['untyçtiç], *adj.* inefficient; incompetent.
unüberlegt ['uny:bərle:kt], *adj.* inconsiderate, thoughtless; rash.
unübersehbar ['uny:bərze:ba:r], *adj.* immense, vast.
unübersteiglich ['uny:bərʃtaikliç], *adj.* insurmountable.
unübertrefflich ['uny:bərtrɛfliç], *adj.* unsurpassable, unequalled, unrivalled.
unübertroffen ['uny:bərtrɔfən], *adj.* unsurpassed.
unüberwindlich ['uny:bərvintliç], *adj.* invincible, unconquerable.
unumgänglich ['unumgɛŋliç], *adj.* indispensable, unavoidable, inevitable.
unumschränkt ['unumʃrɛŋkt], *adj.* unlimited, absolute.
unumstößlich ['unumʃtø:sliç], *adj.* irrefutable.
unumwunden ['unumvundən], *adj.* frank, plain.
ununterbrochen ['ununtərbrɔxən], *adj.* uninterrupted, unremitting.
unveränderlich ['unfɛrɛndərliç], *adj.* unchangeable, unalterable.
unverändert ['unfɛrɛndərt], *adj.* unchanged, unaltered.
unverantwortlich ['unfɛrantvɔrtliç], *adj.* irresponsible, inexcusable, unjustifiable.
unveräußerlich ['unfɛrɔysərliç], *adj.* not for sale; inalienable.
unverbesserlich ['unfɛrbɛsərliç], *adj.* incorrigible.
unverbindlich ['unfɛrbintliç], *adj.* not binding, without prejudice, without obligation.
unverblümt ['unfɛrbly:mt], *adj.* blunt, point-blank.
unverbrennlich ['unfɛrbrɛnliç], *adj.* incombustible.
unverbrüchlich ['unfɛrbryçliç], *adj.* inviolable.
unverbürgt ['unfɛrbyrkt], *adj.* unwarranted, unofficial; unconfirmed.
unverdaulich ['unfɛrdauliç], *adj.* indigestible.
unverdaut ['unfɛrdaut], *adj.* undigested.
unverdient ['unfɛrdi:nt], *adj.* unmerited, undeserved.
unverdientermaßen ['unfɛrdi:ntər-ma:sən], *adv.* undeservedly.
unverdorben ['unfɛrdɔrbən], *adj.* unspoiled, uncorrupted, innocent.
unverdrossen ['unfɛrdrɔsən], *adj.* indefatigable.
unvereidigt ['unfɛraidiçt], *adj.* unsworn.
unvereinbar ['unfɛrainba:r], *adj.* incompatible, inconsistent.

Unvereinbarkeit

Unvereinbarkeit ['unfɛraɪnba:rkaɪt], *f.* (—, *no pl.*) incompatibility, inconsistency.

unverfälscht ['unfɛrfɛlʃt], *adj.* unadulterated, genuine, pure.

unverfänglich ['unfɛrfɛŋlɪç], *adj.* harmless.

unverfroren ['unfɛrfro:rən], *adj.* cheeky, impudent.

unvergeßlich ['unfɛrgɛslɪç], *adj.* memorable, not to be forgotten, unforgettable.

unvergleichlich ['unfɛrglaɪçlɪç], *adj.* incomparable.

unverhältnismäßig ['unfɛrhɛltnɪsmɛ:sɪç], *adj.* disproportionate.

unverheiratet ['unfɛrhaɪra:tət], *adj.* unmarried.

unverhofft ['unfɛrhɔft], *adj.* unexpected.

unverhohlen ['unfɛrho:lən], *adj.* unconcealed, undisguised, candid.

unverkennbar ['unfɛrkɛnba:r], *adj.* unmistakable.

unverlangt ['unfɛrlaŋkt], *adj.* unsolicited, not ordered.

unverletzlich ['unfɛrlɛtslɪç], *adj.* invulnerable; (*fig.*) inviolable.

unverletzt ['unfɛrlɛtst], *adj.* (*persons*) unhurt; (*things*) undamaged, intact.

unvermeidlich ['unfɛrmaɪtlɪç], *adj.* inevitable, unavoidable.

unvermindert ['unfɛrmɪndərt], *adj.* undiminished.

unvermittelt ['unfɛrmɪtəlt], *adj.* sudden, abrupt.

Unvermögen ['unfɛrmø:gən], *n.* (—s, *no pl.*) inability, incapacity.

unvermögend ['unfɛrmø:gənt], *adj.* incapable; impecunious.

unvermutet ['unfɛrmu:tət], *adj.* unexpected, unforeseen.

unverrichtet ['unfɛrrɪçtət], *adj.* *—er Sache*, empty-handed; unsuccessfully.

unverschämt ['unfɛrʃɛ:mt], *adj.* impudent, brazen.

unverschuldet ['unfɛrʃuldət], *adj.* not in debt, unencumbered; (*fig.*) undeserved.

unversehens ['unfɛrze:əns], *adv.* unexpectedly, unawares.

unversehrt ['unfɛrze:rt], *adj.* (*persons*) unhurt, safe; (*things*) undamaged.

unversiegbar ['unfɛrzi:kba:r], *adj.* inexhaustible.

unversiegt ['unfɛrzi:kt], *adj.* unexhausted.

unversöhnlich ['unfɛrzø:nlɪç], *adj.* implacable, irreconcilable.

unversöhnt ['unfɛrzø:nt], *adj.* unreconciled.

unversorgt ['unfɛrzɔrkt], *adj.* unprovided for.

Unverstand ['unfɛrʃtant], *m.* (—(e)s, *no pl.*) want of judgment, indiscretion.

unverständig ['unfɛrʃtɛndɪç], *adj.* foolish, unwise, imprudent.

unverständlich ['unfɛrʃtɛntlɪç], *adj.* unintelligible, incomprehensible.

unversteuert ['unfɛrʃtɔyərt], *adj.* with duty *or* tax unpaid.

unversucht ['unfɛrzu:xt], *adj.* untried; *nichts — lassen*, leave no stone unturned.

unverträglich ['unfɛrtrɛ:klɪç], *adj.* quarrelsome.

unverwandt ['unfɛrvant], *adj.* unrelated; fixed, constant; immovable.

unverwundbar ['unfɛrvuntba:r], *adj.* invulnerable.

unverwüstlich ['unfɛrvy:stlɪç], *adj.* indestructible.

unverzagt ['unfɛrtsa:kt], *adj.* undaunted, intrepid.

unverzeihlich ['unfɛrtsaɪlɪç], *adj.* unpardonable.

unverzinslich ['unfɛrtsɪnslɪç], *adj.* (*money*) gaining no interest.

unverzollt ['unfɛrtsɔlt], *adj.* duty unpaid.

unverzüglich ['unfɛrtsy:klɪç], *adj.* immediate.

unvollendet ['unfɔlɛndət], *adj.* unfinished.

unvollständig ['unfɔlʃtɛndɪç], *adj.* incomplete.

unvorbereitet ['unfo:rbəraɪtət], *adj.* unprepared.

unvordenklich ['unfo:rdɛŋklɪç], *adj.* *seit —en Zeiten*, from time immemorial.

unvorhergesehen ['unfo:rhe:rgəze:ən], *adj.* unforeseen, unlooked for.

unvorsichtig ['unfo:rzɪçtɪç], *adj.* imprudent, incautious, careless.

unvorteilhaft ['unfɔrtaɪlhaft], *adj.* unprofitable, disadvantageous; *— aussehen*, not look o.'s best.

unwägbar ['unvɛ:kba:r], *adj.* imponderable.

unwahr ['unva:r], *adj.* untrue, false.

Unwahrhaftigkeit ['unva:rhaftɪçkaɪt], *f.* (—, *no pl.*) want of truthfulness, unreliability, dishonesty.

Unwahrheit ['unva:rhaɪt], *f.* (—, *pl.* —en) lie, untruth, falsehood.

unwegsam ['unve:kza:m], *adj.* impassable, impracticable.

unweigerlich ['unvaɪgərlɪç], *adj.* unhesitating, unquestioning. — *adv.* without fail.

unweit ['unvaɪt], *prep.* (*Genit.*) not far from, near.

Unwesen ['unve:zən], *n.* (—s, *no pl.*) nuisance; *sein — treiben*, be up to o.'s tricks.

Unwetter ['unvɛtər], *n.* (—s, *pl.* —) bad weather, thunderstorm.

unwichtig ['unvɪçtɪç], *adj.* unimportant; insignificant, of no consequence.

unwiderleglich ['unvi:dərle:klɪç], *adj.* irrefutable.

unwiderruflich ['unvi:dərru:flɪç], *adj.* irrevocable.

unwidersprechlich ['unvi:dərʃprɛçlɪç], *adj.* incontestable.

unwidersprochen ['unvi:dərʃprɔxən], *adj.* uncontradicted.

unwiderstehlich ['unvi:dərʃteːlɪç], *adj.* irresistible.

unwiederbringlich ['unvi:dərbrɪŋlɪç], *adj.* irrecoverable, irretrievable.

Unwille ['unvɪlə], *m.* (—ns, *no pl.*) displeasure, indignation.

unwillkürlich ['unvɪlkyːrlɪç], *adj.* involuntary; instinctive.

unwirsch ['unvɪrʃ], *adj.* petulant, testy; curt, uncivil.

unwirtlich ['unvɪrtlɪç], *adj.* inhospitable.

unwirtschaftlich ['unvɪrtʃaftlɪç], *adj.* not economic, uneconomic.

unwissend ['unvɪsənt], *adj.* illiterate, ignorant.

Unwissenheit ['unvɪsənhaɪt], *f.* (—, *no pl.*) ignorance.

unwissenschaftlich ['unvɪsənʃaftlɪç], *adj.* unscholarly; unscientific.

unwissentlich ['unvɪsəntlɪç], *adv.* unknowingly, unconsciously.

unwohl ['unvoːl], *adj.* unwell, indisposed.

Unwohlsein ['unvoːlzaɪn], *n.* (—s, *no pl.*) indisposition.

unwürdig ['unvyrdɪç], *adj.* unworthy, undeserving.

Unzahl ['untsaːl], *f.* (—, *no pl.*) vast number.

unzählbar [un'tsɛːlbaːr], *adj.* innumerable, numberless.

unzählig [un'tsɛːlɪç], *adj.* innumerable; —*e Male,* over and over again.

unzart ['untsaːrt], *adj.* indelicate, rude, rough; unceremonious.

Unzeit ['untsaɪt], *f.* (—, *no pl.*) *zur* —, out of season, inopportunely.

unzeitgemäß ['untsaɪtgəmɛːs], *adj.* out of date, behind the times; unfashionable.

unzeitig ['untsaɪtɪç], *adj.* unseasonable; untimely, inopportune.

unziemlich ['untsiːmlɪç], *adj.* unseemly, unbecoming.

Unzier ['untsiːr], *f.* (—, *no pl.*) disfigurement; flaw.

Unzucht ['untsuxt], *f.* (—, *no pl.*) unchastity; lewdness; fornication.

unzüchtig ['untsyçtɪç], *adj.* unchaste, lascivious, lewd.

unzufrieden ['untsufriːdən], *adj.* discontented, dissatisfied.

unzugänglich ['untsugɛŋlɪç], *adj.* inaccessible.

unzulänglich ['untsulɛŋlɪç], *adj.* inadequate, insufficient.

Unzulänglichkeit ['untsulɛŋlɪçkaɪt], *f.* (—, *no pl.*) inadequacy.

unzulässig ['untsulɛsɪç], *adj.* inadmissible.

unzurechnungsfähig ['untsurɛçnuŋsfɛːɪç], *adj.* not accountable (for o.'s actions), non compos mentis, insane.

Unzurechnungsfähigkeit ['untsurɛçnuŋsfɛːɪçkaɪt], *f.* (—, *no pl.*) irresponsibility; feeblemindedness.

unzusammenhängend ['untsuzamənhɛŋant], *adj.* incoherent.

unzuständig ['untsuʃtɛndɪç], *adj.* incompetent, not competent (*Law etc.*).

unzuträglich ['untsutrɛːklɪç], *adj.* unwholesome.

unzutreffend ['untsutrɛfənt], *adj.* inapposite; unfounded; inapplicable.

unzuverlässig ['untsufɛrlɛsɪç], *adj.* unreliable.

unzweckmäßig ['untsvɛkmɛːsɪç], *adj.* inexpedient.

unzweideutig ['untsvaɪdɔytɪç], *adj.* unequivocal, explicit, unambiguous.

üppig ['ypɪç], *adj.* abundant; opulent, luxurious, luxuriant, voluptuous.

uralt ['uːralt], *adj.* very old, old as the hills; ancient.

uranfänglich ['uːranfɛŋlɪç], *adj.* primordial, primeval.

Uraufführung ['uːrauffyːruŋ], *f.* (—, *pl.* —en) (*Theat.*) first night, première.

urbar ['uːrbaːr], *adj.* arable, under cultivation; — *machen,* cultivate.

Urbarmachung ['uːrbaːrmaxuŋ], *f.* (—, *no pl.*) cultivation.

Urbild ['uːrbɪlt], *n.* (—(e)s, *pl.* —er) prototype; (*fig.*) ideal.

ureigen ['uːraɪgən], *adj.* quite original; idiosyncratic.

Ureltern ['uːrɛltərn], *pl.* ancestors.

Urenkel ['uːrɛŋkəl], *m.* (—s, *pl.* —) .great-grandson, great-grandchild.

Urenkelin ['uːrɛŋkəlɪn], *f.* (—, *pl.* —nen) great-granddaughter.

Urfehde ['uːrfeːdə], *f.* (—, *no pl.*) oath to keep the peace.

Urform ['uːrfɔrm], *f.* (—, *pl.* —en) primitive form; original form; archetype.

Urgroßmutter ['uːrgroːsmutər], *f.* (—, *pl.* ⸚) great-grandmother.

Urgroßvater ['uːrgroːsfaːtər], *m.* (—s, *pl.* ⸚) great-grandfather.

Urheber ['uːrheːbər], *m.* (—s, *pl.* —) author, originator.

Urheberrecht ['uːrheːbərrɛçt], *n.* (—s, *pl.* —e) copyright.

Urheberschaft ['uːrheːbərʃaft], *f.* (—, *no pl.*) authorship.

Urin [u'riːn], *m.* (—s, *no pl.*) urine.

Urkunde ['uːrkundə], *f.* (—, *pl.* —n) document, deed, charter; *zur — dessen,* (*obs.*) in witness whereof.

Urkundenbeweis ['uːrkundənbəvaɪs], *m.* (—es, *pl.* —e) documentary evidence.

urkundlich ['uːrkuntlɪç], *adj.* documentary.

Urlaub ['uːrlaup], *m.* (—s, *pl.* —e) leave of absence; vacation; (*Mil.*) furlough.

urplötzlich ['uːrplœtslɪç], *adj.* sudden. — *adv.* all at once, suddenly.

Urquell ['uːrkvɛl], *m.* (—s, *pl.* —en) fountain-head, original source.

Ursache ['uːrzaxə], *f.* (—, *pl.* —n) cause; *keine* —, don't mention it.

Urschrift ['uːrʃrɪft], *f.* (—, *pl.* —en) original text.

Ursprache ['uːrʃpraːxə], *f.* (—, *pl.* —n) original language.

Ursprung ['uːrʃpruŋ], *m.* (—s, *pl.* ⸚e) origin; extraction.

ursprünglich

ursprünglich ['u:rʃpryŋlɪç], *adj.* original.

Urteil ['urtaɪl], *n.* (—s, *pl.* —e) opinion; (*Law*) judgment, verdict, sentence; *ein* — *fällen*, pass judgment on; *nach meinem* —, in my opinion.

urteilen ['urtaɪlən], *v.n.* judge.

Urteilsspruch ['urtaɪlsʃprux], *m.* (—s, *pl.* ⁻e) judgment, sentence.

Uruguay [uru'gwaɪ], *n.* Uruguay.

Urureltern ['u:ru:rɛltərn], *pl.* ancestors.

Urvater ['u:rfa:tər], *m.* (—s, *pl.* ⁻) forefather.

Urvolk ['u:rfɔlk], *n.* (—(e)s, *pl.* ⁻er) primitive people, aborigines.

Urwald ['u:rvalt], *m.* (—(e)s, *pl.* ⁻er) primæval forest, virgin forest.

Urwelt ['u:rvɛlt], *f.* (—, *no pl.*) primæval world.

Urzeit ['u:rtsaɪt], *f.* (—, *pl.* —en) prehistoric times.

V

V [fau], *n.* (—s, *pl.* —s) the letter V.

Vagabund [vaga'bunt], *m.* (—en, *pl.* —en) vagabond, tramp; (*Am.*) hobo.

vag ['va:k], *adj.* vague.

Vakuumbremse ['va:kuumbrɛmzə], *f.* (—, *pl.* —n) air-brake, vacuum-brake.

Vase ['va:zə], *f.* (—, *pl.* —n) vase.

Vater ['fa:tər], *m.* (—s, *pl.* ⁻) father.

Vaterland ['fa:tərlant], *n.* (—(e)s, *pl.* ⁻er) mother-country, native country; —*sliebe*, patriotism.

vaterländisch ['fa:tərlɛndɪʃ], *adj.* patriotic.

vaterlandslos ['fa:tərlantslo:s], *adj.* having no mother country; unpatriotic.

väterlich ['fɛ:tərlɪç], *adj.* fatherly, paternal. — *adv.* like a father.

vaterlos ['fa:tərlo:s], *adj.* fatherless.

Vatermord ['fa:tərmɔrt], *m.* (—(e)s, *pl.* —e) parricide; patricide.

Vatermörder ['fa:tərmœrdər], *m.* (—s, *pl.* —) parricide; (*fig.*) high *or* stand-up collar.

Vaterschaft ['fa:tərʃaft], *f.* (—, *no pl.*) paternity.

Vatersname ['fa:tərsna:mə], *m.* (—ns, *pl.* —n) surname, family name.

Vaterstadt ['fa:tərʃtat], *f.* (—, *pl.* ⁻e) native town.

Vaterstelle ['fa:tərʃtɛlə], *f.* (—, *pl.* —n) — *vertreten*, act as a father, be a father (to).

Vaterunser [fa:tər'unzər], *n.* (—s, *pl.* —) Lord's Prayer.

Vatikan [vati'ka:n], *m.* (—s, *no pl.*) Vatican.

vegetieren [vege'ti:rən], *v.n.* vegetate.

Veilchen ['faɪlçən], *n.* (—s, *pl.* — (*Bot.*) violet.

Vene ['ve:nə], *f.* (—, *pl.* —n) vein.

Venezuela [vɛnɛtsu'e:la], *n.* Venezuela.

Ventil [vɛn'ti:l], *n.* (—s, *pl.* —e) valve.

ventilieren [vɛnti'li:rən], *v.a.* ventilate, air; (*fig.*) discuss, ventilate.

verabfolgen [fɛr'apfɔlgən], *v.a.* deliver, hand over, remit; serve.

Verabfolgung [fɛr'apfɔlguŋ], *f.* (—, *no pl.*) delivery.

verabreden [fɛr'apre:dən], *v.a.* agree (upon); stipulate; *etwas mit einem* —, agree on s.th. with s.o. — *v.r. sich mit einem* —, make an appointment with s.o.; (*coll.*) have a date.

Verabredung [fɛr'apre:duŋ], *f.* (—, *pl.* —en) agreement, arrangement, appointment; (*coll.*) date.

verabreichen [fɛr'apraɪçən], *v.a.* deliver, dispense.

verabsäumen [fɛr'apzɔymən], *v.a.* neglect, omit.

verabscheuen [fɛr'apʃɔyən], *v.a.* detest, loathe, abhor.

Verabscheuung [fɛr'apʃɔyuŋ], *f.* (—, *no pl.*) abhorrence, detestation, loathing.

verabscheuungswürdig [fɛr'apʃɔyuŋs-vyrdɪç], *adj.* abominable, detestable.

verabschieden [fɛr'apʃi:dən], *v.a.* dismiss, discharge. — *v.r. sich* —, take leave, say good-bye; (*Pol.*) pass (of an Act).

Verabschiedung [fɛr'apʃi:duŋ], *f.* (—, *no pl.*) dismissal; discharge; (*Pol.*) passing (of an Act).

verachten [fɛr'axtən], *v.a.* despise, scorn.

verächtlich [fɛr'ɛçtlɪç], *adj.* despicable, contemptible; contemptuous, scornful.

Verachtung [fɛr'axtuŋ], *f.* (—, *no pl.*) contempt, disdain, scorn.

verallgemeinern [fɛralgə'maɪnərn], *v.a., v.n.* generalise.

veralten [fɛr'altən], *v.n.* (*aux.* sein) become obsolete, date.

veraltet [fɛr'altat], *adj.* obsolete.

Veranda [ve'randa], *f.* (—, *pl.* —den) verandah, porch.

veränderlich [fɛr'ɛndərlɪç], *adj.* changeable, variable; (*fig.*) inconstant, fickle.

verändern [fɛr'ɛndərn], *v.a.* change, alter. — *v.r. sich* —, change, vary; change o.'s job.

verankern [fɛr'aŋkərn], *v.a.* anchor.

veranlagt [fɛr'anla:kt], *adj.* inclined; gifted; having a propensity (to); *gut* —, talented; (*tax*) assessed.

Veranlagung [fɛr'anla:guŋ], *f.* (—, *pl.* —en) bent; talent · predisposition; (*tax*) assessment.

veranlassen [fɛr'anlasən], *v.a.* bring about, cause, motivate; *einen* —, induce s.o., cause s.o.; *etwas* —, bring s.th. about, cause s.th.

Veranlassung [fɛrˈanlasuŋ], f. (—, no pl.) cause, motive; occasion; inducement; auf seine —, at his suggestion; ohne irgend eine —, without the slightest provocation.

veranschaulichen [fɛrˈanʃaulɪçən], v.a. illustrate, make clear.

veranschlagen [fɛrˈanʃlaːgən], v.a. estimate, assess.

Veranschlagung [fɛrˈanʃlaːguŋ], f. (—, pl. —en) estimate.

veranstalten [fɛrˈanʃtaltən], v.a. organise, arrange.

Veranstalter [fɛrˈanʃtaltər], m. (—s, pl. —) organiser.

Veranstaltung [fɛrˈanʃtaltuŋ], f. (—, pl. —en) arrangement; entertainment; show; event; (sporting) fixture.

verantworten [fɛrˈantvɔrtən], v.a. account for. — v.r. sich —, answer (for), justify o.s.

verantwortlich [fɛrˈantvɔrtlɪç], adj. responsible, answerable, accountable.

Verantwortlichkeit [fɛrˈantvɔrtlɪç-kaɪt], f. (—, no pl.) responsibility.

Verantwortung [fɛrˈantvɔrtuŋ], f. (—, no pl.) responsibility, justification, excuse; defence; auf deine —, at your own risk; einen zur — ziehen, call s.o. to account.

verantwortungsvoll [fɛrˈantvɔrtuŋs-fɔl], adj. responsible.

verarbeiten [fɛrˈarbaItən], v.a. manufacture, process; (fig.) digest.

Verarbeitung [fɛrˈarbaItuŋ], f. (—, no pl.) manufacture; process; finish; (fig.) digestion.

verargen [fɛrˈargən], v.a. einem etwas —, blame or reproach s.o. for s.th.

verärgern [fɛrˈɛrgərn], v.a. annoy, make angry.

Verarmung [fɛrˈarmuŋ], f. (—, no pl.) impoverishment.

verausgaben [fɛrˈausgaːbən], v.r. sich —, overspend, run short of money; spend o.s., wear o.s. out.

veräußern [fɛrˈɔysərn], v.a. dispose of, sell.

Veräußerung [fɛrˈɔysəruŋ], f. (—, no pl.) sale; alienation.

Verband [fɛrˈbant], m. (—s, pl. ⁻e) bandage, dressing; association, union; unit.

verbannen [fɛrˈbanən], v.a. banish, exile, outlaw.

Verbannte [fɛrˈbantə], m. (—n, pl. —n) exile, outlaw.

Verbannung [fɛrˈbanuŋ], f. (—, pl. —en) banishment, exile.

verbauen [fɛrˈbauən], v.n. obstruct; build up; use up or spend in building.

verbeißen [fɛrˈbaIsən], v.a. irr. sich etwas —, suppress s.th.; sich das Lachen —, stifle a laugh. — v.r. sich in etwas —, stick doggedly to s.th.

verbergen [fɛrˈbɛrgən], v.a. irr. conceal, hide.

verbessern [fɛrˈbɛsərn], v.a. improve, correct, mend.

Verbesserung [fɛrˈbɛsəruŋ], f. (—, pl. —en) improvement; correction.

verbeugen [fɛrˈbɔygən], v.r. sich —, bow.

Verbeugung [fɛrˈbɔyguŋ], f. (—, pl. —en) bow, obeisance.

verbiegen [fɛrˈbiːgən], v.a. irr. twist, distort, bend the wrong way.

verbieten [fɛrˈbiːtən], v.a. irr. forbid, prohibit.

verbilligen [fɛrˈbɪlɪgən], v.a. cheapen, reduce the price of.

verbinden [fɛrˈbɪndən], v.a. irr. tie up, bind up, connect; (Med.) dress, bandage; unite, join; die Augen —, blindfold. — v.r. sich —, unite, join; (Chem.) combine.

verbindlich [fɛrˈbɪntlɪç], adj. binding; obligatory; obliging; —en Dank, my best thanks.

Verbindlichkeit [fɛrˈbɪntlɪçkaIt], f. (—, pl. —en) liability, obligation; compliment.

Verbindung [fɛrˈbɪnduŋ], f. (—, pl. —en) connexion, connection, junction; association; alliance; (Railw.) connection; (Chem.) compound.

Verbindungsglied [fɛrˈbɪnduŋsgliːt], n. (—(e)s, pl. —er) connecting link.

Verbindungslinie [fɛrˈbɪnduŋsliːnjə], f. (—, pl. —n) line of communication.

verbissen [fɛrˈbɪsən], adj. obstinate, grim; soured. — adv. doggedly.

verbitten [fɛrˈbɪtən], v.a. irr. sich etwas —, forbid s.th. determinedly; insist on s.th. not being done, object to.

verbittern [fɛrˈbɪtərn], v.a. embitter.

Verbitterung [fɛrˈbɪtəruŋ], f. (—, no pl.) exasperation.

verblassen [fɛrˈblasən], v.n. (aux. sein) turn pale.

Verbleib [fɛrˈblaIp], m. (—(e)s, no pl.) whereabouts.

verbleiben [fɛrˈblaIbən], v.n. irr. (aux. sein) remain.

verblenden [fɛrˈblɛndən], v.a. dazzle, delude, blind.

Verblendung [fɛrˈblɛnduŋ], f. (—, no pl.) infatuation; delusion.

verblüffen [fɛrˈblyfən], v.n. amaze, stagger, dumbfound.

Verblüffung [fɛrˈblyfuŋ], f. (—, no pl.) bewilderment.

verblühen [fɛrˈblyːən], v.n. (aux. sein) wither, fade.

verblümt [fɛrˈblyːmt], adj. veiled.

verbluten [fɛrˈbluːtən], v.n. (aux. sein) bleed to death.

verborgen (1) [fɛrˈbɔrgən], v.a. lend out.

verborgen (2) [fɛrˈbɔrgən], adj. concealed, hidden; im —en, secretly.

Verborgenheit [fɛrˈbɔrgənhaIt], f. (—, no pl.) concealment, seclusion.

Verbot [fɛrˈboːt], n. (—(e)s, pl. —e) prohibition.

verboten [fɛrˈboːtən], adj. forbidden, prohibited.

verbrämen [fɛrˈbrɛːmən], v.a. (garment) edge, border.

verbrauchen

verbrauchen [fɛr'brauxən], *v.a.* consume, use up; spend.
Verbraucher [fɛr'brauxər], *m.* (—s, *pl.* —) consumer.
Verbrechen [fɛr'brɛçən], *n.* (—s, *pl.* —) crime.
verbrechen [fɛr'brɛçən], *v.a. irr.* commit, perpetrate.
Verbrecher [fɛr'brɛçər], *m.* (—s, *pl.* —) criminal.
Verbrecheralbum [fɛr'brɛçəralbum], *n.* (—s, *no pl.*) rogues' gallery.
verbreiten [fɛr'braitən], *v.a.* spread, diffuse.
verbreitern [fɛr'braitərn], *v.a.* widen.
Verbreitung [fɛr'braituŋ], *f.* (—, *no pl.*) spread(ing), propaganda, extension.
verbrennbar [fɛr'brɛnbaːr], *adj.* combustible.
verbrennen [fɛr'brɛnən], *v.a. irr.* burn; cremate; *von der Sonne verbrannt,* sunburnt. — *v.n. (aux.* sein) get burnt. — *v.r. sich* —, scald o.s., burn o.s.
Verbrennung [fɛr'brɛnuŋ], *f.* (—, *pl.* —en) burning, combustion; cremation.
verbrieft [fɛr'briːft], *adj.* vested; documented.
verbringen [fɛr'briŋən], *v.a. irr.* (*time*) spend, pass.
verbrüdern [fɛr'bryːdərn], *v.r. sich* —, fraternise.
verbrühen [fɛr'bryːən], *v.a.* scald.
verbummeln [fɛr'buməln], *v.a. die Zeit* —, fritter the time away.
verbunden [fɛr'bundən], *adj. einem* — *sein,* be obliged to s.o.
verbünden [fɛr'byndən], *v.r. sich* — *mit,* ally o.s. with.
Verbündete [fɛr'byndətə], *m.* (—n, *pl.* —n) ally, confederate.
verbürgen [fɛr'byrgən], *v.a.* warrant, guarantee. — *v.r. sich für etwas* —, vouch for s.th.; guarantee s.th.
Verdacht [fɛr'daxt], *m.* (—(e)s, *no pl.*) suspicion.
verdächtig [fɛr'dɛçtiç], *adj.* suspicious, doubtful, questionable.
verdächtigen [fɛr'dɛçtigən], *v.a.* throw suspicion on, suspect.
verdammen [fɛr'damən], *v.a.* condemn, damn.
verdammenswert [fɛr'damənsveːrt], *adj.* damnable.
Verdammung [fɛr'damuŋ], *f.* (—, *no pl.*) condemnation.
verdampfen [fɛr'dampfən], *v.n. (aux.* sein) evaporate.
verdanken [fɛr'daŋkən], *v.a. einem etwas* —, be indebted to s.o. for s.th.; owe s.th. to s.o.
verdauen [fɛr'dauən], *v.a.* digest.
verdaulich [fɛr'dauliç], *adj.* digestible.
Verdauung [fɛr'dauuŋ], *f.* (—, *no pl.*) digestion.
Verdauungsstörung [fɛr'dauuŋsʃtøː-ruŋ], *f.* (—, *pl.* —en) indigestion.
Verdeck [fɛr'dɛk], *n.* (—s, *pl.* —e) awning; (*Naut.*) deck.

verdecken [fɛr'dɛkən], *v.a.* cover, hide.
verdenken [fɛr'dɛŋkən], *v.a. irr. einem etwas* —, blame s.o. for s.th.
Verderb [fɛr'dɛrp], *m.* (—s, *no pl.*) ruin, decay.
verderben [fɛr'dɛrbən], *v.a. irr.* spoil, corrupt, pervert. — *v.n. (aux.* sein) decay, go bad.
Verderben [fɛr'dɛrbən], *n.* (—s, *no pl.*) corruption, ruin.
Verderber [fɛr'dɛrbər], *m.* (—s, *pl.—*) corrupter, perverter.
verderblich [fɛr'dɛrpliç], *adj.* ruinous, pernicious, destructive; (*goods*) perishable.
Verderbnis [fɛr'dɛrpnis], *f.* (—, *no pl.*) corruption, depravity; perversion; perdition.
Verderbtheit [fɛr'dɛrpthait], *f.* (—, *no pl.*) corruption, perversion, depravity.
verdeutlichen [fɛr'dɔytliçən], *v.a.* illustrate, clarify.
verdichten [fɛr'diçtən], *v.a., v.r.* thicken, condense, liquefy.
Verdichtung [fɛr'diçtuŋ], *f.* (—, *no pl.*) condensation; solidification.
verdicken [fɛr'dikən], *v.a.* thicken; solidify.
verdienen [fɛr'diːnən], *v.a.* earn; deserve.
Verdienst (1) [fɛr'diːnst], *m.* (—es, *pl.* —e) profit, gain, earnings.
Verdienst (2) [fɛr'diːnst], *n.* (—es, *pl.* —e) merit, deserts.
verdienstvoll [fɛr'diːnstfɔl], *adj.* meritorious, deserving; distinguished.
verdient [fɛr'diːnt], *adj. sich* — *machen um,* deserve well of, serve well (a cause etc.).
verdientermaßen [fɛr'diːntərmaːsən], *adv.* deservedly.
verdingen [fɛr'diŋən], *v.r. sich* —, enter service (with), take a situation (with).
verdolmetschen [fɛr'dɔlmɛtʃən], *v.a.* interpret, translate.
verdoppeln [fɛr'dɔpəln], *v.a.* double.
verdorben [fɛr'dɔrbən], *adj.* spoilt; corrupted, depraved, debauched.
verdrängen [fɛr'drɛŋən], *v.a.* crowd out; (*Phys.*) displace; (*fig.*) supplant, supersede; (*Psych.*) inhibit, repress.
Verdrängung [fɛr'drɛŋuŋ], *f.* (—, *no pl.*) supplanting; (*Phys.*) displacement; (*Psych.*) inhibition, repression.
verdrehen [fɛr'dreːən], *v.a.* twist (the wrong way); (*fig.*) misrepresent, distort.
verdreht [fɛr'dreːt], *adj.* cracked, cranky, crazy, queer.
Verdrehtheit [fɛr'dreːthait], *f.* (—, *no pl.*) crankiness.
Verdrehung [fɛr'dreːuŋ], *f.* (—, *pl.* —en) distortion; (*fig.*) misrepresentation.
verdrießen [fɛr'driːsən], *v.a. irr.* vex, annoy.
verdrießlich [fɛr'driːsliç], *adj.* (*thing*) vexatious, tiresome; (*person*) morose, peevish.

verdrossen [fɛr'drɔsən], *adj.* annoyed; fretful, sulky.

Verdrossenheit [fɛr'drɔsənhaɪt], *f.* (—, *no pl.*) annoyance ;fretfulness,sulkiness.

verdrücken [fɛr'drykən], *v.a.* (*sl.*) eat o.'s fill of. — *v.r.* (*coll.*) sich —, slink away ; sneak away.

Verdruß [fɛr'drus], *m.* (**—sses**, *no pl.*) vexation, annoyance; — *bereiten,* give trouble, cause annoyance.

verduften [fɛr'duftən], *v.n.* (*aux.* sein) evaporate. — (*fig.*) (*coll.*) take French leave, clear out.

verdummen [fɛr'dumən], *v.n.* (*aux.* sein) become stupid.

verdunkeln [fɛr'duŋkəln], *v.a.* black-out, obscure; (*fig.*) eclipse.

Verdunk(e)lung [fɛr'duŋk(ə)luŋ], *f.* (—, *no pl.*) darkening, eclipse; black-out.

Verdunk(e)lungsgefahr [vɛr'duŋk(ə)-luŋsɡəfaːr], *f.* (—, *no pl.*) (*Law*) danger of prejudicing the course *or* administration of justice.

verdünnen [fɛr'dynən], *v.a.* thin out, dilute.

Verdünnung [fɛr'dynuŋ], *f.* (—, *no pl.*) attenuation; dilution.

verdunsten [fɛr'dunstən], *v.n.* (*aux.* sein) evaporate.

verdursten [fɛr'durstən], *v.n.* (*aux.* sein) die of thirst, perish with thirst.

verdüstern [fɛr'dyːstərn], *v.a.* darken, make gloomy.

verdutzen [fɛr'dutsən], *v.a.* disconcert, bewilder, nonplus.

Veredlung [fɛr'eːdluŋ], *f.* (—, *no pl.*) improvement, refinement.

verehelichen [fɛr'eːəlɪçən], *v.r.* (*obs.*) sich —, get married.

verehren [fɛr'eːrən], *v.a.* respect, revere, esteem; worship, adore.

Verehrer [fɛr'eːrər], *m.* (**—s,** *pl.* **—**) admirer; lover.

verehrlich [fɛr'eːrlɪç], *adj.* venerable.

verehrt [fɛr'eːrt], *adj.* honoured; *sehr —er Herr,* dear Sir.

Verehrung [fɛr'eːruŋ], *f.* (—, *no pl.*) reverence, veneration; worship, adoration.

verehrungswürdig [fɛr'eːruŋsvyrdɪç], *adj.* venerable.

vereidigt [fɛr'aɪdɪçt], *adj.* sworn in, bound by oath, under oath; *—er Bücherrevisor,* chartered accountant.

Vereidigung [fɛr'aɪdɪɡuŋ], *f.* (—, *no pl.*) swearing in; oathtaking.

Verein [fɛr'aɪn], *m.* (**—s,** *pl.* **—e**) union, association, society; club.

vereinbar [fɛr'aɪnbaːr], *adj.* compatible.

vereinbaren [fɛr'aɪnbaːrən], *v.a.* agree upon, arrange.

Vereinbarung [fɛr'aɪnbaːruŋ], *f.* (—, *pl.* **—en**) arrangement, agreement.

vereinen [fɛr'aɪnən], *v.a.* unite.

vereinfachen [fɛr'aɪnfaxən], *v.a.* simplify.

vereinigen [fɛr'aɪnɪɡən], *v.a.* unite. — *v.r. sich — mit,* associate o.s. with, join with.

Vereinigung [fɛr'aɪnɪɡuŋ], *f.* (—, *pl.* **—en**) union; association.

vereinnahmen [fɛr'aɪnnaːmən], *v.a.* receive, take (*money*).

vereinsamen [fɛr'aɪnzaːmən], *v.n.* (*aux.* sein) become isolated, become lonely.

vereint [fɛr'aɪnt], *adj.* united, joined. — *adv.* in concert, (all) together.

vereinzelt [fɛr'aɪntsəlt], *adj.* sporadic, isolated. — *adv.* here and there, now and then.

Vereinzelung [fɛr'aɪntsəluŋ], *f.* (—, *pl.* **—en**) isolation; individualization.

vereisen [fɛr'aɪzən], *v.n.* become frozen, freeze; congeal.

Vereisung [fɛr'aɪzuŋ], *f.* (—, *pl.* **—en**) freezing, icing (up).

vereiteln [fɛr'aɪtəln], *v.a.* frustrate, thwart.

Vereitelung [fɛr'aɪtəluŋ], *f.* (—, *pl.* **—en**) frustration, thwarting.

vereitern [fɛr'aɪtərn], *v.n.* suppurate.

Vereiterung [fɛr'aɪtəruŋ], *f.* (—, *pl.* **—en**) suppuration.

verenden [fɛr'ɛndən], *v.n.* (*aux.* sein) (*animal*) die.

verengen [fɛr'ɛŋən], *v.a.* narrow, straighten, constrict.

Verengung [fɛr'ɛŋuŋ], *f.* (—, *pl.* **—en**) narrowing, straightening, contrac-tion.

vererben [fɛr'ɛrbən], *v.a.* leave (by will), bequeath. — *v.r. sich — auf,* devolve upon, be hereditary.

vererblich [fɛr'ɛrplɪç],*adj.*(in)heritable, hereditary.

Vererbung [fɛr'ɛrbuŋ], *f.* (—, *no pl.*) heredity.

verewigen [fɛr'eːvɪɡən], *v.a.* immor-talise.

Verewigte [fɛr'eːvɪçtə], *m.* (**—n,** *pl.* **—n**) (*Poet.*) deceased.

Verfahren [fɛr'faːrən], *n.* (**—s,** *pl.* **—**) process; (*Law*) procedure; proceed-ings; *das — einstellen,* quash proceed-ings.

verfahren [fɛr'faːrən], *v.n. irr.* (*aux.* sein) proceed, act, operate. — *v.a.* spend (*money etc.*) on travelling. — *v.r. sich —,* (*Motor.*) lose o.'s way.

Verfall [fɛr'fal], *m.* (**—s,** *no pl.*) decay, decline; downfall, ruin; (*Comm.*) expiration, maturity; *in — geraten,* fall into ruin, decay.

verfallen [fɛr'falən], *v.n. irr.* (*aux.* sein) decay; go to ruin; lapse; (*Comm.*) fall due, expire; (*pledge*) be-come forfeit; *einem —,* become the property of, accrue to, devolve upon s.o.; (*fig.*) become the slave of s.o.; (*health*) decline, fail; *auf etwas —,* hit upon an idea. — *adj.* decayed, ruined.

Verfalltag [fɛr'faltaːk], *m.* (**—s,** *pl.* **—e**) day of payment; maturity.

verfälschen [fɛr'fɛlʃən], *v.a.* falsify; adulterate.

Verfälschung [fɛr'fɛlʃuŋ], *f.* (—, *pl.* **—en**) falsification; adulteration.

verfangen [fɛrˈfaŋən], *v.r. irr.* sich —, get entangled; *sich in ein Lügennetz* —, entangle o.s. in a tissue of lies.

verfänglich [fɛrˈfɛŋlɪç], *adj.* risky; insidious.

verfärben [fɛrˈfɛrbən], *v.r.* sich —, change colour.

verfassen [fɛrˈfasən], *v.a.* compose, write, be the author of.

Verfasser [fɛrˈfasər], *m.* (—s, *pl.* —) author, writer.

Verfassung [fɛrˈfasuŋ], *f.* (—, *pl.* —en) composition; (*state*) constitution; state, condition, disposition.

verfassungsgemäß [fɛrˈfasuŋsɡəmɛːs], *adj.* constitutional.

verfassungswidrig [fɛrˈfasuŋsviːdrɪç], *adj.* unconstitutional.

verfaulen [fɛrˈfaulən], *v.n.* (*aux.* sein) rot, putrefy.

verfechten [fɛrˈfɛçtən], *v.a. irr.* defend, advocate; maintain.

verfehlen [fɛrˈfeːlən], *v.a.* fail, miss; fail to meet; fail to do; *den Weg* —, lose o.'s way.

verfehlt [fɛrˈfeːlt], *adj.* unsuccessful, false, abortive; *eine* —*e Sache*, a failure.

Verfehlung [fɛrˈfeːluŋ], *f.* (—, *pl.* —en) lapse.

verfeinern [fɛrˈfainərn], *v.a.* refine, improve.

Verfeinerung [fɛrˈfainəruŋ], *f.* (—, *pl.* —en) refinement, polish.

verfertigen [fɛrˈfɛrtɪɡən], *v.a.* make, manufacture.

verfilmen [fɛrˈfɪlmən], *v.a.* make a film of, film.

verfinstern [fɛrˈfɪnstərn], *v.r.* sich —, get dark; be eclipsed.

verflechten [fɛrˈflɛçtən], *v.a. irr.* interweave, interlace; — *v.r.* sich —, (*fig.*) become entangled, become involved.

verfließen [fɛrˈfliːsən], *v.n. irr.* (*aux.* sein) flow away; (*time*) elapse, pass.

verflossen [fɛrˈflɔsən], *adj.* past, bygone.

verfluchen [fɛrˈfluːxən], *v.a.* curse, execrate.

verflucht [fɛrˈfluːxt], *excl.* damn!

verflüchtigen [fɛrˈflyçtɪɡən], *v.r.* sich —, become volatile; evaporate; (*coll.*) make off, make o.s. scarce.

Verfluchung [fɛrˈfluːxuŋ], *f.* (—, *pl.* —en) malediction, curse.

Verfolg [fɛrˈfɔlk], *m.* (—(e)s, *no pl.*) progress, course.

verfolgen [fɛrˈfɔlɡən], *v.a.* pursue; persecute; prosecute.

Verfolger [fɛrˈfɔlɡər], *m.* (—s, *pl.* —) pursuer; persecutor.

Verfolgung [fɛrˈfɔlɡuŋ], *f.* (—, *pl.* —en) pursuit; persecution; prosecution.

Verfolgungswahn [fɛrˈfɔlɡuŋsvaːn], *m.* (—s, *no pl.*) persecution mania.

verfrüht [fɛrˈfryːt], *adj.* premature.

verfügbar [fɛrˈfyːkbaːr], *adj.* available.

verfügen [fɛrˈfyːɡən], *v.a.* decree, order. — *v.n.* — *über etwas*, have

control of s.th, have s.th. at o.'s disposal.

Verfügung [fɛrˈfyːɡuŋ], *f.* (—, *pl.* —en) decree, ordinance; disposition, disposal; *einem zur* — *stehen*, be at s.o.'s service or disposal.

verführen [fɛrˈfyːrən], *v.a.* seduce.

verführerisch [fɛrˈfyːrɪʃ], *adj.* seductive, alluring; (*coll.*) fetching.

Verführung [fɛrˈfyːruŋ], *f.* (—, *no pl.*) seduction.

vergällen [fɛrˈɡɛlən], *v.a.* spoil, mar.

vergallopieren [fɛrɡaloˈpiːrən], *v.r.* (*coll.*) sich —, blunder, overshoot the mark.

vergangen [fɛrˈɡaŋən], *adj.* past, gone, last.

Vergangenheit [fɛrˈɡaŋənhait], *f.* (—, *no pl.*) past, time past; (*Gram.*) past tense.

vergänglich [fɛrˈɡɛŋlɪç], *adj.* transient, transitory.

Vergaser [fɛrˈɡaːzər], *m.* (—s, *pl.* —) (*Motor.*) carburettor.

vergeben [fɛrˈɡeːbən], *v.a. irr.* give away; forgive, pardon; confer, bestow.

vergebens [fɛrˈɡeːbəns], *adv.* in vain, vainly.

vergeblich [fɛrˈɡeːplɪç], *adj.* vain, futile, fruitless. — *adv.* in vain.

Vergebung [fɛrˈɡeːbuŋ], *f.* (—, *no pl.*) forgiveness, pardon; (*office*) bestowal.

vergegenwärtigen [fɛrɡeːɡənˈvɛrtɪɡən], *v.a.* bring to mind, imagine.

Vergehen [fɛrˈɡeːən], *n.* (—s, *pl.* —) offence lapse.

vergehen [fɛrˈɡeːən], *v.n. irr.* (*aux.* sein) go away, pass (away); elapse; perish; (*time*) pass. — *v.r.* sich —, go wrong; offend; violate (*Law*, person).

vergelten [fɛrˈɡɛltən], *v.a. irr.* repay, reward, recompense.

Vergeltung [fɛrˈɡɛltuŋ], *f.* (—, *no pl.*) requital, retribution; reward, recompense.

vergessen [fɛrˈɡɛsən], *v.a. irr.* forget; *bei einem* —, leave behind.

Vergessenheit [fɛrˈɡɛsənhait], *f.* (—, *no pl.*) oblivion.

vergeßlich [fɛrˈɡɛslɪç], *adj.* forgetful.

vergeuden [fɛrˈɡɔydən], *v.a.* waste, squander.

vergewaltigen [fɛrɡəˈvaltɪɡən], *v.a.* assault criminally, rape, violate; (*fig.*) coerce, force.

Vergewaltigung [fɛrɡəˈvaltɪɡuŋ], *f.* (—, *no pl.*) criminal assault, rape; (*fig.*) coercion.

vergewissern [fɛrɡəˈvɪsərn], *v.r.* sich —, ascertain, make sure.

vergießen [fɛrˈɡiːsən], *v.a. irr.* spill; shed.

vergiften [fɛrˈɡɪftən], *v.a.* poison.

Vergiftung [fɛrˈɡɪftuŋ], *f.* (—, *pl.* —en) poisoning.

vergilbt [fɛrˈɡɪlpt], *adj.* yellow with age.

Vergißmeinnicht [fɛrˈɡɪsmainnɪçt], *n.* (—s, *pl.* —e) (*Bot.*) forget-me-not.

Vergleich [fɛr'glaɪç], *m.* (—(e)s, *pl.* —e) comparison; agreement; (*Law*) compromise.

vergleichbar [fɛr'glaɪçbaːr], *adj.* comparable.

vergleichen [fɛr'glaɪçən], *v.a. irr.* compare.

vergleichsweise [fɛr'glaɪçsvaɪzə], *adv.* by way of comparison; comparatively; (*Law*) by way of agreement.

Vergnügen [fɛr'gnyːgən], *n.* (—s, *no pl.*) pleasure, enjoyment, fun.

vergnügen [fɛr'gnyːgən], *v.a.* amuse, delight.

Vergnügung [fɛr'gnyːgʊŋ], *f.* (—, *pl.* —en) entertainment, amusement.

vergönnen [fɛr'gœnən], *v.a.* grant, allow; not (be)grudge.

vergöttern [fɛr'gœtərn], *v.a.* idolise, worship.

vergraben [fɛr'graːbən], *v.a. irr.* hide in the ground, bury.

vergrämt [fɛr'grɛːmt], *adj.* careworn.

vergreifen [fɛr'graɪfən], *v.r. irr. sich — an*, lay violent hands on, violate.

vergriffen [fɛr'grɪfən], *adj.* out of stock, out of print.

vergrößern [fɛr'grøːsərn], *v.a.* enlarge, expand; increase; magnify; (*fig.*) exaggerate.

Vergrößerung [fɛr'grøːsərʊŋ], *f.* (—, *pl.* —en) magnification, enlargement, increase.

Vergrößerungsglas [fɛr'grøːsərʊŋsglaːs], *n.* (—es, *pl.* ˙er) magnifying glass.

Vergünstigung [fɛr'gynstɪgʊŋ], *f.* (—, *pl.* —en) privilege, favour, special facility, concession.

vergüten [fɛr'gyːtən], *v.a. einem etwas —*, compensate s.o. for s.th.; reimburse s.o. for s.th.

Vergütung [fɛr'gyːtʊŋ], *f.* (—, *pl.* —en) indemnification, compensation, reimbursement.

verhaften [fɛr'haftən], *v.a.* arrest.

Verhaftung [fɛr'haftʊŋ], *f.* (—, *pl.* —en) arrest.

verhallen [fɛr'halən], *v.n.* (*aux.* sein) (*sound*) fade, die away.

verhalten [fɛr'haltən], *v.r. irr. sich —*, act, behave.

Verhalten [fɛr'haltən], *n.* (—s, *no pl.*) behaviour, conduct, demeanour.

Verhältnis [fɛr'hɛltnɪs], *n.* (—ses, *pl.* —se) (*Maths.*) proportion, ratio; relation; footing; love-affair, liaison; (*coll.*) mistress.

verhältnismäßig [fɛr'hɛltnɪsmɛsɪç], *adj.* proportionate, comparative.

Verhältniswort [fɛr'hɛltnɪsvɔrt], *n.* (—es, *pl.* ˙er) preposition.

Verhältniszahl [fɛr'hɛltnɪstsaːl], *f.* (—, *pl.* —en) proportional number.

Verhaltungsmaßregel [fɛr'haltʊŋsmaːsreːgəl], *f.* (—, *pl.* —n) rule of conduct; instruction.

verhandeln [fɛr'handəln], *v.a.* discuss, transact. — *v.n.* negotiate.

Verhandlung [fɛr'handlʊŋ], *f.* (—, *pl.* —en) discussion, negotiation, transaction; (*Law*) proceedings.

verhängen [fɛr'hɛŋən], *v.a.* cover with; decree; inflict (a penalty) on s.o.

Verhängnis [fɛr'hɛŋnɪs], *n.* (—ses, *pl.* —se) fate, destiny; misfortune.

Verhängnisglaube [fɛr'hɛŋnɪsglaʊbə], *m.* (—ns, *no pl.*) fatalism.

verhängnisvoll [fɛr'hɛŋnɪsfɔl], *adj.* fateful, portentous; fatal.

verhärmt [fɛr'hɛrmt], *adj.* careworn.

verharren [fɛr'harən], *v.n.* remain; persist.

Verhärtung [fɛr'hɛrtʊŋ], *f.* (—, *pl.* —en) hardening, hardened state; (*skin*) callosity; (*fig.*) obduracy.

verhaßt [fɛr'hast], *adj.* hated, odious.

verhätscheln [fɛr'hɛtʃəln], *v.a.* pamper, coddle.

verhauen [fɛr'hauən], *v.a.* beat, thrash.

Verheerung [fɛr'heːrʊŋ], *f.* (—, *pl.* —en) devastation.

verhehlen [fɛr'heːlən], *v.a.* conceal, hide.

verheilen [fɛr'haɪlən], *v.n.* (*aux.* sein) heal.

verheimlichen [fɛr'haɪmlɪçən], *v.a.* keep secret, hush up.

verheiraten [fɛr'haɪraːtən], *v.a.* give in marriage, marry off. — *v.r. sich —*, marry, get married.

verheißen [fɛr'haɪsən], *v.a. irr.* promise.

Verheißung [fɛr'haɪsʊŋ], *f.* (—, *pl.* —en) promise.

verhelfen [fɛr'hɛlfən], *v.n. irr. einem zu etwas —*, help s.o. to s.th.

Verherrlichung [fɛr'hɛrlɪçʊŋ], *f.* (—, *no pl.*) glorification.

Verhetzung [fɛr'hɛtsʊŋ], *f.* (—, *pl.* —en) incitement, instigation.

verhexen [fɛr'hɛksən], *v.a.* bewitch.

verhindern [fɛr'hɪndərn], *v.a.* hinder, prevent.

Verhinderung [fɛr'hɪndərʊŋ], *f.* (—, *pl.* —en) prevention, obstacle.

verhöhnen [fɛr'høːnən], *v.a.* deride, scoff at, jeer at.

Verhöhnung [fɛr'høːnʊŋ], *f.* (—, *pl.* —en) derision.

Verhör [fɛr'høːr], *n.* (—s, *pl.* —e) hearing; (judicial) examination; *ins — nehmen*, question, interrogate, cross-examine.

verhören [fɛr'høːrən], *v.a.* examine judicially, interrogate. — *v.r. sich —*, misunderstand.

verhüllen [fɛr'hylən], *v.a.* cover, wrap up, veil.

verhungern [fɛr'hʊŋərn], *v.n.* (*aux.* sein) starve.

verhungert [fɛr'hʊŋərt], *adj.* famished.

verhunzen [fɛr'hʊntsən], *v.a.* spoil, bungle.

verhüten [fɛr'hyːtən], *v.a.* prevent, avert.

Verhütung [fɛr'hyːtʊŋ], *f.* (—, *no pl.*) prevention, warding off.

verirren [fɛr'ɪrən], *v.r. sich —*, go astray, lose o.'s way.

verirrt

verirrt [fɛrˈɪrt], *adj.* stray, straying, lost.
verjagen [fɛrˈjaːgən], *v.a.* drive away, chase away.
verjährt [fɛrˈjɛːrt], *adj.* statute-barred; prescriptive; obsolete; old.
verjubeln [fɛrˈjuːbəln], *v.a.* play ducks and drakes with; squander.
verjüngen [fɛrˈjʏŋən], *v.a.* make younger; (*Archit.*) taper. — *v.r. sich* —, grow younger.
Verjüngung [fɛrˈjʏŋuŋ], *f.* (—, *pl.* —en) rejuvenation.
verkannt [fɛrˈkant], *adj.* misunderstood.
verkappt [fɛrˈkapt], *adj.* disguised, secret, in disguise.
Verkauf [fɛrˈkauf], *m.* (—(e)s, *pl.* ⸚e) sale.
verkaufen [fɛrˈkaufən], *v.a.* sell.
Verkäufer [fɛrˈkɔyfər], *m.* (—s, *pl.* —) seller; shop assistant, salesman.
verkäuflich [fɛrˈkɔyflɪç], *adj.* for sale, saleable; mercenary.
Verkaufspreis [fɛrˈkaufsprais], *m.* (—es, *pl.* —e) selling-price.
Verkehr [fɛrˈkeːr], *m.* (—s, *no pl.*) traffic; commerce; intercourse; communication; — *mit*, association with; service (*trains, buses etc.*), transport.
verkehren [fɛrˈkeːrən], *v.a.* turn upside down; transform; pervert. — *v.n.* frequent (a place), visit, associate (with); run, operate.
Verkehrsstraße [fɛrˈkeːrsʃtraːsə], *f.* (—, *pl.* —n) thoroughfare.
Verkehrsstockung [fɛrˈkeːrsʃtɔkuŋ], *f.* (—, *pl.* —en) traffic jam.
verkehrt [fɛrˈkeːrt], *adj.* upside down; (*fig.*) wrong.
Verkehrtheit [fɛrˈkeːrthait], *f.* (—, *pl.* —en) absurdity, piece of folly.
Verkehrung [fɛrˈkeːruŋ], *f.* (—, *pl.* —en) turning; inversion; perversion; misrepresentation; (*Gram.*) inversion.
verkennen [fɛrˈkɛnən], *v.a. irr.* mistake, fail to recognize; misjudge (s.o.'s intentions).
verklagen [fɛrˈklaːgən], *v.a.* sue; accuse.
verklären [fɛrˈklɛːrən], *v.a.* transfigure, illumine.
verklärt [fɛrˈklɛːrt], *adj.* transfigured; radiant.
verkleben [fɛrˈkleːbən], *v.a.* paste over.
verkleiden [fɛrˈklaidən], *v.a., v.r.* disguise (o.s.).
Verkleidung [fɛrˈklaiduŋ], *f.* (— *pl.* —en) disguise.
verkleinern [fɛrˈklainərn], *v.a.* make smaller, diminish, reduce; belittle, disparage.
Verkleinerung [fɛrˈklainəruŋ], *f.* (—, *pl.* —en) diminution, reduction; belittling, detraction.
Verkleinerungswort [fɛrˈklainəruŋsvɔrt], *n.* (—s, *pl.* ⸚er) (*Gram.*) diminutive.
verkneifen [fɛrˈknaifən], *v.r. irr.* (*coll.*) *sich etwas* —, deny o.s. s.th.

verkniffen [fɛrˈknɪfən], *adj.* pinched; shrewd; hard-bitten.
verknöchern [fɛrˈknœçərn], *v.n.* (*aux.* sein) ossify; (*fig.*) become fossilised *or* inflexible.
Verknöcherung [fɛrˈknœçəruŋ], *f.* (—, *pl.* —en) ossification; (*fig.*) fossilisation.
verknüpfen [fɛrˈknʏpfən], *v.a.* tie, connect, link.
verkochen [fɛrˈkɔxən], *v.n.* (*aux.* sein) boil away.
verkommen [fɛrˈkɔmən], *v.n. irr.* (*aux.* sein) go from bad to worse, go to seed, decay, become depraved. — *adj.* demoralised, down and out, depraved.
Verkommenheit [fɛrˈkɔmənhait], *f.* (—, *no pl.*) demoralisation; depravity.
verkörpern [fɛrˈkœrpərn], *v.a.* embody.
verkrachen [fɛrˈkraxən], *v.r. sich* —, quarrel, (*coll.*) have a row.
verkriechen [fɛrˈkriːçən], *v.r. irr. sich* —, creep *or* crawl away; slink away, lie low.
verkümmern [fɛrˈkʏmərn], *v.n.* (*aux.* sein) wear away, waste away; pine away.
verkünden [fɛrˈkʏndən], *v.a.* proclaim, announce, publish, prophesy.
Verkündigung [fɛrˈkʏndiguŋ], *f.* (—, *pl.* —en) announcement, proclamation; prediction.
Verkündung [fɛrˈkʏnduŋ], *f.* (—, *pl.* —en) publication, proclamation.
Verkürzung [fɛrˈkʏrtsuŋ], *f.* (—, *pl.* —en) shortening, curtailment.
verlachen [fɛrˈlaxən], *v.a.* laugh at, deride.
verladen [fɛrˈlaːdən], *v.a. irr.* load, ship, freight.
Verladung [fɛrˈlaːduŋ], *f.* (—, *pl.* —en) loading, shipping.
Verlag [fɛrˈlaːk], *m.* (—(e)s, *pl.* —e) publication; publishing-house, (firm of) publishers.
Verlagsrecht [fɛrˈlaːksrɛçt], *n.* (—s, *pl.* —e) copyright.
Verlangen [fɛrˈlaŋən], *n.* (—s, *no pl.*) demand, request; longing, desire.
verlangen [fɛrˈlaŋən], *v.a.* ask, demand, request.
verlängern [fɛrˈlɛŋərn], *v.a.* lengthen, prolong, extend.
Verlängerung [fɛrˈlɛŋəruŋ], *f.* (—, *pl.* —en) lengthening; (*period*) prolongation, extension.
verlangsamen [fɛrˈlaŋzaːmən], *v.a.* slow down, slacken, decelerate.
Verlaß [fɛrˈlas], *m.* (—sses, *no pl.*) *es ist kein* — *auf dich*, you cannot be relied on.
verlassen [fɛrˈlasən], *v.a. irr.* leave, abandon. — *v.r. sich* — *auf*, rely on, depend upon. — *adj.* forlorn, forsaken, deserted, desolate, lonely.
Verlassenheit [fɛrˈlasənhait], *f.* (—, *no pl.*) desolation, loneliness, solitude.
verläßlich [fɛrˈlɛslɪç], *adj.* reliable, trustworthy.

Verlauf [fɛr'lauf], *m.* (—(e)s, *no pl.*) lapse, expiration; course.

verlaufen [fɛr'laufən], *v.n. irr.* (aux. sein) (*time*) pass; (*period*) expire, elapse; develop(e), turn out. — *v.r. sich* —, lose o.s way; (*colour*) run.

verlauten [fɛr'lautən], *v.n.* transpire.

verleben [fɛr'le:bən], *v.a.* pass, spend.

verlebt [fɛr'le:pt], *adj.* worn out; spent; (*Am.*) played out.

verlegen [fɛr'le:gən], *v.a.* (*domicile*) move, remove; (*things*) mislay; (*books*) publish; obstruct; adjourn; change to another date *or* place. — *v.r. sich auf etwas* —, devote o.s. to s.th. — *adj.* embarrassed, ill at ease.

Verlegenheit [fɛr'le:gənhait], *f.* (—, *pl.* —en) embarrassment, perplexity; predicament, difficulty.

Verleger [fɛr'le:gər], *m.* (—s, *pl.* —) publisher.

verleiden [fɛr'laidən], *v.a. einem etwas* —, spoil s.th. for s.o.

verleihen [fɛr'laiən], *v.a. irr.* lend; (*honour, title*) confer; bestow, award.

Verleiher [fɛr'laiər], *m.* (—s, *pl.* —) lender.

Verleihung [fɛr'laiuŋ], *f.* (—, *pl.* —en) lending, loan; (*medal, prize*) investiture; grant, conferring.

verleiten [fɛr'laitən], *v.a.* mislead, entice, induce; seduce.

Verleitung [fɛr'laituŋ], *f.* (—, *no pl.*) misleading, enticement, inducement; seduction.

verlernen [fɛr'lɛrnən], *v.a.* unlearn; forget.

verlesen [fɛr'le:zən], *v.a. irr.* read aloud, read out, recite. — *v.r. sich* —, misread.

verletzen [fɛr'lɛtsən], *v.a.* injure, hurt, wound, violate.

verletzend [fɛr'lɛtsənt], *adj.* offensive, insulting; cutting.

verletzlich [fɛr'lɛtslɪç], *adj.* vulnerable.

Verletzlichkeit [fɛr'lɛtslɪçkait], *f.* (—, *no pl.*) vulnerability.

Verletzung [fɛr'lɛtsuŋ], *f.* (—, *pl.* —en) hurt, wound; (*Law*) violation.

verleugnen [fɛr'lɔygnən], *v.a.* deny, renounce, disown.

Verleugnung [fɛr'lɔygnuŋ], *f.* (—, *pl.* —en) denial, abnegation.

verleumden [fɛr'lɔymdən], *v.a.* slander, calumniate, traduce.

Verleumdung [fɛr'lɔymduŋ], *f.* (—, *pl.* —en) slander, libel, calumny.

verlieben [fɛr'li:bən], *v.r. sich* — *in*, fall in love with.

Verliebte [fɛr'li:ptə], *m. or f.* (—n, *pl.* —n) person in love, lover.

Verliebtheit [fɛr'li:pthait], *f.* (—, *no pl.*) infatuation; amorousness.

verlieren [fɛr'li:rən], *v.a. irr.* lose.

Verlierer [fɛr'li:rər], *m.* (—s, *pl.* —) loser.

Verlies [fɛr'li:s], *n.* (—(s)es, *pl.* —(s)e) dungeon.

verloben [fɛr'lo:bən], *v.r. sich* — *mit*, become engaged to.

Verlöbnis [fɛr'lø:pnɪs], *n.* (—ses, *pl.* —se) (*rare*) engagement.

Verlobte [fɛr'lo:ptə], *m.* (—n, *pl.* —n) and *f.* (—n, *pl.* —n) fiancé(e), betrothed.

Verlobung [fɛr'lo:buŋ], *f.* (—, *pl.* —en) engagement, betrothal.

verlocken [fɛr'lɔkən], *v.a.* tempt, entice.

verlogen [fɛr'lo:gən], *adj.* lying, mendacious.

Verlogenheit [fɛr'lo:gənhait], *f.* (—, *no pl.*) mendacity.

verlohnen [fɛr'lo:nən], *v. impers.* be worth while.

verlöschen [fɛr'lœʃən], *v.a.* extinguish.

verlosen [fɛr'lo:zən], *v.a.* raffle; draw *or* cast lots for.

Verlosung [fɛr'lo:zuŋ], *f.* (—, *pl.* —en) raffle, lottery.

verlöten [fɛr'lø:tən], *v.a.* solder.

verlottern [fɛr'lɔtərn], *v.n.* (aux. sein) go to the dogs.

Verlust [fɛr'lust], *m.* (—es, *pl.* —e) loss; (*death*) bereavement; (*Mil.*) casualty.

verlustig [fɛr'lustɪç], *adj.* — *gehen*, lose s.th., forfeit s.th.

vermachen [fɛr'maxən], *v.a. einem etwas* —, bequeath s.th. to s.o.

Vermächtnis [fɛr'mɛçtnɪs], *n.* (—ses, *pl.* —sse) will; legacy, bequest; (*fig.*) *heiliges* —, sacred trust.

vermahlen [fɛr'ma:lən], *v.a.* grind (down).

Vermählung [fɛr'mɛ:luŋ], *f.* (—, *pl.* —en) marriage, wedding.

Vermahnung [fɛr'ma:nuŋ], *f.* (—, *pl.* —en) admonition, exhortation.

vermauern [fɛr'mauərn], *v.a.* wall up.

vermehren [fɛr'me:rən], *v.a.* augment, multiply, increase. — *v.r. sich* —, multiply.

Vermehrung [fɛr'me:ruŋ], *f.* (—, *pl.* —en) increase, multiplication.

vermeiden [fɛr'maidən], *v.a. irr.* avoid, shun, shirk.

vermeidlich [fɛr'maitlɪç], *adj.* avoidable.

Vermeidung [fɛr'maiduŋ], *f.* (—, *no pl.*) avoidance.

vermeintlich [fɛr'maintlɪç], *adj.* supposed, alleged, pretended; (*heir*) presumptive.

vermelden [fɛr'mɛldən], *v.a.* announce, notify.

vermengen [fɛr'mɛŋən], *v.a.* mingle, mix.

Vermerk [fɛr'mɛrk], *m.* (—s, *pl.* —e) entry, notice, note.

vermerken [fɛr'mɛrkən], *v.a.* observe, jot down.

vermessen [fɛr'mɛsən], *v.a. irr.* measure; (*land*) survey. — *adj.* bold, daring, audacious; arrogant.

Vermessenheit [fɛr'mɛsənhait], *f.* (—, *no pl.*) boldness, audacity; arrogance.

Vermesser [fɛr'mɛsər], *m.* (—s, *pl.* —) (*land*) surveyor.

Vermessung [fɛr'mɛsuŋ], *f.* (—, *pl.* —en) (*land*) survey; measuring.

vermieten [fɛr'mi:tən], *v.a.* let, lease, hire out.

Vermieter [fɛr'mi:tər], *m.* (—s, *pl.* —) landlord; hirer.

vermindern [fɛr'mɪndərn], *v.a.* diminish, lessen.

Verminderung [fɛr'mɪndəruŋ], *f.* (—, *pl.* —en) diminution, reduction, decrease, lessening.

vermischen [fɛr'mɪʃən], *v.a.* mix, mingle, blend.

vermissen [fɛr'mɪsən], *v.a.* miss; *vermißt sein*, be missing; *vermißt werden*, be missed.

vermitteln [fɛr'mɪtəln], *v.n.* mediate. — *v.a.* adjust; negotiate, secure.

Vermittler [fɛr'mɪtlər], *m.* (—s, *pl.* —) mediator; agent, middleman.

Vermittlung [fɛr'mɪtluŋ], *f.* (—, *pl.* —en) mediation, intervention.

vermöbeln [fɛr'mø:bəln], *v.a.* (*sl.*) *einen —*, thrash s.o.

vermodern [fɛr'mo:dərn], *v.n.* (*aux.* sein) moulder, rot.

vermöge [fɛr'mø:gə], *prep.* (*Genit.*) by virtue of, by dint of, on the strength of.

Vermögen [fɛr'mø:gən], *n.* (—s, *pl.* —) faculty, power; means, assets; fortune, wealth, riches; *er hat —*, he is a man of property; *nach bestem —*, to the best of o.'s ability.

vermögen [fɛr'mø:gən], *v.a. irr.* be able to, have the power to, be capable of.

vermögend [fɛr'mø:gənt], *adj.* wealthy.

Vermögensbestand [fɛr'mø:gənsbəʃtant], *m.* (—s, *pl.* ⸗e) assets.

Vermögenssteuer [fɛr'mø:gənsʃtɔyər], *f.* (—, *pl.* —n) property tax.

vermorscht [fɛr'mɔrʃt], *adj.* mouldering, rotten.

vermuten [fɛr'mu:tən], *v.a.* suppose, conjecture, surmise, presume; guess.

vermutlich [fɛr'mu:tlɪç], *adj.* likely, probable.

Vermutung [fɛr'mu:tuŋ], *f.* (—, *pl.* —en) guess, supposition, conjecture.

vernachlässigen [fɛr'naxlɛsɪgən], *v.a.* neglect.

Vernachlässigung [fɛr'naxlɛsɪguŋ], *f.* (—, *pl.* —en) neglect, negligence.

vernarren [fɛr'narən], *v.r. sich — (in, Acc.*), become infatuated (with).

vernarrt [fɛr'nart], *adj.* madly in love.

vernaschen [fɛr'naʃən], *v.a.* squander (money) on sweets.

vernehmbar [fɛr'ne:mba:r], *adj.* audible; *sich — machen*, make o.s. heard.

Vernehmen [fɛr'ne:mən], *n.* (—s, *no pl.*) *dem — nach*, from what o. hears.

vernehmen [fɛr'ne:mən], *v.a. irr.* hear, learn; (*Law*) examine, interrogate.

vernehmlich [fɛr'ne:mlɪç], *adj.* audible, distinct, clear.

Vernehmlichkeit [fɛr'ne:mlɪçkaɪt], *f.* (—, *no pl.*) audibility.

Vernehmung [fɛr'ne:muŋ], *f.* (—, *pl.* —en) (*Law*) interrogation, examination.

verneigen [fɛr'naɪgən], *v.r. sich —*, curts(e)y, bow.

Verneigung [fɛr'naɪguŋ], *f.* (—, *pl.* —en) curts(e)y, bow.

verneinen [fɛr'naɪnən], *v.a.* deny, answer in the negative.

Verneinung [fɛr'naɪnuŋ], *f.* (—, *pl.* —en) negation, denial; (*Gram.*) negation, negative.

vernichten [fɛr'nɪçtən], *v.a.* annihilate, destroy utterly, exterminate.

Vernichtung [fɛr'nɪçtuŋ], *f.* (—, *no pl.*) annihilation, extinction, destruction.

vernieten [fɛr'ni:tən], *v.a.* rivet.

Vernunft [fɛr'nunft], *f.* (—, *no pl.*) reason, sense, intelligence, judgment; *gesunde —*, common sense; *— annehmen*, listen to reason; *einen zur — bringen*, bring s.o. to his senses.

vernünftig [fɛr'nynftɪç], *adj.* sensible, reasonable, rational.

veröden [fɛr'ø:dən], *v.n.* (*aux.* sein) become desolate, become devastated.

Verödung [fɛr'ø:duŋ], *f.* (—, *no pl.*) devastation, desolation.

veröffentlichen [fɛr'œfəntlɪçən], *v.a.* publish.

Veröffentlichung [fɛr'œfəntlɪçuŋ], *f.* (—, *pl.* —en) publication.

verordnen [fɛr'ɔrdnən], *v.a.* order, command, ordain; (*Med.*) prescribe.

Verordnung [fɛr'ɔrdnuŋ], *f.* (—, *pl.* —en) order; (*Law*) decree, edict, statute; (*Med.*) prescription.

verpassen [fɛr'pasən], *v.a.* lose by delay, let slip; (*train etc.*) miss.

verpfänden [fɛr'pfɛndən], *v.a.* pawn, pledge.

Verpfänder [fɛr'pfɛndər], *m.* (—s, *pl.* —) mortgager.

Verpfändung [fɛr'pfɛnduŋ], *f.* (—, *pl.* —en) pawning, pledging.

verpflanzen [fɛr'pflantsən], *v.a.* transplant.

Verpflanzung [fɛr'pflantsuŋ], *f.* (—, *pl.* —en) transplantation.

verpflegen [fɛr'pfle:gən], *v.a.* board, provide food for, feed; nurse.

Verpflegung [fɛr'pfle:guŋ], *f.* (—, *no pl.*) board, catering; food.

Verpflegungskosten [fɛr'pfle:guŋskostən], *f. pl.* (cost of) board and lodging.

verpflichten [fɛr'pflɪçtən], *v.a.* bind, oblige, engage.

verpflichtend [fɛr'pflɪçtənt], *adj.* obligatory.

Verpflichtung [fɛr'pflɪçtuŋ], *f.* (—, *pl.* —en) obligation, duty; liability, engagement.

verplaudern [fɛr'plaudərn], *v.a.* spend (time) chatting.

verplempern [fɛr'plɛmpərn], *v.a.* (*coll.*) spend foolishly, fritter away.

verpönt [fɛr'pø:nt], *adj.* frowned upon; taboo.

verprassen [fɛr'prasən], *v.a.* squander (money) in riotous living.

verpuffen [fɛrˈpufən], *v.n.* (*aux.* sein) (*coll.*) fizzle out.

verpulvern [fɛrˈpulvərn], *v.a.* fritter away.

Verputz [fɛrˈputs], *m.* (**—es,** *no pl.*) plaster.

verquicken [fɛrˈkvɪkən], *v.a.* amalgamate; mix up.

Verrat [fɛrˈraːt], *m.* (**—(e)s,** *no pl.*) treachery, treason.

verraten [fɛrˈraːtən], *v.a. irr.* betray; disclose; *das verrät die Hand des Künstlers,* this proclaims the hand of the artist.

Verräter [fɛrˈrɛːtər], *m.* (**—s,** *pl.* **—**) traitor.

verräterisch [fɛrˈrɛːtərɪʃ], *adj.* treacherous, treasonable, perfidious; (*fig.*) tell-tale.

verrauchen [fɛrˈrauxən], *v.n.* (*aux.* sein) evaporate; (*fig.*) blow over; cool down.

verräuchern [fɛrˈrɔyçərn], *v.a.* smoke, fill with smoke.

verräumen [fɛrˈrɔymən], *v.a.* misplace, mislay.

verrauschen [fɛrˈrauʃən], *v.n.* (*aux.* sein) (*sound*) die away; pass away.

verrechnen [fɛrˈrɛçnən], *v.a.* reckon up. — *v.r. sich —,* miscalculate.

Verrechnung [fɛrˈrɛçnuŋ], *f.* (**—,** *pl.* **— en**) reckoning-up.

Verrechnungsscheck [fɛrˈrɛçnuŋsʃɛk], *m.* (**—s,** *pl.* **—e,** **—s**) crossed cheque, non-negotiable cheque.

verregnen [fɛrˈreːgnən], *v.a.* spoil by rain.

verreiben [fɛrˈraɪbən], *v.a. irr.* rub away; rub hard.

verreisen [fɛrˈraɪzən], *v.n.* (*aux.* sein) go on a journey.

verrenken [fɛrˈrɛŋkən], *v.a.* sprain, dislocate.

Verrenkung [fɛrˈrɛŋkuŋ], *f.* (**—,** *pl.* **—en**) sprain, dislocation.

verrichten [fɛrˈrɪçtən], *v.a.* do, perform, acquit o.s. of; execute; (*prayer*) say.

verriegeln [fɛrˈriːgəln], *v.a.* bolt.

verringern [fɛrˈrɪŋərn], *v.a.* reduce, diminish.

Verringerung [fɛrˈrɪŋəruŋ], *f.* (**—,** *no pl.*) diminution, reduction.

verrinnen [fɛrˈrɪnən], *v.n. irr.* (*aux.* sein) run off; (*fig.*) pass, elapse.

verrosten [fɛrˈrɔstən], *v.n.* (*aux.* sein) rust.

verrottet [fɛrˈrɔtət], *adj.* rotten.

verrucht [fɛrˈruːxt], *adj.* villainous, atrocious, heinous, infamous.

Verruchtheit [fɛrˈruːxthaɪt], *f.* (**—,** *no pl.*) villainy.

verrücken [fɛrˈrykən], *v.a.* shift, displace.

verrückt [fɛrˈrykt], *adj.* crazy, mad.

Verrückte [fɛrˈryktə], *m.* (**—n,** *pl.* **—n**) madman — *f.* (**—n,** *pl.* **—n**) madwoman.

Verrücktheit [fɛrˈrykthaɪt], *f.* (**—,** *pl.* **—en**) craziness; mad act.

Verruf [fɛrˈruːf], *m.* (**—s,** *no pl.*) discredit, ill repute.

verrufen [fɛrˈruːfən], *adj.* notorious, of ill repute.

Vers [fɛrs], *m.* (**—es,** *pl.* **—e**) verse.

versagen [fɛrˈzaːgən], *v.a. einem etwas —,* deny s.o. s.th., refuse s.o. s.th. — *v.n.* fail, break down; (*voice*) falter; *sich etwas —,* abstain from s.th., deny o.s. s.th.

Versager [fɛrˈzaːgər], *m.* (**—s,** *pl.* **—**) misfire; failure, unsuccessful person, flop.

versammeln [fɛrˈzaməln], *v.a.* gather around, convene. — *v.r. sich —,* assemble, meet.

Versammlung [fɛrˈzamluŋ], *f.* (**—,** *pl.* **—en**) assembly, meeting, gathering, convention.

Versand [fɛrˈzant], *m.* (**—s,** *no pl.*) dispatch, forwarding, shipping, shipment.

versanden [fɛrˈzandən], *v.n.* (*aux.* sein) silt up.

Versandgeschäft [fɛrˈzantgəʃɛft], *n.* (**—s,** *pl.* **—e**) export business; mail order business.

Versatzamt [fɛrˈzatsamt], *n.* (**—s,** *pl.* **⸚er**) pawn-shop.

versauen [fɛrˈzauən], *v.a.* (*sl.*) make a mess of.

versauern [fɛrˈzauərn], *v.n.* (*aux.* sein) turn sour; (*fig.*) become morose.

versaufen [fɛrˈzaufən], *v.a. irr.* (*sl.*) squander (money) on drink, drink away.

versäumen [fɛrˈzɔymən], *v.a.* miss, omit, lose by delay; leave undone; neglect.

Versäumnis [fɛrˈzɔymnɪs], *n.* (**—ses,** *pl.* **—se**) neglect, omission; (*time*) loss.

Versbau [ˈfɛrsbau], *m.* (**—s,** *no pl.*) versification; verse structure.

verschachern [fɛrˈʃaxərn], *v.a.* barter away.

verschaffen [fɛrˈʃafən], *v.a.* provide, procure, obtain, get.

verschämt [fɛrˈʃɛːmt], *adj.* shamefaced, bashful.

verschanzen [fɛrˈʃantsən], *v.a.* fortify.

Verschanzung [fɛrˈʃantsuŋ], *f.* (**—,** *pl.* **—en**) fortification, entrenchment.

verschärfen [fɛrˈʃɛrfən], *v.a.* heighten, intensify, sharpen.

verscharren [fɛrˈʃarən], *v.a.* cover with earth; bury hurriedly.

verscheiden [fɛrˈʃaɪdən], *v.n. irr.* (*aux.* sein) die, pass away.

verschenken [fɛrˈʃɛŋkən], *v.a.* make a present of, give away.

verscherzen [fɛrˈʃɛrtsən], *v.a. sich etwas —,* forfeit s.th.

verscheuchen [fɛrˈʃɔyçən], *v.a.* scare away, frighten away; *Sorgen —,* banish care.

verschicken [fɛrˈʃɪkən], *v.a.* send on, send out, forward, transmit; evacuate.

Verschickung [fɛrˈʃɪkuŋ], *f.* (**—,** *no pl.*) forwarding, transmission; evacuation; banishment, exile.

verschieben

verschieben [fɛrˈʃiːbən], *v.a. irr.* shift, move; delay, put off, defer, postpone.

Verschiebung [fɛrˈʃiːbuŋ], *f.* (—, *pl.* —en) removal; postponement; (*fig.*) black marketeering.

verschieden [fɛrˈʃiːdən], *adj.* different, diverse; deceased, departed; (*pl.*) some, several, sundry.

verschiedenartig [fɛrˈʃiːdənaːrtɪç], *adj.* varied, various, heterogeneous.

verschiedenerlei [fɛrˈʃiːdənərlaɪ], *indecl. adj.* diverse, of various kinds.

Verschiedenheit [fɛrˈʃiːdənhaɪt], *f.* (—, *pl.* —en) difference; diversity, variety.

verschiedentlich [fɛrˈʃiːdəntlɪç], *adv.* variously, severally; repeatedly.

verschiffen [fɛrˈʃɪfən], *v.a.* export, ship.

verschimmeln [fɛrˈʃɪməln], *v.n.* (*aux.* sein) go mouldy.

verschlafen [fɛrˈʃlaːfən], *v.a. irr.* sleep through, sleep away. — *v.r. sich* —, oversleep. — *adj.* sleepy, drowsy.

Verschlag [fɛrˈʃlaːk], *m.* (—s, *pl.* ⸚e) partition, box, cubicle.

verschlagen [fɛrˈʃlaːgən], *v.a. irr.* es *verschlägt mir den Atem*, it takes my breath away. — *adj.* cunning, crafty, sly.

verschlechtern [fɛrˈʃlɛçtərn], *v.a.* worsen, make worse. — *v.r. sich* —, deteriorate.

Verschlechterung [fɛrˈʃlɛçtəruŋ], *f.* (—, *no pl.*) deterioration.

verschleiern [fɛrˈʃlaɪərn], *v.a.* veil.

Verschleierung [fɛrˈʃlaɪəruŋ], *f.* (—, *pl.* —en) veiling, concealment; camouflage.

verschleißen [fɛrˈʃlaɪsən], *v.a. irr.* wear out, waste.

verschlemmen [fɛrˈʃlɛmən], *v.a.* squander on eating and drinking.

verschleppen [fɛrˈʃlɛpən], *v.a.* carry off, deport; kidnap; protract, spread; put off, procrastinate.

verschleudern [fɛrˈʃlɔydərn], *v.a.* waste; sell at cut prices.

verschließen [fɛrˈʃliːsən], *v.a. irr.* lock, lock up.

verschlimmern [fɛrˈʃlɪmərn], *v.a.* make worse. — *v.r. sich* —, get worse, worsen, deteriorate.

Verschlimmerung [fɛrˈʃlɪməruŋ], *f.* (—, *no pl.*) worsening, deterioration.

verschlingen [fɛrˈʃlɪŋən], *v.a. irr.* swallow up, devour.

verschlossen [fɛrˈʃlɔsən], *adj.* reserved, uncommunicative, withdrawn.

Verschlossenheit [fɛrˈʃlɔsənhaɪt], *f.* (—, *no pl.*) reserve.

verschlucken [fɛrˈʃlukən], *v.a.* swallow, gulp down; (*fig.*) suppress. — *v.r. sich* —, swallow the wrong way.

verschlungen [fɛrˈʃluŋən], *adj.* intricate, complicated.

Verschluß [fɛrˈʃlus], *m.* (—sses. *pl.* ⸚sse) lock; clasp; fastening; *unter* — *haben*, keep under lock and key.

Verschlußlaut [fɛrˈʃluslaut], *m.* (—s, *pl.* —e) (*Phon.*) explosive, plosive, stop.

verschmachten [fɛrˈʃmaxtən], *v.n.* (*aux.* sein) languish, pine; be parched.

Verschmähung [fɛrˈʃmɛːuŋ], *f.* (—, *no pl.*) disdain, scorn, rejection.

Verschmelzung [fɛrˈʃmɛltsuŋ], *f.* (—, *no pl.*) coalescence, fusion, blending.

verschmerzen [fɛrˈʃmɛrtsən], *v.a.* get over; bear stoically, make the best of.

verschmitzt [fɛrˈʃmɪtst], *adj.* cunning, crafty, mischievous.

verschmutzen [fɛrˈʃmutsən], *v.n.* (*aux.* sein) get dirty.

verschnappen [fɛrˈʃnapən], *v.r. sich* —, blurt out a secret, give o.s. away, let the cat out of the bag.

verschneiden [fɛrˈʃnaɪdən], *v.a. irr.* (*wings*) clip; (*trees*) prune; (*animals*) castrate; (*wine*) blend.

verschneien [fɛrˈʃnaɪən], *v.n.* (*aux.* sein) be snowed up, be covered with snow, be snowbound.

Verschnitt [fɛrˈʃnɪt], *m.* (—s, *no pl.*) blended wine, blend.

Verschnittene [fɛrˈʃnɪtənə], *m.* (—n, *pl.* —n) eunuch.

verschnörkelt [fɛrˈʃnœrkəlt], *adj.* adorned with flourishes.

verschnupft [fɛrˈʃnupft], *adj.* — *sein*, have a cold in the head; (*fig.*) be vexed.

verschnüren [fɛrˈʃnyːrən], *v.a.* (*shoes*) lace up; (*parcel*) tie up.

verschonen [fɛrˈʃoːnən], *v.a.* spare, exempt from.

verschönern [fɛrˈʃøːnərn], *v.a.* embellish, beautify.

Verschönerung [fɛrˈʃøːnəruŋ], *f.* (—, *pl.* —en) embellishment, adornment.

Verschonung [fɛrˈʃoːnuŋ], *f.* (—, *no pl.*) exemption; forbearance.

verschossen [fɛrˈʃɔsən], *adj.* faded, discoloured; (*fig.*) madly in love.

verschreiben [fɛrˈʃraɪbən], *v.a. irr.* prescribe. — *v.r. sich* —, make a mistake in writing.

verschrien [fɛrˈʃriːən], *adj.* notorious.

verschroben [fɛrˈʃroːbən], *adj.* cranky, eccentric.

Verschrobenheit [fɛrˈʃroːbənhaɪt], *f.* (—, *pl.* —en) crankiness, eccentricity.

verschrumpfen [fɛrˈʃrumpfən], *v.n.* (*aux.* sein) shrivel up.

verschüchtern [fɛrˈʃyçtərn], *v.a.* intimidate.

verschulden [fɛrˈʃuldən], *v.a.* bring on, be the cause of; be guilty of.

verschuldet [fɛrˈʃuldət], *adj.* in debt.

Verschuldung [fɛrˈʃulduŋ], *f.* (—, *no pl.*) indebtedness.

verschütten [fɛrˈʃytən], *v.a.* spill; bury alive.

verschwägern [fɛrˈʃvɛːgərn], *v.r. sich* —, become related by marriage.

Verschwägerung [fɛrˈʃvɛːgəruŋ], (—, *no pl.*) relationship by marriage.

verschwatzen [fɛrˈʃvatsən], *v.a.* gossip (the time) away, spend o.'s time gossiping.

verschweigen [fɛrˈʃvaɪgən], *v.a. irr.* keep secret, keep (news) from, hush up.

verschwenden [fɛr'ʃvɛndən], *v.a.* squander, waste.

verschwenderisch [fɛr'ʃvɛndərɪʃ], *adj.* prodigal, profuse, lavish; wasteful.

Verschwendung [fɛr'ʃvɛnduŋ], *f.* (—, *no pl.*) waste, extravagance.

Verschwendungssucht [fɛr'ʃvɛnduŋs-zuxt], *f.* (—, *no pl.*) prodigality; extravagance.

verschwiegen [fɛr'ʃviːgən], *adj.* discreet, close, secretive.

Verschwiegenheit [fɛr'ʃviːgənhaɪt], *f.* (—, *no pl.*) discretion, secrecy.

verschwimmen [fɛr'ʃvɪmən], *v.n.* irr. (*aux.* sein) become blurred.

verschwinden [fɛr'ʃvɪndən], *v.n.* irr. (*aux.* sein) disappear, vanish.

verschwommen [fɛr'ʃvɔmən], *adj.* vague, blurred.

verschwören [fɛr'ʃvøːrən], *v.r.* irr. *sich* —, plot, conspire.

Verschwörer [fɛr'ʃvøːrer], *m.* (—s, *pl.* —) conspirator.

Verschwörung [fɛr'ʃvøːruŋ], *f.* (—, *pl.* —en) conspiracy.

Versehen [fɛr'zeːən], *n.* (—s, *pl.* —) error, mistake, oversight.

versehen [fɛr'zeːən], *v.a.* irr. provide; perform; fill (an office); *einen* — *mit,* furnish s.o. with. — *v.r. sich* —, make a mistake.

versehren [fɛr'zeːrən], *v.a.* wound; disable.

versenden [fɛr'zɛndən], *v.a.* irr. forward, consign, send off.

Versender [fɛr'zɛndər], *m.* (—s, *pl.*—) consigner, exporter.

Versendung [fɛr'zɛnduŋ], *f.* (—, *no pl.*) transmission, shipping.

Versendungskosten [fɛr'zɛnduŋskɔs-tən], *f. pl.* forwarding charges.

versengen [fɛr'zɛŋən], *v.a.* singe, scorch.

versenken [fɛr'zɛŋkən], *v.a.* sink; (*ship*) scuttle.

Versenkung [fɛr'zɛŋkuŋ], *f.* (—, *no pl.*) sinking; hollow; (*ship*) scuttling; (*Theat.*) trap-door.

versessen [fɛr'zɛsən], *adj.* — *sein auf,* be bent upon, be mad on.

versetzen [fɛr'zɛtsən], *v.a.* transplant, remove; give; pawn, pledge; transfer; (*pupil*) promote to a higher form. — *v.r. sich in die Lage eines anderen* —, put o.s. in s.o. else's position.

versichern [fɛr'zɪçərn], *v.a.* assert, declare, aver, assure (s.o. of s.th); insure (s.th.).

Versicherung [fɛr'zɪçəruŋ], *f.* (—, *pl.* —en) assurance, assertion; insurance.

Versicherungsgesellschaft [fɛr'zɪçə-ruŋsgəzɛlʃaft], *f.* (—, *pl.* —en) insurance company.

Versicherungsprämie [fɛr'zɪçəruŋs-prɛːmjə], *f.* (—, *pl.* —n) insurance premium.

versiegbar [fɛr'ziːkbaːr], *adj.* exhaustible.

versiegeln [fɛr'ziːgəln], *v.a.* seal (up).

versiegen [fɛr'ziːgən], *v.n.* (*aux.* sein) dry up, be exhausted.

versilbern [fɛr'zɪlbərn], *v.a.* plate with silver; (*fig.*) convert into money.

versinken [fɛr'zɪŋkən], *v.n.* irr. sink; (*ship*) founder; sink; *versunken sein,* be absorbed (in s.th.).

Versmaß ['fɛrsmaːs], *n.* (—es, *pl.* —e) metre.

versoffen [fɛr'zɔfən], *adj.* (*vulg.*) drunken.

versohlen [fɛr'zoːlən], *v.a.* (*coll.*) thrash (s.o.).

versöhnen [fɛr'zøːnən], *v.r. sich mit einem* —, become reconciled with s.o.

versöhnlich [fɛr'zøːnlɪç], *adj.* propitiatory, conciliatory.

Versöhnung [fɛr'zøːnuŋ], *f.* (—, *no pl.*) reconciliation.

versorgen [fɛr'zɔrgən], *v.a.* provide with; take care of; support, maintain.

Versorger [fɛr'zɔrgər], *m.* (—s, *pl.* —) provider.

Versorgung [fɛr'zɔrguŋ], *f.* (—, *no pl.*) provision, maintenance.

verspäten [fɛr'ʃpɛːtən], *v.r. sich* —, be late, be behind time; (*train*) be overdue.

Verspätung [fɛr'ʃpɛːtuŋ], *f.* (—, *no pl.*) delay; lateness.

verspeisen [fɛr'ʃpaɪzən], *v.a.* eat up.

versperren [fɛr'ʃpɛrən], *v.a.* block up, barricade, close.

verspielen [fɛr'ʃpiːlən], *v.a.* lose (at play); gamble away. — *v.r. sich* —, play wrong.

verspielt [fɛr'ʃpiːlt], *adj.* playful.

verspotten [fɛr'ʃpɔtən], *v.a.* deride, scoff at.

versprechen [fɛr'ʃprɛçən], *v.a.* irr. promise. — *v.r. sich* —, make a slip of the tongue.

Versprechen [fɛr'ʃprɛçən], *n.* (—s, *pl.* —) promise.

versprengen [fɛr'ʃprɛŋən], *v.a.* disperse.

verspüren [fɛr'ʃpyːrən], *v.a.* feel, perceive.

verstaatlichen [fɛr'ʃtaːtlɪçən], *v.a.* nationalise.

Verstand [fɛr'ʃtant], *m.* (—(e)s, *no pl.*) intellect, intelligence, sense; understanding, reason, mind.

verstandesmäßig [fɛr'ʃtandəsmɛːsɪç], *adj.* rational, reasonable.

Verstandesschärfe [fɛr'ʃtandəsʃɛrfə], *f.* (—, *no pl.*) penetration, acumen.

verständig [fɛr'ʃtɛndɪç], *adj.* judicious, sensible, reasonable.

verständigen [fɛr'ʃtɛndɪgən], *v.a.* inform, notify. — *v.r. sich mit einem* —, come to an agreement with s.o.

Verständigung [fɛr'ʃtɛndɪguŋ], *f.* (—, *pl.* —en) understanding, agreement; information; arrangement.

verständlich [fɛr'ʃtɛntlɪç], *adj.* intelligible, clear, understandable.

Verständnis [fɛr'ʃtɛntnɪs], (—ses, *no pl.*) comprehension, understanding, perception, insight.

verständnisinnig [fɛr'ʃtɛntnɪsɪnɪç], *adj.* sympathetic; having profound insight.

verstärken [fɛr'ʃtɛrkən], *v.a.* strengthen, reinforce, intensify.

Verstärker [fɛr'ʃtɛrkər], *m.* (—s, *pl.* —) amplifier; magnifier.

Verstärkung [fɛr'ʃtɛrkuŋ], *f.* (—, *pl.* —en) strengthening, intensification, amplification; (*Mil.*) reinforcements.

verstauben [fɛr'ʃtaubən], *v.n.* (*aux.* sein) get dusty.

verstauchen [fɛr'ʃtauxən], *v.a.* wrench, sprain, dislocate.

verstauen [fɛr'ʃtauən], *v.a.* stow away.

Versteck [fɛr'ʃtɛk], *n.* (—s, *pl.* —e) hiding-place; place of concealment; —(en) *spielen,* play hide-and-seek.

verstecken [fɛr'ʃtɛkən], *v.a.* hide, conceal.

versteckt [fɛr'ʃtɛkt], *adj.* indirect, veiled.

verstehen [fɛr'ʃteːən], *v.a. irr.* understand, comprehend.

versteigen [fɛr'ʃtaigən], *v.r. irr. sich* —, climb too high; (*fig.*) go too far.

versteigern [fɛr'ʃtaigərn], *v.a.* sell by auction.

Versteigerung [fɛr'ʃtaigəruŋ], *f.* (—, *pl.* —en) auction, public sale.

versteinern [fɛr'ʃtainərn], *v.n.* (*aux.* sein) turn into stone, petrify.

verstellbar [fɛr'ʃtɛlbaːr], *adj.* adjustable.

verstellen [fɛr'ʃtɛlən], *v.a.* adjust; (*voice*) disguise. — *v.r. sich* —, sham, pretend.

versterben [fɛr'ʃtɛrbən], *v.n. irr.* (*aux.* sein) (*Poet.*) die.

versteuern [fɛr'ʃtɔyərn], *v.a.* pay tax on.

verstiegen [fɛr'ʃtiːgən], *adj.* eccentric, extravagant.

verstimmen [fɛr'ʃtɪmən], *v.a.* (*Mus.*) put out of tune; (*fig.*) put out of humour, annoy.

Verstimmtheit [fɛr'ʃtɪmthait], *f.* (—, *no pl.*) ill-humour, ill-temper, pique.

Verstimmung [fɛr'ʃtɪmuŋ], *f.* (—, *pl.* —en) bad temper, ill-feeling.

verstockt [fɛr'ʃtɔkt], *adj.* stubborn, obdurate.

Verstocktheit [fɛr'ʃtɔkthait], *f.* (—, *no pl.*) stubbornness, obduracy.

verstohlen [fɛr'ʃtoːlən], *adj.* surreptitious, clandestine, furtive.

verstopfen [fɛr'ʃtɔpfən], *v.a.* stop up; block (up); *verstopft sein,* be constipated.

Verstopfung [fɛr'ʃtɔpfuŋ], *f.* (—, *pl.* —en) obstruction, constipation.

verstorben [fɛr'ʃtɔrbən], *adj.* deceased, late.

verstört [fɛr'ʃtøːrt], *adj.* troubled, worried; distracted.

Verstörtheit [fɛr'ʃtøːrthait], *f.* (—, *no pl.*) consternation, agitation; distraction; haggardness.

Verstoß [fɛr'ʃtoːs], *m.* (—es, *pl.* ⸚e) blunder, mistake; offence.

verstoßen [fɛr'ʃtoːsən], *v.a. irr.* cast off, disown, repudiate. — *v.n.*

gegen, offend against, act in a manner contrary to.

verstreichen [fɛr'ʃtraiçən], *v.n. irr.* (*aux.* sein) (*time*) elapse, pass away.

verstricken [fɛr'ʃtrɪkən], *v.a.* entangle, ensnare.

Verstrickung [fɛr'ʃtrɪkuŋ], *f.* (—, *pl.* —en) entanglement.

verstümmeln [fɛr'ʃtyməln], *v.a.* mutilate, mangle.

verstummen [fɛr'ʃtumən], *v.n.* (*aux.* sein) grow silent; become speechless.

Verstümmlung [fɛr'ʃtymluŋ], *f.* (—, *pl.* —en) mutilation.

Versuch [fɛr'zuːx], *m.* (—s, *pl.* —e) attempt, trial, endeavour; (*science*) experiment; (*Lit.*) essay.

versuchen [fɛr'zuːxən], *v.a.* try, attempt, endeavour; (*food*) taste; *einen* —, tempt s.o.

Versucher [fɛr'zuːxər], *m.* (—s, *pl.* —) tempter.

Versuchskaninchen [fɛr'zuːxskaniːn-çən], *n.* (—s, *pl.* —) (*fig.*) guinea-pig.

Versuchung [fɛr'zuːxuŋ], *f.* (—, *pl.* —en) temptation.

versündigen [fɛr'zyndɪgən], *v.r. sich* —, sin (against).

Versunkenheit [fɛr'zuŋkənhait], *f.* (—, *no pl.*) absorption, preoccupation.

vertagen [fɛr'taːgən], *v.a.* adjourn, prorogue.

Vertagung [fɛr'taːguŋ], *f.* (—, *pl.* —en) adjournment, prorogation.

vertauschen [fɛr'tauʃən], *v.a.* exchange, barter, mistake, confuse.

verteidigen [fɛr'taidɪgən], *v.a.* defend, uphold, vindicate; (*fig.*) maintain.

Verteidiger [fɛr'taidɪgər], *m.* (—s, *pl.* —) defender; (*Law*) counsel for the defence.

Verteidigung [fɛr'taidɪguŋ], *f.* (—, *no pl.*) defence; justification.

Verteidigungskrieg [fɛr'taidɪguŋs-kriːk], *m.* (—(e)s, *pl.* —e) defensive war.

verteilen [fɛr'tailən], *v.a.* distribute, allot, allocate.

Verteilung [fɛr'tailuŋ], *f.* (—, *pl.* —en) distribution, apportionment.

verteuern [fɛr'tɔyərn], *v.a.* make dearer, raise the price of.

verteufelt [fɛr'tɔyfəlt], *adj.* devilish. — *adv.* (*coll.*) awfully, infernally.

vertiefen [fɛr'tiːfən], *v.a.* deepen.

vertieft [fɛr'tiːft], *adj.* absorbed, deep in thought.

Vertiefung [fɛr'tiːfuŋ], *f.* (—, *pl.* —en) cavity, recess, hollow; (*knowledge*) deepening; (*fig.*) absorption.

vertilgen [fɛr'tɪlgən], *v.a.* wipe out, exterminate; (*food*) (*coll.*) polish off.

Vertilgung [fɛr'tɪlguŋ], *f.* (—, *no pl.*) extermination, extirpation.

Vertrag [fɛr'traːk], *m.* (—(e)s, *pl.* ⸚e) contract, agreement; (*Pol.*) treaty, pact, convention.

vertragen [fɛr'traːgən], *v.a. irr.* suffer, endure; (*food*) digest. — *v.r. sich* — *mit,* get on well with.

vertraglich [fɛr'tra:klɪç], *adj.* as per contract, according to agreement.

verträglich [fɛr'trɛ:klɪç], *adj.* accommodating, peaceable.

vertragsmäßig [fɛr'tra:ksmɛ:sɪç], *adj.* according to contract.

vertragswidrig [fɛr'tra:ksvi:drɪç], *adj.* contrary to contract.

vertrauen [fɛr'trauən], *v.n.* rely (upon), trust (in).

Vertrauen [fɛr'trauən], *n.* (—s, *no pl.*) confidence, trust, reliance.

vertrauenerweckend [fɛr'trauənɛrvɛkənt], *adj.* inspiring confidence.

Vertrauensbruch [fɛr'trauənsbrux], *m.* (—es, *pl.* —e) breach of faith.

Vertrauensmann [fɛr'trauənsman], *m.* (—s, *pl.* —e) confidant; delegate; person entrusted with s.th.; (*Ind.*) shop steward.

vertrauensselig [fɛr'trauənsze:lɪç], *adj.* confiding, trusting.

Vertrauensvotum [fɛr'trauənsvo:tum], *n.* (—s, *pl.* —ten) vote of confidence.

vertrauenswürdig [fɛr'trauənsvyrdɪç], *adj.* trustworthy.

vertraulich [fɛr'traulɪç], *adj.* confidential; familiar.

Vertraulichkeit [fɛr'traulɪçkaɪt], *f.* (—, *pl.* —en) familiarity.

verträumt [fɛr'trɔymt], *adj.* dreamy.

vertraut [fɛr'traut], *adj.* intimate, familiar; conversant.

Vertraute [fɛr'trautə], *m.* (—n, *pl.* —n) close friend, confidant.

Vertrautheit [fɛr'trauthaɪt], *f.* (—, *no pl.*) familiarity.

vertreiben [fɛr'traɪbən], *v.a. irr.* drive away, expel; eject; (*person*) banish; (*time*) pass, kill; (*goods*) sell.

Vertreibung [fɛr'traɪbuŋ], *f.* (—, *no pl.*) expulsion; banishment.

vertreten [fɛr'tre:tən], *v.a. irr.* represent (s.o.), deputise for (s.o.).

Vertreter [fɛr'tre:tər], *m.* (—s, *pl.* —) representative, deputy; (*Comm.*) agent.

Vertretung [fɛr'tre:tuŋ], *f.* (—, *pl.* —en) representation, agency.

Vertrieb [fɛr'tri:p], *m.* (—s, *pl.* —e) sale; distribution.

vertrinken [fɛr'trɪŋkən], *v.a. irr.* spend *or* waste money on drink.

vertrocknen [fɛr'trɔknən], *v.n.* (*aux.* sein) dry up, wither.

vertrödeln [fɛr'trø:dəln], *v.a.* fritter (o.'s time) away.

vertrösten [fɛr'trø:stən], *v.a.* console; put off; put (s.o.) off with fine words; fob (s.o.) off with vain hopes.

Vertröstung [fɛr'trø:stuŋ], *f.* (—, *pl.* —en) comfort; empty promises.

vertun [fɛr'tu:n], *v.a. irr.* squander, waste.

vertuschen [fɛr'tuʃən], *v.a.* hush up.

verübeln [fɛr'y:bəln], *v.a.* take amiss.

verüben [fɛr'y:bən], *v.a.* commit, perpetrate.

verunehren [fɛr'une:rən], *v.a.* dishonour, disgrace.

verunglimpfen [fɛr'unglɪmpfən], *v.a.* bring into disrepute; defame, calumniate.

Verunglimpfung [fɛr'unglɪmpfuŋ], *f.* (—, *pl.* —en) defamation, detraction, calumny.

verunglücken [fɛr'unglykən], *v.n.* (*aux.* sein) (*person*) meet with an accident; be killed; (*thing*) misfire, fail.

verunreinigen [fɛr'unraɪnɪgən], *v.a.* contaminate.

Verunreinigung [fɛr'unraɪnɪguŋ], *f.* (—, *pl.* —en) contamination.

verunstalten [fɛr'unʃtaltən], *v.a.* disfigure, deface.

Verunstaltung [fɛr'unʃtaltuŋ], *f.* (—, *pl.* —en) disfigurement.

Veruntreuung [fɛr'untrɔyuŋ], *f.* (—, *pl.* —en) embezzlement, misappropriation.

verunzieren [fɛr'untsi:rən], *v.a.* disfigure, spoil.

verursachen [fɛr'u:rzaxən], *v.a.* cause, occasion.

verurteilen [fɛr'urtaɪlən], *v.a.* condemn; (*Law*) sentence.

Verurteilung [fɛr'urtaɪluŋ], *f.* (—, *no pl.*) condemnation; (*Law*) sentence.

vervielfältigen [fɛr'fi:lfɛltɪgən], *v.a.* multiply; duplicate, make copies of.

Vervielfältigung [fɛr'fi:lfɛltɪguŋ], *f.* (—, *pl.* —en) multiplication; duplication, copying.

vervollkommnen [fɛr'fɔlkɔmnən], *v.a.* improve, perfect.

Vervollkommnung [fɛr'fɔlkɔmnuŋ], *f.* (—, *no pl.*) improvement, perfection.

vervollständigen [fɛr'fɔlʃtɛndɪgən], *v.a.* complete.

Vervollständigung [fɛr'fɔlʃtɛndɪguŋ], *f.* (—, *no pl.*) completion.

verwachsen [fɛr'vaksən], *v.n. irr.* (*aux.* sein) grow together; be overgrown. — *adj.* deformed.

verwahren [fɛr'va:rən], *v.a.* take care of, preserve, secure. — *v.r.* sich — gegen, protest against.

verwahrlosen [fɛr'va:rlo:zən], *v.a.* neglect. — *v.n.* (*aux.* sein) be in need of care and protection, be neglected.

Verwahrlosung [fɛr'va:rlo:zuŋ], *f.* (—, *no pl.*) neglect.

Verwahrung [fɛr'va:ruŋ], *f.* (—, *no pl.*) keeping; charge; *in* — *geben*, deposit, give into s.o.'s charge; — *einlegen gegen*, enter a protest against.

verwalten [fɛr'valtən], *v.a.* manage, administer.

Verwalter [fɛr'valtər], *m.* (—s, *pl.* —) administrator, manager; steward, bailiff.

Verwaltung [fɛr'valtuŋ], *f.* (—, *pl.* —en) administration, management; Civil Service.

Verwaltungsbezirk [fɛr'valtuŋsbətsɪrk], *m.* (—s, *pl.* —e) administrative district.

Verwandlung [fɛr'vandluŋ], *f.* (—, *pl.* —en) alteration, transformation.

Verwandlungskünstler

Verwandlungskünstler [fɛr'vandluŋs-kynstlər], *m.* (—s, *pl.* —) quick-change artist.

verwandt [fɛr'vant], *adj.* related; cognate; congenial.

Verwandte [fɛr'vantə], *m.* (—n, *pl.* —n) relative, relation; kinsman; *der nächste* —, next of kin.

Verwandtschaft [fɛr'vantʃaft], *f.* (—, *pl.* —en) relationship; relations, family; congeniality, sympathy.

verwarnen [fɛr'varnən], *v.a.* admonish, forewarn.

Verwarnung [fɛr'varnuŋ], *f.* (—, *pl.* —en) admonition.

Verwässerung [fɛr'vɛsəruŋ], *f.* (—, *pl.* —en) dilution.

verwechseln [fɛr'vɛksəln], *v.a.* confuse; mistake for.

Verwechslung [fɛr'vɛksluŋ], *f.* (—, *pl.* —en) confusion, mistake.

verwegen [fɛr've:gən], *adj.* bold, audacious.

Verwegenheit [fɛr've:gənhait], *f.* (—, *pl.* —en) boldness, audacity.

verweichlichen [fɛr'vaiçliçən], *v.a.* coddle. — *v.n.* (*aux.* sein) become effeminate.

verweigern [fɛr'vaigərn], *v.a.* refuse, deny; reject.

Verweigerung [fɛr'vaigəruŋ], *f.* (—, *pl.* —en) refusal, denial; rejection.

verweilen [fɛr'vailən], *v.n.* remain; tarry; stay (with), dwell (on).

verweint [fɛr'vaint], *adj.* (eyes) red with weeping.

Verweis [fɛr'vais], *m.* (—es, *pl.* —e) reproof, reprimand, rebuke.

verweisen [fɛr'vaizən], *v.a. irr.* reprimand; banish, exile; — *auf etwas*, refer to s.th., hint at s.th.

Verweisung [fɛr'vaizuŋ], *f.* (—, *pl.* —en) banishment, exile; reference.

verweltlichen [fɛr'vɛltliçən], *v.a.* secularise, profane.

verwenden [fɛr'vɛndən], *v.a.* use, make use of; apply to, employ in, utilize.

Verwendung [fɛr'vɛnduŋ], *f.* (—, *pl.* —en) application, use; expenditure, employment.

verwerfen [fɛr'vɛrfən], *v.a. irr.* reject, disapprove of.

verwerflich [fɛr'vɛrfliç], *adj.* objectionable.

Verwertung [fɛr've:rtuŋ], *f.* (—, *no pl.*) utilisation.

verwesen [fɛr've:zən], *v.a.* administer. — *v.n.* (*aux.* sein) rot, decompose, putrefy.

Verweser [fɛr've:zər], *m.* (—s, *pl.* —) administrator.

Verwesung [fɛr've:zuŋ], *f.* (—, *no pl.*) (*office*) administration; putrefaction, rotting.

verwickeln [fɛr'vikəln], *v.a.* entangle, involve.

verwickelt [fɛr'vikəlt], *adj.* intricate, complicated, involved.

Verwicklung [fɛr'vikluŋ], *f.* (—, *pl.*

—en) entanglement, involvement, complication.

verwildern [fɛr'vildərn], *v.n.* (*aux.* sein) run wild.

verwildert [fɛr'vildərt], *adj.* wild, uncultivated, overgrown; (*fig.*) intractable.

Verwilderung [fɛr'vildəruŋ], *f.* (—, *no pl.*) running wild, growing wild.

verwirken [fɛr'virkən], *v.a.* forfeit.

verwirklichen [fɛr'virkliçən], *v.a.* realise. — *v.r. sich* —, materialise, come true.

Verwirklichung [fɛr'virkliçuŋ], *f.* (—, *no pl.*) realisation, materialisation.

Verwirkung [fɛr'virkuŋ], *f.* (—, *no pl.*) forfeiture.

verwirren [fɛr'virən], *v.a.* disarrange, throw into disorder, entangle; puzzle, bewilder, confuse, disconcert.

Verwirrung [fɛr'viruŋ], *f.* (—, *pl.* —en) bewilderment, confusion.

verwischen [fɛr'viʃən], *v.a.* blot out, smudge, obliterate.

verwittern [fɛr'vitərn], *v.n.* (*aux.* sein) be weather-beaten.

verwöhnen [fɛr'vø:nən], *v.a.* spoil, pamper, coddle.

verworfen [fɛr'vɔrfən], *adj.* profligate; rejected, reprobate.

verworren [fɛr'vɔrən], *adj.* confused, perplexed; intricate; (*speech*) rambling.

verwundbar [fɛr'vuntba:r], *adj.* vulnerable.

verwunden [fɛr'vundən], *v.a.* wound, hurt, injure.

verwundern [fɛr'vundərn], *v.r. sich* —, be surprised, wonder, be amazed.

Verwunderung [fɛr'vundəruŋ], *f.* (—, *no pl.*) surprise, astonishment, amazement.

Verwundung [fɛr'vunduŋ], *f.* (—, *pl.* —en) wounding, wound, injury.

verwunschen [fɛr'vunʃən], *adj.* enchanted, spellbound, bewitched.

verwünschen [fɛr'vynʃən], *v.a.* curse; cast a spell on, bewitch.

verwünscht [fɛr'vynʃt], *excl.* confound it!

Verwünschung [fɛr'vynʃuŋ], *f.* (—, *pl.* —en) curse, malediction.

verwüsten [fɛr'vy:stən], *v.a.* devastate, ravage, lay waste.

Verwüstung [fɛr'vy:stuŋ], *f.* (—, *pl.* —en) devastation.

verzagen [fɛr'tsa:gən], *v.n.* (*aux.* sein) lose heart, lose courage.

verzagt [fɛr'tsa:kt], *adj.* fainthearted, discouraged.

Verzagtheit [fɛr'tsa:kthait], *f.* (—, *no pl.*) faintheartedness.

verzählen [fɛr'tse:lən], *v.r. sich* —, miscount.

verzapfen [fɛr'tsapfən], *v.a.* sell (liquor) on draught; (*fig.*) tell (a story), talk (nonsense).

verzärteln [fɛr'tse:rtəln], *v.a.* pamper, coddle; spoil.

verzaubern [fɛr'tsaubərn], *v.a.* bewitch, charm, put a spell on.

verzehren [fɛrˈtseːrən], *v.a.* consume, eat. — *v.r. sich — in*, pine away with, be consumed with.

Verzehrung [fɛrˈtseːruŋ], *f.* (—, *no pl.*) (*obs.*) consumption, tuberculosis.

verzeichnen [fɛrˈtsaɪçnən], *v.a.* draw badly; note down, register, record.

Verzeichnis [fɛrˈtsaɪçnɪs], *n.* (—ses, *pl.* —se) catalogue, list, register.

verzeihen [fɛrˈtsaɪən], *v.a.* irr. forgive, pardon.

verzeihlich [fɛrˈtsaɪlɪç], *adj.* pardonable, forgivable, excusable, venial.

Verzeihung [fɛrˈtsaɪuŋ], *f.* (—, *no pl.*) pardon, forgiveness; *ich bitte um —*, I beg your pardon.

verzerren [fɛrˈtsɛrən], *v.a.* distort.

Verzerrung [fɛrˈtsɛruŋ], *f.* (—, *pl.* —en) distortion; (*face*) grimace.

verzetteln [fɛrˈtsɛtəln], *v.a.* disperse, scatter.

Verzicht [fɛrˈtsɪçt], *m.* (—(e)s, *no pl.*) renunciation, resignation.

verzichten [fɛrˈtsɪçtən], *v.n.* forgo, renounce.

verziehen [fɛrˈtsiːən], *v.a.* irr. distort; spoil (*child*). — *v.n.* (*aux.* sein) go away, move away.

Verzierung [fɛrˈtsiːruŋ], *f.* (—, *pl.* —en) decoration, ornament.

verzögern [fɛrˈtsøːgərn], *v.a.* delay, defer, retard, protract, procrastinate. — *v.r. sich —*, be delayed.

Verzögerung [fɛrˈtsøːgəruŋ], *f.* (—, *pl.* —en) delay, retardation, procrastination; time-lag.

verzollen [fɛrˈtsɔlən], *v.a.* pay duty on.

Verzücktheit [fɛrˈtsʏkthaɪt], *f.* (—, *no pl.*) ecstasy, rapture.

Verzug [fɛrˈtsuːk], *m.* (—s, *no pl.*) delay.

verzweifeln [fɛrˈtsvaɪfəln], *v.n.* despair, be desperate.

Verzweiflung [fɛrˈtsvaɪfluŋ], *f.* (—, *no pl.*) despair.

verzwickt [fɛrˈtsvɪkt], *adj.* complicated, intricate, tricky.

Vesuv [veˈzuːf], *m.* Mount Vesuvius.

Vetter [ˈvɛtər], *m.* (—s, *pl.* —n) cousin.

Vetternwirtschaft [ˈvɛtərnvɪrtʃaft], *f.* (—, *no pl.*) nepotism.

Vexierbild [vɛˈksiːrbɪlt], *n.* (—s, *pl.* —er) picture-puzzle.

Vexierspiegel [vɛˈksiːrʃpiːgəl], *m.* (—s, *pl.*—) distorting mirror.

vibrieren [viˈbriːrən], *v.n.* vibrate.

Vieh [fiː], *n.* (—s, *no pl.*) cattle, livestock.

Viehfutter [ˈfiːfutər], *n.* (—s, *no pl.*) forage, fodder, feeding-stuff.

viehisch [ˈfiːɪʃ], *adj.* beastly, brutal.

Viehwagen [ˈfiːvaːgən], *m.* (—s, *pl.*—) cattle-truck.

Viehweide [ˈfiːvaɪdə], *f.* (—, *pl.* —n) pasture, pasturage.

Viehzüchter [ˈfiːtsʏçtər], *m.* (—s, *pl.* —) cattle-breeder.

viel [fiːl], *adj.* much, a great deal, a lot; (*pl.*) many.

vielartig [ˈfiːlartɪç], *adj.* multifarious.

vieldeutig [ˈfiːldɔytɪç], *adj.* ambiguous, equivocal.

Vieleck [ˈfiːlɛk], *n.* (—s, *pl.* —e) polygon.

vielerlei [ˈfiːlərlaɪ], *adj.* of many kinds, various.

vielfältig [ˈfiːlfɛltɪç], *adj.* manifold.

vielfarbig [ˈfiːlfarbɪç], *adj.* multicoloured, variegated.

Vielfraß [ˈfiːlfraːs], *m.* (—es, *pl.* —e) glutton.

vielgeliebt [ˈfiːlgəliːpt], *adj.* much loved, well-beloved, dearly loved.

vielgereist [ˈfiːlgəraɪst], *adj.* much travelled.

vielleicht [fiˈlaɪçt], *adv.* perhaps, maybe.

vielmals [ˈfiːlmaːls], *adv.* many times, frequently, much.

Vielmännerei [fiːlmɛnəˈraɪ], *f.* (—, *no pl.*) polyandry.

vielmehr [fiːlˈmeːr], *adv.* rather, much more. — *conj.* rather, on the other hand.

vielsagend [ˈfiːlzaːgənt], *adj.* expressive, full of meaning.

vielseitig [ˈfiːlzaɪtɪç], *adj.* multilateral; (*fig.*) versatile.

Vielseitigkeit [ˈfiːlzaɪtɪçkaɪt], *f.* (—, *no pl.*) versatility.

vielverheißend [ˈfiːlfɛrhaɪsənt], *adj.* promising, auspicious.

Vielweiberei [fiːlvaɪbəˈraɪ], *f.* (—, *no pl.*) polygamy.

vier [fiːr], *num. adj.* four.

Viereck [ˈfiːrɛk], *n.* (—s, *pl.* —e) square, quadrangle.

viereckig [ˈfiːrɛkɪç], *adj.* square.

vierfüßig [ˈfiːrfyːsɪç], *adj.* four-footed.

vierhändig [ˈfiːrhɛndɪç], *adj.* four-handed; — *spielen*, (*piano*) play duets.

vierschrötig [ˈfiːrʃrøːtɪç], *adj.* robust, thick-set, stocky.

vierseitig [ˈfiːrzaɪtɪç], *adj.* quadrilateral.

vierstimmig [ˈfiːrʃtɪmɪç], *adj.* (*Mus.*) four-part; for four voices.

vierteilen [ˈfiːrtaɪlən], *v.a.* quarter, divide into four parts.

Viertel [ˈfɪrtəl], *n.* (—s, *pl.* —) quarter, fourth part.

Viertelstunde [fɪrtəlˈʃtundə], *f.* (—, *pl.* —n) quarter of an hour.

viertens [ˈfiːrtəns], *num. adv.* fourthly, in the fourth place.

Vierwaldstättersee [fiːrˈvaltʃtɛtərzeː], *m.* Lake Lucerne.

vierzehn [ˈfɪrtseːn], *num. adj.* fourteen; — *Tage*, a fortnight.

vierzig [ˈfɪrtsɪç], *num. adj.* forty.

Vietnam [viɛtˈnaːm], *n.* Vietnam.

Violinschlüssel [vioˈliːnʃlʏsəl], *m.* (—s, *pl.* —) (*Mus.*) treble clef.

Virtuosität [vɪrtuoziˈtɛːt], *f.* (—, *no pl.*) mastery, virtuosity.

Visage [viˈzaːʒə], *f.* (—, *pl.* —n) (*coll.*) face.

Visier [viˈziːr], *n.* (—, *pl.* —e) visor; (*gun*) sight.

Vision [viˈzjoːn], *f.* (—, *pl.* —en) vision.

Visionär

Visionär [vizjoʹnɛːr], *m.* (—s, *pl.* —e) visionary.

Visitenkarte [viʹziːtənkartə], *f.* (—, *pl.* —n) card, visiting card.

Visum [ʹviːzum], *n.* (—s, *pl.* **Visa**) visa.

Vizekönig [ʹviːtsəkøːnɪç], *m.* (—s, *pl.* —e) viceroy.

Vlies [fliːs], *n.* (—es, *pl.* —e) fleece.

Vogel [ʹfoːgəl], *m.* (—s, *pl.* ⸚) bird; (*coll.*) fellow; *einen — haben*, be off o.'s head.

Vogelbauer [ʹfoːgəlbauər], *n.* (—s, *pl.* —) bird-cage.

Vogelfänger [ʹfoːgəlfɛŋər], *m.* (—s, *pl.* —) fowler, bird-catcher.

vogelfrei [ʹfoːgəlfrai], *adj.* outlawed, proscribed.

Vogelfutter [ʹfoːgəlfutər], *n.* (—s, *no pl.*) bird-seed.

Vogelhändler [ʹfoːgəlhɛndlər], *m.* (—s, *pl.* —) bird-dealer.

Vogelhaus [ʹfoːgəlhaus], *n.* (—es, *pl.* ⸚er) aviary.

Vogelkenner [ʹfoːgəlkɛnər], *m.* (—s, *pl.* —) ornithologist.

Vogelkunde [ʹfoːgəlkundə], *f.* (—, *no pl.*) ornithology.

Vogelperspektive [ʹfoːgəlpɛrspɛktiːvə], *f.* (—, *no pl.*) bird's-eye view.

Vogelschau [ʹfoːgəlʃau], *f.* (—, *no pl.*) bird's-eye view.

Vogelsteller [ʹfoːgəlʃtɛlər], *m.* (—s, *pl.* —) fowler, bird-catcher.

Vogesen [voʹgeːzən], *pl.* Vosges Mountains.

Vogler [ʹfoːglər], *m.* (—s, *pl.* —) fowler.

Vogt [foːkt], *m.* (—(e)s, *pl.* ⸚e) prefect, bailiff, steward, provost.

Vogtei [foːkʹtai], *f.* (—, *pl.* —en) prefecture, bailiwick.

Vokabel [voʹkaːbəl], *f.* (—, *pl.* —n) word, vocable.

Vokabelbuch [voʹkaːbəlbuːx], *n.* (—(e)s, *pl.* ⸚er) vocabulary (book).

Vokal [voʹkaːl], *m.* (—s, *pl.* —e) vowel.

Vokativ [vokaʹtiːf], *m.* (—s, *pl.* —e) (*Gram.*) vocative.

Volk [fɔlk], *n.* (—(e)s, *pl.* ⸚er) people, nation; *das gemeine —*, mob, the common people.

Völkerkunde [ʹfœlkərkundə], *f.* (—, *no pl.*) ethnology.

Völkerrecht [ʹfœlkərrɛçt], *n.* (—s, *no pl.*) international law.

Völkerschaft [ʹfœlkərʃaft], *f.* (—, *pl.* —en) tribe, people.

Völkerwanderung [ʹfœlkərvandəruŋ], *f.* (—, *pl.* —en) mass migration.

Volksabstimmung [ʹfɔlksapʃtimuŋ], *f.* (—, *pl.* —en) referendum.

Volksausgabe [ʹfɔlksausgaːbə], *f.* (—, *pl.* —n) popular edition.

Volksbeschluß [ʹfɔlksbəʃlus], *m.* (—sses, *pl.* ⸚sse) plebiscite.

Volksbibliothek [ʹfɔlksbibli, oteːk], *f.* (—, *pl.* —en) public library.

Volkscharakter [ʹfɔlkskaraktər], *m.* (—s, *no pl.*) national character.

Volksentscheid [ʹfɔlksɛntʃait], *m.* (—s, *pl.* —e) plebiscite.

Volksführer [ʹfɔlksfyːrər], *m.* (—s, *pl.* —) demagogue.

Volksheer [ʹfɔlksheːr], *n.* (—s, *pl.* —e) national army.

Volksherrschaft [ʹfɔlkshɛrʃaft], *f.* (—, *no pl.*) democracy.

Volkshochschule [ʹfɔlkshoxʃuːlə], *f.* (—, *no pl.*) adult education (classes).

Volksjustiz [ʹfɔlksjustiːts], *f.* (—, *no pl.*) lynch-law.

Volkskunde [ʹfɔlkskundə], *f.* (—, *no pl.*) folklore.

Volkslied [ʹfɔlksliːt], *n.* (—s, *pl.* —er) folk-song.

Volksschicht [ʹfɔlksʃɪçt], *f.* (—, *pl.* —en) class.

Volksschule [ʹfɔlksʃuːlə], *f.* (—, *pl.* —n) primary school; elementary school.

Volkssitte [ʹfɔlksitə], *f.* (—, *pl.* —n) national custom.

Volkssprache [ʹfɔlksʃpraːxə], *f.* (—, *pl.* —n) vernacular.

Volksstamm [ʹfɔlksʃtam], *m.* (—s, *pl.* ⸚e) tribe.

Volkstracht [ʹfɔlkstraxt], *f.* (—, *pl.* —en) national costume.

volkstümlich [ʹfɔlkstyːmlɪç], *adj.* national, popular.

Volksvertretung [ʹfɔlksfɛrtreːtuŋ], *f.* (—, *no pl.*) representation of the people, parliamentary representation.

Volkswirt [ʹfɔlksvɪrt], *m.* (—s, *pl.* —e) political economist.

Volkswirtschaft [ʹfɔlksvɪrtʃaft], *f.* (—, *no pl.*) political economy.

Volkszählung [ʹfɔlkstseːluŋ], *f.* (—, *pl.* —en) census.

voll [fɔl], *adj.* full, filled; whole, complete, entire.

vollauf [ʹfɔlauf], *adv.* abundantly.

Vollbart [ʹfɔlbaːrt], *m.* (—s, *pl.* ⸚e) beard.

vollberechtigt [ʹfɔlbəreçtɪçt], *adj.* fully entitled.

Vollbild [ʹfɔlbɪlt], *n.* (—s, *pl.* —er) full-length portrait, full-page illustration.

Vollblut [ʹfɔlbluːt], *n.* (—s, *pl.* ⸚er) thoroughbred.

vollblütig [ʹfɔlblyːtɪç], *adj.* full-blooded, thoroughbred.

vollbringen [fɔlʹbrɪŋən], *v.a. irr.* accomplish, achieve, complete.

Vollbringung [fɔlʹbrɪŋuŋ], *f.* (—, *no pl.*) achievement.

Volldampf [ʹfɔldampf], *m.* (—es, *no pl.*) full steam.

vollenden [fɔlʹɛndən], *v.a.* finish, complete.

vollendet [fɔlʹɛndət], *adj.* finished; accomplished.

vollends [ʹfɔlɛnts], *adv.* quite, altogether, wholly, entirely, moreover.

Vollendung [fɔlʹɛnduŋ], *f.* (—, *no pl.*) completion; perfection.

Völlerei [fœləʹrai], *f.* (—, *pl.* —en) gluttony.

266

Vorbereitung

voliführen [fɔl'fy:rən], *v.a.* execute, carry out.

Vollgefühl ['fɔlgəfy:l], *n.* (—s, *no pl.*) consciousness, full awareness.

Vollgenuß ['fɔlgənus], *m.* (—sses, *no pl.*) full enjoyment.

vollgültig ['fɔlgyltiç], *adj.* fully valid; unexceptionable.

Vollheit ['fɔlhaɪt], *f.* (—, *no pl.*) fullness, plenitude.

völlig ['fœliç], *adj.* entire, whole, complete.

vollinhaltlich ['fɔlɪnhaltliç], *adv.* to its full extent.

volljährig ['fɔljɛ:riç], *adj.* of age.

Volljährigkeit ['fɔljɛ:riçkaɪt], *f.* (—, *no pl.*) adult years, majority.

vollkommen ['fɔlkɔmən], *adj.* perfect. — *adv.* entirely.

Vollkommenheit [fɔl'kɔmənhaɪt], *f.* (—, *no pl.*) perfection.

Vollmacht ['fɔlmaxt], *f.* (—, *pl.* —en) authority; fullness of power; power of attorney.

vollsaftig ['fɔlzaftiç], *adj.* juicy, succulent.

vollständig ['fɔlʃtɛndiç], *adj.* complete, full. — *adv.* entirely.

vollstrecken [fɔl'ʃtrɛkən], *v.a.* execute, carry out.

Vollstrecker [fɔl'ʃtrɛkər], *m.* (—s, *pl.* —) executor.

volltönig ['fɔltø:niç], *adj.* sonorous.

vollwertig ['fɔlvertiç], *adj.* standard, sterling.

vollzählig ['fɔltsɛ:liç], *adj.* complete.

vollziehen [fɔl'tsi:ən], *v.a. irr.* execute, carry out, ratify.

vollziehend [fɔl'tsi:ənt], *adj.* executive.

Vollziehungsgewalt [fɔl'tsi:unsgəvalt], *f.* (—, *no pl.*) executive power.

Vollzug [fɔl'tsu:k], *m.* (—s, *no pl.*) execution; fulfilment.

Volontär [vɔlɔ'tɛ:r], *m.* (—s, *pl.* —e) volunteer.

von [fɔn] (*von dem* becomes **vom**), *prep.* (*Dat.*) by, from; of; concerning, about; — *Shakespeare*, by Shakespeare; — *Beruf*, by profession; *er kommt — London*, he comes from London; — *fern*, from afar; — *jetzt an*, from now on; — *einem sprechen*, speak of s.o.; *dein Breif vom 15.*, your letter of the 15th.

vonnöten [fɔn'nø:tən], *adv.* — *sein*, be necessary.

vonstatten [fɔn'ʃtatən], *adv.* — *gehen*, progress; go off.

vor [fo:r], *prep.* (*Dat.*, *Acc.*) (*place*) before, ahead of, in front of; (*time*) before, prior to, earlier than; from; of; with; above; in presence of, because of; more than; — *dem Hause*, in front of the house; — *Sonnenaufgang*, before sunrise; — *zwei Tagen*, two days ago; *sich — einem verstecken*, hide from s.o.; *sich hüten* —, beware of; *starr — Kälte*, stiff with cold; — *allem*, above all. — *adv.* before; *nach wie —*, now as before.

Vorabend ['fo:ra:bənt], *m.* (—s, *pl.* —e) eve.

Vorahnung ['fo:ra:nuŋ], *f.* (—, *pl.* —en) presentiment, foreboding.

voran [fo'ran], *adv.* before, in front, forward, on.

vorangehen [fo'range:ən], *v.n. irr.* (*aux.* sein) take the lead, go ahead.

Voranzeige ['fo:rantsaɪgə], *f.* (—, *pl.* —n) advance notice; (*film*) trailer.

Vorarbeiter ['fo:rarbaɪtər], *m.* (—s, *pl.* —) foreman.

voraus [fo'raus], *adv.* before, in front, foremost; in advance; *im* or *zum* —, beforehand; (*thanks*) in anticipation.

vorauseilen [fo'rausaɪlən], *v.n.* (*aux.* sein) run ahead.

vorausgehen [fo'rausge:ən], *v.n. irr.* (*aux.* sein) walk ahead; *einem* —, go before; precede s.o.

voraushaben [fo'rausha:bən], *v.n. irr.* *etwas vor einem* —, have the advantage over s.o.

Voraussage [fo'rauza:gə], *f.* (—, *pl.* —n) prediction, prophecy; (*weather*) forecast.

voraussagen [fo'rauza:gən], *v.a.* predict, foretell; (*weather*) forecast.

voraussehen [fo'rauze:ən], *v.a. irr.* foresee.

voraussetzen [fo'rauzetsən], *v.a.* presuppose, take for granted.

Voraussetzung [fo'rauzetsuŋ], *f.* (—, *pl.* —en) supposition, presupposition; *unter der* —, on the understanding.

Voraussicht [fo'rauziçt], *f.* (—, *no pl.*) foresight, forethought; *aller* — *nach*, in all probability.

voraussichtlich [fo'rauziçtliç], *adj.* prospective, presumptive, probable, expected. — *adv.* probably, presumably.

Vorbau ['fo:rbau], *m.* (—s, *pl.* —ten) frontage.

Vorbedacht ['fo:rbədaxt], *m.* (—s, *no pl.*) premeditation; *mit* —, on purpose, deliberately.

vorbedacht ['fo:rbədaxt], *adj.* premeditated.

Vorbedeutung ['fo:rbədəytuŋ], *f.* (—, *pl.* —en) omen.

Vorbehalt ['fo:rbəhalt], *m.* (—s, *pl.* —e) reservation, proviso.

vorbehalten ['fo:rbəhaltən], *v.a. irr.* reserve; make reservation that.

vorbehaltlich ['fo:rbəhaltliç], *prep.* (*Genit.*) with the proviso that.

vorbei [fo:r'baɪ], *adv.* by; along; past, over, finished, gone.

vorbeigehen [fo:r'baɪge:ən], *v.n. irr.* (*aux.* sein) pass by; go past; march past.

vorbeilassen [fo:r'baɪlasən], *v.a. irr.* let pass.

Vorbemerkung ['fo:rbəmerkuŋ], *f.* (—, *pl.* —en) preface, prefatory note.

vorbereiten ['fo:rbəraɪtən], *v.a.* prepare.

Vorbereitung ['fo:rbəraɪtuŋ], *f.* (—, *pl.* —en) preparation.

267

Vorbesitzer [ˈfoːrbəzɪtsər], *m.* (**—s,** *pl.* **—**) previous owner.

Vorbesprechung [ˈfoːrbəʃprɛçuŋ], *f.* (**—,** *pl.* **—en**) preliminary discussion.

vorbestimmen [ˈfoːrbəʃtɪmən], *v.a.* predestine, predetermine.

Vorbestimmung [ˈfoːrbəʃtɪmuŋ], *f.* (**—,** *no pl.*) predestination.

vorbestraft [ˈfoːrbəʃtraːft], *adj.* previously convicted.

vorbeten [ˈfoːrbeːtən], *v.n.* lead in prayer.

vorbeugen [ˈfoːrbɔygən], *v.n.* prevent, preclude, obviate. — *v.r. sich* —, bend forward.

Vorbeugung [ˈfoːrbɔyguŋ], *f.* (**—,** *no pl.*) prevention; prophylaxis.

Vorbeugungsmaßnahme [ˈfoːrbɔyguŋsmaːsnaːmə], *f.* (**—,** *pl.* **—n**) preventive measure.

Vorbild [ˈfoːrbɪlt], *n.* (**—s,** *pl.* **—er**) model, example, pattern, ideal.

vorbildlich [ˈfoːrbɪltlɪç], *adj.* exemplary; typical; — *sein*, be a model.

Vorbildung [ˈfoːrbɪlduŋ], *f.* (**—,** *no pl.*) preparatory training.

Vorbote [ˈfoːrboːtə], *m.* (**—n,** *pl.* **—n**) herald, precursor, forerunner.

vorbringen [ˈfoːrbrɪŋən], *v.a. irr.* produce, proffer; advance, utter, allege, assert, claim.

vordatieren [ˈfoːrdatiːrən], *v.a.* antedate.

vordem [forˈdeːm], *adv.* (*obs.*) formerly, once.

Vorderachse [ˈfordəraksə], *f.* (**—,** *pl.* **—n**) front axle.

Vorderansicht [ˈfordəranzɪçt], *f.* (**—,** *pl.* **—en**) front view.

Vorderarm [ˈfordərarm], *m.* (**—s,** *pl.* **—e**) forearm.

Vordergrund [ˈfordərgrʊnt], *m.* (**—s,** *pl.* **ⁱe**) foreground.

vorderhand [ˈfordərhant], *adv.* for the present.

Vorderseite [ˈfordərzaɪtə], *f.* (**—,** *pl.* **—n**) front.

vorderst [ˈfordərst], *adj.* foremost, first.

Vordertür [ˈfordərtyːr], *f.* (**—,** *pl.* **—en**) front door.

Vordertreffen [ˈfordərtrɛfən], *n.* (**—s,** *no pl.*) *ins — kommen*, be in the vanguard, come to the fore.

vordrängen [ˈfoːrdrɛŋən], *v.r. sich* —, press forward, jump the queue.

vordringen [ˈfoːrdrɪŋən], *v.n. irr.* (*aux.* sein) advance, push forward.

vordringlich [ˈfoːrdrɪŋlɪç], *adj.* urgent; forward, importunate.

Vordruck [ˈfoːrdruk], *m.* (**—s,** *pl.* **—e**) (*printed*) form.

voreilen [ˈfoːraɪlən], *v.n.* (*aux.* sein) rush forward.

voreilig [ˈfoːraɪlɪç], *adj.* over-hasty, rash.

Voreiligkeit [ˈfoːraɪlɪçkaɪt], *f.* (**—,** *no pl.*) hastiness, rashness.

voreingenommen [ˈfoːraɪngənɔmən], *adj.* biased, prejudiced.

Voreingenommenheit [ˈfoːraɪngənɔmənhaɪt], *f.* (**—,** *no pl.*) bias, prejudice.

Voreltern [ˈfoːrɛltərn], *pl.* forefathers, ancestors.

vorenthalten [ˈfoːrɛnthaltən], *v.a. irr. sep. & insep.* withhold.

Vorentscheidung [ˈfoːrɛntʃaɪduŋ], *f.* (**—,** *pl.* **—en**) preliminary decision.

vorerst [foːrˈeːrst], *adv.* first of all, firstly; for the time being.

vorerwähnt [ˈfoːrɛrvɛːnt], *adj.* aforementioned.

Vorfahr [ˈfoːrfaːr], *m.* (**—en,** *pl.* **—en**) ancestor.

vorfahren [ˈfoːrfaːrən], *v.n. irr.* (*aux.* sein) drive up (to a house *etc.*).

Vorfall [ˈfoːrfal], *m.* (**—s,** *pl.* ⁱe) occurrence, incident.

vorfinden [ˈfoːrfɪndən], *v.a. irr.* find, find present, meet with.

Vorfrage [ˈfoːrfraːgə], *f.* (**—,** *pl.* **—n**) preliminary question.

vorführen [ˈfoːrfyːrən], *v.a.* bring forward, produce.

Vorführung [ˈfoːrfyːruŋ], *f.* (**—,** *pl.* **—en**) production, presentation; performance.

Vorgang [ˈfoːrgaŋ], *m.* (**—s,** *pl.* ⁱe) occurrence, event, happening; proceeding, precedent; procedure.

Vorgänger [ˈfoːrgɛŋər], *m.* (**—s,** *pl.* **—**) predecessor.

Vorgarten [ˈfoːrgartən], *m.* (**—s,** *pl.* ⁱ) front garden.

vorgeben [ˈfoːrgeːbən], *v.a. irr.* pretend; allow (in advance).

Vorgebirge [ˈfoːrgəbɪrgə], *n.* (**—s,** *no pl.*) cape, promontory.

vorgeblich [ˈfoːrgeːplɪç], *adj.* pretended; ostensible.

vorgefaßt [ˈfoːrgəfast], *adj.* preconceived.

Vorgefühl [ˈfoːrgəfyːl], *n.* (**—s,** *pl.* **—e**) presentiment.

vorgehen [ˈfoːrgeːən], *v.n. irr.* (*aux.* sein) advance, walk ahead; proceed; (*clock*) be fast, gain; (*fig.*) take precedence; occur, happen; *was geht hier vor?* what's going on here?

Vorgehen [ˈfoːrgeːən], *n.* (**—s,** *no pl.*) (course of) action, (manner of) procedure.

vorgenannt [ˈfoːrgənant], *adj.* aforenamed.

Vorgericht [ˈfoːrgərɪçt], *n.* (**—s,** *pl.* **—e**) hors d'œuvre, entrée.

Vorgeschichte [ˈfoːrgəʃɪçtə], *f.* (**—,** *no pl.*) prehistory; early history; antecedents.

vorgeschichtlich [ˈfoːrgəʃɪçtlɪç], *adj.* prehistoric.

Vorgeschmack [ˈfoːrgəʃmak], *m.* (**—s,** *no pl.*) foretaste.

Vorgesetzte [ˈfoːrgəzɛtstə], *m.* (**—n,** *pl.* **—n**) superior, senior; boss.

vorgestern [ˈfoːrgɛstərn], *adv.* the day before yesterday.

vorgreifen [ˈfoːrgraɪfən], *v.n. irr.* anticipate, forestall.

Vorhaben ['fo:rha:bən], *m.* (—s, *no pl.*) intention, purpose, design.

vorhaben ['fo:rha:bən], *v.a. irr.* intend; be busy with; *etwas mit einem —*, have designs on s.o.; have plans for s.o.

Vorhalle ['fo:rhalə], *f.* (—, *pl.* —n) vestibule, hall, porch.

vorhalten ['fo:rhaltən], *v.a. irr.* hold s.th. before s.o.; (*fig.*) remonstrate (with s.o. about s.th.); reproach. — *v.n.* last.

Vorhaltungen ['fo:rhaltuŋən], *f. pl.* remonstrances, expostulations.

vorhanden [for'handən], *adj.* at hand, present, in stock, on hand.

Vorhandensein [for'handənzain], *n.* (—s, *no pl.*) existence; availability.

Vorhang ['fo:rhaŋ], *m.* (—s, *pl.* ⁇e) curtain.

Vorhängeschloß ['fo:rhɛŋəʃlɔs], *n.* (—sses, *pl.* ⁇sser) padlock.

vorher ['fo:rhe:r], *adv.* before, beforehand, in advance.

vorhergehen [fo:r'he:rge:ən], *v.n. irr.* (*aux.* sein) go before, precede.

vorhergehend [fo:r'he:rge:ənt], *adj.* foregoing, aforesaid, preceding.

vorherig [fo:r'he:rɪç], *adj.* preceding, previous, former.

vorherrschen ['fo:rhɛrʃən], *v.n.* prevail, predominate.

vorhersagen [fo:r'he:rza:gən], *v.a.* predict, foretell.

vorhersehen [fo:r'he:rze:ən], *v.a. irr.* foresee.

vorheucheln ['fo:rhɔyçəln], *v.a. einem etwas —*, pretend s.th. to s.o.

vorhin [fo:r'hɪn], *adv.* just before, a short while ago.

Vorhof ['fo:rho:f], *m.* (—s, *pl.* ⁇e) forecourt.

Vorhölle ['fo:rhœlə], *f.* (—, *no pl.*) limbo.

Vorhut ['fo:rhu:t], *f.* (—, *no pl.*) vanguard.

vorig ['fo:rɪç], *adj.* former, preceding.

Vorjahr ['fo:rja:r], *n.* (—s, *pl.* ⁇e) preceding year.

vorjammern ['fo:rjamərn], *v.n. einem etwas —*, moan to s.o. about s.th.

Vorkämpfer ['fo:rkɛmpfər], *m.* (—s, *pl.* —) champion; pioneer.

vorkauen ['fo:rkauən], *v.a.* (*fig.*) predigest; spoon-feed.

Vorkaufsrecht ['fo:rkaufsrɛçt], *n.* (—s, *no pl.*) right of first refusal, right of pre-emption.

Vorkehrung ['fo:rke:ruŋ], *f.* (—, *pl.* —en) preparation; precaution; (*pl.*) arrangements.

Vorkenntnisse ['fo:rkɛntnɪsə], *f. pl.* rudiments, elements, grounding; previous knowledge.

vorkommen ['fo:rkɔmən], *v.n. irr.* (*aux.* sein) occur, happen; be found.

Vorkommnis ['fo:rkɔmnɪs], *n.* (—ses, *pl.* —se) occurrence, event, happening.

Vorkriegs- ['fo:rkri:ks], *prefix.* pre-war.

Vorladung ['fo:rla:duŋ], *f.* (—, *pl.* —en) summons, writ, subpœna.

Vorlage ['fo:rla:gə], *f.* (—, *pl.* —n) pattern, master-copy.

vorlagern ['fo:rla:gərn], *v.n.* (*aux.* sein) extend (in front of).

Vorland ['fo:rlant], *n.* (—s, *pl.* ⁇er) cape, foreland, foreshore.

vorlassen ['fo:rlasən], *v.a. irr.* give precedence to; admit, show in.

Vorläufer ['fo:rlɔyfər], *m.* (—s, *pl.* —) forerunner, precursor.

vorläufig ['fo:rlɔyfɪç], *adj.* provisional, preliminary, temporary. — *adv.* for the time being.

vorlaut ['fo:rlaut], *adj.* pert, forward.

Vorleben ['fo:rle:bən], *n.* (—s, *no pl.*) antecedents, past life.

vorlegen ['fo:rle:gən], *v.a.* put before s.o.; submit, propose; (*food*) serve.

Vorleger ['fo:rle:gər], *m.* (—s, *pl.* —) rug, mat.

Vorlegeschloß ['fo:rle:gəʃlɔs], *n.* (—sses, *pl.* ⁇sser) padlock.

vorlesen ['fo:rle:zən], *v.a. irr.* read aloud, read out.

Vorlesung ['fo:rle:zuŋ], *f.* (—, *pl.* —en) lecture.

vorletzte ['fo:rlɛtstə], *adj.* last but one, penultimate.

Vorliebe ['fo:rli:bə], *f.* (—, *no pl.*) predilection, partiality.

vorliebnehmen [fo:r'li:pne:mən], *v.n.* — *mit etwas*, be content with s.th., take pot luck.

vorliegen ['fo:rli:gən], *v.n. irr.* (*aux.* sein) be under consideration.

vorlügen ['fo:rly:gən], *v.a. irr. einem etwas —*, tell lies to s.o.

vormachen ['fo:rmaxən], *v.a. einem etwas —*, show s.o. how a thing is done; (*fig.*) play tricks on s.o., deceive s.o.

vormalig ['fo:rma:lɪç], *adj.* former, erstwhile, late.

vormals ['fo:rma:ls], *adv.* formerly.

Vormarsch ['fo:rmarʃ], *m.* (—es, *pl.* ⁇e) (*Mil.*) advance.

vormerken ['fo:rmɛrkən], *v.a.* make a note of, take down; book.

Vormittag ['fo:rmɪta:k], *m.* (—s, *pl.* —e) morning, forenoon.

vormittags ['fo:rmɪta:ks], *adv.* in the morning; before noon.

Vormund ['fo:rmunt], *m.* (—s, *pl.* ⁇er) guardian.

Vormundschaft ['fo:rmuntʃaft], *f.* (—, *pl.* —en) guardianship.

Vormundschaftsgericht ['fo:rmuntʃaftsgərɪçt], *n.* (—s, *pl.* —e) Court of Chancery.

vorn [forn], *adv.* before, in front of; in front; (*Naut.*) fore.

Vorname ['fo:rna:mə], *m.* (—ns, *pl.* —n) first name, Christian name.

vornehm ['fo:rne:m], *adj.* of noble birth, refined; distinguished, elegant.

vornehmen ['fo:rne:mən], *v.a. irr.* take in hand; *sich etwas —*, undertake s.th.; plan *or* intend to do s.th.

Vornehmheit ['fo:rne:mhaɪt], *f.* (—, *no pl.*) refinement, distinction.

vornehmlich ['fo:rne:mlɪç], *adv.* chiefly, principally, especially.

vornherein ['fɔrnhɛraɪn], *adv. von —*, from the first; from the beginning.

Vorort ['fo:rɔrt], *m.* (—s, *pl.* —e) suburb.

Vorortsbahn ['fo:rɔrtsba:n], *f.* (—, *pl.* —en) suburban (railway) line.

Vorplatz ['fo:rplats], *m.* (—es, *pl.* ⁀e) forecourt.

Vorposten ['fo:rpɔstən], *m.* (—s, *pl.* —) (*Mil.*) outpost, pickets.

Vorpostengefecht ['fo:rpɔstəngəfɛçt], *n.* (—s, *pl.* —e) outpost skirmish.

Vorprüfung ['fo:rpry:fuŋ], *f.* (—, *pl.* —en) preliminary examination.

Vorrang ['fo:rraŋ], *m.* (—s, *no pl.*) precedence, first place, priority.

Vorrat ['fo:rra:t], *m.* (—s, *pl.* ⁀e) store, stock, provision.

Vorratskammer ['fo:rra:tskamər], *f.* (—, *pl.* —n) store-room; larder.

Vorrecht ['fo:rreçt], *n.* (—s, *pl.* —e) privilege, prerogative.

Vorrede ['fo:rre:də], *f.* (—, *pl.* —n) preface; introduction.

Vorredner ['fo:rre:dnər], *m.* (—s, *pl.* —) previous speaker.

vorrichten ['fo:rrɪçtən], *v.a.* prepare, fix up, get ready.

Vorrichtung ['fo:rrɪçtuŋ], *f.* (—, *pl.* —en) appliance, device, contrivance.

vorrücken ['fo:rrykən], *v.a.* move forward, advance; (*clock*) put on. — *v.n.* (*aux.* sein) (*Mil.*) advance.

Vorsaal ['fo:rza:l], *m.* (—s, *pl.* —säle) hall, entrance hall.

Vorsatz ['fo:rzats], *m.* (—es, *pl.* ⁀e) purpose, design, intention.

vorsätzlich ['fo:rzɛtslɪç], *adj.* intentional, deliberate.

Vorschein ['fo:rʃaɪn], *m. zum — kommen*, turn up; appear.

vorschießen ['fo:rʃi:sən], *v.a. irr.* (*money*) advance, lend.

Vorschlag ['fo:rʃla:k], *m.* (—s, *pl.* ⁀e) proposal, offer, proposition.

vorschlagen ['fo:rʃla:gən], *v.a. irr.* put forward, propose, suggest; recommend.

vorschnell ['fo:rʃnɛl], *adj.* hasty, rash, precipitate.

vorschreiben ['fo:rʃraɪbən], *v.a. irr.* write out (for s.o.); (*fig.*) prescribe, order.

Vorschrift ['fo:rʃrɪft], *f.* (—, *pl.* —en) prescription, direction, order, command, regulation.

vorschriftsmäßig ['fo:rʃrɪftsmɛ:sɪç], *adj.* according to regulations.

vorschriftswidrig ['fo:rʃrɪftsvi:drɪç], *adj.* contrary to regulations.

Vorschub ['fo:rʃup], *m.* (—s, *no pl.*) aid, assistance; — *leisten*, countenance, encourage, abet.

Vorschule ['fo:rʃu:lə], *f.* (—, *pl.* —n) preparatory school.

Vorschuß ['fo:rʃus], *m.* (—sses, *pl.* ⁀sse) advance (of cash).

vorschützen ['fo:rʃytsən], *v.a.* use as a pretext, pretend, plead.

vorschweben ['fo:rʃve:bən], *v.n.* be present in o.'s mind.

vorsehen ['fo:rze:ən], *v.r. irr. sich —*, take heed, be careful, look out; beware.

Vorsehung ['fo:rze:uŋ], *f.* (—, *no pl.*) Providence.

vorsetzen ['fo:rzɛtsən], *v.a.* set before; serve; (*word*) prefix.

Vorsicht ['fo:rzɪçt], *f.* (—, *no pl.*) care, precaution, caution, circumspection.

vorsichtig ['fo:rzɪçtɪç], *adj.* cautious, careful, circumspect.

vorsichtshalber ['fo:rzɪçtshalbər], *adv.* as a precautionary measure.

Vorsichtsmaßnahme ['fo:rzɪçtsma:sna:mə], *f.* (—, *pl.* —n) precautionary measure, precaution.

Vorsilbe ['fo:rzɪlbə], *f.* (—, *pl.* —n) prefix.

vorsintflutlich ['fo:rzɪntflu:tlɪç], *adj.* antediluvian; (*fig.*) out-of-date.

Vorsitzende ['fo:rzɪtsəndə], *m.* (—n, *pl.* —n) chairman, president.

Vorsorge ['fo:rzɔrgə], *f.* (—, *no pl.*) care, precaution.

vorsorglich ['fo:rzɔrklɪç], *adj.* provident, careful.

vorspiegeln ['fo:rʃpi:gəln], *v.a. einem etwas —*, deceive s.o.; pretend.

Vorspiegelung ['fo:rʃpi:gəluŋ], *f.* (—, *pl.* —en) pretence; — *falscher Tatsachen*, false pretences.

Vorspiel ['fo:rʃpi:l], *n.* (—s, *pl.* —e) prelude; overture.

vorsprechen ['fo:rʃprɛçən], *v.n. irr. bei einem —*, call on s.o. — *v.a. einem etwas —*, say s.th. for s.o.; repeat.

vorspringen ['fo:rʃprɪŋən], *v.n. irr.* (*aux.* sein) leap forward; jut out, project.

Vorsprung ['fo:rʃpruŋ], *m.* (—s, *pl.* ⁀e) projection, prominence; (*fig.*) advantage (over), start, lead.

Vorstadt ['fo:rʃtat], *f.* (—, *pl.* ⁀e) suburb.

vorstädtisch ['fo:rʃtɛtɪʃ], *adj.* suburban.

Vorstand ['fo:rʃtant], *m.* (—s, *pl.* ⁀e) board of directors; director, principal.

Vorstandssitzung ['fo:rʃtantszɪtsuŋ], *f.* (—, *pl.* —en) board meeting.

vorstehen ['fo:rʃte:ən], *v.n. irr.* project, protrude; (*office*) administer, govern, direct, manage.

vorstehend ['fo:rʃte:ənt], *adj.* projecting, protruding; above-mentioned, foregoing.

Vorsteher ['fo:rʃte:ər], *m.* (—s, *pl.* —) director, manager; supervisor.

Vorsteherdrüse ['fo:rʃte:ərdry:zə], *f.* (—, *pl.* —n) prostate gland.

vorstellbar ['fo:rʃtɛlba:r], *adj.* imaginable.

vorstellen ['fo:rʃtɛlən], *v.a.* (*thing*) put forward; (*person*) present, introduce; (*Theat.*) impersonate; represent; (*clock*) put on; *sich etwas —*, visualise s.th., imagine s.th.

vorstellig ['foːrʃtɛlɪç], *adj.* — *werden*, petition; lodge a complaint.
Vorstellung ['foːrʃtɛluŋ], *f.* (—, *pl.* —en) (*person*) presentation, introduction; (*Theat.*) performance; idea, notion, image; representation.
Vorstellungsvermögen ['foːrʃtɛluŋsfɛrˈmøːɡən], *n.* (—s, *no pl.*) imagination, imaginative faculty.
Vorstoß ['foːrʃtoːs], *m.* (—es, *pl.* ⁼e) (*Mil.*) sudden advance, thrust.
vorstoßen ['foːrʃtoːsən], *v.a. irr.* push forward. — *v.n.* (*aux.* sein) (*Mil.*) advance suddenly.
Vorstrafe ['foːrʃtraːfə], *f.* (—, *pl.* —n) previous conviction.
vorstrecken ['foːrʃtrɛkən], *v.a.* stretch forward, protrude; (*money*) advance.
Vorstufe ['foːrʃtuːfə], *f.* (—, *pl.* —n) first step.
Vortänzerin ['foːrtɛntsərɪn], *f.* (—, *pl.* —nen) prima ballerina.
Vorteil ['fɔrtaɪl], *m.* (—s, *pl.* —e) advantage, profit.
vorteilhaft ['fɔrtaɪlhaft], *adj.* advantageous, profitable, lucrative.
Vortrag ['foːrtraːk], *m.* (—s, *pl.* ⁼e) recitation, delivery, rendering; statement, report; talk, speech, lecture.
vortragen ['foːrtraːɡən], *v.a. irr.* make a report; (*poem*) recite, declaim; make a request; (*Comm.*) carry forward; lecture on.
Vortragskunst ['foːrtraːkskunst], *f.* (—, *no pl.*) elocution; (art of) public speaking.
vortrefflich ['foːrtrɛflɪç], *adj.* excellent, splendid.
Vortrefflichkeit ['foːrtrɛflɪçkaɪt], *f.* (—, *no pl.*) excellence.
vortreten ['foːrtreːtən], *v.n. irr.* (*aux.* sein) step forward.
Vortritt ['foːrtrɪt], *m.* (—s, *no pl.*) precedence.
vorüber [fɔrˈyːbər], *adv.* past, gone, over, finished, done with.
vorübergehen [fɔrˈyːbərɡeːən], *v.n. irr.* (*aux.* sein) pass by, pass, go past.
vorübergehend [fɔrˈyːbərɡeːənt], *adj.* passing, temporary, transitory.
Vorübung ['foːryːbuŋ], *f.* (—, *pl.* —en) preliminary exercise.
Voruntersuchung ['foːruntərzuːxuŋ], *f.* (—, *pl.* —en) preliminary inquiry; trial in magistrate's court.
Vorurteil ['foːrurtaɪl], *n.* (—s, *pl.* —e) bias, prejudice.
vorurteilslos ['foːrurtaɪlsloːs], *adj.* impartial, unprejudiced, unbiased.
Vorvater ['foːrfaːtər], *m.* (—s, *pl.* ⁼) progenitor, ancestor.
Vorverkauf ['foːrfɛrkauf], *m.* (—s, *pl.* ⁼e) booking in advance, advance booking.
vorwagen ['foːrvaːɡən], *v.r. sich* —, dare to go (*or* come) forward.
vorwaltend ['foːrvaltənt], *adj.* prevailing, predominating.

Vorwand ['foːrvant], *m.* (—s, *pl.* ⁼e) pretence, pretext; *unter dem* —, under pretence of.
vorwärts ['foːrvɛrts], *adv.* forward.
vorwärtskommen ['foːrvɛrtskɔmən], *v.n. irr.* (*aux.* sein) make headway, get on.
vorweg [fɔrˈvɛk], *adv.* before.
vorwegnehmen [fɔrˈvɛkneːmən], *v.a. irr.* anticipate.
vorweisen ['foːrvaɪzən], *v.a. irr.* show, produce, exhibit.
Vorwelt ['foːrvɛlt], *f.* (—, *no pl.*) primitive world; former ages.
vorweltlich ['foːrvɛltlɪç], *adj.* primæval, prehistoric.
vorwerfen ['foːrvɛrfən], *v.a. irr. einem etwas* —, blame s.o. for s.th.; charge s.o. with s.th., tax s.o. with s.th.
vorwiegen ['foːrviːɡən], *v.n. irr.* prevail.
vorwiegend ['foːrviːɡənt], *adv.* mostly, for the most part.
Vorwissen ['foːrvɪsən], *n.* (—s, *no pl.*) foreknowledge, prescience.
Vorwitz ['foːrvɪts], *m.* (—es, *no pl.*) pertness.
vorwitzig ['foːrvɪtsɪç], *adj.* forward, pert, meddlesome.
Vorwort (1) ['foːrvɔrt], *n.* (—s, *pl.* —e) preface.
Vorwort (2) ['foːrvɔrt], *n.* (—s, *pl.* ⁼er) (*Gram.*) preposition.
Vorwurf ['foːrvurf], *m.* (—s, *pl.* ⁼e) reproach; theme, subject.
vorwurfsfrei ['foːrvurfsfraɪ], *adj.* free from blame, irreproachable.
vorwurfsvoll ['foːrvurfsfɔl], *adj.* reproachful.
Vorzeichen ['foːrtsaɪxən], *n.* (—s, *pl.* —) omen, token; (*Maths.*) sign.
vorzeigen ['foːrtsaɪɡən], *v.a.* show, produce, exhibit, display.
Vorzeit ['foːrtsaɪt], *f.* (—, *no pl.*) antiquity, olden times.
vorzeiten [foːrˈtsaɪtən], *adv.* (*Poet.*) in olden times, formerly.
vorzeitig ['foːrtsaɪtɪç], *adj.* premature.
vorziehen ['foːrtsiːən], *v.a. irr.* prefer.
Vorzimmer ['foːrtsɪmər], *n.* (—s, *pl.* —) anteroom, antechamber.
Vorzug ['foːrtsuːk], *m.* (—s, *pl.* ⁼e) preference, advantage; excellence, superiority.
vorzüglich [fɔrˈtsyːklɪç], *adj.* superior, excellent, exquisite.
Vorzüglichkeit [fɔrˈtsyːklɪçkaɪt], *f.* (—, *no pl.*) excellence, superiority.
Vorzugsaktie ['foːrtsuːksaktsjə], *f.* (—, *pl.* —n) preference share.
vorzugsweise ['foːrtsuːksvaɪzə], *adv.* for choice, preferably.
vulgär [vulˈɡɛːr], *adj.* vulgar.
Vulkan [vulˈkaːn], *m.* (—s, *pl.* —e) volcano.
vulkanisch [vulˈkaːnɪʃ], *adj.* volcanic.

271

W

W [ve:] *n.* (—s, *pl.* —s) the letter W.

Waage ['va:gə], *f.* (—, *pl.* —n) balance, pair of scales.

waag(e)recht ['va:g(ə)rɛçt], *adj.* horizontal.

Waagschale ['va:kʃa:lə], *f.* (—, *pl.* —n) pan of a balance.

Wabe ['va:bə], *f.* (—, *pl.* —n) honeycomb.

Waberlohe ['va:bərlo:ə], *f.* (—, *no pl.*) (*Poet.*) flickering flames, magic fire.

wach [vax], *adj.* awake; alert; *völlig* —, wide awake.

Wachdienst ['vaxdi:nst], *m.* (—es, *no pl.*) guard, sentry duty.

Wache ['vaxə], *f.* (—, *pl.* —n) guard, watch; (*person*) sentry, sentinel.

wachen ['vaxən], *v.n.* be awake; guard; — *über*, watch, keep an eye on.

Wacholder [va'xɔldər], *m.* (—s, *pl.* —) (*Bot.*) juniper.

wachrufen [vax'ru:fən], *v.a. irr.* (*fig.*) call to mind.

Wachs [vaks], *n.* (—es, *no pl.*) wax.

wachsam ['vaxza:m], *adj.* watchful, vigilant.

Wachsamkeit ['vaxza:mkaIt], *f.* (—, *no pl.*) watchfulness, vigilance.

Wachsbild ['vaksbIlt], *n.* (—s, *pl.* —er) waxen image.

wachsen ['vaksən], *v.n. irr.* (*aux.* sein) grow, increase.

wächsern ['vɛksərn], *adj.* waxen, made of wax.

Wachsfigur ['vaksfigu:r], *f.* (—, *pl.* —en) wax figure.

Wachsfigurenkabinett ['vaksfigu:rənkabinɛt], *n.* (—s, *pl.* —e) waxworks.

Wachsleinwand ['vakslaInvant], *f.* (—, *no pl.*) oil-cloth.

Wachstuch ['vakstu:x], *n.* (—(e)s, *no pl.*) oil-cloth; American cloth.

Wachstum ['vakstu:m], *n.* (—s, *no pl.*) growth, increase.

Wacht [vaxt], *f.* (—, *pl.* —en) watch, guard.

Wachtdienst ['vaxtdi:nst] *see* **Wachdienst**.

Wachtel ['vaxtəl], *f.* (—, *pl.* —n) (*Orn.*) quail.

Wachtelhund ['vaxtəlhunt], *m.* (—(e)s, *pl.* —e) (*Zool.*) spaniel.

Wächter ['vɛçtər], *m.* (—s, *pl.* —) watchman, warder, guard.

wachthabend ['vaxtha:bənt], *adj.* on duty.

Wachtmeister ['vaxtmaIstər], *m.* (—s, *pl.* —) sergeant.

Wachtparade [vaxtpara:də], *f.* (—, *pl.* —n) mounting of the guard.

Wachtposten ['vaxtpɔstən], *m.* (—s, *pl.* —) guard, picket.

Wachtraum ['vaxtraum], *m.* (—s, *pl.* ⁻e) day-dream, waking dream.

Wachtturm ['vaxtturm], *m.* (—s, *pl.* ⁻e) watch-tower.

wackeln ['vakəln], *v.n.* totter, shake, wobble.

wacker ['vakər], *adj.* gallant, brave, valiant; upright.

wacklig ['vaklIç], *adj.* tottering, shaky; (*furniture*) rickety; (*tooth*) loose.

Wade ['va:də], *f.* (—, *pl.* —n) calf (of the leg).

Wadenbein ['va:dənbaIn], *n.* (—s, *pl.* —e) shin-bone.

Waffe ['vafə], *f.* (—, *pl.* —n) weapon, arm; *die —n strecken,* surrender.

Waffel ['vafəl], *f.* (—, *pl.* —n) wafer; waffle.

Waffeleisen ['vafəlaIzən], *n.* (—s, *pl.* —) waffle-iron.

Waffenbruder ['vafənbru:dər], *m.* (—s, *pl.* ⁻) brother-in-arms, comrade.

waffenfähig ['vafənfɛ:Iç], *adj.* able to bear arms.

Waffengewalt ['vafəngəvalt], *f.* (—, *no pl.*) *mit* —, by force of arms.

Waffenglück ['vafənglyk], *n.* (—s, *no pl.*) fortunes of war.

Waffenrock ['vafənrɔk], *m.* (—s, *pl.* ⁻e) tunic.

Waffenruf ['vafənru:f], *m.* (—s, *no pl.*) call to arms.

Waffenschmied [vafənʃmi:t], *m.* (—s, *pl.* —e) armourer.

Waffenstillstand ['vafənʃtIlʃtant], *m.* (—s, *no pl.*) armistice, truce.

waffnen ['vafnən], *v.a.* arm.

Wage *see* **Waage**.

Wagebalken ['va:gəbalkən], *m.* (—s, *pl.* —) scale-beam.

Wagen ['va:gən], *m.* (—s, *pl.* —) vehicle, conveyance, carriage, coach, car, cab, wagon, cart, truck, van, dray.

wagen ['va:gən], *v.a., v.n.* dare, venture, risk.

wägen ['vɛ:gən], *v.a., irr.* weigh, balance; (*words*) consider.

Wagenverkehr ['va:gənferke:r], *m.* (—s, *no pl.*) vehicular traffic.

wagerecht *see* **waagerecht**.

Waggon [va'gõ], *m.* (—s, *pl.* —s) railway car, goods van, freight car.

waghalsig ['va:khalzIç], *adj.* foolhardy, rash, daring.

Wagnis ['va:knIs], *n.* (—ses, *pl.* —se) venture, risky undertaking; risk.

Wagschale *see* **Waagschale**.

Wahl [va:l], *f.* (—, *pl.* —en) choice; election; selection; alternative.

Wahlakt ['va:lakt], *m.* (—s, *pl.* —e) poll, election.

Wahlaufruf /['va:laufru:f], *m.* (—s, *pl.* —e) manifesto, election address.

wählbar ['vɛ:lba:r], *adj.* eligible.

Wählbarkeit ['vɛ:lba:rkaIt], *f.* (—, *no pl.*) eligibility.

wahlberechtigt [ˈvaːlbərɛçtɪçt], *adj.* entitled to vote.

wählen [ˈvɛːlən], *v.a.* choose; *(Parl.)* elect; *(Telephone)* dial.

Wähler [ˈvɛːlər], *m.* (—s, *pl.* —) elector; constituent.

wählerisch [ˈvɛːlərɪʃ], *adj.* fastidious, particular.

Wählerschaft [ˈvɛːlərʃaft], *f.* (—, *pl.* —en) constituency.

wahlfähig [ˈvaːlfɛːɪç], *adj.* eligible.

Wahlliste [ˈvaːllɪstə], *f.* (—, *pl.* —n) electoral list, register (of electors).

wahllos [ˈvaːlloːs], *adj.* indiscriminate.

Wahlrecht [ˈvaːlrɛçt], *n.* (—s, *no pl.*) franchise.

Wahlspruch [ˈvaːlʃprux], *m.* (—s, *pl.* ˝e) device, motto.

wahlunfähig [ˈvaːlunfɛːɪç], *adj.* ineligible.

Wahlurne [ˈvaːlurnə], *f.* (—, *pl.* —n) ballot-box.

Wahlverwandtschaft [ˈvaːlfɛrvantʃaft], *f.* (—, *no pl.*) elective affinity, congeniality.

Wahlzettel [ˈvaːltsɛtəl], *m.* (—s, *pl.* —) ballot-paper.

Wahn [vaːn], *m.* (—(e)s, *no pl.*) delusion.

Wahnbild [ˈvaːnbɪlt], *n.* (—s, *pl.* —er) hallucination, delusion; phantasm.

wähnen [ˈvɛːnən], *v.a.* fancy, believe.

Wahnsinn [ˈvaːnzɪn], *m.* (—s, *no pl.*) madness, lunacy.

wahnsinnig [ˈvaːnzɪnɪç], *adj.* insane, mad, lunatic; *(coll.)* terrific.

Wahnsinnige [ˈvaːnzɪnɪgə], *m.* (—n, *pl.* —n) madman, lunatic.

Wahnwitz [ˈvaːnvɪts], *m.* (—es, *no pl.*) madness.

wahnwitzig [ˈvaːnvɪtsɪç], *adj.* mad.

wahr [vaːr], *adj.* true, real, genuine.

wahren [ˈvaːrən], *v.a.* guard, watch over.

währen [ˈvɛːrən], *v.n.* last.

während [ˈvɛːrənt], *prep.* *(Genit.)* during.— *conj.* while, whilst; whereas.

wahrhaft [ˈvaːrhaft], *adj.* truthful, veracious.

wahrhaftig [vaːrˈhaftɪç], *adv.* truly, really, in truth.

Wahrhaftigkeit [vaːrˈhaftɪçkaɪt], *f.* (—, *no pl.*) truthfulness, veracity.

Wahrheit [ˈvaːrhaɪt], *f.* (—, *pl.* —en) truth; reality; *die — sagen,* tell the truth.

Wahrheitsliebe [ˈvaːrhaɪtsliːbə], *f.* (—, *no pl.*) love of truth, truthfulness.

wahrlich [ˈvaːrlɪç], *adv.* truly, in truth.

wahrnehmbar [ˈvaːrneːmbaːr], *adj.* perceptible.

wahrnehmen [ˈvaːrneːmən], *v.a. irr.* perceive, observe.

Wahrnehmung [ˈvaːrneːmuŋ], *f.* (—, *pl.* —en) perception, observation.

wahrsagen [ˈvaːrzaːgən], *v.n.* prophesy; tell fortunes.

Wahrsager [ˈvaːrzaːgər], *m.* (—s, *pl.* —) fortune-teller, soothsayer.

wahrscheinlich [vaːrˈʃaɪnlɪç], *adj.* likely, probable; *es wird — regnen,* it will probably rain.

Wahrscheinlichkeit [vaːrˈʃaɪnlɪçkaɪt], *f.* (—, *pl.* —en) likelihood, probability.

Wahrung [ˈvaːruŋ], *f.* (—, *no pl.*) protection, preservation, maintenance.

Währung [ˈvɛːruŋ], *f.* (—, *pl.* —en) currency, standard.

Wahrzeichen [ˈvaːrtsaɪçən], *n.* (—s, *pl.* —) landmark; *(fig.)* sign, token.

Waibling(er) [ˈvaɪblɪŋ(ər)], *m.* Ghibelline.

Waidmann [ˈvaɪtman], *m.* (—s, *pl.* ˝er) huntsman, hunter.

waidmännisch [ˈvaɪtmɛnɪʃ], *adj.* sportsmanlike.

Waise [ˈvaɪzə], *f.* (—, *pl.* —n) orphan.

Waisenhaus [ˈvaɪzənhaus], *n.* (—es, *pl.* ˝er) orphanage.

Waisenmutter [ˈvaɪzənmutər], *f.* (—, *pl.* ˝) foster-mother.

Waisenvater [ˈvaɪzənfaːtər], *m.* (—s, *pl.* ˝) foster-father.

Wald [valt], *m.* (—es, *pl.* ˝er) wood, forest; woodland.

Waldbrand [ˈvaltbrant], *m.* (—s, *pl.* ˝e) forest-fire.

Waldlichtung [ˈvaltlɪçtuŋ], *f.* (—, *pl.* —en) forest glade, clearing.

Waldmeister [ˈvaltmaɪstər], *m.* (—s, *no pl.*) *(Bot.)* woodruff.

Waldung [ˈvalduŋ], *f.* (—, *pl.* —en) woods, woodland.

Waldwiese [ˈvaltviːzə], *f.* (—, *pl.* —en) forest-glade.

Walfisch [ˈvaːlfɪʃ], *m.* (—es, *pl.* —e) whale.

Walfischfang [ˈvaːlfɪʃfaŋ], *m.* (—s, *no pl.*) whaling.

Walfischfänger [ˈvaːlfɪʃfɛŋər], *m.* (—s, *pl.* —) whaler, whale fisher.

Walfischtran [ˈvaːlfɪʃtraːn], *m.* (—s, *no pl.*) train-oil.

Walküre [valˈkyːrə], *f.* (—, *pl.* —n) Valkyrie.

Wall [val], *m.* (—(e)s, *pl.* ˝e) rampart, dam, vallum; mound.

Wallach [ˈvalax], *m.* (—s, *pl.* ˝e) castrated horse, gelding.

wallen [ˈvalən], *v.n.* bubble, boil up; wave, undulate.

Wallfahrer [ˈvalfaːrər], *m.* (—s, *pl.* —) pilgrim.

Wallfahrt [ˈvalfaːrt], *f.* (—, *pl.* —en) pilgrimage.

wallfahrten [ˈvalfaːrtən], *v.n.* *(aux. sein)* go on a pilgrimage.

Walnuß [ˈvalnus], *f.* (—, *pl.* ˝sse) *(Bot.)* walnut.

Walpurgisnacht [valˈpurgɪsnaxt], *f.* witches' sabbath.

Walroß [ˈvalrɔs], *n.* (—sses, *pl.* —sse) sea-horse, walrus.

Walstatt [ˈvalʃtat], *f.* (—, *pl.* ˝en) *(Poet.)* battlefield.

walten [ˈvaltən], *v.n.* rule; *seines Amtes —,* do o.'s duty, carry out o.'s duties.

Walze [ˈvaltsə], *f.* (—, *pl.* —n) roller, cylinder.

walzen

walzen ['valtsən], *v.a.* roll. — *v.n.* waltz.

wälzen ['vɛltsən], *v.a.* roll, turn about.

walzenförmig ['valtsənfœrmɪç], *adj.* cylindrical.

Walzer ['valtsər], *m.* (—s, *pl.* —) waltz.

Wälzer ['vɛltsər], *m.* (—s, *pl.* —) tome; thick volume.

Walzwerk ['valtsvɛrk], *n.* (—s, *pl.* —e) rolling-mill.

Wams [vams], *n.* (—es, *pl.* ⁝e) (*obs.*) doublet, jerkin.

Wand [vant], *f.* (—, *pl.* ⁝e) wall; side.

Wandbekleidung ['vantbəklaiduŋ], *f.* (—, *pl.* —en) wainscot, panelling.

Wandel ['vandəl], *m.* (—s, *no pl.*) mutation, change; behaviour, conduct; *Handel und* —, trade and traffic.

wandelbar ['vandəlba:r], *adj.* changeable, inconstant.

Wandelgang ['vandəlgaŋ], *m.* (—s, *pl.* ⁝e) lobby; lounge, foyer; (*in the open*) covered way, covered walk.

wandeln ['vandəln], *v.a.* (*aux.* haben) change. — *v.n.* (*aux.* sein) walk, wander. — *v.r. sich* —, change.

Wanderbursche ['vandərburʃə], *m.* (—n, *pl.* —n) travelling journeyman.

Wanderer ['vandərər], *m.* (—s, *pl.* —) wanderer, traveller; hiker.

Wanderleben ['vandərle:bən], *n.* (—s, *no pl.*) nomadic life.

Wanderlehrer ['vandərle:rər], *m.* (—s, *pl.* —) itinerant teacher.

Wanderlust ['vandərlust], *f.* (—, *no pl.*) urge to travel; call of the open.

wandern ['vandərn], *v.n.* (*aux.* sein) wander, travel; migrate.

Wanderschaft ['vandərʃaft], *f.* (—, *no pl.*) wanderings.

Wandersmann ['vandərsman], *m.* (—s, *pl.* ⁝er) wayfarer.

Wandertruppe ['vandərtrupə], *f.* (—, *pl.* —n) (*Theat.*) strolling players.

Wanderung ['vandəruŋ], *f.* (—, *pl.* —en) walking tour; hike.

Wandervolk ['vandərfɔlk], *n.* (—(e)s, *pl.* ⁝er) nomadic tribe.

Wandgemälde ['vantgəmɛ:ldə], *n.* (—s, *pl.* —) mural painting, mural.

Wandlung ['vandluŋ], *f.* (—, *pl.* —en) transformation; (*Theol.*) transubstantiation.

Wandspiegel ['vantʃpi:gəl], *m.* (—s, *pl.* —) pier-glass.

Wandtafel ['vantta:fəl], *f.* (—, *pl.* —n) blackboard.

Wange ['vaŋə], *f.* (—, *pl.* —n) cheek.

Wankelmut ['vaŋkəlmu:t], *m.* (—s, *no pl.*) fickleness, inconstancy.

wankelmütig ['vaŋkəlmy:tɪç], *adj.* inconstant, fickle.

wanken ['vaŋkən], *v.n.* totter, stagger; (*fig.*) waver, be irresolute.

wann [van], *adv.* when; *dann und* —, now and then, sometimes.

Wanne ['vanə], *f.* (—, *pl.* —n) tub, bath.

wannen ['vanən], *adv.* (*obs.*) *von* —, whence.

Wannenbad ['vanənba:t], *n.* (—s, *pl.* ⁝er) bath.

Wanst [vanst], *m.* (—es, *pl.* ⁝e) belly, paunch.

Wanze ['vantsə], *f.* (—, *pl.* —n) (*Ent.*) bug.

Wappen ['vapən], *n.* (—s, *pl.* —) crest, coat-of-arms.

Wappenbild ['vapənbɪlt], *n.* (—s, *pl.* —er) heraldic figure.

Wappenkunde ['vapənkundə], *f.* (—, *no pl.*) heraldry.

Wappenschild ['vapənʃɪlt], *m.* (—s, *pl.* —e) escutcheon.

Wappenspruch ['vapənʃprux], *m.* (—(e)s, *pl.* ⁝e) motto, device.

wappnen ['vapnən], *v.a.* arm.

Ware ['va:rə], *f.* (—, *pl.* —n) article, commodity; (*pl.*) merchandise, goods, wares.

Warenausfuhr ['va:rənausfu:r], *f.* (—, *no pl.*) exportation, export.

Warenbörse ['va:rənbœrzə], *f.* (—, *pl.* —n) commodity exchange.

Wareneinfuhr ['va:rənainfu:r], *f.* (—, *no pl.*) importation, import.

Warenhaus ['va:rənhaus], *n.* (—es, *pl.* ⁝er) department store, emporium; (*Am.*) store.

Warenlager ['va:rənla:gər], *n.* (—s, *pl.* —) magazine; stock; warehouse.

Warensendung ['va:rənzɛnduŋ], *f.* (—, *pl.* —en) consignment of goods.

Warentausch ['va:rəntauʃ], *m.* (—es, *no pl.*) barter.

warm [varm], *adj.* warm, hot.

warmblütig ['varmbly:tɪç], *adj.* warm-blooded.

Wärme ['vɛrmə], *f.* (—, *no pl.*) warmth; heat.

Wärmeeinheit ['vɛrməainhait], *f.* (—, *pl.* —en) thermal unit; calorie.

Wärmegrad ['vɛrməgra:t], *m.* (—s, *pl.* —e) degree of heat; temperature.

Wärmeleiter ['vɛrməlaitər], *m.* (—s, *pl.* —) conductor of heat.

Wärmemesser ['vɛrməmɛsər], *m.* (—s, *pl.* —) thermometer.

wärmen ['vɛrmən], *v.a.* warm, heat.

Wärmflasche ['vɛrmflaʃə], *f.* (—, *pl.* —n) hot-water bottle.

warnen ['varnən], *v.a.* warn; caution.

Warnung ['varnuŋ], *f.* (—, *pl.* —en) warning, caution, admonition; notice.

Warschau ['varʃau], *n.* Warsaw.

Warte ['vartə], *f.* (—, *pl.* —n) watch-tower, belfry, look-out.

Wartegeld ['vartəgɛlt], *n.* (—s, *pl.* —er) half pay; (*ship*) demurrage charges.

warten ['vartən], *v.n.* wait; — *auf* (*Acc.*), wait for, await. — *v.a.* tend, nurse.

Wärter ['vɛrtər], *m.* (—s, *pl.* —) keeper, attendant; warder; male nurse.

Wartesaal ['vartəza:l], *m.* (—s, *pl.* ⁝säle) (*Railw.*) waiting-room.

Wartung ['vartuŋ], *f.* (—, *no pl.*) nursing, attendance; servicing; maintenance.

warum [va'rum], *adv.*, *conj.* why, for what reason.

Warze ['vartsə], *f.* (—, *pl.* —n) wart.

was [vas], *interr. pron.* what? — *rel. pron.* what, that which.

Waschanstalt ['vaʃanʃtalt], *f.* (—, *pl.* —en) laundry.

waschbar ['vaʃba:r], *adj.* washable.

Waschbär ['vaʃbɛ:r], *m.* (—en, *pl.* —en) (*Zool.*) raccoon.

Waschbecken ['vaʃbɛkən], *n.* (—s, *pl.* —) wash-basin.

Wäsche ['vɛʃə], *f.* (—, *no pl.*) washing, wash, laundry; linen.

waschecht ['vaʃɛçt], *adj.* washable; (*fig.*) genuine.

waschen ['vaʃən], *v.a. irr.* wash.

Wäscherin ['vɛʃərin], *f.* (—, *pl.* —nen) washerwoman, laundress.

Waschhaus ['vaʃhaus], *n.* (—es, *pl.* ·'er) wash-house, laundry; (*reg. trade name*) launderette.

Waschkorb ['vaʃkɔrp], *m.* (—s, *pl.* ·'e) clothes-basket.

Waschküche ['vaʃkyçə], *f.* (—, *pl.* —en) wash-house.

Waschlappen ['vaʃlapən], *m.* (—s, *pl.* —) face-flannel, face-cloth, face-washer; (*fig.*) milksop.

Waschleder ['vaʃle:dər], *n.* (—s, *no pl.*) chamois leather, wash-leather.

Waschmaschine ['vaʃmaʃi:nə], *f.* (—, *pl.* —n) washing-machine.

Waschtisch ['vaʃtiʃ], *m.* (—es, *pl.* —e) wash-stand.

Waschwanne ['vaʃvanə], *f.* (—, *pl.* —n) wash-tub.

Wasser ['vasər], *n.* (—s, *pl.* —) water; *stille — sind tief*, still waters run deep.

wasserarm ['vasərarm], *adj.* waterless, dry, arid.

Wasserbehälter ['vasərbəhɛltər], *m.* (—s, *pl.* —) reservoir, cistern, tank.

Wasserblase ['vasərbla:zə], *f.* (—, *pl.* —en) bubble.

Wässerchen ['vɛsərçən], *n.* (—s, *pl.* —) brook, streamlet; *er sieht aus, als ob er kein — trüben könnte*, he looks as if butter would not melt in his mouth.

Wasserdampf ['vasərdampf], *m.* (—(e)s, *no pl.*) steam.

wasserdicht ['vasərdiçt], *adj.* water-proof.

Wasserdruck ['vasərdruk], *m.* (—s, *no pl.*) hydrostatic pressure, hydraulic pressure.

Wassereimer ['vasəraimər], *m.* (—s, *pl.* —) pail, water-bucket.

Wasserfall ['vasərfal], *m.* (—s, *pl.* ·'e) waterfall, cataract, cascade.

Wasserfarbe ['vasərfarbə], *f.* (—, *pl.* —n) water-colour.

Wasserheilanstalt ['vasərhailanʃtalt], *f.* (—, *pl.* —en) spa.

wässerig ['vɛsəriç], *adj.* watery; (*fig.*) insipid, flat, diluted.

Wasserkanne ['vasərkanə], *f.* (—, *pl.* —n) pitcher, ewer.

Wasserkessel ['vasərkɛsəl], *m.* (—s, *pl.* —) boiler; kettle.

Wasserkopf ['vasərkɔpf], *m.* (—(e)s, *pl.* ·'e) (*Med.*) hydrocephalus.

Wasserkur ['vasərku:r], *f.* (—, *pl.* —en) hydropathic treatment.

Wasserleitung ['vasərlaituŋ], *f.* (—, *pl.* —en) aqueduct; water main.

Wasserlinsen ['vasərlinzən], *f. pl.* (*Bot.*) duck-weed.

Wassermann ['vasərman], *m.* (—s, *no pl.*) (*Astron.*) Aquarius.

wässern ['vɛsərn], *v.a.* water, irrigate, soak.

Wassernixe ['vasərniksə], *f.* (—, *pl.* —n) water nymph.

Wassernot ['vasərno:t], *f.* (—, *no pl.*) drought, scarcity of water.

Wasserrabe ['vasərra:bə], *m.* (—n, *pl.* —n) (*Orn.*) cormorant.

Wasserrinne ['vasərrinə], *f.* (—, *pl.* —n) gutter.

Wasserröhre ['vasərrø:rə], *f.* (—, *pl.* —n) water-pipe.

Wasserscheide ['vasərʃaidə], *f.* (—, *pl.* —n) watershed.

Wasserscheu ['vasərʃɔy], *f.* (—, *no pl.*) hydrophobia.

Wasserspiegel ['vasərʃpi:gəl], *m.* (—s, *pl.* —) water-level.

Wasserspritze ['vasərʃpritsə], *f.* (— *pl.* —n) squirt; sprinkler.

Wasserstand ['vasərʃtant], *m.* (—s, *no pl.*) water-level.

Wasserstiefel ['vasərʃti:fəl], *m.* (—s, *pl.* —) wader, gumboot.

Wasserstoff ['vasərʃtɔf], *m.* (—(e)s, *no pl.*) hydrogen.

Wassersucht ['vasərzuxt], *f.* (—, *no pl.*) dropsy.

Wassersuppe ['vasərzupə], *f.* (—, *pl.* —n) water-gruel.

Wässerung ['vɛsəruŋ], *f.* (—, *pl.* —en) watering, irrigation.

Wasserverdrängung ['vasərfɛrdrɛŋuŋ], *f.* (—, *no pl.*) displacement (of water).

Wasserwaage ['vasərva:gə], *f.* (—, *pl.* —n) water-balance, water-level; hydrometer.

Wasserweg ['vasərve:k], *m.* (—s, *pl.* —e) waterway; *auf dem —*, by water, by sea.

Wasserzeichen ['vasərtsaiçən], *n.* (—s, *pl.* —) watermark.

waten ['va:tən], *v.n.* (*aux.* sein) wade.

watscheln ['va:tʃəln], *v.n.* (*aux.* sein) waddle.

Watt (1) [vat], *n.* (—s, *pl.* —e) sand-bank; (*pl.*) shallows.

Watt (2) [vat], *n.* (—s, *pl.* —) (*Elec.*) watt.

Watte ['vatə], *f.* (—, *no pl.*) wadding, cotton-wool.

wattieren [va'ti:rən], *v.a.* pad.

Webe ['ve:bə], *f.* (—, *pl.* —n) web, weft.

weben ['ve:bən], *v.a.* weave.

Weber ['ve:bər], *m.* (—s, *pl.* —) weaver.

Weberei [ve:bə'rai], *f.* (—, *pl.* —en) weaving-mill.

Weberschiffchen [ˈveːbərʃɪfçən], *n.* (—s, *pl.* —) shuttle.

Wechsel [ˈvɛksəl], *m.* (—s, *pl.* —) change; turn, variation; vicissitude; (*Comm.*) bill of exchange.

Wechselbalg [ˈvɛksəlbalk], *m.* (—s, *pl.* ˇe) changeling.

Wechselbank [ˈvɛksəlbaŋk], *f.* (—, *pl.* ˇe) discount-bank.

Wechselbeziehung [ˈvɛksəlbətsiːuŋ], (—, *pl.* —en) reciprocal relation, correlation.

Wechselfälle [ˈvɛksəlfɛlə], *m. pl.* vicissitudes.

Wechselfieber [ˈvɛksəlfiːbər], *n.* (—s, *pl.* —) intermittent fever.

Wechselfolge [ˈvɛksəlfɔlgə], *f.* (—, *no pl.*) rotation, alternation.

Wechselgeld [ˈvɛksəlgɛlt], *n.* (—(e)s, *no pl.*) change.

wechseln [ˈvɛksəln], *v.a.* change, exchange. — *v.n.* change, alternate, change places.

wechselseitig [ˈvɛksəlzaɪtɪç], *adj.* reciprocal, mutual.

Wechselstrom [ˈvɛksəlʃtroːm], *m.* (—s, *no pl.*) alternating current.

Wechselstube [ˈvɛksəlʃtuːbə], *f.* (—, *pl.* —n) exchange office.

wechselvoll [ˈvɛksəlfɔl], *adj.* eventful, chequered; changeable.

wechselweise [ˈvɛksəlvaɪzə], *adv.* reciprocally, mutually; by turns, alternately.

Wechselwinkel [ˈvɛksəlvɪŋkəl], *m.* (—s, *pl.* —) alternate angle.

Wechselwirkung [ˈvɛksəlvɪrkuŋ], *f.* (—, *pl.* —en) reciprocal effect.

Wechselwirtschaft [ˈvɛksəlvɪrtʃaft], *f.* (—, *no pl.*) rotation of crops.

Wecken [ˈvɛkən], *m.* (—s, *pl.* —) (*dial.*) bread-roll.

wecken [ˈvɛkən], *v.a.* wake, rouse, awaken.

Wecker [ˈvɛkər], *m.* (—s, *pl.* —) alarmclock.

Weckuhr [ˈvɛkuːr], *f.* (—, *pl.* —en) alarm-clock.

Wedel [ˈveːdəl], *m.* (—s, *pl.* —) featherduster, fan; tail.

wedeln [ˈveːdəln], *v.n. mit dem Schwanz* —, wag its tail.

weder [ˈveːdər], *conj.* neither; — ... *noch*, neither ... nor.

Weg [veːk], *m.* (—(e)s, *pl.* —e) way, path, route, road; walk, errand; *am* —, by the wayside.

weg [vɛk], *adv.* away, gone, off, lost.

wegbegeben [ˈvɛkbəgeːbən], *v.r. irr. sich* —, go away, leave.

wegbekommen [ˈvɛkbəkɔmən], *v.a. irr. etwas* —, get the hang of s.th.; get s.th. off *or* away.

Wegbereiter [ˈveːkbəraɪtər], *m.* (—s, *pl.* —) forerunner, pathfinder, pioneer.

wegblasen [ˈvɛkblaːzən], *v.a. irr.* blow away; *wie weggeblasen*, without leaving a trace.

wegbleiben [ˈvɛkblaɪbən], *v.n. irr.* (*aux. sein*) stay away.

wegblicken [ˈvɛkblɪkən], *v.n.* look the other way.

wegbringen [ˈvɛkbrɪŋən], *v.a. irr. einen* —, get s.o. away.

wegdrängen [ˈvɛkdrɛŋən], *v.a.* push away.

Wegebau [ˈveːgəbau], *m.* (—s, *no pl.*) road-making.

wegeilen [ˈvɛkaɪlən], *v.n.* (*aux. sein*) hasten away, hurry off.

wegelagern [ˈveːgəlaːgərn], *v.a.* waylay.

wegen [ˈveːgən], *prep.* (*Genit.*, *Dat.*) because of, on account of, owing to, by reason of.

Wegfall [ˈvɛkfal], *m.* (—s, *no pl.*) omission.

wegfallen [ˈvɛkfalən], *v.n. irr.* (*aux. sein*) fall off; be omitted; cease.

Weggang [ˈvɛkgaŋ], *m.* (—s, *no pl.*) departure, going away.

weggießen [ˈvɛkgiːsən], *v.a. irr.* pour away.

weghaben [ˈvɛkhaːbən], *v.a. irr. etwas* —, understand how to do s.th, have the knack of doing s.th.

wegkommen [ˈvɛkkɔmən], *v.n. irr.* (*aux. sein*) get away; be lost.

wegkönnen [ˈvɛkkœnən], *v.n. irr. nicht* —, not be able to get away.

Weglassung [ˈvɛklasuŋ], *f.* (—, *pl.* —en) omission.

wegmachen [ˈvɛkmaxən], *v.r. sich* —, decamp, make off.

wegmüssen [ˈvɛkmysən], *v.n. irr.* be obliged to go; have to go.

Wegnahme [ˈvɛknaːmə], *f.* (—, *no pl.*) taking, seizure, capture.

Wegreise [ˈvɛkraɪzə], *f.* (—, *no pl.*) departure.

Wegscheide [ˈveːkʃaɪdə], *f.* (—, *pl.* —n) crossroads, crossways.

wegscheren [ˈvɛkʃeːrən], *v.a.* clip; shave off. — *v.r. sich* —, be off.

wegschnappen [ˈvɛkʃnapən], *v.a.* snatch away.

wegsehnen [ˈvɛkzeːnən], *v.r. sich* —, wish o.s. far away; long to get away.

wegsein [ˈvɛkzaɪn], *v.n. irr.* (*aux. sein*) (*person*) be gone, be away; have gone off; (*things*) be lost; *ganz* —, (*coll.*) be beside o.s. *or* amazed.

wegsetzen [ˈvɛkzɛtsən], *v.a.* put away.

wegspülen [ˈvɛkʃpyːlən], *v.a.* wash away.

Wegstunde [ˈveːkʃtundə], *f.* (—, *pl.* —n) an hour's walk.

Wegweiser [ˈveːkvaɪzər], *m.* (—s, *pl.* —) signpost, road-sign.

wegwenden [ˈvɛkvɛndən], *v.r. sich* —, turn away.

wegwerfen [ˈvɛkvɛrfən], *v.a. irr.* throw away.

wegwerfend [ˈvɛkvɛrfənt], *adj.* disparaging, disdainful.

Wegzehrung [ˈveːktseːruŋ], *f.* (—, *no pl.*) food for the journey; (*Eccl.*) viaticum.

wegziehen ['vɛktsiːən], *v.a. irr.* draw away, pull away. — *v.n.* (*aux.* sein) march away; (*fig.*) move, remove.

Wegzug ['vɛktsuːk], *m.* (—s, *no pl.*) removal; moving away.

Weh [veː], *n.* (—s, *no pl.*) pain; grief, pang; misfortune.

weh [veː], *adj.* painful, sore; *mir ist — ums Herz*, I am sick at heart; my heart aches. — *adv.* — *tun*, ache; pain, hurt, offend, distress, grieve. — *int.* — *mir!* woe is me!

Wehen ['veːən], *n. pl.* birth-pangs, labour-pains.

wehen ['veːən], *v.n.* (*wind*) blow.

Wehgeschrei ['veːgəʃraɪ], *n.* (—s, *no pl.*) wailings.

Wehklage ['veːklaːgə], *f.* (—, *pl.* —n) lamentation.

wehklagen ['veːklaːgən], *v.n. insep.* lament, wail.

wehleidig ['veːlaɪdɪç], *adj.* tearful; easily hurt; self-pitying.

wehmütig ['veːmyːtɪç], *adj.* sad, melancholy, wistful.

Wehr (1) [veːr], *n.* (—s, *pl.* —e) weir.

Wehr (2) [veːr], *f.* (—, *pl.* —en) defence, bulwark.

wehren ['veːrən], *v.r. sich* —, defend o.s., offer resistance.

wehrhaft ['veːrhaft], *adj.* capable of bearing arms, able-bodied.

wehrlos ['veːrloːs], *adj.* defenceless, unarmed; (*fig.*) weak, unprotected.

Wehrpflicht ['veːrpflɪçt], *f.* (—, *no pl.*) compulsory military service, conscription.

Wehrstand ['veːrʃtant], *m.* (—s, *no pl.*) the military.

Weib [vaɪp], *n.* (—(e)s, *pl.* —er) woman; (*Poet.*) wife.

Weibchen ['vaɪpçən], *n.* (—s, *pl.* —) (*animal*) female.

Weiberfeind ['vaɪbərfaɪnt], *m.* (—s, *pl.* —e) woman-hater, misogynist.

Weiberherrschaft ['vaɪbərhɛrʃaft], *f.* (—, *no pl.*) petticoat rule.

weibisch ['vaɪbɪʃ], *adj.* womanish, effeminate.

weiblich ['vaɪplɪç], *adj.* female, feminine; womanly.

Weiblichkeit ['vaɪplɪçkaɪt], *f.* (—, *no pl.*) womanliness, femininity.

Weibsbild ['vaɪpsbɪlt], *n.* (—s, *pl.* —er) (*sl.*) female; wench.

weich [vaɪç], *adj.* weak; soft; tender, gentle; effeminate; sensitive; — *machen*, soften; — *werden*, relent.

Weichbild ['vaɪçbɪlt], *n.* (—s, *no pl.*) precincts; city boundaries.

Weiche ['vaɪçə], *f.* (—, *pl.* —n) (*Railw.*) switch, points.

weichen (1) ['vaɪçən], *v.a.* steep, soak, soften.

weichen (2) ['vaɪçən], *v.n. irr.* (*aux.* sein) yield, make way, give ground.

Weichensteller ['vaɪçənʃtɛlər], *m.* (—s, *pl.* —) (*Railw.*) pointsman, signalman.

Weichheit ['vaɪçhaɪt], *f.* (—, *no pl.*) softness; (*fig.*) weakness, tenderness.

weichherzig ['vaɪçhɛrtsɪç], *adj.* soft-hearted, tender-hearted.

weichlich ['vaɪçlɪç], *adj.* soft; (*fig.*) weak, effeminate.

Weichling ['vaɪçlɪŋ], *m.* (—s, *pl.* —e) weakling.

Weichsel ['vaɪksəl], *f.* Vistula.

Weichselkirsche ['vaɪksəlkɪrʃə], *f.* (—, *pl.* —n) sour cherry; morello.

Weide ['vaɪdə], *f.* (—, *pl.* —n) pasture, pasturage; (*Bot.*) willow.

Weideland ['vaɪdəlant], *n.* (—s, *pl.* ˙er) pasture-ground.

weiden ['vaɪdən], *v.a., v.n.* pasture, feed.

Weidenbaum ['vaɪdənbaum], *m.* (—s, *pl.* ˙e) willow-tree.

Weiderich ['vaɪdərɪç], *m.* (—s, *pl.* —e) willow-herb, loose-strife, rose bay.

Weidgenosse ['vaɪtgənɔsə], *m.* (—en, *pl.* —en) fellow huntsman.

weidlich ['vaɪtlɪç], *adv.* (*rare*) greatly, thoroughly.

Weidmann ['vaɪtman], *m.* (—s, *pl.* ˙er) sportsman, huntsman.

Weidmannsheil! ['vaɪtmanshaɪl], *excl.* tally-ho!

weigern ['vaɪgərn], *v.r. sich* —, refuse, decline.

Weigerung ['vaɪgəruŋ], *f.* (—, *pl.* —en) refusal, denial.

Weih [vaɪ], *m.* (—en, *pl.* —en) (*Orn.*) kite.

Weihbischof ['vaɪbɪʃɔf], *m.* (—s, *pl.* ˙e) suffragan bishop.

Weihe ['vaɪə], *f.* (—, *pl.* —en) consecration; (*priest*) ordination; initiation; (*fig.*) solemnity.

weihen ['vaɪən], *v.a.* bless, consecrate; ordain. — *v.r. sich* —, devote o.s. (to).

Weiher ['vaɪər], *m.* (—s, *pl.* —) pond, fishpond.

weihevoll ['vaɪəfɔl], *adj.* solemn.

Weihnachten ['vaɪnaxtən], *n. or f.* Christmas.

Weihnachtsabend ['vaɪnaxtsaːbənt], *m.* (—s, *pl.* —e) Christmas Eve.

Weihnachtsfeiertag ['vaɪnaxtsfaɪərtaːk], *m.* (—s, *pl.* —e) Christmas Day; *zweiter* —, Boxing Day.

Weihnachtsgeschenk ['vaɪnaxtsgəʃɛŋk], *n.* (—s, *pl.* —e) Christmas box, Christmas present.

Weihnachtslied ['vaɪnaxtsliːt], *n.* (—(e)s, *pl.* —er) Christmas carol.

Weihnachtsmann ['vaɪnaxtsman], *m.* (—(e)s, *pl.* ˙er) Santa Claus, Father Christmas.

Weihrauch ['vaɪraux], *m.* (—s, *no pl.*) incense.

Weihwasser ['vaɪvasər], *n.* (—s, *no pl.*) holy water.

weil [vaɪl], *conj.* because, as, since.

weiland ['vaɪlant], *adv.* (*obs.*) formerly, once.

Weile ['vaɪlə], *f.* (—, *no pl.*) while, short time; leisure.

weilen ['vaɪlən], *v.n.* tarry, stay, abide.

Wein [vaɪn], *m.* (—(e)s, *pl.* —e) wine; (*plant*) vine; *einen reinen — einschenken*, tell s.o. the truth.

Weinbau ['vaɪnbau], m. (—s, no pl.) vine growing, viticulture.

Weinbeere ['vaɪnbeːrə], f. (—, pl. —n) grape.

Weinberg ['vaɪnbɛrk], m. (—s, pl. —e) vineyard.

Weinbrand ['vaɪnbrant], m. (—s, no pl.) brandy.

weinen ['vaɪnən], v.n. weep, cry.

Weinernte ['vaɪnɛrntə], f. (—, pl. —n) vintage.

Weinessig ['vaɪnɛsɪç], m. (—s, no pl.) (wine) vinegar.

Weinfaß ['vaɪnfas], n. (—sses, pl. ⁻sser) wine-cask.

Weingeist ['vaɪngaɪst], m. (—es, no pl.) spirits of wine, alcohol.

Weinhändler ['vaɪnhɛndlər], m. (—s, pl. —) wine merchant.

Weinkarte ['vaɪnkartə], f. (—, pl. —n) wine-list.

Weinkeller ['vaɪnkɛlər], m. (—s, pl. —) wine-cellar; wine-tavern.

Weinkellerei ['vaɪnkɛlaraɪ], f. (—, pl. —en) wine-store.

Weinkelter ['vaɪnkɛltər], f. (—, pl. —n) wine-press.

Weinkneipe ['vaɪnknaɪpə], f. (—, pl. —n) wine-tavern.

Weinkoster ['vaɪnkɔstər], m. (—s, pl. —) wine-taster.

Weinlaub ['vaɪnlaup], n. (—s, no pl.) vine-leaves.

Weinlese ['vaɪnleːzə], f. (—, pl. —n) vintage, grape harvest.

Weinranke ['vaɪnraŋkə], f. (—, pl. —n) vine-branch, tendril.

Weinschenke ['vaɪnʃɛŋkə], f. (—, pl. —n) wine-house, tavern.

weinselig ['vaɪnzeːlɪç], adj. tipsy.

Weinstein ['vaɪnʃtaɪn], m. (—s, no pl.) tartar.

Weinsteinsäure ['vaɪnʃtaɪnzɔyrə], f. (—, no pl.) tartaric acid.

Weinstock ['vaɪnʃtɔk], m. (—s, pl. ⁻e) vine.

Weintraube ['vaɪntraubə], f. (—, pl. —n) grape, bunch of grapes.

weinumrankt ['vaɪnumraŋkt], adj. vine-clad.

weise ['vaɪzə], adj. wise, prudent.

Weise (1) ['vaɪzə], m. (—n, pl. —n) wise man, sage.

Weise (2) ['vaɪzə], f. (—, pl. —n) manner, fashion; method, way; tune, melody.

weisen ['vaɪzən], v.a. irr. point to, point out, show.

Weiser ['vaɪzər], m. (—s, pl. —) signpost; indicator; (clock) hand.

Weisheit ['vaɪshaɪt], f. (—, pl. —en) wisdom, prudence.

Weisheitszahn ['vaɪshaɪtstsaːn], m. (—s, pl. ⁻e) wisdom tooth.

weislich ['vaɪslɪç], adv. wisely, prudently, advisedly.

weismachen ['vaɪsmaxən], v.a. einem etwas —, (coll.) spin a yarn to s.o.; laß dir nichts —, don't be taken in.

weissagen ['vaɪsza:gən], v.a. insep. prophesy, foretell.

Weissager ['vaɪssa:gər], m. (—s, pl. —) prophet, soothsayer.

Weissagung ['vaɪssa:guŋ], f. (—, pl. —en) prophecy.

weiß [vaɪs], adj. white, clean, blank.

Weißbuche ['vaɪsbu:xə], f. (—, pl. —n) (Bot.) hornbeam.

Weiße ['vaɪsə], f. (—, no pl.) whiteness; (fig.) (dial.) pale ale.

weißglühend ['vaɪsgly:ənt], adj. at white heat, incandescent, white hot.

Weißnäherin ['vaɪsnɛ:ərɪn], f. (—, pl. —nen) seamstress.

Weißwaren ['vaɪsva:rən], f. pl. linen.

Weisung ['vaɪzuŋ], f. (—, pl. —en) order, direction, instruction; directive.

weit [vaɪt], adj. distant, far, far off; wide, broad, vast, extensive; (clothing) loose, too big.

weitab [vaɪt'ap], adv. far away.

weitaus [vaɪt'aus], adv. by far.

weitblickend ['vaɪtblɪkənt], adj. far-sighted.

Weite ['vaɪtə], f. (—, pl. —n) width, breadth; distance.

weiten ['vaɪtən], v.a. widen, expand.

weiter ['vaɪtər], adj. further, farther, wider.

weiterbefördern ['vaɪtərbəfœrdərn], v.a. send, forward, send on.

weiterbilden ['vaɪtərbɪldən], v.a. improve, develop(e), extend.

Weitere ['vaɪtərə], n. (—n, no pl.) rest, remainder.

weiterführen ['vaɪtərfy:rən], v.a. continue, carry on.

weitergeben ['vaɪtərge:bən], v.a. irr. pass on.

weitergehen ['vaɪtərge:ən], v.n. irr. (aux. sein) walk on.

weiterhin ['vaɪtərhɪn], adv. furthermore; in time to come; in future.

weiterkommen ['vaɪtərkɔmən], v.n. irr. (aux. sein) get on, advance.

Weiterung ['vaɪtəruŋ], f. (—, pl. —en) widening, enlargement.

weitgehend ['vaɪtge:ənt], adj. far-reaching, sweeping.

weitläufig ['vaɪtlɔyfɪç], adj. ample, large; detailed, elaborate; distant, widespread; diffuse, long-winded.

weitschweifig ['vaɪtʃvaɪfɪç], adj. prolix, diffuse, rambling.

weitsichtig ['vaɪtzɪçtɪç], adj. long-sighted.

weittragend ['vaɪttra:gənt], adj. portentous, far-reaching.

weitverbreitet ['vaɪtfɛrbraɪtət], adj. widespread.

Weizen ['vaɪtsən], m. (—s, no pl.) wheat.

Weizengrieß ['vaɪtsəngri:s], m. (—es, no pl.) semolina; grits.

welch [vɛlç], pron. what (a).

welcher, -e, -es ['vɛlçər], interr. pron. which? what? — rel. pron. who, which, that; (indef.) (coll.) some.

welcherlei ['vɛlçərlaɪ], *indecl. adj.* of what kind.

Welfe ['vɛlfə], *m.* (**—n,** *pl.* **—n**) Guelph.

welk [vɛlk], *adj.* faded, withered; — *werden,* fade, wither.

welken ['vɛlkən], *v.n.* (aux. sein) wither, fade, decay.

Wellblech ['vɛlblɛç], *n.* (**—s,** *no pl.*) corrugated iron.

Welle ['vɛlə], *f.* (**—,** *pl.* **—n**) wave, billow.

wellen ['vɛlən], *v.a.* wave.

Wellenbewegung ['vɛlənbəve:guŋ], *f.* (**—,** *pl.* **—en**) undulation.

Wellenlinie ['vɛlənli:njə], *f.* (**—,** *pl.* **—n**) wavy line.

wellig ['vɛlɪç], *adj.* wavy, undulating.

welsch [vɛlʃ], *adj.* foreign; Italian; French.

Welschkohl ['vɛlʃko:l], *m.* (**—s,** *no pl.*) (*Bot.*) savoy cabbage.

Welschkorn ['vɛlʃkɔrn], *n.* (**—s,** *no pl.*) (*Bot.*) Indian corn.

Welt [vɛlt], *f.* (**—,** *pl.* **—en**) world, earth; universe; society.

Weltall ['vɛltal], *n.* (**—s,** *no pl.*) universe, cosmos; (outer) space.

Weltanschauung ['vɛltanʃauuŋ], *f.* (**—,** *pl.* **—en**) view of life, philosophy of life, ideology.

Weltbeschreibung ['vɛltbəʃraɪbuŋ], *f.* (**—,** *no pl.*) cosmography.

Weltbürger ['vɛltbyrgər], *m.* (**—s,** *pl.* **—**) cosmopolitan.

welterschütternd ['vɛltərʃytərnt], *adj.* world-shaking.

weltfremd ['vɛltfrɛmt], *adj.* unwordly, unsophisticated.

Weltgeschichte ['vɛltgəʃɪçtə], *f.* (**—,** *no pl.*) world history.

Weltherrschaft ['vɛlthɛrʃaft], *f.* (**—,** *no pl.*) world dominion.

Weltkenntnis ['vɛltkɛntnɪs], *f.* (**—,** *no pl.*) worldly wisdom.

weltklug ['vɛltklu:k], *adj.* astute, worldly-wise.

Weltkrieg ['vɛltkri:k], *m.* (**—es,** *pl.* **—e**) world war.

weltlich ['vɛltlɪç], *adj.* worldly; (*Eccl.*) temporal, secular.

Weltmacht ['vɛltmaxt], *f.* (**—,** *pl.* **⸚e**) world power, great power.

Weltmeer ['vɛltme:r], *n.* (**—s,** *pl.* **—e**) ocean.

Weltmeisterschaft ['vɛltmaɪstərʃaft], *f.* (**—,** *pl.* **—en**) world championship.

Weltordnung ['vɛltɔrdnuŋ], *f.* (**—** *pl.* **—en**) cosmic order.

Weltraum ['vɛltraum], *m.* (**—s,** *no pl.*) space.

Weltraumflug ['vɛltraumflu:k], *m.* (**—(e)s,** *pl.* **⸚e**) space flight.

Weltraumforschung ['vɛltraumfɔrʃuŋ], *f.* (**—,** *no pl.*) space exploration.

Weltraumgeschoss ['vɛltraumgəʃo:s], *n.* (**—es,** *pl.* **—e**) space rocket.

Weltruf ['vɛltru:f], *m.* (**—s,** *no pl.*) world-wide renown.

Weltschmerz ['vɛltʃmɛrts], *m.* (**—es,** *no pl.*) world-weariness, Wertherism; melancholy.

Weltsprache ['vɛltʃpra:xə], *f.* (**—,** *pl.* **—en**) universal language; world language.

Weltstadt ['vɛltʃtat], *f.* (**—,** *pl.* **⸚e**) metropolis.

Weltumseglung ['vɛltumze:gluŋ], *f.* (**—,** *pl.* **—en**) circumnavigation (of the globe).

Weltuntergang ['vɛltuntərgaŋ], *m.* **—s,** *no pl.*) end of the world.

Weltwirtschaft ['vɛltvɪrtʃaft], *f.* (**—,** *no pl.*) world trade.

wem [ve:m], *pers. pron.* (Dat. of **wer**) to whom — *interr. pron.* to whom?

wen [ve:n], *pers. pron.* (Acc. of **wer**) whom — *interr. pron.* whom?

Wende ['vɛndə], *f.* (**—,** *pl.* **—en**) turn, turning(point).

Wendekreis ['vɛndəkraɪs], *m.* (**—es,** *pl.* **—e**) tropic.

Wendeltreppe ['vɛndəltrɛpə], *f.* (**—,** *pl.* **—n**) spiral staircase.

wenden ['vɛndən], *v.a. reg. & irr.* turn.

Wendepunkt ['vɛndəpuŋkt], *m.* (**—es,** *pl.* **—e**) turning point; crisis.

Wendung ['vɛnduŋ], *f.* (**—,** *pl.* **—en**) turn, turning; crisis; (speech) phrase.

wenig ['ve:nɪç], *adj.* little, few; *ein —,* a little.

weniger ['ve:nɪgər], *adj.* less, fewer.

wenigstens ['ve:nɪçstəns], *adv.* at least.

wenn [vɛn], *conj.* if; when; whenever, in case; — *nicht,* unless.

wenngleich ['vɛnglaɪç], *conj.* though, although.

wer [ve:r], *rel. pron.* who, he who; — *auch,* whoever. — *interr. pron.* who? which? — *da?* who goes there?

Werbekraft ['vɛrbəkraft], *f.* (**—,** *no pl.*) (*Advertising*) attraction; appeal; publicity value.

werben ['vɛrbən], *v.n. irr.* advertise, canvass; court, woo. — *v.a.* (soldiers) recruit.

Werbung ['vɛrbuŋ], *f.* (**—,** *pl.* **—en**) advertising, publicity, propaganda; recruiting; courtship.

Werdegang ['vɛrdəgaŋ], *m.* (**—s,** *no pl.*) evolution, development.

werden ['ve:rdən], *v.n. irr.* (aux. sein) become, get; grow; turn; *Arzt —,* become a doctor; *alt —,* grow old; *bleich —,* turn pale.

werdend ['ve:rdənt], *adj.* becoming; nascent, incipient, budding.

werfen ['vɛrfən], *v.a. irr.* throw, cast.

Werft (1) [vɛrft], *m.* (**—(e)s,** *pl.* **—e**) warp.

Werft (2) [vɛrft], *f.* (**—,** *pl.* **—en**) dockyard, shipyard, wharf.

Werk [vɛrk], *n.* (**—(e)s,** *pl.* **—e**) work, action, deed; undertaking; (*Ind.*) works, plant, mill, factory.

Werkführer ['vɛrkfy:rər], *m.* (**—s,** *pl.* **—**) foreman.

Werkleute ['vɛrkləytə], *pl.* workmen.

Werkmeister ['vɛrkmaɪstər], *m.* (**—s,** *pl.* **—**) overseer.

werktätig ['vɛrktɛ:tɪç], *adj.* active, practical; hard-working.

279

Werkzeug ['vɛrktsɔyk], *n.* (—s, *pl.* —e) implement, tool, jig, instrument.

Wermut ['vɛːrmuːt], *m.* —s, *no pl.*) absinthe, vermouth.

Wert [veːrt], *m.* (—(e)s, *pl.* —e) value, worth, price; use; merit; importance.

wert [veːrt], *adj.* valuable; worth; dear, esteemed.

Wertangabe ['veːrtangaːbə], *f.* (—, *pl.* —n) valuation; declared value.

Wertbestimmung ['veːrtbəʃtɪmuŋ], *f.* (—, *no pl.*) appraisal, assessment, valuation.

Wertbrief ['veːrtbriːf], *m.* (—s, *pl.* —e) registered letter.

werten ['veːrtən], *v.a.* value.

Wertgegenstand ['veːrtgeːgənʃtant], *m.* (—s, *pl.* ∸e) article of value.

Wertmesser ['veːrtmɛsər], *m.* (—s, *pl.* —) standard.

Wertpapiere ['veːrtpapiːrə], *n. pl.* securities.

Wertsachen ['veːrtzaxən], *f. pl.* valuables.

wertschätzen ['veːrtʃɛtsən], *v.a.* esteem (highly).

wertvoll ['veːrtfɔl], *adj.* of great value, valuable.

Wertzeichen ['veːrttsaiçən], *n.* (—s, *pl.* —) stamp; coupon.

wes [vɛs], *pers. pron.* (*obs.*) whose.

Wesen ['veːzən], *n.* (—s, *pl.* —) being, creature; reality; essence, nature, substance; character, demeanour; (*in compounds*) organisation, affairs.

wesenlos ['veːzənlɔːs], *adj.* disembodied, unsubstantial, shadowy; trivial.

wesensgleich ['veːzənsglaiç], *adj.* identical, substantially the same.

wesentlich ['veːzəntlɪç], *adj.* essential, material.

weshalb [vɛs'halp], *conj., adv.* wherefore, why; therefore.

Wespe ['vɛspə], *f.* (—, *pl.* —n) (*Ent.*) wasp.

Wespennest ['vɛspənnɛst], *n.* (—s, *pl.* —er,) wasp's nest; *in ein — stechen,* stir up a hornet's nest.

wessen ['vɛsən], *pers .pron.* (*Genit. of* wer) whose. — *interr. pron.* whose?

Weste ['vɛstə], *f.* (—, *pl.* —n) waistcoat.

Westen ['vɛstən], *m.* (—s, *no pl.*) west; *nach —,* westward.

Westfalen [vɛst'faːlən], *n.* Westphalia.

Westindien [vɛst'ɪndjən], *n.* the West Indies.

weswegen [vɛs've:gən] *see* **weshalb**.

Wettbewerb ['vɛtbəvɛrp], *m.* (—s, *pl.* —e) competition, rivalry; *unlauterer —,* unfair competition.

Wettbewerber ['vɛtbəvɛrbər], *m.* (—s, *pl.* —) rival, competitor.

Wette ['vɛtə], *f.* (—, *pl.* —n) bet, wager; *um die — laufen,* race one another.

Wetteifer ['vɛtaifər], *m.* (—s, *no pl.*) rivalry.

wetteifern ['vɛtaifərn], *v.n. insep.* vie (with), compete.

wetten ['vɛtən], *v.a., v.n.* bet, lay a wager, wager.

Wetter ['vɛtər], *n.* (—s, *pl.* —) weather; bad weather, storm; *schlagende —,* (*Min.*) fire-damp.

Wetterbeobachtung ['vɛtərbəobaxtuŋ], *f.* (—, *pl.* —en) meteorological observation.

Wetterbericht ['vɛtərbəriçt], *m.* —s, *pl.* —e) weather report *or* forecast.

Wetterfahne ['vɛtərfaːnə], *f.* (—, *pl.* —en) weather-cock, vane; (*fig.*) turncoat.

wetterfest ['vɛtərfɛst], *adj.* weatherproof.

Wetterglas ['vɛtərglaːs], *n.* (—es, *pl.* ∸er) barometer.

Wetterhahn ['vɛtərhaːn], *m.* (—s, *pl.* ∸e) weather-cock.

Wetterkunde ['vɛtərkundə], *f.* (—, *no pl.*) meteorology.

Wetterleuchten ['vɛtərlɔyçtən], *n.* (—s, *no pl.*) summer lightning; sheet lightning.

wettern ['vɛtərn], *v.n.* be stormy; (*fig.*) curse, swear, thunder (against), storm.

Wettervorhersage ['vɛtərfoːrheːrzaːgə], *f.* (—, *pl.* —n) weather forecast.

wetterwendisch ['vɛtərvɛndɪʃ], *adj.* changeable; irritable, peevish.

Wettkampf ['vɛtkampf], *m.* (—(e)s, *pl.* ∸e) contest, tournament.

Wettlauf ['vɛtlauf], *m.* (—s, *pl.* ∸e) race.

wettmachen ['vɛtmaxən], *v.a.* make up for.

Wettrennen ['vɛtrɛnən], *n.* (—s, *pl.* —) racing, race.

Wettstreit ['vɛtʃtrait], *m.* —s, *pl.* —e) contest, contention.

wetzen ['vɛtsən], *v.a.* whet, hone, sharpen.

Wichse ['vɪksə], *f.* (—, *pl.* —n) blacking, shoe-polish; (*fig.*) thrashing.

wichsen ['vɪksən], *v.a.* black, shine; (*fig.*) thrash.

Wicht [vɪçt], *m.* (—(e)s, *pl.* —e) creature; (*coll.*) chap.

Wichtelmännchen ['vɪçtəlmɛnçən], *n.* (—s, *pl.* —) pixie, goblin.

wichtig ['vɪçtɪç], *adj.* important; weighty; significant; *sich — machen,* put on airs.

Wichtigkeit ['vɪçtɪçkait], *f.* (—, *no pl.*) importance; s·gnificance.

Wicke ['vɪkə], *f.* (—, *pl.* —n) (*Bot.*) vetch.

Wickel ['vɪkəl], *m.* (—s, *pl.* —) roller; (*hair*) curler; (*Med.*) compress.

Wickelkind ['vɪkəlkɪnt], *n.* (—s, *pl.* —er) babe in arms.

wickeln ['vɪkəln], *v.a.* roll, coil; wind; wrap (up); (*babies*) swaddle; (*hair*) curl.

Widder ['vɪdər], *m.* (—s, *pl.* —) ram; (*Astrol.*) Aries.

wider ['viːdər], *prep.* (*Acc.*) against, in opposition to, contrary to.

widerfahren [vi:dər'fa:rən], *v.n. irr. insep.* (*aux.* sein) happen to s.o.; befall s.o.; *einem Gerechtigkeit — lassen,* give s.o. his due.

Widerhaken ['vi:dərha:kən], *m.* (—s, *pl.* —) barb.

Widerhall ['vi:dərhal], *m.* (—s, *pl.* —e) echo, resonance; (*fig.*) response.

widerlegen [vi:dər'le:gən], *v.a. insep.* refute, disprove, prove (s.o.) wrong.

Widerlegung [vi:dər'le:guŋ], *f.* (—, *pl.* —en) refutation, rebuttal.

widerlich ['vi:dərlıç], *adj.* disgusting, nauseating, repulsive.

widernatürlich ['vi:dərnaty:rlıç], *adj.* unnatural; perverse.

widerraten [vi:dər'ra:tən], *v.a. irr. insep.* advise against; dissuade from.

widerrechtlich ['vi:dərreçtlıç], *adj.* illegal, unlawful.

Widerrede ['vi:dərre:də], *f.* (—, *pl.* —n) contradiction.

Widerruf ['vi:dərru:f], *m.* (—s, *pl.* —e) revocation, recantation.

widerrufen [vi:dər'ru:fən], *v.a. irr. insep.* recant, retract, revoke.

Widersacher ['vi:dərzaxər], *m.* (—s, *pl.* —) adversary, antagonist.

Widerschein ['vi:dərʃaın], *m.* (—s, *no pl.*) reflection.

widersetzen [vi:dər'zɛtsən], *v.r. insep. sich —,* resist, (*Dat.*) oppose.

widersetzlich [vi:dər'zɛtslıç], *adj.* refractory, insubordinate.

Widersinn ['vi:dərzın], *m.* (—s, *no pl.*) nonsense, absurdity; paradox.

widersinnig ['vi:dərzınıç], *adj.* nonsensical, absurd; paradoxical.

widerspenstig ['vi:dərʃpɛnstıç], *adj.* refractory, rebellious, obstinate, stubborn.

widerspiegeln [vi:dər'ʃpi:gəln], *v.a.* reflect, mirror.

widersprechen [vi:dər'ʃprɛçən], *v.n. irr. insep.* (*Dat.*) contradict, gainsay.

Widerspruch ['vi:dərʃprux], *m.* (—es, *pl.* -̈e) contradiction.

widerspruchsvoll ['vi:dərʃpruxsfɔl], *adj.* contradictory.

Widerstand ['vi:dərʃtant], *m.* (—s, *pl.* -̈e) resistance, opposition.

widerstandsfähig ['vi:dərʃtantsfɛ:ıç], *adj.* resistant, hardy.

widerstehen [vi:dər'ʃte:ən], *v.n. irr. insep.* (*Dat.*) resist, withstand; be distasteful (to).

widerstreben [vi:dər'ʃtre:bən], *n.* (—s, *no pl.*) reluctance.

widerstreben [vi:dər'ʃtre:bən], *v.n. insep.* (*Dat.*) strive against, oppose; be distasteful to a p.

Widerstreit ['vi:dərʃtraıt], *m.* (—s, *no pl.*) contradiction, opposition; conflict.

widerwärtig ['vi:dərvɛrtıç], *adj.* unpleasant, disagreeable, repugnant, repulsive; hateful, odious.

Widerwille ['vi:dərvılə], *m.* (—ns, *no pl.*) aversion (to).

widmen ['vıdmən], *v.a.* dedicate.

Widmung ['vıdmuŋ], *f.* (—, *pl.* —en) dedication.

widrig ['vi:drıç], *adj.* contrary, adverse, inimical, unfavourable.

widrigenfalls ['vi:drıgənfals], *adv.* failing this, otherwise, else.

wie [vi:], *adv.* how. — *conj.* as, just as, like; — *geht's?* how are you?

wieder ['vi:dər], *adv.* again, anew, afresh; back, in return.

Wiederabdruck ['vi:dərapdruk], *m.* (—s, *pl.* —e) reprint.

Wiederaufbau [vi:dər'aufbau], *m.* (—s, *no pl.*) rebuilding.

Wiederaufnahme [vi:dər'aufna:mə], *f.* (—, *no pl.*) resumption.

Wiederbelebungsversuch ['vi:dərbə-le:buŋsfɛrzu:x], *m.* (—es, *pl.* —e) attempt at resuscitation.

Wiederbezahlung ['vi:dərbətsa:luŋ], *f.* (—, *pl.* —en) reimbursement.

wiederbringen ['vi:dərbrıŋən], *v.a. irr.* bring back, restore.

Wiedereinrichtung ['vi:dəraınrıçtuŋ], *f.* (—, *no pl.*) reorganisation, re-establishment.

Wiedereinsetzung ['vi:dəraınzɛtsuŋ], *f.* (—, *pl.* —en) restoration, reinstatement, rehabilitation.

wiedererkennen ['vi:dərɛrkɛnən], *v.a. irr.* recognise.

Wiedererstattung ['vi:dərɛrʃtatuŋ], *f.* (—, *no pl.*) restitution.

Wiedergabe ['vi:dərga:bə], *f.* (—, *no pl.*) restitution, return; (*fig.*) rendering, reproduction.

wiedergeben ['vi:dərge:bən], *v.a. irr.* return, give back; (*fig.*) render.

Wiedergeburt ['vi:dərgəbu:rt], *f.* (—, *no pl.*) rebirth, regeneration, renascence.

Wiedergutmachung [vi:dər'gu:t-maxuŋ], *f.* (—, *no pl.*) reparation.

Wiederherstellung [vi:dər'he:rʃtɛluŋ], *f.* (—, *no pl.*) restoration; recovery.

Wiederherstellungsmittel [vi:dər-'he:rʃtɛluŋsmıtəl], *n.* (—s, *pl.* —) restorative, tonic.

wiederholen [vi:dər'ho:lən], *v.a. insep.* repeat, reiterate.

Wiederholung [vi:dər'ho:luŋ], *f.* (—, *pl.* —en) repetition.

Wiederkäuer ['vi:dərkɔyər], *m.* (—s, *pl.* —) ruminant.

Wiederkehr ['vi:dərke:r], *f.* (—, *no pl.*) return; recurrence.

wiederkehren ['vi:dərke:rən], *v.n.* (*aux.* sein) return.

wiederklingen ['vi:dərklıŋən], *v.n. irr.* reverberate.

wiederkommen ['vi:dərkɔmən], *v.n. irr.* (*aux.* sein) return, come back.

Wiedersehen ['vi:dərze:ən], *n.* (—s, *no pl.*) reunion, meeting after separation; *auf —,* good-bye; so long! see you again!

wiedersehen ['vi:dərze:ən], *v.a. irr.* see again, meet again.

281

wiederum ['vi:dǝrum], *adv.* again, anew, afresh.

Wiedervereinigung ['vi:dǝrfɛraɪnɪguŋ], *f.* (—, *pl.* —en) reunion, reunification.

Wiedervergeltung ['vi:dǝrfɛrgɛltuŋ], *f.* (—, *no pl.*) requital, retaliation, reprisal.

Wiederverkauf ['vi:dǝrfɛrkauf], *m.* (—s, *no pl.*) resale.

Wiederverkäufer ['vi:dǝrfɛrkɔyfǝr], *m.* (—s, *pl.* —) retailer.

Wiederversöhnung ['vi:dǝrfɛrzø:nuŋ], *f.* (—, *no pl.*) reconciliation.

Wiederwahl ['vi:dǝrva:l], *f.* (—, *no pl.*) re-election.

Wiege ['vi:gǝ], *f.* (—, *pl.* —n) cradle.

wiegen ['vi:gǝn], *v.a.* rock (the cradle). — *v.r. sich — in,* delude o.s. with. — *v.a., v.n. irr.* weigh.

Wiegenfest ['vi:gǝnfɛst], *n.* (—es, *pl.* —e) (*Poet., Lit.*) birthday.

Wiegenlied ['vi:gǝnli:t], *n.* (—s, *pl.* —er) cradle-song, lullaby.

wiehern ['vi:ǝrn], *v.n.* neigh.

Wien [vi:n], *n.* Vienna.

Wiese ['vi:zǝ], *f.* (—, *pl.* —n) meadow.

Wiesel ['vi:zǝl], *n.* (—s, *pl.* —) (*Zool.*) weasel.

wieso [vi'zo:] *adv.* why? how do you mean? in what way?

wieviel [vi'fi:l], *adv.* how much, how many; *den —ten haben wir heute?* what is the date today?

wiewohl [vi'vo:l], *conj.* although, though.

Wild [vɪlt], *n.* (—(e)s, *no pl.*) game; venison.

wild [vɪlt], *adj.* wild, savage, fierce; furious.

Wildbach ['vɪltbax], *m.* (—s, *pl.* ꞏe) (mountain) torrent.

Wilddieb ['vɪltdi:p], *m.* (—(e)s, *pl.* —e) poacher.

Wilde ['vɪldǝ], *m.* (—n, *pl.* —n) savage.

wildern ['vɪldǝrn], *v.n.* poach.

Wildfang ['vɪltfaŋ], *m.* (—s, *pl.* ꞏe) scamp, tomboy.

wildfremd ['vɪltfrɛmt], *adj.* completely strange.

Wildhüter ['vɪlthy:tǝr], *m.* (—s, *pl.* —) gamekeeper.

Wildleder ['vɪltle:dǝr], *n.* (—s, *no pl.*) suède, doeskin, buckskin.

Wildnis ['vɪltnɪs], *f.* (—, *pl.* —se) wilderness, desert.

Wildpark ['vɪltpark], *m.* (—s, *pl.* —s) game-reserve.

Wildpret ['vɪltprɛt], *n.* (—s, *no pl.*) game; venison.

Wildschwein ['vɪltʃvain], *n.* (—s, *pl.* —e) wild boar.

Wille ['vɪlǝ], *m.* (—ns, *no pl.*) will, wish, design, purpose.

willenlos ['vɪlǝnlo:s], *adj.* weak-minded.

willens ['vɪlǝns], *adv.* — *sein,* be willing, have a mind to.

Willenserklärung ['vɪlǝnsɛrklɛ:ruŋ], *f.* (—, *pl.* —en) (*Law*) declaratory act.

Willensfreiheit ['vflǝnsfraɪhaɪt], *f.* (—, *no pl.*) free will.

Willenskraft ['vɪlǝnskraft], *f.* (—, *no pl.*) strength of will, will-power.

willentlich ['vɪlǝntlɪç], *adv.* purposely, on purpose, intentionally, wilfully.

willfahren [vɪl'fa:rǝn], *v.n. insep.* (*Dat.*) comply with, gratify.

willfährig ['vɪlfɛ:rɪç], *adj.* compliant, complaisant.

willig ['vɪlɪç], *adj.* willing, ready, docile.

willkommen [vɪl'kɔmǝn], *adj.* welcome; — *heißen,* welcome.

Willkür ['vɪlky:r], *f.* (—, *no pl.*) free will; discretion; caprice, arbitrariness.

willkürlich ['vɪlky:rlɪç], *adj.* arbitrary.

wimmeln ['vɪmǝln], *v.n.* swarm, teem (with).

wimmern ['vɪmǝrn], *v.n.* whimper.

Wimpel ['vɪmpǝl], *m.* (—s, *pl.* —) pennon, pennant, streamer.

Wimper ['vɪmpǝr], *f.* (—, *pl.* —n) eyelash; *ohne mit der — zu zucken,* without turning a hair, without batting an eyelid.

Wind [vɪnt], *m.* (—(e)s, *pl.* —e) wind, breeze; *von etwas — bekommen,* get wind of.

Windbeutel ['vɪntbɔytǝl], *m.* (—s, *pl.* —) cream puff; (*fig.*) windbag.

Windbüchse ['vɪntbyksǝ], *f.* (—, *pl.* —n) air-gun.

Winde ['vɪndǝ], *f.* (—, *pl.* —n) (*Tech.*) windlass; (*Bot.*) bindweed.

Windel ['vɪndǝl], *f.* (—, *pl.* —n) (baby's) napkin; (*Am.*) diaper.

windelweich ['vɪndǝlvaiç], *adj.* very soft, limp; *einen — schlagen,* beat s.o. to a jelly.

winden ['vɪndǝn], *v.a. irr.* wind, reel; wring; (*flowers*) make a wreath of. — *v.r. sich —,* writhe.

Windeseile ['vɪndǝsailǝ], *f.* (—, *no pl.*) lightning speed.

Windfahne ['vɪntfa:nǝ], *f.* (—, *pl.* —n) weather-cock, vane.

windfrei ['vɪntfrai], *adj.* sheltered.

Windhund ['vɪnthunt], *m.* (—s, *pl.* —e) greyhound; (*fig.*) windbag.

windig ['vɪndɪç], *adj.* windy.

Windklappe ['vɪntklapǝ], *f.* (—, *pl.* —n) air-valve.

Windlicht ['vɪntlɪçt], *n.* (—s, *pl.* —er) torch; storm lantern.

Windmühle ['vɪntmy:lǝ], *f.* (—, *pl.* —n) windmill.

Windpocken ['vɪntpɔkǝn], *f. pl.* (*Med.*) chicken-pox.

Windrichtung ['vɪntrɪçtuŋ], *f.* (—, *pl.* —en) direction of the wind.

Windrose ['vɪntro:zǝ], *f.* (—, *pl.* —n) compass card; windrose.

Windsbraut ['vɪntsbraut], *f.* (—, *no pl.*) gust of wind, squall; gale.

windschief ['vɪntʃi:f], *adj.* warped, bent.

Windschutzscheibe ['vɪntʃutsʃaibǝ], *f.* (—, *pl.* —n) (*Motor.*) windscreen.

Windseite ['vɪntzaitǝ], *f.* (—, *pl.* —n) windward side.

Windspiel ['vɪntʃpi:l], *n.* (—s, *pl.* —e) greyhound.

windstill ['vɪntʃtɪl], *adj.* calm.

Windung ['vɪnduŋ], *f.* (—, *pl.* —en) winding; convolution; twist, loop; coil; meandering.

Wink [vɪŋk], *m.* (—(e)s, *pl.* —e) sign, nod; (*fig.*) hint, suggestion.

Winkel ['vɪŋkəl], *m.* (—s, *pl.* —) corner; (*Maths.*) angle.

Winkeladvokat ['vɪŋkəlatvoka:t], *m.* (—en, *pl.* —en) quack lawyer.

Winkelmaß ['vɪŋkəlma:s], *n.* (—es, *pl.* —e) set-square.

Winkelmesser ['vɪŋkəlmesər], *m.* (—s, *pl.* —) protractor.

Winkelzug ['vɪŋkəltsu:k], *m.* (—s, *pl.* —e) evasion, trick, shift.

winken ['vɪŋkən], *v.n.* signal, nod, beckon, wave.

winklig ['vɪŋklɪç], *adj.* angular.

winseln ['vɪnzəln], *v.n.* whimper, whine, wail.

Winter ['vɪntər], *m.* (—s, *pl.* —) winter.

Wintergarten ['vɪntərgartən], *m.* (—s, *pl.* ·) conservatory.

Wintergewächs ['vɪntərgəvɛks], *n.* (—es, *pl.* —e) perennial plant.

Wintergrün ['vɪntərgry:n], *n.* (—s, *no pl.*) evergreen; wintergreen.

wintern ['vɪntərn], *v.n.* become wintry.

Winterschlaf ['vɪntərʃla:f], *m.* (—s, *no pl.*) hibernation; den — halten, hibernate.

Winzer ['vɪntsər], *m.* (—s, *pl.* —) vine-grower.

winzig ['vɪntsɪç], *adj.* tiny, diminutive.

Wipfel ['vɪpfəl], *m.* (—s, *pl.* —) top (of a tree), tree-top.

Wippe ['vɪpə], *f.* (—, *pl.* —n) seesaw.

wippen ['vɪpən], *v.n.* balance, see-saw.

wir [vi:r], *pers. pron.* we.

Wirbel ['vɪrbəl], *m.* (—s, *pl.* —) (*water*) whirlpool, eddy; whirlwind; (*drum*) roll; (*head*) crown; (*back*) vertebra.

wirbeln ['vɪrbəln], *v.a., v.n.* whirl.

Wirbelsäule ['vɪrbəlzɔylə], *f.* (—, *pl.* —n) spine, vertebral column.

Wirbelwind ['vɪrbəlvɪnt], *m.* (—s, *pl.* —e) whirlwind.

Wirken ['vɪrkən], *n.* (—s, *no pl.*) activity.

wirken ['vɪrkən], *v.a.* effect, work; bring to pass; (*materials*) weave; (*dough*) knead. — *v.n.* work.

Wirker ['vɪrkər], *m.* (—s, *pl.* —) weaver.

wirklich ['vɪrklɪç], *adj.* real, actual; true, genuine.

Wirklichkeit ['vɪrklɪçkaɪt], *f.* (—, *no pl.*) reality.

wirksam ['vɪrkza:m], *adj.* effective, efficacious.

Wirksamkeit ['vɪrkza:mkaɪt], *f.* (—, *no pl.*) efficacy, efficiency.

Wirkung ['vɪrkuŋ], *f.* (—, *pl.* —en) working, operation; reaction; efficacy; effect, result, consequence; force, in-

fluence; *eine — ausüben auf,* have an effect on; influence s.o. *or* s.th.

Wirkungskreis ['vɪrkuŋskraɪs], *m.* (—es, *pl.* —e) sphere of activity.

wirkungslos ['vɪrkuŋslo:s], *adj.* in-effectual.

wirkungsvoll ['vɪrkuŋsfɔl], *adj.* effective, efficacious; (*fig.*) impressive.

wirr [vɪr], *adj.* tangled, confused; — *durcheinander,* higgledy-piggledy; *mir ist ganz — im Kopf,* my head is going round.

Wirren ['vɪrən], *f. pl.* troubles, disorders, disturbances.

wirrköpfig ['vɪrkœpfɪç], *adj.* muddle-headed.

Wirrsal ['vɪrza:l], *n.* (—s, *pl.* —e) confusion, disorder.

Wirrwarr ['vɪrvar], *m.* (—s, *no pl.*) jumble, hurly-burly, hubbub.

Wirt [vɪrt], *m.* (—(e)s, *pl.* —e) host; innkeeper; landlord.

Wirtin ['vɪrtɪn], *f.* (—, *pl.* —innen) hostess, landlady, innkeeper's wife.

wirtlich ['vɪrtlɪç], *adj.* hospitable.

Wirtschaft ['vɪrtʃaft], *f.* (—, *pl.* —en) housekeeping; administration; economy; household; housekeeping; inn, ale-house; (*coll.*) mess.

wirtschaften ['vɪrtʃaftən], *v.n.* keep house, housekeep; administer, run; (*coll.*) rummage.

Wirtschafterin ['vɪrtʃaftərɪn], *f.* (—, *pl.* —innen) housekeeper.

wirtschaftlich ['vɪrtʃaftlɪç], *adj.* economical, thrifty.

Wirtschaftlichkeit ['vɪrtʃaftlɪçkaɪt], *f.* (—, *no pl.*) economy; profitability.

Wirtschaftsgeld ['vɪrtʃaftsgɛlt], *n.* (—s, *pl.* —er) housekeeping-money.

Wirtshaus ['vɪrtshaus], *n.* (—es, *pl.* ·er) inn.

Wisch [vɪʃ], *m.* (—es, *pl.* —e) scrap of paper, rag.

wischen ['vɪʃən], *v.a.* wipe.

wispern ['vɪspərn], *v.a., v.n.* whisper.

Wißbegier(de) ['vɪsbəgi:r(də)], *f.* (—, *no pl.*) craving for knowledge; curiosity.

Wissen ['vɪsən], *n.* (—s, *no pl.*) knowledge, learning, erudition.

wissen ['vɪsən], *v.a. irr.* know, be aware of (a fact); be able to.

Wissenschaft ['vɪsənʃaft], *f.* (—, *pl.* —en) learning, scholarship; science.

wissenschaftlich ['vɪsənʃaftlɪç], *adj.* learned, scholarly; scientific.

wissenswert ['vɪsənsve:rt], *adj.* worth knowing.

Wissenszweig ['vɪsənstsvaɪk], *m.* (—s, *pl.* —e) branch of knowledge.

wissentlich ['vɪsəntlɪç], *adj.* deliberate, wilful. — *adv.* knowingly.

wittern ['vɪtərn], *v.a.* scent, smell; (*fig.*) suspect.

Witterung ['vɪtəruŋ], *f.* (—, *no pl.*) weather; trail; scent.

Witterungsverhältnisse ['vɪtəruŋsfer-hɛltnɪsə], *n. pl.* atmospheric conditions.

Witterungswechsel

Witterungswechsel [ˈvɪtərʊŋsvɛksəl], *m.* (—s, *no pl.*) change in the weather.

Witwe [ˈvɪtvə], *f.* (—, *pl.* —n) widow.

Witwer [ˈvɪtvər], *m.* (—s, *pl.* —) widower.

Witz [vɪts], *m.* (—es, *pl.* —e) wit, brains; joke, jest, witticism; funny story.

Witzblatt [ˈvɪtsblat], *n.* (—s, *pl.* ⁻er) satirical *or* humorous journal.

Witzbold [ˈvɪtsbɔlt], *m.* (—es, *pl.* —e) wag; wit.

witzeln [ˈvɪtsəln], *v.n.* poke fun (at).

witzig [ˈvɪtsɪç], *adj.* witty; funny, comical; bright.

wo [vo:], *interr. adv.* where? — *conj.* when.

wobei [vo:ˈbaɪ], *adv.* by which, at which, in connection with which; whereby; in doing so.

Woche [ˈvɔxə], *f.* (—, *pl.* —n) week.

Wochenbericht [ˈvɔxənbərɪçt], *m.* (—s, *pl.* —e) weekly report.

Wochenbett [ˈvɔxənbɛt], *n.* (—s, *no pl.*) confinement.

Wochenblatt [ˈvɔxənblat], *n.* (—s, *pl.* ⁻er) weekly (paper).

Wochenlohn [ˈvɔxənlo:n], *m.* (—s, *pl.* ⁻e) weekly wage(s).

Wochenschau [ˈvɔxənʃau], *f.* (—, *no pl.*) newsreel.

Wochentag [ˈvɔxənta:k], *m.* (—s, *pl.* —e) week-day.

wöchentlich [ˈvœçəntlɪç], *adj.* weekly, every week.

wodurch [vo:ˈdurç], *adv.* whereby, by which, through which; (*interr.*) by what?

wofern [vo:ˈfɛrn], *conj.* if, provided that.

wofür [vo:ˈfy:r], *adv.* for what, for which, wherefore.

Woge [ˈvo:gə], *f.* (—, *pl.* —n) wave, billow.

wogegen [vo:ˈge:gən], *adv.* against what, against which, in return for which.

wogen [ˈvo:gən], *v.n.* heave, sway; (*fig.*) fluctuate.

woher [vo:ˈhe:r], *adv.* whence, from what place, how.

wohin [vo:ˈhɪn], *adv.* whither, where.

wohingegen [vo:hɪnˈge:gən], *conj.* (*obs.*) whereas.

Wohl [vo:l], *n.* (—(e)s, *no pl.*) welfare, health; *auf dein* —, your health! cheers!

wohl [vo:l], *adv.* well, fit; indeed, doubtless, certainly; *ja* —, to be sure.

wohlan! [vo:lˈan], *excl.* well! now then!

wohlauf! [vo:lˈauf], *excl.* cheer up! — *sein*, be in good health.

wohlbedacht [ˈvo:lbədaxt], *adj.* well considered.

Wohlbefinden [ˈvo:lbəfɪndən], *n.* (—s, *no pl.*) good health.

Wohlbehagen [ˈvo:lbəha:gən], *n.* (—s, *no pl.*) comfort, ease, wellbeing.

wohlbehalten [ˈvo:lbəhaltən], *adj.* safe.

wohlbekannt [ˈvo:lbəkant], *adj.* well known.

wohlbeleibt [ˈvo:lbəlaipt], *adj.* corpulent, stout.

wohlbestallt [ˈvo:lbəʃtalt], *adj.* duly installed.

Wohlergehen [ˈvo:lɛrge:ən], *n.* (—s, *no pl.*) welfare, wellbeing.

wohlerhalten [ˈvo:lɛrhaltən], *adj.* well preserved.

wohlerzogen [ˈvo:lɛrtso:gən], *adj.* well bred, well brought up.

Wohlfahrt [ˈvo:lfa:rt], *f.* (—, *no pl.*) welfare, prosperity.

wohlfeil [ˈvo:lfail], *adj.* cheap, inexpensive.

Wohlgefallen [ˈvo:lgəfalən], *n.* (—s, *no pl.*) pleasure, delight, approval.

wohlgefällig [ˈvo:lgəfɛlɪç], *adj.* pleasant, agreeable.

Wohlgefühl [ˈvo:lgəfy:l], *n.* (—s, *no pl.*) comfort, ease.

wohlgelitten [ˈvo:lgəlɪtən], *adj.* popular.

wohlgemeint [ˈvo:lgəmaint], *adj.* well meant.

wohlgemerkt [ˈvo:lgəmɛrkt], *adv.* mind you! mark my words!

wohlgemut [ˈvo:lgəmu:t], *adj.* cheerful, merry.

wohlgeneigt [ˈvo:lgənaikt], *adj.* well disposed (towards).

wohlgepflegt [ˈvo:lgəpfle:kt], *adj.* well kept.

wohlgeraten [ˈvo:lgəra:tən], *adj.* successful; well turned out; good, well behaved.

Wohlgeruch [ˈvo:lgəru:x], *m.* (—es, *pl.* ⁻e) sweet scent, perfume, fragrance.

Wohlgeschmack [ˈvo:lgəʃmak], *m.* (—s, *no pl.*) pleasant flavour, agreeable taste.

wohlgesinnt [ˈvo:lgəzɪnt], *adj.* well disposed.

wohlgestaltet [ˈvo:lgəʃtaltət], *adj.* well shaped.

wohlgezielt [ˈvo:lgətsi:lt], *adj.* well aimed.

wohlhabend [ˈvo:lha:bənt], *adj.* well-to-do, wealthy, well off.

wohlig [ˈvo:lɪç], *adj.* comfortable, cosy.

Wohlklang [ˈvo:lklaŋ], *m.* (—s, *pl.* ⁻e) harmony, euphony.

wohlklingend [ˈvo:lklɪŋənt], *adj.* harmonious, euphonious, sweet-sounding.

Wohlleben [ˈvo:lle:bən], *n.* (—s, *no pl.*) luxurious living.

wohllöblich [ˈvo:llø:plɪç], *adj.* worshipful.

wohlmeinend [ˈvo:lmaɪnənt], *adj.* well-meaning.

wohlschmeckend [ˈvo:lʃmɛkənt], *adj.* savoury, tasty, delicious.

Wohlsein [ˈvo:lzaɪn], *n.* (—s, *no pl.*) good health, wellbeing.

Wohlstand [ˈvo:lʃtant], *m.* (—s, *no pl.*) prosperity.

Wohltat [ˈvo:lta:t], *f.* (—, *pl.* —en) benefit; kindness; (*pl.*) benefaction, charity; (*fig.*) treat.

Wohltäter ['vo:ltɛːtər], *m.* (—s, *pl.* —) benefactor.

Wohltätigkeit ['vo:ltɛːtɪçkaɪt], *f.* (—, *no pl.*) charity.

wohltuend ['vo:ltu:ənt], *adj.* soothing.

wohltun ['vo:ltu:n], *v.n. irr.* do good; be comforting.

wohlweislich ['vo:lvaɪslɪç], *adj.* wisely.

Wohlwollen ['vo:lvɔlən], *n.* (—s, *no pl.*) benevolence; favour, patronage.

wohnen ['vo:nən], *v.n.* reside, dwell, live.

wohnhaft ['vo:nhaft], *adj.* domiciled, resident; — *sein*, reside, be domiciled.

Wohnhaus ['vo:nhaus], *n.* (—es, *pl.* ˙er) dwelling-house.

wohnlich ['vo:nlɪç], *adj.* comfortable; cosy.

Wohnort ['vo:nɔrt], *m.* (—s, *pl.* —e) place of residence.

Wohnsitz ['vo:nzɪts], *m.* (—es, *pl.* —e) domicile, abode, residence.

Wohnstätte ['vo:nʃtɛtə], *f.* (—, *pl.* —n) abode, home.

Wohnung ['vo:nuŋ], *f.* (—, *pl.* —en) residence, dwelling; house, flat, lodging; apartment.

Wohnungsmangel ['vo:nuŋsmaŋəl], *m.* (—s, *no pl.*) housing shortage.

Wohnwagen ['vo:nva:gən], *m.* (—s, *pl.* —) caravan.

Wohnzimmer ['vo:ntsɪmər], *n.* (—s, *pl.* —) sitting-room, living-room.

wölben ['vœlbən], *v.r. sich* —, vault, arch.

Wölbung ['vœlbuŋ], *f.* (—, *pl.* —en) vault, vaulting.

Wolf [vɔlf], *m.* (—(e)s, *pl.* ˙e) wolf.

Wolke ['vɔlkə], *f.* (—, *pl.* —n) cloud.

Wolkenbruch ['vɔlkənbrux], *m.* (—s, *pl.* ˙e) cloudburst, violent downpour.

Wolkenkratzer ['vɔlkənkratsər], *m.* (—s, *pl.* —) sky-scraper.

Wolkenkuckucksheim [vɔlkən'kukukshaɪm], *n.* (—s, *no pl.*) Utopia, cloud cuckoo land.

Wolldecke ['vɔldɛkə], *f.* (—, *pl.* —n) blanket.

Wolle ['vɔlə], *f.* (—, *pl.* —n) wool.

wollen (1) ['vɔlən], *v.a., v.n. irr.* wish, want to, be willing, intend; *was — Sie*, what do you want?

wollen (2) ['vɔlən], *ad* . woollen, made of wool.

Wollgarn ['vɔlgarn], *n.* (—s, *pl.* —e) woollen yarn.

Wollhandel ['vɔlhandəl], *m.* (—s, *no pl.*) wool-trade.

wollig ['vɔlɪç], *adj.* woolly.

Wollsamt ['vɔlzamt], *m.* (—s, *no pl.*) ˙ush, velveteen.

Wollust ['vɔlust], *f.* (—, *pl.* ˙e) voluptuousness; lust.

wollüstig ['vɔlystɪç], *adj.* voluptuous.

Wollwaren ['vɔlva:rən], *f. pl.* woollen goods.

Wollzupfen ['vɔltsupfən], *n.* (—s, *no pl.*) wool-picking.

womit [vo:'mɪt], *adv.* wherewith, with which; (*interr.*) with what?

womöglich [vo:'mø:klɪç], *adv.* if possible, perhaps.

wonach [vo:'na:x], *adv.* whereafter, after which; according to which.

Wonne ['vɔnə], *f.* (—, *pl.* —n) delight, bliss, rapture.

wonnetrunken ['vɔnətruŋkən], *adj.* enraptured.

wonnig ['vɔnɪç], *adj.* delightful.

woran [vo:'ran], *adv.* whereat, whereby; (*interr.*) by what? at what?

worauf [vo:'rauf], *adv.* upon which, at which; whereupon; (*interr.*) on what?

woraufhin [vo:rauf'hɪn], *conj.* whereupon.

woraus [vo:'raus], *adv.* (*rel. & interr.*) whence, from which; by or out of which.

worein [vo:'raɪn], *adv.* (*rel. & interr.*) into which; into what.

worin [vo:'rɪn], *adv.* (*rel.*) wherein; (*interr.*) in what?

Wort [vɔrt], *n.* (—(e)s, *pl.* ˙er —e) word, term; expression, saying.

wortarm ['vɔrtarm], *adj.* poor in words, deficient in vocabulary.

Wortarmut ['vɔrtarmu:t], *f.* (—, *no pl.*) paucity of words, poverty of language.

Wortbildung ['vɔrtbɪlduŋ], *f.* (—, *pl.* —en) word-formation.

wortbrüchig ['vɔrtbryçɪç], *adj.* faithless, disloyal.

Wörterbuch ['vœrtərbu:x], *n.* (—(e)s, *pl.* ˙er) dictionary.

Worterklärung ['vɔrtɛrklɛːruŋ], *f.* (—, *pl.* —en) definition.

Wortforschung ['vɔrtfɔrʃuŋ], *f.* (—, *no pl.*) etymology.

Wortfügung ['vɔrtfy:guŋ], *f.* (—, *no pl.*) syntax.

Wortführer ['vɔrtfy:rər], *m.* (—s, *pl.* —) spokesman.

Wortgefecht ['vɔrtgəfɛçt], *n.* (—es, *pl.* —e) verbal battle.

wortgetreu ['vɔrtgətrɔy], *adj.* literal, verbatim.

wortkarg ['vɔrtkark], *adj.* laconic, sparing of words, taciturn.

Wortlaut ['ɔrtlaut], *m.* (—s, *pl.* —e) wording, text.

wörtlich ['vœrtlɪç], *adj.* verbal; literal, word for word.

wortlos ['vɔrtlo:s], *adj.* speechless. — *adv.* without uttering a word.

wortreich ['vɔrtraɪç], *adj.* (*language*) rich in words; (*fig.*) verbose, wordy.

Wortreichtum ['vɔrtraɪçtum], *m.* (—s, *no pl.*) (*language*) wealth of words; (*fig.*) verbosity, wordiness.

Wortschwall ['vɔrtʃval], *m.* (—s, *no pl.*) bombast; torrent of words.

Wortspiel ['vɔrtʃpi:l], *n.* (—s, *pl.* —e) pun.

Wortversetzung ['vɔrtfɛrzetsuŋ], *f.* (—, *pl.* —en) inversion (of words).

Wortwechsel ['vɔrtvɛksəl], *m.* (—s, *pl.* —) dispute, altercation.

worüber [vo'ry:bər], *adv.* (*rel.*) about which, whereof; (*interr.*) about what?

worunter [vo'runtər], *adv.* *(rel.)* whereunder; *(interr.)* under what?

woselbst [vo:'zɛlpst], *adv.* where.

wovon [vo:'fɔn], *adv.* *(rel.)* whereof; *(interr.)* of what?

wovor [vo:'fo:r], *adv.* *(rel.)* before which; *(interr.)* before what?

wozu [vo:'tsu:], *adv.* *(rel.)* whereto; *(interr.)* why? for what purpose? to what end?

Wrack [vrak], *n.* (**—s**, *pl.* **—s**) wreck.

wringen ['vrɪŋən], *v.a.* wring.

Wringmaschine ['vrɪŋmaʃi:nə], *f.* (**—**, *pl.* **—n**) wringer, mangle.

Wucher ['vu:xər], *m.* (**—s**, *no pl.*) usury.

wucherisch ['vu:xərɪʃ], *adj.* usurious, extortionate.

wuchern ['vu:xərn], *v.n.* practise usury; *(plants)* luxuriate, grow profusely.

Wucherungen ['vu:xəruŋən], *f. pl.* *(Med.)* excrescence, growth.

Wuchs [vu:ks], *m.* (**—es**, *no pl.*) growth; shape, build.

Wucht [vuxt], *f.* (**—**, *no pl.*) power, force; weight; impetus.

wuchten ['vuxtən], *v.n.* *(Poet.)* press heavily. — *v.a.* prise up.

wuchtig ['vuxtɪç], *adj.* weighty, forceful.

Wühlarbeit ['vy:larbaɪt], *f.* (**—**, *pl.* **—en**) subversive activity.

wühlen ['vy:lən], *v.a., v.n.* dig, burrow; *(fig.)* agitate.

Wühler ['vy:lər], *m.* (**—s**, *pl.* **—**) agitator, demagogue.

Wühlmaus ['vy:lmaus], *f.* (**—**, *pl.* **⁀e**) *(Zool.)* vole.

Wulst [vulst], *m.* (**—es**, *pl.* **⁀e**) roll, pad; swelling.

wülstig ['vylstɪç], *adj.* padded, stuffed; swollen.

wund [vunt], *adj.* sore, wounded.

Wundarzt ['vuntartst], *m.* (**—es**, *pl.* **⁀e**) *(obs.)* surgeon.

Wundbalsam ['vuntbalzam], *m.* (**—s**, *pl.* **—e**) balm.

Wunde ['vundə], *f.* (**—**, *pl.* **—n**) wound, hurt.

Wunder ['vundər], *n.* (**—s**, *pl.* **—**) marvel, wonder, miracle.

wunderbar ['vundərba:r], *adj.* wonderful, marvellous.

Wunderding ['vundərdɪŋ], *n.* (**—s**, *pl.* **—e**) marvel.

Wunderdoktor ['vundərdɔktər], *m.* (**—s**, *pl.* **—en**) quack doctor.

Wunderglaube ['vundərglaubə], *m.* (**—ns**, *no pl.*) belief in miracles.

wunderhübsch [vundər'hypʃ], *adj.* exceedingly pretty.

Wunderkind ['vundərkɪnt], *n.* (**—s**, *pl.* **—er**) infant prodigy.

Wunderlampe ['vundərlampə], *f.* (**—**, *pl.* **—n**) magic lantern.

wunderlich ['vundərlɪç], *adj.* strange, odd, queer.

wundern ['vundərn], *v.r. sich — über*, be surprised at, be astonished at.

wundersam ['vundərza:m], *adj.* wonderful, strange.

wunderschön ['vundərʃø:n], *adj.* lovely,

gorgeous; exquisite.

Wundertat ['vundərta:t], *f.* (**—**, *pl.* **—en**) miraculous deed.

wundertätig ['vundərtɛ:tɪç], *adj.* miraculous.

Wundertier ['vundərti:r], *n.* (**—s**, *pl.* **—e**) monster; *(fig.)* prodigy.

Wunderwerk ['vundərvɛrk], *n.* (**—s**, *pl.* **—e**) miracle.

Wundmal ['vuntma:l], *n.* (**—s**, *pl.* **—e**) scar.

Wunsch [vunʃ], *m.* (**—es**, *pl.* **⁀e**) wish, desire, aspiration.

Wünschelrute ['vynʃəlru:tə], *f.* (**—**, *pl.* **—n**) divining-rod.

wünschen ['vynʃən], *v.a.* wish, desire, long for.

wünschenswert ['vynʃənsve:rt], *adj.* desirable.

Wunschform ['vunʃfɔrm], *f.* (**—**, *no pl.*) *(Gram.)* optative form.

wuppdich! ['vupdɪç], *excl.* here goes!

Würde ['vyrdə], *f.* (**—**, *pl.* **—n**) dignity, honour.

Würdenträger ['vyrdəntrɛ:gər], *m.* (**—s**, *pl.* **—**) dignitary.

würdevoll ['vyrdəfɔl], *adj.* dignified.

würdig ['vyrdɪç], *adj.* worthy (of), deserving, meritorious.

würdigen ['vyrdɪgən], *v.a.* honour; *ich weiss es zu —*, I appreciate it.

Würdigung ['vyrdɪguŋ], *f.* (**—**, *pl.* **—en**) appreciation.

Wurf [vurf], *m.* (**—(e)s**, *pl.* **⁀e**) cast, throw.

Würfel ['vyrfəl], *m.* (**—s**, *pl.* **—**) die; *(Geom.)* cube; — *spielen*, play at dice.

würfelförmig ['vyrfəlfœrmɪç], *adj.* cubic, cubiform.

würfeln ['vyrfəln], *v.n.* play at dice.

Wurfgeschoß ['vurfgəʃo:s], *n.* (**—sses**, *pl.* **—sse**) missile, projectile.

Wurfmaschine ['vurfmaʃi:nə], *f.* (**—**, *pl.* **—n**) catapult.

Wurfscheibe ['vurfʃaɪbə], *f.* (**—**, *pl.* **—n**) discus, quoit.

Wurfspieß ['vurfʃpi:s], *m.* (**—es**, *pl.* **—e**) javelin.

würgen ['vyrgən], *v.a.* strangle, throttle. — *v.n.* choke.

Würgengel ['vyrgəŋəl], *m.* (**—s**, *no pl.*) avenging angel.

Würger ['vyrgər], *m.* (**—s**, *pl.* **—**) strangler, murderer; *(Poet.)* slayer; *(Orn.)* shrike, butcher-bird.

Wurm [vurm], *m.* (**—(e)s**, *pl.* **⁀er**) worm; *(apple)* maggot.

wurmen ['vurmən], *v.a.* vex.

wurmstichig ['vurmʃtɪçɪç], *adj.* worm-eaten.

Wurst [vurst], *f.* (**—**, *pl.* **⁀e**) sausage.

wurstig ['vurstɪç], *adj.* *(sl.)* quite indifferent.

Wurstigkeit ['vurstɪçkaɪt], *f.* (**—**, *no pl.*) callousness, indifference.

Würze ['vyrtsə], *f.* (**—**, *pl.* **—n**) seasoning, spice, condiment.

Wurzel ['vurtsəl], *f.* (**—**, *pl.* **—n**) root.

wurzeln ['vurtsəln], *v.n.* be rooted.

würzen ['vyrtsən], *v.a.* season, spice.

würzig ['vyrtsɪç], *adj.* spicy, fragrant.

Wust [vust], *m.* (**—es**, *no pl.*) chaos, trash.

wüst [vy:st], *adj.* waste, desert; desolate; dissolute.

Wüste ['vy:stə], *f.* (**—**, *pl.* **—n**) desert, wilderness.

Wüstling ['vy:stlɪŋ], *m.* (**—s**, *pl.* **—e**) profligate, libertine.

Wut [vu:t], *f.* (**—**, *no pl.*) rage, fury, passion.

wüten ['vy:tən], *v.n.* rage, storm, fume.

wutentbrannt ['vu:təntbrant], *adj.* enraged, infuriated.

Wüterich ['vy:tərɪç], *m.* (**—s**, *pl.* **—e**) tyrant; ruthless fellow.

Wutgeschrei ['vu:tgəʃraɪ], *n.* (**—s**, *no pl.*) yell of rage.

wutschnaubend ['vu:tʃnaubənt], *adj.* foaming with rage.

X

X [ɪks], *n.* (**—s**, *pl.* **—s**) the letter X.

X-Beine ['ɪksbaɪnə], *n. pl.* knock-knees.

x-beliebig ['ɪksbəli:bɪç], *adj.* any, whatever (one likes).

Xenie ['kse:njə], *f.* (**—**, *pl.* **—n**) epigram.

Xereswein ['kse:rəsvaɪn], *m.* (**—s**, *pl.* **—e**) sherry.

x-mal ['ɪksma:l], *adv.* (*coll.*) so many times, umpteen times.

X-Strahlen ['ɪksʃtra:lən], *m. pl.* X-rays.

Xylographie [ksylogra'fi:], *f.* (**—**, *no pl.*) wood-engraving.

Xylophon [ksylo'fo:n], *n.* (**—s**, *pl.* **—e**) (*Mus.*) xylophone.

Y

Y ['ypsilɔn], *n.* (**—s**, *pl.* **—s**) the letter Y.

Yak [jak], *m.* (**—s**, *pl.* **—s**) (*Zool.*) yak.

Yamswurzel ['jamsvurtsəl], *f.* (**—**, *pl.* **—n**) yam.

Ysop [y'zo:p], *m.* (**—s**, *no pl.*) hyssop.

Z

Z [tsɛt], *n.* (**—s**, *pl.* **—s**) the letter Z.

Zabel ['tsa:bəl], *m.* (**—s**, *pl.* **—**) (*obs.*) chess-board.

Zacke ['tsakə], *f.* (**—**, *pl.* **—n**) tooth, spike; (*fork*) prong.

zackig ['tsakɪç], *adj.* pronged, toothed, indented; (*rock*) jagged; (*sl.*) smart.

zagen ['tsa:gən], *v.n.* quail, blench, be disheartened, be fainthearted.

zaghaft ['tsa:khaft], *adj.* faint-hearted.

Zaghaftigkeit ['tsa:khaftɪçkaɪt], *f.* (**—**, *no pl.*) faintheartedness, timidity.

zäh [tsɛ:], *adj.* tough.

Zähigkeit ['tsɛ:ɪçkaɪt], *f.* (**—**, *no pl.*) toughness.

Zahl [tsa:l], *f.* (**—**, *pl.* **—en**) number, figure.

zahlbar ['tsa:lba:r], *adj.* payable, due.

zählbar ['tsɛ:lba:r], *adj.* calculable.

zahlen ['tsa:lən], *v.a.* pay; *Ober!* **—**, waiter! the bill, please.

zählen ['tsɛ:lən], *v.a.*, *v.n.* count, number.

Zahlenfolge ['tsa:lənfɔlgə], *f.* (**—**, *no pl.*) numerical order.

Zahlenlehre ['tsa:lənle:rə], *f.* (**—**, *no pl.*) arithmetic.

Zahlenreihe ['tsa:lənraɪə], *f.* (**—**, *pl.* **—n**) numerical progression.

Zahlensinn ['tsa:lənzɪn], *m.* (**—s**, *no pl.*) head for figures.

Zahler ['tsa:lər], *m.* (**—s**, *pl.* **—**) payer.

Zähler ['tsɛ:lər], *m.* (**—s**, *pl.* **—**) counter, teller; meter; (*Maths.*) numerator.

Zahlkellner ['tsa:lkɛlnər], *m.* (**—s**, *pl.* **—**) head waiter.

Zahlmeister ['tsa:lmaɪstər], *m.* (**—s**, *pl.* **—**) paymaster, treasurer, bursar.

zahlreich ['tsa:lraɪç], *adj.* numerous.

Zahltag ['tsa:lta:k], *m.* (**—s**, *pl.* **—e**) pay-day.

Zahlung ['tsa:luŋ], *f.* (**—**, *pl.* **—en**) payment; **—** *leisten*, make payment; *die* **—***en einstellen*, stop payment.

Zählung ['tsɛ:luŋ], *f.* (**—**, *pl.* **—en**) counting, computation; census.

Zahlungseinstellung ['tsa:luŋsaɪnʃtɛluŋ], *f.* (**—**, *pl.* **—en**) suspension of payment.

zahlungsfähig ['tsa:luŋsfɛ:ɪç], *adj.* solvent.

Zahlungsmittel ['tsa:luŋsmɪtəl], *n.* (**—s**, *pl.* **—**) means of payment; *gesetzliches* **—**, legal tender.

Zahlungstermin ['tsa:luŋstermi:n], *m.* (**—s**, *pl.* **—e**) time of payment.

zahlungsunfähig ['tsa:luŋsunfɛ:ɪç], *adj.* insolvent.

Zahlwort ['tsa:lvɔrt], *n.* (**—s**, *pl.* **⁻er**) (*Gram.*) numeral.

zahm [tsa:m], *adj.* tame; domestic(ated); **—** *machen*, tame.

zähmen ['tsɛ:mən], *v.a.* tame, domesticate.

Zähmer ['tsɛ:mər], *m.* (**—s**, *pl.* **—**) tamer.

Zahmheit ['tsa:mhaɪt], *f.* (**—**, *no pl.*) tameness.

Zähmung ['tsɛ:muŋ], *f.* (**—**, *no pl.*) taming, domestication.

Zahn [tsa:n], *m.* (**—(e)s**, *pl.* **⁻e**) tooth; (*wheel*) cog.

Zahnarzt ['tsa:nartst], *m.* (**—es**, *pl.* ⁓e) dentist, dental surgeon.

Zahnbürste ['tsa:nbyrstə], *f.* (**—**, *pl.* **—n**) tooth-brush.

Zähneklappern ['tsɛːnəklapərn], *n.* (**—s**, *no pl.*) chattering of teeth.

Zähneknirschen ['tsɛːnəknɪrʃən], *n.* (**—s**, *no pl.*) gnashing of teeth.

zahnen ['tsa:nən], *v.n.* teethe, cut o.'s teeth.

zähnen ['tsɛ:nən], *v.a.* indent, notch.

Zahnfleisch ['tsa:nflaɪʃ], *n.* (**—es**, *no pl.*) gums.

Zahnfüllung ['tsa:nfylun], *f.* (**—**, *pl.* **—en**) filling, stopping (of tooth).

Zahnheilkunde ['tsa:nhaɪlkundə], *f.* (**—**, *no pl.*) dentistry, dental surgery.

Zahnlücke ['tsa:nlykə], *f.* (**—**, *pl.* **—n**) gap in the teeth.

Zahnpaste ['tsa:npastə], *f.* (**—**, *no pl.*) tooth-paste.

Zahnpulver ['tsa:npulvər], *n.* (**—s**, *no pl.*) tooth-powder.

Zahnrad ['tsa:nra:t], *n.* (**—s**, *pl.* ⁓er) cog-wheel.

Zahnradbahn ['tsa:nra:tba:n], *f.* (**—**, *pl.* **—en**) rack-railway.

Zahnschmerzen ['tsa:nʃmɛrtsən], *m. pl.* toothache.

Zahnstocher ['tsa:nʃtɔxər], *m.* (**—s**, *pl.* **—**) tooth-pick.

Zähre ['tsɛːrə], *f.* (**—**, *pl.* **—n**) (*Poet.*) tear.

Zander ['tsandər], *m.* (**—s**, *pl.* **—**) (*fish*) pike.

Zange ['tsaŋə], *f.* (**—**, *pl.* **—n**) tongs; pincers; tweezers; nippers; (*Med.*) forceps.

Zank [tsaŋk], *m.* (**—es**, *pl.* ⁓ereien) quarrel, altercation, tiff.

Zankapfel ['tsaŋkapfəl], *m.* (**—s**, *pl.* ⁓) bone of contention.

zanken ['tsaŋkən], *v.r. sich —*, quarrel, dispute.

zänkisch ['tsɛnkɪʃ], *adj.* quarrelsome.

Zanksucht ['tsaŋkzuxt], *f.* (**—**, *no pl.*) quarrelsomeness.

zanksüchtig ['tsaŋkzyçtɪç], *adj.* quarrelsome, cantankerous.

Zapfen ['tsapfən], *m.* (**—s**, *pl.* **—**) pin, peg; (*cask*) bung, spigot; (*fir*) cone.

zapfen ['tsapfən], *v.a.* tap, draw.

Zapfenstreich ['tsapfənʃtraɪç], *m.* (**—s**, *no pl.*) (*Mil.*) tattoo, retreat.

zapp(e)lig ['tsap(ə)lɪç], *adj.* fidgety.

zappeln ['tsapəln], *v.n.* kick, struggle, wriggle.

Zar [tsa:r], *m.* (**—en**, *pl.* **—en**) Czar, Tsar.

zart [tsart], *adj.* tender, sensitive, delicate, gentle; *— besaitet*, (*iron.*) sensitive, highly strung.

Zartgefühl ['tsartɡəfy:l], *n.* (**—s**, *no pl.*) delicacy, sensitivity.

Zartheit ['tsarthaɪt], *f.* (**—**, *no pl.*) tenderness, gentleness.

zärtlich ['tsɛ:rtlɪç], *adj.* loving, amorous, tender.

Zärtlichkeit ['tsɛ:rtlɪçkaɪt], *f.* (**—**, *pl.* **—en**) tenderness; caresses.

Zartsinn ['tsartzɪn], *m.* (**—s**, *no pl.*) delicacy.

Zauber ['tsaubər], *m.* (**—s**, *no pl.*) charm, spell, enchantment; magic; fascination.

Zauberei [tsaubə'raɪ], *f.* (**—**, *pl.* **—en**) magic, witchcraft, sorcery.

Zauberer ['tsaubərər], *m.* (**—s**, *pl.* **—**) magician, sorcerer, wizard.

zauberisch ['tsaubərɪʃ], *adj.* magical; (*fig.*) enchanting.

Zauberkraft ['tsaubərkraft], *f.* (**—**, *no pl.*) magic power, witchcraft.

Zaubermittel ['tsaubərmɪtəl], *n.* (**—s**, *pl.* **—**) charm.

zaubern ['tsaubərn], *v.n.* practise magic; conjure.

Zauberspruch ['tsaubərʃprux], *m.* (**—s**, *pl.* ⁓e) spell, charm.

Zauberstab ['tsaubərʃta:p], *m.* (**—s**, *pl.* ⁓e) magic wand.

Zauderer ['tsaudərər], *m.* (**—s**, *pl.* **—**) loiterer, temporizer, procrastinator.

zaudern ['tsaudərn], *v.n.* delay; hesitate, procrastinate.

Zaum [tsaum], *m.* (**—(e)s**, *pl.* ⁓e) bridle; *im — halten*, check, restrain.

zäumen ['tsɔymən], *v.a.* bridle.

Zaun [tsaun], *m.* (**—(e)s**, *pl.* ⁓e) hedge, fence; *einen Streit vom — brechen*, pick a quarrel.

Zaungast ['tsaungast], *m.* (**—s**, *pl.* ⁓e) onlooker, outsider; intruder.

Zaunkönig ['tsaunkø:nɪç], *m.* (**—s**, *pl.* **—e**) (*Orn.*) wren.

Zaunpfahl ['tsaunpfa:l], *m.* (**—s**, *pl.* ⁓e) pale, hedge-pole; *mit dem — winken*, give s.o. a broad hint.

Zaunrebe ['tsaunre:bə], *f.* (**—**, *pl.* **—n**) (*Bot.*) Virginia creeper.

zausen ['tsauzən], *v.a.* tousle; (*hair*) disarrange, ruffle.

Zechbruder ['tsɛçbru:dər], *m.* (**—s**, *pl.* ⁓) tippler, toper.

Zeche ['tsɛçə], *f.* (**—**, *pl.* **—n**) bill (in a restaurant); mine; *die — bezahlen*, foot the bill, pay the piper.

Zeder ['tse:dər], *f.* (**—**, *pl.* **—n**) (*Bot.*) cedar.

zedieren [tsɛ'di:rən], *v.a.* cede.

Zehe ['tse:ə], *f.* (**—**, *pl.* **—n**) toe.

Zehenspitze ['tse:ənʃpɪtsə], *f.* (**—**, *pl.* **—n**) tip of the toe, tiptoe.

zehn [tse:n], *num. adj.* ten.

Zehneck ['tse:nɛk], *n.* (**—s**, *pl.* **—e**) decagon.

Zehnte ['tse:ntə], *m.* (**—n**, *pl.* **—n**) tithe.

zehren ['tse:rən], *v.n. von etwas —*, live on s.th., prey upon s.th.

Zehrfieber ['tse:rfi:bər], *n.* (**—s**, *no pl.*) hectic fever.

Zehrgeld ['tse:rgɛlt], *n.* (**—s**, *pl.* **—er**) subsistence, allowance.

Zehrvorrat ['tse:rfo:rra:t], *m.* (**—s**, *pl.* ⁓e) provisions.

Zehrung ['tse:run], *f.* (**—**, *pl.* **—en**) consumption; victuals; (*Eccl.*) *letzte —*, viaticum.

Zeichen ['tsaɪçən], *n.* (**—s**, *pl.* **—**) sign, token, symptom, omen; indication; badge; signal.

Zeichenbrett ['tsaɪçənbrɛt], *n.* (**—s,** *pl.* **—er**) drawing-board.
Zeichendeuter ['tsaɪçəndɔytər], *m.* (**—s,** *pl.* **—**) astrologer.
Zeichendeuterei [tsaɪçəndɔytəˈraɪ], *f.* (**—,** *no pl.*) astrology.
Zeichenerklärung ['tsaɪçənɛrkleːruŋ], *f.* (**—** *pl.***—en**) legend, key.
Zeichensprache ['tsaɪçənʃpraːxə], *f.* (**—,** *no pl.*) sign-language.
Zeichentinte ['tsaɪçəntɪntə], *f.* (**—,** *no pl.*) marking ink.
zeichnen ['tsaɪçnən], *v.a.* draw; mark; (*money*) subscribe; (*letter*) sign.
Zeichner ['tsaɪçnər], *m.* (**—s,** *pl.* **—**) draughtsman, designer.
Zeichnung ['tsaɪçnuŋ], *f.* (**—,** *pl.* **—en**) drawing.
Zeigefinger ['tsaɪgəfɪŋər], *m.* (**—s,** *pl.* **—**) forefinger, index finger.
zeigen ['tsaɪgən], *v.a.* show, point to, prove.
Zeiger ['tsaɪgər], *m.* (**—s,** *pl.* **—**) indicator; hand (of watch, clock).
zeihen ['tsaɪən], *v.a. irr. einen einer Sache —,* tax s.o. with s.th.
Zeile ['tsaɪlə], *f.* (**—,** *pl.* **—n**) line; furrow; (*pl.*) letter.
Zeisig ['tsaɪzɪç], *m.* (**—s,** *pl.* **—e**) (*Orn.*) siskin.
Zeit [tsaɪt], *f.* (**—,** *pl.* **—en**) time; *zur —,* at present; *auf —,* on credit.
Zeitabschnitt ['tsaɪtapʃnɪt], *m.* (**—s,** *pl.* **—e**) period; epoch.
Zeitalter ['tsaɪtaltər], *n.* (**—s,** *pl.* **—**) age, era.
Zeitdauer ['tsaɪtdauər], *f.* (**—,** *no pl.*) space of time.
Zeitfrage ['tsaɪtfraːgə], *f.* (**—,** *pl.* **—n**) topical question; question of time.
Zeitgeist ['tsaɪtgaɪst], *m.* (**—s,** *no pl.*) spirit of the age.
zeitgemäß ['tsaɪtgəmɛːs], *adj.* timely, seasonable, opportune, modern.
Zeitgenosse ['tsaɪtgənɔsə], *m.* (**—n,** *pl.* **—n**) contemporary.
zeitig ['tsaɪtɪç], *adj.* early, timely.
zeitigen ['tsaɪtɪgən], *v.a.* engender, generate. *— v.n.* mature, ripen.
Zeitkarte ['tsaɪtkartə], *f.* (**—,** *pl.* **—n**) season ticket.
Zeitlauf ['tsaɪtlauf], *m.* (**—s,** *pl.* ᵛe) course of time, conjuncture.
zeitlebens ['tsaɪtleːbəns], *adv.* for life, (for) all his (*or* her) life.
zeitlich ['tsaɪtlɪç], *adj.* temporal, earthly; secular; temporary, transient.
zeitlos ['tsaɪtloːs], *adj.* lasting, permanent.
Zeitmangel ['tsaɪtmaŋəl], *m.* (**—s,** *no pl.*) lack of time.
Zeitmesser ['tsaɪtmɛsər], *m.* (**—s,** *pl.* **—**) chronometer, timepiece; metronome.
Zeitpunkt ['tsaɪtpuŋkt], *m.* (**—s,** *pl.* **—e**) moment, date; point of time.
zeitraubend ['tsaɪtraubənd], *adj.* time-consuming.
Zeitraum ['tsaɪtraum], *m.* (**—s,** *pl.* ᵛe) space of time, period.

Zeitschrift ['tsaɪtʃrɪft], *f.* (**—,** *pl.* **—en**) periodical, journal, magazine.
Zeitung ['tsaɪtuŋ], *f.* (**—,** *pl.* **—en**) newspaper.
Zeitungsente ['tsaɪtuŋsɛntə], *f.* (**—,** *pl.* **—n**) canard, newspaper hoax.
Zeitungskiosk ['tsaɪtuŋskiɔsk], *m.* (**—s,** *pl.* **—e**) newspaper-stall.
Zeitungsnachricht ['tsaɪtuŋsnaːxrɪçt], *f.* (**—,** *pl.* **—en**) newspaper report.
Zeitungswesen ['tsaɪtuŋsveːzən], *n.* (**—s,** *no pl.*) journalism.
Zeitverlust ['tsaɪtferlust], *m.* (**—s,** *no pl.*) loss of time; *ohne —,* without delay.
Zeitvertreib ['tsaɪtfertraɪp], *m.* (**—s,** *no pl.*) pastime, amusement; *zum —,* to pass the time.
zeitweilig ['tsaɪtvaɪlɪç], *adj.* temporary.
zeitweise ['tsaɪtvaɪzə], *adv.* from time to time.
Zeitwort ['tsaɪtvɔrt], *n.* (**—s,** *pl.* ᵛer) (*Gram.*) verb.
Zelle ['tsɛllə], *f.* (**—,** *pl.* **—n**) cell; booth.
Zelt [tsɛlt], *n.* (**—(e)s,** *pl.* **—e**) tent.
Zeltdecke ['tsɛltdɛkə], *f.* (**—,** *pl.* **—n**) awning, marquee.
Zement [tseˈment], *m.* (**—s,** *no pl.*) cement.
Zenit [tseˈniːt], *m.* (**—s,** *no pl.*) zenith.
zensieren [tsɛnˈziːrən], *v.a.* review, censure; (*Sch.*) mark.
Zensor ['tsɛnzɔr], *m.* (**—s,** *pl.* **—en**) censor.
Zensur [tsɛnˈzuːr], *f.* (**—,** *pl.* **—en**) censure; (*Sch.*) report, mark; censorship.
Zentimeter ['tsɛntimeːtər], *m.* (**—s,** *pl.* **—**) centimetre.
Zentner ['tsɛntnər], *m.* (**—s,** *pl.* **—**) hundredweight.
zentral [tsɛnˈtraːl], *adj.* central.
Zentrale [tsɛnˈtraːlə], *f.* (**—,** *pl.* **—n**) control room; head office.
zentralisieren [tsɛntraliˈziːrən], *v.a.* centralise.
Zentrum ['tsɛntrum], *n.* (**—s,** *pl.* **—tren**) centre; (*Am.*) center.
Zephir ['tseːfiːr], *m.* (**—s,** *pl.* **—e**) zephyr.
Zepter ['tsɛptər], *m. & n.* (**—s,** *pl.* **—**) sceptre, mace.
zerbrechen [tsɛrˈbrɛçən], *v.a., v.n. irr.* (*aux.* sein) break to pieces; shatter; *sich den Kopf —,* rack o.'s brains.
zerbrechlich [tsɛrˈbrɛçlɪç], *adj.* brittle, fragile.
zerbröckeln [tsɛrˈbrœkəln], *v.a., v.n.* (*aux.* sein) crumble.
zerdrücken [tsɛrˈdrykən], *v.a.* crush, bruise.
Zeremonie [tseremoˈniː], *f.* (**—,** *pl.* **—n**) ceremony.
zeremoniell [tseremoˈnjel], *adj.* ceremonial, formal.
Zerfahrenheit [tsɛrˈfaːrənhaɪt], *f.* (**—,** *no pl.*) absent-mindedness.
Zerfall [tsɛrˈfal], *m.* (**—s,** *no pl.*) disintegration; decay.
zerfallen [tsɛrˈfalən], *v.n. irr.* (*aux.* sein) fall to pieces. *— adj.* in ruins.

zerfleischen [tsɛrˈflaɪʃən], *v.a.* lacerate, tear to pieces.

zerfließen [tsɛrˈfliːsən], *v.n. irr.* (*aux.* sein) dissolve, melt.

zerfressen [tsɛrˈfrɛsən], *v.a. irr.* gnaw, corrode.

zergehen [tsɛrˈgeːən], *v.n. irr.* (*aux.* sein) dissolve, melt.

zergliedern [tsɛrˈgliːdərn], *v.a.* dissect; (*fig.*) analyse.

zerhauen [tsɛrˈhauən], *v.a.* hew in pieces, chop up.

zerkauen [tsɛrˈkauən], *v.a.* chew.

zerkleinern [tsɛrˈklaɪnərn], *v.a.* cut into small pieces; (*firewood*) chop.

zerklüftet [tsɛrˈklyftət], *adj.* rugged.

zerknirscht [tsɛrˈknɪrʃt], *adj.* contrite.

Zerknirschung [tsɛrˈknɪrʃuŋ], *f.* (—, *no pl.*) contrition.

zerknittern [tsɛrˈknɪtərn], *v.a.* crumple.

zerknüllen [tsɛrˈknylən], *v.a.* rumple.

zerlassen [tsɛrˈlasən], *v.a. irr.* melt, liquefy.

zerlegen [tsɛrˈleːgən], *v.a.* resolve; take to pieces; cut up, carve; (*fig.*) analyse.

zerlumpt [tsɛrˈlumpt], *adj.* ragged, tattered.

zermahlen [tsɛrˈmaːlən], *v.a.* grind to powder.

zermalmen [tsɛrˈmalmən], *v.a.* crush.

zermartern [tsɛrˈmartərn], *v.a.* torment; *sich das Hirn —*, rack o.'s brains.

zernagen [tsɛrˈnaːgən], *v.a.* gnaw (away).

zerquetschen [tsɛrˈkvɛtʃən], *v.a.* squash, crush.

zerraufen [tsɛrˈraufən], *v.a.* dishevel.

Zerrbild [ˈtsɛrbɪlt], *n.* (—s, *pl.* —er) caricature.

zerreiben [tsɛrˈraɪbən], *v.a. irr.* grind to powder, pulverise.

zerreißen [tsɛrˈraɪsən], *v.a. irr.* tear, rend, tear up; break; rupture. — *v.n.* (*aux.* sein) be torn; (*clothes*) wear out.

zerren [ˈtsɛrən], *v.a.* pull, tug, drag; strain.

zerrinnen [tsɛrˈrɪnən], *v.n. irr.* (*aux.* sein) dissolve, melt; (*fig.*) vanish.

zerrütten [tsɛrˈrytən], *v.a.* unsettle, disorder, unhinge; ruin, destroy.

zerschellen [tsɛrˈʃɛlən], *v.n.* (*aux.* sein) be dashed to pieces, be wrecked.

zerschlagen [tsɛrˈʃlaːgən], *v.a. irr.* break, smash to pieces, batter.

zerschmettern [tsɛrˈʃmɛtərn], *v.a.* dash to pieces, break, crush; shatter, overwhelm.

zersetzen [tsɛrˈzɛtsən], *v.a., v.r.* break up; disintegrate.

zerspalten [tsɛrˈʃpaltən], *v.a.* cleave, split, slit.

zersprengen [tsɛrˈʃprɛŋən], *v.a.* explode, burst; (*crowd*) disperse; (*Mil.*) rout.

zerspringen [tsɛrˈʃprɪŋən], *v.n. irr.* (*aux.* sein) crack; fly to pieces, split.

zerstampfen [tsɛrˈʃtampfən], *v.a.* crush, pound.

zerstäuben [tsɛrˈʃtɔybən], *v.a.* spray, atomize.

zerstörbar [tsɛrˈʃtøːrbaːr], *adj.* destructible.

zerstören [tsɛrˈʃtøːrən], *v.a.* destroy, devastate.

Zerstörer [tsɛrˈʃtøːrər], *m.* (—s, *pl.* —) destroyer.

Zerstörung [tsɛrˈʃtøːruŋ], *f.* (—, *pl.* —en) destruction.

Zerstörungswut [tsɛrˈʃtøːruŋsvuːt], *f.* (—, *no pl.*) vandalism.

zerstoßen [tsɛrˈʃtoːsən], *v.a. irr.* bruise, pound.

zerstreuen [tsɛrˈʃtrɔyən], *v.a.* scatter, disperse; divert.

zerstreut [tsɛrˈʃtrɔyt], *adj.* absent-minded.

Zerstreuung [tsɛrˈʃtrɔyuŋ], *f.* (—, *pl.* —en) dispersion; amusement, diversion, distraction.

zerstückeln [tsɛrˈʃtykəln], *v.a.* dismember.

Zerstückelung [tsɛrˈʃtykəluŋ], *f.* (—, *no pl.*) dismemberment.

zerteilen [tsɛrˈtaɪlən], *v.a.* divide, separate; disperse, dissipate. — *v.r. sich —*, dissolve.

Zertifikat [tsɛrtifiˈkaːt], *n.* (—s, *pl.* —e) certificate, attestation.

zertrennen [tsɛrˈtrɛnən], *v.a.* rip up, unstitch.

zertrümmern [tsɛrˈtrymərn], *v.a.* destroy, break up, demolish.

Zerwürfnis [tsɛrˈvyrfnɪs], *n.* (—ses, *pl.* —se) discord, dissension.

zerzausen [tsɛrˈtsauzən], *v.a.* dishevel, tousle.

zerzupfen [tsɛrˈtsupfən], *v.a.* pick to pieces, pluck.

Zession [tsɛsˈjoːn], *f.* (—, *pl.* —en) cession, assignment, transfer.

Zetergeschrei [ˈtseːtərgəʃraɪ], *n.* (—s, *no pl.*) outcry, hullabaloo.

zetern [ˈtseːtərn], *v.n.* yell; (*coll.*) kick up a row.

Zettel [ˈtsɛtəl], *m.* (—s, *pl.* —) slip of paper; label, chit.

Zettelkasten [ˈtsɛtəlkastən], *m.* (—s, *pl.* ⁜) card-index, filing cabinet.

Zeug [tsɔyk], *n.* (—(e)s, *no pl.*) stuff, material; implements, kit, utensils; (*coll.*) things.

Zeuge [ˈtsɔygə], *m.* (—n, *pl.* —n) witness; *zum —n aufrufen*, call to witness.

zeugen [ˈtsɔygən], *v.a.* beget, generate, engender. — *v.n.* give evidence.

Zeugenaussage [ˈtsɔygənausaːgə], *f.* (—, *pl.* —n) evidence, deposition.

Zeugenbeweis [ˈtsɔygənbəvaɪs], *m.* (—es, *pl.* —e) evidence, proof.

Zeugeneid [ˈtsɔygənaɪt], *m.* (—s, *pl.* —e) oath of a witness.

Zeughaus [ˈtsɔykhaus], *n.* (—es, *pl.* ⁜er) (*obs.*) arsenal.

Zeugin [ˈtsɔygɪn], *f.* (—, *pl.* —innen) female witness.

Zeugnis ['tsɔyknɪs], n. (—ses, pl. —se) (Law.) deposition; testimonial, certificate, reference; character; school report; — ablegen, give evidence, bear witness; einem ein gutes — ausstellen, give s.o. a good reference.

Zeugung ['tsɔygʊŋ], f. (—, pl. —en) procreation, generation.

Zeugungskraft ['tsɔygʊŋskraft], f. (—, no pl.) generative power.

Zeugungstrieb ['tsɔygʊŋstriːp], m. (—s, no pl.) procreative instinct.

Zichorie [tsɪ'çoːrjə], f. (—, pl. —n) chicory.

Zicke ['tsɪkə], f. (—, pl. —n) dial. for Ziege.

Ziege ['tsiːgə], f. (—, pl. —n) goat.

Ziegel ['tsiːgəl], m. (—s, pl. —) (roof) tile; (wall) brick.

Ziegelbrenner ['tsiːgəlbrɛnər], m. (—s, pl. —) tile-maker, tiler; brickmaker.

Ziegelbrennerei [tsiːgəlbrɛnə'raɪ], f. (—, pl. —en) tile-kiln; brickyard.

Ziegeldach ['tsiːgəldax], n. (—s, pl. -er) tiled roof.

Ziegeldecker ['tsiːgəldɛkər], m. (—s, pl. —) tiler.

Ziegelei [tsiːgə'laɪ], f. (—, pl. —en) brickyard, brickworks.

Ziegelerde ['tsiːgələːrdə], f. (—, no pl.) brick-clay.

Ziegenbart ['tsiːgənbaːrt], m. (—s, pl. -e) goat's beard; (human) goatee.

Ziegenleder ['tsiːgənleːdər], n. (—s, no pl.) kid (leather).

Ziegenpeter ['tsiːgənpeːtər], m. (—s, no pl.) (Med.) mumps.

ziehen ['tsiːən], v.a. irr. draw, pull, drag; pull out; cultivate; breed; (game) move. — v.n. draw, be an attraction; (aux. sein) go, move. — v.r. sich —, extend.

Ziehkind ['tsiːkɪnt], n. (—s, pl. —er) foster-child.

Ziehmutter ['tsiːmutər], f. (—, pl. -) foster-mother.

Ziehung ['tsiːuŋ], f. (—, pl. —en) draw (in a lottery).

Ziehvater ['tsiːfaːtər], m. (—s, pl. -) foster-father.

Ziel [tsiːl], n. (—s, pl. —e) goal, aim, purpose, intention, end; butt, target; (Mil.) objective; (sports) winning-post.

zielbewußt ['tsiːlbəvust], adj. purposeful; systematic.

zielen ['tsiːlən], v.n. aim (at), take aim (at).

Ziellosigkeit ['tsiːlloːzɪçkaɪt], f. (—, no pl.) aimlessness.

Zielscheibe ['tsiːlʃaɪbə], f. (—, pl. —en) target, butt.

ziemen ['tsiːmən], v.r. sich —, become s.o., behove s.o., be proper for, befit.

Ziemer ['tsiːmər], n. & m. (—s, pl. —) whip.

ziemlich ['tsiːmlɪç], adj. moderate, tolerable, middling, fairly considerable, fair. — adv. rather, fairly.

Zier [tsiːr], f. (—, pl. —den) ornament.

Zieraffe ['tsiːrafə], m. (—n, pl. —n) fop, affected person.

Zierat ['tsiːraːt], m. (—s, no pl.) ornament, finery.

Zierde ['tsiːrdə], f. (—, pl. —n) decoration, embellishment; (fig.) credit, pride.

Ziererei [tsiːrə'raɪ], f. (—, pl. —en) affectation.

Ziergarten ['tsiːrgartən], m. (—s, pl. -) flower-garden, ornamental garden.

zierlich ['tsiːrlɪç], adj. dainty, graceful, pretty.

Zierpflanze ['tsiːrpflantsə], f. (—, pl. —n) ornamental plant.

Zierpuppe ['tsiːrpupə], f. (—, pl. —n) overdressed woman.

Ziffer ['tsɪfər], f. (—, pl. —n) figure, numeral.

Zifferblatt ['tsɪfərblat], n. (—s, pl. -er) dial, face.

ziffernmäßig ['tsɪfərnmɛːsɪç], adj. statistical.

Ziffernschrift ['tsɪfərnʃrɪft], f. (—, pl. —en) code.

Zigarette [tsigaˈrɛtə], f. (—, pl. —n) cigarette.

Zigarettenetui [tsigaˈrɛtənetviː], n. (—s, pl. —s) cigarette-case.

Zigarettenspitze [tsigaˈrɛtənʃpɪtsə], f. (—, pl. —n) cigarette-holder.

Zigarettenstummel [tsigaˈrɛtənʃtuməl], m. (—s, pl. —) cigarette-end.

Zigarre [tsiˈgarə], f. (—, pl. —n) cigar.

Zigarrenkiste [tsiˈgarənkɪstə], f. (—, pl. —n) cigar-box.

Zigarrenstummel [tsiˈgarənʃtuməl], m. (—s, pl. —) cigar-end.

Zigeuner [tsiˈgɔynər], m. (—s, pl. —) gipsy.

Zikade [tsiˈkaːdə], f. (—, pl. —n) (Ent.) grasshopper.

Zimmer ['tsɪmər], n. (—s, pl. —) room.

Zimmermädchen ['tsɪmərmɛːtçən], n. (—s, pl. —) chambermaid.

Zimmermann ['tsɪmərman], m. (—s, pl. Zimmerleute) carpenter, joiner.

zimmern ['tsɪmərn], v.a. carpenter, construct, build.

Zimmernachweis ['tsɪmərnaːxvaɪs], m. (—es, pl. —e) accommodation bureau.

Zimmerreihe ['tsɪmərraɪə], f. (—, pl. —n) suite of rooms.

Zimmervermieter ['tsɪmərfɛrmiːtər], m. (—s, pl. —) landlord.

zimperlich ['tsɪmpərlɪç], adj. simpering; prim; finicky, hypersensitive.

Zimt [tsimt], m. (—(e)s, no pl.) cinnamon.

Zink [tsiŋk], n. (—s, no pl.) zinc.

Zinke ['tsiŋkə], f. (—, pl. —n) prong, tine.

Zinn [tsin], n. (—s, no pl.) tin; pewter.

Zinnblech ['tsinblɛç], n. (—s, no pl.) tin-plate.

Zinne ['tsinə], f. (—, pl. —n) battlement, pinnacle.

zinnern ['tsɪnern], *adj.* made of pewter, of tin.

Zinnober [tsɪn'o:bər], *m.* (—s, *no pl.*) cinnabar; (*coll.*) fuss.

Zinnsäure ['tsɪnzɔyrə], *f.* (—, *no pl.*) stannic acid.

Zins [tsɪns], *m.* (—es, *pl.* —en) duty, tax; rent; (*pl.*) interest.

zinsbar ['tsɪnsba:r], *adj.* tributary; — *anlegen*, invest at interest; — *machen*, force to pay a tribute.

Zinsen ['tsɪnzən], *m. pl.* interest.

zinsentragend ['tsɪnzəntra:gənt], *adj.* interest-bearing.

Zinseszins ['tsɪnzəstsɪns], *m.* (—, *no pl.*) compound interest.

Zinsfuß ['tsɪnsfu:s], *m.* (—es, *pl.* ⸚e) rate of interest.

zinspflichtig ['tsɪnspflɪçtɪç], *adj.* subject to tax.

Zinsrechnung ['tsɪnsrɛçnuŋ], *f.* (—, *pl.* —en) interest account, calculation of interest.

Zinsschein ['tsɪnsʃaɪn], *m.* (—s, *pl.* —e) coupon, dividend warrant.

Zipfel ['tsɪpfəl], *m.* (—s, *pl.* —) tassel, edge, point, tip.

Zipperlein ['tsɪpərlaɪn], *n.* (—s, *no pl.*) (*coll.*) gout.

zirka ['tsɪrka], *adv.* circa, about, approximately.

Zirkel ['tsɪrkəl], *m.* (—s, *pl.* —) circle; (*Maths.*) pair of compasses; gathering.

zirkulieren [tsɪrku'li:rən], *v.n.* circulate; — *lassen*, put in circulation.

Zirkus ['tsɪrkus], *m.* (—, *pl.* —se) circus.

zirpen ['tsɪrpən], *v.n.* chirp.

zischeln ['tsɪʃəln], *v.n.* whisper.

zischen ['tsɪʃən], *v.n.* hiss; sizzle.

Zischlaut ['tsɪʃlaut], *m.* (—s, *pl.* —e) (*Phon.*) sibilant.

Zisterne [tsɪs'tɛrnə], *f.* (—, *pl.* —n) cistern.

Zisterzienser [tsɪstɛr'tsjɛnzər], *m.* (—s, *pl.* —) Cistercian (monk).

Zitadelle [tsɪta'dɛlə], *f.* (—, *pl.* —n) citadel.

Zitat [tsi'ta:t], *n.* (—(e)s, *pl.* —e) quotation, reference; *falsches* —, misquotation.

Zither ['tsɪtər], *f.* (—, *pl.* —n) zither.

zitieren [tsi'ti:rən], *v.a.* cite, quote; *falsch* —, misquote.

Zitronat [tsitro'na:t], *n.* (—s, *no pl.*) candied lemon peel.

Zitrone [tsi'tro:nə], *f.* (—, *pl.* —n) lemon.

Zitronenlimonade [tsi'tro:nənlimona:də], *f.* (—, *pl.* —n) lemonade, lemon drink.

Zitronensaft [tsi'tro:nənzaft], *m.* (—s, *pl.* ⸚e) lemon-juice.

Zitronensäure [tsi'tro:nənzɔyrə], *f.* (—, *no pl.*) citric acid.

Zitronenschale [tsi'tro:nənʃa:lə], *f.* (—, *pl.* —n) lemon-peel.

zitterig ['tsɪtərɪç], *adj.* shaky, shivery.

zittern ['tsɪtərn], *v.n.* tremble, shiver, quake.

Zitterpappel ['tsɪtərpapəl], *f.* (—, *pl.* —n) (*Bot.*) aspen-tree.

Zivil [tsi'vi:l], *n.* (—s, *no pl.*) civilians, *in* —, in plain clothes; (*coll.*) in civvies *or* mufti.

Zivilbeamte [tsi'vi:lbəamtə], *m.* (—n, *pl.* —n) civil servant.

Zivildienst [tsi'vi:ldi:nst], *m.* (—es, *no pl.*) civil service.

Zivilehe [tsi'vi:le:ə], *f.* (—, *pl.* —n) civil marriage.

Zivilgesetzbuch [tsi'vi:lgəzɛtsbu:x], *n.* (—s, *pl.* ⸚er) code of civil law.

Zivilingenieur [tsi'vi:lɪnʒənør], *m.* (—s, *pl.* —e) civil engineer.

Zivilisation [tsiviliza'tsjo:n], *f.* (—, *pl.* —en) civilisation.

zivilisatorisch [tsiviliza'to:rɪʃ], *adj.* civilising.

zivilisieren [tsivili'zi:rən], *v.a.* civilise.

Zivilist [tsivi'lɪst], *m.* (—en, *pl.* —en) civilian.

Zivilkleidung [tsi'vi:lklaɪduŋ], *f.* (—, *no pl.*) civilian dress, plain clothes.

Zobel ['tso:bəl], *m.* (—s, *pl.* —) sable.

Zobelpelz ['tso:bəlpɛlts], *m.* (—es, *pl.* —e) sable fur; sable-coat.

Zofe ['tso:fə], *f.* (—, *pl.* —n) lady's maid.

zögern ['tsø:gərn], *v.n.* hesitate, tarry, delay.

Zögerung ['tsø:gəruŋ], *f.* (—, *pl.* —en) hesitation, delay.

Zögling ['tsø:klɪŋ], *m.* (—s, *pl.* —e) pupil, charge.

Zölibat [tsø:li'ba:t], *m. & n.* (—s, *no pl.*) celibacy.

Zoll (1) [tsɔl], *m.* (—s, *no pl.*) inch.

Zoll (2) [tsɔl], *m.* (—s, *pl.* ⸚e) customs duty; (*bridge*) toll.

Zollabfertigung ['tsɔlapfɛrtɪguŋ], *f.* (—, *no pl.*) customs clearance.

Zollamt ['tsɔlamt], *n.* (—s, *pl.* ⸚er) custom house.

Zollaufschlag ['tsɔlaufʃla:k], *m.* (—s, *pl.* ⸚e) additional duty.

Zollbeamte ['tsɔlbəamtə], *m.* (—n, *pl.* —n) customs officer.

zollbreit ['tsɔlbraɪt], *adj.* one inch wide.

zollen ['tsɔlən], *v.a. Ehrfurcht* —, pay o.'s respects; *Beifall* —, applaud; *Dank* —, show gratitude.

zollfrei ['tsɔlfraɪ], *adj.* duty-free, exempt from duty.

Zöllner ['tsœlnər], *m.* (—s, *pl.* —) tax-gatherer.

zollpflichtig ['tsɔlpflɪçtɪç], *adj.* liable to duty, dutiable.

Zollsatz ['tsɔlzats], *m.* (—es, *pl.* ⸚e) customs tariff.

Zollverein ['tsɔlfəraɪn], *m.* (—s, *no pl.*) customs union.

Zollverschluß ['tsɔlfɛrʃlus], *m.* (—sses, *pl.* ⸚sse) bond.

Zone ['tso:nə], *f.* (—, *pl.* —n) zone.

Zoologe [tso:o'lo:gə], *m.* (—n, *pl.* —n) zoologist.

Zoologie [tso:olo'gi:], *f.* (—, *no pl.*) zoology.

zoologisch [tso:o'lo:gɪʃ], adj. zoological; —er Garten, zoological gardens, zoo.

Zopf [tsɔpf], m. (—(e)s, pl. ⁻e) plait, pigtail; (coll.) (old-fashioned) pedantry.

Zorn [tsɔrn], m. (—(e)s, no pl.) wrath, anger, indignation; seinen — auslassen, vent o.'s anger; in — geraten, get angry.

zornglühend ['tsɔrngly:ənt], adj. boiling with rage.

zornig ['tsɔrnɪç], adj. angry, wrathful, irate; — werden, get angry.

Zote ['tso:tə], f. (—, pl. —n) smutty story, ribaldry, bawdiness.

zotig ['tso:tɪç], adj. loose, ribald, smutty.

zottig ['tsɔtɪç], adj. shaggy.

zu [tsu:], prep. (Dat.) to, towards; in addition to; at, in, on; for; — Anfang. in the beginning; — Fuß, on foot; — Hause, at home; — Wasser, at sea, by sea; — deinem Nutzen, for your benefit. — adv. & prefix, to, towards; closed; too; — sehr, too; — viel, too much.

Zubehör ['tsu:bəhø:r], n. (—s, no pl.) accessory, appurtenance.

zubekommen ['tsu:bəkɔmən], v.a. irr. get in addition.

Zuber ['tsu:bər], m. (—s, pl. —) tub.

zubereiten ['tsu:bəraɪtən], v.a. prepare.

Zubereitung ['tsu:bəraɪtuŋ], f. (—, no pl.) preparation.

zubilligen ['tsu:bɪlɪgən], v.a. allow, grant.

zubleiben ['tsu:blaɪbən], v.n. irr. (aux. sein) remain shut.

zubringen ['tsu:brɪŋən], v.a. irr. die Zeit —, spend the time.

Zubringerdienst ['tsu:brɪŋərdi:nst], m. (—es, pl. —) shuttle-service, tenderservice.

Zubuße ['tsu:bu:sə], f. (—, pl. —n) (additional) contribution.

Zucht [tsuxt], f. (—, no pl.) race, breed; discipline; breeding, rearing; education, discipline; (good) manners; in — halten, keep in hand.

züchten ['tsyçtən], v.a. cultivate; rear, breed; grow.

Züchter ['tsyçtər], m. (—s, pl. —) (plants) nurseryman; (animals) breeder.

Zuchthaus ['tsuxthaus], n. (—es, pl. ⁻er) penitentiary, convict prison.

Zuchthäusler ['tsuxthɔyslər], m. (—s, pl. —) convict.

Zuchthengst ['tsuxthɛŋst], m. (—es, pl. —e) stallion.

züchtig ['tsyçtɪç], adj. modest, chaste.

züchtigen ['tsyçtɪgən], v.a. chastise, lash.

Züchtigkeit ['tsyçtɪçkaɪt], f. (—, no pl.) modesty, chastity.

Züchtigung ['tsyçtɪguŋ], f. (—, pl. —en) chastisement; körperliche —, corporal punishment.

Zuchtlosigkeit ['tsuxtlo:zɪçkaɪt], f. (—, no pl.) want of discipline.

Zuchtmeister ['tsuxtmaɪstər], m. (—s, pl. —) disciplinarian, taskmaster.

Zuchtochse ['tsuxtɔksə], m. (—n, pl. —n) bull.

Zuchtstute ['tsuxtʃtu:tə], f. (—, pl. —n) brood-mare.

Züchtung ['tsyçtuŋ], f. (—, pl. —en) (plants) cultivation; (animals) rearing, breeding.

Zuchtvieh ['tsuxtfi:], n. (—s, no pl.) breeding stock.

Zuchtwahl ['tsuxtva:l], f. (—, no pl.) (breeding) selection.

zucken ['tsukən], v.n. quiver, twitch; wince; start, jerk.

Zucken ['tsukən], n. (—s, no pl.) palpitation, convulsion, twitch, tic.

Zucker ['tsukər], m. (—s, no pl.) sugar.

Zuckerbäcker ['tsukərbɛkər], m. (—s, pl. —) confectioner.

Zuckerguß ['tsukərgus], m. (—es, no pl.) (sugar-)icing.

Zuckerkandis ['tsukərkandɪs], m. (—, no pl.) sugar-candy.

zuckerkrank ['tsukərkraŋk], adj. (Med.) diabetic.

Zuckerkrankheit ['tsukərkraŋkhaɪt], f. (—, no pl.) (Med.) diabetes.

zuckern ['tsukərn], v.a. sugar.

Zuckerpflanzung ['tsukərpflantsuŋ], f. (—, pl. —en) sugar-plantation.

Zuckerraffinerie ['tsukərrafinəri:], f. (—, pl. —n) sugar-refinery.

Zuckerrohr ['tsukərro:r], n. (—s, no pl.) sugar-cane.

Zuckerrübe ['tsukərry:bə], f. (—, pl. —n) sugar-beet.

Zuckerwerk ['tsukərvɛrk], n. (—s, no pl.) confectionery.

Zuckerzange ['tsukərtsaŋə], f. (—, pl. —n) sugar-tongs.

Zuckung ['tsukuŋ], f. (—, pl. —en) convulsion, spasm.

zudecken ['tsu:dɛkən], v.a. cover up.

zudem [tsu'de:m], adv. besides, moreover.

Zudrang ['tsu:draŋ], m. (—s, no pl.) crowd(ing); rush (on), run (on).

zudrehen ['tsu:dre:ən], v.a. turn off.

zudringlich ['tsu:drɪŋlɪç], adj. importunate; intruding.

zudrücken ['tsu:drykən], v.a. close (by pressing), shut.

zueignen ['tsu:aɪgnən], v.a. dedicate.

zuerkennen ['tsu:erkɛnən], v.a. irr. award, adjudicate.

zuerst [tsu'e:rst], adv. at first, first, in the first instance.

Zufahrt ['tsu:fa:rt], f. (—, no pl.) approach, drive.

Zufall ['tsu:fal], m. (—s, pl. ⁻e) chance, coincidence; durch —, by chance.

zufallen ['tsu:falən], v.n. irr. (aux. sein) close, fall shut; einem —, devolve upon s.o., fall to s.o.'s lot.

zufällig ['tsu:fɛlɪç], adj. accidental, casual, fortuitous. — adv. by chance.

Zuflucht ['tsu:fluxt], f. (—, no pl.) refuge, shelter, haven, recourse.

293

Zufluchtsort

Zufluchtsort ['tsu:fluxtsɔrt], *m.* (—(e)s, *pl.* —e) asylum, shelter, place of refuge.

Zufluß ['tsu:flus], *m.* (—sses, *pl.* ˙sse) supply; influx.

zuflüstern ['tsu:flystərn], *v.a. einem etwas* —, whisper s.th. to s.o.

zufolge [tsu'fɔlgə], *prep.* (*Genit., Dat.*) in consequence of, owing to, due to, on account of.

zufrieden [tsu'fri:dən], *adj.* content, contented, satisfied; — *lassen,* leave alone.

zufriedenstellen [tsu'fri:dənʃtɛlən], *v.a.* satisfy.

zufügen ['tsu:fy:gən], *v.a.* add (to); inflict.

Zufuhr ['tsu:fu:r], *f.* (—, *pl.* —en) (*goods*) supplies.

Zug [tsu:k], *m.* (—(e)s, *pl.* ˙e) drawing, pull, tug; draught; march, procession; (*Railw.*) train; (*face*) feature; (*chess*) move; (*character*) trait; (*pen*) stroke; (*birds*) flight; migration; (*mountains*) range.

Zugabe ['tsu:ga:bə], *f.* (—, *pl.* —n) addition, make-weight, extra; (*concert*) encore; as —, into the bargain.

Zugang ['tsu:gaŋ], *m.* (—s, *pl.* ˙e) approach, entry, entrance, admittance, access.

zugänglich ['tsu:gɛŋlɪç], *adj.* accessible, available; (*person*) affable.

Zugbrücke ['tsu:kbrykə], *f.* (—, *pl.* —n) drawbridge.

zugeben ['tsu:ge:bən], *v.a. irr.* give in addition; concede, admit.

zugegen [tsu'ge:gən], *adv.* present.

zugehen ['tsu:ge:ən], *v.n. irr.* (*aux.* sein) (*door*) shut (of itself), close; happen; *auf einen* —, walk towards s.o.; *so geht es im Leben zu,* such is life; *das geht nicht mit rechten Dingen zu,* there is something uncanny about it.

zugehörig ['tsu:gəhø:rɪç], *adj.* belonging, appertaining.

zugeknöpft ['tsu:gəknœpft], *adj.* reserved, taciturn.

Zügel ['tsy:gəl], *m.* (—s, *pl.* —) rein, bridle.

zügeln ['tsy:gəln], *v.a.* bridle, curb, check.

zugesellen ['tsu:gəzɛlən], *v.r. sich* —, associate with, join.

Zugeständnis ['tsu:gəʃtɛntnɪs], *n.* (—sses, *pl.* —sse) admission; concession.

zugestehen ['tsu:gəʃte:ən], *v.a. irr.* admit; concede; *einem etwas* —, allow s.o. s.th.

zugetan ['tsu:gəta:n], *adj.* attached, devoted.

Zugführer ['tsu:kfy:rər], *m.* (—s, *pl.* —) (*Railw.*) guard; (*Mil.*) platoon commander.

zugießen ['tsu:gi:sən], *v.a. irr.* fill up, pour on.

zugig ['tsu:gɪç], *adj.* windy, draughty.

Zugkraft ['tsu:kkraft], *f.* (—, *no pl.*) tractive power, magnetic attraction;

(*fig.*) pull, attraction; publicity value.

zugleich [tsu'glaɪç], *adv.* at the same time; — *mit,* together with.

Zugluft ['tsu:kluft], *f.* (—, *no pl.*) draught (of air).

zugreifen ['tsu:graɪfən], *v.n. irr.* grab; lend a hand; (*at table*) help o.s.

Zugrolle ['tsu:krɔlə], *f.* (—, *pl.* —n) pulley.

zugrunde [tsu'grundə], *adv.* — *gehen,* perish, go to ruin, go to the dogs; — *legen,* base upon.

Zugstück ['tsu:kʃtyk], *n.* (—s, *pl.* —e) (*Theat.*) popular show; (*coll.*) success, hit.

zugucken ['tsu:gukən], *v.n.* look on, watch.

zugunsten [tsu'gunstən], *prep.* (*Genit.*) for the benefit of.

zugute [tsu'gu:tə], *adv.* — *halten,* make allowances.

Zugvogel ['tsu:kfo:gəl], *m.* (—s, *pl.* ˙) bird of passage.

zuhalten ['tsu:haltən], *v.a. irr.* keep closed.

Zuhälter ['tsu:hɛltər], *m.* (—s, *pl.* —) souteneur; pimp.

Zuhilfenahme [tsu'hɪlfəna:mə], *f.* (—, *no pl.*) *unter* —, with the help of, by means of.

zuhören ['tsu:hø:rən], *v.n.* listen to, attend to.

Zuhörerschaft ['tsu:hø:rərʃaft], *f.* (—, *pl.* —en) audience.

zujubeln ['tsu:ju:bəln], *v.n. einem* —, acclaim s.o., cheer s.o.

zukehren ['tsu:ke:rən], *v.a. einem den Rücken* —, turn o.'s back on s.o.

zuknöpfen ['tsu:knœpfən], *v.a.* button (up).

zukommen ['tsu:kɔmən], *v.n. irr.* (*aux.* sein) *auf einen* —, advance towards s.o.; *einem* —, be due to s.o.; become s.o.; reach s.o.

Zukost ['tsu:kɔst], *f.* (—, *no pl.*) (*food*) trimmings, extras.

Zukunft ['tsu:kunft], *f.* (—, *no pl.*) future; prospects.

zukünftig ['tsu:kynftɪç], *adj.* future, prospective.

Zukunftsmusik ['tsu:kunftsmuzi:k], *f.* (—, *no pl.*) daydreams, pipedreams.

zulächeln ['tsu:lɛçəln], *v.a. einem* —, smile at s.o.

Zulage ['tsu:la:gə], *f.* (—, *pl.* —n) addition; increase of salary, rise; (*Am.*) raise.

zulangen ['tsu:laŋən], *v.n.* be sufficient; (*at table*) help o.s.

zulänglich ['tsu:lɛŋlɪç], *adj.* sufficient, adequate.

zulassen ['tsu:lasən], *v.a. irr.* leave unopened; allow; admit; permit.

zulässig ['tsu:lɛsɪç], *adj.* admissible; *das ist nicht* —, that is not allowed.

Zulassung ['tsu:lasuŋ], *f.* (—, *pl.* —en) admission.

Zulauf ['tsu:lauf], *m.* (—s, *no pl.*) run (of customers); crowd, throng.

zulaufen ['tsu:laufən], *v.n. irr. (aux.* sein) *auf einen —,* run towards s.o.; *spitz —,* taper, come to a point.

zulegen ['tsu:le:gən], *v.a.* add; increase; *sich etwas —,* make o.s. a present of s.th.; get s.th.

zuletzt [tsu'lɛtst], *adv.* last, at last, lastly, finally, eventually, in the end.

zuliebe [tsu'li:bə], *adv. einem etwas — tun,* oblige s.o.; do s.th. for s.o.'s sake.

zum — **zu dem**.

zumachen ['tsu:maxən], *v.a.* shut, close.

zumal [tsu'ma:l], *adv.* especially, particularly. — *conj.* especially since.

zumeist [tsu'maɪst], *adv.* mostly, for the most part.

zumute [tsu'mu:tə], *adv. mir ist nicht gut —,* I don't feel well.

zumuten ['tsu:mu:tən], *v.a. einem etwas —,* expect *or* demand s.th. of s.o.

Zumutung ['tsu:mu:tuŋ], *f.* (—, *pl.* —en) unreasonable demand.

zunächst [tsu'nɛ:çst], *adv.* first, above all.

Zunahme ['tsu:na:mə], *f.* (—, *pl.* —n) increase.

Zuname ['tsu:na:mə], *m.* (—ns, *pl.* —n) surname, family name.

zünden ['tsyndən], *v.n.* catch fire, ignite.

Zunder ['tsundər], *m.* (—s, *no pl.*) tinder.

Zünder ['tsyndər], *m.* (—s, *pl.* —) lighter, detonator, fuse.

Zündholz ['tsynthɔlts], *n.* (—es, *pl.* ⁓er) match.

Zündkerze ['tsyntkɛrtsə], *f.* (—, *pl.* —n) (*Motor.*) sparking-plug.

Zündstoff ['tsyntʃtɔf], *m.* (—s, *pl.* —e) fuel.

Zündung ['tsynduŋ], *f.* (—, *pl.* —en) ignition; detonation.

zunehmen ['tsu:ne:mən], *v.n. irr.* increase, put on weight; (*moon*) wax.

zuneigen ['tsu:naɪgən], *v.r. sich —,* incline towards.

Zuneigung ['tsu:naɪguŋ], *f.* (—, *pl.* —en) affection, inclination.

Zunft [tsunft], *f.* (—, *pl.* ⁓e) company, guild, corporation; (*fig.*) brotherhood.

Zunftgenosse ['tsunftgənɔsə], *m.* (—n, *pl.* —n) member of a guild.

zünftig ['tsynftɪç], *adj.* professional; proper.

zunftmäßig ['tsunftmɛ:sɪç], *adj.* professional; competent.

Zunge ['tsuŋə], *f.* (—, *pl.* —n) tongue; (*buckle*) catch; (*fig.*) language; (*fish*) sole.

züngeln ['tsyŋəln], *v.n.* (*flame*) shoot out, lick.

Zungenband ['tsuŋənbant], *n.* (—s, *pl.* ⁓er) ligament of the tongue.

zungenfertig ['tsuŋənfɛrtɪç], *adj.* voluble, glib.

Zungenlaut ['tsuŋənlaut], *m.* (—s, *pl.* —e) (*Phon.*) lingual sound.

Zungenspitze ['tsuŋənʃpɪtsə], *f.* (—, *pl.* —n) tip of the tongue.

zunichte [tsu'nɪçtə], *adv. — machen,* ruin, undo, destroy; — *werden,* come to nothing.

zupfen ['tsupfən], *v.a.* pick, pluck.

zurechnungsfähig ['tsu:rɛçnuŋsfɛ:ɪç], *adj.* accountable, of sane mind, compos mentis.

zurecht [tsu'rɛçt], *adv.* aright, right(ly), in order.

zurechtfinden [tsu'rɛçtfɪndən], *v.r. irr. sich —,* find o.'s way about.

zurechtkommen [tsu'rɛçtkɔmən], *v.n. irr. (aux.* sein) arrive in (good) time; *mit einem gut —,* get on well with s.o.

zurechtlegen [tsu'rɛçtle:gən], *v.a.* put in order, get ready.

zurechtmachen [tsu'rɛçtmaxən], *v.a.* get s.th. ready, prepare s.th. — *v.r. sich —,* prepare o.s.; (*women*) make up; (*coll.*) put on o.'s face.

zurechtweisen [tsu'rɛçtvaɪzən], *v.a. irr.* reprove (s.o.), set (s.o.) right; direct.

Zurechtweisung [tsu'rɛçtvaɪzuŋ], *f.* (—, *pl.* —en) reprimand.

Zureden ['tsu:re:dən], *n.* (—s, *no pl.*) encouragement; entreaties.

zureden ['tsu:re:dən], *v.n.* encourage (s.o.), persuade (s.o.)

zureichen ['tsu:raɪçən], *v.a.* reach, hand. — *v.n.* be sufficient, be enough, suffice.

zurichten ['tsu:rɪçtən], *v.a. etwas (einen) übel —,* maltreat s.th. (s.o.).

zürnen ['tsyrnən], *v.n.* be angry (with).

zurück [tsu'ryk], *adv.* back; behind; backwards; — *excl.* stand back!

zurückbegeben [tsu'rykbəge:bən], *v.r. irr. sich —,* go back, return.

zurückbehalten [tsu'rykbəhaltən], *v.a. irr.* retain, keep back.

zurückbekommen [tsu'rykbəkɔmən], *v.a. irr.* get back, recover (s.th.).

zurückberufen [tsu'rykbəru:fən], *v.a. irr.* recall.

zurückfordern [tsu'rykfɔrdərn], *v.a.* demand back, demand the return of.

zurückführen [tsu'rykfy:rən], *v.a.* lead back; *auf etwas —,* attribute to; trace back to.

zurückgeblieben [tsu'rykgəbli:bən], *adj.* retarded, mentally deficient, backward.

zurückgezogen [tsu'rykgətso:gən], *adj.* secluded, retired.

zurückhalten [tsu'rykhaltən], *v.a. irr.* keep back, retain.

zurückhaltend [tsu'rykhaltənt], *adj.* reserved.

zurückkehren [tsu'rykke:rən], *v.n. (aux.* sein) return.

zurückkommen [tsu'rykkɔmən], *v.n. irr. (aux.* sein) come back.

zurücklassen [tsu'ryklasən], *v.a. irr.* leave behind, abandon.

zurücklegen [tsuˈrykle:gən], *v.a.* lay aside, put by; *eine Strecke —*, cover a distance. — *v.r. sich —*, lean back; *zurückgelegter Gewinn*, undistributed profits.

zurückmüssen [tsuˈrykmysən], *v.n. irr.* be obliged to return.

zurücknehmen [tsuˈrykne:mən], *v.a. irr.* take back.

zurückschrecken [tsuˈrykʃrɛkən], *v.a.* frighten away. — *v.n. irr. (aux. sein)* recoil (from).

zurücksehnen [tsuˈrykze:nən], *v.r. sich —*, long to return, wish o.s. back.

zurücksetzen [tsuˈrykzɛtsən], *v.a.* put back; slight; discriminate against; neglect.

Zurücksetzung [tsuˈrykzɛtsuŋ], *f.* (—, *pl.* **—en**) slight, rebuff.

zurückstrahlen [tsuˈrykʃtra:lən], *v.a.* reflect.

zurücktreten [tsuˈryktre:tən], *v.n. irr. (aux. sein)* stand back, withdraw; resign.

zurückverlangen [tsuˈrykfɛrlaŋən],*v.a.* demand back, request the return of.

zurückversetzen [tsuˈrykfɛrzɛtsən], *v.a.* (*Sch.*) put in a lower form. — *v.r. sich —*, turn o.'s thoughts back (to), hark back.

zurückweichen [tsuˈrykvaɪçən],*v.n.irr.* (*aux. sein*) withdraw, retreat.

zurückweisen [tsuˈrykvaɪzən], *v.a. irr.* refuse, reject, repulse.

zurückwollen [tsuˈrykvɔlən], *v.n.* wish to return.

zurückziehen [tsuˈryktsi:ən], *v.a. irr.* draw back; (*fig.*) withdraw, retract, countermand. — *v.r. sich —*, retire, withdraw.

Zuruf [ˈtsu:ru:f], *m.* (**—s**, *pl.* **—e**) call, acclaim, acclamation.

Zusage [ˈtsu:za:gə], *f.* (—, *pl.* **—n**) promise; acceptance.

zusagen [ˈtsu:za:gən], *v.a.* promise; *es sagt mir zu*, I like it. — *v.n.* accept.

zusagend [ˈtsu:za:gənt], *adj.* affirmative; agreeable.

zusammen [tsuˈzamən], *adv.* together, jointly.

zusammenbeißen [tsuˈzamənbaɪsən], *v.a. irr. die Zähne —*, set o.'s teeth.

zusammenbetteln [tsuˈzamənbɛtəln], *v.a. sich etwas —*, collect (by begging).

zusammenbrechen [tsuˈzamənbrɛçən], *v.n. irr. (aux. sein)* break down, collapse.

Zusammenbruch [tsuˈzamənbrux], *m.* (**—s**, *pl.* **⁓e**) breakdown, collapse, débâcle.

zusammendrängen [tsuˈzaməndreŋən], *v.a.* press together; (*fig.*) abridge, condense.

zusammendrücken [tsuˈzaməndrykən], *v.a.* compress.

zusammenfahren [tsuˈzamənfa:rən], *v.n. irr. (aux. sein)* collide; give a start.

zusammenfallen [tsuˈzamənfalən], *v.n. irr. (aux. sein)* collapse.

zusammenfassen [tsuˈzamənfasən], *v.a.* sum up, summarize.

Zusammenfassung [tsuˈzamənfasuŋ], *f.* (—, *no pl.*) summing-up, summary.

zusammenfinden [tsuˈzamənfɪndən], *v.r. irr. sich —*, discover a mutual affinity, come together.

Zusammenfluß [tsuˈzamənflus], *m.* (**—sses**, *pl.* **⁓sse**) confluence.

zusammengeben [tsuˈzamənge:bən], *v.a. irr.* join in marriage.

Zusammengehörigkeit [tsuˈzaməngəhøːrɪçkaɪt], *f.* (—, *no pl.*) solidarity; (*Am.*) togetherness.

zusammengesetzt [tsuˈzaməngəzɛtst], *adj.* composed (of), consisting (of); complicated; (*Maths.*) composite.

zusammengewürfelt [tsuˈzaməngəvyrfəlt], *adj.* motley, mixed.

Zusammenhalt [tsuˈzamənhalt], *m.* (**—s**, *no pl.*) holding together; unity.

Zusammenhang [tsuˈzamənhaŋ], *m.* (**—s**, *pl.* **⁓e**) coherence, connection, context.

zusammenhängen [tsuˈzamənheŋən], *v.n. irr.* hang together, cohere; (*fig.*) be connected (with).

Zusammenklang [tsuˈzamənklaŋ], *m.* (**—s**, *pl.* **⁓e**) unison, harmony.

Zusammenkunft [tsuˈzamənkunft], *f.* (—, *pl.* **⁓e**) meeting, convention, conference; reunion.

zusammenlaufen [tsuˈzamənlaufən], *v.n. irr. (aux. sein)* crowd together, converge; flock together; (*milk*) curdle; (*material*) shrink.

zusammenlegen [tsuˈzamənle:gən], *v.a.* put together; (*money*) collect; (*letter*) fold up.

zusammennehmen [tsuˈzamənne:mən], *v.a.* gather up. — *v.r. sich —*, get a firm grip on o.s., pull o.s. together.

zusammenpassen [tsuˈzamənpasən], *v.n.* fit together, match; agree; be compatible.

zusammenpferchen [tsuˈzamənpfɛrçən], *v.a.* pen up, crowd together in a small space.

zusammenpressen [tsuˈzamənprɛsən], *v.a.* squeeze together.

zusammenraffen [tsuˈzamənrafən], *v.a.* gather up hurriedly, collect. — *v.r. sich —*, pluck up courage; pull o.s. together.

zusammenrechnen [tsuˈzamənrɛçnən], *v.a.* add up.

zusammenreimen [tsuˈzamənraɪmən], *v.a. sich etwas —*, figure s.th. out.

zusammenrücken [tsuˈzamənrykən], *v.a.* move together, draw closer. — *v.n.* move closer together, move up.

zusammenschießen [tsuˈzamənʃiːsən], *v.a. irr.* shoot to pieces, shoot down; *Geld —*, club together, raise a subscription.

zusammenschlagen [tsuˈzamənʃla:gən], *v.a. irr.* beat up; strike together; clap, fold.

zusammenschließen [tsuˈzamənʃliː-sən], v.r. irr. sich —, join, unite, ally o.s. (with).

zusammenschweißen [tsuˈzamənʃvaɪsən], v.a. weld together.

Zusammensein [tsuˈzamənzaɪn], n. (—s, no pl.) meeting, social gathering.

Zusammensetzung [tsuˈzamənzɛtsuŋ], f. (—, no pl.) construction; composition.

Zusammenspiel [tsuˈzamənʃpiːl], n. (—s, no pl.) (Theat., Mus.) ensemble.

zusammenstellen [tsuˈzamənʃtɛlən], v.a. compose, concoct; put together, compile.

Zusammenstellung [tsuˈzamənʃtɛluŋ], f. (—, pl. —en) combination, compilation; juxtaposition.

zusammenstoppeln [tsuˈzamənʃtɔpəln], v.a. string together, patch up.

Zusammenstoß [tsuˈzamənʃtoːs], m. (—es, pl. ˙e) clash, conflict; collision.

zusammenstoßen [tsuˈzamənʃtoːsən], v.n. irr. (aux. sein) clash; crash, come into collision, collide.

zusammentragen [tsuˈzaməntraːgən], v.a. irr. collect, compile.

zusammentreffen [tsuˈzaməntrɛfən], v.n. irr. meet; coincide.

zusammentreten [tsuˈzaməntreːtən], v.n. irr. (aux. sein) meet.

zusammentun [tsuˈzaməntuːn], v.r. irr. sich — mit, associate with, join.

zusammenwirken [tsuˈzamənvɪrkən], v.n. cooperate, collaborate.

zusammenwürfeln [tsuˈzamənvyrfəln], v.a. jumble up.

zusammenzählen [tsuˈzaməntsɛːlən], v.a. add up.

zusammenziehen [tsuˈzaməntsiːən], v.n. irr. (aux. sein) move in together. — v.a. draw together, contract. — v.r. sich —, shrink; (storm) gather; Zahlen —, add up.

Zusammenziehung [tsuˈzaməntsiːuŋ], f. (—, no pl.) contraction.

Zusatz [ˈtsuːzats], m. (—es, pl. ˙e) addition, supplement, admixture; (will) codicil.

zuschanzen [ˈtsuːʃantsən], v.a. einem etwas —, obtain s.th. for s.o.

zuschauen [ˈtsuːʃauən], v.n. look on, watch.

Zuschauer [ˈtsuːʃauər], m. (—s, pl. —) onlooker, spectator.

Zuschauerraum [ˈtsuːʃauərraum], m. (—s, pl. ˙e) (Theat.) auditorium.

zuschaufeln [ˈtsuːʃaufəln], v.a. shovel in, fill up.

zuschieben [ˈtsuːʃiːbən], v.a. irr. push towards; shut; einem etwas —, shove (blame) on to s.o.

zuschießen [ˈtsuːʃiːsən], v.a. irr. Geld —, put money into (an undertaking).

Zuschlag [ˈtsuːʃlaːk], m. (—s, pl. ˙e) addition; (Railw.) excess fare.

zuschlagen [ˈtsuːʃlaːgən], v.a. irr. add; (door) bang; (auction) knock down to (s.o.). — v.n. strike hard.

zuschlag(s)pflichtig [ˈtsuːʃlaːk(s)pflɪçtɪç], adj. liable to a supplementary charge.

zuschmeißen [ˈtsuːʃmaɪsən], v.a. irr. (door) slam to, bang.

zuschneiden [ˈtsuːʃnaɪdən], v.a. irr. (pattern) cut out; cut up.

Zuschneider [ˈtsuːʃnaɪdər], m. (—s, pl.—) (Tail.) cutter.

Zuschnitt [ˈtsuːʃnɪt], m. (—s, no pl.) (clothing) cut.

zuschreiben [ˈtsuːʃraɪbən], v.a. irr. einem etwas —, impute s.th. to s.o.; attribute or ascribe s.th. to s.o.

Zuschrift [ˈtsuːʃrɪft], f. (—, pl. —en) communication, letter.

Zuschuß [ˈtsuːʃus], m. (—sses, pl. ˙sse) additional money, supplementary allowance, subsidy.

zuschütten [ˈtsuːʃytən], v.a. fill up.

Zusehen [ˈtsuːzeːən], n. (—s, no pl.) das — haben, be left out in the cold.

zusehen [ˈtsuːzeːən], v.n. irr. look on, watch; be a spectator; see to it.

zusehends [ˈtsuːzeːənts], adv. visibly.

zusetzen [ˈtsuːzɛtsən], v.a. add to, admix; lose. — v.n. einem —, pester s.o.; attack s.o.

zusichern [ˈtsuːzɪçərn], v.a. promise, assure.

Zusicherung [ˈtsuːzɪçəruŋ], f. (—, pl. —en) promise, assurance.

Zuspeise [ˈtsuːʃpaɪzə], f. (—, no pl.) (dial.) (food) trimmings; vegetables.

zusperren [ˈtsuːʃpɛrən], v.a. shut, close, lock up.

zuspitzen [ˈtsuːʃpɪtsən], v.a. sharpen to a point. — v.r. sich —, come to a climax.

zusprechen [ˈtsuːʃprɛçən], v.n. irr. dem Wein — drink heavily. — v.a. Mut —, comfort.

Zuspruch [ˈtsuːʃprux], m. (—s, pl. ˙e) exhortation; consolation.

Zustand [ˈtsuːʃtant], m. (—s, pl. ˙e) condition, state of affairs, situation.

zustande [tsuˈʃtandə], adv. — kommen, come off, be accomplished; — bringen, accomplish.

zuständig [ˈtsuːʃtɛndɪç], adj. competent; appropriate.

Zuständigkeit [ˈtsuːʃtɛndɪçkaɪt], f. (—, no pl.) competence.

zustecken [ˈtsuːʃtɛkən], v.a. pin up; einem etwas —, slip s.th. into s.o.'s hand.

zustehen [ˈtsuːʃteːən], v.n. irr. be due to, belong to; be s.o.'s business to.

zustellen [ˈtsuːʃtɛlən], v.a. deliver, hand over; (Law) serve (a writ).

Zustellung [ˈtsuːʃtɛluŋ], f. (—, pl. —en) delivery; (Law) service.

zusteuern [ˈtsuːʃtɔyərn], v.a. contribute. — v.n. (aux. sein) steer for; (fig.) aim at.

zustimmen [ˈtsuːʃtɪmən], v.n. agree to.

Zustimmung [ˈtsuːʃtɪmuŋ], f. (—, pl. —en) assent, consent, agreement.

zustopfen ['tsu:ʃtɔpfən], *v.a.* fill up, stop up, plug; darn, mend.

zustoßen ['tsu:ʃto:sən], *v.a. irr.* push to, shut.

zustürzen ['tsu:ʃtyrtsən], *v.n. (aux. sein) auf einen —*, rush at or towards s.o.

Zutaten ['tsu:ta:tən], *f. pl.* ingredients, garnishings.

zuteil ['tsu:taɪl], *adv. — werden*, fall to s.o.'s share.

zutragen ['tsu:tra:gən], *v.a. irr.* report, tell. *— v.r. sich —*, happen.

Zuträger ['tsu:trɛ:gər], *m.* (**—s,** *pl.* **—**) informer, tale-bearer.

zuträglich ['tsu:trɛ:klɪç], *adj.* advantageous, wholesome.

Zutrauen ['tsu:trauən], *n.* (**—s,** *no pl.*) confidence.

zutrauen ['tsu:trauən], *v.a. einem etwas —*, credit s.o. with s.th.

zutraulich ['tsu:traulɪç], *adj.* trusting; familiar, intimate; tame.

zutreffen ['tsu:trɛfən], *v.n. irr.* prove correct, take place.

zutreffend ['tsu:trɛfənt], *adj.* apposite, pertinent.

Zutritt ['tsu:trɪt], *m.* (**—s,** *no pl.*) entry; access, admittance; *— verboten*, no admittance.

zutunlich ['tsu:ʈu:nlɪç], *adj.* confiding; obliging.

zuverlässig ['tsu:fɛrlɛsɪç], *adj.* reliable; authentic.

Zuversicht ['tsu:fɛrzɪçt], *f.* (**—,** *no pl.*) trust, confidence.

zuversichtlich ['tsu:fɛrzɪçtlɪç], *adj.* confident.

zuvor [tsu'fo:r], *adv.* before, first, formerly.

zuvorkommend [tsu'fo:rkɔmənt], *adj.* obliging, polite.

Zuwachs ['tsu:vaks], *m.* (**—es,** *no pl.*) increase, accretion, growth.

zuwachsen ['tsu:vaksən], *v.n. irr. (aux. sein)* become overgrown.

zuwandern ['tsu:vandərn], *v.n. (aux. sein)* immigrate.

zuwegebringen [tsu've:gəbrɪŋən], *v.a. irr.* bring about, effect.

zuweilen [tsu'vaɪlən], *adv.* sometimes, at times.

zuweisen ['tsu:vaɪzən], *v.a. irr.* assign, apportion.

zuwenden ['tsu:vɛndən], *v.a.* turn towards; give.

zuwerfen ['tsu:vɛrfən], *v.a. irr.* throw towards, cast; *(door)* slam.

zuwider ['tsu:vi:dər], *prep. (Dat.)* against, contrary to. *— adv.* repugnant.

Zuwiderhandlung [tsu'vi:dərhandluŋ], *f.* (**—,** *pl.* **—en**) contravention.

zuwiderlaufen [tsu'vi:dərlaufən], *v.n. irr. (aux. sein)* be contrary to, fly in the face of.

zuzählen ['tsu:tsɛ:lən], *v.a.* add to.

zuziehen ['tsu:tsi:ən], *v.a. irr.* draw together; tighten; consult; *(curtain)* draw. *— v.r. sich eine Krankheit —*, catch a disease.

Zuzug ['tsu:tsu:k], *m.* (**—s,** *no pl.*) immigration; population increase.

zuzüglich ['tsu:tsy:klɪç], *prep. (Genit.)* in addition to, including, plus.

Zwang [tsvaŋ], *m.* (**—s,** *no pl.*) coercion, force; compulsion; *(fig.)* constraint; *sich — auferlegen*, restrain o.s.; *tu deinen Gefühlen keinen — an*, let yourself go.

zwanglos ['tsvaŋlo:s], *adj.* informal, free and easy.

Zwangsarbeit ['tsvaŋsarbaɪt], *f.* (**—, —en**) forced labour.

Zwangsjacke ['tsvaŋsjakə], *f.* (**—,** *pl.* **—en**) strait-jacket.

Zwangsmaßnahme ['tsvaŋsma:sna:mə], *f.* (**—,** *pl.* **—en**) compulsory measure, compulsion.

Zwangsversteigerung ['tsvaŋsfɛrʃtaɪgəruŋ], *f.* (**—,** *pl.* **—en**) enforced sale.

Zwangsvollstreckung ['tsvaŋsfɔlʃtrɛkuŋ], *f.* (**—,** *pl.* **—en**) distraint.

zwangsweise ['tsvaŋsvaɪzə], *adv.* by force, compulsorily.

Zwangswirtschaft ['tsvaŋsvɪrtʃaft], *f.* (**—,** *no pl.*) price control, controlled economy.

zwanzig ['tsvantsɪç], *num. adj.* twenty.

zwar [tsva:r], *adv.* to be sure, indeed, it is true, true; *(Am.)* sure.

Zweck [tsvɛk], *m.* (**—(e)s,** *pl.* **—e**) end, object, purpose.

zweckdienlich ['tsvɛkdi:nlɪç], *adj.* useful, expedient.

Zwecke ['tsvɛkə], *f.* (**—,** *pl.* **—n**) tack, drawing-pin.

zweckentsprechend ['tsvɛkɛntʃprɛçənt], *adj.* suitable, appropriate.

zweckmäßig ['tsvɛkmɛ:sɪç], *adj.* expedient, suitable, proper.

zwecks [tsvɛks], *prep. (Genit.)* for the purpose of.

zwei [tsvaɪ], *num. adj.* two.

zweibändig ['tsvaɪbɛndɪç], *adj.* in two volumes.

zweideutig ['tsvaɪdɔytɪç], *adj.* ambiguous, equivocal; *(fig.)* suggestive.

Zweideutigkeit ['tsvaɪdɔytɪçkaɪt], *f.* (**—,** *pl.* **—en**) ambiguity.

Zweifel ['tsvaɪfəl], *m.* (**—s,** *pl.* **—**) doubt, scruple; *ohne —*, no doubt.

zweifelhaft ['tsvaɪfəlhaft], *adj.* doubtful, dubious.

zweifellos ['tsvaɪfɛllo:s], *adv.* doubtless.

zweifeln ['tsvaɪfəln], *v.n.* doubt, question; *ich zweifle nicht daran*, I have no doubt about it.

Zweifelsfall ['tsvaɪfəlsfal], *m.* (**—s,** *pl.* **-̈e**) doubtful matter; *im —*, in case of doubt.

Zweifler ['tsvaɪflər], *m.* (**—s,** *pl.* **—**) doubter, sceptic.

Zweig [tsvaɪk], *m.* (**—(e)s,** *pl.* **—e**) twig, bough, branch.

zweigen ['tsvaɪgən], *v.r. sich —*, bifurcate, fork, branch.

Zweigniederlassung ['tsvaɪkni:dərlasuŋ], *f.* (**—,** *pl.* **—en**) branch establishment.

zweihändig ['tsvaɪhɛndɪç], adj. two-handed; (keyboard music) solo.

Zweihufer ['tsvaɪhuːfər], m. (—s, pl. —) cloven-footed animal.

zweijährig ['tsvaɪjɛːrɪç], adj. two-year-old; of two years' duration.

zweijährlich ['tsvaɪjɛːrlɪç], adj. biennial. — adv. every two years.

Zweikampf ['tsvaɪkampf], m. (— (e)s, pl. ̈e) duel.

zweimal ['tsvaɪmal], adv. twice; — soviel, twice as much.

zweimotorig ['tsvaɪmotoːrɪç], adj. twin-(or two-) engined.

Zweirad ['tsvaɪraːt], n. (—s, pl. ̈er) bicycle.

zweireihig ['tsvaɪraɪɪç], adj. (suit) double-breasted.

zweischneidig ['tsvaɪʃnaɪdɪç], adj. two-edged.

zweiseitig ['tsvaɪzaɪtɪç], adj. two-sided, bilateral.

zweisprachig ['tsvaɪʃpraːxɪç], adj. bilingual, in two languages.

zweitälteste ['tsvaɪtɛltəstə], adj. second (eldest).

zweitbeste ['tsvaɪtbɛstə], adj. second best.

zweite ['tsvaɪtə], num. adj. second; aus —r Hand, secondhand; zu zweit, in twos, two of (us, them).

Zweiteilung ['tsvaɪtaɪluŋ], f. (—, pl. —en) bisection.

zweitens ['tsvaɪtəns], adv. secondly, in the second place.

zweitletzte ['tsvaɪtlɛtstə], adj. last but one, penultimate.

zweitnächste ['tsvaɪtnɛçstə], adj. next but one.

Zwerchfell ['tsvɛrçfɛl], n. (—s, pl. —e) diaphragm, midriff.

zwerchfellerschütternd ['tsvɛrçfɛlərʃytərnt], adj. side-splitting.

Zwerg [tsvɛrk], m. (—s, pl. —e) dwarf, pigmy.

zwerghaft ['tsvɛrkhaft], adj. dwarfish.

Zwetsche ['tsvɛtʃə], f. (—, pl. —n) (Bot.) damson.

Zwickel ['tsvɪkəl], m. (—s, pl. —) gusset; komischer —, (coll.) queer fish.

zwicken ['tsvɪkən], v.a. pinch, nip.

Zwicker ['tsvɪkər], m. (—s, pl. —) pince-nez.

Zwickmühle ['tsvɪkmyːlə], f. (—, pl. —n) in der — sein, be on the horns of a dilemma, be in a jam.

Zwickzange ['tsvɪktsaŋə], f. (—, pl. —n) pincers.

Zwieback ['tsviːbak], m. (—s, pl. —e) rusk.

Zwiebel ['tsviːbəl], f. (—, pl. —n) onion; bulb.

zwiebelartig ['tsviːbəlaːrtɪç], adj. bulbous.

zwiebeln ['tsviːbəln], v.a. einen —, bully, torment s.o.

Zwielicht ['tsviːlɪçt], n. (—s, no pl.) twilight.

Zwiespalt ['tsviːʃpalt], m. (—s, pl. —e) difference, dissension; schism.

Zwiesprache ['tsviːʃpraːxə], f. (—, pl. —n) dialogue; discussion.

Zwietracht ['tsviːtraxt], f. (—, no pl.) discord, disharmony.

zwieträchtig ['tsviːtrɛçtɪç], adj. discordant, at variance.

Zwillich ['tsvɪlɪç], m. (—s, pl. —e) ticking.

Zwilling ['tsvɪlɪŋ], m. (—s, pl. —e) twin; (pl.) (Astron.) Gemini.

Zwingburg ['tsvɪŋburk], f. (—, pl. —en) stronghold.

Zwinge ['tsvɪŋə], f. (—, pl. —n) ferrule.

zwingen ['tsvɪŋən], v.a. irr. force, compel; master, overcome, get the better of. — v.r. sich —, force o.s. (to), make a great effort (to).

zwingend ['tsvɪŋənt], adj. cogent, imperative, convincing.

Zwinger ['tsvɪŋər], m. (—s, pl. —) keep, donjon, fort; bear-pit.

Zwingherrschaft ['tsvɪŋhɛrʃaft], f. (—, pl. —en) despotism, tyranny.

zwinkern ['tsvɪŋkərn], v.n. wink; (stars) twinkle.

Zwirn [tsvɪrn], m. (—(e)s, pl. —e) thread, sewing cotton.

Zwirnrolle ['tsvɪrnrɔlə], f. (—, pl. —n) ball of thread, reel of cotton.

zwischen ['tsvɪʃən], prep. (Dat., Acc.) between; among, amongst.

Zwischenakt ['tsvɪʃənakt], m. (—s, pl. —e) (Theat.) interval.

Zwischenbemerkung ['tsvɪʃənbəmɛrkuŋ], f. (—, pl. —en) interruption, digression.

Zwischendeck ['tsvɪʃəndɛk], n. (—s, pl. —e) (ship) steerage, between decks.

zwischendurch ['tsvɪʃəndurç], adv. in between, at intervals.

Zwischenfall ['tsvɪʃənfal], m. (—s, pl. ̈e) incident; episode.

Zwischengericht ['tsvɪʃəngərɪçt], n. (—s, pl. —e) (food) entrée, entremets.

Zwischenglied ['tsvɪʃəngliːt], n. (—s, pl. —er) link.

Zwischenhändler ['tsvɪʃənhɛndlər], m. (—s, pl. —) middleman.

Zwischenpause ['tsvɪʃənpauzə], f. (—, pl. —n) interval; pause.

Zwischenraum ['tsvɪʃənraum], m. (—s, pl. ̈e) intermediate space, gap.

Zwischenrede ['tsvɪʃənreːdə], f. (—, pl. —n) interruption.

Zwischenruf ['tsvɪʃənruːf], m. (—s, pl. —e) interruption, interjection.

Zwischensatz ['tsvɪʃənzats], m. (—es, pl. ̈e) parenthesis; interpolation.

Zwischenspiel ['tsvɪʃənʃpiːl], n. (—s, pl. —e) interlude, intermezzo.

Zwischenzeit ['tsvɪʃəntsaɪt], f. (—, no pl.) interval, interim, meantime; in der —, meanwhile.

Zwist [tsvɪst], m. (—es, pl. —e) discord, quarrel, dispute.

Zwistigkeiten ['tsvɪstɪçkaɪtən], f. pl. hostilities.

zwitschern ['tsvɪtʃərn], v.n. chirp, twitter.

Zwitter ['tsvɪtər], *m.* (**—s,** *pl.* **—)** hybrid, cross-breed, mongrel; hermaphrodite.

zwitterhaft ['tsvɪtərhaft], *adj.* hybrid; bisexual.

zwölf [svœlf], *num. adj.* twelve.

Zwölffingerdarm ['tsvœlffɪŋərdarm], *m.* (**—s,** *pl.* ⸚e) duodenum.

Zyankali [tsy:an'ka:li], *n.* (**—s,** *no pl.*) potassium cyanide.

Zyklon [tsy'klo:n], *m.* (**—s,** *pl.* **—e)** cyclone.

Zyklus ['tsyklus], *m.* (**—,** *pl.* **Zyklen)** cycle; course, series.

zylinderförmig [tsy'lɪndərfœrmɪç], *adj.* cylindric(al).

Zylinderhut [tsy'lɪndərhu:t], *m.* (**—s,** *pl.* ⸚e) top-hat, silk-hat.

zylindrisch [tsy'lɪndrɪʃ], *adj.* cylindric(al).

Zyniker ['tsy:nɪkər], *m.* (**—s,** *pl.* **—)** cynic.

zynisch ['tsy:nɪʃ], *adj.* cynical.

Zynismus [tsy'nɪsmus], *m.* (**—,** *no pl.*) cynicism.

Zypern ['tsy:pərn], *n.* Cyprus.

Zypresse [tsy'prɛsə], *f.* (**—,** *pl.* **—n)** (*Bot.*) cypress.

Cassell's English-German Dictionary

A

A [ei]. das A (*also Mus.*).

a [ə, ei] (**an** [ən, æn] *before vowel or silent* h), *indef. art.* ein, eine, ein; *two at a time*, zwei auf einmal; *many a*, mancher; *two shillings a pound*, zwei Schilling das Pfund.

abacus ['æbəkəs], *s.* das Rechenbrett.

abandon [ə'bændən], *v.a.* (*give up*) aufgeben; (*forsake*) verlassen; (*surrender*) preisgeben.

abandonment [ə'bændənmənt], *s.* das Verlassen (*active*); das Verlassensein (*passive*); die Wildheit, das Sichgehenlassen.

abasement [ə'beismənt], *s.* die Demütigung, Erniedrigung.

abash [ə'bæʃ], *v.a.* beschämen.

abate [ə'beit], *v.n.* nachlassen.

abbess ['æbes], *s.* die Äbtissin.

abbey ['æbi], *s.* die Abtei.

abbot ['æbət], *s.* der Abt.

abbreviate [ə'bri:vieit], *v.a.* abkürzen.

abbreviation [əbri:vi'eiʃən], *s.* die Abkürzung.

abdicate ['æbdikeit], *v.a.*, *v.n.* entsagen (*Dat.*), abdanken.

abdomen [æb'doumən, 'æbdəmən], *s.* (*Anat.*) der Unterleib, Bauch.

abdominal [æb'dɔminəl], *adj.* (*Anat.*) Bauch-, Unterleibs-.

abduct [æb'dakt], *v.a.* entführen.

abed [ə'bed], *adv.* zu Bett, im Bett.

aberration [æbə'reiʃən], *s.* die Abirrung; die Verirrung; (*Phys.*) die Strahlenbrechung.

abet [ə'bet], *v.a.* helfen (*Dat.*), unterstützen.

abeyance [ə'beiəns], *s.* die Unentschiedenheit, (der Zustand der) Ungewißheit; *in* —, unentschieden.

abhor [əb'hɔ:], *v.a.* verabscheuen.

abhorrence [əb'hɔrəns], *s.* die Abscheu (*of*, vor, *Dat.*).

abhorrent [əb'hɔrənt], *adj.* widerlich, ekelhaft.

abide [ə'baid], *v.n. irr.* bleiben, verweilen; (*last*) dauern. — *v.a.* aushalten.

ability [ə'biliti], *s.* die Fähigkeit, Tüchtigkeit; (*pl.*) die Geisteskräfte, *f. pl.*

abject ['æbdʒekt], *adj.* elend; (*submissive*) unterwürfig, verächtlich.

ablaze [ə'bleiz], *adj.*, *adv.* in Flammen.

able [eibl], *adj.* fähig; (*clever*) geschickt; (*efficient*) tüchtig.

ablution [ə'blu:ʃən], *s.* die Abwaschung, Waschung.

abnormal [æb'nɔ:məl], *adj.* abnorm, ungewöhnlich.

abnormality [æbnɔ:'mæliti], *s.* die Ungewöhnlichkeit.

aboard [ə'bɔ:d], *adv.* an Bord.

abode [ə'boud], *s.* der Wohnsitz, Wohnort.

abolish [ə'bɔliʃ], *v.a.* aufheben, abschaffen.

abolition [æbo'liʃən], *s.* die Abschaffung, Aufhebung.

abominable [ə'bɔminəbl], *adj.* abscheulich, scheußlich.

abominate [ə'bɔmineit], *v.a.* verabscheuen.

abomination [əbɔmi'neiʃən], *s.* der Abscheu, Greuel.

aboriginal [æbo'ridʒinəl], *adj.* eingeboren, einheimisch. — *s.* der Eingeborene.

aborigines [æbə'ridʒini:z], *s. pl.* die Eingeborenen, Ureinwohner.

abortion [ə'bɔːʃən], *s.* die Fehlgeburt; die Abtreibung.

abortive [ə'bɔːtiv], *adj.* mißlungen.

abound [ə'baund], *v.n.* wimmeln von (*Dat.*).

about [ə'baut], *prep.* um; (*toward*) gegen; *about 3 o'clock*, gegen drei; (*concerning*) über, betreffend. — *adv.* umher, herum; (*round*) rund herum; (*nearly*) etwa, ungefähr; (*everywhere*) überall; *to be* — *to*, im Begriffe sein *or* stehen zu . . .

above [ə'bʌv], *prep.* über; — *all things*, vor allen Dingen; *this is* — *me*, das ist mir zu hoch; — *board*, offen, ehrlich. — *adv.* oben, darüber, *over and* —, obendrein; — *mentioned*, obenerwähnt.

abrade [ə'breid], *v.a.* abschaben, abschürfen.

abrasion [ə'breiʒən], *s.* die Abschürfung; Abnutzung.

abreast [ə'brest], *adj.*, *adv.* nebeneinander, Seite an Seite; *keep* —, (sich) auf dem Laufenden halten; Schritt halten (mit).

abridge [ə'bridʒ], *v.a.* (ab)kürzen.

abridgement [ə'bridʒmənt], *s.* die (Ab)kürzung; (*book etc.*) der Auszug.

abroad [ə'brɔ:d], *adv.* im Ausland, auswärts; *to go* —, ins Ausland reisen.

abrogate ['æbrogeit], *v.a.* abschaffen.

abrogation [æbro'geiʃən], *s.* (*Pol.*) die Abschaffung.

abrupt [ə'brʌpt], *adj.* plötzlich; (*curt*) schroff; kurz; jäh.

abruptness [ə'brʌptnis], *s.* (*speech*) die Schroffheit; (*suddenness*) die Plötzlichkeit; (*drop*) die Steilheit.

abscess ['æbses], *s.* das Geschwür, die Schwellung, der Abszeß.

abscond

abscond [əb'skɔnd], *v.n.* sich davonmachen.

absence ['æbsəns], *s.* die Abwesenheit; *leave of* —, der Urlaub.

absent (1) ['æbsənt], *adj.* abwesend; — *minded*, zerstreut.

absent (2) [æb'sent], *v.r.* — *oneself*, fehlen, fernbleiben; (*go away*) sich entfernen.

absentee [æbsən'ti:], *s.* der Abwesende.

absolute ['æbsəlu:t], *adj.* absolut, unumschränkt.

absolve [əb'zɔlv], *v.a.* freisprechen (*from*, von), lossprechen, entbinden.

absorb [əb'sɔ:b], *v.a.* absorbieren, aufsaugen; (*attention*) in Anspruch nehmen.

absorbed [əb'sɔ:bd], *adj.* versunken.

absorbent [əb'sɔ:bənt], *adj.* absorbierend.

absorption [əb'sɔ:pʃən], *s.* (*Chem.*) die Absorption; (*attention*) das Versunkensein.

abstain [əb'stein], *v.n.* sich enthalten; — *from voting*, sich der Stimme enthalten.

abstainer [əb'steinə], *s.* der Abstinenzler, Antialkoholiker.

abstemious [əb'sti:miəs], *adj.* enthaltsam.

abstention [əb'stenʃən], *s.* die Enthaltung.

abstinence ['æbstinəns], *s.* die Enthaltsamkeit, das Fasten (*food*).

abstract [æb'strækt], *v.a.* abstrahieren, abziehen; (*summarize*) kürzen, ausziehen. —['æbstrækt], *adj.* abstrakt; (*Maths.*) rein. — *s.* der Auszug, Abriß (*of article, book, etc.*).

abstracted [æb'stræktid], *adj.* zerstreut, geistesabwesend.

abstraction [æb'strækʃən], *s.* die Abstraktion; der abstrakte Begriff.

abstruse [æb'stru:s], *adj.* schwerverständlich, tiefsinnig.

absurd [əb'sə:d], *adj.* absurd, töricht; (*unreasonable*) unvernünftig, gegen alle Vernunft; (*laughable*) lächerlich.

absurdity [əb'sə:diti], *s.* die Torheit, Unvernünftigkeit.

abundance [ə'bʌndəns], *s.* die Fülle, der Überfluß.

abundant [ə'bʌndənt], *adj.* reichlich.

abuse [ə'bju:z], *v.a.* mißbrauchen; (*insult*) beschimpfen; (*violate*) schänden. —[ə'bju:s], *s.* der Mißbrauch; (*language*) die Beschimpfung; (*violation*) die Schändung.

abusive [ə'bju:siv], *adj.* (*language*) grob; schimpfend, schmähend.

abut [ə'bʌt], *v.n.* anstoßen, angrenzen.

abysmal [ə'bizməl], *adj.* bodenlos.

abyss [ə'bis], *s.* der Abgrund, Schlund.

Abyssinian [æbi'sinjən], *adj.* abessinisch. — *s.* der Abessinier.

acacia [ə'keiʃə], *s.* (*Bot.*) die Akazie.

academic [ækə'demik], *adj.* akademisch. — *s.* der Akademiker.

academy [ə'kædəmi], *s.* die Akademie.

acajon ['ækəʒu:], *s.* (*Bot.*) der Nierenbaum.

accede [æk'si:d], *v.n.* beistimmen; einwilligen; — *to the throne*, den Thron besteigen.

accelerate [æk'seləreit], *v.a.* beschleunigen. — *v.n.* schneller fahren.

acceleration [æksela'reiʃən], *s.* die Beschleunigung.

accelerator [æk'seləreitə], *s.* (*Motor.*) der Gashebel, das Gaspedal.

accent (1), **accentuate** [æk'sent, æk-'sentjueit], *v.a.* akzentuieren, betonen.

accent (2) ['æksənt], *s.* (*Phon.*) der Ton, Wortton, die Betonung; der Akzent (*dialect*), die Aussprache.

accentuation [æksentju'eiʃən], *s.* die Aussprache, Akzentuierung, Betonung.

accept [æk'sept], *v.a.* annehmen.

acceptable [æk'septəbl], *adj.* angenehm, annehmbar, annehmlich.

acceptance [æk'septəns], *s.* die Annahme; (*Comm.*) das Akzept.

access ['ækses], *s.* der Zugang, Zutritt.

accessible [æk'sesibl], *adj.* erreichbar, zugänglich.

accession [æk'seʃən], *s.* der Zuwachs; — *to the throne*, die Thronbesteigung.

accessory [æk'sesəri], *adj.* zugehörig; hinzukommend; (*Law*) mitschuldig; (*subsidiary*) nebensächlich. — *s.* (*Law*) der Mitschuldige; (*pl.*) das Zubehör.

accidence ['æksidəns], *s.* (*Gram.*) die Flexionslehre.

accident ['æksidənt], *s.* (*chance*) der Zufall; (*mishap*) der Unfall, Unglücksfall.

accidental [æksi'dentəl], *adj.* zufällig; (*inessential*) unwesentlich; durch Unfall.

acclaim [ə'kleim], *v.a.* akklamieren, mit Beifall aufnehmen. — *v.n.* zujubeln. — *s.* der Beifall.

acclamation [æklə'meiʃən], *s.* der Beifall, Zuruf.

acclimatize [ə'klaimətaiz], *v.a.*, *v.r.* akklimatisieren; sich anpassen, eingewöhnen.

accommodate [ə'kɔmədeit], *v.a.* (*adapt*) anpassen; (*lodge*) unterbringen, beherbergen, aufnehmen; einem aushelfen; (*with money*) jemandem Geld leihen. — *v.r.* — *oneself to*, sich an etwas anpassen, sich in etwas fügen.

accommodating [ə'kɔmədeitiŋ], *adj.* gefällig, entgegenkommend.

accommodation [əkɔmə'deiʃən], *s.* (*adaptation*) die Anpassung; (*dispute*) die Beilegung; (*room*) die Unterkunft.

accompaniment [ə'kʌmpənimənt], *s.* die Begleitung.

accompany [ə'kʌmpəni], *v.a.* begleiten.

accomplice [ə'kʌmplis *or* ə'kɔmplis], *s.* der Komplize, Mitschuldige, Mittäter.

accomplish [ə'kʌmpliʃ *or* ə'kɔmpliʃ], *v.a.* vollenden, zustandebringen, vollbringen; (*objective*) erreichen.

accomplished [ə'kʌmpliʃt *or* ə'kɔm-pliʃd], *adj.* vollendet.

accomplishment [əˈkʌmpliʃmənt *or* əˈkɔmpliʃmənt], *s.* (*of project*) die Ausführung; (*of task*) die Vollendung; (*of prophecy*) die Erfüllung; (*pl.*) die Talente, *n. pl.*, Gaben, Kenntnisse, *f. pl.*

accord [əˈkɔːd], *s.* (*agreement*) die Übereinstimmung; (*unison*) die Eintracht. — *v.n.* übereinstimmen (*with*, mit) — *v.a.* bewilligen.

accordance [əˈkɔːdəns], *s.* die Übereinstimmung.

according [əˈkɔːdiŋ], *prep.* — *to*, gemäß, nach, laut.

accordingly [əˈkɔːdiŋli], *adv.* demgemäß, demnach, folglich.

accordion [əˈkɔːdiən], *s.* (*Mus.*) die Ziehharmonika, das Akkordeon.

accost [əˈkɔst], *v.a.* ansprechen, anreden.

account [əˈkaunt], *s.* die Rechnung; (*report*) der Bericht; (*narrative*) die Erzählung; (*importance*) die Bedeutung; (*Fin.*) das Konto, Guthaben; *cash* —, die Kassenrechnung; *on no* —, auf keinen Fall; *on his* —, seinetwegen, um seinetwillen; *on* — *of*, wegen (*Genit.*); *on that* —, darum; *of no* —, unbedeutend. — *v.n.* — *for*, Rechenschaft ablegen über (*Acc.*); (*explain*) erklären.

accountable [əˈkauntəbl], *adj.* verrechenbar (*item*); verantwortlich (*person*).

accountant [əˈkauntənt], *s.* der Bücherrevisor, Rechnungsführer; *junior* —, der Buchhalter.

accredit [əˈkredit], *v.a.* akkreditieren, beglaubigen; (*authorize*) ermächtigen, bevollmächtigen.

accretion [əˈkriːʃən], *s.* der Zuwachs.

accrue [əˈkruː], *v.n.* (*Comm.*) zuwachsen, erwachsen, zufallen.

accumulate [əˈkjuːmjuleit], *v.a., v.n.* anhäufen; sich anhäufen, zunehmen, sich ansammeln.

accumulation [əkjuːmjuˈleiʃən], *s.* die Ansammlung, Anhäufung.

accuracy [ˈækjurəsi], *s.* die Genauigkeit.

accurate [ˈækjurit], *adj.* genau, richtig.

accursed [əˈkəːsid], *adj.* verflucht, verwünscht.

accusation [ækjuˈzeiʃən], *s.* die Anklage.

accusative [əˈkjuːzətiv], *s.* (*Gram.*) der Akkusativ.

accuse [əˈkjuːz], *v.a.* anklagen, beschuldigen (*of*, *Genit.*).

accustom [əˈkʌstəm], *v.a.* gewöhnen (*to*, an, *Acc.*).

ace [eis], *s.* (*Cards*) das As, die Eins.

acerbity [əˈsəːbiti], *s.* die Rauheit, Herbheit; (*manner*) die Grobheit.

acetate [ˈæsiteit], *s.* das Azetat; essigsaures Salz.

acetic [əˈsiːtik, əˈsetik], *adj.* essigsauer.

acetylene [əˈsetiliːn], *s.* das Azetylen.

ache [eik], *s.* der Schmerz. — *v.n.* schmerzen, weh(e)tun.

achieve [əˈtʃiːv], *v.a.* erreichen, erlangen; (*accomplish*) vollenden; (*perform*) ausführen; (*gain*) erlangen, erwerben.

achievement [əˈtʃiːvmənt], *s.* (*accomplishment*) die Leistung, der Erfolg; die Errungenschaft; (*gain*) die Erwerbung.

achromatic [ækroˈmætik], *adj.* achromatisch, farblos.

acid [ˈæsid], *adj.* sauer, scharf. — *s.* (*Chem.*) die Säure.

acidulated [əˈsidjuleitid], *adj.* (*Chem.*) angesäuert.

acknowledge [əkˈnɔlidʒ], *v.a.* anerkennen; (*admit*) zugeben; (*confess*) bekennen; (*letter*) den Empfang bestätigen.

acknowledgement [əkˈnɔlidʒmənt], *s.* die Anerkennung, (*receipt*) Bestätigung, Quittung; (*pl.*) die Dankesbezeigung; die Erkenntlichkeit.

acme [ˈækmi], *s.* der Gipfel, Höhepunkt.

acorn [ˈeikɔːn], *s.* (*Bot.*) die Eichel.

acoustics [əˈkuːstiks], *s. pl.* die Akustik; (*subject*, *study*) die Schallehre.

acquaint [əˈkweint], *v.a.* bekanntmachen; (*inform*) mitteilen (*Dat.*), informieren; unterrichten.

acquaintance [əˈkweintəns], *s.* die Bekanntschaft; der Bekannte, die Bekannte (*person*); die Kenntnis (*with*, von).

acquiesce [ækwiˈes], *v.n.* einwilligen, sich fügen.

acquiescence [ækwiˈesəns], *s.* die Einwilligung (*in*, in, *Acc.*), Zustimmung (*in*, zu, *Dat.*)

acquiescent [ækwiˈesənt], *adj.* fügsam.

acquire [əˈkwaiə], *v.a.* erlangen, erwerben; (*language*) erlernen.

acquisition [ækwiˈziʃən], *s.* die Erlangung, Erwerbung.

acquit [əˈkwit], *v.a.* freisprechen.

acre [ˈeikə], *s.* der Acker (*appr.* 0.4 *Hektar*).

acrid [ˈækrid], *adj.* scharf, beißend.

acrimonious [ækriˈmouniəs], *adj.* scharf, bitter.

across [əˈkrɔs, əˈkrɔːs], *adv.* kreuzweise, (quer) hinüber. — *prep.* quer durch, über; *come* —, (zufällig) treffen, *come* — *a problem*, auf ein Problem stoßen.

act [ækt], *s.* (*deed*) die Tat; (*Theat.*) der Akt; (*Parl. etc.*) die Akte. — *v.a.* (*Theat.*) spielen. — *v.n.* handeln (*do something*); sich benehmen *or* tun, als ob (*act as if*, *pretend*); (*Theat.*) spielen; (*Chem.*) wirken (*react*).

action [ˈækʃən], *s.* die Handlung (*play*, *deed*); Wirkung (*effect*); (*Law*) der Prozeß; der Gang.

active [ˈæktiv], *adj.* (*person*, *Gram.*) aktiv; tätig; rührig (*industrious*); wirksam (*effective*).

activity [ækˈtiviti], *s.* die Tätigkeit; (*Chem.*) Wirksamkeit.

actor [ˈæktə], *s.* der Schauspieler.

actress [ˈæktrəs], die Schauspielerin.

actual [ˈæktjuəl], *adj.* tatsächlich, wirklich.

actuality [æktju'æliti], s. die Wirklichkeit.

actuary ['æktjuəri], s. der Aktuar, Versicherungsbeamte.

actuate ['æktjueit], v.a. betreiben, in Bewegung setzen.

acuity [ə'kju:ti], s. der Scharfsinn (mind), die Schärfe (vision etc.).

acute [ə'kju:t], adj. scharf, scharfsinnig (mind); spitz (angle); fein (sense); — accent, der Akut.

adage ['ædidʒ], s. das Sprichwort.

adamant ['ædəmənt], adj. sehr hart, unerbittlich (inexorable).

adapt [ə'dæpt], v.a. anpassen, angleichen; bearbeiten.

adaptable [ə'dæptəbl], adj. anpassungsfähig.

adaptation [ædæp'teifən], s. die Anpassung, die Bearbeitung (of book).

adaptive [ə'dæptiv], adj. anpassungsfähig.

add [æd], v.a. hinzufügen, (Maths.) addieren.

adder ['ædə], s. (Zool.) die Natter.

addict ['ædikt], s. der Süchtige.

addiction [ə'dikfən], s. die Sucht.

addicted [ə'diktid], adj. verfallen.

addition [ə'difən], s. die Hinzufügung, Zugabe, (Maths.) Addition.

additional [ə'difənəl], adj. zusätzlich, nachträglich.

address [ə'dres], s. die Anschrift, Adresse (letter); die Ansprache (speech). — v.a. (letter) adressieren, richten an (Acc.).

addressee [ædre'si:], s. der Adressat, der Empfänger.

adduce [ə'dju:s], v.a. anführen (proof, Beweis).

adenoid ['ædinɔid], s. (usually pl.) (Med.) die Wucherung.

adept ['ædept], adj. geschickt, erfahren.

adequacy ['ædikwəsi], s. die Angemessenheit, das Gewachsensein, die Zulänglichkeit.

adequate ['ædikwət], adj. gewachsen (Dat.); angemessen, hinreichend (sufficient).

adhere [əd'hiə], v.n. haften, anhängen; — to one's opinion, bei seiner Meinung bleiben.

adherence [əd'hiərəns], s. das Festhalten (an, Dat.).

adhesion [əd'hi:ʒən], s. (Phys.) die Adhäsion; das Anhaften.

adhesive [əd'hi:ziv], adj. haftend, klebrig; — plaster, das Heftpflaster.

adipose ['ædipous], adj. fett, feist.

adjacent [ə'dʒeisənt], adj. naheliegend, benachbart, angrenzend.

adjective ['ædʒəktiv], s. (Gram.) das Adjektiv; Eigenschaftswort.

adjoin [ə'dʒɔin], v.a. anstoßen, angrenzen.

adjourn [ə'dʒə:n], v.a. vertagen, aufschieben.

adjudicate [ə'dʒu:dikeit], v.a. beurteilen, richten.

adjunct ['ædʒʌŋkt], s. der Zusatz.

adjust [ə'dʒʌst], v.a. ordnen; (adapt) anpassen; regulieren, einstellen.

adjustable [ə'dʒʌstəbl], adj. verstellbar, einstellbar.

adjustment [ə'dʒʌstmənt], s. die Einstellung, Anpassung; (Law) Schlichtung; Berichtigung.

administer [əd'm·nistə], v.a. verwalten (an enterprise); verabreichen (medicine); abnehmen (an oath, einen Eid).

administration [ədminis'treifən], s. die Verwaltung, Regierung; die Darreichung (sacraments).

administrative [əd'ministrətiv], adj. Verwaltungs-; verwaltend.

admirable ['ædmirəbl], adj. bewundernswert.

admiral ['ædmirəl], s. der Admiral.

Admiralty ['ædmirəlti], s. die Admiralität.

admiration [ædmi'reifən], s. die Bewunderung.

admire [əd'maiə], v.a. bewundern, verehren.

admirer [əd'maiərə], s. der Bewunderer, Verehrer.

admissible [əd'misibl], adj. zulässig.

admission [əd'mifən], s. die Zulassung; (entry) der Eintritt; Zutritt; (confession) das Eingeständnis, Zugeständnis.

admit [əd'mit], v.a. zulassen; aufnehmen; zugeben (deed); gelten lassen (argument).

admittance [əd'mitəns], s. der Zugang, Eintritt, Zutritt.

admixture [əd'mikstfə], s. die Beimischung, Beigabe.

admonish [əd'mɔnif], v.a. ermahnen, mahnen, warnen.

admonition [ædmə'nifən], s. die Ermahnung, Warnung.

ado [ə'du:], s. der Lärm, das Tun, das Treiben; without further —, ohne weiteres.

adolescence [ædo'lesəns], s. die Adoleszenz, Jugend, Jugendzeit.

adolescent [ædo'lesənt], s. der Jugendliche. — adj. jugendlich.

adopt [ə'dɔpt], v.a. (Law) annehmen, adoptieren.

adoption [ə'dopfən], s. (Law) die Annahme, Adoption.

adoptive [ə'dɔptiv], adj. Adoptiv-, angenommen.

adorable [ə'dɔ:rəbl], adj. anbetungswürdig; (coll.) wunderbar, schön.

adoration [ædo'reifən], s. die Anbetung.

adore [ə'dɔ:], v.a. anbeten; verehren.

adorn [ə'dɔ:n], v.a. (aus)schmücken, zieren.

Adriatic (Sea) [eidri:'ætik (si:)]. das adriatische Meer.

adrift [ə'drift], adv. treibend; cut o.s. —, sich absondern.

adroit [ə'drɔit], adj. gewandt, geschickt.

adroitness [ə'drɔitnis], s. die Gewandtheit, die Geschicklichkeit.

adulation [ædju'leiʃən], *s.* die Schmeichelei.

adulator ['ædjuleitə], *s.* der Schmeichler.

adulatory ['ædjuleitəri], *adj.* schmeichlerisch.

adult [ə'dʌlt *or* 'ædʌlt], *adj.* erwachsen. — *s.* der Erwachsene.

adulterate [ə'dʌltəreit], *v.a.* verfälschen; verwässern.

adulterer [ə'dʌltərə], *s.* der Ehebrecher.

adultery [ə'dʌltəri], *s.* der Ehebruch.

adumbrate [ə'dʌmbreit *or* 'æd-], *v.a.* skizzieren, entwerfen, andeuten.

advance [əd'va:ns], *v.a.* fördern (*a cause*); vorschießen (*money*); geltend machen (*claim*). — *v.n.* vorrücken, vorstoßen; (*make progress, gain promotion*) aufsteigen. — *s.* der Fortschritt (*progress*); der Vorschuß (*money*); in —, im voraus.

advancement [əd'va:nsmənt], *s.* der Fortschritt (*progress*), der Aufstieg, die Beförderung (*promotion*); die Förderung (*of a cause*).

advantage [əd'va:ntidʒ], *s.* der Vorteil, Nutzen; (*superiority*) die Überlegenheit.

Advent ['ædvənt]. (*Eccl.*) der Advent.

advent ['ædvənt], *s.* die Ankunft.

adventitious [ædven'tiʃəs], *adj.* zufällig.

adventure [əd'ventʃə], *s.* das Abenteuer. — *v.n.* auf Abenteuer ausgehen, wagen.

adventurer [əd'ventʃərə], *s.* der Abenteurer.

adventurous [əd'ventʃərəs], *adj.* abenteuerlich, unternehmungslustig.

adverb ['ædvə:b], *s.* (*Gram.*) das Adverb(ium), Umstandswort.

adverbial [əd'və:biəl], *adj.* adverbial.

adversary ['ædvəsəri], *s.* der Gegner, Widersacher.

adverse ['ædvə:s], *adj.* widrig, feindlich, ungünstig.

adversity [əd'və:siti], *s.* das Unglück, Mißgeschick; *in* —, im Unglück.

advert [əd'və:t], *v.n.* hinweisen.

advertise ['ædvətaiz], *v.a.* anzeigen; annoncieren (*in press*), Reklame machen.

advertisement [əd'və:tizmənt], *s.* die Anzeige, Annonce; Reklame.

advertiser ['ædvətaizə], *s.* der Anzeiger.

advice [əd'vais], *s.* der Rat, Ratschlag; die Nachricht (*information*).

advise [əd'vaiz], *v.a.* raten (*Dat.*), beraten; benachrichtigen (*inform*); verständigen.

advisable [əd'vaizəbl], *adj.* ratsam.

advisedly [əd'vaizidli], *adv.* absichtlich, mit Bedacht.

adviser [əd'vaizə], *s.* der Berater.

advisory [əd'vaizəri], *adj.* beratend, ratgebend, Rats-.

advocacy ['ædvəkəsi], *s.* (*Law*) die Verteidigung; die Fürsprache (*championing of*, für, *Acc.*); die Vertretung (*of view*).

Aegean (**Sea**) [i:'dʒi:ən (si:)]. das ägäische Meer.

aerated ['ɛəreitid], *adj.* kohlensauer.

aerial ['ɛəriəl], *s.* (*Rad.*) die Antenne. — *adj.* luftig, Luft-.

aerie ['ɛəri, 'iəri], *s. see* **eyrie**

aerodrome ['ɛərodroum], *s.* der Flugplatz, Flughafen.

aeronautical [ɛəro'nɔ:tikəl], *adj.* aeronautisch.

aeronautics [ɛəro'nɔ:tiks], *s. pl.* die Aeronautik, Luftfahrt.

aeroplane, (*Am.*) **airplane** ['ɛəroplein, 'ɛərplein], *s.* das Flugzeug.

aesthetic(al) [i:s'θetik(əl)], *adj.* ästhetisch.

aesthetics [i:s'θetiks], *s.* die Ästhetik.

afar [ə'fa:], *adv.* fern, weit entfernt; *from* —, von weitem, (von) weit her.

affability [æfə'biliti], *s.* die Leutseligkeit, Freundlichkeit.

affable ['æfəbl], *adj.* freundlich, leutselig.

affair [ə'fɛə], *s.* die Affäre; die Angelegenheit (*matter*); das Anliegen (*concern*).

affect [ə'fekt], *v.a.* beeinflußen; rühren; wirken auf; vortäuschen (*pretend*); zur Schau tragen (*exhibit*).

affectation [æfek'teiʃən], *s.* die Ziererei, das Affektieren, die Affektiertheit.

affected [ə'fektid], *adj.* affektiert, gekünstelt, geziert; befallen, angegriffen (*illness*).

affection [ə'fekʃən], *s.* die Zuneigung, Zärtlichkeit.

affectionate [ə'fekʃənit], *adj.* zärtlich, liebevoll; (*in letters*) *yours* —*ly*, herzlichst.

affinity [ə'finiti], *s.* (*Chem.*) die Affinität; die Verwandtschaft (*relationship*).

affirm [ə'fə:m], *v.a.* behaupten, bestätigen, versichern; bekräftigen (*confirm*).

affirmation [æfə'meiʃən], *s.* die Behauptung, Bekräftigung.

affirmative [ə'fə:mətiv], *adj.* bejahend, positiv; *in the* —, bejahend.

affix [ə'fiks], *v.a.* anheften, aufkleben (*stick*); anbringen (*join to*, an, *Acc.*).

afflict [ə'flikt], *v.a.* quälen, plagen.

affliction [ə'flikʃən], *s.* die Plage, Qual; das Mißgeschick; die Not; das Leiden.

affluence ['æfluəns], *s.* der Überfluß (*abundance*); der Reichtum.

affluent ['æfluənt], *adj.* reich, wohlhabend. — *s.* der Nebenfluß (*tributary*).

afford [ə'fɔ:d], *v.a.* geben, bieten; (*sich*) leisten (*have money for*); gewähren (*give*); hervorbringen (*yield*).

afforest [ə'fɔrist], *v.a.* aufforsten.

affray [ə'frei], *s.* die Schlägerei.

African ['æfrikən], *adj.* afrikanisch. — *s.* der Afrikaner.

affront [ə'frʌnt], *s.* die Beleidigung. — *v.a.* beleidigen.

Afghan ['æfgæn], *adj.* afghanisch. — *s.* der Afghane.

afield [ə'fi:ld], *adj.*, *adv.* im Felde; weit umher; weit weg.

afire [ə'faiə], *adv.*, *adv.* in Flammen.

aflame [ə'fleim], *adj.*, *adv.* in Flammen.
afloat [ə'flout], *adj.*, *adv.* schwimmend, dahintreibend.
afoot [ə'fut], *adj.*, *adv.* im Gange.
afore [ə'fɔː], *adv.* vorher.
aforesaid [ə'fɔːsed], *adj.* the —, das Obengesagte, der Vorhergenannte.
afraid [ə'freid], *adj.* ängstlich, furchtsam; be —, fürchten (of s.th., etwas, Acc.); sich fürchten.
afresh [ə'freʃ], *adv.* von neuem.
aft [ɑːft], *adv.* (Naut.) achtern.
after [ɑːftə], *prep.* nach (time); nach, hinter (place); the day — tomorrow, übermorgen. — *adj.* hinter, später. — *adv.* hinterher, nachher (time); darauf, dahinter (place). — *conj.* nachdem.
afternoon [ɑːftə'nuːn], *s.* der Nachmittag.
afterwards ['ɑːftəwədz], *adv.* nachher, daraufhin, später.
again [ə'gein], *adv.* wieder, abermals, noch einmal, zurück (back); dagegen (however); as much —, noch einmal soviel; — and —, immer wieder.
against [ə'geinst], *prep.* gegen, wider; nahe bei (near, Dat.); bis an (up to, Acc.); — the grain, wider or gegen den Strich.
agate ['ægeit], *s.* der Achat.
agave [ə'geivi], *s.* (Bot.) die Agave.
age [eidʒ], *s.* das Alter (person); das Zeitalter (period); die Reife; come of —, volljährig werden; mündig werden; old —, das Greisenalter; for —s, seit einer Ewigkeit. — *v.n.* altern, alt werden.
aged ['eidʒid], *adj.* bejahrt.
agency ['eidʒənsi], *s.* die Agentur (firm); die Mitwirkung (participation); die Hilfe (assistance); die Vermittlung (mediation).
agenda [ə'dʒendə], *s.* das Sitzungsprogramm; die Tagesordnung.
agent ['eidʒənt], *s.* der Agent, Vertreter.
agglomerate [ə'glɔməreit], *v.a.* zusammenhäufen. — *v.n.* sich zusammenhäufen, sich ballen.
aggrandisement [ə'grændizmənt], *s.* die Überhebung, Übertreibung, Erweiterung.
aggravate ['ægrəveit], *v.a.* verschlimmern; ärgern.
aggravation [ægrə'veiʃən], *s.* die Verschlimmerung (of condition); der Ärger (annoyance).
aggregate ['ægrigit], *adj.* gesamt, vereinigt, vereint. — *s.* das Aggregat.
aggregation [ægri'geiʃən], *s.* (Geol., Chem.) die Vereinigung, Anhäufung, Ansammlung.
aggression [ə'greʃən], *s.* der Angriff, Überfall.
aggressive [ə'gresiv], *adj.* aggressiv, angreifend.
aggressor [ə'gresə], *s.* der Angreifer.
aggrieve [ə'griːv], *v.a.* kränken.

aghast [ə'gɑːst], *adj.* bestürzt; sprachlos; entsetzt.
agile ['ædʒail], *adj.* behend, flink, beweglich.
agitate ['ædʒiteit], *v.a.* bewegen; beunruhigen, aufrühren; stören.
agitation [ædʒi'teiʃən], *s.* (Pol.) die Agitation; die Unruhe (unrest); der Aufruhr (revolt).
agitator ['ædʒiteitə], *s.* (Pol.) der Agitator; der Aufwiegler (inciter).
aglow [ə'glou], *adv.* glühend.
agnostic [æg'nɔstik], *s.* der Agnostiker.
ago [ə'gou], *adv.* vor; long —, vor langer Zeit; not long —, kürzlich; a month —, vor einem Monat.
agog [ə'gɔg], *adj.* erregt, gespannt, neugierig (for, auf, Acc.).
agonize ['ægənaiz], *v.a.* quälen, martern. — *v.n.* Qual erleiden; mit dem Tode ringen or kämpfen.
agonising ['ægənaizɪŋ], *adj.* schmerzhaft, qualvoll.
agony ['ægəni], *s.* die Pein, Qual; der Todeskampf; — column, die Seufzerspalte.
agrarian [ə'greəriən], *adj.* landwirtschaftlich; — party, die Bauernpartei.
agree [ə'griː], *v.n.* übereinstimmen (be in agreement); übereinkommen (come to an agreement), sich einigen.
agreeable [ə'griːəbl], *adj.* angenehm, gefällig.
agreement [ə'griːmənt], *s.* die Übereinstimmung, das Übereinkommen; der Vertrag, die Verständigung (understanding).
agricultural [ægri'kʌltʃərəl], *adj.* landwirtschaftlich.
agriculture ['ægrikʌltʃə], *s.* die Landwirtschaft.
aground [ə'graund], *adj.*, *adv.* (Naut.) gestrandet; to run —, stranden.
ague ['eigjuː], *s.* (Med.) der Schüttelfrost.
ah! [ɑː], *interj.* ach!; aha! (surprise).
aha! [ɑːˈhɑː], *interj.* ach so!
ahead [ə'hed], *adv.* vorwärts, voran (movement), voraus (position), go — (carry on), fortfahren; go — (make progress), vorwärtskommen.
ahoy! [ə'hɔi], *interj.* (Naut.) ahoi!
aid [eid], *v.a.* helfen (Dat.), unterstützen (Acc.), beistehen (Dat.). — *s.* die Hilfe, der Beistand.
aide-de-camp ['eiddə'kɑː], *s.* der Adjutant (eines Generals).
ail [eil], *v.n.* schmerzen; krank sein.
ailing ['eiliŋ], *adj.* kränklich, leidend.
ailment ['eilmənt], *s.* das Leiden.
aim [eim], *v.a.* (weapon, blow etc.) richten (at, auf). — *v.n.* zielen (auf, Acc.); trachten (nach, strive for). — *s.* das Ziel, der Zweck (purpose); die Absicht (intention).
aimless ['eimlis], *adj.* ziellos, zwecklos.

air [εə], s. die Luft; die Melodie (*tune*);
die Miene (*mien*); *air force*, die Luft-
waffe; *air pocket*, das Luftloch; *air
raid*, der Luftangriff; *in the open* —,
im Freien; *on the* —, im Rundfunk; *to
give oneself* —*s*, vornehm tun. — *v.a.*
lüften (*room*); trocknen (*washing*);
aussprechen (*views*).

airbase [ˈεəbeis], s. der Fliegerstütz-
punkt.

airconditioning [ˈεəkəndiʃəniŋ], s. die
Klimaanlage.

aircraft [ˈεəkrɑːft], s. das Luftfahrzeug,
Flugzeug.

airgun [ˈεəgʌn], s. die Windbüchse,
das Luftgewehr.

airiness [ˈεərinis], s. die Luftigkeit,
Leichtigkeit.

airletter [ˈεəletə], s. der Luftpostbrief.

airliner [ˈεəlainə], s. das Verkehrs-
flugzeug.

airmail [ˈεəmeil], s. die Luftpost.

airman [ˈεəmən], s. der Flieger.

airplane *see* **aeroplane**.

airport [ˈεəpɔːt], s. der Flughafen.

airtight [ˈεətait], adj. luftdicht.

airy [ˈεəri], adj. luftig.

aisle [ail], s. das Seitenschiff (*church*);
der Gang.

Aix-la-Chapelle[ˈeiksləˈfæ'pel],Aachen,
n.

ajar [əˈdʒɑː], adv. angelehnt, halb
offen.

akimbo [əˈkimbou], adv. Hände an den
Hüften, Arme in die Seiten gestemmt.

akin [əˈkin], adj. verwandt (*to*, mit,
Dat.).

alack [əˈlæk], interj. ach! oh, weh! *alas
and* —, ach und wehe!

alacrity [əˈlækriti], s. die Bereitwilligkeit; Munterkeit.

alarm [əˈlɑːm], s. der Alarm; Lärm
(*noise*); die Warnung; Angst, Bestürzung; — *clock*, der Wecker. — *v.a.*
erschrecken.

alas! [əˈlæs], interj. ach, wehe!

Albanian [ælˈbeiniən], adj. albanisch.
— s. der Albanier.

album [ˈælbəm], s. das Album.

albumen [ælˈbjuːmən], s. das Eiweiß,
(*Chem.*) der Eiweißstoff.

albuminous [ælˈbjuːminəs], adj. eiweiß-
haltig, Eiweiß-.

alchemist [ˈælkimist], s. der Alchimist.

alchemy [ˈælkimi], s. die Alchimie.

alcohol [ˈælkəhɔl], s. der Alkohol.

alcoholic [ælkəˈhɔlik], adj. alkoholisch.
— s. der Trinker, Alkoholiker.

alcove [ˈælkouv], s. der Alkoven.

alder [ˈɔːldə], s. (*Bot.*) die Erle.

alderman [ˈɔːldəmən], s. der Ratsherr,
der Stadtrat.

ale [eil], s. englisches Bier.

alert [əˈləːt], adj. wachsam, aufmerksam; *on the* —, auf der Hut.

algebra [ˈældʒibrə], s. die Algebra.

Algerian [ælˈdʒiəriən], adj. algerisch.
— s. der Algerier.

Algiers [ælˈdʒiəz], Algier, *n.*

alias [ˈeiliəs], adv. sonst genannt.

alien [ˈeiliən], adj. fremd, ausländisch.
— s. der Fremde, Ausländer.

alienate [ˈeiliəneit], v.a. entfremden.

alienation [eiliəˈneiʃən], s. die Entfremdung; — *of mind*, die Geisteser-
krankung, Geistesgestörtheit.

alienist [ˈeiliənist], s. der Irrenarzt.

alight (1) [əˈlait], v.n. absteigen (*from
horse*); aussteigen (*from carriage etc.*).

alight (2) [əˈlait], adj. brennend, in
Flammen.

alike [əˈlaik], adj. gleich, ähnlich. —
adv. *great and small* —, sowohl große
wie kleine.

alimentary [æliˈmentəri], adj. Nah-
rungs-, Verdauungs-; — *canal*, (*Anat.*)
der Darmkanal.

alimentation [ælimenˈteiʃən], s. die
Beköstigung; (*Law*) der Unterhalt.

alimony [ˈæliməni], s. der Unterhalts-
beitrag; (*pl.*) Alimente. , *n.pl.*

alive [əˈlaiv], adj. lebendig; — *and
kicking*, wohlauf, munter; — *to*,
empfänglich für.

alkali [ˈælkəlai], s. (*Chem.*) das Laugen-
salz, Alkali.

alkaline [ˈælkəlain], adj. (*Chem.*) alka-
lisch, laugensalzig.

all [ɔːl], adj., pron. all, ganz (*whole*);
sämtliche, alle; *above* —, vor allem;
once and for —, ein für allemal; *not
at* —, keineswegs; *All Saints*, Allerheiligen; *All Souls*, Allerseelen. —
adv. ganz, gänzlich, völlig; — *the
same*, trotzdem; — *the better*, umso
besser.

allay [əˈlei], v.a. lindern, beruhigen,
unterdrücken.

allegation [æliˈgeiʃən], s. die Behauptung.

allege [əˈledʒ],v.a. behaupten, aussagen.

allegiance [əˈliːdʒəns], s. die Treue,
Ergebenheit; Untertanenpflicht.

allegorical [æliˈgɔrikəl], adj. allego-
risch, sinnbildlich.

alleviate [əˈliːvieit],ˣ v.a. erleichtern,
mildern.

alleviation [əliːviˈeiʃən], s. die Erleichterung, Milderung.

alley [ˈæli], s. die Gasse; Seitenstraße;
bowling —, die Kegelbahn.

alliance [əˈlaiəns], s. (*Pol.*) die Allianz,
das Bündnis (*treaty*); der · Bund
(*league*).

allied [əˈlaid, ˈælaid], adj. verbündet,
vereinigt; alliiert; verwandt.

alliteration [əlitəˈreiʃən], s. die Alliteration, der Stabreim.

allocate [ˈælokeit], v.a. zuweisen,
zuteilen.

allot [əˈlɔt], v.a. zuteilen (*assign*);
verteilen (*distribute*).

allotment [əˈlɔtmənt], s. der Anteil;
die Zuteilung; die Landparzelle; die
Laubenkolonie, der Schrebergarten
(*garden*).

allow [əˈlau], v.a. gewähren (*grant*);
erlauben (*permit*); zulassen (*admit*). —
v.n. — *for*, Rücksicht nehmen auf
(*Acc.*); in Betracht ziehen.

allowance [əˈlauəns], *s.* die Rente; das Taschengeld (*money*); die Erlaubnis (*permission*); die Genehmigung (*approval*); die Nachsicht (*indulgence*).

alloy [əˈbi, ˈæbi], *s.* die Legierung. — *v.a.* (*Metall.*) legieren.

allude [əˈlu:d], *v.a.* anspielen (*to*, auf).

allure [əˈljuə], *v.a.* locken, anlocken.

allurement [əˈljuəmənt], *s.* der Reiz, die Lockung.

allusion [əˈlu:ʒən], *s.* die Anspielung.

alluvial [əˈlu:viəl], *adj.* angeschwemmt.

alluvium [əˈlu:viəm], *s.* das Schwemmgebiet, Schwemmland.

ally [ˈælai], *s.* der Verbündete, Bundesgenosse, Alliierte. — [əˈlai], *v.a.*, *v.r.* (sich) vereinigen, (sich) verbünden.

almanac [ˈɔːlmənæk], *s.* der Almanach.

almighty [ɔːlˈmaiti], *adj.* allmächtig; *God Almighty!* allmächtiger Gott!

almond [ˈɑːmənd], *s.* (*Bot.*) die Mandel.

almoner [ˈælmənə], *s.* der Wohlfahrtsbeamte, die Fürsorgerin.

almost [ˈɔːlmoust], *adv.* fast, beinahe.

alms [aːmz], *s.* das Almosen.

aloe [ˈælou], *s.* (*Bot.*) die Aloe.

aloft [əˈlɔft], *adv.* droben, (hoch) oben; empor.

alone [əˈloun], *adj.*, *adv.* allein; *all* —, ganz allein; *leave* —, in Ruhe lassen; *let* —, geschweige (denn).

along [əˈlɔŋ], *adv.* längs, der Länge nach; entlang, weiter; *come* —! komm mit!; *get* — (*with*), auskommen. — *prep.* längs; entlang.

alongside [əlɔŋˈsaid], *adv.* nebenan. — [əˈlɔŋsaid], *prep.* neben.

aloof [əˈluːf], *adj.*, *adv.* fern, weitab; *keep* —, sich fernhalten.

aloofness [əˈluːfnis], *s.* das Sichfernhalten; das Vornehmtun.

aloud [əˈlaud], *adj.*, *adv.* laut; hörbar.

alphabet [ˈælfəbet], *s.* das Alphabet, Abc.

Alpine [ˈælpain], *adj.* alpinisch, Alpen-.

Alps, The [ˈælps, ði]. die Alpen, *pl.*

already [ɔːlˈredi], *adv.* schon, bereits.

Alsatian [ælˈseiʃən], *adj.* elsässisch. — *s.* der Elsässer; (*dog*) der Wolfshund, deutscher Schäferhund.

also [ˈɔːlsou], *adv.* (*likewise*) auch, ebenfalls; (*moreover*) ferner.

altar [ˈɔːltə], *s.* der Altar.

alter [ˈɔːltə], *v.a.* ändern, verändern. — *v.n.* sich (ver)ändern.

alterable [ˈɔːltərəbl], *adj.* veränderlich.

alteration [ɔːltəˈreiʃən], *s.* die Änderung, Veränderung.

altercation [ɔːltəˈkeiʃən], *s.* der Zank, Streit; Wortwechsel.

alternate [ˈɔːltəneit], *v.a.*, *v.n.* abwechseln lassen, abwechseln.

alternative [ɔːlˈtəːnətiv], *adj.* abwechselnd, alternativ, zur Wahl gestellt. — *s.* die Alternative, die Wahl.

although [ɔːlˈðou], *conj.* obgleich, obwohl, obschon.

altimeter [ˈæltimiːtə], *s.* der Höhenmesser.

altitude [ˈæltitjuːd], *s.* die Höhe.

alto [ˈæltou], *s.* (*Mus.*) die Altstimme, der Alt.

altogether [ɔːltuˈgeðə], *adv.* zusammen, zusammengenommen, allesamt; (*wholly*) ganz und gar, durchaus.

alum [ˈæləm], *s.* (*Chem.*) der Alaun.

aluminium [æljuˈminjəm], (*Am.*) **aluminum** [əˈluːminəm], *s.* das Aluminium.

always [ˈɔːlweiz], *adv.* immer, stets.

am [æm] *see* **be**.

amalgamate [əˈmælgəmeit], *v.a.* amalgamieren. — *v.n.* sich vereinigen, vermischen.

amalgamation [əmælgəˈmeiʃən], *s.* die Verbindung, Vereinigung.

amass [əˈmæs], *v.a.* anhäufen, zusammentragen.

amateur [æməˈtə:] *or* [ˈæmətjuə], *s.* der Amateur, Liebhaber.

amatory [ˈæmətəri], *adj.* Liebes-, verliebt, sinnlich.

amaze [əˈmeiz], *v.a.* erstaunen, in Erstaunen versetzen; verblüffen (*baffle*).

amazement [əˈmeizmənt], *s.* das Erstaunen, Staunen, die Verwunderung.

amazing [əˈmeiziŋ], *adj.* erstaunlich, wunderbar.

Amazon (1) [ˈæməzən], *s.* (*Myth.*) die Amazone.

Amazon (2) [ˈæməzən], *s.* (*river*) der Amazonas.

ambassador [æmˈbæsədə], *s.* der Botschafter.

ambassadorial [æmbæsəˈdɔ:riəl], *adj.* Botschafts-, gesandtschaftlich.

amber [ˈæmbə], *s.* der Bernstein.

ambidextrous [æmbiˈdekstrəs], *adj.* (mit beiden Händen gleich) geschickt.

ambiguity [æmbiˈgjuːiti], *s.* die Zweideutigkeit, der Doppelsinn.

ambiguous [æmˈbigjuəs], *adj.* zweideutig; dunkel (*sense*).

ambit [ˈæmbit], *s.* der Umkreis, die Umgebung.

ambition [æmˈbiʃən], *s.* die Ambition, der Ehrgeiz.

ambitious [æmˈbiʃəs], *adj.* ehrgeizig.

amble [æmbl], *v.n.* schlendern, (gemächlich) spazieren.

ambulance [ˈæmbjuləns], *s.* der Krankenwagen.

ambush [ˈæmbuʃ], *v.a.* überfallen (*Acc.*), auflauern (*Dat.*). — *s.* die Falle, der Hinterhalt.

ameliorate [əˈmiːliəreit], *v.a.* verbessern.

amenable [əˈmiːnəbl], *adj.* zugänglich; unterworfen.

amend [əˈmend], *v.a.* verbessern, berichtigen; ändern.

amendment [əˈmendmənt], *s.* die Verbesserung, der Zusatz, die zusätzliche Änderung (*proposal*).

amends [əˈmendz], *s. pl.* der Schadenersatz; *make* —, Schadenersatz leisten; wiedergutmachen.

amenity [ə'mi:niti *or* ə'meniti], *s.* die Behaglichkeit, Annehmlichkeit; (*pl.*) die Vorzüge, *m pl.*; die Einrichtungen, *f. pl.*

American [ə'merikən], *adj.* amerikanisch; — *cloth,* das Wachstuch. — *s.* der Amerikaner.

amiability [eimjə'biliti], *s.* die Liebenswürdigkeit.

amiable ['eimjəbl], *adj.* liebenswürdig.

amicable ['æmikəbl], *adj.* freundschaftlich.

amidst [ə'midst], *prep.* mitten in, mitten unter (*Dat.*), inmitten (*Gen.*).

amiss [ə'mis], *adj., adv.* übel; verkehrt; *take* —, übelnehmen.

amity ['æmiti], *s.* die Freundschaft.

ammonia [ə'mouniə], *s.* das Ammoniak; *liquid* —, der Salmiakgeist.

ammunition [æmju'niʃən], *s.* die Munition.

amnesty ['æmnisti], *s.* die Amnestie, Begnadigung.

among(st) [ə'mʌŋ(st)], *prep.* (mitten) unter, zwischen, bei.

amorous ['æmərəs], *adj.* verliebt.

amorphous [ə'mɔ:fəs], *adj.* amorph, gestaltlos, formlos.

amortization [əmɔ:ti'zeiʃən], *s.* die Amortisierung (*debt*); (*Comm.*) Tilgung, Abtragung.

amount [ə'maunt], *s.* der Betrag (*sum of money*); die Menge (*quantity*). — *v.n.* betragen; — *to,* sich belaufen auf (*Acc.*).

amphibian [æm'fibiən], *adj.* amphibisch. — *s.* (*Zool.*) die Amphibie.

amphibious [æm'fibiəs], *adj.* amphibienhaft.

ample [æmpl], *adj.* weit, breit (*scope*); voll, reichlich; ausgebreitet; genügend.

amplification [æmplifi'keiʃən], *s.* die Ausbreitung; Verbreiterung, Erklärung, Erweiterung; (*Elec.*) die Verstärkung (*sound*).

amplifier ['æmplifaiə], *s.* der Verstärker; der Lautsprecher.

amplify ['æmplifai], *v.a.* erweitern, ausführen, vergrößern; verstärken (*sound*).

amputate ['æmpjuteit], *v.a.* amputieren.

amputation [æmpju'teiʃən], *s.* die Amputation.

amuck [ə'mʌk], *adv.* amok.

amulet ['æmjulit], *s.* das Amulett.

amuse [ə'mju:z], *v.a.* unterhalten, amüsieren.

amusement [ə'mju:zmənt], *s.* die Unterhaltung, das Vergnügen.

an *see under* **a.**

Anabaptist [ænə'bæptist], *s.* der Wiedertäufer.

anachronism [ə'nækrənizm], *s.* der Anachronismus.

anaemia [ə'ni:miə], *s.* (*Med.*) die Blutarmut.

anaemic [ə'ni:mik], *adj.* (*Med.*) blutarm.

anaesthetic [ænəs'θetik], *adj.* schmerzbetäubend. — *s.* die Narkose.

analogous [ə'næləgəs], *adj.* analog.

analogy [ə'nælədʒi], *s.* die Analogie.

analyse ['ænəlaiz], *v.a.* analysieren.

analysis [ə'nælisis], *s.* die Analyse.

anarchic(al) [ə'na:kik(əl)], *adj.* anarchisch.

anarchy ['ænəki], *s.* die Anarchie.

anathema [ə'næθimə], *s.* (*Eccl.*) der Kirchenbann.

anatomical [ænə'tɔmikəl], *adj.* anatomisch.

anatomist [ə'nætəmist], *s.* der Anatom.

anatomize [ə'nætəmaiz], *v.a.* zergliedern, zerlegen.

anatomy [ə'nætəmi], *s.* die Anatomie.

ancestor ['ænsəstə], *s.* der Vorfahre, Ahnherr.

ancestry ['ænsəstri], *s.* die Ahnenreihe, Herkunft, der Stammbaum (*family tree*).

anchor ['æŋkə], *s.* der Anker. — *v.a.* verankern. — *v.n.* ankern.

anchorage ['æŋkəridʒ], *s.* die Verankerung; der Ankerplatz.

anchovy [æn'tʃouvi *or* 'æntʃəvi], *s.* (*Zool.*) die Sardelle.

ancient ['einʃənt], *adj.* alt, uralt, antik; althergebracht (*traditional*). — *s.* (*pl.*) die Alten (Griechen und Römer].

and [ænd], *conj.* und.

Andes, the ['ændi:z, ði]. die Anden, *pl.*

anecdote ['ænekdout], *s.* die Anekdote.

anemone [ə'neməni], *s.* (*Bot.*) die Anemone, das Windröschen; (*Zool.*) *sea* —, die Seeanemone.

anew [ə'nju:], *adv.* von neuem.

angel ['eindʒəl], *s.* der Engel.

angelic [æn'dʒelik], *adj.* engelhaft, engelgleich.

anger ['æŋgə], *s.* der Zorn, Unwille, Ärger. — *v.a.* erzürnen, verärgern, ärgerlich machen.

angle ['æŋgl], *s.* (*Geom.*) der Winkel; die Angel (*fishing*). — *v.n.* angeln (*for,* nach).

Angles ['æŋglz], *s. pl.* die Angeln, *m. pl.*

Anglo-Saxon [æŋglou'sæksən], *adj.* angelsächsisch. — *s.* der Angelsachse.

anglicism ['æŋglisizm], *s.* der Anglizismus (*style*).

anguish ['æŋgwiʃ], *s.* die Qual, Pein.

angular ['æŋgjulə], *adj.* winklig, eckig.

anhydrous [æn'haidrəs], *adj.* wasserfrei, (*Chem.*) wasserlos.

aniline ['ænilain], *s.* das Anilin. — *adj.* — *dye,* die Anilinfarbe.

animal ['æniməl], *s.* das Tier, Lebewesen.

animate ['ænimeit], *v.a.* beleben, beseelen; (*fig.*) anregen.

animated ['ænimeitid], *adj.* belebt; munter.

animation [æni'meiʃən], *s.* die Belebung.

animosity [æni'mɔsiti], *s.* die Feindseligkeit, Abneigung, Erbitterung.

anise ['ænis], *s.* (*Bot.*) der Anis.

ankle [æŋkl], s. (*Anat.*) der Fußknöchel; — socks, kurze Socken.

anklet [ˈæŋklit], s. der Fußring.

annalist [ˈænəlist], s. der Chronist, Geschichtsschreiber.

annals [ˈænəlz], s. pl. die Annalen (f. pl.); die Chronik (sing.).

anneal [əˈniːl], v.a. ausglühen.

annex [əˈneks], v.a. annektieren, angliedern, sich aneignen.

annex(e) [ˈæneks], s. der Anhang, der Anbau.

annexation [ænekˈseiʃən], s. die Angliederung, Aneignung.

annihilate [əˈnaiileit], v.a. vernichten, zerstören.

annihilation [ənaiiˈleiʃən], s. die Vernichtung, Zerstörung.

anniversary [æniˈvɔːsəri], s. der Jahrestag, die Jahresfeier.

annotate [ˈænoteit], v.a. anmerken, mit Anmerkungen versehen.

annotation [ænoˈteiʃən], s. die Anmerkung, Notiz.

announce [əˈnauns], v.a. melden, ankündigen; anzeigen; (*Rad.*) ansagen.

announcement [əˈnaunsmənt], s. die Ankündigung, Bekanntmachung; (*Rad.*) die Ansage.

announcer [əˈnaunsə], s. (*Rad.*) der Ansager.

annoy [əˈnɔi], v.a. ärgern; belästigen.

annoyance [əˈnɔiəns], s. das Ärgernis; die Belästigung.

annual [ˈænjuəl], adj. jährlich, Jahres-. — s. der Jahresband (*serial publication*); das Jahrbuch; (*Bot.*) die einjährige Pflanze.

annuity [əˈnjuːiti], s. die Jahresrente, Lebensrente.

annul [əˈnʌl], v.a. annullieren, ungültig machen, für ungültig erklären.

annulment [əˈnʌlmənt], s. die Annullierung, Ungültigkeitserklärung.

Annunciation [ənʌnsiˈeiʃən], s. (*Eccl.*) die Verkündigung.

anode [ˈænoud], s. die Anode.

anodyne [ˈænodain], adj. schmerzstillend.

anoint [əˈnɔint], v.a. salben.

anomalous [əˈnɔmələs], adj. abweichend, unregelmäßig, anomal.

anomaly [əˈnɔməli], s. die Anomalie, Abweichung, Unregelmäßigkeit.

anon [əˈnɔn], adv. sogleich, sofort.

anonymous [əˈnɔniməs], adj. (abbr. anon.) anonym; namenlos; unbekannt.

anonymity [ænoˈnimiti], s. die Anonymität.

another [əˈnʌðə], adj. & pron. ein anderer; ein zweiter; noch einer; one —, einander.

answer [ˈaːnsə], v.a. beantworten. — v.n. antworten. — s. die Antwort, Erwiderung.

answerable [ˈaːnsərəbl], adj. verantwortlich (*responsible*); beantwortbar (*capable of being answered*).

ant [ænt], s. (*Ent.*) die Ameise.

antagonise [ænˈtægənaiz], v.a. sich (*Dat.*) jemanden zum Gegner machen.

antagonism [ænˈtægənizm], s. der Widerstreit, Konflikt; der Antagonismus.

Antarctic [æntˈɑːktik], adj. Südpol-, antarktisch. — s. der südliche Polarkreis.

antecedence [æntiˈsiːdəns], s. der Vortritt (*rank*).

antecedent [æntiˈsiːdənt], s. (*pl.*) das Vorhergehende, die Vorgeschichte.

antedate [ˈæntideit], v.a. vordatieren.

antediluvian [æntidiˈluːviən], adj. vorsintflutlich; (*fig.*) überholt; altmodisch.

antelope [ˈæntiloup], s. (*Zool.*) die Antilope.

antenna [ænˈtenə], s. (*Ent.*) der Fühler; (*Rad.*) die Antenne.

anterior [ænˈtiəriə], adj. vorder (*in space*), älter, vorherig, vorhergehend, (*in time*).

anteroom [ˈæntiruːm], s. das Vorzimmer.

anthem [ˈænθəm], s. die Hymne, der Hymnus.

anther [ˈænθə], s. (*Bot.*) der Staubbeutel.

antic [ˈæntik], s. die Posse; (*pl.*) komisches Benehmen.

anticipate [ænˈtisipeit], v.a. vorwegnehmen; zuvorkommen; ahnen (*guess*); erwarten (*await*); vorgreifen.

anticipation [æntisiˈpeiʃən], s. die Vorwegnahme, die Erwartung.

antidote [ˈæntidout], s. das Gegengift.

antipathy [ænˈtipəθi], s. die Antipathie, der Widerwille.

antipodal [ænˈtipədəl], adj. antipodisch; entgegengesetzt.

antiquarian [æntiˈkwɛəriən], adj. altertümlich; antiquarisch.

antiquary [ˈæntikwəri], s. der Altertumsforscher, Antiquar.

antiquated [ˈæntikweitid], adj. überholt, unmodern, veraltet.

antique [ænˈtiːk], s. die Antike; das alte Kunstwerk. — adj. alt, antik; altmodisch.

antiquity [ænˈtikwiti], s. die Antike, das Altertum; die Vorzeit (*period of history*).

antiseptic [æntiˈseptik], adj. antiseptisch — s. das antiseptische Mittel.

antler [ˈæntlə], s. die Geweihsprosse; (*pl.*) das Geweih.

anvil [ˈænvil], s. der Amboß.

anxiety [æŋˈzaiəti], s. die Angst (*fear*); Besorgnis (*uneasiness*); Unruhe.

anxious [ˈæŋkʃəs], adj. ängstlich (*afraid*); besorgt (*worried*); eifrig bemüht (*keen*, um, on, *Acc.*).

any [ˈeni], adj. & pron. jeder; irgendein; etwas; (*pl.*) einige; (*neg.*) not —, kein.

anybody, anyone [ˈenibɔdi, ˈeniwʌn], pron. irgendeiner, jemand; jeder.

anyhow, anyway [ˈenihau, ˈeniwei], adv. irgendwie, auf irgendeine Weise; auf alle Fälle.

anyone see under **anybody.**

apprentice

anything ['eniθiŋ], *s.* irgend etwas; alles.

anyway *see under* **anyhow.**

anywhere ['enihwɛə], *adv.* irgendwo; überall; *not* —, nirgends.

apace [ə'peis], *adv.* geschwind, hurtig, flink.

apart [ə'pɑːt], *adv.* für sich, abgesondert; einzeln; *poles* —, weit entfernt; *take* —, zerlegen; — *from*, abgesehen von.

apartment [ə'pɑːtmənt], *s.* das Zimmer; *(Am.)* die Wohnung *(flat).*

apathy ['æpəθi], *s.* die Apathie, Interesselosigkeit, Gleichgültigkeit.

apathetic [æpə'θetik], *adj.* apathisch, uninteressiert; teilnahmslos.

ape [eip], *s. (Zool.)* der Affe. — *v.a.* nachäffen, nachahmen.

aperient [ə'piəriənt], *adj. (Med.)* abführend. — *s. (Med.)* das Abführmittel.

aperture ['æpətʃə], *s.* die Öffnung.

apex ['eipeks], *s.* die Spitze, der Gipfel.

aphorism ['æfərizm], *s.* der Aphorismus.

apiary ['eipiəri], *s.* das Bienenhaus.

apiece [ə'piːs], *adv.* pro Stück, pro Person.

apologetic [əpɔlə'dʒetik], *adj.* entschuldigend, reumütig; verteidigend.

apologize [ə'pɔlədʒaiz], *v.n.* sich entschuldigen *(for, wegen; to, bei).*

apology [ə'pɔlədʒi], *s.* die Entschuldigung; Abbitte; Rechtfertigung.

apoplectic [æpə'plektik], *adj. (Med.)* apoplektisch.

apoplexy ['æpəpleksi], *s. (Med.)* der Schlagfluß, Schlaganfall *(fit).*

apostle [ə'pɔsl], *s.* der Apostel.

apostolic [æpəs'tɔlik], *adj.* apostolisch.

apostrophe [ə'pɔstrəfi], *s.* der Apostroph *(punctuation);* die Anrede *(speech).*

apostrophize [ə'pɔstrəfaiz], *v.a.* apostrophieren; anreden *(speak to).*

apotheosis [əpɔθi'ousis], *s.* die Apotheose.

appal [ə'pɔːl], *v.a.* erschrecken.

appalling [ə'pɔːliŋ], *adj.* schrecklich.

apparatus [æpə'reitəs], *s.* das Gerät, die Apparatur; *(coll.)* der Apparat.

apparel [ə'pærəl], *s.* die Kleidung.

apparent [ə'pærənt], *adj.* scheinbar; offensichtlich; augenscheinlich; *heir* —, der rechtmäßige Erbe.

apparition [æpə'riʃən], *s.* die Erscheinung; der Geist, das Gespenst *(ghost).*

appeal [ə'piːl], *v.n.* appellieren *(make an appeal); (Law)* Berufung einlegen; gefallen *(please).* — *s. (public, Mil.)* der Appell; die Bitte *(request).*

appear [ə'piə], *v.n.* erscheinen; scheinen; auftreten.

appearance [ə'piərəns], *s.* die Erscheinung; das Auftreten *(stage, etc.);* der Schein *(semblance); keep up* —*s,* den Schein wahren; *to all* —*s,* allem Anschein nach.

appease [ə'piːz], *v.a.* besänftigen.

appeasement [ə'piːzmənt], *s.* die Besänftigung, *(Pol.)* die Befriedung.

appellation [æpe'leiʃən], *s.* die Benennung.

append [ə'pend], *v.a.* anhängen, beifügen.

appendicitis [əpendi'saitis], *s. (Med.)* die Blinddarmentzündung.

appendix [ə'pendiks], *s.* der Anhang; *(Med.)* der Blinddarm.

appertain [æpə'tein], *v.n.* gehören *(to, zu).*

appetite ['æpitait], *s.* der Appetit.

appetizing ['æpitaiziŋ], *adj.* appetitlich, appetitanregend.

applaud [ə'plɔːd], *v.a., v.n.* applaudieren, Beifall klatschen *(Dat.).*

applause [ə'plɔːz], *s.* der Applaus, Beifall.

apple [æpl], *s.* der Apfel.

appliance [ə'plaiəns], *s.* das Gerät, die Vorrichtung.

applicable ['æplikəbl], *adj.* anwendbar, passend *(to, auf).*

applicant ['æplikənt], *s.* der Bewerber *(for, um).*

application [æpli'keiʃən], *s.* die Bewerbung *(for, um);* das Gesuch; die Anwendung *(to, auf); letter of* —, der Bewerbungsbrief; — *form,* das Bewerbungsformular.

apply [ə'plai], *v.a.* anwenden *(auf, to, Acc.);* gebrauchen. — *v.n.* sich bewerben *(um, for, Acc.); (Dat.) this does not* —, das trifft nicht zu; — *within,* drinnen nachfragen.

appoint [ə'pɔint], *v.a.* bestimmen; ernennen; ausrüsten.

appointment [ə'pɔintmənt], *s.* die Festsetzung; die Ernennung; die Bestellung, die Stellung *(position); make an* —, jemanden ernennen *(fill a post),* sich verabreden *(arrange a meet); by* —, Hoflieferant *(to, Genit.).*

apportion [ə'pɔːʃən], *v.a.* zuteilen, zuweisen, zumessen.

apposite ['æpəzit], *adj.* passend, angemessen.

appositeness ['æpəzitnis], *s.* die Angemessenheit.

appraise [ə'preiz], *v.a.* beurteilen.

appraisal [ə'preizəl], *s.* die Beurteilung, Abschätzung.

appreciable [ə'priːʃəbl], *adj.* merklich; nennenswert.

appreciate [ə'priːʃieit], *v.a.* würdigen, schätzen.

appreciation [əpriːʃi'eiʃən], *s.* die Schätzung, Würdigung.

apprehend [æpri'hend], *v.a.* verhaften, ergreifen *(arrest);* befürchten *(fear).*

apprehension [æpri'henʃən], *s.* die Verhaftung *(arrest);* die Befürchtung *(fear).*

apprehensive [æpri'hensiv], *adj.* besorgt, in Furcht *(for, um),* furchtsam.

apprentice [ə'prentis], *s.* der Lehrling; Praktikant. — *v.a.* in die Lehre geben *(with, bei, Dat.).*

311

apprenticeship [ə'prentiʃip], s. die Lehre, Lehrzeit, Praktikantenzeit; *student* —, die Studentenpraxis.

apprise [ə'praiz], *v.a.* benachrichtigen, informieren.

approach [ə'proutʃ], *v.a., v.n.* sich nähern (*Dat.*). — *s.* die Annäherung, das Herankommen, Näherrücken.

approachable [ə'proutʃəbl], *adj.* zugänglich, freundlich.

approbation [æpro'beiʃən], *s.* die (offizielle) Billigung, Zustimmung.

appropriate [ə'proupriit], *adj.* angemessen, gebührend, geeignet (*suitable*). — [ə'prouprieit], *v.a.* requirieren, sich aneignen.

appropriation [əproupri'eiʃən], *s.* die Requisition, Aneignung, Übernahme, Besitznahme.

approval [ə'pru:vəl], *s.* die Billigung, der Beifall, die Zustimmung.

approve [ə'pru:v], *v.a.* loben, billigen; genehmigen; annehmen (*work*).

approved [ə'pru:vd], *adj.* anerkannt.

approximate [ə'prɔksimit], *adj.* ungefähr, annähernd. —*v.n. & a.*[ə'prɔksimeit], sich nähern.

approximation [əprɔksi'meiʃən], *s.* die Annäherung.

approximative [ə'prɔksimətiv], *adj.* annähernd.

appurtenance [ə'pə:tənəns], *s.* das (*or der*) Zubehör.

appurtenant [ə'pə:tənənt], *adj.* zugehörig.

apricot ['eiprikɔt], *s.* (*Bot.*) die Aprikose.

April ['eipril]. der April.

apron ['eiprən], *s.* die Schürze; der Schurz; — *stage*, die Vorbühne, das Proszenium.

apropos [ɑ:prɔ'pou], *adv.* beiläufig; mit Bezug auf, diesbezüglich.

apse [æps], *s.* (*Archit.*) die Apsis.

apt [æpt], *adj.* geeignet, passend; fähig.

aptitude ['æptitju:d], *s.* die Eignung, Fähigkeit.

aptness ['æptnis], *s.* die Angemessenheit, Eignung.

aquatic [ə'kwɔtik *or* ə'kwætik], *adj.* Wasser-, wasser-; — *display*, Wasserkünste. — *s.* (*pl.*) der Wassersport.

aqueduct ['ækwidʌkt], *s.* die Wasserleitung; der Aquädukt.

aqueous ['eikwiəs], *adj.* (*Chem.*) wässerig.

aquiline ['ækwilain], *adj.* adlerartig, Adler-.

Arab ['ærəb], *s.* der Araber.

Arabian [ə'reibiən], *adj.* arabisch; — *Nights*, Tausend-und-eine-Nacht.

Arabic ['ærəbik], *adj.* arabisch (*language, literature*).

arable ['ærəbl], *adj.* pflügbar, bestellbar.

arbiter ['ɑ:bitə], *s.* der Schiedsrichter.

arbitrary ['ɑ:bitrəri], *adj.* willkürlich.

arbitrate ['ɑ:bitreit], *v.in.* vermitteln.

arbitration [ɑ:bi'treiʃən], *s.* die Vermittlung; Entscheidung; (*Comm.*) Arbitrage.

arboriculture ['ɑ:bɔrikʌltʃə], *s.* die Baumzucht.

arbour ['ɑ:bə], *s.* die Laube, Gartenlaube.

arc [ɑ:k], *s.* (*Geom.*) der Bogen; — *lamp*, die Bogenlampe; — *welding*, das Lichtschweißen.

arcade [ɑ:'keid], *s.* die Arkade.

Arcadian [ɑ:'keidiən], *adj.* arkadisch. — *s.* der Arkadier.

arch [ɑ:tʃ], *s.* der Bogen, die Wölbung; —*way*, der Bogengang. — *v.a., v.n.* wölben, sich wölben. — *adj.* schelmisch, listig. — *prefix* oberst; erst Haupt-; -*enemy*, der Erzfeind.

archaeological [ɑ:kiə'lɔdʒikəl], *adj.* archäologisch.

archaeologist [ɑ:ki'ɔlədʒist], *s.* der Archäologe.

archaeology [ɑ:ki'ɔlədʒi], *s.* die Archäologie.

archaic [ɑ:'keiik], *adj.* altertümlich.

archaism ['ɑ:keiizm], *s.* der Archaismus (*style*).

archbishop [ɑ:tʃ'biʃəp], *s.* der Erzbischof.

archduke [ɑ:tʃ'dju:k], *s.* der Erzherzog.

archer ['ɑ:tʃə], *s.* der Bogenschütze.

archery ['ɑ:tʃəri], *s.* das Bogenschießen.

architect ['ɑ:kitekt], *s.* der Architekt, Baumeister.

architecture ['ɑ:kitektʃə], *s.* die Architektur, Baukunst.

archives ['ɑ:kaivz], *s. pl.* das Archiv.

Arctic ['ɑ:ktik], *adj.* arktisch. — *s.* die Nordpolarländer, *n. pl.*

ardent ['ɑ:dənt], *adj.* heiß, glühend, brennend.

ardour ['ɑ:də], *s.* die Hitze, die Inbrunst, der Eifer.

arduous ['ɑ:djuəs], *adj.* schwierig; mühsam.

area ['ɛəriə], *s.* das Areal (*measurement*); das Gebiet, die Zone; die Fläche (*region*).

arena [ə'ri:nə], *s.* die Arena, der Kampfplatz.

Argentine ['ɑ:dʒəntain], *adj.* argentinisch. — (*Republic*), Argentinien, *n.*

Argentinian [ɑ:dʒən'tiniən], *adj.* argentinisch. — *s.* der Argentin(i)er.

argue ['ɑ:gju:], *v.n.* disputieren, streiten; folgern, schließen.

argument ['ɑ:gjumənt], *s.* das Argument; (*Log.*) der Beweis; der Streit (*dispute*).

argumentative [ɑ:gju'mentətiv], *adj.* streitsüchtig.

arid ['ærid], *adj.* trocken, dürr.

aright [ə'rait], *adv.* richtig, zurecht.

arise [ə'raiz], *v.n. irr.* aufstehen; sich erheben; entstehen (*originate*); *arising from the minutes*, es ergibt sich aus dem Protokoll.

aristocracy [æris'tɔkrəsi], *s.* die Aristokratie, der Adel.

aristocratic [æris'o'krætik], *adj.* aristokratisch, adlig.

arithmetic [ə'riθmətik], *s.* die Arithmetik.

arithmetical [æriθ'metikəl], *adj.* arithmetisch.

ark [ɑːk], *s.* die Arche; — *of the Covenant*, die Bundeslade.

arm (1) [ɑːm], *s.* (*Anat.*) der Arm.

arm (2) [ɑːm], *s.* die Waffe; *up in* —*s*, in Aufruhr. — *v.a., v.n.* bewaffnen, sich bewaffnen, rüsten, sich rüsten.

armament ['ɑːməmənt], *s.* die Rüstung, Bewaffnung.

armature ['ɑːmətiuə], *s.* die Armatur.

armchair ['ɑːmtʃeə], *s.* der Lehnstuhl; der Sessel.

Armenian [ɑː'miːniən], *adj.* armenisch. — *s.* der Armenier.

armistice ['ɑːmistis], *s.* der Waffenstillstand.

armour ['ɑːmə], *s.* die Rüstung, der Harnisch; —*-plated*, gepanzert; —*ed car*, der Panzerwagen.

armourer ['ɑːmərə], *s.* der Waffenschmied.

armoury ['ɑːməri], *s.* die Rüstkammer, Waffenschmiede.

army ['ɑːmi], *s.* die Armee, das Heer.

aroma [ə'roumə], *s.* das Aroma, der Duft.

aromatic [ærə'mætik], *adj.* aromatisch. —*s.* (*Chem.*) das Aromat.

around [ə'raund], *adv.* herum, rundringsherum, umher, im Kreise; *stand* —, herumstehen; *be* —, sich in der Nähe halten. — *prep.* um; bei, um ... herum.

arouse [ə'rauz], *v.a.* aufwecken, aufrütteln.

arraignment [ə'reinmənt], *s.* die Anklage.

arrange [ə'reindʒ], *v.a.* anordnen, arrangieren, einrichten, vereinbaren.

arrangement [ə'reindʒmənt], *s.* die Anordnung; die Einrichtung; die Vereinbarung (*agreement*); (*Law*) die Vergleichung, der Vergleich.

arrant ['ærənt], *adj.* durchtrieben.

array [ə'rei], *v.a.* schmücken, aufstellen. — *s.* die Ordnung; Aufstellung.

arrears [ə'riəz], *s. pl.* der Rückstand, die Schulden.

arrest [ə'rest], *v.a.* (*Law*) festnehmen, verhaften; festhalten; aufhalten (*hinder*). — *s.* die Festnahme; die Festhaltung.

arrival [ə'raivəl], *s.* die Ankunft.

arrive [ə'raiv], *v.n.* ankommen.

arrogance ['ærəgəns], *s.* die Anmaßung, Überheblichkeit.

arrogant ['ærəgənt], *adj.* anmaßend, hochfahrend, überheblich.

arrow ['ærou], *s.* der Pfeil.

arrowroot ['ærouruːt], *s.* (*Bot.*) die Pfeilwurz.

arsenal ['ɑːsinəl], *s.* das Arsenal, Zeughaus.

arsenic ['ɑːsənik], *s.* das Arsen.

arson ['ɑːsən], *s.* die Brandstiftung.

art [ɑːt], *s.* die Kunst; *fine* —, schöne Kunst; (*Univ.*) —*s faculty*, die philosophische Fakultät; —*s* (*subject*), das humanistische Fach, die Geisteswissenschaften.

arterial [ɑː'tiəriəl], *adj.* Pulsader-, Schlagader-; — *road*, die Hauptverkehrsader, die Hauptstraße.

artery ['ɑːtəri], *s.* die Pulsader, Schlagader; der Hauptverkehrsweg.

artesian [ɑː'tiːʒən], *adj.* artesisch.

artful ['ɑːtful], *adj.* listig, schlau.

article ['ɑːtikl], *s.* (*Gram., Law, Press*) der Artikel; der Posten (*item in list*). — *v.a.* — *d to a solicitor*, bei einem Advokaten assistieren.

articulate [ɑː'tikjuleit], *v.a.* artikulieren (*pronounce clearly*). — [—lit], *adj.* deutlich (*speech*).

articulation [ɑːtikju'leiʃən], *s.* die Artikulation, deutliche Aussprache.

artifice ['ɑːtifis], *s.* der Kunstgriff, die List.

artificer [ɑː'tifisə], *s.* der Handwerker.

artificial [ɑːti'fiʃəl], *adj.* künstlich, Kunst-; — *silk*, die Kunstseide.

artillery [ɑː'tiləri], *s.* die Artillerie.

artisan [ɑːti'zæn], *s.* der Handwerker.

artist ['ɑːtist], *s.* der Künstler, die Künstlerin.

artistic [ɑː'tistik], *adj.* künstlerisch.

artless ['ɑːtlis], *adj.* arglos, natürlich, naiv.

Aryan ['ɛəriən], *adj.* arisch. — *s.* der Arier.

as [æz], *adv., conj.* so, als, wie, ebenso; als, während, weil; — *big* —, so groß wie; — *well* —, sowohl als auch; *such* —, wie; — *it were*, gleichsam.

asbestos [æz'bestɔs], *s.* der Asbest.

ascend [ə'send], *v.a., v.n.* ersteigen, besteigen; emporsteigen.

ascendancy, -ency [ə'sendənsi], *s.* der Aufstieg; der Einfluß; das Übergewicht.

ascendant, -ent [ə'sendənt], *s. in the* —, aufsteigend.

ascent [ə'sent], *s.* der Aufstieg, die Besteigung.

ascension [ə'senʃən], *s.* (*Astron.*) das Aufsteigen; *Ascension Day*, Himmelfahrt(stag).

ascertain [æsə'tein], *v.a.* in Erfahrung bringen, erkunden, feststellen.

ascertainable [æsə'teinəbl], *adj.* erkundbar, feststellbar.

ascetic [ə'setik], *adj.* asketisch.

asceticism [ə'setisizm], *s.* die Askese.

ascribe [ə'skraib], *v.a.* zuschreiben.

ascribable [ə'skraibəbl], *adj.* zuzuschreiben, zuschreibbar.

ash (1) [æʃ], *s.* (*Bot.*) die Esche.

ash (2) [æʃ], *s.* die Asche.

ashamed [ə'ʃeimd], *adj.* beschämt; *be* —, sich schämen.

ashcan ['æʃkæn], *(Am.) see* **dustbin**.

ashen ['æʃən], *adj.* aschgrau, aschfarben.

ashore [ə'ʃɔː], *adv.* am Land; am Ufer, ans Ufer *or* Land.

ashtray ['æʃtrei], *s.* der Aschenbecher

Ash Wednesday [æʃ'wenzdei], *s.* der Aschermittwoch.

Asiatic [eiʃi'ætik], *adj.* asiatisch. — *s.* der Asiat.

313

aside

aside [ə'said], *adv.* seitwärts, zur Seite; abseits.

ask [ɑːsk], *v.a.*, *v.n.* fragen (*question*); bitten (*request*); fordern (*demand*); einladen (*invite*).

asleep [ə'sliːp], *pred. adj.*, *adv.* schlafend, im Schlaf; eingeschlafen.

asp [æsp], *s.* (*Zool.*) die Natter.

asparagus [æs'pærəgəs], *s.* (*Bot.*) der Spargel.

aspect ['æspekt], *s.* der Anblick, die Ansicht (*view, angle*); der Gesichtspunkt.

aspen ['æspən], *s.* (*Bot.*) die Espe.

asperity [æs'periti], *s.* die Härte; Rauheit.

aspersion [æs'pəːʃən], *s.* die Verleumdung; Schmähung.

asphalt ['æsfælt], *s.* der Asphalt.

asphyxia [æs'fiksjə], *s.* (*Med.*) die Erstickung.

aspirant [ə'spaiərənt, 'æsp-], *s.* der Bewerber, Anwärter.

aspirate ['æspireit], *v.a.* (*Phon.*) aspirieren. — [—rit] *adj.* aspiriert. — *s.* der Hauchlaut.

aspiration [æspi'reiʃən], *s.* der Atemzug; das Streben (*striving*); (*Phon.*) die Aspiration.

aspire [ə'spaiə], *v.n.* streben, verlangen.

ass [æs], *s.* der Esel.

assail [ə'seil], *v.a.* angreifen, anfallen.

assailable [ə'seiləbl], *adj.* angreifbar.

assassin [ə'sæsin], *s.* der Meuchelmörder.

assassinate [ə'sæsineit], *v.a.* meuchlings ermorden.

assassination [əsæsi'neiʃən], *s.* der Meuchelmord, die Ermordung.

assault [ə'sɔːlt], *v.a.* angreifen, überfallen. — *s.* der Überfall, Angriff.

assay [ə'sei], *s.* die Metallprobe. — *v.a.* (auf Edelmetall hin) prüfen.

assemble [ə'sembl], *v.a.*, *v.n.* versammeln, sich versammeln.

assembly [ə'sembli], *s.* die Versammlung (*assemblage*); — *line*, das laufende Band, die Fließband.

assent [ə'sent], *v.n.* beistimmen (*Dat.*), billigen (*Acc.*). — *s.* die Zustimmung (zu, *Dat.*), Billigung (*Genit.*).

assert [ə'səːt], *v.a.* behaupten.

assertion [ə'səːʃən], *s.* die Behauptung.

assess [ə'ses], *v.a.* schätzen, beurteilen.

assessment [ə'sesmənt], *s.* die Beurteilung, Schätzung, Wertung.

assessor [ə'sesə], *s.* der Beurteiler, Einschätzer, Bewerter, Assessor; der Beisitzer (*second examiner*).

assets ['æsets], *s. pl.* (*Comm.*) die Aktiva; Vorzüge (*personal*).

assiduity [æsi'djuːiti], *s.* der Fleiß, die Emsigkeit.

assiduous [ə'sidjuəs], *adj.* fleißig, unablässig, emsig.

assign [ə'sain], *v.a.* zuteilen, anweisen, zuweisen (*apportion*), festsetzen (*fix*).

assignable [ə'sainəbl], *adj.* zuteilbar; bestimmbar.

assignation [æsig'neiʃən], *s.* die Zuweisung; (*Law*) die Übertragung; die Verabredung.

assignment [ə'sainmənt], *s.* die Zuweisung, Übertragung; die Aufgabe.

assimilate [ə'simileit], *v.a.*, *v.n.* assimilieren, angleichen; sich assimilieren, sich angleichen, ähnlich werden.

assist [ə'sist], *v.a.*, *v.n.* beistehen (*Dat.*), helfen (*Dat.*), unterstützen (*Acc.*).

assistance [ə'sistəns], *s.* der Beistand, die Hilfe; die Aushilfe; (*financial*) der Zuschuß.

assistant [ə'sistənt], *s.* der Assistent, Helfer.

assize [ə'saiz], *s.* die Gerichtssitzung; (*pl.*) das Schwurgericht.

associate [ə'souʃieit], *v.a.* verbinden (*link*). — *v.n.* verkehren (*company*); sich verbinden; (*Comm.*) sich vereinigen. — [—iit], *s.* (*Comm.*) der Partner.

association [əsousi'eiʃən], *s.* die Vereinigung, der Bund, Verein; die Gesellschaft; der Verkehr.

assonance ['æsnəns], *s.* (*Phon.*) die Assonanz, der Gleichlaut.

assort [ə'sɔːt], *v.a.* ordnen, aussuchen, sortieren; —*ed sweets*, gemischte Bonbons.

assortment [ə'sɔːtmənt], *s.* die Sammlung, Mischung, Auswahl.

assuage [ə'sweidʒ], *v.a.* mildern, besänftigen, stillen.

assume [ə'sjuːm], *v.a.* annehmen; übernehmen, ergreifen.

assuming [ə'sjuːmiŋ], *adj.* anmaßend; — *that*, angenommen daß . . ., gesetzt den Fall.

assumption [ə'sʌmpʃən], *s.* die Annahme (*opinion*); Übernahme (*taking up*); Aneignung (*appropriation*); *Assumption of the Blessed Virgin*, Mariä Himmelfahrt.

assurance [ə'ʃuərəns], *s.* die Versicherung; Sicherheit (*manner*).

assure [ə'ʃuə], *v.a.* versichern, sicher stellen, ermutigen.

assuredly [ə'ʃuəridli], *adv.* sicherlich, gewiß.

aster ['æstə], *s.* (*Bot.*) die Aster.

asterisk ['æstərisk], *s.* (*Typ.*) das Sternchen.

astern [ə'stəːn], *adv.* (*Naut.*) achteraus.

asthma ['æsθmə], *s.* das Asthma.

asthmatic [æsθ'mætik], *adj.* asthmatisch.

astir [ə'stəː], *adv.* wach, in Bewegung.

astonish [ə'stɔniʃ], *v.a.* in Erstaunen versetzen, verblüffen.

astonishment [ə'stɔniʃmənt], *s.* das Erstaunen, die Verwunderung; die Bestürzung.

astound [ə'staund], *v.a.* in Erstaunen versetzen, bestürzen.

astounding [ə'staundiŋ], *adj.* erstaunlich, verblüffend.

astral ['æstrəl], *adj.* Stern(en)-, gestirnt.

314

astray [ə'strei], *pred. adj., adv.* irre; go —, sich verirren; (*fig.*) abschweifen.
astride[ə'straid], *pred.adj.,adv.* rittlings.
astringent [ə'strindʒənt], *adj.* zusammenziehend.
astrologer [ə'strɔlədʒə], *s.* der Sterndeuter, Astrolog(e).
astrological [æstrə'lɔdʒikəl], *adj.* astrologisch.
astrology [æ'strɔlədʒi], *s.* die Astrologie, Sterndeuterei.
astronaut ['æstrənɔ:t], *s.* der Astronaut.
astronomer [ə'strɔnəmə], *s.* der Astronom.
astronomical[æstrə'nɔmikəl],*adj.*astronomisch.
astronomy [ə'strɔnəmi], *s.* die Astronomie, Sternkunde.
astute [ə'stju:t], *adj.* listig, schlau.
astuteness [ə'stju:tnis], *s.* die Schlauheit, Listigkeit, der Scharfsinn.
asunder [ə'sʌndə], *adv.* auseinander, entzwei.
asylum [ə'sailəm], *s.* das Asyl, der Zufluchtsort (*refuge*); *lunatic —*, das Irrenhaus.
at [æt], *prep.* an; auf; bei, für; in, nach; mit, gegen; um, über; von, aus, zu; — *my expense*, auf meine Kosten; — *all*, überhaupt; — *first*, zuerst; — *last*, zuletzt, endlich; — *peace*, in Frieden; *what are you driving —?* worauf wollen sie hinaus ?
atheism ['eiθiizm], *s.* der Atheismus.
atheist ['eiθiist], *s.* der Atheist.
atheistic [eiθi'istik], *adj.* atheistisch, gottlos.
Athens ['æθənz]. Athen, *n.*
Athenian [ə'θi:njən], *s.* der Athener. — *adj.* athenisch.
athlete ['æθli:t], *s.* der Athlet.
athletic [æθ'letik], *adj.* athletisch.
athletics [æθ'letiks], *s. pl.* die Leichtathletik, Athletik.
Atlantic (Ocean) [ət'læntik ('ouʃən)]. der Atlantik.
atlas ['ætləs], *s.* der Atlas.
atmosphere ['ætməsfiə], *s.* die Atmosphäre.
atmospheric(al) [ætməs'ferik(əl)], *adj.* atmosphärisch. — *s.* (*pl.*) atmosphärische Störungen, *f. pl.*
atoll[ə'tɔl], *s.* die Koralleninsel,das Atoll.
atom ['ætəm], *s.* das Atom.
atomic [ə'tɔmik], *adj.* (*Phys.*) Atom-, atomisch, atomar; (*theory*) atomistisch; — *bomb*, die Atombombe; — *pile*, der Atomreaktor; — *armament*, die atomare Aufrüstung.
atone [ə'toun], *v.n.* sühnen, büßen.
atonement [ə'tounmənt], *s.* die Buße, Sühne, Versöhnung.
atonic [ei'tɔnik], *adj.* tonlos, unbetont.
atrocious [ə'trouʃəs], *adj.* gräßlich, schrecklich, entsetzlich.
atrocity [ə'trɔsiti], *s.* die Gräßlichkeit, Grausamkeit, Greueltat.
atrophy ['ætrəfi], *s.* (*Med.*) die Abmagerung, Atrophie. — ['ætrəfai], *v.n.* absterben, auszehren.

attach [ə'tætʃ], *v.a.* anheften, beilegen, anhängen; (*fig.*) beimessen (*attribute*).
attachment [ə'tætʃmənt], *s.* das Anhaften (*sticking to*, an, *Acc.*); das Anhängsel (*appendage*); die Freundschaft (*to*, für, *Acc.*); die Anhänglichkeit (*loyalty*, an, *Acc.*).
attack [ə'tæk], *v.a.* angreifen. — *s.* die Attacke, der Angriff; (*Med.*) der Anfall.
attain [ə'tein], *v.a.* erreichen, erlangen.
attainable [ə'teinəbl], *adj.* erreichbar.
attainment [ə'teinmənt], *s.* die Erlangung, Erreichung; Errungenschaft; (*pl.*) Kenntnisse, *f. pl.*
attempt [ə'tempt], *s.* der Versuch. — *v.a.* versuchen.
attend [ə'tend], *v.a., v.n.* begleiten, anwesend sein (*be present*, *at*, bei, *Dat.*); beiwohnen (*be present as guest*); zuhören (*listen to*); bedienen (*customer*); behandeln (*patient*).
attendance [ə'tendəns], *s.* die Begleitung (*accompaniment*); die Anwesenheit (*presence*); die Zuhörerschaft (*audience*); *to be in —*, Dienst tun (*at*, bei); anwesend sein (*be present*).
attendant [ə'tendənt], *s.* der Diener, Wärter.
attention [ə'tenʃən], *s.* die Aufmerksamkeit, Achtung.
attentive [ə'tentiv], *adj.* aufmerksam.
attenuate [ə'tenjueit], *v.a.* verdünnen (*dilute*). — *v.n.* abmagern.
attest [ə'test], *v.a.* attestieren, bezeugen, bescheinigen.
attestation [ætes'teiʃən], *s.* die Bescheinigung; das Zeugnis.
Attic ['ætik], *adj.* attisch, klassisch.
attic ['ætik], *s.* die Dachkammer, die Dachstube.
attire [ə'taiə], *v.a.* ankleiden, kleiden. — *s.* die Kleidung.
attitude ['ætitju:d], *s.* die Haltung, Stellung (*toward*, zu), Einstellung.
attorney [ə'tɔ:ni], *s.* der Anwalt; *Attorney-General*, der Kronanwalt; (*Am.*) der Staatsanwalt; — *at law*, Rechtsanwalt.
attract [ə'trækt], *v.a.* anziehen.
attraction [ə'trækʃən], *s.* die Anziehung; der Reiz (*appeal*); die Anziehungskraft.
attractive [ə'træktiv], *adj.* anziehend, reizvoll.
attribute [ə'tribju:t], *v.a.* zuschreiben, beimessen. — *s.* ['ætribju:t], (*Gram.*) das Attribut, die Eigenschaft.
attributive [ə'tribjutiv], *adj.* (*Gram.*) attributiv; beilegend.
attrition [ə'triʃən], *s.* die Zermürbung, Aufreibung, Reue.
attune [ə'tju:n], *v.a.* (*Mus.*) stimmen, anpassen (*adapt to*, an, *Acc.*).
auburn [ə'bə:n], *adj.* rotbraun.
auction ['ɔ:kʃən], *s.* die Auktion, die Versteigerung.
auctioneer [ɔ:kʃə'niə], *s.* der Auktionator, Versteigerer.

315

audacious

audacious [ɔːˈdeiʃəs], *adj.* waghalsig, kühn, dreist.

audacity [ɔːˈdæsiti], *s.* die Kühnheit (*valour*); Frechheit (*impudence*).

audible [ˈɔːdibl], *adj.* hörbar.

audibility [ɔːdiˈbiliti], *s.* die Hörbarkeit, Vernehmbarkeit.

audience [ˈɔːdjəns], *s.* die Audienz (*of the Pope*, beim Papst); (*Theat.*) das Publikum; (*listeners*) die Zuhörer.

audit [ˈɔːdit], *s.* die Rechnungsprüfung, Revision. — *v.a.* revidieren, prüfen.

auditor [ˈɔːditə], *s.* der Rechnungsrevisor, Buchprüfer.

auditory [ˈɔːditəri], *adj.* Gehör–, Hör–.

auditorium [ɔːdiˈtɔːriəm], *s.* der Hörsaal, Vortragssaal.

auger [ˈɔːgə], *s.* der (große) Bohrer.

aught [ɔːt], *pron.* (*obs.*) irgend etwas (*opp. to* naught).

augment [ɔːgˈment], *v.a.*, *v.n.* vermehren, vergrößern; zunehmen.

augmentation [ɔːgmenˈteiʃən], *s.* die Vergrößerung, Erhöhung, Zunahme.

augur [ˈɔːgə], *v.a.* weissagen, prophezeien.

August [ˈɔːgəst], *s.* der August.

august [ɔːˈgʌst], *adj.* erhaben.

aunt [ɑːnt], *s.* die Tante.

aurora [ɔːˈrɔːrə], *s.* die Morgenröte.

auscultation [ɔːskalˈteiʃən], *s.*(*Med.*) die Auskultation, Leichenschau.

auspices [ˈɔːspisiz], *s.* die Auspizien.

auspicious [ɔːˈspiʃəs], *adj.* unter glücklichem Vorzeichen, verheißungsvoll, günstig.

austere [ɔːsˈtiə], *adj.* streng, ernst, schmucklos.

austerity [ɔːsˈteriti], *s.* die Strenge.

Australian [əˈstreiljən], *adj.* australisch. — *s.* der Australier.

Austrian [ˈɔːstriən], *adj.* österreichisch. — *s.* der Österreicher.

authentic [ɔːˈθentik], *adj.* authentisch, echt.

authenticity [ɔːθenˈtisiti], *s.* die Authentizität, Echtheit.

author, authoress [ˈɔːθə, ɔːθəˈres], *s.* der Autor, die Autorin; der Verfasser, die Verfasserin.

authoritative [ɔːˈθɔritətiv], *adj.* autoritativ, maßgebend.

authority [ɔːˈθɔriti], *s.* die Autorität, Vollmacht (*power of attorney*); das Ansehen; *the authorities*, die Behörden.

authorization [ɔːθɔraiˈzeiʃən], *s.* die Bevollmächtigung, Befugnis.

authorize [ˈɔːθɔraiz], *v.a.* autorisieren, bevollmächtigen, berechtigen.

authorship [ˈɔːθəʃip], *s.* die Autorschaft.

autobiographical [ɔːtobaiəˈgræfikl], *adj.* autobiographisch.

autobiography [ɔːtobaiˈɔgrəfi], *s.* die Autobiographie.

autocracy [ɔːˈtɔkrəsi], *s.* die Selbstherrschaft.

autocrat [ˈɔːtokræt], *s.* der Autokrat, Selbstherrscher.

autograph [ˈɔːtogræf, -grɑːf], *s.* die eigene Handschrift, Unterschrift; das Autogramm.

automatic [ɔːtoˈmætik], *adj.* automatisch.

automatize [ɔːˈtɔmətaiz], *v.a.* automatisieren, auf Automation umstellen.

automation [ɔːtoˈmeiʃən], *s.* (*Engin.*) die Automation; Automatisierung.

automaton [ɔːˈtɔmətən], *s.* der Automat.

automobile [ˈɔːtomobiːl], *s.* der Kraftwagen, das Auto.

autonomous [ɔːˈtɔnəməs], *adj.* autonom, unabhängig.

autonomy [ɔːˈtɔnəmi], *s.* die Autonomie, Unabhängigkeit.

autopsy [ˈɔːtɔpsi], *s.* die Autopsie; Obduktion, Leichenschau.

autumn [ˈɔːtəm], *s.* der Herbst.

autumnal [ɔːˈtʌmnəl], *adj.* herbstlich.

auxiliary [ɔːgˈziljəri], *adj.* Hilfs–.

avail [əˈveil], *v.n.* nützen, helfen, von Vorteil sein. — *v.r.* — *o.s of a th.*, sich einer Sache bedienen. — *s.* der Nutzen; *of no* —, nutzlos.

available [əˈveiləbl], *adj.* vorrätig, verfügbar, zur Verfügung (stehend).

avalanche [ˈævəlɑːnʃ], *s.* die Lawine.

avarice [ˈævəris], *s.* der Geiz, die Habsucht, Gier.

avaricious [ævəˈriʃəs], *adj.* geizig, habsüchtig, habgierig.

avenge [əˈvendʒ], *v.a.* rächen.

avenue [ˈævənjuː], *s.* die Allee; der Zugang.

average [ˈævəridʒ], *adj.* durchschnittlich; *not more than* —, mäßig. — *s.* der Durchschnitt; *on an* —, durchschnittlich, im Durchschnitt. — *v.a.* den Durchschnitt nehmen.

averse [əˈvəːs], *adj.* abgeneigt (*to*, *Dat.*).

aversion [əˈvəːʃən], *s.* die Abneigung, der Widerwille.

avert [əˈvəːt], *v.a.* abwenden.

aviary [ˈeiviəri], *s.* das Vogelhaus.

aviation [eiviˈeiʃən], *s.* das Flugwesen.

aviator [ˈeivieitə], *s.* der Flieger.

avid [ˈævid], *adj.* begierig (*of* or *for*, nach).

avidity [æˈviditi], *s.* die Begierde, Gier (*for*, nach).

avoid [əˈvɔid], *v.a.* vermeiden.

avoidable [əˈvɔidəbl], *adj.* vermeidlich, vermeidbar.

avoidance [əˈvɔidəns], *s.* die Vermeidung, das Meiden.

avow [əˈvau], *v.a.* eingestehen, anerkennen (*acknowledge*).

avowal [əˈvauəl], *s.* das Geständnis; die Erklärung.

await [əˈweit], *v.a.* erwarten, warten auf (*Acc.*).

awake(n) [əˈweik(ən)], *v.a.*, *v.n. irr.* aufwecken, wecken; aufwachen (*wake up*). — *adj. wide awake*, schlau, auf der Hut.

baking

award [ə'wɔːd], *s.* die Zuerkennung, Auszeichnung; Belohnung *(money)*; *(Law)* das Urteil. — *v.a.* zuerkennen; — *damages*, Schadenersatz zusprechen; verleihen *(grant)*.

aware [ə'wɛə], *adj.* gewahr, bewußt *(Genit.)*.

away [ə'wei], *adv.* weg; hinweg, fort.

awe [ɔː], *s.* die Ehrfurcht; Furcht.

awful ['ɔːful], *adj.* furchtbar, schrecklich.

awhile [ə'wail], *adv.* eine Weile, eine kurze Zeit.

awkward ['ɔːkwəd], *adj.* ungeschickt, unbeholfen, ungelenk; unangenehm *(difficult)*; — *situation*, peinliche Situation, Lage.

awkwardness ['ɔːkwədnis], *s.* die Ungeschicklichkeit, Unbeholfenheit.

awl [ɔːl], *s.* die Ahle, der Pfriem.

awning ['ɔːniŋ], *s.* die Plane; das Sonnendach.

awry [ə'rai], *adj.* schief, verkehrt.

axe [æks], *s.* die Axt, das Beil.

axiom ['æksiəm], *s.* das Axiom, der Satz, Lehrsatz, Grundsatz.

axiomatic [æksiə'mætik], *adj.* axiomatisch, grundsätzlich; gewiß.

axis ['æksis], *s.* die Achse.

axle ['æksl], *s.* die Achse.

ay(e) (1) [ai], *adv.* ja, gewiß.

ay(e) (2) [ei], *adv.* ständig, ewig.

azalea [ə'zeiliə], *s.* *(Bot.)* die Azalie.

azure ['æʒə, 'eiʒə], *adj.* himmelblau, azurblau.

B

B [biː]. das B; *(Mus.)* das H.

baa [bɑː], *v.n.* blöken.

babble [bæbl], *v.n.* schwatzen, schwätzen. — *s.* das Geschwätz; das Murmeln *(water)*.

babe, baby [beib, 'beibi], *s.* der Säugling, das Baby, das kleine Kind, das Kindlein.

baboon [bə'buːn], *s.* *(Zool.)* der Pavian.

bachelor ['bætʃələ], *s.* der Junggeselle; *(Univ.)* Bakkalaureus.

back [bæk], *s.* der Rücken, die Rückseite. — *adj.* Hinter-, Rück-; — *door*, die Hintertür; — *stairs*, die Hintertreppe. — *adv.* rückwärts, zurück. — *v.a.* unterstützen; *(Comm.)* indossieren; gegenzeichnen; wetten auf *(Acc.)* *(bet on)*.

backbone ['bækboun], *s.* *(Anat.)* das Rückgrat.

backfire ['bækfaiə], *s.* *(Motor.)* die Frühzündung; *(gun)* die Fehlzündung. — [bæk'faiə], *v.n.* *(Motor.)* frühzünden; *(gun)* fehlzünden.

backgammon [bæk'gæmən], *s.* das Bordspiel, das Puffspiel.

background ['bækgraund], *s.* der Hintergrund.

backhand ['bækhænd], *s.* *(Sport)* die Rückhand; *a —ed compliment*, eine verblümte Grobheit.

backside [bæk'said], *s.* *(vulg.)* der Hintere.

backslide [bæk'slaid], *v.n.* abfallen, abtrünnig werden.

backward ['bækwəd], *adj.* zurückgeblieben. **backward(s)** *adv.* rückwärts, zurück.

backwater ['bækwɔːtə], *s.* das Stauwasser.

backwoods ['bækwudz], *s. pl.* der Hinterwald.

bacon ['beikən], *s.* der Speck.

bad [bæd], *adj.* schlecht, schlimm; böse *(immoral)*; *(coll.)* unwohl *(unwell)*; *not too —*, ganz gut; *from — to worse*, immer schlimmer; — *language*, unanständige Worte, das Fluchen; — *luck*, Unglück, Pech; *want —ly*, nötig brauchen.

badge [bædʒ], *s.* das Abzeichen, Kennzeichen *(mark)*.

badger (1) ['bædʒə], *s.* *(Zool.)* der Dachs.

badger (2) ['bædʒə], *v.a.* ärgern, stören, belästigen.

badness ['bædnis], *s.* die Schlechtigkeit, Bosheit, das schlechte Wesen, die Bösartigkeit.

baffle [bæfl], *v.a.* täuschen, verblüffen. — *s.* *(obs.)* die Täuschung; *(Build.)* Verkleidung; *(Elec.)* Verteilerplatte.

bag [bæg], *s.* der Sack, Beutel; die Tasche; *shopping —*, Einkaufstasche; *travelling —*, Reisehandtasche; — *v.a.* einstecken, als Beute behalten *(hunt)*.

bagatelle [bægə'tel], *s.* die Bagatelle, Lappalie, Kleinigkeit; das Kugelspiel *(pin-table ball-game)*.

baggage ['bægidʒ], *s.* das Gepäck.

bagging ['bægiŋ], *s.* die Sackleinwand.

baggy ['bægi], *adj.* ungebügelt; bauschig.

bagpipe ['bægpaip], *s.* der Dudelsack.

bagpiper ['bægpaipə], *s.* der Dudelsackpfeifer.

bail [beil], *s.* der Bürge; die Bürgschaft; *stand —*, für einen bürgen; *allow —*, Bürgschaft zulassen. — *v.a.* Bürgschaft leisten; — *out*, (durch Kaution) in Freiheit setzen.

bailiff ['beilif], *s.* der Amtmann; Gerichtsvollzieher.

bait [beit], *s.* der Köder. — *v.a.* ködern, locken *(attract)*.

baiter ['beitə], *s.* der Hetzer, Verfolger.

baiting ['beitiŋ], *s.* die Hetze.

bake [beik], *v.a., v.n.* backen.

baker ['beikə], *s.* der Bäcker; *—'s dozen*, 13 Stück.

bakery ['beikəri], *s.* die Bäckerei.

baking ['beikiŋ], *s.* das Backen.

317

balance

balance ['bæləns], *s.* die Waage (*scales*); die Bilanz (*audit*); das Gleichgewicht (*equilibrium*); (*Comm.*) der Saldo, der Überschuß (*profit*); die Unruhe (*watch*). — *v.a.*, *v.n.* wägen, abwägen (*scales*): ausgleichen (— *up*), einen Saldo ziehen (— *an account*); ins Gleichgewicht bringen (*bring into equilibrium*).

balcony ['bælkəni], *s.* der Balkon, der Söller (*castle*); Altan (*villa*).

bald [bɔːld], *adj.* kahl, haarlos; (*fig.*) armselig, schmucklos.

baldness ['bɔːldnis], *s.* die Kahlheit (*hairlessness*); Nacktheit (*bareness*).

bale (1) [beil], *s.* der Ballen.

bale (2) [beil], *v.n.* — *out*, abspringen; aussteigen.

Balearic Islands [bæliˈærik ailəndz], *s. pl.* die Balearen, Balearischen Inseln. — *adj.* balearisch.

baleful ['beilful], *adj.* unheilvoll.

balk [bɔːk], *v.a.* aufhalten, hemmen. — *v.n.* scheuen, zurückscheuen (*at*, vor).

ball (1) [bɔːl], *s.* der Ball; die Kugel; — *cock*, der Absperrhahn; —*point pen*, der Kugelschreiber.

ball (2) [bɔːl], *s.* der Ball (*dance*).

ballad ['bæləd], *s.* die Ballade.

ballast ['bæləst], *s.* der Ballast.

ballet ['bælei], *s.* das Ballett.

balloon [bəˈluːn], *s.* der Ballon.

ballot ['bælət], *s.* die geheime Wahl, Abstimmung; — *box*, die Wahlurne; —*paper*, der Stimmzettel. —*v. n.* wählen, abstimmen.

balm [baːm], *s.* der Balsam.

balsam ['bɔlsəm], *s.* der Balsam.

Baltic ['bɔːltik], *adj.* baltisch. — (*Sea*), die Ostsee; (*Provinces*), das Baltikum.

balustrade ['bæləstreid], *s.* die Balustrade, das Geländer.

bamboo [bæm'buː], *s.* (*Bot.*) der Bambus.

bamboozle [bæm'buːzl], *v.a.* verblüffen; beschwindeln (*cheat*).

ban [bæn], *v.a.* bannen, verbannen; verbieten. — *s.* der Bann, das Verbot.

banal [bæ'næl, 'beinəl], *adj.* banal.

banality [bæ'næliti], *s.* die Banalität, Trivialität.

banana [bə'nɑːnə], *s.* die Banane.

band [bænd], *s.* das Band (*ribbon etc.*); (*Mus.*) die Kapelle; die Bande (*robbers*). — *v.n.* — *together*, sich verbinden; sich zusammentun.

bandage ['bændidʒ], *s.* der Verband, die Bandage.

bandit ['bændit], *s.* der Bandit.

bandmaster ['bændmɑːstə], *s.* der Kapellmeister.

bandstand ['bændstænd], *s.* der Musikpavillon.

bandy ['bændi], *adj.* — *legged*, krummbeinig. — *v.a.* — *words*, Worte wechseln; streiten.

bane [bein], *s.* das Gift; (*fig.*) Verderben.

baneful ['beinful], *adj.* verderblich.

bang [bæŋ], *s.* der Knall (*explosion*), der Krachen (*clap*). — *v.n.* knallen, krachen lassen. — *v.a.* — *a door*, eine Türe zuwerfen.

banish ['bæniʃ], *v.a.* verbannen, bannen.

banisters ['bænistəz], *s. pl.* das Treppengeländer.

bank [bæŋk], *s.* (*Fin.*) die Bank; das Ufer (*river*); der Damm (*dam*). — *v.a.* einlegen, einzahlen, auf die Bank bringen (*sum of money*); eindämmen (*dam up*). — *v.n.* ein Konto haben (*have an account, with*, bei).

banker ['bæŋkə], *s.* der Bankier.

bankrupt ['bæŋkrʌpt], *adj.* bankrott; zahlungsunfähig; (*coll.*) pleite.

bankruptcy ['bæŋkrʌptsi], *s.* der Bankrott.

banns [bænz], *s. pl.* das Heiratsaufgebot.

banquet ['bæŋkwit], *s.* das Banquet, Festessen.

bantam ['bæntəm], *s.* das Bantamhuhn, Zwerghuhn; (*Boxing*) — *weight*, das Bantamgewicht.

banter ['bæntə], *v.n.* scherzen, necken. — *s.* das Scherzen, der Scherz.

baptism ['bæptizm], *s.* die Taufe.

Baptist ['bæptist], *s.* der Täufer; Baptist.

baptize [bæp'taiz], *v.a.* taufen.

bar [baː], *s.* die Barre, Stange (*pole*); der Riegel; Balken; Schlagbaum (*barrier*); (*fig.*) das Hindernis; der Schanktisch (*in public house*); *prisoner at the* —, Gefangener vor (dem) Gericht; *call to the* —, zur Gerichtsadvokatur (*or* als Anwalt) zulassen; (*Mus.*) der Takt. — *v.a.* verriegeln (*door*); (*fig.*) hindern (*from action*); verbieten (*prohibit*); ausschließen (*exclude*).

barb [baːb], *s.* die Spitze (*of wire*); der Widerhaken (*hook*).

barbed [baːbd], *adj.* spitzig; — *remark*, die spitze Bemerkung; — *wire*, der Stacheldraht.

barbarian [baː'bɛəriən], *s.* der Barbar. — *adj.* barbarisch.

barbarism ['baːbərizm], *s.* die Roheit; der Barbarismus.

barber ['baːbə], *s.* der Barbier, Friseur.

barberry ['baːbəri], *s.* (*Bot.*) die Berberitze.

bard [baːd], *s.* der Barde, Sänger.

bare [bɛə], *adj.* nackt, bloß; — *headed*, barhäuptig. — *v.a.* entblößen.

barefaced ['bɛəfeisd], *adj.* schamlos.

barely ['bɛəli], *adv.* kaum.

bargain ['baːgin], *s.* der Kauf, Gelegenheitskauf; der Handel (*trading*); das Geschäft; *into the* —, noch dazu, obendrein. — *v.n.* feilschen, handeln (*haggle*) (*for*, um).

barge [baːdʒ], *s.* der Lastkahn, die Barke. — *v.n.* (*coll.*) — *in*, stören.

bargee [baː'dʒiː], *s.* der Flußschiffer, Bootsmann.

baritone ['bæritoun], *s.* (*Mus.*) der Bariton.

bark (1) [bɑːk], *s.* die Rinde (*of tree*).

bark (2) [bɑːk], *v.n.* bellen (*dog*); — *up the wrong tree*, auf falscher Fährte sein. — *s.* das Gebell (*dog*).

barley ['bɑːli], *s.* (*Bot.*) die Gerste.

barmaid ['bɑːmeid], *s.* die Kellnerin.

barman ['bɑːmən], *s.* der Kellner.

barn [bɑːn], *s.* die Scheune; — *owl*, die Schleiereule.

barnacle ['bɑːnəkl], *s.* die Entenmuschel; die Klette.

barnstormer ['bɑːnstɔːmə], *s.* der Schmierenkomödiant.

barometer [bə'rɔmitə], *s.* das Barometer.

baron ['bærən], *s.* der Baron, Freiherr.

barony ['bærəni], *s.* die Baronswürde.

baroque [bə'rɔk], *adj.* barock. — *s.* das Barock.

barque [bɑːk], *s.* die Bark.

barracks ['bærəks], *s. pl.* die Kaserne.

barrage ['bærɑːʒ, 'bæridʒ], *s.* das Sperrfeuer (*firing*); das Wehr, der Damm.

barrel ['bærəl], *s.* das Faß (*vat*), die Tonne (*tun*); der Gewehrlauf (*rifle*); die Trommel (*cylinder*); — *organ*, die Drehorgel.

barren ['bærən], *adj.* unfruchtbar, dürr.

barrenness ['bærənnis], *s.* die Unfruchtbarkeit.

barricade [bæri'keid], *s.* die Barrikade. — *v.a.* verrammeln, verschanzen.

barrier ['bæriə], *s.* die Barriere, der Schlagbaum; das Hindernis; (*Railw.*) die Schranke.

barrister ['bæristə], *s.* der Rechtsanwalt, Advokat.

barrow (1) ['bærou], *s.* der Schubkarren, Handkarren; — *boy*, der Höker, Schnellverkäufer.

barrow (2) ['bærou], *s.* (*Archaeol.*) das Hünengrab, Heldengrab.

barter ['bɑːtə], *v.a.* tauschen, austauschen. — *s.* der Tauschhandel.

Bartholomew [bɑː'θɔləmju], *m.*; *Massacre of St. Bartholomew's Eve*, Bartholomäusnacht, Pariser Bluthochzeit.

basalt ['bæsɔːlt, bæ'sɔːlt], *s.* der Basalt.

base [beis], *s.* die Basis, Grundlage; der Sockel; (*Chem.*) die Base. — *adj.* niedrig, gemein; (*Metall.*) unedel. — *v.a.* basieren, beruhen, fundieren (*upon*, auf).

baseless ['beislis], *adj.* grundlos.

basement ['beismənt], *s.* das Kellergeschoß.

baseness ['beisnis], *s.* die Gemeinheit, Niedrigkeit.

bashful ['bæʃful], *adj.* verschämt, schamhaft, schüchtern.

basic ['beisik], *adj.* grundlegend.

basin ['beisən], *s.* das Becken.

basis ['beisis], *s.* die Basis, Grundlage.

bask [bɑːsk], *v.n.* sich sonnen.

basket ['bɑːskit], *s.* der Korb.

bass (1) [beis], *s.* (*Mus.*) der Baß, die Baßstimme.

bass (2) [bæs], *s.* (*Zool.*) der Barsch.

bassoon [bə'suːn], *s.* (*Mus.*) das Fagott.

bastard ['bæstəd], *s.* der Bastard.

baste [beist], *v.a.* mit Fett begießen (*roast meat*); (*coll.*) prügeln.

bastion ['bæstiən], *s.* die Bastion, Festung, das Bollwerk.

bat (1) [bæt], *s.* die Fledermaus.

bat (2) [bæt], *s.* der Schläger. — *v.n.* (den Ball) schlagen; (*cricket*) am Schlagen sein (*be batting*).

batch [bætʃ], *s.* der Stoß (*pile*); die Menge (*people*); (*Mil.*) der Trupp.

bath [bɑːθ], *s.* das Bad; (*Am.*) — *robe*, der Schlafrock, Bademantel; — *tub*, die Badewanne.

bathe [beið], *v.n.* baden; *bathing pool*, das Schwimmbad; *bathing suit*, der Badeanzug.

batman ['bætmən], *s.* der Offiziersbursche.

baton ['bætən], *s.* der Stab.

batsman ['bætsmən], *s.* der Schläger (*cricket*).

batten [bætn], *s.* die Holzlatte. — *v.a.* mästen, füttern. — *v.n.* fett werden.

batter ['bætə], *s.* der Schlagteig. — *v.a.* schlagen, zertrümmern; — *ing ram*, (*Mil.*) der Sturmbock.

battery ['bætəri], *s.* die Batterie.

battle [bætl], *s.* die Schlacht; — *cruiser*, der Schlachtkreuzer; — *ship*, das Schlachtschiff. — *v.n.* kämpfen (*for*, um).

Bavarian [bə'vɛəriən], *adj.* bayrisch. — *s.* der Bayer.

bawl [bɔːl], *v.n.* plärren, schreien.

bay (1) [bei], *adj.* rötlich braun.

bay (2) [bei], *s.* die Bucht, Bai; — *window*, das Erkerfenster.

bay (3) [bei], *keep at* —, in Schach halten, *stand at* —, sich zur Wehr setzen.

bay (4) [bei], *s.* (*Bot.*) der Lorbeer.

bay (5) [bei], *v.n.* bellen, heulen; — *for the moon*, das Unmögliche wollen.

bayonet ['beiənet], *s.* das Bajonett.

bazaar [bə'zɑː], *s.* der Basar.

be [biː], *v.n. irr.* sein, existieren; sich befinden; vorhanden sein; — *off*, sich fortmachen (*move*); ungenießbar sein (*meat, food*); nicht mehr da sein (— *off the menu*).

beach [biːtʃ], *s.* der Strand, das Gestade.

beacon ['biːkən], *s.* das Leuchtfeuer; der Leuchtturm; das Lichtsignal.

bead [biːd], *s.* das Tröpfchen (*drop*); die Perle (*pearl*); (*pl.*) die Perlschnur; der Rosenkranz.

beadle [biːdl], *s.* (*Univ.*) der Pedell; (*Eccl.*) Kirchendiener.

beagle ['biːgl], *s.* der Jagdhund, Spürhund.

beak [biːk], *s.* der Schnabel.

beaker ['biːkə], *s.* der Becher.

beam [biːm], *s.* der Balken (*wood*); der Strahl (*ray*), Glanz. — *v.n.* strahlen.

bean

bean [bi:n], *s.* (*Bot.*) die Bohne; *not* ⌐—, keinen Heller *or* Pfennig.

bear (1) [bɛə], *s.* (*Zool.*) der Bär.

bear (2) [bɛə], *v.a. irr.* tragen, ertragen; gebären (*a child*); hegen (*sorrow etc.*). — *v.n.* — *upon*, drücken auf (*pressure*), Einfluß haben (*effect*); — *up*, geduldig sein.

bearable [ʹbɛərəbl], *adj.* tragbar, erträglich.

beard [biəd], *s.* der Bart. — *v.a.* trotzen (*Dat.*).

bearded [ʹbiədid], *adj.* bärtig.

bearer [ʹbɛərə], *s.* der Träger, Überbringer.

bearing [ʹbɛəriŋ], *s.* das Benehmen, die Haltung (*manner*); (*pl.*) (*Geog.*) die Richtung; *lose o.'s* —*s*, sich verlaufen; *ball* —*s*, (*Engin.*) das Kugellager.

bearpit [ʹbɛəpit], *s.* der Bärenzwinger.

beast [bi:st], *s.* das Tier; die Bestie.

beastliness [ʹbi:stlinis], *s.* das tierische Benehmen; die Grausamkeit (*cruelty*); die Gemeinheit.

beastly [ʹbi:stli], *adj.* grausam, (*coll.*) schrecklich.

beat [bi:t], *s.* der Schlag, das Schlagen; (*Mus.*) der Takt; die Runde, das Revier (*patrol district*). — *v.a. irr.* schlagen; — *time*, den Takt schlagen; — *carpets*, Teppich klopfen. — *v.n.* — *it*, sich davonmachen.

beater [ʹbi:tə], *s.* (*Hunt.*) der Treiber.

beatify [bi:ʹætifai], *v.a.* seligsprechen.

beau [bou], *s.* der Stutzer, Geck.

beautiful [ʹbju:tiful], *adj.* schön.

beautify [ʹbju:tifai], *v.a.* schön machen, verschönern.

beauty [ʹbju:ti], *s.* die Schönheit; — *salon*, der Schönheitssalon; *Sleeping Beauty*, das Dornröschen.

beaver [ʹbi:və], *s.* (*Zool.*) der Biber.

becalm [biʹkɑ:m], *v.a.* besänftigen.

because [biʹkɔz], *conj.* weil, da; — *of*, wegen, um … willen.

beck [bek], *s.* der Wink; *be at s.o.'s* — *and call*, jemandem zu Gebote stehen.

beckon [ʹbekən], *v.a., v.n.* winken, heranwinken, zuwinken (*Dat.*).

become [biʹkʌm], *v.n. irr.* werden. — *v.a.* anstehen, sich schicken, passen (*Dat.*).

becoming [biʹkʌmiŋ], *adj.* passend, kleidsam.

bed [bed], *s.* das Bett; Beet (*flowers*); (*Geol.*) das Lager, die Schicht. — *v.a.* betten, einbetten.

bedaub [biʹdɔ:b], *v.a.* beflecken, beschmieren.

bedding [ʹbediŋ], *s.* das Bettzeug.

bedevil [biʹdevəl], *v.a.* behexen, verhexen.

bedew [biʹdju:], *v.a.* betauen.

bedlam [ʹbedləm], *s.* (*coll.*) das Irrenhaus; *this is* —, die Hölle ist los.

Bedouin [ʹbeduin], *s.* der Beduine.

bedpost [ʹbedpoust], *s.* der Bettpfosten.

bedraggle [biʹdrægl], *v.a.* beschmutzen.

bedridden [ʹbedridn], *adj.* bettlägerig, ans Bett gefesselt.

bedroom [ʹbedru:m], *s.* das Schlafzimmer.

bedtime [ʹbedtaim], *s.* die Schlafenszeit.

bee [bi:], *s.* (*Ent.*) die Biene; *have a* — *in o.'s bonnet*, einen Vogel haben.

beech [bi:tʃ], *s.* (*Bot.*) die Buche.

beef [bi:f], *s.* das Rindfleisch; — *tea*, die Fleischbrühe.

beehive [ʹbi:haiv], *s.* der Bienenkorb.

beeline [ʹbi:lain], *s.* die Luftlinie, gerade Linie; *make a* — *for s.th.*, schnurstracks auf etwas losgehen.

beer [biə], *s.* das Bier; *small* —, Dünnbier, (*fig.*) unbedeutend.

beet [bi:t], *s.* (*Bot.*) die Runkelrübe; *sugar* —, die Zuckerrübe.

beetle [ʹbi:tl], *s.* (*Ent.*) der Käfer; — *brows*, buschige Augenbrauen.

beetroot [ʹbi:tru:t], *s.* (*Bot.*) die rote Rübe.

befall [biʹfɔ:l], *v.a. irr.* widerfahren (*Dat.*). — *v.n.* zustoßen (*happen, Dat.*).

befit [biʹfit], *v.a.* sich geziemen, sich gebühren.

befog [biʹfɔg], *v.a.* in Nebel hüllen; umnebeln.

before [biʹfɔ:], *adv.* vorn; voraus, voran; (*previously*) vorher, früher; (*already*) bereits, schon. — *prep.* vor. — *conj.* bevor, ehe.

beforehand [biʹfɔ:hænd], *adv.* im voraus, vorher.

befoul [biʹfaul], *v.a.* beschmutzen.

befriend [biʹfrend], *v.a.* befreunden, unterstützen (*support*).

beg [beg], *v.a., v.n.* betteln (um, *for*); ersuchen, bitten (*request*).

beget [biʹget], *v.a. irr.* zeugen.

beggar [ʹbegə], *s.* der Bettler.

begin [biʹgin], *v.a., v.n. irr.* beginnen, anfangen.

beginner [biʹginə], *s.* der Anfänger.

beginning [biʹginiŋ], *s.* der Anfang.

begone ! [biʹgɔn], *interj.* hinweg! fort! mach dich fort!

begrudge [biʹgrʌdʒ], *v.a.* nicht gönnen, mißgönnen.

beguile [biʹgail], *v.a.* bestricken, betrügen; — *the time*, die Zeit vertreiben.

behalf [biʹhɑ:f], *s. on* — *of*, um … (*Genit.*) willen; im Interesse von, im Namen von.

behave [biʹheiv], *v.n.* sich benehmen, sich betragen.

behaviour [biʹheivjə], *s.* das Benehmen, Gebaren.

behead [biʹhed], *v.a.* enthaupten.

behind [biʹhaind], *adv.* hinten, zurück, hinterher. — *prep.* hinter.

behindhand [biʹhaindhænd], *adj., adv.* im Rückstand (*in arrears*); zurück (*backward*).

behold [biʹhould], *v.a. irr.* ansehen; er blicken; *lo and* —! siehe da!

beholden [biʹhouldən], *adj.* verpflichtet (*to, Dat.*).

beholder [biʹhouldə], *s.* der Zuschauer.

behove [bi'houv], *v.a.* sich geziemen, ziemen, gebühren.

being ['bi:in], *pres. part for the time* —, vorläufig, für jetzt. — *s.* das Sein, die Existenz; das Wesen (*creature*).

belated [bi'leitid], *adj.* verspätet.

belch [beltʃ], *v.n.* rülpsen, aufstoßen.

belfry ['belfri], *s.* der Glockenturm.

Belgian ['beldʒən], *adj.* belgisch. — *s.* der Belgier.

belie [bi'lai], *v.a.* täuschen, Lügen strafen.

belief [bi'li:f], *s.* der Glaube, die Meinung.

believable [bi'li:vəbl], *adj.* glaubhaft, glaublich.

believe [bi'li:v], *v.a., v.n.* glauben (*an, Acc.*), vertrauen (*Dat.*).

believer [bi'li:və], *s.* der Gläubige.

belittle [bi'litl], *v.a.* schmälern, verkleinern, verächtlich machen.

bell [bel], *s.* die Glocke; Schelle, Klingel; — *-founder*, der Glockengießer; — *-boy*, (*Am.*) — *-hop*, der Hotelpage.

belligerent [bi'lidʒərənt], *adj.* kriegführend. — *s.* der Kriegführende.

bellow ['belou], *v.n.* brüllen. — *s.* das Gebrüll.

bellows ['belouz], *s.* der Blasebalg.

belly ['beli], *s.* der Bauch.

belong [bi'lɔŋ], *v.n.* gehören (*Dat.*), angehören (*Dat.*).

belongings [bi'lɔŋiŋz], *s. pl.* die Habe, das Hab und Gut, der Besitz.

beloved [bi'lʌvd, -vid], *adj.* geliebt, lieb.

below [bi'lou], *adv.* unten. — *prep.* unterhalb (*Genit.*), unter.(*Dat.*).

Belshazzar [bel'ʃæzə]. Belsazar, *m.*

belt [belt], *s.* der Gürtel, Gurt; der Riemen; (*Tech.*) Treibriemen; *below the* —, unfair. — *v.a.* umgürten; (*coll.*) prügeln.

bemoan [bi'moun], *v.a.* beklagen.

bench [bentʃ], *s.* die Bank; der Gerichtshof (*court of law*); *Queen's Bench*, der oberste Gerichtshof.

bend [bend], *v.a., v.n. irr.* biegen; beugen; sich krümmen. — *s.* die Biegung, Krümmung, Kurve.

bendable ['bendəbl], *adj.* biegsam.

beneath [bi'ni:θ] *see* **below**.

Benedictine [beni'dikti:n], *s.* der Benediktiner.

benediction [beni'dikʃən], *s.* der Segensspruch, der Segen; die Segnung.

benefaction [beni'fækʃən], *s.* die Wohltat.

benefactor ['benifæktə], *s.* der Wohltäter.

benefactress ['benifæktris], *s.* die Wohltäterin.

beneficent [be'nefisənt], *adj.* wohltätig.

beneficial [beni'fiʃəl], *adj.* vorteilhaft, gut (*for*), wohltuend.

benefit ['benifit], *s.* der Vorteil, Nutzen. — *v.n.* Nutzen ziehen. — *v.a.* nützen.

benevolence [be'nevələns], *s.* das Wohlwollen.

benevolent [be'nevələnt], *adj.* wohlwollend; — *society*, der Unterstützungsverein, — *fund*, der Unterstützungsfond.

Bengali [ben'gɔ:li], *adj.* bengalisch. — *s.* der Bengale.

benign [bi'nain], *adj.* gütig, mild.

bent [bent], *adj.* gebogen, krumm; — *on something*, versessen auf etwas. — *s.* die Neigung, der Hang; — *for*, Vorliebe für.

benzene ['benzi:n], *s.* das Benzol, Kohlenbenzin.

benzine ['benzi:n], *s.* das Benzin.

bequeath [bi'kwi:θ], *v.a.* vermachen, hinterlassen.

bequest [bi'kwest], *s.* das Vermächtnis.

bereave [bi'ri:v], *v.a. irr.* berauben (durch Tod).

bereavement [bi'ri:vmənt], *s.* der Verlust (durch Tod).

beret ['berei], *s.* die Baskenmütze.

Bernard ['bə:nəd]. Bernhard, *m.*; *St.* — *dog*, der Bernhardiner.

berry ['beri], *s.* die Beere.

berth [bə:θ], *s.* (*Naut.*) der Ankerplatz; die Koje. — *v.a., v.n.* anlegen; *vor Anker gehen (boat)*.

beseech [bi'si:tʃ], *v.a. irr.* bitten, anflehen.

beset [bi'set], *v.a. irr.* bedrängen, bedrücken, umringen.

beside [bi'said], *prep.* außer, neben, nahe bei; — *the point*, unwesentlich; *quite* — *the mark*, weit vom Schuß.

besides [bi'saidz], *adv.* überdies, außerdem.

besiege [bi'si:dʒ], *v.a.* belagern.

besmirch [bi'smə:tʃ], *v.a.* besudeln.

besom ['bi:zəm], *s.* der Besen.

bespatter [bi'spætə], *v.a.* bespritzen.

bespeak [bi'spi:k], *v.a. irr.* bestellen; (*Tail.*) *bespoke*, nach Maß gemacht *or* gearbeitet.

best [best], *adj.* (*superl. of* **good**) best; — *adv.* am besten. — *s. want the* — *of both worlds*, alles haben wollen; *to the* — *of my ability*, nach besten Kräften; *to the* — *of my knowledge*, soviel ich weiß.

bestial ['bestjəl], *adj.* bestialisch, tierisch.

bestow [bi'stou], *v.a.* verleihen, erteilen.

bet [bet], *s.* die Wette. — *v.a., v.n. irr.* wetten.

betray [bi'trei], *v.a.* verraten.

betrayal [bi'treiəl], *s.* der Verrat.

betrayer [bi'treiə], *s.* der Verräter.

betroth [bi'trouð], *v.a.* verloben.

betrothal [bi'trouðəl], *s.* die Verlobung.

better ['betə], *adj.* (*comp. of* **good**) besser. — *adv. you had* — *go*, es wäre besser, Sie gingen; *think* — *of it*, sich eines Besseren besinnen, sich's überlegen. — *s. get the* — *of*, überwinden; *so much the* —, desto *or* umso besser. — *v.a.* verbessern; — *oneself*, seine Lage verbessern.

betterment ['betəmənt], *s.* die Verbesserung.

between [bi'twi:n], *adv.* dazwischen. — *prep.* zwischen; unter (*among*).

bevel ['bevəl], *s.* der Winkelpasser; die Schräge. — *v.a.* abkanten.

beverage ['bevəridʒ], *s.* das Getränk.

bevy ['bevi], *s.* die Schar (*of beauties, von Schönen*).

bewail [bi'weil], *v.a., v.n.* betrauern, beweinen; trauern um.

beware [bi'wɛə], *v.n.* sich hüten (*of, vor*).

bewilder [bi'wildə], *v.a.* verwirren.

bewitch [bi'witʃ], *v.a.* bezaubern.

beyond [bi'jɔnd], *adv.* jenseits, drüben. — *prep.* über ... hinaus; jenseits; außer.

biannual [bai'ænjuəl], *adj.* halbjährlich.

bias ['baiəs], *s.* die Neigung; das Vorurteil (*prejudice*). — *v.a.* beeinflussen.

bias(s)ed ['baiəsd], *adj.* voreingenommen.

bib [bib], *s.* der Schürzenlatz; das Lätzchen.

Bible [baibl], *s.* die Bibel.

Biblical ['biblikəl], *adj.* biblisch.

bibliography [bibli'ɔgrəfi], *s.* die Bibliographie.

bibliophile ['bibliɔfail], *s.* der Bücherfreund.

biceps ['baiseps], *s.* der Bizeps, Armmuskel.

bicker ['bikə], *v.n.* zanken, hadern.

bickering ['bikəriŋ], *s.* das Gezänk, Hadern, der Hader.

bicycle ['baisikl], (*coll.*) **bike** [baik], *s.* das Fahrrad.

bicyclist ['baisiklist], *s.* der Radfahrer.

bid [bid], *v.a., v.n. irr.* gebieten, befehlen (*Dat.*) (*order*); bieten (*at auction*); — *farewell*, Lebewohl sagen. — *s.* das Gebot, Angebot (*at auction*).

bidding ['bidiŋ], *s.* der Befehl (*order*); das Bieten (*at auction*); die Einladung (*invitation*).

bide [baid], *v.n. irr.* verbleiben, verharren (*in, by,* bei).

biennial [bai'eniəl], *adj.* zweijährig, alle zwei Jahre.

bier [biə], *s.* die Bahre, Totenbahre.

big [big], *adj.* groß, dick (*fat*); *talking* —, großsprecherisch; *talk* —, prahlen.

bigamy ['bigəmi], *s.* die Bigamie, die Doppelehe.

bigness ['bignis], *s.* die Größe, Dicke.

bigoted ['bigətid], *adj.* bigott, fanatisch.

bigotry ['bigətri], *s.* die Bigotterie.

bigwig ['bigwig], *s.* (*coll.*) die vornehme Person, der Würdenträger.

bike *see* **bicycle**.

bilberry ['bilbəri], *s.* (*Bot.*) die Heidelbeere.

bile [bail], *s.* die Galle.

bilge [bildʒ], *s.* die Bilge, der Schiffsboden; (*coll.*) Unsinn (*nonsense*).

bilious ['biljəs], *adj.* gallig.

bill (1) [bil], *s.* der Schnabel (*bird*).

bill (2) [bil], die Rechnung (*account*); — *of exchange*, der Wechsel; — *of entry*, die Zolldeklaration; — *of fare*, die Speisekarte; (*Parl.*) der Gesetzentwurf; das Plakat (*poster*). — *v.a.* anzeigen.

billboard ['bilbɔ:d], *s.* (*Am.*) das Anschlagbrett.

billet ['bilit], *s.* das Billett (*card*); das Quartier, die Unterkunft (*army*).

billfold ['bilfould], *s.* (*Am.*) die Brieftasche.

billhook ['bilhuk], *s.* die Hippe.

billiards ['biljədz], *s.* das Billardspiel.

billow ['bilou], *s.* die Woge. — *v.n.* wogen.

bin [bin], *s.* der Behälter.

bind [baind], *v.a. irr.* binden, verpflichten; (*Law*) — *over*, zu gutem Benehmen verpflichten.

binder ['baində], *s.* der Binder, Buchbinder.

bindery ['baindəri], *s.* die Buchbinderei, Binderwerkstatt.

binding ['baindiŋ], *s.* der Einband.

binnacle ['binəkl], *s.* das Kompaßhäuschen.

binocular [bi'nɔkjulə], *adj.* für beide Augen. — *s.* (*pl.*) das Fernglas, der Feldstecher.

binomial [bai'noumiəl], *adj.* binomisch. — *s.* (*pl.*) (*Maths.*) das Binom, der zweigliedrige Ausdruck.

biochemical [baio'kemikəl], *adj.* biochemisch.

biochemistry [baio'kemistri], *s.* die Biochemie.

biographer [bai'ɔgrəfə], *s.* der Biograph.

biographical [baio'græfikəl], *adj.* biographisch.

biography [bai'ɔgrəfi], *s.* die Biographie, die Lebensbeschreibung.

biological [baio'lɔdʒikəl], *adj.* biologisch.

biology [bai'ɔlədʒi], *s.* die Biologie.

biometric(al) [baio'metrik(əl)], *adj.* biometrisch.

biometry [bai'ɔmitri], *s.* die Biometrie.

biophysical [baio'fizikəl], *adj.* biophysisch.

biophysics [baio'fiziks], *s.* die Biophysik.

biped ['baiped], *s.* der Zweifüßler.

biplane ['baiplein], *s.* (*Aviat.*) der Doppeldecker.

birch [bə:tʃ], *s.* (*Bot.*) die Birke; die Birkenrute, Rute (*cane*). — *v.a.* (mit der Rute) züchtigen.

bird [bə:d], *s.* der Vogel; — *of passage*, der Wandervogel, Zugvogel; —*cage*, der Vogelkäfig, das Vogelbauer; —*fancier*, der Vogelzüchter; —*'s-eye view*, die Vogelperspektive.

birth [bə:θ], *s.* die Geburt; — *certificate*, der Geburtsschein.

birthday ['bə:θdei], *s.* der Geburtstag.

biscuit ['biskit], *s.* der *or* das Keks; der Zwieback.

bisect [bai'sekt], *v.a.* entzweischneiden, halbieren.

bisection [bai'sekʃən], *s.* die Zweiteilung, Halbierung.

bishop ['biʃəp], *s.* der Bischof; (*Chess*) der Läufer.

bishopric ['biʃəprik], *s.* das Bistum.

bismuth ['bizməθ], *s.* der *or* das Wismut.

bison ['baisən], *s.* (*Zool.*) der Bison.

bit [bit], *s.* der Bissen (*bite*), das Bißchen (*little* —); das Gebiß (*bridle*); der Bart (*of key*).

bitch [bitʃ], *s.* die Hündin.

bite [bait], *v.a.* irr. beißen. — *s.* das Beißen (*mastication*); der Biß (*morsel*).

biting ['baitiŋ], *adj.* (*also fig.*) beißend, scharf. — *adv.* — *cold*, bitterkalt.

bitter ['bitə], *adj.* bitter.

bitterness ['bitənis], *s.* die Bitterkeit.

bittern ['bitə:n], *s.* (*Orn.*) die Rohrdommel.

bitumen [bi'tju:mən], *s.* der Bergteer, Asphalt.

bivouac ['bivuæk], *s.* (*Mil.*) das Biwak, Lager.

bizarre [bi'za:], *adj.* bizarr, wunderlich.

blab [blæb], *v.a., v.n.* schwatzen, ausplaudern (*give away*).

blabber ['blæbə], *s.* (*coll.*) der Schwätzer.

black [blæk], *adj.* schwarz; — *sheep*, der Taugenichts; — *pudding*, die Blutwurst; *Black Forest*, der Schwarzwald; *Black Maria*, der Polizeiwagen; (*coll.*) die grüne Minna; *Black Sea*, das schwarze Meer.

blackberry ['blækbəri], *s.* (*Bot.*) die Brombeere.

blackbird ['blækbə:d], *s.* (*Orn.*) die Amsel.

blackguard ['blæga:d], *s.* der Spitzbube, Schurke.

blackmail ['blækmeil], *v.a.* erpressen. — *s.* die Erpressung.

bladder ['blædə], *s.* (*Anat.*) die Blase.

blacksmith ['blæksmiθ], *s.* der Grobschmied.

blade [bleid], *s.* die Klinge (*razor*); der Halm (*grass*); *shoulder* —, das Schulterblatt.

blamable ['bleiməbl], *adj.* tadelnswert, tadelhaft.

blame [bleim], *s.* der Tadel, die Schuld. — *v.a.* tadeln, beschuldigen, die Schuld zuschreiben (*Dat.*).

blameless ['bleimlis], *adj.* tadellos, schuldlos.

blanch [bla:ntʃ], *v.n.* erbleichen, weiß werden. — *v.a.* weiß machen.

bland [blænd], *adj.* mild, sanft.

blandish ['blændiʃ], *v.a.* schmeicheln (*Dat.*).

blandishment ['blændiʃmənt], *s.* (*mostly in pl.*) die Schmeichelei.

blandness ['blændnis], *s.* die Milde, Sanftheit.

blank [blæŋk], *adj.* blank, leer; reimlos (*verse*); *leave a* —, einen Raum freilassen; — *cartridge*, die Platzpatrone.

blanket ['blæŋkit], *s.* die Decke; (*coll.*) *a wet* —, ein langweiliger Kerl, der Spielverderber.

blare [blɛə], *v.n.* schmettern.

blaspheme [blæs'fi:m], *v.a., v.n.* lästern, fluchen.

blasphemous ['blæsfiməs], *adj.* lästerlich.

blasphemy ['blæsfəmi], *s.* die Gotteslästerung.

blast [bla:st], *v.a.* sprengen, zerstören. — *s.* der Windstoß (*gust*); der Stoß (*trumpets*); die Explosion (*bomb*); — *furnace*, der Hochofen. — *excl.* (*sl.*) — *!* zum Teufel!

blasting ['bla:stiŋ], *s.* das Sprengen.

blatant ['bleitənt], *adj.* laut, lärmend; dreist.

blaze [bleiz], *s.* die Flamme (*flame*); das Feuer; der Glanz (*colour etc.*). — *v.n.* flammen; leuchten (*shine*). — *v.a.* ausposaunen, bekannt machen (*make known*).

blazer ['bleizə], *s.* die Sportjacke, Klubjacke.

blazon ['bleizən], *v.a.* verkünden.

bleach [bli:tʃ], *v.a.* bleichen. — *s.* das Bleichmittel.

bleak [bli:k], *adj.* öde, rauh; trübe, freudlos.

bleakness ['bli:knis], *s.* die Öde (*scenery*); Traurigkeit, Trübheit.

bleary ['bliəri], *adj.* trübe; — *eyed*, triefäugig.

bleat [bli:t], *v.n.* blöken.

bleed [bli:d], *v.n.* irr. bluten. — *v.a.* bluten lassen; erpressen (*blackmail*).

blemish ['blemiʃ], *s.* der Makel, der Fehler. — *v.a.* schänden, entstellen.

blench [blentʃ], *v.n.* zurückweichen, stutzen.

blend [blend], *v.a., v.n.* mischen, vermengen; sich mischen. — *s.* die Mischung, Vermischung.

bless [bles], *v.a.* segnen; beglücken, loben.

blessed [blest, 'blesid], *adj.* gesegnet, selig.

blessing ['blesiŋ], *s.* der Segen.

blight [blait], *s.* der Meltau. — *v.a.* verderben.

blind [blaind], *adj.* blind; — *man's buff*, Blinde Kuh; — *spot*, der schwache Punkt. — *s.* die Blende, das Rouleau; *Venetian* —, die Jalousie. — *v.a.* blind machen, täuschen.

blindfold ['blaindfould], *adj.* mit verbundenen Augen.

blindness ['blaindnis], *s.* die Blindheit.

blindworm ['blaindwə:m], *s.* (*Zool.*) die Blindschleiche.

blink [bliŋk], *s.* das Blinzeln. — *v.n.* blinzeln, blinken. — *v.a.* nicht sehen wollen.

blinkers ['bliŋkəz], *s. pl.* die Scheuklappen.

bliss [blis], *s.* die Wonne, Seligkeit.

blissful ['blisful], *adj.* wonnig, selig.

blister ['blistə], *s.* die Blase. — *v.n.* Blasen ziehen, Blasen bekommen.

blithe

blithe [blaið], *adj.* munter, lustig, fröhlich.
blitheness ['blaiðnis], *s.* die Munterkeit, Fröhlichkeit.
blizzard ['blizəd], *s.* der Schneesturm.
bloated ['bloutid], *adj.* aufgeblasen, aufgedunsen.
bloater ['bloutə], *s.* (Zool.) der Bückling.
blob [blɔb], *s.* der Kleks.
block [blɔk], *s.* der Block, Klotz (*wood*); Häuserblock (*houses*); — *letters*, große Druckschrift. — *v.a.* blockieren, hemmen (*hinder*); sperren (*road*).
blockade [blɔ'keid], *s.* die Blockade.
blockhead ['blɔkhed], *s.* der Dummkopf.
blonde [blɔnd], *adj.* blond. — *s.* die Blondine.
blood [blʌd], *s.* das Blut; — *vessel*, das Blutgefäß.
bloodcurdling ['blʌdkə:dliŋ], *adj.* haarsträubend.
bloodless ['blʌdlis], *adj.* blutlos, unblutig.
bloodthirsty ['blʌdθə:sti], *adj.* blutdürstig.
bloody ['blʌdi], *adj.* blutig; (*vulg.*) verflucht.
bloom [blu:m], *s.* die Blüte; die Blume. — *v.n.* blühen.
bloomers ['blu:məz], *s. pl.* altmodische Unterhosen für Damen.
blooming ['blu:miŋ], *adj.* blühend.
blossom ['blɔsəm], *s.* die Blüte. — *v.n.* blühen, Blüten treiben.
blot [blɔt], *s.* der Klecks; Fleck; (*fig.*) der Schandfleck. — *v.a.* beflecken; löschen (*ink*); — *out*, ausmerzen, austilgen; *blotting paper*, das Löschpapier.
blotch [blɔtʃ], *s.* der Hautfleck; die Pustel; der Klecks (*blot*).
blotter ['blɔtə], *s.* der Löscher.
blouse [blauz], *s.* die Bluse.
blow (1) [blou], *s.* der Schlag.
blow (2) [blou], *v.a. irr.* blasen; wehen; — *o.'s own trumpet*, prahlen; anfachen (*fire*); — *o.'s nose*, sich schneuzen. — *v.n.* schnaufen, keuchen; — *up*, in die Luft sprengen.
blower ['blouə], *s.* das Gebläse; der Bläser.
blowpipe ['bloupaip], *s.* das Lötrohr.
blubber ['blʌbə], *s.* der Walfischspeck, der Tran. — *v.n.* schluchzen, heulen, flennen.
bludgeon ['blʌdʒən], *s.* der Knüppel; die Keule (*club*). — *v.a.* niederschlagen.
blue [blu:], *adj.* blau; schwermütig (*sad*); — *blooded*, aus edlem Geblüte.
bluebell ['blu:bel], *s.* (*Bot.*) die Glockenblume.
bluebottle ['blu:bɔtl], *s.* (*Ent.*) die Schmeißfliege.
bluestocking ['blu:stɔkiŋ], *s.* der Blaustrumpf.

bluff [blʌf], *adj.* grob, schroff. — *s.* der Bluff, die Täuschung, der Trick. — *v.a.*, *v.n.* vortäuschen (*pretend*), bluffen; verblüffen (*deceive*).
blunder ['blʌndə], *s.* der Fehler, Schnitzer. — *v.n.* einen Fehler machen.
blunderer ['blʌndərə], *s.* der Tölpel.
blunderbuss ['blʌndəbʌs], *s.* die Donnerbüchse.
blunt [blʌnt], *adj.* stumpf (*edge*); derb, offen (*speech*). — *v.a.* abstumpfen; verderben (*appetite*).
bluntness ['blʌntnis], *s.* die Stumpfheit (*edge*); die Derbheit (*speech*).
blur [blə:], *s.* der Fleck. — *v.a.* verwischen.
blurt [blə:t], *v.a.* — *out*, herausplatzen.
blush [blʌʃ], *v.n.* erröten. — *s.* die Schamröte, das Erröten.
bluster ['blʌstə], *s.* das Toben, Brausen. — *v.n.* toben, brausen.
blustering ['blʌstəriŋ], *adj.* lärmend, tobend.
boa ['bouə], *s.* (Zool.) die Boa.
boar [bɔ:], *s.* (Zool.) der Eber.
board [bɔ:d], *s.* das Brett (*wood*); die Tafel (*notice* —); die Verpflegung (*food*); — *and lodging*, die Vollpension; die Behörde, der Ausschuß (*officials*). — *v.a.* — *up*, vernageln, zumachen; — *someone*, verpflegen; — *a steamer*, an Bord gehen; —*ing school*, das Internat, das Pensionat.
boarder ['bɔ:də], *s.* der Internatsschüler; der Pensionär.
boast [boust], *v.n.* prahlen, sich rühmen. — *s.* der Stolz (*pride*).
boastful ['boustful], *adj.* prahlerisch.
boat [bout], *s.* das Boot; *rowing-* —, das Ruderboot; der Kahn.
bob [bɔb], *s.* der Knicks; (*coll.*) der Schilling. — *v.n.* baumeln; springen; *bobbed hair*, der Bubikopf.
bobbin ['bɔbin], *s.* die Spule, der Klöppel.
bobsleigh ['bɔbslei], *s.* der Bob(sleigh), Rennschlitten.
bodice ['bɔdis], *s.* das Mieder, Leibchen.
bodied ['bɔdid], *adj. suffix*; *able-* —, gesund, stark.
body ['bɔdi], *s.* der Körper; die Körperschaft (*organisation*).
bodyguard ['bɔdigɑ:d], *s.* die Leibwache.
Boer ['bouə], *s.* der Bure.
bog [bɔg], *s.* der Sumpf. — *v.a.* (*coll.*) — *down*, einsinken.
Bohemian [bo'hi:mjən], *s.* der Böhme. — *adj.* böhmisch; künstlerhaft.
boil (1) [bɔil], *v.a.*, *v.n.* kochen, sieden. — *s.* das Kochen; —*ing point*, der Siedepunkt.
boil (2) [bɔil], *s.* (*Med.*) die Beule, der Furunkel.
boisterous ['bɔistərəs], *adj.* ungestüm; laut (*noisy*).
boisterousness ['bɔistərəsnis], *s.* die Heftigkeit, Lautheit.

bold [bould], *adj.* kühn, dreist; *make* —, sich erkühnen.

boldness ['bouldnis], *s.* die Kühnheit, Dreistigkeit.

Bolivian [bə'livjən], *adj.* bolivianisch. —*s.* der Bolivianer.

bolster ['boulstə], *s.* das Polster, Kissen.

bolt [boult], *s.* der Bolzen, Riegel (*on door*); der Pfeil (*arrow*). — *v.a.* verriegeln (*bar*); verschlingen (*devour*). — *v.n.* davonlaufen (*run away*), durchgehen (*abscond*).

bomb [bom], *s.* die Bombe. — *v.a.* bombardieren.

bombard [bom'ba:d], *v.a.* bombardieren.

bombardment [bom'ba:dmənt], *s.* die Beschießung.

bombastic [bom'bæstik], *adj.* schwülstig, bombastisch (*style*).

bombproof ['bompru:f], *adj.* bombensicher.

bond [bond], *s.* das Band (*link*); die Schuldverschreibung (*debt*); *in* —, unter Zollverschluß; (*pl.*) die Fesseln (*fetters*). — *v.a.* (*Chem.*) binden; (*Comm.*) zollpflichtig erklären (*declare dutiable*).

bondage ['bondidʒ], *s.* die Knechtschaft.

bone [boun], *s.* der Knochen; die Gräte (*fish*); — *china*, feines Geschirr, das Porzellan; — *of contention*, der Zankapfel; — *dry*, staubtrocken; — *idle*, stinkfaul; — *lace*, die Klöppelspitze. — *v.a.* Knochen oder Gräten entfernen.

ɔonfire ['bonfaiə], *s.* das Freudenfeuer.

bonnet ['bonit], *s.* die Haube, das Häubchen.

bonny ['boni], *adj.* hübsch, nett.

bony ['bouni], *adj.* beinern, knöchern.

book [buk], *s.* das Buch. — *v.a.* belegen (*seat*); eine Karte lösen (*ticket*); engagieren (*engage*).

bookbinder ['bukbaində], *s.* der Buchbinder.

bookcase ['bukkeis], *s.* der Bücherschrank.

bookie *see* bookmaker.

booking-office ['bukiɲofis], *s.* der Fahrkartenschalter; die Kasse (*Theat. etc.*)

book-keeper ['bukki:pə], *s.* der Buchhalter.

book-keeping ['bukki:piɲ], *s.* die Buchhaltung; *double entry* —, doppelte Buchführung, *single entry* —, einfache Buchführung.

bookmaker ['bukmeikə] (*abbr.* **bookie** ['buki]), *s.* (*Racing*) der Buchmacher.

bookmark(er) ['bukma:k(ə)], *s.* das Lesezeichen.

bookseller ['bukselə], *s.* der Buchhändler.

bookshop ['bukʃop], *s.* die Buchhandlung.

bookstall ['bukstɔ:l], *s.* der Bücherstand.

bookworm ['bukwə:m], *s.* der Bücherwurm.

boom (1) [bu:m], *s.* der Aufschwung; Boom; (*Comm.*) die Konjunktur; Hausse.

boom (2) [bu:m], *v.n.* dröhnen, (dumpf) schallen.

boon [bu:n], *s.* die Wohltat.

boor [buə], *s.* der Lümmel.

boorish ['buəriʃ], *adj.* lümmelhaft.

boot [bu:t], *s.* der Stiefel, hohe Schuh. — *v.a.* mit dem Stiefel stoßen, kicken.

booth [bu:ð], *s.* die Bude, Zelle (*Teleph.*).

bootlace ['bu:tleis], *s.* der Schnürsenkel, der Schnürriemen.

booty ['bu:ti], *s.* die Beute.

booze [bu:z], *v.n.* (*coll.*) saufen.

boozy ['bu:zi], *adj.* (*coll.*) angeheitert, leicht betrunken.

border ['bo:də], *s.* der Rand; die Grenze. — *v.a.*, *v.n.* angrenzen (*on*); einsäumen (*surround*).

borderer ['bo:dərə], *s.* der Grenzbewohner.

bore [bo:], *v.a.* bohren; langweilen (*be boring*). — *s.* das Bohrloch (*drill-hole*), die Bohrung (*drilling*); der langweilige Kerl (*person*).

boredom ['bo:dəm], *s.* die Langeweile.

borer ['bo:rə], *s.* der Bohrer (*drill*).

born [bo:n], *adj.* geboren.

borrow ['borou], *v.a.* borgen, entlehnen.

borrowing ['borouiɲ], *s.* das Borgen, Entlehnen.

bosom ['buzəm], *s.* der Busen.

boss [bos], *s.* der Beschlag, der Buckel; (*coll.*) der Chef.

botanical [bo'tænikəl], *adj.* botanisch.

botanist ['botənist], *s.* der Botaniker.

botany ['botəni], *s.* die Botanik.

botch [botʃ], *s.* das Flickwerk. — *v.a.* verderben, verhunzen.

both [bouθ], *adj.*, *pron.* beide, beides; — *of them*, beide. — *conj.* — . . . *and*, sowohl . . . als auch.

bother ['boðə], *v.a.* plagen, stören, belästigen; *it!* zum Henker damit! — *v.n.* sich bemühen. — *s.* die Belästigung, das Ärgernis.

bottle ['botl], *s.* die Flasche. — *v.a.* in Flaschen abfüllen.

bottom ['botəm], *s.* der Boden, Grund (*ground*); die Ursache (*cause*); (*Naut.*) der Schiffsboden.

bottomless ['botəmlis], *adj.* grundlos, bodenlos.

bough [bau], *s.* der Zweig, Ast.

boulder ['bouldə], *s.* der Felsblock.

bounce [bauns], *v.a.* aufprallen lassen (*ball*). — *v.n.* aufprallen. — *s.* der Rückprall, Aufprall.

bound (1) [baund], *s.* der Sprung; *by leaps and* —*s*, schr schnell, sprunghaft. — *v.n.* springen, prallen.

bound (2) [baund], *v.a.* begrenzen, einschränken. — *adj.* verpflichtet; — *to* (*inf.*), wird sicherlich . . .

bound (3) [baund], *adj.* — *for*, auf dem Wege nach.

boundary ['baundəri], *s.* die Grenzlinie, Grenze.

bounder ['baundə], *s.* der ungezogene Bursche.

boundless ['baundlis], *adj.* grenzenlos, unbegrenzt.

bounteous ['bauntiəs], *adj.* freigebig; reichlich (*plenty*).

bounty ['baunti], *s.* die Freigebigkeit (*generosity*); (*Comm.*) Prämie.

bouquet [bu'kei], *s.* das Bukett, der Blumenstrauß; die Blume (*wine*).

bourgeois ['buəʒwɑ:], *s.* der Bürger; Philister. — *adj.* kleinbürgerlich, philisterhaft.

bow (1) [bau], *s.* (*Naut.*) der Bug; —*sprit*, das Bugspriet.

bow (2) [bau], *s.* die Verbeugung, Verneigung. — *v.n.* sich verneigen, sich verbeugen. — *v.a.* neigen.

bow (3) [bou], *s.* (*Mus.*) der Bogen; die Schleife (*ribbon*). — *v.a.* streichen (*violin*).

bowel ['bauəl], *s.* der Darm; (*pl.*) die Eingeweide.

bowl (1) [boul], *s.* die Schale, der Napf, die Schüssel.

bowl (2) [boul], *s.* die Holzkugel; (*pl.*) das Rasenkugelspiel, Bowlingspiel. — *v.n.* (*Cricket*) den Ball werfen.

bowler (1) ['boulə], *s.* (*hat*) der steife Hut, die Melone.

bowler (2) ['boulə], *s.* (*Sport*) der Ballmann.

box (1) [bɔks], *s.* (*Bot.*) der Buchsbaum.

box (2) [bɔks], *s.* die Büchse, Dose, Schachtel, der Kasten; (*Theat.*) die Loge; — *office*, die Theaterkasse.

box (3) [bɔks], *s.* der Schlag; — *on the ear*, die Ohrfeige. — *v.n.* boxen.

boxer ['bɔksə], *s.* der Boxer; Boxkämpfer.

Boxing Day ['bɔksiŋ'dei], der zweite Weihnachtstag.

boy [bɔi], *s.* der Junge, Knabe; Diener (*servant*).

boyish ['bɔiiʃ], *adj.* knabenhaft.

boyhood ['bɔihud], *s.* das Knabenalter.

brace [breis], *s.* das Band; die Klammer (*clamp*); — *of partridges*, das Paar Rebhühner; die Spange (*denture*). — *v.a.* spannen, straffen. — *v.r.* — *yourself!* stähle dich!

bracelet ['breislit], *s.* das Armband.

braces ['breisiz], *s. pl.* die Hosenträger.

bracken ['brækən], *s.* (*Bot.*) das Farnkraut.

bracket ['brækit], *s.* die Klammer; *income* —, die Einkommensgruppe. — *v.a.* (ein-)klammern; (*Maths.*) in Klammern setzen.

brackish ['brækiʃ], *adj.* salzig.

brad [bræd], *s.* der kopflose Nagel; — *awl*, der Vorstechbohrer.

brag [bræg], *v.n.* prahlen.

braggart ['brægət], *s.* der Prahlhans.

Brahmin ['brɑːmin], *s.* der Brahmane.

braid [breid], *s.* die Borte; der Saumbesatz. — *v.a.* (mit Borten) besetzen.

Braille [breil], *s.* die Blindenschrift.

brain [brein], *s.* das Gehirn, Hirn; *scatter-* —*ed*, zerstreut.

brainwave ['breinweiv], *s.* der Geistesblitz.

brake [breik], *s.* die Bremse. — *v.a.* bremsen.

bramble [bræmbl], *s.* der (*Bot.*) Brombeerstrauch.

bran [bræn], *s.* die Kleie.

branch [brɑːntʃ], *s.* der Ast, Zweig; (*Comm.*) die Zweigstelle, Filiale. — *v.n.* — *out*, sich verzweigen; — *out into*, sich ausbreiten, etwas Neues anfangen; — *off*, abzweigen.

brand [brænd], *s.* der (Feuer) Brand; das Brandmal (*on skin*); die Sorte, Marke (*make*); — *new*, funkelnagelneu. — *v.a.* brandmarken, kennzeichnen.

brandish ['brændiʃ], *v.a.* schwingen, herumschwenken.

brandy ['brændi], *s.* der Branntwein, Kognac, Weinbrand.

brass [brɑːs], *s.* das Messing; — *band*, die Blechmusik, Militärmusikkapelle; — *founder*, Erzgießer, Gelbgießer; (*sl.*) die Frechheit (*impudence*).

brassiere ['bræsiəə], *s.* der Büstenhalter.

brat [bræt], *s.* (*coll.*) das Kind, der Balg.

brave [breiv], *adj.* tapfer, kühn. — *v.a.* trotzen, standhalten (*Dat.*). — *s.* der Held, Krieger; der Indianer (*redskin*).

bravery ['breivəri], *s.* die Tapferkeit.

brawl [brɔːl], *s.* der Krawall, die Rauferei. — *v.n.* zanken, lärmen.

brawn [brɔːn], *s.* die Sülze; (*fig.*) die Körperkraft, Stärke.

brawny ['brɔːni], *adj.* stark, sehnig.

bray [brei], *v.n.* iah sagen, Eselslaute von sich geben (*donkey*). — *s.* das Iah des Esels, das Eselsgeschrei.

brazen [breizn], *adj.* (*Metall.*) aus Erz; unverschämt (*shameless*).

brazenfaced ['breiznfeisd], *adj.* unverschämt.

brazier ['breiziə], *s.* der Kupferschmied; die Kohlenpfanne.

Brazil [brə'zil]. Brasilien, *n.*; — *nut*, die Paranuß.

Brazilian [brə'ziliən], *adj.* brasilianisch. — *s.* der Brasilianer.

breach [briːtʃ], *s.* die Bresche; der Bruch (*break*); die Verletzung; der Vertragsbruch (*of contract*); der Verstoß (*of*, gegen, *etiquette etc.*).

bread [bred], *s.* das Brot; *brown* —, das Schwarzbrot; — *and butter*, das Butterbrot.

breadth [bretθ], *s.* die Breite, Weite.

break [breik], s. der Bruch (breach); die Lücke (gap); die Chance (chance); a lucky —, ein glücklicher Zufall, ein Glücksfall; die Pause (from work). — v.a., v.n. irr. brechen; — off, Pause machen; — in, unterbrechen (interrupt); — in, (horse) einschulen, zureiten; — up, abbrechen (school, work); — away, sich trennen, absondern; — down, zusammenbrechen (health); (Am.) analysieren; auflösen.

breakage ['breikidʒ], s. der Bruch, der Schaden (damage).

breakdown ['breikdoun], s. der Zusammenbruch (health); die Panne (car); (Am.) die Analyse (analysis).

breaker ['breikə], s. die Brandungswelle, Brandung.

breakfast ['brekfəst], s. das Frühstück. v.n. frühstücken.

breast [brest], s. die Brust.

breath [breθ], s. der Atem; der Hauch (exhalation); with bated —, mit verhaltenem Atem.

breathe [briːð], v.n. atmen.

breathing ['briːðiŋ], s. die Atmung.

breathless ['breθlis], adj. atemlos.

breech [briːtʃ], s. der Boden; — (pl.) die Reithosen, f. pl.

breed [briːd], v.a. irr. zeugen, züchten (cattle, etc.). — v.n. sich vermehren. — s. die Zucht, die Art (type); die Rasse (race).

breeder ['briːdə], s. der Züchter.

breeding ['briːdiŋ], s. die gute Kinderstube (manners); die Erziehung; das Züchten (of plants, cattle etc.).

breeze [briːz], s. die Briese.

breezy ['briːzi], adj. windig; lebhaft (manner), beschwingt (tone).

brethren ['breðrən], s. pl. (obs.) die Brüder.

Breton [bretn], adj. bretonisch. — s. der Bretagner, Bretone.

brevet ['brevit], s. das Patent.

breviary ['briːviəri], s. das Brevier.

brevity ['breviti], s. die Kürze.

brew [bruː], v.a. brauen. — s. das Gebräu, Bräu (beer).

brewer ['bruːə], s. der Brauer, Bierbrauer.

brewery ['bruːəri], s. die Brauerei, das Brauhaus.

briar, brier ['braiə], s. (Bot.) der Dornstrauch, die wilde Rose.

bribe [braib], v.a. bestechen. — s. das Bestechungsgeld.

bribery ['braibəri], s. die Bestechung.

brick [brik], s. der Ziegel, Backstein; drop a —, eine Taktlosigkeit begehen, einen Schnitzer machen.

bricklayer ['brikleiə], s. der Maurer.

bridal [braidl], adj. bräutlich.

bride [braid], s. die Braut.

bridegroom ['braidgruːm], s. der Bräutigam.

bridesmaid ['braidzmeid], s. die Brautjungfer.

bridge [bridʒ], s. die Brücke. — v.a. überbrücken; — the gap, die Lücke füllen.

bridle [braidl], s. der Zaum, Zügel. — v.a. aufzäumen. — v.n. sich brüsten.

brief [briːf], adj. kurz, bündig, knapp. — s. der Schriftsatz, der Rechtsauftrag, die Instruktionen, f. pl. (instructions). — v.a. instruieren, beauftragen; informieren (inform).

brigade [briˈgeid], s. die Brigade.

brigand ['brigənd], s. der Brigant, Straßenräuber.

bright [brait], adj. hell, glänzend (shiny); klug, intelligent (clever).

brighten [braitn], v.a. glänzend machen (polish etc.); erhellen, aufheitern (cheer).

brightness ['braitnis], s. der Glanz; die Helligkeit; die Klugheit (cleverness).

brill [bril], s. (Zool.) der Glattbutt.

brilliance, brilliancy ['briljəns, -jənsi], s. der Glanz, die Pracht.

brim [brim], s. der Rand (glass); die Krempe (hat). — v.n. — (over) with, überfließen von.

brimful ['brimful], adj. übervoll.

brimstone ['brimstoun], s. der Schwefel; — butterfly, der Zitronenfalter.

brindled ['brindld], adj. scheckig, gefleckt.

brine [brain], s. die Salzsole, das Salzwasser.

bring [briŋ], v.a. irr. bringen; — about, zustande bringen; — forth, hervorbringen; gebären; — forward, fördern; anführen; — on, herbeiführen; — up, erziehen, aufziehen.

brink [briŋk], s. (fig.) der Rand, — of a precipice, Rand eines Abgrundes.

briny ['braini], adj. salzig.

brisk [brisk], adj. frisch, munter, feurig (horse).

brisket ['briskit], s. die Brust (eines Tieres).

briskness ['brisknis], s. die Lebhaftigkeit.

bristle [brisl], s. die Borste. — v.n. sich sträuben.

British ['britiʃ], adj. britisch.

Britisher, Briton ['britiʃə, 'britən], s. der Brite.

brittle [britl], adj. zerbrechlich, spröde.

brittleness ['britlnis], s. die Sprödigkeit, Zerbrechlichkeit.

broach [broutʃ], v.a. anzapfen, anschneiden; — a subject, ein Thema berühren.

broad [brɔːd], adj. breit, weit; ordinär, derb (joke); — minded, duldsam, weitherzig.

broadcast ['brɔːdkɑːst], v.a. senden, übertragen (radio). — s. die Sendung, das Programm.

broadcaster ['brɔːdkɑːstə], s. der im Radio Vortragende or Künstler (artist); Ansager.

broadcasting ['brɔːdkɑːstiŋ], s. das Senden, der Rundfunk; — station, der Sender, die Rundfunkstation.

broadcloth

broadcloth ['brɔːdclɔθ], *s.* das feine Tuch.

broaden [brɔːdn], *v.a.* erweitern, verbreitern.

brocade [bro'keid], *s.* der Brokat.

brogue [broug], *s.* der grobe Schuh; der irische Akzent.

broil ['brɔil], *v.a.* braten, rösten.

broke [brouk], *adj.* (coll.) pleite.

broken ['broukən], *adj.* gebrochen; zerbrochen; unterbrochen (*interrupted*).

broker ['broukə], *s.* der Makler.

bronchial ['brɔŋkjəl], *adj.* (*Anat.*) bronchial, in *or* von der Luftröhre, Luftröhren-.

bronchitis [brɔŋ'kaitis], *s.* (*Med.*) die Luftröhrenentzündung, Bronchitis.

bronze [brɔnz], *s.* (*Metall.*) die Bronze, Bronzefarbe.

brooch [broutʃ], *s.* die Brosche.

brood [bruːd], *s.* die Brut. — *v.n.* brüten; grübeln (*meditate*).

brook (1) [bruk], *s.* der Bach.

brook (2) [bruk], *v.a.* ertragen, leiden.

brooklet ['bruklit], *s.* das Bächlein.

broom [bruːm], *s.* der Besen; (*Bot.*) der Ginster.

broth [brɔθ], *s.* die Brühe; *meat* —, Fleischbrühe.

brothel ['brɔθəl], *s.* das Bordell.

brother ['brʌðə], *s.* der Bruder; — *-in-law*, der Schwager.

brotherhood ['brʌðəhud], *s.* die Bruderschaft.

brotherly ['brʌðəli], *adj.* brüderlich.

brow [brau], *s.* die Braue, Augenbraue; der Kamm (*hill*); die Stirn(e) (*forehead*).

browbeat ['braubiːt], *v.a.* einschüchtern.

brown [braun], *adj.* braun; *in a* — *study*, in tiefem Nachsinnen.

browse [brauz], *v.n.* weiden (*cattle*); stöbern, (durch-)blättern (*in books etc.*).

Bruin ['bruːin]. Braun, Meister Petz, der Bär.

bruise [bruːz], *v.a.* quetschen, stoßen; (wund) schlagen. — *s.* die Quetschung.

Brunswick ['brʌnzwik]. Braunschweig, *n.*

brunt [brʌnt], *s.* der Anprall; *bear the* —, der Wucht ausgesetzt sein, den Stoß auffangen.

brush [brʌʃ], *s.* die Bürste (*clothes*); der Pinsel (*paint, painting*); — *stroke*, der Pinselstrich. — *v.a., v.n.* bürsten, abbürsten; — *against s.o.*, mit jemandem zusammenstoßen, streifen (*an, Acc.*); — *up one's English*, das Englisch auffrischen; — *off*, abschütteln.

brushwood ['brʌʃwud], *s.* das Gestrüpp.

brusque [brusk], *adj.* brüsk, barsch.

Brussels ['brʌsəlz]. Brüssel, *n.*; — *sprouts*, (*Bot.*) der Rosenkohl.

brutal [bruːtl], *adj.* brutal, grausam.

brutality [bruː'tæliti], *s.* die Brutalität.

brute [bruːt], *s.* der Unmensch.

bubble [bʌbl], *s.* die Blase; (*fig.*) der Schwindel (*swindle*). — *v.n.* sprudeln, wallen, schäumen.

buccaneer [bʌkə'niə], *s.* der Seeräuber.

buck [bʌk], *s.* (*Zool.*) der Bock; (*Am. sl.*) der Dollar. — *v.a.* — *up*, aufmuntern. — *v.n.* — *up*, sich zusammenraffen.

bucket ['bʌkit], *s.* der Eimer, Kübel.

buckle [bʌkl], *s.* die Schnalle. — *v.a.* zuschnallen; biegen. — *v.n.* sich krümmen.

buckler ['bʌklə], *s.* der Schild.

buckram ['bʌkrəm], *s.* die Steifleinwand.

buckskin ['bʌkskin], *s.* das Wildleder.

buckwheat ['bʌkwiːt], *s.* (*Bot.*) der Buchweizen.

bucolic [bjuː'kɔlik], *adj.* bukolisch, ländlich, Schäfer-.

bud [bʌd], *s.* (*Bot.*) die Knospe. — *v.n.* knospen.

buddy ['bʌdi], *s.*(*coll.Am.*) der Freund, Kamerad.

budge [bʌdʒ], *v.n.* sich rühren, sich regen.

budget ['bʌdʒit], *s.* das Budget; der Haushaltsplan; der Etat; *present the* —, den Staatsetat vorlegen. — *v.n.* voranschlagen (*for*), planen.

buff [bʌf], *adj.* ledergelb.

buffalo ['bʌfəlou], *s.* (*Zool.*) der Büffel.

buffer ['bʌfə], *s.* der Puffer.

buffet (1) ['bʌfit], *s.* der Puff, Faustschlag (*blow*). — *v.a.* schlagen, stoßen.

buffet (2) ['bufei], *s.* das Buffet, der Anrichtetisch.

buffoon [bʌ'fuːn], *s.* der Possenreißer.

buffoonery [bʌ'fuːnəri], *s.* die Possen, *f. pl.*; das Possenreißen.

bug [bʌg], *s.* (*Ent.*) die Wanze; (*Am.*) der Käfer; (*coll.*) das Insekt.

buggy ['bʌgi], *s.* der Einspänner.

bugle [bjuːgl], *s.* (*Mus.*) das Signalhorn, die Militärtrompete.

bugler ['bjuːglə], *s.* (*Mus.*) der Trompeter.

build [bild], *v.a., v.n. irr.* bauen; errichten; — *on*, sich verlassen auf (*rely on*). — *s.* die Statur, Figur (*figure*).

builder ['bildə], *s.* der Bauherr, Baumeister (*employer*); Bauarbeiter (*worker*).

building ['bildiŋ], *s.* das Gebäude, der Bau; — *site*, der Bauplatz.

bulb [bʌlb], *s.* (*Bot.*) der Knollen, die Zwiebel; *Dutch* —, die Tulpe; (*Elec.*) die Birne.

bulbous ['bʌlbəs], *adj.* zwiebelartig; dickbäuchig.

Bulgarian [bʌl'gɛəriən], *adj.* bulgarisch. — *s.* der Bulgare.

bulge [bʌldʒ], *s.* die Ausbauchung; die Ausbuchtung (*in fighting line*). — *v.n.* herausragen, anschwellen.

bulk [bʌlk], *s.* die Masse, Menge; *buy in* —, im Großen einkaufen.

bulky ['bʌlki], *adj.* schwer (*heavy*); massig (*stodgy*); unhandlich.

bull (1) [bul], *s.* (*Zool.*) der Bulle, Stier; —'s *eye,* das Schwarze (*target*).

bull (2) [bul], *s.* (*Papal*) die Bulle, der Erlass.

bulldog ['buldɔg], *s.* der Bullenbeißer.

bullet ['bulit], *s.* die Kugel, das Geschoß.

bulletin ['bulitin], *s.* das Bulletin, der Tagesbericht.

bullfight ['bulfait], *s.* der Stierkampf.

bullfinch ['bulfintʃ], *s.* (*Orn.*) der Dompfaff.

bullfrog ['bulfrɔg], *s.* (*Zool.*) der Ochsenfrosch.

bullion ['buljən], *s.* der Goldbarren, Silberbarren.

bullock ['bulək], *s.* (*Zool.*) der Ochse.

bully ['buli], *s.* der Raufbold, Angeber, Großtuer (*braggart*); der Tyrann. — *v.a.* tyrannisieren, einschüchtern.

bulrush ['bulrʌʃ], *s.* (*Bot.*) die Binse.

bulwark ['bulwək], *s.* das Bollwerk, die Verteidigung.

bump [bʌmp], *s.* der Schlag, der Stoß. — *v.a.* stoßen.

bun [bʌn], *s.* das Rosinenbrötchen; das süße Brötchen; (*hair*) der Knoten.

bunch [bʌntʃ], *s.* der Bund (*keys*); der Strauß (*flowers*); die Traube (*grapes*). — *v a.* zusammenfassen, zusammenbinden, zusammenraffen.

bundle [bʌndl], *s.* das Bündel.

bung [bʌŋ], *s.* der Spund (*in barrel*).

bungle [bʌŋgl], *v.a.* verpfuschen, verderben.

bungler ['bʌŋglə], *s.* der Stümper.

bunion ['bʌnjən], *s.* die Fußschwiele.

bunk (1) [bʌŋk], *s.* die (Schlaf-)Koje.

bunk (2) [bʌŋk], *s.* (*coll.*) der Unsinn.

bunker ['bʌŋkə], *s.* der Kohlenraum, Bunker.

bunting ['bʌntiŋ], *s.* das Flaggentuch.

buoy [bɔi], *s.* die Boje.

buoyant ['bɔiənt], *adj.* schwimmend; lebhaft, heiter.

buoyancy ['bɔiənsi], *s.* die Schwimmkraft; die Schwungkraft.

burden (1) [bə:dn], *s.* die Bürde, Last. — *v.a.* belasten, beladen.

burden (2) [bə:dn], *s.* der Refrain; der Hauptinhalt.

burdensome ['bə:dnsəm], *adj.* beschwerlich.

bureau [bjuə'rou], *s.* der Schreibtisch; das Büro.

bureaucracy [bjuə'rɔkrəsi], *s.* die Bürokratie.

burgess ['bə:dʒis], *s.* der Bürger.

burglar ['bə:glə], *s.* der Einbrecher.

burglary ['bə:gləri], *s.* der Einbruch, der Diebstahl.

burgomaster ['bə:gomɑ:stə], *s.* der Bürgermeister.

Burgundian [bə:'gʌndiən], *adj.* burgundisch. —*s.* der Burgunder.

Burgundy (1) ['bə:gəndi], das Burgund.

Burgundy (2) ['bə:gəndi], *s.* der Burgunder(-wein).

burial ['beriəl], *das Begräbnis; — ground,* der Kirchhof, Friedhof; — *service,* die Totenfeier, Trauerfeier.

burlesque [bə:'lesk], *s.* die Burleske, Posse.

burly ['bə:li], *adj.* dick, stark.

Burmese [bə:'mi:z], *adj.* birmesisch. — *s.* der Birmese.

burn [bə:n], *v.a., v.n. irr.* brennen, verbrennen. — *s.* das Brandmal.

burner ['bə:nə], *s.* der Brenner.

burnish ['bə:niʃ], *v.a.* polieren.

burred [bə:d], *adj.* überliegend; (*Metall.*) ausgehämmert; — *over,* (*Metall.*) breitgeschmiedet.

burrow ['bʌrou], *s.* der Bau, (*rabbits etc.*). —*v.n.* sich eingraben; wühlen.

burst [bə:st], *v.a., v.n. irr.* bersten, platzen, explodieren (*explode*); — *out laughing,* laut auflachen; — *into tears,* in Tränen ausbrechen; — *into flames,* aufflammen; sprengen (*blow up*). — *s.* der Ausbruch; die Explosion.

bury ['beri], *v.a.* begraben, beerdigen.

bus [bʌs], *s.* der Autobus, Omnibus.

busby ['bʌzbi], *s.* (*Mil.*) die Bärenmütze.

bush [buʃ], *s.* der Busch.

bushel [buʃl], *s.* der Scheffel.

bushy ['buʃi], *adj.* buschig.

business ['biznis], *s.* das Geschäft; die Beschäftigung, die Tätigkeit (*activity*); Aufgabe, Obliegenheit; der Handel (*trade*); *on —,* geschäftlich.

businesslike ['biznislaik], *adj.* geschäftsmäßig, nüchtern, praktisch.

businessman ['biznismæn], *s.* der Geschäftsmann.

bust (1) [bʌst], *s.* die Büste.

bust (2) [bʌst], *v.a., v.n.* (*coll.*) sprengen; *go —,* bankrott machen.

bustard ['bʌstəd], *s.* (*Orn.*) die Trappe.

bustle [bʌsl], *s.* der Lärm, die Aufregung. — *v.n.* aufgeregt umherlaufen; rührig sein (*be active*).

busy ['bizi], *adj.* geschäftig (*active*); beschäftigt (*engaged,* mit, *in*); *be —,* zu tun haben.

but [bʌt], *conj.* aber, jedoch; sondern. — *adv.* nur, bloß; — *yesterday,* erst gestern. — *prep.* außer; *all — two,* alle außer zwei.

butcher ['butʃə], *s.* der Metzger, Fleischer; —'s *knife,* das Fleischmesser.

butchery ['butʃəri], *s.* die Schlächterei; das Blutbad, das Gemetzel.

butler ['bʌtlə], *s.* der oberste Diener; Kellermeister.

butt [bʌt], *s.* das dicke Ende; der Kolben (*rifle*); der Stoß (*blow*); die Zielscheibe (*target*). — *v.a.* stoßen, spießen.

butter ['bʌtə], *s.* die Butter. — *v.a.* mit Butter bestreichen; — *up,* schmeicheln (*Dat.*).

butterfly ['bʌtəflai], *s.* (*Ent.*) der Schmetterling.

buttery ['bʌtəri], *s.* die Speisekammer.

buttock(s) ['bʌtək(s)], *s.* der Hintere, das Gesäß (*usually pl.*) (*vulg.*).
button [bʌtn], *s.* der Knopf. — *v.a.* — up, knöpfen, zumachen.
buttress ['bʌtris], *s.* der Strebepfeiler.
buxom ['bʌksəm], *adj.* drall, gesund.
buy [bai], *v.a. irr.* kaufen.
buzz [bʌz], *s.* das Summen. — *v.n.* summen.
buzzard ['bʌzəd], *s.* (*Orn.*) der Bussard.
by [bai], *prep.* (*beside*) neben, an; (*near*) nahe; (*before*) gegen, um, bei; (*about*) bei; (*from, with*) durch, von, mit; — *the way*, nebenbei bemerkt; — *way of*, mittels. — *adv.* (*nearby*) nahe; nebenan.
by-election ['baiilekʃən], *s.* die Nachwahl; Ersatzwahl.
bygone ['baigɔn], *adj.* vergangen.
bylaw, byelaw ['bailɔ:], *s.* die Bestimmung.
Byzantine [bai'zæntain], *adj.* byzantinisch.

C

C [si:]. das C (*also Mus.*).
cab [kæb], *s.* (*horse-drawn*) die Droschke, der Wagen; das Taxi; —*stand*, der Droschkenhalteplatz; (*Motor.*) der Taxiplatz, Taxistand.
cabaret ['kæbərei], *s.* das Kabarett, die Kleinbühne.
cabbage ['kæbidʒ], *s.* (*Bot.*) der Kohl.
cabin ['kæbin], *s.* die Kabine (*boat*); die Hütte (*hut*); — *-boy*, der Schiffsjunge.
cabinet ['kæbinet], *s.* das Kabinett (*government*); der Schrank (*cupboard*); das kleine Zimmer *or* Nebenzimmer (*mainly Austr.*); (*Rad.*) das Gehäuse; — *maker*, der Kunsttischler.
cable [keibl], *s.* das Kabel (*of metal*), das Seil (*metal or rope*); das Telegramm. — *v.a.* kabeln, telegraphieren.
cablegram ['keiblgræm], *s.* die (Kabel-) Depesche.
cabman ['kæbmən], *s.* der Taxichauffeur.
caboose [kə'bu:s], *s.* die Schiffsküche.
cabriolet [kæbrio'lei], *s.* das Kabriolett.
cackle [kækl], *v.n.* gackern (*hens*); schnattern (*geese*); (*fig.*) schwatzen.
cacophony [kæ'kɔfəni], *s.* der Mißklang.
cad [kæd], *s.* der gemeine Kerl, Schuft.
cadaverous [kə'dævərəs], *adj.* leichenhaft.
caddie ['kædi], *s.* der Golfjunge.
caddy ['kædi], *s. tea* —, die Teebüchse, Teedose.
cadence ['keidəns], *s.* (*Phonet.*) der Tonfall; (*Mus.*) die Kadenz.
cadet [kə'det], *s.* (*Mil.*) der Kadett.
cadge [kædʒ], *v.a.* erbetteln.

Caesar ['si:zə]. Cäsar, *m.*
Caesarean [si'zɛəriən], *adj.* cäsarisch; — *operation* or *section*, (*Med.*) der Kaiserschnitt.
cafeteria [kæfə'tiəriə], *s.* das Selbstbedienungsrestaurant.
cage [keidʒ], *s.* (*Zool.*) der Käfig; (*Orn.*) das Vogelbauer. — *v.a.* einfangen, einsperren.
cagey ['keidʒi], *adj.* (*coll.*) argwöhnisch, zurückhaltend; schlau.
cairn [kɛən], *s.* (*Archaeol.*) der Steinhaufen, der Grabhügel.
caitiff ['keitif], *adj.* niederträchtig. — *s.* der Schuft.
cajole [kə'dʒoul], *v.a.* schmeicheln (*Dat.*).
cake [keik], *s.* der Kuchen; — *of soap*, das Stück Seife; *have o.'s — and eat it*, alles haben. — *v.a., v.n.* zusammenbacken; *—d with dirt*, mit Schmutz beschmiert.
calamity [kə'læmiti], *s.* das Unheil, Unglück; Elend.
calcareous [kæl'kɛəriəs], *adj.* (*Geol.*) kalkartig.
calculate ['kælkjuleit], *v.a.* berechnen.
calculation [kælkju'leiʃən], *s.* die Berechnung.
calendar ['kæləndə], *s.* der Kalender.
calf [kɑ:f], *s.* (*Zool.*) das Kalb; (*Anat.*) die Wade; — *love*, die Jugendliebe.
calibre ['kælibə], *s.* das Kaliber.
calico ['kælikou], *s.* der Kaliko, Kattun.
Caliph ['keilif], *s.* der Kalif.
calk (1) [kɔ:k], *v.a.* beschlagen (*horse*).
calk (2), **caulk** [kɔ:k], *v.a.* (*Naut.*) abdichten.
call [kɔ:l], *v.a., v.n.* rufen, herbeirufen; (*Am.*) antelefonieren, anrufen (*ring up*); (*name*) nennen; — *to account*, zur Rechenschaft ziehen; (*summon*) kommen lassen; — *for*, abholen; *this —s for*, das berechtigt zu. — *s.* der Ruf, Anruf; die (innere) Berufung, der Beruf.
callbox ['kɔ:lbɔks] *see* **phone box**.
calling ['kɔ:liŋ], *s.* der Beruf, das Gewerbe (*occupation*).
callous ['kæləs], *adj.* schwielig (*hands*); (*fig.*) unempfindlich, hart, gemein.
callow ['kælou], *adj.* ungefiedert (*bird*); (*fig.*) unerfahren.
calm [kɑ:m], *adj.* ruhig, still; gelassen. — *s.* die Ruhe; (*Naut.*) Windstille. — *v.a.* beruhigen. — *v.n.* — *down*, sich beruhigen, sich legen (*storm etc.*).
caloric [kæ'lɔrik], *adj.* Wärme-, warm; (*Chem.*) kalorisch.
calorie, calory ['kæləri], *s.* die Kalorie.
calumny ['kæləmni], *s.* die Verleumdung.
calve [kɑ:v], *v.n.* kalben, Kälber kriegen.
cambric ['kæmbrik], *s.* der Batist (*textile*).
camel ['kæməl], *s.* (*Zool.*) das Kamel.
cameo ['kæmiou], *s.* die Kamee.
camera ['kæmərə], *s.* (*Phot.*) die Kamera.
camomile ['kæməmail], *s.* (*Bot.*) die Kamille.

camp [kæmp], s. das Lager; Zeltlager. — v.n. sich lagern, ein Lager aufschlagen, zelten.

campaign [kæm'pein], s. der Feldzug. — v.n. einen Feldzug mitmachen; (fig.) Propaganda machen.

camphor ['kæmfə], s. der Kampfer.

camping ['kæmpiŋ], s. die Lagerausrüstung (equipment); das Lagern (activity), das Zelten.

can (1) [kæn], s. die Kanne; die Büchse; watering —, die Gießkanne. — v.a. (Am.) einmachen, einkochen (fruit).

can (2) [kæn], v. aux. irr. können, imstande sein, vermögen.

Canadian [kə'neidiən], adj. kanadisch. — s. der Kanadier.

canal [kə'næl], s. der Kanal; — lock, die Kanalschleuse.

canalize ['kænəlaiz], v.a. kanalisieren, leiten.

cancel ['kænsəl], v.a. widerrufen, absagen (show); aufheben, ungültig machen.

cancellation [kænsə'leiʃən], s. die Aufhebung, Absage, Widerrufung.

cancer ['kænsə], s. (Med., Astron.) der Krebs.

cancerous ['kænsərəs], adj. (Med.) krebsartig.

candelabra [kændi'la:brə], s. der Kandelaber, Leuchter.

candid ['kændid], adj. offen, aufrichtig.

candidate ['kændideit], s. der Kandidat, Bewerber.

candidature ['kændiditʃə], s. die Kandidatur, die Bewerbung.

candied ['kændid], adj. gezuckert, kandiert (fruit).

candle [kændl], s. die Kerze, das Licht.

Candlemas ['kændlməs], (Eccl.) Lichtmeß.

candlestick ['kændlstik], s. der Kerzenleuchter.

candlewick ['kændlwik], s. der Kerzendocht (textile).

candour ['kændə], s. die Offenheit, Aufrichtigkeit.

candy ['kændi], s. (Am.) das Zuckerwerk, (pl.) Süßigkeiten. — v.a. verzuckern.

cane [kein], s. (Bot.) das Rohr, der Rohrstock; Spazierstock. — v.a. (mit dem Stock) schlagen.

canine ['kænain], adj. Hunde-, hündisch; — tooth, der Eckzahn.

canister ['kænistə], s. die Blechbüchse, der Kanister.

canker ['kæŋkə], s. (Bot.) der Brand; (Bot.) der Pflanzenrost; (fig.) eine zerfressende Krankheit.

cannibal ['kænibəl], s. der Kannibale, Menschenfresser.

cannon ['kænən], s. die Kanone, das Geschütz.

canoe [kə'nu:], s. das Kanu.

canon ['kænən], s. (Mus., Eccl.) der Kanon; die Regel; (Eccl.) der Domherr; — law, das kanonische Recht.

canonize ['kænənaiz], v.a. (Eccl.) kanonisieren, heiligsprechen.

canopy ['kænəpi], s. der Baldachin.

cant [kænt], s. die Heuchelei.

can't, cannot [ka:nt,'kænɔt] see **can** (2).

cantankerous [kæn'tæŋkərəs], adj. zänkisch, mürrisch.

cantata [kæn'ta:tə], s. (Mus.) die Kantate.

canteen [kæn'ti:n], s. die Kantine (restaurant); die Besteckgarnitur (set of cutlery).

canter ['kæntə], s. der Galopp, der Kurzgalopp.

canticle ['kæntikl], s. (Eccl.) der Lobgesang, das Loblied.

canto ['kæntou], s. (Lit.) der Gesang.

canton ['kæntən], s. (Pol.) der Kanton, der Bezirk.

canvas ['kænvəs], s. das Segeltuch; (Art) die Malerleinwand; die Zeltplane (tent).

canvass ['kænvəs], v.a., v.n. (Pol.) um Stimmen werben.

canvasser ['kænvəsə], s. (Pol.) der Werber, Stimmensammler.

cap [kæp], s. die Kappe, Mütze; die Haube; der Deckel. — v.a. übertreffen.

capability [keipə'biliti], s. die Fähigkeit.

capable ['keipəbl], adj. fähig (Genit.), imstande (of, zu); tüchtig.

capacious [kə'peiʃəs], adj. geräumig.

capacity [kə'pæsiti], s. der Inhalt, die Geräumigkeit; die Fassungskraft (intellect); die Leistungsfähigkeit (ability); der Fassungsraum (space).

cape (1) [keip], s. (Tail.) der Kragenmantel.

cape (2) [keip], s. (Geog.) das Kap, das Vorgebirge.

caper ['keipə], s. der Sprung, Luftsprung. — v.n. in die Luft springen.

capillary [kə'piləri], adj. haarfein; — tubing, die Haarröhre, die Kapillarröhre.

capital ['kæpitl], s. (Comm.) das Kapital; die Hauptstadt (capital city); — punishment, die Todesstrafe; — letter, der Großbuchstabe. — adj. (coll.) ausgezeichnet, vorzüglich.

capitalize ['kæpitəlaiz], v.a. (Comm.) kapitalisieren; ausnutzen.

capitation [kæpi'teiʃən], s. die Kopfsteuer.

capitulate [kə'pitjuleit], v.n. kapitulieren.

capon ['keipən], s. (Zool.) der Kapaun.

caprice [kə'pri:s], s. die Kaprize, Laune.

capricious [kə'priʃəs], adj. launenhaft, eigensinnig.

Capricorn ['kæprikɔ:n], (Astron.) der Steinbock; tropic of —, der Wendekreis des Steinbocks.

capriole ['kæprioul], s. der Luftsprung.

capsize [kæp'saiz], v.n. umkippen, kentern (boat).

capstan ['kæpstən], s. (Engin.) die Ankerwinde; (Mech.) die Erdwinde; (Naut.) das Gangspill.

capsular ['kæpsjulə], adj. kapselförmig.

capsule ['kæpsju:l], s. die Kapsel.

captain ['kæptin], s. (Naut.) der Kapitän; (Mil.) der Hauptmann.

captious ['kæpʃəs], *adj.* zänkisch, streitsüchtig; verfänglich.

captivate ['kæptiveit], *v.a.* einnehmen, gewinnen.

captive ('kæptiv], *s.* der Gefangene. — *adj.* gefangen.

capture ['kæptʃə], *s.* die Gefangennahme (*men*); Erbeutung (*booty*).

Capuchin ['kæputʃin], *s.* (*Eccl.*) der Kapuziner.

car [ka:], *s.* (*Motor.*) der Wagen; das Auto; (*Am.*) der Eisenbahnwagen.

carafe [kæ'ræf], *s.* die Karaffe, Wasserflasche.

caravan [kærəvæn], *s.* die Karawane; der Wohnwagen.

caraway ['kærəwei], *s.* (*Bot.*) der Kümmel.

carbine ['ka:bain], *s.* der Karabiner.

carbolic [ka:'bɔlik], *adj.* — *acid*, (*Chem.*) die Karbolsäure.

carbon ['ka:bən], *s.* (*Chem.*) der Kohlenstoff.

carbonate ['ka:bəneit], *s.* (*Chem.*) das kohlensaure Salz, Karbonat.

carbonize ['ka:bənaiz], *v.a.* verkohlen. — *v.n.* (*Chem., Geol.*) zu Kohle werden.

carbuncle ['ka:bʌŋkl], *s.* (*Min.*) der Karfunkel; (*Med.*) der Karbunkel.

carburettor [ka:bju'retə], *s.* (*Motor.*) der Vergaser.

carcase, carcass ['ka:kəs], *s.* der Kadaver.

card (1) [ka:d], *s.* die Karte, Postkarte; *playing —*, die Spielkarte; *put your —s on the table*, rück mit der Wahrheit heraus!

card (2) [ka:d], *v.a.* krempeln (*wool*); kardätschen (*cotton*).

cardboard ['ka:dbɔ:d], *s.* die Pappe, der Pappendeckel.

cardiac ['ka:diæk], *adj.* (*Med.*) Herz–.

cardinal ['ka:dinl], *s.* (*Eccl.*) der Kardinal. — *adj.* Kardinal–, grundlegend.

cardiogram ['ka:diogræm], *s.* (*Med.*) das Kardiogramm.

cardsharper ['ka:dʃa:pə], *s.* der Falschspieler.

care [kɛə], *s.* die Sorge (*anxiety*, um, *for*); *with —*, mit Sorgfalt, genau; *care of* (*abbr. c/o on letters*), bei; *take —*, sich in acht nehmen. — *v.n. — for*, sich interessieren, gern haben.

careen [kə'ri:n], *v.a.* (*Naut.*) kielholen, umlegen.

career [kə'riə], *s.* die Karriere, Laufbahn.

careful ['kɛəful], *adj.* sorgfältig, vorsichtig, umsichtig.

carefulness ['kɛəfulnis], *s.* die Vorsicht, Sorgfalt, Umsicht.

careless ['kɛəlis], *adj.* unachtsam, nachlässig.

carelessness ['kɛəlisnis], *s.* die Nachlässigkeit, Unachtsamkeit.

caress [kə'res], *v.a.* liebkosen, herzen. — *s.* die Liebkosung, die Zärtlichkeit.

caretaker ['kɛəteikə], *s.* der Hausmeister.

careworn ['kɛəwɔ:n], *adj.* abgehärmt, von Sorgen gebeugt.

cargo ['ka:gou], *s.* die Fracht, die Ladung.

caricature [kærikə'tjuə *or* 'kærikətʃə], *s.* die Karikatur. — *v.a.* karikieren, verzerren.

Carinthian [kə'rinθjən], *adj.* kärntnerisch.

carmine ['ka:main], *s.* der Karmin.

carnage ['ka:nidʒ], *s.* das Blutbad.

carnal [ka:nl], *adj.* fleischlich, sinnlich.

carnation [ka:'neiʃən], *s.* (*Bot.*) die Nelke.

carnival ['ka:nivl], *s.* der Karneval.

carnivorous [ka:'nivərəs], *adj.* fleischfressend.

carol ['kærəl], *s. Christmas —*, das Weihnachtslied.

carotid [kə'rɔtid], *s.* (*Anat.*) die Halspulsader.

carousal [kə'rauzəl], *s.* das Gelage, das Gezeche.

carouse [kə'rauz], *v.n.* zechen, schmausen.

carp (1) [ka:p], *s.* (*Zool.*) der Karpfen.

carp (2) [ka:p], *v.n.* bekritteln, tadeln.

Carpathian Mountains [ka:'peiθjən 'mauntinz]. die Karpathen, *f. pl.*

carpenter ['ka:pəntə], *s.* der Zimmermann; Tischler.

carpentry ['ka:pəntri], *s.* die Tischlerei, das Zimmerhandwerk.

carpet ['ka:pit], *s.* der Teppich; *— bag*, die Reisetasche.

carriage ['kæridʒ], *s.* der Wagen, Waggon; das Verhalten, die Haltung (*bearing*); (*Comm.*) *— paid*, einschließlich Zustellung; *— way*, der Straßendamm.

carrier ['kæriə], *s.* der Fuhrmann, Fuhrunternehmer.

carrion ['kæriən], *s.* das Aas.

carrot ['kærət], *s.* (*Bot.*) die Mohrrübe; die Karotte.

carry ['kæri], *v.a.* tragen; bringen; führen (*on vehicle*), fahren (*convey*); *— interest*, Zinsen tragen; (*Comm.*) *— forward*, übertragen; *— two* (*in adding up*), zwei weiter; *— on*, weitermachen, fortfahren; *— through*, durchführen, durchhalten; — *v.n.* vernehmbar sein (*of sound*); *— on*, weiterarbeiten, weiterexistieren.

cart [ka:t], *s.* der Karren, Frachtwagen.

cartel [ka:'tel], *s.* (*Comm.*) das Kartell.

Carthage [ka:'θidʒ]. Karthago, *n.*

carthorse ['ka:thɔ:s], *s.* das Zugpferd.

cartilage ['ka:tilidʒ], *s.* der Knorpel.

carton ['ka:tən], *s.* (*cardboard box*) der Karton, die Schachtel.

cartoon [ka:'tu:n], *s.* die Karikatur; *— film*, der Trickfilm.

cartridge ['ka:tridʒ], *s.* die Patrone.

cartwright ['ka:trait], *s.* der Stellmacher, Wagenbauer.

carve [ka:v], *v.a.* schneiden (*cut*); schnitzen (*wood*), meißeln (*stone*), tranchieren (*meat*).

carver ['ka:və], s. der Schnitzer (*wood*); das Tranchiermesser (*carving knife*).

cascade [kæs'keid], s. der Wasserfall.

case (1) [keis], s. der Kasten, Behälter; das Futteral, Etui (*spectacles*); das Gehäuse (*watch*); die Kiste (*wooden box*); (*Typ.*) der Schriftkasten.

case (2) [keis], s. der Fall (*event*); (*Law*) der Rechtsfall, der Umstand (*circumstance*); in —, falls.

casement ['keismənt], s. der Fensterflügel, das Fenster (*frame*).

caseous ['keisjəs], adj. käsig.

cash [kæʃ], s. bares Geld; die Barzahlung; — box, die Kasse. — v.a. einlösen (*cheque*).

cashier [kæ'ʃiə], s. der Kassierer. — v.a. (*Mil.*) entlassen.

cashmere ['kæʃmiə], s. die Kaschmirwolle (*wool*).

casing ['keisiŋ], s. die Hülle; das Gehäuse (*case*); die Haut (*sausage skin*).

cask ['ka:sk], s. das Faß.

casket ['ka:skit], s. das Kästchen; (*Am.*) der Sarg.

Caspian (Sea) ['kæspiən (si:)]. das kaspische Meer.

cassock ['kæsək], s. die Soutane.

cast [ka:st], v.a. irr. werfen (*throw*). (*Metall.*) gießen; (*Theat.*) besetzen; (*plaster*) formen; — off, abwerfen; — anchor, ankern; — o.'s skin, sich häuten; — down, niederschlagen; — a vote, die Stimme abgeben. — s. der Wurf; (*Metall.*) der Guß; (*Theat.*) die Besetzung; der Abguß (plaster). — adj. — iron, das Gusseisen; — steel, der Gußstahl.

castanets [kæstə'nets], s. pl. (*Mus.*) die Kastagnetten, f. pl.

castaway ['ka:stəwei], adj. weggeworfen; (*Naut.*) schiffbrüchig.

caste [ka:st], s. die Kaste.

caster ['ka:stə], s. der Streuer, die Streubüchse; — sugar, Streuzucker.

casting ['ka:stiŋ], s. (*Metall.*) das Gießen, der Guß.

castle [ka:sl], s. die Burg, das Schloß; (*Chess*) der Turm.

castor (1) ['ka:stə], s. (*Zool.*) der Biber.

castor (2) ['ka:stə] see **caster**.

castor (3) **oil** ['ka:stər 'ɔil], s. das Rizinusöl.

castrate [kæs'treit], v.a. kastrieren.

castration [kæs'treiʃən], s. die Kastration.

casual ['kæʒjuəl], adj. zufällig, gelassen (*manner*); gelegentlich; flüchtig.

casualty ['kæʒjuəlti], s. der Unglücksfall; — ward, die Unfallstation; (*pl.*) die Verluste, m. pl.

cat [kæt], s. die Katze; tom —, der Kater; — burglar, der Fassadenkletterer; —'s eye, das Katzenauge, der Rückstrahler; der Reflektor.

cataclysm ['kætəklizm], s. die Sintflut, die Überschwemmung.

catacomb ['kætəku:m], s. die Katakombe.

catalogue ['kætələg], s. der Katalog, das Verzeichnis. — v.a. im Katalog verzeichnen, katalogisieren.

catapult ['kætəpult], s. die Schleuder (*hand*); (*Mil.*) die Wurfmaschine. — v.a. schleudern.

cataract ['kætərækt], s. der Wasserfall (*water*); (*Med.*) der Star.

catarrh [kə'ta:], s. (*Med.*) der Katarrh.

catastrophe [kə'tæstrəfi], s. die Katastrophe, das Unglück.

catastrophic [kætəs'trɔfik], adj. katastrophal, unheilvoll.

catch [kætʃ], v.a. irr. fangen, auffangen, fassen; überfallen (— unawares, ambush); — a cold, sich einen Schnupfen zuziehen, sich erkälten; erreichen (train, etc.); — redhanded, bei frischer Tat ertappen. — s. der Fang (*fish*); die Beute (*prey, booty*); der Haken (*hook*, also fig.).

catchpenny ['kætʃpeni], s. der Flitterkram, Lockartikel. — adj. marktschreierisch.

catchphrase, catchword ['kætʃfreiz, 'kætʃwɑ:d], s. das (billige) Schlagwort.

catechism ['kætikizm], s. der Katechismus.

categorical [kæti'gɔrikəl], adj. kategorisch, entschieden.

category ['kætigəri], s. die Kategorie, Klasse, Gruppe, Gattung.

cater ['keitə], v.n. Lebensmittel einkaufen; verpflegen; (*fig.*) sorgen (*for, für*).

caterer ['keitərə], s. der Lebensmittellieferant.

catering ['keitəriŋ], s. die Verpflegung.

caterpillar ['kætəpilə], s. (*Ent.*) die Raupe; (*Mech.*) der Raupenschlepper.

caterwaul ['kætəwɔ:l], v.n. miauen.

cathedral [kə'θi:drəl], s. der Dom, die Kathedrale.

Catholic ['kæθəlik], adj. katholisch. — s. der Katholik.

catholic ['kæθəlik], adj. allumfassend.

Catholicism [kə'θɔlisizm], s. der Katholizismus.

catkin ['kætkin], s. (*Bot.*) das Kätzchen; pussy-willow —, das Palmkätzchen.

cattle [kætl], s. pl. das Vieh; — plague, die Rinderpest; — show, die Viehausstellung.

caucus ['kɔ:kəs], s. die Wahlversammlung; der Wahlausschuß.

caul [kɔ:l], s. das Haarnetz; (*Anat.*) die Eihaut.

cauldron ['kɔ:ldrən], s. der Kessel.

cauliflower ['kɔliflauə], s. (*Bot.*) der Blumenkohl.

caulk [kɔ:k], v.a. kalfatern (see under calk (2)).

causal ['kɔ:zəl], adj. ursächlich.

causality [kɔ:'zæliti], s. der ursächliche Zusammenhang; (*Log.*) die Kausalität.

cause [kɔ:z], s. die Ursache. — v.a. verursachen.

causeway ['kɔ:zwei], s. der Damm.

caustic ['kɔ:stik], adj. ätzend; beißend.

cauterize [ˈkɔːtəraiz], v.a. (Med.) ätzen, ausbrennen.
caution [ˈkɔːʃən], s. die Vorsicht (care); die Warnung (warning). — v.a. (Law) ermahnen; warnen.
cautionary [ˈkɔːʃənəri], adj. warnend.
cautious [ˈkɔːʃəs], adj. vorsichtig, behutsam.
cautiousness [ˈkɔːʃəsnis], s. die Vorsicht, Behutsamkeit.
cavalcade [kævəlˈkeid], s. die Kavalkade; (Mil.) der Reiterzug.
cavalry [ˈkævəlri], s. die Kavallerie, die Reiterei.
cave [keiv], s. die Höhle. — v.a. aushöhlen. — v.n. — in, einstürzen, einfallen.
caveat [ˈkeiviæt], s. (Law) die Warnung; der Vorbehalt.
cavern [ˈkævən], s. die Höhle.
cavernous [ˈkævənəs], adj. (Geog., Geol.) voll Höhlen.
caviare [kæviˈɑː], s. der Kaviar.
cavil [ˈkævil], v.n. nörgeln (at, über), tadeln (Acc.).
cavity [ˈkæviti], s. die Höhlung.
caw [kɔː], v.n. (Orn.) krächzen.
cease [siːs], v.a. einstellen. — v.n. aufhören.
ceaseless [ˈsiːslis], adj. unaufhörlich.
cedar [ˈsiːdə], s. (Bot.) die Zeder.
cede [siːd], v.a. überlassen. — v.n. nachgeben.
ceiling [ˈsiːliŋ], s. die Decke (room); (Comm.) die Preisgrenze.
celebrate [ˈselibreit], v.a. feiern; zelebrieren.
celebrated [ˈselibreitid], adj. berühmt.
celebration [seliˈbreiʃən], s. die Feier.
celebrity [siˈlebriti], s. die Berühmtheit; der „Star".
celerity [siˈleriti], s. die Behendigkeit, Schnelligkeit.
celery [ˈseləri], s. (Bot.) der Sellerie.
celestial [siˈlestjəl], adj. himmlisch.
celibacy [ˈselibəsi], s. die Ehelosigkeit; (Eccl.) das Zölibat.
celibate [ˈselibit], adj. unverheiratet.
cell [sel], s. die Zelle.
cellar [ˈselə], s. der Keller; salt —, das Salzfaß.
cellarage [ˈseləridʒ], s. die Kellerei; die Einkellerung (storage).
cellarer [ˈselərə], s. der Kellermeister.
cellular [ˈseljulə], adj. zellartig, Zell-.
Celt [kelt, selt], s. der Kelte.
Celtic [ˈkeltik, ˈseltik], adj. keltisch.
cement [siˈment], s. der Zement, Mörtel. — v.a. auszementieren, verkitten.
cemetery [ˈsemətri], s. der Kirchhof, der Friedhof.
cenotaph [ˈsenotæf or -tɑːf], s. das Ehrengrabmal, Ehrendenkmal.
censer [ˈsensə], s. (Eccl.) das Weihrauchfaß.
censor [ˈsensə], s. der Zensor.
censorious [senˈsɔːriəs], adj. kritisch, tadelsüchtig.
censure [ˈsenʃə], s. der Tadel, Verweis. — v.a. tadeln.

census [ˈsensəs], s. die Volkszählung.
cent [sent], s. (Am.) der Cent (coin); (Comm.) per —, das Prozent.
centenarian [sentiˈnɛəriən], adj. hundertjährig. — s. der Hundertjährige.
centenary [senˈtiːnəri], s. die Hundertjahrfeier.
centennial [senˈtenjəl], adj. alle hundert Jahre, hundertjährig.
centipede [ˈsentipiːd], s. (Zool.) der Tausendfüßler.
central [ˈsentrəl], adj. zentral.
centralize [ˈsentrəlaiz], v.a. zentralisieren.
centre [ˈsentə], s. das Zentrum, der Mittelpunkt; die Mitte.
centric(al) [ˈsentrik(əl)], adj. (Engin., Maths.) zentral.
centrifugal [senˈtrifjugəl], adj. zentrifugal.
centrifuge [ˈsentrifjuːdʒ], s. die Zentrifuge.
centripetal [senˈtripitl], adj. zentripetal, zum Mittelpunkt hinstrebend.
century [ˈsentʃuri], s. das Jahrhundert.
cereal [ˈsiəriəl], adj. vom Getreide, Getreide—. — s. die Kornmehlspeise.
cerebral [ˈseribrəl], adj. Gehirn-.
ceremonial [seriˈmounjəl], adj. feierlich, förmlich (formal). — s. das Zeremoniell.
ceremonious [seriˈmounjəs], adj. feierlich, zeremoniell.
ceremony [ˈserimoni], s. die Zeremonie, die Feier.
certain [ˈsəːtin], adj. sicher, gewiß.
certainty [ˈsəːtinti], s. die Gewißheit.
certificate [səːˈtifikit], s. das Zeugnis, die Bescheinigung.
certification [səːtifiˈkeiʃən], s. die Bescheinigung, Bezeugung.
certify [ˈsəːtifai], v.a. bescheinigen, bezeugen, beglaubigen.
certitude [ˈsəːtitjuːd], s. die Gewißheit.
cerulean [siˈruːljən], adj. himmelblau.
cesspool [ˈsespuːl], s. die Senkgrube.
cessation [seˈseiʃən], s. das Aufhören; (of hostilities) der Waffenstillstand.
cession [ˈseʃən], s. die Abtretung, der Verzicht (of, auf).
chafe [tʃeif], v.a. wärmen, warmreiben; erzürnen (annoy); wundreiben (skin). — v.n. toben, wüten.
chafer [ˈtʃeifə], s. (Ent.) der Käfer.
chaff [tʃɑːf], s. die Spreu; die Neckerei (teasing). — v.a. necken.
chaffer [ˈtʃæfə], v.n. handeln, schachern (haggle).
chaffinch [ˈtʃæfintʃ], s. (Orn.) der Buchfink.
chagrin [ʃæˈgriːn], s. der Verdruß, der Ärger.
chain [tʃein], s. die Kette. — v.a. anketten.
chair [tʃɛə], s. der Stuhl; (Univ.) Lehrstuhl. — v.a. vorsitzen (Dat.).
chairman [ˈtʃɛəmən], s. der Vorsitzende.
chalice [ˈtʃælis], s. (Eccl.) der Kelch.

chalk [tʃɔːk], *s.* die Kreide. — *v.a.* — *up*, ankreiden, anschreiben.

chalky ['tʃɔːki], *adj.* (*Geol.*) kreidig, kreideartig.

challenge ['tʃælindʒ], *v.a.* herausfordern; in Frage stellen (*question*); anhalten (*of a sentry*). — *s.* die Herausforderung; das Anhalten (*by a sentry*); die Einwendung.

chalybeate [kə'libiət], *adj.* (*Med.*) eisenhaltig.

chamber ['tʃeimbə], *s.* das Zimmer, die Kammer.

chamberlain ['tʃeimbəlin], *s.* der Kammerherr.

chambermaid ['tʃeimbəmeid], *s.* das Zimmermädchen, Kammermädchen.

chameleon [kə'miːljən], *s.* (*Zool.*) das Chamäleon.

chamois ['ʃæmwaː], *s.* (*Zool.*) die Gemse.

champagne [ʃæm'pein], *s.* der Champagner, der Sekt.

champion ['tʃæmpjən], *s.* der Meister, Verteidiger. — *v.a.* vertreten (*cause*); beschützen (*person*).

chance [tʃɑːns], *s.* der Zufall; die Gelegenheit (*opportunity*); die Möglichkeit (*possibility*); *take a* —, es darauf ankommen lassen; *by* —, zufällig. — *v.a.* zufällig tun, geraten; riskieren (*risk*).

chancel ['tʃɑːnsəl], *s.* (*Eccl.*) der Chor, der Altarplatz.

chancellor ['tʃɑːnsələ], *s.* der Kanzler.

chancery ['tʃɑːnsəri], *s.* das Kanzleigericht.

chandelier [ʃændə'liə], *s.* der Armleuchter, Kronleuchter.

chandler ['tʃɑːndlə], *s.* der Lichtzieher; Krämer; (*corn merchant*) der Kornhändler.

change [tʃeindʒ], *s.* die Änderung; die Umsteigen (*trains*); *small* —, das Kleingeld (*die Veränderung*; Abwechslung. — *v.a.* ändern (*alter*); wechseln (*money*); umsteigen (*trains*); eintauschen, umtauschen (*exchange*); sich umziehen (*clothes*). — *v.n.* sich (ver)ändern, anders werden, umschlagen; (*Railw.*) — *for*, umsteigen nach.

changeable ['tʃeindʒəbl], *adj.* veränderlich.

changeling ['tʃeindʒliŋ], *s.* der Wechselbalg.

changeover ['tʃeindʒouvə], *s.* der Wechsel; der Umschalter; die Umstellung.

channel ['tʃænəl], *s.* der Kanal. — *v.a.* leiten, kanalisieren.

chant [tʃɑːnt], *v.a., v.n.* (*Eccl.*) singen. — *s.* (*Mus.*) der Kantus, der liturgische Gesang.

chaos ['keiɔs], *s.* das Chaos.

chaotic [kei'ɔtik], *adj.* chaotisch.

chap (1) [tʃæp], *s.* der Riss (*skin etc.*). — *v.n.* Risse bekommen.

chap (2) [tʃæp], *s.* (*usually in pl.*) der Kinnbacken.

chap (3) [tʃæp], *s.* (*coll.*) der Kerl, der Bursche.

chapel ['tʃæpəl], *s.* (*Eccl.*) die Kapelle.

chaperon ['ʃæpəroun], *s.* die Anstandsdame. — *v.a.* begleiten, bemuttern.

chaplain ['tʃæplin], *s.* der Kaplan.

chapter ['tʃæptə], *s.* das Kapitel.

char [tʃɑː], *v.a.* verkohlen. — *v.n.* (*coll.*) putzen, Hausarbeit verrichten (*do housework*). — *s.* (*coll.*) die Haushilfe, die Hausgehilfin, Putzfrau.

character ['kærəktə], *s.* der Charakter (*personality*); das Zeichen (*sign, symbol*); (*Maths.*) die Ziffer; das Zeugnis (*testimonial*).

characteristic [kærəktə'ristik], *adj.* charakteristisch, typisch.

characterize ['kærəktəraiz], *v.a.* charakterisieren, kennzeichnen.

charade [ʃəˈrɑːd], *s.* die Scharade, das Silbenrätsel.

charcoal ['tʃɑːkoul], *s.* die Holzkohle; — *burner*, der Köhler.

charge [tʃɑːdʒ], *v.a.* laden, aufladen (*Law*) beschuldigen; (*Mil.*) angreifen; belasten (*with a bill*); — *up to s.o.*, jemandem etwas anrechnen; verlangen (*price*). — *s.* die Ladung, der Auftrag (*order*); die Aufsicht; *to be in* —, die Aufsicht haben; (*Law*) die Beschuldigung, Anklage; das Mündel (*of a guardian*); (*pl.*) die Kosten, Spesen.

chargeable ['tʃɑːdʒəbl], *adj.* anzurechnend; steuerbar (*of objects*).

charger ['tʃɑːdʒə], *s.* das Schlachtroß.

chariness ['tʃɛərinis], *s.* die Behutsamkeit.

chariot ['tʃæriət], *s.* der Kriegswagen.

charioteer [tʃæriə'tiə], *s.* der Wagenlenker.

charitable ['tʃæritəbl], *adj.* wohltätig, mild, mildtätig.

charitableness ['tʃæritəblnis], *s.* die Wohltätigkeit, Milde.

charity ['tʃæriti], *s.* die Güte; Nächstenliebe; Mildtätigkeit (*alms*); die Barmherzigkeit (*charitableness*); der wohltätige Zweck (*cause*); *sister of* —, barmherzige Schwester.

charlatan ['ʃɑːlətən], *s.* der Scharlatan, Pfuscher.

charm [tʃɑːm], *s.* der Zauber (*magic*); der Reiz. — *v.a.* bezaubern.

chart [tʃɑːt], *s.* (*Geog.*) die Karte. — *v.a.* auf der Karte einzeichnen.

charter ['tʃɑːtə], *s.* die Urkunde; (*Naut.*) die Schiffsmiete. — *v.a.* mieten, chartern, heuern (*ship, plane*); ein Privileg geben, berrechtigen.

charwoman ['tʃɑːwumən], *s.* die Putzfrau, Reinemacherin.

chary ['tʃɛəri], *adj.* behutsam; vorsichtig (*cautious*); sparsam (*thrifty*).

chase [tʃeis], *v.a.* jagen, verfolgen. — *s.* die Jagd (*hunt*); das Gehege (*game preserve*).

chaser ['tʃeisə], *s.* der Verfolger (*pursuer*); die Schiffskanone (*gun*).

chasm [kæzm], *s.* die Kluft; der Abgrund.

chassis ['ʃæsi], *s.* (*Motor.*) das Fahrgestell.

335

chaste [tʃeist], *adj.* keusch, züchtig.

chasten [tʃeisn], *v.a.* züchtigen; reinigen.

chastize [tʃæs'taiz], *v.a.* züchtigen.

chastity ['tʃæstiti], *s.* die Keuschheit, Züchtigkeit.

chasuble ['tʃæzjubl], *s.* (*Eccl.*) das Meßgewand.

chat [tʃæt], *v.n.* plaudern. — *s.* das Geplauder.

chattel [tʃætl], *s.* (*usually in pl.*) die Habe; *goods and* —s, Hab und Gut.

chatter ['tʃætə], *v.n.* schwätzen; schnattern. — *s.* das Geschwätz (*talk*).

chatterbox ['tʃætəbɔks], *s.* die Plaudertasche.

chatty ['tʃæti], *adj.* geschwätzig.

chauffeur [ʃoufə, ʃou'fə:], *s.* (*Motor.*) der Fahrer.

chauffeuse [ʃou'fə:z], *s.* die Fahrerin.

chauvinism ['ʃouvinizm], *s.* der Chauvinismus.

cheap [tʃi:p], *adj.* billig.

cheapen ['tʃi:pən], *v.a.* herabsetzen, erniedrigen (*value*).

cheapness ['tʃi:pnis], *s.* die Billigkeit (*price*).

cheat [tʃi:t], *v.a., v.n.* betrügen. — *s.* der Betrüger.

cheating ['tʃi:tiŋ], *s.* das Betrügen; der Betrug.

check [tʃek], *s.* der Einhalt, der Halt; die Kontrolle; das Hindernis (*obstacle*); (*Chess*) Schach; (*Am.*) see **cheque**. — *v.a.* zurückhalten, aufhalten (*stop*); überprüfen. — *v.n.* Schach bieten (*Dat.*).

checker see under **chequer**.

checkmate ['tʃekmeit], *s.* das Schachmatt.

cheek [tʃi:k], *s.* die Wange, die Backe; die Unverschämtheit (*impertinence*). — *v.a.* unverschämt sein *or* handeln (*s.o.*), an jemandem.

cheeky ['tʃi:ki], *adj.* frech, unverschämt.

cheer [tʃiə], *v.a.* anfeuern, anspornen; zujubeln; — *up*, aufmuntern. — *v.n.* — *up*, Mut fassen. — *s.* der Zuruf; der Beifallsruf (*acclaim*); *three* —s, ein dreifaches Hoch (*for*, auf).

cheerful ['tʃiəful], *adj.* fröhlich, froh.

cheerless ['tʃiəlis], *adj.* unfreundlich, freudlos.

cheese [tʃi:z], *s.* der Käse; — *straw*, die Käsestange.

cheesecloth ['tʃi:zklɔθ], *s.* (*Am.*) das Nesseltuch.

cheeseparing ['tʃi:zpɛəriŋ], *adj.* knauserig.

cheesy ['tʃi:zi], *adj.* käsig;(*sl.*) schlecht aussehend.

cheetah ['tʃi:itə], *s.* (*Zool.*) der Jagdleopard.

chemical ['kemikəl], *adj.* chemisch. — *s.* die Chemikalie, das chemische Element; das chemische Produkt.

chemise [ʃi'mi:z], *s.* das Frauenhemd.

chemist ['kemist], *s.* der Chemiker; Drogist; Apotheker (*dispenser*).

chemistry ['kemistri], *s.* die Chemie.

cheque, (*Am.*) **check** [tʃek], *s.* (*Fin.*) der Scheck.

chequer, **checker** ['tʃekə], *s.* das scheckige Muster, Würfelmuster. — *v.a.* würfelig machen, bunt machen.

cherish ['tʃeriʃ], *v.a.* hegen, wertschätzen, lieben.

cherry ['tʃeri], *s.* (*Bot.*) die Kirsche; — *brandy*, das Kirschwasser.

chess [tʃes], *s.* das Schachspiel; —*man*, die Schachfigur; —*board*, das Schachbrett.

chest [tʃest], *s.* die Truhe (*box*); die Kiste; (*Anat.*) Brust; — *of drawers*, die Kommode.

chestnut ['tʃestnʌt], *s.* (*Bot.*) die Kastanie; (*horse*) der Braune. — *adj.* kastanienbraun.

chew [tʃu:], *v.a.* kauen; —*ing gum*, das Kaugummi.

chic [ʃi:k], *adj.* elegant, schick.

chicanery [ʃi'keinəri], *s.* die Schikane, Haarspalterei, Kleinlichkeit.

chicken ['tʃikin], *s.* das Huhn, Kücken; — *soup*, die Hühnersuppe.

chickenpox ['tʃikinpɔks], *s.* (*Med.*) die Windpocken.

chicory ['tʃikəri], *s.* (*Bot.*) die Zichorie.

chide [tʃaid], *v.a. irr.* schelten.

chief [tʃi:f], *s.* der Häuptling (*of tribe*); (*Am. coll.*) der Chef (*boss*). — *adj.* hauptsächlich, Haupt-, oberst.

chieftain ['tʃi:ftin], *s.* der Häuptling (*of tribe*); Anführer (*leader*).

chilblain ['tʃilblein], *s.* die Frostbeule.

child [tʃaild], *s.* das Kind.

childbirth ['tʃaildbə:θ], *s.* die Niederkunft.

childhood ['tʃaildhud], *s.* die Kindheit.

childish ['tʃaildiʃ], *adj.* kindisch.

childlike ['tʃaildlaik], *adj.* kindlich, wie ein Kind.

Chilean ['tʃiliən], *adj.* chilenisch. — *s.* der Chilene.

chill [tʃil], *s.* die Kälte, der Frost; die Erkältung. — *v.a.* kalt machen (*freeze*); erstarren lassen (*make rigid*); entmutigen (*discourage*).

chilly ['tʃili], *adj.* frostig, eisig, eiskalt.

chime [tʃaim], *s.* das Glockengeläute. — *v.n.* klingen, läuten.

chimera [ki'miərə], *s.* das Hirngespinst, das Trugbild.

chimney ['tʃimni], *s.* der Kamin, der Schornstein; —*pot*, —*stack*, der Schornstein; —*sweep*, der Kaminfeger, Schornsteinfeger.

chimpanzee [tʃimpæn'zi:], *s.* (*Zool.*) der Schimpanse.

chin [tʃin], *s.* (*Anat.*) das Kinn.

china ['tʃainə], *s.* das Porzellan; —*ware*, das Küchengeschirr.

chine (1) [tʃain], *s.* das Rückgrat.

chine (2) [tʃain], *s.* (*Geog.*) der Kamm.

Chinaman ['tʃainəmən], *s.* (*obs.*) der Chinese.

Chinese [tʃai'ni:z], *adj.* chinesisch. — *s.* der Chinese.

chink [tʃiŋk], *s.* die Ritze, der Spalt.

chip [tʃip], *v.a.* schnitzeln (*wood*); ausbrechen (*stone*); in kleine Stücke schneiden. — *v.n.* — *off*, abbröckeln; — *in*, (*coll.*) sich hineinmischen. —*s.* der Span (*wood*); der Splitter (*glass, stone*); (*pl.*) Pommes frites (*pl.*) (*potatoes*).

chiromancy [ˈkaiərɔmænsi], *s.* das Handlesen.

chiropodist [kiˈrɔpədist], *s.* der Fußpfleger.

chirp [tʃəːp], *v.n.* zwitschern (*birds*), zirpen (*crickets*).

chirping [ˈtʃəːpiŋ], *s.* das Gezwitscher (*birds*), das Gezirpe (*crickets*).

chisel [tʃizl], *s.* der Meißel. — *v.a.* meißeln.

chit [tʃit], *s.* das Stück Papier; (*coll.*) junges Ding; —*chat*, das Geplauder.

chivalrous [ˈʃivəlrəs], *adj.* ritterlich; tapfer (*brave*).

chivalry [ˈʃivəlri], *s.* die Ritterlichkeit (*courtesy*); Tapferkeit (*bravery*).

chive [tʃaiv], *s.* (*Bot.*) der Schnittlauch.

chlorate [ˈklɔːreit], *s.* (*Chem.*) das Chlorsalz.

chlorine [ˈklɔːriːn], *s.* (*Chem.*) das Chlor, Chlorgas.

chloroform [ˈklɔːrəfɔːm], *s.* das Chloroform. — *v.a.* chloroformieren.

chocolate [ˈtʃɔkəlit], *s.* die Schokolade. — *adj.* schokoladefarben.

choice [tʃɔis], *s.* die Wahl; Auswahl (*selection*). — *adj.* auserlesen.

choir [ˈkwaiə], *s.* der Chor.

choke [tʃouk], *v.a.*, *v.n.* ersticken; verstopfen (*block*). — *s.* (*Elec.*) die Drosselspule; (*Motor.*) die Starterklappe.

choler [ˈkɔlə], *s.* die Galle; (*fig.*) der Zorn (*anger*).

cholera [ˈkɔlərə], *s.* (*Med.*) die Cholera.

choleric [ˈkɔlərik], *adj.* jähzornig, cholerisch.

choose [tʃuːz], *v.a. irr.* wählen, auswählen (*select*).

choosy [ˈtʃuːzi], *adj.* wählerisch.

chop [tʃɔp], *v.a.* abhacken (*cut off*), hacken (*meat*). — *s.* das Kotelett (*meat*).

chopper [ˈtʃɔpə], *s.* das Hackbeil (*axe*); das Hackmesser (*knife*).

choppy [ˈtʃɔpi], *adj.* bewegt (*sea*), stürmisch.

chopstick [ˈtʃɔpstik], *s.* das Eßstäbchen.

choral [ˈkɔːrəl], *adj.* Chor-; — *society*, der Gesangverein.

chorale [kɔˈrɑːl], *s.* (*Eccl.*, *Mus.*) der Choral.

chord [kɔːd], *s.* die Saite; (*Geom.*) die Sehne; (*Mus.*) der Akkord.

chorister [ˈkɔristə], *s.* der Chorknabe (*boy*), Chorsänger.

chorus [ˈkɔːrəs], *s.* der Chor (*opera*); der Refrain (*song*).

Christ [kraist]. Christus, *m.*

christen [krisn], *v.a.* taufen (*baptize*); nennen (*name*).

Christendom [ˈkrisndəm], *s.* die Christenheit.

christening [ˈkrisniŋ], *s.* die Taufe.

Christian [ˈkristjən], *s.* der Christ (*believer in Christ*). — *adj.* christlich; — *name*, der Vorname.

Christianity [kristiˈæniti], *s.* die christliche Religion, das Christentum.

Christmas [ˈkrisməs], *s.* (*die*) Weihnachten; das Weihnachtsfest; — *Eve*, der heilige Abend.

chromatic [kroˈmætik], *adj.* (*Mus.*) chromatisch.

chrome [kroum], *s.* das Chrom.

chronic [ˈkrɔnik], *adj.* chronisch.

chronicle [ˈkrɔnikl], *s.* die Chronik. — *v.a.* (in einer Chronik) verzeichnen.

chronological [krɔnəˈlɔdʒikəl], *adj.* chronologisch.

chronology [krɔˈnɔlədʒi], *s.* die Chronologie.

chronometer [krɔˈnɔmitə], *s.* das Chronometer.

chrysalis [ˈkrisəlis], *s.* (*Ent.*) die Puppe.

chrysanthemum [kriˈzænθəməm], *s.* (*Bot.*) die Chrysantheme.

chub [tʃʌb], *s.* (*Zool.*) der Döbel.

chubby [ˈtʃʌbi], *adj.* pausbäckig, plump.

chuck [tʃʌk], *v.a.* (*coll.*) — *out*, hinauswerfen; — *up*, (*coll.*) glucken (*chicken*).

chuckle [tʃʌkl], *v.n.* kichern. — *s.* das Kichern.

chum [tʃʌm], *s.* (*coll.*) der Freund, Kamerad. — *v.n.* (*coll.*) — *up*, sich befreunden (*with*, mit).

chump [tʃʌmp], *s.* der Klotz (*wood*).

chunk [tʃʌnk], *s.* das große Stück (*meat etc.*).

church [tʃəːtʃ], *s.* die Kirche.

churchwarden [tʃəːtʃˈwɔːdn], *s.* der Kirchenvorsteher.

churchyard [ˈtʃəːtʃjɑːd], *s.* der Friedhof.

churl [tʃəːl], *s.* der Grobian, der grobe Kerl.

churlish [ˈtʃəːliʃ], *adj.* grob, unfein.

churn [tʃəːn], *s.* das Butterfaß. — *v.a.* mischen, schütteln (*butter etc.*); — *up*, aufwühlen (*stir up*).

chute [ʃuːt], *s.* die Gleitbahn.

cider [ˈsaidə], *s.* der Apfelmost.

cigar [siˈgɑː], *s.* die Zigarre; — *case*, das Zigarrenetui.

cigarette [sigəˈret], *s.* die Zigarette; — *holder*, die Zigarettenspitze; — *lighter*, das Feuerzeug.

cinder [ˈsində], *s.* (*usually in pl.*) die Asche (*fire*); die Schlacke (*furnace*).

Cinderella [sindəˈrelə]. das Aschenbrödel, Aschenputtel.

cinema [ˈsinimə], *s.* das Kino.

cinematography [siniməˈtɔgrəfi], *s.* die Filmkunst.

Cingalese *see* **Singhalese.**

cinnamon [ˈsinəmən], *s.* der Zimt.

cipher [ˈsaifə], *s.* die Ziffer; die Geheimschrift (*code*). — *v.n.* rechnen. — *v.a.* chiffrieren (*code*).

Circassian [səːˈkæsiən], *adj.* tscherkessisch. — *s.* der Tscherkesse.

337

circle

circle [ˈsəːkl], *s.* der Zirkel, Kreis; (*social*) Gesellschaftskreis; (*Theat.*) der Rang. — *v.a.* umringen. — *v.n.* umkreisen; sich drehen (*revolve*).

circuit [ˈsəːkit], *s.* der Kreislauf; (*Elec.*) der Stromkreis.

circuitous [səːˈkjuːitəs], *adj.* weitschweifig, weitläufig.

circular [ˈsəːkjulə], *adj.* rund, kreisförmig, Rund-; — *tour*, die Rundreise. — *s.* das Rundschreiben (*letter*); der Werbebrief (*advertising*).

circulate [ˈsəːkjuleit], *v.a.* in Umlauf setzen. — *v.n.* umlaufen, kreisen, zirkulieren.

circulation [səːkjuˈleiʃən], *s.* die Zirkulation, der Kreislauf (*blood*); die Verbreitung, Auflage (*newspaper*); der Umlauf (*banknotes*).

circumcise [ˈsəːkəmsaiz], *v.a.* beschneiden.

circumference [səːˈkʌmfərəns], *s.* der Umfang.

circumscribe [ˈsəːkəmskraib], *v.a.* beschränken, einengen (*narrow down*); umschreiben (*paraphrase*).

circumspect [ˈsəːkəmspekt], *adj.* umsichtig, vorsorglich.

circumspection [səːkəmˈspekʃən], *s.* die Umsicht, Vorsicht.

circumstance [ˈsəːkəmstæns, -stɑːns], *s.* der Umstand; *pomp and* —, großer Aufmarsch.

circumstantial [səːkəmˈstænʃəl], *adj.* umständlich; zu einem Umstand gehörig; eingehend; — *evidence*, der Indizienbeweis.

circumvent [səːkəmˈvent], *v.a.* überlisten, hintergehen.

circus [ˈsəːkəs], *s.* der Zirkus; der Platz.

cirrhus [ˈsirəs], *s.* die Federwolke.

Cistercian [sisˈtəːʃən], *s.* der Zisterzienser (*monk*).

cistern [ˈsistən], *s.* die Zisterne, der Wasserbehälter.

citadel [ˈsitədəl], *s.* die Zitadelle, die Burg.

citation [saiˈteiʃən], *s.* das Zitat; (*Law*) die Zitierung, Vorladung; (*Mil.*) die rühmliche Erwähnung.

cite [sait], *v.a.* zitieren (*quote*); (*Law*) vorladen.

citizen [ˈsitizən], *s.* der Bürger, Staatsbürger (*national*); *fellow* —, der Mitbürger.

citizenship [ˈsitizənʃip], *s.* das Bürgerrecht, die Staatsangehörigkeit.

citrate [ˈsitreit], *s.* (*Chem.*) das Zitrat.

citric [ˈsitrik], *adj.* (*Chem.*) Zitronen-.

citron [ˈsitrən], *s.* die Zitrone. — *adj.* zitronenfarben.

city [ˈsiti], *s.* die Stadt; die Großstadt; die City. — *adj.* städtisch.

civic [ˈsivik], *adj.* Stadt-, städtisch (*ceremonial*); bürgerlich.

civil [ˈsivil], *adj.* zivil; höflich (*polite*); — *engineer*, der Zivilingenieur; — *service*, der Beamtendienst, die Beamtenlaufbahn, der Staatsdienst; — *war*, der Bürgerkrieg.

civilian [siˈviljən], *s.* der Zivilist.

civility [siˈviliti], *s.* die Höflichkeit.

civilization [sivilaiˈzeiʃən], *s.* die Zivilisation.

civilize [ˈsivilaiz], *v.a.* zivilisieren, verfeinern (*refine*).

clack [klæk], *v.n.* klappern (*wood etc.*); plaudern, plappern.

clad [klæd], *adj.* gekleidet.

claim [kleim], *v.a.* Anspruch erheben (*to, auf*); fordern (*demand*); behaupten (*assert*). — *s.* der Anspruch; die Forderung (*demand*); das Recht.

claimant [ˈkleimənt], *s.* der Beanspruchende, Ansprucherheber.

clairvoyance [klɛəˈvɔiəns], *s.* das Hellsehen.

clairvoyant [klɛəˈvɔiənt], *s.* der Hellseher.

clam [klæm], *s.* (*Zool.*) die Venusmuschel; *shut up like a* —, verschwiegen sein.

clamber [ˈklæmbə], *v.n.* klettern.

clamminess [ˈklæminis], *s.* die Feuchtigkeit, Klebrigkeit.

clammy [ˈklæmi], *adj.* feucht, klebrig.

clamorous [ˈklæmərəs], *adj.* lärmend, laut, ungestüm.

clamour [ˈklæmə], *s.* das Geschrei, der Lärm. — *v.n.* laut schreien (*for, nach, Dat.*).

clamp [klæmp], *s.* die Klammer, die Klampe. — *v.a.* festklammern.

clan [klæn], *s.* die Sippe, die Familie.

clandestine [klænˈdestin], *adj.* heimlich, verstohlen.

clang [klæŋ], *s.* der Schall, das Geklirr. — *v.n.* erschallen. — *v.a.* erschallen lassen.

clangour [ˈklæŋə], *s.* das Getöse, der Lärm.

clank [klæŋk], *s.* das Geklirre, das Gerassel (*metal*).

clannish [ˈklæniʃ], *adj.* stammesbewußt; engherzig (*narrow*).

clap [klæp], *v.a.* schlagen, zusammenschlagen (*hands*). — *v.n.* Beifall klatschen (*Dat.*).

clapperboard [ˈklæpəbɔːd], *s.* (*Film*) das Klappbrett, die Klapptafel; der Klöppel (*beater, in lacemaking*).

claptrap [ˈklæptræp], *s.* der billige Effekt, das eitle Geschwätz (*gossip*).

claret [ˈklærit], *s.* der Rotwein.

clarification [klærifiˈkeiʃən], *s.* die Klarstellung, Aufklärung.

clarify [ˈklærifai], *v.a.* klarstellen.

clari(o)net [klæri(ə)ˈnet], *s.* (*Mus.*) die Klarinette.

clarion [ˈklæriən], *s.* (*Mus.*) die Zinke, Trompete; — *call*, der laute Ruf.

clash [klæʃ], *v.a.* zusammenschlagen. — *v.n.* aufeinanderprallen, zusammenfallen (*dates*); widerstreiten (*views*). — *s.* (*fig.*) der Zusammenstoß, der Widerstreit.

clasp [klɑːsp], *v.a.* ergreifen, festhalten. — *s.* der Haken (*hook*); die Schnalle, die Spange (*buckle, brooch*); — *knife*, das Taschenmesser.

class [klɑːs], *s.* die Klasse.
classic(al) ['klæsik(əl)], *adj.* klassisch.
classics ['klæsiks], *s. pl.* die Klassiker, *m. pl.*; die klassische Philologie (*subject of study*).
classification [klæsifi'keiʃən], *s.* die Klassifizierung.
classify ['klæsifai], *v.a.* klassifizieren.
clatter ['klætə], *s.* das Getöse, Geklirr. — *v.a., v.n.* klappern, klirren.
Claus [klɔːz]. Claus, Nicholas, *m.*; *Santa* —, der heilige Nikolaus, Knecht Ruprecht, Weihnachtsmann.
clause [klɔːz], *s.* (*Gram.*) der Nebensatz; die Klausel (*contract*); (*Law*) der Vertragspunkt.
claw [klɔː], *s.* die Klaue, die Kralle. — *v.a.* kratzen.
clay [klei], *s.* der Ton, Lehm.
clayey [kleii], *adj.* lehmig, tonig.
clean [kliːn], *adj.* rein, reinlich (*habits*); sauber; — *shaven*, glattrasiert. — *v.a.* reinigen, putzen.
cleaner ['kliːnə], *s.* die Reinemacherin, die Putzfrau.
cleanliness ['klenlinis], *s.* die Reinlichkeit, Sauberkeit.
cleanse [klenz], *v.a.* reinigen.
clear [kliə], *adj.* klar, hell; deutlich (*meaning*); schuldlos (*not guilty*). — *s. in the* —, nicht betroffen, schuldlos. — *v.a.* (*Chem.*) klären; (*Law*) für unschuldig erklären; verzollen (*pass through customs*); springen (über, *Acc.*). — *v.n.* (— *up*), sich aufklären, aufhellen (*weather*).
clearance ['kliərəns], *s.* die Räumung; — *sale*, der Ausverkauf; die Verzollung (*customs*).
clearing ['kliəriŋ], *s.* die Lichtung (*in wood*); (*Comm.*) die Verrechnung.
clearness ['kliənis], *s.* die Deutlichkeit, die Klarheit, Helle.
cleave [kliːv], *v.a. irr.* spalten (*wood*). — *v.n.* sich spalten.
cleaver ['kliːvə], *s.* das Hackmesser.
cleek [kliːk], *s.* der Golfschläger.
clef [klef], *s.* (*Mus.*) der Schlüssel.
cleft [kleft], *s.* der Spalt. — *adj.* —*palate*, die Gaumenspalte.
clemency ['klemənsi], *s.* die Milde, Gnade (*mercy*).
clement ['klemənt], *adj.* mild (*climate*); gnädig (*merciful*).
clench [klentʃ], *v.a.* zusammenpressen; ballen (*fist*).
clergy ['kləːdʒi], *s.* (*Eccl.*) die Geistlichkeit.
clergyman ['kləːdʒimən], *s.* (*Eccl.*) der Geistliche.
clerical ['klerikl], *adj.* (*Eccl.*) geistlich, beamtlich, Beamten-, Büro- (*office*); — *work*, die Büroarbeit.
clerk [klɑːk], *s.* der Schreiber, der Bürogehilfe (*junior*), der Bürobeamte, Büroangestellte (*senior*); *bank* —, der Bankbeamte.
clever ['klevə], *adj.* klug; intelligent; geschickt (*deft*); gewandt, listig (*cunning*).

cleverness ['klevənis], *s.* die Klugheit (*intelligence*); die Schlauheit (*cunning*); die Begabung (*talent*); die Geschicklichkeit (*skill*).
clew [kluː] *see* **clue**.
click [klik], *v.a., v.n.* einschnappen (*lock*); zusammenschlagen (*o.'s heels*, die Hacken); schnalzen (*o.'s tongue*); (*sl.*) zusammenpassen (*of two people*). — *s.* das Einschnappen (*lock*); das Zusammenschlagen (*heels*); das Schnalzen (*tongue*).
client ['klaiənt], *s.* (*Law*) der Klient; (*Comm.*) der Kunde.
clientele [kliːən'tel], *s.* die Klientel, die Kundschaft.
cliff [klif], *s.* die Klippe.
climate ['klaimit], *s.* das Klima.
climatic [klai'mætik], *adj.* klimatisch.
climax ['klaimæks], *s.* der Höhepunkt.
climb [klaim], *v.a.* erklettern, erklimmen. — *v.n.* klettern, bergsteigen; (*Aviat.*) steigen. — *s.* der Aufstieg, die Ersteigung.
climber ['klaimə], *s.* der Bergsteiger (*mountaineer*); (*Bot.*) die Schlingpflanze.
clinch [klintʃ], *v.a.* vernieten, befestigen; — *a deal*, einen Handel abschließen. — *s.* der feste Griff; die Umklammerung (*boxing*).
cling [kliŋ], *v.n. irr.* sich anklammern, festhalten (*to*, an).
clinic ['klinik], *s.* die Klinik.
clinical ['klinikl], *adj.* klinisch.
clink [kliŋk], *s.* das Geklirre; (*coll.*) das Gefängnis. — *v.a.* — *glasses*, mit den Gläsern anstoßen.
clinker ['kliŋkə], *s.* der Backstein; die Schlacke.
clip (1) [klip], *v.a.* stutzen, beschneiden; lochen (*ticket*).
clip (2) [klip], *v.a.* befestigen. — *s. paper* —, die Büroklammer.
clippings ['klipinz], *s. pl.* die Abschnitte; die Schnitzel (*waste*); Zeitungsausschnitte, *m. pl.*
cloak [klouk], *s.* der Mantel, der Deckmantel (*cover*). — *v.a.* verbergen.
cloakroom ['kloukruːm], *s.* die Garderobe; — *free*, keine Garderobegebühr; (*Railw.*) die Gepäckaufbewahrung.
clock [klɔk], *s.* die (große) Uhr, Wanduhr; — *face*, das Zifferblatt. — *v.n.* — *in*, die Zeitkarte (Kontrollkarte) stempeln lassen, eintreffen (*arrive*).
clockwise ['klɔkwaiz], *adv.* im Uhrzeigersinne.
clod [klɔd], *s.* die Erdscholle, der Erdklumpen; (*sl.*) der Lümmel (*lout*).
clog [klɔg], *v.a.* belasten, hemmen, verstopfen. — *v.n.* sich verstopfen. — *s.* der Holzschuh.
cloisters ['klɔistəz], *s. pl.* (*Eccl., Archit.*) der Kreuzgang.

close

close [klouz], *v.a.* schließen, verschließen; beenden (*meeting etc.*). — *v.n.* — *in on*, über einen hereinbrechen, umzingeln. — *s.* das Ende, der Schluß; [klous] der Domplatz. — [klous], *adj.* nahe (*near*); knapp (*narrow*); nahestehend, vertraut (*friend*); schwül (*weather*); geizig (*miserly*).

closeness ['klousnis], *s.* die Nähe (*nearness*); die Schwüle (*weather*); die Vertrautheit (*familiarity*).

closet ['klɔzit], *s.* der Wandschrank (*cupboard*); das kleine Zimmer; das Klosett (*W.C.*). — *v.r.* — *o.s. with*, sich mit jemandem zurückziehen, sich vertraulich beraten.

closure ['klouʒə], *s.* der Schluß; der Abschluß (einer Debatte).

clot [klɔt], *s.* das Klümpchen. — *v.n.* sich verdicken, gerinnen; —*ted cream*, dicke Sahne.

cloth [klɔθ], *s.* das Tuch; der Stoff; die Leinwand (*bookbinding*); *American* —, das Wachstuch; — *printing*, der Zeugdruck.

clothe [klouð], *v.a.* kleiden. — *v.r.* sich kleiden.

clothes [klouðz], *s. pl.* die Kleider, *n. pl.*; die Kleidung; die Wäsche (*washing*); — *basket*, der Wäschekorb; — *press*, der Kleiderschrank.

clothier ['klouðiə], *s.* der Tuchmacher (*manufacturer*); der Tuchhändler (*dealer*).

clothing ['klouðiŋ], *s.* die Kleidung.

cloud [klaud], *s.* die Wolke; *under a* —, in Ungnade; —*burst*, der Wolkenbruch. — *v.a.* bewölken, verdunkeln. — *v.n.* — *over*, sich umwölken.

cloudiness ['klaudinis], *s.* die Umwölkung, der Wolkenhimmel.

cloudy ['klaudi], *adj.* wolkig, bewölkt, umwölkt.

clout [klaut], *s.* (*obs.*) der Lappen (*rag*); (*coll.*) der Schlag (*hit*). — *v.a.* schlagen (*hit*).

clove [klouv], *s.* die Gewürznelke (*spice*).

clove(n) ['klouv(n)], *adj.* gespalten.

clover ['klouvə], *s.* (*Bot.*) der Klee; *to be in* —, Glück haben, es gut haben.

clown [klaun], *s.* der Hanswurst. — *v.n.* den Hanswurst spielen.

clownish ['klauniʃ], *adj.* tölpelhaft.

clownishness ['klauniʃnis], *s.* die Derbheit, Tölpelhaftigkeit.

cloy [klɔi], *v.n.* übersättigen, anwidern, anekeln.

club (1) [klʌb], *s.* die Keule (*stick*). — *v.a.* (einen) mit einer Keule schlagen.

club (2) [klʌb], *s.* der Klub, der Verein. — *v.n.* — *together*, zusammen beitragen, zusammensteuern (*contribute jointly*).

club (3) [klʌb], *s.* (*cards*) das Treff, die Eichel (*German cards*).

clubfoot ['klʌbfut], *s.* der Klumpfuß.

cluck [klʌk], *v.n.* glucken (*hen*).

clue [klu:], *s.* der Anhaltspunkt, Leitfaden, die Richtlinie, die Angabe (*crossword*); *no* —, keine blasse Ahnung.

clump [klʌmp], *s.* der Klumpen; die Gruppe.

clumsiness ['klʌmzinis], *s.* die Unbeholfenheit, Ungeschicklichkeit.

clumsy ['klʌmzi], *adj.* unbeholfen, schwerfällig, ungeschickt.

Cluniac ['klu:njæk]. (*Eccl.*) der Kluniazenser.

cluster ['klʌstə], *s.* die Traube (*grapes*), der Büschel. — *v.n.* in Büschen wachsen *or* stehen, dicht gruppiert sein.

clutch [klʌtʃ], *v.a.* ergreifen, packen (*grip*). — *s.* der Griff; (*Motor.*) die Kupplung.

coach [koutʃ], *s.* die Kutsche; der Wagen, der Autobus; der Privatlehrer (*teacher*). — *v.a.* unterrichten, vorbereiten (*for examinations etc.*).

coachman ['koutʃmən], *s.* der Kutscher.

coagulate [kou'ægjuleit], *v.a.* gerinnen lassen. — *v.n.* gerinnen.

coagulation [kouægju'leiʃən], *s.* das Gerinnen.

coal [koul], *s.* die Kohle; — *mine*, das Kohlenbergwerk; die Kohlengrube; — *miner*, der Bergmann.

coalesce [kouə'les], *v.n.* zusammenwachsen, sich vereinigen.

coalescence [kouə'lesəns], *s.* die Verschmelzung.

coalition [kouə'liʃən], *s.* (*Pol.*) die Koalition, das Bündnis.

coarse [kɔ:s], *adj.* grob; gemein (*manner*).

coarseness ['kɔ:snis], *s.* die Grobheit, Unfeinheit.

coast [koust], *s.* die Küste. — *v.n.* (an der Küste) entlangfahren; gleiten, rodeln.

coat [kout], *s.* der Mantel, Rock; die Jacke (*jacket*); das Fell (*animal*); — *of arms*, das Wappenschild; — *of mail*, das Panzerhemd; — *of paint*, der Anstrich. — *v.a.* überziehen, bemalen (*paint*).

coathanger ['kouthæŋə], *s.* der Kleiderbügel.

coating ['koutiŋ], *s.* der Überzug.

coax [kouks], *v.a.* beschwatzen; überreden (*persuade*).

cob (1) [kɔb], *s.* der Gaul.

cob (2) [kɔb], *s.* (*Orn.*) der Schwan.

cob (3) [kɔb], *s.* der (Mais)Kolben (*corn on the* —).

cobble [kɔbl], *v.a.* flicken (*shoes*).

cobbled ['kɔbld], *adj.* mit Kopfsteinen gepflastert.

cobbler ['kɔblə], *s.* der Schuhflicker.

cobble(stone) ['kɔbl(stoun)], *s.* das Kopfsteinpflaster.

cobweb ['kɔbweb], *s.* das Spinngewebe.

cock [kɔk], *s.* (*Orn.*) der Hahn; (*Engin.*) der Sperrhahn, Hahn; — *sparrow*, das Sperlingsmännchen; — *-a-doodle-doo*! kikeriki!

cockade [kɔ'keid], *s.* die Kokarde.

cockatoo [kɔkə'tu:], *s.* (*Orn.*) der Kakadu.

cockchafer [ˈkɔktʃeifə], *s.* (*Ent.*) der Maikäfer.
cockerel [ˈkɔkərəl], *s.* (*Orn.*) der junge Hahn.
cockswain [kɔksn] *see* **coxswain.**
cockle [kɔkl], *s.* (*Zool.*) die Herzmuschel.
cockney [ˈkɔkni], *s.* der geborene Londoner.
cockpit [ˈkɔkpit], *s.* (*Aviat.*) der Pilotensitz, die Kanzel, der Führerraum.
cockroach [ˈkɔkroutʃ], *s.* (*Ent.*) die Schabe.
cocksure [ˈkɔkʃuə], *adj.* zuversichtlich, allzu sicher.
cocoa [ˈkoukou], *s.* der Kakao.
coconut [ˈkoukounʌt], *s.* die Kokosnuß.
cocoon [kəˈku:n], *s.* der Kokon, die Puppe (*of silkworm*).
cod [kɔd], *s.* der Kabeljau, Dorsch; — *liver oil*, der Lebertran; *dried* —, der Stockfisch.
coddle [kɔdl], *v.a.* verhätscheln, verweichlichen.
code [koud], *s.* das Gesetzbuch, der Kodex; die Chiffre (*cipher*). — *v.a.* chiffrieren, schlüsseln.
codify [ˈkoudifai], *v.a.* kodifizieren.
coerce [kouˈə:s], *v.a.* zwingen.
coercion [kouˈə:ʃən], *s.* der Zwang.
coercive [kouˈə:siv], *adj.* zwingend.
coeval [kouˈi:vəl], *adj.* gleichaltrig, gleichzeitig.
coexist [kouigˈzist], *v.n.* zugleich existieren, nebeneinander leben.
coffee [ˈkɔfi], *s.* der Kaffee; — *grinder*, die Kaffeemühle; — *grounds*, der Kaffeesatz; — *pot*, die Kaffeekanne; — *set*, das Kaffee service.
coffer [ˈkɔfə], *s.* der Kasten, die Truhe.
coffin [ˈkɔfin], *s.* der Sarg.
cog [kɔg], *s.* der Zahn (*on wheel*); — *wheel*, das Zahnrad.
cogency [ˈkoudʒənsi], *s.* die zwingende Kraft, Triftigkeit.
cogent [ˈkoudʒənt], *adj.* zwingend, triftig.
cogitate [ˈkɔdʒiteit], *v.n.* nachdenken.
cogitation [kɔdʒiˈteiʃən], *s.* die Überlegung, das Nachdenken.
cognate [ˈkɔgneit], *adj.* verwandt.
cognisance [ˈkɔgnizəns], *s.* die Erkenntnis; die Kenntnisnahme; (*Law*) die gerichtliche Kenntnisnahme.
cognisant [ˈkɔgnizənt], *adj.* wissend, in vollem Wissen (*of, Genit.*).
cognition [kɔgˈniʃən], *s.* die Kenntnis, das Erkennen.
cohabit [kouˈhæbit], *v.n.* zusammenleben.
cohabitation [kouhæbiˈteiʃən], *s.* das Zusammenleben.
coheir [kouˈɛə], *s.* der Miterbe.
cohere [kouˈhiə], *v.n.* zusammenhängen.
coherence [kouˈhiərəns], *s.* der Zusammenhang.
coherent [kouˈhiərənt], *adj.* zusammenhängend.

cohesion [kouˈhi:ʒən], *s.* (*Phys.*) die Kohäsion.
coiffure [kwæˈfjuə], *s.* die Frisur, die Haartracht.
coil [kɔil], *s.* (*Elec.*) die Spule; die Windung. — *v.a.* aufwickeln; umwickeln, (auf)spulen. — *v.n.* sich winden.
coin [kɔin], *s.* die Münze, das Geldstück. — *v.a.* münzen, prägen; — *a phrase*, eine Redewendung prägen.
coinage [ˈkɔinidʒ], *s.* die Prägung.
coincide [kouinˈsaid], *v.n.* zusammenfallen, zusammentreffen.
coincidence [kouˈinsidəns], *s.* das Zusammenfallen, Zusammentreffen; der Zufall (*chance*).
coincident [kouˈinsidənt], *adj.* zusammentreffend.
coke [kouk], *s.* der Koks. — *v.a.* (*Chem.*, *Engin.*) verkoken.
cold [kould], *adj.* kalt; gefühllos, kühl. — *s.* die Kälte (*temperature*); die Erkältung (*indisposition*).
coldish [ˈkouldiʃ], *adj.* kühl.
coldness [ˈkouldnis], *s.* die Kälte (*temperature*); die Kaltherzigkeit (*heartlessness*).
colic [ˈkɔlik], *s.* die Kolik.
collaborate [kəˈlæbəreit], *v.n.* zusammenarbeiten.
collaboration [kəlæbəˈreiʃən], *s.* die Zusammenarbeit; die Mitwirkung, Mitarbeit (*assistance*).
collaborator [kəˈlæbəreitə], *s.* der Mitarbeiter.
collapse [kəˈlæps], *s.* der Zusammenbruch. — *v.n.* zusammenbrechen (*disintegrate*); zerfallen, einstürzen.
collapsible [kəˈlæpsibl], *adj.* zerlegbar, zusammenlegbar, zusammenklappbar.
collar [ˈkɔlə], *s.* der Kragen; —*bone*, das Schlüsselbein (*Anat.*); *dog* —, das Halsband; (*coll.*) der Priesterkragen; —*stud*, der Kragenknopf. — *v.a.* beim Kragen fassen, ergreifen.
collate [kɔˈleit], *v.a.* vergleichen (*texts etc.*).
collateral [kɔˈlætərəl], *adj.* Seiten-, von beiden Seiten. — *s.* (*Am.*) die Garantie, Bürgschaft.
collation [kɔˈleiʃən], *s.* die Vergleichung, der Vergleich (*texts etc.*); der Imbiß.
colleague [ˈkɔli:g], *s.* der Kollege, die Kollegin.
collect [kəˈlekt], *v.a.* sammeln, zusammenbringen; — *v.n.* sich versammeln. — [ˈkɔlikt], *s.* (*Eccl.*) die Kollekte.
collection [kəˈlekʃən], *s.* die Sammlung.
collective [kəˈlektiv], *adj.* kollektiv, gemeinsam. — *s.* (*Pol.*) das Kollektiv.
collector [kəˈlektə], *s.* der Sammler.
college [ˈkɔlidʒ], *s.* das Kollegium; das College; die Hochschule, Universität.
collide [kəˈlaid], *v.n.* zusammenstoßen.
collie [ˈkɔli], *s.* der Schäferhund.
collier [ˈkɔliə], *s.* der Kohlenarbeiter; das Kohlenfrachtschiff (*boat*).

341

collision [kə'liʒən], s. der Zusammenstoß, Zusammenprall.
collocate ['kɔləkeit], v.a. ordnen.
collodion [kə'loudjən], s. (Chem.) das Kollodium.
colloquial [kə'loukwiəl], adj. umgangssprachlich, Umgangs-.
colloquy ['kɔləkwi], s. die Unterredung, das Gespräch (formal).
collusion [kə'lu:ʒən], s. das heimliche Einverständnis, die unstatthafte Partnerschaft; die Verdunkelung.
collusive [kə'lu:ziv], adj. abgekartet.
Cologne [kə'loun]. Köln, n.; eau de —, Kölnisch Wasser.
Colombian [kə'lɔmbjən], adj. kolumbisch. — s. der Kolumbier.
colon (1) ['koulən], s. das Kolon, der Doppelpunkt.
colon (2) ['koulən], s. (Med.) der Dickdarm.
colonel [kə:nl], s. (Mil.) der Oberst; — -in-chief, der Generaloberst, der oberste Befehlshaber; lieutenant- —, der Oberstleutnant.
colonial [kə'lounjəl], adj. kolonial, aus den Kolonien.
colonist ['kɔlənist], s. der Siedler; Ansiedler.
colonization [kɔlənai'zeiʃən], s. die Kolonisierung, Besiedelung.
colonize ['kɔlənaiz], v.a. besiedeln, kolonisieren.
colonnade [kɔlə'neid], s. die Kolonnade, der Säulengang.
colony ['kɔləni], s. die Kolonie.
colophony ['kɔ'lɔfəni], s. das Kolophonium (resin).
coloration [kʌlə'reiʃən], s. die Färbung, Tönung.
colossal [kə'lɔsəl], adj. kolossal, riesig, riesenhaft.
colour ['kʌlə], s. die Farbe; (complexion) die Gesichtsfarbe; (paint) die Farbe, der Anstrich; (dye) die Färbung. — v.a. färben; anstreichen (paint house etc.).
colt [koult], s. das Füllen.
columbine ['kɔləmbain], s. (Bot.) die Akelei.
column ['kɔləm], s. die Säule; die Spalte (press); (also Mil.) die Kolonne.
colza ['kɔlzə], s. (Bot.) der Raps.
coma ['koumə], s. (Med.) das Koma, die Schlafsucht.
comb [koum], s. der Kamm. — v.a. kämmen; (fig.) genau untersuchen.
combat ['kʌmbət, 'kɔmbət], s. der Kampf, das Gefecht; in single —, im Duell, Zweikampf. — v.a. kämpfen, bekämpfen.
combatant ['kʌmbətənt, 'kɔmb-], s. der Kämpfer.
comber ['koumə], s. der Wollkämmer.
combination [kɔmbi'neiʃən], s. die Kombination, die Verbindung.
combine [kəm'bain], v.a. kombinieren, verbinden. — v.n. sich verbinden. — ['kɔmbain], s. (Comm.) der Trust, Ring.

combustible [kəm'bʌstibl], adj. verbrennbar; feuergefährlich.
combustion [kəm'bʌstʃən], s. die Verbrennung.
come [kʌm], v.n. irr. kommen; — about, sich ereignen (event); — across, stoßen auf (Acc.); — by (š.th.), ergattern, erwerben; — for, abholen; — forth, forward, hervorkommen, hervortreten; — from, herkommen von, — in, hereinkommen; — off, (object) loskommen, (succeed) glücken; — out (appear), herauskommen; — to o.s., zu sich kommen; — of age, mündig werden; — to o.'s senses, zur Besinnung or Vernunft kommen; that is still to —, das steht uns noch bevor.
comedian [kə'mi:djən], s. der Komödiant, Komiker (stage).
comedy ['kɔmədi], s. die Komödie, das Lustspiel.
comeliness ['kʌmlinis], s. die Anmut, Schönheit.
comely ['kʌmli], adj. anmutig, schön.
comestible [kə'mestibl], s. (usually pl.) die Eßwaren, f. pl.
comet ['kɔmit], s. der Komet.
comfit ['kʌmfit], s. das Konfekt, die Bonbons.
comfort ['kʌmfət], s. der Trost (solace); der Komfort, die Bequemlichkeit. — v.a. trösten.
comforter ['kʌmfətə], s. der Tröster; (Am.) die Steppdecke.
comfortless ['kʌmfətlis], adj. trostlos, unbehaglich.
comic ['kɔmik], adj. komisch; — writer, humoristischer Schriftsteller. — s. die Bilderzeitung (children's paper).
comical ['kɔmikl], adj. lächerlich, zum Lachen, komisch.
comma ['kɔmə], s. das Komma, der Beistrich; inverted —s, die Anführungszeichen.
command [kə'ma:nd], v.a., v.n. (Mil.) kommandieren; über jemanden verfügen (have s.o. at o.'s disposal). — s. der Befehl.
commandant [kɔmən'dænt], s. der Kommandant, Befehlshaber.
commander [kə'ma:ndə], s. der Befehlshaber.
commandment [kə'ma:ndmənt], s. (Rel.) das Gebot.
commemorate [kə'meməreit], v.a. feiern, gedenken (Genit.).
commemoration [kəmemə'reiʃən], s. die Feier, die Gedächtnisfeier.
commemorative [kə'memərətiv], adj. Gedächtnis-.
commence [kə'mens], v.a., v.n. beginnen, anfangen.
commencement [kə'mensmənt], s. der Anfang, der Beginn.
commend [kə'mend], v.a. empfehlen, loben (praise).
commendable [kə'mendəbl], adj. empfehlenswert.

commendation [kɔmen'deiʃən], *s.* die Empfehlung.

commensurable, **commensurate** [kə'menʃərəbl, kə'menʃərit], *adj.* kommensurabel, entsprechend; angemessen.

comment ['kɔment], *v.n.* kommentieren (*on*, zu, *Dat.*). — *s.* der Kommentar; die Bemerkung (*remark*).

commentary ['kɔməntəri], *s.* der Kommentar.

commentator ['kɔmənteitə], *s.* der Kommentator, Berichterstatter.

commerce ['kɔmə:s], *s.* der Handel; *college of* —, die Handelsschule.

commercial [kə'mə:ʃəl], *adj.* kommerziell, kaufmännisch, Handels-; — *traveller*, der Handelsreisende, Vertreter; — *manager*, der geschäftliche Leiter.

commingle [kə'miŋgl], *v.a.* vermischengefühl.

commiserate [kə'mizəreit], *v.n.* bemitleiden; — *with s.o.*, mit einem Mitgefühl haben.

commissariat [kɔmi'sɛəriət], *s.* (*Pol.*) das Kommissariat.

commissary ['kɔmisəri], *s.* der Kommissar. — *adj.* kommissarisch.

commission [kə'miʃən], *s.* die Kommission; (*Mil.*) der Offiziersrang; die Begehung (*of crime*); (*Law*) die (offizielle) Kommission; der Auftrag, die Bestellung (*order*).

commissionaire [kəmiʃən'ɛə], *s.* der Portier.

commissioned [kə'miʃənd], *adj.* bevollmächtigt.

commissioner [kə'miʃənə], *s.* (*Pol.*) der Kommissar, der Bevollmächtigte.

commit [kə'mit], *v.a.* begehen (*do*); übergeben (*give*); anvertrauen (*entrust*). — *v.r.* sich verpflichten.

committal [kə'mitl], *s.* das Übergeben; die Überantwortung.

committee [kə'miti], *s.* das Kommitee, der Ausschuß.

commodious [kə'moudiəs], *adj.* bequem, geräumig.

commodity [kə'mɔditi], *s.* (*Comm.*) die Ware, der Artikel.

commodore ['kɔmədɔ:], *s.* (*Naut.*) der Kommodore, der Kommandant eines Geschwaders.

common ['kɔmən], *adj.* gewöhnlich (*usual*); gemein (*vulgar*); allgemein (*general*); *in* —, gemeinschaftlich; — *sense*, der gesunde Menschenverstand; *the* — *man*, der kleine Mann. — *n. pl. House of Commons*, das Unterhaus.

commoner ['kɔmənə], *s.* der Bürger; (*Parl.*) Mitglied des Unterhauses.

commonness ['kɔmənnis], *s.* die Gemeinheit (*vulgarity*); das häufige Vorkommen (*frequency*).

commonplace ['kɔmənpleis], *adj.* alltäglich. — *s.* der Gemeinplatz.

commonwealth ['kɔmənwelθ], *s.* die Staatengemeinschaft, der Staatenbund; das Commonwealth.

commotion [kə'mouʃən], *s.* die Erschütterung; der Aufruhr; der Lärm.

communal ['kɔmjunəl], *adj.* gemeinschaftlich, allgemein; (*Pol.*) Kommunal-.

commune ['kɔmju:n], *s.* (*Pol.*) die Kommune. — [kə'mju:n], *v.n.* sich unterhalten.

communicable [kə'mju:nikəbl], *adj.* mitteilbar; übertragbar.

communicate [kə'mju:nikeit], *v.a.* mitteilen; verkünden (*proclaim*); benachrichtigen. — *v.n.* in Verbindung stehen.

communication [kəmju:ni'keiʃən], *s.* die Mitteilung; Verlautbarung; die Verkündigung (*proclamation*); die Information; (*Elec.*) die Verbindung; (*pl.*), die Verbindungslinie; —*s engineering*, Fernmeldetechnik.

communion [kə'mju:njən], *s.* (*Eccl.*) die Kommunion; das heilige Abendmahl; die Gemeinschaft (*fellowship*).

Communism ['kɔmjunizm], *s.* (*Pol.*) der Kommunismus.

Communist ['kɔmjunist], *s.* der Kommunist. — *adj.* kommunistisch.

community [kə'mju:niti], *s.* die Gemeinschaft.

commutable [kə'mju:təbl], *adj.* umtauschbar, auswechselbar.

commutation [kɔmju'teiʃən], *s.* der Austausch; (*Law*) die Herabsetzung (*of sentence*).

commutator ['kɔmjuteitə], *s.* (*Elec.*) der Umschalter.

commute [kə'mju:t], *v.n.* hin und her fahren, pendeln, mit Zeitkarte fahren (*travel*). — *v.a.* herabsetzen (*sentence*).

compact ['kɔmpækt], *adj.* kompakt, fest; gedrängt (*succinct*); kurz, bündig (*short*).

companion [kəm'pænjən], *s.* der Gefährte, die Gefährtin.

companionable [kəm'pænjənəbl], *adj.* gesellig, freundlich.

companionship [kəm'pænjənʃip], *s.* die Geselligkeit; die Gesellschaft.

company ['kʌmpəni], *s.* die Gesellschaft; (*Mil.*) die Kompanie; der Freundeskreis (*circle of friends*); (*Comm.*) die Handelsgesellschaft; *limited* (*liability*) —, Gesellschaft mit beschränkter Haftung; *public* (*private*) —, Gesellschaft des öffentlichen (privaten) Rechtes.

comparative [kəm'pærətiv], *adj.* vergleichend, relativ. — *s.* (*Gram.*) der Komparativ.

compare [kəm'pɛə], *v.a.* vergleichen. — *v.n.* sich vergleichen lassen.

comparison [kəm'pærisən], *s.* der Vergleich; das Gleichnis (*simile*).

compartment [kəm'pɑ:tmənt], *s.* (*Railw.*) das Abteil; die Abteilung.

compass ['kʌmpəs], *s.* der Umkreis, Umfang (*scope*); (*Naut.*) der Kompaß; *point of the* —, der Kompaßstrich; (*Engin.*) der Zirkel.

343

compassion

compassion [kəm'pæʃən], s. die Barmherzigkeit, das Mitleid, das Erbarmen.
compassionate [kəm'pæʃənit], adj. mitleidig; (Mil.) — leave, der Sonderurlaub.
compatibility [kəmpæti'biliti], s. die Verträglichkeit, Vereinbarkeit.
compatible [kəm'pætibl], adj. verträglich, vereinbar.
compatriot [kəm'peitriət], s. der Landsmann.
compel [kəm'pel], v.a. zwingen, nötigen.
compendium [kəm'pendjəm], s. das Kompendium, die kurze Schrift, die kurze Darstellung.
compensate ['kɔmpənseit], v.a. kompensieren, einem Ersatz leisten.
compensation [kɔmpən'seiʃən], s. der Ersatz, die Wiedergutmachung.
compensatory [kɔmpən'seitəri], adj. ausgleichend, Ersatz-.
compete [kəm'pi:t], v.n. wetteifern, konkurrieren.
competence, competency ['kɔmpitəns, -nsi], s. die Kompetenz; Zuständigkeit; Befähigung (capability); Tüchtigkeit (ability).
competent ['kɔmpitənt], adj. kompetent; zuständig; fähig (capable); tüchtig (able).
competition [kɔmpi'tiʃən], s. die Konkurrenz; die Mitbewerbung (for job).
competitive [kəm'petitiv], adj. Konkurrenz-, konkurrierend.
competitor [kəm'petitə], s. (Comm.) der Konkurrent; der Mitbewerber (fellow applicant), Teilnehmer (sport).
complacent [kəm'pleisənt], adj. selbstzufrieden, selbstgefällig.
complain [kəm'plein], v.n. sich beklagen (of, über, Acc.).
complaint [kəm'pleint], s. die Klage; Beschwerde (grievance); das Leiden (illness).
complement ['kɔmplimənt], s. die Ergänzung, Gesamtzahl. — [-'ment], v.a. ergänzen.
complementary [kɔmpli'mentəri], adj. Ergänzungs-, ergänzend.
complete [kəm'pli:t], adj. komplett; voll (full up); vollkommen (perfect). — v.a. vollenden (end); ergänzen (make whole).
completeness [kəm'pli:tnis], s. die Vollendung (condition); Ganzheit (wholeness).
completion [kəm'pli:ʃən], s. die Vollendung (fulfilment); die Beendigung (ending); der Abschluß.
complex ['kɔmpleks], adj. (Maths.) komplex; kompliziert (complicated). — s. der Komplex (Archit., Psych.).
complexion [kəm'plekʃən], s. die Gesichtsfarbe; (fig.) das Aussehen.
complexity [kəm'pleksiti], s. die Kompliziertheit; die Schwierigkeit.
compliance [kəm'plaiəns], s. die Willfährigkeit, Einwilligung.
compliant [kəm'plaiənt], adj. willig, willfährig.

complicate ['kɔmplikeit], v.a. komplizieren, erschweren.
complication [kɔmpli'keiʃən], s. die Komplikation, die Erschwerung.
complicity [kəm'plisiti], s. (Law) die Mitschuld.
compliment ['kɔmplimənt], s. das Kompliment. — [-'ment], v.n. Komplimente machen.
complimentary [kɔmpli'mentəri], adj. lobend; — ticket, die Freikarte.
comply [kəm'plai], v.n. einwilligen (with, in, Acc.); sich halten (an, Acc.).
compose [kəm'pouz], v.a., v.n. (Mus.) komponieren; beruhigen (the mind); (Lit.) verfassen; (Typ.) setzen.
composed [kəm'pouzd], adj. ruhig, gefaßt.
composer [kəm'pouzə], s. (Mus.) der Komponist.
composite ['kɔmpəzit], adj. zusammengesetzt.
composition [kɔmpə'ziʃən], s. (Mus. etc.) die Komposition; Beschaffenheit Zusammensetzung.
compositor [kəm'pɔzitə], s. (Typ.) der Schriftsetzer.
compost ['kɔmpɔst], s. (Agr.) der Dünger, Kompost.
composure [kəm'pouʒə], s. die Gelassenheit, die Gemütsruhe, die Fassung.
compound ['kɔmpaund], s. (Chem.) die Verbindung; die Zusammensetzung. — adj. zusammengesetzt; kompliziert; (Comm.) — interest, die Zinseszinsen. — [kəm'paund], v.a. (Chem.) mischen, zusammensetzen.
comprehend [kɔmpri'hend], v.a. verstehen (understand); einschließen (include).
comprehensible [kɔmpri'hensibl], adj. verständlich, begreiflich.
comprehension [kɔmpri'henʃən], s. das Verstehen, das Erfassen; (Psych.) — tests, die Verständnisprüfung.
comprehensive [kɔmpri'hensiv], adj. umfassend.
compress [kəm'pres], v.a. komprimieren; zusammendrücken (press together). — ['kɔmpres], s. (Med.) die Kompresse, der Umschlag (poultice).
compression [kəm'preʃən], s. der Druck; das Zusammendrücken (pressing together); die Kürzung (abridgment).
comprise [kəm'praiz], v.a. umfassen, einschließen.
compromise ['kɔmprəmaiz], v.a. kompromittieren. — v.n. einen Kompromiß schließen. — s. der or das Kompromiß.
compulsion [kəm'pʌlʃən], s. der Zwang.
compulsory [kəm'pʌlsəri], adj. zwingend; Zwangs-; — subject, das obligatorische Fach.
compunction [kəm'pʌŋkʃən], s. die Gewissensbisse, m. pl.
computation [kɔmpju'teiʃən], s. die Berechnung.

compute [kəm'pju:t], *v.a.*, *v.n.* berechnen.

computer [kəm'pju:tə], *s.* die automatische Rechenmaschine.

comrade ['kɔmrid], *s.* der Kamerad.

comradeship ['kɔmridʃip], *s.* die Kameradschaft.

con [kɔn], *v.a.* genau betrachten, studieren; (*ship*) steuern.

concave ['kɔnkeiv], *adj.* (*Phys.*) konkav.

conceal [kən'si:l], *v.a.* verbergen, verstecken.

concealment [kən'si:lmənt], *s.* die Verhehlung, die Verheimlichung (*act of concealing*); *place of —*, das Versteck.

concede [kən'si:d], *v.a.* zugestehen, einräumen.

conceit [kən'si:t], *s.* die Einbildung, der Eigendünkel (*presumption*); (*obs.*) die Idee; (*Lit.*) die (gedankliche) Spielerei.

conceited [kən'si:tid], *adj.* eingebildet, eitel.

conceivable [kən'si:vəbl], *adj.* denkbar; begreiflich (*understandable*).

conceive [kən'si:v], *v.a.*, *v.n.* empfangen (*become pregnant*); begreifen (*understand*).

concentrate ['kɔnsəntreit], *v.a.* konzentrieren. — *v.n.* sich konzentrieren (*on*, auf, *Acc.*). — *s.* (*Chem.*) das Konzentrat.

concentrated ['kɔnsəntreitid], *adj.* konzentriert.

concentration [kɔnsən'treiʃən], *s.* die Konzentration.

concentric [kən'sentrik], *adj.* (*Geom.*) konzentrisch.

conception [kən'sepʃən], *s.* die Vorstellung, der Begriff (*idea*); die Empfängnis (*of a child*).

concern [kən'sə:n], *v.a.* (*affect*) betreffen, angehen; *be concerned with*, zu tun haben (mit, *Dat.*). — *s.* die Angelegenheit (*affair*); die Sorge (*care, business*); das Geschäft, das Unternehmen (*care, business*); *cause —*, tiefe Besorgnis erregen.

concerned [kən'sə:nd], *adj.* (*worried*) besorgt; (*involved*) interessiert (*in*, an, *Dat.*).

concerning [kən'sə:niŋ], *prep.* betreffend (*Acc.*), hinsichtlich (*Genit.*).

concert ['kɔnsət], *s.* (*Mus.*) das Konzert; Einverständnis.

concerted [kən'sə:tid], *adj.* gemeinsam, gemeinschaftlich.

concertina [kɔnsə'ti:nə], *s.* (*Mus.*) die Ziehharmonika.

concerto [kən'tʃə:tou], *s.* (*Mus.*) das Konzert.

concession [kən'seʃən], *s.* die Konzession (*licence*); das Zugeständnis.

conch [kɔŋk], *s.* die (große) Muschel.

conciliate [kən'silieit], *v.a.* versöhnen.

conciliation [kənsili'eiʃən], *s.* die Versöhnung.

conciliatory [kən'siliətəri], *adj.* versöhnlich.

concise [kən'sais], *adj.* kurz, knapp.

conciseness [kən'saisnis], *s.* die Kürze, Knappheit.

conclave ['kɔnkleiv], *s.* (*Eccl.*) das Konklave.

conclude [kən'klu:d], *v.a.*, *v.n.* schließen, beenden (*speech etc.*); (*infer*) folgern (*from*, aus, *Dat.*); abschließen (*treaty*).

conclusion [kən'klu:ʒən], *s.* der Abschluß (*treaty*); die Folgerung (*inference*); der Beschluß (*decision*).

conclusive [kən'klu:siv], *adj.* entscheidend, überzeugend.

concoct [kən'kɔkt], *v.a.* zusammenbrauen, aushecken.

concoction [kən'kɔkʃən], *s.* das Gebräu, die Mischung.

concomitant [kən'kɔmitənt], *adj.* begleitend; Begleit-, Neben-. — *s.* der Begleitumstand.

concord ['kɔnkɔ:d], *s.* die Eintracht, die Harmonie.

concordance [kən'kɔ:dəns], *s.* die Übereinstimmung; die Konkordanz (*of Bible etc.*).

concordant [kən'kɔ:dənt], *adj.* in Eintracht (mit), übereinstimmend (mit) (*Dat.*).

concordat [kən'kɔ:dæt], *s.* (*Eccl.*, *Pol.*) das Konkordat.

concourse ['kɔnkɔ:s], *s.* das Gedränge (*crowd*).

concrete ['kɔnkri:t], *s.* (*Build.*) der Beton; (*Log.*) das Konkrete. — *adj.* konkret, wirklich.

concur [kən'kə:], *v.n.* übereinstimmen (*with*, mit, *Dat.*).

concurrence [kən'kʌrəns], *s.* die Übereinstimmung.

concurrent [kən'kʌrənt], *adj.* gleichzeitig (*simultaneous*); mitwirkend (*accompanying*).

concussion [kən'kʌʃən], *s.* (*Med.*) die (Gehirn)Erschütterung.

condemn [kən'dem], *v.a.* verurteilen, verdammen.

condemnable [kən'demnəbl], *adj.* verwerflich, verdammenswert.

condemnation [kɔndem'neiʃən], *s.* die Verurteilung, die Verdammung.

condensate ['kɔndenseit], *s.* (*Chem.*) das Kondensat, das Ergebnis der Kondensation.

condensation [kɔnden'seiʃən], *s.* die Kondensation; Verdichtung.

condensed [kən'densd], *adj.* (*Chem.*) kondensiert; (*Chem.*, *Engin.*) verdichtet; gekürzt (*abridged*).

condenser [kən'densə], *s.* (*Chem.*, *Engin.*) der Kondensator; (*Elec.*) der Verstärker.

condescend [kɔndi'send], *v.n.* sich herablassen.

condescending [kɔndi'sendiŋ], *adj.* herablassend.

condescension [kɔndi'senʃən], *s.* die Herablassung.

condiment ['kɔndimənt], *s.* die Würze.

condition [kən'diʃən], *s.* der Zustand; Umstand; die Bedingung (*proviso*); der Gesundheitszustand (*physical state*).

conditional [kən'diʃənəl], *adj.* bedingt; unter der Bedingung; konditionell.
conditioned [kən'diʃənd], *adj.* vorbereitet (*for action*); geartet.
condole [kən'doul], *v.n.* Beileid ausdrücken (*with*, Dat.), kondolieren (*with*, Dat.).
condolence [kən'douləns], *s.* das Beileid.
condone [kən'doun], *v.a.* verzeihen.
conducive [kən'dju:siv], *adj.* förderlich, dienlich, nützlich (*to*, Dat.).
conduct [kən'dʌkt], *v.a.* leiten, führen; (*Phys.*) ein Leiter sein; (*Mus.*) dirigieren. — *v.r.* sich aufführen, sich benehmen. — ['kɔndʌkt], *s.* das Benehmen (*behaviour*); — *of a war*, die Kriegsführung.
conductive [kən'dʌktiv], *adj.* (*Elec.*) leitend.
conductor [kən'dʌktə], *s.* der Leiter, Führer (*leader*); (*Phys.*, *Elec.*) der Leiter; (*Am.*) der Schaffner (*train*); (*Mus.*) der Dirigent.
conduit ['kʌn-, 'kɔndit], *s.* die Leitung, die Röhre.
cone [koun], *s.* (*Geom.*) der Kegel; (*Bot.*) der Zapfen.
coney ['kouni], *s.* (*Zool.*) das Kaninchen.
confection [kən'fekʃən], *s.* das Konfekt.
confectioner [kən'fekʃənə], *s.* der Zuckerbäcker, Konditor.
confectionery [kən'fekʃənəri], *s.* die Zuckerwaren, *f.pl.* (*sweets*); Konditoreiwaren, *f.pl.* (*cakes*); die Zuckerbäckerei (*sweet shop*); die Konditorei.
confederacy [kən'fedərəsi], *s.* der Bund (*of states*); das Bündnis (*treaty*).
confederate [kən'fedərit], *s.* der Bundesgenosse, der Verbündete. — *adj.* verbündet; — *state*, der Bundesstaat. — [-reit], *v.n.* sich verbünden (*with*, mit, Dat.).
confederation [kənfedə'reiʃən], *s.* das Bündnis (*treaty*); der Bund (*state*).
confer [kən'fə:], *v.a.* verleihen (*degree*, *title*). — *v.n.* beraten (*with*, mit, Dat.), unterhandeln (*negotiate*).
conference ['kɔnfərəns], *s.* die Konferenz, die Besprechung, die Beratung, Tagung.
confess [kən'fes], *v.a.* bekennen; beichten (*sin*); zugestehen (*acknowledge*).
confession [kən'feʃən], *s.* das Bekenntnis; die Beichte (*sin*); das Glaubensbekenntnis (*creed*).
confessor [kən'fesə], *s.* der Bekenner; *father* —, der Beichtvater.
confidant [kɔnfi'dænt], *s.* der Vertraute.
confide [kən'faid], *v.a.* anvertrauen. — *v.n.* vertrauen (Dat.).
confidence ['kɔnfidəns], *s.* das Vertrauen; die Zuversicht; — *trick*, die Bauernfängerei, der Schwindel.
confident ['kɔnfidənt], *adj.* zuversichtlich; dreist (*bold*).
confidential [kɔnfi'denʃəl], *adj.* vertraulich, privat.

confine [kən'fain], *v.a.* einschränken (*hem in*); einsperren; *be* —*d to bed*, bettlägerig sein.
confinement [kən'fainmənt], *s.* die Einschränkung (*limitation*); das Wochenbett, die Niederkunft (*childbirth*).
confines [kən'fainz], *s. pl.* die Grenzen, *f. pl.* (*physical*); die Einschränkungen, *f. pl.* (*limitations*).
confirm [kən'fə:m], *v.a.* bestätigen, bekräftigen (*corroborate*); (*Eccl.*) firmen, konfirmieren.
confirmation [kɔnfə'meiʃən], *s.* die Bestätigung (*corroboration*); (*Eccl.*) die Firmung, Konfirmation.
confirmed [kən'fə:md], *adj.* eingefleischt; unverbesserlich.
confiscate ['kɔnfiskeit], *v.a.* konfiszieren, einziehen, beschlagnahmen.
confiscation [kɔnfis'keiʃən], *s.* die Konfiszierung, die Einziehung, die Beschlagnahme (*customs etc.*).
conflagration [kɔnflə'greiʃən], *s.* der (große) Brand.
conflict ['kɔnflikt], *s.* der Konflikt, der Zusammenstoß. — [kən'flikt], *v.n.* in Konflikt geraten; in Widerspruch stehen.
confluence ['kɔnfluəns], *s.* (*Geog.*) der Zusammenfluß.
confluent ['kɔnfluənt], *adj.* zusammenfließend. — *s.* der Nebenfluß (*tributary*).
conform [kən'fə:m], *v.n.* sich anpassen.
conformation [kɔnfɔ:'meiʃən], *s.* die Anpassung.
conformist [kən'fɔ:mist], *adj.* fügsam. — *s.* das Mitglied der Staatskirche.
conformity [kən'fɔ:miti], *s.* die Gleichförmigkeit; *in* — *with*, gerade so; gemäß (Dat.); die Gleichheit (*equality*.)
confound [kən'faund], *v.a.* verwirren (*confuse*); vernichten (*overthrow*).
confounded [kən'faundid], *adj.* verdammt, verwünscht.
confront [kən'frʌnt], *v.a.* (*Law*) — *s.o. with*, gegenüberstellen (*put in front of*); gegenüberstehen (*stand in front of*).
confrontation [kɔnfrʌn'teiʃən], *s.* die Gegenüberstellung.
confuse [kən'fju:z], *v.a.* verwirren (*muddle*); bestürzen (*perplex*); verwechseln (*mix up*).
confusion [kən'fju:ʒən], *s.* die Verwirrung, das Durcheinander (*muddle*); die Bestürzung (*astonishment*); die Verlegenheit (*dilemma*).
confutation [kɔnfju:'teiʃən], *s.* die Widerlegung.
confute [kən'fju:t], *v.a.* widerlegen.
congeal [kən'dʒi:l], *v.n.* gefrieren (*freeze*); gerinnen.
congenial [kən'dʒi:niəl], *adj.* geistesverwandt, geistig ebenbürtig, sympathisch.
congeniality [kəndʒi:ni'æliti], *s.* die Geistesverwandtschaft.
conger ['kɔŋgə], *s.* (*Zool.*) der Meeraal.

congest [kən'dʒest], *v.a.* anhäufen, überfüllen.

congestion [kən'dʒestʃən], *s.* die Überfüllung; Stauung; die Übervölkerung (*overpopulation*); (*Med.*) der Blutandrang.

conglomerate [kɔn'glɔməreit], *v.n.* sich zusammenballen. — [-rit], *s.* das Konglomerat, die Ballung.

conglomeration [kɔnglɔmə'reiʃən], *s.* die Zusammenhäufung, Zusammenballung.

Congolese [kɔŋgo'li:z], *adj.* kongolesisch. — *s.* der Kongolese.

congratulate [kən'grætjuleit], *v.n.* gratulieren (*on*, zu, *Dat.*).

congratulation [kəngrætju'leiʃən], *s.* (*usually pl.*) die Glückwünsche.

congratulatory [kən'grætjuleitəri], *adj.* Glückwunsch-.

congregate ['kɔŋgrigeit], *v.a.* versammeln. — *v.n.* sich versammeln, sich scharen (*round*, um, *Acc.*).

congregation [kɔŋgri'geiʃən], *s.* die Versammlung, die Schar; (*Eccl.*) die Gemeinde.

congregational [kɔŋgri'geiʃənəl], *adj.* (*Eccl.*) Gemeinde-; *Congregational Church*, unabhängige Gemeindekirche.

congress ['kɔŋgres], *s.* der Kongreß.

congruence ['kɔŋgruəns], *s.* (*Geom.*) die Kongruenz.

congruent ['kɔŋgruənt], *adj.* (*Geom.*) kongruent.

congruity [kɔŋ'gru:iti], *s.* (*Geom.*) die Übereinstimmung; die Kongruenz.

congruous ['kɔŋgruəs], *adj.* übereinstimmend, angemessen.

conic(al) ['kɔnik(əl)], *adj.* konisch, kegelförmig; (*Geom.*) — *section*, der Kegelschnitt.

conifer ['kɔnifə], *s.* (*Bot.*) der Nadelbaum.

conjecture [kən'dʒektʃə], *s.* die Mutmaßung, die Annahme. — *v.a.* mutmaßen, annehmen.

conjoin [kɔn'dʒɔin], *v.a.* (*Law*) verbinden.

conjugal ['kɔndʒugəl], *adj.* ehelich.

conjugate ['kɔndʒugeit], *v.a.* (*Gram.*) konjugieren.

conjugation [kɔndʒu'geiʃən], *s.* (*Gram.*) die Konjugation.

conjunction [kən'dʒʌŋkʃən], *s.* (*Gram.*) das Bindewort.

conjunctive [kən'dʒʌŋktiv], *adj.* verbindend; (*Gram.*) — *mood*, der Konjunktiv.

conjunctivitis [kən'dʒʌŋktivaitis], *s.* (*Med.*) die Bindehautentzündung.

conjuncture [kən'dʒʌŋktʃə], *s.* der Wendepunkt; die Krise (*of events*).

conjure ['kʌndʒə], *v.a.* beschwören; — *up*, heraufbeschwören. — *v.n.* zaubern.

conjurer ['kʌndʒərə], *s.* der Zauberer.

connect [kə'nekt], *v.a.* verbinden, in Zusammenhang bringen.

connection, connexion [kə'nekʃən], *s.* die Verbindung, der Zusammenhang.

connivance [kə'naivəns], *s.* die Nachsicht, das Gewährenlassen.

connive [kə'naiv], *v.n.* nachsichtig sein (*at*, bei, *Dat.*); gewähren lassen.

connoisseur [kɔne'sə:], *s.* der Kenner.

connubial [kə'nju:biəl], *adj.* ehelich.

conquer ['kɔŋkə], *v.a.* besiegen (*foe*); erobern (*place*).

conqueror ['kɔŋkərə], *s.* der Eroberer, der Sieger.

conquest ['kɔŋkwest], *s.* der Sieg, die Eroberung.

consanguinity [kɔnsæŋ'gwiniti], *s.* die Blutsverwandtschaft.

conscience ['kɔnʃəns], *s.* das Gewissen; *in all* — wahrhaftig.

conscientious [kɔnʃi'enʃəs], *adj.* gewissenhaft.

conscientiousness [kɔnʃi'enʃəsnis], *s.* die Gewissenhaftigkeit.

conscious ['kɔnʃəs], *adj.* bewußt (*Genit.*).

consciousness ['kɔnʃəsnis], *s.* das Bewußtsein.

conscript [kən'skript], *v.a.* (*Mil.*) einziehen, einberufen. — ['kɔnskript], *s.* (*Mil.*) der Rekrut, der Dienstpflichtige.

conscription [kən'skripʃən], *s.* die allgemeine Wehrpflicht.

consecrate ['kɔnsikreit], *v.a.* weihen, widmen.

consecrated ['kɔnsikreitid], *adj.* geweiht (*Dat.*).

consecration [kɔnsi'kreiʃən], *s.* die Weihe, Einweihung (*of church*); die Weihung.

consecutive [kən'sekjutiv], *adj.* aufeinanderfolgend, fortlaufend.

consecutiveness [kən'sekjutivnis], *s.* die Aufeinanderfolge.

consent [kən'sent], *v.n.* zustimmen, beistimmen (*to*, *Dat.*). — *s.* die Zustimmung, die Einwilligung.

consequence ['kɔnsikwəns], *s.* die Konsequenz; (*Log.*) Folgerung; die Folge; die Wichtigkeit (*importance*).

consequent ['kɔnsikwənt], *adj.* folgend, nachfolgend.

consequential [kɔnsi'kwenʃəl], *adj.* wichtigtuend, anmaßend; (*Log.*) folgerichtig.

consequently ['kɔnsikwəntli], *adv.* folglich, infolgedessen.

conservatism [kən'sə:vətizm], *s.* (*Pol.*) der Konservatismus; die konservative Denkweise.

conservative [kən'sə:vətiv], *adj.* (*Pol.*) konservativ.

conservatoire [kən'sə:vatwɑ:], *s.* (*Mus.*) das Konservatorium, die Musikhochschule.

conservatory [kən'sə:vətəri], *s.* (*Bot.*) das Gewächshaus.

conserve [kən'sə:v], *v.a.* konservieren, erhalten, einmachen. — *s.* (*fruit*) das Eingemachte.

consider [kən'sidə], *v.a.* betrachten, in Betracht ziehen (*think over, look at*); berücksichtigen (*have regard to*); nachdenken über (*Acc.*) (*ponder*).

considerable

considerable [kən'sidərəbl], *adj.* beträchtlich, ansehnlich.
considerate [kən'sidərit], *adj.* rücksichtsvoll (*thoughtful*).
consideration [kənsidə'reiʃən], *s.* die Betrachtung (*contemplation*); die Rücksicht (*regard*) (*for*, auf, *Acc.*); die Entschädigung (*compensation*); die Belohnung (*reward*).
considering [kən'sidəriŋ], *prep.* in Anbetracht (*Genit.*).
consign [kən'sain], *v.a.* überliefern (*hand over*); übersenden (*remit*).
consignee [kɔnsai'niː], *s.* (*Comm.*) der Empfänger, der Adressat (*recipient*).
consigner [kən'sainə], *s.* der Absender (*of goods*).
consignment [kən'sainmənt], *s.* die Sendung (*of goods*).
consist [kən'sist], *v.n.* bestehen (*of*, aus, *Dat.*).
consistency [kən'sistənsi], *s.* die Festigkeit, Dichtigkeit; (*Chem.*) die Konsistenz.
consistent [kən'sistənt], *adj.* konsequent; — *with*, übereinstimmend, gemäß (*Dat.*); (*Chem.*) dicht, fest.
consistory [kən'sistəri], *s.* (*Eccl.*) das Konsistorium.
consolable [kən'souləbl], *adj.* tröstlich, zu trösten.
consolation [kɔnso'leiʃən], *s.* der Trost; *draw* —, Trost schöpfen.
console (1) [kən'soul], *v.a.* trösten.
console (2) ['kɔnsoul], *s.* (*Archit.*) die Konsole.
consolidate [kən'sɔlideit], *v.a.* befestigen, konsolidieren. — *v.n.* fest werden.
consolidation [kənsɔli'deiʃən], *s.* die Befestigung; Festigung, Bestärkung (*confirmation*).
consonance ['kɔnsənəns], *s.* (*Phonet.*) die Konsonanz; der Einklang, die Harmonie.
consonant ['kɔnsənənt], *adj.* in Einklang (*with*, mit, *Dat.*). — *s.* der Konsonant.
consort ['kɔnsɔːt], *s.* der Gemahl, Gatte; die Gemahlin, die Gattin. — [kən'sɔːt], *v.n.* verkehren (*with*, mit, *Dat.*).
conspicuous [kən'spikjuəs], *adj.* auffallend, deutlich sichtbar, hervorragend.
conspiracy [kən'spirəsi], *s.* die Verschwörung.
conspirator [kən'spirətə], *s.* der Verschwörer.
conspire [kən'spaiə], *v.n.* sich verschwören.
constable ['kʌnstəbl], *s.* der Polizist, der Schutzmann.
Constance ['kɔnstəns]. Konstanze *f.* (*name*); Konstanz (*town*); *Lake* —, der Bodensee.
constancy ['kɔnstənsi], *s.* die Beständigkeit, Treue.
constant ['kɔnstənt], *adj.* (*Chem.*) konstant; treu, beständig.

constellation [kɔnste'leiʃən], *s.* die Konstellation; das Sternbild.
consternation [kɔnstə'neiʃən], *s.* die Bestürzung.
constipation [kɔnsti'peiʃən], *s.* die Verstopfung.
constituency [kən'stitjuənsi], *s.* der Wahlkreis (*electoral district*); die Wählerschaft (*voters*).
constituent [kən'stitjuənt], *adj.* wesentlich. — *s.* der Bestandteil (*component*); (*Pol.*) der Wähler.
constitute ['kɔnstitjuːt], *v.a.* ausmachen (*make up*); bilden (*form*); festsetzen (*establish*); (*Pol.*) errichten (*set up*).
constitution [kɔnsti'tjuːʃən], *s.* die Konstitution (*physique*); die Errichtung (*establishment*); die Beschaffenheit, Natur (*nature*); (*Pol.*) die Verfassung.
constitutional [kɔnsti'tjuːʃənəl], *adj.* körperlich bedingt; (*Pol.*) verfassungsmäßig.
constrain [kən'strein], *v.a.* nötigen, zwingen.
constraint [kən'streint], *s.* der Zwang.
constrict [kən'strikt], *v.a.* zusammenziehen.
constriction [kən'strikʃən], *s.* die Zusammenziehung, Beengtheit.
construct [kən'strʌkt], *v.a.* errichten, bauen, konstruieren.
construction [kən'strʌkʃən], *s.* die Errichtung, der Bau, die Konstruktion.
constructive [kən'strʌktiv], *adj.* (*Engin.*) konstruktiv; behilflich (*positive*).
constructor [kən'strʌktə], *s.* der Strukteur, der Erbauer (*builder*).
construe [kən'struː], *v.a.* konstruieren, deuten (*interpret*).
consul ['kɔnsəl], *s.* der Konsul; — *general*, der Generalkonsul.
consular ['kɔnsjulə], *adj.* konsularisch.
consulate ['kɔnsjulit], *s.* das Konsulat; — *general*, das Generalkonsulat.
consult [kən'sʌlt], *v.a.* konsultieren, zu Rate ziehen; nachschlagen (*a book*). — *v.n.* sich beraten (*with*, mit, *Dat.*); (*Comm.*) als Berater hinzuziehen.
consultant [kən'sʌltənt], *s.* (*Med.*) der Facharzt; der Berater.
consultation [kɔnsəl'teiʃən], *s.* die Beratung (*advice*); die Besprechung (*discussion*); (*Med.*, *Engin.*) die Konsultation.
consume [kən'sjuːm], *v.a.* verzehren (*eat up*); verbrauchen (*use up*).
consumer [kən'sjuːmə], *s.* der Verbraucher; (*Comm.*) der Konsument.
consummate [kən'sʌmit], *adj.* vollendet. — ['kɔnsəmeit], *v.a.* vollenden, vollziehen.
consummation [kɔnsə'meiʃən], *s.* die Vollziehung, Vollendung.
consumption [kən'sʌmpʃən], *s.* (*Comm.*) der Verbrauch; (*Med.*) die Schwindsucht.
consumptive [kən'sʌmptiv], *adj.* (*Med.*) schwindsüchtig.

contact ['kɔntækt], *v.a.* berühren (*touch*); in Verbindung treten (mit) (*get into touch (with)*). — *s.* (*Elec.*) der Kontakt; die Berührung (*touch*); die Verbindung (*connexion*).

contagion [kən'teidʒən], *s.* (*Med.*) die Ansteckung.

contagious[kən'teidʒəs],*adj.*ansteckend.

contain [kən'tein], *v.a.* enthalten (*hold*); zurückhalten (*restrain*).

container [kən'teinə], *s.* der Behälter.

contaminate [kən'tæmineit], *v.a.* verunreinigen; vergiften.

contemplate ['kɔntəmpleit], *v.a.* betrachten (*consider*). — *v.n.* nachdenken (*ponder*).

contemplation [kɔntəm'pleiʃən], *s.* die Betrachtung (*consideration*); das Sinnen (*pondering*).

contemplative ['kɔn'templətiv], *adj.* nachdenklich, kontemplativ.

contemporaneous [kɔntempə'reiniəs], *adj.* gleichzeitig.

contemporary [kən'tempərəri], *adj.* zeitgenössich. — *s.* der Zeitgenosse.

contempt [kən'tempt], *s.* die Verachtung; — *of court*, die Gerichtsbeleidigung.

contemptible [kən'temptibl], *adj.* verächtlich, verachtungswert.

contemptibleness [kən'temptiblnis], *s.* die Verächtlichkeit.

contemptuous [kən'temptjuəs], *adj.* höhnisch, verachtungsvoll.

contemptuousness [kən'temptjuəsnis], *s.* der Hohn, der verachtungsvolle Ton, der Hochmut.

contend [kən'tend], *v.n.* streiten; bestreiten, behaupten.

content [kən'tent], *adj.* zufrieden. — *v.a.* zufriedenstellen. — ['kɔntent], *s.* (*often pl.*) der Inhalt.

contented [kən'tentid], *adj.* zufrieden.

contentedness, contentment [kən'tentidnis, kən'tentmənt], *s.* die Zufriedenheit.

contention [kən'tenʃən], *s.* der Streit, die Behauptung.

contentious [kən'tenʃəs], *adj.* streitsüchtig (*person*); strittig (*question*).

contest ['kɔntest], *s.* der Streit, Wettstreit, Wettkampf. — [kən'test], *v.a.* um etwas streiten, bestreiten.

context ['kɔntekst], *s.* der Zusammenhang.

contexture [kən'tekstʃə], *s.* (*Engin.*) der Bau, die Zusammensetzung; das Gewebe (*textile*).

contiguity [kɔnti'gju:iti], *s.* die Berührung; die Nachbarschaft.

contiguous [kən'tigjuəs], *adj.* anstossend, anliegend.

continence ['kɔntinəns], *s.* die Mäßigung (*moderation*); die Enthaltsamkeit (*abstemiousness*).

continent (1) ['kɔntinənt], *adj.* enthaltsam, mässig.

continent (2) ['kɔntinənt], *s.* das Festland, der Kontinent.

contingency [kən'tindʒənsi], *s.* der Zufall; die Möglichkeit (*possibility*).

contingent [kən'tindʒənt], *s.* der Beitrag, das Kontingent (*share*). — *adj.* möglich.

continual [kən'tinjuəl], *adj.* fortwährend, beständig.

continuance [kən'tinjuəns], *s.* die Fortdauer.

continuation [kɔntinju'eiʃən], *s.* die Fortsetzung.

continue [kən'tinju:], *v.a.* fortsetzen (*go on with*); verlängern (*prolong*). — *v.n.* weitergehen, weiterführen (*of story*).

continuity [kɔnti'nju:iti], *s.* der Zusammenhang, die ununterbrochene Folge, Kontinuität (*Film*); — *girl*, die Drehbuchsekretärin.

continuous [kən'tinjuəs], *adj.* zusammenhängend, ununterbrochen, andauernd.

contort [kən'tɔ:t], *v.a.* verdrehen.

contortion [kən'tɔ:ʃən], *s.* die Verdrehung, Verkrümmung, Verzerrung.

contortionist [kən'tɔ:ʃənist], *s.* der Schlangenmensch.

contour ['kɔntuə], *s.* die Kontur, der Umriß.

contraband ['kɔntrəbænd], *adj.* Schmuggel-, geschmuggelt. — *s.* die Bannware, Schmuggelware.

contract [kən'trækt], *v.a.* zusammenziehen (*pull together*); verengen (*narrow down*); verkürzen (*shorten*); sich eine Krankheit zuziehen (— *a disease*); Schulden machen (— *debts*). — *v.n.* sich zusammenziehen, kürzer werden; einen Kontrakt abschließen (*come to terms*). — ['kɔntrækt], *s.* der Vertrag (*pact*; (*Comm.*) der Kontrakt.

contraction [kən'trækʃən], *s.* die Zusammenziehung; (*Phonet.*) die Kürzung.

contractor [kən'træktə], *s.* (*Comm.*) der Kontrahent; der Lieferant (*supplier*); *building* —, der Bauunternehmer.

contradict [kɔntrə'dikt], *v.n.* widersprechen (*Dat.*).

contradiction [kɔntrə'dikʃən], *s.* der Widerspruch.

contradictory [kɔntrə'diktəri], *adj.* in Widerspruch stehend, widersprechend.

contrarily ['kɔntrərili], *adv.* im Gegensatz dazu, hingegen, dagegen.

contrary ['kɔntrəri], *adj.* entgegengesetzt, *on the* —, im Gegenteil; [kən'trɛəri], widersprechend.

contrast [kən'trɑ:st], *v.a.* einander entgegenstellen, gegenüberstellen. — *v.n.* einen Gegensatz darstellen *or* bilden. — ['kɔntrɑ:st], *s.* der Kontrast (*colours*); der Gegensatz.

contravene [kɔntrə'vi:n], *v.a.* übertreten, zuwiderhandeln (*Dat.*).

contribute [kən'tribju:t], *v.a.* beitragen; beisteuern (*money, energy*).

contribution [kɔntri'bju:ʃən], *s.* der Beitrag.

contributive, contributory [kən'tri-bjutiv, kən'tribjutəri], *adj.* beitragend, Beitrags-.

contributor [kən'tribjutə], *s.* der Beitragende, der Spender (*of money*); der Mitarbeiter (*journalist etc.*).

contrite ['kɔntrait], *adj.* zerknirscht, reuevoll.

contrition [kən'triʃən], *s.* die Zerknirschung, die Reue.

contrivance [kən'traivəns], *s.* die Vorrichtung, die Erfindung.

contrive [kən'traiv], *v.a.* ausdenken, erfinden; fertigbringen (*accomplish*).

control [kən'troul], *v.a.* kontrollieren (*check*); die Leitung haben (*have command of*); die Aufsicht führen (*supervise*). — *s.* die Kontrolle; die Aufsicht; die Leitung; (*pl.*) (*Motor.*) die Steuerung; (*Aviat.*) das Leitwerk.

controller [kən'troulə], *s.* der Aufseher (*supervisor*); der Direktor (*of corporation*); der Revisor (*examiner, auditor*).

controversial [kɔntro'vəːʃəl], *adj.* umstritten, strittig.

controversy ['kɔntrovəːsi], *s.* die Kontroverse, die Streitfrage.

controvert ['kɔntrovəːt], *v.a.* bestreiten, widersprechen (*Dat.*).

contumacious [kɔntju'meiʃəs], *adj.* widerspenstig, halsstarrig.

contumacy ['kɔntjuməsi], *s.* die Widerspenstigkeit (*obstreperousness*); der Ungehorsam (*disobedience*).

contumelious [kɔntju'miːliəs], *adj.* frech, unverschämt (*insolent*).

contuse [kən'tjuːz], *v.a.* quetschen.

conundrum [kə'nʌndrəm], *s.* das Scherzrätsel.

convalescence [kɔnvə'lesəns], *s.* die Gesundung, die Genesung.

convalescent [kɔnvə'lesənt], *adj.* genesend. — *s.* der Genesende, der Rekonvaleszent.

convene [kən'viːn], *v.a.* zusammenrufen, versammeln. — *v.n.* zusammentreten, sich versammeln.

convenience [kən'viːniəns], *s.* die Bequemlichkeit; *at your early —*, umgehend; *public —*, öffentliche Bedürfnisanstalt.

convenient [kən'viːniənt], *adj.* bequem, gelegen; passend (*time*).

convent ['kɔnvənt], *s.* das (Nonnen)-Kloster.

convention [kən'venʃən], *s.* die Konvention, der Kongress (*meeting*); der Vertrag (*treaty*); die Sitte (*tradition, custom*).

conventional [kən'venʃənəl], *adj.* herkömmlich, traditionell.

conventual [kən'ventjuəl], *adj.* klösterlich.

conversation [kɔnvə'seiʃən], *s.* die Konversation, Unterhaltung; das Gespräch.

conversational [kɔnvə'seiʃənəl], *adj.* gesprächig, umgangssprachlich.

converse (1) [kən'vəːs], *v.n.* sich unterhalten (*with*, mit, *Dat.*).

converse (2) ['kɔnvəːs], *adj.* umgekehrt.

conversely ['kɔnvəːsli], *adv.* hingegen, dagegen.

conversion [kən'vəːʃən], *s.* die Umkehrung (*reversal*); (*Rel.*) die Bekehrung; (*Comm.*) die Umwechslung.

convert ['kɔnvəːt], *s.* (*Rel.*) der Bekehrte, die Bekehrte; der Konvertit. — [kən'vəːt], *v.a.* (*Rel.*) bekehren; (*Comm.*) umwechseln.

converter [kən'vəːtə], *s.* (*Rel.*) der Bekehrer; (*Metall., Elec.*) der Umformer.

convertible [kən'vəːtibl], *adj.* umwandelbar. — *s.* (*Motor.*) der *or* das Konvertible.

convex ['kɔnveks], *adj.* (*Phys.*) konvex.

convey [kən'vei], *v.a.* transportieren; führen (*bear, carry*); mitteilen (*impart*).

conveyance [kən'veiəns], *s.* die Beförderung (*transport*); das Fuhrwerk (*vehicle*); die Übertragung; (*Law*) das Übertragungsdokument.

conveyancing [kən'veiənsiŋ], *s.* (*Law*) die legale *or* rechtliche Übertragung.

convict ['kɔnvikt], *s.* der Sträfling. — [kən'vikt], *v.a.* für schuldig erklären.

conviction [kən'vikʃən], *s.* die Überzeugung; (*Law*) die Überführung, die Schuldigsprechung.

convince [kən'vins], *v.a.* überzeugen.

convivial [kən'viviəl], *adj.* gesellig (*sociable*).

conviviality [kənvivi'æliti], *s.* die Geselligkeit.

convocation [kɔnvə'keiʃən], *s.* die Zusammenberufung, Festversammlung; (*Eccl.*) die Synode.

convoke [kən'vouk], *v.a.* zusammenberufen.

convolvulus [kən'vɔlvjuləs], *s.* (*Bot.*) die Winde.

convoy ['kɔnvɔi], *s.* das Geleit, die Bedeckung; (*Mil.*) der Begleitzug. — [kən'vɔi], *v.a.* geleiten; (*Mil.*) im Geleitzug mitführen.

convulse [kən'vʌls], *v.a.* erschüttern.

convulsion [kən'vʌlʃən], *s.* der Krampf, die Zuckung.

convulsive [kən'vʌlsiv], *adj.* krampfhaft, zuckend.

coo [kuː], *v.n.* girren (*of birds*); *bill and —*, schnäbeln.

cook [kuk], *v.a., v.n.* kochen; (*coll.*) — *the books*, die Bücher(Bilanz)fälschen *or* frisieren. — *s.* der Koch, die Köchin; *too many cooks* (*spoil the broth*), zu viele Köche (verderben den Brei).

cookery ['kukəri], *s.* die Kochkunst; — *school*, die Kochschule.

cool [kuːl], *adj.* kühl (*climate*); kaltblütig (*coldblooded*); unverschämt (*brazen*). — *s.* die Kühle. — *v.a.* abkühlen; (*fig.*) besänftigen. — *v.n.* sich abkühlen.

cooler ['kuːlə], *s.* (*Chem.*) das Kühlfaß; (*coll.*) das Gefängnis; (*sl.*) das Kittchen.

coop [ku:p], *s.* die Kufe; das Faß; *hen* —, der Hühnerkorb. — *v.a.* — *up*, einsperren.

cooper ['ku:pə], *s.* der Böttcher, der Faßbinder.

cooperate [kou'ɔpəreit], *v.n.* zusammenarbeiten; mitarbeiten, mitwirken.

cooperation [kouɔpə'reiʃən], *s.* die Zusammenarbeit, die Mitarbeit.

cooperative [kou'ɔpərətiv], *adj.* willig; mitwirkend. — *s.* die Konsumgenossenschaft, der Konsum.

coordinate [kou'ɔ:dineit], *v.a.* koordinieren, beiordnen. — [-nit], *adj.* (*Gram.*) koordiniert.

coordination [kouɔ:di'neiʃən], *s.* die Koordinierung.

coot [ku:t], *s.* (*Orn.*) das Wasserhuhn.

copartnership [kou'pɑ:tnəʃip], *s.* die Teilhaberschaft; die Partnerschaft in der Industrie.

cope (1) [koup], *s.* (*Eccl.*) das Pluviale, der Priesterrock; (*Build.*) die Decke.

cope (2) [koup], *v.n.* — *with s.th.*, mit etwas fertig werden, es schaffen.

coping ['koupiŋ], *s.* (*Build.*) die Kappe; — *-stone* or *copestone*, der Firststein, Schlußstein, Kappstein.

copious ['koupiəs], *adj.* reichlich; wortreich (*style*).

copiousness ['koupiəsnis], *s.* die Reichhaltigkeit, Fülle.

copper ['kɔpə], *s.* (*Metall.*) das Kupfer; (*sl.*) der Polizist; (*coll.*) der Penny, das Pennystück. — *adj.* kupfern.

copperplate ['kɔpəpleit], *s.* der Kupferstich (*etching*); (*Typ.*) die Kupferplatte.

coppery ['kɔpəri], *adj.* Kupfer-, kupfern, kupferfarben (*colour*).

coppice, copse ['kɔpis, kɔps], *s.* das Unterholz, das Dickicht.

copulate ['kɔpjuleit], *v.n.* sich paaren, begatten.

copulation [kɔpju'leiʃən], *s.* die Paarung; der Beischlaf (*human*).

copy ['kɔpi], *v.a.* kopieren, abschreiben (*write*); imitieren, nachahmen (*imitate*). — *s.* die Kopie; *carbon* —, die Durchschrift; Abschrift; die Nachahmung (*imitation*); die Fälschung (*forgery*).

copybook ['kɔpibuk], *s.* das Heft.

copyist ['kɔpiist], *s.* der Kopist.

coquet, coquette (1) [kɔ'ket], *v.n.* kokettieren.

coquette (2) [kɔ'ket], *s.* die Kokette.

coquettish [kɔ'ketiʃ], *adj.* kokett.

coral ['kɔrəl], *s.* die Koralle. — *adj.* Korallen-.

cord [kɔ:d], *s.* die Schnur, der Strick (*rope*); (*Am.*) der Bindfaden (*string*); die Klafter (*wood measure*); der Kordstoff (*textile*); *vocal* —, das Stimmband.

cordage ['kɔ:didʒ], *s.* (*Naut.*) das Tauwerk.

cordial (1) ['kɔ:diəl], *adj.* herzlich.

cordial (2) ['kɔ:diəl], *s.* der Fruchtsaft (konzentriert), Magenlikör.

cordiality [kɔ:di'æliti], *s.* die Herzlichkeit.

corduroy ['kɔ:djurɔi], *s.* der Kordsamt.

core [kɔ:], *s.* der Kern; das Innere (*innermost part*).

cork [kɔ:k], *s.* der Kork, der Korken. — *v.a.* verkorken.

corkscrew ['kɔ:kskru:], *s.* der Korkzieher.

cormorant ['kɔ:mərənt], *s.* (*Orn.*) der Kormoran, die Scharbe.

corn (1) [kɔ:n], *s.* das Korn, das Getreide (*wheat etc.*); (*Am.*) *sweet* —, der Mais.

corn (2) [kɔ:n], *s.* das Hühnerauge (*on foot*).

corned [kɔ:nd], *adj.* eingesalzt; — *beef*, das Pökelrindfleisch.

cornea ['kɔ:niə], *s.* (*Anat.*) die Hornhaut.

cornel-tree ['kɔ:nəltri:], *s.* (*Bot.*) der Kornelkirschbaum.

cornelian [kɔ:'ni:liən], *s.* (*Geol.*) der Karneol.

corner ['kɔ:nə], *s.* die Ecke; (*Footb.*) der Eckstoß. — *v.a.* in eine Ecke treiben; in die Enge treiben (*force*).

cornered ['kɔ:nəd], *adj.* eckig (*angular*); in die Enge getrieben, gefangen (*caught*).

cornet ['kɔ:nit], *s.* (*Mus.*) die Zinke, das Flügelhorn; (*Mil.*) der Kornett, der Fähnrich.

cornflower ['kɔ:nflauə], *s.* (*Bot.*) die Kornblume.

cornice ['kɔ:nis], *s.* (*Archit.*) das Gesims.

cornucopia [kɔ:nju'koupjə], *s.* das Füllhorn.

corollary [kə'rɔləri], *s.* (*Log.*) der Folgesatz; die Folgeerscheinung (*consequence*).

corona [kə'rounə], *s.* (*Astron.*) der Hof, Lichtkranz.

coronation [kɔrə'neiʃən], *s.* die Krönung.

coroner ['kɔrənə], *s.* der Leichenbeschauer.

coronet ['kɔrənet], *s.* die Adelskrone.

corporal (1) ['kɔ:pərəl], *s.* (*Mil.*) der Korporal, der Unteroffizier, Obergefreite.

corporal (2) ['kɔ:pərəl], *adj.* körperlich; — *punishment*, die Züchtigung.

corporate ['kɔ:pərit], *adj.* (*Law, Comm.*) als Körperschaft; gemeinschaftlich, einheitlich (*as a group or unit*).

corporation [kɔ:pə'reiʃən], *s.* (*Law, Comm.*) die Körperschaft; die Korporation; die Gemeinde (*municipal*); (*sl.*) der Schmerbauch (*stoutness*).

corps [kɔ:], *s.* das Korps.

corpse [kɔ:ps], *s.* der Leichnam.

corpulence [kɔ:pjuləns], *s.* die Korpulenz, die Beleibtheit.

corpulent ['kɔ:pjulənt], *adj.* korpulent, dick.

Corpus Christi ['kɔ:pəs 'kristi], (der) Fronleichnam, das Fronleichnamsfest.

corpuscle ['kɔ:pʌsl], *s.* (*Anat.*) das Körperchen.

correct

correct [kəˈrekt], v.a. korrigieren (*remove mistakes*); verbessern; tadeln (*reprove*); berichtigen (*rectify*). — adj. korrekt, tadellos, richtig.
correction [kəˈrekʃən], s. die Korrektur (*of mistakes*); die Verbesserung (*improvement*); die Richtigstellung (*restoration*); der Verweis (*censure*).
corrective [kəˈrektiv], adj. zur Besserung. — s. das Korrektiv.
correctness [kəˈrektnis], s. die Korrektheit (*of manner, action etc.*).
corrector [kəˈrektə], s. der Korrektor (*proof reader etc.*).
correlate [ˈkɔrileit], v.a. in Beziehung setzen, aufeinander beziehen. — [-lit], s. (*Log.*) das Korrelat.
correlative [kɔˈrelativ], adj. in Wechselbeziehung stehend.
correspond [kɔrisˈpɔnd], v.n. korrespondieren (*exchange letters*); entsprechen (*to, Dat.*).
correspondence [kɔrisˈpɔndəns], s. die Korrespondenz; der Briefwechsel (*letters*); die Übereinstimmung (*harmony*).
correspondent [kɔrisˈpɔndənt], s. der Korrespondent (*letter-writer*); der Journalist, Berichterstatter (*newspaper*).
corridor [ˈkɔridɔ:], s. der Korridor; der Gang.
corrigible [ˈkɔridʒibl], adj. verbesserlich.
corroborate [kəˈrɔbəreit], v.a. bestätigen (*confirm*); bestärken (*strengthen*).
corroboration [kərɔbəˈreiʃən], s. die Bestätigung, die Bekräftigung.
corroborative [kəˈrɔbərətiv], adj. bekräftigend.
corrode [kəˈroud], v.a. zerfressen, zersetzen, ätzen (*acid*).
corrosion [kəˈrouʒən], s. die Anfressung, Ätzung.
corrosive [kəˈrouziv], adj. ätzend.
corrugated [ˈkɔrugeitid], adj. gewellt, Well-; — iron, das Wellblech; — paper, die Wellpappe.
corrupt [kəˈrʌpt], v.a. verderben (*spoil*); bestechen (*bribe*). — adj. korrupt (*morals*); verdorben (*spoilt*).
corruptible [kəˈrʌptibl], adj. verderblich; bestechlich.
corruption [kəˈrʌpʃən], s. die Korruption; die Bestechung (*bribery*).
corruptness [kəˈrʌptnis], s. die Verdorbenheit, der Verfall.
corsair [ˈkɔ:seə], s. der Korsar, der Seeräuber.
corset [ˈkɔ:sit], s. das Korsett.
coruscate [ˈkɔrəskeit], v.n. schimmern, leuchten.
corvette [kɔ:ˈvet], s. (*Naut.*) die Korvette.
cosine [ˈkousain], s. (*Maths.*) der Kosinus.
cosiness [ˈkouzinis], s. die Bequemlichkeit, die Behaglichkeit (*comfort*).

cosmetic [kɔzˈmetik], adj. kosmetisch. — s. (*pl.*) das or die (*pl.*) Schönheitsmittel.
cosmic [ˈkɔzmik], adj. kosmisch.
cosmopolitan [kɔzmoˈpɔlitən], adj. kosmopolitisch, weltbürgerlich. — s. der Kosmopolit, der Weltbürger.
Cossack [ˈkɔsæk], s. der Kosak.
cost [kɔst], v.a. irr. kosten. — v.n. irr. zu stehen kommen. —s. die Kosten, f. pl. (*expenses*); at all —s, um jeden Preis.
costermonger [ˈkɔstəmʌŋgə], s. der Straßenhändler.
costly [ˈkɔstli], adj. kostspielig.
costume [ˈkɔstju:m], s. das Kostüm; — play, das Zeitstück.
cosy [ˈkouzi], adj. behaglich, bequem.
cot (1) [kɔt], s. das Bettchen, Kinderbett.
cot (2) [kɔt], s. (*obs.*) die Hütte (*hut*).
cottage [ˈkɔtidʒ], s. die Hütte, das Häuschen.
cottager [ˈkɔtidʒə], s. der Kleinhäusler.
cotton [kɔtn], s. die Baumwolle. — v.n. — on to, (*coll.*) sich anhängen, sich anschließen (*Dat.*); — on, folgen können (*understand*).
couch [kautʃ], s. die Chaiselongue; der Diwan. — v.a. (*express*) in Worte fassen.
cough [kɔf], v.n. husten. — s. der Husten; whooping —, der Keuchhusten.
council [ˈkaunsil], s. der Rat (*body*); die Ratsversammlung.
councillor [ˈkaunsilə], s. der Rat, das Ratsmitglied; der Stadtrat.
counsel [ˈkaunsəl], s. der Rat (*advice*); der Berater (*adviser*); der Anwalt (*lawyer*). — v.a. einen Rat geben, beraten (*Acc.*).
counsellor [ˈkaunsələ], s. der Ratgeber; der Ratsherr; (*Am.*) der Anwalt (*lawyer*).
count (1) [kaunt], v.a., v.n. zählen; — on s.o., sich auf jemanden verlassen. — s. die Zählung.
count (2) [kaunt], s. der Graf.
countenance [ˈkauntənəns], s. das Gesicht, die Miene. — v.a. begünstigen, unterstützen, zulassen.
counter (1) [ˈkauntə], s. der Rechner, der Zähler (*chip*); die Spielmarke; der Zahltisch (*desk*); Ladentisch (*in shop*); Schalter (*in office*).
counter (2) [ˈkauntə], adv. entgegen.
counteract [kauntəˈrækt], v.a. entgegenwirken (*Dat.*).
counteraction [kauntəˈrækʃən], s. die Gegenwirkung; der Widerstand (*resistance*).
counterbalance [ˈkauntəbæləns], s. das Gegengewicht. — [-ˈbæləns], v.a. ausbalancieren, ausgleichen.
countercharge [ˈkauntətʃa:dʒ], s. die Gegenklage.
counterfeit [ˈkauntəfi:t, -fit], s. die Fälschung (*forgery*); die Nachahmung (*imitation*). — adj. gefälscht, falsch.

counterfoil ['kauntəfɔil], *s.* das Kontrollblatt; der Kupon.

counter–intelligence ['kauntərintelidʒəns], *s.* die Spionageabwehr.

countermand [kauntə'mɑːnd], *v.a.* widerrufen.

counterpane ['kauntəpein], *s.* die Steppdecke.

counterpart ['kauntəpɑːt], *s.* das Gegenbild, das Gegenstück.

counterplot ['kauntəplɔt], *s.* der Gegenplan. — *v.n.* einen Gegenplan machen.

counterpoint ['kauntəpɔint], *s.* (*Mus.*) der Kontrapunkt.

counterpoise ['kauntəpɔiz], *s.* das Gegengewicht. — *v.a.* die Gleichgewicht halten.

countersign ['kauntəsain], *v.a.* gegenzeichnen, mitunterschreiben. — *s.* das Gegenzeichen.

countess ['kauntes], *s.* die Gräfin.

counting-house ['kauntiŋhaus], *s.* das Kontor.

countless ['kauntlis], *adj.* zahllos.

country ['kʌntri], *s.* das Land. — *adj.* Land-, ländlich, Bauern-.

county ['kaunti], *s.* die Grafschaft (*British*); der Landbezirk (*U.S.A.*).

couple [kʌpl], *s.* das Paar. — *v.a.* paaren, verbinden. — *v.n.* sich paaren (*pair*); sich verbinden.

couplet ['kʌplit], *s.* das Verspaar.

coupling ['kʌpliŋ], *s.* (*Mech.*) die Kupplung.

courage ['kʌridʒ], *s.* der Mut.

courageous [kə'reidʒəs], *adj.* mutig, tapfer.

courier ['kuriə], *s.* der Eilbote (*messenger*); der Reisebegleiter (*tour leader*).

course [kɔːs], *s.* der Kurs; der Lauf (*time*); der Ablauf (*lapse of a period etc.*); die Bahn (*racing track*); *in due —*, zu gegebener Zeit; *of —*, natürlich.

courser ['kɔːsə], *s.* das schnelle Pferd.

court [kɔːt], *s.* der Hof (*royal etc.*); (*Law*) der Gerichtshof. — *v.a.* (*a lady*) den Hof machen (*Dat.*); — *disaster*, das Unglück herausfordern.

courteous ['kɔːtiəs], *adj.* höflich.

courtesan ['kɔːtizən or kɔːti'zæn], *s.* die Kurtisane, die Buhlerin.

courtesy ['kɔːtəsi], *s.* die Höflichkeit; *by — of*, mit freundlicher Erlaubnis von.

courtier ['kɔːtiə], *s.* der Höfling.

courtly ['kɔːtli], *adj.* höfisch, Hof-.

court-martial [kɔːt'mɑːʃəl], *s.* das Kriegsgericht.

courtship ['kɔːtʃip], *s.* das Werben, die Werbung, das Freien.

courtyard ['kɔːtjɑːd], *s.* der Hof, der Hofraum.

cousin [kʌzn], *s.* der Vetter (*male*); die Kusine (*female*).

cove [kouv], *s.* die (kleine) Bucht.

covenant ['kʌvənənt], *s.* (*Bibl.*) der Bund; (*Comm.*) der Vertrag.

cover ['kʌvə], *v.a.* decken, bedecken (*table etc.*); schützen (*protect*); — *up*, bemänteln. — *s.* die Decke (*blanket*); der Deckel (*lid*); der Einband (*book*); das Gedeck (*table*); (*Comm.*) die Deckung; — *point*, (*Cricket*) die Deckstellung; *under —*, (*Mil.*) verdeckt, unter Deckung; — *girl*, das Mädchen auf dem Titelblatt (einer Illustrierten.)

covering ['kʌvəriŋ], *s.* die Bedeckung, die Bekleidung (*clothing*).

coverlet, coverlid ['kʌvəlit, 'kʌvəlid], *s.* die Bettdecke.

covert ['kʌvəːt], *s.* der Schlupfwinkel (*hideout*); das Dickicht (*thicket*). — *adj.* verborgen, bedeckt (*covered*); heimlich (*secret*).

covet ['kʌvit], *v.a., v.n.* begehren (*Acc.*), gelüsten (nach (*Dat.*)).

covetous ['kʌvitəs], *adj.* begierig, habsüchtig.

covetousness ['kʌvitəsnis], *s.* die Begierde, die Habsucht.

covey ['kʌvi], *s.* der Flug *or* die Kette (Rebhühner, *partridges*).

cow (1) [kau], *s.* die Kuh; — *-shed*, der Kuhstall.

cow (2) [kau], *v.a.* einschüchtern.

coward ['kauəd], *s.* der Feigling.

cowardice ['kauədis], *s.* die Feigheit.

cower ['kauə], *v.n.* kauern.

cowherd ['kauhɔːd], *s.* der Kuhhirt.

cowl [kaul], *s.* die Kappe (*of monk*), die Kapuze (*hood*).

cowslip ['kauslip], *s.* (*Bot.*) die Primel, die Schlüsselblume.

coxswain [kɔksn], *s.* (*Naut.*) der Steuermann.

coy [kɔi], *adj.* scheu, spröde, zurückhaltend.

coyness ['kɔinis], *s.* die Sprödigkeit.

crab [kræb], *s.* (*Zool.*) die Krabbe; — *apple*, (*Bot.*) der Holzapfel.

crabbed [kræbd], *adj.* mürrisch (*temper*); unleserlich (*handwriting*).

crack [kræk], *s.* der Riß (*fissure*); der Krach, Schlag; der Sprung; die komische Bemerkung (*remark*). — *adj.* (*coll.*) erstklassig; —*shot*, der Meisterschütze. — *v.a.* aufbrechen; aufknacken (*nut, safe*); — *a joke*, einen witzige Bemerkung machen. — *v.n.* — *under strain*, unter einer Anstrengung zusammenbrechen; bersten (*break*).

cracked, crackers [krækd, 'krækəz], *adj.* (*coll.*) verrückt.

cracker ['krækə], *s.* der Keks; der Frosch (*firework*).

crackle [krækl], *v.n.* knistern, prasseln (*fire*); knallen, platzen (*rocket*).

cracknel ['kræknəl], *s.* die Brezel.

crackpot ['krækpɔt], *s.* (*coll.*) der verrückte Kerl.

cradle [kreidl], *s.* die Wiege. — *v.a.* einwiegen.

craft [krɑːft], *s.* die Fertigkeit (*skill*); das Handwerk (*trade*); die List (*cunning*); *arts and —s*, die Handwerkskünste.

craftsman ['krɑːftsmən], s. der (gelernte) Handwerker.

crafty ['krɑːfti], adj. listig, schlau.

crag [kræg], s. die Klippe.

cragged, craggy [krægd, 'krægi], adj. felsig, schroff.

cram [kræm], v.a. vollstopfen (stuff full); (coll.) pauken (coach). — v.n. büffeln.

crammer ['kræmə], s. (coll.) der Einpauker, Privatlehrer (tutor).

cramp [kræmp], s. (Med.) der Krampf; die Klammer (tool). — v.a. einengen (narrow); verkrampfen.

cramped [kræmpd], adj. krampfhaft; eingeengt, beengt (enclosed).

cranberry ['krænbəri], s. (Bot.) die Preiselbeere.

crane [krein], s. (Orn.) der Kranich; (Engin.) der Kran. — v.a. — o.'s neck, den Hals ausrecken.

crank (1) [kræŋk], s. (Motor.) die Kurbel; — -handle, die Andrehwelle; (Motor., Engin.) -shaft, die Kurbelwelle, die Kurbel.

crank (2) [kræŋk], s. der Sonderling, der sonderbare Kauz (eccentric).

cranky ['kræŋki], adj. sonderbar.

cranny ['kræni], s. der Spalt, der Riß; nook and —, Eck und Spalt.

crape [kreip], s. der Krepp, Flor.

crash [kræʃ], s. der Krach; (Motor.) Zusammenstoß; (Aviat.) Absturz. — v.n. krachen (noise); stürzen, abstürzen (fall).

crass [kræs], adj. derb, grob, kraß.

crate [kreit], s. der Packkorb (basket); die Kiste (wood).

crater ['kreitə], s. (Geol.) der Krater.

cravat [krə'væt], s. die breite Halsbinde, das Halstuch (scarf); die Krawatte.

crave [kreiv], v.a. (dringend) verlangen (for, nach, Dat.).

craven ['kreivn], adj. feig, mutlos. — s. der Feigling.

craving ['kreiviŋ], s. das starke Verlangen.

craw [krɔː], s. (Zool.) der Vogelkropf.

crawl [krɔːl], v.n. kriechen; kraulen (swim).

crawling ['krɔːliŋ], s. das Kriechen; das Kraulschwimmen.

crayon ['kreiən], s. der Farbstift, der Pastellstift.

craze [kreiz], s. die Manie; die verrückte Mode (fashion).

craziness ['kreizinis], s. die Verrücktheit.

crazy ['kreizi], adj. verrückt.

creak [kriːk], v.n. knarren.

cream [kriːm], s. der Rahm, die Sahne; whipped —, die Schlagsahne, (Austr.) der Schlagobers. — v.a. — off, (die Sahne) abschöpfen; (fig.) das Beste abziehen.

creamery ['kriːməri], s. die Molkerei.

creamy ['kriːmi], adj. sahnig.

crease [kriːs], s. die Falte (trousers etc.); — -resistant, knitterfrei. — v.a. falten (fold). — v.n. knittern.

create [kriˈeit], v.a. erschaffen, schaffen.

creation [kriˈeiʃən], s. die Schöpfung.

creative [kriˈeitiv], adj. schöpferisch.

creator [kriˈeitə], s. der Schöpfer.

creature ['kriːtʃə], s. das Geschöpf.

credence ['kriːdəns], s. der Glaube.

credentials [kriˈdenʃəlz], s. pl. das Zeugnis, das Beglaubigungsschreiben; die Legitimation (proof of identity).

credibility [kredi'biliti], s. die Glaubwürdigkeit.

credible ['kredibl], adj. glaubwürdig, glaublich.

credit ['kredit], s. (Comm.) der Kredit; der gute Ruf (reputation); das Guthaben (assets). — v.a. — s.o. with s.th., jemandem etwas gutschreiben; glauben (believe).

creditable ['kreditəbl], adj. ehrenwert, lobenswert.

creditor ['kreditə], s. (Comm.) der Gläubiger.

credulity [kreˈdjuːliti], s. die Leichtgläubigkeit.

credulous ['kredjuləs], adj. leichtgläubig.

creed [kriːd], s. das Glaubensbekenntnis.

creek [kriːk], s. die kleine Bucht; das Flüßchen (small river).

creel [kriːl], s. der Fischkorb.

creep [kriːp], s. (Geol.) der Rutsch; (pl., coll.) the —s, die Gänsehaut, das Gruseln. — v.n.irr. kriechen; (furtively) sich einschleichen.

creeper ['kriːpə], s. die Schlingpflanze, das Rankengewächs; (Sch.) der Kriecher; Virginia —, der wilde Wein.

creepy ['kriːpi], adj. kriechend; gruselig (frightening).

cremate [kriˈmeit], v.a. einäschern.

cremation [kriˈmeiʃən], s. die Verbrennung, Einäscherung.

crematorium, (Am.) crematory [kreməˈtɔːriəm, 'kremətəri], s. das Krematorium.

Creole ['kriːoul], s. der Kreole.

crepuscular [kriˈpʌskjulə], adj. dämmerig.

crescent ['kresənt], adj. wachsend, zunehmend. — s. der (zunehmende) Mond, die Mondsichel; das Hörnchen.

cress [kres], s. (Bot.) die Kresse; mustard and —, die Gartenkresse.

crest [krest], s. der Kamm (cock); der Gipfel (hill); der Kamm (wave); der Busch (helmet); das Wappenschild (Heraldry).

crestfallen ['krestfɔːlən], adj. entmutigt, mutlos, niedergeschlagen.

Cretan ['kriːtən], adj. kretisch. — s. der Kreter, die Kreterin.

cretonne ['kretɔn], s. die Kretonne.

crevasse [krə'væs], s. die Gletscherspalte.

crevice ['krevis], s. der Riß.

crew (1) [kruː], s. (Naut., Aviat.) die Besatzung; (Naut.) die Schiffsmannschaft; die Mannschaft (team); (Am.) — cut, die Bürstenfrisur.

crew (2) [kru:] *see* **crow**.

crib [krib], *s.* die Krippe (*Christmas*); die Wiege (*cradle*); (*Sch.*) die Eselsbrücke. — *v.a.* (*Sch.*) abschreiben (*copy*).

crick [krik], *s.* (*in neck*) der steife Hals.

cricket ['krikit], *s.* (*Ent.*) das Heimchen, die Grille; (*Sport*) das Cricket(spiel).

crime [kraim], *s.* das Verbrechen; — *fiction*, die Detektivromane, *m. pl.*

criminal ['kriminəl], *s.* der Verbrecher. — *adj.* — *case*, der Kriminalfall; verbrecherisch (*act*); — *investigation*, die Fahndung.

crimp [krimp], *v.a.* kräuseln (*hair*).

crimson ['krimzən], *adj.* karmesinrot.

cringe [krindʒ], *v.n.* kriechen.

crinkle ['kriŋkl], *v.a.*, *v.n.* kräuseln. — *s.* die Falte.

crinoline ['krinəlin], *s.* der Reifrock.

cripple [kripl], *s.* der Krüppel. — *v.a.* verkrüppeln; lahmlegen (*immobilize*).

crisis ['kraisis], *s.* die Krise, der Wendepunkt; die Notlage.

crisp [krisp], *adj.* kraus (*hair*); knusperig (*bread*); frisch.

criss-cross ['kriskrɔs], *adv.* kreuz und quer.

criterion [krai'tiəriən], *s.* das Kennzeichen, das Kriterium.

critic ['kritik], *s.* der Kritiker; Rezensent (*reviewer*).

critical ['kritikəl], *adj.* kritisch.

criticism ['kritisizm], *s.* die Kritik (*of*, *an*, *Dat.*); Rezension, Besprechung (*review*).

criticize ['kritisaiz], *v.a.* kritisieren.

croak [krouk], *v.n.* krächzen (*raven*); quaken (*frog*).

croaking ['kroukiŋ], *s.* das Krächzen, das Gekrächze (*raven*); das Quaken (*frog*).

Croat ['krouæt], *s.* der Kroate.

Croatian [krou'eiʃən], *adj.* kroatisch.

crochet ['krouʃei], *s.* die Häkelei; — *hook*, die Häkelnadel. — *v.a.*, *v.n.* häkeln.

crock [krɔk], *s.* der Topf, der irdene Krug; der alte Topf; (*coll.*) old —, der Invalide, Krüppel.

crockery ['krɔkəri], *s.* (*Comm.*) die Töpferware; das Geschirr (*household*).

crocodile ['krɔkədail], *s.* das Krokodil.

crocus ['kroukəs], *s.* (*Bot.*) der Krokus, die Safranblume.

croft [krɔft], *s.* das Kleinbauerngut.

crofter ['krɔftə], *s.* der Kleinbauer.

crone [kroun], *s.* das alte Weib; die Hexe (*witch*).

crony ['krouni], *s.* (*coll.*) old —, der alte Freund.

crook [kruk], *s.* der Krummstab (*staff*); der Schwindler (*cheat*). — *v.a.* krümmen, biegen.

crooked ['krukid], *adj.* krumm; (*fig.*) schwindlerisch, verbrecherisch.

crookedness ['krukidnis], *s.* die Krummheit; die Durchtriebenheit (*slyness*).

croon [kru:n], *v.n.* leise singen; (*Am.*) im modernen Stil singen.

crooner ['kru:nə], *s.* der Jazzsänger.

crop [krɔp], *s.* der Kropf (*bird*); die Ernte (*harvest*); der (kurze) Haarschnitt; *riding* —, die Reitpeitsche. — *v.a.* stutzen (*cut short*). — *v.n.* — *up*, auftauchen.

crosier ['krouziə], *s.* (*Eccl.*) der Bischofsstab.

cross [krɔs], *s.* das Kreuz. — *v.a.* (*Zool.*, *Bot.*) kreuzen; überqueren (*road*, *on foot*); — *s.o.'s path*, einem in die Quere kommen. — *v.n.* überfahren (*übers Wasser*); hinübergehen; — *over*, übersetzen (*on boat or ferry*). — *v.r.* sich bekreuzigen. — *adj.* mürrisch (*grumpy*), verstimmt; *at — purposes*, ohne einander zu verstehen; *make* —, verstimmen. — *adv.* kreuzweise; — *-eyed*, schielend; — *-grained*, wider den Strich, schlecht aufgelegt.

crossbow ['krɔsbou], *s.* die Armbrust.

crossbreed ['krɔsbri:d], *s.* die Mischrasse, der Mischling.

cross-examine [krɔsig'zæmin], *v.a.*, *v.n.* (*Law*) ins (Kreuz–)Verhör nehmen.

crossing ['krɔsiŋ], *s.* die Straßenkreuzung; (*Naut.*) die Überfahrt; der Straßenübergang; Kreuzweg.

crossroads ['krɔsroudz], *s.* der Kreuzweg, die Kreuzung.

crossword ['krɔswɔ:d], *s.* das Kreuzworträtsel.

crotch [krɔtʃ], *s.* der Haken.

crotchet ['krɔtʃit], *s.* (*Mus.*) die Viertelnote; die Grille (*mood*).

crotchety ['krɔtʃiti], *adj.* grillenhaft, verschroben.

crouch [krautʃ], *v.n.* sich ducken (*squat*); sich demütigen (*cringe*).

croup (1) [kru:p], *s.* (*Med.*) der Krupp.

croup (2) [kru:p], *s.* die Kruppe.

crow [krou], *s.* (*Orn.*) die Krähe; das Krähen (*of cock*). — *v.n. irr.* krähen (*cock*).

crowbar ['kroubɑ:], *s.* das Brecheisen.

crowd [kraud], *s.* die Menge (*multitude*); das Gedränge (*throng*). — *v.n.* — *in*, sich hineindrängen, dazudrängen; — *around*, sich herumscharen um (*Acc.*).

crown [kraun], *s.* die Krone (*diadem or coin*); der Gipfel (*mountain*); (*Anat.*) der Scheitel; — *lands*, Krongüter (*n. pl.*), Landeigentum der Krone, *n.*; — *prince*, der Kronprinz; — *of thorns*, die Dornenkrone. — *v.a.* krönen.

crucial ['kru:ʃəl], *adj.* entscheidend, kritisch.

crucifix ['kru:sifiks], *s.* das Kruzifix.

crucify ['kru:sifai], *v.a.* kreuzigen.

crude [kru:d], *adj.* roh, ungekocht, unreif; grob (*manners*); ungeschliffen.

crudity ['kru:diti], *s.* die Rohheit; Grobheit (*manners*).

cruel ['kru:əl], *adj.* grausam.

cruelty ['kru:əlti], *s.* die Grausamkeit.

cruet ['kru:it], *s.* das Salz- oder Pfefferfäßchen; das Fläschchen.

cruise [kru:z], *v.n.* (*Naut.*) kreuzen. — *s.* die Seehfahrt, die Seereise; *pleasure* —, die Vergnügungsreise (zu Wasser).

cruiser ['kru:zə], *s.* (*Naut.*) der Kreuzer; *battle* —, der Panzerkreuzer.

crumb [krʌm], *s.* die Krume. — *v.a.* zerbröckeln, zerkrümeln.

crumble [krʌmbl], *v.n.* zerfallen, zerbröckeln.

crumpet ['krʌmpit], *s.* das Teebrötchen, das Teeküchlein.

crumple [krʌmpl], *v.a.* zerknittern (*material*). — *v.n.* — *up*, zusammenbrechen.

crunch [krʌntʃ], *v.a.* zerstoßen, zermalmen. — *v.n.* knirschen.

crusade [kru:'seid], *s.* der Kreuzzug.

crusader [kru:'seidə], *s.* der Kreuzfahrer.

crush [krʌʃ], *v.a.* zerdrücken; zerstoßen (*pulverize*); drängen (*crowd*); zertreten (*tread down*); (*fig.*) vernichten. — *s.* das Gedränge (*throng*); (*coll.*) *have a* — *on*, verknallt sein, in einen verliebt sein.

crust [krʌst], *s.* die Kruste, die Rinde (*bread*). — *v.a.* mit einer Kruste bedecken — *v.n.* verkrusten.

crustaceous [krʌs'teiʃəs], *adj.* (*Zool.*) krustenartig, Krustentier-.

crusty ['krʌsti], *adj.* krustig, knusperig (*pastry, bread*); mürrisch (*grumpy*).

crutch [krʌtʃ], *s.* die Krücke.

crux [krʌks], *s.* der entscheidende Punkt, der springende Punkt, die Schwierigkeit.

cry [krai], *v.n.* schreien, rufen; weinen (*weep*). — *v.a.* — *down*, niederschreien. — *s.* der Schrei; der Zuruf (*call*).

crypt [kript], *s.* (*Eccl.*) die Krypta, die Gruft.

crystal ['kristəl], *s.* der Kristall.

crystallize ['kristəlaiz], *v.n.* sich kristallisieren, Kristalle bilden.

cub [kʌb], *s.* (*Zool.*) das Junge. — *v.n.* Junge haben, Junge werfen.

Cuban ['kju:bən], *adj.* kubanisch. — *s.* der Kubaner.

cube [kju:b], *s.* der Würfel; (*Maths.*) *root*, die Kubikwurzel. — *v.a.* zur Dritten (Potenz) erheben; kubieren (*Maths.*).

cubic(al) ['kju:bik(əl)], *adj.* kubisch, zur dritten Potenz.

cubit ['kju:bit], *s.* die Elle.

cuckoo ['kuku:], *s.* (*Orn.*) der Kuckuck.

cucumber ['kju:kʌmbə], *s.* (*Bot.*) die Gurke; *cool as a* —, ruhig und gelassen.

cud [kʌd], *s.* das wiedergekäute Futter; *chew the* —, wiederkäuen (*also fig.*).

cuddle [kʌdl], *v.a.* liebkosen, an sich drücken. — *v.n.* sich anschmiegen.

cudgel ['kʌdʒəl], *s.* der Knüttel; *take up the* —*s for*, sich für etwas einsetzen.

cue (1) [kju:], *s.* (*Theat.*) das Stichwort. — *v.a.* einem (*Theat.*) das Stichwort or (*Mus.*) den Einsatz geben.

cue (2) [kju:], *s.* der Billardstock. — *v.a* (*Billiards*) abschießen.

cuff (1) [kʌf], *s.* die Manschette, der Aufschlag (*shirt*); —*links*, die Manschettenknöpfe.

cuff (2) [kʌf], *s.* der Schlag. — *v.a.* schlagen, puffen.

culinary ['kju:linəri], *adj.* kulinarisch; Küchen-, Eß-, Speisen-.

cull [kʌl], *v.a.* auswählen, auslesen (*from books*).

culminate ['kʌlmineit], *v.n.* kulminieren, den Höhepunkt erreichen.

culpable ['kʌlpəbl], *adj.* schuldig; strafbar.

culprit ['kʌlprit], *s.* der Schuldige, Verbrecher.

cult [kʌlt], *s.* der Kult, die Verehrung; der Kultus.

cultivate ['kʌltiveit], *v.a.* kultivieren; (*Agr.*) anbauen; pflegen (*acquaintance*); bilden (*mind*).

cultivation [kʌlti'veiʃən], *s.* (*Agr.*) der Anbau; die Bildung (*mind*).

culture ['kʌltʃə], *s.* die Kultur, die Bildung.

cumbersome ['kʌmbəsəm], *adj.* beschwerlich, lästig.

cunning ['kʌniŋ], *s.* die List, die Schlauheit. — *adj.* listig, schlau.

cup [kʌp], *s.* die Tasse (*tea*—); der Becher (*handleless*); (*Eccl.*) der Kelch; der Pokal (*sports*); — *final*, das Endspiel. — *v.a.* (*Med.*) schröpfen.

cupboard ['kʌbəd], *s.* der Schrank.

cupola ['kju:polə], *s.* (*Archit., Metall.*) die Kuppel.

cur [kə:], *s.* der Köter; (*fig*) der Schurke.

curable ['kjuərəbl], *adj.* heilbar.

curate ['kjuərit], *s.* der Hilfsgeistliche.

curative ['kjuərətiv], *adj.* heilsam, heilend.

curator [kjuə'reitə], *s.* der Kurator, Verwalter, Direktor.

curb [kə:b], *v.a.* zügeln, bändigen. — *s.* der Zaum (*bridle*).

curd [kə:d], *s.* der Rahmkäse, der Milchkäse; (*pl.*) der Quark.

curdle [kə:dl], *v.a.* gerinnen lassen. — *v.n.* gerinnen; erstarren.

cure [kjuə], *v.a.* die Kur, die Heilung. — *v.a.* kurieren, wieder gesundmachen; einpökeln (*foodstuffs*).

curfew ['kə:fju:], *s.* die Abendglocke (*bells*); das Ausgehverbot, die Polizeistunde (*police*).

curio ['kjuəriou], *s.* die Kuriosität, das Sammlerstück; die Rarität.

curiosity [kjuəri'ositi], *s.* die Neugier; Merkwürdigkeit.

curious ['kjuəriəs], *adj.* neugierig (*inquisitive*); seltsam, sonderbar (*strange*).

curl [kə:l], *v.a.* kräuseln, (in Locken) wickeln. — *v.n.* sich kräuseln. — *s.* die Haarlocke.

curler ['kə:lə], *s.* der Lockenwickler.

curlew ['kə:lju:], *s.*(*Orn.*) der Brachvogel.

curly ['kə:li], *adj.* lockig.

currant ['kʌrənt], *s.* (*Bot.*) die Korinthe, die Johannisbeere.

currency ['kʌrənsi], s. die Währung (*money*); der Umlauf (*circulation*).

current ['kʌrənt], adj. im Umlauf; allgemein gültig, eben gültig; jetzig (*modern*). — s. (*Elect.*) der Strom; die Strömung (*river*); der Zug (*air*).

curry (1) ['kʌri], v.a. gerben (*tan*); — *comb*, der Pferdestriegel; — *favour*, sich einschmeicheln.

curry (2) ['kʌri], s. das indische Ragout. — v.a. würzen.

curse [kə:s], v.a., v.n. verfluchen; verwünschen. — s. der Fluch; die Verwünschung.

cursive ['kə:siv], adj. kursiv, Kursiv-.

cursory ['kə:səri], adj. kursorisch, oberflächlich.

curt [kə:t], adj. kurz angebunden (*speech, manner*).

curtail [kə:'teil], v.a. stutzen, beschränken (*scope*); verkürzen (*time*).

curtain ['kə:tin], s. die Gardine, der Vorhang; (*Mil.*) — *fire*, das Sperrfeuer; — *lecture*, die Gardinenpredigt; — *speech*, die Ansprache vor dem Vorhang. — v.a. verhüllen (*hide*); mit Vorhängen versehen (*hang curtains*).

curtness ['kə:tnis], s. die Kürze; die Barschheit.

curts(e)y ['kə:tsi], s. der Knicks. — v.n. knicksen, einen Knicks machen.

curve [kə:v], s. die Krümmung; (*Geom.*) die Kurve. — v.a. krümmen, biegen. — v.n. sich biegen.

curved [kə:vd], adj. krumm, gebogen.

cushion ['kuʃən], s. das Kissen. — v.a. polstern.

custody ['kʌstədi], s. die Obhut; Bewachung, Haft.

custom ['kʌstəm], s. die Sitte, die Tradition; der Gebrauch, Brauch (*usage*); die Kundschaft (*trade*); (*pl.*) der Zoll (*duty*).

customary ['kʌstəməri], adj. gewohnt, althergebracht, gebräuchlich.

customer ['kʌstəmə], s. der Kunde, die Kundin.

cut [kʌt], v.a. irr. schneiden; — (*s.o.*), ignorieren; — *o.'s teeth*, zahnen; *this won't — any ice*, das wird nicht viel nützen; — *both ways*, das ist ein zweischneidiges Schwert; — *a lecture*, eine Vorlesung schwänzen; — *short*, unterbrechen. — adj. — *out for*, wie gerufen zu or für; — *to the quick*, aufs tiefste verletzt; — *glass*, das geschliffene Glas; — *price*, verbilligt. — s. der Schnitt (*section*); der Hieb (*gash*); (*Art*) der Stich; — *in salary*, eine Gehaltskürzung; die Abkürzung; die Kürzung (*abridgement*).

cute [kju:t], adj. klug, aufgeweckt; (*Am.*) süß; niedlich.

cutler ['kʌtlə], s. der Messerschmied.

cutlery ['kʌtləri], s. das Besteck (*tableware*); (*Comm.*) die Messerschmiedwaren, *f. pl.*

cutlet ['kʌtlit], s. das Kotelett, das Rippchen.

cut-throat ['kʌtθrout], s. der Halsabschneider; — *competition*, Konkurrenz auf Leben und Tod.

cuttle [kʌtl], s. (*Zool.*) der Tintenfisch.

cyanide ['saiənaid], s. (*Chem.*) zyanidsaures Salz; das Zyanid, die Blausäure.

cyclamen ['sikləmən], s. (*Bot.*) das Alpenveilchen.

cycle [saikl], s. (*Geom.*) der Kreis; (*Mus., Zool.*) der Zyklus; (*coll.*) das Fahrrad. — v.n. (*coll.*) radfahren; zirkulieren (*round*, um, *Acc.*).

cyclone ['saikloun], s. der Wirbelwind, der Wirbelsturm.

cyclopaedia [saiklo'pi:djə] *see* **encyclopaedia**.

cylinder ['silində], s. der Zylinder; die Walze.

cymbal ['simbəl], s. (*Mus.*) die Zimbel, das Becken.

cynic ['sinik], s. der Zyniker.

cynical ['sinikəl], adj. zynisch.

cypress ['saiprəs], s. (*Bot.*) die Zypresse.

Cypriot ['sipriət], adj. zyprisch. — s. der Zypriote.

czar [zɑ:], s. der Zar.

Czech, Czechoslovak(ian) [tʃek, tʃeko'slouvæk, tʃekoslo'vækjən], adj. tschechisch. — s. der Tscheche.

D

D [di:]. das D (*also Mus.*).

dab [dæb], v.a. leicht berühren. — s. der leichte Schlag (*blow*).

dabble [dæbl], v.n. sich in etwas versuchen, pfuschen (*in*, in, *Dat.*).

dabbler ['dæblə], s. der Pfuscher, Stümper.

dace [deis], s. (*Zool.*) der Weißfisch.

dad, daddy [dæd, 'dædi], s. der Papa; Vati; *daddy longlegs*, die Bachmücke, die langbeinige Mücke.

dado ['deidou], s. die Täfelung.

daffodil ['dæfədil], s. (*Bot.*) die Narzisse.

dagger ['dægə], s. der Dolch; *at —s drawn*, spinnefeind; *look* —s, mit Blicken durchbohren.

dahlia ['deiliə], s. (*Bot.*) die Dahlie, die Georgine.

daily ['deili], adj. täglich; Tages-. — s. (*newspaper*) die Tageszeitung; (*woman*) die Putzfrau.

dainties ['deintiz], s. pl. das Backwerk, das kleine Gebäck, das Teegebäck.

daintiness ['deintinis], s. die Feinheit; die Kleinheit; die Leckerhaftigkeit.

dainty ['deinti], adj. fein, klein, zierlich; lecker (*food*).

dairy ['dɛəri], s. die Molkerei, die Meierei.

dairyman ['dɛərimən], s. der Milchmann; der Senne (*in Alps*).

dais [deis, 'deiis], s. das Podium.

daisy ['deizi], *s.* (*Bot.*) das Gänseblümchen, das Marienblümchen.
dale [deil], *s.* das Tal.
dalliance ['dæliəns], *s.* die Tändelei, Liebelei; Verzögerung.
dally ['dæli], *v.n.* die Zeit vertrödeln.
dam (1) [dæm], *s.* der Damm. — *v.a.* eindämmen, abdämmen.
dam (2) [dæm], *s.* (*Zool.*) die Tiermutter.
damage ['dæmidʒ], *s.* der Schaden; der Verlust (*loss*); (*pl.*) (*Law*) der Schadenersatz. — *v.a.* beschädigen.
damageable ['dæmidʒəbl], *adj.* leicht zu beschädigen.
damask ['dæməsk], *s.* der Damast (*textile*). — *adj.* damasten, aus Damast.
dame [deim], *s.* die Dame (*title*); (*Am.*) (*coll.*) die junge Dame, das Fräulein.
damn [dæm], *v.a.* verdammen.
damnable ['dæmnəbl], *adj.* verdammenswert, verdammt.
damnation [dæm'neiʃən], *s.* die Verdammung, Verdammnis.
damn(ed) [dæm(d)], *adj. & adv.* verwünscht, verdammt.
damp [dæmp], *adj.* feucht, dumpfig. — *s.* die Feuchtigkeit; (*Build.*) — *course*, die Schutzschicht. — *v.a.* dämpfen, befeuchten; — *the spirits*, die gute Laune verderben.
damsel ['dæmzəl], *s.* die Jungfer; das Mädchen.
damson ['dæmzən], *s.* (*Bot.*) die Damaszenerpflaume.
dance [dɑ:ns], *v.a., v.n.* tanzen. — *s.* der Tanz; *lead s.o. a —*, einem viel Mühe machen.
dandelion ['dændilaiən], *s.* (*Bot.*) der Löwenzahn.
dandle [dændl], *v.a.* hätscheln; schaukeln.
dandy ['dændi], *s.* der Geck, der Stutzer.
Dane [dein], *s.* der Däne.
dane [dein], *s. great —*, die Dogge.
Danish ['deiniʃ], *adj.* dänisch.
danger ['deindʒə], *s.* die Gefahr.
dangerous ['deindʒərəs], *adj.* gefährlich.
dangle [dæŋgl], *v.a.* baumeln lassen. — *v.n.* baumeln, hängen.
dank [dæŋk], *adj.* feucht, naßkalt.
Danube ['dænju:b]. die Donau.
dapper ['dæpə], *adj.* schmuck; niedlich; elegant.
dappled [dæpld], *adj.* scheckig, bunt.
Dardanelles, The [dɑ:də'nelz]. die Dardanellen, *pl.*
dare [deə], *v.n. irr.* wagen; *I — say*, das meine ich wohl, ich gebe zu.
daredevil ['deədevl], *s.* der Wagehals, der Draufgänger.
daring ['deəriŋ], *s.* die Kühnheit.
dark [dɑ:k], *adj.* dunkel, finster. — *s.* die Dunkelheit; *shot in the —*, ein Schuß aufs Geratewohl, ins Blaue.
darken ['dɑ:kən], *v.a.* verdunkeln, verfinstern. — *v.n.* dunkel werden.

darkish ['dɑ:kiʃ], *adj.* nahezu dunkel.
darkness ['dɑ:knis], *s.* die Dunkelheit, Finsternis.
darkroom ['dɑ:kru:m], *s.* die Dunkelkammer.
darling ['dɑ:liŋ], *s.* der Liebling. — *adj.* lieb, teuer.
darn (1) [dɑ:n], *v.a.* stopfen.
darn (2) [dɑ:n], *v.a.* verdammen.
darn(ed) [dɑ:n(d)], (*excl.*) verdammt.
darning ['dɑ:niŋ], *s.* das Stopfen; — *needle*, die Stopfnadel.
dart [dɑ:t], *s.* der Pfeil; der Spieß (*spear*); (*pl.*) das Pfeilwurfspiel. — *v.n.* losstürmen, sich stürzen.
dash [dæʃ], *v.a.* zerschmettern, zerstören (*hopes*). — *v.n.* stürzen. — *s.* der Schlag (*blow*); die Eleganz; (*Typ.*) der Gedankenstrich; (*Motor.*) — *-board*, das Schaltbrett, Armaturenbrett.
dashing ['dæʃiŋ], *adj.* schneidig.
dastard ['dæstəd], *s.* der Feigling, die Memme.
dastardly ['dæstədli], *adj., adv.* feige.
data ['deitə], *s. pl.* (*Science*) die Angaben, die Daten.
date (1) [deit], *s.* das Datum; (*Am.*) die Verabredung; *out of —*, vertetal (*antiquated*), altmodisch (*out of fashion*). — *v.a.* datieren; (*Am.*) ausführen. — *v.n.* das Datum tragen.
date (2) [deit], *s.* (*Bot.*) die Dattel.
dative ['deitiv], *s.* (*Gram.*) der Dativ.
daub [dɔ:b], *v.a.* beschmieren; (*coll.*) bemalen. — *s.* die Kleckserei; (*coll.*) die Malerei.
daughter ['dɔ:tə], *s.* die Tochter; — *-in-law*, die Schwiegertochter.
daunt [dɔ:nt], *v.a.* einschüchtern.
dauphin ['dɔ:fin], *s.* der Dauphin.
daw [dɔ:], *s.* (*Orn.*) die Dohle.
dawdle ['dɔ:dl], *v.n.* trödeln, die Zeit vertrödeln.
dawdler ['dɔ:dlə], *s.* der Trödler, Tagedieb, die Schlafmütze.
dawn [dɔ:n], *s.* das Morgengrauen, die Morgendämmerung. — *v.n.* dämmern, tagen.
day [dei], *s.* der Tag; *the other —*, neulich; *every —*, täglich; *one —*, eines Tages; *by —*, bei or am Tage.
daybreak ['deibreik], *s.* der Tagesanbruch.
daytime ['deitaim], *s. in the —*, bei Tage.
daze [deiz], *v.a.* blenden (*dazzle*); betäuben (*stupefy*).
dazzle [dæzl], *v.a.* blenden.
deacon ['di:kən], *s.* (*Eccl.*) der Diakon.
deaconess ['di:kənes], *s.* (*Eccl.*) die Diakonisse.
dead [ded], *adj.* tot; *stop —*, plötzlich anhalten; *as — as mutton*, mausetot; *— from the neck up*, (*coll.*) dumm wie die Nacht. — *adv. — beat*, erschöpft; (*Am.*) *— sure*, ganz sicher. — *s. in the — of night*, in tiefster Nacht; (*pl.*) die Toten.

decompose

deaden [dedn], *v.a.* abschwächen (*weaken*); abtöten (*anæsthetise*).
deadly ['dedli], *adj.* tödlich.
deadness ['dednis], *s.* die Leblosigkeit; Mattheit (*tiredness*).
deaf [def], *adj.* taub; — *and dumb*, taubstumm.
deafen [defn], *v.a.* betäuben.
deafmute ['defmju:t], *s.* der Taubstumme.
deal (1) [di:l], *s.* das Geschäft; die Anzahl; *a fair or square* —, eine anständige Behandlung; *a good* —, beträchtlich; *a great* — *of*, sehr viel; *make a* —, ein Geschäft abschliessen; *it's a* —! abgemacht! — *v.n. irr.* austeilen; Karten geben (*cards*); — *a blow*, einen Schlag erteilen. — *v.n. irr.* — *with s.th.*, etwas behandeln.
deal (2) [di:l], *s.* (*Bot.*) das Kiefernholz, die Kiefer; — *board*, das Kiefernholzbrett.
dealer ['di:lə], *s.* der Händler.
dean [di:n], *s.* der Dekan.
dear [diə], *adj.* teuer, lieb (*beloved*); teuer, kostspielig (*expensive*); — *me!* ach, Du lieber Himmel! —! du liebe Zeit! *John!* Lieber Hans!
dearness ['diənis], *s.* die Teuerung, das Teuersein.
dearth [də:θ], *s.* der Mangel (*of*, an, *Dat.*).
death [deθ], *s.* der Tod; der Todesfall; — *penalty*, die Todesstrafe; — *warrant*, das Todesurteil.
deathbed ['deθbed], *s.* das Totenbett, Sterbebett.
deathblow ['deθblou], *s.* der Todesstoß.
deathless ['deθlis], *adj.* unsterblich.
debar [di'ba:], *v.a.* ausschließen (*from*, von, *Dat.*).
debase [di'beis], *v.a.* erniedrigen, verschlechtern.
debatable [di'beitəbl], *adj.* strittig.
debate [di'beit], *s.* die Debatte. — *v.a.*, *v.n.* debattieren.
debauch [di'bɔ:tʃ], *v.a.*, *v.n.* verführen; verderben.
debauchee [di'bɔ:tʃi:], *s.* der Schwelger, der Wüstling.
debenture [di'bentʃə], *s.* der Schuldschein.
debilitate [di'biliteit], *v.a.* schwächen.
debit ['debit], *s.* die Schuldseite, das Soll (*in account*). — *v.a.* belasten.
debt [det], *s.* die Schuld; *run into* — or *incur* — *s*, Schulden machen.
debtor ['detə], *s.* der Schuldner.
decade ['dekəd, 'dekeid], *s.* das Jahrzehnt; die Dekade.
decadence ['dekədəns], *s.* die Dekadenz, der Verfall.
decalogue ['dekələg], *s.* (*Bibl.*) die zehn Gebote.
decamp [di'kæmp], *v.n.* aufbrechen, ausreißen.
decant [di'kænt], *v.a.* abfüllen, abgießen.
decanter [di'kæntə], *s.* die Karaffe.

decapitate [di'kæpiteit], *v.a.* enthaupten köpfen.
decapitation [di:kæpi'teiʃən], *s.* die Enthauptung.
decay [di'kei], *v.n.* in Verfall geraten. — *s.* der Verfall, die Verwesung.
decease [di'si:s], *s.* das Hinscheiden, der Tod. — *v.n.* sterben, dahinscheiden, verscheiden.
deceit [di'si:t], *s.* der Betrug; die List (*cunning*).
deceive [di'si:v], *v.a.* betrügen.
deceiver [di'si:və], *s.* der Betrüger.
December [di'sembə]. der Dezember.
decency ['di:sənsi], *s.* der Anstand; die Anständigkeit, Ehrlichkeit; die Schicklichkeit.
decent [di'sənt], *adj.* anständig.
decentralize [di:'sentrəlaiz], *v.a.* dezentralisieren.
deception [di'sepʃən], *s.* der Betrug.
deceptive [di'septiv], *adj.* trügerisch.
decide [di'said], *v.a.*, *v.n.* entscheiden; bestimmen (*determine*).
decimal ['desiməl], *adj.* dezimal.
decimate ['desimeit], *v.a.* dezimieren, herabsetzen (*reduce*).
decipher [di'saifə], *v.a.* entziffern (*read*); dechiffrieren (*decode*).
decision [di'siʒən], *s.* die Entscheidung, der Beschluß (*resolution*); die Entschlossenheit (*decisiveness*).
decisive [di'saisiv], *adj.* entscheidend.
decisiveness [di'saisivnis], *s.* die Entschiedenheit.
deck [dek], *s.* (*Naut.*) das Deck; — *chair*, der Liegestuhl. — *v.a.* — (*out*), ausschmücken.
declaim [di'kleim], *v.a.* deklamieren.
declamation [deklə'meiʃən], *s.* die Deklamation.
declamatory [di'klæmətəri], *adj.* Deklamations-, deklamatorisch, Vortrags-.
declaration [deklə'reiʃən], *s.* die Erklärung; die Deklaration.
declare [di'kleə], *v.a.* erklären. — *v.n.* sich erklären.
declared [di'kleəd], *adj.* erklärt, offen.
declension [di'klenʃən], *s.* (*Gram.*) die Deklination, die Abwandlung.
declinable [di'klainəbl], *adj.* (*Gram.*) deklinierbar.
declination [dekli'neiʃən], *s.* (*Phys.*) die Abweichung, Deklination.
decline [di'klain], *v.n.* abweichen (*deflect*); abnehmen (*decrease*); sich weigern (*refuse*); fallen (*price*). — *v.a.* (*Gram.*) deklinieren; ablehnen (*turn down*). — *s.* die Abnahme (*decrease*); der Verfall (*decadence*); der Abhang (*slope*).
declivity [di'kliviti], *s.* der Abhang.
decode [di:'koud], *v.a.* entziffern, dechiffrieren.
decompose [di:kəm'pouz], *v.n.* verwesen; zerfallen, sich zersetzen. — *v.a.* auflösen.

359

decorate

decorate ['dekəreit], *v.a.* dekorieren (*honour*); ausschmücken (*beautify*); ausmalen (*paint*).

decoration [dekə'reiʃən], *s.* die Dekoration, der Orden (*medal*); die Ausschmückung (*ornamentation*); die Ausmalung (*décor*).

decorator ['dekəreitə], *s.* der Zimmermaler.

decorous ['dekərəs *or* di'kɔ:rəs], *adj.* anständig, sittsam.

decorum [di'kɔ:rəm], *s.* das Dekorum, das anständige Benehmen.

decoy [di'kɔi], *s.* der Köder (*bait*). — *v.a.* locken, verlocken.

decrease [di'kri:s], *v.a.* vermindern, verringern. — *v.n.* abnehmen. — ['di:kri:s], *s.* die Abnahme, die Verringerung.

decree [di'kri:], *s.* der Beschluß (*resolution*); (*Law*) das Urteil; — *nisi,* das provisorische Scheidungsurteil. — *v.a., v.n.* eine Verordnung erlassen; beschließen (*decide*).

decrepit [di'krepit], *adj.* abgelebt; gebrechlich (*frail*).

decry [di'krai], *v.a.* verrufen; in Verruf bringen.

dedicate ['dedikeit], *v.a.* widmen, weihen, zueignen (*to, Dat.*).

dedication [dedi'keiʃən], *s.* die Widmung, Weihung; die Zueignung.

dedicatory ['dedikeitəri], *adj.* zueignend.

deduce [di'dju:s], *v.a.* schließen (*conclude*); ableiten (*derive*).

deduct [di'dʌkt], *v.a.* abziehen (*subtract*); abrechnen (*take off*).

deduction [di'dʌkʃən], *s.* der Abzug (*subtraction*); die Folgerung (*inference*); der Rabatt (*in price*).

deductive [di'dʌktiv], *adj.* (*Log.*) deduktiv.

deed [di:d], *s.* die Tat, die Handlung (*action*); (*Law*) die Urkunde, das Dokument.

deem [di:m], *v.a.* erachten, halten für.

deep [di:p], *adj.* tief; — *freeze,* die Tiefkühlung; (*fig.*) dunkel. — *s.* die Tiefe (*des Meeres*).

deepen [di:pn], *v.a.* vertiefen. — *v.n.* tiefer werden; sich vertiefen.

deer [diə], *s.* (*Zool.*) das Rotwild, der Hirsch; — *stalking,* die Pirsch.

deface [di'feis], *v.a.* entstellen, verunstalten.

defalcate [di'fælkeit], *v.n.* Gelder unterschlagen.

defamation [defə'meiʃən], *s.* die Verleumdung.

defamatory [di'fæmətəri], *adj.* verleumderisch.

defame [di'feim], *v.a.* verleumden.

default [di'fɔ:lt], *v.n.* (*vor Gericht*) ausbleiben. — *s.* der Fehler (*error*); die Unterlassung (*omission*).

defaulter [di'fɔ:ltə], *s.* der Pflichtvergessene; (*Law*) der Schuldige.

defeat [di'fi:t], *v.a.* schlagen, besiegen. — *s.* die Niederlage.

defect [di'fekt], *s.* der Fehler, Makel. — *v.n.* abfallen (*desert, from,* von, *Dat.*).

defection [di'fekʃən], *s.* der Abfall.

defective [di'fektiv], *adj.* fehlerhaft, mangelhaft.

defectiveness [di'fektivnis], *s.* die Mangelhaftigkeit, die Fehlerhaftigkeit.

defence [di'fens], *s.* die Verteidigung.

defenceless [di'fenslis], *adj.* wehrlos.

defencelessness [di'fenslisnis], *s.* die Wehrlosigkeit.

defend [di'fend], *v.a.* verteidigen.

defendant [di'fendənt], *s.* (*Law*) der Angeklagte.

defensive [di'fensiv], *adj.* verteidigend. — *s.* die Defensive; *be on the* —, sich verteidigen.

defer [di'fə:], *v.a.* aufschieben (*postpone*). — *v.n.* sich unterordnen, sich fügen (*to, Dat.*).

deference ['defərəns], *s.* der Respekt, die Achtung (*to,* vor, *Dat.*).

deferential [defə'renʃəl], *adj.* ehrerbietig, respektvoll.

defiance [di'faiəns], *s.* der Trotz, die Herausforderung.

defiant [di'faiənt], *adj.* trotzig, herausfordernd.

deficiency [di'fiʃənsi], *s.* die Unzulänglichkeit, der Mangel (*quantity*); die Fehlerhaftigkeit (*quality*).

deficient [di'fiʃənt], *adj.* unzulänglich (*quantity*); fehlerhaft (*quality*).

deficit ['defisit], *s.* das Defizit, der Fehlbetrag.

defile (1) [di'fail], *v.a.* schänden, beflecken.

defile (2) ['di:fail], *v.n.* vorbeimarschieren (*march past*) (an, *Dat.*). — *s.* der Engpaß.

defilement [di'failmənt], *s.* die Schändung.

define [di'fain], *v.a.* definieren, begrenzen; bestimmen (*determine*).

definite ['definit], *adj.* bestimmt (*certain*); klar, deutlich (*clear*); endgültig (*final*).

definition [defi'niʃən], *s.* die Definition, die Klarheit; (*Maths.*) die Bestimmung.

definitive [di'finitiv], *adj.* definitiv, endgültig (*final*); bestimmt (*certain*).

deflect [di'flekt], *v.a.* ablenken (*divert*). — *v.n.* abweichen (von, *Dat.*).

defoliation [di:fouli'eiʃən], *s.* der Blätterfall.

deform [di'fɔ:m], *v.a.* verunstalten, entstellen. — *v.n.* (*Metall.*) sich verformen.

deformity [di'fɔ:miti], *s.* die Entstellung; die Häßlichkeit (*ugliness*).

defraud [di'frɔ:d], *v.a.* betrügen.

defray [di'frei], *v.a.* bestreiten, bezahlen (*costs*).

deft [deft], *adj.* geschickt, gewandt.

deftness ['deftnis], *s.* die Gewandtheit, die Geschicktheit.

defunct [di'fʌŋkt], *adj.* verstorben. — *s.* der Verstorbene.

defy [di'fai], v.a. trotzen (*Dat.*).

degenerate [di'dʒenəreit], v.n. entarten; herabsinken (*sink low*). —[-rit], adj. degeneriert, entartet.

degradation [degri'deiʃən], s. die Absetzung, Entsetzung, Degradierung.

degrade [di'greid], v.a. (*Mil.*) degradieren; entwürdigen; vermindern.

degraded [di'greidid], adj. heruntergekommen.

degrading [di'greidiŋ], adj. entehrend.

degree [di'gri:], s. (*Meas.*, *Univ.*) der Grad; (*Univ.*) die akademische Würde; die Stufe (*step*, *stage*); die Ordnung, die Klasse (*order*, *class*); by —s, nach und nach, allmählich.

deify ['di:ifai], v.a. vergöttern.

deign [dein], v.n. geruhen, belieben.

deity ['di:iti], s. die Gottheit.

dejected [di'dʒektid], adj. niedergeschlagen.

dejection [di'dʒekʃən], s. die Niedergeschlagenheit.

delay [di'lei], v.a., v.n. aufschieben (*put off*); verzögern (*retard*). — s. der Aufschub; die Verzögerung.

delectable [di'lektəbl], adj. erfreulich, köstlich.

delectation [delek'teiʃən], s. die Freude, das Ergötzen (*in*, an, *Dat.*).

delegate [di'deligit], s. der Delegierte, Abgeordnete; der Vertreter. — ['deligeit], v.a. delegieren, entsenden.

delegation [deli'geiʃən], s. die Delegation, die Abordnung.

delete [di'li:t], v.a. tilgen, (aus-)streichen, auslöschen (*writing*).

deletion [di'li:ʃən], s. die Tilgung, die Auslöschung.

deleterious [deli'tiəriəs], adj. schädlich.

delf [delf], s. das Delfter Porzellan.

deliberate [di'libərit], adj. absichtlich (*intentional*); vorsichtig (*careful*); bedächtig (*thoughtful*). — [-reit], v.n. beratschlagen, Rat halten. — v.a. überlegen, bedenken.

deliberateness [di'libəritnis], s. die Bedächtigkeit (*thoughtfulness*); die Absichtlichkeit (*intention*).

deliberation [dilibə'reiʃən], s. die Überlegung, die Beratung.

delicacy ['delikəsi], s. die Feinheit, Zartheit (*manner*); der Leckerbissen (*luxury food*); die Schwächlichkeit (*health*).

delicate ['delikit], adj. fein (*manner*); schwächlich (*sickly*); kitzlig, heikel (*difficult*).

delicious [di'liʃəs], adj. köstlich (*food*).

deliciousness [di'liʃəsnis], s. die Köstlichkeit.

delight [di'lait], s. das Entzücken, das Vergnügen; *Turkish* —, türkisches Konfekt; *take* — *in*, an etwas Gefallen finden, sich freuen (*an*, über). — v.a., v.n. entzücken, erfreuen (*in*, an, *Dat.*).

delightful [di'laitful], adj. entzückend, bezaubernd.

delimit [di:'limit], v.a. abgrenzen, begrenzen.

delimitation [di:limi'teiʃən], s. die Begrenzung, Abgrenzung.

delineate [di'linieit], v.a. umreißen, entwerfen, skizzieren (*draft*, *sketch*); schildern, beschreiben (*describe*).

delineation [dilini'eiʃən], s. die Skizze, der Entwurf (*sketch*, *draft*); die Schilderung (*description*).

delinquency [di'liŋkwənsi], s. das Verbrechen.

delinquent [di'liŋkwənt], adj. verbrecherisch. — s. der Verbrecher, Missetäter (*criminal*).

deliquesce [deli'kwes], v.n. (*Chem.*) zergehen, zerschmelzen.

deliquescence [deli'kwesəns], s. das Zerschmelzen, die Schmelzbarkeit.

deliquescent [deli'kwesənt], adj. leicht schmelzbar (*melting*); leicht zerfliessend (*butter etc.*).

delirious [di'liriəs], adj. (*Med.*) phantasierend, wahnsinnig.

delirium [di'liriəm], s. (*Med.*) das Delirium; der Wahnsinn (*madness*); das Phantasieren (*raving*); — *tremens*, der Säuferwahnsinn.

deliver [di'livə], v.a. abliefern, überreichen (*hand over*); liefern (*goods*); befreien (*free*); erlösen (*redeem*); zustellen (*letters etc.*); entbinden (*woman of child*).

deliverance [di'livərəns], s. die Erlösung (*redemption*); die Befreiung (*liberation*); die Übergabe.

delivery [di'livəri], s. die Befreiung (*liberation*); (*Med.*) die Niederkunft, Entbindung; der Vortrag (*speech*); die Lieferung, die Zustellung (*goods*); — *man*, der Zustellbote; — *van*, der Lieferwagen.

dell [del], s. das enge Tal.

delude [di'lu:d], v.a. betrügen, täuschen.

deluge ['delju:dʒ], s. die Überschwemmung. — v.a. überschwemmen.

delusion [di'lu:ʒən], s. die Täuschung, das Blendwerk.

delusive, delusory [di'lu:ziv, di'lu:zəri], adj. täuschend, trügerisch.

delve [delv], v.n. graben.

demagogic(al) [demə'gɔdʒik(əl)], adj. demagogisch.

demagogue ['deməgɔg], s. der Demagoge, der Aufrührer.

demand [di'ma:nd], v.a. verlangen, fordern. — s. die Forderung, das Begehren (*desire*); *on* —, auf Verlangen; *in great* —, viel gefragt; *supply and* —, Angebot und Nachfrage.

demarcate [di:'ma:keit], v.a. abgrenzen, abstecken (*field*).

demarcation [di:ma:'keiʃən], s. die Abgrenzung; — *line*, die Grenzlinie.

demeanour [di'mi:nə], s. das Benehmen.

demented [di'mentid], adj. wahnsinnig, von Sinnen, toll.

demerit [di:'merit], s. der Fehler.

demesne

demesne [di'mi:n *or* -'mein], *s.* das Erbgut; die Domäne.

demi- ['demi], *prefix.* halb-.

demigod ['demigɔd], *s.* der Halbgott.

demijohn ['demidʒɔn], *s.* der Glasballon.

demise [di'maiz], *s.* der Tod, das Hinscheiden. — *v.a.* (*Law*) vermachen.

demisemiquaver ['demisemikweivə], *s.* (*Mus.*) die Zweiunddreißigstelnote.

demobilize [di:'moubilaiz], *v.a.* demobilisieren.

democracy [di'mɔkrəsi], *s.* die Demokratie.

democratic [demo'krætik], *adj.* demokratisch.

demolish [di'mɔliʃ], *v.a.* demolieren, zerstören, niederreißen.

demon ['di:mən], *s.* der Dämon, der Teufel; *a* — *for work,* ein unersättlicher Arbeiter.

demoniac [di'mouniæk], **demoniacal** [di:mə'naiəkl], *adj.* besessen, teuflisch.

demonstrable [di'mɔnstrəbl], *adj.* beweisbar, nachweislich (*verifiable*).

demonstrate ['demənstreit], *v.a., v.n.* beweisen (*prove*); demonstrieren.

demonstration [demən'streiʃən], *s.* der Beweis (*theoretical*); die Demonstration (*practical*); (*Pol.*) Kundgebung.

demonstrative [di'mɔnstrətiv], *adj.* (*Gram.*) demonstrativ; überschwenglich (*emotional*).

demoralize [di:'mɔrəlaiz], *v.a.* demoralisieren.

demote [di:'mout], *v.a.* (*Mil., official*) degradieren.

demotion [di:'mouʃən], *s.* (*Mil., official*) die Degradierung.

demur [di'mə:], *v.n.* Anstand nehmen; Einwendungen machen (*raise objections*); zögern, zaudern (*hesitate*). — *s.* der Zweifel, der Skrupel.

demure [di'mjuə], *adj.* sittsam, zimperlich; spröde (*prim*).

demureness [di'mjuənis], *s.* die Sittsamkeit; die Sprödigkeit (*primness*).

den [den], *s.* die Höhle, Grube; *lion's* —, die Löwengrube.

denial [di'naiəl], *s.* die Verneinung, das Dementi (*negation*); das Ableugnen (*disclaimer*); die Absage (*refusal*).

denizen ['denizən], *s.* der Bürger, der Alteingesessene.

denominate [di'nɔmineit], *v.a.* nennen, benennen (*name*).

denomination [dinɔmi'neiʃən], *s.* die Bezeichnung; der Nennwert (*currency*); (*Rel.*) das Bekenntnis.

denominational [dinɔmi'neiʃənəl], *adj.* konfessionell.

denominator [di'nɔmineitə], *s.* (*Maths.*) der Nenner.

denote [di'nout], *v.a.* bezeichnen, kennzeichnen.

dénouement [dei'nu:mã], *s.* die Entwicklung, die Darlegung, die Lösung.

denounce [di'nauns], *v.a.* denunzieren, angeben, (*Law*) anzeigen.

dense [dens], *adj.* dicht; (*coll.*) beschränkt (*stupid*).

density ['densiti], *s.* die Dichte; — *of population,* die Bevölkerungsdichte.

dent (1) [dent], *s.* die Beule.

dent (2) [dent], *s.* die Kerbe (*in wood*); der Einschnitt (*cut*).

dental [dentl], *adj.* Zahn-; — *studies,* zahnärztliche Studien; — *treatment,* die Zahnbehandlung. — *s.* (*Phonet.*) der Zahnlaut.

dentist ['dentist], *s.* der Zahnarzt.

dentistry ['dentistri], *s.* die Zahnheilkunde.

denude [di'nju:d], *v.a.* entblößen; berauben (*of, Genit.*).

denunciation [dinʌnsi'eiʃən], *s.* die Denunzierung, die Anzeige.

deny [di'nai], *v.a.* verneinen (*negate*); abschlagen (*refuse*); verleugnen (*refuse to admit*).

deodorant, deodorizer [di:'oudərənt, di:'oudəraizə], *s.* der Geruchsentzieher (*apparatus*); der Deodorant.

deodorize [di:'oudəraiz], *v.a.* geruchlos machen.

depart [di'pa:t], *v.n.* abreisen, abfahren (*for, nach, Dat.*); scheiden.

department [di'pa:tmənt], *s.* die Abteilung; — *store,* das Kaufhaus.

departmental [di:pa:t'mentl], *adj.* Abteilungs-.

departure [di'pa:tʃə], *s.* die Abreise, die Abfahrt.

depend [di'pend], *v.n.* abhängen, abhängig sein (*upon, von, Dat.*); sich verlassen (*upon, auf, Acc.*); *that* —*s,* das kommt darauf an.

dependable [di'pendəbl], *adj.* verläßlich, zuverlässig.

dependant [di'pendənt], *s.* das abhängige Familienmitglied (*member of family*); der Angehörige, Abhängige.

dependence [di'pendəns], *s.* die Abhängigkeit (*need*); das Vertrauen, der Verlaß (*reliance*).

dependency [di'pendənsi], *s.* (*Pol.*) die abhängige Kolonie.

dependent [di'pendənt], *adj.* abhängig (*upon, von, Dat.*).

depict [di'pikt], *v.a.* schildern, beschreiben.

deplete [di'pli:t], *v.a.* entleeren (*make empty*); erschöpfen (*exhaust*).

depletion [di'pli:ʃən], *s.* die Entleerung.

deplorable [di'plɔ:rəbl], *adj.* bedauernswert, bedauerlich.

deplore [di'plɔ:], *v.a.* beklagen.

deploy [di'plɔi], *v.a.* entfalten. — *v.n.* sich entfalten; (*Mil.*) aufmarschieren.

deployment [di'plɔimənt], *s.* (*Mil.*) das Deployieren, die Entfaltung.

deponent [di'pounənt], *s.* (*Law*) der vereidigte Zeuge. — *adj.* (*Gram.*) (*verb*) das Deponens.

depopulate [di:'pɔpjuleit], *v.a.* entvölkern.

deport [di'pɔ:t], *v.a.* deportieren.

deportation [di:pɔ:'teiʃən], *s.* die Deportation.

deportment [di'pɔ:tmənt], *s.* die körperliche Haltung (*physical*); das Benehmen (*social*).

depose [di'pouz], *v.a.* absetzen (*remove from office*); (*Law*) zu Papier bringen (*write down*); schriftlich erklären (*declare in writing*).

deposit [di'pɔzit], *s.* (*Comm.*) die Anzahlung; (*Geol., Chem.*) der Niederschlag; (*Geol.*) die Ablagerung; (*Comm.*) — *account*, das Depositenkonto. — *v.a.* (*Geol., Chem.*) absetzen; (*Comm.*) anzahlen, einzahlen.

deposition [di:pə'ziʃən], *s.* die Niederschrift, die schriftliche Erklärung; die Absetzung (*removal from office*).

depositor [di'pɔzitə], *s.* (*Comm.*) der Einzahler.

depository [di'pɔzitəri], *s.* das Lagerhaus.

depot [depou], *s.* das Depot, das Lagerhaus (*store*); (*Am.*) der Bahnhof.

deprave [di'preiv], *v.a.* verderben.

depraved [di'preivd], *adj.* (*moralisch*) verdorben.

depravity [di'præviti], *s.* die Verdorbenheit, die Verworfenheit.

deprecate ['deprikeit], *v.a.* mißbilligen (*disapprove of*; *Acc.*); sich verbitten.

deprecation [depri'keiʃən], *s.* die Abbitte; die Mißbilligung (*disapproval*).

depreciate [di'pri:ʃieit], *v.a.* abwerten, herabwürdigen. — *v.n.* an Wert verlieren, im Wert sinken.

depreciation [dipri:ʃi'eiʃən], *s.* die Abwertung; der Verlust (*loss*); (*Pol., Comm.*) die Entwertung.

depredation [depri'deiʃən], *s.* das Plündern, der Raub.

depress [di'pres], *v.a.* niederdrücken (*press down*); deprimieren (*morale*).

depressed [di'prest], *adj.* niedergeschlagen.

depression [di'preʃən], *s.* das Niederdrücken (*action*); (*Pol.*) die Depression; die Niedergeschlagenheit (*despondency*); das Tief (*weather*).

deprivation [depri'veiʃən], *s.* der Verlust (*lack*); die Beraubung (*robbery*).

deprive [di'praiv], *v.a.* berauben (*of*, *Genit.*); wegnehmen (*of*, *Acc.*).

depth [depθ], *s.* die Tiefe; — *charge*, die Unterwasserbombe; *in the* —*s of night*, in tiefster Nacht; (*Phys.*) — *of focus*, die Tiefenschärfe; *be out of o.'s* —, den Grund unter seinen Füßen verloren haben, ratlos sein (*be helpless*); — *sounder*, das Echolot.

deputation [depju'teiʃən], *s.* die Deputation, die Abordnung.

depute [di'pju:t], *v.a.* abordnen, entsenden.

deputize ['depjutaiz], *v.n.* vertreten (*for*, *Acc.*).

deputy ['depjuti], *s.* der Abgeordnete, der Deputierte (*delegate*); der Vertreter (*replacement*).

derail [di:'reil], *v.a.* zum Entgleisen bringen. — *v.n.* entgleisen.

derailment [di:'reilmənt], *s.* die Entgleisung.

derange [di'reindʒ], *v.a.* verwirren, stören.

derangement [di'reindʒmənt], *s.* die Verwirrung; die Geistesstörung (*madness*).

derelict ['derilikt], *adj.* verlassen.

dereliction [deri'likʃən], *s.* das Verlassen; — *of duty*, die Pflichtvergessenheit.

deride [di'raid], *v.a.* verlachen, verhöhnen.

derision [di'riʒən], *s.* die Verhöhnung.

derisive [di'raisiv], *adj.* höhnisch, spöttisch.

derivable [di'raivəbl], *adj.* ableitbar.

derivation [deri'veiʃən], *s.* die Ableitung.

derivative [di'rivətiv], *adj.* abgeleitet. — *s.* das abgeleitete Wort.

derive [di'raiv], *v.a., v.n.* ableiten, herleiten.

derogation [derо'geiʃən], *s.* die Herabsetzung.

derrick ['derik], *s.* der Ladebaum.

dervish ['də:viʃ], *s.* der Derwisch.

descant ['deskænt], *s.* (*Mus.*) der Diskant *or* der Sopran. — [dis'kænt], *v.n.* sich verbreiten (*on*, über, *Acc.*).

descend [di'send], *v.n.* hinab- *or* herabsteigen (*go down*); abstammen (*stem from*).

descendant [di'sendənt], *s.* der Nachkomme.

descent [di'sent], *s.* der Abstieg (*going down*); der Fall (*decline*); die Abstammung (*forebears*); der Abhang (*slope*); (*Aviat.*) die Landung.

describable [dis'kraibəbl], *adj.* zu beschreiben, beschreibbar.

describe [dis'kraib], *v.a.* beschreiben, schildern.

description [dis'kripʃən], *s.* die Beschreibung; *of any* —, jeder Art.

descriptive [dis'kriptiv], *adj.* schildernd, beschreibend.

desecrate ['desikreit], *v.a.* entweihen, entheiligen.

desecration [desi'kreiʃən], *s.* die Entweihung, die Schändung.

desert (1) ['dezət], *s.* die Wüste.

desert (2) [di'zə:t], *v.a.* verlassen, im Stiche lassen. — *v.n.* desertieren.

desert (3) [di'zə:t], *s.* (*usually pl.*) das Verdienst.

desertion [di'zə:ʃən], *s.* (*Mil.*) die Fahnenflucht.

deserve [di'zə:v], *v.a.* verdienen.

deserving [di'zə:viŋ], *adj.* verdienstvoll.

design [di'zain], *v.a.* entwerfen (*plan*); vorhaben (*intend*); bestimmen (*determine*). — *s.* der Entwurf (*sketch*); der Plan (*draft*); die Absicht, das Vorhaben (*intention*); das Muster (*pattern*).

designate

designate ['dezigneit], *v.a.* bezeichnen
(*mark*); ernennen (*appoint*). — [-nit],
adj. ernannt; *chairman* —, der künf-
tige Vorsitzende.
designation [dezig'neiʃən], *s.* die
Bestimmung, Ernennung (*appointment*); die Bezeichnung (*mark*).
designer [di'zainə], *s.* der Zeichner, der
Graphiker (*artist*); der Ränkeschmied
(*schemer*).
designing [di'zainiŋ], *adj.* hinterlistig,
schlau.
desirable [di'zaiərəbl], *adj.* erwünscht,
wünschenswert.
desire [di'zaiə], *s.* der Wunsch, die
Begierde; das Verlangen, die Sehnsucht (*longing*). — *v.a.* verlangen,
begehren.
desirous [di'zaiərəs], *adj.* begierig (*of,
inf.*).
desist [di'zist], *v.n.* ablassen, aufhören.
desk [desk], *s.* der Schreibtisch; das
Pult; — *lamp*, die Tischlampe *or*
Bürolampe.
desolate ['desəlit], *adj.* verlassen, öde;
trostlos (*sad*). — [-leit], *v.a.* verwüsten
(*lay waste*).
desolation [desə'leiʃən], *s.* die Verwüstung (*of land*); die Trostlosigkeit
(*sadness*).
despair [dis'pɛə], *v.n.* verzweifeln (*of,
an, Dat.*). — *s.* die Verzweiflung.
despatch, dispatch [dis'pætʃ], *v.a.*
absenden, befördern (*post*); abfertigen
(*send*); erledigen (*deal with*); töten
(*kill*). — *s.* die Abfertigung (*clearance*);
die Eile (*speed*); die Depesche (*message*).
desperado [despə'reidou, -'raːdou], *s.*
der Wagehals, der Draufgänger.
desperate ['despərit], *adj.* verzweifelt.
desperation [despə'reiʃən], *s.* die
Verzweiflung.
despicable ['despikəbl], *adj.* verächtlich.
despise [dis'paiz], *v.a.* verachten.
despite [dis'pait], *prep.* trotz (*Genit.,
Dat.*).
despoil [dis'pɔil], *v.a.* plündern, aus-
rauben.
despondency [dis'pɔndənsi], *s.* die
Verzweiflung, Verzagtheit.
despondent [dis'pɔndənt], *adj.* ver-
zagend, verzweifelnd, mutlos.
despot ['despɔt], *s.* der Despot, der
Tyrann.
despotic [des'pɔtik], *adj.* despotisch.
despotism ['despətizm], *s.* (*Pol.*) der
Despotismus.
dessert [di'zəːt], *s.* das Dessert, der
Nachtisch.
destination [desti'neiʃən], *s.* die Bestimmung, das Ziel; der Bestimmungsort
(*address*); das Reiseziel (*journey*).
destine [di'stein], *v.a.* bestimmen.
destiny ['destini], *s.* das Geschick; das
Schicksal, das Verhängnis (*fate*).
destitute ['destitjuːt], *adj.* verlassen
(*deserted*); hilflos, mittellos (*poor*);
in bitterer Not (*in great distress*).

destitution [desti'tjuːʃən], *s.* die Notlage, die bittere Not.
destroy [dis'trɔi], *v.a.* zerstören (*buildings*); verwüsten; vernichten (*lives*).
destroyer [dis'trɔiə], *s.* der Zerstörer.
destructible [dis'trʌktibl], *adj.* zerstörbar.
destruction [dis'trʌkʃən], *s.* die Zerstörung (*of buildings*), die Verwüstung;
die Vernichtung.
destructive [dis'trʌktiv], *adj.* zer-
störend, verderblich.
destructiveness [dis'trʌktivnis], *s.* die
Zerstörungswut, der Zerstörungs-
sinn.
desultory ['desəltəri], *adj.* unmetho-
disch, sprunghaft; oberflächlich (*superficial*).
detach [di'tætʃ], *v.a.* absondern, trennen.
detachment [di'tætʃmənt], *s.* die
Absonderung (*separation*); (*Mil.*) das
Kommando.
detail [di'teil], *v.a.* im einzelnen beschreiben (*describe minutely*); (*Mil.*)
abkommandieren. — ['diːteil], *s.* die
Einzelheit.
detailed ['diːteild], *adj.* ausführlich;
detailliert, ins Einzelne gehend (*report etc.*); [di'teild], (*Mil.*) abkom-
mandiert.
detain [di'tein], *v.a.* aufhalten, zurückhalten; festhalten (*in prison*).
detect [di'tekt], *v.a.* entdecken, aufdecken.
detection [di'tekʃən], *s.* die Entdeckung,
die Aufdeckung.
detective [di'tektiv], *s.* der Detektiv.
detention [di'tenʃən], *s.* (*Law*) die Haft;
die Vorenthaltung (*of articles*).
deter [di'təː], *v.a.* abschrecken.
detergent [di'təːdʒənt], *s.* das Rei-
nigungsmittel.
deteriorate [di'tiəriəreit], *v.n.* sich verschlimmern, verschlechtern.
deterioration [ditiəriə'reiʃən], *s.* die
Verschlimmerung.
determinable [di'təːminəbl], *adj.* bestimmbar.
determinate [ditə:minit], *adj.* fest-
gesetzt, bestimmt.
determination [di'təːmi'neiʃən], *s.* die
Entschlossenheit (*resoluteness*); die
Bestimmung (*identification*); der Entschluß (*resolve*).
determine [di'təːmin], *v.a.* bestimmen (*ascertain*); beschließen (*resolve*).
deterrent [di'terənt], *s.* das Ab-
schreckungsmittel.
detest [di'test], *v.a.* verabscheuen.
detestable [di'testəbl], *adj.* abscheulich.
detestation [detes'teiʃən], *s.* der Abscheu (*of, vor, Dat.*).
dethrone [di'θroun], *v.a.* entthronen,
vom Thron verdrängen.
detonate ['diː- *or* 'detoneit], *v.n.* detonieren, explodieren. — *v.a.* explodieren, detonieren lassen, zum
Detonieren bringen.

detonation [deto'neiʃən], s. die Detonation, die Explosion.

detonator ['detoneitə], s. der Zünder, die Zündpatrone; (Railw.) die Knallpatrone.

detour ['deituə or di'tuə], s. der Umweg; (Civil Engin.) die Umleitung. — v.n. (Am.) einen Umweg machen. — v.a. (Am.) umleiten (re-route).

detract [di'trækt], v.a., v.n. abziehen; schmälern.

detraction [di'trækʃən], s. die Schmälerung, die Verleumdung (slander).

detractive [di'træktiv], adj. verleumderisch.

detractor [di'træktə], s. der Verleumder.

detriment ['detrimənt], s. der Nachteil, der Schaden.

detrimental [detri'mentl], adj. nachteilig; abträglich; schädlich (harmful).

deuce (1) [dju:s], s. die Zwei (game); (Tennis) der Einstand.

deuce (2) [dju:s], s. (coll.) der Teufel.

devastate ['devəsteit], v.a. verwüsten, verheeren.

devastating ['devəsteitiŋ], adj. schrecklich, verheerend.

devastation [devəs'teiʃən], s. die Verheerung, die Verwüstung.

develop [di'veləp], v.a. entwickeln. — v.n. sich entwickeln; sich entfalten (prove, turn out).

developer [di'veləpə], s. (Phot.) das Entwicklungsmittel.

development [di'veləpmənt], s. die Entwicklung.

developmental [diveləp'mentl], adj. Entwicklungs-.

deviate ['di:vieit], v.n. abweichen.

deviation [di:vi'eiʃən], s. die Abweichung.

device [di'vais], s. die Vorrichtung (equipment); der Kunstgriff (trick).

devil [devl], s. der Teufel; der Lehrling, Laufbursche (printer's, lawyer's); the — take the hindmost! der Teufel hol was dann kommt! — v.n. in der Lehre sein (for, bei, Dat.).

devilish ['deviliʃ], adj. teuflisch.

devilment ['devlmənt], **devilry** ['devəlri], s. die Teufelei, die Teufelslaune.

devious ['di:viəs], adj. abweichend; abgelegen; abwegig.

deviousness ['di:viəsnis], s. die Abschweifung, Verirrung.

devise [di'vaiz], v.a. erfinden (invent); ersinnen (think out).

deviser, devisor [di'vaizə], s. der Erfinder (inventor); der Erblasser (testator).

devoid [di'void], adj. frei (of, von, Dat.); ohne (Acc.).

devolve [di'volv], v.a. übertragen (transfer); abwälzen (pass on burden) (to, auf, Acc.). — v.n. zufallen (Dat.).

devote [di'vout], v.a. widmen; aufopfern (sacrifice).

devoted [di'voutid], adj. ergeben (affectionate); geweiht (consecrated).

devotee [devo'ti:], s. der Anhänger; der Verehrer (fan).

devotion [di'vouʃən], s. die Hingabe; die Aufopferung (sacrifice); die Andacht (prayer).

devotional [di'vouʃənəl], adj. Andachts–.

devour [di'vauə], v.a. verschlingen.

devout [di'vaut], adj. andächtig, fromm.

devoutness [di'vautnis], s. die Frömmigkeit.

dew [dju:], s. der Tau.

dewy [dju:i], adj. betaut, taufeucht.

dexterity [deks'teriti], s. die Gewandtheit, die Fertigkeit.

dexterous ['dekstərəs], adj. gewandt, geschickt.

diabetes [daiə'bi:ti:z], s. (Med.) die Zuckerkrankheit.

diabetic [daiə'betik], s. (Med.) der Zuckerkranke. — adj. zuckerkrank.

diabolic(al) [daiə'bolik(əl)], adj. teuflisch.

diadem ['daiədem], s. das Diadem, das Stirnband.

diæresis [dai'iərəsis], s. die Diärese.

diagnose [daiəg'nouz], v.a. diagnostizieren, als Diagnose finden, befinden.

diagnosis [daiəg'nousis], s. die Diagnose, der Befund.

diagonal [dai'ægənəl], adj. diagonal, schräg. — s. (Geom.) die Diagonale.

diagram ['daiəgræm], s. das Diagramm.

dial ['daiəl], s. das Zifferblatt; (Teleph.) die Wählerscheibe. — v.a., v.n. (Teleph.) wählen.

dialect ['daiəlekt], s. der Dialekt, die Mundart.

dialectic [daiə'lektik], s. (Phil.) die Dialektik.

dialektical [daiə'lektikəl], adj. dialektisch, logisch.

dialogue ['daiəlɔg], s. der Dialog, das Zwiegespräch.

diameter [dai'æmitə], s. der Durchmesser.

diametrical [daiə'metrikəl], adj. diametral; gerade entgegengesetzt.

diamond ['daiəmənd], s. der Diamant; (Cards) das Karo.

diaper ['daiəpə], s. (Am.) die Windel.

diaphragm ['daiəfræm], s. (Anat.) das Zwerchfell; (Phys.) die Membran.

diarrhœa [daiə'riə], s. (Med.) der Durchfall.

diary ['daiəri], s. das Tagebuch, der Kalender.

diatribe ['daiətraib], s. der Tadel, der Angriff (verbal), die Schmähschrift (written).

dibble [dibl], s. der Pflanzstock. — v.n. Pflanzen stecken, anpflanzen.

dice [dais], s. pl. die Würfel (sing. **die**). — v.a. würfeln, werfen.

dicker ['dikə], *v.n.* (*Am.*) feilschen, handeln.

dicky ['diki], *s.* das Vorhemd.

dictate [dik'teit], *v.a.*, *v.n.* diktieren, vorschreiben.

dictation [dik'teifən], *s.* (*Sch.*) das Diktat.

dictator [dik'teitə], *s.* der Diktator.

dictatorship [dik'teitəfip], *s.* die Diktatur.

diction ['dikfən], *s.* die Ausdrucksweise (*speech*).

dictionary ['dikfənri], *s.* das Wörterbuch.

didactic [di'dæktik], *adj.* lehrhaft, Lehr-.

die (1) [dai], *v.n.* sterben (*of*, an, *Dat.*); — *away*, verebben.

die (2) [dai], *s.* der Würfel (*cube*); die Gießform (*mould*); der Stempel (*punch*); (*Metall.*) das Gesenk (*swage*); — *casting*, der Spritzguß; — *castings*, die Spritzgußteile, Gußteile; — *forging*, das Gesenkschmiedestück.

die (3) [dai] *see under* **dice**.

dielectric [daii'lektrik], *adj.* dielektrisch.

diet (1) ['daiət], *s.* (*Pol.*) der Landtag, Reichstag.

diet (2) ['daiət], *s.* (*Med.*) die Diät. — *v.n.* (*Med.*) eine Diät halten. — *v.a.* (*Med.*) eine Diät vorschreiben.

dietary, dietetic ['daiətəri, daiə'tetik], *adj.* diätetisch.

differ ['difə], *v.n.* sich unterscheiden (*be different from*, von, *Dat.*); anderer Meinung sein (*be of different opinion*).

difference ['difərəns], *s.* (*Maths.*) die Differenz; der Unterschied (*discrepancy*); die Meinungsverschiedenheit (*divergence of opinion*).

different ['difərənt], *adj.* verschieden, verschiedenartig.

differentiate [difə'renfieit], *v.n.* (*Maths.*) differenzieren; einen Unterschied machen (*between*, zwischen, *Dat.*).

difficult ['difikəlt], *adj.* schwierig, schwer.

difficulty ['difikəlti], *s.* die Schwierigkeit.

diffidence ['difidəns], *s.* die Schüchternheit.

diffident ['difidənt], *adj.* schüchtern.

diffraction [di'frækfən], *s.* die Ablenkung, (*Phys.*, *Optics*) die Brechung.

diffuse [di'fju:z], *v.a.* ausgießen (*pour*); verbreiten (*spread*). — [di'fju:s], *adj.* verbreitet, weitschweifig (*style*); zerstreut.

diffuseness [di'fju:snis], *s.* die Weitläufigkeit (*style*).

diffusion [di'fju:ʒən], *s.* (*Phys.*) die Diffusion, die Zerstreuung, die Verbreitung.

dig (1) [dig], *v.a.* *irr.* graben; — *in the ribs*, in die Rippen stoßen. — *v.n.* (*coll.*) wohnen (*live in lodgings*).

dig (2) [dig], *v.a.* (*coll.*) verstehen.

digger ['digə], *s.* der Gräber; (*coll.*) der Australier.

digest [di'dʒest], *v.a.* (*Anat.*) verdauen. — ['daidʒest], *s.* (*Am.*) die Sammlung von Auszügen; (*pl.*) Pandekten.

digestibility [didʒesti'biliti], *s.* die Verdaulichkeit.

digestible [di'dʒestibl], *adj.* verdaulich.

digestion [di'dʒestfən], *s.* die Verdauung.

digestive [di'dʒestiv], *adj.* Verdauungs-; — *biscuit*, das Kornmehlkeks; — *organs*, die Verdauungsorgane.

digit ['didʒit], *s.* (*Maths.*) die (einstellige) Zahl; der Zahlenwert.

digitalis [didʒi'teilis], *s.* (*Bot.*) der Fingerhut.

dignified ['dignifaid], *adj.* würdig, würdevoll.

dignify ['dignifai], *v.a.* ehren (*honour*); zieren (*decorate*).

dignitary ['dignitari], *s.* der Würdenträger.

dignity ['digniti], *s.* die Würde.

digress [dai'gres], *v.n.* abweichen, abschweifen.

digression [dai'grefən], *s.* die Abweichung, die Abschweifung.

digressive [dai'gresiv], *adj.* abschweifend (*style*).

digs [digz], *s. pl.* (*coll.*) das (möblierte) Zimmer, die Wohnung.

dike [daik], *s.* der Graben, der Deich. — *v.a.* eindeichen, eindämmen.

dilapidated [di'læpideitid], *adj.* baufällig.

dilapidation [dilæpi'deifən], *s.* die Baufälligkeit, der Verfall.

dilate [d(a)i'leit], *v.a.* erweitern, ausdehnen. — *v.n.* sich ausdehnen; sich auslassen (*speak*) (*on*, über, *Acc.*).

dilation [d(a)i'leifən], *s.* die Erweiterung (*expansion*); die Auslassung (*speaking*).

dilatoriness ['dilətərinis], *s.* die Saumseligkeit.

dilatory ['dilətəri], *adj.* zögernd, aufschiebend, saumselig.

dilemma [d(a)i'lemə], *s.* das Dilemma, die Klemme.

diligence ['dilidʒəns], *s.* der Fleiß, die Emsigkeit.

diligent ['dilidʒənt], *adj.* fleißig, arbeitsam.

dilly-dally ['dili'dæli], *v.n.* tändeln, zaudern, Zeit vertrödeln.

dilute [d(a)i'lju:t], *v.a.* (*Chem.*) verdünnen; schwächen (*weaken*).

dilution [d(a)i'lju:fən], *s.* die Verdünnung.

diluvial, diluvian [d(a)i'lju:viəl, -iən], *adj.* Diluvial-, des Diluviums; sintflutlich.

dim [dim], *adj.* trübe, unklar; (*Phys.*) abgeblendet. — *v.a.* abdunkeln, abblenden.

dimension [d(a)i'menfən], *s.* die Dimension, das Maß.

dimensional [d(a)i'menfənəl], *adj.* dimensional.

diminish [di'miniʃ], *v.a.* vermindern.
— *v.n.* sich vermindern.

diminution [dimi'nju:ʃən], *s.* die Verringerung, die Verminderung.

diminutive [di'minjutiv], *adj.* verkleinernd, klein. — *s.* (*Gram.*) das Verkleinerungswort.

dimness ['dimnis], *s.* die Trübheit; die Düsterkeit (*dark*).

dimple [dimpl], *s.* das Grübchen.

dimpled [dimpld], *adj.* mit einem Grübchen.

din [din], *s.* das Getöse, der Lärm.

dine [dain], *v.n.* speisen, essen.

dinginess ['dindʒinis], *s.* die Dunkelheit, die Schäbigkeit.

dingy ['dindʒi], *adj.* dunkel, schäbig.

dinner ['dinə], *s.* das Essen; das Festessen (*formal*); — *jacket*, der Smoking.

dint [dint], *s.* der Nachdruck, der Schlag; *by* — *of*, mittels (*Genit.*).

diocesan [dai'ɔsisən], *adj.* (*Eccl.*) einer Diözese, Diözesan–.

diocese ['daiəsis], *s.* (*Eccl.*) die Diözese.

dip [dip], *v.a.* eintauchen, eintunken; abblenden (*lights*). — *v.n.* (unter)tauchen; sinken; sich flüchtig einlassen (*into*, in). — *s.* die Senke; der Abhang (*slope*).

diphtheria [dif'θiəriə], *s.* (*Med.*) die Diphtherie.

diphthong ['difθɔŋ], *s.* (*Phonet.*) der Diphthong.

diploma [di'ploumə], *s.* das Diplom; *teaching* —, das Lehrerdiplom.

diplomacy [di'plouməsi], *s.* die Diplomatie.

diplomatic [diplo'mætik], *adj.* diplomatisch, taktvoll; urkundlich (*documents*). — *s.* (*pl.*) das Studium der Urkunden.

diplomat(ist) ['diplomæt, di'ploumətist], *s.* (*Pol.*) der Diplomat.

dipper ['dipə], *s.* der Taucher.

dire [daiə], *adj.* fürchterlich, schrecklich; — *necessity*, bittere Not.

direct [d(a)i'rekt], *adj.* direkt, unmittelbar. — *v.a.* leiten (*be in charge of*); hinweisen, hinlenken; (den Weg zeigen (*tell the way to*); anordnen (*arrange for*).

direction [d(a)i'rekʃən], *s.* die Leitung (*management*); (*Geog.*) die Richtung, Himmelsrichtung; die Anordnung (*arrangement*, *order*); —*s for use*, die Gebrauchsanweisung.

director [d(a)i'rektə], *s.* der Direktor; der Leiter.

directory [d(a)i'rektəri], *s.* das Adreßbuch; das Telephonbuch.

dirge [də:dʒ], *s.* der Trauergesang.

dirigible ['diridʒibl], *adj.* lenkbar, leitbar.

dirt [də:t], *s.* der Schmutz, der Kot, Dreck. — *adj.* — *cheap*, spottbillig.

dirty ['də:ti], *adj.* schmutzig; gemein (*joke*).

disability [disə'biliti], *s.* die Unfähigkeit, das Unvermögen (*inability*); die Schädigung (*impairment of health*).

disable [dis'eibl], *v.a.* unfähig *or* untauglich machen.

disablement [dis'eiblmənt], *s.* die Versehrung, die Verkrüppelung.

disabuse [disə'bju:z], *v.a.* aufklären, eines Besseren belehren.

disaccustom [disə'kʌstəm], *v.a.* entwöhnen, abgewöhnen.

disadvantage [disəd'va:ntidʒ], *s.* der Nachteil.

disaffection [disə'fekʃən], *s.* die Abneigung; der Widerwille.

disagree [disə'gri:], *v.n.* nicht übereinstimmen, nicht einer Meinung sein.

disagreeable [disə'griəbl], *adj.* unangenehm, verdrießlich; unfreundlich.

disagreement [disə'gri:mənt], *s.* die Uneinigkeit (*disunity*); die Meinungsverschiedenheit (*difference of opinion*).

disallow [disə'lau], *v.a.* nicht gestatten; in Abrede stellen.

disappear [disə'piə], *v.n.* verschwinden.

disappearance [disə'piərəns], *s.* das Verschwinden.

disappoint [disə'pɔint], *v.a.* enttäuschen.

disappointment [disə'pɔintmənt], *s.* die Enttäuschung.

disapprobation [disæpro'beiʃən], *s.* die Mißbilligung.

disapproval [disə'pru:vəl], *s.* die Mißbilligung.

disapprove [disə'pru:v], *v.a.* mißbilligen (*of*, *Acc.*).

disarm [dis'a:m], *v.a.* entwaffnen. —*v.n.* abrüsten.

disarmament [dis'a:məmənt], *s.* die Abrüstung.

disarray [disə'rei], *v.a.* in Unordnung bringen. — *s.* die Unordnung (*disorder*); die Verwirrung (*confusion*).

disaster [di'za:stə], *s.* das Unglück; das Unheil, die Katastrophe.

disastrous [di'za:strəs], *adj.* unheilvoll, schrecklich.

disavow [disə'vau], *v.a.* ableugnen.

disavowal [disə'vauəl], *s.* das Ableugnen.

disband [dis'bænd], *v.a.* entlassen (*dismiss*); auflösen (*dissolve*).

disbar [dis'ba:], *v.a.* (*Law*) von der Rechtspraxis ausschließen.

disbelief [disbi'li:f], *s.* der Unglaube (*incredulity*); der Zweifel (*doubt*).

disbelieve [disbi'li:v], *v.a.* nicht glauben; bezweifeln.

disburse [dis'bə:s], *v.a.* auszahlen, ausgeben.

disbursement [dis'bə:smənt], *s.* die Auszahlung, die Ausgabe.

disc [disk], *s.* (*also Med.*) die Scheibe; die Platte (*record*).

discard [dis'ka:d], *v.a.* ablegen, beiseite legen, aufgeben.

discern [di'zə:n *or* di'sə:n], *v.a.* unterscheiden; wahrnehmen, bemerken.

discernment [di'sə:nmənt], *s.* die Urteilskraft (*powers of judgment*); die Einsicht.

discharge

discharge [dis'tʃɑ:dʒ], *v.a.* entlassen (*dismiss*); abfeuern (*pistol*); abladen, ausladen (*cargo*); bezahlen (*debt*); tun, erfüllen (*duty*). — *s.* die Entladung (*gun*); die Entlassung (*dismissal*); die Bezahlung (*debt*); die Erfüllung (*duty*).

disciple [di'saipl], *s.* (*Bibl.*) der Jünger; der Schüler.

disciplinarian [disipli'neəriən], *s.* der Zuchtmeister.

disciplinary ['disiplinəri], *adj.* disziplinarisch.

discipline ['disiplin], *s.* die Disziplin, die Zucht. — *v.a.* disziplinieren, züchtigen.

disclaim [dis'kleim], *v.a.* verleugnen (*deny*); nicht anerkennen (*refuse to acknowledge*); verzichten (*renounce*).

disclaimer [dis'kleimə], *s.* der Widerruf.

disclose [dis'klouz], *v.a.* eröffnen, enthüllen.

disclosure [dis'klouʒə], *s.* die Eröffnung, die Enthüllung.

discoloration [diskʌlə'reiʃən], *s.* die Entfärbung, Verfärbung.

discomfiture [dis'kʌmfitʃə], *s.* die Verwirrung.

discomfort [dis'kʌmfət], *s.* das Unbehagen; die Beschwerde.

disconcert [diskən'sə:t], *v.a.* außer Fassung bringen (*upset*); vereiteln (*frustrate*).

disconnect [diskə'nekt], *v.a.* trennen (*separate*); abstellen.

disconsolate [dis'kɔnsəlit], *adj.* trostlos, untröstlich.

discontent [diskən'tent], *s.* die Unzufriedenheit, das Mißvergnügen. — *v.a.* mißvergnügt stimmen.

discontinuance [diskən'tinjuəns], *s.* die Beendigung (*finish*); das Aufhören (*suspension*); die Unterbrechung (*interruption*).

discontinue [diskən'tinju:], *v.a.* nicht fortsetzen; unterbrechen (*interrupt*); einstellen.

discord ['diskɔ:d], *s.* die Zwietracht (*disagreement*); (*Mus.*) der Mißklang.

discordance [dis'kɔ:dəns], *s.* die Uneinigkeit.

discordant [dis'kɔ:dənt], *adj.* uneinig, widersprechend.

discount ['diskaunt], *s.* (*Comm.*) der Abzug, der Rabatt; *allow a* —, einen Rabatt gewähren; *be at a* —, unbeliebt sein, nicht geschätzt sein; *sell at a* —, unter dem Preis verkaufen. — [dis'kaunt], *v.a.* (*Comm.*) diskontieren, einen Rabatt gewähren; nur mit Vorsicht aufnehmen (*accept with doubt*).

discountable [dis'kauntəbl], *adj.* diskontierbar, in Abzug zu bringen.

discountenance [dis'kauntinəns], *v.a.* mißbilligen.

discourage [dis'kʌridʒ], *v.a.* entmutigen; abraten (*from*, von, *Dat.*).

discouragement [dis'kʌridʒmənt], *s.* die Entmutigung.

discourse [dis'kɔ:s], *v.n.* einen Vortrag halten (*on*, über, *Acc.*); sprechen. — ['diskɔ:s], *s.* der Vortrag; das Gespräch, die Rede.

discourteous [dis'kə:tiəs], *adj.* unhöflich.

discourtesy [dis'kə:təsi], *s.* die Unhöflichkeit.

discover [dis'kʌvə], *v.a.* entdecken.

discovery [dis'kʌvəri], *s.* die Entdeckung.

discredit [dis'kredit], *s.* der üble Ruf; die Schande. — *v.a.* in schlechten Ruf bringen; diskreditieren.

discreditable [dis'kreditəbl], *adj.* schimpflich.

discreet [dis'kri:t], *adj.* diskret, verschwiegen; vorsichtig (*cautious*).

discrepancy [dis'krepənsi], *s.* die Diskrepanz, der Widerspruch; der Unterschied (*difference*).

discretion [dis'kreʃən], *s.* die Diskretion; die Klugheit; der Takt (*tact*); die Verschwiegenheit (*silence*); *at your* —, nach Ihrem Belieben; *use your* —, handle nach deinem Ermessen; handeln Sie nach Ihrem Ermessen.

discretionary [dis'kreʃənəri], *adj.* willkürlich, uneingeschränkt.

discriminate [dis'krimineit], *v.a., v.n.* unterscheiden (*distinguish*); absondern (*separate*).

discriminating [dis'krimineitiŋ], *adj.* scharfsinnig; einsichtig.

discriminatory [dis'krimineitəri], *adj.* einen Unterschied machend; — *legislation*, das Ausnahmegesetz.

discursive [dis'kə:siv], *adj.* diskursiv, ohne Zusammenhang.

discuss [dis'kʌs], *v.a.* besprechen, erörtern.

discussion [dis'kʌʃən], *s.* die Diskussion, das Gespräch.

disdain [dis'dein], *s.* die Verachtung. — *v.a.* verachten, verschmähen; herabsetzen (*belittle*).

disdainful [dis'deinful], *adj.* geringschätzig, verächtlich.

disease [di'zi:z], *s.* die Krankheit.

diseased [di'zi:zd], *adj.* krank.

disembark [disim'bɑ:k], *v.n.* aussteigen, landen. — *v.a.* aussteigen lassen, ausschiffen.

disembarkation [disembɑ:'keiʃən], *s.* die Ausschiffung, die Landung.

disenchant [disin'tʃɑ:nt], *v.a.* ernüchtern.

disenchantment [disin'tʃɑ:ntmənt], *s.* die Ernüchterung.

disengage [disin'geidʒ], *v.a.* losmachen, befreien (*release*); freigeben. — *v.n.* (*Mil.*) sich absetzen.

disengaged [disin'geidʒd], *adj.* frei (*unoccupied*).

disentangle [disin'tæŋgl], *v.a.* entwirren; befreien (*free*).

disentanglement [disin'tæŋglmənt], *s.* die Entwirrung, die Befreiung.

disfavour [dis'feivə], *s.* die Ungunst, die Ungnade.

disfigure [dis'figə], *v.a.* entstellen, verunstalten.

disfiguration [disfigjuə'reiʃən], *s.* die Entstellung, die Verunstaltung.

disfranchise [dis'fræntʃaiz], *v.a.* das Wahlrecht entziehen (*Dat.*).

disgorge [dis'gɔːdʒ], *v.a.* ausspeien.

disgrace [dis'greis], *v.a.* entehren, Schande bringen. — *s.* die Ungnade, Schande (*shame*); die Entehrung (*putting to shame*).

disgraceful [dis'greisful], *adj.* schändlich, entehrend.

disgruntled [dis'grʌntld], *adj.* verstimmt, unzufrieden.

disguise [dis'gaiz], *v.a.* verkleiden (*dress*); (*fig.*) verstellen. — *s.* die Verkleidung; die Verstellung.

disgust [dis'gʌst], *s.* der Ekel, der Widerwille. — *v.a.* anekeln; *be —ed,* sehr ärgerlich sein; *be —ed with s. th.,* etwas verabscheuen.

dish [diʃ], *s.* die Schüssel (*bowl*); das Gericht (*food*). — *v.a.* (*coll.*) abtun (*frustrate*); — *up,* auftragen (*food*).

dishcloth ['diʃklɔθ], *s.* das Wischtuch; der Abwaschlappen.

dishearten [dis'hɑːtn], *v.a.* entmutigen, verzagt machen.

dishevelled [di'ʃevəld], *adj.* aufgelöst (*hair*); zerzaust (*hair, clothes*).

dishonest [dis'ɔnist], *adj.* unehrlich.

dishonesty [dis'ɔnisti], *s.* die Unehrlichkeit.

dishonour [dis'ɔnə], *s.* die Schande. — *v.a.* schänden, Schande bringen (*über, Acc.*).

dishonourable [dis'ɔnərəbl], *adj.* ehrlos, schimpflich.

dishwater ['diʃwɔːtə], *s.* das Spülwasser.

disillusion [disi'luːʒən], *s.* die Enttäuschung, die Ernüchterung. — *v.a.* enttäuschen, ernüchtern.

disinclination [disinkli'neiʃən], *s.* die Abneigung.

disincline [disin'klain], *v.a.* abgeneigt machen (*Dat.*).

disinfect [disin'fekt], *v.a.* desinfizieren.

disinfectant [disin'fektənt], *s.* das Desinfektionsmittel.

disinfection [disin'fekʃən], *s.* die Desinfektion.

disingenuous [disin'dʒenjuəs], *adj.* unaufrichtig, unredlich.

disinherit [disin'herit], *v.a.* enterben.

disinter [disin'təː], *v.a.* exhumieren, ausgraben.

disinterested [dis'intrəstid], *adj.* uneigennützig.

disinterestedness [dis'intrəstidnis], *s.* die Selbstlosigkeit, die Uneigennützigkeit.

disjoin [dis'dʒɔin], *v.a.* trennen.

disjoint [dis'dʒɔint], *v.a.* zerlegen, zerstückeln.

disjointedness [dis'dʒɔintidnis], *s.* die Zerstücktheit, die Zusammenhangslosigkeit (*style of writing etc.*).

disjunction [dis'dʒʌŋkʃən], *s.* die Trennung, die Abtrennung.

disjunctive [dis'dʒʌŋktiv], *adj.* (*Gram.*) trennend, disjunktiv.

disk [disk] *see* **disc.**

dislike [dis'laik], *v.a.* nicht leiden mögen, nicht gerne haben. — *s.* die Abneigung (*of, gegen, Acc.*).

dislocate ['dislokeit], *v.a.* verrenken (*bone*); (*fig.*) in Unordnung bringen.

dislocation [dislo'keiʃən], *s.* (*Med.*) die Verrenkung; die Verwirrung (*traffic etc.*).

dislodge [dis'lɔdʒ], *v.a.* vertreiben (*drive out*); entfernen (*remove*).

disloyal [dis'lɔiəl], *adj.* ungetreu; verräterisch.

disloyalty [dis'lɔiəlti], *s.* die Untreue (*sentiment*); der Verrat (*act*).

dismal ['dizməl], *adj.* trostlos, traurig (*mood*); düster, trüb (*weather*).

dismantle [dis'mæntl], *v.a.* niederreißen, zerlegen; abbauen.

dismay [dis'mei], *v.a.* erschrecken, entmutigen. — *s.* die Furcht, der Schrecken, die Bangigkeit.

dismember [dis'membə], *v.a.* zerstückeln.

dismemberment [dis'membəmənt], *s.* die Zerstückelung, die Aufteilung.

dismiss [dis'mis], *v.a.* entlassen (*person*); aufgeben (*idea*).

dismissal [dis'misəl], *s.* die Entlassung; (*Law*) die Abweisung.

dismount [dis'maunt], *v.n.* vom Pferd absteigen. — *v.a.* (die Truppen) absteigen lassen.

disobedience [diso'biːdjəns], *s.* der Ungehorsam.

disobedient [diso'biːdjənt], *adj.* ungehorsam.

disobey [diso'bei], *v.a., v.n.* nicht gehorchen.

disoblige [diso'blaidʒ], *v.a.* verletzen, unhöflich behandeln.

disorder [dis'ɔːdə], *s.* die Unordnung; der Aufruhr (*riot*). — *v.a.* verwirren, in Unordnung bringen.

disorderliness [dis'ɔːdəlinis], *s.* die Unordentlichkeit.

disorderly [dis'ɔːdəli], *adj.* unordentlich (*unsystematic*); aufrührerisch, liederlich.

disorganization [disɔːgəni'zeiʃən *or* -nai'zeiʃən], *s.* die Zerrüttung, die Auflösung (*dissolution*).

disorganize [dis'ɔːgənaiz], *v.a.* auflösen.

disown [dis'oun], *v.a.* verleugnen.

disparage [dis'pæridʒ], *v.a.* verunglimpfen (*slight*); herabsetzen (*minimize*).

disparagement [dis'pæridʒmənt], *s.* die Herabsetzung.

disparity [dis'pæriti], *s.* die Ungleichheit.

dispatch [dis'pætʃ] *see* **despatch.**

dispel [dis'pel], *v.a.* vertreiben, verscheuchen.

dispensable [dis'pensəbl], *adj.* erläßlich, entbehrlich.

dispensation [dispen'seiʃən], *s.* die Austeilung; (*Eccl.*) die Dispensation.

dispensary [dis'pensəri], *s.* die Apotheke.

dispense [dis'pens], *v.a.* ausgeben, austeilen (*distribute*); — *with*, entbehren können, verzichten (auf, *Acc.*).

dispenser [dis'pensə], *s.* der Apotheker, der Pharmazeut.

dispersal [dis'pə:səl], *s.* das Zerstreuen, die Verteilung.

disperse [dis'pə:s], *v.a.* zerstreuen. — *v.n.* sich zerstreuen, sich verteilen.

dispirit [dis'pirit], *v.a.* mutlos machen, entmutigen.

displace [dis'pleis], *v.a.* verlegen, versetzen; (*Phys.*) verdrängen; —*d person*, der Heimatlose, der Verschleppte, der Flüchtling.

displacement [dis'pleismənt], *s.* die Versetzung (*from one place to another*); die Entwurzelung (*uprooting*); (*Phys.*) die Verdrängung; (*Naut.*) das Deplacement.

display [dis'plei], *v.a.* entfalten, ausstellen, zur Schau stellen (*show*). — *s.* die Entfaltung (*showing*), die Schaustellung, Ausstellung (*exhibition*).

displease [dis'pli:z], *v.a.* mißfallen (*Dat.*).

displeased [dis'pli:zd], *adj.* ungehalten (*at*, über, *Acc.*).

displeasure [dis'pleʒə], *s.* das Mißvergnügen, das Mißfallen (— *at*, an, *Dat.*).

disposable [dis'pouzəbl], *adj.* (*Comm.*) disponibel; zur Verfügung stehend.

disposal [dis'pouzl], *s.* die Verfügung (*ordering*); die Übergabe (*handing over*); *at o.'s* —, zur Verfügung; *bomb* —, die Unschädlichmachung der Bomben.

dispose [dis'pouz], *v.a.* einrichten (*thing*); geneigt machen (*person*); — *of*, etwas loswerden (*Acc.*). — *v.n.* anordnen (*ordain*).

disposed [dis'pouzd], *adj.* geneigt; *be well — towards s.o.*, jemandem zugeneigt sein *or* wohlwollend gegenüberstehen; *well* —, (in) guter Laune.

disposition [dispə'ziʃən], *s.* (*Psych.*) die Anlage, die Gemütsart (*temperament*); die Anordnung (*sequence*); der Plan, die Anlage (*of book etc.*); die Verfügung (*arrangement*).

dispossess [dispə'zes], *v.a.* enteignen, (des Besitzes) berauben (*Genit.*).

disproof [dis'pru:f], *s.* die Widerlegung.

disproportion [disprə'pɔ:ʃən], *s.* das Mißverhältnis.

disproportionate [disprə'pɔ:sənit], *adj.* unverhältnismäßig.

disprove [dis'pru:v], *v.a.* widerlegen.

disputable [dis'pju:təbl], *adj.* bestreitbar.

disputant ['dispjutənt], *s.* der Opponent, der Disputant.

disputation [dispju'teiʃən], *s.* der gelehrte Streit, die Disputation.

dispute [dis'pju:t], *s.* der Disput, die Meinungsverschiedenheit. — *v.a.*, *v.n.* streiten, verschiedener Ansicht sein; disputieren (*debate*); mit Worten streiten (*argue*).

disqualification [diskwɔlifi'keiʃən], *s.* die Disqualifikation.

disqualify [dis'kwɔlifai], *v.a.* disqualifizieren, ausschließen.

disquiet [dis'kwaiət], *v.a.* beunruhigen, stören. — *s.* die Unruhe, die Störung.

disquisition [diskwi'ziʃən], *s.* die (lange) Abhandlung *or* Rede.

disregard [disri'gɑ:d], *v.a.* mißachten, nicht beachten. — *s.* die Außerachtlassung, die Mißachtung.

disreputable [dis'repjutəbl], *adj.* verrufen, in üblem Rufe stehend.

disrepute [disri'pju:t], *s.* der schlechte Name, der üble Ruf.

disrespect [disris'pekt], *s.* die Geringschätzung, der Mangel an Respekt. — *v.a.* (*obs.*) mißachten, geringschätzen, respektlos behandeln.

disrespectful [disris'pektful], *adj.* respektlos, unhöflich.

disrobe [dis'roub], *v.a.* entkleiden. — *v.n.* sich entkleiden.

disrupt [dis'rʌpt], *v.a.* abreißen, unterbrechen, stören (*disturb*).

disruption [dis'rʌpʃən], *s.* die Störung, die Unterbrechung (*interruption*); der Bruch.

dissatisfaction [dissætis'fækʃən], *s.* die Unzufriedenheit.

dissatisfied [dis'sætisfaid], *adj.* unzufrieden, unbefriedigt.

dissatisfy [dis'sætisfai], *v.a.* unzufrieden lassen.

dissect [di'sekt], *v.a.* zergliedern, zerlegen; (*Anat.*) sezieren.

dissection [di'sekʃən], *s.* die Zergliederung; (*Anat.*) die Sektion.

dissemble [di'sembl], *v.a.*, *v.n.* heucheln; sich verstellen.

disseminate [di'semineit], *v.a.* verbreiten.

dissemination [disemi'neiʃən], *s.* die Verbreitung.

dissension [di'senʃən], *s.* die Uneinigkeit, der Zwist (*conflict*).

dissent [di'sent], *v.n.* anderer Meinung sein; abweichen (*from*, von, *Dat.*). — *s.* die Abweichung, die abweichende Meinung.

dissenter [di'sentə], *s.* der Dissenter, das Mitglied der Freikirche.

dissertation [disə'teiʃən], *s.* die Dissertation, die Abhandlung.

dissever [di'sevə], *v.a.* trennen (*separate*); zerteilen (*divide*).

dissidence ['disidəns], *s.* die Uneinigkeit.

dissident ['disidənt], *adj.* uneinig, anders denkend.

dissimilar [di'similə], *adj.* unähnlich, ungleichartig.

dissimilarity [disimi'læriti], *s.* die Unähnlichkeit, die Ungleichartigkeit.

dissimulate [di'simjuleit], *v.a.* verhehlen (*conceal*). — *v.n.* sich verstellen, heucheln.

dissimulation [disimju'leifən], *s.* die Verstellung, Heuchelei, das Vorgeben (*pretence*).

dissipate ['disipeit], *v.a.* zerstreuen (*spread*); verschwenden (*waste*).

dissipation [disi'peifən], *s.* die Zerstreuung, die Verschwendung; die Ausschweifung.

dissociate [di'soufieit], *v.a.* trennen, lösen. — *v.r.* abrücken (von).

dissociation [disoufi'eifən], *s.* die Trennung; die Dissoziation.

dissolubility [disəlju'biliti], *s.* die Auflösbarkeit.

dissoluble [di'səljubl], *adj.* auflösbar.

dissolute ['disəlju:t], *adj.* ausschweifend, lose, liederlich.

dissolution [disə'lju:fən], *s.* die Auflösung; der Tod (*death*).

dissolvable [di'zɔlvəbl], *adj.* auflösbar, löslich.

dissolve [di'zɔlv], *v.a.* auflösen; lösen. — *v.n.* sich auflösen, zergehen (*melt*).

dissonance ['disənəns], *s.* die Dissonanz, der Mißklang.

dissonant ['disənənt], *adj.* (*Mus.*) dissonant; mißhellig (*discordant*).

dissuade [di'sweid], *v.a.* abraten (*from*, von, *Dat.*).

dissuasion [di'sweiʒən], *s.* das Abraten.

dissuasive [di'sweisiv], *adj.* abratend.

distaff ['distɑ:f], *s.* der Spinnrocken (*spinning*); - *on the* — *side*, auf der weiblichen Linie.

distance ['distəns], *s.* die Entfernung; die Ferne (*remoteness*). — *v.a.* hinter sich lassen, sich distanzieren (von, *Dat.*).

distant ['distənt], *adj.* entfernt, fern (*space*); kühl (*manner*).

distaste [dis'teist], *s.* die Abneigung (vor, *Dat.*); der Widerwille (gegen, *Acc.*).

distasteful [dis'teistful], *adj.* widerwärtig, zuwider.

distastefulness [dis'teistfulnis], *s.* die Widerwärtigkeit.

distemper (1) [dis'tempə], *s.* die Krankheit; die Staupe (*dogs*).

distemper (2) [dis'tempə], *s.* die Wasserfarbe (*paint*). — *v.a.* mit Wasserfarbe streichen.

distend [dis'tend], *v.a.* (*Med.*) ausdehnen, strecken. — *v.n.* sich ausdehnen.

distension, distention [dis'tenfən], *s.* das Dehnen; (*Med.*) die Ausdehnung, die Streckung.

distich ['distik], *s.* (*Poet.*) das Distichon.

distil [dis'til], *v.a.* destillieren. — *v.n.* (*Chem.*) destillieren, herauströpfeln.

distillation [disti'leifən], *s.* die Destillierung, (*Chem.*) der Destilliervorgang.

distiller [dis'tilə], *s.* der Branntweinbrenner.

distillery [dis'tiləri], *s.* die (Branntwein)brennerei.

distinct [dis'tiŋkt], *adj.* deutlich, klar; — *from*, verschieden von (*Dat.*).

distinction [dis'tiŋkfən], *s.* der Unterschied, die Unterscheidung (*differentiation*); die Auszeichnung (*eminence*).

distinctive [dis'tiŋktiv], *adj.* unterscheidend (*differentiating*); deutlich (*clear*); leicht zu unterscheiden (*easy to distinguish*).

distinctiveness [dis'tiŋktivnis], *s.* die Deutlichkeit (*of voice etc.*); die Eigenart, Eigentümlichkeit (*peculiarity*).

distinguish [dis'tiŋgwif], *v.a.* unterscheiden. — *v.r.* — *o.s.*, sich auszeichnen.

distinguishable [dis'tiŋgwifəbl], *adj.* unterscheidbar.

distinguished [dis'tiŋgwifd], *adj.* berühmt, vornehm.

distort [dis'tɔ:t], *v.a.* verdrehen; verzerren, verrenken.

distortion [dis'tɔ:fən], *s.* die Verdrehung, Verzerrung; (*fig.*) die Entstellung (*of truth etc.*).

distract [dis'trækt], *v.a.* abziehen, ablenken (*divert*); stören (*disturb*).

distracted [dis'træktid], *adj.* zerstreut; verrückt (*mentally deranged*).

distraction [dis'trækfən], *s.* die Ablenkung; die Störung (*disturbance*); *to* —, bis zur Raserei.

distrain [dis'trein], *v.a.* beschlagnahmen, in Beschlag nehmen.

distraint [dis'treint], *s.* die Beschlagnahme.

distress [dis'tres], *s.* die Not, die Trübsal. — *v.a.* betrüben (*sadden*); quälen (*torture*).

distribute [dis'tribju:t], *v.a.* verteilen, austeilen (*among*, unter, *Acc.*).

distribution [dis'tribju:fən], *s.* die Verteilung; die Austeilung (*giving out*), (*Comm.*) der Vertrieb.

distributive [dis'tribjutiv], *adj.* (*Gram.*) distributiv; — *trades*, die Vertriebsgewerbe.

district ['distrikt], *s.* (*Geog., Pol.*) der Bezirk; die Gegend (*region*); der Kreis (*administrative*); — *commissioner*, der Kreisbeamte, Kreisvorsteher.

distrust [dis'trʌst], *v.a.* mißtrauen (*Dat.*). — *s.* das Mißtrauen (*of*, gegen, *Acc.*).

distrustful [dis'trʌstful], *adj.* mißtrauisch (*of*, gegen, *Acc.*).

disturb [dis'tə:b], *v.a.* stören (*trouble*); in Unordnung bringen (*disorder*).

disturbance [dis'tə:bəns], *s.* die Störung (*interruption etc.*); der Aufruhr (*riot*).

disunion [dis'ju:njən], *s.* die Entzweiung, die Zwietracht.

disunite [disju'nait], *v.a.* entzweien, Zwietracht säen zwischen. — *v.n.* sich trennen.

371

disuse

disuse [dis'ju:z], *v.a.* außer Gebrauch setzen. — [-'ju:s], *s.* der Nichtgebrauch (*abeyance*); die Entwöhnung (*cessation of practice*).

ditch [ditʃ], *s.* der Graben; *dull as —water*, uninteressant, langweilig. — *v.a.* mit einem Graben umgeben (*dig around*); graben.

ditto ['ditou], *adv.* desgleichen, dito.

ditty ['diti], *s.* das Liedchen.

diurnal [dai'ə:nəl], *adj.* täglich.

divan [di'væn], *s.* der Diwan.

dive [daiv], *v.n.* tauchen, springen (ins Wasser); (*Aviat.*) sturzfliegen, einen Sturzflug machen. — *s.* der Hechtsprung (ins Wasser); der Wassersprung; der Kopfsprung; (*Aviat.*) der Sturzflug.

diver ['daivə], *s.* (*Sport, Orn.*) der Taucher.

diverge [dai'və:dʒ], *v.n.* abweichen, auseinandergehen.

divergence [dai'və:dʒəns], *s.* die Abweichung, die Divergenz, Meinungsverschiedenheit.

divergent [dai'və:dʒənt], *adj.* auseinandergehend, abweichend.

divers ['daivəz], *adj. pl.* etliche, verschiedene.

diverse [dai'və:s], *adj.* verschieden, mannigfaltig.

diversify [dai'və:sifai], *v.a.* verschieden machen.

diversion [dai'və:ʃən], *s.* die Zerstreuung; (*Traffic*) die Umleitung.

diversity [dai'və:siti], *s.* die Verschiedenheit; die Ungleichheit (*disparity*).

divert [dai'və:t], *v.a.* ablenken, zerstreuen.

divest [di'vest *or* dai'-], *v.a.* entkleiden, berauben (*of office*, eines Amtes). — *v.r.* — *o.s. of*, auf etwas verzichten (*give up*).

divide [di'vaid], *v.a.* (*Maths.*) dividieren; teilen (*share*); aufteilen (*proportion*); sondern, trennen (*separate*). — *v.n.* sich teilen; (*Maths.*) sich dividieren lassen.

dividend ['dividənd], *s.* (*Comm.*) die Dividende; (*Maths.*) der Dividend.

dividers [di'vaidəz], *s.pl.* der Stechzirkel.

divination [divi'neiʃən], *s.* die Wahrsagung (*prophecy*); die Ahnung.

divine [di'vain], *v.a.* weissagen (*prophesy*); erraten (*guess*). — *adj.* göttlich; (*coll.*) herrlich. —*s.* (*obs.*) der Geistliche (*clergyman*).

divinity [di'viniti], *s.* die Göttlichkeit; die Gottheit (*deity*); die Theologie.

divisibility [divizi'biliti], *s.* (*Maths.*) die Teilbarkeit.

divisible [di'vizibl], *adj.* teilbar.

division [di'viʒən], *s.* (*Maths., Mil.*) die Division; die Teilung (*partition*); die Abteilung (*department*); (*Parl.*) die Abstimmung.

divisor [di'vaizə], *s.* (*Maths.*) der Divisor; der Teiler.

divorce [di'vɔ:s], *s.* (*Law*) die Scheidung; die Trennung (*separation*). — *v.a.* sich von einem scheiden lassen.

divulge [dai'vʌldʒ], *v.a.* ausplaudern; verraten (*betray*); verbreiten (*spread*).

dizziness ['dizinis], *s.* der Schwindel.

dizzy ['dizi], *adj.* schwindlig.

do [du:], *v.a. irr.* tun, machen; — *o.'s duty*, seine Pflicht erfüllen; — *o.'s bit*, das Seinige leisten; — *o.'s homework*, seine Aufgaben machen; — *a favour*, einen Gefallen erweisen; vollbringen (*accomplish*); — *away with*, abschaffen (*Acc.*); einpacken. — *v.n. this will —*, das genügt; *this won't —*, so geht's nicht; — *without*, ohne etwas auskommen; *how — you —?* sehr angenehm (*on introduction to people*).

docile ['dousail], *adj.* gelehrig, lenksam, fügsam.

docility [do'siliti], *s.* die Gelehrigkeit, die Fügsamkeit.

dock (1) [dɔk], *s.* (*Bot.*) das Ampferkraut; — *leaf*, das Ampferblatt.

dock (2) [dɔk], *s.* (*Naut.*) das Dock; —*yard*, die Schiffswerft; (*Law*) die Anklagebank. — *v.a.* (*Naut.*) ein Schiff ins Dock bringen.

dock (3) [dɔk], *v.a.* stutzen (*clip*); kürzen (*wages*).

docket ['dɔkit], *s.* der Zettel (*chit*); der Lieferschein.

doctor ['dɔktə], *s.* (*Med.*) der Arzt, der Doktor. — *v.a.* operieren, kastrieren (*a cat etc.*).

doctorate ['dɔktərit], *s.* das Doktorat, die Doktorwürde.

doctrinaire [dɔktri'neə], *s.* der Doktrinär. — *adj.* doktrinär.

doctrinal [dɔk'trainəl], *adj.* Lehr-.

doctrine ['dɔktrin], *s.* die Lehre, die Doktrin.

document ['dɔkjumənt], *s.* das Dokument, die Urkunde.

documentary [dɔkju'mentəri], *adj.* Dokumentar- (*film*); dokumentarisch (*evidence*).

documentation [dɔkjumen'teiʃən], *s.* die Dokumentation, Heranziehung von Dokumenten.

dodge [dɔdʒ], *v.a.* ausweichen (*Dat.*). — *s.* der Kniff.

dodger ['dɔdʒə], *s.* der Schwindler.

doe [dou], *s.* (*Zool.*) das Reh.

doeskin ['douskin], *s.* das Rehleder.

doff [dɔf], *v.a.* abnehmen, ablegen (*clothes*).

dog [dɔg], *s.* der Hund; —*'s ear*, das Eselsohr (*in book*). — *v.a.* verfolgen, auf Schritt und Tritt folgen (*Dat.*) (*follow closely*).

dogfish ['dɔgfiʃ], *s.* (*Zool.*) der Dornhai.

dogged ['dɔgid], *adj.* unverdrossen, zäh.

doggedness ['dɔgidnis], *s.* die Zähigkeit.

doggerel ['dɔgərəl], *s.* der Knüttelvers.

dogma ['dɔgmə], *s.* das Dogma, der Glaubenssatz.

dogmatic [dɔg'mætik], *adj.* dogmatisch.
dogmatism ['dɔgmətizm], *s.* der Dogmatismus.
dogmatize ['dɔgmətaiz], *v.n.* dogmatisieren.
doldrums ['douldrəmz], *s. pl.* die Schwermut, die Depression; (*Naut.*) die Windstillen, *f.pl.*
dole [doul], *s.* das Almosen; die Arbeitslosenunterstützung (*unemployment benefit*); *be on the* —, stempeln gehen, Arbeitslosenunterstützung beziehen. — *v.a.* — *out*, austeilen, verteilen.
doleful ['doulful], *adj.* traurig, bekümmert.
doll [dɔl], *s.* die Puppe.
dollar ['dɔlə], *s.* der Dollar.
dolman ['dɔlmən], *s.* der Dolman.
dolorous ['dɔlərəs], *adj.* (*Lit.*) schmerzlich, schmerzhaft.
dolphin ['dɔlfin], *s.* (*Zool.*) der Delphin.
dolt [doult], *s.* der Tölpel.
doltish ['doultiʃ], *adj.* tölpelhaft.
doltishness ['doultiʃnis], *s.* die Tölpelhaftigkeit.
domain [do'mein], *s.* das Gebiet, der Bereich.
dome [doum], *s.* (*Archit.*) die Kuppel, die Wölbung; der Dom.
domed [doumd], *adj.* gewölbt.
domestic [do'mestik], *adj.* Haus-, häuslich; — *animal*, das Haustier.
domesticate [do'mestikeit], *v.a.* zähmen (*tame*), zivilisieren.
domesticity [dɔmes'tisiti], *s.* die Häuslichkeit.
domicile ['dɔmisail], *s.* das Domizil; der Wohnort.
domiciled ['dɔmisaild], *adj.* wohnhaft (*at*, in, *Dat.*).
dominant ['dɔminənt], *adj.* vorherrschend. — *s.* (*Mus.*) die Dominante.
dominate ['dɔmineit], *v.a.* beherrschen. — *v.n.* herrschen.
domination [dɔmi'neiʃən], *s.* die Herrschaft.
domineer [dɔmi'niə], *v.n.* tyrannisieren.
domineering [dɔmi'niəriŋ], *adj.* überheblich, gebieterisch.
Dominican [do'minikən], *s.* der Dominikaner (*friar*).
dominion [do'minjən], *s.* die Herrschaft (*rule*); das Dominion (*Br. Commonwealth*).
domino ['dɔminou], *s.* (*pl.* —**noes**) der Domino (*mask*); (*pl.*) das Domino (*game*).
don (1) [dɔn], *s.* der Universitätsgelehrte, Universitätsdozent (*scholar*); Don (*Spanish nobleman*).
don (2) [dɔn], *v.a.* anziehen.
donate [do'neit], *v.a.* schenken, stiften.
donation [do'neiʃən], *s.* die Schenkung, die Stiftung; die Gabe (*gift*).
donkey ['dɔŋki], *s.* (*Zool.*) der Esel; — *engine*, die Hilfsmaschine.
donor ['dounə], *s.* der Spender, der Stifter; *blood* —, der Blutspender.

doom [du:m], *s.* die Verurteilung (*judgment*); der Untergang; das jüngste Gericht.
doomed [du:md], *adj.* verurteilt, verdammt (*to*, zu, *Dat.*).
Doomsday ['du:msdei]. der jüngste Tag, der Tag des jüngsten Gerichtes.
door [dɔ:], *s.* die Tür(e); *next* —, nebenan; *out of* —*s*, draußen, im Freien; —*bell*, die Türklingel; —*latch*, die Klinke.
doorman ['dɔ:mæn], *s.* der Türsteher, der Pförtner.
dormant ['dɔ:mənt], *adj.* schlafend; unbenutzt.
dormer window ['dɔ:mə 'windou], *s.* das Dachfenster.
dormitory ['dɔmitri], *s.* der Schlafsaal.
dormouse ['dɔ:maus], *s.* (*Zool.*) die Haselmaus.
dose [dous], *s.* (*Med.*) die Dosis. — *v.a.* dosieren.
dot [dɔt], *s.* der Punkt, das Tüpfel. — *v.a.* punktieren; *sign on the* —*ted line*, unterschreiben; — *the i's and cross the t's*, äußerst genau sein.
dotage ['doutidʒ], *s.* die Altersschwäche, das Greisenalter.
dotard ['doutəd], *s.* der alte Dummkopf.
dote [dout], *v.n.* vernarrt sein (*on*, in, *Acc.*).
double [dʌbl], *adj.* (*Maths.*) doppelt; zweideutig (*meaning*); falsch (*false*); — *entry book-keeping*, doppelte Buchführung. — *s.* der Doppelgänger, die Doppelgängerin; *at the* —, im Sturmschritt. — *v.a.* (*Maths.*) verdoppeln; zusammenlegen (*fold in two*). — *v.n.* — *up with pain*, sich vor Schmerzen winden *or* krümmen.
doublet ['dʌblit], *s.* der Wams; — *and hose*, Wams und Hosen; der Pasch (*dice*); (*Ling.*) die Dublette, Doppelform.
doubt [daut], *s.* der Zweifel. — *v.a.* zweifeln (*an*, *Dat.*); bezweifeln.
doubtful ['dautful], *adj.* zweifelhaft, fraglich (*uncertain*).
doubtless ['dautlis], *adj.* zweifellos, ohne Zweifel.
douche [du:ʃ], *s.* die Dusche.
dough [dou], *s.* der Teig.
doughnut ['dounʌt], *s.* der Krapfen, Pfannkuchen.
doughy ['doui], *adj.* weich, teigig.
douse [daus], *v.a.* begießen, mit Wasser beschütten.
dove [dʌv], *s.* (*Orn.*) die Taube.
dovecote ['dʌvkɔt], *s.* der Taubenschlag.
dovetail ['dʌvteil], *v.a., v.n.* einpassen; fügen; —*ing*, die Einpassung, die Verzinkung.
dowager ['dauədʒə], *s.* die Witwe (*of noble family*, von Stande).
dowdy ['daudi], *adj.* schlampig, unordentlich, unelegant.
dower ['dauə], *s.* die Mitgift, die Ausstattung.

down (1) [daun], *s.* der Flaum, die Daune.

down (2) [daun], *s.* das Hügelland.

down (3) [daun], *adv.* hinunter, herunter; nieder; unter; hinab. — *prep.* herab; hinunter. — *adj. the — train*, der Zug aus London. — *v.a.* niederzwingen, hinunterstürzen.

downcast ['daunkɑ:st], *adj.* niedergeschlagen.

downfall ['daunfɔ:l], *s.* der Sturz.

downhill [daun'hil], *adv.* bergab. — ['daunhil], *adj.* abschüssig.

downpour ['daunpɔ:], *s.* der Platzregen.

downright ['daunrait], *adj.* völlig. — *adv.* geradezu.

downward ['daunwəd], *adj.* abschüssig. — *adv.* (*also* **downwards**) *see* **down**.

dowry ['dauri] *see* **dower**.

doze [douz], *v.n.* dösen, schlummern.

dozen [dazn], *s.* das Dutzend.

drab [dræb], *adj.* eintönig; langweilig (*boring*).

draft [drɑ:ft], *s.* (*Comm.*) die Tratte; der Entwurf (*sketch*); (*Mil.*) das Detachement — *v.a.* entwerfen (*sketch*); (*Mil.*) abordnen; (*Am.*) einziehen.

drag [dræg], *v.a.* schleppen. — *s.* (*Engin.*) die Schleppbremse, der Dreghaken; der Hemmschuh (*wedge*); —*net*, das Schleppnetz; —*wheel*, das Schlepprad.

dragoman ['drægomən], *s.* der Dolmetscher.

dragon ['drægən], *s.* der Drache.

dragonfly ['drægənflai], *s.* (*Ent.*) die Libelle.

dragoon [drə'gu:n], *v.a.* unterdrücken. — *s.* (*Mil.*) der Dragoner.

drain [drein], *v.a.* entwässern, austrocknen; trockenlegen. — *v.n.* ablaufen, abfließen, auslaufen. — *s.* der Abguß, Abzug, die Gosse (*in street*); (*Engin.*) die Dränage; —*ing board*, das Ablauf- *or* Abwaschbrett; (*Phot.*) —*ing rack*, der Trockenständer; *a — on o.'s income*, eine Belastung des Einkommens.

drainage ['dreinidʒ], *s.* die Trockenlegung, die Kanalisierung.

drainpipe ['dreinpaip], *s.* das Abflußrohr; — *trousers*, die Röhrenhosen, *f. pl.*

drake [dreik], *s.* (*Orn.*) der Enterich.

dram [dræm], *s.* der Trunk; Schluck (*spirits*).

drama ['drɑ:mə], *s.* das Drama, das Schauspiel.

dramatic [drə'mætik], *adj.* dramatisch.

dramatist ['drɑ:m- *or* 'dræmatist], *s.* der Dramatiker.

dramatize ['dræmətaiz], *v.a.* dramatisieren.

drape [dreip], *v.a.* drapieren, bedecken; einhüllen (*wrap*). — *s.* (*Am.*) der Vorhang.

draper ['dreipə], *s.* der Stoffhändler, der Tuchhändler.

drapery ['dreipəri], *s.* — *department*, die Stoff- *or* Tuchabteilung; die Tuchhandlung (*shop*).

drastic ['drɑ:stik *or* 'dræstik], *adj.* drastisch, radikal.

draught [drɑ:ft], *s.* der Zug (*air*); der Tiefgang (— *of ship*); der Schluck (*drink*); der Schlaftrunk (*sleeping* —); — *horse*, das Zugpferd; — *beer*, das Faßbier; —*board*, das Damespielbrett; (*pl.*) das Damespiel.

draw [drɔ:], *v.a. irr.* ziehen (*pull*); zeichnen (*sketch*); anlocken (*attract*); ausschreiben (*cheque*); —*well*, der Ziehbrunnen; — (*Sport*) das Unentschieden.

drawback ['drɔ:bæk], *s.* der Nachteil, die Schattenseite.

drawbridge ['drɔ:bridʒ], *s.* die Zugbrücke.

drawer ['drɔ:ə], *s.* die Schublade; *chest of* —*s*, die Kommode; (*pl.*) die Unterhosen, *f. pl.*

drawing ['drɔ:iŋ], *s.* (*Art*) die Zeichnung; —*board*, das Reißbrett; —*office*, das Zeichenbüro, der Zeichensaal.

drawing room ['drɔ:iŋ rum], *s.* das Wohnzimmer, der Salon.

drawl [drɔ:l], *v.n.* gedehnt sprechen. — *s.* die gedehnte Sprechweise.

drawn [drɔ:n], *adj.* (*Sport*) unentschieden.

dray [drei], *s.* der Rollwagen, der Karren; —*man*, der Kutscher, der Fuhrmann.

dread [dred], *s.* der Schrecken. — *adj.* schrecklich. — *v.a.* fürchten. — *v.n.* sich fürchten (vor, *Dat.*).

dreadful ['dredful], *adj.* schrecklich, furchtbar.

dreadnought ['drednɔ:t], *s.* (*Naut.*) das große Schlachtschiff.

dream [dri:m], *s.* der Traum. — *v.n. irr.* träumen; *I would not — of it*, es würde mir nicht im Traum einfallen, ich denke nicht daran.

dreamt [dremt] *see* **dream**.

dreamy ['dri:mi], *adj.* verträumt, träumerisch.

dreariness ['driərinis], *s.* die Öde.

dreary ['driəri], *adj.* traurig, öde.

dredge [dredʒ], *s.* das Schleppnetz. — *v.a.* (*Engin.*) ausbaggern; (*Naut.*) dreggen.

dredger ['dredʒə], *s.* der Bagger, das Baggerschiff; (*Cul.*) die Streubüchse.

dregs [dregz], *s. pl.* der Bodensatz (*in cup etc.*); die Hefe (*yeast*).

drench [drentʃ], *v.a.* durchnässen, tränken.

Dresden ['drezdən]. (*china*) das Meißner Porzellan.

dress [dres], *s.* das Kleid; die Kleidung; *evening* —, die Abendkleidung; *full* —, die Gala(kleidung); — *circle*, erster Rang; —*maker*, die Schneiderin; — *rehearsal*, die Generalprobe; — *shirt*, das Frackhemd; — *suit*, der Frackanzug. — *v.a., v.n.* (sich) anziehen.

dresser ['dresə], *s.* der Ankleider (*valet*); der Anrichtetisch (*table*).

dressing ['dresiŋ], *s.* (*Build.*) die Verkleidung; der Verband (*bandage*); der Verputz (*interior decoration*); — *gown*, der Schlafrock, Bademantel; (*Theat.*) — *room*, das Künstlerzimmer; Ankleidezimmer; — *table*, der Toilettentisch.

dressy ['dresi], *adj.* elegant; modesüchtig.

dribble [dribl], *v.n.* tröpfeln (*trickle*); geifern (*slaver*); (*Footb.*) dribbeln.

driblet ['driblit], *s.* die Kleinigkeit, die Lappalie.

drift [drift], *s.* die Richtung (*direction*); die Strömung (*stream*); das Treiben; Gestöber (*snow*). — *v.a.* treiben. — *v.n.* dahintreiben.

drill (1) [dril], *v.a.* drillen, bohren (*bore*); (*Mil.*) exerzieren (*Agr.*) eine Furche ziehen; einstudieren (*coach*). — *s.* (*Mil.*) das Exerzieren; (*Agr.*) die Furche; der Bohrer (*tool*); — *hall*, die Übungs- or Exerzierhalle.

drill (2) [dril], *s.* der Drillich (*textile*).

drily ['draili], *adv.* trocken.

drink [driŋk], *v.a., v.n. irr.* trinken. — *s.* das Getränk, der Trank (*potion*); etwas zum Trinken (*a* —); *come, have a* —; trinken wir ein Glas (zusammen); *strong* —, geistiges Getränk.

drinkable ['driŋkəbl], *adj.* trinkbar; zum Trinken.

drinker ['driŋkə], *s.* der Trinker, Säufer; der Zecher; der Trunkenbold (*drunkard*).

drip [drip], *v.n.* tröpfeln. — *s.* das Tröpfeln.

dripping ['dripiŋ], *s.* (*Cul.*) das Bratenfett, das Schmalz.

drive [draiv], *v.a. irr.* treiben (*sheep etc.*); fahren (*a car*). — *v.n.* fahren; dahinfahren (— *along*). — *s.* die Ausfahrt, die Fahrt (*trip*); die Einfahrt (*approach to house*).

driving ['draiviŋ], *s.* das Fahren; — *licence*, der Führerschein; — *school*, die Fahrschule; — *test*, die Fahrprüfung.

drivel [drivl], *s.* der Geifer; der Unsinn (*nonsense*). —, *v.n.* Unsinn reden.

driver ['draivə], *s.* der Fahrer, der Chauffeur; (*Railw.*) Führer; (*Hunt.*) der Treiber.

drizzle [drizl], *v.n.* rieseln; leicht regnen. — *s.* das Rieseln, der feine Regen, der Sprühregen.

droll [droul], *adj.* drollig, possierlich.

drollery ['drouləri], *s.* die Possierlichkeit; die Schnurre.

dromedary ['drʌmədəri or 'drəm-], *s.* (*Zool.*) das Dromedar.

drone (1) [droun], *s.* das Gedröhn, das Gesumme (*noise*). — *v.n.* dröhnen, summen (*hum loudly*).

drone (2) [droun], *s.* (*Ent.*) die Drohne; der Faulpelz (*lazybones*).

droop [dru:p], *v.a.* hängen lassen. — *v.n.* herabhängen; verwelken (*flowers*); ermatten (*tire*).

drop [drɔp], *s.* der Tropfen (*liquid*); das Fallen (*fall*). — *v.a.* fallen lassen; — *a brick*, eine taktlose Bemerkung machen; — *a hint*, andeuten, auf etwas hindeuten. — *v.n.* fallen.

droppings ['drɔpiŋz], *s. pl.* der Mist, Dünger (*of animals*).

dropsical ['drɔpsikəl], *adj.* (*Med.*) wassersüchtig.

dropsy ['drɔpsi], *s.* (*Med.*) die Wassersucht.

dross [drɔs], *s.* (*Metall.*) die Schlacke; der Unrat, das wertlose Zeug.

drought [draut], *s.* die Dürre, die Trockenheit.

drove [drouv], *s.* die Herde, die Trift (*cattle*).

drover ['drouvə], *s.* der Viehtreiber.

drown [draun], *v.a.* ertränken; überschwemmen (*flood*); übertönen (*noise*). — *v.n.* ertrinken.

drowse [drauz], *v.n.* schlummern, schläfrig sein.

drowsy ['drauzi], *adj.* schläfrig.

drub [drʌb], *v.a.* prügeln.

drudge [drʌdʒ], *s.* das Packtier; der Sklave, der Knecht.

drudgery ['drʌdʒəri], *s.* die Plackerei, die Plagerei (*hard toil*).

drug [drʌg], *s.* die Droge; die Medizin; das Rauschgift (*flood*). — *v.a.* betäuben.

drugget ['drʌgit], *s.* der (grobe) Wollstoff.

drum [drʌm], *s.* die Trommel. — *v.n.* trommeln, austrommeln.

drunk [drʌŋk], *adj.* betrunken.

drunkard ['drʌŋkəd], *s.* der Trunkenbold.

drunkenness ['drʌŋkənnis], *s.* die Trunkenheit.

dry [drai], *adj.* trocken, dürr; ausgetrocknet, durstig (*thirsty*). — *v.a.* austrocknen, trocken machen, dörren. — *v.n.* trocken werden, trocknen.

dryad ['draiæd], *s.* die Baumnymphe Dryade.

dryness ['drainis], *s.* die Trockenheit, die Dürre.

dual ['dju:əl], *adj.* doppelt; Zwei-.

dub (1) [dʌb], *v.a.* zum Ritter schlagen; nennen (*name*).

dub (2) [dʌb], *v.a.* (*Films*) synchronisieren.

dubious ['dju:bjəs], *adj.* zweifelhaft.

ducal ['dju:kəl], *adj.* herzoglich.

duchess ['dʌtʃis], *s.* die Herzogin.

duchy ['dʌtʃi], *s.* das Herzogtum.

duck (1) [dʌk], *s.* (*Orn.*) die Ente.

duck (2) [dʌk], *v.n.* sich ducken, sich bücken; untertauchen (*in water*).— *v.a.* untertauchen, ins Wasser tauchen.

duckling ['dʌkliŋ], *s.* (*Orn.*) das Entchen.

duct [dʌkt], *s.* (*Anat.*) der Kanal; die Röhre.

ductile ['dʌktail], *adj.* dehnbar; fügsam.

dud [dʌd], *s.* (*Mil.*) der Blindgänger; der Fehlschlag.

dude [dju:d], *s.* (*Am.*) der Geck.

dudgeon ['dʌdʒən], *s.* der Groll, der Unwille; *in high —*, sehr aufgebracht.

due [dju:], *adj.* gebührend, fällig, schuldig (*to, Dat.*); angemessen, recht; *this is — to carelessness*, das ist auf Nachlässigkeit zurückzuführen. — *adv.* direkt, gerade. — *s.* (*pl.*) die Gebühren.

duel ['dju:əl], *s.* das Duell. — *v.n.* sich duellieren (mit, *Dat.*).

duet [dju'et], *s.* (*Mus.*) das Duett.

duffer ['dʌfə], *s.* der Tölpel; (*obs.*) der Hausierer.

duffle, duffel [dʌfl], *s.* der Düffel, das Düffeltuch.

dug [dʌg], *s.* die Zitze.

dug-out ['dʌg-aut], *s.* der Unterstand, der Bunker.

duke [dju:k], *s.* der Herzog; *Grand Duke*, der Großherzog.

dukedom ['dju:kdəm], *s.* das Herzogtum.

dull [dʌl], *adj.* fade, langweilig (*boring*); träge, schwerfällig (*slow to grasp*); stumpfsinnig (*obtuse*), abgeschmackt (*tasteless*); schwach (*perception*); dumpf (*thud, noise*); matt (*colour*); trüb, überwölkt (*weather*); flau (*trade*). — *v.a.* abstumpfen (*senses*).

dullness ['dʌlnis], *s.* die Stumpfheit (*senses*); die Langeweile (*boredom*); die Schwerfälligkeit (*stolidity*); die Schwäche (*vision etc.*); die Stumpfsinnigkeit (*stupidity*).

dumb [dʌm], *adj.* stumm; (*sl.*) dumm; *—founded*, verblüfft; *— show*, die Pantomime; *—bell* (*Gymn.*) die Hantel.

dumbness ['dʌmnis], *s.* die Stummheit.

dummy ['dʌmi], *s.* der Strohmann (*cards*); die Kleiderpuppe (*wax figure*); der Blindgänger (*dud shell*); der Schnuller (*baby's*).

dump [dʌmp], *v.a.* kippen, abladen; *—ing ground*, der Abladeplatz. — *s.* (*Am. coll.*) das Bumslokal.

dumpling ['dʌmpliŋ], *s.* der Kloß, (*Austr.*) der Knödel.

dumps [dʌmps], *s. pl.* der Unmut, der Mißmut, die Depression.

dumpy ['dʌmpi], *adj.* untersetzt, kurz und dick.

dun (1) [dʌn], *adj.* schwarzbraun.

dun (2) [dʌn], *s.* der Gläubiger. — *v.a.* energisch mahnen.

dunce [dʌns], *s.* der Dummkopf.

dune [dju:n], *s.* die Düne.

dung [dʌŋ], *s.* der Dünger. — *v.n.* düngen.

dungeon ['dʌndʒən], *s.* der Kerker.

dupe [dju:p], *s.* der Betrogene. — *v.a.* betrügen.

duplicate ['dju:plikeit], *v.a.* verdoppeln; doppelt schreiben *or* ausfüllen (*write twice*); vervielfältigen (*stencil*). — [-kit], *s.* das Duplikat.

duplicity [dju:'plisiti], *s.* die Falschheit, die Doppelzüngigkeit.

durability [djuərə'biliti] *s.* die Dauerhaftigkeit.

durable ['djuərəbl], *adj.* dauerhaft.

duration [djuə'reiʃən], *s.* die Dauer, die Länge (*time*).

duress [djuə'res], *s.* der Zwang; *under —*, zwangsweise.

during ['djuəriŋ], *prep.* während.

dusk [dʌsk], *s.* die Dämmerung.

dusky ['dʌski], *adj.* dunkel, trüb; düster.

dust [dʌst], *s.* der Staub. — *v.a.* abstauben (*clean*); bestäuben (*pollinate*); bestreuen.

dustbin ['dʌstbin], *s.* der Mülleimer.

dusty ['dʌsti], *adj.* staubig; *not so —*, (*coll.*) nicht so übel.

Dutch [dʌtʃ], *adj.* holländisch; niederländisch; — *treat*, auf getrennte Kosten; *double —*, Kauderwelsch, Unsinn.

Dutchman ['dʌtʃmən], *s.* der Holländer, der Niederländer.

dutiful ['dju:tiful], *adj.* gehorsam, pflichttreu, pflichtbewußt.

duty ['dju:ti], *s.* die Pflicht; die Abgabe (*tax*); *customs —*, der Zoll; *be on —*, Dienst haben; (*being*) *on —*, diensthabend; *off —*, dienstfrei; *— free*, zollfrei; *in — bound*, von Rechts wegen, pflichtgemäß.

dwarf [dwɔ:f], *s.* der Zwerg. — *v.a.* am Wachstum hindern (*stunt*); klein erscheinen lassen (*overshadow*).

dwell [dwel], *v.n. irr.* wohnen (*be domiciled*); verweilen (*remain*).

dwelling ['dweliŋ], *s.* die Wohnung; *— place*, der Wohnort.

dwindle [dwindl], *v.n.* abnehmen, kleiner werden.

dye [dai], *v.a.* färben. — *s.* die Farbe; (*Chem.*) der Farbstoff.

dyeing ['daiiŋ], *s.* das Färben; Färbereigewerbe.

dyer ['daiə], *s.* der Färber.

dying ['daiiŋ], *s.* das Sterben; *the —*, (*pl.*) die Sterbenden, *pl.* — *adj.* sterbend.

dynamic [dai'næmik], *adj.* dynamisch.

dynamics [dai'næmiks], *s. pl.* die Dynamik.

dynamite ['dainəmait], *s.* das Dynamit.

dynamo ['dainəmou], *s.* der Dynamo, die Dynamomaschine.

dynasty ['dinəsti], *s.* die Dynastie.

dysentery ['disəntri], *s.* (*Med.*) die Ruhr.

dyspepsia [dis'pepsiə], *s.* (*Med.*) die Magenverstimmung.

dyspeptic [dis'peptik], *adj.* mit verstimmtem Magen; schlecht aufgelegt (*grumpy*).

E

E [i:]. das E (*also Mus.*); *E flat*, Es; *E sharp*, Eis; *E minor*, E-moll.

each [i:tʃ], *adj.*, *pron.* jeder, jede, jedes; — *other*, einander; — *one*, jeder einzelne.

eager [´i:gə], *adj.* eifrig, begierig.

eagerness [´i:gənis], *s.* der Eifer, die Begierde.

eagle [i:gl], *s.* (*Orn.*) der Adler; (*Am.*) das Zehndollarstück.

ear [iə], *s.* das Ohr; —*lap*, das Ohrläppchen; —*phones*, die Kopfhörer; — *piece*, die Hörmuschel; (*fig.*) —*drum*, das Trommelfell; — *of corn*, die Ähre.

earl [ə:l], *s.* der Graf.

earldom [´ə:ldəm], *s.* die (englische) Grafschaft.

early [´ə:li], *adj.* früh, frühzeitig.

earmark [´iəma:k], *v.a.* kennzeichnen, bezeichnen.

earn [ə:n], *v.a.* verdienen; erwerben.

earnest [´ə:nist], *s.* der Ernst; der ernste Beweis, das Handgeld; (*Comm.*) die Anzahlung; (*fig.*) der Vorgeschmack; — *adj.* ernst, ernsthaft.

earnings [´ə:niŋz], *s.* das Einkommen.

earshot [´iəʃɔt], *s.* die Hörweite.

earth [ə:θ], *s.* die Erde; der Erdboden (*soil*); der Fuchsbau (*of fox*); *down to* —, praktisch denkend; *move heaven and* —, alles daransetzen; *where on* —, wo in aller Welt.

earthen [´ə:θən], *adj.* irden, aus Erde; —*ware*, das Steingut.

earthquake [´ə:θkweik], *s.* das Erdbeben.

earthly [´ə:θli], *adj.* irdisch.

earthworm [´ə:θwə:m], *s.* (*Zool.*) der Regenwurm.

earthy [´ə:θi], *adj.* erdig; irdisch.

earwig [´iəwig], *s.* (*Ent.*) der Ohrwurm.

ease [i:z], *s.* die Leichtigkeit (*facility*); die Bequemlichkeit (*comfort*); *feel at* —, sich wie zu Hause fühlen; (*Mil.*) *stand at* —! rührt euch! *ill at* —, unbehaglich. — *v.a.* erleichtern, leichter machen; lindern (*pain*). — *v.n.* — *off*, (*Mil.*) sich auflockern.

easel [i:zl], *s.* das Gestell; die Staffelei.

easiness [´i:zinis], *s.* die Leichtigkeit, die Ungezwungenheit.

east [i:st], *adj.*, *adv.* Ost-, ostwärts (*direction*). — *s.* der Osten, der Orient.

Easter [´i:stə], das *or* (*n.* or *f. pl.*) die Ostern.

eastern [´i:stən], *adj.* östlich; morgenländisch, orientalisch (*oriental*).

easy [´i:zi], *adj.* leicht, frei; — *chair*, der Lehnstuhl, Sessel; *stand* —! rührt Euch! *take it* —, nimm's nicht so ernst; *es sich* (*Dat.*) *bequem machen* (*make o.s. comfortable*); (*Comm.*) — *terms*, Zahlungserleichterungen; — -*going*, gemütlich.

eat [i:t], *v.a.*, *v.n. irr.* essen, speisen (*dine*); fressen (*of animals*); — *humble pie*, sich demütigen; — *hat*, einen Besen fressen; — *o.'s words* seine Worte bereuen.

eatable [´i:təbl], *adj.* genießbar, eßbar.

eaves [i:vz], *s. pl.* die Dachrinne, die Traufe.

eavesdrop [´i:vzdrɔp], *v.n.* belauschen (*on s.o.*, *Acc.*).

eavesdropper [´i:vzdrɔpə], *s.* der Lauscher.

ebb [eb], *s.* die Ebbe; — *v.n.* nachlassen, abebben, abfließen.

ebonize [´ebənaiz], *v.a.* wie Ebenholz *or* schwarz beizen.

ebony [´ebəni], *s.* das Ebenholz.

ebullient [i´bʌljənt], *adj.* aufwallend.

eccentric [ik´sentrik], *adj.* exzentrisch, überspannt, wunderlich.

eccentricity [eksen´trisiti], *s.* die Exzentrizität, die Überspanntheit.

ecclesiastic [ikli:zi´æstik], *s.* der Geistliche. — *adj.* (*also* -**ical**) geistlich, kirchlich.

echo [´ekou], *s.* das Echo, der Widerhall. — *v.a.*, *v.n.* widerhallen (*resound*); wiederholen (*repeat*).

eclectic [i´klektik], *adj.* eklektisch. — *s.* der Eklektiker.

eclecticism [i´klektisizm], *s.* (*Phil.*) der Eklektizismus.

eclipse [i´klips], *s.* die Verfinsterung, Finsternis (*darkness*); die Verdunklung (*darkening*). — *v.a.* verdunkeln.

ecliptic [i´kliptik], *s.* die Ekliptik, die Sonnenbahn.

economic [i:kə´nɔmik], *adj.* ökonomisch, wirtschaftlich.

economical [i:kə´nɔmikl], *adj.* (*frugal*) sparsam, wirtschaftlich.

economics [i:kə´nɔmiks], *s.* (*pl.*) die Wirtschaftslehre, die Ökonomie.

economist [i:´kɔnəmist], *s.* der Ökonom der Wirtschaftsfachmann.

economize [i:´kɔnəmaiz], *v.n.* sparen (*on*, mit, *Dat.*); sparsam sein mit (*Dat.*).

economy [i:´kɔnəmi], *s.* die Wirtschaft; *political* —, die Nationalekonomie, Staatswirtschaftslehre.

ecstasy [´ekstəsi], *s.* die Ekstase, die Entzückung, die Verzückung.

ecstatic [iks´tætik], *adj.* ekstatisch, verzückt; entzückt (*delighted*).

Ecuadorean [ekwə´dɔ:riən], *adj.* ekuadorianisch. — *n.* der Ekuadorianer.

ecumenical [i:kju´menikəl], *adj.* ökumenisch.

eddy [´edi], *s.* der Wirbel, Strudel. — *v.n.* wirbeln.

edge [edʒ], *s.* die Schärfe, die Schneide (*blade*); die Kante (*ledge*); der Rand (*brink*); der Saum (*border*); die Ecke (*corner*); der Schnitt (*book*); die Schärfe (*wit, keenness*); *put an* — *on*, schärfen; *be on* —, nervös sein. — *v.a.* besetzen (*decorate*); umgeben; *double*- —*d*, zweischneidig; *two*- —*d*, zweischneidig, zweikantig; —*d with lace*, mit Spitze eingefaßt. — *v.n.* sich bewegen; — *forward*, langsam vorrücken; — *off*, sich abseits halten, sich abrücken; — *away from*, abrücken.

edgy [´edʒi], *adj.* kantig, eckig; (*fig.*) nervös, reizbar.

edible [´edibl], *adj.* eßbar.

edict ['i:dikt], *s.* die Verordnung.
edification [edifi'keiʃən], *s.* die Erbauung.
edifice ['edifis], *s.* der Bau, das Gebäude.
edify ['edifai], *v.a.* erbauen.
edit ['edit], *v.a.* herausgeben (*book etc.*).
edition [i'diʃən], *s.* die Ausgabe.
editor ['editə], *s.* der Herausgeber, der Schriftleiter; (*newspaper*) der Redakteur.
editorial [edi'tɔ:riəl], *adj.* Redaktions–. — *s.* der Leitartikel.
editorship ['editəʃip], *s.* die Redaktion; die Schriftleitung.
educate ['edjukeit], *v.a.* erziehen, (heran)bilden.
education [edju'keiʃən], *s.* die Erziehung (*upbringing*); die Bildung (*general culture*); das Bildungswesen, das Schulwesen (*educational system*); *primary* —, die Grundschulung, das Volksschulwesen; *secondary* —, das Mittelschulwesen, das höhere Schulwesen; *university* —, das Hochschulwesen (*system*), die Universitätsbildung (*of individual*); *local* —*authority*, das Schulamt, die Schulbehörde; *Professor of Education*, Professor der Pädagogik; *further* —, *adult* —, weitere Ausbildung, Erwachsenenbildung.
educational [edju'keiʃənəl], *adj.* erzieherisch (*educative*); Bildungs–, Unterrichts– (*for education*); — *attainment*, der Bildungsgrad, die Schulstufe (*grade*); — *facilities*, die Lehrmittel, Bildungs– *or* Schulungsmöglichkeiten, *f. pl.*
education(al)ist [edju'keiʃən(əl)ist], *s.* der Erzieher, der Pädagoge; der Erziehungsfachmann (*theorist*).
eel [i:l], *s.* (*Zool.*) der Aal.
eerie ['iəri], *adj.* gespenstisch, unheimlich.
efface [i'feis], *v.a.* auslöschen, austilgen.
effacement [i'feismənt], *s.* die Austilgung; *self* —, die Selbstaufopferung.
effect [i'fekt], *s.* die Wirkung; die Folge, das Ergebnis (*consequence*); der Eindruck (*impression*); *of no* —, ohne jede Wirkung; *carry into* —, ausführen; *take* — *from*, vom ... in Kraft treten. — *v.a.* bewirken (*bring about*).
effective [i'fektiv], *adj.* wirksam (*having an effect*); gültig (*in force*); dienstfähig (*usable*); wirklich (*actual*).
effectual [i'fektjuəl], *adj.* wirksam (*effective*); kräftig, energisch (*strong*).
effectuate [i'fektjueit], *v.a.* bewerkstelligen (*get done*); bewirken (*bring about*).
effeminacy [i'feminəsi], *s.* die Verweichlichung.
effeminate [i'feminit], *adj.* weichlich, verweichlicht.
effervescence [efə'vesəns], *s.* das Aufbrausen, Schäumen.
effervescent [efə'vesənt], *adj.* aufbrausend, aufschäumend.

effete [i'fi:t], *adj.* abgenutzt, erschöpft.
efficacious [efi'keiʃəs], *adj.* wirksam, energisch.
efficacy ['efikəsi], *s.* die Wirksamkeit, die Energie.
efficiency [i'fiʃənsi], *s.* die Tüchtigkeit (*of person*); die Wirksamkeit; die Leistung.
efficient [i'fiʃənt], *adj.* tüchtig; leistungsfähig; wirksam (*drug etc.*).
effigy ['efidʒi], *s.* das Bild, das Abbild.
efflorescent [eflɔ:'resənt], *adj.* aufblühend.
effluent ['efluənt], *adj.* ausfließend.
effluvium [i'flu:viəm], *s.* die Ausdünstung.
effort ['efət], *s.* die Anstrengung, die Bemühung; *make an* —, sich bemühen, sich anstrengen; *make every* —, alle Kräfte anspannen.
effrontery [i'frʌntəri], *s.* die Frechheit (*cheek*); die Unverschämtheit (*impertinence*).
effortless ['efətlis], *adj.* mühelos.
effulgence [i'fʌldʒəns], *s.* der Glanz, das Strahlen.
effulgent [i'fʌldʒənt], *adj.* schimmernd, strahlend.
effusion [i'fju:ʒən], *s.* die Ausgießung; der Erguß (*verse etc.*); der Überschwang.
effusive [i'fju:ziv], *adj.* überschwenglich.
egg [eg], *s.* das Ei; *fried* —, das Spiegelei; *scrambled* —, das Rührei; *flip*, der Eierpunsch; —*shell*, die Eierschale. — *v.a.* — *on*, anspornen, anreizen.
eglantine ['egləntain], *s.* (*Bot.*) die wilde Rose.
egoism ['egouizm], *s.* der Egoismus.
ego(t)ist ['ego(t)ist], *s.* der Egoist.
egregious [i'gri:dʒəs], *adj.* ungeheuer(lich).
egress ['i:gres], *s.* der Ausgang, der Ausfluß (*water etc.*).
Egyptian [i'dʒipʃən], *adj.* ägyptisch. — *s.* der Ägypter.
eiderdown ['aidədaun], *s.* die Daunendecke, Steppdecke.
eiderduck ['aidədʌk], *s.* (*Orn.*) die Eidergans.
eight [eit], *num. adj.* acht.
eighteen [ei'ti:n], *num. adj.* achtzehn.
eighty ['eiti], *num. adj.* achtzig.
either ['aiðə], *adj.*, *pron.* einer von beiden. — *conj.* entweder (*or*, oder).
ejaculate [i'dʒækjuleit], *v.a.*, *v.n.* ausstoßen.
eject [i'dʒekt], *v.a.* hinauswerfen; ausstoßen.
ejection [i'dʒekʃən], *s.* die Ausstoßung.
eke [i:k], *v.a.* — *out*, verlängern, ergänzen; — *out an existence*, ein spärliches Auskommen finden.
elaborate [i'læbəreit], *v.a.* ausarbeiten, im einzelnen ausarbeiten. — [-rit], *adj.* detailliert, ausgearbeitet; kunstvoll (*intricate*); umständlich (*involved*).

elaboration [ilæbə'reiʃən], *s.* die Ausar-
beitung (im einzelnen); die Detailar-
beit.

elapse [i'læps], *v.n.* verstreichen, verfließen (*time*).

elastic [i'læstik], *adj.* elastisch. — *s.*
das Gummiband.

elasticity [elæs'tisiti], *s.* (*Phys.*) die
Elastizität.

elate [i'leit], *v.a.* stolz machen; ermutigen.

elated [i'leitid], *adj.* in gehobener
Stimmung.

elation [i'leiʃən], *s.* der Stolz; die
Begeisterung.

elbow ['elbou], *s.* (*Anat.*) der Ellen-
bogen; *at o.'s* —, bei der Hand; —
room, der Spielraum. — *v.a.* — *o.'s
way through*, sich durchdrängen.

elder (1) ['eldə], *comp. adj.* älter. — *s.*
der Alte, der Älteste; Kirchenälteste.

elder (2) ['eldə], *s.* (*Bot.*) der Holunder.

elderly ['eldəli], *adj.* älter; alt; ältlich.

elect [i'lekt], *v.a.* erwählen (*to, zu,
Dat.*); auswählen (*choose*). — *adj.*
erwählt, auserwählt; *chairman* —, der
gewählte Vorsitzende.

election [i'lekʃən], *s.* die Auswahl
(*selection*); (*Pol.*) die Wahlen, *f. pl.*; die
Wahl (*choice*); *by(e)* — —, die Bezirks-
wahl, die Neuwahl; — *broadcast*, eine
Radiowahlrede.

electioneering [ilekʃən'iəriŋ], *s.* das
Wahlmanöver, die Wahlpropaganda,
der Wahlkampf.

elective [i'lektiv], *adj.* durch Wahl
bestimmt; Wahl—.

elector [i'lektə], *s.* (*Pol.*) der Wähler;
das Mitglied eines Wahlausschusses
(*academic etc.*); der Kurfürst (*prince*).

electorate [i'lektərit], *s.* die Wählerschaft.

electress [i'lektrəs], *s.* die Kurfürstin
(*princess*).

electric(al) [i'lektrik(əl)], *adj.* elektrisch;
electrical engineer, der Elektrotechni-
ker; der Student der Elektrotechnik
(*trainee*); *electric switch*, der elek-
trische Schalter; — *razor*, der elek-
trische Rasierapparat.

electrician [elek'triʃən], *s.* der Elek-
triker.

electricity [ilek- *or* elek'trisiti], *s.* die
Elektrizität.

electrocution [ilektro'kju:ʃən], *s.* die
Hinrichtung *or* der Unfall (*accidental*)
durch Elektrizität.

electron [i'lektrən], *s.* das Elektron.

electroplate [i'lektropleit], *v.a.* galvanisch versilbern.

electrotype [i'lektrotaip], *s.* der galva-
nische Abdruck, die Galvanographie.

elegance ['eligəns], *s.* die Eleganz.

elegant ['eligənt], *adj.* elegant, fein.

elegy ['elidʒi], *s.* (*Lit.*) die Elegie.

element ['elimənt], *s.* das Element; der
Bestandteil (*component*).

elemental [eli'mentl], *adj.* elementar.

elementary [eli'mentri], *adj.* einfach
(*simple*); elementar (*for beginners*).

elephant ['elifənt], *s.* (*Zool.*) der
Elefant.

elevate ['eliveit], *v.a.* erheben, erhöhen.

elevation [eli'veiʃən], *s.* die Erhebung
(*lifting*); (*Geom.*) die Elevation; die
Erhöhung (*rise*); der Aufriß (*Engin.
drawing*).

elevator ['eliveitə], *s.* (*Am.*) der Lift,
der Aufzug, der Fahrstuhl; (*Agr.*) der
Getreideheber.

eleven [i'levn], *num. adj.* elf.

elf [elf], *s.* der Elf, der Kobold.

elfin ['elfin], *adj.* Elfen-, elfenhaft.

elicit [i'lisit], *v.a.* herauslocken, entlocken.

eligibility [elidʒi'biliti], *s.* die Wählbarkeit.

eligible ['elidʒibl], *adj.* wählbar, passend.

eliminate [i'limineit], *v.a.* ausschalten,
ausscheiden, eliminieren.

elimination [ilimi'neiʃən], *s.* die Aus-
schaltung, die Ausscheidung.

elision [i'liʒən], *s.* (*Phonet.*) die Auslassung, die Weglassung.

elixir [i'liksə], *s.* das Elixier.

elk [elk], *s.* (*Zool.*) der Elch.

ell [el], *s.* die Elle.

ellipse [i'lips], *s.* (*Geom.*) die Ellipse.

ellipsis [i'lipsis], *s.* (*Gram.*) die
Ellipse.

elliptic(al) [i'liptik(əl)], *adj.* (*Gram.,
Geom.*) elliptisch.

elm [elm], *s.* (*Bot.*) die Ulme.

elocution [elə'kju:ʃən], *s.* der Vortrag
(*delivery*); die Vortragskunst.

elocutionist [elə'kju:ʃənist], *s.* der
Vortragskünstler.

elongate ['i:lɔŋgeit], *v.a.* verlängern.

elongation [i:lɔŋ'geiʃən], *s.* die Verlängerung.

elope [i'loup], *v.n.* entlaufen, von
zu Hause fliehen.

elopement [i'loupmənt], *s.* das Entlaufen, die Flucht von zu Hause.

eloquence ['eləkwəns], *s.* die Bered-
samkeit.

eloquent ['eləkwənt], *adj.* beredt,
redegewandt.

else [els], *adv.* sonst, außerdem, anders;
or —, sonst . . .; *how* — ? wie denn
sonst? *nobody* —, sonst niemand;
anyone — ? sonst noch jemand? — *conj.*
sonst.

elsewhere [els'wɛə], *adv.* anderswo;
anderswohin.

Elsinore ['elsinɔ:], Helsingör, *n.*

elucidate [i'lju:sideit], *v.a.* erläutern,
erklären (*to s.o., Dat.*).

elucidation [ilju:si'deiʃən], *s.* die
Erläuterung, die Erklärung.

elude [i'lju:d], *v.a.* ausweichen, entgehen (*Dat.*).

elusive [i'lju:siv], *adj.* schwer faßbar,
täuschend.

Elysian [i'liziən], *adj.* elysisch.

emaciate [i'meiʃieit], *v.a.* abmagern,
dünn werden.

emaciation [imeiʃi'eiʃən], *s.* die Abmagerung.

379

emanate

emanate ['emǝneit], *v.n.* ausgehen, herrühren (*derive*); ausstrahlen (*radiate*).

emancipate [i'mænsipeit], *v.a.* befreien, emanzipieren.

emancipation [imænsi'peiʃǝn], *s.* die Emanzipation.

embalm [im'ba:m], *v.a.* einbalsamieren.

embankment [im'bæŋkmǝnt], *s.* der Flußdamm, der Eisenbahndamm; die Eindämmung.

embarcation *see* **embarkation**.

embargo [im'ba:gou], *s.* die Handelssperre.

embark [im'ba:k], *v.a.* einschiffen. — *v.n.* sich einschiffen; — *upon s.th.*, an etwas herangehen, unternehmen.

embarkation [emba:'keiʃǝn], *s.* die Einschiffung.

embarrass [im'bærǝs], *v.a.* verlegen machen, in Verlegenheit bringen.

embarrassment [im'bærǝsmǝnt], *s.* die Verlegenheit.

embassy ['embǝsi], *s.* (Pol.) die Botschaft, die Gesandtschaft.

embed [im'bed], *v.a.* einbetten.

embellish [im'beliʃ], *v.a.* verschönern, ausschmücken; ausmalen (*story*).

embers ['embǝz], *s. pl.* die glühende Asche; die Kohlen, *f. pl.*; *Ember Days*, (*Eccl.*) die Quatembertage, *m. pl.*

embezzle [im'bezl], *v.a.* veruntreuen, unterschlagen.

embitter [im'bitǝ], *v.a.* verbittern.

emblazon [im'bleizn], *v.a.* ausmalen, auf ein Schild setzen.

emblem ['emblǝm], *s.* das Emblem, das Abzeichen.

emblematic(al) [embla'mætik(ǝl)], *adj.* sinnbildlich, symbolisch.

embodiment [im'bɔdimǝnt], *s.* die Verkörperung.

embody [im'bɔdi], *v.a.* verkörpern.

embolden [im'bouldn], *v.a.* erkühnen, anfeuern, anspornen; *be emboldened*, sich erkühnen.

emboss [im'bɔs], *v.a.* in getriebener Arbeit verfertigen, prägen.

embossed [im'bɔst], *adj.* getrieben, in erhabener Arbeit; gestanzt.

embrace [im'breis], *v.a.* (*fig.*) umarmen, umfassen. — *s.* die Umarmung.

embrasure [im'breiʒǝ], *s.* die Schießscharte.

embrocation [embro'keiʃǝn], *s.* die Einreibung (*act*); (*Pharm.*) die Einreibsalbe.

embroider [im'brɔidǝ], *v.a.* sticken, verzieren, ausschmücken (*adorn*).

embroidery [im'brɔidǝri], *s.* die Stickerei; die Verzierung, Ausschmückung (*of story etc.*).

embroil [im'brɔil], *v.a.* verwickeln.

embryo ['embriou], *s.* der Keim; Embryo.

embryonic [embri'ɔnik], *adj.* im Embryostadium, im Werden.

emend [i'mend], *v.a.* verbessern (*text*), berichtigen.

emendation [i:men'deiʃǝn], *s.* die Textverbesserung.

emendator ['i:mendeitǝ], *s.* der Berichtiger.

emerald ['emǝrǝld], *s.* der Smaragd.

emerge [i'mǝ:dʒ], *v.n.* auftauchen, hervortreten, an den Tag kommen.

emergence [i'mǝ:dʒǝns], *s.* das Auftauchen, das Hervortreten.

emergency [i'mǝ:dʒǝnsi], *s.* der Notfall; die kritische Lage; *in case of* —, im Notfalle; — *exit*, der Notausgang; — *landing*, die Notlandung; — *measures*, Notmaßnahmen; — *brake*, die Notbremse.

emery ['emǝri], *s.* — *paper*, das Schmirgelpapier.

emetic [i'metik], *s.* das Brechmittel.

emigrant ['emigrǝnt], *s.* der Auswanderer.

emigrate ['emigreit], *v.n.* auswandern.

emigration [emi'greiʃǝn], *s.* die Auswanderung.

eminence ['eminǝns], *s.* die Anhöhe; die Eminenz, der hohe Ruf (*fame*); die eminente Stellung, die Autorität (*authority*); *Your Eminence*, Eure Eminenz.

eminent ['eminǝnt], *adj.* eminent, hervorragend.

emissary ['emisǝri], *s.* der Abgesandte, der Sendbote.

emission [i'miʃǝn], *s.* die Aussendung (*sending out*); die Ausstrahlung (*radiation*).

emit [i'mit], *v.a.* aussenden; ausstrahlen; ausströmen.

emolument [i'mɔljumǝnt], *s.* das (Neben)einkommen, das Zusatzgehalt, das Honorar (*fee*).

emotion [i'mouʃǝn], *s.* die Rührung, die Bewegung, das Gefühl, die Gemütsbewegung.

emotional [i'mouʃǝnǝl], *adj.* gefühlvoll.

emperor ['empǝrǝ], *s.* der Kaiser.

emphasis ['emfǝsis], *s.* der Nachdruck.

emphasize ['emfǝsaiz], *v.a.* betonen.

empire [empaiǝ], *s.* das Reich, das Kaiserreich.

empiric(al) [emp'irik(ǝl)], *adj.* (*Phil.*) empirisch.

empiricism [em'pirisizm], *s.* (*Phil.*) der Empirizismus.

employ [im'plɔi], *v.a.* benutzen (*thing*); beschäftigen, anstellen (*person*).

employee [im'plɔii:], *s.* der Angestellte.

employer [im'plɔiǝ], *s.* der Arbeitgeber.

employment [im'plɔimǝnt], *s.* die Beschäftigung, die Arbeit.

emporium [em'pɔ:riǝm], *s.* der Handelsplatz; (*Naut.*) der Stapelplatz; das Warenhaus (*stores*).

empower [em'pauǝ], *v.a.* bevollmächtigen.

empress ['empres], *s.* die Kaiserin.

emptiness ['emptinis], *s.* die Leere, die Öde.

empty ['empti], *adj.* leer; — -*headed*, geistlos.

emulate ['emjuleit], *v.a.* nacheifern (*Dat.*).

emulation [emju'leiʃən], *s.* der Wetteifer, das Nacheifern.

emulous ['emjuləs], *adj.* nacheifernd, wetteifernd; eifersüchtig (*jealous*).

emulsion [i'mʌlʃən], *s.* (*Pharm.*) die Emulsion.

enable [i'neibl], *v.a.* befähigen; ermächtigen (*empower*).

enact [i'nækt], *v.a.* (*Pol.*) verordnen; verfügen (*order*); darstellen, aufführen (*on stage*).

enactment [i'næktmənt], *s.* die Verordnung.

enamel [i'næml], *v.a.* emaillieren. — *s.* die Emaille; (*Med.*) der Schmelz.

enamour [i'næmə], *v.a.* verliebt machen.

encamp [in'kæmp], *v.n.* (sich) lagern, das Lager aufschlagen.

encampment [in'kæmpmənt], *s.* das Lager.

encase [in'keis], *v.a.* einschließen, in ein Gehäuse schließen.

encashment [in'kæʃmənt], *s.* (*Comm.*) das Inkasso, die Einkassierung.

enchain [in'tʃein], *v.a.* in Ketten legen, anketten.

enchant [in'tʃɑ:nt], *v.a.* bezaubern.

enchantment [in'tʃɑ:ntmənt], *s.* die Bezauberung; der Zauber (*spell*).

encircle [in'sə:kl], *v.a.* umringen, umkreisen; (*Mil.*) einkreisen.

encirclement [in'sə:klmənt], *s.* die Einkreisung.

enclose [in'klouz], *v.a.* einschließen; einlegen (*in letter*).

enclosure [in'klouʒə], *s.* die Einfriedigung; die Beilage, Einlage (*in letter*).

encompass [in'kʌmpəs], *v.a.* umfassen, umspannen (*comprise*).

encore [ɔŋkɔ:, ɔn'kɔ:], *int.* noch einmal! — *s.* die Wiederholung, Zugabe.

encounter [in'kauntə], *v.a.* treffen; begegnen (*Dat.*). — *s.* das Zusammentreffen.

encourage [in'kʌridʒ], *v.a.* ermutigen, anspornen.

encouragement [in'kʌridʒmənt], *s.* die Ermutigung; die Förderung (*promotion*).

encroach [in'kroutʃ], *v.n.* eingreifen (*interfere*); übergreifen.

encroachment [in'kroutʃmənt], *s.* der Eingriff, der Übergriff.

encrust [in'krʌst], *v.a.* inkrustieren; verkrusten.

encumber [in'kʌmbə], *v.a.* belasten.

encumbrance [in'kʌmbrəns], *s.* die Belastung, das Hindernis.

encyclical [en'siklikl], *s.* das (päpstliche) Rundschreiben, die Enzyklika.

encylopaedia [insaiklo'pi:djə], *s.* das Lexikon, die Enzyklopädie.

encyclopaedic [insaiklo'pi:dik], *adj.* enzyklopädisch.

end [end], *s.* das Ende; der Schluß; das Ziel (*aim*); die Absicht (*intention*); *in the* —, am Ende, letzten Endes; *to*

that —, zu dem Zweck; *put an* — *to*, einer Sache ein Ende machen; *make* —*s meet*, sein Auskommen finden; *burn the candle at both* —*s*, seine Kräfte verschwenden. — *v.a.* beenden. — *v.n.* enden, Schluß machen.

ending ['endiŋ], *s.* das Ende (*of play etc.*); (*Gram.*) die Endung.

endanger [in'deindʒə], *v.a.* gefährden, in Gefahr bringen.

endear [in'diə], *v.a.* beliebt machen. — *v.r.* — *o.s. to*, sich lieb Kind machen bei.

endearment [in'diəmənt], *s.* term of —, ein Kosewort.

endeavour [in'devə], *v.n.* sich bemühen, sich bestreben. — *s.* das Streben, die Bestrebung, die Bemühung.

endemic(al) [en'demik(əl)], *adj.* einheimisch; endemisch.

endive ['endiv], *s.* (*Bot.*) die Endivie.

endless ['endlis], *adj.* unendlich, endlos.

endorse [in'dɔ:s], *v.a.* bestätigen (*confirm*); beipflichten; (*Fin.*) indossieren (*cheque*).

endorsement [in'dɔ:smənt], *s.* die Bestätigung (*confirmation*); (*Fin.*) das Indossament (*cheque*).

endow [en'dau], *v.a.* begaben (*talents*); ausstatten (*equip*); stiften.

endowment [en'daumənt], *s.* die Begabung (*talents*); die Stiftung; — *policy*, die abgekürzte Lebensversicherung.

endurable [in'djuərəbl], *adj.* erträglich.

endurance [in'djuərəns], *s.* die Ausdauer (*toughness*); die Dauer, Fortdauer (*time*); das Ertragen (*suffering*); — *test*, die Dauerprüfung; (*fig.*) die Geduldsprobe (*patience*).

endure [in'djuə], *v.a.* aushalten, ertragen; leiden (*suffer*).

endways, endwise ['endweiz, -waiz], *adv.* mit dem Ende nach vorne: aufrecht (*vertical*).

enemy ['enəmi], *s.* der Feind, der Gegner.

energetic [enə'dʒetik], *adj.* energisch, tatkräftig.

energy ['enədʒi], *s.* die Energie, die Tatkraft; der Nachdruck (*vehemence*).

enervate ['enə:veit], *v.a.* entkräften, schwächen.

enervation [enə:'veiʃən], *s.* die Entkräftigung, die Schwächung.

enfeeble [in'fi:bl], *v.a.* entkräften, schwächen.

enfold [in'fould], *v.a.* umschließen, umfassen; einhüllen (*veil*).

enforce [in'fɔ:s], *v.a.* erzwingen, durchsetzen.

enforcement [in'fɔ:smənt], *s.* die Erzwingung, die Durchsetzung.

enfranchise [in'fræntʃaiz], *v.a.* freilassen, befreien (*emancipate*); (*Pol.*) das Stimmrecht geben.

enfranchisement [in'fræntʃizmənt], *s.* die Befreiung, die Gewährung des Stimmrechts.

engage

engage [in'geidʒ], *v.a.* verpflichten, engagieren (*pledge, bind*); anstellen (*employ*); verwickeln (*in conversation*); *become* —*d*, sich verloben. — *v.n.* — *in*, sich einlassen in (*Acc.*), sich befassen mit (*Dat.*).

engagement [in'geidʒmənt], *s.* die Verpflichtung (*pledge*); die Verlobung (*betrothal*); die Verabredung (*appointment*); das Gefecht (*with enemy*).

engaging [in'geidʒiŋ], *adj.* freundlich, verbindlich (*smile etc.*); einnehmend.

engender [in'dʒendə], *v.a.* erzeugen, hervorrufen (*cause*).

engine ['endʒin], *s.* die Maschine; der Motor; (*Railw.*) die Lokomotive; *fire* —, die Feuerspritze; — *driver*, (*Railw.*) der Lokomotivführer.

engineer [endʒi'niə], *s.* der Ingenieur (*professional*); der Techniker (*technician*); (*Am.*) der Lokomotivführer (*engine driver*).

engineering [endʒi'niəriŋ], *s.* das Ingenieurwesen; der Maschinenbau; *chemical* —, die chemische Technik or Technologie; *civil* —, das Zivilingenieurwesen; *electrical* —, die Elektrotechnik or die Elektrotechnologie; *mechanical* —, der Maschinenbau, die Strukturtechnik; — *laboratory*, das technische Labor; — *workshop*, die technische Werkstatt.

English ['iŋgliʃ], *adj.* englisch; britisch. — *s.* die englische Sprache, das Englisch; (*pl.*) *the* —, die Engländer, *m.pl.*

Englishman ['iŋgliʃmən], *s.* der Engländer.

Englishwoman ['iŋgliʃwumən], *s.* die Engländerin.

engrain [in'grein], *v.a.* tief einprägen.

engrave [in'greiv], *v.a.* gravieren, eingravieren (*art*); einprägen (*impress*).

engraver [in'greivə], *s.* der Graveur, der Kupferstecher.

engraving [in'greiviŋ], *s.* der Kupferstich.

engross [in'grous], *v.a.* ganz in Anspruch nehmen, gefangen halten(*mind*).

engulf [in'gʌlf], *v.a.* verschlingen.

enhance [in'hɑːns], *v.a.* erhöhen (*raise*); steigern (*increase*).

enhancement [in'hɑːnsmənt], *s.* die Erhöhung (*pleasure*); die Steigerung (*growth*).

enigma [i'nigmə], *s.* das Rätsel.

enigmatic(al) [enig'mætik(əl)], *adj.* rätselhaft (*puzzling*); dunkel (*obscure*).

enjoin[in'dʒɔin], *v.a.* (an)befehlen (*s.o., Dat.*), einschärfen (*s.o., Dat.*).

enjoy [in'dʒɔi], *v.a.* genießen (*Acc.*); sich freuen (über, *Acc.*). — *v.r.* — *o.s.*, sich amüsieren.

enjoyable [in'dʒɔiəbl], *adj.* erfreulich, angenehm, genießbar.

enjoyment [in'dʒɔimənt], *s.* der Genuß, die Freude (*of*, an, *Dat.*).

enlarge [in'lɑːdʒ], *v.a.* vergrößern (*premises etc.*); erweitern (*expand*). —

v.n. sich verbreiten (*on* or *upon*, über, *Acc.*).

enlargement [in'lɑːdʒmənt], *s.* die Vergrößerung (*also Phot.*).

enlighten [in'laitn], *v.a.* erleuchten, aufklären (*explain to*).

enlightenment [in'laitnmənt], *s.* (*Eccl.*) die Erleuchtung;(*Phil.*)die Aufklärung.

enlist [in'list], *v.a.* anwerben (*Mil.*); gewinnen (*cooperation*). — *v.n.* (*Mil.*) sich anwerben lassen.

enliven [in'laivn], *v.a.* beleben, aufmuntern.

enmity ['enmiti], *s.* die Feindschaft.

ennoble [i'noubl], *v.a.* adeln; veredeln.

enormity [i'nɔːmiti], *s.* die Ungeheuerlichkeit.

enormous [i'nɔːməs], *adj.* ungeheuer; ungeheuerlich.

enough [i'nʌf], *adj., adv.* genug; ausreichend; *sure* —, gewiß!; *well* —, ziemlich gut.

enquire *see under* **inquire**.

enquiry *see under* **inquiry**.

enrage [in'reidʒ], *v.a.* wütend machen.

enraged [in'reidʒd], *adj.* wütend, entrüstet.

enrapture [in'ræptʃə], *v.a.* in Entzückung versetzen, entzücken (*delight*).

enrich [in'ritʃ], *v.a.* bereichern; (*Chem.*) verbessern.

enrol [in'roul], *v.a.* einschreiben (*inscribe*); (*Mil.*) anwerben. — *v.n.* sich einschreiben; beitreten (*Dat.*).

enrolment [in'roulmənt], *s.* die Einschreibung; — *form*, das Einschreibeformular.

ensconce [in'skɔns], *v.r.* — *o.s.*, sich niederlassen.

enshrine [in'ʃrain], *v.a.* umhüllen, einschließen; in einem Schrein aufbewahren.

enshroud [in'ʃraud], *v.a.* einhüllen.

ensign ['ensin *or* 'enzən, 'ensain], *s.* (*Naut.*) die Fahne, die Flagge; (*Mil. rank*) der Fähnrich.

enslave [in'sleiv], *v.a.* unterjochen, versklaven.

ensnare [in'snɛə], *v.a.* umgarnen, verführen (*seduce*).

ensue [in'sjuː], *v.n.* folgen.

ensure [in'ʃuə], *v.a.* versichern (*assure*); sicherstellen (*make sure*).

entail [in'teil], *v.a.* zur Folge haben, mit sich bringen.

entangle [in'tæŋgl], *v.a.* verwickeln, verwirren (*confuse*).

entanglement [in'tæŋglmənt], *s.* die Verwicklung; die Verwirrung (*confusion*).

enter ['entə], *v.a.* betreten; eintreten; — *o.'s name*, seinen Namen einschreiben. — *v.n.* eintreten (*in*, in, *Acc.*); — *into agreement*, einen Vertrag eingehen; — *on*, sich einlassen in (*Acc.*); — *upon a career*, eine Laufbahn antreten.

enterprise ['entəpraiz], *s.* das Unternehmen; das Wagnis (*daring*); *private* —, das Privatunternehmen; (*Econ.*)

die freie Wirtschaft; *public* —, das staatliche *or* Staatsunternehmen.

enterprising ['entəpraiziŋ], *adj.* unternehmungslustig.

entertain [entə'tein], *v.a.* unterhalten (*amuse*); zu Tisch haben (*person*); hegen (*opinion*).

entertaining [entə'teiniŋ], *adj.* amüsant, unterhaltend.

entertainment [entə'teinmənt], *s.* die Unterhaltung, Vergnügung.

enthral [in'θrɔːl], *v.a.* fesseln, bannen.

enthrone [in'θroun], *v.a.* auf den Thron bringen *or* setzen.

enthusiasm [in'θjuːziæzm], *s.* die Begeisterung, die Schwärmerei.

enthusiast [in'θjuːziæst], *s.* der Enthusiast, der Schwärmer.

enthusiastic [inθjuːzi'æstik], *adj.* enthusiastisch, begeistert, schwärmerisch.

entice [in'tais], *v.a.* locken, anlocken, verlocken (*lure*).

enticement [in'taismənt], *s.* die Lockung.

entire [in'taiə], *adj.* gesamt, ganz; völlig; vollständig (*complete*).

entirety [in'taiəriti], *s.* die Gesamtheit (*totality*); das Ganze (*total*).

entitle [in'taitl], *v.a.* berechtigen; betiteln (*title*).

entitlement [in'taitlmənt], *s.* die Berechtigung.

entity [in'titi], *s.* das Wesen.

entomb [in'tuːm], *v.a.* begraben.

entomologist [entə'mɔlədʒist], *s.* der Entomologe.

entomology [entə'mɔlədʒi], *s.* die Entomologie.

entrails ['entreilz], *s. pl.* die Eingeweide, *n. pl.*

entrain [in'trein], *v.a.* (*Railw., Mil.*) einsteigen lassen. — *v.n.* (*Railw.*) (in den Zug) einsteigen.

entrance (1) ['entrəns], *s.* der Eingang (*door*); — *fee*, der Eintritt; — *hall*, der Hausflur, die Vorhalle; *university* —, Zulassung zur Universität.

entrance (2) [in'trɑːns], *v.a.* entzücken, hinreißen.

entrant ['entrənt], *s.* (*to school, university etc.*) der (neu) Zugelassene; Teilnehmer.

entrap [in'træp], *v.a.* fangen, verstricken.

entreat [in'triːt], *v.a.* anflehen, ersuchen.

entreaty [in'triːti], *s.* die flehentliche *or* dringende Bitte, (*obs.*) das Ansuchen.

entrench [in'trentʃ], *v.a.* verschanzen, festsetzen.

entrenchment [in'trentʃmənt], *s.* (*Mil.*) die Verschanzung.

entrust [in'trʌst], *v.a.* anvertrauen (*s. th.*); betreuen (*s.o. with*, mit, *Dat.*).

entry ['entri], *s.* das Eintreten, der Eintritt; der Eingang (*house*); (*Comm.*) die Eintragung (*book-keeping*); *double* —, doppelte Buchführung; die Einfuhr (*import*); — *permit*, die

Einreisebewilligung; *no* —, Eintritt verboten!

entwine [in'twain], *v.a.* verflechten, herumwickeln.

enumerate [i'njuːməreit], *v.a.* aufzählen.

enumeration [injuːmə'reiʃən], *s.* die Aufzählung.

enunciate [i'nʌnsieit], *v.a.* aussprechen.

enunciation [inʌnsi'eiʃən], *s.* (*Phonet.*) die Aussprache; die Kundgebung (*declaration*).

envelop [in'veləp], *v.a.* einhüllen, umhüllen.

envelope ['enviloup, 'ɔnvələup], *s.* die Hülle; der Umschlag, Briefumschlag (*letter*).

enviable ['enviəbl], *adj.* beneidenswert.

envious ['enviəs], *adj.* neidisch (*of s.o.*, auf, *Acc.*).

environment [in'vaiərənmənt], *s.* die Umgebung, (*Geog., Zool.*) die Umwelt.

environs [in'vairənz], *s. pl.* die Umgebung, die Umgegend.

envisage [in'vizidʒ], *v.a.* sich vorstellen.

envoy ['envɔi], *s.* (*Pol.*) der Gesandte, der Bote.

envy ['envi], *s.* der Neid. — *v.a.* beneiden.

epaulette [epɔ:'let], *s.* (*Mil.*) das Achselstück, die Epaulette.

ephemeral [i'femərəl], *adj.* Eintags-, Tages-; eintägig, vergänglich (*transient*).

epic ['epik], *adj.* episch. — *s.* das Epos.

epicure ['epikjuə], *s.* der Epikureer, der Feinschmecker, der Genießer.

epidemic [epi'demik], *s.* die Epidemie.

epigram ['epigræm], *s.* das Epigramm.

epigrammatic [epigrə'mætik], *adj.* epigrammatisch, kurz; treffend (*apt*).

epilepsy ['epilepsi], *s.* (*Med.*) die Epilepsie, die Fallsucht.

epileptic [epi'leptik], *s.* (*Med.*) der Epileptiker.

epilogue ['epilɔg], *s.* der Epilog.

Epiphany [i'pifəni], *s.* (*Eccl.*) das Fest der heiligen drei Könige, Epiphanias.

episcopal [i'piskəpəl], *adj.* bischöflich.

episcopate [i'piskəpit], *s.* die Bischofswürde, das Episkopat (*collective*).

episode ['episoud], *s.* die Episode.

epistle [i'pisl], *s.* die Epistel, das Sendschreiben.

epistolary [i'pistələri], *adj.* brieflich, Brief-.

epitaph ['epitɑːf], *s.* die Grabschrift.

epithet ['epiθet], *s.* das Beiwort, die Benennung.

epitome [i'pitəmi], *s.* die Epitome, der Auszug; der Abriß (*summary*).

epitomize [i'pitəmaiz], *v.a.* kürzen; einen Auszug machen von (*Dat.*).

epoch ['iːpɔk], *s.* die Epoche. — *making*, bahnbrechend.

equable ['ekwəbl], *adj.* gleich, gleichmäßig; gleichmütig (*tranquil*).

equal ['iːkwəl], *adj.* gleich, ebenbürtig (*to*, *Dat.*).

equality [i'kwɔliti], *s.* die Gleichheit, Ebenbürtigkeit.

equalization [i:kwəlai'zeiʃən], *s.* der Ausgleich; — *of burdens,* der Lastenausgleich.

equalize ['i:kwəlaiz], *v.a.* gleichmachen. — *v.n.* (*Footb.*) ausgleichen.

equanimity [i:kwə'nimiti], *s.* der Gleichmut.

equate [i'kweit], *v.a.* (*Maths.*) gleichsetzen.

equation [i'kweiʃən], *s.* die Gleichung.

equator [i'kweitə], *s.* (*Geog.*) der Äquator.

equatorial [ekwə'tɔ:riəl], *adj.* (*Geog.*) äquatorial.

equerry ['ekwəri], *s.* der Stallmeister; diensttuender Kammerherr (*of King*).

equestrian [i'kwestriən], *adj.* beritten; Reit-; — *art,* die Reitkunst.

equidistant [i:kwi'distənt], *adj.* gleich weit entfernt.

equilateral [i:kwi'lætərəl], *adj.* gleichseitig.

equilibrium [i:kwi'libriəm], *s.* das Gleichgewicht.

equine ['i:kwain], *adj.* Pferd-, pferdeartig.

equinoctial [i:kwi'nɔkʃəl], *adj.* äquinoktial.

equinox ['i:kwinɔks], *s.* die Tag- und Nachtgleiche.

equip [i'kwip], *v.a.* (*Mil.*) ausrüsten; ausstatten (*furnish*).

equipment [i'kwipmənt], *s.* die Ausrüstung, die Ausstattung; das Zeug.

equitable ['ekwitəbl], *adj.* unparteiisch, gerecht, billig.

equity ['ekwiti], *s.* die Billigkeit, die Unparteilichkeit.

equivalence [i'kwivələns], *s.* die Gleichwertigkeit, die Gleichheit.

equivalent [i'kwivələnt], *adj.* gleichwertig. — *s.* das Äquivalent, der gleiche Wert, der Gegenwert.

equivocal [i'kwivəkəl], *adj.* zweideutig, doppelsinnig, zweifelhaft.

era ['iərə], *s.* die Ära, die Zeitrechnung.

eradicate [i'rædikeit], *v.a.* ausrotten, austilgen, vertilgen.

eradication [irædi'keiʃən], *s.* die Ausrottung, die Vertilgung.

erase [i'reiz], *v.a.* ausradieren.

eraser [i'reizə], *s.* der Radiergummi (*India rubber*).

erasure [i'reiʒiə], *s.* die Ausradierung; die Auskratzung (*scratching*).

ere [ɛə], *prep.* (*obs.*) vor. — *conj.* (*obs.*) ehe, bevor.

erect [i'rekt], *adj.* aufrecht, gerade. — *v.a.* aufrichten; errichten (*build*).

erection [i'rekʃən], *s.* die Errichtung (*structure*); die Aufrichtung (*putting up*).

ermine ['ə:min], *s.* der *or* das Hermelin.

erode [i'roud], *v.a.* (*Geog., Geol.*) ausfressen.

erosion [i'rouʒən], *s.* die Erosion.

erotic [i'rɔtik], *adj.* erotisch.

err [ə:], *v.n.* irren.

errand ['erənd], *s.* der Auftrag, Gang;

der Botengang; — *boy,* der Laufbursche.

errant ['erənt], *adj.* herumstreifend; *knight* —, fahrender Ritter.

errata *see under* **erratum.**

erratic [i'rætik], *adj.* regellos, unberechenbar, ohne Verlaß.

erratum [e'reitəm, e'ra:təm], *s.* (*pl.* **errata** [e'reitə, e'ra:tə]) der Druckfehler.

erroneous [i'rouniəs], *adj.* irrig, irrtümlich.

error ['erə], *s.* der Irrtum, der Fehler.

erudite ['erudait], *adj.* gelehrt.

erudition [eru'diʃən], *s.* die Gelehrsamkeit.

erupt [i'rʌpt], *v.n.* ausbrechen.

eruption [i'rʌpʃən], *s.* der Ausbruch.

eruptive [i'rʌptiv], *adj.* Ausbruchs-, ausbrechend.

escalator ['eskəleitə], *s.* die Rolltreppe.

escapade [eskə'peid], *s.* der Streich (*prank*).

escape [is'keip], *v.a., v.n.* entkommen, entgehen, entfliehen.

escapism [is'keipizm], *s.* die Philosophie der Weltflucht.

escapist [is'keipist], *s.* der Weltflüchtling.

escarpment [is'ka:pmənt], *s.* die Böschung.

eschew [is'tʃu:], *v.a.* vermeiden.

escort [is'kɔ:t], *v.a.* geleiten; decken (*cover*). — ['eskɔ:t], *s.* (*Mil.*) die Garde, die Deckung; Begleitung (*persons*); (*Mil.*) das Geleit (*conduct*).

escutcheon [is'kʌtʃən], *s.* das Wappenschild.

esoteric [eso'terik], *adj.* (*Phil.*) esoterisch, geheim, dunkel.

espalier [es'pæljə], *s.* (*Mil.*) das Spalier.

especial [is'peʃəl], *adj.* besonder, außergewöhnlich.

espionage ['espiəna:ʒ *or* -nidʒ], *s.* die Spionage, das Spionieren.

espouse [is'pauz], *v.a.* (ver)-heiraten; (*fig.*) eintreten (für, *Acc.*).

espy [is'pai], *v.a.* ausspähen, erspähen.

essay [e'sei], *v.a.* versuchen, probieren. — ['esei], *s.* der Versuch; der Aufsatz, Essay (*composition*).

essayist ['eseiist], *s.* der Essayist.

essence ['esəns], *s.* (*Phil., Chem.*) die Essenz.

essential [i'senʃəl], *adj.* wesentlich; wichtig (*important*).

establish [is'tæbliʃ], *v.a.* feststellen, (*ascertain*); gründen (*found*); —*ed Church,* die englische Staatskirche.

establishment [is'tæbliʃmənt], *s.* die Feststellung (*ascertainment*); die Gründung (*foundation*); die Unternehmung, das Geschäft (*business*); (*Mil.*) die Aufstellung, der Bestand; (*Eccl.*) die Staatskirche.

estate [is'teit], *s.* (*Pol.*) der Stand; das Vermögen, das Gut; (*property*) — *duty,* die Vermögenssteuer; — *manager,* der Gutsverwalter; — *agent,* der

Grundstückmakler; *real* —, der Grundbesitz; (*pl.*) Immobilien, *pl.*

esteem [is'ti:m], *v.a.* schätzen (*value*); achten (*respect*). — *s.* die Wertschätzung, die Achtung.

estimable ['estiməbl], *adj.* schätzenswert.

estimate ['estimeit], *v.a.* schätzen (*evaluate*); berechnen (*calculate*). — ['estimit], *s.* die Schätzung, der Voranschlag.

estimation [esti'meifən], *s.* die Wertschätzung; die Achtung (*respect*).

Estonian [es'touniən], *adj.* estnisch, estländisch. — *s.* der Este, Estländer.

estrange [is'treindʒ], *v.a.* entfremden.

estrangement [is'treindʒmənt], *s.* die Entfremdung.

estuary ['estjuəri], *s.* die Mündung (*river*); der Meeresarm (*bay*).

etch [etʃ], *v.a.* (*Metall.*) ätzen; (*Art*) radieren.

etching ['etʃiŋ], *s.* (*Art*) die Radierung.

eternal [i'tə:nl], *adj.* ewig; immerwährend.

eternity [i'tə:niti], *s.* die Ewigkeit.

ether ['i:θə], *s.* der Äther.

ethereal [i'θiəriəl], *adj.* ätherisch, luftig.

ethical ['eθikl], *adj.* ethisch, sittlich.

ethics ['eθiks], *s. pl.* die Ethik, die Sittenlehre; *professional* —, das Berufsethos.

Ethiopian [i:θi'oupiən], *adj.* äthiopisch. — *s.* der Äthiopier.

ethnography [eθ'nɔgrəfi], *s.* die Ethnographie, die Völkerkunde.

etymology [eti'mɔlədʒi], *s.* die Etymologie, die Wortableitung.

eucharist ['ju:karist], *s.* (*Eccl.*) die Eucharistie; das heilige Abendmahl.

eulogize ['ju:lədʒaiz], *v.a.* loben, preisen.

euphonium [ju'founiəm], *s.* (*Mus.*) das Bombardon; Baritonhorn.

euphony ['ju:fəni], *s.* der Wohlklang.

European [juərə'piən], *adj.* europäisch. — *s.* der Europäer.

euphemism ['ju:fimizm], *s.* der Euphemismus.

euphuism ['ju:fjuizm], *s.* (*Lit.*) der gezierte Stilart.

evacuate [i'vækjueit], *v.a.* evakuieren, räumen.

evacuation [ivækju'eifən], *s.* die Evakuierung, die Räumung.

evade [i'veid], *v.a.* ausweichen (*Dat.*); entgehen (*escape, Dat.*).

evanescent [evə'nesənt], *adj.* verschwindend.

evangelical [i:væn'dʒelikəl], *adj.* evangelisch.

evangelist [i'vændʒəlist], *s.* der Evangelist.

evangelize [i'vændʒəlaiz], *v.a., v.n.* das Evangelium lehren *or* predigen.

evaporate [i'væpəreit], *v.a.* verdunsten lassen, verdampfen lassen. — *v.n.* (*Chem.*) verdunsten.

evaporation [ivæpə'reifən], *s.* die Verdampfung, die Verdunstung.

evasion [i'veiʒən], *s.* die Flucht (*escape*) (*from*, von, *Dat.*); die Ausflucht, das Ausweichen.

evasive [i'veiziv], *adj.* ausweichend.

eve, even (1) [i:v, i:vn], *s.* (*Poet.*) der Vorabend; Abend.

even (2) [i:vn], *adj.* eben, glatt (*smooth*); gerade (*number*); quitt (*quits*); gelassen (*temper*); gleich (*equal*). — *v.a.* — *out*, gleichmachen, ebnen.

even (3) [i:vn], *adv.* gerade, selbst, sogar (*emphatic*); *not* —, nicht einmal; — *though*, obwohl.

evening ['i:vniŋ], *s.* der Abend; — *gown*, das Abendkleid; — *dress*, der Abendanzug; der Smoking (*dinner jacket*); der Frack (*tails*).

evenness ['i:vənnis], *s.* die Ebenheit (*of surface*); die Gelassenheit (*of temper*).

event [i'vent], *s.* die Begebenheit, der Vorfall (*happening*); das große Ereignis (*state occasion*); *at all* —s, auf alle Fälle; *in the* —, im Falle, daß.

eventful [i'ventful], *adj.* ereignisreich.

eventual [i'ventjuəl], *adj.* schließlich, endlich.

ever ['evə], *adv.* je; immer, stets; nur, überhaupt; *for* —, für immer; — *so*, so sehr, soho; — *since*, seitdem.

evergreen ['evəgri:n], *adj.* immergrün. — *s.* (*Bot.*) das Immergrün.

everlasting [evə'la:stiŋ], *adj.ewig*; dauernd; fortwährend (*continual*).

every ['evri], *adj.* jeder, jeder einzelne (*pl.* alle); — *one*, jeder einzelne; — *now and then*, dann und wann; — *other day*, jeden zweiten Tag; — *day*, alle Tage.

everybody, everyone ['evribɔdi, 'evriwʌn], *s.* jedermann, ein jeder.

everyday ['evridei], *adj.* alltäglich.

everyone *see under* **everybody.**

everything ['evriθiŋ], *s.* alles.

everywhere ['evrihwɛə], *adv.* überall.

evict [i'vikt], *v.a.* vertreiben (*eject*); (*Law*) (gerichtlich) kündigen (*Dat.*).

eviction [i'vikfən], *s.* die Kündigung, die Vertreibung.

evidence ['evidəns], *s.* der Beweis (*proof*); (*Law*) das Zeugnis; *documentary* —, (*Law*) das Beweisstück; (*Law*) *give* —, eine Zeugenaussage machen.

evident ['evidənt], *adj.* klar, deutlich (*obvious*); augenscheinlich (*visible*); *self*- —, selbstverständlich.

evil ['i:vil], *s.* das Übel, das Böse. — *adj.* übel, böse; — *speaking*, die üble Nachrede.

evildoer ['i:vildu:ə], *s.* der Übeltäter.

evince [i'vins], *v.a.* zeigen, dartun, an den Tag legen.

evocation [i:vo'keifən], *s.* die Beschwörung (*magic*); das Hervorrufen.

evocative [i'vɔkativ], *adj.* hervorrufend, voll Erinnerungen (*of, Genit.*).

evoke [i'vouk], *v.a.* hervorrufen (*call forth*); beschwören (*conjure up*).

evolution [i:və'lju:fən, ev-], *s.* die Entwicklung, Evolution.

385

evolutionary [i:və'lju:ʃənri], *adj.* Evolutions-, Entwicklungs-.

evolve [i'vɔlv], *v.a.* entwickeln. — *v.n.* sich entwickeln.

ewe [ju:], *s.* (*Zool.*) das Mutterschaf.

ewer ['juə], *s.* die Wasserkanne.

exact [ig'zækt], *adj.* genau, gewissenhaft, exakt. — *v.a.* fordern; erpressen; eintreiben (*dept.*).

exacting [ig'zæktiŋ], *adj.* genau, anspruchsvoll.

exactitude [ig'zæktitju:d], *s.* die Genauigkeit.

exactly [ig'zæktli], *adv.* (*coll.*) ganz richtig!

exactness [ig'zæktnis], *s.* die Genauigkeit.

exaggerate [ig'zædʒəreit], *v.a.* übertreiben.

exaggeration [igzædʒə'reiʃən], *s.* die Übertreibung.

exalt [ig'zɔ:lt], *v.a.* erhöhen, erheben.

exaltation [egzɔ:l'teiʃən], *s.* die Erhöhung, die Erhebung.

exalted [ig'zɔ:ltid], *adj.* erhaben, hoch.

examination [igzæmi'neiʃən], *s.* die Prüfung; (*Med.*) die Untersuchung; (*Law*) das Verhör, das Untersuchungsverhör; die Ausfragung (*scrutiny*); — *board*, die Prüfungskommission.

examine [ig'zæmin], *v.a.* prüfen; (*Med.*) untersuchen; (*Law*) verhören; ausfragen.

examiner [ig'zæminə], *s.* der Examinator.

example [ig'za:mpl], *s.* das Beispiel; *for* —, zum Beispiel; *set an* —, ein Beispiel geben.

exasperate [ig'zæspəreit], *v.a.* aufreizen; ärgern, aufbringen.

exasperation [igzæspə'reiʃən], *s.* die Entrüstung, die Erbitterung.

excavate ['ekskəveit], *v.a.* ausgraben.

excavation [ekskə'veiʃən], *s.* die Ausgrabung.

exceed [ik'si:d], *v.a.* überschreiten (*go beyond*); übertreffen (*surpass*). — *v.n.* zu weit gehen.

exceeding [ik'si:diŋ], *adj.* (*obs.*) übermäßig, übertrieben.

exceedingly [ik'si:diŋli], *adv.* außerordentlich; äußerst.

excel [ik'sel], *v.a.* übertreffen. — *v.n.* sich auszeichnen (*in*, in, *Dat.*).

excellence ['eksələns], *s.* die Vortrefflichkeit.

excellent ['eksələnt], *adj.* ausgezeichnet, hervorragend.

except [ik'sept], *v.a.* ausnehmen, ausschließen. — *conj.* außer (es sei denn) daß. — *prep.* ausgenommen, mit Ausnahme von (*Dat.*).

exception [ik'sepʃən], *s.* die Ausnahme (*exemption*); der Einwand, Einwurf (*objection*).

exceptionable [ik'sepʃənəbl], *adj.* anfechtbar (*disputable*); anstößig.

exceptional [ik'sepʃənəl], *adj.* außergewöhnlich.

exceptionally [ik'sepʃənəli], *adv.* ausnahmsweise.

excerpt [ik'sə:pt], *v.a.* ausziehen, exzerpieren. — ['eksə:pt], *s.* der Auszug, das Exzerpt.

excess [ik'ses], *s.* das Übermaß; *carry to* —, übertreiben; — *fare*, der Zuschlag; — *luggage*, das Übergewicht.

excessive [ik'sesiv], *adj.* übermäßig, allzuviel.

exchange [iks'tʃeindʒ], *s.* der Austausch; *stock* —, die Börse; *rate of* —, der Kurs; *bill of* —, der Wechsel; der Tausch (*barter*). — *v.a.* wechseln; tauschen (*barter*) (*against*, für, *Acc.*); austauschen (*messages etc.*).

exchangeable [iks'tʃeindʒəbl], *adj.* (*Comm.*) austauschbar.

exchequer [iks'tʃekə], *s.* die Staatskasse; das Finanzamt (*office*); *Chancellor of the Exchequer*, der Schatzkanzler.

excise (1) ['eksaiz], *s.* die Aksize; *customs and* —, das Zollamt, der Zoll; — *officer*, der Zollbeamte, Steuerbeamte.

excise (2) [ek'saiz], *v.a.* (her)ausschneiden.

excision [ek'siʒən], *s.* das Ausschneiden, die Entfernung.

excitable [ik'saitəbl], *adj.* erregbar, reizbar.

excitation [eksi'teiʃən], *s.* (*Phys.*, *Chem.*) die Erregung.

excitement [ik'saitmənt], *s.* die Erregung, Aufregung (*mood*).

exciting [ik'saitiŋ], *adj.* erregend, aufregend, packend (*thrilling*).

exclaim [iks'kleim], *v.a.* ausrufen.

exclamation [eksklə'meiʃən], *s.* der Ausruf (*interjection*); das Geschrei (*shouting*).

exclude [iks'klu:d], *v.a.* ausschließen.

exclusion [iks'klu:ʒən], *s.* der Ausschluß.

exclusive [iks'klu:siv], *adj.* ausschließlich (*sole*); exklusiv (*select*).

exclusiveness [iks'klu:sivnis], *s.* der exklusive Charakter, die Exklusivität.

excommunicate [ekskə'mju:nikeit], *v.a.* (*Eccl.*) von der Kirchengemeinde ausschließen, bannen, exkommunizieren.

excommunication [ekskəmju:ni'keiʃən], *s.* (*Eccl.*) die Exkommunikation, der Bann.

excoriate [eks'kɔ:rieit], *v.a.* häuten; abschälen (*peel*).

excrement [eks'krimənt], *s.* das Exkrement, der Kot.

excrescence [iks'kresəns], *s.* der Auswuchs.

excretion [eks'kri:ʃən], *s.* die Ausscheidung, der Auswurf.

excruciate [iks'kru:ʃieit], *v.a.* martern, peinigen; *excruciatingly funny*, furchtbar komisch.

exculpate ['ekskʌlpeit], *v.a.* rechtfertigen, entschuldigen.

exculpation [ekskʌl'peiʃən], *s.* die Entschuldigung, die Rechtfertigung.

excursion [iks'kə:ʃən], *s.* der Ausflug, die Exkursion (*outing*); die Digression (*irrelevance*); der Abstecher (*deviation*).

excusable [iks'kju:zəbl], *adj.* entschuldbar, verzeihlich.

excuse [iks'kju:s], *s.* die Entschuldigung. — [-'kju:z], *v.a.* entschuldigen (*Acc.*), verzeihen (*Dat.*).

execrable ['eksikrəbl], *adj.* abscheulich.

execrate ['eksikreit], *v.a.* verfluchen, verwünschen.

execute ['eksikju:t], *v.a.* ausführen (*carry out*); (*Law*) hinrichten (*kill*).

execution [eksi'kju:ʃən], *s.* die Ausführung (*of an order*); (*Law*) die Hinrichtung; die Pfändung (*official forfeit*).

executioner [eksi'kju:ʃənə], *s.* der Henker, der Scharfrichter.

executive [ik'sekjutiv], *adj.* ausübend, vollziehend (*of power etc.*). — *s.* (*Pol.*) die Exekutive; (*Comm.*) das Direktionsmitglied.

executor [ik'sekjutə], *s.* der Testamentsvollstrecker (*of a will*).

exemplar [ig'zemplə], *s.* das Muster, das Beispiel.

exemplary [ig'zempləri], *adj.* musterhaft, vorbildlich.

exemplify [ig'zemplifai], *v.a.* durch Beispiel(e) erläutern.

exempt [ig'zempt], *v.a.* ausnehmen, befreien, verschonen (*spare*).

exemption [ig'zempʃən], *s.* die Ausnahme.

exequies ['eksikwiz], *s. pl.* das Leichenbegängnis, die Totenfeier.

exercise ['eksəsaiz], *s.* die Übung (*practice*); die körperliche Betätigung (*exertion*). — *v.a.* üben; — *o.'s rights*, von seinen Rechten Gebrauch machen; — *discretion*, Diskretion walten lassen; (*Mil.*) — *troops*, exerzieren.

exert [ig'zə:t], *v.a.* ausüben; — *pressure*, Druck ausüben (*upon*, auf, *Acc.*). — *v.r.* — *o.s.*, sich anstrengen.

exertion [ig'zə:ʃən], *s.* die Anstrengung, die Bemühung.

exhale [eks'heil], *v.a.* ausatmen; aushauchen; ausdünsten.

exhalation [ekshə'leiʃən], *s.* die Ausatmung, die Ausdünstung.

exhaust [ig'zɔ:st], *v.a.* erschöpfen. — *s.* (*Motor.*) der Auspuff.

exhaustible [ig'zɔ:stibl], *adj.* erschöpflich.

exhaustion [ig'zɔ:stʃən], *s.* die Erschöpfung.

exhibit [ig'zibit], *v.a.* ausstellen (*display*); zeigen (*demonstrate*). — ['eksibit], *s.* das Ausstellungsobjekt; (*Law*) das Beweisstück.

exhibition [eksi'biʃən], *s.* die Ausstellung (*display*); (*Films*) die Vorführung (*showing*); das Stipendium (*scholarship*).

exhibitioner [eksi'biʃənə], *s.* der Stipendiat.

exhilarate [ig'ziləreit], *v.a.* aufheitern.

exhilaration [igzilə'reiʃən], *s.* die Aufheiterung.

exhort [ig'zɔ:t], *v.a.* ermahnen.

exhortation [egzɔ:'teiʃən], *s.* die Ermahnung.

exigence, exigency ['eksidʒəns, -si], *s.* das Bedürfnis, Erfordernis (*necessity*); der dringende Notfall (*emergency*).

exigent ['eksidʒənt], *adj.* dringend.

exile ['eksail], *s.* der Verbannte (*person*); das Exil, die Verbannung (*state*). — *v.a.* verbannen; des Landes verweisen.

exist [ig'zist], *v.n.* existieren.

existence [ig'zistəns], *s.* das Dasein, die Existenz.

existent [ig'zistənt], *adj.* seiend, wirklich, existierend.

existentialism [egzis'tenʃəlizm], *s.* der Existentialismus.

exit ['eksit], *s.* der Ausgang; (*Theat.*) der Abgang.

exonerate [ig'zɔnəreit], *v.a.* entlasten.

exorbitant [ig'zɔ:bitənt], *adj.* übertrieben, übermäßig.

exorcise ['eksɔ:saiz], *v.a.* bannen, beschwören.

exorcism ['eksɔ:sizm], *s.* die Geisterbeschwörung.

exotic [ig'zɔtik], *adj.* exotisch.

expand [iks'pænd], *v.a.* erweitern, ausbreiten, ausdehnen. — *v.n.* sich erweitern (*broaden*); sich ausdehnen (*stretch*).

expansion [iks'pænʃən], *s.* die Ausdehnung, die Ausbreitung.

expansive [iks'pænsiv], *adj.* ausgedehnt; Ausdehnungs- (*forces*); (*fig.*) mitteilsam.

expatiate [iks'peiʃieit], *v.n.* sich verbreiten (*on*, über, *Acc.*).

expatriate [eks'peitrieit], *v.a.* verbannen.

expect [iks'pekt], *v.a.* erwarten (*wait for*); glauben (*believe*); hoffen (*hope for*); — *a baby*, ein Kind erwarten.

expectant [iks'pektənt], *adj.* schwanger (*with child*); voll Erwartung.

expectation [ekspek'teiʃən], *s.* die Erwartung, die Hoffnung.

expedience, expediency [iks'pi:diəns, -si], *s.* die Zweckmäßigkeit, die Schicklichkeit.

expedient [iks'pi:diənt], *adj.* zweckmäßig, schicklich, ratsam. — *s.* das Mittel; der Ausweg.

expedite ['ekspidait], *v.a.* beschleunigen.

expedition [ekspi'diʃən], *s.* (*Mil. etc.*) die Expedition; die schnelle Abfertigung.

expeditious [ekspi'diʃəs], *adj.* schleunig, schnell.

expel [iks'pel], *v.a.* vertreiben, austreiben; (*Sch.*) verweisen (*from*, von, aus).

expend [iks'pend], *v.a.* ausgeben.

expenditure [iks'penditʃə], *s.* (*Comm.*) die Ausgabe; der Aufwand (*of energy*).

expense [iks'pens], *s.* die Ausgabe; (*pl.*) die Kosten, Auslagen, Spesen, *f. pl.*

expensive [iks'pensiv], *adj.* teuer, kostspielig.

experience [iks'piəriəns], *s.* die Erfahrung, das Erlebnis. — *v.a.* erfahren.

experienced [iks'piəriənsd], *adj.* erfahren.

experiment [iks'perimənt], *s.* das Experiment, der Versuch. — *v.n.* experimentieren, Versuche machen.

experimental [iksperi'mentl], *adj.* Probe-, probeweise, experimentell.

expert ['ekspə:t], *s.* der Fachmann; der Sachverständige.

expertise [ekspə'ti:z], *s.* die Expertise, die Fachkenntnis.

expertness [iks'pə:tnis], *s.* die Gewandtheit.

expiable ['ekspiəbl], *adj.* sühnbar.

expiation [ekspi'eiʃən], *s.* die Sühnung, die Sühne.

expiration [ekspi'reiʃən], *s.* das Ausatmen; (*fig.*) der Tod; der Ablauf (*time*); die Verfallszeit (*lapse of validity*).

expire [iks'paiə], *v.n.* aushauchen (*breathe*); ablaufen (*run out*); sterben (*die*).

expiry [iks'pairi], *s.* die Ablaufsfrist (*of papers*).

explain [iks'plein], *v.a.* erklären, erläutern.

explanation [eksplə'neiʃən], *s.* die Erklärung, Erläuterung.

expletive [iks'pli:tiv], *s.* das Fluchwort, der Kraftausdruck.

explicable ['eksplikəbl], *adj.* erklärlich, erklärbar.

explication [ekspli'keiʃən], *s.* die Erklärung.

explicit [iks'plisit], *adj.* ausdrücklich, deutlich.

explicitness [iks'plisitnis], *s.* die Deutlichkeit, die Bestimmtheit.

explode [iks'ploud], *v.n.* explodieren; (*Mil.*) platzen (*of a shell*). — *v.a.* explodieren lassen.

exploit [iks'plɔit], *v.a.* ausbeuten; ausnützen (*utilize*). — ['eksplɔit], *s.* die Heldentat, die Großtat.

exploitation [eksplɔi'teiʃən], *s.* die Ausbeutung, die Ausnützung.

exploration [eksplɔ:'reiʃən], *s.* die Erforschung.

explore [iks'plɔ:], *v.a.* erforschen, untersuchen (*investigate*).

explosion [iks'plouʒən], *s.* die Explosion.

explosive [iks'plousiv], *adj.* explosiv. — *s.* der Sprengstoff.

exponent [eks'pounənt], *s.* (*Maths.*) der Exponent; der Vertreter (*of a theory*).

export [eks'pɔ:t], *v.a.* ausführen, exportieren. — ['ekspɔ:t], *s.* der Export, die Ausfuhr.

exporter [eks'pɔ:tə], *s.* der Exporteur, der Ausfuhrhändler, der Exportkaufmann.

expose [iks'pouz], *v.a.* entblößen; aussetzen (*to cold etc.*); bloßstellen (*display*); (*Phot.*) belichten; darlegen (*set forth*); ausstellen (*exhibit*).

exposition [ekspo'ziʃən], *s.* die Aussetzung; die Auslegung (*interpretation*); die Darlegung (*deposition, declaration*); die Ausstellung (*exhibition*).

exposure [iks'pouʒə], *s.* die Aussetzung (*to cold etc.*); die Bloßstellung; (*Phot.*) die Belichtung.

expostulate [iks'pɔstjuleit], *v.n.* zur Rede stellen.

expound [iks'paund], *v.a.* auslegen, darlegen.

express [iks'pres], *v.a.* ausdrücken; zum Ausdruck bringen. — *adj.* ausdrücklich, eilig, Eil-; besonders; — *letter*, der Eilbrief; — *train*, der Schnellzug. — *s.* der Eilzug.

expression [iks'preʃən], *s.* der Ausdruck.

expressive [iks'presiv], *adj.* ausdrucksvoll.

expressly [iks'presli], *adv.* ausdrücklich, besonders.

expropriate [eks'prouprieit], *v.a.* enteignen.

expropriation [eksproupri'eiʃən], *s.* die Enteignung.

expulsion [iks'pʌlʃən], *s.* die Ausstoßung; der Ausschluß; die Vertreibung (*of a large number*).

expunge [iks'pʌndʒ], *v.a.* austilgen, auslöschen.

expurgate ['ekspə:geit], *v.a.* reinigen.

exquisite ['ekskwizit], *adj.* auserlesen, vortrefflich.

extant ['ekstənt, ek'stænt], *adj.* noch vorhanden, existierend.

extempore [eks'tempəri], *adv.* aus dem Stegreif, extemporiert.

extemporize [eks'tempəraiz], *v.a.* extemporieren, improvisieren.

extend [iks'tend], *v.a.* ausdehnen (*boundaries etc.*); ausstrecken (*a helping hand*); verlängern (*time*); bieten (*a welcome*); erweitern (*enlarge*). — *v.n.* sich erstrecken, sich ausdehnen; dauern (*time*).

extensible [iks'tensibl], *adj.* ausdehnbar.

extension [iks'tenʃən], *s.* die Ausdehnung; die Verlängerung (*time*); *university — classes*, Abendkurse, *m. pl.* (der Erwachsenenbildung); (*Telephone*) der Apparat.

extensive [iks'tensiv], *adj.* ausgedehnt, umfassend.

extent [iks'tent], *s.* die Ausdehnung, die Weite, die Größe (*size*); *to a certain —*, bis zu einem gewissen Grade; *to the — of £x*, bis zu einem Betrage von x Pfund.

extenuate [iks'tenjueit], *v.a.* beschönigen; mildern; *extenuating circumstances*, (*Law*) mildernde Umstände, *m. pl.*

extenuation [ikstenju'eiʃən], *s.* die Beschönigung, die Abschwächung.

factor

exterior [eks'tiəriə], *adj.* äußerlich. — *s.* das Äußere.
exterminate [iks'tə:mineit], *v.a.* ausrotten, vertilgen.
extermination [iksta:mi'neiʃən], *s.* die Ausrottung, die Vertilgung.
external [eks'tə:nl], *adj.* äußerlich; auswärtig.
extinct [iks'tiŋkt], *adj.* ausgestorben.
extinction [iks'tiŋkʃən], *s.* die Erlöschen (*dying*); die Vernichtung (*annihilation*); das Aussterben.
extinguish [iks'tiŋgwiʃ], *v.a.* auslöschen; vernichten (*annihilate*). — *v.n.* auslöschen, ausgehen (*of fire or life*).
extirpate ['eksta:peit], *v.a.* ausrotten.
extol [iks'toul], *v.a.* preisen, erheben.
extort [iks'tɔ:t], *v.a.* erpressen.
extortion [iks'tɔ:ʃən], *s.* die Erpressung.
extortionate [iks'tɔ:ʃənit], *adj.* erpresserisch.
extra ['ekstrə], *adj.* zusätzlich. — *s.* (*pl.*) die Nebenausgaben, *f. pl.*
extract [iks'trækt], *v.a.* (aus)ziehen (*pull out*). — ['ekstrækt], *s.* (*Chem.*) der Extrakt; der Auszug (*book*).
extraction [iks'trækʃən], *s.* das Ausziehen (*pulling out*); das Zahnziehen (*tooth*); das Verfertigen eines Auszuges (*book*); die Herkunft (*origin*).
extradite ['ekstrədait], *v.a.* (*Pol.*) ausliefern.
extradition [ekstrə'diʃən], *s.* (*Pol.*) die Auslieferung.
extraneous [eks'treiniəs], *adj.* nicht zur Sache gehörig, unwesentlich.
extraordinary [iks'trɔ:dnəri], *adj.* außerordentlich.
extravagance [iks'trævəgəns], *s.* die Extravaganz; die Verschwendung (*waste*).
extravagant [iks'trævəgənt], *adj.* extravagant; verschwenderisch.
extravaganza [ikstrævə'gænzə], *s.* fantastisches Werk, die Burleske, Posse.
extreme [iks'tri:m], *adj.* äußerst (*uttermost*); höchst (*highest*); extrem (*stringent*); letzt (*last*); — *unction*, (*Eccl.*) die Letzte Ölung; *in the* —, äußerst.
extremity [iks'tremiti], *s.* die äußerste Grenze (*limit*); die Notlage (*straits, emergency*); (*pl.*) die Extremitäten, *f. pl.*
extricate ['ekstrikeit], *v.a.* herauswinden, herauswickeln (*disentangle*), befreien.
extrude [eks'tru:d], *v.a.* ausstoßen (*Metall.*) ausziehen.
extrusion [eks'tru:ʒən], *s.* die Ausstoßung; die Ausziehung (*of steel etc.*).
exuberant [ig'zju:bərənt], *adj.* überschwenglich, überschäumend.
exude [ik'sju:d], *v.a.* ausschwitzen; von sich geben (*give out*).
exult [ig'zʌlt], *v.n.* frohlocken.
exultant [ig'zʌltənt], *adj.* triumphierend.
exultation [egzʌl'teiʃən], *s.* das Frohlocken, der Jubel.
eye [ai], *v.a.* ansehen, betrachten. — *s.* das Auge, — *of a needle*, das Nadelöhr; *an* — *for an* —, Aug' um Auge; — *witness*, der Augenzeuge.

eyeball ['aibɔ:l], *s.* der Augapfel.
eyebrow ['aibrau], *s.* die Augenbraue.
eyeglass ['aiglɑ:s], *s.* der Zwicker, Klemmer.
eyelash ['ailæʃ], *s.* die Augenwimper.
eyelid ['ailid], *s.* das Augenlid.
eyesight ['aisait], *s.* die Sehkraft, das Augenlicht.
eyrie ['ɛəri, 'iəri], *s.* der Adlerhorst.

F

F [ef]. das F (*also Mus.*).
fable [feibl], *s.* die Fabel; das Märchen.
fabric ['fæbrik], *s.* das Gewebe, der Stoff.
fabricate ['fæbrikeit], *v.a.* herstellen; (*fig.*) fabrizieren; erfinden.
fabrication [fæbri'keiʃən], *s.* (*fig.*) die Erdichtung, die Erfindung.
fabulous ['fæbjuləs], *adj.* fabelhaft; wunderbar.
façade [fə'sɑ:d], *s.* die Fassade.
face [feis], *v.a.* jemandem ins Gesicht sehen (*s.o.*); gegenüberstehen, gegenüberliegen (*lie opposite, Dat.*); — *west*, nach Westen gehen (*of house, window*). — *v.n.* — *about*, sich umdrehen. — *s.* das Gesicht, (*Poet.*) das Angesicht; — *to* — *with*, gegenüber (*Dat.*); *on the* — *of it*, auf den ersten Blick; *lose* —, sich blamieren; *have the* — *to*, die Frechheit haben etwas zu tun.
facet ['fæsit], *s.* die Facette; der Zug (*feature*).
facetious [fə'si:ʃəs], *adj.* scherzhaft.
facetiousness [fə'si:ʃəsnis], *s.* die Scherzhaftigkeit, die Witzigkeit.
facile ['fæsail], *adj.* leicht.
facilitate [fə'siliteit], *v.a.* erleichtern, leicht machen.
facility [fə'siliti], *s.* die Leichtigkeit (*ease*); die Gewandtheit (*deftness*); die Möglichkeit (*possibility*); (*pl.*) die Einrichtungen, die Möglichkeiten, *f. pl.* (*amenities*).
facing ['feisiŋ], *s.* (*Tail.*) der Besatz, der Aufschlag; (*Build.*) die Verkleidung; (*Mil.*) die Schwenkung, die Wendung.
facsimile ['fæk'simili], *s.* das Faksimile.
fact [fækt], *s.* die Tatsache; *as a matter of* —, tatsächlich, in Wirklichkeit; —*s and figures*, der Bericht mit Tatsachen und Zahlen; *in* —, tatsächlich; *in point of* —, in der Tat, in Wirklichkeit.
faction ['fækʃən], *s.* (*Pol.*) die Partei, die Faktion.
factitious [fæk'tiʃəs], *adj.* nachgemacht, künstlich.
factor ['fæktə], *s.* der Faktor; (*Comm.*) der Agent; der Umstand (*fact*).

389

factory ['fæktəri], *s.* die Fabrik; — *hand,* der Fabrikarbeiter.

factual ['fæktjuəl], *adj.* Tatsachen-, tatsächlich.

faculty ['fækəlti], *s.* (*Univ.*) die Fakultät; die Fähigkeit (*sense*); (*pl.*) die Talente, *n. pl.,* die Begabung; Kräfte *f. pl.*

fad [fæd], *s.* die Grille, die Laune; die Marotte.

faddy ['fædi], *adj.* schrullig.

fade [feid], *v.n.* verschießen (*colour*); verwelken (*flower*); vergehen.

fag [fæg], *v.a.* ermüden. — *v.n.* (*Sch.*) Dienste tun, Diener sein (*for,* für). — *s.* die Plackerei; (*coll.*) die Zigarette; (*Sch.*) der Fuchs, der neue Schüler; — *end,* der Zigarettenstummel; (*Naut.*) das offene Tauende; der letze Rest (*remnant*).

faggot ['fægət], *s.* das Reisigbündel.

fail [feil], *v.a.* im Stiche lassen (*let down*); (*Sch.*) durchfallen (*an examination,* in einer Prüfung). — *v.n.* — *to do,* etwas nicht tun, fehlgehen, scheitern; versagen.

failing ['feiliŋ], *adj.* schwach, versagend. — *s.* der Mangel, Fehler.

failure ['feiljə], *s.* der Fehlschlag; das Versagen (*weakness*); das Nichteinhalten (*non-compliance*); der Durchfallen (*in examinations*); der Versager (*person*).

fain [fein], *adv.* (*obs.*) gern, gerne.

faint [feint], *v.n.* in Ohnmacht fallen, ohnmächtig werden. — *adj.* leise, schwach (*noise etc.*); — *hearted,* kleinmütig.

fair (1) [feə], *adj.* hübsch, schön (*beautiful*); unparteiisch, fair (*impartial*); anständig, angemessen (*equitable*); blond.

fair (2) [feə], *s.* der Jahrmarkt (*market*); (*Comm.*) die Messe, die Handelsmesse.

fairness ['fɛənis], *s.* die Schönheit (*beauty*); die Unparteilichkeit, Fairneß (*objectivity*); die Sportlichkeit (*sportsmanship*); die Anständigkeit (*equity*).

fairy ['fɛəri], *s.* die Fee.

faith [feiθ], *s.* der Glaube; die Treue (*loyalty*); das Vertrauen (*trust*).

faithful ['feiθful], *adj.* (*Rel.*) gläubig; treu (*loyal*); ergeben (*devoted*).

faithless ['feiθlis], *adj.* (*Rel.*) ungläubig; treulos, untreu (*disloyal*).

fake [feik], *s.* der Schwindel.

falcon ['fɔ:(l)kən], *s.* (*Orn.*) der Falke.

falconer ['fɔ:(l)knə], *s.* der Falkner.

falconry ['fɔ:(l)kənri], *s.* die Falknerei.

fall [fɔ:l], *v.n. irr.* fallen, abfallen (*leaves*); einbrechen (*night*); sich legen (*wind*); heruntergehen, sinken (*price*); geboren werden (*pigs, lambs*); — *through,* mißlingen, zunichte werden. — *s.* der Fall; (*Am.*) der Herbst (*autumn*); der Abhang (*precipice*); der Verfall (*decay*); der Untergang (*decline*).

fallacious [fə'leiʃəs], *adj.* trügerisch, trüglich, falsch (*assumption etc.*).

fallacy ['fæləsi], *s.* die Täuschung, der Irrtum, Trugschluß.

fallible ['fælibl], *adj.* fehlbar.

falling ['fɔ:liŋ], *s.* das Fallen; — *sickness,* die Fallsucht; — *off,* das Abnehmen (*decrease*); — *out,* der Zwist, der Streit (*disunity*). — *adj.* — *star,* die Sternschnuppe.

fallow ['fælou], *adj.* brach, fahl.

false [fɔ:ls], *adj.* falsch, unrichtig (*untrue*); — *alarm,* der blinde Alarm; — *bottom,* der Doppelboden; — *start,* der Fehlstart; — *step,* der Fehltritt; — *verdict,* das Fehlurteil; — *pretences,* die Vorspiegelung falscher Tatsachen.

falsehood ['fɔ:lshud], *s.* die Lüge, die Unwahrheit.

falseness ['fɔ:lsnis], *s.* die Falschheit; die Unaufrichtigkeit (*insincerity*).

falsify ['fɔ:lsifai], *v.a.* fälschen, verfälschen.

falsity ['fɔ:lsiti] *see* falseness.

falter ['fɔ:ltə], *v.n.* straucheln (*stumble*); stammeln (*stammer*).

fame [feim], *s.* der Ruhm; der Ruf; *ill —,* der üble Ruf.

familiar [fə'miljə], *adj.* vertraut, wohlbekannt, intim; gewohnt (*habitual*); *be on — terms,* auf vertrautem Fuß stehen.

familiarity [fəmili'æriti], *s.* die Vertrautheit, die Vertraulichkeit (*intimacy*).

familiarize [fə'miljəraiz], *v.a.* vertraut machen, bekannt machen.

family ['fæmili], *s.* die Familie; — *doctor,* der Hausarzt; (*Chem.*) die Gruppe; *be in the — way,* in anderen Umständen sein, guter Hoffnung sein, schwanger sein; — *tree,* der Stammbaum.

famine ['fæmin], *s.* die Hungersnot; — *relief,* Hilfe für die Hungernden.

famish ['fæmiʃ], *v.n.* verhungern, hungern; verschmachten.

famous ['feiməs], *adj.* berühmt, wohlbekannt (*for,* wegen).

fan [fæn], *s.* der Fächer (*lady's*); der Ventilator; (*sl.*) der leidenschaftliche Anhänger, der Fan; (*coll.*) Fanatiker (*admirer*). — *v.a.* fächeln; anfachen (*flames*); entfachen (*hatred*). — *v.n.* (*Mil.*) — *out,* sich ausbreiten, ausschwärmen.

fanatic [fə'nætik], *s.* der Fanatiker.

fanatical [fə'nætikəl], *adj.* fanatisch.

fanaticism [fə'nætisizm], *s.* der Fanatismus, die Schwärmerei.

fancier ['fænsiə], *s. — pigeon —,* der Taubenzüchter; *bird —,* der Vogelzüchter.

fanciful ['fænsiful], *adj.* schwärmerisch, wunderlich.

fancy ['fænsi], *s.* die Vorliebe (*preference*); die Phantasie; die Laune (*whim*); *take a — to,* liebgewinnen. — *adj.* — *dress,* der Maskenanzug, das Kostüm; — *goods,* Galanteriewaren; — *cakes,* Torten, *f.pl.*; das Feingebäck. — *v.a.* denken, gern haben; (*coll.*) — *oneself as,* sich einbilden, man sei; *just —!* denk doch mal! denk mal an!

fanfare ['fænfɛə], *s.* (*Mus.*) die Fanfare, der Tusch.

fang [fæŋ], *s.* (*Zool.*) der Hauzahn, der Giftzahn (*of snake*); (*Engin.*) der Zapfen. — *v.a.* (*Engin.*) vollpumpen, aufpumpen und in Tätigkeit setzen.

fanlight ['fænlait], *s.* die Lünette, das Lichtfenster.

fantastic(al) [fæn'tæstik(əl)], *adj.* fantastisch.

fantasy ['fæntəsi], *s.* (*Poet.*, *Mus.*) die Phantasie; das Hirngespinst (*chimæra*).

far [fɑ:], *adj.* weit; fern, entfernt (*distant*). — *adv.* — *and wide*, weit und breit; *by* —, bei weitem; *go too* —, zu weit gehen; *he will go* —, er wird seinen Weg machen; — *sighted*, weitsichtig.

farce [fɑ:s], *s.* die Farce, die Posse.

fare [fɛə], *s.* das Fahrgeld; der Fahrpreis (*of taxi etc.*); der Fahrgast (*one travelling in taxi*); — *stage*, die Fahr or Teilstrecke; das Essen, die Kost (*food*); *bill of* —, die Speisekarte. — *v.n.* ergehen (*Dat.*); daran sein.

farewell [fɛə'wel], *interj.* lebewohl! — *dinner*, das Abschiedsessen; — *party*, die Abschiedsgesellschaft.

farinaceous [færi'neiʃəs], *adj.* mehlig, aus Mehl.

farm [fɑ:m], *s.* der Pachthof, der Bauernhof; die Farm; — *hand*, der Landarbeiter, der Farmarbeiter; — *bailiff*, der Gutsverwalter. — *v.a.* bebauen; — *out*, verpachten. — *v.n.* Landwirt sein.

farmer ['fɑ:mə], *s.* der Bauer, Landwirt; der Pächter (*tenant*).

farmland ['fɑ:mlænd], *s.* das Ackerland.

farmyard ['fɑ:mjɑ:d], *s.* der Bauernhof, Gutshof.

farrier ['færiə], *s.* der Hufschmid.

farrow ['færou], *s.* der Wurf (*pigs*). — *v.n.* ferkeln, Junge haben.

farther ['fɑ:ðə], *comp. adj.*, *adv.* ferner, weiter.

farthest ['fɑ:ðist], *superl. adj.*, *adv.* fernst, weitest.

farthing ['fɑ:ðiŋ], *s.* der Farthing, der Heller.

fascinate ['fæsineit], *v.a.* bezaubern, faszinieren.

fascination [fæsi'neiʃən], *s.* die Bezauberung; der Reiz, der Zauberbann (*spell*).

fascism ['fæʃizm], *s.* (*Pol.*) der Faschismus.

fashion ['fæʃən], *s.* die Mode; *out of* —, außer Mode; die Art und Weise (*manner*). — *v.a.* gestalten, bilden (*shape*); *fully* —*ed*, vollgeformt *or* geformt, angepaßt.

fashionable ['fæʃnəbl], *adj.* modisch, modern; elegant.

fast (1) [fɑ:st], *adj.* schnell (*runner*); fest (*firm*); *my watch is* —, meine Uhr geht vor; *a* — *woman*, eine leichtlebige Frau; — *train*, der Schnellzug; — *and furious*, schnell wie der Wind. — *adv.* fest.

fast (2) [fɑ:st], *v.n.* (*Rel.*) fasten; (*Rel.*) — *day*, der Fasttag.

fasten [fɑ:sn], *v.a.* festbinden, festmachen (*fix*). — *v.n.* sich festhalten (*on to*, an, *Dat.*).

fastidious [fəs'tidiəs], *adj.* wählerisch, anspruchsvoll.

fastidiousness [fəs'tidiəsnis], *s.* die anspruchsvolle Art.

fat [fæt], *adj.* fett; dick (*person*). — *s.* das Fett; (*Cul.*) das Speisefett.

fatal ['feitəl], *adj.* tödlich (*lethal*); verhängnisvoll.

fatalism ['feitəlizm], *s.* der Fatalismus.

fatality [fə'tæliti], *s.* das Verhängnis; der Todesfall; der tödliche Unfall.

fate [feit], *s.* das Schicksal, Geschick; das Verhängnis (*doom*, *destiny*).

fated ['feitid], *adj.* dem Verderben (Untergang) geweiht.

fateful ['feitful], *adj.* verhängnisvoll, unselig.

father ['fɑ:ðə], *s.* der Vater; (*Eccl.*) Pater; — *in-law*, der Schwiegervater. — *v.a.* Vater sein *or* werden von (*Dat.*); zeugen (*procreate*).

fatherland ['fɑ:ðəlænd], *s.* das Vaterland.

fatherly ['fɑ:ðəli], *adj.* väterlich; wie ein Vater.

fathom ['fæðəm], *s.* die Klafter. — *v.a.* ergründen, erforschen.

fatigue [fə'ti:g], *s.* die Ermüdung, die Erschöpfung; (*Mil.*) der Arbeitsdienst. — *v.a.* ermüden, erschöpfen.

fatling ['fætliŋ], *s.* (*Agr.*) das Mastvieh.

fatness ['fætnis], *s.* die Beleibtheit (*person*); die Fettheit (*animals*).

fatten [fætn], *v.a.* — *up*, mästen (*animals*); fett werden lassen. — *v.n.* fett werden, sich mästen (an, *Dat.*).

fatty ['fæti], *adj.* (*Chem.*) fett, fettig. — *s.* (*coll.*) der Dickwanst.

fatuity [fə'tju:iti], *s.* die Albernheit, die Dummheit.

fatuous ['fætjuəs], *adj.* albern, dumm, nichtssagend.

faucet ['fɔ:sit], *s.* der Zapfen, der Hahn.

fault [fɔ:lt], *s.* der Fehler; die Schuld; *find* — *with*, etwas kritisieren; tadeln; *it is my* —, es ist meine Schuld; *at* —, im Irrtum.

faultless ['fɔ:ltlis], *adj.* fehlerlos, fehlerfrei.

faultlessness ['fɔ:ltlisnis], *s.* die Fehlerlosigkeit, die fehlerlose Ausführung.

faulty ['fɔ:lti], *adj.* fehlerhaft, mangelhaft.

faun [fɔ:n], *s.* (*Myth.*) der Faun.

fauna ['fɔ:nə], *s.* die Fauna, die Tierwelt.

favour ['feivə], *s.* die Gunst, das Wohlwollen; (*Comm.*) *in* — *of*, zugunsten; *do a* —, einen Gefallen tun *or* erweisen; *be in* —, sehr begehrt sein, in hoher Gunst stehen. — *v.a.* bevorzugen, begünstigen, wohlwollend gegenüberstehen (*Dat.*).

favourable ['feivərəbl], *adj.* günstig, vorteilhaft.

favourite [ˈfeivərit], *s.* der Favorit, der Liebling; der Günstling (*of kings*). — *adj.* Lieblings-, bevorzugt.

fawn (1) [fɔːn], *s.* (*Zool.*) das junge Reh, das Rehkalb; — *coloured*, rehfarben. — *adj.* rehfarben, hellbraun.

fawn (2) [fɔːn], *v.n.* schmeicheln, kriecherisch sein ((*up*)*on*, *Dat.*).

fawning [ˈfɔːniŋ], *adj.* kriecherisch, kriechend.

fear [fiə], *s.* die Furcht, die Angst; *stand in — of s.o.*, vor jemandem fürchten; *for — of*, aus Angst vor (*Dat.*). — *v.a.* fürchten, befürchten.

fearful [ˈfiəful], *adj.* furchtsam (*full of fear*); furchtbar (*causing fear*).

fearless [ˈfiəlis], *adj.* furchtlos (*of*, vor, *Dat.*).

fearlessness [ˈfiəlisnis], *s.* die Furchtlosigkeit.

feasibility [fiːziˈbiliti], *s.* die Tunlichkeit, die Möglichkeit.

feasible [ˈfiːzibl], *adj.* tunlich, möglich.

feast [fiːst], *s.* das Fest, der Festtag; der Schmaus (*good meal*). — *v.n.* schmausen (*upon*, von, *Dat.*). — *v.a.* festlich bewirten.

feat [fiːt], *s.* die Tat, die Heldentat; das Kunststück.

feather [ˈfeðə], *s.* die Feder; *show the white —*, Feigheit an den Tag legen; — *bed*, das Federbett. — *v.a.* federn; — *o.'s nest*, sein Schäfchen ins Trockene bringen.

feature [ˈfiːtʃə], *s.* der Zug (*characteristic*); der Gesichtszug (*facial*). — *v.a.* charakterisieren; (*Film*) in der Hauptrolle zeigen.

February [ˈfebruəri], *s.* der Februar.

feckless [ˈfeklis], *adj.* hilflos, unfähig.

feculence [ˈfekjuləns], *s.* (*Chem.*) der Bodensatz, der Hefesatz.

fecund [ˈfekənd], *adj.* fruchtbar.

fecundate [ˈfekəndeit], *v.a.* fruchtbar machen, befruchten.

fecundity [fiˈkʌnditi], *s.* die Fruchtbarkeit.

federacy [ˈfedərəsi], *s.* der Bund, die Föderation.

federal [ˈfedərəl], *adj.* Bundes-, föderativ.

federalism [ˈfedərəlizm], *s.* der Föderalismus.

federalize [ˈfedərəlaiz], *v.a.* verbünden.

federation [fedəˈreiʃən], *s.* die Föderation, die Verbündung; (*Pol.*) der Bund.

fee [fiː], *s.* die Gebühr (*official dues*); das Honorar (*of doctor etc.*); (*pl.*) (*Sch.*) das Schulgeld.

feeble [ˈfiːbl], *adj.* schwach, matt; — *minded*, schwachsinnig.

feed [fiːd], *v.a. irr.* füttern; verköstigen (*humans*); unterhalten (*maintain*); zuführen (*into machine*, *Dat.*); *be fed up with*, etwas satt haben; — *pipe*, die Speiseröhre. — *v.n.* sich nähren (*on*, von, *Dat.*); weiden (*graze*).

feeder [ˈfiːdə], *s.* der Kinderlatz (*bib*); (*Tech.*) der Zubringer.

feel [fiːl], *v.n. irr.* sich fühlen (*sense*); meinen (*think*). — *v.a.* berühren, betasten (*touch*); empfinden (*be aware of*).

feeler [ˈfiːlə], *s.* der Fühler; *put out a —*, einen Fühler ausstrecken.

feeling [ˈfiːliŋ], *s.* das Gefühl; *with —*, bewegt, gerührt (*moved*); grimmig (*in anger*).

feign [fein], *v.a.* vortäuschen, heucheln.

feint [feint], *s.* die Verstellung (*disguise*); die Finte (*fencing*).

felicitate [fiˈlisiteit], *v.a.* Glück wünschen (*upon*, zu, *Dat.*), beglückwünschen (*Acc.*).

felicitation [filisiˈteiʃən], *s.* die Beglückwünschung, der Glückwunsch.

felicitous [fiˈlisitəs], *adj.* glücklich ausgedrückt, gut gesagt (*in speaking*).

felicity [fiˈlisiti], *s.* die Glückseligkeit; die glückliche Ausdrucksweise (*style*).

feline [ˈfiːlain], *adj.* Katzen-, katzenartig.

fell (1) [fel], *adj.* grausam; *at one — swoop*, mit einem wilden Schwung.

fell (2) [fel], *v.a.* fällen (*timber*); töten (*kill*).

fell (3) [fel], *s.* das Gebirge, das Felsengelände.

fell (4) [fel], *s.* das Fell, die Haut (*skin*).

fellow [ˈfelou], *s.* der Gefährte, Genosse (*companion*); das Mitglied eines College *or* einer Universität; (*coll.*) der Kerl; *queer —*, seltsamer Kauz; — *feeling*, das Mitgefühl; — *traveller*, der Weggenosse (*Pol.*) der Mitläufer.

fellowship [ˈfelouʃip], *s.* die Mitgliedschaft (einer Hochschule etc.) (*membership*); die Freundschaft (*friendship*); *good —*, die Geselligkeit.

felly, felloe [ˈfeli, ˈfelou], *s.* die Radfelge.

felon [ˈfelən], *s.* der Verbrecher.

felonious [fiˈlouniəs], *adj.* verbrecherisch.

felt [felt], *s.* der Filz.

female [ˈfiːmeil], *adj.* weiblich. — *s.* (*Zool.*) das Weibchen.

feminine [ˈfeminin], *adj.* weiblich. — *s.* (*Gram.*) das weibliche Geschlecht; das Weibliche.

fen [fen], *s.* das Moor, das Marschland.

fence [fens], *s.* der Zaun, das Staket. — *v.a.* umzäunen, einzäunen (*enclose*). — *v.n.* fechten (*fight with rapiers*).

fencing [ˈfensiŋ], *s.* die Einzäunung (*fence*); das Fechten (*with rapiers*); — *master*, der Fechtmeister.

fend [fend], *v.a.* — *off*, abwehren, parieren. — *v.n.* — *for oneself*, sich allein behelfen.

fennel [ˈfenl], *s.* (*Bot.*) der Fenchel.

ferment [fəˈment], *v.a.* zur Gärung bringen. — *v.n.* gären, fermentieren. — [ˈfəːment], *s.* das Gärmittel (*also fig.*); (*Chem.*) das Gärungsprodukt.

fermentation [fəːmenˈteiʃən], *s.* die Gärung.

fern [fəːn], *s.* (*Bot.*) das Farnkraut.

ferocious [fəˈrouʃəs], *adj.* wild, grimmig.

ferocity [fəˈrɔsiti], *s.* die Wildheit.
ferret [ˈferit], *s.* (*Zool.*) das Frett, das Frettchen. — *v.a.* — *out*, ausspüren.
ferry [ˈferi], *s.* die Fähre. — *v.a.* — *across*, hinüberrudern, hinüberfahren, übersetzen.
fertile [ˈfəːtail], *adj.* fruchtbar.
fertility [fəˈtiliti], *s.* die Fruchtbarkeit.
fertilize [ˈfəːtilaiz], *v.a.* befruchten.
fertilizer [ˈfəːtilaizə], *s.* das Düngemittel, der Dünger.
fervent [ˈfəːvənt], *adj.* inbrünstig (*prayer*); heiß (*wish*).
fervid [ˈfəːvid], *adj.* glühend, heiß (*with zeal*).
fervour [ˈfəːvə], *s.* die Inbrunst (*prayer*); die Sehnsucht (*wish*).
fester [ˈfestə], *v.n.* schwären, eitern.
festival [ˈfestivəl], *s.* das Fest, die Festspiele, *n. pl.*
festive [ˈfestiv], *adj.* festlich, Fest-.
festivity [fesˈtiviti], *s.* die Festlichkeit.
festoon [fesˈtuːn], *s.* die Girlande. — *v.a.* behängen, mit Girlanden verzieren, schmücken.
fetch [fetʃ], *v.a.* holen, bringen.
fetching [ˈfetʃiŋ], *adj.* einnehmend.
fetter [ˈfetə], *v.a.* fesseln, binden. — *s.* (*pl.*) die Fesseln, *f. pl.*
feud [fjuːd], *s.* die Fehde.
feudal [ˈfjuːdl], *adj.* feudal, Lehns-.
fever [ˈfiːvə], *s.* das Fieber.
few [fjuː], *adj.* einige; wenige; *a* —, ein paar.
fiancé [fiˈɔːnsei], *s.* der Verlobte, Bräutigam.
fiancée [fiˈɔːnsei], *s.* die Verlobte, Braut.
fib [fib], *s.* (*coll.*) die Lüge. — *v.n.* (*coll.*) lügen.
fibre [ˈfaibə], *s.* die Fiber, Faser.
fibrous [ˈfaibrəs], *adj.* faserartig.
fickle [fikl], *adj.* unbeständig, wankelmütig.
fiction [ˈfikʃən], *s.* die Erdichtung (*figment*) (*Lit.*) die Romanliteratur.
fictitious [fikˈtiʃəs], *adj.* erdichtet, in der Phantasie.
fiddle [fidl], *s.* (*coll.*) die Geige, Fiedel, Violine. — *v.n.* (*coll.*, *Mus.*) geigen; schwindeln (*cheat*).
fiddlesticks! [ˈfidlstiks], *int.* Unsinn!
fidelity [fiˈdeliti], *s.* die Treue (*loyalty*); Genauigkeit; (*Engin.*) *high* —, Präzision, High Fidelity.
fidget [ˈfidʒit], *v.n.* unruhig sein.
fidgety [ˈfidʒiti], *adj.* nervös.
fie! [fai], *int.* pfui!
field [fiːld], *s.* das Feld; (*fig.*) das Gebiet; — *glass*, der Feldstecher; (*Hunt.*) — *sports*, die Feldübungen, der Jagdsport. — *v.a.*, *v.n.* abfangen, abpassen (*cricket*).
fiend [fiːnd], *s.* der Unhold, böse Geist; *fresh air* —, ein Freund der frischen Luft.
fiendish [ˈfiːndiʃ], *adj.* teuflisch, boshaft.
fierce [fiəs], *adj.* wild, wütend (*beast*); — *weather*, — *cold*, die grimmige Kälte, der grimmige Winter.

fiery [ˈfaiəri], *adj.* feurig; hitzig.
fife [faif], *s.* (*Mus.*) die Querpfeife.
fifteen [fifˈtiːn], *num. adj.* fünfzehn.
fifth [fifθ], *num. adj.* der fünfte.
fifty [ˈfifti], *num. adj.* fünfzig.
fig [fig], *s.* (*Bot.*) die Feige.
fight [fait], *v.a.*, *v.n.* ~ *irr.* kämpfen, bekämpfen (*in battle*); raufen (*of boys*). — *s.* der Kampf; die Rauferei.
figment [ˈfigmənt], *s.* die Erdichtung.
figurative [ˈfigjuərətiv], *adj.* bildlich (*style*).
figure [ˈfigə], *s.* die Figur (*body*); die Gestalt, Form (*shape*); (*Maths.*) die Zahl, die Ziffer; *cut a* —, einen Eindruck machen; *a fine* — *of a man!* ein fabelhafter Kerl! — *v.a.* — *out*, ausdenken, ausrechnen. — *v.n.* eine Rolle spielen, rangieren.
figured [ˈfigəd], *adj.* figuriert.
figurehead [ˈfigəhed], *s.* der scheinbare Leiter, die Representationsfigur.
filament [ˈfiləmənt], *s.* der Faden, der Glühfaden (*bulb*).
filbert [ˈfilbəːt], *s.* (*Bot.*) die Haselnuß.
filch [filtʃ], *v.a.* stehlen, klauen.
file [fail], *s.* (*Engin.*) die Feile; (*Mil.*) die Reihe; (*Comm.*) der Aktenstoß, das Aktenbündel, der Ordner; (*pl.*) die Akten, *f. pl.*; *single* —, im Gänsemarsch; *rank and* —, die große Masse; *on the* —, in den Akten. — *v.a.* feilen (*metal*); zu den Akten legen (*papers*); einreichen (*petition*).
filial [ˈfiliəl], *adj.* kindlich.
filibuster [ˈfilibastə], *s.* der Freibeuter; (*Am.*) (*Pol.*) die Obstruktion.
filigree [ˈfiligriː], *s.* die Filigranarbeit.
filing [ˈfailiŋ], *s.* (*pl.*) die Feilspäne, die Einheften (*of papers*); — *cabinet*, die Kartei.
fill [fil], *v.a.* füllen; ausfüllen (*place*, *job*); plombieren (*tooth*); — *up*, tanken (*with petrol*). — *s.* das volle Maß; *eat o.'s* —, sich satt essen.
fillet [ˈfilit], *s.* das Filet (*meat*); das Band, die Binde (*band*).
filling [ˈfiliŋ], *s.* die Plombe (*in tooth*); — *station*, die Tankstelle.
filly [ˈfili], *s.* das Füllen.
film [film], *s.* der Film (*cinema*, *Phot.*); die Haut, das Häutchen (*skin*); der Belag (*coating*). — *v.a.* aufnehmen, verfilmen, filmen (*photograph*).
filter [ˈfiltə], *v.a.* filtrieren, filtern. — *v.n.* durchfiltern. — *s.* das Filter.
filth [filθ], *s.* der Schmutz.
filthy [ˈfilθi], *adj.* schmutzig.
filtration [filˈtreiʃən], *s.* das Filtrieren, das Durchsickern.
fin [fin], *s.* (*Zool.*) die Finne, die Flosse.
final [fainl], *adj.* letzt, endlich; endgültig. — *s.* (*Sport*) die Endrunde, das Endspiel.
finale [fiˈnɑːli], *s.* (*Mus.*) das Finale.
finality [faiˈnæliti], *s.* die Endgültigkeit.
finance [fiˈnæns *or* ˈfai-], *s.* die Finanz, das Finanzwesen. — *v.a.* finanzieren.

financial [fi'nænʃəl], *adj.* finanziell, Geld-, Finanz-.

finch [fintʃ], *s.* (*Orn.*) der Fink.

find [faind], *v.a. irr.* finden; — *fault with*, jemanden kritisieren; *all found*, volle Verpflegung (inbegriffen). — *s.* der Fund.

finding ['faindiŋ], *s.* das Finden, der Befund; (*Law*) der Wahrspruch.

fine (1) [fain], *adj.* fein (*delicate*); dünn (*thin*); schön (*beautiful*); scharf (*distinct*); großartig(*splendid*).

fine (2) [fain], *v.a.* zu einer Geldstrafe verurteilen. — *s.* die Geldstrafe.

finery ['fainəri], *s.* der Putz; (*Engin.*) der Frischofen.

finger ['fiŋgə], *s.* der Finger; *have a — in the pie*, die Hand im Spiel haben. — *v.a.* berühren, antasten.

finish ['finiʃ], *v.a.* beenden, fertig machen, vollenden; —*ing touch*, die lezte Hand. — *v.n.* aufhören, enden. — *s.* das Ende (*end*); der letzte Schliff; die Appretur, die Fertigung.

finite ['fainait], *adj.* endlich.

Finn [fin], *s.* der Finne.

Finnish ['finiʃ], *adj.* finnisch.

fir [fə:], *s.* (*Bot.*) die Föhre, die Tanne; — *cone*, der Tannenzapfen.

fire [faiə], *s.* das Feuer; — *brigade*, die Feuerwehr; — *damp*, (*Min.*) schlagende Wetter, *n.pl.*; — *engine*, die Feuerspritze; — *extinguisher*, der Löschapparat, Feuerlöscher; — *escape*, die Rettungsleiter. — *v.a.* brennen (*clay*); anzünden, in Gang setzen (*furnace*); anspornen (*enthuse*); (*coll.*) entlassen (*dismiss*). — *v.n.* feuern (*at*, *Acc.*).

firebrand ['faiəbrænd], *s.* der Aufwiegler.

fireman ['faiəmən], *s.* der Heizer.

fireplace ['faiəpleis], *s.* der Kamin.

fireproof ['faiəpru:f], *adj.* feuerfest.

fireside ['faiəsaid], *s.* der (häusliche) Herd, der Kamin.

firewood ['faiəwud], *s.* das Brennholz.

firework ['faiəwə:k], *s.* (*usually pl.*) das Feuerwerk.

firm [fə:m], *adj.* fest, hart (*solid*); entschlossen (*decided*). — *s.* die Firma.

firmament ['fə:məmənt], *s.* das Firmament, Himmelsgewölbe, der Sternenhimmel.

firmness ['fə:mnis], *s.* die Festigkeit, Entschlossenheit.

first [fə:st], *num. adj., adv.* erst; zuerst; — *of all*, zuallererst; — *born*, erstgeboren; — *rate*, erstklassig. — *s. from the* —, von Anfang an.

fiscal ['fiskəl], *adj.* fiskalisch, von der Staatskasse, Finanz-.

fish [fiʃ], *s.* der Fisch; *like a — out of water*, nicht in seinem Element; *a queer —*, ein seltsamer Kauz; —*bone*, die Gräte. — *v.n.* fischen; — *for compliments*, nach Lob haschen, nach Komplimenten fischen.

fisherman ['fiʃəmən], *s.* der Fischer.

fishery ['fiʃəri], *s.* der Fischfang.

fishing ['fiʃiŋ], *s.* das Fischen, der Fischfang; — *fly*, die Angelfliege; — *line*, die Angelschnur; — *rod*, die Angelrute; — *tackle*, das Angelgerät.

fishy ['fiʃi], *adj.* (*coll.*) anrüchig, verdächtig.

fissile ['fisail], *adj.* (*Phys.*) spaltbar.

fission ['fiʃ(ə)n], *s.* (*Phys.*) die Spaltung.

fist [fist], *s.* die Faust; *hand over —*, im Überfluß; *tight —ed*, geizig.

fisticuffs ['fistikʌfs], *s.* die Schlägerei, das Raufen.

fistula ['fistjulə], *s.* (*Anat.*) die Fistel.

fit (1) [fit], *v.a.* passen, anpassen (*Dat.*); einfügen (— *into s.th.*); — *in*, hineinpassen; — *on a suit*, einen Anzug anprobieren (*Dat.*); — *for a career*, zu einer Laufbahn vorbereiten; — *out*, ausrüsten. — *v.n.* passen, sich fügen (— *into*); — *in*, passen (*in*, *zu*, *Dat.*). — *adj.* geeignet, fähig (*suitable*); — *to drop*, todmüde; gesund, stark (*healthy*); schicklich (*proper*); (*Sport*) in guter Form.

fit (2) [fit], *s.* der Anfall; *by —s and starts*, ruckweise.

fitful ['fitful], *adj.* launenhaft; unbeständig.

fitness ['fitnis], *s.* die Tauglichkeit (*health*); die Schicklichkeit (*propriety*); die Fähigkeit (*ability*); (*Sport*) die gute Form.

fitter ['fitə], *s.* der Monteur.

fitting, fitment ['fitiŋ, 'fitmənt], *s.* die Armatur; die Montage. — *adj.* passend (*suitable*); geeignet (*appropriate*).

five [faiv], *num. adj.* fünf.

fiver ['faivə], *s.* (*coll.*) die Fünfpfundnote.

fix [fiks], *v.a.* festmachen, befestigen (*make firm*); festsetzen (*a time*); (*Am.*) herrichten, anrichten (*a meal*); — *with a glare* or *stare*, mit den Augen fixieren, scharf ansehen; — *up* (*coll.*), etwas erledigen (*something*); bedienen (*serve s.o.*). — *s.* (*coll.*) die Klemme, die Schwierigkeit, das Dilemma.

fixture ['fikstʃə], *s.* (*Sport*) die Veranstaltung; das Inventarstück (*furniture*).

fizz [fiz], *v.n.* brausen (*drink*).

fizzle ['fizl], *v.n.* zischen (*flame*); — *out*, verebben, ausgehen, zunichte werden; (*Am.*, *coll.*) durchfallen (*fail in school*).

fizzy ['fizi], *adj.* mit Kohlensäure, sprudelnd.

flabbergast ['flæbəga:st], *v.a.* (*coll.*) verblüffen.

flabby ['flæbi], *adj.* schlaff.

flaccid ['flæksid], *adj.* schlapp, schlaff.

flag (1) [flæg], *s.* (*Mil.*) die Flagge; die Fahne; — *officer*, der Flaggoffizier; —*staff*, die Fahnenstange.

flag (2) [flæg], *v.n.* ermatten, erschlaffen.

flag (3) [flæg], *s.* (—*stone*) der Fliesstein, die Fliese. — *v.a.* mit Fliesen auslegen, mit Fliessteinen pflastern.

flop

flagon ['flægən], *s.* die Doppelflasche.
flagrant ['fleigrənt], *adj.* entsetzlich (*shocking*); schamlos (*impudent*).
flail [fleil], *s.* der Dreschflegel.
flair [fleə], *s.* der Instinkt; (*coll.*) die Nase (*for*, für, *Acc.*).
flake [fleik], *s.* die Flocke. — *v.n.* — *off*, abblättern.
flame [fleim], *s.* die Flamme. (*coll.*) *old* —, die (alte) Liebe, Geliebte(r), die Flamme. — *v.n.* flammen, lodern.
flamingo [flə'miŋgou], *s.* (*Orn.*) der Flamingo.
flange [flændʒ], *s.* (*Engin.*) der Flan(t)sch.
flank [flæŋk], *s.* die Flanke, die Seite; die Weiche (*of animal*). — *v.a.* flankieren.
flannel [flænl], *s.* der Flanell.
flap [flæp], *s.* die Klappe; das Ohrläppchen (*earlobe*); der Flügelschlag (— *of wings*).
flare [fleə], *v.n.* flammen, flackern; — *up*, aufbrausen (*in temper*). — *s.* das Aufflammen, das Aufflackern; die Leuchtkugel.
flash [flæʃ], *s.* der Blitz (*of lightning*); das Aufflammen; (*Phot.*) —*light*, das Blitzlicht. — *v.a.* aufflammen lassen, aufblitzen lassen. — *v.n.* aufflammen, aufblitzen.
flashy ['flæʃi], *adj.* großtuend, angeberisch (*bragging*); buntfarbig (*gaudy*).
flask [fla:sk], *s.* die kleine Flasche, das Fläschchen.
flat [flæt], *adj.* flach, eben; abgestanden, schal (*drink*). — *footed*, plattfüßig; (*Mus.*) zu tief, vermindert; platt; albern (*conversation*); — *tyre*, die Panne. — *adv.* — *out*, ausgepumpt, erschöpft. — *s.* die Mietwohnung, Wohnung (*lodgings*); (*Mus.*) das B; (*pl.*) das Flachland; (*Theat.*) (*pl.*) die Bühnenbilder.
flatness ['flætnis], *s.* die Flachheit, die Plattheit (*of conversation etc.*).
flatten [flætn], *v.a.* flach machen; glätten (*smooth*).
flatter ['flætə], *v.a.* schmeicheln (*Dat.*).
flattery ['flætəri], *s.* die Schmeichelei.
flaunt [flɔ:nt], *v.a.* prahlen, prunken (*s.th.*, mit, *Dat.*).
flavour ['fleivə], *s.* der Geschmack, die Würze; das Aroma; die Blume (*bouquet of wine*). — *v.a.* würzen.
flaw [flɔ:], *s.* der Riß (*chink*); der Fehler (*fault*).
flawless ['flɔ:lis], *adj.* fehlerlos.
flax [flæks], *s.* (*Bot.*) der Flachs.
flay [flei], *v.a.* schinden, die Haut abziehen (*Dat.*).
flea [fli:], *s.* (*Ent.*) der Floh.
fleck [flek], *v.a.* sprenkeln.
fledge [fledʒ], *v.a.* befiedern; *fully* —*d*, flügge; selbständig.
fledgling ['fledʒliŋ], *s.* der Grünschnabel, der Novize.
flee [fli:], *v.a.*, *v.n. irr.* fliehen, entfliehen (*from*, von, *Dat.*); flüchten (*vor*, *Dat.*).

fleece [fli:s], *s.* das Vlies. — *v.a.* scheren (*sheep*); ausnützen (*exploit*); berauben.
fleet [fli:t], *s.* die Flotte. — *adj.* (*Poet.*) schnellfüßig.
Fleming ['flemiŋ], *s.* der Flame.
Flemish ['flemiʃ], *adj.* flämisch.
flesh [fleʃ], *s.* das (lebende) Fleisch; die Frucht (*of fruit*).
flex [fleks], *s.* (*Elec.*) die Kontaktschnur.
flexible ['fleksibl], *adj.* biegsam; (*fig.*) anpassungsfähig.
flexion ['flekʃən], *s.* (*Gram.*) die Flexion, die Biegung.
flick [flik], *s.* der leichte Schlag. — *v.a.* leicht schlagen, berühren.
flicker ['flikə], *s.* das Flackern, das Flimmern. — *v.n.* flackern, flimmern.
flight [flait], *s.* (*Aviat.*) der Flug; die Flucht (*escape*); — *of stairs*, die Treppe, Treppenflucht.
flimsy ['flimzi], *adj.* hauchdünn (*material*); schwach (*argument*).
flinch [flintʃ], *v.n.* zurückweichen, zurückzucken (*from*, vor, *Dat.*).
fling [fliŋ], *v.a. irr.* schleudern, werfen. — *s.* der Wurf; *highland* —, schottischer Tanz; *have a last* —, sich zum letzten Mal austoben.
flint [flint], *s.* der Feuerstein.
flippancy ['flipənsi], *s.* die Leichtfertigkeit.
flippant ['flipənt], *adj.* leichtfertig, leichtsinnig, schnippisch.
flirt [flə:t], *v.n.* flirten, liebeln, (*with*, *Dat.*).
flirtation [flə:'teiʃən], *s.* die Liebelei.
flit [flit], *v.n.* hin und her flitzen, huschen.
flitch [flitʃ], *s.* die Speckseite.
flitter ['flitə], *v.n.* flattern.
float [flout], *v.n.* obenauf schwimmen, dahingleiten; —*ing ice*, das Treibeis. — *v.a.* schwimmen lassen; (*Naut.*) flott machen; (*Comm.*) gründen (*a company*); ausgeben (*a loan*). — *s.* das Floß (*raft*); der ausgeschmückte Wagen (*decorated vehicle*).
flock [flɔk], *s.* die Herde (*sheep*). — *v.n.* zusammenlaufen, sich scharen.
floe [flou], *s.* die Eisscholle.
flog [flɔg], *v.a.* peitschen (*whip*); antreiben; — *a dead horse*, sich umsonst bemühen; (*coll.*) verkaufen.
flood [flʌd], *s.* die Flut; das Hochwasser, die Überschwemmung (*flooding*); (*fig.*) die Fülle; — *gate*, die Schleuse. — *v.a.* überfluten, überschütten (*with requests*). — *v.n.* überschwemmen (*of river*).
floodlight ['flʌdlait], *s.* das Flutlicht, Scheinwerferlicht.
floor [flɔ:], *s.* der Boden, der Fußboden; das Stockwerk, der Stock (*storey*); *from the* —, aus dem Plenum; —*walker*, die Aufsicht (*in stores*). — *v.a.* zu Boden strecken, überrumpeln (*surprise*).
flop [flɔp], *v.n.* (*coll.*) hinsinken, hinplumpsen; versagen (*fail*). — *s.* das Hinfallen; der Versager (*play, film etc.*).

395

Florentine

Florentine ['florəntain], *adj.* florentinisch. — *s.* der Florentiner.

florid ['florid], *adj.* blühend; überladen.

florin ['florin], *s.* das Zweischillingstück.

florist ['florist], *s.* der Blumenhändler.

flotsam ['flotsəm], *s.* das Strandgut, Wrackgut.

flounce (1) [flauns], *v.n.* hastig bewegen.

flounce (2) [flauns], *v.a.* mit Falbeln besetzen (*dress*). — *s.* die Falbel (*on dress*).

flounder (1) ['flaundə], *v.n.* umhertappen, unsicher sein.

flounder (2) ['flaundə], *s.* (*Zool.*) die Flunder.

flour ['flauə], *s.* das Mehl.

flourish ['flɔriʃ], *v.n.* blühen; wirken; gedeihen (*thrive*); schnörkeln, verzieren (*in writing*); Fanfaren blasen, schmettern (*trumpets*). — *s.* der Schnörkel; der Trompetenstoß, Tusch (*of trumpets*).

flout [flaut], *v.a.* verhöhnen, verspotten. — *s.* der Hohn, der Spott.

flow [flou], *v.n. irr.* fließen, strömen. — *s.* der Fluß (*of water, goods etc.*); — *of words*, der Redeschwall.

flower ['flauə], *s.* die Blume; die Blüte (*blossom*). — *v.n.* blühen, in Blüte stehen.

flowery ['flauəri], *adj.* gewählt, umständlich, geziert (*style*).

fluctuate ['flʌktjueit], *v.n.* schwanken.

fluctuation [flʌktju'eiʃən], *s.* das Schwanken.

flue [flu:], *s.* der Rauchfang (*of chimney*).

fluency ['flu:ənsi], *s.* das fließende Sprechen, die Geläufigkeit.

fluent ['flu:ənt], *adj.* geläufig, fließend.

fluid ['flu:id], *adj.* fließend, flüssig (*liquid*). — *s.* die Flüssigkeit.

fluke [flu:k], *s.* der glückliche Zufall (*chance*).

flunkey ['flʌŋki], *s.* der Diener, der Bediente.

flurry ['flʌri], *s.* die Unruhe; die Aufregung (*excitement*).

flush (1) [flʌʃ], *s.* das Erröten (*blushing*); die Aufwallung (*of anger*). — *v.a.* nachspülen (*basin*); erröten machen (*make blush*). — *v.n.* erröten.

flush (2) [flʌʃ], *adj.* in gleicher Ebene, eben.

flush (3) [flʌʃ], *v.a.* (*Hunt.*) aufscheuchen.

fluster ['flʌstə], *v.a.* verwirren (*muddle*); aufregen (*excite*).

flute [flu:t], *s.* (*Mus.*) die Flöte; (*Carp.*) die Hohlkehle. — *v.a.* (*Carp., Archit.*) aushöhlen. — *v.n.* (*Mus.*) flöten, Flöte spielen.

flutter ['flʌtə], *v.n.* flattern, unruhig sein. — *s.* die Unruhe.

flux [flʌks], *s.* das Fließen; *be in* —, in der Schwebe sein.

fly [flai], *v.a. irr.* wehen lassen, hissen (*flag*). — *v.n. irr.* (*Aviat.*) fliegen

fliehen (*escape*); eilen (*hurry*). — *s.* (*Ent.*) die Fliege.

flyleaf ['flaili:f], *s.* das Vorsatzblatt.

flying ['flaiiŋ], *adj.* fliegend, Flug-; — *squad*, das Überfallkommando.

flyover ['flaiouvə], *s.* die Brückenkreuzung, Überführung.

flywheel ['flaiwi:l], *s.* das Schwungrad.

foal [foul], *s.* (*Zool.*) das Füllen. — *v.n.* fohlen.

foam [foum], *s.* der Schaum; — *rubber*, das Schaumgummi. — *v.n.* schäumen.

fob [fob], *v.a.* — *off*, abfertigen, abspeisen.

focus ['foukəs], *s.* der Brennpunkt; der Mittelpunkt (*of interest*). — *v.a.* (*Phot.*) einstellen. — *v.n.* — *upon*, sich konzentrieren auf (*Acc.*).

fodder ['fodə], *s.* das Futter.

foe [fou], *s.* der Feind.

fog [fog], *s.* der Nebel.

fogey ['fougi], *s.* der Kerl, Kauz.

foible ['foibl], *s.* die Schwäche, die schwache Seite.

foil (1) [foil], *v.a.* vereiteln. — *s.* das Florett (*fencing rapier*).

foil (2) [foil], *s.* die Folie; der Hintergrund (*background*).

foist [foist], *v.a.* aufschwatzen (*upon, Dat.*).

fold (1) [fould], *v.a.* falten (*clothes etc.*); umarmen (*in o.'s arms*). — *v.n.* schließen, sich falten. — *s.* die Falte; (*Geol.*) die Vertiefung.

fold (2) [fould], *s.* die Herde (*sheep*); *return to the* —, zu den Seinen zurückkehren.

folder ['fouldə], *s.* die Mappe (*papers*); das Falzbein.

folding ['fouldiŋ], *adj.* Klapp-; — *chair*, der Klappstuhl; — *door*, die Flügeltür.

foliage ['fouliidʒ], *s.* (*Bot.*) das Laub.

folio ['fouliou], *s.* das Folio, der Foliant.

folk [fouk], *s.* (*also pl.*) die Leute; (*pl.*) (*Am.*) Freunde (*mode of address*).

folklore ['fouklɔ:], *s.* die Volkskunde.

folksong ['fouksɔŋ], *s.* das Volkslied.

follow ['folou], *v.a., v.n.* folgen (*Dat.*); — *suit*, dasselbe tun, Farbe bekennen.

follower ['folouə], *s.* der Anhänger (*supporter*); der Nachfolger (*successor*); *camp* —, der Mitläufer.

folly ['foli], *s.* die Narrheit; die törichte Handlung (*action*).

foment [fo'ment], *v.a.* anregen (*stimulate*); pflegen (*cultivate*); warm baden.

fond [fond], *adj.* zärtlich, lieb; *be* — *of*, gern haben.

fondle [fondl], *v.a.* liebkosen.

fondness ['fondnis], *s.* die Zärtlichkeit, die (Vor)liebe.

font [font], *s.* der Taufstein (*baptismal*).

food [fu:d], *s.* die Nahrung, Speise (*nourishment*); Lebensmittel (*n. pl.*); das Futter (*for animals*); *some* —, etwas zum Essen; — *store*, das Lebensmittelgeschäft.

fool [fu:l], *s.* der Narr, Tor. — *v.a.* zum Narren halten, übertölpeln.

foolish [ˈfuːliʃ], *adj.* töricht, albern, närrisch (*person*); unsinnig (*act*).

foolscap [ˈfuːlskæp], *s.* das Kanzleipapier.

foot [fut], *s.* der Fuß; *on* —, zu Fuß; — *board*, das Trittbrett; *put o.'s* — *in it*, eine taktlose Bemerkung fallen lassen, ins Fettnäpfchen treten. — *v.a.* — *the bill*, bezahlen.

footage [ˈfutidʒ], *s.* die Länge in Fuß.

football [ˈfutbɔːl], *s.* der Fußball.

footbridge [ˈfutbridʒ], *s.* der Steg.

footing [ˈfutiŋ], *s.* die Grundlage, Basis.

footlight [ˈfutlait], *s.* (*usually pl.*) die Rampenlichter, *n. pl.*

footman [ˈfutmən], *s.* der Bediente.

footprint [ˈfutprint], *s.* die Fußstapfe.

footstool [ˈfutstuːl], *s.* der Schemel.

fop [fɔp], *s.* der Geck.

for [fɔː], *prep.* für (*Acc.*); anstatt (*Genit.*) (*instead of*); *in exchange* —, für, um; — *example*, zum Beispiel; — *heaven's sake*, um Himmels willen; — *two days*, zwei Tage lang; auf zwei Tage; seit zwei Tagen; *now you are* — *it!* jetzt has du's! *as* — *me*, meinetwegen, was mich anbelangt; — *all that*, trotz alledem. — *conj.* denn, weil.

forage [ˈfɔridʒ], *s.* das Futter. — *v.n.* furagieren.

forasmuch [fɔrəzˈmʌtʃ], *conj.* (*obs.*) — *as*, insofern als.

foray [ˈfɔrei], *s.* der Raubzug.

forbear [fɔˈbɛə], *v.a. irr.* vermeiden, unterlassen (*avoid*); sich enthalten (*abstain*). — *v.n.* (geduldig) hinnehmen, ertragen.

forbid [fəˈbid], *v.a. irr.* verbieten; *God* — *!* Gott behüte!

forbidding [fəˈbidiŋ], *adj.* abschreckend.

force [fɔːs], *s.* (*Phys.*) die Kraft; die Macht (*might*); die Gewalt (*brute* —); (*pl.*) die Streitkräfte, *f. pl.*; (*Phys.*) die Kräfte. — *v.a.* zwingen, nötigen.

forceful [ˈfɔːsful], *adj.* kräftig, energisch, kraftvoll.

forceps [ˈfɔːseps], *s.* (*Med.*) die Zange; die Pinzette.

forcible [ˈfɔːsibl], *adj.* heftig, stark (*strong*); gewaltsam (*violent*).

ford [fɔːd], *s.* die Furt.

fore- [fɔː], *pref.* Vorder-, vorder.

forebear [ˈfɔːbɛə], *s.* der Vorfahre.

forebode [fɔːˈboud], *v.a.* voraussagen, vorbedeuten.

forecast [fɔːˈkɑːst], *v.a.* vorhersagen, voraussagen. — [ˈfɔːkɑːst], *s.* die Vorhersage.

foreclose [fɔːˈklouz], *v.a.* ausschließen.

forefather [ˈfɔːfɑːðə], *s.* der Ahne, der Vorvater.

forefinger [ˈfɔːfiŋgə], *s.* (*Anat.*) der Zeigefinger.

forego [fɔːˈgou], *v.a. irr.* vorhergehen.

foreground [ˈfɔːgraund], *s.* der Vordergrund.

forehead [ˈfɔrid], *s.* die Stirne.

foreign [ˈfɔrin], *adj.* fremd; ausländisch.

foreigner [ˈfɔrinə], *s.* der Fremde, der Ausländer.

foreland [ˈfɔːlənd], *s.* das Vorgebirge.

foreman [ˈfɔːmən], *s.* der Werkführer, Vorarbeiter.

foremast [ˈfɔːmɑːst], *s.* (*Naut.*) der Fockmast.

foremost [ˈfɔːmoust], *adj.* vorderst, vornehmlichst, führend. — *adv.* zuerst; *first and* —, zuallererst.

forenoon [ˈfɔːnuːn], *s.* der Vormittag.

forensic [fɔˈrensik], *adj.* forensisch, gerichtsmedizinisch.

forerunner [ˈfɔːrʌnə], *s.* der Vorläufer.

foresail [ˈfɔːseil, ˈfɔːsəl], *s.* (*Naut.*) das Focksegel.

foresee [fɔːˈsiː], *v.a. irr.* vorhersehen.

foreshadow [fɔːˈʃædou], *v.a.* vorher andeuten.

foreshorten [fɔːˈʃɔːtn], *v.a.* verkürzen.

foresight [ˈfɔːsait], *s.* die Vorsorge, der Vorbedacht.

forest [ˈfɔrist], *s.* der Wald; der Urwald (*jungle*).

forestall [fɔːˈstɔːl], *v.a.* vorwegnehmen, zuvorkommen (*Dat.*).

forester [ˈfɔristə], *s.* der Förster.

forestry [ˈfɔristri], *s.* die Forstwissenschaft (*science*); das Forstwesen (*management*).

foretaste [ˈfɔːteist], *s.* der Vorgeschmack.

foretell [fɔːˈtel], *v.a. irr.* voraussagen.

forethought [ˈfɔːθɔːt], *s.* der Vorbedacht.

forewarn [fɔːˈwɔːn], *v.a.* warnen.

forfeit [ˈfɔːfit], *s.* das Pfand (*pledge*); die Einbuße (*fine*); (*pl.*) das Pfänderspiel. — *v.a.* verlieren, verwirken.

forfeiture [ˈfɔːfitʃə], *s.* die Verwirkung, die Einbuße, der Verlust.

forge [fɔːdʒ], *v.a.* schmieden (*iron*); fälschen (*falsify*). — *v.n.* — *ahead*, sich vorwärtsarbeiten. — *s.* die Schmiede (*iron*); der Eisenhammer (*hammer*).

forget [fəˈget], *v.a., v.n. irr.* vergessen; — *me-not*, das Vergißmeinnicht.

forgetful [fəˈgetful], *adj.* vergeßlich.

forgive [fəˈgiv], *v.a., v.n. irr.* vergeben, verzeihen.

forgo [fɔːˈgou], *v.a. irr.* verzichten; aufgeben.

fork [fɔːk], *s.* die Gabel; die Abzweigung (*road*). — *v.n.* sich gabeln, sich spalten.

forlorn [fɔːˈlɔːn], *adj.* verlassen, verloren, elend.

form [fɔːm], *s.* die Form, die Gestalt (*shape*); die Formalität (*formality*); das Formular (*document*); *in good* —, (*Sport*) in guter Form; *bad* —, gegen den guten Ton; *a matter of* —, eine Formsache. — *v.a.* formen, gestalten (*shape*); bilden (*an association etc. of*, über, *Acc.*).

formal [ˈfɔːməl], *adj.* formal, äußerlich; formell.

formality [fɔːˈmæliti], *s.* die Formalität.

formation

formation [fɔːˈmeiʃən], s. (*Mil.*) die Formation; (*Geol.*) die Bildung; die Formung; die Aufstellung (*sports team*).

former [ˈfɔːmə], *adj.* früher, vorig.

formidable [ˈfɔːmidəbl], *adj.* schrecklich, furchtbar.

formula [ˈfɔːmjulə], s. die Formel.

formulate [ˈfɔːmjuleit], *v.a.* formulieren.

forsake [fɔːˈseik], *v.a. irr.* verlassen, im Stich lassen.

forsooth [fɔːˈsuːθ], *adv.* (*Poet.*) wahrlich, wirklich!

forswear [fɔːˈswɛə], *v.a. irr.* abschwören; — *oneself*, einen Meineid schwören.

fort, fortress [fɔːt, ˈfɔːtris], s. das Fort, die Festung.

forth [fɔːθ], *adv.* vorwärts; weiter (*further*); *and so* —, und so weiter (u.s.w.); fort (*away*).

forthcoming [ˈfɔːθˈkʌmiŋ], *adj.* bevorstehend.

forthwith [fɔːθˈwiθ], *adv.* sogleich.

fortieth [ˈfɔːtiəθ], *num. adj.* vierzigst. — *s.* der Vierzigste.

fortification [fɔːtifiˈkeiʃən], s. die Befestigung.

fortify [ˈfɔːtifai], *v.a.* befestigen; bestärken.

fortitude [ˈfɔːtitjuːd], s. die Tapferkeit.

fortnight [ˈfɔːtnait], s. vierzehn Tage, *m. pl.*

fortuitous [fɔːˈtjuːitəs], *adj.* zufällig.

fortunate [ˈfɔːtʃənit], *adj.* glücklich, günstig.

fortune [ˈfɔːtjuːn], s. das Glück, das Schicksal; das Vermögen (*wealth*); — *teller*, die Wahrsagerin.

forty [ˈfɔːti], *num. adj.* vierzig.

forward [ˈfɔːwəd], *adj.* vorder (*in front*); voreilig, vorlaut (*rash*); früh (*early*). — *adv.* vorne; — *march!* vorwärts! *carry* —, (*Comm.*) übertragen. — *s.* (*Footb.*) der Stürmer; — *line*, der Angriff. — *v.a.* weiterleiten, expedieren; (*letter*) *please* —, bitte nachsenden.

forwardness [ˈfɔːwədnis], s. die Frühreife; die Voreiligkeit, Dreistigkeit.

fossil [ˈfɔsil], s. das Fossil.

foster [ˈfɔstə], *v.a.* nähren (*feed*); aufziehen (*bring up*); — *a thought*, einen Gedanken hegen; — *mother*, die Pflegemutter; — *brother*, der Pflegebruder.

foul [faul], *adj.* schmutzig; faul (*rotten*). — *v.a.* beschmutzen. — *v.n.* (*Footb.*) einen Verstoß begehen. — *s.* (*Footb.*) der Verstoß.

found (1) [faund], *v.a.* gründen, begründen.

found (2) [faund], *v.a.* (*Metall.*) gießen (*cast*).

foundation [faunˈdeiʃən], s. das Fundament; die Unterlage; die Begründung, die Gründung (*initiation*); die Stiftung (*establishment*); — *stone*, der Grundstein.

founder (1) [ˈfaundə], s. der Gründer, Stifter.

founder (2) [ˈfaundə], *v.n.* scheitern, Schiffbruch erleiden (*on*, an, *Dat.*).

foundling [ˈfaundliŋ], s. das Findelkind, der Findling.

foundry [ˈfaundri], s. (*Metall.*) die Gießerei.

fount (1) [faunt], s. (*Typ.*) der Schriftguss.

fount (2) [faunt] (*Poet.*) *see* **fountain**.

fountain [ˈfauntin], s. die Quelle, der Brunnen; der Springbrunnen; — *pen*, die Füllfeder; — *head*, der Urquell.

four [fɔː], *num. adj.* vier; — *-in-hand*, das Viergespann.

fowl [faul], s. (*Orn.*) das Huhn, das Geflügel.

fowler [ˈfaulə], s. der Vogelsteller, Vogelfänger.

fox [fɔks], s. (*Zool.*) der Fuchs; (*fig.*) der listige Kauz, Schlauberger (*cunning fellow*). — *v.a.* (*coll.*) überlisten, täuschen.

fraction [ˈfrækʃən], s. (*Maths.*) der Bruch; (*Mech.*) der Bruchteil.

fractional [ˈfrækʃənəl], *adj.* (*Maths.*) Bruch-, gebrochen.

fractionate [ˈfrækʃəneit], *v.a.* (*Chem.*) fraktionieren (*oil*).

fractious [ˈfrækʃəs], *adj.* zänkisch, streitsüchtig.

fracture [ˈfræktʃə], s. (*Med.*) der Bruch. — *v.a.* brechen; — *o.'s leg*, sich das Bein brechen.

fragile [ˈfrædʒail], *adj.* zerbrechlich; gebrechlich (*feeble*).

fragment [ˈfrægmənt], s. das Bruchstück, das Fragment.

fragrance [ˈfreigrəns], s. der Wohlgeruch, Duft.

fragrant [ˈfreigrənt], *adj.* wohlriechend, duftend.

frail [freil], *adj.* gebrechlich, schwach (*feeble*).

frailty [ˈfreilti], s. die Schwäche.

frame [freim], s. der Rahmen (*of picture*); das Gerüst (*scaffold*); die Form (*shape*). — *v.a.* einrahmen (*a picture*); (*Am.*) in die Enge treiben, reinlegen (*get s.o. wrongly blamed*); (*Comm.*) entwerfen (*a letter*).

framework [ˈfreimwəːk], s. der Rahmen (*outline*); das Fachwerk (*construction*).

franchise [ˈfræntʃaiz], s. das Wahlrecht.

Franciscan [frænˈsiskən], s. der Franziskaner (*friar*).

frank [fræŋk], *adj.* offen, aufrichtig. — *v.a.* frankieren (*letter*). — *s.* der Frankovermerk.

frankincense [ˈfræŋkinsens], s. der Weihrauch.

frantic [ˈfræntik], *adj.* wahnsinnig, außer sich.

fraternal [frəˈtəːnəl], *adj.* brüderlich.

fraternity [frəˈtəːniti], s. die Bruderschaft; (*Am.*) der Studentenbund, -klub.

fraternize ['frætənaiz], v.n. sich verbrüdern, fraternisieren.

fraud [frɔːd], s. der Betrug.

fraudulent ['frɔːdjulənt], adj. betrügerisch.

fraught [frɔːt], adj. voll (with, von, Dat.).

fray (1) [frei], v.a. abnutzen; — the nerves, auf die Nerven gehen (Dat.).

fray (2) [frei], s. der Kampf, die Schlägerei.

freak [friːk], s. das Monstrum, die Mißgeburt.

freakish ['friːkiʃ], adj. seltsam; grotesk.

freckle [frekl], s. die Sommersprosse.

freckled [frekld], adj. sommersprossig.

free [friː], adj. frei; offen (frank); — trade area, die Freihandelszone; of my own — will, aus freien Stücken. — v.a. befreien.

freebooter ['friːbuːtə], s. der Freibeuter.

freedom ['friːdəm], s. die Freiheit; — of a city, das Ehrenbürgerrecht.

freehold ['friːhould], s. der freie Grundbesitz, der Freigrundbesitz.

freeholder ['friːhouldə], s. der (freie) Grundbesitzer.

freeman ['friːmən], s. der Freibürger, Ehrenbürger.

freemason ['friːmeisn], s. der Freimaurer.

freewheel ['friː'wiːl], s. der Freilauf, das Freilaufrad. — v.n. mit Freilauf fahren.

freeze [friːz], v.a. irr. gefrieren lassen. — v.n. frieren, gefrieren; — up, zufrieren.

freight [freit], s. die Fracht. — v.a. verfrachten.

freighter ['freitə], s. (Naut.) der Frachtdampfer.

French [frentʃ], adj. französisch; — bean, die Schnittbohne; — horn, (Mus.) das Horn.

Frenchman ['frentʃmən], s. der Franzose.

Frenchwoman ['frentʃwumən], s. die Französin.

frenzied ['frenzid], adj. wahnsinnig, außer sich.

frequency ['friːkwənsi], s. (Phys.) die Frequenz; die Häufigkeit (of occurrence).

frequent ['friːkwənt], adj. häufig. — [fri'kwent], v.a. (häufig) besuchen.

fresh [freʃ], adj. frisch, neu; ungesalzen (water); (sl.) frech; — water, das Süßwasser.

fresher, freshman ['freʃə, 'freʃmən], s. der Neuankömmling; (Univ.) der Fuchs, Anfänger.

fret (1) [fret], s. (Carp.) das Gitterwerk, Laubsägewerk. — v.a. (Carp.) durchbrochen verzieren.

fret (2) [fret], s. der Verdruß, Ärger. — v.n. sich Sorgen machen.

fretful ['fretful], adj. verdrießlich, ärgerlich, mißmutig.

fretsaw ['fretsɔː], s. (Carp.) die Laubsäge.

friar ['fraiə], s. (Eccl.) der Mönch, Bettelmönch.

friction ['frikʃən], s. die Reibung; (fig.) die Unstimmigkeit.

Friday ['fraid(e)i], s. der Freitag; Good —, der Karfreitag.

friend [frend], s. der (die) Freund(in).

friendly ['frendli], adj. freundlich.

friendship ['frendʃip], s. die Freundschaft.

frigate ['frigit], s. (Naut.) die Fregatte.

fright [frait], s. die Furcht, der Schreck, das Entsetzen.

frighten ['fraitn], v.a. erschrecken (s.o.).

frightful ['fraitful], adj. schrecklich.

frigid ['fridʒid], adj. kalt, frostig; kühl.

frill [fril], s. die Krause; die Ausschmückung (style).

frilly ['frili], adj. gekräuselt, geziert.

fringe [frindʒ], s. die Franse (fringed edge); der Rand (edge, brink). — v.a. mit Fransen besetzen, einsäumen. — v.n. — on, grenzen an (Acc.).

Frisian ['friːʒən], adj. friesisch.

frisk [frisk], v.a. (sl.) durchsuchen (search). — v.n. hüpfen (of animals). — s. der Sprung (of animals).

frisky ['friski], adj. lebhaft, munter.

fritter ['fritə], s. die Franse (fringed apple —, Äpfel im Schlafrock; — v.a. zerstückeln (cut up); vertrödeln (waste), vergeuden.

frivolity [fri'vɔliti], s. der Leichtsinn, die Leichtfertigkeit.

frivolous ['frivələs], adj. leichtsinnig, leichtfertig.

fro [frou], adv. to and —, auf und ab, hin und her.

frock [frɔk], s. der Kittel, das Kleid; (Eccl.) die Soutane, Kutte.

frog [frɔg], s. (Zool.) der Frosch.

frogman ['frɔgmən], s. der Tauchschwimmer, Froschmann.

frolic ['frɔlik], s. der Scherz; der Spaß. — v.n. scherzen; ausgelassen sein.

from [frɔm], prep. von; von . . . her (hence); aus . . . heraus (out of); von . . . an (starting—); vor (in the face of).

front [frʌnt], s. die Stirn; die Vorderseite; (Mil.) die Front; in — of, vor (Dat.); — door, die Haustür.

frontage ['frʌntidʒ], s. die Front, Vorderfront (of building).

frontal ['frʌntl], adj. Stirn-, Vorder-; (Mil.) — attack, der Frontalangriff. — s. (Eccl.) die Altardecke.

frontier ['frʌntiə], s. die Grenze; — police, die Grenzpolizei.

frontispiece ['frʌntispiːs], s. das Titelbild.

frost [frɔst], s. der Frost, der Reif.

frostbite ['frɔstbait], s. die Frostbeule.

frosted ['frɔstid], adj. bereift.

froth [frɔθ], s. der Schaum. — v.n. schäumen.

frown

frown [fraun], *v.n.* die Stirn runzeln, finster dreinschauen. — *s.* das Stirnrunzeln.

frugal ['fru:gəl], *adj.* frugal, sparsam, einfach.

fruit [fru:t], *s.* die Frucht (*singular*); das Obst (*plural or collective*). — *v.n.* (*Bot.*) Früchte tragen.

frustrate [frʌs'treit], *v.a.* verhindern; vereiteln (*bring to nought*).

fry (1) [frai], *v.a.* braten; *fried potatoes*, Bratkartoffeln, *f. pl.*

fry (2) [frai], *s.* der Rogen (*of fish*); (*fig.*) die Brut, Menge.

frying pan ['fraiiŋpæn], *s.* die Bratpfanne; *out of the — into the fire*, vom Regen in die Traufe.

fuchsia ['fju:ʃə], *s.* (*Bot.*) die Fuchsie.

fudge [fʌdʒ], *s.* weiches Zuckerwerk; (*coll.*) Unsinn!

fuel ['fjuəl], *s.* der Brennstoff, Treibstoff; das Heizmaterial. — *v.a., v.n.* tanken.

fugitive ['fju:dʒitiv], *adj.* flüchtig, auf der Flucht. — *s.* der Flüchtling.

fugue [fju:g], *s.* (*Mus.*) die Fuge.

fulcrum ['fʌlkrəm], *s.* der Stützpunkt, Hebelpunkt.

fulfil [ful'fil], *v.a.* erfüllen; — *a requirement*, einem Gesetz genüge tun.

full [ful], *adj.* voll; vollständig (*complete*); — *time*, hauptberuflich.

fuller ['fulə], *s.* der Walker.

fullness ['fulnis], *s.* die Fülle.

fulsome ['fulsəm], *adj.* widerlich, ekelhaft; übermäßig.

fumble [fʌmbl], *v.n.* tappen (*for*, nach, *Dat.*).

fume [fju:m], *s.* der Rauch, Dunst; der Zorn (*anger*). — *v.n.* zornig sein, wüten (*be angered*).

fun [fʌn], *s.* der Spaß, Scherz; *have —*, sich gut unterhalten, sich amüsieren; *make — of*, zum besten haben.

function ['fʌŋkʃən], *s.* (*also Maths.*) die Funktion; das Amt (*office*); die Feier(lichkeit) (*formal occasion*). — *v.n.* funktionieren (*be in working order*); fungieren (*officiate*).

fund [fʌnd], *s.* der Fonds (*financial*); (*fig.*) die Fülle (*of*, an); *public —s*, die Staatsgelder.

fundamental [fʌndə'mentl], *adj.* grundsätzlich, wesentlich. — *s.* (*pl.*) die Grundlagen, *f.pl.*

funeral ['fju:nərəl], *s.* die Bestattung, Beerdigung.

funereal [fju:'niəriəl], *adj.* wie bei einem Begräbnis, betrübt, traurig.

fungus ['fʌŋgəs], *s.* (*Bot.*) der Pilz; der Schwamm (*mushroom*).

funk [fʌŋk], *s.* (*sl.*) die Angst, Panik. — *v.a.* fürchten.

funnel [fʌnl], *s.* der Trichter.

funny ['fʌni], *adj.* spaßhaft, komisch.

fur [fə:], *s.* der Pelz, das Fell (*coat of animal*); (*Med.*) der Belag (*on tongue*).

furbelow ['fə:bilou], *s.* die Falbel.

furbish ['fə:biʃ], *v.a.* aufputzen.

furious ['fjuəriəs], *adj.* wild, rasend, wütend.

furl [fə:l], *v.a.* (zusammen-)rollen; (*Naut.*) aufrollen.

furlong ['fə:loŋ], *s.* ein Achtel einer englischen Meile.

furlough ['fə:lou], *s.* der Urlaub.

furnace ['fə:nis], *s.* der Ofen, Hochofen (*steel*); (*Metall.*) der Schmelzofen.

furnish ['fə:niʃ], *v.a.* ausstatten, versehen (*equip*); möblieren (*a room etc.*).

furnisher ['fə:niʃə], *s.* der Möbelhändler; der Lieferant.

furniture ['fə:nitʃə], *s.* die Möbel, *n. pl.*; die Einrichtung.

furrier ['fʌriə], *s.* der Kürschner.

furrow ['fʌrou], *s.* die Furche (*field*); die Runzel (*brow*). — *v.a.* runzeln (*brow*); Furchen ziehen (*plough up*).

further ['fə:ðə], *comp. adj., adv. see* **farther**. — *v.a.* fördern (*advance*).

furtherance ['fə:ðərəns], *s.* die Förderung (*advancement*).

furthermore ['fə:ðəmɔ:], *adv.* ferner.

furthest ['fə:ðist], *superl. adj., adv. see* **farthest**.

furtive ['fə:tiv], *adj.* verstohlen, heimlich.

fury ['fjuəri], *s.* die Wut; (*Myth.*) die Furie.

furze [fə:z], *s.* (*Bot.*) der Stechginster.

fuse [fju:z], *v.a., v.n.* schmelzen (*melt*); vereinigen (*unite*). — *s.* (*Elec.*) die Sicherung; *blow a —*, eine Sicherung durchbrennen; — *box*, der Sicherungskasten; — *wire*, der Schmelzdraht.

fuselage ['fju:zila:ʒ *or* -lidʒ], *s.* (*Aviat.*) der (Flugzeug-)rumpf.

fusible ['fju:zibl], *adj.* schmelzbar.

fusilier [fju:zi'liə], *s.* (*Mil.*) der Füsilier.

fusion ['fju:ʒən], *s.* die Verschmelzung; die Vereinigung.

fuss [fʌs], *s.* das Getue, die Umständlichkeit; *make a — about*, viel Aufhebens machen.

fussy ['fʌsi], *adj.* übertrieben genau; umständlich; geschäftig (*busy*); — *about*, genau in (*Dat.*).

fusty ['fʌsti], *adj.* moderig, muffig.

futile ['fju:tail], *adj.* nutzlos, vergeblich.

futility [fju:'tiliti], *s.* die Nutzlosigkeit.

future ['fju:tʃə], *s.* die Zukunft. — *adj.* (zu-)künftig.

fuzzy ['fʌzi], *adj.* kraus.

G

G [dʒi:]. das G (*also Mus.*); — *sharp*, das Gis; — *flat*, das Ges; *key of —*, der G Schlüssel, Violinschlüssel.

gab [gæb], s. das Geschwätz; *the gift of the* —, ein gutes Mundwerk.

gabble [gæbl], v.n. schwatzen.

gable [geibl], s. der Giebel.

gad [gæd], v.n. — *about*, umherstreifen.

gadfly ['gædflai], s. (Ent.) die Bremse.

gag [gæg], s. der Knebel; (sl.) der Witz. — v.a. knebeln.

gaiety ['geiəti], s. die Fröhlichkeit.

gain [gein], v.a. gewinnen, erwerben (earn); — possession, Besitz ergreifen. — s. der Gewinn, Vorteil.

gainful ['geinful], adj. — employment, die einträgliche Beschäftigung.

gainsay ['geinsei or gein'sei], v.a. widersprechen (pers., Dat.).

gait [geit], s. das Schreiten, der Schritt, Gang.

gaiter ['geitə], s. die Gamasche.

galaxy ['gæləksi], s. (Astron.) die Milchstraße; (fig.) die glänzende Versammlung.

gale [geil], s. der Sturm.

gall [gɔ:l], s. die Galle. — v.a. verbittern, ärgern.

gallant ['gælənt], adj. tapfer (of soldier); gallant, höflich (polite).

gallantry ['gæləntri], s. die Tapferkeit; die Höflichkeit, Galanterie.

gallery ['gæləri], s. die Gallerie.

galley ['gæli], s. (Naut.) die Galeere; (Typ.) — proof, der Fahnenabzug.

gallon ['gælən], s. die Gallone.

gallop ['gæləp], v.n. galoppieren. — s. der Galopp.

gallows ['gælouz], s. der Galgen.

galosh [gə'lɔʃ], s. die Galosche.

galvanic [gæl'vænik], adj. galvanisch.

galvanize ['gælvənaiz], v.a. galvanisieren.

gamble [gæmbl], v.n. um Geld spielen; — away, verspielen. — s. das Risiko.

gambol [gæmbl], v.n. herumspringen.

game [geim], s. das Spiel (play); das Wild, Wildbret (pheasants etc.); fair —, Freiwild, n., offene Beute, f.

gamecock ['geimkɔk], s. (Orn.) der Kampfhahn.

gamekeeper ['geimki:pə], s. der Wildhüter.

gammon ['gæmən], s. der (geräucherte) Schinken (bacon).

gamut ['gæmət], s. die Tonleiter.

gander ['gændə], s. (Orn.) der Gänserich.

gang [gæŋ], s. die Bande; die Mannschaft (workmen). — up, — up, eine Bande bilden; — up on s.o., sich gegen jemanden verbünden.

gangrene ['gæŋgri:n], s. (Med.) der Brand; die Fäulnis.

gangway ['gæŋwei], s. die Planke, der Laufgang (on boat); der Durchgang.

gaol, jail [dʒeil], s. das Gefängnis. — v.a. einsperren.

gaoler, jailer ['dʒeilə], s. der Kerkermeister.

gap [gæp], s. die Lücke; die Bresche (breach).

gape [geip], v.n. gähnen, (fig.) klaffen.

garage ['gærɑ:ʒ or 'gæridʒ], s. die Garage, die Tankstelle.

garb [gɑ:b], s. die Tracht, Kleidung.

garbage ['gɑ:bidʒ], s. der Abfall; (Am.) — can, der Mülleimer.

garble [gɑ:bl], v.a. verstümmeln.

garden ['gɑ:dn], s. der Garten. — v.n. im Garten arbeiten.

gardener ['gɑ:dnə], s. der Gärtner.

gargle [gɑ:gl], v.n. gurgeln, spülen.

gargoyle ['gɑ:gɔil], s. (Archit.) der Wasserspeier.

garish ['gɛəriʃ], adj. grell, auffallend.

garland ['gɑ:lənd], s. der Blumenkranz, die Girlande.

garlic ['gɑ:lik], s. (Bot.) der Knoblauch.

garment ['gɑ:mənt], s. das Gewand.

garner ['gɑ:nə], v.a. aufspeichern (store).

garnet ['gɑ:nit], s. der Granat.

garnish ['gɑ:niʃ], v.a. ausschmücken, verzieren.

garret ['gærət], s. die Dachkammer.

garrison ['gærisən], s. (Mil.) die Garnison. — v.a. stationieren.

garrulity [gæ'ru:liti], s. die Schwatzhaftigkeit.

garter ['gɑ:tə], s. das Strumpfband, das Hosenband; Order of the Garter, der Hosenbandorden.

gas [gæs], s. das Gas; (Am.) see gasoline.

gaseous ['geisiəs], adj. gasförmig, gasartig.

Gascon ['gæskən], s. der Gaskogner.

gasoline ['gæsoli:n], s. (Am.) das Benzin.

gash [gæʃ], s. die Schnittwunde.

gasp [gɑ:sp], v.n. keuchen; nach Luft schnappen. — s. das Keuchen, das Luftschnappen.

gastric ['gæstrik], adj. (Anat.) gastrisch; — ulcer, das Magengeschwür.

gate [geit], s. das Tor, der Eingang. — v.a. einsperren, Hausarrest geben (Dat.).

gateway ['geitwei], s. die Einfahrt.

gather ['gæðə], v.a. sammeln, einsammeln (collect); versammeln (assemble). — v.n. entnehmen, schließen (infer); sich versammeln (come together); aufziehen (storm).

gathering ['gæðəriŋ], s. die Versammlung (meeting).

gauche [gouʃ], adj. linkisch, ungeschickt.

gaudy ['gɔ:di], adj. übertrieben, grell, prunkhaft.

gauge [geidʒ], v.a. (Engin.) ausmessen, kalibrieren; eichen (officially). — s. der Maßstab (scale); (Railw.) die Spurweite.

gauger ['geidʒə], s. der Eichmeister.

Gaul [gɔ:l], s. der Gallier.

gaunt [gɔ:nt], adj. mager; hager.

gauntlet ['gɔ:ntlit], s. der (Panzer)handschuh.

gauze [gɔ:z], s. die Gaze.

gavotte [gə'vɔt], s. (Mus.) die Gavotte.

gay [gei], *adj.* fröhlich, heiter; bunt (*colour*).

gaze [geiz], *v.n.* starren.

gazelle [gə'zel], *s.* (*Zool.*) die Gazelle.

gazette [gə'zet], *s.* die (amtliche) Zeitung; das Amtsblatt.

gear [giə], *s.* das Gerät; (*Mech.*) das Triebwerk; (*Naut.*) das Geschirr; *switch*—, das Schaltgerät; (*Motor.*) der Gang; — *ratio*, die Übersetzung; *differential* —, der Achsenantrieb; *steering* —, die Lenkung (*of car*); — *box*, das Schaltgetriebe, die Gangschaltung; *out of* —, in Unordnung; *in top* —, mit Höchstgeschwindigkeit; *change to bottom* —, auf erste Geschwindigkeit (*or*, auf langsam) einschalten. — *v.a.* — *down*, herabsetzen. (*Engin.*) — *up*, übersetzen; — *to*, anpassen.

gelatine ['dʒeləti:n], *s.* die Gallerte, die Geleemasse.

gem [dʒem], *s.* die Gemme, der Edelstein.

gender ['dʒendə], *s.* (*Gram.*) das Geschlecht.

gene [dʒi:n], *s.* (*Biol.*) das Gen.

geneaology [dʒi:ni'ælədʒi], *s.* die Genealogie; der Stammbaum (*family tree*).

general ['dʒenərəl], *s.* (*Mil.*) der General; *lieutenant* —, der Generalleutnant. — *adj.* allgemein, General-; — *purpose*, für alle Zwecke; *Allzweck*-.

generalization [dʒenərəlai'zeiʃən], *s.* die Verallgemeinerung.

generalize ['dʒenərəlaiz], *v.a.* verallgemeinern.

generate ['dʒenəreit], *v.a.* erzeugen; (*Elec.*) Strom erzeugen.

generation [dʒenə'reiʃən], *s.* die Generation (*contemporaries*); das Zeugen (*production*); (*Elec.*) die Stromerzeugung.

generosity [dʒenə'rositi], *s.* die Großmut (*magnanimity*); die Freigebigkeit (*liberality*).

generous ['dʒenərəs], *adj.* großmütig; freigebig (*with gifts*).

Genevan [dʒi'ni:vən], *adj.* genferisch. — *s.* der Genfer.

genitive ['dʒenitiv], *s.* (*Gram.*) der Wesfall, Genitiv.

genial [dʒi:niəl], *adj.* freundlich, mild.

geniality [dʒi:ni'æliti], *s.* die Freundlichkeit, Leutseligkeit.

genital [dʒenitəl], *adj.* Zeugungs-. — *s.* (*pl.*) die Geschlechtsteile, Genitalien, *pl.*

genius ['dʒi:niəs], *s.* das Genie; der Genius.

Genoese [dʒenou'i:z], *adj.* genuesisch. — *s.* der Genuese.

Gentile ['dʒentail], *s.* heidnisch; nicht jüdisch.

gentility [dʒen'tiliti], *s.* die Herkunft aus vornehmem Haus, Vornehmheit.

gentle [dʒentl], *adj.* sanft, mild; gelind (*breeze*).

gentlefolk ['dʒentlfouk], *s.* bessere *or* vornehme Leute, *pl.*

gentleman ['dʒentlmən], *s.* der Gentleman, Herr; feiner Herr.

gentleness ['dʒentlnis], *s.* die Milde, Sanftheit.

gentry ['dʒentri], *s.* der niedere Adel.

genuine ['dʒenjuin], *adj.* echt.

genus ['dʒenəs], *s.* (*Biol.*) die Gattung.

geographer [dʒi'ɔgrəfə], *s.* der Geograph.

geographical [dʒi:o'græfikəl], *adj.* geographisch.

geography [dʒi'ɔgrəfi], die Geographie, Erdkunde.

geological [dʒi:o'lɔdʒikəl], *adj.* geologisch.

geologist [dʒi'ɔlədʒist], *s.* der Geologe.

geology [dʒi'ɔlədʒi], *s.* (*Biol.*) die Geologie.

geometric(al) [dʒi:o'metrik(əl)], *adj.* geometrisch.

geometrist [dʒi'ɔmətrist], *s.* der Geometer.

geometry [dʒi'ɔmətri], *s.* die Geometrie.

geranium [dʒə'reiniəm], *s.* (*Bot.*) die Geranie, das Germaniu.

germ [dʒə:m], *s.* der Keim; (*pl.*) die Bakterien, *f. pl.*

German ['dʒə:mən], *adj.* deutsch. — *s.* der, die Deutsche.

germane [dʒə:'mein], *adj.* zur Sache gehörig, zugehörig.

germinate ['dʒə:mineit], *v.n.* keimen.

Germanic [dʒə:'mænik], *adj.* germanisch.

gerund ['dʒerənd], *s.* (*Gram.*) das Gerundium.

gerundive [dʒe'rʌndiv], *s.* (*Gram.*) das Gerundiv(um).

gesticulate [dʒes'tikjuleit], *v.n.* Gebärden machen, gestikulieren.

gesture ['dʒestʃə], *s.* die Geste; der Gebärde.

get [get], *v.a.* irr. bekommen, (*coll.*) kriegen; erhalten (*receive*); erwischen (*catch up with*); einholen (*fetch*); — *over* or *across*, klar machen. — *v.n.* gelangen (*arrive*); werden (*become*); — *along*, weiterkommen; — *on* or (*Am.*) *along with s.o.*, mit jemandem auskommen; — *on in the world*, Karriere machen; — *away*, entkommen; — *down to it*, zur Sache kommen; — *in*, hineinkommen; — *off*, aussteigen; *show s.o. where he* — *s off*, jemandem seine Meinung sagen; (*Sch.*) — *through*, durchkommen (*in examination*); — *up*, aufstehen.

get-up ['getʌp], *s.* das Kostüm; die Ausstattung (*attire*).

Ghanaian [gɑ:'neiən], *adj.* ghanaisch. — *s.* der Ghanaer.

ghastly ['gɑ:stli], *adj.* furchtbar, schrecklich.

gherkin ['gə:kin], *s.* (*Bot.*) die Essiggurke.

ghost [goust], *s.* der Geist, das Gespenst.

giant ['dʒaiənt], *s.* der Riese.

gibberish ['dʒibəriʃ], *s.* das Kauderwelsch.

gibbet ['dʒibit], *s.* der Galgen.

gibe [dʒaib], *v.n.* spotten, höhnen (*at*, über, *Acc.*). — *s.* der Spott, Hohn; die spöttische Bemerkung (*remark*).

giblets [ˈdʒiblits], *s. pl.* das Gänseklein.

giddiness [ˈgidinis], *s.* das Schwindelgefühl.

giddy [ˈgidi], *adj.* schwindelig.

gift [gift], *s.* die Gabe, das Geschenk.

gifted [ˈgiftid], *adj.* begabt.

gig [gig], *s.* der leichte Wagen; (*Naut.*) der Nachen, das Gig.

gigantic [dʒaiˈgæntik], *adj.* riesig, riesengroß.

giggle [gigl], *v.n.* kichern. — *s.* das Kichern, Gekicher.

gild [gild], *v.a.* vergolden; verschönern; —*ing the pill*, etwas Unangenehmes (die Pille) versüßen.

gill (1) [gil], *s.* (*Biol.*) die Kieme.

gill (2) [dʒil], *s.* das Viertel einer Pinte (0.14 *l.*).

gilt [gilt], *s.* die Vergoldung; — *edged*, mit Goldschnitt; (*Comm.*) hochwertige *or* mündelsichere Staatspapiere.

gimlet [ˈgimlit], *s.* (*Carp.*) der Handbohrer.

gin [dʒin], *s.* der Gin, der Wachholderbranntwein; — *and tonic*, Gin und Tonic.

ginger [ˈdʒindʒə], *s.* der Ingwer; — *haired*, rothaarig; — *nut*, das Ingwer- *or* Pfeffernüßchen, Ingwerkeks; — *beer*, Ingwerbier. — *v.a.* — *up*, aufstacheln, anreizen.

gingerbread [ˈdʒindʒəbred], *s.* der Lebkuchen, Pfefferkuchen.

gipsy [ˈdʒipsi], *s.* der Zigeuner.

giraffe [dʒiˈrɑːf], *s.* (*Zool.*) die Giraffe.

gird [gəːd], *v.a. reg. & irr.* (*Poet.*) gürten.

girder [ˈgəːdə], *s.* der Balken, Träger.

girdle [ˈgəːdl], *v.a.* gürten, umgürten; — *the earth*, die Erde umkreisen.

girl [gəːl], *s.* das Mädchen.

girlhood [ˈgəːlhud], *s.* die Mädchenzeit, die Mädchenjahre, *n. pl.*

girlish [ˈgəːliʃ], *adj.* mädchenhaft, wie ein Mädchen.

gist [dʒist], *s.* das Wesentliche.

give [giv], *v.a. irr.* geben; — *out*, bekanntgeben, bekanntmachen; — *up*, aufgeben; — *way to*, Platz machen. — *v.n.* sich dehnen, sich strecken (*of wood, metal etc.*); — *in*, nachgeben (*to*, *Dat.*).

glacial [ˈgleisəl], *adj.* eisig, Gletscher-.

glacier [ˈglæsiə], *s.* der Gletscher.

glad [glæd], *adj.* froh, erfreut (*at*, über, *Acc.*).

gladden [glædn], *v.a.* erheitern, erfreuen.

glade [gleid], *s.* die Lichtung.

glamorous [ˈglæmərəs], *adj.* bezaubernd, blendend glanzvoll.

glamour [ˈglæmə], *s.* der Zauber; der Glanz.

glance [glɑːns], *s.* der Blick; *at a* —, auf den ersten Blick. — *v.n.* flüchtig blicken.

gland [glænd], *s.* (*Anat.*) die Drüse.

glandular [ˈglændjulə], *adj.* Drüsen-, drüsig.

glare [glɛə], *s.* der blendende Glanz, das Schimmern; der (scharf durchbohrende Blick (*stare*).

glaring [ˈglɛəriŋ], *adj.* schreiend (*of colour*); auffallend (*obvious*).

glass [glɑːs], *s.* das Glas; der Spiegel (*mirror*); das Wetterglas (*barometer*); (*pl.*) die Brille (*spectacles*).

glassblower [ˈglɑːsbləuə], *s.* der Glasbläser.

glassworks [ˈglɑːswəːks], *s.* die Glashütte.

glassy [ˈglɑːsi], *adj.* gläsern.

glaze [gleiz], *s.* die Glasur. — *v.a.* glasieren; verglasen.

glazier [ˈgleiziə], *s.* der Glaser.

gleam [gliːm], *v.n.* strahlen, glänzen (*with*, vor, *Dat.*). — *s.* der Glanz, das Strahlen.

glean [gliːn], *v.a.* auflesen; erfahren (*learn*).

glebe [gliːb], *s.* das Pfarrgut.

glee (1) [gliː], *s.* die Freude, Heiterkeit.

glee (2) [gliː], *s.* (*Mus.*) der Rundgesang; — *club*, die Liedertafel.

glen [glen], *s.* das enge Tal.

glib [glib], *adj.* glatt, geläufig, zungenfertig.

glide [glaid], *v.n.* gleiten. — *s.* das Gleiten.

glider [ˈglaidə], *s.* (*Aviat.*) das Segelflugzeug.

glimmer [ˈglimə], *s.* der Schimmer, Glimmer. — *v.n.* schimmern, glimmen.

glimpse [glimps], *s.* der (flüchtige) Blick; *catch a* —, einen Blick erhaschen. — *v.a.* flüchtig blicken (auf, *Acc.*).

glisten [glisn], *v.n.* glitzern, glänzen.

glitter [ˈglitə], *v.n.* glänzen, schimmern.

gloaming [ˈgloumin], *s.* die Dämmerung.

globe [gloub], *s.* der Globus, der Erdball; die Kugel.

globular [ˈglobjulə], *adj.* kugelförmig.

gloom [gluːm], *s.* das Dunkel; der Trübsinn, die Traurigkeit.

gloomy [ˈgluːmi], *adj.* deprimiert, trübsinnig, düster.

glorify [ˈglɔːrifai], *v.a.* verherrlichen.

glorious [ˈglɔːriəs], *adj.* herrlich; (*Mil.*) glorreich.

glory [ˈglɔːri], *s.* die Herrlichkeit, der Ruhm. — *v.n.* frohlocken (*in*, über, *Acc.*).

gloss [glos], *s.* der Glanz; (*Lit.*) die Glosse, Anmerkung. — *v.a.* — *over*, beschönigen; (*Lit.*) glossieren, mit Anmerkungen versehen.

glossary [ˈglosəri], *s.* das Glossar, die Spezialwörterliste; das Wörterbuch.

glossy [ˈglosi], *adj.* glänzend.

glove [glʌv], *s.* der Handschuh.

glow [glou], *v.n.* glühen. — *s.* die Glut, das Glühen; Wohlbehagen.

glower [ˈglauə], *v.n.* — *at*, feindselig ansehen, anstarren.

glue

glue [glu:], *s.* der Leim. — *v.a.* leimen, zusammenleimen.

glum [glʌm], *adj.* mürrisch, finster.

glut [glʌt], *s.* die Überfülle. — *v.a.* überladen, überfüllen.

glutinous ['glu:tinəs], *adj.* zähe, klebrig.

glutton [glʌtn], *s.* der Vielfraß.

gluttony ['glʌtəni], *s.* die Schwelgerei, Gefräßigkeit.

glycerine ['glisəri:n], *s.* das Glyzerin.

gnarled [nɑ:ld], *adj.* knorrig.

gnash [næʃ], *v.a.* knirschen (*teeth*).

gnat [næt], *s.* (*Ent.*) die Mücke.

gnaw [nɔ:], *v.a., v.n.* nagen (an, *Dat.*), zernagen, zerfressen (at, *Acc.*).

gnome [noum], *s.* der Erdgeist, der Zwerg, Gnom.

go [gou], *v.n. irr.* gehen, fahren, laufen; arbeiten (*engine*); verlaufen (*event*); sich erstrecken (*distance*); — *down in the general esteem*, in der Achtung sinken; — *on*, fortfahren; — *mad*, verrückt werden; — *bald*, die Haare verlieren; — *without*, leer ausgehen, entbehren; *let* —, loslassen; — *for*, auf jemanden losgehen; — *in for*, sich interessieren für (*Acc.*); — *all out for*, energisch unternehmen; *a* —*ing concern*, ein gutgehendes Unternehmen; —*ing on for 20*, fast 20 Jahre. — *s.* der Versuch; (*coll.*) *plenty of* —, recht lebhaft, voller Schwung.

goad [goud], *v.a.* anstacheln.

goal [goul], *s.* das Ziel; (*Footb.*) das Tor.

goalkeeper ['goulki:pə], *s.* der Torwart.

goalpost ['goulpoust], *s.* der Torpfosten.

goat [gout], *s.* (*Zool.*) die Geiß, Ziege; *billy* —, der Ziegenbock; *nanny* —, die Geiß.

gobble [gɔbl], *v.a.* verschlingen, gierig essen.

goblet ['gɔblit], *s.* der Becher.

goblin ['gɔblin], *s.* der Kobold, der Gnom; der Schelm.

go-cart ['gouka:t], *s.* der Kinderwagen, Gängelwagen.

God [gɔd], *s.* Gott.

god [gɔd], *s.* der Gott.

godchild ['gɔdtʃaild], *s.* das Patenkind.

goddess ['gɔdes], *s.* die Göttin.

godfather ['gɔdfɑ:ðə], *s.* der Pate.

godhead ['gɔdhed], *s.* die Gottheit.

godless ['gɔdlis], *adj.* gottlos, ungläubig.

godmother ['gɔdmʌðə], *s.* die Patin.

goggle [gɔgl], *v.n.* glotzen, starren (*stare*). — *s.* (*pl.*) die Schutzbrille.

going ['gouiŋ], *s.* das Gehen, das Funktionieren (*of machinery*); *while the* — *is good*, zur rechten Zeit.

gold [gould], *s.* das Gold; (*Fin.*) — *standard*, die Goldwährung.

goldfinch ['gouldfintʃ], *s.* (*Orn.*) der Stieglitz.

goldsmith ['gouldsmiθ], *s.* der Goldschmied.

gondola ['gɔndələ], *s.* die Gondel.

good [gud], *adj.* gut; artig, brav; *for* —, auf immer; *in* — *time*, rechtzeitig; — *and proper*, (*coll.*) wie es sich gehört, anständig; *as* — *as*, so gut wie; — *looking*, hübsch; — *natured*, gutmütig. — *s. for your own* —, in Ihrem eigenen Interesse; *that's no* —, das taugt nichts; (*pl.*) die Güter, *n.pl.*, Waren, *f.pl.*; *goods station*, der Frachbahnhof; *goods train*, der Güterzug; *goods yard*, der Güterstapelplatz.

goodbye [gud'bai], *interj.*, *s.*—! leb wohl! auf Wiedersehen!

goodness ['gudnis], *s.* die Güte.

goodwill [gud'wil], *s.* das Wohlwollen; (*Comm.*) die Kundschaft.

goose [gu:s], *s.* (*Orn.*) die Gans.

gooseberry ['guzbəri], *s.* (*Bot.*) die Stachelbeere.

gore [gɔ:], *s.* das geronnene Blut. — *v.a.* durchbohren (*pierce, stab*).

gorge [gɔ:dʒ], *s.* die Felsenschlucht (*ravine*); (*Anat.*) die Kehle. — *v.a.* gierig verschlingen.

gorgeous ['gɔ:dʒəs], *adj.* prachtvoll, prächtig.

gorse [gɔ:s], *s.* (*Bot.*) der Stechginster.

gory ['gɔ:ri], *adj.* blutig.

goshawk ['gɔshɔ:k], *s.* (*Orn.*) der Hühnerhabicht.

gosling ['gɔzliŋ], *s.* (*Orn.*) das Gänschen.

gospel ['gɔspəl], *s.* das Evangelium; *the*— *according to*, das Evangelium des . . .

gossamer ['gɔsəmə], *s.* das feine Gewebe; die Sommerfäden.

gossip ['gɔsip], *v.n.* klatschen; schwatzen, plaudern. — *s.* der Klatsch; der Schwätzer; die Klatschbase.

Gothic ['gɔθik], *adj.* gotisch.

gouge [gaudʒ], *s.* der Hohlmeißel. — *v.a.* aushöhlen, ausstechen.

gourd [guəd], *s.* der Kürbis.

gout [gaut], *s.* (*Med.*) die Gicht.

govern ['gʌvən], *v.a., v.n.* (*Pol.*) regieren; beherrschen; (*fig.*) leiten, herrschen.

governable ['gʌvənəbl], *adj.* lenkbar, lenksam.

governess ['gʌvənis], *s.* die Erzieherin, die Gouvernante.

government ['gʌvənmənt], *s.* die Regierung; (*Pol.*) — *benches*, die Regierungssitze; — *loan*, die Staatsanleihe.

governor ['gʌvənə], *s.* der Gouverneur, Statthalter.

gown [gaun], *s.* das Kleid (*lady's*); (*Univ.*) der Talar; (*official robe*) die Amtstracht.

grab [græb], *v.a.* packen, ergreifen. — *s.* der Zugriff.

grace [greis], *s.* die Gnade; Gunst (*favour*); die Anmut (*gracefulness*); *Your Grace*, Euer Gnaden; das Tischgebet (*prayer at table*); (*Mus.*) — *note*, die Fermate; *ten minutes'* —, zehn Minuten Aufschub. — *v.a.* schmücken, zieren, ehren.

graceful ['greisful], *adj.* anmutig, reizend; graziös (*movement*).

great

graceless ['greislis], *adj.* ungraziös.
gracious ['greiʃəs],*adj.*gnädig,huldreich.
gradation [grə'deiʃən], *s.* die Abstufung, die Stufenleiter.
grade [greid], *s.* der Grad, Rang (*rank*); (*Am.*) (*Sch.*) die Klasse. — *v.a.* sortieren, ordnen.
gradient ['greidiənt], *s.* (*Geog.*) die Steigung (*angle*).
gradual ['grædjuəl], *adj.* allmählich.
graduate ['grædjueit], *v.n.* promovieren (*receive degree*); — *as a doctor*, als Doktor promovieren, den Doktor machen.—[-djuit], *s.* der Akademiker, Graduierte.
graft (1) [grɑ:ft], *s.* (*Hort., Med.*) die (Haut)übertragung. — *v.a.* (*Hort., Med.*) übertragen, anheften (*on to*, auf, *Acc.*).
graft (2) [grɑ:ft], *s.* (*Am.*) der unerlaubte Gewinn; das Schmiergeld; der Betrug (*swindle*).
grain [grein], *s.* das Korn, Samenkorn; das Getreide; das Gran (= 0·065 *gramme*); die Maserung (*in wood*); *against the* —, gegen den Strich.
grammar ['græmə], *s.* die Grammatik; — *school*, das Gymnasium.
grammatical [grə'mætikəl], *adj.* grammatisch.
gramme [græm], *s.* das Gramm.
gramophone ['græməfoun], *s.* das Grammophon.
granary ['grænəri], *s.* der (Korn-)speicher, die Kornkammer.
grand [grænd], *adj.* groß, großartig; wunderbar; *Grand Duke*, der Großherzog. — *s.* (*Am.*) (*sl.*) 1000 Dollar; (*piano*) der Flügel; *baby* —, der Stutzflügel.
grandchild ['grændtʃaild], *s.* der Enkel, die Enkelin.
grandee [græn'di:], *s.* der spanische Grande.
grandeur ['grændjə], *s.* die Größe, Pracht.
grandfather ['grændfɑ:ðə], *s.* der Großvater.
grandiloquent [græn'dilokwənt], *adj.* großsprecherisch.
grandmother ['grændmʌðə], *s.* die Großmutter.
grange [greindʒ], *s.* der Meierhof, das Landhaus.
granite ['grænit], *s.* der Granit.
grannie, granny ['græni], *s.* (*coll.*) die Oma.
grant [grɑ:nt], *s.* die Gewährung (*of permission etc.*); die Zuwendung (*subsidy*); (*Sch.*) das Stipendium. — *v.a.* geben, gewähren; *take for* —*ed*, als selbstverständlich hinnehmen.
granular ['grænjulə], *adj.* körnig.
granulated ['grænjuleitid], *adj.* feinkörnig, Kristall- (*sugar*).
grape [greip], *s.* (*Bot.*) die Weinbeere; die Traube; — *sugar*, der Traubenzucker; *bunch of* —*s*,Weintrauben, *f. pl.*
grapefruit ['greipfru:t], *s.* die Pampelmuse.

graphic ['græfik], *adj.* (*Art*) graphisch; deutlich, bildhaft, anschaulich.
grapnel ['græpnəl], *s.* (*Naut.*) der Dreganker.
grapple [græpl], *v.n.* — *with*, raufen, (miteinander) ringen.
grasp [grɑ:sp], *v.a.* (mit der Hand) ergreifen, erfassen. — *s.* das Fassungsvermögen, die Auffassung; der Griff (*hand*).
grasping ['grɑ:spiŋ], *adj.* habgierig, gewinnsüchtig.
grass [grɑ:s], *s.* (*Bot.*) das Gras; der Rasen (*lawn*); — *widow*, die Strohwitwe.
grasshopper ['grɑ:shopə], *s.* (*Ent.*) die Heuschrecke.
grate (1) [greit], *s.* der Feuerrost, der Kamin.
grate (2) [greit], *v.a.* reiben (*cheese*); schaben, kratzen. — *v.n.* knirschen; auf die Nerven gehen.
grateful ['greitful], *adj.* dankbar.
grater ['greitə], *s.* das Reibeisen; die Reibe (*electrical*).
gratification [grætifi'keiʃən], *s.* die Genugtuung, Befriedigung.
gratify ['grætifai], *v.a.* befriedigen, erfreuen.
grating ['greitiŋ], *s.* das Gitter.
gratis ['greitis], *adv.* gratis, umsonst, frei, unentgeltlich.
gratitude ['grætitju:d], *s.* die Dankbarkeit.
gratuitous [grə'tju:itəs], *adj.* frei, freiwillig (*voluntary*); unentgeltlich (*free of charge*); grundlos (*baseless*).
gratuity [grə'tju:iti], *s.* das Trinkgeld (*tip*); die Gratifikation.
grave (1) [greiv], *adj.* schwer, ernst (*serious*); feierlich (*solemn*). —*s.* (*Mus.*) das Grave.
grave (2) [greiv], *s.* das Grab (*tomb*).
gravel [grævl], *s.* der Kies.
graveyard ['greivjɑ:d], *s.* der Friedhof.
gravitate ['græviteit], *v.n.* gravitieren, hinstreben.
gravitation [grævi'teiʃən], *s.* die Schwerkraft.
gravitational [grævi'teiʃənəl], *adj.* (*Phys.*) Schwerkrafts-.
gravity ['græviti], *s.* der Ernst (*seriousness*); (*Phys.*) die Schwere, Schwerkraft.
gravy ['greivi], *s.* die Sauce, Soße; der Saft des Fleisches, des Bratens; — *boat*, die Sauciere.
gray, grey [grei], *adj.* grau.
graze (1) [greiz], *v.n.* weiden.
graze (2) [greiz], *v.a.* streifen (*pass closely*), abschürfen.
grazier ['greiziə], *s.* der Viehzüchter.
grease [gri:s], *s.* das Fett; das Schmieröl (*machine*). — *v.a.* einfetten (*pans*); schmieren, einschmieren (*machinery*).
greasy ['gri:si], *adj.* fett, schmierig, ölig.
great [greit], *adj.* groß, bedeutend, wichtig; (*Am.*) wundervoll, wunderbar.

405

greatcoat ['greitcout], *s.* der Wintermantel.

great-grandfather [greit'grændfɑːðə], *s.* der Urgroßvater.

greatly ['greitli], *adv.* stark, sehr.

greatness ['greitnis], *s.* die Größe, Bedeutung.

greedy ['griːdi], *adj.* gierig; gefräßig (*eater*).

Greek [griːk], *adj.* griechisch. — *s.* der Grieche.

green [griːn], *adj.* grün; neu (*new*), frisch (*fresh*).

greengage ['griːngeidʒ], *s.* (*Bot.*) die Reineclaude.

greengrocer ['griːngrousə], *s.* der Grünwarenhändler, Gemüsehändler.

greenhorn ['griːnhɔːn], *s.* der Grünschnabel.

greenhouse ['griːnhaus], *s.* das Gewächshaus, Treibhaus.

Greenlander ['griːnləndə], *s.* der Grönländer.

greet [griːt], *v.a.* grüßen, begrüßen.

greeting ['griːtiŋ], *s.* die Begrüßung; (*pl.*) Grüße, *m. pl.*

gregarious [gri'gɛəriəs], *adj.* gesellig.

grenade [gri'neid], *s.* die Granate.

grey *see under* **gray**.

greyhound ['greihaund], *s.* (*Zool.*) der Windspiel, der Windhund.

grid [grid], *s.* (*Elec.*) das Stromnetz; (*Phys.*) das Gitter.

gridiron ['gridaiən], *s.* der Bratrost, das Bratrostgitter.

grief [griːf], *s.* der Kummer, die Trauer.

grievance ['griːvəns], *s.* die Klage, Beschwerde.

grieve [griːv], *v.a.* kränken. — *v.n.* sich grämen, sich kränken (*over*, über, *Acc.*, wegen, *Genit.*).

grievous ['griːvəs], *adj.* schmerzlich.

grill [gril], *s.* der Rostbraten, Bratrost. — *v.a.* grillieren, rösten (*meat*); verhören (*question closely*).

grilling ['griliŋ], *s.* das Verhör.

grim [grim], *adj.* grimmig, finster.

grimace [gri'meis], *s.* die Grimasse, die Fratze.

grime [graim], *s.* der Schmutz, der Ruß.

grimy ['graimi], *adj.* schmutzig, rußig.

grin [grin], *v.n.* grinsen; (*coll.*) — *and bear it*, mach gute Miene zum bösen Spiel. — *s.* das Grinsen.

grind [graind], *v.a. irr.* zerreiben (*rub*); schleifen (*sharpen*); mahlen (*pulverize*); — *o.'s teeth*, mit den Zähnen knirschen. — *s.* (*coll.*) die ungeheure Anstrengung, die Plackerei.

grinder ['graində], *s. coffee* —, die Kaffeemühle; *knife* —, der Schleifer, Wetzer; der Backzahn (*molar*).

grindstone ['graindstoun], *s.* der Schleifstein; *keep o.'s nose to the* —, fest bei der Arbeit bleiben.

grip [grip], *s.* der Griff; *lose o.'s* —, nicht mehr bewältigen können (wie bisher); (*Tech.*) der Handgriff (*handle*). — *v.a.* ergreifen, festhalten.

gripe [graip], *v.n.* (*sl.*) meckern.

gripes [graips], *s. pl.* (*Med.*) das Bauchgrimmen, die Kolik.

gripping ['gripiŋ], *adj.* fesselnd (*story*).

grisly ['grizli], *adj.* scheußlich, gräßlich.

grist [grist], *s.* das Mahlgut, Gemahlene; — *to o.'s mill*, Wasser auf seine Mühle.

gristle ['grisl], *s.* der Knorpel.

grit [grit], *s.* das Schrot, der Kies; der Mut (*courage*).

gritty ['griti], *adj.* körnig, kiesig, sandig.

grizzled [grizld], *adj.* grau, graumeliert.

groan [groun], *v.n.* stöhnen.

groats [grouts], *s. pl.* die Hafergrütze.

grocer ['grousə], *s.* der Kolonialwarenhändler, Feinkosthändler.

groin [grɔin], *s.* (*Anat.*) die Leiste; (*Archit.*) die Gewölbekante, Rippe.

groom [gruːm], *s.* der Stallknecht (*stables*); (*obs.*) der Junge (*inn*). — *v.a.* schniegeln, bürsten; schön machen.

groove [gruːv], *s.* die Rinne; die Rille (*of gramophone record*). — *v.a.* rillen; furchen (*dig a furrow*).

grope [group], *v.n.* tappen, tasten (*around*, umher).

gross [grous], *adj.* dick (*fat*); plump (*heavy-handed*); grob (*ill-mannered*); — *weight*, das Bruttogewicht; ungeheuer (*error*).

grotto ['grotou], *s.* die Grotte.

ground [graund], *s.* der Grund, Boden (*also pl.*); die Ursache (*cause*); — *floor*, das Erdgeschoß. — *v.n.* stranden (*of ship*).

groundwork ['graundwəːk], *s.* die Grundlagen, *f. pl.*

group [gruːp], *s.* die Gruppe. — *v.a.* gruppieren, anordnen.

grouse (1) [graus], *v.n.* (*coll.*) meckern, sich beklagen. — *s.* der Grund zur Klage, die Beschwerde.

grouse (2) [graus], *s.* (*Orn.*) das Birkhuhn, Moorhuhn.

grove [grouv], *s.* der Hain, das Wäldchen.

grovel [grɔvl], *v.n.* kriechen, schöntun (*Dat.*).

grow [grou], *v.n. irr.* wachsen, sich mehren (*increase*); werden (*become*). — *v.a.* anbauen, anpflanzen.

growl [graul], *v.n.* brummen, knurren. — *s.* das Gebrumme, Geknurre.

grown-up [groun'ʌp], *s.* der Erwachsene. — *adj.* erwachsen.

growth [grouθ], *s.* das Anwachsen (*increase*); das Wachstum (*growing*).

grub [grʌb], *s.* (*Zool.*) die Larve; (*coll.*) das Essen. — *about*, wühlen.

grudge [grʌdʒ], *s.* der Groll; Neid (*jealousy*). — *v.a.* mißgönnen (*envy*). — *v.n.* — *doing s.th.*, etwas ungerne tun.

gruel ['gruːəl], *s.* der Haferschleim.

gruesome ['gruːsəm], *adj.* schauerlich, schrecklich.

gruff [grʌf], *adj.* mürrisch.

grumble [grʌmbl], *v.n.* murren, klagen.

grumbler ['grʌmblə], s. der Unzufriedene, Nörgler.

grunt [grʌnt], v.n. grunzen. — s. das Grunzen.

guarantee [gærən'ti:], v.a. bürgen, garantieren. — s. die Bürgschaft; (Comm.) die Garantie.

guarantor ['gærəntɔ:], s. der Bürge; der Garant.

guard [ga:d], s. die Wache (watch or watchman); (Railw.) der Schaffner; die Schutzvorrichtung (protective device); (fire) —, das Kamingitter ; (for sword) das Stichblatt. — v.a. bewachen; behüten (protect). — v.n. auf der Hut sein; — against, sich hüten (vor, Dat.); vorbeugen.

guarded ['ga:did], adj. behutsam, vorsichtig.

guardian ['ga:djən], s. der Vormund (of child); der Wächter.

guardianship ['ga:djənʃip], s. (Law) die Vormundschaft.

Guatemalan [gwæti'ma:lən], adj. guatemaltekisch. — s. der Guatemalteke.

Guelph [gwelf], s. der Welfe.

guess [ges], v.a. raten (a riddle). — v.n. (Am.) glauben, meinen. — s. die Vermutung; have a —, rate mal!

guest [gest], s. der Gast; paying —, der Pensionär.

guffaw [gʌ'fɔ:], s. das (laute) Gelächter.

guidance ['gaidəns], s. die Führung, Anleitung.

guide [gaid], s. der Führer, Wegweiser, Reiseführer; (Phot.) die Führung. — v.a. führen, anleiten.

guided ['gaidid], adj. gelenkt; — missile, das Ferngeschoß, die Rakete.

guild [gild], s. die Gilde, Zunft, Innung.

guildhall ['gildhɔ:l], s. das Rathaus.

guile [gail], s. der Betrug, die Arglist.

guileless ['gaillis], adj. arglos.

guilt [gilt], s. die Schuld.

guilty ['gilti], adj. schuldig.

guinea ['gini], s. die Guinee (21 shillings); — fowl, das Perlhuhn; — pig, das Meerschweinchen.

guise [gaiz], s. die Verkleidung (costume); die Erscheinung (appearance).

guitar [gi'ta:], s. (Mus.) die Gitarre.

gulf [gʌlf], s. der Meerbusen, Golf; der Abgrund (abyss).

gull [gʌl], s. (Orn.) die Möwe.

gullet ['gʌlit], s. (Anat.) der Schlund, die Gurgel.

gullible ['gʌlibl], adj. leichtgläubig.

gully ['gʌli], s. die Schlucht (abyss).

gulp [gʌlp], v.a. schlucken. — s. der Schluck, Zug.

gum (1) [gʌm], s. (Bot.) das Gummi. — v.a. gummieren, (coll.) — up, verderben (spoil).

gum (2) [gʌm], s. (Anat.) das Zahnfleisch.

gun [gʌn], s. das Gewehr (rifle); die Kanone (cannon); — carriage, die Lafette.

gunpowder ['gʌnpaudə], s. das Schießpulver.

gunsmith ['gʌnsmiθ], s. der Büchsenmacher.

gurgle [gə:gl], v.n. glucksen.

gush [gʌʃ], v.n. sich ergießen; schwärmen.

gusset ['gʌsit], s. (Tail.) der Zwickel.

gust [gʌst], s. der Windstoß.

gut [gʌt], s. (Anat.) der Darm; (pl.) die Eingeweide, n. pl.; (coll.) der Mut. — v.a. ausnehmen; ausleeren.

gutter ['gʌtə], s. die Rinne, Gosse.

guttersnipe ['gʌtəsnaip], s. der Lausbube.

guttural ['gʌtərəl], adj. Kehl-. — s. (Phon.) der Kehllaut.

guy [gai], s. die Vogelscheuche, die verkleidete Puppe; (Am.) der Kerl.

guzzle [gʌzl], v.n. schlemmen.

gymnasium [dʒim'neiziəm], s. die Turnhalle.

gymnastics [dʒim'næstiks], s. pl. das Turnen; die Gymnastik.

gypsum ['dʒipsəm], s. der Gips; der schwefelsaure Kalk.

gyrate [dʒaiə'reit], v.n. sich im Kreise bewegen, sich drehen, kreisen.

H

H [eitʃ], das H.

haberdasher ['hæbədæʃə], s. der Kurzwarenhändler.

haberdashery ['hæbədæʃəri], s. die Kurzwarenhandlung.

habit ['hæbit], s. die Gewohnheit (custom); force of —, aus Gewohnheit, die Macht der Gewohnheit; die Kleidung (costume); riding —, das Reitkostüm.

habitable ['hæbitəbl], adj. bewohnbar.

habitation [hæbi'teiʃən], s. die Wohnung.

habitual [hə'bitjuəl], adj. gewohnheitsmäßig.

habituate [hə'bitjueit], v.a. gewöhnen.

hack (1) [hæk], v.a. hacken (wood); treten.

hack (2) [hæk], s. der Lohnschreiber; der (alte) Gaul, das Mietpferd (horse).

hackle [hækl], v.a. hecheln.

hackney ['hækni], s. — carriage, die Mietskutsche; das Taxi.

haddock ['hædək], s. (Zool.) der Schellfisch.

haemorrhage ['heməridʒ], s. (Med.) die Blutung, der Blutsturz.

haemorrhoids ['hemərɔidz], s.pl.(Med.) die Hämorrhoiden, f. pl.

hag [hæg], s. das alte Weib; die Hexe (witch).

haggard

haggard ['hægəd], *adj.* hager (*lean*); häßlich, abgehärmt.

haggle [hægl], *v.n.* feilschen.

haggler ['hæglə], *s.* der Feilscher. — *v.n.*

hail (1) [heil], *s.* der Hagel. — *v.n.* hageln.

hail (2) [heil], *v.a.* (mit einem Ruf) begrüßen; rufen. — *interj.* Heil, willkommen! — *s.* der Zuruf, Gruß.

hair [hɛə], *s.* das Haar; *split* —*s*, Haarspalterei treiben.

haircut ['hɛəkʌt], *s.* der Haarschnitt.

hairdresser ['hɛədresə], *s.* der Friseur.

hale [heil], *adj.* — *and hearty*, frisch und gesund, rüstig.

half [hɑːf], *adj.* halb. — *adv.* —*baked*, unreif; unterentwickelt (*stupid*); (*coll.*) *not* —, und wie! sehr gern. — *s.* die Hälfte; *too clever by* —, allzu gescheit.

halfcaste ['hɑːfkɑːst], *s.* der Mischling.

halfpenny ['heipni], *s.* der halbe Penny.

halfwit ['hɑːfwit], *s.* der Dummkopf.

halibut ['hælibət], *s.* (*Zool.*) der Heilbutt.

hall [hɔːl], *s.* der Saal; die Halle; der Hausflur (*entrance* —); (*Univ.*) — (*of residence*), das Studentenheim; — *porter*, der Portier.

hallmark ['hɔːlmɑːk], *s.* das Kennzeichen.

hallow ['hælou], *v.a.* weihen, heiligen.

Halloween [hælou'iːn]. der Allerheiligenabend.

halo ['heilou], *s.* der Heiligenschein (*of saint*); der Hof (*round the moon*).

hallucination [həluːsi'neiʃən], *s.* die Halluzination.

halt [hɔːlt], *v.n.* halten, haltmachen; —*!* Halt! zögern (*tarry*); —*ing speech*, die Sprechhemmung. — *v.a.* anhalten, zum Halten bringen. — *s.* (*Railw.*) die (kleine) Haltestelle.

halve [hɑːv], *v.a.* halbieren.

ham [hæm], *s.* (*Cul.*) der Schinken; (*Anat.*) der Schenkel; — *acting*, das Schmierentheater.

hammer ['hæmə], *s.* der Hammer. — *v.a., v.n.* hämmern; — *away at*, an etwas emsig arbeiten; — *out a problem*, ein Problem zur Lösung bringen.

hammock ['hæmək], *s.* die Hängematte.

hamper (1) ['hæmpə], *s.* der Packkorb.

hamper (2) ['hæmpə], *v.a.* behindern.

hand [hænd], *s.* die Hand; *a fair* —, eine gute Handschrift; der Uhrzeiger (*on watch, clock*); die Seite (*right, left* —); die Karten, *f. pl.* (*card game*); *play a strong* —, starke Karten halten oder spielen; *on* —, vorrätig, auf Lager; *get out of* —, unkontrollierbar werden. — *v.a.* — *in*, einhändigen, einreichen; — *out*, austeilen; — *over*, übergeben, abgeben.

handbag ['hændbæg], *s.* die Handtasche.

handbill ['hændbil], *s.* der Zettel, Reklamezettel (*advertising*).

handful ['hændful], *s.* die Handvoll; *to be quite a* —, genug zu schaffen geben; das Sorgenkind.

handicap ['hændikæp], *s.* das Hindernis. — *v.a.* hindern, behindern.

handicraft ['hændikrɑːft], *s.* das Handwerk; Kunsthandwerk.

handkerchief ['hæŋkətʃif], *s.* das Taschentuch.

handle [hændl], *s.* der Griff; der Henkel (*pot, vase*). — *v.a.* handhaben (*machine*); behandeln (*person*); anpacken (*problem*).

handlebar ['hændlbɑː], *s.* die Lenkstange (*bicycle*).

handmaid(en) ['hændmeid(n)], *s.* (*obs.*) die Magd.

handrail ['hændreil], *s.* das Geländer.

handshake ['hændʃeik], *s.* der Händedruck.

handsome ['hænsəm], *adj.* hübsch, schön, stattlich.

handy ['hændi], *adj.* geschickt; — *man*, der Gelegenheitsarbeiter, Mann für alles.

hang [hæŋ], *v.a. reg. & irr.* hängen; aufhängen (*suspend*); — *it!* zum Henker; — *paper*, ein Zimmer austapezieren; — *dog expression*, den Kopf hängen lassen, die betrübte Miene. — *v.n.* hängen; (*coll.*) — *on!* warte einen Moment! — *about*, herumstehen; herumlungern (*loiter*).

hanger-on [hæŋər'ɔn], *s.* der Anhänger, Mitläufer.

hangman ['hæŋmən], *s.* der Henker.

hanker ['hæŋkə], *v.n.* sich sehnen.

Hanoverian [hæno'viəriən], *adj.* hannöversch. — *s.* der Hannoveraner.

hansom ['hænsəm], *s.* die zweirädrige Droschke.

haphazard [hæp'hæzəd], *s.* der Zufall, das Geratewohl.

hapless ['hæplis], *adj.* unglücklich.

happen ['hæpn], *v.n.* sich ereignen, passieren; — *to* . . ., zufällig . . .

happiness ['hæpinis], *s.* das Glück; die Glückseligkeit.

happy ['hæpi], *adj.* glücklich, glückselig.

harangue [hə'ræŋ], *s.* die Ansprache. — *v.a.* einsprechen (auf, *Acc.*); anreden.

harass ['hærəs], *v.a.* plagen, quälen.

harbinger [hɑː'bindʒə], *s.* der Vorbote, Bote.

harbour ['hɑːbə], *s.* der Hafen. — *v.a.* beherbergen (*shelter*); hegen (*cherish*).

hard [hɑːd], *adj.* schwer (*difficult*); hart (*tough*); hartherzig (*miserly*); — *up*, in Not, in Geldverlegenheit; — *of hearing*, schwerhörig.

harden [hɑːdn], *v.a.* härten. — *v.n.* hart werden.

hardiness ['hɑːdinis], *s.* die Kraft, Stärke; die Rüstigkeit.

hardly ['hɑːdli], *adv.* kaum.

hardship ['hɑːdʃip], *s.* die Not, Bedrängnis (*need*); die Beschwerde (*complaint*).

hardware ['hɑ:dwɛə], *s.* die Eisenware(n).

hardy ['hɑ:di], *adj.* abgehärtet, stark; (*Bot.*) — *annual*, ein widerstandsfähiges Jahresgewächs.

hare [hɛə], *s.* (*Zool.*) der Hase; — *brained*, unbedacht, gedankenlos; — *lip*, die Hasenscharte.

harebell ['hɛəbel], *s.* (*Bot.*) die Glockenblume.

haricot ['hærikou], *s.* (*Bot.*) — *bean*, die welsche Bohne.

hark [hɑ:k], *v.n.* horchen.

harlequin ['hɑ:likwin], *s.* der Harlekin.

harlot ['hɑ:lət], *s.* die Hure.

harm [hɑ:m], *s.* das Leid, Unrecht; *do — to*, Schaden zufügen (*Dat.*). — *v.a.* verletzen (*hurt*); schaden (*damage, Dat.*).

harmful ['hɑ:mful], *adj.* schädlich.

harmless ['hɑ:mlis], *adj.* harmlos.

harmonious [hɑ:'mouniəs], *adj.* harmonisch; einmütig (*of one mind*).

harmonize ['hɑ:mənaiz], *v.a.* in Einklang bringen. — *v.n.* harmonieren, in Einklang stehen.

harmony ['hɑ:məni], *s.* (*Mus.*) die Harmonie; (*fig.*) der Einklang, die Einmütigkeit.

harness ['hɑ:nis], *s.* der Harnisch. — *v.a.* anschirren, anspannen (*horse*); (*fig.*) nutzbar machen.

harp [hɑ:p], *s.* (*Mus.*) die Harfe. — *v.n.* (*coll.*) — *upon*, herumreiten auf (*Dat.*).

harpoon [hɑ:'pu:n], *s.* die Harpune. — *v.a.* harpunieren.

harrow ['hærou], *s.* die Egge, Harke. — *v.a.* harken, eggen; quälen.

harry ['hæri], *v.a.* verheeren, quälen.

harsh [hɑ:ʃ], *adj.* herb, rauh (*rough*); streng (*severe*).

hart [hɑ:t], *s.* (*Zool.*) der Hirsch.

harvest ['hɑ:vist], *s.* die Ernte; — *home*, das Erntefest.

hash [hæʃ], *v.a.* zerhacken; vermischen (*mix up*). — *s.* das Hackfleisch; *make a — of things*, verpfuschen, alles verderben.

hasp [hæsp or hɑ:sp], *s.* der Haken, die Spange.

haste [heist], *s.* die Hast, Eile (*hurry*); die Voreiligkeit (*rashness*).

hasten [heisn], *v.n.* eilen, sich beeilen.

hasty ['heisti], *adj.* voreilig.

hat [hæt], *s.* der Hut; (*coll.*) *talk through o.'s —*, Unsinn reden.

hatch (1) [hætʃ], *s.* die Brut (*chickens*). — *v.a., v.n.* (aus-)brüten; aushecken (*cunning*).

hatch (2) [hætʃ], *s.* das Servierfenster (*for serving food*); (*Naut.*) die Luke.

hatch (3) [hætʃ], *v.a.* (*Art*) schraffieren.

hatchet ['hætʃit], *s.* das Beil, die Axt; *bury the —*, das Kriegsbeil begraben.

hate [heit], *v.a., v.n.* hassen; — *to ...*, nicht ... wollen. — *s.* der Haß, Widerwille, die Abneigung.

hateful ['heitful], *adj.* verhaßt (*hated*); gehässig (*hating*).

hatred ['heitrid], *s.* der Haß.

hatter ['hætə], *s.* der Hutmacher.

haughty ['hɔ:ti], *adj.* übermütig (*supercilious*); hochmütig, stolz (*proud*); hochnäsig (*giving o.s. airs*).

haul [hɔ:l], *v.a.* schleppen, ziehen. — *s.* das Schleppen; (*coll.*) die Beute.

haulage ['hɔ:lidʒ], *s.* der Schleppdienst, die Spedition.

haunch [hɔ:ntʃ], *s.* (*Anat.*) die Hüfte; der Schenkel (*horse*); die Keule (*venison*).

haunt [hɔ:nt], *v.a.* heimsuchen, spuken (in, *Dat.*); *it is —ed*, hier spuktes.

have [hæv], *v.a. irr.* haben, besitzen (*possess*); erhalten; lassen; — *to*, müssen; — *s.th. made, done*, etwas machen lassen.

haven [heivn], *s.* der Zufluchtsort.

haversack ['hævəsæk], *s.* der Brotbeutel.

havoc ['hævək], *s.* die Verwüstung, Verheerung.

hawk (1) [hɔ:k], *s.* (*Orn.*) der Habicht; der Falke (*falcon*).

hawk (2) [hɔ:k], *v.a.* hausieren.

hawker ['hɔ:kə], *s.* der Hausierer.

hawthorn ['hɔ:θɔ:n], *s.* (*Bot.*) der Hagedorn.

hay [hei], *s.* das Heu; — *fever*, der Heuschnupfen; — *loft*, der Heuboden; — *rick*, der Heuschober.

hazard ['hæzəd], *s.* der Zufall (*chance*); die Gefahr (*danger*); das Risiko (*risk*). — *v.a.* aufs Spiel setzen, riskieren.

hazardous ['hæzədəs], *adj.* gefährlich, gewagt.

haze [heiz], *s.* der Dunst, Nebeldunst.

hazel [heizl], *s.* (*Bot.*) die Haselstaude; — *nut*, die Haselnuß.

hazy ['heizi], *adj.* dunstig, nebelig.

he [hi:] *pers. pron.* er; — *who*, derjenige, welcher, wer.

head [hed], *s.* der Kopf; die Spitze (*of arrow*); der Leiter (*of firm*); (*Sch.*) der Direktor; die Überschrift (*heading*); die Krisis (*climax*); (*Pol.*) der Führer, das (Staats-)Oberhaupt. — *v.a.* anführen, führen; (*Mil.*) befehligen; — *v.n.* (*Naut.*) — *for*, Kurs nehmen auf (*Acc.*).

headache ['hedeik], *s.* (*Med.*) die Kopfschmerzen, *m. pl.*

headlamp ['hedlæmp], *s.* der Scheinwerfer.

headphone ['hedfoun], *s.* (*usually pl.*) der Kopfhörer.

headstrong ['hedstrɔŋ], *adj.* halsstarrig.

heady ['hedi], *adj.* hastig, ungestüm; berauschend (*liquor*).

heal [hi:l], *v.a.* heilen. — *v.n.* (zu)heilen, verheilen.

health [helθ], *s.* die Gesundheit; — *resort*, der Kurort; *your (good) —!* Gesundheit! auf Ihr Wohl! Prosit! (*drinking toast*).

healthy ['helθi], *adj.* gesund.

heap [hi:p], *s.* der Haufen, die Menge. — *v.a.* häufen, aufhäufen.

hear

hear [hiə], *v.a.*, *v.n. irr.* hören; erfahren (*learn*); (*Law*) verhören (*evidence*).

hearing [ˈhiəriŋ], *s.* das Gehör (*auditory perception*); *within* —, in Hörweite; (*Law*) das Verhör.

hearsay [ˈhiəsei], *s.* das Hörensagen.

hearse [həːs], *s.* der Leichenwagen.

heart [haːt], *s.* das Herz; der Mut (*courage*); das Innerste (*core*); *by* —, auswendig; *take to* —, beherzigen; *take* — *from*, Mut fassen (aus, *Dat.*).

heartburn [ˈhaːtbəːn], *s.* (*Med.*) das Sodbrennen.

heartfelt [ˈhaːtfelt], *adj.* herzlich.

hearth [haːθ], *s.* der Herd.

hearty [ˈhaːti], *adj.* herzlich; aufrichtig (*sincere*); herzhaft.

heat [hiːt], *s.* die Hitze, Wärme; die Brunst (*animals*). — *v.a.* heizen (*fuel*); erhitzen (*make hot*).

heath [hiːθ], *s.* die Heide.

heathen [ˈhiːðən], *s.* der Heide, Ungläubige.

heather [ˈheðə], *s.* (*Bot.*) das Heidekraut.

heating [ˈhiːtiŋ], *s.* die Heizung.

heave [hiːv], *v.a. reg. & irr.* heben, hieben. — *v.n.* sich heben und senken.

heaven [hevn], *s.* der Himmel; *good* —*s!* ach, du lieber Himmel!

heaviness [ˈhevinis], *s.* die Schwere.

heavy [ˈhevi], *adj.* schwer; schwerwiegend (*grave*).

Hebrew [ˈhiːbruː], *adj.* hebräisch. — *s.* der Hebräer, der Jude.

hectic [ˈhektik], *adj.* hektisch, aufgeregt.

hector [ˈhektə], *v.a.* tyrannisieren (*bully*). — *v.n.* renommieren, prahlen.

hedge [hedʒ], *s.* die Hecke. — *v.a.* einhegen, einzäunen.

hedgehog [ˈhedʒhɔg], *s.* (*Zool.*) der Igel.

hedgerow [ˈhedʒrou], *s.* die Baumhecke.

heed [hiːd], *s.* die Hut, Aufmerksamkeit. — *v.a.* beachten.

heedless [ˈhiːdlis], *adj.* unachtsam.

heel [hiːl], *s.* die Ferse (*foot*); der Absatz (*shoe*); *take to o.'s* —s, die Flucht ergreifen; (*Am. sl.*) der Lump.

heifer [ˈhefə], *s.* (*Zool.*) die junge Kuh.

height [hait], *s.* die Höhe, Anhöhe; die Größe (*tallness*); der Hügel (*hill*).

heighten [haitn], *v.a.* erhöhen.

heir [ɛə], *s.* der Erbe (*to, Genit.*).

heiress [ˈɛəres], *s.* die Erbin.

heirloom [ˈɛəluːm], *s.* das Erbstück.

helicopter [ˈhelikɔptə], *s.* (*Aviat.*) der Hubschrauber.

hell [hel], *s.* die Hölle. — *interj.* zum Teufel!

hellish [ˈheliʃ], *adj.* höllisch.

helm [helm], *s.* das Steuer, Steuerruder.

helmet [ˈhelmit], *s.* der Helm.

helmsman [ˈhelmzmən], *s.* (*Naut.*) der Steuermann.

help [help], *v.a.*, *v.n.* helfen (*Dat.*); *I cannot* — *laughing*, ich muß lachen; *I cannot* — *it*, ich kann nichts dafür. — *v. r.*, o.'s., sich bedienen. — *s.* die Hilfe, Unterstützung.

helpful [ˈhelpful], *adj.* behilflich, hilfreich.

helping [ˈhelpiŋ], *s.* die Portion.

helpless [ˈhelplis], *adj.* hilflos.

helpmate, helpmeet [ˈhelpmeit, -miːt], *s.* der Gehilfe, die Gehilfin.

helter-skelter [ˈheltəˈskeltə], *adv.* Hals über Kopf.

hem [hem], *s.* der Saum. — *v.a.* (*Tail.*) einsäumen, säumen.

hemisphere [ˈhemisfiə], *s.* die Halbkugel, Hemisphäre.

hemlock [ˈhemlɔk], *s.* der Schierling.

hemp [hemp], *s.* der Hanf.

hemstitch [ˈhemstitʃ], *s.* der Hohlsaum.

hen [hen], *s.* die Henne (*poultry*); das Weibchen (*other birds*).

hence [hens], *adv.* von hier; von jetzt an.

henceforth [ˈhensˈfɔːθ], *adv.* fortan, von nun an.

henpecked [ˈhenpekd], *adj.* unter dem Pantoffel stehend.

her [həː], *pers. pron.* sie (*Acc.*), ihr (*Dat.*). — *poss. adj.* ihr.

herald [ˈherəld], *s.* der Herold. — *v.a.* ankündigen.

heraldry [ˈherəldri], *s.* die Wappenkunde.

herb [həːb], *s.* (*Bot.*) das Kraut.

herbaceous [həːˈbeiʃəs], *adj.* krautartig.

herbage [ˈhəːbidʒ], *s.* das Gras; (*Law*) das Weiderecht.

herbal [ˈhəːbəl], *adj.* krautartig, Kräuter-, Kraut-.

herd [həːd], *s.* die Herde. — *v.n.* sich zusammenfinden.

here [hiə], *adv.* hier.

hereafter [hiərˈaːftə], *adv.* hernach, künftig. — *s.* die Zukunft; das Jenseits.

hereby [hiəˈbai], *adv.* hiermit.

hereditary [hiˈreditəri], *adj.* erblich.

heredity [hiˈrediti], *s.* (*Biol.*) die Erblichkeit, Vererbung.

heresy [ˈherisi], *s.* die Ketzerei.

heretic [ˈheritik], *s.* der Ketzer.

heretofore [ˈhiətufɔː], *adv.* zuvor, vormals.

heritage [ˈheritidʒ], *s.* die Erbschaft.

hermetic [həːˈmetik], *adj.* luftdicht.

hermit [ˈhəːmit], *s.* der Eremit, Einsiedler.

hero [ˈhiərou], *s.* der Held.

heroic [hiˈrouik], *adj.* heldenhaft, heldenmütig.

heroine [ˈheroin], *s.* die Heldin.

heroism [ˈheroizm], *s.* der Heldenmut.

heron [ˈherən], *s.* (*Orn.*) der Reiher.

herring [ˈheriŋ], *s.* (*Zool.*) der Hering; *red* —, die Ablenkungsfinte, das Ablenkungsmanöver; — *bone*, die Gräte; *pickled* —, der eingemachte Hering.

hers [həːz], *poss. pron.* ihr, der ihre, der ihrige.

herself [həːˈself], *pers. pron.* sich; sie selbst.

hesitate [ˈheziteit], *v.n.* zögern, zaudern; unschlüssig sein (*be undecided*).

hesitation [hezi'teiʃən], *s.* das Zögern, Zaudern; das Bedenken (*deliberation*).

Hessian ['heʃən], *adj.* hessisch. — *s.* der Hesse.

hessian ['hesiən], *s.* die Sackleinwand (*textile*).

heterodox ['hetərədɔks], *adj.* irrgläubig.

heterogeneous [hetəro'dʒi:niəs], *adj.* heterogen, ungleichartig.

hew [hju:], *v.a. irr.* hauen.

hexagonal [hek'sægənəl], *adj.* sechseckig.

hiatus [hai'eitəs], *s.* die Lücke.

hibernate ['haibəneit], *v.n.* überwintern.

hibernation [haibə'neiʃən], *s.* der Winterschlaf.

hiccup ['hikʌp], *s.* (*usually pl.*) (*Med.*) der Schlucken, Schluckauf.

hickory ['hikəri], *s.* (*Bot.*) das Hickoryholz.

hide (1) [haid], *v.a. irr.* verstecken, verbergen. — *v.n. irr.* sich verbergen; — *and seek,* das Versteckspiel.

hide (2) [haid], *s.* die Haut (*of animal*), das Fell, (*tanned*) das Leder.

hideous ['hidiəs], *adj.* häßlich, scheußlich, furchtbar.

hiding (1) ['haidiŋ], *s.* das Versteck.

hiding (2) ['haidiŋ], *s.* die Tracht Prügel.

hierarchy ['haiərɑ:ki], *s.* die Hierarchie.

higgle [higl] *see* **haggle**.

higgledy-piggledy ['higldi'pigldi], *adv.* wüst durcheinander.

high [hai], *adj.* hoch; erhaben, vornehm; angegangen (*meat*); — *school,* die höhere Schule; — *time,* höchste Zeit; (*Am.*) vergnügliche Zeit; *High Church,* die Hochkirche. — *s.* (*Meteor.*) das Hoch.

Highness ['hainis], *s.* die Hoheit (*title*).

highroad, highway ['hairoud, 'haiwei], *s.* die Haupt- *or* Landstraße.

highwayman ['haiweimən], *s.* der Straßenräuber.

hike [haik], *v.n.* wandern, einen Ausflug machen. — *s.* die Wanderung, der Ausflug.

hilarious [hi'lɛəriəs], *adj.* fröhlich, lustig, ausgelassen.

hill [hil], *s.* der Hügel, Berg.

hilt [hilt], *s.* der Griff.

him [him], *pers. pron.* ihn, ihm.

himself [him'self], *pers. pron.* sich; er selbst.

hind [haind], *s.* (*Zool.*) die Hirschkuh, Hindin.

hinder ['hində], *v.a.* hindern.

hindmost ['haindmoust], *adj.* hinterst; *the devil take the* —, den letzten hol der Teufel! nach mir die Sintflut!

hindrance ['hindrəns], *s.* das Hindernis; (*Law*) *without let or* —, ohne Hinderung.

Hindu [hin'du:], *s.* der Hindu.

hinge [hindʒ], *s.* die Angel, der Angelpunkt. — *v.n.* sich um etwas drehen; von etwas abhängen (on, *Dat.*).

hint [hint], *v.n.* zu verstehen geben, auf etwas hindeuten (at, auf, *Acc.*), andeuten. — *s.* die Andeutung, der Fingerzeig.

hip (1) [hip], *s.* (*Anat.*) die Hüfte.

hip (2) [hip], *s.* (*Bot.*) die Hagebutte.

hire ['haiə], *v.a.* (ver-)mieten (*car etc.*); anstellen (*man etc.*). — *s.* die Miete; der Lohn (*wage*); — *purchase,* der Abzahlungskauf, die Ratenzahlung.

hireling ['haiəliŋ], *s.* der Mietling.

hirsute ['hə:sju:t], *adj.* behaart, haarig.

his [hiz], *poss. adj.* sein, seine. — *poss. pron.* sein, der seinige oder der seine.

hiss [his], *v.n.* zischen (at, auf, *Acc.*). — *s.* das Zischen.

historian [his'tɔ:riən], *s.* der Historiker, der Geschichtsschreiber.

historical [his'tɔrikəl], *adj.* historisch, geschichtlich.

history ['histəri], *s.* die Geschichte, die Geschichtswissenschaft.

histrionic [histri'ɔnik], *adj.* schauspielerisch.

hit [hit], *v.a. irr.* schlagen, stoßen. — *s.* der Schlag, der Treffer (*on the target*); (*Am.*) der Schlager, Erfolg (*success*); — *parade,* die Schlagerparade.

hitch [hitʃ], *v.a.* anhaken (*hook*); anhängen; — *a lift,* — *hike,* per Anhalter fahren. — *s.* der Nachteil, der Haken.

hither ['hiðə], *adv.* hierher.

hitherto [hiðə'tu:], *adv.* bisher.

hive [haiv], *s.* der Bienenkorb; Bienenstock; — *of bees,* der Schwarm.

hoar [hɔ:], *adj.* eisgrau, weißlich; — *frost,* der Reif.

hoard [hɔ:d], *v.a.* hamstern. — *s.* der Vorrat, Schatz.

hoarding ['hɔ:diŋ], *s.* die Umzäunung, die Bretterwand; die Reklamewand.

hoarse [hɔ:s], *adj.* heiser.

hoarseness ['hɔ:snis], *s.* die Heiserkeit.

hoax [houks], *s.* der Betrug, die Irreführung; der Schabernack (*in fun*). — *v.a.* betrügen; foppen (*in fun*).

hobble [hɔbl], *v.n.* humpeln. — *v.a.* an den Füßen fesseln.

hobby ['hɔbi], *s.* das Steckenpferd, Hobby, die Liebhaberei.

hobgoblin [hɔb'gɔblin], *s.* der Kobold.

hobnail ['hɔbneil], *s.* der Hufnagel.

hobnailed ['hɔbneild], *adj.* — *boots,* genagelte Stiefel, *m. pl.*

hobnob [hɔb'nɔb], *v.n.* (*coll.*) vertraulich sein.

hock (1) [hɔk], *s.* (*Anat.*) das Sprunggelenk.

hock (2) [hɔk], *s.* (*wine*) der Rheinwein.

hod [hɔd], *s.* (*Build.*) der Trog; der Eimer (*coal*).

hodge-podge *see under* **hotchpotch**.

hoe [hou], *s.* die Hacke, Harke. — *v.a., v.n.* hacken, harken.

hog [hɔg], *s.* das Schwein. — *v.a.* verschlingen (*food*); an sich reißen (*grasp*).

hogshead ['hɔgzhed], *s.* das Oxhoft.

hoist [hɔist], *v.a.* hissen.

hold

hold [hould], *v.a.*, *v.n. irr.* halten (*keep*); enthalten (*contain*); behaupten (*assert*); meinen (*think*); gelten (*be valid*); — *forth*, deklamieren; — *good*, sich bewähren; — *out*, hinhalten (*hope*); (*endure*) aushalten; — *up*, aufhalten. — *s.* (*Naut.*) der Schiffsraum; die Macht (*power*).

holder ['houldə], *s.* der Inhaber, Besitzer.

holding ['houldin], *s.* das Pachtgut (*farm*); der Besitz (*property*); (*Comm.*) der Trust.

hole [houl], *s.* das Loch; die Höhle (*cavity*). — *v.a.* aushöhlen; (*Golf*) ins Loch spielen.

holiday ['hɔlidei], *s.* der Feiertag; der Urlaub (*vacation*); (*pl.*) die Ferien, *pl.*

holiness ['houlinis], *s.* die Heiligkeit.

hollow ['hɔlou], *adj.* hohl. — *s.* die Höhlung; die Höhle.

holly ['hɔli], *s.* (*Bot.*) die Stechpalme.

hollyhock ['hɔlihɔk], *s.* (*Bot.*) die Stockrose.

holocaust ['hɔlokɔːst], *s.* das Brandopfer; die Katastrophe.

holster ['houlstə], *s.* die Pistolentasche, die Halfter.

holy ['houli], *adj.* heilig; *Holy Week,* die Karwoche.

homage ['hɔmidʒ], *s.* die Huldigung; *pay — to,* huldigen (*Dat.*).

home [houm], *s.* das Heim, die Wohnung; die Heimat; *at —,* zu Hause; *Home Office,* das Innenministerium; — *Rule,* (*Pol.*) die Selbstverwaltung.

homer ['houmə] (*Am.*) *see* **homing pigeon.**

homesick ['houmsik], *adj.* an Heimweh leidend.

homestead ['houmsted], *s.* der Bauernhof.

homicide ['hɔmisaid], *s.* der Mord (*crime*); der Mörder (*killer*).

homily ['hɔmili], *s.* die Predigt; Moralpredigt.

homing pigeon ['houmiŋ'pidʒən], *s.* die Brieftaube.

homogeneous [hɔmə'dʒiːniəs], *adj.* homogen; gleichartig.

hone [houn], *s.* der Wetzstein. — *v.a.* (*blade, knife*) abziehen.

honest ['ɔnist], *adj.* ehrlich, aufrichtig.

honesty ['ɔnisti], *s.* die Ehrlichkeit.

honey ['hʌni], *s.* der Honig; (*Am., coll.*) Liebling!

honeycomb ['hʌnikoum], *s.* die Honigwabe.

honeymoon ['hʌnimuːn], *s.* die Flitterwochen.

honorarium [ɔnə'rɛəriəm], *s.* das Honorar.

honorary ['ɔnərəri], *adj.* Ehren-, ehrenamtlich.

honour ['ɔnə], *s.* die Ehre; *your —,* Euer Ehrwürden, Euer Gnaden (*title*). — *v.a.* ehren, auszeichnen.

honourable ['ɔnərəbl], *adj.* ehrenwert, ehrenvoll; Hochwohlgeboren (*title*).

hood [hud], *s.* die Kapuze; das akademische Gradabzeichen über dem Talar; (*Hunt.*) die Haube; —*ed falcon,* der Jagdfalke (mit Haube).

hoodwink ['hudwiŋk], *v.a.* täuschen.

hoof [huːf *or* huf], *s.* der Huf (*horse*); die Klaue.

hook [huk], *s.* der Haken; *by — or by crook,* mit allen Mitteln. — *v.a.* angeln, fangen.

hooked [hukd], *adj.* gekrümmt, hakenförmig.

hooligan ['huːligən], *s.* der Rowdy.

hoop [huːp], *s.* der Reifen. — *v.a.* (ein Faß) binden.

hooper ['huːpə], *s.* der Böttcher.

hoopoe ['huːpou], *s.* (*Orn.*) der Wiedehopf.

hoot [huːt], *v.n.* schreien (*owl*); ertönen (*siren*); hupen (*car*).

hooter ['huːtə], *s.* die Sirene (*siren*); die Hupe (*car*).

hop (1) [hɔp], *v.n.* hüpfen, tanzen; —*ping mad,* ganz verrückt.

hop (2) [hɔp], *s.* (*Bot.*) der Hopfen. — *v.a.* (*beer*) hopfen, Hopfen zusetzen (*Dat.*). — *v.n.* Hopfen ernten.

hope [houp], *s.* die Hoffnung. — *v.n.* hoffen (*for, auf, Acc.*).

hopeless ['houplis], *adj.* hoffnungslos.

horizon [hə'raizən], *s.* der Horizont.

horizontal [hɔri'zɔntl], *adj.* horizontal, waagrecht.

horn [hɔːn], *s.* das Horn; (*Mus.*) *French —,* das Waldhorn, Horn; (*Motor.*) die Hupe.

hornet ['hɔːnit], *s.* (*Ent.*) die Hornisse.

hornpipe ['hɔːnpaip], *s.* (*Mus.*) der Matrosentanz; die Hornpfeife.

horrible ['hɔribl], *adj.* schrecklich.

horrid ['hɔrid], *adj.* abscheulich.

horrific [hɔ'rifik], *adj.* schrecklich, schreckenerregend.

horror ['hɔrə], *s.* der Schrecken, das Entsetzen; (*fig.*) der Greuel.

horse [hɔːs], *s.* das Pferd, Roß; *on —back,* zu Pferd.

horseman ['hɔːsmən], *s.* der Reiter.

horsepower ['hɔːspauə], *s.* die Pferdestärke.

horseradish ['hɔːsrædiʃ], *s.* der Meerrettich.

horseshoe ['hɔːsʃuː], *s.* das Hufeisen.

horticulture ['hɔːtikʌltʃə], *s.* der Gartenbau.

hose [houz], *s.* die Strümpfe, *m. pl.* (*stockings*); der Schlauch (*water pipe*).

hosiery ['houʒəri], *s.* die Strumpfwarenindustrie; die Strumpfwaren.

hospitable ['hɔs'pitəbl], *adj.* gastlich, gastfreundlich.

hospital ['hɔspitl], *s.* das Krankenhaus.

hospitality [hɔspi'tæliti], *s.* die Gastlichkeit, Gastfreundschaft.

host (1) [houst], *s.* der Gastwirt (*landlord*); der Gastgeber.

host (2) [houst], *s.* (*Rel.*) *angelic —,* die Engelschar; (*Mil.*) das Heer, die Heerschar.

host (3) [houst], *s.* (*Eccl.*) die Hostie.

hurried

hostage ['hɔstidʒ], *s.* die Geisel.
hostess ['houstis *or* -tes], *s.* die Gastgeberin; *air —,* die StewardeB.
hostile ['hɔstail], *adj.* feindlich; feindselig (*inimical*).
hot [hɔt], *adj.* heiß; hitzig (*temperament*); scharf, gewürzt (*of spices*); (*fig.*) heftig, erbittert.
hotchpotch, hodge-podge ['hɔtʃpɔtʃ, 'hɔdʒpɔdʒ], *s.* das Mischmasch.
— *v.a.* hetzen.
hotel [ho(u)'tel],*s.*das Hotel,der Gasthof.
hothouse ['hɔthaus], *s.* das Treibhaus.
hound [haund], *s.* (*Zool.*) der Jagdhund.
— *v.a.* hetzen.
hour ['auə], *s.* die Stunde; — *hand,* der Stundenzeiger; *for —s,* studenlang; *keep early (late) —s,* früh (spät) zu Bett gehen.
hourglass ['auəglɑ:s], *s.* die Sanduhr.
hourly ['auəli], *adj., adv.,* stündlich.
house [haus], *s.* das Haus; (*Comm.*) die Firma. — [hauz], *v.a.* beherbergen, unterbringen.
houseboat ['hausbout], *s.* das Wohnboot.
housebreaking ['hausbreikiŋ], *s.* der Einbruch.
household ['haushould], *s.* der Haushalt.
housekeeper ['hauski:pə], *s.* die Haushälterin.
housewife ['hauswaif], *s.* die Hausfrau.
housing ['hauziŋ], *s.* die Unterbringung; — *department,* das Wohnungsamt.
hovel ['hɔvl *or* hʌvl], *s.* die Hütte.
hover ['hɔvə *or* 'hʌvə], *v.n.* schweben, schwanken.
how [hau], *adv.* wie; — *do you do?* (*in introduction*) sehr angenehm; — *are you?* wie geht es Ihnen, Dir?
however [hau'evə], *adv.* wie immer, wie auch immer, wie auch. — *conj.* doch, jedoch, dennoch.
howl [haul], *v.n.* heulen. — *s.* das Geheul.
hoyden [hɔidn], *s.* das wilde Mädchen.
hub [hʌb], *s.* die Nabe (am Rad); — *of the universe,* der Mitte der Welt.
hubbub ['hʌbʌb], *s.* der Tumult, Lärm.
huckaback ['hʌkəbæk], *s.* der Zwillich (*textile*).
huckle ['hʌkl], *s.* die Hüfte.
huddle ['hʌdl], *v.n.* sich drängen, sich zusammenducken. — *s.* das Gedränge.
hue [hju:], *s.* der Farbton, die Tönung.
huff [hʌf], *s.* die schlechte Laune, die Mißstimmung.
huffy ['hʌfi], *adj.* mißmutig, übel gelaunt.
hug [hʌg], *v.a.* umarmen. — *s.* die Umarmung.
huge [hju:dʒ], *adj.* riesig, groß, ungeheuer.
Huguenot ['hju:gənou *or* -nɔt], *s.* der Hugenote. — *adj.* hugenottisch, Hugenotten-.

hulk [hʌlk], *s.* (*Naut.*) das Schiffsinnere, der Schiffsrumpf; der schwerfällige Mensch.
hull [hʌl], *s.* die Hülse, Schale; (*Naut., Aviat.*) der Rumpf. — *v.a.* (*Engin.*) hülsen.
hullo! [hə'lou], *interj.* hallo!
hum [hʌm], *v.n.* summen, brummen. — *s.* das Summen, Brummen, Gemurmel (*murmuring*).
human ['hju:mən], *adj.* menschlich. — *s.* der Mensch.
humane [hju:'mein], *adj.* menschenfreundlich.
humanity [hju:'mæniti], *s.* die Menschheit (*mankind*); (*compassion*); (*pl.*) die klassischen Fächer, *n. pl.,* die humanistischen Wissenschaften, *f. pl.*
humanize ['hju:mənaiz], *v.a.* menschlich oder gesittet machen.
humble [hʌmbl], *adj.* demütig; bescheiden (*modest*); unterwürfig (*servile*). — *v.a.* erniedrigen (*humiliate*).
humbug ['hʌmbʌg], *s.* die Schwindelei (*swindle*); der Schwindler (*crook*); der Unsinn (*nonsense*).
humdrum ['hʌmdrʌm], *adj.* langweilig, eintönig.
humid ['hju:mid], *adj.* feucht.
humidity [hju:'miditi], *s.* die Feuchtigkeit.
humiliate [hju:'milieit], *v.a.* erniedrigen.
humility [hju:'militi], *s.* die Demut.
humming-bird ['hʌmiŋbə:d], *s.* (*Orn.*) der Kolibri.
humming-top ['hʌmiŋtɔp], *s.* der Brummkreisel.
humorous ['hju:mərəs], *adj.* humoristisch, spaßhaft, komisch.
humour ['hju:mə], *s.* der Humor, die (gute) Laune. — *v.a.* in guter Laune erhalten, gut stimmen; willfahren (*Dat.*).
hump [hʌmp], *s.* der Buckel, der Höcker.
hunch [hʌntʃ], *s.* der Buckel; *have a —,* das Gefühl haben.
hunchback ['hʌntʃbæk], *s.* der Bucklige.
hundred ['hʌndrəd], *num. adj.* a —, hundert.
hundredweight ['hʌndrədweit], *s.* der (englische) Zentner.
Hungarian [hʌŋ'gɛəriən],*adj.*ungarisch. — *s.* der Ungar.
hunger ['hʌŋgə], *s.* der Hunger.
hungry ['hʌŋgri], *adj.* hungrig.
hunt [hʌnt], *s.* die Jagd. — *v.a., v.n.* jagen.
hunter ['hʌntə], *s.* der Jäger.
hurdle ['hə:dl], *s.* die Hürde.
hurdy-gurdy ['hə:digə:di], *s.* der Leierkasten.
hurl [hə:l], *v.a.* schleudern, werfen.
hurly-burly ['hə:libə:li], *s.* der Wirrwarr.
hurricane ['hʌrikin], *s.* der Orkan; — *lamp,* die Sturmlaterne.
hurried ['hʌrid], *adj.* eilig, hastig.

413

hurry [ˈhʌri], v.n. eilen, sich beeilen; — to do, eiligst tun. — v.a. beschleunigen. — s. die Eile, Hast, Beschleunigung.

hurt [həːt], v.a. irr. verletzen; wehetun (Dat.); (verbally) kränken. — s. die Verletzung, Kränkung.

hurtful [ˈhəːtful], adj. schädlich, kränkend.

husband [ˈhʌzbənd], s. der Mann, Ehemann, Gemahl. — v.a. verwalten, sparsam verfahren mit (Dat.).

husbandman [ˈhʌzbəndmən], s. der Landwirt.

husbandry [ˈhʌzbəndri], s. die Landwirtschaft.

hush [hʌʃ], v.a. zum Schweigen bringen. — s. die Stille; — money, das Schweigegeld.

husky (1) [ˈhʌski], adj. heiser (voice).

husky (2) [ˈhʌski], s. (Zool.) der Eskimohund.

hussy [ˈhʌzi], s. (coll.) das Frauenzimmer.

hustings [ˈhʌstiŋz], s. die Wahltribüne.

hustle [ˈhʌsl], v.a. drängen, stoßen. — s. das Gedränge.

hut [hʌt], s. die Hütte, Baracke.

hutch [hʌtʃ], s. der Trog, Kasten (chest).

hybrid [ˈhaibrid], adj. Bastard-. — s. der Bastard.

hydraulic [haiˈdrɔːlik], adj. hydraulisch.

hydrogen [ˈhaidrədʒən], s. der Wasserstoff.

hydroelectric [haidrouiˈlektrik], adj. hydroelektrisch.

hyena [haiˈiːnə], s. (Zool.) die Hyäne.

hygiene [ˈhaidʒiːn], s. die Hygiene, Gesundheitslehre.

hymn [him], s. die Hymne, das Kirchenlied.

hymnal [ˈhimnəl], s. das Gesangbuch.

hyper- [ˈhaipə], prefix. über-.

hyperbole [haiˈpəːbəli], s. die Übertreibung.

hyphen [ˈhaifən], s. der Bindestrich.

hypnosis [hipˈnousis], s. die Hypnose.

hypochondriac [haipoˈkɔndriæk], adj. hypochondrisch. — s. der Hypochonder.

hypocrisy [hiˈpɔkrisi], s. die Heuchelei.

hypocrite [ˈhipəkrit], s. der Heuchler.

hypothesis [haiˈpɔθisis], s. die Hypothese.

hypothetical [haipəˈθetikəl], adj. hypothetisch, angenommen.

hysteria [hisˈtiəriə], s. die Hysterie.

I

I [ai]. das I.

I [ai], pers. pron. ich.

ice [ais], s. das Eis; — bound, eingefroren; (Naut.) — breaker, der Eisbrecher; (Am.) — box, der Kühlschrank; — cream, das Eis; das Gefrorene. — v.a. (confectionery) verzuckern; (cake) glasieren.

Icelander [ˈaislændə], s. der Isländer.

Icelandic [aisˈlændik], adj. isländisch.

icicle [ˈaisikl], s. der Eiszapfen.

icy [ˈaisi], adj. eisig.

idea [aiˈdiə], s. die Idee.

ideal [aiˈdiəl], adj. ideal. — s. das Ideal.

idealize [aiˈdiəlaiz], v.a. idealisieren.

identical [aiˈdentikəl], adj. identisch, gleich.

identification [aidentifiˈkeiʃən], s. die Gleichsetzung, Identifizierung.

identify [aiˈdentifai], v.a. identifizieren, gleichsetzen.

identity [aiˈdentiti], s. die Identität, Gleichheit.

idiocy [ˈidiəsi], s. der Blödsinn.

idiom [ˈidiəm], s. das Idiom, die sprachliche Eigentümlichkeit.

idiomatic [idioˈmætik], adj. idiomatisch.

idiosyncrasy [idioˈsiŋkrəsi], s. die Empfindlichkeit; die Abneigung (gegen, Acc.); die Idiosynkrasie.

idle [aidl], adj. unnütz (useless); müßig, faul (lazy). — v.n. träge sein.

idleness [ˈaidlnis], s. der Müßiggang, die Faulheit.

idiot [ˈidiət], s. der Idiot.

idol [aidl], s. das Götzenbild; das Idol.

idolatry [aiˈdɔlətri], s. die Götzenverehrung.

idolize [ˈaidolaiz], v.a. vergöttern, abgöttisch lieben.

idyll [ˈaidil or ˈidil], s. die Idylle, das Idyll.

idyllic [aiˈdilik or iˈdilik], adj. idyllisch.

if [if], conj. wenn, falls (in case); ob (whether).

igneous [ˈigniəs], adj. feurig.

ignite [igˈnait], v.a. entzünden. — v.n. zur Entzündung kommen, sich entzünden.

ignition [igˈniʃən], s. die Zündung.

ignoble [igˈnoubl], adj. unedel, gemein.

ignominious [ignoˈminiəs], adj. schimpflich, schmählich.

ignominy [ˈignomini], s. die Schande, Schmach.

ignoramus [ignəˈreiməs], s. der Unwissende.

ignorance [ˈignərəns], s. die Unwissenheit, Unkenntnis.

ignorant [ˈignərənt], adj. unwissend.

ignore [igˈnɔː], v.a. ignorieren, nicht beachten.

ill [il], adj. böse, schlimm (bad); krank (sick); — feeling, die Verstimmung. — adv. — at ease, unbequem, verlegen; can — afford, kann sich kaum leisten …; —-timed, zu unrechter Zeit.

illbred [ilˈbred], adj. ungezogen.

illegal [iˈliːgəl], adj. illegal, ungesetzlich.

illegibility [iledʒiˈbiliti], s. die Unleserlichkeit.

illegible [i'ledʒibl], *adj.* unleserlich.

illegitimacy [ili'dʒitiməsi], *s.* die Un-ehelichkeit, Illegitimität.

illegitimate [ili'dʒitimit], *adj.* illegi-tim, unehelich.

illicit [[i'lisit], *adj.* unerlaubt.

illiteracy [i'litərəsi], *s.* die Unkenntnis des Schreibens und Lesens, das Analphabetentum.

illiterate [i'litərit], *s.* der Analphabet.

illness ['ilnis], *s.* die Krankheit.

illogical [i'lɔdʒikəl], *adj.* unlogisch.

illuminate [i'lju:mineit], *v.a.* erleuch-ten; (*fig.*) aufklären.

illuminating [i'lju:mineitiŋ], *adj.* auf-schlußreich.

illumination [ilju:mi'neiʃən], *s.* die Erleuchtung; die Erklärung (*explana-tion*).

illusion [i'lju:ʒən], *s.* die Illusion, Täuschung.

illusive, illusory [i'lju:ziv, i'lju:zəri], *adj.* trügerisch, täuschend.

illustrate ['iləstreit], *v.a.* erläutern; illustrieren (*with pictures*).

illustration [iləs'treiʃən], *s.* die Illu-stration (*pictorial*); Erläuterung, Er-klärung; das Beispiel (*instance*).

illustrious [i'lʌstriəs], *adj.* glänzend, berühmt.

image ['imidʒ], *s.* das Bild; das Eben-bild; die Erscheinung (*appearance*).

imagery ['imidʒəri], *s.* der Gebrauch von Stilbildern (*style*), die Bilder-sprache.

imaginable [i'mædʒinəbl], *adj.* denk-bar.

imaginary [i'mædʒinəri], *adj.* ein-gebildet, nicht wirklich, vermeintlich.

imagination [imædʒi'neiʃən], *s.* die Einbildung; die Vorstellung; die Phantasie.

imaginative [i'mædʒinətiv], *adj.* erfin-derisch, voll Phantasie.

imagine [i'mædʒin], *v.a.* sich vorstel-len, sich denken.

imbecile ['imbisail *or* 'imbisi:l], *adj.* schwachsinnig. — *s.* der Idiot.

imbecility [imbi'siliti], *s.* der Schwach-sinn.

imbibe [im'baib], *v.a.* trinken; (*fig.*) in sich aufnehmen.

imbroglio [im'brouliou], *s.* die Ver-wicklung.

imbue [im'bju:], *v.a.* erfüllen, sättigen (*fig.*).

imitate ['imiteit], *v.a.* nachahmen, imitieren.

imitation [imi'teiʃən], *s.* die Nachah-mung, Imitation; — *leather*, das Kunstleder.

immaculate [i'mækjulit], *adj.* unbe-fleckt, makellos.

immaterial [imə'tiəriəl], *adj.* unwesent-lich, unwichtig.

immature [imə'tjuə], *adj.* unreif.

immeasurable [i'meʒərəbl], *adj.* uner-meßlich, unmeßbar.

immediate [i'mi:djit], *adj.* unmittel-bar, direkt, sofortig.

immediately [i'mi:djətli], *adv.* sofort.

immemorial [imi'mɔ:riəl], *adj.* un-denklich, ewig.

immense [i'mens], *adj.* unermeßlich, ungeheuer.

immerse [i'mə:s], *v.a.* eintauchen.

immersion [i'mə:ʃən], *s.* das Eintau-chen, die Versenkung; — *heater*, der Tauchsieder.

immigrant ['imigrənt], *s.* der Ein-wanderer.

imminent ['iminənt], *adj.* bevor-stehend.

immobile [i'moubail], *adj.* unbeweg-lich.

immoderate [i'mɔdərit], *adj.* unmäßig.

immodest [i'mɔdist], *adj.* unbeschei-den; unsittlich, unanständig (*immoral*).

immodesty [i'mɔdisti], *s.* die Unan-ständigkeit (*indecency*); Unbeschei-denheit (*presumption*).

immolate ['iməleit], *v.a.* opfern.

immoral [i'mɔrəl], *adj.* unsittlich, unmoralisch.

immortal [i'mɔ:tl], *adj.* unsterblich.

immortalize [i'mɔ:təlaiz], *v.a.* ver-ewigen, unsterblich machen.

immovable [i'mu:vəbl], *adj.* unbeweg-lich (*fig.*).

immunity [i'mju:niti], *s.* die Freiheit, Straffreiheit; Immunität.

immutable [i'mju:təbl], *adj.* unabän-derlich; unveränderlich.

imp [imp], *s.* der Knirps, Kobold, kleine Schelm.

impair [im'peə], *v.a.* beeinträchtigen; vermindern (*reduce*).

impale [im'peil], *v.a.* aufspießen; durchbohren.

impalpable [im'pælpəbl], *adj.* unfühl-bar, unmerklich.

impart [im'pa:t], *v.a.* erteilen; ver-leihen (*confer*); mitteilen (*inform*).

impartial [im'pa:ʃəl], *adj.* unpartei-isch.

impartiality [impa:ʃi'æliti], *s.* die Unparteilichkeit, Objektivität.

impassable [im'pa:səbl], *adj.* unweg-sam, unpassierbar.

impasse [im'pæs], *s.* der völlige Still-stand.

impassioned [im'pæʃənd], *adj.* leiden-schaftlich.

impassive [im'pæsiv], *adj.* unempfind-lich.

impatience [im'peiʃəns], *s.* die Unge-duld.

impatient [im'peiʃənt], *adj.* ungedul-dig.

impeach [im'pi:tʃ], *v.a.* anklagen.

impeachment [im'pi:tʃmənt], *s.* die Anklage.

impecunious [impi'kju:niəs], *adj.* un-bemittelt, mittellos.

impede [im'pi:d], *v.a.* behindern, ver-hindern.

impediment [im'pedimənt], *s.* das Hindernis.

impel [im'pel], *v.a.* antreiben; zwingen (*force*).

impending

impending [im'pendiŋ], *adj.* bevorstehend, drohend.
impenetrable [im'penitrəbl], *adj.* undurchdringlich, unerforschlich.
impenitent [im'penitənt], *adj.* reuelos, unbußfertig.
imperative [im'perətiv], *adj.* zwingend (*cogent*); dringend notwendig. — *s.* (*Gram.*) der Imperativ, die Befehlsform.
imperceptible [impə'septibl], *adj.* unmerklich.
imperfect [im'pə:fikt], *adj.* unvollständig, unvollkommen; fehlerhaft (*goods etc.*). — *s.* (*Gram.*) das Imperfekt.
imperial [im'piəriəl], *adj.* kaiserlich, Kaiser-, Reichs-.
imperil [im'peril], *v.a.* gefährden; in Gefahr bringen, einer Gefahr aussetzen.
imperious [im'piəriəs], *adj.* gebieterisch.
imperishable [im'periʃəbl], *adj.* unverwüstlich, unvergänglich.
impermeable [im'pə:miəbl], *adj.* undurchdringlich.
impersonal [im'pə:sənəl], *adj.* unpersönlich.
impersonate [im'pə:səneit], *v.a.* verkörpern, darstellen; sich ausgeben als.
impertinence [im'pə:tinəns], *s.* die Anmaßung, Frechheit, Unverschämtheit.
impertinent [im'pə:tinənt], *adj.* anmaßend, frech, unverschämt.
imperturbable [impə'tə:bəbl], *adj.* unerschütterlich, ruhig, gelassen.
impervious [im'pə:viəs], *adj.* unwegsam, undurchdringlich.
impetuous [im'petjuəs], *adj.* ungestüm, heftig.
impetus ['impitəs], *s.* die Triebkraft, der Antrieb.
impinge [im'pindʒ], *v.n.* verstoßen (*on,* gegen); übergreifen (*on,* in).
implacable [im'plækəbl], *adj.* unversöhnlich.
implement ['implimənt], *s.* das Gerät. — [impli'ment], *v.a.* (*Law*) erfüllen, in Wirkung setzen, in Kraft treten lassen.
implementation [implimen'teiʃən], *s.* das Inkrafttreten, die Erfüllung, Ausführung.
implicate ['implikeit], *v.a.* verwickeln.
implicit [im'plisit], *adj.* unbedingt; einbegriffen.
implore [im'plɔ:], *v.a.* anflehen.
imply [im'plai], *v.a.* besagen, meinen; andeuten.
impolite [impə'lait], *adj.* unhöflich, grob.
impolitic [im'pɔlitik], *adj.* unklug, unpolitisch, undiplomatisch.
imponderable [im'pɔndərəbl], *adj.* unwägbar. — *s. pl.* unwägbare, unvorhersehbare Umstände, *m.pl.*
import [im'pɔ:t], *v.a.* einführen, importieren; bedeuten, besagen. —

['impɔ:t], *s.* (*Comm.*) die Einfuhr, der Import; die Bedeutung (*importance, meaning*), Wichtigkeit (*significance*); (*Comm.*) — *licence,* die Einfuhrgenehmigung.
importance [im'pɔ:təns], *s.* die Bedeutung, Wichtigkeit.
important [im'pɔ:tənt], *adj.* bedeutend, wichtig.
importation [impɔ:'teiʃən], *s.* die Einfuhr.
importune [impɔ:'tju:n], *v.a.* belästigen, angehen, dringend bitten.
impose [im'pouz], *v.a.* aufbürden, auferlegen. — *v.n.* — *upon s.o.,* einen belästigen.
imposition [impə'ziʃən], *s.* die Belästigung; (*Sch.*) die Strafarbeit.
impossible [im'pɔsibl], *adj.* unmöglich.
impostor [im'pɔstə], *s.* der Schwindler, Betrüger.
impotent ['impətənt], *adj.* schwach, machtlos; impotent (*sexually*).
impound [im'paund], *v.a.* beschlagnahmen, in Beschlag nehmen.
impoverish [im'pɔvəriʃ], *v.a.* arm machen.
impoverished [im'pɔvəriʃd], *adj.* verarmt, armselig.
impracticability [impræktikə'biliti], *s.* die Unmöglichkeit, Unausführbarkeit.
impracticable [im'præktikəbl], *adj.* unausführbar.
imprecate ['imprikeit], *v.a.* verwünschen.
impregnable [im'pregnəbl], *adj.* uneinnehmbar, unbezwinglich.
impregnate [im'pregneit], *v.a.* impregnieren; (*Chem.*) sättigen.
impress [im'pres], *v.a.* beeindrucken, imponieren (*fig.*); einprägen, einpressen (*print*). — ['impres], *s.* der Eindruck, (*Typ.*) Abdruck.
impression [im'preʃən], *s.* (*fig.*) der Eindruck; die Auflage (*books*).
impressionable [im'preʃənəbl], *adj.* eindrucksfähig, empfänglich.
impressive [im'presiv], *adj.* ergreifend, eindrucksvoll.
imprint ['imprint], *s.* der Name des Verlags oder Druckers. — [im'print], *v.a.* drucken.
imprison [im'prizn], *v.a.* gefangensetzen, in Haft nehmen.
imprisonment [im'priznmənt], *s.* die Haft; (*Law*) der Arrest.
improbability [imprɔbə'biliti], *s.* die Unwahrscheinlichkeit.
improbable [im'prɔbəbl], *adj.* unwahrscheinlich.
improbity [im'proubiti], *s.* die Unredlichkeit.
impromptu [im'prɔmptju:], *adj., adv.* aus dem Stegreif, unvorbereitet.
improper [im'prɔpə], *adj.* unpassend; unanständig (*indecent*).
impropriety [impro'praiiti], *s.* die Unanständigkeit (*indecency*); die Ungehörigkeit.

improve [im′pru:v], *v.a.* verbessern; (*Hort.*) veredeln. — *v.n.* besser werden, sich bessern; (*Med.*) sich erholen.

improvement [im′pru:vmənt], *s.* die Verbesserung; (*Med.*) die Besserung, der Fortschritt.

improvident [im′prɔvidənt], *adj.* unvorsichtig, nicht auf die Zukunft bedacht.

improvise [′imprəvaiz], *v.a.* improvisieren.

imprudent [im′pru:dənt], *adj.* unklug, unvorsichtig.

impudent [′impjudənt], *adj.* unverschämt.

impugn [im′pju:n], *v.a.* anfechten, angreifen.

impulse [′impʌls], *s.* der Impuls; der Anstoß.

impulsive [im′pʌlsiv], *adj.* impulsiv.

impunity [im′pju:niti], *s.* die Straffreiheit.

impure [im′pjuə], *adj.* (*also Metall.*, *Chem.*) unrein, unedel; unsauber.

impute [im′pju:t], *v.a.* beimessen; zurechnen, die Schuld geben für.

in [in], *prep.* in; an; zu, auf; bei; nach, unter; über; von; mit; — *the morning*, vormittags; — *case*, falls; — *any case*, auf jeden Fall; — *German*, auf deutsch; — *my opinion*, meiner Meinung nach; — *the street*, auf der Straße; — *time*, rechtzeitig. — *adv.* drinnen, innen; herein, hinein; zu Hause.

inability [inə′biliti], *s.* die Unfähigkeit.

inaccessible [inæk′sesibl], *adj.* unzugänglich.

inaccurate [i′nækjurit], *adj.* ungenau.

inaction [i′nækʃən], *s.* die Untätigkeit.

inactive [i′næktiv], *adj.* untätig.

inadequate [i′nædikwit], *adj.* unzulänglich.

inadmissible [inəd′misibl], *adj.* unzulässig.

inadvertent [inəd′və:tənt], *adj.* unbeabsichtigt; unachtsam.

inadvertently [inəd′və:təntli], *adv.* unversehens; versehentlich.

inalienable [in′eiliənəbl], *adj.* unveräußerlich.

inane [i′nein], *adj.* hohl, leer, sinnlos.

inanimate [i′nænimit], *adj.* unbeseelt, leblos.

inanity [i′næniti], *s.* die Leere, Nichtigkeit.

inapplicable [i′næplikəbl], *adj.* unanwendbar; unzutreffend.

inappropriate [inə′proupriit], *adj.* unpassend.

inarticulate [ina:′tikjulit], *adj.* unartikuliert.

inasmuch [inəz′mʌtʃ], *adv.* insofern(als).

inattentive [inə′tentiv], *adj.* unaufmerksam.

inaudible [i′nɔ:dibl], *adj.* unhörbar.

inaugural [i′nɔ:gjurəl], *adj.* Inaugural-, Eröffnungs-, Antritts-.

inaugurate [i′nɔ:gjureit], *v.a.* einweihen, eröffnen.

inauspicious [inɔ:′spiʃəs], *adj.* ungünstig.

inborn [′inbɔ:n], *adj.* angeboren.

inbred [′inbred], *adj.* in Inzucht geboren; angeboren, ererbt.

inbreeding [′inbri:din], *s.* die Inzucht.

incalculable [in′kælkjuləbl], *adj.* unberechenbar.

incandescence [inkæn′desəns], *s.* die Weißglut.

incandescent [inkæn′desənt], *adj.* weißglühend.

incantation [inkæn′teiʃən], *s.* die Beschwörung.

incapable [in′keipəbl], *adj.* unfähig (*of doing s.th.*, etwas zu tun).

incapacitate [inkə′pæsiteit], *v.a.* unfähig machen.

incapacity [inkə′pæsiti], *s.* die Unfähigkeit.

incarcerate [in′ka:səreit], *v.a.* einkerkern, einsperren.

incarnate [in′ka:nit], *adj.* eingefleischt; (*Theol.*) verkörpert.

incarnation [inka:′neiʃən], *s.* die Verkörperung; (*Theol.*) Menschwerdung.

incautious [in′kɔ:ʃəs], *adj.* unvorsichtig.

incendiary [in′sendjəri], *adj.* Brand-, brennend. — *s.* der Brandstifter.

incense [in′sens], *v.a.* aufregen, erzürnen (*make angry*); (*Eccl.*) beweihräuchern. — [′insens], *s.* (*Eccl.*) der Weihrauch.

incentive [in′sentiv], *adj.* Ansporn-, Anreiz-. — *s.* der Ansporn, Anreiz; (*Comm.*) — *scheme*, das Inzentivsystem, Akkordsystem.

incessant [in′sesənt], *adj.* unaufhörlich, ununterbrochen.

incest [′insest], *s.* die Blutschande.

incestuous [in′sestjuəs], *adj.* blutschänderisch.

inch [intʃ], *s.* der Zoll. — *v.n.* — *away*, abrücken.

incident [′insidənt], *s.* der Vorfall, Zwischenfall; das Ereignis.

incidental [insi′dentl], *adj.* zufällig. — *s.* (*pl.*) zufällige Ausgaben, *f. pl.*; das Zusätzliche, Nebenausgaben, *f. pl.*

incipient [in′sipiənt], *adj.* beginnend, anfangend.

incise [in′saiz], *v.a.* einschneiden, (*Med.*) einen Einschnitt machen.

incision [in′siʒən], *s.* der Einschnitt.

incisive [in′saisiv], *adj.* einschneidend; energisch (*person*).

incite [in′sait], *v.a.* aufreizen, anspornen.

incivility [insi′viliti], *s.* die Unhöflichkeit.

inclement [in′klemənt], *adj.* unfreundlich (*weather, climate*).

inclination [inkli′neiʃən], *s.* die Neigung (*also fig.*).

incline [in′klain], *v.n.* neigen, sich neigen. — [′inklain], *s.* der Neigungswinkel; der Abhang.

include [in′klu:d], *v.a.* einschließen (*contain*); umfassen (*enclose*).

including

including [in'klu:diŋ], *prep.* einschließlich.

inclusive [in'klu:siv], *adj.* einschließlich, mitgerechnət.

incoherent [inko'hiərənt], *adj.* unzusammenhängend.

incombustible [inkəm'bʌstibl], *adj.*
unverbrennbar.

income ['inkʌm], *s.* das Einkommen.

**incommensurable, incommensu-
rate** [inkə'menʃərəbl, inkə'menʃərit],
adj. unvereinbar, unmeßbar.

incomparable [in'kɔmpərəbl], *adj.* unvergleichlich.

incompatible [inkəm'pætibl], *adj.* unvereinbar.

incompetence, incompetency [in-
'kɔmpitəns, -tənsi], *s.* die Inkompe-
tenz; Unzulänglichkeit.

incompetent [in'kɔmpitənt], *adj.* unzuständig, inkompetent; unzulänglich.

incomplete [inkəm'pli:t], *adj.* unvollständig.

incomprehensible [inkɔmpri'hensibl],
adj. unverständlich.

inconceivable [inkən'si:vəbl], *adj.* unbegreiflich.

inconclusive [inkən'klu:siv], *adj.* unvollständig (*incomplete*); unüberzeu-
gend; ergebnislos.

incongruity [inkən'gru:iti], *s.* (*Maths.*)
die Inkongruenz; (*fig.*) die Unan-
gemessenheit.

incongruous [in'kɔŋgruəs], *adj.* in-
kongruent; unangemessen.

inconsequent [in'kɔnsikwənt], *adj.* folg-
ewidrig.

inconsequential [inkɔnsi'kwenʃəl], *adj.*
inkonsequent (*inconsistent*); unzusammenhängend.

inconsiderate [inkən'sidərit], *adj.* rücksichtslos, unbedachtsam.

inconsistent [inkən'sistənt], *adj.* inkonsequent.

inconsolable [inkən'souləbl], *adj.* untröstlich.

inconstancy [in'kɔnstənsi], *s.* die Unbeständigkeit; Untreue (*fickleness*).

incontestable [inkən'testəbl], *adj.* unanfechtbar, unbestreitbar.

incontinent [in'kɔntinənt], *adj.* unent-
haltsam.

incontrovertible [inkɔntro'və:tibl], *adj.*
unstreitig, unanfechtbar.

inconvenience [inkən'vi:niəns], *s.* die
Unbequemlichkeit, Unannehmlich-
keit.

inconvenient [inkən'vi:niənt], *adj.* unangenehm, unpassend.

inconvertible [inkən'və:tibl], *adj.* unveränderlich; (*Comm.*) unumsetzbar.

incorporate [in'kɔ:pəreit], *v.a.* einverleiben (*Dat.*), eingliedern (*Acc.*).

incorporated [in'kɔ:pəreitid], *adj.*
(*Am.*) eingetragene Körperschaft,
eingetragener Verein.

incorrect [inkə'rekt], *adj.* unrichtig,
fehlerhaft; unschicklich, unpassend.

incorrigible [in'kɔridʒibl], *adj.* unverbesserlich.

incorruptible [inkə'rʌptibl], *adj.* unbestechlich.

increase [in'kri:s], *v.a.* vermehren,
vergrößern (*size, volume*); steigern
(*heat, intensity*); erhöhen (*price*). —
v.n. sich vermehren, sich erhöhen;
wachsen (*grow*). — ['inkri:s], *s.* die
Zunahme; der Zuwachs (*family*); die
Erhöhung.

incredible [in'kredibl], *adj.* unglaublich.

incredulity [inkre'dju:liti], *s.* die
Ungläubigkeit, der Unglaube.

incredulous [in'kredjuləs], *adj.* ungläubig, schwer zu überzeugen.

increment ['inkrimənt], *s.* (*Comm.*) die
Zulage, Gehaltserhöhung.

incriminate [in'krimineit], *v.a.* beschuldigen, inkriminieren.

incubate ['inkjubeit], *v.a.* brüten, ausbrüten. — *v.n.* brüten.

incubator ['inkjubeitə], *s.* der Brutap-
parat.

inculcate ['inkʌlkeit], *v.a.* einprägen.

inculpate ['inkʌlpeit], *v.a.* beschuldigen.

incumbent [in'kʌmbənt], *adj.* (*upon,
Dat.*) obliegend, nötig. — *s.* der
Pfründner, Amtsinhaber.

incur [in'kə:], *v.a.* auf sich laden, sich
zuziehen.

incurable [in'kjuərəbl], *adj.* unheilbar.

incursion [in'kə:ʃən], *s.* der Einfall,
Streifzug.

indebted [in'detid], *adj.* verpflichtet,
dankbar (*grateful*); verschuldet (*in
debt*).

indecent [in'di:sənt], *adj.* unschicklich,
unanständig.

indecision [indi'siʒən], *s.* die Unentschlossenheit.

indecisive [indi'saisiv], *adj.* unentschlossen.

indeclinable [indi'klainəbl], *adj.*
(*Gram.*) undeklinierbar.

indecorous [indi'kɔ:rəs *or* in'dekərəs],
adj. unrühmlich, unanständig.

indeed [in'di:d], *adv.* in der Tat,
tatsächlich.

indefatigable [indi'fætigəbl], *adj.* unermüdlich.

indefensible [indi'fensibl], *adj.* unhaltbar; unverzeihlich (*unforgivable*).

indefinable [indi'fainəbl], *adj.* unbestimmbar, undefinierbar.

indefinite [in'definit], *adj.* unbestimmt.

indelible [in'delibl], *adj.* unauslöschlich.

indelicate [in'delikit], *adj.* unfein.

indemnify [in'demnifai], *v.a.* entschädigen.

indemnity [in'demniti], die Entschädigung.

indent [in'dent], *v.a.* auszacken, einschneiden.

indenture [in'dentʃə], *s.* der Lehrbrief
(*apprentice*); Vertrag.

independence [indi'pendəns], *s.* die
Unabhängigkeit, Freiheit.

independent [indi'pendənt], *adj.* unabhängig, frei.

indescribable [indi'skraibəbl], *adj.* unbeschreiblich.

indestructible [indi'strʌktibl], *adj.* unverwüstlich; unzerstörbar.

indeterminable [indi'tə:minəbl], *adj.* unbestimmbar.

indeterminate [indi'tə:minit], *adj.* unbestimmt.

index ['indeks], *s.* (*pl.* **indexes**) das Inhaltsverzeichnis; (*pl.* **indices**) (*Maths.*) der Exponent; — *finger*, der Zeigefinger; (*pl.*) die Finger, Zeiger, *m. pl.* (*pointers*).

India ['indjə], das Indien; — *paper*, das Dünnpapier.

Indian ['indjən], *adj.* indisch; — *ink*, die Tusche. — *s.* der Ind(i)er.

indiarubber ['indjə'rʌbə], *s.* der Radiergummi.

indicate ['indikeit], *v.a.* anzeigen, angeben.

indication [indi'keiʃən], *s.* das Anzeichen, Merkmal, der Hinweis.

indicative [in'dikətiv], *adj.* bezeichnend (für, *Acc.*). — *s.* (*Gram.*) der Indikativ.

indict [in'dait], *v.a.* anklagen.

indictment [in'daitmənt], *s.* die Anklage.

indifference [in'difrəns], *s.* die Gleichgültigkeit.

indifferent [in'difrənt], *adj.* gleichgültig.

indigence ['indidʒəns], *s.* die Armut.

indigenous [in'didʒinəs], *adj.* eingeboren, einheimisch.

indigent ['indidʒənt], *adj.* arm, dürftig.

indigestible [indi'dʒestibl], *adj.* unverdaulich.

indigestion [indi'dʒestʃən], *s.* die Magenbeschwerden, *f. pl.*; die Magenverstimmung.

indignant [in'dignənt], *adj.* empört, unwillig, entrüstet.

indignation [indig'neiʃən], *s.* die Entrüstung, der Unwille.

indignity [in'digniti], *s.* die Schmach, der Schimpf.

indirect [indi'rekt], *adj.* indirekt, mittelbar.

indiscreet [indis'kri:t], *adj.* indiskret, unvorsichtig; unbescheiden (*immodest*); taktlos.

indiscretion [indis'kreʃən], *s.* die Indiskretion, Taktlosigkeit.

indiscriminate [indis'kriminit], *adj.* ohne Unterschied, wahllos, kritiklos.

indispensable [indis'pensəbl], *adj.* unerläßlich, unentbehrlich.

indisposed [indis'pouzd], *adj.* unwohl (*health*); unwillig (*unwilling*).

indisposition [indispə'ziʃən], *s.* das Unwohlsein (*health*); das Abgeneigtsein (*disinclination*).

indisputable [indis'pju:təbl], *adj.* unbestreitbar.

indissoluble [indi'sɔljubl], *adj.* unauflöslich.

indistinct [indis'tiŋkt], *adj.* undeutlich.

indistinguishable [indis'tiŋgwiʃəbl], *adj.* nicht zu unterscheiden, ununterscheidbar.

individual [indi'vidjuəl], *adj.* individuell, persönlich; einzeln (*single*). — *s.* das Individuum, Einzelwesen.

individuality [individju'æliti], *s.* die Individualität.

indivisible [indi'vizibl], *adj.* unteilbar.

Indo-Chinese [indotʃai'ni:z], *adj.* hinterindisch. — *s.* der Hinterind(i)er.

indolent ['indələnt], *adj.* indolent, träge.

Indonesian [indo'ni:ʒən], *adj.* indonesisch. — *s.* der Indonesier.

indoor ['indɔ:], *adj.* im Haus; drinnen (*inside*).

indoors [in'dɔ:z], *adv.* im Hause, zu Hause.

indubitable [in'dju:bitəbl], *adj.* zweifellos, unzweifelhaft.

induce [in'dju:s], *v.a.* veranlassen, bewegen, verleiten (*incite*).

inducement [in'dju:smənt], *s.* der Beweggrund (*cause*); der Anlaß (*reason*); die Verleitung (*incitement*).

induction [in'dʌkʃən], *s.* die Einführung; (*Elec.*) die Induktion.

inductive [in'dʌktiv], *adj.* (*Log.*, *Elec.*) induktiv.

indulge [in'dʌldʒ], *v.a.* nachgeben (*Dat.*); verwöhnen. — *v.n.* — *in*, frönen (*Dat.*).

indulgence [in'dʌldʒəns], *s.* die Nachsicht; das Wohlleben; (*Eccl.*) der Ablaß.

industrial [in'dʌstriəl], *adj.* industriell, Industrie-.

industrious [in'dʌstriəs], *adj.* fleißig, arbeitsam.

industry ['indəstri], *s.* die Industrie (*production*); der Fleiß (*industriousness*).

inebriate [i'ni:brieit], *v.a.* berauschen. — [-iit], *adj.* berauscht.

ineffable [i'nefəbl], *adj.* unaussprechlich.

ineffective, ineffectual [ini'fektiv, ini'fektjuəl], *adj.* unwirksam, wirkungslos; unfähig.

inefficiency [ini'fiʃənsi], *s.* die Erfolglosigkeit, Untauglichkeit.

inefficient [ini'fiʃənt], *adj.* untauglich, untüchtig.

ineligible [in'elidʒibl], *adj.* nicht wählbar.

inept [i'nept], *adj.* untüchtig, albern, dumm.

ineptitude [i'neptitju:d], *s.* die Unfähigkeit; die Dummheit (*stupidity*).

inequality [ini'kwɔliti], *s.* die Ungleichheit.

inert [i'nə:t], *adj.* träg.

inestimable [in'estiməbl], *adj.* unschätzbar.

inevitable [in'evitəbl], *adj.* unumgänglich, unvermeidlich.

inexcusable [iniks'kju:zəbl], *adj.* unverzeihlich, unentschuldbar.

inexhaustible [inig'zɔ:stibl], *adj.* unerschöpflich.

inexpedient [iniks'pi:djənt], *adj.* unzweckmäßig, unpraktisch, unpassend.

inexpensive [iniks'pensiv], *adj.* billig, nicht kostspielig.

inexperience [iniks'piəriəns], *s.* die Unerfahrenheit, Naivität.

inexpert [iniks'pə:t], *adj.* ungeübt, unerfahren.

inexpiable [i'nekspiəbl], *adj.* unsühnbar, nicht wieder gut zu machen.

inexplicable [i'neksplikəbl], *adj.* unerklärlich.

inexpressible [iniks'presibl], *adj.* unaussprechlich.

inexpressive [iniks'presiv], *adj.* ausdruckslos.

inextinguishable [iniks'tiŋgwiʃəbl], *adj.* unauslöschlich.

inextricable [i'nekstrikəbl], *adj.* unentwirrbar.

infallible [in'fælibl], *adj.* unfehlbar.

infamous ['infəməs], *adj.* verrufen, abscheulich, berüchtigt.

infamy ['infəmi], *s.* die Schande; Ehrlosigkeit (*dishonour*).

infancy ['infənsi], *s.* die Kindheit, Unmündigkeit; (*fig.*) der Anfang.

infant ['infənt], *s.* das Kind; (*Law*) der Unmündige, das Mündel.

infantry ['infəntri], *s.* die Infanterie.

infatuate [in'fætjueit], *v.a.* betören.

infect [in'fekt], *v.a.* anstecken, infizieren.

infection [in'fekʃən], *s.* (*Med.*) die Ansteckung, Infektion.

infectious [in'fekʃəs], *adj.* (*Med.*) ansteckend.

infer [in'fə:], *v.a.* schließen, herleiten, folgern.

inference ['infərəns], *s.* die Folgerung.

inferior [in'fiəriə], *comp. adj.* geringer; untergeordnet (*subordinate*); schlechter (*worse*).

inferiority [infiəri'oriti], *s.* die Inferiorität, Minderwertigkeit.

infernal [in'fə:nəl], *adj.* höllisch.

infest [in'fest], *v.a.* heimsuchen, plagen.

infidel ['infidəl], *adj.* ungläubig. — *s.* der Heide, Ungläubige.

infiltrate ['infiltreit], *v.n.* durchsickern, durchdringen, infiltrieren.

infinite ['infinit], *adj.* unendlich.

infinitive [in'finitiv], *s.* (*Gram.*) der Infinitiv, die Nennform.

infirm [in'fə:m], *adj.* gebrechlich, schwach; siech (*sick*).

infirmary [in'fə:məri], *s.* das Krankenhaus.

infirmity [in'fə:miti], *s.* die Schwäche, Gebrechlichkeit.

inflame [in'fleim], *v.a.* entzünden.

inflammation [inflə'meiʃən], *s.* die Entzündung.

inflate [in'fleit], *v.a.* aufblasen, aufblähen; (*Comm.*) künstlich erhöhen (*values*).

inflation [in'fleiʃən], *s.* die Aufblähung; (*Comm.*) die Inflation.

inflect [in'flekt], *v.a.* (*Gram.*) biegen, flektieren, deklinieren, konjugieren.

inflection [in'flekʃən], *s.* (*Gram.*) die Biegung; (*Phonet.*) der Tonfall.

inflexible [in'fleksibl], *adj.* unbiegsam.

inflexion *see* **inflection**.

inflict [in'flikt], *v.a.* auferlegen (*impose*); beibringen (*administer*).

infliction [in'flikʃən], *s.* die Verhängung, das Beibringen.

influence ['influəns], *v.a.* beeinflussen. — *s.* der Einfluß.

influential [influ'enʃəl], *adj.* einflußreich.

influenza [influ'enzə], *s.* (*Med.*) die Grippe.

inform [in'fo:m], *v.a., v.n.* informieren, benachrichtigen; — *against*, jemanden denunzieren.

informal [in'fo:məl], *adj.* nicht formell; ungezwungen, zwanglos.

informant [in'fo:mənt], *s.* der Angeber.

information [infə'meiʃən], *s.* die Information, Nachricht, Auskunft.

infrequent [in'fri:kwənt], *adj.* selten.

infringe [in'frindʒ], *v.a.* übertreten.

infuriate [in'fjuərieit], *v.a.* wütend machen.

infuse [in'fju:z], *v.a.* einflößen, aufgießen, begießen.

infusion [in'fju:ʒən], *s.* die Eingießung; der Aufguß (*tea*); (*Chem.*) die Infusion.

ingenious [in'dʒi:niəs], *adj.* geistreich, genial.

ingenuity [indʒi'nju:iti], *s.* der Scharfsinn.

ingenuous [in'dʒenjuəs], *adj.* offen, unbefangen, arglos.

ingot ['iŋgət], *s.* der Barren.

ingrained [in'greind], *adj.* eingefleischt.

ingratiate [in'greiʃieit], *v.r.* — *o.s.*, sich beliebt machen, sich einschmeicheln (*with*, bei).

ingratitude [in'grætitju:d], *s.* die Undankbarkeit.

ingredient [in'gri:diənt], *s.* der Bestandteil, die Zutat.

inhabit [in'hæbit], *v.a.* bewohnen.

inhabitant [in'hæbitənt], *s.* der Bewohner; Einwohner.

inhale [in'heil], *v.a.* einatmen.

inherent [in'hiərənt], *adj.* eigen, angeboren (*innate*); in der Sache selbst (*intrinsic*).

inherit [in'herit], *v.a.* erben.

inheritance [in'heritəns], *s.* die Erbschaft, das Erbgut (*patrimony*); (*fig.*) das Erbe.

inhibit [in'hibit], *v.a.* hindern; —*ing factor*, der Hemmfaktor.

inhibition [ini'biʃən], *s.* (*Psych.*) die Hemmung.

inhospitable [in'hɔs'pitəbl], *adj.* ungastlich, ungastfreundlich.

inhuman [in'hju:mən], *adj.* unmenschlich.

inhume [in'hju:m], *v.a.* beerdigen.

inimical [i'nimikəl], *adj.* feindlich (gesinnt), feindselig.

inimitable [i'nimitəbl], *adj.* unnachahmlich.

iniquitous [i'nikwitəs], *adj.* ungerecht, schlecht, boshaft.

iniquity [i'nikwiti], *s.* die Ungerechtigkeit (*injustice*); die Schändlichkeit (*shame*).

initial [i'niʃəl], *adj.* anfänglich. — *s.* (*Typ.*) der Anfangsbuchstabe.

initiate [i'niʃieit], *v.a.* einweihen, anfangen.

initiative [i'niʃiətiv], *s.* die Initiative; der erste Anstoß (*impulse*).

injection [in'dʒekʃən], *s.* (*Med.*) die Einspritzung, Injektion.

injudicious [indʒu'diʃəs], *adj.* unbedacht, unbesonnen; übereilt (*rash*).

injunction [in'dʒʌŋkʃən], *s.* die Vorschrift, (*Law*) die gerichtliche Verfügung.

injure ['indʒə], *v.a.* verletzen.

injurious [in'dʒuəriəs], *adj.* verletzend; schädlich (*harmful*).

injury ['indʒəri], *s.* die Verletzung, Verwundung; der Schaden (*damage*).

injustice [in'dʒʌstis], *s.* die Ungerechtigkeit.

ink [iŋk], *s.* die Tinte.

inkling ['iŋkliŋ], *s.* die Ahnung.

inkstand ['iŋkstænd], *s.* das Schreibzeug.

inlaid [in'leid], *adj.* eingelegt.

inland [in'lænd], *adj.* inländisch, Binnen-; — *revenue office*, das Steueramt, Finanzamt.

inlet ['inlit], *s.* (*Geog.*) die kleine Bucht.

inmate ['inmeit], *s.* der Insasse, Bewohner.

inmost ['inmoust], *adj.* innerst.

inn [in], *s.* der Gasthof, das Wirtshaus; *Inns of Court*, die Londoner Rechtskammern, *f. pl.*

innate [i'neit], *adj.* angeboren.

inner ['inə], *adj.* inner; geheim (*secret*).

innings ['iniŋz], *s.* das Daransein (*in Cricket*); die Reihe.

innocence ['inəsəns], *s.* die Unschuld.

innocuous [i'nɔkjuəs], *adj.* unschädlich.

innovate ['inoveit], *v.a., v.n.* als Neuerung einführen, Neuerungen machen.

innovation [ino'veiʃən], *s.* die Neuerung.

innuendo [inju'endou], *s.* das Innuendo, die Anspielung.

innumerable [i'nju:mərəbl], *adj.* unzählig, unzählbar.

inoculate [i'nɔkjuleit], *v.a.* impfen.

inoffensive [ino'fensiv], *adj.* harmlos, unschädlich.

inopportune [in'ɔpətju:n], *adj.* ungelegen.

inordinate [in'ɔ:dinit], *adj.* unmäßig.

inorganic [inɔ:'gænik], *adj.* anorganisch.

inquest ['inkwest], *s.* die gerichtliche Untersuchung (*Law*); *coroner's* —, die Leichenschau.

inquire, enquire [in'kwaiə], *v.n.* sich erkundigen (*after*, nach, *Dat.*), nachfragen.

inquiry, enquiry [in'kwaiəri], *s.* die Nachfrage; — *office*, die Auskunftsstelle.

inquisition [inkwi'ziʃən], *s.* (*Eccl.*) die Inquisition; die gerichtliche Untersuchung.

inquisitive [in'kwizitiv], *adj.* neugierig.

inquisitiveness [in'kwizitivnis], *s.* die Neugier(de).

inroad ['inroud], *s.* der Eingriff, Überfall.

insane [in'sein], *adj.* wahnsinnig.

insanity [in'sæniti], *s.* der Wahnsinn.

insatiable [in'seiʃəbl], *adj.* unersättlich.

inscribe [in'skraib], *v.a.* einschreiben (*enrol*); widmen (*book*).

inscription [in'skripʃən], *s.* die Inschrift.

inscrutable [in'skru:təbl], *adj.* unergründlich, unerforschlich.

insect ['insekt], *s.* das Insekt, Kerbtier.

insecure [insi'kjuə], *adj.* unsicher.

insensate [in'sensit], *adj.* unsinnig (*senseless*); gefühllos..

insensible [in'sensibl], *adj.* unempfindlich; gefühllos.

insensitive [in'sensitiv], *adj.* ohne feineres Gefühl, unempfindlich.

inseparable [in'sepərəbl], *adj.* unzertrennlich, untrennbar.

insert [in'sə:t], *v.a.* einsetzen, einschalten (*add*); inserieren (*in newspaper*).

insertion [in'sə:ʃən], *s.* die Einschaltung (*addition*); die Annonce, das Inserat (*press*).

inside [in'said], *adj.* inner. — *adv.* im Innern. — *prep.* innerhalb. — *s.* das Innere.

insidious [in'sidiəs], *adj.* heimtückisch.

insight ['insait], *s.* der Einblick.

insignia [in'signiə], *s. pl.* die Insignien.

insignificance [insig'nifikəns], *s.* die Geringfügigkeit, Bedeutungslosigkeit.

insignificant [insig'nifikənt], *adj.* unbedeutend, geringfügig.

insincere [insin'siə], *adj.* unaufrichtig.

insincerity [insin'seriti], *s.* die Unaufrichtigkeit.

insinuate [in'sinjueit], *v.a.* zu verstehen geben, andeuten, anspielen auf (*Acc.*).

insinuation [insinju'eiʃən], *s.* der Wink, die Andeutung, Anspielung.

insipid [in'sipid], *adj.* schal, geschmacklos.

insist [in'sist], *v.n.* bestehen (*upon*, auf, *Dat.*).

insistence [in'sistəns], *s.* das Bestehen, Beharren.

insolence ['insələns], *s.* die Frechheit.

insolent ['insələnt], *adj.* frech, unverschämt.

insoluble [in'sɔljubl], *adj.* unlösbar; (*Chem.*) unlöslich.

insolvent [in'sɔlvənt], *adj.* insolvent, zahlungsunfähig, bankrott.

inspect [in'spekt], *v.a.* inspizieren; besichtigen.

inspection [in'spekʃən], *s.* die Inspektion; Besichtigung.

inspiration [inspi'reiʃən], *s.* die Inspiration, Erleuchtung, Begeisterung.

inspire [in'spaiə], *v.a.* inspirieren, begeistern.

instability [instə'biliti], *s.* die Unbeständigkeit, Labilität.

install [in'stɔ:l], *v.a.* einsetzen (*in office*); einbauen.

installation [instə'leiʃən], *s.* die Einsetzung (*inauguration*); die Installation.

instalment [in'stɔ:lmənt], *s.* die Rate; *by* —*s,* auf Abzahlung; die Fortsetzung (*serial*).

instance ['instəns], *s.* das Beispiel (*example*); (*Law*) die Instanz; *at my* —, auf meine dringende Bitte; *for* —, zum Beispiel. — *v.a.* als Beispiel anführen.

instant ['instənt], *s.* der Augenblick. — *adj.* gegenwärtig; sofortig; laufend (*current month*).

instantaneous [instən'teiniəs], *adj.* augenblicklich, sofortig.

instead [in'sted], *adv.* dafür, stattdessen; — *of,* (an)statt (*Genit.*).

instep [in'step], *s.* (*Anat.*) der Rist.

instigate ['instigeit], *v.a.* aufhetzen, anreizen, anstiften.

instil [in'stil], *v.a.* einflößen.

instinct ['instiŋkt], *s.* der Instinkt, Naturtrieb.

institute ['institju:t], *s.* das Institut. — *v.a.* einrichten (*install*); stiften (*found*).

institution [insti'tju:ʃən], *s.* die Stiftung (*foundation*); die Anstalt (*establishment*).

instruct [in'strʌkt], *v.a.* unterrichten, unterweisen.

instruction [in'strʌkʃən], *s.* der Unterricht (*in schools etc.*); (*pl.*) die Instruktionen, *f. pl.*; die Direktive.

instructive [in'strʌktiv], *adj.* instruktiv, lehrreich.

instrument ['instrumənt], *s.* das Instrument; Werkzeug (*tool*).

insubordination [insəbɔ:di'neiʃən], *s.* der Ungehorsam.

insufferable [in'sʌfərəbl], *adj.* unerträglich.

insufficient [insə'fiʃənt], *adj.* ungenügend, unzulänglich.

insular ['insjulə], *adj.* Insel-; insular (*narrow-minded*).

insulate ['insjuleit], *v.a.* absondern (*separate*); (*Elec.*) isolieren; *insulating tape,* das Isolierband.

insult [in'sʌlt], *v.a.* beleidigen.

insuperable [in'sju:pərəbl], *adj.* unüberwindlich.

insupportable [insə'pɔ:təbl], *adj.* unhaltbar (*argument*); unerträglich (*insufferable*).

insurance [in'ʃuərəns], *s.* die Versicherung; — *policy,* die Police; — *premium,* die Prämie; — *broker,* der Versicherungsmakler.

insure [in'ʃuə], *v.a.* versichern.

insurgent [in'sə:dʒənt], *s.* der Aufständische, Aufrührer.

insurmountable [insə'mauntəbl], *adj.* unüberwindlich.

insurrection [insə'rekʃən], *s.* der Aufstand, Aufruhr; die Empörung.

intact [in'tækt], *adj.* unversehrt, intakt.

intangible [in'tændʒibl], *adj.* unberührbar (*untouchable*); (*Log.*) abstrakt. — *s. pl.* (*Log.*) die Intangibilien, *pl.*

integer ['intidʒə], *s.* (*Maths.*) das Ganze, die ganze Zahl.

integral ['intigrəl], *adj.* wesentlich; vollständig. — *s.* (*Maths.*) das Integral.

integrate ['intigreit], *v.a.* (*Maths.*) integrieren.

integration [inti'greiʃən], *s.* (*Maths.*) die Integrierung; (*fig.*) die Integration, das völlige Aufgehen.

integrity [in'tegriti], *s.* die Rechtschaffenheit, Redlichkeit (*probity*).

intellect ['intilekt], *s.* der Geist, Intellekt, Verstand.

intellectual [inti'lektjuəl], *adj.* intellektuell. — *s.* der Intellektuelle.

intelligence [in'telidʒəns], *s.* die Intelligenz; die Nachricht (*news*).

intelligent [in'telidʒənt], *adj.* intelligent.

intelligible [in'telidʒibl], *adj.* verständlich.

intemperance [in'tempərəns], *s.* die Unmäßigkeit.

intemperate [in'tempərit], *adj.* unmäßig.

intend [in'tend], *v.a.* beabsichtigen, vorhaben.

intendant [in'tendənt], *s.* der Intendant, Verwalter.

intense [in'tens], *adj.* intensiv, heftig.

intent [in'tent], *adj.* gespannt, begierig, bedacht (*on,* auf, *Acc.*). — *s.* die Absicht.

intention [in'tenʃən], *s.* die Absicht.

intentioned [in'tenʃənd], *adj. well-* —, wohlgesinnt.

inter [in'tə:], *v.a.* beerdigen.

intercede [intə'si:d], *v.n.* vermitteln (*between*); sich verwenden (*on behalf of,* für, *Acc.*).

intercept [intə'sept], *v.a.* abfangen, auffangen, hemmen.

intercession [intə'seʃən], *s.* die Vermittlung, Fürsprache, Fürbitte.

interchange [intə'tʃeindʒ], *s.* der Austausch. — [-'tʃeindʒ], *v.a.* austauschen.

intercourse ['intəkɔ:s], *s.* der Verkehr, Umgang.

interdict [intə'dikt], *v.a.* untersagen, verbieten.

interest ['intrəst], *s.* das Interesse; die Beteiligung; (*Comm.*) die Zinsen, *m. pl.*; *compound* —, die Zinseszinsen, *m. pl.* — *v.a.* interessieren.

interested ['intrəstid], *adj.* (*in,* an, *Dat.*) interessiert; *be* — *in,* sich interessieren für.

interesting ['intrəstiŋ], *adj.* interessant.

interfere [intə'fiə], *v.n.* sich einmischen, eingreifen (*in*, in, *Acc.*)

interference [intə'fiərəns], *s.* die Einmischung; (*Rad.*) die Störung.

interim ['intərim], *adj.* vorläufig, Zwischen-.

interior [in'tiəriə], *adj.* innerlich. — *s.* das Innere; das Binnenland; — *decorator*, der Innenraumgestalter, der Innenarchitekt; *Ministry of the Interior*, das Innenministerium.

interjection [intə'dʒekʃən], *s.* die Interjektion; der Ausruf.

interlace [intə'leis], *v.a.* einflechten.

interleave [intə'liːv], *v.a.* durchschießen (*a book*).

interlinear [intə'liniə], *adj.* zwischenzeilig.

interlocutor [intə'lɔkjutə], *s.* der Gesprächspartner.

interloper ['intəloupə], *s.* der Eindringling.

interlude ['intəljuːd], *s.* das Zwischenspiel.

intermarry [intə'mæri], *v.n.* untereinander heiraten.

intermediate [intə'miːdiːt], *adj.* Mittel-; (*Sch.*) — *certificate*, das Mittelstufenzeugnis.

interment [in'təːmənt], *s.* die Beerdigung.

interminable [in'təːminəbl], *adj.* endlos, langwierig.

intermingle [intə'miŋgl], *v.n.* sich vermischen.

intermission [intə'miʃən], *s.* die Pause, Unterbrechung.

intermit [intə'mit], *v.a.* unterbrechen.

intermittent [intə'mitənt], *adj.* Wechsel-, aussetzend.

internal [in'təːnl], *adj.* intern, innerlich.

international [intə'næʃənəl], *adj.* international; — *law*, das Völkerrecht.

interpolate [in'təːpoleit], *v.a.* interpolieren, einschalten.

interpose [intə'pouz], *v.a.* dazwischenstellen. — *v.n.* vermitteln (*mediate*).

interpret [in'təːprit], *v.a.* verdolmetschen; erklären (*explain*); auslegen, interpretieren.

interpretation [intəːpri'teiʃən], *s.* die Auslegung, Interpretation.

interpreter [in'təːpritə], *s.* der Dolmetscher.

interrogate [in'terogeit], *v.a.* ausfragen, befragen, vernehmen.

interrogation [intero'geiʃən], *s.* die Befragung; (*Law*) das Verhör, die Vernehmung.

interrogative [intə'rɔgətiv], *adj.* (*Gram.*) Frage-, Interrogativ-.

interrupt [intə'rʌpt], *v.a.* unterbrechen; stören (*disturb*).

interruption [intə'rʌpʃən], *s.* die Unterbrechung; Störung (*disturbance*).

intersect [intə'sekt], *v.a.* durchschneiden.

intersperse [intə'spəːs], *v.a.* untermengen, vermischen, einstreuen.

intertwine [intə'twain], *v.a.*, *v.n.* (sich) durchflechten.

interval ['intəvəl], *s.* der Zwischenraum; die Pause; (*Mus.*) das Interval.

intervene [intə'viːn], *v.n.* eingreifen; als Vermittler dienen (*act as mediator*).

intervention [intə'venʃən], *s.* die Vermittlung, Intervention.

interview ['intəvjuː], *v.a.* zur Vorsprache einladen (*a candidate*); interviewen. — *s.* die Vorsprache, das Interview.

intestate [in'testit], *adj.* ohne Testament.

intestines [in'testinz], *s. pl.* (*Anat.*) die Eingeweide, *n. pl.*

intimacy ['intiməsi], *s.* die Vertraulichkeit, Intimität.

intimate ['intimit], *adj.* intim, vertraut, vertraulich. — [-meit], *v.a.* andeuten, zu verstehen geben.

intimation [inti'meiʃən], *s.* der Wink, die Andeutung.

intimidate [in'timideit], *v.a.* einschüchtern.

into ['intu], *prep.* (*Acc.*) in, in ... hinein (*towards*).

intolerable [in'tɔlərəbl], *adj.* unerträglich.

intolerance [in'tɔlərəns], *s.* die Unduldsamkeit, Intoleranz.

intonation [into'neiʃən], *s.* (*Phonet.*) die Intonation; (*Mus.*) das Anstimmen, der Tonansatz (*of instruments*).

intoxicate [in'tɔksikeit], *v.a.* berauschen.

intractable [in'træktəbl], *adj.* unbändig, unlenksam.

intransitive [in'trænsitiv *or* in'trɑːns-], *adj.* (*Gram.*) intransitiv.

intrepid [in'trepid], *adj.* unerschrocken, furchtlos.

intricacy ['intrikəsi], *s.* die Verwicklung (*tangle*), Schwierigkeit (*difficulty*).

intricate ['intrikit], *adj.* verwickelt, schwierig.

intrigue [in'triːg], *s.* die Intrige. — *v.n.* intrigieren.

intrinsic [in'trinsik], *adj.* wesentlich; innerlich (*inner*).

introduce [intrə'djuːs], *v.a.* einführen, einleiten (*book etc.*); vorstellen (*person*).

introduction [intrə'dʌkʃən], *s.* die Einführung, das Bekanntmachen; die Einleitung (*preface*); die Vorstellung (*presentation to s.o.*, *Dat.*).

introductory [intrə'dʌktəri], *adj.* einführend.

introspection [intrə'spekʃən], *s.* die Selbstbetrachtung, Introspektion.

introspective [intrə'spektiv], *adj.* nachdenklich, beschaulich.

intrude [in'truːd], *v.n.* eindringen, sich eindrängen; stören (*be in the way*).

intrusion [in'truːʒən], *s.* das Eindringen.

intuition

intuition [intju'iʃən], *s.* die Intuition, Eingebung.

intuitive [in'tju:itiv], *adj.* intuitiv, gefühlsmäßig.

inundate ['inʌndeit], *v.a.* überschwemmen.

inure [i'njuə], *v.a.* gewöhnen; abhärten (*harden*).

invade [in'veid], *v.a.* angreifen, einfallen (in, *Dat.*).

invalid [in'vælid], *adj.* ungültig (*void*); ['invəlid] krank (*sick*). — *s.* der Kranke, Invalide.

invalidate [in'vælideit], *v.a.* ungültig machen, für ungültig erklären.

invalidity [invə'liditi], *s.* die Ungültigkeit.

invaluable [in'væljuəbl], *adj.* von hohem Wert, wertvoll, unschätzbar.

invariable [in'vɛəriəbl], *adj.* unveränderlich. — *s.* (*Maths.*) die unveränderliche Größe, die Konstante, Unveränderliche.

invasion [in'veiʒən], *s.* die Invasion, der Einfall; Angriff (*of*, auf, *Acc.*).

invective [in'vektiv], *adj.* schmähend. — *s.* die Schmähung.

inveigh [in'vei], *v.n.* schmähen, losziehen (gegen); schimpfen (auf, *Acc.*).

inveigle [in'veigl], *v.a.* verleiten, verführen.

invent [in'vent], *v.a.* erfinden.

invention [in'venʃən], *s.* die Erfindung.

inventor [in'ventə], *s.* der Erfinder.

inventory ['invəntri], *s.* der Bestand, das Inventar; die Liste (*list*).

inverse [in'və:s,'invə:s], *adj.* umgekehrt.

inversion [in'və:ʃən], *s.* die Umkehrung; (*Gram., Maths.*) die Inversion.

invert [in'və:t], *v.a.* umstellen, umkehren. — ['invə:t], *s.* (*Chem.*) — *sugar*, der Invertzucker.

invest [in'vest], *v.a.* bekleiden; bedecken; (*Comm.*) investieren, anlegen.

investigate [in'vestigeit], *v.a.* untersuchen, erforschen.

investiture [in'vestitʃə], *s.* die Investitur; die Belehnung.

investment [in'vestmənt], *s.* die Investierung, Kapitalanlage.

inveterate [in'vetərit], *adj.* eingewurzelt, eingefleischt.

invidious [in'vidiəs], *adj.* neiderregend, verhaßt.

invigorate [in'vigəreit], *v.a.* stärken, beleben.

invincible [in'vinsibl], *adj.* unbesiegbar, unüberwindlich.

inviolable [in'vaiələbl], *adj.* unverletzlich.

invisible [in'vizibl], *adj.* unsichtbar.

invitation [invi'teiʃən], *s.* die Einladung.

invite [in'vait], *v.a.* einladen.

invocation [invo'keiʃən], *s.* die Anrufung.

invoice ['invois], *s.* die Rechnung, Faktura. — *v.a.* fakturieren.

invoke [in'vouk], *v.a.* anrufen.

involuntary [in'vɔləntri], *adj.* unfreiwillig (*unwilling*); unwillkürlich (*reflex*).

involve [in'vɔlv], *v.a.* verwickeln.

involved [in'vɔlvd], *adj.* schwierig, verwickelt, kompliziert.

invulnerable [in'vʌlnərəbl], *adj.* unverwundbar, unverletzlich.

inward ['inwəd], *adj.* inner(lich). — *adv.* (*also* **inwards**) einwärts, nach innen, ins Innere.

iodine ['aiədain *or* 'aiədi:n], *s.* (*Chem.*) das Jod.

Iraki, Iraqi [i'ra:ki], *adj.* irakisch. — *s.* der Iraker.

Iranian [i'reinjən], *adj.* iranisch. — *s.* der Iranier.

irascible [i'ræsibl], *adj.* jähzornig, aufbrausend.

irate [ai'reit], *adj.* erzürnt, zornig.

ire [aiə], *s.* (*Poet.*) der Zorn.

iridescent [iri'desənt], *adj.* irisierend, schillernd.

iris ['aiəris], *s.* (*Anat.*) die Regenbogenhaut; (*Bot.*) die Schwertlilie.

Irish ['airiʃ], *adj.* irisch, ersisch. — *s.* (*pl.*) *the* —, die Irländer, Iren, *pl.*

Irishman ['airiʃmən], *s.* der Irländer, Ire.

irk [ə:k], *v.a.* verdrießen, verärgern.

irksome ['ə:ksəm], *adj.* lästig, ärgerlich.

iron ['aiən], *s.* (*Metall.*) das Eisen; (*pl.*) die eisernen Fesseln. — *adj.* eisern, Eisen-. — *v.a.* bügeln, plätten; — *out*, schlichten, beilegen.

ironical [ai'rɔnikəl], *adj.* ironisch.

ironmonger ['aiənmʌŋgə], *s.* der Eisenhändler.

ironmould ['aiənmould], *s.* der Rostfleck.

irony ['aiərəni], *s.* die Ironie.

irradiate [i'reidieit], *v.a.* bestrahlen.

irrational [i'ræʃənəl], *adj.* (*Log., Maths.*) irrational; unvernünftig (*without reason*).

irreconcilable [irekən'sailəbl], *adj.* unversöhnlich; unvereinbar (*incompatible*).

irregular [i'regjulə], *adj.* unregelmäßig, gegen die Regel.

irrelevant [i'reləvənt], *adj.* belanglos.

irremediable [iri'mi:diəbl], *adj.* unheilbar; nicht wieder gut zu machen.

irreparable [i'repərəbl], *adj.* unersetzlich.

irrepressible [iri'presibl], *adj.* nicht zu unterdrücken, unbezähmbar.

irreproachable [iri'proutʃəbl], *adj.* untadelhaft, tadellos.

irresistible [iri'zistibl], *adj.* unwiderstehlich.

irresolute [i'rezolju:t], *adj.* unschlüssig, unentschlossen.

irrespective [iris'pektiv], *adj.* ohne Rücksicht (*of*, auf, *Acc.*).

irresponsible [iris'pɔnsibl], *adj.* unverantwortlich.

irretrievable [iri'tri:vəbl], *adj.* unersetzlich, unwiederbringlich.

irreverent [i'revərənt], *adj.* unehrerbietig.

irrevocable [i'revəkəbl], *adj.* unwiderruflich.

irrigate ['irigeit], v.a. bewässern.
irritable ['iritəbl], adj. reizbar.
irritant ['iritənt], s. das Reizmittel.
irritation [iri'teiʃən], s. die Reizung, das Reizen; die Erzürnung.
irruption [i'rʌpʃən], s. der Einbruch.
island ['ailənd], s. die Insel.
isle [ail], s. (Poet.) die Insel.
isolate ['aisəleit], v.a. (Med.) isolieren; absondern; (Chem.) darstellen.
isolation [aisə'leiʃən], s. die Absonderung, Isolierung.
Israeli [iz'reili], adj. den Staat Israel betreffend. — s. der Israeli.
Israelite ['izreiəlait], adj. israelitisch. — s. der Israelit.
issue ['isju: or 'iʃu:], s. der Ausgang, Erfolg (result); main —, der Hauptpunkt; die Nachkommenschaft (children); die Ausgabe (edition); Herausgabe (publication). — v.a. herausgeben; erlassen (proclaim); veröffentlichen (publish). — v.n. herrühren, stammen (from).
isthmus ['isθməs], s. die Landenge.
it [it], pron. es; with —, damit.
Italian [i'tæljən], adj. italienisch. — s. der Italiener.
italics [i'tæliks], s. pl. (Typ.) der Kursivdruck, die Kursivschrift.
itch [itʃ], s. das Jucken. — v.n. jucken; — to do s.th., (coll.) darauf brennen, etwas zu tun.
item ['aitəm], s. der Posten (in bill); der Programmpunkt (agenda); die Einzelheit.
itemize ['aitəmaiz], v.a. (Comm.) aufführen; verzeichnen.
iterate ['itəreit], v.a. wiederholen.
itinerant [i'tinərənt], adj. wandernd.
its [its], poss. adj. sein, ihr; dessen, deren.
itself [it'self], pron. selber, sich; of —, von selbst.
ivory ['aivəri], s. das Elfenbein. — adj. aus Elfenbein, elfenbeinern.
ivy ['aivi], s. (Bot.) der Efeu.

J

J [dʒei]. das J.
jabber ['dʒæbə], v.n. schnattern.
Jack [dʒæk]. Hans; Union —, die britische Flagge; (Cards) der Bube.
jack [dʒæk], s. (Motor.) der Wagenheber. — v.a. — up, (Motor.) hochwinden.
jackal ['dʒækɔ:l], s. (Zool.) der Schakal.
jackass ['dʒækæs], s. (Zool.) der Esel.
jackdaw ['dʒækdɔ:], s. (Orn.) die Dohle.
jacket ['dʒækit], s. das Jackett, die Jacke; dinner —, der Smoking;

potatoes in their —s, Kartoffeln in der Schale, f. pl.
jade [dʒeid], s. der Nierenstein.
jaded ['dʒeidid], adj. abgeplagt, abgehärmt, ermüdet.
jag [dʒæg], s. die Kerbe. — v.a. kerben, zacken.
jagged ['dʒægid], adj. zackig.
jail see under gaol.
jailer see under gaoler.
jam (1) [dʒæm], s. die Marmelade, Konfitüre.
jam (2) [dʒæm], s. traffic —, die Verkehrsstauung; (coll.) in a —, in der Klemme. — v.a. zusammenpressen (press together); (Rad.) stören.
Jamaican [dʒə'meikən], adj. jamaikanisch. — s. der Jamaikaner.
jamb [dʒæm], s. der Türpfosten.
jangle ['dʒæŋgl], v.n. klirren, rasseln. — s. das Geklirr, Gerassel.
janitor ['dʒænitə], s. der Portier.
January ['dʒænjuəri], s. der Januar.
japan [dʒə'pæn], s. lackierte Arbeit. — v.a. lackieren.
Japanese [dʒæpə'ni:z], adj. japanisch. — s. der Japaner.
jar (1) [dʒɑ:], s. der Topf, das Glas (preserves).
jar (2) [dʒɑ:], v.n. offenstehen (door); mißtönen, knarren.
jargon ['dʒɑ:gən], s. der Jargon.
jasmine ['dʒæzmin], s. (Bot.) der Jasmin.
jasper ['dʒæspə], s. der Jaspis.
jaundice ['dʒɔ:ndis], s. (Med.) die Gelbsucht; (fig.) der Neid (envy); —d outlook, die Verbitterung, Mißstimmung.
jaunt [dʒɔ:nt], s. der Ausflug, Spaziergang. — v.n. herumstreifen, spazieren.
jaunty ['dʒɔ:nti], adj. leicht, munter, lebhaft.
jaw [dʒɔ:], s. (Anat.) der Kinnbacken; der Rachen (animals).
jay [dʒei], s. (Orn.) der Häher.
jazz [dʒæz], s. die Jazzmusik.
jealous ['dʒeləs], adj. eifersüchtig.
jealousy ['dʒeləsi], s. die Eifersucht.
jeer ['dʒiə], v.a., v.n. spotten, verhöhnen.
jejune [dʒi'dʒu:n], adj. nüchtern, trocken.
jelly ['dʒeli], s. das Gelee.
jellyfish ['dʒelifiʃ], s. (Zool.) die Qualle.
jeopardize ['dʒepədaiz], v.a. gefährden.
jeopardy ['dʒepədi], s. die Gefahr.
jerk [dʒə:k], v.a. rucken, stoßen (push); plötzlich bewegen (move suddenly). — v.n. zusammenzucken. — s. (Am. coll.) der Kerl; der Ruck, Stoß.
jersey ['dʒə:zi], s. die Wolljacke.
jessamine ['dʒesəmin], s. (Bot.) der Jasmin.
jest [dʒest], s. der Spaß, Scherz. — v.n. scherzen.
jester ['dʒestə], s. der Spaßmacher, Hofnarr.

jet

jet (1) [dʒet], s. der Strahl, Wasserstrahl; (Aviat.) die Düse; — engine, der Düsenmotor; — plane, das Düsenflugzeug. — v.n. hervorspringen.

jet (2) [dʒet], s. der Gagat; — black, pechschwarz.

jetsam ['dʒetsəm], s. das Strandgut.

jetty ['dʒeti], s. der Hafendamm, die Landungsbrücke (landing stage).

Jew [dʒu:], s. der Jude.

jewel ['dʒuəl], s. das Juwel, der Edelstein.

jewel(le)ry ['dʒuəlri], s. der Schmuck; die Juwelen, n. pl.

Jewish ['dʒu:iʃ], adj. jüdisch.

Jewry ['dʒuəri], s. die Judenschaft, das Judentum.

jiffy ['dʒifi], s. (coll.) der Augenblick.

jig (1) [dʒig], s. die Gigue (dance).

jig (2) [dʒig], s. das Werkzeug (tool); —saw, die Säge; —saw puzzle, das Zusammenlegspiel, -setzspiel.

jilt [dʒilt], v.a. sitzen lassen.

jingle [dʒingl], v.a. klimpern, klimpern lassen (coins etc.). — s. das Geklimper.

job [dʒɔb], s. die Arbeit, Anstellung; die Stellung; das Geschäft; — in hand, die Beschäftigung.

jobber ['dʒɔbə], s. der Makler, Spekulant (stock exchange).

jockey ['dʒɔki], s .der Jockei, Reiter.

jocular ['dʒɔkjulə], adj. scherzhaft, lustig.

jocund ['dʒɔkənd], adj. munter, heiter.

jog [dʒɔg], v.a. stoßen, antreiben. — v.n. gemächlich traben, trotten. — s. der Trott.

join [dʒɔin], v.a. verbinden, zusammenfügen; (club etc.) beitreten (Dat.). — v.n. (rivers) zusammenfließen (mit, Dat.); (Comm.) sich vereinigen (mit, Dat.).

joiner ['dʒɔinə], s. der Tischler, Schreiner.

joint [dʒɔint], s. (Anat.) das Gelenk; das Stück Fleisch, der Braten (meat); (sl.) das Lokal, die Spelunke. — adj. vereint, gemeinsam; (Comm.) — stock company, die Aktiengesellschaft; — heir, der Miterbe.

joist [dʒɔist], s. (Carp.) der Querbalken.

joke [dʒouk], s. der Scherz, Witz.

jollity ['dʒɔliti], s. die Heiterkeit.

jolly ['dʒɔli], adj. fröhlich, heiter, lustig.

jolt [dʒoult], v.a. schütteln, erschüttern (shake up). — s. der Stoß.

jostle [dʒɔsl], v.a. stoßen, drängen. — v.n. drängeln.

jot [dʒɔt], s. der Punkt, das Iota. — v.a. — (down), notieren, niederschreiben.

journal ['dʒə:nəl], s. die Zeitschrift (periodical).

journalism ['dʒə:nəlizm], s. das Zeitungswesen, der Journalistenberuf.

journalist ['dʒə:nəlist], s. der Journalist.

journey ['dʒə:ni], s. die Reise.

joust [dʒu:st], s. dəs Turnier.

jovial ['dʒouviəl], adj. jovial, freundlich; lustig (gay).

joy [dʒɔi], s. die Freude.

jubilant ['dʒu:bilant], adj. frohlockend.

jubilation [dʒu:bi'leiʃən], s. der Jubel.

jubilee ['dʒu:bili:], s. das Jubiläum.

Judaism ['dʒu'deiizm], s. das Judentum.

judge [dʒʌdʒ], s. der Richter. — v.a. richten, beurteilen, entscheiden.

judgment ['dʒʌdʒmənt], s. das Urteil; das Urteilsvermögen (discretion), die Urteilskraft.

judicial [dʒu:'diʃəl], adj. richterlich, gerichtlich.

judicious [dʒu:'diʃəs], adj. klug, scharfsinnig.

jug [dʒʌg], s. der Krug.

juggle [dʒʌgl], v.n. jonglieren, gaukeln.

juggler ['dʒʌglə], s. der Jongleur.

Jugoslav see Yugoslav.

jugular ['dʒu:g- or 'dʒʌgjulə], adj. Kehl-, Hals-, Gurgel-. — s. (vein) die Halsader.

juice [dʒu:s], s. der Saft.

July [dʒu'lai], der Juli.

jumble [dʒʌmbl], v.a. zusammenmischen, vermischen. — s. das gemischte Zeug; — sale, der Verkauf, Ausverkauf gebrauchter Dinge, Ramschverkauf.

jump [dʒʌmp], v.n. springen. — s. der Sprung.

junction ['dʒʌnkʃən], s. (Railw.) der Knotenpunkt; die Kreuzung.

juncture ['dʒʌnktʃə], s. der (kritische) Zeitpunkt.

June [dʒu:n], der Juni.

jungle [dʒʌngl], s. der Dschungel.

junior ['dʒu:njə], adj. jünger; Unter-.

juniper ['dʒu:nipə], s. (Bot.) der Wacholder.

junk [dʒʌnk], s. (coll.) das alte Zeug, alte Möbelstücke, n. pl.

junket ['dʒʌnkit], s. der Schmaus, das Fest; (Cul.) dicke Milch mit Sahne. — v.n. schmausen, feiern (celebrate).

juridical [dʒuə'ridikəl], adj. rechtlich; gerichtlich (in Court).

jurisdiction [dʒuəriz'dikʃən], s. die Gerichtsbarkeit.

juror ['dʒuərə], s. der, die Geschworene.

jury ['dʒuəri], s. die Jury, das Geschworenengericht.

just [dʒʌst], adj. gerecht; réchtschaffen (decent); gehörig (proper). — adv. soeben,eben; —as,eben als,gerade wie.

justice ['dʒʌstis], s. die Gerechtigkeit; der Richter (judge).

justifiable ['dʒʌstifaiəbl], adj. zu rechtfertigen, berechtigt.

justify ['dʒʌstifai], v.a. rechtfertigen.

jut [dʒʌt], v.n. — (out), hervorragen. — s. der Vorsprung.

jute [dʒu:t], s. die Jute.

juvenile ['dʒu:vənail], adj. jugendlich, unreif.

juxtaposition [dʒʌkstəpə'ziʃən], s. die Nebeneinanderstellung, Gegenüberstellung.

K

K [kei]. das K.

kale [keil], *s.* (*Bot.*) der Krauskohl.

kaleidoscope [kə'laidəskoup], *s.* das Kaleidoskop.

kangaroo [kæŋgə'ru:], *s.* (*Zool.*) das Känguruh.

keel [ki:l], *s.* der Kiel; *on an even —*, bei ruhiger See; (*also fig.*) ruhig. — *v.n. — over*, umkippen.

keen [ki:n], *adj.* eifrig (*intent*); scharfsinnig (*perspicacious*); scharf (*blade*).

keenness ['ki:nnis], *s.* der Eifer; Scharfsinn; die Schärfe (*blade*).

keep [ki:p], *v.a. irr.* halten (*hold*); behalten (*retain*); führen (*a shop*); hüten (*gate, dog etc.*). — *v.n. — doing,* in etwas fortfahren; *— going,* weitergehen; *— away,* sich fernhalten; *— in, indoors,* zu Hause bleiben; *— off,* abhalten; sich fernhalten; *— out,* draußen bleiben; *— up,* aufrechterhalten. — *s.* das Burgverlies; der Unterhalt.

keeper ['ki:pə], *s.* der Hüter, Wärter; Museumsbeamte.

keeping ['ki:piŋ], *s.* die Verwahrung; *in safe —,* in guten Händen, in guter Obhut.

keepsake ['ki:pseik], *s.* das Andenken.

keg [keg], *s.* das Fäßchen.

ken [ken], *s.* die Kenntnis; *in my —,* meines Wissens. — *v.a.* (*Scottish*) kennen.

kennel [kenl], *s.* die Hundehütte.

kerb(stone) ['kə:b(stoun)], *s.* der Prellstein.

kerchief ['kə:tʃif], *s.* das Kopftuch, Halstuch.

kernel [kə:nl], *s.* der Kern.

kettle [ketl], *s.* der Kessel; *— drum,* die Kesselpauke.

key [ki:], *s.* der Schlüssel; (*Mus.*) die Tonart; die Taste (*on piano etc.*); *— man,* eine wichtige Person, Person in einer Schlüsselstellung. — *v.a. — (in),* einfügen, befestigen.

keyboard ['ki:bo:d], *s.* die Klaviatur; Tastatur (*typewriter*); *— instrument,* das Tasteninstrument.

keyhole ['ki:houl], *s.* das Schlüsselloch.

keystone ['ki:stoun], *s.* der Schlußstein.

kick [kik], *v.a., v.n.* mit dem Fuße stoßen *or* treten; *— against s.th.,* sich wehren. — *s.* der Fußstoß, Tritt; (*Footb.*) *— off,* der Ankick; *free —,* der Freistoß; *penalty —,* der Strafstoß, der Elfmeterstoß.

kid (1) [kid], *s.* (*Zool.*) das Geißlein, Zicklein; *with — gloves,* mit Glacéhandschuhen; (*coll.*) das Kind.

kid (2) [kid], *v.a.* (*Am. coll.*) zum Narren haben, aufziehen (*tease*).

kidnap ['kidnæp], *v.a.* entführen.

kidney ['kidni], *s.* (*Anat.*) die Niere; *— bean,* die französische Bohne.

kill [kil], *v.a.* töten; schlachten (*animal*).

kiln [kiln], *s.* der Darrofen; der Ziegelofen (*tiles, bricks*).

kilt [kilt], *s.* der Schottenrock.

kin [kin], *s.* die Verwandtschaft; *kith and —,* die Verwandten, *m. pl.*

kind [kaind], *s.* die Art, Gattung, Art und Weise. — *adj.* freundlich, gütig, liebenswürdig.

kindle [kindl], *v.a.* anzünden, anfachen.

kindliness, kindness ['kaindlinis, 'kaindnis], *s.* die Güte, Freundlichkeit.

kindred ['kindrid], *adj.* verwandt.

king [kiŋ], *s.* der König.

kingdom ['kiŋdəm], *s.* das Königreich.

kink [kiŋk], *s.* der Knoten; (*coll.*) der Vogel, die Grille (*obsession etc.*).

kinship ['kinʃip], *s.* die Sippe, Verwandtschaft.

kipper ['kipə], *s.* der geräucherte Hering.

kiss [kis], *v.a.* küssen. — *s.* der Kuß.

kit [kit], *s.* (*Mil.*) die Ausrüstung.

kitbag ['kitbæg], *s.* der Tornister.

kitchen ['kitʃən], *s.* die Küche; *— garden,* der Gemüsegarten.

kite [kait], *s.* der Drache, Papierdrache; *fly a —,* einen Drachen steigen lassen; (*Orn.*) der Gabelweih, der (rote) Milan; (*sl.*) der Schwindler.

kith [kiθ], *s.* now only in *— and kin,* die Verwandten, *m. pl.*

kitten [kitn], *s.* das Kätzchen.

knack [næk], *s.* der Kniff, Kunstgriff.

knacker ['nækə], *s.* der Abdecker (*horse*).

knapsack ['næpsæk], *s.* der Rucksack, Tornister.

knave [neiv], *s.* der Kerl, Schurke; Bube (*cards*).

knead [ni:d], *v.a.* kneten.

knee [ni:], *s.* (*Anat.*) das Knie.

kneel [ni:l], *v.n. irr.* knieen, niederknieen.

knell [nel], *s.* die Totenglocke.

knick-knack ['niknæk], *s.* die Nippsache.

knife [naif], *s.* das Messer. — *v.a.* erstechen.

knight [nait], *s.* der Ritter; der Springer (*chess*).

knit [nit], *v.a., v.n. reg. & irr.* stricken; *knitting needle,* die Stricknadel.

knob [nɔb], *s.* der (Tür)knopf, die Türklinke; der Knorren (*wood*).

knock [nɔk], *v.n.* klopfen, schlagen. — *s.* der Schlag, Stoß.

knoll [noul], *s.* der kleine Hügel.

knot [nɔt], *s.* der Knoten; die Schwierigkeit (*difficulty*).

know [nou], *v.a. irr.* kennen (*be acquainted with*); wissen (*possess knowledge (of)*).

knowing ['nouiŋ], *adj.* wissend.

knowledge ['nɔlidʒ], *s.* die Kenntnis (*acquaintance with*); das Wissen (*by*

study, *information etc.*); die Kenntnisse (*of language etc.*).
knuckle [nʌkl], *s.* (*Anat.*) der Knöchel. — *v.n.* — *under*, sich fügen.
Kremlin ['kremlin], *s.* der Kreml.
kudos ['kjuːdɔs], *s.* der Ruhm, das Ansehen.

L

L [el]. das L.
label [leibl], *s.* die Etikette, das Schildchen.
labial ['leibiəl], *adj.* (*Phonet.*) labial, Lippen-. — *s.* (*Phonet.*) der Lippenlaut.
laboratory [lə'bɔrətəri, (*Am.*) 'læbərətəri], *s.* das Laboratorium, (*coll.*) das Labor.
laborious [lə'bɔːriəs], *adj.* mühsam.
labour ['leibə], *s.* die Arbeit, Mühe; *Labour Party*, die Arbeiterpartei; (*Med.*) die Geburtswehen, *f. pl.* — *v.n.* sich abmühen, leiden; sich anstrengen.
labourer ['leibərə], *s.* der Arbeiter, Taglöhner.
lace [leis], *s.* die Spitze, Tresse. — *v.a.* verbrämen (*trim with lace*); zuschnüren (*shoe*); stärken (*coffee with rum etc.*).
lacerate ['læsəreit], *v.a.* zerreißen.
lack [læk], *v.a.* ermangeln (*Genit.*). — *v.n.* fehlen (an, *Dat.*). — *s.* der Mangel, das Fehlen.
lackadaisical [lækə'deizikəl], *adj.* schlaff, (*coll.*) schlapp, unbekümmert.
lackey ['læki], *s.* der Lakai, Diener, Bediente.
laconic [lə'kɔnik], *adj.* lakonisch.
lacquer ['lækə], *s.* der Lack. — *v.a.* lackieren.
lad [læd], *s.* der Bursche, Junge.
ladder ['lædə], *s.* die Leiter.
lading ['leidiŋ], *s.* (*Comm.*) das Laden; die Fracht; *bill of —*, der Frachtbrief.
ladle [leidl], *s.* der Schöpflöffel, Suppenlöffel; die Kelle. — *v.a.* ausschöpfen, austeilen.
lady ['leidi], *s.* die Dame; *— -in-waiting*, die Hofdame.
ladybird ['leidibəːd], *s.* (*Ent.*) der Marienkäfer.
ladyship ['leidiʃip], *s.* (*Title*) gnädige Frau.
lag [læg], *v.n.* zurückbleiben. — *v.a.* verkleiden, isolieren (*tank*).
laggard ['lægəd], *s.* der Zauderer. — *adj.* zögernd, zaudernd.
lagoon [lə'guːn], *s.* die Lagune.
lair [lɛə], *s.* das Lager (*of animal*).
laird [lɛəd], *s.* der schottische Gutsherr.

laity ['leiiti], *s.* die Laien, *m. pl.*
lake [leik], *s.* der See.
lamb [læm], *s.* (*Zool.*) das Lamm. — *v.n.* lammen.
lambent ['læmbənt], *adj.* brennend, lodernd, strahlend.
lame [leim], *adj.* lahm. — *v.a.* lähmen.
lament [lə'ment], *v.a.*, *v.n.* betrauern, beweinen. — *s.* das Klagelied, die Wehklage.
lamp [læmp], *s.* die Lampe; *— -post*, der Laternenpfahl.
lampoon [læm'puːn], *v.a.* schmähen, lächerlich machen. — *s.* die Schmähschrift.
lamprey ['læmpri], *s.* (*Zool.*) das Neunauge.
lance [lɑːns], *s.* (*Mil.*) die Lanze. — *v.a.* durchbohren; (*Med.*) lancieren.
lancer ['lɑːnsə], *s.* (*Mil.*) der Ulan.
lancet ['lɑːnsit], *s.* (*Med.*) die Lanzette.
land [lænd], *s.* das Land; das Grundstück (*plot*); *— tax*, die Grundsteuer. — *v.a.* ans Land bringen, fangen (*fish*). — *v.n.* landen.
landlord ['lændlɔːd], *s.* der Eigentümer, der Hausherr; Wirt (*pub*).
landmark ['lændmɑːk], *s.* der Grenzstein, das Wahrzeichen.
landscape ['lændskeip], *s.* die Landschaft.
landslide, landslip ['lændslaid, 'lændslip], *s.* der Erdrutsch.
lane [lein], *s.* der Heckenweg, Pfad; die Gasse; (*Motor.*) die Fahrbahn.
language ['læŋgwidʒ], *s.* die Sprache.
languid ['læŋgwid], *adj.* flau, matt.
languor ['læŋgə], *s.* die Mattigkeit, Flauheit.
lank [læŋk], *adj.* mager, schlank.
lantern ['læntən], *s.* die Laterne.
Laotian ['lauʃən], *adj.* laotisch. — *s.* der Laote.
lap (1) [læp], *s.* der Schoß.
lap (2) [læp], *s.* das Plätschern (*of waves*). — *v.a.* auflecken (*lick up*). — *v.n.* plätschern.
lapel [lə'pel], *s.* der Aufschlag (*of jacket*).
lapidary ['læpidəri], *adj.* lapidarisch; wuchtig.
lapse [læps], *v.n.* gleiten, fallen; verlaufen (*time*). — *s.* der Verlauf (*time*); der Fehler (*mistake*); das Verfallen (*into laziness etc.*).
lapwing ['læpwiŋ], *s.* (*Orn.*) der Kiebitz.
larceny ['lɑːsəni], *s.* der Diebstahl.
larch [lɑːtʃ], *s.* (*Bot.*) die Lärche.
lard [lɑːd], *s.* das Schweinefett, Schweineschmalz.
larder ['lɑːdə], *s.* die Speisekammer.
large [lɑːdʒ], *adj.* groß; weit; dick, stark.
largesse [lɑː'dʒes], *s.* die Freigebigkeit (*generosity*); die Schenkung (*donation*).
lark (1) [lɑːk], *s.* (*Orn.*) die Lerche.
lark (2) [lɑːk], *s.* (*coll.*) der Scherz. — *v.n.* scherzen.
larkspur ['lɑːkspəː], *s.* (*Bot.*) der Rittersporn.
larva ['lɑːvə], *s.* (*Zool.*) die Larve.

larynx ['lærɪŋks], *s.* (*Anat.*) der Kehlkopf.
lascivious [lə'sɪvɪəs], *adj.* wollüstig.
lash [læʃ], *s.* die Wimper (*eye*); die Peitschenschnur (*whip*), der Peitschenhieb (*stroke of whip*). — *v.a.* peitschen.
lass [læs], *s.* (*coll.*) das Mädchen.
lassitude ['læsɪtjuːd], *s.* die Mattigkeit.
lasso [lə'suː or 'læsoʊ], *s.* das Lasso. — *v.a.* mit einem Lasso fangen.
last (1) [lɑːst], *adj.* letzt, vorig, äußerst; *at long* —, endlich.
last (2) [lɑːst], *s.* der Leisten (*shoemaking*).
last (3) [lɑːst], *v.n.* dauern, anhalten; hinreichen (*be sufficient*).
lastly ['lɑːstlɪ], *adv.* zuletzt.
latch [lætʃ], *v.a.* verschließen.
latchkey ['lætʃkiː], *s.* der Hausschlüssel.
late [leɪt], *adj.* spät; verspätet; verstorben, selig (*deceased*); neulich (*recent*); *the train is* —, der Zug hat Verspätung; *of late*, jüngst.
latent ['leɪtənt], *adj.* (*Med.*) latent; verborgen.
lateral ['lætərəl], *adj.* seitlich, Seiten-.
lath [lɑːθ], *s.* die Latte.
lathe [leɪð], *s.* die Drehbank.
lather ['lɑːðə], *s.* der Seifenschaum. — *v.n.*, *v.a.* (sich) einseifen.
Latin ['lætɪn], *adj.* lateinisch. — *s.* das Latein, die lateinische Sprache.
latitude ['lætɪtjuːd], *s.* die geographische Breite; die Weite (*width*); (*fig.*) der Spielraum (*scope*).
latter ['lætə], *adj.* letzter; später (*later*). — *s.* der Letztere.
latterly ['lætəlɪ], *adv.* neulich, neuerdings.
lattice ['lætɪs], *s.* das Gitter. — *v.a.* vergittern.
Latvian ['lætvɪən], *adj.* lettisch. — *s.* der Lette.
laud [lɔːd], *v.a.* loben, preisen.
laudable ['lɔːdəbl], *adj.* lobenswert.
laudatory ['lɔːdətərɪ], *adj.* belobend.
laugh [lɑːf], *v.n.* lachen; —*ing stock*, der Gegenstand des Gelächters.
laughter ['lɑːftə], *s.* das Lachen, Gelächter.
launch [lɔːntʃ], *s.* die Barkasse. — *v.a.* vom Stapel lassen.
launching ['lɔːntʃɪŋ], *s.* der Stapellauf.
laundress ['lɔːndrɪs], *s.* die Wäscherin.
laundry ['lɔːndrɪ], *s.* die Wäsche (*clothes*); Wäscherei (*place*).
laureate ['lɔːriːt], *s.* der Hofdichter.
laurel ['lɔrəl], *s.* (*Bot.*) der Lorbeer.
lavatory ['lævətrɪ], *s.* das W.C., der Abort, Waschraum; die Toilette; *public* —, die Bedürfnisanstalt.
lavender ['lævəndə], *s.* (*Bot.*) der Lavendel.
lavish ['lævɪʃ], *adj.* freigebig, verschwenderisch. — *v.a.* vergeuden.
lavishness ['lævɪʃnɪs], *s.* die Freigebigkeit, Verschwendung.
law [lɔː], *s.* das Gesetz (*statute*); das Recht (*justice*); die Jura, Jurisprudenz (*subject of study*).
lawful ['lɔːful], *adj.* gesetzlich, gesetzmäßig.
lawless ['lɔːlɪs], *adj.* gesetzlos; unrechtmäßig (*illegal*).
lawn (1) [lɔːn], *s.* der Rasen.
lawn (2) [lɔːn], *s.* der Batist.
lawsuit ['lɔːsuːt], *s.* der Prozeß.
lawyer ['lɔːjə], *s.* der Advokat, Rechtsanwalt, Jurist.
lax [læks], *adj.* locker, lax.
laxative ['læksətɪv], *s.* das Abführmittel.
laxity ['læksɪtɪ], *s.* die Schlaffheit, Lockerheit (*of rope etc.*).
lay (1) [leɪ], *v.a.* irr. legen; setzen (*put*); stellen (*place*); bannen (*ghost*); — *up*, sammeln. — *v.n.* legen (*eggs*); wetten (*wager*); — *about one*, um sich schlagen.
lay (2) [leɪ], *s.* (*Poet.*) das Lied.
lay (3) [leɪ], *adj.* Laien-.
layer ['leɪə], *s.* die Schicht; — *cake*, die Cremetorte.
layman ['leɪmən], *s.* der Laie.
laziness ['leɪzɪnɪs], *s.* die Faulheit.
lazy ['leɪzɪ], *adj.* faul, träge.
lea [liː], *s.* (*Poet.*) die Aue.
lead (1) [liːd], *v.a.*, *v.n.* irr. führen, leiten; ausspielen (*cards*). — *s.* die Führung; (*Elec.*) Leitung.
lead (2) [led], *s.* das Blei; Bleilot (*plumbline*).
leader ['liːdə], *s.* der Führer; (*Mus.*) der Konzertmeister; der Leitartikel (*leading article*).
leaf [liːf], *s.* (*Bot.*) das Blatt; (*Build.*) der Türflügel. — *v.a.* (*coll.*) — *through*, durchblättern.
leafy ['liːfɪ], *adj.* belaubt.
league (1) [liːg], *s.* drei englische Meilen, *f.pl.*
league (2) [liːg], *s.* das Bündnis (*pact*); *be in* —, verbündet sein; *League of Nations*, der Völkerbund.
leak [liːk], *v.n.* lecken, ein Loch haben. — *s.* das Loch; (*Naut.*) das Leck.
leaky ['liːkɪ], *adj.* leck.
lean (1) [liːn], *v.n. irr.* (sich) lehnen (an, *Acc.*), stützen (auf, *Acc.*).
lean (2) [liːn], *adj.* mager, hager.
leap [liːp], *v.n. irr.* springen. — *s.* der Sprung; — *year*, das Schaltjahr.
learn [lɜːn], *v.a. irr.* lernen, erfahren.
learned ['lɜːnɪd], *adj.* gelehrt.
learning ['lɜːnɪŋ], *s.* die Gelehrsamkeit.
lease [liːs], *s.* die Pacht, der Mietvertrag (*of house*). — *v.a.* (ver)pachten.
leasehold ['liːshoʊld], *s.* die Pachtung.
leash [liːʃ], *v.a.* koppeln, anbinden. — *s.* die Koppel.
least [liːst], *adj.* wenigst, geringst, mindest, kleinst. — *s. at* (*the*) —, wenigstens, mindestens.
leather ['leðə], *s.* das Leder. — *adj.* Leder-, ledern.
leave [liːv], *v.a. irr.* verlassen (*quit*); lassen (*let*); hinterlassen (*bequeath*). — *v.n.* Abschied nehmen, abreisen. — *s.* der Urlaub; der Abschied (*farewell*); die Erlaubnis (*permission*).

leaven [levn], *s.* der Sauerteig. — *v.a.* säuern.

Lebanese [lebə'ni:z], *adj.* libanesisch. — *s.* der Libanese.

lecture ['lektʃə], *s.* die Vorlesung; der Vortrag.

lecturer ['lektʃərə], *s.* (*Univ.*) der Dozent; der Vortragende (*speaker*).

ledge [ledʒ], *s.* der Sims (*window*).

ledger ['ledʒə], *s.* (*Comm.*) das Hauptbuch.

lee [li:], *s.* die Leeseite (*shelter*).

leech [li:tʃ], *s.* (*Zool.*) der Blutegel.

leek [li:k], *s.* (*Bot.*) der Lauch.

leer ['liə], *s.* das Starren; der Seitenblick. — *v.n.* schielen (*at*, auf, nach); starren.

lees [li:z], *s. pl.* der Bodensatz, die Hefe.

left [left], *adj.* link. — *adv.* inks. — *s.* die linke Seite.

leg [leg], *s.* (*Anat.*) das Bein; der Schaft.

legacy ['legəsi], *s.* das Vermächtnis, das Erbe, Erbgut.

legal ['li:gəl], *adj.* gesetzlich.

legality [li'gæliti], *s.* die Gesetzlichkeit.

legatee [legə'ti:], *s.* (*Law*) der Erbe, die Erbin.

legation [li'geiʃən], *s.* die Gesandtschaft.

legend ['ledʒənd], *s.* die Legende, Sage; die Inschrift (*inscription*).

legendary ['ledʒəndəri], *adj.* legendär, sagenhaft.

leggings ['leginz], *s. pl.* die Gamaschen.

legible ['ledʒibl], *adj.* leserlich.

legislation [ledʒis'leiʃən], *s.* die Gesetzgebung.

legislative ['ledʒislətiv], *adj.* gesetzgebend.

legislator ['ledʒisleitə], *s.* der Gesetzgeber.

legitimacy [li'dʒitiməsi], *s.* die Gesetzmäßigkeit; (*Law*) die eheliche Geburt (*of birth*).

legitimate [li'dʒitimit], *adj.* gesetzmäßig; (*Law*) ehelich (*child*). — [-meit], *v.a.* für gesetzlich erklären.

legitimize [li'dʒitimaiz], *v.a.* legitimieren.

leguminous [li'gju:minəs], *adj.* Hülsen-; hülsentragend.

leisure ['leʒə], *s.* die Freizeit, Muße.

leisurely ['leʒəli], *adj.*, *adv.* gelassen, gemächlich.

lemon ['lemən], *s.* (*Bot.*) die Zitrone.

lemonade [lemən'eid], *s.* die Limonade.

lend [lend], *v.a. irr.* leihen; —*ing library*, die Leihbibliothek.

length [leŋθ], *s.* die Länge (*extent*); die Dauer (*duration*); *at* —, ausführlich.

lengthen ['leŋθən], *v.a.*, *v.n.* (sich) verlängern.

lengthy ['leŋθi], *adj.* langwierig, lang.

lenient ['li:niənt], *adj.* nachsichtig, milde.

lens [lenz], *s.* die Linse (*optics*); das Objektiv.

Lent [lent]. die Fastenzeit.

lentil ['lentil], *s.* (*Bot.*) die Linse.

leprosy ['leprəsi], *s.* der Aussatz, die Leprakrankheit.

leprous ['leprəs], *adj.* aussätzig.

lesion ['li:ʒən], *s.* die Verletzung.

less [les], *comp. adj.*, *adv.* weniger, kleiner.

lessee [le'si:], *s.* der Pächter, Mieter.

lessen [lesn], *v.a.*, *v.n.* (sich) verringern, vermindern.

lesser ['lesə], *comp. adj.* geringer; kleiner.

lesson [lesn], *s.* die Lehrstunde, Lektion; (*pl.*) der Unterricht; (*Rel.*) der Bibeltext.

lessor ['lesə], *s.* der Eigentümer, Vermieter.

lest [lest], *conj.* damit nicht; aus Furcht, daß.

let [let], *v.a. irr.* lassen; zulassen; vermieten; (*room*); — *down*, blamieren, enttäuschen; *off*, abschießen. — *s. without* — *or hindrance*, ohne Hinderung.

lethal ['li:θəl], *adj.* tödlich.

letter ['letə], *s.* der Brief; der Buchstabe (*character*); — *box*, der Briefkasten; (*pl.*) die Literatur.

letterpress ['letəpres], *s.* die Kopierpresse.

lettuce ['letis], *s.* (*Bot.*) der Salat.

level [levl], *adj.* eben, gleich. — *s.* die Ebene; das Niveau. — *v.a.* ebnen, ausgleichen; (*Build.*) planieren.

lever ['li:və], *s.* der Hebel.

levity ['leviti], *s.* der Leichtsinn.

levy ['levi], *v.a.* erheben (*tax*); auferlegen (*penalty*). — *s.* die Steuer.

lewd [lju:d *or* lu:d], *adj.* liederlich, gemein, unzüchtig.

liability [laiə'biliti], *s.* die Verantwortlichkeit; *limited* —, beschränkte Haftung; die Steuerpflichtigkeit (*to tax*), Zollpflichtigkeit (*to duty*).

liable ['laiəbl], *adj.* haftbar, zahlungspflichtig.

liar ['laiə], *s.* der Lügner.

libel ['laibəl], *s.* die Verleumdung. — *v.a.* verleumden, schmähen.

libellous ['laibələs], *adj.* verleumderisch.

liberal ['libərəl], *adj.* (*Pol.*) liberal; freigebig (*generous*); — *arts*, Geisteswissenschaften, *f. pl.*

liberate ['libəreit], *v.a.* befreien, freisetzen; (*Law*) in Freiheit setzen.

Liberian [lai'biriən], *adj.* liberisch. — *s.* der Liberier.

libertine ['libəti:n], *s.* der Wüstling.

liberty ['libəti], *s.* die Freiheit; die Erlaubnis (*permission*).

librarian [lai'brɛəriən], *s.* der Bibliothekar, die Bibliothekarin.

library ['laibrəri], *s.* die Bibliothek.

Libyan ['libjən], *adj.* libysch. — *s.* der Libyer.

licence ['laisəns], *s.* die Genehmigung, Erlaubnis (*permit*); *driving* —, der Führerschein; die Zügellosigkeit (*licentiousness*).

license ['laisəns], *v.a.* genehmigen, bewilligen; *licensing laws*, Ausschanksgesetze, *n. pl.* (*for alcohol*).

licentiate [lai'senʃiit], s. der Lizenziat (*degree*).

licentious [lai'senʃəs], adj. ausschweifend, liederlich, locker (*in morals*).

lichen ['laikən, 'litʃən], s. (*Bot.*) die Flechte.

lichgate ['litʃgeit], s. das Friedhofstor.

lick [lik], v.a. lecken; (*Am.*) prügeln, verhauen.

lid [lid], s. das Augenlid; der Deckel.

lie [lai], (1) v.n. lügen. — s. die Lüge (*untruth*).

lie [lai], (2) v.n. irr. liegen; — *down*, sich legen, hinlegen; sich fügen (*fig.*).

lieu [lju:], s. in —, an Stelle, anstatt (*Genit.*).

lieutenant [lef'tenənt], s. der Leutnant.

life [laif], s. das Leben.

lifebelt ['laifbelt], s. der Rettungsgürtel.

lifeboat ['laifbout], s. das Rettungsboot.

lifetime ['laiftaim], s. die Lebenszeit, Zeit seines Lebens.

lift [lift], s. der Aufzug, Fahrstuhl; (*coll.*) *give a — to*, mitnehmen (im Auto). — v.a. heben; aufheben (*abolish*); (*coll.*) klauen, stehlen.

ligament ['ligəmənt], s. das Band; (*Anat.*) die Flechse, die Sehne.

ligature ['ligətʃə], s. (*Typ.*) die Ligatur; die Verbindung.

light [lait], adj. hell, licht; blond (*hair*); leicht (*weight*). — s. das Licht; *give a —*, ein Streichholz geben, Feuer geben. — v.a. irr. beleuchten (*room*); anzünden (*fire*). — v.n. irr. — (*up*), hell werden, leuchten; (*fig.*) aufleuchten.

lighten [laitn], v.a. erhellen (*brighten*); erleichtern (*ease*).

lighter ['laitə], s. das Feuerzeug (*smoker's*); (*Naut.*) das Lichterschiff.

lighthouse ['laithaus], s. der Leuchtturm.

lightning ['laitniŋ], s. der Blitz; — *conductor*, der Blitzableiter; — *speed*, die Blitzesschnelle.

ligneous ['ligniəs], adj. holzig.

lignite ['lignait], s. die Braunkohle.

like (1) [laik], v.a. gern haben; *I — to sing*, ich singe gern. — v.n. belieben, wollen; *as you —*, wie Sie wollen. — s. *his —s and dislikes*, seine Wünsche und Abneigungen.

like (2) [laik], adj. gleich, ähnlich. — s. *his —*, seinesgleichen. — prep. gleich, wie; *just — him!* das sieht ihm ähnlich! *feel —*, möchte gern; *what is it —?* wie sieht es aus?

likelihood ['laiklihud], s. die Möglichkeit; Wahrscheinlichkeit (*probability*).

likely ['laikli], adj. möglich; wahrscheinlich (*probable*).

liken ['laikən], v.a. vergleichen.

likeness ['laiknis], s. die Ähnlichkeit.

likewise ['laikwaiz], adv. ebenso, gleichfalls, auch.

liking ['laikiŋ], s. die Vorliebe (*for*, für, *Acc.*); Neigung (*for*, zu, *Dat.*); *to my*

—, nach meinem Geschmack or Wunsch.

lilac ['lailək], s. (*Bot.*) der Flieder.

lilt [lilt], v.a., v.n. trällern, summen. — s. die Melodie, Weise.

lily ['lili], (*Bot.*) s. die Lilie; — *of the valley*, das Maiglöckchen.

limb [lim], s. das Glied.

limber ['limbə], adj. geschmeidig.

lime (1) [laim], s. der Leim, Kalk (*chalk*).

lime (2) [laim], s. (*Bot.*) die Linde (*tree*); die Limone (*fruit*); — *juice*, der Limonensaft.

limestone ['laimstoun], s. der Kalkstein.

limit ['limit], s. die Grenze, das Ende. — v.a. begrenzen, beschränken.

limitation [limi'teiʃən], s. die Begrenzung.

limn [lim], v.a. (*Art.*) zeichnen, malen.

limp [limp], v.n. hinken. — adj. müde, schlaff.

limpid ['limpid], adj. klar, durchsichtig.

linden ['lindən], s. (*Bot.*) die Linde.

line (1) [lain], s. die Linie, Eisenbahnlinie (*Railw.*); die Zeile; der Strich; (*Mil.*) der Reihe; — *of business*, die Geschäftsbranche; — (*Genealogy*) die Abstammung; *take a strong —*, entschlossen auftreten.

line (2) [lain], v.a. füttern (a *garment*).

lineage ['liniidʒ], s. die Abstammung.

lineament ['liniəmənt], s. der Gesichtszug.

linear ['liniə], adj. linear, geradlinig.

linen ['linin], s. die Leinwand; *bed —*, die Laken, Bettwäsche. — adj. leinen.

liner ['lainə], s. (*Naut.*) das Passagierschiff.

linger ['liŋgə], v.n. zögern; verweilen.

lingerie ['lɛ̃ʒəri:], s. die Damenunterwäsche.

linguist ['liŋgwist], s. der Sprachkundige, Philologe, Linguist.

liniment ['linimənt], s. (*Med.*) die Salbe.

lining ['lainiŋ], s. das Futter (*of garment*).

link [liŋk], s. das Glied (*in chain*); die Verbindung (*connexion*). — v.a. verbinden, verknüpfen.

linnet ['linit], s. (*Orn.*) der Hänfling.

linseed ['linsi:d], s. der Leinsamen; — *oil*, das Leinöl.

lint [lint], s. die Scharpie, das Verbandzeug.

lion ['laiən], s. (*Zool.*) der Löwe.

lioness ['laiənes], s. (*Zool.*) die Löwin.

lip [lip], s. (*Anat.*, *Bot.*) die Lippe (*mouth*); der Rand (*of jug*).

lipstick ['lipstik], s. der Lippenstift.

liquefy ['likwifai], v.a., v.n. flüssig machen or werden.

liqueur [li'kjuə], s. der Likör.

liquid ['likwid], adj. flüssig. — s. die Flüssigkeit.

liquidate ['likwideit], v.a. liquidieren; (*Comm.*) flüssig machen (*assets*); bezahlen (*pay off*).

431

liquor

liquor ['likə], *s.* der Alkohol.
liquorice ['likəris], *s.* die Lakritze.
lisp [lisp], *v.n.* lispeln. — *s.* der Sprachfehler, das Anstoßen, Lispeln.
list [list], *s.* die Liste, das Verzeichnis; (*Naut.*) die Schlagseite.
listen [lisn], *v.n.* horchen, zuhören.
listless ['listlis], *adj.* teilnahmslos.
litany ['litəni], *s.* (*Eccl.*) die Litanei.
literal ['litərəl], *adj.* buchstäblich.
literary ['litərəri], *adj.* literarisch, Literatur-.
literature ['litrətʃə], *s.* die Literatur.
lithe [laið], *adj.* geschmeidig.
Lithuanian [liθju'einiən], *adj.* litauisch. — *s.* der Litauer.
litigate ['litigeit], *v.n.* einen Prozeß anstrengen, litigieren, prozessieren.
litigation [liti'geiʃən], *s.* die Litigation, der Prozeß.
litter ['litə], *s.* (*Zool.*) die Jungen, *n. pl.*; die Brut; die Sänfte (*carriage*); der Abfall, die Abfälle (*waste paper etc.*). — *v.n.* (*Zool.*) Junge haben, werfen. — *v.a.* Abfälle wegwerfen, unsauber machen.
little [litl], *adj.* klein (*size, value*); gering (*value*); — *by* —, nach und nach.
liturgy ['litədʒi], *s.* (*Eccl.*) die Liturgie.
live [liv], *v.n.* leben; wohnen (*dwell*).
livelihood ['laivlihud], *s.* der Lebensunterhalt.
liveliness ['laivlinis], *s.* die Lebhaftigkeit.
lively ['laivli], *adj.* lebhaft.
liven [laivn], *v.a.* — *up*, beleben.
liver ['livə], *s.* (*Anat.*) die Leber.
livery ['livəri], *s.* die Livree (*uniform*); — *company* die Zunftgenossenschaft.
livid ['livid], *adj.* bleich, blaß.
living ['liviŋ], *s.* das Auskommen, der Unterhalt; die Lebensweise; (*Eccl.*) die Pfründe, Pfarrstelle.
lizard ['lizəd], *s.* (*Zool.*) die Eidechse.
lo! [lou], *excl.* (*obs.*) sieh, da! siehe!
load [loud], *s.* die Last, Belastung. — *v.a.* beladen, belasten. — *v.n.* laden, aufladen.
loadstone *see* **lodestone**.
loaf [louf], *s.* der Laib (*bread*); *sugar* —, der Zuckerhut. — *v.n.* herumlungern, nichts tun.
loafer ['loufə], *s.* der Faulenzer, Drückeberger.
loam [loum], *s.* der Lehm.
loan [loun], *s.* die Anleihe. — *v.a.* leihen.
loath [louθ], *adj.* unwillig, abgeneigt.
loathe [louð], *v.a.* verabscheuen, hassen.
loathing ['louðiŋ], *s.* der Abscheu, Ekel.
loathsome ['louθsəm], *adj.* abscheulich, ekelhaft.
lobby ['lɔbi], *s.* die Vorhalle. — *v.a.* (*Pol.*) einen beeinflussen.
lobe [loub], *s.* das Läppchen.
lobster ['lɔbstə], *s.* (*Zool.*) der Hummer.
local ['loukəl], *adj.* lokal, örtlich. — *s.* (*coll.*) das Stammgasthaus (*pub*).

locality [lo'kæliti], *s.* die Lokalität, die Örtlichkeit, der Ort.
localize ['loukəlaiz], *v.a.* lokalisieren, auf einen Ort beschränken.
locate [lo'keit], *v.a.* finden (*find*); ausfindig machen.
location [lo'keiʃən], *s.* die Plazierung (*position*); die Lage; der Standort; *on* —, auf dem Gelände, auf Außenaufnahme (*film*).
loch [lɔx], *s.* (*Scot.*) der See.
lock [lɔk], *s.* das Schloß (*on door*); die Schleuse (*on waterway*); die Locke (*hair*). — *v.a.* schließen, abschließen (*door*); hemmen (*wheel*). — *v.n.* sich schließen; — *in*, ineinandergreifen (*cogs*).
locker ['lɔkə], *s.* der Schließschrank, das Schließfach.
locket ['lɔkit], *s.* das Medaillon.
locksmith ['lɔksmiθ], *s.* der Schlosser.
lock-up ['lɔkʌp], *s.* der Arrest, die Haftzelle; (*coll.*) die Garage.
locust ['loukəst], *s.* (*Ent.*) die Heuschrecke.
lodestone ['loudstoun], *s.* der Magnetstein, Magnet.
lodge [lɔdʒ], *v.n.* wohnen, logieren (*temporary*). — *v.a.* beherbergen (*accommodate*); einbringen (*a complaint, protest*). — *s.* das Haus, das Häuschen; die Loge (*Freemasons*).
lodger ['lɔdʒə], *s.* der (Unter)mieter.
lodgings ['lɔdʒiŋz], *s. pl.* das möblierte Zimmer, die Wohnung.
loft [lɔft], *s.* der Boden, Dachboden.
lofty ['lɔfti], *adj.* hoch; erhaben; stolz (*proud*).
log [lɔg], *s.* der Holzklotz, das Scheit; —*cabin*, —*house*, das Blockhaus; (*Naut.*) das Log, das Schiffstagebuch. — *v.a.* (*Naut.*) eintragen.
loggerheads ['lɔgəhedz], *s. pl. at* —, in Widerspruch, Widerstreit, im Konflikt.
logic ['lɔdʒik], *s.* die Logik.
logical ['lɔdʒikəl], *adj.* logisch.
loin [lɔin], *s.* (*Anat.*) die Lende.
loincloth ['lɔinklɔθ], *s.* der Lendenschurz.
loiter ['lɔitə], *v.n.* herumlungern; bummeln.
loiterer ['lɔitərə], *s.* der Lungerer, Faulenzer.
loitering ['lɔitəriŋ], *s.* das Herumlungern, Herumstehen, Faulenzen.
loll [lɔl], *v.n.* herumlungern.
lollipop ['lɔlipɔp], *s.* das Zuckerwerk, die Süßigkeit; (*fig.*) der Leckerbissen.
loneliness ['lounlinis], *s.* die Einsamkeit.
lonely, (*Am.*) **lonesome** ['lounli, 'lounsəm], *adj.* einsam.
long [lɔŋ], *adj.* lang. — *adv.* — *ago*, vor langer Zeit; *before* —, in kurzer Zeit. — *v.n.* sich sehnen (*for*, nach, *Dat.*).
longitude ['lɔndʒitjuːd], *s.* die Länge; (*Geog.*) der Längengrad.

longitudinal [lɔndʒiˈtjuːdinəl], *adj.* in der geographischen Länge, Längen-.

look [luk], *v.n.* blicken, sehen, schauen (*at*, auf, *Acc.*); — *to it*, dafür sorgen; — *out for*, Ausschau halten nach (*Dat.*); — *out!* paß auf! — *after s.o.*, sich um jemanden kümmern; — *into*, prüfen, untersuchen; — *forward to*, sich freuen (auf, *Acc.*); — *over, durchsehen. — s.* der Blick (*glance*); das Aussehen (*appearance*).

looking-glass [ˈlukiŋglaːs], *s.* der Spiegel.

look-out [ˈlukaut], *s.* der Ausblick; die Ausschau.

loom [luːm], *s.* der Webstuhl. — *v.n.* in der Ferne auftauchen (*emerge*).

loon [luːn], *s.* (*Orn.*) der Eisvogel, Eistaucher; (*coll.*) der Narr.

loony [ˈluːni], *adj.* (*coll.*) wahnsinnig, närrisch.

loop [luːp], *s.* die Schlinge, das Schlingband; (*Railw.*) — *line*, die Schleife.

loophole [ˈluːphoul], *s.* der Ausweg, die Hintertür.

loose [luːs], *adj.* locker, lose; liederlich (*morals*). — *v.a.* lösen.

loosen [ˈluːsn], *v.a.* auflockern, locker machen.

lop [lɔp], *v.a.* stutzen (*trees*).

lopsided [lɔpˈsaidid], *adj.* einseitig.

loquacious [loˈkweiʃəs], *adj.* geschwätzig.

loquacity [loˈkwæsiti], *s.* die Schwatzhaftigkeit.

Lord [lɔːd], *s.* (*Rel.*) the —, Gott der Herr; der Lord (*nobleman's title*); — Mayor, der Oberbürgermeister.

lord [lɔːd], *s.* der Herr.

lordly [ˈlɔːdli], *adj.* vornehm, stolz.

lore [lɔː], *s.* die Kunde.

lose [luːz], *v.a., v.n. irr.* verlieren; nachgehen (*of timepiece*).

loser [ˈluːzə], *s.* der Verlierende.

loss [lɔs], *s.* der Verlust.

lot [lɔt], *s.* das Los; der Anteil (*share*); die Menge (*quantity*); die Partie (*auction*); (*Am.*) das Stück Land.

loth see **loath.**

lotion [ˈlouʃən], *s.* das Waschmittel, das Wasser.

loud [laud], *adj.* laut; grell (*colour*).

lounge [laundʒ], *s.* der Gesellschaftsraum; (*Obs.*) die Chaiselongue; — *suit*, der Straßenanzug. — *v.n.* nichts tun, herumlungern, herumsitzen.

louse [laus], *s.* (*Zool.*) die Laus.

lout [laut], *s.* der Tölpel.

lovable [ˈlʌvəbl], *adj.* liebenswürdig, liebenswert.

love [lʌv], *s.* die Liebe; *for the — of God*, um Gottes Willen; *for —*, um nichts; *not for — nor money*, weder für Geld noch gute Worte, auf keinen Fall. — *v.a., v.n.* lieben; — *to*, gern tun.

lover [ˈlʌvə], *s.* der Liebhaber, der *or* die Geliebte.

low [lou], *adj.* niedrig; nieder, tief; leise; (*Mus.*) tief; (*spirits*) niedergeschlagen. — *v.n.* muhen (*of cattle*).

lowlands [ˈloulandz], *s. pl.* die Niederungen, *f.pl.*; die Ebene; das Unterland.

lowliness [ˈloulinis], *s.* die Demut, Bescheidenheit.

lowness [ˈlounis], *s.* die Niedrigkeit; Tiefe.

loyal [ˈlɔiəl], *adj.* treu, ergeben, loyal.

loyalty [ˈlɔiəlti], *s.* die Treue, Ergebenheit, Loyalität.

lozenge [ˈlɔzindʒ], *s.* die Pastille; (*Geom.*) die Raute.

lubricant [ˈluːbrikənt], *s.* das Schmiermittel, Schmieröl.

lubricate [ˈluːbrikeit], *v.a.* ölen, schmieren.

lucid [ˈluːsid], *adj.* klar, deutlich.

lucidity [luːˈsiditi], *s.* die Klarheit.

luck [lʌk], *s.* das Glück, der Glücksfall.

luckily [ˈlʌkili], *adv.* glücklicherweise.

lucky [ˈlʌki], *adj.* mit Glück gesegnet, glücklich.

lucrative [ˈluːkrətiv], *adj.* einträglich.

lucre [ˈluːkə], *s.* der Gewinn.

ludicrous [ˈluːdikrəs], *adj.* lächerlich, komisch.

lug [lʌg], *v.a.* schleifen, zerren; (*burden*) schleppen.

luggage [ˈlʌgidʒ], *s.* das Gepäck.

lugger [ˈlʌgə], *s.* (*Naut.*) der Logger, Lugger.

lugubrious [luːˈgjuːbriəs], *adj.* traurig.

lukewarm [ˈluːkwoːm], *adj.* lauwarm.

lull [lʌl], *s.* die (Wind)stille. — *v.a.* einlullen, beschwichtigen.

lullaby [ˈlʌləbai], *s.* das Wiegenlied.

lumbago [lʌmˈbeigou], *s.* (*Med.*) der Hexenschuß.

lumbar [ˈlʌmbə], *adj.* (*Anat.*) zu den Lenden gehörig, Lenden-.

lumber [ˈlʌmbə], *s.* der Kram, das alte Zeug; (*timber*) das Bauholz; — *room*, die Rumpelkammer.

luminous [ˈluːminəs], *adj.* leuchtend, Leucht-.

lump [lʌmp], *s.* der Klumpen, Haufen; — *sugar*, der Würfelzucker; — *sum*, die Pauschalsumme. — *v.a.* — (*together*), zusammenwerfen.

lumpy [ˈlʌmpi], *adj.* klumpig.

lunacy [ˈluːnəsi], *s.* der Wahnsinn.

lunatic [ˈluːnətik], *adj.* wahnsinnig. — *s.* der Wahnsinnige; — *asylum*, das Irrenhaus, die Irrenanstalt.

lunch [lʌntʃ], *v.n.* zu Mittag essen. — *s.* (*also* **luncheon** [ˈlʌntʃən]) das Mittagessen.

lung [lʌŋ], *s.* (*Anat.*) die Lunge.

lunge [lʌndʒ], *v.n.* stoßen, stürzen. — *s.* der Stoß.

lurch [ləːtʃ], *s. leave in the —*, im Stiche lassen. — *v.n.* taumeln.

lure [luə], *v.a.* locken, ködern (*bait*). — *s.* der Köder (*bait*); die Lockung.

lurid [ˈljuərid], *adj.* unheimlich, grell.

lurk [ləːk], *v.n.* lauern.

luscious [ˈlʌʃəs], *adj.* saftig, süß.

lush [lʌʃ], *adj.* üppig (*vegetation*); übermäßig.

lust [lʌst], *s.* die Wollust, Sucht. — *v.n.* gelüsten (*for*, nach, *Dat.*).

lustre ['lʌstə], *s.* der Glanz.

lusty ['lʌsti], *adj.* kräftig, laut.

lute [lu:t], *s.* (*Mus.*) die Laute.

lutanist ['lu:tənist], *s.* (*Mus.*) der Lautenspieler.

Lutheran ['lu:θərən], *adj.* lutherisch. — *s.* der Lutheraner.

luxuriate [lʌg'zjuərieit, lʌk'sjuə-], *v.n.* schwelgen; (*Bot.*) üppig wachsen.

luxurious [lʌg'zjuəriəs, lʌk'sjuə-], *adj.* üppig; (*rich*) reich ausgeschmückt, prächtig, luxuriös.

luxury ['lʌkʃəri], *s.* der Luxus, Aufwand.

lymph [limf], *s.* die Lymphe.

lynx [links], *s.* (*Zool.*) der Luchs.

lyric ['lirik], *s.* die Lyrik.

lyrical ['lirikəl], *adj.* lyrisch.

M

M [em]. das M.

macaroon [mækə'ru:n], *s.* die Makrone.

mace [meis], *s.* das Zepter.

macerate ['mæsəreit], *v.a.* abzehren.

machination [mæki'neiʃən], *s.* die Machenschaft, Ränke, *m.pl.*

machine [mə'ʃi:n], *s.* die Maschine.

mackerel ['mækərəl], *s.* (*Zool.*) die Makrele.

mackintosh ['mækintəʃ], *s.* der Regenmantel.

mad [mæd], *adj.* verrückt, wahnsinnig.

madam ['mædəm], *s.* (*addr.*) gnädige Frau.

madden [mædn], *v.a.* verrückt machen.

madman ['mædmən], *s.* der Wahnsinnige.

madness ['mædnis], *s.* der Wahnsinn.

magazine [mægə'zi:n], *s.* die (illustrierte) Zeitschrift; (*gun*) der Ladestock; der Lagerraum (*storeroom*).

maggot ['mægət], *s.* (*Ent.*) die Made.

magic ['mædʒik], *adj.* zauberhaft; — *lantern*, die Laterna Magica. — *s.* der Zauber; die Magie, Zauberei.

magician [mə'dʒiʃən], *s.* der Zauberer.

magistracy ['mædʒistrəsi], *s.* die Obrigkeit (*authority*).

magistrate ['mædʒistr(e)it], *s.* der Richter.

magnanimity [mægnə'nimiti], *s.* der Großmut.

magnanimous [mæg'næniməs], *adj.* großmütig.

magnate ['mægneit], *s.* der Magnat, Großunternehmer.

magnet ['mægnit], *s.* der Magnet.

magnetic [mæg'netik], *adj.* magnetisch.

magnetize ['mægnitaiz], *v.a.* magnetisieren.

magnificence [mæg'nifisəns], *s.* die Herrlichkeit.

magnificent [mæg'nifisənt], *adj.* herrlich, großartig.

magnify ['mægnifai], *v.a.* vergrößern (*make larger*); (*Rel.*) verherrlichen.

magnitude ['mægnitju:d], *s.* die Größe; *order of —*, die Größenordnung.

magpie ['mægpai], *s.* (*Orn.*) die Elster.

Magyar ['mægjɔ:], *adj.* madjarisch. — *s.* der Magyar, Madjar.

mahogany [mə'hɔgəni], *s.* das Mahagoni(holz).

maid [meid], *s.* (*Poet.*) das Mädchen; das Stubenmädchen (*servant*).

maiden [meidn], *s.* (*Poet.*) die Jungfrau, das Mädchen; — *aunt*, die unverheiratete Tante.

mail (1) [meil], *s.* die Post. — *v.a.* aufgeben, mit der Post senden.

mail (2) [meil], *s.* (*Mil.*) der Panzer.

maim [meim], *v.a.* verstümmeln, lähmen.

main (1) [mein], *adj.* hauptsächlich, Haupt-; (*Railw.*) — *line*, die Hauptstrecke. — *s.* der Hauptteil; *in the —*, hauptsächlich; (*Poet.*) das Weltmeer; (*pl.*) das Hauptrohr, die Hauptleitung.

main (2) [mein], *s. with might and —*, mit allen Kräften.

mainstay ['meinstei], *s.* die Hauptgrundlage, Hauptstütze.

maintain [mein'tein], *v.a.* erhalten, unterhalten (*keep*); behaupten (*assert*).

maintenance ['meintənəns], *s.* der Unterhalt, die Unterhaltskosten, *pl.* die Erhaltung.

maize [meiz], *s.* (*Bot.*) der Mais.

majestic [mə'dʒestik], *adj.* majestätisch, prunkvoll.

majesty ['mædʒəsti], *s.* die Majestät.

major ['meidʒə], *adj.* größer, älter (*elder brother*); wichtig (*more important*). — *s.* (*Mil.*) der Major; (*Law*) der Mündige. — *v.n.* (*Am.*) sich spezialisieren.

majority [mə'dʒɔriti], *s.* die Mehrheit (*in numbers*); (*Law*) die Mündigkeit; (*Mil.*) der Majorsrang.

make [meik], *v.a. irr.* machen, schaffen, herstellen (*produce*); (*coll.*) verdienen (*money*); *he has made it* (*coll.*) er hat's geschafft!; — *out*, ausfüllen (*cheque etc.*); entziffern (*decipher*); — *up*, erfinden (*invent*); schminken (*o.'s face*). — *v.n. what do you — of him?* was halten Sie von ihm? — *s.* die Marke.

make-believe ['meikbəli:v], *s.* der Vorwand. — *adj.* vorgeblich.

maladjustment [mælə'dʒʌstmənt], *s.* die Unfähigkeit sich anzupassen; die falsche Einstellung; das Missverhältnis.

maladroit [mælə'drɔit], *adj.* ungeschickt, ungewandt.

malady ['mælədi], *s.* das Leiden, die Krankheit.

Malagasy [mæləˈgæsi], *adj.* madagassich. — *s.* der Madagasse.

Malaysian [məˈleiziən], *adj.* malaysisch. — *s.* der Malaysier.

malcontent [ˈmælkəntent], *adj.* mißvergnügt.

male [meil], *adj.* männlich; — *screw*, die Schraubenspindel. — *s.* der Mann; (*Zool.*) das Männchen.

malefactor [ˈmælifæktə], *s.* der Übeltäter.

malice [ˈmælis], *s.* die Bosheit.

malicious [məˈliʃəs], *adj.* boshaft, böswillig.

malign [məˈlain], *v.a.* lästern, verleumden.

malignant [məˈlignənt], *adj.* bösartig.

malignity [məˈligniti], *s.* die Bösartigkeit.

malinger [məˈliŋgə], *v.n.* sich krank stellen.

malleable [ˈmæliəbl], *adj.* (*Metall.*) leicht zu hämmern; (*fig.*) geschmeidig.

mallet [ˈmælit], *s.* der Schlegel, Holzhammer.

mallow [ˈmælou], *s.* (*Bot.*) die Malve.

malpractice [mælˈpræktis], *s.* das gesetzwidrige Handeln, der Mißbrauch; die Amtsvergehung.

malt [mɔːlt], *s.* das Malz.

Maltese [mɔːlˈtiːz], *adj.* maltesisch. — *s.* der Malteser.

maltreat [mælˈtriːt], *v.a.* mißhandeln.

mammal [ˈmæməl], *s.* (*Zool.*) das Säugetier.

man [mæn], *s.* der Mann (*adult male*); der Mensch (*human being*); — *of war*, das Kriegschiff. — *v.a.* bemannen.

manacle [ˈmænəkl], *s.* die Handschelle. — *v.a.* fesseln.

manage [ˈmænidʒ], *v.a.* leiten, handhaben, verwalten; *how did you — it?* wie haben Sie's fertiggebracht?

management [ˈmænidʒmənt], *s.* die Leitung, Führung.

manager [ˈmænədʒə], *s.* der Leiter, Geschäftsführer, Manager.

mandatary *see* **mandatory**.

mandate [ˈmændeit], *s.* das Mandat.

mandatory [ˈmændətəri], *adj.* befehlend, bevollmächtigt, beauftragt. — *s.* der Bevollmächtigte, Beauftragte.

mandrake [ˈmændreik], *s.* der Alraun.

mane [mein], *s.* die Mähne.

manganese [ˈmæŋgəniːz], *s.* (*Chem.*) das Mangan.

mange [meindʒ], *s.* die Räude.

manger [ˈmeindʒə], *s.* die Krippe.

mangle (1) [mæŋgl], *s.* der Mangel. — *v.a.* rollen; mangeln (*laundry*).

mangle (2) [mæŋgl], *v.a.* verstümmeln (*disfigure*).

mango [ˈmæŋgou], *s.* (*Bot.*) die Mangofrucht.

manhood [ˈmænhud], *s.* die Mannbarkeit, das Mannesalter.

mania [ˈmeiniə], *s.* der Wahnsinn, die Manie.

maniac [ˈmeiniæk], *s.* der Wahnsinnige. — *adj.* wahnsinnig.

manifest [ˈmænifest], *adj.* deutlich, klar, offenbar.

manifestation [mænifesˈteiʃən], *s.* die Offenbarung.

manifesto [mæniˈfestou], *s.* das Manifest.

manifold [ˈmænifould], *adj.* mannigfach.

manipulate [məˈnipjuleit], *v.a.* manipulieren, handhaben.

mankind [mænˈkaind], *s.* die Menschheit.

manly [ˈmænli], *adj.* mannhaft, männlich.

manner [ˈmænə], *s.* die Art, Sitte (*custom*); die Manier (*bearing*); das Benehmen (*behaviour*); (*pl.*) gute Sitten.

mannered [ˈmænəd], *adj.* gesittet, geartet; manieriert, gekünstelt (*artificial*).

manor [ˈmænə], *s.* — *house*, das Herrenhaus, Schloß.

manorial [məˈnɔːriəl], *adj.* des Herrenhauses, herrschaftlich.

manservant [ˈmænsəːvənt], *s.* der Bediente, Diener.

mansion [ˈmænʃən], *s.* das (herrschaftliche) Wohnhaus, Herrenhaus.

manslaughter [ˈmænslɔːtə], *s.* der Totschlag.

mantelpiece [ˈmæntlpiːs], *s.* der Kaminsims.

mantle [mæntl], *s.* (*gas*) der Glühstrumpf; (*Tail.*) der Mantel. — *v.a.* verhüllen (*cloak*).

manual [ˈmænjuəl], *s.* das Handbuch; (*Mus.*) das Handregister. — *adj.* Hand-.

manufacture [mænjuˈfæktʃə], *s.* die Herstellung, Erzeugung (*production*); (*Comm.*) das Fabrikat (*product*).

manufacturer [mænjuˈfæktʃərə], *s.* der Fabrikant, Erzeuger.

manure [məˈnjuə], *s.* der Dünger; der Mist. — *v.a.* düngen.

manuscript [ˈmænjuskript], *s.* die Handschrift, das Manuskript.

many [ˈmeni], *adj.* viele; — *as — as*, ganze ... (*emphatically*); — *a*, mancher.

map [mæp], *s.* die Landkarte. — *v.a.* —(*out*), nach der Karte planen.

maple [meipl], *s.* (*Bot.*) der Ahorn.

mar [mɑː], *v.a.* verderben.

marauder [məˈrɔːdə], *s.* der Plünderer.

marble [mɑːbl], *s.* der Marmor (*rock*); (*pl.*) die Murmel (*game*). — *adj.* marmorn.

March [mɑːtʃ], *s.* der März.

march [mɑːtʃ], *s.* der Marsch. — *v.n.* marschieren; *steal a — on s.o.*, jemandem zuvorkommen.

marchioness [mɑːʃəˈnes], *s.* die Marquise.

mare [mɛə], *s.* (*Zool.*) die Stute.

margin [ˈmɑːdʒin], *s.* der Rand.

marginal [ˈmɑːdʒinəl], *adj.* Rand-, am Rande gelegen.

marigold [ˈmærigould], *s.* (*Bot.*) die Dotterblume.

marine

marine [məˈriːn], *adj.* Marine-, See-. — *s.* (*Mil.*) der Seesoldat; *tell that to the Marines!* der Großmutter erzählen.

mariner [ˈmærinə], *s.* der Seemann.

marital [ˈmæritəl], *adj.* ehelich.

maritime [ˈmæritaim], *adj.* Meeres-, See-.

mark [maːk], *s.* das Zeichen (*sign*); (*Sch.*) die Zensur, Note; (*Comm.*) die Marke; *wide of the* —, auf dem Holzwege. — *v.a.* markieren (*make sign on*); — *my words*, merk dir das! paß auf! (*Comm.*) — *down*, den Preis heruntersetzen; ins Auge fassen (*observe closely*); *a* —*ed man*, ein Gezeichneter.

market [ˈmaːkit], *s.* der Markt. — *v.a.* auf den Markt bringen.

marksman [ˈmaːksmən], *s.* der Schütze.

marl [maːl], *s.* der Mergel.

marmalade [ˈmaːməleid], *s.* die Orangenmarmelade.

marmot [ˈmaːmət], *s.* (*Zool.*) das Murmeltier.

maroon (1) [məˈruːn], *adj.* kastanienbraun, rotbraun.

maroon (2) [məˈruːn], *v.a.* aussetzen.

marquee [maːˈkiː], *s.* das große Zelt.

marquess, marquis [ˈmaːkwis], *s.* der Marquis.

marriage [ˈmæridʒ], *s.* die Ehe, Heirat; die Hochzeit (*wedding*).

marriageable [ˈmæridʒəbl], *adj.* heiratsfähig.

married [ˈmærid], *adj.* verheiratet.

marrow [ˈmærou], *s.* (*Anat.*) das Mark; (*Bot.*) der Kürbis.

marry [ˈmæri], *v.a.* heiraten; trauen (*perform marriage ceremony*); — *off*, verheiraten (*o.'s daughter*). — *v.n.* sich verheiraten.

marsh [maːʃ], *s.* der Morast, Sumpf.

marshal [ˈmaːʃəl], *s.* der Marschall.

marshy [ˈmaːʃi], *adj.* morastig, sumpfig.

marten [ˈmaːtin], *s.* (*Zool.*) der Marder.

martial [ˈmaːʃəl], *adj.* Kriegs-, kriegerisch.

martin [ˈmaːtin], *s.* (*Orn.*) die Mauerschwalbe.

martyr [ˈmaːtə], *s.* der Märtyrer.

martyrdom [ˈmaːtədəm], *s.* das Märtyrertum, der Märtyrertod.

marvel [ˈmaːvl], *v.n.* staunen (*at*, über, *Acc.*).

marvellous [ˈmaːv(ə)ləs], *adj.* wunderbar, erstaunlich.

masculine [ˈmæskjulin], *adj.* männlich. — *s.* (*Gram.*) das Maskulinum, das männliche Geschlecht.

mash [mæʃ], *v.a.* zerquetschen, zerdrücken. — *s.* der Brei.

mask [maːsk], *v.a., v.n.* maskieren, sich vermummen. — *s.* die Maske.

mason [ˈmeisən], *s.* der Maurer.

masonic [məˈsɔnik], *adj.* freimaurerisch.

masonry [ˈmeisənri], *s.* das Mauerwerk.

masquerade [mæskəˈreid], *s.* der Mummenschanz, die Maskerade.

Mass [mæs, maːs], *s.* (*Eccl.*) die Messe; *Low Mass*, die stille Messe; *High*

Mass, das Hochamt; *Requiem Mass*, die Seelenmesse.

mass [mæs], *s.* die Masse; die Menge. — *v.a., v.n.* (sich) massen, ansammeln.

massacre [ˈmæsəkə], *s.* das Blutbad.

massive [ˈmæsiv], *adj.* massiv, schwer.

mast [maːst], *s.* der Mast. — *v.a.* (*Naut.*) bemasten.

Master [ˈmaːstə], *s.* (*Univ.*) der Magister; der junge Herr (*before boy's name*).

master [ˈmaːstə], *s.* der Meister (*of a craft*); der Herr, Arbeitgeber (*employer*); — *key*, der Hauptschlüssel. — *v.a.* meistern, beherrschen.

masticate [ˈmæstikeit] *v.a.* kauen.

mastiff [ˈmæstif], *s.* (*Zool.*) der Kettenhund, Mastiff.

mat [mæt], *s.* die Matte.

match (1) [mætʃ], *s.* das Streichholz, Zündholz.

match (2) [mætʃ], *s.* der ebenbürtige Partner (*suitable partner*); *find o.'s* —, seinesgleichen finden; (*Sport*) das Wettspiel, der Wettkampf; Fußballkampf; (*Cricket*) das Cricketspiel. — *v.a., v.n.* passen zu, anpassen; ebenbürtig sein (*be equal*).

matchless [ˈmætʃlis], *adj.* unvergleichlich, ohnegleichen.

mate (1) [meit], *s.* der Gefährte, Genosse; (*Naut.*) der Maat, Steuermann; (*coll.*) Freund. — *v.n.* sich paaren, sich verheiraten.

mate (2) [meit], *v.a.* (*Chess*) matt setzen.

material [məˈtiəriəl], *s.* das Material, der Stoff. — *adj.* wesentlich (*essential*); materiell (*tangible*).

materialism [məˈtiəriəlizm], *s.* der Materialismus.

maternal [məˈtəːnəl], *adj.* mütterlich.

maternity [məˈtəːniti], *s.* die Mutterschaft; — *ward*, die Geburtsklinik.

mathematical [mæθəˈmætikəl], *adj.* mathematisch.

mathematics [mæθəˈmætiks], *s.* die Mathematik.

matins [ˈmætinz], *s.* (*Eccl.*) die Frühmette.

matriculate [məˈtrikjuleit], *v.n.* sich immatrikulieren (lassen).

matrimonial [mætriˈmouniəl], *adj.* Ehe-, ehelich.

matrimony [ˈmætriməni], *s.* die Ehe.

matron [ˈmeitrən], *s.* die Oberschwester, Oberin (*in hospital etc.*); die Matrone (*older woman*).

matter [ˈmætə], *s.* der Stoff (*substance*); die Sache, der Gegenstand (*subject*); die Angelegenheit (*case*); *printed* —, Drucksache; *what is the* —? was ist los?; *the heart of the* —, des Pudels Kern; *as a* — *of fact*, tatsächlich, ernst gesprochen. — *v.n.* bedeutsam sein, wichtig sein.

mattock [ˈmætək], *s.* die Haue.

mattress [ˈmætrəs], *s.* die Matratze.

mature [məˈtjuə], *adj.* reif; (*fig.*) gereift. — *v.a., v.n.* reifen, zur Reife bringen; (*Comm.*) fällig werden.

436

matured [məˈtjuəd], *adj.* abgelagert.
maturity [məˈtjuəriti], *s.* die Reife; (*Comm.*) die Fälligkeit.
maudlin [ˈmɔːdlin], *adj.* rührselig, sentimental.
maul [mɔːl], *v.a.* mißhandeln.
Maundy Thursday [ˈmɔːndiˈθəːzd(e)i]. der Gründonnerstag.
mauve [mouv], *adj.* malvenfarbig; violett.
maw [mɔː], *s.* (*Zool.*) der Magen.
mawkish [ˈmɔːkiʃ], *adj.* abgeschmackt, sentimental, rührselig.
maxim [ˈmæksim], *s.* der Grundsatz.
May [mei]. der Mai.
may (1) [mei], *v.n. aux. irr.* mögen, können; (*permissive*) dürfen.
may (2) [mei], *s.* (*Bot.*) der Weißdorn.
mayor [mɛə], *s.* der Bürgermeister.
maypole [ˈmeipoul], *s.* der Maibaum.
maze [meiz], *s.* das Labyrinth.
me [miː], *pers. pron.* (*Acc.*) mich; (*Dat.*) mir.
mead [miːd], *s.* der Met.
meadow [ˈmedou], *s.* die Wiese.
meagre [ˈmiːgə], *adj.* mager, karg (*lean, poor*); dürftig.
meal (1) [miːl], *s.* das Mahl, Essen, die Mahlzeit.
meal (2) [miːl], *s.* das Mehl (*flour*).
mealy [ˈmiːli], *adj.* mehlig; — *-mouthed*, frömmelnd; kleinlaut (*shy*).
mean (1) [miːn], *v.a. irr.* bedeuten (*signify*); meinen (*wish to express*); vorhaben (*intend*).
mean (2) [miːn], *adj.* mittelmäßig, Mittel– (*average*). — *s.* die Mitte.
mean (3) [miːn], *adj.* gemein, niedrig (*despicable*); geizig.
meander [miˈændə], *s.* die Windung, das Wellenmuster. — *v.n.* sich winden, sich schlängeln.
meaning [ˈmiːniŋ], *s.* die Bedeutung (*significance, connotation*); der Sinn.
meaningless [ˈmiːniŋlis], *adj.* bedeutungslos.
means [miːnz], *s.* das Mittel; *by all* —, auf jeden Fall, unbedingt; *by no* —, keinesfalls; *by*—*of*, mittels (*Genit.*).
meantime, meanwhile [ˈmiːntaim, ˈmiːnwail], *s.* die Zwischenzeit.—*adv.* in der Zwischenzeit, indessen.
measles [ˈmiːnz], *s.* (*Med.*) die Masern, *f. pl.*; *German* —, die Röteln, *m. pl.*
measurable [ˈmeʒərəbl], *adj.* meßbar.
measure [ˈmeʒə], *s.* das Maß; der Maßstab (*scale*); (*Mus.*) der Takt; das Zeitmaß.—*v.a.* messen, abmessen.
meat [miːt], *s.* das Fleisch.
mechanic [miˈkænik], *s.* der Mechaniker.
mechanical [miˈkænikəl], *adj.* mechanisch, automatisch; — *engineering*, der Maschinenbau.
mechanics [miˈkæniks], *s.* die Mechanik.
medal [medl], *s.* die Medaille, der Orden.
meddle [medl], *v.n.* sich einmischen (in, *in, Acc.*).

mediæval, medieval [mediˈiːvəl], *adj.* mittelalterlich.
mediate [ˈmiːdieit], *v.n.* vermitteln, intervenieren. — *adj.* mittelbar.
mediator [ˈmiːdieitə], *s.* der Vermittler.
medical [ˈmedikəl], *adj.* medizinisch, ärztlich; — *orderly*, der Krankenwärter.
medicate [ˈmedikeit], *v.a.* medizinisch behandeln.
medicine [ˈmedsən], *s.* die Medizin, Arznei.
medieval *see* **mediæval**.
mediocre [ˈmiːdioukə], *adj.* mittelmäßig.
mediocrity [miːdiˈɔkriti], *s.* die Mittelmäßigkeit.
meditate [ˈmediteit], *v.n.* nachdenken, sinnen.
meditation [mediˈteiʃən], *s.* das Sinnen, Nachdenken.
Mediterranean [meditəˈreiniən], *adj.* mittelländisch. — *s.* das Mittelmeer, mittelländische Meer.
medium [ˈmiːdjəm], *s.* das Medium; das Mittel (*means*). — *adj.* mittelgroß.
medlar [ˈmedlə], *s.* (*Bot.*) die Mispel.
medley [ˈmedli], *s.* (*Mus.*) das Potpourri; das Gemisch (*mixture*).
meek [miːk], *adj.* sanft, mild.
meet [miːt], *v.a., v.n. irr.* treffen (*Acc.*), sich treffen (mit, *Dat.*), begegnen (*Dat.*). — *s.* (*Hunt.*) die Jagd.
meeting [ˈmiːtiŋ], *s.* das Zusammentreffen; die Tagung, Sitzung (*conference*).
melancholy [ˈmelənkɔli], *adj.* melancholisch, schwermütig. — *s.* die Melancholie, die Schwermut.
mellifluous [meˈlifluəs], *adj.* lieblich, süß (*of sounds*).
mellow [ˈmelou], *adj.* mild, weich, mürbe (*fruit etc.*); freundlich (*mood*). — *v.a.* mürbe machen, reifen lassen. — *v.n.* weich werden.
melodious [məˈloudiəs], *adj.* klangvoll, wohlklingend, melodisch.
melodrama [ˈmelədrɑːmə], *s.* das Melodrama.
melody [ˈmelədi], *s.* die Melodie.
melon [ˈmelən], *s.* (*Bot.*) die Melone.
melt [melt], *v.a., v.n. reg. & irr.* schmelzen.
member [ˈmembə], *s.* das Mitglied (*of club*); (*Parl.*) der Abgeordnete, das Glied.
membrane [ˈmembrein], *s.* die Membran; (*Anat.*) das Häutchen.
memento [miˈmentou], *s.* das Andenken.
memoir [ˈmemwɑː], *s.* die Denkschrift; (*pl.*) die Memoiren, *n. pl.*
memorable [ˈmemərəbl], *adj.* denkwürdig.
memorandum [meməˈrændəm], *s.* das Memorandum, die Denkschrift.
memorial [miˈmɔːriəl], *s.* das Denkmal (*monument*). — *adj.* Gedenk-, zum Gedenken, Gedächtnis–.

memory

memory ['meməri], *s.* die Erinnerung; das Gedächtnis (*faculty*); das Andenken (*remembrance*).

menace ['menis], *s.* die Drohung. — *v.a.* bedrohen.

mend [mend], *v.a.* reparieren; verbessern, ausbessern. — *v.n.* sich bessern.

mendacious [men'deiʃəs], *adj.* lügnerisch, verlogen (*lying*).

mendacity [men'dæsiti], *s.* die Lügenhaftigkeit, Verlogenheit.

mendicant ['mendikənt], *adj.* bettlerisch. — *s.* der Bettler.

mendicity [men'disiti], *s.* die Bettelei.

menial ['mi:niəl], *adj.* gemein, grob (*job*).

mental [mentl], *adj.* geistig; (*coll.*) geisteskrank.

mention ['menʃən], *v.a.* erwähnen; *don't — it,* gern geschehen! — *s.* die Erwähnung.

mentor ['mentə], *s.* der Ratgeber.

menu ['menju:], *s.* die Speisekarte.

mercantile ['mə:kəntail], *adj.* Handels-, kaufmännisch.

mercenary ['mə:sənəri], *adj.* für Geld zu haben, käuflich, feil; materiell eingestellt. — *s.* der Söldner.

mercer ['mə:sə], *s.* der Seidenhändler.

mercerised ['mə:səraizd], *adj.* (*Textile*) merzerisiert.

merchandise ['mə:tʃəndaiz], *s.* die Ware.

merchant ['mə:tʃənt], *s.* der Kaufmann.

merchantman ['mə:tʃəntmən], *s.* (*Naut.*) das Handelsschiff, Frachtschiff.

merciful ['mə:siful], *adj.* barmherzig, gnädig.

Mercury ['mə:kjuəri]. (*Myth.*) Merkur, *m.*

mercury ['mə:kjuəri], *s.* (*Chem.*) das Quecksilber.

mercy ['mə:si], *s.* die Barmherzigkeit, Gnade.

mere (1) [miə], *adj.* bloß, allein.

mere (2) [miə], *s.* der Teich.

meretricious [meri'triʃəs], *adj.* falsch, täuschend.

merge [mə:dʒ], *v.n.* aufgehen lassen, verschmelzen (*combine*).

merger ['mə:dʒə], *s.* (*Comm.*) die Fusion, Vereinigung, Zusammenlegung.

meridian [mə'ridiən], *s.* der Meridian; (*fig.*) der Gipfel.

merit ['merit], *s.* das Verdienst, der Wert. — *v.a.* verdienen.

meritorious [meri'tɔ:riəs], *adj.* verdienstlich.

mermaid ['mə:meid], *s.* die Wasserjungfer, Nixe.

merriment ['merimənt], *s.* die Belustigung, das Fröhlichsein, die Fröhlichkeit.

merry ['meri], *adj.* froh, fröhlich; *—go-round,* das Karussel.

mesh [meʃ], *s.* das Netz; die Masche (*knitting*). — *v.a.* einfangen.

mess (1) [mes], *s.* (*Mil.*) die Offiziersmesse.

mess (2) [mes], *s.* die Unordnung (*disorder*).

message ['mesidʒ], *s.* die Nachricht, Mitteilung, Botschaft.

messenger ['mesindʒə], *s.* der Bote.

Messiah [mi'saiə], *s.* der Messias.

metal [metl], *s.* das Metall.

metallurgy ['metələ:dʒi], *s.* die Metallurgie, Hüttenkunde.

metaphor ['metəfɔ:], *s.* die Metapher.

metaphorical [metə'fɔrikəl], *adj.* bildlich.

meter ['mi:tə], *s.* der Messer, Zähler (*gauge*); (*Am.*) see **metre** (1).

methinks [mi'θiŋks], *v. impers.* (*obs.*) mich dünkt, ich meine, mir scheint.

method ['meθəd], *s.* die Methode.

methodical [mi'θɔdikəl], *adj.* methodisch, systematisch.

methylate ['meθileit], *v.a.* (*Chem.*) denaturieren.

metre (1) ['mi:tə], *s.* der or das Meter (*unit of measurement*).

metre (2) ['mi:tə], *s.* (*Poet.*) das Versmaß.

metric ['metrik], *adj.* metrisch (*system of measurement*).

metrical ['metrikəl], *adj.* (*Poet.*) im Metrum, metrisch, Vers-.

metropolis [mi'trɔpəlis], *s.* die Metropole.

metropolitan [metrə'pɔlitən], *adj.* hauptstädtisch. — *s.* (*Eccl.*) der Erzbischof.

mettle [metl], *s.* der Mut (*courage*); *put s.o. on his —,* einen anspornen.

mew [mju:], *s.* das Miauen (*of cat*). — *v.n.* miauen.

mews [mju:z], *s. pl.* die Stallung.

Mexican ['meksikən], *adj.* mexikanisch. — *s.* der Mexikaner.

microphone ['maikrəfoun], *s.* das Mikrophon.

mid- [mid], *prefix.* mittel, Mittel-, mittler.

midday [mid'dei], *s.* der Mittag.

middle [midl], *s.* die Mitte, das Zentrum.

middling ['midliŋ], *adj.* (*coll.*) mittelmäßig.

midget ['midʒit], *s.* der Zwerg (*dwarf*).

midnight ['midnait], *s.* die Mitternacht.

midriff ['midrif], *s.* das Zwerchfell.

midshipman ['midʃipmən], *s.* (*Naut.*) der Seekadett.

midwife ['midwaif], *s.* die Hebamme.

mien [mi:n], *s.* die Miene.

might [mait], *s.* die Macht, Gewalt.

mighty ['maiti], *adj.* mächtig, stark.

mignonette [minjə'net], *s.* (*Bot.*) die Reseda.

migrate [mai'greit], *v.n.* wandern, migrieren; (*birds*) ziehen.

migratory ['maigrətəri], *adj.* Zug-, Wander-.

Milanese [milə'n:iz], *adj.* mailändisch. — *s.* der Mailänder.

mild [maild], *adj.* mild, sanft.

mildew ['mildju:], *s.* der Meltau.

mile [mail], *s.* die (englische) Meile.

mileage ['mailidʒ], *s.* die Meilenzahl.

milfoil ['milfɔil], *s.* (*Bot.*) die Schafgarbe (*yarrow*).

military ['militəri], *adj.* militärisch. — *s.* das Militär.

militia [mi'liʃə], *s.* die Miliz.

milk [milk], *v.a.* melken. — *s.* die Milch.

milksop ['milksɔp], *s.* die Memme.

milky ['milki], *adj.* milchig; *Milky Way*, die Milchstraße.

mill [mil], *s.* die Mühle; die Spinnerei (*textile*); *rolling* —, das Walzwerk; *run of the* —, gewöhnlich; *through the* —, wohl erfahren, lebenserfahren. — *v.a.* mahlen (*flour*); rollen, walzen (*steel*); rändern (*coins*); —*ed edge*, die Rändelkante. —*v.n.* — (*around*), sich drängen.

miller ['milə], *s.* der Müller.

millet ['milit], *s.* die Hirse.

milliner ['milinə], *s.* die Modistin, Putzmacherin.

millinery ['milinəri], *s.* die Putzwaren, Modewaren, *f. pl.*

million ['miljən], *s.* die Million.

milt [milt], *s.* die Fischmilch; (*Anat.*) die Milz.

mimic ['mimik], *s.* der Mimiker. — *v.a.* nachahmen.

mimicry ['mimikri], *s.* die Nachahmung; (*Zool.*) die Anpassung (*in colour*).

mince [mins], *v.a.* kleinhacken (*meat*); — *o.'s words*, affektiert sprechen; *not* — *o.'s words*, kein Blatt vor den Mund nehmen. — *s.* gehacktes Fleisch; — *pie*, die Dörrobstpastete.

mincemeat ['minsmi:t], *s.* die (gehackte) Dörrobstmischung.

mincing ['minsiŋ], *adj.* affektiert; — *steps*, trippelnde Schritte.

mind [maind], *s.* der Geist, das Gemüt; die Meinung; der Sinn; der Verstand; *what is on your* —? was bedrückt Sie?; *bear in* —, daran denken; *have a* —, Lust haben; *make up o.'s* —, sich entschließen; *with an open* —, unparteiisch. — *v.a.* beachten, achten (auf, *Acc.*). — *v.n. do you* —? macht es Ihnen etwas aus? *never* —, macht nichts; *I don't* —, mir ist's recht, meinetwegen.

minded ['maindid], *adj.* gesinnt, eingestellt.

mine (1) [main], *poss. pron.* mein, meinig.

mine (2) [main], *s.* das Bergwerk (*general*), die Grube (*coal*). — *v.a.* abbauen, graben (*Acc.*, nach, *Dat.*).

miner ['mainə], *s.* der Bergmann, Bergarbeiter; (*coll.*) der Kumpel.

mineral ['minərəl], *s.* das Mineral; (*pl.*) Mineralwasser.

mingle [miŋgl], *v.a., v.n.* (sich) mischen.

minimize ['minimaiz], *v.a.* (möglichst) klein machen.

mining ['mainiŋ], *s.* die Hüttenkunde (*theory*); der Bergbau.

minion ['minjən], *s.* der Liebling.

minister ['ministə], *s.* (*Pol.*) der Minister; *Prime Minister*, der Ministerpräsident; (*Eccl.*) der Geistliche, Pfarrer. — *v.n.* einen Gottesdienst abhalten; dienen (*to*, *Dat.*).

ministration [minis'treiʃən], *s.* der Dienst, die Dienstleistung.

ministry ['ministri], *s.* das Ministerium (*department of state*); (*Eccl.*) der Beruf *or* das Amt des Geistlichen.

minnow ['minou], *s.* (*Zool.*) die Elritze.

minor ['mainə], *adj.* kleiner, geringer; (*Sch.*) jünger (*after boy's name*). — *s.* (*Law*) der Minderjährige, Unmündige.

minority [mai'nɔriti], *s.* die Minorität (*in numbers*); (*Law*) die Unmündigkeit.

minster ['minstə], *s.* (*Eccl.*) das Münster.

minstrel ['minstrəl], *s.* der Spielmann.

mint (1) [mint], *s.* (*Bot.*) die Minze.

mint (2) [mint], *s.* die Münzstätte. — *v.a.* münzen.

minuet [minju'et], *s.* (*Mus.*) das Menuett.

minute (1) ['minit], *s.* die Minute (*time*); (*pl.*) das Protokoll (*of meeting*). — *v.a.* zu Protokoll nehmen, protokollieren.

minute (2) [mai'nju:t], *adj.* winzig, klein.

minutiae [mi'nju:ʃii], *s.pl.* die Details, *n. pl.*; die Einzelheiten, *f.pl.*

miracle ['mirəkl], *s.* das Wunder.

miraculous [mi'rækjuləs], *adj.* wunderbar; wundertätig.

mirage [mi'ra:ʒ], *s.* die Luftspiegelung, die Fata Morgana.

mire [maiə], *s.* der Schlamm, Kot.

mirror ['mirə], *s.* der Spiegel. — *v.a.* reflektieren, spiegeln.

mirth [mə:θ], *s.* der Frohsinn.

misadventure [misəd'ventʃə], *s.* das Mißgeschick.

misalliance [misə'laiəns], *s.* die Mißheirat, Mesalliance.

misapply [misə'plai], *v.a.* falsch anwenden.

misapprehend [misæpri'hend], *v.a.* mißverstehen.

misapprehension [misæpri'henʃən], *s.* das Mißverständnis.

misappropriate [misə'prouprieit], *v.a.* unrechtmäßig erwerben, unterschlagen.

misbehave [misbi'heiv], *v.n.* sich schlecht benehmen.

miscalculate [mis'kælkjuleit], *v.a., v.n.* sich verrechnen.

miscarriage [mis'kæridʒ], *s.* das Mißlingen; (*Med.*) die Fehlgeburt.

miscarry [mis'kæri], *v.n.* mißlingen; (*Med.*) fehlgebären.

miscellaneous [misə'leiniəs], *adj.* vermischt.

miscellany

miscellany [mi'seləni], s. der Sammelband (of writers); die Mischung, das Gemisch.

mischief ['mistʃif], s. der Unfug; out to make —, darauf aus, Unfug zu stiften; — maker, der Unheilstifter.

mischievous ['mistʃivəs], adj. boshaft.

misconceive [miskən'si:v], v.a. mißverstehen.

misconception [miskən'sepʃən], s. das Mißverständnis.

misconduct [mis'kɔndʌkt], s. das unkorrekte Verhalten; der Fehltritt.

misconstruction [miskən'strʌkʃən], s. die Mißdeutung.

misconstrue [miskən'stru:], v.a. mißdeuten.

misdeed [mis'di:d], s. die Missetat.

misdemeanour [misdi'mi:nə], s. (Law.) das Vergehen; die Missetat.

miser ['maizə], s. der Geizhals.

miserable ['mizərəbl], adj. elend, kläglich (wretched); nichtswürdig (base).

miserly ['maizəli], adj. geizig.

misery ['mizəri], s. das Elend, die Not.

misfortune [mis'fɔ:tʃən], s. das Unglück.

misgiving [mis'giviŋ], s. die Befürchtung, der Zweifel (doubt).

misguide [mis'gaid], v.a. irreführen, verleiten.

mishap [mis'hæp], s. der Unfall.

misinform [misin'fɔ:m], v.a. falsch informieren, falsch unterrichten.

misinterpret [misin'tə:prit], v.a. mißdeuten.

misjudge [mis'dʒʌdʒ], v.a. falsch beurteilen.

mislay [mis'lei], v.a. irr. verlegen.

mislead [mis'li:d], v.a. irr. verführen, irreführen.

misnomer [mis'noumə], s. der falsche Name.

misogynist [mi'sɔdʒinist], s. der Weiberfeind.

misplace [mis'pleis], v.a. übel anbringen (remark); verlegen (thing).

misprint [mis'print], v.a. verdrucken, falsch drucken. — ['misprint], s. der Druckfehler.

misquote [mis'kwout], v.a. falsch zitieren.

misrepresent [misrepri'zent], v.a. falsch darstellen.

misrule [mis'ru:l], s. die schlechte Regierung; die Unordnung (disorder).

miss (1) [mis], s. das Fräulein.

miss (2) [mis], v.a. vermissen (yearn for); versäumen (a train, lesson etc.); verfehlen (target); — the boat, den Anschluß verpassen; be missing, fehlen.

missal [misl], s. (Eccl.) das Meßbuch.

misshapen [mis'ʃeipən], adj. mißgestaltet.

missile ['misail], s. das Geschoß; ballistic —, das Raketengeschoß; guided —, ferngesteuertes Raketengeschoss.

mission ['miʃən], s. die Mission; Sendung; der Auftrag (task).

missionary ['miʃənəri], adj. Missions-. — s. der Missionar.

missive ['misiv], s. das Sendschreiben.

misspell [mis'spel], v.a. falsch buchstabieren, falsch schreiben.

mist [mist], s. der Dunst; Nebel (fog).

mistake [mis'teik], s. der Fehler. — v.a. irr. verkennen.

mistaken [mis'teikn], adj. im Unrecht; irrig; be —, sich irren.

mistimed [mis'taimd], adj. zur Unzeit, unzeitig.

mistletoe ['misltou], s. (Bot.) die Mistel, der Mistelzweig.

mistress ['mistrəs], s. die Herrin; Hausfrau; Geliebte (paramour); Lehrerin (Sch.).

mistrust [mis'trʌst], v.a. mißtrauen.

misunderstand [misʌndə'stænd], v.a. irr. mißverstehen.

misuse [mis'ju:z], v.a. mißbrauchen.

mite (1) [mait], s. (Zool.) die Milbe.

mite (2) [mait], s. das Scherflein (coin); (coll.) das Kindchen, das Kerlchen.

mitigate ['mitigeit], v.a. mildern.

mitre ['maitə], s. die Bischofsmütze, Mitra.

mitten [mitn], s. der Fäustling, Fausthandschuh.

mix [miks], v.a. mischen, vermischen. — v.n. verkehren.

mixed [mikst], adj. a — blessing, eine fragliche Wohltat.

mizzle [mizl], v.n. sprühen, rieseln.

mnemonics [ni'mɔniks], s. die Gedächtniskunst.

moan [moun], v.n. stöhnen (wail); klagen (complain). — s. (coll.) die Klage.

moat [mout], s. der Burggraben, Wassergraben.

mob [mɔb], s. der Pöbel.

mobility [mo'biliti], s. die Beweglichkeit.

mobilize ['moubilaiz], v.a. mobilisieren.

mock [mɔk], v.a. verspotten (tease); täuschen (mislead). — v.n. spotten. — s. der Spott, die Täuschung. — adj. Schein-; — heroic, komischheroisch.

modal ['moudl], adj. (Gram.) modal, der Aussageweise nach; (Mus.) dem Modus nach.

mode [moud], s. (Mus.) der Modus, die Art; die Mode (fashion).

model ['mɔdl], s. das Modell; das Muster (pattern). — v.a., v.n. modellieren.

moderate ['mɔdərit], adj. mäßig; (climate) gemäßigt. — [-reit], v.a. mäßigen; abändern.

modern ['mɔdən], adj. modern.

modernize ['mɔdənaiz], v.a. modernisieren.

modest ['mɔdist], adj. bescheiden.

modesty ['mɔdisti], s. die Bescheidenheit.

modify ['mɔdifai], v.a. abändern, modifizieren.

modish ['moudiʃ], *adj.* nach der neuesten Mode, modisch.

modulate ['mɔdjuleit], *v.a.* modulieren.

moil [mɔil], *v.n.* sich plagen.

moist [mɔist], *adj.* feucht.

moisten [mɔisn], *v.a.* befeuchten.

moisture ['mɔistʃə], *s.* die Feuchtigkeit.

molasses [mo'læsiz], *s.* die Melasse.

mole (1) [moul], *s.* (*Zool.*) der Maulwurf.

mole (2) [moul], *s.* das Muttermal (*skin mark*).

mole (3) [moul], *s.* der Seedamm, Hafendamm.

molecular [mo'lekjulə], *adj.* molekular.

molecule ['mɔl-, 'moulikju:l], *s.* das Molekül.

molest [mo'lest], *v.a.* belästigen.

mollify ['mɔlifai], *v.a.* besänftigen.

mollusc ['mɔləsk], *s.* (*Zool.*) die Molluske.

molt *see under* **moult**.

molten ['moultən], *adj.* geschmolzen.

moment ['moumənt], *s.* der Augenblick, Moment (*instant*); die Wichtigkeit (*importance*).

momentary ['moumentəri], *adj.* momentan, einen Augenblick lang.

momentum [mo'mentəm], *s.* das Moment, die Triebkraft.

monarch ['mɔnək], *s.* der Monarch.

monarchy ['mɔnəki], *s.* die Monarchie.

monastery ['mɔnəstri], *s.* das (Mönchs-)kloster.

monastic [mə'næstik], *adj.* klösterlich.

Monday ['mʌndi], *s.* der Montag.

money ['mʌni], *s.* das Geld; *ready* —, bares Geld; *make* —, Geld verdienen; — *order*, die Postanweisung.

Mongolian [mɔŋ'goulian], *adj.* mongolisch. — *s.* der Mongole.

mongrel ['mʌŋgrəl], *s.* (*Zool.*) der Mischling.

monitor ['mɔnitə], *s.* der Ermahner; (*Rad.*) der Abhörer.

monitoring ['mɔnitəriŋ], *adj.* — *service*, der Abhördienst.

monk [mʌŋk], *s.* (*Eccl.*) der Mönch.

monkey ['mʌŋki], *s.* (*Zool.*) der Affe.

monomania [mɔno'meiniə], *s.* die Monomanie, fixe Idee.

monopolize [mə'nɔpəlaiz], *v.a.* monopolisieren.

monopoly [mə'nɔpəli], *s.* das Monopol.

monosyllabic [mɔnəsi'læbik], *adj.* einsilbig.

monotonous [mə'nɔtənəs], *adj.* monoton, eintönig.

monsoon [mɔn'su:n], *s.* der Monsun.

monster ['mɔnstə], *s.* das Ungeheuer.

monstrance ['mɔnstrəns], *s.* (*Eccl.*) die Monstranz.

monstrosity [mɔns'trɔsiti], *s.* die Ungeheuerlichkeit.

monstrous ['mɔnstrəs], *adj.* ungeheuerlich.

month [mʌnθ], *s.* der Monat.

monthly ['mʌnθli], *adj.* monatlich, Monats-.

mood [mu:d], *s.* die Stimmung, Laune; (*Gram., Mus.*) der Modus.

moodiness ['mu:dinis], *s.* die Launenhaftigkeit.

moody ['mu:di], *adj.* launenhaft.

moon [mu:n], *s.* der Mond.

moonlight ['mu:nlait], *s.* das Mondlicht, der Mondschein.

moonshine ['mu:nʃain], *s.* der Mondschein; (*fig.*) Unsinn.

moonstruck ['mu:nstrʌk], *adj.* mondsüchtig; verliebt.

Moor [muə], *s.* der Mohr.

moor [muə], *s.* das Moor, Heideland.

moorage ['muəridʒ], *s.* der Ankerplatz.

moorhen ['mɔ:hen], *s.* (*Orn.*) das Moorhuhn, Wildhuhn.

moorish ['muəriʃ], *adj.* maurisch.

moot [mu:t], *v.a.* erörtern, besprechen. — *adj.* a — *point*, ein strittiger Punkt.

mop [mɔp], *s.* der Wischlappen, Mop. — *v.a.* aufwischen (*floor*), wischen (*brow*).

mope [moup], *v.n.* traurig sein.

moral ['mɔrəl], *adj.* moralisch (*high principled*); sittlich (*decent*). — *s.* die Moral (*precept*); (*pl.*) die Sitten, *f. pl.*; die Sittlichkeit.

moralize ['mɔrəlaiz], *v.n.* moralisieren, Moral predigen (*Dat.*).

morass [mo'ræs], *s.* der Morast.

morbid ['mɔ:bid], *adj.* krankhaft.

more [mɔ:], *comp. adj., adv.* mehr; *once* —, noch einmal; *all the* —, umso mehr; *the* — *the better*, je mehr desto besser.

moreover [mɔ:'rouvə], *adv.* zudem, überdies, weiterhin.

morning ['mɔ:niŋ], *s.* der Morgen, Vormittag; — *coat*, der Cutaway, Frack.

Moroccan [mə'rɔkən], *adj.* marokkanisch. — *s.* der Marokkaner.

Morocco [mə'rɔkou]. Marokko, *n.*

morocco [mə'rɔkou], *s.* der Saffian, das Maroquinleder.

moron ['mɔ:rɔn], *s.* der Schwachsinnige.

morose [mə'rous], *adj.* mürrisch.

morrow ['mɔrou], *s.* (*Poet.*) der Morgen.

morsel ['mɔ:sl], *s.* der Bissen, das Stück.

mortal ['mɔ:tl], *adj.* sterblich, tödlich; — *sin*, die Todsünde. — *s.* der Sterbliche, der Mensch.

mortality [mɔ:'tæliti], *s.* die Sterblichkeit.

mortar ['mɔ:tə], *s.* (*Build.*) der Mörtel; (*Mil.*) der Mörser.

mortgage ['mɔ:gidʒ], *s.* die Hypothek. — *v.a.* verpfänden; eine Hypothek aufnehmen (auf, *Acc.*).

mortgagee [mɔ:gi'dʒi:], *s.* der Hypothekengläubiger.

mortician [mɔ:'tiʃən], *s.* (*Am.*) *see* **undertaker**.

mortify ['mɔ:tifai], *v.a.* kasteien (*chasten*); kränken (*humiliate*).

mortise ['mɔ:tis], *s.* (*Build.*) das Zapfenloch.

mortuary ['mɔːtjuəri], s. die Leichenhalle.

mosque [mɔsk], s. (Rel.) die Moschee.

mosquito [mɔs'kiːtou], s. (Ent.) der Moskito.

moss [mɔs], s. (Bot.) das Moos.

most [moust], superl. adj. meist; (pl.) die meisten. — adv. meist, meistens; höchst (before adjectives).

mostly ['moustli], adv. meistenteils.

mote [mout], s. das Stäubchen.

moth [mɔθ], s. (Ent.) die Motte.

mother ['mʌðə], s. die Mutter; — -in-law, die Schwiegermutter; —-of-pearl, die Perlmutter.

motherly ['mʌðəli], adj. mütterlich.

motion ['mouʃən], s. die Bewegung, der Gang; (Parl., Rhet.) der Antrag. — v.a. bewegen. — v.n. zuwinken (Dat.).

motive ['moutiv], s. das Motiv, der Beweggrund.

motley ['mɔtli], adj. scheckig, bunt.

motor ['moutə], s. der Motor.

motoring ['moutəriŋ], s. das Autofahren, der Autosport.

mottled [mɔtld], adj. gescheckt, gesprenkelt.

motto ['mɔtou], s. das Motto, der Wahlspruch.

mould (1) [mould], s. die Form; Gußform (casting); die Schablone. — v.a. formen; (Metall.) gießen, formen.

mould (2) [mould], s. der Schimmel (fungus); (Hort.) die Gartenerde. — v.n. schimmeln.

moulder (1) ['mouldə], s. der Bildner; (Metall.) der Gießer.

moulder (2) ['mouldə], v.n. vermodern.

mouldy ['mouldi], adj. moderig, schimmelig.

moult, (Am.) **molt** [moult], v.n. (Zool.) sich mausern.

mound [maund], s. der Erdhügel.

mount [maunt], v.a. besteigen (horse, hill); montieren, anbringen (apparatus). — v.n. sich belaufen (bill), betragen. — s. (Poet.) der Berg.

mountain ['mauntin], s. der Berg.

mountaineer [maunti'niə], s. der Bergsteiger.

mountainous ['mauntinəs], adj. gebirgig.

mourn [mɔːn], v.a., v.n. (be)trauern.

mourner ['mɔːnə], s. der Leidtragende.

mournful ['mɔːnful], adj. traurig.

mourning ['mɔːniŋ], s. die Trauer.

mouse [maus], s. (Zool.) die Maus.

moustache [mə'stɑːʃ], s. der Schnurrbart.

mouth [mauθ], s. (Anat.) der Mund; (Geog.) die Mündung.

movable ['muːvəbl], adj. beweglich, verschiebbar.

move [muːv], v.a. bewegen; (emotionally) rühren; den Antrag stellen (a motion). — v.n. umziehen; übersiedeln (change residence).

movement ['muːvmənt], s. die Bewegung (motion); (Mus.) der Satz; das Gehwerk (mechanism).

movies ['muːviz], s. pl. (coll.) das Kino, der Film.

mow [mou], v.a. irr. mähen.

much [mʌtʃ], adj. viel. — adv. sehr, bei weitem; as — as, ganze ...; as — again, noch einmal so viel.

mud [mʌd], s. der Schmutz, Schlamm.

muddle [mʌdl], v.a. verwirren. — s. die Verwirrung.

muff (1) [mʌf], s. der Muff.

muff (2) [mʌf], v.a. verderben (mar).

muffin ['mʌfin], s. der dünne Kuchen, der Butterkuchen.

muffle ['mʌfl], v.a. umwickeln; dämpfen (a sound).

muffler ['mʌflə], s. das Halstuch; (Motor.) der Schalldämpfer.

mug [mʌg], s. der Krug; (coll.) der Tölpel.

muggy ['mʌgi], adj. schwül; feucht (humid).

mulatto [mju'lætou], s. der Mulatte.

mulberry ['mʌlbəri], s. (Bot.) die Maulbeere.

mule [mjuːl], s. (Zool.) das Maultier, der Maulesel.

muleteer [mjuːli'tiə], s. der Mauleseltreiber.

mulish ['mjuːliʃ], adj. störrisch.

mull (1) [mʌl], v.a. würzen (add spices to); mulled wine, der Glühwein.

mull (2) [mʌl], v.a., v.n. — over, überlegen, überdenken.

multifarious [mʌlti'fɛəriəs], adj. mannigfaltig.

multiple ['mʌltipl], s. das Vielfache. — adj. vielfach.

multiply ['mʌltiplai], v.a., v.n. multiplizieren, (sich) vervielfachen.

multitude ['mʌltitjuːd], s. die Menge.

multitudinous [mʌlti'tjuːdinəs], adj. zahlreich, massenhaft.

mumble [mʌmbl], v.a., v.n. murmeln.

mummery ['mʌməri], s. der Mummenschanz.

mummy (1) ['mʌmi], s. die Mumie.

mummy (2) ['mʌmi], s. (coll.) die Mutti.

mumps [mʌmps], s. (Med.) der Ziegenpeter.

munch [mʌntʃ], v.a., v.n. kauen.

mundane ['mʌndein], adj. weltlich.

municipal [mju'nisipəl], adj. städtisch.

municipality [mjunisi'pæliti], s. die Stadtgemeinde.

munificence [mju'nifisəns], s. die Freigebigkeit.

munificent [mju'nifisənt], adj. freigebig.

mural ['mjuərəl], s. die Wandmalerei; das Wandgemälde. — adj. Wand-.

murder ['mɔːdə], s. der Mord. — v.a. ermorden, morden.

murderer ['mɔːdərə], s. der Mörder.

murderous ['mɔːdərəs], adj. mörderisch.

murky ['mɔːki], adj. trübe, unklar.

murmur ['mɔːmə], s. das Gemurmel.

muscle [mʌsl], s. (Anat.) der Muskel.

muscular ['mʌskjulə], adj. (Anat.) muskulös, Muskel-.

muse (1) [mju:z], *v.n.* nachdenken, sinnen.

muse (2) [mju:z], *s.* (*Myth.*) die Muse.

museum [mju:'ziəm], *s.* das Museum.

mushroom ['mʌʃrum], *s.* (*Bot.*) der (eßbare) Pilz.

music ['mju:zik], *s.* die Musik; — *stand,* das Notenpult.

musician [mju:'ziʃən], *s.* der Musiker.

musk [mʌsk], *s.* der Moschus, Bisam.

musket ['mʌskit], *s.* die Muskete, Flinte.

muslin ['mʌzlin], *s.* der Musselin.

mussel ['mʌsl], *s.* (*Zool.*) die Muschel.

must [mʌst], *v. aux. irr.* müssen; (*with neg.*) dürfen.

mustard ['mʌstəd], *s.* der Senf.

muster ['mʌstə], *v.a.* mustern. — *v.n.* sich sammeln. — *s.* die Musterung; *pass —,* die Prüfung bestehen.

musty ['mʌsti], *adj.* dumpf, dumpfig, muffig.

mutable ['mju:təbl], *adj.* veränderlich.

mutation [mju:'teiʃən], *s.* die Veränderung; (*Maths., Genetics*) die Mutation.

mute [mju:t], *adj.* stumm. — *v.a.* (*Mus.*) dämpfen. — *s.* (*Mus.*) der Dämpfer.

mutilate ['mju:tileit], *v.a.* verstümmeln.

mutinous ['mju:tinəs], *adj.* aufrührerisch.

mutiny ['mju:tini], *s.* die Meuterei.

mutter ['mʌtə], *v.a., v.n.* murmeln.

mutton [mʌtn], *s.* das Hammelfleisch; — *chop,* das Hammelkotelett.

mutual ['mju:tjuəl], *adj.* gegenseitig.

muzzle [mʌzl], *s.* der Maulkorb (*of dog*); die Mündung (*of rifle*).

my [mai], *poss. adj.* mein.

myrrh [mə:], *s.* die Myrrhe.

myrtle ['mə:tl], *s.* (*Bot.*) die Myrte.

myself [mai'self], *pron.* ich selbst; (*refl.*) mir, mich.

mysterious [mis'tiəriəs], *adj.* geheimnisvoll.

mystery ['mistəri], *s.* das Geheimnis.

mystic ['mistik], *s.* der Mystiker.

mystic(al) ['mistik(əl)], *adj.* mystisch, geheimnisvoll, dunkel.

mystification [mistifi'keiʃən], *s.* die Täuschung, Irreführung.

mystify ['mistifai], *v.a.* täuschen, verblüffen.

myth [miθ], *s.* der Mythos, die Mythe, Sage.

N

N [en]. das N.

nag (1) [næg], *v.a.* nörgeln.

nag (2) [næg], *s.* der Gaul.

nail [neil], *s.* der Nagel. — *v.a.* annageln.

naïve ['naii:v], *adj.* naiv.

naïveté, naïvety [nai'i:vti], *s.* die Naivität, Einfalt.

naked ['neikid], *adj.* nackt.

name [neim], *s.* der Name. — *v.a.* nennen, heißen.

nameless ['neimlis], *adj.* namenlos.

namely ['neimli], *adv.* nämlich.

namesake ['neimseik], *s.* der Namensvetter.

nap [næp], *s.* das Schläfchen. — *v.n.* schlummern, einnicken.

nape [neip], *s.* (*Anat.*) das Genick.

napkin ['næpkin], *s.* die Serviette; Windel (*baby's*).

narrate [nə'reit], *v.a.* erzählen.

narrative ['nærətiv], *s.* die Erzählung, Geschichte.

narrator [nə'reitə], *s.* der Erzähler; (*Rad.*) der Sprecher.

narrow ['nærou], *adj.* eng, schmal; — *gauge,* die Schmalspur; — *minded,* engstirnig.

nasty ['nɑ:sti], *adj.* widerlich, unangenehm.

natal [neitl], *adj.* Geburts-.

nation ['neiʃən], *s.* die Nation, das Volk.

nationality [næʃə'næliti], *s.* die Staatsangehörigkeit, Nationalität.

native ['neitiv], *adj.* einheimisch, eingeboren. — *s.* der Eingeborene.

natural ['nætʃərəl], *adj.* natürlich.

naturalist ['nætʃərəlist], *s.* der Naturforscher.

naturalization [nætʃərəlai'zeiʃən], *s.* die Naturalisierung, Einbürgerung.

naturalize ['nætʃərəlaiz], *v.a., v.n.* naturalisieren, einbürgern.

nature ['neitʃə], *s.* die Natur, das Wesen.

naught [nɔ:t], *s.* die Null.

naughty ['nɔ:ti], *adj.* unartig.

nausea ['nɔ:siə], *s.* (*Med.*) der Brechreiz, das Erbrechen.

nautical ['nɔ:tikəl], *adj.* nautisch, Schiffs-.

naval ['neivəl], *adj.* Marine-.

nave [neiv], *s.* (*Archit.*) das Schiff.

navigable ['nævigəbl], *adj.* schiffbar.

navigate ['nævigeit], *v.a., v.n.* steuern.

navigation [nævi'geiʃən], *s.* die Schiffahrt (*shipping*); das Steuern, die Navigation.

navy ['neivi], *s.* die Flotte, Marine.

Neopolitan [niə'pɔlitən], *adj.* neapolitanisch. — *s.* der Neapolitaner.

near [niə], *adj., adv.* nahe, in der Nähe. — *prep.* nahe (an *or* bei).

nearly ['niəli], *adv.* beinahe, fast.

nearness ['niənis], *s.* die Nähe.

neat [ni:t], *adj.* nett, sauber (*tidy*); rein, unvermischt, pur (*unmixed*).

neatness ['ni:tnis], *s.* die Sauberkeit.

necessary ['nesəsəri], *adj.* notwendig.

necessity [ni'sesiti], *s.* die Not, Notwendigkeit; (*pl.*) das zum Leben Nötige.

neck [nek], *s.* (*Anat.*) der Hals; *stick o.'s — out,* es riskieren. — *v.n.* (*Am. sl.*) knutschen.

necklace ['neklis], *s.* das Halsband, die Halskette.

necktie ['nektai], *s.* der Schlips, die Krawatte.

need [ni:d], *s.* die Not, der Bedarf. — *v.a.* brauchen, nötig haben.

needful ['ni:dful], *adj.* notwendig.

needle [ni:dl], *s.* die Nadel. — *v.a.* (*coll.*) sticheln, ärgern (*annoy*).

needy ['ni:di], *adj.* in Not befindlich, arm, bedürftig.

nefarious [ni'fɛəriəs], *adj.* nichtswürdig, schändlich.

negative ['negativ], *adj.* negativ, verneinend. — *s.* (*Phot.*) das Negativ; die Verneinung (*denial*); *in the* —, verneinend.

neglect [ni'glekt], *v.a.* vernachlässigen, außer acht lassen. — *s.* die Vernachlässigung.

neglectful [ni'glektful], *adj.* nachlässig.

negligence ['neglidʒəns], *s.* die Nachlässigkeit.

negotiate [ni'gouʃieit], *v.a., v.n.* verhandeln, unterhandeln.

negotiation [nigouʃi'eiʃən], *s.* die Unterhandlung.

Negro ['ni:grou], *s.* der Neger.

neigh [nei], *v.n.* wiehern.

neighbour ['neibə], *s.* der Nachbar.

neighbourhood ['neibəhud], *s.* die Nachbarschaft, Umgebung.

neighbouring ['neibəriŋ], *adj.* Nachbar-, benachbart.

neighbourliness ['neibəlinis], *s.* das gute nachbarliche Verhältnis, die Geselligkeit.

neither ['naiðə *or* 'ni:ðə], *adj., pron.* keiner (von beiden). — *conj.* auch nicht; — *nor*, weder . . . noch.

Nepalese [nepə'li:z], *adj.* nepalesisch. — *s.* der Nepalese.

nephew ['nefju *or* 'nevju], *s.* der Neffe.

nerve [nə:v], *s.* der Nerv; der Mut (*courage*); die Frechheit (*impudence*); (*pl.*) die Angst, Nervosität.

nervous ['nə:vəs], *adj.* nervös; — *of*, furchtsam vor (*Dat.*), ängstlich wegen (*Genit.*).

nest [nest], *s.* das Nest; (*fig.*) — *egg*, die Ersparnisse, *f.pl.* — *v.n.* nisten.

nestle [nesl], *v.n.* sich anschmiegen.

net (1) [net], *s.* das Netz. — *v.a.* (Fische) fangen, im Netz bekommen.

net (2) [net], *adj.* netto; ohne Verpackung; — *weight*, das Nettogewicht.

nettle [netl], *s.* (*Bot.*) die Nessel. — *v.a.* sticheln, ärgern.

neurosis [njuə'rousis], *s.* (*Med.*) die Neurose.

neutrality [nju:'træliti], *s.* die Neutralität.

never ['nevə], *adv.* nie, niemals; — *mind*, mach Dir (machen Sie sich) nichts draus!

nevertheless [nevəðə'les], *conj.* trotzdem, nichtsdestoweniger.

new [nju:], *adj.* neu; *New Year's Day*, der Neujahrstag; *New Zealander*, der Neuseeländer. — *s.* (*pl.*) die Nachrichten, *f. pl.*

newspaper ['nju:speipə], *s.* die Zeitung.

next [nekst], *adj.* nächst. — *adv.* danach.

nib [nib], *s.* die Spitze (*of pen*).

nibble [nibl], *v.a., v.n.* knabbern, nagen (*at, an, Dat.*).

nice [nais], *adj.* fein (*scrupulous*); nett, angenehm (*pleasant*).

nicety ['naisəti], *s.* die Feinheit (*of distinction etc.*).

nickel [nikl], *s.* das Nickel; (*Am.*) das Fünfcentstück.

nickname ['nikneim], *s.* der Spitzname.

niece [ni:s], *s.* die Nichte.

Nigerian [nai'dʒiəriən], *adj.* nigerisch. — *s.* der Nigerier.

niggardly ['nigədli], *adj.* geizig.

nigh [nai], *adj., adv.* (*Poet.*) nahe.

night [nait], *s.* die Nacht; *last* —, gestern abend; *the* — *before last*, vorgestern abend; *at* —, nachts.

nightingale ['naitiŋgeil], *s.* (*Orn.*) die Nachtigall.

nightmare ['naitmɛə], *s.* der Alpdruck.

nimble [nimbl], *adj.* flink; geschickt (*deft*).

nine [nain], *num. adj.* neun.

nineteen [nain'ti:n], *num. adj.* neunzehn.

ninety ['nainti], *num. adj.* neunzig.

ninth [nainθ], *num. adj.* neunte.

nip [nip], *v.a.* zwicken.

nipple [nipl], *s.* (*Anat.*) die Brustwarze.

nitrogen ['naitrədʒən], *s.* (*Chem.*) der Stickstoff.

no [nou], *part.* nein. — *adj.* kein. — *adv.* nicht; — *one*, niemand.

nobility [no'biliti], *s.* der Adel.

noble [noubl], *adj.* edel; großmütig (*magnanimous*); adlig (*well born*).

nobody ['noubədi], *pron.* niemand.

nod [nod], *v.n.* nicken.

noise [noiz], *s.* der Lärm, das Geräusch.

noiseless ['noizlis], *adj.* geräuschlos.

noisy ['noizi], *adj.* laut, lärmend.

nominal ['nominəl], *adj.* nominell.

nominate ['nomineit], *v.a.* nennen (*name*); ernennen (*appoint*).

nomination [nomi'neiʃən], *s.* die Nennung, Ernennung.

none [nʌn], *pron.* keiner, niemand.

nonsense ['nonsəns], *s.* der Unsinn.

nook [nuk], *s.* die Ecke, der Winkel.

noon [nu:n], *s.* der Mittag.

noose [nu:s], *s.* die Schlinge.

nor [no:], *conj.* auch nicht; *neither* . . . —, weder . . . noch.

normal ['no:məl], *adj.* normal.

normalize ['no:məlaiz], *v.a.* normalisieren.

Norman ['no:mən], *adj.* normannisch. — *s.* der Normanne.

north [no:θ], *s.* der Norden. — *adj.* nördlich.

northerly, northern ['no:ðəli, 'no:ðən], *adj.* nördlich, von Norden.

Norwegian [no:'wi:dʒən], *adj.* norwegisch. — *s.* der Norweger.

nose [nouz], *s.* (*Anat.*) die Nase; — *dive*, der Sturzflug.

nosey ['nouzi], *adj. (coll.)* neugierig.
nostalgia [nɔs'tældʒə], *s.* das Heimweh, die Sehnsucht.
nostril ['nɔstril], *s. (Anat.)* das Nasenloch.
not [nɔt], *adv.* nicht; — *at all*, keineswegs.
notable ['noutəbl], *adj.* berühmt, wohlbekannt; bemerkenswert.
notary ['noutəri], *s.* der Notar.
notch [nɔtʃ], *s.* die Kerbe. — *v.a.* kerben, einkerben.
note [nout], *s.* die Notiz, der Zettel; (*Mus.*) die Note; die Bedeutung; *take* —*s*, Notizen machen; *take* — *of*, zur Kenntnis nehmen. — *v.a.* notieren, aufzeichnen.
notepaper ['noutpeipə], *s.* das Briefpapier.
noteworthy ['noutwə:ði], *adj.* beachtenswert.
nothing ['nʌθiŋ], *pron. s.* nichts; *for* —, umsonst; *good for* —, der Taugenichts.
notice ['noutis], *s.* die Kenntnis (*attention*); die Anzeige (*in press etc.*); Notiz; Bekanntmachung; *give* —, kündigen. — *v.a.* bemerken.
noticeable ['noutisəbl], *adj.* bemerkbar.
notification [noutifi'keiʃən], *s.* die Benachrichtigung, Bekanntmachung.
notify ['noutifai], *v.a.* benachrichtigen, informieren.
notion ['nouʃən], *s.* der Begriff (*concept*); die Idee (*idea*); die Meinung (*opinion*).
notoriety [noutə'raiiti], *s.* der üble Ruf.
notorious [nou'tɔ:riəs], *adj.* berüchtigt.
notwithstanding [nɔtwið'stændiŋ], *prep.* ungeachtet (*Genit.*). — *adv.* trotzdem, dennoch. — *conj.* — *that*, obgleich.
nought [nɔ:t], *s.* die Null (*figure 0*); nichts (*nothing*).
noun [naun], *s. (Gram.)* das Hauptwort, Substantiv.
nourish ['nʌriʃ], *v.a.* nähren; ernähren.
nourishment ['nʌriʃmənt], *s.* die Nahrung.
Nova Scotian ['nouvə'skouʃən], *adj.* neuschottisch. [Neuschottland]
novel [nɔvl], *s. (Lit.)* der Roman. — *adj.* neu; neuartig (*modern*).
novelty ['nɔvlti], *s.* die Neuheit.
November [nou'vembə], der November.
novice ['nɔvis], *s.* der Neuling (*greenhorn*); (*Eccl.*) der, die Novize.
novitiate [no'viʃiit], *s.* die Lehrzeit; (*Eccl.*) das Noviziat.
now [nau], *adv.* nun, jetzt; — *and then*, dann und wann, hin und wieder. — *conj.* — (*that*), da nun.
nowadays ['nauədeiz], *adv.* heutzutage.
nowhere ['nouhwεə], *adv.* nirgends.
noxious ['nɔkʃəs], *adj. (Med., Bot.)* schädlich.
nozzle [nɔzl], *s.* die Düse; (*sl.*) die Schnauze.
nuclear ['nju:kliə], *adj. (Phys.)* nuklear, Kern-.
nucleus ['nju:kliəs], *s.* der Kern.

nude [nju:d], *adj.* nackt, bloß.
nudge [nʌdʒ], *v.a.* leicht anstoßen.
nudity ['nju:diti], *s.* die Nacktheit.
nugget ['nʌgit], *s.* der Klumpen.
nuisance ['nju:səns], *s.* die Plage, Lästigkeit; das Ärgernis (*annoyance*).
null [nʌl], *adj.* null und nichtig; ungültig.
nullify ['nʌlifai], *v.a.* annullieren, ungültig machen.
nullity ['nʌliti], *s.* die Ungültigkeit.
numb [nʌm], *adj.* erstarrt, gefühllos. — *v.a.* erstarren lassen.
number ['nʌmbə], *s.* die Zahl, Nummer (*telephone etc.*); die Anzahl (*quantity*); *cardinal* —, die Grundzahl; *ordinal* —, die Ordnungszahl. — *v.a.* nummerieren; zählen (*count*).
numbness ['nʌmnis], *s.* die Erstarrung.
numeral ['nju:mərəl], *s. (Gram.)* das Zahlwort.
numerical [nju:'merikəl], *adj. (Maths.)* Zahlen-, numerisch.
numerous ['nju:mərəs], *adj.* zahlreich.
numismatics [nju:miz'mætiks], *s.* die Münzkunde.
numskull ['nʌmskʌl], *s.* der Dummkopf.
nun [nʌn], *s. (Eccl.)* die Nonne.
nunnery ['nʌnəri], *s. (Eccl.)* das Nonnenkloster.
nuptials ['nʌpʃəlz], *s. pl. (Lit., Poet.)* die Hochzeit, das Hochzeitsfest.
nurse [nə:s], *s.* die Krankenschwester, Pflegerin; die Amme (*wet nurse*). — *v.a.* pflegen.
nursery ['nə:səri], *s.* das Kinderzimmer; (*Bot.*) die Pflanzschule, Baumschule (*for trees*); — *school*, der Kindergarten.
nurture ['nə:tʃə], *v.a.* nähren, aufziehen.
nut [nʌt], *s. (Bot.)* die Nuß; (*Tech.*) die Schraubenmutter; (*Am. coll.*) *nuts*, verrückt.
nutcracker ['nʌtkrækə], *s. (usually pl.)* der Nußknacker.
nutmeg ['nʌtmeg], *s. (Cul.)* die Muskatnuß.
nutriment ['nju:trimənt], *s.* die Nahrung; (*animals*) das Futter.
nutrition [nju:'triʃən], *s.* die Ernährung.
nutritious [nju:'triʃəs], *adj.* nahrhaft.
nutshell ['nʌtʃel], *s.* die Nußschale; (*fig.*) *put in a* —, kurz ausdrücken.
nymph [nimf], *s. (Myth.)* die Nymphe.

O

O [ou]. das O. — *int.* oh!
oaf [ouf], *s.* der Tölpel.
oak [ouk], *s. (Bot.)* die Eiche.
oaken ['oukən], *adj.* eichen, aus Eichenholz.

oar [ɔ:], *s.* das Ruder; *put o.'s — in*, sich einmengen.

oasis [ou'eisis], *s.* die Oase.

oath [ouθ], *s.* der Eid; der Fluch (*curse*); *commissioner for —s*, der öffentliche Notar; *take an —*, einen Eid schwören *or* leisten.

oats [outs], *s. pl.* (*Bot.*) der Hafer; *sow o.'s wild —s*, sich austoben, sich die Hörner ablaufen.

obdurate ['ɔbdjurit], *adj.* halsstarrig.

obedience [o'bi:djəns], *s.* der Gehorsam.

obedient [o'bi:djənt], *adj.* gehorsam.

obeisance [o'beisəns], *s.* die Verbeugung, Ehrfurchtsbezeigung.

obese [o'bi:s], *adj.* fettleibig, beleibt.

obey [o'bei], *v.a., v.n.* gehorchen (*Dat.*).

obituary [o'bitjuəri], *s.* der Nachruf, der Nekrolog.

object ['ɔbdʒikt], *s.* der Gegenstand (*thing*); (*Gram.*) das Objekt; der Zweck (*objective, purpose*). — [əb-'dʒekt], *v.n. — to*, einwenden (*gainsay*); vorhalten (*remonstrate*).

objection [əb'dʒekʃən], *s.* der Einwand.

objectionable [əb'dʒekʃənəbl], *adj.* anstößig.

objective [əb'dʒektiv], *adj.* objektiv, unparteiisch. — *s.* das Ziel (*aim*).

obligation [ɔbli'geiʃən], *s.* die Verpflichtung.

obligatory [o'bligətəri, 'ɔblig-], *adj.* verbindlich, obligatorisch.

oblige [o'blaidʒ], *v.a.* verpflichten; *much obliged*, vielen Dank; *can you — me?* können Sie mir aushelfen?

obliging [o'blaidʒiŋ], *adj.* gefällig, zuvorkommend.

oblique [o'bli:k], *adj.* schräg, schief; (*fig.*) indirekt.

obliterate [o'blitəreit], *v.a.* auslöschen (*extinguish*); vertilgen (*destroy*).

oblivion [o'bliviən], *s.* die Vergessenheit.

oblivious [o'bliviəs], *adj.* vergeßlich.

oblong ['ɔblɔŋ], *adj.* länglich. — *s.* das Rechteck.

obloquy ['ɔblɔkwi], *s.* die Schmähung, Schande.

obnoxious [ɔb'nɔkʃəs], *adj.* verhaßt, scheußlich.

obscene [ɔb'si:n], *adj.* anstößig, obszön.

obscenity [ɔb'sen-, ɔb'si:niti], *s.* die Obszönität.

obscure [əb'skjuə], *adj.* dunkel (*dark*); unbekannt (*unknown*).

obscurity [əb'skjuəriti], *s.* die Dunkelheit (*darkness*); die Unbekanntheit.

obsequies ['ɔbsikwiz], *s. pl.* das Leichenbegängnis.

obsequious [əb'si:kwiəs], *adj.* unterwürfig.

observance [əb'zə:vəns], *s.* die Befolgung, Beobachtung, das Einhalten (*Law etc.*).

observant [əb'zə:vənt], *adj.* aufmerksam; achtsam.

observation [ɔbzə'veiʃən], *s.* die Beobachtung (*watching*); die Bemerkung (*remark*).

observatory [əb'zə:vətri], *s.* die Sternwarte.

observe [əb'zə:v], *v.a.* beobachten (*watch*); bemerken (*notice, remark on*).

obsession [əb'seʃən], *s.* die Besessenheit, fixe Idee.

obsolete ['ɔbsəli:t], *adj.* veraltet.

obstacle ['ɔbstəkl], *s.* das Hindernis.

obstinacy ['ɔbstinəsi], *s.* die Hartnäckigkeit.

obstinate ['ɔbstinit], *adj.* hartnäckig.

obstruct [əb'strʌkt], *v.a.* hemmen, hindern.

obstruction [əb'strʌkʃən], *s.* das Hindernis, die Hemmung, Verstopfung.

obtain [əb'tein], *v.a.* erhalten, erlangen; bekommen (*get*).

obtrude [əb'tru:d], *v.n.* sich aufdrängen. — *v.a.* aufdrängen.

obtrusive [əb'tru:siv], *adj.* aufdringlich.

obtuse [əb'tju:s], *adj.* stumpf; dumm (*stupid*).

obviate ['ɔbvieit], *v.a.* vorbeugen (*Dat.*).

obvious ['ɔbviəs], *adj.* klar, offenbar, selbstverständlich.

occasion [o'keiʒən], *s.* die Gelegenheit (*chance*); der Anlaß; die Veranlassung (*cause*). — *v.a.* veranlassen; verursachen (*cause*).

occasional [o'keiʒənəl], *adj.* gelegentlich.

occident ['ɔksidənt], *s.* das Abendland, der Westen.

occult [ɔ'kʌlt], *adj.* geheim, Okkult-.

occupancy ['ɔkjupənsi], *s.* der Besitz, das Innehaben (*holding*).

occupant ['ɔkjupənt], *s.* der Inhaber; der Bewohner (*of house*), Insasse.

occupation [ɔkju'peiʃən], *s.* die Besetzung; (*Mil.*) *army of —*, die Besatzung; der Beruf, die Beschäftigung (*job*); — *with*, das Befassen mit (*Dat.*).

occupy ['ɔkjupai], *v.a.* (*Mil.*) besetzen, in Besitz nehmen; beschäftigen (*engage*); bekleiden (*office*).

occur [ə'kə:], *v.n.* geschehen, sich ereignen; — *to s.o.*, jemandem einfallen.

occurrence [ə'kʌrəns], *s.* das Geschehen, Ereignis, der Vorfall.

ocean ['ouʃən], *s.* der Ozean, die See, das Meer. — *adj.* Meeres-.

octagon ['ɔktəgən], *s.* das Achteck.

octagonal [ɔk'tægənəl], *adj.* achteckig.

October [ɔk'toubə]. der Oktober.

octogenarian [ɔktodʒi'nɛəriən], *s.* der Achtzigjährige.

ocular ['ɔkjulə], *adj.* Augen-.

oculist ['ɔkjulist], *s.* (*Med.*) der Augenarzt.

odd [ɔd], *adj.* ungerade; seltsam (*queer*); einzeln (*solitary*). — *s.* (*pl.*) die Wahrscheinlichkeit.

oddity ['ɔditi], *s.* die Seltenheit, Sonderbarkeit.

oddment ['ɔdmənt], *s.* (*pl.*) die Reste, *m. pl.*

ode [oud], *s.* (*Poet.*) die Ode.

odious ['oudiəs], *adj.* verhaßt, widerwärtig.

odium ['oudiəm], *s.* der Haß.

odorous ['oudərəs], *adj.* duftend, duftig.

odour ['oudə], *s.* der Geruch, Duft.

of [ɔv], *prep.* von (*Dat.*); aus (*out of*) (*Dat.*); — *course,* natürlich.

off [ɔf, ɔːf], *adv.* fort, weg; entfernt; *make* —, sich davonmachen; *far* —, weit weg; — *and on,* ab und zu; *well* —, wohlhabend. — *prep.* von (*from*); fort von; entfernt von (*distant from*).

offal [ɔfl], *s.* der Abfall.

offence [o'fens], *s.* (*Law*) das Vergehen; die Beleidigung (*insult*).

offend [o'fend], *v.a.* beleidigen (*insult*). — *v.n.* (*Law*) sich vergehen (gegen, *Acc.*).

offensive [o'fensiv], *adj.* beleidigend (*insulting*); anstößig (*indecent*). — *s.* die Offensive, der Angriff (*against,* auf, *Acc.*).

offer ['ɔfə], *v.a.* bieten (*auction*); anbieten (*hold out*). — *s.* das Anerbieten; (*Comm.*) das Angebot, der Antrag.

offering ['ɔfəriŋ], *s.* das Opfer.

office ['ɔfis], *s.* das Amt; die Stellung (*position*); die Funktion (*duties*); das Büro; (*Eccl.*) der Gottesdienst; *high* —, das hohe Amt; — *bearer,* der Amtswalter.

officer ['ɔfisə], *s.* (*Mil.*) der Offizier; der Beamte (*functionary*); *honorary* —, der ehrenamtliche Beamte, der Beamte im Ehrenamt.

official [o'fiʃəl], *adj.* offiziell, amtlich. — *s.* der Beamte.

officiate [o'fiʃieit], *v.n.* amtieren; fungieren.

officious [o'fiʃəs], *adj.* zudringlich, (übertrieben) dienstfertig.

offing ['ɔfiŋ], *s.* (*Naut.*) die hohe See; *in the* —, bevorstehend.

offset [ɔf'set], *v.a.* (*Comm.*) ausgleichen; (*Typ.*) offset drucken, im Offset drucken; (*fig.*) unschädlich machen, wettmachen. — ['ɔfset], *s.* (*Comm.*) die Gegenrechnung, der Ausgleich; (*Typ.*) der Offsetdruck.

offshoot ['ɔfʃuːt], *s.* der Sprößling.

offspring ['ɔfspriŋ], *s.* die Nachkommenschaft.

often, (*Poet.*) **oft** [ɔfn,ɔft], *adv.* oft, häufig.

ogle [ougl], *v.a., v.n.* äugeln, beäugeln, glotzen, anglotzen.

ogre ['ougə], *s.* der Menschenfresser.

oil [ɔil], *s.* das Öl. — *v.a.* einölen, einschmieren.

oilcloth ['ɔilklɔθ], *s.* das Wachstuch.

ointment ['ɔintmənt], *s.* die Salbe.

old [ould], *adj.* alt; —*fashioned,* altmodisch.

olive ['ɔliv], *s.* (*Bot.*) die Olive; *the Mount of Olives,* der Ölberg.

Olympic [o'limpik], *adj.* olympisch; *the* — *Games,* die Olympischen Spiele.

omelette ['ɔməlit], *s.* (*Cul.*) das Omelett, der Eierkuchen.

omen ['oumən], *s.* das (böse) Vorzeichen, das Omen.

ominous ['ɔminəs], *adj.* von schlimmer Vorbedeutung, ominös.

omission [o'miʃən], *s.* die Unterlassung; (*Typ.*) die Auslassung.

omit [o'mit], *v.a.* unterlassen (*leave undone*); auslassen (*leave out*).

omnibus ['ɔmnibəs], *s.* der Omnibus, der Autobus.

omnipotent [ɔm'nipətənt], *adj.* allmächtig.

omniscient [ɔm'nisiənt], *adj.* allwissend.

on [ɔn], *prep.* an; auf; über; vor; bei; zu; nach; um; *call* — (*s.o.*), vorsprechen (bei, *Dat.*); — *fire,* in Flammen; — *condition,* unter der Bedingung (*Comm.*); — *account,* a Konto; — *high,* hoch oben; — *my honour,* auf mein Ehrenwort; — *purpose,* absichtlich; — *sale,* zum Verkauf. — *adv.* weiter, fort (*forward*); gültig, zutreffend (*correct, valid*); *get* —, vorwärtskommen; *get* — *with s.th.,* weitermachen; *get* — *with s.o.,* auskommen (mit, *Dat.*).

once [wʌns], *adv.* einmal; einst (*long ago*); — *more,* nochmals, noch einmal; — *and for all,* ein für alle Mal; *at* —, sogleich; — *in a while,* ab und zu. — *conj.* sobald.

one [wʌn], *num. adj.* ein, eine, ein; — *way street,* die Einbahnstraße. — *pron.* man (*impersonal*). — *s. little* —, der Kleine; — *by* —, eins nach dem anderen, einzeln.

onerous ['ɔnərəs], *adj.* beschwerlich.

onion ['ʌnjən], *s.* (*Bot.*) die Zwiebel.

onlooker ['ɔnlukə], *s.* der Zuschauer.

only ['ounli], *adj.* einzig, allein. — *adv.* nur, bloß. — *conj.* jedoch.

onset ['ɔnset], *s.* der Angriff (*attack*); der Anfang (*beginning*).

onslaught ['ɔnslɔːt], *s.* der Angriff, Überfall.

onward ['ɔnwəd], *adj.* fortschreitend. — *adv.* (*also* **onwards**) vorwärts.

ooze [uːz], *s.* der Schlamm. — *v.n.* träufeln, sickern.

opacity [o'pæsiti], *s.* (*Phys.*) die Dunkelheit, Undurchsichtigkeit.

opal [oupl], *s.* der Opal.

opaque [o'peik], *adj.* (*Phys.*) dunkel, undurchsichtig.

open [oupn], *adj.* offen; offenherzig (*frank*); — *to suggestions,* einem Vorschlag zugänglich. — *v.a.* öffnen; eröffnen (*start*); — *an account,* ein Konto eröffnen. — *v.n.* sich öffnen, sich auftun.

opening ['oupniŋ], *s.* das Öffnen; die freie Stelle; die Gelegenheit (*opportunity*). — *adj.* einleitend; — *gambit,* (*Chess*) der Eröffnungszug.

openness ['oupənnis], *s.* die Offenheit, Ehrlichkeit (*frankness*).

opera ['ɔpərə], *s.* (*Mus.*) die Oper; *comic* —, die komische Oper; — *hat,* der Zylinderhut, Klapphut.

operatic [ɔpə'rætik], *adj.* (*Mus.*) Opern-.

operate ['ɔpəreit], *v.a.*, *v.n.* (*Engin.*) bedienen; (*Med.*) operieren (*on*, *Acc.*).
operation [ɔpə'reiʃən], *s.* (*Med.*, *Mil.*) die Operation; die Bedienung (*of engine etc.*).
operative ['ɔpərətiv], *adj.* wirksam (*effective*). — *s.* der Arbeiter.
opiate ['oupiit], *s.* das Schlafmittel. — *adj.* einschläfernd.
opine [o'pain], *v.n.* meinen.
opinion [o'pinjən], *s.* die Meinung; *in my —*, meiner Meinung nach.
opinionated [o'pinjəneitid], *adj.* von sich eingenommen, selbstgefällig.
opium ['oupjəm], *s.* das Opium.
opponent [ə'pounənt], *s.* der Gegner.
opportune ['ɔpətju:n], *adj.* gelegen, günstig.
opportunity [ɔpə'tju:niti], *s.* die Gelegenheit, Chance; die Möglichkeit.
oppose [ə'pouz], *v.a.* bekämpfen; widerstehen, entgegentreten (*Dat.*).
opposite [ɔpəzit], *adj.* entgegengesetzt; gegenüberliegend; gegensätzlich (*contrary*). — *prep.* gegenüber (*Dat.*). — *s.* das Gegenteil.
opposition [ɔpə'ziʃən], *s.* (*Parl.*) die Opposition; der Widerstand.
oppress [ə'pres], *v.a.* unterdrücken.
oppression [ə'preʃən], *s.* die Unterdrückung.
oppressive [ə'presiv], *adj.* drückend, tyrannisch.
opprobrious [ə'proubriəs], *adj.* schändlich, schimpflich.
opprobrium [ə'proubriəm], *s.* die Schande.
optician [ɔp'tiʃən], *s.* der Optiker.
optics ['ɔptiks], *s.* die Optik.
optimism ['ɔptimizm], *s.* der Optimismus.
option ['ɔpʃən], *s.* die Wahl.
optional ['ɔpʃənl], *adj.* Wahl-, frei, beliebig.
opulence ['ɔpjuləns], *s.* der Reichtum (*an*, *Dat.*), die Üppigkeit.
opulent ['ɔpjulənt], *adj.* reich, üppig.
or [ɔ:], *conj.* oder; noch (*after neg.*); *either . . . —*, entweder . . . oder.
oracle ['ɔrəkl], *s.* das Orakel.
oral ['ɔ:rəl], *adj.* mündlich. — *s.* die mündliche Prüfung.
orange ['ɔrindʒ],] *s.* (*Bot.*) die Orange, Apfelsine.
oration [ɔ'reiʃən], *s.* die feierliche Rede, Ansprache.
orator ['ɔrətə], *s.* der Redner.
oratorio [ɔrə'tɔ:riou], *s.* (*Mus.*) das Oratorium.
oratory ['ɔrətəri], *s.* (*Eccl.*) die Kapelle; (*Rhet.*) die Redekunst.
orb [ɔ:b], *s.* die Kugel; der Reichsapfel; (*Poet.*) der Himmelskörper.
orbit ['ɔ:bit], *s.* (*Astron.*) die Bahn (der Gestirne), Planetenbahn.
orchard ['ɔ:tʃəd], *s.* der Obstgarten.
orchestra ['ɔ:kistrə], *s.* (*Mus.*) das Orchester.
ordain [ɔ:'dein], *v.a.* ordinieren, anordnen; (*Eccl.*) zum Priester weihen.

ordeal ['ɔ:diəl], *s.* die Feuerprobe; Heimsuchung.
order ['ɔ:də], *s.* die Ordnung (*system*); die Verordnung (*command etc.*); (*Mil.*) der Befehl; (*Comm.*) die Bestellung; (*Biol.*) die Ordnung; der Orden (*Eccl.*; *also decoration*); *take (holy) —s*, ordiniert werden, Priester werden; *in — to*, um zu; *in — that*, so daß; *by —*, auf (den) Befehl. — *v.a.* befehlen, verordnen, anordnen; (*Comm.*) bestellen.
orderly ['ɔ:dəli], *adj.* ordentlich, ruhig. — *s.* (*Mil.*) die Ordonanz; (*Med.*) der Gehilfe, Krankenwärter.
ordinal ['ɔ:dinl], *adj.*, *s.* (*number*) die Ordnungszahl.
ordinance ['ɔ:dinəns], *s.* die Verordnung.
ordinary ['ɔ:dinəri], *adj.* gewöhnlich.
ordnance ['ɔ:dnəns], *s.* das schwere Geschütz; (*Mil.*, *Geog.*) — *survey*, die Landesvermessung.
ore [ɔ:], *s.* das Erz, Metall.
organ ['ɔ:gən], *s.* das Organ; (*Mus.*) die Orgel; *— grinder*, der Leierkastenmann.
organic [ɔ:'gænik], *adj.* organisch.
organisation [ɔ:gənai'zeiʃən], *s.* die Organisation.
organise ['ɔ:gənaiz], *v.a.* organisieren.
organism ['ɔ:gənizm], *s.* (*Biol.*) der Organismus.
organist ['ɔ:gənist], *s.* (*Mus.*) der Organist.
orgy ['ɔ:dʒi], *s.* die Orgie.
oriel ['ɔ:riəl], *s.* der Erker; *— window*, das Erkerfenster.
orient ['ɔ:riənt], *s.* der Orient, Osten.
oriental [ɔ:ri'entl], *adj.* östlich.
orifice ['ɔrifis], *s.* die Öffnung, Mündung.
origin ['ɔridʒin], *s.* der Ursprung, die Herkunft.
original [ə'ridʒinl], *adj.* Ursprungs-, ursprünglich; originell (*creative*). — *s.* das Original.
originality [əridʒi'næliti], *s.* die Originalität.
originate [ə'ridʒineit], *v.n.* entstehen, entspringen. — *v.a.* hervorbringen, entstehen lassen.
ornament ['ɔ:nəmənt], *s.* das Ornament; die Verzierung (*decoration*).
ornate [ɔ:'neit], *adj.* geziert, geschmückt.
orphan ['ɔ:fən], *s.* der, die Waise.
orphanage ['ɔ:fənidʒ], *s.* das Waisenhaus.
orthodoxy ['ɔ:θədɔksi], *s.* die Orthodoxie, die Rechtgläubigkeit.
orthography [ɔ:'θɔgrəfi], *s.* die Rechtschreibung.
orthopaedic [ɔ:θə'pi:dik], *adj.* orthopädisch.
oscillate ['ɔsileit], *v.n.* oszillieren, schwingen.
oscillatory ['ɔsileitəri], *adj.* schwingend, oszillierend.
osier ['ouʒiə], *s.* (*Bot.*) die Korbweide.
osprey ['ɔsprei], *s.* (*Orn.*) der Seeadler.

ossify ['ɔsifai], *v.a.* verknöchern lassen; versteinern lassen (*stone*). — *v.n.* verknöchern; versteinern (*stone*).

ostensible [ɔs'tensibl], *adj.* scheinbar, anscheinend, vorgeblich.

ostentation [ɔsten'teiʃən], *s.* die Großtuerei, der Prunk.

ostentatious [ɔsten'teiʃəs], *adj.* großtuerisch, prahlerisch, protzig.

ostler ['ɔslə], *s.* (*obs.*) der Stallknecht.

ostracize ['ɔstrəsaiz], *v.a.* verbannen, ausschließen.

ostrich ['ɔstritʃ], *s.* (*Orn.*) der Strauß.

other ['ʌðə], *adj.* ander. — *pron.*, *s.* *the* —, der, die, das andere.

otherwise ['ʌðəwaiz], *conj.* sonst. — *adv.* andernfalls.

otter ['ɔtə], *s.* (*Zool.*) die Otter.

ought [ɔːt], *v. aux. defect.* sollte, müßte.

ounce [auns], *s.* die Unze.

our ['auə], *poss. adj.* unser, uns(e)re, unser.

ours ['auəz], *poss. pron.* unsrig, unser, uns(e)re, unser.

ourselves [auə'selvz], *pers. pron.* wir, wir selbst, uns selbst; (*refl.*) uns.

ousel [uːzl], *s.* (*Orn.*) die Amsel.

out [aut], *adv.* aus; draußen (*outside*); außerhalb (*outside, externally*); heraus; hinaus (*outward, away from the speaker*).—*prep.—of*, aus, von (*Dat.*).

outer ['autə], *adj.* äußer.

outfit ['autfit], *s.* die Ausrüstung.

outing ['autiŋ], *s.* der Ausflug.

outhouse ['authaus], *s.* das Nebengebäude, der Anbau.

outlaw ['autlɔː], *s.* der Verbannte, der Vogelfreie.

outlay ['autlei], *s.* (*Comm.*) die Auslagen, die Spesen, *f. pl.*

outlet ['autlit], *s.* der Ausfluß, Abfluß; (*fig.*) das Ventil.

outline ['autlain], *s.* der Umriß, Entwurf. — [aut'lain], *v.a.* skizzieren, umreißen, kurz beschreiben.

outlive [aut'liv], *v.a.* überleben.

outlook ['autluk], *s.* die Aussicht, der Ausblick; die Weltanschauung (*philosophy*).

outlying ['autlaiiŋ], *adj.* außenliegend, außerhalb liegend, entlegen.

outnumber [aut'nʌmbə], *v.a.* an Zahl übertreffen.

outpatient ['autpeiʃənt], *s.* der ambulante Patient.

outrage ['autreidʒ], *s.* die Beleidigung (*insult*); die Gewalttat. — [aut'reidʒ], *v.a.* verletzen, beleidigen, schänden.

outrageous [aut'reidʒəs], *adj.* schändlich, schimpflich, unerhört; übertrieben (*exaggerated*).

outright ['autrait], *adj.* völlig. — [aut'rait], *adv.* gerade heraus, gänzlich.

outrun [aut'rʌn], *v.a. irr.* überholen, einholen.

outset ['autset], *s.* der Anfang.

outshine [aut'ʃain], *v.a. irr.* übertreffen.

outside [aut'said], *adv.* außen, draußen. — ['autsaid], *prep.* außerhalb (*Genit.*).

— *adj.* äußere, außenstehend. — *s.* das Äußere, die Außenseite.

outskirts ['autskəːts], *s. pl.* die Umgebung, Vorstadt.

outstanding [aut'stændiŋ], *adj.* hervorragend (*excellent*); noch unbeglichen (*unpaid*); unerledigt (*undone*).

outstay [aut'stei], *v.a.* länger bleiben, zu lange bleiben.

outvote [aut'vout], *v.a.* überstimmen.

outward ['autwəd], *adj.* äußere, äußerlich, außerhalb befindlich. — *adv.* (*also* **outwards**) auswärts, nach außen.

outweigh [aut'wei], *v.a.* schwerer wiegen als, überwiegen.

outwit [aut'wit], *v.a.* überlisten.

oval [ouvl], *adj.* oval. — *s.* das Oval.

ovary ['ouvəri], *s.* (*Anat.*) der Eierstock.

ovation [o'veiʃən], *s.* die Huldigung, Ovation.

oven [ʌvn], *s.* der Backofen; (*kleine*) Schmelzofen.

over ['ouvə], *prep.* über; oberhalb. — *adv.* über; herüber; drüben; — *there*, drüben; hinüber (*across*); vorüber (*past*).

overact [ouvər'ækt], *v.n.* übertreiben.

overawe [ouvər'ɔː], *v.a.* einschüchtern.

overbalance [ouvə'bæləns], *v.a.* überwiegen. — *v.n.* überkippen.

overbear [ouvə'bεə], *v.a. irr.* überwältigen.

overbearing [ouvə'bεəriŋ], *adj.* anmaßend.

overboard ['ouvəbɔːd], *adv.* über Bord.

overburden [ouvə'bəːdn], *v.a.* überlasten.

overcast [ouvə'kaːst], *adj.* bewölkt.

overcharge [ouvə'tʃaːdʒ], *v.a.* zu viel berechnen (*pers., Dat.*), übervorteilen; überladen (*overload*). — *s.* die Übervorteilung; (*Tech.*) der Überdruck.

overcoat ['ouvəkout], *s.* der Mantel; *light* —, der Überzieher.

overcome [ouvə'kʌm], *v.a., v.n. irr.* überwinden.

overdo [ouvə'duː], *v.a. irr.* übertreiben.

overdone [ouvə'dʌn], *adj.* übergar, zu lange gekocht.

overdrive [ouvə'draiv], *v.a. irr.* abhetzen, zu weit treiben. — ['ouvədraiv] *s.* (*Motor.*) der Schnellgang.

overdue [ouvə'djuː], *adj.* überfällig, verfallen.

overflow [ouvə'flou], *v.a., v.n.* überfließen; überfluten (*banks*). — ['ouvəflou], *s.* der Überfluß (*flood*); die Überschwemmung.

overgrow [ouvə'grou], *v.a. irr.* überwachsen, überwuchern. — *v.n.* zu groß werden.

overhang [ouvə'hæŋ], *v.a. irr.* überhängen.

overhaul [ouvə'hɔːl], *v.a.* überholen. — ['ouvəhɔːl], *s.* die Überholung.

overhead [ouvə'hed], *adv.* droben; oben (*above*). — ['ouvəhed], *s.* (*pl.*) (*Comm.*) laufende Unkosten, *pl.*

overhear [ouvə'hiə], *v.a.* irr. zufällig hören.

overjoyed [ouvə'dʒɔid], *adj.* entzückt.

overlap [ouvə'læp], *v.n.* überschneiden, zusammenfallen (*dates etc.*). — ['ouvə-læp], *s.* die Überschneidung, das Zusammenfallen.

overload [ouvə'loud], *v.a.* überlasten; (*Elec.*) überladen.

overlook [ouvə'luk], *v.a.* übersehen; verzeihen (*disregard*).

overmuch [ouvə'mʌtʃ], *adv.* allzusehr.

overpay [ouvə'pei], *v.a., v.n.* zu viel bezahlen.

overpopulated [ouvə'pɔpjuleitid], *adj.* übervölkert.

overpower [ouvə'pauə], *v.a.* überwältigen.

overrate [ouvə'reit], *v.a.* überschätzen.

overreach [ouvə'ri:tʃ], *v.a.* übervorteilen.

override [ouvə'raid], *v.a.* irr. überreiten; unterdrücken (*suppress*).

overrule [ouvə'ru:l], *v.a.* nicht gelten lassen, verwerfen.

overseer ['ouvəsiə], *s.* der Aufseher.

oversleep [ouvə'sli:p], *v.n.* irr. sich verschlafen.

overstep [ouvə'step], *v.a.* überschreiten.

overstrain [ouvə'strein], *v.a., v.n.* (sich) zu sehr anstrengen, überanstrengen.

overt ['ouvə:t], *adj.* offenkundig; öffentlich (*public*).

overtake [ouvə'teik], *v.a.* irr. einholen; (*Mot.*) überholen.

overtax [ouvə'tæks], *v.a.* zu hoch besteuern; (*fig.*) überanstrengen (*strain*).

overthrow [ouvə'θrou], *v.a.* irr. umstürzen; (*Pol.*) stürzen. — ['ouvəθrou], *s.* der Sturz.

overtime ['ouvətaim], *s.* Überstunden, *f. pl.*

overture ['ouvətjuə], *s.* die Ouvertüre.

overturn [ouvə'tə:n], *v.a.* umstürzen. — *v.n.* überschlagen.

overweening [ouvə'wi:niŋ], *adj.* eingebildet.

overweight [ouvə'weit], *s.* das Übergewicht.

overwhelm [ouvə'welm], *v.a.* überwältigen.

overwork [ouvə'wə:k], *v.n.* sich überarbeiten.

overwrought [ouvə'rɔ:t], *adj.* übermäßig erregt, aufgeregt, überreizt.

owe [ou], *v.a.* schulden. — *v.n.* verdanken (*be in debt*).

owing ['ouiŋ], *pred. adj.* — *to*, dank (*Dat.*), zufolge (*Dat.*).

owl [aul], *s.* (*Orn.*) die Eule.

own (1) [oun], *v.a.* besitzen (*possess*). — *adj.* eigen.

own (2) [oun], *v.a.* anerkennen (*acknowledge*).

owner ['ounə], *s.* der Besitzer, Eigentümer.

ox [ɔks], *s.* (*Zool.*) der Ochse.

oxidate ['ɔksideit] *see* **oxidise**.

oxide ['ɔksaid], *s.* (*Chem.*) das Oxyd.

oxidise ['ɔksidaiz], *v.a., v.n.* (*Chem.*) oxydieren.

oxtail ['ɔksteil], *s.* der Ochsenschwanz.

oxygen ['ɔksidʒən], *s.* (*Chem.*) der Sauerstoff.

oyster ['ɔistə], *s.* (*Zool.*) die Auster.

ozone ['ouzoun], *s.* (*Chem.*) das Ozon.

P

P [pi:]. das P.

pa [pɑ:], *s.* (*coll.*) Papa, der Vater.

pace [peis], *s.* der Gang, Schritt (*step*); das Tempo (*rate*). — *v.n.* — *up and down*, auf- und abschreiten. — *v.a.* einschulen (*horse*).

Pacific, The [pə'sifik, θə]. der Stille Ozean.

pacific [pə'sifik], *adj.* friedlich, still.

pacify ['pæsifai], *v.a.* Frieden stiften, beruhigen.

pack [pæk], *s.* das *or* der Pack; der Ballen (*bale*); das Rudel (*wolves*); das Spiel (*cards*); das Paket, die Packung. — *v.a.* packen (*a case*); parteiisch zusammensetzen; die Karten schlecht mischen (*cheat at cards*); *packed like sardines*, dichtgedrängt, eingepfercht. — *v.n.* packen; seine Sachen einpacken.

package ['pækidʒ], *s.* der Ballen (*bale*); das Gepäckstück, Paket.

packet ['pækit], *s.* das Paket; (*Naut.*) — *boat*, das Paketboot, Postschiff.

pact [pækt], *s.* der Pakt, Vertrag.

pad [pæd], *s.* das Polster, Kissen; der Notizblock (*writing block*). — *v.a.* auspolstern; *padded cell*, die Gummizelle.

padding ['pædiŋ], *s.* (*Tail.*) das Futter; (*fig.*) die (nichtssagende) Ausfüllung, das leere Geschwätz.

paddle ['pædl], *v.a., v.n.* rudern, paddeln. — *s.* das Paddel, (Doppel)ruder, das Schaufelruder; — *steamer*, der Raddampfer.

paddock ['pædək], *s.* der Sattelplatz; das Gehege.

padlock ['pædlɔk], *s.* das Vorhängeschloß, Vorlegeschloß.

pagan ['peigən], *adj.* heidnisch. — *s.* der Heide.

paganism ['peigənizm], *s.* das Heidentum.

page (1) [peidʒ], *s.* der Page (*court attendant*); Hoteljunge (*hotel boy*). — *v.a.* durch Pagen suchen lassen.

page (2) [peidʒ], die Seite (*of book*). — *v.a.* paginieren (*book*).

pageant ['pædʒənt], *s.* der Aufzug, der Prunkzug; das Schaustück (*dramatic*).

pail [peil], *s.* der Eimer.

pain [pein], *s.* der Schmerz, die Pein;
(*pl.*) die Mühe; *go to a lot of —s*, sich
große Mühe geben.— *v.a.* schmerzen;
bekümmern (*mentally*).

paint [peint], *s.* die Farbe (*dye*); die
Schminke (*make-up*). — *v.a.* anstreichen, malen.

painter [ˈpeintə], *s.* der Maler.

painting [ˈpeintiŋ], *s.* das Gemälde.

pair [pɛə], *s.* das Paar; *two —s of shoes*,
zwei Paar Schuhe; *a — of spectacles*,
die Brille; *a — of scissors*, die Schere.
— *v.a.* paaren. — *v.n.* sich paaren.

pajamas [pəˈdʒɑːməz] *see under*
pyjamas.

Pakistani [pɑːkiˈstɑːni], *adj.* paki-
stanisch. — *s.* der Pakistaner.

palace [ˈpæləs], *s.* der Palast.

palatable [ˈpælətəbl], *adj.* schmackhaft.

palatal [ˈpælətl], *adj.* (*Phonet.*) palatal,
Gaumen-, Vordergaumen-. — *s.*
(*Phonet.*) der Gaumenlaut.

palate [ˈpælit], *s.* der Gaumen.

Palatinate, The [pəˈlætinit, ðə]. die
Pfalz, Pfalzgrafschaft.

palaver [pəˈlɑːvə], *s.* die Unterredung;
das Palaver.

pale (1) [peil], *adj.* blaß, bleich.

pale (2) [peil], *s.* der Pfahl; *beyond the
—*, unkultiviert.

Palestinian [pælisˈtiniən], *adj.* palä-
stinisch. — *s.* der Palästiner.

palette [ˈpælit], *s.* die Palette (*see also*
pallet (1)).

paling [ˈpeiliŋ], *s.* der Lattenzaun; (*pl.*)
der Pfahlbau.

pall (1) [pɔːl], *s.* das Leichentuch.

pall (2) [pɔːl], *v.n.* schal werden (*become stale*).

pallet (1) [ˈpælit], *s.* die Palette (*painter's*); — *knife*, das Streichmesser
(*potter's* etc.).

pallet (2) [ˈpælit], *s.* der Strohsack.

palliative [ˈpæliətiv], *s.* linderndes
Mittel; (*fig.*) die Beschönigung.

pallid [ˈpælid], *adj.* blaß, bleich.

pallor [ˈpælə], *s.* die Blässe.

palm (1) [pɑːm], *s.* die Handfläche. —
v.a. — (*off*) *on to s.o.*, an jemanden
loswerden, jemandem etwas andrehen.

palm (2) [pɑːm], *s.* (*Bot.*) die Palme;
Palm Sunday, Palmsonntag.

palmer [ˈpɑːmə], *s.* (*obs.*) der Pilger
(*pilgrim*).

palmist [ˈpɑːmist], *s.* der Handleser,
Wahrsager.

palmistry [ˈpɑːmistri], *s.* die Hand-
wahrsagerei.

palmy [ˈpɑːmi], *adj.* glorreich.

palpable [ˈpælpəbl], *adj.* handgreiflich,
greifbar, klar.

palpitate [ˈpælpiteit], *v.n.* klopfen (*of
heart*).

palsied [ˈpɔːlzid], *adj.* (*Med.*) gelähmt.

palsy [ˈpɔːlzi], *s.* (*Med.*) die Lähmung.

paltry [ˈpɔːltri], *adj.* erbärmlich, armselig.

pamper [ˈpæmpə], *v.a.* verwöhnen.

pan (1) [pæn], *s.* die Pfanne. — *v.n.* —

out, sich ausbreiten, sich weiten.

pan (2) [pæn], *v.a.* (*Phot.*) kreisen, im
Bogen führen.

panacea [pænəˈsiə], *s.* das Universalmittel.

pancake [ˈpænkeik], *s.* der Pfannkuchen.

pander [ˈpændə], *v.n.* fröhnen (*Dat.*),
nachgeben.

pane [pein], *s.* die Glasscheibe.

panel [pænl], *s.* die Holzfüllung,
Täfelung (*in room*); die Liste; die
Kommission (*of experts etc.*).

pang [pæŋ], *s.* die Angst, Pein; der
Schmerz, Stich (*stab of pain*).

panic [ˈpænik], *s.* die Panik, der
Schrecken.

panoply [ˈpænəpli], *s.* (*Poet.*) die
Rüstung.

pansy [ˈpænzi], *s.* (*Bot.*) das Stiefmütterchen; (*sl.*) der Weichling,
Feigling.

pant [pænt], *v.n.* keuchen, schwer
atmen.

pantaloons [pæntəˈluːnz] (*usually abbr.*
pants [pænts]), *s. pl.* die Unterhosen,
Hosen, *f.pl.*

panther [ˈpænθə], *s.* (*Zool.*) der
Panther.

pantomime [ˈpæntəmaim], *s.* die Pantomime, das Weihnachtsstück.

pantry [ˈpæntri], *s.* die Speisekammer.

pap [pæp], *s.* der Kinderbrei.

papacy [ˈpeipəsi], *s.* das Papsttum.

papal [ˈpeipəl], *adj.* päpstlich.

paper [ˈpeipə], *s.* das Papier (*material*);
die Zeitung (*daily —*); die Abhand-
lung (*essay*); — *knife*, der Brieföffner.
— *v.a.* tapezieren (*a room*).

paperhanger [ˈpeipəhæŋə], *s.* der
Tapezierer.

paperweight [ˈpeipəweit], *s.* der Briefbeschwerer.

par [pɑː], *s.* die Gleichheit, das Pari.

parable [ˈpærəbl], *s.* die Parabel, das
Gleichnis.

parabola [pəˈræbələ], *s.* (*Geom.*) die
Parabel.

parabolic [pærəˈbɔlik], *adj.* para-
bolisch, gleichnishaft.

parachute [ˈpærəʃuːt], *s.* (*Aviat.*) der
Fallschirm.

parade [pəˈreid], *s.* die Parade, der Auf-
marsch. — *v.a.* herausstellen; zur
Schau tragen (*show off*). — *v.n.*
(*Mil.*) vorbeimarschieren.

paradise [ˈpærədais], *s.* das Paradies.

paraffin [ˈpærəfin], *s.* das Paraffin.

paragon [ˈpærəgən], *s.* das Musterkind,
Musterbeispiel, Vorbild.

paragraph [ˈpærəgrɑːf], *s.* der Abschnitt, Absatz, Paragraph.

Paraguayan [pærəˈgwaiən], *adj.* para-
guayisch. — *s.* der Paraguayer.

parallel [ˈpærəlel], *adj.* parallel. — *s.*
die Parallele.

paralyse [ˈpærəlaiz], *v.a.* lähmen.

paralysis [pəˈrælisis], *s.* die Lähmung.

paramount [ˈpærəmaunt], *adj.* oberst.

paramour [ˈpærəmuə], *s.* der *or* die
Geliebte.

451

parapet ['pærəpit], s. das Geländer, die Brüstung.

paraphrase ['pærəfreiz], s. die Umschreibung. — v.a. umschreiben.

parasite ['pærəsait], s. der Schmarotzer, Parasit.

parasol ['pærəsɔl], s. der Sonnenschirm.

parboil ['pɑ:bɔil], v.a. aufkochen lassen.

parcel [pɑ:sl], s. das Paket; Bündel (bundle). — v.a. — up, einpacken.

parch [pɑ:tʃ], v.a. austrocknen.

parchment ['pɑ:tʃmənt], s. das Pergament.

pardon [pɑ:dn], v.a. vergeben, verzeihen (Dat.); begnadigen (Acc.) (give amnesty). — s. der Pardon, die Verzeihung; — !, I beg your — ! bitte um Entschuldigung; I beg your — ? wie bitte?

pare [pɛə], v.a. beschneiden (nails); schälen (fruit).

parent ['pɛərənt], s. der Vater, die Mutter, (pl.) die Eltern, pl.

parentage ['pɛərəntidʒ], s. die Abkunft, Herkunft.

parenthesis [pə'renθisis], s. die Parenthese, die Klammer.

parish ['pæriʃ], s. das Kirchspiel, die Gemeinde, die Pfarre.

parishioner [pə'riʃənə], s. das Gemeindemitglied.

Parisian [pə'riziən], adj. parisisch. — s. der Pariser.

park [pɑ:k], s. der Park; (Motor.) der Wagenpark, Parkplatz. — v.a., v.n. parken.

parking ['pɑ:kiŋ], s. (Motor.) das Parken; — meter, die Parkuhr, Parkometer.

parley ['pɑ:li], s. die Unterredung, Verhandlung. — v.n. verhandeln.

parliament ['pɑ:ləmənt], s. das Parlament.

parlour ['pɑ:lə], s. das Wohnzimmer, die gute Stube; —maid, das Dienstmädchen; — trick, das Kunststück.

parochial [pə'roukiəl], adj. Pfarr-, Gemeinde-; (fig.) engstirnig.

parody ['pærədi], s. die Parodie. — v.a. parodieren.

parole [pə'roul], s. das Ehrenwort; (Mil.) das Losungswort.

paroxysm ['pærəksizm], s. der heftige Anfall.

parquet ['pɑ:ki], s. das Parkett; — floor, der Parkettfußboden.

parrot ['pærət], s. (Orn.) der Papagei.

parry ['pæri], v.a. parieren, abwehren.

parse [pɑ:s, pɑ:z], v.a. (Gram.) analysieren.

parsimony ['pɑ:siməni], s. die Sparsamkeit.

parsley ['pɑ:sli], s. (Bot.) die Petersilie.

parson [pɑ:sn], s. der Pastor, Pfarrer.

parsonage ['pɑ:sənidʒ], s. das Pfarrhaus.

part [pɑ:t], s. der Teil; Anteil (share); (Theat.) die Rolle; (Mus.) die Stimme; (Geog.) die Gegend; for his —, seinerseits. — v.n. — (with), sich trennen (von, Dat.); — company, auseinandergehen.

partake [pɑ:'teik], v.n. teilnehmen, teilhaben (in, an, Dat.).

partial [pɑ:ʃl], adj. Teil-; parteiisch (subjective); — to, eingenommen für.

participate [pɑ:'tisipeit], v.n. teilnehmen (in, an, Dat.).

participation [pɑ:tisi'peiʃən], s. die Teilnahme.

participle ['pɑ:tisipl], s. (Gram.) das Mittelwort, Partizip(ium).

particle ['pɑ:tikl], s. die Partikel, das Teilchen.

particular [pə'tikjulə], adj. besonder (special); einzel (individual); sonderbar (queer); ungewöhnlich; genau. — s. (pl.) die Details, n. pl., Einzelheiten, f. pl.

parting ['pɑ:tiŋ], s. der Abschied (taking leave); der Scheitel (hair).

partisan [pɑ:ti'zæn], s. der Partisane, Parteigänger.

partition [pɑ:'tiʃən], s. die Teilung (division); die Scheidewand (dividing wall). — v.a. teilen; aufteilen (divide up).

partly ['pɑ:tli], adv. zum Teil, teils.

partner ['pɑ:tnə], s. der Partner; Teilhaber (in business etc.).

partnership ['pɑ:tnəʃip], s. die Partnerschaft.

partridge ['pɑ:tridʒ], s. (Orn.) das Rebhuhn.

party ['pɑ:ti], s. (Pol.) die Partei; (Law) die Partei, Seite; die Gesellschaft, die Party (social gathering); throw or give a —, einen Gesellschaftsabend (or eine Party) geben; guilty —, der schuldige Teil; (Build.) — wall, die Brandmauer.

Paschal ['pɑ:skəl], adj. Oster-.

pass [pɑ:s], v.a. passieren, vorbeigehen (an, Dat.); durchlassen (let through); (Law) — sentence, das Urteil fällen. — v.n. fortgehen, vergehen, geschehen (happen); vorübergehen (of time); — for, gelten; (Sch.) durchkommen (exam); come to —, sich ereignen. — s. der Paß; (Theat.) die Freikarte.

passable ['pɑ:səbl], adj. gangbar; (fig.) leidlich, erträglich.

passage ['pæsidʒ], s. der Durchgang (thoroughfare); das Vergehen (of time); die Seereise; die Stelle (book).

passenger ['pæsindʒə], s. der Reisende, Passagier; — train, der Personenzug.

passer-by ['pɑ:səbai], s. der Passant, Vorübergehende.

passing ['pɑ:siŋ], s. das Vorbeigehen, das Vorübergehen; (Parl.) das Durchgehen; das Hinscheiden (death). — adj. vorübergehend, zeitweilig.

Passion ['pæʃən], s. das Leiden; (Mus.) die Passion; — Week, die Karwoche; — flower, die Passionsblume.

passion ['pæʃən], s. die Leidenschaft;

fly into a —, aufbrausen.

passive ['pæsiv], *adj.* passiv. — *s.* (*Gram.*) das Passiv(um).

Passover ['pɑːsouvə], *s.* (*Rel.*) das Passahfest.

passport ['pɑːspɔːt], *s.* der Reisepaß.

past [pɑːst], *adj.* vergangen. — *adv.* vorbei. — *prep.* nach (*time*). — *s.* die Vergangenheit; (*Gram.*) das Imperfekt, Präteritum.

paste [peist], *s.* die Paste, der Brei; der Kleister (*glue*). — *v.a.* kleben, kleistern.

pasteboard ['peistbɔːd], *s.* die Pappe.

pastime ['pɑːstaim], *s.* der Zeitvertreib.

pastor ['pɑːstə], *s.* (*Rel.*) der Seelsorger, Pfarrer.

pastoral ['pɑːstərəl], *adj.* Hirten-, pastoral. — *s.* (*Poet*). das Hirtengedicht.

pastry ['peistri], *s.* (*Cul.*) die Pastete; das Gebäck; — *cook*, der Konditor, Zuckerbäcker.

pasture ['pɑːstʃə], *s.* die Weide, das Grasland. — *v.n.* weiden, grasen.

pasty ['pɑːsti, 'pæsti], *s.* (*Cul.*) die Pastete. — ['peisti], *adj.* teigig.

pat [pæt], *s.* der Klaps; der Schlag (*slap*). — *v.a.* leicht schlagen, streicheln (*gently*).

patch [pætʃ], *v.a.* flicken, ausbessern. — *s.* der Fleck (*mending material*); der Flecken (*land*); (*coll.*) *no — on him,* kein Vergleich mit ihm; *nicht zu vergleichen mit ihm.*

patent ['peitənt *or* 'pætənt], *adj.* offen, klar, patent; — *leather,* das Glanzleder. — *s.* das Patent.

patentee [peitən'tiː], *s.* der Patentinhaber.

paternal [pə'təːnəl], *adj.* väterlich.

path [pɑːθ], *s.* der Pfad, Weg, Fußsteig.

pathetic [pə'θetik], *adj.* pathetisch, rührend; armselig.

pathology [pə'θɔlədʒi], *s.* (*Med.*) die Pathologie.

pathway ['pɑːθwei], *s.* der Fußweg, Fußsteig.

patience ['peiʃəns], *s.* die Geduld; die Patience (*card game*).

patient ['peiʃənt], *adj.* geduldig. — *s.* (*Med.*) der Patient.

patrician [pə'triʃən], *s.* (*Med.*) der Patrizier.

patrimony ['pætriməni], *s.* das (väterliche) Erbgut.

patriot ['peitriət, 'pætriət], *s.* der Patriot.

patriotism ['peitriətizm, 'pæt-], *s.* die Vaterlandsliebe, der Patriotismus.

patrol [pə'troul], *s.* die Patrouille, Streife. — *v.n.* auf Patrouille sein.

patron ['peitrən], *s.* der Schutzherr, der Gönner; (*Comm.*) der Kunde; — *saint,* der Schutzheilige.

patronage ['pætrənidʒ], *s.* die Gönnerschaft, Huld.

patronize ['pætrənaiz], *v.a.* besuchen (*frequent*); begünstigen (*favour*).

patronizing ['pætrənaiziŋ], *adj.* herablassend.

patten [pætn], *s.* (*Archit.*) der Sockel; der Holzschuh (*clog*).

patter (1) ['pætə], *s.* das Geplätscher (*rain etc.*). — *v.n.* plätschern.

patter (2) ['pætə], *s.* das Geplauder (*chatter*). — *v.n.* schwätzen.

pattern ['pætən], *s.* das Muster; die Schablone (*in material*).

paucity ['pɔːsiti], *s.* die geringe Anzahl, der Mangel.

paunch [pɔːntʃ], *s.* der Wanst.

pauper ['pɔːpə], *s.* der Arme.

pauperize ['pɔːpəraiz], *v.a.* arm machen, verarmen lassen.

pause [pɔːz], *s.* die Pause. — *v.n.* innehalten.

pave [peiv], *v.a.* pflastern.

pavement ['peivmənt], *s.* das Pflaster; der Bürgersteig, Gehsteig.

pavilion [pə'viljən], *s.* das Gartenhaus; der Pavillon.

paw [pɔː], *s.* die Pfote; die Tatze. — *v.a.* streicheln, betasten.

pawn (1) [pɔːn], *s.* das Pfand. — *v.a.* verpfänden.

pawn (2) [pɔːn], *s.* (*Chess*) der Bauer.

pawnbroker ['pɔːnbroukə], *s.* der Pfandleiher.

pay [pei], *v.a. irr.* zahlen; bezahlen, begleichen (*bill*); — *attention,* aufpassen, Aufmerksamkeit schenken; — *o.'s respects,* Respekt zollen. — *v.n. irr.* sich bezahlt machen, sich lohnen (*it —s to . . .*). — *s.* (*Mil.*) der Sold; (*Comm.*) der Lohn (*wage*), die Bezahlung (*payment*).

payable ['peiəbl], *adj.* zahlbar, zu bezahlen.

payee [pei'iː], *s.* der Empfänger, Präsentant.

payer ['peiə], *s.* der Zahler; (*Comm.*) der Trassat.

payment ['peimənt], *s.* die Bezahlung, Begleichung (*of sum*).

pea [piː], *s.* (*Bot.*) die Erbse (*see also* **peas**(e)).

peace [piːs], *s.* der Friede(n); die Ruhe (*restfulness*).

peaceable ['piːsəbl], *adj.* friedlich; friedliebend.

peaceful ['piːsful], *adj.* friedlich, ruhig (*restful*).

peach [piːtʃ], *s.* (*Bot.*) der *or* (*Austr.*) die Pfirsich.

peacock ['piːkɔk], *s.* (*Orn.*) der Pfau.

peahen ['piːhen], *s.* (*Orn.*) die Pfauhenne.

peak [piːk], *s.* der Gipfel, die Spitze; der Schirm (*of cap*); — *hour,* die Stunde des Hochbetriebs, Hauptverkehrsstunde.

peal [piːl], *v.a.* läuten. — *v.n.* erschallen. — *s.* das Läuten, Geläute.

peanut ['piːnʌt], *s.* (*Bot.*) die Erdnuß.

pear [pɛə], *s.* (*Bot.*) die Birne.

pearl [pəːl], *s.* die Perle; — *barley,* die Perlgraupen, *f. pl.*; *mother of* —, die Perlmutter.

peasant ['pezənt], s. der Bauer.
peasantry ['pezəntri], s. das Bauern-volk, die Bauernschaft.
peas(e) [pi:z], s. pl. pease pudding, der Erbsenbrei, das Erbsenpüree.
peat [pi:t], s. der Torf.
pebble [pebl], s. der Kiesel(stein).
peck (1) [pek], s. der Viertelscheffel (=9 litres.)
peck (2) [pek], s. das Picken (of hen); (coll.) der Kuß. — v.a. hacken, hauen.
pecker ['pekə], s. die Picke, Haue; keep your — up! Mut bewahren!
peckish ['pekiʃ], adj. hungrig.
pectoral ['pektərəl], adj. Brust-. — s. das Brustmittel.
peculiar [pi'kju:liə], adj. eigenartig, eigentümlich (strange); — to, eigen (Dat.); besonder (special).
peculiarity [pikju:li'æriti], s. die Eigen-tümlichkeit, Eigenartigkeit.
pecuniary [pi'kju:niəri], adj. Geld-, geldlich, finanziell, pekuniär.
pedagogue ['pedəgɔg], s. der Päda-gog(e), Erzieher.
pedal [pedl] s. das Pedal; (Motor.) der Fußhebel. — v.n. radfahren; (coll.) radeln.
pedant ['pedənt], s. der Pedant.
pedantic [pi'dæntik], adj. pedantisch.
pedantry ['pedəntri], s. die Pedanterie.
peddle [pedl], v.a. hausieren.
peddling ['pedliŋ], adj. kleinlich, un-bedeutend.
pedestal ['pedistl], s. der Sockel.
pedestrian [pi'destriən], s. der Fuß-gänger. — adj. Fuß-, Fußgänger-.
pedigree ['pedigri:], s. der Stamm-baum.
pediment ['pedimənt], s. (Archit.) der Ziergiebel.
pedlar ['pedlə], s. der Hausierer.
peel [pi:l], s. die Schale (of fruit). — v.a. schälen. — v.n. sich schälen.
peep [pi:p], v.n. gucken. — s. der (schnelle) Blick, das Gucken; — show, der Guckkasten.
peer (1) [piə], s. (Parl.) der Pair, Lord; der Ebenbürtige (equal).
peer (2) [piə], v.n. gucken, blicken, schauen.
peerage ['piəridʒ], s. der (Reichs)adel.
peeress ['piəres], s. die Gattin eines Pairs.
peerless ['piəlis], adj. unvergleichlich.
peevish ['pi:viʃ], adj. mürrisch.
pe(e)wit ['pi:wit], s. (Orn.) der Kiebitz.
peg ['peg], s. der Pflock (stake); der Holzstift (in wall); clothes —, die Wäscheklammer. — v.a. anpflocken (to ground).
pelican ['pelikən], s. (Orn.) der Pelikan.
pellet ['pelit], s. das Kügelchen.
pell-mell ['pel'mel], adv. durchein-ander.
pelt (1) [pelt], v.a. — with, bewerfen mit, — a person with, werfen nach einem (Acc.). — v.n. strömen (rain etc.); rennen (hasten).
pelt (2) [pelt], s. der Pelz (of animal).

pen (1) [pen], s. quill —, die Feder; fountain —, die Füllfeder; ballpoint —, der Kugelschreiber. — v.a. schrei-ben; verfassen (compose).
pen (2) [pen], s. das Gehege. — v.a. einschliessen (sheep).
penal ['pi:nəl], adj. Straf-; — servitude, die Zuchthausstrafe.
penalize ['pi:nəlaiz], v.a. bestrafen.
penalty ['penəlti], s. die Strafe.
penance ['penəns], s. die Buße.
pence [pens] see under **penny**.
pencil ['pensl], s. der Bleistift; der Stift; (Geom.) der Strahl. — v.a. niederschreiben, notieren.
pendant ['pendənt], s. das Ohrgehänge; (fig.) das Gegenstück.
pendent ['pendənt], adj. hängend, schwebend.
pending ['pendiŋ], adj. in der Schwebe; unentschieden (undecided). — prep. während (during); bis (zu) (until).
pendulum ['pendjuləm], s. das Pendel.
penetrate ['penitreit], v.a. durch-dringen.
peninsula [pi'ninsjulə], s. die Halb-insel.
penitent ['penitənt], s. der Büßer. — adj. bußfertig.
penitentiary [peni'tenʃəri], s. (Am.) das Zuchthaus (prison).
penknife ['pennaif], s. das Taschen-messer.
pennant ['penənt], s. der Wimpel, das Fähnchen.
penniless ['penilis], adj. mittellos, ohne einen Heller Geld, arm.
pennon ['penən] see **pennant**.
penny ['peni], s. (pl. pence [pens], pennies ['peniz]) der Penny; (Am.) das Centstück; — farthing, das Hoch-rad; — whistle, die Blechpfeife; a pretty —, hübsches Geld.
pension ['penʃən], s. die Pension; das Ruhegehalt. — v.a. (off) pensionieren, in den Ruhestand versetzen.
pensive ['pensiv], adj. nachdenklich.
Pentecost ['pentikɔst]. das or (pl.) die Pfingsten.
penthouse ['penthaus], s. das Wetter-dach.
penurious [pi'njuəriəs], adj. unbe-mittelt, arm (poor); dürftig, karg (meagre).
penury ['penjuəri], s. die Not, Armut.
peony ['piəni], s. (Bot.) die Päonie, Pfingstrose.
people [pi:pl], s. pl. das Volk (nation); die Leute, Menschen (pl.). — v.a. bevölkern.
pepper ['pepə], s. der Pfeffer. — v.a. pfeffern.
per [pə:], prep. pro; per; durch; as — account, laut Rechnung.
peradventure [pə:rəd'ventʃə], adv. (obs.) von ungefähr; vielleicht (per-haps).
perambulator [pə'ræmbjuleitə] (abbr. coll.) pram [præm], s. der Kinder-wagen.

perceive [pə'si:v], *v.a.* wahrnehmen, merken.

percentage [pə'sentidʒ], *s.* der Prozentsatz (*of interest*); Prozente, *n. pl.*

perceptible [pə'septibl], *adj.* wahrnehmbar, merklich.

perception [pə'sepʃən], *s.* die Wahrnehmung, Empfindung.

perch (1) [pə:tʃ], *v.n.* aufsitzen; sitzen (*of birds*). — *s.* die Stange.

perch (2) [pə:tʃ], *s.* (*Zool.*) der Barsch.

perchance [pə'tʃɑ:ns], *adv.* vielleicht.

percolate ['pə:kəleit], *v.n.* durchsickern, durchtröpfeln.

percolator ['pə:kəleitə], *s.* die Kaffeemaschine.

percussion [pə'kʌʃən], *s.* (*Mus.*) das Schlagzeug.

peremptory ['perəmptəri, pə'remptəri], *adj.* entschieden, bestimmt (*decided*); absprechend.

perennial [pə'reniəl], *adj.* (*Bot.*) perennierend; Dauer-.

perfect ['pə:fikt], *adj.* vollkommen, vollendet, perfekt. — *s.* (*tense*) (*Gram.*) das Perfekt(um). — [pə'fekt], *v.a.* vollenden.

perfection [pə'fekʃən], *s.* die Vollendung, Vollkommenheit; *to —,* vollkommen.

perfidious [pə'fidiəs], *adj.* treulos, untreu; tückisch.

perfidy ['pə:fidi], *s.* die Treulosigkeit.

perforate ['pə:fəreit], *v.a.* durchlöchern, perforieren (*paper*); durchbohren (*pierce*).

perforce [pə'fɔ:s], *adv.* mit Gewalt, notgedrungen.

perform [pə'fɔ:m], *v.a.* ausführen (*carry out*); (*Theat.*) aufführen. — *v.n.* spielen, auftreten (*of actor*).

performance [pə'fɔ:məns], *s.* die Ausführung, Verrichtung (*execution of duty etc.*); (*Theat.*) die Aufführung.

perfume ['pə:fju:m], *s.* das Parfüm; der Duft (*scent*). — *v.a.* parfümieren.

perfunctory [pə'fʌŋktəri], *adj.* nachlässig, oberflächlich, flüchtig.

perhaps [pə'hæps], *adv.* vielleicht.

peril ['peril], *s.* die Gefahr.

period ['piəriəd], *s.* die Periode (*time*); der Zeitraum (*span*); (*Am.*) der Punkt (*full stop*).

periodical [piəri'ɔdikəl], *adj.* periodisch. — *s.* die Zeitschrift.

perish ['periʃ], *v.n.* zugrunde gehen, umkommen.

perishable ['periʃəbl], *adj.* vergänglich; (*leicht*) verderblich (*of food*).

periwig ['periwig], *s.* die Perücke.

periwinkle (1) ['periwiŋkl], *s.* (*Zool.*) die Uferschnecke.

periwinkle (2) ['periwiŋkl], (*Bot.*) das Immergrün.

perjure ['pə:dʒə], *v.r.* meineidig werden.

perjurer ['pə:dʒərə], *s.* der Meineidige.

perjury ['pə:dʒəri], *s.* der Meineid.

permanence, permanency ['pə:mə-

nəns, 'pə:mənənsi], *s.* die Dauer, Beständigkeit.

permanent ['pə:mənənt], *adj.* Dauer-, dauerhaft, beständig; — *wave*, die Dauerwelle.

permeability [pə:miə'biliti], *s.* die Durchdringbarkeit, Durchlässigkeit.

permeable ['pə:miəbl], *adj.* durchdringlich.

permeate ['pə:mieit], *v.a.* durchdringen.

permissible [pə'misibl], *adj.* zulässig, statthaft.

permission [pə'miʃən], *s.* die Erlaubnis.

permit [pə'mit], *v.a.* zulassen, erlauben. — ['pə:mit], *s.* die Erlaubnis; (*official*) die Genehmigung.

permutation [pə:mju'teiʃən], *s.* (*Maths.*) die Permutation.

pernicious [pə'niʃəs], *adj.* verderblich, schädlich, bösartig.

perorate ['perəreit], *v.n.* eine (lange) Rede beschließen.

perpendicular [pə:pən'dikjulə], *adj.* senkrecht. — *s.* die Senkrechte.

perpetrate ['pə:pitreit], *v.a.* begehen (*commit*).

perpetration [pə:pi'treiʃən], *s.* die Verübung, Begehung.

perpetrator ['pə:pitreitə], *s.* der Begeher, Täter.

perpetual [pə'petjuəl], *adj.* (an-) dauernd; ewig.

perpetuate [pə'petjueit], *v.a.* verewigen.

perpetuity [pə:pi'tju:iti], *s.* die Ewigkeit.

perplex [pə'pleks], *v.a.* bestürzen, verblüffen.

perplexity [pə'pleksiti], *s.* die Bestürzung, Verwirrung.

persecute ['pə:sikju:t], *v.a.* verfolgen.

persecution [pə:si'kju:ʃən], *s.* die Verfolgung.

perseverance [pə:si'viərəns], *s.* die Ausdauer, Beharrlichkeit.

persevere [pə:si'viə], *v.n.* beharren (*in, bei, Dat.*).

Persian ['pə:ʃən], *adj.* persisch. — *s.* der Perser.

persist [pə'sist], *v.n.* beharren (*in, auf, Dat.*).

persistence [pə'sistəns], *s.* die Beharrlichkeit.

person ['pə:sən], *s.* die Person; *in —,* persönlich.

personal ['pə:sənəl], *adj.* persönlich.

personality [pə:sə'næliti], *s.* die Persönlichkeit.

personify [pə'sɔnifai], *v.a.* verkörpern.

personnel [pə:sə'nel], *s.* das Personal; (*Comm.*) — *manager,* der Personalchef.

perspective [pə'spektiv], *s.* die Perspektive. — *adj.* perspektivisch.

perspicacious [pə:spi'keiʃəs], *adj.* scharfsichtig, scharfsinnig.

perspicacity [pə:spi'kæsiti], *s.* der Scharfblick, Scharfsinn.

perspicuity [pə:spi'kju:iti], *s.* die Durchsichtigkeit, Klarheit.

perspicuous [pə'spikjuəs], *adj.* deutlich, klar.

perspiration [pə:spi'reiʃən], *s.* der Schweiß.

perspire [pə'spaiə], *v.n.* schwitzen.

persuade [pə'sweid], *v.a.* überreden.

persuasion [pə'sweiʒən], *s.* die Überredung.

persuasive [pə'sweiziv], *adj.* überzeugend, überredend.

pert [pə:t], *adj.* naseweis, keck.

pertain [pə'tein], *v.n.* (an)gehören (*to Dat.*).

pertinacious [pə:ti'neiʃəs], *adj.* beharrlich, halsstarrig.

pertinacity [pə:ti'næsiti], *s.* die Beharrlichkeit, Halsstarrigkeit.

pertinence, pertinency ['pə:tinəns, 'pə:tinənsi], *s.* die Angemessenheit.

pertinent ['pə:tinənt], *adj.* angemessen, passend.

pertness ['pə:tnis], *s.* die Keckheit, der Vorwitz.

perturb [pə'tə:b], *v.a.* verwirren, stören, beunruhigen.

perturbation [pə:tə'beiʃən], *s.* die Verwirrung, Störung, Beunruhigung.

peruke [pə'ru:k], *s.* die Perücke.

peruse [pə'ru:z], *v.a.* durchlesen.

Peruvian [pə'ru:viən], *adj.* peruanisch. — *s.* der Peruaner.

pervade [pə'veid], *v.a.* durchdringen.

perverse [pə'və:s], *adj.* verkehrt.

perversion [pə'və:ʃən], *s.* die Perversion.

perversity [pə'və:siti], *s.* die Verdorbenheit, Widernatürlichkeit.

pervert [pə'və:t], *v.a.* verkehren, verderben. — ['pə:və:t], *s.* der Verdorbene, der perverse Mensch.

perverted [pə'və:tid], *adj.* pervers (*sexually*).

pervious ['pə:viəs], *adj.* zugänglich, passierbar; durchlässig.

pessimist ['pesimist], *s.* der Pessimist.

pest [pest], *s.* (*Med.*) die Pest; (*fig.*) die Plage.

pester ['pestə], *v.a.* quälen, auf die Nerven gehen (*Dat.*).

pestiferous [pes'tifərəs], *adj.* verpestend.

pestilence ['pestiləns], *s.* (*Med.*) die Pest, Seuche.

pestle [pesl], *s.* die Mörserkeule.

pet [pet], *s.* das Haustier; der Liebling; — *name*, der Kosename. — *v.a.* liebkosen, streicheln.

petition [pi'tiʃən], *s.* die Bittschrift. — *v.a.* mit einer Bittschrift herantreten an (*Acc.*).

petrel ['petrəl], *s.* (*Orn.*) der Sturmvogel.

petrification [petrifi'keiʃən], *s.* die Versteinerung.

petrify ['petrifai], *v.a.* versteinern; (*fig.*) starr machen, bestürzen; *petrified with fright*, starr vor Entsetzen. — *v.n.* zu Stein werden.

petrol ['petrəl], *s.* das Benzin; (*crude oil*) das Petroleum; — *station*, die Tankstelle.

petticoat ['petikout], *s.* der Unterrock.

pettifogging ['petifɔgiŋ], *adj.* Winkel-, kleinlich, schikanös (*petty*).

pettiness ['petinis], *s.* die Kleinlichkeit.

pettish ['petiʃ], *adj.* verdrießlich.

petty ['peti], *adj.* klein, gering, kleinlich.

petulance ['petjuləns], *s.* die Launenhaftigkeit, Gereiztheit.

petulant ['petjulənt], *adj.* launenhaft.

pew [pju:], *s.* (*Eccl.*) der Kirchensitz; (*coll.*) der Sitz, Stuhl.

pewit ['pi:wit] *see* **pe(e)wit**.

pewter ['pju:tə], *s.* das Zinn; die Zinnwaren, *f. pl.* (*wares*).

pewterer ['pju:tərə], *s.* die Zinngießer.

phantom ['fæntəm], *s.* das Phantom, Trugbild; das Gespenst (*ghost*).

Pharisee ['færisi:], *s.* der Pharisäer.

pharmaceutical [fɑ:mə'sju:tikəl], *adj.* pharmazeutisch.

pharmacy ['fɑ:məsi], *s.* die Apothekerkunst (*dispensing*); die Apotheke (*dispensary*); die Pharmazeutik (*discipline*).

phase [feiz], *s.* die Phase.

pheasant ['fezənt], *s.* (*Orn.*) der Fasan.

phenomenal [fi'nɔminəl], *adj.* außerordentlich, phänomenal.

phenomenon [fi'nɔminən], *s.* das Phänomen.

phial ['faiəl], *s.* die Phiole, das Fläschchen.

philanthropist [fi'lænθrəpist], *s.* der Philanthrop.

philanthropy [fi'lænθrəpi], *s.* die Philanthropie.

philatelist [fi'lætəlist], *s.* der Philatelist, Markensammler.

philately [fi'lætəli], *s.* das Markensammeln, die Philatelie, Briefmarkenkunde.

Philippine ['filipi:n], *adj.* philippinisch.

Philistine ['filistain], *s.* der Philister; (*fig.*) der Spießbürger.

philologist [fi'lɔlədʒist], *s.* der Philologe.

philology [fi'lɔlədʒi], *s.* die Philologie.

philosopher [fi'lɔsəfə], *s.* der Philosoph.

philosophize [fi'lɔsəfaiz], *v.n.* philosophieren.

philosophy [fi'lɔsəfi], *s.* die Philosophie.

phlegm [flem], *s.* das Phlegma (*mood*); (*Med.*) der Schleim.

phlegmatic [fleg'mætik], *adj.* phlegmatisch, gelassen.

phone [foun] *see under* **telephone**.

phonetics [fə'netiks], *s.* die Phonetik.

phosphorescent [fɔsfə'resənt], *adj.* phosphoreszierend, leuchtend.

phosphorus ['fɔsfərəs], *s.* (*Chem.*) der Phosphor.

photograph ['foutəgræf *or* -grɑ:f], *s.* die Photographie, das Lichtbild (*picture*). — *v.a.* photographieren, aufnehmen, (*coll.*) knipsen.

photographer [fə'tɔgrəfə], *s.* der Photograph.

photography [fə'tɔgrəfi], s. die Photographie.

phrase [freiz], s. die Phrase. — v.a. phrasieren, fassen, ausdrücken.

phrenology [fre'nɔlədʒi], s. die Phrenologie, Schädellehre.

phthisis ['θaisis], s. (Med.) die Schwindsucht.

physic ['fizik], s. (obs.) die Medizin, Arznei.

physical ['fizikəl], adj. körperlich (bodily); physikalisch (of physics).

physician [fi'zifən], s. der Arzt.

physics ['fiziks], s. die Physik.

physiognomy [fizi'ɔnəmi or -'ɔgnəmi], s. die Physiognomie, die Gesichtsbildung.

physiologist [fizi'ɔlədʒist], s. der Physiolog.

physiology [fizi'ɔlədʒi], s. die Physiologie.

piano(forte) ['pjænou('fɔːti)], s. das Klavier.

pick [pik], v.a. pflücken (flowers); hacken (hack); — up, auflesen; auswählen (select); gewaltsam öffnen (a lock); anfangen (a quarrel). — v.n. why — on me? warum gerade mich auswählen? — s. die Picke, Spitzhacke (axe); die Auswahl; — of the bunch, (coll.) das Beste von allen.

picket ['pikit], s. die Wache; der Streikposten (of strikers); der Pflock (wood). — v.a. bewachen. — v.n. Wache stehen.

pickle [pikl], s. (Cul.) der Pökel, das Gepökelte; (coll.) die unangenehme Lage (calamity). — v.a. einpökeln.

pickpocket ['pikpɔkit], s. der Taschendieb.

picnic ['piknik], s. das Picknick. — v.n. picknicken.

pictorial [pik'tɔːriəl], adj. illustriert.

picture ['piktʃə], s. das Bild; — book, das Bilderbuch; — postcard, die Ansichtskarte; pretty as a —, bildhübsch; der Film; (pl.) das Kino. — v.a. sich vorstellen.

picturesque [piktʃə'resk], adj. pittoresk, malerisch.

pie [pai], s. (Cul.) die Pastete (savoury); das Törtchen (sweet).

piebald ['paibɔːld], adj. scheckig. — s. der Schecke (horse).

piece [piːs], s. das Stück. — v.a. — together, zusammenflicken (mend), zusammensetzen (compose).

piecemeal ['piːsmiːl], adv. stückweise.

pied [paid] see **piebald**.

pier [piə], s. der Hafendamm; der Pfeiler (column).

pierce [piəs], v.a. durchstechen, durchbohren.

pierglass ['piəglɑːs], s. der Pfeilerspiegel.

piety ['paiəti], s. die Pietät, Frömmigkeit.

pig [pig], s. (Zool.) das Schwein.

pigeon ['pidʒən], s. (Orn.) die Taube.

pigeonhole ['pidʒənhoul], s. das Fach.

pigheaded [pig'hedid], adj. starrköpfig, dickköpfig.

piglet ['piglit], s. (Zool.) das Ferkel.

pigment ['pigmənt], s. das Pigment, der (natürliche) Farbstoff.

pigtail ['pigteil], s. der Haarzopf.

pike [paik], s. (Zool.) der Hecht; die Pike (weapon).

pile (1) [pail], s. der Haufen, Stoß (paper). — v.a. aufhäufen.

pile (2) [pail], s. (Archit.) der Pfahl; Pfeiler (stone).

pile (3) [pail], s. (Text.) der Teppichflausch (carpet), die Noppe (cloth).

piles [pailz], s. pl. (Med. coll.) die Haemorrhoiden, pl.

pilfer ['pilfə], v.a. stehlen, mausen.

pilferer ['pilfərə], s. der Dieb.

pilgrim ['pilgrim], s. der Pilger.

pill [pil], s. (Med.) die Pille.

pillage ['pilidʒ], s. die Plünderung. — v.a. ausplündern.

pillar ['pilə], s. der Pfeiler, die Säule; — box, der Briefkasten.

pillion ['piljən], s. der zweite Sitz, Sozius (motorcycle).

pillory ['piləri], s. der Pranger. — v.a. anprangern.

pillow ['pilou], s. das Kopfkissen.

pilot ['pailət], s. der Pilot; (Naut.) der Lotse. — v.a. (Aviat.) steuern, (Naut.) lotsen.

pimento [pi'mentou], s. (Bot.) der Jamaikapfeffer.

pimp [pimp], s. der Kuppler.

pimple [pimpl], s. der Pickel; (pl.) der Ausschlag.

pin [pin], s. die Stecknadel; (Engin.) der Bolzen, Stift; (skittles) der Kegel. — v.a. — down, festlegen.

pinafore ['pinəfɔː], s. die Schürze, Kinderschürze.

pincers ['pinsəz], s. pl. die Kneifzange, Zange.

pinch [pintʃ], v.a. kneifen, zwicken; (coll.) klauen, stehlen. — v.n. sparen, darben. — s. die Prise (tobacco); at a —, wenn es sein muß.

pine (1) [pain], s. (Bot.) die Kiefer, Föhre.

pine (2) [pain], v.n. — for, schmachten (nach, Dat.), sich sehnen.

pineapple ['painæpl], s. (Bot.) die Ananas.

pinion ['pinjən], s. der Flügel (wing); (Poet.) die Schwinge; (Mech.) das Zahnrad; — shaft, die Ritzelwelle; — spindle, die Zahnradwelle. — v.a. binden, fesseln.

pink [piŋk], adj. rosa. — s. (Bot.) die (rosa) Nelke; (Hunt.) der (rote) Jagdrock; in the — (of condition), in bester Gesundheit, in bester Form.

pinnacle ['pinəkl], s. die Zinne, Spitze; (fig.) der Gipfel.

pint [paint], s. die Pinte (0.57 litre); (beer) der Schoppen.

pioneer [paiə'niə], s. der Pionier. — v.a. bahnbrechend sein, bahnen.

pious ['paiəs], adj. fromm.

pip [pip], s. der Obstkern; (*Mil. coll.*) der Leutnantsstern.

pipe [paip], s. die Pfeife; (*Engin.*) das Rohr; die Röhre; (*Mus.*) die Pfeife. — *v.a.* pfeifen; durch Rohre leiten.

piping ['paipiŋ], *adj.* — *hot*, kochend heiß.

pipkin ['pipkin], s. das Töpfchen.

piquant ['pi:kənt], *adj.* pikant; scharf (*taste*).

pique [pi:k], s. der Groll. — *v.a.* reizen.

piracy ['pairəsi], s. die Seeräuberei.

pirate ['pairit], s. der Pirat, Seeräuber. — [pai'reit], *v.a.* (*fig.*) plagiieren, ohne Erlaubnis drucken (*books*).

pistil ['pistil], s. (*Bot.*) der Stempel.

pistol ['pistəl], s. die Pistole.

piston ['pistən], s. (*Mech.*) der Kolben.

pit [pit], s. die Grube; (*Min.*) der Schacht, das Bergwerk; (*Theat., Mus.*) der Orchesterraum; (*Theat.*) das Parterre.

pitch (1) [pitʃ], s. der Grad, Gipfel (*height*); (*Mus.*) der Ton, die Tonhöhe (*level*); (*Sport*) das Spielfeld. — *v.a.* werfen; feststecken; (*Mus.*) stimmen; befestigen; (*tent*) (ein Zelt) aufschlagen; — *in*, sich ins Zeug legen.

pitch (2) [pitʃ], s. das Pech (*tar*); — *dark*, pechschwarz.

pitchblende ['pitʃblend], s. die Pechblende.

pitcher ['pitʃə], s. der Krug.

pitchfork ['pitʃfɔ:k], s. die Heugabel.

piteous ['pitiəs], *adj.* erbärmlich.

pitfall ['pitfɔ:l], s. die Falle.

pith [piθ], s. das Mark; (*fig.*) der Kern, das Wesentliche; die Kraft (*strength*).

pithy ['piθi], *adj.* markig, kräftig; prägnant.

pitiable ['pitiəbl], *adj.* erbärmlich.

pitiful ['pitiful], *adj.* erbärmlich (*pitiable*); mitleidig (*sympathetic*).

pitiless ['pitilis], *adj.* erbarmungslos, grausam.

pittance ['pitəns], s. der Hungerlohn, das Bißchen, die Kleinigkeit.

pity ['piti], s. das Mitleid. — *v.a.* bemitleiden, bedauern.

pivot ['pivət], s. (*Mech.*) der Drehpunkt, Zapfen; (*fig.*) der Mittelpunkt, Angelpunkt. — *v.n.* zum Mittelpunkt haben, sich drehen (um).

placard ['plækɑ:d], s. das Plakat.

placate [plə'keit], *v.a.* versöhnen.

place [pleis], s. der Platz, Ort, die Stelle; — *name*, der Ortsname; (*rank*) der Rang, die Rangstufe. — *v.a.* plazieren (*in a job*); legen, setzen, stellen; — *an order*, einen Auftrag geben.

placid ['plæsid], *adj.* gelassen, sanft, gutmütig.

plagiarism ['pleidʒiərizm], s. das Plagiat, das Plagiieren.

plague [pleig], s. (*Med.*) die Pest, Seuche; (*fig.*) die Plage. — *v.a.* belästigen, plagen.

plaice [pleis], s. (*Zool.*) die Scholle.

plain [plein], s. die Ebene, Fläche. — *adj.* eben, flach (*even*); schlicht,

einfach, klar; — *dealing*, ehrliche Handlungsweise; — *speaking*, offenes Sprechen, aufrichtiges Reden; (*Mus.*) — *song*, der einstimmige Chorgesang, die gregorianische Kirchenmusik.

plaintiff ['pleintif], s. (*Law*) der Kläger.

plaintive ['pleintiv], *adj.* klagend.

plait [plæt], s. der Zopf, die Flechte. — — *v.a.* flechten (*hair*); falten.

plan [plæn], s. der Plan, Grundriß. — *v.a.* planen, entwerfen.

plane (1) [plein], *v.a.* hobeln (*wood*). — s. die Fläche (*surface*); die Stufe (*level*); (*coll.*) das Flugzeug (*aeroplane*).

plane (2) see **plane-tree**.

planet ['plænit], s. (*Astron.*) der Planet.

plane-tree ['pleintri:], s. (*Bot.*) die Platane.

planish ['plæniʃ], *v.a.* (*woodwork*) polieren, glätten.

plank [plæŋk], s. die Planke; (*Pol.*) der Programmpunkt.

plant [plɑ:nt], s. (*Bot.*) die Pflanze; (*Ind.*) die Anlage, der Betrieb. — *v.a.* anpflanzen, anlegen; — *suspicion*, Verdacht einflößen (*of, against*, gegen, *Acc.*).

plantain ['plæntein], s. (*Bot.*) der Wegerich; der Pisang.

plantation [plæn'teiʃən], s. die Pflanzung, Plantage.

plaster ['plɑ:stə], s. das Pflaster (*adhesive*); (*Build.*) der Mörtel, der Mauerbewurf; — *cast*, der Gipsabdruck; — *of Paris*, der Stuck, der feine Gipsmörtel. — *v.a.* bepflastern, verputzen; (*fig.*) dick auftragen.

plastic ['plæstik], *adj.* plastisch; (*malleable*) formbar; — *surgery*, plastische Chirurgie. — s. der Kunststoff.

Plate, River [pleit, 'rivə], der La Plata Strom.

plate [pleit], s. der Teller (*dish*), die Platte, Scheibe; (*coll.*) — *glass*, das Spiegelglas; das Geschirr (*service of crockery*); *gold*, — das Goldgeschirr. — *v.a.* überziehen, versilbern, verchromen.

platform ['plætfɔ:m], s. (*Railw.*) der Bahnsteig; die Bühne, das Podium.

platinum ['plætinəm], s. das Platin.

platitude ['plætitju:d], s. die Plattheit, der Gemeinplatz.

platitudinous [plæti'tju:dinəs], *adj.* nichtssagend.

platoon [plə'tu:n], s. (*Mil.*) der Zug.

plaudit ['plɔ:dit], s. der Beifall.

plausible ['plɔ:zibl], *adj.* wahrscheinlich, glaubwürdig, einleuchtend.

play [plei], s. das Spiel (*game*); (*Theat.*) das Stück. — *v.a., v.n.* spielen.

player ['pleiə], s. der Spieler; (*Theat.*) der Schauspieler.

playful ['pleiful], *adj.* spielerisch, spielend.

playground ['pleigraund], s. der Spielplatz.

playhouse ['pleihaus], s. das Schauspielhaus.

playmate ['pleimeit], *s.* der Spielgefährte.

playwright ['pleirait], *s.* der Dramatiker, Schauspieldichter.

plea [pli:], *s.* die Bitte; das Gesuch; der Vorwand.

plead [pli:d], *v.a., v.n.* plädieren, sich berufen auf; vorschützen (*claim*).

pleasant ['plezənt], *adj.* angenehm, freundlich.

pleasantry ['plezəntri], *s.* das freundliche Wort, der Scherz (*joke*).

please [pli:z], *v.a., v.n.* gefallen; einen Gefallen tun (*do a favour*); — ! bitte, haben Sie die Güte!; *if you* —, wenn Sie nichts dagegen haben.

pleasing ['pli:ziŋ], *adj.* einnehmend, angenehm.

pleasure ['pleʒə], *s.* das Vergnügen; *at your* —, nach Belieben; *take* — *in*, Vergnügen finden an (*Dat.*).

pleat [pli:t], *v.a.* plissieren. — *s.* die Falte, das Plissee.

pledge [pledʒ], *s.* das Pfand, die Bürgschaft (*guarantee*); das Versprechen (*promise*). — *v.a.* sich verbürgen, versprechen; zutrinken (*drink to*).

plenary ['pli:nəri], *adj.* Plenar-, vollständig.

plenipotentiary [plenipo'tenʃəri], *s.* der Bevollmächtigte.

plenitude ['plenitju:d], *s.* die Fülle.

plenteous, plentiful ['plentiəs, 'plentiful], *adj.* reichlich, in Fülle.

plenty ['plenti], *s.* die Fülle.

pleurisy ['pluərəsi], *s.* (*Med.*) die Brustfellentzündung.

pliable, pliant ['plaiəbl, 'plaiənt], *adj.* geschmeidig, biegsam.

pliers ['plaiəz], *s. pl.* die Drahtzange.

plight (1) [plait], *s.* die Notlage.

plight (2) [plait], *v.a.* feierlich versprechen.

plod [plɔd], *v.n.* schwerfällig gehen (*walk*); sich plagen (*work hard*).

plot (1) [plɔt], *s.* das Stück Land, der Bauplatz.

plot (2) [plɔt], *s.* das Komplott, die Verschwörung; die Handlung (*book, play etc.*). — *v.a.* aushecken (*ambush etc.*), planen.

plough, plow [plau], *s.* der Pflug. — *v.a.* pflügen; (*coll.*) *be* —*ed*, durchfallen (*in*, in, *Dat.*).

ploughshare ['plauʃeə], *s.* die Pflugschar.

plover ['plʌvə], *s.* (*Orn.*) der Kiebitz, Regenpfeifer.

plow *see under* **plough**.

pluck (1) [plʌk], *v.a.* pflücken (*flowers*); rupfen (*feathers*); — *up courage*, Mut fassen.

pluck (2) [plʌk], *s.* (*coll.*) der Mut.

plucky ['plʌki], *adj.* mutig.

plug [plʌg], *s.* (*Elec.*) der Stecker; der Stöpsel (*stopper*); *sparking* —, (*Motor.*) die Zündkerze. — *v.a.* stöpseln, zustopfen (*block*); (*fig.*) betonen, herausstellen (*repeat for advertisement*).

plum [plʌm], *s.* (*Bot.*) die Pflaume; (*coll.*) das Beste.

plumage ['plu:midʒ], *s.* (*Orn.*) das Gefieder.

plumb [plʌm], *s.* das Senkblei, Lot; — *-rule*, die Senkwaage. — *adv.* senkrecht, gerade, lotrecht.

plume [plu:m], *s.* die (Schmuck) feder.

plump [plʌmp], *adj.* dick, drall.

plunder ['plʌndə], *v.a., v.n.* plündern. — *s.* die Beute, der Raub.

plunge [plʌndʒ], *v.a., v.n.* untertauchen, stoßen, hinabstürzen.

plunger ['plʌndʒə], *s.* der Taucher; (*Engin.*) der Tauchkolben.

pluperfect [plu:'pə:fikt], *s.* (*Gram.*) das Plusquamperfektum.

plural ['pluərəl], *s.* (*Gram.*) der Plural, die Mehrzahl.

plurality [pluə'ræliti], *s.* die Mehrzahl, der Plural.

plus [plʌs], *prep.* plus, zuzüglich.

plush [plʌʃ], *s.* (*Text.*) der Plüsch.

ply [plai], *s.* die Falte (*fold*), Lage (*layer*). — *v.a.* ausüben (*trade*).

plywood ['plaiwud], *s.* das Sperrholz, die Sperrholzplatte.

pneumonia [nju'mouniə], *s.* (*Med.*) die Lungenentzündung.

poach (1) [poutʃ], *v.n.* wildern; — *on*, übergreifen auf.

poach (2) [poutʃ], *v.a.* ohne Schale kochen; *poached eggs*, verlorene Eier, *n. pl.*

poacher ['poutʃə], *s.* der Wilderer, Wilddieb.

pocket ['pɔkit], *s.* die Tasche; — *book*, die Brieftasche; das Taschenbuch; — *money*, das Taschengeld.

pod [pɔd], *s.* (*Bot.*) die Schote.

poem ['pouim], *s.* das Gedicht.

poet ['pouit], *s.* der Dichter.

poetic(al) [pou'etik(l)], *adj.* dichterisch.

poignancy ['pɔinjənsi], *s.* die Schärfe.

poignant ['pɔinjənt], *adj.* scharf, beißend, schmerzlich.

point [pɔint], *s.* der Punkt (*of remark, sentence*); die Sache; der Zweck; die Spitze (*of pencil etc.*); *make a* —, es sich zur Aufgabe machen; *in* — *of fact*, tatsächlich; *come to the* —, zur Sache kommen. — *v.a., v.n.* spitzen, zuspitzen (*pencil*); — *out*, zeigen, (hin)deuten, — *to*, hinweisen auf; — *the moral*, die Moral erklären.

pointblank ['pɔint'blæŋk], *adj., adv.* schnurgerade, direkt.

pointed ['pɔintid], *adj.* scharf, spitzig, deutlich (*remark*).

pointer ['pɔintə], *s.* der Zeiger; (*fig.*) der Fingerzeig (*hint*).

poise [pɔiz], *s.* das Gleichgewicht; (*fig.*) angemessenes Benehmen, die Grazie. — *v.a.* abwägen; im Gleichgewicht halten. — *v.n.* schweben; —*d for action*, tatbereit.

poison [pɔizn], *s.* das Gift. — *v.a.* vergiften.

poke

poke (1) [pouk], *v.a.* schüren (*fire*); stoßen; — *fun at*, sich lustig machen über. — *s.* der Stoß; — *in the ribs*, ein Rippenstoß.

poke (2) [pouk], *s.* der Sack; *a pig in a* —, die Katze im Sack.

poker (1) ['poukə], *s.* der Schürhaken, das Schüreisen.

poker (2) ['poukə], *s.* (*Cards*) das Pokerspiel.

polar ['poulə], *adj.* (*Geog.*) Polar-; (*Phys.*) polar.

polarity [po'læriti], *s.* die Polarität.

Pole [poul], *s.* der Pole.

pole (1) [poul], *s.* (*Geog.*) der Pol.

pole (2) [poul], *s.* die Stange (*rod*); der Pfahl (*upright*).

poleaxe ['poulæks], *s.* die Streitaxt.

polecat ['poulkæt], *s.* (*Zool.*) der Iltis.

polemic [pə'lemik], *s.* die Polemik, der Streit.

police [pə'li:s], *s.* die Polizei. — *v.a.* polizeilich beaufsichtigen.

policeman [pə'li:smən], *s.* der Polizist.

policy (1) ['pɔlisi], *s.* die Politik.

policy (2) ['pɔlisi], *s.* (*Insurance*) die Police.

Polish ['pouliʃ], *adj.* polnisch.

polish ['pɔliʃ], *v.a.* polieren. — *s.* die Politur, der Glanz.

polished ['pɔliʃd], *adj.* glatt (*smooth*); (*fig.*) wohlerzogen, fein (*manners*).

polite [pə'lait], *adj.* höflich.

politeness [pə'laitnis], *s.* die Höflichkeit.

politic ['pɔlitik], *adj.* politisch; schlau (*cunning*).

political [pə'litikəl], *adj.* politisch; staatskundig.

politician [pɔli'tiʃən], *s.* der Politiker, Staatsmann.

politics ['pɔlitiks], *s.* (*sometimes pl.*) die Politik, politische Staatskunst.

poll [poul], *s.* die Wahl (*election*). — *v.n.* abstimmen, wählen, seine Stimme abgeben.

pollard ['pɔləd], *s.* (*Bot.*) der gekappte Baum; (*Zool.*) das hornlose Tier.

pollen ['pɔlən], *s.* (*Bot.*) der Blütenstaub.

pollinate ['pɔlineit], *v.a.* (*Bot.*) bestäuben.

polling ['poulin], *s.* die Wahl, der Wahlgang (*election*); — *station*, das Wahllokal.

pollute [pə'lju:t], *v.a.* verunreinigen.

pollution [pə'lju:ʃən], *s.* die Verunreinigung.

poltroon [pɔl'tru:n], *s.* die Memme.

poly- ['pɔli], *pref.* viel-.

Polynesian [pɔli'ni:ziən], *adj.* polynesisch. — *s.* der Polynesier.

polytechnic [pɔli'teknik], *s.* das Technikum; polytechnische Fachschule.

pomegranate ['pɔm-, 'pʌmgrænit], *s.* (*Bot.*) der Granatapfel.

Pomeranian [pɔmə'reiniən], *adj.* pommersch. — *s.* der Pommer; der Spitz (*dog*).

pommel [pʌml], *s.* der Sattelknopf; der Knauf (*sword*). — *v.a.* schlagen.

pomp [pɔmp], *s.* der Pomp, das Gepränge.

pompous ['pɔmpəs], *adj.* hochtrabend, prahlerisch; (*manner*) schwerfällig, wichtigtuerisch.

pond [pɔnd], *s.* der Teich.

ponder ['pɔndə], *v.a.*, *v.n.* bedenken, überlegen.

ponderous ['pɔndərəs], *adj.* schwer, schwerfällig.

pontiff ['pɔntif], *s.* der Hohepriester; der Papst.

pontifical [pɔn'tifikəl], *adj.* bischöflich, päpstlich; — *s. pl.* die bischöfliche Amtstracht.

pontificate [pɔn'tifikit], *s.* das (*or der*) Pontifikat. — [-keit], *v.n.* (*coll.*) predigen.

pontoon (1) [pɔn'tu:n], *s.* die Schiffsbrücke, der Brückenkahn.

pontoon (2) [pɔn'tu:n], *s.* (*cards*) das Einundzwanzig, Vingt-et-un.

pony ['pouni], *s.* (*Zool.*) der *or* das Pony.

poodle [pu:dl], *s.* (*Zool.*) der Pudel.

pooh-pooh [pu:'pu:], *v.a.* verspotten.

pool (1) [pu:l], *s.* die Lache, der Pfuhl.

pool (2) [pu:l], *s.* (*fig.*) der gemeinsame Einsatz (*money, forces etc.*). — *v.a.* zusammenschließen.

poop [pu:p], *s.* (*Naut.*) das Heck, Hinterteil.

poor [puə], *adj.* arm, dürftig; *in — health*, bei schwacher Gesundheit; (*fig.*) armselig, schlecht.

pop [pɔp], *v.n.* knallen, explodieren. — *v.a.* (*coll.*) schnell versetzen, verpfänden.

Pope [poup], *s.* (*Eccl.*) der Papst.

poplar ['pɔplə], *s.* (*Bot.*) die Pappel.

poppy ['pɔpi], *s.* (*Bot.*) der Mohn.

populace ['pɔpjulis], *s.* der Pöbel.

popular ['pɔpjulə], *adj.* volkstümlich, beliebt.

popularity [pɔpju'læriti], *s.* die Beliebtheit.

populate ['pɔpjuleit], *v.a.* bevölkern.

population [pɔpju'leiʃən], *s.* die Bevölkerung.

populous ['pɔpjuləs], *adj.* dicht bevölkert.

porcelain ['pɔ:slin], *s.* das Porzellan, das Geschirr.

porch [pɔ:tʃ], *s.* die Eingangshalle, Vorhalle.

porcupine ['pɔ:kjupain], *s.* (*Zool.*) das Stachelschwein.

pore (1) [pɔ:], *s.* die Pore.

pore (2) [pɔ:], *v.n.* sich vertiefen (*over, in*), brüten (*über*).

pork [pɔ:k], *s.* das Schweinefleisch.

porosity [pɔ:'rɔsiti], *s.* die Porosität.

porous ['pɔ:rəs], *adj.* porös.

porpoise ['pɔ:pəs], *s.* (*Zool.*) der Tümmler, das Meerschwein.

porridge ['pɔridʒ], *s.* (*Cul.*) der Haferbrei.

porringer ['pɔrindʒə], *s.* (*Cul.*) der Napf.

port (1) [pɔ:t], *s.* der Hafen.

port (2) [pɔ:t], *s.* der Portwein (*wine*).

portable ['pɔ:təbl], *adj.* tragbar; Koffer- *(radio etc.).*

portcullis [pɔ:'tʃʌlis], *s.* das Fallgatter.

portend [pɔ:'tend], *v.a.* vorbedeuten, ahnen lassen.

portent ['pɔ:tent], *s.* die Vorbedeutung.

porter ['pɔ:tə], *s.* *(Railw.)* der Gepäckträger; der Pförtner, Portier *(caretaker, janitor)*; das Porterbier *(beer).*

porterage ['pɔ:təridʒ], *s.* der Trägerlohn, die Zustellkosten, *f. pl.*

portfolio [pɔ:'fouliou], *s.* die Mappe; *(Pol.)* das Ressort; das Portefeuille.

portico ['pɔ:tikou], *s.* *(Archit.)* die Säulenhalle.

portion ['pɔ:ʃən], *s.* die Portion, der Anteil. — *v.a.* aufteilen, austeilen *(share out).*

portliness ['pɔ:tlinis], *s.* die Stattlichkeit *(dignity)*; Behäbigkeit *(corpulence).*

portly ['pɔ:tli], *adj.* stattlich *(dignified)*; behäbig *(corpulent).*

portmanteau [pɔ:t'mæntou], *s.* der Handkoffer.

portrait ['pɔ:trit], *s.* *(Art)* das Bildnis, Porträt.

portray [pɔ:'trei], *v.a.* im Bilde darstellen, porträtieren; *(fig.)* schildern, darstellen *(describe).*

Portuguese [pɔ:tju'gi:z], *adj.* portugiesisch. — *s.* der Portugiese.

pose [pouz], *s.* die Haltung, Stellung *(of model etc.).* — *v.a.* in Pose stellen; aufwerfen *(question).* — *v.n. (as model)* stehen, sitzen; — *as,* posieren, sich ausgeben als *(pretend to be).*

poser ['pouzə], *s.* die schwierige Frage.

position [pə'ziʃən], *s.* die Lage *(situation)*; die Stellung *(job)*; der Stand, Rang *(rank)*; *(Astron., Mil.)* die Position.

positive ['pɔzitiv], *adj.* positiv; *(fig.)* ausdrücklich, sicher *(sure).*

possess [pə'zes], *v.a.* besitzen.

possession [pə'zeʃən], *s.* der Besitz, Besitztum.

possessive [pə'zesiv], *adj.* *(Gram.)* besitzanzeigend, possessiv; *(fig.)* besitzgierig.

possibility [pɔsi'biliti], *s.* die Möglichkeit.

possible ['pɔsibl], *adj.* möglich.

post (1) [poust], *s.* der Pfosten *(pillar).*

post (2) [poust], *s.* die Post *(mail)*; der Posten *(job).* — *v.a.* zur Post geben; *(coll.)* einstecken *(letter).*

postage ['poustidʒ], *s.* das Porto; — *stamp,* die Briefmarke.

postal [poustl], *adj.* Post-.

poster ['poustə], *s.* das Plakat.

posterity [pɔs'teriti], *s.* die Nachwelt.

posthumous ['pɔstjuməs], *adj.* hinterlassen, nach dem Tode, postum.

postman ['poustmən], *s.* der Briefträger.

postmark ['poustma:k], *s.* der Poststempel.

post-mortem [poust'mɔ:təm], *s.* — — —

(examination), die Obduktion, Leichenschau.

post-office ['poustɔfis], *s.* das Postamt.

postpone [poust'poun], *v.a.* verschieben, aufschieben.

postscript ['poustskript], *s.* die Nachschrift.

postulate ['pɔstjuleit], *v.a.* postulieren, voraussetzen.

posture ['pɔstʃə], *s.* die Positur, Haltung *(of body).*

pot [pɔt], *s.* der Topf; die Kanne *(beer)*; *(coll.) go to —,* zugrunde gehen. — *v.a.* einkochen, einmachen; *(fig.)* kürzen.

potash ['pɔtæʃ], *s.* *(Chem.)* die Pottasche.

potassium [pə'tæsiəm], *s.* *(Chem.)* das Kalium.

potato [pə'teitou], *s.* *(Bot.)* die Kartoffel.

potent ['poutənt], *adj.* kräftig, stark, wirksam.

potential [pə'tenʃəl], *s.* das Potential. — *adj.* möglich, potentiell *(possible).*

potter ['pɔtə], *s.* der Töpfer.

pottery ['pɔtəri], *s.* die Töpferei; die Töpferwaren, Tonwaren, *f. pl. (goods).*

pouch [pautʃ], *s.* der Beutel.

poulterer ['poultərə], *s.* der Geflügelhändler.

poultice ['poultis], *s.* der Umschlag.

poultry ['poultri], *s.* das Geflügel.

pounce (1) [pauns], *s. (obs.)* die Klaue. — *v.n. — upon,* herfallen (über, *Acc.*).

pounce (2) [pauns], *s.* das Bimssteinpulver. — *v.a.* (mit Bimsstein) abreiben.

pound (1) [paund], *s.* das Pfund; das Pfund Sterling.

pound (2) [paund], *v.a.* zerstoßen.

poundage ['paundidʒ], *s.* das Pfundgeld, die Gebühr pro Pfund.

pour [pɔ:], *v.a.* gießen, schütten, einschenken. — *v.n.* strömen.

pout [paut], *v.n.* schmollen.

poverty ['pɔvəti], *s.* die Armut.

powder ['paudə], *s.* *(Mil.)* das Pulver; der Puder *(face etc.).* — *v.a.* zu Pulver machen, stoßen; *(face)* pudern.

power [pauə], *s.* die Macht, Gewalt; Kraft; Fähigkeit; — *of attorney,* die Vollmacht; *(Maths.)* die Potenz; *(Elec.)* der Strom; — *house,* — *station,* das Elektrizitätswerk; — *cut,* die Stromstörung.

powerful ['pauəful], *adj.* kräftig, mächtig, einflußreich.

powerless ['pauəlis], *adj.* kraftlos, machtlos.

pox [pɔks], *s.* *(Med.)* die Pocken, *f. pl.*; die Syphilis.

practicable ['præktikəbl], *adj.* ausführbar, tunlich.

practical ['præktikəl], *adj.* praktisch.

practice ['præktis], *s.* die Ausübung *(doing, carrying out)*; die Praxis.

practise ['præktis], *v.a.* ausführen, ausüben *(a profession etc.)*; üben *(rehearse).* — *v.n.* sich üben.

practised ['præktisd], *adj.* geübt, geschult (in).

practitioner [præk'tiʃənə], *s.* (*Med.*) praktischer Arzt; (*Law*) Advokat.

pragmatic [præg'mætik], *adj.* pragmatisch.

prairie ['prɛəri], *s.* die Prärie.

praise [preiz], *v.a.* preisen, loben. — *s.* das Lob.

pram *see under* **perambulator**.

prance [pra:ns], *v.n.* sich bäumen; (*fig.*) sich brüsten (*brag*).

prank [prænk], *s.* der Streich.

prate [preit], *v.n.* plappern, schwatzen.

prattle [prætl], *v.n.* plaudern, schwatzen. — *s.* das Geschwätz.

prawn [prɔ:n], *s.* (*Zool.*) die Steingarnele.

pray [prei], *v.n.* beten. — *v.a.* bitten, ersuchen (*beseech*).

prayer [prɛə], *s.* das Gebet.

preach [pri:tʃ], *v.a., v.n.* predigen.

preacher ['pri:tʃə], *s.* der Prediger.

preamble [pri:'æmbl], *s.* die Vorrede, der Einleitungsparagraph.

precarious [pri'kɛəriəs], *adj.* unsicher, prekär.

precaution [pri'kɔ:ʃən], *s.* die Vorsichtsmaßregel.

precede [pri'si:d], *v.a., v.n.* vorausgehen, den Vortritt haben.

precedence ['presidəns *or* pri'si:dəns], *s.* der Vortritt, Vorrang.

precedent ['president], *s.* der Präzedenzfall.

precept ['pri:sept], *s.* die Vorschrift, Regel.

preceptor [pri'septə], *s.* der Lehrer, Lehrmeister.

precinct ['pri:siŋkt], *s.* das Gebiet, der Bezirk; (*pl.*) die Grenzen, *f. pl.*

precious ['preʃəs], *adj.* wertvoll, kostbar; — *metal*, das Edelmetall.

precipice ['presipis], *s.* der Abgrund.

precipitous [pri'sipitəs], *adj.* jäh, abschüssig.

precise [pri'sais], *adj.* genau, bestimmt.

precision [pri'siʒən], *s.* die Präzision, Genauigkeit; (*Engin.*) — *tool*, das Präzisionswerkzeug.

preclude [pri'klu:d], *v.a.* ausschließen.

precocious [pri'kouʃəs], *adj.* frühreif.

preconceive [pri:kən'si:v], *v.a.* vorher denken.

preconceived [pri:kən'si:vd], *adj.* vorgefaßt.

preconception [pri:kən'sepʃən], *s.* das Vorurteil.

precursor [pri'kə:sə], *s.* der Vorläufer.

predatory ['predətəri], *adj.* räuberisch, Raub-.

predecessor ['pri:disesə], *s.* der Vorgänger.

predestin(at)e [pri:'destin(eit)], *v.a.* vorher bestimmen; (*Theol.*) prädestinieren.

predicament [pri'dikəmənt], *s.* die Verlegenheit.

predicate ['predikit], *s.* (*Gram.*) das Prädikat. — [-keit], *v.a.* behaupten.

predict [pri'dikt], *v.a.* voraussagen, vorhersagen.

prediction [pri'dikʃən], *s.* die Vorhersage (*weather etc.*); die Weissagung (*prophecy*).

predilection [pri:di'lekʃən], *s.* die Vorliebe.

predispose [pri:dis'pouz], *v.a.* vorbereiten; empfänglich machen.

predominant [pri'dɔminənt], *adj.* vorherrschend.

predominate [pri'dɔmineit], *v.n.* vorherrschen.

pre-eminence [pri:'eminəns], *s.* der Vorrang.

prefabricate [pri:'fæbrikeit], *v.a.* vorfabrizieren, als Fertigteil herstellen, in der Fabrik herstellen.

prefabrication [pri:fæbri'keiʃən], *s.* die Vorfabrizierung.

preface ['prefis], *s.* das Vorwort.

prefatory ['prefətəri], *adj.* einleitend.

prefect ['pri:fekt], *s.* der Präfekt.

prefer [pri'fə:], *v.a.* vorziehen.

preference ['prefərəns], *s.* der Vorzug (*Comm.*) — *share*, die Vorzugsaktie.

preferment [pri'fə:mənt], *s.* die Beförderung.

prefix ['pri:fiks], *s.* die Vorsilbe. — [pri:'fiks], *v.a.* vorsetzen.

pregnancy ['pregnənsi], *s.* die Schwangerschaft.

pregnant ['pregnənt], *adj.* schwanger.

prejudge [pri:'dʒʌdʒ], *v.a.* vorher urteilen, voreilig urteilen.

prejudice ['predʒudis], *s.* das Vorurteil. — *v.a.* beeinträchtigen.

prejudicial [predʒu'diʃəl], *adj.* schädlich.

prelate ['prelit], *s.* (*Eccl.*) der Prälat.

preliminary [pri'liminəri], *adj.* vorläufig, Präliminar-. —*s.* (*pl.*) die Vorbereitungen, *f. pl.*

prelude ['prelju:d], *s.* das Vorspiel.

premature ['prematʃə], *adj.* vorschnell, übereilt, vorzeitig.

premeditate [pri:'mediteit], *v.a.* (*Law*) vorher überlegen.

Premier ['premiə], *s.* der Premierminister.

premise (1) ['premis], *s.* (*Log.*) die Prämisse; (*pl.*) das Haus, Grundstück; die Stätte, der Ort; das Lokal (*inn etc.*).

premise (2) [pri:'maiz], *v.a.* vorausschicken.

premium ['pri:miəm], *s.* die Prämie.

premonition [pri:mə'niʃən], *s.* die Vorahnung.

preoccupation [pri:ɔkju'peiʃən], *s.* die Zerstreutheit.

preoccupied [pri:'ɔkjupaid], *adj.* besorgt; zerstreut (*absent-minded*).

preparation [prepə'reiʃən], *s.* die Vorbereitung; Zubereitung (*of meals*).

preparatory [pri'pærətri], *adj.* vorbereitend; — *school*, die Vorschule.

prepare [pri'pɛə], *v.a., v.n.* vorbereiten (*for*, auf); zubereiten (*meals*).

prepay [pri:'pei], *v.a. irr.* vorausbezahlen; (*post*) frankieren.

preponderant [pri'pɒndərənt], *adj.*
überwiegend.
preponderate [pri'pɒndəreit], *v.a.*,
v.n. überwiegen.
preposition [prepə'ziʃən], *s.* (*Gram.*)
die Präposition.
prepossess [pri:pə'zes], *v.a.* einnehmen,
beeindrucken.
preposterous [pri'pɒstərəs], *adj.* töricht,
lächerlich, unerhört.
prerogative [pri'rɒgətiv], *s.* das Vorrecht.
presage [pri'seidʒ], *v.a.* prophezeien.
— ['presidʒ], *s.* die Prophezeiung.
prescient ['preʃiənt, 'pri:–], *adj.* vorahnend, vorherwissend.
prescribe [pri'skraib], *v.a.*, *v.n.* vorschreiben; (*Med.*) verschreiben,
verordnen.
prescription [pri'skripʃən], *s.* die
Vorschrift (*precept*); (*Med.*) das Rezept.
presence ['prezəns], *s.* die Gegenwart,
Anwesenheit (*attendance*); das Äußere
(*appearance*); — *of mind*, die Geistesgegenwart.
present (1) ['prezənt], *adj.* anwesend,
gegenwärtig; jetzig. — *s.* (*Gram.*) das
Präsens, die Gegenwart; (*time*) die
Gegenwart, heutige Zeit.
present (2) [pri'zent], *v.a.* darstellen
(*on stage*); vorstellen (*introduce*);
präsentieren (*arms*); schenken, geben
(*gifts*). — ['prezənt], *s.* das Geschenk
(*gift*).
presentation [prezən'teiʃən], *s.* die
Darstellung (*stage*, *art*); die Vorstellung (*introduction*); die Überreichung (*of gift*).
presentiment [pri'zentimənt], *s.* das
Vorgefühl, die Vorahnung.
presently ['prezəntli], *adv.* bald, sogleich.
preservation [prezə'veiʃən], *s.* die
Erhaltung, Bewahrung.
preservative [pri'zɜːvətiv], *s.* das Konservierungsmittel.
preserve [pri'zɜːv], *v.a.* bewahren,
erhalten; (*fruit*) einmachen. — *s.*
(*Hunt.*) das Jagdgehege, Jagdrevier,
(*pl.*) die Konserven, *f. pl.*
preside [pri'zaid], *v.n.* (*over*) den
Vorsitz führen.
president ['prezidənt], *s.* der Präsident.
press [pres], *v.a.*, *v.n.* drücken (*push*);
bügeln, plätten (*iron*); nötigen (*force*);
dringend bitten (*entreat*). — *s.* die
Presse (*newspapers*, *printing*); der
Schrank (*cupboard*); das Gedränge
(*crowd*).
pressing ['presiŋ], *adj.* dringend.
pressure ['preʃə], *s.* der Druck.
prestige [pres'ti:ʒ], *s.* das Prestige,
Ansehen.
presumable [pri'zju:məbl], *adj.* mutmaßlich, vermutlich.
presume [pri'zju:m], *v.a.*, *v.n.* vermuten; — *on*, sich anmaßen.
presumption [pri'zʌmpʃən], *s.* die
Annahme; die Anmaßung (*arrogance*).
presumptive [pri'zʌmptiv], *adj.* mutmaßlich.

presumptuous [pri'zʌmptjuəs], *adj.*
anmaßend, dreist, vermessen.
presuppose [pri:sə'pouz], *v.a.* voraussetzen.
pretence [pri'tens], *s.* der Vorwand.
pretend [pri'tend], *v.a.*, *v.n.* vortäuschen, vorgeben.
pretension [pri'tenʃən], *s.* die Anmaßung, der Anspruch (*to*, auf).
pretentious [pri'tenʃəs], *adj.* anspruchsvoll.
preterite ['pretərit], *s.* (*Gram.*) das
Präteritum.
pretext ['pri:tekst], *s.* der Vorwand.
pretty ['priti], *adj.* hübsch, nett. —
adv. (*coll.*) ziemlich.
prevail [pri'veil], *v.n.* vorherrschen, die
Oberhand gewinnen.
prevalence ['prevələns], *s.* das Vorherrschen.
prevaricate [pri'værikeit], *v.n.* Ausflüchte machen.
prevent [pri'vent], *v.a.* verhindern.
prevention [pri'venʃən], *s.* die Verhinderung.
preventive [pri'ventiv], *adj.* vorbeugend.
previous ['pri:viəs], *adj.* vorhergehend.
prey [prei], *s.* die Beute, der Raub. —
v.n. rauben, nachstellen.
price [prais], *s.* der Preis, Wert.
priceless ['praislis], *adj.* unschätzbar,
unbezahlbar.
prick [prik], *s.* der Stachel, Stich (*stab*).
— *v.a.* stechen (*stab*); punktieren
(*puncture*).
prickle [prikl], *s.* (*Bot.*) der Stachel.
pride [praid], *s.* der Stolz. — *v.r.* — *o.s.*,
sich brüsten, stolz sein (*on*, auf, *Acc.*).
priest [pri:st], *s.* (*Eccl.*) der Priester.
prig [prig], *s.* der eingebildete Tropf;
Tugendheld.
priggish ['prigiʃ], *adj.* dünkelhaft,
selbstgefällig.
prim [prim], *adj.* steif, spröde.
primacy ['praiməsi], *s.* der, das Primat.
primæval [prai'mi:vəl], *adj.* Ur-, anfänglich, ursprünglich.
primary ['praiməri], *adj.* erst, ursprünglich; Haupt— (*main*). — *s.* (*pl.*)
(*Am.*) die Vorwahlen, *f. pl.* (*Presidential elections*).
prime [praim], *adj.* erst, wichtigst. —
s. die Blüte, Vollendung, Vollkraft.
primer ['praimə], *s.* das Elementarbuch,
die Fibel.
primitive ['primitiv], *adj.* primitiv;
ursprünglich (*original*).
primness ['primnis], *s.* die Geziertheit,
Steifheit.
primrose ['primrouz], *s.* (*Bot.*) die
Primel.
prince [prins], *s.* der Prinz; Fürst
(*rank*).
princess [prin'ses], *s.* die Prinzessin.
principal ['prinsipl], *s.* der Direktor
(*business*); Rektor (*school etc.*);
(*Comm.*) das Kapital; (*Mus.*) der erste
Spieler. — *adj.* erst, Haupt-.
principality [prinsi'pæliti], *s.* das
Fürstentum.

principle

principle ['prinsipl], *s.* das Prinzip, der Grundsatz.

print [print], *v.a.* drucken, abdrucken. — *s.* (*Typ.*, *Art*) der Druck; *out of* —, vergriffen.

printer ['printə], *s.* der (Buch-)drucker.

prior [praiə], *adj.* früher, eher; — *to*, vor (*Dat.*). — *s.* (*Eccl.*) der Prior.

priority [prai'ɔriti], *s.* die Priorität, der Vorrang.

prise [praiz], *v.a.* — *open*, gewaltsam öffnen, aufbrechen.

prism [prizm], *s.* das Prisma.

prison [prizn], *s.* das Gefängnis.

prisoner ['prizənə], *s.* der Gefangene, Sträfling.

pristine ['pristain] *adj.* ehemalig, vormalig, ursprünglich.

privacy ['praivəsi *or* 'privəsi], *s.* die Zurückgezogenheit, Stille.

private ['praivit], *adj.* privat, persönlich, vertraulich (*confidential*). — *s.* (*Mil.*) der Gemeine, Landser.

privation [prai'veiʃən], *s.* der Mangel, die Entbehrung (*lack*); die Beraubung (*deprivation*).

privilege ['privilidʒ], *s.* das Privileg, Vorrecht. — *v.a.* ausnehmen, privilegieren.

privy ['privi], *s.* der Abtritt, Abort. — *adj.* —, mitwissend; *Privy Council*, der Staatsrat.

prize [praiz], *s.* der Preis, die Belohnung; — *v.a.* hochschätzen.

prizewinner ['praizwinə], *s.* der Preisträger; *Nobel* —, der Nobelpreisträger.

probability [prɔbə'biliti], *s.* die Wahrscheinlichkeit.

probable ['prɔbəbl], *adj.* wahrscheinlich.

probate ['proubeit], *s.* (*Law*) die Testamentsbestätigung.

probation [pro'beiʃən], *s.* die Bewährung, Bewährungsfrist (*period*).

probationary [pro'beiʃənəri], *adj.* Bewährungs-.

probe [proub], *v.a.* sondieren, untersuchen. — *s.* die Sonde, Prüfung.

probity ['proubiti], *s.* die Redlichkeit, Anständigkeit.

problem ['prɔbləm], *s.* das Problem.

problematic [prɔblə'mætik], *adj.* zweifelhaft, problematisch.

proboscis [pro'bɔsis],*s.*(*Ent.*) der Rüssel.

procedure [prə'si:dʒə], *s.* der Vorgang, das Verfahren.

proceed [prə'si:d], *v.n.* vorgehen, verfahren.

proceeds ['prousi:dz], *s. pl.* der Ertrag.

process (1) ['prouses], *s.* der Vorgang, Prozeß. — *v.a.* verarbeiten, fertigen.

process (2) [pro'ses], *v.n.* in einem Zuge gehen.

procession [prə'seʃən], *s.* der (feierliche) Umzug, die Prozession.

proclaim [prə'kleim], *v.a.* (*Pol.*) proklamieren, ausrufen.

proclamation [prɔklə'meiʃən], *s.* (*Pol.*) die Ausrufung, Proklamation.

proclivity [prə'kliviti], *s.* der Hang, die Neigung (*tendency*).

procrastinate [prə'kræstineit], *v.a.* aufschieben. — *v.n.* zögern, zaudern.

procreate ['proukrieit], *v.a.* zeugen, hervorbringen.

procurable [prə'kjuərəbl], *adj.* zu verschaffen, erhältlich.

procure [prə'kjuə], *v.a.* verschaffen, besorgen.

prod [prɔd], *v.a.* stoßen.

prodigal ['prɔdigəl], *adj.* verschwenderisch, vergeudend; — *son*, der verlorene Sohn.

prodigious [prə'didʒəs], *adj.* erstaunlich, ungeheuer.

prodigy ['prɔdidʒi], *s.* das Wunderkind.

produce [prə'dju:s], *v.a.* erzeugen, produzieren. — ['prɔdju:s], *s.* das Produkt, Erzeugnis.

producer [prə'dju:sə], *s.* der Erzeuger; (*Theat.*, *Cinema*) der Regisseur.

product ['prɔdʌkt], *s.* das Produkt, Erzeugnis.

production [prə'dʌkʃən], *s.* die Produktion; die Erzeugung (*industrial*); das Zeigen, Vorweisen (*of documents*); (*Theat.*) die Regie.

productive [prə'dʌktiv], *adj.* produktiv, schöpferisch (*mind*); fruchtbar (*soil*).

profane [prə'fein], *adj.* profan; ruchlos.

profanity [prə'fæniti], *s.* die Profanierung; das Lästern.

profess [prə'fes], *v.a.*, *v.n.* bekennen, erklären, sich bekennen zu.

profession [prə'feʃən], *s.* der (höhere) Beruf; (*Eccl.*) das Bekenntnis; die Beteuerung (*protestation*).

professional [prə'feʃənəl], *adj.* beruflich, berufsmäßig.

professor [prə'fesə], *s.* der (Universitäts) Professor.

professorship [prə'fesəʃip], *s.* die Professur.

proffer ['prɔfə], *v.a.* anbieten (*offer*).

proficiency [prə'fiʃənsi], *s.* die Tüchtigkeit; (*skill*) die Beherrschung.

proficient [prə'fiʃənt], *adj.* bewandert, tüchtig; (*in language*) fließend.

profile ['proufail], *s.* das Profil.

profit ['prɔfit], *s.* der Profit, Gewinn, Nutzen. — *v.n.* Nutzen ziehen. — *v.a.* von Nutzen sein (*Dat.*).

profound [prə'faund], *adj.* tief; gründlich (*thorough*).

profuse [prə'fju:s], *adj.* reichlich, verschwenderisch.

profusion [prə'fju:ʒen], *s.* der Überfluß.

progeny ['prɔdʒəni], *s.* der Nachkomme; die Nachkommenschaft.

prognosticate [prɔg'nɔstikeit], *v.a.* vorhersagen.

prognostication [prɔgnɔsti'keiʃən], *s.* die Voraussage.

programme, (*Am.*) **program** ['prougræm], *s.* das Programm.

progress ['prougres], *s.* der Fortschritt. — [prou'gres], *v.n.* fortschreiten, Fortschritte machen.

464

progression [pro'greʃən], s. (Maths.) die Reihe, Progression.

progressive [pro'gresiv], adj. fortschrittlich (modern); fortschreitend (continuous); progressiv.

prohibit [prou'hibit], v.a. verbieten.

prohibition [proui'biʃən], s. das Verbot.

project [prə'dʒekt], v.a. projizieren; entwerfen. — ['prɔdʒekt], s. das Projekt, der Plan.

projectile [prə'dʒektail], s. das Geschoß.

projection [prə'dʒekʃən], s. die Projektion (film); der Entwurf (plan); der Vorsprung (jutting out).

proletarian [prouli'tɛəriən], adj. proletarisch. — s. der Prolet(arier).

prolific [prə'lifik], adj. fruchtbar.

prolix ['prouliks], adj. weitschweifig.

prologue ['proulɔg], s. der Prolog.

prolong [prə'lɔŋ], v.a. verlängern, prolongieren.

prominent ['prɔminənt], adj. prominent, hervorragend.

promiscuous [prə'miskjuəs], adj. unterschiedslos (indiscriminate); vermischt (mixed).

promise ['prɔmis], v.a. versprechen. — v.n. Erwartungen erwecken. — s. das Versprechen.

promissory ['prɔmisəri], adj. versprechend; (Comm.) — note, der Schuldschein.

promontory ['prɔməntəri], s. das Vorgebirge.

promote [prə'mout], v.a. befördern; fördern (foster).

promotion [prə'mouʃən], s. die Beförderung (advancement); Förderung (fostering); (Am.) die Reklame (publicity).

prompt [prɔmpt], adj. prompt, pünktlich. — v.a. (Theat.) soufflieren; treiben (inspire).

prompter ['prɔmptə], s. (Theat.) der Souffleur.

promptitude ['prɔmptitju:d], s. die Promptheit, Pünktlichkeit.

promulgate ['prɔməlgeit], v.a. bekanntmachen, verbreiten.

prone [proun], adj. geneigt, neigend.

prong [prɔŋ], s. die Zinke, Gabel.

pronominal [pro'nɔminəl], adj. (Gram.) pronominal.

pronoun ['prounaun], s. das Fürwort, Pronomen.

pronounce [prə'nauns], v.a., v.n. aussprechen (words); feierlich erklären (proclaim).

pronunciation [prənʌnsi'eiʃən], s. die Aussprache.

proof [pru:f], s. der Beweis, die Probe; (Typ.) der Korrekturbogen. — v.a. (Engin., Chem.) impregnieren.

prop [prɔp], s. die Stütze, der Stützpfahl. — v.a. stützen.

propaganda [prɔpə'gændə], s. die Propaganda, Reklame.

propagate ['prɔpəgeit], v.a. propagieren; (Bot.) fortpflanzen.

propel [prə'pel], v.a. forttreiben, vorwärtstreiben.

propeller [prə'pelə], s. der Propeller, die Schraube.

propensity [prə'pensiti], s. die Neigung, der Hang.

proper ['prɔpə], adj. schicklich (manners); eigentümlich, eigen (peculiar).

property ['prɔpəti], s. das Eigentum (possession); die Eigenschaft (quality).

prophecy ['prɔfisi], s. die Prophezeiung, Weissagung.

prophesy ['prɔfisai], v.a. prophezeien.

propitiate [prə'piʃieit], v.a. versöhnen.

propitiation [prəpiʃi'eiʃən], s. die Versöhnung.

propitious [prə'piʃəs], adj. gnädig, günstig, geneigt.

proportion [prə'pɔ:ʃən], s. das Verhältnis; die Proportion; der Anteil (portion); das Ebenmaß (in art).

proportionate [prə'pɔ:ʃənit], adj. im Verhältnis, verhältnismäßig, proportioniert.

proposal [prə'pouzəl], s. der Vorschlag, Antrag.

propose [prə'pouz], v.a. antragen, beantragen, vorschlagen. — v.n. — to a lady, einen Heiratsantrag machen.

proposition [prɔpə'ziʃən], s. der Vorschlag, Antrag; die Idee.

propound [prə'paund], v.a. vorlegen, vorbringen (a theory etc.).

proprietor [prə'praiətə], s. der Eigentümer.

propriety [prə'praiəti], s. die Schicklichkeit.

propulsion [prə'pʌlʃən], s. der Antrieb.

prorogue [prə'roug], v.a. vertagen.

prosaic [pro'zeiik], adj. prosaisch, nüchtern.

proscribe [pro'skraib], v.a. verbieten, ächten.

proscription [pro'skripʃən], s. die Verbannung, das Verbot.

prose [prouz], s. die Prosa.

prosecute ['prɔsikju:t], v.a. verfolgen; (Law) gerichtlich verfolgen, anklagen.

prosecutor ['prɔsikju:tə], s. (public) der Staatsanwalt; der Kläger.

proselyte ['prɔsəlait], s. der Neubekehrte, Proselyt.

prospect ['prɔspekt], s. die Aussicht; (pl.) die Aussichten, Chancen, f.pl. — [prɔs'pekt], v.n. suchen (for, nach, Dat.).

prospectus [prə'spektəs], s. der Prospekt.

prosper ['prɔspə], v.n. gedeihen, blühen. — v.a. segnen.

prosperity [prɔs'periti], s. der Wohlstand; der Reichtum; das Gedeihen (thriving).

prosperous ['prɔspərəs], adj. glücklich, wohlhabend.

prostitute ['prɔstitju:t], s. die Prostituierte, Dirne. — v.a. erniedrigen.

prostrate ['prɔstreit], adj. hingestreckt, niedergeworfen, fußfällig. — [prɔs'treit], v.a. niederwerfen.

prosy ['prouzi], *adj.* prosaisch, weitschweifig, langweilig.
protect [prə'tekt], *v.a.* beschützen.
protection [prə'tekʃən], *s.* der Schutz; die Protektion (*favour*).
protective [prə'tektiv], *adj.* Schutz-, schützend.
protector [prə'tektə], *s.* der Beschützer; (*Engin.*) der Schutz.
protest [prə'test], *v.a.*, *v.n.* protestieren, einwenden. — ['proutest], *s.* der Protest, Einspruch.
Protestant ['prɔtistənt], *adj.* protestantisch. — *s.* der Protestant.
protestation [prɔtes'teiʃən], *s.* die Beteuerung, Verwahrung.
protocol ['proutəkɔl], *s.* das Protokoll.
prototype ['proutotaip], *s.* das Urbild, Modell, das Prototyp.
protract [prə'trækt], *v.a.* in die Länge ziehen; hinausziehen.
protractor [prə'træktə], *s.* der Winkelmesser, Transporteur, die Schmiege.
protrude [prə'tru:d], *v.n.* herausragen, hervorstehen, vordringen.
protuberance [prə'tju:bərəns], *s.* der Höcker, der Auswuchs, die Protuberanz.
proud [praud], *adj.* stolz (*of*, auf, *Acc.*).
prove [pru:v], *v.a.* beweisen. — *v.n.* sich erweisen (*turn out*).
provender ['prɔvində], *s.* das Viehfutter.
proverb ['prɔvə:b], *s.* das Sprichwort.
proverbial [prə'və:biəl], *adj.* sprichwörtlich.
provide [prə'vaid], *v.a.*, *v.n.* vorsehen, versorgen, verschaffen.
provided [prə'vaidid], *conj.* vorausgesetzt.
providence ['prɔvidəns], *s.* die Vorsehung.
provident ['prɔvidənt], *adj.* vorsorglich.
providential [prɔvi'denʃəl], *adj.* von der Vorsehung bestimmt.
province ['prɔvins], *s.* die Provinz, das Gebiet (*also fig.*).
provincial [prə'vinʃəl], *adj.* ländlich, Provinz-; provinziell.
provision [prə'viʒən], *s.* die Versorgung (*supply*); der Vorrat (*stock*); (*pl.*) die Lebensmittel (*victuals*).
provisional [prə'viʒənəl], *adj.* vorläufig.
proviso [prə'vaizou], *s.* der Vorbehalt.
provocation [prɔvə'keiʃən], *s.* die Herausforderung.
provoke [prə'vouk], *v.a.* herausfordern, provozieren.
prow [prau], *s.* (*Naut.*) der Bug.
prowess ['praues], *s.* die Stärke (*physical*); die körperliche Tüchtigkeit; Tapferkeit.
prowl [praul], *v.n.* herumstreichen.
proximity [prɔk'simiti], *s.* die Nähe.
proxy ['prɔksi], *s.* der Stellvertreter.
prudence ['pru:dəns], *s.* die Klugheit, Vorsicht.
prudent ['pru:dənt], *adj.* klug, vorsichtig.

prudery ['pru:dəri], *s.* die Sprödigkeit.
prudish ['pru:diʃ], *adj.* prüde, spröde, zimperlich.
prune (1) [pru:n], *s.* (*Cul.*) die Backpflaume.
prune (2) [pru:n], *v.a.* beschneiden, stutzen.
Prussian ['prʌʃən], *adj.* preußisch; — *blue*, das Berlinerblau. — *s.* der Preuße.
prussic ['prʌsik], *adj.* blausauer; — *acid*, die Blausäure.
pry [prai], *v.n.* spähen, ausforschen.
psalm [sɑ:m], *s.* der Psalm.
psychology [sai'kɔlədʒi], *s.* die Psychologie.
pub [pʌb], *s.* das Wirtshaus, die Kneipe.
puberty ['pju:bəti], *s.* die Pubertät, Mannbarkeit.
public ['pʌblik], *adj.* öffentlich. — *s.* das Publikum; die Öffentlichkeit.
publican ['pʌblikən], *s.* der Gastwirt.
publication [pʌbli'keiʃən], *s.* die Veröffentlichung, Herausgabe.
publicity [pʌb'lisiti], *s.* die Werbung, die Reklame; — *manager*, der Reklamechef, Werbeleiter.
publicize ['pʌblisaiz], *v.a.* weithin bekannt machen, publizieren.
publish ['pʌbliʃ], *v.a.* veröffentlichen; verlegen (*books*); —*ing house*, der Verlag.
publisher ['pʌbliʃə], *s.* der Verleger.
pucker ['pʌkə], *v.a.* falten; runzeln (*wrinkle*). — *s.* die Falte.
pudding ['pudiŋ], *s.* der Pudding.
puddle [pʌdl], *s.* die Pfütze. — *v.a.* puddeln (*iron*).
puerile ['pjuərail], *adj.* kindisch, knabenhaft.
puff [pʌf], *v.a.*, *v.n.* puffen, paffen, blasen; —*ed-up*, aufgebläht, stolz. — *s.* der Windstoß; — *pastry*, der Blätterteig.
pug [pʌg], *s.* (*Zool.*) der Mops.
pugnacious [pʌg'neiʃəs], *adj.* kampfsüchtig, zankflustig.
puisne ['pju:ni], *adj.* (*Law*) jünger, Unter-.
puissant ['pwi:sənt], *adj.* mächtig, stark.
puke [pju:k], *v.n.* sich erbrechen.
pull [pul], *v.a.*, *v.n.* ziehen, reißen; zerren. — *s.* der Zug, Ruck.
pullet ['pulit], *s.* (*Orn.*) das Hühnchen.
pulley ['puli], *s.* der Flaschenzug.
pulmonary, pulmonic ['pʌlmənəri, pʌl'mɔnik], *adj.* Lungen-.
pulp [pʌlp], *s.* der Brei; das Fleisch (*of fruit*); das Mark (*marrow*); die Pulpa (*tooth*). — *v.a.* zerstampfen, zu Brei stampfen.
pulpit ['pulpit], *s.* (*Eccl.*) die Kanzel.
pulsate [pʌl'seit], *v.n.* pulsieren, schlagen.
pulse (1) [pʌls], *s.* der Puls.
pulse (2) [pʌls], *s.* (*Bot.*) die Hülsenfrüchte, *f. pl.*
pulverize ['pʌlvəraiz], *v.a.* zu Pulver stoßen, zerstoßen.

pumice ['pʌmis], *s.* der Bimsstein.
pump (1) [pʌmp], *s.* die Pumpe. — *v.a.*, *v.n.* pumpen; ausfragen (*question*).
pump (2) [pʌmp], *s.* der Tanzschuh (*dancing shoe*).
pumpkin ['pʌmpkin], *s.* (*Bot.*) der Kürbis.
pun [pʌn], *s.* das Wortspiel. — *v.n.* Wortspiele machen.
Punch [pʌntʃ]. das Kasperle; — *and Judy*, Hanswurst und seine Frau.
punch (1) [pʌntʃ], *v.a.* schlagen, boxen (*box*). — *s.* der Schlag (*hit*); der Faustschlag (*boxing*).
punch (2) [pʌntʃ], *v.a.* lochen (*card*). — *s.* der Pfriem (*tool*).
punch (3) [pʌntʃ], *s.* der Punsch (*drink*).
punchy ['pʌntʃi], *adj.* kurz, dick, untersetzt.
punctilious [pʌŋk'tiliəs], *adj.* sorgfältig, spitzfindig.
punctual ['pʌŋktjuəl], *adj.* pünktlich.
punctuate ['pʌŋktjueit], *v.a.* (*Gram.*) interpunktieren; (*fig.*) betonen.
punctuation [pʌŋktju'eiʃən], *s.* (*Gram.*) die Interpunktion.
puncture ['pʌŋktʃə], *s.* (*Motor.*) der Reifendefekt, die Panne; (*Med.*) die Punktur, der Einstich. — *v.a.* (*Med.*) punktieren.
pungent ['pʌndʒənt], *adj.* scharf, stechend.
punish ['pʌniʃ], *v.a.* bestrafen (*s.o.*); strafen.
punishable ['pʌniʃəbl], *adj.* strafbar.
punishment ['pʌniʃmənt], *s.* die Strafe, Bestrafung.
punt [pʌnt], *s.* das kleine Boot, Flachboot.
puny ['pjuːni], *adj.* schwach, winzig.
pup [pʌp], *s.* der junge Hund; *be sold a* —, einen schlechten Kauf machen. — *v.n.* Junge werfen.
pupil (1) ['pjuːpil], *s.* der Schüler.
pupil (2) ['pjuːpil], *s.* die Pupille (*eye*).
pupil(l)age ['pjuːpilidʒ], *s.* die Minderjährigkeit (*of minor*).
puppet ['pʌpit], *s.* die Puppe, Marionette; der Strohmann (*human tool*).
puppy ['pʌpi] *see* **pup**.
purblind ['pəːblaind], *adj.* halbblind.
purchase ['pəːtʃis], *s.* der Kauf, Einkauf. — *v.a.* kaufen.
pure ['pjuə], *adj.* pur, rein.
purge [pəːdʒ], *v.a.* reinigen. — *s.* die Reinigung; (*Pol.*) die Säuberung.
purify ['pjuərifai], *v.a.* läutern, reinigen.
purl (1) [pəːl], *s.* die Borte; (*knitting*) die Häkelkante.
purl (2) [pəːl], *v.n.* sich drehen, wirbeln; (*sl.*) umkippen.
purl (3) [pəːl], *s.* das Murmeln, Rieseln (*of brook*). — *v.n.* murmeln, rieseln.
purloin [pəː'lɔin], *v.a.* stehlen.
purple [pəːpl], *adj.* purpurn; — *patch*, die Glanzstelle. — *s.* der Purpur.
purport [pəː'pɔːt], *v.a.* bedeuten, Sinn haben. — ['pəːpət], *s.* der Sinn, die Bedeutung.
purpose ['pəːpəs], *s.* die Absicht, der Zweck.

purposeful ['pəːpəsful], *adj.* zweckbewußt, energisch, zielbewußt.
purr [pəː], *v.n.* schnurren (*of cat*).
purse [pəːs], *s.* die Börse, Geldtasche; das Portemonnaie.
pursuance [pə'sjuːəns], *s.* (*Law*) die Verfolgung, Ausführung.
pursuant [pə'sjuːənt], *adj.* (*Law*) zufolge, gemäß (*to, Dat.*).
pursue [pə'sjuː], *v.a.* verfolgen.
pursuit [pə'sjuːt], *s.* die Verfolgung; (*pl.*) die Geschäfte, *n. pl.*; Beschäftigung.
purvey [pə'vei], *v.a.* versorgen, liefern.
purview ['pəːvjuː], *s.* der Spielraum; das Blickfeld.
push [puʃ], *v.a.* stoßen, drücken, schieben, drängen; *be —ed for*, in der Klemme sein. — *s.* der Stoß, Schub, das Drängen; *at a —*, wenn absolut nötig.
pusillanimous [pjuːsi'læniməs], *adj.* kleinmütig.
puss, pussy [pus, 'pusi], *s.* (*coll.*) die Katze, das Kätzchen, Miezchen.
put [put], *v.a. irr.* setzen (*set*), legen (*lay*), stellen (*stand*), — *off*, aufschieben, aus der Fassung bringen (*deflect*); — *on*, anziehen, auflegen; — *it on thickly*, es dick auftragen. — *v.n.* (*Naut.*) — *in*, anlegen.
putrefy ['pjuːtrifai], *v.a.*, *v.n.* faul werden (*rot*), verwesen.
putrid ['pjuːtrid], *adj.* faul (*rotten*).
puttee [pʌti:], *s.* (*Mil.*) die Wickelgamasche.
putty ['pʌti], *s.* der Kitt.
puzzle [pʌzl], *s.* das Rätsel. — *v.a.* zu denken geben (*Dat.*).
pygmy ['pigmi], *s.* der Pygmäe.
pyjamas, (*Am.*) **pajamas** [pi'dʒaːməz, pə-], *s. pl.* der Schlafanzug.
pyramid ['pirəmid], *s.* die Pyramide.
pyre [paiə], *s.* der Scheiterhaufen.
pyrotechnics [paiərə'tekniks], *s. pl.* das Feuerwerk, die Feuerwerkskunst.
python ['paiθən], *s.* (*Zool.*) die Riesenschlange.

Q

Q [kjuː]. das Q.
qua [kwei], *conj.* als.
quack [kwæk], *v.n.* quaken; (*coll.*) quacksalbern. — *s.* der Quacksalber.
quadrangle ['kwɔdræŋgl], *s.* (*abbr.* **quad** [kwɔd]), das Viereck; der Hof (*in college etc*).
quadrant ['kwɔdrənt], *s.* der Quadrant, Viertelkreis; (*Engin.*) der Winkelmesser.
quadrille [kwɔ'dril], *s.* die Quadrille, der Kontertanz.

quadruped

quadruped ['kwɔdruped], *s.* (*Zool.*) das vierfüßige Tier.

quadruple ['kwɔdrupl], *adj.* vierfach.

quaff [kwæf], *v.a.* schlucken. — *v.n.* zechen (*drink heavily*).

quagmire ['kwægmaiə], *s.* der Sumpf.

quail (1) [kweil], *s.* (*Orn.*) die Wachtel.

quail (2) [kweil], *v.n.* verzagen.

quaint [kweint], *adj.* seltsam, wunderlich, eigenartig.

quake [kweik], *v.n.* erzittern, beben.

Quaker ['kweikə], *s.* der Quäker.

qualification [kwɔlifi'keiʃən], *s.* die Befähigung, Qualifikation (*ability*); die Einschränkung (*proviso*).

qualify ['kwɔlifai], *v.a.* befähigen (*make able*); beschränken, mäßigen, qualifizieren (*modify*). — *v.n.* sich qualifizieren, das Studium abschließen.

qualitative ['kwɔlitətiv], *adj.* qualitätsmäßig, Wert-, qualitativ.

quality ['kwɔliti], *s.* die Qualität (*high class*); der Wert (*standard*).

qualm [kwɑːm], *s.* der Skrupel.

quantitative ['kwɔntitətiv], *adj.* quantitativ.

quantity ['kwɔntiti], *s.* die Quantität, Menge.

quantum ['kwɔntəm], *s.* die Menge; das Quantum; — *theory*, die Quantentheorie.

quarantine ['kwɔrəntiːn], *s.* die Quarantäne.

quarrel ['kwɔrəl], *s.* der Streit, Zwist. — *v.n.* streiten, zanken.

quarry (1) ['kwɔri], *s.* der Steinbruch.

quarry (2) ['kwɔri], *s.* die Beute (*prey*).

quart [kwɔːt], *s.* das Viertelmaß (*1.15 litre*).

quarter ['kwɔːtə], *s.* das Viertel (jahr); (*Arith.*) das Viertel (*also of town*); (*pl.*) das Quartier.

quartermaster ['kwɔːtəmɑːstə], *s.* (*Mil.*) der Feldzeugmeister.

quartet(te) [kwɔːˈtet], *s.* das Quartett.

quarto ['kwɔːtou], *s.* das Quartformat.

quartz [kwɔːts], *s.* der Quartz.

quash [kwɔʃ], *v.a.* unterdrücken (*suppress*); (*Law*) annullieren.

quaver ['kweivə], *s.* (*Mus.*) die Achtelnote; der Triller (*trill*). — *v.n.* tremolieren, trillern.

quay [kiː], *s.* der Kai, Hafendamm.

queen [kwiːn], *s.* die Königin.

queer [kwiə], *adj.* seltsam, sonderlich.

quell [kwel], *v.a.* unterdrücken.

quench [kwentʃ], *v.a.* löschen; stillen (*thirst*).

querulous ['kweruləs], *adj.* mürrisch, jämmerlich; zänkisch.

query ['kwiəri], *s.* die Frage. — *v.a.* in Frage stellen.

quest [kwest], *s.* das Suchen, Streben; die Suche.

question ['kwestʃən], *s.* die Frage; — *mark*, das Fragezeichen. — *v.a.* fragen, in Frage stellen; ausfragen (*s.o.*).

questionable ['kwestʃənəbl], *adj.* zweifelhaft, fraglich, bedenklich.

queue [kjuː], *s.* die Schlange, das Anstellen. — *v.n.* Schlange stehen.

quibble [kwibl], *s.* das Wortspiel, die Ausflucht. — *v.n.* um Worte streiten.

quick [kwik], *adj.* schnell (*fast*); lebendig (*live*).

quicken ['kwikən], *v.a.* beleben, anfeuern.

quicklime ['kwiklaim], *s.* der ungelöschte Kalk.

quicksand ['kwiksænd], *s.* der Flugsand.

quicksilver ['kwiksilvə], *s.* (*Chem.*) das Quecksilber.

quid (1) [kwid], *s.* (*sl.*) das Pfund Sterling.

quid (2) [kwid], *s.* (*Lat.*) etwas; — *pro quo*, Gleiches mit Gleichem.

quiescence [kwi'esəns], *s.* die Ruhe.

quiet ['kwaiət], *adj.* ruhig.

quietism ['kwaiətizm], *s.* der Quietismus.

quietness ['kwaiətnis], *s.* die Ruhe, Stille.

quill [kwil], *s.* der Federkiel, die Feder. — *v.a.* falten, fälteln.

quilt [kwilt], *s.* die Steppdecke.

quince [kwins], *s.* (*Bot.*) die Quitte.

quinine [kwi'niːn], *s.* (*Med.*) das Chinin.

quinquennial [kwin'kweniəl], *adj.* fünfjährig, fünfjährlich, alle fünf Jahre.

quinsy ['kwinzi], *s.* (*Med.*) die Bräune.

quint [kwint], *s.* (*Mus.*) die Quinte.

quintessence [kwin'tesəns], *s.* die Quintessenz, der Kern, der Inbegriff.

quintuple ['kwintjupl], *adj.* fünffach.

quip [kwip], *s.* die Stichelei; die witzige Bemerkung.

quire [kwaiə], *s.* das Buch Papier.

quirk [kwəːk], *s.* die (unerwartete) Wendung; Spitzfindigkeit.

quit [kwit], *v.a.*, *v.n.* verlassen; weggehen; (*Am.*) aufhören. — *adj.* (*pl.*) (**quits**) quitt, bezahlt.

quite [kwait], *adv.* ganz, völlig.

quiver (1) ['kwivə], *s.* der Köcher.

quiver (2) ['kwivə], *v.n.* erzittern, schauern.

quiz [kwiz], *s.* das Fragespiel, Quizprogramm (*Radio etc.*).

quoit [kɔit], *s.* die Wurfscheibe.

quorum ['kwɔːrəm], *s.* die beschlußfähige Anzahl.

quota ['kwoutə], *s.* die Quote.

quotation [kwo'teiʃən], *s.* das Zitat; (*Comm.*) der Kostenanschlag, die Notierung.

quote [kwout], *v.a.* zitieren; (*Comm.*) einen Preis zitieren, notieren.

R

R [ɑː(r)]. das R.

rabbet ['ræbit], *s.* die Fuge, Nute. — *v.a.* einfugen.

rabbi ['ræbai], *s.* (*Rel.*) der Rabbiner.
rabbit ['ræbit], *s.* (*Zool.*) das Kaninchen.
rabble [ræbl], *s.* der Pöbel.
rabid ['ræbid], *adj.* wütend, rasend.
race (1) [reis], *s.* die Rasse; das Geschlecht (*stock*).
race (2) [reis], *s.* das Rennen (*horses etc.*); der Wettlauf (*run*); — *course*, die Rennbahn. — *v.a.*, *v.n.* um die Wette laufen.
racial ['reiʃəl], *adj.* rassisch.
raciness ['reisinis], *s.* das Rassige, die Urwüchsigkeit.
rack [ræk], *s.* die Folterbank; das Reck (*gymnasium*); (*Railw.*) das Gepäcknetz. — *v.a.* recken, strecken; — *o.'s brains*, sich den Kopf zerbrechen.
racket (1), **racquet** ['rækit], *s.* der Tennisschläger.
racket (2) ['rækit], *s.* der Lärm (*noise*, *din*).
racket (3) ['rækit], *s.* (*coll.*) der Schwindel.
racketeer [ræki'tiə], *s.* der Schwindler.
racy ['reisi], *adj.* stark; pikant.
radar, ['reidɑ:], *s.* das Radar.
radiance ['reidiəns], *s.* der Glanz, das Strahlen.
radiant ['reidiənt], *adj.* strahlend.
radiate ['reidieit], *v.a.*, *v.n.* strahlen, ausstrahlen.
radiator ['reidieitə], *s.* der Heizapparat, Heizkörper; (*Motor.*) der Kühler.
radical ['rædikəl], *adj.* (*Pol.*) radikal; gründlich (*thorough*). — *s.* (*Pol.*) der Radikale; (*Phonet.*) der Grundlaut, Wurzellaut.
radio ['reidiou], *s.* das Radio, der Rundfunk.
radioactive [reidiou'æktiv], *adj.* radioaktiv.
radish ['rædiʃ], *s.* (*Bot.*) der Rettich.
radius ['reidiəs], *s.* der Radius, Halbmesser; (*Phys.*, *Maths.*) der Strahl (*line*).
raffle [ræfl], *s.* die Auslosung. — *v.a.* auslosen, ausspielen.
raft [rɑ:ft], *s.* das Floß.
rafter ['rɑ:ftə], *s.* der Dachsparren.
rag (1) [ræg], *s.* der Lumpen.
rag (2) [ræg], *v.a.* necken, zum Besten haben (*tease*).
ragamuffin ['rægəmʌfin], *s.* der Lumpenkerl.
rage [reidʒ], *s.* die Wut, Raserei; die Manie, Mode (*fashion*). — *v.n.* wüten, rasen.
ragged ['rægid], *adj.* zerlumpt; zackig, rauh (*rough*).
ragout [ræ'gu:], *s.* (*Cul.*) das Ragout.
raid [reid], *s.* der Streifzug, die Razzia; der Angriff. — *v.a.* überfallen.
rail (1) [reil], *s.* (*Railw.*) die Schiene; *by* —, mit der Eisenbahn.
rail (2) [reil], *v.n.* schmähen; spotten (*Genit.*).
railing ['reilin], *s.* das Geländer, Gitter.
raillery ['reiləri], *s.* die Spötterei, das Schmähen.

railway, (*Am.*) **railroad** ['reilwei, 'reilroud], *s.* die Eisenbahn.
raiment ['reimənt], *s.* (*Poet.*) die Kleidung.
rain [rein], *s.* der Regen. — *v.n.* regnen.
rainbow ['reinbou], *s.* der Regenbogen.
raincoat ['reinkout], *s.* der Regenmantel.
raise [reiz], *v.a.* heben (*lift*); steigern (*prices*); aufbringen (*army*, *money*); züchten (*breed*); aufziehen (*children*). — *s.* (*Am.*) die Steigerung, Erhöhung (*salary*).
raisin ['reizin], *s.* (*Bot.*) die Rosine.
rake (1) [reik], *s.* der Rechen (*tool*). — *v.a.* zusammenrechen, harken; bestreichen (*fire at*).
rake (2) [reik], *s.* der Schlemmer (*roué*).
rakish ['reikiʃ], *adj.* liederlich.
rally ['ræli], *v.a.* sammeln, versammeln. — *v.n.* sich versammeln, sich scharen. — *s.* die Massenversammlung, Kundgebung; das Treffen.
ram [ræm], *s.* der Widder; (*Mil.*) die Ramme. — *v.a.* rammen.
ramble [ræmbl], *v.n.* (im Grünen) wandern; herumschweifen; einen Ausflug machen. — *s.* der Ausflug.
rambler ['ræmblə], *s.* der Wanderer (*hiker*); (*Bot.*) die Heckenrose.
ramification [ræmifi'keiʃən], *s.* die Verzweigung, Verästelung (*also fig.*); (*pl.*) Zweige, *m. pl.* (*also fig.*).
ramp [ræmp], *v.n.* sich ranken (*of plants*). — *s.* die Rampe.
rampant ['ræmpənt], *adj.* zügellos, grassierend (*wild*); (*Her.*) sich bäumend.
rampart ['ræmpɑ:t], *s.* der Wall.
ramshackle ['ræmʃækl], *adj.* wackelig, baufällig.
rancid ['rænsid], *adj.* ranzig.
rancour ['ræŋkə], *s.* der Groll, die Erbitterung.
random ['rændəm], *s. at* —, aufs Geratewohl. — *adj.* zufällig, Zufalls-.
range [reindʒ], *s.* die Reihe (*row*, *series*); (*Geog.*) die Bergkette; der Küchenherd (*stove*); (*Mil.*) die Schießstätte (*shooting ground*); die Schußweite, Reichweite (*distance*). — *v.n.* sich reihen; sich erstrecken (*stretch*). — *v.a.* rangieren, anordnen, durchstreifen.
rangefinder ['reindʒfaində], *s.* (*Phot.*) der Entfernungsmesser.
ranger ['reindʒə], *s.* der Förster, Forstgehilfe; (*Mil.*) der leichte Reiter.
rank (1) [ræŋk], *s.* die Klasse; der Rang (*order*); — *and file*, die Mannschaft (*of members*); die Mitgliedschaft, Masse. — *v.n.* sich reihen; gelten.
rank (2) [ræŋk], *adj.* übermäßig, üppig, allzu stark; ranzig (*of fat etc.*).
rankle [ræŋkl], *v.n.* nagen.
ransack ['rænsæk], *v.a.* plündern.
ransom ['rænsəm], *s.* das Lösegeld; *hold to* —, (gegen Lösegeld) gefangen halten. — *v.a.* loskaufen.

rant [rænt], *v.n.* wüten; großtun; großsprechen.

rap [ræp], *v.a., v.n.* schlagen, klopfen.

rapacious [rə'peiʃəs], *adj.* raubgierig.

rape (1) [reip], *v.a.* vergewaltigen. — *s.* die Vergewaltigung.

rape (2) [reip], *s.* (*Bot.*) der Raps.

rapid ['ræpid], *adj.* rasch, schnell, reißend (*river*). — *s.* (*pl.*) die Stromschnelle.

rapier ['reipiə], *s.* der Degen; (*fencing*) das Rapier.

rapine ['ræpain], *s.* (*Poet.*) der Raub.

rapt [ræpt], *adj.* entzückt; versunken.

rapture ['ræptʃə], *s.* das Entzücken.

rare (1) [rɛə], *adj.* selten.

rare (2) [rɛə], *adj.* (*meat*) rar.

rarity ['rɛəriti], *s.* die Seltenheit.

rascal ['rɑːskəl], *s.* der Schurke.

rash (1) [ræʃ], *adj.* unbesonnen.

rash (2) [ræʃ], *s.* der Ausschlag (*skin*).

rasher ['ræʃə], *s.* die Speckschnitte.

rasp [rɑːsp], *s.* die Raspel, Feile. — *v.a., v.n.* raspeln; heiser sein (*speech*).

raspberry ['rɑːzbəri], *s.* (*Bot.*) die Himbeere.

rat [ræt], *s.* (*Zool.*) die Ratte; (*fig.*) der Verräter.

ratable ['reitəbl], *adj.* steuerpflichtig.

rate (1) [reit], *s.* das Mass; der Tarif; die Geschwindigkeit (*speed*); Gemeindeabgabe (*tax*); das Verhältnis (*proportion*). — *v.a.* schätzen (*estimate*); (*Am.*) einschätzen, halten für.

rate (2) [reit], *v.a.* schelten (*berate*).

rather ['rɑːðə], *adv.* vielmehr, eher, lieber (*in comparisons*); — *good,* ziemlich gut.

ratification [rætifi'keiʃən], *s.* die Bestätigung; (*Pol.*) die Ratifizierung.

ratify ['rætifai], *v.a.* bestätigen; (*Pol.*) ratifizieren.

ratio ['reiʃiou], *s.* das Verhältnis.

ration ['ræʃən], *s.* die Ration.

rational ['ræʃənəl], *adj.* Vernunfts-, rationell, vernunftgemäß.

rattle ['rætl], *s.* das Geklapper (*noise*); die Klapper (*toy etc.*); *death* —, das Todesröcheln. — *v.a.* klappern, Lärm machen; (*fig.*) aus der Fassung bringen; — *off,* herunterleiern. — *v.n.* rasseln, klappern.

raucous ['rɔːkəs], *adj.* heiser, rauh.

ravage ['rævidʒ], *v.a.* verheeren. — *s.* (*pl.*) die Verheerung, Verwüstung.

rave [reiv], *v.n.* vernarrt sein (*about,* in); schwärmen (*für*).

raven [reivn], *s.* (*Orn.*) der Rabe.

ravenous ['rævənəs], *adj.* gefräßig, gierig.

ravine [rə'viːn], *s.* die Schlucht.

ravish ['ræviʃ], *v.a.* schänden, entehren; (*delight*) entzücken.

raw [rɔː], *adj.* rauh (*rough*); roh (*meat*); jung, grün (*novice*); *a* — *deal,* die unfaire Behandlung.

ray (1) [rei], *s.* (*Phys.*) der Strahl. — *v.n.* strahlen.

ray (2) [rei], *s.* (*Zool.*) der Rochen.

raze [reiz], *v.a.* radieren (*erase*); zer-

stören (*destroy*).

razor ['reizə], *s.* der Rasierapparat; — *strop,* der Streichriemen.

re* [riː], *pref.* wieder —, noch einmal, zurück-.

* In the following pages, only those compounds are listed in which the meaning is different from the root word or where no simple stem exists.

reach [riːtʃ], *v.a.* reichen, erlangen (*attain*); reichen (*hand*); erreichen. — *s.* der Bereich, (*fig.*) die Weite.

react [ri'ækt], *v.n.* reagieren (*to,* auf, *Acc.*).

read (1) [riːd], *v.a., v.n. irr.* lesen; anzeigen (*meter etc.*); — *for a degree,* studieren.

read (2) [red], *adj. well*—, belesen.

readable ['riːdəbl], *adj.* gut zu lesen, lesenswert; leserlich (*legible*).

reader ['riːdə], *s.* der Leser; (*Univ.*) der außerordentliche Professor; (*fig.*) das Lesebuch.

readiness ['redinis], *s.* die Bereitschaft, Bereitwilligkeit.

ready ['redi], *adj.* bereit, fertig; prompt; — *money,* das Bargeld.

real [riəl], *adj.* wirklich, wahr, tatsächlich; echt; *estate,* der Grundbesitz.

realistic [riə'listik], *adj.* realistisch.

reality [ri'æliti], *s.* die Wirklichkeit.

realize ['riəlaiz], *v.a.* (*understand*) begreifen;(*sell*) veräußern;verwirklichen.

realm [relm], *s.* das Reich.

reap [riːp], *v.a.* ernten.

rear (1) [riə], *adj.* hinter, nach-. — *s.* der Hintergrund; (*Mil.*) die Nachhut.

rear (2) [riə], *v.a.* aufziehen, erziehen (*bring up*). — *v.n.* sich bäumen.

reason ['riːzən], *s.* die Ursache, der Grund (*cause*); die Vernunft (*reasonableness*). — *v.n.* argumentieren, debattieren.

reasonable ['riːzənəbl], *adj.* vernünftig; verständig.

reasonably ['riːzənəbli], *adv.* ziemlich, verhältnismäßig.

rebate ['riːbeit], *s.* der Rabatt.

rebel [rebl], *s.* der Rebell. — [ri'bel], *v.n.* sich empören.

rebound [ri'baund], *v.n.* zurückprallen. —['riːbaund], *s.* der Rückprall.

rebuff [ri'bʌf], *s.* die Abweisung. — *v.a.* abweisen, zurückweisen.

rebuke [ri'bjuːk], *v.a.* zurechtweisen, tadeln. — *s.* der Tadel, die Kritik (an).

rebut [ri'bʌt], *v.a.* zurückweisen.

rebuttal [ri'bʌtl], *s.* die Widerlegung.

recalcitrant [ri'kælsitrənt], *adj.* widerspenstig, störrisch.

recall [ri'kɔːl], *v.a.* zurückrufen; (*remember*) sich erinnern.

recant [ri'kænt], *v.a., v.n.* widerrufen.

recapitulate [riːkə'pitjuleit], *v.a.* rekapitulieren, wiederholen.

recast [riː'kɑːst], *v.a.* neu fassen, umarbeiten.

recede [ri'siːd], *v.n.* zurückgehen; heruntergehen (*prices etc.*).

receipt [ri'si:t], *s.* die Empfangsbestätigung, Quittung. — *v.a.* quittieren.

receive [ri'si:v], *v.a.* erhalten, empfangen; (*Law*) Diebesgut annehmen.

receiver [ri'si:və], *s.* der Empfänger; (*Law*) der Hehler; (*Telephone*) der Hörer; (*Rad.*) der Apparat.

recent ['ri:sənt], *adj.* jüngst, neuest.

recently ['ri:səntli], *adv.* vor kurzem.

reception [ri'sepʃən], *s.* der Empfang.

receptive [ri'septiv], *adj.* empfänglich.

recess [ri'ses], *s.* (*Parl.*) die Ferien, *pl.*; die Pause; die Nische (*nook*).

recession [ri'seʃən], *s.* (*Econ.*) die Rezession, die Baisse.

recipe ['resipi], *s.* (*Cul.*) das Rezept.

recipient [ri'sipiənt], *s.* der Empfänger (*of donation etc.*).

reciprocal [ri'siprəkəl], *adj.* gegenseitig, wechselseitig.

reciprocate [ri'siprəkeit], *v.a., v.n.* erwidern, vergelten.

recital [ri'saitl], *s.* der Vortrag; (*Mus.*) das Solokonzert, Kammerkonzert.

recite [ri'sait], *v.a.* vortragen; (*story*) erzählen, aufsagen.

reckless ['reklis], *adj.* leichtsinnig.

reckon ['rekən], *v.n.* rechnen (*on*, mit, *Dat.*); dafür halten, denken (*think*).

reclamation [reklə'meiʃən], *s.* (*Agr.*) die Urbarmachung; (*fig.*) die Beschwerde, Reklamation.

recline [ri'klain], *v.n.* sich zurücklehnen.

recluse [ri'klu:s], *s.* der Einsiedler.

recognition [rekəg'niʃən], *s.* die Anerkennung.

recognize ['rekəgnaiz], *v.a.* anerkennen (als) (*acknowledge*); erkennen (*know again*).

recoil [ri'kɔil], *v.n.* zurückprallen, zurückfahren.

recollect [rekə'lekt], *v.a.* sich erinnern (an, *Acc.*).

recollection [rekə'lekʃən], *s.* die Erinnerung, das Gedächtnis.

recommend [rekə'mend], *v.a.* empfehlen.

recompense ['rekəmpens], *v.a.* vergelten, entschädigen, belohnen.

reconcile ['rekənsail], *v.a.* versöhnen.

reconciliation [rekənsili'eiʃən], *s.* die Versöhnung.

recondite ['rekəndait], *adj.* dunkel, verborgen, wenig bekannt.

reconnoitre [rekə'nɔitə], *v.a.* auskundschaften.

record [ri'kɔ:d], *v.a.* notieren, eintragen (*enter*), festhalten; aufnehmen (*tape etc.*). — ['rekɔ:d], *s.* die Aufzeichnung (*in writing*); die Schallplatte (*gramophone*); (*Sports*) der Rekord.

recorder [ri'kɔ:də], *s.* der Protokollführer; (*Law*) der Richter; Syndikus, Registrator; (*Mus.*) die Blockflöte.

recount [ri'kaunt], *v.a.* erzählen

recourse [ri'kɔ:s], *s.* die Zuflucht.

recover [ri'kʌvə], *v.a.* wiedererlangen. — *v.n.* sich erholen.

recovery [ri'kʌvəri], *s.* die Wiedererlangung (*regaining*); (*Med.*) die Genesung, Erholung.

recreation [rekri'eiʃən], *s.* die Erholung.

recrimination [rekrimi'neiʃən], *s.* die Gegenklage.

recruit [ri'kru:t], *v.a.* rekrutieren, anwerben. — *s.* der Rekrut.

rectangle ['rektæŋgl], *s.* das Rechteck.

rectify ['rektifai], *v.a.* richtigstellen; (*Elec.*) gleichrichten, umformen.

rectilinear [rekti'liniə], *adj.* geradlinig.

rectitude ['rektitju:d], *s.* die Aufrichtigkeit.

rector ['rektə], *s.* (*Eccl.*) der Pfarrer; der Rektor, Vorstand (*institution*).

recuperate [ri'kju:pəreit], *v.n.* sich erholen.

recur [ri'kə:], *v.n.* sich wieder ereignen, sich wiederholen.

recurrence [ri'kʌrəns], *s.* die Wiederholung.

red [red], *adj.* rot; — *hot*, glühend heiß.

redbreast ['redbrest], *s.* (*Orn.*) das Rotkehlchen.

redeem [ri'di:m], *v.a.* erlösen.

redemption [ri'dempʃən], *s.* die Erlösung.

redolent ['redolənt], *adj.* duftend.

redound [ri'daund], *v.n.* gereichen, sich erweisen.

redress [ri'dres], *v.a.* abhelfen (*Dat.*); wieder herstellen. — *s.* die Abhilfe.

reduce [ri'dju:s], *v.a.* vermindern, herabsetzen; (*fig.*) degradieren. — *v.n.* (*weight*) abnehmen.

reduction [ri'dʌkʃən], *s.* die Herabsetzung (*price etc.*); die Verminderung (*decrease*); (*Chem.*) die Reduktion.

redundant [ri'dʌndənt], *adj.* überflüssig.

reduplicate [ri:'dju:plikeit], *v.a.* verdoppeln.

reed [ri:d], *s.* (*Bot.*) das Schilfrohr; (*Mus.*) die Rohrpfeife.

reef [ri:f], *s.* das Riff, Felsenriff; (*Naut.*) das Reff.

reek [ri:k], *v.n.* rauchen, dampfen, riechen. — *s.* der Rauch, Dampf, der Gestank.

reel [ri:l], *s.* die Spule, Rolle, Haspel. — *v.a.* — *off*, abrollen; (*fig.*) mechanisch hersagen. — *v.n.* taumeln.

refectory [ri'fektəri], *s.* der Speisesaal; das Refektorium (*in monastery etc.*).

refer [ri'fə:], *v.n.* — *to s.th.*, weiterleiten; überweisen; — *to*, sich beziehen (auf, *Acc.*).

referee [refə'ri:], *s.* der Referent; (*Sport*) der Schiedsrichter.

reference ['refərəns], *s.* with — *to*, in or mit Bezug auf; die Referenz, Empfehlung; Verweisung (*to*, auf); — *library*, die Nachschlagebibliothek; — *index*, das (Nachschlags)verzeichnis.

refine [ri'fain], *v.a.* (*Chem.*) raffinieren; (*manners*) verfeinern; (*products*) läutern, veredeln.

reflect [ri'flekt], *v.a.* widerspiegeln (*mirror*); ein Licht werfen (auf, *Acc.*). — *v.n.* — *on*, überlegen (*think over*).

reflection, reflexion [ri'flekʃən], *s.* die Überlegung, das Nachdenken; die Spiegelung, Reflexion.

reform [ri:'fɔ:m], *s.* die Reform, Verbesserung. — *v.a.* reformieren; ['ri:'fɔ:m] (sich) neu bilden. — *v.n.* sich bessern.

refractory [ri'fræktəri], *adj.* widerspenstig.

refrain (1) [ri'frein], *v.n.* — *from*, sich enthalten (*Genit.*); absehen von (*Dat.*).

refrain (2) [ri'frein], *s.* (*Mus., Poet.*) der Kehrreim.

refresh [ri'freʃ], *v.a.* erfrischen.

refrigerator [ri'fridʒəreitə], *s.* der Kühlschrank.

refuge ['refju:dʒ], *s.* die Zuflucht.

refugee [refju'dʒi:], *s.* der Flüchtling. — *adj.* Flüchtlings-.

refund [ri:'fʌnd], *v.a.* ersetzen, zurückzahlen. — ['ri:fʌnd], *s.* die Rückvergütung.

refusal [ri'fju:zəl], *s.* die Verweigerung.

refuse [ri'fju:z], *v.a.* verweigern, abschlagen. — *v.n.* — *to*, sich weigern. — ['refju:s], *s.* der Müll.

refute [ri'fju:t], *v.a.* widerlegen.

regal ['ri:gəl], *adj.* königlich.

regale [ri'geil], *v.a.* bewirten.

regalia [ri'geiliə], *s. pl.* die Kronjuwelen, *n. pl.*; (*fig.*) die Amtstracht, der Amtsschmuck.

regard [ri'ga:d], *v.a.* ansehen (*as*, als); beachten (*heed*); *as* —*s*, was . . . betrifft. — *s.* die Hochachtung, Achtung (*esteem*);(*pl.*)die Grüsse,*m.pl.*

regarding [ri'ga:diŋ], *prep.* bezüglich, mit Bezug auf.

regardless [ri'ga:dlis], *adj.* rücksichtslos, ohne Rücksicht auf.

regency ['ri:dʒənsi], *s.* die Regentschaft.

regent ['ri:dʒənt], *s.* der Regent.

regiment ['redʒimənt], *s.* (*Mil.*) das Regiment. — [-ment], *v.a.* (*fig.*) regimentieren.

region ['ri:dʒən], *s.* die Gegend.

regional ['ri:dʒənəl], *adj.* örtlich, lokal, Bezirks-.

register ['redʒistə], *s.* das Register, die Liste. — *v.n.* sich eintragen.

registrar ['redʒistra:], *s.* der Registrator; der Standesbeamte (*births etc.*); der Kanzleidirektor (*institution*).

registry ['redʒistri], *s.* die Registratur.

regret [ri'gret], *v.a.* bereuen, bedauern. — *s.* die Reue; das Bedauern (*in formal apology*); *with* —, mit Bedauern.

regular ['regjulə], *adj.* regelmäßig; (*Am.*) anständig. — *s.* (*Mil.*) der Berufssoldat.

regulate ['regjuleit], *v.a.* regulieren, regeln.

regulation [regju'leiʃən], *s.* die Regelung; die Anordung (*order*).

rehabilitate [ri:hə'biliteit], *v.a.* rehabilitieren.

rehearsal [ri'hə:sl], *s.* (*Theat., Mus.*) die Probe.

rehearse [ri'hə:s], *v.a.* proben, wiederholen.

reign [rein], *v.n.* herrschen, regieren. — *s.* die Herrschaft, Regierung.

rein [rein], *s.* der Zügel, der Zaum.

reindeer ['reindiə], *s.* (*Zool.*) das Ren, Rentier.

reinforce [ri:in'fɔ:s], *v.a.* betonen, verstärken.

reinforced [ri:in'fɔ:sd], *adj.* verstärkt; — *concrete*, der Eisenbeton.

reject [ri'dʒekt], *v.a.* ausschlagen, verwerfen.

rejection [ri'dʒekʃən], *s.* die Ablehnung, Verwerfung.

rejoice [ri'dʒɔis], *v.n.* sich freuen.

rejoin ['ri:'dʒɔin],*v.a.* wiedervereinigen. — [ri'dʒɔin], *v.n.* erwidern.

rejoinder [ri'dʒɔində], *s.* die Erwiderung.

relapse [ri'læps], *s.* der Rückfall. — *v.n.* fallen, zurückfallen.

relation [ri'leiʃən], *s.* die Beziehung (*connexion*); der Verwandte (*relative*); (*pl.*) die Verwandtschaft (*family*).

relative ['relətiv], *adj.* relativ; verhältnismäßig (*in proportion*). — *s.* der, die Verwandte.

relax [ri'læks], *v.n.* sich ausruhen; nachlassen. — *v.a.* entspannen.

relay [ri'lei], *v.a.* (*Rad.*) übertragen. — ['ri:lei], *s.* — *race*, der Staffellauf.

release [ri'li:s], *v.a.* freilassen, freisetzen (*prisoner*); freigeben (*news*). — *s.* die Freigabe (*news etc.*); die Freisetzung (*liberation*).

relegate ['religeit], *v.a.* verweisen, zurückweisen.

relent [ri'lent], *v.n.* nachgeben.

relentless [ri'lentlis], *adj.* unerbittlich, unnachgiebig.

relevance ['reləvəns], *s.* die Wichtigkeit.

relevant ['reləvənt], *adj.* wichtig, sachdienlich.

reliable [ri'laiəbl], *adj.* verläßlich, zuverlässig.

reliance [ri'laiəns], *s.* das Vertrauen.

relic ['relik], *s.* das Überbleibsel; das Andenken; (*Eccl.*) die Reliquie.

relief (1) [ri'li:f], *s.* die Erleichterung, Linderung, (*easement*); die Ablösung (*guard etc.*); die Aushilfe (*extra staff etc.*).

relief (2) [ri'li:f], *s.* (*Art*) das Relief.

relieve [ri'li:v], *v.a.* erleichtern; lindern (*pain*); ablösen (*from duty*).

religion [ri'lidʒən], *s.* die Religion.

religious [ri'lidʒəs], *adj.* religiös, gläubig, fromm.

relinquish [ri'liŋkwiʃ], *v.a.* verlassen, aufgeben.

relish [ˈreliʃ], v.a. Geschmack finden an. — v.n. schmecken. — s. der Geschmack, die Würze.

reluctance [riˈlʌktəns], s. der Widerwille, das Zögern.

reluctant [riˈlʌktənt], adj. widerwillig, widerstrebend.

rely [riˈlai], v.n. sich verlassen (on, auf); vertrauen (auf).

remain [riˈmein], v.n. bleiben, zurückbleiben, übrigbleiben.

remainder [riˈmeində], s. der Rest.

remand [riˈmaːnd], v.a. — in custody, in die Untersuchungshaft zurückschicken. — s. — home, die Besserungsanstalt.

remark [riˈmaːk], s. die Bemerkung. — v.a. bemerken.

remarkable [riˈmaːkəbl], adj. bemerkenswert, außerordentlich.

remedial [rəˈmiːdiəl], adj. Heil-, abhelfend.

remedy [ˈremədi], s. das Heilmittel, Hilfsmittel. — v.a. abhelfen (Dat.).

remember [riˈmembə], v.a. sich erinnern an; — s.o. to s.o. else, jemanden von jemandem grüßen lassen.

remembrance [riˈmembrəns], s. die Erinnerung.

remind [riˈmaind], v.a. erinnern (of, an), mahnen.

reminiscence [remiˈnisəns], s. die Erinnerung.

remiss [riˈmis], adj. nachlässig.

remission [riˈmiʃən], s. der Nachlaß; (Rel.) die Vergebung (sins).

remit [riˈmit], v.a. (Comm.) überweisen, einsenden; erlassen (forgive).

remittance [riˈmitəns], s. (Comm.) die Rimesse, die Überweisung.

remnant [ˈremnənt], s. der Überrest.

remonstrate [ˈremənstreit], v.n. Vorstellungen machen.

remorse [riˈmɔːs], s. die Reue.

remote [riˈmout], adj. fern, entlegen.

removal [riˈmuːvəl], s. das Wegschaffen (taking away); die Übersiedlung, der Umzug.

remove [riˈmuːv], v.a. entfernen. — v.n. umziehen. — s. (Sch.) die Versetzungsklasse; der Verwandtschaftsgrad (relationship).

removed [riˈmuːvd], adj. entfernt; cousin once —, der Vetter ersten Grades.

remuneration [rimjuːnəˈreiʃən], s. die Besoldung, Entlohnung.

rend [rend], v.a. reißen, zerreißen.

render [ˈrendə], v.a. leisten (service); übersetzen (translate); wiedergeben; (Comm.) — account, Rechnung vorlegen.

rendering [ˈrendəriŋ], s. die Wiedergabe, der Vortrag (of song etc.); (Comm.) die Vorlage; die Übersetzung (translation).

renegade [ˈrenigeid], s. der Abtrünnige.

renewal [riˈnjuːəl], s. die Erneuerung; die Verlängerung (extension).

rennet [ˈrenit], s. das Lab.

renounce [riˈnauns], v.a. entsagen (Dat.), verzichten auf (Acc.).

renown [riˈnaun], s. der Ruhm.

rent (1) [rent], v.a. mieten, pachten. — s. die Miete, Pacht (of land, farm).

rent (2) [rent], s. der Riß (tear).

rental [rentl], s. die Miete.

renunciation [rinʌnsiˈeiʃən], s. die Entsagung, der Verzicht.

repair [riˈpɛə], v.a. ausbessern, reparieren. — s. die Reparatur; beyond —, nicht reparierbar.

reparations [repəˈreiʃənz], s. pl. (Pol.) die Reparationen, Wiedergutmachungskosten, f. pl.

repartee [repaːˈtiː], s. die treffende Antwort.

repast [riˈpaːst], s. die Mahlzeit.

repeal [riˈpiːl], v.a. (Parl.) aufheben, widerrufen. — s. die Aufhebung.

repeat [riˈpiːt], v.a. wiederholen.

repent [riˈpent], v.a. bereuen.

repercussion [riːpəˈkʌʃən], s. der Rückstoß, die Rückwirkung.

repertory [ˈrepətəri], s. (Theat. etc.) das Repertoire, der Spielplan.

repetition [repiˈtiʃən], s. die Wiederholung.

replace [riˈpleis], v.a. ersetzen.

replete [riˈpliːt], adj. voll, angefüllt.

reply [riˈplai], v.n. antworten, erwidern. — s. die Antwort.

report [riˈpɔːt], v.a., v.n. berichten. — s. der Bericht; (Sch.) das Zeugnis; der Knall (of explosion).

repose [riˈpouz], v.n. ruhen. — v.a. setzen (in, auf). — s. die Ruhe, der Friede.

repository [riˈpɔzitəri], s. die Niederlage, Aufbewahrungsstätte, Fundstätte.

reprehensible [repriˈhensibl], adj. tadelnswert.

represent [repriˈzent], v.a. repräsentieren, vertreten.

representative [repriˈzentətiv], adj. repräsentativ, typisch. — s. der Stellvertreter; (Pol.) der Repräsentant.

repress [riˈpres], v.a. unterdrücken.

reprieve [riˈpriːv], v.a. begnadigen. — s. die Gnadenfrist.

reprimand [repriˈmaːnd], v.a. verweisen, tadeln. — s. der Tadel.

reprint [riːˈprint], v.a. neu drucken. — [ˈriːprint], s. der Neudruck.

reprisal [riˈpraizəl], s. die Vergeltungsmaßregel; (pl.) die Repressalien, f. pl.

reproach [riˈproutʃ], v.a. vorwerfen (Dat.), tadeln. — s. der Vorwurf, Tadel.

reprobate [ˈreprəbeit], adj. ruchlos, verworfen.

reproduce [riːprəˈdjuːs], v.a. reproduzieren, erzeugen.

reproof [riˈpruːf], s. der Vorwurf, Tadel.

reprove [riˈpruːv], v.a. tadeln, rügen (a person), mißbilligen (a practice).

republic [ri'pʌblik], s. die Republik.
repudiate [ri'pju:dieit], v.a. zurückweisen, verwerfen.
repugnant [ri'pʌgnənt], adj. widerwärtig, ekelhaft.
repulse [ri'pʌls], v.a. (Mil.) zurückschlagen; abweisen (s.o.). — s. (Mil.) das Zurückschlagen; (fig.) die Zurückweisung.
repulsive [ri'pʌlsiv], adj. widerwärtig.
reputation [repju'teiʃən], s. der (gute) Ruf.
request [ri'kwest], v.a. ersuchen. — s. das Ersuchen, Ansuchen, die Bitte.
requiem ['rekwiəm], s. (Eccl.) das Requiem, die Totenmesse.
require [ri'kwaiə], v.a. fordern, verlangen, brauchen.
requirement [ri'kwaiəmənt], s. die Anforderung, das Erfordernis.
requisite ['rekwizit], adj. erforderlich.
requisition [rekwi'ziʃən], s. (Mil.) die Requisition; die Forderung.
requite [ri'kwait], v.a. vergelten.
rescind [ri'sind], v.a. für ungültig erklären, aufheben.
rescue ['reskju:], v.a. retten. — s. die Rettung.
research [ri'sə:tʃ], v.n. forschen, Forschung treiben. — s. die Forschung.
resemble [ri'zembl], v.a. ähnlich sein (Dat.), gleichen (Dat.).
resent [ri'zent], v.a. übelnehmen.
resentful [ri'zentful], adj. nachträgerisch; empfindlich (over–sensitive).
resentment [ri'zentmənt], s. die Empfindlichkeit; der Groll (spite).
reservation [rezə'veiʃən], s. die Reservierung (of seat); der Vorbehalt (doubt).
reserve [ri'zə:v], v.a. reservieren, belegen (seat); (fig.) vorbehalten (o.'s position). — s. die Reserve, die Verschlossenheit (shyness); die Einschränkung (limitation); die Reserven, f. pl. (money).
reside [ri'zaid], v.n. wohnen.
resident ['rezidənt], adj. wohnhaft. — s. der Ansässige.
residual [ri'zidjuəl], adj. übrig bleibend.
residue ['rezidju:], s. der Rückstand, Rest.
resign [ri'zain], v.a. abtreten, aufgeben; (ein Amt) niederlegen. — v.n. abdanken. — v.r. — o.s. to, sich in etwas fügen, zurücktreten.
resignation [rezig'neiʃən], s. die Resignation, der Rücktritt (from office); die Fügung, Resignation (attitude).
resin ['rezin], s. das Harz.
resist [ri'zist], v.a., v.n. widerstehen, Widerstand leisten (Dat.).
resistance [ri'zistəns], s. der Widerstand.
resolute ['rezəlju:t], adj. entschlossen.
resolution [rezə'lju:ʃən], s. die Entschlossenheit (determination); die Entscheidung (decision); der Vorsatz, Entschluß (vow).

resolve [ri'zɔlv], v.a. auflösen (solve); beschließen (conclude). — v.n. entscheiden (decide). — s. der Beschluß, die Entscheidung.
resonance ['rezənəns], s. die Resonanz.
resort [ri'zɔ:t], v.n. — to, seine Zuflucht nehmen (zu). — s. seaside —, das Seebad, health —, der Kurort (spa).
resound [ri'zaund], v.n. widerhallen.
resource [ri'sɔ:s], s. das Hilfsmittel; (pl.) die Mittel, n. pl.
respect [ri'spekt], v.a. respektieren, achten; berücksichtigen (have regard to). — s. der Respekt, die Achtung; with — to, mit Bezug auf; in — of, bezüglich (Genit.).
respectability [rispektə'biliti], s. die Anständigkeit; Achtbarkeit.
respective [ris'pektiv], adj. respektiv.
respectively [ris'pektivli], adv. beziehungsweise.
respiration [respi'reiʃən], s. die Atmung.
respiratory [ris'paiərətri or 'respireitəri], adj. Atmungs-.
respire [ri'spaiə], v.n. atmen.
respite ['respit], s. die Frist, der Aufschub.
resplendent [ri'splendənt], adj. glänzend.
respond [ri'spɔnd], v.n. antworten, eingehen (to, auf).
respondent [ri'spɔndənt], s. (Law) der Beklagte.
response [ri'spɔns], s. die Antwort, Aufnahme, Reaktion; (fig.) der Widerhall.
responsibility [risponsi'biliti], s. die Verantwortung, Verantwortlichkeit.
responsible [ri'spɔnsibl], adj. verantwortlich.
responsive [ri'spɔnsiv], adj. empfänglich, zugänglich.
rest (1) [rest], v.n. ruhen, rasten. — s. die Ruhe, Rast; (Mus.) die Pause.
rest (2) [rest], v.n. bleiben (stay); — assured, sei (seien Sie) versichert. — s. der Rest; die übrigen, pl.
restaurant ['restərã], s. das Restaurant.
restful ['restful], adj. ruhig.
restitution [resti'tju:ʃən], s. die Wiedergutmachung.
restive ['restiv], adj. unruhig, ruhelos.
restless ['restlis], adj. rastlos, unruhig.
restoration [restɔ:'reiʃən], s. die Wiederherstellung; (Hist.) die Restauration.
restore [ri'stɔ:], v.a. wiederherstellen.
restrain [ri'strein], v.a. zurückhalten, einschränken.
restraint [ri'streint], s. die Zurückhaltung.
restrict [ri'strikt], v.a. beschränken.
restriction [ri'strikʃən], s. die Einschränkung.
restrictive [ri'striktiv], adj. einschränkend.

result [ri'zʌlt], *v.n.* folgen, sich ergeben; (*come about*) erfolgen. — *s.* das Ergebnis, Resultat; (*consequence*) die Folge.

resume [ri'zju:m], *v.a.* wiederaufnehmen; (*narrative*) fortsetzen. — *v.n.* fortfahren.

résumé ['rezjumei], *s.* das Resümee, die Zusammenfassung.

resumption [ri'zʌmpʃən], *s.* die Wiederaufnahme.

resurrection [rezə'rekʃən], *s.* (*Rel.*) die Auferstehung.

resuscitate [ri'sʌsiteit], *v.a.* wiederbeleben.

retail ['ri:teil], *s.* der Kleinhandel, Einzelhandel. — [ri'teil], *v.a.* im Detail handeln, verkaufen.

retain [ri'tein], *v.a.* behalten.

retainer [ri'teinə], *s.* der Diener; Gefolgsmann; der Vorschuß (*fee*).

retake [ri:'teik], *v.a. irr.* (*Mil.*) wieder erobern; (*Phot., Film*) noch einmal aufnehmen. — *s.* (*Am.*) die Neuaufnahme (*Phot., Film*).

retaliate [ri'tælieit], *v.n.* sich rächen, vergelten.

retard [ri'ta:d], *v.a.* verzögern, verlangsamen.

retch [retʃ], *v.n.* sich erbrechen.

retentive [ri'tentiv], *adj.* behaltend, gut (*memory*).

reticent ['retisənt], *adj.* schweigsam, einsilbig.

retina ['retinə], *s.* (*Anat.*) die Netzhaut.

retinue ['retinju:], *s.* das Gefolge.

retire [ri'taiə], *v.n.* sich zurückziehen (*withdraw*); in den Ruhestand treten (*from work*). — *v.a.* pensionieren.

retirement [ri'taiəmənt], *s.* die Pension, der Ruhestand; die Zurückgezogenheit (*seclusion*).

retort [ri'to:t], *s.* (*Chem.*) die Retorte; die scharfe Antwort (*debate*). — *v.n.* scharf erwidern.

retouch [ri:'tʌtʃ], *v.a.* (*Phot.*) retouchieren.

retrace [ri:'treis], *v.a.* zurückverfolgen.

retreat [ri'tri:t], *v.n.* sich zurückziehen. — *s.* der Rückzug (*Mil.*); Zufluchtsort.

retrench [ri'trentʃ], *v.a.* einschränken (*restrict*); verkürzen (*shorten*). — *v.n.* sich einschränken.

retribution [retri'bju:ʃən], *s.* die Vergeltung.

retrieve [ri'tri:v], *v.a.* wieder bekommen, wieder gewinnen.

retriever [ri'tri:və], *s.* (*Zool.*) der Apportierhund, Stöberhund.

retrograde ['retrogreid], *adj.* rückgängig, rückwärts.

retrospect ['retrospekt], *s.* der Rückblick.

retrospective [retro'spektiv], *adj.* rückblickend.

return [ri'tə:n], *v.a.* zurückgeben; erwidern (*reciprocate*); abordnen, entsenden (*to Parl.*); (*figures*) einsenden. — *v.n.* zurückkehren, zurückkommen.

— *s.* die Rückkehr; (*Fin.*) der Gewinn; (*Parl.*) die Entsendung, Mandatierung; (*pl.*) (*figures*) die Einsendung; *by* — *of post*, umgehend, postwendend; — *ticket*, die Rückfahrkarte.

reunion [ri:'ju:niən], *s.* die Wiedervereinigung.

reveal [ri'vi:l], *v.a.* enthüllen, offenbaren (*show*); verraten (*betray*).

reveille [ri'væli], *s.* (*Mil.*) das Wecken, Wecksignal.

revel [revl], *v.n.* schwelgen.

revelation [revə'leiʃən], *s.* die Offenbarung.

revelry ['revəlri], *s.* die Schwelgerei.

revenge [ri'vendʒ], *s.* die Rache, Revanche. — *v.r.* (*also be revenged*) sich rächen (*on*, an, *Dat.*).

revenue ['revənju:], *s.* das Einkommen; *Inland* —, die Steuereinnahmen.

reverberate [ri'və:bəreit], *v.n.* widerhallen.

revere [ri'viə], *v.a.* verehren.

reverence ['revərəns], *s.* die Ehrerbietung, der Respekt; *show* —, Ehrerbietung zollen.

Reverend ['revərənd]. (*abbr.* **Rev.**) (*Eccl.*) *The* —, Seine Ehrwürden; *The Very* —, Seine Hochwürden.

reverent, reverential ['revərənt, revə'renʃəl], *adj.* ehrerbietig.

reverie ['revəri], *s.* die Träumerei.

reversal [ri'və:səl], *s.* die Umkehrung, Umstoßung.

reverse [ri'və:s], *v.a., v.n.* umkehren, umdrehen. — *s.* das Gegenteil (*contrary*); die Kehrseite (*of coin*).

revert [ri'və:t], *v.a., v.n.* umkehren, zurückkehren.

review [ri'vju:], *v.a.* durchsehen, prüfen (*examine*); rezensieren (*book etc.*). — *s.* die Revision; (*Mil.*) die Parade, Truppenmusterung; die Rezension, Besprechung (*book etc.*).

revile [ri'vail], *v.a., v.n.* schmähen.

revise [ri'vaiz], *v.a.* korrigieren (*correct*); wiederholen (*recapitulate*); umarbeiten (*modify*).

revision [ri'viʒən], *s.* die Revision; Korrektur; Umarbeitung; Wiederholung (*recapitulation*).

revolt [ri'voult], *v.n.* sich empören, revoltieren. — *v.a.* empören. — *s.* die Empörung.

revolting [ri'voultiŋ], *adj.* ekelhaft, empörend.

revolution [revə'lju:ʃən], *s.* (*Pol.*) die Revolution; (*Motor.*) die Umdrehung.

revolve [ri'vɔlv], *v.n.* rotieren, sich drehen.

revolver [ri'vɔlvə], *s.* der Revolver.

revue [ri'vju:], *s.* (*Theat.*) die Revue.

revulsion [ri'vʌlʃən], *s.* der Ekel; der Umschwung.

reward [ri'wɔ:d], *v.a.* belohnen (*person*); vergelten (*deed*). — *s.* die Belohnung.

rheumatic [ru:'mætik], *adj.* (*Med.*) rheumatisch.

475

rheumatism

rheumatism [ˈruːmətizm], *s.* (*Med.*) der Rheumatismus.

rhetoric [ˈretərik], *s.* die Redekunst.

Rhodesian [roˈdiːʃən, -ˈdiːʒən], *adj.* rhodesisch. — *s.* der Rhodesier.

rhododendron [roudəˈdendrən], *s.* (*Bot.*) die Alpenrose.

rhubarb [ˈruːbɑːb], *s.* (*Bot.*) der Rhabarber.

rhyme [raim], *s.* der Reim; *no — nor reason*, sinnlos.

rhythm [riðm], *s.* der Rhythmus.

rib [rib], *s.* (*Anat.*) die Rippe.

ribald [ˈribəld], *adj.* liederlich; (*joke*) unanständig.

ribbon [ˈribən], *s.* das Band.

rice [rais], *s.* der Reis.

rich [ritʃ], *adj.* reich; fruchtbar (*fertile*).

rick [rik], *s.* der Schober.

rickets [ˈrikits], *s.* (*Med.*) die englische Krankheit, die Rachitis.

rickety [ˈrikiti], *adj.* gebrechlich, wackelig, baufällig.

rid [rid], *v.a. irr.* befreien, freimachen (*of*, von); — *o.s.*, sich entledigen (*of, Genit.*); *get — of*, loswerden (*Acc.*); *be — of*, los sein (*Acc.*).

riddance [ˈridəns], *s.* die Befreiung, das Loswerden.

riddle (1) [ridl], *s.* das Rätsel (*puzzle*).

riddle (2) [ridl], *s.* das grobe Sieb (*sieve*). — *v.a.* sieben (*sieve*); durchlöchern.

ride [raid], *v.a., v.n. irr.* reiten (*on horse*), fahren (*on bicycle etc.*); — *at anchor*, vor Anker liegen. — *s.* der Ritt (*on horse*), die Fahrt (*in vehicle*).

rider [ˈraidə], *s.* der Reiter (*horseman*); der Fahrer (*cyclist etc.*); der Zusatz (*addition*).

ridge [ridʒ], *s.* der Rücken (*edge*); die Bergkette; die Furche (*furrow*). — *v.a.* furchen.

ridicule [ˈridikjuːl], *s.* der Spott. — *v.a.* lächerlich machen.

ridiculous [riˈdikjuləs], *adj.* lächerlich.

rife [raif], *adj.* häufig, weitverbreitet.

rifle (1) [raifl], *s.* die Büchse, das Gewehr.

rifle (2) [raifl], *v.a.* ausplündern.

rift [rift], *s.* der Riß, Spalt, die Spalte. — *v.a.* spalten.

rig [rig], *s.* (*Naut.*) die Takelung; (*fig.*) — *out*, die Ausstattung. — *v.a.* (*Naut.*) (auf)takeln; (*Am.*) fälschen (*fake*); — *out*, ausstatten.

right [rait], *adj.* recht; richtig; wahr; gesund; korrekt; — *hand*, rechtsseitig; *you are* —, Sie haben recht; *that's* —, das stimmt. — *s.* das Recht; *by right(s)*, rechtmäßig; *drive on the* —, rechts fahren.

righteous [ˈraitʃəs], *adj.* rechtschaffen, aufrecht.

rightful [ˈraitful], *adj.* rechtmäßig.

rigid [ˈridʒid], *adj.* steif; unbeugsam; streng (*severe*).

rigidity [riˈdʒiditi], *s.* die Steifheit, Unnachgiebigkeit; die Strenge.

rigmarole [ˈrigməroul], *s.* die Salbaderei, das Gewäsch.

rigorous [ˈrigərəs], *adj.* streng; genau.

rigour [ˈrigə], *s.* die Strenge; die Härte.

rill [ril], *s.* (*Poet.*) das Bächlein.

rim [rim], *s.* der Rand, die Felge.

rime [raim], *s.* (*Poet.*) der Reif.

rind [raind], *s.* die Rinde.

ring (1) [riŋ], *s.* der Ring.

ring (2) [riŋ], *s.* der Schall, das Läuten (*bell*); der Anruf (*telephone*); das Geläute (*bells*). — *v.a. irr.* läuten, klingeln (*bell*). — *v.n.* läuten; ertönen, tönen (*call, voice*).

ringleader [ˈriŋliːdə], *s.* der Rädelsführer.

rink [riŋk], *s.* die Eisbahn; Rollschuhbahn.

rinse [rins], *v.a.* spülen, waschen. — *s.* das Abspülen.

riot [ˈraiət], *s.* der Aufruhr. — *v.n.* Aufruhr stiften; meutern.

rip [rip], *v.a.* reißen, aufreißen. — *s.* der Riß.

ripe [raip], *adj.* reif.

ripen [ˈraipən], *v.n.* reifen. — *v.a.* reifen lassen.

ripple [ripl], *s.* die Welle, Kräuselwelle (*water*). — *v.n.* kräuseln (*water*); (*Bot.*) riffeln.

rise [raiz], *v.n. irr.* aufstehen (*get up*); aufsteigen (*ascend*); anschwellen (*swell*); steigen (*price*). — *s.* die Erhöhung; (*Comm.*) der Anstieg; die Steigerung; Erhöhung (*salary*); der Ursprung (*origin*).

rising [ˈraiziŋ], *s.* der Aufstand (*rebellion*).

risk [risk], *s.* das Risiko. — *v.a.* wagen, riskieren.

rite [rait], *s.* der Ritus.

ritual [ˈritjuəl], *s.* das Ritual.

rival [raivl], *s.* der Rivale, Nebenbuhler. — *adj.* nebenbuhlerisch, konkurrierend. — *v.a.* konkurrieren, wetteifern.

river [ˈrivə], *s.* der Fluß.

rivet [ˈrivit], *s.* die Niete. — *v.a.* nieten.

roach [routʃ], *s.* (*Zool.*) die Plötze.

road [roud], *s.* die Straße; der Weg.

roam [roum], *v.n.* herumstreifen.

roan [roun], *s.* der Rotschimmel (*horse*).

roar [rɔː], *v.n.* brüllen (*animals*); brausen (*storm*). — *s.* das Gebrüll (*animal*); das Getöse, Brausen, Rauschen.

roast [roust], *v.a., v.n.* braten, rösten. — *s.* der Braten.

rob [rɔb], *v.a.* berauben.

robbery [ˈrɔbəri], *s.* der Raub, die Räuberei.

robe [roub], *s.* die Robe.

robin [ˈrɔbin], *s.* (*Orn.*) das Rotkehlchen.

rock [rɔk], *s.* der Felsen, die Klippe. — *v.a.* schaukeln, wiegen. — *v.n.* wackeln, taumeln.

rocket [ˈrɔkit], *s.* die Rakete; (*sl.*) die Rüge. — *v.n.* hochfliegen; hochgehen (*prices*).

rocky [ˈrɔki], *adj.* felsig.

rod [rɔd], *s.* die Rute; (*fishing*) die Angelrute; die Stange (*pole*).

rodent [ˈroudənt], *s.* (*Zool.*) das Nagetier.

roe (1) [rou], *s.* der Fischrogen.

roe (2) [rou], *s.* (*Zool.*) das Reh, die Hirschkuh.

rogation [roˈgeiʃən], *s.* das Gebet, die Litanei; *Rogation Sunday*, der Sonntag Rogate.

rogue [roug], *s.* der Schelm.

role [roul]. *s.* (*Theat.*, *fig.*) die Rolle.

roll [roul], *s.* die Liste; — *call*, der Aufruf, die Parade; die Rolle; die Semmel, das Brötchen (*bread*). — *v.a.* rollen; wälzen. — *v.n.* rollen; sich wälzen; sich drehen; schlingen (*ship*); schlenkern (*person*).

roller [ˈroulə], *s.* die Rolle; — *bandage*, das Wickelband; — *skates*, die Rollschuhe.

rollick [ˈrɔlik], *v.n.* herumtollen, lustig sein.

rolling stock [ˈrouliŋ stɔk], *s.* (*Railw.*) der Wagenbestand.

romance [rouˈmæns], *s.* die Romanze.

romantic [rouˈmæntik], *adj.* romantisch.

romp [rɔmp], *s.* der Wildfang, das Tollen. — *v.n.* toben.

roof [ru:f], *s.* das Dach. — *v.a.* decken.

rook (1) [ruk], *s.* (*Orn.*) die Saatkrähe.

rook (2) [ruk], *s.* (*Chess*) der Turm.

room [ru:m, rum], *s.* der Raum, das Zimmer. — *v.n.* (*Am.*) ein Zimmer teilen (*with*, mit).

roomy [ˈru:mi], *adj.* geräumig.

roost [ru:st], *s.* der Hühnerstall. — *v.n.* aufsitzen, schlafen.

root [ru:t], *s.* die Wurzel. — *v.n.* wurzeln.

rooted [ˈru:tid], *adj.* eingewurzelt.

rope [roup], *s.* das Seil. — *v.a.* anseilen (*in climbing*); (*coll.*) — *in*, verwickeln, hereinziehen.

rosary [ˈrouzəri], *s.* (*Rel.*) der Rosenkranz.

rose [rouz], *s.* (*Bot.*) die Rose.

Rosemary [ˈrouzməri]. Rosemarie.

rosemary [ˈrouzməri], *s.* (*Bot.*) der Rosmarin.

rosin [ˈrɔzin] *see* **resin**.

rosy [ˈrouzi], *adj.* rosig.

rot [rɔt], *v.n.* faulen, modern. — *s.* die Fäulnis, Verwesung; (*coll.*) der Unsinn.

rotate [roˈteit], *v.a.*, *v.n.* (sich) drehen, rotieren.

rote [rout], *s. by* —, mechanisch, auswendig.

rotten [rɔtn], *adj.* faul, verdorben, schlecht.

rotund [roˈtʌnd], *adj.* rundlich, rund.

rough [rʌf], *adj.* rauh, grob; flüchtig, ungefähr (*approximate*); ungehobelt (*ill-mannered*).

roughshod [ˈrʌfʃɔd], *adj.* rücksichtslos.

round [raund], *adj.* rund. — *s.* die Runde. — *prep.* (rund) um; um . . ., herum. — *adv.* (rings)herum; (*around*) ungefähr; etwa (*approximately*).

roundabout [ˈraundəbaut], *s.* das Karussel. — *adj.* umständlich.

Roundhead [ˈraundhed], *s.* (*Eng. Hist.*) der Puritaner.

rouse [rauz], *v.a.* erwecken.

rout [raut], *s.* (*Mil.*) die wilde Flucht. — *v.a.* in die Flucht jagen.

route [ru:t], *s.* der Weg; die Route.

rover [ˈrouvə], *s.* der Wanderer, ältere Pfadfinder (*scout*); der Seeräuber (*pirate*).

row (1) [rou], *s.* die Reihe.

row (2) [rau], *s.* der Lärm, Streit. → *v.n.* (*coll.*) lärmend streiten, zanken.

row (3) [rou], *v.n.* rudern.

rowdy [ˈraudi], *s.* der Raufbold. — *adj.* laut, lärmend.

royal [ˈrɔiəl], *adj.* königlich.

royalty [ˈrɔiəlti], *s.* das Mitglied des Königshauses, die königliche Hoheit; (*pl.*) (*Law*) die Tantieme.

rub [rʌb], *v.a.*, *v.n.* (sich) reiben. — *s.* die Reibung; die heikle Stelle, das Problem.

rubber (1) [ˈrʌbə], *s.* der Gummi; Radiergummi.

rubber (2) [ˈrʌbə], *s.* (*Whist*) der Robber.

rubbish [ˈrʌbiʃ], *s.* der Abfall, Mist; (*fig.*) der Schund (*book*), der Unsinn (*nonsense*).

ruby [ˈru:bi], *s.* der Rubin.

rudder [ˈrʌdə], *s.* das Steuerruder.

ruddy [ˈrʌdi], *adj.* rötlich.

rude [ru:d], *adj.* roh; grob; ungebildet; unhöflich.

rudiment [ˈru:dimənt], *s.* die Anfangsgründe, die Grundlage.

rue (1) [ru:], *s.* (*Bot.*) die Raute.

rue (2) [ru:], *v.a.* beklagen, bereuen.

ruff [rʌf], *s.* die Halskrause.

ruffian [ˈrʌfiən], *s.* der Raufbold.

ruffle [rʌfl], *v.a.* zerzausen (*hair*); verwirren (*muddle*). — *s.* die Krause (*on dress*); die Aufregung.

rug [rʌg], *s.* die Wolldecke, der Vorleger.

rugged [ˈrʌgid], *adj.* rauh; uneben.

ruin [ˈru:in], *s.* die Ruine; (*fig.*) der Zusammenbruch. — *v.a.* ruinieren.

rule [ru:l], *s.* die Regel, Vorschrift; die Herrschaft; *slide* —, der Rechenschieber. — *v.a.* beherrschen; regeln; lin(i)ieren (*draw lines on*). — *v.n.* herrschen (*reign*; *be valid*); lin(i)ieren (*draw lines*); entscheiden (*decide*).

ruling [ˈru:liŋ], *s.* die Regelung, Entscheidung.

rum (1) [rʌm], *s.* der Rum.

rum (2) [rʌm], *adj.* (*sl.*) seltsam.

Rumanian [ru:ˈmeiniən], *adj.* rumänisch. — *s.* der Rumäne.

rumble [rʌmbl], *v.n.* poltern, rasseln, rumpeln; (*stomach*) knurren.

ruminate [ˈru:mineit], *v.n.* wiederkäuen; nachsinnen.

rummage [ˈrʌmidʒ], *v.a.*, *v.n.* durchstöbern.

rumour [ˈru:mə], *s.* das Gerücht.

rump [rʌmp], *s.* der Rumpf, Steiß; — *steak*, das Rumpsteak.

run

run [rʌn], *v.n. irr.* laufen, rennen; eilen; verkehren (*bus*); fließen (*flow*); (*Theat.*) gegeben werden; lauten (*text*). — *s.* der Lauf, das Rennen; (*Theat.*) die Spieldauer; *in the long* —, am Ende, auf die Dauer.

runaway ['rʌnəwei], *adj.* entlaufen. — *s.* der Ausreißer.

rung [rʌŋ], *s.* die Sprosse.

runway ['rʌnwei], *s.* (*Aviat.*) die Rollbahn, Startbahn, Landebahn.

rupture ['rʌptʃə], *s.* (*Med.*) der Leistenbruch.

rural ['ruərəl], *adj.* ländlich.

rush (1) [rʌʃ], *s.* (*Bot.*) die Binse.

rush (2) [rʌʃ], *s.* der Ansturm, Andrang; die Hetze; der Hochbetrieb. — *v.n.* stürzen, in Eile sein.

Russian ['rʌʃən], *adj.* russisch. — *s.* der Russe.

rust [rʌst], *s.* der Rost. — *v.n.* verrosten.

rustic ['rʌstik], *adj.* ländlich.

rut (1) [rʌt], *s.* die Spur; das Geleise.

rut (2) [rʌt], *s.* (*animals*) die Brunst.

ruthless ['ruːθlis], *adj.* grausam, rücksichtslos.

rye [rai], *s.* (*Bot.*) der Roggen.

S

S [es]. das S.

sable [seibl], *s.* der Zobel. — *adj.* schwarz.

sabotage ['sæbɔtɑːʒ], *s.* die Sabotage. — *v.a.* sabotieren.

sabre ['seibə], *s.* der Säbel.

sack (1) [sæk], *s.* der Sack; (*coll.*) die Entlassung (*get the* —). — *v.a.* (*coll.*) entlassen.

sack (2) [sæk], *v.a.* plündern (*pillage*).

sack (3) [sæk], *s.* (*obs.*) der Weißwein.

sacrament ['sækrəmənt], *s.* das Sakrament.

sacred ['seikrid], *adj.* heilig.

sacrifice ['sækrifais], *s.* das Opfer. — *v.a.* opfern.

sacrilege ['sækrilidʒ], *s.* das Sakrileg, der Frevel.

sad [sæd], *adj.* traurig.

sadden [sædn], *v.a.* betrüben.

saddle [sædl], *s.* der Sattel. — *v.a.* satteln; (*coll.*) — *s.o. with s.th.*, einem etwas aufhalsen.

safe [seif], *adj.* sicher (*secure*); wohlbehalten (*arrival etc.*). — *s.* der Geldschrank, das Safe.

safeguard ['seifgɑːd], *v.a.* beschützen, garantieren. — *s.* der Schutz, die Sicherheit.

safety ['seifti], *s.* die Sicherheit.

saffron ['sæfrən], *s.* der Safran. — *adj.* safrangelb.

sagacious [sə'geiʃəs], *adj.* scharfsinnig.

sagacity [sə'gæsiti], *s.* der Scharfsinn.

sage (1) [seidʒ], *s.* (*Bot.*) der, die Salbei.

sage (2) [seidʒ], *s.* der Weise. — *adj.* weise, klug.

sail [seil], *s.* das Segel. — *v.n.* segeln, (*Naut.*) fahren.

sailor ['seilə], *s.* der Matrose, Seemann.

Saint [seint, sənt]. (*abbr.* **S.** *or* **St.**) Sankt (*before name*).

saint [seint], *s.* der *or* die Heilige.

sake [seik], *s. for my son's* —, um meines Sohnes willen; *for the* — *of peace*, um des Friedens willen.

salacious [sə'leiʃəs], *adj.* geil; zotig (*joke*).

salad ['sæləd], *s.* der Salat.

salary ['sæləri], *s.* das Gehalt.

sale [seil], *s.* der Verkauf; *annual* —, (*Comm.*) der Ausverkauf.

salesman ['seilzmən], *s.* der Verkäufer.

salient ['seiliənt], *adj.* hervorspringend, wichtig, Haupt-.

saline ['seilain], *s.* die Salzquelle. — *adj.* salzhaltig.

saliva [sə'laivə], *s.* der Speichel.

sallow ['sælou], *adj.* blaß, bleich.

sally ['sæli], *s.* der Ausfall, (*fig.*) der komische Einfall. — *v.n.* ausfallen; — *forth*, losgehen.

salmon ['sæmən], *s.* (*Zool.*) der Lachs.

saloon [sə'luːn], *s.* der Salon; (*Am.*) das Wirtshaus, die Kneipe.

salt [sɔːlt], *s.* das Salz; — *cellar*, das Salzfäßchen; (*coll.*) *old* —, der alte Matrose. — *v.a.* salzen.

saltpetre [sɔːlt'piːtə], *s.* der Salpeter.

salubrious [sə'ljuːbriəs], *adj.* gesund (*climate, neighbourhood*).

salutary ['sæljutəri], *adj.* heilsam (*lesson, experience*).

salute [sə'ljuːt], *v.a.* grüßen. — *s.* der Gruß, (*Mil.*) Salut.

salvage ['sælvidʒ], *s.* die Bergung, Rettung; das Bergegut. — *v.a.* retten, bergen.

salvation [sæl'veiʃən], *s.* die Rettung; (*Rel.*) die Erlösung, das Heil.

salve [sælv, sɑːv], *v.a.* einsalben; heilen. — *s.* die Salbe.

salver ['sælvə], *s.* der Präsentierteller.

salvo ['sælvou], *s.* (*Mil.*) die Salve.

Samaritan [sə'mæritən], *s.* der Samariter; (*fig.*) der Wohltäter.

same [seim], *adj.* der-, die-, dasselbe.

sample [sɑːmpl], *s.* die Probe, das Muster (*test, pack etc.*). — *v.a.* probieren; kosten (*food*).

sampler ['sɑːmplə], *s.* das Stickmuster.

sanctify ['sæŋktifai], *v.a.* heiligen.

sanctimonious [sæŋkti'mouniəs], *adj.* scheinheilig.

sanction ['sæŋkʃən], *s.* (*Pol.*) die Sanktion; (*fig.*) Genehmigung. — *v.a.* genehmigen, sanktionieren.

sanctuary ['sæŋktjuəri], *s.* das Heiligtum.

sand [sænd], *s.* der Sand. — *v.a.* sanden, bestreuen; (*floors*) abreiben.

sandal [sændl], *s.* die Sandale.

sandwich ['sænwitʃ], s. das belegte (Butter)brot.
sane [sein], adj. gesund (mind); vernünftig.
sanguine ['sæŋgwin], adj. optimistisch.
sanitary ['sænitəri], adj. Gesundheits-, Sanitäts-; — towel, die (Damen)binde.
sanity ['sæniti], s. die Vernunft, der gesunde Menschenverstand; (Law) die Zurechnungsfähigkeit.
Santa Claus [sæntə'klɔ:z]. der heilige Nikolaus, Knecht Ruprecht.
sap (1) [sæp], s. der Saft; (fig.) die Lebenskraft.
sap (2) [sæp], v.a. untergraben, schwächen.
sapling ['sæpliŋ], s. (Bot.) das Bäumchen, der junge Baum.
sapper ['sæpə], s. (Mil.) der Sappeur; der Schanzgräber, Pionier.
sapphire ['sæfaiə], s. der Saphir.
sarcasm ['sɑ:kæzm], s. der Sarkasmus.
sarcastic [sɑ:'kæstik], adj. sarkastisch.
sash (1) [sæʃ], s. die Schärpe.
sash (2) [sæʃ], s.— window, das Schiebefenster; — cord, die Fensterschnur.
Satan ['seitən]. der Satan.
satchel ['sætʃəl], s. die Leder(schul)-tasche.
sate [seit], v.a. sättigen.
satellite ['sætəlait], s. der Satellit, Trabant.
satin ['sætin], s. (Text.) der Atlas.
satire ['sætaiə], s. die Satire.
satisfaction [sætis'fækʃən], s. die Befriedigung, Zufriedenheit.
satisfactory [sætis'fæktri], adj. befriedigend, genügend; zufriedenstellend.
satisfy ['sætisfai], v.a. befriedigen, sättigen; (fig.) zufriedenstellen.
saturate ['sætʃəreit], v.a. (Chem.) saturieren, sättigen.
Saturday ['sætədei]. der Samstag, Sonnabend.
sauce [sɔ:s], s. (Cul.) die Sauce, Tunke; (coll.) die Unverschämtheit.
saucepan ['sɔ:spæn], s. (Cul.) der Kochtopf.
saucer ['sɔ:sə], s. die Untertasse.
saucy ['sɔ:si], adj. (coll.) unverschämt, frech.
saunter ['sɔ:ntə], v.n. schlendern, spazieren.
sausage ['sɔsidʒ], s. die Wurst.
savage ['sævidʒ], adj. wild. — s. der Wilde.
save [seiv], v.a. retten (life); (Theol.) erlösen; sparen (money); sich ersparen (trouble, labour); aufheben (keep). — v.n. sparen, sparsam sein. — prep., conj. außer, außer daß, ausgenommen.
saving ['seiviŋ], s. das Ersparnis; savings bank, die Sparkasse.
saviour ['seivjə], s. der Retter; (Rel.) der Heiland.
savour ['seivə], s. der Geschmack; die Würze. — v.n. schmecken (of, nach, Dat.).

savoury ['seivəri], adj. schmackhaft. — s. pikantes Vor- or Nachgericht.
saw (1) [sɔ:], v.a. sägen. — s. die Säge.
saw (2) [sɔ:], s. (obs.) das Sprichwort.
sawyer ['sɔ:jə], s. der Sägearbeiter, Säger.
Saxon ['sæksən], adj. sächsisch. — s. der Sachse.
say [sei], v.a. irr. sagen; (lines, prayer) hersagen. — v.n. (Am. coll.) — ! sagen Sie mal! — s. das entscheidende Wort.
saying ['seiiŋ], s. das Sprichwort, der Spruch.
scab [skæb], s. der Schorf, die Krätze.
scabbard ['skæbəd], s. die Degenscheide.
scaffold ['skæfəld], s. (Build.) das Gerüst; das Schafott (place of execution).
scald [skɔ:ld], v.a. verbrühen; —ing hot, brühheiß.
scale (1) [skeil], s. die Waagschale (balance).
scale (2) [skeil], s. (Mus.) die Skala, Tonleiter.
scale (3) [skeil], s. (Geog. etc.) die Skala, das Ausmaß, der Maßstab; on a large —, im großen (Maßstabe). — v.a. erklettern (climb); — down, im Maßstab verringern.
scale (4) [skeil], s. (fish etc.) die Schuppe. — v.a. schuppen, abschälen (remove —s).
scallop ['skɔləp], s. (Zool.) die Kammuschel.
scalp [skælp], s. (Anat.) die Kopfhaut. — v.a. skalpieren, die Kopfhaut abziehen.
scamp [skæmp], s. (coll.) der Taugenichts.
scan [skæn], v.a. (Poet.) skandieren; (Rad.) absuchen.
scandalize ['skændəlaiz], v.a. empören, verärgern.
scant [skænt], adj. selten; knapp, sparsam.
Scandinavian [skændi'neivjən], adj. skandinavisch. — s. der Skandinavier.
scanty ['skænti], adj. spärlich, knapp.
scapegoat ['skeipgout], s. der Sündenbock.
scar [skɑ:], s. die Narbe.
scarce [skɛəs], adj. selten, spärlich.
scarcely ['skɛəsli], adv. kaum.
scarcity ['skɛəsiti], s. die Seltenheit, Knappheit.
scare [skɛə], v.a. erschrecken, ängstigen. — s. der Schreck.
scarecrow ['skɛəkrou], s. die Vogelscheuche.
scarf [skɑ:f], s. der Schal, das Halstuch.
scarlet ['skɑ:lit], adj. scharlachrot. — s. der Scharlach.
scarp [skɑ:p], s. die Böschung.
scatter ['skætə], v.a., v.n. (sich) zerstreuen, (sich) verbreiten; streuen.
scavenge ['skævindʒ], v.a. ausreinigen, auswaschen; säubern.
scavenger ['skævindʒə], s. der Straßenkehrer; Aasgeier.

scene [si:n], *s.* die Szene, der Schauplatz; *behind the —s,* hinter den Kulissen; — *shifter,* der Kulissenschieber.

scenery ['si:nəri], *s.* die Landschaft (*nature*); (*Theat.*) das Bühnenbild, die Kulissen, *f. pl.*

scent [sent], *s.* der Geruch, Duft, das Parfüm (*perfume*); die Witterung, Fährte (*trail of hunted animal*).

sceptic ['skeptik], *s.* der Skeptiker.

sceptre ['septə], *s.* das Zepter.

schedule ['ʃedju:l, (*Am.*) 'ske-], *s.* der Plan; die Liste; der (Fahr-, Stunden-) plan; (*Law*) der Zusatz (*in documents*). — *v.a.* (*Am.*) einteilen, zuteilen (*apportion*); aufzeichnen.

scheme [ski:m], *s.* das Schema; der Plan; — *of things,* in der Gesamtplanung. — *v.n.* aushecken; Ränke schmieden.

scholar ['skɔlə], *s.* der Gelehrte, der Wissenschaftler; der Schuljunge, Schüler; (*Univ.*) der Stipendiat.

scholarly ['skɔləli], *adj.* gelehrt.

scholarship ['skɔləʃip], *s.* die Gelehrsamkeit (*learning*); das Stipendium (*award*).

scholastic [skɔ'læstik], *adj.* scholastisch. — *s.* der Scholastiker.

school [sku:l], *s.* die Schule. — *v.a.* abrichten; schulen; erziehen.

schoolboy ['sku:lbɔi], *s.* der Schüler.

schoolgirl ['sku:lgə:l], *s.* die Schülerin.

schoolmaster ['sku:lma:stə], *s.* der Lehrer.

schoolmistress ['sku:lmistrəs], *s.* die Lehrerin.

schooner ['sku:nə], *s.* (*Naut.*) der Schoner.

science ['saiəns], *s.* die Wissenschaft, Naturwissenschaft (*natural — s*).

scientific [saiən'tifik], *adj.* wissenschaftlich, naturwissenschaftlich.

scientist ['saiəntist], *s.* der Gelehrte; Naturwissenschaftler, Naturforscher.

scintillate ['sintileit], *v.n.* funkeln, glänzen.

scion ['saiən], *s.* der Sprößling.

scissors ['sizəz], *s. pl.* die Schere.

scoff [skɔf], *v.a.* verspotten, verhöhnen. — *v.n.* spotten. —*s.* der Spott, Hohn.

scold [skould], *v.a.* schelten. — *v.n.* zanken.

scoop [sku:p], *v.a.* aushöhlen (*hollow out*); ausschöpfen (*ladle out*). — *s.* die Schippe, Schöpfkelle; (*fig.*) die Sensation, Erstmeldung.

scope [skoup], *s.* der Wirkungskreis, Spielraum.

scooter ['sku:tə], *s.* der (Motor)roller.

scorch [skɔ:tʃ], *v.a.* versengen, verbrennen. — *v.n.* versengt werden; (*coll.*) dahinrasen (*speed*).

score [skɔ:], *s.* die Zwanzig; die Rechnung; (*Mus.*) die Partitur; das Spielergebnis (*in game*).

scorn [skɔ:n], *v.a.* verachten. — *s.* der Spott (*scoffing*); die Geringschätzung, Verachtung.

Scot, Scotsman [skɔt, 'skɔtsmən], *s.* der Schotte.

Scotch [skɔtʃ], *s.* der Whisky.

scotch [skɔtʃ], *v.a.* ritzen; (*fig.*) vernichten.

Scotswoman ['skɔtswumən], *s.* die Schottin.

Scottish ['skɔtiʃ], *adj.* schottisch.

scoundrel ['skaundrəl], *s.* der Schurke.

scour ['skauə], *v.a.* scheuern, reinigen.

scourge [skə:dʒ], *s.* die Geißel. — *v.a.* geißeln.

scout [skaut], *s.* der Kundschafter; (*Boy Scout*) der Pfadfinder.

scowl [skaul], *v.n.* finster dreinsehen. — *s.* das finstere Gesicht.

scraggy ['skrægi], *adj.* hager, dürr.

scramble ['skræmbl], *v.n.* klettern. — *v.a.* verrühren; *scrambled eggs,* das Rührei.

scrap [skræp], *s.* das Stückchen, der Brocken, Fetzen; — *merchant,* der Altwarenhändler. — *v.a.* zum alten Eisen werfen, verschrotten.

scrapbook ['skræpbuk], *s.* das Sammelbuch, Bilderbuch.

scrape [skreip], *v.a., v.n.* (sich) schaben, kratzen; — *up,* auflesen. — *s.* (*coll.*) die Klemme (*difficulty*).

scraper ['skreipə], *s.* der Fußabstreifer.

scratch [skrætʃ], *v.a., v.n.* kratzen; sich kratzen; (*Sport*) zurückziehen. — *s.* der Kratzer; *come up to —,* seinen Mann stellen.

scrawl [skrɔ:l], *v.a., v.n.* kritzeln (*scribble*); (*coll.*) unleserlich schreiben. — *s.* das Gekritzel.

scream [skri:m], *v.n.* schreien; kreischen. — *s.* der Schrei; (*coll.*) zum Schreien, zum Lachen.

screech [skri:tʃ], *v.n.* schreien, kreischen (*hoarsely*). — *s.* das Gekreisch.

screen [skri:n], *s.* der Schirm (*protection*); (*Cinema*) die Leinwand. — *v.a.* abschirmen (*shade*); (*Film*) durchspielen, vorführen; (*question*) untersuchen; ausfragen.

screening ['skri:niŋ], *s.* (*Cinema*) die Vorführung, (*Pol.*) die Befragung, Untersuchung.

screw [skru:], *v.a.* schrauben. — *s.* die Schraube.

screwdriver ['skru:draivə], *s.* der Schraubenzieher.

scribble [skribl], *v.a., v.n.* kritzeln (unleserlich) schreiben. — *s.* das Gekritzel.

scribe [skraib], *s.* der Schreiber.

script [skript], *s.* das Manuskript; (*Film*) das Drehbuch.

scripture ['skriptʃə], *s.* die Heilige Schrift.

scroll [skroul], *s.* die Schriftrolle; (*Typ.*) der Schnörkel; die Urkunde (*document etc.*).

scrub [skrʌb], *v.a.* schrubben, reiben, scheuern.

scruff [skrʌf], *s.* (*of the neck*) das Genick.

scruple [skru:pl], *s.* der Skrupel.

scrupulous ['skru:pjuləs], *adj.* genau, gewissenhaft; allzu bedenklich.

scrutinize ['skru:tinaiz], *v.a.* genau prüfen, untersuchen.
scrutiny ['skru:tini], *s.* die genaue Prüfung; die Untersuchung.
scuffle [skʌfl], *v.n.* sich raufen. — *s.* die Balgerei, Rauferei.
scull [skʌl], *s.* das kurze Ruder.
scullery ['skʌləri], *s.* die Abwaschküche.
scullion ['skʌliən], *s.* (*obs.*) der Küchenjunge.
sculptor ['skʌlptə], *s.* der Bildhauer.
sculpture ['skʌlptʃə], *s.* die Bildhauerei (*activity*); die Skulptur (*piece*).
scum [skʌm], *s.* der Abschaum.
scurf [skə:f], *s.* der Schorf, Grind.
scurrilous ['skʌrilǝs], *adj.* gemein.
scurvy ['skǝ:vi], *s.* (*Med.*) der Skorbut. — *adj.* niederträchtig.
scutcheon ['skʌtʃǝn] *see* **escutcheon.**
scuttle (1) [skʌtl], *s.* (*Naut.*) die Springluke. — *v.a.* (*Naut.*) ein Schiff zum Sinken bringen, versenken.
scuttle (2) [skʌtl], *s.* der Kohleneimer.
scuttle (3) [skʌtl], *v.n.* eilen (*hurry*).
scythe [saið], *s.* die Sense.
sea [si:], *s.* die See, das Meer.
seal (1) [si:l], *s.* das Siegel, Petschaft. — *v.a.* (be)siegeln.
seal (2) [si:l], *s.* (*Zool.*) der Seehund, die Robbe.
seam [si:m], *s.* der Saum; die Naht; (*Min.*) die Ader, das Flöz; (*Metall.*) die Naht. — *v.a. see* **sere.**
seamstress ['si:mstrǝs], *s.* die Näherin.
sear [siǝ], *v.a.* sengen (*burn*); trocknen; verdorren. — *adj. see* **sere.**
search [sǝ:tʃ], *v.n.* suchen (*for*, nach, *Dat.*); forschen (*for*, nach, *Dat.*). — *v.a.* untersuchen, durchsuchen (*house, case etc.*). — *s.* die Suche (*for person*); die Untersuchung (*of house etc.*).
searchlight ['sǝ:tʃlait], *s.* der Scheinwerfer.
seasick ['si:sik], *adj.* seekrank.
seaside ['si:said], *s.* die Küste, der Strand.
season [si:zn], *s.* die Jahreszeit, Saison; — *ticket*, die Dauerkarte. — *v.a.* würzen (*spice*). — *v.n.* reifen (*mature*).
seasoning ['si:zniŋ], *s.* die Würze.
seat [si:t], *s.* der Sitz, Sitzplatz, Stuhl. — *v.a.* setzen; fassen (*of room capacity*); *be —ed*, Platz nehmen.
seaweed ['si:wi:d], *s.* (*Bot.*) der Seetang.
secession [si'seʃǝn], *s.* die Loslösung, Trennung, Spaltung.
seclude [si'klu:d], *v.a.* abschließen, absondern.
seclusion [si'klu:ʒǝn], *s.* die Abgeschlossenheit.
second ['sekǝnd], *num. adj.* zweit; (*repeat*) noch ein. — *s.* die Sekunde (*time*); (*Sport*) der Sekundant. — *v.a.* sekundieren (*Dat.*), beipflichten; [si'kɔnd] abkommandieren (zu).
secondary ['sekǝndri], *adj.* zweitrangig, sekundär.
secondhand ['sekǝndhænd], *adj.* antiquarisch, gebraucht.

secrecy ['si:krǝsi], *s.* die Heimlichkeit; *pledge to —*, die Verschwiegenheit.
secret ['si:krit], *s.* das Geheimnis. — *adj.* geheim.
secretary ['sekrǝtǝri], *s.* der Sekretär, die Sekretärin.
secrete [si'kri:t], *v.a.* ausscheiden, absondern.
secretion [si'kri:ʃǝn], *s.* die Ausscheidung; (*Med.*) das Sekret.
sect [sekt], *s.* die Sekte.
section ['sekʃǝn], *s.* die Sektion, Abteilung (*department*); der Teil (*part*); Abschnitt (*in book etc.*).
secular ['sekjulǝ], *adj.* weltlich, säkulär.
secure [sǝ'kjuǝ], *adj.* sicher, gesichert. — *v.a.* sichern (*make safe*); besorgen (*obtain*).
security [sǝ'kjuǝriti], *s.* die Sicherheit; (*Comm.*) die Garantie, Bürgschaft; (*pl.*) die Staatspapiere, Wertpapiere, *n. pl.*, Aktien, *f. pl.*
sedate [si'deit], *adj.* gesetzt, ruhig (*placid*).
sedative ['sedǝtiv], *adj.* beruhigend. — *s.* das Beruhigungsmittel.
sedentary ['sedǝntri], *adj.* sitzend, Sitz-.
sediment ['sedimǝnt], *s.* der Bodensatz; (*Geol.*) das Sediment.
sedition [si'diʃǝn], *s.* der Aufstand.
seditious [si'diʃǝs], *adj.* aufrührerisch.
seduce [si'dju:s], *v.a.* verführen.
sedulous ['sedjulǝs], *adj.* emsig, fleißig.
see (1) [si:], *s.* (*Eccl.*) das (Erz)bistum; *Holy See*, der Heilige Stuhl.
see (2) [si:], *v.a., v.n. irr.* sehen; einsehen, verstehen (*understand*).
seed [si:d], *s.* die Saat; der Same (*grain*). — *v.a.* (*Sport*) aussetzen, setzen.
seediness ['si:dinis], *s.* die Schäbigkeit; Armseligkeit, das Elend.
seedy ['si:di], *adj.* elend; schäbig.
seeing ['si:iŋ], *conj. — that*, da doch.
seek [si:k], *v.a. irr.* suchen (*object*). — *v.n.* trachten (*to, infin.*).
seem [si:m], *v.n.* scheinen, erscheinen.
seemly ['si:mli], *adj.* schicklich, anständig.
seer [siǝ], *s.* der Prophet.
seesaw ['si:sɔ:], *s.* die Schaukel.
seethe [si:ð], *v.n.* kochen, (*fig.*) sieden.
segment ['segmǝnt], *s.* (*Geom.*) der Abschnitt.
segregate ['segrigeit], *v.a.* absondern.
segregation [segri'geiʃǝn], *s. racial —*, die Rassentrennung.
seize [si:z], *v.a.* ergreifen, packen (*arrest, grasp*); beschlagnahmen (*impound*).
seizure [si:ʒǝ], *s.* die Beschlagnahme (*of goods*); (*Med.*) der Anfall.
seldom ['seldǝm], *adv.* selten.
select [si'lekt], *v.a.* auswählen; auslesen. — *adj.* auserlesen.
selection [si'lekʃǝn], *s.* die Wahl, Auswahl.
self [self], *s.* das Selbst; — *— consciousness*, die Befangenheit; — *— denial*, die Selbstverleugnung, Selbstaufopferung.

481

selfish ['selfiʃ], *adj.* egoistisch, selbstsüchtig.

sell [sel], *v.a. irr.* verkaufen; (*sl.*) — (*s.o.*) *out*, jemanden verraten.

semblance ['sembləns], *s.* der Anschein, die Ähnlichkeit.

semi- ['semi], *pref.* halb.

semibreve ['semibri:v], *s.* (*Mus.*) die ganze Note.

semicircle ['semisə:kl], *s.* der Halbkreis.

semicolon ['semikoulən], *s.* der Strichpunkt.

semiquaver ['semikweivə], *s.* (*Mus.*) die Sechzehntelnote.

senate ['senit], *s.* der Senat.

send [send], *v.a. irr.* senden, schicken; — *for*, holen lassen; — *-off*, die Abschiedsfeier.

Senegalese [senigə'li:z], *adj.* senegal-. — *s.* der Senegalese.

senile ['si:nail], *adj.* altersschwach.

senior ['si:njə], *adj.* älter; dienstälter (*in position*).

seniority [si:ni'ɔriti], *s.* der Rangvortritt, das Dienstalter.

sensation [sen'seiʃən], *s.* die Empfindung; Sensation.

sensational [sen'seiʃənəl], *adj.* sensationell.

sense [sens], *v.a.* fühlen, empfinden. — *s.* der Sinn; das Empfinden, Gefühl; *common* —, gesunder Menschenverstand.

senseless ['senslis], *adj.* sinnlos.

sensibility [sensi'biliti], *s.* die Empfindlichkeit.

sensible ['sensibl], *adj.* vernünftig.

sensitive ['sensitiv], *adj.* feinfühlend, empfindlich.

sensitize ['sensitaiz], *v.a.* (*Phot. etc.*) empfindlich machen.

sensual ['sensjuəl], *adj.* sinnlich, wollüstig.

sensuous ['sensjuəs], *adj.* sinnlich.

sentence ['sentəns], *s.* (*Gram.*) der Satz; (*Law*) das Urteil. — *v.a.* verurteilen.

sententious [sen'tenʃəs], *adj.* spruchreich; affektiert.

sentiment ['sentimənt], *s.* die Empfindung, das Gefühl; die Meinung (*opinion*).

sentimental [senti'mentl], *adj.* sentimental, gefühlvoll; empfindsam.

sentinel ['sentinəl], *s.* (*Mil.*) die Schildwache, Wache.

separable ['sepərəbl], *adj.* trennbar.

separate ['sepəreit], *v.a.* trennen. — [-rit], *adj.* getrennt.

separation [sepə'reiʃən], *s.* die Trennung.

September [sep'tembə]. der September.

sequel ['si:kwəl], *s.* die Folge, Fortsetzung (*serial*).

sequence ['si:kwəns], *s.* die Ordnung, Reihenfolge, Aufeinanderfolge.

sequester [si'kwestə], *v.a.* absondern, entfernen.

sere [siə], *adj.* trocken, dürr.

serene [si'ri:n], *adj.* heiter; gelassen, ruhig (*quiet*).

serf [sə:f], *s.* der Leibeigene.

sergeant ['sɑ:dʒənt], *s.* (*Mil.*) der Feldwebel.

series ['siəri:z *or* 'siərii:z], *s.* die Reihe.

serious ['siəriəs], *adj.* ernst, seriös.

sermon ['sə:mən], *s.* die Predigt.

serpent ['sə:pənt], *s.* (*Zool.*) die Schlange.

serpentine ['sə:pəntain], *adj.* schlangenartig, sich schlängelnd.

serrated [se'reitid], *adj.* (*Bot., Engin.*) zackig, gezackt.

serried ['serid], *adj.* dichtgedrängt.

servant ['sə:vənt], *s.* der Bediente, Diener; die Magd, das Mädchen, Dienstmädchen.

serve [sə:v], *v.a., v.n.* dienen (*Dat.*); (*Law*) abbüßen, absitzen (*sentence*); servieren (*food*); (*Tennis*) angeben.

service ['sə:vis], *s.* der Dienst, die Bedienung; (*Mil.*) der Militärdienst; das Service, Geschirr, Porzellan (*china*).

serviceable ['sə:visəbl], *adj.* brauchbar, dienlich, benutzbar.

servile ['sə:vail], *adj.* knechtisch.

servility [sə:'viliti], *s.* die Kriecherei.

servitude ['sə:vitju:d], *s.* die Knechtschaft.

session ['seʃən], *s.* die Sitzung; das Studienjahr, Hochschuljahr.

set [set], *v.a. irr.* setzen; stellen (*stand*); legen (*lay*); ordnen (— *out*); — *a saw*, eine Sage schärfen, wetzen; fassen (*stone*); — *fire to*, in Brand setzen; — *aside*, beiseitelegen; — *to music*, vertonen; — *about*, anfangen, sich anschicken; herfallen über (*s.o.*); — *up*, einrichten. — *v.n.* — *forth, forward*, aufbrechen; — *out to*, streben, trachten; (*sun*) untergehen; fest werden (*solidify*). — *s.* der Satz (*complete collection*); die Garnitur (*garments*); der Kreis, die Clique (*circle of people*); (*Theat.*) das Bühnenbild.

settee [se'ti:], *s.* das Sofa.

setter ['setə], *s.* (*Zool.*) der Vorstehhund; *red* —, der Hühnerhund.

setting ['setiŋ], *s.* das Setzen; die Szene (*of play etc.*); der Sonnenuntergang (*of the sun*); (*Typ.*) — *up*, die Auslegung, Aufstellung.

settle (1) [setl], *v.a.* ordnen, schlichten; (*Comm.*) begleichen, bezahlen. — *v.n.* sich niederlassen, siedeln; (*weather*) sich aufklären.

settle (2) [setl], *s.* der Ruhesitz.

settlement ['setlmənt], *s.* (*Comm.*) die Begleichung; die Siedlung (*habitation*).

seven [sevn], *num. adj.* sieben.

seventeen ['sevnti:n], *num. adj.* siebzehn.

seventh [sevnθ], *num. adj.* siebente.

seventy ['sevnti], *num. adj.* siebzig.

sever ['sevə], *v.a.* trennen.

several ['sevərəl], *adj. pl.* verschiedene, mehrere.

severance ['sevərəns], *s.* die Trennung.
severe [si'viə], *adj.* streng.
severity [si'veriti], *s.* die Strenge.
sew [sou], *v.a., v.n.* nähen.
sewage ['sju:idʒ], *s.* das Abfuhrwasser, Kloakenwasser, Kanalwasser.
sewer (1) ['sjuːə], *s.* die Kanalanlage, der Abzugskanal.
sewer (2) ['souə], *s.* der Näher, die Näherin.
sewing ['souiŋ], *s.* das Nähen; — *machine*, die Nähmaschine.
sex [seks], *s.* das Geschlecht.
sexagenarian [seksədʒə'neəriən], *s.* der Sechzigjährige.
sextant ['sekstənt], *s.* der Sextant.
sexton ['sekstən], *s.* (*Eccl.*) der Küster, Totengräber.
sexual ['seksjuəl], *adj.* geschlechtlich, sexuell.
shabby ['ʃæbi], *adj.* schäbig; (*fig.*) erbärmlich.
shackle [ʃækl], *v.a.* fesseln. — *s.* (*usually pl.*) die Fesseln, *f. pl.*
shade [ʃeid], *s.* der Schatten; (*pl.*) (*Am.*) die Jalousien, *f. pl.* (*blinds*). — *v.a.* beschatten; (*Art*) schattieren, verdunkeln.
shadow ['ʃædou], *s.* der Schatten. — *v.a.* verfolgen.
shady ['ʃeidi], *adj.* schattig; (*fig.*) verdächtig.
shaft [ʃɑ:ft], *s.* der Schaft (*handle*); (*Min.*) der Schacht; die Deichsel (*cart*); der Pfeil (*arrow*).
shag [ʃæg], *s.* der Tabak.
shaggy ['ʃægi], *adj.* zottig.
shake [ʃeik], *v.a. irr.* schütteln; rütteln; (*fig.*) erschüttern. — *v.n.* zittern (*tremble*); wanken (*waver*). — *s.* das Zittern, Beben; (*Mus.*) der Triller.
shaky ['ʃeiki], *adj.* zitternd, wankend; rissig, wackelig (*wobbly*); (*fig.*) unsicher (*insecure*).
shall [ʃæl], *v. aux.* sollen (*be supposed to*); werden (*future*).
shallow ['ʃælou], *adj.* flach, seicht. — *s.* die Untiefe (*sea*).
sham [ʃæm], *adj.* falsch, unecht. — *v.a.* vortäuschen.
shambles [ʃæmblz], *s.* die Unordnung; (*fig.*) das Schlachtfeld.
shame [ʃeim], *s.* die Scham (*remorse*); die Schande (*dishonour*); *what a* —! wie schade! — *v.a.* beschämen.
shamefaced ['ʃeimfeisd], *adj.* verschämt.
shameful ['ʃeimful], *adj.* schändlich (*despicable*).
shampoo [ʃæm'pu:], *s.* das Haarwaschmittel. — *v.a.* das Haar waschen.
shamrock ['ʃæmrɔk], *s.* (*Bot.*) der irische Klee.
shank [ʃæŋk], *s.* der Unterschenkel; (*coll.*) *on Shanks's pony*, zu Fuß.
shanty (1) ['ʃænti], *s.* die Hütte.
shanty (2) ['ʃænti], *s.* *sea* —, das Matrosenlied.
shape [ʃeip], *s.* die Gestalt, Figur, Form. — *v.a.* gestalten, formen. — *v.n.* Gestalt annehmen.

shapely ['ʃeipli], *adj.* wohlgestaltet, schön gestaltet.
share [ʃeə], *v.a., v.n.* (sich) teilen. — *s.* der Teil, Anteil; (*Comm.*) die Aktie (*in company*).
shareholder ['ʃeəhouldə], *s.* der Aktionär.
shark [ʃɑːk], *s.* (*Zool.*) der Haifisch, Hai; (*fig.*) der Wucherer (*profiteer*), Hochstapler.
sharp [ʃɑːp], *adj.* scharf; (*fig.*) intelligent. — *s.* (*Mus.*) das Kreuz.
sharpen [ʃɑːpn], *v.a.* schärfen; spitzen (*pencil*).
sharpener ['ʃɑːpnə], *s.* *pencil* —, der Bleistiftspitzer.
shatter ['ʃætə], *v.a.* zerschmettern. — *v.n.* zerbrechen.
shave [ʃeiv], *v.a., v.n.* (sich) rasieren; abschaben (*pare*). — *s.* die Rasur, das Rasieren.
shavings ['ʃeivinz], *s. pl.* die Hobelspäne, *m. pl.*
shawl [ʃɔːl], *s.* der Schal, das Umschlagetuch.
she [ʃiː], *pers. pron.* sie.
sheaf [ʃiːf], *s.* die Garbe.
shear [ʃiə], *v.a. irr.* scheren (*sheep etc.*).
shears [ʃiəz], *s. pl.* die Schere.
sheath [ʃiːθ], *s.* die Scheide.
sheathe [ʃiːð], *v.a.* in die Scheide stecken.
shed (1) [ʃed], *s.* der Schuppen.
shed (2) [ʃed], *v.a. irr.* vergießen (*blood, tears*); ausschütten.
sheen [ʃiːn], *s.* der Glanz.
sheep [ʃiːp], *s.* (*Zool.*) das Schaf.
sheer (1) [ʃiə], *adj.* rein, lauter; senkrecht.
sheer (2) [ʃiə], *v.n.* (*Naut.*) gieren, abgieren.
sheet [ʃiːt], *s.* das Bettuch; das Blatt, der Bogen (*paper*); die Platte (*metal*); — *metal*, — *iron*, das Eisenblech; — *lightning*, das Wetterleuchten.
shelf [ʃelf], *s.* das Brett, Regal; der Sims (*mantel*); (*Geog.*) die Sandbank; (*coll.*) *on the* —, sitzengeblieben.
shell [ʃel], *s.* die Schale (*case*); die Muschel (*mussel*); (*Mil.*) die Bombe, Granate. — *v.a.* schälen (*peas*); bombardieren, beschiessen (*town*).
shelter ['ʃeltə], *s.* das Obdach (*lodging*); der Unterstand, Schuppen; der Schutz (*protection*). — *v.a.* Obdach gewähren (*Dat.*); beschützen (*protect*). — *v.n.* sich schützen, unterstellen.
shelve [ʃelv], *v.a.* auf ein Brett legen; (*fig.*) aufschieben (*postpone*).
shelving ['ʃelviŋ], *s.* das Regal.
shepherd ['ʃepəd], *s.* der Schäfer, Hirt.
sheriff ['ʃerif], *s.* der Sheriff.
shew [ʃou] *see* **show**.
shield [ʃiːld], *s.* der Schild. — *v.a.* schützen.
shift [ʃift], *v.a.* verschieben. — *v.n.* die Lage ändern. — *s.* die Veränderung, der Wechsel; (*Industry*) die Schicht.
shifty ['ʃifti], *adj.* unstet; durchtrieben.

shin [ʃin], *s.* (*Anat.*) das Schienbein.
shindy [ʃindi], *s.* der Lärm.
shine [ʃain], *v.n. irr.* scheinen (*sun*); glänzen. — *s.* der Glanz.
shingle (1) [ʃiŋgl], *s.* (*Build.*) die Schindel; (*Hair*) der Herrenschnitt.
shingle (2) [ʃiŋgl], *s.* (*Geol.*) der Kiesel.
shingles [ʃiŋglz], *s. pl.* (*Med.*) die Gürtelrose.
ship [ʃip], *s.* das Schiff. — *v.a.* verschiffen, (*Comm.*) versenden.
shipping [ʃipiŋ], *s.* die Schiffahrt; (*Comm.*) der Versand, die Verfrachtung, Verschiffung.
shire [ʃaiə], *s.* die Grafschaft.
shirk [ʃəːk], *v.a.* vermeiden, sich drücken (vor, *Dat.*).
shirt [ʃəːt], *s.* das Hemd.
shirting [ʃəːtiŋ], *s.* der Hemdenstoff.
shiver [ʃivə], *v.n.* zittern, beben. — *s.* der Schauer, Schauder.
shoal [ʃoul], *s.* der Schwarm; (*Naut.*) die Untiefe.
shock (1) [ʃɔk], *v.a.* entsetzen; erschrecken; schockieren. — *s.* der Schock, das Entsetzen.
shock (2) [ʃɔk], *s.* — *of hair,* zottiges Haar.
shoddy [ʃɔdi], *adj.* schlecht, wertlos.
shoe [ʃuː], *s.* der Schuh. — *v.a.* beschuhen; (*horse*) beschlagen.
shoelace, shoestring [ʃuːleis, ʃuːstriŋ], *s.* der Schuhsenkel, (*Austr.*) das Schuhschnürl; *on a shoestring,* fast ohne Geld.
shoeshine [ʃuːʃain], *s.* (*Am.*) der Schuhputzer.
shoestring *see under* **shoelace**.
shoot [ʃuːt], *v.a. irr.* schießen. — *v.n.* sprossen, hervorschießen; (*film*) aufnehmen. — *s.* (*Bot.*) der Sproß.
shooting [ʃuːtiŋ], *s.* das Schießen; — *range,* der Schießstand. — *adj.* — *star,* die Sternschnuppe.
shop [ʃɔp], *s.* der Laden, das Geschäft; (*work*) die Werkstatt; *talk* —, fachsimpeln; — *window,* das Schaufenster. — *v.n.* einkaufen.
shopkeeper [ʃɔpkiːpə], *s.* der Kaufmann, Krämer.
shoplifter [ʃɔpliftə], *s.* der Ladendieb.
shore [ʃɔː], *s.* das Gestade, die Küste; die Stütze. — *v.a.* — *up,* stützen.
short [ʃɔːt], *adj.* kurz, klein, knapp; (*curt*) kurz angebunden; — *of money,* in Geldnot; *run* —, knapp werden; — *sighted,* kurzsichtig; *be on* — *time working,* kurz arbeiten. — *s.* (*Elect.*) (*coll.*) der Kurzschluß (*short circuit*); (*pl.*) die Kniehose, kurze Hose.
shortcoming [ʃɔːtkʌmiŋ], *s.* der Fehler, Mangel.
shorten [ʃɔːtn], *v.a.* verkürzen, abkürzen. — *v.n.* kürzer werden.
shorthand [ʃɔːthænd], *s.* die Stenographie; — *typist,* die Stenotypistin.
shot [ʃɔt], *s.* der Schuß; (*man*) der Schütze.

shoulder [ʃouldə], *s.* (*Anat.*) die Schulter. — *v.a.* schultern, auf sich nehmen, auf die Achsel nehmen.
shout [ʃaut], *v.n.* schreien, rufen. — *s.* der Schrei, Ruf.
shove [ʃʌv], *v.a.* schieben, stoßen. — *s.* der Schub, Stoß.
shovel [ʃʌvl], *s.* die Schaufel. — *v.a.* schaufeln.
show [ʃou], *v.a. irr.* zeigen; (*fig.*) dartun. — *v.n.* sich zeigen, zu sehen sein; — *off,* prahlen, protzen. — *v.r.* — *o.s. to be,* sich erweisen als. — *s.* (*Theat.*) die Schau, Aufführung.
shower [ʃauə], *s.* der Schauer (*rain*); (*fig.*) die Fülle, der Überfluß; — (*bath*), die Dusche; *take a* —(*bath*), brausen. — *v.a., v.n.* herabregnen; überschütten.
showing [ʃouiŋ], *s.* die Vorführung, der Beweis.
showy [ʃoui], *adj.* protzig, angeberisch.
shred [ʃred], *s.* der Fetzen; (*fig.*) die Spur (*of evidence*). — *v.a.* zerreißen, zerfetzen.
shrew [ʃruː], *s.* die Spitzmaus; (*fig.*) das zänkische Weib.
shrewd [ʃruːd], *adj.* schlau, verschlagen, listig.
shriek [ʃriːk], *v.n.* kreischen. — *s.* der Schrei, das Gekreisch.
shrift [ʃrift], *s. give s.o. short* —, mit einem kurzen Prozeß machen.
shrill [ʃril], *adj.* schrill, gellend, durchdringend.
shrimp [ʃrimp], *s.* (*Zool.*) die Garnele.
shrine [ʃrain], *s.* der (Reliquien)-schrein; der Altar.
shrink [ʃriŋk], *v.n. irr.* eingehen, einschrumpfen. — *v.a.* eingehen lassen.
shrinkage [ʃriŋkidʒ], *s.* das Eingehen (*fabric*); (*Geol.*) die Schrumpfung.
shrivel [ʃrivl], *v.n.* einschrumpfen, sich runzeln.
shroud [ʃraud], *s.* das Leichentuch. — *v.a.* einhüllen.
Shrove [ʃrouv] **Tuesday.** die Fastnacht.
shrub [ʃrʌb], *s.* (*Bot.*) der Strauch, die Staude.
shrug [ʃrʌg], *v.a.* (*shoulders*) die Achseln zucken. — *s.* das Achselzucken.
shudder [ʃʌdə], *s.* der Schauder. — *v.n.* schaudern.
shuffle [ʃʌfl], *v.a.* (*cards*) mischen. — *v.n.* schlürfen, schleppend gehen.
shun [ʃʌn], *v.a.* meiden.
shunt [ʃʌnt], *v.a., v.n.* rangieren.
shut [ʃʌt], *v.a. irr.* schließen. — *v.n.* sich schließen, zugehen; (*coll.*) — *up!* halt's Maul!
shutter [ʃʌtə], *s.* der Fensterladen.
shuttle [ʃʌtl], *s.* (*Mech.*) das Weberschiff.
shuttlecock [ʃʌtlkɔk], *s.* der Federball.
shy (1) [ʃai], *adj.* scheu, schüchtern; — *v.n.* scheuen (*of horses*).
shy (2) [ʃai], *s.* der Wurf.
sick [sik], *adj.* krank; unwohl, übel; leidend (*suffering*); (*fig.*) — *of,* überdrüssig (*Genit.*).

sicken [sikn], *v.n.* krank werden *or* sein; sich ekeln (*be nauseated*). — *v.a.* anekeln.

sickle [sikl], *s.* die Sichel.

sickness ['siknis], *s.* die Krankheit.

side [said], *s.* die Seite. — *v.n.* — *with*, Partei ergreifen für.

sideboard ['saidbɔ:d], *s.* das Büffet, die Anrichte.

sidereal [sai'diəriəl], *adj.* (*Maths., Phys.*) Sternen-, Stern-.

sidewalk ['saidwɔ:k] (*Am.*) *see* **pavement**.

siding ['saidiŋ], *s.* (*Railw.*) das Nebengleis.

sidle [saidl], *v.n.* — *up to*, sich heranmachen.

siege [si:dʒ], *s.* die Belagerung.

sieve [siv], *s.* das Sieb. — *v.a.* sieben.

sift [sift], *v.a.* sieben; (*fig.*) prüfen.

sigh [sai], *v.n.* seufzen. — *s.* der Seufzer.

sight [sait], *s.* die Sicht (*view*); die Sehkraft (*sense of*); der Anblick; *at* —, auf den ersten Blick; *out of* —, *out of mind*, aus den Augen, aus dem Sinn; (*pl.*) die Sehenswürdigkeiten, *f. pl.*; —*seeing*, die Besichtigung (der Sehenswürdigkeiten). — *v.a.* sichten.

sign [sain], *s.* das Zeichen; der Wink (*hint*); das Aushängeschild (*of pub, shop etc.*). — *v.a.* unterschreiben, unterzeichnen. — *v.n.* winken.

signal ['signəl], *s.* das Signal.

signboard ['sainbɔ:d], *s.* das Aushängeschild.

signet ['signit], *s.* das Siegel; — *ring*, der Siegelring.

significance [sig'nifikəns], *s.* die Bedeutung, der Sinn.

significant [sig'nifikənt], *adj.* bedeutend, wichtig.

signify ['signifai], *v.a.* bedeuten (*mean*); anzeigen (*denote*).

silence ['sailəns], *s.* das Schweigen, die Ruhe.

silent ['sailənt], *adj.* still; schweigsam (*taciturn*).

Silesian [sai'li:ʃən], *adj.* schlesisch. — *s.* der Schlesier.

silk [silk], *s.* (*Text.*) die Seide.

silkworm ['silkwə:m], *s.* (*Ent.*) die Seidenraupe.

sill [sil], *s.* die Schwelle; *window* —, das Fensterbrett.

silly ['sili], *adj.* albern, dumm.

silver ['silvə], *s.* das Silber. — *v.a.* versilbern. — *adj.* silbern.

similar ['similə], *adj.* ähnlich.

simile ['simili], *s.* (*Lit.*) das Gleichnis.

simmer ['simə], *v.n.*, *v.a.* langsam kochen.

simper ['simpə], *v.n.* lächeln, grinsen.

simple [simpl], *adj.* einfach; (*fig.*) einfältig.

simpleton ['simpltən], *s.* der Einfaltspinsel, Tor.

simplicity [sim'plisiti], *s.* die Einfachheit; (*fig.*) die Einfalt.

simplify ['simplifai], *v.a.* vereinfachen.

simulate ['simjuleit], *v.a.* nachahmen, heucheln, vortäuschen.

simultaneous [siməl'teinjəs], *adj.* gleichzeitig.

sin [sin], *s.* die Sünde. — *v.n.* sündigen.

since [sins], *prep.* seit (*Dat.*). — *conj.* seit (*time*); weil, da (*cause*). — *adv.* seither, seitdem.

sincere [sin'siə], *adj.* aufrichtig.

sincerely [sin'siəli], *adv.* yours —, Ihr ergebener (*letters*).

sincerity [sin'seriti], *s.* die Aufrichtigkeit.

sine [sain], *s.* (*Maths.*) der Sinus, die Sinuskurve.

sinecure ['sainikjuə], *s.* der Ruheposten, die Sinekure.

sinew ['sinju:], *s.* (*Anat.*) die Sehne, der Nerv.

sinful ['sinful], *adj.* sündig, sündhaft.

sing [siŋ], *v.a.*, *v.n. irr.* singen; — *of*, besingen.

singe [sindʒ], *v.a.* sengen.

Singhalese [siŋgə'li:z], *adj.* singhalesisch. — *s.* der Singhalese, die Singhalesin.

single [siŋgl], *adj.* einzeln; ledig (*unmarried*; *single-handed*, allein. — *v.a.* — *out*, auswählen.

singlet ['siŋglit], *s.* die Unterjacke.

singly ['siŋgli], *adv.* einzeln (*one by one*).

singular ['siŋgjulə], *adj.* einzigartig, einzig. — *s.* (*Gram.*) die Einzahl.

sinister ['sinistə], *adj.* böse, unheimlich, finster.

sink [siŋk], *v.a. irr.* versenken; (*fig.*) (*differences etc.*) begraben. — *v.n.* versinken; (*Naut.*) sinken, versinken. — *s.* das Abwaschbecken, Ausgußbecken.

sinker ['siŋkə], *s.* der Schachtarbeiter (*man*); (*Naut.*) das Senkblei.

sinuous ['sinjuəs], *adj.* gewunden.

sinus ['sainəs], *s.* (*Anat.*) die Knochenhöhle; die Bucht.

sip [sip], *v.a.* schlürfen, nippen. — *s.* das Schlückchen.

siphon ['saifən], *s.* (*Phys.*) der Heber; die Siphonflasche. — *v.a.* auspumpen.

Sir (1) [sə:] (*title preceding Christian name*) Herr von... (*baronet or knight*).

sir (2) [sə:], *s.* Herr (*respectful form of address*); *dear* —, sehr geehrter Herr (*in letters*).

sire [saiə], *s.* der Ahnherr, Vater. — *v.a.* zeugen (*horses etc.*).

siren ['saiərən], *s.* die Sirene.

sirloin ['sə:lɔin], *s.* die Lendenstück.

siskin ['siskin], *s.* (*Orn.*) der Zeisig.

sister ['sistə], *s.* die Schwester; (*Eccl.*) Nonne; —*in-law*, die Schwägerin.

sit [sit], *v.n. irr.* sitzen. — *v.a.* — *an examination*, eine Prüfung machen.

site [sait], *s.* die Lage, der Platz.

sitting ['sitiŋ], *s.* die Sitzung; — *room*, das Wohnzimmer.

situated ['sitjueitid], *adj.* gelegen.

situation [sitju'eiʃən], *s.* die Lage, Situation; der Posten, die Stellung (*post*).

six [siks], *num. adj.* sechs; *be at —es and sevens*, durcheinander, uneinig sein.

sixteen [siks'ti:n], *num. adj.* sechzehn.

sixth [siksθ], *num. adj.* sechste.

sixty ['siksti], *num. adj.* sechzig.

size [saiz], *s.* die Größe, das Maß; (*fig.*) der Umfang.

skate (1) [skeit], *s.* der Schlittschuh. — *v.n.* Schlittschuh laufen.

skate (2) [skeit], *s.* (*Zool.*) der Glattrochen.

skeleton ['skelitən], *s.* das Skelett, Knochengerüst; — *key*, der Dietrich.

sketch [sketʃ], *s.* die Skizze, der Entwurf. — *v.a.* skizzieren, entwerfen. — *v.n.* Skizzen entwerfen.

sketchy ['sketʃi], *adj.* flüchtig.

skew [skju:], *adj.* schief, schräg.

skewer ['skjuːə], *s.* der Fleischspieß.

ski [ski:], *s.* der Schi.

skid [skid], *v.n.* gleiten, schleudern, rutschen. — *v.a.* hemmen, bremsen (*wheel*). — *s.* der Hemmschuh, die Bremse (*of wheel*).

skiff [skif], *s.* (*Naut.*) der Nachen, Kahn.

skilful ['skilful], *adj.* geschickt, gewandt; (*fig.*) erfahren.

skill [skil], *s.* die Geschicklichkeit, Gewandtheit; (*fig.*) die Erfahrung.

skim [skim], *v.a.* abschöpfen, abschäumen.

skimp [skimp], *v.a.* knausern, sparsam sein (mit, *Dat.*).

skimpy ['skimpi], *adj.* knapp.

skin [skin], *s.* die Haut; die Schale (*fruit*); — *deep*, oberflächlich. — *v.a.* häuten, schinden.

skinflint ['skinflint], *s.* der Geizhals.

skinner ['skinə], *s.* der Kürschner.

skip [skip], *v.n.* springen, hüpfen. — *v.a.* (*coll.*) auslassen, überspringen. — *s.* der Sprung.

skipper ['skipə], *s.* (*Naut.*) der Kapitän; (*coll.*) der Chef.

skipping rope ['skipiŋ roup], *s.* das Springseil.

skirmish ['skə:miʃ], *s.* das Scharmützel. — *v.n.* scharmützeln.

skirt [skə:t], *s.* der Rock, Rockschoß (*woman's garment*); der Saum (*edge*). — *v.a.* einsäumen (*seam, edge*); grenzen, am Rande entlang gehen.

skirting (board) ['skə:tiŋ (bɔːd)], *s.* die Fußleiste.

skit [skit], *s.* die Stichelei, die Parodie, Satire.

skittish ['skitiʃ], *adj.* leichtfertig.

skulk [skʌlk], *v.n.* lauern, herumlungern.

skull [skʌl], *s.* der Schädel; — *and crossbones*, der Totenkopf.

skunk [skʌŋk], *s.* (*Zool.*) das Stinktier; (*coll.*) der Schuft.

sky [skai], *s.* der (sichtbare) Himmel.

skylark ['skailɑːk], *s.* (*Orn.*) die Feldlerche.

skylarking ['skailɑːkiŋ], *s.* das Possenreißen, die Streiche.

skyline ['skailain], *s.* der Horizont.

skyscraper ['skaiskreipə], *s.* der Wolkenkratzer.

slab [slæb], *s.* die Platte (*stone*); die Tafel, das Stück.

slack [slæk], *adj.* schlaff (*feeble*); locker (*loose*). — *s.* der Kohlengrus. — *v.n.* nachlassen, locker werden, faulenzen.

slacken [slækn], *v.a., v.n.* locker werden, nachlassen.

slackness ['slæknis], *s.* die Schlaffheit, Faulheit.

slag [slæg], *s.* die Schlacke.

slake [sleik], *v.a.* dämpfen, löschen, stillen.

slam (1) [slæm], *v.a.* zuwerfen, zuschlagen (*door*). — *s.* der Schlag.

slam (2) [slæm], *v.a.* (*Cards*) Schlemm ansagen, Schlemm machen. — *s.* (*Cards*) der Schlag.

slander ['slɑːndə], *v.a.* verleumden. — *s.* die Verleumdung.

slanderer ['slɑːndərə], *s.* der Verleumder.

slang [slæŋ], *s.* der Slang.

slant [slɑːnt], *s.* die schräge Richtung, der Winkel (*angle*).

slap [slæp], *v.a.* schlagen. — *s.* der Klaps, Schlag.

slapdash ['slæpdæʃ], *adj.* oberflächlich.

slash [slæʃ], *v.a.* schlitzen, aufschlitzen; (*coll.*) (*Comm.*) herunterbringen (*prices*). — *s.* der Hieb, Schlag.

slate [sleit], *s.* der Schiefer. — *v.a.* mit Schiefer decken; (*fig.*) ankreiden, ausschelten (*scold*).

slattern ['slætə:n], *s.* die Schlampe.

slaughter ['slɔːtə], *v.a.* schlachten; niedermetzeln. — *s.* das Schlachten; das Gemetzel.

slave [sleiv], *s.* der Sklave; — *driver*, der Sklavenaufseher. — *v.n.* (*away*), sich placken, sich rackern.

slavery ['sleivəri], *s.* die Sklaverei.

slavish ['sleiviʃ], *adj.* sklavisch.

slay [slei], *v.a.* erschlagen, töten.

sled, sledge [sled, sledʒ], *s.* der Schlitten.

sleek [sli:k], *adj.* glatt. — *v.a.* glätten.

sleep [sli:p], *v.n. irr.* schlafen. — *s.* der Schlaf.

sleeper ['sli:pə], *s.* der Schläfer; (*Railw.*) die Bahnschwelle; der Schlafwagen (*sleeping car*).

sleepwalker ['sli:pwɔːkə], *s.* der Nachtwandler.

sleet [sli:t], *s.* der Graupelregen.

sleeve [sli:v], *s.* der Ärmel; der Umschlag (*of record*); *have up o.'s —*, die Überraschung bereithalten; *laugh in o.'s —*, sich ins Fäustchen lachen.

sleigh [slei], *s.* der Schlitten; — *ride*, die Schlittenfahrt.

sleight [slait], *s.* —*of hand*, der Taschenspielerstreich; der Trick.

slender ['slendə], *adj.* schlank, dünn, gering.

slice [slais], *s.* die Schnitte, Scheibe. — *v.a.* in Scheiben schneiden.

slick [slik], *adj.* glatt.

slide [slaid], *v.n. irr.* gleiten, rutschen (*glide*). — *v.a.* einschieben. — *s.* die Rutschbahn; (*Phot.*) das Dia, Diapositiv; — *rule*, der Rechenschieber.

slight [slait], *adj.* leicht (*light*), gering (*small*); (*fig.*) schwach, dünn(*weak*). — *s.* die Geringschätzung, Respektlosigkeit. — *v.a.* mißachten, geringschätzig behandeln.

slim [slim], *adj.* schlank.

slime [slaim], *s.* der Schleim (*phlegm*); der Schlamm (*mud*).

sling [sliŋ], *v.a. irr.* schléudern, werfen. — *s.* die Schleuder; (*Med.*) die Binde; der Wurf (*throw*).

slink [sliŋk], *v.n. irr.* schleichen.

slip [slip], *v.n.* ausgleiten; — *away*, entschlüpfen; — *up*, einen Fehltritt begehen (*err*). — *v.a.* gleiten lassen, schieben. — *s.* das Ausgleiten; (*fig.*) der Fehltritt; der Fehler (*mistake*); der Unterrock (*petticoat*); *give s.o. the* —, einem entgehen, entschlüpfen.

slipper ['slipə], *s.* der Pantoffel, Hausschuh.

slippery ['slipəri], *adj.* schlüpfrig, glatt.

slipshod ['slipʃɔd], *adj.* nachlässig.

slit [slit], *v.a.* schlitzen, spalten. — *s.* der Schlitz, Spalt.

slither ['sliðə], *v.n.* gleiten, rutschen.

sloe [slou], *s.* (*Bot.*) die Schlehe.

slogan ['slougən], *s.* das Schlagwort.

sloop [slu:p], *s.* (*Naut.*) die Schaluppe.

slop [slɔp], *s.* das Spülicht, Spülwasser.

slope [sloup], *s.* der Abhang, die Abdachung. — *v.n.* sich neigen. — *v.a.* abschrägen.

sloppy ['slɔpi], *adj.* unordentlich, nachlässig.

slot [slɔt], *s.* der Spalt, Schlitz (*slit*); die Kerbe (*notch*); — *machine*, der Automat.

sloth [slouθ], *s.* die Trägheit; (*Zool.*) das Faultier.

slouch [slautʃ], *v.n.* umherschlendern; sich schlaff halten.

slough [slau], *s.* der Morast, Sumpf.

slovenly ['slʌvnli], *adj.* schlampig, schmutzig.

slow [slou], *adj.* langsam; (*Phot.*) *motion*, die Zeitlupenaufnahme. — *v.n.* — *down*, langsamer fahren *or* laufen.

slow-worm ['slouwə:m], *s.* (*Zool.*) die Blindschleiche.

sludge [slʌdʒ], *s.* der Schlamm, Schmutz.

slug [slʌg], *s.* (*Zool.*) die Wegschnecke; (*Am.*) die Kugel.

sluggish ['slʌgiʃ], *adj.* träg(e).

sluice [slu:s], *s.* die Schleuse. — *v.a.* ablassen (*drain*); begießen (*water*).

slum [slʌm], *s.* das Elendsviertel; Haus im Elendsviertel.

slumber ['slʌmbə], *s.* der Schlummer. — *v.n.* schlummern.

slump [slʌmp], *s.* (*Comm.*) der Tiefstand der Konjunktur; der Preissturz. — *v.n.* stürzen.

slur [slə:], *v.a.* undeutlich sprechen. — *s.* der Schandfleck, die Beleidigung; das Bindezeichen.

slush [slʌʃ], *s.* der Matsch, Schlamm; (*Lit.*) der Kitsch, die Schundliteratur.

slut [slʌt], *s.* die Schlampe.

sly [slai], *adj.* schlau, listig.

smack [smæk], *v.n.* schmecken (*of, nach, Dat.*). — *v.a.* schmatzen, lecken. — *s.* der Klaps. — *adv.* (*coll.*) — *in the middle*, gerade in der Mitte.

small [smɔ:l], *adj.* klein; (*fig.*) kleinlich (*petty*); — *talk*, das Geplauder.

smallpox ['smɔ:lpɔks], *s.* (*Med.*) die Blattern, *f. pl.*

smart [smɑ:t], *adj.* schneidig; elegant, schick (*well-dressed*). — *v.n.* schmerzen. — *s.* der Schmerz.

smash [smæʃ], *v.a.* zertrümmern, in Stücke schlagen. — *v.n.* zerschmettern; (*fig.*) zusammenbrechen. — *s.* der Krach.

smattering ['smætəriŋ], *s.* die oberflächliche Kenntnis.

smear [smiə], *v.a.* beschmieren; (*Am. coll.*) den Charakter angreifen, verleumden. — *s.* die Beschmierung, Befleckung.

smell [smel], *v.a. irr.* riechen. — *v.n.* riechen (*nach, Dat.*). — *s.* der Geruch.

smelt (1) [smelt], *v.a.* (*Metall.*) schmelzen.

smelt (2) [smelt], *s.* (*Zool.*) der Stintfisch.

smile [smail], *v.n.* lächeln. — *s.* das Lächeln.

smirk [smə:k], *v.n.* grinsen. — *s.* das Grinsen, die Grimasse.

smite [smait], *v.a. irr.* treffen, schlagen.

smith [smiθ], *s.* der Schmied.

smitten [smitn], *adj.* verliebt.

smock [smɔk], *s.* der Arbeitskittel.

smoke [smouk], *v.a., v.n.* rauchen; räuchern (*fish etc.*). — *s.* der Rauch.

smoked [smoukd], *adj.* — *ham*, der Räucherschinken.

smooth [smu:ð], *adj.* glatt, sanft (*to touch*); (*fig.*) glatt, geschmeidig, wendig. — *v.a.* glätten, ebnen.

smother ['smʌðə], *v.a.* ersticken.

smoulder ['smouldə], *v.n.* schwelen.

smudge [smʌdʒ], *v.a.* beschmutzen. — *v.n.* schmieren, schmutzen. — *s.* der Schmutzfleck, Schmutz.

smug [smʌg], *adj.* selbstgefällig.

smuggle [smʌgl], *v.a.* schmuggeln.

smuggler ['smʌglə], *s.* der Schmuggler.

smut [smʌt], *v.a., v.n.* beschmutzen. — *s.* (*fig.*) der Schmutz.

snack [snæk], *s.* der Imbiß.

snaffle [snæfl], *s.* die Trense.

snag [snæg], *s.* die Schwierigkeit; der Haken.

snail [sneil], *s.* (*Zool.*) die Schnecke.

snake [sneik], *s.* (*Zool.*) die Schlange.

snap [snæp], *v.n.* schnappen (*at, nach, Dat.*); (*fig.*) einen anfahren (*shout at s.o.*). — *v.a.* (er)schnappen; (*Phot.*) knipsen. — *s.* (*abbr. for* **snapshot** ['snæpʃɔt]) (*Phot.*) das Photo.

snare [snɛə], *s.* die Schlinge. — *v.a. see* **ensnare**.

snarl [snɑ:l], *v.n.* knurren (*dog*); — *at s.o.*, einen anfahren, anschnauzen.

snatch [snætʃ], *v.a.* erschnappen, erhaschen.

sneak [sni:k], *v.n.* kriechen, schleichen. — *s.* der Kriecher.

sneer [sniə], *v.n.* höhnen, verhöhnen (*at, Acc.*). — *s.* der Spott.

sneeze [sni:z], *v.n.* niesen. — *s.* das Niesen.

sniff [snif], *v.a.,* *v.n.* schnüffeln.

snigger [ˈsnigə], *v.n.* kichern. — *s.* das Kichern.

snip [snip], *v.a.* schneiden, schnippeln.

snipe (1) [snaip], *s.* (*Orn.*) die Schnepfe.

snipe (2) [snaip], *v.n.* schießen.

snivel [snivl], *v.n.* schluchzen (*from weeping*); verschnupft sein (*with a cold*).

snob [snɔb], *s.* der Snob.

snobbish [ˈsnɔbiʃ], *adj.* vornehm tuend; protzig, snobistisch.

snooze [snu:z], *s.* das Schläfchen. — *v.n.* einschlafen, ein Schläfchen machen.

snore [snɔ:], *v.n.* schnarchen. — *s.* das Schnarchen.

snort [snɔ:t], *v.n.* schnaufen; schnarchen (*snore*).

snout [snaut], *s.* die Schnauze, der Rüssel.

snow [snou], *s.* der Schnee. — *v.n.* schneien.

snowdrift [ˈsnoudrift], *s.* das Schneegestöber.

snowdrop [ˈsnoudrɔp], *s.* (*Bot.*) das Schneeglöckchen.

snub [snʌb], *v.a.* kurz abfertigen; (*fig.*) schneiden (*ignore*). — *adj.* — *nosed*, stumpfnasig. — *s.* die Geringschätzung, das Ignorieren.

snuff [snʌf], *s.* der Schnupftabak. — *v.a.* ausblasen (*candle*).

snug [snʌg], *adj.* behaglich; geborgen (*protected*).

so [sou], *adv.* so, also; *not* — *as*, nicht so wie. — *conj.* so.

soak [souk], *v.a.* einweichen, durchtränken. — *v.n.* weichen, durchsickern (*in*(*to*), in, *Acc.*). — *s.* der Regenguß.

soap [soup], *s.* die Seife. — *v.a.* einseifen.

soar [sɔ:], *v.n.* sich aufschwingen, schweben.

sob [sɔb], *v.n.* schluchzen. — *s.* das Schluchzen.

sober [ˈsoubə], *adj.* nüchtern. — *v.a.,* *v.n.* — (*down*), (sich) ernüchtern.

sobriety [soˈbraiəti], *s.* die Nüchternheit.

soccer [ˈsɔkə], *s.* (*Sport*) das Fußballspiel.

sociable [ˈsouʃəbl], *adj.* gesellig.

social [ˈsouʃəl], *adj.* sozial, gesellschaftlich. — *s.* die Gesellschaft (*party*).

socialism [ˈsouʃəlizm], *s.* (*Pol.*) der Sozialismus.

socialist [ˈsouʃəlist], *adj.* (*Pol.*) sozialistisch, Sozial-. — *s.* der Sozialist.

society [səˈsaiəti], *s.* die Gesellschaft (*human* —); der Verein (*association*); (*Comm.*) die (Handels)gesellschaft.

sock (1) [sɔk], *s.* der Strumpf.

sock (2) [sɔk], *v.a.* (*sl.*) schlagen, boxen.

socket [ˈsɔkit], *s.* *eye* —, die Augenhöhle; (*Elec.*) die Steckdose.

sod [sɔd], *s.* der Rasen, die Erde.

sodden [sɔdn], *adj.* durchweicht.

sofa [ˈsoufə], *s.* das Sofa.

soft [sɔft], *adj.* weich, sanft; einfältig (*stupid*).

soften [sɔfn], *v.a.* weich machen, erweichen. — *v.n.* weich werden, erweichen.

soil [sɔil], *s.* der Boden, die Erde. — *v.a.* beschmutzen.

sojourn [ˈsʌdʒən *or* ˈsɔdʒən], *s.* der Aufenthalt. — *v.n.* sich aufhalten.

solace [ˈsɔlis], *s.* der Trost.

solar [ˈsoulə], *adj.* Sonnen-.

solder [ˈsɔldə *or* ˈsɔːdə], *v.a.* löten. — *s.* das Lötmittel.

soldier [ˈsouldʒə], *s.* der Soldat. — *v.n.* dienen, Soldat sein.

sole (1) [soul], *s.* (*Zool.*) die Seezunge.

sole (2) [soul], *s.* die Sohle (*foot*).

sole (3) [soul], *adj.* allein, einzig.

solecism [ˈsɔlisizm], *s.* der Sprachschnitzer.

solemn [ˈsɔləm], *adj.* feierlich.

solemnize [ˈsɔləmnaiz], *v.a.* feiern, feierlich begehen.

solicit [səˈlisit], *v.a.* direkt erbitten, angehen, anhalten (*for*, um).

solicitor [səˈlisitə], *s.* (*Law*) der Anwalt, Rechtsanwalt.

solicitous [səˈlisitəs], *adj.* besorgt.

solid [ˈsɔlid], *adj.* fest; solide; (*fig.*) gediegen, massiv (*bulky*).

solidify [səˈlidifai], *v.a.* verdichten, fest machen. — *v.n.* sich verfestigen.

soliloquy [səˈliləkwi], *s.* das Selbstgespräch, der Monolog.

solitaire [sɔliˈtɛə], *s.* der Solitär; (*Am.*) die Patience.

solitary [ˈsɔlitəri], *adj.* einzeln (*single*); einsam (*lonely*).

solitude [ˈsɔlitju:d], *s.* die Einsamkeit.

solstice [ˈsɔlstis], *s.* die Sonnenwende.

soluble [ˈsɔljubl], *adj.* (*Chem.*) löslich; lösbar.

solution [səˈlju:ʃən], *s.* die Lösung.

solvable [ˈsɔlvəbl], *adj.* (auf)lösbar (*problem*, *puzzle*).

solve [sɔlv], *v.a.* lösen (*problem*, *puzzle*).

solvent [ˈsɔlvənt], *adj.* (*Chem.*) auflösend; (*Comm.*) zahlungsfähig. — *s.* das Lösungsmittel.

sombre [ˈsɔmbə], *adj.* düster; schwermütig, traurig.

some [sʌm], *adj.* irgend ein, etwas; (*pl.*) einige, manche, etliche.

somebody [ˈsʌmbədi], *s.* jemand.

somersault [ˈsʌməsɔːlt], *s.* der Purzelbaum.

sometimes [ˈsʌmtaimz], *adv.* manchmal, zuweilen.

somewhat [ˈsʌmwɔt], *adv.* etwas, ziemlich.

somewhere [ˈsʌmwɛə], *adv.* irgendwo(hin).

somnambulist [som'næmbjulist], *s.* der Nachtwandler.

somnolent ['somnələnt], *adj.* schläfrig, schlafsüchtig.

son [sʌn], *s.* der Sohn; —-*in-law*, der Schwiegersohn.

song [soŋ], *s.* (*Mus.*) das Lied; der Gesang; *for a* —, spottbillig.

sonnet ['sonit], *s.* (*Poet.*) das Sonett.

sonorous ['sonərəs], *adj.* wohlklingend.

soon [su:n], *adv.* bald.

sooner ['su:nə], *comp. adv.* lieber (*rather*); früher, eher (*earlier*), *no* — *said than done*, gesagt, getan.

soot [sut], *s.* der Ruß.

soothe [su:ð], *v.a.* besänftigen.

soothsayer ['su:θseiə], *s.* der Wahrsager.

sop [sop], *s.* der eingetunkte Bissen; (*fig.*) die Bestechung (*bribe*).

soporific [sopə'rifik], *adj.* einschläfernd.

soprano [sə'prɑ:nou], *s.* (*Mus.*) der Sopran.

sorcerer ['so:sərə], *s.* der Zauberer.

sorceress ['so:sərəs], *s.* die Hexe.

sorcery ['so:səri], *s.* die Zauberei, Hexerei.

sordid ['so:did], *adj.* schmutzig; gemein.

sore [so:], *adj.* wund, schmerzhaft; empfindlich. — *s.* die wunde Stelle.

sorrel (1) ['sorəl], *s.* (*Bot.*) der Sauerampfer.

sorrel (2) ['sorəl], *s.* (*Zool.*) der Rotfuchs.

sorrow ['sorou], *s.* der Kummer, das Leid, der Gram.

sorry ['sori], *adj.* traurig; *I am* —, es tut mir leid.

sort [so:t], *s.* die Art, Gattung, Sorte. — *v.a.* aussortieren.

sortie ['so:ti:], *s.* (*Mil.*) der Ausfall.

sot [sot], *s.* der Trunkenbold.

soul [soul], *s.* die Seele; *not a* —, niemand, keine Menschenseele.

sound (1) [saund], *v.n.*, *v.a.* tönen, klingen, erklingen lassen. — *s.* der Klang, Ton, Laut.

sound (2) [saund], *adj.* gesund; (*fig.*) vernünftig (*plan etc.*); solide.

soup [su:p], *s.* die Suppe.

sour [sauə], *adj.* sauer; (*fig.*) mürrisch.

source [so:s], *s.* die Quelle; der Ursprung (*origin*).

souse [saus], *v.a.* einpökeln, einsalzen.

south [sauθ], *s.* der Süden.

South African [sauθ 'æfrikən], *adj.* südafrikanisch. — *s.* der Südafrikaner.

southern ['sʌðən], *adj.* südlich, Süd-.

sou(th)-wester [sauθ(θ)'westə], *s.* (*Naut.*) der Südwester.

souvenir ['su:vəniə], *s.* das Andenken.

sovereign ['sovrin], *s.* der Herrscher (*ruler*); das Goldstück (£1 *coin*). — *adj.* allerhöchst, souverän.

Soviet ['souviit], *adj.* sowjetisch. — *s.* der Sowjet.

sow (1) [sau], *s.* (*Zool.*) die Sau.

sow (2) [sou], *v.a. irr.* säen, ausstreuen (*cast*).

spa [spɑ:], *s.* das Bad; der Kurort.

space [speis], *s.* der Zwischenraum (*interval*); der Raum, das Weltall, der Kosmos (*interplanetary*); der Platz (*room*). — *v.a.* sperren, richtig plazieren.

spacious ['speiʃəs], *adj.* geräumig.

spade [speid], *s.* der Spaten; *call a* — *a* —, das Kind beim rechten Namen nennen; (*Cards*) das Pik.

span [spæn], *s.* die Spanne (*time*); die Spannweite. — *v.a.* überspannen (*bridge*); ausmessen.

spangle ['spæŋgl], *s.* der Flitter. — *v.a.* beflittern, schmücken.

Spaniard ['spænjəd], *s.* der Spanier.

spaniel ['spænjəl], *s.*(*Zool.*) der Wachtelhund.

Spanish ['spæniʃ], *adj.* spanisch.

spanner ['spænə], *s.* der Schraubenschlüssel.

spar (1) [spɑ:], *s.* (*Naut.*) der Sparren.

spar (2) [spɑ:], *s.* (*Geol.*) der Spat.

spar (3) [spɑ:], *v.n.* boxen.

spare [spɛə], *v.a.* schonen (*save*); sparsam sein; übrig haben. — *v.n.* sparen; sparsam sein. — *adj.* übrig (*extra*); mager, hager (*lean*); Reserve- (*tyre etc.*).

sparing ['spɛəriŋ], *adj.* sparsam, karg.

spark [spɑ:k], *s.* der Funken; (*fig.*) der helle Kopf.

sparkle [spɑ:kl], *v.n.* glänzen, funkeln. — *s.* das Funkeln.

sparrow ['spærou], *s.* (*Orn.*) der Sperling.

sparrowhawk ['spærouhɔ:k], *s.* (*Orn.*) der Sperber.

sparse [spɑ:s], *adj.* spärlich, dünn.

spasm [spæzm], *s.* der Krampf.

spasmodic [spæz'modik], *adj.* krampfhaft; (*fig.*) ab und zu auftretend.

spats [spæts], *s. pl.* die Gamaschen, *f.pl.*

spatter ['spætə], *v.a.* bespritzen, besudeln.

spatula ['spætjulə], *s.* der Spachtel.

spawn [spo:n], *s.* der Laich, die Brut.

speak [spi:k], *v.a.*, *v.n. irr.* sprechen, reden; — *out*, frei heraussprechen.

speaker ['spi:kə], *s.* der Sprecher.

spear [spiə], *s.* der Spieß, Speer, die Lanze. — *v.a.* aufspießen.

special [speʃl], *adj.* besonder, speziell, Sonder-.

specific [spi'sifik], *adj.* spezifisch, eigentümlich.

specify ['spesifai], *v.a.* spezifizieren.

specimen ['spesimən], *s.* die Probe; (*Comm.*) das Muster.

specious ['spi:ʃəs], *adj.* bestechend, trügerisch.

speck [spek], *s.* der Fleck.

speckle [spekl], *s.* der Tüpfel, Sprenkel. — *v.a.* sprenkeln.

spectacle ['spektəkl], *s.* das Schauspiel, der Anblick; (*pl.*) die Brille.

spectator [spek'teitə], *s.* der Zuschauer.

spectre ['spektə], *s.* das Gespenst.

speculate ['spekjuleit], *v.n.* nachsinnen, grübeln (*ponder*); spekulieren.

speculative

speculative [ˈspekjulətiv], *adj.* spekulativ; sinnend.

speech [spiːtʃ], *s.* die Rede, Ansprache; das Sprechen (*articulation*); *figure of* —, die Redewendung; *make a —,* eine Rede halten.

speechify [ˈspiːtʃifai], *v.n.* viele Worte machen, unermüdlich reden.

speed [spiːd], *s.* die Eile; die Geschwindigkeit (*velocity*); (*Mus.*) das Tempo. — *v.a.* (eilig) fortschicken. — *v.n.* eilen, schnell fahren; — *up,* sich beeilen.

spell (1) [spel], *s.* der Zauber (*enchantment*). — *v.a.* buchstabieren (*verbally*); richtig schreiben (*in writing*).

spell (2) [spel], *s.* die Zeitlang, Zeit (*period*).

spellbound [ˈspelbaund], *adj.* bezaubert, gebannt.

spend [spend], *v.a. irr.* ausgeben (*money*); verbringen (*time*); aufwenden (*energy*); erschöpfen (*exhaust*).

spendthrift [ˈspendθrift], *s.* der Verschwender.

spew [spjuː], *v.a.* speien; ausspeien.

sphere [sfiə], *s.* die Sphäre (*also fig.*); (*Geom.*) die Kugel.

spice [spais], *s.* die Würze (*seasoning*); das Gewürz (*herb*). — *v.a.* würzen.

spider [ˈspaidə], *s.* (*Zool.*) die Spinne.

spigot [ˈspigət], *s.* (*Mech.*) der Zapfen.

spike [spaik], *s.* die Spitze, der lange Nagel; (*fig.*) der Dorn. — *v.a.* durchbohren, spießen; (*Mil.*) vernageln (*a gun*).

spill (1) [spil], *v.a. irr.* ausschütten, vergießen; (*Am. coll.*) — *the beans,* mit der Sprache herausrücken, alles verraten; *it's no good crying over spilt milk,* was geschehen ist, ist geschehen.

spill (2) [spil], *s.* der Fidibus.

spin [spin], *v.a. irr.* spinnen, drehen, wirbeln; — *v.n.* wirbeln, sich schnell drehen; — *dry,* schleudern. — *s.* die schnelle Drehung; — *drier,* die Wäscheschleuder.

spinach [ˈspinidʒ], *s.* (*Bot.*) der Spinat.

spinal [ˈspainal], *adj.* Rückgrats–.

spine [spain], *s.* (*Anat.*) die Wirbelsäule; der Rücken (*of book*).

spinney [ˈspini], *s.* das Gestrüpp.

spinster [ˈspinstə], *s.* die (alte) Jungfer; die unverheiratete Dame.

spiral [ˈspaiərəl], *adj.* Spiral–, gewunden. — *s.* (*Geom.*) die Spirale.

spirant [ˈspaiərənt], *s.* (*Phonet.*) der Spirant.

spire [spaiə], *s.* (*Archit.*) die Turmspitze.

spirit [ˈspirit], *s.* der Geist; das Gespenst (*ghost*); der Mut (*courage*); die Stimmung, Verfassung (*mood*); das geistige Getränk (*drink*), (*pl.*) Spirituosen, *pl.*; *in high —s,* in guter Stimmung, Laune. — *v.a.* — *away,* entführen, verschwinden lassen.

spiritual [ˈspirituəl], *adj.* geistig (*mental*); (*Rel.*) geistlich. — *s.* (*Mus.*) das Negerlied.

spit (1) [spit], *s.* der Spieß, Bratspieß. — *v.a.* aufspießen.

spit (2) [spit], *v.n. irr.* ausspucken. — *s.* die Spucke.

spite [spait], *s.* der Groll; *in — of,* trotz (*Genit.*). — *v.a.* ärgern.

spiteful [ˈspaitful], *adj.* boshaft.

spittle [spitl], *s.* der Speichel.

spittoon, [spiˈtuːn], *s.* der Spucknapf.

splash [splæʃ], *s.* der Spritzer; *make a —,* Aufsehen erregen. — *v.a., v.n.* spritzen; (*fig.*) um sich werfen (*money etc.*).

splay [splei], *v.a.* ausrenken, verrenken.

spleen [spliːn], *s.* (*Anat.*) die Milz; (*fig.*) der Spleen, die Laune, Marotte.

splendour [ˈsplendə], *s.* die Pracht, der Glanz.

splice [splais], *v.a.* splissen; (*Naut.*) — *the mainbrace,* das Hauptfaß öffnen!

splint [splint], *s.* (*Med.*) die Schiene.

splinter [ˈsplintə], *s.* der Span; der Splitter (*fragment*).

split [split], *v.a. irr.* spalten; (*fig.*) verteilen, teilen (*divide*). — *v.n.* sich trennen; (*coll.*) — *on s.o.,* einen verraten. — *adj.* — *second timing,* auf den Bruchteil einer Sekunde. — *s.* die Spaltung.

splutter [ˈsplatə], *v.n.* sprudeln. — *s.* das Sprudeln.

spoil [spɔil], *v.a. irr.* verderben; (*child*) verwöhnen; (*Mil.*) plündern, berauben. — *v.n.* verderben. — *s.* (*pl.*) die Beute.

spoilsport [ˈspɔilspɔːt], *s.* der Spielverderber.

spoke [spouk], *s.* die Speiche; die Sprosse.

spokesman [ˈspouksmən], *s.* der Wortführer, Sprecher.

sponge [spandʒ], *s.* der Schwamm; — *cake,* die Sandtorte. — *v.a.* mit dem Schwamm wischen; — *v.n.* (*coll.*) schmarotzen (*on,* bei, *Dat.*).

sponger [ˈspandʒə], *s.* (*coll.*) der Schmarotzer (*parasite*).

sponsor [ˈspɔnsə], *s.* der Bürge (*guarantor*); der Förderer; Pate. — *v.a.* fördern, unterstützen.

spontaneous [spɔnˈteiniəs], *adj.* spontan, freiwillig.

spook [spuk], *s.* der Spuk, Geist, das Gespenst.

spool [spuːl], *s.* die Spule. — *v.a.* aufspulen.

spoon [spuːn], *s.* der Löffel. — *v.a.* mit dem Löffel essen, löffeln.

sport [spɔːt], *s.* der Sport; (*fig.*) der Scherz. — *v.a.* tragen (*wear*). — *v.n.* scherzen.

spot [spɔt], *s.* die Stelle, der Ort, Platz; (*stain*) der Fleck; (*fig.*) der Schandfleck (*on o.'s honour*); *on the —,* sogleich; auf der Stelle; *in a —,* (*Am. coll.*) in Verlegenheit; — *cash,* Barzahlung, *f.* — *v.a.* entdecken, finden.

spotted [ˈspɔtid], *adj.* fleckig, gefleckt; befleckt; pickelig.

spouse [spauz], *s.* der Gatte; die Gattin.

490

spout [spaut], *v.a.*, *v.n.* ausspeien, sprudeln, sprudeln lassen; (*sl.*) predigen, schwatzen. — *s.* die Tülle (*teapot etc.*); die Abflußröhre.

sprain [sprein], *v.a.* (*Med.*) verrenken. — *s.* die Verrenkung.

sprat [spræt], *s.* (*Zool.*) die Sprotte.

sprawl [sprɔːl], *v.n.* sich spreizen, ausbreiten.

spray [sprei], *s.*, *v.n.* sprühen spritzen. — *s.* die Sprühe; der Sprühregen.

spread [spred], *v.a.*, *v.n.* *irr.* ausbreiten; verbreiten (*get abroad*); streichen (*overlay with*). — *s.* die Ausbreitung; Verbreitung.

spree [spriː], *s.* das Vergnügen, der lustige Abend, Bummel.

sprig [sprig], *s.* der Zweig, Sprößling.

sprightly [ˈspraitli], *adj.* munter, lebhaft.

spring [spriŋ], *s.* die Quelle (*water*); der Ursprung (*origin*); der Frühling (*season*); (*Mech.*) die Feder, Sprungfeder, Spirale. — *v.n. irr.* springen (*jump*); entspringen (*originate*). — *v.a.* — *a surprise*, eine Überraschung bereiten.

springe [sprindʒ], *s.* der Sprenkel.

sprinkle [spriŋkl], *v.a.* (be)sprengen; (*Hort.*) berieseln.

sprint [sprint], *s.* der Kurzstreckenlauf, Wettlauf.

sprite [sprait], *s.* der Geist, Kobold.

sprout [spraut], *s.* (*Bot.*) die Sprosse, der Sprößling; *Brussels —s*, der Rosenkohl.

spruce (1) [spruːs], *adj.* sauber, geputzt; schmuck.

spruce (2) [spruːs], *s.* (*Bot.*) die Fichte, Rottanne.

spume [spjuːm], *s.* der Schaum.

spur [spəː], *s.* der Sporn (*goad*); (*fig.*) der Stachel; der Ansporn, Antrieb; (*Geog.*) der Ausläufer (*of range*). — *v.a.* anspornen.

spurious [ˈspjuəriəs], *adj.* unecht, falsch.

spurn [spəːn], *v.a.* verschmähen, verachten.

spurt [spəːt], *v.a.* spritzen. — *v.n.* sich anstrengen. — *s.* die Anstrengung.

sputter [ˈspʌtə], *v.a.* herausprudeln. — *v.n.* sprühen, sprudeln.

spy [spai], *s.* der Spion. — *v.n.* spionieren (*on*, bei, *Dat.*).

squabble [skwɔbl], *v.n.* zanken. — *s.* der Zank, Streit.

squad [skwɔd], *s.* der Trupp.

squadron [ˈskwɔdrən], *s.* die Schwadron, das Geschwader.

squalid [ˈskwɔlid], *adj.* schmutzig, elend, eklig.

squall [skwɔːl], *s.* der Windstoß.

squalor [ˈskwɔlə], *s.* der Schmutz.

squander [skwɔndə], *v.a.* verschwenden, vergeuden.

square [skwɛə], *s.*, das Quadrat; der Platz; (*coll.*) der Philister, Spießer. — *v.a.* ausrichten; (*coll.*) ins Reine bringen. — *adj.* viereckig; quadratisch; redlich (*honest*); quitt (*quits*).

squash (1) [skwɔʃ], *v.a.* zerquetschen, zerdrücken (*press together*). — *s.* das Gedränge (*crowd*); der Fruchtsaft (*drink*).

squash (2) [skwɔʃ], *s.* (*Sport*) eine Art Racketspiel.

squat [skwɔt], *v.n.* kauern; sich niederlassen. — *adj.* stämmig, untersetzt.

squatter [ˈskwɔtə], *s.* der Ansiedler.

squaw [skwɔː], *s.* die Indianerfrau.

squeak [skwiːk], *v.n.* quieken, quietschen. — *s.* das Gequiek.

squeal [skwiːl], *v.n.* quieken; (*Am. coll.*) verraten, preisgeben.

squeamish [ˈskwiːmiʃ], *adj.* empfindlich, zimperlich.

squeeze [skwiːz], *v.a.* drücken, quetschen. — *s.* das Gedränge.

squib [skwib], *s.* der Frosch (*firework*); (*Lit.*) das Spottgedicht.

squint [skwint], *v.n.* schielen. — *s.* das Schielen.

squire [skwaiə], *s.* der Landedelmann, Junker.

squirrel [ˈskwirəl], *s.* (*Zool.*) das Eichhörnchen.

squirt [skwəːt], *v.a.* spritzen. — *s.* der Spritzer, Wasserstrahl; (*sl.*) der Wicht.

stab [stæb], *v.a.* erstechen, erdolchen. — *s.* der Dolchstich, Dolchstoß.

stability [stəˈbiliti], *s.* die Beständigkeit, Stabilität.

stable (1) [steibl], *adj.* fest, beständig; (*Phys.*) stabil.

stable (2) [steibl], *s.* der Stall.

stack [stæk], *s.* der Stoß (*pile*); der Schornstein (*chimneys*). — *v.a.* aufschichten.

staff [stɑːf], *s.* der Stab, Stock; (*Mil.*) der Stab, Generalstab; (*Sch.*) der Lehrkörper; das Personal. — *v.a.* besetzen.

stag [stæg], *s.* (*Zool.*) der Hirsch; *— party*, die Herrengesellschaft.

stage [steidʒ], *s.* (*Theat.*) die Bühne; die Stufe, das Stadium (*phase*); (*fig.*) der Schauplatz; *fare —*, die Teilstrecke. — *v.a.* (*Theat.*) inszenieren, abhalten (*hold*).

stagecoach [ˈsteidʒkoutʃ], *s.* die Postkutsche.

stagger [ˈstægə], *v.n.* schwanken, wanken, taumeln. — *v.a.* (*coll.*) verblüffen (*astonish*); staffeln (*graduate*).

stagnate [stægˈneit], *v.n.* stocken, stillstehen.

staid [steid], *adj.* gesetzt, gelassen.

stain [stein], *s.* der Fleck, Makel. — *v.a.* beflecken; beizen; färben (*dye*).

stained [steind], *adj.* — *glass window*, buntes Fenster.

stainless [ˈsteinlis], *adj.* rostfrei.

stair [stɛə], *s.* die Stufe, Stiege.

staircase [ˈstɛəkeis], *s.* das Treppenhaus; die Treppe.

stake [steik], *s.* der Pfahl, Pfosten; Scheiterhaufen; (*Gambling*) der Einsatz; *at —*, auf dem Spiel. — *v.a.* aufs Spiel setzen.

stale [steil], *adj.* abgestanden, schal.

stalemate ['steilmeit], s. (Chess) das Patt; der Stillstand.
stalk (1) [stɔ:k], s. (Bot.) der Stengel, Halm.
stalk (2) [stɔ:k], v.n. stolzieren, steif gehen. — v.a. pirschen (hunt).
stall [stɔ:l], s. die Bude (booth), der Stand (stand); (Eccl.) der Chorstuhl; (Theat.) der Sperrsitz; Parterresitz. — v.n. (Motor.) stehenbleiben.
stallion ['stæljən], s. (Zool.) der Hengst.
stalwart ['stɔ:lwət], adj. kräftig, stark, verläßlich.
stamina ['stæminə], s. die Ausdauer, Widerstandskraft.
stammer ['stæmə], v.n. stammeln, stottern.
stamp [stæmp], s. der Stempel (rubber —); die Marke (postage); die Stampfe, Stanze (die —). — v.a. stempeln; (Mech.) stanzen; frankieren (letters). — v.n. stampfen.
stampede [stæm'pi:d], s. die wilde Flucht. — v.n. in wilder Flucht davonlaufen.
stand [stænd], v.n. irr. stehen. — v.a. aushalten, standhalten (Dat.). — s. der Ständer (hats etc.); der Stand (stall); (fig.) die Stellung.
standard ['stændəd], s. der Standard (level); (Mil.) die Standarte; der Maßstab (yardstick). — adj. normal.
standing ['stændiŋ], s. der Rang, das Ansehen. — adj. — orders, die Geschäftsordnung; (Mil.) die Vorschriften, f. pl., (Mil.) die Dauerbefehle, m. pl.
standpoint ['stændpɔint], s. der Standpunkt (point of view).
standstill ['stændstil], s. der Stillstand.
stanza ['stænzə], s. (Poet.) die Stanze, Strophe.
staple [steipl], s. das Haupterzeugnis; der Stapelplatz. — adj. Haupt-. — v.a. stapeln; heften (paper).
stapler ['steiplə], s. die Heftmaschine.
star [stɑ:], s. der Stern; (Theat. etc.) der Star. — v.n. (Theat. etc.) die Hauptrolle spielen.
starboard ['stɑ:bəd], s. das Steuerbord.
starch [stɑ:tʃ], s. die Stärke (laundry). — v.a. stärken.
stare [steə], v.n. starren. — s. der starre Blick, das Starren.
stark [stɑ:k], adj. völlig, ganz.
starling ['stɑ:liŋ], s. (Orn.) der Star.
start [stɑ:t], v.n. anfangen; aufbrechen; auffahren, aufspringen; stutzen (jerk); abfahren (depart). — v.a. starten (car etc.), in Gang setzen. — s. der Anfang; (Sport) der Start, Anlauf; der Aufbruch (departure); by fits and —s, ruckweise.
starter ['stɑ:tə], s. (Sport) der Starter, Teilnehmer (participant); das Rennpferd (horse); (Motor.) der Anlasser.
startle [stɑ:tl], v.a. erschrecken.
starve [stɑ:v], v.n. verhungern, hungern. — v.a. aushungern.
state [steit], s. der Zustand, die Lage;

(Pol.) der Staat; (personal) der Stand (single etc.). — v.a. erklären, darlegen.
stately ['steitli], adj. stattlich, prachtvoll.
statement ['steitmənt], s. die Feststellung; bank —, der Kontoauszug.
statesman ['steitsmən], s. der Staatsmann, Politiker.
statics ['stætiks], s. die Statik.
station ['steiʃən], s. (Railw.) die Station; der Bahnhof; die Stellung, der Rang (position); (Mil.) die Stationierung. — v.a. (Mil.) aufstellen, stationieren; (fig.) hinstellen.
stationary ['steiʃənri], adj. stationär, stillstehend.
stationer ['steiʃənə], s. der Papierhändler.
stationery ['steiʃənri], s. das Briefpapier, Schreibpapier; die Papierwaren, f. pl.
statuary ['stætjuəri], s. die Bildhauerkunst.
statue ['stætju:], s. das Standbild.
status ['steitəs], s. die Stellung (rank, position).
statute ['stætju:t], s. das Statut; — law, das Landesrecht, Gesetzesrecht.
staunch [stɔ:ntʃ], adj. zuverlässig.
stave [steiv], s. die Faßdaube (of vat); (Poet.) die Strophe; (Mus.) die Linie. — v.a. — off, abwehren.
stay [stei], v.n. bleiben, verweilen, wohnen. — v.a. hindern, aufhalten. — s. der Aufenthalt; (pl.) das Korsett.
stead [sted], s. die Stelle; in his —, an seiner Statt.
steadfast ['stedfa:st], adj. standhaft, fest.
steadiness ['stedinis], s. die Beständigkeit.
steady ['stedi], adj. fest, sicher; beständig, treu.
steak [steik], s. das Steak.
steal [sti:l], v.a. irr. stehlen. — v.n. sich stehlen, schleichen.
stealth [stelθ], s. die Heimlichkeit.
stealthy ['stelθi], adj. heimlich, verstohlen.
steam [sti:m], s. der Dampf; get up —, in Gang bringen or kommen; — boiler, der Dampfkessel. — v.n. dampfen; davondampfen. — v.a. dämpfen, (Cul.) dünsten.
steed [sti:d], s. das Schlachtroß.
steel [sti:l], s. der Stahl. — adj. stählern. — v.n. — o.s., sich stählen.
steep (1) [sti:p], adj. steil; (fig.) hoch; (coll.) gesalzen (price).
steep (2) [sti:p], v.a. einweichen, sättigen.
steeple [sti:pl], s. (Archit.) der Kirchturm.
steeplechase ['sti:pltʃeis], s. das Hindernisrennen.
steeplejack ['sti:pldʒæk], s. der Turmdecker.
steer (1) [stiə], s. (Zool.) der junge Stier.
steer (2) [stiə], v.a. steuern (guide).
steerage ['stiəridʒ], s. die Steuerung; (Naut.) das Zwischendeck.

stellar ['stelə], *adj.* Stern-, Sternen-.

stem (1) [stem], *s.* der Stamm; (*Phonet.*) der Stamm; der Stiel, die Wurzel. — *v.n.* — *from*, kommen von, abstammen.

stem (2) [stem], *v.a.* sich entgegenstemmen (*Dat.*); (*fig.*) eindämmen.

stench [stentʃ], *s.* der Gestank.

stencil ['stensil], *s.* die Schablone, Matrize; *cut a* —, auf Matrize schreiben.

step [step], *s.* der Schritt, Tritt; (*of ladder*) die Sprosse; (*of stairs*) die Stufe. — *v.n.* treten, schreiten (*stride*). — *v.a.* (*coll.*) — *up*, beschleunigen.

step- [step], *pref.* Stief- (*brother, mother etc.*).

stereo- ['stiariou], *pref.* Stereo-.

sterile ['sterail], *adj.* steril.

sterling ['stə:liŋ], *adj.* echt, vollwertig; *pound* —, ein Pfund Sterling.

stern (1) [stə:n], *adj.* streng.

stern (2) [stə:n], *s.* (*Naut.*) das Heck.

stevedore ['sti:vədɔ:], *s.* der Hafenarbeiter.

stew [stju:], *s.* (*Cul.*) das Schmorfleisch, das Gulasch.

steward ['stju:əd], *s.* der Verwalter; der Haushofmeister; (*Naut.*) der Steward.

stick [stik], *s.* der Stock, Stecken. — *v.a.* stecken (*insert*); kleben (*glue*). — *v.n.* stecken, haften bleiben; (*fig., coll.*) — *to s.o.*, zu jemandem halten (*be loyal*).

sticky ['stiki], *adj.* klebrig; (*fig.*) prekär, schwierig (*difficult*); *come to a* — *end*, ein böses Ende nehmen.

stiff [stif], *adj.* steif; schwer, schwierig (*examination*); formell (*manner*).

stiffen [stifn], *v.a.* steifen, versteifen. — *v.n.* steif werden, sich versteifen.

stifle [staifl], *v.a., v.n.* ersticken; (*fig.*) unterdrücken.

stigmatize ['stigmətaiz], *v.a.* stigmatisieren, brandmarken.

stile [stail], *s.* der Zauntritt, Übergang.

still (1) [stil], *adj.* still, ruhig. — *adv.* immer noch. — *conj.* doch, dennoch. — *v.a.* stillen, beruhigen.

still (2) [stil], *s.* die Destillierflasche, der Destillierkolben.

stilt [stilt], *s.* die Stelze.

stilted ['stiltid], *adj.* auf Stelzen; (*fig.*) hochtrabend, geschraubt.

stimulant ['stimjulənt], *s.* das Reizmittel. — *adj.* anreizend, anregend.

stimulate ['stimjuleit], *v.a.* anreizen, stimulieren, anregen.

stimulus ['stimjuləs], *s.* der Reiz, die Anregung.

sting [stiŋ], *v.a. irr.* stechen; (*fig.*) kränken, verwunden. — *v.n. irr.* stechen, brennen, schmerzen. — *s.* der Stachel (*prick*); der Stich (*stab*).

stink [stiŋk], *v.n. irr.* stinken. — *s.* der Gestank.

stint [stint], *s.* die Einschränkung (*limit*); das Maß, Tagespensum. — *v.a.* beschränken, einschränken.

stipend ['staipend], *s.* die Besoldung, das Gehalt.

stipendiary [stai'pendiəri], *adj.* besoldet, bezahlt.

stipulate ['stipjuleit], *v.a.* festsetzen, ausbedingen.

stir [stə:], *v.a.* rühren, bewegen. — *v.n.* sich rühren. — *s.* die Aufregung; *cause a* —, Aufsehen erregen.

stirrup ['stirəp], *s.* der Steigbügel.

stitch [stitʃ], *v.a.* sticken, nähen. — *s.* der Stich; der stechende Schmerz, der Seitenstich (*pain*).

stoat [stout], *s.* (*Zool.*) das Hermelin.

stock [stɔk], *s.* das Lager; *in* —, auf Lager; vorrätig; der Stamm, die Familie; (*Fin.*) das Kapital; — *exchange*, die Börse; (*pl.*) die Börsenpapiere, *n. pl.*, Aktien, *f. pl.* — *v.a.* halten, führen.

stockade [stɔ'keid], *s.* das Staket.

stockbroker ['stɔkbroukə], *s.* (*Fin.*) der Börsenmakler.

stockholder ['stɔkhouldə], *s.* (*Fin., Am.*) der Aktionär.

stocking ['stɔkiŋ], *s.* der Strumpf.

stocktaking ['stɔkteikiŋ], *s.* die Inventuraufnahme.

stoical ['stouikəl], *adj.* stoisch.

stoke [stouk], *v.a.* schüren.

stoker ['stoukə], *s.* der Heizer.

stole [stoul], *s.* (*Eccl.*) die Stola; der Pelzkragen (*fur*).

stolid ['stɔlid], *adj.* schwerfällig, gleichgültig.

stomach ['stʌmək], *s.* der Magen; (*fig.*) der Appetit.

stone [stoun], *s.* der Stein; der Kern (*fruit*). — *v.a.* steinigen (*throw* —*s at*); entsteinen (*fruit*).

stony ['stouni], *adj.* steinig; (*sl.*) — *broke*, pleite.

stool [stu:l], *s.* der Schemel, Hocker; (*Med.*) der Stuhlgang.

stoop [stu:p], *v.n.* sich bücken; (*fig.*) sich herablassen.

stooping ['stu:piŋ], *adj.* gebückt.

stop [stɔp], *v.a.* halten, stoppen; aufhören; aufhalten (*halt*); — *up*, verstopfen, versperren (*block*); (*tooth*) plombieren. — *v.n.* stehen bleiben (*stand*); sich aufhalten (*stay*). — *s.* der Halt, die Haltestelle (*of bus etc.*); das Aufhalten, Innehalten (*stoppage*); das Register (*organ*); (*Gram.*) der Punkt.

stoppage ['stɔpidʒ], *s.* die Stockung, Hemmung (*hindrance*); die Arbeitseinstellung (*strike*).

stopper ['stɔpə], *s.* der Stöpsel.

storage ['stɔ:ridʒ], *s.* das Lagern.

store [stɔ:], *s.* der Vorrat, das Lagerhaus, Magazin; (*Am.*) das Kaufhaus; (*fig.*) die Menge (*of anecdotes etc.*). — *v.a.* lagern.

storey ['stɔ:ri], *s.* das Stockwerk.

stork [stɔ:k], *s.* (*Orn.*) der Storch.

storm [stɔ:m], *s.* der Sturm, das Gewitter.

story ['stɔ:ri], *s.* die Geschichte, Erzählung (*narrative*).

stout [staut], *adj.* fest; stark, kräftig. — *s.* das starke Bier.

stove [stouv], *s.* der Ofen.

stow [stou], *v.a.* verstauen, packen. — *v.n.* — *away*, als blinder Passagier fahren.

stowaway ['stouəwei], *s.* der blinde Passagier.

straddle [strædl], *v.n.* rittlings sitzen.

straggle [strægl], *v.n.* umherschweifen, streifen, (*Bot.*) wuchern.

straight [streit], *adj.* gerade, offen. — *adv.* — *away*, sofort, sogleich.

straighten [streitn], *v.a.* ausrichten, gerade richten. — *v.n.* sich ausrichten.

strain [strein], *s.* die Anstrengung, Anspannung; (*Mus.*) der Ton, Stil; der Hang. — *v.a.* anstrengen, filtrieren; seihen. — *v.n.* sich anstrengen.

strainer ['streinə], *s.* der Seiher, der Filter, das Sieb.

strait [streit], *adj.* eng. — *s.* (*usually pl.*) die Enge, Meerenge.

strand (1) [strænd], *s.* der Strand.

strand (2) [strænd], *s.* die Litze (*of rope, string*).

strange [streindʒ], *adj.* fremd (*unknown*); seltsam (*queer*).

stranger ['streindʒə], *s.* der Fremdling, Fremde; der Unbekannte.

strangle [strængl], *v.a.* erdrosseln, erwürgen.

strangulation [stræŋgju'leiʃən], *s.* die Erdrosselung, Erwürgung.

strap [stræp], *v.a.* festschnallen, anschnallen. — *s.* der Gurt, Riemen.

strapping ['stræpiŋ], *adj.* stark, stämmig.

strata *see under* **stratum**.

stratagem ['strætədʒəm], *s.* die List; (*Mil.*) der Plan.

strategy ['strætədʒi], *s.* die Strategie.

stratification [strætifi'keiʃən], *s.* die Schichtung, (*Geol.*) die Lagerung.

stratum ['streitəm], *s.* (*pl.* **strata** ['streitə]) die Schicht, Lage.

straw [strɔː], *s.* das Stroh; *that's the last* —, das ist die Höhe!

strawberry ['strɔːbəri], *s.* (*Bot.*) die Erdbeere.

stray [strei], *v.n.* irregehen, schweifen; sich verirren. — *adj.* irr, verirrt.

streak [striːk], *s.* der Strich; der Streifen; (*fig.*) der Anflug.

streaky ['striːki], *adj.* gestreift; (*bacon*) durchwachsen.

stream [striːm], *v.n.* strömen, wehen (*in the wind*). — *s.* die Strömung (*flow*); der Bach (*brook*), der Strom (*river*).

streamer ['striːmə], *s.* der Wimpel, das Band, die Papierschlange.

street [striːt], *s.* die Straße; —*s ahead*, weit voraus.

streetcar ['striːtkaː], *s.* (*Am.*) see **tram**.

streetlamp ['striːtlæmp], *s.* die Straßenlaterne.

strength [streŋθ], *s.* die Stärke; die Kraft.

strengthen ['streŋθən], *v.a.* stärken; (*fig.*) bekräftigen (*support*).

strenuous ['strenjuəs], *adj.* anstrengend.

stress [stres], *v.a.* (*Phonet.*) betonen; (*fig.*) hervorheben. — *s.* die Betonung (*emphasis*); der Druck (*pressure*).

stretch [stretʃ], *v.a.* spannen; strecken, ausstrecken; — *a point*, eine Ausnahme machen. — *s.* die Strecke (*distance*); (*coll.*) die Zuchthausstrafe (*penal sentence*).

stretcher ['stretʃə], *s.* die Tragbahre.

strew [struː], *v.a.* streuen, ausstreuen.

strict [strikt], *adj.* streng (*severe*); genau (*exact*).

stricture ['striktʃə], *s.* der Tadel, die Kritik; (*pl.*) die kritische Rede.

stride [straid], *v.n. irr.* schreiten. — *s.* der Schritt; *take in o.'s* —, leicht bewältigen.

strident ['straidənt], *adj.* laut, lärmend, grell.

strife [straif], *s.* der Streit, Zank.

strike [straik], *v.a.*, *v.n. irr.* schlagen; abmachen (*bargain*); (*Mus.*) — *up*, anstimmen (*song*), aufspielen (*instrument*); beginnen; — *the eye*, auffallen; streiken, in Streik treten. — *s.* der Streik, die Arbeitseinstellung.

striking ['straikiŋ], *adj.* auffallend.

string [striŋ], *s.* die Schnur; (*Mus.*) die Saite; — *quartet*, das Streichquartett; die Reihe (*series*). — *v.a.* anreihen (*beads etc.*); — *together*, verbinden. — *v.n.* — *along*, sich anschließen.

stringency ['strindʒənsi], *s.* die Strenge (*severity*); die Knappheit (*shortage*).

stringent ['strindʒənt], *adj.* streng (*severe*); knapp (*short*).

strip [strip], *s.* der Streifen. — *v.a.*, *v.n.* abstreifen, (sich) entkleiden; (sich) entblößen.

stripe [straip], *s.* der (Farb)streifen; die Strieme (*mark on body*). — *v.a.* streifen, bestreifen.

strive [straiv], *v.n. irr.* sich bemühen (*for*, um, *Acc.*), streben (*for*, nach, *Dat.*).

stroke (1) [strouk], *v.a.* streicheln.

stroke (2) [strouk], *s.* der Strich (*brush*); der Streich (*sword*), der Stoß (*blow*); (*Med.*) der Schlaganfall.

stroll [stroul], *v.n.* schlendern.

strolling ['strouliŋ], *adj.* — *players*, die Wandertruppe.

strong [strɔŋ], *adj.* stark.

strongbox ['strɔŋbɔks], *s.* die Geldkassette.

strongroom ['strɔŋrum], *s.* der Geldtresor.

strop [strɔp], *s.* der Streichriemen.

structure ['strʌktʃə], *s.* der Bau, Aufbau; die Struktur.

struggle [strʌgl], *s.* der Kampf, das Ringen. — *v.n.* kämpfen, ringen.

strut [strʌt], *v.n.* stolzieren.

stub [stʌb], *s.* der Stumpf, Stummel (*cigarette*). — *v.a.* — *out*, ausmachen, auslöschen (*cigarette etc.*).

stubble [stʌbl], *s.* die Stoppel, das Stoppelfeld; die (Bart)stoppeln, *f. pl.* (*beard*).

stubborn [ˈstʌbən], *adj.* eigensinnig, hartnäckig.

stucco [ˈstʌkou], *s.* die Stuckarbeit.

stud (1) [stʌd], *s.* der Hemdenknopf, Kragenknopf (*collar* —). — *v.a.* beschlagen (*nail*); besetzen (*bejewel*).

stud (2) [stʌd], *s.* das Gestüt (*horses*).

student [ˈstjuːdənt], *s.* der Student.

studied [ˈstʌdid], *adj.* geziert, absichtlich (*deliberate*); gelehrt (*learned*).

studio [ˈstjuːdiou], *s.* (*Phot.*) das Atelier; (*Film, Rad.*) das Studio.

studious [ˈstjuːdiəs], *adj.* beflissen, fleißig, lernbegierig.

study [ˈstʌdi], *v.a., v.n.* studieren. — *s.* das Studium; das Arbeitszimmer (*room*); (*Mus. etc.*) die Studie; (*Art*) der Entwurf; die Untersuchung (*investigation*).

stuff [stʌf], *s.* der Stoff, das Material; (*coll.*) das Zeug (*rubbish*). — *v.a.* stopfen, ausstopfen (*animals*); (*Cul.*) füllen.

stuffing [ˈstʌfiŋ], *s.* die Füllung, das Füllsel.

stultify [ˈstʌltifai], *v.a.* dumm machen.

stumble [stʌmbl], *v.n.* stolpern; — *upon*, zufällig stoßen (auf, *Acc.*).

stumbling [ˈstʌmbliŋ], *s.* das Stolpern; — *block*, das Hindernis, der Stein des Anstoßes.

stump [stʌmp], *s.* der Stumpf. — *v.a.* verblüffen; abstumpfen. — *v.n.* schwerfällig gehen.

stun [stʌn], *v.a.* betäuben, verdutzen.

stunning [ˈstʌniŋ], *adj.* betörend, fabelhaft, überwältigend.

stunt (1) [stʌnt], *v.a.* am Wachstum behindern, klein halten.

stunt (2) [stʌnt], *s.* der Trick, das Kunststück; (*Aviat.*) der Kunstflug.

stupefy [ˈstjuːpifai], *v.a.* betäuben.

stupendous [stjuːˈpendəs], *adj.* erstaunlich.

stupid [ˈstjuːpid], *adj.* dumm.

stupor [ˈstjuːpə], *s.* die Erstarrung, Lähmung (*of mind*).

sturdy [ˈstəːdi], *adj.* derb, stark, stämmig.

sturgeon [ˈstəːdʒən], *s.* (*Zool.*) der Stör.

stutter [ˈstʌtə], *v.n.* stottern.

sty [stai], *s.* der Schweinestall.

sty(e) [stai], *s.* (*Med.*) das Gerstenkorn (*on eyelid*).

style [stail], *s.* (*Lit.*) der Stil; der Griffel (*stylus*); die Mode (*fashion*); die Anrede (*address*). — *v.a.* anreden.

stylish [ˈstailiʃ], *adj.* elegant, modern.

suave [sweiv, swaːv], *adj.* höflich, gewinnend.

sub- [sʌb], *pref.* Unter–.

subaltern [ˈsʌbəltən], *s.* (*Mil.*) der Leutnant, Oberleutnant.

subject [ˈsʌbdʒikt], *s.* (*Gram.*) das Subjekt; (*Pol.*) der Untertan; der Gegenstand. — *adj.* untertan (*to,*

Dat.); — *to*, abhängig von. — [səbˈdʒekt], *v.a.* unterwerfen (*to, Dat.*); aussetzen (*Dat.*).

subjunctive [səbˈdʒʌŋktiv], *s.* (*Gram.*) der Konjunktiv.

sublet [sʌbˈlet], *v.a.* in Untermiete vermieten, untervermieten.

sublimate [ˈsʌblimeit], *v.a.* sublimieren.

submarine [ˈsʌbməriːn], *s.* das Unterseeboot.

submission [səbˈmiʃən], *s.* die Unterwerfung (*subjection*); der Vorschlag (*suggestion*).

submit [səbˈmit], *v.a.* unterwerfen (*subjugate*); vorlegen. — *v.n.* sich beugen (*to, Dat.*).

suborn [sʌˈbɔːn], *v.a.* anstiften; bestechen (*corrupt*).

subpoena [sʌbˈpiːnə], *s.* (*Law*) die Vorladung.

subscribe [səbˈskraib], *v.a.* unterschreiben. — *v.n.* zeichnen (*to,* zu); abonnieren (*paper*).

subscription [səbˈskripʃən], *s.* das Abonnement (*to, Genit.*); (*club*) der Beitrag.

subsequent [ˈsʌbsikwənt], *adj.* folgend.

subservient [sʌbˈsəːviənt], *adj.* unterwürfig.

subside [səbˈsaid], *v.n.* sinken; abnehmen (*decrease*).

subsidence [sʌbˈsaidəns, ˈsʌbsidəns], *s.* das Sinken, Sichsetzen.

subsidiary [sʌbˈsidjəri], *adj.* Hilfs-, Neben-.

subsidize [ˈsʌbsidaiz], *v.a.* unterstützen (*with money*), subventionieren.

subsidy [ˈsʌbsidi], *s.* die Unterstützung, Subvention.

subsist [səbˈsist], *v.n.* leben, existieren.

subsistence [səbˈsistəns], *s.* das Dasein, Auskommen; der Lebensunterhalt.

substance [ˈsʌbstəns], *s.* das Wesen, der Stoff, die Substanz.

substantial [səbˈstænʃəl], *adj.* wesentlich, beträchtlich.

substantiate [səbˈstænʃieit], *v.a.* dartun, nachweisen, bestätigen.

substantive [ˈsʌbstəntiv], *s.* (*Gram.*) das Substantiv, Hauptwort. — *adj.* (*Mil.*) effektiv, wirklich.

substitute [ˈsʌbstitjuːt], *v.a.* ersetzen, an die Stelle setzen. — *s.* der Ersatzmann, Vertreter.

subterfuge [ˈsʌbtəfjuːdʒ], *s.* die Ausflucht.

subtle [sʌtl], *adj.* fein, schlau, subtil.

subtract [səbˈtrækt], *v.a.* abziehen; (*Maths.*) subtrahieren.

suburb [ˈsʌbəːb], *s.* die Vorstadt, der Vorort.

subversion [səbˈvəːʃən], *s.* (*Pol.*) der Umsturz.

subversive [səbˈvəːsiv], *adj.* umstürzlerisch, umstürzend.

subway [ˈsʌbwei], *s.* die Unterführung; (*Am.*) die Untergrundbahn.

succeed [səkˈsiːd], *v.n.* erfolgreich sein, Erfolg haben. — *v.a.* nachfolgen (*Dat.*) (*follow*).

success [sək'ses], *s*. der Erfolg.
successful [sək'sesful], *adj*. erfolgreich.
succession [sək'seʃən], *s*. die Nachfolge.
successive [sək'sesiv], *adj*. der Reihe nach, aufeinanderfolgend.
succinct [sək'siŋkt], *adj*. bündig, kurz.
succour ['sakə], *v.a.* beistehen (*Dat.*), helfen (*Dat.*).
succulent ['sakjulənt], *adj*. saftig.
succumb [sə'kam], *v.n.* unterliegen (*to, Dat.*).
such [satʃ], *adj*. solch, derartig. — *pron*. ein solcher; — *as*, diejenigen, alle die.
suchlike ['satʃlaik], *pron*. (*coll.*) dergleichen.
suck [sak], *v.a., v.n.* saugen.
suckle [sakl], *v.a.* säugen, stillen.
suction ['sakʃən], *s*. das Saugen; (*Engin.*) Saug-.
Sudanese [su:də'ni:z], *adj*. sudanisch, sudanesisch. — *s*. der Sudan(es)er.
sudden [sadn], *adj*. plötzlich.
suds [sadz], *s. pl*. das Seifenwasser.
sue [sju:], *v.a.* gerichtlich belangen, verklagen.
suède [sweid], *s*. das Wildleder.
suet ['su:it], *s*. das Nierenfett.
suffer ['safə], *v.a.* ertragen, dulden. — *v.n.* leiden (*from*, an).
sufferance ['safərəns], *s*. die Duldung; *on* —, nur widerwillig.
suffice [sə'fais], *v.n.* genügen, langen, (aus)reichen.
sufficient [sə'fiʃənt], *adj*. genügend, hinreichend.
suffocate ['safəkeit], *v.a., v.n.* ersticken.
suffragan ['safrəgən], *s*. (*Eccl.*) der Weihbischof.
suffrage ['safridʒ], *s*. das Wahlrecht, Stimmrecht.
suffuse [sə'fju:z], *v.a.* übergießen, überfließen.
sugar ['ʃugə], *s*. der Zucker; — *basin*, die Zuckerdose.
suggest [sə'dʒest], *v.a.* vorschlagen, anregen.
suggestion [sə'dʒestʃən], *s*. der Vorschlag.
suggestive [sə'dʒestiv], *adj*. zweideutig.
suicide ['sju:isaid], *s*. der Selbstmord, Freitod.
suit [su:t], *s*. das Gesuch, die Bitte (*request*); die Farbe (*cards*); (*Law*) der Prozeß; der Anzug (*clothes*). — *v.n.* passen (*Dat.*) (*be convenient to*); passen zu (*look well with*). — *v.a.* anpassen (*match*).
suitcase ['su:tkeis], *s*. der Handkoffer.
suitable ['su:təbl], *adj*. passend.
suite [swi:t], *s*. das Gefolge (*following*); die Zimmerflucht (*rooms*); die Reihe (*cards*).
suitor ['su:tə], *s*. der Brautwerber, Freier.
sulk [salk], *v.n.* schmollen.
sullen ['salən], *adj*. düster, mürrisch.
sully ['sali], *v.a.* beschmutzen.
sulphur ['salfə], *s*. (*Chem.*) der Schwefel.

Sultan ['saltən], *s*. der Sultan.
Sultana [sal'ta:nə], *s*. die Sultanin.
sultana [sal'ta:nə], *s*. (*Bot.*) die Sultanine.
sultry ['saltri], *adj*. schwül.
sum [sam], *s*. die Summe; (*fig.*) der Inbegriff. — *v.a., v.n.* — *up*, zusammenfassen.
summary ['saməri], *s*. die Zusammenfassung, der Auszug. — *adj*. summarisch.
summer ['samə], *s*. der Sommer; *Indian* —, der Spätsommer, Altweibersommer, Nachsommer.
summit ['samit], *s*. der Gipfel, die Spitze.
summon(s) ['samən(z)], *v.a.* (*Law*) vorladen. — *s*. (**summons**) die Vorladung.
sump [samp], *s*. (*Motor.*) die Ölwanne.
sumptuous ['samptjuəs], *adj*. prächtig, mit Aufwand, kostbar.
sun [san], *s*. die Sonne. — *v.r.* sich sonnen.
sunburn ['sanbə:n], *s*. der Sonnenbrand.
Sunday ['sand(e)i]. der Sonntag.
sundial ['sandaiəl], *s*. die Sonnenuhr.
sundown ['sandaun] *see* **sunset**.
sundry ['sandri], *adj*. mehrere, verschiedene. — *s*. (*pl.*) Gemischtwaren, *f. pl.*
sunny ['sani], *adj*. sonnig.
sunrise ['sanraiz], *s*. der Sonnenaufgang.
sunset ['sanset], *s*. der Sonnenuntergang.
sunshade ['sanʃeid], *s*. das Sonnendach, der Sonnenschirm (*parasol*).
super ['su:pə], *s*. (*Theat.*) der Statist. — *adj*. (*coll.*) fein, famos.
super- ['su:pə], *pref.* über-, hinzu-.
superannuation [su:pərænju'eiʃən], *s*. die Pensionierung.
superb [su'pə:b], *adj*. hervorragend, herrlich.
supercilious [su:pə'siliəs], *adj*. hochmütig, anmaßend.
superficial [su:pə'fiʃəl], *adj*. oberflächlich.
superfluous [su:'pə:fluəs], *adj*. überflüssig.
superintendent [su:pərin'tendənt], *s*. der Oberaufseher.
superior [su:'piəriə], *adj*. ober, höher. — *s*. der Vorgesetzte.
superiority [su:piəri'oriti], *s*. die Überlegenheit.
superlative [su:'pə:lətiv], *s*. (*Gram.*) der Superlativ. — *adj*. ausnehmend gut.
supermarket ['su:pəma:kit], *s*. das Selbstbedienungsgeschäft, SB-Geschäft, der grosse Lebensmittelladen.
supersede [su:pə'si:d], *v.a.* verdrängen.
superstition [su:pə'stiʃən], *s*. der Aberglaube.
superstitious [su:pə'stiʃəs], *adj*. abergläubisch.
supervise ['su:pəvaiz], *v.a.* beaufsichtigen, überwachen.

supine [su'pain], *adj.* auf dem Rücken liegend. — ['su:pain], *s.* (*Gram.*) das Supinum.

supper ['sʌpə], *s.* das Abendessen; *Last Supper*, das Heilige Abendmahl.

supplant [sə'plɑ:nt], *v.a.* verdrängen.

supple [sʌpl], *adj.* geschmeidig, biegsam.

supplement ['sʌplimənt], *s.* die Beilage (*paper*); der Zusatz.

supplementary [sʌpli'mentri], *adj.* zusätzlich.

supplier [sə'plaiə], *s.* der Lieferant.

supply [sə'plai], *v.a.* liefern (*s. th.*); beliefern, versorgen (*s.o.*). — *s.* die Versorgung.

support [sə'pɔ:t], *v.a.* unterstützen. — *s.* die Stütze (*prop*); die Unterstützung (*financial etc.*).

suppose [sə'pouz], *v.a.* annehmen, vermuten.

supposition [sʌpə'ziʃən], *s.* die Annahme, Vermutung, Voraussetzung.

suppress [sə'pres], *v.a.* unterdrücken.

suppurate ['sʌpjureit], *v.n.* eitern.

supremacy [su'preməsi], *s.* die Überlegenheit (*pre-eminence*); Obergewalt (*power*).

supreme [su'pri:m], *adj.* höchst, oberst.

surcharge ['sə:tʃɑ:dʒ], *s.* die Sonderzahlung, der Aufschlag, Zuschlag.

sure [ʃuə], *adj.* sicher; *to be* —, sicherlich; *make* —, sich überzeugen.

surety ['ʃuəti], *s.* (*Law*) die Kaution.

surf [sə:f], *s.* die Brandung.

surface ['sə:fis], *s.* die Oberfläche.

surfeit ['sə:fit], *s.* die Übersättigung, das Übermaß. — *v.a.* übersättigen.

surge [sə:dʒ], *v.n.* wogen, rauschen. — *s.* die Woge, das Aufwallen.

surgeon ['sə:dʒən], *s.* (*Med.*) der Chirurg.

surgery ['sə:dʒəri], *s.* (*Med.*) die Chirurgie (*subject*); — *hours*, die Sprechstunde.

surgical ['sə:dʒikəl], *adj.* chirurgisch.

surly ['sə:li], *adj.* mürrisch.

surmise [sə:'maiz], *v.a.* mutmaßen, vermuten. — *s.* die Mutmaßung, Vermutung.

surmount [sə'maunt], *v.a.* übersteigen; überwinden (*overcome*).

surname [sə:neim], *s.* der Zuname.

surpass [sə'pɑ:s], *v.a.* übertreffen.

surplice ['sə:plis], *s.* das Chorhemd.

surplus ['sə:pləs], *s.* der Überfluß.

surprise [sə'praiz], *s.* die Überraschung. — *v.a.* überraschen.

surrender [sə'rendə], *v.a.* übergeben, aufgeben. — *v.n.* sich ergeben. — *s.* die Waffenstreckung, Kapitulation.

surreptitious [sʌrəp'tiʃəs], *adj.* heimlich.

surround [sə'raund], *v.a.* umgeben, einschließen.

surroundings [sə'raundiɲz], *s. pl.* die Umgegend, Umgebung.

survey ['sə:vei], *s.* die Übersicht; die Vermessung. — [sə'vei], *v.a.* überblicken; vermessen.

surveyor [sə'veiə], *s.* der Vermesser, Feldmesser.

survival [sə'vaivəl], *s.* das Überleben.

survive [sə'vaiv], *v.a., v.n.* überleben, überstehen.

susceptibility [səsepti'biliti], *s.* die Empfänglichkeit.

susceptible [sə'septibl], *adj.* empfänglich, empfindlich.

suspect [səs'pekt], *v.a.* verdächtigen. — ['sʌspekt], *adj.* verdächtig. — *s.* die Verdachtsperson, der Verdächtige.

suspend [səs'pend], *v.a.* aufhängen; unterbrechen (*procedure*); einstellen (*work*).

suspense [səs'pens], *s.* die Spannung (*tension*); Ungewißheit (*uncertainty*).

suspension [səs'penʃən], *s.* (*Law*) die Suspension; die Einstellung (*stoppage*); die Aufhängung, Suspension (*Motor.*) die Federung; — *bridge*, die Kettenbrücke, Hängebrücke.

suspicion [səs'piʃən], *s.* der Verdacht, Argwohn.

suspicious [səs'piʃəs], *adj.* verdächtig; argwöhnisch.

sustain [səs'tein], *v.a.* erleiden (*suffer*); ertragen (*bear*); aufrechterhalten (*maintain*).

sustenance ['sʌstinəns], *s.* der Unterhalt (*maintenance*); die Nahrung (*food*).

suture ['sju:tʃə], *s.* (*Med.*) die Naht.

suzerain ['sju:zərein], *s.* der Oberherr, Oberlehnsherr.

swab [swɔb], *s.* (*Med.*) die Laborprobe, der Abstrich; der Schrubber (*scrubber*). — *v.a.* (*Med.*) eine Probe entnehmen; schrubben (*scrub*).

swaddle [swɔdl], *s.* die Windel.

swaddling ['swɔdliɲ], *adj.* — *clothes*, die Windeln, *f. pl.*

swagger ['swægə], *v.n.* großtun. — *s.* das Großtun, Renommieren.

swallow (1) ['swɔlou], *s.* (*Orn.*) die Schwalbe.

swallow (2) ['swɔlou], *v.a.* schlucken; verschlingen (*devour*).

swamp [swɔmp], *s.* der Sumpf. — *v.a.* versenken; (*fig.*) überschütten.

swan [swɔn], *s.* (*Orn.*) der Schwan.

swank [swæɲk], *v.n.* großtun, angeben, aufschneiden. — *s.* der Großtuer.

swap, **swop** [swɔp], *v.a.* eintauschen, tauschen. — *v.n.* tauschen. — *s.* der Tausch.

sward [swɔ:d], *s.* (*Poet.*) der Rasen.

swarm [swɔ:m], *v.n.* schwärmen. — *s.* der Schwarm.

swarthy ['swɔ:ði], *adj.* dunkel, dunkelbraun.

swashbuckler ['swɔʃbʌklə], *s.* der Aufschneider, Angeber, Renommist.

swastika ['swɔstikə], *s.* das Hakenkreuz.

swathe [sweið], *v.a.* einhüllen, einwickeln.

sway [swei], *v.a.* schwenken; beeinflußen. — *v.n.* schwanken, sich schwingen. — *s.* der Einfluß, die Macht.

swear [swɛə], *v.a.*, *v.n. irr.* schwören (*an oath*); fluchen (*curse*).

sweat [swet], *v.n.* schwitzen. — *s.* der Schweiß.

Swede [swi:d], *s.* der Schwede.

Swedish ['swi:diʃ], *adj.* schwedisch.

sweep [swi:p], *v.a.*, *v.n. irr.* fegen, kehren; *a new broom —s clean*, neue Besen kehren gut. — *s.* der Schornsteinfeger (*chimney —*).

sweet [swi:t], *adj.* süß. — *s.* der Nachtisch; (*pl.*) Süßigkeiten, *f. pl.*

swell [swel], *v.a. irr.* anschwellen lassen. — *v.n.* anschwellen. — *adj.*, *adv.* (*Am. sl.*) ausgezeichnet. — *s.* (*sl.*) der feine Kerl.

swelter ['sweltə], *v.n.* vor Hitze vergehen.

swerve [swə:v], *v.n.* abschweifen, abbiegen.

swift (1) [swift], *adj.* schnell, behende, rasch.

swift (2) [swift], *s.* (*Orn.*) die Turmschwalbe.

swill [swil], *v.a.* spülen (*rinse*); (*sl.*) saufen (*drink heavily*). — *s.* das Spülicht (*dishwater*); (*coll.*) das Gesöff.

swim [swim], *v.n. irr.* schwimmen. — *s.* das Schwimmen.

swindle [swindl], *v.a.* beschwindeln. — *s.* der Schwindel.

swine [swain], *s. pl.* die Schweine; (*sing.*) der Schweinehund, das Schwein.

swing [swiŋ], *v.a.*, *v.n. irr.* schwingen, schaukeln. — *s.* der Schwung; die Schaukel.

swipe [swaip], *v.a.* schlagen; (*fig.*) stehlen. — *s.* der Schlag.

swirl [swə:l], *v.a.*, *v.n.* wirbeln (*in air*). — *s.* der Wirbel.

Swiss [swis], *s.* der Schweizer. — *adj.* schweizerisch, Schweizer-.

switch [switʃ], *v.a.* (*Elec.*) — *on*, andrehen, einschalten; — *off*, abschalten; (*fig.*) wechseln, vertauschen (*change*). — *v.n.* umstellen, umschalten. — *s.* (*Elec.*) der Schalter.

switchboard ['switʃbɔ:d], *s.* die Telephonzentrale, das Schaltbrett.

switchgear ['switʃgiə], *s.* (*Elec.*) das Schaltgerät, die Schaltung.

swivel [swivl], *v.n.* drehen. — *s.* der Drehring; — *chair*, der Drehstuhl.

swoon [swu:n], *v.n.* in Ohnmacht fallen. — *s.* die Ohnmacht.

swoop [swu:p], *s.* der Stoß. — *v.n.* (*herab*)stoßen; stürzen; (*nieder*)schießen.

swop *see* **swap**.

sword [sɔ:d], *s.* das Schwert.

syllable ['siləbl], *s.* die Silbe.

syllabus ['siləbəs], *s.* das Verzeichnis, der Lehrplan.

symbol ['simbəl], *s.* das Symbol, Sinnbild.

sympathetic [simpə'θetik], *adj.* mitfühlend, teilnehmend; sympathisch.

sympathy ['simpəθi], *s.* die Sympathie, das Mitgefühl.

symphony ['simfəni], *s.* (*Mus.*) die Symphonie.

synchronize ['siŋkrənaiz], *v.a.* synchronisieren.

syndicate ['sindikit], *s.* die Arbeitsgruppe, das Syndikat.

synod ['sinəd], *s.* die Synode, Kirchentagung.

synonymous [si'nɔniməs], *adj.* synonym.

synopsis [si'nɔpsis], *s.* die Zusammenfassung, Übersicht.

Syrian ['siriən], *adj.* syrisch. — *s.* der Syrer.

syringe ['sirindʒ], *s.* die Spritze.

syrup ['sirəp], *s.* der Sirup.

system ['sistəm], *s.* das System.

systematize ['sistəmətaiz], *v.a.* ordnen, in ein System bringen.

T

T [ti:]. das T.

tab [tæb], *s.* das Schildchen, der Streifen.

tabard ['tæbəd], *s.* der Wappenrock, Heroldsrock.

tabby ['tæbi], *s.* (*cat*) die getigerte Katze.

table [teibl], *s.* der Tisch; (*Maths.*) die Tabelle, das Einmaleins. — *v.a.* (*Parl.*) einen Entwurf einbringen; (*Am.*) auf die lange Bank schieben.

tablecloth ['teiblklɔθ], *s.* das Tischtuch.

tablemat ['teiblmæt], *s.* der Untersatz.

tablenapkin ['teiblnæpkin], *s.* die Serviette.

tablespoon ['teiblspu:n], *s.* der Eßlöffel.

tablet ['tæblit], *s.* die Tablette (*pill*); die Schreibtafel, der Block (*writing*).

taboo [tə'bu:], *s.* das Verbot, Tabu.

tabular ['tæbjulə], *adj.* tabellarisch; wie eine Tafel.

tacit ['tæsit], *adj.* stillschweigend.

taciturn ['tæsitə:n], *adj.* schweigsam, einsilbig.

tack [tæk], *s.* der Stift; der Stich (*sewing*). — *v.a.* nageln; heften (*sew*).

tackle [tækl], *v.a.* (*Naut.*) takeln; (*Footb.*, *fig.*) angreifen. — *s.* (*Naut.*) das Takel; (*fig.*) das Zeug; (*Footb.*) das Angreifen.

tact [tækt], *s.* der Takt; das Zartgefühl.

tactics ['tæktiks], *s. pl.* die Taktik.

tadpole ['tædpoul], *s.* (*Zool.*) die Kaulquappe.

taffeta ['tæfitə], *s.* (*Text.*) der Taft.

tag [tæg], *s.* der Anhängezettel; das Sprichwort (*saying*). — *v.a.* anhängen. — *v.n.* — *on to*, sich anschließen.

tail [teil], *s.* der Schwanz; (*fig.*) das Ende; (*pl.*) der Frack (*tailcoat*). — *v.a.* (*Am.*) folgen (*Dat.*).

tailor ['teilə], *s.* der Schneider; —*made*, geschneidert, nach Maß gemacht. — *v.a.* schneidern.

taint [teint], *v.a.* beflecken; verderben (*corrupt*). — *s.* der Fleck.

take [teik], *v.a. irr.* nehmen; bringen, ergreifen (*seize*); erfordern (*require*); — *up*, aufnehmen, beginnen; ertragen (*suffer, tolerate*); — *breath*, Atem holen; — *care*, sich in acht nehmen; — *offence at*, Anstoß nehmen an; — *place*, stattfinden; — *for*, halten für. — *v.n.* wirken (*be effective*); — *to*, Gefallen finden (an, *Dat.*); — *to flight* or *o.'s heels*, sich aus dem Staube machen; — *after*, ähnlich sein.

takings ['teikiŋz], *s.* (*pl.*) die Einnahmen, *f. pl.*

tale [teil], *s.* das Märchen, die Geschichte.

talent ['tælənt], *s.* das Talent, die Begabung.

talented ['tæləntid], *adj.* talentiert, begabt.

talk [tɔ:k], *v.a., v.n.* reden, sprechen. — *s.* das Gespräch (*discussion*); der Vortrag (*lecture*); das Reden, Gerede (*speaking*).

talkative ['tɔ:kətiv], *adj.* geschwätzig, redselig, gesprächig.

tall [tɔ:l], *adj.* hoch (*high*); groß (*grown high*); *a — order*, eine schwierige Aufgabe; *a — story*, eine Aufschneiderei, die Seemannsgarn.

tallow ['tælou], *s.* der Talg.

tally ['tæli], *v.n.* passen (*match*); stimmen (*be correct*).

talon ['tælən], *s.* die Klaue, Kralle.

tame [teim], *adj.* zahm. — *v.a.* zähmen.

tamper ['tæmpə], *v.n.* hineinpfuschen (*with*, in, *Acc.*).

tan [tæn], *s.* die Lohe; die braune Farbe; der Sonnenbrand (*sun*). — *v.a.* bräunen; (*leather*) gerben; (*fig.*) verbleuen (*beat*).

tang [tæŋ], *s.* der Seetang; (*fig.*) der Beigeschmack.

tangible ['tændʒibl], *adj.* greifbar.

tangle ['tæŋgl], *v.a.* verwickeln (*entangle*). — *s.* die Verwirrung, Verwicklung.

tank [tæŋk], *s.* der Tank; (*Mil.*) der Panzer; der Wasserspeicher (*cistern*). — *v.a., v.n.* tanken.

tankard ['tæŋkəd], *s.* der Maßkrug, Bierkrug.

tanner (1) ['tænə], *s.* der Gerber.

tanner (2) ['tænə], *s.* (*sl.*) das Sechspencestück.

tantalize ['tæntəlaiz], *v.a.* quälen.

tantamount ['tæntəmaunt], *adj.* gleich, gleichwertig.

tap [tæp], *v.a.* anzapfen (*barrel*); klopfen; tippen (*on shoulder etc.*); (*fig.*) anpumpen (*for money*). — *s.* der Hahn; der Zapfen (*barrel*); der leichte Schlag (*on shoulder etc.*).

tape [teip], *s.* das Band; *red —*, die Bürokratie, der Bürokratismus; — *measure*, das Bandmaß; — *recorder*, das Tonbandgerät.

taper ['teipə], *v.n.* spitz zulaufen. — *v.a.* spitzen. — *s.* die (spitze) Kerze.

tapestry ['tæpistri], *s.* die Tapete, der Wandteppich.

tapeworm ['teipwə:m], *s.* der Bandwurm.

taproot ['tæpru:t], *s.* die Pfahlwurzel, Hauptwurzel.

tar [ta:], *s.* der Teer; (*Naut. sl.*) der Matrose. — *v.a.* teeren.

tardy ['ta:di], *adj.* träge (*sluggish*), langsam.

tare (1) [tɛə], *s.* das Taragewicht, die Tara (*weight*). — *v.a.* auswägen, tarieren.

tare (2) [tɛə], *s.* (*Bot.*) die Wicke.

target ['ta:git], *s.* das Ziel; die Zielscheibe (*board*).

tariff ['tærif], *s.* der Tarif.

tarnish ['ta:niʃ], *v.a.* trüben. — *v.n.* anlaufen.

tarpaulin [ta:'pɔ:lin], *s.* die Persenning.

tarry (1) ['tæri], *v.n.* zögern (*hesitate*); warten (*wait*).

tarry (2) ['ta:ri], *adj.* teerig.

tart (1) [ta:t], *s.* die Torte.

tart (2) [ta:t], *adj.* herb, sauer.

tart (3) [ta:t], *s.* (*sl.*) die Dirne.

Tartar ['ta:tə], *s.* der Tatar; (*fig.*) der Tyrann.

tartar ['ta:tə], *s.* (*Chem.*) der Weinstein.

task [ta:sk], *s.* die Aufgabe, das Tagewerk; *take to —*, zur Rechenschaft ziehen.

tassel [tæsl], *s.* die Quaste.

taste [teist], *v.a.* schmecken; versuchen, kosten. — *s.* die Probe (*tasting*); der Geschmack (*flavour*).

tasteful ['teistful], *adj.* geschmackvoll.

tasteless ['teistlis], *adj.* geschmacklos.

tasty ['teisti], *adj.* schmackhaft.

tatter ['tætə], *s.* der Lumpen. — *v.a.* in Fetzen reißen, zerfetzen.

tattle [tætl], *v.n.* schwatzen. — *s.* das Geschwätz.

tattoo (1) [tə'tu:], *s.* (*Mil.*) der Zapfenstreich, das militärische Schaustück, die Parade.

tattoo (2) [tə'tu:], *v.a.* tätowieren. — *s.* die Tätowierung.

taunt [tɔ:nt], *v.a.* höhnen, schmähen. — *s.* der Hohn, Spott.

tavern ['tævən], *s.* die Schenke.

tawdry ['tɔ:dri], *adj.* kitschig, flitterhaft.

tawny ['tɔ:ni], *adj.* braungelb, lohfarbig.

tax [tæks], *s.* die Abgabe, Steuer; Besteuerung (*taxation*). — *v.a.* besteuern; (*fig.*) anstrengen, ermüden (*strain*).

taxi ['tæksi], *s.* das Taxi.

tea [ti:], *s.* der Tee.

teach [ti:tʃ], *v.a., v.n. irr.* lehren, unterrichten.

teacher ['ti:tʃə], *s.* der Lehrer; die Lehrerin.

team [ti:m], *s.* (*Sport*) die Mannschaft; das Gespann (*horses*); (*fig.*) der Stab; — *spirit*, der Korpsgeist.

tear (1) [tɛə], *s.* der Riß (*rent*). — *v.a. irr.* zerreißen (*rend*).

tear (2) [tiə], *s.* die Träne.

tearing ['tɛəriŋ], *adj.* — *hurry*, rasende Eile.

tease [ti:z], *v.a.* necken (*mock*); aufrauhen (*roughen*).

teat [ti:t], *s.* die Brustwarze, Zitze.

technical ['teknikəl], *adj.* technisch.

technique [tek'ni:k], *s.* die Technik, Methode.

techy *see* **tetchy**.

tedious ['ti:diəs], *adj.* langweilig, lästig.

tedium ['ti:diəm], *s.* der Überdruß, die Langeweile.

tee [ti:], *s.* (*Sport*) der Golfballhalter.

teem [ti:m], *v.n.* wimmeln.

teenager ['ti:neidʒə], *s.* der, die Jugendliche; Teenager.

teeth *see under* **tooth**.

teethe [ti:ð], *v.n.* Zähne bekommen, zahnen.

teetotal [ti:'toutl], *adj.* abstinent, antialkoholisch.

teetotaller [ti:'toutlə], *s.* der Antialkoholiker.

telegram ['teligræm], *s.* das Telegramm.

telephone ['telifoun], *s.* (*abbr.* **phone**) das Telephon; – *booth*, die Fernsprechzelle; — *exchange*, das Fernsprechamt.

television [teli'viʒən], *s.* das Fernsehen; — *set*, der Fernsehapparat.

tell [tel], *v.a. irr.* erzählen, berichten (*relate*); verraten (*reveal*).

tell-tale ['telteil], *s.* der Angeber, Zuträger. — *adj.* sprechend; Warnungs-.

teller ['telə], *s.* der Zähler; der Kassier (*cashier*).

temerity [ti'meriti], *s.* die Verwegenheit, Tollkühnheit.

temper ['tempə], *v.a.* vermischen (*mix*); mäßigen (*moderate*); (*Metall.*) härten. — *s.* die üble Stimmung, Wut, Laune; (*Metall.*) die Härte.

temperance ['tempərəns], *s.* die Mäßigkeit, Enthaltsamkeit.

temperate ['tempərit], *adj.* gemäßigt, temperiert.

temperature ['temprətʃə], *s.* die Temperatur.

tempest ['tempist], *s.* der Sturm.

tempestuous [tem'pestjuəs], *adj.* stürmisch.

temple (1) [templ], *s.* der Tempel.

temple (2) [templ], *s.* (*Anat.*) die Schläfe (*side of brow*).

temporal ['tempərəl], *adj.* weltlich, zeitlich.

temporary ['tempərəri], *adj.* zeitweilig, vorläufig, provisorisch.

temporize ['tempəraiz], *v.n.* zögern, Zeit zu gewinnen suchen.

tempt [tempt], *v.a.* versuchen.

temptation [temp'teiʃən], *s.* die Versuchung.

ten [ten], *num. adj.* zehn.

tenth [tenθ], *num. adj.* zehnte. — *s.* der Zehnte.

tenable ['tenəbl], *adj.* haltbar.

tenacious [ti'neiʃəs], *adj.* zähe, festhaltend, hartnäckig.

tenacity [ti'næsiti], *s.* die Zähigkeit, Ausdauer.

tenancy ['tenənsi], *s.* das Mietverhältnis; die Mietdauer.

tenant ['tenənt], *s.* der Mieter, Pächter.

tench [tentʃ], *s.* (*Zool.*) die Schleie.

tend (1) [tend], *v.a., v.n.* warten, pflegen (*nurse*).

tend (2) [tend], *v.n.* neigen, gerichtet sein (*be inclined*).

tendency ['tendənsi], *s.* die Tendenz, Neigung.

tender (1) ['tendə], *s.* das Angebot (*offer*); *legal* —, das Zahlungsmittel. — *v.a.* einreichen.

tender (2) ['tendə], *adj.* sanft (*affectionate*); zart, zärtlich, weich (*delicate*).

tender (3) ['tendə], *s.* (*Railw.*) der Tender.

tendon ['tendən], *s.* (*Anat.*) die Sehne, Flechse.

tendril ['tendril], *s.* (*Bot.*) die Ranke.

tenement ['tenimənt], *s.* die Mietswohnung, die Mietskaserne.

tenet ['tenit], *s.* der Grundsatz (*principle*); die Lehre (*doctrine*).

tenfold ['tenfould], *adj.* zehnfach.

tennis ['tenis], *s.* das Tennis.

tenor ['tenə], *s.* (*Mus.*) der Tenor; der Sinn, Inhalt (*meaning*).

tense (1) [tens], *adj.* gespannt; straff (*taut*).

tense (2) [tens], *s.* (*Gram.*) die Zeitform.

tension ['tenʃən], *s.* die Spannung.

tent [tent], *s.* das Zelt.

tentacle ['tentəkl], *s.* (*Zool.*) das Fühlhorn, der Fühler.

tentative ['tentətiv], *adj.* versuchend, vorsichtig; (*fig.*) vorläufig.

tenterhooks ['tentəhuks], *s. pl.* die Spannhaken, *m. pl.*; *be on* —, in größter Spannung sein.

tenuous ['tenjuəs], *adj.* dünn, fadenscheinig, spärlich.

tenure ['tenjuə], *s.* der Mietbesitz, die Mietvertragslänge, das Mietrecht; — *of office*, die Amtsdauer.

tepid ['tepid], *adj.* lau, lauwarm.

term [tə:m], *s.* der Ausdruck (*expression*); die Bedingung (*condition*); der Termin, die Frist (*period*); (*Sch.*) das Semester, Trimester; *be on good* — *with* (*s.o.*), auf gutem Fuß stehen mit. — *v.a.* benennen, bezeichnen.

terminate ['tə:mineit], *v.a.* beenden, zu Ende bringen. — *v.n.* zu Ende kommen.

terminus ['tə:minəs], *s.* die Endstation.

terrace ['teris], *s.* die Terrasse.

terrestrial [tə'restriəl], *adj.* irdisch.

terrible ['teribl], *adj.* schrecklich, furchtbar.

terrific [tə'rifik], *adj.* fürchterlich; (*coll.*) ungeheuer.

terrify ['terifai], *v.a.* erschrecken.
territory ['teritəri], *s.* das Gebiet.
terror ['terə], *s.* der Schrecken.
terse [tə:s], *adj.* bündig, kurz.
tertiary ['tə:ʃəri], *adj.* tertiär.
test [test], *s.* die Prüfung; (*Chem.*) die Probe; — *-tube*, das Reagensglas *or* Reagenzglas. — *v.a.* prüfen.
testament ['testəmənt], *s.* das Testament.
testator [tes'teitə], *s.* der Erblasser.
testicle ['testikl], *s.* (*Anat.*) die Hode.
testify ['testifai], *v.a.* bezeugen.
testimonial [testi'mouniəl], *s.* das Zeugnis.
testimony ['testiməni], *s.* das Zeugnis, die Zeugenaussage (*oral*).
testiness ['testinis], *s.* die Verdrießlichkeit.
testy ['testi], *adj.* verdrießlich, reizbar.
tetanus ['tetənəs], *s.* (*Med.*) der Starrkrampf.
tetchy, techy ['tetʃi], *adj.* mürrisch, reizbar.
tether ['teðə], *s.* das Spannseil; (*fig.*) *at the end of o.'s —*, am Ende seiner Geduld. — *v.a.* anbinden.
text ['tekst], *s.* der Text, Wortlaut.
textile ['tekstail], *s.* die Textilware, der Webstoff.
textual ['tekstjuəl], *adj.* textlich, Text-.
texture ['tekstʃə], *s.* das Gewebe, die Struktur.
Thai [tai], *adj.* Thai-, siamesisch. — *s. pl.* die Thaivölker, *pl.*
than [ðæn], *conj.* als (*after comparatives*).
thank [θæŋk], *v.a.* danken (*Dat.*). — *s.* (*pl.*) der Dank.
that [ðæt], *dem. adj.* der, die, das, jener. — *dem. pron.* der, die, das; (*absolute, no pl.*) das. — *rel. pron.* der, die, das, welcher, was. — *conj.* daß; damit (*in order —*).
thatch [θætʃ], *v.a.* decken (mit Stroh). — *s.* das Strohdach.
thaw [θɔ:], *v.n.* tauen; auftauen. — *s.* das Tauwetter.
the [ðə, *before vowel* ði], *def. art.* der, die, das. — *adv.* — *bigger* — *better*, je grösser desto *or* umso besser.
theatre ['θiətə], *s.* das Theater; (*fig.*) der Schauplatz.
theatrical [θi'ætrikəl], *adj.* bühnenhaft (*of the stage*); theatralisch; Bühnen-, Theater-.
theft [θeft], *s.* der Diebstahl.
their [ðɛə], *poss. adj.* ihr.
theirs [ðɛəz], *poss. pron.* der, die, das ihrige, der, die, das ihre.
them [ðem], *pers. pron.* sie, ihnen.
theme [θi:m], *s.* das Thema; (*Mus.*) das Thema, Motiv.
then [ðen], *adv.* dann, damals; *by —, till —*, bis dahin. — *conj.* dann, denn. — *adj.* damalig.
thence [ðens], *adv.* von da; daher.
theology [θi'ɔlədʒi], *s.* die Theologie.
theorem ['θiərəm], *s.* (*Maths.*) der Lehrsatz, Grundsatz.
theorize ['θiəraiz], *v.n.* theoretisieren.

therapeutics [θerə'pju:tiks], *s. pl.* die Heilkunde.
therapy ['θerəpi], *s.* die Therapie.
there [ðɛə], *adv.* dort, da; dorthin, dahin (*thereto*); — *is*, — *are*, es gibt; *here and —*, hier und da.
thereabout(s) [ðɛərəbaut(s)], *adv.* ungefähr, da herum.
thereafter [ðɛər'ɑ:ftə], *adv.* hernach, danach.
thereby [ðɛə'bai], *adv.* dadurch.
therefore ['ðɛəfɔ:], *adv.* darum, deshalb.
thermal, thermic ['θə:məl, 'θə:mik], *adj.* thermisch; warm; Wärme-.
thermometer [θə'mɔmitə], *s.* das Thermometer.
these [ði:z], *dem. adj. & pron. pl.* diese.
thesis ['θi:sis], *s.* die These; die Dissertation.
they [ðei], *pers. pron. pl.* sie.
thick [θik], *adj.* dick; dicht; (*fig.*) dick befreundet; — *as thieves*, wie eine Diebsbande.
thicken ['θikən], *v.a.* verdicken. — *v.n.* dick werden.
thicket ['θikit], *s.* das Dickicht.
thickness ['θiknis], *s.* die Dicke.
thief [θi:f], *s.* der Dieb.
thieve [θi:v], *v.n.* stehlen.
thigh [θai], *s.* (*Anat.*) der Oberschenkel.
thimble [θimbl], *s.* der Fingerhut.
thin [θin], *adj.* dünn. — *v.a., v.n.* (sich) verdünnen.
thine [ðain], *poss. pron.* (*Poet.*) dein, der, die, das deinige.
thing [θiŋ], *s.* das Ding; die Sache (*matter*).
think [θiŋk], *v.a., v.n. irr.* denken; meinen, glauben.
thinker ['θiŋkə], *s.* der Denker.
third [θə:d], *num. adj.* der, die, das dritte. — *s.* das Drittel.
thirdly ['θə:dli], *adv.* drittens.
thirst [θə:st], *s.* der Durst (*for*, nach). — *v.n.* dürsten.
thirsty ['θə:sti], *adj.* durstig; *be —*, Durst haben.
thirteen [θə:'ti:n], *num. adj.* dreizehn.
thirty ['θə:ti], *num. adj.* dreißig.
this [ðis], *dem. adj.* dieser, diese, dieses. — *dem. pron.* dieser, diese, dieses; dies.
thistle [θisl], *s.* (*Bot.*) die Distel.
thither ['ðiðə], *adv.* dahin, dorthin.
tho' [ðou] *see under* **though**.
thong [θɔŋ], *s.* der Riemen (*strap*); die Peitschenschnur.
thorn [θɔ:n], *s.* (*Bot.*) der Dorn.
thorough ['θʌrə], *adj.* gründlich; völlig (*complete*).
thoroughbred ['θʌrəbred], *s.* das Vollblut, der Vollblüter. — *adj.* Vollblut-.
thoroughfare ['θʌrəfɛə], *s.* der Durchgang (*path*); die Durchfahrt.
those [ðouz], *dem. adj. pl.* die, jene. — *dem. pron. pl.* jene, diejenigen.
thou [ðau], *pers. pron.* (*Poet.*) du.
though [ðou], *conj.* (*abbr.* **tho'**) obgleich, obwohl, wenn auch (*even if*). — *adv.* doch, zwar.

thought [θɔ:t], *s.* der Gedanke; *also past tense and participle of* **think** *q.v.*

thoughtful ['θɔ:tful], *adj.* rücksichtsvoll, nachdenklich.

thoughtless ['θɔ:tlis], *adj.* gedankenlos.

thousand ['θauzənd], *num. adj. a* —, tausend. — *s.* das Tausend.

thrash [θræʃ], *v.a.* dreschen (*corn*); prügeln (*s.o.*).

thread [θred], *s.* der Faden. — *v.a.* einfädeln. — *v.n.* sich schlängeln, sich winden.

threadbare ['θredbɛə], *adj.* fadenscheinig.

threat [θret], *s.* die Drohung.

threaten [θretn], *v.a.* drohen, androhen (*Dat.*).

three [θri:], *num. adj.* drei.

threescore ['θri:skɔ:], *num. adj.* sechzig.

thresh [θreʃ], *v.a.* dreschen (*corn*). — *See also* **thrash**.

threshold ['θreʃould], *s.* die Schwelle (*of door*).

thrice [θrais], *num. adv.* dreimal.

thrift [θrift], *s.* die Sparsamkeit; (*Bot.*) die Grasnelke, Meernelke.

thrill [θril], *v.a.* packen (*grip*). — *v.n.* erschauern, zittern (vor, *Dat.*). — *s.* der Schauer; die Spannung.

thriller ['θrilə], *s.* der Thriller, der spannende Roman *or* Film etc.

thrive [θraiv], *v.n.* gedeihen (*also fig.*); (*fig.*) gut weiterkommen, Glück haben.

thriving ['θraiviŋ], *adj.* blühend, (*Comm.*) gut gehend.

throat [θrout], *s.* (*Anat.*) der Schlund, die Kehle.

throb [θrɔb], *v.n.* pochen, klopfen.

throes [θrouz], *s. pl.* die Wehen, *f. pl.*; die Schmerzen, *m. pl.*

throne [θroun], *s.* der Thron.

throng [θrɔŋ], *s.* die Menge, das Gedränge. — *v.a., v.n.* drängen.

throttle [θrɔtl], *s.* die Kehle, Luftröhre; (*Mech.*) das Drosselventil; (*Motor.*) *open the* —, Gas geben.

through [θru:], *prep.* durch (*Acc.*); mittels (*Genit.*) (*by means of*). — *adv.* (mitten) durch.

throughout [θru:'aut], *prep.* ganz (hin)durch (*space*); während, hindurch (*time*). — *adv.* durchaus, in jeder Beziehung.

throw [θrou], *v.a. irr.* werfen; — *open,* eröffnen. — *s.* der Wurf.

thrush [θrʌʃ], *s.* (*Orn.*) die Drossel.

thrust [θrʌst], *v.a.* stoßen, drängen. — *v.n.* stoßen (*at, nach*); sich drängen. — *s.* der Stoß, Angriff; *cut and* —, Hieb und Gegenhieb.

thud [θʌd], *s.* der Schlag, das Dröhnen, der dumpfe Ton. — *v.n.* dröhnen, aufschlagen.

thumb [θʌm], *s.* (*Anat.*) der Daumen; *rule of* —, die Faustregel; (*Am.*) *tack* see **drawing pin**. — *v.a.* durchblättern (*book*); — *a lift,* per Anhalter fahren.

thump [θʌmp], *v.a.* schlagen, puffen. —

v.n. schlagen (*on,* auf; *against,* gegen). — *s.* der Schlag, Stoß.

thunder ['θʌndə], *s.* der Donner. — *v.n.* donnern.

thunderstruck ['θʌndəstrʌk], *adj.* wie vom Donner gerührt.

Thursday ['θə:zdi]. der Donnerstag.

Thuringian [θuə'rindʒiən], *adj.* thüringisch. — *s.* der Thüringer.

thus [ðʌs], *adv.* so, auf diese Weise (*in this way*).

thwart [θwɔ:t], *v.a.* vereiteln, durchkreuzen.

thy [ðai], *poss. adj.* (*Poet.*) dein, deine, dein.

thyme [taim], *s.* (*Bot.*) der Thymian.

tic [tik], *s.* (*Med.*) das Zucken.

tick (1) [tik], *s.* das Ticken (*watch*). — *v.n.* ticken.

tick (2) [tik], *s.* (*coll.*) der Kredit, Borg.

ticket ['tikit], *s.* die Fahrkarte (*travel*); die Eintrittskarte (*entry*); (*Am.*) der Strafzettel (*driving*).

ticking (1) ['tikiŋ], *s.* das Ticken (*of watch*).

ticking (2) ['tikiŋ], *s.* (*Text.*) der Zwillich.

tickle [tikl], *v.a., v.n.* kitzeln. — *s.* das Kitzeln.

ticklish ['tikliʃ], *adj.* kitzlig.

tidal [taidl], *adj.* Gezeiten-, Ebbe-, Flut-.

tide [taid], *s.* die Gezeiten, *f.pl.*, die Ebbe und Flut. — *v.a.* — *over,* hinweghelfen (über, *Acc.*).

tidiness ['taidinis], *s.* die Sauberkeit, Ordnung.

tidings ['taidiŋz], *s. pl.* (*Poet.*) die Nachricht.

tidy ['taidi], *adj.* nett, sauber, ordentlich. — *v.a.* up, sauber machen.

tie [tai], *v.a.* binden, knüpfen. — *v.n.* (*Sport*) unentschieden sein. — *s.* die Binde, Krawatte; (*Sport*) das Unentschieden.

tier [tiə], *s.* der Rang, die Reihe, Sitzreihe.

tiger ['taigə], *s.* (*Zool.*) der Tiger.

tight [tait], *adj.* fest, eng, dicht (*close*); (*coll.*) betrunken (*drunk*); — *fisted,* geizig (*stingy*). — *s. pl.* die Trikothosen, *f.pl.*

tighten [taitn], *v.a.* festziehen.

tile [tail], *s.* der Ziegel (*roof etc.*); die Kachel (*glazed*). — *v.a.* kacheln, ziegeln.

till (1) [til], *prep., conj.* bis.

till (2) [til], *v.a.* aufbauen, beackern (*land*).

till (3) [til], *s.* die Ladenkasse.

tilt [tilt], *v.a.* kippen, neigen, umschlagen (*tip over*). — *v.n.* sich neigen, kippen, kentern. — *s.* die Neigung.

timber ['timbə], *s.* das Holz, Bauholz.

time [taim], *s.* die Zeit; (*Mus.*) das Tempo, Zeitmaß; *in* —, zur rechten Zeit; *every* —, jedesmal; *what is the* —? wievel Uhr ist es? — *v.a.* zeitlich messen, rechtzeitig einrichten.

timely ['taimli], *adj.* rechtzeitig.

timetable ['taimteibl], *s.* (*Railw.*) der Fahrplan; (*Sch.*) der Stundenplan.

timid ['timid], *adj.* furchtsam.

timpani ['timpəni], *s. pl.* (*Mus.*) die Kesselpauken, *f. pl.*

tin [tin], *s.* das Zinn, Weißblech; die Dose, Büchse (*preserved foods*); — *opener,* der Büchsenöffner.

tincture ['tiŋktʃə], *s.* die Tinktur, das Färbungsmittel.

tinder ['tində], *s.* der Zunder.

tinfoil ['tinfɔil], *s.* das Stanniol.

tinge [tindʒ], *v.a.* färben, anfärben. — *s.* die Färbung, leichte Farbe; (*fig.*) die Spur.

tingle [tiŋgl], *v.n.* klingen (*bells*); (*Anat.*) prickeln. — *s.* das Klingen; Prickeln.

tinker ['tiŋkə], *s.* der Kesselflicker. — *v.n.* basteln.

tinkle [tiŋkl], *v.a.* klingeln.

tinsel ['tinsəl], *s.* das Lametta, Flittergold.

tint [tint], *v.a.* färben. — *s.* die Farbe; der Farbton.

tiny ['taini], *adj.* winzig.

tip (1) [tip], *v.a.* kippen; (*coll.*) ein Trinkgeld geben (*Dat.*). — *s.* (*Sport etc.*) (*coll.*) der Tip; das Trinkgeld (*gratuity*).

tip (2) [tip], *s.* die Spitze; das Mundstück (*cigarette*).

tipple [tipl], *v.n.* (viel) trinken, zechen.

tipsy ['tipsi], *adj.* beschwipst.

tiptoe ['tiptou], *s. on* —, auf Zehenspitzen.

tiptop ['tiptɔp], *adj.* (*coll.*) erstklassig.

tirade [ti'reid *or* tai'reid], *s.* der Wortschwall, die Tirade.

tire (1) [taiə], *v.a., v.n.* ermüden.

tire (2) *see under* **tyre**.

tired ['taiəd], *adj.* müde.

tiresome ['taiəsəm], *adj.* langweilig (*boring*); auf die Nerven gehend (*annoying*).

tissue ['tiʃju:], *s.* das Gewebe; —*paper,* das Seidenpapier.

titbit ['titbit], *s.* der Leckerbissen.

tithe [taið], *s.* der Zehnte.

title [taitl], *s.* der Titel, die Überschrift; (*fig.*) der Anspruch (*claim*).

titmouse ['titmaus], *s.* (*Orn.*) die Meise.

titter ['titə], *v.n.* kichern. — *s.* das Kichern.

tittle [titl], *s.* das Tüpfelchen; — *tattle,* das Geschwätz.

titular ['titjulə], *adj.* Titular-.

to [tu], *prep. zu* (*Dat.*), gegen (*Acc.*); bis (*until, as far as*), nach, an, auf; *in order* —, um zu. — [tu:], *adv.* zu; — *and fro,* hin und her.

toad [toud], *s.* (*Zool.*) die Kröte.

toadstool ['toudstu:l], *s.* (*Bot.*) der Giftpilz.

toady ['toudi], *v.n.* kriechen. — *s.* der Kriecher.

toast [toust], *s.* der Toast, das Röstbrot; der Trinkspruch. — *v.a.* toasten,

rösten; trinken auf; — *s.o.,* einen Trinkspruch ausbringen auf einen.

tobacco [tə'bækou], *s.* der Tabak.

toboggan [tə'bɔgən], *s.* der Rodel, der Schlitten. — *v.n.* rodeln, Schlitten fahren.

tocsin ['tɔksin], *s.* die Sturmglocke.

today [tə'dei], *adv.* heute.

toddle [tɔdl], *v.n.* watscheln; abschieben (— *off*).

toddler ['tɔdlə], *s.* (*coll.*) das kleine Kind (das gehen lernt).

toe [tou], *s.* (*Anat.*) die Zehe.

toffee ['tɔfi], *s.* der Sahnebonbon.

together [tə'geðə], *adv.* zusammen.

toil [tɔil], *v.n.* hart arbeiten. — *s.* die schwere, harte Arbeit.

toilet ['tɔilit], *s.* das Anziehen, Ankleiden; die Toilette, der Abort, das Klosett (*lavatory*).

token ['toukən], *s.* das Zeichen (*sign*); der Beweis (*proof*); das Andenken (*keepsake*).

tolerable ['tɔlərəbl], *adj.* erträglich, leidlich.

tolerance ['tɔlərəns], *s.* die Toleranz, Duldsamkeit; (*Tech.*) die Toleranz.

tolerant ['tɔlərənt], *adj.* tolerant, duldsam.

tolerate ['tɔləreit], *v.a.* ertragen, dulden.

toll [toul], *v.n.* läuten. — *s.* der Zoll; — *gate,* — *bar,* der Schlagbaum.

tomato [tə'ma:tou], *s.* (*Bot.*) die Tomate.

tomb [tu:m], *s.* das Grab, Grabmal.

tomboy ['tɔmbɔi], *s.* der Wildfang.

tomcat ['tɔmkæt], *s.* (*Zool.*) der Kater.

tome [toum], *s.* der große Band, (*coll.*) der Wälzer.

tomfoolery [tɔm'fu:ləri], *s.* die Narretei.

Tommy ['tɔmi], *s.* (*Mil.*) (*coll.*) der englische Soldat.

tomorrow [tə'mɔrou], *adv.* morgen; — *morning,* morgen früh; *the day after* —, übermorgen.

ton [tʌn], *s.* die Tonne.

tone [toun], *s.* der Ton, Klang; (*fig.*) die Stimmung (*mood*). — *v.a.* — *down,* abtönen, abstimmen.

tongs [tɔŋz], *s. pl.* die Zange.

tongue [tʌŋ], *s.* (*Anat.*) die Zunge.

tonic ['tɔnik], *s.* das Stärkungsmittel. — *adj.* tonisch, stärkend.

tonight [tə'nait], *adv.* heute abend, heute nacht.

tonnage ['tʌnidʒ], *s.* die Tonnage, das Tonnengeld.

tonsil ['tɔnsil], *s.* (*Anat.*) die Mandel.

tonsilitis [tɔnsi'laitis], *s.* (*Med.*) die Mandelentzündung.

tonsure ['tɔnʃə], *s.* die Tonsur.

too [tu:], *adv.* allzu, zu, allzusehr; auch (*also*).

tool [tu:l], *s.* das Werkzeug, das Gerät; *machine* —, die Werkzeugmaschine.

tooth [tu:θ], *s.* (*pl.* **teeth** [ti:θ]) der Zahn.

toothache ['tu:θeik], *s.* das Zahnweh.

toothbrush ['tu:θbrʌʃ], *s.* die Zahnbürste.

toothpaste

toothpaste ['tu:θpeist], *s.* die Zahnpaste.

top (1) [tɔp], *s.* die Spitze; der Gipfel
(*mountain*); der Wipfel (*tree*); der
Giebel (*house*); die Oberfläche (*sur-*
face); *big* —, das Zirkuszeltdach; —
hat, der Zylinder. — *v.a.* übertreffen
(*surpass*); bedecken (*cover*).

top (2) [tɔp], *s.* der Kreisel (*spinning* —).

topaz ['toupæz], *s.* der Topas.

tope [toup], *v.n.* zechen, saufen.

toper ['toupə], *s.* der Zecher.

topic ['tɔpik], *s.* das Thema, der
Gegenstand.

topical ['tɔpikəl], *adj.* aktuell (*up to date*).

topmost ['tɔpmoust], *adj.* höchst,
oberst.

topsy-turvy ['tɔpsi 'tə:vi], *adv.* durcheinander, auf den Kopf gestellt.

torch [tɔ:tʃ], *s.* die Fackel; (*Elec.*) die
Taschenlampe.

torment ['tɔ:mənt], *s.* die Qual, Marter.
— [tɔ:'ment], *v.a.* quälen, martern,
peinigen.

tornado [tɔ:'neidou], *s.* der Wirbelsturm.

torpid ['tɔ:pid], *adj.* starr, betäubt;
(*fig.*) stumpfsinnig.

torpor ['tɔ:pə], *s.* die Starre; die
Stumpfheit, Stumpfsinnigkeit.

torrent ['tɔrənt], *s.* der Gießbach, der
(reißende) Strom.

torrid ['tɔrid], *adj.* brennend heiß,
verbrannt.

torsion ['tɔ:ʃən], *s.* die Drehung,
Windung.

tortoise ['tɔ:təs], *s.* (*Zool.*) die Schildkröte.

tortoiseshell ['tɔ:təʃel], *s.* das Schildpatt.

tortuous ['tɔ:tjuəs], *adj.* gewunden.

torture ['tɔ:tʃə], *s.* die Folter; (*fig.*) die
Folterqualen, *f. pl.* — *v.a.* foltern.

Tory ['tɔ:ri], *s.* (*Pol.*) der englische
Konservative.

toss [tɔs], *s.* der Wurf (*of coin, etc.*);
argue the —, sich streiten. — *v.a.*
werfen. — *v.n.* — *up*, losen.

total [toutl], *adj.* ganz, gänzlich, total.
— *s.* die Gesamtsumme. — *v.a.* sich
(im ganzen) belaufen auf.

totality [tou'tæliti], *s.* die Gesamtheit.

totter ['tɔtə], *v.n.* wanken, schwanken,
torkeln.

touch [tʌtʃ], *v.a.* berühren; anfassen;
(*coll.*) anpumpen (*for money*); — *up*,
auffrischen. — *s.* die Berührung
(*contact*); (*Mus.*) der Anschlag.

touching ['tʌtʃiŋ], *adj.* rührend, ergreifend.

touchline ['tʌtʃlain], *s.* (*Sport*) der Rand
des Spielfeldes, die Seitenlinie.

touchy ['tʌtʃi], *adj.* empfindlich.

tough [tʌf], *adj.* zäh, widerstandsfähig
(*resistant*); *get* —, grob werden; —
luck, Pech! — *s.* (*Am. coll.*) der
Grobian.

tour [tuə], *s.* die Tour, Reise; (*Theat.*)
die Tournee. — *v.a., v.n.* touren,
bereisen.

tourist ['tuərist], *s.* der Tourist.

tournament ['tuə- *or* 'tɔ:nəmənt], *s.* der
Wettkampf, das Turnier.

tout [taut], *v.n.* Kunden suchen,
anlocken. — *s.* der Kundenfänger.

tow [tou], *s.* das Schlepptau. — *v.a.*
ziehen, schleppen.

toward(s) [tu'wɔ:d(z), tɔ:d(z)], *prep.*
gegen; gegenüber; zu ... hin; auf ...
zu; für.

towel ['tauəl], *s.* das Handtuch.

towelling ['tauəliŋ], *s.* der Hand-
tuchdrell; *Turkish* —, das Frottiertuch.

tower [tauə], *s.* der Turm, Zwinger. —
v.n. emporragen, hervorragen
(*über*).

towing path ['tou(iŋ) pɑ:θ] *see*
towpath.

town [taun], *s.* die Stadt; — *crier*, der
Ausrufer; — *hall*, das Rathaus (*offices*).

townsman ['taunzmən], *s.* der Städter.

towpath ['toupɑ:θ], *s.* der Treidelpfad.

toy [tɔi], *s.* das Spielzeug; (*pl.*) Spiel-
sachen, Speilwaren, *f. pl.*; — *shop*, der
Speilwarenladen. — *v.n.* spielen.

trace [treis], *s.* die Spur. — *v.a.* suchen,
aufspüren; pausen (*through paper*).

track [træk], *s.* die Spur, Fährte (*path*);
(*Railw.*) das Geleis(e).

tract [trækt], *s.* der Traktat (*pamphlet*);
die Strecke (*stretch*).

traction ['trækʃən], *s.* das Ziehen
(*pulling*); (*Tech.*) der Zug.

tractor ['træktə], *s.* der Traktor.

trade [treid], *s.* der Handel (*commerce*);
das Gewerbe (*craft*); — *wind*, der Passatwind; — *union*, die Gewerkschaft.
— *v.a.* — *in*, in Zahlung geben. —
v.n. handeln, Handel treiben; — *in*,
eintauschen.

trademark ['treidmɑ:k], *s.* die (Schutz)-
marke, das Warenzeichen.

tradesman ['treidzmən], *s.* der Lieferant.

traduce [trə'dju:s], *v.a.* verleumden.

traffic ['træfik], *s.* der Verkehr; (*Comm.*)
der Handel; — *light*, die Verkehrs-
ampel.

trafficator ['træfikeitə], *s.* (*Motor.*) der
Winker.

tragedy ['trædʒədi], *s.* die Tragödie,
das Trauerspiel.

tragic ['trædʒik], *adj.* tragisch.

tradition [trə'diʃən], *s.* die Tradition.

traditional [trə'diʃənəl], *adj.* traditionell.

trail [treil], *s.* die Spur, Fährte; (*Am.*)
der Pfad. — *v.a.* nach sich ziehen,
schleppen; (*Am.*) nachfolgen (*Dat.*).

trailer ['treilə], *s.* (*Motor.*) der Anhänger; (*Film*) die Voranzeige.

train [trein], *v.a.* ausbilden; (*Sport*)
trainieren, abrichten, dressieren
(*animal*). — *v.n.* (*Sport*) sich vorbereiten; sich ausbilden (*for pro-*
fession). — *s.* (*Railw.*) der Zug; (*Mil.*)
der Zug, Transport; die Schleppe
(*bridal gown, etc.*); — *of thought*, die
Gedankenfolge.

training ['treiniŋ], *s.* die Erziehung; Ausbildung; — *college*, das Lehrerseminar, die pädagogische Hochschule.

trait [trei, treit], *s.* der Zug, Wesenszug.

traitor ['treitə], *s.* der Verräter.

tram(car) ['træm(ka:)], *s.* die Straßenbahn, der Strassenbahnwagen.

trammelled [træmld], *adj.* gebunden, gefesselt.

tramp [træmp], *s.* der Landstreicher, Strolch. — *v.n.* trampeln; (zu Fuß) wandern.

trample [træmpl], *v.a.* niedertrampeln. — *v.n.* trampeln, treten.

tramway ['træmwei], *s.* die Strassenbahn.

trance [tra:ns], *s.* die Verzückung.

tranquil ['træŋkwil], *adj.* ruhig, still, friedlich.

tranquillizer ['træŋkwilaizə], *s.* (*Med.*) das Beruhigungsmittel.

transact [træn'zækt], *v.a.* abmachen; verrichten (*conclude*), erledigen.

transaction [træn'zækʃən], *s.* die Verhandlung, Abmachung, Durchführung.

transcend [træn'send], *v.a.* übersteigen.

transcendental [trænsen'dentl], *adj.* transzendental.

transcribe [træn'skraib], *v.a.* übertragen; umschreiben (*cipher etc.*); abschreiben.

transcription [træn'skripʃən], *s.* die Umschrift; die Abschrift (*copy*).

transept ['trænsept], *s.* (*Archit.*) das Querschiff.

transfer [træns'fə:], *v.a.* versetzen, überführen; übertragen; überweisen (*money*). — *v.n.* verlegt werden. —['trænsfə:], *s.* der Wechsel, Transfer; die Versetzung; Überweisung.

transfigure [træns'figə], *v.a.* verklären.

transfix [træns'fiks], *v.a.* durchbohren.

transform [træns'fɔ:m], *v.a.* verändern, umwandeln. — *v.r.* sich verwandeln.

transgress [træns'gres], *v.a.* überschreiten (*trespass on*). — *v.n.* sich vergehen.

transient ['trænsiənt], *adj.* vergänglich.

transit ['trænsit, 'trænzit], *s.* der Durchgang; die Durchfahrt, Durchfuhr (*travel*); (*Comm.*) der Transit. — *v.n.* (*Am.*) durchfahren (*of goods*).

transitive ['trænsitiv], *adj.* (*Gram.*) transitiv.

transitory ['trænsitəri], *adj.* vergänglich, flüchtig.

translate [træns'leit], *v.a.* übersetzen; versetzen (*office*).

translation [træns'leiʃən], *s.* die Übersetzung, die Übertragung.

translucent [trænz'lju:sənt], *adj.* durchscheinend.

transmission [trænz'miʃən], *s.* die Übersendung, Übermittlung; (*Rad.*) die Sendung; (*Motor.*) die Transmission.

transmit [trænz'mit], *v.a.* übersenden,

übermitteln; (*Rad., T.V.*) übertragen, senden.

transmutation [trænzmju'teiʃən], *s.* die Verwandlung.

transparent [træns'pɛərənt], *adj.* durchsichtig.

transpire [træns'paiə, trænz–], *v.n.* bekannt werden.

transplant [træns'pla:nt, trænz–], *v.a.* verpflanzen; (*Med.*) übertragen.

transport [træns'pɔ:t], *v.a.* transportieren; (*fig.*) entzücken. — ['trænspɔ:t], *s.* der Transport; die Versendung (*sending*); (*fig.*) die Entzückung.

transpose [træns'pouz], *v.a.* (*Mus.*) transponieren.

transverse [trænz'və:s], *adj.* quer; schräg (*oblique*).

trap [træp], *v.a.* in eine Falle führen; ertappen (*detect*). — *s.* die Falle; der Einspänner (*gig*).

trapeze [trə'pi:z], *s.* das Trapez.

trapper ['træpə], *s.* der Fallensteller.

trappings ['træpiŋz], *s.pl.* der Schmuck; (*fig.*) die Äußerlichkeiten, *f. pl.*

trash [træʃ], *s.* (*Lit.*) der Schund; der Kitsch; das wertlose Zeug.

trashy ['træʃi], *adj.* wertlos, kitschig.

travail ['træveil], *s.* die Wehen, Sorgen, die Mühe.

travel [trævl], *v.n.* reisen. — *v.a.* bereisen. — *s.* das Reisen; — *agency*, das Reisebüro.

traveller ['trævələ], *s.* der Reisende; (*Comm.*) der Handelsreisende, Vertreter.

traverse ['trævə:s], *adj.* quer. — *s.* die Traverse, der Querbalken. — [trə–'və:s], *v.a.* durchqueren; (*fig.*) durchwandern.

trawl [trɔ:l], *v.n.* (mit Schleppnetz) fischen.

trawler ['trɔ:lə], *s.* das Fischerboot, der Fischdampfer.

tray [trei], *s.* das Tablett.

treacherous ['tretʃərəs], *adj.* verräterisch; (*fig.*) gefährlich.

treachery ['tretʃəri], *s.* der Verrat.

treacle [tri:kl], *s.* der Sirup.

tread [tred], *v.a., v.n. irr.* (be)treten, auftreten. — *s.* der Tritt, Schritt; die Lauffläche (*of a tyre*).

treason [tri:zn], *s.* der Verrat.

treasure ['treʒə], *s.* der Schatz.

treasurer ['treʒərə], *s.* der Schatzmeister.

treasury ['treʒəri], *s.* die Schatzkammer; (*U.K.*) *the Treasury*, das Schatzamt, Finanzministerium.

treat [tri:t], *v.a.* behandeln; bewirten (*as host*). — *v.n.* (*Pol.*) unterhandeln (*negotiate*). — *s.* der Genuß (*pleasure*).

treatise ['tri:tis], *s.* die Abhandlung.

treatment ['tri:tmənt], *s.* die Behandlung.

treaty ['tri:ti], *s.* der Vertrag.

treble [trebl], *s.* (*Mus.*) die Sopranstimme, Knabenstimme, der Diskant; (*Maths.*) das Dreifache. — *v.a.* verdreifachen.

tree [tri:], *s.* (*Bot.*) der Baum.
trefoil ['tri:foil], *s.* (*Bot.*) der dreiblätt(e)rige Klee; das Dreiblatt.
trellis ['trelis], *s.* das Gitter.
tremble [trembl], *v.n.* zittern. — *s.* das Zittern.
tremendous [tri'mendəs], *adj.* ungeheuer (*groß*); schrecklich.
tremor ['tremə], *s.* das Zittern; (*Geol.*) das Beben; (*Med.*) das Zucken.
trench [trentʃ], *s.* der Graben.
trenchant ['trentʃənt], *adj.* einschneidend, scharf.
trend [trend], *s.* die Tendenz; (*Comm.*) der Trend.
trepidation [trepi'deiʃən], *s.* die Angst, das Zittern.
trespass ['trespəs], *v.n.* sich vergehen, übertreten (*law*); — *on*, unbefugt betreten. — *s.* die Übertretung.
tress [tres], *s.* die Flechte, Haarlocke.
trestle [tresl], *s.* das Gestell; — *table*, der Klapptisch.
trial ['traiəl], *s.* die Probe, der Versuch; (*Law*) die Verhandlung, der Prozeß, das Verhör.
triangle ['traiæŋgl], *s.* das Dreieck; (*Mus.*) der Triangel.
tribe [traib], *s.* der Stamm.
tribulation [tribju'leiʃən], *s.* die Trübsal, Drangsal.
tribunal [trai'bju:nəl], *s.* das Tribunal, der Gerichtshof.
tributary ['tribjutəri], *adj.* Neben-. — *s.* der Nebenfluß.
tribute ['tribju:t], *s.* der Tribut.
trice [trais], *s. in a* —, im Nu.
trick [trik], *s.* der Kniff, Trick. — *v.a.* betrügen.
trickery ['trikəri], *s.* der Betrug.
trickle [trikl], *v.n.* tröpfeln, sickern. — *s.* das Tröpfeln.
tricky ['triki], *adj.* verwickelt; (*fig.*) bedenklich, heikel.
tricycle ['traisikl], *s.* das Dreirad.
tried [traid], *adj.* erprobt, bewährt.
triennial [trai'eniəl], *adj.* dreijährlich.
trifle [traifl], *v.n.* scherzen, spielen. — *s.* die Kleinigkeit; (*Cul.*) der süße Auflauf.
trigger ['trigə], *s.* der Drücker. — *v.a.* — *off*, auslösen.
trilateral [trai'lætərəl], *adj.* dreiseitig.
trill [tril], *s.* (*Mus.*) der Triller. — *v.a.*, *v.n.* trillern.
trim [trim], *adj.* niedlich, schmuck; nett (*dress*). — *v.a.* beschneiden; (*Naut.*) — *sails*, einziehen. — *s.* die Ausrüstung; (*Naut.*) das Gleichgewicht.
trimmer ['trimə], *s.* der Putzmacherin; (*fig.*) der Opportunist.
trimmings ['triminz], *s. pl.* (*fig.*) der Kleinkram (*Tail.*) der Besatz.
Trinity ['triniti], *s.* (*Theol.*) die Dreifaltigkeit, Dreieinigkeit.
trinket ['triŋkit], *s.* das Geschmeide; (*pl.*) Schmucksachen, *f. pl.*
trip [trip], *s.* der Ausflug, die Reise. —

v.a. — *up*, ein Bein stellen (*Dat.*). — *v.n.* stolpern.
tripe ['traip], *s.* die Kaldaunen, *f. pl.*; (*fig.*) der Unsinn.
triple [tripl], *adj.* dreifach.
triplet ['triplit], *s.* der Drilling; (*Mus.*) die Triole; (*Poet.*) der Dreireim.
tripod ['traipɔd], *s.* der Dreifuß.
tripos ['traipɔs], *s.* das Schlußexamen (*Cambridge Univ.*).
trite [trait], *adj.* abgedroschen.
triumph ['traiʌmf], *s.* der Triumph. — *v.n.* triumphieren.
triumphant [trai'ʌmfənt], *adj.* triumphierend.
trivial ['triviəl], *adj.* trivial, platt, alltäglich.
troll (1) [troul], *v.n.* trällern (*hum*); fischen. — *s.* der Rundgesang (*song*).
troll (2) [troul], *s.* der Kobold (*gnome*).
trolley ['trɔli], *s.* der Teewagen (*furniture*); (*Tech.*) die Dräsine, der Karren.
trollop ['trɔləp], *s.* die Schlampe.
trombone [trɔm'boun], *s.* (*Mus.*) die Posaune.
troop [tru:p], *s.* der Haufe; (*Mil.*) die Truppe, der Trupp. — *v.n.* sich sammeln. — *v.a. Trooping the Colour*, die Fahnenparade.
trophy ['troufi], *s.* die Trophäe, das Siegeszeichen.
tropic ['trɔpik], *s.* (*Geog.*) der Wendekreis; (*pl.*) die Tropen, *f. pl.*
tropical ['trɔpikəl], *adj.* tropisch.
trot [trɔt], *v.n.* traben. — *s.* der Trab, Trott.
troth [trouθ], *s.* (*obs.*) die Treue; *pledge o.'s* —, Treue geloben.
trouble [trʌbl], *s.* die Mühe, Sorge (*worry*); der Kummer (*sadness*); die Störung (*disturbance*). — *v.a.* bemühen (*ask favour of*); bekümmern (*worry*); stören (*disturb*).
troublesome ['trʌblsəm], *adj.* ärgerlich, schwierig, unangenehm.
trough [trɔf], *s.* der Trog; (*Met.*) das Tief.
trounce [trauns], *v.a.* verprügeln.
trouncing ['traunsiŋ], *s.* die Tracht Prügel.
trousers ['trauzəz], *s. pl.* die Hosen, *f.pl.*
trout [traut], *s.* (*Zool.*) die Forelle.
trowel ['trauəl], *s.* die Kelle.
troy(weight) ['trɔi(weit)], *s.* das Troygewicht.
truant ['tru:ənt], *s.* (*Sch.*) der Schulschwänzer; *play* —, die Schule schwänzen.
truce [tru:s], *s.* der Waffenstillstand.
truck (1) [trʌk], *s.* (*Rail.*) der Güterwagen; (*Am.*) *see* **lorry**.
truck (2) [trʌk], *s. have no* — *with*, nichts zu tun haben mit.
truculent ['trʌkjulənt], *adj.* streitsüchtig.
trudge [trʌdʒ], *v.n.* sich schleppen.
true [tru:], *adj.* wahr; treu (*faithful*); echt (*genuine*); richtig (*correct*).

truffle [trʌfl], *s.* die Trüffel.

truism ['tru:izm], *s.* der Gemeinplatz, die Binsenwahrheit.

truly ['tru:li], *adv. yours* —, Ihr ergebener.

trump [trʌmp], *s.* der Trumpf; — *card*, die Trumpfkarte. — *v.a.* — *up*, erfinden, erdichten.

trumpery ['trʌmpəri], *s.* der Plunder, Schund. — *adj.* wertlos, belanglos.

trumpet ['trʌmpit], *s.* (*Mus.*) die Trompete. — *v.a.* stolz austrompeten, ausposaunen. — *v.n.* trompeten.

truncate [trʌŋ'keit], *v.a.* verstümmeln, stutzen.

truncheon [trʌnʃən], *s.* der Knüppel. — *v.a.* durchprügeln.

trundle [trʌndl], *v.n.* trudeln; sich wälzen. — *v.a.* — *a hoop*, Reifen schlagen.

trunk [trʌŋk], *s.* der Stamm (*tree*); der Rüssel (*of elephant*); der (große) Koffer (*chest*); — *call*, das Ferngespräch.

truss [trʌs], *s.* das Band, Bruchband. — *v.a.* zäumen, stützen; aufschürzen.

trust [trʌst], *v.a., v.n.* trauen (*Dat.*), vertrauen (*Dat.*); anvertrauen (*Dat., Acc.*). — *s.* das Vertrauen; *in* —, zu treuen Händen, als Treuhänder; (*Comm.*) der Trust.

trustworthy ['trʌstwə:ði], *adj.* zuverlässig.

truth [tru:θ], *s.* die Wahrheit.

truthful ['tru:θful], *adj.* wahrhaftig.

try [trai], *v.a., v.n.* versuchen (*s. th.*); (*Law*) verhören; — *on* (*clothes*), anprobieren; — *out*, ausprobieren. — *v.n.* versuchen, sich bemühen. — *s.* der Versuch (*attempt*); (*Rugby*) der Try.

Tsar [zɑ:], *s.* der Zar.

tub [tʌb], *s.* das Faß; die Wanne (*bath*); (*Naut.*) das Übungsboot.

tube [tju:b], *s.* die Tube (*paste etc.*); die Röhre (*pipe, also Elec.*); der Schlauch (*tyre*); das Rohr (*tubing*); (*Transport*) die Londoner Untergrundbahn.

tuberous ['tju:bərəs], *adj.* knollenartig, knollig.

tubular ['tju:bjulə], *adj.* röhrenförmig.

tuck [tʌk], *s.* (*Tail.*) die Falte; (*Sch. sl.*) der Leckerbissen. — *v.a.* — *up*, zudecken; — *in*, einschlagen. — *v.n.* (*sl.*) — *in*, tüchtig zugreifen.

tucker ['tʌkə], *s.* (*sl.*) das Essen.

tuckshop ['tʌkʃɔp], *s.* der Schulladen.

Tuesday ['tju:zdi], der Dienstag.

tuft [tʌft], *s.* der Büschel.

tug [tʌg], *v.a.* ziehen, zerren. — *s.* (*Naut.*) der Schlepper; — *of war*, das Tauziehen.

tuition [tju:'iʃən], *s.* der Unterricht, Privatunterricht.

tulip ['tju:lip], *s.* (*Bot.*) die Tulpe.

tumble [tʌmbl], *v.n.* purzeln. — *s.* der Sturz, Fall.

tumbril ['tʌmbril], *s.* der Karren.

tumid ['tju:mid], *adj.* geschwollen.

tumour ['tju:mə], *s.* (*Med.*) die Geschwulst, der Tumor.

tumult ['tju:mʌlt], *s.* der Tumult, Auflauf; der Lärm (*noise*).

tun [tʌn], *s.* die Tonne, das Faß.

tune [tju:n], *s.* die Melodie. — *v.a.* stimmen; (*Rad.*) — *in* (*to*), einstellen (auf).

tuneful ['tju:nful], *adj.* melodisch.

tuner ['tju:nə], *s.* der (Klavier)stimmer.

tunic ['tju:nik], *s.* der Kittel.

tuning ['tju:niŋ], *s.* das Stimmen; die Abstimmung (*also Rad.*); — *fork*, die Stimmgabel.

tunnel [tʌnl], *s.* der Tunnel. — *v.n.* graben, einen Tunnel bauen.

turbid ['tə:bid], *adj.* trüb, dick.

turbot ['tə:bət], *s.* (*Zool.*) der Steinbutt.

turbulence ['tə:bjuləns], *s.* der Sturm, das Ungestüm; (*Aviat.*) die Turbulenz.

tureen [tjuə'ri:n], *s.* die Suppenterrine, Suppenschüssel.

turf [tə:f], *s.* der Rasen; (*Sport*) die Rennbahn, der Turf. — *v.a.* mit Rasen belegen; (*sl.*) — *out*, hinausschmeißen.

turgid ['tə:dʒid], *adj.* schwülstig (*style*).

Turk [tə:k], *s.* der Türke.

turkey ['tə:ki], *s.* (*Orn.*) der Truthahn.

Turkish ['tə:kiʃ], *adj.* türkisch.

turmoil ['tə:mɔil], *s.* die Unruhe, der Aufruhr.

turn [tə:n], *v.a.* wenden, drehen, kehren (*to*); — *down*, ablehnen; (*coll.*) — *in*, abgeben (*hand over*); — *on*, andrehen (*tap etc.*); — *off*, ausdrehen; — *out*, produzieren. — *v.n.* sich drehen, sich ändern; werden; — *on s.o.*, jemanden verraten; (*coll.*) — *out*, ausrücken; (*coll.*) — *up*, auftauchen. — *s.* die Drehung, Windung; der Hang; die Reihe; die Nummer (*act*); *it is my* —, ich bin an der Reihe.

turncoat ['tə:nkout], *s.* der Überläufer.

turner ['tə:nə], *s.* der Drechsler.

turnip ['tə:nip], *s.* (*Bot.*) die Rübe.

turnpike ['tə:npaik], *s.* der Schlagbaum.

turnstile ['tə:nstail], *s.* das Drehkreuz.

turntable ['tə:nteibl], *s.* die Drehscheibe.

turpentine ['tə:pəntain], *s.* der *or* das Terpentin.

turquoise ['tə:kwɔiz *or* 'tə:kɔiz], *s.* der Türkis.

turret ['tʌrit], *s.* (*Archit.*) der Turm, das Türmchen.

turtle [tə:tl], *s.* (*Zool.*) die Schildkröte; (*Orn.*) -*dove*, die Turteltaube.

tusk [tʌsk], *s.* (*Zool.*) der Stoßzahn.

tussle [tʌsl], *s.* der Streit, die Rauferei.

tutelage ['tju:tilidʒ], *s.* die Vormundschaft.

tutor ['tju:tə], *s.* der Privatlehrer; der Tutor, Studienleiter. — *v.a.* unterrichten.

twaddle [twɔdl], *s.* das Geschwätz. — *v.n.* schwätzen.

twang [twæŋ], *s.* der scharfe Ton. — *v.n.* scharf klingen.

tweed [twi:d], *s.* (*Text.*) der Tweed.

twelfth [twelfθ], *num.adj.* zwölft; *Twelfth Night*, das Fest der Heiligen Drei Könige (*6th January*).

twelve

twelve [twelv], *num. adj.* zwölf.
twenty ['twenti], *num. adj.* zwanzig.
twice [twais], *num. adv.* zweimal, doppelt.
twig [twig], *s.* (*Bot.*) der Zweig, die Rute.
twilight ['twailait], *s.* das Zwielicht, die Dämmerung.
twill [twil], *s.* (*Text.*) der Köper. — *v.a.* köpern.
twin [twin], *s.* der Zwilling.
twine [twain], *s.* der Bindfaden, die Schnur. — *v.a.* drehen, zwirnen. — *v.n.* sich verflechten; sich winden (*plant*).
twinge [twindʒ], *s.* der Zwick, Stich.
twinkle ['twiŋkl], *v.n.* blinzeln, blinken. — *s.* das Zwinkern, der Blick.
twirl [twəːl], *s.* der Wirbel. — *v.a.* schnell drehen, wirbeln.
twist [twist], *v.a.* flechten, drehen; verdrehen. — *s.* die Drehung, Krümmung; das Geflecht; (*fig.*) die Wendung (*sudden change*).
twitch [twitʃ], *v.a.* zupfen, zucken. — *v.n.* zucken. — *s.* das Zucken, der Krampf.
twitter ['twitə], *v.n.* zwitschern; (*fig.*) zittern. — *s.* das Gezwitscher; (*fig.*) die Angst.
two [tuː], *num. adj.* zwei; — -faced, falsch.
twofold ['tuːfould], *adj.* zweifach.
tympanum ['timpənəm], *s.* (*Med.*) das Trommelfell.
type [taip], *s.* (*Typ.*) die Type; (*Psych.*) der Typ, Typus. — *v.a., v.n.* tippen; mit der Maschine schreiben.
typewriter ['taipraitə], *s.* die Schreibmaschine.
typhoid ['taifɔid], *s.* (*Med.*) der (Unterleibs)typhus. — *adj.* typhusartig.
typist ['taipist], *s.* der (die) Maschinenschreiber(in).
typhoon [tai'fuːn], *s.* der Taifun.
typical ['tipikəl], *adj.* typisch, charakteristisch.
typography [tai'pɔgrəfi], *s.* die Typographie, Buchdruckerkunst.
tyrannical [ti'rænikəl], *adj.* tyrannisch.
tyranny ['tirəni], *s.* die Tyrannei.
tyrant ['taiərənt], *s.* der Tyrann.
tyre, (*Am.*) tire [taiə], *s.* der Reifen.
tyro ['taiərou], *s.* der Anfänger.
Tyrolese [tiro'liːz], *adj.* tirolisch, Tiroler-. — *s.* der Tiroler.

U

U [juː]. das U.
ubiquitous [juː'bikwitəs], *adj.* überall da, überall zu finden.
udder ['ʌdə], *s.* (*Zool.*) das Euter.
ugly ['ʌgli], *adj.* häßlich.

Ukrainian [juː'kreiniən],*adj.*ukrainisch. — *s.* der Ukrainer.
ulcer ['ʌlsə], *s.* (*Med.*) das Geschwür.
ulcerate ['ʌlsəreit], *v.n.* (*Med.*) schwären.
ulcerous ['ʌlsərəs], *adj.* (*Med.*) geschwürig.
ulterior [ʌl'tiəriə], *adj.* weiter, ferner, weiterliegend.
ultimate ['ʌltimit], *adj.* letzt, endlich, äußerst.
ultimatum [ʌlti'meitəm], *s.* das Ultimatum.
umbrage ['ʌmbridʒ], *s.* der Schatten; take —, Anstoß nehmen (an, *Dat.*).
umbrella [ʌm'brelə], *s.* der Schirm, Regenschirm.
umpire ['ʌmpaiə], *s.* (*Sport*) der Schiedsrichter.
umpteen ['ʌmptiːn], *adj.* zahlreiche, verschiedene.
un- [ʌn], *negating pref.* un-, nicht-; with *verbs*, auf-, ent-, los-, ver-; *where a word is not given, see the simple form.*
unable [ʌn'eibl], *adj.* unfähig; be —, nicht können.
unaccustomed [ʌnə'kʌstəmd], *adj.* ungewohnt.
unaided [ʌn'eidid], *adj.* allein, ohne Hilfe.
unaware [ʌnə'wɛə], *adj.* unbewußt.
uncertain [ʌn'səːtin], *adj.* unsicher.
uncle [ʌŋkl], *s.* der Onkel.
unconscious [ʌn'kɔnʃəs], *adj.* bewußtlos; unbewußt.
uncouth [ʌn'kuːθ], *adj.* ungehobelt, roh.
unction ['ʌŋkʃən], *s.* die Salbung (*anointing*); die Salbe; *Extreme Unction*, (*Eccl.*) die Letzte Ölung.
unctuous ['ʌŋktjuəs], *adj.* salbungsvoll.
under ['ʌndə], *prep.* unter. — *adv.* darunter, unten (*underneath*); *pref.* (*compounds*) unter-.
undercarriage ['ʌndəkæridʒ],*s.*(*Aviat.*) das Fahrwerk.
underfed [ʌndə'fed], *adj.* unterernährt.
undergo [ʌndə'gou], *v.a. irr.* durchmachen, erdulden.
undergraduate [ʌndə'grædjuit], *s.* (*Univ.*) der Student.
underground ['ʌndəgraund], *adj.* unterirdisch; — *railway* die Untergrundbahn. — [ʌndə'graund], *adv.* unterirdisch.
underhand [ʌndə'hænd], *adj.* heimlich, hinterlistig.
underline [ʌndə'lain], *v.a.* unterstreichen.
undermine [ʌndə'main], *v.a.* untergraben.
underneath [ʌndə'niːθ], *adv.* unten, darunter. — ['ʌndəniːθ], *prep.* unter.
undersigned [ʌndə'saind], *adj.* unterzeichnet. —*s.* der Unterzeichnete.
understand [ʌndə'stænd], *v.a. irr.* verstehen, begreifen.
understatement ['ʌndəsteitmənt], *s.* die zu bescheidene Festellung, Unterbewertung.

undertaker ['ʌndəteikə], s. der Leichenbestatter.

undertaking [ʌndə'teikiŋ], s. das Unternehmen (*business*); das Versprechen (*promise*).

undertone ['ʌndətoun], s. der Unterton.

underwrite [ʌndə'rait], v.a. irr. (*Comm.*) versichern.

underwriter ['ʌndəraitə], s. (*Comm.*) der Assekurant, Versicherer, Mitversicherer.

undeserved [ʌndi'zə:vd], adj. unverdient.

undeserving [ʌndi'zə:viŋ], adj. unwürdig.

undignified [ʌn'dignifaid], adj. würdelos.

undiscerning [ʌndi'zə:niŋ], adj. geschmacklos.

undiscriminating [ʌndis'krimineitiŋ], adj. unterschiedslos, unkritisch.

undisputed [ʌndis'pju:tid], adj. unbestritten.

undo [ʌn'du:], v.a. irr. zerstören (*destroy*); öffnen (*open*).

undoubted [ʌn'dautid], adj. zweifellos.

undress [ʌn'dres], v.a., v.n. — (sich)ausziehen. — ['ʌndres], s. das Hauskleid.

undue [ʌn'dju:], adj. unangemessen.

undulate ['ʌndjuleit], v.n. wallen, Wellen schlagen.

unduly [ʌn'dju:li], adv. ungebührlich, übermäßig.

unearth [ʌn'ə:θ], v.a. ausgraben.

unearthly [ʌn'ə:θli], adj. überirdisch.

uneasy [ʌn'i:zi], adj. unruhig, unbehaglich.

unemployed [ʌnim'plɔid], adj. arbeitslos.

unemployment [ʌnim'plɔimənt], s. die Arbeitslosigkeit.

unending [ʌn'endiŋ], adj. endlos.

uneven [ʌn'i:vən], adj. uneben; ungerade.

unexceptionable [ʌnik'sepʃənəbl], adj. tadellos.

unexpired [ʌniks'paiəd], adj. noch nicht abgelaufen, noch gültig.

unfair [ʌn'feə], adj. unfair; unehrlich.

unfeeling [ʌn'fi:liŋ], adj. gefühllos.

unfit [ʌn'fit], adj. (*Mil.*, *Med.*) untauglich, schwach; (*food etc.*) ungenießbar.

unfold [ʌn'fould], v.a. entfalten.

unforeseen [ʌnfɔ:'si:n], adj. unerwartet.

unfounded [ʌn'faundid], adj. grundlos.

unfurnished [ʌn'fə:niʃd], adj. unmöbliert.

ungrudging [ʌn'grʌdʒiŋ], adj. bereitwillig.

unhappy [ʌn'hæpi], adj. unglücklich.

unhinge [ʌn'hindʒ], v.a. aus den Angeln heben.

unicorn ['ju:nikɔ:n], s. (*Myth.*) das Einhorn.

uniform ['ju:nifɔ:m], s. die Uniform. — adj. gleichförmig, einförmig.

union ['ju:niən], s. die Vereinigung; *trade* —, die Gewerkschaft; *Union Jack*, die britische Nationalflagge.

unique [ju'ni:k], adj. einzigartig.

unison ['ju:nisən], s. (*Mus.*) der Einklang, die Harmonie.

unit ['ju:nit], s. die Einheit (*measure etc.*).

unite [ju'nait], v.a. vereinen. — v.n. sich vereinen, verbünden.

unity ['ju:niti], s. die Einigkeit.

universal [ju:ni'və:səl], adj. allgemein.

universe ['ju:nivə:s], s. das Weltall.

university [ju:ni'və:siti], s. die Universität, Hochschule; — *degree*, der akademische Grad.

unkempt [ʌn'kempt], adj. ungekämmt, ungepflegt.

unleavened [ʌn'levənd], adj. ungesäuert.

unless [ʌn'les], conj. außer, wenn nicht, es sei denn.

unlettered [ʌn'letəd], adj. ungebildet.

unlicensed [ʌn'laisənsd], adj. nicht (für Alkoholverkauf) lizenziert.

unlike [ʌn'laik], adj. ungleich. — ['ʌnlaik], prep. anders als, verschieden von.

unlikely [ʌn'laikli], adj., adv. unwahrscheinlich.

unlock [ʌn'lɔk], v.a. aufschließen.

unmask [ʌn'mɑ:sk], v.a. entlarven.

unpack [ʌn'pæk], v.a., v.n. auspacken.

unpleasant [ʌn'plεznt], adj. unangenehm.

unreliable [ʌnri'laiəbl], adj. unzuverlässig.

unremitting [ʌnri'mitiŋ], adj. unablässig.

unrepentant [ʌnri'pentənt], adj.reuelos.

unrest [ʌn'rest], s. die Unruhe.

unsafe [ʌn'seif], adj. unsicher.

unscathed [ʌn'skeiðd], adj. unversehrt.

unscrew [ʌn'skru:], v.a. abschrauben.

unscrupulous [ʌn'skru:pjuləs], adj. skrupellos, gewissenlos.

unseat [ʌn'si:t], v.a. aus dem Sattel heben; absetzen.

unselfish [ʌn'selfiʃ], adj. selbstlos.

unsettle [ʌn'setl], v.a. verwirren; (*fig.*) aus dem Konzept bringen.

unsew [ʌn'sou], v.a. auftrennen.

unshrinking [ʌn'ʃrinkiŋ], adj. unverzagt.

unsophisticated [ʌnsə'fistikeitid], adj. naiv, natürlich.

unsparing [ʌn'spεəriŋ], adj. schonungslos.

unstable [ʌn'steibl], adj. unsicher; labil.

unstitch [ʌn'stitʃ], v.a. auftrennen.

unstop [ʌn'stɔp], v.a. aufstöpseln, öffnen (*a bottle*).

unstudied [ʌn'stʌdid], adj. ungekünstelt.

unsuccessful [ʌnsək'sesful], adj. erfolglos.

unsuspecting [ʌnsə'spektiŋ], adj. arglos.

untie [ʌn'tai], v.a. losbinden.

until [ʌn'til], prep., conj. bis.

untimely

untimely [ʌn'taimli], *adj.* vorzeitig, unzeitig.

untiring [ʌn'taiəriŋ], *adj.* unermüdlich.

unto ['ʌntu], *prep.* (*Poet.*) zu.

untold [ʌn'tould], *adj.* ungezählt, unermeßlich.

untoward [ʌn'tɔːd *or* ʌn'touəd], *adj.* unangenehm; widerspenstig (*recalcitrant*).

untrustworthy [ʌn'trʌstwəːði], *adj.* unzuverlässig.

unveil [ʌn'veil], *v.a.* enthüllen.

unwieldy [ʌn'wiːldi], *adj.* sperrig, schwerfällig.

unwind [ʌn'waind], *v.a.* abwickeln.

unwitting [ʌn'witiŋ], *adj.* unwissentlich, unbewusst.

unwonted [ʌn'wountid], *adj.* ungewohnt.

unwrap [ʌn'ræp], *v.a.* auspacken, auswickeln.

unyielding [ʌn'jiːldiŋ], *adj.* unnachgiebig; hartnäckig.

unyoke [ʌn'jouk], *v.a.* ausspannen.

up [ʌp], *adv.* auf, aufwärts (*upward*); aufgestanden (*out of bed*); — (*there*), oben; *what's up?* was ist los? — *to*, bis zu; *be — to s.th.*, auf etwas aus sein, etwas im Schilde führen; *it's — to you*, es liegt an dir. — *prep.* auf, hinauf. — *s. ups and downs*, das wechselnde Schicksal, Auf und Ab.

upbraid [ʌp'breid], *v.a.* tadeln.

upheaval [ʌp'hiːvl], *s.* das Chaos, Durcheinander, die Umwälzung.

uphill [ʌp'hil], *adv.* bergauf(wärts). — ['ʌphil], *adj.* (an)steigend; (*fig.*) mühsam.

uphold [ʌp'hould], *v.a.* aufrechterhalten.

upholster [ʌp'houlstə], *v.a.* polstern.

upholstery [ʌp'houlstəri], *s.* die Polsterung.

upon [ʌ'pɔn] *see* on.

upper ['ʌpə], *adj.* ober, höher; — *hand*, die Oberhand.

uppish ['ʌpiʃ], *adj.* anmaßend.

upright ['ʌprait], *adj.* aufrecht, gerade; (*fig.*) aufrichtig, rechtschaffen.

uproar ['ʌprɔː], *s.* der Lärm, Aufruhr.

uproot [ʌp'ruːt], *v.a.* entwurzeln.

upset [ʌp'set], *v.a.* umwerfen; (*fig.*) aus der Fassung bringen. — ['ʌpset], *s.* das Umwerfen; (*fig.*) die Bestürzung.

upshot ['ʌpʃɔt], *s.* der Ausgang, das Ergebnis.

upside ['ʌpsaid], *s.* die Oberseite; — *down*, auf den Kopf gestellt.

upstairs [ʌp'steəz], *adv.* oben, nach oben.

upstart ['ʌpstaːt], *s.* der Parvenü, Emporkömmling.

upward ['ʌpwəd], *adj.* steigend, aufwärtsgehend. — *adv.* (*also* upwards) aufwärts; — *of*, mehr als.

urban ['əːbən], *adj.* städtisch.

urbane [əː'bein], *adj.* zivilisiert.

urbanity [əː'bæniti], *s.* die Bildung, der Schliff.

urchin ['əːtʃin], *s.* der Schelm; (*Zool.*) *sea* —, der Seeigel.

urge [əːdʒ], *v.a.* drängen. — *s.* der Drang.

urgent ['əːdʒənt], *adj.* dringend, drängend, dringlich.

urine ['juərin], *s.* der Urin.

urn [əːn], *s.* die Urne.

Uruguayan [juːruˈgwaiən], *adj.* uruguayisch. — *s.* der Uruguayer.

us [ʌs], *pers. pron.* uns.

usage ['juːsidʒ], *s.* der (Sprach)gebrauch; die Sitte.

use [juːz], *v.a.* gebrauchen, benutzen. — [juːs], *s.* der Gebrauch, die Benutzung; der Nutzen (*usefulness*).

usher ['ʌʃə], *s.* der Türhüter, Platzanweiser. — *v.a.* — *in*, anmelden, einführen.

usherette [ʌʃə'ret], *s.* die Platzanweiserin, Programmverkäuferin.

usual ['juːʒəl], *adj.* gewöhnlich, üblich.

usurer ['juːʒərə *or* 'juːzjuərə], *s.* der Wucherer.

usurp [juːˈzəːp], *v.a.* an sich reißen, usurpieren.

usury ['juːʒjuəri], *s.* der Wucher.

utensil [juːˈtensil], *s.* das Gerät, Werkzeug.

utility [juːˈtiliti], *s.* die Nützlichkeit (*usefulness*); der Nutzen; *public* —, (die) öffentliche Einrichtung.

utilize ['juːtilaiz], *v.a.* nutzbar machen, ausbeuten, ausnützen.

utmost ['ʌtmoust], *adj.* äußerst, weitest, höchst. — *s.* das Höchste, Äußerste.

utter ['ʌtə], *adj.* äußerst, gänzlich. — *v.a.* äußern, aussprechen.

utterly ['ʌtəli], *adv.* äußerst, völlig.

uvula ['juːvjulə], *s.* (*Anat.*) das Zäpfchen.

V

V [viː]. das V.

vacancy ['veikənsi], *s.* die freie Stelle, die Vakanz.

vacant ['veikənt], *adj.* frei; leer.

vacate [vəˈkeit], *v.a.* frei machen.

vacation [vəˈkeiʃən], *s.* die Niederlegung (*of a post*); die Ferien, *pl.* (*school*); der Urlaub (*holiday*).

vaccinate ['væksineit], *v.a.* (*Med.*) impfen.

vaccine ['væksiːn], *s.* (*Med.*) der Impfstoff.

vacillate ['væsileit], *v.n.* schwanken.

vacuity [væˈkjuːiti], *s.* die Leere.

vacuous ['vækjuəs], *adj.* leer.

vacuum ['vækjuəm], *s.* das Vakuum; — *cleaner*, der Staubsauger.

vagabond ['vægəbɔnd], *s.* der Landstreicher.

vagary [vəˈgeəri], *s.* die Laune, Grille.

vagrant ['veigrənt], *adj.* herumstreichend. — *s.* der Landstreicher.

vague [veig], *adj.* vage, unbestimmt, unklar.

vain [vein], *adj.* nichtig, vergeblich, eitel; *in* —, vergebens, umsonst.

vale [veil], *s.* (*Poet.*) das Tal.

valerian [və'liəriən], *s.* (*Bot.*) der Baldrian.

valet ['vælei, 'vælit], *s.* der Diener.

valiant ['væljənt], *adj.* mutig, tapfer.

valid ['vælid], *adj.* gültig, stichhaltig.

valley ['væli], *s.* das Tal.

valuable ['væljuəbl], *adj.* wertvoll, kostbar.

valuation [vælju'eiʃən], *s.* die Schätzung.

value ['vælju:], *s.* der Wert. — *v.a.* wertschätzen, schätzen.

valve [vælv], *s.* (*Mech.*) das Ventil; (*Rad.*) die Röhre.

vamp (1) [væmp], *s.* das Oberleder.

vamp (2) [væmp], *s.* (*Am. coll.*) der Vamp.

vampire ['væmpaiə], *s.* der Vampir.

van [væn], *s.* der Lieferwagen.

vane [vein], *s.* die Wetterfahne.

vanguard ['vænga:d], *s.* die Vorhut, der Vortrupp.

vanilla [və'nilə], *s.* die Vanille.

vanish ['væniʃ], *v.n.* verschwinden.

vanity ['væniti], *s.* die Nichtigkeit; die Eitelkeit (*conceit*).

vanquish ['væŋkwiʃ], *v.a.* besiegen.

vantage ['va:ntidʒ], *s.* der Vorteil; — *point*, die günstige Position.

vapid ['væpid], *adj.* leer, schal.

vapour ['veipə], *s.* der Dunst; (*Chem.*) der Dampf.

variable ['vɛəriəbl], *adj.* variabel, veränderlich.

variance ['vɛəriəns], *s.* die Uneinigkeit.

variation [vɛəri'eiʃən], *s.* die Variation; die Veränderung, Abweichung.

varicose ['værikəs], *adj.* Krampf-, krampfaderig.

variegated ['vɛərigeitid], *adj.* bunt, vielfarbig.

variety [və'raiəti], *s.* die Mannigfaltigkeit; (*Bot.*) die Varietät, Abart; (*Theat.*) das Varieté, das Varietétheater.

various ['vɛəriəs], *adj.* verschieden, mannigfaltig.

varnish ['va:niʃ], *s.* der Firnis, der Lack. — *v.a.* mit Firnis anstreichen, lackieren.

vary ['vɛəri], *v.a.* abändern. — *v.n.* sich ändern, variieren.

vase [va:z], *s.* die Vase.

vassal [væsl], *s.* der Vasall, Lehnsmann.

vast [va:st], *adj.* ungeheuer, groß.

vat [væt], *s.* die Kufe, das große Faß.

vault [vɔ:lt], *s.* das Gewölbe; die Gruft (*grave*); (*Sport*) der Sprung, *pole* —, der Stabhochsprung. — *v.n.* springen.

vaunt [vɔ:nt], *v.a.* rühmen. — *v.n.* prahlen, sich rühmen. — *s.* die Prahlerei.

veal [vi:l], *s.* das Kalbfleisch.

veer [viə], *v.n.* sich drehen.

vegetable ['vedʒitəbl], *s.* das Gemüse.

vegetarian [vedʒi'tɛəriən], *adj.* vegetarisch. — *s.* der Vegetarier.

vegetate ['vedʒiteit], *v.n.* vegetieren.

vehemence ['vi:əməns], *s.* die Vehemenz, Heftigkeit.

vehicle ['vi:ikl], *s.* das Fahrzeug, Fuhrwerk; (*Motor.*) der Wagen.

veil [veil], *s.* der Schleier. — *v.a.* verschleiern.

vein [vein], *s.* die Ader.

vellum ['veləm], *s.* das feine Pergamentpapier.

velocity [vi'lɔsiti], *s.* die Geschwindigkeit, Schnelligkeit.

velvet ['velvit], *s.* (*Text.*) der Samt.

venal ['vi:nəl], *adj.* käuflich.

vend [vend], *v.a.* verkaufen; —*ing machine*, der Automat.

veneer [və'niə], *s.* das Furnier. — *v.a.* furnieren.

venerable ['venərəbl], *adj.* ehrwürdig.

venerate ['venəreit], *v.a.* verehren.

venereal [və'niəriəl], *adj.* Geschlechts-.

Venezuelan [veni'zweilən], *adj.* venezolanisch. — *s.* der Venezolaner.

vengeance ['vendʒəns], *s.* die Rache.

venison ['venizn *or* venzn], *s.* das Wildpret.

venom ['venəm], *s.* das Gift.

vent [vent], *v.a.* Luft machen (*Dat.*). — *s.* das Luftloch, die Öffnung.

ventilate ['ventileit], *v.a.* ventilieren, lüften.

ventricle ['ventrikl], *s.* (*Anat.*) die Herzkammer.

ventriloquist [ven'triləkwist], *s.* der Bauchredner.

venture ['ventʃə], *s.* das Wagnis, Unternehmen. — *v.a.* wagen, riskieren. — *v.n.* sich erlauben, (sich) wagen.

venue ['venju:], *s.* der Treffpunkt, Versammlungsort.

veracity [və'ræsiti], *s.* die Glaubwürdigkeit, Wahrhaftigkeit.

verbose [və:'bous], *adj.* wortreich, weitschweifig.

verdant ['və:dənt], *adj.* grünend, grün.

verdict ['və:dikt], *s.* das Urteil, die Entscheidung.

verdigris ['və:digri:s], *s.* der Grünspan.

verdure ['və:djə], *s.* das Grün.

verge [və:dʒ], *s.* der Rand, die Einfassung. — *v.n.* grenzen (*on*, an, *Acc.*).

verify ['verifai], *v.a.* bestätigen; (*Law*) beglaubigen.

verily ['verili], *adv.* (*Bibl.*) wahrlich.

veritable ['veritəbl], *adj.* wahr, echt.

vermicelli [və:mi'seli], *s.* die Nudeln, *f. pl.*

vermilion [və'miljən], *s.* das Zinnober (*paint*).

vermin ['və:min], *s. pl.* das Ungeziefer.

vermouth ['və:mu:θ, -mu:t], *s.* der Wermut.

vernacular [və'nækjulə], *s.* die Landessprache. — *adj.* einheimisch.

vernal ['və:nəl], *adj.* frühlingsartig, Frühlings-.

versatile [ˈvəːsətail], *adj.* gewandt; vielseitig.

verse [vəːs], *s.* der Vers; (*Poet.*) die Strophe.

versed [vəːsd], *adj.* bewandert.

version [ˈvəːʃən], *s.* die Version, Fassung, Lesart; (*fig.*) die Darstellung.

vertebrate [ˈvəːtibrət], *s.* (*Zool.*) das Wirbeltier. — *adj.* mit Rückenwirbeln versehen.

vertex [ˈvəːteks], *s.* der Zenit.

vertigo [ˈvəːtigou], *s.* (*Med.*) der Schwindel, das Schwindelgefühl.

verve [vəːv], *s.* der Schwung.

very [ˈveri], *adv.* sehr. — *adj.* echt, wirklich, wahrhaftig.

vespers [ˈvespəz], *s. pl.* (*Eccl.*) der Abendgottesdienst, die Vesper.

vessel [vesl], *s.* das Gefäß (*container*); (*Naut.*) das Fahrzeug, Schiff.

vest [vest], *s.* das Gewand; (*Tail.*) die Weste; das Unterhemd (*undergarment*). — *v.a.* übertragen.

vested [ˈvestid], *adj.* — *interests*, das Eigeninteresse.

vestige [ˈvestidʒ], *s.* die Spur.

vestment [ˈvestmənt], *s.* (*Eccl.*) das Meßgewand.

vestry [ˈvestri], *s.* (*Eccl.*) die Sakristei.

vetch [vetʃ], *s.* (*Bot.*) die Wicke.

veterinary [ˈvetərinri], *adj.* tierärztlich; — *surgeon*, der Tierarzt.

veto [ˈviːtou], *s.* (*Pol.*) der Einspruch, das Veto.

vex [veks], *v.a.* quälen, plagen.

vexation [vekˈseiʃən], *s.* die Plage, der Verdruß.

via [vaiə], *prep.* über.

vibrate [vaiˈbreit], *v.n.* schwingen, vibrieren.

vicar [ˈvikə], *s.* (*Eccl.*) der Pfarrer, Vikar.

vicarious [viˈkɛəriəs], *adj.* stellvertretend.

vice (1) [vais], *s.* das Laster (*immorality*).

vice (2) [vais], *s.* (*Mech.*) der Schraubstock.

vice- [vais], *pref.* Vize-, zweiter (*chairman etc.*).

vicinity [viˈsiniti], *s.* die Nachbarschaft, Nähe.

vicious [ˈviʃəs], *adj.* böse, bösartig.

vicissitude [viˈsisitjuːd], *s.* der Wechsel, Wandel; (*pl.*) Wechselfälle, *m. pl.*

victim [ˈviktim], *s.* das Opfer.

victuals [vitlz], *s. pl.* die Lebensmittel, *n. pl.*

vie [vai], *v.n.* wetteifern.

Vietnamese [vjetnəˈmiːz], *adj.* vietnamesisch. — *s.* der Vietnamese.

view [vjuː], *s.* der Anblick, die Aussicht (*panorama*); die Ansicht (*opinion*); die Absicht (*intention*). — *v.a.* betrachten; besichtigen (*inspect*).

vigil [ˈvidʒil], *s.* die Nachtwache.

vigilance [ˈvidʒiləns], *s.* die Wachsamkeit.

vigorous [ˈvigərəs], *adj.* kräftig, rüstig, energisch.

vigour [ˈvigə], *s.* die Kraft, Energie.

vile [vail], *adj.* schlecht, niedrig.

vilify [ˈvilifai], *v.a.* beschimpfen, erniedrigen.

villa [ˈvilə], *s.* das Landhaus, die Villa.

village [ˈvilidʒ], *s.* das Dorf.

villain [ˈvilən], *s.* der Schurke.

villainous [ˈvilənəs], *adj.* niederträchtig.

villainy [ˈviləni], *s.* die Niedertracht, Schändlichkeit.

vindicate [ˈvindikeit], *v.a.* behaupten, verteidigen; rechtfertigen (*justify*).

vindictive [vinˈdiktiv], *adj.* rachsüchtig.

vine [vain], *s.* (*Bot.*) der Weinstock, die Rebe.

vinegar [ˈvinigə], *s.* der Essig.

vintage [ˈvintidʒ], *s.* die Weinernte; der Jahrgang (*also fig.*).

vintner [ˈvintnə], *s.* der Weinbauer, Winzer.

viola [viˈoulə], *s.* (*Mus.*) die Viola, Bratsche.

violate [ˈvaiəleit], *v.a.* verletzen, schänden.

violence [ˈvaiələns], *s.* die Gewalt; die Gewalttätigkeit.

violent [ˈvaiələnt], *adj.* gewalttätig (*brutal*); heftig (*vehement*).

violet [ˈvaiəlit], *s.* (*Bot.*) das Veilchen. — *adj.* veilchenblau, violett.

violin [vaiəˈlin], *s.* (*Mus.*) die Violine, Geige.

viper [ˈvaipə], *s.* (*Zool.*) die Viper, Natter.

virago [viˈrɑːgou], *s.* das Mannweib.

virgin [ˈvəːdʒin], *s.* die Jungfrau.

virile [ˈvirail], *adj.* männlich, kräftig.

virtual [ˈvəːtjuəl], *adj.* eigentlich.

virtue [ˈvəːtjuː], *s.* die Tugend; *by — of*, kraft (*Genit.*).

virtuoso [vəːtjuˈousou], *s.* der Virtuose.

virtuous [ˈvəːtjuəs], *adj.* tugendhaft.

virulent [ˈvirulənt], *adj.* bösartig, giftig.

virus [ˈvaiərəs], *s.* (*Med.*) das Gift, Virus.

viscosity [visˈkɔsiti], *s.* die Zähigkeit, Zähflüssigkeit.

viscount [ˈvaikaunt], *s.* der Vicomte.

viscous [ˈviskəs], *adj.* zähflüssig, klebrig.

visibility [viziˈbiliti], *s.* die Sichtbarkeit, Sicht.

visible [ˈvizibl], *adj.* sichtbar.

vision [ˈviʒən], *s.* die Sehkraft; (*fig.*) die Vision (*dream*); die Erscheinung (*apparition*).

visionary [ˈviʒənri], *s.* der Träumer, (*Poet.*) der Seher. — *adj.* visionär, phantastisch, seherisch.

visit [ˈvizit], *s.* der Besuch. — *v.a.* besuchen.

visitation [viziˈteiʃən], *s.* die Heimsuchung.

visor [ˈvaizə], *s.* das Visier.

vista [ˈvistə], *s.* (*Art*) die Aussicht, der Ausblick.

visual [ˈvizjuəl], *adj.* visuell, Seh-.

vital [vaitl], *adj.* lebenswichtig; (*fig.*) wesentlich.

vitality [vaiˈtæliti], *s.* die Lebenskraft, Vitalität.

vitiate ['viʃieit], v.a. verderben, umstoßen.
vitreous ['vitriəs], adj. gläsern, glasartig.
vitrify ['vitrifai], v.a. verglasen.
vivacious [vi'veiʃəs], adj. lebhaft, munter.
viva (voce) ['vaivə ('vousi)], s. die mündliche Prüfung.
vivacity [vi'væsiti], s. die Lebhaftigkeit.
vivid ['vivid], adj. lebhaft.
vixen ['viksən], s. (Zool.) die Füchsin; (fig.) das zänkische Weib.
vizier [vi'ziə], s. der Wesir.
vocabulary [vo'kæbjuləri], s. das Vokabular; der Wortschatz.
vocal ['voukəl], adj. laut; (Mus.) Stimm-, Sing-.
vocation [vo'keiʃən], s. die Berufung (call); der Beruf (occupation).
vociferous [vo'sifərəs], adj. schreiend, laut.
vogue [voug], s. die Mode.
voice [vɔis], s. die Stimme.
void [vɔid], adj. leer (empty); ungültig, (invalid); null and —, null und nichtig. — s. die Leere.
volatile ['vɔlətail], adj. flüchtig.
volcanic [vɔl'kænik], adj. vulkanisch.
volcano [vɔl'keinou], s. der Vulkan.
volition [vo'liʃən], s. der Wille.
volley ['vɔli], s. (Mil.) die Salve; (Footb.) der Volleyschuß; (Tennis) der Flugball.
volt [voult], s. (Elec.) das Volt.
voltage ['voultidʒ], s. die Spannung.
voluble ['vɔljubl], adj. gesprächig, zungenfertig.
volume ['vɔlju:m], s. (Phys.) das Volumen; der Band (book); (fig.) der Umfang.
voluminous [və'lju:minəs], adj. umfangreich.
voluntary ['vɔləntri], adj. freiwillig. — s. (Mus.) das Orgelsolo.
volunteer [vɔlən'tiə], s. der Freiwillige. — v.n. sich freiwillig melden.
voluptuous [və'lʌptjuəs], adj. wollüstig, lüstern.
vomit ['vɔmit], v.a., v.n. (sich) erbrechen, übergeben.
voracious [vɔ'reiʃəs], adj. gierig, gefräßig.
vortex ['vɔ:teks], s. der Wirbel, Strudel.
vote [vout], v.n. (Pol.) wählen, abstimmen, die Stimme abgeben. — s. (Pol.) die Stimme.
voter ['voutə], s. der Wähler.
votive ['voutiv], adj. (Eccl.) geweiht, gelobt; Votiv-.
vouch [vautʃ], v.a., v.n. (sich) verbürgen, einstehen(für).
voucher ['vautʃə], s. der Beleg; (Comm.) der Gutschein.
vouchsafe [vautʃ'seif], v.a. bewilligen, gewähren. — v.n. geruhen, sich herablassen.
vow [vau], s. das Gelübde. — v.a. schwören, geloben.

vowel ['vauəl], s. der Vokal.
voyage ['vɔiidʒ], s. die Seereise. — v.n. zur See reisen.
vulcanize ['vʌlkənaiz], v.a. vulkanisieren.
vulgar ['vʌlgə], adj. gemein, pöbelhaft, ordinär, vulgär.
vulnerable ['vʌlnərəbl], adj. verwundbar, verletzbar.
vulture ['vʌltʃə], s. (Orn.) der Geier.

W

W ['dʌblju:]. das W.
wabble see **wobble**.
wad [wɔd], s. das Bündel (notes); der Bausch (cotton wool).
waddle ['wɔdl], v.n. watscheln.
wade [weid], v.n. waten, durchwaten.
wafer ['weifə], s. die Oblate, die Waffel; (Eccl.) die Hostie.
waffle [wɔfl], s. (Cul.) die Waffel. — v.n. (coll.) schwafeln.
waft [wæft], v.a. wegwehen.
wag (1) [wæg], v.a. wedeln, schütteln.
wag (2) [wæg], s. der Spaßvogel.
wage (1) [weidʒ], v.a. unternehmen; — war, Krieg führen.
wage (2) ['weidʒ], s. (often in pl.) der Lohn.
wager ['weidʒə], v.a. wetten. — s. die Wette.
waggish ['wægiʃ], adj. spaßhaft, mutwillig, schelmisch.
wag(g)on ['wægən], s. der Wagen, Güterwagen.
wagtail ['wægteil], s. (Orn.) die Bachstelze.
waif [weif], s. das verwahrloste Kind; das herrenlose Gut.
wail [weil], v.n. wehklagen. — s. das Wehklagen, die Klage.
waist [weist], s. (Anat.) die Taille.
waistcoat ['weiskout, 'weskət], s. die Weste, das Wams.
wait [weit], v.n. warten; — for, warten auf; — upon, bedienen. — v.a. erwarten.
waiter ['weitə], s. der Kellner; head —, der Oberkellner, (coll.) der Ober.
waiting room ['weitiŋ rum], s. das Wartezimmer; (Railw.) der Wartesaal.
waive [weiv], v.a. aufgeben, verzichten (auf, Acc.).
wake (1) [weik], v.n. irr. wachen, aufwachen, wach sein. — v.a. aufwecken.
wake (2) [weik], s. (Naut.) das Kielwasser; (fig.) die Spur; in the — of, in den Fußstapfen (Genit.).
waken ['weikən], v.a. aufwecken. — v.n. aufwachen.
walk [wɔ:k], v.n. (zu Fuß) gehen. — s. der Gang (gait); der Spaziergang.

wall

wall [wɔːl], s. die Wand, Mauer.

wallet ['wɔlit], s. die Brieftasche.

wallflower ['wɔːlflauə], s. (Bot.) der Goldlack; (fig.) das Mauerblümchen.

wallow ['wɔlou], v.n. schwelgen; sich wälzen.

walnut ['wɔːlnʌt], s. (Bot.) die Walnuß.

walrus ['wɔːlrəs], s. (Zool.) das Walroß.

waltz [wɔːlts], s. der Walzer.

wan [wɔn], adj. blaß, bleich.

wand [wɔnd], s. der Stab.

wander ['wɔndə], v.n. wandern, durchwandern; (fig.) — from the subject, vom Thema abkommen.

wane [wein], v.n. abnehmen, verfallen.

want [wɔnt], v.a. brauchen, wollen, nötig haben, wünschen. — v.n. mangeln, fehlen. — s. die Not.

wanton ['wɔntən], adj. mutwillig, ausgelassen.

war [wɔː], s. der Krieg.

warble [wɔːbl], v.a., v.n. singen; (Mus.) trillern.

warbler ['wɔːblə], s. (Orn.) der Singvogel.

ward [wɔːd], s. die Verwahrung; das or der Mündel (child in care); (Pol.) der Wahlbezirk, die Station (hospital). — v.a. — off, abwehren.

warden [wɔːdn], s. der Vorstand, Vorsteher; Rektor.

warder ['wɔːdə], s. der Wächter; (in prison) der Wärter, Gefängniswärter.

wardrobe ['wɔːdroub], s. der Kleiderschrank.

ware [wɛə], s. die Ware.

warehouse ['wɛəhaus], s. das Warenlager.

warfare ['wɔːfɛə], s. der Krieg, die Kriegsführung.

warlike ['wɔːlaik], adj. kriegerisch.

warm [wɔːm], adj. warm.

warn [wɔːn], v.a. warnen, ermahnen.

warning ['wɔːniŋ], s. die Warnung.

warp [wɔːp], v.a. krümmen, verziehen (of wood); (fig.) verderben; verzerren, verdrehen. — v.n. sich werfen, krümmen.

warrant ['wɔrənt], s. (Law) der Haftbefehl; — officer, der Unteroffizier; (Comm.) die Vollmacht, Bürgschaft. — v.a. garantieren (vouch for); versichern (assure).

warranty ['wɔrənti], s. (Law) die Gewähr; Garantie.

warren ['wɔrən], s. das Gehege.

warrior ['wɔriə], s. der Krieger.

wart [wɔːt], s. (Med.) die Warze.

wary ['wɛəri], adj. vorsichtig, achtsam (careful).

wash [wɔʃ], v.a., v.n. (sich) waschen; — up, spülen, abwaschen. — s. die Wäsche (laundry).

wasp [wɔsp], s. (Ent.) die Wespe.

waspish ['wɔspiʃ], adj. reizbar, zänkisch, bissig.

wassail [wɔsl], s. das Trinkgelage. — v.n. zechen.

waste [weist], v.a. zerstören, verwüsten; verschwenden. — adj. wüst, öde. — s. die Verschwendung (process); der Abfall (product); — paper, die Makulatur; — paper basket, der Papierkorb.

wasteful ['weistful], adj. verschwenderisch.

watch [wɔtʃ], v.a. bewachen; beobachten (observe); hüten (guard). — s. die Wache (guard); die Uhr, Taschenuhr (time-piece).

watchful ['wɔtʃful], adj. wachsam.

watchman ['wɔtʃmən], s. der Nachtwächter.

water ['wɔːtə], s. das Wasser; (pl.) die Kur; — colour, das Aquarell; — gauge, der Pegel. — v.a. wässern; begießen (flowers).

watercress ['wɔːtəkres], s. (Bot.) die Brunnenkresse.

waterproof ['wɔːtəpruːf], adj. wasserdicht.

watt [wɔt], s. (Elec.) das Watt.

wattle [wɔtl], s. (Bot.) die Hürde.

wave [weiv], s. die Welle; permanent —, die Dauerwelle. — v.n. zuwinken (Dat.); wehen; winken. — v.a. schwenken (handkerchief).

waver ['weivə], v.n. schwanken, unentschlossen sein.

wax [wæks], s. das Wachs, der Siegellack. — v.a. wachsen, bohnern.

waxen [wæksn], adj. aus Wachs, wächsern.

way [wei], s. der Weg (road etc.); die Strecke; Richtung; in no —, keineswegs; (pl.) die Art und Weise; Milky Way, die Milchstraße.

wayward ['weiwəd], adj. eigensinnig.

we [wiː], pers. pron. wir.

weak [wiːk], adj. schwach, kraftlos.

weaken ['wiːkən], v.a. schwächen. — v.n. schwach werden.

weakling ['wiːkliŋ], s. der Schwächling.

wealth [welθ], s. der Wohlstand, Reichtum.

wealthy ['welθi], adj. wohlhabend, reich.

wean [wiːn], v.a. entwöhnen.

weapon ['wepən], s. die Waffe.

wear [wɛə], v.a. irr. tragen (clothes). — v.n. — off, sich abtragen, schäbig werden; — out, sich erschöpfen. — s. die Abnutzung.

weariness ['wiərinis], s. die Müdigkeit, der Überdruß.

weary ['wiəri], adj. müde, überdrüssig.

weasel [wiːzl], s. (Zool.) das Wiesel.

weather ['weðə], s. das Wetter. — v.a. überstehen. — v.n. (Geol.) verwittern.

weatherbeaten ['weðəbiːtn], adj. abgehärtet, wetterhart.

weathercock ['weðəkɔk], s. der Wetterhahn; (fig.) wetterwendischer Mensch.

weave [wiːv], v.a. irr. (Text.) weben, — s. das Gewebe.

web [web], s. das Gewebe.

wed [wed], v.a. heiraten; trauen (a couple). — v.n. (sich ver)heiraten.

wedding ['wediŋ], s. die Hochzeit; Trauung (ceremony).

wedge [wedʒ], *s.* der Keil. — *v.a.*
keilen.

wedlock ['wedlɔk], *s.* die Ehe.

Wednesday ['wenzd(e)i]. der Mittwoch.

wee [wi:], *adj.* (*Scot.*) winzig, klein.

weed [wi:d], *s.* das Unkraut. — *v.a.*
ausjäten, jäten.

week [wi:k], *s.* die Woche.

weep [wi:p], *v.n. irr.* weinen; —*ing
willow*, die Trauerweide.

weigh [wei], *v.a.* wiegen, wägen; (*fig.*)
abwägen, beurteilen; (*Naut.*) —
anchor, den Anker lichten. — *v.n.*
wiegen.

weighing machine ['weiiŋ mə'ʃi:n],
s. die Waage.

weight [weit], *s.* das Gewicht; *gross* —,
das Bruttogewicht; *net* —, das Nettogewicht.

weighty ['weiti], *adj.* (ge)wichtig;
(*fig.*) schwer.

weir [wiə], *s.* das Wehr.

weird [wiəd], *adj.* unheimlich.

welcome ['welkəm], *adj.* willkommen.
— *s.* der *or* das Willkommen. — *v.a.*
willkommen heißen, begrüßen.

weld [weld], *v.a.* schweißen.

welfare ['welfɛə], *s.* die Wohlfahrt,
soziale Fürsorge.

well (1) [wel], *s.* der Brunnen. — *v.n.*
hervorsprudeln.

well (2) [wel], *adv.* gut, wohl; durchaus; — *bred*, wohlerzogen. — *pred.
adj.* gesund, wohl.

Welsh [welʃ], *adj.* walisisch. — *s. pl.* die
Waliser, *m.pl.*

Welshman ['welʃmən], *s.* der Waliser.

welt [welt], *s.* der Rand, die Einfassung.

welter ['weltə], *s.* die Masse, das
Chaos. — *v.n.* sich wälzen.

wen [wen], *s.* (*Med.*) die Schwellung.

wench [wentʃ], *s.* die Magd, das Mädchen.

west [west], *s.* der Westen. — *adj.*
(*also* **westerly**, **western** ['westəli,
'westən]) westlich.

Westphalian [west'feiliən], *adj.* westfälisch. — *s.* der Westfale.

wet [wet], *adj.* naß, feucht; — *paint*,
frisch gestrichen. — *v.a.* anfeuchten,
benetzen, naß machen.

whack [hwæk], *v.a.* durchprügeln. —
s. die Tracht Prügel, der Schlag.

whale [hweil], *s.* (*Zool.*) der Walfisch.

whalebone ['hweilboun], *s.* das Fischbein.

wharf [hwɔ:f], *s.* der Kai.

wharfinger ['hwɔ:findʒə], *s.* der Kaimeister.

what [hwɔt], *rel. & interr. pron.* was;
welcher, welche, welches; was für.

what(so)ever [hwɔt(sou)'evə], *rel. pron.*
was auch immer. — *adj.* einerlei
welche-r, -s, -n.

wheat [hwi:t], *s.* (*Bot.*) der Weizen.

wheedle ['hwi:dl], *v.a.* beschwatzen.

wheel [hwi:l], *s.* das Rad; die Umdrehung, Drehung. — *v.a., v.n.* drehen,
sich drehen, schieben.

wheelbarrow ['hwi:lbærou], *s.* der
Schubkarren.

wheeze [hwi:z], *v.n.* keuchen, schnaufen. — *s.* das Keuchen.

whelp [hwelp], *s.* (*Zool.*) das Junge, der
junge Hund. — *v.n.* Junge werfen.

when [hwen], *adv.* (*interr.*) wann ?
— *conj.* als (*in past*), wenn, während.

whence [hwens], *adv.* woher, von wo.

where [hwɛə], *adv.* wo, wohin; (*interr.*)
wo ? wohin ?

whereabout(s) ['hwɛərəbaut(s)], *adv.*
wo, wo etwa. — *s.* (**whereabouts**)
der zeitweilige Aufenthalt *or* Wohnort.

whereas [hwɛər'æz], *conj.* wohingegen,
während.

whereupon [hwɛərə'pɔn], *conj.* woraufhin.

wherewithal ['hwɛəwiðɔ:l], *s.* die gesamte Habe, das Nötige. — *adv.*
(*obs.*) womit.

whet [hwet], *v.a.* wetzen, schleifen.

whether ['hweðə], *conj.* ob.

whey [hwei], *s.* die Molke.

which [hwitʃ], *rel. & interr. pron.*
welcher, welche, welches; der, die,
das.

whiff [hwif], *s.* der Hauch, Luftzug.

while [hwail], *s.* die Weile, Zeit. —
v.a. — *away the time*, dahinbringen,
vertreiben. — *conj.* (*also* **whilst**) während, so lange als.

whim [hwim], *s.* die Laune, Grille.

whimper ['hwimpə], *v.n.* winseln.

whimsical ['hwimzikəl], *adj.* grillenhaft.

whine [hwain], *v.n.* weinen, wimmern,
klagen. — *s.* das Gewimmer, Gejammer.

whinny ['hwini], *v.n.* wiehern.

whip [hwip], *s.* die Peitsche; (*Pol.*) der
Einpeitscher. — *v.a.* peitschen.

whir [hwə:], *v.n.* schwirren. — *s.* das
Schwirren.

whirl [hwə:l], *s.* der Wirbel, Strudel. —
v.a., v.n. wirbeln.

whirligig ['hwə:ligig], *s.* der Karussel.

whirlpool ['hwə:lpu:l], *s.* der Strudel.

whirr *see* **whir**.

whisk [hwisk], *v.a.* fegen; schlagen; —*away*
or off, schnell wegtun (*a th.*), schnell
fortnehmen (*a p.*). — *v.n.* — *away*,
dahinhuschen. — *s.* der Schläger.

whiskers ['hwiskəz], *s.* der Backenbart,
Bart.

whisky ['hwiski], *s.* der Whisky.

whisper ['hwispə], *s.* das Geflüster.
v.a., v.n. flüstern.

whistle [hwisl], *s.* die Pfeife (*instrument*); der Pfiff (*sound*). — *v.a., v.n.*
pfeifen.

whit [hwit], *s.* die Kleinigkeit; *not a* —,
nicht im geringsten.

white [hwait], *adj.* weiß; — *lead*, das
Bleiweiß; — *lie*, die Notlüge.

whitebait ['hwaitbeit], *s.* (*Zool.*) der
Breitling.

whiten [hwaitn], *v.a.* weißen, bleichen.

whitewash ['hwaitwɔʃ], *s.* die Tünche.
— *v.a.* reinwaschen.

whither ['hwiðə], *adv.* wohin; dahin wo.

whiting ['hwaitiŋ], *s.* (*Zool.*) der Weißfisch; die Schlämmkreide (*chalk*).

whitlow ['hwitlou], *s.* (*Med.*) das Nagelgeschwür.

Whitsun(tide) ['hwitsən(taid)], *s.* (das) Pfingsten; *Whit Sunday*, der Pfingstsonntag.

whittle [hwitl], *v.a.* schnitzen, abschaben.

whiz [hwiz], *v.n.* zischen; (*fig.*) vorbeiflitzen.

who [hu:], *interr. pron.* wer ?, welcher ?, welche ? — *rel. pron.* welcher, welche, welches, der, die, das.

whoever [hu:'evə], *rel. pron.* wer auch immer.

whole [houl], *adj.* ganz, völlig. — *s.* das Ganze.

wholesale ['houlseil], *adv.* im Engros. — *adj.* Engros-, Großhandels-.

wholesome ['houlsəm], *adj.* gesund.

whoop [hu:p], *s.* das Geschrei; — *v.n.* laut keuchen; —*ing cough*, der Keuchhusten.

whortleberry ['hwə:tlbəri], *s.* (*Bot.*) die Heidelbeere.

whose [hu:z], *pron.* wessen, dessen, deren.

whosoever [hu:sou'evə] *see* **whoever**.

why [hwai], *rel. & interr. adv.* warum ?

wick [wik], *s.* der Docht.

wicked ['wikid], *adj.* böse, schlecht.

wicker ['wikə], *adj.* Rohr-, geflochten.

wicket ['wikit], *s.* das Pförtchen.

wide [waid], *adj.* weit, breit; (*fig.*) umfangreich, groß, reich(*experience*).- *adv.* far and —, weit und breit; — *awake*, völlig wach.

widen [waidn], *v.a.*, erweitern.

widgeon ['widʒən], *s.* die Pfeifente.

widow ['widou], *s.* die Witwe.

widower ['widouə], *s.* der Witwer.

width [widθ], *s.* die Weite, Breite.

wield [wi:ld], *v.a.* schwingen; — *power*, die Macht ausüben.

wife [waif], *s.* die Frau, Gattin.

wig [wig], *s.* die Perücke.

wild [waild], *adj.* wild.

wilderness ['wildənis], *s.* die Wildnis.

wildfire ['waildfaiə], *s.* das Lauffeuer.

wilful ['wilful], *adj.* absichtlich; vorsätzlich.

wiliness ['wailinis], *s.* die Schlauheit, Arglist.

will [wil], *s.* der Wille; (*Law*) das letzte Testament. — *v.n.* wollen. — *v.a.* (*Law*) vermachen, hinterlassen.

willing ['wiliŋ], *adj.* bereitwillig.

will-o'-the-wisp [wiləð'wisp], *s.* das Irrlicht.

willow ['wilou], *s.* (*Bot.*) die Weide.

wily ['waili], *adj.* schlau, verschmitzt.

wimple [wimpl], *s.* der Schleier.

win [win], *v.a.*, *v.n. irr.* gewinnen, siegen, erringen.

wince [wins], *v.n.* zucken, zusammenzucken.

winch [wintʃ], *s.* die Kurbel, Winde.

wind (1) [wind], *s.* der Wind; der Atem (*breath*); *get — of s.th.*, von etwas hören.

wind (2) [waind], *v.a. irr.* winden; wenden, drehen (*turn*); —(*up*), aufziehen (*timepiece*); — *up*, (*business*, *debate*) beenden. — *v.n.* sich schlängeln, winden.

windfall ['windfɔ:l], *s.* das Fallobst (*fruit*); (*fig.*) der Glücksfall.

windlass ['windləs], *s.* die Winde.

window ['windou], *s.* das Fenster; — *sill*, das Fensterbrett.

windpipe ['windpaip], *s.* (*Anat.*) die Luftröhre.

windscreen ['windskri:n], *s.* (*Motor.*) die Windschutzscheibe.

windshield ['windʃi:ld] (*Am.*) *see* **windscreen.**

windy ['windi], *adj.* windig.

wine [wain], *s.* der Wein; — *merchant*, der Weinhändler.

wing [wiŋ], *s.* der Flügel; (*Poet.*) die Schwinge.

wink [wiŋk], *s.* das Zwinkern; der Augenblick.—*v.n.* blinzeln, zwinkern.

winner ['winə], *s.* der Sieger, Gewinner.

winning ['winiŋ], *adj.* einnehmend.

winsome ['winsəm], *adj.* reizend, einnehmend.

winter ['wintə], *s.* der Winter.

wintry ['wintri], *adj.* winterlich.

wipe [waip], *v.a.* wischen, abwischen.

wire [waiə], *s.* der Draht; (*coll.*) das Telegramm; *barbed* —, der Stacheldraht. — *v.a.* verbinden; (*fig.*) telegraphieren. — *v.n.* telegraphieren.

wireless ['waiəlis], *s.* das Radio. — *adj.* drahtlos.

wirepuller ['waiəpulə], *s.* der Puppenspieler; (*fig.*) der Intrigant.

wiry ['waiəri], *adj.* zäh, stark.

wisdom ['wizdəm], *s.* die Weisheit.

wise [waiz], *adj.* weise, verständig, klug.

wiseacre ['waizeikə], *s.* der Allzuschlaue, Naseweis.

wish [wiʃ], *v.a.*, *v.n.* wünschen. — *s.* der Wunsch.

wistful ['wistful], *adj.* nachdenklich (*pensive*); wehmütig (*sad*).

wit [wit], *s.* der Witz; Geist; Verstand; der witzige Mensch; der Witzbold.

witch [witʃ], *s.* die Hexe, Zauberin.

witchcraft ['witʃkra:ft], *s.* die Zauberkunst, Hexerei.

with [wið], *prep.* mit, mitsamt, bei, durch, von.

withal [wi'ðɔ:l], *adv.* obendrein.

withdraw [wið'drɔ:], *v.a.*, *v.n. irr.* (sich) zurückziehen; widerrufen; abheben (*money from bank*).

withdrawal [wið'drɔ:əl], *s.* der Rückzug; (*Comm. etc.*) die Widerrufung; Abhebung (*bank*).

wither [wiðə], *v.a.* welk machen. — *v.n.* verwelken; ausdorren, verdorren (*dry up*); (*fig.*) vergehen.

withhold [wið'hould], *v.a. irr.* zurückhalten, vorenthalten.

within [wi'ðin], *prep.* innerhalb; (*time*) binnen (*Genit.*). — *adv.* darin, drinnen.

without [wi'ðaut], *prep.* ohne; (*obs.*) außerhalb (*outside*); *do* —, entbehren. — *adv.* draußen, außen.

withstand [wið'stænd], *v.a. irr.* widerstehen (*Dat.*).

withy ['wiθi], *s.* der Weidenzweig.

witless ['witlis], *adj.* einfältig.

witness ['witnis], *s.* der Zeuge. — *v.a.* bezeugen, Zeuge sein von. — *v.n.* zeugen, Zeuge sein.

witticism ['witisizm], *s.* das Bonmot, die witzige Bemerkung.

witty ['witi], *adj.* witzig, geistreich.

wizard ['wizəd], *s.* der Zauberer.

wizened ['wizənd], *adj.* verwelkt, vertrocknet, runzlig.

wobble ['wɔbl], *v.n.* wackeln.

woe [wou], *s.* (*Poet.*) das Weh, Leid.

wolf [wulf], *s.* (*Zool.*) der Wolf.

woman ['wumən], *s.* die Frau, das Weib.

womanly ['wumənli], *adj.* weiblich.

womb [wu:m], *s.* der Mutterleib, Schoß; (*Anat.*) die Gebärmutter.

wonder ['wʌndə], *s.* das Wunder. — *v.n.* sich wundern (*be amazed*); gern wissen mögen (*like to know*); sich fragen.

wonderful ['wʌndəful], *adj.* wunderbar.

wondrous ['wʌndrəs], *adj.* (*Poet.*) wunderbar.

wont [wount], *s.* die Gewohnheit. — *pred. adj.* gewohnt.

won't [wount] = **will not**.

woo [wu:], *v.a.* freien, werben (um).

wood [wud], *s.* das Holz (*timber*); der Wald (*forest*).

woodbine ['wudbain], *s.* das Geißblatt.

woodcock ['wudkɔk], *s.* (*Orn.*) die Waldschnepfe.

woodcut ['wudkʌt], *s.* (*Art*) der Holzschnitt.

wooded ['wudid], *adj.* bewaldet.

wooden [wudn], *adj.* hölzern, Holz–.

woodlark ['wudla:k], *s.* (*Orn.*) die Heidelerche.

woodpecker ['wudpekə], *s.* (*Orn.*) der Specht.

woodruff ['wudrʌf], *s.* (*Bot.*) der Waldmeister.

woof [wu:f], *s.* (*Text.*) der Einschlag, das Gewebe.

wool [wul], *s.* die Wolle; — *gathering*, zerstreut.

woollen ['wulən], *adj.* wollen, aus Wolle.

woolly ['wuli], *adj.* wollig; (*fig.*) unklar, verschwommen.

word [wə:d], *s.* das Wort; *send* —, Botschaft senden. — *v.a.* ausdrücken.

wording ['wə:diŋ], *s.* die Fassung, der Stil.

work [wə:k], *s.* die Arbeit; *out of* —, arbeitslos; das Werk (*opus*); (*pl.*) die Fabrik. — *v.a., v.n.* arbeiten, bearbeiten; (*engine*) funktionieren.

worker ['wə:kə], *s.* der Arbeiter.

workhouse ['wə:khaus], *s.* das Armenhaus.

workshop ['wə:kʃɔp], *s.* die Werkstatt.

world [wə:ld], *s.* die Welt.

worldly ['wə:ldli], *adj.* weltlich, zeitlich.

worm [wə:m], *s.* (*Zool.*) der Wurm. — *v.a.* — *o.'s way*, sich einschleichen. — *v.n.* sich einschleichen.

wormeaten ['wə:mi:tn], *adj.* wurmstichig.

worry ['wʌri], *v.a., v.n.* plagen, quälen, sorgen, ängstigen; sich beunruhigen; *don't* —, bitte machen Sie sich keine Mühe. — *s.* die Plage, Mühe, Qual, Sorge (*about*, um, Acc.).

worse [wə:s], *comp. adj., adv.* schlechter, schlimmer.

worship ['wə:ʃip], *s.* die Verehrung; der Gottesdienst (*divine* —).

worst [wə:st], *superl. adj.* schlechtest, schlimmst. — *adv.* am schlimmsten *or* schlechtesten. — *s.* das Schlimmste.

worsted ['wustid], *s.* (*Text.*) das Kammgarn.

worth [wə:θ], *adj.* wert. — *s.* der Wert.

worthy ['wə:ði], *adj.* würdig, wert, verdient.

would [wud] *past tense of* **will**, *q.v.*

wound [wu:nd], *s.* die Wunde. — *v.a.* verwunden.

wraith [reiθ], *s.* das Gespenst.

wrangle [ræŋgl], *v.n.* zanken, streiten. — *s.* der Zank, Streit.

wrap [ræp], *v.a.* einwickeln, einhüllen. — *s.* (*Am.*) der Mantel (*coat*), Pelz (*fur*), Schal (*stole*).

wrapper ['ræpə], *s.* der Umschlag, die Hülle.

wrath [rɔ:θ], *s.* der Zorn, Grimm.

wreak ˌ[ri:k], *v.a.* (*Lit.*) auslassen, üben.

wreath [ri:θ], *s.* der Kranz.

wreathe [ri:ð], *v.a.* winden, bekränzen.

wreck [rek], *s.* der Schiffbruch; das Wrack (*debris*). — *v.a.* zerstören, zertrümmern, (*fig.*) verderben.

wren [ren], *s.* (*Orn.*) der Zaunkönig.

wrench [rentʃ], *v.a.* entreißen (*tear from*); verdrehen; *s.* heftiger Ruck; (*fig.*) der (Trennungs)schmerz.

wrest [rest], *v.a.* zerren.

wrestle [resl], *v.n.* ringen, im Ringkampf kämpfen.

wrestling ['resliŋ], *s.* der Ringkampf.

wretch [retʃ], *s.* der Schuft, Lump (*scoundrel*).

wretched ['retʃid], *adj.* elend.

wriggle [rigl], *v.n.* sich winden, schlängeln.

wring [riŋ], *v.a. irr.* auswinden, ausringen.

wrinkle [riŋkl], ˎs. die Hautfalte, Runzel. — *v.a.* runzeln (*brow*); rümpfen (*nose*).

wrist [rist], *s.* (*Anat.*) das Handgelenk.

wristwatch ['ristwɔtʃ], *s.* die Armbanduhr.

writ [rit], *s.* die Schrift; (*Law*) die Vorladung.

write [rait], v.a., v.n. irr. schreiben, verfassen.
writer ['raitə], s. der Schreiber; (Lit.) der Schriftsteller.
writhe [raið], v.n. sich winden.
writing ['raitiŋ], s. die Schrift; der Stil (style).
wrong [rɔŋ], adj. falsch, verkehrt; to be —, unrecht haben. — s. das Unrecht. — v.a. Unrecht or Schaden tun (Dat.).
wrongful ['rɔŋful], adj. unrechtmäßig.
wrongheaded [rɔŋ'hedid], adj. querköpfig.
wroth [rouθ], adj. (Lit.) zornig.
wrought [rɔːt], adj. (work) gearbeitet; — iron, das Schmiedeeisen.
wry [rai], adj. verkehrt, krumm, schief, verdreht.

X

X [eks], das X.
X-ray ['eksrei], s. (der) Röntgenstrahl.
xylophone ['zailəfoun], s. (Mus.) das Xylophon.

Y

Y [wai], das Y, Ypsilon.
yacht [jɔt], s. (Naut.) die Jacht.
yachtsman ['jɔtsmən], s. (Naut.) der Segelsportler.
yap [jæp], v.n. kläffen.
yard (1) [jɑːd], s. der Hof.
yard (2) [jɑːd], s. die englische Elle, der Yard.
yarn [jɑːn], s. das Garn; (coll.) die Geschichte (tale).
yarrow ['jærou], s. (Bot.) die Schafgarbe.
yawl [jɔːl], s. (Naut.) die Yawl.
yawn [jɔːn], v.n. gähnen. — s. das Gähnen.
ye [jiː], pron. (obs.) see you.
year [jə: or jiə], s. das Jahr; every other —, alle zwei Jahre.
yearly ['jiəli], adj., adv. jährlich.
yearn [jəːn], v.n. sich sehnen (nach, Dat.).
yeast [jiːst], s. die Hefe.
yell [jel], v.n. gellen, schreien. — s. der Schrei.
yellow ['jelou], adj. gelb; (sl.) feige.
yelp [jelp], v.n. kläffen, bellen. — s. das Gebelle.
yeoman ['joumən], s. der Freisasse; (Mil.) der Leibgardist (Yeoman of the Guard).

yes [jes], adv. ja; jawohl.
yesterday ['jestəd(e)i], adv. gestern; the day before —, vorgestern.
yet [jet], conj. doch, dennoch. — adv. noch, außerdem; as —, bisher; not —, noch nicht.
yew [juː], s. (Bot.) die Eibe.
yield [jiːld], v.a. hervorbringen, ergeben; abwerfen (profit). — v.n. nachgeben (to, Dat.). — s. der Ertrag.
yoke [jouk], s. das Joch (Ochsen). — v.a. einspannen, anspannen.
yolk [jouk], s. das Eidotter.
yon, yonder [jɔn, 'jɔndə], dem. adj. (obs.) jener, jene, jenes; der or die or das da drüben.
yore [jɔː], adv. (obs.) of —, von damals; ehemals.
you [juː], pers. pron. du, dich, ihr, euch; (formal) sie (in letters, Du, Dich etc.).
young [jʌŋ], adj. jung. — s. (Zool.) das Junge.
your [juə], poss. adj. dein, deine, dein; euer, eure, euer; (formal) ihr, ihre, ihr (in letters Dein, Euer etc.).
yours [jɔːz], poss. pron. deinig, eurig; der, die or das ihrige (in letters Deinig, der Ihrige etc.).
yourself [juə'self], pers. pron. du selbst, Sie selbst; ihr selbst; dich (selbst), euch (selbst) (in letters Du selbst, Dich (selbst) etc.).
youth [juːθ], s. die Jugend.
youthful ['juːθful], adj. jugendlich.
Yugoslav [juːgo'slɑːv], adj. jugoslawisch. — s. der Jugoslawe.
Yule, Yuletide [juːl, 'juːltaid], s. das Julfest, die Weihnachtszeit.

Z

Z [zed, (Am.) ziː]. das Z.
zany ['zeini], s. der Hanswurst.
zeal [ziːl], s. der Eifer.
zealous ['zeləs], adj. eifrig.
zebra ['ziːbrə], s. (Zool.) das Zebra.
zenith ['zeniθ], s. der Zenit, Scheitelpunkt.
zero ['ziərou], s. der Nullpunkt, die (Ziffer) Null; — hour, die festgesetzte Stunde; festgesetzter Zeitpunkt.
zest [zest], s. die Lust; der Genuß; die Würze.
zigzag ['zigzæg], s. der Zickzack. — adj. Zickzack-.
zinc [ziŋk], s. das Zink.
zip(per) ['zip(ə)], s. der Reißverschluß (zip fastener).
zone [zoun], s. die Zone.
zoological gardens [zouə'lɔdʒikəl gɑ:dnz], s. (abbr. zoo [zuː]) zoologischer Garten, der Zoo, Tiergarten.

German Irregular Verbs

Note: *Where a compound irregular verb is not given, its forms are identical with those of the simple irregular verb as listed.*

Infin.	Pres. Indic. 3rd Pers. Sing.	Imperf. Indic.	Imperf. Subj.
backen	bäckt	backte (buk)	backte
befehlen	befiehlt	befahl	beföhle
beginnen	beginnt	begann	begönne
beißen	beißt	biß	bisse
bergen	birgt	barg	bürge
bersten	birst	barst	börste
bewegen	bewegt	bewog	bewöge
biegen	biegt	bog	böge
bieten	bietet	bot	böte
binden	bindet	band	bände
bitten	bittet	bat	bäte
blasen	bläst	blies	bliese
bleiben	bleibt	blieb	bliebe
braten	brät	briet	briete
brechen	bricht	brach	bräche
brennen	brennt	brannte	brennte
bringen	bringt	brachte	brächte
denken	denkt	dachte	dächte
dreschen	drischt	drosch	dräsche
dringen	dringt	drang	dränge
dürfen	darf	durfte	dürfte
empfangen	empfängt	empfing	empfinge
empfehlen	empfiehlt	empfahl	empföhle
empfinden	empfindet	empfand	empfände
erlöschen	erlischt	erlosch	erlösche

Imper.	Past Participle	English
backe	gebacken	bake
befiehl	befohlen	order, command
beginn(e)	begonnen	begin
beiß(e)	gebissen	bite
birg	geborgen	save, conceal
birst	geborsten	burst
beweg(e)	bewogen	induce
bieg(e)	gebogen	bend
biet(e)	geboten	offer
bind(e)	gebunden	tie, bind
bitte	gebeten	request
blas(e)	geblasen	blow
bleib(e)	geblieben	remain
brat(e)	gebraten	roast
brich	gebrochen	break
brenne	gebrannt	burn
bring(e)	gebracht	bring
denk(e)	gedacht	think
drisch	gedroschen	thrash
dring(e)	gedrungen	press forward
	gedurft	be permitted
empfang(e)	empfangen	receive
empfiehl	empfohlen	(re)commend
empfind(e)	empfunden	feel, perceive
erlisch	erloschen	extinguish

German Irregular Verbs

Infin.	Pres. Indic. 3rd Pers. Sing.	Imperf. Indic.	Imperf. Subj.
erschrecken (*v.n.*)	erschrickt	erschrak	erschräke
essen	ißt	aß	äße
fahren	fährt	fuhr	führe
fallen	fällt	fiel	fiele
fangen	fängt	fing	finge
fechten	ficht	focht	föchte
finden	findet	fand	fände
flechten	flicht	flocht	flöchte
fliegen	fliegt	flog	flöge
fliehen	flieht	floh	flöhe
fließen	fließt	floß	flösse
fressen	frißt	fraß	fräße
frieren	friert	fror	fröre
gebären	gebiert	gebar	gebäre
geben	gibt	gab	gäbe
gedeihen	gedeiht	gedieh	gediehe
gehen	geht	ging	ginge
gelingen (*impers.*)	(mir) gelingt	gelang	gelänge
gelten	gilt	galt	gälte
genesen	genest	genas	genäse
genießen	genießt	genoß	genösse
geschehen (*impers.*)	(mir) geschieht	geschah	geschähe
gewinnen	gewinnt	gewann	gewönne
gießen	gießt	goß	gösse
gleichen	gleicht	glich	gliche
gleiten	gleitet	glitt	glitte
graben	gräbt	grub	grübe
greifen	greift	griff	griffe

German Irregular Verbs

Imper.	Past Participle	English
erschrick	erschrocken	be frightened
iß	gegessen	eat
fahr(e)	gefahren	travel
fall(e)	gefallen	fall
fang(e)	gefangen	catch
ficht	gefochten	fight
find(e)	gefunden	find
flicht	geflochten	twine together
flieg(e)	geflogen	fly
flieh(e)	geflohen	flee
fließ(e)	geflossen	flow
friß	gefressen	eat (of animals)
frier(e)	gefroren	freeze
gebier	geboren	give birth to
gib	gegeben	give
gedeih(e)	gediehen	thrive
geh(e)	gegangen	go
geling(e)	gelungen	succeed
gilt	gegolten	be worth, be valid
genese	genesen	recover
genieß(e)	genossen	enjoy
	geschehen	happen
gewinn(e)	gewonnen	win
gieß(e)	gegossen	pour
gleich(e)	geglichen	equal, resemble
gleit(e)	geglitten	glide
grab(e)	gegraben	dig
greif(e)	gegriffen	grasp

German Irregular Verbs

Infin.	Pres. Indic. 3rd Pers. Sing.	Imperf. Indic.	Imperf. Subj.
haben	hat	hatte	hätte
halten	hält	hielt	hielte
hangen (v.n.)	hängt	hing	hinge
heben	hebt	hob	höbe
heißen	heißt	hieß	hieße
helfen	hilft	half	hülfe
kennen	kennt	kannte	kennte
klimmen	klimmt	klomm	klömme
klingen	klingt	klang	klänge
kneifen	kneift	kniff	kniffe
kommen	kommt	kam	käme
können	kann	konnte	könnte
kriechen	kriecht	kroch	kröche
laden	lädt	lud	lüde
lassen	läßt	ließ	ließe
laufen	läuft	lief	liefe
leiden	leidet	litt	litte
leihen	leiht	lieh	liehe
lesen	liest	las	läse
liegen	liegt	lag	läge
lügen	lügt	log	löge
mahlen	mahlt	mahlte	mahlte
meiden	meidet	mied	miede
messen	mißt	maß	mäße
mißlingen (impers.)	(mir) mißlingt	mißlang	mißlänge
mögen	mag	mochte	möchte
müssen	muß	mußte	müßte
nehmen	nimmt	nahm	nähme

Imper.	Past Participle	English
habe	gehabt	have
halt(e)	gehalten	hold
häng(e)	gehangen	hang
hebe	gehoben	lift
heiß(e)	geheißen	be called
hilf	geholfen	help
kenn(e)	gekannt	know
klimm(e)	geklommen	climb
kling(e)	geklungen	ring, sound
kneif(e)	gekniffen	pinch
komm(e)	gekommen	come
	gekonnt	be able
kriech(e)	gekrochen	creep
lad(e)	geladen	load
laß	gelassen	let
lauf(e)	gelaufen	run
leid(e)	gelitten	suffer
leih(e)	geliehen	lend
lies	gelesen	read
lieg(e)	gelegen	lie
lüg(e)	gelogen	lie, be untruthful
mahle	gemahlen	grind
meid(e)	gemieden	avoid
miß	gemessen	measure
	mißlungen	fail
	gemocht	wish, be willing
	gemußt	have to
nimm	genommen	take

German Irregular Verbs

Infin.	Pres. Indic. 3rd Pers. Sing.	Imperf. Indic.	Imperf. Subj.
nennen	nennt	nannte	nennte
pfeifen	pfeift	pfiff	pfiffe
preisen	preist	pries	priese
quellen (v.n.)	quillt	quoll	quölle
raten	rät	riet	riete
reiben	reibt	rieb	riebe
reißen	reißt	riß	risse
reiten	reitet	ritt	ritte
rennen	rennt	rannte	rennte
riechen	riecht	roch	röche
ringen	ringt	rang	ränge
rinnen	rinnt	rann	rönne
rufen	ruft	rief	riefe
saufen	säuft	soff	söffe
saugen	saugt	sog	söge
schaffen	schafft	schuf	schüfe
scheiden	scheidet	schied	schiede
scheinen	scheint	schien	schiene
schelten	schilt	schalt	schölte
schieben	schiebt	schob	schöbe
schießen	schießt	schoß	schösse
schinden	schindet	schund	schünde
schlafen	schläft	schlief	schliefe
schlagen	schlägt	schlug	schlüge
schleichen	schleicht	schlich	schliche
schleifen	schleift	schliff	schliffe
schließen	schließt	schloß	schlösse
schlingen	schlingt	schlang	schlänge

Imper.	Past Participle	English
nenne	genannt	name
pfeif(e)	gepfiffen	whistle
preis(e)	gepriesen	praise
quill	gequollen	spring
rat(e)	geraten	counsel
reib(e)	gerieben	rub
reiß(e)	gerissen	tear
reit(e)	geritten	ride
renn(e)	gerannt	run
riech(e)	gerochen	smell
ring(e)	gerungen	struggle
rinn(e)	geronnen	flow
ruf(e)	gerufen	call
sauf(e)	gesoffen	drink (to excess)
saug(e)	gesogen	suck
schaff(e)	geschaffen	create
scheid(e)	geschieden	separate
schein(e)	geschienen	appear
schilt	gescholten	scold
schieb(e)	geschoben	shove
schieß(e)	geschossen	shoot
schind(e)	geschunden	skin
schlaf(e)	geschlafen	sleep
schlag(e)	geschlagen	beat
schleich(e)	geschlichen	slink, creep
schleif(e)	geschliffen	slide, polish
schließ(e)	geschlossen	shut, close
schling(e)	geschlungen	wind, devour

German Irregular Verbs

Infin.	Pres. Indic. 3rd Pers. Sing.	Imperf. Indic.	Imperf. Subj.
schmeißen	schmeißt	schmiß	schmisse
schmelzen (v.n.)	schmilzt	schmolz	schmölze
schneiden	schneidet	schnitt	schnitte
schrecken (v.n.)	schrickt	schrak	schräke
schreiben	schreibt	schrieb	schriebe
schreien	schreit	schrie	schriee
schreiten	schreitet	schritt	schritte
schweigen	schweigt	schwieg	schwiege
schwellen	schwillt	schwoll	schwölle
schwimmen	schwimmt	schwamm	schwömme
schwinden	schwindet	schwand	schwände
schwingen	schwingt	schwang	schwänge
schwören	schwört	schwur	schwüre
sehen	sieht	sah	sähe
sein	ist	war	wäre
senden	sendet	sandte or sendete	sendete
singen	singt	sang	sänge
sinken	sinkt	sank	sänke
sinnen	sinnt	sann	sänne
sitzen	sitzt	saß	säße
sollen	soll	sollte	sollte
speien	speit	spie	spiee
spinnen	spinnt	spann	spönne
sprechen	spricht	sprach	spräche
sprießen	sprießt	sproß	sprösse
springen	springt	sprang	spränge
stechen	sticht	stach	stäche
stehen	steht	stand	stände

Imper.	Past Participle	English
schmeiß(e)	geschmissen	hurl
schmilz	geschmolzen	melt
schneid(e)	geschnitten	cut
schrick	(erschrocken)	frighten
schreib(e)	geschrieben	write
schrei(e)	geschrien	cry
schreit(e)	geschritten	stride
schweig(e)	geschwiegen	be silent
schwill	geschwollen	swell
schwimm(e)	geschwommen	swim
schwind(e)	geschwunden	vanish
schwing(e)	geschwungen	swing
schwör(e)	geschworen	swear
sieh	gesehen	see
sei	gewesen	be
send(e)	gesandt or gesendet	send
sing(e)	gesungen	sing
sink(e)	gesunken	sink
sinn(e)	gesonnen	meditate
sitz(e)	gesessen	sit
	gesollt	be obliged
spei(e)	gespieen	spit
spinn(e)	gesponnen	spin
sprich	gesprochen	speak
sprieß(e)	gesprossen	sprout
spring(e)	gesprungen	leap
stich	gestochen	prick
steh(e)	gestanden	stand

German Irregular Verbs

Infin.	Pres. Indic. 3rd Pers. Sing.	Imperf. Indic.	Imperf. Subj.
stehlen	stiehlt	stahl	stöhle
steigen	steigt	stieg	stiege
sterben	stirbt	starb	stürbe
stinken	stinkt	stank	stänke
stoßen	stößt	stieß	stieße
streichen	streicht	strich	striche
streiten	streitet	stritt	stritte
tragen	trägt	trug	trüge
treffen	trifft	traf	träfe
treiben	treibt	trieb	triebe
treten	tritt	trat	träte
trinken	trinkt	trank	tränke
trügen	trügt	trog	tröge
tun	tut	tat	täte
verderben	verdirbt	verdarb	verdürbe
verdrießen	verdrießt	verdroß	verdrösse
vergessen	vergißt	vergaß	vergäße
verlieren	verliert	verlor	verlöre
wachsen	wächst	wuchs	wüchse
wägen	wägt	wog	wöge
waschen	wäscht	wusch	wüsche
weichen	weicht	wich	wiche
weisen	weist	wies	wiese
werben	wirbt	warb	würbe
werden	wird	wurde	würde
werfen	wirft	warf	würfe
wiegen	wiegt	wog	wöge
winden (v.a.)	windet	wand	wände

Imper.	Past Participle	English
stiehl	gestohlen	steal
steig(e)	gestiegen	climb
stirb	gestorben	die
stink(e)	gestunken	stink
stoß(e)	gestoßen	push
streich(e)	gestrichen	stroke, touch
streit(e)	gestritten	quarrel, fight
trag(e)	getragen	carry
triff	getroffen	meet
treib(e)	getrieben	drive
tritt	getreten	step
trink(e)	getrunken	drink
trüg(e)	getrogen	deceive
tu(e)	getan	do
verdirb	verdorben (and verderbt)	spoil
verdrieß(e)	verdrossen	grieve
vergiß	vergessen	forget
verlier(e)	verloren	lose
wachs(e)	gewachsen	grow
wäg(e)	gewogen	weigh
wasch(e)	gewaschen	wash
weich(e)	gewichen	yield
weis(e)	gewiesen	show
wirb	geworben	court
werde	geworden	become
wirf	geworfen	throw
wieg(e)	gewogen	weigh
wind(e)	gewunden	wind

German Irregular Verbs

Infin.	Pres. Indic. 3rd. Pers. Sing.	Imperf. Indic.	Imperf. Subj.
wissen	weiß	wußte	wüßte
wollen	will	wollte	wollte
zeihen	zeiht	zieh	ziehe
ziehen	zieht	zog	zöge
zwingen	zwingt	zwang	zwänge

German Irregular Verbs

Imper.	Past Participle	English
wisse	gewußt	know
wolle	gewollt	wish, want
zeih(e)	geziehen	accuse
zieh(e)	gezogen	draw, pull
zwing(e)	gezwungen	force, compel

English Irregular Verbs

Infin.	Past Indic.	Past Participle	German
abide	abode	abode	bleiben
arise	arose	arisen	aufstehen
awake	awoke	awoke	aufwecken
be	was, were	been	sein
bear	bore	borne	tragen
beat	beat	beaten	schlagen
become	became	become	werden
beget	begot	begotten	zeugen
begin	began	begun	beginnen
bend	bent	bent	biegen
bereave	bereaved, bereft	bereaved, bereft	berauben
beseech	besought	besought	bitten
bid	bade, bid	bidden, bid	gebieten
bide	bided, bode	bided	verbleiben
bind	bound	bound	binden
bite	bit	bitten	beißen
bleed	bled	bled	bluten
blow	blew	blown	blasen
break	broke	broken	brechen
breed	bred	bred	zeugen
bring	brought	brought	bringen
build	built	built	bauen
burn	burnt, burned	burnt, burned	brennen
burst	burst	burst	bersten
buy	bought	bought	kaufen

English Irregular Verbs

Infin.	Past Indic.	Past Participle	German
can (*pres. indic.*)	could	—	können
cast	cast	cast	werfen
catch	caught	caught	fangen
chide	chid	chidden, chid	schelten
choose	chose	chosen	wählen
cleave	cleft, clove	cleft, cloven	spalten
cling	clung	clung	sich anklammern
clothe	clothed, clad	clothed, clad	kleiden
come	came	come	kommen
cost	cost	cost	kosten
creep	crept	crept	kriechen
crow	crowed, crew	crowed	krähen
cut	cut	cut	schneiden
dare	dared, durst	dared	wagen
deal	dealt	dealt	austeilen, handeln
dig	dug	dug	graben
do	did	done	tun
draw	drew	drawn	ziehen
dream	dreamt, dreamed	dreamt, dreamed	träumen
drink	drank	drunk	trinken
drive	drove	driven	treiben
dwell	dwelt	dwelt	wohnen
eat	ate	eaten	essen
fall	fell	fallen	fallen
feed	fed	fed	füttern
feel	felt	felt	fühlen
fight	fought	fought	kämpfen
find	found	found	finden

English Irregular Verbs

Infin.	Past Indic.	Past Participle	German
flee	fled	fled	fliehen
fling	flung	flung	schleudern
fly	flew	flown	fliegen
forbid	forbad(e)	forbidden	verbieten
forget	forgot	forgotten	vergessen
forgive	forgave	forgiven	vergeben
forsake	forsook	forsaken	verlassen
freeze	froze	frozen	frieren
get	got	got	bekommen
gird	girded, girt	girden, girt	gürten
give	gave	given	geben
go	went	gone	gehen
grind	ground	ground	mahlen
grow	grew	grown	wachsen
hang	hung	hung	hängen
have	had	had	haben
hear	heard	heard	hören
heave	heaved, hove	heaved, hove	heben
hew	hewed	hewn, hewed	hauen
hide	hid	hidden, hid	verstecken
hit	hit	hit	schlagen
hold	held	held	halten
hurt	hurt	hurt	verletzen
keep	kept	kept	halten
kneel	knelt	knelt	knien
knit	knitted, knit	knitted, knit	stricken
know	knew	known	kennen, wissen
lay	laid	laid	legen

Infin.	Past Indic.	Past Participle	German
lead	led	led	führen
lean	leant, leaned	leant, leaned	lehnen
leap	leaped, leapt	leaped, leapt	springen
learn	learned, learnt	learned, learnt	lernen
leave	left	left	lassen
lend	lent	lent	leihen
let	let	let	lassen
lie (= recline)	lay	lain	liegen
light	lit, lighted	lit, lighted	beleuchten
lost	lost	lost	verlieren
make	made	made	machen
may (*pres. indic.*)	might	—	mögen
mean	meant	meant	meinen
meet	met	met	treffen, begegnen
melt	melted	melted, molten	schmelzen
mow	mowed	mown	mähen.
must (*pres. indic.*)	—	—	müssen
pay	paid	paid	zahlen
put	put	put	stellen
quit	quit(ted)	quit(ted)	verlassen
—	quoth	—	sagte
read	read	read	lesen
rend	rent	rent	reissen
rid	rid	rid	befreien
ride	rode	ridden	reiten, fahren
ring	rang	rung	klingeln
rise	rose	risen	aufstehen
run	ran	run	laufen

English Irregular Verbs

Infin.	Past Indic.	Past Participle	German
saw	sawed	sawn	sägen
say	said	said	sagen
see	saw	seen	sehen
seek	sought	sought	suchen
sell	sold	sold	verkaufen
send	sent	sent	senden
set	set	set	setzen
shake	shook	shaken	schütteln
shall (*pres. indic.*)	should	—	werden, sollen
shape	shaped	shaped, shapen	formen
shear	sheared	shorn	scheren
shed	shed	shed	vergiessen
shine	shone	shone	scheinen
shoe	shod	shod	beschuhen
shoot	shot	shot	schiessen
show	showed	shown	zeigen
shrink	shrank	shrunk	schrumpfen
shut	shut	shut	schliessen
sing	sang	sung	singen
sink	sank	sunk	sinken
sit	sat	sat	sitzen
slay	slew	slain	erschlagen
sleep	slept	slept	schlafen
slide	slid	slid	gleiten
sling	slung	slung	schleudern
slink	slunk	slunk	schleichen
slit	slit	slit	schlitzen
smell	smelt, smelled	smelt, smelled	riechen

Infin.	Past Indic.	Past Participle	German
smit	smote	smitten	schlagen
sow	sowed	sown, sowed	säen
speak	spoke	spoken	sprechen
speed	sped, speeded	sped, speeded	eilen
spell	spelt, spelled	spelt, spelled	buchstabieren
spend	spent	spent	ausgeben
spill	spilled, spilt	spilled, spilt	verschütten
spin	spun, span	spun	spinnen
spit	spat	spat	speien
split	split	split	spalten
spread	spread	spread	ausbreiten
spring	sprang	sprung	springen
stand	stood	stood	stehen
steal	stole	stolen	stehlen
stick	stuck	stuck	stecken
sting	stung	stung	stechen
stink	stank, stunk	stunk	stinken
strew	strewed	strewed, strewn	streuen
stride	strode	stridden	schreiten
strike	struck	struck, stricken	schlagen
string	strung	strung	(auf)reihen
strive	strove	striven	streben
swear	swore	sworn	schwören
sweep	swept	swept	kehren
swell	swelled	swollen, swelled	schwellen
swim	swam	swum	schwimmen
swing	swung	swung	schwingen
take	took	taken	nehmen

English Irregular Verbs

Infin.	Past Indic.	Past Participle	German
teach	taught	taught	lehren
tear	tore	torn	zerreißen
tell	told	told	erzählen
think	thought	thought	denken
thrive	thrived, throve	thrived, thriven	gedeihen
throw	threw	thrown	werfen
thrust	thrust	thrust	stoßen
tread	trod	trodden	treten
wake	woke, waked	waked, woken woke	wachen
wear	wore	worn	tragen
weave	wove	woven	weben
weep	wept	wept	weinen
will	would	—	wollen
win	won	won	gewinnen
wind	wound	wound	winden
work	worked, wrought	worked, wrought	arbeiten
wring	wrung	wrung	ringen
write	wrote	written	schreiben

Numerical Tables

Cardinal Numbers

0	nought, zero	null
1	one	eins
2	two	zwei
3	three	drei
4	four	vier
5	five	fünf
6	six	sechs
7	seven	sieben
8	eight	acht
9	nine	neun
10	ten	zehn
11	eleven	elf
12	twelve	zwölf
13	thirteen	dreizehn
14	fourteen	vierzehn
15	fifteen	fünfzehn
16	sixteen	sechzehn
17	seventeen	siebzehn
18	eighteen	achtzehn
19	nineteen	neunzehn
20	twenty	zwanzig
21	twenty-one	einundzwanzig
22	twenty-two	zweiundzwanzig
25	twenty-five	fünfundzwanzig
30	thirty	dreißig
36	thirty-six	sechsunddreißig
40	forty	vierzig
50	fifty	fünfzig
60	sixty	sechzig
70	seventy	siebzig
80	eighty	achtzig
90	ninety	neunzig
100	(one)hundred	hundert
101	(a)hundred and one	hundert(und)eins
102	(a)hundred and two	hundert(und)zwei
200	two hundred	zweihundert
300	three hundred	dreihundert
600	six hundred	sechshundert
625	six hundred and twenty-five	sechshundertfünfundzwanzig
1000	(a)thousand	tausend
1965	nineteen hundred and sixty-five	neunzehnhundertfünfundsechzig
2000	two thousand	zweitausend
1,000,000	a million	eine Million
2,000,000	two million	zwei Millionen

Various suffixes may be added to German numerals, the commonest of which are cited in the following examples:

zehnfach	tenfold
dreisilbig	trisyllabic
vierstimmig	four-part (*i.e.* for four voices)
sechsteilig	in six parts

Ordinal Numbers

1st	first	erste (abbr. 1.)
2nd	second	zweite (abbr. 2.)
3rd	third	dritte (abbr. 3.)
4th	fourth	vierte
5th	fifth	fünfte
6th	sixth	sechste
7th	seventh	siebte
8th	eighth	achte
9th	ninth	neunte
10th	tenth	zehnte
11th	eleventh	elfte
12th	twelfth	zwölfte
13th	thirteenth	dreizehnte
14th	fourteenth	vierzehnte
15th	fifteenth	fünfzehnte
16th	sixteenth	sechzehnte
17th	seventeenth	siebzehnte
18th	eighteenth	achtzehnte
19th	nineteenth	neunzehnte
20th	twentieth	zwanzigste
21st	twenty-first	einundzwanzigste
22nd	twenty-second	zweiundzwanzigste
25th	twenty-fifth	fünfundzwanzigste
30th	thirtieth	dreißigste
40th	fortieth	vierzigste
50th	fiftieth	fünfzigste
60th	sixtieth	sechzigste
70th	seventieth	siebzigste
80th	eightieth	achtzigste
90th	ninetieth	neunzigste
100th	hundredth	hundertste
102nd	hundred and second	hundert(und)zweite
200th	two hundredth	zweihundertste
300th	three hundredth	dreihundertste
625th	six hundred and twenty-fifth	sechshundertfünfundzwanzigste
1000th	thousandth	tausendste
2000th	two thousandth	zweitausendste
1,000,000th	millionth	millionste

Fractions etc.

$\frac{1}{4}$	a quarter	ein Viertel
$\frac{1}{3}$	a third	ein Drittel
$\frac{1}{2}$	a half	(ein)halb
$\frac{2}{3}$	two thirds	zwei Drittel
$\frac{3}{4}$	three quarters	drei Viertel
$1\frac{1}{4}$	one and a quarter	ein und ein Viertel
$1\frac{1}{2}$	one and a half	anderthalb
$5\frac{1}{2}$	five and a half	fünfeinhalb
$7\frac{2}{5}$	seven and two-fifths	sieben zwei Fünftel
$\frac{15}{20}$	fifteen-twentieths	fünfzehn Zwanzigstel
.7	point seven	0,7 Null Komma sieben

541